2010

ICD-9-CM Professional

for Physicians
Volumes 1 & 2

International Classification of Diseases
9th Revision
Clinical Modification

Sixth Edition

Edited by:
Anita C. Hart, RHIA, CCS, CCS-P
Melinda S. Stegman, MBA, CCS
Beth Ford, RHIT, CCS

Ingenix is committed to providing you with the ICD-9-CM code update information you need
to code accurately and to be in compliance with HIPAA regulations. In case of adoption of
additional ICD-9-CM code changes effective April 1, 2010, Ingenix will provide these code
changes to you at no additional cost! Just check back at www.shopingenix.com/productalerts
to review the latest information concerning any new code changes.

Codes Valid October 1, 2009, through September 30, 2010

First Printing — August 2009
Made in the USA

This book, or parts hereof, may not be reproduced in any form without permission.
Additional copies may be ordered from:
Your local bookstore
or
1-800-INGENIX (464-3649)

IPP ISBN 978-1-60151-259-8

PUBLISHER'S NOTICE

All codes, indexes, and other material in the ICD-9-CM are compiled from official ICD-9-CM codes and instructions as well as the Medicare regulations and manuals issued or authorized by the Centers for Medicare and Medicaid Services. The code book is designed to provide accurate and authoritative information in regard to the subject covered, and every reasonable effort has been made to ensure the accuracy of the information within these pages. However, the ultimate responsibility for correct coding lies with the provider of services.

Ingenix, its employees, agents and staff make no representation, warranty or guarantee that this compilation of codes and narratives is error-free or that the use of this code book will prevent differences of opinion or disputes with Medicare or other third-party payers as to the codes that are accepted or the amounts that will be paid to providers for services, and will bear no responsibility or liability for the results or consequences of the use of this code book.

OUR COMMITMENT TO ACCURACY

Ingenix is committed to producing accurate and reliable materials. To report corrections, please visit www.ingenixonline.com/accuracy or email accuracy@ingenix.com. You can also reach customer service by calling 1.800.INGENIX (464.3649), option 1.

Preface

ICD-9-CM for Physicians has been designed with the physician office professional in mind. The most recent official government versions of volumes 1 and 2 have been combined to provide physicians and their office staff with an ICD-9-CM book that is easy to use.

In addition, our technical experts have drawn upon their extensive hands-on experience to enhance the government's official version with valuable features essential to correct coding and reimbursement. With these enhancements, physician office health information professionals will increase the efficiency and timeliness of claim submission for both Medicare and other third-party payers.

As you review the content, you'll find the following:

- All the official ICD-9-CM codes, indexes, notes, footnotes and symbols
- Complete official coding guidelines
- Our exclusive color coding, symbols, and footnotes that alert coders to coding and reimbursement issues. Medicare outpatient code edits, such as invalid fourth or fifth digit for diagnosis codes are identified.
- Illustrations and clinically oriented definitions to aid in correct code assignment
- Coding tips based upon the official coding guidelines and advice found in AHA's *Coding Clinic for ICD-9-CM*
- Symbols identifying new codes and text revisions; pages are dated to indicate when the changes were made
- Exclusive QuickFlip Color Tabs for quick, easy location of terms and codes in the Alphabetic Index and Tabular List

Use of Official Sources

This *ICD-9-CM for Physicians* contains the official U.S. Department of Health and Human Services, ICD-9-CM codes, effective for the current year.

The color coding, footnotes and symbols, which identify coding and reimbursement issues, are derived from official federal government sources, including the Medicare Outpatient Code Editor as well as the knowledge of our technical experts.

The American Hospital Association's (AHA) *Coding Clinic for ICD-9-CM* references are used with permission of the AHA.

Important Information About Your Subscription Service

If you have purchased the updateable *ICD-9-CM for Physicians*, your subscription includes an updating service throughout the year to keep the code book current and accurate. Whenever CMS issues changes or corrections to the ICD-9-CM codes, We will issue an update to the book. In July you will receive a list of all new, revised, and invalid codes for the upcoming year.

Technical Editors

Anita C. Hart, RHIA, CCS, CCS-P, *Product Manager, Ingenix*
Ms. Hart's experience includes conducting and publishing research in clinical medicine and human genetics for Yale University, Massachusetts General Hospital, and Massachusetts Institute of Technology. In addition, Ms. Hart has supervised medical records management, health information management, coding and reimbursement, and worker's compensation issues as the office manager for a physical therapy rehabilitation clinic. Ms. Hart is an expert in physician and facility coding, reimbursement systems, and compliance issues. Ms. Hart has developed and has served as technical consultant for numerous other publications for hospital and physician practices. Currrently, Ms. Hart is the Product Manager and Technical Editor for the ICD-9-CM and ICD-10-CM/PCS product lines.

Melinda S. Stegman, MBA, CCS, *Clinical/Technical Editor, Ingenix*
Ms. Stegman has more than 25 years of experience in the HIM profession and has been responsible for managing the clinical aspects of the HSS/Ingenix HIM Consulting practice in the Washington, DC area office. Her areas of specialization include training on inpatient and DRG coding, outpatient coding, and Ambulatory Payment Classifications (APCs) for HIM professionals, software developers, and other clients; developing an outpatient billing/coding compliance tool for a major accounting firm; and managing HIM consulting practices. Ms. Stegman is a regular contributing author for *Advance for Health Information Management Professionals* and for the *Journal of Health Care Compliance*. She has performed coding assessments and educational sessions throughout the country. Ms. Stegman is credentialed by the American Health Information Management Association (AHIMA) as a Certified Coding Specialist (CCS) and holds a Master of Business Administration degree with a concentration in health care management from the University of New Mexico—Albuquerque.

Beth Ford, RHIT, CCS, *Clinical/Technical Editor, Ingenix*
Ms. Ford is a clinical/technical editor for Ingenix. She has extensive background in both physician and facility ICD-9-CM and CPT/HCPCS coding. Ms. Ford has served as a coding specialist, coding manager, coding trainer/educator and coding consultant, as well as a health information management director. She is an active member of the American Heath Information Management Association (AHIMA).

In addition to the editors, the following people have contributed to this book:

Stacy Perry, *Manager, Desktop Publishing*
Tracy Betzler, *Desktop Publishing Specialist*
Hope Dunn, *Desktop Publishing Specialist*
Toni Stewart, *Desktop Publishing Specialist*
Kate Holden, *Editor*

What to Do If You Have Questions

If you have any questions call our customer service department toll-free at 800-INGENIX (464-3649), option 1.

If you have comments on the content of this book, please e-mail them to customerservice@ingenix.com or fax to 801-982-4033.

Additional Copies

Contact the customer service order department toll-free at 800-INGENIX (464-3649), option 1.

Introduction

HISTORY AND FUTURE OF ICD-9

The International Classification of Diseases, Ninth Revision, Clinical Modification (ICD-9-CM) is based on the official version of the World Health Organization's Ninth Revision, International Classification of Diseases (ICD-9). ICD-9-CM classifies morbidity and mortality information for statistical purposes, indexing of hospital records by disease and operations, data storage, and retrieval.

This modification of ICD-9 supplants the Eighth Revision International Classification of Diseases, Adapted for Use in the United States (ICDA-8) and the Hospital Adaptation of ICDA (H-ICDA).

The concept of extending the International Classification of Diseases for use in hospital indexing was originally developed in response to a need for a more efficient basis for storage and retrieval of diagnostic data. In 1950, the U.S. Public Health Service and the Veterans Administration began independent tests of the International Classification of Diseases for hospital indexing purposes. The following year, the Columbia Presbyterian Medical Center in New York City adopted the International Classification of Diseases, Sixth Revision, with some modifications for use in its medical record department. A few years later, the Commission on Professional and Hospital Activities (CPHA) in Ann Arbor, Mich., adopted the International Classification of Diseases with similar modifications for use in hospitals participating in the Professional Activity Study.

The problem of adapting ICD for indexing hospital records was addressed by the U.S. National Committee on Vital and Health Statistics through its subcommittee on hospital statistics. The subcommittee reviewed the modifications made by the various users of ICD and proposed that uniform changes be made. This was done by a small working party.

In view of the growing interest in the use of the International Classification of Diseases for hospital indexing, a study was undertaken in 1956 by the American Hospital Association and the American Medical Record Association (then the American Association of Medical Record Librarians) of the relative efficiencies of coding systems for diagnostic indexing. This study indicated the International Classification of Diseases provided a suitable and efficient framework for indexing hospital records. The major users of the International Classification of Diseases for hospital indexing purposes then consolidated their experiences, and an adaptation was first published in December 1959. A revision was issued in 1962 and the first "Classification of Operations and Treatments" was included.

In 1966, the international conference for revising the International Classification of Diseases noted the eighth revision of ICD had been constructed with hospital indexing in mind and considered the revised classification suitable, in itself, for hospital use in some countries. However, it was recognized that the basic classification might provide inadequate detail for diagnostic indexing in other countries. A group of consultants was asked to study the eighth revision of ICD (ICD-8) for applicability to various users in the United States. This group recommended that further detail be provided for coding of hospital and morbidity data. The American Hospital Association was requested to develop the needed adaptation proposals. This was done by an advisory committee (the Advisory Committee to the Central Office on ICDA). In 1968 the United States Public Health Service published the product, Eighth Revision International Classification of Diseases, Adapted for Use in the United States. This became commonly known as ICDA-8, and beginning in 1968 it served as the basis for coding diagnostic data for both official morbidity and mortality statistics in the United States.

In 1968, the CPHA published the Hospital Adaptation of ICDA (H-ICDA) based on both the original ICD-8 and ICDA-8. In 1973, CPHA published a revision of H-ICDA, referred to as H-ICDA-2. Hospitals throughout the United States were divided in their use of these classifications until January 1979, when ICD-9-CM was made the single classification intended primarily for use in the United States, replacing these earlier related, but somewhat dissimilar, classifications.

Physicians have been required by law to submit diagnosis codes for Medicare reimbursement since the passage of the Medicare Catastrophic Coverage Act of 1988. This act requires physician offices to include the appropriate diagnosis codes when billing for services provided to Medicare beneficiaries on or after April 1, 1989. The Centers for Medicare and Medicaid Services (CMS) designated ICD-9-CM as the coding system physicians must use.

In 1993 the World Health Organization published the newest version of International Classification of Diseases, Tenth Revision, ICD-10. This version contains the greatest number of changes in the history of ICD. There are more codes (5,500 more than ICD-9) to allow more specific reporting of diseases and newly recognized conditions. ICD-10 consists of three volumes; Tabular List (volume I), instructions (volume 2) and the Alphabetic Index (volume 3). It contains 21 chapters including two supplementary ones. The codes are alphanumeric (A00–T98, V01–Y98 and Z00–Z99). Currently ICD-10 is being used in some European countries with an implementation date of October 1, 2013, in the United States.

ICD-9-CM BACKGROUND

In February 1977, a steering committee was convened by the National Center for Health Statistics to provide advice and counsel in developing a clinical modification of ICD-9. The organizations represented on the steering committee included the following:

- American Association of Health Data Systems
- American Hospital Association
- American Medical Record Association
- Association for Health Records
- Council on Clinical Classifications
- Centers for Medicare and Medicaid Services, Department of Health and Human Services
- WHO Center for Classification of Diseases for North America, sponsored by the National Center for Health Statistics, Department of Health and Human Services

The Council on Clinical Classifications was sponsored by the following:

- American Academy of Pediatrics
- American College of Obstetricians and Gynecologists
- American College of Physicians
- American College of Surgeons
- American Psychiatric Association
- Commission on Professional and Hospital Activities

The steering committee met periodically in 1977. Clinical guidance and technical input were provided by task forces on classification from the Council on Clinical Classification's sponsoring organizations.

ICD-9-CM is a clinical modification of the World Health Organization's ICD-9. The term "clinical" is used to emphasize the modification's intent: to serve as a useful tool to classify morbidity data for indexing medical records, medical care review, and ambulatory and other medical care programs, as well as for basic health statistics. To describe the clinical picture of the patient, the codes must be more precise than those needed only for statistical groupings and trend analysis.

CHARACTERISTICS OF ICD-9-CM

ICD-9-CM far exceeds its predecessors in the number of codes provided. The disease classification has been expanded to include health-related conditions and to provide greater specificity at the fifth-digit level of detail. These fifth digits are not optional; they are intended for use in recording the information substantiated in the clinical record.

Volume I (Tabular List) of ICD-9-CM contains four appendixes:

Appendix A: Morphology of Neoplasms

Appendix B: Deleted effective October 1, 2004

Appendix C: Classification of Drugs by American Hospital Formulary Service List Number and Their ICD-9-CM Equivalents

Appendix D: Classification of Industrial Accidents According to Agency

Appendix E: List of Three-Digit Categories

These appendixes are included as a reference to provide further information about the patient's clinical picture, to further define a diagnostic statement, to aid in classifying new drugs or to reference three-digit categories.

Volume 2 (Alphabetic Index) of ICD-9-CM contains many diagnostic terms that do not appear in volume I since the index includes most diagnostic terms currently in use.

THE DISEASE CLASSIFICATION

ICD-9-CM is totally compatible with its parent system, ICD-9, thus meeting the need for comparability of morbidity and mortality statistics at the international level. A few fourth-digit codes were created in existing three-digit rubrics only when the necessary detail could not be accommodated by the use of a fifth-digit subclassification. To ensure that each rubric of ICD-9-CM collapses back to its ICD-9 counterpart the following specifications governed the ICD-9-CM disease classification:

Specifications for the Tabular List:

1. Three-digit rubrics and their contents are unchanged from ICD-9.

2. The sequence of three-digit rubrics is unchanged from ICD-9.

3. Three-digit rubrics are not added to the main body of the classification.

4. Unsubdivided three-digit rubrics are subdivided where necessary to
   - add clinical detail
   - isolate terms for clinical accuracy

5. The modification in ICD-9-CM is accomplished by adding a fifth digit to existing ICD-9 rubrics, except as noted under #7 below.

6. The optional dual classification in ICD-9 is modified.
   - Duplicate rubrics are deleted:
     - four-digit manifestation categories duplicating etiology entries
     - manifestation inclusion terms duplicating etiology entries[2]
   - Manifestations of disease are identified, to the extent possible, by creating five-digit codes in the etiology rubrics.
   - When the manifestation of a disease cannot be included in the etiology rubrics, provision for its identification is made by retaining the ICD-9 rubrics used for classifying manifestations of disease.

7. The format of ICD-9-CM is revised from that used in ICD-9.
   - American spelling of medical terms is used.
   - Inclusion terms are indented beneath the titles of codes.
   - Codes not to be used for primary tabulation of disease are printed in italics with the notation, "code first underlying disease."

Specifications for the Alphabetic Index:

1. The format of the Alphabetic Index follows that of ICD-9.

2. When two codes are required to indicate etiology and manifestation, the manifestation code appears in brackets (e.g., diabetic cataract 250.5 [*366.41*]).

THE ICD-9-CM COORDINATION AND MAINTENANCE COMMITTEE

The four cooperating parties involved in maintaining the ICD-9-CM classification system include representatives of the American Hospital Association (AHA), the Centers for Medicare and Medicaid Services (CMS), the National Center for Health Statistics (NCHS), and the American Health Information Management Association (AHIMA).

Proposals for changes to the ICD-9-CM classification system are submitted and discussed in two open forum meetings held in March and September of each year at the Headquarters of the Centers for Medicare and Medicaid Services, Baltimore, Maryland. Comments received during and after the meetings are then discussed by the Committee. A notice of the new codes and code revisions approved by the Committee are published in the *Federal Register* as part of the proposed and final rule for the changes to the inpatient prospective payment system. The complete official document of changes to the classification system is released as the Addenda for the *International Classification of Diseases, Ninth Revision, Clinical Modification, Sixth Edition, Volumes 1, 2, and 3.*

How to Use the ICD-9-CM for Physicians (Volume 1 & 2)

ICD-9-CM for Physicians is based on the official version of the International Classification of Diseases, Ninth Revision, Clinical Modification, Sixth Edition, issued by the U.S. Department of Health and Human Services. Annual code changes are implemented by the government and are effective Oct. 1 and valid through Sept. 30 of the following year.

To accommodate the coder's approach to coding, the Alphabetic Index (Volume 2) has been placed before the Tabular List (Volume 1). This allows the user to locate the term in the index, then confirm the accuracy of the code in the Tabular List.

10 STEPS TO CORRECT CODING

To code accurately, it is necessary to have a working knowledge of medical terminology and to understand the characteristics, terminology and conventions of ICD-9-CM. Transforming descriptions of diseases, injuries, conditions and procedures into numerical designations (coding) is a complex activity and should not be undertaken without proper training.

Originally, coding allowed retrieval of medical information by diagnoses and operations for medical research, education and administration. Coding today is used to describe the medical necessity of a procedure and facilitate payment of health services, to evaluate utilization patterns and to study the appropriateness of health care costs. Coding provides the basis for epidemiological studies and research into the quality of health care. Incorrect or inaccurate coding can lead to investigations of fraud and abuse. Therefore, coding must be performed correctly and consistently to produce meaningful statistics to aid in planning for the health needs of the nation.

Follow the steps below to code correctly:

Step 1: Identify the reason for the visit (e.g., sign, symptom, diagnosis, condition to be coded).

Physicians describe the patient's condition using terminology that includes specific diagnoses as well as symptoms, problems or reasons for the encounter. If symptoms are present but a definitive diagnosis has not yet been determined, code the symptoms. Do not code conditions that are referred to as "rule out," "suspected," "probable" or "questionable."

Step 2: Always consult the Alphabetic Index, Volume 2, before turning to the Tabular List.

The most critical rule is to begin a code search in the index. Never turn first to the Tabular List (Volume 1), as this will lead to coding errors and less specificity in code assignments. To prevent coding errors, use both the Alphabetic Index and the Tabular List when locating and assigning a code.

Step 3: Locate the main entry term.

The Alphabetic Index is arranged by condition. Conditions may be expressed as nouns, adjectives and eponyms. Some conditions have multiple entries under their synonyms. Main terms are identified using boldface type.

Step 4: Read and interpret any notes listed with the main term

Notes are identified using italicized type.

Step 5: Review entries for modifiers

Nonessential modifiers are in parentheses. These parenthetical terms are supplementary words or explanatory information that may either be present or absent in the diagnostic statement and do not affect code assignment.

Step 6: Interpret abbreviations, cross-references, symbols and brackets

Cross-references used are "*see*," "*see* category," or "*see* also." The abbreviation NEC may follow main terms or subterms. NEC (not elsewhere classified) indicates that there is no specific code for the condition even though the medical documentation may be very specific. The ☑ box indicates the code requires an additional digit. If the appropriate digits are not found in the index, in a box beneath the main term, you MUST refer to the Tabular

List. Italicized brackets [ ], are used to enclose a second code number that must be used with the code immediately preceding it and in that sequence.

Step 7: Choose a tentative code and locate it in the Tabular List.

Be guided by any inclusion or exclusion terms, notes or other instructions, such as "*code first*" and "use additional code," that would direct the use of a different or additional code from that selected in the index for a particular diagnosis, condition or disease.

Step 8: Determine whether the code is at the highest level of specificity.

Assign three-digit codes (category codes) if there are no four-digit codes within the code category. Assign four-digit codes (subcategory codes) if there are no five-digit codes for that category. Assign five-digit codes (fifth-digit subclassification codes) for those categories where they are available.

Step 9: Consult the color coding and reimbursement prompts, including the age and sex edits.

Consult the official ICD-9-CM guidelines for coding and reporting, and refer to the AHA's *Coding Clinic for ICD-9-CM* for coding guidelines governing the use of specific codes.

Step 10: Assign the code.

ORGANIZATION

Introduction

The introductory material in this book includes the history and future of ICD-9-CM as well as an overview of the classification system

Official ICD-9-CM Conventions

This section provides a full explanation of all the official footnotes, symbols, instructional notes, and conventions found in the official government version

Additional Conventions

Exclusive color-coding, symbols, and notations have been included in the *ICD-9-CM for Physicians, Volumes 1 and 2* to alert coders to important coding and reimbursement issues. This section provides a full explanation of the additional conventions used throughout this book.

Summary of Code Changes

This section includes a complete listing of all code changes for the current year.

Summary of AHA's *Coding Clinic for ICD-9-CM* Topics

This is a brief summary of the official advice concerning coding topics covered in the latest issues of AHA's *Coding Clinic for ICD-9-CM* and is found **ONLY** in the *ICD-9-CM Expert for Physicians* updateable edition.

ICD-9-CM Code Changes for 2010: An Insider's View

Chapter-by-chapter detailed clinical and coding information with coding scenarios for all new codes adopted for 2010 located in one resource for quick reference and training. This section is found **only** in the Expert editions.

Coding Guidelines

Included in this book are the official ICD-9-CM coding guidelines as approved by the four cooperating parties of the ICD-9-CM Coordination and Maintenance Committee. Failure to comply with these official coding guidelines may result in denied or delayed claims.

Disease Classification: Alphabetic Index to Diseases

The Alphabetic Index to Diseases is separated by tabs labeled with the letters of the alphabet, contains diagnostic terms for illnesses, injuries and reasons for encounters with health care professionals. Both the Table of

Drugs and Chemicals and the Alphabetic Index to External Causes of Injury and Poisoning are easily located with the tabs in this section.

The warning statement at the bottom of every page of the index, ⬇ Subterms under main terms may continue to next column or page, is a reminder to always check for additional subterms before making final selection.

Disease Classification: Tabular List of Diseases

The Tabular List of Diseases arranges the ICD-9-CM codes and descriptors numerically. Tabs divide this section into chapters, identified by the code range on the tab.

The Tabular List includes two supplementary classifications:

- V Codes–Supplementary Classification of Factors Influencing Health Status and Contact with Health Services (V01–V89)
- E Codes–Supplementary Classification of External Causes of Injury and Poisoning (E000–E999)

ICD-9-CM includes four official appendixes.

- Appendix A   Morphology of Neoplasms
- Appendix B   Deleted effective October 1, 2004
- Appendix C   Classification of Drugs by AHFS List
- Appendix D   Classification of Industrial Accidents According to Agency
- Appendix E   List of Three-digit Categories

These appendixes are included as a reference to provide further information about the patient's circumstances, help further define a diagnostic statement, maintain a tumor registry and aid in classifying new drugs.

RESOURCES

Listed below are the exclusive resources found **ONLY** in the *ICD-9-CM Expert for Physicians, Volumes 1 & 2*.

10 Steps to Correct Coding

This is a valuable resource that takes the coder step by step through the coding process with detailed explanations accompanied by coding examples that demonstrate the practical application of ICD-9-CM conventions and coding guidelines in 10 steps.

Valid Three-digit Code Table

ICD-9-CM is composed of codes with either 3, 4, or 5 digits. A code is invalid if it has not been coded to the full number of digits required for that code. There are a certain number codes that are valid for reporting as three digit codes. A list of these valid three-digit code is included as a convenient reference when auditing claims.

Code Tables

Exclusive coding tables covering abortion, burns, complications, diabetes, hernia, pregnancy, and others are provided to simplify those complex coding issues.

ICD-9-CM Official Conventions

ICD-9-CM FOOTNOTES, SYMBOLS, INSTRUCTIONAL NOTES AND CONVENTIONS

This *ICD-9-CM for Physicians* preserves all the footnotes, symbols, instructional notes and conventions found in the government's official version. Accurate coding depends upon understanding the meaning of these elements.

The following appear in the disease Tabular List, unless otherwise noted.

OFFICIAL GOVERNMENT SYMBOLS

§   The section mark preceding a code denotes a footnote on the page. This symbol is used in the Tabular List of Diseases.

ICD-9-CM CONVENTIONS USED IN THE TABULAR LIST

In addition to the symbols and footnotes above, the ICD-9-CM disease tabular has certain abbreviations, punctuation, symbols and other conventions. Our *ICD-9-CM for Physicians* preserves these conventions. Proper use of the conventions will lead to efficient and accurate coding.

Abbreviations

NEC   Not elsewhere classifiable
This abbreviation is used when the ICD-9-CM system does not provide a code specific for the patient's condition.

NOS   Not otherwise specified
This abbreviation is the equivalent of "unspecified" and is used only when the coder lacks the information necessary to code to a more specific four-digit subcategory.

[ ]   Brackets enclose synonyms, alternative terminology or explanatory phrases:

482.2   Pneumonia due to Hemophilus influenzae [H. influenzae]

Brackets that appear beneath a code indicate the fifth digits that are considered valid fifth digits for the code. This convention is applied for those instances in ICD-9-CM where not all common fifth digits are considered valid for each subcategory within a category.

715.0   Osteoarthrosis, generalized
[0,4,9]

Generalized arthrosis can only be assigned in cases for which the degenerative joint disease involves multiple joints. Therefore, this code is considered for arthrosis in the sites described as unspecified, hand (which consists of multiple joints), or multiple sites. Therefore, only fifth digits 0, 4, and 9 are valid with subcategory 715.0.

[ ]   Slanted brackets that appear in the Alphabetic Index indicate mandatory multiple coding. Both codes must be assigned to fully describe the condition and are sequenced in the order listed.

Tachycardia
ventricular (paroxysmal)
    psychogenic 316 *[427.1]*

Psychogenic paroxysmal tachycardia is reported using both 316, Psychogenic factors associated with diseases classified elsewhere, and 427.1, Paroxysmal ventricular tachydcardia.

( )   Parentheses enclose supplementary words, called nonessential modifiers, that may be present in the narrative description of a disease without affecting the code assignment:

198.4   Other parts of nervous system
Meninges (cerebral) (spinal)

:   Colons are used in the Tabular List after an incomplete term that needs one or more of the modifiers that follow in order to make it assignable to a given category:

021.1   Enteric tularemia
Tularemia:
    cryptogenic
    intestinal
    typhoidal

}   Braces enclose a series of terms, each of which is modified by the statement appearing to the right of the brace:

560.2   Volvulus
Knotting
Strangulation   } of intestine, bowel, or colon
Torsion
Twist

OTHER CONVENTIONS

Boldface   Boldface type is used for all codes and titles in the Tabular List.

Italicized   Italicized type is used for all exclusion notes and to identify codes that should not be used for describing the primary diagnosis.

GENERAL NOTES USED IN THE TABULAR LIST

These notes appear only in the Tabular List of Diseases:

Includes   An includes note further defines or clarifies the content of the chapter, subchapter, category, subcategory or subclassification. The includes note in the example below applies only to category 461.

Excludes   following the word "Excludes" are not classified to the chapter, subchapter, category, subcategory or specific subclassification code under which it is found. The note also may provide the location of the excluded diagnosis. Excludes notes are italicized.

461   Acute sinusitis
INCLUDES   abscess
     empyema   acute, of sinus
     infection   (accessory)
     inflammation   (nasal)
     suppuration
EXCLUDES   *chronic or unspecified sinusitis (473.0-473.9)*

INSTRUCTIONAL NOTES

The following official instructional notes are critical to correct coding practices. The instructional notes appear in red type in the Tabular List.

Use additional code:
This instruction signals the coder that an additional code should be used if the information is available to provide a more complete picture of that diagnosis.

362.13   Changes in vascular appearance
Vascular sheathing of retina
Use additional code for any associated
    atherosclerosis (440.8)

For emphasis this instructional note appears in red type in the tabular section.

There are coding circumstances outside of the etiology/manifestation convention when multiple coding for a single condition is required. The "Use additional code" note will be found under the associated condition code in the tabular. In the index, the multiple coding requirement is indicated by the use of the slanted bracket. The two codes are to be sequenced as listed in the index. For example, retinal arteriosclerosis must be coded using two codes sequenced as listed in the index.

Arteriosclerosis, arteriosclerotic
retinal (vascular) 440.8 [362.13]

Code first underlying disease:

The *"Code first underlying"* instructional note found under certain codes is a sequencing rule. Most often this sequencing rule applies to the etiology/manifestation convention and is found under the manifestation code. The manifestation code may never be used alone or as a primary diagnosis (i.e., sequenced first). The instructional note, the code and its descriptor appear in italics in the Tabular List.

590.81 Pyelitis or pyelonephritis in diseases classified elsewhere
Code first underlying disease as:
tuberculosis (016.0)

Not all codes with a "Code first underlying disease" instructional note are part of the etiology/manifestation convention. The `Code first' note will appear, but the title of the code and the instructional note are not in italics. These codes may be reported alone or as the secondary diagnosis. For example, disseminated chorioretinitis may be reported as a principal diagnosis. However, if the underlying condition that caused disseminated chorioretinitis is known, such as tuberculous disseminated chorioretinitis, two codes are required and sequenced as listed in the index.

363.13 Disseminated choroiditis and chorioretinitis, generalized
Code first underlying disease as:
tuberculosis (017.3)

For emphasis this instructional note appears in red type in the tabular section.

Code, if applicable, any causal condition first:

A code with this note indicates that this code may be assigned as a principal diagnosis when the causal condition is unknown or not applicable. If a causal condition is known, then the code for that condition should be sequenced as the principal or first-listed diagnosis.

590.0 Chronic pyelonephritis
Chronic pyelitis
Chronic pyonephrosis
Code, if applicable, any causal condition first

For emphasis this instructional note appears in red type in the tabular section.

INSTRUCTIONAL NOTES USED IN THE INDEX

Omit code:

"Omit code" is used to instruct the coder that no code is to be assigned. When this instruction is found in the Alphabetic Index to Diseases the medical term should not be coded as a diagnosis.

Metaplasia
cervix — *omit code*

See Condition:

The "see condition" note found in the Alphabetic Index to Disease instructs the coder to refer to a main term for the condition. This note will follow index terms that are nouns for anatomical sites or adjectival forms of disease term. In the example below, the index terms "Cervix" and "Diffuse" are followed by the — see condition. Coders should search the index using a condition term such as atrophy or prolapse.

Cervix — *see* condition
Diffuse — *see* condition

Morphology Codes:

For each neoplastic disease listed in the index, a morphology code is provided that identifies histological type and behavior.

Example:

Myelolipoma (M8870/0) — *see* Neoplasm, by site, benign

The histology is identified by the first four digits and the behavior is identified by the digit following the slash. Appendix A of Volume 1 contains a listing of morphology codes. This appendix is helpful when the pathology report identifies the neoplasm by using an M code. The coder may refer to Appendix A to determine the nomenclature of the neoplasm that will be the main term to search in the Index. The behavior classification is as follows:

0   Benign

1   Uncertain behavior

2   Carcinoma in situ

3   Malignant, primary site

Additional Conventions

SYMBOLS AND NOTATIONS

New and Revised Text Symbols

●   A bullet at a code or line of text indicates that the entry is new.

▲   A triangle in the Tabular List indicates that the code title is revised. In the Alphabetic Index the triangle indicates that a code has changed.

►◄   These symbols appear at the beginning and at the end of a section of new or revised text.

When these symbols appear on a page there will be a date on the lower outside corner of the page indicating the date of the change, (e.g., October 2009).

Additional Digits Required

✓4ᵗʰ   This symbol indicates that the code requires a fourth digit.

✓5ᵗʰ   This symbol indicates that a code requires a fifth digit.

✓   This symbol found only in the Alphabetic Index sections and the Table of Drugs and Chemicals indicates that an additional digit is required. Referring to the tabular section is essential to locate the appropriate additional digit.

AHA's Coding Clinic for ICD-9-CM References
The four cooperating parties have designated the AHA's *Coding Clinic for ICD-9-CM* as the official publication for coding guidelines. The references are identified by the notation **AHA:** followed by the issue, year and page number.

In the example below, AHA's *Coding Clinic for ICD-9-CM*, third quarter 1991, page 15, contains a discussion on code assignment for vitreous hemorrhage:

379.23 Vitreous hemorrhage
AHA: 3Q, '91, 15

The table below explains the abbreviations in the *Coding Clinic* references:

J-F	January/February
M-A	March/April
M-J	May/June
J-A	July/August
S-O	September/October
N-D	November/December
1Q	First quarter
2Q	Second quarter
3Q	Third quarter
4Q	Fourth quarter

AHA's *Coding Clinic for ICD-9-CM* references appear in blue type in the Tabular List.

Age and Sex Edit Symbols
The age edits below address OCE edits and are used to detect inconsistencies between the patient's age and diagnosis. They appear in the Tabular List of Diseases to the right of the code description.

Newborn Age: 0   N
These diagnoses are intended for newborns and neonates and the patient's age must be 0 years.

Pediatric Age: 0-17   P
These diagnoses are intended for children and the patient's age must between 0 and 17 years.

Maternity Age: 12-55   M
These diagnoses are intended for the patients between the age of 12 and 55 years.

Adult Age: 15-124   A
These diagnoses are intended for the patients between the age of 15 and 124 years.

The sex symbols below address OCE edits and are used to detect inconsistencies between the patient's sex and diagnosis. They appear in the Tabular List of Diseases to the right of the code description:

♂   **Male diagnosis only**
This symbol appears to the right of the code description. This reference appears in the disease Tabular List.

♀   **Female diagnosis only**
This symbol appears to the right of the code description. This reference appears in the disease Tabular List.

COLOR CODING
To alert the coder to Medicare outpatient code edits and other important reimbursement issues, color bars have been added over the code descriptors in the Tabular List. Some codes carry more than one color.

Carriers use the Medicare Outpatient Code Editor (OCE) to examine claims for coding and billing accuracy and completeness. Color codes in this book signify Medicare code edits for manifestation codes not to be reported as a primary diagnosis, and when a more specific diagnosis code should be used.

Manifestation Code
These codes will appear in italic type as well as with a blue color bar over the code title. A manifestation code is not allowed to be reported as a primary diagnosis because each describes a manifestation of some other underlying disease, not the disease itself. This is referred to as mandatory multiple coding of etiology and manifestation. Code the underlying disease first. A *Code first underlying disease* instructional note will appear with underlying disease codes identified. In the Alphabetic Index these codes are listed as the secondary code in slanted brackets with the code for the underlying disease listed first.

Other Specified Code
These codes will appear with a gray color bar over the code title. Use these codes when the documentation indicates a specified diagnosis, but the ICD-9-CM system does not have a specific code that describes the diagnosis. These codes are may be stated as "Other" or "Not elsewhere classified (NEC)."

Unspecified Code
These codes will have a yellow color bar over the code title. Use these codes when the neither the diagnostic statement nor the documentation provides enough information to assign a more specified diagnosis code. These codes may be stated as "Unspecified" or "Not otherwise specified (NOS)." Note: Do not assign these codes when a more specific diagnosis has been determined.

OTHER NOTATIONS

DEF: This symbol indicates a definition of disease term. The definition will appear in blue type in the Disease Tabular Lists.

TIPS: This symbol precedes official coding advice found in the official coding guidelines and AHA's *Coding Clinic for ICD-9-CM*. Coding tips appear in blue type in the Tabular List.

I-10   In preparation for the transition to coding using the ICD-10-CM classification system, examples of ICD-10-CM codes have been provided for selected ICD-9-CM diagnosis codes. This symbol indicates that the code provided is an ICD-10-CM code to which the selected ICD-9-CM code is mapped.

Note: Coding professionals should keep in mind the following points when referring to the ICD-10-CM codes provided:

- ICD-10-CM codes are not currently valid for reporting purposes.

- The ICD-10-CM code may represent only one possible coding option. Since mappings between ICD-9-CM and ICD-10-CM are not always straightforward one-to-one correspondences due to the differences in terminology and clinical concepts, the mapping may result in a one-to-many code option. Not all code options for a particular ICD-9-CM code are provided. For cases in which many code alternatives are possible in ICD-10-CM, only one example is provided.

- The ICD-10-CM code examples are provided only for the most frequently reported ICD-9-CM codes in each chapter.

- The ICD-10-CM codes are examples only and are provided to ease the transition to the new classification system.

PDx This symbol identifies a V code that generally is for use as a first listed diagnosis only but may be used as an additional diagnosis if the patient has more than one encounter on one day or there is more than one reason for the encounter.

SDx This symbol identifies a V code that can only be used as a secondary diagnosis.

Note: A V code without a symbol may be used as either a primary or secondary diagnosis.

Note: Please note that the symbols indicating the V code "primary only" and "secondary only" designation and the V Code Table included in the official coding guidelines [Section 1.C.18.e] are consistent with reporting guidelines for healthcare encounters *excluding acute care inpatient admissions*. These V code edits are often in conflict with the inpatient prospective payment system (IPPS) edits. For example, V22.0, Encounter for supervision of a normal first pregnancy, may be an appropriate primary reason for an outpatient encounter. However, supervision for a normal pregnancy is not an acceptable principal diagnosis for an inpatient admission and will have an unacceptable prinicpal diagnosis edit under IPPS.

Medicare as Secondary Payer (MSP)

Note: This edit is no longer included in the official Medicare Code Editor (MCE).The Medicare as Secondary Payer (MSP) alert identified trauma diagnoses that may be covered under automobile insurance, no-fault insurance, workmen's compensation or other types of liability insurance for which Medicare should be a secondary payer. Providers must verify MSP information prior to submitting the claim to Medicare.

Wrong Surgery Edit

When a particular surgical or other invasive procedure is indicated to treat a medical condition and the wrong procedure is performed, the procedure is not considered reasonable and necessary. Assign E codes to report these wrong surgery incidents. A Wrong Surgery edit associated with the E code will be triggered and the claim will be denied and returned to the provider. The wrong surgery E codes are identified with an asterisk (*) and a footnote.

Alphabetic Indexes

Subterms under main terms may continue to next column/page.
This warning statement is a reminder to always check for additional subterms and information that may continue on to the next page or column before making a final selection.

Summary of Code Changes

DIAGNOSIS TABULAR (VOLUME 1)

001-139	INFECTIOUS AND PARASITIC DISEASES
	Exclusion term revised
008.63	Inclusion note added
▲ 008.65	Calicivirus
035	Exclusion term revised
037	Exclusion term revised
▲ 041.3	Friedländer's bacillus Klebsiella pneumoniae
	Inclusion note deleted
▲ 041.86	Helicobacter pylori (H. pylori) ▶[H. pylori]◀
046.1	Use additional code note added
▲ 050-059	VIRAL DISEASES ▶GENERALLY◀ ACCOMPANIED BY EXANTHEM
078.89	Inclusion note deleted
190	Exclusion notes added
196	Exclusion note added
197	Exclusion notes added
198	Exclusion note added
199	Exclusion note added
	Exclusion terms revised
199.2	Use additional code note revised
200-208	MALIGNANT NEOPLASM OF LYMPHATIC AND HEMATOPOIETIC TISSUE
	Exclusion note added
202.0	Inclusion term revised
202.1	Exclusion note added
209	Exclusion note added
	Exclusion term revised
209.30	Exclusion note added
● 209.31	Merkel cell carcinoma of the face
	Inclusion notes added
● 209.32	Merkel cell carcinoma of the scalp and neck
● 209.33	Merkel cell carcinoma of the upper limb
● 209.34	Merkel cell carcinoma of the lower limb
● 209.35	Merkel cell carcinoma of the trunk
● 209.36	Merkel cell carcinoma of other sites
	Inclusion notes added
● 209.7	Secondary neuroendocrine tumors
	Inclusion note added
● 209.70	Secondary neuroendocrine tumor, unspecified site
● 209.71	Secondary neuroendocrine tumor of distant lymph nodes
	Inclusion note added
● 209.72	Secondary neuroendocrine tumor of liver
● 209.73	Secondary neuroendocrine tumor of bone
● 209.74	Secondary neuroendocrine tumor of peritoneum
● 209.75	Secondary Merkel cell carcinoma
	Inclusion notes added
● 209.79	Secondary neuroendocrine tumor of other sites
	238.72 Inclusion note added
	238.73 Inclusion note deleted
● 239.81	Retina and choroid
	Inclusion notes added
● 239.89	Other specified sites
251.3	Use additional code notes added
	Exclusion notes added
269.8	Exclusion term revised
270	Exclusion term revised

272.2	Inclusion notes added
272.4	Inclusion note deleted
● 274.00	Gouty arthropathy, unspecified
● 274.01	Acute gouty arthropathy
	Inclusion notes added
● 274.02	Chronic gouty arthropathy without mention of tophus (tophi)
	Inclusion note added
● 274.03	Chronic gouty arthropathy with tophus (tophi)
	Inclusion notes added
274.82	Exclusion notes added
277.2	Exclusion term revised
● 277.88	Tumor lysis syndrome
	Inclusion notes added
	Use additional code note added
279.4	Inclusion note deleted
● 279.41	Autoimmune lymphoproliferative syndrome
	Inclusion note added
● 279.49	Autoimmune disease, not elsewhere classified
	Inclusion note added
279.5	Code first notes revised
285.2	Inclusion term revised
285.22	Exclusion note added
● 285.3	Antineoplastic chemotherapy induced anemia
	Inclusion note added
	Exclusion notes added
290.0	Exclusion term revised
294.1	Code first note revised
294.8	Exclusion term revised
307.0	Exclusion note added
	Exclusion term revised
310.1	Exclusion notes added
	Exclusion note deleted
310.8	Exclusion note added
331.7	Exclusion term revised
331.83	Exclusion note added
333.2	Inclusion note added
	Inclusion notes deleted
	Exclusion notes added
345	Fifth-digit subclassification
	inclusion notes added
	Exclusion notes added
345.1	Inclusion notes added
348.8	Inclusion notes deleted
● 348.81	Temporal sclerosis
	Inclusion notes added
● 348.89	Other conditions of brain
	Inclusion notes added
359.22	Inclusion note added
359.29	Inclusion note deleted
● 359.7	Inflammatory and immune myopathies, NEC
● 359.71	Inclusion body myositis
	Inclusion note added
● 359.79	Other inflammatory and immune myopathies, NEC
	Inclusion note added
● 372.06	Acute chemical conjunctivitis
	Inclusion note added
	Use additional code note added
	Exclusion notes added
372.34	Exclusion note added
372.51	Exclusion note added
403	Exclusion term revised
413.9	Inclusion note added
	Use additional code note added

415.1	Exclusion notes added
● 416.2	Chronic pulmonary embolism
	Use additional code note added
	Exclusion note added
● 438.13	Dysarthria
● 438.14	Fluency disorder
	Inclusion note added
445.81	Use additional code note revised
453	Exclusion note deleted
▲ 453.2	▶Of inferior◀ vena cava
▲ 453.4	▶Acute◀ venous embolism and thrombosis of deep vessels of lower extremity
▲ 453.40	▶Acute◀ venous embolism and thrombosis of unspecified deep vessels of lower extremity
▲ 453.41	▶Acute◀ venous embolism and thrombosis of deep vessels of proximal lower extremity
▲ 453.42	▶Acute◀ venous embolism and thrombosis of deep vessels of distal lower extremity
● 453.5	Chronic venous embolism and thrombosis of deep vessels of lower extremity
	Use additional code note added
	Exclusion note added
● 453.50	Chronic venous embolism and thrombosis of unspecified deep vessels of lower extremity
● 453.51	Chronic venous embolism and thrombosis of deep vessels of proximal lower extremity
● 453.52	Chronic venous embolism and thrombosis of deep vessels of distal lower extremity
● 453.6	Venous embolism and thrombosis of superficial vessels of lower extremity
	Inclusion note added
● 453.7	Chronic venous embolism and thrombosis of other specified vessels
	Use additional code note added
	Exclusion note added
● 453.71	Chronic venous embolism and thrombosis of superficial veins of upper extremity
	Inclusion notes added
● 453.72	Chronic venous embolism and thrombosis of deep veins of upper extremity
	Inclusion notes added
● 453.73	Chronic venous embolism and thrombosis of upper extremity, unspecified
● 453.74	Chronic venous embolism and thrombosis of axillary veins
● 453.75	Chronic venous embolism and thrombosis of subclavian veins
● 453.76	Chronic venous embolism and thrombosis of internal jugular veins
● 453.77	Chronic venous embolism and thrombosis of other thoracic veins
	Inclusion notes added
● 453.79	Chronic venous embolism and thrombosis of other specified veins

---

▶◀ Revised Text   ● New Code   ▲ Revised Code Title

▲ 453.8	►Acute venous embolism and thrombosis of◄ other specified veins
● 453.81	Acute venous embolism and thrombosis of superficial veins of upper extremity
	Inclusion notes added
● 453.82	Acute venous embolism and thrombosis of deep veins of upper extremity
	Inclusion notes added
● 453.83	Acute venous embolism and thrombosis of upper extremity, unspecified
● 453.84	Acute venous embolism and thrombosis of axillary veins
● 453.85	Acute venous embolism and thrombosis of subclavian veins
● 453.86	Acute venous embolism and thrombosis of internal jugular veins
● 453.87	Acute venous embolism and thrombosis of other thoracic veins
	Inclusion notes added
● 453.89	Acute venous embolism and thrombosis of other specified veins
487	Inclusion note added
	Exclusion notes added
	Exclusion term revised
▲ 488	Influenza due to ►certain◄ identified avian influenza ►viruses◄
	Instructional note deleted
	Exclusion term revised
● 488.0	Influenza due to identified avian influenza virus
	Inclusion notes added
● 488.1	Influenza due to identified novel H1N1 influenza virus
	Inclusion notes added
536.2	Exclusion notes added
567	Exclusion term revised
● 569.7	Complications of intestinal pouch
● 569.71	Pouchitis
	Inclusion note added
● 569.79	Other complications of intestinal pouch
● 569.87	Vomiting of fecal matter
▲ 572.2	Hepatic coma ►encephalopathy◄
	Inclusion note added
	Inclusion note deleted
▲ 584	Acute renal ►kidney◄ failure
	Inclusion note added
▲ 584.5	►Acute kidney failure◄ Wwith lesion of tubular necrosis
▲ 584.6	►Acute kidney failure◄ Wwith lesion of renal cortical necrosis
▲ 584.7	►Acute kidney failure◄ Wwith lesion of renal medullary [papillary] necrosis
▲ 584.8	►Acute kidney failure◄ Wwith other specified pathological lesion in kidney
▲ 584.9	►Acute kidney failure◄ Acute renal failure, unspecified
587	Inclusion term revised
	Inclusion note deleted
611.82	Exclusion note added
614	Exclusion term revised
615	Exclusion terms revised
621.3	Inclusion notes deleted
621.30	Inclusion notes added
621.31	Exclusion note added
621.32	Exclusion note added
621.33	Exclusion note added

● 621.34	Benign endometrial hyperplasia
● 621.35	Endometrial intraepithelial neoplasia [EIN]
	Exclusion note added
624	Exclusion term revised
▲ 639.3	Renal ►Kidney◄ failure
	Inclusion term revised
646.6	Exclusion term revised
649.3	Instructional note revised
	Use additional code note revised
▲ 669.3	Acute renal ►kidney◄ failure following labor and delivery
[0,2,4]	
670	Major puerperal infection
	Use 0 as fourth digit note deleted
	Inclusion notes deleted
▲ 670.00	Major puerperal infection ►, unspecified,◄ unspecified as to episode of care or not applicable
▲ 670.02	Major puerperal infection ►, unspecified,◄ delivered with mention of postpartum complication
▲ 670.04	Major puerperal infection ►, unspecified,◄ postpartum condition or complication
● 670.10	Puerperal endometritis, unspecified as to episode of care or not applicable
● 670.12	Puerperal endometritis, delivered with mention of postpartum complication
● 670.14	Puerperal endometritis, postpartum condition or complication
● 670.20	Puerperal sepsis, unspecified as to episode of care or not applicable
	Inclusion note added
● 670.22	Puerperal sepsis , delivered with mention of postpartum complication
	Inclusion note added
● 670.24	Puerperal sepsis, postpartum condition or complication
	Inclusion note added
● 670.30	Puerperal septic thrombophlebitis, unspecified as to episode of care or not applicable
● 670.32	Puerperal septic thrombophlebitis, delivered with mention of postpartum complication
● 670.34	Puerperal septic thrombophlebitis, postpartum condition or complication
● 670.80	Other major puerperal infection, unspecified as to episode of care or not applicable
	Inclusion notes added
● 670.82	Other major puerperal infection, delivered with mention of postpartum complication
	Inclusion notes added
● 670.84	Other major puerperal infection, postpartum condition or complication
	Inclusion notes added
671	Exclusion notes added
671.2	Inclusion notes added
671.3	Use additional code notes added
671.4	Use additional code notes added
671.9	Inclusion notes deleted
680-686	INFECTIONS OF SKIN AND SUBCUTANEOUS TISSUE
	Exclusion term revised
707.03	Inclusion note added
712	Exclusion term revised

713.0	Exclusion term revised
727.01	Exclusion term revised
733.1	Inclusion note added
● 756.72	Omphalocele
	Inclusion note added
● 756.73	Gastroschisis
756.79	Inclusion notes deleted
▲ 757.6	Specified ►congenital◄ anomalies of breast
	Inclusion term revised
	Exclusion note added
762.3	Use additional code note revised
768.5	Exclusion term revised
768.6	Exclusion term revised
● 768.70	Hypoxic-ischemic encephalopathy, unspecified
● 768.71	Mild hypoxic-ischemic encephalopathy
● 768.72	Moderate hypoxic-ischemic encephalopathy
● 768.73	Severe hypoxic-ischemic encephalopathy
772	Exclusion note added
▲ 772.0	Fetal blood loss ►affecting newborn◄
776	Inclusion term revised
▲ 776.9	Unspecified hematological disorder specific to fetus or newborn
777.5	Inclusion note deleted
777.51	Inclusion note added
▲ 779.3	►Disorder of stomach function and ◄ feeding problems in newborn
	Inclusion notes deleted
● 779.31	Feeding problems in newborn
	Inclusion note added
	Exclusion note added
● 779.32	Bilious vomiting in newborn
	Exclusion note added
● 779.33	Other vomiting in newborn
	Inclusion note added
	Exclusion note added
● 779.34	Failure to thrive in newborn
	Exclusion note added
780.0	Exclusion notes added
780.93	Exclusion notes added
	Exclusion term revised
783.3	Exclusion term revised
783.41	Exclusion note added
▲ 784.4	Voice disturbance ►and resonance disorders◄
▲ 784.40	Voice disturbance ►and resonance disorder◄, unspecified
● 784.42	Dysphonia
	Inclusion note added
● 784.43	Hypernasality
● 784.44	Hyponasality
▲ 784.49	Other ►voice and resonance disorders◄
	Inclusion notes deleted
784.5	Inclusion notes deleted
	Exclusion note added
● 784.51	Dysarthria
	Exclusion note added
● 784.59	Other speech disturbance
	Inclusion notes added
787.0	Exclusion notes added
	Exclusion term revised
● 787.04	Bilious emesis
	Inclusion note added
	Exclusion note added
789.00	Inclusion notes deleted
	Exclusion note deleted

►◄ **Revised Text**   ● **New Code**   ▲ **Revised Code Title**

789.01	Inclusion notes deleted		969.0	Inclusion notes deleted	● V20.32	Health supervision for newborn 8 to 28 days old
	Exclusion note deleted		● 969.00	Antidepressant, unspecified		Inclusion notes added
789.02	Inclusion notes deleted		● 969.01	Monoamine oxidase inhibitors	V23.86	Exclusion term revised
	Exclusion note deleted			Inclusion note added	● V26.42	Encounter for fertility preservation counseling
789.03	Inclusion notes deleted		● 969.02	Selective serotonin and norepinephrine reuptake inhibitors		Inclusion notes added
	Exclusion note deleted			Inclusion note added	● V26.82	Encounter for fertility preservation procedure
789.04	Inclusion notes deleted		● 969.03	Selective serotonin reuptake inhibitors		Inclusion notes added
	Exclusion note deleted			Inclusion note added	V45.71	Exclusion note added
789.05	Inclusion notes deleted		● 969.04	Tetracyclic antidepressants	▲ V53.5	Other ▶gastrointestinal◀ appliance ▶and device◀
	Exclusion note deleted		● 969.05	Tricyclic antidepressants		
789.06	Inclusion notes deleted		● 969.09	Other antidepressants	● V53.50	Fitting and adjustment of intestinal appliance and device
	Exclusion note deleted		969.7	Inclusion notes added		
789.07	Inclusion notes deleted		● 969.70	Psychostimulant, unspecified	● V53.51	Fitting and adjustment of gastric lap band
	Exclusion note deleted		● 969.71	Caffeine		
789.09	Inclusion notes deleted		● 969.72	Amphetamines	● V53.59	Fitting and adjustment of other gastrointestinal appliance and device
	Exclusion note deleted			Inclusion note added		
● 789.7	Colic		● 969.73	Methylphenidate		
	Inclusion notes added		● 969.79	Other psychostimulants	V54.1	Exclusion note added
	Exclusion notes added		974.1	Exclusion term revised	V54.2	Exclusion note added
790.01	Inclusion note added		● 995.24	Failed moderate sedation during procedure	▲ V57.3	Speech ▶-language◀ therapy
▲ 793	Nonspecific ▶(abnormal)◀ findings on radiological and other examination of body structure			Inclusion note added	● V60.81	Foster care (status)
			995.92	Use additional code note revised	● V60.89	Other specified housing or economic circumstances
● 793.82	Inconclusive mammogram		995.94	Use additional code note revised		
	Inclusion notes added		▲ 996.43	~~Prosthetic joint implant failure~~ ▶Broken prosthetic joint implant◀	V61.01	Exclusion note added
▲ 793.89	Other ▶(abnormal)◀ findings on radiological examination of breast				● V61.07	Family disruption due to death of family member
			996.47	Inclusion note added		
▲ 793.99	Other nonspecific ▶(abnormal)◀ findings on radiological examination and other examinations of body structure		996.7	Use additional code note added		Exclusion note added
			997.31	Inclusion note added	● V61.08	Family disruption due to other extended absence of family member
			997.4	Exclusion notes added		
795.0	Exclusion term revised		997.5	Inclusion term revised		
795.39	Exclusion note added		999.6	Exclusion notes added		Exclusion note added
796.7	Exclusion term revised		V07.52	Inclusion term revised	● V61.23	Counseling for parent-biological child problem
▲ 799.2	~~Nervousness~~ ▶Signs and symptoms involving emotional state◀		V10	Code first note deleted		
			V10.0	Exclusion notes added		Inclusion notes added
	Inclusion note deleted		V10.1	Exclusion notes added	● V61.24	Counseling for parent-adopted child problem
	Exclusion notes added		V10.8	Exclusion notes added		
● 799.21	Nervousness		▲ V10.9	▶Other and◀ ~~U~~unspecified personal history of malignant neoplasm		Inclusion notes added
	Inclusion note added				● V61.25	Counseling for parent (guardian)-foster child problem
● 799.22	Irritability					
	Inclusion note added		● V10.90	Personal history of unspecified malignant neoplasm		Inclusion notes added
● 799.23	Impulsiveness				▲ V61.29	Other ▶parent-child problems◀
	Inclusion note added			Inclusion note added		Inclusion note deleted
	Exclusion note added			Exclusion notes added	● V61.42	Substance abuse in family
● 799.24	Emotional lability		● V10.91	Personal history of malignant neuroendocrine tumor	V62.82	Exclusion note added
● 799.25	Demoralization and apathy				▲ V65.11	Pediatric pre-birth visit for ▶expectant◀ ~~mother~~ ▶parent(s)◀
	Inclusion note added			Inclusion notes added		
● 799.29	Other signs and symptoms involving emotional state			Code first note added		Inclusion note added
			V12.54	Exclusion note added	V70.0	Exclusion notes added
● 799.82	Apparent life threatening event in infant		▲ V15.06	Allergy to insects ▶and arachnids◀		Exclusion term revised
					V72	Exclusion notes added
	Inclusion notes added		● V15.52	History of traumatic brain injury		Exclusion term revised
	Exclusion notes added			Exclusion note added	V72.5	Exclusion note deleted
	Use additional code note added		● V15.80	History of failed moderate sedation		Exclusion note added
800-804	FRACTURE OF SKULL			Inclusion note added	V72.6	Inclusion note added
	Inclusion note added		● V15.83	Underimmunization status		Exclusion note deleted
▲ 813.45	Torus fracture of radius ▶(alone)◀			Inclusion notes added	● V72.60	Laboratory examination, unspecified
	Exclusion note added		▲ V15.84	▶Contact with and (suspected)◀ exposure to asbestos		
● 813.46	Torus fracture of ulna (alone)				● V72.61	Antibody response examination
	Exclusion note added		▲ V15.85	▶Contact with and (suspected)◀ exposure to potentially hazardous body fluids		Inclusion note added
● 813.47	Torus fracture of radius and ulna					Exclusion note added
832	Fifth-digit subclassification note revised				● V72.62	Laboratory examination ordered as part of a routine general medical examination
			▲ V15.86	▶Contact with and (suspected)◀ exposure to lead		
● 832.2	Nursemaid's elbow		V20.2	Inclusion note added		Inclusion note added
	Inclusion note added			Inclusion note deleted	● V72.63	Pre-procedural laboratory examination
850-854	INTRACRANIAL INJURY, EXCLUDING THOSE WITH SKULL FRACTURE			Exclusion notes added		
			● V20.3	Newborn health supervision		Inclusion notes added
				Inclusion note added	● V72.69	Other laboratory examination
	Inclusion note added			Exclusion note added	V72.8	Exclusion note added
854	Inclusion note added		● V20.31	Health supervision for newborn under 8 days old	V72.83	Inclusion note added
	Inclusion terms revised				● V80.01	Traumatic brain injury
870-897	OPEN WOUNDS			Inclusion note added		
	Use additional code note deleted					

- V80.09 Other neurological conditions
- V87.32 Contact with and (suspected) exposure to algae bloom
- V87.43 Personal history of estrogen therapy
- V87.44 Personal history of inhaled steroid therapy
- V87.45 Personal history of systemic steroid therapy
  Inclusion note added
- V87.46 Personal history of immunosuppression therapy
  Exclusion note added
- E000-E999 SUPPLEMENTARY CLASSIFICATION OF EXTERNAL CAUSES OF INJURY AND POISONING ▶(E000-E999)◄
  Revised section introduction
- EXTERNAL CAUSE STATUS (E000)
  Instructional note added
- E000 External cause status
- E000.0 Civilian activity done for income or pay
  Inclusion note added
  Exclusion note added
- E000.1 Military activity
  Exclusion note added
- E000.8 Other external cause status
  Inclusion notes added
  Exclusion notes added
- E000.9 Unspecified external cause status
- ACTIVITY (E001-E030)
  Instructional note added
- E001 Activities involving walking and running
  Exclusion notes added
- E001.0 Walking, marching and hiking
  Inclusion note added
  Exclusion note added
- E001.1 Running
- E002 Activities involving water and water craft
  Exclusion note added
- E002.0 Swimming
- E002.1 Springboard and platform diving
- E002.2 Water polo
- E002.3 Water aerobics and water exercise
- E002.4 Underwater diving and snorkeling
  Inclusion note added
- E002.5 Rowing, canoeing, kayaking, rafting and tubing
  Inclusion note added
- E002.6 Water skiing and wake boarding
- E002.7 Surfing, windsurfing and boogie boarding
- E002.8 Water sliding
- E002.9 Other activity involving water and watercraft
  Inclusion notes added
- E003 Activities involving ice and snow
  Exclusion note added
- E003.0 Ice skating
  Inclusion notes added
  Exclusion note added
- E003.1 Ice hockey
- E003.2 Snow (alpine) (downhill) skiing, snow boarding, sledding, tobogganing and snow tubing
  Exclusion note added
- E003.3 Cross country skiing
  Inclusion note added
- E003.9 Other activity involving ice and snow
  Inclusion note added

- E004 Activities involving climbing, rappelling and jumping off
  Exclusion notes added
- E004.0 Mountain climbing, rock climbing and wall climbing
- E004.1 Rappelling
- E004.2 BASE jumping
  Inclusion note added
- E004.3 Bungee jumping
- E004.4 Hang gliding
- E004.9 Other activity involving climbing, rappelling and jumping off
- E005 Activities involving dancing and other rhythmic movement
  Exclusion note added
- E005.0 Dancing
- E005.1 Yoga
- E005.2 Gymnastics
  Inclusion note added
  Exclusion note added
- E005.3 Trampoline
- E005.4 Cheerleading
- E005.9 Other activity involving dancing and other rhythmic movements
- E006 Activities involving other sports and athletics played individually
  Exclusion notes added
- E006.0 Roller skating (inline) and skateboarding
- E006.1 Horseback riding
- E006.2 Golf
- E006.3 Bowling
- E006.4 Bike riding
  Exclusion note added
- E006.5 Jumping rope
- E006.6 Non-running track and field events
  Exclusion note added
- E006.9 Other activity involving other sports and athletics played individually
  Exclusion notes added
- E007 Activities involving other sports and athletics played as a team or group
  Exclusion notes added
- E007.0 American tackle football
  Inclusion note added
- E007.1 American flag or touch football
- E007.2 Rugby
- E007.3 Baseball
  Inclusion note added
- E007.4 Lacrosse and field hockey
- E007.5 Soccer
- E007.6 Basketball
- E007.7 Volleyball (beach) (court)
- E007.8 Physical games generally associated with school recess, summer camp and children
  Inclusion notes added
- E007.9 Other activity involving other sports and athletics played as a team or group
  Inclusion note added
- E008 Activities involving other specified sports and athletics
- E008.0 Boxing
- E008.1 Wrestling
- E008.2 Racquet and hand sports
  Inclusion notes added
- E008.3 Frisbee
  Inclusion note added
- E008.4 Martial arts
  Inclusion note added

- E008.9 Other specified sports and athletics activity
  Exclusion note added
- E009 Activity involving other cardiorespiratory exercise
  Inclusion note added
- E009.0 Exercise machines primarily for cardiorespiratory conditioning
  Inclusion notes added
- E009.1 Calisthenics
  Inclusion notes added
- E009.2 Aerobic and step exercise
- E009.3 Circuit training
- E009.4 Obstacle course
  Inclusion notes added
- E009.5 Grass drills
  Inclusion note added
- E009.9 Other activity involving other cardiorespiratory exercise
  Exclusion note added
- E010 Activity involving other muscle strengthening exercises
- E010.0 Exercise machines primarily for muscle strengthening
- E010.1 Push-ups, pull-ups, sit-ups
- E010.2 Free weights
  Inclusion notes added
- E010.3 Pilates
- E010.9 Other activity involving other muscle strengthening exercises
  Exclusion note added
- E011 Activities involving computer technology and electronic devices
  Exclusion note added
- E011.0 Computer keyboarding
  Inclusion note added
- E011.1 Hand held interactive electronic device
  Inclusion notes added
  Exclusion notes added
- E011.9 Other activity involving computer technology and electronic devices
- E012 Activities involving arts and handcrafts
  Exclusion note added
- E012.0 Knitting and crocheting
- E012.1 Sewing
- E012.2 Furniture building and finishing
  Inclusion note added
- E012.9 Activity involving other arts and handcrafts
- E013 Activities involving personal hygiene and household maintenance
  Exclusion notes added
- E013.0 Personal bathing and showering
- E013.1 Laundry
- E013.2 Vacuuming
- E013.3 Ironing
- E013.4 Floor mopping and cleaning
- E013.5 Residential relocation
  Inclusion note added
- E013.8 Other personal hygiene activity
- E013.9 Other household maintenance
- E014 Activities involving person providing caregiving
- E014.0 Caregiving involving bathing
- E014.1 Caregiving involving lifting
- E014.9 Other activity involving person providing caregiving
- E015 Activities involving food preparation, cooking and grilling
- E015.0 Food preparation and clean up
  Inclusion note added
- E015.1 Grilling and smoking food

● E015.2   Cooking and baking
          Inclusion note added
● E015.9   Other activity involving cooking
          and grilling
● E016   Activities involving property and
          land maintenance, building and
          construction
● E016.0   Digging, shoveling and raking
          Inclusion notes added
● E016.1   Gardening and landscaping
          Inclusion note added
● E016.2   Building and construction
● E016.9   Other activity involving property
          and land maintenance, building
          and construction
● E017   Activities involving roller coasters
          and other types of external motion
● E017.0   Roller coaster riding
● E017.9   Other activity involving external
          motion
● E018   Activities involving playing musical
          instrument
          Inclusion note added
● E018.0   Piano playing
          Inclusion note added
● E018.1   Drum and other percussion
          instrument playing
● E018.2   String instrument playing
● E018.3   Wind and brass instrument playing
● E019   Activities involving animal care
          Exclusion note added
● E019.0   Walking an animal
● E019.1   Milking an animal
● E019.2   Grooming and shearing an animal
● E019.9   Other activity involving animal
          care
● E029   Other activity
● E029.0   Refereeing a sports activity
● E029.1   Spectator at an event
● E029.2   Rough housing and horseplay
● E029.9   Other activity
● E030   Unspecified activity
● TRANSPORT ACCIDENTS (E800-E848)
          Instructional note added
  E830-E838 WATER TRANSPORT ACCIDENTS
          Fourth-digit subdivision added
● E830.7   Accident to watercraft causing
          submersion, Occupant of military
          watercraft, any type
● E831.7   Accident to watercraft causing
          other injury, Occupant of military
          watercraft, any type
● E832.7   Other accidental submersion or
          drowning in water transport
          accident, Occupant of military
          watercraft, any type
● E833.7   Fall on stairs or ladders in water
          transport, Occupant of military
          watercraft, any type
● E834.7   Other fall from one level to another
          in water transport, Occupant of
          military watercraft, any type
● E835.7   Other and unspecified fall in water
          transport, Occupant of military
          watercraft, any type
● E836.7   Machinery accident in water
          transport, Occupant of military
          watercraft, any type
● E837.7   Explosion, fire, or burning in
          watercraft, Occupant of military
          watercraft, any type

● E838.7   Other and unspecified water
          transport accident, Occupant of
          military watercraft, any type
▲ E876.5   Performance of ~~inappropriate~~
          ►wrong◄ operation ►(procedure)
          on correct patient◄
          Inclusion note added
          Exclusion note added
● E876.6   Performance of operation
          (procedure) on patient not
          scheduled for surgery
          Inclusion notes added
● E876.7   Performance of correct operation
          (procedure) on wrong side/body
          part
          Inclusion notes added
  E918   Exclusion note added
  E919   Exclusion note added
  E920   Exclusion note added
  E922   Exclusion note added
  E923   Exclusion note added
  E927   Use additional code note added
● E928.7   Mechanism or component of
          firearm and air gun
          Inclusion notes added
          Exclusion note added
  E930-E949 DRUGS, MEDICINAL AND
          BIOLOGICAL SUBSTANCES
          CAUSING ADVERSE EFFECTS IN
          THERAPEUTIC USE
          Exclusion term revised
  E990-E999 INJURY RESULTING FROM
          OPERATIONS OF WAR
          Inclusion term revised
  E990.0   Inclusion note added
● E990.1   From flamethrower
● E990.2   From incendiary bullet
● E990.3   From fire caused indirectly from
          conventional weapon
          Exclusion note added
  E991   Exclusion notes added
● E991.4   Fragments from munitions
          Inclusion notes added
● E991.5   Fragments from person-borne
          improvised explosive device [IED]
● E991.6   Fragments from vehicle-borne
          improvised explosive device [IED]
          Inclusion note added
● E991.7   Fragments from other improvised
          explosive device [IED]
          Inclusion note added
● E991.8   Fragments from weapons
          Inclusion notes added
  E991.9   Inclusion notes deleted
          Inclusion term revised
  E992   Inclusion notes deleted
● E992.0   Torpedo
● E992.1   Depth charge
● E992.2   Marine mines
          Inclusion notes added
● E992.3   Sea-based artillery shell
● E992.8   Other marine weapons
● E992.9   Unspecified marine weapon
          Inclusion note added
  E993   Inclusion notes added
          Inclusion notes deleted
          Exclusion notes added
● E993.0   Aerial bomb
● E993.1   Guided missile
● E993.2   Mortar
          Inclusion notes added
● E993.3   Person-borne improvised
          explosive device [IED]

● E993.4   Vehicle-borne improvised
          explosive device [IED]
          Inclusion notes added
● E993.5   Other improvised explosive device
          [IED]
          Inclusion note added
● E993.6   Unintentional detonation of own
          munitions
          Inclusion notes added
● E993.7   Unintentional discharge of own
          munitions launch device
          Inclusion notes added
● E993.8   Other specified explosion
          Inclusion notes added
● E993.9   Unspecified explosion
          Inclusion notes added
  E994   Inclusion notes deleted
● E994.0   Destruction of aircraft due to
          enemy fire or explosives
          Inclusion notes added
● E994.1   Unintentional destruction of
          aircraft due to own onboard
          explosives
● E994.2   Destruction of aircraft due to
          collision with other aircraft
● E994.3   Destruction of aircraft due to
          onboard fire
● E994.8   Other destruction of aircraft
● E994.9   Unspecified destruction of aircraft
  E995   Inclusion notes deleted
● E995.0   Unarmed hand-to-hand combat
          Exclusion note added
● E995.1   Struck by blunt object
          Inclusion notes added
● E995.2   Piercing object
          Inclusion notes added
● E995.3   Intentional restriction of air and
          airway
          Inclusion notes added
● E995.4   Unintentional drowning due to
          inability to surface or obtain air
          Inclusion note added
● E995.8   Other forms of conventional
          warfare
● E995.9   Unspecified form of conventional
          warfare
  E996   Inclusion notes deleted
          Inclusion note added
          Exclusion note added
● E996.0   Direct blast effect of nuclear
          weapon
          Inclusion notes added
● E996.1   Indirect blast effect of nuclear
          weapon
          Inclusion notes added
● E996.2   Thermal radiation effect of nuclear
          weapon
          Inclusion notes added
● E996.3   Nuclear radiation effects
          Inclusion notes added
● E996.8   Other effects of nuclear weapons
● E996.9   Unspecified effect of nuclear
          weapon
● E997.3   Weapon of mass destruction
          [WMD], unspecified
● E998.0   Explosion of mines
● E998.1   Explosion of bombs
● E998.8   Injury due to other war operations
          but occurring after cessation of
          hostilities
● E998.9   Injury due to unspecified war
          operations but occurring after
          cessation of hostilities

►◄ **Revised Text**   ● **New Code**   ▲ **Revised Code Title**

Coding Guidelines

Effective October 1, 2008
Note: The revised guidelines effective October 1, 2009 were not released in time to be included in this publication. The complete revised guidelines effective October 1, 2009 will be available on our Web site. Please log on to: www.ShopIngenix.com/productalerts to view and download the latest revisions to the official coding guidelines.

The Centers for Medicare and Medicaid Services (CMS) and the National Center for Health Statistics (NCHS), two departments within the U.S. Federal Government's Department of Health and Human Services (DHHS) provide the following guidelines for coding and reporting using the International Classification of Diseases, 9th Revision, Clinical Modification (ICD-9-CM). These guidelines should be used as a companion document to the official version of the ICD-9-CM as published on CD-ROM by the U.S. Government Printing Office (GPO).

These guidelines have been approved by the four organizations that make up the Cooperating Parties for the ICD-9-CM: the American Hospital Association (AHA), the American Health Information Management Association (AHIMA), CMS, and NCHS. These guidelines are included on the official government version of the ICD-9-CM, and also appear in *"Coding Clinic for ICD-9-CM"* published by the AHA.

These guidelines are a set of rules that have been developed to accompany and complement the official conventions and instructions provided within the ICD-9-CM itself. These guidelines are based on the coding and sequencing instructions in Volumes I, II and III of ICD-9-CM, but provide additional instruction. Adherence to these guidelines when assigning ICD-9-CM diagnosis and procedure codes is required under the Health Insurance Portability and Accountability Act (HIPAA). The diagnosis codes (Volumes 1-2) have been adopted under HIPAA for all healthcare settings. Volume 3 procedure codes have been adopted for inpatient procedures reported by hospitals. A joint effort between the healthcare provider and the coder is essential to achieve complete and accurate documentation, code assignment, and reporting of diagnoses and procedures. These guidelines have been developed to assist both the healthcare provider and the coder in identifying those diagnoses and procedures that are to be reported. The importance of consistent, complete documentation in the medical record cannot be overemphasized. Without such documentation accurate coding cannot be achieved. The entire record should be reviewed to determine the specific reason for the encounter and the conditions treated.

The term encounter is used for all settings, including hospital admissions. In the context of these guidelines, the term provider is used throughout the guidelines to mean physician or any qualified health care practitioner who is legally accountable for establishing the patient's diagnosis. Only this set of guidelines, approved by the Cooperating Parties, is official.

The guidelines are organized into sections. Section I includes the structure and conventions of the classification and general guidelines that apply to the entire classification, and chapter-specific guidelines that correspond to the chapters as they are arranged in the classification. Section II includes guidelines for selection of principal diagnosis for non-outpatient settings. Section III includes guidelines for reporting additional diagnoses in non-outpatient settings. Section IV is for outpatient coding and reporting.

Section I. Conventions, general coding guidelines and chapter specific guidelines

A. Conventions for the ICD-9-CM
1. Format:
2. Abbreviations
   a. Index abbreviations
   b. Tabular abbreviations
3. Punctuation
4. Includes and Excludes Notes and Inclusion terms
5. Other and Unspecified codes
   a. "Other" codes
   b. "Unspecified" codes
6. Etiology/manifestation convention ("code first", "use additional code" and "in diseases classified elsewhere" notes)
7. "And"
8. "With"
9. "See" and "See Also"

B. General Coding Guidelines
1. Use of Both Alphabetic Index and Tabular List
2. Locate each term in the Alphabetic Index
3. Level of Detail in Coding
4. Code or codes from 001.0 through V89
5. Selection of codes 001.0 through 999.9
6. Signs and symptoms
7. Conditions that are an integral part of a disease process
8. Conditions that are not an integral part of a disease process
9. Multiple coding for a single condition
10. Acute and Chronic Conditions
11. Combination Code
12. Late Effects
13. Impending or Threatened Condition
14. Reporting Same Diagnosis Code more than Once
15. Admissions/Encounters for Rehabilitation
16. Documentation for BMI and Pressure Ulcer Stages

C. Chapter-Specific Coding Guidelines
1. Chapter 1: Infectious and Parasitic Diseases (001-139)
   a. Human Immunodeficiency Virus (HIV) Infections
   b. Septicemia, Systemic Inflammatory Response Syndrome (SIRS), Sepsis, Severe Sepsis and Septic Shock
   c. Methicillin Resistant *Staphylococcus aureus* (MRSA) Conditions
2. Chapter 2: Neoplasms (140-239)
   a. Treatment directed at the malignancy
   b. Treatment of secondary site
   c. Coding and sequencing of complications
   d. Primary malignancy previously excised
   e. Admissions/Encounters involving chemotherapy, immunotherapy and radiation therapy
   f. Admission/encounter to determine extent of malignancy
   g. Symptoms, signs, and ill-defined conditions listed in Chapter 16 associated with neoplasms
   h. Admission/encounter for pain control/management
   i. Malignant neoplasm associated with transplanted organ
3. Chapter 3: Endocrine, Nutritional, and Metabolic Diseases and Immunity Disorders (240-279)
   a. Diabetes mellitus
4. Chapter 4: Diseases of Blood and Blood Forming Organs (280-289)
   a. Anemia of chronic disease
5. Chapter 5: Mental Disorders (290-319)
   Reserved for future guideline expansion
6. Chapter 6: Diseases of Nervous System and Sense Organs (320-389)
   a. Pain - Category 338
7. Chapter 7: Diseases of Circulatory System (390-459)
   a. Hypertension
   b. Cerebral infarction/stroke/cerebrovascular accident (CVA)
   c. Postoperative cerebrovascular accident
   d. Late Effects of Cerebrovascular Disease
   e. Acute myocardial infarction (AMI)
8. Chapter 8: Diseases of Respiratory System (460-519)
   a. Chronic Obstructive Pulmonary Disease [COPD] and Asthma
   b. Chronic Obstructive Pulmonary Disease [COPD] and Bronchitis
   c. Acute Respiratory Failure
   d. Influenza due to identified avian influenza virus (avian influenza)
9. Chapter 9: Diseases of Digestive System (520-579)
   Reserved for future guideline expansion
10. Chapter 10: Diseases of Genitourinary System (580-629)
    a. Chronic kidney disease
11. Chapter 11: Complications of Pregnancy, Childbirth, and the Puerperium (630-679)
    a. General Rules for Obstetric Cases
    b. Selection of OB Principal or First-listed Diagnosis
    c. Fetal Conditions Affecting the Management of the Mother
    d. HIV Infection in Pregnancy, Childbirth and the Puerperium
    e. Current Conditions Complicating Pregnancy
    f. Diabetes mellitus in pregnancy
    g. Gestational diabetes
    h. Normal Delivery, Code 650
    i. The Postpartum and Peripartum Periods
    j. Code 677, Late effect of complication of pregnancy
    k. Abortions
12. Chapter 12: Diseases Skin and Subcutaneous Tissue (680-709)
    a. Pressure ulcer stage codes

Section II. Selection of Principal Diagnosis

Section III. Reporting Additional Diagnoses

Section IV. Diagnostic Coding and Reporting Guidelines for Outpatient Services

Appendix I: Present on Admission Reporting Guidelines

SECTION I. CONVENTIONS, GENERAL CODING GUIDELINES AND CHAPTER SPECIFIC GUIDELINES

The conventions, general guidelines and chapter-specific guidelines are applicable to all health care settings unless otherwise indicated.

A. **Conventions for the ICD-9-CM**

The conventions for the ICD-9-CM are the general rules for use of the classification independent of the guidelines. These conventions are incorporated within the index and tabular of the ICD-9-CM as instructional notes. The conventions are as follows:

1. **Format:**

    The ICD-9-CM uses an indented format for ease in reference

2. **Abbreviations**

    a. **Index abbreviations**

        NEC   "Not elsewhere classifiable"
        This abbreviation in the index represents "other specified" when a specific code is not available for a condition the index directs the coder to the "other specified" code in the tabular.

    b. **Tabular abbreviations**

        NEC   "Not elsewhere classifiable"
        This abbreviation in the tabular represents "other specified". When a specific code is not available for a condition the tabular includes an NEC entry under a code to identify the code as the "other specified" code.
        See Section I.A.5.a. "Other" codes

        NOS   "Not otherwise specified"
        This abbreviation is the equivalent of unspecified.
        See Section I.A.5.b., "Unspecified" codes

3. **Punctuation**

    [ ]   Brackets are used in the tabular list to enclose synonyms, alternative wording or explanatory phrases. Brackets are used in the index to identify manifestation codes.
    See Section I.A.6. "Etiology/manifestations"

    ( )   Parentheses are used in both the index and tabular to enclose supplementary words that may be present or absent in the statement of a disease or procedure without affecting the code number to which it is assigned. The terms within the parentheses are referred to as nonessential modifiers.

    :   Colons are used in the Tabular list after an incomplete term which needs one or more of the modifiers following the colon to make it assignable to a given category.

4. **Includes and Excludes Notes and Inclusion terms**

    Includes: This note appears immediately under a three-digit code title to further define, or give examples of, the content of the category.

    Excludes: An excludes note under a code indicates that the terms excluded from the code are to be coded elsewhere. In some cases the codes for the excluded terms should not be used in conjunction with the code from which it is excluded. An example of this is a congenital condition excluded from an acquired form of the same condition. The congenital and acquired codes should not be used together. In other cases, the excluded terms may be used together with an excluded code. An example of this is when fractures of different bones are coded to different codes. Both codes may be used together if both types of fractures are present.

Inclusion terms: List of terms is included under certain four and five digit codes. These terms are the conditions for which that code number is to be used. The terms may be synonyms of the code title, or, in the case of "other specified" codes, the terms are a list of the various conditions assigned to that code. The inclusion terms are not necessarily exhaustive. Additional terms found only in the index may also be assigned to a code.

5. **Other and Unspecified codes**
   a. **"Other" codes**
      Codes titled "other" or "other specified" (usually a code with a 4th digit 8 or fifth-digit 9 for diagnosis codes) are for use when the information in the medical record provides detail for which a specific code does not exist. Index entries with NEC in the line designate "other" codes in the tabular. These index entries represent specific disease entities for which no specific code exists so the term is included within an "other" code.
   b. **"Unspecified" codes**
      Codes (usually a code with a 4th digit 9 or 5th digit 0 for diagnosis codes) titled "unspecified" are for use when the information in the medical record is insufficient to assign a more specific code.

6. **Etiology/manifestation convention ("Code first," "Use additional code" and "In diseases classified elsewhere" notes)**
   Certain conditions have both an underlying etiology and multiple body system manifestations due to the underlying etiology. For such conditions, the ICD-9-CM has a coding convention that requires the underlying condition be sequenced first followed by the manifestation. Wherever such a combination exists, there is a "Use additional code" note at the etiology code, and a "Code first" note at the manifestation code. These instructional notes indicate the proper sequencing order of the codes, etiology followed by manifestation.

   In most cases the manifestation codes will have in the code title, "In diseases classified elsewhere." Codes with this title are a component of the etiology/manifestation convention. The code title indicates that it is a manifestation code. "In diseases classified elsewhere" codes are never permitted to be used as first listed or principal diagnosis codes. They must be used in conjunction with an underlying condition code and they must be listed following the underlying condition.

   There are manifestation codes that do not have "In diseases classified elsewhere" in the title. For such codes a "Use additional code" note will still be present and the rules for sequencing apply.

   In addition to the notes in the tabular, these conditions also have a specific index entry structure. In the index both conditions are listed together with the etiology code first followed by the manifestation codes in brackets. The code in brackets is always to be sequenced second.

   The most commonly used etiology/manifestation combinations are the codes for Diabetes mellitus, category 250. For each code under category 250 there is a use additional code note for the manifestation that is specific for that particular diabetic manifestation. Should a patient have more than one manifestation of diabetes, more than one code from category 250 may be used with as many manifestation codes as are needed to fully describe the patient's complete diabetic condition. The category 250 diabetes codes should be sequenced first, followed by the manifestation codes.

   "Code first" and "Use additional code" notes are also used as sequencing rules in the classification for certain codes that are not part of an etiology/manifestation combination.

   See - Section I.B.9. "Multiple coding for a single condition."

7. **"And"**
   The word "and" should be interpreted to mean either "and" or "or" when it appears in a title.

8. **"With"**
   The word "with" in the alphabetic index is sequenced immediately following the main term, not in alphabetical order.

9. **"See" and "See Also"**
   The "see" instruction following a main term in the index indicates that another term should be referenced. It is necessary to go to the main term referenced with the "see" note to locate the correct code.

   A "see also" instruction following a main term in the index instructs that there is another main term that may also be referenced that may provide

additional index entries that may be useful. It is not necessary to follow the "see also" note when the original main term provides the necessary code.

B. **General Coding Guidelines**
   1. **Use of Both Alphabetic Index and Tabular List**
      Use both the Alphabetic Index and the Tabular List when locating and assigning a code. Reliance on only the Alphabetic Index or the Tabular List leads to errors in code assignments and less specificity in code selection.
   2. **Locate each term in the Alphabetic Index**
      Locate each term in the Alphabetic Index and verify the code selected in the Tabular List. Read and be guided by instructional notations that appear in both the Alphabetic Index and the Tabular List.
   3. **Level of Detail in Coding**
      Diagnosis and procedure codes are to be used at their highest number of digits available.

      ICD-9-CM diagnosis codes are composed of codes with 3, 4, or 5 digits. Codes with three digits are included in ICD-9-CM as the heading of a category of codes that may be further subdivided by the use of fourth and/or fifth-digits, which provide greater detail.

      A three-digit code is to be used only if it is not further subdivided. Where fourth-digit subcategories and/or fifth-digit subclassifications are provided, they must be assigned. A code is invalid if it has not been coded to the full number of digits required for that code. For example, Acute myocardial infarction, code 410, has fourth-digits that describe the location of the infarction (e.g., 410.2, Of inferolateral wall), and fifth-digits that identify the episode of care. It would be incorrect to report a code in category 410 without a fourth and fifth-digit.

      ICD-9-CM Volume 3 procedure codes are composed of codes with either 3 or 4 digits. Codes with two digits are included in ICD-9-CM as the heading of a category of codes that may be further subdivided by the use of third and/or fourth-digits, which provide greater detail.
   4. **Code or codes from 001.0 through V89.09**
      The appropriate code or codes from 001.0 through V89.09 must be used to identify diagnoses, symptoms, conditions, problems, complaints or other reason(s) for the encounter/visit.
   5. **Selection of codes 001.0 through 999.9**
      The selection of codes 001.0 through 999.9 will frequently be used to describe the reason for the admission/encounter. These codes are from the section of ICD-9-CM for the classification of diseases and injuries (e.g., infectious and parasitic diseases; neoplasms; symptoms, signs, and ill-defined conditions, etc.).
   6. **Signs and symptoms**
      Codes that describe symptoms and signs, as opposed to diagnoses, are acceptable for reporting purposes when a related definitive diagnosis has not been established (confirmed) by the provider. Chapter 16 of ICD-9-CM, Symptoms, Signs, and Ill-Defined conditions (codes 780.0 - 799.9) contain many, but not all codes for symptoms.
   7. **Conditions that are an integral part of a disease process**
      Signs and symptoms that are associated routinely with a disease process should not be assigned as additional codes, unless otherwise instructed by the classification.
   8. **Conditions that are not an integral part of a disease process**
      Additional signs and symptoms that may not be associated routinely with a disease process should be coded when present.
   9. **Multiple coding for a single condition**
      In addition to the etiology/manifestation convention that requires two codes to fully describe a single condition that affects multiple body systems, there are other single conditions that also require more than one code. "Use additional code" notes are found in the tabular at codes that are not part of an etiology/manifestation pair where a secondary code is useful to fully describe a condition. The sequencing rule is the same as the etiology/manifestation pair - , "Use additional code" indicates that a secondary code should be added.

      For example, for infections that are not included in chapter 1, a secondary code from category 041, Bacterial infection in conditions classified elsewhere and of unspecified site, may be required to identify the bacterial organism causing the infection. A "Use additional code" note will normally be found at the infectious disease code, indicating a need for the organism code to be added as a secondary code.

      "Code first" notes are also under certain codes that are not specif- ically manifestation codes but may be due to an underlying cause. When a "Code first" note is present and an underlying condition is present the underlying condition should be sequenced first.

      "Code, if applicable, any causal condition first", notes indicate that this code may be assigned as a principal diagnosis when the causal condition is unknown or not applicable. If a causal condition is known, then the code for that condition should be sequenced as the principal or first-listed diagnosis. Multiple codes may be needed for late effects, complication codes and obstetric codes to more fully describe a condition. See the specific guidelines for these conditions for further instruction.

10. Acute and Chronic Conditions

If the same condition is described as both acute (subacute) and chronic, and separate subentries exist in the Alphabetic Index at the same indentation level, code both and sequence the acute (subacute) code first.

11. Combination Code

A combination code is a single code used to classify:
- Two diagnoses, or
- A diagnosis with an associated secondary process (manifestation)
- A diagnosis with an associated complication

Combination codes are identified by referring to subterm entries in the Alphabetic Index and by reading the inclusion and exclusion notes in the Tabular List.

Assign only the combination code when that code fully identifies the diagnostic conditions involved or when the Alphabetic Index so directs. Multiple coding should not be used when the classification provides a combination code that clearly identifies all of the elements documented in the diagnosis. When the combination code lacks necessary specificity in describing the manifestation or complication, an additional code should be used as a secondary code.

12. Late Effects

A late effect is the residual effect (condition produced) after the acute phase of an illness or injury has terminated. There is no time limit on when a late effect code can be used. The residual may be apparent early, such as in cerebrovascular accident cases, or it may occur months or years later, such as that due to a previous injury. Coding of late effects generally requires two codes sequenced in the following order: The condition or nature of the late effect is sequenced first. The late effect code is sequenced second.

An exception to the above guidelines are those instances where the code for late effect is followed by a manifestation code identified in the Tabular List and title, or the late effect code has been expanded (at the fourth and fifth-digit levels) to include the manifestation(s). The code for the acute phase of an illness or injury that led to the late effect is never used with a code for the late effect.

13. Impending or Threatened Condition

Code any condition described at the time of discharge as "impending" or "threatened" as follows:

If it did occur, code as confirmed diagnosis. If it did not occur, reference the Alphabetic Index to determine if the condition has a subentry term for "impending" or "threatened" and also reference main term entries for "Impending" and for "Threatened." If the subterms are listed, assign the given code. If the subterms are not listed, code the existing underlying condition(s) and not the condition described as impending or threatened.

14. Reporting Same Diagnosis Code more than Once

Each unique ICD-9-CM diagnosis code may be reported only once for an encounter. This applies to bilateral conditions or two different conditions classified to the same ICD-9-CM diagnosis code.

15. Admissions/Encounters for Rehabilitation

When the purpose for the admission/encounter is rehabilitation, sequence the appropriate V code from category V57, Care involving use of rehabilitation procedures, as the principal/first-listed diagnosis. The code for the condition for which the service is being performed should be reported as an additional diagnosis.

Only one code from category V57 is required. Code V57.89, Other specified rehabilitation procedures, should be assigned if more than one type of rehabilitation is performed during a single encounter. A procedure code should be reported to identify each type of rehabilitation therapy actually performed.

16. Documentation for BMI and Pressure Ulcer Stages

For the Body Mass Index (BMI) and pressure ulcer stage codes, code assignment may be based on medical record documentation from clinicians who are not the patient's provider (i.e., physician or other qualified healthcare practitioner legally accountable for establishing the patient's diagnosis), since this information is typically documented by other clinicians involved in the care of the patient (e.g., a dietitian often documents the BMI and nurses often documents the pressure ulcer stages). However, the associated diagnosis (such as overweight, obesity, or pressure ulcer) must be documented by the patient's provider. If there is conflicting medical record documentation, either from the same clinician or different clinicians, the patient's attending provider should be queried for clarification.

The BMI and pressure ulcer stage codes should only be reported as secondary diagnoses. As with all other secondary diagnosis codes, the BMI and pressure ulcer stage codes should only be assigned when they meet the definition of a reportable additional diagnosis.
See Section III, Reporting Additional Diagnoses.

C. Chapter-Specific Coding Guidelines

In addition to general coding guidelines, there are guidelines for specific diagnoses and/or conditions in the classification. Unless otherwise indicated, these guidelines apply to all health care settings. Please refer to Section II for guidelines on the selection of principal diagnosis.

1. Chapter 1: Infectious and Parasitic Diseases (001–139)

a. Human Immunodeficiency Virus (HIV) Infections

1) Code only confirmed cases

Code only confirmed cases of HIV infection/illness. This is an exception to the hospital inpatient guideline Section II, H.

In this context, "confirmation" does not require documentation of positive serology or culture for HIV; the provider's diagnostic statement that the patient is HIV positive, or has an HIV-related illness is sufficient.

2) Selection and sequencing of HIV codes

(a) Patient admitted for HIV-related condition

If a patient is admitted for an HIV-related condition, the principal diagnosis should be 042, followed by additional diagnosis codes for all reported HIV-related conditions.

(b) Patient with HIV disease admitted for unrelated condition

If a patient with HIV disease is admitted for an unrelated condition (such as a traumatic injury), the code for the unrelated condition (e.g., the nature of injury code) should be the principal diagnosis. Other diagnoses would be 042 followed by additional diagnosis codes for all reported HIV-related conditions.

(c) Whether the patient is newly diagnosed

Whether the patient is newly diagnosed or has had previous admissions/encounters for HIV conditions is irrelevant to the sequencing decision.

(d) Asymptomatic human immunodeficiency virus

V08 Asymptomatic human immunodeficiency virus [HIV] infection, is to be applied when the patient without any documentation of symptoms is listed as being "HIV positive," "known HIV," "HIV test positive," or similar terminology. Do not use this code if the term "AIDS" is used or if the patient is treated for any HIV-related illness or is described as having any condition(s) resulting from his/her HIV positive status; use 042 in these cases.

(e) Patients with inconclusive HIV serology

Patients with inconclusive HIV serology, but no definitive diagnosis or manifestations of the illness, may be assigned code 795.71, Inconclusive serologic test for Human Immunodeficiency Virus [HIV].

(f) Previously diagnosed HIV-related illness

Patients with any known prior diagnosis of an HIV-related illness should be coded to 042. Once a patient has developed an HIV-related illness, the patient should always be assigned code 042 on every subsequent admission/encounter. Patients previously diagnosed with any HIV illness (042) should never be assigned to 795.71 or V08.

(g) HIV Infection in Pregnancy, Childbirth and the Puerperium

During pregnancy, childbirth or the puerperium, a patient admitted (or presenting for a health care encounter) because of an HIV-related illness should receive a principal diagnosis code of 647.6x, Other specified infectious and parasitic diseases in the mother classifiable elsewhere, but complicating the pregnancy, childbirth or the puerperium, followed by 042 and the code(s) for the HIV-related illness(es). Codes from Chapter 15 always take sequencing priority.

Patients with asymptomatic HIV infection status admitted (or presenting for a health care encounter) during pregnancy, childbirth, or the puerperium should receive codes of 647.6x and V08.

(h) Encounters for testing for HIV

If a patient is being seen to determine his/her HIV status, use code V73.89, Screening for other specified viral disease. Use code V69.8, Other problems related to lifestyle, as a secondary code if an asymptomatic patient is in a known high risk group for HIV. Should a patient with signs or symptoms or illness, or a confirmed HIV related diagnosis be tested for HIV, code the signs and symptoms or the diagnosis. An additional counseling code V65.44 may be used if counseling is provided during the encounter for the test.

When a patient returns to be informed of his/her HIV test results use code V65.44, HIV counseling, if the results of the test are negative.

If the results are positive but the patient is asymptomatic use code V08, Asymptomatic HIV infection. If the results are positive and the patient is symptomatic use code 042, HIV infection, with codes for the HIV related symptoms or diagnosis. The HIV counseling code may also be used if counseling is provided for patients with positive test results.

b. **Septicemia, Systemic Inflammatory Response Syndrome (SIRS), Sepsis, Severe Sepsis, and Septic Shock**

1) **SIRS, Septicemia, and Sepsis**

   (a) The terms *septicemia* and *sepsis* are often used interchangeably by providers, however they are not considered synonymous terms. The following descriptions are provided for reference but do not preclude querying the provider for clarification about terms used in the documentation:

       (i) Septicemia generally refers to a systemic disease associated with the presence of pathological microorganisms or toxins in the blood, which can include bacteria, viruses, fungi or other organisms.

       (ii) Systemic inflammatory response syndrome (SIRS) generally refers to the systemic response to infection, trauma/burns, or other insult (such as cancer) with symptoms including fever, tachycardia, tachypnea, and leukocytosis.

       (iii) Sepsis generally refers to SIRS due to infection.

       (iv) Severe sepsis generally refers to sepsis with associated acute organ dysfunction.

   (b) **The coding of SIRS, sepsis and severe sepsis**
       The coding of SIRS, sepsis and severe sepsis requires a minimum of 2 codes: a code for the underlying cause (such as infection or trauma) and a code from subcategory 995.9 Systemic inflammatory response syndrome (SIRS).

       (i) The code for the underlying cause (such as infection or trauma) must be sequenced before the code from subcategory 995.9 Systemic inflammatory response syndrome (SIRS).

       (ii) Sepsis and severe sepsis require a code for the systemic infection (038.xx, 112.5, etc.) and either code 995.91, Sepsis, or 995.92, Severe sepsis. If the causal organism is not documented, assign code 038.9, Unspecified septicemia.

       (iii) Severe sepsis requires additional code(s) for the associated acute organ dysfunction(s).

       (iv) If a patient has sepsis with multiple organ dysfunctions, follow the instructions for coding severe sepsis.

       (v) Either the term sepsis or SIRS must be documented to assign a code from subcategory 995.9.

       (vi) *See Section I.C.17.g, Injury and poisoning, for information regarding systemic inflammatory response syndrome (SIRS) due to trauma/burns and other non-infectious processes.*

   (c) Due to the complex nature of sepsis and severe sepsis, some cases may require querying the provider prior to assignment of the codes.

2) **Sequencing sepsis and severe sepsis**

   (a) **Sepsis and severe sepsis as principal diagnosis**
       If sepsis or severe sepsis is present on admission, and meets the definition of principal diagnosis, the systemic infection code (e.g., 038.xx, 112.5, etc) should be assigned as the principal diagnosis, followed by code 995.91, Sepsis, or 995.92, Severe sepsis, as required by the sequencing rules in

the Tabular List. Codes from subcategory 995.9 can never be assigned as a principal diagnosis. A code should also be assigned for any localized infection, if present.

If the sepsis or severe sepsis is due to a postprocedural infection, *see Section I.C.10 for guidelines related to sepsis due to postprocedural infection.*

   (b) **Sepsis and severe sepsis as secondary diagnoses**
       When sepsis or severe sepsis develops during the encounter (it was not present on admission), the systemic infection code and code 995.91 or 995.92 should be assigned as secondary diagnoses.

   (c) **Documentation unclear as to whether sepsis or severe sepsis is present on admission**
       Sepsis or severe sepsis may be present on admission but the diagnosis may not be confirmed until sometime after admission. If the documentation is not clear whether the sepsis or severe sepsis was present on admission, the provider should be queried.

3) **Sepsis/SIRS with Localized Infection**
   If the reason for admission is both sepsis, severe sepsis, or SIRS and a localized infection, such as pneumonia or cellulitis, a code for the systemic infection (038.xx, 112.5, etc) should be assigned first, then code 995.91 or 995.92, followed by the code for the localized infection. If the patient is admitted with a localized infection, such as pneumonia, and sepsis/SIRS doesn't develop until after admission, see guideline I.C.1.b.2.b).

   If the localized infection is postprocedural, *see Section I.C.10 for guidelines related to sepsis due to postprocedural infection.*

   Note: The term urosepsis is a nonspecific term. If that is the only term documented then only code 599.0 should be assigned based on the default for the term in the ICD-9-CM index, in addition to the code for the causal organism if known.

4) **Bacterial Sepsis and Septicemia**
   In most cases, it will be a code from category 038, Septicemia, that will be used in conjunction with a code from subcategory 995.9 such as the following:

   (a) **Streptococcal sepsis**
       If the documentation in the record states streptococcal sepsis, codes 038.0, Streptococcal septicemia, and code 995.91 should be used, in that sequence.

   (b) **Streptococcal septicemia**
       If the documentation states streptococcal septicemia, only code 038.0 should be assigned, however, the provider should be queried whether the patient has sepsis, an infection with SIRS.

5) **Acute organ dysfunction that is not clearly associated with the sepsis**
   If a patient has sepsis and an acute organ dysfunction, but the medical record documentation indicates that the acute organ dysfunction is related to a medical condition other than the sepsis, do not assign code 995.92, Severe sepsis. An acute organ dysfunction must be associated with the sepsis in order to assign the severe sepsis code. If the documentation is not clear as to whether an acute organ dysfunction is related to the sepsis or another medical condition, query the provider.

6) **Septic shock**
   (a) **Sequencing of septic shock**
       Septic shock generally refers to circulatory failure associated with severe sepsis, and, therefore, it represents a type of acute organ dysfunction.

       For all cases of septic shock, the code for the systemic infection should be sequenced first, followed by codes 995.92 and 785.52. Any additional codes for other acute organ dysfunctions should also be assigned. As noted in the sequencing instructions in the Tabular List, the code for septic shock cannot be assigned as a principal diagnosis.

   (b) **Septic Shock without documentation of severe sepsis**
       Septic shock indicates the presence of severe sepsis.

       Code 995.92, Severe sepsis, must be assigned with code 785.52, Septic shock, even if the term severe sepsis is not documented in the record. The "Use additional code" note and the "Code first" note in the tabular support this guideline.

7) **Sepsis and septic shock complicating abortion and pregnancy**
Sepsis and septic shock complicating abortion, ectopic pregnancy, and molar pregnancy are classified to category codes in Chapter 11 (630-639).
See section I.C.11.

8) **Negative or inconclusive blood cultures**
Negative or inconclusive blood cultures do not preclude a diagnosis of septicemia or sepsis in patients with clinical evidence of the condition, however, the provider should be queried.

9) **Newborn sepsis**
See Section I.C.15.j for information on the coding of newborn sepsis.

10) **Sepsis due to a postprocedural infection**
(a) **Documentation of causal relationship**
As with all postprocedural complications, code assignment is based on the provider's documentation of the relationship between the infection and the procedure.

(b) **Sepsis due to postprocedural infection**
In cases of postprocedural sepsis, the complication code, such as code 998.59, Other postoperative infection, or 674.3x, Other complications of obstetrical surgical wounds should be coded first followed by the appropriate sepsis codes (systemic infection code and either code 995.91or 995.92). An additional code(s) for any acute organ dysfunction should also be assigned for cases of severe sepsis.

11) **External cause of injury codes with SIRS**
Refer to Section I.C.19.a.7 for instruction on the use of external cause of injury codes with codes for SIRS resulting from trauma.

12) **Sepsis and severe sepsis associated with noninfectious process**
In some cases, a non-infectious process, such as trauma, may lead to an infection which can result in sepsis or severe sepsis. If sepsis or severe sepsis is documented as associated with a non-infectious condition, such as a burn or serious injury, and this condition meets the definition for principal diagnosis, the code for the noninfectious condition should be sequenced first, followed by the code for the systemic infection and either code 995.91, Sepsis, or 995.92, Severe sepsis. Additional codes for any associated acute organ dysfunction(s) should also be assigned for cases of severe sepsis. If the sepsis or severe sepsis meets the definition of principal diagnosis, the systemic infection and sepsis codes should be sequenced before the non-infectious condition. When both the associated non-infectious condition and the sepsis or severe sepsis meet the definition of principal diagnosis, either may be assigned as principal diagnosis.

See Section I.C.1.b.2) (a) for guidelines pertaining to sepsis or severe sepsis as the principal diagnosis.

Only one code from subcategory 995.9 should be assigned. Therefore, when a non-infectious condition leads to an infection resulting in sepsis or severe sepsis, assign either code 995.91 or 995.92. Do not additionally assign code 995.93, Systemic inflammatory response syndrome due to non-infectious process without acute organ dysfunction, or 995.94, Systemic inflammatory response syndrome with acute organ dysfunction.

See Section I.C.17.g for information on the coding of SIRS due to trauma/burns or other non-infectious disease processes.

c. **Methicillin Resistant *Staphylococcus aureus* (MRSA) Conditions**

1) **Selection and sequencing of MRSA codes**
(a) **Combination codes for MRSA infection**
When a patient is diagnosed with an infection that is due to methicillin resistant Staphylococcus aureus (MRSA), and that infection has a combination code that includes the causal organism (e.g., septicemia, pneumonia) assign the appropriate code for the condition (e.g., code 038.12, Methicillin resistant Staphylococcus aureus septicemia or code 482.42, Methicillin resistant pneumonia due to Staphylococcus aureus). Do not assign code 041.12, Methicillin resistant Staphylococcus aureus, as an additional code because the code includes the type of infection

and the MRSA organism. Do not assign a code from subcategory V09.0, Infection with microorganisms resistant to penicillins, as an additional diagnosis.

See Section C.1.b.1 for instructions on coding and sequencing of septicemia.

(b) **Other codes for MRSA infection**
When there is documentation of a current infection (e.g., wound infection, stitch abscess, urinary tract infection) due to MRSA, and that infection does not have a combination code that includes the causal organism, select the appropriate code to identify the condition along with code 041.12, Methicillin resistant Staphylococcus aureus, for the MRSA infection. Do not assign a code from subcategory V09.0, Infection with microorganisms resistant to penicillins.

(c) **Methicillin susceptible *Staphylococcus aureus* (MSSA) and MRSA colonization**
The condition or state of being colonized or carrying MSSA or MRSA is called colonization or carriage, while an individual person is described as being colonized or being a carrier. Colonization means that MSSA or MSRA is present on or in the body without necessarily causing illness. A positive MRSA colonization test might be documented by the provider as "MRSA screen positive" or "MRSA nasal swab positive".

Assign code V02.54, Carrier or suspected carrier, Methicillin resistant Staphylococcus aureus, for patients documented as having MRSA colonization. Assign code V02.53, Carrier or suspected carrier, Methicillin susceptible Staphylococcus aureus, for patient documented as having MSSA colonization. Colonization is not necessarily indicative of a disease process or as the cause of a specific condition the patient may have unless documented as such by the provider.

Code V02.59, Other specified bacterial diseases, should be assigned for other types of staphylococcal colonization (e.g., S. epidermidis, S. saprophyticus). Code V02.59 should not be assigned for colonization with any type of Staphylococcus aureus (MRSA, MSSA).

(d) **MRSA colonization and infection**
If a patient is documented as having both MRSA colonization and infection during a hospital admission, code V02.54, Carrier or suspected carrier, Methicillin resistant Staphylococcus aureus, and a code for the MRSA infection may both be assigned.

2. **Chapter 2: Neoplasms (140-239)**
General guidelines
Chapter 2 of the ICD-9-CM contains the codes for most benign and all malignant neoplasms. Certain benign neoplasms, such as prostatic adenomas, may be found in the specific body system chapters. To properly code a neoplasm it is necessary to determine from the record if the neoplasm is benign, in-situ, malignant, or of uncertain histologic behavior. If malignant, any secondary (metastatic) sites should also be determined.

The neoplasm table in the Alphabetic Index should be referenced first. However, if the histological term is documented, that term should be referenced first, rather than going immediately to the Neoplasm Table, in order to determine which column in the Neoplasm Table is appropriate. For example, if the documentation indicates "adenoma," refer to the term in the Alphabetic Index to review the entries under this term and the instructional note to "see also neoplasm, by site, benign." The table provides the proper code based on the type of neoplasm and the site. It is important to select the proper column in the table that corresponds to the type of neoplasm. The tabular should then be referenced to verify that the correct code has been selected from the table and that a more specific site code does not exist.

See Section I. C. 18.d.4. for information regarding V codes for genetic susceptibility to cancer.

a. **Treatment directed at the malignancy**

If the treatment is directed at the malignancy, designate the malignancy as the principal diagnosis.

The only exception to this guideline is if a patient admission/encounter is solely for the administration of chemotherapy, immunotherapy or radiation therapy, assign the appropriate V58.x code as the first-listed or principal diagnosis, and the diagnosis or problem for which the service is being performed as a secondary diagnosis.

b. **Treatment of secondary site**

When a patient is admitted because of a primary neoplasm with metastasis and treatment is directed toward the secondary site only, the secondary neoplasm is designated as the principal diagnosis even though the primary malignancy is still present.

c. **Coding and sequencing of complications**

Coding and sequencing of complications associated with the malignancies or with the therapy thereof are subject to the following guidelines:

1) **Anemia associated with malignancy**

When admission/encounter is for management of an anemia associated with the malignancy, and the treatment is only for anemia, the appropriate anemia code (such as code 285.22, Anemia in neoplastic disease) is designated as the principal diagnosis and is followed by the appropriate code(s) for the malignancy.

Code 285.22 may also be used as a secondary code if the patient suffers from anemia and is being treated for the malignancy.

2) **Anemia associated with chemotherapy, immunotherapy and radiation therapy**

When the admission/encounter is for management of an anemia associated with chemotherapy, immunotherapy or radiotherapy and the only treatment is for the anemia, the anemia is sequenced first followed by code E933.1. The appropriate neoplasm code should be assigned as an additional code.

3) **Management of dehydration due to the malignancy**

When the admission/encounter is for management of dehydration due to the malignancy or the therapy, or a combination of both, and only the dehydration is being treated (intravenous rehydration), the dehydration is sequenced first, followed by the code(s) for the malignancy.

4) **Treatment of a complication resulting from a surgical procedure**

When the admission/encounter is for treatment of a complication resulting from a surgical procedure, designate the complication as the principal or first-listed diagnosis if treatment is directed at resolving the complication.

d. **Primary malignancy previously excised**

When a primary malignancy has been previously excised or eradicated from its site and there is no further treatment directed to that site and there is no evidence of any existing primary malignancy, a code from category V10, Personal history of malignant neoplasm, should be used to indicate the former site of the malignancy. Any mention of extension, invasion, or metastasis to another site is coded as a secondary malignant neoplasm to that site. The secondary site may be the principal or first-listed with the V10 code used as a secondary code.

e. **Admissions/Encounters involving chemotherapy, immunotherapy and radiation therapy**

1) **Episode of care involves surgical removal of neoplasm**

When an episode of care involves the surgical removal of a neoplasm, primary or secondary site, followed by adjunct chemotherapy or radiation treatment during the same episode of care, the neoplasm code should be assigned as principal or first-listed diagnosis, using codes in the 140-198 series or where appropriate in the 200-203 series.

2) **Patient admission/encounter solely for administration of chemotherapy, immunotherapy and radiation therapy**

If a patient admission/encounter is solely for the administration of chemotherapy, immunotherapy or radiation therapy assign code V58.0, Encounter for radiation therapy, or V58.11, Encounter for antineoplastic chemotherapy, or V58.12, Encounter for antineoplastic immunotherapy as the first-listed or principal diagnosis. If a patient receives more than one of these therapies during the same admission more than one of these codes may be assigned, in any sequence.

The malignancy for which the therapy is being administered should be assigned as a secondary diagnosis.

3) **Patient admitted for radiotherapy/chemotherapy and immunotherapy and develops complications**

When a patient is admitted for the purpose of radiotherapy, immunotherapy or chemotherapy and develops complications such as uncontrolled nausea and vomiting or dehydration, the principal or first-listed diagnosis is V58.0, Encounter for radiotherapy, or V58.11, Encounter for antineoplastic chemotherapy, or V58.12, Encounter for antineoplastic immunotherapy followed by any codes for the complications.

f. **Admission/encounter to determine extent of malignancy**

When the reason for admission/encounter is to determine the extent of the malignancy, or for a procedure such as paracentesis or thoracentesis, the primary malignancy or appropriate metastatic site is designated as the principal or first-listed diagnosis, even though chemotherapy or radiotherapy is administered.

g. **Symptoms, signs, and ill-defined conditions listed in Chapter 16 associated with neoplasms**

Symptoms, signs, and ill-defined conditions listed in Chapter 16 characteristic of, or associated with, an existing primary or secondary site malignancy cannot be used to replace the malignancy as principal or first-listed diagnosis, regardless of the number of admissions or encounters for treatment and care of the neoplasm.

See section I.C.18.d.14, Encounter for prophylactic organ removal.

h. **Admission/encounter for pain control/management**

See Section I.C.6.a.5 for information on coding admission/encounter for pain control/management.

i. **Malignant neoplasm associated with transplanted organ**

A malignant neoplasm of a transplanted organ should be coded as a transplant complication. Assign first the appropriate code from subcategory 996.8, Complications of transplanted organ, followed by code 199.2, Malignant neoplasm associated with transplanted organ. Use an additional code for the specific malignancy.

3. **Chapter 3: Endocrine, Nutritional, and Metabolic Diseases and Immunity Disorders (240-279)**

a. **Diabetes mellitus**

Codes under category 250, Diabetes mellitus, identify complications/manifestations associated with diabetes mellitus. A fifth-digit is required for all category 250 codes to identify the type of diabetes mellitus and whether the diabetes is controlled or uncontrolled.

See I.C.3.a.7 for secondary diabetes

1) **Fifth-digits for category 250:**

The following are the fifth-digits for the codes under category 250:

0   type II or unspecified type, not stated as uncontrolled

1   type I, [juvenile type], not stated as uncontrolled

2   type II or unspecified type, uncontrolled

3   type I, [juvenile type], uncontrolled

The age of a patient is not the sole determining factor, though most type I diabetics develop the condition before reaching puberty. For this reason type I diabetes mellitus is also referred to as juvenile diabetes.

2) **Type of diabetes mellitus not documented**

If the type of diabetes mellitus is not documented in the medical record the default is type II.

3) **Diabetes mellitus and the use of insulin**

All type I diabetics must use insulin to replace what their bodies do not produce. However, the use of insulin does not mean that a patient is a type I diabetic. Some patients with type II diabetes mellitus are unable to control their blood sugar through diet and oral medication alone and do require insulin.

If the documentation in a medical record does not indicate the type of diabetes but does indicate that the patient uses insulin, the appropriate fifth-digit for type II must be used. For type II patients who routinely use insulin, code V58.67, Long-term (current) use of insulin, should also be assigned to indicate that the patient uses insulin. Code V58.67 should not be assigned if insulin is given temporarily to bring a type II patient's blood sugar under control during an encounter.

4) **Assigning and sequencing diabetes codes and associated conditions**

When assigning codes for diabetes and its associated conditions, the code(s) from category 250 must be sequenced before the codes for the associated conditions. The diabetes codes and the secondary codes that correspond to them are paired codes that follow the etiology/manifestation convention of the classification (*See Section I.A.6., Etiology/manifestation convention*). Assign as many codes from category 250 as needed to identify all of the associated conditions that the patient has. The corresponding secondary codes are listed under each of the diabetes codes.

(a) Diabetic retinopathy/diabetic macular edema

Diabetic macular edema, code 362.07, is only present with diabetic retinopathy. Another code from subcategory 362.0, Diabetic retinopathy, must be used with code 362.07. Codes under subcategory 362.0 are diabetes manifestation codes, so they must be used following the appropriate diabetes code.

5) Diabetes mellitus in pregnancy and gestational diabetes

(a) For diabetes mellitus complicating pregnancy, *see Section I.C.11.f, Diabetes mellitus in pregnancy.*

(b) For gestational diabetes, *see Section I.C.11, g., Gestational diabetes.*

6) Insulin pump malfunction

(a) Underdose of insulin due insulin pump failure

An underdose of insulin due to an insulin pump failure should be assigned 996.57, Mechanical complication due to insulin pump, as the principal or first listed code, followed by the appropriate diabetes mellitus code based on documentation.

(b) Overdose of insulin due to insulin pump failure

The principal or first listed code for an encounter due to an insulin pump malfunction resulting in an overdose of insulin, should also be 996.57, Mechanical complication due to insulin pump, followed by code 962.3, Poisoning by insulins and antidiabetic agents, and the appropriate diabetes mellitus code based on documentation.

7) Secondary Diabetes Mellitus

Codes under category 249, Secondary diabetes mellitus, identify complications/manifestations associated with secondary diabetes mellitus. Secondary diabetes is always caused by another condition or event (e.g., cystic fibrosis, malignant neoplasm of pancreas, pancreatectomy, adverse effect of drug, or poisoning).

(a) Fifth-digits for category 249:

A fifth-digit is required for all category 249 codes to identify whether the diabetes is controlled or uncontrolled.

(b) Secondary diabetes mellitus and the use of insulin

For patients who routinely use insulin, code V58.67, Long-term (current) use of insulin, should also be assigned. Code V58.67 should not be assigned if insulin is given temporarily to bring a patient's blood sugar under control during an encounter.

(c) Assigning and sequencing secondary diabetes codes and associated conditions

When assigning codes for secondary diabetes and its associated conditions (e.g. renal manifestations), the code(s) from category 249 must be sequenced before the codes for the associated conditions. The secondary diabetes codes and the diabetic manifestation codes that correspond to them are paired codes that follow the etiology/manifestation convention of the classification. Assign as many codes from category 249 as needed to identify all of the associated conditions that the patient has. The corresponding codes for the associated conditions are listed under each of the secondary diabetes codes. For example, secondary diabetes with diabetic nephrosis is assigned to code 249.40, followed by 581.81.

(d) Assigning and sequencing secondary diabetes codes and its causes

The sequencing of the secondary diabetes codes in relationship to codes for the cause of the diabetes is based on the reason for the encounter, applicable ICD-9-CM sequencing conventions, and chapter-specific guidelines.

If a patient is seen for treatment of the secondary diabetes or one of its associated conditions, a code from category 249 is sequenced as the principal or first-listed diagnosis, with the cause of the secondary diabetes (e.g. cystic fibrosis) sequenced as an additional diagnosis.

If, however, the patient is seen for the treatment of the condition causing the secondary diabetes (e.g. malignant neoplasm of pancreas), the code for the cause of the secondary diabetes should be sequenced as the principal or first-listed diagnosis followed by a code from category 249.

(i) Secondary diabetes mellitus due to pancreatectomy

For postpancreatectomy diabetes mellitus (lack of insulin due to the surgical removal of all or part of the pancreas), assign code 251.3, Postsurgical hypoinsulinemia. A code from subcategory 249 should not be assigned for secondary diabetes mellitus due to pancreatectomy. Code also any diabetic manifestations (e.g. diabetic nephrosis 581.81).

(ii) Secondary diabetes due to drugs

Secondary diabetes may be caused by an adverse effect of correctly administered medications, poisoning or late effect of poisoning.

See Section I.C.17.e for coding of adverse effects and poisoning, and section I.C.19 for E code reporting.

4. Chapter 4: Diseases of Blood and Blood Forming Organs (280-289)

a. Anemia of chronic disease

Subcategory 285.2, Anemia in chronic illness, has codes for anemia in chronic kidney disease, code 285.21; anemia in neoplastic disease, code 285.22; and anemia in other chronic illness, code 285.29. These codes can be used as the principal/first listed code if the reason for the encounter is to treat the anemia. They may also be used as secondary codes if treatment of the anemia is a component of an encounter, but not the primary reason for the encounter. When using a code from subcategory 285 it is also necessary to use the code for the chronic condition causing the anemia.

1) Anemia in chronic kidney disease

When assigning code 285.21, Anemia in chronic kidney disease, it is also necessary to assign a code from category 585, Chronic kidney disease, to indicate the stage of chronic kidney disease. *See I.C.10.a. Chronic kidney disease (CKD).*

2) Anemia in neoplastic disease

When assigning code 285.22, Anemia in neoplastic disease, it is also necessary to assign the neoplasm code that is responsible for the anemia. Code 285.22 is for use for anemia that is due to the malignancy, not for anemia due to antineoplastic chemotherapy drugs, which is an adverse effect. *See Section I.C.2.c.1 Anemia associated with malignancy. See Section I.C.2.c.2 Anemia associated with chemotherapy, immunotherapy and radiation therapy. See Section I.C.17.e.1. Adverse effects.*

5. Chapter 5: Mental Disorders (290-319)

Reserved for future guideline expansion

6. Chapter 6: Diseases of Nervous System and Sense Organs (320-389)

a. Pain - Category 338

1) General coding information

Codes in category 338 may be used in conjunction with codes from other categories and chapters to provide more detail about acute or chronic pain and neoplasm- related pain, unless otherwise indicated below.

If the pain is not specified as acute or chronic, do not assign codes from category 338, except for post-thoracotomy pain, postoperative pain, neoplasm related pain, or central pain syndrome.

A code from subcategories 338.1 and 338.2 should not be assigned if the underlying (definitive) diagnosis is known, unless the reason for the encounter is pain control/ management and not management of the underlying condition.

(a) Category 338 codes as principal or first-listed diagnosis

Category 338 codes are acceptable as principal diagnosis or the first-listed code:

- When pain control or pain management is the reason for the admission/encounter (e.g., a patient with displaced intervertebral disc, nerve impingement and severe back pain presents for injection of steroid into the spinal canal). The underlying cause of the pain should be reported as an additional diagnosis, if known.

- When an admission or encounter is for a procedure aimed at treating the underlying condition (e.g., spinal fusion, kyphoplasty), a code for the underlying condition (e.g., vertebral fracture, spinal stenosis) should be assigned as the principal diagnosis. No code from category 338 should be assigned.

- When a patient is admitted for the insertion of a neurostimulator for pain control, assign the appropriate pain code as the principal or first listed diagnosis. When an admission or encounter is for a procedure aimed at treating the underlying condition and a neurostimulator is inserted for pain control during the same admission/encounter, a code for the underlying condition should be assigned as the principal diagnosis and the appropriate pain code should be assigned as a secondary diagnosis.

(b) **Use of category 338 codes in conjunction with site specific pain codes**

   (i) **Assigning category 338 codes and site-specific pain codes**

   Codes from category 338 may be used in conjunction with codes that identify the site of pain (including codes from chapter 16) if the category 338 code provides additional information. For example, if the code describes the site of the pain, but does not fully describe whether the pain is acute or chronic, then both codes should be assigned.

   (ii) **Sequencing of category 338 codes with site-specific pain codes**

   The sequencing of category 338 codes with site-specific pain codes (including chapter 16 codes), is dependent on the circumstances of the encounter/admission as follows:

   - If the encounter is for pain control or pain management, assign the code from category 338 followed by the code identifying the specific site of pain (e.g., encounter for pain management for acute neck pain from trauma is assigned code 338.11, Acute pain due to trauma, followed by code 723.1, Cervicalgia, to identify the site of pain).

   - If the encounter is for any other reason except pain control or pain management, and a related definitive diagnosis has not been established (confirmed) by the provider, assign the code for the specific site of pain first, followed by the appropriate code from category 338.

2) **Pain due to devices, implants and grafts**

   Pain associated with devices, implants or grafts left in a surgical site (for example painful hip prosthesis) is assigned to the appropriate code(s) found in Chapter 17, Injury and Poisoning. Use additional code(s) from category 338 to identify acute or chronic pain due to presence of the device, implant or graft (338.18- 338.19 or 338.28-338.29).

3) **Postoperative pain**

   Post-thoracotomy pain and other postoperative pain are classified to subcategories 338.1 and 338.2, depending on whether the pain is acute or chronic. The default for post-thoracotomy and other postoperative pain not specified as acute or chronic is the code for the acute form.

   Routine or expected postoperative pain immediately after surgery should not be coded.

   (a) **Postoperative pain not associated with specific postoperative complication**

   Postoperative pain not associated with a specific postoperative complication is assigned to the appropriate postoperative pain code in category 338.

   (b) **Postoperative pain associated with specific postoperative complication**

   Postoperative pain associated with a specific postoperative complication (such as painful wire sutures) is assigned to the appropriate code(s) found in Chapter 17, Injury and Poisoning. If appropriate, use additional code(s) from category 338 to identify acute or chronic pain (338.18 or 338.28). If pain control/management is the reason for the encounter, a code from category 338 should be assigned as the principal or first-listed diagnosis in accordance with *Section I.C.6.a.1.a above.*

   (c) **Postoperative pain as principal or first-listed diagnosis**

   Postoperative pain may be reported as the principal or first-listed diagnosis when the stated reason for the admission/encounter is documented as postoperative pain control/management.

   (d) **Postoperative pain as secondary diagnosis**

   Postoperative pain may be reported as a secondary diagnosis code when a patient presents for outpatient surgery and develops an unusual or inordinate amount of postoperative pain.

   The provider's documentation should be used to guide the coding of postoperative pain, as well as *Section III. Reporting Additional Diagnoses* and *Section IV. Diagnostic Coding and Reporting in the Outpatient Setting.*

   See Section II.I.2 for information on sequencing of diagnoses for patients admitted to hospital inpatient care following post-operative observation.

   See Section II.J for information on sequencing of diagnoses for patients admitted to hospital inpatient care from outpatient surgery.

   See Section IV.A.2 for information on sequencing of diagnoses for patients admitted for observation.

4) **Chronic pain**

   Chronic pain is classified to subcategory 338.2. There is no time frame defining when pain becomes chronic pain. The provider's documentation should be used to guide use of these codes.

5) **Neoplasm related pain**

   Code 338.3 is assigned to pain documented as being related, associated or due to cancer, primary or secondary malignancy, or tumor. This code is assigned regardless of whether the pain is acute or chronic.

   This code may be assigned as the principal or first-listed code when the stated reason for the admission/encounter is documented as pain control/pain management. The underlying neoplasm should be reported as an additional diagnosis.

   When the reason for the admission/encounter is management of the neoplasm and the pain associated with the neoplasm is also documented, code 338.3 may be assigned as an additional diagnosis.

   See Section I.C.2 for instructions on the sequencing of neoplasms for all other stated reasons for the admission/encounter (except for pain control/pain management).

6) **Chronic pain syndrome**

   This condition is different than the term "chronic pain," and therefore this code should only be used when the provider has specifically documented this condition.

7. **Chapter 7: Diseases of Circulatory System (390-459)**

   a. **Hypertension**

   Hypertension Table

   The Hypertension Table, found under the main term, "Hypertension," in the Alphabetic Index, contains a complete listing of all conditions due to or associated with hypertension and classifies them according to malignant, benign, and unspecified.

   1) **Hypertension, essential, or NOS**

   Assign hypertension (arterial) (essential) (primary) (systemic) (NOS) to category code 401 with the appropriate fourth-digit to indicate malignant (.0), benign (.1), or unspecified (.9). Do not use either .0 malignant or .1 benign unless medical record documentation supports such a designation.

   2) **Hypertension with heart disease**

   Heart conditions (425.8, 429.0-429.3, 429.8, 429.9) are assigned to a code from category 402 when a causal relationship is stated (due to hypertension) or implied (hypertensive). Use an additional code from category 428 to identify the type of heart failure in those patients with heart failure. More than one code from category 428 may be assigned if the patient has systolic or diastolic failure and congestive heart failure.

   The same heart conditions (425.8, 429.0-429.3, 429.8, 429.9) with hypertension, but without a stated causal relationship, are coded separately. Sequence according to the circumstances of the admission/encounter.

   3) **Hypertensive chronic kidney disease**

   Assign codes from category 403, Hypertensive chronic kidney disease, when conditions classified to categories 585-587 are present. Unlike hypertension with heart disease, ICD-9-CM presumes a cause-and-effect relationship and classifies chronic kidney disease (CKD) with hypertension as hypertensive chronic kidney disease.

Fifth-digits for category 403 should be assigned as follows:

- 0 with CKD stage I through stage IV, or unspecified.
- 1 with CKD stage V or end stage renal disease.

The appropriate code from category 585, Chronic kidney disease, should be used as a secondary code with a code from category 403 to identify the stage of chronic kidney disease.

See Section I.C.10.a for information on the coding of chronic kidney disease.

4) **Hypertensive heart and chronic kidney disease**
Assign codes from combination category 404, Hypertensive heart and chronic kidney disease, when both hypertensive kidney disease and hypertensive heart disease are stated in the diagnosis. Assume a relationship between the hypertension and the chronic kidney disease, whether or not the condition is so designated. Assign an additional code from category 428, to identify the type of heart failure. More than one code from category 428 may be assigned if the patient has systolic or diastolic failure and congestive heart failure.

Fifth-digits for category 404 should be assigned as follows:

- 0 without heart failure and with chronic kidney disease (CKD) stage I through stage IV, or unspecified
- 1 with heart failure and with CKD stage I through stage IV, or unspecified
- 2 without heart failure and with CKD stage V or end stage renal disease
- 3 with heart failure and with CKD stage V or end stage renal disease

The appropriate code from category 585, Chronic kidney disease, should be used as a secondary code with a code from category 404 to identify the stage of kidney disease.

See Section I.C.10.a for information on the coding of chronic kidney disease.

5) **Hypertensive cerebrovascular disease**
First assign codes from 430-438, Cerebrovascular disease, then the appropriate hypertension code from categories 401-405.

6) **Hypertensive retinopathy**
Two codes are necessary to identify the condition. First assign the code from subcategory 362.11, Hypertensive retinopathy, then the appropriate code from categories 401-405 to indicate the type of hypertension.

7) **Hypertension, secondary**
Two codes are required: one to identify the underlying etiology and one from category 405 to identify the hypertension. Sequencing of codes is determined by the reason for admission/encounter.

8) **Hypertension, transient**
Assign code 796.2, Elevated blood pressure reading without diagnosis of hypertension, unless patient has an established diagnosis of hypertension. Assign code 642.3x for transient hypertension of pregnancy.

9) **Hypertension, controlled**
Assign appropriate code from categories 401-405. This diagnostic statement usually refers to an existing state of hypertension under control by therapy.

10) **Hypertension, uncontrolled**
Uncontrolled hypertension may refer to untreated hypertension or hypertension not responding to current therapeutic regimen. In either case, assign the appropriate code from categories 401-405 to designate the stage and type of hypertension. Code to the type of hypertension.

11) **Elevated blood pressure**
For a statement of elevated blood pressure without further specificity, assign code 796.2, Elevated blood pressure reading without diagnosis of hypertension, rather than a code from category 401.

b. **Cerebral infarction/stroke/cerebrovascular accident (CVA)**
The terms stroke and CVA are often used interchangeably to refer to a cerebral infarction. The terms stroke, CVA, and cerebral infarction NOS are all indexed to the default code 434.91, Cerebral artery occlusion,

unspecified, with infarction. Code 436, Acute, but ill-defined, cerebrovascular disease, should not be used when the documentation states stroke or CVA.

See Section I.C.18.d.3 for information on coding status post administration of tPA in a different facility within the last 24 hours.

c. **Postoperative cerebrovascular accident**
A cerebrovascular hemorrhage or infarction that occurs as a result of medical intervention is coded to 997.02, Iatrogenic cerebrovascular infarction or hemorrhage. Medical record documentation should clearly specify the cause- and-effect relationship between the medical intervention and the cerebrovascular accident in order to assign this code. A secondary code from the code range 430-432 or from a code from subcategories 433 or 434 with a fifth-digit of "1" should also be used to identify the type of hemorrhage or infarct.

This guideline conforms to the use additional code note instruction at category 997. Code 436, Acute, but ill-defined, cerebrovascular disease, should not be used as a secondary code with code 997.02.

d. **Late Effects of cerebrovascular disease**
1) **Category 438, late effects of cerebrovascular disease**
Category 438 is used to indicate conditions classifiable to categories 430-437 as the causes of late effects (neurologic deficits), themselves classified elsewhere. These "late effects" include neurologic deficits that persist after initial onset of conditions classifiable to 430-437. The neurologic deficits caused by cerebrovascular disease may be present from the onset or may arise at any time after the onset of the condition classifiable to 430-437.

2) **Codes from category 438 with codes from 430-437**
Codes from category 438 may be assigned on a health care record with codes from 430-437, if the patient has a current cerebrovascular accident (CVA) and deficits from an old CVA.

3) **Code V12.54**
Assign code V12.54, Transient ischemic attack (TIA), and cerebral infarction without residual deficits (and not a code from category 438) as an additional code for history of cerebrovascular disease when no neurologic deficits are present.

e. **Acute myocardial infarction (AMI)**
1) **ST elevation myocardial infarction (STEMI) and non ST elevation myocardial infarction (NSTEMI)**
The ICD-9-CM codes for acute myocardial infarction (AMI) identify the site, such as anterolateral wall or true posterior wall. Subcategories 410.0-410.6 and 410.8 are used for ST elevation myocardial infarction (STEMI). Subcategory 410.7, Subendocardial infarction, is used for non ST elevation myocardial infarction (NSTEMI) and nontransmural MIs.

2) **Acute myocardial infarction, unspecified**
Subcategory 410.9 is the default for the unspecified term acute myocardial infarction. If only STEMI or transmural MI without the site is documented, query the provider as to the site, or assign a code from subcategory 410.9.

3) **AMI documented as nontransmural or subendocardial but site provided**
If an AMI is documented as nontransmural or subendocardial, but the site is provided, it is still coded as a subendocardial AMI. If NSTEMI evolves to STEMI, assign the STEMI code. If STEMI converts to NSTEMI due to thrombolytic therapy, it is still coded as STEMI.

See Section I.C.18.d.3 for information on coding status post administration of tPA in a different facility within the last 24 hours.

8. **Chapter 8: Diseases of Respiratory System (460-519)**
See I.C.17.f. for ventilator-associated pneumonia.
a. **Chronic obstructive pulmonary disease [COPD] and asthma**
1) **Conditions that comprise COPD and asthma**
The conditions that comprise COPD are obstructive chronic bronchitis, subcategory 491.2, and emphysema, category 492. All asthma codes are under category 493, Asthma. Code 496, Chronic airway obstruction, not elsewhere classified, is a nonspecific code that should only be used when the documentation in a medical record does not specify the type of COPD being treated.

2) **Acute exacerbation of chronic obstructive bronchitis and asthma**
The codes for chronic obstructive bronchitis and asthma distinguish between uncomplicated cases and those in acute exacerbation. An acute exacerbation is a worsening or a decompensation of a chronic condition. An acute exacerbation is

not equivalent to an infection superimposed on a chronic condition, though an exacerbation may be triggered by an infection.

3) Overlapping nature of the conditions that comprise COPD and asthma

Due to the overlapping nature of the conditions that make up COPD and asthma, there are many variations in the way these conditions are documented. Code selection must be based on the terms as documented. When selecting the correct code for the documented type of COPD and asthma, it is essential to first review the index, and then verify the code in the tabular list. There are many instructional notes under the different COPD subcategories and codes. It is important that all such notes be reviewed to assure correct code assignment.

4) Acute exacerbation of asthma and status asthmaticus

An acute exacerbation of asthma is an increased severity of the asthma symptoms, such as wheezing and shortness of breath. Status asthmaticus refers to a patient's failure to respond to therapy administered during an asthmatic episode and is a life threatening complication that requires emergency care. If status asthmaticus is documented by the provider with any type of COPD or with acute bronchitis, the status asthmaticus should be sequenced first. It supersedes any type of COPD including that with acute exacerbation or acute bronchitis. It is inappropriate to assign an asthma code with 5th digit 2, with acute exacerbation, together with an asthma code with 5th digit 1, with status asthmatics. Only the 5th digit 1 should be assigned.

b. Chronic obstructive pulmonary disease [COPD] and bronchitis

1) Acute bronchitis with COPD

Acute bronchitis, code 466.0, is due to an infectious organism. When acute bronchitis is documented with COPD, code 491.22, Obstructive chronic bronchitis with acute bronchitis, should be assigned. It is not necessary to also assign code 466.0. If a medical record documents acute bronchitis with COPD with acute exacerbation, only code 491.22 should be assigned. The acute bronchitis included in code 491.22 supersedes the acute exacerbation. If a medical record documents COPD with acute exacerbation without mention of acute bronchitis, only code 491.21 should be assigned.

c. Acute Respiratory Failure

1) Acute respiratory failure as principal diagnosis

Code 518.81, Acute respiratory failure, may be assigned as a principal diagnosis when it is the condition established after study to be chiefly responsible for occasioning the admission to the hospital, and the selection is supported by the Alphabetic Index and Tabular List. However, chapter-specific coding guidelines (such as obstetrics, poisoning, HIV, newborn) that provide sequencing direction take precedence.

2) Acute respiratory failure as secondary diagnosis

Respiratory failure may be listed as a secondary diagnosis if it occurs after admission, or if it is present on admission, but does not meet the definition of principal diagnosis.

3) Sequencing of acute respiratory failure and another acute condition

When a patient is admitted with respiratory failure and another acute condition, (e.g., myocardial infarction, cerebrovascular accident, aspiration pneumonia), the principal diagnosis will not be the same in every situation. This applies whether the other acute condition is a respiratory or nonrespiratory condition. Selection of the principal diagnosis will be dependent on the circumstances of admission. If both the respiratory failure and the other acute condition are equally responsible for occasioning the admission to the hospital, and there are no chapter-specific sequencing rules, the guideline regarding two or more diagnoses that equally meet the definition for principal diagnosis (Section II, C.) may be applied in these situations.

If the documentation is not clear as to whether acute respiratory failure and another condition are equally responsible for occasioning the admission, query the provider for clarification.

d. Influenza due to identified avian influenza virus (avian influenza)

Code only confirmed cases of avian influenza. This is an exception to the hospital inpatient guideline Section II, H. (Uncertain Diagnosis).

In this context, "confirmation" does not require documentation of positive laboratory testing specific for avian influenza. However, coding should be based on the provider's diagnostic statement that the patient has avian influenza.

If the provider records "suspected or possible or probable avian influenza," the appropriate influenza code from category 487 should be assigned. Code 488, Influenza due to identified avian influenza virus, should not be assigned.

9. Chapter 9: Diseases of Digestive System (520-579)

Reserved for future guideline expansion

10. Chapter 10: Diseases of Genitourinary System (580-629)

a. Chronic kidney disease

1) Stages of chronic kidney disease (CKD)

The ICD-9-CM classifies CKD based on severity. The severity of CKD is designated by stages I-V. Stage II, code 585.2, equates to mild CKD; stage III, code 585.3, equates to moderate CKD; and stage IV, code 585.4, equates to severe CKD. Code 585.6, End stage renal disease (ESRD), is assigned when the provider has documented end-stage-renal disease (ESRD).

If both a stage of CKD and ESRD are documented, assign code 585.6 only.

2) Chronic kidney disease and kidney transplant status

Patients who have undergone kidney transplant may still have some form of CKD, because the kidney transplant may not fully restore kidney function. Therefore, the presence of CKD alone does not constitute a transplant complication. Assign the appropriate 585 code for the patient's stage of CKD and code V42.0. If a transplant complication such as failure or rejection is documented, see section I.C.17.f.1.b for information on coding complications of a kidney transplant. If the documentation is unclear as to whether the patient has a complication of the transplant, query the provider.

3) Chronic kidney disease with other conditions

Patients with CKD may also suffer from other serious conditions, most commonly diabetes mellitus and hypertension. The sequencing of the CKD code in relationship to codes for other contributing conditions is based on the conventions in the tabular list.

See Section I.C.3.a.4 for sequencing instructions for diabetes.
See Section I.C.4.a.1 for anemia in CKD.
See Section I.C.7.a.3 for hypertensive chronic kidney disease.
See Section I.C.17.f.1.b, Kidney transplant complications, for instructions on coding of documented rejection or failure.

11. Chapter 11: Complications of Pregnancy, Childbirth, and the Puerperium (630-679)

a. General Rules for Obstetric Cases

1) Codes from chapter 11 and sequencing priority

Obstetric cases require codes from chapter 11, codes in the range 630-679, Complications of Pregnancy, Childbirth, and the Puerperium. Chapter 11 codes have sequencing priority over codes from other chapters. Additional codes from other chapters may be used in conjunction with chapter 11 codes to further specify conditions. Should the provider document that the pregnancy is incidental to the encounter, then code V22.2 should be used in place of any chapter 11 codes. It is the provider's responsibility to state that the condition being treated is not affecting the pregnancy.

2) Chapter 11 codes used only on the maternal record

Chapter 11 codes are to be used only on the maternal record, never on the record of the newborn.

3) Chapter 11 fifth-digits

Categories 640-648, 651-676 have required fifth-digits, which indicate whether the encounter is antepartum, postpartum and whether a delivery has also occurred.

4) Fifth-digits, appropriate for each code

The fifth-digits, which are appropriate for each code number, are listed in brackets under each code. The fifth-digits on each code should all be consistent with each other. That is, should a delivery occur all of the fifth-digits should indicate the delivery.

b. Selection of OB Principal or First-listed Diagnosis

1) Routine outpatient prenatal visits

For routine outpatient prenatal visits when no complications are present codes V22.0, Supervision of normal first pregnancy, and

V22.1, Supervision of other normal pregnancy, should be used as the first-listed diagnoses. These codes should not be used in conjunction with chapter 11 codes.

2) Prenatal outpatient visits for high-risk patients

For prenatal outpatient visits for patients with high-risk pregnancies, a code from category V23, Supervision of high-risk pregnancy, should be used as the first-listed diagnosis. Secondary Chapter 11 codes may be used in conjunction with these codes if appropriate.

3) Episodes when no delivery occurs

In episodes when no delivery occurs, the principal diagnosis should correspond to the principal complication of the pregnancy, which necessitated the encounter. Should more than one complication exist, all of which are treated or monitored, any of the complications codes may be sequenced first.

4) When a delivery occurs

When a delivery occurs, the principal diagnosis should correspond to the main circumstances or complication of the delivery. In cases of cesarean delivery, the selection of the principal diagnosis should correspond to the reason the cesarean delivery was performed unless the reason for admission/encounter was unrelated to the condition resulting in the cesarean delivery.

5) Outcome of delivery

An outcome of delivery code, V27.0-V27.9, should be included on every maternal record when a delivery has occurred. These codes are not to be used on subsequent records or on the newborn record.

c. Fetal conditions affecting the management of the mother

1) Codes from category 655

Known or suspected fetal abnormality affecting management of the mother, and category 656, Other fetal and placental problems affecting the management of the mother, are assigned only when the fetal condition is actually responsible for modifying the management of the mother, i.e., by requiring diagnostic studies, additional observation, special care, or termination of pregnancy. The fact that the fetal condition exists does not justify assigning a code from this series to the mother's record.

See I.C.18.d. for suspected maternal and fetal conditions not found

2) In utero surgery

In cases when surgery is performed on the fetus, a diagnosis code from category 655, Known or suspected fetal abnormalities affecting management of the mother, should be assigned identifying the fetal condition. Procedure code 75.36, Correction of fetal defect, should be assigned on the hospital inpatient record.

No code from Chapter 15, the perinatal codes, should be used on the mother's record to identify fetal conditions. Surgery performed in utero on a fetus is still to be coded as an obstetric encounter.

d. HIV infection in pregnancy, childbirth and the puerperium

During pregnancy, childbirth or the puerperium, a patient admitted because of an HIV-related illness should receive a principal diagnosis of 647.6x, Other specified infectious and parasitic diseases in the mother classifiable elsewhere, but complicating the pregnancy, childbirth or the puerperium, followed by 042 and the code(s) for the HIV-related illness(es).

Patients with asymptomatic HIV infection status admitted during pregnancy, childbirth, or the puerperium should receive codes of 647.6x and V08.

e. Current conditions complicating pregnancy

Assign a code from subcategory 648.x for patients that have current conditions when the condition affects the management of the pregnancy, childbirth, or the puerperium. Use additional secondary codes from other chapters to identify the conditions, as appropriate.

f. Diabetes mellitus in pregnancy

Diabetes mellitus is a significant complicating factor in pregnancy. Pregnant women who are diabetic should be assigned code 648.0x, Diabetes mellitus complicating pregnancy, and a secondary code from category 250, Diabetes mellitus, or category 249, Secondary diabetes to identify the type of diabetes.

Code V58.67, Long-term (current) use of insulin, should also be assigned if the diabetes mellitus is being treated with insulin.

g. Gestational diabetes

Gestational diabetes can occur during the second and third trimester of pregnancy in women who were not diabetic prior to pregnancy.

Gestational diabetes can cause complications in the pregnancy similar to those of pre-existing diabetes mellitus. It also puts the woman at greater risk of developing diabetes after the pregnancy. Gestational diabetes is coded to 648.8x, Abnormal glucose tolerance. Codes 648.0x and 648.8x should never be used together on the same record. Code V58.67, Long-term (current) use of insulin, should also be assigned if the gestational diabetes is being treated with insulin.

h. Normal delivery, Code 650

1) Normal delivery

Code 650 is for use in cases when a woman is admitted for a full-term normal delivery and delivers a single, healthy infant without any complications antepartum, during the delivery, or postpartum during the delivery episode. Code 650 is always a principal diagnosis. It is not to be used if any other code from chapter 11 is needed to describe a current complication of the antenatal, delivery, or perinatal period. Additional codes from other chapters may be used with code 650 if they are not related to or are in any way complicating the pregnancy.

2) Normal delivery with resolved antepartum complication

Code 650 may be used if the patient had a complication at some point during her pregnancy, but the complication is not present at the time of the admission for delivery.

3) V27.0, Single liveborn, outcome of delivery

V27.0, Single liveborn, is the only outcome of delivery code appropriate for use with 650.

i. The postpartum and peripartum periods

1) Postpartum and peripartum periods

The postpartum period begins immediately after delivery and continues for six weeks following delivery. The peripartum period is defined as the last month of pregnancy to five months postpartum.

2) Postpartum complication

A postpartum complication is any complication occurring within the six-week period.

3) Pregnancy-related complications after 6 week period

Chapter 11 codes may also be used to describe pregnancy-related complications after the six-week period should the provider document that a condition is pregnancy related.

4) Postpartum complications occurring during the same admission as delivery

Postpartum complications that occur during the same admission as the delivery are identified with a fifth-digit of "2." Subsequent admissions/encounters for postpartum complications should be identified with a fifth-digit of "4."

5) Admission for routine postpartum care following delivery outside hospital

When the mother delivers outside the hospital prior to admission and is admitted for routine postpartum care and no complications are noted, code V24.0, Postpartum care and examination immediately after delivery, should be assigned as the principal diagnosis.

6) Admission following delivery outside hospital with postpartum conditions

A delivery diagnosis code should not be used for a woman who has delivered prior to admission to the hospital. Any postpartum conditions and/or postpartum procedures should be coded.

j. Code 677, Late effect of complication of pregnancy

1) Code 677

Code 677, Late effect of complication of pregnancy, childbirth, and the puerperium is for use in those cases when an initial complication of a pregnancy develops a sequelae requiring care or treatment at a future date.

2) After the initial postpartum period

This code may be used at any time after the initial postpartum period.

3) Sequencing of Code 677

This code, like all late effect codes, is to be sequenced following the code describing the sequelae of the complication.

k. Abortions

1) Fifth-digits required for abortion categories

Fifth-digits are required for abortion categories 634-637.

Fifth-digit 1, incomplete, indicates that all of the products of conception have not been expelled from the uterus. fifth-digit 2, complete, indicates that all products of conception have been expelled from the uterus prior to the episode of care.

2) **Code from categories 640-648 and 651-659**
A code from categories 640-648 and 651-659 may be used as additional codes with an abortion code to indicate the complication leading to the abortion.

Fifth-digit 3 is assigned with codes from these categories when used with an abortion code because the other fifth-digits will not apply. Codes from the 660-669 series are not to be used for complications of abortion.

3) **Code 639 for complications**
Code 639 is to be used for all complications following abortion. Code 639 cannot be assigned with codes from categories 634-638.

4) **Abortion with liveborn fetus**
When an attempted termination of pregnancy results in a liveborn fetus assign code 644.21, Early onset of delivery, with an appropriate code from category V27, Outcome of Delivery. The procedure code for the attempted termination of pregnancy should also be assigned.

5) **Retained products of conception following an abortion**
Subsequent admissions for retained products of conception following a spontaneous or legally induced abortion are assigned the appropriate code from category 634, Spontaneous abortion, or 635 Legally induced abortion, with a fifth-digit of "1" (incomplete). This advice is appropriate even when the patient was discharged previously with a discharge diagnosis of complete abortion.

12. **Chapter 12: Diseases of Skin and Subcutaneous Tissue (680-709)**
a. **Pressure ulcer stage codes**
1) **Pressure ulcer stages**
Two codes are needed to completely describe a pressure ulcer: A code from subcategory 707.0, Pressure ulcer, to identify the site of the pressure ulcer and a code from subcategory 707.2, Pressure ulcer stages.

The codes in subcategory 707.2, Pressure ulcer stages, are to be used as an additional diagnosis with a code(s) from subcategory 707.0, Pressure Ulcer. Codes from 707.2, Pressure ulcer stages, may not be assigned as a principal or first-listed diagnosis. The pressure ulcer stage codes should only be used with pressure ulcers and not with other types of ulcers (e.g., stasis ulcer).

The ICD-9-CM classifies pressure ulcer stages based on severity, which is designated by stages I-IV and unstageable.

2) **Unstageable pressure ulcers**
Assignment of code 707.25, Pressure ulcer, unstageable, should be based on the clinical documentation. Code 707.25 is used for pressure ulcers whose stage cannot be clinically determined (e.g., the ulcer is covered by eschar or has been treated with a skin or muscle graft) and pressure ulcers that are documented as deep tissue injury but not documented as due to trauma. This code should not be confused with code 707.20, Pressure ulcer, stage unspecified. Code 707.20 should be assigned when there is no documentation regarding the stage of the pressure ulcer.

3) **Documented pressure ulcer stage**
Assignment of the pressure ulcer stage code should be guided by clinical documentation of the stage or documentation of the terms found in the index. For clinical terms describing the stage that are not found in the index, and there is no documentation of the stage, the provider should be queried.

4) **Bilateral pressure ulcers with same stage**
When a patient has bilateral pressure ulcers (e.g., both buttocks) and both pressure ulcers are documented as being the same stage, only the code for the site and one code for the stage should be reported.

5) **Bilateral pressure ulcers with different stages**
When a patient has bilateral pressure ulcers at the same site (e.g., both buttocks) and each pressure ulcer is documented as being at a different stage, assign one code for the site and the appropriate codes for the pressure ulcer stage.

6) **Multiple pressure ulcers of different sites and stages**
When a patient has multiple pressure ulcers at different sites (e.g., buttock, heel, shoulder) and each pressure ulcer is documented as

being at different stages (e.g., stage 3 and stage 4), assign the appropriate codes for each different site and a code for each different pressure ulcer stage.

7) **Patients admitted with pressure ulcers documented as healed**
No code is assigned if the documentation states that the pressure ulcer is completely healed.

8) **Patients admitted with pressure ulcers documented as healing**
Pressure ulcers described as healing should be assigned the appropriate pressure ulcer stage code based on the documentation in the medical record. If the documentation does not provide information about the stage of the healing pressure ulcer, assign code 707.20, Pressure ulcer stage, unspecified.

If the documentation is unclear as to whether the patient has a current (new) pressure ulcer or if the patient is being treated for a healing pressure ulcer, query the provider.

9) **Patient admitted with pressure ulcer evolving into another stage during the admission**
If a patient is admitted with a pressure ulcer at one stage and it progresses to a higher stage, assign the code for highest stage reported for that site.

13. **Chapter 13: Diseases of Musculoskeletal and Connective Tissue (710-739)**
a. **Coding of pathologic fractures**
1) **Acute fractures vs. aftercare**
Pathologic fractures are reported using subcategory 733.1, when the fracture is newly diagnosed. Subcategory 733.1 may be used while the patient is receiving active treatment for the fracture. Examples of active treatment are: surgical treatment, emergency department encounter, evaluation and treatment by a new physician.

Fractures are coded using the aftercare codes (subcategories V54.0, V54.2, V54.8 or V54.9) for encounters after the patient has completed active treatment of the fracture and is receiving routine care for the fracture during the healing or recovery phase. Examples of fracture aftercare are: cast change or removal, removal of external or internal fixation device, medication adjustment, and follow up visits following fracture treatment.

Care for complications of surgical treatment for fracture repairs during the healing or recovery phase should be coded with the appropriate complication codes.

Care of complications of fractures, such as malunion and nonunion, should be reported with the appropriate codes.

See Section I. C. 17.b for information on the coding of traumatic fractures.

14. **Chapter 14: Congenital Anomalies (740-759)**
a. **Codes in categories 740-759, congenital anomalies**
Assign an appropriate code(s) from categories 740-759, Congenital Anomalies, when an anomaly is documented. A congenital anomaly may be the principal/first listed diagnosis on a record or a secondary diagnosis.

When a congenital anomaly does not have a unique code assignment, assign additional code(s) for any manifestations that may be present. When the code assignment specifically identifies the congenital anomaly, manifestations that are an inherent component of the anomaly should not be coded separately. Additional codes should be assigned for manifestations that are not an inherent component.

Codes from Chapter 14 may be used throughout the life of the patient. If a congenital anomaly has been corrected, a personal history code should be used to identify the history of the anomaly. Although present at birth, a congenital anomaly may not be identified until later in life. Whenever the condition is diagnosed by the physician, it is appropriate to assign a code from codes 740-759.

For the birth admission, the appropriate code from category V30, Liveborn infants, according to type of birth should be sequenced as the principal diagnosis, followed by any congenital anomaly codes, 740-759.

15. **Chapter 15: Newborn (Perinatal) Guidelines (760-779)**
For coding and reporting purposes the perinatal period is defined as before birth through the 28th day following birth. The following guidelines are provided for reporting purposes. Hospitals may record other diagnoses as needed for internal data use.

a. General perinatal rules

1) Chapter 15 Codes

They are <u>never</u> for use on the maternal record. Codes from Chapter 11, the obstetric chapter, are never permitted on the newborn record. Chapter 15 code may be used throughout the life of the patient if the condition is still present.

2) Sequencing of perinatal codes

Generally, codes from Chapter 15 should be sequenced as the principal/first-listed diagnosis on the newborn record, with the exception of the appropriate V30 code for the birth episode, followed by codes from any other chapter that provide additional detail. The "use additional code" note at the beginning of the chapter supports this guideline. If the index does not provide a specific code for a perinatal condition, assign code 779.89, Other specified conditions originating in the perinatal period, followed by the code from another chapter that specifies the condition. Codes for signs and symptoms may be assigned when a definitive diagnosis has not been established.

3) Birth process or community acquired conditions

If a newborn has a condition that may be either due to the birth process or community acquired and the documentation does not indicate which it is, the default is due to the birth process and the code from Chapter 15 should be used. If the condition is community-acquired, a code from Chapter 15 should not be assigned.

4) Code all clinically significant conditions

All clinically significant conditions noted on routine newborn examination should be coded. A condition is clinically significant if it requires:

*   clinical evaluation; or
*   therapeutic treatment; or
*   diagnostic procedures; or
*   extended length of hospital stay; or
*   increased nursing care and/or monitoring; or
*   has implications for future health care needs

Note: The perinatal guidelines listed above are the same as the general coding guidelines for "additional diagnoses", except for the final point regarding implications for future health care needs. Codes should be assigned for conditions that have been specified by the provider as having implications for future health care needs. Codes from the perinatal chapter should not be assigned unless the provider has established a definitive diagnosis.

b. Use of codes V30-V39

When coding the birth of an infant, assign a code from categories V30-V39, according to the type of birth. A code from this series is assigned as a principal diagnosis, and assigned only once to a newborn at the time of birth.

c. Newborn transfers

If the newborn is transferred to another institution, the V30 series is not used at the receiving hospital.

d. Use of category V29

1) Assigning a code from category V29

Assign a code from category V29, Observation and evaluation of newborns and infants for suspected conditions not found, to identify those instances when a healthy newborn is evaluated for a suspected condition that is determined after study not to be present. Do not use a code from category V29 when the patient has identified signs or symptoms of a suspected problem; in such cases, code the sign or symptom.

A code from category V29 may also be assigned as a principal code for readmissions or encounters when the V30 code no longer applies. Codes from category V29 are for use only for healthy newborns and infants for which no condition after study is found to be present.

2) V29 code on a birth record

A V29 code is to be used as a secondary code after the V30, Outcome of delivery, code.

e. Use of other V codes on perinatal records

V codes other than V30 and V29 may be assigned on a perinatal or newborn record code. The codes may be used as a principal or first-listed diagnosis for specific types of encounters or for readmissions or encounters when the V30 code no longer applies.

See Section I.C.18 for information regarding the assignment of V codes.

f. Maternal causes of perinatal morbidity

Codes from categories 760-763, Maternal causes of perinatal morbidity and mortality, are assigned only when the maternal condition has actually affected the fetus or newborn. The fact that the mother has an associated medical condition or experiences some complication of pregnancy, labor or delivery does not justify the routine assignment of codes from these categories to the newborn record.

g. Congenital anomalies in newborns

For the birth admission, the appropriate code from category V30, Liveborn infants according to type of birth, should be used, followed by any congenital anomaly codes, categories 740-759. Use additional secondary codes from other chapters to specify conditions associated with the anomaly, if applicable.

Also, see Section I.C.14 for information on the coding of congenital anomalies.

h. Coding additional perinatal diagnoses

1) Assigning codes for conditions that require treatment

Assign codes for conditions that require treatment or further investigation, prolong the length of stay, or require resource utilization.

2) Codes for conditions specified as having implications for future health care needs

Assign codes for conditions that have been specified by the provider as having implications for future health care needs.

Note: This guideline should not be used for adult patients.

3) Codes for newborn conditions originating in the perinatal period

Assign a code for newborn conditions originating in the perinatal period (categories 760-779), as well as complications arising during the current episode of care classified in other chapters, only if the diagnoses have been documented by the responsible provider at the time of transfer or discharge as having affected the fetus or newborn.

i. Prematurity and fetal growth retardation

Providers utilize different criteria in determining prematurity. A code for prematurity should not be assigned unless it is documented. The 5th digit assignment for codes from category 764 and subcategories 765.0 and 765.1 should be based on the recorded birth weight and estimated gestational age.

A code from subcategory 765.2, Weeks of gestation, should be assigned as an additional code with category 764 and codes from 765.0 and 765.1 to specify weeks of gestation as documented by the provider in the record.

j. Newborn sepsis

Code 771.81, Septicemia [sepsis] of newborn, should be assigned with a secondary code from category 041, Bacterial infections in conditions classified elsewhere and of unspecified site, to identify the organism. It is not necessary to use a code from subcategory 995.9, Systemic inflammatory response syndrome (SIRS), on a newborn record. Do not assign code 995.91, Sepsis, as code 771.81 describes the sepsis. If applicable, use additional codes to identify severe sepsis (995.92) and any associated acute organ dysfunction.

16. Chapter 16: Signs, Symptoms and Ill-Defined Conditions (780-799)

Reserved for future guideline expansion

17. Chapter 17: Injury and Poisoning (800-999)

a. Coding of injuries

When coding injuries, assign separate codes for each injury unless a combination code is provided, in which case the combination code is assigned. Multiple injury codes are provided in ICD-9-CM, but should not be assigned unless information for a more specific code is not available. These codes are not to be used for normal, healing surgical wounds or to identify complications of surgical wounds.

The code for the most serious injury, as determined by the provider and the focus of treatment, is sequenced first.

1) Superficial injuries

Superficial injuries such as abrasions or contusions are not coded when associated with more severe injuries of the same site.

2) Primary injury with damage to nerves/blood vessels

When a primary injury results in minor damage to peripheral nerves or blood vessels, the primary injury is sequenced first with additional code(s) from categories 950-957, Injury to nerves and spinal cord, and/or 900-904, Injury to blood vessels. When the primary injury is to the blood vessels or nerves, that injury should be sequenced first.

b. **Coding of traumatic fractures**

The principles of multiple coding of injuries should be followed in coding fractures. Fractures of specified sites are coded individually by site in accordance with both the provisions within categories 800-829 and the level of detail furnished by medical record content. Combination categories for multiple fractures are provided for use when there is insufficient detail in the medical record (such as trauma cases transferred to another hospital), when the reporting form limits the number of codes that can be used in reporting pertinent clinical data, or when there is insufficient specificity at the fourth-digit or fifth-digit level. More specific guidelines are as follows:

1) **Acute fractures vs. aftercare**

Traumatic fractures are coded using the acute fracture codes (800-829) while the patient is receiving active treatment for the fracture. Examples of active treatment are: surgical treatment, emergency department encounter, and evaluation and treatment by a new physician.

Fractures are coded using the aftercare codes (subcategories V54.0, V54.1, V54.8, or V54.9) for encounters after the patient has completed active treatment of the fracture and is receiving routine care for the fracture during the healing or recovery phase. Examples of fracture aftercare are: cast change or removal, removal of external or internal fixation device, medication adjustment, and follow up visits following fracture treatment.

Care for complications of surgical treatment for fracture repairs during the healing or recovery phase should be coded with the appropriate complication codes.

Care of complications of fractures, such as malunion and nonunion, should be reported with the appropriate codes. Pathologic fractures are not coded in the 800-829 range, but instead are assigned to subcategory 733.1. *See Section I.C.13.a for additional information.*

2) **Multiple fractures of same limb**

Multiple fractures of same limb classifiable to the same three-digit or four-digit category are coded to that category.

3) **Multiple unilateral or bilateral fractures of same bone**

Multiple unilateral or bilateral fractures of same bone(s) but classified to different fourth-digit subdivisions (bone part) within the same three-digit category are coded individually by site.

4) **Multiple fracture categories 819 and 828**

Multiple fracture categories 819 and 828 classify bilateral fractures of both upper limbs (819) and both lower limbs (828), but without any detail at the fourth-digit level other than open and closed type of fractures.

5) **Multiple fractures sequencing**

Multiple fractures are sequenced in accordance with the severity of the fracture. The provider should be asked to list the fracture diagnoses in the order of severity.

c. **Coding of burns**

Current burns (940-948) are classified by depth, extent and by agent (E code). Burns are classified by depth as first degree (erythema), second degree (blistering), and third degree (full-thickness involvement).

1) **Sequencing of burn and related condition codes**

Sequence first the code that reflects the highest degree of burn when more than one burn is present.

a. When the reason for the admission or encounter is for treatment of external multiple burns, sequence first the code that reflects the burn of the highest degree.

b. When a patient has both internal and external burns, the circumstances of admission govern the selection of the principal diagnosis or first-listed diagnosis.

c. When a patient is admitted for burn injuries and other related conditions such as smoke inhalation and/or respiratory failure, the circumstances of admission govern the selection of the principal or first-listed diagnosis.

2) **Burns of the same local site**

Classify burns of the same local site (three-digit category level, 940-947) but of different degrees to the subcategory identifying the highest degree recorded in the diagnosis.

3) **Non-healing burns**

Non-healing burns are coded as acute burns.

Necrosis of burned skin should be coded as a non-healed burn.

4) **Code 958.3, posttraumatic wound infection**

Assign code 958.3, Posttraumatic wound infection, not elsewhere classified, as an additional code for any documented infected burn site.

5) **Assign separate codes for each burn site**

When coding burns, assign separate codes for each burn site. Category 946, Burns of Multiple specified sites, should only be used if the location of the burns are not documented.

Category 949, Burn, unspecified, is extremely vague and should rarely be used.

6) **Assign codes from category 948, burns**

Burns classified according to extent of body surface involved, when the site of the burn is not specified or when there is a need for additional data. It is advisable to use category 948 as additional coding when needed to provide data for evaluating burn mortality, such as that needed by burn units. It is also advisable to use category 948 as an additional code for reporting purposes when there is mention of a third-degree burn involving 20 percent or more of the body surface.

In assigning a code from category 948:

Fourth-digit codes are used to identify the percentage of total body surface involved in a burn (all degree).

Fifth-digits are assigned to identify the percentage of body surface involved in third-degree burn.

Fifth-digit zero (0) is assigned when less than 10 percent or when no body surface is involved in a third-degree burn.

Category 948 is based on the classic "rule of nines" in estimating body surface involved: head and neck are assigned nine percent, each arm nine percent, each leg 18 percent, the anterior trunk 18 percent, posterior trunk 18 percent, and genitalia one percent. Providers may change these percentage assignments where necessary to accommodate infants and children who have proportionately larger heads than adults and patients who have large buttocks, thighs, or abdomen that involve burns.

7) **Encounters for treatment of late effects of burns**

Encounters for the treatment of the late effects of burns (i.e., scars or joint contractures) should be coded to the residual condition (sequelae) followed by the appropriate late effect code (906.5-906.9). A late effect E code may also be used, if desired.

8) **Sequelae with a late effect code and current burn**

When appropriate, both a sequelae with a late effect code, and a current burn code may be assigned on the same record (when both a current burn and sequelae of an old burn exist).

d. **Coding of debridement of wound, infection, or burn**

Excisional debridement involves surgical removal or cutting away, as opposed to a mechanical (brushing, scrubbing, washing) debridement. For coding purposes, excisional debridement is assigned to code 86.22. Nonexcisional debridement is assigned to code 86.28.

e. **Adverse effects, poisoning and toxic effects**

The properties of certain drugs, medicinal and biological substances or combinations of such substances, may cause toxic reactions. The occurrence of drug toxicity is classified in ICD-9-CM as follows:

1) **Adverse effect**

When the drug was correctly prescribed and properly administered, code the reaction plus the appropriate code from the E930-E949 series. Codes from the E930-E949 series must be used to identify the causative substance for an adverse effect of drug, medicinal and biological substances, correctly prescribed and properly administered. The effect, such as tachycardia, delirium, gastrointestinal hemorrhaging, vomiting, hypokalemia, hepatitis, renal failure, or respiratory failure, is coded and followed by the appropriate code from the E930-E949 series.

Adverse effects of therapeutic substances correctly prescribed and properly administered (toxicity, synergistic reaction, side effect, and idiosyncratic reaction) may be due to (1) differences among patients, such as age, sex, disease, and genetic factors, and (2) drug-related factors, such as type of drug, route of administration, duration of therapy, dosage, and bioavailability.

2) **Poisoning**

(a) **Error was made in drug prescription**

Errors made in drug prescription or in the administration of the drug by provider, nurse, patient, or other person, use the appropriate poisoning code from the 960-979 series.

(b) **Overdose of a drug intentionally taken**

If an overdose of a drug was intentionally taken or administered and resulted in drug toxicity, it would be coded as a poisoning (960-979 series).

(c) **Nonprescribed drug taken with correctly prescribed and properly administered drug**

If a nonprescribed drug or medicinal agent was taken in combination with a correctly prescribed and properly administered drug, any drug toxicity or other reaction resulting from the interaction of the two drugs would be classified as a poisoning.

(d) **Sequencing of poisoning**

When a reaction results from the interaction of a drug(s) and alcohol, this would be classified as poisoning.

(e) **Sequencing of poisoning**

When coding a poisoning or reaction to the improper use of a medication (e.g., wrong dose, wrong substance, wrong route of administration) the poisoning code is sequenced first, followed by a code for the manifestation. If there is also a diagnosis of drug abuse or dependence to the substance, the abuse or dependence is coded as an additional code.

See Section I.C.3.a.6.b. if poisoning is the result of insulin pump malfunctions and Section I.C.19 for general use of E-codes.

3) **Toxic effects**

(a) **Toxic effect codes**

When a harmful substance is ingested or comes in contact with a person, this is classified as a toxic effect. The toxic effect codes are in categories 980-989.

(b) **Sequencing toxic effect codes**

A toxic effect code should be sequenced first, followed by the code(s) that identify the result of the toxic effect.

(c) **External cause codes for toxic effects**

An external cause code from categories E860-E869 for accidental exposure, codes E950.6 or E950.7 for intentional self-harm, category E962 for assault, or categories E980-E982, for undetermined, should also be assigned to indicate intent.

f. **Complications of care**

1) **Complications of care**

(a) **Documentation of complications of care**

As with all procedural or postprocedural complications, code assignment is based on the provider's documentation of the relationship between the condition and the procedure.

2) **Transplant complications**

(a) **Transplant complications other than kidney**

Codes under subcategory 996.8, Complications of transplanted organ, are for use for both complications and rejection of transplanted organs. A transplant complication code is only assigned if the complication affects the function of the transplanted organ. Two codes are required to fully describe a transplant complication, the appropriate code from subcategory 996.8 and a secondary code that identifies the complication.

Pre-existing conditions or conditions that develop after the transplant are not coded as complications unless they affect the function of the transplanted organs.

See I.C.18.d.3) for transplant organ removal status

See I.C.2.i for malignant neoplasm associated with transplanted organ.

(b) **Chronic kidney disease and kidney transplant complications**

Patients who have undergone kidney transplant may still have some form of chronic kidney disease (CKD) because the kidney transplant may not fully restore kidney function. Code 996.81 should be assigned for documented complications of a kidney transplant, such as transplant failure or rejection or other transplant complication. Code 996.81 should not be assigned for post kidney transplant patients who have chronic kidney (CKD) unless a transplant complication such as transplant failure or rejection is documented. If the documentation is unclear as to whether the patient has a complication of the transplant, query the provider.

For patients with CKD following a kidney transplant, but who do not have a complication such as failure or rejection, see

section I.C.10.a.2, *Chronic kidney disease and kidney transplant status.*

3) **Ventilator associated pneumonia**

(a) **Documentation of Ventilator associated Pneumonia**

As with all procedural or postprocedural complications, code assignment is based on the provider's documentation of the relationship between the condition and the procedure.

Code 997.31, Ventilator associated pneumonia, should be assigned only when the provider has documented ventilator associated pneumonia (VAP). An additional code to identify the organism (e.g., Pseudomonas aeruginosa, code 041.7) should also be assigned. Do not assign an additional code from categories 480-484 to identify the type of pneumonia.

Code 997.31 should not be assigned for cases where the patient has pneumonia and is on a mechanical ventilator but the provider has not specifically stated that the pneumonia is ventilator-associated pneumonia.

If the documentation is unclear as to whether the patient has a pneumonia that is a complication attributable to the mechanical ventilator, query the provider.

(b) **Patient admitted with pneumonia and develops VAP**

A patient may be admitted with one type of pneumonia (e.g., code 481, Pneumococcal pneumonia) and subsequently develop VAP. In this instance, the principal diagnosis would be the appropriate code from categories 480-484 for the pneumonia diagnosed at the time of admission. Code 997.31, Ventilator associated pneumonia, would be assigned as an additional diagnosis when the provider has also documented the presence of ventilator associated pneumonia.

g. **SIRS due to non-infectious process**

The systemic inflammatory response syndrome (SIRS) can develop as a result of certain non-infectious disease processes, such as trauma, malignant neoplasm, or pancreatitis. When SIRS is documented with a noninfectious condition, and no subsequent infection is documented, the code for the underlying condition, such as an injury, should be assigned, followed by code 995.93, Systemic inflammatory response syndrome due to noninfectious process without acute organ dysfunction, or 995.94, Systemic inflammatory response syndrome due to non-infectious process with acute organ dysfunction. If an acute organ dysfunction is documented, the appropriate code(s) for the associated acute organ dysfunction(s) should be assigned in addition to code 995.94. If acute organ dysfunction is documented, but it cannot be determined if the acute organ dysfunction is associated with SIRS or due to another condition (e.g., directly due to the trauma), the provider should be queried.

When the non-infectious condition has led to an infection that results in SIRS, *see Section I.C.1.b.12 for the guideline for sepsis and severe sepsis associated with a non-infectious process.*

18. **Classification of Factors Influencing Health Status and Contact with Health Service (Supplemental V01-V89)**

Note: The chapter specific guidelines provide additional information about the use of V codes for specified encounters.

a. **Introduction**

ICD-9-CM provides codes to deal with encounters for circumstances other than a disease or injury. The Supplementary Classification of Factors Influencing Health Status and Contact with Health Services (V01.0 - V89.09) is provided to deal with occasions when circumstances other than a disease or injury (codes 001-V89.09) are recorded as a diagnosis or problem.

There are four primary circumstances for the use of V codes:

1) A person who is not currently sick encounters the health services for some specific reason, such as to act as an organ donor, to receive prophylactic care, such as inoculations or health screenings, or to receive counseling on health related issues.

2) A person with a resolving disease or injury, or a chronic, long-term condition requiring continuous care, encounters the health care system for specific aftercare of that disease or injury (e.g., dialysis for renal disease; chemotherapy for malignancy; cast change). A diagnosis/symptom code should be used whenever a current, acute, diagnosis is being treated or a sign or symptom is being studied.

3) Circumstances or problems influence a person's health status but are not in themselves a current illness or injury.

4)   Newborns, to indicate birth status

b.   V codes use in any healthcare setting
V codes are for use in any healthcare setting. V codes may be used as either a first listed (principal diagnosis code in the inpatient setting) or secondary code, depending on the circumstances of the encounter. Certain V codes may only be used as first listed, others only as secondary codes.
See Section I.C.18.e, V Code Table.

c.   V Codes indicate a reason for an encounter
They are not procedure codes. A corresponding procedure code must accompany a V code to describe the procedure performed.

d.   Categories of V codes

1)   Contact/exposure
Category V01 indicates contact with or exposure to communicable diseases. These codes are for patients who do not show any sign or symptom of a disease but have been exposed to it by close personal contact with an infected individual or are in an area where a disease is epidemic. These codes may be used as a first listed code to explain an encounter for testing, or, more commonly, as a secondary code to identify a potential risk.

2)   Inoculations and vaccinations
Categories V03-V06 are for encounters for inoculations and vaccinations. They indicate that a patient is being seen to receive a prophylactic inoculation against a disease. The injection itself must be represented by the appropriate procedure code. A code from V03-V06 may be used as a secondary code if the inoculation is given as a routine part of preventive health care, such as a well-baby visit.

3)   Status
Status codes indicate that a patient is either a carrier of a disease or has the sequelae or residual of a past disease or condition. This includes such things as the presence of prosthetic or mechanical devices resulting from past treatment. A status code is informative, because the status may affect the course of treatment and its outcome. A status code is distinct from a history code. The history code indicates that the patient no longer has the condition.

A status code should not be used with a diagnosis code from one of the body system chapters, if the diagnosis code includes the information provided by the status code. For example, code V42.1, Heart transplant status, should not be used with code 996.83, Complications of transplanted heart. The status code does not provide additional information. The complication code indicates that the patient is a heart transplant patient.

The status V codes/categories are:

V02   Carrier or suspected carrier of infectious diseases
Carrier status indicates that a person harbors the specific organisms of a disease without manifest symptoms and is capable of transmitting the infection.

V07.5x   Prophylactic use of agents affecting estrogen receptors and estrogen level
This code indicates when a patient is receiving a drug that affects estrogen receptors and estrogen levels for prevention of cancer.

V08   Asymptomatic HIV infection status
This code indicates that a patient has tested positive for HIV but has manifested no signs or symptoms of the disease.

V09   Infection with drug-resistant microorganisms
This category indicates that a patient has an infection that is resistant to drug treatment. Sequence the infection code first.

V21   Constitutional states in development

V22.2   Pregnant state, incidental
This code is a secondary code only for use when the pregnancy is in no way complicating the reason for visit. Otherwise, a code from the obstetric chapter is required.

V26.5x   Sterilization status

V42   Organ or tissue replaced by transplant

V43   Organ or tissue replaced by other means

V44   Artificial opening status

V45   Other postsurgical states

Assign code V45.87, Transplant organ removal status, to indicate that a transplanted organ has been previously removed. This code should not be assigned for the encounter in which the transplanted organ is removed. The complication necessitating removal of the transplant organ should be assigned for that encounter.
See section I.C17.f.2. for information on the coding of organ transplant complications.

Assign code V45.88, Status post administration of tPA (rtPA) in a different facility within the last 24 hours prior to admission to the current facility, as a secondary diagnosis when a patient is received by transfer into a facility and documentation indicates they were administered tissue plasminogen activator (tPA) within the last 24 hours prior to admission to the current facility.

This guideline applies even if the patient is still receiving the tPA at the time they are received into the current facility.

The appropriate code for the condition for which the tPA was administered (such as cerebrovascular disease or myocardial infarction) should be assigned first.

Code V45.88 is only applicable to the receiving facility record and not to the transferring facility record.

V46   Other dependence on machines

V49.6   Upper limb amputation status

V49.7   Lower limb amputation status
Note: Categories V42-V46, and subcategories V49.6, V49.7 are for use only if there are no complications or malfunctions of the organ or tissue replaced, the amputation site or the equipment on which the patient is dependent.

V49.81   Postmenopausal status

V49.82   Dental sealant status

V49.83   Awaiting organ transplant status

V58.6x   Long-term (current) drug use
Codes from this subcategory indicate a patient's continuous use of a prescribed drug (including such things as aspirin therapy) for the long-term treatment of a condition or for prophylactic use. It is not for use for patients who have addictions to drugs. This subcategory is not for use of medications for detoxification or maintenance programs to prevent withdrawal symptoms in patients with drug dependence (e.g., methadone maintenance for opiate dependence). Assign the appropriate code for the drug dependence instead.

Assign a code from subcategory V58.6, Long-term (current) drug use, if the patient is receiving a medication for an extended period as a prophylactic measure (such as for the prevention of deep vein thrombosis) or as treatment of a chronic condition (such as arthritis) or a disease requiring a lengthy course of treatment (such as cancer). Do not assign a code from subcategory V58.6 for medication being administered for a brief period of time to treat an acute illness or injury (such as a course of antibiotics to treat acute bronchitis).

V83   Genetic carrier status
Genetic carrier status indicates that a person carries a gene, associated with a particular disease, which may be passed to offspring who may develop that disease. The person does not have the disease and is not at risk of developing the disease.

V84   Genetic susceptibility status
Genetic susceptibility indicates that a person has a gene that increases the risk of that person developing the disease.

Codes from category V84, Genetic susceptibility to disease, should not be used as principal or first-listed codes. If the patient has the condition to which he/she is susceptible, and that condition is the reason for the encounter, the code for the current condition should be sequenced first. If the patient is being seen for follow-up after completed treatment for this condition, and the condition no longer exists, a follow-up code should be sequenced first, followed by the appropriate personal history and genetic susceptibility codes. If the purpose of the encounter is genetic counseling associated with procreative management, a code from subcategory V26.3, Genetic counseling and testing, should be assigned as the first-listed code, followed by a code from category V84. Additional codes should be assigned for any applicable family or personal history.

See Section I.C. 18.d.14 for information on prophylactic organ removal due to a genetic susceptibility.

V86	Estrogen receptor status
V88	Acquired absence of other organs and tissue

4) History (of)

There are two types of history V codes, personal and family. Personal history codes explain a patient's past medical condition that no longer exists and is not receiving any treatment, but that has the potential for recurrence, and therefore may require continued monitoring. The exceptions to this general rule are category V14, Personal history of allergy to medicinal agents, and subcategory V15.0, Allergy, other than to medicinal agents. A person who has had an allergic episode to a substance or food in the past should always be considered allergic to the substance.

Family history codes are for use when a patient has a family member(s) who has had a particular disease that causes the patient to be at higher risk of also contracting the disease.

Personal history codes may be used in conjunction with follow-up codes and family history codes may be used in conjunction with screening codes to explain the need for a test or procedure. History codes are also acceptable on any medical record regardless of the reason for visit. A history of an illness, even if no longer present, is important information that may alter the type of treatment ordered.

The history V code categories are:

V10	Personal history of malignant neoplasm
V12	Personal history of certain other diseases
V13	Personal history of other diseases
	Except: V13.4, Personal history of arthritis, and V13.6, Personal history of congenital malformations. These conditions are life-long so are not true history codes.
V14	Personal history of allergy to medicinal agents
V15	Other personal history presenting hazards to health
	Except: V15.7, Personal history of contraception.
V16	Family history of malignant neoplasm
V17	Family history of certain chronic disabling diseases
V18	Family history of certain other specific diseases
V19	Family history of other conditions
V87	Other specified personal exposures and history presenting hazards to health

5) Screening

Screening is the testing for disease or disease precursors in seemingly well individuals so that early detection and treatment can be provided for those who test positive for the disease. Screenings that are recommended for many subgroups in a population include: routine mammograms for women over 40, a fecal occult blood test for everyone over 50, an amniocentesis to rule out a fetal anomaly for pregnant women over 35, because the incidence of breast cancer and colon cancer in these subgroups is higher than in the general population, as is the incidence of Down's syndrome in older mothers.

The testing of a person to rule out or confirm a suspected diagnosis because the patient has some sign or symptom is a diagnostic examination, not a screening. In these cases, the sign or symptom is used to explain the reason for the test.

A screening code may be a first listed code if the reason for the visit is specifically the screening exam. It may also be used as an additional code if the screening is done during an office visit for other health problems. A screening code is not necessary if the screening is inherent to a routine examination, such as a pap smear done during a routine pelvic examination.

Should a condition be discovered during the screening then the code for the condition may be assigned as an additional diagnosis.

The V code indicates that a screening exam is planned. A procedure code is required to confirm that the screening was performed.

The screening V code categories:

V28	Antenatal screening
V73-V82	Special screening examinations

6) Observation

There are three observation V code categories. They are for use in very limited circumstances when a person is being observed for a suspected condition that is ruled out. The observation codes are not for use if an injury or illness or any signs or symptoms related to the suspected condition are present. In such cases the diagnosis/symptom code is used with the corresponding E code to identify any external cause.

The observation codes are to be used as principal diagnosis only. The only exception to this is when the principal diagnosis is required to be a code from the V30, Live born infant, category. Then the V29 observation code is sequenced after the V30 code. Additional codes may be used in addition to the observation code but only if they are unrelated to the suspected condition being observed.

Codes from subcategory V89.0, Suspected maternal and fetal conditions not found, may either be used as a first listed or as an additional code assignment depending on the case. They are for use in very limited circumstances on a maternal record when an encounter is for a suspected maternal or fetal condition that is ruled out during that encounter (for example, a maternal or fetal condition may be suspected due to an abnormal test result). These codes should not be used when the condition is confirmed. In those cases, the confirmed condition should be coded. In addition, these codes are not for use if an illness or any signs or symptoms related to the suspected condition or problem are present. In such cases the diagnosis/symptom code is used.

Additional codes may be used in addition to the code from subcategory V89.0, but only if they are unrelated to the suspected condition being evaluated.

Codes from subcategory V89.0 may not be used for encounters for antenatal screening of mother.

See Section I.C.18.d., Screening.

For encounters for suspected fetal condition that are inconclusive following testing and evaluation, assign the appropriate code from category 655, 656, 657 or 658.

The observation V code categories:

V29	Observation and evaluation of newborns for suspected condition not found
	For the birth encounter, a code from category V30 should be sequenced before the V29 code.
V71	Observation and evaluation for suspected condition not found
V89	Suspected maternal and fetal conditions not found

7) Aftercare

Aftercare visit codes cover situations when the initial treatment of a disease or injury has been performed and the patient requires continued care during the healing or recovery phase, or for the long-term consequences of the disease. The aftercare V code should not be used if treatment is directed at a current, acute disease or injury. The diagnosis code is to be used in these cases. Exceptions to this rule are codes V58.0, Radiotherapy, and codes from subcategory V58.1, Encounter for chemotherapy and immunotherapy for neoplastic conditions. These codes are to be first listed, followed by the diagnosis code when a patient's encounter is solely to receive radiation therapy or chemotherapy for the treatment of a neoplasm. Should a patient receive both chemotherapy and radiation therapy during the same encounter code V58.0 and V58.1 may be used together on a record with either one being sequenced first.

The aftercare codes are generally first listed to explain the specific reason for the encounter. An aftercare code may be used as an additional code when some type of aftercare is provided in addition to the reason for admission and no diagnosis code is applicable. An example of this would be the closure of a colostomy during an encounter for treatment of another condition.

Aftercare codes should be used in conjunction with any other aftercare codes or other diagnosis codes to provide better detail on the specifics of an aftercare encounter visit, unless otherwise directed by the classification. The sequencing of multiple aftercare codes is discretionary.

Certain aftercare V code categories need a secondary diagnosis code to describe the resolving condition or sequelae, for others, the condition is inherent in the code title.

Additional V code aftercare category terms include, fitting and adjustment, and attention to artificial openings.

Status V codes may be used with aftercare V codes to indicate the nature of the aftercare. For example code V45.81, Aortocoronary bypass status, may be used with code V58.73, Aftercare following surgery of the circulatory system, NEC, to indicate the surgery for which the aftercare is being performed. Also, a transplant status code may be used following code V58.44, Aftercare following organ transplant, to identify the organ transplanted. A status code should not be used when the aftercare code indicates the type of status, such as using V55.0, Attention to tracheostomy with V44.0, Tracheostomy status.

See Section I. B.16 Admissions/Encounter for Rehabilitation

The aftercare V category/codes:

V51.0	Encounter for breast reconstruction following mastectomy
V52	Fitting and adjustment of prosthetic device and implant
V53	Fitting and adjustment of other device
V54	Other orthopedic aftercare
V55	Attention to artificial openings
V56	Encounter for dialysis and dialysis catheter care
V57	Care involving the use of rehabilitation procedures
V58.0	Radiotherapy
V58.11	Encounter for antineoplastic chemotherapy
V58.12	Encounter for antineoplastic immunotherapy
V58.3x	Attention to dressings and sutures
V58.41	Encounter for planned post-operative wound closure
V58.42	Aftercare, surgery, neoplasm
V58.43	Aftercare, surgery, trauma
V58.44	Aftercare involving organ transplant
V58.49	Other specified aftercare following surgery
V58.7x	Aftercare following surgery
V58.81	Fitting and adjustment of vascular catheter
V58.82	Fitting and adjustment of non-vascular catheter
V58.83	Monitoring therapeutic drug
V58.89	Other specified aftercare

8) **Follow-up**

The follow-up codes are used to explain continuing surveillance following completed treatment of a disease, condition, or injury. They imply that the condition has been fully treated and no longer exists. They should not be confused with aftercare codes that explain current treatment for a healing condition or its sequelae. Follow-up codes may be used in conjunction with history codes to provide the full picture of the healed condition and its treatment. The follow-up code is sequenced first, followed by the history code.

A follow-up code may be used to explain repeated visits. Should a condition be found to have recurred on the follow-up visit, then the diagnosis code should be used in place of the follow-up code. The follow-up V code categories:

V24	Postpartum care and evaluation
V67	Follow-up examination

9) **Donor**

Category V59 is the donor codes. They are used for living individuals who are donating blood or other body tissue. These codes are only for individuals donating for others, not for self donations. They are not for use to identify cadaveric donations.

10) **Counseling**

Counseling V codes are used when a patient or family member receives assistance in the aftermath of an illness or injury, or when support is required in coping with family or social problems. They

are not necessary for use in conjunction with a diagnosis code when the counseling component of care is considered integral to standard treatment.

The counseling V categories/codes:

V25.0	General counseling and advice for contraceptive management
V26.3	Genetic counseling
V26.4	General counseling and advice for procreative management
V61.x	Other family circumstances
V65.1	Person consulted on behalf of another person
V65.3	Dietary surveillance and counseling
V65.4	Other counseling, not elsewhere classified

11) **Obstetrics and related conditions**

See Section I.C.11., the Obstetrics guidelines for further instruction on the use of these codes.

V codes for pregnancy are for use in those circumstances when none of the problems or complications included in the codes from the Obstetrics chapter exist (a routine prenatal visit or postpartum care). Codes V22.0, Supervision of normal first pregnancy, and V22.1, Supervision of other normal pregnancy, are always first listed and are not to be used with any other code from the OB chapter.

The outcome of delivery, category V27, should be included on all maternal delivery records. It is always a secondary code.

V codes for family planning (contraceptive) or procreative management and counseling should be included on an obstetric record either during the pregnancy or the postpartum stage, if applicable.

Obstetrics and related conditions V code categories:

V22	Normal pregnancy
V23	Supervision of high-risk pregnancy Except: V23.2, Pregnancy with history of abortion. Code 646.3, Habitual aborter, from the OB chapter is required to indicate a history of abortion during a pregnancy.
V24	Postpartum care and evaluation
V25	Encounter for contraceptive management Except V25.0x *See Section I.C.18.d.11, Counseling*
V26	Procreative management Except V26.5x, Sterilization status, V26.3 and V26.4 *See Section I.C.18.d.11., Counseling*
V27	Outcome of delivery
V28	Antenatal screening *See Section I.C.18.d.6., Screening*

12) **Newborn, infant and child**

See Section I.C.15, the Newborn guidelines for further instruction on the use of these codes.

Newborn V code categories:

V20	Health supervision of infant or child
V29	Observation and evaluation of newborns for suspected condition not found *See Section I.C.18.d.7, Observation*
V30-V39	Liveborn infant according to type of birth

13) **Routine and administrative examinations**

The V codes allow for the description of encounters for routine examinations, such as, a general check-up, or, examinations for administrative purposes, such as, a pre-employment physical. The codes are not to be used if the examination is for diagnosis of a suspected condition or for treatment purposes. In such cases the diagnosis code is used. During a routine exam, should a diagnosis or condition be discovered, it should be coded as an additional code. Pre-existing and chronic conditions and history codes may also be included as additional codes as long as the examination is for administrative purposes and not focused on any particular condition.

Pre-operative examination V codes are for use only in those situations when a patient is being cleared for surgery and no treatment is given.

The V codes categories/code for routine and administrative examinations:

V20.2   Routine infant or child health check

Any injections given should have a corresponding procedure code.

V70   General medical examination

V72   Special investigations and examinations

Codes V72.5 and V72.6 may be used if the reason for the patient encounter is for routine laboratory/radiology testing in the absence of any signs, symptoms, or associated diagnosis. If routine testing is performed during the same encounter as a test to evaluate a sign, symptom, or diagnosis, it is appropriate to assign both the V code and the code describing the reason for the non-routine test.

14) Miscellaneous V codes

The miscellaneous V codes capture a number of other health care encounters that do not fall into one of the other categories. Certain of these codes identify the reason for the encounter, others are for use as additional codes that provide useful information on circumstances that may affect a patient's care and treatment.

Prophylactic organ removal

For encounters specifically for prophylactic removal of breasts, ovaries, or another organ due to a genetic susceptibility to cancer or a family history of cancer, the principal or first listed code should be a code from subcategory V50.4, Prophylactic organ removal, followed by the appropriate genetic susceptibility code and the appropriate family history code.

If the patient has a malignancy of one site and is having prophylactic removal at another site to prevent either a new primary malignancy or metastatic disease, a code for the malignancy should also be assigned in addition to a code from subcategory V50.4. A V50.4 code should not be assigned if the patient is having organ removal for treatment of a malignancy, such as the removal of the testes for the treatment of prostate cancer.

Miscellaneous V code categories/codes:

V07   Need for isolation and other prophylactic measures

Except V07.5, Prophylactic use of agents affecting estrogen receptors and estrogen levels

V50   Elective surgery for purposes other than remedying health states

V58.5   Orthodontics

V60   Housing, household, and economic circumstances

V62   Other psychosocial circumstances

V63   Unavailability of other medical facilities for care

V64   Persons encountering health services for specific procedures, not carried out

V66   Convalescence and palliative care

V68   Encounters for administrative purposes

V69   Problems related to lifestyle

V85   Body Mass Index

15) Nonspecific V codes

Certain V codes are so non-specific, or potentially redundant with other codes in the classification, that there can be little justification for their use in the inpatient setting. Their use in the outpatient setting should be limited to those instances when there is no further documentation to permit more precise coding. Otherwise, any sign or symptom or any other reason for visit that is captured in another code should be used.

Nonspecific V code categories/codes:

V11   Personal history of mental disorder A code from the mental disorders chapter, with an in remission fifth-digit, should be used.

V13.4   Personal history of arthritis

V13.6   Personal history of congenital malformations

V15.7   Personal history of contraception

V23.2   Pregnancy with history of abortion

V40   Mental and behavioral problems

V41   Problems with special senses and other special functions

V47   Other problems with internal organs

V48   Problems with head, neck, and trunk

V49   Problems with limbs and other problems

Exception:

V49.6   Upper limb amputation status

V49.7   Lower limb amputation status

V49.81   Postmenopausal status

V49.82   Dental sealant status

V49.83   Awaiting organ transplant status

V51.8   Other aftercare involving the use of plastic surgery

V58.2   Blood transfusion, without reported diagnosis

V58.9   Unspecified aftercare

See Section IV.K. and Section IV.L. of the Outpatient guidelines.

V CODE TABLE

October 1, 2008 (FY2009)

The following V code table contains columns for 1st listed, 1st or additional, additional only, and non-specific. Each code or category is listed on the left hand column and the allowable sequencing of the code or codes within the category is noted under the appropriate column.

As indicated by the footnote in the "1st Dx Only" column, the V codes designated as first-listed only are generally intended to be limited for use as a first-listed only diagnosis, but may be reported as an additional diagnosis in those situations when the patient has more than one encounter on a single day and the codes for the multiple encounters are combined, or when there is more than one V code that meets the definition of principal diagnosis (e.g., a patient is admitted to home healthcare for both aftercare and rehabilitation and they equally meet the definition of principal diagnosis). The V codes designated as first-listed only should not be reported if they do not meet the definition of principal or first-listed diagnosis.

See Section II and Section IV.A for information on selection of principal and first-listed diagnosis.

See Section II.C for information on two or more diagnoses that equally meet the definition for principal diagnosis.

Code(s)	Description	1st Dx Only[1]	1st or Add'l Dx[2]	Add'l Dx Only[3]	Non-Specific Diagnosis[4]
V01.X	Contact with or exposure to communicable diseases		X		
V02.X	Carrier or suspected carrier of infectious diseases		X		
V03.X	Need for prophylactic vaccination and inoculation against bacterial diseases		X		
V04.X	Need for prophylactic vaccination and inoculation against certain diseases		X		
V05.X	Need for prophylactic vaccination and inoculation against single diseases		X		
V06.X	Need for prophylactic vaccination and inoculation against combinations of diseases		X		
V07.0	Isolation		X		
V07.1	Desensitization to allergens		X		
V07.2	Prophylactic immunotherapy		X		
V07.3X	Other prophylactic chemotherapy		X		
V07.4	Hormone replacement therapy (postmenopausal)			X	
V07.5X	Prophylactic use of agents affecting estrogen receptors and estrogen levels			X	
V07.8	Other specified prophylactic measure		X		

1. Generally for use as first listed only but may be used as additional if patient has more than one encounter on one day or there is more than one reason for the encounter
2. These codes may be used as first listed or additional codes
3. These codes are only for use as additional codes
4. These codes are primarily for use in the nonacute setting and should be limited to encounters for which no sign or symptom or reason for visit is documented in the record. Their use may be as either a first listed or additional code.

Code(s)	Description	1st Dx Only[1]	1st or Add'l Dx[2]	Add'l Dx Only[3]	Non-Specific Diagnosis[4]
V07.9	Unspecified prophylactic measure				X
V08	Asymptomatic HIV infection status		X		
V09.X	Infection with drug resistant organisms			X	
V10.X	Personal history of malignant neoplasm		X		
V11.X	Personal history of mental disorder				X
V12.X	Personal history of certain other diseases		X		
V13.0X	Personal history of other disorders of urinary system		X		
V13.1	Personal history of trophoblastic disease		X		
V13.2X	Personal history of other genital system and obstetric disorders		X		
V13.3	Personal history of diseases of skin and subcutaneous tissue		X		
V13.4	Personal history of arthritis				X
V13.5X	Personal history of other musculoskeletal disorders		X		
V13.61	Personal history of hypospadias			X	
V13.69	Personal history of congenital malformations				X
V13.7	Personal history of perinatal problems		X		
V13.8	Personal history of other specified diseases		X		
V13.9	Personal history of unspecified disease				X
V14.X	Personal history of allergy to medicinal agents			X	
V15.0X	Personal history of allergy, other than to medicinal agents			X	
V15.1	Personal history of surgery to heart and great vessels			X	
V15.2X	Personal history of surgery to other organs			X	
V15.3	Personal history of irradiation			X	
V15.4X	Personal history of psychological trauma			X	
V15.5X	Personal history of injury			X	
V15.6	Personal history of poisoning			X	
V15.7	Personal history of contraception				X
V15.81	Personal history of noncompliance with medical treatment			X	
V15.82	Personal history of tobacco use			X	
V15.84	Personal history of exposure to asbestos			X	
V15.85	Personal history of exposure to potentially hazardous body fluids			X	
V15.86	Personal history of exposure to lead			X	
V15.87	Personal history of extracorporeal membrane oxygenation [ECMO]			X	
V15.88	History of fall		X		
V15.89	Other specified personal history presenting hazards to health			X	
V16.X	Family history of malignant neoplasm		X		
V17.X	Family history of certain chronic disabling diseases		X		
V18.X	Family history of certain other specific conditions		X		
V19.X	Family history of other conditions		X		
V20.X	Health supervision of infant or child	X			
V21.X	Constitutional states in development			X	
V22.0	Supervision of normal first pregnancy	X			
V22.1	Supervision of other normal pregnancy	X			
V22.2	Pregnancy state, incidental			X	
V23.X	Supervision of high-risk pregnancy		X		
V24.X	Postpartum care and examination	X			
V25.X	Encounter for contraceptive management		X		
V26.0	Tuboplasty or vasoplasty after previous sterilization		X		
V26.1	Artificial insemination		X		
V26.2X	Procreative management investigation and testing		X		
V26.3X	Procreative management, genetic counseling and testing		X		
V26.4X	Procreative management, genetic counseling and advice		X		
V26.5X	Procreative management, sterilization status			X	
V26.81	Encounter for assisted reproductive fertility procedure cycle	X			
V26.89	Other specified procreative management		X		
V26.9	Unspecified procreative management		X		
V27.X	Outcome of delivery			X	
V28.X	Encounter for antenatal screening of mother		X		
V29.X	Observation and evaluation of newborns for suspected condition not found		X		
V30.X	Single liveborn	X			

1. Generally for use as first listed only but may be used as additional if patient has more than one encounter on one day or there is more than one reason for the encounter
2. These codes may be used as first listed or additional codes
3. These codes are only for use as additional codes
4. These codes are primarily for use in the nonacute setting and should be limited to encounters for which no sign or symptom or reason for visit is documented in the record. Their use may be as either a first listed or additional code.

Code(s)	Description	1st Dx Only[1]	1st or Add'l Dx[2]	Add'l Dx Only[3]	Non-Specific Diagnosis[4]
V31.X	Twin, mate liveborn	X			
V32.X	Twin, mate stillborn	X			
V33.X	Twin, unspecified	X			
V34.X	Other multiple, mates all liveborn	X			
V35.X	Other multiple, mates all stillborn	X			
V36.X	Other multiple, mates live- and stillborn	X			
V37.X	Other multiple, unspecified	X			
V39.X	Unspecified	X			
V40.X	Mental and behavioral problems				X
V41.X	Problems with special senses and other special functions				X
V42.X	Organ or tissue replaced by transplant			X	
V43.0	Organ or tissue replaced by other means, eye globe			X	
V43.1	Organ or tissue replaced by other means, lens			X	
V43.21	Organ or tissue replaced by other means, heart assist device			X	
V43.22	Fully implantable artificial heart status		X		
V43.3	Organ or tissue replaced by other means, heart valve			X	
V43.4	Organ or tissue replaced by other means, blood vessel			X	
V43.5	Organ or tissue replaced by other means, bladder			X	
V43.6X	Organ or tissue replaced by other means, joint			X	
V43.7	Organ or tissue replaced by other means, limb			X	
V43.8X	Other organ or tissue replaced by other means			X	
V44.X	Artificial opening status			X	
V45.0X	Cardiac device in situ			X	
V45.1X	Renal dialysis status			X	
V45.2	Presence of cerebrospinal fluid drainage device			X	
V45.3	Intestinal bypass or anastomosis status			X	
V45.4	Arthrodesis status			X	
V45.5X	Presence of contraceptive device			X	
V45.6X	States following surgery of eye and adnexa			X	
V45.7X	Acquired absence of organ		X		
V45.8X	Other postprocedural status			X	
V46.0	Other dependence on machines, aspirator			X	
V46.11	Dependence on respiratory, status			X	
V46.12	Encounter for respirator dependence during power failure	X			
V46.13	Encounter for weaning from respirator [ventilator]	X			
V46.14	Mechanical complication of respirator [ventilator]		X		
V46.2	Other dependence on machines, supplemental oxygen			X	
V46.3	Wheelchair dependence			X	
V46.8	Other dependence on other enabling machines			X	
V46.9	Unspecified machine dependence				X
V47.X	Other problems with internal organs				X
V48.X	Problems with head, neck and trunk				X
V49.0	Deficiencies of limbs				X
V49.1	Mechanical problems with limbs				X
V49.2	Motor problems with limbs				X
V49.3	Sensory problems with limbs				X
V49.4	Disfigurements of limbs				X
V49.5	Other problems with limbs				X
V49.6X	Upper limb amputation status		X		
V49.7X	Lower limb amputation status		X		
V49.81	Asymptomatic postmenopausal status (age-related) (natural)		X		
V49.82	Dental sealant status			X	
V49.83	Awaiting organ transplant status			X	
V49.84	Bed confinement status		X		
V49.85	Dual sensory impairment			X	
V49.89	Other specified conditions influencing health status		X		
V49.9	Unspecified condition influencing health status				X
V50.X	Elective surgery for purposes other than remedying health states		X		
V51.0	Encounter for breast reconstruction following mastectomy	X			

1.   Generally for use as first listed only but may be used as additional if patient has more than one encounter on one day or there is more than one reason for the encounter
2.   These codes may be used as first listed or additional codes
3.   These codes are only for use as additional codes
4.   These codes are primarily for use in the nonacute setting and should be limited to encounters for which no sign or symptom or reason for visit is documented in the record. Their use may be as either a first listed or additional code.

Code(s)	Description	1st Dx Only[1]	1st or Add'l Dx[2]	Add'l Dx Only[3]	Non-Specific Diagnosis[4]
V51.8	Other aftercare involving the use of plastic surgery				X
V52.X	Fitting and adjustment of prosthetic device and implant		X		
V53.X	Fitting and adjustment of other device		X		
V54.X	Other orthopedic aftercare		X		
V55.X	Attention to artificial openings		X		
V56.0	Extracorporeal dialysis	X			
V56.1	Encounter for fitting and adjustment of extracorporeal dialysis catheter		X		
V56.2	Encounter for fitting and adjustment of peritoneal dialysis catheter		X		
V56.3X	Encounter for adequacy testing for dialysis		X		
V56.8	Encounter for other dialysis and dialysis catheter care		X		
V57.X	Care involving use of rehabilitation procedures	X			
V58.0	Radiotherapy	X			
V58.11	Encounter for antineoplastic chemotherapy	X			
V58.12	Encounter for antineoplastic immunotherapy	X			
V58.2	Blood transfusion without reported diagnosis				X
V58.3X	Attention to dressings and sutures		X		
V58.4X	Other aftercare following surgery		X		
V58.5	Encounter for orthodontics				X
V58.6X	Long term (current) drug use			X	
V58.7X	Aftercare following surgery to specified body systems, not elsewhere classified		X		
V58.8X	Other specified procedures and aftercare		X		
V58.9	Unspecified aftercare				X
V59.X	Donors	X			
V60.X	Housing, household, and economic circumstances			X	
V61.X	Other family circumstances		X		
V62.X	Other psychosocial circumstances			X	
V63.X	Unavailability of other medical facilities for care		X		
V64.X	Persons encountering health services for specified procedure, not carried out			X	
V65.X	Other persons seeking consultation without complaint or sickness		X		
V66.0	Convalescence and palliative care following surgery	X			
V66.1	Convalescence and palliative care following radiotherapy	X			
V66.2	Convalescence and palliative care following chemotherapy	X			
V66.3	Convalescence and palliative care following psychotherapy and other treatment for mental disorder	X			
V66.4	Convalescence and palliative care following treatment of fracture	X			
V66.5	Convalescence and palliative care following other treatment	X			
V66.6	Convalescence and palliative care following combined treatment	X			
V66.7	Encounter for palliative care			X	
V66.9	Unspecified convalescence	X			
V67.X	Follow-up examination		X		
V68.X	Encounters for administrative purposes	X			
V69.X	Problems related to lifestyle		X		
V70.0	Routine general medical examination at a health care facility	X			
V70.1	General psychiatric examination, requested by the authority	X			
V70.2	General psychiatric examination, other and unspecified	X			
V70.3	Other medical examination for administrative purposes	X			
V70.4	Examination for medicolegal reasons	X			
V70.5	Health examination of defined subpopulations	X			
V70.6	Health examination in population surveys	X			
V70.7	Examination of participant in clinical trial		X		
V70.8	Other specified general medical examinations	X			
V70.9	Unspecified general medical examination	X			
V71.X	Observation and evaluation for suspected conditions not found	X			
V72.0	Examination of eyes and vision		X		
V72.1X	Examination of ears and hearing		X		
V72.2	Dental examination		X		
V72.3X	Gynecological examination		X		
V72.4X	Pregnancy examination or test		X		
V72.5	Radiological examination, NEC		X		

1.   Generally for use as first listed only but may be used as additional if patient has more than one encounter on one day or there is more than one reason for the encounter
2.   These codes may be used as first listed or additional codes
3.   These codes are only for use as additional codes
4.   These codes are primarily for use in the nonacute setting and should be limited to encounters for which no sign or symptom or reason for visit is documented in the record. Their use may be as either a first listed or additional code.

Code(s)	Description	1st Dx Only[1]	1st or Add'l Dx[2]	Add'l Dx Only[3]	Non-Specific Diagnosis[4]
V72.6	Laboratory examination		X		
V72.7	Diagnostic skin and sensitization tests		X		
V72.81	Preoperative cardiovascular examination		X		
V72.82	Preoperative respiratory examination		X		
V72.83	Other specified preoperative examination		X		
V72.84	Preoperative examination, unspecified		X		
V72.85	Other specified examination		X		
V72.86	Encounter for blood typing		X		
V72.9	Unspecified examination				X
V73.X	Special screening examination for viral and chlamydial diseases		X		
V74.X	Special screening examination for bacterial and spirochetal diseases		X		
V75.X	Special screening examination for other infectious diseases		X		
V76.X	Special screening examination for malignant neoplasms		X		
V77.X	Special screening examination for endocrine, nutritional, metabolic and immunity disorders		X		
V78.X	Special screening examination for disorders of blood and blood-forming organs		X		
V79.X	Special screening examination for mental disorders and developmental handicaps		X		
V80.X	Special screening examination for neurological, eye, and ear diseases		X		
V81.X	Special screening examination for cardiovascular, respiratory, and genitourinary diseases		X		
V82.X	Special screening examination for other conditions		X		
V83.X	Genetic carrier status		X		
V84.X	Genetic susceptibility to disease			X	
V85	Body mass index			X	
V86	Estrogen receptor status			X	
V87.0X	Contact with and (suspected) exposure to hazardous metals		X		
V87.1X	Contact with and (suspected) exposure to hazardous aromatic compounds		X		
V87.2	Contact with and (suspected) exposure to other potentially hazardous chemicals		X		
V87.3X	Contact with and (suspected) exposure to other potentially hazardous substances		X		
V87.4X	Personal history of drug therapy			X	
V88.0X	Acquired absence of cervix and uterus			X	
V89.0X	Suspected maternal and fetal anomalies not found		X		

1. Generally for use as first listed only but may be used as additional if patient has more than one encounter on one day or there is more than one reason for the encounter
2. These codes may be used as first listed or additional codes
3. These codes are only for use as additional codes
4. These codes are primarily for use in the nonacute setting and should be limited to encounters for which no sign or symptom or reason for visit is documented in the record. Their use may be as either a first listed or additional code.

19. **Supplemental Classification of External Causes of Injury and Poisoning (E codes, E800-E999)**

    Introduction: These guidelines are provided for those who are currently collecting E codes in order that there will be standardization in the process. If your institution plans to begin collecting E codes, these guidelines are to be applied. The use of E codes is supplemental to the application of ICD-9-CM diagnosis codes. E codes are never to be recorded as principal diagnoses (first-listed in non-inpatient setting) and are not required for reporting to CMS.

    External causes of injury and poisoning codes (E codes) are intended to provide data for injury research and evaluation of injury prevention strategies. E codes capture how the injury or poisoning happened (cause), the intent (unintentional or accidental; or intentional, such as suicide or assault), and the place where the event occurred.

    Some major categories of E codes include:
    - transport accidents
    - poisoning and adverse effects of drugs, medicinal substances and biologicals
    - accidental falls
    - accidents caused by fire and flames
    - accidents due to natural and environmental factors
    - late effects of accidents, assaults or self injury
    - assaults or purposely inflicted injury
    - suicide or self inflicted injury

    These guidelines apply for the coding and collection of E codes from records in hospitals, outpatient clinics, emergency departments, other ambulatory care settings and provider offices, and nonacute care settings, except when other specific guidelines apply.

a. **General E code coding guidelines**

   1) **Used with any code in the range of 001-V89**
      An E code may be used with any code in the range of 001-V89, which indicates an injury, poisoning, or adverse effect due to an external cause.

   2) **Assign the appropriate E code for all initial treatments**
      Assign the appropriate E code for the initial encounter of an injury, poisoning, or adverse effect of drugs, not for subsequent treatment.

      External cause of injury codes (E-codes) may be assigned while the acute fracture codes are still applicable.
      See Section I.C.17.b.1 for coding of acute fractures.

   3) **Use the full range of E codes**
      Use the full range of E codes to completely describe the cause, the intent and the place of occurrence, if applicable, for all injuries, poisonings, and adverse effects of drugs.

   4) **Assign as many E codes as necessary**
      Assign as many E codes as necessary to fully explain each cause. If only one E code can be recorded, assign the E code most related to the principal diagnosis.

   5) **The selection of the appropriate E code**
      The selection of the appropriate E code is guided by the Index to External Causes, which is located after the alphabetical index to diseases and by Inclusion and Exclusion notes in the Tabular List.

   6) **E code can never be a principal diagnosis**
      An E code can never be a principal (first listed) diagnosis.

   7) **External cause code(s) with systemic inflammatory response syndrome (SIRS)**
      An external cause code is not appropriate with a code from subcategory 995.9, unless the patient also has an injury, poisoning, or adverse effect of drugs.

b. **Place of occurrence guideline**

Use an additional code from category E849 to indicate the Place of Occurrence for injuries and poisonings. The Place of Occurrence describes the place where the event occurred and not the patient's activity at the time of the event.

Do not use E849.9 if the place of occurrence is not stated.

c. **Adverse effects of drugs, medicinal and biological substances guidelines**

1) **Do not code directly from the Table of Drugs**

Do not code directly from the Table of Drugs and Chemicals. Always refer back to the Tabular List.

2) **Use as many codes as necessary to describe**

Use as many codes as necessary to describe completely all drugs, medicinal or biological substances.

3) **If the same E code would describe the causative agent**

If the same E code would describe the causative agent for more than one adverse reaction, assign the code only once.

4) **If two or more drugs, medicinal or biological substances**

If two or more drugs, medicinal or biological substances are reported, code each individually unless the combination code is listed in the Table of Drugs and Chemicals. In that case, assign the E code for the combination.

5) **When a reaction results from the interaction of a drug(s)**

When a reaction results from the interaction of a drug(s) and alcohol, use poisoning codes and E codes for both.

6) **If the reporting format limits the number of E codes**

If the reporting format limits the number of E codes that can be used in reporting clinical data, code the one most related to the principal diagnosis. Include at least one from each category (cause, intent, place) if possible.

If there are different fourth-digit codes in the same three digit category, use the code for "Other specified" of that category. If there is no "Other specified" code in that category, use the appropriate "Unspecified" code in that category.

If the codes are in different three digit categories, assign the appropriate E code for other multiple drugs and medicinal substances.

7) **Codes from the E930-E949 series**

Codes from the E930-E949 series must be used to identify the causative substance for an adverse effect of drug, medicinal and biological substances, correctly prescribed and properly administered. The effect, such as tachycardia, delirium, gastrointestinal hemorrhaging, vomiting, hypokalemia, hepatitis, renal failure, or respiratory failure, is coded and followed by the appropriate code from the E930-E949 series.

d. **Multiple cause E code coding guidelines**

If two or more events cause separate injuries, an E code should be assigned for each cause. The first listed E code will be selected in the following order:

E codes for child and adult abuse take priority over all other E codes.

See Section I.C.19.e., Child and Adult abuse guidelines.

E codes for terrorism events take priority over all other E codes except child and adult abuse.

E codes for cataclysmic events take priority over all other E codes except child and adult abuse and terrorism.

E codes for transport accidents take priority over all other E codes except cataclysmic events and child and adult abuse and terrorism.

The first-listed E code should correspond to the cause of the most serious diagnosis due to an assault, accident, or self-harm, following the order of hierarchy listed above.

e. **Child and adult abuse guideline**

1) **Intentional injury**

When the cause of an injury or neglect is intentional child or adult abuse, the first listed E code should be assigned from categories E960-E968, Homicide and injury purposely inflicted by other persons, (except category E967). An E code from category E967, Child and adult battering and other maltreatment, should be added as an additional code to identify the perpetrator, if known.

2) **Accidental intent**

In cases of neglect when the intent is determined to be accidental E code E904.0, Abandonment or neglect of infant and helpless person, should be the first listed E code.

f. **Unknown or suspected intent guideline**

1) **If the intent (accident, self-harm, assault) of the cause of an injury or poisoning is unknown**

If the intent (accident, self-harm, assault) of the cause of an injury or poisoning is unknown or unspecified, code the intent as undetermined E980-E989.

2) **If the intent (accident, self-harm, assault) of the cause of an injury or poisoning is questionable**

If the intent (accident, self-harm, assault) of the cause of an injury or poisoning is questionable, probable or suspected, code the intent as undetermined E980-E989.

g. **Undetermined cause**

When the intent of an injury or poisoning is known, but the cause is unknown, use codes: E928.9, Unspecified accident, E958.9, Suicide and self-inflicted injury by unspecified means, and E968.9, Assault by unspecified means.

These E codes should rarely be used, as the documentation in the medical record, in both the inpatient outpatient and other settings, should normally provide sufficient detail to determine the cause of the injury.

h. **Late effects of external cause guidelines**

1) **Late effect E codes**

Late effect E codes exist for injuries and poisonings but not for adverse effects of drugs, misadventures and surgical complications.

2) **Late effect E codes (E929, E959, E969, E977, E989, or E999.1)**

A late effect E code (E929, E959, E969, E977, E989, or E999.1) should be used with any report of a late effect or sequela resulting from a previous injury or poisoning (905-909).

3) **Late effect E code with a related current injury**

A late effect E code should never be used with a related current nature of injury code.

4) **Use of late effect E codes for subsequent visits**

Use a late effect E code for subsequent visits when a late effect of the initial injury or poisoning is being treated. There is no late effect E code for adverse effects of drugs. Do not use a late effect E code for subsequent visits for follow-up care (e.g., to assess healing, to receive rehabilitative therapy) of the injury or poisoning when no late effect of the injury has been documented.

i. **Misadventures and complications of care guidelines**

1) **Code range E870-E876**

Assign a code in the range of E870-E876 if misadventures are stated by the provider.

2) **Code range E878-E879**

Assign a code in the range of E878-E879 if the provider attributes an abnormal reaction or later complication to a surgical or medical procedure, but does not mention misadventure at the time of the procedure as the cause of the reaction.

j. **Terrorism guidelines**

1) **Cause of injury identified by the Federal Government (FBI) as terrorism**

When the cause of an injury is identified by the Federal Government (FBI) as terrorism, the first-listed E-code should be a code from category E979, Terrorism. The definition of terrorism employed by the FBI is found at the inclusion note at E979. The terrorism E-code is the only E-code that should be assigned. Additional E codes from the assault categories should not be assigned.

2) **Cause of an injury is suspected to be the result of terrorism**

When the cause of an injury is suspected to be the result of terrorism a code from category E979 should not be assigned. Assign a code in the range of E codes based circumstances on the documentation of intent and mechanism.

3) **Code E979.9, Terrorism, secondary effects**

Assign code E979.9, Terrorism, secondary effects, for conditions occurring subsequent to the terrorist event. This code should not be assigned for conditions that are due to the initial terrorist act.

4) **Statistical tabulation of terrorism codes**

For statistical purposes these codes will be tabulated within the category for assault, expanding the current category from E960-E969 to include E979 and E999.1.

SECTION II. SELECTION OF PRINCIPAL DIAGNOSIS

The circumstances of inpatient admission always govern the selection of principal diagnosis. The principal diagnosis is defined in the Uniform Hospital Discharge Data Set (UHDDS) as "that condition established after study to be chiefly responsible for occasioning the admission of the patient to the hospital for care."

The UHDDS definitions are used by hospitals to report inpatient data elements in a standardized manner. These data elements and their definitions can be found in the July 31, 1985, Federal Register (Vol. 50, No, 147), pp. 31038-40.

Since that time the application of the UHDDS definitions has been expanded to include all non-outpatient settings (acute care, short term, long term care and psychiatric hospitals; home health agencies; rehab facilities; nursing homes, etc).

In determining principal diagnosis the coding conventions in the ICD-9-CM, Volumes I and II take precedence over these official coding guidelines.

(See Section I.A., Conventions for the ICD-9-CM)

The importance of consistent, complete documentation in the medical record cannot be overemphasized. Without such documentation the application of all coding guidelines is a difficult, if not impossible, task.

A. Codes for symptoms, signs, and ill-defined conditions

Codes for symptoms, signs, and ill-defined conditions from Chapter 16 are not to be used as principal diagnosis when a related definitive diagnosis has been established.

B. Two or more interrelated conditions, each potentially meeting the definition for principal diagnosis

When there are two or more interrelated conditions (such as diseases in the same ICD-9-CM chapter or manifestations characteristically associated with a certain disease) potentially meeting the definition of principal diagnosis, either condition may be sequenced first, unless the circumstances of the admission, the therapy provided, the Tabular List, or the Alphabetic Index indicate otherwise.

C. Two or more diagnoses that equally meet the definition for principal diagnosis

In the unusual instance when two or more diagnoses equally meet the criteria for principal diagnosis as determined by the circumstances of admission, diagnostic workup and/or therapy provided, and the Alphabetic Index, Tabular List, or another coding guidelines does not provide sequencing direction, any one of the diagnoses may be sequenced first.

D. Two or more comparative or contrasting conditions

In those rare instances when two or more contrasting or comparative diagnoses are documented as "either/or" (or similar terminology), they are coded as if the diagnoses were confirmed and the diagnoses are sequenced according to the circumstances of the admission. If no further determination can be made as to which diagnosis should be principal, either diagnosis may be sequenced first.

E. A symptom(s) followed by contrasting/comparative diagnoses

When a symptom(s) is followed by contrasting/comparative diagnoses, the symptom code is sequenced first. All the contrasting/comparative diagnoses should be coded as additional diagnoses.

F. Original treatment plan not carried out

Sequence as the principal diagnosis the condition, which after study occasioned the admission to the hospital, even though treatment may not have been carried out due to unforeseen circumstances.

G. Complications of surgery and other medical care

When the admission is for treatment of a complication resulting from surgery or other medical care, the complication code is sequenced as the principal diagnosis. If the complication is classified to the 996-999 series and the code lacks the necessary specificity in describing the complication, an additional code for the specific complication should be assigned.

H. Uncertain diagnosis

If the diagnosis documented at the time of discharge is qualified as "probable", "suspected", "likely", "questionable", "possible", or "still to be ruled out", or other similar terms indicating uncertainty, code the condition as if it existed or was established. The bases for these guidelines are the diagnostic workup, arrangements for further workup or observation, and initial therapeutic approach that correspond most closely with the established diagnosis.

Note: This guideline is applicable only to inpatient admissions to short-term, acute, long-term care and psychiatric hospitals.

I. Admission from observation unit

1. Admission following medical observation

When a patient is admitted to an observation unit for a medical condition, which either worsens or does not improve, and is subsequently admitted as an inpatient of the same hospital for this same medical condition, the principal diagnosis would be the medical condition which led to the hospital admission.

2. Admission following post-operative observation

When a patient is admitted to an observation unit to monitor a condition (or complication) that develops following outpatient surgery, and then is subsequently admitted as an inpatient of the same hospital, hospitals should apply the Uniform Hospital Discharge Data Set (UHDDS) definition of principal diagnosis as "that condition established after study to be chiefly responsible for occasioning the admission of the patient to the hospital for care."

J. Admission from outpatient surgery

When a patient receives surgery in the hospital's outpatient surgery department and is subsequently admitted for continuing inpatient care at the same hospital, the following guidelines should be followed in selecting the principal diagnosis for the inpatient admission:

- If the reason for the inpatient admission is a complication, assign the complication as the principal diagnosis.
- If no complication, or other condition, is documented as the reason for the inpatient admission, assign the reason for the outpatient surgery as the principal diagnosis.
- If the reason for the inpatient admission is another condition unrelated to the surgery, assign the unrelated condition as the principal diagnosis.

SECTION III. REPORTING ADDITIONAL DIAGNOSES

GENERAL RULES FOR OTHER (ADDITIONAL) DIAGNOSES

For reporting purposes the definition for "other diagnoses" is interpreted as additional conditions that affect patient care in terms of requiring:

clinical evaluation; or
therapeutic treatment; or
diagnostic procedures; or
extended length of hospital stay; or
increased nursing care and/or monitoring.

The UHDDS item #11-b defines Other Diagnoses as "all conditions that coexist at the time of admission, that develop subsequently, or that affect the treatment received and/or the length of stay. Diagnoses that relate to an earlier episode which have no bearing on the current hospital stay are to be excluded." UHDDS definitions apply to inpatients in acute care, short-term, long term care and psychiatric hospital setting. The UHDDS definitions are used by acute care short-term hospitals to report inpatient data elements in a standardized manner. These data elements and their definitions can be found in the July 31, 1985, Federal Register (Vol. 50, No, 147), pp. 31038-40**.**

Since that time the application of the UHDDS definitions has been expanded to include all non-outpatient settings (acute care, short term, long term care and psychiatric hospitals; home health agencies; rehab facilities; nursing homes, etc).

The following guidelines are to be applied in designating "other diagnoses" when neither the Alphabetic Index nor the Tabular List in ICD-9-CM provide direction. The listing of the diagnoses in the patient record is the responsibility of the attending provider.

A. Previous conditions

If the provider has included a diagnosis in the final diagnostic statement, such as the discharge summary or the face sheet, it should ordinarily be coded. Some providers include in the diagnostic statement resolved conditions or diagnoses and status-post procedures from previous admission that have no bearing on the current stay. Such conditions are not to be reported and are coded only if required by hospital policy.

However, history codes (V10-V19) may be used as secondary codes if the historical condition or family history has an impact on current care or influences treatment.

B. Abnormal findings

Abnormal findings (laboratory, x-ray, pathologic, and other diagnostic results) are not coded and reported unless the provider indicates their clinical significance. If the findings are outside the normal range and the attending provider has ordered other tests to evaluate the condition or prescribed treatment, it is appropriate to ask the provider whether the abnormal finding should be added.

Please note: This differs from the coding practices in the outpatient setting for coding encounters for diagnostic tests that have been interpreted by a provider.

C. Uncertain diagnosis

If the diagnosis documented at the time of discharge is qualified as "probable", "suspected", "likely", "questionable", "possible", or "still to be ruled out" or other similar terms indicating uncertainty, code the condition as if it existed or was established. The bases for these guidelines are the diagnostic workup, arrangements for further workup or observation, and initial therapeutic approach that correspond most closely with the established diagnosis.

Note: This guideline is applicable only to inpatient admissions to short-term, acute, long-term care and psychiatric hospitals.

SECTION IV. DIAGNOSTIC CODING AND REPORTING GUIDELINES FOR OUTPATIENT SERVICES

These coding guidelines for outpatient diagnoses have been approved for use by hospitals/ providers in coding and reporting hospital-based outpatient services and provider-based office visits.

Information about the use of certain abbreviations, punctuation, symbols, and other conventions used in the ICD-9-CM Tabular List (code numbers and titles), can be found in Section IA of these guidelines, under "Conventions Used in the Tabular List." Information about the correct sequence to use in finding a code is also described in Section I.

The terms encounter and visit are often used interchangeably in describing outpatient service contacts and, therefore, appear together in these guidelines without distinguishing one from the other.

Though the conventions and general guidelines apply to all settings, coding guidelines for outpatient and provider reporting of diagnoses will vary in a number of instances from those for inpatient diagnoses, recognizing that:

The Uniform Hospital Discharge Data Set (UHDDS) definition of principal diagnosis applies only to inpatients in acute, short-term, long-term care and psychiatric hospitals.

Coding guidelines for inconclusive diagnoses (probable, suspected, rule out, etc.) were developed for inpatient reporting and do not apply to outpatients.

A. Selection of first-listed condition

In the outpatient setting, the term first-listed diagnosis is used in lieu of principal diagnosis.

In determining the first-listed diagnosis the coding conventions of ICD-9-CM, as well as the general and disease specific guidelines take precedence over the outpatient guidelines.

Diagnoses often are not established at the time of the initial encounter/visit. It may take two or more visits before the diagnosis is confirmed.

The most critical rule involves beginning the search for the correct code assignment through the Alphabetic Index. Never begin searching initially in the Tabular List as this will lead to coding errors.

1. Outpatient surgery

When a patient presents for outpatient surgery, code the reason for the surgery as the first-listed diagnosis (reason for the encounter), even if the surgery is not performed due to a contraindication.

2. Observation stay

When a patient is admitted for observation for a medical condition, assign a code for the medical condition as the first-listed diagnosis.

When a patient presents for outpatient surgery and develops complications requiring admission to observation, code the reason for the surgery as the first reported diagnosis (reason for the encounter), followed by codes for the complications as secondary diagnoses.

B. Codes from 001.0 through V89

The appropriate code or codes from 001.0 through **V89** must be used to identify diagnoses, symptoms, conditions, problems, complaints, or other reason(s) for the encounter/visit.

C. Accurate reporting of ICD-9-CM diagnosis codes

For accurate reporting of ICD-9-CM diagnosis codes, the documentation should describe the patient's condition, using terminology which includes specific diagnoses as well as symptoms, problems, or reasons for the encounter. There are ICD-9-CM codes to describe all of these.

D. Selection of codes 001.0 through 999.9

The selection of codes 001.0 through 999.9 will frequently be used to describe the reason for the encounter. These codes are from the section of ICD-9-CM for the classification of diseases and injuries (e.g. infectious and parasitic diseases; neoplasms; symptoms, signs, and ill-defined conditions, etc.).

E. Codes that describe symptoms and signs

Codes that describe symptoms and signs, as opposed to diagnoses, are acceptable for reporting purposes when a diagnosis has not been established (confirmed) by the provider. Chapter 16 of ICD-9-CM, Symptoms, Signs, and Ill-defined conditions (codes 780.0-799.9) contain many, but not all codes for symptoms.

F. Encounters for circumstances other than a disease or injury

ICD-9-CM provides codes to deal with encounters for circumstances other than a disease or injury. The Supplementary Classification of factors Influencing Health Status and Contact with Health Services (V01.0-**V89**) is provided to deal with occasions when circumstances other than a disease or injury are recorded as diagnosis or problems. *See Section I.C. 18 for information on V-codes*

G. Level of detail in coding

1. ICD-9-CM codes with 3, 4, or 5 digits

ICD-9-CM is composed of codes with either 3, 4, or 5 digits. Codes with three digits are included in ICD-9-CM as the heading of a category of codes that may be further subdivided by the use of fourth and/or fifth-digits, which provide greater specificity.

2. Use of full number of digits required for a code

A three-digit code is to be used only if it is not further subdivided. Where fourth-digit subcategories and/or fifth-digit subclassifications are provided, they must be assigned. A code is invalid if it has not been coded to the full number of digits required for that code.

See also discussion under Section I.b.3., General Coding Guidelines, Level of Detail in Coding.

H. ICD-9-CM code for the diagnosis, condition, problem, or other reason for encounter/visit

List first the ICD-9-CM code for the diagnosis, condition, problem, or other reason for encounter/visit shown in the medical record to be chiefly responsible for the services provided. List additional codes that describe any coexisting conditions. In some cases the first-listed diagnosis may be a symptom when a diagnosis has not been established (confirmed) by the physician.

I. Uncertain diagnosis

Do not code diagnoses documented as "probable", "suspected," "questionable," "rule out," or "working diagnosis" or other similar terms indicating uncertainty. Rather, code the condition(s) to the highest degree of certainty for that encounter/visit, such as symptoms, signs, abnormal test results, or other reason for the visit.

Please note: This differs from the coding practices used by short-term, acute care, long-term care and psychiatric hospitals.

J. Chronic diseases

Chronic diseases treated on an ongoing basis may be coded and reported as many times as the patient receives treatment and care for the condition(s)

K. Code all documented conditions that coexist

Code all documented conditions that coexist at the time of the encounter/visit, and require or affect patient care treatment or management. Do not code conditions that were previously treated and no longer exist. However, history codes (V10-V19) may be used as secondary codes if the historical condition or family history has an impact on current care or influences treatment.

L. Patients receiving diagnostic services only

For patients receiving diagnostic services only during an encounter/visit, sequence first the diagnosis, condition, problem, or other reason for encounter/visit shown in the medical record to be chiefly responsible for the outpatient services provided during the encounter/visit. Codes for other diagnoses (e.g., chronic conditions) may be sequenced as additional diagnoses.

For encounters for routine laboratory/radiology testing in the absence of any signs, symptoms, or associated diagnosis, assign V72.5 and V72.6. If routine testing is performed during the same encounter as a test to evaluate a sign, symptom, or diagnosis, it is appropriate to assign both the V code and the code describing the reason for the non-routine test.

For outpatient encounters for diagnostic tests that have been interpreted by a physician, and the final report is available at the time of coding, code any confirmed or definitive diagnosis(es) documented in the interpretation. Do not code related signs and symptoms as additional diagnoses.

Please note: This differs from the coding practice in the hospital inpatient setting regarding abnormal findings on test results.

M. Patients receiving therapeutic services only

For patients receiving therapeutic services only during an encounter/visit, sequence first the diagnosis, condition, problem, or other reason for encounter/visit shown in the medical record to be chiefly responsible for the outpatient services provided during the encounter/visit. Codes for other diagnoses (e.g., chronic conditions) may be sequenced as additional diagnoses.

The only exception to this rule is that when the primary reason for the admission/encounter is chemotherapy, radiation therapy, or rehabilitation, the appropriate V code for the service is listed first, and the diagnosis or problem for which the service is being performed listed second.

N. Patients receiving preoperative evaluations only

For patients receiving preoperative evaluations only, sequence first a code from category V72.8, Other specified examinations, to describe the pre-op consultations. Assign a code for the condition to describe the reason for the surgery as an additional diagnosis. Code also any findings related to the pre-op evaluation.

O. Ambulatory surgery

For ambulatory surgery, code the diagnosis for which the surgery was performed. If the postoperative diagnosis is known to be different from the preoperative diagnosis at the time the diagnosis is confirmed, select the postoperative diagnosis for coding, since it is the most definitive.

P. Routine outpatient prenatal visits

For routine outpatient prenatal visits when no complications are present, codes V22.0, Supervision of normal first pregnancy, or V22.1, Supervision of other normal pregnancy, should be used as the principal diagnosis. These codes should not be used in conjunction with chapter 11 codes.

APPENDIX I. PRESENT ON ADMISSION REPORTING GUIDELINES

Introduction

These guidelines are to be used as a supplement to the *ICD-9-CM Official Guidelines for Coding and Reporting* to facilitate the assignment of the Present on Admission (POA) indicator for each diagnosis and external cause of injury code reported on claim forms (UB-04 and 837 Institutional).

These guidelines are not intended to replace any guidelines in the main body of the *ICD-9-CM Official Guidelines for Coding and Reporting*. The POA guidelines are not intended to provide guidance on when a condition should be coded, but rather, how to apply the POA indicator to the final set of diagnosis codes that have been assigned in accordance with Sections I, II, and III of the official coding guidelines. Subsequent to the assignment of the ICD-9-CM codes, the POA indicator should then be assigned to those conditions that have been coded.

As stated in the Introduction to the ICD-9-CM Official Guidelines for Coding and Reporting, a joint effort between the healthcare provider and the coder is essential to achieve complete and accurate documentation, code assignment, and reporting of diagnoses and procedures. The importance of consistent, complete documentation in the medical record cannot be overemphasized. Medical record documentation from any provider involved in the care and treatment of the patient may be used to support the determination of whether a condition was present on admission or not. In the context of the official coding guidelines, the term "provider" means a physician or any qualified healthcare practitioner who is legally accountable for establishing the patient's diagnosis.

These guidelines are not a substitute for the provider's clinical judgment as to the determination of whether a condition was/was not present on admission. The provider should be queried regarding issues related to the linking of signs/symptoms, timing of test results, and the timing of findings.

General Reporting Requirements

All claims involving inpatient admissions to general acute care hospitals or other facilities that are subject to a law or regulation mandating collection of present on admission information.

Present on admission is defined as present at the time the order for inpatient admission occurs. Conditions that develop during an outpatient encounter, including emergency department, observation, or outpatient surgery, are considered as present on admission.

POA indicator is assigned to principal and secondary diagnoses (as defined in Section II of the Official Guidelines for Coding and Reporting) and the external cause of injury codes.

Issues related to inconsistent, missing, conflicting or unclear documentation must still be resolved by the provider.

If a condition would not be coded and reported based on UHDDS definitions and current official coding guidelines, then the POA indicator would not be reported.

Reporting Options

Y - Yes

N - No

U - Unknown

W – Clinically undetermined

Unreported/Not used (or "1" for Medicare usage) – (Exempt from POA reporting)

For more specific instructions on Medicare POA indicator reporting options, refer to http://www.cms.hhs.gov/HospitalAcqCond/02_Statute_Regulations_Program_Instructions.asp#TopOfPage

Reporting Definitions

Y = present at the time of inpatient admission

N = not present at the time of inpatient admission

U = documentation is insufficient to determine if condition is present on admission

W = provider is unable to clinically determine whether condition was present on admission or not

Timeframe for POA Identification and Documentation

There is no required timeframe as to when a provider (per the definition of "provider" used in these guidelines) must identify or document a condition to be present on admission. In some clinical situations, it may not be possible for a provider to make a definitive diagnosis (or a condition may not be recognized or reported by the patient) for a period of time after admission. In some cases it may be several days before the provider arrives at a definitive diagnosis. This does not mean that the condition was not present on admission. Determination of whether the condition was present on admission or not will be based on the

applicable POA guideline as identified in this document, or on the provider's best clinical judgment.

If at the time of code assignment the documentation is unclear as to whether a condition was present on admission or not, it is appropriate to query the provider for clarification.

Assigning the POA Indicator

Condition is on the "Exempt from Reporting" list Leave the "present on admission" field blank if the condition is on the list of ICD-9-CM codes for which this field is not applicable. This is the only circumstance in which the field may be left blank.

POA explicitly documented

Assign Y for any condition the provider explicitly documents as being present on admission.

Assign N for any condition the provider explicitly documents as not present at the time of admission.

Conditions diagnosed prior to inpatient admission

Assign "Y" for conditions that were diagnosed prior to admission (example: hypertension, diabetes mellitus, asthma)

Conditions diagnosed during the admission but clearly present before admission

Assign "Y" for conditions diagnosed during the admission that were clearly present but not diagnosed until after admission occurred.

Diagnoses subsequently confirmed after admission are considered present on admission if at the time of admission they are documented as suspected, possible, rule out, differential diagnosis, or constitute an underlying cause of a symptom that is present at the time of admission.

Condition develops during outpatient encounter prior to inpatient admission

Assign Y for any condition that develops during an outpatient encounter prior to a written order for inpatient admission.

Documentation does not indicate whether condition was present on admission

Assign "U" when the medical record documentation is unclear as to whether the condition was present on admission. "U" should not be routinely assigned and used only in very limited circumstances. Coders are encouraged to query the providers when the documentation is unclear.

Documentation states that it cannot be determined whether the condition was or was not present on admission

Assign "W" when the medical record documentation indicates that it cannot be clinically determined whether or not the condition was present on admission.

Chronic condition with acute exacerbation during the admission

If the code is a combination code that identifies both the chronic condition and the acute exacerbation, see POA guidelines pertaining to combination codes.

If the combination code only identifies the chronic condition and not the acute exacerbation (e.g., acute exacerbation of CHF), assign "Y."

Conditions documented as possible, probable, suspected, or rule out at the time of discharge

If the final diagnosis contains a possible, probable, suspected, or rule out diagnosis, and this diagnosis was suspected at the time of inpatient admission, assign "Y."

If the final diagnosis contains a possible, probable, suspected, or rule out diagnosis, and this diagnosis was based on symptoms or clinical findings that were not present on admission, assign "N".

Conditions documented as impending or threatened at the time of discharge

If the final diagnosis contains an impending or threatened diagnosis, and this diagnosis is based on symptoms or clinical findings that were present on admission, assign "Y".

If the final diagnosis contains an impending or threatened diagnosis, and this diagnosis is based on symptoms or clinical findings that were not present on admission, assign "N".

Acute and chronic conditions

Assign "Y" for acute conditions that are present at time of admission and N for acute conditions that are not present at time of admission.

Assign "Y" for chronic conditions, even though the condition may not be diagnosed until after admission.

If a single code identifies both an acute and chronic condition, see the POA guidelines for combination codes.

Combination codes

Assign "N" if any part of the combination code was not present on admission (e.g., obstructive chronic bronchitis with acute exacerbation and the exacerbation was not present on admission; gastric ulcer that does not start bleeding until after admission; asthma patient develops status asthmaticus after admission)

Assign "Y" if all parts of the combination code were present on admission (e.g., patient with diabetic nephropathy is admitted with uncontrolled diabetes)

If the final diagnosis includes comparative or contrasting diagnoses, and both were present, or suspected, at the time of admission, assign "Y".

For infection codes that include the causal organism, assign "Y" if the infection (or signs of the infection) was present on admission, even though the culture results may not be known until after admission (e.g., patient is admitted with pneumonia and the provider documents pseudomonas as the causal organism a few days later).

Same Diagnosis Code for Two or More Conditions

When the same ICD-9-CM diagnosis code applies to two or more conditions during the same encounter (e.g. bilateral condition, or two separate conditions classified to the same ICD-9-CM diagnosis code):

Assign "Y" if all conditions represented by the single ICD-9-CM code were present on admission (e.g. bilateral fracture of the same bone, same site, and both fractures were present on admission)

Assign "N" if any of the conditions represented by the single ICD-9-CM code was not present on admission (e.g. dehydration with hyponatremia is assigned to code 276.1, but only one of these conditions was present on admission).

Obstetrical conditions

Whether or not the patient delivers during the current hospitalization does not affect assignment of the POA indicator. The determining factor for POA assignment is whether the pregnancy complication or obstetrical condition described by the code was present at the time of admission or not.

If the pregnancy complication or obstetrical condition was present on admission (e.g., patient admitted in preterm labor), assign "Y".

If the pregnancy complication or obstetrical condition was not present on admission (e.g., 2nd degree laceration during delivery, postpartum hemorrhage that occurred during current hospitalization, fetal distress develops after admission), assign "N".

If the obstetrical code includes more than one diagnosis and any of the diagnoses identified by the code were not present on admission (e.g., Code 642.7, Pre-eclampsia or eclampsia superimposed on preexisting hypertension) assign "N".

If the obstetrical code includes information that is not a diagnosis, do not consider that information in the POA determination. Example, code 652.1x, Breech or other malpresentation successfully converted to cephalic presentation, should be reported as present on admission if the fetus was breech on admission but was converted to cephalic presentation after admission. Since the conversion to cephalic presentation does not represent a diagnosis, the fact that the conversion occurred after admission has no bearing on the POA determination.

Perinatal conditions

Newborns are not considered to be admitted until after birth. Therefore, any condition present at birth or that developed in utero is considered present at admission and should be assigned "Y". This includes conditions that occur during delivery (e.g., injury during delivery, meconium aspiration, exposure to streptococcus B in the vaginal canal).

Congenital conditions and anomalies

Assign "Y" for congenital conditions and anomalies. Congenital conditions are always considered present on admission.

External cause of injury codes

Assign "Y" for any E code representing an external cause of injury or poisoning that occurred prior to inpatient admission (e.g., patient fell out of bed at home, patient fell out of bed in emergency room prior to admission)

Assign "N" for any E code representing an external cause of injury or poisoning that occurred during inpatient hospitalization (e.g., patient fell out of hospital bed during hospital stay, patient experienced an adverse reaction to a medication administered after inpatient admission)

Categories and Codes Exempt from Diagnosis Present on Admission Requirement

Note: *"Diagnosis present on admission" for these code categories are exempt because they represent circumstances regarding the healthcare encounter or factors influencing health status that do not represent a current disease or injury or are always present on admission*

137-139	Late effects of infectious and parasitic diseases
268.1	Rickets, late effect
326	Late effects of intracranial abscess or pyogenic infection
412	Old myocardial infarction
438	Late effects of cerebrovascular disease
650	Normal delivery

660.7	Failed forceps or vacuum extractor, unspecified
677	Late effect of complication of pregnancy, childbirth, and the puerperium
905-909	Late effects of injuries, poisonings, toxic effects, and other external causes
V02	Carrier or suspected carrier of infectious diseases
V03	Need for prophylactic vaccination and inoculation against bacterial diseases
V04	Need for prophylactic vaccination and inoculation against certain viral diseases
V05	Need for other prophylactic vaccination and inoculation against single diseases
V06	Need for prophylactic vaccination and inoculation against combinations of diseases
V07	Need for isolation and other prophylactic measures
V10	Personal history of malignant neoplasm
V11	Personal history of mental disorder
V12	Personal history of certain other diseases
V13	Personal history of other diseases
V14	Personal history of allergy to medicinal agents
V15.01-V15.09	Other personal history, Allergy, other than to medicinal agents
V15.1	Other personal history, Surgery to heart and great vessels
V15.2	Other personal history, Surgery to other major organs
V15.3	Other personal history, Irradiation
V15.4	Other personal history, Psychological trauma
V15.5	Other personal history, Injury
V15.6	Other personal history, Poisoning
V15.7	Other personal history, Contraception
V15.81	Other personal history, Noncompliance with medical treatment
V15.82	Other personal history, History of tobacco use
V15.88	Other personal history, History of fall
V15.89	Other personal history, Other
V15.9	Unspecified personal history presenting hazards to health
V16	Family history of malignant neoplasm
V17	Family history of certain chronic disabling diseases
V18	Family history of certain other specific conditions
V19	Family history of other conditions
V20	Health supervision of infant or child
V21	Constitutional states in development
V22	Normal pregnancy
V23	Supervision of high-risk pregnancy
V24	Postpartum care and examination
V25	Encounter for contraceptive management
V26	Procreative management
V27	Outcome of delivery
V28	Antenatal screening
V29	Observation and evaluation of newborns for suspected condition not found
V30-V39	Liveborn infants according to type of birth
V42	Organ or tissue replaced by transplant
V43	Organ or tissue replaced by other means
V44	Artificial opening status
V45	Other postprocedural states
V46	Other dependence on machines
V49.60-V49.77	Upper and lower limb amputation status
V49.81-V49.84	Other specified conditions influencing health status
V50	Elective surgery for purposes other than remedying health states
V51	Aftercare involving the use of plastic surgery
V52	Fitting and adjustment of prosthetic device and implant
V53	Fitting and adjustment of other device
V54	Other orthopedic aftercare
V55	Attention to artificial openings
V56	Encounter for dialysis and dialysis catheter care
V57	Care involving use of rehabilitation procedures
V58	Encounter for other and unspecified procedures and aftercare
V59	Donors
V60	Housing, household, and economic circumstances
V61	Other family circumstances
V62	Other psychosocial circumstances
V64	Persons encountering health services for specific procedures, not carried out
V65	Other persons seeking consultation
V66	Convalescence and palliative care
V67	Follow-up examination
V68	Encounters for administrative purposes
V69	Problems related to lifestyle

V70	General medical examination
V71	Observation and evaluation for suspected condition not found
V72	Special investigations and examinations
V73	Special screening examination for viral and chlamydial diseases
V74	Special screening examination for bacterial and spirochetal diseases
V75	Special screening examination for other infectious diseases
V76	Special screening for malignant neoplasms
V77	Special screening for endocrine, nutritional, metabolic, and immunity disorders
V78	Special screening for disorders of blood and blood-forming organs
V79	Special screening for mental disorders and developmental handicaps
V80	Special screening for neurological, eye, and ear diseases
V81	Special screening for cardiovascular, respiratory, and genitourinary diseases
V82	Special screening for other conditions
V83	Genetic carrier status
V84	Genetic susceptibility to disease
V85	Body Mass Index
V86	Estrogen receptor status
V87.4	Personal history of drug therapy
V88	Acquired absence of cervix and uterus
V89	Suspected maternal and fetal conditions not found
E800-E807	Railway accidents
E810-E819	Motor vehicle traffic accidents
E820-E825	Motor vehicle nontraffic accidents E826-E829, Other road vehicle accidents
E830-E838	Water transport accidents
E840-E845	Air and space transport accidents
E846-E848	Vehicle accidents not elsewhere classifiable
E849.0-E849.6	Place of occurrence
E849.8-E849.9	Place of occurrence
E883.1	Accidental fall into well
E883.2	Accidental fall into storm drain or manhole
E884.0	Fall from playground equipment
E884.1	Fall from cliff
E885.0	Fall from (nonmotorized) scooter
E885.1	Fall from roller skates
E885.2	Fall from skateboard
E885.3	Fall from skis
E885.4	Fall from snowboard
E886.0	Fall on same level from collision, pushing, or shoving, by or with other person, In sports
E890.0-E890.9	Conflagration in private dwelling
E893.0	Accident caused by ignition of clothing, from controlled fire in private dwelling
E893.2	Accident caused by ignition of clothing, from controlled fire not in building or structure
E894	Ignition of highly inflammable material
E895	Accident caused by controlled fire in private dwelling
E897	Accident caused by controlled fire not in building or structure
E898.0-E898.1	Accident caused by other specified fire and flames
E917.0	Striking against or struck accidentally by objects or persons, in sports without subsequent fall
E917.1	Striking against or struck accidentally by objects or persons, caused by a crowd, by collective fear or panic without subsequent fall
E917.2	Striking against or struck accidentally by objects or persons, in running water without subsequent fall
E917.5	Striking against or struck accidentally by objects or persons, object in sports with subsequent fall
E917.6	Striking against or struck accidentally by objects or persons, caused by a crowd, by collective fear or panic with subsequent fall
E919.0-E919.1	Accidents caused by machinery
E919.3-E919.9	Accidents caused by machinery
E921.0-E921.9	Accident caused by explosion of pressure vessel
E922.0-E922.9	Accident caused by firearm and air gun missile
E924.1	Caustic and corrosive substances
E926.2	Visible and ultraviolet light sources
E928.0-E928.8	Other and unspecified environmental and accidental causes
E929.0-E929.9	Late effects of accidental injury
E959	Late effects of self-inflicted injury
E970-E978	Legal intervention
E979	Terrorism

E981.0-E981.8	Poisoning by gases in domestic use, undetermined whether accidentally or purposely inflicted
E982.0-E982.9	Poisoning by other gases, undetermined whether accidentally or purposely inflicted
E985.0-E985.7	Injury by firearms, air guns and explosives, undetermined whether accidentally or purposely inflicted
E987.0	Falling from high place, undetermined whether accidentally or purposely inflicted, residential premises
E987.2	Falling from high place, undetermined whether accidentally or purposely inflicted, natural sites
E989	Late effects of injury, undetermined whether accidentally or purposely inflicted
E990-E999	Injury resulting from operations of war

POA Examples
General Medical Surgical

1. Patient is admitted for diagnostic work-up for cachexia. The final diagnosis is malignant neoplasm of lung with metastasis.

   Assign "Y" on the POA field for the malignant neoplasm. The malignant neoplasm was clearly present on admission, although it was not diagnosed until after the admission occurred.

2. A patient undergoes outpatient surgery. During the recovery period, the patient develops atrial fibrillation and the patient is subsequently admitted to the hospital as an inpatient.

   Assign "Y" on the POA field for the atrial fibrillation since it developed prior to a written order for inpatient admission.

3. A patient is treated in observation and while in Observation, the patient falls out of bed and breaks a hip. The patient is subsequently admitted as an inpatient to treat the hip fracture.

   Assign "Y" on the POA field for the hip fracture since it developed prior to a written order for inpatient admission.

4. A patient with known congestive heart failure is admitted to the hospital after he develops decompensated congestive heart failure.

   Assign "Y" on the POA field for the congestive heart failure. The ICD-9-CM code identifies the chronic condition and does not specify the acute exacerbation.

5. A patient undergoes inpatient surgery. After surgery, the patient develops fever and is treated aggressively. The physician's final diagnosis documents "possible postoperative infection following surgery."

   Assign "N" on the POA field for the postoperative infection since final diagnoses that contain the terms "possible", "probable", "suspected" or "rule out" and that are based on symptoms or clinical findings that were not present on admission should be reported as "N".

6. A patient with severe cough and difficulty breathing was diagnosed during his hospitalization to have lung cancer.

   Assign "Y" on the POA field for the lung cancer. Even though the cancer was not diagnosed until after admission, it is a chronic condition that was clearly present before the patient's admission.

7. A patient is admitted to the hospital for a coronary artery bypass surgery. Postoperatively he developed a pulmonary embolism.

   Assign "N" on the POA field for the pulmonary embolism. This is an acute condition that was not present on admission.

8. A patient is admitted with a known history of coronary atherosclerosis, status post myocardial infarction five years ago is now admitted for treatment of impending myocardial infarction. The final diagnosis is documented as "impending myocardial infarction."

   Assign "Y" to the impending myocardial infarction because the condition is present on admission.

9. A patient with diabetes mellitus developed uncontrolled diabetes on day 3 of the hospitalization.

   Assign "N" to the diabetes code because the "uncontrolled" component of the code was not present on admission.

10. A patient is admitted with high fever and pneumonia. The patient rapidly deteriorates and becomes septic. The discharge diagnosis lists sepsis and pneumonia. The documentation is unclear as to whether the sepsis was present on admission or developed shortly after admission.

    Query the physician as to whether the sepsis was present on admission, developed shortly after admission, or it cannot be clinically determined as to whether it was present on admission or not.

11. A patient is admitted for repair of an abdominal aneurysm. However, the aneurysm ruptures after hospital admission.

    Assign "N" for the ruptured abdominal aneurysm. Although the aneurysm was present on admission, the "ruptured" component of the code description did not occur until after admission.

12. A patient with viral hepatitis B progresses to hepatic coma after admission.

    Assign "N" for the viral hepatitis B with hepatic coma because part of the code description did not develop until after admission.

13. A patient with a history of varicose veins and ulceration of the left lower extremity strikes the area against the side of his hospital bed during an inpatient hospitalization. It bleeds profusely. The final diagnosis lists varicose veins with ulcer and hemorrhage.

    Assign "Y" for the varicose veins with ulcer. Although the hemorrhage occurred after admission, the code description for varicose veins with ulcer does not mention hemorrhage.

14. The nursing initial assessment upon admission documents the presence of a decubitus ulcer. There is no mention of the decubitus ulcer in the physician documentation until several days after admission.

    Query the physician as to whether the decubitus ulcer was present on admission, or developed after admission. Both diagnosis code assignment and determination of whether a condition was present on admission must be based on provider documentation in the medical record (per the definition of "provider" found at the beginning of these POA guidelines and in the introductory section of the ICD-9-CM Official Guidelines for Coding and Reporting). If it cannot be determined from the provider documentation whether or not a condition was present on admission, the provider should be queried.

15. A urine culture is obtained on admission. The provider documents urinary tract infection when the culture results become available a few days later.

    Assign "Y" to the urinary tract infection since the diagnosis is based on test results from a specimen obtained on admission. It may not be possible for a provider to make a definitive diagnosis for a period of time after admission. There is no required timeframe as to when a provider must identify or document a condition to be present on admission.

16. A patient tested positive for Methicillin resistant Staphylococcus (MRSA) on routine nasal culture on admission to the hospital. During the hospitalization, he underwent insertion of a central venous catheter and later developed an infection and was diagnosed with MRSA sepsis due to central venous catheter infection.

    Assign "Y" to the positive MRSA colonization. Assign "N" for the MRSA sepsis due to central venous catheter infection since the patient did not have a MRSA infection at the time of admission.

Obstetrics

1. A female patient was admitted to the hospital and underwent a normal delivery.

    Leave the "present on admission" (POA) field blank. Code 650, Normal delivery, is on the "exempt from reporting" list.

2. Patient admitted in late pregnancy due to excessive vomiting and dehydration. During admission patient goes into premature labor

    Assign "Y" for the excessive vomiting and the dehydration.
    Assign "N" for the premature labor

3. Patient admitted in active labor. During the stay, a breast abscess is noted when mother attempted to breast feed. Provider is unable to determine whether the abscess was present on admission

    Assign "W" for the breast abscess.

4. Patient admitted in active labor. After 12 hours of labor it is noted that the infant is in fetal distress and a Cesarean section is performed

    Assign "N" for the fetal distress.

5. Pregnant female was admitted in labor and fetal nuchal cord entanglement was diagnosed. Physician is queried, but is unable to determine whether the cord entanglement was present on admission or not.

    Assign "W" for the fetal nuchal cord entanglement.

Newborn

1. A single liveborn infant was delivered in the hospital via Cesarean section. The physician documented fetal bradycardia during labor in the final diagnosis in the newborn record.

    Assign "Y" because the bradycardia developed prior to the newborn admission (birth).

2. A newborn developed diarrhea which was believed to be due to the hospital baby formula.

    Assign "N" because the diarrhea developed after admission.

3. A newborn born in the hospital, birth complicated by nuchal cord entanglement.

    Assign "Y" for the nuchal cord entanglement on the baby's record. Any condition that is present at birth or that developed in utero is considered present at admission, including conditions that occur during delivery.

A

AAT (alpha-1 antitrypsin) deficiency 273.4
AAV (disease) (illness) (infection) — *see* Human immunodeficiency virus (disease) (illness) (infection)
Abactio — *see* Abortion, induced
Abactus venter — *see* Abortion, induced
Abarognosis 781.99
Abasia (-astasia) 307.9
  atactica 781.3
  choreic 781.3
  hysterical 300.11
  paroxysmal trepidant 781.3
  spastic 781.3
  trembling 781.3
  trepidans 781.3
Abderhalden-Kaufmann-Lignac syndrome (cystinosis) 270.0
Abdomen, abdominal — *see also* condition
  accordion 306.4
  acute 789.0 ☑
  angina 557.1
  burst 868.00
  convulsive equivalent (*see also* Epilepsy) 345.5 ☑
  heart 746.87
  muscle deficiency syndrome 756.79
  obstipum 756.79
Abdominalgia 789.0 ☑
  periodic 277.31
Abduction contracture, hip or other joint — *see* Contraction, joint
Abercrombie's syndrome (amyloid degeneration) 277.39
Aberrant (congenital) — *see also* Malposition, congenital
  adrenal gland 759.1
  blood vessel NEC 747.60
    arteriovenous NEC 747.60
    cerebrovascular 747.81
    gastrointestinal 747.61
    lower limb 747.64
    renal 747.62
    spinal 747.82
    upper limb 747.63
  breast 757.6
  endocrine gland NEC 759.2
  gastrointestinal vessel (peripheral) 747.61
  hepatic duct 751.69
  lower limb vessel (peripheral) 747.64
  pancreas 751.7
  parathyroid gland 759.2
  peripheral vascular vessel NEC 747.60
  pituitary gland (pharyngeal) 759.2
  renal blood vessel 747.62
  sebaceous glands, mucous membrane, mouth 750.26
  spinal vessel 747.82
  spleen 759.0
  testis (descent) 752.51
  thymus gland 759.2
  thyroid gland 759.2
  upper limb vessel (peripheral) 747.63
Aberratio
  lactis 757.6
  testis 752.51
Aberration — *see also* Anomaly
  chromosome — *see* Anomaly, chromosome(s)
  distantial 368.9
  mental (*see also* Disorder, mental, nonpsychotic) 300.9
Abetalipoproteinemia 272.5
Abionarce 780.79
Abiotrophy 799.89
Ablatio
  placentae — *see* Placenta, ablatio
  retinae (*see also* Detachment, retina) 361.9
Ablation
  pituitary (gland) (with hypofunction) 253.7
  placenta — *see* Placenta, ablatio
  uterus 621.8
Ablepharia, ablepharon, ablephary 743.62
Ablepsia — *see* Blindness
Ablepsy — *see* Blindness
Ablutomania 300.3

Abnormal, abnormality, abnormalities — *see also* Anomaly
acid-base balance 276.4
  fetus or newborn — *see* Distress, fetal
adaptation curve, dark 368.63
alveolar ridge 525.9
amnion 658.9 ☑
  affecting fetus or newborn 762.9
anatomical relationship NEC 759.9
apertures, congenital, diaphragm 756.6
auditory perception NEC 388.40
autosomes NEC 758.5
  13 758.1
  18 758.2
  21 or 22 758.0
  D_1 758.1
  E_3 758.2
  G 758.0
ballistocardiogram 794.39
basal metabolic rate (BMR) 794.7
biosynthesis, testicular androgen 257.2
blood level (of)
  cobalt 790.6
  copper 790.6
  iron 790.6
  lead 790.6
  lithium 790.6
  magnesium 790.6
  mineral 790.6
  zinc 790.6
blood pressure
  elevated (without diagnosis of hypertension) 796.2
  low (*see also* Hypotension) 458.9
    reading (incidental) (isolated) (nonspecific) 796.3
blood sugar 790.29
bowel sounds 787.5
breathing behavior — *see* Respiration
caloric test 794.19
cervix (acquired) NEC 622.9
  congenital 752.40
  in pregnancy or childbirth 654.6 ☑
    causing obstructed labor 660.2 ☑
      affecting fetus or newborn 763.1
chemistry, blood NEC 790.6
chest sounds 786.7
chorion 658.9 ☑
  affecting fetus or newborn 762.9
chromosomal NEC 758.89
  analysis, nonspecific result 795.2
  autosomes (*see also* Abnormal, autosomes NEC) 758.5
  fetal, (suspected) affecting management of pregnancy 655.1 ☑
  sex 758.81
clinical findings NEC 796.4
communication — *see* Fistula
configuration of pupils 379.49
coronary
  artery 746.85
  vein 746.9
cortisol-binding globulin 255.8
course, Eustachian tube 744.24
creatinine clearance 794.4
dentofacial NEC 524.9
  functional 524.50
  specified type NEC 524.89
development, developmental NEC 759.9
  bone 756.9
  central nervous system 742.9
direction, teeth 524.30
Dynia (*see also* Defect, coagulation) 286.9
Ebstein 746.2
echocardiogram 793.2
echoencephalogram 794.01
echogram NEC — *see* Findings, abnormal, structure
electrocardiogram (ECG) (EKG) 794.31
electroencephalogram (EEG) 794.02
electromyogram (EMG) 794.17
  ocular 794.14
electro-oculogram (EOG) 794.12
electroretinogram (ERG) 794.11
erythrocytes 289.9

Abnormal, abnormality, abnormalities — *see also* Anomaly — *continued*
erythrocytes — *continued*
  congenital, with perinatal jaundice 282.9 [774.0]
Eustachian valve 746.9
excitability under minor stress 301.9
fat distribution 782.9
feces 787.7
fetal heart rate — *see* Distress, fetal
fetus NEC
  affecting management of pregnancy — *see* Pregnancy, management affected by, fetal
  causing disproportion 653.7 ☑
    affecting fetus or newborn 763.1
    causing obstructed labor 660.1 ☑
      affecting fetus or newborn 763.1
findings without manifest disease — *see* Findings, abnormal
fluid
  amniotic 792.3
  cerebrospinal 792.0
  peritoneal 792.9
  pleural 792.9
  synovial 792.9
  vaginal 792.9
forces of labor NEC 661.9 ☑
  affecting fetus or newborn 763.7
form, teeth 520.2
function studies
  auditory 794.15
  bladder 794.9
  brain 794.00
  cardiovascular 794.30
  endocrine NEC 794.6
  kidney 794.4
  liver 794.8
  nervous system
    central 794.00
    peripheral 794.19
  oculomotor 794.14
  pancreas 794.9
  placenta 794.9
  pulmonary 794.2
  retina 794.11
  special senses 794.19
  spleen 794.9
  thyroid 794.5
  vestibular 794.16
gait 781.2
  hysterical 300.11
gastrin secretion 251.5
globulin
  cortisol-binding 255.8
  thyroid-binding 246.8
glucagon secretion 251.4
glucose 790.29
  in pregnancy, childbirth, or puerperium 648.8 ☑
    fetus or newborn 775.0
  non-fasting 790.29
gravitational (G) forces or states 994.9
hair NEC 704.2
hard tissue formation in pulp 522.3
head movement 781.0
heart
  rate
    fetus, affecting liveborn infant
      before the onset of labor 763.81
      during labor 763.82
      unspecified as to time of onset 763.83
    intrauterine
      before the onset of labor 763.81
      during labor 763.82
      unspecified as to time of onset 763.83
    newborn
      before the onset of labor 763.81
      during labor 763.82
      unspecified as to time of onset 763.83
  shadow 793.2
  sounds NEC 785.3

Abnormal, abnormality, abnormalities — *see also* Anomaly — *continued*
hemoglobin (*see also* Disease, hemoglobin) 282.7
  trait — *see* Trait, hemoglobin, abnormal
hemorrhage, uterus — *see* Hemorrhage, uterus
histology NEC 795.4
increase
  in
    appetite 783.6
    development 783.9
involuntary movement 781.0
jaw closure 524.51
karyotype 795.2
knee jerk 796.1
labor NEC 661.9 ☑
  affecting fetus or newborn 763.7
laboratory findings — *see* Findings, abnormal
length, organ or site, congenital — *see* Distortion
liver function test 790.6
loss of height 781.91
loss of weight 783.21
lung shadow 793.1
mammogram 793.80
  calcification 793.89
  calculus 793.89
  microcalcification 793.81
Mantoux test 795.5
membranes (fetal)
  affecting fetus or newborn 762.9
  complicating pregnancy 658.8 ☑
menstruation — *see* Menstruation
metabolism (*see also* condition) 783.9
movement 781.0
  disorder NEC 333.90
    sleep related, unspecified 780.58
    specified NEC 333.99
  head 781.0
  involuntary 781.0
  specified type NEC 333.99
muscle contraction, localized 728.85
myoglobin (Aberdeen) (Annapolis) 289.9
narrowness, eyelid 743.62
optokinetic response 379.57
organs or tissues of pelvis NEC
  in pregnancy or childbirth 654.9 ☑
    affecting fetus or newborn 763.89
    causing obstructed labor 660.2 ☑
      affecting fetus or newborn 763.1
origin — *see* Malposition, congenital
palmar creases 757.2
Papanicolaou (smear)
  anus 796.70
    with
      atypical squamous cells
        cannot exclude high grade squamous intraepithelial lesion (ASC-H) 796.72
        of undetermined significance (ASC-US) 796.71
      cytologic evidence of malignancy 796.76
      high grade squamous intraepithelial lesion (HGSIL) 796.74
      low grade squamous intraepithelial lesion (LGSIL) 796.73
  glandular 796.70
  specified finding NEC 796.79
  cervix 795.00
    with
      atypical squamous cells
        cannot exclude high grade squamous intraepithelial lesion (ASC-H) 795.02
        of undetermined significance (ASC-US) 795.01
      cytologic evidence of malignancy 795.06
      high grade squamous intraepithelial lesion (HGSIL) 795.04
      low grade squamous intraepithelial lesion (LGSIL) 795.03
      nonspecific finding NEC 795.09
  other site 796.9

☑ Additional Digit Required — Refer to the Tabular List for Digit Selection   Subterms under main terms may continue to next column or page

2010 ICD-9-CM   ▶◀ Revised Text   ● New Line   ▲ Revised Code   **Volume 2 — 1**

AAT — Abnormal, abnormality, abnormalities

Index

Abnormal, abnormalities, abnormalities — Abortion

Abnormal, abnormality, abnormalities — *see also* Anomaly — *continued*
Papanicolaou — *continued*
vagina 795.10
with
atypical squamous cells
cannot exclude high grade
squamous intraepithelial
lesion (ASC-H) 795.12
of undetermined significance
(ASC-US) 795.11
cytologic evidence of malignancy
795.16
high grade squamous intraepithelial lesion (HGSIL) 795.14
low grade squamous intraepithelial
lesion (LGSIL) 795.13
glandular 795.10
specified finding NEC 795.19
parturition
affecting fetus or newborn 763.9
mother — *see* Delivery, complicated
pelvis (bony) — *see* Deformity, pelvis
percussion, chest 786.7
periods (grossly) (*see also* Menstruation) 626.9
phonocardiogram 794.39
placenta — *see* Placenta, abnormal
plantar reflex 796.1
plasma protein — *see* Deficiency, plasma,
protein
pleural folds 748.8
position (*see also* Malposition)
gravid uterus 654.4 ☑
causing obstructed labor 660.2 ☑
affecting fetus or newborn 763.1
posture NEC 781.92
presentation (fetus) — *see* Presentation, fetus,
abnormal
product of conception NEC 631
puberty — *see* Puberty
pulmonary
artery 747.3
function, newborn 770.89
test results 794.2
ventilation, newborn 770.89
hyperventilation 786.01
pulsations in neck 785.1
pupil reflexes 379.40
quality of milk 676.8 ☑
radiological examination 793.99
abdomen NEC 793.6
biliary tract 793.3
breast 793.89
mammogram NOS 793.80
mammographic
calcification 793.89
calculus 793.89
microcalcification 793.81
gastrointestinal tract 793.4
genitourinary organs 793.5
head 793.0
image test inconclusive due to excess body
fat 793.91
intrathoracic organ NEC 793.2
lung (field) 793.1
musculoskeletal system 793.7
retroperitoneum 793.6
skin and subcutaneous tissue 793.99
skull 793.0
red blood cells 790.09
morphology 790.09
volume 790.09
reflex NEC 796.1
renal function test 794.4
respiration signs — *see* Respiration
response to nerve stimulation 794.10
retinal correspondence 368.34
rhythm, heart (*see also* Arrhythmia)
fetus — *see* Distress, fetal
saliva 792.4
scan
brain 794.09
kidney 794.4
liver 794.8
lung 794.2
thyroid 794.5

Abnormal, abnormality, abnormalities — *see also* Anomaly — *continued*
secretion
gastrin 251.5
glucagon 251.4
semen 792.2
serum level (of)
acid phosphatase 790.5
alkaline phosphatase 790.5
amylase 790.5
enzymes NEC 790.5
lipase 790.5
shape
cornea 743.41
gallbladder 751.69
gravid uterus 654.4 ☑
affecting fetus or newborn 763.89
causing obstructed labor 660.2 ☑
affecting fetus or newborn 763.1
head (*see also* Anomaly, skull) 756.0
organ or site, congenital NEC — *see* Distortion
sinus venosus 747.40
size
fetus, complicating delivery 653.5 ☑
causing obstructed labor 660.1 ☑
gallbladder 751.69
head (*see also* Anomaly, skull) 756.0
organ or site, congenital NEC — *see* Distortion
teeth 520.2
skin and appendages, congenital NEC 757.9
soft parts of pelvis — *see* Abnormal, organs
or tissues of pelvis
spermatozoa 792.2
sputum (amount) (color) (excessive) (odor)
(purulent) 786.4
stool NEC 787.7
bloody 578.1
occult 792.1
bulky 787.7
color (dark) (light) 792.1
content (fat) (mucus) (pus) 792.1
occult blood 792.1
synchondrosis 756.9
test results without manifest disease — *see*
Findings, abnormal
thebesian valve 746.9
thermography — *see* Findings, abnormal,
structure
threshold, cones or rods (eye) 368.63
thyroid-binding globulin 246.8
thyroid product 246.8
toxicology (findings) NEC 796.0
tracheal cartilage (congenital) 748.3
transport protein 273.8
ultrasound results — *see* Findings, abnormal,
structure
umbilical cord
affecting fetus or newborn 762.6
complicating delivery 663.9 ☑
specified NEC 663.8 ☑
union
cricoid cartilage and thyroid cartilage 748.3
larynx and trachea 748.3
thyroid cartilage and hyoid bone 748.3
urination NEC 788.69
psychogenic 306.53
stream
intermittent 788.61
slowing 788.62
splitting 788.61
weak 788.62
urgency 788.63
urine (constituents) NEC 791.9
uterine hemorrhage (*see also* Hemorrhage,
uterus) 626.9
climacteric 627.0
postmenopausal 627.1
vagina (acquired) (congenital)
in pregnancy or childbirth 654.7 ☑
affecting fetus or newborn 763.89
causing obstructed labor 660.2 ☑
affecting fetus or newborn 763.1
vascular sounds 785.9
vectorcardiogram 794.39

Abnormal, abnormality, abnormalities — *see also* Anomaly — *continued*
visually evoked potential (VEP) 794.13
vulva (acquired) (congenital)
in pregnancy or childbirth 654.8 ☑
affecting fetus or newborn 763.89
causing obstructed labor 660.2 ☑
affecting fetus or newborn 763.1
weight
gain 783.1
of pregnancy 646.1 ☑
with hypertension — *see* Toxemia,
of pregnancy
loss 783.21
x-ray examination — *see* Abnormal, radiological examination
Abnormally formed uterus — *see* Anomaly,
uterus
Abnormity (any organ or part) — *see* Anomaly
ABO
hemolytic disease 773.1
incompatibility reaction 999.6
Abocclusion 524.20
Abolition, language 784.69
Aborter, habitual or recurrent NEC
without current pregnancy 629.81
current abortion (*see also* Abortion, spontaneous) 634.9 ☑
affecting fetus or newborn 761.8
observation in current pregnancy 646.3 ☑
Abortion (complete) (incomplete) (inevitable)
(with retained products of conception)
637.9 ☑

Note — Use the following fifth-digit subclassification with categories 634–637:
0 *unspecified*
1 *incomplete*
2 *complete*

with
complication(s) (any) following previous
abortion — *see* category 639
damage to pelvic organ (laceration) (rupture) (tear) 637.2 ☑
embolism (air) (amniotic fluid) (blood clot)
(pulmonary) (pyemic) (septic)
(soap) 637.6 ☑
genital tract and pelvic infection 637.0 ☑
hemorrhage, delayed or excessive 637.1 ☑
metabolic disorder 637.4 ☑
renal failure (acute) 637.3 ☑
sepsis (genital tract) (pelvic organ)
637.0 ☑
urinary tract 637.7 ☑
shock (postoperative) (septic) 637.5 ☑
specified complication NEC 637.7 ☑
toxemia 637.3 ☑
unspecified complication(s) 637.8 ☑
urinary tract infection 637.7 ☑
accidental — *see* Abortion, spontaneous
artificial — *see* Abortion, induced
attempted (failed) — *see* Abortion, failed
criminal — *see* Abortion, illegal
early — *see* Abortion, spontaneous
elective — *see* Abortion, legal
failed (legal) 638.9
with
damage to pelvic organ (laceration)
(rupture) (tear) 638.2
embolism (air) (amniotic fluid) (blood
clot) (pulmonary) (pyemic)
(septic) (soap) 638.6
genital tract and pelvic infection 638.0
hemorrhage, delayed or excessive
638.1
metabolic disorder 638.4
renal failure (acute) 638.3
sepsis (genital tract) (pelvic organ)
638.0
urinary tract 638.7
shock (postoperative) (septic) 638.5
specified complication NEC 638.7
toxemia 638.3
unspecified complication(s) 638.8

Abortion — *continued*
failed — *continued*
with — *continued*
urinary tract infection 638.7
fetal indication — *see* Abortion, legal
fetus 779.6
following threatened abortion — *see* Abortion,
by type
habitual or recurrent (care during pregnancy)
646.3 ☑
with current abortion (*see also* Abortion,
spontaneous) 634.9 ☑
affecting fetus or newborn 761.8
without current pregnancy 629.81
homicidal — *see* Abortion, illegal
illegal 636.9 ☑
with
damage to pelvic organ (laceration)
(rupture) (tear) 636.2 ☑
embolism (air) (amniotic fluid) (blood
clot) (pulmonary) (pyemic)
(septic) (soap) 636.6 ☑
genital tract and pelvic infection
636.0 ☑
hemorrhage, delayed or excessive
636.1 ☑
metabolic disorder 636.4 ☑
renal failure 636.3 ☑
sepsis (genital tract) (pelvic organ)
636.0 ☑
urinary tract 636.7 ☑
shock (postoperative) (septic) 636.5 ☑
specified complication NEC 636.7 ☑
toxemia 636.3 ☑
unspecified complication(s) 636.8 ☑
urinary tract infection 636.7 ☑
fetus 779.6
induced 637.9 ☑
illegal — *see* Abortion, illegal
legal indications — *see* Abortion, legal
medical indications — *see* Abortion, legal
therapeutic — *see* Abortion, legal
late — *see* Abortion, spontaneous
legal (legal indication) (medical indication)
(under medical supervision) 635.9 ☑
with
damage to pelvic organ (laceration)
(rupture) (tear) 635.2 ☑
embolism (air) (amniotic fluid) (blood
clot) (pulmonary) (pyemic)
(septic) (soap) 635.6 ☑
genital tract and pelvic infection
635.0 ☑
hemorrhage, delayed or excessive
635.1 ☑
metabolic disorder 635.4 ☑
renal failure (acute) 635.3 ☑
sepsis (genital tract) (pelvic organ)
635.0 ☑
urinary tract 635.7 ☑
shock (postoperative) (septic) 635.5 ☑
specified complication NEC 635.7 ☑
toxemia 635.3 ☑
unspecified complication(s) 635.8 ☑
urinary tract infection 635.7 ☑
fetus 779.6
medical indication — *see* Abortion, legal
mental hygiene problem — *see* Abortion, legal
missed 632
operative — *see* Abortion, legal
psychiatric indication — *see* Abortion, legal
recurrent — *see* Abortion, spontaneous
self-induced — *see* Abortion, illegal
septic — *see* Abortion, by type, with sepsis
spontaneous 634.9 ☑
with
damage to pelvic organ (laceration)
(rupture) (tear) 634.2 ☑
embolism (air) (amniotic fluid) (blood
clot) (pulmonary) (pyemic)
(septic) (soap) 634.6 ☑
genital tract and pelvic infection
634.0 ☑
hemorrhage, delayed or excessive
634.1 ☑

Abortion — *continued*
  spontaneous — *continued*
    with — *continued*
      metabolic disorder 634.4 ✓
      renal failure 634.3 ✓
      sepsis (genital tract) (pelvic organ) 634.0 ✓
      urinary tract 634.7 ✓
      shock (postoperative) (septic) 634.5 ✓
      specified complication NEC 634.7 ✓
      toxemia 634.3 ✓
      unspecified complication(s) 634.8 ✓
      urinary tract infection 634.7 ✓
    fetus 761.8
    threatened 640.0 ✓
      affecting fetus or newborn 762.1
  surgical — *see* Abortion, legal
  therapeutic — *see* Abortion, legal
  threatened 640.0 ✓
    affecting fetus or newborn 762.1
  tubal — *see* Pregnancy, tubal
  voluntary — *see* Abortion, legal
Abortus fever 023.9
Aboulomania 301.6
Abrachia 755.20
Abrachiatism 755.20
Abrachiocephalia 759.89
Abrachiocephalus 759.89
Abrami's disease (acquired hemolytic jaundice) 283.9
Abramov-Fiedler myocarditis (acute isolated myocarditis) 422.91
Abrasion — *see also* Injury, superficial, by site
  cornea 918.1
  dental 521.20
    extending into
      dentine 521.22
      pulp 521.23
    generalized 521.25
    limited to enamel 521.21
    localized 521.24
  teeth, tooth (dentifrice) (habitual) (hard tissues) (occupational) (ritual) (traditional) (wedge defect) (*see also* Abrasion, dental) 521.20
Abrikossov's tumor (M9580/0) — *see also* Neoplasm, connective tissue, benign
  malignant (M9580/3) — *see* Neoplasm, connective tissue, malignant
Abrism 988.8
Abruption, placenta — *see* Placenta, abruptio
Abruptio placentae — *see* Placenta, abruptio
Abscess (acute) (chronic) (infectional) (lymphangitic) (metastatic) (multiple) (pyogenic) (septic) (with lymphangitis) — *see also* Cellulitis 682.9
  abdomen, abdominal
    cavity 567.22
    wall 682.2
  abdominopelvic 567.22
  accessory sinus (chronic) (*see also* Sinusitis) 473.9
  adrenal (capsule) (gland) 255.8
  alveolar 522.5
    with sinus 522.7
  amebic 006.3
    bladder 006.8
    brain (with liver or lung abscess) 006.5
    liver (without mention of brain or lung abscess) 006.3
      with
        brain abscess (and lung abscess) 006.5
        lung abscess 006.4
    lung (with liver abscess) 006.4
      with brain abscess 006.5
    seminal vesicle 006.8
    specified site NEC 006.8
    spleen 006.8
  anaerobic 040.0
  ankle 682.6
  anorectal 566
  antecubital space 682.3
  antrum (chronic) (Highmore) (*see also* Sinusitis, maxillary) 473.0
  anus 566

Abscess — *see also* Cellulitis — *continued*
  apical (tooth) 522.5
    with sinus (alveolar) 522.7
  appendix 540.1
  areola (acute) (chronic) (nonpuerperal) 611.0
    puerperal, postpartum 675.1 ✓
  arm (any part, above wrist) 682.3
  artery (wall) 447.2
  atheromatous 447.2
  auditory canal (external) 380.10
  auricle (ear) (staphylococcal) (streptococcal) 380.10
  axilla, axillary (region) 682.3
    lymph gland or node 683
  back (any part) 682.2
  Bartholin's gland 616.3
    with
      abortion — *see* Abortion, by type, with sepsis
      ectopic pregnancy (*see also* categories 633.0–633.9) 639.0
      molar pregnancy (*see also* categories 630–632) 639.0
    complicating pregnancy or puerperium 646.6 ✓
    following
      abortion 639.0
      ectopic or molar pregnancy 639.0
  bartholinian 616.3
  Bezold's 383.01
  bile, biliary, duct or tract (*see also* Cholecystitis) 576.8
  bilharziasis 120.1
  bladder (wall) 595.89
    amebic 006.8
  bone (subperiosteal) (*see also* Osteomyelitis) 730.0 ✓
    accessory sinus (chronic) (*see also* Sinusitis) 473.9
    acute 730.0 ✓
    chronic or old 730.1 ✓
    jaw (lower) (upper) 526.4
    mastoid — *see* Mastoiditis, acute
    petrous (*see also* Petrositis) 383.20
    spinal (tuberculous) (*see also* Tuberculosis) 015.0 ✓ *[730.88]*
      nontuberculous 730.08
  bowel 569.5
  brain (any part) 324.0
    amebic (with liver or lung abscess) 006.5
    cystic 324.0
    late effect — *see* category 326
    otogenic 324.0
    tuberculous (*see also* Tuberculosis) 013.3 ✓
  breast (acute) (chronic) (nonpuerperal) 611.0
    newborn 771.5
    puerperal, postpartum 675.1 ✓
    tuberculous (*see also* Tuberculosis) 017.9 ✓
  broad ligament (chronic) (*see also* Disease, pelvis, inflammatory) 614.4
    acute 614.3
  Brodie's (chronic) (localized) (*see also* Osteomyelitis) 730.1 ✓
  bronchus 519.19
  buccal cavity 528.3
  bulbourethral gland 597.0
  bursa 727.89
    pharyngeal 478.29
  buttock 682.5
  canaliculus, breast 611.0
  canthus 372.20
  cartilage 733.99
  cecum 569.5
    with appendicitis 540.1
  cerebellum, cerebellar 324.0
    late effect — *see* category 326
  cerebral (embolic) 324.0
    late effect — *see* category 326
  cervical (neck region) 682.1
    lymph gland or node 683
    stump (*see also* Cervicitis) 616.0
  cervix (stump) (uteri) (*see also* Cervicitis) 616.0
  cheek, external 682.0
    inner 528.3

Abscess — *see also* Cellulitis — *continued*
  chest 510.9
    with fistula 510.0
    wall 682.2
  chin 682.0
  choroid 363.00
  ciliary body 364.3
  circumtonsillar 475
  cold (tuberculous) (*see also* Tuberculosis, abscess)
    articular — *see* Tuberculosis, joint
  colon (wall) 569.5
  colostomy or enterostomy 569.61
  conjunctiva 372.00
  connective tissue NEC 682.9
  cornea 370.55
    with ulcer 370.00
  corpus
    cavernosum 607.2
    luteum (*see also* Salpingo-oophoritis) 614.2
  Cowper's gland 597.0
  cranium 324.0
  cul-de-sac (Douglas') (posterior) (*see also* Disease, pelvis, inflammatory) 614.4
    acute 614.3
  dental 522.5
    with sinus (alveolar) 522.7
  dentoalveolar 522.5
    with sinus (alveolar) 522.7
  diaphragm, diaphragmatic 567.22
  digit NEC 681.9
  Douglas' cul-de-sac or pouch (*see also* Disease, pelvis, inflammatory) 614.4
    acute 614.3
  Dubois' 090.5
  ductless gland 259.8
  ear
    acute 382.00
    external 380.10
    inner 386.30
    middle — *see* Otitis media
  elbow 682.3
  endamebic — *see* Abscess, amebic
  entamebic — *see* Abscess, amebic
  enterostomy 569.61
  epididymis 604.0
  epidural 324.9
    brain 324.0
    late effect — *see* category 326
    spinal cord 324.1
  epiglottis 478.79
  epiploon, epiploic 567.22
  erysipelatous (*see also* Erysipelas) 035
  esophagostomy 530.86
  esophagus 530.19
  ethmoid (bone) (chronic) (sinus) (*see also* Sinusitis, ethmoidal) 473.2
  external auditory canal 380.10
  extradural 324.9
    brain 324.0
    late effect — *see* category 326
    spinal cord 324.1
  extraperitoneal — *see* Abscess, peritoneum
  eye 360.00
  eyelid 373.13
  face (any part, except eye) 682.0
  fallopian tube (*see also* Salpingo-oophoritis) 614.2
  fascia 728.89
  fauces 478.29
  fecal 569.5
  femoral (region) 682.6
  filaria, filarial (*see also* Infestation, filarial) 125.9
  finger (any) (intrathecal) (periosteal) (subcutaneous) (subcuticular) 681.00
  fistulous NEC 682.9
  flank 682.2
  foot (except toe) 682.7
  forearm 682.3
  forehead 682.0
  frontal (sinus) (chronic) (*see also* Sinusitis, frontal) 473.1
  gallbladder (*see also* Cholecystitis, acute) 575.0
  gastric 535.0 ✓
  genital organ or tract NEC
    female 616.9

Abscess — *see also* Cellulitis — *continued*
  genital organ or tract — *continued*
    female — *continued*
      with
        abortion — *see* Abortion, by type, with sepsis
        ectopic pregnancy (*see also* categories 633.0–633.9) 639.0
        molar pregnancy (*see also* categories 630–632) 639.0
      following
        abortion 639.0
        ectopic or molar pregnancy 639.0
      puerperal, postpartum, childbirth 670.8 ✓   ▲
    male 608.4
  genitourinary system, tuberculous (*see also* Tuberculosis) 016.9 ✓
  gingival 523.30
  gland, glandular (lymph) (acute) NEC 683
  glottis 478.79
  gluteal (region) 682.5
  gonorrheal NEC (*see also* Gonococcus) 098.0
  groin 682.2
  gum 523.30
  hand (except finger or thumb) 682.4
  head (except face) 682.8
  heart 429.89
  heel 682.7
  helminthic (*see also* Infestation, by specific parasite) 128.9
  hepatic 572.0
    amebic (*see also* Abscess, liver, amebic) 006.3
    duct 576.8
  hip 682.6
    tuberculous (active) (*see also* Tuberculosis) 015.1 ✓
  ileocecal 540.1
  ileostomy (bud) 569.61
  iliac (region) 682.2
    fossa 540.1
  iliopsoas 567.31
    nontuberculous 728.89
    tuberculous (*see also* Tuberculosis) 015.0 ✓ *[730.88]*
  infraclavicular (fossa) 682.3
  inguinal (region) 682.2
    lymph gland or node 683
  intersphincteric (anus) 566
  intestine, intestinal 569.5
    rectal 566
  intra-abdominal (*see also* Abscess, peritoneum) 567.22
    postoperative 998.59
  intracranial 324.0
    late effect — *see* category 326
  intramammary — *see* Abscess, breast
  intramastoid (*see also* Mastoiditis, acute) 383.00
  intraorbital 376.01
  intraperitoneal 567.22
  intraspinal 324.1
    late effect — *see* category 326
  intratonsillar 475
  iris 364.3
  ischiorectal 566
  jaw (bone) (lower) (upper) 526.4
    skin 682.0
  joint (*see also* Arthritis, pyogenic) 711.0 ✓
    vertebral (tuberculous) (*see also* Tuberculosis) 015.0 ✓ *[730.88]*
      nontuberculous 724.8
  kidney 590.2
    with
      abortion — *see* Abortion, by type, with urinary tract infection
      calculus 592.0
      ectopic pregnancy (*see also* categories 633.0–633.9) 639.8
      molar pregnancy (*see also* categories 630–632) 639.8
    complicating pregnancy or puerperium 646.6 ✓
    affecting fetus or newborn 760.1

✓ Additional Digit Required — Refer to the Tabular List for Digit Selection   Subterms under main terms may continue to next column or page

2010 ICD-9-CM   ▶◀ Revised Text   ● New Line   ▲ Revised Code   **October 2009 · Volume 2 — 3**

Abortion — Abscess

Abscess — *see also* Cellulitis — *continued*
  kidney — *continued*
    following
      abortion 639.8
      ectopic or molar pregnancy 639.8
    knee 682.6
      joint 711.06
      tuberculous (active) (*see also* Tuberculosis) 015.2 ☑
    labium (majus) (minus) 616.4
      complicating pregnancy, childbirth, or puerperium 646.6 ☑
    lacrimal (passages) (sac) (*see also* Dacryocystitis) 375.30
      caruncle 375.30
      gland (*see also* Dacryoadenitis) 375.00
    lacunar 597.0
    larynx 478.79
    lateral (alveolar) 522.5
      with sinus 522.7
    leg, except foot 682.6
    lens 360.00
    lid 373.13
    lingual 529.0
      tonsil 475
    lip 528.5
    Littre's gland 597.0
    liver 572.0
      amebic 006.3
        with
          brain abscess (and lung abscess) 006.5
          lung abscess 006.4
        due to Entamoeba histolytica 006.3
        dysenteric (*see also* Abscess, liver, amebic) 006.3
        pyogenic 572.0
        tropical (*see also* Abscess, liver, amebic) 006.3
    loin (region) 682.2
    lumbar (tuberculous) (*see also* Tuberculosis) 015.0 ☑ [730.88]
      nontuberculous 682.2
    lung (miliary) (putrid) 513.0
      amebic (with liver abscess) 006.4
        with brain abscess 006.5
    lymphangitic, acute — *see* Cellulitis
    lymph, lymphatic, gland or node (acute) 683
      any site, except mesenteric 683
      mesentery 289.2
    malar 526.4
    mammary gland — *see* Abscess, breast
    marginal (anus) 566
    mastoid (process) (*see also* Mastoiditis, acute) 383.00
      subperiosteal 383.01
    maxilla, maxillary 526.4
      molar (tooth) 522.5
        with sinus 522.7
      premolar 522.5
      sinus (chronic) (*see also* Sinusitis, maxillary) 473.0
    mediastinum 513.1
    meibomian gland 373.12
    meninges (*see also* Meningitis) 320.9
    mesentery, mesenteric 567.22
    mesosalpinx (*see also* Salpingo-oophoritis) 614.2
    milk 675.1 ☑
    Monro's (psoriasis) 696.1
    mons pubis 682.2
    mouth (floor) 528.3
    multiple sites NEC 682.9
    mural 682.2
    muscle 728.89
      psoas 567.31
    myocardium 422.92
    nabothian (follicle) (*see also* Cervicitis) 616.0
    nail (chronic) (with lymphangitis) 681.9
      finger 681.02
      toe 681.11
    nasal (fossa) (septum) 478.19
      sinus (chronic) (*see also* Sinusitis) 473.9
    nasopharyngeal 478.29
    nates 682.5
    navel 682.2

Abscess — *see also* Cellulitis — *continued*
  navel — *continued*
    newborn NEC 771.4
  neck (region) 682.1
    lymph gland or node 683
  nephritic (*see also* Abscess, kidney) 590.2
  nipple 611.0
    puerperal, postpartum 675.0 ☑
  nose (septum) 478.19
    external 682.0
  omentum 567.22
  operative wound 998.59
  orbit, orbital 376.01
  ossifluent — *see* Abscess, bone
  ovary, ovarian (corpus luteum) (*see also* Salpingo-oophoritis) 614.2
  oviduct (*see also* Salpingo-oophoritis) 614.2
  palate (soft) 528.3
    hard 526.4
  palmar (space) 682.4
  pancreas (duct) 577.0
  paradontal 523.30
  parafrenal 607.2
  parametric, parametrium (chronic) (*see also* Disease, pelvis, inflammatory) 614.4
    acute 614.3
  paranephric 590.2
  parapancreatic 577.0
  parapharyngeal 478.22
  pararectal 566
  parasinus (*see also* Sinusitis) 473.9
  parauterine (*see also* Disease, pelvis, inflammatory) 614.4
    acute 614.3
  paravaginal (*see also* Vaginitis) 616.10
  parietal region 682.8
  parodontal 523.30
  parotid (duct) (gland) 527.3
    region 528.3
  parumbilical 682.2
    newborn 771.4
  pectoral (region) 682.2
  pelvirectal 567.22
  pelvis, pelvic
    female (chronic) (*see also* Disease, pelvis, inflammatory) 614.4
      acute 614.3
    male, peritoneal (cellular tissue) — *see* Abscess, peritoneum
    tuberculous (*see also* Tuberculosis) 016.9 ☑
  penis 607.2
    gonococcal (acute) 098.0
      chronic or duration of 2 months or over 098.2
  perianal 566
  periapical 522.5
    with sinus (alveolar) 522.7
  periappendiceal 540.1
  pericardial 420.99
  pericecal 540.1
  pericemental 523.30
  pericholecystic (*see also* Cholecystitis, acute) 575.0
  pericoronal 523.30
  peridental 523.30
  perigastric 535.0 ☑
  perimetric (*see also* Disease, pelvis, inflammatory) 614.4
    acute 614.3
  perinephric, perinephritic (*see also* Abscess, kidney) 590.2
  perineum, perineal (superficial) 682.2
    deep (with urethral involvement) 597.0
    urethra 597.0
  periodontal (parietal) 523.31
    apical 522.5
  periosteum, periosteal (*see also* Periostitis) 730.3 ☑
    with osteomyelitis (*see also* Osteomyelitis) 730.2 ☑
      acute or subacute 730.0 ☑
      chronic or old 730.1 ☑
  peripleuritic 510.9
    with fistula 510.0
  periproctic 566

Abscess — *see also* Cellulitis — *continued*
  periprostatic 601.2
  perirectal (staphylococcal) 566
  perirenal (tissue) (*see also* Abscess, kidney) 590.2
  perisinuous (nose) (*see also* Sinusitis) 473.9
  peritoneum, peritoneal (perforated) (ruptured) 567.22
    with
      abortion — *see* Abortion, by type, with sepsis
      appendicitis 540.1
      ectopic pregnancy (*see also* categories 633.0–633.9) 639.0
      molar pregnancy (*see also* categories 630–632) 639.0
    following
      abortion 639.0
      ectopic or molar pregnancy 639.0
    pelvic, female (*see also* Disease, pelvis, inflammatory) 614.4
      acute 614.3
    postoperative 998.59
    puerperal, postpartum, childbirth 670.8 ☑ ▲
    tuberculous (*see also* Tuberculosis) 014.0 ☑
  peritonsillar 475
  perityphlic 540.1
  periureteral 593.89
  periurethral 597.0
    gonococcal (acute) 098.0
      chronic or duration of 2 months or over 098.2
  periuterine (*see also* Disease, pelvis, inflammatory) 614.4
    acute 614.3
  perivesical 595.89
  pernicious NEC 682.9
  petrous bone — *see* Petrositis
  phagedenic NEC 682.9
    chancroid 099.0
  pharynx, pharyngeal (lateral) 478.29
  phlegmonous NEC 682.9
  pilonidal 685.0
  pituitary (gland) 253.8
  pleura 510.9
    with fistula 510.0
  popliteal 682.6
  postanal 566
  postcecal 540.1
  postlaryngeal 478.79
  postnasal 478.19
  postpharyngeal 478.24
  posttonsillar 475
  posttyphoid 002.0
  Pott's (*see also* Tuberculosis) 015.0 ☑ [730.88]
  pouch of Douglas (chronic) (*see also* Disease, pelvis, inflammatory) 614.4
  premammary — *see* Abscess, breast
  prepatellar 682.6
  prostate (*see also* Prostatitis) 601.2
    gonococcal (acute) 098.12
      chronic or duration of 2 months or over 098.32
  psoas 567.31
    nontuberculous 728.89
    tuberculous (*see also* Tuberculosis) 015.0 ☑ [730.88]
  pterygopalatine fossa 682.8
  pubis 682.2
  puerperal — *see* Puerperal, abscess, by site
  pulmonary — *see* Abscess, lung
  pulp, pulpal (dental) 522.0
    finger 681.01
    toe 681.10
  pyemic — *see* Septicemia
  pyloric valve 535.0 ☑
  rectovaginal septum 569.5
  rectovesical 595.89
  rectum 566
  regional NEC 682.9
  renal (*see also* Abscess, kidney) 590.2
  retina 363.00
  retrobulbar 376.01
  retrocecal 567.22

Abscess — *see also* Cellulitis — *continued*
  retrolaryngeal 478.79
  retromammary — *see* Abscess, breast
  retroperineal 682.2
  retroperitoneal 567.38
    postprocedural 998.59
  retropharyngeal 478.24
    tuberculous (*see also* Tuberculosis) 012.8 ☑
  retrorectal 566
  retrouterine (*see also* Disease, pelvis, inflammatory) 614.4
    acute 614.3
  retrovesical 595.89
  root, tooth 522.5
    with sinus (alveolar) 522.7
  round ligament (*see also* Disease, pelvis, inflammatory) 614.4
    acute 614.3
  rupture (spontaneous) NEC 682.9
  sacrum (tuberculous) (*see also* Tuberculosis) 015.0 ☑ [730.88]
    nontuberculous 730.08
  salivary duct or gland 527.3
  scalp (any part) 682.8
  scapular 730.01
  sclera 379.09
  scrofulous (*see also* Tuberculosis) 017.2 ☑
  scrotum 608.4
  seminal vesicle 608.0
    amebic 006.8
  septal, dental 522.5
    with sinus (alveolar) 522.7
  septum (nasal) 478.19
  serous (*see also* Periostitis) 730.3 ☑
  shoulder 682.3
  side 682.2
  sigmoid 569.5
  sinus (accessory) (chronic) (nasal) (*see also* Sinusitis) 473.9
    intracranial venous (any) 324.0
    late effect — *see* category 326
  Skene's duct or gland 597.0
  skin NEC 682.9
    tuberculous (primary) (*see also* Tuberculosis) 017.0 ☑
  sloughing NEC 682.9
  specified site NEC 682.8
    amebic 006.8
  spermatic cord 608.4
  sphenoidal (sinus) (*see also* Sinusitis, sphenoidal) 473.3
  spinal
    cord (any part) (staphylococcal) 324.1
      tuberculous (*see also* Tuberculosis) 013.5 ☑
    epidural 324.1
  spine (column) (tuberculous) (*see also* Tuberculosis) 015.0 ☑ [730.88]
    nontuberculous 730.08
  spleen 289.59
    amebic 006.8
  staphylococcal NEC 682.9
  stitch 998.59
  stomach (wall) 535.0 ☑
  strumous (tuberculous) (*see also* Tuberculosis) 017.2 ☑
  subarachnoid 324.9
    brain 324.0
    cerebral 324.0
    late effect — *see* category 326
    spinal cord 324.1
  subareolar (*see also* Abscess, breast)
    puerperal, postpartum 675.1 ☑
  subcecal 540.1
  subcutaneous NEC 682.9
  subdiaphragmatic 567.22
  subdorsal 682.2
  subdural 324.9
    brain 324.0
    late effect — *see* category 326
    spinal cord 324.1
  subgaleal 682.8
  subhepatic 567.22
  sublingual 528.3
    gland 527.3

☑ Additional Digit Required — Refer to the Tabular List for Digit Selection   ◤ Subterms under main terms may continue to next column or page

4 — Volume 2 • October 2009   ▶◀ Revised Text   ● New Line   ▲ Revised Code   2010 ICD-9-CM

Absence — *continued*
- jejunum — *continued*
  - congenital 751.1
- joint, congenital NEC 755.8
- kidney(s) (acquired) V45.73
  - congenital 753.0
- labium (congenital) (majus) (minus) 752.49
- labyrinth, membranous 744.05
- lacrimal apparatus (congenital) 743.65
- larynx (congenital) 748.3
- leg (acquired) V49.70
  - above knee V49.76
  - below knee V49.75
  - congenital (partial) (unilateral) (*see also* Deformity, reduction, lower limb) 755.31
    - lower (complete) (partial) (with absence of distal elements, incomplete) 755.35
      - with
        - complete absence of distal elements (foot and toes) 755.31
        - thigh (incomplete) 755.33
          - with complete absence of distal elements 755.31
    - upper — *see* Absence, femur
- lens (congenital) 743.35
  - acquired 379.31
- ligament, broad (congenital) 752.19
- limb (acquired)
  - congenital (complete) (partial) (*see also* Deformity, reduction) 755.4
    - lower 755.30
      - complete 755.31
      - incomplete 755.32
      - longitudinal — *see* Deficiency, lower limb, longitudinal
      - transverse 755.31
    - upper 755.20
      - complete 755.21
      - incomplete 755.22
      - longitudinal — *see* Deficiency, upper limb, longitudinal
      - transverse 755.21
  - lower NEC V49.70
  - upper NEC V49.60
- lip 750.26
- liver (congenital) (lobe) 751.69
- lumbar (congenital) (vertebra) 756.13
  - isthmus 756.11
  - pars articularis 756.11
- lumen — *see* Atresia
- lung (bilateral) (congenital) (fissure) (lobe) (unilateral) 748.5
  - acquired (any part) V45.76
- mandible (congenital) 524.09
- maxilla (congenital) 524.09
- menstruation 626.0
- metacarpal(s), congenital (complete) (partial) (with absence of distal elements, incomplete) (*see also* Deformity, reduction, upper limb) 755.28
  - with all fingers, complete 755.21
- metatarsal(s), congenital (complete) (partial) (with absence of distal elements, incomplete) (*see also* Deformity, reduction, lower limb) 755.38
  - with complete absence of distal elements 755.31
- muscle (congenital) (pectoral) 756.81
  - ocular 743.69
- musculoskeletal system (congenital) NEC 756.9
- nail(s) (congenital) 757.5
- neck, part 744.89
- nerve 742.8
- nervous system, part NEC 742.8
- neutrophil 288.00
- nipple (congenital) 757.6
  - acquired V45.71
- nose (congenital) 748.1
  - acquired 738.0
- nuclear 742.8
- ocular muscle (congenital) 743.69

Absence — *continued*
- organ
  - of Corti (congenital) 744.05
  - or site
    - acquired V45.79
    - congenital NEC 759.89
- osseous meatus (ear) 744.03
- ovary (acquired) V45.77
  - congenital 752.0
- oviduct (acquired) V45.77
  - congenital 752.19
- pancreas (congenital) 751.7
  - acquired (postoperative) (posttraumatic) V45.79
- parathyroid gland (congenital) 759.2
- parotid gland(s) (congenital) 750.21
- patella, congenital 755.64
- pelvic girdle (congenital) 755.69
- penis (congenital) 752.69
  - acquired V45.77
- pericardium (congenital) 746.89
- perineal body (congenital) 756.81
- phalange(s), congenital 755.4
  - lower limb (complete) (intercalary) (partial) (terminal) (*see also* Deformity, reduction, lower limb) 755.39
    - meaning all toes (complete) (partial) 755.31
    - transverse 755.31
  - upper limb (complete) (intercalary) (partial) (terminal) (*see also* Deformity, reduction, upper limb) 755.29
    - meaning all digits (complete) (partial) 755.21
    - transverse 755.21
- pituitary gland (congenital) 759.2
- postoperative — *see* Absence, by site, acquired
- prostate (congenital) 752.89
  - acquired V45.77
- pulmonary
  - artery 747.3
  - trunk 747.3
  - valve (congenital) 746.01
  - vein 747.49
- punctum lacrimale (congenital) 743.65
- radius, congenital (complete) (partial) (with absence of distal elements, incomplete) 755.26
  - with
    - complete absence of distal elements 755.21
    - ulna 755.25
      - with
        - complete absence of distal elements 755.21
        - humerus (incomplete) 755.23
- ray, congenital 755.4
  - lower limb (complete) (partial) (*see also* Deformity, reduction, lower limb) 755.38
    - meaning all rays 755.31
    - transverse 755.31
  - upper limb (complete) (partial) (*see also* Deformity, reduction, upper limb) 755.28
    - meaning all rays 755.21
    - transverse 755.21
- rectum (congenital) 751.2
  - acquired V45.79
- red cell 284.9
  - acquired (secondary) 284.81
  - congenital 284.01
  - hereditary 284.01
  - idiopathic 284.9
- respiratory organ (congenital) NEC 748.9
- rib (acquired) 738.3
  - congenital 756.3
- roof of orbit (congenital) 742.0
- round ligament (congenital) 752.89
- sacrum, congenital 756.13
- salivary gland(s) (congenital) 750.21
- scapula 755.59
- scrotum, congenital 752.89
- seminal tract or duct (congenital) 752.89
  - acquired V45.77

Absence — *continued*
- septum (congenital) (*see also* Imperfect, closure, septum)
  - atrial 745.69
    - and ventricular 745.7
  - between aorta and pulmonary artery 745.0
  - ventricular 745.3
    - and atrial 745.7
- sex chromosomes 758.81
- shoulder girdle, congenital (complete) (partial) 755.59
- skin (congenital) 757.39
- skull bone 756.0
  - with
    - anencephalus 740.0
    - encephalocele 742.0
    - hydrocephalus 742.3
      - with spina bifida (*see also* Spina bifida) 741.0 ☑
    - microcephalus 742.1
- spermatic cord (congenital) 752.89
- spinal cord 742.59
- spine, congenital 756.13
- spleen (congenital) 759.0
  - acquired V45.79
- sternum, congenital 756.3
- stomach (acquired) (partial) (postoperative) V45.75
  - with postgastric surgery syndrome 564.2
  - congenital 750.7
- submaxillary gland(s) (congenital) 750.21
- superior vena cava (congenital) 747.49
- tarsal(s), congenital (complete) (partial) (with absence of distal elements, incomplete) (*see also* Deformity, reduction, lower limb) 755.38
- teeth, tooth (congenital) 520.0
  - with abnormal spacing 524.30
  - acquired 525.10
    - with malocclusion 524.30
    - due to
      - caries 525.13
      - extraction 525.10
      - periodontal disease 525.12
      - trauma 525.11
- tendon (congenital) 756.81
- testis (congenital) 752.89
  - acquired V45.77
- thigh (acquired) 736.89
- thumb (acquired) V49.61
  - congenital 755.29
- thymus gland (congenital) 759.2
- thyroid (gland) (surgical) 246.8
  - with hypothyroidism 244.0
  - cartilage, congenital 748.3
  - congenital 243
- tibia, congenital (complete) (partial) (with absence of distal elements, incomplete) (*see also* Deformity, reduction, lower limb) 755.36
  - with
    - complete absence of distal elements 755.31
    - fibula 755.35
      - with
        - complete absence of distal elements 755.31
        - femur (incomplete) 755.33
          - with complete absence of distal elements 755.31
- toe (acquired) V49.72
  - congenital (complete) (partial) 755.39
    - meaning all toes 755.31
    - transverse 755.31
  - great V49.71
- tongue (congenital) 750.11
- tooth, teeth (congenital) 520.0
  - with abnormal spacing 524.30
  - acquired 525.10
    - with malocclusion 524.30
    - due to
      - caries 525.13
      - extraction 525.10
      - periodontal disease 525.12
      - trauma 525.11

Absence — *continued*
- trachea (cartilage) (congenital) (rings) 748.3
- transverse aortic arch (congenital) 747.21
- tricuspid valve 746.1
- ulna, congenital (complete) (partial) (with absence of distal elements, incomplete) (*see also* Deformity, reduction, upper limb) 755.27
  - with
    - complete absence of distal elements 755.21
    - radius 755.25
      - with
        - complete absence of distal elements 755.21
        - humerus (incomplete) 755.23
- umbilical artery (congenital) 747.5
- ureter (congenital) 753.4
  - acquired V45.74
- urethra, congenital 753.8
  - acquired V45.74
- urinary system, part NEC, congenital 753.8
  - acquired V45.74
- uterus (acquired) V88.01
  - with remaining cervical stump V88.02
  - and cervix V88.01
  - congenital 752.3
- uvula (congenital) 750.26
- vagina, congenital 752.49
  - acquired V45.77
- vas deferens (congenital) 752.89
  - acquired V45.77
- vein (congenital) (peripheral) NEC (*see also* Anomaly, peripheral vascular system) 747.60
  - brain 747.81
  - great 747.49
  - portal 747.49
  - pulmonary 747.49
- vena cava (congenital) (inferior) (superior) 747.49
- ventral horn cell 742.59
- ventricular septum 745.3
- vermis of cerebellum 742.2
- vertebra, congenital 756.13
- vulva, congenital 752.49

Absentia epileptica — *see also* Epilepsy 345.0 ☑
Absinthemia — *see also* Dependence 304.6 ☑
Absinthism — *see also* Dependence 304.6 ☑
Absorbent system disease 459.89
Absorption
- alcohol, through placenta or breast milk 760.71
- antibiotics, through placenta or breast milk 760.74
- anticonvulsants, through placenta or breast milk 760.77
- antifungals, through placenta or breast milk 760.74
- anti-infective, through placenta or breast milk 760.74
- antimetabolics, through placenta or breast milk 760.78
- chemical NEC 989.9
  - specified chemical or substance — *see* Table of Drugs and Chemicals
  - through placenta or breast milk (fetus or newborn) 760.70
    - alcohol 760.71
    - anticonvulsants 760.77
    - antifungals 760.74
    - anti-infective agents 760.74
    - antimetabolics 760.78
    - cocaine 760.75
    - "crack" 760.75
    - diethylstilbestrol [DES] 760.76
    - hallucinogenic agents 760.73
    - medicinal agents NEC 760.79
    - narcotics 760.72
    - obstetric anesthetic or analgesic drug 763.5
    - specified agent NEC 760.79
    - suspected, affecting management of pregnancy 655.5 ☑
- cocaine, through placenta or breast milk 760.75
- drug NEC (*see also* Reaction, drug)

☑ Additional Digit Required — Refer to the Tabular List for Digit Selection

Subterms under main terms may continue to next column or page

Absorption — *continued*
  drug (*see also* Reaction, drug) — *continued*
    through placenta or breast milk (fetus or newborn) 760.70
      alcohol 760.71
      anticonvulsants 760.77
      antifungals 760.74
      anti-infective agents 760.74
      antimetabolics 760.78
      cocaine 760.75
      "crack" 760.75
      diethylstilbestrol [DES] 760.76
      hallucinogenic agents 760.73
      medicinal agents NEC 760.79
      narcotics 760.72
      obstetric anesthetic or analgesic drug 763.5
      specified agent NEC 760.79
      suspected, affecting management of pregnancy 655.5 ☑
  fat, disturbance 579.8
  hallucinogenic agents, through placenta or breast milk 760.73
  immune sera, through placenta or breast milk 760.79
  lactose defect 271.3
  medicinal agents NEC, through placenta or breast milk 760.79
  narcotics, through placenta or breast milk 760.72
  noxious substance — *see* Absorption, chemical
  protein, disturbance 579.8
  pus or septic, general — *see* Septicemia
  quinine, through placenta or breast milk 760.74
  toxic substance — *see* Absorption, chemical
  uremic — *see* Uremia

Abstinence symptoms or syndrome
  alcohol 291.81
  drug 292.0
  neonatal 779.5 ●

Abt-Letterer-Siwe syndrome (acute histiocytosis X) (M9722/3) 202.5 ☑

Abulia 799.89

Abulomania 301.6

Abuse
  adult 995.80
    emotional 995.82
    multiple forms 995.85
    neglect (nutritional) 995.84
    physical 995.81
    psychological 995.82
    sexual 995.83
  alcohol — *see also* Alcoholism 305.0 ☑
    dependent 303.9 ☑
    non-dependent 305.0 ☑
  child 995.50
    counseling
      perpetrator
        non-parent V62.83
        parent V61.22
      victim V61.21
    emotional 995.51
    multiple forms 995.59
    neglect (nutritional) 995.52
    physical 995.54
      shaken infant syndrome 995.55
    psychological 995.51
    sexual 995.53
  drugs, nondependent 305.9 ☑

> *Note* — *Use the following fifth-digit subclassification with the following codes: 305.0, 305.2–305.9:*
>
> 0   *unspecified*
>
> 1   *continuous*
>
> 2   *episodic*
>
> 3   *in remission*

    amphetamine type 305.7 ☑
    antidepressants 305.8 ☑
    anxiolytic 305.4 ☑
    barbiturates 305.4 ☑

Abuse — *continued*
  drugs, nondependent — *continued*
    caffeine 305.9 ☑
    cannabis 305.2 ☑
    cocaine type 305.6 ☑
    hallucinogens 305.3 ☑
    hashish 305.2 ☑
    hypnotic 305.4 ☑
    inhalant 305.9 ☑
    LSD 305.3 ☑
    marijuana 305.2 ☑
    mixed 305.9 ☑
    morphine type 305.5 ☑
    opioid type 305.5 ☑
    phencyclidine (PCP) 305.9 ☑
    sedative 305.4 ☑
    specified NEC 305.9 ☑
    tranquilizers 305.4 ☑
  spouse 995.80
  tobacco 305.1

Acalcerosis 275.40

Acalcicosis 275.40

Acalculia 784.69
  developmental 315.1

Acanthocheilonemiasis 125.4

Acanthocytosis 272.5

Acanthokeratodermia 701.1

Acantholysis 701.8
  bullosa 757.39

Acanthoma (benign) (M8070/0) — *see also* Neoplasm, by site, benign
  malignant (M8070/3) — *see* Neoplasm, by site, malignant

Acanthosis (acquired) (nigricans) 701.2
  adult 701.2
  benign (congenital) 757.39
  congenital 757.39
  glycogenic
    esophagus 530.89
  juvenile 701.2
  tongue 529.8

Acanthrocytosis 272.5

Acapnia 276.3

Acarbia 276.2

Acardia 759.89

Acardiacus amorphus 759.89

Acardiotrophia 429.1

Acardius 759.89

Acariasis 133.9
  sarcoptic 133.0

Acaridiasis 133.9

Acarinosis 133.9

Acariosis 133.9

Acarodermatitis 133.9
  urticarioides 133.9

Acarophobia 300.29

Acatalasemia 277.89

Acatalasia 277.89

Acatamathesia 784.69

Acataphasia 784.59 ▲

Acathisia 781.0
  due to drugs 333.99

Acceleration, accelerated
  atrioventricular conduction 426.7
  idioventricular rhythm 427.89

Accessory (congenital)
  adrenal gland 759.1
  anus 751.5
  appendix 751.5
  atrioventricular conduction 426.7
  auditory ossicles 744.04
  auricle (ear) 744.1
  autosome(s) NEC 758.5
    21 or 22 758.0
  biliary duct or passage 751.69
  bladder 753.8
  blood vessels (peripheral) (congenital) NEC (*see also* Anomaly, peripheral vascular system) 747.60
    cerebral 747.81
    coronary 746.85
  bone NEC 756.9
    foot 755.67
  breast tissue, axilla 757.6
  carpal bones 755.56
  cecum 751.5

Accessory — *continued*
  cervix 752.49
  chromosome(s) NEC 758.5
    13-15 758.1
    16-18 758.2
    21 or 22 758.0
    autosome(s) NEC 758.5
    D_1 758.1
    E_3 758.2
    G 758.0
    sex 758.81
  coronary artery 746.85
  cusp(s), heart valve NEC 746.89
    pulmonary 746.09
  cystic duct 751.69
  digits 755.00
  ear (auricle) (lobe) 744.1
  endocrine gland NEC 759.2
  external os 752.49
  eyelid 743.62
  eye muscle 743.69
  face bone(s) 756.0
  fallopian tube (fimbria) (ostium) 752.19
  fingers 755.01
  foreskin 605
  frontonasal process 756.0
  gallbladder 751.69
  genital organ(s)
    female 752.89
      external 752.49
      internal NEC 752.89
    male NEC 752.89
      penis 752.69
  genitourinary organs NEC 752.89
  heart 746.89
    valve NEC 746.89
      pulmonary 746.09
  hepatic ducts 751.69
  hymen 752.49
  intestine (large) (small) 751.5
  kidney 753.3
  lacrimal canal 743.65
  leaflet, heart valve NEC 746.89
    pulmonary 746.09
  ligament, broad 752.19
  liver (duct) 751.69
  lobule (ear) 744.1
  lung (lobe) 748.69
  muscle 756.82
  navicular of carpus 755.56
  nervous system, part NEC 742.8
  nipple 757.6
  nose 748.1
  organ or site NEC — *see* Anomaly, specified type NEC
  ovary 752.0
  oviduct 752.19
  pancreas 751.7
  parathyroid gland 759.2
  parotid gland (and duct) 750.22
  pituitary gland 759.2
  placental lobe — *see* Placenta, abnormal
  preauricular appendage 744.1
  prepuce 605
  renal arteries (multiple) 747.62
  rib 756.3
    cervical 756.2
  roots (teeth) 520.2
  salivary gland 750.22
  sesamoids 755.8
  sinus — *see* condition
  skin tags 757.39
  spleen 759.0
  sternum 756.3
  submaxillary gland 750.22
  tarsal bones 755.67
  teeth, tooth 520.1
    causing crowding 524.31
  tendon 756.89
  thumb 755.01
  thymus gland 759.2
  thyroid gland 759.2
  toes 755.02
  tongue 750.13
  tragus 744.1
  ureter 753.4

Accessory — *continued*
  urethra 753.8
  urinary organ or tract NEC 753.8
  uterus 752.2
  vagina 752.49
  valve, heart NEC 746.89
    pulmonary 746.09
  vertebra 756.19
  vocal cords 748.3
  vulva 752.49

Accident, accidental — *see also* condition
  birth NEC 767.9
  cardiovascular (*see also* Disease, cardiovascular) 429.2
  cerebral (*see also* Disease, cerebrovascular, acute) 434.91
  cerebrovascular (current) (CVA) (*see also* Disease, cerebrovascular, acute) 434.91
    aborted 434.91
    embolic 434.11
    healed or old V12.54
    hemorrhagic — *see* Hemorrhage, brain
    impending 435.9
    ischemic 434.91
    late effect — *see* Late effect(s) (of) cerebrovascular disease
    postoperative 997.02
    thrombotic 434.01
  coronary (*see also* Infarct, myocardium) 410.9 ☑
  craniovascular (*see also* Disease, cerebrovascular, acute) 436
  during pregnancy, to mother, affecting fetus or newborn 760.5
  heart, cardiac (*see also* Infarct, myocardium) 410.9 ☑
  intrauterine 779.89
  vascular — *see* Disease, cerebrovascular, acute

Accommodation
  disorder of 367.51
    drug-induced 367.89
    toxic 367.89
  insufficiency of 367.4
  paralysis of 367.51
    hysterical 300.11
  spasm of 367.53

Accouchement — *see* Delivery

Accreta placenta (without hemorrhage) 667.0 ☑
  with hemorrhage 666.0 ☑

Accretio cordis (nonrheumatic) 423.1

Accretions on teeth 523.6

Accumulation secretion, prostate 602.8

Acephalia, acephalism, acephaly 740.0

Acephalic 740.0

Acephalobrachia 759.89

Acephalocardia 759.89

Acephalocardius 759.89

Acephalochiria 759.89

Acephalochirus 759.89

Acephalogaster 759.89

Acephalostomus 759.89

Acephalothorax 759.89

Acephalus 740.0

Acetonemia 790.6
  diabetic 250.1 ☑
    due to secondary diabetes 249.1 ☑

Acetonglycosuria 982.8

Acetonuria 791.6

Achalasia 530.0
  cardia 530.0
  digestive organs congenital NEC 751.8
  esophagus 530.0
  pelvirectal 751.3
  psychogenic 306.4
  pylorus 750.5
  sphincteral NEC 564.89

Achard-Thiers syndrome (adrenogenital) 255.2

Ache(s) — *see* Pain

Acheilia 750.26

Acheiria 755.21

Achillobursitis 726.71

Achillodynia 726.71

Achlorhydria, achlorhydric 536.0
  anemia 280.9
  diarrhea 536.0
  neurogenic 536.0

☑ Additional Digit Required — Refer to the Tabular List for Digit Selection   ▽ Subterms under main terms may continue to next column or page

2010 ICD-9-CM   ►◄ Revised Text   ● New Line   ▲ Revised Code   October 2009 • Volume 2 — 7

Achlorhydria, achlorhydric — *continued*
  postvagotomy 564.2
  psychogenic 306.4
  secondary to vagotomy 564.2
Achloroblepsia 368.52
Achloropsia 368.52
Acholia 575.8
Acholuric jaundice (familial) (splenomegalic) —
  see also Spherocytosis 282.0
  acquired 283.9
Achondroplasia 756.4
Achrestic anemia 281.8
Achroacytosis, lacrimal gland 375.00
  tuberculous (*see also* Tuberculosis) 017.3 ☑
Achroma, cutis 709.00
Achromate (congenital) 368.54
Achromatopia 368.54
Achromatopsia (congenital) 368.54
Achromia
  congenital 270.2
  parasitica 111.0
  unguium 703.8
Achylia
  gastrica 536.8
    neurogenic 536.3
    psychogenic 306.4
  pancreatica 577.1
Achylosis 536.8
Acid
  burn (*see also* Burn, by site)
    from swallowing acid — *see* Burn, internal
      organs
  deficiency
    amide nicotinic 265.2
    amino 270.9
    ascorbic 267
    folic 266.2
    nicotinic (amide) 265.2
    pantothenic 266.2
  intoxication 276.2
  peptic disease 536.8
  stomach 536.8
    psychogenic 306.4
Acidemia 276.2
  arginosuccinic 270.6
  fetal
    affecting management of pregnancy
      656.3 ☑
    before onset of labor, in liveborn infant
      768.2
    during labor and delivery in liveborn infant
      768.3
    intrauterine 656.3 ☑
    unspecified as to time of onset, in liveborn
      infant 768.4
  newborn 775.81
  pipecolic 270.7
Acidity, gastric (high) (low) 536.8
  psychogenic 306.4
Acidocytopenia 288.59
Acidocytosis 288.3
Acidopenia 288.59
Acidosis 276.2
  diabetic 250.1 ☑
    due to secondary diabetes 249.1 ☑
  fetal, affecting management of pregnancy
    756.8 ☑
  fetal, affecting newborn 775.81
  kidney tubular 588.89
    newborn 775.81
  lactic 276.2
  metabolic NEC 276.2
    with respiratory acidosis 276.4
      of newborn 775.81
    late, of newborn 775.7
  newborn 775.81
  renal
    hyperchloremic 588.89
    tubular (distal) (proximal) 588.89
  respiratory 276.2
    complicated by
      metabolic acidosis 276.4
        of newborn 775.81
      metabolic alkalosis 276.4
Aciduria 791.9
  arginosuccinic 270.6

Aciduria — *continued*
  beta-aminoisobutyric (BAIB) 277.2
  glutaric
    type I 270.7
    type II (type IIA, IIB, IIC) 277.85
    type III 277.86
  glycolic 271.8
  methylmalonic 270.3
    with glycinemia 270.7
  organic 270.9
  orotic (congenital) (hereditary) (pyrimidine
    deficiency) 281.4
Acladiosis 111.8
  skin 111.8
Aclasis
  diaphyseal 756.4
  tarsoepiphyseal 756.59
Acleistocardia 745.5
Aclusion 524.4
Acmesthesia 782.0
Acne (pustular) (vulgaris) 706.1
  agminata (*see also* Tuberculosis) 017.0 ☑
  artificialis 706.1
  atrophica 706.0
  cachecticorum (Hebra) 706.1
  conglobata 706.1
  conjunctiva 706.1
  cystic 706.1
  decalvans 704.09
  erythematosa 695.3
  eyelid 706.1
  frontalis 706.0
  indurata 706.1
  keloid 706.1
  lupoid 706.0
  necrotic, necrotica 706.0
    miliaris 704.8
  neonatal 706.1
  nodular 706.1
  occupational 706.1
  papulosa 706.1
  rodens 706.0
  rosacea 695.3
  scorbutica 267
  scrofulosorum (Bazin) (*see also* Tuberculosis)
    017.0 ☑
  summer 692.72
  tropical 706.1
  varioliformis 706.0
Acneiform drug eruptions 692.3
Acnitis (primary) — *see also* Tuberculosis
  017.0 ☑
Acomia 704.00
Acontractile bladder 344.61
Aconuresis — *see also* Incontinence 788.30
Acosta's disease 993.2
Acousma 780.1
Acoustic — *see* condition
Acousticophobia 300.29
Acquired — *see* condition
Acquired immune deficiency syndrome —
  see Human immunodeficiency virus (dis-
  ease) (illness) (infection)
Acquired immunodeficiency syndrome — *see*
  Human immunodeficiency virus (disease)
  (illness) (infection)
Acragnosis 781.99
Acrania 740.0
Acroagnosis 781.99
Acroasphyxia, chronic 443.89
Acrobrachycephaly 756.0
Acrobystiolith 608.89
Acrobystitis 607.2
Acrocephalopolysyndactyly 755.55
Acrocephalosyndactyly 755.55
Acrocephaly 756.0
Acrochondrohyperplasia 759.82
Acrocyanosis 443.89
  newborn 770.83
    meaning transient blue hands and feet —
      omit code
Acrodermatitis 686.8
  atrophicans (chronica) 701.8
  continua (Hallopeau) 696.1
  enteropathica 686.8
  Hallopeau's 696.1

Acrodermatitis — *continued*
  perstans 696.1
  pustulosa continua 696.1
  recalcitrant pustular 696.1
Acrodynia 985.0
Acrodysplasia 755.55
Acrohyperhidrosis — *see also* Hyperhidrosis
  780.8
Acrokeratosis verruciformis 757.39
Acromastitis 611.0
Acromegaly, acromegalia (skin) 253.0
Acromelalgia 443.82
Acromicria, acromikria 756.59
Acronyx 703.0
Acropachyderma 757.39
Acropachy, thyroid — *see also* Thyrotoxicosis
  242.9 ☑
Acroparesthesia 443.89
  simple (Schultz's type) 443.89
  vasomotor (Nothnagel's type) 443.89
Acropathy thyroid — *see also* Thyrotoxicosis
  242.9 ☑
Acrophobia 300.29
Acroposthitis 607.2
Acroscleriasis — *see also* Scleroderma 710.1
Acroscleroderma — *see also* Scleroderma 710.1
Acrosclerosis — *see also* Scleroderma 710.1
Acrosphacelus 785.4
Acrosphenosyndactylia 755.55
Acrospiroma, eccrine (M8402/0) — *see* Neo-
  plasm, skin, benign
Acrostealgia 732.9
Acrosyndactyly — *see also* Syndactylism 755.10
Acrotrophodynia 991.4
Actinic — *see also* condition
  cheilitis (due to sun) 692.72
    chronic NEC 692.74
    due to radiation, except from sun 692.82
  conjunctivitis 370.24
  dermatitis (due to sun) (*see also* Dermatitis,
    actinic) 692.70
  due to
    roentgen rays or radioactive substance
      692.82
    ultraviolet radiation, except from sun
      692.82
    sun NEC 692.70
  elastosis solare 692.74
  granuloma 692.73
  keratitis 370.24
  ophthalmia 370.24
  reticuloid 692.73
Actinobacillosis, general 027.8
Actinobacillus
  lignieresii 027.8
  mallei 024
  muris 026.1
Actinocutitis NEC — *see also* Dermatitis, actinic
  692.70
Actinodermatitis NEC — *see also* Dermatitis,
  actinic 692.70
Actinomyces
  israelii (infection) — *see* Actinomycosis
  muris-ratti (infection) 026.1
Actinomycosis, actinomycotic 039.9
  with
    pneumonia 039.1
  abdominal 039.2
  cervicofacial 039.3
  cutaneous 039.0
  pulmonary 039.1
  specified site NEC 039.8
  thoracic 039.1
Actinoneuritis 357.89
Action, heart
  disorder 427.9
    postoperative 997.1
  irregular 427.9
    postoperative 997.1
    psychogenic 306.2
Active — *see* condition
Activity decrease, functional 780.99
Acute — *see also* condition
  abdomen NEC 789.0 ☑
  gallbladder (*see also* Cholecystitis, acute) 575.0
Acyanoblepsia 368.53

Acyanopsia 368.53
Acystia 753.8
Acystinervia — *see* Neurogenic, bladder
Acystineuria — *see* Neurogenic, bladder
Adactylia, adactyly (congenital) 755.4
  lower limb (complete) (intercalary) (partial)
    (terminal) (*see also* Deformity, reduc-
    tion, lower limb) 755.39
    meaning all digits (complete) (partial)
      755.31
    transverse (complete) (partial) 755.31
  upper limb (complete) (intercalary) (partial)
    (terminal) (*see also* Deformity, reduc-
    tion, upper limb) 755.29
    meaning all digits (complete) (partial)
      755.21
    transverse (complete) (partial) 755.21
Adair-Dighton syndrome (brittle bones and
  blue sclera, deafness) 756.51
Adamantinoblastoma (M9310/0) — *see*
  Ameloblastoma
Adamantinoma (M9310/0) — *see* Ameloblas-
  toma
Adamantoblastoma (M9310/0) — *see*
  Ameloblastoma
Adams-Stokes (-Morgagni) disease or syn-
  drome (syncope with heart block) 426.9
Adaptation reaction — *see also* Reaction, adjustment 309.9
Addiction — *see also* Dependence
  absinthe 304.6 ☑
  alcoholic (ethyl) (methyl) (wood) 303.9 ☑
    complicating pregnancy, childbirth, or
      puerperium 648.4 ☑
      affecting fetus or newborn 760.71
    suspected damage to fetus affecting
      management of pregnancy
      655.4 ☑
  drug (*see also* Dependence) 304.9 ☑
  ethyl alcohol 303.9 ☑
  heroin 304.0 ☑
  hospital 301.51
  methyl alcohol 303.9 ☑
  methylated spirit 303.9 ☑
  morphine (-like substances) 304.0 ☑
  nicotine 305.1
  opium 304.0 ☑
  tobacco 305.1
  wine 303.9 ☑
Addison's
  anemia (pernicious) 281.0
  disease (bronze) (primary adrenal insufficiency)
    255.41
    tuberculous (*see also* Tuberculosis)
      017.6 ☑
  keloid (morphea) 701.0
  melanoderma (adrenal cortical hypofunction)
    255.41
Addison-Biermer anemia (pernicious) 281.0
Addison-Gull disease — *see* Xanthoma
Addisonian crisis or melanosis (acute adrenocortical insufficiency) 255.41
Additional — *see also* Accessory
  chromosome(s) 758.5
    13-15 758.1
    16-18 758.2
    21 758.0
    autosome(s) NEC 758.5
    sex 758.81
Adduction contracture, hip or other joint —
  see Contraction, joint
ADEM (acute disseminated encephalomyelitis)
  (postinfectious) 136.9 *[323.61]*
  infectious 136.9 *[323.61]*
  noninfectious 323.81
Adenasthenia gastrica 536.0
Aden fever 061
Adenitis — *see also* Lymphadenitis 289.3
  acute, unspecified site 683
    epidemic infectious 075
  axillary 289.3
    acute 683
    chronic or subacute 289.1
  Bartholin's gland 616.89
  bulbourethral gland (*see also* Urethritis) 597.89
  cervical 289.3

☑ Additional Digit Required — Refer to the Tabular List for Digit Selection

▼ Subterms under main terms may continue to next column or page

►◄ Revised Text   ● New Line   ▲ Revised Code

Adenitis — *see also* Lymphadenitis — *continued*
  cervical — *continued*
    acute 683
    chronic or subacute 289.1
  chancroid (Ducrey's bacillus) 099.0
  chronic (any lymph node, except mesenteric) 289.1
    mesenteric 289.2
  Cowper's gland (*see also* Urethritis) 597.89
  epidemic, acute 075
  gangrenous 683
  gonorrheal NEC 098.89
  groin 289.3
    acute 683
    chronic or subacute 289.1
  infectious 075
  inguinal (region) 289.3
    acute 683
    chronic or subacute 289.1
  lymph gland or node, except mesenteric 289.3
    acute 683
    chronic or subacute 289.1
    mesenteric (acute) (chronic) (nonspecific) (subacute) 289.2
  mesenteric (acute) (chronic) (nonspecific) (subacute) 289.2
    due to Pasteurella multocida (P. septica) 027.2
  parotid gland (suppurative) 527.2
  phlegmonous 683
  salivary duct or gland (any) (recurring) (suppurative) 527.2
  scrofulous (*see also* Tuberculosis) 017.2 ☑
  septic 289.3
  Skene's duct or gland (*see also* Urethritis) 597.89
  strumous, tuberculous (*see also* Tuberculosis) 017.2 ☑
  subacute, unspecified site 289.1
  sublingual gland (suppurative) 527.2
  submandibular gland (suppurative) 527.2
  submaxillary gland (suppurative) 527.2
  suppurative 683
  tuberculous — *see* Tuberculosis, lymph gland
  urethral gland (*see also* Urethritis) 597.89
  venereal NEC 099.8
  Wharton's duct (suppurative) 527.2
Adenoacanthoma (M8570/3) — *see* Neoplasm, by site, malignant
Adenoameloblastoma (M9300/0) 213.1
  upper jaw (bone) 213.0
Adenocarcinoma (M8140/3) — *see also* Neoplasm, by site, malignant

Note — The list of adjectival modifiers below is not exhaustive. A description of adenocarcinoma that does not appear in this list should be coded in the same manner as carcinoma with that description. Thus, "mixed acidophil-basophil adenocarcinoma," should be coded in the same manner as "mixed acidophil-basophil carcinoma," which appears in the list under "Carcinoma."

Except where otherwise indicated, the morphological varieties of adenocarcinoma in the list below should be coded by site as for "Neoplasm, malignant."

  with
    apocrine metaplasia (M8573/3)
    cartilaginous (and osseous) metaplasia (M8571/3)
    osseous (and cartilaginous) metaplasia (M8571/3)
    spindle cell metaplasia (M8572/3)
    squamous metaplasia (M8570/3)
  acidophil (M8280/3)
    specified site — *see* Neoplasm, by site, malignant
    unspecified site 194.3
  acinar (M8550/3)
  acinic cell (M8550/3)
  adrenal cortical (M8370/3) 194.0

Adenocarcinoma — *see also* Neoplasm, by site, malignant — *continued*
  alveolar (M8251/3)
    and
      epidermoid carcinoma, mixed (M8560/3)
      squamous cell carcinoma, mixed (M8560/3)
  apocrine (M8401/3)
    breast — *see* Neoplasm, breast, malignant
    specified site NEC — *see* Neoplasm, skin, malignant
    unspecified site 173.9
  basophil (M8300/3)
    specified site — *see* Neoplasm, by site, malignant
    unspecified site 194.3
  bile duct type (M8160/3)
    liver 155.1
    specified site NEC — *see* Neoplasm, by site, malignant
    unspecified site 155.1
  bronchiolar (M8250/3) — *see* Neoplasm, lung, malignant
  ceruminous (M8420/3) 173.2
  chromophobe (M8270/3)
    specified site — *see* Neoplasm, by site, malignant
    unspecified site 194.3
  clear cell (mesonephroid type) (M8310/3)
  colloid (M8480/3)
  cylindroid type (M8200/3)
  diffuse type (M8145/3)
    specified site — *see* Neoplasm, by site, malignant
    unspecified site 151.9
  duct (infiltrating) (M8500/3)
    with Paget's disease (M8541/3) — *see* Neoplasm, breast, malignant
    specified site — *see* Neoplasm, by site, malignant
    unspecified site 174.9
  embryonal (M9070/3)
  endometrioid (M8380/3) — *see* Neoplasm, by site, malignant
  eosinophil (M8280/3)
    specified site — *see* Neoplasm, by site, malignant
    unspecified site 194.3
  follicular (M8330/3)
    and papillary (M8340/3) 193
    moderately differentiated type (M8332/3) 193
    pure follicle type (M8331/3) 193
    specified site — *see* Neoplasm, by site, malignant
    trabecular type (M8332/3) 193
    unspecified type 193
    well differentiated type (M8331/3) 193
  gelatinous (M8480/3)
  granular cell (M8320/3)
  Hürthle cell (M8290/3) 193
  in
    adenomatous
      polyp (M8210/3)
    polyposis coli (M8220/3) 153.9
    polypoid adenoma (M8210/3)
    tubular adenoma (M8210/3)
    villous adenoma (M8261/3)
  infiltrating duct (M8500/3)
    with Paget's disease (M8541/3) — *see* Neoplasm, breast, malignant
    specified site — *see* Neoplasm, by site, malignant
    unspecified site 174.9
  inflammatory (M8530/3)
    specified site — *see* Neoplasm, by site, malignant
    unspecified site 174.9
  in situ (M8140/2) — *see* Neoplasm, by site, in situ
  intestinal type (M8144/3)
    specified site — *see* Neoplasm, by site, malignant
    unspecified site 151.9

Adenocarcinoma — *see also* Neoplasm, by site, malignant — *continued*
  intraductal (noninfiltrating) (M8500/2)
    papillary (M8503/2)
      specified site — *see* Neoplasm, by site, in situ
      unspecified site 233.0
    specified site — *see* Neoplasm, by site, in situ
    unspecified site 233.0
  islet cell (M8150/3)
    and exocrine, mixed (M8154/3)
      specified site — *see* Neoplasm, by site, malignant
      unspecified site 157.9
    pancreas 157.4
    specified site NEC — *see* Neoplasm, by site, malignant
    unspecified site 157.4
  lobular (M8520/3)
    specified site — *see* Neoplasm, by site, malignant
    unspecified site 174.9
  medullary (M8510/3)
  mesonephric (M9110/3)
  mixed cell (M8323/3)
  mucinous (M8480/3)
  mucin-producing (M8481/3)
  mucoid (M8480/3) (*see also* Neoplasm, by site, malignant)
    cell (M8300/3)
      specified site — *see* Neoplasm, by site, malignant
      unspecified site 194.3
  nonencapsulated sclerosing (M8350/3) 193
  oncocytic (M8290/3)
  oxyphilic (M8290/3)
  papillary (M8260/3)
    and follicular (M8340/3) 193
    intraductal (noninfiltrating) (M8503/2)
      specified site — *see* Neoplasm, by site, in situ
      unspecified site 233.0
    serous (M8460/3)
      specified site — *see* Neoplasm, by site, malignant
      unspecified site 183.0
  papillocystic (M8450/3)
    specified site — *see* Neoplasm, by site, malignant
    unspecified site 183.0
  pseudomucinous (M8470/3)
    specified site — *see* Neoplasm, by site, malignant
    unspecified site 183.0
  renal cell (M8312/3) 189.0
  sebaceous (M8410/3)
  serous (M8441/3) (*see also* Neoplasm, by site, malignant)
    papillary
      specified site — *see* Neoplasm, by site, malignant
      unspecified site 183.0
  signet ring cell (M8490/3)
  superficial spreading (M8143/3)
  sweat gland (M8400/3) — *see* Neoplasm, skin, malignant
  trabecular (M8190/3)
  tubular (M8211/3)
  villous (M8262/3)
  water-clear cell (M8322/3) 194.1
Adenofibroma (M9013/0)
  clear cell (M8313/0) — *see* Neoplasm, by site, benign
  endometrioid (M8381/0) 220
    borderline malignancy (M8381/1) 236.2
    malignant (M8381/3) 183.0
  mucinous (M9015/0)
    specified site — *see* Neoplasm, by site, benign
    unspecified site 220
  prostate 600.20
    with
      other lower urinary tract symptoms (LUTS) 600.21

Adenofibroma — *continued*
  prostate — *continued*
    with — *continued*
      urinary
        obstruction 600.21
        retention 600.21
  serous (M9014/0)
    specified site — *see* Neoplasm, by site, benign
    unspecified site 220
  specified site — *see* Neoplasm, by site, benign
  unspecified site 220
Adenofibrosis
  breast 610.2
  endometrioid 617.0
Adenoiditis 474.01
  acute 463
  chronic 474.01
    with chronic tonsillitis 474.02
Adenoids (congenital) (of nasal fossa) 474.9
  hypertrophy 474.12
  vegetations 474.2
Adenolipomatosis (symmetrical) 272.8
Adenolymphoma (M8561/0)
  specified site — *see* Neoplasm, by site, benign
  unspecified 210.2
Adenomatosis (M8220/0)
  endocrine (multiple) (M8360/1)
    single specified site — *see* Neoplasm, by site, uncertain behavior
    two or more specified sites 237.4
    unspecified site 237.4
  erosive of nipple (M8506/0) 217
  pluriendocrine — *see* Adenomatosis, endocrine
  pulmonary (M8250/1) 235.7
    malignant (M8250/3) — *see* Neoplasm, lung, malignant
  specified site — *see* Neoplasm, by site, benign
  unspecified site 211.3
Adenomatous
  cyst, thyroid (gland) — *see* Goiter, nodular
  goiter (nontoxic) (*see also* Goiter, nodular) 241.9
    toxic or with hyperthyroidism 242.3 ☑
Adenoma (sessile) (M8140/0) — *see also* Neoplasm, by site, benign

Note — Except where otherwise indicated, the morphological varieties of adenoma in the list below should be coded by site as for "Neoplasm, benign."

  acidophil (M8280/0)
    specified site — *see* Neoplasm, by site, benign
    unspecified site 227.3
  acinar (cell) (M8550/0)
  acinic cell (M8550/0)
  adrenal (cortex) (cortical) (functioning) (M8370/0) 227.0
    clear cell type (M8373/0) 227.0
    compact cell type (M8371/0) 227.0
    glomerulosa cell type (M8374/0) 227.0
    heavily pigmented variant (M8372/0) 227.0
    mixed cell type (M8375/0) 227.0
  alpha cell (M8152/0)
    pancreas 211.7
    specified site NEC — *see* Neoplasm, by site, benign
    unspecified site 211.7
  alveolar (M8251/0)
  apocrine (M8401/0)
    breast 217
    specified site NEC — *see* Neoplasm, skin, benign
    unspecified site 216.9
  basal cell (M8147/0)
  basophil (M8300/0)
    specified site — *see* Neoplasm, by site, benign
    unspecified site 227.3
  beta cell (M8151/0)
    pancreas 211.7
    specified site NEC — *see* Neoplasm, by site, benign
    unspecified site 211.7
  bile duct (M8160/0) 211.5

☑ Additional Digit Required — Refer to the Tabular List for Digit Selection
▽ Subterms under main terms may continue to next column or page
10 — Volume 2
▶◀ Revised Text ● New Line ▲ Revised Code
2010 ICD-9-CM

Adhesion(s), adhesive — continued
  peritoneum, peritoneal — continued
    female (postoperative) (postinfective)
        614.6
      pelvic, female 614.6
      pelvic, male 568.0
      postpartal, pelvic 614.6
      to uterus 614.6
    peritubal 614.6
    periureteral 593.89
    periuterine 621.5
    perivesical 596.8
    perivesicular (seminal vesicle) 608.89
    pleura, pleuritic 511.0
      tuberculous (see also Tuberculosis, pleura)
          012.0 ☑
    pleuropericardial 511.0
    postoperative (gastrointestinal tract) (see also
        Adhesions, peritoneum) 568.0
      eyelid 997.99
        surgically created V45.69
      pelvic female 614.9
      pelvic male 568.0
      urethra 598.2
    postpartal, old 624.4
    preputial, prepuce 605
    pulmonary 511.0
    pylorus (see also Adhesions, peritoneum) 568.0
    Rosenmüller's fossa 478.29
    sciatic nerve 355.0
    seminal vesicle 608.89
    shoulder (joint) 726.0
    sigmoid flexure (see also Adhesions, peri-
        toneum) 568.0
    spermatic cord (acquired) 608.89
      congenital 752.89
    spinal canal 349.2
      nerve 355.9
        root 724.9
            cervical NEC 723.4
            lumbar NEC 724.4
            lumbosacral 724.4
            thoracic 724.4
    stomach (see also Adhesions, peritoneum)
        568.0
    subscapular 726.2
    tendonitis 726.90
      shoulder 726.0
    testicle 608.89
    tongue (congenital) (to gum or roof of mouth)
        750.12
      acquired 529.8
    trachea 519.19
    tubo-ovarian 614.6
    tunica vaginalis 608.89
    ureter 593.89
    uterus 621.5
      to abdominal wall 614.6
        in pregnancy or childbirth 654.4 ☑
          affecting fetus or newborn 763.89
    vagina (chronic) (postoperative) (postradia-
        tion) 623.2
    vaginitis (congenital) 752.49
    vesical 596.8
    vitreous 379.29
Adie (-Holmes) syndrome (tonic pupillary reac-
    tion) 379.46
Adiponecrosis neonatorum 778.1
Adiposa dolorosa 272.8
Adiposalgia 272.8
Adiposis
  cerebralis 253.8
  dolorosa 272.8
  tuberosa simplex 272.8
Adiposity 278.02
  heart (see also Degeneration, myocardial) 429.1
  localized 278.1
Adiposogenital dystrophy 253.8
Adjustment
  prosthesis or other device — see Fitting of
  reaction — see Reaction, adjustment
Administration, prophylactic
  antibiotics V07.39
  antitoxin, any V07.2
  antivenin V07.2
  chemotherapeutic agent NEC V07.39

Administration, prophylactic — continued
  chemotherapy NEC V07.39
  diphtheria antitoxin V07.2
  fluoride V07.31
  gamma globulin V07.2
  immune sera (gamma globulin) V07.2
  passive immunization agent V07.2
  RhoGAM V07.2
Admission (encounter)
  as organ donor — see Donor
  by mistake V68.9
  for
    adequacy testing (for)
      hemodialysis V56.31
      peritoneal dialysis V56.32
    adjustment (of)
      artificial
        arm (complete) (partial) V52.0
        eye V52.2
        leg (complete) (partial) V52.1
      brain neuropacemaker V53.02
      breast
        implant V52.4
          exchange (different material)
              (different size) V52.4
        prosthesis V52.4
      cardiac device V53.39
        defibrillator, automatic implantable
            V53.32
        pacemaker V53.31
          carotid sinus V53.39
      catheter
        non-vascular V58.82
        vascular V58.81
      cerebral ventricle (communicating)
          shunt V53.01
      colostomy belt V55.3
      contact lenses V53.1
      cystostomy device V53.6
      dental prosthesis V52.3
      device, unspecified type V53.90
        abdominal V53.59   ▲
        cardiac V53.39
          defibrillator, automatic im-
              plantable V53.32
          pacemaker V53.31
        carotid sinus V53.39
        cerebral ventricle (communicating)
            shunt V53.01
        gastrointestinal NEC V53.59   ●
        insulin pump V53.91
        intestinal V53.50   ●
        intrauterine contraceptive V25.1
        nervous system V53.09
        orthodontic V53.4
        other device V53.99
        prosthetic V52.9
          breast V52.4
          dental V52.3
          eye V52.2
          specified type NEC V52.8
        special senses V53.09
        substitution
          auditory V53.09
          nervous system V53.09
          visual V53.09
        urinary V53.6
      dialysis catheter
        extracorporeal V56.1
        peritoneal V56.2
      diaphragm (contraceptive) V25.02
      gastric lap band V53.51   ●
      gastrointestinal appliance and device ●
          NEC V53.59   ●
      growth rod V54.02
      hearing aid V53.2
      ileostomy device V55.2
      intestinal appliance ▶and◀ device
          V53.50   ▲
      intrauterine contraceptive device V25.1
      neuropacemaker (brain) (peripheral
          nerve) (spinal cord) V53.02
      orthodontic device V53.4
      orthopedic (device) V53.7
        brace V53.7
        cast V53.7

Admission — continued
  for — continued
    adjustment — continued
      orthopedic — continued
        shoes V53.7
      pacemaker
        brain V53.02
        cardiac V53.31
        carotid sinus V53.39
        peripheral nerve V53.02
        spinal cord V53.02
      prosthesis V52.9
        arm (complete) (partial) V52.0
        breast V52.4
        dental V52.3
        eye V52.2
        leg (complete) (partial) V52.1
        specified type NEC V52.8
      spectacles V53.1
      wheelchair V53.8
    adoption referral or proceedings V68.89
    aftercare (see also Aftercare) V58.9
      cardiac pacemaker V53.31
      chemotherapy ▶(oral) (intravenous)◀
          V58.11
      dialysis
        extracorporeal (renal) V56.0
        peritoneal V56.8
        renal V56.0
      fracture (see also Aftercare, fracture)
          V54.9
      medical NEC V58.89
      organ transplant V58.44
      orthopedic V54.9
        specified care NEC V54.89
      pacemaker device
        brain V53.02
        cardiac V53.31
        carotid sinus V53.39
        nervous system V53.02
        spinal cord V53.02
      postoperative NEC V58.49
        wound closure, planned V58.41
      postpartum
        immediately after delivery V24.0
        routine follow-up V24.2
      postradiation V58.0
      radiation therapy V58.0
      removal of
        non-vascular catheter V58.82
        vascular catheter V58.81
      specified NEC V58.89
      surgical NEC V58.49
        wound closure, planned V58.41
    antineoplastic
      chemotherapy ▶(oral) (intravenous)◀
          V58.11
      immunotherapy V58.12
    artificial insemination V26.1
    assisted reproductive fertility procedure
        cycle V26.81
    attention to artificial opening (of) V55.9
      artificial vagina V55.7
      colostomy V55.3
      cystostomy V55.5
      enterostomy V55.4
      gastrostomy V55.1
      ileostomy V55.2
      jejunostomy V55.4
      nephrostomy V55.6
      specified site NEC V55.8
        intestinal tract V55.4
        urinary tract V55.6
      tracheostomy V55.0
      ureterostomy V55.6
      urethrostomy V55.6
    battery replacement
      cardiac pacemaker V53.31
    blood typing V72.86
      Rh typing V72.86
    boarding V65.0
    breast
      augmentation or reduction V50.1
      implant exchange (different material)
          (different size) V52.4

Admission — continued
  for — continued
    breast — continued
      reconstruction following mastectomy
          V51.0
      removal
        prophylactic V50.41
        tissue expander without syn-
            chronous insertion of perma-
            nent implant V52.4
    change of
      cardiac pacemaker (battery) V53.31
      carotid sinus pacemaker V53.39
      catheter in artificial opening — see At-
          tention to, artificial, opening
      drains V58.49
      dressing
        wound V58.30
          nonsurgical V58.30
          surgical V58.31
      fixation device
        external V54.89
        internal V54.01
      Kirschner wire V54.89
      neuropacemaker device (brain) (periph-
          eral nerve) (spinal cord) V53.02
      nonsurgical wound dressing V58.30
      pacemaker device
        brain V53.02
        cardiac V53.31
        carotid sinus V53.39
        nervous system V53.02
      plaster cast V54.89
      splint, external V54.89
      Steinmann pin V54.89
      surgical wound dressing V58.31
      traction device V54.89
      wound packing V58.30
        nonsurgical V58.30
        surgical V58.31
    checkup only V70.0
    chemotherapy, ▶(oral) (intravenous)◀
        antineoplastic V58.11
    circumcision, ritual or routine (in absence
        of medical indication) V50.2
    clinical research investigation (control)
        (normal comparison) (participant)
        V70.7
    closure of artificial opening — see Atten-
        tion to, artificial, opening
    contraceptive
      counseling V25.09
        emergency V25.03
        postcoital V25.03
      management V25.9
        specified type NEC V25.8
    convalescence following V66.9
      chemotherapy V66.2
      psychotherapy V66.3
      radiotherapy V66.1
      surgery V66.0
      treatment (for) V66.5
        combined V66.6
        fracture V66.4
        mental disorder NEC V66.3
        specified condition NEC V66.5
    cosmetic surgery NEC V50.1
      breast reconstruction following mastec-
          tomy V51.0
      following healed injury or operation
          V51.8
    counseling (see also Counseling) V65.40
      without complaint or sickness V65.49
      contraceptive management V25.09
        emergency V25.03
        postcoital V25.03
      dietary V65.3
      exercise V65.41
      fertility preservation (prior to cancer ●
          therapy) (prior to surgical re- ●
          moval of gonads) V26.42   ●
      for
        nonattending third party V65.19
        pediatric
          pre-adoption visit for adop- ●
              tive parent(s) V65.11   ●

Admission — *continued*
  for — *continued*
    counseling (*see also* Counseling) — *continued*
      for — *continued*
        pediatric — *continued*
          pre-birth visit for expectant ●
            parent(s) V65.11 ●
        victim of abuse
          child V61.21
          partner or spouse V61.11
      genetic V26.33
      gonorrhea V65.45
      HIV V65.44
      human immunodeficiency virus V65.44
      injury prevention V65.43
      insulin pump training V65.46
      natural family planning
        procreative V26.41
        to avoid pregnancy V25.04
      procreative management V26.49
        using natural family planning V26.41
      sexually transmitted disease NEC V65.45
        HIV V65.44
      specified reason NEC V65.49
      substance use and abuse V65.42
      syphilis V65.45
      victim of abuse
        child V61.21
        partner or spouse V61.11
    desensitization to allergens V07.1
    dialysis V56.0
      catheter
        fitting and adjustment
          extracorporeal V56.1
          peritoneal V56.2
        removal or replacement
          extracorporeal V56.1
          peritoneal V56.2
      extracorporeal (renal) V56.0
      peritoneal V56.8
      renal V56.0
    dietary surveillance and counseling V65.3
    drug monitoring, therapeutic V58.83
    ear piercing V50.3
    elective surgery V50.9
      breast
        augmentation or reduction V50.1
        reconstruction following mastectomy V51.0
        removal, prophylactic V50.41
      circumcision, ritual or routine (in absence of medical indication) V50.2
      cosmetic NEC V50.1
        breast reconstruction following mastectomy V51.0
        following healed injury or operation V51.8
      ear piercing V50.3
      face-lift V50.1
      hair transplant V50.0
      plastic
        breast reconstruction following mastectomy V51.0
        cosmetic NEC V50.1
        following healed injury or operation V51.8
      prophylactic organ removal V50.49
        breast V50.41
        ovary V50.42
      repair of scarred tissue (following healed injury or operation) V51.8
      specified type NEC V50.8
    end-of-life care V66.7
    examination (*see also* Examination) V70.9
      administrative purpose NEC V70.3
      adoption V70.3
      allergy V72.7
      antibody response V72.61 ●
      at health care facility V70.0
      athletic team V70.3 ·
      camp V70.3

Admission — *continued*
  for — *continued*
    examination (*see also* Examination) — *continued*
      cardiovascular, preoperative V72.81
      clinical research investigation (control) (participant) V70.7
      dental V72.2
      developmental testing (child) (infant) V20.2
      donor (potential) V70.8
      driver's license V70.3
      ear V72.19
      employment V70.5
      eye V72.0
      fertility preservation (prior to cancer ●
        therapy) (prior to surgical re- ●
        moval of gonads) V26.82
      follow-up (routine) — *see* Examination, follow-up
      for admission to
        old age home V70.3
        school V70.3
      general V70.9
        specified reason NEC V70.8
      gynecological V72.31
      health supervision
        child (over 28 days old) V20.2 ●
        infant (over 28 days old) V20.2 ●
        newborn
          8 to 28 days old V20.32 ●
          under 8 days old V20.31 ●
      hearing V72.19
        following failed hearing screening V72.11
      immigration V70.3
      infant
        8 to 28 days old V20.32 ●
        over 28 days old, routine V20.2 ●
        under 8 days old V20.31 ●
      insurance certification V70.3
      laboratory V72.60 ▲
        ordered as part of a routine gen- ●
          eral medical examination ●
          V72.62 ●
        pre-operative V72.63 ●
        pre-procedural V72.63 ●
        specified NEC V72.69 ●
      marriage license V70.3
      medical (general) (*see also* Examination, medical) V70.9
      medicolegal reasons V70.4
      naturalization V70.3
      pelvic (annual) (periodic) V72.31
      postpartum checkup V24.2
      pregnancy (possible) (unconfirmed) V72.40
        negative result V72.41
        positive result V72.42
      preoperative V72.84
        cardiovascular V72.81
        respiratory V72.82
        specified NEC V72.83
      preprocedural V72.84
        cardiovascular V72.81
        general physical V72.83
        respiratory V72.82
        specified NEC V72.83
      prior to chemotherapy V72.83 ●
      prison V70.3
      psychiatric (general) V70.2
        requested by authority V70.1
      radiological NEC V72.5
      respiratory, preoperative V72.82
      school V70.3
      screening — *see* Screening
      skin hypersensitivity V72.7
      specified type NEC V72.85
      sport competition V70.3
      vision V72.0
      well baby and child care V20.2
    exercise therapy V57.1
    face-lift, cosmetic reason V50.1
    fertility preservation (prior to cancer ●
      therapy) (prior to surgical re- ●
      moval of gonads) V26.82 ●

Admission — *continued*
  for — *continued*
    fitting (of)
      artificial
        arm (complete) (partial) V52.0
        eye V52.2
        leg (complete) (partial) V52.1
      biliary drainage tube V58.82
      brain neuropacemaker V53.02
      breast V52.4
        implant V52.4
        prosthesis V52.4
      cardiac pacemaker V53.31
      catheter
        non-vascular V58.82
        vascular V58.81
      cerebral ventricle (communicating) shunt V53.01
      chest tube V58.82
      colostomy belt V55.2
      contact lenses V53.1
      cystostomy device V53.6
      dental prosthesis V52.3
      device, unspecified type V53.90
        abdominal V53.59 ▲
        cerebral ventricle (communicating) shunt V53.01
        gastrointestinal NEC V53.59 ●
        insulin pump V53.91
        intestinal V53.50 ●
        intrauterine contraceptive V25.1
        nervous system V53.09
        orthodontic V53.4
        other device V53.99
        prosthetic V52.9
          breast V52.4
          dental V52.3
          eye V52.2
        special senses V53.09
        substitution
          auditory V53.09
          nervous system V53.09
          visual V53.09
      diaphragm (contraceptive) V25.02
      fistula (sinus tract) drainage tube V58.82
      gastric lap band V53.51 ●
      gastrointestinal appliance and device ●
        NEC V53.59 ●
      growth rod V54.02
      hearing aid V53.2
      ileostomy device V55.2
      intestinal appliance ►and◄ device V53.50 ▲
      intrauterine contraceptive device V25.1
      neuropacemaker (brain) (peripheral nerve) (spinal cord) V53.02
      orthodontic device V53.4
      orthopedic (device) V53.7
        brace V53.7
        cast V53.7
        shoes V53.7
      pacemaker
        brain V53.02
        cardiac V53.31
        carotid sinus V53.39
        spinal cord V53.02
      pleural drainage tube V58.82
      portacath V58.81
      prosthesis V52.9
        arm (complete) (partial) V52.0
        breast V52.4
        dental V52.3
        eye V52.2
        leg (complete) (partial) V52.1
        specified type NEC V52.8
      spectacles V53.1
      wheelchair V53.8
    follow-up examination (routine) (following) V67.9
      cancer chemotherapy V67.2
      chemotherapy V67.2
      high-risk medication NEC V67.51
      injury NEC V67.59
      psychiatric V67.3
      psychotherapy V67.3

Admission — *continued*
  for — *continued*
    follow-up examination — *continued*
      radiotherapy V67.1
      specified surgery NEC V67.09
      surgery V67.00
        vaginal pap smear V67.01
      treatment (for) V67.9
        combined V67.6
        fracture V67.4
        involving high-risk medication NEC V67.51
        mental disorder V67.3
        specified NEC V67.59
    hair transplant, for cosmetic reason V50.0
    health advice, education, or instruction V65.4 ☑
    hearing conservation and treatment V72.12
    hormone replacement therapy (post-menopausal) V07.4
    hospice care V66.7
    immunizations (childhood) appropriate ●
      for age V20.2 ●
    immunotherapy, antineoplastic V58.12
    insertion (of)
      subdermal implantable contraceptive V25.5
    insulin pump titration V53.91
    insulin pump training V65.46
    intrauterine device
      insertion V25.1
      management V25.42
    investigation to determine further disposition V63.8
    in vitro fertilization cycle V26.81
    isolation V07.0
    issue of
      disability examination certificate V68.01
      medical certificate NEC V68.09
      repeat prescription NEC V68.1
        contraceptive device NEC V25.49
    kidney dialysis V56.0
    lengthening of growth rod V54.02
    mental health evaluation V70.2
      requested by authority V70.1
    natural family planning counseling and advice
      procreative V26.41
      to avoid pregnancy V25.04
    nonmedical reason NEC V68.89
    nursing care evaluation V63.8
    observation (without need for further medical care) (*see also* Observation) V71.9
      accident V71.4
      alleged rape or seduction V71.5
      criminal assault V71.6
      following accident V71.4
        at work V71.3
      foreign body ingestion V71.89
      growth and development variations, childhood V21.0
      inflicted injury NEC V71.6
      ingestion of deleterious agent or foreign body V71.89
      injury V71.6
      malignant neoplasm V71.1
      mental disorder V71.09
      newborn — *see* Observation, suspected, condition, newborn
      rape V71.5
      specified NEC V71.89
      suspected
        abuse V71.81
        accident V71.4
          at work V71.3
        benign neoplasm V71.89
        cardiovascular V71.7
        disorder V71.9
        exposure
          anthrax V71.82
          biological agent NEC V71.83
          SARS V71.83
        heart V71.7
        inflicted injury NEC V71.6

Admission — *continued*
  for — *continued*
    observation (*see also* Observation) — *continued*
      suspected — *continued*
        malignant neoplasm V71.1
        maternal and fetal problem not found
          amniotic cavity and membrane V89.01
          cervical shortening V89.05
          fetal anomaly V89.03
          fetal growth V89.04
          oligohydramnios V89.01
          other specified NEC V89.09
          placenta V89.02
          polyhydramnios V89.01
        mental NEC V71.09
        neglect V71.81
        specified condition NEC V71.89
        tuberculosis V71.2
      tuberculosis V71.2
    occupational therapy V57.21
    organ transplant, donor — *see* Donor
    ovary, ovarian removal, prophylactic V50.42
    palliative care V66.7
    Papanicolaou smear
      cervix V76.2
        for suspected malignant neoplasm V76.2
        no disease found V71.1
        routine, as part of gynecological examination V72.31
        to confirm findings of recent normal smear following initial abnormal smear V72.32
      vaginal V76.47
        following hysterectomy for malignant condition V67.01
    passage of sounds or bougie in artificial opening — *see* Attention to, artificial, opening
    paternity testing V70.4
    peritoneal dialysis V56.32
    physical therapy NEC V57.1
    plastic surgery
      breast reconstruction following mastectomy V51.0
      cosmetic NEC V50.1
      following healed injury or operation V51.8
    postmenopausal hormone replacement therapy V07.4
    postpartum observation
      immediately after delivery V24.0
      routine follow-up V24.2
    poststerilization (for restoration) V26.0
    procreative management V26.9
      assisted reproductive fertility procedure cycle V26.81
      in vitro fertilization cycle V26.81
      specified type NEC V26.89
    prophylactic
      administration of
        antibiotics V07.39
        antitoxin, any V07.2
        antivenin V07.2
        chemotherapeutic agent NEC V07.39
        chemotherapy NEC V07.39
        diphtheria antitoxin V07.2
        fluoride V07.31
        gamma globulin V07.2
        immune sera (gamma globulin) V07.2
        RhoGAM V07.2
        tetanus antitoxin V07.2
      breathing exercises V57.0
      chemotherapy NEC V07.39
        fluoride V07.31
      measure V07.9
        specified type NEC V07.8
      organ removal V50.49
        breast V50.41
        ovary V50.42
    psychiatric examination (general) V70.2

Admission — *continued*
  for — *continued*
    psychiatric examination — *continued*
      requested by authority V70.1
    radiation management V58.0
    radiotherapy V58.0
    reconstruction following mastectomy V51.0
    reforming of artificial opening — *see* Attention to, artificial, opening
    rehabilitation V57.9
      multiple types V57.89
      occupational V57.21
      orthoptic V57.4
      orthotic V57.81
      physical NEC V57.1
      specified type NEC V57.89
      speech ▶(-language)◀ V57.3
      vocational V57.22
    removal of
      breast tissue expander without synchronous insertion of permanent implant V52.4
      cardiac pacemaker V53.31
      cast (plaster) V54.89
      catheter from artificial opening — *see* Attention to, artificial, opening
      cerebral ventricle (communicating) shunt V53.01
      cystostomy catheter V55.5
      device
        cerebral ventricle (communicating) shunt V53.01
        fixation
          external V54.89
          internal V54.01
        intrauterine contraceptive V25.42
        traction, external V54.89
      drains V58.49
      dressing
        wound V58.30
          nonsurgical V58.30
          surgical V58.31
      fixation device
        external V54.89
        internal V54.01
      intrauterine contraceptive device V25.42
      Kirschner wire V54.89
      neuropacemaker (brain) (peripheral nerve) (spinal cord) V53.02
      nonsurgical wound dressing V58.30
      orthopedic fixation device
        external V54.89
        internal V54.01
      pacemaker device
        brain V53.02
        cardiac V53.31
        carotid sinus V53.39
        nervous system V53.02
      plaster cast V54.89
      plate (fracture) V54.01
      rod V54.01
      screw (fracture) V54.01
      splint, traction V54.89
      staples V58.32
      Steinmann pin V54.89
      subdermal implantable contraceptive V25.43
      surgical wound dressing V58.31
      sutures V58.32
      traction device, external V54.89
      ureteral stent V53.6
      wound packing V58.30
        nonsurgical V58.30
        surgical V58.31
    repair of scarred tissue (following healed injury or operation) V51.8
    reprogramming of cardiac pacemaker V53.31
    respirator [ventilator] dependence during
      mechanical failure V46.14
      power failure V46.12
      for weaning V46.13

Admission — *continued*
  for — *continued*
    restoration of organ continuity (poststerilization) (tuboplasty) (vasoplasty) V26.0
    Rh typing V72.86
    routine infant and child vision and hearing testing V20.2 ●
    sensitivity test (*see also* Test, skin)
      allergy NEC V72.7
      bacterial disease NEC V74.9
      Dick V74.8
      Kveim V82.89
      Mantoux V74.1
      mycotic infection NEC V75.4
      parasitic disease NEC V75.8
      Schick V74.3
      Schultz-Charlton V74.8
    social service (agency) referral or evaluation V63.8
    speech ▶(-language)◀ therapy V57.3
    sterilization V25.2
    suspected disorder (ruled out) (without need for further care) — *see* Observation
    terminal care V66.7
    tests only — *see* Test
    therapeutic drug monitoring V58.83
    therapy
      blood transfusion, without reported diagnosis V58.2
      breathing exercises V57.0
      chemotherapy, antineoplastic V58.11
        prophylactic NEC V07.39
          fluoride V07.31
      dialysis (intermittent) (treatment)
        extracorporeal V56.0
        peritoneal V56.8
        renal V56.0
        specified type NEC V56.8
      exercise (remedial) NEC V57.1
        breathing V57.0
      immunotherapy, antineoplastic V58.12
      long-term (current) drug use NEC V58.69
        antibiotics V58.62
        anticoagulants V58.61
        anti-inflammatories, non-steroidal (NSAID) V58.64
        antiplatelets V58.63
        antithrombotics V58.63
        aspirin V58.66
        high-risk medications NEC V58.69
        insulin V58.67
        methadone V58.69
        opiate analgesic V58.69
        steroids V58.65
      occupational V57.21
      orthoptic V57.4
      physical NEC V57.1
      radiation V58.0
      speech ▶(-language)◀ V57.3
      vocational V57.22
    toilet or cleaning
      of artificial opening — *see* Attention to, artificial, opening
      of non-vascular catheter V58.82
      of vascular catheter V58.81
    tubal ligation V25.2
    tuboplasty for previous sterilization V26.0
    ultrasound, routine fetal V28.3
    vaccination, prophylactic (against)
      arthropod-borne virus, viral NEC V05.1
        disease NEC V05.1
        encephalitis V05.0
      Bacille Calmette Guérin (BCG) V03.2
      BCG V03.2
      chickenpox V05.4
      cholera alone V03.0
        with typhoid-paratyphoid (cholera + TAB) V06.0
      common cold V04.7
      dengue V05.1
      diphtheria alone V03.5
      diphtheria-tetanus-pertussis (DTP) (DTaP) V06.1

Admission — *continued*
  for — *continued*
    vaccination, prophylactic — *continued*
      diphtheria-tetanus-pertussis — *continued*
        with
          poliomyelitis (DTP + polio) V06.3
          typhoid-paratyphoid (DTP + TAB) V06.2
      diphtheria-tetanus [Td] [DT] without pertussis V06.5
      disease (single) NEC V05.9
        bacterial NEC V03.9
          specified type NEC V03.89
        combinations NEC V06.9
          specified type NEC V06.8
        specified type NEC V05.8
        viral NEC V04.89
      encephalitis, viral, arthropod-borne V05.0
      Hemophilus influenzae, type B [Hib] V03.81
      hepatitis, viral V05.3
      human papillomavirus (HPV) V04.89
      immune sera (gamma globulin) V07.2
      influenza V04.81
        with
          Streptococcus pneumoniae [pneumococcus] V06.6
      Leishmaniasis V05.2
      measles alone V04.2
      measles-mumps-rubella (MMR) V06.4
      mumps alone V04.6
        with measles and rubella (MMR) V06.4
      not done because of contraindication V64.09
      pertussis alone V03.6
      plague V03.3
      pneumonia V03.82
      poliomyelitis V04.0
        with diphtheria-tetanus-pertussis (DTP+ polio) V06.3
      rabies V04.5
      respiratory syncytial virus (RSV) V04.82
      rubella alone V04.3
        with measles and mumps (MMR) V06.4
      smallpox V04.1
      specified type NEC V05.8
      Streptococcus pneumoniae [pneumococcus] V03.82
        with
          influenza V06.6
      tetanus toxoid alone V03.7
        with diphtheria [Td] [DT] V06.5
        and pertussis (DTP) (DTaP) V06.1
      tuberculosis (BCG) V03.2
      tularemia V03.4
      typhoid alone V03.1
        with diphtheria-tetanus-pertussis (TAB + DTP) V06.2
      typhoid-paratyphoid alone (TAB) V03.1
      typhus V05.8
      varicella (chicken pox) V05.4
      viral encephalitis, arthropod-borne V05.0
      viral hepatitis V05.3
      yellow fever V04.4
    vasectomy V25.2
    vasoplasty for previous sterilization V26.0
    vision examination V72.0
    vocational therapy V57.22
    waiting period for admission to other facility V63.2
    undergoing social agency investigation V63.8
    well baby and child care V20.2
    x-ray of chest
      for suspected tuberculosis V71.2
      routine V72.5
Adnexitis (suppurative) — *see also* Salpingo-oophoritis 614.2
Adolescence NEC V21.2

☑ Additional Digit Required — Refer to the Tabular List for Digit Selection   ▽ Subterms under main terms may continue to next column or page

2010 ICD-9-CM   ▶◀ Revised Text   ● New Line   ▲ Revised Code   October 2009 • Volume 2 — 13

Admission — Adolescence

Adoption
  agency referral V68.89
  examination V70.3
  held for V68.89
Adrenal gland — *see* condition
Adrenalism 255.9
  tuberculous (*see also* Tuberculosis) 017.6 ☑
Adrenalitis, adrenitis 255.8
  meningococcal hemorrhagic 036.3
Adrenarche, precocious 259.1
Adrenocortical syndrome 255.2
Adrenogenital syndrome (acquired) (congenital) 255.2
  iatrogenic, fetus or newborn 760.79
Adrenoleukodystrophy 277.86
  neonatal 277.86
  x-linked 277.86
Adrenomyeloneuropathy 277.86
Adventitious bursa — *see* Bursitis
Adynamia (episodica) (hereditary) (periodic) 359.3
Adynamic
  ileus or intestine (*see also* Ileus) 560.1
  ureter 753.22
Aeration lung, imperfect, newborn 770.5
Aerobullosis 993.3
Aerocele — *see* Embolism, air
Aerodermectasia
  subcutaneous (traumatic) 958.7
    surgical 998.81
  surgical 998.81
Aerodontalgia 993.2
Aeroembolism 993.3
Aerogenes capsulatus infection — *see also* Gangrene, gas 040.0
Aero-otitis media 993.0
Aerophagy, aerophagia 306.4
  psychogenic 306.4
Aerosinusitis 993.1
Aerotitis 993.0
Affection, affections — *see also* Disease
  sacroiliac (joint), old 724.6
  shoulder region NEC 726.2
Afibrinogenemia 286.3
  acquired 286.6
  congenital 286.3
  postpartum 666.3 ☑
African
  sleeping sickness 086.5
  tick fever 087.1
  trypanosomiasis 086.5
    Gambian 086.3
    Rhodesian 086.4
Aftercare V58.9
  amputation stump V54.89
  artificial openings — *see* Attention to, artificial, opening
  blood transfusion without reported diagnosis V58.2
  breathing exercise V57.0
  cardiac device V53.39
    defibrillator, automatic implantable V53.32
    pacemaker V53.31
      carotid sinus V53.39
  carotid sinus pacemaker V53.39
  cerebral ventricle (communicating) shunt V53.01
  chemotherapy ▶(oral) (intravenous)◀ session (adjunctive) (maintenance) V58.11
  defibrillator, automatic implantable cardiac V53.32
  exercise (remedial) (therapeutic) V57.1
    breathing V57.0
  extracorporeal dialysis (intermittent) (treatment) V56.0
  following surgery NEC V58.49
    for
      injury V58.43
      neoplasm V58.42
      organ transplant V58.44
      trauma V58.43
    joint replacement V54.81
    of
      circulatory system V58.73
      digestive system V58.75
      genital organs V58.76

Aftercare — *continued*
  following surgery — *continued*
    of — *continued*
      genitourinary system V58.76
      musculoskeletal system V58.78
      nervous system V58.72
      oral cavity V58.75
      respiratory system V58.74
      sense organs V58.71
      skin V58.77
      subcutaneous tissue V58.77
      teeth V58.75
      urinary system V58.76
    spinal — *see* Aftercare, following surgery, of, specified body system
    wound closure, planned V58.41
  fracture V54.9
    healing V54.89
      pathologic
        ankle V54.29
        arm V54.20
          lower V54.22
          upper V54.21
        finger V54.29
        foot V54.29
        hand V54.29
        hip V54.23
        leg V54.24
          lower V54.26
          upper V54.25
        pelvis V54.29
        specified site NEC V54.29
        toe(s) V54.29
        vertebrae V54.27
        wrist V54.29
      traumatic
        ankle V54.19
        arm V54.10
          lower V54.12
          upper V54.11
        finger V54.19
        foot V54.19
        hand V54.19
        hip V54.13
        leg V54.14
          lower V54.16
          upper V54.15
        pelvis V54.19
        specified site NEC V54.19
        toe(s) V54.19
        vertebrae V54.17
        wrist V54.19
    removal of
      external fixation device V54.89
      internal fixation device V54.01
    specified care NEC V54.89
  gait training V57.1
    for use of artificial limb(s) V57.81
  internal fixation device V54.09
  involving
    dialysis (intermittent) (treatment)
      extracorporeal V56.0
      peritoneal V56.8
      renal V56.0
    gait training V57.1
      for use of artificial limb(s) V57.81
    growth rod
      adjustment V54.02
      lengthening V54.02
    internal fixation device V54.09
    orthoptic training V57.4
    orthotic training V57.81
    radiotherapy session V58.0
    removal of
      drains V58.49
      dressings
        wound V58.30
          nonsurgical V58.30
          surgical V58.31
      fixation device
        external V54.89
        internal V54.01
      fracture plate V54.01
      nonsurgical wound dressing V58.30
      pins V54.01
      plaster cast V54.89

Aftercare — *continued*
  involving — *continued*
    removal of — *continued*
      rods V54.01
      screws V58.32
      staples V58.32
      surgical wound dressings V58.31
      sutures V58.32
      traction device, external V54.89
      wound packing V58.30
        nonsurgical V58.30
        surgical V58.31
    neuropacemaker (brain) (peripheral nerve) (spinal cord) V53.02
    occupational therapy V57.21
    orthodontic V58.5
    orthopedic V54.9
      change of external fixation or traction device V54.89
      following joint replacement V54.81
      internal fixation device V54.09
      removal of fixation device
        external V54.89
        internal V54.01
      specified care NEC V54.89
    orthoptic training V57.4
    orthotic training V57.81
    pacemaker
      brain V53.02
      cardiac V53.31
      carotid sinus V53.39
      peripheral nerve V53.02
      spinal cord V53.02
    peritoneal dialysis (intermittent) (treatment) V56.8
    physical therapy NEC V57.1
      breathing exercises V57.0
    radiotherapy session V58.0
    rehabilitation procedure V57.9
      breathing exercises V57.0
      multiple types V57.89
      occupational V57.21
      orthoptic V57.4
      orthotic V57.81
      physical therapy NEC V57.1
      remedial exercises V57.1
      specified type NEC V57.89
      speech ▶(-language)◀ V57.3
      therapeutic exercises V57.1
      vocational V57.22
    renal dialysis (intermittent) (treatment) V56.0
    specified type NEC V58.89
      removal of non-vascular catheter V58.82
      removal of vascular catheter V58.81
    speech ▶(-language)◀ therapy V57.3
    stump, amputation V54.89
    vocational rehabilitation V57.22
After-cataract 366.50
  obscuring vision 366.53
  specified type, not obscuring vision 366.52
Agalactia 676.4 ☑
Agammaglobulinemia 279.00
  with lymphopenia 279.2
  acquired (primary) (secondary) 279.06
  Bruton's X-linked 279.04
  infantile sex-linked (Bruton's) (congenital) 279.04
  Swiss-type 279.2
Aganglionosis (bowel) (colon) 751.3
Age (old) — *see also* Senile 797
Agenesis — *see also* Absence, by site, congenital
  acoustic nerve 742.8
  adrenal (gland) 759.1
  alimentary tract (complete) (partial) NEC 751.8
    lower 751.2
    upper 750.8
  anus, anal (canal) 751.2
  aorta 747.22
  appendix 751.2
  arm (complete) (partial) (*see also* Deformity, reduction, upper limb) 755.20
  artery (peripheral) NEC (*see also* Anomaly, peripheral vascular system) 747.60
    brain 747.81
    coronary 746.85
    pulmonary 747.3

Agenesis — *see also* Absence, by site, congenital — *continued*
  artery (*see also* Anomaly, peripheral vascular system) — *continued*
    umbilical 747.5
  auditory (canal) (external) 744.01
  auricle (ear) 744.01
  bile, biliary duct or passage 751.61
  bone NEC 756.9
  brain 740.0
    specified part 742.2
  breast 757.6
  bronchus 748.3
  canaliculus lacrimalis 743.65
  carpus NEC (*see also* Deformity, reduction, upper limb) 755.28
  cartilage 756.9
  cecum 751.2
  cerebellum 742.2
  cervix 752.49
  chin 744.89
  cilia 743.63
  circulatory system, part NEC 747.89
  clavicle 755.51
  clitoris 752.49
  coccyx 756.13
  colon 751.2
  corpus callosum 742.2
  cricoid cartilage 748.3
  diaphragm (with hernia) 756.6
  digestive organ(s) or tract (complete) (partial) NEC 751.8
    lower 751.2
    upper 750.8
  ductus arteriosus 747.89
  duodenum 751.1
  ear NEC 744.09
    auricle 744.01
    lobe 744.21
  ejaculatory duct 752.89
  endocrine (gland) NEC 759.2
  epiglottis 748.3
  esophagus 750.3
  Eustachian tube 744.24
  extrinsic muscle, eye 743.69
  eye 743.00
    adnexa 743.69
  eyelid (fold) 743.62
  face
    bones NEC 756.0
    specified part NEC 744.89
  fallopian tube 752.19
  femur NEC (*see also* Absence, femur, congenital) 755.34
  fibula NEC (*see also* Absence, fibula, congenital) 755.37
  finger NEC (*see also* Absence, finger, congenital) 755.29
  foot (complete) (*see also* Deformity, reduction, lower limb) 755.31
  gallbladder 751.69
  gastric 750.8
  genitalia, genital (organ)
    female 752.89
      external 752.49
      internal NEC 752.89
    male 752.89
      penis 752.69
  glottis 748.3
  gonadal 758.6
  hair 757.4
  hand (complete) (*see also* Deformity, reduction, upper limb) 755.21
  heart 746.89
    valve NEC 746.89
      aortic 746.89
      mitral 746.89
      pulmonary 746.01
  hepatic 751.69
  humerus NEC (*see also* Absence, humerus, congenital) 755.24
  hymen 752.49
  ileum 751.1
  incus 744.04
  intestine (small) 751.1
    large 751.2

Agenesis — *see also* Absence, by site, congenital — *continued*
- iris (dilator fibers) 743.45
- jaw 524.09
- jejunum 751.1
- kidney(s) (partial) (unilateral) 753.0
- labium (majus) (minus) 752.49
- labyrinth, membranous 744.05
- lacrimal apparatus (congenital) 743.65
- larynx 748.3
- leg NEC (*see also* Deformity, reduction, lower limb) 755.30
- lens 743.35
- limb (complete) (partial) (*see also* Deformity, reduction) 755.4
  - lower NEC 755.30
  - upper 755.20
- lip 750.26
- liver 751.69
- lung (bilateral) (fissures) (lobe) (unilateral) 748.5
- mandible 524.09
- maxilla 524.09
- metacarpus NEC 755.28
- metatarsus NEC 755.38
- muscle (any) 756.81
- musculoskeletal system NEC 756.9
- nail(s) 757.5
- neck, part 744.89
- nerve 742.8
- nervous system, part NEC 742.8
- nipple 757.6
- nose 748.1
- nuclear 742.8
- organ
  - of Corti 744.05
  - or site not listed — *see* Anomaly, specified type NEC
- osseous meatus (ear) 744.03
- ovary 752.0
- oviduct 752.19
- pancreas 751.7
- parathyroid (gland) 759.2
- patella 755.64
- pelvic girdle (complete) (partial) 755.69
- penis 752.69
- pericardium 746.89
- perineal body 756.81
- pituitary (gland) 759.2
- prostate 752.89
- pulmonary
  - artery 747.3
  - trunk 747.3
  - vein 747.49
- punctum lacrimale 743.65
- radioulnar NEC (*see also* Absence, forearm, congenital) 755.25
- radius NEC (*see also* Absence, radius, congenital) 755.26
- rectum 751.2
- renal 753.0
- respiratory organ NEC 748.9
- rib 756.3
- roof of orbit 742.0
- round ligament 752.89
- sacrum 756.13
- salivary gland 750.21
- scapula 755.59
- scrotum 752.89
- seminal duct or tract 752.89
- septum
  - atrial 745.69
  - between aorta and pulmonary artery 745.0
  - ventricular 745.3
- shoulder girdle (complete) (partial) 755.59
- skull (bone) 756.0
  - with
    - anencephalus 740.0
    - encephalocele 742.0
    - hydrocephalus 742.3
      - with spina bifida (*see also* Spina bifida) 741.0 ☑
    - microcephalus 742.1
- spermatic cord 752.89
- spinal cord 742.59
- spine 756.13

Agenesis — *see also* Absence, by site, congenital — *continued*
- spine — *continued*
  - lumbar 756.13
    - isthmus 756.11
    - pars articularis 756.11
- spleen 759.0
- sternum 756.3
- stomach 750.7
- tarsus NEC 755.38
- tendon 756.81
- testicular 752.89
- testis 752.89
- thymus (gland) 759.2
- thyroid (gland) 243
  - cartilage 748.3
- tibia NEC (*see also* Absence, tibia, congenital) 755.36
- tibiofibular NEC 755.35
- toe (complete) (partial) (*see also* Absence, toe, congenital) 755.39
- tongue 750.11
- trachea (cartilage) 748.3
- ulna NEC (*see also* Absence, ulna, congenital) 755.27
- ureter 753.4
- urethra 753.8
- urinary tract NEC 753.8
- uterus 752.3
- uvula 750.26
- vagina 752.49
- vas deferens 752.89
- vein(s) (peripheral) NEC (*see also* Anomaly, peripheral vascular system) 747.60
  - brain 747.81
  - great 747.49
  - portal 747.49
  - pulmonary 747.49
- vena cava (inferior) (superior) 747.49
- vermis of cerebellum 742.2
- vertebra 756.13
  - lumbar 756.13
    - isthmus 756.11
    - pars articularis 756.11
- vulva 752.49

Ageusia — *see also* Disturbance, sensation 781.1

Aggressiveness 301.3

Aggressive outburst — *see* Disturbance, conduct 312.0 ☑
- in children or adolescents 313.9

Aging skin 701.8

Agitated — *see* condition

Agitation 307.9
- catatonic (*see also* Schizophrenia) 295.2 ☑

Aglossia (congenital) 750.11

Aglycogenosis 271.0

Agnail (finger) (with lymphangitis) 681.02

Agnosia (body image) (tactile) 784.69
- verbal 784.69
  - auditory 784.69
    - secondary to organic lesion 784.69
  - developmental 315.8
    - secondary to organic lesion 784.69
- visual 368.16
  - object 368.16

Agoraphobia 300.22
- with panic disorder 300.21

Agrammatism 784.69

Agranulocytopenia — *see also* Agranulocytosis 288.09

Agranulocytosis ► — *see also* Neutropenia ◄ 288.09
- chronic 288.09
- cyclical 288.02
- due to infection 288.04   ●
- genetic 288.01
- infantile 288.01
- periodic 288.02
- pernicious 288.09

Agraphia (absolute) 784.69
- with alexia 784.61
- developmental 315.39

Agrypnia (*see also* Insomnia) 780.52

Ague — *see also* Malaria 084.6
- brass-founders' 985.8
- dumb 084.6

Ague — *see also* Malaria — *continued*
- tertian 084.1

Agyria 742.2

Ahumada-del Castillo syndrome (nonpuerperal galactorrhea and amenorrhea) 253.1

AIDS 042

AIDS-associated retrovirus (disease) (illness) 042
- infection — *see* Human immunodeficiency virus, infection

AIDS-associated virus (disease) (illness) 042
- infection — *see* Human immunodeficiency virus, infection

AIDS-like disease (illness) (syndrome) 042

AIDS-related complex 042

AIDS-related conditions 042

AIDS-related virus (disease) (illness) 042
- infection — *see* Human immunodeficiency virus, infection

AIDS virus (disease) (illness) 042
- infection — *see* Human immunodeficiency virus, infection

Ailment, heart — *see* Disease, heart

Ailurophobia 300.29

Ainhum (disease) 136.0

AIN I [anal intraepithelial neoplasia I] (histologically confirmed) 569.44

AIN II [anal intraepithelial neoplasia II] (histologically confirmed) 569.44

AIN III [anal intraepithelial neoplasia III] 230.6
- anal canal 230.5

Air
- anterior mediastinum 518.1
- compressed, disease 993.3
- embolism (any site) (artery) (cerebral) 958.0
  - with
    - abortion — *see* Abortion, by type, with embolism
    - ectopic pregnancy (*see also* categories 633.0–633.9) 639.6
    - molar pregnancy (*see also* categories 630–632) 639.6
  - due to implanted device — *see* Complications, due to (presence of) any device, implant, or graft classified to 996.0–996.5 NEC
  - following
    - abortion 639.6
    - ectopic or molar pregnancy 639.6
  - infusion, perfusion, or transfusion 999.1
  - in pregnancy, childbirth, or puerperium 673.0 ☑
  - traumatic 958.0
- hunger 786.09
  - psychogenic 306.1
- leak (lung) (pulmonary) (thorax) 512.8
  - iatrogenic 512.1
  - postoperative 512.1
- rarefied, effects of — *see* Effect, adverse, high altitude
- sickness 994.6

Airplane sickness 994.6

Akathisia, acathisia 781.0
- due to drugs 333.99
- neuroleptic-induced acute 333.99

Akinesia algeria 352.6

Akiyami 100.89

Akureyri disease (epidemic neuromyasthenia) 049.8

Alacrima (congenital) 743.65

Alactasia (hereditary) 271.3

Alagille syndrome 759.89

Alalia 784.3
- developmental 315.31
  - receptive-expressive 315.32
- secondary to organic lesion 784.3

Alaninemia 270.8

Alastrim 050.1

Albarrán's disease (colibacilluria) 791.9

Albers-Schönberg's disease (marble bones) 756.52

Albert's disease 726.71

Albinism, albino (choroid) (cutaneous) (eye) (generalized) (isolated) (ocular) (oculocutaneous) (partial) 270.2

Albinismus 270.2

Albright (-Martin) (-Bantam) disease (pseudohypoparathyroidism) 275.49

Albright (-McCune) (-Sternberg) syndrome (osteitis fibrosa disseminata) 756.59

Albuminous — *see* condition

Albuminuria, albuminuric (acute) (chronic) (subacute) 791.0
- Bence-Jones 791.0
- cardiac 785.9
- complicating pregnancy, childbirth, or puerperium 646.2 ☑
  - with hypertension — *see* Toxemia, of pregnancy
  - affecting fetus or newborn 760.1
- cyclic 593.6
- gestational 646.2 ☑
- gravidarum 646.2 ☑
  - with hypertension — *see* Toxemia, of pregnancy
  - affecting fetus or newborn 760.1
- heart 785.9
- idiopathic 593.6
- orthostatic 593.6
- postural 593.6
- pre-eclamptic (mild) 642.4 ☑
  - affecting fetus or newborn 760.0
  - severe 642.5 ☑
    - affecting fetus or newborn 760.0
- recurrent physiologic 593.6
- scarlatinal 034.1

Albumosuria 791.0
- Bence-Jones 791.0
- myelopathic (M9730/3) 203.0 ☑

Alcaptonuria 270.2

Alcohol, alcoholic
- abstinence 291.81
- acute intoxication 305.0 ☑
  - with dependence 303.0 ☑
- addiction (*see also* Alcoholism) 303.9 ☑
  - maternal
    - with suspected fetal damage affecting management of pregnancy 655.4 ☑
    - affecting fetus or newborn 760.71
- amnestic disorder, persisting 291.1
- anxiety 291.89
- brain syndrome, chronic 291.2
- cardiopathy 425.5
- chronic (*see also* Alcoholism) 303.9 ☑
- cirrhosis (liver) 571.2
- delirium 291.0
  - acute 291.0
  - chronic 291.1
  - tremens 291.0
  - withdrawal 291.0
- dementia NEC 291.2
- deterioration 291.2
- drunkenness (simple) 305.0 ☑
- hallucinosis (acute) 291.3
- induced
  - circadian rhythm sleep disorder 291.82
  - hypersomnia 291.82
  - insomnia 291.82
  - mental disorder 291.9
    - anxiety 291.89
    - mood 291.89
    - sexual 291.89
    - sleep 291.82
    - specified type 291.89
  - parasomnia 291.82
  - persisting
    - amnestic disorder 291.1
    - dementia 291.2
  - psychotic disorder
    - with
      - delusions 291.5
      - hallucinations 291.3
    - sleep disorder 291.82
- insanity 291.9
- intoxication (acute) 305.0 ☑
  - with dependence 303.0 ☑
  - pathological 291.4
- jealousy 291.5
- Korsakoff's, Korsakov's, Korsakow's 291.1
- liver NEC 571.3
  - acute 571.1

☑ Additional Digit Required — Refer to the Tabular List for Digit Selection   ▽ Subterms under main terms may continue to next column or page

2010 ICD-9-CM   ►◄ Revised Text   ● New Line   ▲ Revised Code   October 2009 • Volume 2 — 15

Alcohol, alcoholic — continued
  liver — continued
    chronic 571.2
  mania (acute) (chronic) 291.9
  mood 291.89
  paranoia 291.5
  paranoid (type) psychosis 291.5
  pellagra 265.2
  poisoning, accidental (acute) NEC 980.9
    specified type of alcohol — see Table of Drugs and Chemicals
  psychosis (see also Psychosis, alcoholic) 291.9
    Korsakoff's, Korsakov's, Korsakow's 291.1
    polyneuritic 291.1
      with
        delusions 291.5
        hallucinations 291.3
  related disorder 291.9
  withdrawal symptoms, syndrome NEC 291.81
    delirium 291.0
    hallucinosis 291.3
Alcoholism 303.9 ☑

> Note — Use the following fifth-digit subclassification with category 303:
>
> 0   unspecified
> 1   continuous
> 2   episodic
> 3   in remission

  with psychosis (see also Psychosis, alcoholic) 291.9
  acute 303.0 ☑
  chronic 303.9 ☑
    with psychosis 291.9
  complicating pregnancy, childbirth, or puerperium 648.4 ☑
    affecting fetus or newborn 760.71
  history V11.3
  Korsakoff's, Korsakov's, Korsakow's 291.1
  suspected damage to fetus affecting management of pregnancy 655.4 ☑
Alder's anomaly or syndrome (leukocyte granulation anomaly) 288.2
Alder-Reilly anomaly (leukocyte granulation) 288.2
Aldosteronism (primary) 255.10
  congenital 255.10
  familial type I 255.11
  glucocorticoid-remediable 255.11
  secondary 255.14
Aldosteronoma (M8370/1) 237.2
Aldrich (-Wiskott) syndrome (eczema-thrombocytopenia) 279.12
Aleppo boil 085.1
Aleukemic — see condition
Aleukia
  congenital 288.09
  hemorrhagica 284.9
    acquired (secondary) 284.89
    congenital 284.09
    idiopathic 284.9
  splenica 289.4
Alexia (congenital) (developmental) 315.01
  secondary to organic lesion 784.61
Algoneurodystrophy 733.7
Algophobia 300.29
Alibert-Bazin disease (M9700/3) 202.1 ☑
Alibert's disease (mycosis fungoides) (M9700/3) 202.1 ☑
Alice in Wonderland syndrome 293.89
Alienation, mental — see also Psychosis 298.9
Alkalemia 276.3
Alkalosis 276.3
  metabolic 276.3
    with respiratory acidosis 276.4
  respiratory 276.3
Alkaptonuria 270.2
Allen-Masters syndrome 620.6
Allergic bronchopulmonary aspergillosis 518.6
Allergy, allergic (reaction) 995.3
  air-borne substance — see also Fever, hay 477.9
    specified allergen NEC 477.8
  alveolitis (extrinsic) 495.9

Allergy, allergic — continued
  alveolitis — continued
    due to
      Aspergillus clavatus 495.4
      cryptostroma corticale 495.6
      organisms (fungal, thermophilic actinomycete, other) growing in ventilation (air conditioning systems) 495.7
      specified type NEC 495.8
  anaphylactic shock 999.4
    due to food — see Anaphylactic shock, due to, food
  angioneurotic edema 995.1
  animal (cat) (dog) (epidermal) 477.8
    dander 477.2
    hair 477.2
  arthritis (see also Arthritis, allergic) 716.2 ☑
  asthma — see Asthma
  bee sting (anaphylactic shock) 989.5
  biological — see Allergy, drug
  bronchial asthma — see Asthma
  conjunctivitis (eczematous) 372.14
  dander, animal (cat) (dog) 477.2
  dandruff 477.8
  dermatitis (venenata) — see Dermatitis
  diathesis V15.09
  drug, medicinal substance, and biological (any) (correct medicinal substance properly administered) (external) (internal) 995.27
    wrong substance given or taken NEC 977.9
      specified drug or substance — see Table of Drugs and Chemicals
  dust (house) (stock) 477.8
  eczema — see Eczema
  endophthalmitis 360.19
  epidermal (animal) 477.8
  existing dental restorative material 525.66
  feathers 477.8
  food (any) (ingested) 693.1
    atopic 691.8
    in contact with skin 692.5
  gastritis 535.4 ☑
  gastroenteritis 558.3
  gastrointestinal 558.3
  grain 477.0
  grass (pollen) 477.0
    asthma (see also Asthma) 493.0 ☑
    hay fever 477.0
  hair, animal (cat) (dog) 477.2
  hay fever (grass) (pollen) (ragweed) (tree) (see also Fever, hay) 477.9
  history (of) V15.09
    to
      arachnid bite V15.06 ●
      eggs V15.03
      food additives V15.05
      insect bite V15.06
      latex V15.07
      milk products V15.02
      nuts V15.05
        peanuts V15.01
      radiographic dye V15.08
      seafood V15.04
      specified food NEC V15.05
      spider bite V15.06
    horse serum — see Allergy, serum
    inhalant 477.9
      dust 477.8
      pollen 477.0
      specified allergen other than pollen 477.8
    kapok 477.8
    medicine — see Allergy, drug
    migraine 339.00
    milk protein 558.3
    pannus 370.62
    pneumonia 518.3
    pollen (any) (hay fever) 477.0
      asthma (see also Asthma) 493.0 ☑
    primrose 477.0
    primula 477.0
    purpura 287.0
    ragweed (pollen) (Senecio jacobae) 477.0
      asthma (see also Asthma) 493.0 ☑
      hay fever 477.0

Allergy, allergic — continued
  respiratory (see also Allergy, inhalant) 477.9
    due to
      drug — see Allergy, drug
      food — see Allergy, food
    rhinitis (see also Fever, hay) 477.9
      due to food 477.1
    rose 477.0
    Senecio jacobae 477.0
    serum (prophylactic) (therapeutic) 999.5
      anaphylactic shock 999.4
    shock (anaphylactic) (due to adverse effect of correct medicinal substance properly administered) 995.0
      food — see Anaphylactic shock, due to, food
      from serum or immunization 999.5
        anaphylactic 999.4
    sinusitis (see also Fever, hay) 477.9
    skin reaction 692.9
      specified substance — see Dermatitis, due to
    tree (any) (hay fever) (pollen) 477.0
      asthma (see also Asthma) 493.0 ☑
    upper respiratory (see also Fever, hay) 477.9
    urethritis 597.89
    urticaria 708.0
    vaccine — see Allergy, serum
Allescheriosis 117.6
Alligator skin disease (ichthyosis congenita) 757.1
  acquired 701.1
Allocheiria, allochiria — see also Disturbance, sensation 782.0
Almeida's disease (Brazilian blastomycosis) 116.1
Alopecia (atrophicans) (pregnancy) (premature) (senile) 704.00
  adnata 757.4
  areata 704.01
  celsi 704.01
  cicatrisata 704.09
  circumscripta 704.01
  congenital, congenitalis 757.4
  disseminata 704.01
  effluvium (telogen) 704.02
  febrile 704.09
  generalisata 704.09
  hereditaria 704.09
  marginalis 704.01
  mucinosa 704.09
  postinfectional 704.09
  seborrheica 704.09
  specific 091.82
  syphilitic (secondary) 091.82
  telogen effluvium 704.02
  totalis 704.09
  toxica 704.09
  universalis 704.09
  x-ray 704.09
Alpers' disease 330.8
Alpha-lipoproteinemia 272.4
Alpha thalassemia 282.49
Alphos 696.1
Alpine sickness 993.2
Alport's syndrome (hereditary hematuria-nephropathy-deafness) 759.89
ALPS (autoimmune lymphoproliferative syndrome) 279.41 ●
ALTE (apparent life threatening event) **in newborn and infant** 799.82 ●
Alteration (of), altered
  awareness 780.09
    transient 780.02
  consciousness 780.09
    persistent vegetative state 780.03
    transient 780.02
  mental status 780.97
    amnesia (retrograde) 780.93
    memory loss 780.93
Alternaria (infection) 118
Alternating — see condition
Altitude, high (effects) — see Effect, adverse, high altitude
Aluminosis (of lung) 503
Alvarez syndrome (transient cerebral ischemia) 435.9

Alveolar capillary block syndrome 516.3
Alveolitis
  allergic (extrinsic) 495.9
    due to organisms (fungal, thermophilic actinomycete, other) growing in ventilation (air conditioning systems) 495.7
    specified type NEC 495.8
  due to
    Aspergillus clavatus 495.4
    Cryptostroma corticale 495.6
  fibrosing (chronic) (cryptogenic) (lung) 516.3
    idiopathic 516.3
    rheumatoid 714.81
  jaw 526.5
  sicca dolorosa 526.5
Alveolus, alveolar — see condition
Alymphocytosis (pure) 279.2
Alymphoplasia, thymic 279.2
Alzheimer's
  dementia (senile)
    with behavioral disturbance 331.0 [294.11]
    without behavioral disturbance 331.0 [294.10]
  disease or sclerosis 331.0
    with dementia — see Alzheimer's, dementia
Amastia — see also Absence, breast 611.89
Amaurosis (acquired) (congenital) — see also Blindness 369.00
  fugax 362.34
  hysterical 300.11
  Leber's (congenital) 362.76
  tobacco 377.34
  uremic — see Uremia
Amaurotic familial idiocy (infantile) (juvenile) (late) 330.1
Ambisexual 752.7
Amblyopia (acquired) (congenital) (partial) 368.00
  color 368.59
    acquired 368.55
  deprivation 368.02
  ex anopsia 368.00
  hysterical 300.11
  nocturnal 368.60
    vitamin A deficiency 264.5
  refractive 368.03
  strabismic 368.01
  suppression 368.01
  tobacco 377.34
  toxic NEC 377.34
  uremic — see Uremia
Ameba, amebic (histolytica) — see also Amebiasis
  abscess 006.3
    bladder 006.8
    brain (with liver and lung abscess) 006.5
    liver 006.3
      with
        brain abscess (and lung abscess) 006.5
        lung abscess 006.4
    lung (with liver abscess) 006.4
      with brain abscess 006.5
    seminal vesicle 006.8
    spleen 006.8
  carrier (suspected of) V02.2
  meningoencephalitis
    due to Naegleria (gruberi) 136.29
    primary 136.29
Amebiasis NEC 006.9
  with
    brain abscess (with liver or lung abscess) 006.5
    liver abscess (without mention of brain or lung abscess) 006.3
    lung abscess (with liver abscess) 006.4
      with brain abscess 006.5
  acute 006.0
  bladder 006.8
  chronic 006.1
  cutaneous 006.6
  cutis 006.6
  due to organism other than Entamoeba histolytica 007.8

☑ Additional Digit Required — Refer to the Tabular List for Digit Selection   〰 Subterms under main terms may continue to next column or page

16 — Volume 2 • October 2009   ▶◀ Revised Text   ● New Line   ▲ Revised Code   2010 ICD•9•CM

Amebiasis — *continued*
hepatic (*see also* Abscess, liver, amebic) 006.3
nondysenteric 006.2
seminal vesicle 006.8
specified
organism NEC 007.8
site NEC 006.8
Ameboma 006.8
Amelia 755.4
lower limb 755.31
upper limb 755.21
Ameloblastoma (M9310/0) 213.1
jaw (bone) (lower) 213.1
upper 213.0
long bones (M9261/3) — *see* Neoplasm, bone, malignant
malignant (M9310/3) 170.1
jaw (bone) (lower) 170.1
upper 170.0
mandible 213.1
tibial (M9261/3) 170.7
Amelogenesis imperfecta 520.5
nonhereditaria (segmentalis) 520.4
Amenorrhea (primary) (secondary) 626.0
due to ovarian dysfunction 256.8
hyperhormonal 256.8
Amentia — *see also* Retardation, mental 319
Meynert's (nonalcoholic) 294.0
alcoholic 291.1
nevoid 759.6
American
leishmaniasis 085.5
mountain tick fever 066.1
trypanosomiasis — *see* Trypanosomiasis, American
Ametropia — *see also* Disorder, accommodation 367.9
Amianthosis 501
Amimia 784.69
Amino acid
deficiency 270.9
anemia 281.4
metabolic disorder (*see also* Disorder, amino acid) 270.9
Aminoaciduria 270.9
imidazole 270.5
Amnesia (retrograde) 780.93
auditory 784.69
developmental 315.31
secondary to organic lesion 784.69
dissociative 300.12
hysterical or dissociative type 300.12
psychogenic 300.12
transient global 437.7
Amnestic (confabulatory) **syndrome** 294.0
alcohol-induced persisting 291.1
drug-induced persisting 292.83
posttraumatic 294.0
Amniocentesis screening (for) V28.2
alphafetoprotein level, raised V28.1
chromosomal anomalies V28.0
Amnion, amniotic — *see also* condition
nodosum 658.8 ☑
Amnionitis (complicating pregnancy) 658.4 ☑
affecting fetus or newborn 762.7
Amoral trends 301.7
Amotio retinae — *see also* Detachment, retina 361.9
Ampulla
lower esophagus 530.89
phrenic 530.89
Amputation
any part of fetus, to facilitate delivery 763.89
cervix (supravaginal) (uteri) 622.8
in pregnancy or childbirth 654.6 ☑
affecting fetus or newborn 763.89
clitoris — *see* Wound, open, clitoris
congenital
lower limb 755.31
upper limb 755.21
neuroma (traumatic) (*see also* Injury, nerve, by site)
surgical complication (late) 997.61
penis — *see* Amputation, traumatic, penis
status (without complication) — *see* Absence, by site, acquired

Amputation — *continued*
stump (surgical) (posttraumatic)
abnormal, painful, or with complication (late) 997.60
healed or old NEC (*see also* Absence, by site, acquired)
lower V49.70
upper V49.60
traumatic (complete) (partial)

> *Note* — "Complicated" includes traumatic amputation with delayed healing, delayed treatment, foreign body, or infection.

arm 887.4
at or above elbow 887.2
complicated 887.3
below elbow 887.0
complicated 887.1
both (bilateral) (any level(s)) 887.6
complicated 887.7
complicated 887.5
finger(s) (one or both hands) 886.0
with thumb(s) 885.0
complicated 885.1
complicated 886.1
foot (except toe(s) only) 896.0
and other leg 897.6
complicated 897.7
both (bilateral) 896.2
complicated 896.3
complicated 896.1
toe(s) only (one or both feet) 895.0
complicated 895.1
genital organ(s) (external) NEC 878.8
complicated 878.9
hand (except finger only) 887.0
and other arm 887.6
complicated 887.7
both (bilateral) 887.6
complicated 887.7
complicated 887.1
finger(s) (one or both hands) 886.0
with thumb(s) 885.0
complicated 885.1
complicated 886.1
thumb(s) (with fingers of either hand) 885.0
complicated 885.1
head 874.9
late effect — *see* Late, effects (of), amputation
leg 897.4
and other foot 897.6
complicated 897.7
at or above knee 897.2
complicated 897.3
below knee 897.0
complicated 897.1
both (bilateral) 897.6
complicated 897.7
complicated 897.5
lower limb(s) except toe(s) — *see* Amputation, traumatic, leg
nose — *see* Wound, open, nose
penis 878.0
complicated 878.1
sites other than limbs — *see* Wound, open, by site
thumb(s) (with finger(s) of either hand) 885.0
complicated 885.1
toe(s) (one or both feet) 895.0
complicated 895.1
upper limb(s) — *see* Amputation, traumatic, arm
Amputee (bilateral) (old) — *see also* Absence, by site, acquired V49.70
Amusia 784.69
developmental 315.39
secondary to organic lesion 784.69
Amyelencephalus 740.0
Amyelia 742.59
Amygdalitis — *see* Tonsillitis
Amygdalolith 474.8
Amyloid disease or degeneration 277.30
heart 277.39 *[425.7]*

Amyloidosis (familial) (general) (generalized) (genetic) (primary) 277.30
with lung involvement 277.39 *[517.8]*
cardiac, hereditary 277.39
heart 277.39 *[425.7]*
nephropathic 277.39 *[583.81]*
neuropathic (Portuguese) (Swiss) 277.39 *[357.4]*
pulmonary 277.39 *[517.8]*
secondary 277.39
systemic, inherited 277.39
Amylopectinosis (brancher enzyme deficiency) 271.0
Amylophagia 307.52
Amyoplasia, congenita 756.89
Amyotonia 728.2
congenita 358.8
Amyotrophia, amyotrophy, amyotrophic 728.2
congenita 756.89
diabetic 250.6 ☑ *[353.5]*
due to secondary diabetes 249.6 ☑ *[353.5]*
lateral sclerosis (syndrome) 335.20
neuralgic 353.5
sclerosis (lateral) 335.20
spinal progressive 335.21
Anacidity, gastric 536.0
psychogenic 306.4
Anaerosis of newborn 770.88
Analbuminemia 273.8
Analgesia — *see also* Anesthesia 782.0
Analphalipoproteinemia 272.5
Anaphylactic shock or reaction (correct substance properly administered) 995.0
due to
food 995.60
additives 995.66
crustaceans 995.62
eggs 995.68
fish 995.65
fruits 995.63
milk products 995.67
nuts (tree) 995.64
peanuts 995.61
seeds 995.64
specified NEC 995.69
tree nuts 995.64
vegetables 995.63
immunization 999.4
overdose or wrong substance given or taken 977.9
specified drug — *see* Table of Drugs and Chemicals
serum 999.4
following sting(s) 989.5
purpura 287.0
serum 999.4
Anaphylactoid shock or reaction — *see* Anaphylactic shock
Anaphylaxis — *see* Anaphylactic shock
Anaplasia, cervix 622.10
Anarthria 784.51
Anarthritic rheumatoid disease 446.5 ▲
Anasarca 782.3
cardiac (*see also* Failure, heart) 428.0
fetus or newborn 778.0
lung 514
nutritional 262
pulmonary 514
renal (*see also* Nephrosis) 581.9
Anaspadias 752.62
Anastomosis
aneurysmal — *see* Aneurysm
arteriovenous, congenital NEC (*see also* Anomaly, arteriovenous) 747.60
ruptured, of brain (*see also* Hemorrhage, subarachnoid) 430
intestinal 569.89
complicated NEC 997.4
involving urinary tract 997.5
retinal and choroidal vessels 743.58
acquired 362.17
Anatomical narrow angle (glaucoma) 365.02
Ancylostoma (infection) (infestation) 126.9
americanus 126.1
braziliense 126.2
caninum 126.8

Ancylostoma — *continued*
ceylanicum 126.3
duodenale 126.0
Necator americanus 126.1
Ancylostomiasis (intestinal) 126.9
ancylostoma
americanus 126.1
caninum 126.8
ceylanicum 126.3
duodenale 126.0
braziliense 126.2
Necator americanus 126.1
Anders' disease or syndrome (adiposis tuberosa simplex) 272.8
Andersen's glycogen storage disease 271.0
Anderson's disease 272.7
Andes disease 993.2
Andrews' disease (bacterid) 686.8
Androblastoma (M8630/1)
benign (M8630/0)
specified site — *see* Neoplasm, by site, benign
unspecified site
female 220
male 222.0
malignant (M8630/3)
specified site — *see* Neoplasm, by site, malignant
unspecified site
female 183.0
male 186.9
specified site — *see* Neoplasm, by site, uncertain behavior
tubular (M8640/0)
with lipid storage (M8641/0)
specified site — *see* Neoplasm, by site, benign
unspecified site
female 220
male 222.0
specified site — *see* Neoplasm, by site, benign
unspecified site
female 220
male 222.0
unspecified site
female 236.2
male 236.4
Android pelvis 755.69
with disproportion (fetopelvic) 653.3 ☑
affecting fetus or newborn 763.1
causing obstructed labor 660.1 ☑
affecting fetus or newborn 763.1
Anectasis, pulmonary (newborn or fetus) 770.5
Anemia 285.9
with
disorder of
anaerobic glycolysis 282.3
pentose phosphate pathway 282.2
koilonychia 280.9
6-phosphogluconic dehydrogenase deficiency 282.2
achlorhydric 280.9
achrestic 281.8
Addison's (pernicious) 281.0
Addison-Biermer (pernicious) 281.0
agranulocytic 288.09
amino acid deficiency 281.4
antineoplastic chemotherapy induced 285.3 ●
aplastic 284.9
acquired (secondary) 284.89
congenital 284.01
constitutional 284.01
due to
antineoplastic chemotherapy 284.89
chronic systemic disease 284.89
drugs 284.89
infection 284.89
radiation 284.89
idiopathic 284.9
myxedema 244.9
of or complicating pregnancy 648.2 ☑
red cell (acquired) (adult) (with thymoma) 284.81
congenital 284.01
pure 284.01

☑ Additional Digit Required — Refer to the Tabular List for Digit Selection   ▽ Subterms under main terms may continue to next column or page

2010 ICD-9-CM   ►◄ Revised Text   ● New Line   ▲ Revised Code   **October 2009 • Volume 2 — 17**

Amebiasis — Anemia

Anemia — *continued*
  aplastic — *continued*
    specified type NEC 284.89
    toxic (paralytic) 284.89
  aregenerative 284.9
    congenital 284.01
  asiderotic 280.9
  atypical (primary) 285.9
  autohemolysis of Selwyn and Dacie (type I) 282.2
  autoimmune hemolytic 283.0
  Baghdad Spring 282.2
  Balantidium coli 007.0
  Biermer's (pernicious) 281.0
  blood loss (chronic) 280.0
    acute 285.1
  bothriocephalus 123.4
  brickmakers' (*see also* Ancylostomiasis) 126.9
  cerebral 437.8
  childhood 282.9
  chlorotic 280.9
  chronica congenita aregenerativa 284.01
  chronic simple 281.9
  combined system disease NEC 281.0 *[336.2]*
    due to dietary deficiency 281.1 *[336.2]*
  complicating pregnancy or childbirth 648.2 ☑
  congenital (following fetal blood loss) 776.5
    aplastic 284.01
    due to isoimmunization NEC 773.2
    Heinz-body 282.7
    hereditary hemolytic NEC 282.9
    nonspherocytic
      Type I 282.2
      Type II 282.3
    pernicious 281.0
    spherocytic (*see also* Spherocytosis) 282.0
  Cooley's (erythroblastic) 282.49
  crescent — *see* Disease, sickle-cell
  cytogenic 281.0
  Dacie's (nonspherocytic)
    type I 282.2
    type II 282.3
  Davidson's (refractory) 284.9
  deficiency 281.9
    2, 3 diphosphoglycurate mutase 282.3
    2, 3 PG 282.3
    6-PGD 282.2
    6-phosphogluronic dehydrogenase 282.2
    amino acid 281.4
    combined B₁₂ and folate 281.3
    enzyme, drug-induced (hemolytic) 282.2
    erythrocytic glutathione 282.2
    folate 281.2
      dietary 281.2
      drug-induced 281.2
    folic acid 281.2
      dietary 281.2
      drug-induced 281.2
    G-6-PD 282.2
    GGS-R 282.2
    glucose-6-phosphate dehydrogenase (G-6-PD) 282.2
    glucose-phosphate isomerase 282.3
    glutathione peroxidase 282.2
    glutathione reductase 282.2
    glyceraldehyde phosphate dehydrogenase 282.3
    GPI 282.3
    G SH 282.2
    hexokinase 282.3
    iron (Fe) 280.9
      specified NEC 280.8
    nutritional 281.9
      with
        poor iron absorption 280.9
        specified deficiency NEC 281.8
      due to inadequate dietary iron intake 280.1
      specified type NEC 281.8
    of or complicating pregnancy 648.2 ☑
    pentose phosphate pathway 282.2
    PFK 282.3
    phosphofructo-aldolase 282.3
    phosphofructokinase 282.3
    phosphoglycerate kinase 282.3
    PK 282.3

Anemia — *continued*
  deficiency — *continued*
    protein 281.4
    pyruvate kinase (PK) 282.3
    TPI 282.3
    triosephosphate isomerase 282.3
    vitamin B₁₂ NEC 281.1
      dietary 281.1
      pernicious 281.0
  Diamond-Blackfan (congenital hypoplastic) 284.01
  dibothriocephalus 123.4
  dimorphic 281.9
  diphasic 281.8
  diphtheritic 032.89
  Diphyllobothrium 123.4
  drepanocytic (*see also* Disease, sickle-cell) 282.60
  due to
    antineoplastic chemotherapy 285.3 ●
    blood loss (chronic) 280.0
      acute 285.1
    chemotherapy, antineoplastic 285.3 ●
    defect of Embden-Meyerhof pathway glycolysis 282.3
    disorder of glutathione metabolism 282.2
    drug — *see* Anemia, by type (*see also* Table of Drugs and Chemicals)
      chemotherapy, antineoplastic 285.3●
    fetal blood loss 776.5
    fish tapeworm (D. latum) infestation 123.4
    glutathione metabolism disorder 282.2
    hemorrhage (chronic) 280.0
      acute 285.1
    hexose monophosphate (HMP) shunt deficiency 282.2
    impaired absorption 280.9
    loss of blood (chronic) 280.0
      acute 285.1
    myxedema 244.9
    Necator americanus 126.1
    prematurity 776.6
    selective vitamin B₁₂ malabsorption with proteinuria 281.1
  Dyke-Young type (secondary) (symptomatic) 283.9
  dyserythropoietic (congenital) (types I, II, III) 285.8
  dyshemopoietic (congenital) 285.8
  Egypt (*see also* Ancylostomiasis) 126.9
  elliptocytosis (*see also* Elliptocytosis) 282.1
  enzyme deficiency, drug-induced 282.2
  epidemic (*see also* Ancylostomiasis) 126.9
  EPO resistant 285.21
  erythroblastic
    familial 282.49
    fetus or newborn (*see also* Disease, hemolytic) 773.2
      late 773.5
  erythrocytic glutathione deficiency 282.2
  erythropoietin-resistant (EPO resistant anemia) 285.21
  essential 285.9
  Faber's (achlorhydric anemia) 280.9
  factitious (self-induced blood letting) 280.0
  familial erythroblastic (microcytic) 282.49
  Fanconi's (congenital pancytopenia) 284.09
  favism 282.2
  fetal 678.0 ☑
    following blood loss, affecting newborn 776.5
  fetus or newborn
    due to
      ABO
        antibodies 773.1
        incompatibility, maternal/fetal 773.1
        isoimmunization 773.1
      Rh
        antibodies 773.0
        incompatibility, maternal/fetal 773.0
        isoimmunization 773.0
    following fetal blood loss 776.5
  fish tapeworm (D. latum) infestation 123.4
  folate (folic acid) deficiency 281.2

Anemia — *continued*
  folate deficiency — *continued*
    dietary 281.2
    drug-induced 281.2
  folate malabsorption, congenital 281.2
  folic acid deficiency 281.2
    dietary 281.2
    drug-induced 281.2
  G-6-PD 282.2
  general 285.9
  glucose-6-phosphate dehydrogenase deficiency 282.2
  glutathione-reductase deficiency 282.2
  goat's milk 281.2
  granulocytic 288.09
  Heinz-body, congenital 282.7
  hemoglobin deficiency 285.9
  hemolytic 283.9
    acquired 283.9
      with hemoglobinuria NEC 283.2
      autoimmune (cold type) (idiopathic) (primary) (secondary) (symptomatic) (warm type) 283.0
      due to
        cold reactive antibodies 283.0
        drug exposure 283.0
        warm reactive antibodies 283.0
      fragmentation 283.19
      idiopathic (chronic) 283.9
      infectious 283.19
        autoimmune 283.0
      non-autoimmune 283.10
      toxic 283.19
      traumatic cardiac 283.19
    acute 283.9
      due to enzyme deficiency NEC 282.3
      fetus or newborn (*see also* Disease, hemolytic) 773.2
        late 773.5
      Lederer's (acquired infectious hemolytic anemia) 283.19
    autoimmune (acquired) 283.0
    chronic 282.9
      idiopathic 283.9
    cold type (secondary) (symptomatic) 283.0
    congenital (spherocytic) (*see also* Spherocytosis) 282.0
      nonspherocytic — *see* Anemia, hemolytic, nonspherocytic, congenital
    drug-induced 283.0
      enzyme deficiency 282.2
    due to
      cardiac conditions 283.19
      drugs 283.0
      enzyme deficiency NEC 282.3
        drug-induced 282.2
      presence of shunt or other internal prosthetic device 283.19
      thrombotic thrombocytopenic purpura 446.6
    elliptocytotic (*see also* Elliptocytosis) 282.1
    familial 282.9
    hereditary 282.9
      due to enzyme deficiency NEC 282.3
      specified NEC 282.8
    idiopathic (chronic) 283.9
    infectious (acquired) 283.19
    mechanical 283.19
    microangiopathic 283.19
    non-autoimmune NEC 283.10
    nonspherocytic
      congenital or hereditary NEC 282.3
        glucose-6-phosphate dehydrogenase deficiency 282.2
        pyruvate kinase (PK) deficiency 282.3
        type I 282.2
        type II 282.3
      type I 282.2
      type II 282.3
    of or complicating pregnancy 648.2 ☑
    resulting from presence of shunt or other internal prosthetic device 283.19
    secondary 283.19
      autoimmune 283.0

Anemia — *continued*
  hemolytic — *continued*
    sickle-cell — *see* Disease, sickle-cell
    Stransky-Regala type (Hb-E) (*see also* Disease, hemoglobin) 282.7
    symptomatic 283.19
      autoimmune 283.0
    toxic (acquired) 283.19
    uremic (adult) (child) 283.11
    warm type (secondary) (symptomatic) 283.0
  hemorrhagic (chronic) 280.0
    acute 285.1
  HEMPAS 285.8
  hereditary erythroblast multinuclearity-positive acidified serum test 285.8
  Herrick's (hemoglobin S disease) 282.61
  hexokinase deficiency 282.3
  high A₂ 282.49
  hookworm (*see also* Ancylostomiasis) 126.9
  hypochromic (idiopathic) (microcytic) (normoblastic) 280.9
    with iron loading 285.0
    due to blood loss (chronic) 280.0
      acute 285.1
    familial sex linked 285.0
    pyridoxine-responsive 285.0
  hypoplasia, red blood cells 284.81
    congenital or familial 284.01
  hypoplastic (idiopathic) 284.9
    congenital 284.01
    familial 284.01
    of childhood 284.09
  idiopathic 285.9
    hemolytic, chronic 283.9
  in ▶(due to) (with)◀
    chronic illness NEC 285.29
    chronic kidney disease 285.21
    end-stage renal disease 285.21
    neoplastic disease 285.22
  infantile 285.9
  infective, infectional 285.9
  intertropical (*see also* Ancylostomiasis) 126.9
  iron (Fe) deficiency 280.9
    due to blood loss (chronic) 280.0
      acute 285.1
    of or complicating pregnancy 648.2 ☑
    specified NEC 280.8
  Jaksch's (pseudoleukemia infantum) 285.8
  Joseph-Diamond-Blackfan (congenital hypoplastic) 284.01
  labyrinth 386.50
  Lederer's (acquired infectious hemolytic anemia) 283.19
  leptocytosis (hereditary) 282.49
  leukoerythroblastic 284.2
  macrocytic 281.9
    nutritional 281.2
    of or complicating pregnancy 648.2 ☑
    tropical 281.2
  malabsorption (familial), selective B₁₂ with proteinuria 281.1
  malarial (*see also* Malaria) 084.6
  malignant (progressive) 281.0
  malnutrition 281.9
  marsh (*see also* Malaria) 084.6
  Mediterranean (with hemoglobinopathy) 282.49
  megaloblastic 281.9
    combined B₁₂ and folate deficiency 281.3
    nutritional (of infancy) 281.2
    of infancy 281.2
    of or complicating pregnancy 648.2 ☑
    refractory 281.3
    specified NEC 281.3
  megalocytic 281.9
  microangiopathic hemolytic 283.19
  microcytic (hypochromic) 280.9
    due to blood loss (chronic) 280.0
      acute 285.1
    familial 282.49
    hypochromic 280.9
  microdrepanocytosis 282.49
  miners' (*see also* Ancylostomiasis) 126.9
  myelopathic 285.8
  myelophthisic (normocytic) 284.2

☑ Additional Digit Required — Refer to the Tabular List for Digit Selection   ▽ Subterms under main terms may continue to next column or page

Anemia — *continued*
  newborn (*see also* Disease, hemolytic) 773.2
    due to isoimmunization (*see also* Disease,
      hemolytic) 773.2
    late, due to isoimmunization 773.5
    posthemorrhagic 776.5
  nonregenerative 284.9
  nonspherocytic hemolytic — *see* Anemia,
    hemolytic, nonspherocytic
  normocytic (infectional) (not due to blood
    loss) 285.9
    due to blood loss (chronic) 280.0
      acute 285.1
    myelophthisic 284.2
  nutritional (deficiency) 281.9
    with
      poor iron absorption 280.9
      specified deficiency NEC 281.8
    due to inadequate dietary iron intake 280.1
    megaloblastic (of infancy) 281.2
  of childhood 282.9
  of chronic
    disease NEC 285.29
    illness NEC 285.29
  of or complicating pregnancy 648.2 ☑
    affecting fetus or newborn 760.8
  of prematurity 776.6
  orotic aciduric (congenital) (hereditary) 281.4
  osteosclerotic 289.89
  ovalocytosis (hereditary) (*see also* Elliptocyto-
    sis) 282.1
  paludal (*see also* Malaria) 084.6
  pentose phosphate pathway deficiency 282.2
  pernicious (combined system disease) (con-
    genital) (dorsolateral spinal degenera-
    tion) (juvenile) (myelopathy) (neuropa-
    thy) (posterior sclerosis) (primary)
    (progressive) (spleen) 281.0
    of or complicating pregnancy 648.2 ☑
  pleochromic 285.9
    of sprue 281.8
  portal 285.8
  posthemorrhagic (chronic) 280.0
    acute 285.1
    newborn 776.5
  postoperative
    due to (acute) blood loss 285.1
      chronic blood loss 280.0
    other 285.9
  postpartum 648.2 ☑
  pressure 285.9
  primary 285.9
  profound 285.9
  progressive 285.9
    malignant 281.0
    pernicious 281.0
  protein-deficiency 281.4
  pseudoleukemica infantum 285.8
  puerperal 648.2 ☑
  pure red cell 284.81
    congenital 284.01
  pyridoxine-responsive (hypochromic) 285.0
  pyruvate kinase (PK) deficiency 282.3
  refractoria sideroblastica 238.72
  refractory (primary) 238.72
    with
      excess
        blasts-1 (RAEB-1) 238.72 ▲
        blasts-2 (RAEB-2) 238.73
      hemochromatosis 238.72
      ringed sideroblasts (RARS) 238.72
    due to
      drug 285.0
      myelodysplastic syndrome 238.72
      toxin 285.0
    hereditary 285.0
    idiopathic 238.72
    megaloblastic 281.3
    sideroblastic 238.72
      hereditary 285.0
    sideropenic 280.9
  Rietti-Greppi-Micheli (thalassemia minor)
    282.49
  scorbutic 281.8
  secondary (to) 285.9
    blood loss (chronic) 280.0

Anemia — *continued*
  secondary — *continued*
    blood loss — *continued*
      acute 285.1
    hemorrhage 280.0
      acute 285.1
    inadequate dietary iron intake 280.1
  semiplastic 284.9
  septic 285.9
  sickle-cell (*see also* Disease, sickle-cell) 282.60
  sideroachrestic 285.0
  sideroblastic (acquired) (any type) (congenital)
    (drug-induced) (due to disease)
    (hereditary) (primary) (secondary) (sex-
    linked hypochromic) (vitamin B_6 re-
    sponsive) 285.0
    refractory 238.72
      congenital 285.0
      drug-induced 285.0
      hereditary 285.0
      sex-linked hypochromic 285.0
      vitamin B_6-responsive 285.0
  sideropenic (refractory) 280.9
    due to blood loss (chronic) 280.0
      acute 285.1
  simple chronic 281.9
  specified type NEC 285.8
  spherocytic (hereditary) (*see also* Spherocyto-
    sis) 282.0
  splenic 285.8
    familial (Gaucher's) 272.7
  splenomegalic 285.8
  stomatocytosis 282.8
  syphilitic 095.8
  target cell (oval) 282.49
  thalassemia 282.49
  thrombocytopenic (*see also* Thrombocytope-
    nia) 287.5
  toxic 284.89
  triosephosphate isomerase deficiency 282.3
  tropical, macrocytic 281.2
  tuberculous (*see also* Tuberculosis) 017.9 ☑
  vegan's 281.1
  vitamin
    B_6-responsive 285.0
    B_{12} deficiency (dietary) 281.1
      pernicious 281.0
  von Jaksch's (pseudoleukemia infantum) 285.8
  Witts' (achlorhydric anemia) 280.9
  Zuelzer (-Ogden) (nutritional megaloblastic
    anemia) 281.2
Anencephalus, anencephaly 740.0
  fetal, affecting management of pregnancy
    655.0 ☑
Anergasia — *see also* Psychosis, organic 294.9
  senile 290.0
Anesthesia, anesthetic 782.0
  complication or reaction NEC 995.22
    due to
      correct substance properly adminis-
        tered 995.22
      overdose or wrong substance given
        968.4
        specified anesthetic — *see* Table
          of Drugs and Chemicals
  cornea 371.81
  death from
    correct substance properly administered
      995.4
    during delivery 668.9 ☑
    overdose or wrong substance given 968.4
    specified anesthetic — *see* Table of Drugs
      and Chemicals
  eye 371.81
  functional 300.11
  hyperesthetic, thalamic 338.0
  hysterical 300.11
  local skin lesion 782.0
  olfactory 781.1
  sexual (psychogenic) 302.72
  shock
    due to
      correct substance properly adminis-
        tered 995.4

Anesthesia, anesthetic — *continued*
  shock — *continued*
    due to — *continued*
      overdose or wrong substance given
        968.4
      specified anesthetic — *see* Table of
        Drugs and Chemicals
  skin 782.0
  tactile 782.0
  testicular 608.9
  thermal 782.0
Anetoderma (maculosum) 701.3
Aneuploidy NEC 758.5
Aneurin deficiency 265.1
Aneurysm (anastomotic) (artery) (cirsoid) (diffuse)
  (false) (fusiform) (multiple) (ruptured)
  (saccular) (varicose) 442.9
  abdominal (aorta) 441.4
    ruptured 441.3
    syphilitic 093.0
  aorta, aortic (nonsyphilitic) 441.9
    abdominal 441.4
      dissecting 441.02
      ruptured 441.3
      syphilitic 093.0
    arch 441.2
      ruptured 441.1
    arteriosclerotic NEC 441.9
      ruptured 441.5
    ascending 441.2
      ruptured 441.1
    congenital 747.29
    descending 441.9
      abdominal 441.4
        ruptured 441.3
      ruptured 441.5
      thoracic 441.2
        ruptured 441.1
    dissecting 441.00
      abdominal 441.02
      thoracic 441.01
      thoracoabdominal 441.03
    due to coarctation (aorta) 747.10
    ruptured 441.5
    sinus, right 747.29
    syphilitic 093.0
    thoracoabdominal 441.7
      ruptured 441.6
    thorax, thoracic (arch) (nonsyphilitic) 441.2
      dissecting 441.01
      ruptured 441.1
      syphilitic 093.0
    transverse 441.2
      ruptured 441.1
    valve (heart) (*see also* Endocarditis, aortic)
      424.1
  arteriosclerotic NEC 442.9
    cerebral 437.3
      ruptured (*see also* Hemorrhage, sub-
        arachnoid) 430
  arteriovenous (congenital) (peripheral) NEC
    (*see also* Anomaly, arteriovenous)
    747.60
    acquired NEC 447.0
      brain 437.3
        ruptured (*see also* Hemorrhage,
          subarachnoid) 430
      coronary 414.11
      pulmonary 417.0
    brain (cerebral) 747.81
      ruptured (*see also* Hemorrhage, sub-
        arachnoid) 430
      coronary 746.85
      pulmonary 747.3
      retina 743.58
      specified site NEC 747.89
        acquired 447.0
      traumatic (*see also* Injury, blood vessel, by
        site) 904.9
  basal — *see* Aneurysm, brain
  berry (congenital) (ruptured) (*see also* Hemor-
    rhage, subarachnoid) 430
  brain 437.3
    arteriosclerotic 437.3
      ruptured (*see also* Hemorrhage, sub-
        arachnoid) 430

Aneurysm — *continued*
  brain — *continued*
    arteriovenous 747.81
      acquired 437.3
        ruptured (*see also* Hemorrhage,
          subarachnoid) 430
      ruptured (*see also* Hemorrhage, sub-
        arachnoid) 430
    berry (congenital) (ruptured) (*see also*
      Hemorrhage, subarachnoid) 430
    congenital 747.81
      ruptured (*see also* Hemorrhage, sub-
        arachnoid) 430
    meninges 437.3
      ruptured (*see also* Hemorrhage, sub-
        arachnoid) 430
    miliary (congenital) (ruptured) (*see also*
      Hemorrhage, subarachnoid) 430
    mycotic 421.0
      ruptured (*see also* Hemorrhage, sub-
        arachnoid) 430
    nonruptured 437.3
    ruptured (*see also* Hemorrhage, subarach-
      noid) 430
    syphilitic 094.87
    syphilitic (hemorrhage) 094.87
    traumatic — *see* Injury, intracranial
  cardiac (false) (*see also* Aneurysm, heart)
    414.10
  carotid artery (common) (external) 442.81
    internal (intracranial portion) 437.3
      extracranial portion 442.81
      ruptured into brain (*see also* Hemor-
        rhage, subarachnoid) 430
    syphilitic 093.89
      intracranial 094.87
  cavernous sinus (*see also* Aneurysm, brain)
    437.3
    arteriovenous 747.81
      ruptured (*see also* Hemorrhage, sub-
        arachnoid) 430
    congenital 747.81
      ruptured (*see also* Hemorrhage, sub-
        arachnoid) 430
  celiac 442.84
  central nervous system, syphilitic 094.89
  cerebral — *see* Aneurysm, brain
  chest — *see* Aneurysm, thorax
  circle of Willis (*see also* Aneurysm, brain) 437.3
    congenital 747.81
      ruptured (*see also* Hemorrhage, sub-
        arachnoid) 430
    ruptured (*see also* Hemorrhage, subarach-
      noid) 430
  common iliac artery 442.2
  congenital (peripheral) NEC 747.60
    brain 747.81
      ruptured (*see also* Hemorrhage, sub-
        arachnoid) 430
    cerebral — *see* Aneurysm, brain, congeni-
      tal
    coronary 746.85
    gastrointestinal 747.61
    lower limb 747.64
    pulmonary 747.3
    renal 747.62
    retina 743.58
    specified site NEC 747.89
    spinal 747.82
    upper limb 747.63
  conjunctiva 372.74
  conus arteriosus (*see also* Aneurysm, heart)
    414.10
  coronary (arteriosclerotic) (artery) (vein) (*see*
    also Aneurysm, heart) 414.11
    arteriovenous 746.85
    congenital 746.85
    syphilitic 093.89
  cylindrical 441.9
    ruptured 441.5
    syphilitic 093.9
  dissecting 442.9
    aorta 441.00
      abdominal 441.02
      thoracic 441.01
      thoracoabdominal 441.03

☑ Additional Digit Required — Refer to the Tabular List for Digit Selection   ᴺᴱᶜ Subterms under main terms may continue to next column or page

2010 ICD-9-CM   ▶◀ Revised Text   ● New Line   ▲ Revised Code   **October 2009 · Volume 2 — 19**

Aneurysm — *continued*
  dissecting — *continued*
    syphilitic 093.9
  ductus arteriosus 747.0
  embolic — *see* Embolism, artery
  endocardial, infective (any valve) 421.0
  femoral 442.3
  gastroduodenal 442.84
  gastroepiploic 442.84
  heart (chronic or with a stated duration of over
    8 weeks) (infectional) (wall) 414.10
    acute or with a stated duration of 8 weeks
      or less (*see also* Infarct, myocardi-
      um) 410.9 ✓
    congenital 746.89
    valve — *see* Endocarditis
  hepatic 442.84
  iliac (common) 442.2
  infective (any valve) 421.0
  innominate (nonsyphilitic) 442.89
    syphilitic 093.89
  interauricular septum (*see also* Aneurysm,
    heart) 414.10
  interventricular septum (*see also* Aneurysm,
    heart) 414.10
  intracranial — *see* Aneurysm, brain
  intrathoracic (nonsyphilitic) 441.2
    ruptured 441.1
    syphilitic 093.0
  jugular vein 453.89   ▲
  lower extremity 442.3
  lung (pulmonary artery) 417.1
  malignant 093.9
  mediastinal (nonsyphilitic) 442.89
    syphilitic 093.89
  miliary (congenital) (ruptured) (*see also* Hem-
    orrhage, subarachnoid) 430
  mitral (heart) (valve) 424.0
  mural (arteriovenous) (heart) (*see also*
    Aneurysm, heart) 414.10
  mycotic, any site 421.0
    without endocarditis — *see* Aneurysm by
      site
    ruptured, brain (*see also* Hemorrhage,
      subarachnoid) 430
  myocardium (*see also* Aneurysm, heart) 414.10
  neck 442.81
  pancreaticoduodenal 442.84
  patent ductus arteriosus 747.0
  peripheral NEC 442.89
    congenital NEC (*see also* Aneurysm, con-
      genital) 747.60
  popliteal 442.3
  pulmonary 417.1
    arteriovenous 747.3
      acquired 417.0
    syphilitic 093.89
    valve (heart) (*see also* Endocarditis, pul-
      monary) 424.3
  racemose 442.9
    congenital (peripheral) NEC 747.60
  radial 442.0
  Rasmussen's (*see also* Tuberculosis) 011.2 ✓
  renal 442.1
  retinal (acquired) 362.17
    congenital 743.58
    diabetic 250.5 ✓ *[362.01]*
      due to secondary diabetes
        249.5 ✓ *[362.01]*
  sinus, aortic (of Valsalva) 747.29
  specified site NEC 442.89
  spinal (cord) 442.89
    congenital 747.82
    syphilitic (hemorrhage) 094.89
  spleen, splenic 442.83
  subclavian 442.82
    syphilitic 093.89
  superior mesenteric 442.84
  syphilitic 093.9
    aorta 093.0
    central nervous system 094.89
    congenital 090.5
    spine, spinal 094.89
  thoracoabdominal 441.7
    ruptured 441.6
  thorax, thoracic (arch) (nonsyphilitic) 441.2

Aneurysm — *continued*
  thorax, thoracic — *continued*
    dissecting 441.01
    ruptured 441.1
    syphilitic 093.0
  traumatic (complication) (early) — *see* Injury,
    blood vessel, by site
  tricuspid (heart) (valve) — *see* Endocarditis,
    tricuspid
  ulnar 442.0
  upper extremity 442.0
  valve, valvular — *see* Endocarditis
  venous 456.8
    congenital NEC (*see also* Aneurysm, con-
      genital) 747.60
  ventricle (arteriovenous) (*see also* Aneurysm,
    heart) 414.10
  visceral artery NEC 442.84
Angiectasis 459.89
Angiectopia 459.9
Angiitis 447.6
  allergic granulomatous 446.4
  hypersensitivity 446.20
    Goodpasture's syndrome 446.21
    specified NEC 446.29
  necrotizing 446.0
  Wegener's (necrotizing respiratory granulo-
    matosis) 446.4
Angina (attack) (cardiac) (chest) (effort) (heart)
  (pectoris) (syndrome) (vasomotor) 413.9
  abdominal 557.1
  accelerated 411.1
  agranulocytic 288.03
  aphthous 074.0
  catarrhal 462
  crescendo 411.1
  croupous 464.4
  cruris 443.9
    due to atherosclerosis NEC (*see also* Arte-
      riosclerosis, extremities) 440.20
  decubitus 413.0
  diphtheritic (membranous) 032.0
  equivalent 413.9   ●
  erysipelatous 034.0
  erythematous 462
  exudative, chronic 476.0
  faucium 478.29
  gangrenous 462
    diphtheritic 032.0
  infectious 462
  initial 411.1
  intestinal 557.1
  ludovici 528.3
  Ludwig's 528.3
  malignant 462
    diphtheritic 032.0
  membranous 464.4
    diphtheritic 032.0
  mesenteric 557.1
  monocytic 075
  nocturnal 413.0
  phlegmonous 475
    diphtheritic 032.0
  preinfarctional 411.1
  Prinzmetal's 413.1
  progressive 411.1
  pseudomembranous 101
  psychogenic 306.2
  pultaceous, diphtheritic 032.0
  scarlatinal 034.1
  septic 034.0
  simple 462
  stable NEC 413.9
  staphylococcal 462
  streptococcal 034.0
  stridulous, diphtheritic 032.3
  syphilitic 093.9
    congenital 090.5
  tonsil 475
  trachealis 464.4
  unstable 411.1
  variant 413.1
  Vincent's 101
Angioblastoma (M9161/1) — *see* Neoplasm,
  connective tissue, uncertain behavior

Angiocholecystitis — *see also* Cholecystitis,
  acute 575.0
Angiocholitis — *see also* Cholecystitis, acute
  576.1
Angiodysgensis spinalis 336.1
Angiodysplasia (intestinalis) (intestine) 569.84
  with hemorrhage 569.85
  duodenum 537.82
    with hemorrhage 537.83
  stomach 537.82
    with hemorrhage 537.83
Angioedema (allergic) (any site) (with urticaria)
  995.1
  hereditary 277.6
Angioendothelioma (M9130/1) — *see also*
  Neoplasm, by site, uncertain behavior
  benign (M9130/0) (*see also* Hemangioma, by
    site) 228.00
  bone (M9260/3) — *see* Neoplasm, bone, ma-
    lignant
  Ewing's (M9260/3) — *see* Neoplasm, bone,
    malignant
  nervous system (M9130/0) 228.09
Angiofibroma (M9160/0) — *see also* Neoplasm,
  by site, benign
  juvenile (M9160/0) 210.7
    specified site — *see* Neoplasm, by site,
      benign
    unspecified site 210.7
Angiohemophilia (A) (B) 286.4
Angioid streaks (choroid) (retina) 363.43
Angiokeratoma (M9141/0) — *see also* Neoplasm,
  skin, benign
  corporis diffusum 272.7
Angiokeratosis
  diffuse 272.7
Angioleiomyoma (M8894/0) — *see* Neoplasm,
  connective tissue, benign
Angioleucitis 683
Angiolipoma (M8861/0) — *see also* Lipoma, by
  site 214.9
  infiltrating (M8861/1) — *see* Neoplasm, con-
    nective tissue, uncertain behavior
Angioma (M9120/0) — *see also* Hemangioma,
  by site 228.00
  capillary 448.1
  hemorrhagicum hereditaria 448.0
  malignant (M9120/3) — *see* Neoplasm, con-
    nective tissue, malignant
  pigmentosum et atrophicum 757.33
  placenta — *see* Placenta, abnormal
  plexiform (M9131/0) — *see* Hemangioma, by
    site
  senile 448.1
  serpiginosum 709.1
  spider 448.1
  stellate 448.1
Angiomatosis 757.32
  bacillary 083.8
  corporis diffusum universale 272.7
  cutaneocerebral 759.6
  encephalocutaneous 759.6
  encephalofacial 759.6
  encephalotrigeminal 759.6
  hemorrhagic familial 448.0
  hereditary familial 448.0
  heredofamilial 448.0
  meningo-oculofacial 759.6
  multiple sites 228.09
  neuro-oculocutaneous 759.6
  retina (Hippel's disease) 759.6
  retinocerebellosa 759.6
  retinocerebral 759.6
  systemic 228.09
Angiomyolipoma (M8860/0)
  specified site — *see* Neoplasm, connective
    tissue, benign
  unspecified site 223.0
Angiomyoliposarcoma (M8860/3) — *see* Neoplasm, connective tissue, malignant
Angiomyoma (M8894/0) — *see* Neoplasm, connective tissue, benign
Angiomyosarcoma (M8894/3) — *see* Neoplasm,
  connective tissue, malignant
Angioneurosis 306.2

Angioneurotic edema (allergic) (any site) (with
  urticaria) 995.1
  hereditary 277.6
Angiopathia, angiopathy 459.9
  diabetic (peripheral) 250.7 ✓ *[443.81]*
    due to secondary diabetes
      249.7 ✓ *[443.81]*
  peripheral 443.9
    diabetic 250.7 ✓ *[443.81]*
      due to secondary diabetes
        249.7 ✓ *[443.81]*
    specified type NEC 443.89
  retinae syphilitica 093.89
  retinalis (juvenilis) 362.18
    background 362.10
    diabetic 250.5 ✓ *[362.01]*
      due to secondary diabetes
        249.5 ✓ *[362.01]*
    proliferative 362.29
    tuberculous (*see also* Tuberculosis)
      017.3 ✓ *[362.18]*
Angiosarcoma (M9120/3) — *see* Neoplasm,
  connective tissue, malignant
Angiosclerosis — *see* Arteriosclerosis
Angioscotoma, enlarged 368.42
Angiospasm 443.9
  brachial plexus 353.0
  cerebral 435.9
  cervical plexus 353.2
  nerve
    arm 354.9
      axillary 353.0
      median 354.1
      ulnar 354.2
    autonomic (*see also* Neuropathy, peripher-
      al, autonomic) 337.9
    axillary 353.0
    leg 355.8
      plantar 355.6
    lower extremity — *see* Angiospasm, nerve,
      leg
    median 354.1
    peripheral NEC 355.9
    spinal NEC 355.9
    sympathetic (*see also* Neuropathy, periph-
      eral, autonomic) 337.9
    ulnar 354.2
    upper extremity — *see* Angiospasm, nerve,
      arm
  peripheral NEC 443.9
  traumatic 443.9
    foot 443.9
    leg 443.9
  vessel 443.9
Angiospastic disease or edema 443.9
Angle's
  class I 524.21
  class II 524.22
  class III 524.23
Anguillulosis 127.2
Angulation
  cecum (*see also* Obstruction, intestine) 560.9
  coccyx (acquired) 738.6
    congenital 756.19
  femur (acquired) 736.39
    congenital 755.69
  intestine (large) (small) (*see also* Obstruction,
    intestine) 560.9
  sacrum (acquired) 738.5
    congenital 756.19
  sigmoid (flexure) (*see also* Obstruction, intes-
    tine) 560.9
  spine (*see also* Curvature, spine) 737.9
  tibia (acquired) 736.89
    congenital 755.69
  ureter 593.3
  wrist (acquired) 736.09
    congenital 755.59
Angulus infectiosus 686.8
Anhedonia 780.99
Anhidrosis (lid) (neurogenic) (thermogenic) 705.0
Anhydration 276.51
  with
    hypernatremia 276.0
    hyponatremia 276.1
Anhydremia 276.52

✓ Additional Digit Required — Refer to the Tabular List for Digit Selection   ▽ Subterms under main terms may continue to next column or page

Anhydremia — continued
with
hypernatremia 276.0
hyponatremia 276.1
Anidrosis 705.0
Aniridia (congenital) 743.45
Anisakiasis (infection) (infestation) 127.1
Anisakis larva infestation 127.1
Aniseikonia 367.32
Anisocoria (pupil) 379.41
congenital 743.46
Anisocytosis 790.09
Anisometropia (congenital) 367.31
Ankle — see condition
Ankyloblepharon (acquired) (eyelid) 374.46
filiforme (adnatum) (congenital) 743.62
total 743.62
Ankylodactly — see also Syndactylism 755.10
Ankyloglossia 750.0
Ankylosis (fibrous) (osseous) 718.50
ankle 718.57
any joint, produced by surgical fusion V45.4
cricoarytenoid (cartilage) (joint) (larynx) 478.79
dental 521.6
ear ossicle NEC 385.22
malleus 385.21
elbow 718.52
finger 718.54
hip 718.55
incostapedial joint (infectional) 385.22
joint, produced by surgical fusion NEC V45.4
knee 718.56
lumbosacral (joint) 724.6
malleus 385.21
multiple sites 718.59
postoperative (status) V45.4
sacroiliac (joint) 724.6
shoulder 718.51
specified site NEC 718.58
spine NEC 724.9
surgical V45.4
teeth, tooth (hard tissues) 521.6
temporomandibular joint 524.61
wrist 718.53
Ankylostoma — see Ancylostoma
Ankylostomiasis (intestinal) — see Ancylostomiasis
Ankylurethria — see also Stricture, urethra 598.9
Annular — see also condition
detachment, cervix 622.8
organ or site, congenital NEC — see Distortion
pancreas (congenital) 751.7
Anodontia (complete) (partial) (vera) 520.0
with abnormal spacing 524.30
acquired 525.10
causing malocclusion 524.30
due to
caries 525.13
extraction 525.10
periodontal disease 525.12
trauma 525.11
Anomaly, anomalous (congenital) (unspecified type) 759.9
abdomen 759.9
abdominal wall 756.70
acoustic nerve 742.9
adrenal (gland) 759.1
Alder (-Reilly) (leukocyte granulation) 288.2
alimentary tract 751.9
lower 751.5
specified type NEC 751.8
upper (any part, except tongue) 750.9
tongue 750.10
specified type NEC 750.19
alveolar 524.70
ridge (process) 525.8
specified NEC 524.79
ankle (joint) 755.69
anus, anal (canal) 751.5
aorta, aortic 747.20
arch 747.21
coarctation (postductal) (preductal) 747.10
cusp or valve NEC 746.9
septum 745.0
specified type NEC 747.29
aorticopulmonary septum 745.0

Anomaly, anomalous — continued
apertures, diaphragm 756.6
appendix 751.5
aqueduct of Sylvius 742.3
with spina bifida (see also Spina bifida) 741.0 ☑
arm 755.50
reduction (see also Deformity, reduction, upper limb) 755.20
arteriovenous (congenital) (peripheral) NEC 747.60
brain 747.81
cerebral 747.81
coronary 746.85
gastrointestinal 747.61
acquired — see Angiodysplasia
lower limb 747.64
renal 747.62
specified site NEC 747.69
spinal 747.82
upper limb 747.63
artery (see also Anomaly, peripheral vascular system) NEC 747.60
brain 747.81
cerebral 747.81
coronary 746.85
eye 743.9
pulmonary 747.3
renal 747.62
retina 743.9
umbilical 747.5
arytenoepiglottic folds 748.3
atrial
bands 746.9
folds 746.9
septa 745.5
atrioventricular
canal 745.69
common 745.69
conduction 426.7
excitation 426.7
septum 745.4
atrium — see Anomaly, atrial
auditory canal 744.3
specified type NEC 744.29
with hearing impairment 744.02
auricle
ear 744.3
causing impairment of hearing 744.02
heart 746.9
septum 745.5
autosomes, autosomal NEC 758.5
Axenfeld's 743.44
back 759.9
band
atrial 746.9
heart 746.9
ventricular 746.9
Bartholin's duct 750.9
biliary duct or passage 751.60
atresia 751.61
bladder (neck) (sphincter) (trigone) 753.9
specified type NEC 753.8
blood vessel 747.9
artery — see Anomaly, artery
peripheral vascular — see Anomaly, peripheral vascular system
vein — see Anomaly, vein
bone NEC 756.9
ankle 755.69
arm 755.50
chest 756.3
cranium 756.0
face 756.0
finger 755.50
foot 755.67
forearm 755.50
frontal 756.0
head 756.0
hip 755.63
leg 755.60
lumbosacral 756.10
nose 748.1
pelvic girdle 755.60
rachitic 756.4
rib 756.3

Anomaly, anomalous — continued
bone — continued
shoulder girdle 755.50
skull 756.0
with
anencephalus 740.0
encephalocele 742.0
hydrocephalus 742.3
with spina bifida (see also Spina bifida) 741.0 ☑
microcephalus 742.1
toe 755.66
brain 742.9
multiple 742.4
reduction 742.2
specified type NEC 742.4
vessel 747.81
branchial cleft NEC 744.49
cyst 744.42
fistula 744.41
persistent 744.41
sinus (external) (internal) 744.41
breast 757.6 ▲
broad ligament 752.10
specified type NEC 752.19
bronchus 748.3
bulbar septum 745.0
bulbus cordis 745.9
persistent (in left ventricle) 745.8
bursa 756.9
canal of Nuck 752.9
canthus 743.9
capillary NEC (see also Anomaly, peripheral vascular system) 747.60
cardiac 746.9
septal closure 745.9
acquired 429.71
valve NEC 746.9
pulmonary 746.00
specified type NEC 746.89
cardiovascular system 746.9
complicating pregnancy, childbirth, or puerperium 648.5 ☑
carpus 755.50
cartilage, trachea 748.3
cartilaginous 756.9
caruncle, lacrimal, lachrymal 743.9
cascade stomach 750.7
cauda equina 742.59
cecum 751.5
cerebral (see also Anomaly, brain vessels) 747.81
cerebrovascular system 747.81
cervix (uterus) 752.40
with doubling of vagina and uterus 752.2
in pregnancy or childbirth 654.6 ☑
affecting fetus or newborn 763.89
causing obstructed labor 660.2 ☑
affecting fetus or newborn 763.1
Chédiak-Higashi (-Steinbrinck) (congenital gigantism of peroxidase granules) 288.2
cheek 744.9
chest (wall) 756.3
chin 744.9
specified type NEC 744.89
chordae tendineae 746.9
choroid 743.9
plexus 742.9
chromosomes, chromosomal 758.9
13 (13-15) 758.1
18 (16-18) 758.2
21 or 22 758.0
autosomes NEC (see also Abnormal, autosomes) 758.5
deletion 758.39
Christchurch 758.39
D_1 758.1
E_3 758.2
G 758.0
mitochondrial 758.9
mosaics 758.89
sex 758.81
complement, XO 758.6
complement, XXX 758.81
complement, XXY 758.7
complement, XYY 758.81

Anomaly, anomalous — continued
chromosomes, chromosomal — continued
sex — continued
gonadal dysgenesis 758.6
Klinefelter's 758.7
Turner's 758.6
trisomy 21 758.0
cilia 743.9
circulatory system 747.9
specified type NEC 747.89
clavicle 755.51
clitoris 752.40
coccyx 756.10
colon 751.5
common duct 751.60
communication
coronary artery 746.85
left ventricle with right atrium 745.4
concha (ear) 744.3
connection
renal vessels with kidney 747.62
total pulmonary venous 747.41
connective tissue 756.9
specified type NEC 756.89
cornea 743.9
shape 743.41
size 743.41
specified type NEC 743.49
coronary
artery 746.85
vein 746.89
cranium — see Anomaly, skull
cricoid cartilage 748.3
cushion, endocardial 745.60
specified type NEC 745.69
cystic duct 751.60
dental arch 524.20
specified NEC 524.29
dental arch relationship 524.20
angle's class I 524.21
angle's class II 524.22
angle's class III 524.23
articulation
anterior 524.27
posterior 524.27
reverse 524.27
disto-occlusion 524.22
division I 524.22
division II 524.22
excessive horizontal overlap 524.26
interarch distance (excessive) (inadequate) 524.28
mesio-occlusion 524.23
neutro-occlusion 524.21
open
anterior occlusal relationship 524.24
posterior occlusal relationship 524.25
specified NEC 524.29
dentition 520.6
dentofacial NEC 524.9
functional 524.50
specified type NEC 524.89
dermatoglyphic 757.2
Descemet's membrane 743.9
specified type NEC 743.49
development
cervix 752.40
vagina 752.40
vulva 752.40
diaphragm, diaphragmatic (apertures) NEC 756.6
digestive organ(s) or system 751.9
lower 751.5
specified type NEC 751.8
upper 750.9
distribution, coronary artery 746.85
ductus
arteriosus 747.0
Botalli 747.0
duodenum 751.5
dura 742.9
brain 742.4
spinal cord 742.59
ear 744.3
causing impairment of hearing 744.00

Anomaly, anomalous — *continued*
  ear — *continued*
    causing impairment of hearing — *continued*
      specified type NEC 744.09
    external 744.3
      causing impairment of hearing 744.02
      specified type NEC 744.29
    inner (causing impairment of hearing) 744.05
    middle, except ossicles (causing impairment of hearing) 744.03
      ossicles 744.04
    ossicles 744.04
    prominent auricle 744.29
    specified type NEC 744.29
      with hearing impairment 744.09
  Ebstein's (heart) 746.2
    tricuspid valve 746.2
  ectodermal 757.9
  Eisenmenger's (ventricular septal defect) 745.4
  ejaculatory duct 752.9
    specified type NEC 752.89
  elbow (joint) 755.50
  endocardial cushion 745.60
    specified type NEC 745.69
  endocrine gland NEC 759.2
  epididymis 752.9
  epiglottis 748.3
  esophagus 750.9
    specified type NEC 750.4
  Eustachian tube 744.3
    specified type NEC 744.24
  eye (any part) 743.9
    adnexa 743.9
      specified type NEC 743.69
    anophthalmos 743.00
    anterior
      chamber and related structures 743.9
        angle 743.9
          specified type NEC 743.44
        specified type NEC 743.44
      segment 743.9
        combined 743.48
        multiple 743.48
        specified type NEC 743.49
    cataract (*see also* Cataract) 743.30
    glaucoma (*see also* Buphthalmia) 743.20
    lid 743.9
      specified type NEC 743.63
    microphthalmos (*see also* Microphthalmos) 743.10
    posterior segment 743.9
      specified type NEC 743.59
      vascular 743.58
      vitreous 743.9
        specified type NEC 743.51
    ptosis (eyelid) 743.61
    retina 743.9
      specified type NEC 743.59
    sclera 743.9
      specified type NEC 743.47
    specified type NEC 743.8
  eyebrow 744.89
  eyelid 743.9
    specified type NEC 743.63
  face (any part) 744.9
    bone(s) 756.0
    specified type NEC 744.89
  fallopian tube 752.10
    specified type NEC 752.19
  fascia 756.9
    specified type NEC 756.89
  femur 755.60
  fibula 755.60
  finger 755.50
    supernumerary 755.01
    webbed (*see also* Syndactylism, fingers) 755.11
  fixation, intestine 751.4
  flexion (joint) 755.9
    hip or thigh (*see also* Dislocation, hip, congenital) 754.30
  folds, heart 746.9
  foot 755.67

Anomaly, anomalous — *continued*
  foramen
    Botalli 745.5
    ovale 745.5
  forearm 755.50
  forehead (*see also* Anomaly, skull) 756.0
  form, teeth 520.2
  fovea centralis 743.9
  frontal bone (*see also* Anomaly, skull) 756.0
  gallbladder 751.60
  Gartner's duct 752.41
  gastrointestinal tract 751.9
    specified type NEC 751.8
    vessel 747.61
  genitalia, genital organ(s) or system
    female 752.9
      external 752.40
        specified type NEC 752.49
      internal NEC 752.9
    male (external and internal) 752.9
      epispadias 752.62
      hidden penis 752.65
      hydrocele, congenital 778.6
      hypospadias 752.61
      micropenis 752.64
      testis, undescended 752.51
        retractile 752.52
      specified type NEC 752.89
  genitourinary NEC 752.9
  Gerbode 745.4
  globe (eye) 743.9
  glottis 748.3
  granulation or granulocyte, genetic 288.2
    constitutional 288.2
    leukocyte 288.2
  gum 750.9
  gyri 742.9
  hair 757.9
    specified type NEC 757.4
  hand 755.50
  hard tissue formation in pulp 522.3
  head (*see also* Anomaly, skull) 756.0
  heart 746.9
    auricle 746.9
    bands 746.9
    fibroelastosis cordis 425.3
    folds 746.9
    malposition 746.87
    maternal, affecting fetus or newborn 760.3
    obstructive NEC 746.84
    patent ductus arteriosus (Botalli) 747.0
    septum 745.9
      acquired 429.71
      aortic 745.0
      aorticopulmonary 745.0
      atrial 745.5
      auricular 745.5
      between aorta and pulmonary artery 745.0
      endocardial cushion type 745.60
        specified type NEC 745.69
      interatrial 745.5
      interventricular 745.4
        with pulmonary stenosis or atresia, dextraposition of aorta, and hypertrophy of right ventricle 745.2
        acquired 429.71
      specified type NEC 745.8
      ventricular 745.4
        with pulmonary stenosis or atresia, dextraposition of aorta, and hypertrophy of right ventricle 745.2
        acquired 429.71
    specified type NEC 746.89
    tetralogy of Fallot 745.2
    valve NEC 746.9
      aortic 746.9
        atresia 746.89
        bicuspid valve 746.4
        insufficiency 746.4
        specified type NEC 746.89
        stenosis 746.3
          subaortic 746.81
          supravalvular 747.22

Anomaly, anomalous — *continued*
  heart — *continued*
    valve — *continued*
      mitral 746.9
        atresia 746.89
        insufficiency 746.6
        specified type NEC 746.89
        stenosis 746.5
      pulmonary 746.00
        atresia 746.01
        insufficiency 746.09
        stenosis 746.02
          infundibular 746.83
          subvalvular 746.83
      tricuspid 746.9
        atresia 746.1
        stenosis 746.1
      ventricle 746.9
  heel 755.67
  Hegglin's 288.2
  hemianencephaly 740.0
  hemicephaly 740.0
  hemicrania 740.0
  hepatic duct 751.60
  hip (joint) 755.63
  hourglass
    bladder 753.8
    gallbladder 751.69
    stomach 750.7
  humerus 755.50
  hymen 752.40
  hypersegmentation of neutrophils, hereditary 288.2
  hypophyseal 759.2
  ileocecal (coil) (valve) 751.5
  ileum (intestine) 751.5
  ilium 755.60
  integument 757.9
    specified type NEC 757.8
  interarch distance (excessive) (inadequate) 524.28
  intervertebral cartilage or disc 756.10
  intestine (large) (small) 751.5
    fixational type 751.4
  iris 743.9
    specified type NEC 743.46
  ischium 755.60
  jaw NEC 524.9
    closure 524.51
    size (major) NEC 524.00
    specified type NEC 524.89
  jaw-cranial base relationship 524.10
    specified NEC 524.19
  jejunum 751.5
  joint 755.9
    hip
      dislocation (*see also* Dislocation, hip, congenital) 754.30
      predislocation (*see also* Subluxation, congenital, hip) 754.32
      preluxation (*see also* Subluxation, congenital, hip) 754.32
      subluxation (*see also* Subluxation, congenital, hip) 754.32
    lumbosacral 756.10
      spondylolisthesis 756.12
      spondylosis 756.11
    multiple arthrogryposis 754.89
    sacroiliac 755.69
  Jordan's 288.2
  kidney(s) (calyx) (pelvis) 753.9
    vessel 747.62
  Klippel-Feil (brevicollis) 756.16
  knee (joint) 755.64
  labium (majus) (minus) 752.40
  labyrinth, membranous (causing impairment of hearing) 744.05
  lacrimal
    apparatus, duct or passage 743.9
      specified type NEC 743.65
    gland 743.9
      specified type NEC 743.64
  Langdon Down (mongolism) 758.0
  larynx, laryngeal (muscle) 748.3
    web, webbed 748.2
  leg (lower) (upper) 755.60

Anomaly, anomalous — *continued*
  leg — *continued*
    reduction NEC (*see also* Deformity, reduction, lower limb) 755.30
  lens 743.9
    shape 743.36
    specified type NEC 743.39
  leukocytes, genetic 288.2
    granulation (constitutional) 288.2
  lid (fold) 743.9
  ligament 756.9
    broad 752.10
    round 752.9
  limb, except reduction deformity 755.9
    lower 755.60
      reduction deformity (*see also* Deformity, reduction, lower limb) 755.30
      specified type NEC 755.69
    upper 755.50
      reduction deformity (*see also* Deformity, reduction, upper limb) 755.20
      specified type NEC 755.59
  lip 750.9
    harelip (*see also* Cleft, lip) 749.10
    specified type NEC 750.26
  liver (duct) 751.60
    atresia 751.69
  lower extremity 755.60
    vessel 747.64
  lumbosacral (joint) (region) 756.10
  lung (fissure) (lobe) NEC 748.60
    agenesis 748.5
    specified type NEC 748.69
  lymphatic system 759.9
  Madelung's (radius) 755.54
  mandible 524.9
    size NEC 524.00
  maxilla 524.9
    size NEC 524.00
  May (-Hegglin) 288.2
  meatus urinarius 753.9
    specified type NEC 753.8
  meningeal bands or folds, constriction of 742.8
  meninges 742.9
    brain 742.4
    spinal 742.59
  meningocele (*see also* Spina bifida) 741.9 ☑
    acquired 349.2
  mesentery 751.9
  metacarpus 755.50
  metatarsus 755.67
  middle ear, except ossicles (causing impairment of hearing) 744.03
    ossicles 744.04
  mitral (leaflets) (valve) 746.9
    atresia 746.89
    insufficiency 746.6
    specified type NEC 746.89
    stenosis 746.5
  mouth 750.9
    specified type NEC 750.26
  multiple NEC 759.7
    specified type NEC 759.89
  muscle 756.9
    eye 743.9
      specified type NEC 743.69
    specified type NEC 756.89
  musculoskeletal system, except limbs 756.9
    specified type NEC 756.9
  nail 757.9
    specified type NEC 757.5
  narrowness, eyelid 743.62
  nasal sinus or septum 748.1
  neck (any part) 744.9
    specified type NEC 744.89
  nerve 742.9
    acoustic 742.9
      specified type NEC 742.8
    optic 742.9
      specified type NEC 742.8
    specified type NEC 742.8
  nervous system NEC 742.9
    brain 742.9
      specified type NEC 742.4

Anomaly, anomalous — *continued*
nervous system — *continued*
  specified type NEC 742.8
neurological 742.9
nipple 757.6
nonteratogenic NEC 754.89
nose, nasal (bone) (cartilage) (septum) (sinus) 748.1
ocular muscle 743.9
omphalomesenteric duct 751.0
opening, pulmonary veins 747.49
optic
  disc 743.9
    specified type NEC 743.57
  nerve 742.9
opticociliary vessels 743.9
orbit (eye) 743.9
  specified type NEC 743.66
organ
  of Corti (causing impairment of hearing) 744.05
  or site 759.9
    specified type NEC 759.89
origin
  both great arteries from same ventricle 745.11
  coronary artery 746.85
  innominate artery 747.69
  left coronary artery from pulmonary artery 746.85
  pulmonary artery 747.3
  renal vessels 747.62
  subclavian artery (left) (right) 747.21
osseous meatus (ear) 744.03
ovary 752.0
oviduct 752.10
palate (hard) (soft) 750.9
  cleft (*see also* Cleft, palate) 749.00
pancreas (duct) 751.7
papillary muscles 746.9
parathyroid gland 759.2
paraurethral ducts 753.9
parotid (gland) 750.9
patella 755.64
Pelger-Huët (hereditary hyposegmentation) 288.2
pelvic girdle 755.60
  specified type NEC 755.69
pelvis (bony) 755.60
  complicating delivery 653.0 ☑
  rachitic 268.1
    fetal 756.4
penis (glans) 752.69
pericardium 746.89
peripheral vascular system NEC 747.60
  gastrointestinal 747.61
  lower limb 747.64
  renal 747.62
  specified site NEC 747.69
  spinal 747.82
  upper limb 747.63
Peter's 743.44
pharynx 750.9
  branchial cleft 744.41
  specified type NEC 750.29
Pierre Robin 756.0
pigmentation 709.00
  congenital 757.33
  specified NEC 709.09
pituitary (gland) 759.2
pleural folds 748.8
portal vein 747.40
position tooth, teeth 524.30
  crowding 524.31
  displacement 524.30
    horizontal 524.33
    vertical 524.34
  distance
    interocclusal
      excessive 524.37
      insufficient 524.36
  excessive spacing 524.32
  rotation 524.35
  specified NEC 524.39
preauricular sinus 744.46
prepuce 752.9

Anomaly, anomalous — *continued*
prostate 752.9
pulmonary 748.60
  artery 747.3
  circulation 747.3
  specified type NEC 748.69
  valve 746.00
    atresia 746.01
    insufficiency 746.09
    specified type NEC 746.09
    stenosis 746.02
      infundibular 746.83
      subvalvular 746.83
  vein 747.40
  venous
    connection 747.49
      partial 747.42
      total 747.41
    return 747.49
      partial 747.42
      total (TAPVR) (complete) (subdiaphragmatic) (supradiaphragmatic) 747.41
pupil 743.9
pylorus 750.9
  hypertrophy 750.5
  stenosis 750.5
rachitic, fetal 756.4
radius 755.50
rectovaginal (septum) 752.40
rectum 751.5
refraction 367.9
renal 753.9
  vessel 747.62
respiratory system 748.9
  specified type NEC 748.8
rib 756.3
  cervical 756.2
Rieger's 743.44
rings, trachea 748.3
rotation (*see also* Malrotation)
  hip or thigh (*see also* Subluxation, congenital, hip) 754.32
round ligament 752.9
sacroiliac (joint) 755.69
sacrum 756.10
saddle
  back 754.2
  nose 754.0
    syphilitic 090.5
salivary gland or duct 750.9
  specified type NEC 750.26
scapula 755.50
sclera 743.9
  specified type NEC 743.47
scrotum 752.9
sebaceous gland 757.9
seminal duct or tract 752.9
sense organs 742.9
  specified type NEC 742.8
septum
  heart — *see* Anomaly, heart, septum
  nasal 748.1
sex chromosomes NEC (*see also* Anomaly, chromosomes) 758.81
shoulder (girdle) (joint) 755.50
  specified type NEC 755.59
sigmoid (flexure) 751.5
sinus of Valsalva 747.29
site NEC 759.9
skeleton generalized NEC 756.50
skin (appendage) 757.9
  specified type NEC 757.39
skull (bone) 756.0
  with
    anencephalus 740.0
    encephalocele 742.0
    hydrocephalus 742.3
      with spina bifida (*see also* Spina bifida) 741.0 ☑
    microcephalus 742.1
specified type NEC
  adrenal (gland) 759.1
  alimentary tract (complete) (partial) 751.8
    lower 751.5
    upper 750.8

Anomaly, anomalous — *continued*
specified type — *continued*
  ankle 755.69
  anus, anal (canal) 751.5
  aorta, aortic 747.29
    arch 747.21
  appendix 751.5
  arm 755.59
  artery (peripheral) NEC (*see also* Anomaly, peripheral vascular system) 747.60
    brain 747.81
    coronary 746.85
    eye 743.58
    pulmonary 747.3
    retinal 743.58
    umbilical 747.5
  auditory canal 744.29
    causing impairment of hearing 744.02
  bile duct or passage 751.69
  bladder 753.8
    neck 753.8
  bone(s) 756.9
    arm 755.59
    face 756.0
    leg 755.69
    pelvic girdle 755.69
    shoulder girdle 755.59
    skull 756.0
      with
        anencephalus 740.0
        encephalocele 742.0
        hydrocephalus 742.3
          with spina bifida (*see also* Spina bifida) 741.0 ☑
        microcephalus 742.1
  brain 742.4
  breast 757.6
  broad ligament 752.19
  bronchus 748.3
  canal of Nuck 752.89
  cardiac septal closure 745.8
  carpus 755.59
  cartilaginous 756.9
  cecum 751.5
  cervix 752.49
  chest (wall) 756.3
  chin 744.89
  ciliary body 743.46
  circulatory system 747.89
  clavicle 755.51
  clitoris 752.49
  coccyx 756.19
  colon 751.5
  common duct 751.69
  connective tissue 756.89
  cricoid cartilage 748.3
  cystic duct 751.69
  diaphragm 756.6
  digestive organ(s) or tract 751.8
    lower 751.5
    upper 750.8
  duodenum 751.5
  ear 744.29
    auricle 744.29
      causing impairment of hearing 744.02
    causing impairment of hearing 744.09
    inner (causing impairment of hearing) 744.05
    middle, except ossicles 744.03
      ossicles 744.04
  ejaculatory duct 752.89
  endocrine 759.2
  epiglottis 748.3
  esophagus 750.4
  Eustachian tube 744.24
  eye 743.8
    lid 743.63
    muscle 743.69
  face 744.89
    bone(s) 756.0
  fallopian tube 752.19
  fascia 756.89
  femur 755.69
  fibula 755.69

Anomaly, anomalous — *continued*
specified type — *continued*
  finger 755.59
  foot 755.67
  fovea centralis 743.55
  gallbladder 751.69
  Gartner's duct 752.89
  gastrointestinal tract 751.8
  genitalia, genital organ(s)
    female 752.89
      external 752.49
      internal NEC 752.89
    male 752.89
      penis 752.69
      scrotal transposition 752.81
  genitourinary tract NEC 752.89
  glottis 748.3
  hair 757.4
  hand 755.59
  heart 746.89
    valve NEC 746.89
      pulmonary 746.09
  hepatic duct 751.69
  hydatid of Morgagni 752.89
  hymen 752.49
  integument 757.8
  intestine (large) (small) 751.5
    fixational type 751.4
  iris 743.46
  jejunum 751.5
  joint 755.8
  kidney 753.3
  knee 755.64
  labium (majus) (minus) 752.49
  labyrinth, membranous 744.05
  larynx 748.3
  leg 755.69
  lens 743.39
  limb, except reduction deformity 755.8
    lower 755.69
      reduction deformity (*see also* Deformity, reduction, lower limb) 755.30
    upper 755.59
      reduction deformity (*see also* Deformity, reduction, upper limb) 755.20
  lip 750.26
  liver 751.69
  lung (fissure) (lobe) 748.69
  meatus urinarius 753.8
  metacarpus 755.59
  mouth 750.26
  muscle 756.89
    eye 743.69
  musculoskeletal system, except limbs 756.9
  nail 757.5
  neck 744.89
  nerve 742.8
    acoustic 742.8
    optic 742.8
  nervous system 742.8
  nipple 757.6
  nose 748.1
  organ NEC 759.89
    of Corti 744.05
  osseous meatus (ear) 744.03
  ovary 752.0
  oviduct 752.19
  pancreas 751.7
  parathyroid 759.2
  patella 755.64
  pelvic girdle 755.69
  penis 752.69
  pericardium 746.89
  peripheral vascular system NEC (*see also* Anomaly, peripheral vascular system) 747.60
  pharynx 750.29
  pituitary 759.2
  prostate 752.89
  radius 755.59
  rectum 751.5
  respiratory system 748.8
  rib 756.3

Anomaly, anomalous — *continued*
specified type — *continued*
round ligament 752.89
sacrum 756.19
salivary duct or gland 750.26
scapula 755.59
sclera 743.47
scrotum 752.89
transposition 752.81
seminal duct or tract 752.89
shoulder girdle 755.59
site NEC 759.89
skin 757.39
skull (bone(s)) 756.0
with
anencephalus 740.0
encephalocele 742.0
hydrocephalus 742.3
with spina bifida (*see also* Spina
bifida) 741.0 ☑
microcephalus 742.1
specified organ or site NEC 759.89
spermatic cord 752.89
spinal cord 742.59
spine 756.19
spleen 759.0
sternum 756.3
stomach 750.7
tarsus 755.67
tendon 756.89
testis 752.89
thorax (wall) 756.3
thymus 759.2
thyroid (gland) 759.2
cartilage 748.3
tibia 755.69
toe 755.66
tongue 750.19
trachea (cartilage) 748.3
ulna 755.59
urachus 753.7
ureter 753.4
obstructive 753.29
urethra 753.8
obstructive 753.6
urinary tract 753.8
uterus 752.3
uvula 750.26
vagina 752.49
vascular NEC (*see also* Anomaly, peripheral
vascular system) 747.60
brain 747.81
vas deferens 752.89
vein(s) (peripheral) NEC (*see also* Anomaly,
peripheral vascular system) 747.60
brain 747.81
great 747.49
portal 747.49
pulmonary 747.49
vena cava (inferior) (superior) 747.49
vertebra 756.19
vulva 752.49
spermatic cord 752.9
spine, spinal 756.10
column 756.10
cord 742.9
meningocele (*see also* Spina bifida)
741.9 ☑
specified type NEC 742.59
spina bifida (*see also* Spina bifida)
741.9 ☑
vessel 747.82
meninges 742.59
nerve root 742.9
spleen 759.0
Sprengel's 755.52
sternum 756.3
stomach 750.9
specified type NEC 750.7
submaxillary gland 750.9
superior vena cava 747.40
talipes — *see* Talipes
tarsus 755.67
with complete absence of distal elements
755.31
teeth, tooth NEC 520.9

Anomaly, anomalous — *continued*
teeth, tooth — *continued*
position 524.30
crowding 524.31
displacement 524.30
horizontal 524.33
vertical 524.34
distance
interocclusal
excessive 524.37
insufficient 524.36
excessive spacing 524.32
rotation 524.35
specified NEC 524.39
spacing 524.30
tendon 756.9
specified type NEC 756.89
termination
coronary artery 746.85
testis 752.9
thebesian valve 746.9
thigh 755.60
flexion (*see also* Subluxation, congenital,
hip) 754.32
thorax (wall) 756.3
throat 750.9
thumb 755.50
supernumerary 755.01
thymus gland 759.2
thyroid (gland) 759.2
cartilage 748.3
tibia 755.60
saber 090.5
toe 755.66
supernumerary 755.02
webbed (*see also* Syndactylism, toes)
755.13
tongue 750.10
specified type NEC 750.19
trachea, tracheal 748.3
cartilage 748.3
rings 748.3
tragus 744.3
transverse aortic arch 747.21
trichromata 368.59
trichromatopsia 368.59
tricuspid (leaflet) (valve) 746.9
atresia 746.1
Ebstein's 746.2
specified type NEC 746.89
stenosis 746.1
trunk 759.9
Uhl's (hypoplasia of myocardium, right ventricle) 746.84
ulna 755.50
umbilicus 759.9
artery 747.5
union, trachea with larynx 748.3
unspecified site 759.9
upper extremity 755.50
vessel 747.63
urachus 753.7
specified type NEC 753.7
ureter 753.9
obstructive 753.20
specified type NEC 753.4
obstructive 753.29
urethra (valve) 753.9
obstructive 753.6
specified type NEC 753.8
urinary tract or system (any part, except
urachus) 753.9
specified type NEC 753.8
urachus 753.7
uterus 752.3
with only one functioning horn 752.3
in pregnancy or childbirth 654.0 ☑
affecting fetus or newborn 763.89
causing obstructed labor 660.2 ☑
affecting fetus or newborn 763.1
uvula 750.9
vagina 752.40
valleculae 748.3
valve (heart) NEC 746.9
formation, ureter 753.29
pulmonary 746.00

Anomaly, anomalous — *continued*
valve — *continued*
specified type NEC 746.89
vascular NEC (*see also* Anomaly, peripheral
vascular system) 747.60
ring 747.21
vas deferens 752.9
vein(s) (peripheral) NEC (*see also* Anomaly,
peripheral vascular system) 747.60
brain 747.81
cerebral 747.81
coronary 746.89
great 747.40
specified type NEC 747.49
portal 747.40
pulmonary 747.40
retina 743.9
vena cava (inferior) (superior) 747.40
venous — *see* Anomaly, vein
venous return (pulmonary) 747.49
partial 747.42
total 747.41
ventricle, ventricular (heart) 746.9
bands 746.9
folds 746.9
septa 745.4
vertebra 756.10
vesicourethral orifice 753.9
vessels NEC (*see also* Anomaly, peripheral vascular system) 747.60
optic papilla 743.9
vitelline duct 751.0
vitreous humor 743.9
specified type NEC 743.51
vulva 752.40
wrist (joint) 755.50
Anomia 784.69
Anonychia 757.5
acquired 703.8
Anophthalmos, anophthalmus (clinical) (congenital) (globe) 743.00
acquired V45.78
Anopsia (altitudinal) (quadrant) 368.46
Anorchia 752.89
Anorchism, anorchidism 752.89
Anorexia 783.0
hysterical 300.11
nervosa 307.1
Anosmia — *see also* Disturbance, sensation 781.1
hysterical 300.11
postinfectional 478.9
psychogenic 306.7
traumatic 951.8
Anosognosia 780.99
Anosphrasia 781.1
Anosteoplasia 756.50
Anotia 744.09
Anovulatory cycle 628.0
Anoxemia 799.02
newborn 770.88
Anoxia 799.02
altitude 993.2
cerebral 348.1
with
abortion — *see* Abortion, by type, with
specified complication NEC
ectopic pregnancy (*see also* categories
633.0–633.9) 639.8
molar pregnancy (*see also* categories
630–632) 639.8
complicating
delivery (cesarean) (instrumental)
669.4 ☑
ectopic or molar pregnancy 639.8
obstetric anesthesia or sedation
668.2 ☑
during or resulting from a procedure
997.01
following
abortion 639.8
ectopic or molar pregnancy 639.8
newborn (*see also* Distress, fetal, liveborn
infant) 770.88
due to drowning 994.1
fetal, affecting newborn 770.88
heart — *see* Insufficiency, coronary

Anoxia — *continued*
high altitude 993.2
intrauterine
fetal death (before onset of labor) 768.0
during labor 768.1
liveborn infant — *see* Distress, fetal, liveborn infant
myocardial — *see* Insufficiency, coronary
newborn 768.9
mild or moderate 768.6
severe 768.5
pathological 799.02
Anteflexion — *see* Anteversion
Antenatal
care, normal pregnancy V22.1
first V22.0
sampling
chorionic villus V28.89
screening of mother (for) V28.9
based on amniocentesis NEC V28.2
chromosomal anomalies V28.0
raised alphafetoprotein levels V28.1
chromosomal anomalies V28.0
fetal growth retardation using ulatrasonics
V28.4
genomic V28.89
isoimmunization V28.5
malformations using ulatrasonics V28.3
proteomic V28.89
raised alphafetoprotein levels in amniotic
fluid V28.1
risk
pre-term labor V28.82
specified condition NEC V28.89
Streptococcus B V28.6
survey
fetal anatomic V28.81
testing
nuchal translucency V28.89
Antepartum — *see* condition
Anterior — *see also* condition
spinal artery compression syndrome 721.1
Antero-occlusion 524.24
Anteversion
cervix — *see* Anteversion, uterus
femur (neck), congenital 755.63
uterus, uterine (cervix) (postinfectional) (postpartal, old) 621.6
congenital 752.3
in pregnancy or childbirth 654.4 ☑
affecting fetus or newborn 763.89
causing obstructed labor 660.2 ☑
affecting fetus or newborn 763.1
Anthracosilicosis (occupational) 500
Anthracosis (lung) (occupational) 500
lingua 529.3
Anthrax 022.9
with pneumonia 022.1 [*484.5*]
colitis 022.2
cutaneous 022.0
gastrointestinal 022.2
intestinal 022.2
pulmonary 022.1
respiratory 022.1
septicemia 022.3
specified manifestation NEC 022.8
Anthropoid pelvis 755.69
with disproportion (fetopelvic) 653.2 ☑
affecting fetus or newborn 763.1
causing obstructed labor 660.1 ☑
affecting fetus or newborn 763.1
Anthropophobia 300.29
Antibioma, breast 611.0
Antibodies
maternal (blood group) (*see also* Incompatibility) 656.2 ☑
anti-D, cord blood 656.1 ☑
fetus or newborn 773.0
Antibody deficiency syndrome
agammaglobulinemic 279.00
congenital 279.04
hypogammaglobulinemic 279.00
Anticoagulant, ▶intrinsic,◀ circulating,
▶causing hemorrhagic disorder◀ —
see also Circulating anticoagulants 286.5
Antimongolism syndrome 758.39

Antimonial cholera 985.4
Antisocial personality 301.7
Antithrombinemia — *see also* Circulating anticoagulants 286.5
Antithromboplastinemia — *see also* Circulating anticoagulants 286.5
Antithromboplastinogenemia — *see also* Circulating anticoagulants 286.5
Antitoxin complication or reaction — *see* Complications, vaccination
Anton (-Babinski) syndrome (hemiasomatognosia) 307.9
Antritis (chronic) 473.0
  maxilla 473.0
    acute 461.0
  stomach 535.4 ☑
Antrum, antral — *see* condition
Anuria 788.5
  with
    abortion — *see* Abortion, by type, with renal failure
    ectopic pregnancy (*see also* categories 633.0–633.9) 639.3
    molar pregnancy (*see also* categories 630–632) 639.3
  calculus (impacted) (recurrent) 592.9
    kidney 592.0
    ureter 592.1
  congenital 753.3
  due to a procedure 997.5
  following
    abortion 639.3
    ectopic or molar pregnancy 639.3
  newborn 753.3
  postrenal 593.4
  puerperal, postpartum, childbirth 669.3 ☑
  specified as due to a procedure 997.5
  sulfonamide
    correct substance properly administered 788.5
    overdose or wrong substance given or taken 961.0
  traumatic (following crushing) 958.5
Anus, anal — *see also* condition
  high risk human papillomavirus (HPV) DNA test positive 796.75
  low risk human papillomavirus (HPV) DNA test positive 796.79
Anusitis 569.49
Anxiety (neurosis) (reaction) (state) 300.00
  alcohol-induced 291.89
  depression 300.4
  drug-induced 292.89
  due to or associated with physical condition 293.84
  generalized 300.02
  hysteria 300.20
  in
    acute stress reaction 308.0
    transient adjustment reaction 309.24
  panic type 300.01
  separation, abnormal 309.21
  syndrome (organic) (transient) 293.84
Aorta, aortic — *see* condition
Aortectasia 441.9
Aortitis (nonsyphilitic) 447.6
  arteriosclerotic 440.0
  calcific 447.6
  Döhle-Heller 093.1
  luetic 093.1
  rheumatic (*see also* Endocarditis, acute, rheumatic) 391.1
  rheumatoid — *see* Arthritis, rheumatoid
  specific 093.1
  syphilitic 093.1
    congenital 090.5
Apathetic 799.25 ▲
  thyroid storm (*see also* Thyrotoxicosis) 242.9 ☑ ●
Apathy 799.25 ●
Apepsia 536.8
  achlorhydric 536.0
  psychogenic 306.4
Aperistalsis, esophagus 530.0
Apert-Gallais syndrome (adrenogenital) 255.2
Apertognathia 524.20

Apert's syndrome (acrocephalosyndactyly) 755.55
Aphagia 787.20
  psychogenic 307.1
Aphakia (acquired) (bilateral) (postoperative) (unilateral) 379.31
  congenital 743.35
Aphalangia (congenital) 755.4
  lower limb (complete) (intercalary) (partial) (terminal) 755.39
    meaning all digits (complete) (partial) 755.31
    transverse 755.31
  upper limb (complete) (intercalary) (partial) (terminal) 755.29
    meaning all digits (complete) (partial) 755.21
    transverse 755.21
Aphasia (amnestic) (ataxic) (auditory) (Broca's) (choreatic) (classic) (expressive) (global) (ideational) (ideokinetic) (ideomotor) (jargon) (motor) (nominal) (receptive) (semantic) (sensory) (syntactic) (verbal) (visual) (Wernicke's) 784.3
  developmental 315.31
  syphilis, tertiary 094.89
  uremic — *see* Uremia
Aphemia 784.3
  uremic — *see* Uremia
Aphonia 784.41
  clericorum 784.49
  hysterical 300.11
  organic 784.41
  psychogenic 306.1
Aphthae, aphthous — *see also* condition
  Bednar's 528.2
  cachectic 529.0
  epizootic 078.4
  fever 078.4
  oral 528.2
  stomatitis 528.2
  thrush 112.0
  ulcer (oral) (recurrent) 528.2
    genital organ(s) NEC
      female 616.50
      male 608.89
    larynx 478.79
Apical — *see* condition
Apical ballooning syndrome 429.83
Aplasia — *see also* Agenesis
  alveolar process (acquired) 525.8
    congenital 750.26
  aorta (congenital) 747.22
  aortic valve (congenital) 746.89
  axialis extracorticalis (congenital) 330.0
  bone marrow (myeloid) 284.9
    acquired (secondary) 284.89
    congenital 284.01
    idiopathic 284.9
  brain 740.0
    specified part 742.2
  breast 757.6
  bronchus 748.3
  cementum 520.4
  cerebellar 742.2
  congenital (pure) red cell 284.01
  corpus callosum 742.2
  erythrocyte 284.81
    congenital 284.01
  extracortical axial 330.0
  eye (congenital) 743.00
  fovea centralis (congenital) 743.55
  germinal (cell) 606.0
  iris 743.45
  labyrinth, membranous 744.05
  limb (congenital) 755.4
    lower NEC 755.30
    upper NEC 755.20
  lung (bilateral) (congenital) (unilateral) 748.5
  nervous system NEC 742.8
  nuclear 742.8
  ovary 752.0
  Pelizaeus-Merzbacher 330.0
  prostate (congenital) 752.89
  red cell (with thymoma) (adult) 284.81
    acquired (secondary) 284.81

Aplasia — *see also* Agenesis — *continued*
  red cell — *continued*
    congenital 284.01
    hereditary 284.01
    of infants 284.01
    primary 284.01
    pure 284.01
  round ligament (congenital) 752.89
  salivary gland 750.21
  skin (congenital) 757.39
  spinal cord 742.59
  spleen 759.0
  testis (congenital) 752.89
  thymic, with immunodeficiency 279.2
  thyroid 243
  uterus 752.3
  ventral horn cell 742.59
Apleuria 756.3
Apnea, apneic (spells) 786.03
  newborn, neonatorum 770.81
    essential 770.81
    obstructive 770.82
    primary 770.81
    sleep 770.81
    specified NEC 770.82
  psychogenic 306.1
  sleep, unspecified 780.57
    with
      hypersomnia, unspecified 780.53
      hyposomnia, unspecified 780.51
      insomnia, unspecified 780.51
      sleep disturbance 780.57
    central, in conditions classified elsewhere 327.27
    obstructive (adult) (pediatric) 327.23
    organic 327.20
      other 327.29
    primary central 327.21
Apneumatosis newborn 770.4
Apodia 755.31
Aponeurosis 726.90
Apophysitis (bone) — *see also* Osteochondrosis 732.9
  calcaneus 732.5
  juvenile 732.6
Apoplectiform convulsions — *see also* Disease, cerebrovascular, acute 436
Apoplexia, apoplexy, apoplectic — *see also* Disease, cerebrovascular, acute 436
  abdominal 569.89
  adrenal 036.3
  attack 436
  basilar (*see also* Disease, cerebrovascular, acute) 436
  brain (*see also* Disease, cerebrovascular, acute) 436
  bulbar (*see also* Disease, cerebrovascular, acute) 436
  capillary (*see also* Disease, cerebrovascular, acute) 436
  cardiac (*see also* Infarct, myocardium) 410.9 ☑
  cerebral (*see also* Disease, cerebrovascular, acute) 436
  chorea (*see also* Disease, cerebrovascular, acute) 436
  congestive (*see also* Disease, cerebrovascular, acute) 436
    newborn 767.4
  embolic (*see also* Embolism, brain) 434.1 ☑
  fetus 767.0
  fit (*see also* Disease, cerebrovascular, acute) 436
  healed or old V12.54
  heart (auricle) (ventricle) (*see also* Infarct, myocardium) 410.9 ☑
  heat 992.0
  hemiplegia (*see also* Disease, cerebrovascular, acute) 436
  hemorrhagic (stroke) (*see also* Hemorrhage, brain) 432.9
  ingravescent (*see also* Disease, cerebrovascular, acute) 436
  late effect — *see* Late effect(s) (of) cerebrovascular disease
  lung — *see* Embolism, pulmonary

Apoplexia, apoplexy, apoplectic — *see also* Disease, cerebrovascular, acute — *continued*
  meninges, hemorrhagic (*see also* Hemorrhage, subarachnoid) 430
  neonatorum 767.0
  newborn 767.0
  pancreatitis 577.0
  placenta 641.2 ☑
  progressive (*see also* Disease, cerebrovascular, acute) 436
  pulmonary (artery) (vein) — *see* Embolism, pulmonary
  sanguineous (*see also* Disease, cerebrovascular, acute) 436
  seizure (*see also* Disease, cerebrovascular, acute) 436
  serous (*see also* Disease, cerebrovascular, acute) 436
  spleen 289.59
  stroke (*see also* Disease, cerebrovascular, acute) 436
  thrombotic (*see also* Thrombosis, brain) 434.0 ☑
  uremic — *see* Uremia
  uteroplacental 641.2 ☑
Appendage
  fallopian tube (cyst of Morgagni) 752.11
  intestine (epiploic) 751.5
  preauricular 744.1
  testicular (organ of Morgagni) 752.89
Appendicitis 541
  with
    perforation, peritonitis (generalized), or rupture 540.0
      with peritoneal abscess 540.1
    peritoneal abscess 540.1
  acute (catarrhal) (fulminating) (gangrenous) (inflammatory) (obstructive) (retrocecal) (suppurative) 540.9
    with
      perforation, peritonitis, or rupture 540.0
        with peritoneal abscess 540.1
      peritoneal abscess 540.1
  amebic 006.8
  chronic (recurrent) 542
  exacerbation — *see* Appendicitis, acute
  fulminating — *see* Appendicitis, acute
  gangrenous — *see* Appendicitis, acute
  healed (obliterative) 542
  interval 542
  neurogenic 542
  obstructive 542
  pneumococcal 541
  recurrent 542
  relapsing 542
  retrocecal 541
  subacute (adhesive) 542
  subsiding 542
  suppurative — *see* Appendicitis, acute
  tuberculous (*see also* Tuberculosis) 014.8 ☑
Appendiclausis 543.9
Appendicolithiasis 543.9
Appendicopathia oxyurica 127.4
Appendix, appendicular — *see also* condition
  Morgagni (male) 752.89
    fallopian tube 752.11
Appetite
  depraved 307.52
  excessive 783.6
    psychogenic 307.51
  lack or loss (*see also* Anorexia) 783.0
    nonorganic origin 307.59
  perverted 307.52
    hysterical 300.11
Apprehension, apprehensiveness (abnormal) (state) 300.00
  specified type NEC 300.09
Approximal wear 521.10
Apraxia (classic) (ideational) (ideokinetic) (ideomotor) (motor) 784.69
  oculomotor, congenital 379.51
  verbal 784.69
Aptyalism 527.7
Aqueous misdirection 365.83

☑ Additional Digit Required — Refer to the Tabular List for Digit Selection   Subterms under main terms may continue to next column or page

2010 ICD-9-CM   ▶◀ Revised Text   ● New Line   ▲ Revised Code   **October 2009 · Volume 2 — 25**

Antimonial cholera — Aqueous misdirection

Arabicum elephantiasis — Arthralgia

Index

Arabicum elephantiasis — *see also* Infestation, filarial 125.9
Arachnidism 989.5
Arachnitis — *see* Meningitis
Arachnodactyly 759.82
Arachnoidism 989.5
Arachnoiditis (acute) (adhesive) (basic) (brain) (cerebrospinal) (chiasmal) (chronic) (spinal) — *see also* Meningitis 322.9
　meningococcal (chronic) 036.0
　syphilitic 094.2
　tuberculous (*see also* Tuberculosis, meninges) 013.0 ☑
Araneism 989.5
Arboencephalitis, Australian 062.4
Arborization block (heart) 426.6
Arbor virus, arbovirus (infection) NEC 066.9
ARC 042
Arches — *see* condition
Arcuatus uterus 752.3
Arcus (cornea)
　juvenilis 743.43
　　interfering with vision 743.42
　senilis 371.41
Arc-welders' lung 503
Arc-welders' syndrome (photokeratitis) 370.24
Areflexia 796.1
Areola — *see* condition
Argentaffinoma (M8241/1) — *see also* Neoplasm, by site, uncertain behavior
　benign (M8241/0) — *see* Neoplasm, by site, benign
　malignant (M8241/3) — *see* Neoplasm, by site, malignant
　syndrome 259.2
Argentinian hemorrhagic fever 078.7
Arginosuccinicaciduria 270.6
Argonz-Del Castillo syndrome (nonpuerperal galactorrhea and amenorrhea) 253.1
Argyll-Robertson phenomenon, pupil, or syndrome (syphilitic) 094.89
　atypical 379.45
　nonluetic 379.45
　nonsyphilitic 379.45
　reversed 379.45
Argyria, argyriasis NEC 985.8
　conjunctiva 372.55
　cornea 371.16
　from drug or medicinal agent
　　correct substance properly administered 709.09
　　overdose or wrong substance given or taken 961.2
Arhinencephaly 742.2
Arias-Stella phenomenon 621.30
Ariboflavinosis 266.0
Arizona enteritis 008.1
Arm — *see* condition
Armenian disease 277.31
Arnold-Chiari obstruction or syndrome — *see also* Spina bifida 741.0 ☑
　type I 348.4
　type II (*see also* Spina bifida) 741.0 ☑
　type III 742.0
　type IV 742.2
Arousals
　confusional 327.41
Arrest, arrested
　active phase of labor 661.1 ☑
　　affecting fetus or newborn 763.7
　any plane in pelvis
　　complicating delivery 660.1 ☑
　　　affecting fetus or newborn 763.1
　bone marrow (*see also* Anemia, aplastic) 284.9
　cardiac 427.5
　　with
　　　abortion — *see* Abortion, by type, with specified complication NEC
　　　ectopic pregnancy (*see also* categories 633.0–633.9) 639.8
　　　molar pregnancy (*see also* categories 630–632) 639.8
　　complicating
　　　anesthesia
　　　　correct substance properly administered 427.5

Arrest, arrested — *continued*
　cardiac — *continued*
　　complicating — *continued*
　　　anesthesia — *continued*
　　　　obstetric 668.1 ☑
　　　　overdose or wrong substance given 968.4
　　　　specified anesthetic — *see* Table of Drugs and Chemicals
　　　delivery (cesarean) (instrumental) 669.4 ☑
　　　ectopic or molar pregnancy 639.8
　　　surgery (nontherapeutic) (therapeutic) 997.1
　　fetus or newborn 779.85
　　following
　　　abortion 639.8
　　　ectopic or molar pregnancy 639.8
　　personal history, successfully resuscitated V12.53
　　postoperative (immediate) 997.1
　　　long-term effect of cardiac surgery 429.4
　cardiorespiratory (*see also* Arrest, cardiac) 427.5
　deep transverse 660.3 ☑
　　affecting fetus or newborn 763.1
　development or growth
　　bone 733.91
　　child 783.40
　　fetus 764.9 ☑
　　　affecting management of pregnancy 656.5 ☑
　　tracheal rings 748.3
　epiphyseal 733.91
　granulopoiesis 288.09
　heart — *see* Arrest, cardiac
　respiratory 799.1
　　newborn 770.87
　sinus 426.6
　transverse (deep) 660.3 ☑
　　affecting fetus or newborn 763.1
Arrhenoblastoma (M8630/1)
　benign (M8630/0)
　　specified site — *see* Neoplasm, by site, benign
　　unspecified site
　　　female 220
　　　male 222.0
　malignant (M8630/3)
　　specified site — *see* Neoplasm, by site, malignant
　　unspecified site
　　　female 183.0
　　　male 186.9
　specified site — *see* Neoplasm, by site, uncertain behavior
　unspecified site
　　female 236.2
　　male 236.4
Arrhinencephaly 742.2
　due to
　　trisomy 13 (13-15) 758.1
　　trisomy 18 (16-18) 758.2
Arrhythmia (auricle) (cardiac) (cordis) (gallop rhythm) (juvenile) (nodal) (reflex) (sinus) (supraventricular) (transitory) (ventricle) 427.9
　bigeminal rhythm 427.89
　block 426.9
　bradycardia 427.89
　contractions, premature 427.60
　coronary sinus 427.89
　ectopic 427.89
　extrasystolic 427.60
　postoperative 997.1
　psychogenic 306.2
　vagal 780.2
Arrillaga-Ayerza syndrome (pulmonary artery sclerosis with pulmonary hypertension) 416.0
Arsenical
　dermatitis 692.4
　keratosis 692.4
　pigmentation 985.1

Arsenical — *continued*
　pigmentation — *continued*
　　from drug or medicinal agent
　　　correct substance properly administered 709.09
　　　overdose or wrong substance given or taken 961.1
Arsenism 985.1
　from drug or medicinal agent
　　correct substance properly administered 692.4
　　overdose or wrong substance given or taken 961.1
Arterial — *see* condition
Arteriectasis 447.8
Arteriofibrosis — *see* Arteriosclerosis
Arteriolar sclerosis — *see* Arteriosclerosis
Arteriolith — *see* Arteriosclerosis
Arteriolitis 447.6
　necrotizing, kidney 447.5
　renal — *see* Hypertension, kidney
Arteriolosclerosis — *see* Arteriosclerosis
Arterionephrosclerosis — *see also* Hypertension, kidney 403.90
Arteriopathy 447.9
Arteriosclerosis, arteriosclerotic (artery) (deformans) (diffuse) (disease) (endarteritis) (general) (obliterans) (obliterative) (occlusive) (senile) (with calcification) 440.9
　with
　　gangrene 440.24
　　psychosis (*see also* Psychosis, arteriosclerotic) 290.40
　　ulceration 440.23
　aorta 440.0
　arteries of extremities — *see* Arteriosclerosis, extremities
　basilar (artery) (*see also* Occlusion, artery, basilar) 433.0 ☑
　brain 437.0
　bypass graft
　　coronary artery 414.05
　　　autologous artery (gastroepiploic) (internal mammary) 414.04
　　　autologous vein 414.02
　　　nonautologous biological 414.03
　　　of transplanted heart 414.07
　　extremity 440.30
　　　autologous vein 440.31
　　　nonautologous biological 440.32
　cardiac — *see* Arteriosclerosis, coronary
　cardiopathy — *see* Arteriosclerosis, coronary
　cardiorenal (*see also* Hypertension, cardiorenal) 404.90
　cardiovascular (*see also* Disease, cardiovascular) 429.2
　carotid (artery) (common) (internal) (*see also* Occlusion, artery, carotid) 433.1 ☑
　central nervous system 437.0
　cerebral 437.0
　　late effect — *see* Late effect(s) (of) cerebrovascular disease
　cerebrospinal 437.0
　cerebrovascular 437.0
　coronary (artery) 414.00
　　due to lipid rich plaque 414.3
　　graft — *see* Arteriosclerosis, bypass graft
　　native artery 414.01
　　　of transplanted heart 414.06
　extremities (native artery) NEC 440.20
　　bypass graft 440.30
　　　autologous vein 440.31
　　　nonautologous biological 440.32
　　claudication (intermittent) 440.21
　　　and
　　　　gangrene 440.24
　　　　rest pain 440.22
　　　　　and
　　　　　　gangrene 440.24
　　　　　　ulceration 440.23
　　　　　　　and gangrene 440.24
　　　ulceration 440.23
　　　　and gangrene 440.24
　　gangrene 440.24
　　rest pain 440.22

Arteriosclerosis, arteriosclerotic — *continued*
　extremities — *continued*
　　rest pain — *continued*
　　　and
　　　　gangrene 440.24
　　　　ulceration 440.23
　　　　　and gangrene 440.24
　　specified site NEC 440.29
　　ulceration 440.23
　　　and gangrene 440.24
　heart (disease) (*see also* Arteriosclerosis, coronary)
　　valve 424.99
　　　aortic 424.1
　　　mitral 424.0
　　　pulmonary 424.3
　　　tricuspid 424.2
　kidney (*see also* Hypertension, kidney) 403.90
　labyrinth, labyrinthine 388.00
　medial NEC (*see also* Arteriosclerosis, extremities) 440.20
　mesentery (artery) 557.1
　Mönckeberg's (*see also* Arteriosclerosis, extremities) 440.20
　myocarditis 429.0
　nephrosclerosis (*see also* Hypertension, kidney) 403.90
　peripheral (of extremities) — *see* Arteriosclerosis, extremities
　precerebral 433.9 ☑
　　specified artery NEC 433.8 ☑
　pulmonary (idiopathic) 416.0
　renal (*see also* Hypertension, kidney) 403.90
　　arterioles (*see also* Hypertension, kidney) 403.90
　　artery 440.1
　retinal (vascular) 440.8 *[362.13]*
　specified artery NEC 440.8
　　with gangrene 440.8 *[785.4]*
　spinal (cord) 437.0
　vertebral (artery) (*see also* Occlusion, artery, vertebral) 433.2 ☑
Arteriospasm 443.9
Arteriovenous — *see* condition
Arteritis 447.6
　allergic (*see also* Angiitis, hypersensitivity) 446.20
　aorta (nonsyphilitic) 447.6
　　syphilitic 093.1
　aortic arch 446.7
　brachiocephalica 446.7
　brain 437.4
　　syphilitic 094.89
　branchial 446.7
　cerebral 437.4
　　late effect — *see* Late effect(s) (of) cerebrovascular disease
　　syphilitic 094.89
　coronary (artery) (*see also* Arteriosclerosis, coronary)
　　rheumatic 391.9
　　　chronic 398.99
　　syphilitic 093.89
　cranial (left) (right) 446.5
　deformans — *see* Arteriosclerosis
　giant cell 446.5
　necrosing or necrotizing 446.0
　nodosa 446.0
　obliterans (*see also* Arteriosclerosis)
　　subclaviocarotica 446.7
　pulmonary 417.8
　retina 362.18
　rheumatic — *see* Fever, rheumatic
　senile — *see* Arteriosclerosis
　suppurative 447.2
　syphilitic (general) 093.89
　　brain 094.89
　　coronary 093.89
　　spinal 094.89
　temporal 446.5
　young female, syndrome 446.7
Artery, arterial — *see* condition
Arthralgia (*see also* Pain, joint) 719.4 ☑
　allergic (*see also* Pain, joint) 719.4 ☑
　in caisson disease 993.3

☑ Additional Digit Required — Refer to the Tabular List for Digit Selection　　　　　　　　　　　　　　　　　　　〽 Subterms under main terms may continue to next column or page

26 — Volume 2　　　　　▶◀ Revised Text　　　　● New Line　　　▲ Revised Code　　　　　　**2010 ICD-9-CM**

Arthralgia — *see also* Pain, joint — *continued*
psychogenic 307.89
rubella 056.71
Salmonella 003.23
temporomandibular joint 524.62
Arthritis, arthritic (acute) (chronic) (subacute)
716.9 ☑
meaning Osteoarthritis — *see* Osteoarthrosis

Note — Use the following fifth-digit subclassification with categories 711–712, 715–716:

0   *site unspecified*
1   *shoulder region*
2   *upper arm*
3   *forearm*
4   *hand*
5   *pelvic region and thigh*
6   *lower leg*
7   *ankle and foot*
8   *other specified sites*
9   *multiple sites*

allergic 716.2 ☑
ankylosing (crippling) (spine) 720.0
sites other than spine 716.9 ☑
atrophic 714.0
spine 720.9
back (*see also* Arthritis, spine) 721.90
Bechterew's (ankylosing spondylitis) 720.0
blennorrhagic 098.50
cervical, cervicodorsal (*see also* Spondylosis, cervical) 721.0
Charcôt's 094.0 [713.5]
diabetic 250.6 ☑ [713.5]
due to secondary diabetes
249.6 ☑ [713.5]
syringomyelic 336.0 [713.5]
tabetic 094.0 [713.5]
chylous (*see also* Filariasis) 125.9 [711.7] ☑
climacteric NEC 716.3 ☑
coccyx 721.8
cricoarytenoid 478.79
crystal (-induced) — *see* Arthritis, due to crystals
deformans (*see also* Osteoarthrosis) 715.9 ☑
spine 721.90
with myelopathy 721.91
degenerative (*see also* Osteoarthrosis) 715.9 ☑
idiopathic 715.09
polyarticular 715.09
spine 721.90
with myelopathy 721.91
dermatoarthritis, lipoid 272.8 [713.0]
due to or associated with
acromegaly 253.0 [713.0]
actinomycosis 039.8 [711.4] ☑
amyloidosis 277.39 [713.7]
bacterial disease NEC 040.89 [711.4] ☑
Behçet's syndrome 136.1 [711.2] ☑
blastomycosis 116.0 [711.6] ☑
brucellosis (*see also* Brucellosis)
023.9 [711.4] ☑
caisson disease 993.3
coccidioidomycosis 114.3 [711.6] ☑
coliform (Escherichia coli) 711.0 ☑
colitis, ulcerative (*see also* Colitis, ulcerative)
556.9 [713.1]
cowpox 051.01 [711.5] ☑
crystals (*see also* Gout)
dicalcium phosphate 275.49 [712.1] ☑
pyrophosphate 275.49 [712.2] ☑
specified NEC 275.49 [712.8] ☑
dermatoarthritis, lipoid 272.8 [713.0]
dermatological disorder NEC 709.9 [713.3]
diabetes 250.6 ☑ [713.5]
due to secondary diabetes
249.6 ☑ [713.5]
diphtheria 032.89 [711.4] ☑
dracontiasis 125.7 [711.7] ☑
dysentery 009.0 [711.3] ☑
endocrine disorder NEC 259.9 [713.0]
enteritis NEC 009.1 [711.3] ☑

Arthritis, arthritic — *continued*
due to or associated with — *continued*
enteritis — *continued*
infectious (*see also* Enteritis, infectious)
009.0 [711.3] ☑
specified organism NEC
008.8 [711.3] ☑
regional (*see also* Enteritis, regional)
555.9 [713.1]
specified organism NEC
008.8 [711.3] ☑
epiphyseal slip, nontraumatic (old)
716.8 ☑
erysipelas 035 [711.4] ☑
erythema
epidemic 026.1
multiforme 695.10 [713.3]
nodosum 695.2 [713.3]
Escherichia coli 711.0 ☑
filariasis NEC 125.9 [711.7] ☑
gastrointestinal condition NEC
569.9 [713.1]
glanders 024 [711.4] ☑
Gonococcus 098.50
gout 274.00   ▲
helminthiasis NEC 128.9 [711.7] ☑
hematological disorder NEC 289.9 [713.2]
hemochromatosis 275.0 [713.0]
hemoglobinopathy NEC (*see also* Disease, hemoglobin) 282.7 [713.2]
hemophilia (*see also* Hemophilia)
286.0 [713.2]
Hemophilus influenzae (H. influenzae)
711.0 ☑
Henoch (-Schönlein) purpura 287.0 [713.6]
H. influenzae 711.0 ☑
histoplasmosis NEC (*see also* Histoplasmosis) 115.99 [711.6] ☑
human parvovirus 079.83 [711.5] ☑
hyperparathyroidism 252.00 [713.0]
hypersensitivity reaction NEC 995.3 [713.6]
hypogammaglobulinemia (*see also* Hypogamma-globulinemia)
279.00 [713.0]
hypothyroidism NEC 244.9 [713.0]
infection (*see also* Arthritis, infectious)
711.9 ☑
infectious disease NEC 136.9 [711.8] ☑
leprosy (*see also* Leprosy) 030.9 [711.4] ☑
leukemia NEC (M9800/3) 208.9 [713.2]
lipoid dermatoarthritis 272.8 [713.0]
Lyme disease 088.81 [711.8] ☑
Mediterranean fever, familial 277.31 [713.7]
meningococcal infection 036.82
metabolic disorder NEC 277.9 [713.0]
multiple myelomatosis (M9730/3) 203.0
[713.2]
mumps 072.79 [711.5] ☑
mycobacteria 031.8 [711.4] ☑
mycosis NEC 117.9 [711.6] ☑
neurological disorder NEC 349.9 [713.5]
ochronosis 270.2 [713.0]
O'Nyong Nyong 066.3 [711.5] ☑
parasitic disease NEC 136.9 [711.8] ☑
paratyphoid fever (*see also* Fever, paratyphoid) 002.9 [711.3] ☑
parvovirus B19 079.83 [711.5] ☑
Pneumococcus 711.0 ☑
poliomyelitis (*see also* Poliomyelitis)
045.9 [711.5] ☑
Pseudomonas 711.0 ☑
psoriasis 696.0
pyogenic organism (E. coli) (H. influenzae)
(Pseudomonas) (Streptococcus)
711.0 ☑
rat-bite fever 026.1 [711.4] ☑
regional enteritis (*see also* Enteritis, regional) 555.9 [713.1]
Reiter's disease 099.3 [711.1] ☑
respiratory disorder NEC 519.9 [713.4]
reticulosis, malignant (M9720/3) 202.3
[713.2]
rubella 056.71
salmonellosis 003.23
sarcoidosis 135 [713.7]

Arthritis, arthritic — *continued*
due to or associated with — *continued*
serum sickness 999.5 [713.6]
Staphylococcus 711.0 ☑
Streptococcus 711.0 ☑
syphilis (*see also* Syphilis) 094.0 [711.4] ☑
syringomyelia 336.0 [713.5]
thalassemia 282.49 [713.2]
tuberculosis (*see also* Tuberculosis, arthritis)
015.9 ☑ [711.4] ☑
typhoid fever 002.0 [711.3] ☑
ulcerative colitis (*see also* Colitis, ulcerative)
556.9 [713.1]
urethritis
nongonococcal (*see also* Urethritis, nongonococcal)
099.40 [711.1] ☑
nonspecific (*see also* Urethritis, nongonococcal) 099.40 [711.1] ☑
Reiter's 099.3
viral disease NEC 079.99 [711.5] ☑
erythema epidemic 026.1
gonococcal 098.50
gouty 274.00   ▲
acute 274.01   ●
hypertrophic (*see also* Osteoarthrosis) 715.9 ☑
spine 721.90
with myelopathy 721.91
idiopathic, blennorrheal 099.3
in caisson disease 993.3 [713.8]
infectious or infective (acute) (chronic) (subacute) NEC 711.9 ☑
nonpyogenic 711.9 ☑
spine 720.9
inflammatory NEC 714.9
juvenile rheumatoid (chronic) (polyarticular)
714.30
acute 714.31
monoarticular 714.33
pauciarticular 714.32
lumbar (*see also* Spondylosis, lumbar) 721.3
meningococcal 036.82
menopausal NEC 716.3 ☑
migratory — *see* Fever, rheumatic
neuropathic (Charcôt's) 094.0 [713.5]
diabetic 250.6 ☑ [713.5]
due to secondary diabetes
249.6 ☑ [713.5]
nonsyphilitic NEC 349.9 [713.5]
syringomyelic 336.0 [713.5]
tabetic 094.0 [713.5]
nodosa (*see also* Osteoarthrosis) 715.9 ☑
spine 721.90
with myelopathy 721.91
nonpyogenic NEC 716.9 ☑
spine 721.90
with myelopathy 721.91
ochronotic 270.2 [713.0]
palindromic (see also Rheumatism, palindromic) 719.3 ☑
pneumococcal 711.0 ☑
postdysenteric 009.0 [711.3] ☑
postrheumatic, chronic (Jaccoud's) 714.4
primary progressive 714.0
spine 720.9
proliferative 714.0
spine 720.0
psoriatic 696.0
purulent 711.0 ☑
pyogenic or pyemic 711.0 ☑
rheumatic 714.0
acute or subacute — *see* Fever, rheumatic
chronic 714.0
spine 720.9
rheumatoid (nodular) 714.0
with
splenoadenomegaly and leukopenia
714.1
visceral or systemic involvement 714.2
aortitis 714.89
carditis 714.2
heart disease 714.2
juvenile (chronic) (polyarticular) 714.30
acute 714.31
monoarticular 714.33
pauciarticular 714.32

Arthritis, arthritic — *continued*
rheumatoid — *continued*
spine 720.0
rubella 056.71
sacral, sacroiliac, sacrococcygeal (*see also* Spondylosis, sacral) 721.3
scorbutic 267
senile or senescent (*see also* Osteoarthrosis)
715.9 ☑
spine 721.90
with myelopathy 721.91
septic 711.0 ☑
serum (nontherapeutic) (therapeutic)
999.5 [713.6]
specified form NEC 716.8 ☑
spine 721.90
with myelopathy 721.91
atrophic 720.9
degenerative 721.90
with myelopathy 721.91
hypertrophic (with deformity) 721.90
with myelopathy 721.91
infectious or infective NEC 720.9
Marie-Strümpell 720.0
nonpyogenic 721.90
with myelopathy 721.91
pyogenic 720.9
rheumatoid 720.0
traumatic (old) 721.7
tuberculous (*see also* Tuberculosis)
015.0 ☑ [720.81]
staphylococcal 711.0 ☑
streptococcal 711.0 ☑
suppurative 711.0 ☑
syphilitic 094.0 [713.5]
congenital 090.49 [713.5]
syphilitica deformans (Charcôt) 094.0 [713.5]
temporomandibular joint 524.69
thoracic (*see also* Spondylosis, thoracic) 721.2
toxic of menopause 716.3 ☑
transient 716.4 ☑
traumatic (chronic) (old) (post) 716.1 ☑
current injury — *see* nature of injury
tuberculous (*see also* Tuberculosis, arthritis)
015.9 ☑ [711.4] ☑
urethritica 099.3 [711.1] ☑
urica, uratic 274.00   ▲
venereal 099.3 [711.1] ☑
vertebral (*see also* Arthritis, spine) 721.90
villous 716.8 ☑
von Bechterew's 720.0
Arthrocele — *see also* Effusion, joint 719.0 ☑
Arthrochondritis — *see* Arthritis
Arthrodesis status V45.4
Arthrodynia — *see also* Pain, joint 719.4 ☑
psychogenic 307.89
Arthrodysplasia 755.9
Arthrofibrosis joint — *see also* Ankylosis
718.5 ☑
Arthrogryposis 728.3
multiplex, congenita 754.89
Arthrokatadysis 715.35
Arthrolithiasis 274.00   ▲
Arthro-onychodysplasia 756.89
Arthro-osteo-onychodysplasia 756.89
Arthropathy — *see also* Arthritis 716.9 ☑

Note — Use the following fifth-digit subclassification with categories 711–712, 716:

0   *site unspecified*
1   *shoulder region*
2   *upper arm*
3   *forearm*
4   *hand*
5   *pelvic region and thigh*
6   *lower leg*
7   *ankle and foot*
8   *other specified sites*
9   *multiple sites*

Behçet's 136.1 [711.2] ☑
Charcôt's 094.0 [713.5]

☑ Additional Digit Required — Refer to the Tabular List for Digit Selection   ▽ Subterms under main terms may continue to next column or page

Arthropathy — *see also* Arthritis — *continued*
  Charcôt's — *continued*
    diabetic 250.6 ☑ *[713.5]*
      due to secondary diabetes 249.6 ☑ *[713.5]*
    syringomyelic 336.0 *[713.5]*
    tabetic 094.0 *[713.5]*
  crystal (-induced) — *see* Arthritis, due to crystals
  gouty 274.00 ▲
    acute 274.01 ●
    chronic (without mention of tophus (tophi)) 274.02 ●
      with tophus (tophi) 274.03 ●
  neurogenic, neuropathic (Charcôt's) (tabetic) 094.0 *[713.5]*
    diabetic 250.6 ☑ *[713.5]*
      due to secondary diabetes 249.6 ☑ *[713.5]*
    nonsyphilitic NEC 349.9 *[713.5]*
    syringomyelic 336.0 *[713.5]*
  postdysenteric NEC 009.0 *[711.3]* ☑
  postrheumatic, chronic (Jaccoud's) 714.4
  psoriatic 696.0
  pulmonary 731.2
  specified NEC 716.8 ☑
  syringomyelia 336.0 *[713.5]*
  tabes dorsalis 094.0 *[713.5]*
  tabetic 094.0 *[713.5]*
  transient 716.4 ☑
  traumatic 716.1 ☑
  uric acid 274.00 ▲
Arthrophyte — *see also* Loose, body, joint 718.1 ☑
Arthrophytis 719.80
  ankle 719.87
  elbow 719.82
  foot 719.87
  hand 719.84
  hip 719.85
  knee 719.86
  multiple sites 719.89
  pelvic region 719.85
  shoulder (region) 719.81
  specified site NEC 719.88
  wrist 719.83
Arthropyosis — *see also* Arthritis, pyogenic 711.0 ☑
Arthroscopic surgical procedure converted to open procedure V64.43
Arthrosis (deformans) (degenerative) — *see also* Osteoarthrosis 715.9 ☑
  Charcôt's 094.0 *[713.5]*
  polyarticular 715.09
  spine (*see also* Spondylosis) 721.90
Arthus phenomenon 995.21
  due to
    correct substance properly administered 995.21
    overdose or wrong substance given or taken 977.9
      specified drug — *see* Table of Drugs and Chemicals
    serum 999.5
Articular — *see also* condition
  disc disorder (reducing or non-reducing) 524.63
  spondylolisthesis 756.12
Articulation
  anterior 524.27
  posterior 524.27
  reverse 524.27
Artificial
  device (prosthetic) — *see* Fitting, device
  insemination V26.1
  menopause (states) (symptoms) (syndrome) 627.4
  opening status (functioning) (without complication) V44.9
    anus (colostomy) V44.3
    colostomy V44.3
    cystostomy V44.50
      appendico-vesicostomy V44.52
      cutaneous-vesicostomy V44.51
      specified type NEC V44.59

Artificial — *continued*
  opening status — *continued*
    enterostomy V44.4
    gastrostomy V44.1
    ileostomy V44.2
    intestinal tract NEC V44.4
    jejunostomy V44.4
    nephrostomy V44.6
    specified site NEC V44.8
    tracheostomy V44.0
    ureterostomy V44.6
    urethrostomy V44.6
    urinary tract NEC V44.6
    vagina V44.7
  vagina status V44.7
ARV (disease) (illness) (infection) — *see* Human immunodeficiency virus (disease) (illness) (infection)
Arytenoid — *see* condition
Asbestosis (occupational) 501
Asboe-Hansen's disease (incontinentia pigmenti) 757.33
Ascariasis (intestinal) (lung) 127.0
Ascaridiasis 127.0
Ascaridosis 127.0
Ascaris 127.0
  lumbricoides (infestation) 127.0
  pneumonia 127.0
Ascending — *see* condition
ASC-H (atypical squamous cells cannot exclude high grade squamous intraepithelial lesion)
  anus 796.72
  cervix 795.02
  vagina 795.12
Aschoff's bodies — *see also* Myocarditis, rheumatic 398.0
Ascites 789.59
  abdominal NEC 789.59
  cancerous (M8000/6) 789.51
  cardiac 428.0
  chylous (nonfilarial) 457.8
    filarial (*see also* Infestation, filarial) 125.9
  congenital 778.0
  due to S. japonicum 120.2
  fetal, causing fetopelvic disproportion 653.7 ☑
  heart 428.0
  joint (*see also* Effusion, joint) 719.0 ☑
  malignant (M8000/6) 789.51
  pseudochylous 789.59
  syphilitic 095.2
  tuberculous (*see also* Tuberculosis) 014.0 ☑
Ascorbic acid (vitamin C) **deficiency** (scurvy) 267
ASC-US (atypical squamous cells of undetermined significance)
  anus 796.71
  cervix 795.01
  vagina 795.11
ASCVD (arteriosclerotic cardiovascular disease) 429.2
Aseptic — *see* condition
Asherman's syndrome 621.5
Asialia 527.7
Asiatic cholera — *see also* Cholera 001.9
Asocial personality or trends 301.7
Asomatognosia 781.8
Aspergillosis 117.3
  with pneumonia 117.3 *[484.6]*
  allergic bronchopulmonary 518.6
  nonsyphilitic NEC 117.3
Aspergillus (flavus) (fumigatus) (infection) (terreus) 117.3
Aspermatogenesis 606.0
Aspermia (testis) 606.0
Asphyxia, asphyxiation (by) 799.01
  antenatal — *see* Distress, fetal
  bedclothes 994.7
  birth (*see also* Asphyxia, newborn) 768.9
  bunny bag 994.7
  carbon monoxide 986
  caul (*see also* Asphyxia, newborn) 768.9
  cave-in 994.7
    crushing — *see* Injury, internal, intrathoracic organs
  constriction 994.7

Asphyxia, asphyxiation — *continued*
  crushing — *see* Injury, internal, intrathoracic organs
  drowning 994.1
  fetal, affecting newborn 768.9
  food or foreign body (in larynx) 933.1
    bronchioles 934.8
    bronchus (main) 934.1
    lung 934.8
    nasopharynx 933.0
    nose, nasal passages 932
    pharynx 933.0
    respiratory tract 934.9
      specified part NEC 934.8
    throat 933.0
    trachea 934.0
  gas, fumes, or vapor NEC 987.9
    specified — *see* Table of Drugs and Chemicals
  gravitational changes 994.7
  hanging 994.7
  inhalation — *see* Inhalation
  intrauterine
    fetal death (before onset of labor) 768.0
      during labor 768.1
    liveborn infant — *see* Distress, fetal, liveborn infant
  local 443.0
  mechanical 994.7
    during birth (*see also* Distress, fetal) 768.9
  mucus 933.1
    bronchus (main) 934.1
    larynx 933.1
    lung 934.8
    nasal passages 932
    newborn 770.18
    pharynx 933.0
    respiratory tract 934.9
      specified part NEC 934.8
    throat 933.0
    trachea 934.0
    vaginal (fetus or newborn) 770.18
  newborn 768.9
    with neurologic involvement 768.5
    blue 768.6
    livida 768.6
    mild or moderate 768.6
    pallida 768.5
    severe 768.5
    white 768.5
  pathological 799.01
  plastic bag 994.7
  postnatal (*see also* Asphyxia, newborn) 768.9
    mechanical 994.7
  pressure 994.7
  reticularis 782.61
  strangulation 994.7
  submersion 994.1
  traumatic NEC — *see* Injury, internal, intrathoracic organs
  vomiting, vomitus — *see* Asphyxia, food or foreign body
Aspiration
  acid pulmonary (syndrome) 997.39
    obstetric 668.0 ☑
  amniotic fluid 770.13
    with respiratory symptoms 770.14
  bronchitis 507.0
  clear amniotic fluid 770.13
    with
      pneumonia 770.14
      pneumonitis 770.14
      respiratory symptoms 770.14
  contents of birth canal 770.17
    with respiratory symptoms 770.18
  fetal 770.10
    blood 770.15
      with
        pneumonia 770.16
        pneumonitis 770.16
    pneumonitis 770.18
  food, foreign body, or gasoline (with asphyxiation) — *see* Asphyxia, food or foreign body
  meconium 770.11

Aspiration — *continued*
  meconium — *continued*
    with
      pneumonia 770.12
      pneumonitis 770.12
      respiratory symptoms 770.12
    below vocal cords 770.11
      with respiratory symptoms 770.12
    mucus 933.1
      into
        bronchus (main) 934.1
        lung 934.8
        respiratory tract 934.9
          specified part NEC 934.8
        trachea 934.0
      newborn 770.17
      vaginal (fetus or newborn) 770.17
    newborn 770.10
      with respiratory symptoms 770.18
      blood 770.15
        with
          pneumonia 770.16
          pneumonitis 770.16
          respiratory symptoms 770.16
    pneumonia 507.0
      fetus or newborn 770.18
        meconium 770.12
    pneumonitis 507.0
      fetus or newborn 770.18
        meconium 770.12
      obstetric 668.0 ☑
    postnatal stomach contents 770.85
      with
        pneumonia 770.86
        pneumonitis 770.86
        respiratory symptoms 770.86
    syndrome of newborn (massive) 770.18
      meconium 770.12
    vernix caseosa 770.12
Asplenia 759.0
  with mesocardia 746.87
Assam fever 085.0
Assimilation, pelvis
  with disproportion 653.2 ☑
    affecting fetus or newborn 763.1
    causing obstructed labor 660.1 ☑
      affecting fetus or newborn 763.1
Assmann's focus — *see also* Tuberculosis 011.0 ☑
Astasia (-abasia) 307.9
  hysterical 300.11
Asteatosis 706.8
  cutis 706.8
Astereognosis 780.99
Asterixis 781.3
  in liver disease 572.8
Asteroid hyalitis 379.22
Asthenia, asthenic 780.79
  cardiac (*see also* Failure, heart) 428.9
    psychogenic 306.2
  cardiovascular (*see also* Failure, heart) 428.9
    psychogenic 306.2
  heart (*see also* Failure, heart) 428.9
    psychogenic 306.2
  hysterical 300.11
  myocardial (*see also* Failure, heart) 428.9
    psychogenic 306.2
  nervous 300.5
  neurocirculatory 306.2
  neurotic 300.5
  psychogenic 300.5
  psychoneurotic 300.5
  psychophysiologic 300.5
  reaction, psychoneurotic 300.5
  senile 797
  Stiller's 780.79
  tropical anhidrotic 705.1
Asthenopia 368.13
  accommodative 367.4
  hysterical (muscular) 300.11
  psychogenic 306.7
Asthenospermia 792.2

Asthma, asthmatic (bronchial) (catarrh) (spasmodic) 493.9 ☑

Note — Use the following fifth-digit subclassification with codes 493.0–493.2, 493.9:

0   *without mention of status asthmaticus or acute exacerbation or unspecified*

1   *with status asthmaticus*

2   *with acute exacerbation*

with
    chronic obstructive pulmonary disease (COPD) 493.2 ☑
    hay fever 493.0 ☑
    rhinitis, allergic 493.0 ☑
allergic 493.9 ☑
    stated cause (external allergen) 493.0 ☑
atopic 493.0 ☑
cardiac (*see also* Failure, ventricular, left) 428.1
cardiobronchial (*see also* Failure, ventricular, left) 428.1
cardiorenal (*see also* Hypertension, cardiorenal) 404.90
childhood 493.0 ☑
Colliers' 500
cough variant 493.82
croup 493.9 ☑
detergent 507.8
due to
    detergent 507.8
    inhalation of fumes 506.3
    internal immunological process 493.0 ☑
endogenous (intrinsic) 493.1 ☑
eosinophilic 518.3
exercise induced bronchospasm 493.81
exogenous (cosmetics) (dander or dust) (drugs) (dust) (feathers) (food) (hay) (platinum) (pollen) 493.0 ☑
extrinsic 493.0 ☑
grinders' 502
hay 493.0 ☑
heart (*see also* Failure, ventricular, left) 428.1
IgE 493.0 ☑
infective 493.1 ☑
intrinsic 493.1 ☑
Kopp's 254.8
late-onset 493.1 ☑
meat-wrappers' 506.9
Millar's (laryngismus stridulus) 478.75
millstone makers' 502
miners' 500
Monday morning 504
New Orleans (epidemic) 493.0 ☑
platinum 493.0 ☑
pneumoconiotic (occupational) NEC 505
potters' 502
psychogenic 316 *[493.9]* ☑
pulmonary eosinophilic 518.3
red cedar 495.8
Rostan's (*see also* Failure, ventricular, left) 428.1
sandblasters' 502
sequoiosis 495.8
stonemasons' 502
thymic 254.8
tuberculous (*see also* Tuberculosis, pulmonary) 011.9 ☑
Wichmann's (laryngismus stridulus) 478.75
wood 495.8

Astigmatism (compound) (congenital) 367.20
irregular 367.22
regular 367.21

Astroblastoma (M9430/3)
nose 748.1
specified site — *see* Neoplasm, by site, malignant
unspecified site 191.9

Astrocytoma (cystic) (M9400/3)
anaplastic type (M9401/3)
    specified site — *see* Neoplasm, by site, malignant
    unspecified site 191.9
fibrillary (M9420/3)
    specified site — *see* Neoplasm, by site, malignant

Astrocytoma — *continued*
fibrillary — *continued*
    unspecified site 191.9
fibrous (M9420/3)
    specified site — *see* Neoplasm, by site, malignant
    unspecified site 191.9
gemistocytic (M9411/3)
    specified site — *see* Neoplasm, by site, malignant
    unspecified site 191.9
juvenile (M9421/3)
    specified site — *see* Neoplasm, by site, malignant
    unspecified site 191.9
nose 748.1
pilocytic (M9421/3)
    specified site — *see* Neoplasm, by site, malignant
    unspecified site 191.9
piloid (M9421/3)
    specified site — *see* Neoplasm, by site, malignant
    unspecified site 191.9
protoplasmic (M9410/3)
    specified site — *see* Neoplasm, by site, malignant
    unspecified site 191.9
specified site — *see* Neoplasm, by site, malignant
subependymal (M9383/1) 237.5
    giant cell (M9384/1) 237.5
unspecified site 191.9

Astroglioma (M9400/3)
nose 748.1
specified site — *see* Neoplasm, by site, malignant
unspecified site 191.9

Asymbolia 784.60

Asymmetrical breathing 786.09

Asymmetry — *see also* Distortion
breast, between native and reconstructed 612.1
chest 786.9
face 754.0
jaw NEC 524.12
    maxillary 524.11
pelvis with disproportion 653.0 ☑
    affecting fetus or newborn 763.1
    causing obstructed labor 660.1 ☑
        affecting fetus or newborn 763.1

Asynergia 781.3

Asynergy 781.3
ventricular 429.89

Asystole (heart) — *see also* Arrest, cardiac 427.5

Ataxia, ataxy, ataxic 781.3
acute 781.3
brain 331.89
cerebellar 334.3
    hereditary (Marie's) 334.2
    in
        alcoholism 303.9 ☑ *[334.4]*
        myxedema (*see also* Myxedema) 244.9 *[334.4]*
        neoplastic disease NEC 239.9 *[334.4]*
cerebral 331.89
family, familial 334.2
    cerebral (Marie's) 334.2
    spinal (Friedreich's) 334.0
Friedreich's (hereofamilial) (spinal) 334.0
frontal lobe 781.3
gait 781.2
    hysterical 300.11
general 781.3
hereditary NEC 334.2
    cerebellar 334.2
    spastic 334.1
    spinal 334.0
heredofamilial (Marie's) 334.2
hysterical 300.11
locomotor (progressive) 094.0
    diabetic 250.6 ☑ *[337.1]*
        due to secondary diabetes 249.6 ☑ *[337.1]*
Marie's (cerebellar) (heredofamilial) 334.2
nonorganic origin 307.9

Ataxia, ataxy, ataxic — *continued*
partial 094.0
postchickenpox 052.7
progressive locomotor 094.0
psychogenic 307.9
Sanger-Brown's 334.2
spastic 094.0
    hereditary 334.1
    syphilitic 094.0
spinal
    hereditary 334.0
    progressive locomotor 094.0
telangiectasia 334.8

Ataxia-telangiectasia 334.8

Atelectasis (absorption collapse) (complete) (compression) (massive) (partial) (postinfective) (pressure collapse) (pulmonary) (relaxation) 518.0
newborn (congenital) (partial) 770.5
    primary 770.4
primary 770.4
tuberculous (*see also* Tuberculosis, pulmonary) 011.9 ☑

Ateleiosis, ateliosis 253.3

Atelia — *see* Distortion

Ateliosis 253.3

Atelocardia 746.9

Atelomyelia 742.59

Athelia 757.6

Atheroembolism
extremity
    lower 445.02
    upper 445.01
kidney 445.81
specified site NEC 445.89

Atheroma, atheromatous — *see also* Arteriosclerosis 440.9
aorta, aortic 440.0
    valve (*see also* Endocarditis, aortic) 424.1
artery — *see* Arteriosclerosis
basilar (artery) (*see also* Occlusion, artery, basilar) 433.0 ☑
carotid (artery) (common) (internal) (*see also* Occlusion, artery, carotid) 433.1 ☑
cerebral (arteries) 437.0
coronary (artery) — *see* Arteriosclerosis, coronary
degeneration — *see* Arteriosclerosis
heart, cardiac — *see* Arteriosclerosis, coronary
mitral (valve) 424.0
myocardium, myocardial — *see* Arteriosclerosis, coronary
pulmonary valve (heart) (*see also* Endocarditis, pulmonary) 424.3
skin 706.2
tricuspid (heart) (valve) 424.2
valve, valvular — *see* Endocarditis
vertebral (artery) (*see also* Occlusion, artery, vertebral) 433.2 ☑

Atheromatosis — *see also* Arteriosclerosis
arterial, congenital 272.8

Atherosclerosis — *see* Arteriosclerosis

Athetosis (acquired) 781.0
bilateral 333.79
congenital (bilateral) 333.6
double 333.71
unilateral 781.0

Athlete's
foot 110.4
heart 429.3

Athletic team examination V70.3

Athrepsia 261

Athyrea (acquired) — *see also* Hypothyroidism 244.9
congenital 243

Athyreosis (congenital) 243
acquired — *see* Hypothyroidism

Athyroidism (acquired) — *see also* Hypothyroidism 244.9
congenital 243

Atmospheric pyrexia 992.0

Atonia, atony, atonic
abdominal wall 728.2
bladder (sphincter) 596.4
    neurogenic NEC 596.54
        with cauda equina syndrome 344.61

Atonia, atony, atonic — *continued*
capillary 448.9
cecum 564.89
    psychogenic 306.4
colon 564.89
    psychogenic 306.4
congenital 779.89
dyspepsia 536.3
    psychogenic 306.4
intestine 564.89
    psychogenic 306.4
stomach 536.3
    neurotic or psychogenic 306.4
    psychogenic 306.4
uterus 661.2 ☑
    with hemorrhage (postpartum) 666.1 ☑
    without hemorrhage
        intrapartum 661.2 ☑
        postpartum 669.8 ☑
vesical 596.4

Atopy NEC V15.09

Atransferrinemia, congenital 273.8

Atresia, atretic (congenital) 759.89
alimentary organ or tract NEC 751.8
    lower 751.2
    upper 750.8
ani, anus, anal (canal) 751.2
aorta 747.22
    with hypoplasia of ascending aorta and defective development of left ventricle (with mitral valve atresia) 746.7
    arch 747.11
    ring 747.21
aortic (orifice) (valve) 746.89
    arch 747.11
aqueduct of Sylvius 742.3
    with spina bifida (*see also* Spina bifida) 741.0 ☑
artery NEC (*see also* Atresia, blood vessel) 747.60
    cerebral 747.81
    coronary 746.85
    eye 743.58
    pulmonary 747.3
    umbilical 747.5
auditory canal (external) 744.02
bile, biliary duct (common) or passage 751.61
    acquired (*see also* Obstruction, biliary) 576.2
bladder (neck) 753.6
blood vessel (peripheral) NEC 747.60
    cerebral 747.81
    gastrointestinal 747.61
    lower limb 747.64
    pulmonary artery 747.3
    renal 747.62
    spinal 747.82
    upper limb 747.63
bronchus 748.3
canal, ear 744.02
cardiac
    valve 746.89
        aortic 746.89
        mitral 746.89
        pulmonary 746.01
        tricuspid 746.1
cecum 751.2
cervix (acquired) 622.4
    congenital 752.49
    in pregnancy or childbirth 654.6 ☑
        affecting fetus or newborn 763.89
        causing obstructed labor 660.2 ☑
            affecting fetus or newborn 763.1
choana 748.0
colon 751.2
cystic duct 751.61
    acquired 575.8
        with obstruction (*see also* Obstruction, gallbladder) 575.2
digestive organs NEC 751.8
duodenum 751.1
ear canal 744.02
ejaculatory duct 752.89
epiglottis 748.3
esophagus 750.3

Index

Atresia, atretic — Atrophy, atrophic

Atresia, atretic — *continued*
Eustachian tube 744.24
fallopian tube (acquired) 628.2
   congenital 752.19
follicular cyst 620.0
foramen of
   Luschka 742.3
      with spina bifida (*see also* Spina bifida)
         741.0 ☑
   Magendie 742.3
      with spina bifida (*see also* Spina bifida)
         741.0 ☑
gallbladder 751.69
genital organ
   external
      female 752.49
      male NEC 752.89
         penis 752.69
   internal
      female 752.89
      male 752.89
glottis 748.3
gullet 750.3
heart
   valve NEC 746.89
      aortic 746.89
      mitral 746.89
      pulmonary 746.01
      tricuspid 746.1
hymen 752.42
   acquired 623.3
   postinfective 623.3
ileum 751.1
intestine (small) 751.1
   large 751.2
iris, filtration angle (*see also* Buphthalmia)
      743.20
jejunum 751.1
kidney 753.3
lacrimal, apparatus 743.65
   acquired — *see* Stenosis, lacrimal
larynx 748.3
ligament, broad 752.19
lung 748.5
meatus urinarius 753.6
mitral valve 746.89
   with atresia or hypoplasia of aortic orifice
      or valve, with hypoplasia of ascend-
      ing aorta and defective develop-
      ment of left ventricle 746.7
nares (anterior) (posterior) 748.0
nasolacrimal duct 743.65
nasopharynx 748.8
nose, nostril 748.0
   acquired 738.0
organ or site NEC — *see* Anomaly, specified
      type NEC
osseous meatus (ear) 744.03
oviduct (acquired) 628.2
   congenital 752.19
parotid duct 750.23
   acquired 527.8
pulmonary (artery) 747.3
   valve 746.01
   vein 747.49
pulmonic 746.01
pupil 743.46
rectum 751.2
salivary duct or gland 750.23
   acquired 527.8
sublingual duct 750.23
   acquired 527.8
submaxillary duct or gland 750.23
   acquired 527.8
trachea 748.3
tricuspid valve 746.1
ureter 753.29
ureteropelvic junction 753.21
ureterovesical orifice 753.22
urethra (valvular) 753.6
urinary tract NEC 753.29
uterus 752.3
   acquired 621.8
vagina (acquired) 623.2
   congenital 752.49
      postgonococcal (old) 098.2

Atresia, atretic — *continued*
vagina — *continued*
   postinfectional 623.2
   senile 623.2
vascular NEC (*see also* Atresia, blood vessel)
      747.60
   cerebral 747.81
vas deferens 752.89
vein NEC (*see also* Atresia, blood vessel) 747.60
   cardiac 746.89
   great 747.49
   portal 747.49
   pulmonary 747.49
vena cava (inferior) (superior) 747.49
vesicourethral orifice 753.6
vulva 752.49
   acquired 624.8
Atrichia, atrichosis 704.00
   congenital (universal) 757.4
Atrioventricularis commune 745.69
At risk for falling V15.88
Atrophia — *see also* Atrophy
   alba 709.09
   cutis 701.8
      idiopathica progressiva 701.8
      senilis 701.8
   dermatological, diffuse (idiopathic) 701.8
   flava hepatis (acuta) (subacuta) (*see also*
      Necrosis, liver) 570
   gyrata of choroid and retina (central) 363.54
      generalized 363.57
   senilis 797
      dermatological 701.8
   unguium 703.8
      congenita 757.5
Atrophoderma, atrophodermia 701.9
   diffusum (idiopathic) 701.8
   maculatum 701.3
      et striatum 701.3
         due to syphilis 095.8
      syphilitic 091.3
   neuriticum 701.8
   pigmentosum 757.33
   reticulatum symmetricum faciei 701.8
   senile 701.8
   symmetrical 701.8
   vermiculata 701.8
Atrophy, atrophic
   adrenal (autoimmune) (capsule) (cortex)
      (gland) 255.41
      with hypofunction 255.41
   alveolar process or ridge (edentulous) 525.20
      mandible 525.20
         minimal 525.21
         moderate 525.22
         severe 525.23
      maxilla 525.20
         minimal 525.24
         moderate 525.25
         severe 525.26
   appendix 543.9
   Aran-Duchenne muscular 335.21
   arm 728.2
   arteriosclerotic — *see* Arteriosclerosis
   arthritis 714.0
      spine 720.9
   bile duct (any) 576.8
   bladder 596.8
   blanche (of Milian) 701.3
   bone (senile) 733.99
      due to
         disuse 733.7
         infection 733.99
         tabes dorsalis (neurogenic) 094.0
      posttraumatic 733.99
   brain (cortex) (progressive) 331.9
      with dementia 290.10
      Alzheimer's 331.0
         with dementia — *see* Alzheimer's, de-
            mentia
      circumscribed (Pick's) 331.11
         with dementia
            with behavioral disturbance
               331.11 *[294.11]*
            without behavioral disturbance
               331.11 *[294.10]*

Atrophy, atrophic — *continued*
brain — *continued*
   congenital 742.4
   hereditary 331.9
   senile 331.2
breast 611.4
   puerperal, postpartum 676.3 ☑
buccal cavity 528.9
cardiac (brown) (senile) (*see also* Degeneration,
      myocardial) 429.1
cartilage (infectional) (joint) 733.99
cast, plaster of Paris 728.2
cerebellar — *see* Atrophy, brain
cerebral — *see* Atrophy, brain
cervix (endometrium) (mucosa) (myometrium)
      (senile) (uteri) 622.8
   menopausal 627.8
Charcôt-Marie-Tooth 356.1
choroid 363.40
   diffuse secondary 363.42
   hereditary (*see also* Dystrophy, choroid)
      363.50
      gyrate
         central 363.54
         diffuse 363.57
         generalized 363.57
      senile 363.41
ciliary body 364.57
colloid, degenerative 701.3
conjunctiva (senile) 372.89
corpus cavernosum 607.89
cortical (*see also* Atrophy, brain) 331.9
Cruveilhier's 335.21
cystic duct 576.8
dacryosialadenopathy 710.2
degenerative
   colloid 701.3
   senile 701.3
Déjérine-Thomas 333.0
diffuse idiopathic, dermatological 701.8
disuse
   bone 733.7
   muscle 728.2
   pelvic muscles and anal sphincter 618.83
Duchenne-Aran 335.21
ear 388.9
edentulous alveolar ridge 525.20
      mandible 525.20
         minimal 525.21
         moderate 525.22
         severe 525.23
      maxilla 525.20
         minimal 525.24
         moderate 525.25
         severe 525.26
emphysema, lung 492.8
endometrium (senile) 621.8
   cervix 622.8
enteric 569.89
epididymis 608.3
eyeball, cause unknown 360.41
eyelid (senile) 374.50
facial (skin) 701.9
facioscapulohumeral (Landouzy-Déjérine)
      359.1
fallopian tube (senile), acquired 620.3
fatty, thymus (gland) 254.8
gallbladder 575.8
gastric 537.89
gastritis (chronic) 535.1 ☑
gastrointestinal 569.89
genital organ, male 608.89
glandular 289.3
globe (phthisis bulbi) 360.41
gum (*see also* Recession, gingival) 523.20
hair 704.2
heart (brown) (senile) (*see also* Degeneration,
      myocardial) 429.1
hemifacial 754.0
   Romberg 349.89
hydronephrosis 591
infantile 261
   paralysis, acute (*see also* Poliomyelitis, with
      paralysis) 045.1 ☑
intestine 569.89

Atrophy, atrophic — *continued*
iris (generalized) (postinfectional) (sector
      shaped) 364.59
   essential 364.51
   progressive 364.51
   sphincter 364.54
kidney (senile) (*see also* Sclerosis, renal) 587
   with hypertension (*see also* Hypertension,
      kidney) 403.90
   congenital 753.0
   hydronephrotic 591
   infantile 753.0
lacrimal apparatus (primary) 375.13
   secondary 375.14
Landouzy-Déjérine 359.1
laryngitis, infection 476.0
larynx 478.79
Leber's optic 377.16
lip 528.5
liver (acute) (subacute) (*see also* Necrosis, liver)
      570
   chronic (yellow) 571.8
   yellow (congenital) 570
      with
         abortion — *see* Abortion, by type,
            with specified complication
            NEC
         ectopic pregnancy (*see also* cate-
            gories 633.0–633.9) 639.8
         molar pregnancy (*see also* cate-
            gories 630–632) 639.8
   chronic 571.8
   complicating pregnancy 646.7 ☑
   following
      abortion 639.8
      ectopic or molar pregnancy 639.8
   from injection, inoculation or transfu-
      sion (onset within 8 months af-
      ter administration) — *see* Hep-
      atitis, viral
   healed 571.5
   obstetric 646.7 ☑
   postabortal 639.8
   postimmunization — *see* Hepatitis, vi-
      ral
   posttransfusion — *see* Hepatitis, viral
   puerperal, postpartum 674.8 ☑
lung (senile) 518.89
   congenital 748.69
macular (dermatological) 701.3
   syphilitic, skin 091.3
      striated 095.8
muscle, muscular 728.2
   disuse 728.2
   Duchenne-Aran 335.21
   extremity (lower) (upper) 728.2
   familial spinal 335.11
   general 728.2
   idiopathic 728.2
   infantile spinal 335.0
   myelopathic (progressive) 335.10
   myotonic 359.21
   neuritic 356.1
   neuropathic (peroneal) (progressive) 356.1
   peroneal 356.1
   primary (idiopathic) 728.2
   progressive (familial) (hereditary) (pure)
      335.21
      adult (spinal) 335.19
      infantile (spinal) 335.0
      juvenile (spinal) 335.11
      spinal 335.10
         adult 335.19
         hereditary or familial 335.11
         infantile 335.0
   pseudohypertrophic 359.1
   spinal (progressive) 335.10
      adult 335.19
      Aran-Duchenne 335.21
      familial 335.11
      hereditary 335.11
      infantile 335.0
      juvenile 335.11
   syphilitic 095.6
myocardium (*see also* Degeneration, myocar-
      dial) 429.1

☑ Additional Digit Required — Refer to the Tabular List for Digit Selection

▽ Subterms under main terms may continue to next column or page

►◄ Revised Text   ● New Line   ▲ Revised Code

Atrophy, atrophic — *continued*
 myometrium (senile) 621.8
  cervix 622.8
 myotatic 728.2
 myotonia 359.21
 nail 703.8
  congenital 757.5
 nasopharynx 472.2
 nerve (*see also* Disorder, nerve)
  abducens 378.54
  accessory 352.4
  acoustic or auditory 388.5
  cranial 352.9
   first (olfactory) 352.0
   second (optic) (*see also* Atrophy, optic
    nerve) 377.10
   third (oculomotor) (partial) 378.51
    total 378.52
   fourth (trochlear) 378.53
   fifth (trigeminal) 350.8
   sixth (abducens) 378.54
   seventh (facial) 351.8
   eighth (auditory) 388.5
   ninth (glossopharyngeal) 352.2
   tenth (pneumogastric) (vagus) 352.3
   eleventh (accessory) 352.4
   twelfth (hypoglossal) 352.5
  facial 351.8
  glossopharyngeal 352.2
  hypoglossal 352.5
  oculomotor (partial) 378.51
   total 378.52
  olfactory 352.0
  peripheral 355.9
  pneumogastric 352.3
  trigeminal 350.8
  trochlear 378.53
  vagus (pneumogastric) 352.3
 nervous system, congenital 742.8
 neuritic (*see also* Disorder, nerve) 355.9
 neurogenic NEC 355.9
  bone
   tabetic 094.0
 nutritional 261
 old age 797
 olivopontocerebellar 333.0
 optic nerve (ascending) (descending) (infectional) (nonfamilial) (papillomacular
   bundle) (postretinal) (secondary NEC)
   (simple) 377.10
  associated with retinal dystrophy 377.13
  dominant hereditary 377.16
  glaucomatous 377.14
  hereditary (dominant) (Leber's) 377.16
  Leber's (hereditary) 377.16
  partial 377.15
  postinflammatory 377.12
  primary 377.11
  syphilitic 094.84
   congenital 090.49
   tabes dorsalis 094.0
  orbit 376.45
 ovary (senile), acquired 620.3
 oviduct (senile), acquired 620.3
 palsy, diffuse 335.20
 pancreas (duct) (senile) 577.8
 papillary muscle 429.81
 paralysis 355.9
 parotid gland 527.0
 patches skin 701.3
  senile 701.8
 penis 607.89
 pharyngitis 472.1
 pharynx 478.29
 pluriglandular 258.8
 polyarthritis 714.0
 prostate 602.2
 pseudohypertrophic 359.1
 renal (*see also* Sclerosis, renal) 587
 reticulata 701.8
 retina (*see also* Degeneration, retina) 362.60
  hereditary (*see also* Dystrophy, retina)
   362.70
 rhinitis 472.0
 salivary duct or gland 527.0
 scar NEC 709.2

Atrophy, atrophic — *continued*
 sclerosis, lobar (of brain) 331.0
  with dementia
   with behavioral disturbance
    331.0 [294.11]
   without behavioral disturbance
    331.0 [294.10]
 scrotum 608.89
 seminal vesicle 608.89
 senile 797
  degenerative, of skin 701.3
 skin (patches) (senile) 701.8
 spermatic cord 608.89
 spinal (cord) 336.8
  acute 336.8
  muscular (chronic) 335.10
   adult 335.19
   familial 335.11
   juvenile 335.10
  paralysis 335.10
   acute (*see also* Poliomyelitis, with
    paralysis) 045.1 ☑
 spine (column) 733.99
 spleen (senile) 289.59
 spots (skin) 701.3
  senile 701.8
 stomach 537.89
 striate and macular 701.3
  syphilitic 095.8
 subcutaneous 701.9
  due to injection 999.9
 sublingual gland 527.0
 submaxillary gland 527.0
 Sudeck's 733.7
 suprarenal (autoimmune) (capsule) (gland)
   255.41
  with hypofunction 255.41
 tarso-orbital fascia, congenital 743.66
 testis 608.3
 thenar, partial 354.0
 throat 478.29
 thymus (fat) 254.8
 thyroid (gland) 246.8
  with
   cretinism 243
   myxedema 244.9
  congenital 243
 tongue (senile) 529.8
  papillae 529.4
  smooth 529.4
 trachea 519.19
 tunica vaginalis 608.89
 turbinate 733.99
 tympanic membrane (nonflaccid) 384.82
  flaccid 384.81
 ulcer (*see also* Ulcer, skin) 707.9
 upper respiratory tract 478.9
 uterus, uterine (acquired) (senile) 621.8
  cervix 622.8
  due to radiation (intended effect) 621.8
 vagina (senile) 627.3
 vascular 459.89
 vas deferens 608.89
 vertebra (senile) 733.99
 vulva (primary) (senile) 624.1
 Werdnig-Hoffmann 335.0
 yellow (acute) (congenital) (liver) (subacute)
   (*see also* Necrosis, liver) 570
  chronic 571.8
  resulting from administration of blood,
    plasma, serum, or other biological
    substance (within 8 months of ad-
    ministration) — *see* Hepatitis, viral

Attack
 akinetic (*see also* Epilepsy) 345.0 ☑
 angina — *see* Angina
 apoplectic (*see also* Disease, cerebrovascular,
   acute) 436
 benign shuddering 333.93
 bilious — *see* Vomiting
 cataleptic 300.11
 cerebral (*see also* Disease, cerebrovascular,
   acute) 436
 coronary (*see also* Infarct, myocardium)
   410.9 ☑
 cyanotic, newborn 770.83

Attack — *continued*
 epileptic (*see also* Epilepsy) 345.9 ☑
 epileptiform 780.39
 heart (*see also* Infarct, myocardium) 410.9 ☑
 hemiplegia (*see also* Disease, cerebrovascular,
   acute) 436
 hysterical 300.11
 jacksonian (*see also* Epilepsy) 345.5 ☑
 myocardium, myocardial (*see also* Infarct, myocardium) 410.9 ☑
 myoclonic (*see also* Epilepsy) 345.1 ☑
 panic 300.01
 paralysis (*see also* Disease, cerebrovascular,
   acute) 436
 paroxysmal 780.39
 psychomotor (*see also* Epilepsy) 345.4 ☑
 salaam (*see also* Epilepsy) 345.6 ☑
 schizophreniform (*see also* Schizophrenia)
   295.4 ☑
 sensory and motor 780.39
 syncope 780.2
 toxic, cerebral 780.39
 transient ischemic (TIA) 435.9
 unconsciousness 780.2
  hysterical 300.11
 vasomotor 780.2
 vasovagal (idiopathic) (paroxysmal) 780.2
Attention to
 artificial opening (of) V55.9
  digestive tract NEC V55.4
  specified site NEC V55.8
  urinary tract NEC V55.6
  vagina V55.7
 colostomy V55.3
 cystostomy V55.5
 dressing
  wound V58.30
   nonsurgical V58.30
   surgical V58.31
 gastrostomy V55.1
 ileostomy V55.2
 jejunostomy V55.4
 nephrostomy V55.6
 surgical dressings V58.31
 sutures V58.32
 tracheostomy V55.0
 ureterostomy V55.6
 urethrostomy V55.6
Attrition
 gum (*see also* Recession, gingival) 523.20
 teeth (hard tissues) 521.10
  excessive 521.10
   extending into
    dentine 521.12
    pulp 521.13
   generalized 521.15
   limited to enamel 521.11
   localized 521.14
Atypical — *see also* condition
 cells
  endocervical 795.00
  endometrial 795.00
  glandular
   anus 796.70
   cervical 795.00
   vaginal 795.10
  distribution, vessel (congenital) (peripheral)
   NEC 747.60
  endometrium 621.9
  kidney 593.89
Atypism, cervix 622.10
Audible tinnitus — *see also* Tinnitus 388.30
Auditory — *see* condition
Audry's syndrome (acropachyderma) 757.39
Aujeszky's disease 078.89
Aura
 jacksonian (*see also* Epilepsy) 345.5 ☑
 persistent migraine 346.5 ☑
  with cerebral infarction 346.6 ☑
  without cerebral infarction 346.5 ☑
Aurantiasis, cutis 278.3
Auricle, auricular — *see* condition
Auriculotemporal syndrome 350.8
Australian
 Q fever 083.0
 X disease 062.4

Autism, autistic (child) (infantile) 299.0 ☑
Autodigestion 799.89
Autoerythrocyte sensitization 287.2
Autographism 708.3
Autoimmune
 cold sensitivity 283.0
 disease NEC 279.49 ▲
 hemolytic anemia 283.0
 lymphoproliferative syndrome (ALPS) 279.41 ●
 thyroiditis 245.2
Autoinfection, septic — *see* Septicemia
Autointoxication 799.89
Automatism 348.89 ▲
 epileptic (*see also* Epilepsy) 345.4 ☑
 paroxysmal, idiopathic (*see also* Epilepsy)
   345.4 ☑
Autonomic, autonomous
 bladder 596.54
  neurogenic 596.54
   with cauda equina 344.61
 dysreflexia 337.3
 faciocephalalgia (*see also* Neuropathy, peripheral, autonomic) 337.9
 hysterical seizure 300.11
 imbalance (*see also* Neuropathy, peripheral,
   autonomic) 337.9
Autophony 388.40
Autosensitivity, erythrocyte 287.2
Autotopagnosia 780.99
Autotoxemia 799.89
Autumn — *see* condition
Avellis' syndrome 344.89
Aviators
 disease or sickness (*see also* Effect, adverse,
   high altitude) 993.2
 ear 993.0
 effort syndrome 306.2
Avitaminosis (multiple NEC) — *see also* Deficiency, vitamin 269.2
 A 264.9
 B 266.9
  with
   beriberi 265.0
   pellagra 265.2
 B₁ 265.1
 B₂ 266.0
 B₆ 266.1
 B₁₂ 266.2
 C (with scurvy) 267
 D 268.9
  with
   osteomalacia 268.2
   rickets 268.0
 E 269.1
 G 266.0
 H 269.1
 K 269.0
 multiple 269.2
 nicotinic acid 265.2
 P 269.1
Avulsion (traumatic) 879.8
 blood vessel — *see* Injury, blood vessel, by site
 cartilage (*see also* Dislocation, by site)
  knee, current (*see also* Tear, meniscus)
   836.2
  symphyseal (inner), complicating delivery
   665.6 ☑
 complicated 879.9
 diaphragm — *see* Injury, internal, diaphragm
 ear — *see* Wound, open, ear
 epiphysis of bone — *see* Fracture, by site
 external site other than limb — *see* Wound,
   open, by site
 eye 871.3
 fingernail — *see* Wound, open, finger
 fracture — *see* Fracture, by site
 genital organs, external — *see* Wound, open,
   genital organs
 head (intracranial) NEC (*see also* Injury, intracranial, with open intracranial wound)
  complete 874.9
  external site NEC 873.8
   complicated 873.9
 internal organ or site — *see* Injury, internal, by
   site

☑ Additional Digit Required — Refer to the Tabular List for Digit Selection   Subterms under main terms may continue to next column or page

2010 ICD-9-CM   ▶◀ Revised Text   ● New Line   ▲ Revised Code   October 2009 • Volume 2 — 31

Avulsion — continued
  joint (see also Dislocation, by site)
    capsule — see Sprain, by site
    ligament — see Sprain, by site
  limb (see also Amputation, traumatic, by site)
    skin and subcutaneous tissue — see
      Wound, open, by site
  muscle — see Sprain, by site
  nerve (root) — see Injury, nerve, by site
  scalp — see Wound, open, scalp
  skin and subcutaneous tissue — see Wound,
    open, by site
  symphyseal cartilage (inner), complicating
    delivery 665.6 ☑
  tendon (see also Sprain, by site)
    with open wound — see Wound, open,
      by site
  toenail — see Wound, open, toe(s)
  tooth 873.63
    complicated 873.73
Awaiting organ transplant status V49.83
Awareness of heart beat 785.1
Axe grinders' disease 502
Axenfeld's anomaly or syndrome 743.44
Axilla, axillary — see also condition
  breast 757.6
Axonotmesis — see Injury, nerve, by site
Ayala's disease 756.89
Ayerza's disease or syndrome (pulmonary
  artery sclerosis with pulmonary hyperten-
  sion) 416.0
Azoospermia 606.0
Azorean disease (of the nervous system) 334.8
Azotemia 790.6
  meaning uremia (see also Uremia) 586
Aztec ear 744.29
Azygos lobe, lung (fissure) 748.69

B

Baader's syndrome (erythema multiforme ex-
  udativum) 695.19
Baastrup's syndrome 721.5
Babesiasis 088.82
Babesiosis 088.82
Babington's disease (familial hemorrhagic
  telangiectasia) 448.0
Babinski-Fröhlich syndrome (adiposogenital
  dystrophy) 253.8
Babinski-Nageotte syndrome 344.89
Babinski's syndrome (cardiovascular syphilis)
  093.89
Bacillary — see condition
Bacilluria 791.9
  asymptomatic, in pregnancy or puerperium
    646.5 ☑
  tuberculous (see also Tuberculosis) 016.9 ☑
Bacillus — see also Infection, bacillus
  abortus infection 023.1
  anthracis infection 022.9
  coli
    infection 041.4
      generalized 038.42
      intestinal 008.00
    pyemia 038.42
    septicemia 038.42
  Flexner's 004.1
  fusiformis infestation 101
  mallei infection 024
  Shiga's 004.0
  suipestifer infection (see also Infection,
    Salmonella) 003.9
Back — see condition
Backache (postural) 724.5
  psychogenic 307.89
  sacroiliac 724.6
Backflow (pyelovenous) — see also Disease, renal
  593.9
Backknee — see also Genu, recurvatum 736.5
Bacteremia 790.7
  newborn 771.83
Bacteria
  in blood (see also Bacteremia) 790.7
  in urine (see also Bacteriuria) 599.0
Bacterial — see condition
Bactericholia — see also Cholecystitis, acute
  575.0

Bacterid, bacteride (Andrews' pustular) 686.8
Bacteriuria, bacteruria 791.9
  with
    urinary tract infection 599.0
  asymptomatic 791.9
    in pregnancy or puerperium 646.5 ☑
      affecting fetus or newborn 760.1
Bad
  breath 784.99
  heart — see Disease, heart
  trip (see also Abuse, drugs, nondependent)
    305.3 ☑
Baehr-Schiffrin disease (thrombotic thrombocytopenic purpura) 446.6
Baelz's disease (cheilitis glandularis apostematosa) 528.5
Baerensprung's disease (eczema marginatum)
  110.3
Bagassosis (occupational) 495.1
Baghdad boil 085.1
Bagratuni's syndrome (temporal arteritis) 446.5
Baker's
  cyst (knee) 727.51
    tuberculous (see also Tuberculosis)
      015.2 ☑
  itch 692.89
Bakwin-Krida syndrome (craniometaphyseal
  dysplasia) 756.89
Balanitis (circinata) (gangraenosa) (infectious)
  (vulgaris) 607.1
  amebic 006.8
  candidal 112.2
  chlamydial 099.53
  due to Ducrey's bacillus 099.0
  erosiva circinata et gangraenosa 607.1
  gangrenous 607.1
  gonococcal (acute) 098.0
    chronic or duration of 2 months or over
      098.2
  nongonococcal 607.1
  phagedenic 607.1
  venereal NEC 099.8
  xerotica obliterans 607.81
Balanoposthitis 607.1
  chlamydial 099.53
  gonococcal (acute) 098.0
    chronic or duration of 2 months or over
      098.2
  ulcerative NEC 099.8
Balanorrhagia — see Balanitis
Balantidiasis 007.0
Balantidiosis 007.0
Balbuties, balbutio 307.0
Bald
  patches on scalp 704.00
  tongue 529.4
Baldness — see also Alopecia 704.00
Balfour's disease (chloroma) 205.3 ☑
Balint's syndrome (psychic paralysis of visual
  fixation) 368.16
Balkan grippe 083.0
Ball
  food 938
  hair 938
Ballantyne (-Runge) syndrome (postmaturity)
  766.22
Balloon disease — see also Effect, adverse, high
  altitude 993.2
Ballooning posterior leaflet syndrome 424.0
Baló's disease or concentric sclerosis 341.1
Bamberger's disease (hypertrophic pulmonary
  osteoarthropathy) 731.2
Bamberger-Marie disease (hypertrophic pul-
  monary osteoarthropathy) 731.2
Bamboo spine 720.0
Bancroft's filariasis 125.0
Band(s)
  adhesive (see also Adhesions, peritoneum)
    568.0
  amniotic 658.8 ☑
    affecting fetus or newborn 762.8
  anomalous or congenital (see also Anomaly,
    specified type NEC)
    atrial 746.9
    heart 746.9
    intestine 751.4

Band(s) — continued
  anomalous or congenital (see also Anomaly,
    specified type) — continued
    omentum 751.4
    ventricular 746.9
  cervix 622.3
  gallbladder (congenital) 751.69
  intestinal (adhesive) (see also Adhesions, peri-
    toneum) 568.0
    congenital 751.4
    obstructive (see also Obstruction, intestine)
      560.81
    periappendiceal (congenital) 751.4
  peritoneal (adhesive) (see also Adhesions,
    peritoneum) 568.0
    with intestinal obstruction 560.81
    congenital 751.4
  uterus 621.5
  vagina 623.2
Bandemia (without diagnosis of specific infection) 288.66
Bandl's ring (contraction)
  complicating delivery 661.4 ☑
    affecting fetus or newborn 763.7
Bang's disease (Brucella abortus) 023.1
Bangkok hemorrhagic fever 065.4
Bannister's disease 995.1
Bantam-Albright-Martin disease (pseudohypoparathyroidism) 275.49
Banti's disease or syndrome (with cirrhosis)
  (with portal hypertension) — see Cirrhosis,
  liver
Bar
  calcaneocuboid 755.67
  calcaneonavicular 755.67
  cubonavicular 755.67
  prostate 600.90
    with
      other lower urinary tract symptoms
        (LUTS) 600.91
      urinary
        obstruction 600.91
        retention 600.91
  talocalcaneal 755.67
Baragnosis 780.99
Barasheh, barashek 266.2
Barcoo disease or rot — see also Ulcer, skin
  707.9
Bard-Pic syndrome (carcinoma, head of pancreas) 157.0
Bärensprung's disease (eczema marginatum)
  110.3
Baritosis 503
Barium lung disease 503
Barlow (-Möller) disease or syndrome (mean-
  ing infantile scurvy) 267
Barlow's syndrome (meaning mitral valve pro-
  lapse) 424.0
Barodontalgia 993.2
Baron Münchausen syndrome 301.51
Barosinusitis 993.1
Barotitis 993.0
Barotrauma 993.2
  odontalgia 993.2
  otitic 993.0
  sinus 993.1
Barraquer's disease or syndrome (progressive
  lipodystrophy) 272.6
Barré-Guillain syndrome 357.0
Barrel chest 738.3
Barré-Liéou syndrome (posterior cervical sym-
  pathetic) 723.2
Barrett's esophagus 530.85
Barrett's syndrome or ulcer (chronic peptic ul-
  cer of esophagus) 530.85
Bársony-Polgár syndrome (corkscrew esopha-
  gus) 530.5
Bársony-Teschendorf syndrome (corkscrew
  esophagus) 530.5
Bartholin's
  adenitis (see also Bartholinitis) 616.89
  gland — see condition
Bartholinitis (suppurating) 616.89
  gonococcal (acute) 098.0
    chronic or duration of 2 months or over
      098.2

Barth syndrome 759.89
Bartonellosis 088.0
Bartter's syndrome (secondary hyperaldostero-
  nism with juxtaglomerular hyperplasia)
  255.13
Basal — see condition
Basan's (hidrotic) **ectodermal dysplasia** 757.31
Baseball finger 842.13
Basedow's disease or syndrome (exophthalmic
  goiter) 242.0 ☑
Basic — see condition
Basilar — see condition
Bason's (hidrotic) **ectodermal dysplasia** 757.31
Basopenia 288.59
Basophilia 288.65
Basophilism (corticoadrenal) (Cushing's) (pitu-
  itary) (thymic) 255.0
Bassen-Kornzweig syndrome (abetalipopro-
  teinemia) 272.5
Bat ear 744.29
Bateman's
  disease 078.0
  purpura (senile) 287.2
Bathing cramp 994.1
Bathophobia 300.23
Batten's disease, retina 330.1 [362.71]
Batten-Mayou disease 330.1 [362.71]
Batten-Steinert syndrome 359.21
Battered
  adult (syndrome) 995.81
  baby or child (syndrome) 995.54
  spouse (syndrome) 995.81
Battey mycobacterium infection 031.0
Battledore placenta — see Placenta, abnormal
Battle exhaustion — see also Reaction, stress,
  acute 308.9
Baumgarten-Cruveilhier (cirrhosis) **disease, or
  syndrome** 571.5
Bauxite
  fibrosis (of lung) 503
  workers' disease 503
Bayle's disease (dementia paralytica) 094.1
Bazin's disease (primary) — see also Tuberculosis
  017.1 ☑
Beach ear 380.12
Beaded hair (congenital) 757.4
Beals syndrome 759.82
Beard's disease (neurasthenia) 300.5
Bearn-Kunkel (-Slater) syndrome (lupoid hepatitis) 571.49
Beat
  elbow 727.2
  hand 727.2
  knee 727.2
Beats
  ectopic 427.60
  escaped, heart 427.60
    postoperative 997.1
  premature (nodal) 427.60
    atrial 427.61
    auricular 427.61
    postoperative 997.1
    specified type NEC 427.69
    supraventricular 427.61
    ventricular 427.69
Beau's
  disease or syndrome (see also Degeneration,
    myocardial) 429.1
  lines (transverse furrows on fingernails) 703.8
Bechterew's disease (ankylosing spondylitis)
  720.0
Bechterew-Strümpell-Marie syndrome (ankylosing spondylitis) 720.0
Becker's
  disease
    idiopathic mural endomyocardial disease
      425.2
    myotonia congenita, recessive form 359.22
  dystrophy 359.22
Beck's syndrome (anterior spinal artery occlu-
  sion) 433.8 ☑
Beckwith (-Wiedemann) syndrome 759.89
Bedbugs bite(s) — see Injury, superficial, by site
Bedclothes, asphyxiation or suffocation by
  994.7
Bed confinement status V49.84

☑ Additional Digit Required — Refer to the Tabular List for Digit Selection   ▽ Subterms under main terms may continue to next column or page

32 — Volume 2   ▶◀ Revised Text   ● New Line   ▲ Revised Code   2010 ICD-9-CM

Bednar's aphthae 528.2
Bedsore (*see also* Ulcer, pressure) 707.00
  with gangrene 707.00 *[785.4]*
Bedwetting — *see also* Enuresis 788.36
Beer-drinkers' heart (disease) 425.5
Bee sting (with allergic or anaphylactic shock) 989.5
Begbie's disease (exophthalmic goiter) 242.0 ☑
Behavior disorder, disturbance — *see also* Disturbance, conduct
  antisocial, without manifest psychiatric disorder
    adolescent V71.02
    adult V71.01
    child V71.02
  dyssocial, without manifest psychiatric disorder
    adolescent V71.02
    adult V71.01
    child V71.02
  high risk — *see* Problem
Behçet's syndrome 136.1
Behr's disease 362.50
Beigel's disease or morbus (white piedra) 111.2
Bejel 104.0
Bekhterev's disease (ankylosing spondylitis) 720.0
Bekhterev-Strümpell-Marie syndrome (ankylosing spondylitis) 720.0
Belching — *see also* Eructation 787.3
Bell's
  disease (*see also* Psychosis, affective) 296.0 ☑
  mania (*see also* Psychosis, affective) 296.0 ☑
  palsy, paralysis 351.0
    infant 767.5
    newborn 767.5
    syphilitic 094.89
  spasm 351.0
Bence-Jones albuminuria, albuminosuria, or proteinuria 791.0
Bends 993.3
Benedikt's syndrome (paralysis) 344.89
Benign — *see also* condition
  cellular changes, cervix 795.09
  prostate
    with
      other lower urinary tract symptoms (LUTS) 600.21
      urinary
        obstruction 600.21
        retention 600.21
    hyperplasia 600.20
    neoplasm 222.2
Bennett's
  disease (leukemia) 208.9 ☑
  fracture (closed) 815.01
    open 815.11
Benson's disease 379.22
Bent
  back (hysterical) 300.11
  nose 738.0
    congenital 754.0
Bereavement V62.82
  as adjustment reaction 309.0
Bergeron's disease (hysteroepilepsy) 300.11
Berger's paresthesia (lower limb) 782.0
Beriberi (acute) (atrophic) (chronic) (dry) (subacute) (wet) 265.0
  with polyneuropathy 265.0 *[357.4]*
  heart (disease) 265.0 *[425.7]*
  leprosy 030.1
  neuritis 265.0 *[357.4]*
Berlin's disease or edema (traumatic) 921.3
Berloque dermatitis 692.72
Bernard-Horner syndrome — *see also* Neuropathy, peripheral, autonomic 337.9
Bernard-Sergent syndrome (acute adrenocortical insufficiency) 255.41
Bernard-Soulier disease or thrombopathy 287.1
Bernhardt's disease or paresthesia 355.1
Bernhardt-Roth disease or syndrome (paresthesia) 355.1
Bernheim's syndrome — *see also* Failure, heart 428.0
Bertielliasis 123.8

Bertolotti's syndrome (sacralization of fifth lumbar vertebra) 756.15
Berylliosis (acute) (chronic) (lung) (occupational) 503
Besnier's
  lupus pernio 135
  prurigo (atopic dermatitis) (infantile eczema) 691.8
Besnier-Boeck disease or sarcoid 135
Besnier-Boeck-Schaumann disease (sarcoidosis) 135
Best's disease 362.76
Bestiality 302.1
Beta-adrenergic hyperdynamic circulatory state 429.82
Beta-aminoisobutyric aciduria 277.2
Beta-mercaptolactate-cysteine disulfiduria 270.0
Beta thalassemia (major) (minor) (mixed) 282.49
Beurmann's disease (sporotrichosis) 117.1
Bezoar 938
  intestine 936
  stomach 935.2
Bezold's abscess — *see also* Mastoiditis 383.01
Bianchi's syndrome (aphasia-apraxia-alexia) 784.69
Bicornuate or bicornis uterus 752.3
  in pregnancy or childbirth 654.0 ☑
    with obstructed labor 660.2 ☑
      affecting fetus or newborn 763.1
    affecting fetus or newborn 763.89
Bicuspid aortic valve 746.4
Biedl-Bardet syndrome 759.89
Bielschowsky's disease 330.1
Bielschowsky-Jansky
  amaurotic familial idiocy 330.1
  disease 330.1
Biemond's syndrome (obesity, polydactyly, and mental retardation) 759.89
Biermer's anemia or disease (pernicious anemia) 281.0
Biett's disease 695.4
Bifid (congenital) — *see also* Imperfect, closure
  apex, heart 746.89
  clitoris 752.49
  epiglottis 748.3
  kidney 753.3
  nose 748.1
  patella 755.64
  scrotum 752.89
  toe 755.66
  tongue 750.13
  ureter 753.4
  uterus 752.3
  uvula 749.02
    with cleft lip (*see also* Cleft, palate, with cleft lip) 749.20
Biforis uterus (suprasimplex) 752.3
Bifurcation (congenital) — *see also* Imperfect, closure
  gallbladder 751.69
  kidney pelvis 753.3
  renal pelvis 753.3
  rib 756.3
  tongue 750.13
  trachea 748.3
  ureter 753.4
  urethra 753.8
  uvula 749.02
    with cleft lip (*see also* Cleft, palate, with cleft lip) 749.20
  vertebra 756.19
Bigeminal pulse 427.89
Bigeminy 427.89
Big spleen syndrome 289.4
Bilateral — *see* condition
Bile duct — *see* condition
Bile pigments in urine 791.4
Bilharziasis — *see also* Schistosomiasis 120.9
  chyluria 120.0
  cutaneous 120.3
  galacturia 120.0
  hematochyluria 120.0
  intestinal 120.1
  lipemia 120.9
  lipuria 120.0

Bilharziasis — *see also* Schistosomiasis — *continued*
  Oriental 120.2
  piarhemia 120.9
  pulmonary 120.2
  tropical hematuria 120.0
  vesical 120.0
Biliary — *see* condition
Bilious (attack) — *see also* Vomiting
  fever, hemoglobinuric 084.8
Bilirubinuria 791.4
Biliuria 791.4
Billroth's disease
  meningocele (*see also* Spina bifida) 741.9 ☑
Bilobate placenta — *see* Placenta, abnormal
Bilocular
  heart 745.7
  stomach 536.8
Bing-Horton syndrome (histamine cephalgia) 339.00
Binswanger's disease or dementia 290.12
Biörck (-Thorson) syndrome (malignant carcinoid) 259.2
Biparta, bipartite — *see also* Imperfect, closure
  carpal scaphoid 755.59
  patella 755.64
  placenta — *see* Placenta, abnormal
  vagina 752.49
Bird
  face 756.0
  fanciers' lung or disease 495.2
  flu 488.0   ●
Bird's disease (oxaluria) 271.8
Birth
  abnormal fetus or newborn 763.9
  accident, fetus or newborn — *see* Birth, injury
  complications in mother — *see* Delivery, complicated
  compression during NEC 767.9
  defect — *see* Anomaly
  delayed, fetus 763.9
  difficult NEC, affecting fetus or newborn 763.9
  dry, affecting fetus or newborn 761.1
  forced, NEC, affecting fetus or newborn 763.89
  forceps, affecting fetus or newborn 763.2
  hematoma of sternomastoid 767.8
  immature 765.1 ☑
    extremely 765.0 ☑
  inattention, after or at 995.52
  induced, affecting fetus or newborn 763.89
  infant — *see* Newborn
  injury NEC 767.9
    adrenal gland 767.8
    basal ganglia 767.0
    brachial plexus (paralysis) 767.6
    brain (compression) (pressure) 767.0
    cerebellum 767.0
    cerebral hemorrhage 767.0
    conjunctiva 767.8
    eye 767.8
    fracture
      bone, any except clavicle or spine 767.3
      clavicle 767.2
      femur 767.3
      humerus 767.3
      long bone 767.3
      radius and ulna 767.3
      skeleton NEC 767.3
      skull 767.3
      spine 767.4
      tibia and fibula 767.3
    hematoma 767.8
      liver (subcapsular) 767.8
      mastoid 767.8
      skull 767.19
      sternomastoid 767.8
      testes 767.8
      vulva 767.8
    intracranial (edema) 767.0
    laceration
      brain 767.0
      by scalpel 767.8
      peripheral nerve 767.7
      liver 767.8
    meninges
      brain 767.0

Birth — *continued*
  injury — *continued*
    meninges — *continued*
      spinal cord 767.4
    nerves (cranial, peripheral) 767.7
      brachial plexus 767.6
      facial 767.5
    paralysis 767.7
      brachial plexus 767.6
      Erb (-Duchenne) 767.6
      facial nerve 767.5
      Klumpke (-Déjérine) 767.6
      radial nerve 767.6
      spinal (cord) (hemorrhage) (laceration) (rupture) 767.4
    rupture
      intracranial 767.0
      liver 767.8
      spinal cord 767.4
      spleen 767.8
      viscera 767.8
    scalp 767.19
    scalpel wound 767.8
    skeleton NEC 767.3
    specified NEC 767.8
    spinal cord 767.4
    spleen 767.8
    subdural hemorrhage 767.0
    tentorial, tear 767.0
    testes 767.8
    vulva 767.8
  instrumental, NEC, affecting fetus or newborn 763.2
  lack of care, after or at 995.52
  multiple
    affected by maternal complications of pregnancy 761.5
    healthy liveborn — *see* Newborn, multiple
  neglect, after or at 995.52
  newborn — *see* Newborn
  palsy or paralysis NEC 767.7
  precipitate, fetus or newborn 763.6
  premature (infant) 765.1 ☑
  prolonged, affecting fetus or newborn 763.9
  retarded, fetus or newborn 763.9
  shock, newborn 779.89
  strangulation or suffocation
    due to aspiration of clear amniotic fluid 770.13
      with respiratory symptoms 770.14
    mechanical 767.8
  trauma NEC 767.9
  triplet
    affected by maternal complications of pregnancy 761.5
    healthy liveborn — *see* Newborn, multiple
  twin
    affected by maternal complications of pregnancy 761.5
    healthy liveborn — *see* Newborn, twin
  ventouse, affecting fetus or newborn 763.3
Birthmark 757.32
Birt-Hogg-Dube syndrome 759.89
Bisalbuminemia 273.8
Biskra button 085.1
Bite(s)
  with intact skin surface — *see* Contusion
  animal — *see* Wound, open, by site
    intact skin surface — *see* Contusion
  bedbug — *see* Injury, superficial, by site
  centipede 989.5
  chigger 133.8
  fire ant 989.5
  flea — *see* Injury, superficial, by site
  human (open wound) (*see also* Wound, open, by site)
    intact skin surface — *see* Contusion
  insect
    nonvenomous — *see* Injury, superficial, by site
    venomous 989.5
  mad dog (death from) 071
  open
    anterior 524.24
    posterior 524.25
  poisonous 989.5

Bite(s) — *continued*
  red bug 133.8
  reptile 989.5
    nonvenomous — *see* Wound, open, by
      site
  snake 989.5
    nonvenomous — *see* Wound, open, by
      site
  spider (venomous) 989.5
    nonvenomous — *see* Injury, superficial, by
      site
  venomous 989.5
Biting
  cheek or lip 528.9
  nail 307.9
Black
  death 020.9
  eye NEC 921.0
  hairy tongue 529.3
  heel 924.20
  lung disease 500
  palm 923.20
Blackfan-Diamond anemia or syndrome
  (congenital hypoplastic anemia) 284.01
Blackhead 706.1
Blackout 780.2
Blackwater fever 084.8
Bladder — *see* condition
Blast
  blindness 921.3
  concussion — *see* Blast, injury
  injury 869.0
    with open wound into cavity 869.1
    abdomen or thorax — *see* Injury, internal,
      by site
    brain (*see also* Concussion, brain) 850.9
      with skull fracture — *see* Fracture, skull
    ear (acoustic nerve trauma) 951.5
      with perforation, tympanic membrane
        — *see* Wound, open, ear, drum
    lung (*see also* Injury, internal, lung) 861.20
    otitic (explosive) 388.11
Blastomycosis, blastomycotic (chronic) (cutaneous) (disseminated) (lung) (pulmonary)
  (systemic) 116.0
  Brazilian 116.1
  European 117.5
  keloidal 116.2
  North American 116.0
  primary pulmonary 116.0
  South American 116.1
Bleb(s) 709.8
  emphysematous (bullous) (diffuse) (lung)
    (ruptured) (solitary) 492.0
  filtering, eye (postglaucoma) (status) V45.69
    with complication 997.99
    postcataract extraction (complication)
      997.99
  lung (ruptured) 492.0
    congenital 770.5
  subpleural (emphysematous) 492.0
Bleeder (familial) (hereditary) — *see also* Defect,
  coagulation 286.9
  nonfamilial 286.9
Bleeding — *see also* Hemorrhage 459.0
  anal 569.3
  anovulatory 628.0
  atonic, following delivery 666.1 ☑
  capillary 448.9
  due to subinvolution 621.1
    puerperal 666.2 ☑
  ear 388.69
  excessive, associated with menopausal onset
    627.0
  familial (*see also* Defect, coagulation) 286.9
  following intercourse 626.7
  gastrointestinal 578.9
  gums 523.8
  hemorrhoids — *see* Hemorrhoids, bleeding
  intermenstrual
    irregular 626.6
    regular 626.5
  intraoperative 998.11
  irregular NEC 626.4
  menopausal 627.0
  mouth 528.9

Bleeding — *see also* Hemorrhage —
  continued
  nipple 611.79
  nose 784.7
  ovulation 626.5
  postclimacteric 627.1
  postcoital 626.7
  postmenopausal 627.1
    following induced menopause 627.4
  postoperative 998.11
  preclimacteric 627.0
  puberty 626.3
    excessive, with onset of menstrual periods
      626.3
  rectum, rectal 569.3
  tendencies (*see also* Defect, coagulation) 286.9
  throat 784.8
  umbilical stump 772.3
  umbilicus 789.9
  unrelated to menstrual cycle 626.6
  uterus, uterine 626.9
    climacteric 627.0
    dysfunctional 626.8
    functional 626.8
    unrelated to menstrual cycle 626.6
  vagina, vaginal 623.8
    functional 626.8
  vicarious 625.8
Blennorrhagia, blennorrhagic — *see* Blennorrhea
Blennorrhea (acute) 098.0
  adultorum 098.40
  alveolaris 523.40
  chronic or duration of 2 months or over 098.2
  gonococcal (neonatorum) 098.40
  inclusion (neonatal) (newborn) 771.6
  neonatorum 098.40
Blepharelosis — *see also* Entropion 374.00
Blepharitis (eyelid) 373.00
  angularis 373.01
  ciliaris 373.00
    with ulcer 373.01
  marginal 373.00
    with ulcer 373.01
  scrofulous (*see also* Tuberculosis)
    017.3 ☑ *[373.00]*
  squamous 373.02
  ulcerative 373.01
Blepharochalasis 374.34
  congenital 743.62
Blepharoclonus 333.81
Blepharoconjunctivitis — *see also* Conjunctivitis
  372.20
  angular 372.21
  contact 372.22
Blepharophimosis (eyelid) 374.46
  congenital 743.62
Blepharoplegia 374.89
Blepharoptosis 374.30
  congenital 743.61
Blepharopyorrhea 098.49
Blepharospasm 333.81
  due to drugs 333.85
Blessig's cyst 362.62
Blighted ovum 631
Blind
  bronchus (congenital) 748.3
  eye (*see also* Blindness)
    hypertensive 360.42
    hypotensive 360.41
  loop syndrome (postoperative) 579.2
  sac, fallopian tube (congenital) 752.19
  spot, enlarged 368.42
  tract or tube (congenital) NEC — *see* Atresia
Blindness (acquired) (congenital) (both eyes)
  369.00
  with deafness V49.85
  blast 921.3
    with nerve injury — *see* Injury, nerve, optic
  Bright's — *see* Uremia
  color (congenital) 368.59
    acquired 368.55
    blue 368.53
    green 368.52
    red 368.51
    total 368.54

Blindness — *continued*
  concussion 950.9
  cortical 377.75
  day 368.10
    acquired 368.10
    congenital 368.10
    hereditary 368.10
    specified type NEC 368.10
  due to
    injury NEC 950.9
    refractive error — *see* Error, refractive
  eclipse (total) 363.31
  emotional 300.11
  face 368.16
  hysterical 300.11
  legal (both eyes) (USA definition) 369.4
    with impairment of better (less impaired)
      eye
      near-total 369.02
      with
        lesser eye impairment 369.02
          near-total 369.04
          total 369.03
      profound 369.05
      with
        lesser eye impairment 369.05
          near-total 369.07
          profound 369.08
          total 369.06
    severe 369.21
      with
        lesser eye impairment 369.21
          blind 369.11
          near-total 369.13
          profound 369.14
          severe 369.22
          total 369.12
    total
      with lesser eye impairment
        total 369.01
  mind 784.69
  moderate
    both eyes 369.25
      with impairment of lesser eye (speci-
        fied as)
        blind, not further specified 369.15
        low vision, not further specified
          369.23
        near-total 369.17
        profound 369.18
        severe 369.24
        total 369.16
    one eye 369.74
      with vision of other eye (specified as)
        near-normal 369.75
        normal 369.76
  near-total
    both eyes 369.04
      with impairment of lesser eye (speci-
        fied as)
        blind, not further specified 369.02
        total 369.03
    one eye 369.64
      with vision of other eye (specified as)
        near-normal 369.65
        normal 369.66
  night 368.60
    acquired 368.62
    congenital (Japanese) 368.61
    hereditary 368.61
    specified type NEC 368.69
    vitamin A deficiency 264.5
  nocturnal — *see* Blindness, night
  one eye 369.60
    with low vision of other eye 369.10
  profound
    both eyes 369.08
      with impairment of lesser eye (speci-
        fied as)
        blind, not further specified 369.05
        near-total 369.07
        total 369.06
    one eye 369.67
      with vision of other eye (specified as)
        near-normal 369.68
        normal 369.69

Blindness — *continued*
  psychic 784.69
  severe
    both eyes 369.22
      with impairment of lesser eye (speci-
        fied as)
        blind, not further specified 369.11
        low vision, not further specified
          369.21
        near-total 369.13
        profound 369.14
        total 369.12
    one eye 369.71
      with vision of other eye (specified as)
        near-normal 369.72
        normal 369.73
  snow 370.24
  sun 363.31
  temporary 368.12
  total
    both eyes 369.01
    one eye 369.61
      with vision of other eye (specified as)
        near-normal 369.62
        normal 369.63
  transient 368.12
  traumatic NEC 950.9
  word (developmental) 315.01
    acquired 784.61
    secondary to organic lesion 784.61
Blister — *see also* Injury, superficial, by site
  beetle dermatitis 692.89
  due to burn — *see* Burn, by site, second de-
    gree
  fever 054.9
  multiple, skin, nontraumatic 709.8
Bloating 787.3
Bloch-Siemens syndrome (incontinentia pigmenti) 757.33
Bloch-Stauffer dyshormonal dermatosis
  757.33
Bloch-Sulzberger disease or syndrome (incontinentia pigmenti) (melanoblastosis) 757.33
Block
  alveolar capillary 516.3
  arborization (heart) 426.6
  arrhythmic 426.9
  atrioventricular (AV) (incomplete) (partial)
    426.10
    with
      2:1 atrioventricular response block
        426.13
      atrioventricular dissociation 426.0
      first degree (incomplete) 426.11
      second degree (Mobitz type I) 426.13
        Mobitz (type) II 426.12
      third degree 426.0
    complete 426.0
      congenital 746.86
    congenital 746.86
    Mobitz (incomplete)
      type I (Wenckebach's) 426.13
      type II 426.12
    partial 426.13
  auriculoventricular (*see also* Block, atrioventric-
    ular) 426.10
    complete 426.0
      congenital 746.86
    congenital 746.86
  bifascicular (cardiac) 426.53
  bundle branch (complete) (false) (incomplete)
    426.50
    bilateral 426.53
    left (complete) (main stem) 426.3
      with right bundle branch block 426.53
      anterior fascicular 426.2
      with
        posterior fascicular block 426.3
        right bundle branch block
          426.52
      hemiblock 426.2
      incomplete 426.2
        with right bundle branch block
          426.53
      posterior fascicular 426.2

☑ Additional Digit Required — Refer to the Tabular List for Digit Selection   ⬙ Subterms under main terms may continue to next column or page

34 — Volume 2   ▶◀ Revised Text   ● New Line   ▲ Revised Code   **2010 ICD-9-CM**

Index

Bite(s) — Block

Block — *continued*
- bundle branch — *continued*
  - left — *continued*
    - posterior fascicular — *continued*
      - with
        - anterior fascicular block 426.3
        - right bundle branch block 426.51
    - right 426.4
      - with
        - left bundle branch block (incomplete) (main stem) 426.53
        - left fascicular block 426.53
          - anterior 426.52
          - posterior 426.51
    - Wilson's type 426.4
  - cardiac 426.9
  - conduction 426.9
    - complete 426.0
  - Eustachian tube (*see also* Obstruction, Eustachian tube) 381.60
  - fascicular (left anterior) (left posterior) 426.2
  - foramen Magendie (acquired) 331.3
    - congenital 742.3
      - with spina bifida (*see also* Spina bifida) 741.0 ☑
  - heart 426.9
    - first degree (atrioventricular) 426.11
    - second degree (atrioventricular) 426.13
    - third degree (atrioventricular) 426.0
    - bundle branch (complete) (false) (incomplete) 426.50
      - bilateral 426.53
        - left (*see also* Block, bundle branch, left) 426.3
        - right (*see also* Block, bundle branch, right) 426.4
    - complete (atrioventricular) 426.0
    - congenital 746.86
    - incomplete 426.13
    - intra-atrial 426.6
    - intraventricular NEC 426.6
    - sinoatrial 426.6
    - specified type NEC 426.6
  - hepatic vein 453.0
  - intraventricular (diffuse) (myofibrillar) 426.6
    - bundle branch (complete) (false) (incomplete) 426.50
      - bilateral 426.53
        - left (*see also* Block, bundle branch, left) 426.3
        - right (*see also* Block, bundle branch, right) 426.4
  - kidney (*see also* Disease, renal) 593.9
    - postcystoscopic 997.5
  - myocardial (*see also* Block, heart) 426.9
  - nodal 426.10
  - optic nerve 377.49
  - organ or site (congenital) NEC — *see* Atresia
  - parietal 426.6
  - peri-infarction 426.6
  - portal (vein) 452
  - sinoatrial 426.6
  - sinoauricular 426.6
  - spinal cord 336.9
  - trifascicular 426.54
  - tubal 628.2
  - vein NEC 453.9

Blocq's disease or syndrome (astasia-abasia) 307.9

Blood
- constituents, abnormal NEC 790.6
- disease 289.9
  - specified NEC 289.89
- donor V59.01
  - other blood components V59.09
  - stem cells V59.02
  - whole blood V59.01
- dyscrasia 289.9
  - with
    - abortion — *see* Abortion, by type, with hemorrhage, delayed or excessive
    - ectopic pregnancy (*see also* categories 633.0–633.9) 639.1

Blood — *continued*
- dyscrasia — *continued*
  - with — *continued*
    - molar pregnancy (*see also* categories 630–632) 639.1
    - following
      - abortion 639.1
      - ectopic or molar pregnancy 639.1
    - newborn NEC 776.9 ●
    - puerperal, postpartum 666.3 ☑
  - flukes NEC (*see also* Infestation, Schistosoma) 120.9
  - in
    - feces (*see also* Melena) 578.1
      - occult 792.1
    - urine (*see also* Hematuria) 599.70
  - mole 631
  - occult 792.1
  - poisoning (*see also* Septicemia) 038.9
  - pressure
    - decreased, due to shock following injury 958.4
    - fluctuating 796.4
    - high (*see also* Hypertension) 401.9
      - incidental reading (isolated) (nonspecific), without diagnosis of hypertension 796.2
    - low (*see also* Hypotension) 458.9
      - incidental reading (isolated) (nonspecific), without diagnosis of hypotension 796.3
  - spitting (*see also* Hemoptysis) 786.3
  - staining cornea 371.12
  - transfusion
    - without reported diagnosis V58.2
    - donor V59.01
      - stem cells V59.02
    - reaction or complication — *see* Complications, transfusion
  - tumor — *see* Hematoma
  - vessel rupture — *see* Hemorrhage
  - vomiting (*see also* Hematemesis) 578.0

Blood-forming organ disease 289.9
Bloodgood's disease 610.1
Bloodshot eye 379.93
Bloom (-Machacek) (-Torre) syndrome 757.39
Blotch, palpebral 372.55
Blount-Barber syndrome (tibia vara) 732.4
Blount's disease (tibia vara) 732.4
Blue
- baby 746.9
- bloater 491.20
  - with
    - acute bronchitis 491.22
    - exacerbation (acute) 491.21
- diaper syndrome 270.0
- disease 746.9
- dome cyst 610.0
- drum syndrome 381.02
- sclera 743.47
  - with fragility of bone and deafness 756.51
- toe syndrome 445.02

Blueness — *see also* Cyanosis 782.5
Blurring, visual 368.8
Blushing (abnormal) (excessive) 782.62
BMI (body mass index)
- adult
  - 25.0-25.9 V85.21
  - 26.0-26.9 V85.22
  - 27.0-27.9 V85.23
  - 28.0-28.9 V85.24
  - 29.0-29.9 V85.25
  - 30.0-30.9 V85.30
  - 31.0-31.9 V85.31
  - 32.0-32.9 V85.32
  - 33.0-33.9 V85.33
  - 34.0-34.9 V85.34
  - 35.0-35.9 V85.35
  - 36.0-36.9 V85.36
  - 37.0-37.9 V85.37
  - 38.0-38.9 V85.38
  - 39.0-39.9 V85.39
  - 40 and over V85.4
  - between 19-24 V85.1
  - less than 19 V85.0

BMI — *continued*
- pediatric
  - 5th percentile to less than 85th percentile for age V85.52
  - 85th percentile to less than 95th percentile for age V85.53
  - greater than or equal to 95th percentile for age V85.54
  - less than 5th percentile for age V85.51
Boarder, hospital V65.0
- infant V65.0
Bockhart's impetigo (superficial folliculitis) 704.8
Bodechtel-Guttmann disease (subacute sclerosing panencephalitis) 046.2
Boder-Sedgwick syndrome (ataxia-telangiectasia) 334.8
Body, bodies
- Aschoff (*see also* Myocarditis, rheumatic) 398.0
- asteroid, vitreous 379.22
- choroid, colloid (degenerative) 362.57
  - hereditary 362.77
- cytoid (retina) 362.82
- drusen (retina) (*see also* Drusen) 362.57
  - optic disc 377.21
- fibrin, pleura 511.0
- foreign — *see* Foreign body
- Hassall-Henle 371.41
- loose
  - joint (*see also* Loose, body, joint) 718.1 ☑
    - knee 717.6
  - knee 717.6
  - sheath, tendon 727.82
- Mallory's 034.1
- mass index (BMI)
  - adult
    - 25.0-25.9 V85.21
    - 26.0-26.9 V85.22
    - 27.0-27.9 V85.23
    - 28.0-28.9 V85.24
    - 29.0-29.9 V85.25
    - 30.0-30.9 V85.30
    - 31.0-31.9 V85.31
    - 32.0-32.9 V85.32
    - 33.0-33.9 V85.33
    - 34.0-34.9 V85.34
    - 36.0-36.9 V85.36
    - 37.0-37.9 V85.37
    - 38.0-38.9 V85.38
    - 39.0-39.9 V85.39
    - 40 and over V85.4
    - between 19-24 V85.1
    - less than 19 V85.0
  - pediatric
    - 5th percentile to less than 85th percentile for age V85.52
    - 85th percentile to less than 95th percentile for age V85.53
    - greater than or equal to 95th percentile for age V85.54
    - less than 5th percentile for age V85.51
- Mooser 081.0
- Negri 071
- rice (joint) (*see also* Loose, body, joint) 718.1 ☑
  - knee 717.6
- rocking 307.3
Boeck's
- disease (sarcoidosis) 135
- lupoid (miliary) 135
- sarcoid 135
Boerhaave's syndrome (spontaneous esophageal rupture) 530.4
Boggy
- cervix 622.8
- uterus 621.8
Boil — *see also* Carbuncle 680.9
- abdominal wall 680.2
- Aleppo 085.1
- ankle 680.6
- anus 680.5
- arm (any part, above wrist) 680.3
- auditory canal, external 680.0
- axilla 680.3
- back (any part) 680.2
- Baghdad 085.1
- breast 680.2
- buttock 680.5

Boil — *see also* Carbuncle — *continued*
- chest wall 680.2
- corpus cavernosum 607.2
- Delhi 085.1
- ear (any part) 680.0
- eyelid 373.13
- face (any part, except eye) 680.0
- finger (any) 680.4
- flank 680.2
- foot (any part) 680.7
- forearm 680.3
- Gafsa 085.1
- genital organ, male 608.4
- gluteal (region) 680.5
- groin 680.2
- hand (any part) 680.4
- head (any part, except face) 680.8
- heel 680.7
- hip 680.6
- knee 680.6
- labia 616.4
- lacrimal (*see also* Dacryocystitis) 375.30
  - gland (*see also* Dacryoadenitis) 375.00
  - passages (duct) (sac) (*see also* Dacryocystitis) 375.30
- leg, any part, except foot 680.6
- multiple sites 680.9
- natal 085.1
- neck 680.1
- nose (external) (septum) 680.0
- orbit, orbital 376.01
- partes posteriores 680.5
- pectoral region 680.2
- penis 607.2
- perineum 680.2
- pinna 680.0
- scalp (any part) 680.8
- scrotum 608.4
- seminal vesicle 608.0
- shoulder 680.3
- skin NEC 680.9
- specified site NEC 680.8
- spermatic cord 608.4
- temple (region) 680.0
- testis 608.4
- thigh 680.6
- thumb 680.4
- toe (any) 680.7
- tropical 085.1
- trunk 680.2
- tunica vaginalis 608.4
- umbilicus 680.2
- upper arm 680.3
- vas deferens 608.4
- vulva 616.4
- wrist 680.4
Bold hives — *see also* Urticaria 708.9
Bolivian hemorrhagic fever 078.7
Bombé, iris 364.74
Bomford-Rhoads anemia (refractory) 238.72
Bone — *see* condition
Bonnevie-Ullrich syndrome 758.6
Bonnier's syndrome 386.19
Bonvale Dam fever 780.79
Bony block of joint 718.80
- ankle 718.87
- elbow 718.82
- foot 718.87
- hand 718.84
- hip 718.85
- knee 718.86
- multiple sites 718.89
- pelvic region 718.85
- shoulder (region) 718.81
- specified site NEC 718.88
- wrist 718.83
BOOP (bronchiolitis obliterans organized pneumonia) 516.8
Borderline
- intellectual functioning V62.89
- osteopenia 733.90
- pelvis 653.1 ☑
  - with obstruction during labor 660.1 ☑
    - affecting fetus or newborn 763.1
- psychosis (*see also* Schizophrenia) 295.5 ☑

☑ Additional Digit Required — Refer to the Tabular List for Digit Selection   ⏍ Subterms under main terms may continue to next column or page

2010 ICD-9-CM   ▶◀ Revised Text   ● New Line   ▲ Revised Code   **October 2009 • Volume 2 — 35**

Borderline — continued
- psychosis (see also Schizophrenia) — continued
  - of childhood (see also Psychosis, childhood) 299.8 ☑
  - schizophrenia (see also Schizophrenia) 295.5 ☑
Borna disease 062.9
Bornholm disease (epidemic pleurodynia) 074.1
Borrelia vincentii (mouth) (pharynx) (tonsils) 101
Bostock's catarrh — see also Fever, hay 477.9
Boston exanthem 048
Botalli, ductus (patent) (persistent) 747.0
Bothriocephalus latus infestation 123.4
Botulism 005.1
- food poisoning 005.1
- infant 040.41
- non-foodborne 040.42
- wound 040.42
Bouba — see also Yaws 102.9
Bouffée délirante 298.3
Bouillaud's disease or syndrome (rheumatic heart disease) 391.9
Bourneville's disease (tuberous sclerosis) 759.5
Boutonneuse fever 082.1
Boutonniere
- deformity (finger) 736.21
- hand (intrinsic) 736.21
Bouveret (-Hoffmann) disease or syndrome (paroxysmal tachycardia) 427.2
Bovine heart — see Hypertrophy, cardiac
Bowel — see condition
Bowen's
- dermatosis (precancerous) (M8081/2) — see Neoplasm, skin, in situ
- disease (M8081/2) — see Neoplasm, skin, in situ
- epithelioma (M8081/2) — see Neoplasm, skin, in situ
- type
  - epidermoid carcinoma in situ (M8081/2) — see Neoplasm, skin, in situ
  - intraepidermal squamous cell carcinoma (M8081/2) — see Neoplasm, skin, in situ
Bowing
- femur 736.89
  - congenital 754.42
- fibula 736.89
  - congenital 754.43
- forearm 736.09
  - away from midline (cubitus valgus) 736.01
  - toward midline (cubitus varus) 736.02
- leg(s), long bones, congenital 754.44
- radius 736.09
  - away from midline (cubitus valgus) 736.01
  - toward midline (cubitus varus) 736.02
- tibia 736.89
  - congenital 754.43
Bowleg(s) 736.42
- congenital 754.44
- rachitic 268.1
Boyd's dysentery 004.2
Brachial — see condition
Brachman-de Lange syndrome (Amsterdam dwarf, mental retardation, and brachycephaly) 759.89
Brachycardia 427.89
Brachycephaly 756.0
Brachymorphism and ectopia lentis 759.89
Bradley's disease (epidemic vomiting) 078.82
Bradycardia 427.89
- chronic (sinus) 427.81
- newborn 779.81
- nodal 427.89
- postoperative 997.1
- reflex 337.09
- sinoatrial 427.89
  - with paroxysmal tachyarrhythmia or tachycardia 427.81
  - chronic 427.81
- sinus 427.89
  - with paroxysmal tachyarrhythmia or tachycardia 427.81
  - chronic 427.81
  - persistent 427.81

Bradycardia — continued
- sinus — continued
  - severe 427.81
  - tachycardia syndrome 427.81
  - vagal 427.89
Bradykinesia 781.0 ●
Bradypnea 786.09
Brailsford's disease 732.3
- radial head 732.3
- tarsal scaphoid 732.5
Brailsford-Morquio disease or syndrome (mucopolysaccharidosis IV) 277.5
Brain — see also condition
- death 348.89 ▲
- syndrome (acute) (chronic) (nonpsychotic) (organic) (with neurotic reaction) (with behavioral reaction) (see also Syndrome, brain) 310.9
  - with
    - presenile brain disease 290.10
    - psychosis, psychotic reaction (see also Psychosis, organic) 294.9
  - congenital (see also Retardation, mental) 319
Branched-chain amino-acid disease 270.3
Branchial — see condition
Brandt's syndrome (acrodermatitis enteropathica) 686.8
Brash (water) 787.1
Brass-founders' ague 985.8
Bravais-Jacksonian epilepsy — see also Epilepsy 345.5 ☑
Braxton Hicks contractions 644.1 ☑
Braziers' disease 985.8
Brazilian
- blastomycosis 116.1
- leishmaniasis 085.5
BRBPR (bright red blood per rectum) 569.3
Break
- cardiorenal — see Hypertension, cardiorenal
- retina (see also Defect, retina) 361.30
Breakbone fever 061
Breakdown
- device, implant, or graft — see Complications, mechanical
- nervous (see also Disorder, mental, nonpsychotic) 300.9
- perineum 674.2 ☑
Breast — see also condition
- buds 259.1
  - in newborn 779.89
- dense 793.82
- nodule 793.89
Breast feeding difficulties 676.8 ☑
Breath
- foul 784.99
- holder, child 312.81
- holding spells 786.9
- shortness 786.05
Breathing
- asymmetrical 786.09
- bronchial 786.09
- exercises V57.0
- labored 786.09
- mouth 784.99
  - causing malocclusion 524.59
- periodic 786.09
  - high altitude 327.22
- tic 307.20
Breathlessness 786.09
Breda's disease — see also Yaws 102.9
Breech
- delivery, affecting fetus or newborn 763.0
- extraction, affecting fetus or newborn 763.0
- presentation (buttocks) (complete) (frank) 652.2 ☑
  - with successful version 652.1 ☑
  - before labor, affecting fetus or newborn 761.7
  - during labor, affecting fetus or newborn 763.0
Breisky's disease (kraurosis vulvae) 624.09
Brennemann's syndrome (acute mesenteric lymphadenitis) 289.2
Brenner's
- tumor (benign) (M9000/0) 220

Brenner's — continued
- tumor — continued
  - borderline malignancy (M9000/1) 236.2
  - malignant (M9000/3) 183.0
  - proliferating (M9000/1) 236.2
Bretonneau's disease (diphtheritic malignant angina) 032.0
Breus' mole 631
Brevicollis 756.16
Bricklayers' itch 692.89
Brickmakers' anemia 126.9
Bridge
- myocardial 746.85
Bright's
- blindness — see Uremia
- disease (see also Nephritis) 583.9
  - arteriosclerotic (see also Hypertension, kidney) 403.90
Bright red blood per rectum (BRBPR) 569.3
Brill's disease (recrudescent typhus) 081.1
- flea-borne 081.0
- louse-borne 081.1
Brill-Symmers disease (follicular lymphoma) (M9690/3) 202.0 ☑
Brill-Zinsser disease (recrudescent typhus) 081.1
Brinton's disease (linitis plastica) (M8142/3) 151.9
Brion-Kayser disease — see also Fever, paratyphoid 002.9
Briquet's disorder or syndrome 300.81
Brissaud's
- infantilism (infantile myxedema) 244.9
- motor-verbal tic 307.23
Brissaud-Meige syndrome (infantile myxedema) 244.9
Brittle
- bones (congenital) 756.51
- nails 703.8
  - congenital 757.5
Broad — see also condition
- beta disease 272.2
- ligament laceration syndrome 620.6
Brock's syndrome (atelectasis due to enlarged lymph nodes) 518.0
Brocq's disease 691.8
- atopic (diffuse) neurodermatitis 691.8
- lichen simplex chronicus 698.3
- parakeratosis psoriasiformis 696.2
- parapsoriasis 696.2
Brocq-Duhring disease (dermatitis herpetiformis) 694.0
Brodie's
- abscess (localized) (chronic) (see also Osteomyelitis) 730.1 ☑
- disease (joint) (see also Osteomyelitis) 730.1 ☑
Broken
- arches 734
  - congenital 755.67
- back — see Fracture, vertebra, by site
- bone — see Fracture, by site
- compensation — see Disease, heart
- heart syndrome 429.83
- implant or internal device — see listing under Complications, mechanical
- neck — see Fracture, vertebra, cervical
- nose 802.0
  - open 802.1
- tooth, teeth 873.63
  - complicated 873.73
Bromhidrosis 705.89
Bromidism, bromism
- acute 967.3
  - correct substance properly administered 349.82
  - overdose or wrong substance given or taken 967.3
- chronic (see also Dependence) 304.1 ☑
Bromidrosiphobia 300.23
Bromidrosis 705.89
Bronchi, bronchial — see condition
Bronchiectasis (cylindrical) (diffuse) (fusiform) (localized) (moniliform) (postinfectious) (recurrent) (saccular) 494.0
- with acute exacerbation 494.1
- congenital 748.61
- tuberculosis (see also Tuberculosis) 011.5 ☑

Bronchiolectasis — see Bronchiectasis
Bronchiolitis (acute) (infectious) (subacute) 466.19
- with
  - bronchospasm or obstruction 466.19
  - influenza, flu, or grippe 487.1
- catarrhal (acute) (subacute) 466.19
- chemical 506.0
  - chronic 506.4
- chronic (obliterative) 491.8
- due to external agent — see Bronchitis, acute, due to
- fibrosa obliterans 491.8
- influenzal 487.1
- obliterans 491.8
  - with organizing pneumonia (BOOP) 516.8
  - status post lung transplant 996.84
- obliterative (chronic) (diffuse) (subacute) 491.8
  - due to fumes or vapors 506.4
- respiratory syncytial virus 466.11
- vesicular — see Pneumonia, broncho-
Bronchitis (diffuse) (hypostatic) (infectious) (inflammatory) (simple) 490
- with
  - emphysema — see Emphysema
  - influenza, flu, or grippe 487.1
  - obstruction airway, chronic 491.20
    - with
      - acute bronchitis 491.22
      - exacerbation (acute) 491.21
  - tracheitis 490
    - acute or subacute 466.0
      - with bronchospasm or obstruction 466.0
    - chronic 491.8
- acute or subacute 466.0
  - with
    - bronchiectasis 494.1
    - bronchospasm 466.0
    - obstruction 466.0
    - tracheitis 466.0
  - chemical (due to fumes or vapors) 506.0
  - due to
    - fumes or vapors 506.0
    - radiation 508.8
- allergic (acute) (see also Asthma) 493.9 ☑
- arachidic 934.1
- aspiration 507.0
  - due to fumes or vapors 506.0
- asthmatic (acute) 493.90
  - with
    - acute exacerbation 493.92
    - status asthmaticus 493.91
  - chronic 493.2 ☑
- capillary 466.19
  - with bronchospasm or obstruction 466.19
  - chronic 491.8
- caseous (see also Tuberculosis) 011.3 ☑
- Castellani's 104.8
- catarrhal 490
  - acute — see Bronchitis, acute
  - chronic 491.0
- chemical (acute) (subacute) 506.0
  - chronic 506.4
  - due to fumes or vapors (acute) (subacute) 506.0
    - chronic 506.4
- chronic 491.9
  - with
    - tracheitis (chronic) 491.8
  - asthmatic 493.2 ☑
  - catarrhal 491.0
  - chemical (due to fumes and vapors) 506.4
  - due to
    - fumes or vapors (chemical) (inhalation) 506.4
    - radiation 508.8
    - tobacco smoking 491.0
  - mucopurulent 491.1
  - obstructive 491.20
    - with
      - acute bronchitis 491.22
      - exacerbation (acute) 491.21
  - purulent 491.1
  - simple 491.0
  - specified type NEC 491.8

Bronchitis — *continued*
  croupous 466.0
    with bronchospasm or obstruction 466.0
    due to fumes or vapors 506.0
  emphysematous 491.20
    with
      acute bronchitis 491.22
      exacerbation (acute) 491.21
  exudative 466.0
  fetid (chronic) (recurrent) 491.1
  fibrinous, acute or subacute 466.0
    with bronchospasm or obstruction 466.0
  grippal 487.1
  influenzal 487.1
  membranous, acute or subacute 466.0
    with bronchospasm or obstruction 466.0
  moulders' 502
  mucopurulent (chronic) (recurrent) 491.1
    acute or subacute 466.0
  obliterans 491.8
  obstructive (chronic) 491.20
    with
      acute bronchitis 491.22
      exacerbation (acute) 491.21
  pituitous 491.1
  plastic (inflammatory) 466.0
  pneumococcal, acute or subacute 466.0
    with bronchospasm or obstruction 466.0
  pseudomembranous 466.0
  purulent (chronic) (recurrent) 491.1
    acute or subacute 466.0
      with bronchospasm or obstruction 466.0
  putrid 491.1
  scrofulous (*see also* Tuberculosis) 011.3 ☑
  senile 491.9
  septic, acute or subacute 466.0
    with bronchospasm or obstruction 466.0
  smokers' 491.0
  spirochetal 104.8
  suffocative, acute or subacute 466.0
  summer (*see also* Asthma) 493.9 ☑
  suppurative (chronic) 491.1
    acute or subacute 466.0
  tuberculous (*see also* Tuberculosis) 011.3 ☑
  ulcerative 491.8
    Vincent's 101
  Vincent's 101
  viral, acute or subacute 466.0
Bronchoalveolitis 485
Bronchoaspergillosis 117.3
Bronchocele
  meaning
    dilatation of bronchus 519.19
    goiter 240.9
Bronchogenic carcinoma 162.9
Bronchohemisporosis 117.9
Broncholithiasis 518.89
  tuberculous (*see also* Tuberculosis) 011.3 ☑
Bronchomalacia 748.3
Bronchomoniliasis 112.89
Bronchomycosis 112.89
Bronchonocardiosis 039.1
Bronchopleuropneumonia — *see* Pneumonia, broncho-
Bronchopneumonia — *see* Pneumonia, broncho-
Bronchopneumonitis — *see* Pneumonia, broncho-
Bronchopulmonary — *see* condition
Bronchopulmonitis — *see* Pneumonia, broncho-
Bronchorrhagia 786.3
  newborn 770.3
  tuberculous (*see also* Tuberculosis) 011.3 ☑
Bronchorrhea (chronic) (purulent) 491.0
  acute 466.0
Bronchospasm 519.11
  with
    asthma — *see* Asthma
    bronchiolitis, acute 466.19
      due to respiratory syncytial virus 466.11
    bronchitis — *see* Bronchitis
    chronic obstructive pulmonary disease (COPD) 496
    emphysema — *see* Emphysema

Bronchospasm — *continued*
  with — *continued*
    emphysema — *see* Emphysema — *continued*
      due to external agent — *see* Condition, respiratory, acute, due to
    acute 519.11
    exercise induced 493.81
Bronchospirochetosis 104.8
Bronchostenosis 519.19
Bronchus — *see* condition
Bronze, bronzed
  diabetes 275.0
  disease (Addison's) (skin) 255.41
    tuberculous (*see also* Tuberculosis) 017.6 ☑
Brooke's disease or tumor (M8100/0) — *see* Neoplasm, skin, benign
Brown enamel of teeth (hereditary) 520.5
Brown-Séquard's paralysis (syndrome) 344.89
Brown's tendon sheath syndrome 378.61
Brow presentation complicating delivery 652.4 ☑
Brucella, brucellosis (infection) 023.9
  abortus 023.1
  canis 023.3
  dermatitis, skin 023.9
  melitensis 023.0
  mixed 023.8
  suis 023.2
Bruck-de Lange disease or syndrome (Amsterdam dwarf, mental retardation, and brachycephaly) 759.89
Bruck's disease 733.99
Brugada syndrome 746.89
Brug's filariasis 125.1
Brugsch's syndrome (acropachyderma) 757.39
Bruhl's disease (splenic anemia with fever) 285.8
Bruise (skin surface intact) — *see also* Contusion
  with
    fracture — *see* Fracture, by site
    open wound — *see* Wound, open, by site
  internal organ (abdomen, chest, or pelvis) — *see* Injury, internal, by site
  umbilical cord 663.6 ☑
    affecting fetus or newborn 762.6
Bruit 785.9
  arterial (abdominal) (carotid) 785.9
  supraclavicular 785.9
Brushburn — *see* Injury, superficial, by site
Bruton's X-linked agammaglobulinemia 279.04
Bruxism 306.8
  sleep related 327.53
Bubbly lung syndrome 770.7
Bubo 289.3
  blennorrhagic 098.89
  chancroidal 099.0
  climatic 099.1
  due to Hemophilus ducreyi 099.0
  gonococcal 098.89
  indolent NEC 099.8
  inguinal NEC 099.8
    chancroidal 099.0
    climatic 099.1
    due to H. ducreyi 099.0
  scrofulous (*see also* Tuberculosis) 017.2 ☑
  soft chancre 099.0
  suppurating 683
  syphilitic 091.0
    congenital 090.0
  tropical 099.1
  venereal NEC 099.8
  virulent 099.0
Bubonic plague 020.0
Bubonocele — *see* Hernia, inguinal
Buccal — *see* condition
Buchanan's disease (juvenile osteochondrosis of iliac crest) 732.1
Buchem's syndrome (hyperostosis corticalis) 733.3
Buchman's disease (osteochondrosis, juvenile) 732.1
Bucket handle fracture (semilunar cartilage) — *see also* Tear, meniscus 836.2

Budd-Chiari syndrome (hepatic vein thrombosis) 453.0
Budgerigar-fanciers' disease or lung 495.2
Büdinger-Ludloff-Läwen disease 717.89
Buds
  breast 259.1
    in newborn 779.89
Buerger's disease (thromboangiitis obliterans) 443.1
Bulbar — *see* condition
Bulbus cordis 745.9
  persistent (in left ventricle) 745.8
Bulging fontanels (congenital) 756.0
Bulimia 783.6
  nervosa 307.51
  nonorganic origin 307.51
Bulky uterus 621.2
Bulla(e) 709.8
  lung (emphysematous) (solitary) 492.0
Bullet wound — *see also* Wound, open, by site
  fracture — *see* Fracture, by site, open
  internal organ (abdomen, chest, or pelvis) — *see* Injury, internal, by site, with open wound
  intracranial — *see* Laceration, brain, with open wound
Bullis fever 082.8
Bullying — *see also* Disturbance, conduct 312.0 ☑
Bundle
  branch block (complete) (false) (incomplete) 426.50
    bilateral 426.53
    left (*see also* Block, bundle branch, left) 426.3
      hemiblock 426.2
    right (*see also* Block, bundle branch, right) 426.4
  of His — *see* condition
  of Kent syndrome (anomalous atrioventricular excitation) 426.7
Bungpagga 040.81
Bunion 727.1
Bunionette 727.1
Bunyamwera fever 066.3
Buphthalmia, buphthalmos (congenital) 743.20
  associated with
    keratoglobus, congenital 743.22
    megalocornea 743.22
    ocular anomalies NEC 743.22
  isolated 743.21
  simple 743.21
Bürger-Grütz disease or syndrome (essential familial hyperlipemia) 272.3
Buried roots 525.3
Burke's syndrome 577.8
Burkitt's
  tumor (M9750/3) 200.2 ☑
  type malignant, lymphoma, lymphoblastic, or undifferentiated (M9750/3) 200.2 ☑
Burn (acid) (cathode ray) (caustic) (chemical) (electric heating appliance) (electricity) (fire) (flame) (hot liquid or object) (irradiation) (lime) (radiation) (steam) (thermal) (x-ray) 949.0

Note — Use the following fifth-digit subclassification with category 948 to indicate the percent of body surface with third degree burn:

0	*Less than 10% or unspecified*
1	*10–19%*
2	*20–29%*
3	*30–39%*
4	*40–49%*
5	*50–59%*
6	*60–69%*
7	*70–79%*
8	*80–89%*
9	*90% or more of body surface*

---

  with
    blisters — *see* Burn, by site, second degree

Burn — *continued*
  with — *continued*
    erythema — *see* Burn, by site, first degree
    skin loss (epidermal) (*see also* Burn, by site, second degree)
    full thickness (*see also* Burn, by site, third degree)
      with necrosis of underlying tissues — *see* Burn, by site, third degree, deep
  first degree — *see* Burn, by site, first degree
  second degree — *see* Burn, by site, second degree
  third degree — *see* Burn, by site, third degree
    deep — *see* Burn, by site, third degree, deep
  abdomen, abdominal (muscle) (wall) 942.03
    with
      trunk — *see* Burn, trunk, multiple sites
    first degree 942.13
    second degree 942.23
    third degree 942.33
      deep 942.43
        with loss of body part 942.53
  ankle 945.03
    with
      lower limb(s) — *see* Burn, leg, multiple sites
    first degree 945.13
    second degree 945.23
    third degree 945.33
      deep 945.43
        with loss of body part 945.53
  anus — *see* Burn, trunk, specified site NEC
  arm(s) 943.00
    first degree 943.10
    second degree 943.20
    third degree 943.30
      deep 943.40
        with loss of body part 943.50
    lower — *see* Burn, forearm(s)
    multiple sites, except hand(s) or wrist(s) 943.09
      first degree 943.19
      second degree 943.29
      third degree 943.39
        deep 943.49
          with loss of body part 943.59
    upper 943.03
      first degree 943.13
      second degree 943.23
      third degree 943.33
        deep 943.43
          with loss of body part 943.53
  auditory canal (external) — *see* Burn, ear
  auricle (ear) — *see* Burn, ear
  axilla 943.04
    with
      upper limb(s), except hand(s) or wrist(s) — *see* Burn, arm(s), multiple sites
    first degree 943.14
    second degree 943.24
    third degree 943.34
      deep 943.44
        with loss of body part 943.54
  back 942.04
    with
      trunk — *see* Burn, trunk, multiple sites
    first degree 942.14
    second degree 942.24
    third degree 942.34
      deep 942.44
        with loss of body part 942.54
  biceps
    brachii — *see* Burn, arm(s), upper
    femoris — *see* Burn, thigh
  breast(s) 942.01
    with
      trunk — *see* Burn, trunk, multiple sites
    first degree 942.11
    second degree 942.21
    third degree 942.31
      deep 942.41
        with loss of body part 942.51
  brow — *see* Burn, forehead

☑ Additional Digit Required — Refer to the Tabular List for Digit Selection   ▽ Subterms under main terms may continue to next column or page

2010 ICD-9-CM   ►◄ Revised Text   ● New Line   ▲ Revised Code   **Volume 2 — 37**

Burn — *continued*
buttock(s) — *see* Burn, back
canthus (eye) 940.1
chemical 940.0
cervix (uteri) 947.4
cheek (cutaneous) 941.07
with
face or head — *see* Burn, head, multiple sites
first degree 941.17
second degree 941.27
third degree 941.37
deep 941.47
with loss of body part 941.57
chest wall (anterior) 942.02
with
trunk — *see* Burn, trunk, multiple sites
first degree 942.12
second degree 942.22
third degree 942.32
deep 942.42
with loss of body part 942.52
chin 941.04
with
face or head — *see* Burn, head, multiple sites
first degree 941.14
second degree 941.24
third degree 941.34
deep 941.44
with loss of body part 941.54
clitoris — *see* Burn, genitourinary organs, external
colon 947.3
conjunctiva (and cornea) 940.4
chemical
acid 940.3
alkaline 940.2
cornea (and conjunctiva) 940.4
chemical
acid 940.3
alkaline 940.2
costal region — *see* Burn, chest wall
due to ingested chemical agent — *see* Burn, internal organs
ear (auricle) (canal) (drum) (external) 941.01
with
face or head — *see* Burn, head, multiple sites
first degree 941.11
second degree 941.21
third degree 941.31
deep 941.41
with loss of a body part 941.51
elbow 943.02
with
hand(s) and wrist(s) — *see* Burn, multiple specified sites
upper limb(s), except hand(s) or wrist(s) (*see also* Burn, arm(s), multiple sites)
first degree 943.12
second degree 943.22
third degree 943.32
deep 943.42
with loss of body part 943.52
electricity, electric current — *see* Burn, by site
entire body — *see* Burn, multiple, specified sites
epididymis — *see* Burn, genitourinary organs, external
epigastric region — *see* Burn, abdomen
epiglottis 947.1
esophagus 947.2
extent (percent of body surface)
less than 10 percent 948.0 ☑
10-19 percent 948.1 ☑
20-29 percent 948.2 ☑
30-39 percent 948.3 ☑
40-49 percent 948.4 ☑
50-59 percent 948.5 ☑
60-69 percent 948.6 ☑
70-79 percent 948.7 ☑
80-89 percent 948.8 ☑
90 percent or more 948.9 ☑

Burn — *continued*
extremity
lower — *see* Burn, leg
upper — *see* Burn, arm(s)
eye(s) (and adnexa) (only) 940.9
with
face, head, or neck 941.02
first degree 941.12
second degree 941.22
third degree 941.32
deep 941.42
with loss of body part 941.52
other sites (classifiable to more than one category in 940–945) — *see* Burn, multiple, specified sites
resulting rupture and destruction of eyeball 940.5
specified part — *see* Burn, by site
eyeball (*see also* Burn, eye)
with resulting rupture and destruction of eyeball 940.5
eyelid(s) 940.1
chemical 940.0
face — *see* Burn, head
finger (nail) (subungual) 944.01
with
hand(s) — *see* Burn, hand(s), multiple sites
other sites — *see* Burn, multiple, specified sites
thumb 944.04
first degree 944.14
second degree 944.24
third degree 944.34
deep 944.44
with loss of body part 944.54
first degree 944.11
second degree 944.21
third degree 944.31
deep 944.41
with loss of body part 944.51
multiple (digits) 944.03
with thumb — *see* Burn, finger, with thumb
first degree 944.13
second degree 944.23
third degree 944.33
deep 944.43
with loss of body part 944.53
flank — *see* Burn, abdomen
foot 945.02
with
lower limb(s) — *see* Burn, leg, multiple sites
first degree 945.12
second degree 945.22
third degree 945.32
deep 945.42
with loss of body part 945.52
forearm(s) 943.01
with
upper limb(s), except hand(s) or wrist(s) — *see* Burn, arm(s), multiple sites
first degree 943.11
second degree 943.21
third degree 943.31
deep 943.41
with loss of body part 943.51
forehead 941.07
with
face or head — *see* Burn, head, multiple sites
first degree 941.17
second degree 941.27
third degree 941.37
deep 941.47
with loss of body part 941.57
fourth degree — *see* Burn, by site, third degree, deep
friction — *see* Injury, superficial, by site
from swallowing caustic or corrosive substance NEC — *see* Burn, internal organs

Burn — *continued*
full thickness — *see* Burn, by site, third degree
gastrointestinal tract 947.3
genitourinary organs
external 942.05
with
trunk — *see* Burn, trunk, multiple sites
first degree 942.15
second degree 942.25
third degree 942.35
deep 942.45
with loss of body part 942.55
internal 947.8
globe (eye) — *see* Burn, eyeball
groin — *see* Burn, abdomen
gum 947.0
hand(s) (phalanges) (and wrist) 944.00
first degree 944.10
second degree 944.20
third degree 944.30
deep 944.40
with loss of body part 944.50
back (dorsal surface) 944.06
first degree 944.16
second degree 944.26
third degree 944.36
deep 944.46
with loss of body part 944.56
multiple sites 944.08
first degree 944.18
second degree 944.28
third degree 944.38
deep 944.48
with loss of body part 944.58
head (and face) 941.00
first degree 941.10
second degree 941.20
third degree 941.30
deep 941.40
with loss of body part 941.50
eye(s) only 940.9
specified part — *see* Burn, by site
multiple sites 941.09
with eyes — *see* Burn, eyes, with face, head, or neck
first degree 941.19
second degree 941.29
third degree 941.39
deep 941.49
with loss of body part 941.59
heel — *see* Burn, foot
hip — *see* Burn, trunk, specified site NEC
iliac region — *see* Burn, trunk, specified site NEC
infected 958.3
inhalation (*see also* Burn, internal organs) 947.9
internal organs 947.9
from caustic or corrosive substance (swallowing) NEC 947.9
specified NEC (*see also* Burn, by site) 947.8
interscapular region — *see* Burn, back
intestine (large) (small) 947.3
iris — *see* Burn, eyeball
knee 945.05
with
lower limb(s) — *see* Burn, leg, multiple sites
first degree 945.15
second degree 945.25
third degree 945.35
deep 945.45
with loss of body part 945.55
labium (majus) (minus) — *see* Burn, genitourinary organs, external
lacrimal apparatus, duct, gland, or sac 940.1
chemical 940.0
larynx 947.1
late effect — *see* Late, effects (of), burn
leg 945.00
first degree 945.10
second degree 945.20
third degree 945.30
deep 945.40
with loss of body part 945.50
lower 945.04

Burn — *continued*
leg — *continued*
lower — *continued*
with other part(s) of lower limb(s) — *see* Burn, leg, multiple sites
first degree 945.14
second degree 945.24
third degree 945.34
deep 945.44
with loss of body part 945.54
multiple sites 945.09
first degree 945.19
second degree 945.29
third degree 945.39
deep 945.49
with loss of body part 945.59
upper — *see* Burn, thigh
lightning — *see* Burn, by site
limb(s)
lower (including foot or toe(s)) — *see* Burn, leg
upper (except wrist and hand) — *see* Burn, arm(s)
lip(s) 941.03
with
face or head — *see* Burn, head, multiple sites
first degree 941.13
second degree 941.23
third degree 941.33
deep 941.43
with loss of body part 941.53
lumbar region — *see* Burn, back
lung 947.1
malar region — *see* Burn, cheek
mastoid region — *see* Burn, scalp
membrane, tympanic — *see* Burn, ear
midthoracic region — *see* Burn, chest wall
mouth 947.0
multiple (*see also* Burn, unspecified) 949.0
specified sites classifiable to more than one category in 940-945 ☑, 946.0
first degree 946.1
second degree 946.2
third degree 946.3
deep 946.4
with loss of body part 946.5
muscle, abdominal — *see* Burn, abdomen
nasal (septum) — *see* Burn, nose
neck 941.08
with
face or head — *see* Burn, head, multiple sites
first degree 941.18
second degree 941.28
third degree 941.38
deep 941.48
with loss of body part 941.58
nose (septum) 941.05
with
face or head — *see* Burn, head, multiple sites
first degree 941.15
second degree 941.25
third degree 941.35
deep 941.45
with loss of body part 941.55
occipital region — *see* Burn, scalp
orbit region 940.1
chemical 940.0
oronasopharynx 947.0
palate 947.0
palm(s) 944.05
with
hand(s) and wrist(s) — *see* Burn, hand(s), multiple sites
first degree 944.15
second degree 944.25
third degree 944.35
deep 944.45
with loss of a body part 944.55
parietal region — *see* Burn, scalp
penis — *see* Burn, genitourinary organs, external
perineum — *see* Burn, genitourinary organs, external

Burn — *continued*
  periocular area 940.1
    chemical 940.0
  pharynx 947.0
  pleura 947.1
  popliteal space — *see* Burn, knee
  prepuce — *see* Burn, genitourinary organs, external
  pubic region — *see* Burn, genitourinary organs, external
  pudenda — *see* Burn, genitourinary organs, external
  rectum 947.3
  sac, lacrimal 940.1
    chemical 940.0
  sacral region — *see* Burn, back
  salivary (ducts) (glands) 947.0
  scalp 941.06
    with
      face or neck — *see* Burn, head, multiple sites
    first degree 941.16
    second degree 941.26
    third degree 941.36
      deep 941.46
        with loss of body part 941.56
  scapular region 943.06
    with
      upper limb(s), except hand(s) or wrist(s) — *see* Burn, arm(s), multiple sites
    first degree 943.16
    second degree 943.26
    third degree 943.36
      deep 943.46
        with loss of body part 943.56
  sclera — *see* Burn, eyeball
  scrotum — *see* Burn, genitourinary organs, external
  septum, nasal — *see* Burn, nose
  shoulder(s) 943.05
    with
      hand(s) and wrist(s) — *see* Burn, multiple, specified sites
      upper limb(s), except hand(s) or wrist(s) — *see* Burn, arm(s), multiple sites
    first degree 943.15
    second degree 943.25
    third degree 943.35
      deep 943.45
        with loss of body part 943.55
  skin NEC (*see also* Burn, unspecified) 949.0
  skull — *see* Burn, head
  small intestine 947.3
  sternal region — *see* Burn, chest wall
  stomach 947.3
  subconjunctival — *see* Burn, conjunctiva
  subcutaneous — *see* Burn, by site, third degree
  submaxillary region — *see* Burn, head
  submental region — *see* Burn, chin
  sun — *see* Sunburn
  supraclavicular fossa — *see* Burn, neck
  supraorbital — *see* Burn, forehead
  temple — *see* Burn, scalp
  temporal region — *see* Burn, scalp
  testicle — *see* Burn, genitourinary organs, external
  testis — *see* Burn, genitourinary organs, external
  thigh 945.06
    with
      lower limb(s) — *see* Burn, leg, multiple sites
    first degree 945.16
    second degree 945.26
    third degree 945.36
      deep 945.46
        with loss of body part 945.56
  thorax (external) — *see* Burn, chest wall
  throat 947.0
  thumb(s) (nail) (subungual) 944.02
    with
      finger(s) — *see* Burn, finger, with other sites, thumb

Burn — *continued*
  thumb(s) — *continued*
    with — *continued*
      hand(s) and wrist(s) — *see* Burn, hand(s), multiple sites
    first degree 944.12
    second degree 944.22
    third degree 944.32
      deep 944.42
        with loss of body part 944.52
  toe (nail) (subungual) 945.01
    with
      lower limb(s) — *see* Burn, leg, multiple sites
    first degree 945.11
    second degree 945.21
    third degree 945.31
      deep 945.41
        with loss of body part 945.51
  tongue 947.0
  tonsil 947.0
  trachea 947.1
  trunk 942.00
    first degree 942.10
    second degree 942.20
    third degree 942.30
      deep 942.40
        with loss of body part 942.50
    multiple sites 942.09
      first degree 942.19
      second degree 942.29
      third degree 942.39
        deep 942.49
          with loss of body part 942.59
    specified site NEC 942.09
      first degree 942.19
      second degree 942.29
      third degree 942.39
        deep 942.49
          with loss of body part 942.59
  tunica vaginalis — *see* Burn, genitourinary organs, external
  tympanic membrane — *see* Burn, ear
  tympanum — *see* Burn, ear
  ultraviolet 692.82
  unspecified site (multiple) 949.0
    with extent of body surface involved specified
      less than 10 percent 948.0 ☑
      10-19 percent 948.1 ☑
      20-29 percent 948.2 ☑
      30-39 percent 948.3 ☑
      40-49 percent 948.4 ☑
      50-59 percent 948.5 ☑
      60-69 percent 948.6 ☑
      70-79 percent 948.7 ☑
      80-89 percent 948.8 ☑
      90 percent or more 948.9 ☑
    first degree 949.1
    second degree 949.2
    third degree 949.3
      deep 949.4
        with loss of body part 949.5
  uterus 947.4
  uvula 947.0
  vagina 947.4
  vulva — *see* Burn, genitourinary organs, external
  wrist(s) 944.07
    with
      hand(s) — *see* Burn, hand(s), multiple sites
    first degree 944.17
    second degree 944.27
    third degree 944.37
      deep 944.47
        with loss of body part 944.57
Burnett's syndrome (milk-alkali) 275.42
Burnier's syndrome (hypophyseal dwarfism) 253.3
Burning
  feet syndrome 266.2
  sensation (*see also* Disturbance, sensation) 782.0
  tongue 529.6

Burns' disease (osteochondrosis, lower ulna) 732.3
Bursa — *see also* condition
  pharynx 478.29
Bursitis NEC 727.3
  Achilles tendon 726.71
  adhesive 726.90
    shoulder 726.0
  ankle 726.79
  buttock 726.5
  calcaneal 726.79
  collateral ligament
    fibular 726.63
    tibial 726.62
  Duplay's 726.2
  elbow 726.33
  finger 726.8
  foot 726.79
  gonococcal 098.52
  hand 726.4
  hip 726.5
  infrapatellar 726.69
  ischiogluteal 726.5
  knee 726.60
  occupational NEC 727.2
  olecranon 726.33
  pes anserinus 726.61
  pharyngeal 478.29
  popliteal 727.51
  prepatellar 726.65
  radiohumeral 727.3
  scapulohumeral 726.19
    adhesive 726.0
  shoulder 726.10
    adhesive 726.0
  subacromial 726.19
    adhesive 726.0
  subcoracoid 726.19
  subdeltoid 726.19
    adhesive 726.0
  subpatellar 726.69
  syphilitic 095.7
  Thornwaldt's, Tornwaldt's (pharyngeal) 478.29
  toe 726.79
  trochanteric area 726.5
  wrist 726.4
Burst stitches or sutures (complication of surgery) (external) (*see also* Dehiscence) 998.32
  internal 998.31
Buruli ulcer 031.1
Bury's disease (erythema elevatum diutinum) 695.89
Buschke's disease or scleredema (adultorum) 710.1
Busquet's disease (osteoperiostitis) — *see also* Osteomyelitis 730.1 ☑
Busse-Buschke disease (cryptococcosis) 117.5
Buttock — *see* condition
Button
  Biskra 085.1
  Delhi 085.1
  oriental 085.1
Buttonhole hand (intrinsic) 736.21
Bwamba fever (encephalitis) 066.3
Byssinosis (occupational) 504
Bywaters' syndrome 958.5

C

Cacergasia 300.9
Cachexia 799.4
  cancerous (*see also* Neoplasm, by site, malignant) 799.4
  cardiac — *see* Disease, heart
  dehydration 276.51
    with
      hypernatremia 276.0
      hyponatremia 276.1
  due to malnutrition 799.4
  exophthalmic 242.0 ☑
  heart — *see* Disease, heart
  hypophyseal 253.2
  hypopituitary 253.2
  lead 984.9
    specified type of lead — *see* Table of Drugs and Chemicals

Cachexia — *continued*
  malaria 084.9
  malignant (*see also* Neoplasm, by site, malignant) 799.4
  marsh 084.9
  nervous 300.5
  old age 797
  pachydermic — *see* Hypothyroidism
  paludal 084.9
  pituitary (postpartum) 253.2
  renal (*see also* Disease, renal) 593.9
  saturnine 984.9
    specified type of lead — *see* Table of Drugs and Chemicals
  senile 797
  Simmonds' (pituitary cachexia) 253.2
  splenica 289.59
  strumipriva (*see also* Hypothyroidism) 244.9
  tuberculous NEC (*see also* Tuberculosis) 011.9 ☑
Café au lait spots 709.09
Caffey's disease or syndrome (infantile cortical hyperostosis) 756.59
Caisson disease 993.3
Caked breast (puerperal, postpartum) 676.2 ☑
Cake kidney 753.3
Calabar swelling 125.2
Calcaneal spur 726.73
Calcaneoapophysitis 732.5
Calcaneonavicular bar 755.67
Calcareous — *see* condition
Calcicosis (occupational) 502
Calciferol (vitamin D) **deficiency** 268.9
  with
    osteomalacia 268.2
    rickets (*see also* Rickets) 268.0
Calcification
  adrenal (capsule) (gland) 255.41
    tuberculous (*see also* Tuberculosis) 017.6 ☑
  aorta 440.0
  artery (annular) — *see* Arteriosclerosis
  auricle (ear) 380.89
  bladder 596.8
    due to S. hematobium 120.0
  brain (cortex) — *see* Calcification, cerebral
  bronchus 519.19
  bursa 727.82
  cardiac (*see also* Degeneration, myocardial) 429.1
  cartilage (postinfectional) 733.99
  cerebral (cortex) 348.89 ▲
    artery 437.0
  cervix (uteri) 622.8
  choroid plexus 349.2
  conjunctiva 372.54
  corpora cavernosa (penis) 607.89
  cortex (brain) — *see* Calcification, cerebral
  dental pulp (nodular) 522.2
  dentinal papilla 520.4
  disc, intervertebral 722.90
    cervical, cervicothoracic 722.91
    lumbar, lumbosacral 722.93
    thoracic, thoracolumbar 722.92
  fallopian tube 620.8
  falx cerebri — *see* Calcification, cerebral
  fascia 728.89
  gallbladder 575.8
  general 275.40
  heart (*see also* Degeneration, myocardial) 429.1
    valve — *see* Endocarditis
  intervertebral cartilage or disc (postinfectional) 722.90
    cervical, cervicothoracic 722.91
    lumbar, lumbosacral 722.93
    thoracic, thoracolumbar 722.92
  intracranial — *see* Calcification, cerebral
  intraspinal ligament 728.89
  joint 719.80
    ankle 719.87
    elbow 719.82
    foot 719.87
    hand 719.84
    hip 719.85
    knee 719.86
    multiple sites 719.89

☑ Additional Digit Required — Refer to the Tabular List for Digit Selection   ▽ Subterms under main terms may continue to next column or page

Calcification — *continued*
  joint — *continued*
    pelvic region 719.85
    shoulder (region) 719.81
    specified site NEC 719.88
    wrist 719.83
  kidney 593.89
    tuberculous (*see also* Tuberculosis)
      016.0 ☑
  larynx (senile) 478.79
  lens 366.8
  ligament 728.89
    intraspinal 728.89
    knee (medial collateral) 717.89
  lung 518.89
    active 518.89
    postinfectional 518.89
    tuberculous (*see also* Tuberculosis, pulmonary) 011.9 ☑
  lymph gland or node (postinfectional) 289.3
    tuberculous (*see also* Tuberculosis, lymph gland) 017.2 ☑
  mammographic 793.89
  massive (paraplegic) 728.10
  medial NEC (*see also* Arteriosclerosis, extremities) 440.20
  meninges (cerebral) 349.2
  metastatic 275.40
  Mönckeberg's — *see* Arteriosclerosis
  muscle 728.10
    heterotopic, postoperative 728.13
  myocardium, myocardial (*see also* Degeneration, myocardial) 429.1
  ovary 620.8
  pancreas 577.8
  penis 607.89
  periarticular 728.89
  pericardium (*see also* Pericarditis) 423.8
  pineal gland 259.8
  pleura 511.0
    postinfectional 518.89
    tuberculous (*see also* Tuberculosis, pleura) 012.0 ☑
  pulp (dental) (nodular) 522.2
  renal 593.89
  Rider's bone 733.99
  sclera 379.16
  semilunar cartilage 717.89
  spleen 289.59
  subcutaneous 709.3
  suprarenal (capsule) (gland) 255.41
  tendon (sheath) 727.82
    with bursitis, synovitis or tenosynovitis 727.82
  trachea 519.19
  ureter 593.89
  uterus 621.8
  vitreous 379.29
Calcified — *see also* Calcification
  hematoma NEC 959.9
Calcinosis (generalized) (interstitial) (tumoral) (universalis) 275.49
  circumscripta 709.3
  cutis 709.3
  intervertebralis 275.49 [722.90]
  Raynaud's phenomenonsclerodactylytelangiectasis (CRST) 710.1
Calciphylaxis — *see also* Calcification, by site 275.49
Calcium
  blood
    high (*see also* Hypercalcemia) 275.42
    low (*see also* Hypocalcemia) 275.41
  deposits (*see also* Calcification, by site)
    in bursa 727.82
    in tendon (sheath) 727.82
      with bursitis, synovitis or tenosynovitis 727.82
  salts or soaps in vitreous 379.22
Calciuria 791.9
Calculi — *see* Calculus
Calculosis, intrahepatic — *see* Choledocholithiasis
Calculus, calculi, calculous 592.9
  ampulla of Vater — *see* Choledocholithiasis
  anuria (impacted) (recurrent) 592.0

Calculus, calculi, calculous — *continued*
  appendix 543.9
  bile duct (any) — *see* Choledocholithiasis
  biliary — *see* Cholelithiasis
  bilirubin, multiple — *see* Cholelithiasis
  bladder (encysted) (impacted) (urinary) 594.1
    diverticulum 594.0
  bronchus 518.89
  calyx (kidney) (renal) 592.0
    congenital 753.3
  cholesterol (pure) (solitary) — *see* Cholelithiasis
  common duct (bile) — *see* Choledocholithiasis
  conjunctiva 372.54
  cystic 594.1
    duct — *see* Cholelithiasis
  dental 523.6
    subgingival 523.6
    supragingival 523.6
  epididymis 608.89
  gallbladder (*see also* Cholelithiasis)
    congenital 751.69
  hepatic (duct) — *see* Choledocholithiasis
  intestine (impaction) (obstruction) 560.39
  kidney (impacted) (multiple) (pelvis) (recurrent) (staghorn) 592.0
    congenital 753.3
  lacrimal (passages) 375.57
  liver (impacted) — *see* Choledocholithiasis
  lung 518.89
  mammographic 793.89
  nephritic (impacted) (recurrent) 592.0
  nose 478.19
  pancreas (duct) 577.8
  parotid gland 527.5
  pelvis, encysted 592.0
  prostate 602.0
  pulmonary 518.89
  renal (impacted) (recurrent) 592.0
    congenital 753.3
  salivary (duct) (gland) 527.5
  seminal vesicle 608.89
  staghorn 592.0
  Stensen's duct 527.5
  sublingual duct or gland 527.5
    congenital 750.26
  submaxillary duct, gland, or region 527.5
  suburethral 594.8
  tonsil 474.8
  tooth, teeth 523.6
  tunica vaginalis 608.89
  ureter (impacted) (recurrent) 592.1
  urethra (impacted) 594.2
  urinary (duct) (impacted) (passage) (tract) 592.9
    lower tract NEC 594.9
      specified site 594.8
  vagina 623.8
  vesical (impacted) 594.1
  Wharton's duct 527.5
Caliectasis 593.89
California
  disease 114.0
  encephalitis 062.5
Caligo cornea 371.03
Callositas, callosity (infected) 700
Callus (infected) 700
  bone 726.91
  excessive, following fracture (*see also* Late, effect (of), fracture)
Calvé (-Perthes) disease (osteochondrosis, femoral capital) 732.1
Calvities — *see also* Alopecia 704.00
Cameroon fever — *see also* Malaria 084.6
Camptocormia 300.11
Camptodactyly (congenital) 755.59
Camurati-Engelmann disease (diaphyseal sclerosis) 756.59
Canal — *see* condition
Canaliculitis (lacrimal) (acute) 375.31
  Actinomyces 039.8
  chronic 375.41
Canavan's disease 330.0

Cancer (M8000/3) — *see also* Neoplasm, by site, malignant

> *Note* — The term "cancer" when modified by an adjective or adjectival phrase indicating a morphological type should be coded in the same manner as "carcinoma" with that adjective or phrase. Thus, "squamous-cell cancer" should be coded in the same manner as "squamous-cell carcinoma," which appears in the list under "Carcinoma."

  bile duct type (M8160/3), liver 155.1
  hepatocellular (M8170/3) 155.0
Cancerous (M8000/3) — *see* Neoplasm, by site, malignant
Cancerphobia 300.29
Cancrum oris 528.1
Candidiasis, candidal 112.9
  with pneumonia 112.4
  balanitis 112.2
  congenital 771.7
  disseminated 112.5
  endocarditis 112.81
  esophagus 112.84
  intertrigo 112.3
  intestine 112.85
  lung 112.4
  meningitis 112.83
  mouth 112.0
  nails 112.3
  neonatal 771.7
  onychia 112.3
  otitis externa 112.82
  otomycosis 112.82
  paronychia 112.3
  perionyxis 112.3
  pneumonia 112.4
  pneumonitis 112.4
  skin 112.3
  specified site NEC 112.89
  systemic 112.5
  urogenital site NEC 112.2
  vagina 112.1
  vulva 112.1
  vulvovaginitis 112.1
Candidiosis — *see* Candidiasis
Candiru infection or infestation 136.8
Canities (premature) 704.3
  congenital 757.4
Canker (mouth) (sore) 528.2
  rash 034.1
Cannabinosis 504
Canton fever 081.9
Cap
  cradle 690.11
Capillariasis 127.5
Capillary — *see* condition
Caplan-Colinet syndrome 714.81
Caplan's syndrome 714.81
Capsule — *see* condition
Capsulitis (joint) 726.90
  adhesive (shoulder) 726.0
  hip 726.5
  knee 726.60
  labyrinthine 387.8
  thyroid 245.9
  wrist 726.4
Caput
  crepitus 756.0
  medusae 456.8
  succedaneum 767.19
Carapata disease 087.1
Carate — *see* Pinta
Carbohydrate-deficient glycoprotein syndrome (CGDS) 271.8
Carboxyhemoglobinemia 986
Carbuncle 680.9
  abdominal wall 680.2
  ankle 680.6
  anus 680.5
  arm (any part, above wrist) 680.3
  auditory canal, external 680.0
  axilla 680.3
  back (any part) 680.2
  breast 680.2
  buttock 680.5
  chest wall 680.2

Carbuncle — *continued*
  corpus cavernosum 607.2
  ear (any part) (external) 680.0
  eyelid 373.13
  face (any part, except eye) 680.0
  finger (any) 680.4
  flank 680.2
  foot (any part) 680.7
  forearm 680.3
  genital organ (male) 608.4
  gluteal (region) 680.5
  groin 680.2
  hand (any part) 680.4
  head (any part, except face) 680.8
  heel 680.7
  hip 680.6
  kidney (*see also* Abscess, kidney) 590.2
  knee 680.6
  labia 616.4
  lacrimal
    gland (*see also* Dacryoadenitis) 375.00
    passages (duct) (sac) (*see also* Dacryocystitis) 375.30
  leg, any part except foot 680.6
  lower extremity, any part except foot 680.6
  malignant 022.0
  multiple sites 680.9
  neck 680.1
  nose (external) (septum) 680.0
  orbit, orbital 376.01
  partes posteriores 680.5
  pectoral region 680.2
  penis 607.2
  perineum 680.2
  pinna 680.0
  scalp (any part) 680.8
  scrotum 608.4
  seminal vesicle 608.0
  shoulder 680.3
  skin NEC 680.9
  specified site NEC 680.8
  spermatic cord 608.4
  temple (region) 680.0
  testis 608.4
  thigh 680.6
  thumb 680.4
  toe (any) 680.7
  trunk 680.2
  tunica vaginalis 608.4
  umbilicus 680.2
  upper arm 680.3
  urethra 597.0
  vas deferens 608.4
  vulva 616.4
  wrist 680.4
Carbunculus — *see also* Carbuncle 680.9
Carcinoid (tumor) (M8240/1) — *see* Tumor, carcinoid
Carcinoidosis 259.2
Carcinomaphobia 300.29
Carcinomatosis
  peritonei (M8010/6) 197.6
  specified site NEC (M8010/3) — *see* Neoplasm, by site, malignant
  unspecified site (M8010/6) 199.0
Carcinoma (M8010/3) — *see also* Neoplasm, by site, malignant

> *Note* — Except where otherwise indicated, the morphological varieties of carcinoma in the list below should be coded by site as for "Neoplasm, malignant."

  with
    apocrine metaplasia (M8573/3)
    cartilaginous (and osseous) metaplasia (M8571/3)
    osseous (and cartilaginous) metaplasia (M8571/3)
    productive fibrosis (M8141/3)
    spindle cell metaplasia (M8572/3)
    squamous metaplasia (M8570/3)
  acidophil (M8280/3)
    specified site — *see* Neoplasm, by site, malignant
    unspecified site 194.3

Carcinoma — *see also* Neoplasm, by site, malignant — *continued*
  acidophil-basophil, mixed (M8281/3)
    specified site — *see* Neoplasm, by site, malignant
    unspecified site 194.3
  acinar (cell) (M8550/3)
  acinic cell (M8550/3)
  adenocystic (M8200/3)
  adenoid
    cystic (M8200/3)
    squamous cell (M8075/3)
  adenosquamous (M8560/3)
  adnexal (skin) (M8390/3) — *see* Neoplasm, skin, malignant
  adrenal cortical (M8370/3) 194.0
  alveolar (M8251/3)
    cell (M8250/3) — *see* Neoplasm, lung, malignant
  anaplastic type (M8021/3)
  apocrine (M8401/3)
    breast — *see* Neoplasm, breast, malignant
    specified site NEC — *see* Neoplasm, skin, malignant
    unspecified site 173.9
  basal cell (pigmented) (M8090/3) (*see also* Neoplasm, skin, malignant)
    fibro-epithelial type (M8093/3) — *see* Neoplasm, skin, malignant
    morphea type (M8092/3) — *see* Neoplasm, skin, malignant
    multicentric (M8091/3) — *see* Neoplasm, skin, malignant
  basaloid (M8123/3)
  basal-squamous cell, mixed (M8094/3) — *see* Neoplasm, skin, malignant
  basophil (M8300/3)
    specified site — *see* Neoplasm, by site, malignant
    unspecified site 194.3
  basophil-acidophil, mixed (M8281/3)
    specified site — *see* Neoplasm, by site, malignant
    unspecified site 194.3
  basosquamous (M8094/3) — *see* Neoplasm, skin, malignant
  bile duct type (M8160/3)
    and hepatocellular, mixed (M8180/3) 155.0
    liver 155.1
    specified site NEC — *see* Neoplasm, by site, malignant
    unspecified site 155.1
  branchial or branchiogenic 146.8
  bronchial or bronchogenic — *see* Neoplasm, lung, malignant
  bronchiolar (terminal) (M8250/3) — *see* Neoplasm, lung, malignant
  bronchiolo-alveolar (M8250/3) — *see* Neoplasm, lung, malignant
  bronchogenic (epidermoid) 162.9
  C cell (M8510/3)
    specified site — *see* Neoplasm, by site, malignant
    unspecified site 193
  ceruminous (M8420/3) 173.2
  chorionic (M9100/3)
    specified site — *see* Neoplasm, by site, malignant
    unspecified site
      female 181
      male 186.9
  chromophobe (M8270/3)
    specified site — *see* Neoplasm, by site, malignant
    unspecified site 194.3
  clear cell (mesonephroid type) (M8310/3)
  cloacogenic (M8124/3)
    specified site — *see* Neoplasm, by site, malignant
    unspecified site 154.8
  colloid (M8480/3)
  cribriform (M8201/3)
  cylindroid type (M8200/3)
  diffuse type (M8145/3)
    specified site — *see* Neoplasm, by site, malignant

Carcinoma — *see also* Neoplasm, by site, malignant — *continued*
  diffuse type — *continued*
    unspecified site 151.9
  duct (cell) (M8500/3)
    with Paget's disease (M8541/3) — *see* Neoplasm, breast, malignant
    infiltrating (M8500/3)
      specified site — *see* Neoplasm, by site, malignant
      unspecified site 174.9
  ductal (M8500/3)
  ductular, infiltrating (M8521/3)
  embryonal (M9070/3)
    and teratoma, mixed (M9081/3)
    combined with choriocarcinoma (M9101/3) — *see* Neoplasm, by site, malignant
    infantile type (M9071/3)
    liver 155.0
    polyembryonal type (M9072/3)
  endometrioid (M8380/3)
  eosinophil (M8280/3)
    specified site — *see* Neoplasm, by site, malignant
    unspecified site 194.3
  epidermoid (M8070/3) (*see also* Carcinoma, squamous cell)
    and adenocarcinoma, mixed (M8560/3)
    in situ, Bowen's type (M8081/2) — *see* Neoplasm, skin, in situ
    intradermal — *see* Neoplasm, skin, in situ
    fibroepithelial type basal cell (M8093/3) — *see* Neoplasm, skin, malignant
  follicular (M8330/3)
    and papillary (mixed) (M8340/3) 193
    moderately differentiated type (M8332/3) 193
    pure follicle type (M8331/3) 193
    specified site — *see* Neoplasm, by site, malignant
    trabecular type (M8332/3) 193
    unspecified site 193
    well differentiated type (M8331/3) 193
  gelatinous (M8480/3)
  giant cell (M8031/3)
    and spindle cell (M8030/3)
  granular cell (M8320/3)
  granulosa cell (M8620/3) 183.0
  hepatic cell (M8170/3) 155.0
  hepatocellular (M8170/3) 155.0
    and bile duct, mixed (M8180/3) 155.0
  hepatocholangiolitic (M8180/3) 155.0
  Hürthle cell (thyroid) 193
  hypernephroid (M8311/3)
  in
    adenomatous
      polyp (M8210/3)
      polyposis coli (M8220/3) 153.9
    pleomorphic adenoma (M8940/3)
    polypoid adenoma (M8210/3)
    situ (M8010/3) — *see* Carcinoma, in situ
    tubular adenoma (M8210/3)
    villous adenoma (M8261/3)
  infiltrating duct (M8500/3)
    with Paget's disease (M8541/3) — *see* Neoplasm, breast, malignant
    specified site — *see* Neoplasm, by site, malignant
    unspecified site 174.9
  inflammatory (M8530/3)
    specified site — *see* Neoplasm, by site, malignant
    unspecified site 174.9
  in situ (M8010/2) (*see also* Neoplasm, by site, in situ)
    epidermoid (M8070/2) (*see also* Neoplasm, by site, in situ)
      with questionable stromal invasion (M8076/2)
      specified site — *see* Neoplasm, by site, in situ
      unspecified site 233.1
    Bowen's type (M8081/2) — *see* Neoplasm, skin, in situ

Carcinoma — *see also* Neoplasm, by site, malignant — *continued*
  in situ (*see also* Neoplasm, by site, in situ) — *continued*
    intraductal (M8500/2)
      specified site — *see* Neoplasm, by site, in situ
      unspecified site 233.0
    lobular (M8520/2)
      specified site — *see* Neoplasm, by site, in situ
      unspecified site 233.0
    papillary (M8050/2) — *see* Neoplasm, by site, in situ
    squamous cell (M8070/2) (*see also* Neoplasm, by site, in situ)
      with questionable stromal invasion (M8076/2)
      specified site — *see* Neoplasm, by site, in situ
      unspecified site 233.1
    transitional cell (M8120/2) — *see* Neoplasm, by site, in situ
  intestinal type (M8144/3)
    specified site — *see* Neoplasm, by site, malignant
    unspecified site 151.9
  intraductal (noninfiltrating) (M8500/2)
    papillary (M8503/2)
      specified site — *see* Neoplasm, by site, in situ
      unspecified site 233.0
    specified site — *see* Neoplasm, by site, in situ
    unspecified site 233.0
  intraepidermal (M8070/2) (*see also* Neoplasm, skin, in situ)
    squamous cell, Bowen's type (M8081/2) — *see* Neoplasm, skin, in situ
  intraepithelial (M8010/2) (*see also* Neoplasm, by site, in situ)
    squamous cell (M8072/2) — *see* Neoplasm, by site, in situ
  intraosseous (M9270/3) 170.1
    upper jaw (bone) 170.0
  islet cell (M8150/3)
    and exocrine, mixed (M8154/3)
      specified site — *see* Neoplasm, by site, malignant
      unspecified site 157.9
    pancreas 157.4
    specified site NEC — *see* Neoplasm, by site, malignant
    unspecified site 157.4
  juvenile, breast (M8502/3) — *see* Neoplasm, breast, malignant
  Kulchitsky's cell (carcinoid tumor of intestine) 259.2
  large cell (M8012/3)
    squamous cell, non-keratinizing type (M8072/3)
  Leydig cell (testis) (M8650/3)
    specified site — *see* Neoplasm, by site, malignant
    unspecified site 186.9
      female 183.0
      male 186.9
  liver cell (M8170/3) 155.0
  lobular (infiltrating) (M8520/3)
    non-infiltrating (M8520/3)
      specified site — *see* Neoplasm, by site, in situ
      unspecified site 233.0
    specified site — *see* Neoplasm, by site, malignant
    unspecified site 174.9
  lymphoepithelial (M8082/3)
  medullary (M8510/3)
    with
      amyloid stroma (M8511/3)
        specified site — *see* Neoplasm, by site, malignant
        unspecified site 193
      lymphoid stroma (M8512/3)
        specified site — *see* Neoplasm, by site, malignant

Carcinoma — *see also* Neoplasm, by site, malignant — *continued*
  medullary — *continued*
    with — *continued*
      lymphoid stroma — *continued*
        unspecified site 174.9
  Merkel cell 209.36 ●
    buttock 209.36 ●
    ear 209.31 ●
    eyelid, including canthus 209.31 ●
    face 209.31 ●
    genitals 209.36 ●
    lip 209.31 ●
    lower limb 209.34 ●
    neck 209.32 ●
    nodal presentation 209.75 ●
    scalp 209.32 ●
    secondary (any site) 209.75 ●
    specified site NEC 209.36 ●
    trunk 209.35 ●
    unknown primary site 209.75 ●
    upper limb 209.33 ●
    visceral metastatic presentation 209.75 ●
  mesometanephric (M9110/3)
  mesonephric (M9110/3)
  metastatic (M8010/6) — *see* Metastasis, cancer
  metatypical (M8095/3) — *see* Neoplasm, skin, malignant
  morphea type basal cell (M8092/3) — *see* Neoplasm, skin, malignant
  mucinous (M8480/3)
  mucin-producing (M8481/3)
  mucin-secreting (M8481/3)
  mucoepidermoid (M8430/3)
  mucoid (M8480/3)
    cell (M8300/3)
      specified site — *see* Neoplasm, by site, malignant
      unspecified site 194.3
  mucous (M8480/3)
  neuroendocrine
    high grade (M8240/3) 209.30
    malignant poorly differentiated (M8240/3) 209.30
  nonencapsulated sclerosing (M8350/3) 193
  noninfiltrating
    intracystic (M8504/2) — *see* Neoplasm, by site, in situ
    intraductal (M8500/2)
      papillary (M8503/2)
        specified site — *see* Neoplasm, by site, in situ
        unspecified site 233.0
      specified site — *see* Neoplasm, by site, in situ
      unspecified site 233.0
    lobular (M8520/2)
      specified site — *see* Neoplasm, by site, in situ
      unspecified site 233.0
  oat cell (M8042/3)
    specified site — *see* Neoplasm, by site, malignant
    unspecified site 162.9
  odontogenic (M9270/3) 170.1
    upper jaw (bone) 170.0
  onocytic (M8290/3)
  oxyphilic (M8290/3)
  papillary (M8050/3)
    and follicular (mixed) (M8340/3) 193
    epidermoid (M8052/3)
    intraductal (noninfiltrating) (M8503/2)
      specified site — *see* Neoplasm, by site, in situ
      unspecified site 233.0
    serous (M8460/3)
      specified site — *see* Neoplasm, by site, malignant
    surface (M8461/3)
      specified site — *see* Neoplasm, by site, malignant
      unspecified site 183.0
    unspecified site 183.0

☑ Additional Digit Required — Refer to the Tabular List for Digit Selection   ▼ Subterms under main terms may continue to next column or page

2010 ICD-9-CM   ▶◀ Revised Text   ● New Line   ▲ Revised Code   October 2009 • Volume 2 — 41

Carcinoma — see also Neoplasm, by site, malignant — continued
  papillary — continued
    squamous cell (M8052/3)
    transitional cell (M8130/3)
  papillocystic (M8450/3)
    specified site — see Neoplasm, by site, malignant
    unspecified site 183.0
  parafollicular cell (M8510/3)
    specified site — see Neoplasm, by site, malignant
    unspecified site 193
  pleomorphic (M8022/3)
  polygonal cell (M8034/3)
  prickle cell (M8070/3)
  pseudoglandular, squamous cell (M8075/3)
  pseudomucinous (M8470/3)
    specified site — see Neoplasm, by site, malignant
    unspecified site 183.0
  pseudosarcomatous (M8033/3)
  regaud type (M8082/3) — see Neoplasm, nasopharynx, malignant
  renal cell (M8312/3) 189.0
  reserve cell (M8041/3)
  round cell (M8041/3)
  Schmincke (M8082/3) — see Neoplasm, nasopharynx, malignant
  Schneiderian (M8121/3)
    specified site — see Neoplasm, by site, malignant
    unspecified site 160.0
  scirrhous (M8141/3)
  sebaceous (M8410/3) — see Neoplasm, skin, malignant
  secondary (M8010/6) — see Neoplasm, by site, malignant, secondary
  secretory, breast (M8502/3) — see Neoplasm, breast, malignant
  serous (M8441/3)
    papillary (M8460/3)
      specified site — see Neoplasm, by site, malignant
      unspecified site 183.0
    surface, papillary (M8461/3)
      specified site — see Neoplasm, by site, malignant
      unspecified site 183.0
  Sertoli cell (M8640/3)
    specified site — see Neoplasm, by site, malignant
    unspecified site 186.9
  signet ring cell (M8490/3)
    metastatic (M8490/6) — see Neoplasm, by site, secondary
  simplex (M8231/3)
  skin appendage (M8390/3) — see Neoplasm, skin, malignant
  small cell (M8041/3)
    fusiform cell type (M8043/3)
    squamous cell, non-keratinizing type (M8073/3)
  solid (M8230/3)
    with amyloid stroma (M8511/3)
      specified site — see Neoplasm, by site, malignant
      unspecified site 193
  spheroidal cell (M8035/3)
  spindle cell (M8032/3)
    and giant cell (M8030/3)
  spinous cell (M8070/3)
  squamous (cell) (M8070/3)
    adenoid type (M8075/3)
    and adenocarcinoma, mixed (M8560/3)
    intraepidermal, Bowen's type — see Neoplasm, skin, in situ
    keratinizing type (large cell) (M8071/3)
    large cell, non-keratinizing type (M8072/3)
    microinvasive (M8076/3)
      specified site — see Neoplasm, by site, malignant
      unspecified site 180.9

Carcinoma — see also Neoplasm, by site, malignant — continued
  squamous — continued
    non-keratinizing type (M8072/3)
    papillary (M8052/3)
    pseudoglandular (M8075/3)
    small cell, non-keratinizing type (M8073/3)
    spindle cell type (M8074/3)
    verrucous (M8051/3)
  superficial spreading (M8143/3)
  sweat gland (M8400/3) — see Neoplasm, skin, malignant
  theca cell (M8600/3) 183.0
  thymic (M8580/3) 164.0
  trabecular (M8190/3)
  transitional (cell) (M8120/3)
    papillary (M8130/3)
    spindle cell type (M8122/3)
  tubular (M8211/3)
  undifferentiated type (M8020/3)
  urothelial (M8120/3)
  ventriculi 151.9
  verrucous (epidermoid) (squamous cell) (M8051/3)
  villous (M8262/3)
  water-clear cell (M8322/3) 194.1
  wolffian duct (M9110/3)
Carcinosarcoma (M8980/3) — see also Neoplasm, by site, malignant
  embryonal type (M8981/3) — see Neoplasm, by site, malignant
Cardiac — see also condition
  death — see Disease, heart
  device
    defibrillator, automatic implantable V45.02
    in situ NEC V45.00
    pacemaker
      cardiac
        fitting or adjustment V53.31
        in situ V45.01
      carotid sinus
        fitting or adjustment V53.39
        in situ V45.09
  pacemaker — see Cardiac, device, pacemaker
  tamponade 423.3
Cardia, cardial — see condition
Cardialgia — see also Pain, precordial 786.51
Cardiectasis — see Hypertrophy, cardiac
Cardiochalasia 530.81
Cardiomalacia — see also Degeneration, myocardial 429.1
Cardiomegalia glycogenica diffusa 271.0
Cardiomegaly — see also Hypertrophy, cardiac 429.3
  congenital 746.89
  glycogen 271.0
  hypertensive (see also Hypertension, heart) 402.90
  idiopathic 429.3
Cardiomyoliposis — see also Degeneration, myocardial 429.1
Cardiomyopathy (congestive) (constrictive) (familial) (infiltrative) (obstructive) (restrictive) (sporadic) 425.4
  alcoholic 425.5
  amyloid 277.39 [425.7]
  beriberi 265.0 [425.7]
  cobalt-beer 425.5
  congenital 425.3
  due to
    amyloidosis 277.39 [425.7]
    beriberi 265.0 [425.7]
    cardiac glycogenosis 271.0 [425.7]
    Chagas' disease 086.0
    Friedreich's ataxia 334.0 [425.8]
    hypertension — see Hypertension, with, heart involvement
    mucopolysaccharidosis 277.5 [425.7]
    myotonia atrophica 359.21 [425.8]
    progressive muscular dystrophy 359.1 [425.8]
    sarcoidosis 135 [425.8]
    glycogen storage 271.0 [425.7]
  hypertensive — see Hypertension, with, heart involvement

Cardiomyopathy — continued
  hypertrophic
    nonobstructive 425.4
    obstructive 425.1
      congenital 746.84
  idiopathic (concentric) 425.4
  in
    Chagas' disease 086.0
    sarcoidosis 135 [425.8]
  ischemic 414.8
  metabolic NEC 277.9 [425.7]
    amyloid 277.39 [425.7]
    thyrotoxic (see also Thyrotoxicosis) 242.9 ✔ [425.7]
    thyrotoxicosis (see also Thyrotoxicosis) 242.9 ✔ [425.7]
  newborn 425.4
    congenital 425.3
  nutritional 269.9 [425.7]
    beriberi 265.0 [425.7]
  obscure of Africa 425.2
  peripartum 674.5 ✔
  postpartum 674.5 ✔
  primary 425.4
  secondary 425.9
  stress inuced 429.83
  takotsubo 429.83
  thyrotoxic (see also Thyrotoxicosis) 242.9 ✔ [425.7]
  toxic NEC 425.9
  tuberculous (see also Tuberculosis) 017.9 ✔ [425.8]
Cardionephritis — see Hypertension, cardiorenal
Cardionephropathy — see Hypertension, cardiorenal
Cardionephrosis — see Hypertension, cardiorenal
Cardioneurosis 306.2
Cardiopathia nigra 416.0
Cardiopathy — see also Disease, heart 429.9
  hypertensive (see also Hypertension, heart) 402.90
  idiopathic 425.4
  mucopolysaccharidosis 277.5 [425.7]
Cardiopericarditis — see also Pericarditis 423.9
Cardiophobia 300.29
Cardioptosis 746.87
Cardiorenal — see condition
Cardiorrhexis — see also Infarct, myocardium 410.9 ✔
Cardiosclerosis — see Arteriosclerosis, coronary
Cardiosis — see Disease, heart
Cardiospasm (esophagus) (reflex) (stomach) 530.0
  congenital 750.7
Cardiostenosis — see Disease, heart
Cardiosymphysis 423.1
Cardiothyrotoxicosis — see Hyperthyroidism
Cardiovascular — see condition
Carditis (acute) (bacterial) (chronic) (subacute) 429.89
  Coxsackie 074.20
  hypertensive (see also Hypertension, heart) 402.90
  meningococcal 036.40
  rheumatic — see Disease, heart, rheumatic
  rheumatoid 714.2
Care (of)
  child (routine) V20.1
  convalescent following V66.9
    chemotherapy V66.2
    medical NEC V66.5
    psychotherapy V66.3
    radiotherapy V66.1
    surgery V66.0
    surgical NEC V66.0
    treatment (for) V66.5
      combined V66.6
      fracture V66.4
      mental disorder NEC V66.3
      specified type NEC V66.5
  end-of-life V66.7
  family member (handicapped) (sick)
    creating problem for family V61.49
    provided away from home for holiday relief V60.5

Care — continued
  family member — continued
    unavailable, due to
      absence (person rendering care) (sufferer) V60.4
      inability (any reason) of person rendering care V60.4
  holiday relief V60.5
  hospice V66.7
  lack of (at or after birth) (infant) (child) 995.52
    adult 995.84
  lactation of mother V24.1
  palliative V66.7
  postpartum
    immediately after delivery V24.0
    routine follow-up V24.2
  prenatal V22.1
    first pregnancy V22.0
    high-risk pregnancy V23.9
      specified problem NEC V23.89
  terminal V66.7
  unavailable, due to
    absence of person rendering care V60.4
    inability (any reason) of person rendering care V60.4
  well baby V20.1
Caries (bone) — see also Tuberculosis, bone 015.9 ✔ [730.8] ✔
  arrested 521.04
  cementum 521.03
  cerebrospinal (tuberculous) 015.0 ✔ [730.88]
  dental (acute) (chronic) (incipient) (infected) 521.00
    with pulp exposure 521.03
    extending to
      dentine 521.02
      pulp 521.03
    other specified NEC 521.09
    pit and fissure 521.06
    primary
      pit and fissure origin 521.06
      root surface 521.08
      smooth surface origin 521.07
    root surface 521.08
    smooth surface 521.07
  dentin (acute) (chronic) 521.02
  enamel (acute) (chronic) (incipient) 521.01
  external meatus 380.89
  hip (see also Tuberculosis) 015.1 ✔ [730.85]
  initial 521.01
  knee 015.2 ✔ [730.86]
  labyrinth 386.8
  limb NEC 015.7 ✔ [730.88]
  mastoid (chronic) (process) 383.1
  middle ear 385.89
  nose 015.7 ✔ [730.88]
  orbit 015.7 ✔ [730.88]
  ossicle 385.24
  petrous bone 383.20
  sacrum (tuberculous) 015.0 ✔ [730.88]
  spine, spinal (column) (tuberculous) 015.0 ✔ [730.88]
  syphilitic 095.5
    congenital 090.0 [730.8] ✔
  teeth (internal) 521.00
    initial 521.01
  vertebra (column) (tuberculous) 015.0 ✔ [730.88]
Carini's syndrome (ichthyosis congenita) 757.1
Carious teeth 521.00
Carneous mole 631
Carnosinemia 270.5
Carotid body or sinus syndrome 337.01
Carotidynia 337.01
Carotinemia (dietary) 278.3
Carotinosis (cutis) (skin) 278.3
Carpal tunnel syndrome 354.0
Carpenter's syndrome 759.89
Carpopedal spasm — see also Tetany 781.7
Carpoptosis 736.05
Carrier (suspected) of
  amebiasis V02.2
  bacterial disease (meningococcal, staphylococcal) NEC V02.59
  cholera V02.0
  cystic fibrosis gene V83.81

✔ Additional Digit Required — Refer to the Tabular List for Digit Selection

▽ Subterms under main terms may continue to next column or page

▶◀ Revised Text   ● New Line   ▲ Revised Code

☑ Additional Digit Required — Refer to the Tabular List for Digit Selection   ᴺᴱᵂ Subterms under main terms may continue to next column or page

2010 ICD-9-CM   ▶◀ Revised Text   ● New Line   ▲ Revised Code   Volume 2 — 43

Index

Cellulitis — Change(s)

Cellulitis — see also Abscess — continued
  arm (any part, above wrist) 682.3
  auditory canal (external) 380.10
  axilla 682.3
  back (any part) 682.2
  breast 611.0
    postpartum 675.1 ☑
  broad ligament (see also Disease, pelvis, inflammatory) 614.4
    acute 614.3
  buttock 682.5
  cervical (neck region) 682.1
  cervix (uteri) (see also Cervicitis) 616.0
  cheek, external 682.0
    internal 528.3
  chest wall 682.2
  chronic NEC 682.9
  colostomy 569.61
  corpus cavernosum 607.2
  digit 681.9
  Douglas' cul-de-sac or pouch (chronic) (see also Disease, pelvis, inflammatory) 614.4
    acute 614.3
  drainage site (following operation) 998.59
  ear, external 380.10
  enterostomy 569.61
  erysipelar (see also Erysipelas) 035
  esophagostomy 530.86
  eyelid 373.13
  face (any part, except eye) 682.0
  finger (intrathecal) (periosteal) (subcutaneous) (subcuticular) 681.00
  flank 682.2
  foot (except toe) 682.7
  forearm 682.3
  gangrenous (see also Gangrene) 785.4
  genital organ NEC
    female — see Abscess, genital organ, female
    male 608.4
  glottis 478.71
  gluteal (region) 682.5
  gonococcal NEC 098.0
  groin 682.2
  hand (except finger or thumb) 682.4
  head (except face) NEC 682.8
  heel 682.7
  hip 682.6
  jaw (region) 682.0
  knee 682.6
  labium (majus) (minus) (see also Vulvitis) 616.10
  larynx 478.71
  leg, except foot 682.6
  lip 528.5
  mammary gland 611.0
  mouth (floor) 528.3
  multiple sites NEC 682.9
  nasopharynx 478.21
  navel 682.2
    newborn NEC 771.4
  neck (region) 682.1
  nipple 611.0
  nose 478.19
    external 682.0
  orbit, orbital 376.01
  palate (soft) 528.3
  pectoral (region) 682.2
  pelvis, pelvic
    with
      abortion — see Abortion, by type, with sepsis
      ectopic pregnancy (see also categories 633.0–633.9) 639.0
      molar pregnancy (see also categories 630–632) 639.0
    female (see also Disease, pelvis, inflammatory) 614.4
      acute 614.3
    following
      abortion 639.0
      ectopic or molar pregnancy 639.0
    male 567.21
    puerperal, postpartum, childbirth
      670.8 ☑   ▲

Cellulitis — see also Abscess — continued
  penis 607.2
  perineal, perineum 682.2
  perirectal 566
  peritonsillar 475
  periurethral 597.0
  periuterine (see also Disease, pelvis, inflammatory) 614.4
    acute 614.3
  pharynx 478.21
  phlegmonous NEC 682.9
  rectum 566
  retromammary 611.0
  retroperitoneal (see also Peritonitis) 567.2 ☑, 567.38
  round ligament (see also Disease, pelvis, inflammatory) 614.4
    acute 614.3
  scalp (any part) 682.8
    dissecting 704.8
  scrotum 608.4
  seminal vesicle 608.0
  septic NEC 682.9
  shoulder 682.3
  specified sites NEC 682.8
  spermatic cord 608.4
  submandibular (region) (space) (triangle) 682.0
    gland 527.3
  submaxillary 528.3
    gland 527.3
  submental (pyogenic) 682.0
    gland 527.3
  suppurative NEC 682.9
  testis 608.4
  thigh 682.6
  thumb (intrathecal) (periosteal) (subcutaneous) (subcuticular) 681.00
  toe (intrathecal) (periosteal) (subcutaneous) (subcuticular) 681.10
  tonsil 475
  trunk 682.2
  tuberculous (primary) (see also Tuberculosis) 017.0 ☑
  tunica vaginalis 608.4
  umbilical 682.2
    newborn NEC 771.4
  vaccinal 999.39
  vagina — see Vaginitis
  vas deferens 608.4
  vocal cords 478.5
  vulva (see also Vulvitis) 616.10
  wrist 682.4
Cementoblastoma, benign (M9273/0) 213.1
  upper jaw (bone) 213.0
Cementoma (M9273/0) 213.1
  gigantiform (M9276/0) 213.1
    upper jaw (bone) 213.0
  upper jaw (bone) 213.0
Cementoperiostitis 523.40
  acute 523.33
  apical 523.40
Cephalgia, cephalagia — see also Headache 784.0
  histamine 339.00
  nonorganic origin 307.81
  other trigeminal autonomic (TACS) 339.09
  psychogenic 307.81
  tension 307.81
Cephalhematocele, cephalematocele
  due to birth injury 767.19
  fetus or newborn 767.19
  traumatic (see also Contusion, head) 920
Cephalhematoma, cephalematoma (calcified)
  due to birth injury 767.19
  fetus or newborn 767.19
  traumatic (see also Contusion, head) 920
Cephalic — see condition
Cephalitis — see Encephalitis
Cephalocele 742.0
Cephaloma — see Neoplasm, by site, malignant
Cephalomenia 625.8
Cephalopelvic — see condition
Cercomoniasis 007.3
Cerebellitis — see Encephalitis
Cerebellum (cerebellar) — see condition
Cerebral — see condition

Cerebritis — see Encephalitis
Cerebrohepatorenal syndrome 759.89
Cerebromacular degeneration 330.1
Cerebromalacia — see also Softening, brain 434.9 ☑
Cerebrosidosis 272.7
Cerebrospasticity — see Palsy, cerebral
Cerebrospinal — see condition
Cerebrum — see condition
Ceroid storage disease 272.7
Cerumen (accumulation) (impacted) 380.4
Cervical — see also condition
  auricle 744.43
  high risk human papillomavirus (HPV) DNA test positive 795.05
  intraepithelial glandular neoplasia 233.1
  low risk human papillomavirus (HPV) DNA test positive 795.09
  rib 756.2
  shortening — see Short, cervical
Cervicalgia 723.1
Cervicitis (acute) (chronic) (nonvenereal) (subacute) (with erosion or ectropion) 616.0
  with
    abortion — see Abortion, by type, with sepsis
    ectopic pregnancy (see also categories 633.0–633.9) 639.0
    molar pregnancy (see also categories 630–632) 639.0
    ulceration 616.0
  chlamydial 099.53
  complicating pregnancy or puerperium 646.6 ☑
    affecting fetus or newborn 760.8
  following
    abortion 639.0
    ectopic or molar pregnancy 639.0
  gonococcal (acute) 098.15
    chronic or duration of 2 months or more 098.35
  senile (atrophic) 616.0
  syphilitic 095.8
  trichomonal 131.09
  tuberculous (see also Tuberculosis) 016.7 ☑
Cervicoaural fistula 744.49
Cervicocolpitis (emphysematosa) — see also Cervicitis 616.0
Cervix — see condition
Cesarean delivery, operation or section NEC 669.7 ☑
  affecting fetus or newborn 763.4
  post mortem, affecting fetus or newborn 761.6
  previous, affecting management of pregnancy 654.2 ☑
Céstan-Chenais paralysis 344.89
Céstan-Raymond syndrome 433.8 ☑
Céstan's syndrome 344.89
Cestode infestation NEC 123.9
  specified type NEC 123.8
Cestodiasis 123.9
CGF (congenital generalized fibromatosis) 759.89
Chabert's disease 022.9
Chacaleh 266.2
Chafing 709.8
Chagas' disease — see also Trypanosomiasis, American 086.2
  with heart involvement 086.0
Chagres fever 084.0
Chalasia (cardiac sphincter) 530.81
Chalazion 373.2
Chalazoderma 757.39
Chalcosis 360.24
  cornea 371.15
  crystalline lens 360.24 [366.34]
  retina 360.24
Chalicosis (occupational) (pulmonum) 502
Chancre (any genital site) (hard) (indurated) (infecting) (primary) (recurrent) 091.0
  congenital 090.0
  conjunctiva 091.2
  Ducrey's 099.0
  extragenital 091.2
  eyelid 091.2
  Hunterian 091.0
  lip (syphilis) 091.2

Chancre — continued
  mixed 099.8
  nipple 091.2
  Nisbet's 099.0
  of
    carate 103.0
    pinta 103.0
    yaws 102.0
  palate, soft 091.2
  phagedenic 099.0
  Ricord's 091.0
  Rollet's (syphilitic) 091.0
  seronegative 091.0
  seropositive 091.0
  simple 099.0
  soft 099.0
    bubo 099.0
  urethra 091.0
  yaws 102.0
Chancriform syndrome 114.1
Chancroid 099.0
  anus 099.0
  penis (Ducrey's bacillus) 099.0
  perineum 099.0
  rectum 099.0
  scrotum 099.0
  urethra 099.0
  vulva 099.0
Chandipura fever 066.8
Chandler's disease (osteochondritis dissecans, hip) 732.7
Change(s) (of) — see also Removal of
  arteriosclerotic — see Arteriosclerosis
  battery
    cardiac pacemaker V53.31
  bone 733.90
    diabetic 250.8 ☑ [731.8]
      due to secondary diabetes 249.8 ☑ [731.8]
    in disease, unknown cause 733.90
  bowel habits 787.99
  cardiorenal (vascular) (see also Hypertension, cardiorenal) 404.90
  cardiovascular — see Disease, cardiovascular
  circulatory 459.9
  cognitive or personality change of other type, nonpsychotic 310.1
  color, teeth, tooth
    during formation 520.8
    extrinsic 523.6
    intrinsic posteruptive 521.7
  contraceptive device V25.42
  cornea, corneal
    degenerative NEC 371.40
    membrane NEC 371.30
    senile 371.41
  coronary (see also Ischemia, heart) 414.9
  degenerative
    chamber angle (anterior) (iris) 364.56
    ciliary body 364.57
    spine or vertebra (see also Spondylosis) 721.90
  dental pulp, regressive 522.2
  drains V58.49
  dressing
    wound V58.30
      nonsurgical V58.30
      surgical V58.31
  fixation device V54.89
    external V54.89
    internal V54.01
  heart (see also Disease, heart)
  hip joint 718.95
  hyperplastic larynx 478.79
  hypertrophic
    nasal sinus (see also Sinusitis) 473.9
    turbinate, nasal 478.0
    upper respiratory tract 478.9
  inflammatory — see Inflammation
  joint (see also Derangement, joint) 718.90
    sacroiliac 724.6
  Kirschner wire V54.89
  knee 717.9
  macular, congenital 743.55

Change(s) — *see also* Removal of —
  continued
  malignant (M — — /3) (*see also* Neoplasm,
    by site, malignant)

> *Note* — for malignant change occurring in
> a neoplasm, use the appropriate M code
> with behavior digit /3 e.g., malignant
> change in uterine fibroid — M8890/3. For
> malignant change occurring in a nonneo-
> plastic condition (e.g., gastric ulcer) use the
> M code M8000/3.

  mental (status) NEC 780.97
    due to or associated with physical condi-
      tion — *see* Syndrome, brain
  myocardium, myocardial — *see* Degeneration,
    myocardial
  of life (*see also* Menopause) 627.2
  pacemaker battery (cardiac) V53.31
  peripheral nerve 355.9
  personality (nonpsychotic) NEC 310.1
  plaster cast V54.89
  refractive, transient 367.81
  regressive, dental pulp 522.2
  retina 362.9
    myopic (degenerative) (malignant) 360.21
    vascular appearance 362.13
  sacroiliac joint 724.6
  scleral 379.19
    degenerative 379.16
  senile (*see also* Senility) 797
  sensory (*see also* Disturbance, sensation) 782.0
  skin texture 782.8
  spinal cord 336.9
  splint, external V54.89
  subdermal implantable contraceptive V25.5
  suture V58.32
  traction device V54.89
  trophic 355.9
    arm NEC 354.9
    leg NEC 355.8
    lower extremity NEC 355.8
    upper extremity NEC 354.9
  vascular 459.9
  vasomotor 443.9
  voice 784.49
    psychogenic 306.1
  wound packing V58.30
    nonsurgical V58.30
    surgical V58.31
Changing sleep-work schedule, affecting
  sleep 327.36
Changuinola fever 066.0
Chapping skin 709.8
Character
  depressive 301.12
Charcôt's
  arthropathy 094.0 *[713.5]*
  cirrhosis — *see* Cirrhosis, biliary
  disease 094.0
    spinal cord 094.0
  fever (biliary) (hepatic) (intermittent) — *see*
    Choledocholithiasis
  joint (disease) 094.0 *[713.5]*
    diabetic 250.6 ☑ *[713.5]*
      due to secondary diabetes
        249.6 ☑ *[713.5]*
    syringomyelic 336.0 *[713.5]*
  syndrome (intermittent claudication) 443.9
    due to atherosclerosis 440.21
Charcôt-Marie-Tooth disease, paralysis, or
  syndrome 356.1
CHARGE association (syndrome) 759.89
Charleyhorse (quadriceps) 843.8
  muscle, except quadriceps — *see* Sprain, by
    site
Charlouis' disease — *see also* Yaws 102.9
Chauffeur's fracture — *see* Fracture, ulna, lower
  end
Cheadle (-Möller) (-Barlow) disease or syn-
  drome (infantile scurvy) 267
Checking (of)
  contraceptive device (intrauterine) V25.42
  device
    fixation V54.89
      external V54.89
      internal V54.09

Checking — *continued*
  device — *continued*
    traction V54.89
    Kirschner wire V54.89
    plaster cast V54.89
    splint, external V54.89
Checkup
  following treatment — *see* Examination
  health V70.0
  infant ▶(over 28 days old)◀ (not sick) V20.2
  newborn, routine
    8 to 28 days old V20.32 ●
    over 28 days old, routine V20.2 ●
    under 8 days old V20.31 ●
    weight V20.32 ●
  pregnancy (normal) V22.1
    first V22.0
    high-risk pregnancy V23.9
      specified problem NEC V23.89
Chédiak-Higashi (-Steinbrinck) anomaly, dis-
  ease, or syndrome (congenital gigantism
    of peroxidase granules) 288.2
Cheek — *see also* condition
  biting 528.9
Cheese itch 133.8
Cheese washers' lung 495.8
Cheilitis 528.5
  actinic (due to sun) 692.72
    chronic NEC 692.74
      due to radiation, except from sun
        692.82
    due to radiation, except from sun 692.82
  acute 528.5
  angular 528.5
  catarrhal 528.5
  chronic 528.5
  exfoliative 528.5
  gangrenous 528.5
  glandularis apostematosa 528.5
  granulomatosa 351.8
  infectional 528.5
  membranous 528.5
  Miescher's 351.8
  suppurative 528.5
  ulcerative 528.5
  vesicular 528.5
Cheilodynia 528.5
Cheilopalatoschisis — *see also* Cleft, palate, with
  cleft lip 749.20
Cheilophagia 528.9
Cheiloschisis — *see also* Cleft, lip 749.10
Cheilosis 528.5
  with pellagra 265.2
  angular 528.5
  due to
    dietary deficiency 266.0
    vitamin deficiency 266.0
Cheiromegaly 729.89
Cheiropompholyx 705.81
Cheloid — *see also* Keloid 701.4
Chemical burn — *see also* Burn, by site
  from swallowing chemical — *see* Burn, inter-
    nal organs
Chemodectoma (M8693/1) — *see* Paragan-
  glioma, nonchromaffin
Chemoprophylaxis NEC V07.39
Chemosis, conjunctiva 372.73
Chemotherapy
  convalescence V66.2
  encounter (for) ▶(oral) (intravenous)◀ V58.11
  maintenance ▶(oral) (intravenous)◀ V58.11
  prophylactic NEC V07.39
    fluoride V07.31
Cherubism 526.89
Chest — *see* condition
Cheyne-Stokes respiration (periodic) 786.04
Chiari's
  disease or syndrome (hepatic vein thrombosis)
    453.0
  malformation
    type I 348.4
    type II (*see also* Spina bifida) 741.0 ☑
    type III 742.0
    type IV 742.2
  network 746.89
Chiari-Frommel syndrome 676.6 ☑

Chicago disease (North American blastomycosis)
  116.0
Chickenpox — *see also* Varicella 052.9
  exposure to V01.71
  vaccination and inoculation (prophylactic)
    V05.4
Chiclero ulcer 085.4
Chiggers 133.8
Chignon 111.2
  fetus or newborn (from vacuum extraction)
    767.19
Chigoe disease 134.1 ●
Chikungunya fever 066.3 ●
Chilaiditi's syndrome (subphrenic displacement,
  colon) 751.4
Chilblains 991.5
  lupus 991.5
Child
  behavior causing concern V61.20
    adopted child V61.24 ●
    biological child V61.23 ●
    foster child V61.25 ●
Childbed fever 670.8 ☑ ▲
Childbirth — *see also* Delivery
  puerperal complications — *see* Puerperal
Childhood, period of rapid growth V21.0
Chill(s) 780.64
  with fever 780.60
  without fever 780.64
  congestive 780.99
    in malarial regions 084.6
  septic — *see* Septicemia
  urethral 599.84
Chilomastigiasis 007.8
Chin — *see* condition
Chinese dysentery 004.9
Chiropractic dislocation — *see also* Lesion,
  nonallopathic, by site 739.9
Chitral fever 066.0
Chlamydia, chlamydial — *see* condition
Chloasma 709.09
  cachecticorum 709.09
  eyelid 374.52
    congenital 757.33
    hyperthyroid 242.0 ☑
  gravidarum 646.8 ☑
  idiopathic 709.09
  skin 709.09
  symptomatic 709.09
Chloroma (M9930/3) 205.3 ☑
Chlorosis 280.9
  Egyptian (*see also* Ancylostomiasis) 126.9
  miners' (*see also* Ancylostomiasis) 126.9
Chlorotic anemia 280.9
Chocolate cyst (ovary) 617.1
Choked
  disk or disc — *see* Papilledema
  on food, phlegm, or vomitus NEC (*see also* As-
    phyxia, food) 933.1
  phlegm 933.1
  while vomiting NEC (*see also* Asphyxia, food)
    933.1
Chokes (resulting from bends) 993.3
Choking sensation 784.99
Cholangiectasis — *see also* Disease, gallbladder
  575.8
Cholangiocarcinoma (M8160/3)
  and hepatocellular carcinoma, combined
    (M8180/3) 155.0
  liver 155.1
  specified site NEC — *see* Neoplasm, by site,
    malignant
  unspecified site 155.1
Cholangiohepatitis 575.8
  due to fluke infestation 121.1
Cholangiohepatoma (M8180/3) 155.0
Cholangiolitis (acute) (chronic) (extrahepatic)
  (gangrenous) 576.1
  intrahepatic 575.8
  paratyphoidal (*see also* Fever, paratyphoid)
    002.9
  typhoidal 002.0
Cholangioma (M8160/0) 211.5
  malignant — *see* Cholangiocarcinoma

Cholangitis (acute) (ascending) (catarrhal)
  (chronic) (infective) (malignant) (primary)
  (recurrent) (sclerosing) (secondary)
  (stenosing) (suppurative) 576.1
  chronic nonsuppurative destructive 571.6
  nonsuppurative destructive (chronic) 571.6
Cholecystdocholithiasis — *see* Choledocholithiasis
Cholecystitis 575.10
  with
    calculus, stones in
      bile duct (common) (hepatic) — *see*
        Choledocholithiasis
      gallbladder — *see* Cholelithiasis
  acute 575.0
  acute and chronic 575.12
  chronic 575.11
  emphysematous (acute) (*see also* Cholecystitis,
    acute) 575.0
  gangrenous (*see also* Cholecystitis, acute) 575.0
  paratyphoidal, current (*see also* Fever, paraty-
    phoid) 002.9
  suppurative (*see also* Cholecystitis, acute) 575.0
  typhoidal 002.0
Choledochitis (suppurative) 576.1
Choledocholith — *see* Choledocholithiasis
Choledocholithiasis 574.5 ☑

> *Note* — Use the following fifth-digit subclas-
> sification with category 574:
>
> 0   without mention of obstruction
>
> 1   with obstruction

  with
    cholecystitis 574.4 ☑
      acute 574.3 ☑
      chronic 574.4 ☑
    cholelithiasis 574.9 ☑
      with
        cholecystitis 574.7 ☑
          acute 574.6 ☑
          and chronic 574.8 ☑
          chronic 574.7 ☑
Cholelithiasis (impacted) (multiple) 574.2 ☑

> *Note* — Use the following fifth-digit subclas-
> sification with category 574:
>
> 0   without mention of obstruction
>
> 1   with obstruction

  with
    cholecystitis 574.1 ☑
      acute 574.0 ☑
      chronic 574.1 ☑
    choledocholithiasis 574.9 ☑
      with
        cholecystitis 574.7 ☑
          acute 574.6 ☑
          and chronic 574.8 ☑
          chronic cholecystitis 574.7 ☑
Cholemia — *see also* Jaundice 782.4
  familial 277.4
  Gilbert's (familial nonhemolytic) 277.4
Cholemic gallstone — *see* Cholelithiasis
Choleperitoneum, choleperitonitis — *see also*
  Disease, gallbladder 567.81
Cholera (algid) (Asiatic) (asphyctic) (epidemic)
  (gravis) (Indian) (malignant) (morbus)
  (pestilential) (spasmodic) 001.9
  antimonial 985.4
  carrier (suspected) of V02.0
  classical 001.0
  contact V01.0
  due to
    Vibrio
      cholerae (Inaba, Ogawa, Hikojima
        serotypes) 001.0
      El Tor 001.1
  El Tor 001.1
  exposure to V01.0
  vaccination, prophylactic (against) V03.0
Cholerine — *see also* Cholera 001.9
Cholestasis 576.8
  due to total parenteral nutrition (TPN) 573.8
Cholesteatoma (ear) 385.30
  attic (primary) 385.31

☑ Additional Digit Required — Refer to the Tabular List for Digit Selection   ⬚ Subterms under main terms may continue to next column or page

2010 ICD-9-CM   ▶◀ Revised Text   ● New Line   ▲ Revised Code   October 2009 • Volume 2 — 45

Cholesteatoma — continued
  diffuse 385.35
  external ear (canal) 380.21
  marginal (middle ear) 385.32
    with involvement of mastoid cavity 385.33
    secondary (with middle ear involvement) 385.33
  mastoid cavity 385.30
  middle ear (secondary) 385.32
    with involvement of mastoid cavity 385.33
  postmastoidectomy cavity (recurrent) 383.32
  primary 385.31
  recurrent, postmastoidectomy cavity 383.32
  secondary (middle ear) 385.32
    with involvement of mastoid cavity 385.33
Cholesteatosis (middle ear) — see also Cholesteatoma 385.30
  diffuse 385.35
Cholesteremia 272.0
Cholesterin
  granuloma, middle ear 385.82
  in vitreous 379.22
Cholesterol
  deposit
    retina 362.82
    vitreous 379.22
  elevated (high) 272.0
    with elevated (high) triglycerides 272.2
  imbibition of gallbladder (see also Disease, gallbladder) 575.6
Cholesterolemia 272.0
  essential 272.0
  familial 272.0
  hereditary 272.0
Cholesterosis, cholesterolosis (gallbladder) 575.6
  with
    cholecystitis — see Cholecystitis
    cholelithiasis — see Cholelithiasis
  middle ear (see also Cholesteatoma) 385.30
Cholocolic fistula — see also Fistula, gallbladder 575.5
Choluria 791.4
Chondritis (purulent) 733.99
  auricle 380.03
  costal 733.6
    Tietze's 733.6
  patella, posttraumatic 717.7
  pinna 380.03
  posttraumatica patellae 717.7
  tuberculous (active) (see also Tuberculosis) 015.9 ☑
    intervertebral 015.0 ☑ [730.88]
Chondroangiopathia calcarea seu punctate 756.59
Chondroblastoma (M9230/0) — see also Neoplasm, bone, benign
  malignant (M9230/3) — see Neoplasm, bone, malignant
Chondrocalcinosis (articular) (crystal deposition) (dihydrate) — see also Arthritis, due to, crystals 275.49 [712.3] ☑
  due to
    calcium pyrophosphate 275.49 [712.2] ☑
    dicalcium phosphate crystals 275.49 [712.1] ☑
    pyrophosphate crystals 275.49 [712.2] ☑
Chondrodermatitis nodularis helicis 380.00
Chondrodysplasia 756.4
  angiomatose 756.4
  calcificans congenita 756.59
  epiphysialis punctata 756.59
  hereditary deforming 756.4
  rhizomelic punctata 277.86
Chondrodystrophia (fetalis) 756.4
  calcarea 756.4
  calcificans congenita 756.59
  fetalis hypoplastica 756.59
  hypoplastica calcinosa 756.59
  punctata 756.59
  tarda 277.5
Chondrodystrophy (familial) (hypoplastic) 756.4
  myotonic (congenital) 359.23
Chondroectodermal dysplasia 756.55
Chondrolysis 733.99

Chondroma (M9220/0) — see also Neoplasm, cartilage, benign
  juxtacortical (M9221/0) — see Neoplasm, bone, benign
  periosteal (M9221/0) — see Neoplasm, bone, benign
Chondromalacia 733.92
  epiglottis (congenital) 748.3
  generalized 733.92
  knee 717.7
  larynx (congenital) 748.3
  localized, except patella 733.92
  patella, patellae 717.7
  systemic 733.92
  tibial plateau 733.92
  trachea (congenital) 748.3
Chondromatosis (M9220/1) — see Neoplasm, cartilage, uncertain behavior
Chondromyxosarcoma (M9220/3) — see Neoplasm, cartilage, malignant
Chondro-osteodysplasia (Morquio-Brailsford type) 277.5
Chondro-osteodystrophy 277.5
Chondro-osteoma (M9210/0) — see Neoplasm, bone, benign
Chondropathia tuberosa 733.6
Chondrosarcoma (M9220/3) — see also Neoplasm, cartilage, malignant
  juxtacortical (M9221/3) — see Neoplasm, bone, malignant
  mesenchymal (M9240/3) — see Neoplasm, connective tissue, malignant
Chordae tendineae rupture (chronic) 429.5
Chordee (nonvenereal) 607.89
  congenital 752.63
  gonococcal 098.2
Chorditis (fibrinous) (nodosa) (tuberosa) 478.5
Chordoma (M9370/3) — see Neoplasm, by site, malignant
Chorea (gravis) (minor) (spasmodic) 333.5
  with
    heart involvement — see Chorea with rheumatic heart disease
    rheumatic heart disease (chronic, inactive, or quiescent) (conditions classifiable to 393–398) (see rheumatic heart condition involved)
      active or acute (conditions classifiable to 391) 392.0
  acute — see Chorea, Sydenham's
  apoplectic (see also Disease, cerebrovascular, acute) 436
  chronic 333.4
  electric 049.8
  gravidarum — see Eclampsia, pregnancy
  habit 307.22
  hereditary 333.4
  Huntington's 333.4
  posthemiplegic 344.89
  pregnancy — see Eclampsia, pregnancy
  progressive 333.4
    chronic 333.4
    hereditary 333.4
  rheumatic (chronic) 392.9
    with heart disease or involvement — see Chorea, with rheumatic heart disease
  senile 333.5
  Sydenham's 392.9
    with heart involvement — see Chorea, with rheumatic heart disease
    nonrheumatic 333.5
  variabilis 307.23
Choreoathetosis (paroxysmal) 333.5
Chorioadenoma (destruens) (M9100/1) 236.1
Chorioamnionitis 658.4 ☑
  affecting fetus or newborn 762.7
Chorioangioma (M9120/0) 219.8
Choriocarcinoma (M9100/3)
  combined with
    embryonal carcinoma (M9101/3) — see Neoplasm, by site, malignant
    teratoma (M9101/3) — see Neoplasm, by site, malignant
  specified site — see Neoplasm, by site, malignant

Choriocarcinoma — continued
  unspecified site
    female 181
    male 186.9
Chorioencephalitis, lymphocytic (acute) (serous) 049.0
Chorioepithelioma (M9100/3) — see Choriocarcinoma
Choriomeningitis (acute) (benign) (lymphocytic) (serous) 049.0
Chorionepithelioma (M9100/3) — see Choriocarcinoma
Chorionitis — see also Scleroderma 710.1
Chorioretinitis 363.20
  disseminated 363.10
    generalized 363.13
    in
      neurosyphilis 094.83
      secondary syphilis 091.51
    peripheral 363.12
    posterior pole 363.11
    tuberculous (see also Tuberculosis) 017.3 ☑ [363.13]
  due to
    histoplasmosis (see also Histoplasmosis) 115.92
    toxoplasmosis (acquired) 130.2
      congenital (active) 771.2
  focal 363.00
    juxtapapillary 363.01
    peripheral 363.04
    posterior pole NEC 363.03
  juxtapapillaris, juxtapapillary 363.01
  progressive myopia (degeneration) 360.21
  syphilitic (secondary) 091.51
    congenital (early) 090.0 [363.13]
    late 090.5 [363.13]
    late 095.8 [363.13]
  tuberculous (see also Tuberculosis) 017.3 ☑ [363.13]
Choristoma — see Neoplasm, by site, benign
Choroid — see condition
Choroideremia, choroidermia (initial stage) (late stage) (partial or total atrophy) 363.55
Choroiditis — see also Chorioretinitis 363.20
  leprous 030.9 [363.13]
  senile guttate 363.41
  sympathetic 360.11
  syphilitic (secondary) 091.51
    congenital (early) 090.0 [363.13]
    late 090.5 [363.13]
    late 095.8 [363.13]
  Tay's 363.41
  tuberculous (see also Tuberculosis) 017.3 ☑ [363.13]
Choroidopathy NEC 363.9
  degenerative (see also Degeneration, choroid) 363.40
  hereditary (see also Dystrophy, choroid) 363.50
  specified type NEC 363.8
Choroidoretinitis — see Chorioretinitis
Choroidosis, central serous 362.41
Choroidretinopathy, serous 362.41
Christian's syndrome (chronic histiocytosis X) 277.89
Christian-Weber disease (nodular nonsuppurative panniculitis) 729.30
Christmas disease 286.1
Chromaffinoma (M8700/0) — see also Neoplasm, by site, benign
  malignant (M8700/3) — see Neoplasm, by site, malignant
Chromatopsia 368.59
Chromhidrosis, chromidrosis 705.89
Chromoblastomycosis 117.2
Chromomycosis 117.2
Chromophytosis 111.0
Chromotrichomycosis 111.8
Chronic — see condition
Churg-Strauss syndrome 446.4
Chyle cyst, mesentery 457.8
Chylocele (nonfilarial) 457.8
  filarial (see also Infestation, filarial) 125.9
  tunica vaginalis (nonfilarial) 608.84
    filarial (see also Infestation, filarial) 125.9

Chylomicronemia (fasting) (with hyperprebetal-ipoproteinemia) 272.3
Chylopericardium (acute) 420.90
Chylothorax (nonfilarial) 457.8
  filarial (see also Infestation, filarial) 125.9
Chylous
  ascites 457.8
  cyst of peritoneum 457.8
  hydrocele 603.9
  hydrothorax (nonfilarial) 457.8
    filarial (see also Infestation, filarial) 125.9
Chyluria 791.1
  bilharziasis 120.0
  due to
    Brugia (malayi) 125.1
    Wuchereria (bancrofti) 125.0
      malayi 125.1
  filarial (see also Infestation, filarial) 125.9
  filariasis (see also Infestation, filarial) 125.9
  nonfilarial 791.1
Cicatricial (deformity) — see Cicatrix
Cicatrix (adherent) (contracted) (painful) (vicious) 709.2
  adenoid 474.8
  alveolar process 525.8
  anus 569.49
  auricle 380.89
  bile duct (see also Disease, biliary) 576.8
  bladder 596.8
  bone 733.99
  brain 348.89   ▲
  cervix (postoperative) (postpartal) 622.3
    in pregnancy or childbirth 654.6 ☑
      causing obstructed labor 660.2 ☑
  chorioretinal 363.30
    disseminated 363.35
    macular 363.32
    peripheral 363.34
    posterior pole NEC 363.33
  choroid — see Cicatrix, chorioretinal
  common duct (see also Disease, biliary) 576.8
  congenital 757.39
  conjunctiva 372.64
  cornea 371.00
    tuberculous (see also Tuberculosis) 017.3 ☑ [371.05]
  duodenum (bulb) 537.3
  esophagus 530.3
  eyelid 374.46
    with
      ectropion — see Ectropion
      entropion — see Entropion
  hypopharynx 478.29
  knee, semilunar cartilage 717.5
  lacrimal
    canaliculi 375.53
    duct
      acquired 375.56
      neonatal 375.55
    punctum 375.52
    sac 375.54
  larynx 478.79
  limbus (cystoid) 372.64
  lung 518.89
  macular 363.32
    disseminated 363.35
    peripheral 363.34
  middle ear 385.89
  mouth 528.9
  muscle 728.89
  nasolacrimal duct
    acquired 375.56
    neonatal 375.55
  nasopharynx 478.29
  palate (soft) 528.9
  penis 607.89
  prostate 602.8
  rectum 569.49
  retina 363.30
    disseminated 363.35
    macular 363.32
    peripheral 363.34
    posterior pole NEC 363.33
  semilunar cartilage — see Derangement, meniscus
  seminal vesicle 608.89

☑ Additional Digit Required — Refer to the Tabular List for Digit Selection   ⬙ Subterms under main terms may continue to next column or page

Cicatrix — *continued*
skin 709.2
  infected 686.8
  postinfectional 709.2
  tuberculous (*see also* Tuberculosis)
    017.0 ☑
specified site NEC 709.2
throat 478.29
tongue 529.8
tonsil (and adenoid) 474.8
trachea 478.9
tuberculous NEC (*see also* Tuberculosis)
  011.9 ☑
ureter 593.89
urethra 599.84
uterus 621.8
vagina 623.4
  in pregnancy or childbirth 654.7 ☑
    causing obstructed labor 660.2 ☑
vocal cord 478.5
wrist, constricting (annular) 709.2
CIDP (chronic inflammatory demyelinating polyneuropathy) 357.81
CIN I [cervical intraepithelial neoplasia I] 622.11
CIN II [cervical intraepithelial neoplasia II] 622.12
CIN III [cervical intraepithelial neoplasia III] 233.1
Cinchonism
correct substance properly administered 386.9
overdose or wrong substance given or taken 961.4
Circine herpes 110.5
Circle of Willis — *see* condition
Circular — *see also* condition
hymen 752.49
Circulating, ▶intrinsic◀ anticoagulants ▶causing hemorrhagic disorder◀ 286.5
following childbirth 666.3 ☑
postpartum 666.3 ☑
Circulation
collateral (venous), any site 459.89
defective 459.9
  congenital 747.9
  lower extremity 459.89
embryonic 747.9
failure 799.89
  fetus or newborn 779.89
  peripheral 785.59
fetal, persistent 747.83
heart, incomplete 747.9
Circulatory system — *see* condition
Circulus senilis 371.41
Circumcision
in absence of medical indication V50.2
ritual V50.2
routine V50.2
status (post), female 629.20
Circumscribed — *see* condition
Circumvallata placenta — *see* Placenta, abnormal
Cirrhosis, cirrhotic 571.5
with alcoholism 571.2
alcoholic (liver) 571.2
atrophic (of liver) — *see* Cirrhosis, portal
Baumgarten-Cruveilhier 571.5
biliary (cholangiolitic) (cholangitic) (cholestatic) (extrahepatic) (hypertrophic) (intrahepatic) (nonobstructive) (obstructive) (pericholangiolitic) (posthepatic) (primary) (secondary) (xanthomatous) 571.6
  due to
    clonorchiasis 121.1
    flukes 121.3
brain 331.9
capsular — *see* Cirrhosis, portal
cardiac 571.5
  alcoholic 571.2
central (liver) — *see* Cirrhosis, liver
Charcôt's 571.6
cholangiolitic — *see* Cirrhosis, biliary
cholangitic — *see* Cirrhosis, biliary
cholestatic — *see* Cirrhosis, biliary
clitoris (hypertrophic) 624.2
coarsely nodular 571.5
congestive (liver) — *see* Cirrhosis, cardiac

Cirrhosis, cirrhotic — *continued*
Cruveilhier-Baumgarten 571.5
cryptogenic (of liver) 571.5
  alcoholic 571.2
dietary (*see also* Cirrhosis, portal) 571.5
due to
  bronzed diabetes 275.0
  congestive hepatomegaly — *see* Cirrhosis, cardiac
  cystic fibrosis 277.00
  hemochromatosis 275.0
  hepatolenticular degeneration 275.1
  passive congestion (chronic) — *see* Cirrhosis, cardiac
  Wilson's disease 275.1
  xanthomatosis 272.2
extrahepatic (obstructive) — *see* Cirrhosis, biliary
fatty 571.8
  alcoholic 571.0
florid 571.2
Glisson's — *see* Cirrhosis, portal
Hanot's (hypertrophic) — *see* Cirrhosis, biliary
hepatic — *see* Cirrhosis, liver
hepatolienal — *see* Cirrhosis, liver
hobnail — *see* Cirrhosis, portal
hypertrophic (*see also* Cirrhosis, liver)
  biliary — *see* Cirrhosis, biliary
  Hanot's — *see* Cirrhosis, biliary
infectious NEC — *see* Cirrhosis, portal
insular — *see* Cirrhosis, portal
intrahepatic (obstructive) (primary) (secondary) — *see* Cirrhosis, biliary
juvenile (*see also* Cirrhosis, portal) 571.5
kidney (*see also* Sclerosis, renal) 587
Laennec's (of liver) 571.2
  nonalcoholic 571.5
liver (chronic) (hepatolienal) (hypertrophic) (nodular) (splenomegalic) (unilobar) 571.5
  with alcoholism 571.2
  alcoholic 571.2
  congenital (due to failure of obliteration of umbilical vein) 777.8
  cryptogenic 571.5
    alcoholic 571.2
  fatty 571.8
    alcoholic 571.0
  macronodular 571.5
    alcoholic 571.2
  micronodular 571.5
    alcoholic 571.2
  nodular, diffuse 571.5
    alcoholic 571.2
  pigmentary 275.0
  portal 571.5
    alcoholic 571.2
  postnecrotic 571.5
    alcoholic 571.2
  syphilitic 095.3
lung (chronic) (*see also* Fibrosis, lung) 515
macronodular (of liver) 571.5
  alcoholic 571.2
malarial 084.9
metabolic NEC 571.5
micronodular (of liver) 571.5
  alcoholic 571.2
monolobular — *see* Cirrhosis, portal
multilobular — *see* Cirrhosis, portal
nephritis (*see also* Sclerosis, renal) 587
nodular — *see* Cirrhosis, liver
nutritional (fatty) 571.5
obstructive (biliary) (extrahepatic) (intrahepatic) — *see* Cirrhosis, biliary
ovarian 620.8
paludal 084.9
pancreas (duct) 577.8
pericholangiolitic — *see* Cirrhosis, biliary
periportal — *see* Cirrhosis, portal
pigment, pigmentary (of liver) 275.0
portal (of liver) 571.5
  alcoholic 571.2
posthepatitic (*see also* Cirrhosis, postnecrotic) 571.5
postnecrotic (of liver) 571.5
  alcoholic 571.2

Cirrhosis, cirrhotic — *continued*
primary (intrahepatic) — *see* Cirrhosis, biliary
pulmonary (*see also* Fibrosis, lung) 515
renal (*see also* Sclerosis, renal) 587
septal (*see also* Cirrhosis, postnecrotic) 571.5
spleen 289.51
splenomegalic (of liver) — *see* Cirrhosis, liver
stasis (liver) — *see* Cirrhosis, liver
stomach 535.4 ☑
Todd's (*see also* Cirrhosis, biliary) 571.6
toxic (nodular) — *see* Cirrhosis, postnecrotic
trabecular — *see* Cirrhosis, postnecrotic
unilobar — *see* Cirrhosis, liver
vascular (of liver) — *see* Cirrhosis, liver
xanthomatous (biliary) (*see also* Cirrhosis, biliary) 571.6
  due to xanthomatosis (familial) (metabolic) (primary) 272.2
Cistern, subarachnoid 793.0
Citrullinemia 270.6
Citrullinuria 270.6
Ciuffini-Pancoast tumor (M8010/3) (carcinoma, pulmonary apex) 162.3
Civatte's disease or poikiloderma 709.09
CJD (Creutzfeldt-Jakob disease) 046.19
variant (vCJD) 046.11
Clam diggers' itch 120.3
Clap — *see* Gonorrhea
Clarke-Hadfield syndrome (pancreatic infantilism) 577.8
Clark's paralysis 343.9
Clastothrix 704.2
Claude Bernard-Horner syndrome — *see also* Neuropathy, peripheral, autonomic 337.9
Claude's syndrome 352.6
Claudication, intermittent 443.9
cerebral (artery) (*see also* Ischemia, cerebral, transient) 435.9
due to atherosclerosis 440.21
spinal cord (arteriosclerotic) 435.1
  syphilitic 094.89
spinalis 435.1
venous (axillary) 453.89   ▲
Claudicatio venosa intermittens 453.89   ▲
Claustrophobia 300.29
Clavus (infected) 700
Clawfoot (congenital) 754.71
acquired 736.74
Clawhand (acquired) 736.06
congenital 755.59
Clawtoe (congenital) 754.71
acquired 735.5
Clay eating 307.52
Clay shovelers' fracture — *see* Fracture, vertebra, cervical
Cleansing of artificial opening — *see also* Attention to artificial opening V55.9
Cleft (congenital) — *see also* Imperfect, closure
alveolar process 525.8
branchial (persistent) 744.41
  cyst 744.42
clitoris 752.49
cricoid cartilage, posterior 748.3
facial (*see also* Cleft, lip) 749.10
lip 749.10
  with cleft palate 749.20
    bilateral (lip and palate) 749.24
      with unilateral lip or palate 749.25
      complete 749.23
      incomplete 749.24
    unilateral (lip and palate) 749.22
      with bilateral lip or palate 749.25
      complete 749.21
      incomplete 749.22
  bilateral 749.14
    with cleft palate, unilateral 749.25
    complete 749.13
    incomplete 749.14
  unilateral 749.12
    with cleft palate, bilateral 749.25
    complete 749.11
    incomplete 749.12
nose 748.1
palate 749.00
  with cleft lip 749.20
    bilateral (lip and palate) 749.24

Cleft — *see also* Imperfect, closure — *continued*
palate — *continued*
  with cleft lip — *continued*
    bilateral — *continued*
      with unilateral lip or palate 749.25
      complete 749.23
      incomplete 749.24
    unilateral (lip and palate) 749.22
      with bilateral lip or palate 749.25
      complete 749.21
      incomplete 749.22
  bilateral 749.04
    with cleft lip, unilateral 749.25
    complete 749.03
    incomplete 749.04
  unilateral 749.02
    with cleft lip, bilateral 749.25
    complete 749.01
    incomplete 749.02
penis 752.69
posterior, cricoid cartilage 748.3
scrotum 752.89
sternum (congenital) 756.3
thyroid cartilage (congenital) 748.3
tongue 750.13
uvula 749.02
  with cleft lip (*see also* Cleft, lip, with cleft palate) 749.20
water 366.12
Cleft hand (congenital) 755.58
Cleidocranial dysostosis 755.59
Cleidotomy, fetal 763.89
Cleptomania 312.32
Clérambault's syndrome 297.8
erotomania 302.89
Clergyman's sore throat 784.49
Click, clicking
systolic syndrome 785.2
Clifford's syndrome (postmaturity) 766.22
Climacteric — *see also* Menopause 627.2
arthritis NEC (*see also* Arthritis, climacteric) 716.3 ☑
depression (*see also* Psychosis, affective) 296.2 ☑
disease 627.2
  recurrent episode 296.3 ☑
  single episode 296.2 ☑
female (symptoms) 627.2
male (symptoms) (syndrome) 608.89
melancholia (*see also* Psychosis, affective) 296.2 ☑
  recurrent episode 296.3 ☑
  single episode 296.2 ☑
paranoid state 297.2
paraphrenia 297.2
polyarthritis NEC 716.39
  male 608.89
symptoms (female) 627.2
Clinical research investigation (control) (participant) V70.7
Clinodactyly 755.59
Clitoris — *see* condition
Cloaca, persistent 751.5
Clonorchiasis 121.1
Clonorchiosis 121.1
Clonorchis infection, liver 121.1
Clonus 781.0
Closed bite 524.20
Closed surgical procedure converted to open procedure
arthroscopic V64.43
laparoscopic V64.41
thoracoscopic V64.42
Closure
artificial opening (*see also* Attention to artificial opening) V55.9
congenital, nose 748.0
cranial sutures, premature 756.0
defective or imperfect NEC — *see* Imperfect, closure
fistula, delayed — *see* Fistula
fontanelle, delayed 756.0
foramen ovale, imperfect 745.5
hymen 623.3
interauricular septum, defective 745.5

☑ Additional Digit Required — Refer to the Tabular List for Digit Selection   Subterms under main terms may continue to next column or page

2010 ICD-9-CM   ▶◀ Revised Text   ● New Line   ▲ Revised Code   October 2009 • Volume 2 — 47

Cicatrix — Closure

Closure — continued
- interventricular septum, defective 745.4
- lacrimal duct 375.56
  - congenital 743.65
  - neonatal 375.55
- nose (congenital) 748.0
  - acquired 738.0
- vagina 623.2
- valve — see Endocarditis
- vulva 624.8

Clot (blood)
- artery (obstruction) (occlusion) (see also Embolism) 444.9
- atrial appendage 429.89
- bladder 596.7
- brain (extradural or intradural) (see also Thrombosis, brain) 434.0
  - late effect — see Late effect(s) (of) cerebrovascular disease
- circulation 444.9
- heart (see also Infarct, myocardium) 410.9
  - without myocardial infarction 429.89
- vein (see also Thrombosis) 453.9

Clotting defect NEC — see also Defect, coagulation 286.9

Clouded state 780.09
- epileptic (see also Epilepsy) 345.9
- paroxysmal (idiopathic) (see also Epilepsy) 345.9

Clouding
- corneal graft 996.51

Cloudy
- antrum, antra 473.0
- dialysis effluent 792.5

Clouston's (hidrotic) ectodermal dysplasia 757.31

Clubbing of fingers 781.5

Clubfinger 736.29
- acquired 736.29
- congenital 754.89

Clubfoot (congenital) 754.70
- acquired 736.71
- equinovarus 754.51
- paralytic 736.71

Club hand (congenital) 754.89
- acquired 736.07

Clubnail (acquired) 703.8
- congenital 757.5

Clump kidney 753.3

Clumsiness 781.3
- syndrome 315.4

Cluttering 307.0

Clutton's joints 090.5

Coagulation, intravascular (diffuse) (disseminated) — see also Fibrinolysis 286.6
- newborn 776.2

Coagulopathy — see also Defect, coagulation 286.9
- consumption 286.6
- intravascular (disseminated) NEC 286.6
  - newborn 776.2

Coalition
- calcaneoscaphoid 755.67
- calcaneus 755.67
- tarsal 755.67

Coal miners'
- elbow 727.2
- lung 500

Coal workers' lung or pneumoconiosis 500

Coarctation
- aorta (postductal) (preductal) 747.10
- pulmonary artery 747.3

Coated tongue 529.3

Coats' disease 362.12

Cocainism — see also Dependence 304.2

Coccidioidal granuloma 114.3

Coccidioidomycosis 114.9
- with pneumonia 114.0
- cutaneous (primary) 114.1
- disseminated 114.3
- extrapulmonary (primary) 114.1
- lung 114.5
  - acute 114.0
  - chronic 114.4
  - primary 114.0
- meninges 114.2

Coccidioidomycosis — continued
- primary (pulmonary) 114.0
  - acute 114.0
- prostate 114.3
- pulmonary 114.5
  - acute 114.0
  - chronic 114.4
  - primary 114.0
- specified site NEC 114.3

Coccidioidosis 114.9
- lung 114.5
  - acute 114.0
  - chronic 114.4
  - primary 114.0
- meninges 114.2

Coccidiosis (colitis) (diarrhea) (dysentery) 007.2

Cocciuria 791.9

Coccus in urine 791.9

Coccydynia 724.79

Coccygodynia 724.79

Coccyx — see condition

Cochin-China
- diarrhea 579.1
  - anguilluliasis 127.2
- ulcer 085.1

Cockayne's disease or syndrome (microcephaly and dwarfism) 759.89

Cockayne-Weber syndrome (epidermolysis bullosa) 757.39

Cocked-up toe 735.2

Cock's peculiar tumor 706.2

Codman's tumor (benign chondroblastoma) (M9230/0) — see Neoplasm, bone, benign

Coenurosis 123.8

Coffee workers' lung 495.8

Cogan's syndrome 370.52
- congenital oculomotor apraxia 379.51
- nonsyphilitic interstitial keratitis 370.52

Coiling, umbilical cord — see Complications, umbilical cord

Coitus, painful (female) 625.0
- male 608.89
- psychogenic 302.76

Cold 460
- with influenza, flu, or grippe 487.1
- abscess (see also Tuberculosis, abscess)
  - articular — see Tuberculosis, joint
- agglutinin
  - disease (chronic) or syndrome 283.0
    - hemoglobinuria 283.0
      - paroxysmal (cold) (nocturnal) 283.2
- allergic (see also Fever, hay) 477.9
- bronchus or chest — see Bronchitis
  - with grippe or influenza 487.1
- common (head) 460
  - vaccination, prophylactic (against) V04.7
- deep 464.10
- effects of 991.9
  - specified effect NEC 991.8
- excessive 991.9
  - specified effect NEC 991.8
- exhaustion from 991.8
- exposure to 991.9
  - specified effect NEC 991.8
- grippy 487.1
- head 460
- injury syndrome (newborn) 778.2
- intolerance 780.99
- on lung — see Bronchitis
- rose 477.0
- sensitivity, autoimmune 283.0
- virus 460

Coldsore — see also Herpes, simplex 054.9

Colibacillosis 041.4
- generalized 038.42

Colibacilluria 791.9

Colic (recurrent) 789.7 ▲
- abdomen 789.7 ▲
  - psychogenic 307.89
- appendicular 543.9
- appendix 543.9
- bile duct — see Choledocholithiasis
- biliary — see Cholelithiasis
- bilious — see Cholelithiasis
- common duct — see Choledocholithiasis
- Devonshire NEC 984.9

Colic — continued
- Devonshire — continued
  - specified type of lead — see Table of Drugs and Chemicals
- flatulent 787.3
- gallbladder or gallstone — see Cholelithiasis
- gastric 536.8
- hepatic (duct) — see Choledocholithiasis
- hysterical 300.11
- in ●
  - adult 789.0 ●
  - child over 12 months old 789.0 ●
  - infant 789.7 ●
- infantile 789.7 ▲
- intestinal 789.7 ▲
- kidney 788.0
- lead NEC 984.9
  - specified type of lead — see Table of Drugs and Chemicals
- liver (duct) — see Choledocholithiasis
- mucous 564.9
  - psychogenic 316 [564.9]
- nephritic 788.0
- painter's NEC 984.9
- pancreas 577.8
- psychogenic 306.4
- renal 788.0
- saturnine NEC 984.9
  - specified type of lead — see Table of Drugs and Chemicals
- spasmodic 789.7 ▲
- ureter 788.0
- urethral 599.84
  - due to calculus 594.2
- uterus 625.8
  - menstrual 625.3
- vermicular 543.9
- virus 460
- worm NEC 128.9

Colicystitis — see also Cystitis 595.9

Colitis (acute) (catarrhal) (croupous) (cystica superficialis) (exudative) (hemorrhagic) (noninfectious) (phlegmonous) (presumed noninfectious) 558.9
- adaptive 564.9
- allergic 558.3
- amebic (see also Amebiasis) 006.9
  - nondysenteric 006.2
- anthrax 022.2
- bacillary (see also Infection, Shigella) 004.9
- balantidial 007.0
- chronic 558.9
  - ulcerative (see also Colitis, ulcerative) 556.9
- coccidial 007.2
- dietetic 558.9
- due to radiation 558.1
- eosinophilic 558.42 ▲
- functional 558.9
- gangrenous 009.0
- giardial 007.1
- granulomatous 555.1
- gravis (see also Colitis, ulcerative) 556.9
- infectious (see also Enteritis, due to, specific organism) 009.0
  - presumed 009.1
- ischemic 557.9
  - acute 557.0
  - chronic 557.1
  - due to mesenteric artery insufficiency 557.1
- membranous 564.9
  - psychogenic 316 [564.9]
- mucous 564.9
  - psychogenic 316 [564.9]
- necrotic 009.0
- polyposa (see also Colitis, ulcerative) 556.9
- protozoal NEC 007.9
- pseudomembranous 008.45
- pseudomucinous 564.9
- regional 555.1
- segmental 555.1
- septic (see also Enteritis, due to, specific organism) 009.0
- spastic 564.9
  - psychogenic 316 [564.9]
- Staphylococcus 008.41

Colitis — continued
- Staphylococcus — continued
  - food 005.0
- thromboulcerative 557.0
- toxic 558.2
- transmural 555.1
- trichomonal 007.3
- tuberculous (ulcerative) 014.8
- ulcerative (chronic) (idiopathic) (nonspecific) 556.9
  - entero- 556.0
  - fulminant 557.0
  - ileo- 556.1
  - left-sided 556.5
  - procto- 556.2
  - proctosigmoid 556.3
  - psychogenic 316 [556]
  - specified NEC 556.8
  - universal 556.6

Collagen disease NEC 710.9
- nonvascular 710.9
- vascular (allergic) (see also Angiitis, hypersensitivity) 446.20

Collagenosis — see also Collagen disease 710.9
- cardiovascular 425.4
- mediastinal 519.3

Collapse 780.2
- adrenal 255.8
- cardiorenal (see also Hypertension, cardiorenal) 404.90
- cardiorespiratory 785.51
  - fetus or newborn 779.85
- cardiovascular (see also Disease, heart) 785.51
  - fetus or newborn 779.85
- circulatory (peripheral) 785.59
  - with
    - abortion — see Abortion, by type, with shock
    - ectopic pregnancy (see also categories 633.0–633.9) 639.5
    - molar pregnancy (see also categories 630–632) 639.5
  - during or after labor and delivery 669.1
  - fetus or newborn 779.85
  - following
    - abortion 639.5
    - ectopic or molar pregnancy 639.5
  - during or after labor and delivery 669.1
  - fetus or newborn 779.89
- external ear canal 380.50
  - secondary to
    - inflammation 380.53
    - surgery 380.52
    - trauma 380.51
- general 780.2
- heart — see Disease, heart
- heat 992.1
- hysterical 300.11
- labyrinth, membranous (congenital) 744.05
- lung (massive) (see also Atelectasis) 518.0
  - pressure, during labor 668.0
- myocardial — see Disease, heart
- nervous (see also Disorder, mental, nonpsychotic) 300.9
- neurocirculatory 306.2
- nose 738.0
- postoperative (cardiovascular) 998.0
- pulmonary (see also Atelectasis) 518.0
  - fetus or newborn 770.5
    - partial 770.5
    - primary 770.4
- thorax 512.8
  - iatrogenic 512.1
  - postoperative 512.1
- trachea 519.19
- valvular — see Endocarditis
- vascular (peripheral) 785.59
  - with
    - abortion — see Abortion, by type, with shock
    - ectopic pregnancy (see also categories 633.0–633.9) 639.5
    - molar pregnancy (see also categories 630–632) 639.5
  - cerebral (see also Disease, cerebrovascular, acute) 436

☑ Additional Digit Required –- Refer to the Tabular List for Digit Selection

▽ Subterms under main terms may continue to next column or page

▶◀ Revised Text   ● New Line   ▲ Revised Code

Index

Closure — Collapse

Collapse — continued
  vascular — continued
    during or after labor and delivery 669.1 ☑
    fetus or newborn 779.89
    following
      abortion 639.5
      ectopic or molar pregnancy 639.5
  vasomotor 785.59
  vertebra 733.13
Collateral — see also condition
  circulation (venous) 459.89
  dilation, veins 459.89
Colles' fracture (closed) (reversed) (separation) 813.41
  open 813.51
Collet-Sicard syndrome 352.6
Collet's syndrome 352.6
Colliculitis urethralis — see also Urethritis 597.89
Colliers'
  asthma 500
  lung 500
  phthisis (see also Tuberculosis) 011.4 ☑
Collodion baby (ichthyosis congenita) 757.1
Colloid milium 709.3
Coloboma NEC 743.49
  choroid 743.59
  fundus 743.52
  iris 743.46
  lens 743.36
  lids 743.62
  optic disc (congenital) 743.57
    acquired 377.23
  retina 743.56
  sclera 743.47
Coloenteritis — see Enteritis
Colon — see condition
Colonization
  MRSA (methicillin resistant Staphylococcus aureus) V02.54
  MSSA (methicillin susceptible Staphylococcus aureus) V02.53
Coloptosis 569.89
Color
  amblyopia NEC 368.59
    acquired 368.55
  blindness NEC (congenital) 368.59
    acquired 368.55
Colostomy
  attention to V55.3
  fitting or adjustment V55.3
  malfunctioning 569.62
  status V44.3
Colpitis — see also Vaginitis 616.10
Colpocele 618.6
Colpocystitis — see also Vaginitis 616.10
Colporrhexis 665.4 ☑
Colpospasm 625.1
Column, spinal, vertebral — see condition
Coma 780.01
  apoplectic (see also Disease, cerebrovascular, acute) 436
  diabetic (with ketoacidosis) 250.3 ☑
    due to secondary diabetes 249.3 ☑
    hyperosmolar 250.2 ☑
      due to secondary diabetes 249.2 ☑
  eclamptic (see also Eclampsia) 780.39
  epileptic 345.3
  hepatic 572.2
  hyperglycemic 250.3 ☑
    due to secondary diabetes 249.3 ☑
  hyperosmolar (diabetic) (nonketotic) 250.2 ☑
    due to secondary diabetes 249.2 ☑
  hypoglycemic 251.0
    diabetic 250.3 ☑
      due to secondary diabetes 249.3 ☑
  insulin 250.3 ☑
    due to secondary diabetes 249.3 ☑
    hyperosmolar 250.2 ☑
      due to secondary diabetes 249.2 ☑
    non-diabetic 251.0
    organic hyperinsulinism 251.0
  Kussmaul's (diabetic) 250.3 ☑
    due to secondary diabetes 249.3 ☑
  liver 572.2
  newborn 779.2
  prediabetic 250.2 ☑

Coma — continued
  prediabetic — continued
    due to secondary diabetes 249.2 ☑
  uremic — see Uremia
Combat fatigue — see also Reaction, stress, acute 308.9
Combined — see condition
Comedo 706.1
Comedocarcinoma (M8501/3) — see also Neoplasm, breast, malignant
  noninfiltrating (M8501/2)
    specified site — see Neoplasm, by site, in situ
    unspecified site 233.0
Comedomastitis 610.4
Comedones 706.1
  lanugo 757.4
Comma bacillus, carrier (suspected) of V02.3
Comminuted fracture — see Fracture, by site
Common
  aortopulmonary trunk 745.0
  atrioventricular canal (defect) 745.69
  atrium 745.69
  cold (head) 460
    vaccination, prophylactic (against) V04.7
  truncus (arteriosus) 745.0
  ventricle 745.3
Commotio (current)
  cerebri (see also Concussion, brain) 850.9
    with skull fracture — see Fracture, skull, by site
  retinae 921.3
  spinalis — see Injury, spinal, by site
Commotion (current)
  brain (without skull fracture) (see also Concussion, brain) 850.9
    with skull fracture — see Fracture, skull, by site
  spinal cord — see Injury, spinal, by site
Communication
  abnormal (see also Fistula)
    between
      base of aorta and pulmonary artery 745.0
      left ventricle and right atrium 745.4
      pericardial sac and pleural sac 748.8
      pulmonary artery and pulmonary vein 747.3
    congenital, between uterus and anterior abdominal wall 752.3
      bladder 752.3
      intestine 752.3
      rectum 752.3
    left ventricular — right atrial 745.4
    pulmonary artery — pulmonary vein 747.3
Compartment syndrome — see Syndrome, compartment
Compensation
  broken — see Failure, heart
  failure — see Failure, heart
  neurosis, psychoneurosis 300.11
Complaint — see also Disease
  bowel, functional 564.9
    psychogenic 306.4
  intestine, functional 564.9
    psychogenic 306.4
  kidney (see also Disease, renal) 593.9
  liver 573.9
  miners' 500
Complete — see condition
Complex
  cardiorenal (see also Hypertension, cardiorenal) 404.90
  castration 300.9
  Costen's 524.60
  ego-dystonic homosexuality 302.0
  Eisenmenger's (ventricular septal defect) 745.4
  homosexual, ego-dystonic 302.0
  hypersexual 302.89
  inferiority 301.9
  jumped process
    spine — see Dislocation, vertebra
  primary, tuberculosis (see also Tuberculosis) 010.0 ☑
  regional pain syndrome 355.9
    type I 337.20

Complex — continued
  regional pain syndrome — continued
    type I — continued
      lower limb 337.22
      specified site NEC 337.29
      upper limb 337.21
    type II
      lower limb 355.71
      upper limb 354.4
  Taussig-Bing (transposition, aorta and overriding pulmonary artery) 745.11
Complications
  abortion NEC — see categories 634-639 ☑
  accidental puncture or laceration during a procedure 998.2
  amniocentesis, fetal 679.1 ☑
  amputation stump (late) (surgical) 997.60
    traumatic — see Amputation, traumatic
  anastomosis (and bypass) (see also Complications, due to (presence of) any device, implant, or graft classified to 996.0–996.5 NEC)
    hemorrhage NEC 998.11
    intestinal (internal) NEC 997.4
      involving urinary tract 997.5
    mechanical — see Complications, mechanical, graft
    urinary tract (involving intestinal tract) 997.5
  anesthesia, anesthetic NEC (see also Anesthesia, complication) 995.22
    in labor and delivery 668.9 ☑
      affecting fetus or newborn 763.5
      cardiac 668.1 ☑
      central nervous system 668.2 ☑
      pulmonary 668.0 ☑
      specified type NEC 668.8 ☑
  aortocoronary (bypass) graft 996.03
    atherosclerosis — see Arteriosclerosis, coronary
    embolism 996.72
    occlusion NEC 996.72
    thrombus 996.72
  arthroplasty (see also Complications, prosthetic joint) 996.49
  artificial opening
    cecostomy 569.60
    colostomy 569.60
    cystostomy 997.5
    enterostomy 569.60
    esophagostomy 530.87
      infection 530.86
      mechanical 530.87
    gastrostomy 536.40
    ileostomy 569.60
    jejunostomy 569.60
    nephrostomy 997.5
    tracheostomy 519.00
    ureterostomy 997.5
    urethrostomy 997.5
  bariatric surgery 997.4
  bile duct implant (prosthetic) NEC 996.79
    infection or inflammation 996.69
    mechanical 996.59
  bleeding (intraoperative) (postoperative) 998.11
  blood vessel graft 996.1
    aortocoronary 996.03
      atherosclerosis — see Arteriosclerosis, coronary
      embolism 996.72
      occlusion NEC 996.72
      thrombus 996.72
    atherosclerosis — see Arteriosclerosis, extremities
    embolism 996.74
    occlusion NEC 996.74
    thrombus 996.74
  bone growth stimulator NEC 996.78
    infection or inflammation 996.67
  bone marrow transplant 996.85
  breast implant (prosthetic) NEC 996.79
    infection or inflammation 996.69
    mechanical 996.54
  bypass (see also Complications, anastomosis)
    aortocoronary 996.03

Complications — continued
  bypass (see also Complications, anastomosis) — continued
    aortocoronary — continued
      atherosclerosis — see Arteriosclerosis, coronary
      embolism 996.72
      occlusion NEC 996.72
      thrombus 996.72
    carotid artery 996.1
      atherosclerosis — see Arteriosclerosis, extremities
      embolism 996.74
      occlusion NEC 996.74
      thrombus 996.74
  cardiac (see also Disease, heart) 429.9
    device, implant, or graft NEC 996.72
      infection or inflammation 996.61
      long-term effect 429.4
      mechanical (see also Complications, mechanical, by type) 996.00
      valve prosthesis 996.71
        infection or inflammation 996.61
    postoperative NEC 997.1
    long-term effect 429.4
  cardiorenal (see also Hypertension, cardiorenal) 404.90
  carotid artery bypass graft 996.1
    atherosclerosis — see Arteriosclerosis, extremities
    embolism 996.74
    occlusion NEC 996.74
    thrombus 996.74
  cataract fragments in eye 998.82
  catheter device NEC (see also Complications, due to (presence of) any device, implant, or graft classified to 996.0–996.5 NEC)
    mechanical — see Complications, mechanical, catheter
  cecostomy 569.60
  cesarean section wound 674.3 ☑
  chemotherapy (antineoplastic) 995.29
  chin implant (prosthetic) NEC 996.79
    infection or inflammation 996.69
    mechanical 996.59
  colostomy (enterostomy) 569.60
    specified type NEC 569.69
  contraceptive device, intrauterine NEC 996.76
    infection 996.65
    inflammation 996.65
    mechanical 996.32
  cord (umbilical) — see Complications, umbilical cord
  cornea
    due to
      contact lens 371.82
  coronary (artery) bypass (graft) NEC 996.03
    atherosclerosis — see Arteriosclerosis, coronary
    embolism 996.72
    infection or inflammation 996.61
    mechanical 996.03
    occlusion NEC 996.72
    specified type NEC 996.72
    thrombus 996.72
  cystostomy 997.5
  delivery 669.9 ☑
    procedure (instrumental) (manual) (surgical) 669.4 ☑
    specified type NEC 669.8 ☑
  dialysis (hemodialysis) (peritoneal) (renal) NEC 999.9
    catheter NEC (see also Complications, due to (presence of) any device, implant, or graft classified to 996.0–996.5 NEC)
      infection or inflammation 996.62
        peritoneal 996.68
      mechanical 996.1
        peritoneal 996.56
  drug NEC 995.29
  due to (presence of) any device, implant, or graft classified to 996.0–996.5 NEC 996.70

☑ Additional Digit Required — Refer to the Tabular List for Digit Selection   ⤷ Subterms under main terms may continue to next column or page

2010 ICD-9-CM   ▶◀ Revised Text   ● New Line   ▲ Revised Code   **Volume 2 — 49**

Complications — *continued*
  due to any device, implant, or graft classified
    to 996.0–996.5 — *continued*
    with infection or inflammation — *see*
      Complications, infection or inflam-
      mation, due to (presence of) any
      device, implant, or graft classified
      to 996.0–996.5 NEC
  arterial NEC 996.74
    coronary NEC 996.03
      atherosclerosis — *see* Arteriosclero-
        sis, coronary
      embolism 996.72
      occlusion NEC 996.72
      specified type NEC 996.72
      thrombus 996.72
    renal dialysis 996.73
  arteriovenous fistula or shunt NEC 996.74
  bone growth stimulator 996.78
  breast NEC 996.79
  cardiac NEC 996.72
    defibrillator 996.72
    pacemaker 996.72
    valve prosthesis 996.71
  catheter NEC 996.79
    spinal 996.75
    urinary, indwelling 996.76
    vascular NEC 996.74
      renal dialysis 996.73
    ventricular shunt 996.75
  coronary (artery) bypass (graft) NEC 996.03
    atherosclerosis — *see* Arteriosclerosis,
      coronary
    embolism 996.72
    occlusion NEC 996.72
    thrombus 996.72
  electrodes
    brain 996.75
    heart 996.72
  esophagostomy 530.87
  gastrointestinal NEC 996.79
  genitourinary NEC 996.76
  heart valve prosthesis NEC 996.71
  infusion pump 996.74
  insulin pump 996.57
  internal
    joint prosthesis 996.77
    orthopedic NEC 996.78
    specified type NEC 996.79
  intrauterine contraceptive device NEC
    996.76
  joint prosthesis, internal NEC 996.77
  mechanical — *see* Complications, mechan-
    ical
  nervous system NEC 996.75
  ocular lens NEC 996.79
  orbital NEC 996.79
  orthopedic NEC 996.78
    joint, internal 996.77
  renal dialysis 996.73
  specified type NEC 996.79
  urinary catheter, indwelling 996.76
  vascular NEC 996.74
  ventricular shunt 996.75
  during dialysis NEC 999.9
  ectopic or molar pregnancy NEC 639.9
  electroshock therapy NEC 999.9
  enterostomy 569.60
    specified type NEC 569.69
  esophagostomy 530.87
    infection 530.86
    mechanical 530.87
  external (fixation) device with internal compo-
    nent(s) NEC 996.78
    infection or inflammation 996.67
    mechanical 996.49
  extracorporeal circulation NEC 999.9
  eye implant (prosthetic) NEC 996.79
    infection or inflammation 996.69
    mechanical
      ocular lens 996.53
      orbital globe 996.59
  fetal, from amniocentesis 679.1 ☑
  gastrointestinal, postoperative NEC (*see also*
    Complications, surgical procedures)
    997.4

Complications — *continued*
  gastrostomy 536.40
    specified type NEC 536.49
  genitourinary device, implant or graft NEC
    996.76
    infection or inflammation 996.65
      urinary catheter, indwelling 996.64
    mechanical (*see also* Complications, me-
      chanical, by type) 996.30
      specified NEC 996.39
  graft (bypass) (patch) (*see also* Complications,
    due to (presence of) any device, im-
    plant, or graft classified to 996.0–996.5
    NEC)
    bone marrow 996.85
    corneal NEC 996.79
      infection or inflammation 996.69
      rejection or reaction 996.51
    mechanical — *see* Complications, mechan-
      ical, graft
    organ (immune or nonimmune cause)
      (partial) (total) 996.80
      bone marrow 996.85
      heart 996.83
      intestines 996.87
      kidney 996.81
      liver 996.82
      lung 996.84
      pancreas 996.86
      specified NEC 996.89
    skin NEC 996.79
      infection or inflammation 996.69
      rejection 996.52
        artificial 996.55
        decellularized allodermis 996.55
  heart (*see also* Disease, heart transplant (im-
    mune or nonimmune cause)) 996.83
  hematoma (intraoperative) (postoperative)
    998.12
  hemorrhage (intraoperative) (postoperative)
    998.11
  hyperalimentation therapy NEC 999.9
  immunization (procedure) — *see* Complica-
    tions, vaccination
  implant (*see also* Complications, due to (pres-
    ence of) any device, implant, or graft
    classified to 996.0–996.5 NEC)
    dental placement, hemorrhagic 525.71
    mechanical — *see* Complications, mechan-
      ical, implant
  infection and inflammation
    due to (presence of) any device, implant
      or graft classified to 996.0–996.5
      NEC 996.60
      arterial NEC 996.62
        coronary 996.61
        renal dialysis 996.62
      arteriovenous fistula or shunt 996.62
      artificial heart 996.61
      bone growth stimulator 996.67
      breast 996.69
      cardiac 996.61
      catheter NEC 996.69
        central venous 999.31
        Hickman 999.31
        peripherally inserted central (PICC)
          999.31
        peritoneal 996.68
        portacath (port-a-cath) 999.31
        spinal 996.63
        triple lumen 999.31
        umbilical venous 999.31
        urinary, indwelling 996.64
        vascular (arterial) (dialysis) (periph-
          eral venous) NEC 996.62
        ventricular shunt 996.63
      central venous catheter 999.31
      coronary artery bypass 996.61
      electrodes
        brain 996.63
        heart 996.61
      gastrointestinal NEC 996.69
      genitourinary NEC 996.65
        indwelling urinary catheter 996.64
      heart assist device 996.61
      heart valve 996.61

Complications — *continued*
  infection and inflammation — *continued*
    due to any device, implant or graft classi-
      fied to 996.0–996.5 — *contin-
      ued*
      Hickman catheter 999.31
      infusion pump 996.62
      insulin pump 996.69
      intrauterine contraceptive device
        996.65
      joint prosthesis, internal 996.66
      ocular lens 996.69
      orbital (implant) 996.69
      orthopedic NEC 996.67
        joint, internal 996.66
      peripherally inserted central catheter
        (PICC) 999.31
      portacath (port-a-cath) 999.31
      specified type NEC 996.69
      triple lumen catheter 999.31
      umbilical venous catheter 999.31
      urinary catheter, indwelling 996.64
      ventricular shunt 996.63
  infusion (procedure) 999.88
    blood — *see* Complications, transfusion
    infection NEC 999.39
    sepsis NEC 999.39
  inhalation therapy NEC 999.9
  injection (procedure) 999.9
    drug reaction (*see also* Reaction, drug)
      995.27
    infection NEC 999.39
    sepsis NEC 999.39
    serum (prophylactic) (therapeutic) — *see*
      Complications, vaccination
    vaccine (any) — *see* Complications, vacci-
      nation
  inoculation (any) — *see* Complications, vacci-
    nation
  insulin pump 996.57
  internal device (catheter) (electronic) (fixation)
    (prosthetic) (*see also* Complications,
    due to (presence of) any device, im-
    plant, or graft classified to 996.0–996.5
    NEC)
    mechanical — *see* Complications, mechan-
      ical
  intestinal pouch, specified NEC 569.79 ●
  intestinal transplant (immune or nonimmune
    cause) 996.87
  intraoperative bleeding or hemorrhage 998.11
  intrauterine contraceptive device (*see also*
    Complications, contraceptive device)
    996.76
    with fetal damage affecting management
      of pregnancy 655.8 ☑
    infection or inflammation 996.65
  in utero procedure
    fetal 679.1 ☑
    maternal 679.0 ☑
  jejunostomy 569.60
  kidney transplant (immune or nonimmune
    cause) 996.81
  labor 669.9 ☑
    specified condition NEC 669.8 ☑
  liver transplant (immune or nonimmune
    cause) 996.82
  lumbar puncture 349.0
  mechanical
    anastomosis — *see* Complications, me-
      chanical, graft
    artificial heart 996.09
    bypass — *see* Complications, mechanical,
      graft
    catheter NEC 996.59
      cardiac 996.09
      cystostomy 996.39
      dialysis (hemodialysis) 996.1
        peritoneal 996.56
      during a procedure 998.2
      urethral, indwelling 996.31
    colostomy 569.62
    device NEC 996.59
      balloon (counterpulsation), intra-aortic
        996.1
      cardiac 996.00

Complications — *continued*
  mechanical — *continued*
    device — *continued*
      cardiac — *continued*
        automatic implantable defibrillator
          996.04
        long-term effect 429.4
        specified NEC 996.09
      contraceptive, intrauterine 996.32
      counterpulsation, intra-aortic 996.1
      fixation, external, with internal compo-
        nents 996.49
      fixation, internal (nail, rod, plate) 996.40
      genitourinary 996.30
        specified NEC 996.39
      insulin pump 996.57
      nervous system 996.2
      orthopedic, internal 996.40
        prosthetic joint (*see also* Complica-
          tions, mechanical, device,
          orthopedic, prosthetic, joint)
          996.47
      prosthetic NEC 996.59
        joint 996.47
          articular bearing surface wear
            996.46
          aseptic loosening 996.41
          breakage 996.43
          dislocation 996.42
          failure 996.47   ▲
          fracture 996.43
            around prosthetic 996.44
            peri-prosthetic 996.44
          instability 996.42
          loosening 996.41
          peri-prosthetic osteolysis 996.45
          subluxation 996.42
          wear 996.46
      umbrella, vena cava 996.1
      vascular 996.1
    dorsal column stimulator 996.2
    electrode NEC 996.59
      brain 996.2
      cardiac 996.01
      spinal column 996.2
    enterostomy 569.62
    esophagostomy 530.87
    fistula, arteriovenous, surgically created
      996.1
    gastrostomy 536.42
    graft NEC 996.52
      aortic (bifurcation) 996.1
      aortocoronary bypass 996.03
      blood vessel NEC 996.1
      bone 996.49
      cardiac 996.00
      carotid artery bypass 996.1
      cartilage 996.49
      corneal 996.51
      coronary bypass 996.03
      decellularized allodermis 996.55
      genitourinary 996.30
        specified NEC 996.39
      muscle 996.49
      nervous system 996.2
      organ (immune or nonimmune cause)
        996.80
        heart 996.83
        intestines 996.87
        kidney 996.81
        liver 996.82
        lung 996.84
        pancreas 996.86
        specified NEC 996.89
      orthopedic, internal 996.49
      peripheral nerve 996.2
      prosthetic NEC 996.59
      skin 996.52
        artificial 996.55
      specified NEC 996.59
      tendon 996.49
      tissue NEC 996.52
      tooth 996.59
      ureter, without mention of resection
        996.39
      vascular 996.1

☑ Additional Digit Required — Refer to the Tabular List for Digit Selection   ▼ Subterms under main terms may continue to next column or page

50 — Volume 2 · October 2009   ▶◀ Revised Text   ● New Line   ▲ Revised Code   **2010 ICD·9·CM**

Complications — *continued*
mechanical — *continued*
    heart valve prosthesis 996.02
      long-term effect 429.4
    implant NEC 996.59
      cardiac 996.00
        automatic implantable defibrillator 996.04
        long-term effect 429.4
        specified NEC 996.09
      electrode NEC 996.59
        brain 996.2
        cardiac 996.01
        spinal column 996.2
      genitourinary 996.30
      nervous system 996.2
      orthopedic, internal 996.49
      prosthetic NEC 996.59
        in
          bile duct 996.59
          breast 996.54
          chin 996.59
          eye
            ocular lens 996.53
            orbital globe 996.59
          vascular 996.1
    insulin pump 996.57
    nonabsorbable surgical material 996.59
    pacemaker NEC 996.59
      brain 996.2
      cardiac 996.01
      nerve (phrenic) 996.2
    patch — *see* Complications, mechanical, graft
    prosthesis NEC 996.59
      bile duct 996.59
      breast 996.54
      chin 996.59
      ocular lens 996.53
      reconstruction, vas deferens 996.39
    reimplant NEC 996.59
      extremity (*see also* Complications, reattached, extremity) 996.90
      organ (*see also* Complications, transplant, organ, by site) 996.80
    repair — *see* Complications, mechanical, graft
    respirator [ventilator] V46.14
    shunt NEC 996.59
      arteriovenous, surgically created 996.1
      ventricular (communicating) 996.2
    stent NEC 996.59
    tracheostomy 519.02
    vas deferens reconstruction 996.39
    ventilator [respirator] V46.14
medical care NEC 999.9
    cardiac NEC 997.1
    gastrointestinal NEC 997.4
    nervous system NEC 997.00
    peripheral vascular NEC 997.2
    respiratory NEC 997.39
    urinary NEC 997.5
    vascular
      mesenteric artery 997.71
      other vessels 997.79
      peripheral vessels 997.2
      renal artery 997.72
nephrostomy 997.5
nervous system
    device, implant, or graft NEC 349.1
      mechanical 996.2
    postoperative NEC 997.00
obstetric 669.9 ☑
    procedure (instrumental) (manual) (surgical) 669.4 ☑
    specified NEC 669.8 ☑
    surgical wound 674.3 ☑
ocular lens implant NEC 996.79
    infection or inflammation 996.69
    mechanical 996.53
organ transplant — *see* Complications, transplant, organ, by site
orthopedic device, implant, or graft
    internal (fixation) (nail) (plate) (rod) NEC 996.78
      infection or inflammation 996.67

Complications — *continued*
orthopedic device, implant, or graft — *continued*
    internal — *continued*
      joint prosthesis 996.77
        infection or inflammation 996.66
        mechanical 996.40
pacemaker (cardiac) 996.72
    infection or inflammation 996.61
    mechanical 996.01
pancreas transplant (immune or nonimmune cause) 996.86
perfusion NEC 999.9
perineal repair (obstetrical) 674.3 ☑
    disruption 674.2 ☑
pessary (uterus) (vagina) — *see* Complications, contraceptive device
phototherapy 990
postcystoscopic 997.5
postmastoidectomy NEC 383.30
postoperative — *see* Complications, surgical procedures
pregnancy NEC 646.9 ☑
    affecting fetus or newborn 761.9
prosthetic device, internal (*see also* Complications, due to (presence of) any device, implant or graft classified to 996.0–996.5 NEC)
    mechanical NEC (*see also* Complications, mechanical) 996.59
puerperium NEC (*see also* Puerperal) 674.9 ☑
puncture, spinal 349.0
pyelogram 997.5
radiation 990
radiotherapy 990
reattached
    body part, except extremity 996.99
    extremity (infection) (rejection) 996.90
      arm(s) 996.94
      digit(s) (hand) 996.93
        foot 996.95
      finger(s) 996.93
      foot 996.95
      forearm 996.91
      hand 996.92
      leg 996.96
      lower NEC 996.96
      toe(s) 996.95
      upper NEC 996.94
reimplant NEC (*see also* Complications, due to (presence of) any device, implant, or graft classified to 996.0–996.5 NEC)
    bone marrow 996.85
    extremity (*see also* Complications, reattached, extremity) 996.90
      due to infection 996.90
    mechanical — *see* Complications, mechanical, reimplant
    organ (immune or nonimmune cause) (partial) (total) (*see also* Complications, transplant, organ, by site) 996.80
renal allograft 996.81
renal dialysis — *see* Complications, dialysis
respirator [ventilator], mechanical V46.14
respiratory 519.9
    device, implant or graft NEC 996.79
      infection or inflammation 996.69
      mechanical 996.59
    distress syndrome, adult, following trauma or surgery 518.5
    insufficiency, acute, postoperative 518.5
    postoperative NEC 997.39
    therapy NEC 999.9
sedation during labor and delivery 668.9 ☑
    affecting fetus or newborn 763.5
    cardiac 668.1 ☑
    central nervous system 668.2 ☑
    pulmonary 668.0 ☑
    specified type NEC 668.8 ☑
seroma (intraoperative) (postoperative) (noninfected) 998.13
    infected 998.51
shunt (*see also* Complications, due to (presence of) any device, implant or graft classified to 996.0–996.5 NEC)

Complications — *continued*
shunt (*see also* Complications, due to any device, implant, or graft classified to 996.0–996.5) — *continued*
    mechanical — *see* Complications, mechanical, shunt
specified body system NEC
    device, implant, or graft — *see* Complications, due to (presence of) any device, implant, or graft classified to 996.0–996.5 NEC
    postoperative NEC 997.99
spinal puncture or tap 349.0
stomach banding 997.4
stomach stapling 997.4
stoma, external
    gastrointestinal tract
      colostomy 569.60
      enterostomy 569.60
      esophagostomy 530.87
        infection 530.86
        mechanical 530.87
      gastrostomy 536.40
    urinary tract 997.5
surgical procedures 998.9
    accidental puncture or laceration 998.2
    amputation stump (late) 997.60
    anastomosis — *see* Complications, anastomosis
    burst stitches or sutures (external) (*see also* Dehiscence) 998.32
      internal 998.31
    cardiac 997.1
      long-term effect following cardiac surgery 429.4
    cataract fragments in eye 998.82
    catheter device — *see* Complications, catheter device
    cecostomy malfunction 569.62
    colostomy malfunction 569.62
    cystostomy malfunction 997.5
    dehiscence (of incision) (external) (*see also* Dehiscence) 998.32
      internal 998.31
    dialysis NEC (*see also* Complications, dialysis) 999.9
    disruption (*see also* Dehiscence)
      anastomosis (internal) — *see* Complications, mechanical, graft
      internal suture (line) 998.31
      wound (external) 998.32
        internal 998.31
    dumping syndrome (postgastrectomy) 564.2
    elephantiasis or lymphedema 997.99
      postmastectomy 457.0
    emphysema (surgical) 998.81
    enterostomy malfunction 569.62
    esophagostomy malfunction 530.87
    evisceration 998.32
    fistula (persistent postoperative) 998.6
    foreign body inadvertently left in wound (sponge) (suture) (swab) 998.4
      from nonabsorbable surgical material (Dacron) (mesh) (permanent suture) (reinforcing) (Teflon) — *see* Complications, due to (presence of) any device, implant, or graft classified to 996.0–996.5 NEC
    gastrointestinal NEC 997.4
    gastrostomy malfunction 536.42
    hematoma 998.12
    hemorrhage 998.11
    ileostomy malfunction 569.62
    internal prosthetic device NEC (*see also* Complications, internal device) 996.70
      hemolytic anemia 283.19
      infection or inflammation 996.60
      malfunction — *see* Complications, mechanical
      mechanical complication — *see* Complications, mechanical
      thrombus 996.70
    jejunostomy malfunction 569.62
    nervous system NEC 997.00

Complications — *continued*
surgical procedures — *continued*
    obstruction, internal anastomosis — *see* Complications, mechanical, graft
    other body system NEC 997.99
    peripheral vascular 997.2
    postcardiotomy syndrome 429.4
    postcholecystectomy syndrome 576.0
    postcommissurotomy syndrome 429.4
    postgastrectomy dumping syndrome 564.2
    postmastectomy lymphedema syndrome 457.0
    postmastoidectomy 383.30
      cholesteatoma, recurrent 383.32
      cyst, mucosal 383.31
      granulation 383.33
      inflammation, chronic 383.33
    postvagotomy syndrome 564.2
    postvalvulotomy syndrome 429.4
    reattached extremity (infection) (rejection) (*see also* Complications, reattached, extremity) 996.90
    respiratory NEC 997.39
    seroma 998.13
    shock (endotoxic) (hypovolemic) (septic) 998.0
    shunt, prosthetic (thrombus) (*see also* Complications, due to (presence of) any device, implant, or graft classified to 996.0–996.5 NEC)
      hemolytic anemia 283.19
    specified complication NEC 998.89
    stitch abscess 998.59
    transplant — *see* Complications, graft
    ureterostomy malfunction 997.5
    urethrostomy malfunction 997.5
    urinary NEC 997.5
    vascular
      mesenteric artery 997.71
      other vessels 997.79
      peripheral vessels 997.2
      renal artery 997.72
    wound infection 998.59
therapeutic misadventure NEC 999.9
    surgical treatment 998.9
tracheostomy 519.00
transfusion (blood) (lymphocytes) (plasma) NEC 999.89
    acute lung injury (TRALI) 518.7
    atrophy, liver, yellow, subacute (within 8 months of administration) — *see* Hepatitis, viral
    bone marrow 996.85
    embolism
      air 999.1
      thrombus 999.2
    hemolysis NEC 999.89
      bone marrow 996.85
    hepatitis (serum) (type B) (within 8 months after administration) — *see* Hepatitis, viral
    incompatibility reaction
      ABO 999.6   ●
      minor blood group 999.89   ●
      Rh (factor) 999.7
    infection 999.39
    jaundice (serum) (within 8 months after administration) — *see* Hepatitis, viral
    sepsis 999.39
    shock or reaction NEC 999.89
      bone marrow 996.85
    subacute yellow atrophy of liver (within 8 months after administration) — *see* Hepatitis, viral
    thromboembolism 999.2
transplant NEC (*see also* Complications, due to (presence of) any device, implant, or graft classified to 996.0–996.5 NEC)
    bone marrow 996.85
    organ (immune or nonimmune cause) (partial) (total) 996.80
      bone marrow 996.85
      heart 996.83
      intestines 996.87

☑ Additional Digit Required — Refer to the Tabular List for Digit Selection   ⬚ Subterms under main terms may continue to next column or page

2010 ICD-9-CM   ▶◀ Revised Text   ● New Line   ▲ Revised Code   October 2009 · Volume 2 — 51

Complications — continued
  transplant (see also Complications, due to any device, implant, or graft classified to 996.0–996.5) — continued
    organ — continued
      kidney 996.81
      liver 996.82
      lung 996.84
      pancreas 996.86
      specified NEC 996.89
  trauma NEC (early) 958.8
  ultrasound therapy NEC 999.9
  umbilical cord
    affecting fetus or newborn 762.6
    complicating delivery 663.9 ☑
      affecting fetus or newborn 762.6
      specified type NEC 663.8 ☑
  urethral catheter NEC 996.76
    infection or inflammation 996.64
    mechanical 996.31
  urinary, postoperative NEC 997.5
  vaccination 999.9
    anaphylaxis NEC 999.4
    cellulitis 999.39
    encephalitis or encephalomyelitis 323.51
    hepatitis (serum) (type B) (within 8 months after administration) — see Hepatitis, viral
    infection (general) (local) NEC 999.39
    jaundice (serum) (within 8 months after administration) — see Hepatitis, viral
    meningitis 997.09 [321.8]
    myelitis 323.52
    protein sickness 999.5
    reaction (allergic) 999.5
      Herxheimer's 995.0
      serum 999.5
    sepsis 999.39
    serum intoxication, sickness, rash, or other serum reaction NEC 999.5
    shock (allergic) (anaphylactic) 999.4
    subacute yellow atrophy of liver (within 8 months after administration) — see Hepatitis, viral
    vaccinia (generalized) 999.0
      localized 999.39
  vascular
    device, implant, or graft NEC 996.74
      infection or inflammation 996.62
      mechanical NEC 996.1
        cardiac (see also Complications, mechanical, by type) 996.00
    following infusion, perfusion, or transfusion 999.2
    postoperative NEC 997.2
      mesenteric artery 997.71
      other vessels 997.79
      peripheral vessels 997.2
      renal artery 997.72
  ventilation therapy NEC 999.9
  ventilator [respirator], mechanical V46.14
Compound presentation, complicating delivery 652.8 ☑
  causing obstructed labor 660.0 ☑
Compressed air disease 993.3
Compression
  with injury — see specific injury
  arm NEC 354.9
  artery 447.1
    celiac, syndrome 447.4
  brachial plexus 353.0
  brain (stem) 348.4
    due to
      contusion, brain — see Contusion, brain
      injury NEC (see also Hemorrhage, brain, traumatic)
        birth — see Birth, injury, brain
      laceration, brain — see Laceration, brain
    osteopathic 739.0
  bronchus 519.19
  by cicatrix — see Cicatrix
  cardiac 423.9
  cauda equina 344.60

Compression — continued
  cauda equina — continued
    with neurogenic bladder 344.61
  celiac (artery) (axis) 447.4
  cerebral — see Compression, brain
  cervical plexus 353.2
  cord (umbilical) — see Compression, umbilical cord
  cranial nerve 352.9
    second 377.49
    third (partial) 378.51
      total 378.52
    fourth 378.53
    fifth 350.8
    sixth 378.54
    seventh 351.8
  divers' squeeze 993.3
  duodenum (external) (see also Obstruction, duodenum) 537.3
  during birth 767.9
  esophagus 530.3
    congenital, external 750.3
  Eustachian tube 381.63
  facies (congenital) 754.0
  fracture — see Fracture, by site
  heart — see Disease, heart
  intestine (see also Obstruction, intestine) 560.9
    with hernia — see Hernia, by site, with obstruction
  laryngeal nerve, recurrent 478.79
  leg NEC 355.8
  lower extremity NEC 355.8
  lumbosacral plexus 353.1
  lung 518.89
  lymphatic vessel 457.1
  medulla — see Compression, brain
  nerve NEC (see also Disorder, nerve)
    arm NEC 354.9
    autonomic nervous system (see also Neuropathy, peripheral, autonomic) 337.9
    axillary 353.0
    cranial NEC 352.9
    due to displacement of intervertebral disc 722.2
      with myelopathy 722.70
      cervical 722.0
        with myelopathy 722.71
      lumbar, lumbosacral 722.10
        with myelopathy 722.73
      thoracic, thoracolumbar 722.11
        with myelopathy 722.72
    iliohypogastric 355.79
    ilioinguinal 355.79
    leg NEC 355.8
    lower extremity NEC 355.8
    median (in carpal tunnel) 354.0
    obturator 355.79
    optic 377.49
    plantar 355.6
    posterior tibial (in tarsal tunnel) 355.5
    root (by scar tissue) NEC 724.9
      cervical NEC 723.4
      lumbar NEC 724.4
      lumbosacral 724.4
      thoracic 724.4
    saphenous 355.79
    sciatic (acute) 355.0
    sympathetic 337.9
    traumatic — see Injury, nerve
    ulnar 354.2
    upper extremity NEC 354.9
  peripheral — see Compression, nerve
  spinal (cord) (old or nontraumatic) 336.9
    by displacement of intervertebral disc — see Displacement, intervertebral disc
    nerve
      root NEC 724.9
        postoperative 722.80
          cervical region 722.81
          lumbar region 722.83
          thoracic region 722.82
        traumatic — see Injury, nerve, spinal
      traumatic — see Injury, nerve, spinal

Compression — continued
  spinal — continued
    spondylogenic 721.91
      cervical 721.1
      lumbar, lumbosacral 721.42
      thoracic 721.41
    traumatic (see also Injury, spinal, by site)
      with fracture, vertebra — see Fracture, vertebra, by site, with spinal cord injury
  spondylogenic — see Compression, spinal cord, spondylogenic
  subcostal nerve (syndrome) 354.8
  sympathetic nerve NEC 337.9
  syndrome 958.5
  thorax 512.8
    iatrogenic 512.1
    postoperative 512.1
  trachea 519.19
    congenital 748.3
  ulnar nerve (by scar tissue) 354.2
  umbilical cord
    affecting fetus or newborn 762.5
      cord prolapsed 762.4
    complicating delivery 663.2 ☑
      cord around neck 663.1 ☑
      cord prolapsed 663.0 ☑
  upper extremity NEC 354.9
  ureter 593.3
  urethra — see Stricture, urethra
  vein 459.2
  vena cava (inferior) (superior) 459.2
  vertebral NEC — see Compression, spinal (cord)
Compulsion, compulsive
  eating 307.51
  neurosis (obsessive) 300.3
  personality 301.4
  states (mixed) 300.3
  swearing 300.3
    in Gilles de la Tourette's syndrome 307.23
  tics and spasms 307.22
  water drinking NEC (syndrome) 307.9
Concato's disease (pericardial polyserositis) 423.2
  peritoneal 568.82
  pleural — see Pleurisy
Concavity, chest wall 738.3
Concealed
  hemorrhage NEC 459.0
  penis 752.65
Concentric fading 368.12
Concern (normal) **about sick person in family** V61.49
Concrescence (teeth) 520.2
Concretio cordis 423.1
  rheumatic 393
Concretion — see also Calculus
  appendicular 543.9
  canaliculus 375.57
  clitoris 624.8
  conjunctiva 372.54
  eyelid 374.56
  intestine (impaction) (obstruction) 560.39
  lacrimal (passages) 375.57
  prepuce (male) 605
    female (clitoris) 624.8
  salivary gland (any) 527.5
  seminal vesicle 608.89
  stomach 537.89
  tonsil 474.8
Concussion (current) 850.9
  with
    loss of consciousness 850.5
      brief (less than one hour)
        30 minutes or less 850.11
        31-59 minutes 850.12
      moderate (1-24 hours) 850.2
      prolonged (more than 24 hours) (with complete recovery) (with return to pre-existing conscious level) 850.3
        without return to pre-existing conscious level 850.4
    mental confusion or disorientation (without loss of consciousness) 850.0

Concussion — continued
  with — continued
    mental confusion or disorientation — continued
      with loss of consciousness — see Concussion, with, loss of consciousness
    without loss of consciousness 850.0
  blast (air) (hydraulic) (immersion) (underwater) 869.0
    with open wound into cavity 869.1
    abdomen or thorax — see Injury, internal, by site
    brain — see Concussion, brain
    ear (acoustic nerve trauma) 951.5
      with perforation, tympanic membrane — see Wound, open, ear drum
    thorax — see Injury, internal, intrathoracic organs NEC
  brain or cerebral (without skull fracture) 850.9
    with
      loss of consciousness 850.5
        brief (less than one hour)
          30 minutes or less 850.11
          31-59 minutes 850.12
        moderate (1-24 hours) 850.2
        prolonged (more than 24 hours)
          (with complete recovery)
          (with return to pre-existing conscious level) 850.3
          without return to pre-existing conscious level 850.4
      mental confusion or disorientation (without loss of consciousness) 850.0
        with loss of consciousness — see Concussion, brain, with, loss of consciousness
      skull fracture — see Fracture, skull, by site
    without loss of consciousness 850.0
  cauda equina 952.4
  cerebral — see Concussion, brain
  conus medullaris (spine) 952.4
  hydraulic — see Concussion, blast
  internal organs — see Injury, internal, by site
  labyrinth — see Injury, intracranial
  ocular 921.3
  osseous labyrinth — see Injury, intracranial
  spinal (cord) (see also Injury, spinal, by site)
    due to
      broken
        back — see Fracture, vertebra, by site, with spinal cord injury
        neck — see Fracture, vertebra, cervical, with spinal cord injury
      fracture, fracture dislocation, or compression fracture of spine or vertebra — see Fracture, vertebra, by site, with spinal cord injury
  syndrome 310.2
  underwater blast — see Concussion, blast
Condition — see also Disease
  fetal hematologic 678.0 ☑
  psychiatric 298.9
  respiratory NEC 519.9
    acute or subacute NEC 519.9
      due to
        external agent 508.9
          specified type NEC 508.8
        fumes or vapors (chemical) (inhalation) 506.3
        radiation 508.0
    chronic NEC 519.9
      due to
        external agent 508.9
          specified type NEC 508.8
        fumes or vapors (chemical) (inhalation) 506.4
        radiation 508.1
    due to
      external agent 508.9
        specified type NEC 508.8
      fumes or vapors (chemical) (inhalation) 506.9

☑ Additional Digit Required — Refer to the Tabular List for Digit Selection   ⩒ Subterms under main terms may continue to next column or page

Index   **Complications — Condition**

52 — Volume 2   ▶◀ Revised Text   ● New Line   ▲ Revised Code   **2010 ICD-9-CM**

Conduct disturbance — *see also* Disturbance, conduct 312.9
  adjustment reaction 309.3
  hyperkinetic 314.2
Condyloma NEC 078.11
  acuminatum 078.11
  gonorrheal 098.0
  latum 091.3
  syphilitic 091.3
    congenital 090.0
  venereal, syphilitic 091.3
Confinement — *see* Delivery
Conflagration — *see also* Burn, by site
  asphyxia (by inhalation of smoke, gases, fumes, or vapors) 987.9
    specified agent — *see* Table of Drugs and Chemicals
Conflict
  family V61.9
    specified circumstance NEC V61.8
  interpersonal NEC V62.81
  marital V61.10
    involving
      divorce V61.03
      estrangement V61.09
  parent ▶(guardian)◀ child V61.20
    adopted child V61.24 ●
    biological child V61.23 ●
    foster child V61.25 ●
  partner V61.10
Confluent — *see* condition
Confusional arousals 327.41
Confusion, confused (mental) (state) — *see also* State, confusional 298.9
  acute 293.0
  epileptic 293.0
  postoperative 293.9
  psychogenic 298.2
  reactive (from emotional stress, psychological trauma) 298.2
  subacute 293.1
Congelation 991.9
Congenital — *see also* condition
  aortic septum 747.29
  generalized fibromatosis (CGF) 759.89
  intrinsic factor deficiency 281.0
  malformation — *see* Anomaly
Congestion, congestive
  asphyxia, newborn 768.9
  bladder 596.8
  bowel 569.89
  brain (*see also* Disease, cerebrovascular NEC) 437.8
    malarial 084.9
  breast 611.79
  bronchi 519.19
  bronchial tube 519.19
  catarrhal 472.0
  cerebral — *see* Congestion, brain
  cerebrospinal — *see* Congestion, brain
  chest 786.9
  chill 780.99
    malarial (*see also* Malaria) 084.6
  circulatory NEC 459.9
  conjunctiva 372.71
  due to disturbance of circulation 459.9
  duodenum 537.3
  enteritis — *see* Enteritis
  eye 372.71
  fibrosis syndrome (pelvic) 625.5
  gastroenteritis — *see* Enteritis
  general 799.89
  glottis 476.0
  heart (*see also* Failure, heart) 428.0
  hepatic 573.0
  hypostatic (lung) 514
  intestine 569.89
  intracranial — *see* Congestion, brain
  kidney 593.89
  labyrinth 386.50
  larynx 476.0
  liver 573.0
  lung 786.9
    active or acute (*see also* Pneumonia) 486
      congenital 770.0
    chronic 514

Congestion, congestive — *continued*
  lung — *continued*
    hypostatic 514
    idiopathic, acute 518.5
    passive 514
  malaria, malarial (brain) (fever) (*see also* Malaria) 084.6
  medulla — *see* Congestion, brain
  nasal 478.19
  nose 478.19
  orbit, orbital 376.33
    inflammatory (chronic) 376.10
    acute 376.00
  ovary 620.8
  pancreas 577.8
  pelvic, female 625.5
  pleural 511.0
  prostate (active) 602.1
  pulmonary — *see* Congestion, lung
  renal 593.89
  retina 362.89
  seminal vesicle 608.89
  spinal cord 336.1
  spleen 289.51
    chronic 289.51
  stomach 537.89
  trachea 464.11
  urethra 599.84
  uterus 625.5
    with subinvolution 621.1
  viscera 799.89
Congestive — *see* Congestion
Conical
  cervix 622.6
  cornea 371.60
  teeth 520.2
Conjoined twins 759.4
  causing disproportion (fetopelvic) 678.1 ☑
  fetal 678.1 ☑
Conjugal maladjustment V61.10
  involving
    divorce V61.03
    estrangement V61.09
Conjunctiva — *see* condition
Conjunctivitis (exposure) (infectious) (nondiphtheritic) (pneumococcal) (pustular) (staphylococcal) (streptococcal) NEC 372.30
  actinic 370.24
  acute 372.00
    atopic 372.05
    chemical 372.06 ●
    contagious 372.03
    follicular 372.02
    hemorrhagic (viral) 077.4
    toxic 372.06 ●
  adenoviral (acute) 077.3
  allergic (chronic) 372.14
    with hay fever 372.05
  anaphylactic 372.05
  angular 372.03
  Apollo (viral) 077.4
  atopic 372.05
  blennorrhagic (neonatorum) 098.40
  catarrhal 372.03
  chemical 372.06 ▲
    allergic 372.05
    meaning corrosion — *see* Burn, conjunctiva
  chlamydial 077.98
    due to
      Chlamydia trachomatis — *see* Trachoma
      paratrachoma 077.0
  chronic 372.10
    allergic 372.14
    follicular 372.12
    simple 372.11
    specified type NEC 372.14
    vernal 372.13
  diphtheritic 032.81
  due to
    dust 372.05
    enterovirus type 70 077.4
    erythema multiforme 695.10 *[372.33]*
    filariasis (*see also* Filariasis) 125.9 *[372.15]*

Conjunctivitis — *continued*
  due to — *continued*
    mucocutaneous
      disease NEC 372.33
      leishmaniasis 085.5 *[372.15]*
    Reiter's disease 099.3 *[372.33]*
    syphilis 095.8 *[372.10]*
    toxoplasmosis (acquired) 130.1
      congenital (active) 771.2
    trachoma — *see* Trachoma
  dust 372.05
  eczematous 370.31
  epidemic 077.1
    hemorrhagic 077.4
  follicular (acute) 372.02
    adenoviral (acute) 077.3
    chronic 372.12
  glare 370.24
  gonococcal (neonatorum) 098.40
  granular (trachomatous) 076.1
    late effect 139.1
  hemorrhagic (acute) (epidemic) 077.4
  herpetic (simplex) 054.43
    zoster 053.21
  inclusion 077.0
  infantile 771.6
  influenzal 372.03
  Koch-Weeks 372.03
  light 372.05
  medicamentosa 372.05
  membranous 372.04
  meningococcic 036.89
  Morax-Axenfeld 372.02
  mucopurulent NEC 372.03
  neonatal 771.6
    gonococcal 098.40
  Newcastle's 077.8
  nodosa 360.14
  of Beal 077.3
  parasitic 372.15
    filariasis (*see also* Filariasis) 125.9 *[372.15]*
    mucocutaneous leishmaniasis 085.5 *[372.15]*
  Parinaud's 372.02
  petrificans 372.39
  phlyctenular 370.31
  pseudomembranous 372.04
    diphtheritic 032.81
  purulent 372.03
  Reiter's 099.3 *[372.33]*
  rosacea 695.3 *[372.31]*
  serous 372.01
  simple chronic 372.11
  specified NEC 372.39
  sunlamp 372.04
  swimming pool 077.0
  toxic 372.06 ●
  trachomatous (follicular) 076.1
    acute 076.0
    late effect 139.1
  traumatic NEC 372.39
  tuberculous (*see also* Tuberculosis) 017.3 ☑ *[370.31]*
  tularemic 021.3
  tularensis 021.3
  vernal 372.13
    limbar 372.13 *[370.32]*
  viral 077.99
    acute hemorrhagic 077.4
    specified NEC 077.8
Conjunctivochalasis 372.81
Conjunctoblepharitis — *see* Conjunctivitis
Connective tissue — *see* condition
Conn (-Louis) syndrome (primary aldosteronism) 255.12
Conradi (-Hünermann) syndrome or disease (chondrodysplasia calcificans congenita) 756.59
Consanguinity V19.7
Consecutive — *see* condition
Consolidated lung (base) — *see* Pneumonia, lobar
Constipation 564.00
  atonic 564.09

Constipation — *continued*
  drug induced
    correct substance properly administered 564.09
    overdose or wrong substance given or taken 977.9
      specified drug — *see* Table of Drugs and Chemicals
  neurogenic 564.09
  other specified NEC 564.09
  outlet dysfunction 564.02
  psychogenic 306.4
  simple 564.00
  slow transit 564.01
  spastic 564.09
Constitutional — *see also* condition
  arterial hypotension (*see also* Hypotension) 458.9
  obesity 278.00
    morbid 278.01
  psychopathic state 301.9
  short stature in childhood 783.43
  state, developmental V21.9
    specified development NEC V21.8
  substandard 301.6
Constitutionally substandard 301.6
Constriction
  anomalous, meningeal bands or folds 742.8
  aortic arch (congenital) 747.10
  asphyxiation or suffocation by 994.7
  bronchus 519.19
  canal, ear (*see also* Stricture, ear canal, acquired) 380.50
  duodenum 537.3
  gallbladder (*see also* Obstruction, gallbladder) 575.2
    congenital 751.69
  intestine (*see also* Obstruction, intestine) 560.9
  larynx 478.74
    congenital 748.3
  meningeal bands or folds, anomalous 742.8
  organ or site, congenital NEC — *see* Atresia
  prepuce (congenital) 605
  pylorus 537.0
    adult hypertrophic 537.0
    congenital or infantile 750.5
    newborn 750.5
  ring (uterus) 661.4 ☑
    affecting fetus or newborn 763.7
  spastic (*see also* Spasm)
    ureter 593.3
    urethra — *see* Stricture, urethra
  stomach 537.89
  ureter 593.3
  urethra — *see* Stricture, urethra
  visual field (functional) (peripheral) 368.45
Constrictive — *see* condition
Consultation
  without complaint or sickness V65.9
    feared complaint unfounded V65.5
    specified reason V65.8
  medical (*see also* Counseling, medical)
  specified reason NEC V65.8
Consumption — *see* Tuberculosis
Contact
  with
    AIDS virus V01.79
    anthrax V01.81
    asbestos V15.84 ●
    cholera V01.0
    communicable disease V01.9
      specified type NEC V01.89
      viral NEC V01.79
    Escherichia coli (E. coli) V01.83
    German measles V01.4
    gonorrhea V01.6
    HIV V01.79
    human immunodeficiency virus V01.79
    lead V15.86 ●
    meningococcus V01.84
    parasitic disease NEC V01.89
    poliomyelitis V01.2
    potentially hazardous body fluids V15.85 ●
    rabies V01.5
    rubella V01.4
    SARS-associated coronavirus V01.82

☑ Additional Digit Required — Refer to the Tabular List for Digit Selection   ▶◀ Revised Text   ● New Line   ▲ Revised Code   Subterms under main terms may continue to next column or page

2010 ICD-9-CM   October 2009 • Volume 2 — 53

Contact — *continued*
with — *continued*
smallpox V01.3
syphilis V01.6
tuberculosis V01.1
varicella V01.71
venereal disease V01.6
viral disease NEC V01.79
dermatitis — *see* Dermatitis
Contamination, food — *see also* Poisoning, food 005.9
Contraception, contraceptive
advice NEC V25.09
family planning V25.09
fitting of diaphragm V25.02
prescribing or use of
oral contraceptive agent V25.01
specified agent NEC V25.02
counseling NEC V25.09
emergency V25.03
family planning V25.09
fitting of diaphragm V25.02
prescribing or use of
oral contraceptive agent V25.01
emergency V25.03
postcoital V25.03
specified agent NEC V25.02
device (in situ) V45.59
causing menorrhagia 996.76
checking V25.42
complications 996.32
insertion V25.1
intrauterine V45.51
reinsertion V25.42
removal V25.42
subdermal V45.52
fitting of diaphragm V25.02
insertion
intrauterine contraceptive device V25.1
subdermal implantable V25.5
maintenance V25.40
examination V25.40
oral contraceptive V25.41
specified method NEC V25.49
subdermal implantable V25.43
intrauterine device V25.42
intrauterine device V25.42
oral contraceptive V25.41
specified method NEC V25.49
subdermal implantable V25.43
management NEC V25.49
prescription
oral contraceptive agent V25.01
emergency V25.03
postcoital V25.03
repeat V25.41
specified agent NEC V25.02
repeat V25.49
sterilization V25.2
surveillance V25.40
intrauterine device V25.42
oral contraceptive agent V25.41
subdermal implantable V25.43
specified method NEC V25.49
Contraction, contracture, contracted
Achilles tendon (*see also* Short, tendon, Achilles) 727.81
anus 564.89
axilla 729.90
bile duct (*see also* Disease, biliary) 576.8
bladder 596.8
neck or sphincter 596.0
bowel (*see also* Obstruction, intestine) 560.9
Braxton Hicks 644.1 ☑
breast implant, capsular 611.83
bronchus 519.19
burn (old) — *see* Cicatrix
capsular, of breast implant 611.83
cecum (*see also* Obstruction, intestine) 560.9
cervix (*see also* Stricture, cervix) 622.4
congenital 752.49
cicatricial — *see* Cicatrix
colon (*see also* Obstruction, intestine) 560.9
conjunctiva trachomatous, active 076.1
late effect 139.1
Dupuytren's 728.6

Contraction, contracture, contracted — *continued*
eyelid 374.41
eye socket (after enucleation) 372.64
face 729.90
fascia (lata) (postural) 728.89
Dupuytren's 728.6
palmar 728.6
plantar 728.71
finger NEC 736.29
congenital 755.59
joint (*see also* Contraction, joint) 718.44
flaccid, paralytic
joint (*see also* Contraction, joint) 718.4 ☑
muscle 728.85
ocular 378.50
gallbladder (*see also* Obstruction, gallbladder) 575.2
hamstring 728.89
tendon 727.81
heart valve — *see* Endocarditis
Hicks' 644.1 ☑
hip (*see also* Contraction, joint) 718.4 ☑
hourglass
bladder 596.8
congenital 753.8
gallbladder (*see also* Obstruction, gallbladder) 575.2
congenital 751.69
stomach 536.8
congenital 750.7
psychogenic 306.4
uterus 661.4 ☑
affecting fetus or newborn 763.7
hysterical 300.11
infantile (*see also* Epilepsy) 345.6 ☑
internal os (*see also* Stricture, cervix) 622.4
intestine (*see also* Obstruction, intestine) 560.9
joint (abduction) (acquired) (adduction) (flexion) (rotation) 718.40
ankle 718.47
congenital NEC 755.8
generalized or multiple 754.89
lower limb joints 754.89
hip (*see also* Subluxation, congenital, hip) 754.32
lower limb (including pelvic girdle) not involving hip 754.89
upper limb (including shoulder girdle) 755.59
elbow 718.42
foot 718.47
hand 718.44
hip 718.45
hysterical 300.11
knee 718.46
multiple sites 718.49
pelvic region 718.45
shoulder (region) 718.41
specified site NEC 718.48
wrist 718.43
kidney (granular) (secondary) (*see also* Sclerosis, renal) 587
congenital 753.3
hydronephritic 591
pyelonephritic (*see also* Pyelitis, chronic) 590.00
tuberculous (*see also* Tuberculosis) 016.0 ☑
ligament 728.89
congenital 756.89
liver — *see* Cirrhosis, liver
muscle (postinfectional) (postural) NEC 728.85
congenital 756.89
sternocleidomastoid 754.1
extraocular 378.60
eye (extrinsic) (*see also* Strabismus) 378.9
paralytic (*see also* Strabismus, paralytic) 378.50
flaccid 728.85
hysterical 300.11
ischemic (Volkmann's) 958.6
paralytic 728.85
posttraumatic 958.6
psychogenic 306.0
specified as conversion reaction 300.11

Contraction, contracture, contracted — *continued*
myotonic 728.85
neck (*see also* Torticollis) 723.5
congenital 754.1
psychogenic 306.0
ocular muscle (*see also* Strabismus) 378.9
paralytic (*see also* Strabismus, paralytic) 378.50
organ or site, congenital NEC — *see* Atresia
outlet (pelvis) — *see* Contraction, pelvis
palmar fascia 728.6
paralytic
joint (*see also* Contraction, joint) 718.4 ☑
muscle 728.85
ocular (*see also* Strabismus, paralytic) 378.50
pelvis (acquired) (general) 738.6
affecting fetus or newborn 763.1
complicating delivery 653.1 ☑
causing obstructed labor 660.1 ☑
generally contracted 653.1 ☑
causing obstructed labor 660.1 ☑
inlet 653.2 ☑
causing obstructed labor 660.1 ☑
midpelvic 653.8 ☑
causing obstructed labor 660.1 ☑
midplane 653.8 ☑
causing obstructed labor 660.1 ☑
outlet 653.3 ☑
causing obstructed labor 660.1 ☑
plantar fascia 728.71
premature
atrial 427.61
auricular 427.61
auriculoventricular 427.61
heart (junctional) (nodal) 427.60
supraventricular 427.61
ventricular 427.69
prostate 602.8
pylorus (*see also* Pylorospasm) 537.81
rectosigmoid (*see also* Obstruction, intestine) 560.9
rectum, rectal (sphincter) 564.89
psychogenic 306.4
ring (Bandl's) 661.4 ☑
affecting fetus or newborn 763.7
scar — *see* Cicatrix
sigmoid (*see also* Obstruction, intestine) 560.9
socket, eye 372.64
spine (*see also* Curvature, spine) 737.9
stomach 536.8
hourglass 536.8
congenital 750.7
psychogenic 306.4
tendon (sheath) (*see also* Short, tendon) 727.81
toe 735.8
ureterovesical orifice (postinfectional) 593.3
urethra 599.84
uterus 621.8
abnormal 661.9 ☑
affecting fetus or newborn 763.7
clonic, hourglass or tetanic 661.4 ☑
affecting fetus or newborn 763.7
dyscoordinate 661.4 ☑
affecting fetus or newborn 763.7
hourglass 661.4 ☑
affecting fetus or newborn 763.7
hypotonic NEC 661.2 ☑
affecting fetus or newborn 763.7
incoordinate 661.4 ☑
affecting fetus or newborn 763.7
inefficient or poor 661.2 ☑
affecting fetus or newborn 763.7
irregular 661.2 ☑
affecting fetus or newborn 763.7
tetanic 661.4 ☑
affecting fetus or newborn 763.7
vagina (outlet) 623.2
vesical 596.8
neck or urethral orifice 596.0
visual field, generalized 368.45
Volkmann's (ischemic) 958.6
Contusion (skin surface intact) 924.9

Contusion — *continued*
with
crush injury — *see* Crush
dislocation — *see* Dislocation, by site
fracture — *see* Fracture, by site
internal injury (*see also* Injury, internal, by site)
heart — *see* Contusion, cardiac
kidney — *see* Contusion, kidney
liver — *see* Contusion, liver
lung — *see* Contusion, lung
spleen — *see* Contusion, spleen
intracranial injury — *see* Injury, intracranial
nerve injury — *see* Injury, nerve
open wound — *see* Wound, open, by site
abdomen, abdominal (muscle) (wall) 922.2
organ(s) NEC 868.00
adnexa, eye NEC 921.9
ankle 924.21
with other parts of foot 924.20
arm 923.9
lower (with elbow) 923.10
upper 923.03
with shoulder or axillary region 923.09
auditory canal (external) (meatus) (and other part(s) of neck, scalp, or face, except eye) 920
auricle, ear (and other part(s) of neck, scalp, or face except eye) 920
axilla 923.02
with shoulder or upper arm 923.09
back 922.31
bone NEC 924.9
brain (cerebral) (membrane) (with hemorrhage) 851.8 ☑

Note — Use the following fifth-digit subclassification with categories 851–854:

0   *unspecified state of consciousness*

1   *with no loss of consciousness*

2   *with brief [less than one hour] loss of consciousness*

3   *with moderate [1–24 hours] loss of consciousness*

4   *with prolonged [more than 24 hours] loss of consciousness and return to pre-existing conscious level*

5   *with prolonged [more than 24 hours] loss of consciousness, without return to pre-existing conscious level*

Use fifth-digit 5 to designate when a patient is unconscious and dies before regaining consciousness, regardless of the duration of the loss of consciousness

6   *with loss of consciousness of unspecified duration*

9   *with concussion, unspecified*

with
open intracranial wound 851.9 ☑
skull fracture — *see* Fracture, skull, by site
cerebellum 851.4 ☑
with open intracranial wound 851.5 ☑
cortex 851.0 ☑
with open intracranial wound 851.1 ☑
occipital lobe 851.4 ☑
with open intracranial wound 851.5 ☑
stem 851.4 ☑
with open intracranial wound 851.5 ☑
breast 922.0
brow (and other part(s) of neck, scalp, or face, except eye) 920
buttock 922.32
canthus 921.1
cardiac 861.01
with open wound into thorax 861.11
cauda equina (spine) 952.4
cerebellum — *see* Contusion, brain, cerebellum
cerebral — *see* Contusion, brain
cheek(s) (and other part(s) of neck, scalp, or face, except eye) 920

Contusion — *continued*
chest (wall) 922.1
chin (and other part(s) of neck, scalp, or face, except eye) 920
clitoris 922.4
conjunctiva 921.1
conus medullaris (spine) 952.4
cornea 921.3
corpus cavernosum 922.4
cortex (brain) (cerebral) — *see* Contusion, brain, cortex
costal region 922.1
ear (and other part(s) of neck, scalp, or face except eye) 920
elbow 923.11
   with forearm 923.10
epididymis 922.4
epigastric region 922.2
eye NEC 921.9
eyeball 921.3
eyelid(s) (and periocular area) 921.1
face (and neck, or scalp, any part, except eye) 920
femoral triangle 922.2
fetus or newborn 772.6
finger(s) (nail) (subungual) 923.3
flank 922.2
foot (with ankle) (excluding toe(s)) 924.20
forearm (and elbow) 923.10
forehead (and other part(s) of neck, scalp, or face, except eye) 920
genital organs, external 922.4
globe (eye) 921.3
groin 922.2
gum(s) (and other part(s) of neck, scalp, or face, except eye) 920
hand(s) (except fingers alone) 923.20
head (any part, except eye) (and face) (and neck) 920
heart — *see* Contusion, cardiac
heel 924.20
hip 924.01
   with thigh 924.00
iliac region 922.2
inguinal region 922.2
internal organs (abdomen, chest, or pelvis) NEC — *see* Injury, internal, by site
interscapular region 922.33
iris (eye) 921.3
kidney 866.01
   with open wound into cavity 866.11
knee 924.11
   with lower leg 924.10
labium (majus) (minus) 922.4
lacrimal apparatus, gland, or sac 921.1
larynx (and other part(s) of neck, scalp, or face, except eye) 920
late effect — *see* Late, effects (of), contusion
leg 924.5
   lower (with knee) 924.10
lens 921.3
lingual (and other part(s) of neck, scalp, or face, except eye) 920
lip(s) (and other part(s) of neck, scalp, or face, except eye) 920
liver 864.01
   with
      laceration — *see* Laceration, liver
      open wound into cavity 864.11
lower extremity 924.5
   multiple sites 924.4
lumbar region 922.31
lung 861.21
   with open wound into thorax 861.31
malar region (and other part(s) of neck, scalp, or face, except eye) 920
mandibular joint (and other part(s) of neck, scalp, or face, except eye) 920
mastoid region (and other part(s) of neck, scalp, or face, except eye) 920
membrane, brain — *see* Contusion, brain
midthoracic region 922.1
mouth (and other part(s) of neck, scalp, or face, except eye) 920
multiple sites (not classifiable to same three-digit category) 924.8

Contusion — *continued*
multiple sites — *continued*
   lower limb 924.4
   trunk 922.8
   upper limb 923.8
muscle NEC 924.9
myocardium — *see* Contusion, cardiac
nasal (septum) (and other part(s) of neck, scalp, or face, except eye) 920
neck (and scalp or face, any part, except eye) 920
nerve — *see* Injury, nerve, by site
nose (and other part(s) of neck, scalp, or face, except eye) 920
occipital region (scalp) (and neck or face, except eye) 920
   lobe — *see* Contusion, brain, occipital lobe
orbit (region) (tissues) 921.2
palate (soft) (and other part(s) of neck, scalp, or face, except eye) 920
parietal region (scalp) (and neck, or face, except eye) 920
   lobe — *see* Contusion, brain
penis 922.4
pericardium — *see* Contusion, cardiac
perineum 922.4
periocular area 921.1
pharynx (and other part(s) of neck, scalp, or face, except eye) 920
popliteal space (*see also* Contusion, knee) 924.11
prepuce 922.4
pubic region 922.4
pudenda 922.4
pulmonary — *see* Contusion, lung
quadriceps femoralis 924.00
rib cage 922.1
sacral region 922.32
salivary ducts or glands (and other part(s) of neck, scalp, or face, except eye) 920
scalp (and neck, or face any part, except eye) 920
scapular region 923.01
   with shoulder or upper arm 923.09
sclera (eye) 921.3
scrotum 922.4
shoulder 923.00
   with upper arm or axillar regions 923.09
skin NEC 924.9
skull 920
spermatic cord 922.4
spinal cord (*see also* Injury, spinal, by site)
   cauda equina 952.4
   conus medullaris 952.4
spleen 865.01
   with open wound into cavity 865.11
sternal region 922.1
stomach — *see* Injury, internal, stomach
subconjunctival 921.1
subcutaneous NEC 924.9
submaxillary region (and other part(s) of neck, scalp, or face, except eye) 920
submental region (and other part(s) of neck, scalp, or face, except eye) 920
subperiosteal NEC 924.9
supraclavicular fossa (and other part(s) of neck, scalp, or face, except eye) 920
supraorbital (and other part(s) of neck, scalp, or face, except eye) 920
temple (region) (and other part(s) of neck, scalp, or face, except eye) 920
testis 922.4
thigh (and hip) 924.00
thorax 922.1
   organ — *see* Injury, internal, intrathoracic
throat (and other part(s) of neck, scalp, or face, except eye) 920
thumb(s) (nail) (subungual) 923.3
toe(s) (nail) (subungual) 924.3
tongue (and other part(s) of neck, scalp, or face, except eye) 920
trunk 922.9
   multiple sites 922.8
   specified site — *see* Contusion, by site
tunica vaginalis 922.4

Contusion — *continued*
tympanum (membrane) (and other part(s) of neck, scalp, or face, except eye) 920
upper extremity 923.9
   multiple sites 923.8
uvula (and other part(s) of neck, scalp, or face, except eye) 920
vagina 922.4
vocal cord(s) (and other part(s) of neck, scalp, or face, except eye) 920
vulva 922.4
wrist 923.21
   with hand(s), except finger(s) alone 923.20
Conus (any type) (congenital) 743.57
acquired 371.60
medullaris syndrome 336.8
Convalescence (following) V66.9
chemotherapy V66.2
medical NEC V66.5
psychotherapy V66.3
radiotherapy V66.1
surgery NEC V66.0
treatment (for) NEC V66.5
   combined V66.6
   fracture V66.4
   mental disorder NEC V66.3
   specified disorder NEC V66.5
Conversion
closed surgical procedure to open procedure
   arthroscopic V64.43
   laparoscopic V64.41
   thoracoscopic V64.42
hysteria, hysterical, any type 300.11
neurosis, any 300.11
reaction, any 300.11
Converter, tuberculosis (test reaction) 795.5
Convulsions (idiopathic) 780.39
apoplectiform (*see also* Disease, cerebrovascular, acute) 436
brain 780.39
cerebral 780.39
cerebrospinal 780.39
due to trauma NEC — *see* Injury, intracranial
eclamptic (*see also* Eclampsia) 780.39
epileptic (*see also* Epilepsy) 345.9 ☑
epileptiform (*see also* Seizure, epileptiform) 780.39
epileptoid (*see also* Seizure, epileptiform) 780.39
ether
   anesthetic
      correct substance properly administered 780.39
      overdose or wrong substance given 968.2
   other specified type — *see* Table of Drugs and Chemicals
febrile (simple) 780.31
   complex 780.32
generalized 780.39
hysterical 300.11
infantile 780.39
   epilepsy — *see* Epilepsy
internal 780.39
jacksonian (*see also* Epilepsy) 345.5 ☑
myoclonic 333.2
newborn 779.0
paretic 094.1
pregnancy (nephritic) (uremic) — *see* Eclampsia, pregnancy
psychomotor (*see also* Epilepsy) 345.4 ☑
puerperal, postpartum — *see* Eclampsia, pregnancy
recurrent 780.39
   epileptic — *see* Epilepsy
reflex 781.0
repetitive 780.39
   epileptic — *see* Epilepsy
salaam (*see also* Epilepsy) 345.6 ☑
scarlatinal 034.1
spasmodic 780.39
tetanus, tetanic (*see also* Tetanus) 037
thymic 254.8
uncinate 780.39
uremic 586
Convulsive — *see also* Convulsions

Convulsive — *see also* Convulsions — *continued*
disorder or state 780.39
   epileptic — *see* Epilepsy
equivalent, abdominal (*see also* Epilepsy) 345.5 ☑
Cooke-Apert-Gallais syndrome (adrenogenital) 255.2
Cooley's anemia (erythroblastic) 282.49
Coolie itch 126.9
Cooper's
disease 610.1
hernia — *see* Hernia, Cooper's
Coordination disturbance 781.3
Copper wire arteries, retina 362.13
Copra itch 133.8
Coprolith 560.39
Coprophilia 302.89
Coproporphyria, hereditary 277.1
Coprostasis 560.39
with hernia (*see also* Hernia, by site, with obstruction)
   gangrenous — *see* Hernia, by site, with gangrene
Cor
biloculare 745.7
bovinum — *see* Hypertrophy, cardiac
bovis (*see also* Hypertrophy, cardiac)
pulmonale (chronic) 416.9
   acute 415.0
triatriatum, triatrium 746.82
triloculare 745.8
   biatriatum 745.3
   biventriculare 745.69
Corbus' disease 607.1
Cord — *see also* condition
around neck (tightly) (with compression)
   affecting fetus or newborn 762.5
   complicating delivery 663.1 ☑
      without compression 663.3 ☑
        affecting fetus or newborn 762.6
bladder NEC 344.61
   tabetic 094.0
prolapse
   affecting fetus or newborn 762.4
   complicating delivery 663.0 ☑
Cord's angiopathy — *see also* Tuberculosis 017.3 ☑ *[362.18]*
Cordis ectopia 746.87
Corditis (spermatic) 608.4
Corectopia 743.46
Cori type glycogen storage disease — *see* Disease, glycogen storage
Cork-handlers' disease or lung 495.3
Corkscrew esophagus 530.5
Corlett's pyosis (impetigo) 684
Corn (infected) 700
Cornea — *see also* condition
donor V59.5
guttata (dystrophy) 371.57
plana 743.41
Cornelia de Lange's syndrome (Amsterdam dwarf, mental retardation, and brachycephaly) 759.89
Cornual gestation or pregnancy — *see* Pregnancy, cornual
Cornu cutaneum 702.8
Coronary (artery) — *see also* condition
arising from aorta or pulmonary trunk 746.85
Corpora — *see also* condition
amylacea (prostate) 602.8
cavernosa — *see* condition
Corpulence — *see* Obesity
Corpus — *see* condition
Corrigan's disease — *see* Insufficiency, aortic
Corrosive burn — *see* Burn, by site
Corsican fever — *see also* Malaria 084.6
Cortical — *see also* condition
blindness 377.75
necrosis, kidney (bilateral) 583.6
Corticoadrenal — *see* condition
Corticosexual syndrome 255.2
Coryza (acute) 460
with grippe or influenza 487.1
syphilitic 095.8
   congenital (chronic) 090.0

☑ Additional Digit Required — Refer to the Tabular List for Digit Selection   ▽ Subterms under main terms may continue to next column or page

2010 ICD-9-CM   ►◄ Revised Text   ● New Line   ▲ Revised Code   Volume 2 — 55

Index

Costen's syndrome or complex — Croup, croupous

Costen's syndrome or complex 524.60
Costiveness — *see also* Constipation 564.00
Costochondritis 733.6
Cotard's syndrome (paranoia) 297.1
Cot death 798.0
Cotia virus 059.8
Cotungo's disease 724.3
Cough 786.2
  with hemorrhage (*see also* Hemoptysis) 786.3
  affected 786.2
  bronchial 786.2
    with grippe or influenza 487.1
  chronic 786.2
  epidemic 786.2
  functional 306.1
  hemorrhagic 786.3
  hysterical 300.11
  laryngeal, spasmodic 786.2
  nervous 786.2
  psychogenic 306.1
  smokers' 491.0
  tea tasters' 112.89
Counseling NEC V65.40
  without complaint or sickness V65.49
  abuse victim NEC V62.89
    child V61.21
    partner V61.11
    spouse V61.11
  child abuse, maltreatment, or neglect V61.21
  contraceptive NEC V25.09
    device (intrauterine) V25.02
    maintenance V25.40
      intrauterine contraceptive device
        V25.42
      oral contraceptive (pill) V25.41
      specified type NEC V25.49
      subdermal implantable V25.43
    management NEC V25.9
    oral contraceptive (pill) V25.01
      emergency V25.03
      postcoital V25.03
    prescription NEC V25.02
      oral contraceptive (pill) V25.01
        emergency V25.03
        postcoital V25.03
        repeat prescription V25.41
      repeat prescription V25.40
    subdermal implantable V25.43
    surveillance NEC V25.40
  dietary V65.3
  exercise V65.41
  expectant ▶parent(s)◀
    pediatric pre-adoption visit V65.11 ●
    pediatric pre-birth visit V65.11 ●
  explanation of
    investigation finding NEC V65.49
    medication NEC V65.49
  family planning V25.09
    natural
      procreative V26.41
      to avoid pregnancy V25.04
  for nonattending third party V65.19
  genetic V26.33
  gonorrhea V65.45
  health (advice) (education) (instruction) NEC
    V65.49
  HIV V65.44
  human immunodeficiency virus V65.44
  injury prevention V65.43
  insulin pump training V65.46
  marital V61.10
  medical (for) V65.9
    boarding school resident V60.6
    condition not demonstrated V65.5
    feared complaint and no disease found
      V65.5
    institutional resident V60.6
    on behalf of another V65.19
    person living alone V60.3
  natural family planning
    procreative V26.41
    to avoid pregnancy V25.04
  parent ▶(guardian)◀-child conflict V61.20
    adopted child V61.24 ●
    biological child V61.23 ●
    foster child V61.25 ●

Counseling — *continued*
  parent -child conflict — *continued*
    specified problem NEC V61.29
  partner abuse
    perpetrator V61.12
    victim V61.11
  pediatric
    pre-adoption visit for adoptive parent(s) ●
      V65.11
    pre-birth visit for expectant parents ●
      V65.11 ●
  perpetrator of
    child abuse V62.83
      parental V61.22
    partner abuse V61.12
    spouse abuse V61.12
  procreative V65.49
  sex NEC V65.49
    transmitted disease NEC V65.45
      HIV V65.44
  specified reason NEC V65.49
  spousal abuse
    perpetrator V61.12
    victim V61.11
  substance use and abuse V65.42
  syphilis V65.45
  victim (of)
    abuse NEC V62.89
    child abuse V61.21
    partner abuse V61.11
    spousal abuse V61.11
Coupled rhythm 427.89
Couvelaire uterus (complicating delivery) — *see*
  Placenta, separation
Cowper's gland — *see* condition
Cowperitis — *see also* Urethritis 597.89
  gonorrheal (acute) 098.0
    chronic or duration of 2 months or over
      098.2
Cowpox (abortive) 051.01
  due to vaccination 999.0
  eyelid 051.01 *[373.5]*
    postvaccination 999.0 *[373.5]*
Coxa
  plana 732.1
  valga (acquired) 736.31
    congenital 755.61
    late effect of rickets 268.1
  vara (acquired) 736.32
    congenital 755.62
    late effect of rickets 268.1
Coxae malum senilis 715.25
Coxalgia (nontuberculous) 719.45 ●
  tuberculous (*see also* Tuberculosis)
    015.1 ☑ *[730.85]*
Coxalgic pelvis 736.30
Coxitis 716.65
Coxsackie (infection) (virus) 079.2
  central nervous system NEC 048
  endocarditis 074.22
  enteritis 008.67
  meningitis (aseptic) 047.0
  myocarditis 074.23
  pericarditis 074.21
  pharyngitis 074.0
  pleurodynia 074.1
  specific disease NEC 074.8
Crabs, meaning pubic lice 132.2
Crack baby 760.75
Cracked
  nipple 611.2
    puerperal, postpartum 676.1 ☑
  tooth 521.81
Cradle cap 690.11
Craft neurosis 300.89
Craigiasis 007.8
Cramp(s) 729.82
  abdominal 789.0 ☑
  bathing 994.1
  colic 789.7
    infantile 789.7
    psychogenic 306.4
  due to immersion 994.1
  extremity (lower) (upper) NEC 729.82
  fireman 992.2
  heat 992.2

Cramp(s) — *continued*
  hysterical 300.11
  immersion 994.1
  intestinal 789.0 ☑
    psychogenic 306.4
  linotypist's 300.89
    organic 333.84
  muscle (extremity) (general) 729.82
    due to immersion 994.1
    hysterical 300.11
  occupational (hand) 300.89
    organic 333.84
  psychogenic 307.89
  salt depletion 276.1
  sleep related leg 327.52
  stoker 992.2
  stomach 789.0 ☑
  telegraphers' 300.89
    organic 333.84
  typists' 300.89
    organic 333.84
  uterus 625.8
    menstrual 625.3
  writers' 333.84
    organic 333.84
    psychogenic 300.89
Cranial — *see* condition
Cranioclasis, fetal 763.89
Craniocleidodysostosis 755.59
Craniofenestria (skull) 756.0
Craniolacunia (skull) 756.0
Craniopagus 759.4
Craniopathy, metabolic 733.3
Craniopharyngeal — *see* condition
Craniopharyngioma (M9350/1) 237.0
Craniorachischisis (totalis) 740.1
Cranioschisis 756.0
Craniostenosis 756.0
Craniosynostosis 756.0
Craniotabes (cause unknown) 733.3
  rachitic 268.1
  syphilitic 090.5
Craniotomy, fetal 763.89
Cranium — *see* condition
Craw-craw 125.3
CRBSI (catheter-related bloodstream infection)
  999.31
Creaking joint 719.60
  ankle 719.67
  elbow 719.62
  foot 719.67
  hand 719.64
  hip 719.65
  knee 719.66
  multiple sites 719.69
  pelvic region 719.65
  shoulder (region) 719.61
  specified site NEC 719.68
  wrist 719.63
Creeping
  eruption 126.9
  palsy 335.21
  paralysis 335.21
Crenated tongue 529.8
Creotoxism 005.9
Crepitus
  caput 756.0
  joint 719.60
    ankle 719.67
    elbow 719.62
    foot 719.67
    hand 719.64
    hip 719.65
    knee 719.66
    multiple sites 719.69
    pelvic region 719.65
    shoulder (region) 719.61
    specified site NEC 719.68
    wrist 719.63
▲ **Crescent or conus choroid, congenital** 743.57
● **Cretin, cretinism** (athyrotic) (congenital) (endemic) (metabolic) (nongoitrous) (sporadic) 243
  goitrous (sporadic) 246.1
  pelvis (dwarf type) (male type) 243
    with disproportion (fetopelvic) 653.1 ☑
      affecting fetus or newborn 763.1

Cretin, cretinism — *continued*
  pelvis — *continued*
    with disproportion — *continued*
      causing obstructed labor 660.1 ☑
        affecting fetus or newborn 763.1
  pituitary 253.3
Cretinoid degeneration 243
Creutzfeldt-Jakob disease (CJD) (syndrome)
  046.19
  with dementia
    with behavioral disturbance
      046.19 *[294.11]*
    without behavioral disturbance
      046.19 *[294.10]*
  familial 046.19
  iatrogenic 046.19
  specified NEC 046.19
  sporadic 046.19
  variant (vCJD) 046.11
    with dementia
      with behavioral disturbance
        046.11 *[294.11]*
      without behavioral disturbance
        046.11 *[294.10]*
Crib death 798.0
Cribriform hymen 752.49
Cri-du-chat syndrome 758.31
Crigler-Najjar disease or syndrome (congenital
  hyperbilirubinemia) 277.4
Crimean hemorrhagic fever 065.0
Criminalism 301.7
Crisis
  abdomen 789.0 ☑
  addisonian (acute adrenocortical insufficiency)
    255.41
  adrenal (cortical) 255.41
  asthmatic — *see* Asthma
  brain, cerebral (*see also* Disease, cerebrovascu-
    lar, acute) 436
  celiac 579.0
  Dietl's 593.4
  emotional NEC 309.29
    acute reaction to stress 308.0
    adjustment reaction 309.9
    specific to childhood or adolescence 313.9
  gastric (tabetic) 094.0
  glaucomatocyclitic 364.22
  heart (*see also* Failure, heart) 428.9
  hypertensive — *see* Hypertension
  nitritoid
    correct substance properly administered
      458.29
    overdose or wrong substance given or
      taken 961.1
  oculogyric 378.87
    psychogenic 306.7
  Pel's 094.0
  psychosexual identity 302.6
  rectum 094.0
  renal 593.81
  sickle cell 282.62
  stomach (tabetic) 094.0
  tabetic 094.0
  thyroid (*see also* Thyrotoxicosis) 242.9 ☑
  thyrotoxic (*see also* Thyrotoxicosis) 242.9 ☑
  vascular — *see* Disease, cerebrovascular, acute
Crocq's disease (acrocyanosis) 443.89
Crohn's disease — *see also* Enteritis, regional
  555.9
Cronkhite-Canada syndrome 211.3
Crooked septum, nasal 470
Cross
  birth (of fetus) complicating delivery 652.3 ☑
    with successful version 652.1 ☑
    causing obstructed labor 660.0 ☑
  bite, anterior or posterior 524.27
  eye (*see also* Esotropia) 378.00
Crossed ectopia of kidney 753.3
Crossfoot 754.50
Croup, croupous (acute) (angina) (catarrhal) (infective) (inflammatory) (laryngeal) (membranous) (nondiphtheritic) (pseudomembranous) 464.4
  asthmatic (*see also* Asthma) 493.9 ☑
  bronchial 466.0
  diphtheritic (membranous) 032.3

Croup, croupous — *continued*
false 478.75
spasmodic 478.75
diphtheritic 032.3
stridulous 478.75
diphtheritic 032.3
Crouzon's disease (craniofacial dysostosis) 756.0
Crowding, teeth 524.31
CRST syndrome (cutaneous systemic sclerosis) 710.1
Cruchet's disease (encephalitis lethargica) 049.8
Cruelty in children — *see also* Disturbance, conduct 312.9
Crural ulcer — *see also* Ulcer, lower extremity 707.10
Crush, crushed, crushing (injury) 929.9
abdomen 926.19
internal — *see* Injury, internal, abdomen
ankle 928.21
with other parts of foot 928.20
arm 927.9
lower (and elbow) 927.10
upper 927.03
with shoulder or axillary region 927.09
axilla 927.02
with shoulder or upper arm 927.09
back 926.11
breast 926.19
buttock 926.12
cheek 925.1
chest — *see* Injury, internal, chest
ear 925.1
elbow 927.11
with forearm 927.10
face 925.1
finger(s) 927.3
with hand(s) 927.20
and wrist(s) 927.21
flank 926.19
foot, excluding toe(s) alone (with ankle) 928.20
forearm (and elbow) 927.10
genitalia, external (female) (male) 926.0
internal — *see* Injury, internal, genital organ NEC
hand, except finger(s) alone (and wrist) 927.20
head — *see* Fracture, skull, by site
heel 928.20
hip 928.01
with thigh 928.00
internal organ (abdomen, chest, or pelvis) — *see* Injury, internal, by site
knee 928.11
with leg, lower 928.10
labium (majus) (minus) 926.0
larynx 925.2
late effect — *see* Late, effects (of), crushing
leg 928.9
lower 928.10
and knee 928.11
upper 928.00
limb
lower 928.9
multiple sites 928.8
upper 927.9
multiple sites 927.8
multiple sites NEC 929.0
neck 925.2
nerve — *see* Injury, nerve, by site
nose 802.0
open 802.1
penis 926.0
pharynx 925.2
scalp 925.1
scapular region 927.01
with shoulder or upper arm 927.09
scrotum 926.0
shoulder 927.00
with upper arm or axillary region 927.09
skull or cranium — *see* Fracture, skull, by site
spinal cord — *see* Injury, spinal, by site
syndrome (complication of trauma) 958.5
testis 926.0
thigh (with hip) 928.00
throat 925.2
thumb(s) (and fingers) 927.3
toe(s) 928.3

Crush, crushed, crushing — *continued*
toe(s) — *continued*
with foot 928.20
and ankle 928.21
tonsil 925.2
trunk 926.9
chest — *see* Injury, internal, intrathoracic organs NEC
internal organ — *see* Injury, internal, by site
multiple sites 926.8
specified site NEC 926.19
vulva 926.0
wrist 927.21
with hand(s), except fingers alone 927.20
Crusta lactea 690.11
Crusts 782.8
Crutch paralysis 953.4
Cruveilhier-Baumgarten cirrhosis, disease, or syndrome 571.5
Cruveilhier's disease 335.21
Cruz-Chagas disease — *see also* Trypanosomiasis 086.2
Crying
constant, continuous
adolescent 780.95
adult 780.95
baby 780.92
child 780.95
infant 780.92
newborn 780.92
excessive
adolescent 780.95
adult 780.95
baby 780.92
child 780.95
infant 780.92
newborn 780.92
Cryofibrinogenemia 273.2
Cryoglobulinemia (mixed) 273.2
Crypt (anal) (rectal) 569.49
Cryptitis (anal) (rectal) 569.49
Cryptococcosis (European) (pulmonary) (systemic) 117.5
Cryptococcus 117.5
epidermicus 117.5
neoformans, infection by 117.5
Cryptopapillitis (anus) 569.49
Cryptophthalmos (eyelid) 743.06
Cryptorchid, cryptorchism, cryptorchidism 752.51
Cryptosporidiosis 007.4
hepatobiliary 136.8 ●
respiratory 136.8 ●
Cryptotia 744.29
Crystallopathy
calcium pyrophosphate (*see also* Arthritis) 275.49 [712.2] ☑
dicalcium phosphate (*see also* Arthritis) 275.49 [712.1] ☑
gouty 274.00 ▲
pyrophosphate NEC (*see also* Arthritis) 275.49 [712.2] ☑
uric acid 274.00 ▲
Crystalluria 791.9
Csillag's disease (lichen sclerosis et atrophicus) 701.0
Cuban itch 050.1
Cubitus
valgus (acquired) 736.01
congenital 755.59
late effect of rickets 268.1
varus (acquired) 736.02
congenital 755.59
late effect of rickets 268.1
Cultural deprivation V62.4
Cupping of optic disc 377.14
Curling esophagus 530.5
Curling's ulcer — *see* Ulcer, duodenum
Curschmann (-Batten) (-Steinert) disease or syndrome 359.21
Curvature
organ or site, congenital NEC — *see* Distortion
penis (lateral) 752.69
Pott's (spinal) (*see also* Tuberculosis) 015.0 ☑ [737.43]

Curvature — *continued*
radius, idiopathic, progressive (congenital) 755.54
spine (acquired) (angular) (idiopathic) (incorrect) (postural) 737.9
congenital 754.2
due to or associated with
Charcôt-Marie-Tooth disease 356.1 [737.40]
mucopolysaccharidosis 277.5 [737.40]
neurofibromatosis 237.71 [737.40]
osteitis
deformans 731.0 [737.40]
fibrosa cystica 252.01 [737.40]
osteoporosis (*see also* Osteoporosis) 733.00 [737.40]
poliomyelitis (*see also* Poliomyelitis) 138 [737.40]
tuberculosis (Pott's curvature) (*see also* Tuberculosis) 015.0 ☑ [737.43]
kyphoscoliotic (*see also* Kyphoscoliosis) 737.30
kyphotic (*see also* Kyphosis) 737.10
late effect of rickets 268.1 [737.40]
Pott's 015.0 ☑ [737.40]
scoliotic (*see also* Scoliosis) 737.30
specified NEC 737.8
tuberculous 015.0 ☑ [737.40]
Cushing's
basophilism, disease, or syndrome (iatrogenic) (idiopathic) (pituitary basophilism) (pituitary dependent) 255.0
ulcer — *see* Ulcer, peptic
Cushingoid due to steroid therapy
correct substance properly administered 255.0
overdose or wrong substance given or taken 962.0
Cut (external) — *see* Wound, open, by site
Cutaneous — *see also* condition
hemorrhage 782.7
horn (cheek) (eyelid) (mouth) 702.8
larva migrans 126.9
Cutis — *see also* condition
hyperelastic 756.83
acquired 701.8
laxa 756.83
senilis 701.8
marmorata 782.61
osteosis 709.3
pendula 756.83
acquired 701.8
rhomboidalis nuchae 701.8
verticis gyrata 757.39
acquired 701.8
Cyanopathy, newborn 770.83
Cyanosis 782.5
autotoxic 289.7
common atrioventricular canal 745.69
congenital 770.83
conjunctiva 372.71
due to
endocardial cushion defect 745.60
nonclosure, foramen botalli 745.5
patent foramen botalli 745.5
persistent foramen ovale 745.5
enterogenous 289.7
fetus or newborn 770.83
ostium primum defect 745.61
paroxysmal digital 443.0
retina, retinal 362.10
Cycle
anovulatory 628.0
menstrual, irregular 626.4
Cyclencephaly 759.89
Cyclical vomiting 536.2
associated with migraine 346.2 ☑
psychogenic 306.4
Cyclitic membrane 364.74
Cyclitis — *see also* Iridocyclitis 364.3
acute 364.00
primary 364.01
recurrent 364.02
chronic 364.10
in
sarcoidosis 135 [364.11]

Cyclitis — *see also* Iridocyclitis — *continued*
chronic — *continued*
in — *continued*
tuberculosis (*see also* Tuberculosis) 017.3 ☑ [364.11]
Fuchs' heterochromic 364.21
granulomatous 364.10
lens induced 364.23
nongranulomatous 364.00
posterior 363.21
primary 364.01
recurrent 364.02
secondary (noninfectious) 364.04
infectious 364.03
subacute 364.00
primary 364.01
recurrent 364.02
Cyclokeratitis — *see* Keratitis
Cyclophoria 378.44
Cyclopia, cyclops 759.89
Cycloplegia 367.51
Cyclospasm 367.53
Cyclosporiasis 007.5
Cyclothymia 301.13
Cyclothymic personality 301.13
Cyclotropia 378.33
Cyesis — *see* Pregnancy
Cylindroma (M8200/3) — *see also* Neoplasm, by site, malignant
eccrine dermal (M8200/0) — *see* Neoplasm, skin, benign
skin (M8200/0) — *see* Neoplasm, skin, benign
Cylindruria 791.7
Cyllosoma 759.89
Cynanche
diphtheritic 032.3
tonsillaris 475
Cynorexia 783.6
Cyphosis — *see* Kyphosis
Cyprus fever — *see also* Brucellosis 023.9
Cyriax's syndrome (slipping rib) 733.99
Cyst (mucus) (retention) (serous) (simple)

Note — In general, cysts are not neoplastic and are classified to the appropriate category for disease of the specified anatomical site. This generalization does not apply to certain types of cysts which are neoplastic in nature, for example, dermoid, nor does it apply to cysts of certain structures, for example, branchial cleft, which are classified as developmental anomalies.

The following listing includes some of the most frequently reported sites of cysts as well as qualifiers which indicate the type of cyst. The latter qualifiers usually are not repeated under the anatomical sites. Since the code assignment for a given site may vary depending upon the type of cyst, the coder should refer to the listings under the specified type of cyst before consideration is given to the site.

accessory, fallopian tube 752.11
adenoid (infected) 474.8
adrenal gland 255.8
congenital 759.1
air, lung 518.89
allantoic 753.7
alveolar process (jaw bone) 526.2
amnion, amniotic 658.8 ☑
anterior chamber (eye) 364.60
exudative 364.62
implantation (surgical) (traumatic) 364.61
parasitic 360.13
anterior nasopalatine 526.1
antrum 478.19
anus 569.49
apical (periodontal) (tooth) 522.8
appendix 543.9
arachnoid, brain 348.0
arytenoid 478.79
auricle 706.2
Baker's (knee) 727.51
tuberculous (*see also* Tuberculosis) 015.2 ☑
Bartholin's gland or duct 616.2

☑ Additional Digit Required — Refer to the Tabular List for Digit Selection

☟ Subterms under main terms may continue to next column or page

Cyst — *continued*
bile duct (*see also* Disease, biliary) 576.8
bladder (multiple) (trigone) 596.8
Blessig's 362.62
blood, endocardial (*see also* Endocarditis) 424.90
blue dome 610.0
bone (local) 733.20
aneurysmal 733.22
jaw 526.2
developmental (odontogenic) 526.0
fissural 526.1
latent 526.89
solitary 733.21
unicameral 733.21
brain 348.0
congenital 742.4
hydatid (*see also* Echinococcus) 122.9
third ventricle (colloid) 742.4
branchial (cleft) 744.42
branchiogenic 744.42
breast (benign) (blue dome) (pedunculated) (solitary) (traumatic) 610.0
involution 610.4
sebaceous 610.8
broad ligament (benign) 620.8
embryonic 752.11
bronchogenic (mediastinal) (sequestration) 518.89
congenital 748.4
buccal 528.4
bulbourethral gland (Cowper's) 599.89
bursa, bursal 727.49
pharyngeal 478.26
calcifying odontogenic (M9301/0) 213.1
upper jaw (bone) 213.0
canal of Nuck (acquired) (serous) 629.1
congenital 752.41
canthus 372.75
carcinomatous (M8010/3) — *see* Neoplasm, by site, malignant
cartilage (joint) — *see* Derangement, joint
cauda equina 336.8
cavum septi pellucidi NEC 348.0
celomic (pericardium) 746.89
cerebellopontine (angle) — *see* Cyst, brain
cerebellum — *see* Cyst, brain
cerebral — *see* Cyst, brain
cervical lateral 744.42
cervix 622.8
embryonal 752.41
nabothian (gland) 616.0
chamber, anterior (eye) 364.60
exudative 364.62
implantation (surgical) (traumatic) 364.61
parasitic 360.13
chiasmal, optic NEC (*see also* Lesion, chiasmal) 377.54
chocolate (ovary) 617.1
choledochal (congenital) 751.69
acquired 576.8
choledochus 751.69
chorion 658.8 ☑
choroid plexus 348.0
chyle, mesentery 457.8
ciliary body 364.60
exudative 364.64
implantation 364.61
primary 364.63
clitoris 624.8
coccyx (*see also* Cyst, bone) 733.20
colloid
third ventricle (brain) 742.4
thyroid gland — *see* Goiter
colon 569.89
common (bile) duct (*see also* Disease, biliary) 576.8
congenital NEC 759.89
adrenal glands 759.1
epiglottis 748.3
esophagus 750.4
fallopian tube 752.11
kidney 753.10
multiple 753.19
single 753.11
larynx 748.3

Cyst — *continued*
congenital — *continued*
liver 751.62
lung 748.4
mediastinum 748.8
ovary 752.0
oviduct 752.11
pancreas 751.7
periurethral (tissue) 753.8
prepuce NEC 752.69
penis 752.69
sublingual 750.26
submaxillary gland 750.26
thymus (gland) 759.2
tongue 750.19
ureterovesical orifice 753.4
vulva 752.41
conjunctiva 372.75
cornea 371.23
corpora quadrigemina 348.0
corpus
albicans (ovary) 620.2
luteum (ruptured) 620.1
Cowper's gland (benign) (infected) 599.89
cranial meninges 348.0
craniobuccal pouch 253.8
craniopharyngeal pouch 253.8
cystic duct (*see also* Disease, gallbladder) 575.8
Cysticercus (any site) 123.1
Dandy-Walker 742.3
with spina bifida (*see also* Spina bifida) 741.0 ☑
dental 522.8
developmental 526.0
eruption 526.0
lateral periodontal 526.0
primordial (keratocyst) 526.0
root 522.8
dentigerous 526.0
mandible 526.0
maxilla 526.0
dermoid (M9084/0) (*see also* Neoplasm, by site, benign)
with malignant transformation (M9084/3) 183.0
implantation
external area or site (skin) NEC 709.8
iris 364.61
skin 709.8
vagina 623.8
vulva 624.8
mouth 528.4
oral soft tissue 528.4
sacrococcygeal 685.1
with abscess 685.0
developmental of ovary, ovarian 752.0
dura (cerebral) 348.0
spinal 349.2
ear (external) 706.2
echinococcal (*see also* Echinococcus) 122.9
embryonal
cervix uteri 752.41
genitalia, female external 752.41
uterus 752.3
vagina 752.41
endometrial 621.8
ectopic 617.9
endometrium (uterus) 621.8
ectopic — *see* Endometriosis
enteric 751.5
enterogenous 751.5
epidermal (inclusion) (*see also* Cyst, skin) 706.2
epidermoid (inclusion) (*see also* Cyst, skin) 706.2
mouth 528.4
not of skin — *see* Cyst, by site
oral soft tissue 528.4
epididymis 608.89
epiglottis 478.79
epiphysis cerebri 259.8
epithelial (inclusion) (*see also* Cyst, skin) 706.2
epoophoron 752.11
eruption 526.0
esophagus 530.89
ethmoid sinus 478.19
eye (retention) 379.8

Cyst — *continued*
eye — *continued*
congenital 743.03
posterior segment, congenital 743.54
eyebrow 706.2
eyelid (sebaceous) 374.84
infected 373.13
sweat glands or ducts 374.84
falciform ligament (inflammatory) 573.8
fallopian tube 620.8
congenital 752.11
female genital organs NEC 629.89
fimbrial (congenital) 752.11
fissural (oral region) 526.1
follicle (atretic) (graafian) (ovarian) 620.0
nabothian (gland) 616.0
follicular (atretic) (ovarian) 620.0
dentigerous 526.0
frontal sinus 478.19
gallbladder or duct 575.8
ganglion 727.43
Gartner's duct 752.41
gas, of mesentery 568.89
gingiva 523.8
gland of moll 374.84
globulomaxillary 526.1
graafian follicle 620.0
granulosal lutein 620.2
hemangiomatous (M9121/0) (*see also* Hemangioma) 228.00
hydatid (*see also* Echinococcus) 122.9
fallopian tube (Morgagni) 752.11
liver NEC 122.8
lung NEC 122.9
Morgagni 752.89
fallopian tube 752.11
specified site NEC 122.9
hymen 623.8
embryonal 752.41
hypopharynx 478.26
hypophysis, hypophyseal (duct) (recurrent) 253.8
cerebri 253.8
implantation (dermoid)
anterior chamber (eye) 364.61
external area or site (skin) NEC 709.8
iris 364.61
vagina 623.8
vulva 624.8
incisor, incisive canal 526.1
inclusion (epidermal) (epithelial) (epidermoid) (mucous) (squamous) (*see also* Cyst, skin) 706.2
not of skin — *see* Neoplasm, by site, benign
intestine (large) (small) 569.89
intracranial — *see* Cyst, brain
intraligamentous 728.89
knee 717.89
intrasellar 253.8
iris (idiopathic) 364.60
exudative 364.62
implantation (surgical) (traumatic) 364.61
miotic pupillary 364.55
parasitic 360.13
Iwanoff's 362.62
jaw (bone) (aneurysmal) (extravasation) (hemorrhagic) (traumatic) 526.2
developmental (odontogenic) 526.0
fissural 526.1
keratin 706.2
kidney (congenital) 753.10
acquired 593.2
calyceal (*see also* Hydronephrosis) 591
multiple 753.19
pyelogenic (*see also* Hydronephrosis) 591
simple 593.2
single 753.11
solitary (not congenital) 593.2
labium (majus) (minus) 624.8
sebaceous 624.8
lacrimal
apparatus 375.43
gland or sac 375.12
larynx 478.79
lens 379.39

Cyst — *continued*
lens — *continued*
congenital 743.39
lip (gland) 528.5
liver 573.8
congenital 751.62
hydatid (*see also* Echinococcus) 122.8
granulosis 122.0
multilocularis 122.5
lung 518.89
congenital 748.4
giant bullous 492.0
lutein 620.1
lymphangiomatous (M9173/0) 228.1
lymphoepithelial
mouth 528.4
oral soft tissue 528.4
macula 362.54
malignant (M8000/3) — *see* Neoplasm, by site, malignant
mammary gland (sweat gland) (*see also* Cyst, breast) 610.0
mandible 526.2
dentigerous 526.0
radicular 522.8
maxilla 526.2
dentigerous 526.0
radicular 522.8
median
anterior maxillary 526.1
palatal 526.1
mediastinum (congenital) 748.8
meibomian (gland) (retention) 373.2
infected 373.12
membrane, brain 348.0
meninges (cerebral) 348.0
spinal 349.2
meniscus knee 717.5
mesentery, mesenteric (gas) 568.89
chyle 457.8
gas 568.89
mesonephric duct 752.89
mesothelial
peritoneum 568.89
pleura (peritoneal) 568.89
milk 611.5
miotic pupillary (iris) 364.55
Morgagni (hydatid) 752.89
fallopian tube 752.11
mouth 528.4
Müllerian duct 752.89
appendix testis 608.89
cervix (embryonal) 752.41
fallopian tube 752.11
prostatic utricle 599.89
vagina (embryonal) 752.41
multilocular (ovary) (M8000/1) 239.5
myometrium 621.8
nabothian (follicle) (ruptured) 616.0
nasal sinus 478.19
nasoalveolar 528.4
nasolabial 528.4
nasopalatine (duct) 526.1
anterior 526.1
nasopharynx 478.26
neoplastic (M8000/1) (*see also* Neoplasm, by site, unspecified nature)
benign (M8000/0) — *see* Neoplasm, by site, benign
uterus 621.8
nervous system — *see* Cyst, brain
neuroenteric 742.59
neuroepithelial ventricle 348.0
nipple 610.0
nose 478.19
skin of 706.2
odontogenic, developmental 526.0
omentum (lesser) 568.89
congenital 751.8
oral soft tissue (dermoid) (epidermoid) (lymphoepithelial) 528.4
ora serrata 361.19
orbit 376.81
ovary, ovarian (twisted) 620.2
adherent 620.2
chocolate 617.1

☑ Additional Digit Required — Refer to the Tabular List for Digit Selection
58 — Volume 2
▶◀ Revised Text
● New Line
▲ Revised Code
▽ Subterms under main terms may continue to next column or page
2010 ICD-9-CM

Cyst — continued
  ovary, ovarian — continued
    corpus
      albicans 620.2
      luteum 620.1
    dermoid (M9084/0) 220
    developmental 752.0
    due to failure of involution NEC 620.2
    endometrial 617.1
    follicular (atretic) (graafian) (hemorrhagic)
      620.0
    hemorrhagic 620.2
    in pregnancy or childbirth 654.4 ☑
      affecting fetus or newborn 763.89
      causing obstructed labor 660.2 ☑
        affecting fetus or newborn 763.1
    multilocular (M8000/1) 239.5
    pseudomucinous (M8470/0) 220
    retention 620.2
    serous 620.2
    theca lutein 620.2
    tuberculous (see also Tuberculosis)
      016.6 ☑
    unspecified 620.2
  oviduct 620.8
  palatal papilla (jaw) 526.1
  palate 526.1
    fissural 526.1
    median (fissural) 526.1
  palatine, of papilla 526.1
  pancreas, pancreatic 577.2
    congenital 751.7
    false 577.2
    hemorrhagic 577.2
    true 577.2
  paralabral
    hip 718.85
    shoulder 840.7
  paramesonephric duct — see Cyst, Müllerian
    duct
  paranephric 593.2
  para ovarian 752.11
  paraphysis, cerebri 742.4
  parasitic NEC 136.9
  parathyroid (gland) 252.8
  paratubal (fallopian) 620.8
  paraurethral duct 599.89
  paroophoron 752.11
  parotid gland 527.6
    mucous extravasation or retention 527.6
  parovarian 752.11
  pars planus 364.60
    exudative 364.64
    primary 364.63
  pelvis, female
    in pregnancy or childbirth 654.4 ☑
      affecting fetus or newborn 763.89
      causing obstructed labor 660.2 ☑
        affecting fetus or newborn 763.1
  penis (sebaceous) 607.89
  periapical 522.8
  pericardial (congenital) 746.89
    acquired (secondary) 423.8
  pericoronal 526.0
  perineural (Tarlov's) 355.9
  periodontal 522.8
    lateral 526.0
  peripancreatic 577.2
  peripelvic (lymphatic) 593.2
  peritoneum 568.89
    chylous 457.8
  pharynx (wall) 478.26
  pilonidal (infected) (rectum) 685.1
    with abscess 685.0
    malignant (M9084/3) 173.5
  pituitary (duct) (gland) 253.8
  placenta (amniotic) — see Placenta, abnormal
  pleura 519.8
  popliteal 727.51
  porencephalic 742.4
    acquired 348.0
  postanal (infected) 685.1
    with abscess 685.0
  posterior segment of eye, congenital 743.54
  postmastoidectomy cavity 383.31
  preauricular 744.47

Cyst — continued
  prepuce 607.89
    congenital 752.69
  primordial (jaw) 526.0
  prostate 600.3
  pseudomucinous (ovary) (M8470/0) 220
  pudenda (sweat glands) 624.8
  pupillary, miotic 364.55
    sebaceous 624.8
  radicular (residual) 522.8
  radiculodental 522.8
  ranular 527.6
  Rathke's pouch 253.8
  rectum (epithelium) (mucous) 569.49
  renal — see Cyst, kidney
  residual (radicular) 522.8
  retention (ovary) 620.2
  retina 361.19
    macular 362.54
    parasitic 360.13
    primary 361.13
    secondary 361.14
  retroperitoneal 568.89
  sacrococcygeal (dermoid) 685.1
    with abscess 685.0
  salivary gland or duct 527.6
    mucous extravasation or retention 527.6
  Sampson's 617.1
  sclera 379.19
  scrotum (sebaceous) 706.2
    sweat glands 706.2
  sebaceous (duct) (gland) 706.2
    breast 610.8
    eyelid 374.84
    genital organ NEC
      female 629.89
      male 608.89
    scrotum 706.2
  semilunar cartilage (knee) (multiple) 717.5
  seminal vesicle 608.89
  serous (ovary) 620.2
  sinus (antral) (ethmoidal) (frontal) (maxillary)
    (nasal) (sphenoidal) 478.19
  Skene's gland 599.89
  skin (epidermal) (epidermoid, inclusion) (ep-
    ithelial) (inclusion) (retention) (seba-
    ceous) 706.2
    breast 610.8
    eyelid 374.84
    genital organ NEC
      female 629.89
      male 608.89
    neoplastic 216.3
    scrotum 706.2
    sweat gland or duct 705.89
  solitary
    bone 733.21
    kidney 593.2
  spermatic cord 608.89
  sphenoid sinus 478.19
  spinal meninges 349.2
  spine (see also Cyst, bone) 733.20
  spleen NEC 289.59
    congenital 759.0
    hydatid (see also Echinococcus) 122.9
  spring water (pericardium) 746.89
  subarachnoid 348.0
    intrasellar 793.0
  subdural (cerebral) 348.0
    spinal cord 349.2
  sublingual gland 527.6
    mucous extravasation or retention 527.6
  submaxillary gland 527.6
    mucous extravasation or retention 527.6
  suburethral 599.89
  suprarenal gland 255.8
  suprasellar — see Cyst, brain
  sweat gland or duct 705.89
  sympathetic nervous system 337.9
  synovial 727.40
    popliteal space 727.51
  Tarlov's 355.9
  tarsal 373.2
  tendon (sheath) 727.42
  testis 608.89
  theca-lutein (ovary) 620.2

Cyst — continued
  Thornwaldt's, Tornwaldt's 478.26
  thymus 254.8
  thyroglossal (duct) (infected) (persistent) 759.2
  thyroid (gland) 246.2
    adenomatous — see Goiter, nodular
    colloid (see also Goiter) 240.9
  thyrolingual duct (infected) (persistent) 759.2
  tongue (mucous) 529.8
  tonsil 474.8
  tooth (dental root) 522.8
  tubo-ovarian 620.8
    inflammatory 614.1
  tunica vaginalis 608.89
  turbinate (nose) (see also Cyst, bone) 733.20
  Tyson's gland (benign) (infected) 607.89
  umbilicus 759.89
  urachus 753.7
  ureter 593.89
  ureterovesical orifice 593.89
    congenital 753.4
  urethra 599.84
  urethral gland (Cowper's) 599.89
  uterine
    ligament 620.8
      embryonic 752.11
    tube 620.8
  uterus (body) (corpus) (recurrent) 621.8
    embryonal 752.3
  utricle (ear) 386.8
    prostatic 599.89
  utriculus masculinus 599.89
  vagina, vaginal (squamous cell) (wall) 623.8
    embryonal 752.41
    implantation 623.8
    inclusion 623.8
  vallecula, vallecular 478.79
  ventricle, neuroepithelial 348.0
  verumontanum 599.89
  vesical (orifice) 596.8
  vitreous humor 379.29
  vulva (sweat glands) 624.8
    congenital 752.41
    implantation 624.8
    inclusion 624.8
    sebaceous gland 624.8
  vulvovaginal gland 624.8
  wolffian 752.89
Cystadenocarcinoma (M8440/3) — see also
    Neoplasm, by site, malignant
  bile duct type (M8161/3) 155.1
  endometrioid (M8380/3) — see Neoplasm, by
    site, malignant
  mucinous (M8470/3)
    papillary (M8471/3)
      specified site — see Neoplasm, by site,
        malignant
      unspecified site 183.0
    specified site — see Neoplasm, by site,
      malignant
    unspecified site 183.0
  papillary (M8450/3)
    mucinous (M8471/3)
      specified site — see Neoplasm, by site,
        malignant
      unspecified site 183.0
    pseudomucinous (M8471/3)
      specified site — see Neoplasm, by site,
        malignant
      unspecified site 183.0
    serous (M8460/3)
      specified site — see Neoplasm, by site,
        malignant
      unspecified site 183.0
    specified site — see Neoplasm, by site,
      malignant
    unspecified 183.0
  pseudomucinous (M8470/3)
    papillary (M8471/3)
      specified site — see Neoplasm, by site,
        malignant
      unspecified site 183.0
    specified site — see Neoplasm, by site,
      malignant
    unspecified site 183.0

Cystadenocarcinoma — see also Neoplasm, by
    site, malignant — continued
  serous (M8441/3)
    papillary (M8460/3)
      specified site — see Neoplasm, by site,
        malignant
      unspecified site 183.0
    specified site — see Neoplasm, by site,
      malignant
    unspecified site 183.0
Cystadenofibroma (M9013/0)
  clear cell (M8313/0) — see Neoplasm, by site,
    benign
  endometrioid (M8381/0) 220
    borderline malignancy (M8381/1) 236.2
    malignant (M8381/3) 183.0
  mucinous (M9015/0)
    specified site — see Neoplasm, by site,
      benign
    unspecified site 220
  serous (M9014/0)
    specified site — see Neoplasm, by site,
      benign
    unspecified site 220
  specified site — see Neoplasm, by site, benign
  unspecified site 220
Cystadenoma (M8440/0) — see also Neoplasm,
    by site, benign
  bile duct (M8161/0) 211.5
  endometrioid (M8380/0) (see also Neoplasm,
    by site, benign)
    borderline malignancy (M8380/1) — see
      Neoplasm, by site, uncertain behav-
      ior
  malignant (M8440/3) — see Neoplasm, by
    site, malignant
  mucinous (M8470/0)
    borderline malignancy (M8470/1)
      specified site — see Neoplasm, uncer-
        tain behavior
      unspecified site 236.2
    papillary (M8471/0)
      borderline malignancy (M8471/1)
        specified site — see Neoplasm, by
          site, uncertain behavior
        unspecified site 236.2
      specified site — see Neoplasm, by site,
        benign
      unspecified site 220
    specified site — see Neoplasm, by site,
      benign
    unspecified site 220
  papillary (M8450/0)
    borderline malignancy (M8450/1)
      specified site — see Neoplasm, by site,
        uncertain behavior
      unspecified site 236.2
    lymphomatosum (M8561/0) 210.2
    mucinous (M8471/0)
      borderline malignancy (M8471/1)
        specified site — see Neoplasm, by
          site, uncertain behavior
        unspecified site 236.2
      specified site — see Neoplasm, by site,
        benign
      unspecified site 220
    pseudomucinous (M8471/0)
      borderline malignancy (M8471/1)
        specified site — see Neoplasm, by
          site, uncertain behavior
        unspecified site 236.2
      specified site — see Neoplasm, by site,
        benign
      unspecified site 220
    serous (M8460/0)
      borderline malignancy (M8460/1)
        specified site — see Neoplasm, by
          site, uncertain behavior
        unspecified site 236.2
      specified site — see Neoplasm, by site,
        benign
      unspecified site 220
    specified site — see Neoplasm, by site,
      benign
    unspecified site 220

Cystadenoma — *see also* Neoplasm, by site,
benign — *continued*
  pseudomucinous (M8470/0)
    borderline malignancy (M8470/1)
      specified site — *see* Neoplasm, by site,
        uncertain behavior
      unspecified site 236.2
    papillary (M8471/0)
      borderline malignancy (M8471/1)
        specified site — *see* Neoplasm, by
          site, uncertain behavior
        unspecified site 236.2
      specified site — *see* Neoplasm, by site,
        benign
      unspecified site 220
    specified site — *see* Neoplasm, by site,
      benign
    unspecified site 220
  serous (M8441/0)
    borderline malignancy (M8441/1)
      specified site — *see* Neoplasm, by site,
        uncertain behavior
      unspecified site 236.2
    papillary (M8460/0)
      borderline malignancy (M8460/1)
        specified site — *see* Neoplasm, by
          site, uncertain behavior
        unspecified site 236.2
      specified site — *see* Neoplasm, by site,
        benign
      unspecified site 220
    specified site — *see* Neoplasm, by site,
      benign
    unspecified site 220
  thyroid 226
Cystathioninemia 270.4
Cystathioninuria 270.4
Cystic — *see also* condition
  breast, chronic 610.1
  corpora lutea 620.1
  degeneration, congenital
    brain 742.4
    kidney (*see also* Cystic, disease, kidney)
      753.10
  disease
    breast, chronic 610.1
    kidney, congenital 753.10
      medullary 753.16
      multiple 753.19
      polycystic — *see* Polycystic, kidney
      single 753.11
      specified NEC 753.19
    liver, congenital 751.62
    lung 518.89
      congenital 748.4

Cystic — *see also* condition — *continued*
  disease — *continued*
    pancreas, congenital 751.7
    semilunar cartilage 717.5
  duct — *see* condition
  eyeball, congenital 743.03
  fibrosis (pancreas) 277.00
    with
      manifestations
        gastrointestinal 277.03
        pulmonary 277.02
        specified NEC 277.09
      meconium ileus 277.01
      pulmonary exacerbation 277.02
  hygroma (M9173/0) 228.1
  kidney, congenital 753.10
    medullary 753.16
    multiple 753.19
    polycystic — *see* Polycystic, kidney
    single 753.11
    specified NEC 753.19
  liver, congenital 751.62
  lung 518.89
    congenital 748.4
  mass — *see* Cyst
  mastitis, chronic 610.1
  ovary 620.2
  pancreas, congenital 751.7
Cysticerciasis 123.1
Cysticercosis (mammary) (subretinal) 123.1
Cysticercus 123.1
  cellulosae infestation 123.1
Cystinosis (malignant) 270.0
Cystinuria 270.0
Cystitis (bacillary) (colli) (diffuse) (exudative)
    (hemorrhagic) (purulent) (recurrent) (sep-
    tic) (suppurative) (ulcerative) 595.9
  with
    abortion — *see* Abortion, by type, with
      urinary tract infection
    ectopic pregnancy (*see also* categories
      633.0–633.9) 639.8
    fibrosis 595.1
    leukoplakia 595.1
    malakoplakia 595.1
    metaplasia 595.1
    molar pregnancy (*see also* categories
      630–632) 639.8
  actinomycotic 039.8 *[595.4]*
  acute 595.0
    of trigone 595.3
  allergic 595.89
  amebic 006.8 *[595.4]*
  bilharzial 120.9 *[595.4]*
  blennorrhagic (acute) 098.11

Cystitis — *continued*
  blennorrhagic — *continued*
    chronic or duration of 2 months or more
      098.31
  bullous 595.89
  calculus 594.1
    chlamydial 099.53
  chronic 595.2
    interstitial 595.1
    of trigone 595.3
  complicating pregnancy, childbirth, or puer-
    perium 646.6 ☑
    affecting fetus or newborn 760.1
  cystic(a) 595.81
  diphtheritic 032.84
  echinococcal
    granulosus 122.3 *[595.4]*
    multilocularis 122.6 *[595.4]*
  emphysematous 595.89
  encysted 595.81
  follicular 595.3
  following
    abortion 639.8
    ectopic or molar pregnancy 639.8
  gangrenous 595.89
  glandularis 595.89
  gonococcal (acute) 098.11
    chronic or duration of 2 months or more
      098.31
  incrusted 595.89
  interstitial 595.1
  irradiation 595.82
  irritation 595.89
  malignant 595.89
  monilial 112.2
  of trigone 595.3
  panmural 595.1
  polyposa 595.89
  prostatic 601.3
  radiation 595.82
  Reiter's (abacterial) 099.3
  specified NEC 595.89
  subacute 595.2
  submucous 595.1
  syphilitic 095.8
  trichomoniasis 131.09
  tuberculous (*see also* Tuberculosis) 016.1 ☑
  ulcerative 595.1
Cystocele
  female (without uterine prolapse) 618.01
    with uterine prolapse 618.4
      complete 618.3
      incomplete 618.2
    lateral 618.02
    midline 618.01

Cystocele — *continued*
  female — *continued*
    paravaginal 618.02
  in pregnancy or childbirth 654.4 ☑
    affecting fetus or newborn 763.89
    causing obstructed labor 660.2 ☑
      affecting fetus or newborn 763.1
  male 596.8
Cystoid
  cicatrix limbus 372.64
  degeneration macula 362.53
Cystolithiasis 594.1
Cystoma (M8440/0) — *see also* Neoplasm, by
    site, benign
  endometrial, ovary 617.1
  mucinous (M8470/0)
    specified site — *see* Neoplasm, by site,
      benign
    unspecified site 220
  serous (M8441/0)
    specified site — *see* Neoplasm, by site,
      benign
    unspecified site 220
  simple (ovary) 620.2
Cystoplegia 596.53
Cystoptosis 596.8
Cystopyelitis — *see also* Pyelitis 590.80
Cystorrhagia 596.8
Cystosarcoma phyllodes (M9020/1) 238.3
  benign (M9020/0) 217
  malignant (M9020/3) — *see* Neoplasm, breast,
    malignant
Cystostomy status V44.50
  with complication 997.5
  appendico-vesicostomy V44.52
  cutaneous-vesicostomy V44.51
  specified type NEC V44.59
Cystourethritis — *see also* Urethritis 597.89
Cystourethrocele — *see also* Cystocele
  female (without uterine prolapse) 618.09
    with uterine prolapse 618.4
      complete 618.3
      incomplete 618.2
  male 596.8
Cytomegalic inclusion disease 078.5
  congenital 771.1
Cytomycosis, reticuloendothelial — *see also*
    Histoplasmosis, American 115.00
Cytopenia 289.9
  refractory
    with
      multilineage dysplasia (RCMD) 238.72
      and ringed sideroblasts (RCMD-RS)
        238.72

☑ Additional Digit Required — Refer to the Tabular List for Digit Selection

Subterms under main terms may continue to next column or page

►◄ Revised Text   ● New Line   ▲ Revised Code

D

Daae (-Finsen) disease (epidemic pleurodynia) 074.1
Dabney's grip 074.1
Da Costa's syndrome (neurocirculatory asthenia) 306.2
Dacryoadenitis, dacryadenitis 375.00
  acute 375.01
  chronic 375.02
Dacryocystitis 375.30
  acute 375.32
  chronic 375.42
  neonatal 771.6
  phlegmonous 375.33
  syphilitic 095.8
    congenital 090.0
  trachomatous, active 076.1
    late effect 139.1
  tuberculous (see also Tuberculosis) 017.3 ☑
Dacryocystoblenorrhea 375.42
Dacryocystocele 375.43
Dacryolith, dacryolithiasis 375.57
Dacryoma 375.43
Dacryopericystitis (acute) (subacute) 375.32
  chronic 375.42
Dacryops 375.11
Dacryosialadenopathy, atrophic 710.2
Dacryostenosis 375.56
  congenital 743.65
Dactylitis
  bone (see also Osteomyelitis) 730.2 ☑
  sickle-cell 282.62
    Hb-C 282.64
    Hb-SS 282.62
    specified NEC 282.69
  syphilitic 095.5
  tuberculous (see also Tuberculosis) 015.5 ☑
Dactylolysis spontanea 136.0
Dactylosymphysis — see also Syndactylism 755.10
Damage
  arteriosclerotic — see Arteriosclerosis
  brain 348.9
    anoxic, hypoxic 348.1
      during or resulting from a procedure 997.01
    ischemic, in newborn 768.70 ▲
      mild 768.71 ●
      moderate 768.72 ●
      severe 768.73 ●
    child NEC 343.9
    due to birth injury 767.0
    minimal (child) (see also Hyperkinesia) 314.9
    newborn 767.0
  cardiac (see also Disease, heart)
  cardiorenal (vascular) (see also Hypertension, cardiorenal) 404.90
  central nervous system — see Damage, brain
  cerebral NEC — see Damage, brain
  coccyx, complicating delivery 665.6 ☑
  coronary (see also Ischemia, heart) 414.9
  eye, birth injury 767.8
  heart (see also Disease, heart)
    valve — see Endocarditis
  hypothalamus NEC 348.9
  liver 571.9
    alcoholic 571.3
  medication 995.20
  myocardium (see also Degeneration, myocardial) 429.1
  pelvic
    joint or ligament, during delivery 665.6 ☑
    organ NEC
      with
        abortion — see Abortion, by type, with damage to pelvic organs
        ectopic pregnancy (see also categories 633.0–633.9) 639.2
        molar pregnancy (see also categories 630–632) 639.2
      during delivery 665.5 ☑
      following
        abortion 639.2

Damage — continued
  pelvic — continued
    organ — continued
      following — continued
        ectopic or molar pregnancy 639.2
  renal (see also Disease, renal) 593.9
  skin, solar 692.79
    acute 692.72
    chronic 692.74
  subendocardium, subendocardial (see also Degeneration, myocardial) 429.1
  vascular 459.9
Dameshek's syndrome (erythroblastic anemia) 282.49
Dana-Putnam syndrome (subacute combined sclerosis with pernicious anemia) 281.0 [336.2]
Danbolt (-Closs) syndrome (acrodermatitis enteropathica) 686.8
Dandruff 690.18
Dandy fever 061
Dandy-Walker deformity or syndrome (atresia, foramen of Magendie) 742.3
  with spina bifida (see also Spina bifida) 741.0 ☑
Dangle foot 736.79
Danielssen's disease (anesthetic leprosy) 030.1
Danlos' syndrome 756.83
Darier's disease (congenital) (keratosis follicularis) 757.39
  due to vitamin A deficiency 264.8
  meaning erythema annulare centrifugum 695.0
Darier-Roussy sarcoid 135
Dark area on retina 239.81 ●
Darling's
  disease (see also Histoplasmosis, American) 115.00
  histoplasmosis (see also Histoplasmosis, American) 115.00
Dartre 054.9
Darwin's tubercle 744.29
Davidson's anemia (refractory) 284.9
Davies-Colley syndrome (slipping rib) 733.99
Davies' disease 425.0
Dawson's encephalitis 046.2
Day blindness — see also Blindness, day 368.60
Dead
  fetus
    retained (in utero) 656.4 ☑
      early pregnancy (death before 22 completed weeks gestation) 632
      late (death after 22 completed weeks gestation) 656.4 ☑
    syndrome 641.3 ☑
  labyrinth 386.50
  ovum, retained 631
Deaf and dumb NEC 389.7
Deaf mutism (acquired) (congenital) NEC 389.7
  endemic 243
  hysterical 300.11
  syphilitic, congenital 090.0
Deafness (acquired) (complete) (congenital) (hereditary) (middle ear) (partial) 389.9
  with
    blindness V49.85
    blue sclera and fragility of bone 756.51
  auditory fatigue 389.9
  aviation 993.0
    nerve injury 951.5
  boilermakers' 951.5
  central 389.14
    with conductive hearing loss 389.20
      bilateral 389.22
      unilateral 389.21
  conductive (air) 389.00
    with sensorineural hearing loss 389.20
      bilateral 389.22
      unilateral 389.21
    bilateral 389.06
    combined types 389.08
    external ear 389.01
    inner ear 389.04
    middle ear 389.03
    multiple types 389.08

Deafness — continued
  conductive — continued
    tympanic membrane 389.02
    unilateral 389.05
  emotional (complete) 300.11
  functional (complete) 300.11
  high frequency 389.8
  hysterical (complete) 300.11
  injury 951.5
  low frequency 389.8
  mental 784.69
  mixed conductive and sensorineural 389.20
    bilateral 389.22
    unilateral 389.21
  nerve
    with conductive hearing loss 389.20
      bilateral 389.22
      unilateral 389.21
    bilateral 389.12
    unilateral 389.13
  neural
    with conductive hearing loss 389.20
      bilateral 389.22
      unilateral 389.21
    bilateral 389.12
    unilateral 389.13
  noise-induced 388.12
  nerve injury 951.5
  nonspeaking 389.7
  perceptive 389.10
    with conductive hearing loss 389.20
      bilateral 389.22
      unilateral 389.21
    central 389.14
    neural
      bilateral 389.12
      unilateral 389.13
    sensorineural 389.10
      asymmetrical 389.16
      bilateral 389.18
      unilateral 389.15
    sensory
      bilateral 389.11
      unilateral 389.17
  psychogenic (complete) 306.7
  sensorineural (see also Deafness, perceptive) 389.10
    asymmetrical 389.16
    bilateral 389.18
    unilateral 389.15
  sensory
    with conductive hearing loss 389.20
      bilateral 389.22
      unilateral 389.21
    bilateral 389.11
    unilateral 389.17
  specified type NEC 389.8
  sudden NEC 388.2
  syphilitic 094.89
  transient ischemic 388.02
  transmission — see Deafness, conductive
  traumatic 951.5
  word (secondary to organic lesion) 784.69
    developmental 315.31
Death
  after delivery (cause not stated) (sudden) 674.9 ☑
  anesthetic
    due to
      correct substance properly administered 995.4
      overdose or wrong substance given 968.4
        specified anesthetic — see Table of Drugs and Chemicals
    during delivery 668.9 ☑
  brain 348.89 ▲
  cardiac (sudden) (SCD) — code to underlying condition
    family history of V17.41
    personal history of, successfully resuscitated V12.53
  cause unknown 798.2
  cot (infant) 798.0
  crib (infant) 798.0

Death — continued
  fetus, fetal (cause not stated) (intrauterine) 779.9
    early, with retention (before 22 completed weeks gestation) 632
    from asphyxia or anoxia (before labor) 768.0
      during labor 768.1
    late, affecting management of pregnancy (after 22 completed weeks gestation) 656.4 ☑
  from pregnancy NEC 646.9 ☑
  instantaneous 798.1
  intrauterine (see also Death, fetus) 779.9
    complicating pregnancy 656.4 ☑
  maternal, affecting fetus or newborn 761.6
  neonatal NEC 779.9
  sudden (cause unknown) 798.1
    cardiac (SCD)
      family history of V17.41
      personal history of, successfully resuscitated V12.53
    during delivery 669.9 ☑
      under anesthesia NEC 668.9 ☑
    infant, syndrome (SIDS) 798.0
    puerperal, during puerperium 674.9 ☑
  unattended (cause unknown) 798.9
  under anesthesia NEC
    due to
      correct substance properly administered 995.4
      overdose or wrong substance given 968.4
        specified anesthetic — see Table of Drugs and Chemicals
    during delivery 668.9 ☑
  violent 798.1
de Beurmann-Gougerot disease (sporotrichosis) 117.1
Debility (general) (infantile) (postinfectional) 799.3
  with nutritional difficulty 269.9
  congenital or neonatal NEC 779.9
  nervous 300.5
  old age 797
  senile 797
Débove's disease (splenomegaly) 789.2
Decalcification
  bone (see also Osteoporosis) 733.00
  teeth 521.89
Decapitation 874.9
  fetal (to facilitate delivery) 763.89
Decapsulation, kidney 593.89
Decay
  dental 521.00
  senile 797
  tooth, teeth 521.00
Decensus, uterus — see Prolapse, uterus
Deciduitis (acute)
  with
    abortion — see Abortion, by type, with sepsis
    ectopic pregnancy (see also categories 633.0–633.9) 639.0
    molar pregnancy (see also categories 630–632) 639.0
  affecting fetus or newborn 760.8
  following
    abortion 639.0
    ectopic or molar pregnancy 639.0
  in pregnancy 646.6 ☑
  puerperal, postpartum 670.1 ☑ ▲
Deciduoma malignum (M9100/3) 181
Deciduous tooth (retained) 520.6
Decline (general) — see also Debility 799.3
Decompensation
  cardiac (acute) (chronic) (see also Disease, heart) 429.9
    failure — see Failure, heart
  cardiorenal (see also Hypertension, cardiorenal) 404.90
  cardiovascular (see also Disease, cardiovascular) 429.2
  heart (see also Disease, heart) 429.9
    failure — see Failure, heart
  hepatic 572.2

☑ Additional Digit Required — Refer to the Tabular List for Digit Selection   ⊌ Subterms under main terms may continue to next column or page

2010 ICD-9-CM   ►◄ Revised Text   ● New Line   ▲ Revised Code   October 2009 • Volume 2 — 61

Index

Decompensation — Deficiency, deficient

Decompensation — *continued*
  myocardial (acute) (chronic) (*see also* Disease, heart) 429.9
    failure — *see* Failure, heart
  respiratory 519.9
Decompression sickness 993.3
Decrease, decreased
  blood
    platelets (*see also* Thrombocytopenia) 287.5
    pressure 796.3
      due to shock following
        injury 958.4
        operation 998.0
    white cell count 288.50
      specified NEC 288.59
  cardiac reserve — *see* Disease, heart
  estrogen 256.39
    postablative 256.2
  fetal movements 655.7 ☑
  fragility of erythrocytes 289.89
  function
    adrenal (cortex) 255.41
      medulla 255.5
    ovary in hypopituitarism 253.4
    parenchyma of pancreas 577.8
    pituitary (gland) (lobe) (anterior) 253.2
      posterior (lobe) 253.8
  functional activity 780.99
  glucose 790.29
  haptoglobin (serum) NEC 273.8
  leukocytes 288.50
  libido 799.81
  lymphocytes 288.51
  platelets (*see also* Thrombocytopenia) 287.5
  pulse pressure 785.9
  respiration due to shock following injury 958.4
  sexual desire 799.81
  tear secretion NEC 375.15
  tolerance
    fat 579.8
    salt and water 276.9
  vision NEC 369.9
  white blood cell count 288.50
Decubital gangrene — *see also* Ulcer, pressure 707.00 [785.4]
Decubiti — *see also* Ulcer, pressure 707.00
Decubitus (ulcer) — *see also* Ulcer, pressure 707.00
  with gangrene 707.00 [785.4]
  ankle 707.06
  back
    lower 707.03
    upper 707.02
  buttock 707.05
  coccyx 707.03
  elbow 707.01
  head 707.09
  heel 707.07
  hip 707.04
  other site 707.09
  sacrum 707.03
  shoulder blades 707.02
Deepening acetabulum 718.85
Defect, defective 759.9
  3-beta-hydroxysteroid dehydrogenase 255.2
  11-hydroxylase 255.2
  21-hydroxylase 255.2
  abdominal wall, congenital 756.70
  aorticopulmonary septum 745.0
  aortic septal 745.0
  atrial septal (ostium secundum type) 745.5
    acquired 429.71
    ostium primum type 745.61
    sinus venosus 745.8
  atrioventricular
    canal 745.69
    septum 745.4
      acquired 429.71
  atrium secundum 745.5
    acquired 429.71
  auricular septal 745.5
    acquired 429.71
  bilirubin excretion 277.4
  biosynthesis, testicular androgen 257.2
  bridge 525.60

Defect, defective — *continued*
  bulbar septum 745.0
  butanol-insoluble iodide 246.1
  chromosome — *see* Anomaly, chromosome
  circulation (acquired) 459.9
    congenital 747.9
    newborn 747.9
  clotting NEC (*see also* Defect, coagulation) 286.9
  coagulation (factor) (*see also* Deficiency, coagulation factor) 286.9
    with
      abortion — *see* Abortion, by type, with hemorrhage
      ectopic pregnancy (*see also* categories 634–638) 639.1
      molar pregnancy (*see also* categories 630–632) 639.1
    acquired (any) 286.7
    antepartum or intrapartum 641.3 ☑
      affecting fetus or newborn 762.1
    causing hemorrhage of pregnancy or delivery 641.3 ☑
    complicating pregnancy, childbirth, or puerperium 649.3 ☑
    due to
      liver disease 286.7
      vitamin K deficiency 286.7
    newborn, transient 776.3
    postpartum 666.3 ☑
    specified type NEC 286.9
  conduction (heart) 426.9
    bone (*see also* Deafness, conductive) 389.00
  congenital, organ or site NEC (*see also* Anomaly)
    circulation 747.9
    Descemet's membrane 743.9
      specified type NEC 743.49
    diaphragm 756.6
    ectodermal 757.9
    esophagus 750.9
    pulmonic cusps — *see* Anomaly, heart valve
    respiratory system 748.9
      specified type NEC 748.8
  crown 525.60
  cushion endocardial 745.60
  dental restoration 525.60
  dentin (hereditary) 520.5
  Descemet's membrane (congenital) 743.9
    acquired 371.30
    specific type NEC 743.49
  deutan 368.52
  developmental (*see also* Anomaly, by site)
    cauda equina 742.59
    left ventricle 746.9
      with atresia or hypoplasia of aortic orifice or valve, with hypoplasia of ascending aorta 746.7
      in hypoplastic left heart syndrome 746.7
    testis 752.9
    vessel 747.9
  diaphragm
    with elevation, eventration, or hernia — *see* Hernia, diaphragm
    congenital 756.6
      with elevation, eventration, or hernia 756.6
      gross (with elevation, eventration, or hernia) 756.6
  ectodermal, congenital 757.9
  Eisenmenger's (ventricular septal defect) 745.4
  endocardial cushion 745.60
    specified type NEC 745.69
  esophagus, congenital 750.9
  extensor retinaculum 728.9
  fibrin polymerization (*see also* Defect, coagulation) 286.3
  filling
    biliary tract 793.3
    bladder 793.5
    dental 525.60
    gallbladder 793.3
    kidney 793.5

Defect, defective — *continued*
  filling — *continued*
    stomach 793.4
    ureter 793.5
  fossa ovalis 745.5
  gene, carrier (suspected) of V83.89
  Gerbode 745.4
  glaucomatous, without elevated tension 365.89
  Hageman (factor) (*see also* Defect, coagulation) 286.3
  hearing (*see also* Deafness) 389.9
  high grade 317
  homogentisic acid 270.2
  interatrial septal 745.5
    acquired 429.71
  interauricular septal 745.5
    acquired 429.71
  interventricular septal 745.4
    with pulmonary stenosis or atresia, dextraposition of aorta, and hypertrophy of right ventricle 745.2
    acquired 429.71
    in tetralogy of Fallot 745.2
  iodide trapping 246.1
  iodotyrosine dehalogenase 246.1
  kynureninase 270.2
  learning, specific 315.2
  major osseous 731.3
  mental (*see also* Retardation, mental) 319
  osseous, major 731.3
  osteochondral NEC 738.8
  ostium
    primum 745.61
    secundum 745.5
  pericardium 746.89
  peroxidase-binding 246.1
  placental blood supply — *see* Placenta, insufficiency
  platelet (qualitative) 287.1
    constitutional 286.4
  postural, spine 737.9
  protan 368.51
  pulmonic cusps, congenital 746.00
  renal pelvis 753.9
    obstructive 753.29
    specified type NEC 753.3
  respiratory system, congenital 748.9
    specified type NEC 748.8
  retina, retinal 361.30
    with detachment (*see also* Detachment, retina, with retinal defect) 361.00
    multiple 361.33
      with detachment 361.02
    nerve fiber bundle 362.85
    single 361.30
      with detachment 361.01
  septal (closure) (heart) NEC 745.9
    acquired 429.71
    atrial 745.5
    specified type NEC 745.8
  speech NEC 784.59 ▲
    developmental 315.39
    late effect of cerebrovascular disease — ●
      see Late effect(s) (of) cerebrovas-●
      cular disease, speech and lan- ●
      guage deficit ●
    secondary to organic lesion 784.59 ▲
  Taussig-Bing (transposition, aorta and overriding pulmonary artery) 745.11
  teeth, wedge 521.20
  thyroid hormone synthesis 246.1
  tritan 368.53
  ureter 753.9
    obstructive 753.29
  vascular (acquired) (local) 459.9
    congenital (peripheral) NEC 747.60
      gastrointestinal 747.61
      lower limb 747.64
      renal 747.62
      specified NEC 747.69
      spinal 747.82
      upper limb 747.63
  ventricular septal 745.4

Defect, defective — *continued*
  ventricular septal — *continued*
    with pulmonary stenosis or atresia, dextraposition of aorta, and hypertrophy of right ventricle 745.2
    acquired 429.71
    atrioventricular canal type 745.69
    between infundibulum and anterior portion 745.4
    in tetralogy of Fallot 745.2
    isolated anterior 745.4
  vision NEC 369.9
  visual field 368.40
    arcuate 368.43
    heteronymous, bilateral 368.47
    homonymous, bilateral 368.46
    localized NEC 368.44
    nasal step 368.44
    peripheral 368.44
    sector 368.43
  voice ▶and resonance◀ 784.40
  wedge, teeth (abrasion) 521.20
Defeminization syndrome 255.2
Deferentitis 608.4
  gonorrheal (acute) 098.14
    chronic or duration of 2 months or over 098.34
Defibrination syndrome — *see also* Fibrinolysis 286.6
Deficiency, deficient
  3-beta-hydroxysteroid dehydrogenase 255.2
  6-phosphogluconic dehydrogenase (anemia) 282.2
  11-beta-hydroxylase 255.2
  17-alpha-hydroxylase 255.2
  18-hydroxysteroid dehydrogenase 255.2
  20-alpha-hydroxylase 255.2
  21-hydroxylase 255.2
  AAT (alpha-1 antitrypsin) 273.4
  abdominal muscle syndrome 756.79
  accelerator globulin (Ac G) (blood) (*see also* Defect, coagulation) 286.3
  AC globulin (congenital) (*see also* Defect, coagulation) 286.3
    acquired 286.7
  activating factor (blood) (*see also* Defect, coagulation) 286.3
  adenohypophyseal 253.2
  adenosine deaminase 277.2
  aldolase (hereditary) 271.2
  alpha-1-antitrypsin 273.4
  alpha-1-trypsin inhibitor 273.4
  alpha-fucosidase 271.8
  alpha-lipoprotein 272.5
  alpha-mannosidase 271.8
  amino acid 270.9
  anemia — *see* Anemia, deficiency
  aneurin 265.1
    with beriberi 265.0
  antibody NEC 279.00
  antidiuretic hormone 253.5
  antihemophilic
    factor (A) 286.0
      B 286.1
      C 286.2
    globulin (AHG) NEC 286.0
  antithrombin III 289.81
  antitrypsin 273.4
  argininosuccinate synthetase or lyase 270.6
  ascorbic acid (with scurvy) 267
  autoprothrombin
    I (*see also* Defect, coagulation) 286.3
    II 286.1
    C (*see also* Defect, coagulation) 286.3
  bile salt 579.8
  biotin 266.2
  biotinidase 277.6
  bradykinase-1 277.6
  brancher enzyme (amylopectinosis) 271.0
  calciferol 268.9
    with
      osteomalacia 268.2
      rickets (*see also* Rickets) 268.0
  calcium 275.40
    dietary 269.3
  calorie, severe 261

Deficiency, deficient — Deficiency, deficient

☑ Additional Digit Required — Refer to the Tabular List for Digit Selection   ▽ Subterms under main terms may continue to next column or page

2010 ICD-9-CM   ▶◀ Revised Text   ● New Line   ▲ Revised Code   October 2009 · Volume 2 — 63

Deficiency, deficient — *continued*
　riboflavin (vitamin B$_2$) 266.0
　saccadic eye movements 379.57
　salivation 527.7
　salt 276.1
　secretion
　　ovary 256.39
　　salivary gland (any) 527.7
　　urine 788.5
　selenium 269.3
　serum
　　antitrypsin, familial 273.4
　　protein (congenital) 273.8
　short chain acyl CoA dehydrogenase (SCAD) 277.85
　short stature homeobox gene (SHOX)
　　with
　　　dyschondrosteosis 756.89
　　　short stature (idiopathic) 783.43
　　　Turner's syndrome 758.6
　smooth pursuit movements (eye) 379.58
　sodium (Na) 276.1
　SPCA (*see also* Defect, coagulation) 286.3
　specified NEC 269.8
　stable factor (congenital) (*see also* Defect, co-agulation) 286.3
　　acquired 286.7
　Stuart (-Prower) factor (*see also* Defect, coagulation) 286.3
　sucrase 271.3
　sucrase-isomaltase 271.3
　sulfite oxidase 270.0
　syndrome, multiple 260
　thiamine, thiaminic (chloride) 265.1
　thrombokinase (*see also* Defect, coagulation) 286.3
　　newborn 776.0
　thrombopoieten 287.39
　thymolymphatic 279.2
　thyroid (gland) 244.9
　tocopherol 269.1
　toe — *see* Absence, toe
　tooth bud (*see also* Anodontia) 520.0
　trunk V48.1
　UDPG-glycogen transferase 271.0
　upper limb V49.0
　　congenital 755.20
　　　with complete absence of distal elements 755.21
　　　longitudinal (complete) (partial) (with distal deficiencies, incomplete) 755.22
　　　　carpal(s) 755.28
　　　　combined humeral, radial, ulnar (incomplete) 755.23
　　　　humeral 755.24
　　　　metacarpal(s) 755.28
　　　　phalange(s) 755.29
　　　　　meaning all digits 755.21
　　　　radial 755.26
　　　　radioulnar 755.25
　　　　ulnar 755.27
　　　transverse (complete) (partial) 755.21
　vascular 459.9
　vasopressin 253.5
　viosterol (*see also* Deficiency, calciferol) 268.9
　vitamin (multiple) NEC 269.2
　　A 264.9
　　　with
　　　　Bitôt's spot 264.1
　　　　corneal 264.2
　　　　　with corneal ulceration 264.3
　　　　keratomalacia 264.4
　　　　keratosis, follicular 264.8
　　　　night blindness 264.5
　　　　scar of cornea, xerophthalmic 264.6
　　　　specified manifestation NEC 264.8
　　　　ocular 264.7
　　　　xeroderma 264.8
　　　　xerophthalmia 264.7
　　　　xerosis
　　　　　conjunctival 264.0
　　　　　　with Bitôt's spot 264.1
　　　　　corneal 264.2

Deficiency, deficient — *continued*
　vitamin — *continued*
　　A — *continued*
　　　with — *continued*
　　　　xerosis — *continued*
　　　　　corneal — *continued*
　　　　　　with corneal ulceration 264.3
　　B (complex) NEC 266.9
　　　with
　　　　beriberi 265.0
　　　　pellagra 265.2
　　　　specified type NEC 266.2
　　B$_1$ NEC 265.1
　　　beriberi 265.0
　　B$_2$ 266.0
　　B$_6$ 266.1
　　B$_{12}$ 266.2
　　B$_c$ (folic acid) 266.2
　　C (ascorbic acid) (with scurvy) 267
　　D (calciferol) (ergosterol) 268.9
　　　with
　　　　osteomalacia 268.2
　　　　rickets (*see also* Rickets) 268.0
　　E 269.1
　　folic acid 266.2
　　G 266.0
　　H 266.2
　　K 269.0
　　　of newborn 776.0
　　nicotinic acid 265.2
　　P 269.1
　　PP 265.2
　　specified NEC 269.1
　zinc 269.3
Deficient — *see also* Deficiency
　blink reflex 374.45
　craniofacial axis 756.0
　number of teeth (*see also* Anodontia) 520.0
　secretion of urine 788.5
Deficit
　neurologic NEC 781.99
　　due to
　　　cerebrovascular lesion (*see also* Disease, cerebrovascular, acute) 436
　　　late effect — *see* Late effect(s) (of) cerebrovascular disease
　　　transient ischemic attack 435.9
　　ischemic
　　　reversible (RIND) 434.91
　　　　history of (personal) V12.54
　　　prolonged (PRIND) 434.91
　　　　history of (personal) V12.54
　oxygen 799.02
Deflection
　radius 736.09
　septum (acquired) (nasal) (nose) 470
　spine — *see* Curvature, spine
　turbinate (nose) 470
Defluvium
　capillorum (*see also* Alopecia) 704.00
　ciliorum 374.55
　unguium 703.8
Deformity 738.9
　abdomen, congenital 759.9
　abdominal wall
　　acquired 738.8
　　congenital 756.70
　　muscle deficiency syndrome 756.79
　acquired (unspecified site) 738.9
　　specified site NEC 738.8
　adrenal gland (congenital) 759.1
　alimentary tract, congenital 751.9
　　lower 751.5
　　specified type NEC 751.8
　　upper (any part, except tongue) 750.9
　　　specified type NEC 750.8
　　　tongue 750.10
　　　　specified type NEC 750.19
　ankle (joint) (acquired) 736.70
　　abduction 718.47
　　congenital 755.69
　　contraction 718.47
　　specified NEC 736.79
　anus (congenital) 751.5

Deformity — *continued*
　anus — *continued*
　　acquired 569.49
　aorta (congenital) 747.20
　　acquired 447.8
　　arch 747.21
　　　acquired 447.8
　　coarctation 747.10
　aortic
　　arch 747.21
　　　acquired 447.8
　　cusp or valve (congenital) 746.9
　　　acquired (*see also* Endocarditis, aortic) 424.1
　　ring 747.21
　appendix 751.5
　arm (acquired) 736.89
　　congenital 755.50
　arteriovenous (congenital) (peripheral) NEC 747.60
　　gastrointestinal 747.61
　　lower limb 747.64
　　renal 747.62
　　specified NEC 747.69
　　spinal 747.82
　　upper limb 747.63
　artery (congenital) (peripheral) NEC (*see also* Deformity, vascular) 747.60
　　acquired 447.8
　　cerebral 747.81
　　coronary (congenital) 746.85
　　　acquired (*see also* Ischemia, heart) 414.9
　　retinal 743.9
　　umbilical 747.5
　atrial septal (congenital) (heart) 745.5
　auditory canal (congenital) (external) (*see also* Deformity, ear) 744.3
　　acquired 380.50
　auricle
　　ear (congenital) (*see also* Deformity, ear) 744.3
　　　acquired 380.32
　　heart (congenital) 746.9
　back (acquired) — *see* Deformity, spine
　Bartholin's duct (congenital) 750.9
　bile duct (congenital) 751.60
　　acquired 576.8
　　　with calculus, choledocholithiasis, or stones — *see* Choledocholithiasis
　biliary duct or passage (congenital) 751.60
　　acquired 576.8
　　　with calculus, choledocholithiasis, or stones — *see* Choledocholithiasis
　bladder (neck) (sphincter) (trigone) (acquired) 596.8
　　congenital 753.9
　bone (acquired) NEC 738.9
　　congenital 756.9
　　turbinate 738.0
　boutonniere (finger) 736.21
　brain (congenital) 742.9
　　acquired 348.89　　　　　　　　　　▲
　　multiple 742.4
　　reduction 742.2
　　vessel (congenital) 747.81
　breast (acquired) 611.89
　　congenital 757.6　　　　　　　　　　▲
　　reconstructed 612.0
　bronchus (congenital) 748.3
　　acquired 519.19
　bursa, congenital 756.9
　canal of Nuck 752.9
　canthus (congenital) 743.9
　　acquired 374.89
　capillary (acquired) 448.9
　　congenital NEC (*see also* Deformity, vascular) 747.60
　cardiac — *see* Deformity, heart
　cardiovascular system (congenital) 746.9
　caruncle, lacrimal (congenital) 743.9
　　acquired 375.69
　cascade, stomach 537.6
　cecum (congenital) 751.5

Deformity — *continued*
　cecum — *continued*
　　acquired 569.89
　cerebral (congenital) 742.9
　　acquired 348.89　　　　　　　　　　▲
　cervix (acquired) (uterus) 622.8
　　congenital 752.40
　cheek (acquired) 738.19
　　congenital 744.9
　chest (wall) (acquired) 738.3
　　congenital 754.89
　　late effect of rickets 268.1
　chin (acquired) 738.19
　　congenital 744.9
　choroid (congenital) 743.9
　　acquired 363.8
　　plexus (congenital) 742.9
　　　acquired 349.2
　cicatricial — *see* Cicatrix
　cilia (congenital) 743.9
　　acquired 374.89
　circulatory system (congenital) 747.9
　clavicle (acquired) 738.8
　　congenital 755.51
　clitoris (congenital) 752.40
　　acquired 624.8
　clubfoot — *see* Clubfoot
　coccyx (acquired) 738.6
　　congenital 756.10
　colon (congenital) 751.5
　　acquired 569.89
　concha (ear) (congenital) (*see also* Deformity, ear) 744.3
　　acquired 380.32
　congenital, organ or site not listed (*see also* Anomaly) 759.9
　cornea (congenital) 743.9
　　acquired 371.70
　coronary artery (congenital) 746.85
　　acquired (*see also* Ischemia, heart) 414.9
　cranium (acquired) 738.19
　　congenital (*see also* Deformity, skull, congenital) 756.0
　cricoid cartilage (congenital) 748.3
　　acquired 478.79
　cystic duct (congenital) 751.60
　　acquired 575.8
　Dandy-Walker 742.3
　　with spina bifida (*see also* Spina bifida) 741.0 ☑
　diaphragm (congenital) 756.6
　　acquired 738.8
　digestive organ(s) or system (congenital) NEC 751.9
　　specified type NEC 751.8
　ductus arteriosus 747.0
　duodenal bulb 537.89
　duodenum (congenital) 751.5
　　acquired 537.89
　dura (congenital) 742.9
　　brain 742.4
　　　acquired 349.2
　　spinal 742.59
　　　acquired 349.2
　ear (congenital) 744.3
　　acquired 380.32
　　auricle 744.3
　　　causing impairment of hearing 744.02
　　causing impairment of hearing 744.00
　　external 744.3
　　　causing impairment of hearing 744.02
　　internal 744.05
　　lobule 744.3
　　middle 744.03
　　　ossicles 744.04
　　ossicles 744.04
　ectodermal (congenital) NEC 757.9
　　specified type NEC 757.8
　ejaculatory duct (congenital) 752.9
　　acquired 608.89
　elbow (joint) (acquired) 736.00
　　congenital 755.50
　　contraction 718.42
　endocrine gland NEC 759.2
　epididymis (congenital) 752.9
　　acquired 608.89

☑ Additional Digit Required — Refer to the Tabular List for Digit Selection　　　　　　　　　　　　　　　　　　　　　　　　␥ Subterms under main terms may continue to next column or page

64 — Volume 2 · October 2009　　　▶◀ Revised Text　　　● New Line　　　▲ Revised Code　　　　　　　　　　**2010 ICD-9-CM**

☑ Additional Digit Required — Refer to the Tabular List for Digit Selection

▼ Subterms under main terms may continue to next column or page

2010 ICD-9-CM

▶◀ Revised Text   ● New Line   ▲ Revised Code

October 2009 • Volume 2 — 65

Deformity — Deformity

Deformity — *continued*
  reduction — *continued*
    lower limb — *continued*
      longitudinal — *continued*
        fibular 755.37
        metatarsal(s) 755.38
        phalange(s) 755.39
          meaning all digits 755.31
        tarsal(s) 755.38
        tibia 755.36
        tibiofibular 755.35
        transverse 755.31
      upper limb 755.20
        with complete absence of distal elements 755.21
        longitudinal (complete) (partial) (with distal deficiencies, incomplete) 755.22
          with complete absence of distal elements 755.21
          carpal(s) 755.28
          combined humeral, radial, ulnar (incomplete) 755.23
          humeral 755.24
          metacarpal(s) 755.28
          phalange(s) 755.29
            meaning all digits 755.21
          radial 755.26
          radioulnar 755.25
          ulnar 755.27
        transverse (complete) (partial) 755.21
  renal — *see* Deformity, kidney
  respiratory system (congenital) 748.9
    specified type NEC 748.8
  rib (acquired) 738.3
    congenital 756.3
      cervical 756.2
  rotation (joint) (acquired) 736.9
    congenital 755.9
    hip or thigh 736.39
      congenital (*see also* Subluxation, congenital, hip) 754.32
  sacroiliac joint (congenital) 755.69
    acquired 738.5
  sacrum (acquired) 738.5
    congenital 756.10
  saddle
    back 737.8
    nose 738.0
      syphilitic 090.5
  salivary gland or duct (congenital) 750.9
    acquired 527.8
  scapula (acquired) 736.89
    congenital 755.50
  scrotum (congenital) 752.9
    acquired 608.89
  sebaceous gland, acquired 706.8
  seminal tract or duct (congenital) 752.9
    acquired 608.89
  septum (nasal) (acquired) 470
    congenital 748.1
  shoulder (joint) (acquired) 736.89
    congenital 755.50
      specified type NEC 755.59
    contraction 718.41
  sigmoid (flexure) (congenital) 751.5
    acquired 569.89
  sinus of Valsalva 747.29
  skin (congenital) 757.9
    acquired NEC 709.8
  skull (acquired) 738.19
    congenital 756.0
      with
        anencephalus 740.0
        encephalocele 742.0
        hydrocephalus 742.3
          with spina bifida (*see also* Spina bifida) 741.0 ☑
        microcephalus 742.1
      due to intrauterine malposition and pressure 754.0
  soft parts, organs or tissues (of pelvis)
    in pregnancy or childbirth NEC 654.9 ☑
      affecting fetus or newborn 763.89
      causing obstructed labor 660.2 ☑
        affecting fetus or newborn 763.1

Deformity — *continued*
  spermatic cord (congenital) 752.9
    acquired 608.89
      torsion 608.22
        extravaginal 608.21
        intravaginal 608.22
  spinal
    column — *see* Deformity, spine
    cord (congenital) 742.9
      acquired 336.8
      vessel (congenital) 747.82
    nerve root (congenital) 742.9
      acquired 724.9
  spine (acquired) NEC 738.5
    congenital 756.10
      due to intrauterine malposition and pressure 754.2
    kyphoscoliotic (*see also* Kyphoscoliosis) 737.30
    kyphotic (*see also* Kyphosis) 737.10
    lordotic (*see also* Lordosis) 737.20
    rachitic 268.1
    scoliotic (*see also* Scoliosis) 737.30
  spleen
    acquired 289.59
    congenital 759.0
  Sprengel's (congenital) 755.52
  sternum (acquired) 738.3
    congenital 756.3
  stomach (congenital) 750.9
    acquired 537.89
  submaxillary gland (congenital) 750.9
    acquired 527.8
  swan neck (acquired)
    finger 736.22
    hand 736.09
  talipes — *see* Talipes
  teeth, tooth NEC 520.9
  testis (congenital) 752.9
    acquired 608.89
      torsion 608.20
  thigh (acquired) 736.89
    congenital 755.60
  thorax (acquired) (wall) 738.3
    congenital 754.89
    late effect of rickets 268.1
  thumb (acquired) 736.20
    congenital 755.50
  thymus (tissue) (congenital) 759.2
  thyroid (gland) (congenital) 759.2
    cartilage 748.3
      acquired 478.79
  tibia (acquired) 736.89
    congenital 755.60
    saber 090.5
  toe (acquired) 735.9
    congenital 755.66
    specified NEC 735.8
  tongue (congenital) 750.10
    acquired 529.8
  tooth, teeth NEC 520.9
  trachea (rings) (congenital) 748.3
    acquired 519.19
  transverse aortic arch (congenital) 747.21
  tricuspid (leaflets) (valve) (congenital) 746.9
    acquired — *see* Endocarditis, tricuspid
    atresia or stenosis 746.1
    specified type NEC 746.89
  trunk (acquired) 738.3
    congenital 759.9
  ulna (acquired) 736.00
    congenital 755.50
  upper extremity — *see* Deformity, arm
  urachus (congenital) 753.7
  ureter (opening) (congenital) 753.9
    acquired 593.89
  urethra (valve) (congenital) 753.9
    acquired 599.84
  urinary tract or system (congenital) 753.9
    urachus 753.7
  uterus (congenital) 752.3
    acquired 621.8
  uvula (congenital) 750.9
    acquired 528.9
  vagina (congenital) 752.40
    acquired 623.8

Deformity — *continued*
  valve, valvular (heart) (congenital) 746.9
    acquired — *see* Endocarditis
    pulmonary 746.00
    specified type NEC 746.89
  vascular (congenital) (peripheral) NEC 747.60
    acquired 459.9
    gastrointestinal 747.61
    lower limb 747.64
    renal 747.62
    specified site NEC 747.69
    spinal 747.82
    upper limb 747.63
  vas deferens (congenital) 752.9
    acquired 608.89
  vein (congenital) NEC (*see also* Deformity, vascular) 747.60
    brain 747.81
    coronary 746.9
    great 747.40
  vena cava (inferior) (superior) (congenital) 747.40
  vertebra — *see* Deformity, spine
  vesicourethral orifice (acquired) 596.8
  vesicourethral orifice (acquired) 596.8
    congenital NEC 753.9
      specified type NEC 753.8
  vessels of optic papilla (congenital) 743.9
  visual field (contraction) 368.45
  vitreous humor (congenital) 743.9
    acquired 379.29
  vulva (congenital) 752.40
    acquired 624.8
  wrist (joint) (acquired) 736.00
    congenital 755.50
    contraction 718.43
    valgus 736.03
      congenital 755.59
    varus 736.04
      congenital 755.59

Degeneration, degenerative
  adrenal (capsule) (gland) 255.8
    with hypofunction 255.41
    fatty 255.8
    hyaline 255.8
    infectional 255.8
    lardaceous 277.39
  amyloid (any site) (general) 277.39
  anterior cornua, spinal cord 336.8
  anterior labral 840.8
  aorta, aortic 440.0
    fatty 447.8
    valve (heart) (*see also* Endocarditis, aortic) 424.1
  arteriovascular — *see* Arteriosclerosis
  artery, arterial (atheromatous) (calcareous) (*see also* Arteriosclerosis)
    amyloid 277.39
    lardaceous 277.39
    medial NEC (*see also* Arteriosclerosis, extremities) 440.20
  articular cartilage NEC (*see also* Disorder, cartilage, articular) 718.0 ☑
    elbow 718.02
    knee 717.5
    patella 717.7
    shoulder 718.01
    spine (*see also* Spondylosis) 721.90
  atheromatous — *see* Arteriosclerosis
  bacony (any site) 277.39
  basal nuclei or ganglia NEC 333.0
  bone 733.90
  brachial plexus 353.0
  brain (cortical) (progressive) 331.9
    arteriosclerotic 437.0
    childhood 330.9
      specified type NEC 330.8
    congenital 742.4
    cystic 348.0
      congenital 742.4
    familial NEC 331.89
    grey matter 330.8
    heredofamilial NEC 331.89
    in
      alcoholism 303.9 ☑ *[331.7]*
      beriberi 265.0 *[331.7]*
      cerebrovascular disease 437.9 *[331.7]*

Degeneration, degenerative — *continued*
  brain — *continued*
    in — *continued*
      congenital hydrocephalus 742.3 *[331.7]*
        with spina bifida (*see also* Spina bifida) 741.0 ☑ *[331.7]*
      Fabry's disease 272.7 *[330.2]*
      Gaucher's disease 272.7 *[330.2]*
      Hunter's disease or syndrome 277.5 *[330.3]*
      lipidosis
        cerebral 330.1
        generalized 272.7 *[330.2]*
      mucopolysaccharidosis 277.5 *[330.3]*
      myxedema (*see also* Myxedema) 244.9 *[331.7]*
      neoplastic disease NEC (M8000/1) 239.9 *[331.7]*
      Niemann-Pick disease 272.7 *[330.2]*
      sphingolipidosis 272.7 *[330.2]*
      vitamin B$_{12}$ deficiency 266.2 *[331.7]*
    motor centers 331.89
    senile 331.2
    specified type NEC 331.89
  breast — *see* Disease, breast
  Bruch's membrane 363.40
  bundle of His 426.50
    left 426.3
    right 426.4
  calcareous NEC 275.49
  capillaries 448.9
    amyloid 277.39
    fatty 448.9
    lardaceous 277.39
  cardiac (brown) (calcareous) (fatty) (fibrous) (hyaline) (mural) (muscular) (pigmentary) (senile) (with arteriosclerosis) (*see also* Degeneration, myocardial) 429.1
    valve, valvular — *see* Endocarditis
  cardiorenal (*see also* Hypertension, cardiorenal) 404.90
  cardiovascular (*see also* Disease, cardiovascular) 429.2
    renal (*see also* Hypertension, cardiorenal) 404.90
  cartilage (joint) — *see* Derangement, joint
  cerebellar NEC 334.9
    primary (hereditary) (sporadic) 334.2
  cerebral — *see* Degeneration, brain
  cerebromacular 330.1
  cerebrovascular 437.1
    due to hypertension 437.2
    late effect — *see* Late effect(s) (of) cerebrovascular disease
  cervical plexus 353.2
  cervix 622.8
    due to radiation (intended effect) 622.8
      adverse effect or misadventure 622.8
  changes, spine or vertebra (*see also* Spondylosis) 721.90
  chitinous 277.39
  chorioretinal 363.40
    congenital 743.53
    hereditary 363.50
  choroid (colloid) (drusen) 363.40
    hereditary 363.50
    senile 363.41
      diffuse secondary 363.42
  cochlear 386.8
  collateral ligament (knee) (medial) 717.82
    lateral 717.81
  combined (spinal cord) (subacute) 266.2 *[336.2]*
    with anemia (pernicious) 281.0 *[336.2]*
      due to dietary deficiency 281.1 *[336.2]*
      due to vitamin B$_{12}$ deficiency anemia (dietary) 281.1 *[336.2]*
  conjunctiva 372.50
    amyloid 277.39 *[372.50]*
  cornea 371.40
    calcerous 371.44
    familial (hereditary) (*see also* Dystrophy, cornea) 371.50
      macular 371.55
      reticular 371.54
    hyaline (of old scars) 371.41

Index

Deformity — Degeneration, degenerative

☑ Additional Digit Required — Refer to the Tabular List for Digit Selection   Subterms under main terms may continue to next column or page

2010 ICD-9-CM   ▶◀ Revised Text   ● New Line   ▲ Revised Code   Volume 2 — 67

Degeneration, degenerative — continued
  vascular (see also Arteriosclerosis) — contin-
      ued
    hypertensive — see Hypertension
    vitreoretinal (primary) 362.73
      secondary 362.66
    vitreous humor (with infiltration) 379.21
    wallerian NEC — see Disorder, nerve
    waxy (any site) 277.39
    Wilson's hepatolenticular 275.1
Deglutition
  paralysis 784.99
    hysterical 300.11
  pneumonia 507.0
Degos' disease or syndrome 447.8
**Degradation disorder, branched-chain amino
  acid** 270.3
Dehiscence
  anastomosis — see Complications, anastomo-
      sis
  cesarean wound 674.1 ☑
  closure of
    cornea 998.32
    fascia, superficial or muscular 998.31
    internal organ 998.31
    mucosa 998.32
    muscle or muscle flap 998.31
    ribs or rib cage 998.31
    skin 998.32
    skull or craniotomy 998.31
    sternum or sternotomy 998.31
    subcutaneous tissue 998.32
    tendon or ligament 998.31
    traumatic laceration (external) (internal)
        998.33
  episiotomy 674.2 ☑
  operation wound 998.32
    deep 998.31
    external 998.32
    internal 998.31
    superficial 998.32
  perineal wound (postpartum) 674.2 ☑
  postoperative 998.32
    abdomen 998.32
      internal 998.31
    internal 998.31
  traumatic injury wound repair 998.33
  uterine wound 674.1 ☑
Dehydration (cachexia) 276.51
  with
    hypernatremia 276.0
    hyponatremia 276.1
  newborn 775.5
Deiters' nucleus syndrome 386.19
Déjérine's disease 356.0
Déjérine-Klumpke paralysis 767.6
Déjérine-Roussy syndrome 338.0
Déjérine-Sottas disease or neuropathy (hypertrophic) 356.0
Déjérine-Thomas atrophy or syndrome 333.0
de Lange's syndrome (Amsterdam dwarf, mental
  retardation, and brachycephaly) 759.89
Delay, delayed
  adaptation, cones or rods 368.63
  any plane in pelvis
    affecting fetus or newborn 763.1
    complicating delivery 660.1 ☑
  birth or delivery NEC 662.1 ☑
    affecting fetus or newborn 763.89
    second twin, triplet, or multiple mate
        662.3 ☑
  closure (see also Fistula)
    cranial suture 756.0
    fontanel 756.0
  coagulation NEC 790.92
  conduction (cardiac) (ventricular) 426.9
  delivery NEC 662.1 ☑
    second twin, triplet, etc. 662.3 ☑
      affecting fetus or newborn 763.89
  development
    in childhood 783.40
      physiological 783.40
      intellectual NEC 315.9
      learning NEC 315.2
      reading 315.00
    sexual 259.0

Delay, delayed — continued
  development — continued
    speech 315.39
      and language due to hearing loss
          315.34
      associated with hyperkinesis 314.1
    spelling 315.09
  gastric emptying 536.8
  menarche 256.39
    due to pituitary hypofunction 253.4
  menstruation (cause unknown) 626.8
  milestone in childhood 783.42
  motility — see Hypomotility
  passage of meconium (newborn) 777.1
  primary respiration 768.9
  puberty 259.0
  separation of umbilical cord 779.83
  sexual maturation, female 259.0
  vaccination V64.00
Del Castillo's syndrome (germinal aplasia) 606.0
Déleage's disease 359.89
Deletion syndrome
  5p 758.31
  22q11.2 758.32
  autosomal NEC 758.39
  constitutional 5q deletion 758.39
Delhi (boil) (button) (sore) 085.1
Delinquency (juvenile) 312.9
  group (see also Disturbance, conduct) 312.2 ☑
  neurotic 312.4
Delirium, delirious 780.09
  acute (psychotic) 293.0
  alcoholic 291.0
    acute 291.0
    chronic 291.1
  alcoholicum 291.0
  chronic (see also Psychosis) 293.89
    due to or associated with physical condi-
        tion — see Psychosis, organic
  drug-induced 292.81
  due to conditions classified elsewhere 293.0
  eclamptic (see also Eclampsia) 780.39
  exhaustion (see also Reaction, stress, acute)
      308.9
  hysterical 300.11
  in
    presenile dementia 290.11
    senile dementia 290.3
  induced by drug 292.81
  manic, maniacal (acute) (see also Psychosis,
      affective) 296.0 ☑
    recurrent episode 296.1 ☑
    single episode 296.0 ☑
  puerperal 293.9
  senile 290.3
  subacute (psychotic) 293.1
  thyroid (see also Thyrotoxicosis) 242.9 ☑
  traumatic (see also Injury, intracranial)
    with
      lesion, spinal cord — see Injury, spinal,
          by site
      shock, spinal — see Injury, spinal, by
          site
  tremens (impending) 291.0
  uremic — see Uremia
  withdrawal
    alcoholic (acute) 291.0
      chronic 291.1
    drug 292.0
Delivery

Note — Use the following fifth-digit subclassification with categories 640–649, 651–676:

0   unspecified as to episode of care

1   delivered, with or without mention
     of antepartum condition

2   delivered, with mention of postpar-
     tum complication

3   antepartum condition or complica-
     tion

4   postpartum condition or complica-
     tion

  breech (assisted) (buttocks) (complete) (frank)
      (spontaneous) 652.2 ☑

Delivery — continued
  breech — continued
    affecting fetus or newborn 763.0
    extraction NEC 669.6 ☑
  cesarean (for) 669.7 ☑
    abnormal
      cervix 654.6 ☑
      pelvic organs or tissues 654.9 ☑
      pelvis (bony) (major) NEC 653.0 ☑
      presentation or position 652.9 ☑
        in multiple gestation 652.6 ☑
      size, fetus 653.5 ☑
      soft parts (of pelvis) 654.9 ☑
      uterus, congenital 654.0 ☑
      vagina 654.7 ☑
      vulva 654.8 ☑
    abruptio placentae 641.2 ☑
    acromion presentation 652.8 ☑
    affecting fetus or newborn 763.4
    anteversion, cervix or uterus 654.4 ☑
    atony, uterus 661.2 ☑
      with hemorrhage 666.1 ☑
    bicornis or bicornuate uterus 654.0 ☑
    breech presentation (buttocks) (complete)
        (frank) 652.2 ☑
    brow presentation 652.4 ☑
    cephalopelvic disproportion (normally
        formed fetus) 653.4 ☑
    chin presentation 652.4 ☑
    cicatrix of cervix 654.6 ☑
    contracted pelvis (general) 653.1 ☑
      inlet 653.2 ☑
      outlet 653.3 ☑
    cord presentation or prolapse 663.0 ☑
    cystocele 654.4 ☑
    deformity (acquired) (congenital)
      pelvic organs or tissues NEC 654.9 ☑
      pelvis (bony) NEC 653.0 ☑
    displacement, uterus NEC 654.4 ☑
    disproportion NEC 653.9 ☑
    distress
      fetal 656.8 ☑
      maternal 669.0 ☑
    eclampsia 642.6 ☑
    face presentation 652.4 ☑
    failed
      forceps 660.7 ☑
      trial of labor NEC 660.6 ☑
      vacuum extraction 660.7 ☑
      ventouse 660.7 ☑
    fetal deformity 653.7 ☑
    fetal-maternal hemorrhage 656.0 ☑
    fetus, fetal
      distress 656.8 ☑
      prematurity 656.8 ☑
    fibroid (tumor) (uterus) 654.1 ☑
    footling 652.8 ☑
      with successful version 652.1 ☑
    hemorrhage (antepartum) (intrapartum)
        NEC 641.9 ☑
    hydrocephalic fetus 653.6 ☑
    incarceration of uterus 654.3 ☑
    incoordinate uterine action 661.4 ☑
    inertia, uterus 661.2 ☑
      primary 661.0 ☑
      secondary 661.1 ☑
    lateroversion, uterus or cervix 654.4 ☑
    mal lie 652.9 ☑
    malposition
      fetus 652.9 ☑
        in multiple gestation 652.6 ☑
      pelvic organs or tissues NEC 654.9 ☑
      uterus NEC or cervix 654.4 ☑
    malpresentation NEC 652.9 ☑
      in multiple gestation 652.6 ☑
    maternal
      diabetes mellitus (conditions classifi-
          able to 249 and 250) 648.0 ☑
      heart disease NEC 648.6 ☑
    meconium in liquor 656.8 ☑
      staining only 792.3
    oblique presentation 652.3 ☑
    oversize fetus 653.5 ☑
    pelvic tumor NEC 654.9 ☑

Delivery — continued
  cesarean — continued
    placental insufficiency 656.5 ☑
    placenta previa 641.0 ☑
      with hemorrhage 641.1 ☑
    poor dilation, cervix 661.0 ☑
    pre-eclampsia 642.4 ☑
      severe 642.5 ☑
    previous
      cesarean delivery, section 654.2 ☑
      surgery (to)
        cervix 654.6 ☑
        gynecological NEC 654.9 ☑
        rectum 654.8 ☑
        uterus NEC 654.9 ☑
          previous cesarean delivery, sec-
              tion 654.2 ☑
        vagina 654.7 ☑
    prolapse
      arm or hand 652.7 ☑
      uterus 654.4 ☑
    prolonged labor 662.1 ☑
    rectocele 654.4 ☑
    retroversion, uterus or cervix 654.3 ☑
    rigid
      cervix 654.6 ☑
      pelvic floor 654.4 ☑
      perineum 654.8 ☑
      vagina 654.7 ☑
      vulva 654.8 ☑
    sacculation, pregnant uterus 654.4 ☑
    scar(s)
      cervix 654.6 ☑
      cesarean delivery, section 654.2 ☑
      uterus NEC 654.9 ☑
        due to previous cesarean delivery,
            section 654.2 ☑
    Shirodkar suture in situ 654.5 ☑
    shoulder presentation 652.8 ☑
    stenosis or stricture, cervix 654.6 ☑
    transverse presentation or lie 652.3 ☑
    tumor, pelvic organs or tissues NEC
        654.4 ☑
    umbilical cord presentation or prolapse
        663.0 ☑
  completely normal case — see category 650
  complicated (by) NEC 669.9 ☑
    abdominal tumor, fetal 653.7 ☑
      causing obstructed labor 660.1 ☑
    abnormal, abnormality of
      cervix 654.6 ☑
        causing obstructed labor 660.2 ☑
      forces of labor 661.9 ☑
      formation of uterus 654.0 ☑
      pelvic organs or tissues 654.9 ☑
        causing obstructed labor 660.2 ☑
      pelvis (bony) (major) NEC 653.0 ☑
        causing obstructed labor 660.1 ☑
      presentation or position NEC 652.9 ☑
        causing obstructed labor 660.0 ☑
      size, fetus 653.5 ☑
        causing obstructed labor 660.1 ☑
      soft parts (of pelvis) 654.9 ☑
        causing obstructed labor 660.2 ☑
      uterine contractions NEC 661.9 ☑
      uterus (formation) 654.0 ☑
        causing obstructed labor 660.2 ☑
      vagina 654.7 ☑
        causing obstructed labor 660.2 ☑
    abnormally formed uterus (any type)
        (congenital) 654.0 ☑
      causing obstructed labor 660.2 ☑
    acromion presentation 652.8 ☑
      causing obstructed labor 660.0 ☑
    adherent placenta 667.0 ☑
      with hemorrhage 666.0 ☑
    adhesions, uterus (to abdominal wall)
        654.4 ☑
    advanced maternal age NEC 659.6 ☑
      multigravida 659.6 ☑
      primigravida 659.5 ☑
    air embolism 673.0 ☑
    amnionitis 658.4 ☑

☑ Additional Digit Required — Refer to the Tabular List for Digit Selection   ⌐ʀᴇᴠ Subterms under main terms may continue to next column or page

68 — Volume 2   ▶◀ Revised Text   ● New Line   ▲ Revised Code   2010 ICD-9-CM

Delivery — *continued*
  complicated — *continued*
    amniotic fluid embolism 673.1 ☑
    anesthetic death 668.9 ☑
    annular detachment, cervix 665.3 ☑
    antepartum hemorrhage — *see* Delivery, complicated, hemorrhage
    anteversion, cervix or uterus 654.4 ☑
      causing obstructed labor 660.2 ☑
    apoplexy 674.0 ☑
      placenta 641.2 ☑
    arrested active phase 661.1 ☑
    asymmetrical pelvis bone 653.0 ☑
      causing obstructed labor 660.1 ☑
    atony, uterus with hemorrhage (hypotonic) (inertia) 666.1 ☑
      hypertonic 661.4 ☑
    Bandl's ring 661.4 ☑
    battledore placenta — *see* Placenta, abnormal
    bicornis or bicornuate uterus 654.0 ☑
      causing obstructed labor 660.2 ☑
    birth injury to mother NEC 665.9 ☑
    bleeding (*see also* Delivery, complicated, hemorrhage) 641.9 ☑
    breech presentation (assisted) (buttocks) (complete) (frank) (spontaneous) 652.2 ☑
      with successful version 652.1 ☑
    brow presentation 652.4 ☑
    cephalopelvic disproportion (normally formed fetus) 653.4 ☑
      causing obstructed labor 660.1 ☑
    cerebral hemorrhage 674.0 ☑
    cervical dystocia 661.2 ☑
    chin presentation 652.4 ☑
      causing obstructed labor 660.0 ☑
    cicatrix
      cervix 654.6 ☑
        causing obstructed labor 660.2 ☑
      vagina 654.7 ☑
        causing obstructed labor 660.2 ☑
    coagulation defect 649.3 ☑
    colporrhexis 665.4 ☑
      with perineal laceration 664.0 ☑
    compound presentation 652.8 ☑
      causing obstructed labor 660.0 ☑
    compression of cord (umbilical) 663.2 ☑
      around neck 663.1 ☑
      cord prolapsed 663.0 ☑
    contraction, contracted pelvis 653.1 ☑
      causing obstructed labor 660.1 ☑
      general 653.1 ☑
        causing obstructed labor 660.1 ☑
      inlet 653.2 ☑
        causing obstructed labor 660.1 ☑
      midpelvic 653.8 ☑
        causing obstructed labor 660.1 ☑
      midplane 653.8 ☑
        causing obstructed labor 660.1 ☑
      outlet 653.3 ☑
        causing obstructed labor 660.1 ☑
    contraction ring 661.4 ☑
    cord (umbilical) 663.9 ☑
      around neck, tightly or with compression 663.1 ☑
        without compression 663.3 ☑
      bruising 663.6 ☑
      complication NEC 663.9 ☑
        specified type NEC 663.8 ☑
      compression NEC 663.2 ☑
      entanglement NEC 663.3 ☑
        with compression 663.2 ☑
      forelying 663.0 ☑
      hematoma 663.6 ☑
      marginal attachment 663.8 ☑
      presentation 663.0 ☑
      prolapse (complete) (occult) (partial) 663.0 ☑
      short 663.4 ☑
      specified complication NEC 663.8 ☑
      thrombosis (vessels) 663.6 ☑
      vascular lesion 663.6 ☑

Delivery — *continued*
  complicated — *continued*
    cord — *continued*
      velamentous insertion 663.8 ☑
    Couvelaire uterus 641.2 ☑
    cretin pelvis (dwarf type) (male type) 653.1 ☑
      causing obstructed labor 660.1 ☑
    crossbirth 652.3 ☑
      with successful version 652.1 ☑
      causing obstructed labor 660.0 ☑
    cyst (Gartner's duct) 654.7 ☑
    cystocele 654.4 ☑
      causing obstructed labor 660.2 ☑
    death of fetus (near term) 656.4 ☑
      early (before 22 completed weeks gestation) 632
    deformity (acquired) (congenital)
      fetus 653.7 ☑
        causing obstructed labor 660.1 ☑
      pelvic organs or tissues NEC 654.9 ☑
        causing obstructed labor 660.2 ☑
      pelvis (bony) NEC 653.0 ☑
        causing obstructed labor 660.1 ☑
    delay, delayed
      delivery in multiple pregnancy 662.3 ☑
        due to locked mates 660.5 ☑
      following rupture of membranes (spontaneous) 658.2 ☑
        artificial 658.3 ☑
    depressed fetal heart tones 659.7 ☑
    diastasis recti 665.8 ☑
    dilatation
      bladder 654.4 ☑
        causing obstructed labor 660.2 ☑
      cervix, incomplete, poor or slow 661.0 ☑
    diseased placenta 656.7 ☑
    displacement uterus NEC 654.4 ☑
      causing obstructed labor 660.2 ☑
    disproportion NEC 653.9 ☑
      causing obstructed labor 660.1 ☑
    disruptio uteri — *see* Delivery, complicated, rupture, uterus
    distress
      fetal 656.8 ☑
      maternal 669.0 ☑
    double uterus (congenital) 654.0 ☑
      causing obstructed labor 660.2 ☑
    dropsy amnion 657.0 ☑
    dysfunction, uterus 661.9 ☑
      hypertonic 661.4 ☑
      hypotonic 661.2 ☑
        primary 661.0 ☑
        secondary 661.1 ☑
      incoordinate 661.4 ☑
    dystocia
      cervical 661.2 ☑
      fetal — *see* Delivery, complicated, abnormal, presentation
      maternal — *see* Delivery, complicated, prolonged labor
      pelvic — *see* Delivery, complicated, contraction pelvis
      positional 652.8 ☑
      shoulder girdle 660.4 ☑
    eclampsia 642.6 ☑
    ectopic kidney 654.4 ☑
      causing obstructed labor 660.2 ☑
    edema, cervix 654.6 ☑
      causing obstructed labor 660.2 ☑
    effusion, amniotic fluid 658.1 ☑
    elderly multigravida 659.6 ☑
    elderly primigravida 659.5 ☑
    embolism (pulmonary) 673.2 ☑
      air 673.0 ☑
      amniotic fluid 673.1 ☑
      blood clot 673.2 ☑
      cerebral 674.0 ☑
      fat 673.8 ☑
      pyemic 673.3 ☑
      septic 673.3 ☑
    entanglement, umbilical cord 663.3 ☑

Delivery — *continued*
  complicated — *continued*
    entanglement, umbilical cord — *continued*
      with compression 663.2 ☑
      around neck (with compression) 663.1 ☑
    eversion, cervix or uterus 665.2 ☑
    excessive
      fetal growth 653.5 ☑
        causing obstructed labor 660.1 ☑
      size of fetus 653.5 ☑
        causing obstructed labor 660.1 ☑
    face presentation 652.4 ☑
      causing obstructed labor 660.0 ☑
      to pubes 660.3 ☑
    failure, fetal head to enter pelvic brim 652.5 ☑
      causing obstructed labor 660.0 ☑
    female genital mutilation 660.8 ☑
    fetal
      acid-base balance 656.8 ☑
      death (near term) NEC 656.4 ☑
        early (before 22 completed weeks gestation) 632
      deformity 653.7 ☑
        causing obstructed labor 660.1 ☑
      distress 656.8 ☑
      heart rate or rhythm 659.7 ☑
      reduction of multiple fetuses reduced to single fetus 651.7 ☑
    fetopelvic disproportion 653.4 ☑
      causing obstructed labor 660.1 ☑
    fever during labor 659.2 ☑
    fibroid (tumor) (uterus) 654.1 ☑
      causing obstructed labor 660.2 ☑
    fibromyomata 654.1 ☑
      causing obstructed labor 660.2 ☑
    forelying umbilical cord 663.0 ☑
    fracture of coccyx 665.6 ☑
    hematoma 664.5 ☑
      broad ligament 665.7 ☑
      ischial spine 665.7 ☑
      pelvic 665.7 ☑
      perineum 664.5 ☑
      soft tissues 665.7 ☑
      subdural 674.0 ☑
      umbilical cord 663.6 ☑
      vagina 665.7 ☑
      vulva or perineum 664.5 ☑
    hemorrhage (uterine) (antepartum) (intrapartum) (pregnancy) 641.9 ☑
      accidental 641.2 ☑
      associated with
        afibrinogenemia 641.3 ☑
        coagulation defect 641.3 ☑
          hyperfibrinolysis 641.3 ☑
          hypofibrinogenemia 641.3 ☑
      cerebral 674.0 ☑
      due to
        low-lying placenta 641.1 ☑
        placenta previa 641.1 ☑
        premature separation of placenta (normally implanted) 641.2 ☑
        retained placenta 666.0 ☑
        trauma 641.8 ☑
        uterine leiomyoma 641.8 ☑
      marginal sinus rupture 641.2 ☑
      placenta NEC 641.9 ☑
      postpartum (atonic) (immediate) (within 24 hours) 666.1 ☑
        with retained or trapped placenta 666.0 ☑
        delayed 666.2 ☑
        secondary 666.2 ☑
        third stage 666.0 ☑
    hourglass contraction, uterus 661.4 ☑
    hydramnios 657.0 ☑
    hydrocephalic fetus 653.6 ☑
      causing obstructed labor 660.1 ☑
    hydrops fetalis 653.7 ☑
      causing obstructed labor 660.1 ☑

Delivery — *continued*
  complicated — *continued*
    hypertension — *see* Hypertension, complicating pregnancy
    hypertonic uterine dysfunction 661.4 ☑
    hypotonic uterine dysfunction 661.2 ☑
    impacted shoulders 660.4 ☑
    incarceration, uterus 654.3 ☑
      causing obstructed labor 660.2 ☑
    incomplete dilation (cervix) 661.0 ☑
    incoordinate uterus 661.4 ☑
    indication NEC 659.9 ☑
      specified type NEC 659.8 ☑
    inertia, uterus 661.2 ☑
      hypertonic 661.4 ☑
      hypotonic 661.2 ☑
      primary 661.0 ☑
      secondary 661.1 ☑
    infantile
      genitalia 654.4 ☑
        causing obstructed labor 660.2 ☑
      uterus (os) 654.4 ☑
        causing obstructed labor 660.2 ☑
    injury (to mother) NEC 665.9 ☑
    intrauterine fetal death (near term) NEC 656.4 ☑
      early (before 22 completed weeks gestation) 632
    inversion, uterus 665.2 ☑
    kidney, ectopic 654.4 ☑
      causing obstructed labor 660.2 ☑
    knot (true), umbilical cord 663.2 ☑
    labor, premature (before 37 completed weeks gestation) 644.2 ☑
    laceration 664.9 ☑
      anus (sphincter) (healed) (old) 654.8 ☑
        with mucosa 664.3 ☑
        not associated with third-degree perineal laceration 664.6 ☑
      bladder (urinary) 665.5 ☑
      bowel 665.5 ☑
      central 664.4 ☑
      cervix (uteri) 665.3 ☑
      fourchette 664.0 ☑
      hymen 664.0 ☑
      labia (majora) (minora) 664.0 ☑
      pelvic
        floor 664.1 ☑
        organ NEC 665.5 ☑
      perineum, perineal 664.4 ☑
        first degree 664.0 ☑
        second degree 664.1 ☑
        third degree 664.2 ☑
        fourth degree 664.3 ☑
        central 664.4 ☑
        extensive NEC 664.4 ☑
        muscles 664.1 ☑
        skin 664.0 ☑
        slight 664.0 ☑
      peritoneum 665.5 ☑
      periurethral tissue 664.8 ☑
      rectovaginal (septum) (without perineal laceration) 665.4 ☑
        with perineum 664.2 ☑
          with anal or rectal mucosa 664.3 ☑
      skin (perineum) 664.0 ☑
      specified site or type NEC 664.8 ☑
      sphincter ani (healed) (old) 654.8 ☑
        with mucosa 664.3 ☑
        not associated with third-degree perineal laceration 664.6 ☑
      urethra 665.5 ☑
      uterus 665.1 ☑
        before labor 665.0 ☑
      vagina, vaginal (deep) (high) (sulcus) (wall) (without perineal laceration) 665.4 ☑
        with perineum 664.0 ☑
          muscles, with perineum 664.1 ☑
      vulva 664.0 ☑
    lateroversion, uterus or cervix 654.4 ☑
      causing obstructed labor 660.2 ☑
    locked mates 660.5 ☑

☑ Additional Digit Required — Refer to the Tabular List for Digit Selection   ▽ Subterms under main terms may continue to next column or page

2010 ICD-9-CM   ▶◀ Revised Text   ● New Line   ▲ Revised Code   Volume 2 — 69

Delivery — *continued*
  multiple gestation — *continued*
    specified type — *continued*
      following (elective) fetal reduction 651.7 ☑
  nonviable infant 656.4 ☑
  normal — *see* category 650
  precipitate 661.3 ☑
    affecting fetus or newborn 763.6
  premature NEC (before 37 completed weeks gestation) 644.2 ☑
  previous, affecting management of pregnancy V23.41
  quadruplet NEC 651.2 ☑
    with fetal loss and retention of one or more fetus(es) 651.5 ☑
    following (elective) fetal reduction 651.7 ☑
  quintuplet NEC 651.8 ☑
    with fetal loss and retention of one or more fetus(es) 651.6 ☑
    following (elective) fetal reduction 651.7 ☑
  sextuplet NEC 651.8 ☑
    with fetal loss and retention of one or more fetus(es) 651.6 ☑
    following (elective) fetal reduction 651.7 ☑
  specified complication NEC 669.8 ☑
  stillbirth (near term) NEC 656.4 ☑
    early (before 22 completed weeks gestation) 632
  term pregnancy (live birth) NEC — *see* category 650
    stillbirth NEC 656.4 ☑
  threatened premature 644.2 ☑
  triplets NEC 651.1 ☑
    with fetal loss and retention of one or more fetus(es) 651.4 ☑
    delayed delivery (one or more mates) 662.3 ☑
    following (elective) fetal reduction 651.7 ☑
    locked mates 660.5 ☑
  twins NEC 651.0 ☑
    with fetal loss and retention of one fetus 651.3 ☑
    delayed delivery (one or more mates) 662.3 ☑
    locked mates 660.5 ☑
  uncomplicated — *see* category 650
  vacuum extractor NEC 669.5 ☑
    affecting fetus or newborn 763.3
  ventouse NEC 669.5 ☑
    affecting fetus or newborn 763.3
Dellen, cornea 371.41
Delusions (paranoid) 297.9
  grandiose 297.1
  parasitosis 300.29
  systematized 297.1
Dementia 294.8
  alcohol-induced persisting (*see also* Psychosis, alcoholic) 291.2
  Alzheimer's — *see* Alzheimer's, dementia
  arteriosclerotic (simple type) (uncomplicated) 290.40
    with
      acute confusional state 290.41
      delirium 290.41
      delusions 290.42
      depressed mood 290.43
    depressed type 290.43
    paranoid type 290.42
  Binswanger's 290.12
  catatonic (acute) (*see also* Schizophrenia) 295.2 ☑
  congenital (*see also* Retardation, mental) 319
  degenerative 290.9
    presenile-onset — *see* Dementia, presenile
    senile-onset — *see* Dementia, senile
  developmental (*see also* Schizophrenia) 295.9 ☑
  dialysis 294.8
    transient 293.9

Dementia — *continued*
  drug-induced persisting (*see also* Psychosis, drug) 292.82
  due to or associated with condition(s) classified elsewhere
    Alzheimer's
      with behavioral disturbance 331.0 [294.11]
      without behavioral disturbance 331.0 [294.10]
    cerebral lipidoses
      with behavioral disturbance 330.1 [294.11]
      without behavioral disturbance 330.1 [294.10]
    epilepsy
      with behavioral disturbance 345.9 ☑ [294.11]
      without behavioral disturbance 345.9 ☑ [294.10]
    hepatolenticular degeneration
      with behavioral disturbance 275.1 [294.11]
      without behavioral disturbance 275.1 [294.10]
    HIV
      with behavioral disturbance 042 [294.11]
      without behavioral disturbance 042 [294.10]
    Huntington's chorea
      with behavioral disturbance 333.4 [294.11]
      without behavioral disturbance 333.4 [294.10]
    Jakob-Creutzfeldt disease (CJD)
      with behavioral disturbance 046.19 [294.11]
      without behavioral disturbance 046.19 [294.10]
      variant (vCJD) 046.11
        with dementia
          with behavioral disturbance 046.11 [294.11]
          without behavioral disburbance 046.11 [294.10]
    Lewy bodies
      with behavioral disturbance 331.82 [294.11]
      without behavioral disturbance 331.82 [294.10]
    multiple sclerosis
      with behavioral disturbance 340 [294.11]
      without behavioral disturbance 340 [294.10]
    neurosyphilis
      with behavioral disturbance 094.9 [294.11]
      without behavioral disturbance 094.9 [294.10]
    Parkinsonism
      with behavioral disturbance 331.82 [294.11]
      without behavioral disturbance 331.82 [294.10]
    Pelizaeus-Merzbacher disease
      with behavioral disturbance 333.0 [294.11]
      without behavioral disturbance 333.0 [294.10]
    Pick's disease
      with behavioral disturbance 331.11 [294.11]
      without behavioral disturbance 331.11 [294.10]
    polyarteritis nodosa
      with behavioral disturbance 446.0 [294.11]
      without behavioral disturbance 446.0 [294.10]
    syphilis
      with behavioral disturbance 094.1 [294.11]
      without behavioral disturbance 094.1 [294.10]

Dementia — *continued*
  due to or associated with condition(s) classified elsewhere — *continued*
    Wilson's disease
      with behavioral disturbance 275.1 [294.11]
      without behavioral disturbance 275.1 [294.10]
  frontal 331.19
    with behavioral disturbance 331.19 [294.11]
    without behavioral disturbance 331.19 [294.10]
  frontotemporal 331.19
    with behavioral disturbance 331.19 [294.11]
    without behavioral disturbance 331.19 [294.10]
  hebephrenic (acute) 295.1 ☑
  Heller's (infantile psychosis) (*see also* Psychosis, childhood) 299.1 ☑
  idiopathic 290.9
    presenile-onset — *see* Dementia, presenile
    senile-onset — *see* Dementia, senile
  in
    arteriosclerotic brain disease 290.40
    senility 290.0
  induced by drug 292.82
  infantile, infantilia (*see also* Psychosis, childhood) 299.0 ☑
  Lewy body 331.82
    with behavioral disturbance 331.82 [294.11]
    without behavioral disturbance 331.82 [294.10]
  multi-infarct (cerebrovascular) (*see also* Dementia, arteriosclerotic) 290.40
  old age 290.0
  paralytica, paralytic 094.1
    juvenilis 090.40
    syphilitic 094.1
      congenital 090.40
    tabetic form 094.1
  paranoid (*see also* Schizophrenia) 295.3 ☑
  paraphrenic (*see also* Schizophrenia) 295.3 ☑
  paretic 094.1
  praecox (*see also* Schizophrenia) 295.9 ☑
  presenile 290.10
    with
      acute confusional state 290.11
      delirium 290.11
      delusional features 290.12
      depressive features 290.13
    depressed type 290.13
    paranoid type 290.12
    simple type 290.10
    uncomplicated 290.10
  primary (acute) (*see also* Schizophrenia) 295.0 ☑
  progressive, syphilitic 094.1
  puerperal — *see* Psychosis, puerperal
  schizophrenic (*see also* Schizophrenia) 295.9 ☑
  senile 290.0
    with
      acute confusional state 290.3
      delirium 290.3
      delusional features 290.20
      depressive features 290.21
    depressed type 290.21
    exhaustion 290.0
    paranoid type 290.20
  simple type (acute) (*see also* Schizophrenia) 295.0 ☑
  simplex (acute) (*see also* Schizophrenia) 295.0 ☑
  syphilitic 094.1
  uremic — *see* Uremia
  vascular 290.40
    with
      delirium 290.41
      delusions 290.42
      depressed mood 290.43
Demerol dependence — *see also* Dependence 304.0 ☑

Demineralization, ankle — *see also* Osteoporosis 733.00
Demodex folliculorum (infestation) 133.8
Demoralization 799.25
de Morgan's spots (senile angiomas) 448.1
Demyelinating
  polyneuritis, chronic inflammatory 357.81
Demyelination, demyelinization
  central nervous system 341.9
    specified NEC 341.8
  corpus callosum (central) 341.8
  global 340
Dengue (fever) 061
  sandfly 061
  vaccination, prophylactic (against) V05.1
  virus hemorrhagic fever 065.4
Dens
  evaginatus 520.2
  in dente 520.2
  invaginatus 520.2
Dense
  breast(s) — *omit code*
Density
  increased, bone (disseminated) (generalized) (spotted) 733.99
  lung (nodular) 518.89
Dental — *see also* condition
  examination only V72.2
Dentia praecox 520.6
Denticles (in pulp) 522.2
Dentigerous cyst 526.0
Dentin
  irregular (in pulp) 522.3
  opalescent 520.5
  secondary (in pulp) 522.3
  sensitive 521.89
Dentinogenesis imperfecta 520.5
Dentinoma (M9271/0) 213.1
  upper jaw (bone) 213.0
Dentition 520.7
  abnormal 520.6
  anomaly 520.6
  delayed 520.6
  difficult 520.7
  disorder of 520.6
  precocious 520.6
  retarded 520.6
Denture sore (mouth) 528.9
Dependence

> *Note* — *Use the following fifth-digit subclassification with category 304:*
>
> 0   *unspecified*
>
> 1   *continuous*
>
> 2   *episodic*
>
> 3   *in remission*

  with
    withdrawal symptoms
      alcohol 291.81
      drug 292.0
  14-hydroxy-dihydromorphinone 304.0 ☑
  absinthe 304.6 ☑
  acemorphan 304.0 ☑
  acetanilid(e) 304.6 ☑
  acetophenetidin 304.6 ☑
  acetorphine 304.0 ☑
  acetyldihydrocodeine 304.0 ☑
  acetyldihydrocodeinone 304.0 ☑
  Adalin 304.1 ☑
  Afghanistan black 304.3 ☑
  agrypnal 304.1 ☑
  alcohol, alcoholic (ethyl) (methyl) (wood) 303.9 ☑
    maternal, with suspected fetal damage affecting management of pregnancy 655.4 ☑
  allobarbitone 304.1 ☑
  allonal 304.1 ☑
  allylisopropylacetylurea 304.1 ☑
  alphaprodine (hydrochloride) 304.0 ☑
  Alurate 304.1 ☑
  Alvodine 304.0 ☑
  amethocaine 304.6 ☑
  amidone 304.0 ☑

☑ Additional Digit Required — Refer to the Tabular List for Digit Selection   Subterms under main terms may continue to next column or page

2010 ICD-9-CM   ▶◀ Revised Text   ● New Line   ▲ Revised Code   October 2009 • Volume 2 — 71

Delivery — Dependence

Dependence — *continued*

amidopyrine 304.6 ✓
aminopyrine 304.6 ✓
amobarbital 304.1 ✓
amphetamine(s) (type) (drugs classifiable to 969.7) 304.4 ✓
amylene hydrate 304.6 ✓
amylobarbitone 304.1 ✓
amylocaine 304.6 ✓
Amytal (sodium) 304.1 ✓
analgesic (drug) NEC 304.6 ✓
   synthetic with morphine-like effect 304.0 ✓
anesthetic (agent) (drug) (gas) (general) (local) NEC 304.6 ✓
Angel dust 304.6 ✓
anileridine 304.0 ✓
antipyrine 304.6 ✓
anxiolytic 304.1 ✓
aprobarbital 304.1 ✓
aprobarbitone 304.1 ✓
atropine 304.6 ✓
Avertin (bromide) 304.6 ✓
barbenyl 304.1 ✓
barbital(s) 304.1 ✓
barbitone 304.1 ✓
barbiturate(s) (compounds) (drugs classifiable to 967.0) 304.1 ✓
barbituric acid (and compounds) 304.1 ✓
benzedrine 304.4 ✓
benzylmorphine 304.0 ✓
Beta-chlor 304.1 ✓
bhang 304.3 ✓
blue velvet 304.0 ✓
Brevital 304.1 ✓
bromal (hydrate) 304.1 ✓
bromide(s) NEC 304.1 ✓
bromine compounds NEC 304.1 ✓
bromisovalum 304.1 ✓
bromoform 304.1 ✓
Bromo-seltzer 304.1 ✓
bromural 304.1 ✓
butabarbital (sodium) 304.1 ✓
butabarpal 304.1 ✓
butallylonal 304.1 ✓
butethal 304.1 ✓
buthalitone (sodium) 304.1 ✓
Butisol 304.1 ✓
butobarbitone 304.1 ✓
butyl chloral (hydrate) 304.1 ✓
caffeine 304.4 ✓
cannabis (indica) (sativa) (resin) (derivatives) (type) 304.3 ✓
carbamazepine 304.6 ✓
Carbrital 304.1 ✓
carbromal 304.1 ✓
carisoprodol 304.6 ✓
Catha (edulis) 304.4 ✓
chloral (betaine) (hydrate) 304.1 ✓
chloralamide 304.1 ✓
chloralformamide 304.1 ✓
chloralose 304.1 ✓
chlordiazepoxide 304.1 ✓
Chloretone 304.1 ✓
chlorobutanol 304.1 ✓
chlorodyne 304.1 ✓
chloroform 304.6 ✓
Cliradon 304.0 ✓
coca (leaf) and derivatives 304.2 ✓
cocaine 304.2 ✓
   hydrochloride 304.2 ✓
   salt (any) 304.2 ✓
codeine 304.0 ✓
combination of drugs (excluding morphine or opioid type drug) NEC 304.8 ✓
   morphine or opioid type drug with any other drug 304.7 ✓
croton-chloral 304.1 ✓
cyclobarbital 304.1 ✓
cyclobarbitone 304.1 ✓
dagga 304.3 ✓
Delvinal 304.1 ✓
Demerol 304.0 ✓

Dependence — *continued*

desocodeine 304.0 ✓
desomorphine 304.0 ✓
desoxyephedrine 304.4 ✓
DET 304.5 ✓
dexamphetamine 304.4 ✓
dexedrine 304.4 ✓
dextromethorphan 304.0 ✓
dextromoramide 304.0 ✓
dextronorpseudoephedrine 304.4 ✓
dextrorphan 304.0 ✓
diacetylmorphine 304.0 ✓
Dial 304.1 ✓
diallylbarbituric acid 304.1 ✓
diamorphine 304.0 ✓
diazepam 304.1 ✓
dibucaine 304.6 ✓
dichloroethane 304.6 ✓
diethyl barbituric acid 304.1 ✓
diethylsulfone-diethylmethane 304.1 ✓
difencloxazine 304.0 ✓
dihydrocodeine 304.0 ✓
dihydrocodeinone 304.0 ✓
dihydrohydroxycodeinone 304.0 ✓
dihydroisocodeine 304.0 ✓
dihydromorphine 304.0 ✓
dihydromorphinone 304.0 ✓
dihydroxcodeinone 304.0 ✓
Dilaudid 304.0 ✓
dimenhydrinate 304.6 ✓
dimethylmeperidine 304.0 ✓
dimethyltriptamine 304.5 ✓
Dionin 304.0 ✓
diphenoxylate 304.6 ✓
dipipanone 304.0 ✓
d-lysergic acid diethylamide 304.5 ✓
DMT 304.5 ✓
Dolophine 304.0 ✓
DOM 304.2 ✓
Doriden 304.1 ✓
dormiral 304.1 ✓
Dormison 304.1 ✓
Dromoran 304.0 ✓
drug NEC 304.9 ✓
   analgesic NEC 304.6 ✓
   combination (excluding morphine or opioid type drug) NEC 304.8 ✓
      morphine or opioid type drug with any other drug 304.7 ✓
   complicating pregnancy, childbirth, or puerperium 648.3 ✓
      affecting fetus or newborn 779.5
   hallucinogenic 304.5 ✓
   hypnotic NEC 304.1 ✓
   narcotic NEC 304.9 ✓
   psychostimulant NEC 304.4 ✓
   sedative 304.1 ✓
   soporific NEC 304.1 ✓
   specified type NEC 304.6 ✓
   suspected damage to fetus affecting management of pregnancy 655.5 ✓
   synthetic, with morphine-like effect 304.0 ✓
   tranquilizing 304.1 ✓
duboisine 304.6 ✓
ectylurea 304.1 ✓
Endocaine 304.6 ✓
Equanil 304.1 ✓
Eskabarb 304.1 ✓
ethchlorvynol 304.1 ✓
ether (ethyl) (liquid) (vapor) (vinyl) 304.6 ✓
ethidene 304.6 ✓
ethinamate 304.1 ✓
ethoheptazine 304.6 ✓
ethyl
   alcohol 303.9 ✓
   bromide 304.6 ✓
   carbamate 304.6 ✓
   chloride 304.6 ✓
   morphine 304.0 ✓
ethylene (gas) 304.6 ✓
   dichloride 304.6 ✓

Dependence — *continued*

ethylidene chloride 304.6 ✓
etilfen 304.1 ✓
etorphine 304.0 ✓
etoval 304.1 ✓
eucodal 304.0 ✓
euneryl 304.1 ✓
Evipal 304.1 ✓
Evipan 304.1 ✓
fentanyl 304.0 ✓
ganja 304.3 ✓
gardenal 304.1 ✓
gardenpanyl 304.1 ✓
gelsemine 304.6 ✓
Gelsemium 304.6 ✓
Gemonil 304.1 ✓
glucochloral 304.1 ✓
glue (airplane) (sniffing) 304.6 ✓
glutethimide 304.1 ✓
hallucinogenics 304.5 ✓
hashish 304.3 ✓
headache powder NEC 304.6 ✓
Heavenly Blue 304.5 ✓
hedonal 304.1 ✓
hemp 304.3 ✓
heptabarbital 304.1 ✓
Heptalgin 304.0 ✓
heptobarbitone 304.1 ✓
heroin 304.0 ✓
   salt (any) 304.0 ✓
hexethal (sodium) 304.1 ✓
hexobarbital 304.1 ✓
Hycodan 304.0 ✓
hydrocodone 304.0 ✓
hydromorphinol 304.0 ✓
hydromorphinone 304.0 ✓
hydromorphone 304.0 ✓
hydroxycodeine 304.0 ✓
hypnotic NEC 304.1 ✓
Indian hemp 304.3 ✓
inhalant 304.6 ✓
intranarcon 304.1 ✓
Kemithal 304.1 ✓
ketobemidone 304.0 ✓
khat 304.4 ✓
kif 304.3 ✓
Lactuca (virosa) extract 304.1 ✓
lactucarium 304.1 ✓
laudanum 304.0 ✓
Lebanese red 304.3 ✓
Leritine 304.0 ✓
lettuce opium 304.1 ✓
Levanil 304.1 ✓
Levo-Dromoran 304.0 ✓
levo-iso-methadone 304.0 ✓
levorphanol 304.0 ✓
Librium 304.1 ✓
Lomotil 304.6 ✓
Lotusate 304.1 ✓
LSD (-25) (and derivatives) 304.5 ✓
Luminal 304.1 ✓
lysergic acid 304.5 ✓
   amide 304.5 ✓
maconha 304.3 ✓
magic mushroom 304.5 ✓
marihuana 304.3 ✓
MDA (methylene dioxyamphetamine) 304.4 ✓
Mebaral 304.1 ✓
Medinal 304.1 ✓
Medomin 304.1 ✓
megahallucinogenics 304.5 ✓
meperidine 304.0 ✓
mephobarbital 304.1 ✓
meprobamate 304.1 ✓
mescaline 304.5 ✓
methadone 304.0 ✓
methamphetamine(s) 304.4 ✓
methaqualone 304.1 ✓
metharbital 304.1 ✓
methitural 304.1 ✓
methobarbitone 304.1 ✓
methohexital 304.1 ✓

Dependence — *continued*

methopholine 304.6 ✓
methyl
   alcohol 303.9 ✓
   bromide 304.6 ✓
   morphine 304.0 ✓
   sulfonal 304.1 ✓
methylaparafynol 304.1 ✓
methylated spirit 303.9 ✓
methylbutinol 304.6 ✓
methyldihydromorphinone 304.0 ✓
methylene
   chloride 304.6 ✓
   dichloride 304.6 ✓
   dioxyamphetamine (MDA) 304.4 ✓
methylphenidate 304.4 ✓
methyprylone 304.1 ✓
metopon 304.0 ✓
Miltown 304.1 ✓
morning glory seeds 304.5 ✓
morphinan(s) 304.0 ✓
morphine (sulfate) (sulfite) (type) (drugs classifiable to 965.00–965.09) 304.0 ✓
morphine or opioid type drug (drugs classifiable to 965.00–965.09) with any other drug 304.7 ✓
morphinol(s) 304.0 ✓
morphinon 304.0 ✓
morpholinylethylmorphine 304.0 ✓
mylomide 304.1 ✓
myristicin 304.5 ✓
narcotic (drug) NEC 304.9 ✓
nealbarbital 304.1 ✓
nealbarbitone 304.1 ✓
Nembutal 304.1 ✓
Neonal 304.1 ✓
Neraval 304.1 ✓
Neravan 304.1 ✓
neurobarb 304.1 ✓
nicotine 305.1
Nisentil 304.0 ✓
nitrous oxide 304.6 ✓
Noctec 304.1 ✓
Noludar 304.1 ✓
nonbarbiturate sedatives and tranquilizers with similar effect 304.1 ✓
noptil 304.1 ✓
normorphine 304.0 ✓
noscapine 304.0 ✓
Novocaine 304.6 ✓
Numorphan 304.0 ✓
nunol 304.1 ✓
Nupercaine 304.6 ✓
Oblivon 304.1 ✓
on
   aspirator V46.0
   hemodialysis V45.11
   hyperbaric chamber V46.8
   iron lung V46.11
   machine (enabling) V46.9
      specified type NEC V46.8
   peritoneal dialysis V45.11
   Possum (Patient-Operated-Selector-Mechanism) V46.8
   renal dialysis machine V45.11
   respirator [ventilator] V46.11
      encounter
         during
            mechanical failure V46.14
            power failure V46.12
         for weaning V46.13
   supplemental oxygen V46.2
   wheelchair V46.3
opiate 304.0 ✓
opioids 304.0 ✓
opioid type drug 304.0 ✓
   with any other drug 304.7 ✓
opium (alkaloids) (derivatives) (tincture) 304.0 ✓
ortal 304.1 ✓
Oxazepam 304.1 ✓
oxycodone 304.0 ✓
oxymorphone 304.0 ✓
Palfium 304.0 ✓

Dependence — continued
Panadol 304.6 ☑
pantopium 304.0 ☑
pantopon 304.0 ☑
papaverine 304.0 ☑
paracetamol 304.6 ☑
paracodin 304.0 ☑
paraldehyde 304.1 ☑
paregoric 304.0 ☑
Parzone 304.0 ☑
PCP (phencyclidine) 304.6 ☑
Pearly Gates 304.5 ☑
pentazocine 304.0 ☑
pentobarbital 304.1 ☑
pentobarbitone (sodium) 304.1 ☑
Pentothal 304.1 ☑
Percaine 304.6 ☑
Percodan 304.0 ☑
Perichlor 304.1 ☑
Pernocton 304.1 ☑
Pernoston 304.1 ☑
peronine 304.0 ☑
pethidine (hydrochloride) 304.0 ☑
petrichloral 304.1 ☑
peyote 304.5 ☑
Phanodron 304.1 ☑
phenacetin 304.6 ☑
phenadoxone 304.0 ☑
phenaglycodol 304.1 ☑
phenazocine 304.0 ☑
phencyclidine 304.6 ☑
phenmetrazine 304.4 ☑
phenobal 304.1 ☑
phenobarbital 304.1 ☑
phenobarbitone 304.1 ☑
phenomorphan 304.0 ☑
phenonyl 304.1 ☑
phenoperidine 304.0 ☑
pholcodine 304.0 ☑
piminodine 304.0 ☑
Pipadone 304.0 ☑
Pitkin's solution 304.6 ☑
Placidyl 304.1 ☑
polysubstance 304.8 ☑
Pontocaine 304.6 ☑
pot 304.3 ☑
potassium bromide 304.1 ☑
Preludin 304.4 ☑
Prinadol 304.0 ☑
probarbital 304.1 ☑
procaine 304.6 ☑
propanal 304.1 ☑
propoxyphene 304.6 ☑
psilocibin 304.5 ☑
psilocin 304.5 ☑
psilocybin 304.5 ☑
psilocyline 304.5 ☑
psilocyn 304.5 ☑
psychedelic agents 304.5 ☑
psychostimulant NEC 304.4 ☑
psychotomimetic agents 304.5 ☑
pyrahexyl 304.3 ☑
Pyramidon 304.6 ☑
quinalbarbitone 304.1 ☑
racemoramide 304.0 ☑
racemorphan 304.0 ☑
Rela 304.6 ☑
scopolamine 304.6 ☑
secobarbital 304.1 ☑
Seconal 304.1 ☑
sedative NEC 304.1 ☑
   nonbarbiturate with barbiturate effect
      304.1 ☑
Sedormid 304.1 ☑
sernyl 304.1 ☑
sodium bromide 304.1 ☑
Soma 304.6 ☑
Somnal 304.1 ☑
Somnos 304.1 ☑
Soneryl 304.1 ☑
soporific (drug) NEC 304.1 ☑
specified drug NEC 304.6 ☑
speed 304.4 ☑

Dependence — continued
spinocaine 304.6 ☑
Stovaine 304.6 ☑
STP 304.5 ☑
stramonium 304.6 ☑
Sulfonal 304.1 ☑
sulfonethylmethane 304.1 ☑
sulfonmethane 304.1 ☑
Surital 304.1 ☑
synthetic drug with morphine-like effect
   304.0 ☑
talbutal 304.1 ☑
tetracaine 304.6 ☑
tetrahydrocannabinol 304.3 ☑
tetronal 304.1 ☑
THC 304.3 ☑
thebacon 304.0 ☑
thebaine 304.0 ☑
thiamil 304.1 ☑
thiamylal 304.1 ☑
thiopental 304.1 ☑
tobacco 305.1
toluene, toluol 304.6 ☑
tranquilizer NEC 304.1 ☑
   nonbarbiturate with barbiturate effect
      304.1 ☑
tribromacetaldehyde 304.6 ☑
tribromethanol 304.6 ☑
tribromomethane 304.6 ☑
trichloroethanol 304.6 ☑
trichoroethyl phosphate 304.1 ☑
triclofos 304.1 ☑
Trional 304.1 ☑
Tuinal 304.1 ☑
Turkish Green 304.3 ☑
urethan(e) 304.6 ☑
Valium 304.1 ☑
Valmid 304.1 ☑
veganin 304.0 ☑
veramon 304.1 ☑
Veronal 304.1 ☑
versidyne 304.6 ☑
vinbarbital 304.1 ☑
vinbarbitone 304.1 ☑
vinyl bitone 304.1 ☑
vitamin B₆ 266.1
wine 303.9 ☑
Zactane 304.6 ☑
Dependency
   passive 301.6
   reactions 301.6
Depersonalization (episode, in neurotic state)
   (neurotic) (syndrome) 300.6
Depletion
   carbohydrates 271.9
   complement factor 279.8
   extracellular fluid 276.52
   plasma 276.52
   potassium 276.8
      nephropathy 588.89
   salt or sodium 276.1
      causing heat exhaustion or prostration
         992.4
      nephropathy 593.9
   volume 276.50
      extracellular fluid 276.52
      plasma 276.52
Deployment (military) ●
   personal history of V62.22 ●
   returned from V62.22 ●
   status V62.21 ●
Deposit
   argentous, cornea 371.16
   bone, in Boeck's sarcoid 135
   calcareous, calcium — see Calcification
   cholesterol
      retina 362.82
      skin 709.3
      vitreous (humor) 379.22
   conjunctival 372.56
   cornea, corneal NEC 371.10
      argentous 371.16
      in
         cystinosis 270.0 [371.15]

Deposit — continued
   cornea, corneal — continued
      in — continued
         mucopolysaccharidosis 277.5 [371.15]
   crystalline, vitreous (humor) 379.22
   hemosiderin, in old scars of cornea 371.11
   metallic, in lens 366.45
   skin 709.3
   teeth, tooth (betel) (black) (green) (materia
      alba) (orange) (soft) (tobacco) 523.6
   urate, in kidney (see also Disease, renal) 593.9
Depraved appetite 307.52
Depression 311
   acute (see also Psychosis, affective) 296.2 ☑
      recurrent episode 296.3 ☑
      single episode 296.2 ☑
   agitated (see also Psychosis, affective) 296.2 ☑
      recurrent episode 296.3 ☑
      single episode 296.2 ☑
   anaclitic 309.21
   anxiety 300.4
   arches 734
      congenital 754.61
   autogenous (see also Psychosis, affective)
      296.2 ☑
      recurrent episode 296.3 ☑
      single episode 296.2 ☑
   basal metabolic rate (BMR) 794.7
   bone marrow 289.9
   central nervous system 799.1
      newborn 779.2
   cerebral 331.9
      newborn 779.2
   cerebrovascular 437.8
      newborn 779.2
   chest wall 738.3
   endogenous (see also Psychosis, affective)
      296.2 ☑
      recurrent episode 296.3 ☑
      single episode 296.2 ☑
   functional activity 780.99
   hysterical 300.11
   involutional, climacteric, or menopausal (see
      also Psychosis, affective) 296.2 ☑
      recurrent episode 296.3 ☑
      single episode 296.2 ☑
   manic (see also Psychosis, affective) 296.80
   medullary 348.89   ▲
      newborn 779.2
   mental 300.4
   metatarsal heads — see Depression, arches
   metatarsus — see Depression, arches
   monopolar (see also Psychosis, affective)
      296.2 ☑
      recurrent episode 296.3 ☑
      single episode 296.2 ☑
   nervous 300.4
   neurotic 300.4
   nose 738.0
   postpartum 648.4 ☑
   psychogenic 300.4
      reactive 298.0
   psychoneurotic 300.4
   psychotic (see also Psychosis, affective)
      296.2 ☑
      reactive 298.0
      recurrent episode 296.3 ☑
      single episode 296.2 ☑
   reactive 300.4
      neurotic 300.4
      psychogenic 298.0
      psychoneurotic 300.4
      psychotic 298.0
   recurrent 296.3 ☑
   respiratory center 348.89   ▲
      newborn 770.89
   scapula 736.89
   senile 290.21
   situational (acute) (brief) 309.0
      prolonged 309.1
   skull 754.0
   sternum 738.3
   visual field 368.40
Depressive reaction — see also Reaction, depressive

Depressive reaction — see also Reaction,
   depressive — continued
   acute (transient) 309.0
      with anxiety 309.28
   prolonged 309.1
   situational (acute) 309.0
      prolonged 309.1
Deprivation
   cultural V62.4
   emotional V62.89
      affecting
         adult 995.82
         infant or child 995.51
   food 994.2
      specific substance NEC 269.8
   protein (familial) (kwashiorkor) 260
   sleep V69.4
   social V62.4
      affecting
         adult 995.82
         infant or child 995.51
   symptoms, syndrome
      alcohol 291.81
      drug 292.0
   vitamins (see also Deficiency, vitamin) 269.2
   water 994.3
de Quervain's
   disease (tendon sheath) 727.04
   syndrome 259.51
   thyroiditis (subacute granulomatous thyroidi-
      tis) 245.1
Derangement
   ankle (internal) 718.97
      current injury (see also Dislocation, ankle)
         837.0
      recurrent 718.37
   cartilage (articular) NEC (see also Disorder,
      cartilage, articular) 718.0 ☑
      knee 717.9
         recurrent 718.36
      recurrent 718.3 ☑
   collateral ligament (knee) (medial) (tibial)
      717.82
      current injury 844.1
         lateral (fibular) 844.0
      lateral (fibular) 717.81
         current injury 844.0
   cruciate ligament (knee) (posterior) 717.84
      anterior 717.83
         current injury 844.2
      current injury 844.2
   elbow (internal) 718.92
      current injury (see also Dislocation, elbow)
         832.00
      recurrent 718.32
   gastrointestinal 536.9
   heart — see Disease, heart
   hip (joint) (internal) (old) 718.95
      current injury (see also Dislocation, hip)
         835.00
      recurrent 718.35
   intervertebral disc — see Displacement, inter-
      vertebral disc
   joint (internal) 718.90
      ankle 718.97
      current injury (see also Dislocation, by site)
         knee, meniscus or cartilage (see also
             Tear, meniscus) 836.2
      elbow 718.92
      foot 718.97
      hand 718.94
      hip 718.95
      knee 717.9
      multiple sites 718.99
      pelvic region 718.95
      recurrent 718.30
         ankle 718.37
         elbow 718.32
         foot 718.37
         hand 718.34
         hip 718.35
         knee 718.36
         multiple sites 718.39
         pelvic region 718.35
         shoulder (region) 718.31
         specified site NEC 718.38

☑ Additional Digit Required — Refer to the Tabular List for Digit Selection   Subterms under main terms may continue to next column or page

2010 ICD-9-CM   ▶◀ Revised Text   ● New Line   ▲ Revised Code   October 2009 • Volume 2 — 73

Index

Derangement — Dermatitis

Derangement — continued
  joint — continued
    recurrent — continued
      temporomandibular (old) 524.69
        wrist 718.33
      shoulder (region) 718.91
      specified site NEC 718.98
      spine NEC 724.9
      temporomandibular 524.69
      wrist 718.93
  knee (cartilage) (internal) 717.9
    current injury (see also Tear, meniscus)
        836.2
    ligament 717.89
      capsular 717.85
      collateral — see Derangement, collateral ligament
      cruciate — see Derangement, cruciate ligament
      specified NEC 717.85
    recurrent 718.36
  low back NEC 724.9
  meniscus NEC (knee) 717.5
    current injury (see also Tear, meniscus)
        836.2
    lateral 717.40
      anterior horn 717.42
      posterior horn 717.43
      specified NEC 717.49
    medial 717.3
      anterior horn 717.1
      posterior horn 717.2
    recurrent 718.3 ☑
    site other than knee — see Disorder, cartilage, articular
  mental (see also Psychosis) 298.9
  rotator cuff (recurrent) (tear) 726.10
    current 840.4
  sacroiliac (old) 724.6
    current — see Dislocation, sacroiliac
  semilunar cartilage (knee) 717.5
    current injury 836.2
      lateral 836.1
      medial 836.0
    recurrent 718.3 ☑
  shoulder (internal) 718.91
    current injury (see also Dislocation, shoulder) 831.00
    recurrent 718.31
  spine (recurrent) NEC 724.9
    current — see Dislocation, spine
  temporomandibular (internal) (joint) (old)
      524.69
    current — see Dislocation, jaw
Dercum's disease or syndrome (adiposis dolorosa) 272.8
Derealization (neurotic) 300.6
Dermal — see condition
Dermaphytid — see Dermatophytosis
Dermatergosis — see Dermatitis
Dermatitis (allergic) (contact) (occupational)
      (venenata) 692.9
  ab igne 692.82
  acneiform 692.9
  actinic (due to sun) 692.70
    acute 692.72
    chronic NEC 692.74
    other than from sun NEC 692.82
  ambustionis
    due to
      burn or scald — see Burn, by site
      sunburn (see also Sunburn) 692.71
  amebic 006.6
  ammonia 691.0
  anaphylactoid NEC 692.9
  arsenical 692.4
  artefacta 698.4
    psychogenic 316 [698.4]
  asthmatic 691.8
  atopic (allergic) (intrinsic) 691.8
    psychogenic 316 [691.8]
  atrophicans 701.8
    diffusa 701.8
    maculosa 701.3
  autoimmune progesterone 279.49   ●
  berlock, berloque 692.72

Dermatitis — continued
  blastomycetic 116.0
  blister beetle 692.89
  Brucella NEC 023.9
  bullosa 694.9
    striata pratensis 692.6
  bullous 694.9
    mucosynechial, atrophic 694.60
      with ocular involvement 694.61
    seasonal 694.8
  calorica
    due to
      burn or scald — see Burn, by site
      cold 692.89
      sunburn (see also Sunburn) 692.71
  caterpillar 692.89
  cercarial 120.3
  combustionis
    due to
      burn or scald — see Burn, by site
      sunburn (see also Sunburn) 692.71
  congelationis 991.5
  contusiformis 695.2
  diabetic 250.8 ☑
  diaper 691.0
  diphtheritica 032.85
  due to
    acetone 692.2
    acids 692.4
    adhesive plaster 692.4
    alcohol (skin contact) (substances classifiable to 980.0–980.9) 692.4
      taken internally 693.8
    alkalis 692.4
    allergy NEC 692.9
    ammonia (household) (liquid) 692.4
    animal
      dander (cat) (dog) 692.84
      hair (cat) (dog) 692.84
    arnica 692.3
    arsenic 692.4
      taken internally 693.8
    blister beetle 692.89
    cantharides 692.3
    carbon disulphide 692.2
    caterpillar 692.89
    caustics 692.4
    cereal (ingested) 693.1
      contact with skin 692.5
    chemical(s) NEC 692.4
      internal 693.8
      irritant NEC 692.4
        taken internally 693.8
    chlorocompounds 692.2
    coffee (ingested) 693.1
      contact with skin 692.5
    cold weather 692.89
    cosmetics 692.81
    cyclohexanes 692.2
    dander, animal (cat) (dog) 692.84
    deodorant 692.81
    detergents 692.0
    dichromate 692.4
    drugs and medicinals (correct substance properly administered) (internal use) 693.0
      external (in contact with skin) 692.3
        wrong substance given or taken
            976.9
        specified substance — see Table of Drugs and Chemicals
      wrong substance given or taken 977.9
        specified substance — see Table of Drugs and Chemicals
    dyes 692.89
      hair 692.89
    epidermophytosis — see Dermatophytosis
    esters 692.2
    external irritant NEC 692.9
      specified agent NEC 692.89
    eye shadow 692.81
    fish (ingested) 693.1
      contact with skin 692.5
    flour (ingested) 693.1
      contact with skin 692.5

Dermatitis — continued
  due to — continued
    food (ingested) 693.1
      in contact with skin 692.5
    fruit (ingested) 693.1
      contact with skin 692.5
    fungicides 692.3
    furs 692.84
    glycols 692.2
    greases NEC 692.1
    hair, animal (cat) (dog) 692.84
    hair dyes 692.89
    hot
      objects and materials — see Burn, by site
      weather or places 692.89
    hydrocarbons 692.2
    infrared rays, except from sun 692.82
      solar NEC (see also Dermatitis, due to, sun) 692.70
    ingested substance 693.9
      drugs and medicinals (see also Dermatitis, due to, drugs and medicinals) 693.0
      food 693.1
      specified substance NEC 693.8
    ingestion or injection of chemical 693.8
      drug (correct substance properly administered) 693.0
      wrong substance given or taken 977.9
        specified substance — see Table of Drugs and Chemicals
    insecticides 692.4
    internal agent 693.9
      drugs and medicinals (see also Dermatitis, due to, drugs and medicinals) 693.0
      food (ingested) 693.1
        in contact with skin 692.5
      specified agent NEC 693.8
    iodine 692.3
    iodoform 692.3
    irradiation 692.82
    jewelry 692.83
    keratolytics 692.3
    ketones 692.2
    lacquer tree (Rhus verniciflua) 692.6
    light (sun) NEC (see also Dermatitis, due to, sun) 692.70
      other 692.82
    low temperature 692.89
    mascara 692.81
    meat (ingested) 693.1
      contact with skin 692.5
    mercury, mercurials 692.3
    metals 692.83
    milk (ingested) 693.1
      contact with skin 692.5
    Neomycin 692.3
    nylon 692.4
    oils NEC 692.1
    paint solvent 692.2
    pediculocides 692.3
    petroleum products (substances classifiable to 981) 692.4
    phenol 692.3
    photosensitiveness, photosensitivity (sun) 692.72
      other light 692.82
    plants NEC 692.6
    plasters, medicated (any) 692.3
    plastic 692.4
    poison
      ivy (Rhus toxicodendron) 692.6
      oak (Rhus diversiloba) 692.6
      plant or vine 692.6
      sumac (Rhus venenata) 692.6
      vine (Rhus radicans) 692.6
    preservatives 692.89
    primrose (primula) 692.6
    primula 692.6
    radiation 692.82
      sun NEC (see also Dermatitis, due to, sun) 692.70
      tanning bed 692.82
    radioactive substance 692.82

Dermatitis — continued
  due to — continued
    radium 692.82
    ragweed (Senecio jacobae) 692.6
    Rhus (diversiloba) (radicans) (toxicodendron) (venenata) (verniciflua) 692.6
    rubber 692.4
    scabicides 692.3
    Senecio jacobae 692.6
    solar radiation — see Dermatitis, due to, sun
    solvents (any) (substances classifiable to 982.0–982.8) 692.2
      chlorocompound group 692.2
      cyclohexane group 692.2
      ester group 692.2
      glycol group 692.2
      hydrocarbon group 692.2
      ketone group 692.2
      paint 692.2
    specified agent NEC 692.89
    sun 692.70
      acute 692.72
      chronic NEC 692.74
      specified NEC 692.79
    sunburn (see also Sunburn) 692.71
    sunshine NEC (see also Dermatitis, due to, sun) 692.70
    tanning bed 692.82
    tetrachlorethylene 692.2
    toluene 692.2
    topical medications 692.3
    turpentine 692.2
    ultraviolet rays, except from sun 692.82
      sun NEC (see also Dermatitis, due to, sun) 692.70
    vaccine or vaccination (correct substance properly administered) 693.0
      wrong substance given or taken
        bacterial vaccine 978.8
          specified — see Table of Drugs and Chemicals
        other vaccines NEC 979.9
          specified — see Table of Drugs and Chemicals
    varicose veins (see also Varicose, vein, inflamed or infected) 454.1
    x-rays 692.82
  dyshidrotic 705.81
  dysmenorrheica 625.8
  eczematoid NEC 692.9
    infectious 690.8
  eczematous NEC 692.9
  epidemica 695.89
  erysipelatosa 695.81
  escharotica — see Burn, by site
  exfoliativa, exfoliative 695.89
    generalized 695.89
    infantum 695.81
    neonatorum 695.81
  eyelid 373.31
    allergic 373.32
    contact 373.32
    eczematous 373.31
    herpes (zoster) 053.20
      simplex 054.41
    infective 373.5
      due to
        actinomycosis 039.3 [373.5]
        herpes
          simplex 054.41
          zoster 053.20
        impetigo 684 [373.5]
        leprosy (see also Leprosy)
            030.0 [373.4]
        lupus vulgaris (tuberculous) (see also Tuberculosis)
            017.0 ☑ [373.4]
        mycotic dermatitis (see also Dermatomycosis) 111.9 [373.5]
        vaccinia 051.02 [373.5]
          postvaccination 999.0 [373.5]
        yaws (see also Yaws) 102.9 [373.4]
  facta, factitia 698.4
    psychogenic 316 [698.4]
  ficta 698.4

☑ Additional Digit Required — Refer to the Tabular List for Digit Selection   ▽ Subterms under main terms may continue to next column or page

74 — Volume 2 • October 2009   ▶◀ Revised Text   ● New Line   ▲ Revised Code   **2010 ICD-9-CM**

Dermatitis — continued
ficta — continued
psychogenic 316 [698.4]
flexural 691.8
follicularis 704.8
friction 709.8
fungus 111.9
specified type NEC 111.8
gangrenosa, gangrenous (infantum) (see also Gangrene) 785.4
gestationis 646.8 ✓
gonococcal 098.89
gouty 274.89
harvest mite 133.8
heat 692.89
herpetiformis (bullous) (erythematous) (pustular) (vesicular) 694.0
juvenile 694.2
senile 694.5
hiemalis 692.89
hypostatic, hypostatica 454.1
with ulcer 454.2
impetiginous 684
infantile (acute) (chronic) (intertriginous) (intrinsic) (seborrheic) 690.12
infectiosa eczematoides 690.8
infectious (staphylococcal) (streptococcal) 686.9
eczematoid 690.8
infective eczematoid 690.8
Jacquet's (diaper dermatitis) 691.0
leptus 133.8
lichenified NEC 692.9
lichenoid, chronic 701.0
lichenoides purpurica pigmentosa 709.1
meadow 692.6
medicamentosa (correct substance properly administered) (internal use) (see also Dermatitis, due to, drugs or medicinals) 693.0
due to contact with skin 692.3
mite 133.8
multiformis 694.0
juvenile 694.2
senile 694.5
napkin 691.0
neuro 698.3
neurotica 694.0
nummular NEC 692.9
osteatosis, osteatotic 706.8
papillaris capillitii 706.1
pellagrous 265.2
perioral 695.3
perstans 696.1
photosensitivity (sun) 692.72
other light 692.82
pigmented purpuric lichenoid 709.1
polymorpha dolorosa 694.0
primary irritant 692.9
pruriginosa 694.0
pruritic NEC 692.9
psoriasiform nodularis 696.2
psychogenic 316
purulent 686.00
pustular contagious 051.2
pyococcal 686.00
pyocyaneus 686.09
pyogenica 686.00
radiation 692.82
repens 696.1
Ritter's (exfoliativa) 695.81
Schamberg's (progressive pigmentary dermatosis) 709.09
schistosome 120.3
seasonal bullous 694.8
seborrheic 690.10
infantile 690.12
sensitization NEC 692.9
septic (see also Septicemia) 686.00
gonococcal 098.89
solar, solare NEC (see also Dermatitis, due to, sun) 692.70
stasis 454.1
due to
postphlebitic syndrome 459.12
with ulcer 459.13

Dermatitis — continued
stasis — continued
due to — continued
varicose veins — see Varicose
ulcerated or with ulcer (varicose) 454.2
sunburn (see also Sunburn) 692.71
suppurative 686.00
traumatic NEC 709.8
trophoneurotica 694.0
ultraviolet, except from sun 692.82
due to sun NEC (see also Dermatitis, due to, sun) 692.82
varicose 454.1
with ulcer 454.2
vegetans 686.8
verrucosa 117.2
xerotic 706.8
Dermatoarthritis, lipoid 272.8 [713.0]
Dermatochalasia, dermatochalasis 374.87
Dermatofibroma (lenticulare) (M8832/0) — see also Neoplasm, skin, benign
protuberans (M8832/1) — see Neoplasm, skin, uncertain behavior
Dermatofibrosarcoma (protuberans) (M8832/3) — see Neoplasm, skin, malignant
Dermatographia 708.3
Dermatolysis (congenital) (exfoliativa) 757.39
acquired 701.8
eyelids 374.34
palpebrarum 374.34
senile 701.8
Dermatomegaly NEC 701.8
Dermatomucomyositis 710.3
Dermatomycosis 111.9
furfuracea 111.0
specified type NEC 111.8
Dermatomyositis (acute) (chronic) 710.3
Dermatoneuritis of children 985.0
Dermatophiliasis 134.1
Dermatophytide — see Dermatophytosis
Dermatophytosis (Epidermophyton) (infection) (microsporum) (tinea) (Trichophyton) 110.9
beard 110.0
body 110.5
deep seated 110.6
fingernails 110.1
foot 110.4
groin 110.3
hand 110.2
nail 110.1
perianal (area) 110.3
scalp 110.0
scrotal 110.8
specified site NEC 110.8
toenails 110.1
vulva 110.8
Dermatopolyneuritis 985.0
Dermatorrhexis 756.83
acquired 701.8
Dermatosclerosis — see also Scleroderma 710.1
localized 701.0
Dermatosis 709.9
Andrews' 686.8
atopic 691.8
Bowen's (M8081/2) — see Neoplasm, skin, in situ
bullous 694.9
specified type NEC 694.8
erythematosquamous 690.8
exfoliativa 695.89
factitial 698.4
gonococcal 098.89
herpetiformis 694.0
juvenile 694.2
senile 694.5
hysterical 300.11
linear IgA 694.8
menstrual NEC 709.8
neutrophilic, acute febrile 695.89
occupational (see also Dermatitis) 692.9
papulosa nigra 709.8
pigmentary NEC 709.00
progressive 709.09
Schamberg's 709.09
Siemens-Bloch 757.33
progressive pigmentary 709.09

Dermatosis — continued
psychogenic 316
pustular subcorneal 694.1
Schamberg's (progressive pigmentary) 709.09
senile NEC 709.3
specified NEC 702.8
Unna's (seborrheic dermatitis) 690.10
Dermographia 708.3
Dermographism 708.3
Dermoid (cyst) (M9084/0) — see also Neoplasm, by site, benign
with malignant transformation (M9084/3) 183.0
Dermopathy
infiltrative, with thyrotoxicosis 242.0 ✓
nephrogenic fibrosing 701.8
senile NEC 709.3
Dermophytosis — see Dermatophytosis
Descemet's membrane — see condition
Descemetocele 371.72
Descending — see condition
Descensus uteri (complete) (incomplete) (partial) (without vaginal wall prolapse) 618.1
with mention of vaginal wall prolapse — see Prolapse, uterovaginal
Desensitization to allergens V07.1
Desert
rheumatism 114.0
sore (see also Ulcer, skin) 707.9
Desertion (child) (newborn) 995.52
adult 995.84
Desmoid (extra-abdominal) (tumor) (M8821/1) — see also Neoplasm, connective tissue, uncertain behavior
abdominal (M8822/1) — see Neoplasm, connective tissue, uncertain behavior
Despondency 300.4
Desquamative dermatitis NEC 695.89
Destruction
articular facet (see also Derangement, joint) 718.9 ✓
vertebra 724.9
bone 733.90
syphilitic 095.5
joint (see also Derangement, joint) 718.9 ✓
sacroiliac 724.6
kidney 593.89
live fetus to facilitate birth NEC 763.89
ossicles (ear) 385.24
rectal sphincter 569.49
septum (nasal) 478.19
tuberculous NEC (see also Tuberculosis) 011.9 ✓
tympanic membrane 384.82
tympanum 385.89
vertebral disc — see Degeneration, intervertebral disc
Destructiveness — see also Disturbance, conduct 312.9
adjustment reaction 309.3
Detachment
cartilage (see also Sprain, by site)
knee — see Tear, meniscus
cervix, annular 622.8
complicating delivery 665.3 ✓
choroid (old) (postinfectional) (simple) (spontaneous) 363.70
hemorrhagic 363.72
serous 363.71
knee, medial meniscus (old) 717.3
current injury 836.0
ligament — see Sprain, by site
placenta (premature) — see Placenta, separation
retina (recent) 361.9
with retinal defect (rhegmatogenous) 361.00
giant tear 361.03
multiple 361.02
partial
with
giant tear 361.03
multiple defects 361.02
retinal dialysis (juvenile) 361.04
single defect 361.01
retinal dialysis (juvenile) 361.04

Detachment — continued
retina — continued
with retinal defect — continued
single 361.01
subtotal 361.05
total 361.05
delimited (old) (partial) 361.06
old
delimited 361.06
partial 361.06
total or subtotal 361.07
pigment epithelium (RPE) (serous) 362.42
exudative 362.42
hemorrhagic 362.43
rhegmatogenous (see also Detachment, retina, with retinal defect) 361.00
serous (without retinal defect) 361.2
specified type NEC 361.89
traction (with vitreoretinal organization) 361.81
vitreous humor 379.21
Detergent asthma 507.8
Deterioration
epileptic
with behavioral disturbance 345.9 ✓ [294.11]
without behavioral disturbance 345.9 ✓ [294.10]
heart, cardiac (see also Degeneration, myocardial) 429.1
mental (see also Psychosis) 298.9
myocardium, myocardial (see also Degeneration, myocardial) 429.1
senile (simple) 797
transplanted organ — see Complications, transplant, organ, by site
de Toni-Fanconi syndrome (cystinosis) 270.0
Deuteranomaly 368.52
Deuteranopia (anomalous trichromat) (complete) (incomplete) 368.52
Deutschländer's disease — see Fracture, foot
Development
abnormal, bone 756.9
arrested 783.40
bone 733.91
child 783.40
due to malnutrition (protein-calorie) 263.2
fetus or newborn 764.9 ✓
tracheal rings (congenital) 748.3
defective, congenital (see also Anomaly)
cauda equina 742.59
left ventricle 746.9
with atresia or hypoplasia of aortic orifice or valve with hypoplasia of ascending aorta 746.7
in hypoplastic left heart syndrome 746.7
delayed (see also Delay, development) 783.40
arithmetical skills 315.1
language (skills) 315.31
and speech due to hearing loss 315.34
expressive 315.31
mixed receptive-expressive 315.32
learning skill, specified NEC 315.2
mixed skills 315.5
motor coordination 315.4
reading 315.00
specified
learning skill NEC 315.2
type NEC, except learning 315.8
speech 315.39
and language due to hearing loss 315.34
associated with hyperkinesia 314.1
phonological 315.39
spelling 315.09
written expression 315.2
imperfect, congenital (see also Anomaly)
heart 746.9
lungs 748.60
improper (fetus or newborn) 764.9 ✓
incomplete (fetus or newborn) 764.9 ✓
affecting management of pregnancy 656.5 ✓
bronchial tree 748.3
organ or site not listed — see Hypoplasia

✓ Additional Digit Required — Refer to the Tabular List for Digit Selection   ▽ Subterms under main terms may continue to next column or page

2010 ICD-9-CM   ►◄ Revised Text   ● New Line   ▲ Revised Code   **Volume 2 — 75**

Dermatitis — Development

Development — *continued*
  incomplete — *continued*
    respiratory system 748.9
  sexual, precocious NEC 259.1
  tardy, mental (*see also* Retardation, mental)
    319
Developmental — *see* condition
Devergie's disease (pityriasis rubra pilaris) 696.4
Deviation
  conjugate (eye) 378.87
    palsy 378.81
    spasm, spastic 378.82
  esophagus 530.89
  eye, skew 378.87
  mandible, opening and closing 524.53
  midline (jaw) (teeth) 524.29
    specified site NEC — *see* Malposition
  occlusal plane 524.76
  organ or site, congenital NEC — *see* Malposition, congenital
  septum (acquired) (nasal) 470
    congenital 754.0
  sexual 302.9
    bestiality 302.1
    coprophilia 302.89
    ego-dystonic
      homosexuality 302.0
      lesbianism 302.0
    erotomania 302.89
      Clérambault's 297.8
    exhibitionism (sexual) 302.4
    fetishism 302.81
      transvestic 302.3
    frotteurism 302.89
    homosexuality, ego-dystonic 302.0
      pedophilic 302.2
    lesbianism, ego-dystonic 302.0
    masochism 302.83
    narcissism 302.89
    necrophilia 302.89
    nymphomania 302.89
    pederosis 302.2
    pedophilia 302.2
    sadism 302.84
    sadomasochism 302.84
    satyriasis 302.89
    specified type NEC 302.89
    transvestic fetishism 302.3
    transvestism 302.3
    voyeurism 302.82
    zoophilia (erotica) 302.1
  teeth, midline 524.29
  trachea 519.19
  ureter (congenital) 753.4
Devic's disease 341.0
Device
  cerebral ventricle (communicating) in situ V45.2
  contraceptive — *see* Contraceptive, device
  drainage, cerebrospinal fluid V45.2
Devil's
  grip 074.1
  pinches (purpura simplex) 287.2
Devitalized tooth 522.9
Devonshire colic 984.9
  specified type of lead — *see* Table of Drugs and Chemicals
Dextraposition, aorta 747.21
  with ventricular septal defect, pulmonary stenosis or atresia, and hypertrophy of right ventricle 745.2
  in tetralogy of Fallot 745.2
Dextratransposition, aorta 745.11
Dextrinosis, limit (debrancher enzyme deficiency) 271.0
Dextrocardia (corrected) (false) (isolated) (secondary) (true) 746.87
  with
    complete transposition of viscera 759.3
    situs inversus 759.3
Dextroversion, kidney (left) 753.3
Dhobie itch 110.3

Diabetes, diabetic (brittle) (congenital) (familial) (mellitus) (severe) (slight) (without complication) 250.0 ☑

Note — Use the following fifth-digit subclassification with category 250:

0   type II or unspecified type, not stated as uncontrolled

Fifth-digit 0 is for use for type II patients, even if the patient requires insulin

1   type I [juvenile type], not stated as uncontrolled

2   type II or unspecified type, uncontrolled

Fifth-digit 2 is for use for type II patients, even if the patient requires insulin

3   type I [juvenile type], uncontrolled

  with
    coma (with ketoacidosis) 250.3 ☑
      due to secondary diabetes 249.3 ☑
      hyperosmolar (nonketotic) 250.2 ☑
        due to secondary diabetes 249.2 ☑
    complication NEC 250.9 ☑
      due to secondary diabetes 249.9 ☑
      specified NEC 250.8 ☑
        due to secondary diabetes 249.8 ☑
    gangrene 250.7 ☑ *[785.4]*
      due to secondary diabetes 249.7 ☑ *[785.4]*
    hyperglycemia — code to Diabetes, by type, with 5th digit for not stated as uncontrolled
    hyperosmolarity 250.2 ☑
      due to secondary diabetes 249.2 ☑
    ketosis, ketoacidosis 250.1 ☑
      due to secondary diabetes 249.1 ☑
    osteomyelitis 250.8 ☑ *[731.8]*
      due to secondary diabetes 249.8 ☑ *[731.8]*
    specified manifestations NEC 250.8 ☑
      due to secondary diabetes 249.8 ☑
  acetonemia 250.1 ☑
    due to secondary diabetes 249.1 ☑
  acidosis 250.1 ☑
    due to secondary diabetes 249.1 ☑
  amyotrophy 250.6 ☑ *[353.5]*
    due to secondary diabetes 249.6 ☑ *[353.5]*
  angiopathy, peripheral 250.7 ☑ *[443.81]*
    due to secondary diabetes 249.7 ☑ *[443.81]*
  asymptomatic 790.29
  autonomic neuropathy (peripheral) 250.6 ☑ *[337.1]*
    due to secondary diabetes 249.6 ☑ *[337.1]*
  bone change 250.8 ☑ *[731.8]*
    due to secondary diabetes 249.8 ☑ *[731.8]*
  bronze, bronzed 275.0
  cataract 250.5 ☑ *[366.41]*
    due to secondary diabetes 249.5 ☑ *[366.41]*
  chemical induced — *see* Diabetes, secondary
  complicating pregnancy, childbirth, or puerperium 648.0 ☑
  coma (with ketoacidosis) 250.3 ☑
    due to secondary diabetes 249.3 ☑
    hyperglycemic 250.3 ☑
      due to secondary diabetes 249.3 ☑
    hyperosmolar (nonketotic) 250.2 ☑
      due to secondary diabetes 249.2 ☑
    hypoglycemic 250.3 ☑
      due to secondary diabetes 249.3 ☑
    insulin 250.3 ☑
      due to secondary diabetes 249.3 ☑
  complicating pregnancy, childbirth, or puerperium (maternal) (conditions classifiable to 249 and 250) 648.0 ☑
    affecting fetus or newborn 775.0
  complication NEC 250.9 ☑
    due to secondary diabetes 249.9 ☑
    specified NEC 250.8 ☑
      due to secondary diabetes 249.8 ☑

Diabetes, diabetic — *continued*
  dorsal sclerosis 250.6 ☑ *[340]*
    due to secondary diabetes 249.6 ☑ *[340]*
  drug-induced — *see also* Diabetes, secondary
    overdose or wrong substance given or taken — *see* Table of Drugs and Chemicals
  due to
    cystic fibrosis — *see* Diabetes, secondary
    infection — *see* Diabetes, secondary
  dwarfism-obesity syndrome 258.1
  gangrene 250.7 ☑ *[785.4]*
    due to secondary diabetes 249.7 ☑ *[785.4]*
  gastroparesis 250.6 ☑ *[536.3]*
    due to secondary diabetes 249.6 ☑ *[536.3]*
  gestational 648.8 ☑
    complicating pregnancy, childbirth, or puerperium 648.8 ☑
  glaucoma 250.5 ☑ *[365.44]*
    due to secondary diabetes 249.5 ☑ *[365.44]*
  glomerulosclerosis (intercapillary) 250.4 ☑ *[581.81]*
    due to secondary diabetes 249.4 ☑ *[581.81]*
  glycogenosis, secondary 250.8 ☑ *[259.8]*
    due to secondary diabetes 249.8 ☑ *[259.8]*
  hemochromatosis 275.0
  hyperosmolar coma 250.2 ☑
    due to secondary diabetes 249.2 ☑
  hyperosmolarity 250.2 ☑
    due to secondary diabetes 249.2 ☑
  hypertension-nephrosis syndrome 250.4 ☑ *[581.81]*
    due to secondary diabetes 249.4 ☑ *[581.81]*
  hypoglycemia 250.8 ☑
    due to secondary diabetes 249.8 ☑
  hypoglycemic shock 250.8 ☑
    due to secondary diabetes 249.8 ☑
  inadequately controlled — code to Diabetes, by type, with 5th digit for not stated as uncontrolled
  insipidus 253.5
    nephrogenic 588.1
    pituitary 253.5
    vasopressin-resistant 588.1
  intercapillary glomerulosclerosis 250.4 ☑ *[581.81]*
    due to secondary diabetes 249.4 ☑ *[581.81]*
  iritis 250.5 ☑ *[364.42]*
    due to secondary diabetes 249.5 ☑ *[364.42]*
  ketosis, ketoacidosis 250.1 ☑
    due to secondary diabetes 249.1 ☑
  Kimmelstiel (-Wilson) disease or syndrome (intercapillary glomerulosclerosis) 250.4 ☑ *[581.81]*
    due to secondary diabetes 249.4 ☑ *[581.81]*
  Lancereaux's (diabetes mellitus with marked emaciation) 250.8 ☑ *[261]*
    due to secondary diabetes 249.8 ☑ *[261]*
  latent (chemical) — *see* Diabetes, secondary
  complicating pregnancy, childbirth, or puerperium 648.0 ☑
  lipoidosis 250.8 ☑ *[272.7]*
    due to secondary diabetes 249.8 ☑ *[272.7]*
  macular edema 250.5 ☑ *[362.07]*
    due to secondary diabetes 249.5 ☑ *[362.07]*
  maternal
    with manifest disease in the infant 775.1
    affecting fetus or newborn 775.0
  microaneurysms, retinal 250.5 ☑ *[362.01]*
    due to secondary diabetes 249.5 ☑ *[362.01]*
  mononeuropathy 250.6 ☑ *[355.9]*
    due to secondary diabetes 249.6 ☑ *[355.9]*
  neonatal, transient 775.1
  nephropathy 250.4 ☑ *[583.81]*
    due to secondary diabetes 249.4 ☑ *[583.81]* ▲

Diabetes, diabetic — *continued*
  nephrosis (syndrome) 250.4 ☑ *[581.81]*
    due to secondary diabetes 249.4 ☑ *[581.81]*
  neuralgia 250.6 ☑ *[357.2]*
    due to secondary diabetes 249.6 ☑ *[357.2]*
  neuritis 250.6 ☑ *[357.2]*
    due to secondary diabetes 249.6 ☑ *[357.2]*
  neurogenic arthropathy 250.6 ☑ *[713.5]*
    due to secondary diabetes 249.6 ☑ *[713.5]*
  neuropathy 250.6 ☑ *[357.2]*
    autonomic (peripheral) 250.6 ☑ *[337.1]* ●
      due to secondary diabetes 249.6 ☑ *[337.1]* ●
    due to secondary diabetes 249.6 ☑ *[357.2]*
  nonclinical 790.29
  osteomyelitis 250.8 ☑ *[731.8]*
    due to secondary diabetes 249.8 ☑ *[731.8]*
  out of control — code to Diabetes, by type, with 5th digit for uncontrolled
  peripheral autonomic neuropathy 250.6 ☑ *[337.1]*
    due to secondary diabetes 249.6 ☑ *[337.1]*
  phosphate 275.3
  polyneuropathy 250.6 ☑ *[357.2]*
    due to secondary diabetes 249.6 ☑ *[357.2]*
  poorly controlled — code to Diabetes, by type, with 5th digit for not stated as uncontrolled
  renal (true) 271.4
  retinal
    edema 250.5 ☑ *[362.07]*
      due to secondary diabetes 249.5 ☑ *[362.07]*
    hemorrhage 250.5 ☑ *[362.01]*
      due to secondary diabetes 249.5 ☑ *[362.01]*
    microaneurysms 250.5 ☑ *[362.01]*
      due to secondary diabetes 249.5 ☑ *[362.01]*
  retinitis 250.5 ☑ *[362.01]*
    due to secondary diabetes 249.5 ☑ *[362.01]*
  retinopathy 250.5 ☑ *[362.01]*
    background 250.5 ☑ *[362.01]*
      due to secondary diabetes 249.5 ☑ *[362.01]*
    due to secondary diabetes 249.5 ☑ *[362.01]*
    nonproliferative 250.5 ☑ *[362.03]*
      due to secondary diabetes 249.5 ☑ *[362.03]*
    mild 250.5 ☑ *[362.04]*
      due to secondary diabetes 249.5 ☑ *[362.04]*
    moderate 250.5 ☑ *[362.05]*
      due to secondary diabetes 249.5 ☑ *[362.05]*
    severe 250.5 ☑ *[362.06]*
      due to secondary diabetes 249.5 ☑ *[362.06]*
    proliferative 250.5 ☑ *[362.02]*
      due to secondary diabetes 249.5 ☑ *[362.02]*
  secondary (chemical-induced) (due to chronic condition) (due to infection) (drug-induced) 249.0 ☑
    with
      coma (with ketoacidosis) 249.3 ☑
        hyperosmolar (nonketotic) 249.2 ☑
      complication NEC 249.9 ☑
        specified NEC 249.8 ☑
      gangrene 249.7 ☑ *[785.4]*
      hyperosmolarity 249.2 ☑
      ketosis, ketoacidosis 249.1 ☑
      osteomyelitis 249.8 ☑ *[731.8]*
      specified manifestations NEC 249.8 ☑
    acetonemia 249.1 ☑
    acidosis 249.1 ☑
    amyotrophy 249.6 ☑ *[353.5]*
    angiopathy, peripheral 249.7 ☑ *[443.81]*
    autonomic neuropathy (peripheral) 249.6 ☑ *[337.1]*

☑ Additional Digit Required — Refer to the Tabular List for Digit Selection   ⩊ Subterms under main terms may continue to next column or page

76 — Volume 2 • October 2009   ▶◀ Revised Text   ● New Line   ▲ Revised Code   2010 ICD-9-CM

Diabetes, diabetic — *continued*
　secondary — *continued*
　　bone change 249.8 ☑ [731.8]
　　cataract 249.5 ☑ [366.41]
　　coma (with ketoacidosis) 249.3 ☑
　　　hyperglycemic 249.3 ☑
　　　hyperosmolar (nonketotic) 249.2 ☑
　　　hypoglycemic 249.3 ☑
　　　insulin 249.3 ☑
　　complicating pregnancy, childbirth, or
　　　　puerperium (maternal) 648.0 ☑
　　　affecting fetus or newborn 775.0
　　complication NEC 249.9 ☑
　　　specified NEC 249.8 ☑
　　dorsal sclerosis 249.6 ☑ [340]
　　due to overdose or wrong substance given
　　　　or taken — *see* Table of Drugs and
　　　　Chemicals
　　gangrene 249.7 ☑ [785.4]
　　gastroparesis 249.6 ☑ [536.3]
　　glaucoma 249.5 ☑ [365.44]
　　glomerulosclerosis (intercapillary)
　　　　249.4 ☑ [581.81]
　　glycogenosis, secondary 249.8 ☑ [259.8]
　　hyperosmolar coma 249.2 ☑
　　hyperosmolarity 249.2 ☑
　　hypertension-nephrosis syndrome
　　　　249.4 ☑ [581.81]
　　hypoglycemia 249.8 ☑
　　hypoglycemic shock 249.8 ☑
　　intercapillary glomerulosclerosis
　　　　249.4 ☑ [581.81]
　　iritis 249.5 ☑ [364.42]
　　ketosis, ketoacidosis 249.1 ☑
　　Kimmelstiel (-Wilson) disease or syndrome
　　　　(intercapillary glomerulosclerosis)
　　　　249.4 ☑ [581.81]
　　Lancereaux's (diabetes mellitus with
　　　　marked emaciation) 249.8 ☑ [261]
　　lipoidosis 249.8 ☑ [272.7]
　　macular edema 249.5 ☑ [362.07]
　　maternal
　　　with manifest disease in the infant
　　　　775.1
　　　affecting fetus or newborn 775.0
　　microaneurysms, retinal 249.5 ☑ [362.01]
　　mononeuropathy 249.6 ☑ [355.9]
　　nephropathy 249.4 ☑ [583.81]　▲
　　nephrosis (syndrome) 249.4 ☑ [581.81]
　　neuralgia 249.6 ☑ [357.2]
　　neuritis 249.6 ☑ [357.2]
　　neurogenic arthropathy 249.6 ☑ [713.5]
　　neuropathy 249.6 ☑ [357.2]
　　　autonomic (peripheral)　　　　　●
　　　　249.6 ☑ [337.1]　　　　　　　●
　　osteomyelitis 249.8 ☑ [731.8]
　　peripheral autonomic neuropathy
　　　　249.6 ☑ [337.1]
　　polyneuropathy 249.6 ☑ [357.2]
　　retinal
　　　edema 249.5 ☑ [362.07]
　　　hemorrhage 249.5 ☑ [362.01]
　　　microaneurysms 249.5 ☑ [362.01]
　　retinitis 249.5 ☑ [362.01]
　　retinopathy 249.5 ☑ [362.01]
　　　background 249.5 ☑ [362.01]
　　　nonproliferative 249.5 ☑ [362.03]
　　　　mild 249.5 ☑ [362.04]
　　　　moderate 249.5 ☑ [362.05]
　　　　severe 249.5 ☑ [362.06]
　　　proliferative 249.5 ☑ [362.02]
　　ulcer (skin) 249.8 ☑ [707.9]
　　　lower extremity 249.8 ☑ [707.10]
　　　　ankle 249.8 ☑ [707.13]
　　　　calf 249.8 ☑ [707.12]
　　　　foot 249.8 ☑ [707.15]
　　　　heel 249.8 ☑ [707.14]
　　　　knee 249.8 ☑ [707.19]
　　　　specified site NEC 249.8 ☑ [707.19]
　　　　thigh 249.8 ☑ [707.11]
　　　　toes 249.8 ☑ [707.15]
　　　specified site NEC 249.8 ☑ [707.8]
　　xanthoma 249.8 ☑ [272.2]

Diabetes, diabetic — *continued*
　steroid induced — *see also* Diabetes, sec-
　　　ondary
　　overdose or wrong substance given or
　　　　taken 962.0
　stress 790.29
　subclinical 790.29
　subliminal 790.29
　sugar 250.0 ☑
　ulcer (skin) 250.8 ☑ [707.9]
　　due to secondary diabetes 249.8 ☑ [707.9]
　　lower extremity 250.8 ☑ [707.10]
　　　ankle 250.8 ☑ [707.13]
　　　　due to secondary diabetes
　　　　　249.8 ☑ [707.13]
　　　calf 250.8 ☑ [707.12]
　　　　due to secondary diabetes
　　　　　249.8 ☑ [707.12]
　　　due to secondary diabetes
　　　　249.8 ☑ [707.10]
　　　foot 250.8 ☑ [707.15]
　　　　due to secondary diabetes
　　　　　249.8 ☑ [707.15]
　　　heel 250.8 ☑ [707.14]
　　　　due to secondary diabetes
　　　　　249.8 ☑ [707.14]
　　　knee 250.8 ☑ [707.19]
　　　　due to secondary diabetes
　　　　　249.8 ☑ [707.19]
　　　specified site NEC 250.8 ☑ [707.19]
　　　　due to secondary diabetes
　　　　　249.8 ☑ [707.19]
　　　thigh 250.8 ☑ [707.11]
　　　　due to secondary diabetes
　　　　　249.8 ☑ [707.11]
　　　toes 250.8 ☑ [707.15]
　　　　due to secondary diabetes
　　　　　249.8 ☑ [707.15]
　　specified site NEC 250.8 ☑ [707.8]
　　　due to secondary diabetes
　　　　249.8 ☑ [707.8]
　　xanthoma 250.8 ☑ [272.2]
　　　due to secondary diabetes 249.8 ☑ [272.2]
Diacyclothrombopathia 287.1
Diagnosis deferred 799.9
Dialysis (intermittent) (treatment)
　anterior retinal (juvenile) (with detachment)
　　　361.04
　extracorporeal V56.0
　hemodialysis V56.0
　　status only V45.11
　peritoneal V56.8
　　status only V45.11
　renal V56.0
　　status only V45.11
　specified type NEC V56.8
Diamond-Blackfan anemia or syndrome
　　(congenital hypoplastic anemia) 284.01
Diamond-Gardener syndrome (autoerythrocyte
　　sensitization) 287.2
Diaper rash 691.0
Diaphoresis (excessive) NEC — *see* Hyper-
　　hidrosis) 780.8
Diaphragm — *see* condition
Diaphragmalgia 786.52
Diaphragmitis 519.4
Diaphyseal aclasis 756.4
Diaphysitis 733.99
Diarrhea, diarrheal (acute) (autumn) (bilious)
　　(bloody) (catarrhal) (choleraic) (chronic)
　　(gravis) (green) (infantile) (lienteric) (non-
　　infectious) (presumed noninfectious) (pu-
　　trefactive) (secondary) (sporadic) (summer)
　　(symptomatic) (thermic) 787.91
　achlorhydric 536.0
　allergic 558.3
　amebic (*see also* Amebiasis) 006.9
　　with abscess — *see* Abscess, amebic
　　acute 006.0
　　chronic 006.1
　　nondysenteric 006.2
　bacillary — *see* Dysentery, bacillary
　bacterial NEC 008.5
　balantidial 007.0
　bile salt-induced 579.8

Diarrhea, diarrheal — *continued*
　cachectic 787.91
　chilomastix 007.8
　choleriformis 001.1
　coccidial 007.2
　Cochin-China 579.1
　　anguilluliasis 127.2
　　psilosis 579.1
　Dientamoeba 007.8
　dietetic 787.91
　due to
　　achylia gastrica 536.8
　　Aerobacter aerogenes 008.2
　　Bacillus coli — *see* Enteritis, E. coli
　　bacteria NEC 008.5
　　bile salts 579.8
　　Capillaria
　　　hepatica 128.8
　　　philippinensis 127.5
　　Clostridium perfringens (C) (F) 008.46
　　Enterobacter aerogenes 008.2
　　enterococci 008.49
　　Escherichia coli — *see* Enteritis, E. coli
　　Giardia lamblia 007.1
　　Heterophyes heterophyes 121.6
　　irritating foods 787.91
　　Metagonimus yokogawai 121.5
　　Necator americanus 126.1
　　Paracolobactrum arizonae 008.1
　　Paracolon bacillus NEC 008.47
　　　Arizona 008.1
　　Proteus (bacillus) (mirabilis) (Morganii)
　　　008.3
　　Pseudomonas aeruginosa 008.42
　　S. japonicum 120.2
　　specified organism NEC 008.8
　　　bacterial 008.49
　　　viral NEC 008.69
　　Staphylococcus 008.41
　　Streptococcus 008.49
　　　anaerobic 008.46
　　Strongyloides stercoralis 127.2
　　Trichuris trichiuria 127.3
　　virus NEC (*see also* Enteritis, viral) 008.69
　dysenteric 009.2
　　due to specified organism NEC 008.8
　dyspeptic 787.91
　endemic 009.3
　　due to specified organism NEC 008.8
　epidemic 009.2
　　due to specified organism NEC 008.8
　fermentative 787.91
　flagellate 007.9
　Flexner's (ulcerative) 004.1
　functional 564.5
　　following gastrointestinal surgery 564.4
　　psychogenic 306.4
　giardial 007.1
　Giardia lamblia 007.1
　hill 579.1
　hyperperistalsis (nervous) 306.4
　infectious 009.2
　　due to specified organism NEC 008.8
　　presumed 009.3
　inflammatory 787.91
　　due to specified organism NEC 008.8
　malarial (*see also* Malaria) 084.6
　mite 133.8
　mycotic 117.9
　nervous 306.4
　neurogenic 564.5
　parenteral NEC 009.2
　postgastrectomy 564.4
　postvagotomy 564.4
　prostaglandin induced 579.8
　protozoal NEC 007.9
　psychogenic 306.4
　septic 009.2
　　due to specified organism NEC 008.8
　specified organism NEC 008.8
　　bacterial 008.49
　　viral NEC 008.69
　Staphylococcus 008.41
　Streptococcus 008.49
　　anaerobic 008.46
　toxic 558.2

Diarrhea, diarrheal — *continued*
　travelers' 009.2
　　due to specified organism NEC 008.8
　trichomonal 007.3
　tropical 579.1
　tuberculous 014.8 ☑
　ulcerative (chronic) (*see also* Colitis, ulcerative)
　　556.9
　viral (*see also* Enteritis, viral) 008.8
　zymotic NEC 009.2
Diastasis
　cranial bones 733.99
　　congenital 756.0
　joint (traumatic) — *see* Dislocation, by site
　muscle 728.84
　　congenital 756.89
　recti (abdomen) 728.84
　　complicating delivery 665.8 ☑
　　congenital 756.79
Diastema, teeth, tooth 524.30
Diastematomyelia 742.51
Diataxia, cerebral, infantile 343.0
Diathesis
　allergic V15.09
　bleeding (familial) 287.9
　cystine (familial) 270.0
　gouty 274.9
　hemorrhagic (familial) 287.9
　　newborn NEC 776.0
　oxalic 271.8
　scrofulous (*see also* Tuberculosis) 017.2 ☑
　spasmophilic (*see also* Tetany) 781.7
　ulcer 536.9
　uric acid 274.9
Diaz's disease or osteochondrosis 732.5
Dibothriocephaliasis 123.4
　larval 123.5
Dibothriocephalus (infection) (infestation) (latus)
　　123.4
　larval 123.5
Dicephalus 759.4
Dichotomy, teeth 520.2
Dichromat, dichromata (congenital) 368.59
Dichromatopsia (congenital) 368.59
Dichuchwa 104.0
Dicroceliasis 121.8
Didelphys, didelphic — *see also* Double uterus
　　752.2
Didymitis — *see also* Epididymitis 604.90
Died — *see also* Death
　without
　　medical attention (cause unknown) 798.9
　　sign of disease 798.2
Dientamoeba diarrhea 007.8
Dietary
　inadequacy or deficiency 269.9
　surveillance and counseling V65.3
Dietl's crisis 593.4
Dieulafoy lesion (hemorrhagic)
　of
　　duodenum 537.84
　　esophagus 530.82
　　intestine 569.86
　　stomach 537.84
Difficult
　birth, affecting fetus or newborn 763.9
　delivery NEC 669.9 ☑
Difficulty
　feeding 783.3
　　adult 783.3
　　breast 676.8 ☑
　　child 783.3
　　elderly 783.3
　　infant 783.3
　　newborn 779.31　　　　　　　　　　▲
　　nonorganic (infant) NEC 307.59
　mechanical, gastroduodenal stoma 537.89
　reading 315.00
　specific, spelling 315.09
　swallowing (*see also* Dysphagia) 787.20
　walking 719.7
Diffuse — *see* condition
Diffused ganglion 727.42
Di George's syndrome (thymic hypoplasia)
　　279.11
Digestive — *see* condition

☑ Additional Digit Required — Refer to the Tabular List for Digit Selection　　　　　　　▽ Subterms under main terms may continue to next column or page

2010 ICD-9-CM　　　　　▶◀ Revised Text　　　● New Line　　▲ Revised Code　　　　October 2009 • Volume 2 — 77

Di Guglielmo's disease or syndrome (M9841/3)
207.0 ☑

Diktyoma (M9051/3) — *see* Neoplasm, by site, malignant

Dilaceration, tooth 520.4

Dilatation
anus 564.89
 venule — *see* Hemorrhoids
aorta (focal) (general) (*see also* Aneurysm, aorta) 441.9
 congenital 747.29
 infectional 093.0
 ruptured 441.5
 syphilitic 093.0
appendix (cystic) 543.9
artery 447.8
bile duct (common) (cystic) (congenital) 751.69
 acquired 576.8
bladder (sphincter) 596.8
 congenital 753.8
 in pregnancy or childbirth 654.4 ☑
 causing obstructed labor 660.2 ☑
 affecting fetus or newborn 763.1
blood vessel 459.89
bronchus, bronchi 494.0
 with acute exacerbation 494.1
calyx (due to obstruction) 593.89
capillaries 448.9
cardiac (acute) (chronic) (*see also* Hypertrophy, cardiac) 429.3
 congenital 746.89
 valve NEC 746.89
 pulmonary 746.09
 hypertensive (*see also* Hypertension, heart) 402.90
cavum septi pellucidi 742.4
cecum 564.89
 psychogenic 306.4
cervix (uteri) (*see also* Incompetency, cervix)
 incomplete, poor, slow
 affecting fetus or newborn 763.7
 complicating delivery 661.0 ☑
 affecting fetus or newborn 763.7
colon 564.7
 congenital 751.3
 due to mechanical obstruction 560.89
 psychogenic 306.4
common bile duct (congenital) 751.69
 acquired 576.8
 with calculus, choledocholithiasis, or stones — *see* Choledocholithiasis
cystic duct 751.69
 acquired (any bile duct) 575.8
duct, mammary 610.4
duodenum 564.89
esophagus 530.89
 congenital 750.4
 due to
 achalasia 530.0
 cardiospasm 530.0
Eustachian tube, congenital 744.24
fontanel 756.0
gallbladder 575.8
 congenital 751.69
gastric 536.8
 acute 536.1
 psychogenic 306.4
heart (acute) (chronic) (*see also* Hypertrophy, cardiac) 429.3
 congenital 746.89
 hypertensive (*see also* Hypertension, heart) 402.90
 valve (*see also* Endocarditis)
 congenital 746.89
ileum 564.89
 psychogenic 306.4
inguinal rings — *see* Hernia, inguinal
jejunum 564.89
 psychogenic 306.4
kidney (calyx) (collecting structures) (cystic) (parenchyma) (pelvis) 593.89
lacrimal passages 375.69
lymphatic vessel 457.1
mammary duct 610.4

Dilatation — *continued*
Meckel's diverticulum (congenital) 751.0
meningeal vessels, congenital 742.8
myocardium (acute) (chronic) (*see also* Hypertrophy, cardiac) 429.3
organ or site, congenital NEC — *see* Distortion
pancreatic duct 577.8
pelvis, kidney 593.89
pericardium — *see* Pericarditis
pharynx 478.29
prostate 602.8
pulmonary
 artery (idiopathic) 417.8
 congenital 747.3
 valve, congenital 746.09
pupil 379.43
rectum 564.89
renal 593.89
saccule vestibularis, congenital 744.05
salivary gland (duct) 527.8
sphincter ani 564.89
stomach 536.8
 acute 536.1
 psychogenic 306.4
submaxillary duct 527.8
trachea, congenital 748.3
ureter (idiopathic) 593.89
 congenital 753.20
 due to obstruction 593.5
urethra (acquired) 599.84
vasomotor 443.9
vein 459.89
ventricular, ventricle (acute) (chronic) (*see also* Hypertrophy, cardiac) 429.3
 cerebral, congenital 742.4
 hypertensive (*see also* Hypertension, heart) 402.90
venule 459.89
 anus — *see* Hemorrhoids
vesical orifice 596.8

Dilated, dilation — *see* Dilatation

Diminished
hearing (acuity) (*see also* Deafness) 389.9
pulse pressure 785.9
vision NEC 369.9
vital capacity 794.2

Diminuta taenia 123.6

Diminution, sense or sensation (cold) (heat) (tactile) (vibratory) — *see also* Disturbance, sensation 782.0

Dimitri-Sturge-Weber disease (encephalocutaneous angiomatosis) 759.6

Dimple
parasacral 685.1
 with abscess 685.0
pilonidal 685.1
 with abscess 685.0
postanal 685.1
 with abscess 685.0

Dioctophyma renale (infection) (infestation) 128.8

Dipetalonemiasis 125.4

Diphallus 752.69

Diphtheria, diphtheritic (gangrenous) (hemorrhagic) 032.9
carrier (suspected) of V02.4
cutaneous 032.85
cystitis 032.84
faucial 032.0
infection of wound 032.85
inoculation (anti) (not sick) V03.5
laryngeal 032.3
myocarditis 032.82
nasal anterior 032.2
nasopharyngeal 032.1
neurological complication 032.89
peritonitis 032.83
specified site NEC 032.89

Diphyllobothriasis (intestine) 123.4
larval 123.5

Diplacusis 388.41

Diplegia (upper limbs) 344.2
brain or cerebral 437.8
 congenital 343.0
facial 351.0
 congenital 352.6

Diplegia — *continued*
infantile or congenital (cerebral) (spastic) (spinal) 343.0
lower limbs 344.1
syphilitic, congenital 090.49

Diplococcus, diplococcal — *see* condition

Diplomyelia 742.59

Diplopia 368.2
refractive 368.15

Dipsomania — *see also* Alcoholism 303.9 ☑
with psychosis (*see also* Psychosis, alcoholic) 291.9

Dipylidiasis 123.8
intestine 123.8

Direction, teeth, abnormal 524.30

Dirt-eating child 307.52

Disability
heart — *see* Disease, heart
learning NEC 315.2
special spelling 315.09

Disarticulation — *see also* Derangement, joint 718.9 ☑
meaning
 amputation
 status — *see* Absence, by site
 traumatic — *see* Amputation, traumatic
 dislocation, traumatic or congenital — *see* Dislocation

Disaster, cerebrovascular — *see also* Disease, cerebrovascular, acute 436

Discharge
anal NEC 787.99
breast (female) (male) 611.79
conjunctiva 372.89
continued locomotor idiopathic (*see also* Epilepsy) 345.5 ☑
diencephalic autonomic idiopathic (*see also* Epilepsy) 345.5 ☑
ear 388.60
 blood 388.69
 cerebrospinal fluid 388.61
excessive urine 788.42
eye 379.93
nasal 478.19
nipple 611.79
patterned motor idiopathic (*see also* Epilepsy) 345.5 ☑
penile 788.7
postnasal — *see* Sinusitis
sinus, from mediastinum 510.0
umbilicus 789.9
urethral 788.7
 bloody 599.84
vaginal 623.5

Discitis 722.90
cervical, cervicothoracic 722.91
lumbar, lumbosacral 722.93
thoracic, thoracolumbar 722.92

Discogenic syndrome — *see* Displacement, intervertebral disc

Discoid
kidney 753.3
meniscus, congenital 717.5
semilunar cartilage 717.5

Discoloration
mouth 528.9
nails 703.8
teeth 521.7
 due to
 drugs 521.7
 metals (copper) (silver) 521.7
 pulpal bleeding 521.7
 during formation 520.8
 extrinsic 523.6
 intrinsic posteruptive 521.7

Discomfort
chest 786.59
visual 368.13

Discomycosis — *see* Actinomycosis

Discontinuity, ossicles, ossicular chain 385.23

Discrepancy
centric occlusion
 maximum intercuspation 524.55
 of teeth 524.55
leg length (acquired) 736.81

Discrepancy — *continued*
leg length — *continued*
 congenital 755.30
 uterine size-date 649.6 ☑

Discrimination
political V62.4
racial V62.4
religious V62.4
sex V62.4

Disease, diseased — *see also* Syndrome
Abrami's (acquired hemolytic jaundice) 283.9
absorbent system 459.89
accumulation — *see* Thesaurismosis
acid-peptic 536.8
Acosta's 993.2
Adams-Stokes (-Morgagni) (syncope with heart block) 426.9
Addison's (bronze) (primary adrenal insufficiency) 255.41
 anemia (pernicious) 281.0
 tuberculous (*see also* Tuberculosis) 017.6 ☑
Addison-Gull — *see* Xanthoma
adenoids (and tonsils) (chronic) 474.9
adrenal (gland) (capsule) (cortex) 255.9
 hyperfunction 255.3
 hypofunction 255.41
 specified type NEC 255.8
ainhum (dactylolysis spontanea) 136.0
akamushi (scrub typhus) 081.2
Akureyri (epidemic neuromyasthenia) 049.8
Albarrán's (colibacilluria) 791.9
Albers-Schönberg's (marble bones) 756.52
Albert's 726.71
Albright (-Martin) (-Bantam) 275.49
Alibert's (mycosis fungoides) (M9700/3) 202.1 ☑
Alibert-Bazin (M9700/3) 202.1 ☑
alimentary canal 569.9
alligator skin (ichthyosis congenita) 757.1
 acquired 701.1
Almeida's (Brazilian blastomycosis) 116.1
Alpers' 330.8
alpine 993.2
altitude 993.2
alveoli, teeth 525.9
Alzheimer's — *see* Alzheimer's
amyloid (any site) 277.30
anarthritic rheumatoid 446.5
Anders' (adiposis tuberosa simplex) 272.8
Andersen's (glycogenosis IV) 271.0
Anderson's (angiokeratoma corporis diffusum) 272.7
Andes 993.2
Andrews' (bacterid) 686.8
angiospastic, angiospasmodic 443.9
 cerebral 435.9
 with transient neurologic deficit 435.9
 vein 459.89
anterior
 chamber 364.9
 horn cell 335.9
 specified type NEC 335.8
antral (chronic) 473.0
 acute 461.0
anus NEC 569.49
aorta (nonsyphilitic) 447.9
 syphilitic NEC 093.89
aortic (heart) (valve) (*see also* Endocarditis, aortic) 424.1
apollo 077.4
aponeurosis 726.90
appendix 543.9
aqueous (chamber) 364.9
arc-welders' lung 503
Armenian 277.31
Arnold-Chiari (*see also* Spina bifida) 741.0 ☑
arterial 447.9
 occlusive (*see also* Occlusion, by site) 444.22
 with embolus or thrombus — *see* Occlusion, by site
 due to stricture or stenosis 447.1
 specified type NEC 447.8
arteriocardiorenal (*see also* Hypertension, cardiorenal) 404.90

Disease, diseased — *see also* Syndrome — *continued*

arteriolar (generalized) (obliterative) 447.9
  specified type NEC 447.8
arteriorenal — *see* Hypertension, kidney
arteriosclerotic (*see also* Arteriosclerosis)
  cardiovascular 429.2
  coronary — *see* Arteriosclerosis, coronary
  heart — *see* Arteriosclerosis, coronary
  vascular — *see* Arteriosclerosis
  artery 447.9
    cerebral 437.9
    coronary — *see* Arteriosclerosis, coronary
    specified type NEC 447.8
arthropod-borne NEC 088.9
  specified type NEC 088.89
Asboe-Hansen's (incontinentia pigmenti) 757.33
atticoantral, chronic (with posterior or superior marginal perforation of ear drum) 382.2
auditory canal, ear 380.9
Aujeszky's 078.89
auricle, ear NEC 380.30
Australian X 062.4
autoimmune NEC 279.49 ▲
  hemolytic (cold type) (warm type) 283.0
  parathyroid 252.1
  thyroid 245.2
aviators' (*see also* Effect, adverse, high altitude) 993.2
ax(e)-grinders' 502
Ayala's 756.89
Ayerza's (pulmonary artery sclerosis with pulmonary hypertension) 416.0
Azorean (of the nervous system) 334.8
Babington's (familial hemorrhagic telangiectasia) 448.0
back bone NEC 733.90
bacterial NEC 040.89
  zoonotic NEC 027.9
  specified type NEC 027.8
Baehr-Schiffrin (thrombotic thrombocytopenic purpura) 446.6
Baelz's (cheilitis glandularis apostematosa) 528.5
Baerensprung's (eczema marginatum) 110.3
Balfour's (chloroma) 205.3 ☑
balloon (*see also* Effect, adverse, high altitude) 993.2
Baló's 341.1
Bamberger (-Marie) (hypertrophic pulmonary osteoarthropathy) 731.2
Bang's (Brucella abortus) 023.1
Bannister's 995.1
Banti's (with cirrhosis) (with portal hypertension) — *see* Cirrhosis, liver
Barcoo (*see also* Ulcer, skin) 707.9
barium lung 503
Barlow (-Möller) (infantile scurvy) 267
barometer makers' 985.0
Barraquer (-Simons) (progressive lipodystrophy) 272.6
basal ganglia 333.90
  degenerative NEC 333.0
  specified NEC 333.89
Basedow's (exophthalmic goiter) 242.0 ☑
basement membrane NEC 583.89
  with
    pulmonary hemorrhage (Goodpasture's syndrome) 446.21 [583.81]
Bateman's 078.0
  purpura (senile) 287.2
Batten's 330.1 [362.71]
Batten-Mayou (retina) 330.1 [362.71]
Batten-Steinert 359.21
Battey 031.0
Baumgarten-Cruveilhier (cirrhosis of liver) 571.5
bauxite-workers' 503
Bayle's (dementia paralytica) 094.1
Bazin's (primary) (*see also* Tuberculosis) 017.1 ☑
Beard's (neurasthenia) 300.5
Beau's (*see also* Degeneration, myocardial) 429.1

Disease, diseased — *see also* Syndrome — *continued*

Bechterew's (ankylosing spondylitis) 720.0
Becker's
  idiopathic mural endomyocardial disease 425.2
  myotonia congenita, recessive form 359.22
Begbie's (exophthalmic goiter) 242.0 ☑
Behr's 362.50
Beigel's (white piedra) 111.2
Bekhterev's (ankylosing spondylitis) 720.0
Bell's (*see also* Psychosis, affective) 296.0 ☑
Bennett's (leukemia) 208.9 ☑
Benson's 379.22
Bergeron's (hysteroepilepsy) 300.11
Berlin's 921.3
Bernard-Soulier (thrombopathy) 287.1
Bernhardt (-Roth) 355.1
beryllium 503
Besnier-Boeck (-Schaumann) (sarcoidosis) 135
Best's 362.76
Beurmann's (sporotrichosis) 117.1
Bielschowsky (-Jansky) 330.1
Biermer's (pernicious anemia) 281.0
Biett's (discoid lupus erythematosus) 695.4
bile duct (*see also* Disease, biliary) 576.9
biliary (duct) (tract) 576.9
  with calculus, choledocholithiasis, or stones — *see* Choledocholithiasis
Billroth's (meningocele) (*see also* Spina bifida) 741.9 ☑
Binswanger's 290.12
Bird's (oxaluria) 271.8
bird fanciers' 495.2
black lung 500
bladder 596.9
  specified NEC 596.8
bleeder's 286.0
Bloch-Sulzberger (incontinentia pigmenti) 757.33
Blocq's (astasia-abasia) 307.9
blood (-forming organs) 289.9
  specified NEC 289.89
  vessel 459.9
Bloodgood's 610.1
Blount's (tibia vara) 732.4
blue 746.9
Bodechtel-Guttmann (subacute sclerosing panencephalitis) 046.2
Boeck's (sarcoidosis) 135
bone 733.90
  fibrocystic NEC 733.29
    jaw 526.2
  marrow 289.9
  Paget's (osteitis deformans) 731.0
  specified type NEC 733.99
  von Recklinghausen's (osteitis fibrosa cystica) 252.01
Bonfils' — *see* Disease, Hodgkin's
Borna 062.9
Bornholm (epidemic pleurodynia) 074.1
Bostock's (*see also* Fever, hay) 477.9
Bouchard's (myopathic dilatation of the stomach) 536.1
Bouillaud's (rheumatic heart disease) 391.9
Bourneville (-Brissaud) (tuberous sclerosis) 759.5
Bouveret (-Hoffmann) (paroxysmal tachycardia) 427.2
bowel 569.9
  functional 564.9
    psychogenic 306.4
Bowen's (M8081/2) — *see* Neoplasm, skin, in situ
Bozzolo's (multiple myeloma) (M9730/3) 203.0 ☑
Bradley's (epidemic vomiting) 078.82
Brailsford's 732.3
  radius, head 732.3
  tarsal, scaphoid 732.5
Brailsford-Morquio (mucopolysaccharidosis IV) 277.5
brain 348.9
  Alzheimer's 331.0
    with dementia — *see* Alzheimer's, dementia

Disease, diseased — *see also* Syndrome — *continued*

brain — *continued*
  arterial, artery 437.9
  arteriosclerotic 437.0
  congenital 742.9
  degenerative — *see* Degeneration, brain
  inflammatory (*see also* Encephalitis)
    late effect — *see* category 326
  organic 348.9
    arteriosclerotic 437.0
  parasitic NEC 123.9
  Pick's 331.11
    with dementia
      with behavioral disturbance 331.11 [294.11]
      without behavioral disturbance 331.11 [294.10]
  senile 331.2
braziers' 985.8
breast 611.9
  cystic (chronic) 610.1
  fibrocystic 610.1
  inflammatory 611.0
  Paget's (M8540/3) 174.0
  puerperal, postpartum NEC 676.3 ☑
  specified NEC 611.89
Breda's (*see also* Yaws) 102.9
Breisky's (kraurosis vulvae) 624.09
Bretonneau's (diphtheritic malignant angina) 032.0
Bright's (*see also* Nephritis) 583.9
  arteriosclerotic (*see also* Hypertension, kidney) 403.90
Brill's (recrudescent typhus) 081.1
  flea-borne 081.0
  louse-borne 081.1
Brill-Symmers (follicular lymphoma) (M9690/3) 202.0 ☑
Brill-Zinsser (recrudescent typhus) 081.1
Brinton's (leather bottle stomach) (M8142/3) 151.9
Brion-Kayser (*see also* Fever, paratyphoid) 002.9
broad
  beta 272.2
  ligament, noninflammatory 620.9
    specified NEC 620.8
Brocq's 691.8
  meaning
    atopic (diffuse) neurodermatitis 691.8
    dermatitis herpetiformis 694.0
    lichen simplex chronicus 698.3
    parapsoriasis 696.2
    prurigo 698.2
Brocq-Duhring (dermatitis herpetiformis) 694.0
Brodie's (joint) (*see also* Osteomyelitis) 730.1 ☑
bronchi 519.19
bronchopulmonary 519.19
bronze (Addison's) 255.41
  tuberculous (*see also* Tuberculosis) 017.6 ☑
Brown-Séquard 344.89
Bruck's 733.99
Bruck-de Lange (Amsterdam dwarf, mental retardation and brachycephaly) 759.89
Bruhl's (splenic anemia with fever) 285.8
Bruton's (X-linked agammaglobulinemia) 279.04
buccal cavity 528.9
Buchanan's (juvenile osteochondrosis, iliac crest) 732.1
Buchman's (osteochondrosis juvenile) 732.1
Budgerigar-Fanciers' 495.2
Büdinger-Ludloff-Läwen 717.89
Buerger's (thromboangiitis obliterans) 443.1
Bürger-Grütz (essential familial hyperlipemia) 272.3
Burns' (lower ulna) 732.3
bursa 727.9
Bury's (erythema elevatum diutinum) 695.89
Buschke's 710.1
Busquet's (*see also* Osteomyelitis) 730.1 ☑
Busse-Buschke (cryptococcosis) 117.5
C_2 (*see also* Alcoholism) 303.9 ☑
Caffey's (infantile cortical hyperostosis) 756.59

Disease, diseased — *see also* Syndrome — *continued*

caisson 993.3
calculus 592.9
California 114.0
Calvé (-Perthes) (osteochondrosis, femoral capital) 732.1
Camurati-Engelmann (diaphyseal sclerosis) 756.59
Canavan's 330.0
capillaries 448.9
Carapata 087.1
cardiac — *see* Disease, heart
cardiopulmonary, chronic 416.9
cardiorenal (arteriosclerotic) (hepatic) (hypertensive) (vascular) (*see also* Hypertension, cardiorenal) 404.90
cardiovascular (arteriosclerotic) 429.2
  congenital 746.9
  hypertensive (*see also* Hypertension, heart) 402.90
    benign 402.10
    malignant 402.00
  renal (*see also* Hypertension, cardiorenal) 404.90
  syphilitic (asymptomatic) 093.9
carotid gland 259.8
Carrión's (Bartonellosis) 088.0
cartilage NEC 733.90
  specified NEC 733.99
Castellani's 104.8
cat-scratch 078.3
Cavare's (familial periodic paralysis) 359.3
Cazenave's (pemphigus) 694.4
cecum 569.9
celiac (adult) 579.0
  infantile 579.0
cellular tissue NEC 709.9
central core 359.0
cerebellar, cerebellum — *see* Disease, brain
cerebral (*see also* Disease, brain) 348.9
  arterial, artery 437.9
  degenerative — *see* Degeneration, brain
cerebrospinal 349.9
cerebrovascular NEC 437.9
  acute 436
    embolic — *see* Embolism, brain
    late effect — *see* Late effect(s) (of) cerebrovascular disease
    puerperal, postpartum, childbirth 674.0 ☑
    thrombotic — *see* Thrombosis, brain
  arteriosclerotic 437.0
  embolic — *see* Embolism, brain
  ischemic, generalized NEC 437.1
  late effect — *see* Late effect(s) (of) cerebrovascular disease
  occlusive 437.1
  puerperal, postpartum, childbirth 674.0 ☑
  specified type NEC 437.8
  thrombotic — *see* Thrombosis, brain
ceroid storage 272.7
cervix (uteri)
  inflammatory 616.0
  noninflammatory 622.9
    specified NEC 622.8
Chabert's 022.9
Chagas' (*see also* Trypanosomiasis, American) 086.2
Chandler's (osteochondritis dissecans, hip) 732.7
Charcot-Marie-Tooth 356.1
Charcôt's (joint) 094.0 [713.5]
  spinal cord 094.0
Charlouis' (*see also* Yaws) 102.9
Cheadle (-Möller) (-Barlow) (infantile scurvy) 267
Chédiak-Steinbrinck (-Higashi) (congenital gigantism of peroxidase granules) 288.2
cheek, inner 528.9
chest 519.9
Chiari's (hepatic vein thrombosis) 453.0
Chicago (North American blastomycosis) 116.0
chignon (white piedra) 111.2
chigoe, chigo (jigger) 134.1
childhood granulomatous 288.1

☑ Additional Digit Required — Refer to the Tabular List for Digit Selection

Subterms under main terms may continue to next column or page

Disease, diseased — *see also* Syndrome — *continued*

Chinese liver fluke 121.1
chlamydial NEC 078.88
cholecystic (*see also* Disease, gallbladder) 575.9
choroid 363.9
  degenerative (*see also* Degeneration, choroid) 363.40
  hereditary (*see also* Dystrophy, choroid) 363.50
  specified type NEC 363.8
Christian's (chronic histiocytosis X) 277.89
Christian-Weber (nodular nonsuppurative panniculitis) 729.30
Christmas 286.1
ciliary body 364.9
  specified NEC 364.89
circulatory (system) NEC 459.9
  chronic, maternal, affecting fetus or newborn 760.3
  specified NEC 459.89
  syphilitic 093.9
    congenital 090.5
Civatte's (poikiloderma) 709.09
climacteric 627.2
  male 608.89
coagulation factor deficiency (congenital) (*see also* Defect, coagulation) 286.9
Coats' 362.12
coccidioidal pulmonary 114.5
  acute 114.0
  chronic 114.4
  primary 114.0
  residual 114.4
Cockayne's (microcephaly and dwarfism) 759.89
Cogan's 370.52
cold
  agglutinin 283.0
    or hemoglobinuria 283.0
      paroxysmal (cold) (nocturnal) 283.2
  hemagglutinin (chronic) 283.0
collagen NEC 710.9
  nonvascular 710.9
  specified NEC 710.8
  vascular (allergic) (*see also* Angiitis, hypersensitivity) 446.20
colon 569.9
  functional 564.9
    congenital 751.3
  ischemic 557.0
combined system (of spinal cord) 266.2 *[336.2]*
  with anemia (pernicious) 281.0 *[336.2]*
compressed air 993.3
Concato's (pericardial polyserositis) 423.2
  peritoneal 568.82
  pleural — *see* Pleurisy
congenital NEC 799.89
conjunctiva 372.9
  chlamydial 077.98
    specified NEC 077.8
  specified type NEC 372.89
  viral 077.99
    specified NEC 077.8
connective tissue, diffuse (*see also* Disease, collagen) 710.9
Conor and Bruch's (boutonneuse fever) 082.1
Conradi (-Hünermann) 756.59
Cooley's (erythroblastic anemia) 282.49
Cooper's 610.1
Corbus' 607.1
cork-handlers' 495.3
cornea (*see also* Keratopathy) 371.9
coronary (*see also* Ischemia, heart) 414.9
  congenital 746.85
  ostial, syphilitic 093.20
    aortic 093.22
    mitral 093.21
    pulmonary 093.24
    tricuspid 093.23
Corrigan's — *see* Insufficiency, aortic
Cotugno's 724.3
Coxsackie (virus) NEC 074.8
cranial nerve NEC 352.9
Creutzfeldt-Jakob (CJD) 046.19

Disease, diseased — *see also* Syndrome — *continued*

Creutzfeldt-Jakob — *continued*
  with dementia
    with behavioral disturbance 046.19 *[294.11]*
    without behavioral disturbance 046.19 *[294.10]*
  familial 046.19
  iatrogenic 046.19
  specified NEC 046.19
  sporadic 046.19
  variant (vCJD) 046.11
    with dementia
      with behavioral disturbance 046.11 *[294.11]*
      without behavioral disturbance 046.11 *[294.10]*
Crigler-Najjar (congenital hyperbilirubinemia) 277.4
Crocq's (acrocyanosis) 443.89
Crohn's (intestine) (*see also* Enteritis, regional) 555.9
Crouzon's (craniofacial dysostosis) 756.0
Cruchet's (encephalitis lethargica) 049.8
Cruveilhier's 335.21
Cruz-Chagas (*see also* Trypanosomiasis, American) 086.2
crystal deposition (*see also* Arthritis, due to, crystals) 712.9 ☑
Csillag's (lichen sclerosus et atrophicus) 701.0
Curschmann's 359.21
Cushing's (pituitary basophilism) 255.0
cystic
  breast (chronic) 610.1
  kidney, congenital (*see also* Cystic, disease, kidney) 753.10
  liver, congenital 751.62
  lung 518.89
    congenital 748.4
  pancreas 577.2
    congenital 751.7
  renal, congenital (*see also* Cystic, disease, kidney) 753.10
  semilunar cartilage 717.5
cysticercus 123.1
cystine storage (with renal sclerosis) 270.0
cytomegalic inclusion (generalized) 078.5
  with
    pneumonia 078.5 *[484.1]*
  congenital 771.1
Daae (-Finsen) (epidemic pleurodynia) 074.1
dancing 297.8
Danielssen's (anesthetic leprosy) 030.1
Darier's (congenital) (keratosis follicularis) 757.39
  erythema annulare centrifugum 695.0
  vitamin A deficiency 264.8
Darling's (histoplasmosis) (*see also* Histoplasmosis, American) 115.00
Davies' 425.0
de Beurmann-Gougerot (sporotrichosis) 117.1
Débove's (splenomegaly) 789.2
deer fly (*see also* Tularemia) 021.9
deficiency 269.9
degenerative (*see also* Degeneration)
  disc — *see* Degeneration, intervertebral disc
Degos' 447.8
Déjérine (-Sottas) 356.0
Déleage's 359.89
demyelinating, demyelinizating (brain stem) (central nervous system) 341.9
  multiple sclerosis 340
  specified NEC 341.8
de Quervain's (tendon sheath) 727.04
  thyroid (subacute granulomatous thyroiditis) 245.1
Dercum's (adiposis dolorosa) 272.8
Deutschländer's — *see* Fracture, foot
Devergie's (pityriasis rubra pilaris) 696.4
Devic's 341.0
diaphorase deficiency 289.7
diaphragm 519.4
diarrheal, infectious 009.2
diatomaceous earth 502

Disease, diseased — *see also* Syndrome — *continued*

Diaz's (osteochondrosis astragalus) 732.5
digestive system 569.9
Di Guglielmo's (erythemic myelosis) (M9841/3) 207.0 ☑
Dimitri-Sturge-Weber (encephalocutaneous angiomatosis) 759.6
disc, degenerative — *see* Degeneration, intervertebral disc
discogenic (*see also* Disease, intervertebral disc) 722.90
diverticular — *see* Diverticula
Down's (mongolism) 758.0
Dubini's (electric chorea) 049.8
Dubois' (thymus gland) 090.5
Duchenne's 094.0
  locomotor ataxia 094.0
  muscular dystrophy 359.1
  paralysis 335.22
  pseudohypertrophy, muscles 359.1
Duchenne-Griesinger 359.1
ductless glands 259.9
Duhring's (dermatitis herpetiformis) 694.0
Dukes (-Filatov) 057.8
duodenum NEC 537.9
  specified NEC 537.89
Duplay's 726.2
Dupré's (meningism) 781.6
Dupuytren's (muscle contracture) 728.6
Durand-Nicolas-Favre (climatic bubo) 099.1
Duroziez's (congenital mitral stenosis) 746.5
Dutton's (trypanosomiasis) 086.9
Eales' 362.18
ear (chronic) (inner) NEC 388.9
  middle 385.9
    adhesive (*see also* Adhesions, middle ear) 385.10
    specified NEC 385.89
Eberth's (typhoid fever) 002.0
Ebstein's
  heart 746.2
  meaning diabetes 250.4 ☑ *[581.81]*
    due to secondary diabetes 249.4 ☑ *[581.81]*
Echinococcus (*see also* Echinococcus) 122.9
ECHO virus NEC 078.89
Economo's (encephalitis lethargica) 049.8
Eddowes' (brittle bones and blue sclera) 756.51
Edsall's 992.2
Eichstedt's (pityriasis versicolor) 111.0
Ellis-van Creveld (chondroectodermal dysplasia) 756.55
endocardium — *see* Endocarditis
endocrine glands or system NEC 259.9
  specified NEC 259.8
endomyocardial, idiopathic mural 425.2
Engelmann's (diaphyseal sclerosis) 756.59
Engel-von Recklinghausen (osteitis fibrosa cystica) 252.01
English (rickets) 268.0
Engman's (infectious eczematoid dermatitis) 690.8
enteroviral, enterovirus NEC 078.89
  central nervous system NEC 048
epidemic NEC 136.9
epididymis 608.9
epigastric, functional 536.9
  psychogenic 306.4
Erb (-Landouzy) 359.1
Erb-Goldflam 358.00
Erdheim-Chester (ECD) 277.89 ●
Erichsen's (railway spine) 300.16
esophagus 530.9
  functional 530.5
  psychogenic 306.4
Eulenburg's (congenital paramyotonia) 359.29
Eustachian tube 381.9
Evans' (thrombocytopenic purpura) 287.32
external auditory canal 380.9
extrapyramidal NEC 333.90
eye 379.90
  anterior chamber 364.9
  inflammatory NEC 364.3
  muscle 378.9

Disease, diseased — *see also* Syndrome — *continued*

eyeball 360.9
eyelid 374.9
eyeworm of Africa 125.2
Fabry's (angiokeratoma corporis diffusum) 272.7
facial nerve (seventh) 351.9
  newborn 767.5
Fahr-Volhard (malignant nephrosclerosis) 403.00
fallopian tube, noninflammatory 620.9
  specified NEC 620.8
familial periodic 277.31
  paralysis 359.3
Fanconi's (congenital pancytopenia) 284.09
Farber's (disseminated lipogranulomatosis) 272.8
fascia 728.9
  inflammatory 728.9
Fauchard's (periodontitis) 523.40
Favre-Durand-Nicolas (climatic bubo) 099.1
Favre-Racouchot (elastoidosis cutanea nodularis) 701.8
Fede's 529.0
Feer's 985.0
Felix's (juvenile osteochondrosis, hip) 732.1
Fenwick's (gastric atrophy) 537.89
Fernels' (aortic aneurysm) 441.9
fibrocaseous, of lung (*see also* Tuberculosis, pulmonary) 011.9 ☑
fibrocystic (*see also* Fibrocystic, disease) newborn 277.01
Fiedler's (leptospiral jaundice) 100.0
fifth 057.0
Filatoff's (infectious mononucleosis) 075
Filatov's (infectious mononucleosis) 075
file-cutters' 984.9
  specified type of lead — *see* Table of Drugs and Chemicals
filterable virus NEC 078.89
fish skin 757.1
  acquired 701.1
Flajani (-Basedow) (exophthalmic goiter) 242.0 ☑
Flatau-Schilder 341.1
flax-dressers' 504
Fleischner's 732.3
flint 502
fluke — *see* Infestation, fluke
Følling's (phenylketonuria) 270.1
foot and mouth 078.4
foot process 581.3
Forbes' (glycogenosis III) 271.0
Fordyce's (ectopic sebaceous glands) (mouth) 750.26
Fordyce-Fox (apocrine miliaria) 705.82
Fothergill's
  meaning scarlatina anginosa 034.1
  neuralgia (*see also* Neuralgia, trigeminal) 350.1
Fournier's 608.83
fourth 057.8
Fox (-Fordyce) (apocrine miliaria) 705.82
Francis' (*see also* Tularemia) 021.9
Franklin's (heavy chain) 273.2
Frei's (climatic bubo) 099.1
Freiberg's (flattening metatarsal) 732.5
Friedländer's (endarteritis obliterans) — *see* Arteriosclerosis
Friedreich's
  combined systemic or ataxia 334.0
  facial hemihypertrophy 756.0
  myoclonia 333.2
Fröhlich's (adiposogenital dystrophy) 253.8
Frommel's 676.6 ☑
frontal sinus (chronic) 473.1
  acute 461.1
Fuller's earth 502
fungus, fungous NEC 117.9
Gaisböck's (polycythemia hypertonica) 289.0
gallbladder 575.9
  congenital 751.60
Gamna's (siderotic splenomegaly) 289.51
Gamstorp's (adynamia episodica hereditaria) 359.3

☑ Additional Digit Required -— Refer to the Tabular List for Digit Selection   ▽ Subterms under main terms may continue to next column or page

Disease, diseased — *see also* Syndrome — *continued*

Gandy-Nanta (siderotic splenomegaly) 289.51
Gannister (occupational) 502
Garré's (*see also* Osteomyelitis) 730.1 ☑
gastric (*see also* Disease, stomach) 537.9
gastroesophageal reflux (GERD) 530.81
gastrointestinal (tract) 569.9
    amyloid 277.39
    functional 536.9
        psychogenic 306.4
Gaucher's (adult) (cerebroside lipidosis) (infantile) 272.7
Gayet's (superior hemorrhagic polioencephalitis) 265.1
Gee (-Herter) (-Heubner) (-Thaysen) (nontropical sprue) 579.0
generalized neoplastic (M8000/6) 199.0
genital organs NEC
    female 629.9
        specified NEC 629.89
    male 608.9
Gerhardt's (erythromelalgia) 443.82
Gerlier's (epidemic vertigo) 078.81
Gibert's (pityriasis rosea) 696.3
Gibney's (perispondylitis) 720.9
Gierke's (glycogenosis I) 271.0
Gilbert's (familial nonhemolytic jaundice) 277.4
Gilchrist's (North American blastomycosis) 116.0
Gilford (-Hutchinson) (progeria) 259.8
Gilles de la Tourette's (motor-verbal tic) 307.23
Giovannini's 117.9
gland (lymph) 289.9
Glanzmann's (hereditary hemorrhagic thrombasthenia) 287.1
glassblowers' 527.1
Glénard's (enteroptosis) 569.89
Glisson's (*see also* Rickets) 268.0
glomerular
    membranous, idiopathic 581.1
    minimal change 581.3
glycogen storage (Andersen's) (Cori types 1-7) (Forbes') (McArdle-Schmid-Pearson) (Pompe's) (types I-VII) 271.0
    cardiac 271.0 *[425.7]*
    generalized 271.0
    glucose–6–phosphatase deficiency 271.0
    heart 271.0 *[425.7]*
    hepatorenal 271.0
    liver and kidneys 271.0
    myocardium 271.0 *[425.7]*
    von Gierke's (glycogenosis I) 271.0
Goldflam-Erb 358.00
Goldscheider's (epidermolysis bullosa) 757.39
Goldstein's (familial hemorrhagic telangiectasia) 448.0
gonococcal NEC 098.0
Goodall's (epidemic vomiting) 078.82
Gordon's (exudative enteropathy) 579.8
Gougerot's (trisymptomatic) 709.1
Gougerot-Carteaud (confluent reticulate papillomatosis) 701.8
Gougerot-Hailey-Hailey (benign familial chronic pemphigus) 757.39
graft-versus-host 279.50
    acute 279.51
        on chronic 279.53
    chronic 279.52
grain-handlers' 495.8
Grancher's (splenopneumonia) — *see* Pneumonia
granulomatous (childhood) (chronic) 288.1
graphite lung 503
Graves' (exophthalmic goiter) 242.0 ☑
Greenfield's 330.0
green monkey 078.89
Griesinger's (*see also* Ancylostomiasis) 126.9
grinders' 502
Grisel's 723.5
Gruby's (tinea tonsurans) 110.0
Guertin's (electric chorea) 049.8
Guillain-Barré 357.0
Guinon's (motor-verbal tic) 307.23
Gull's (thyroid atrophy with myxedema) 244.8
Gull and Sutton's — *see* Hypertension, kidney

Disease, diseased — *see also* Syndrome — *continued*

gum NEC 523.9
Günther's (congenital erythropoietic porphyria) 277.1
gynecological 629.9
    specified NEC 629.89
H 270.0
Haas' 732.3
Habermann's (acute parapsoriasis varioliformis) 696.2
Haff 985.1
Hageman (congenital factor XII deficiency) (*see also* Defect, congenital) 286.3
Haglund's (osteochondrosis os tibiale externum) 732.5
Hagner's (hypertrophic pulmonary osteoarthropathy) 731.2
Hailey-Hailey (benign familial chronic pemphigus) 757.39
hair (follicles) NEC 704.9
    specified type NEC 704.8
Hallervorden-Spatz 333.0
Hal(peau's (lichen sclerosus et atrophicus) 701.0
Hamman's (spontaneous mediastinal emphysema) 518.1
hand, foot, and mouth 074.3
Hand-Schüller-Christian (chronic histiocytosis X) 277.89
Hanot's — *see* Cirrhosis, biliary
Hansen's (leprosy) 030.9
    benign form 030.1
    malignant form 030.0
Harada's 363.22
Harley's (intermittent hemoglobinuria) 283.2
Hartnup (pellagra-cerebellar ataxia-renal aminoaciduria) 270.0
Hart's (pellagra-cerebellar ataxia-renal aminoaciduria) 270.0
Hashimoto's (struma lymphomatosa) 245.2
Hb — *see* Disease, hemoglobin
heart (organic) 429.9
    with
        acute pulmonary edema (*see also* Failure, ventricular, left) 428.1
        hypertensive 402.91
            with renal failure 404.93
            benign 402.11
                with renal failure 404.13
            malignant 402.01
                with renal failure 404.03
        kidney disease — *see* Hypertension, cardiorenal
        rheumatic fever (conditions classifiable to 390)
            active 391.9
                with chorea 392.0
            inactive or quiescent (with chorea) 398.90
    amyloid 277.39 *[425.7]*
    aortic (valve) (*see also* Endocarditis, aortic) 424.1
    arteriosclerotic or sclerotic (minimal) (senile) — *see* Arteriosclerosis, coronary
    artery, arterial — *see* Arteriosclerosis, coronary
    atherosclerotic — *see* Arteriosclerosis, coronary
    beer drinkers' 425.5
    beriberi 265.0 *[425.7]*
    black 416.0
    congenital NEC 746.9
        cyanotic 746.9
        maternal, affecting fetus or newborn 760.3
        specified type NEC 746.89
    congestive (*see also* Failure, heart) 428.0
    coronary 414.9
    cryptogenic 429.9
    due to
        amyloidosis 277.39 *[425.7]*
        beriberi 265.0 *[425.7]*
        cardiac glycogenosis 271.0 *[425.7]*
        Friedreich's ataxia 334.0 *[425.8]*

Disease, diseased — *see also* Syndrome — *continued*

heart — *continued*
    due to — *continued*
        gout 274.82
        mucopolysaccharidosis 277.5 *[425.7]*
        myotonia atrophica 359.21 *[425.8]*
        progressive muscular dystrophy 359.1 *[425.8]*
        sarcoidosis 135 *[425.8]*
    fetal 746.9
        inflammatory 746.89
    fibroid (*see also* Myocarditis) 429.0
    functional 427.9
        postoperative 997.1
        psychogenic 306.2
    glycogen storage 271.0 *[425.7]*
    gonococcal NEC 098.85
    gouty 274.82
    hypertensive (*see also* Hypertension, heart) 402.90
        benign 402.10
        malignant 402.00
    hyperthyroid (*see also* Hyperthyroidism) 242.9 ☑ *[425.7]*
    incompletely diagnosed — *see* Disease, heart
    ischemic (chronic) (*see also* Ischemia, heart) 414.9
        acute (*see also* Infarct, myocardium) 410.9 ☑
            without myocardial infarction 411.89
                with coronary (artery) occlusion 411.81
        asymptomatic 412
        diagnosed on ECG or other special investigation but currently presenting no symptoms 412
    kyphoscoliotic 416.1
    mitral (*see also* Endocarditis, mitral) 394.9
    muscular (*see also* Degeneration, myocardial) 429.1
    postpartum 674.8 ☑
    psychogenic (functional) 306.2
    pulmonary (chronic) 416.9
        acute 415.0
        specified NEC 416.8
    rheumatic (chronic) (inactive) (old) (quiescent) (with chorea) 398.90
        active or acute 391.9
            with chorea (active) (rheumatic) (Sydenham's) 392.0
            specified type NEC 391.8
        maternal, affecting fetus or newborn 760.3
    rheumatoid — *see* Arthritis, rheumatoid
    sclerotic — *see* Arteriosclerosis, coronary
    senile (*see also* Myocarditis) 429.0
    specified type NEC 429.89
    syphilitic 093.89
        aortic 093.1
            aneurysm 093.0
        asymptomatic 093.89
        congenital 090.5
    thyroid (gland) (*see also* Hyper-thyroidism) 242.9 ☑ *[425.7]*
    thyrotoxic (*see also* Thyrotoxicosis) 242.9 ☑ *[425.7]*
    tuberculous (*see also* Tuberculosis) 017.9 ☑ *[425.8]*
    valve, valvular (obstructive) (regurgitant) (*see also* Endocarditis)
        congenital NEC (*see also* Anomaly, heart, valve) 746.9
            pulmonary 746.00
            specified type NEC 746.89
    vascular — *see* Disease, cardiovascular
heavy-chain (gamma G) 273.2
Heberden's 715.04
Hebra's
    dermatitis exfoliativa 695.89
    erythema multiforme exudativum 695.19
    pityriasis
        maculata et circinata 696.3
        rubra 695.89

Disease, diseased — *see also* Syndrome — *continued*

Hebra's — *continued*
    pityriasis — *continued*
        rubra — *continued*
            pilaris 696.4
        prurigo 698.2
Heerfordt's (uveoparotitis) 135
Heidenhain's 290.10
    with dementia 290.10
Heilmeyer-Schöner (M9842/3) 207.1 ☑
Heine-Medin (*see also* Poliomyelitis) 045.9 ☑
Heller's (*see also* Psychosis, childhood) 299.1 ☑
Heller-Döhle (syphilitic aortitis) 093.1
hematopoietic organs 289.9
hemoglobin (Hb) 282.7
    with thalassemia 282.49
    abnormal (mixed) NEC 282.7
        with thalassemia 282.49
    AS genotype 282.5
    Bart's 282.49
    C (Hb-C) 282.7
        with other abnormal hemoglobin NEC 282.7
        elliptocytosis 282.7
        Hb-S (without crisis) 282.63
            with
                crisis 282.64
                    vaso-occlusive pain 282.64
        sickle-cell (without crisis) 282.63
            with
                crisis 282.64
                    vaso-occlusive pain 282.64
        thalassemia 282.49
    constant spring 282.7
    D (Hb-D) 282.7
        with other abnormal hemoglobin NEC 282.7
        Hb-S (without crisis) 282.68
            with crisis 282.69
        sickle-cell (without crisis) 282.68
            with crisis 282.69
        thalassemia 282.49
    E (Hb-E) 282.7
        with other abnormal hemoglobin NEC 282.7
        Hb-S (without crisis) 282.68
            with crisis 282.69
        sickle-cell (without crisis) 282.68
            with crisis 282.69
        thalassemia 282.49
    elliptocytosis 282.7
    F (Hb-F) 282.7
    G (Hb-G) 282.7
    H (Hb-H) 282.49
    hereditary persistence, fetal (HPFH) ("Swiss variety") 282.7
    high fetal gene 282.7
    I thalassemia 282.49
    M 289.7
    S (*see also* Disease, sickle-cell, Hb-S)
        thalassemia (without crisis) 282.41
            with
                crisis 282.42
                    vaso-occlusive pain 282.42
    spherocytosis 282.7
    unstable, hemolytic 282.7
    Zurich (Hb-Zurich) 282.7
hemolytic (fetus) (newborn) 773.2
    autoimmune (cold type) (warm type) 283.0
    due to or with
        incompatibility
            ABO (blood group) 773.1
            blood (group) (Duffy) (Kell) (Kidd) (Lewis) (M) (S) NEC 773.2
            Rh (blood group) (factor) 773.0
                Rh negative mother 773.0
    unstable hemoglobin 282.7
hemorrhagic 287.9
    newborn 776.0
Henoch (-Schönlein) (purpura nervosa) 287.0
hepatic — *see* Disease, liver
hepatolenticular 275.1
heredodegenerative NEC
    brain 331.89

Index

Disease, diseased — Disease, diseased

Disease, diseased — *see also* Syndrome — *continued*

heredodegenerative — *continued*
    spinal cord 336.8
Hers' (glycogenosis VI) 271.0
Herter (-Gee) (-Heubner) (nontropical sprue) 579.0
Herxheimer's (diffuse idiopathic cutaneous atrophy) 701.8
Heubner's 094.89
Heubner-Herter (nontropical sprue) 579.0
high fetal gene or hemoglobin thalassemia 282.49
Hildenbrand's (typhus) 081.9
hip (joint) NEC 719.95
    congenital 755.63
    suppurative 711.05
    tuberculous (*see also* Tuberculosis) 015.1 ☑ *[730.85]*
Hippel's (retinocerebral angiomatosis) 759.6
Hirschfeld's (acute diabetes mellitus) (*see also* Diabetes) 250.0 ☑
    due to secondary diabetes 249.0 ☑
Hirschsprung's (congenital megacolon) 751.3
His (-Werner) (trench fever) 083.1
HIV 042
Hodgkin's (M9650/3) 201.9 ☑

Note — Use the following fifth-digit sub-classification with category 201:

0	*unspecified site*
1	*lymph nodes of head, face, and neck*
2	*intrathoracic lymph nodes*
3	*intra-abdominal lymph nodes*
4	*lymph nodes of axilla and upper limb*
5	*lymph nodes of inguinal region and lower limb*
6	*intrapelvic lymph nodes*
7	*spleen*
8	*lymph nodes of multiple sites*

    lymphocytic
        depletion (M9653/3) 201.7 ☑
            diffuse fibrosis (M9654/3) 201.7 ☑
            reticular type (M9655/3) 201.7 ☑
        predominance (M9651/3) 201.4 ☑
    lymphocytic-histiocytic predominance (M9651/3) 201.4 ☑
    mixed cellularity (M9652/3) 201.6 ☑
    nodular sclerosis (M9656/3) 201.5 ☑
        cellular phase (M9657/3) 201.5 ☑
Hodgson's 441.9
    ruptured 441.5
Hoffa (-Kastert) (liposynovitis prepatellaris) 272.8
Holla (*see also* Spherocytosis) 282.0
homozygous-Hb-S 282.61
hoof and mouth 078.4
hookworm (*see also* Ancylostomiasis) 126.9
Horton's (temporal arteritis) 446.5
host-versus-graft (immune or nonimmune cause) 279.50
HPFH (hereditary persistence of fetal hemoglobin) ("Swiss variety") 282.7
Huchard's disease (continued arterial hypertension) 401.9
Huguier's (uterine fibroma) 218.9
human immunodeficiency (virus) 042
hunger 251.1
Hunt's
    dyssynergia cerebellaris myoclonica 334.2
    herpetic geniculate ganglionitis 053.11
Huntington's 333.4
Huppert's (multiple myeloma) (M9730/3) 203.0 ☑
Hurler's (mucopolysaccharidosis I) 277.5
Hutchinson-Boeck (sarcoidosis) 135
Hutchinson-Gilford (progeria) 259.8
Hutchinson's, meaning
    angioma serpiginosum 709.1
    cheiropompholyx 705.81
    prurigo estivalis 692.72
hyaline (diffuse) (generalized) 728.9

Disease, diseased — *see also* Syndrome — *continued*

hyaline — *continued*
    membrane (lung) (newborn) 769
hydatid (*see also* Echinococcus) 122.9
Hyde's (prurigo nodularis) 698.3
hyperkinetic (*see also* Hyperkinesia) 314.9
    heart 429.82
hypertensive (*see also* Hypertension) 401.9
hypophysis 253.9
    hyperfunction 253.1
    hypofunction 253.2
Iceland (epidemic neuromyasthenia) 049.8
I cell 272.7
ill-defined 799.89
immunologic NEC 279.9
immunoproliferative 203.8 ☑
inclusion 078.5
    salivary gland 078.5
infancy, early NEC 779.9
infective NEC 136.9
inguinal gland 289.9
internal semilunar cartilage, cystic 717.5
intervertebral disc 722.90
    with myelopathy 722.70
    cervical, cervicothoracic 722.91
        with myelopathy 722.71
    lumbar, lumbosacral 722.93
        with myelopathy 722.73
    thoracic, thoracolumbar 722.92
        with myelopathy 722.72
intestine 569.9
    functional 564.9
        congenital 751.3
        psychogenic 306.4
    lardaceous 277.39
    organic 569.9
    protozoal NEC 007.9
iris 364.9
    specified NEC 364.89
iron
    metabolism 275.0
    storage 275.0
Isambert's (*see also* Tuberculosis, larynx) 012.3 ☑
Iselin's (osteochondrosis, fifth metatarsal) 732.5
island (scrub typhus) 081.2
itai-itai 985.5
Jadassohn's (maculopapular erythroderma) 696.2
Jadassohn-Pellizari's (anetoderma) 701.3
Jakob-Creutzfeldt (CJD) 046.19
    with dementia
        with behavioral disturbance 046.19 *[294.11]*
        without behavioral disturbance 046.19 *[294.10]*
    familial 046.19
    iatrogenic 046.19
    specified NEC 046.19
    sporadic 046.19
    variant (vCJD) 046.11
        with dementia
            with behavioral disturbance 046.11 *[294.11]*
            without behavioral disturbance 046.11 *[294.10]*
Jaksch (-Luzet) (pseudoleukemia infantum) 285.8
Janet's 300.89
Jansky-Bielschowsky 330.1
jaw NEC 526.9
    fibrocystic 526.2
Jensen's 363.05
Jeune's (asphyxiating thoracic dystrophy) 756.4
jigger 134.1
Johnson-Stevens (erythema multiforme exudativum) 695.13
joint NEC 719.9 ☑
    ankle 719.97
    Charcôt 094.0 *[713.5]*
    degenerative (*see also* Osteoarthrosis) 715.9 ☑
        multiple 715.09
        spine (*see also* Spondylosis) 721.90

Disease, diseased — *see also* Syndrome — *continued*

joint — *continued*
    elbow 719.92
    foot 719.97
    hand 719.94
    hip 719.95
    hypertrophic (chronic) (degenerative) (*see also* Osteoarthrosis) 715.9 ☑
        spine (*see also* Spondylosis) 721.90
    knee 719.96
    Luschka 721.90
    multiple sites 719.99
    pelvic region 719.95
    sacroiliac 724.6
    shoulder (region) 719.91
    specified site NEC 719.98
    spine NEC 724.9
        pseudarthrosis following fusion 733.82
        sacroiliac 724.6
    wrist 719.93
Jourdain's (acute gingivitis) 523.00
Jüngling's (sarcoidosis) 135
Kahler (-Bozzolo) (multiple myeloma) (M9730/3) 203.0 ☑
Kalischer's 759.6
Kaposi's 757.33
    lichen ruber 697.8
        acuminatus 696.4
        moniliformis 697.8
    xeroderma pigmentosum 757.33
Kaschin-Beck (endemic polyarthritis) 716.00
    ankle 716.07
    arm 716.02
        lower (and wrist) 716.03
        upper (and elbow) 716.02
    foot (and ankle) 716.07
    forearm (and wrist) 716.03
    hand 716.04
    leg 716.06
        lower 716.06
        upper 716.05
    multiple sites 716.09
    pelvic region (hip) (thigh) 716.05
    shoulder region 716.01
    specified site NEC 716.08
Katayama 120.2
Kawasaki 446.1
Kedani (scrub typhus) 081.2
kidney (functional) (pelvis) (*see also* Disease, renal) 593.9
    chronic 585.9
        requiring chronic dialysis 585.6
        stage
            I 585.1
            II (mild) 585.2
            III (moderate) 585.3
            IV (severe) 585.4
            V 585.5
    cystic (congenital) 753.10
        multiple 753.19
        single 753.11
        specified NEC 753.19
    fibrocystic (congenital) 753.19
    in gout 274.10
    polycystic (congenital) 753.12
        adult type (APKD) 753.13
        autosomal dominant 753.13
        autosomal recessive 753.14
        childhood type (CPKD) 753.14
        infantile type 753.14
Kienböck's (carpal lunate) (wrist) 732.3
Kimmelstiel (-Wilson) (intercapillary glomerulosclerosis) 250.4 ☑ *[581.81]*
    due to secondary diabetes 249.4 ☑ *[581.81]*
Kinnier Wilson's (hepatolenticular degeneration) 275.1
kissing 075
Kleb's (*see also* Nephritis) 583.9
Klinger's 446.4
Klippel's 723.8
Klippel-Feil (brevicollis) 756.16
knight's 911.1
Köbner's (epidermolysis bullosa) 757.39
Koenig-Wichmann (pemphigus) 694.4

Disease, diseased — *see also* Syndrome — *continued*

Köhler's
    first (osteoarthrosis juvenilis) 732.5
    second (Freiberg's infraction, metatarsal head) 732.5
    patellar 732.4
    tarsal navicular (bone) (osteoarthrosis juvenilis) 732.5
Köhler-Freiberg (infraction, metatarsal head) 732.5
Köhler-Mouchet (osteoarthrosis juvenilis) 732.5
Köhler-Pellegrini-Stieda (calcification, knee joint) 726.62
Kok 759.89
König's (osteochondritis dissecans) 732.7
Korsakoff's (nonalcoholic) 294.0
    alcoholic 291.1
Kostmann's (infantile genetic agranulocytosis) 288.01
Krabbe's 330.0
Kraepelin-Morel (*see also* Schizophrenia) 295.9 ☑
Kraft-Weber-Dimitri 759.6
Kufs' 330.1
Kugelberg-Welander 335.11
Kuhnt-Junius 362.52
Kümmell's (-Verneuil) (spondylitis) 721.7
Kundrat's (lymphosarcoma) 200.1 ☑
kuru 046.0
Kussmaul (-Meier) (polyarteritis nodosa) 446.0
Kyasanur Forest 065.2
Kyrle's (hyperkeratosis follicularis in cutem penetrans) 701.1
labia
    inflammatory 616.10
    noninflammatory 624.9
        specified NEC 624.8
labyrinth, ear 386.8
lacrimal system (apparatus) (passages) 375.9
    gland 375.00
    specified NEC 375.89
Lafora's 333.2
Lagleyze-von Hippel (retinocerebral angiomatosis) 759.6
Lancereaux-Mathieu (leptospiral jaundice) 100.0
Landry's 357.0
Lane's 569.89
lardaceous (any site) 277.39
Larrey-Weil (leptospiral jaundice) 100.0
Larsen (-Johansson) (juvenile osteopathia patellae) 732.4
larynx 478.70
Lasègue's (persecution mania) 297.9
Leber's 377.16
Lederer's (acquired infectious hemolytic anemia) 283.19
Legg's (capital femoral osteochondrosis) 732.1
Legg-Calvé-Perthes (capital femoral osteochondrosis) 732.1
Legg-Calvé-Waldenström (femoral capital osteochondrosis) 732.1
Legg-Perthes (femoral capital osteochondrosis) 732.1
Legionnaires' 482.84
Leigh's 330.8
Leiner's (exfoliative dermatitis) 695.89
Leloir's (lupus erythematosus) 695.4
Lenegre's 426.0
lens (eye) 379.39
Leriche's (osteoporosis, posttraumatic) 733.7
Letterer-Siwe (acute histiocytosis X) (M9722/3) 202.5 ☑
Lev's (acquired complete heart block) 426.0
Lewandowski's (*see also* Tuberculosis) 017.0 ☑
Lewandowski-Lutz (epidermodysplasia verruciformis) 078.19
Lewy body 331.82
    with dementia
        with behavioral disturbance 331.82 *[294.11]*
        without behavioral disturbance 331.82 *[294.10]*
Leyden's (periodic vomiting) 536.2

Disease, diseased — Disease, diseased

Disease, diseased — *see also* Syndrome — *continued*
Libman-Sacks (verrucous endocarditis) 710.0 *[424.91]*
Lichtheim's (subacute combined sclerosis with pernicious anemia) 281.0 *[336.2]*
ligament 728.9
light chain 203.0 ☑
Lightwood's (renal tubular acidosis) 588.89
Lignac's (cystinosis) 270.0
Lindau's (retinocerebral angiomatosis) 759.6
Lindau-von Hippel (angiomatosis retinocere-bellosa) 759.6
lip NEC 528.5
lipidosis 272.7
lipoid storage NEC 272.7
Lipschütz's 616.50
Little's — *see* Palsy, cerebral
liver 573.9
    alcoholic 571.3
        acute 571.1
        chronic 571.3
    chronic 571.9
        alcoholic 571.3
    cystic, congenital 751.62
    drug-induced 573.3
    due to
        chemicals 573.3
        fluorinated agents 573.3
        hypersensitivity drugs 573.3
        isoniazids 573.3
    end stage NEC 572.8
        due to hepatitis — *see* Hepatitis
    fibrocystic (congenital) 751.62
    glycogen storage 271.0
    organic 573.9
    polycystic (congenital) 751.62
Lobo's (keloid blastomycosis) 116.2
Lobstein's (brittle bones and blue sclera) 756.51
locomotor system 334.9
Lorain's (pituitary dwarfism) 253.3
Lou Gehrig's 335.20
Lucas-Championnière (fibrinous bronchitis) 466.0
Ludwig's (submaxillary cellulitis) 528.3
luetic — *see* Syphilis
lumbosacral region 724.6
lung NEC 518.89
    black 500
    congenital 748.60
    cystic 518.89
        congenital 748.4
    fibroid (chronic) (*see also* Fibrosis, lung) 515
    fluke 121.2
        oriental 121.2
    in
        amyloidosis 277.39 *[517.8]*
        polymyositis 710.4 *[517.8]*
        sarcoidosis 135 *[517.8]*
        Sjögren's syndrome 710.2 *[517.8]*
        syphilis 095.1
        systemic lupus erythematosus 710.0 *[517.8]*
        systemic sclerosis 710.1 *[517.2]*
    interstitial (chronic) 515
        acute 136.3
    nonspecific, chronic 496
    obstructive (chronic) (COPD) 496
        with
            acute
                bronchitis 491.22
                    exacerbation NEC 491.21
                alveolitis, allergic (*see also* Alveolitis, allergic) 495.9
                asthma (chronic) (obstructive) 493.2 ☑
                bronchiectasis 494.0
                    with acute exacerbation 494.1
                bronchitis (chronic) 491.20
                    with
                        acute bronchitis 491.22
                        exacerbation (acute) 491.21
                decompensated 491.21
                    with exacerbation 491.21
                emphysema NEC 492.8

Disease, diseased — *see also* Syndrome — *continued*
lung — *continued*
    obstructive — *continued*
        diffuse (with fibrosis) 496
    polycystic 518.89
        asthma (chronic) (obstructive) 493.2 ☑
        congenital 748.4
        purulent (cavitary) 513.0
    restrictive 518.89
    rheumatoid 714.81
        diffuse interstitial 714.81
    specified NEC 518.89
Lutembacher's (atrial septal defect with mitral stenosis) 745.5
Lutz-Miescher (elastosis perforans serpiginosa) 701.1
Lutz-Splendore-de Almeida (Brazilian blasto-mycosis) 116.1
Lyell's (toxic epidermal necrolysis) 695.15
    due to drug
        correct substance properly adminis-tered 695.15
        overdose or wrong substance given or taken 977.9
            specific drug — *see* Table of Drugs and Chemicals
Lyme 088.81
lymphatic (gland) (system) 289.9
    channel (noninfective) 457.9
    vessel (noninfective) 457.9
        specified NEC 457.8
lymphoproliferative (chronic) (M9970/1) 238.79
Machado-Joseph 334.8
Madelung's (lipomatosis) 272.8
Madura (actinomycotic) 039.9
    mycotic 117.4
Magitot's 526.4
Majocchi's (purpura annularis telangiectodes) 709.1
malarial (*see also* Malaria) 084.6
Malassez's (cystic) 608.89
Malibu 919.8
    infected 919.9
malignant (M8000/3) (*see also* Neoplasm, by site, malignant)
    previous, affecting management of preg-nancy V23.89
Manson's 120.1
maple bark 495.6
maple syrup (urine) 270.3
Marburg (virus) 078.89
Marchiafava (-Bignami) 341.8
Marfan's 090.49
    congenital syphilis 090.49
    meaning Marfan's syndrome 759.82
Marie-Bamberger (hypertrophic pulmonary osteoarthropathy) (secondary) 731.2
    primary or idiopathic (acropachyderma) 757.39
    pulmonary (hypertrophic osteoarthropa-thy) 731.2
Marie-Strümpell (ankylosing spondylitis) 720.0
Marion's (bladder neck obstruction) 596.0
Marsh's (exophthalmic goiter) 242.0 ☑
Martin's 715.27
mast cell 757.33
    systemic (M9741/3) 202.6 ☑
mastoid (*see also* Mastoiditis) 383.9
    process 385.9
maternal, unrelated to pregnancy NEC, affect-ing fetus or newborn 760.9
Mathieu's (leptospiral jaundice) 100.0
Mauclaire's 732.3
Mauriac's (erythema nodosum syphiliticum) 091.3
Maxcy's 081.0
McArdle (-Schmid-Pearson) (glycogenosis V) 271.0
mediastinum NEC 519.3
Medin's (*see also* Poliomyelitis) 045.9 ☑
Mediterranean (with hemoglobinopathy) 282.49
medullary center (idiopathic) (respiratory) 348.89 ▲

Disease, diseased — *see also* Syndrome — *continued*
Meige's (chronic hereditary edema) 757.0
Meleda 757.39
Ménétrier's (hypertrophic gastritis) 535.2 ☑
Ménière's (active) 386.00
    cochlear 386.02
    cochleovestibular 386.01
    inactive 386.04
    in remission 386.04
    vestibular 386.03
meningeal — *see* Meningitis
mental (*see also* Psychosis) 298.9
Merzbacher-Pelizaeus 330.0
mesenchymal 710.9
mesenteric embolic 557.0
metabolic NEC 277.9
metal polishers' 502
metastatic — *see* Metastasis
Mibelli's 757.39
microdrepanocytic 282.49
microvascular — code to condition
Miescher's 709.3
Mikulicz's (dryness of mouth, absent or de-creased lacrimation) 527.1
Milkman (-Looser) (osteomalacia with pseud-ofractures) 268.2
Miller's (osteomalacia) 268.2
Mills' 335.29
Milroy's (chronic hereditary edema) 757.0
Minamata 985.0
Minor's 336.1
Minot's (hemorrhagic disease, newborn) 776.0
Minot-von Willebrand-Jürgens (angiohe-mophilia) 286.4
Mitchell's (erythromelalgia) 443.82
mitral — *see* Endocarditis, mitral
Mljet (mal de Meleda) 757.39
Möbius', Moebius' 346.2 ☑
Moeller's 267
Möller (-Barlow) (infantile scurvy) 267
Mönckeberg's (*see also* Arteriosclerosis, extrem-ities) 440.20
Mondor's (thrombophlebitis of breast) 451.89
Monge's 993.2
Morel-Kraepelin (*see also* Schizophrenia) 295.9 ☑
Morgagni's (syndrome) (hyperostosis frontalis interna) 733.3
Morgagni-Adams-Stokes (syncope with heart block) 426.9
Morquio (-Brailsford) (-Ullrich) (mucopolysac-charidosis IV) 277.5
Morton's (with metatarsalgia) 355.6
Morvan's 336.0
motor neuron (bulbar) (mixed type) 335.20
Mouchet's (juvenile osteochondrosis, foot) 732.5
mouth 528.9
Moyamoya 437.5
Mucha's (acute parapsoriasis varioliformis) 696.2
mu-chain 273.2
mucolipidosis (I) (II) (III) 272.7
Münchmeyer's (exostosis luxurians) 728.11
Murri's (intermittent hemoglobinuria) 283.2
muscle 359.9
    inflammatory 728.9
    ocular 378.9
musculoskeletal system 729.90
mushroom workers' 495.5
Myà's (congenital dilation, colon) 751.3
mycotic 117.9
myeloproliferative (chronic) (M9960/1) 238.79
myocardium, myocardial (*see also* Degenera-tion, myocardial) 429.1
    hypertensive (*see also* Hypertension, heart 402.90
    primary (idiopathic) 425.4
myoneural 358.9
Naegeli's 287.1
nail 703.9
    specified type NEC 703.8
Nairobi sheep 066.1
nasal 478.19
    cavity NEC 478.19

Disease, diseased — *see also* Syndrome — *continued*
nasal — *continued*
    sinus (chronic) — *see* Sinusitis
navel (newborn) NEC 779.89
    delayed separation of umbilical cord 779.83
nemaline body 359.0
neoplastic, generalized (M8000/6) 199.0
nerve — *see* Disorder, nerve
nervous system (central) 349.9
    autonomic, peripheral (*see also* Neuropa-thy, peripheral, autonomic) 337.9
    congenital 742.9
    inflammatory — *see* Encephalitis
    parasympathetic (*see also* Neuropathy, peripheral, autonomic) 337.9
    peripheral NEC 355.9
    prion NEC 046.79
    specified NEC 349.89
    sympathetic (*see also* Neuropathy, periph-eral, autonomic) 337.9
    vegetative (*see also* Neuropathy, peripheral, autonomic) 337.9
Nettleship's (urticaria pigmentosa) 757.33
Neumann's (pemphigus vegetans) 694.4
neurologic (central) NEC (*see also* Disease, nervous system) 349.9
    peripheral NEC 355.9
neuromuscular system NEC 358.9
Newcastle 077.8
Nicolas (-Durand) — Favre (climatic bubo) 099.1
Niemann-Pick (lipid histiocytosis) 272.7
nipple 611.9
    Paget's (M8540/3) 174.0
Nishimoto (-Takeuchi) 437.5
nonarthropod-borne NEC 078.89
    central nervous system NEC 049.9
    enterovirus NEC 078.89
nonautoimmune hemolytic NEC 283.10
Nonne-Milroy-Meige (chronic hereditary ede-ma) 757.0
Norrie's (congenital progressive oculoacoustic-ocerebral degeneration) 743.8
nose 478.19
nucleus pulposus — *see* Disease, intervertebral disc
nutritional 269.9
    maternal, affecting fetus or newborn 760.4
oasthouse, urine 270.2
obliterative vascular 447.1
Odelberg's (juvenile osteochondrosis) 732.1
Oguchi's (retina) 368.61
Ohara's (*see also* Tularemia) 021.9
Ollier's (chondrodysplasia) 756.4
Opitz's (congestive splenomegaly) 289.51
Oppenheim's 358.8
Oppenheim-Urbach (necrobiosis lipoidica dia-beticorum) 250.8 ☑ *[709.3]*
    due to secondary diabetes 249.8 ☑ *[709.3]*
optic nerve NEC 377.49
orbit 376.9
    specified NEC 376.89
Oriental liver fluke 121.1
Oriental lung fluke 121.2
Ormond's 593.4
Osgood-Schlatter 732.4
Osgood's tibia (tubercle) 732.4
Osler (-Vaquez) (polycythemia vera) (M9950/1) 238.4
Osler-Rendu (familial hemorrhagic telangiec-tasia) 448.0
osteofibrocystic 252.01
Otto's 715.35
outer ear 380.9
ovary (noninflammatory) NEC 620.9
    cystic 620.2
    polycystic 256.4
    specified NEC 620.8
Owren's (congenital) (*see also* Defect, coagula-tion) 286.3
Paas' 756.59
Paget's (osteitis deformans) 731.0

Disease, diseased — *see also* Syndrome — *continued*

Paget's — *continued*
  with infiltrating duct carcinoma of the breast (M8541/3) — *see* Neoplasm, breast, malignant
  bone 731.0
    osteosarcoma in (M9184/3) — *see* Neoplasm, bone, malignant
  breast (M8540/3) 174.0
  extramammary (M8542/3) (*see also* Neoplasm, skin, malignant)
    anus 154.3
    skin 173.5
  malignant (M8540/3)
    breast 174.0
    specified site NEC (M8542/3) — *see* Neoplasm, skin, malignant
    unspecified site 174.0
  mammary (M8540/3) 174.0
  nipple (M8540/3) 174.0
palate (soft) 528.9
Paltauf-Sternberg 201.9 ☑
pancreas 577.9
  cystic 577.2
    congenital 751.7
  fibrocystic 277.00
Panner's 732.3
  capitellum humeri 732.3
  head of humerus 732.3
  tarsal navicular (bone) (osteochondrosis) 732.5
panvalvular — *see* Endocarditis, mitral
parametrium 629.9
parasitic NEC 136.9
  cerebral NEC 123.9
  intestinal NEC 129
  mouth 112.0
  skin NEC 134.9
  specified type — *see* Infestation
  tongue 112.0
parathyroid (gland) 252.9
  specified NEC 252.8
Parkinson's 332.0
parodontal 523.9
Parrot's (syphilitic osteochondritis) 090.0
Parry's (exophthalmic goiter) 242.0 ☑
Parson's (exophthalmic goiter) 242.0 ☑
Pavy's 593.6
Paxton's (white piedra) 111.2
Payr's (splenic flexure syndrome) 569.89
pearl-workers' (chronic osteomyelitis) (*see also* Osteomyelitis) 730.1 ☑
Pel-Ebstein — *see* Disease, Hodgkin's
Pelizaeus-Merzbacher 330.0
  with dementia
    with behavioral disturbance 330.0 [294.11]
    without behavioral disturbance 330.0 [294.10]
Pellegrini-Stieda (calcification, knee joint) 726.62
pelvis, pelvic
  female NEC 629.9
    specified NEC 629.89
  gonococcal (acute) 098.19
    chronic or duration of 2 months or over 098.39
  infection (*see also* Disease, pelvis, inflammatory) 614.9
  inflammatory (female) (PID) 614.9
    with
      abortion — *see* Abortion, by type, with sepsis
      ectopic pregnancy (*see also* categories 633.0–633.9) 639.0
      molar pregnancy (*see also* categories 630–632) 639.0
    acute 614.3
    chronic 614.4
    complicating pregnancy 646.6 ☑
      affecting fetus or newborn 760.8
    following
      abortion 639.0
      ectopic or molar pregnancy 639.0
    peritonitis (acute) 614.5

Disease, diseased — *see also* Syndrome — *continued*

pelvis, pelvic — *continued*
  inflammatory — *continued*
    peritonitis — *continued*
      chronic NEC 614.7
      puerperal, postpartum, childbirth 670.8 ☑ ▲
      specified NEC 614.8
    organ, female NEC 629.9
      specified NEC 629.89
    peritoneum, female NEC 629.9
      specified NEC 629.89
penis 607.9
  inflammatory 607.2
peptic NEC 536.9
  acid 536.8
periapical tissues NEC 522.9
pericardium 423.9
  specified type NEC 423.8
perineum
  female
    inflammatory 616.9
      specified NEC 616.89
    noninflammatory 624.9
      specified NEC 624.8
  male (inflammatory) 682.2
periodic (familial) (Reimann's) NEC 277.31
  paralysis 359.3
periodontal NEC 523.9
  specified NEC 523.8
periosteum 733.90
peripheral
  arterial 443.9
  autonomic nervous system (*see also* Neuropathy, autonomic) 337.9
  nerve NEC (*see also* Neuropathy) 356.9
    multiple — *see* Polyneuropathy
  vascular 443.9
    specified type NEC 443.89
peritoneum 568.9
  pelvic, female 629.9
    specified NEC 629.89
Perrin-Ferraton (snapping hip) 719.65
persistent mucosal (middle ear) (with posterior or superior marginal perforation of ear drum) 382.2
Perthes' (capital femoral osteochondrosis) 732.1
Petit's (*see also* Hernia, lumbar) 553.8
Peutz-Jeghers 759.6
Peyronie's 607.85
Pfeiffer's (infectious mononucleosis) 075
pharynx 478.20
Phocas' 610.1
photochromogenic (acid-fast bacilli) (pulmonary) 031.0
  nonpulmonary 031.9
Pick's
  brain 331.11
    with dementia
      with behavioral disturbance 331.11 [294.11]
      without behavioral disturbance 331.11 [294.10]
  cerebral atrophy 331.11
    with dementia
      with behavioral disturbance 331.11 [294.11]
      without behavioral disturbance 331.11 [294.10]
  lipid histiocytosis 272.7
  liver (pericardial pseudocirrhosis of liver) 423.2
  pericardium (pericardial pseudocirrhosis of liver) 423.2
  polyserositis (pericardial pseudocirrhosis of liver) 423.2
Pierson's (osteochondrosis) 732.1
pigeon fanciers' or breeders' 495.2
pineal gland 259.8
pink 985.1
Pinkus' (lichen nitidus) 697.1
pinworm 127.4
pituitary (gland) 253.9
  hyperfunction 253.1

Disease, diseased — *see also* Syndrome — *continued*

pituitary — *continued*
  hypofunction 253.2
pituitary snuff-takers' 495.8
placenta
  affecting fetus or newborn 762.2
  complicating pregnancy or childbirth 656.7 ☑
pleura (cavity) (*see also* Pleurisy) 511.0
Plummer's (toxic nodular goiter) 242.3 ☑
pneumatic
  drill 994.9
  hammer 994.9
policeman's 729.2
Pollitzer's (hidradenitis suppurativa) 705.83
polycystic (congenital) 759.89
  congenital 748.4
  kidney or renal 753.12
    adult type (APKD) 753.13
    autosomal dominant 753.13
    autosomal recessive 753.14
    childhood type (CPKD) 753.14
    infantile type 753.14
  liver or hepatic 751.62
  lung or pulmonary 518.89
  ovary, ovaries 256.4
  spleen 759.0
Pompe's (glycogenosis II) 271.0
Poncet's (tuberculous rheumatism) (*see also* Tuberculosis) 015.9 ☑
Posada-Wernicke 114.9
Potain's (pulmonary edema) 514
Pott's (*see also* Tuberculosis) 015.0 ☑ [730.88]
  osteomyelitis 015.0 ☑ [730.88]
  paraplegia 015.0 ☑ [730.88]
  spinal curvature 015.0 ☑ [737.43]
  spondylitis 015.0 ☑ [720.81]
Potter's 753.0
Poulet's 714.2
pregnancy NEC (*see also* Pregnancy) 646.9 ☑
Preiser's (osteoporosis) 733.09
Pringle's (tuberous sclerosis) 759.5
Profichet's 729.90
prostate 602.9
  specified type NEC 602.8
protozoal NEC 136.8
  intestine, intestinal NEC 007.9
pseudo-Hurler's (mucolipidosis III) 272.7
psychiatric (*see also* Psychosis) 298.9
psychotic (*see also* Psychosis) 298.9
Puente's (simple glandular cheilitis) 528.5
puerperal NEC (*see also* Puerperal) 674.9 ☑
pulmonary (*see also* Disease, lung)
  amyloid 277.39 [517.8]
  artery 417.9
  circulation, circulatory 417.9
    specified NEC 417.8
  diffuse obstructive (chronic) 496
    with
      acute bronchitis 491.22
      asthma (chronic) (obstructive) 493.2 ☑
      exacerbation NEC (acute) 491.21
  heart (chronic) 416.9
    specified NEC 416.8
  hypertensive (vascular) 416.0
    cardiovascular 416.0
  obstructive diffuse (chronic) 496
    with
      acute bronchitis 491.22
      asthma (chronic) (obstructive) 493.2 ☑
      bronchitis (chronic) 491.20
        with
          exacerbation (acute) 491.21
        acute 491.22
        exacerbation NEC (acute) 491.21
      decompensated 491.21
        with exacerbation 491.21
  valve (*see also* Endocarditis, pulmonary) 424.3
  pulp (dental) NEC 522.9
pulseless 446.7

Disease, diseased — *see also* Syndrome — *continued*

Putnam's (subacute combined sclerosis with pernicious anemia) 281.0 [336.2]
Pyle (-Cohn) (craniometaphyseal dysplasia) 756.89
pyramidal tract 333.90
Quervain's
  tendon sheath 727.04
  thyroid (subacute granulomatous thyroiditis) 245.1
Quincke's — *see* Edema, angioneurotic
Quinquaud (acne decalvans) 704.09
rag sorters' 022.1
Raynaud's (paroxysmal digital cyanosis) 443.0
reactive airway — *see* Asthma
Recklinghausen's (M9540/1) 237.71
  bone (osteitis fibrosa cystica) 252.01
Recklinghausen-Applebaum (hemochromatosis) 275.0
Reclus' (cystic) 610.1
rectum NEC 569.49
Refsum's (heredopathia atactica polyneuritiformis) 356.3
Reichmann's (gastrosuccorrhea) 536.8
Reimann's (periodic) 277.31
Reiter's 099.3
renal (functional) (pelvis) (*see also* Disease, kidney) 593.9
  with
    edema (*see also* Nephrosis) 581.9
    exudative nephritis 583.89
    lesion of interstitial nephritis 583.89
    stated generalized cause — *see* Nephritis
  acute 593.9
  basement membrane NEC 583.89
    with
      pulmonary hemorrhage (Goodpasture's syndrome) 446.21 [583.81]
  chronic (*see also* Disease, kidney, chronic) 585.9
  complicating pregnancy or puerperium NEC 646.2 ☑
    with hypertension — *see* Toxemia, of pregnancy
    affecting fetus or newborn 760.1
  cystic, congenital (*see also* Cystic, disease, kidney) 753.10
  diabetic 250.4 ☑ [583.81]
    due to secondary diabetes 249.4 ☑ [581.81]
  due to
    amyloidosis 277.39 [583.81]
    diabetes mellitus 250.4 ☑ [583.81]
      due to secondary diabetes 249.4 ☑ [581.81]
    systemic lupus erythematosis 710.0 [583.81]
  end-stage 585.6
  exudative 583.89
  fibrocystic (congenital) 753.19
  gonococcal 098.19 [583.81]
  gouty 274.10
  hypertensive (*see also* Hypertension, kidney) 403.90
  immune complex NEC 583.89
  interstitial (diffuse) (focal) 583.89
  lupus 710.0 [583.81]
  maternal, affecting fetus or newborn 760.1
    hypertensive 760.0
  phosphate-losing (tubular) 588.0
  polycystic (congenital) 753.12
    adult type (APKD) 753.13
    autosomal dominant 753.13
    autosomal recessive 753.14
    childhood type (CPKD) 753.14
    infantile type 753.14
  specified lesion or cause NEC (*see also* Glomerulonephritis) 583.89
  subacute 581.9
  syphilitic 095.4
  tuberculous (*see also* Tuberculosis) 016.0 ☑ [583.81]
  tubular (*see also* Nephrosis, tubular) 584.5

☑ Additional Digit Required — Refer to the Tabular List for Digit Selection

⬇ Subterms under main terms may continue to next column or page

Disease, diseased — *see also* Syndrome —
    continued
  Rendu-Osler-Weber (familial hemorrhagic
      telangiectasia) 448.0
  renovascular (arteriosclerotic) (*see also* Hyper-
      tension, kidney) 403.90
  respiratory (tract) 519.9
    acute or subacute (upper) NEC 465.9
      due to fumes or vapors 506.3
      multiple sites NEC 465.8
      noninfectious 478.9
      streptococcal 034.0
    chronic 519.9
      arising in the perinatal period 770.7
      due to fumes or vapors 506.4
    due to
      aspiration of liquids or solids 508.9
      external agents NEC 508.9
        specified NEC 508.8
      fumes or vapors 506.9
        acute or subacute NEC 506.3
        chronic 506.4
    fetus or newborn NEC 770.9
    obstructive 496
    specified type NEC 519.8
    upper (acute) (infectious) NEC 465.9
      multiple sites NEC 465.8
      noninfectious NEC 478.9
      streptococcal 034.0
  retina, retinal NEC 362.9
    Batten's or Batten-Mayou 330.1 *[362.71]*
    degeneration 362.89
    vascular lesion 362.17
  rheumatic (*see also* Arthritis) 716.8 ☑
    heart — *see* Disease, heart, rheumatic
  rheumatoid (heart) — *see* Arthritis, rheuma-
      toid
  rickettsial NEC 083.9
    specified type NEC 083.8
  Riedel's (ligneous thyroiditis) 245.3
  Riga (-Fede) (cachectic aphthae) 529.0
  Riggs' (compound periodontitis) 523.40
  Ritter's 695.81
  Rivalta's (cervicofacial actinomycosis) 039.3
  Robles' (onchocerciasis) 125.3 *[360.13]*
  Roger's (congenital interventricular septal de-
      fect) 745.4
  Rokitansky's (*see also* Necrosis, liver) 570
  Romberg's 349.89
  Rosenthal's (factor XI deficiency) 286.2
  Rossbach's (hyperchlorhydria) 536.8
    psychogenic 306.4
  Roth (-Bernhardt) 355.1
  Runeberg's (progressive pernicious anemia)
      281.0
  Rust's (tuberculous spondylitis) (*see also* Tuber-
      culosis) 015.0 ☑ *[720.81]*
  Rustitskii's (multiple myeloma) (M9730/3)
      203.0 ☑
  Ruysch's (Hirschsprung's disease) 751.3
  Sachs (-Tay) 330.1
  sacroiliac NEC 724.6
  salivary gland or duct NEC 527.9
    inclusion 078.5
      streptococcal 034.0
    virus 078.5
  Sander's (paranoia) 297.1
  Sandhoff's 330.1
  sandworm 126.9
  Savill's (epidemic exfoliative dermatitis) 695.89
  Schamberg's (progressive pigmentary dermato-
      sis) 709.09
  Schaumann's (sarcoidosis) 135
  Schenck's (sporotrichosis) 117.1
  Scheuermann's (osteochondrosis) 732.0
  Schilder (-Flatau) 341.1
  Schimmelbusch's 610.1
  Schlatter-Osgood 732.4
  Schlatter's tibia (tubercle) 732.4
  Schmorl's 722.30
    cervical 722.39
    lumbar, lumbosacral 722.32
    specified region NEC 722.39
    thoracic, thoracolumbar 722.31
  Scholz's 330.0

Disease, diseased — *see also* Syndrome —
    continued
  Schönlein (-Henoch) (purpura rheumatica)
      287.0
  Schottmüller's (*see also* Fever, paratyphoid)
      002.9
  Schüller-Christian (chronic histiocytosis X)
      277.89
  Schultz's (agranulocytosis) 288.09
  Schwalbe-Ziehen-Oppenheimer 333.6
  Schwartz-Jampel 359.23
  Schweninger-Buzzi (macular atrophy) 701.3
  sclera 379.19
  scrofulous (*see also* Tuberculosis) 017.2 ☑
  scrotum 608.9
  sebaceous glands NEC 706.9
  Secretan's (posttraumatic edema) 782.3
  semilunar cartilage, cystic 717.5
  seminal vesicle 608.9
  Senear-Usher (pemphigus erythematosus)
      694.4
  serum NEC 999.5
  Sever's (osteochondrosis calcaneum) 732.5
  sexually transmitted — *see* Disease, venereal
  Sézary's (reticulosis) (M9701/3) 202.2 ☑
  Shaver's (bauxite pneumoconiosis) 503
  Sheehan's (postpartum pituitary necrosis)
      253.2
  shimamushi (scrub typhus) 081.2
  shipyard 077.1
  sickle cell 282.60
    with
      crisis 282.62
      Hb-S disease 282.61
      other abnormal hemoglobin (Hb-D)
          (Hb-E) (Hb-G) (Hb-J) (Hb-K)
          (Hb-O) (Hb-P) (high fetal gene)
          (without crisis) 282.68
        with crisis 282.69
    elliptocytosis 282.60
    Hb-C (without crisis) 282.63
      with
        crisis 282.64
        vaso-occlusive pain 282.64
    Hb-S 282.61
      with
        crisis 282.62
        Hb-C (without crisis) 282.63
          with
            crisis 282.64
            vaso-occlusive pain 282.64
        other abnormal hemoglobin (Hb-
            D) (Hb-E) (Hb-G) (Hb-J) (Hb-
            K) (Hb-O) (Hb-P) (high fetal
            gene) (without crisis) 282.68
          with crisis 282.69
    spherocytosis 282.60
    thalassemia (without crisis) 282.41
      with
        crisis 282.42
        vaso-occlusive pain 282.42
  Siegal-Cattan-Mamou (periodic) 277.31
  silo fillers' 506.9
  Simian B 054.3
  Simmonds' (pituitary cachexia) 253.2
  Simons' (progressive lipodystrophy) 272.6
  Sinding-Larsen (juvenile osteopathia patellae)
      732.4
  sinus (*see also* Sinusitis)
    brain 437.9
    specified NEC 478.19
  Sirkari's 085.0
  sixth (*see also* Exanthem subitum) 058.10
  Sjögren (-Gougerot) 710.2
    with lung involvement 710.2 *[517.8]*
  Skevas-Zerfus 989.5
  skin NEC 709.9
    due to metabolic disorder 277.9
    specified type NEC 709.8
  sleeping (*see also* Narcolepsy) 347.00
    meaning sleeping sickness (*see also* Try-
        panosomiasis) 086.5
  small vessel 443.9
  Smith-Strang (oasthouse urine) 270.2
  Sneddon-Wilkinson (subcorneal pustular der-
      matosis) 694.1

Disease, diseased — *see also* Syndrome —
    continued
  South African creeping 133.8
  Spencer's (epidemic vomiting) 078.82
  Spielmeyer-Stock 330.1
  Spielmeyer-Vogt 330.1
  spine, spinal 733.90
    combined system (*see also* Degeneration,
        combined) 266.2 *[336.2]*
      with pernicious anemia 281.0 *[336.2]*
    cord NEC 336.9
      congenital 742.9
    demyelinating NEC 341.8
    joint (*see also* Disease, joint, spine) 724.9
      tuberculous 015.0 ☑ *[730.8]* ☑
  spinocerebellar 334.9
    specified NEC 334.8
  spleen (organic) (postinfectional) 289.50
    amyloid 277.39
    lardaceous 277.39
    polycystic 759.0
    specified NEC 289.59
  sponge divers' 989.5
  Stanton's (melioidosis) 025
  Stargardt's 362.75
  Startle 759.89
  Steinert's 359.21
  Sternberg's — *see* Disease, Hodgkin's
  Stevens-Johnson (erythema multiforme exuda-
      tivum) 695.13
  Sticker's (erythema infectiosum) 057.0
  Stieda's (calcification, knee joint) 726.62
  Still's (juvenile rheumatoid arthritis) 714.30
    adult onset 714.2
  Stiller's (asthenia) 780.79
  Stokes' (exophthalmic goiter) 242.0 ☑
  Stokes-Adams (syncope with heart block)
      426.9
  Stokvis (-Talma) (enterogenous cyanosis) 289.7
  stomach NEC (organic) 537.9
    functional 536.9
      psychogenic 306.4
    lardaceous 277.39
  stonemasons' 502
  storage
    glycogen (*see also* Disease, glycogen stor-
        age) 271.0
    lipid 272.7
    mucopolysaccharide 277.5
  striatopallidal system 333.90
    specified NEC 333.89
  Strümpell-Marie (ankylosing spondylitis) 720.0
  Stuart's (congenital factor X deficiency) (*see*
      also Defect, coagulation) 286.3
  Stuart-Prower (congenital factor X deficiency)
      (*see also* Defect, coagulation) 286.3
  Sturge (-Weber) (-Dimitri) (encephalocuta-
      neous angiomatosis) 759.6
  Stuttgart 100.89
  Sudeck's 733.7
  supporting structures of teeth NEC 525.9
  suprarenal (gland) (capsule) 255.9
    hyperfunction 255.3
    hypofunction 255.41
  Sutton's 709.09
  Sutton and Gull's — *see* Hypertension, kidney
  sweat glands NEC 705.9
    specified type NEC 705.89
  sweating 078.2
  Sweeley-Klionsky 272.4
  Swift (-Feer) 985.0
  swimming pool (bacillus) 031.1
  swineherd's 100.89
  Sylvest's (epidemic pleurodynia) 074.1
  Symmers (follicular lymphoma) (M9690/3)
      202.0 ☑
  sympathetic nervous system (*see also* Neuropa-
      thy, peripheral, autonomic) 337.9
  synovium 727.9
  syphilitic — *see* Syphilis
  systemic tissue mast cell (M9741/3) 202.6 ☑
  Taenzer's 757.4
  Takayasu's (pulseless) 446.7
  Talma's 728.85
  Tangier (familial high-density lipoprotein defi-
      ciency) 272.5

Disease, diseased — *see also* Syndrome —
    continued
  Tarral-Besnier (pityriasis rubra pilaris) 696.4
  Taylor's 701.8
  Tay-Sachs 330.1
  tear duct 375.69
  teeth, tooth 525.9
    hard tissues 521.9
      specified NEC 521.89
    pulp NEC 522.9
  tendon 727.9
    inflammatory NEC 727.9
  terminal vessel 443.9
  testis 608.9
  Thaysen-Gee (nontropical sprue) 579.0
  Thomsen's 359.22
  Thomson's (congenital poikiloderma) 757.33
  Thornwaldt's, Tornwaldt's (pharyngeal bursitis)
      478.29
  throat 478.20
    septic 034.0
  thromboembolic (*see also* Embolism) 444.9
  thymus (gland) 254.9
    specified NEC 254.8
  thyroid (gland) NEC 246.9
    heart (*see also* Hyperthyroidism)
        242.9 ☑ *[425.7]*
    lardaceous 277.39
    specified NEC 246.8
  Tietze's 733.6
  Tommaselli's
    correct substance properly administered
        599.70
    overdose or wrong substance given or
        taken 961.4
  tongue 529.9
  tonsils, tonsillar (and adenoids) (chronic) 474.9
    specified NEC 474.8
  tooth, teeth 525.9
    hard tissues 521.9
      specified NEC 521.89
    pulp NEC 522.9
  Tornwaldt's (pharyngeal bursitis) 478.29
  Tourette's 307.23
  trachea 519.19
  tricuspid — *see* Endocarditis, tricuspid
  triglyceride-storage, type I, II, III 272.7
  triple vessel (coronary arteries) — *see* Arte-
      riosclerosis, coronary
  trisymptomatic, Gougerot's 709.1
  trophoblastic (*see also* Hydatidiform mole) 630
    previous, affecting management of preg-
        nancy V23.1
  tsutsugamushi (scrub typhus) 081.2
  tube (fallopian), noninflammatory 620.9
    specified NEC 620.8
    tuberculous NEC (*see also* Tuberculosis)
        011.9 ☑
  tubo-ovarian
    inflammatory (*see also* Salpingo-oophoritis)
        614.2
    noninflammatory 620.9
      specified NEC 620.8
  tubotympanic, chronic (with anterior perfora-
      tion of ear drum) 382.1
  tympanum 385.9
  Uhl's 746.84
  umbilicus (newborn) NEC 779.89
    delayed separation 779.83
  Underwood's (sclerema neonatorum) 778.1
  undiagnosed 799.9
  Unna's (seborrheic dermatitis) 690.18
  unstable hemoglobin hemolytic 282.7
  Unverricht (-Lundborg) 345.1 ☑   ▲
  Urbach-Oppenheim (necrobiosis lipoidica dia-
      beticorum) 250.8 ☑ *[709.3]*
    due to secondary diabetes 249.8 ☑ *[709.3]*
  Urbach-Wiethe (lipoid proteinosis) 272.8
  ureter 593.9
  urethra 599.9
    specified type NEC 599.84
  urinary (tract) 599.9
    bladder 596.9
      specified NEC 596.8
    maternal, affecting fetus or newborn 760.1

☑ Additional Digit Required — Refer to the Tabular List for Digit Selection   ⟅Ⓜ⟆ Subterms under main terms may continue to next column or page

2010 ICD-9-CM   ▶◀ Revised Text   ● New Line   ▲ Revised Code   October 2009 • Volume 2 — 85

Disease, diseased — *see also* Syndrome — *continued*
Usher-Senear (pemphigus erythematosus) 694.4
uterus (organic) 621.9
infective (*see also* Endometritis) 615.9
inflammatory (*see also* Endometritis) 615.9
noninflammatory 621.9
specified type NEC 621.8
uveal tract
anterior 364.9
posterior 363.9
vagabonds' 132.1
vagina, vaginal
inflammatory 616.10
noninflammatory 623.9
specified NEC 623.8
Valsuani's (progressive pernicious anemia, puerperal) 648.2 ☑
complicating pregnancy or puerperium 648.2 ☑
valve, valvular — *see also* Endocarditis
congenital NEC (*see also* Anomaly, heart, valve) 746.9
pulmonary 746.00
specified type NEC 746.89
van Bogaert-Nijssen (-Peiffer) 330.0
van Creveld-von Gierke (glycogenosis I) 271.0
van den Bergh's (enterogenous cyanosis) 289.7
van Neck's (juvenile osteochondrosis) 732.1
Vaquez (-Osler) (polycythemia vera) (M9950/1) 238.4
vascular 459.9
arteriosclerotic — *see* Arteriosclerosis
hypertensive — *see* Hypertension
obliterative 447.1
peripheral 443.9
occlusive 459.9
peripheral (occlusive) 443.9
in ▶(due to) (with)◀ diabetes mellitus 250.7 ☑ *[443.81]*
▶in (due to) (with)◀ secondary diabetes 249.7 ☑ *[443.81]*
specified type NEC 443.89
vas deferens 608.9
vasomotor 443.9
vasospastic 443.9
vein 459.9
venereal 099.9
chlamydial NEC 099.50
anus 099.52
bladder 099.53
cervix 099.53
epididymis 099.54
genitourinary NEC 099.55
lower 099.53
specified NEC 099.54
pelvic inflammatory disease 099.54
perihepatic 099.56
peritoneum 099.56
pharynx 099.51
rectum 099.52
specified site NEC 099.59
testis 099.54
vagina 099.53
vulva 099.53
complicating pregnancy, childbirth, or puerperium 647.2 ☑
fifth 099.1
sixth 099.1
specified nature or type NEC 099.8
chlamydial — *see* Disease, venereal, chlamydial
Verneuil's (syphilitic bursitis) 095.7
Verse's (calcinosis intervertebralis) 275.49 *[722.90]*
vertebra, vertebral NEC 733.90
disc — *see* Disease, Intervertebral disc
vibration NEC 994.9
Vidal's (lichen simplex chronicus) 698.3
Vincent's (trench mouth) 101
Virchow's 733.99
virus (filterable) NEC 078.89
arbovirus NEC 066.9
arthropod-borne NEC 066.9
central nervous system NEC 049.9

Disease, diseased — *see also* Syndrome — *continued*
virus — *continued*
central nervous system — *continued*
specified type NEC 049.8
complicating pregnancy, childbirth, or puerperium 647.6 ☑
contact (with) V01.79
varicella V01.71
exposure to V01.79
varicella V01.71
Marburg 078.89
maternal
with fetal damage affecting management of pregnancy 655.3 ☑
nonarthropod-borne NEC 078.89
central nervous system NEC 049.9
specified NEC 049.8
vaccination, prophylactic (against) V04.89
vitreous 379.29
vocal cords NEC 478.5
Vogt's (Cecile) 333.71
Vogt-Spielmeyer 330.1
Volhard-Fahr (malignant nephrosclerosis) 403.00
Volkmann's
acquired 958.6
von Bechterew's (ankylosing spondylitis) 720.0
von Economo's (encephalitis lethargica) 049.8
von Eulenburg's (congenital paramyotonia) 359.29
von Gierke's (glycogenosis I) 271.0
von Graefe's 378.72
von Hippel's (retinocerebral angiomatosis) 759.6
von Hippel-Lindau (angiomatosis retinocerebellosa) 759.6
von Jaksch's (pseudoleukemia infantum) 285.8
von Recklinghausen's (M9540/1) 237.71
bone (osteitis fibrosa cystica) 252.01
von Recklinghausen-Applebaum (hemochromatosis) 275.0
von Willebrand (-Jürgens) (angiohemophilia) 286.4
von Zambusch's (lichen sclerosus et atrophicus) 701.0
Voorhoeve's (dyschondroplasia) 756.4
Vrolik's (osteogenesis imperfecta) 756.51
vulva
inflammatory 616.10
noninflammatory 624.9
specified NEC 624.8
Wagner's (colloid milium) 709.3
Waldenström's (osteochondrosis capital femoral) 732.1
Wallgren's (obstruction of splenic vein with collateral circulation) 459.89
Wardrop's (with lymphangitis) 681.9
finger 681.02
toe 681.11
Wassilieff's (leptospiral jaundice) 100.0
wasting NEC 799.4
due to malnutrition 261
paralysis 335.21
Waterhouse-Friderichsen 036.3
waxy (any site) 277.39
Weber-Christian (nodular nonsuppurative panniculitis) 729.30
Wegner's (syphilitic osteochondritis) 090.0
Weil's (leptospiral jaundice) 100.0
of lung 100.0
Weir Mitchell's (erythromelalgia) 443.82
Werdnig-Hoffmann 335.0
Werlhof's (*see also* Purpura, thrombocytopenic) 287.39
Wermer's 258.01
Werner's (progeria adultorum) 259.8
Werner-His (trench fever) 083.1
Werner-Schultz (agranulocytosis) 288.09
Wernicke's (superior hemorrhagic polioencephalitis) 265.1
Wernicke-Posadas 114.9
Whipple's (intestinal lipodystrophy) 040.2
whipworm 127.3
White's (congenital) (keratosis follicularis) 757.39

Disease, diseased — *see also* Syndrome — *continued*
white
blood cell 288.9
specified NEC 288.8
spot 701.0
Whitmore's (melioidosis) 025
Widal-Abrami (acquired hemolytic jaundice) 283.9
Wilkie's 557.1
Wilkinson-Sneddon (subcorneal pustular dermatosis) 694.1
Willis' (diabetes mellitus) (*see also* Diabetes) 250.0 ☑
due to secondary diabetes 249.0 ☑
Wilson's (hepatolenticular degeneration) 275.1
Wilson-Brocq (dermatitis exfoliativa) 695.89
winter vomiting 078.82
Wise's 696.2
Wohlfart-Kugelberg-Welander 335.11
Woillez's (acute idiopathic pulmonary congestion) 518.5
Wolman's (primary familial xanthomatosis) 272.7
wool-sorters' 022.1
Zagari's (xerostomia) 527.7
Zahorsky's (exanthem subitum) 058.10
Ziehen-Oppenheim 333.6
zoonotic, bacterial NEC 027.9
specified type NEC 027.8
Disfigurement (due to scar) 709.2
head V48.6
limb V49.4
neck V48.7
trunk V48.7
Disgerminoma — *see* Dysgerminoma
Disinsertion, retina 361.04
Disintegration, complete, of the body 799.89
traumatic 869.1
Disk kidney 753.3
Dislocatable hip, congenital — *see also* Dislocation, hip, congenital 754.30
Dislocation (articulation) (closed) (displacement) (simple) (subluxation) 839.8

> Note — "Closed" includes simple, complete, partial, uncomplicated, and unspecified dislocation.
>
> "Open" includes dislocation specified as infected or compound and dislocation with foreign body.
>
> "Chronic," "habitual," "old," or "recurrent" dislocations should be coded as indicated under the entry "Dislocation, recurrent," and "pathological" as indicated under the entry "Dislocation, pathological."
>
> For late effect of dislocation see Late, effect, dislocation.

with fracture — *see* Fracture, by site
acromioclavicular (joint) (closed) 831.04
open 831.14
anatomical site (closed)
specified NEC 839.69
open 839.79
unspecified or ill-defined 839.8
open 839.9
ankle (scaphoid bone) (closed) 837.0
open 837.1
arm (closed) 839.8
open 839.9
astragalus (closed) 837.0
open 837.1
atlanto-axial (closed) 839.01
open 839.11
atlas (closed) 839.01
open 839.11
axis (closed) 839.02
open 839.12
back (closed) 839.8
open 839.9
Bell-Daly 723.8
breast bone (closed) 839.61
open 839.71
capsule, joint — *see* Dislocation, by site
carpal (bone) — *see* Dislocation, wrist

Dislocation — *continued*
carpometacarpal (joint) (closed) 833.04
open 833.14
cartilage (joint) (*see also* Dislocation, by site)
knee — *see* Tear, meniscus
cervical, cervicodorsal, or cervicothoracic (spine) (vertebra) — *see* Dislocation, vertebra, cervical
chiropractic (*see also* Lesion, nonallopathic) 739.9
chondrocostal — *see* Dislocation, costochondral
chronic — *see* Dislocation, recurrent
clavicle (closed) 831.04
open 831.14
coccyx (closed) 839.41
open 839.51
collar bone (closed) 831.04
open 831.14
compound (open) NEC 839.9
congenital NEC 755.8
hip (*see also* Dislocation, hip, congenital) 754.30
lens 743.37
rib 756.3
sacroiliac 755.69
spine NEC 756.19
vertebra 756.19
coracoid (closed) 831.09
open 831.19
costal cartilage (closed) 839.69
open 839.79
costochondral (closed) 839.69
open 839.79
cricoarytenoid articulation (closed) 839.69
open 839.79
cricothyroid (cartilage) articulation (closed) 839.69
open 839.79
dorsal vertebrae (closed) 839.21
open 839.31
ear ossicle 385.23
elbow (closed) 832.00
anterior (closed) 832.01
open 832.11
congenital 754.89
divergent (closed) 832.09
open 832.19
lateral (closed) 832.04
open 832.14
medial (closed) 832.03
open 832.13
open 832.10
posterior (closed) 832.02
open 832.12
recurrent 718.32
specified type NEC 832.09
open 832.19
eye 360.81
lateral 376.36
eyeball 360.81
lateral 376.36
femur
distal end (closed) 836.50
anterior 836.52
open 836.62
lateral 836.54 ▲
open 836.64 ▲
medial 836.53 ▲
open 836.63 ▲
open 836.60
posterior 836.51
open 836.61
proximal end (closed) 835.00
anterior (pubic) 835.03
open 835.13
obturator 835.02
open 835.12
posterior 835.01
open 835.11
fibula
distal end (closed) 837.0
open 837.1
proximal end (closed) 836.59
open 836.69

☑ Additional Digit Required — Refer to the Tabular List for Digit Selection

▽ Subterms under main terms may continue to next column or page

Dislocation — Dislocation

Dislocation — *continued*
vertebra — *continued*
cervical, cervicodorsal or cervicothoracic — *continued*
open 839.10
congenital 756.19
dorsal 839.21
open 839.31
recurrent 724.9
lumbar, lumbosacral 839.20
open 839.30
non-traumatic — *see* Displacement, intervertebral disc
open NEC 839.50
recurrent 724.9
specified region NEC 839.49
open 839.59
thoracic 839.21
open 839.31
wrist (carpal bone) (scaphoid) (semilunar) (closed) 833.00
carpometacarpal (joint) 833.04
open 833.14
metacarpal bone, proximal end 833.05
open 833.15
midcarpal (joint) 833.03
open 833.13
open 833.10
radiocarpal (joint) 833.02
open 833.12
radioulnar (joint) 833.01
open 833.11
recurrent 718.33
specified site NEC 833.09
open 833.19
xiphoid cartilage (closed) 839.61
open 839.71

Dislodgement
artificial skin graft 996.55
decellularized allodermis graft 996.55

Disobedience, hostile (covert) (overt) — *see also*
Disturbance, conduct 312.0 ☑

Disorder — *see also* Disease
academic underachievement, childhood and
adolescence 313.83
accommodation 367.51
drug-induced 367.89
toxic 367.89
adjustment (*see also* Reaction, adjustment)
309.9
with
anxiety 309.24
anxiety and depressed mood 309.28
depressed mood 309.0
disturbance of conduct 309.3
disturbance of emotions and conduct
309.4
adrenal (capsule) (cortex) (gland) 255.9
specified type NEC 255.8
adrenogenital 255.2
affective (*see also* Psychosis, affective) 296.90
atypical 296.81
aggressive, unsocialized (*see also* Disturbance,
conduct) 312.0 ☑
alcohol, alcoholic (*see also* Alcohol) 291.9
allergic — *see* Allergy
amino acid (metabolic) (*see also* Disturbance,
metabolism, amino acid) 270.9
albinism 270.2
alkaptonuria 270.2
argininosuccinicaciduria 270.6
beta-amino-isobutyricaciduria 277.2
cystathioninuria 270.4
cystinosis 270.0
cystinuria 270.0
glycinuria 270.0
homocystinuria 270.4
imidazole 270.5
maple syrup (urine) disease 270.3
neonatal, transitory 775.89
oasthouse urine disease 270.2
ochronosis 270.2
phenylketonuria 270.1
phenylpyruvic oligophrenia 270.1
purine NEC 277.2
pyrimidine NEC 277.2

Disorder — *see also* Disease — *continued*
amino acid (*see also* Disturbance, metabolism,
amino acid) — *continued*
renal transport NEC 270.0
specified type NEC 270.8
transport NEC 270.0
renal 270.0
xanthinuria 277.2
amnestic (*see also* Amnestic syndrome) 294.8
alcohol-induced persisting 291.1
drug-induced persisting 292.83
in conditions classified elsewhere 294.0
anaerobic glycolysis with anemia 282.3
anxiety (*see also* Anxiety) 300.00
due to or associated with physical condition 293.84
arteriole 447.9
specified type NEC 447.8
artery 447.9
specified type NEC 447.8
articulation — *see* Disorder, joint
Asperger's 299.8 ☑
attachment of infancy or early childhood
313.89
attention deficit 314.00
with hyperactivity 314.01
predominantly
combined hyperactive/inattentive
314.01
hyperactive/impulsive 314.01
inattentive 314.00
residual type 314.8
auditory processing disorder 388.45
acquired 388.45
developmental 315.32
autistic 299.0 ☑
autoimmune NEC 279.49 ▲
hemolytic (cold type) (warm type) 283.0
parathyroid 252.1
thyroid 245.2
avoidant, childhood or adolescence 313.21
balance
acid-base 276.9
mixed (with hypercapnia) 276.4
electrolyte 276.9
fluid 276.9
behavior NEC (*see also* Disturbance, conduct)
312.9
disruptive 312.9
bilirubin excretion 277.4
bipolar (affective) (alternating) 296.80

Note — *Use the following fifth-digit sub-classification with categories 296.0–296.6:*

0   *unspecifed*

1   *mild*

2   *moderate*

3   *severe, without mention of psychotic behavior*

4   *severe, specified as with psychotic behavior*

5   *in partial or unspecified remission*

6   *in full remission*

---

atypical 296.7
currently
depressed 296.5 ☑
hypomanic 296.4 ☑
manic 296.4 ☑
mixed 296.6 ☑
specified type NEC 296.89
type I 296.7
most recent episode (or current)
depressed 296.5 ☑
hypomanic 296.4 ☑
manic 296.4 ☑
mixed 296.6 ☑
unspecified 296.7
single manic episode 296.0 ☑
type II (recurrent major depressive
episodes with hypomania) 296.89
bladder 596.9
functional NEC 596.59
specified NEC 596.8

Disorder — *see also* Disease — *continued*
bleeding 286.9
bone NEC 733.90
specified NEC 733.99
brachial plexus 353.0
branched-chain amino-acid degradation 270.3
breast 611.9
puerperal, postpartum 676.3 ☑
specified NEC 611.89
Briquet's 300.81
bursa 727.9
shoulder region 726.10
carbohydrate metabolism, congenital 271.9
cardiac, functional 427.9
postoperative 997.1
psychogenic 306.2
cardiovascular, psychogenic 306.2
cartilage NEC 733.90
articular 718.00
ankle 718.07
elbow 718.02
foot 718.07
hand 718.04
hip 718.05
knee 717.9
multiple sites 718.09
pelvic region 718.05
shoulder region 718.01
specified
site NEC 718.08
type NEC 733.99
wrist 718.03
catatonic — *see* Catatonia
central auditory processing 315.32
acquired 388.45
developmental 315.32
cervical region NEC 723.9
cervical root (nerve) NEC 353.2
character NEC (*see also* Disorder, personality)
301.9
ciliary body 364.9
specified NEC 364.89
coagulation (factor) (*see also* Defect, coagulation) 286.9
factor VIII (congenital) (functional) 286.0
factor IX (congenital) (functional) 286.1
neonatal, transitory 776.3
coccyx 724.70
specified NEC 724.79
cognitive 294.9
colon 569.9
functional 564.9
congenital 751.3
communication 307.9
conduct (*see also* Disturbance, conduct) 312.9
adjustment reaction 309.3
adolescent onset type 312.82
childhood onset type 312.81
compulsive 312.30
specified type NEC 312.39
hyperkinetic 314.2
onset unspecified 312.89
socialized (type) 312.20
aggressive 312.23
unaggressive 312.21
specified NEC 312.89
conduction, heart 426.9
specified NEC 426.89
conflict
sexual orientation 302.0
congenital
glycosylation (CDG) 271.8
convulsive (secondary) (*see also* Convulsions)
780.39
due to injury at birth 767.0
idiopathic 780.39
coordination 781.3
cornea NEC 371.89
due to contact lens 371.82
corticosteroid metabolism NEC 255.2
cranial nerve — *see* Disorder, nerve, cranial
cyclothymic 301.13
degradation, branched-chain amino acid 270.3
delusional 297.1
dentition 520.6
depersonalization 300.6

Disorder — *see also* Disease — *continued*
depressive NEC 311
atypical 296.82
major (*see also* Psychosis, affective)
296.2 ☑
recurrent episode 296.3 ☑
single episode 296.2 ☑
development, specific 315.9
associated with hyperkinesia 314.1
coordination 315.4
language 315.31
and speech due to hearing loss 315.34
learning 315.2
arithmetical 315.1
reading 315.00
mixed 315.5
motor coordination 315.4
specified type NEC 315.8
speech 315.39
and language due to hearing loss
315.34
diaphragm 519.4
digestive 536.9
fetus or newborn 777.9
specified NEC 777.8
psychogenic 306.4
disintegrative, childhood 299.1 ☑
dissociative 300.15
identity 300.14
nocturnal 307.47
drug-related 292.9
dysmorphic body 300.7
dysthymic 300.4
ear 388.9
degenerative NEC 388.00
external 380.9
specified 380.89
pinna 380.30
specified type NEC 388.8
vascular NEC 388.00
eating NEC 307.50
electrolyte NEC 276.9
with
abortion — *see* Abortion, by type, with
metabolic disorder
ectopic pregnancy (*see also* categories
633.0–633.9) 639.4
molar pregnancy (*see also* categories
630–632) 639.4
acidosis 276.2
metabolic 276.2
respiratory 276.2
alkalosis 276.3
metabolic 276.3
respiratory 276.3
following
abortion 639.4
ectopic or molar pregnancy 639.4
neonatal, transitory NEC 775.5
emancipation as adjustment reaction 309.22
emotional (*see also* Disorder, mental, nonpsychotic) V40.9
endocrine 259.9
specified type NEC 259.8
esophagus 530.9
functional 530.5
psychogenic 306.4
explosive
intermittent 312.34
isolated 312.35
expressive language 315.31
eye 379.90
globe — *see* Disorder, globe
ill-defined NEC 379.99
limited duction NEC 378.63
specified NEC 379.8
eyelid 374.9
degenerative 374.50
sensory 374.44
specified type NEC 374.89
vascular 374.85
factitious (with combined psychological and
physical signs and symptoms) (with
predominantly physical signs and
symptoms) 300.19

Disorder — *see also* Disease — *continued*
factitious — *continued*
    with predominantly psychological signs
      and symptoms 300.16
  factor, coagulation (*see also* Defect, coagulation) 286.9
    IX (congenital) (funcitonal) 286.1
    VIII (congenital) (functional) 286.0
  fascia 728.9
  fatty acid oxidation 277.85
  feeding — *see* Feeding
  female sexual arousal 302.72
  fluid NEC 276.9
  gastric (functional) 536.9
    motility 536.8
    psychogenic 306.4
    secretion 536.8
  gastrointestinal (functional) NEC 536.9
    newborn (neonatal) 777.9
      specified NEC 777.8
    psychogenic 306.4
  gender (child) 302.6
    adult 302.85
  gender identity (childhood) 302.6
    adolescents 302.85
    adults (-life) 302.85
  genitourinary system, psychogenic 306.50
  globe 360.9
    degenerative 360.20
      specified NEC 360.29
    specified type NEC 360.89
  hearing (*see also* Deafness)
    conductive type (air) (*see also* Deafness, conductive) 389.00
    mixed conductive and sensorineural 389.20
      bilateral 389.22
      unilateral 389.21
    nerve
      bilateral 389.12
      unilateral 389.13
    perceptive (*see also* Deafness, perceptive) 389.10
    sensorineural type NEC (*see also* Deafness, sensorineural 389.10
  heart action 427.9
    postoperative 997.1
  hematological, transient neonatal 776.9
    specified type NEC 776.8
  hematopoietic organs 289.9
  hemorrhagic NEC 287.9
    due to intrinsic circulating anticoagulants 286.5
    specified type NEC 287.8
  hemostasis (*see also* Defect, coagulation) 286.9
  homosexual conflict 302.0
  hypomanic (chronic) 301.11
  identity
    childhood and adolescence 313.82
      gender 302.6
  immune mechanism (immunity) 279.9
    single complement (C1-C9) 279.8
    specified type NEC 279.8
  impulse control (*see also* Disturbance, conduct, compulsive) 312.30
  infant sialic acid storage 271.8
  integument, fetus or newborn 778.9
    specified type NEC 778.8
  interactional psychotic (childhood) (*see also* Psychosis, childhood) 299.1 ☑
  intermittent explosive 312.34
  intervertebral disc 722.90
    cervical, cervicothoracic 722.91
    lumbar, lumbosacral 722.93
    thoracic, thoracolumbar 722.92
  intestinal 569.9
    functional NEC 564.9
      congenital 751.3
      postoperative 564.4
    psychogenic 306.4
  introverted, of childhood and adolescence 313.22
  involuntary emotional expression (IEED) 310.8
  iris 364.9
    specified NEC 364.89
  iron, metabolism 275.0

Disorder — *see also* Disease — *continued*
  isolated explosive 312.35
  joint NEC 719.90
    ankle 719.97
    elbow 719.92
    foot 719.97
    hand 719.94
    hip 719.95
    knee 719.96
    multiple sites 719.99
    pelvic region 719.95
    psychogenic 306.0
    shoulder (region) 719.91
    specified site NEC 719.98
    temporomandibular 524.60
      sounds on opening or closing 524.64
      specified NEC 524.69
    wrist 719.93
  kidney 593.9
    functional 588.9
      specified NEC 588.89
  labyrinth, labyrinthine 386.9
    specified type NEC 386.8
  lactation 676.9 ☑
  language (developmental) (expressive) 315.31
    mixed receptive-expressive 315.32
  learning 315.9
  ligament 728.9
  ligamentous attachments, peripheral (*see also* Enthesopathy)
    spine 720.1
  limb NEC 729.90
    psychogenic 306.0
  lipid
    metabolism, congenital 272.9
    storage 272.7
  lipoprotein deficiency (familial) 272.5
  low back NEC 724.9
    psychogenic 306.0
  lumbosacral
    plexus 353.1
    root (nerve) NEC 353.4
  lymphoproliferative (chronic) NEC (M9970/1) 238.79
    post-transplant (PTLD) 238.77
  major depressive (*see also* Psychosis, affective) 296.2 ☑
    recurrent episode 296.3 ☑
    single episode 296.2 ☑
  male erectile 607.84
    nonorganic origin 302.72
  manic (*see also* Psychosis, affective) 296.0 ☑
    atypical 296.81
  mathematics 315.1
  meniscus NEC (*see also* Disorder, cartilage, articular) 718.0 ☑
  menopausal 627.9
    specified NEC 627.8
  menstrual 626.9
    psychogenic 306.52
    specified NEC 626.8
  mental (nonpsychotic) 300.9
    affecting management of pregnancy, childbirth, or puerperium 648.4 ☑
    drug-induced 292.9
      hallucinogen persisting perception 292.89
      specified type NEC 292.89
    due to or associated with
      alcoholism 291.9
      drug consumption NEC 292.9
        specified type NEC 292.89
      physical condition NEC 293.9
    induced by drug 292.9
      specified type NEC 292.89
    neurotic (*see also* Neurosis) 300.9
    of infancy, childhood or adolescence 313.9
    persistent
      other
        due to conditions classified elsewhere 294.8
      unspecified
        due to conditions classified elsewhere 294.9
    presenile 310.1
      psychotic NEC 290.10

Disorder — *see also* Disease — *continued*
  mental — *continued*
    previous, affecting management of pregnancy V23.89
    psychoneurotic (*see also* Neurosis) 300.9
    psychotic (*see also* Psychosis) 298.9
      brief 298.8
      senile 290.20
    specific, following organic brain damage 310.9
      cognitive or personality change of other type 310.1
      frontal lobe syndrome 310.0
      postconcussional syndrome 310.2
      specified type NEC 310.8
    transient
      in conditions classified elsewhere 293.9
  metabolism NEC 277.9
    with
      abortion — *see* Abortion, by type, with metabolic disorder
      ectopic pregnancy (*see also* categories 633.0–633.9) 639.4
      molar pregnancy (*see also* categories 630–632) 639.4
    alkaptonuria 270.2
    amino acid (*see also* Disorder, amino acid) 270.9
      specified type NEC 270.8
    ammonia 270.6
    arginine 270.6
    argininosuccinic acid 270.6
    basal 794.7
    bilirubin 277.4
    calcium 275.40
    carbohydrate 271.9
      specified type NEC 271.8
    cholesterol 272.9
    citrulline 270.6
    copper 275.1
    corticosteroid 255.2
    cystine storage 270.0
    cystinuria 270.0
    fat 272.9
    fatty acid oxidation 277.85
    following
      abortion 639.4
      ectopic or molar pregnancy 639.4
    fructosemia 271.2
    fructosuria 271.2
    fucosidosis 271.8
    galactose-1-phosphate uridyl transferase 271.1
    glutamine 270.7
    glycine 270.7
    glycogen storage NEC 271.0
      hepatorenal 271.0
    hemochromatosis 275.0
    in labor and delivery 669.0 ☑
    iron 275.0
    lactose 271.3
    lipid 272.9
      specified type NEC 272.8
      storage 272.7
    lipoprotein (*see also* Hyperlipemia deficiency (familial)) 272.5
    lysine 270.7
    magnesium 275.2
    mannosidosis 271.8
    mineral 275.9
      specified type NEC 275.8
    mitochondrial 277.87
    mucopolysaccharide 277.5
    nitrogen 270.9
    ornithine 270.6
    oxalosis 271.8
    pentosuria 271.8
    phenylketonuria 270.1
    phosphate 275.3
    phosphorous 275.3
    plasma protein 273.9
      specified type NEC 273.8
    porphyrin 277.1
    purine 277.2
    pyrimidine 277.2
    serine 270.7

Disorder — *see also* Disease — *continued*
  metabolism — *continued*
    sodium 276.9
    specified type NEC 277.89
    steroid 255.2
    threonine 270.7
    urea cycle 270.6
    xylose 271.8
  micturition NEC 788.69
    psychogenic 306.53
  misery and unhappiness, of childhood and adolescence 313.1
  mitochondrial metabolism 277.87
  mitral valve 424.0
  mood (*see also* Disorder, bipolar) 296.90
    episodic 296.90
      specified NEC 296.99
    in conditions classified elsewhere 293.83
  motor tic 307.20
    chronic 307.22
    transient (childhood) 307.21
  movement NEC 333.90
    hysterical 300.11
    medication-induced 333.90
    periodic limb 327.51
    sleep related, unspecified 780.58
      other organic 327.59
    specified type NEC 333.99
    stereotypic 307.3
  mucopolysaccharide 277.5
  muscle 728.9
    psychogenic 306.0
    specified type NEC 728.3
  muscular attachments, peripheral (*see also* Enthesopathy)
    spine 720.1
  musculoskeletal system NEC 729.90
    psychogenic 306.0
  myeloproliferative (chronic) NEC (M9960/1) 238.79
  myoneural 358.9
    due to lead 358.2
    specified type NEC 358.8
    toxic 358.2
  myotonic 359.29
  neck region NEC 723.9
  nerve 349.9
    abducens NEC 378.54
    accessory 352.4
    acoustic 388.5
    auditory 388.5
    auriculotemporal 350.8
    axillary 353.0
    cerebral — *see* Disorder, nerve, cranial
    cranial 352.9
      first 352.0
      second 377.49
      third
        partial 378.51
        total 378.52
      fourth 378.53
      fifth 350.9
      sixth 378.54
      seventh NEC 351.9
      eighth 388.5
      ninth 352.2
      tenth 352.3
      eleventh 352.4
      twelfth 352.5
      multiple 352.6
    entrapment — *see* Neuropathy, entrapment
    facial 351.9
      specified NEC 351.8
    femoral 355.2
    glossopharyngeal NEC 352.2
    hypoglossal 352.5
    iliohypogastric 355.79
    ilioinguinal 355.79
    intercostal 353.8
    lateral
      cutaneous of thigh 355.1
      popliteal 355.3
    lower limb NEC 355.8
    medial, popliteal 355.4
    median NEC 354.1

Disorder — *see also* Disease — *continued*
- nerve — *continued*
  - obturator 355.79
  - oculomotor
    - partial 378.51
    - total 378.52
  - olfactory 352.0
  - optic 377.49
    - hypoplasia 377.43
    - ischemic 377.41
    - nutritional 377.33
    - toxic 377.34
  - peroneal 355.3
  - phrenic 354.8
  - plantar 355.6
  - pneumogastric 352.3
  - posterior tibial 355.5
  - radial 354.3
  - recurrent laryngeal 352.3
  - root 353.9
    - specified NEC 353.8
  - saphenous 355.79
  - sciatic NEC 355.0
  - specified NEC 355.9
    - lower limb 355.79
    - upper limb 354.8
  - spinal 355.9
  - sympathetic NEC 337.9
  - trigeminal 350.9
    - specified NEC 350.8
  - trochlear 378.53
  - ulnar 354.2
  - upper limb NEC 354.9
  - vagus 352.3
- nervous system NEC 349.9
  - autonomic (peripheral) (*see also* Neuropathy, peripheral, autonomic) 337.9
  - cranial 352.9
  - parasympathetic (*see also* Neuropathy, peripheral, autonomic) 337.9
  - specified type NEC 349.89
  - sympathetic (*see also* Neuropathy, peripheral, autonomic) 337.9
  - vegetative (*see also* Neuropathy, peripheral, autonomic) 337.9
- neurohypophysis NEC 253.6
- neurological NEC 781.99
  - peripheral NEC 355.9
- neuromuscular NEC 358.9
  - hereditary NEC 359.1
  - specified NEC 358.8
  - toxic 358.2
- neurotic 300.9
  - specified type NEC 300.89
- neutrophil, polymorphonuclear (functional) 288.1
- nightmare 307.47
- night terror 307.46
- obsessive-compulsive 300.3
- oppositional defiant, childhood and adolescence 313.81
- optic
  - chiasm 377.54
    - associated with
      - inflammatory disorders 377.54
      - neoplasm NEC 377.52
        - pituitary 377.51
      - pituitary disorders 377.51
      - vascular disorders 377.53
  - nerve 377.49
  - radiations 377.63
  - tracts 377.63
- orbit 376.9
  - specified NEC 376.89
- orgasmic
  - female 302.73
  - male 302.74
- overanxious, of childhood and adolescence 313.0
- oxidation, fatty acid 277.85
- pancreas, internal secretion (other than diabetes mellitus) 251.9
  - specified type NEC 251.8
- panic 300.01
  - with agoraphobia 300.21
- papillary muscle NEC 429.81

Disorder — *see also* Disease — *continued*
- paranoid 297.9
  - induced 297.3
  - shared 297.3
- parathyroid 252.9
  - specified type NEC 252.8
- paroxysmal, mixed 780.39
- pentose phosphate pathway with anemia 282.2
- periodic limb movement 327.51
- peroxisomal 277.86
- personality 301.9
  - affective 301.10
  - aggressive 301.3
  - amoral 301.7
  - anancastic, anankastic 301.4
  - antisocial 301.7
  - asocial 301.7
  - asthenic 301.6
  - avoidant 301.82
  - borderline 301.83
  - compulsive 301.4
  - cyclothymic 301.13
  - dependent-passive 301.6
  - dyssocial 301.7
  - emotional instability 301.59
  - epileptoid 301.3
  - explosive 301.3
  - following organic brain damage 310.1
  - histrionic 301.50
  - hyperthymic 301.11
  - hypomanic (chronic) 301.11
  - hypothymic 301.12
  - hysterical 301.50
  - immature 301.89
  - inadequate 301.6
  - introverted 301.21
  - labile 301.59
  - moral deficiency 301.7
  - narcissistic 301.81
  - obsessional 301.4
  - obsessive-compulsive 301.4
  - overconscientious 301.4
  - paranoid 301.0
  - passive (-dependent) 301.6
  - passive-aggressive 301.84
  - pathological NEC 301.9
  - pseudosocial 301.7
  - psychopathic 301.9
  - schizoid 301.20
    - introverted 301.21
    - schizotypal 301.22
  - schizotypal 301.22
  - seductive 301.59
  - type A 301.4
  - unstable 301.59
- pervasive developmental 299.9 ☑
  - childhood-onset 299.8 ☑
  - specified NEC 299.8 ☑
- phonological 315.39
- pigmentation, choroid (congenital) 743.53
- pinna 380.30
  - specified type NEC 380.39
- pituitary, thalamic 253.9
  - anterior NEC 253.4
  - iatrogenic 253.7
  - postablative 253.7
  - specified NEC 253.8
- pityriasis-like NEC 696.8
- platelets (blood) 287.1
- polymorphonuclear neutrophils (functional) 288.1
- porphyrin metabolism 277.1
- postmenopausal 627.9
  - specified type NEC 627.8
- post-transplant lymphoproliferative (PTLD) 238.77
- posttraumatic stress 309.81
- post-traumatic stress (PTSD) 309.81
  - acute 309.81
  - brief 309.81
  - chronic 309.81
- premenstrual dysphoric (PMDD) 625.4
- psoriatic-like NEC 696.8
- psychic, with diseases classified elsewhere 316
- psychogenic NEC (*see also* condition) 300.9

Disorder — *see also* Disease — *continued*
- psychogenic (*see also* condition) — *continued*
  - allergic NEC
    - respiratory 306.1
  - anxiety 300.00
    - atypical 300.00
    - generalized 300.02
  - appetite 307.59
  - articulation, joint 306.0
  - asthenic 300.5
  - blood 306.8
  - cardiovascular (system) 306.2
  - compulsive 300.3
  - cutaneous 306.3
  - depressive 300.4
  - digestive (system) 306.4
  - dysmenorrheic 306.52
  - dyspneic 306.1
  - eczematous 306.3
  - endocrine (system) 306.6
  - eye 306.7
  - feeding 307.59
  - functional NEC 306.9
  - gastric 306.4
  - gastrointestinal (system) 306.4
  - genitourinary (system) 306.50
  - heart (function) (rhythm) 306.2
  - hemic 306.8
  - hyperventilatory 306.1
  - hypochondriacal 300.7
  - hysterical 300.10
  - intestinal 306.4
  - joint 306.0
  - learning 315.2
  - limb 306.0
  - lymphatic (system) 306.8
  - menstrual 306.52
  - micturition 306.53
  - monoplegic NEC 306.0
  - motor 307.9
  - muscle 306.0
  - musculoskeletal 306.0
  - neurocirculatory 306.2
  - obsessive 300.3
  - occupational 300.89
  - organ or part of body NEC 306.9
  - organs of special sense 306.7
  - paralytic NEC 306.0
  - phobic 300.20
  - physical NEC 306.9
  - pruritic 306.3
  - rectal 306.4
  - respiratory (system) 306.1
  - rheumatic 306.0
  - sexual (function) 302.70
    - specified type NEC 302.79
  - sexual orientation conflict 302.0
  - skin (allergic) (eczematous) (pruritic) 306.3
  - sleep 307.40
    - initiation or maintenance 307.41
      - persistent 307.42
      - transient 307.41
    - movement 780.58
    - sleep terror 307.46
    - specified type NEC 307.49
  - specified part of body NEC 306.8
  - stomach 306.4
- psychomotor NEC 307.9
  - hysterical 300.11
- psychoneurotic (*see also* Neurosis) 300.9
  - mixed NEC 300.89
- psychophysiologic (*see also* Disorder, psychosomatic) 306.9
- psychosexual identity (childhood) 302.6
  - adult-life 302.85
- psychosomatic NEC 306.9
  - allergic NEC
    - respiratory 306.1
  - articulation, joint 306.0
  - cardiovascular (system) 306.2
  - cutaneous 306.3
  - digestive (system) 306.4
  - dysmenorrheic 306.52
  - dyspneic 306.1
  - endocrine (system) 306.6

Disorder — *see also* Disease — *continued*
- psychosomatic — *continued*
  - eye 306.7
  - gastric 306.4
  - gastrointestinal (system) 306.4
  - genitourinary (system) 306.50
  - heart (functional) (rhythm) 306.2
  - hyperventilatory 306.1
  - intestinal 306.4
  - joint 306.0
  - limb 306.0
  - lymphatic (system) 306.8
  - menstrual 306.52
  - micturition 306.53
  - monoplegic NEC 306.0
  - muscle 306.0
  - musculoskeletal 306.0
  - neurocirculatory 306.2
  - organs of special sense 306.7
  - paralytic NEC 306.0
  - pruritic 306.3
  - rectal 306.4
  - respiratory (system) 306.1
  - rheumatic 306.0
  - sexual (function) 302.70
  - skin 306.3
  - specified part of body NEC 306.8
  - specified type NEC 302.79
  - stomach 306.4
- psychotic (*see also* Psychosis) 298.9
  - brief 298.8
- purine metabolism NEC 277.2
- pyrimidine metabolism NEC 277.2
- reactive attachment of infancy or early childhood 313.89
- reading, developmental 315.00
- reflex 796.1
- REM sleep behavior 327.42
- renal function, impaired 588.9
  - specified type NEC 588.89
- renal transport NEC 588.89
- respiration, respiratory NEC 519.9
  - due to
    - aspiration of liquids or solids 508.9
    - inhalation of fumes or vapors 506.9
  - psychogenic 306.1
- retina 362.9
  - specified type NEC 362.89
- rumination 307.53
- sacroiliac joint NEC 724.6
- sacrum 724.6
- schizo-affective (*see also* Schizophrenia) 295.7 ☑
- schizoid, childhood or adolescence 313.22
- schizophreniform 295.4 ☑
- schizotypal personality 301.22
- secretion, thyrocalcitonin 246.0
- seizure 345.9 ☑
  - recurrent 345.9 ☑
    - epileptic — *see* Epilepsy
- semantic pragmatic 315.39
  - with autism 299.0 ☑
- sense of smell 781.1
  - psychogenic 306.7
- separation anxiety 309.21
- sexual (*see also* Deviation, sexual) 302.9
  - aversion 302.79
  - desire, hypoactive 302.71
  - function, psychogenic 302.70
- shyness, of childhood and adolescence 313.21
- single complement (C1-C9) 279.8
- skin NEC 709.9
  - fetus or newborn 778.9
    - specified type 778.8
  - psychogenic (allergic) (eczematous) (pruritic) 306.3
  - specified type NEC 709.8
  - vascular 709.1
- sleep 780.50
  - with apnea — *see* Apnea, sleep
  - alcohol induced 291.82
  - arousal 307.46
    - confusional 327.41
  - circadian rhythm 327.30
    - advanced sleep phase type 327.32
    - alcohol induced 291.82

☑ Additional Digit Required — Refer to the Tabular List for Digit Selection

▽ Subterms under main terms may continue to next column or page

▶◀ Revised Text   ● New Line   ▲ Revised Code   2010 ICD-9-CM

Disorder — *see also* Disease — *continued*
  sleep — *continued*
    circadian rhythm — *continued*
      delayed sleep phase type 327.31
      drug induced 292.85
      free running type 327.34
      in conditions classified elsewhere 327.37
      irregular sleep-wake type 327.33
      jet lag type 327.35
      other 327.39
      shift work type 327.36
    drug induced 292.85
    initiation or maintenance (*see also* Insomnia) 780.52
      nonorganic origin (transient) 307.41
        persistent 307.42
    nonorganic origin 307.40
      specified type NEC 307.49
    organic specified type NEC 327.8
    periodic limb movement 327.51
    specified NEC 780.59
    wake
      cycle — *see* Disorder, sleep, circadian rhythm
      schedule — *see* Disorer, sleep, circadian rhythm
  social, of childhood and adolescence 313.22
  soft tissue 729.90
    specified type NEC 729.99
  somatization 300.81
  somatoform (atypical) (undifferentiated) 300.82
    severe 300.81
    specified type NEC 300.89
  speech NEC 784.59 ▲
    nonorganic origin 307.9
  spine NEC 724.9
    ligamentous or muscular attachments, peripheral 720.1
  steroid metabolism NEC 255.2
  stomach (functional) (*see also* Disorder, gastric) 536.9
    psychogenic 306.4
  storage, iron 275.0
  stress (*see also* Reaction, stress, acute) 308.3
    posttraumatic
      acute 309.81
      brief 309.81
      chronic 309.81
  substitution 300.11
  suspected — *see* Observation
  synovium 727.9
  temperature regulation, fetus or newborn 778.4
  temporomandibular joint NEC 524.60
    sounds on opening or closing 524.64
    specified NEC 524.69
  tendon 727.9
    shoulder region 726.10
  thoracic root (nerve) NEC 353.3
  thyrocalcitonin secretion 246.0
  thyroid (gland) NEC 246.9
    specified type NEC 246.8
  tic 307.20
    chronic (motor or vocal) 307.22
    motor-verbal 307.23
    organic origin 333.1
    transient (of childhood) 307.21
  tooth NEC 525.9
    development NEC 520.9
      specified type NEC 520.8
    eruption 520.6
    specified type NEC 525.8
  Tourette's 307.23
  transport, carbohydrate 271.9
    specified type NEC 271.8
  tubular, phosphate-losing 588.0
  tympanic membrane 384.9
  unaggressive, unsocialized (*see also* Disturbance, conduct) 312.1 ☑
  undersocialized, unsocialized (*see also* Disturbance, conduct)
    aggressive (type) 312.0 ☑
    unaggressive (type) 312.1 ☑
  vision, visual NEC 368.9

Disorder — *see also* Disease — *continued*
  vision, visual — *continued*
    binocular NEC 368.30
    cortex 377.73
      associated with
        inflammatory disorders 377.73
        neoplasms 377.71
        vascular disorders 377.72
    pathway NEC 377.63
      associated with
        inflammatory disorders 377.63
        neoplasms 377.61
        vascular disorders 377.62
  vocal tic
    chronic 307.22
  wakefulness (*see also* Hypersomnia) 780.54
    nonorganic origin (transient) 307.43
      persistent 307.44
  written expression 315.2
Disorganized globe 360.29
Displacement, displaced

> Note — *For acquired displacement of bones, cartilage, joints, tendons, due to injury, see also Dislocation.*
>
> *Displacements at ages under one year should be considered congenital, provided there is no indication the condition was acquired after birth.*

  acquired traumatic of bone, cartilage, joint, tendon NEC (without fracture) (*see also* Dislocation) 839.8
    with fracture — *see* Fracture, by site
  adrenal gland (congenital) 759.1
  alveolus and teeth, vertical 524.75
  appendix, retrocecal (congenital) 751.5
  auricle (congenital) 744.29
  bladder (acquired) 596.8
    congenital 753.8
  brachial plexus (congenital) 742.8
  brain stem, caudal 742.4
  canaliculus lacrimalis 743.65
  cardia, through esophageal hiatus 750.6
  cerebellum, caudal 742.4
  cervix — *see* Displacement, uterus
  colon (congenital) 751.4
  device, implant, or graft — *see* Complications, mechanical
  epithelium
    columnar of cervix 622.10
    cuboidal, beyond limits of external os (uterus) 752.49
  esophageal mucosa into cardia of stomach, congenital 750.4
  esophagus (acquired) 530.89
    congenital 750.4
  eyeball (acquired) (old) 376.36
    congenital 743.8
    current injury 871.3
    lateral 376.36
  fallopian tube (acquired) 620.4
    congenital 752.19
    opening (congenital) 752.19
  gallbladder (congenital) 751.69
  gastric mucosa 750.7
    into
      duodenum 750.7
      esophagus 750.7
      Meckel's diverticulum, congenital 750.7
  globe (acquired) (lateral) (old) 376.36
    current injury 871.3
  graft
    artificial skin graft 996.55
    decellularized allodermis graft 996.55
  heart (congenital) 746.87
    acquired 429.89
  hymen (congenital) (upward) 752.49
  internal prosthesis NEC — *see* Complications, mechanical
  intervertebral disc (with neuritis, radiculitis, sciatica, or other pain) 722.2
    with myelopathy 722.70
    cervical, cervicodorsal, cervicothoracic 722.0
      with myelopathy 722.71

Displacement, displaced — *continued*
  intervertebral disc — *continued*
    cervical, cervicodorsal, cervicothoracic — *continued*
      due to major trauma — *see* Dislocation, vertebra, cervical
    due to trauma — *see* Dislocation, vertebra
    lumbar, lumbosacral 722.10
      with myelopathy 722.73
      due to major trauma — *see* Dislocation, vertebra, lumbar
    thoracic, thoracolumbar 722.11
      with myelopathy 722.72
      due to major trauma — *see* Dislocation, vertebra, thoracic
  intrauterine device 996.32
  kidney (acquired) 593.0
    congenital 753.3
  lacrimal apparatus or duct (congenital) 743.65
  macula (congenital) 743.55
  Meckel's diverticulum (congenital) 751.0
  nail (congenital) 757.5
    acquired 703.8
  opening of Wharton's duct in mouth 750.26
  organ or site, congenital NEC — *see* Malposition, congenital
  ovary (acquired) 620.4
    congenital 752.0
    free in peritoneal cavity (congenital) 752.0
    into hernial sac 620.4
  oviduct (acquired) 620.4
    congenital 752.19
  parathyroid (gland) 252.8
  parotid gland (congenital) 750.26
  punctum lacrimale (congenital) 743.65
  sacroiliac (congenital) (joint) 755.69
    current injury — *see* Dislocation, sacroiliac
    old 724.6
  spine (congenital) 756.19
  spleen, congenital 759.0
  stomach (congenital) 750.7
    acquired 537.89
  subglenoid (closed) 831.01
  sublingual duct (congenital) 750.26
  teeth, tooth 524.30
    horizontal 524.33
    vertical 524.34
  tongue (congenital) (downward) 750.19
  trachea (congenital) 748.3
  ureter or ureteric opening or orifice (congenital) 753.4
  uterine opening of oviducts or fallopian tubes 752.19
  uterus, uterine (*see also* Malposition, uterus) 621.6
    congenital 752.3
  ventricular septum 746.89
    with rudimentary ventricle 746.89
  xyphoid bone (process) 738.3
Disproportion 653.9 ☑
  affecting fetus or newborn 763.1
  breast, reconstructed 612.1
    between native and reconstructed 612.1
  caused by
    conjoined twins 678.1 ☑
    contraction, pelvis (general) 653.1 ☑
      inlet 653.2 ☑
      midpelvic 653.8 ☑
      midplane 653.8 ☑
      outlet 653.3 ☑
    fetal
      ascites 653.7 ☑
      hydrocephalus 653.6 ☑
      hydrops 653.7 ☑
      meningomyelocele 653.7 ☑
      sacral teratoma 653.7 ☑
      tumor 653.7 ☑
    hydrocephalic fetus 653.6 ☑
    pelvis, pelvic, abnormality (bony) NEC 653.0 ☑
    unusually large fetus 653.5 ☑
  causing obstructed labor 660.1 ☑
  cephalopelvic, normally formed fetus 653.4 ☑
    causing obstructed labor 660.1 ☑
  fetal NEC 653.5 ☑
    causing obstructed labor 660.1 ☑

Disproportion — *continued*
  fetopelvic, normally formed fetus 653.4 ☑
    causing obstructed labor 660.1 ☑
  mixed maternal and fetal origin, normally formed fetus 653.4 ☑
  pelvis, pelvic (bony) NEC 653.1 ☑
    causing obstructed labor 660.1 ☑
  specified type NEC 653.8 ☑
Disruption
  cesarean wound 674.1 ☑
  family V61.09
    due to
      child in
        care of non-parental family member V61.06
        foster care V61.06
        welfare custody V61.05
      death of family member V61.07 ●
      divorce V61.03
      estrangement V61.09
        parent-child V61.04
      extended absence of family member ● NEC V61.08 ●
      family member
        on military deployment V61.01
        return from military deployment V61.02
      legal separation V61.03
  gastrointestinal anastomosis 997.4
  ligament(s) (*see also* Sprain)
    knee
      current injury — *see* Dislocation, knee
      old 717.89
        capsular 717.85
        collateral (medial) 717.82
          lateral 717.81
        cruciate (posterior) 717.84
          anterior 717.83
        specified site NEC 717.85
    marital V61.10
      involving
        divorce V61.03
        estrangement V61.09
  operation wound (external) (*see also* Dehiscence) 998.32
    internal 998.31
  organ transplant, anastomosis site — *see* Complications, transplant, organ, by site
  ossicles, ossicular chain 385.23
    traumatic — *see* Fracture, skull, base
  parenchyma
    liver (hepatic) — *see* Laceration, liver, major
    spleen — *see* Laceration, spleen, parenchyma, massive
  phase-shift, of 24-hour sleep-wake cycle, unspecified 780.55
    nonorganic origin 307.45
  sleep-wake cycle (24-hour), unspecified 780.55
    circadian rhythm 327.33
    nonorganic origin 307.45
  suture line (external) (*see also* Dehiscence) 998.32
    internal 998.31
  wound 998.30
    cesarean operation 674.1 ☑
    episiotomy 674.2 ☑
    operation (surgical) 998.32
      cesarean 674.1 ☑
      internal 998.31
    perineal (obstetric) 674.2 ☑
    uterine 674.1 ☑
Disruptio uteri — *see also* Rupture, uterus
  complicating delivery — *see* Delivery, complicated, rupture, uterus
Dissatisfaction with
  employment V62.29
  school environment V62.3
Dissecting — *see* condition
Dissection
  aorta 441.00
    abdominal 441.02
    thoracic 441.01
    thoracoabdominal 441.03

☑ Additional Digit Required — Refer to the Tabular List for Digit Selection   Subterms under main terms may continue to next column or page

2010 ICD-9-CM   ▶◀ Revised Text   ● New Line   ▲ Revised Code   October 2009 · Volume 2 — 91

Index

Dissection — Disturbance

Dissection — continued
  artery, arterial
    carotid 443.21
    coronary 414.12
    iliac 443.22
    renal 443.23
    specified NEC 443.29
    vertebral 443.24
  vascular 459.9
  wound — see Wound, open, by site
Disseminated — see condition
Dissociated personality NEC 300.15
Dissociation
  auriculoventricular or atrioventricular (any degree) (AV) 426.89
    with heart block 426.0
  interference 426.89
  isorhythmic 426.89
  rhythm
    atrioventricular (AV) 426.89
    interference 426.89
Dissociative
  identity disorder 300.14
  reaction NEC 300.15
Dissolution, vertebra — see also Osteoporosis 733.00
Distention
  abdomen (gaseous) 787.3
  bladder 596.8
  cecum 569.89
  colon 569.89
  gallbladder 575.8
  gaseous (abdomen) 787.3
  intestine 569.89
  kidney 593.89
  liver 573.9
  seminal vesicle 608.89
  stomach 536.8
    acute 536.1
    psychogenic 306.4
  ureter 593.5
  uterus 621.8
Distichia, distichiasis (eyelid) 743.63
Distoma hepaticum infestation 121.3
Distomiasis 121.9
  bile passages 121.3
    due to Clonorchis sinensis 121.1
  hemic 120.9
  hepatic (liver) 121.3
    due to Clonorchis sinensis (clonorchiasis) 121.1
  intestinal 121.4
  liver 121.3
    due to Clonorchis sinensis 121.1
  lung 121.2
  pulmonary 121.2
Distomolar (fourth molar) 520.1
  causing crowding 524.31
Disto-occlusion (division I) (division II) 524.22
Distortion (congenital)
  adrenal (gland) 759.1
  ankle (joint) 755.69
  anus 751.5
  aorta 747.29
  appendix 751.5
  arm 755.59
  artery (peripheral) NEC (see also Distortion, peripheral vascular system) 747.60
    cerebral 747.81
    coronary 746.85
    pulmonary 747.3
    retinal 743.58
    umbilical 747.5
  auditory canal 744.29
    causing impairment of hearing 744.02
  bile duct or passage 751.69
  bladder 753.8
  brain 742.4
  bronchus 748.3
  cecum 751.5
  cervix (uteri) 752.49
  chest (wall) 756.3
  clavicle 755.51
  clitoris 752.49
  coccyx 756.19
  colon 751.5

Distortion — continued
  common duct 751.69
  cornea 743.41
  cricoid cartilage 748.3
  cystic duct 751.69
  duodenum 751.5
  ear 744.29
    auricle 744.29
      causing impairment of hearing 744.02
    causing impairment of hearing 744.09
    external 744.29
      causing impairment of hearing 744.02
    inner 744.05
    middle, except ossicles 744.03
      ossicles 744.04
    ossicles 744.04
  endocrine (gland) NEC 759.2
  epiglottis 748.3
  Eustachian tube 744.24
  eye 743.8
    adnexa 743.69
  face bone(s) 756.0
  fallopian tube 752.19
  femur 755.69
  fibula 755.69
  finger(s) 755.59
  foot 755.67
  gallbladder 751.69
  genitalia, genital organ(s)
    female 752.89
      external 752.49
      internal NEC 752.89
    male 752.89
      penis 752.69
  glottis 748.3
  gyri 742.4
  hand bone(s) 755.59
  heart (auricle) (ventricle) 746.89
    valve (cusp) 746.89
  hepatic duct 751.69
  humerus 755.59
  hymen 752.49
  ileum 751.5
  intestine (large) (small) 751.5
    with anomalous adhesions, fixation or malrotation 751.4
  jaw NEC 524.89
  jejunum 751.5
  kidney 753.3
  knee (joint) 755.64
  labium (majus) (minus) 752.49
  larynx 748.3
  leg 755.69
  lens 743.36
  liver 751.69
  lumbar spine 756.19
    with disproportion (fetopelvic) 653.0 ☑
      affecting fetus or newborn 763.1
    causing obstructed labor 660.1 ☑
  lumbosacral (joint) (region) 756.19
  lung (fissures) (lobe) 748.69
  nerve 742.8
  nose 748.1
  organ
    of Corti 744.05
    of site not listed — see Anomaly, specified type NEC
  ossicles, ear 744.04
  ovary 752.0
  oviduct 752.19
  pancreas 751.7
  parathyroid (gland) 759.2
  patella 755.64
  peripheral vascular system NEC 747.60
    gastrointestinal 747.61
    lower limb 747.64
    renal 747.62
    spinal 747.82
    upper limb 747.63
  pituitary (gland) 759.2
  radius 755.59
  rectum 751.5
  rib 756.3
  sacroiliac joint 755.69
  sacrum 756.19
  scapula 755.59

Distortion — continued
  shoulder girdle 755.59
  site not listed — see Anomaly, specified type NEC
  skull bone(s) 756.0
    with
      anencephalus 740.0
      encephalocele 742.0
      hydrocephalus 742.3
        with spina bifida (see also Spina bifida) 741.0 ☑
      microcephalus 742.1
  spinal cord 742.59
  spine 756.19
  spleen 759.0
  sternum 756.3
  thorax (wall) 756.3
  thymus (gland) 759.2
  thyroid (gland) 759.2
    cartilage 748.3
  tibia 755.69
  toe(s) 755.66
  tongue 750.19
  trachea (cartilage) 748.3
  ulna 755.59
  ureter 753.4
    causing obstruction 753.20
  urethra 753.8
    causing obstruction 753.6
  uterus 752.3
  vagina 752.49
  vein (peripheral) NEC (see also Distortion, peripheral vascular system) 747.60
    great 747.49
    portal 747.49
    pulmonary 747.49
  vena cava (inferior) (superior) 747.49
  vertebra 756.19
  visual NEC 368.15
    shape or size 368.14
  vulva 752.49
  wrist (bones) (joint) 755.59
Distress
  abdomen 789.0 ☑
  colon 564.9
  emotional V40.9
  epigastric 789.0 ☑
  fetal (syndrome) 768.4
    affecting management of pregnancy or childbirth 656.8 ☑
    liveborn infant 768.4
      first noted
        before onset of labor 768.2
        during labor and delivery 768.3
      stillborn infant (death before onset of labor) 768.0
        death during labor 768.1
  gastrointestinal (functional) 536.9
    psychogenic 306.4
  intestinal (functional) NEC 564.9
    psychogenic 306.4
  intrauterine — see Distress, fetal
  leg 729.5
  maternal 669.0 ☑
  mental V40.9
  respiratory 786.09
    acute (adult) 518.82
    adult syndrome (following shock, surgery, or trauma) 518.5
      specified NEC 518.82
    fetus or newborn 770.89
    syndrome (idiopathic) (newborn) 769
  stomach 536.9
    psychogenic 306.4
Distribution vessel, atypical NEC 747.60
  coronary artery 746.85
  spinal 747.82
Districhiasis 704.2
Disturbance — see also Disease
  absorption NEC 579.9
    calcium 269.3
    carbohydrate 579.8
    fat 579.8
    protein 579.8
    specified type NEC 579.8
    vitamin (see also Deficiency, vitamin) 269.2

Disturbance — see also Disease — continued
  acid-base equilibrium 276.9
  activity and attention, simple, with hyperkinesis 314.01
  amino acid (metabolic) (see also Disorder, amino acid) 270.9
    imidazole 270.5
    maple syrup (urine) disease 270.3
    transport 270.0
  assimilation, food 579.9
  attention, simple 314.00
    with hyperactivity 314.01
  auditory, nerve, except deafness 388.5
  behavior (see also Disturbance, conduct) 312.9
  blood clotting (hypoproteinemia) (mechanism) (see also Defect, coagulation) 286.9
  central nervous system NEC 349.9
  cerebral nerve NEC 352.9
  circulatory 459.9
  conduct 312.9

Note — Use the following fifth-digit subclassification with categories 312.0–312.2:

0   unspecified

1   mild

2   moderate

3   severe

    adjustment reaction 309.3
    adolescent onset type 312.82
    childhood onset type 312.81
    compulsive 312.30
      intermittent explosive disorder 312.34
      isolated explosive disorder 312.35
      kleptomania 312.32
      pathological gambling 312.31
      pyromania 312.33
    hyperkinetic 314.2
    intermittent explosive 312.34
    isolated explosive 312.35
    mixed with emotions 312.4
    socialized (type) 312.20
      aggressive 312.23
      unaggressive 312.21
    specified type NEC 312.89
    undersocialized, unsocialized
      aggressive (type) 312.0 ☑
      unaggressive (type) 312.1 ☑
  coordination 781.3
  cranial nerve NEC 352.9
  deep sensibility — see Disturbance, sensation
  digestive 536.9
    psychogenic 306.4
  electrolyte — see Imbalance, electrolyte
  emotions specific to childhood or adolescence 313.9
    with
      academic underachievement 313.83
      anxiety and fearfulness 313.0
      elective mutism 313.23
      identity disorder 313.82
      jealousy 313.3
      misery and unhappiness 313.1
      oppositional defiant disorder 313.81
      overanxiousness 313.0
      sensitivity 313.21
      shyness 313.21
      social withdrawal 313.22
      withdrawal reaction 313.22
    involving relationship problems 313.3
    mixed 313.89
    specified type NEC 313.89
  endocrine (gland) 259.9
    neonatal, transitory 775.9
      specified NEC 775.89
  equilibrium 780.4
  feeding (elderly) (infant) 783.3
    newborn 779.31   ▲
    nonorganic origin NEC 307.59
    psychogenic NEC 307.59
  fructose metabolism 271.2
  gait 781.2
    hysterical 300.11
  gastric (functional) 536.9
    motility 536.8

Disturbance — *see also* Disease — *continued*
gastric — *continued*
  psychogenic 306.4
  secretion 536.8
gastrointestinal (functional) 536.9
  psychogenic 306.4
habit, child 307.9
hearing, except deafness 388.40
heart, functional (conditions classifiable to 426, 427, 428)
  due to presence of (cardiac) prosthesis 429.4
  postoperative (immediate) 997.1
    long-term effect of cardiac surgery 429.4
  psychogenic 306.2
hormone 259.9
innervation uterus, sympathetic, parasympathetic 621.8
keratinization NEC
  gingiva 523.10
  lip 528.5
  oral (mucosa) (soft tissue) 528.79
    residual ridge mucosa
      excessive 528.72
      minimal 528.71
  tongue 528.79
labyrinth, labyrinthine (vestibule) 386.9
learning, specific NEC 315.2
memory (*see also* Amnesia) 780.93
  mild, following organic brain damage 310.8
mental (*see also* Disorder, mental) 300.9
  associated with diseases classified elsewhere 316
metabolism (acquired) (congenital) (*see also* Disorder, metabolism) 277.9
  with
    abortion — *see* Abortion, by type, with metabolic disorder
    ectopic pregnancy (*see also* categories 633.0–633.9) 639.4
    molar pregnancy (*see also* categories 630–632) 639.4
  amino acid (*see also* Disorder, amino acid) 270.9
    aromatic NEC 270.2
    branched-chain 270.3
    specified type NEC 270.8
    straight-chain NEC 270.7
    sulfur-bearing 270.4
    transport 270.0
  ammonia 270.6
  arginine 270.6
  argininosuccinic acid 270.6
  carbohydrate NEC 271.9
  cholesterol 272.9
  citrulline 270.6
  cystathionine 270.4
  fat 272.9
  following
    abortion 639.4
    ectopic or molar pregnancy 639.4
  general 277.9
    carbohydrate 271.9
    iron 275.0
    phosphate 275.3
    sodium 276.9
  glutamine 270.7
  glycine 270.7
  histidine 270.5
  homocystine 270.4
  in labor or delivery 669.0 ☑
  iron 275.0
  isoleucine 270.3
  leucine 270.3
  lipoid 272.9
    specified type NEC 272.8
  lysine 270.7
  methionine 270.4
  neonatal, transitory 775.9
    specified type NEC 775.89
  nitrogen 788.99
  ornithine 270.6
  phosphate 275.3
  phosphatides 272.7

Disturbance — *see also* Disease — *continued*
metabolism (*see also* Disorder, metabolism) — *continued*
  serine 270.7
  sodium NEC 276.9
  threonine 270.7
  tryptophan 270.2
  tyrosine 270.2
  urea cycle 270.6
  valine 270.3
motor 796.1
nervous functional 799.21 ▲
neuromuscular mechanism (eye) due to syphilis 094.84
nutritional 269.9
  nail 703.8
ocular motion 378.87
  psychogenic 306.7
oculogyric 378.87
  psychogenic 306.7
oculomotor NEC 378.87
  psychogenic 306.7
olfactory nerve 781.1
optic nerve NEC 377.49
oral epithelium, including tongue 528.79
  residual ridge mucosa
    excessive 528.72
    minimal 528.71
personality (pattern) (trait) (*see also* Disorder, personality) 301.9
  following organic brain damage 310.1
polyglandular 258.9
psychomotor 307.9
pupillary 379.49
reflex 796.1
rhythm, heart 427.9
  postoperative (immediate) 997.1
    long-term effect of cardiac surgery 429.4
  psychogenic 306.2
salivary secretion 527.7
sensation (cold) (heat) (localization) (tactile discrimination localization) (texture) (vibratory) NEC 782.0
  hysterical 300.11
  skin 782.0
  smell 781.1
  taste 781.1
sensory (*see also* Disturbance, sensation) 782.0
  innervation 782.0
situational (transient) (*see also* Reaction, adjustment) 309.9
  acute 308.3
sleep 780.50
  with apnea — *see* Apnea, sleep
  initiation or maintenance (*see also* Insomnia) 780.52
    nonorganic origin 307.41
  nonorganic origin 307.40
    specified type NEC 307.49
  specified NEC 780.59
    nonorganic origin 307.49
  wakefulness (*see also* Hypersomnia) 780.54
    nonorganic origin 307.43
sociopathic 301.7
speech NEC 784.59 ▲
  developmental 315.39
    associated with hyperkinesis 314.1
  secondary to organic lesion 784.59 ▲
stomach (functional) (*see also* Disturbance, gastric) 536.9
sympathetic (nerve) (*see also* Neuropathy, peripheral, autonomic) 337.9
temperature sense 782.0
  hysterical 300.11
tooth
  eruption 520.6
  formation 520.4
  structure, hereditary NEC 520.5
touch (*see also* Disturbance, sensation) 782.0
vascular 459.9
  arteriosclerotic — *see* Arteriosclerosis
vasomotor 443.9
vasospastic 443.9
vestibular labyrinth 386.9
vision, visual NEC 368.9

Disturbance — *see also* Disease — *continued*
vision, visual — *continued*
  psychophysical 368.16
  specified NEC 368.8
  subjective 368.10
voice ▶and resonance◀ 784.40
wakefulness (initiation or maintenance) (*see also* Hypersomnia) 780.54
  nonorganic origin 307.43

Disulfiduria, beta-mercaptolactate-cysteine 270.0
Disuse atrophy, bone 733.7 ▲
Ditthomska syndrome 307.81
Diuresis 788.42
Divers'
palsy or paralysis 993.3
squeeze 993.3
Diverticula, diverticulosis, diverticulum (acute) (multiple) (perforated) (ruptured) 562.10
with diverticulitis 562.11
aorta (Kommerell's) 747.21
appendix (noninflammatory) 543.9
bladder (acquired) (sphincter) 596.3
  congenital 753.8
broad ligament 620.8
bronchus (congenital) 748.3
  acquired 494.0
    with acute exacerbation 494.1
calyx, calyceal (kidney) 593.89
cardia (stomach) 537.1
cecum 562.10
  with
    diverticulitis 562.11
      with hemorrhage 562.13
    hemorrhage 562.12
  congenital 751.5
colon (acquired) 562.10
  with
    diverticulitis 562.11
      with hemorrhage 562.13
    hemorrhage 562.12
  congenital 751.5
duodenum 562.00
  with
    diverticulitis 562.01
      with hemorrhage 562.03
    hemorrhage 562.02
  congenital 751.5
epiphrenic (esophagus) 530.6
esophagus (congenital) 750.4
  acquired 530.6
  epiphrenic 530.6
  pulsion 530.6
  traction 530.6
  Zenker's 530.6
Eustachian tube 381.89
fallopian tube 620.8
gallbladder (congenital) 751.69
gastric 537.1
heart (congenital) 746.89
ileum 562.00
  with
    diverticulitis 562.01
      with hemorrhage 562.03
    hemorrhage 562.02
intestine (large) 562.10
  with
    diverticulitis 562.11
      with hemorrhage 562.13
    hemorrhage 562.12
  congenital 751.5
  small 562.00
    with
      diverticulitis 562.01
        with hemorrhage 562.03
      hemorrhage 562.02
    congenital 751.5
jejunum 562.00
  with
    diverticulitis 562.01
      with hemorrhage 562.03
    hemorrhage 562.02
kidney (calyx) (pelvis) 593.89
  with calculus 592.0
Kommerell's 747.21
laryngeal ventricle (congenital) 748.3

Diverticula, diverticulosis, diverticulum — *continued*
Meckel's (displaced) (hypertrophic) 751.0
midthoracic 530.6
organ or site, congenital NEC — *see* Distortion
pericardium (conginital) (cyst) 746.89
  acquired (true) 423.8
pharyngoesophageal (pulsion) 530.6
pharynx (congenital) 750.27
pulsion (esophagus) 530.6
rectosigmoid 562.10
  with
    diverticulitis 562.11
      with hemorrhage 562.13
    hemorrhage 562.12
  congenital 751.5
rectum 562.10
  with
    diverticulitis 562.11
      with hemorrhage 562.13
    hemorrhage 562.12
renal (calyces) (pelvis) 593.89
  with calculus 592.0
Rokitansky's 530.6
seminal vesicle 608.0
sigmoid 562.10
  with
    diverticulitis 562.11
      with hemorrhage 562.13
    hemorrhage 562.12
  congenital 751.5
small intestine 562.00
  with
    diverticulitis 562.01
      with hemorrhage 562.03
    hemorrhage 562.02
stomach (cardia) (juxtacardia) (juxtapyloric) (acquired) 537.1
  congenital 750.7
subdiaphragmatic 530.6
trachea (congenital) 748.3
  acquired 519.19
traction (esophagus) 530.6
ureter (acquired) 593.89
  congenital 753.4
ureterovesical orifice 593.89
urethra (acquired) 599.2
  congenital 753.8
ventricle, left (congenital) 746.89
vesical (urinary) 596.3
  congenital 753.8
Zenker's (esophagus) 530.6
Diverticulitis (acute) — *see also* Diverticula 562.11
with hemorrhage 562.13
bladder (urinary) 596.3
cecum (perforated) 562.11
  with hemorrhage 562.13
colon (perforated) 562.11
  with hemorrhage 562.13
duodenum 562.01
  with hemorrhage 562.03
esophagus 530.6
ileum (perforated) 562.01
  with hemorrhage 562.03
intestine (large) (perforated) 562.11
  with hemorrhage 562.13
  small 562.01
    with hemorrhage 562.03
jejunum (perforated) 562.01
  with hemorrhage 562.03
Meckel's (perforated) 751.0
pharyngoesophageal 530.6
rectosigmoid (perforated) 562.11
  with hemorrhage 562.13
rectum 562.11
  with hemorrhage 562.13
sigmoid (old) (perforated) 562.11
  with hemorrhage 562.13
small intestine (perforated) 562.01
  with hemorrhage 562.03
vesical (urinary) 596.3
Diverticulosis — *see* Diverticula
Division
cervix uteri 622.8

☑ Additional Digit Required — Refer to the Tabular List for Digit Selection   ⟲ Subterms under main terms may continue to next column or page

2010 ICD-9-CM   ▶◀ Revised Text   ● New Line   ▲ Revised Code   October 2009 • Volume 2 — 93

Division — continued
  cervix uteri — continued
    external os into two openings by frenum 752.49
    external (cervical) into two openings by frenum 752.49
    glans penis 752.69
    hymen 752.49
    labia minora (congenital) 752.49
    ligament (partial or complete) (current) (see also Sprain, by site)
      with open wound — see Wound, open, by site
    muscle (partial or complete) (current) (see also Sprain, by site)
      with open wound — see Wound, open, by site
    nerve — see Injury, nerve, by site
    penis glans 752.69
    spinal cord — see Injury, spinal, by site
    vein 459.9
      traumatic — see Injury, vascular, by site
Divorce V61.03
Dix-Hallpike neurolabyrinthitis 386.12
Dizziness 780.4
  hysterical 300.11
  psychogenic 306.9
Doan-Wiseman syndrome (primary splenic neutropenia) 289.53
Dog bite — see Wound, open, by site
Döhle body-panmyelopathic syndrome 288.2
Döhle-Heller aortitis 093.1
Dolichocephaly, dolichocephalus 754.0
Dolichocolon 751.5
Dolichostenomelia 759.82
Donohue's syndrome (leprechaunism) 259.8
Donor
  blood V59.01
    other blood components V59.09
    stem cells V59.02
    whole blood V59.01
  bone V59.2
    marrow V59.3
  cornea V59.5
  egg (oocyte) (ovum) V59.70
    over age 35 V59.73
      anonymous recipient V59.73
      designated recipient V59.74
    under age 35 V59.71
      anonymous recipient V59.71
      designated recipient V59.72
  heart V59.8
  kidney V59.4
  liver V59.6
  lung V59.8
  lymphocyte V59.8
  organ V59.9
    specified NEC V59.8
  potential, examination of V70.8
  skin V59.1
  specified organ or tissue NEC V59.8
  sperm V59.8
  stem cells V59.02
  tissue V59.9
    specified type NEC V59.8
Donovanosis (granuloma venereum) 099.2
DOPS (diffuse obstructive pulmonary syndrome) 496
Double
  albumin 273.8
  aortic arch 747.21
  auditory canal 744.29
  auricle (heart) 746.82
  bladder 753.8
  external (cervical) os 752.49
  kidney with double pelvis (renal) 753.3
  larynx 748.3
  meatus urinarius 753.8
  organ or site NEC — see Accessory
  orifice
    heart valve NEC 746.89
      pulmonary 746.09
  outlet, right ventricle 745.11
  pelvis (renal) with double ureter 753.4
  penis 752.69
  tongue 750.13

Double — continued
  ureter (one or both sides) 753.4
    with double pelvis (renal) 753.4
  urethra 753.8
  urinary meatus 753.8
  uterus (any degree) 752.2
    with doubling of cervix and vagina 752.2
    in pregnancy or childbirth 654.0 ☑
      affecting fetus or newborn 763.89
  vagina 752.49
    with doubling of cervix and uterus 752.2
  vision 368.2
  vocal cords 748.3
  vulva 752.49
  whammy (syndrome) 360.81
Douglas' pouch, cul-de-sac — see condition
Down's disease or syndrome (mongolism) 758.0
Down-growth, epithelial (anterior chamber) 364.61
Dracontiasis 125.7
Dracunculiasis 125.7
Dracunculosis 125.7
Drainage
  abscess (spontaneous) — see Abscess
  anomalous pulmonary veins to hepatic veins or right atrium 747.41
  stump (amputation) (surgical) 997.62
  suprapubic, bladder 596.8
Dream state, hysterical 300.13
Drepanocytic anemia — see also Disease, sickle cell 282.60
Dresbach's syndrome (elliptocytosis) 282.1
Dreschlera (infection) 118
  hawaiiensis 117.8
Dressler's syndrome (postmyocardial infarction) 411.0
Dribbling (post-void) 788.35
Drift, ulnar 736.09
Drinking (alcohol) — see also Alcoholism
  excessive, to excess NEC (see also Abuse, drugs, nondependent) 305.0 ☑
    bouts, periodic 305.0 ☑
    continual 303.9 ☑
    episodic 305.0 ☑
    habitual 303.9 ☑
    periodic 305.0 ☑
Drip, postnasal (chronic) 784.91
  due to
    allergic rhinitis — see Rhinitis, allergic
    common cold 460
    gastroesophageal reflux — see Reflux, gastroesophageal
    nasopharyngitis — see Nasopharyngitis
    other known condition — code to condition
    sinusitis — see Sinusitis
Drivers' license examination V70.3
Droop
  Cooper's 611.81
  facial 781.94
Drop
  finger 736.29
  foot 736.79
  hematocrit (precipitous) 790.01
  hemoglobin 790.01
  toe 735.8
  wrist 736.05
Dropped
  dead 798.1
  heart beats 426.6
Dropsy, dropsical — see also Edema 782.3
  abdomen 789.59
  amnion (see also Hydramnios) 657.0 ☑
  brain — see Hydrocephalus
  cardiac (see also Failure, heart) 428.0
  cardiorenal (see also Hypertension, cardiorenal) 404.90
  chest 511.9
  fetus or newborn 778.0
    due to isoimmunization 773.3
  gangrenous (see also Gangrene) 785.4
  heart (see also Failure, heart) 428.0
  hepatic — see Cirrhosis, liver
  infantile — see Hydrops, fetalis
  kidney (see also Nephrosis) 581.9
  liver — see Cirrhosis, liver

Dropsy, dropsical — see also Edema — continued
  lung 514
  malarial (see also Malaria) 084.9
  neonatorum — see Hydrops, fetalis
  nephritic 581.9
  newborn — see Hydrops, fetalis
  nutritional 269.9
  ovary 620.8
  pericardium (see also Pericarditis) 423.9
  renal (see also Nephrosis) 581.9
  uremic — see Uremia
Drowned, drowning (near) 994.1
  lung 518.5
Drowsiness 780.09
Drug — see also condition
  addiction (see also listing under Dependence) 304.9 ☑
  adverse effect NEC, correct substance properly administered 995.20
  allergy 995.27
  dependence (see also listing under Dependence) 304.9 ☑
  habit (see also listing under Dependence) 304.9 ☑
  hypersensitivity 995.27
  induced
    circadian rhythm sleep disorder 292.85
    hypersomnia 292.85
    insomnia 292.85
    mental disorder 292.9
      anxiety 292.89
      mood 292.84
      sexual 292.89
      sleep 292.85
      specified type 292.89
    parasomnia 292.85
    persisting
      amnestic disorder 292.83
      dementia 292.82
    psychotic disorder
      with
        delusions 292.11
        hallucinations 292.12
    sleep disorder 292.85
  intoxication 292.89
  overdose — see Table of Drugs and Chemicals
  poisoning — see Table of Drugs and Chemicals
  therapy (maintenance) status NEC
    chemotherapy, antineoplastic V58.11
    immunotherapy, antineoplastic V58.12
    long-term (current) use V58.69
      antibiotics V58.62
      anticoagulants V58.61
      anti-inflammatories, non-steroidal (NSAID) V58.64
      antiplatelets V58.63
      antithrombotics V58.63
      aspirin V58.66
      high-risk medications NEC V58.69
      insulin V58.67
      methadone V58.69
      opiate analgesic V58.69
      steroids V58.65
  wrong substance given or taken in error — see Table of Drugs and Chemicals
Drunkenness — see also Abuse, drugs, nondependent 305.0 ☑
  acute in alcoholism (see also Alcoholism) 303.0 ☑
  chronic (see also Alcoholism) 303.9 ☑
  pathologic 291.4
  simple (acute) 305.0 ☑
    in alcoholism 303.0 ☑
  sleep 307.47
Drusen
  optic disc or papilla 377.21
  retina (colloid) (hyaloid degeneration) 362.57
    hereditary 362.77
Drusenfieber 075
Dry, dryness — see also condition
  eye 375.15
    syndrome 375.15
  larynx 478.79
  mouth 527.7

Dry, dryness — see also condition — continued
  nose 478.19
  skin syndrome 701.1
  socket (teeth) 526.5
  throat 478.29
DSAP (disseminated superficial actinic porokeratosis) 692.75
Duane's retraction syndrome 378.71
Duane-Stilling-Türk syndrome (ocular retraction syndrome) 378.71
Dubini's disease (electric chorea) 049.8
Dubin-Johnson disease or syndrome 277.4
Dubois' abscess or disease 090.5
Duchenne's
  disease 094.0
    locomotor ataxia 094.0
    muscular dystrophy 359.1
    pseudohypertrophy, muscles 359.1
  paralysis 335.22
  syndrome 335.22
Duchenne-Aran myelopathic, muscular atrophy (nonprogressive) (progressive) 335.21
Duchenne-Griesinger disease 359.1
Ducrey's
  bacillus 099.0
  chancre 099.0
  disease (chancroid) 099.0
Duct, ductus — see condition
Duengero 061
Duhring's disease (dermatitis herpetiformis) 694.0
Dukes (-Filatov) disease 057.8
Dullness
  cardiac (decreased) (increased) 785.3
Dumb ague — see also Malaria 084.6
Dumbness — see also Aphasia 784.3
Dumdum fever 085.0
Dumping syndrome (postgastrectomy) 564.2
  nonsurgical 536.8
Duodenitis (nonspecific) (peptic) 535.60
  with hemorrhage 535.61
  due to
    Strongyloides stercoralis 127.2
Duodenocholangitis 575.8
Duodenum, duodenal — see condition
Duplay's disease, periarthritis, or syndrome 726.2
Duplex — see also Accessory
  kidney 753.3
  placenta — see Placenta, abnormal
  uterus 752.2
Duplication — see also Accessory
  anus 751.5
  aortic arch 747.21
  appendix 751.5
  biliary duct (any) 751.69
  bladder 753.8
  cecum 751.5
    and appendix 751.5
  clitoris 752.49
  cystic duct 751.69
  digestive organs 751.8
  duodenum 751.5
  esophagus 750.4
  fallopian tube 752.19
  frontonasal process 756.0
  gallbladder 751.69
  ileum 751.5
  intestine (large) (small) 751.5
  jejunum 751.5
  kidney 753.3
  liver 751.69
  nose 748.1
  pancreas 751.7
  penis 752.69
  respiratory organs NEC 748.9
  salivary duct 750.22
  spinal cord (incomplete) 742.51
  stomach 750.7
  ureter 753.4
  vagina 752.49
  vas deferens 752.89
  vocal cords 748.3
Dupré's disease or syndrome (meningism) 781.6

☑ Additional Digit Required — Refer to the Tabular List for Digit Selection   ▽ Subterms under main terms may continue to next column or page

94 — Volume 2 • October 2009   ▶◀ Revised Text   ● New Line   ▲ Revised Code   2010 ICD-9-CM

Dupuytren's
  contraction 728.6
  disease (muscle contracture) 728.6
  fracture (closed) 824.4
    ankle (closed) 824.4
      open 824.5
    fibula (closed) 824.4
      open 824.5
    open 824.5
    radius (closed) 813.42
      open 813.52
  muscle contracture 728.6
Durand-Nicolas-Favre disease (climatic bubo) 099.1
Durotomy, incidental (inadvertent) — *see also* Tear, dural 349.31
Duroziez's disease (congenital mitral stenosis) 746.5
Dust
  conjunctivitis 372.05
  reticulation (occupational) 504
Dutton's
  disease (trypanosomiasis) 086.9
  relapsing fever (West African) 087.1
Dwarf, dwarfism 259.4
  with infantilism (hypophyseal) 253.3
  achondroplastic 756.4
  Amsterdam 759.89
  bird-headed 759.89
  congenital 259.4
  constitutional 259.4
  hypophyseal 253.3
  infantile 259.4
  Levi type 253.3
  Lorain-Levi (pituitary) 253.3
  Lorain type (pituitary) 253.3
  metatropic 756.4
  nephrotic-glycosuric, with hypophosphatemic rickets 270.0
  nutritional 263.2
  ovarian 758.6
  pancreatic 577.8
  pituitary 253.3
  polydystrophic 277.5
  primordial 253.3
  psychosocial 259.4
  renal 588.0
    with hypertension — *see* Hypertension, kidney
  Russell's (uterine dwarfism and craniofacial dysostosis) 759.89
Dyke-Young anemia or syndrome (acquired macrocytic hemolytic anemia) (secondary) (symptomatic) 283.9
Dynia abnormality — *see also* Defect, coagulation 286.9
Dysacousis 388.40
Dysadrenocortism 255.9
  hyperfunction 255.3
  hypofunction 255.41
Dysarthria 784.51 ▲
  due to late effect of cerebrovascular disease ●
    (*see also* Late effect(s) (of) cerebrovascular disease) 438.13 ●
Dysautonomia — *see also* Neuropathy, peripheral, autonomic 337.9
  familial 742.8
Dysbarism 993.3
Dysbasia 719.7
  angiosclerotica intermittens 443.9
    due to atherosclerosis 440.21
  hysterical 300.11
  lordotica (progressiva) 333.6
  nonorganic origin 307.9
  psychogenic 307.9
Dysbetalipoproteinemia (familial) 272.2
Dyscalculia 315.1
Dyschezia — *see also* Constipation 564.00
Dyschondroplasia (with hemangiomata) 756.4
  Voorhoeve's 756.4
Dyschondrosteosis 756.59
Dyschromia 709.00
Dyscollagenosis 710.9
Dyscoria 743.41
Dyscraniopyophalangy 759.89

Dyscrasia
  blood 289.9
    with antepartum hemorrhage 641.3 ☑
    hemorrhage, subungual 287.8
    puerperal, postpartum 666.3 ☑
  ovary 256.8
  plasma cell 273.9
  pluriglandular 258.9
  polyglandular 258.9
Dysdiadochokinesia 781.3
Dysectasia, vesical neck 596.8
Dysendocrinism 259.9
Dysentery, dysenteric (bilious) (catarrhal) (diarrhea) (epidemic) (gangrenous) (hemorrhagic) (infectious) (sporadic) (tropical) (ulcerative) 009.0
  abscess, liver (*see also* Abscess, amebic) 006.3
  amebic (*see also* Amebiasis) 006.9
    with abscess — *see* Abscess, amebic
    acute 006.0
    carrier (suspected) of V02.2
    chronic 006.1
  arthritis (*see also* Arthritis, due to, dysentery) 009.0 [711.3] ☑
    bacillary 004.9 [711.3] ☑
  asylum 004.9
  bacillary 004.9
    arthritis 004.9 [711.3] ☑
    Boyd 004.2
    Flexner 004.1
    Schmitz (-Stutzer) 004.0
    Shiga 004.0
    Shigella 004.9
      group A 004.0
      group B 004.1
      group C 004.2
      group D 004.3
      specified type NEC 004.8
    Sonne 004.3
    specified type NEC 004.8
  bacterium 004.9
  balantidial 007.0
  Balantidium coli 007.0
  Boyd's 004.2
  Chilomastix 007.8
  Chinese 004.9
  choleriform 001.1
  coccidial 007.2
  Dientamoeba fragilis 007.8
  due to specified organism NEC — *see* Enteritis, due to, by organism
  Embadomonas 007.8
  Endolimax nana — *see* Dysentery, amebic
  Entamoba, entamebic — *see* Dysentery, amebic
  Flexner's 004.1
  Flexner-Boyd 004.2
  giardial 007.1
  Giardia lamblia 007.1
  Hiss-Russell 004.1
  lamblia 007.1
  leishmanial 085.0
  malarial (*see also* Malaria) 084.6
  metazoal 127.9
  Monilia 112.89
  protozoal NEC 007.9
  Russell's 004.8
  salmonella 003.0
  schistosomal 120.1
  Schmitz (-Stutzer) 004.0
  Shiga 004.0
  Shigella NEC (*see also* Dysentery, bacillary) 004.9
    boydii 004.2
    dysenteriae 004.0
      Schmitz 004.0
      Shiga 004.0
    flexneri 004.1
    group A 004.0
    group B 004.1
    group C 004.2
    group D 004.3
    Schmitz 004.0
    Shiga 004.0
    Sonnei 004.3
  Sonne 004.3

Dysentery, dysenteric — *continued*
  strongyloidiasis 127.2
  trichomonal 007.3
  tuberculous (*see also* Tuberculosis) 014.8 ☑
  viral (*see also* Enteritis, viral) 008.8
Dysequilibrium 780.4
Dysesthesia 782.0
  hysterical 300.11
Dysfibrinogenemia (congenital) — *see also* Defect, coagulation 286.3
Dysfunction
  adrenal (cortical) 255.9
    hyperfunction 255.3
    hypofunction 255.41
  associated with sleep stages or arousal from sleep 780.56
    nonorganic origin 307.47
  bladder NEC 596.59
  bleeding, uterus 626.8
  brain, minimal (*see also* Hyperkinesia) 314.9
  cerebral 348.30
  colon 564.9
    psychogenic 306.4
  colostomy or enterostomy 569.62
  cystic duct 575.8
  diastolic 429.9
    with heart failure — *see* Failure, heart
    due to
      cardiomyopathy — *see* Cardiomyopathy
      hypertension — *see* Hypertension, heart
  endocrine NEC 259.9
  endometrium 621.8
  enteric stoma 569.62
  enterostomy 569.62
  erectile 607.84
    nonorganic origin 302.72
  esophagostomy 530.87
  Eustachian tube 381.81
  gallbladder 575.8
  gastrointestinal 536.9
  gland, glandular NEC 259.9
  heart 427.9
    postoperative (immediate) 997.1
      long-term effect of cardiac surgery 429.4
  hemoglobin 289.89
  hepatic 573.9
  hepatocellular NEC 573.9
  hypophysis 253.9
    hyperfunction 253.1
    hypofunction 253.2
    posterior lobe 253.6
      hypofunction 253.5
  kidney (*see also* Disease, renal) 593.9
  labyrinthine 386.50
    specified NEC 386.58
  liver 573.9
    constitutional 277.4
  minimal brain (child) (*see also* Hyperkinesia) 314.9
  ovary, ovarian 256.9
    hyperfunction 256.1
      estrogen 256.0
    hypofunction 256.39
      postablative 256.2
    postablative 256.2
    specified NEC 256.8
  papillary muscle 429.81
    with myocardial infarction 410.8 ☑
  parathyroid 252.8
    hyperfunction 252.00
    hypofunction 252.1
  pineal gland 259.8
  pituitary (gland) 253.9
    hyperfunction 253.1
    hypofunction 253.2
    posterior 253.6
      hypofunction 253.5
  placental — *see* Placenta, insufficiency
  platelets (blood) 287.1
  polyglandular 258.9
    specified NEC 258.8
  psychosexual 302.70

Dysfunction — *continued*
  psychosexual — *continued*
    with
      dyspareunia (functional) (psychogenic) 302.76
      frigidity 302.72
      impotence 302.72
      inhibition
        orgasm
          female 302.73
          male 302.74
        sexual
          desire 302.71
          excitement 302.72
      premature ejaculation 302.75
      sexual aversion 302.79
      specified disorder NEC 302.79
      vaginismus 306.51
  pylorus 537.9
  rectum 564.9
    psychogenic 306.4
  segmental (*see also* Dysfunction, somatic) 739.9
  senile 797
  sexual 302.70
  sinoatrial node 427.81
  somatic 739.9
    abdomen 739.9
    acromioclavicular 739.7
    cervical 739.1
    cervicothoracic 739.1
    costochondral 739.8
    costovertebral 739.8
    extremities
      lower 739.6
      upper 739.7
    head 739.0
    hip 739.5
    lumbar, lumbosacral 739.3
    occipitocervical 739.0
    pelvic 739.5
    pubic 739.5
    rib cage 739.8
    sacral 739.4
    sacrococcygeal 739.4
    sacroiliac 739.4
    specified site NEC 739.9
    sternochondral 739.8
    sternoclavicular 739.7
    temporomandibular 739.0
    thoracic, thoracolumbar 739.2
  stomach 536.9
    psychogenic 306.4
  suprarenal 255.9
    hyperfunction 255.3
    hypofunction 255.41
  symbolic NEC 784.60
    specified type NEC 784.69
  systolic 429.9
    with heart failure — *see* Failure, heart
  temporomandibular (joint) (joint-pain-syndrome) NEC 524.60
    sounds on opening or closing 524.64
    specified NEC 524.69
  testicular 257.9
    hyperfunction 257.0
    hypofunction 257.2
    specified type NEC 257.8
  thymus 254.9
  thyroid 246.9
    complicating pregnancy, childbirth, or puerperium 648.1 ☑
    hyperfunction — *see* Hyperthyroidism
    hypofunction — *see* Hypothyroidism
  uterus, complicating delivery 661.9 ☑
    affecting fetus or newborn 763.7
    hypertonic 661.4 ☑
    hypotonic 661.2 ☑
      primary 661.0 ☑
      secondary 661.1 ☑
  velopharyngeal (acquired) 528.9
    congenital 750.29
  ventricular 429.9
    with congestive heart failure (*see also* Failure, heart) 428.0

☑ Additional Digit Required — Refer to the Tabular List for Digit Selection   ▽ Subterms under main terms may continue to next column or page

2010 ICD-9-CM   ▶◀ Revised Text   ● New Line   ▲ Revised Code   October 2009 • Volume 2 — 95

Dysfunction — *continued*
　ventricular — *continued*
　　due to
　　　cardiomyopathy — *see* Cardiomyopathy
　　　hypertension — *see* Hypertension, heart
　　left, reversible following sudden emotional stress 429.83
　vesicourethral NEC 596.59
　vestibular 386.50
　　specified type NEC 386.58
Dysgammaglobulinemia 279.06
Dysgenesis
　gonadal (due to chromosomal anomaly) 758.6
　　pure 752.7
　kidney(s) 753.0
　ovarian 758.6
　renal 753.0
　reticular 279.2
　seminiferous tubules 758.6
　tidal platelet 287.31
Dysgerminoma (M9060/3)
　specified site — *see* Neoplasm, by site, malignant
　unspecified site
　　female 183.0
　　male 186.9
Dysgeusia 781.1
Dysgraphia 781.3
Dyshidrosis 705.81
Dysidrosis 705.81
Dysinsulinism 251.8
Dyskaryotic cervical smear 795.09
Dyskeratosis — *see also* Keratosis 701.1
　bullosa hereditaria 757.39
　cervix 622.10
　congenital 757.39
　follicularis 757.39
　　vitamin A deficiency 264.8
　gingiva 523.8
　oral soft tissue NEC 528.79
　tongue 528.79
　uterus NEC 621.8
Dyskinesia 781.3
　biliary 575.8
　esophagus 530.5
　hysterical 300.11
　intestinal 564.89
　neuroleptic-induced tardive 333.85
　nonorganic origin 307.9
　orofacial 333.82
　　due to drugs 333.85
　psychogenic 307.9
　subacute, due to drugs 333.85
　tardive (oral) 333.85
Dyslalia 784.59 ▲
　developmental 315.39
Dyslexia 784.61
　developmental 315.02
　secondary to organic lesion 784.61
Dyslipidemia 272.4
Dysmaturity — *see also* Immaturity 765.1 ☑
　lung 770.4
　pulmonary 770.4
Dysmenorrhea (essential) (exfoliative) (functional) (intrinsic) (membranous) (primary) (secondary) 625.3
　psychogenic 306.52
Dysmetabolic syndrome X 277.7
Dysmetria 781.3
Dysmorodystrophia mesodermalis congenita 759.82
Dysnomia 784.3
Dysorexia 783.0
　hysterical 300.11
Dysostosis
　cleidocranial, cleidocranialis 755.59
　craniofacial 756.0
　Fairbank's (idiopathic familial generalized osteophytosis) 756.50
　mandibularis 756.0
　mandibulofacial, incomplete 756.0
　multiplex 277.5
　orodigitofacial 759.89
Dyspareunia (female) 625.0

Dyspareunia — *continued*
　male 608.89
　psychogenic 302.76
Dyspepsia (allergic) (congenital) (fermentative) (flatulent) (functional) (gastric) (gastrointestinal) (neurogenic) (occupational) (reflex) 536.8
　acid 536.8
　atonic 536.3
　　psychogenic 306.4
　diarrhea 787.91
　　psychogenic 306.4
　intestinal 564.89
　　psychogenic 306.4
　nervous 306.4
　neurotic 306.4
　psychogenic 306.4
Dysphagia 787.20
　cervical 787.29
　functional 300.11
　hysterical 300.11
　nervous 300.11
　neurogenic 787.29
　oral phase 787.21
　oropharyngeal phase 787.22
　pharyngeal phase 787.23
　pharyngoesophageal phase 787.24
　psychogenic 306.4
　sideropenic 280.8
　spastica 530.5
　specified NEC 787.29
Dysphagocytosis, congenital 288.1
Dysphasia 784.59 ▲
Dysphonia 784.42 ▲
　clericorum 784.49
　functional 300.11
　hysterical 300.11
　psychogenic 306.1
　spastica 478.79
Dyspigmentation — *see also* Pigmentation
　eyelid (acquired) 374.52
Dyspituitarism 253.9
　hyperfunction 253.1
　hypofunction 253.2
　posterior lobe 253.6
Dysplasia — *see also* Anomaly
　anus 569.44
　　intraepithelial neoplasia I [AIN I] (histologically confirmed) 569.44
　　intraepithelial neoplasia II [AIN II] (histologically confirmed) 569.44
　　intraepithelial neoplasia III [AIN III] 230.6
　　anal canal 230.5
　　mild (histologically confirmed) 569.44
　　moderate (histologically confirmed) 569.44
　　severe 230.6
　　　anal canal 230.5
　artery
　　fibromuscular NEC 447.8
　　　carotid 447.8
　　　renal 447.3
　bladder 596.8
　bone (fibrous) NEC 733.29
　　diaphyseal, progressive 756.59
　　jaw 526.89
　　monostotic 733.29
　　polyostotic 756.54
　　solitary 733.29
　brain 742.9
　bronchopulmonary, fetus or newborn 770.7
　cervix (uteri) 622.10
　　cervical intraepithelial neoplasia I [CIN I] 622.11
　　cervical intraepithelial neoplasia II [CIN II] 622.12
　　cervical intraepithelial neoplasia III [CIN III] 233.1
　　CIN I 622.11
　　CIN II 622.12
　　CIN III 233.1
　　mild 622.11
　　moderate 622.12
　　severe 233.1
　chondroectodermal 756.55
　chondromatose 756.4
　colon 211.3

Dysplasia — *see also* Anomaly — *continued*
　craniocarpotarsal 759.89
　craniometaphyseal 756.89
　dentinal 520.5
　diaphyseal, progressive 756.59
　ectodermal (anhidrotic) (Bason) (Clouston's) (congenital) (Feinmesser) (hereditary) (hidrotic) (Marshall) (Robinson's) 757.31
　epiphysealis 756.9
　　multiplex 756.56
　　punctata 756.59
　epiphysis 756.9
　　multiple 756.56
　epithelial
　　epiglottis 478.79
　　uterine cervix 622.10
　erythroid NEC 289.89
　eye (*see also* Microphthalmos) 743.10
　familial metaphyseal 756.89
　fibromuscular, artery NEC 447.8
　　carotid 447.8
　　renal 447.3
　fibrous
　　bone NEC 733.29
　　diaphyseal, progressive 756.59
　　jaw 526.89
　　monostotic 733.29
　　polyostotic 756.54
　　solitary 733.29
　high-grade, focal — *see* Neoplasm, by site, benign
　hip (congenital) 755.63
　　with dislocation (*see also* Dislocation, hip, congenital) 754.30
　hypohidrotic ectodermal 757.31
　joint 755.8
　kidney 753.15
　leg 755.69
　linguofacialis 759.89
　lung 748.5
　macular 743.55
　mammary (benign) (gland) 610.9
　　cystic 610.1
　　specified type NEC 610.8
　metaphyseal 756.9
　　familial 756.89
　monostotic fibrous 733.29
　muscle 756.89
　myeloid NEC 289.89
　nervous system (general) 742.9
　neuroectodermal 759.6
　oculoauriculovertebral 756.0
　oculodentodigital 759.89
　olfactogenital 253.4
　osteo-onycho-arthro (hereditary) 756.89
　periosteum 733.99
　polyostotic fibrous 756.54
　progressive diaphyseal 756.59
　prostate 602.3
　　intraepithelial neoplasia I [PIN I] 602.3
　　intraepithelial neoplasia II [PIN II] 602.3
　　intraepithelial neoplasia III [PIN III] 233.4
　renal 753.15
　renofacialis 753.0
　retinal NEC 743.56
　retrolental (*see also* Retinopathy of prematurity) 362.21
　skin 709.8
　spinal cord 742.9
　thymic, with immunodeficiency 279.2
　vagina 623.0
　　mild 623.0
　　moderate 623.0
　　severe 233.31
　vocal cord 478.5
　vulva 624.8
　　intraepithelial neoplasia I [VIN I] 624.01
　　intraepithelial neoplasia II [VIN II] 624.02
　　intraepithelial neoplasia III [VIN III] 233.32
　　mild 624.01
　　moderate 624.02
　　severe 233.32
　　VIN I 624.01
　　VIN II 624.02
　　VIN III 233.32
Dyspnea (nocturnal) (paroxysmal) 786.09

Dyspnea — *continued*
　asthmatic (bronchial) (*see also* Asthma) 493.9 ☑
　　with bronchitis (*see also* Asthma) 493.9 ☑
　　　chronic 493.2 ☑
　　cardiac (*see also* Failure, ventricular, left) 428.1
　cardiac (*see also* Failure, ventricular, left) 428.1
　functional 300.11
　hyperventilation 786.01
　hysterical 300.11
　Monday morning 504
　newborn 770.89
　psychogenic 306.1
　uremic — *see* Uremia
Dyspraxia 781.3
　syndrome 315.4
Dysproteinemia 273.8
　transient with copper deficiency 281.4
Dysprothrombinemia (constitutional) — *see also* Defect, coagulation 286.3
Dysreflexia, autonomic 337.3
Dysrhythmia
　cardiac 427.9
　　postoperative (immediate) 997.1
　　　long-term effect of cardiac surgery 429.4
　　specified type NEC 427.89
　cerebral or cortical 348.30
Dyssecretosis, mucoserous 710.2
Dyssocial reaction, without manifest psychiatric disorder
　adolescent V71.02
　adult V71.01
　child V71.02
Dyssomnia NEC 780.56
　nonorganic origin 307.47
Dyssplenism 289.4
Dyssynergia
　biliary (*see also* Disease, biliary) 576.8
　cerebellaris myoclonica 334.2
　detrusor sphincter (bladder) 596.55
　ventricular 429.89
Dystasia, hereditary areflexic 334.3
Dysthymia 300.4
Dysthymic disorder 300.4
Dysthyroidism 246.9
Dystocia 660.9 ☑
　affecting fetus or newborn 763.1
　cervical 661.2 ☑
　　affecting fetus or newborn 763.7
　contraction ring 661.4 ☑
　　affecting fetus or newborn 763.7
　fetal 660.9 ☑
　　abnormal size 653.5 ☑
　　　affecting fetus or newborn 763.1
　　deformity 653.7 ☑
　maternal 660.9 ☑
　　affecting fetus or newborn 763.1
　positional 660.0 ☑
　　affecting fetus or newborn 763.1
　shoulder (girdle) 660.4 ☑
　　affecting fetus or newborn 763.1
　uterine NEC 661.4 ☑
　　affecting fetus or newborn 763.7
Dystonia
　acute
　　due to drugs 333.72
　　neuroleptic-induced acute 333.72
　deformans progressiva 333.6
　lenticularis 333.6
　musculorum deformans 333.6
　torsion (idiopathic) 333.6
　　acquired 333.79
　　fragments (of) 333.89
　　genetic 333.6
　　symptomatic 333.79
Dystonic
　movements 781.0
Dystopia kidney 753.3
Dystrophia myotonica 359.2 ☑
Dystrophy, dystrophia 783.9
　adiposogenital 253.8
　asphyxiating thoracic 756.4
　Becker's type 359.22
　brevicollis 756.16

☑ Additional Digit Required — Refer to the Tabular List for Digit Selection　　　　　　　▽ Subterms under main terms may continue to next column or page

96 — Volume 2 • October 2009　　　▶◀ Revised Text　　　● New Line　　　▲ Revised Code　　　2010 ICD-9-CM

Dystrophy, dystrophia — *continued*
 Bruch's membrane 362.77
 cervical (sympathetic) NEC 337.09
 chondro-osseus with punctate epiphyseal
  dysplasia 756.59
 choroid (hereditary) 363.50
  central (areolar) (partial) 363.53
   total (gyrate) 363.54
  circinate 363.53
  circumpapillary (partial) 363.51
   total 363.52
  diffuse
   partial 363.56
   total 363.57
  generalized
   partial 363.56
   total 363.57
  gyrate
   central 363.54
   generalized 363.57
  helicoid 363.52
  peripapillary — *see* Dystrophy, choroid,
   circumpapillary
  serpiginous 363.54
 cornea (hereditary) 371.50
  anterior NEC 371.52
  Cogan's 371.52
  combined 371.57
  crystalline 371.56
  endothelial (Fuchs') 371.57
  epithelial 371.50
   juvenile 371.51
   microscopic cystic 371.52
  granular 371.53
  lattice 371.54
  macular 371.55
  marginal (Terrien's) 371.48
  Meesman's 371.51
  microscopic cystic (epithelial) 371.52
  nodular, Salzmann's 371.46
  polymorphous 371.58
  posterior NEC 371.58
  ring-like 371.52
  Salzmann's nodular 371.46
  stromal NEC 371.56
 dermatochondrocorneal 371.50
 Duchenne's 359.1
 due to malnutrition 263.9
 Erb's 359.1
 familial
  hyperplastic periosteal 756.59
  osseous 277.5
 foveal 362.77
 Fuchs', cornea 371.57
 Gowers' muscular 359.1
 hair 704.2
 hereditary, progressive muscular 359.1
 hypogenital, with diabetic tendency 759.81
 Landouzy-Déjérine 359.1
 Leyden-Möbius 359.1
 mesodermalis congenita 759.82
 muscular 359.1
  congenital (hereditary) 359.0
   myotonic 359.22
  distal 359.1
  Duchenne's 359.1
  Erb's 359.1
  fascioscapulohumeral 359.1
  Gowers' 359.1
  hereditary (progressive) 359.1
  Landouzy-Déjérine 359.1
  limb-girdle 359.1
  myotonic 359.21
  progressive (hereditary) 359.1
   Charcôt-Marie-Tooth 356.1
  pseudohypertrophic (infantile) 359.1
 myocardium, myocardial (*see also* Degeneration, myocardial) 429.1
 myotonic 359.21
 myotonica 359.21
 nail 703.8
  congenital 757.5
 neurovascular (traumatic) (*see also* Neuropathy, peripheral, autonomic) 337.9
 nutritional 263.9
 ocular 359.1

Dystrophy, dystrophia — *continued*
 oculocerebrorenal 270.8
 oculopharyngeal 359.1
 ovarian 620.8
 papillary (and pigmentary) 701.1
 pelvicrural atrophic 359.1
 pigmentary (*see also* Acanthosis) 701.2
 pituitary (gland) 253.8
 polyglandular 258.8
 posttraumatic sympathetic — *see* Dystrophy,
  sympathetic
 progressive ophthalmoplegic 359.1
 reflex neuromuscular — *see* Dystrophy, sympathetic
 retina, retinal (hereditary) 362.70
  albipunctate 362.74
  Bruch's membrane 362.77
  cone, progressive 362.75
  hyaline 362.77
  in
   Bassen-Kornzweig syndrome
    272.5 [362.72]
   cerebroretinal lipidosis 330.1 [362.71]
   Refsum's disease 356.3 [362.72]
   systemic lipidosis 272.7 [362.71]
  juvenile (Stargardt's) 362.75
  pigmentary 362.74
  pigment epithelium 362.76
  progressive cone (-rod) 362.75
  pseudoinflammatory foveal 362.77
  rod, progressive 362.75
  sensory 362.75
  vitelliform 362.76
 Salzmann's nodular 371.46
 scapuloperoneal 359.1
 skin NEC 709.9
 sympathetic (posttraumatic) (reflex) 337.20
  lower limb 337.22
  specified site NEC 337.29
  upper limb 337.21
 tapetoretinal NEC 362.74
 thoracic asphyxiating 756.4
 unguium 703.8
  congenital 757.5
 vitreoretinal (primary) 362.73
  secondary 362.66
 vulva 624.09
Dysuria 788.1
 psychogenic 306.53

E

Eagle-Barrett syndrome 756.71
Eales' disease (syndrome) 362.18
Ear — *see also* condition
 ache 388.70
  otogenic 388.71
  referred 388.72
 lop 744.29
 piercing V50.3
 swimmers' acute 380.12
 tank 380.12
 tropical 111.8 [380.15]
 wax 380.4
Earache 388.70
 otogenic 388.71
 referred 388.72
Early satiety 780.94
Eaton-Lambert syndrome — *see also* Neoplasm,
 by site, malignant 199.1 [358.1]
Eberth's disease (typhoid fever) 002.0
Ebstein's
 anomaly or syndrome (downward displacement, tricuspid valve into right ventricle) 746.2
 disease (diabetes) 250.4 ☑ [581.81]
  due to secondary diabetes
   249.4 ☑ [581.81]
Eccentro-osteochondrodysplasia 277.5
Ecchondroma (M9210/0) — *see* Neoplasm, bone,
 benign
Ecchondrosis (M9210/1) 238.0
Ecchordosis physaliphora 756.0
Ecchymosis (multiple) 459.89
 conjunctiva 372.72
 eye (traumatic) 921.0
 eyelids (traumatic) 921.1

Ecchymosis — *continued*
 newborn 772.6
 spontaneous 782.7
 traumatic — *see* Contusion
ECD (Erdheim-Chester disease) 277.89 ●
Echinococciasis — *see* Echinococcus
Echinococcosis — *see* Echinococcus
Echinococcus (infection) 122.9
 granulosus 122.4
  liver 122.0
  lung 122.1
  orbit 122.3 [376.13]
  specified site NEC 122.3
  thyroid 122.2
 liver NEC 122.8
  granulosus 122.0
  multilocularis 122.5
 lung NEC 122.9
  granulosus 122.1
  multilocularis 122.6
 multilocularis 122.7
  liver 122.5
  specified site NEC 122.6
 orbit 122.9 [376.13]
  granulosus 122.3 [376.13]
  multilocularis 122.6 [376.13]
 specified site NEC 122.9
  granulosus 122.3
  multilocularis 122.6 [376.13]
 thyroid NEC 122.9
  granulosus 122.2
  multilocularis 122.6
Echinorhynchiasis 127.7
Echinostomiasis 121.8
Echolalia 784.69
ECHO virus infection NEC 079.1
Eclampsia, eclamptic (coma) (convulsions)
 (delirium) 780.39
 female, child-bearing age NEC — *see*
  Eclampsia, pregnancy
 gravidarum — *see* Eclampsia, pregnancy
 male 780.39
 not associated with pregnancy or childbirth
  780.39
 pregnancy, childbirth, or puerperium 642.6 ☑
  with pre-existing hypertension 642.7 ☑
   affecting fetus or newborn 760.0
 uremic 586
Eclipse blindness (total) 363.31
Economic circumstance affecting care V60.9
 specified type NEC V60.89 ▲
Economo's disease (encephalitis lethargica)
 049.8
Ectasia, ectasis
 aorta (*see also* Aneurysm, aorta) 441.9
  ruptured 441.5
 breast 610.4
 capillary 448.9
 cornea (marginal) (postinfectional) 371.71
 duct (mammary) 610.4
 gastric antral vascular (GAVE) 537.82
  with hemorrhage 537.83
  without hemorrhage 537.82
 kidney 593.89
 mammary duct (gland) 610.4
 papillary 448.9
 renal 593.89
 salivary gland (duct) 527.8
 scar, cornea 371.71
 sclera 379.11
Ecthyma 686.8
 contagiosum 051.2
 gangrenosum 686.09
 infectiosum 051.2
Ectocardia 746.87
Ectodermal dysplasia, congenital 757.31
Ectodermosis erosiva pluriorificialis 695.19
Ectopic, ectopia (congenital) 759.89
 abdominal viscera 751.8
  due to defect in anterior abdominal wall
   756.79
 ACTH syndrome 255.0
 adrenal gland 759.1
 anus 751.5
 auricular beats 427.61
 beats 427.60

Ectopic, ectopia — *continued*
 bladder 753.5
 bone and cartilage in lung 748.69
 brain 742.4
 breast tissue 757.6
 cardiac 746.87
 cerebral 742.4
 cordis 746.87
 endometrium 617.9
 gallbladder 751.69
 gastric mucosa 750.7
 gestation — *see* Pregnancy, ectopic
 heart 746.87
 hormone secretion NEC 259.3
 hyperparathyroidism 259.3
 kidney (crossed) (intrathoracic) (pelvis) 753.3
  in pregnancy or childbirth 654.4 ☑
   causing obstructed labor 660.2 ☑
 lens 743.37
 lentis 743.37
 mole — *see* Pregnancy, ectopic
 organ or site NEC — *see* Malposition, congenital
 ovary 752.0
 pancreas, pancreatic tissue 751.7
 pregnancy — *see* Pregnancy, ectopic
 pupil 364.75
 renal 753.3
 sebaceous glands of mouth 750.26
 secretion
  ACTH 255.0
  adrenal hormone 259.3
  adrenalin 259.3
  adrenocorticotropin 255.0
  antidiuretic hormone (ADH) 259.3
  epinephrine 259.3
  hormone NEC 259.3
  norepinephrine 259.3
  pituitary (posterior) 259.3
 spleen 759.0
 testis 752.51
 thyroid 759.2
 ureter 753.4
 ventricular beats 427.69
 vesicae 753.5
Ectrodactyly 755.4
 finger (*see also* Absence, finger, congenital)
  755.29
 toe (*see also* Absence, toe, congenital) 755.39
Ectromelia 755.4
 lower limb 755.30
 upper limb 755.20
Ectropion 374.10
 anus 569.49
 cervix 622.0
  with mention of cervicitis 616.0
 cicatricial 374.14
 congenital 743.62
 eyelid 374.10
  cicatricial 374.14
  congenital 743.62
  mechanical 374.12
  paralytic 374.12
  senile 374.11
  spastic 374.13
 iris (pigment epithelium) 364.54
 lip (congenital) 750.26
  acquired 528.5
 mechanical 374.12
 paralytic 374.12
 rectum 569.49
 senile 374.11
 spastic 374.13
 urethra 599.84
 uvea 364.54
Eczema (acute) (allergic) (chronic) (erythematous)
 (fissum) (occupational) (rubrum) (squa-
 mous) 692.9
 asteatotic 706.8
 atopic 691.8
 contact NEC 692.9
 dermatitis NEC 692.9
 due to specified cause — *see* Dermatitis, due
  to
 dyshidrotic 705.81
 external ear 380.22

Eczema — *continued*
flexural 691.8
gouty 274.89
herpeticum 054.0
hypertrophicum 701.8
hypostatic — *see* Varicose, vein
impetiginous 684
infantile (acute) (chronic) (due to any substance) (intertriginous) (seborrheic)
690.12
intertriginous NEC 692.9
infantile 690.12
intrinsic 691.8
lichenified NEC 692.9
marginatum 110.3
nummular 692.9
pustular 686.8
seborrheic 690.18
infantile 690.12
solare 692.72
stasis (lower extremity) 454.1
ulcerated 454.2
vaccination, vaccinatum 999.0
varicose (lower extremity) — *see* Varicose, vein
verrucosum callosum 698.3
Eczematoid, exudative 691.8
Eddowes' syndrome (brittle bones and blue
sclera) 756.51
Edema, edematous 782.3
with nephritis (*see also* Nephrosis) 581.9
allergic 995.1
angioneurotic (allergic) (any site) (with urticaria) 995.1
hereditary 277.6
angiospastic 443.9
Berlin's (traumatic) 921.3
brain 348.5
due to birth injury 767.8
fetus or newborn 767.8
cardiac (*see also* Failure, heart) 428.0
cardiovascular (*see also* Failure, heart) 428.0
cerebral — *see* Edema, brain
cerebrospinal vessel — *see* Edema, brain
cervix (acute) (uteri) 622.8
puerperal, postpartum 674.8 ☑
chronic hereditary 757.0
circumscribed, acute 995.1
hereditary 277.6
complicating pregnancy (gestational) 646.1 ☑
with hypertension — *see* Toxemia, of
pregnancy
conjunctiva 372.73
connective tissue 782.3
cornea 371.20
due to contact lenses 371.24
idiopathic 371.21
secondary 371.22
cystoid macular 362.53
due to
lymphatic obstruction — *see* Edema, lymphatic
salt retention 276.0
epiglottis — *see* Edema, glottis
essential, acute 995.1
hereditary 277.6
extremities, lower — *see* Edema, legs
eyelid NEC 374.82
familial, hereditary (legs) 757.0
famine 262
fetus or newborn 778.5
genital organs
female 629.89
male 608.86
gestational 646.1 ☑
with hypertension — *see* Toxemia, of
pregnancy
glottis, glottic, glottides (obstructive) (passive)
478.6
allergic 995.1
hereditary 277.6
due to external agent — *see* Condition,
respiratory, acute, due to specified
agent
heart (*see also* Failure, heart) 428.0
newborn 779.89
heat 992.7

Edema, edematous — *continued*
hereditary (legs) 757.0
inanition 262
infectious 782.3
intracranial 348.5
due to injury at birth 767.8
iris 364.89
joint (*see also* Effusion, joint) 719.0 ☑
larynx (*see also* Edema, glottis) 478.6
legs 782.3
due to venous obstruction 459.2
hereditary 757.0
localized 782.3
due to venous obstruction 459.2
lower extremity 459.2
lower extremities — *see* Edema, legs
lung 514
acute 518.4
with heart disease or failure (*see also*
Failure, ventricular, left) 428.1
congestive 428.0
chemical (due to fumes or vapors)
506.1
due to
external agent(s) NEC 508.9
specified NEC 508.8
fumes and vapors (chemical) (inhalation) 506.1
radiation 508.0
chemical (acute) 506.1
chronic 506.4
chronic 514
chemical (due to fumes or vapors)
506.4
due to
external agent(s) NEC 508.9
specified NEC 508.8
fumes or vapors (chemical) (inhalation) 506.4
radiation 508.1
due to
external agent 508.9
specified NEC 508.8
high altitude 993.2
near drowning 994.1
postoperative 518.4
terminal 514
lymphatic 457.1
due to mastectomy operation 457.0
macula 362.83
cystoid 362.53
diabetic 250.5 ☑ *[362.07]*
due to secondary diabetes
249.5 ☑ *[362.07]*
malignant (*see also* Gangrene, gas) 040.0
Milroy's 757.0
nasopharynx 478.25
neonatorum 778.5
nutritional (newborn) 262
with dyspigmentation, skin and hair 260
optic disc or nerve — *see* Papilledema
orbit 376.33
circulatory 459.89
palate (soft) (hard) 528.9
pancreas 577.8
penis 607.83
periodic 995.1
hereditary 277.6
pharynx 478.25
pitting 782.3
pulmonary — *see* Edema, lung
Quincke's 995.1
hereditary 277.6
renal (*see also* Nephrosis) 581.9
retina (localized) (macular) (peripheral) 362.83
cystoid 362.53
diabetic 250.5 ☑ *[362.07]*
due to secondary diabetes
249.5 ☑ *[362.07]*
salt 276.0
scrotum 608.86
seminal vesicle 608.86
spermatic cord 608.86
spinal cord 336.1
starvation 262
stasis (*see also* Hypertension, venous) 459.30

Edema, edematous — *continued*
subconjunctival 372.73
subglottic (*see also* Edema, glottis) 478.6
supraglottic (*see also* Edema, glottis) 478.6
testis 608.86
toxic NEC 782.3
traumatic NEC 782.3
tunica vaginalis 608.86
vas deferens 608.86
vocal cord — *see* Edema, glottis
vulva (acute) 624.8
Edentia (complete) (partial) — *see also* Absence,
tooth 520.0
acquired (*see also* Edentulism) 525.40
due to
caries 525.13
extraction 525.10
periodontal disease 525.12
specified NEC 525.19
trauma 525.11
causing malocclusion 524.30
congenital (deficiency of tooth buds) 520.0
Edentulism 525.40
complete 525.40
class I 525.41
class II 525.42
class III 525.43
class IV 525.44
partial 525.50
class I 525.51
class II 525.52
class III 525.53
class IV 525.54
Edsall's disease 992.2
Educational handicap V62.3
Edwards' syndrome 758.2
Effect, adverse NEC
abnormal gravitational (G) forces or states
994.9
air pressure — *see* Effect, adverse, atmospheric
pressure
altitude (high) — *see* Effect, adverse, high altitude
anesthetic
in labor and delivery NEC 668.9 ☑
affecting fetus or newborn 763.5
antitoxin — *see* Complications, vaccination
atmospheric pressure 993.9
due to explosion 993.4
high 993.3
low — *see* Effect, adverse, high altitude
specified effect NEC 993.8
biological, correct substance properly administered (*see also* Effect, adverse, drug)
995.20
blood (derivatives) (serum) (transfusion) —
see Complications, transfusion
chemical substance NEC 989.9
specified — *see* Table of Drugs and
Chemicals
cobalt, radioactive (*see also* Effect, adverse, radioactive substance) 990
cold (temperature) (weather) 991.9
chilblains 991.5
frostbite — *see* Frostbite
specified effect NEC 991.8
drugs and medicinals 995.20
correct substance properly administered
995.20
overdose or wrong substance given or
taken 977.9
specified drug — *see* Table of Drugs
and Chemicals
electric current (shock) 994.8
burn — *see* Burn, by site
electricity (electrocution) (shock) 994.8
burn — *see* Burn, by site
exertion (excessive) 994.5
exposure 994.9
exhaustion 994.4
external cause NEC 994.9
fallout (radioactive) NEC 990
fluoroscopy NEC 990
foodstuffs
allergic reaction (*see also* Allergy, food)
693.1

Effect, adverse — *continued*
foodstuffs — *continued*
allergic reaction (*see also* Allergy, food) —
continued
anaphylactic shock due to food NEC
995.60
noxious 988.9
specified type NEC (*see also* Poisoning,
by name of noxious foodstuff)
988.8
gases, fumes, or vapors — *see* Table of Drugs
and Chemicals
glue (airplane) sniffing 304.6 ☑
heat — *see* Heat
high altitude NEC 993.2
anoxia 993.2
on
ears 993.0
sinuses 993.1
polycythemia 289.0
hot weather — *see* Heat
hunger 994.2
immersion, foot 991.4
immunization — *see* Complications, vaccination
immunological agents — *see* Complications,
vaccination
implantation (removable) of isotope or radium
NEC 990
infrared (radiation) (rays) NEC 990
burn — *see* Burn, by site
dermatitis or eczema 692.82
infusion — *see* Complications, infusion
ingestion or injection of isotope (therapeutic)
NEC 990
irradiation NEC (*see also* Effect, adverse, radiation) 990
isotope (radioactive) NEC 990
lack of care (child) (infant) (newborn) 995.52
adult 995.84
lightning 994.0
burn — *see* Burn, by site
Lirugin — *see* Complications, vaccination
medicinal substance, correct, properly administered (*see also* Effect, adverse, drugs)
995.20
mesothorium NEC 990
motion 994.6
noise, inner ear 388.10
other drug, medicinal and biological substance
995.29
overheated places — *see* Heat
polonium NEC 990
psychosocial, of work environment V62.1
radiation (diagnostic) (fallout) (infrared) (natural source) (therapeutic) (tracer) (ultraviolet) (x-ray) NEC 990
with pulmonary manifestations
acute 508.0
chronic 508.1
dermatitis or eczema 692.82
due to sun NEC (*see also* Dermatitis,
due to, sun) 692.70
fibrosis of lungs 508.1
maternal with suspected damage to fetus
affecting management of pregnancy 655.6 ☑
pneumonitis 508.0
radioactive substance NEC 990
dermatitis or eczema 692.82
radioactivity NEC 990
radiotherapy NEC 990
dermatitis or eczema 692.82
radium NEC 990
reduced temperature 991.9
frostbite — *see* Frostbite
immersion, foot (hand) 991.4
specified effect NEC 991.8
roentgenography NEC 990
roentgenoscopy NEC 990
roentgen rays NEC 990
serum (prophylactic) (therapeutic) NEC 999.5
specified NEC 995.89
external cause NEC 994.9
strangulation 994.7
submersion 994.1

☑ Additional Digit Required — Refer to the Tabular List for Digit Selection

🔻 Subterms under main terms may continue to next column or page

▶◀ Revised Text   ● New Line   ▲ Revised Code

Effect, adverse — continued
  teletherapy NEC 990
  thirst 994.3
  transfusion — see Complications, transfusion
  ultraviolet (radiation) (rays) NEC 990
    burn (see also Burn, by site)
      from sun (see also Sunburn) 692.71
      dermatitis or eczema 692.82
        due to sun NEC (see also Dermatitis, due to, sun) 692.70
  uranium NEC 990
  vaccine (any) — see Complications, vaccination
  weightlessness 994.9
  whole blood (see also Complications, transfusion)
    overdose or wrong substance given (see also Table of Drugs and Chemicals) 964.7
  working environment V62.1
  x-rays NEC 990
    dermatitis or eczema 692.82
Effect, remote
  of cancer — see condition
Effects, late — see Late, effect (of)
Effluvium, telogen 704.02
Effort
  intolerance 306.2
  syndrome (aviators) (psychogenic) 306.2
Effusion
  amniotic fluid (see also Rupture, membranes, premature) 658.1 ☑
  brain (serous) 348.5
  bronchial (see also Bronchitis) 490
  cerebral 348.5
  cerebrospinal (see also Meningitis) 322.9
    vessel 348.5
  chest — see Effusion, pleura
  intracranial 348.5
  joint 719.00
    ankle 719.07
    elbow 719.02
    foot 719.07
    hand 719.04
    hip 719.05
    knee 719.06
    multiple sites 719.09
    pelvic region 719.05
    shoulder (region) 719.01
    specified site NEC 719.08
    wrist 719.03
  meninges (see also Meningitis) 322.9
  pericardium, pericardial (see also Pericarditis) 423.9
    acute 420.90
  peritoneal (chronic) 568.82
  pleura, pleurisy, pleuritic, pleuropericardial 511.9
    bacterial, nontuberculous 511.1
    fetus or newborn 511.9
    malignant 511.81
    nontuberculous 511.9
      bacterial 511.1
    pneumococcal 511.1
    staphylococcal 511.1
    streptococcal 511.1
    traumatic 862.29
      with open wound 862.39
    tuberculous (see also Tuberculosis, pleura) 012.0 ☑
      primary progressive 010.1 ☑
  pulmonary — see Effusion, pleura
  spinal (see also Meningitis) 322.9
  thorax, thoracic — see Effusion, pleura
Egg (oocyte) (ovum)
  donor V59.70
    over age 35 V59.73
      anonymous recipient V59.73
      designated recipient V59.74
    under age 35 V59.71
      anonymous recipient V59.71
      designated recipient V59.72
Eggshell nails 703.8
  congenital 757.5
Ego-dystonic
  homosexuality 302.0

Ego-dystonic — continued
  lesbianism 302.0
  sexual orientation 302.0
Egyptian splenomegaly 120.1
Ehlers-Danlos syndrome 756.83
Ehrlichiosis 082.40
  chaffeensis 082.41
  specified type NEC 082.49
Eichstedt's disease (pityriasis versicolor) 111.0
EIN (endometrial intraepithelial neoplasia) ●
  621.35 ●
Eisenmenger's complex or syndrome (ventricular septal defect) 745.4
Ejaculation, semen
  painful 608.89
    psychogenic 306.59
  premature 302.75
  retrograde 608.87
Ekbom syndrome (restless legs) 333.94
Ekman's syndrome (brittle bones and blue sclera) 756.51
Elastic skin 756.83
  acquired 701.8
Elastofibroma (M8820/0) — see Neoplasm, connective tissue, benign
Elastoidosis
  cutanea nodularis 701.8
  cutis cystica et comedonica 701.8
Elastoma 757.39
  juvenile 757.39
  Miescher's (elastosis perforans serpiginosa) 701.1
Elastomyofibrosis 425.3
Elastosis 701.8
  atrophicans 701.8
  perforans serpiginosa 701.1
  reactive perforating 701.1
  senilis 701.8
  solar (actinic) 692.74
Elbow — see condition
Electric
  current, electricity, effects (concussion) (fatal) (nonfatal) (shock) 994.8
    burn — see Burn, by site
  feet (foot) syndrome 266.2
  shock from electroshock gun (taser) 994.8
Electrocution 994.8
Electrolyte imbalance 276.9
  with
    abortion — see Abortion, by type, with metabolic disorder
    ectopic pregnancy (see also categories 633.0–633.9) 639.4
    hyperemesis gravidarum (before 22 completed weeks gestation) 643.1 ☑
    molar pregnancy (see also categories 630–632) 639.4
  following
    abortion 639.4
    ectopic or molar pregnancy 639.4
Elephantiasis (nonfilarial) 457.1
  arabicum (see also Infestation, filarial) 125.9
  congenita hereditaria 757.0
  congenital (any site) 757.0
  due to
    Brugia (malayi) 125.1
    mastectomy operation 457.0
    Wuchereria (bancrofti) 125.0
      malayi 125.1
  eyelid 374.83
  filarial (see also Infestation, filarial) 125.9
  filariensis (see also Infestation, filarial) 125.9
  gingival 523.8
  glandular 457.1
  graecorum 030.9
  lymphangiectatic 457.1
  lymphatic vessel 457.1
    due to mastectomy operation 457.0
  neuromatosa 237.71
  postmastectomy 457.0
  scrotum 457.1
  streptococcal 457.1
  surgical 997.99
    postmastectomy 457.0
  telangiectodes 457.1
  vulva (nonfilarial) 624.8

Elephant man syndrome 237.71
Elevated — see Elevation
Elevated — see Elevation
  findings on laboratory examination — see ●
    Findings, abnormal, without diagno- ●
    sis (examination) (laboratory test) ●
  GFR (glomerular filtration rate) — see Find- ●
    ings, abnormal, without diagnosis ●
    (examination) (laboratory test) ●
Elevation
  17-ketosteroids 791.9
  acid phosphatase 790.5
  alkaline phosphatase 790.5
  amylase 790.5
  antibody titers 795.79
  basal metabolic rate (BMR) 794.7
  blood pressure (see also Hypertension) 401.9
    reading (incidental) (isolated) (nonspecific), no diagnosis of hypertension 796.2
  blood sugar 790.29
  body temperature (of unknown origin) (see also Pyrexia) 780.60
  cancer antigen 125 [CA 125] 795.82
  carcinoembryonic antigen [CEA] 795.81
  cholesterol 272.0
    with high triglycerides 272.2
  conjugate, eye 378.81
  C-reactive protein (CRP) 790.95
  CRP (C-reactive protein) 790.95
  diaphragm, congenital 756.6
  GFR (glomerular filtration rate) — see Find- ●
    ings, abnormal, without diagnosis ●
    (examination) (laboratory test) ●
  glucose
    fasting 790.21
    tolerance test 790.22
  immunoglobulin level 795.79
  indolacetic acid 791.9
  lactic acid dehydrogenase (LDH) level 790.4
  leukocytes 288.60
  lipase 790.5
  lipoprotein a level 272.8
  liver function test (LFT) 790.6
    alkaline phosphatase 790.5
    aminotransferase 790.4
    bilirubin 782.4
    hepatic enzyme NEC 790.5
    lactate dehydrogenase 790.4
  lymphocytes 288.61
  prostate specific antigen (PSA) 790.93
  renin 790.99
    in hypertension (see also Hypertension, renovascular) 405.91
  Rh titer 999.7
  scapula, congenital 755.52
  sedimentation rate 790.1
  SGOT 790.4
  SGPT 790.4
  transaminase 790.4
  triglycerides 272.1
    with high cholesterol 272.2
  vanillylmandelic acid 791.9
  venous pressure 459.89
  VMA 791.9
  white blood cell count 288.60
    specified NEC 288.69
Elliptocytosis (congenital) (hereditary) 282.1
  Hb-C (disease) 282.7
  hemoglobin disease 282.7
  sickle-cell (disease) 282.60
    trait 282.5
Ellison-Zollinger syndrome (gastric hypersecretion with pancreatic islet cell tumor) 251.5
Ellis-van Creveld disease or syndrome (chondroectodermal dysplasia) 756.55
Elongation, elongated (congenital) — see also Distortion
  bone 756.9
  cervix (uteri) 752.49
    acquired 622.6
    hypertrophic 622.6
  colon 751.5
  common bile duct 751.69
  cystic duct 751.69
  frenulum, penis 752.69
  labia minora, acquired 624.8
  ligamentum patellae 756.89

Elongation, elongated — see also Distortion — continued
  petiolus (epiglottidis) 748.3
  styloid bone (process) 733.99
  tooth, teeth 520.2
  uvula 750.26
    acquired 528.9
Elschnig bodies or pearls 366.51
El Tor cholera 001.1
Emaciation (due to malnutrition) 261
Emancipation disorder 309.22
Embadomoniasis 007.8
Embarrassment heart, cardiac — see Disease, heart
Embedded tooth, teeth 520.6
  root only 525.3
Embolic — see condition
Embolism 444.9
  with
    abortion — see Abortion, by type, with embolism
    ectopic pregnancy (see also categories 633.0–633.9) 639.6
    molar pregnancy (see also categories 630–632) 639.6
  air (any site) 958.0
    with
      abortion — see Abortion, by type, with embolism
      ectopic pregnancy (see also categories 633.0–633.9) 639.6
      molar pregnancy (see also categories 630–632) 639.6
    due to implanted device — see Complications, due to (presence of) any device, implant, or graft classified to 996.0–996.5 NEC
    following
      abortion 639.6
      ectopic or molar pregnancy 639.6
    infusion, perfusion, or transfusion 999.1
    in pregnancy, childbirth, or puerperium 673.0 ☑
    traumatic 958.0
  amniotic fluid (pulmonary) 673.1 ☑
    with
      abortion — see Abortion, by type, with embolism
      ectopic pregnancy (see also categories 633.0–633.9) 639.6
      molar pregnancy (see also categories 630–632) 639.6
    following
      abortion 639.6
      ectopic or molar pregnancy 639.6
  aorta, aortic 444.1
    abdominal 444.0
    bifurcation 444.0
    saddle 444.0
    thoracic 444.1
  artery 444.9
    auditory, internal 433.8 ☑
    basilar (see also Occlusion, artery, basilar) 433.0 ☑
    bladder 444.89
    carotid (common) (internal) (see also Occlusion, artery, carotid) 433.1 ☑
    cerebellar (anterior inferior) (posterior inferior) (superior) 433.8 ☑
    cerebral (see also Embolism, brain) 434.1 ☑
    choroidal (anterior) 433.8 ☑
    communicating posterior 433.8 ☑
    coronary (see also Infarct, myocardium) 410.9 ☑
      without myocardial infarction 411.81
    extremity 444.22
      lower 444.22
      upper 444.21
    hypophyseal 433.8 ☑
    mesenteric (with gangrene) 557.0
    ophthalmic (see also Occlusion, retina) 362.30
    peripheral 444.22
    pontine 433.8 ☑

Embolism — *continued*
  artery — *continued*
    precerebral NEC — *see* Occlusion, artery,
        precerebral
    pulmonary — *see* Embolism, pulmonary
    pyemic 449
      pulmonary 415.12
    renal 593.81
    retinal (*see also* Occlusion, retina) 362.30
    septic 449
      pulmonary 415.12
    specified site NEC 444.89
    vertebral (*see also* Occlusion, artery, verte-
        bral) 433.2 ☑
  auditory, internal 433.8 ☑
  basilar (artery) (*see also* Occlusion, artery,
      basilar) 433.0 ☑
  birth, mother — *see* Embolism, obstetrical
  blood-clot
    with
      abortion — *see* Abortion, by type, with
          embolism
      ectopic pregnancy (*see also* categories
          633.0–633.9) 639.6
      molar pregnancy (*see also* categories
          630–632) 639.6
    following
      abortion 639.6
      ectopic or molar pregnancy 639.6
    in pregnancy, childbirth, or puerperium
        673.2 ☑
  brain 434.1 ☑
    with
      abortion — *see* Abortion, by type, with
          embolism
      ectopic pregnancy (*see also* categories
          633.0–633.9) 639.6
      molar pregnancy (*see also* categories
          630–632) 639.6
    following
      abortion 639.6
      ectopic or molar pregnancy 639.6
    late effect — *see* Late effect(s) (of) cere-
        brovascular disease
    puerperal, postpartum, childbirth 674.0 ☑
  capillary 448.9
  cardiac (*see also* Infarct, myocardium) 410.9 ☑
  carotid (artery) (common) (internal) (*see also*
      Occlusion, artery, carotid) 433.1 ☑
  cavernous sinus (venous) — *see* Embolism,
      intracranial venous sinus
  cerebral (*see also* Embolism, brain) 434.1 ☑
  cholesterol — *see* Atheroembolism
  choroidal (anterior) (artery) 433.8 ☑
  coronary (artery or vein) (systemic) (*see also*
      Infarct, myocardium) 410.9 ☑
    without myocardial infarction 411.81
  due to (presence of) any device, implant, or
      graft classifiable to 996.0–996.5 — *see*
      Complications, due to (presence of)
      any device, implant, or graft classified
      to 996.0–996.5 NEC
  encephalomalacia (*see also* Embolism, brain)
      434.1 ☑
  extremities 444.22
    lower 444.22
    upper 444.21
  eye 362.30
  fat (cerebral) (pulmonary) (systemic) 958.1
    with
      abortion — *see* Abortion, by type, with
          embolism
      ectopic pregnancy (*see also* categories
          633.0–633.9) 639.6
      molar pregnancy (*see also* categories
          630–632) 639.6
      complicating delivery or puerperium
          673.8 ☑
    following
      abortion 639.6
      ectopic or molar pregnancy 639.6
    in pregnancy, childbirth, or the puerperium
        673.8 ☑
  femoral (artery) 444.22
    vein 453.6   ▲
      deep 453.41

Embolism — *continued*
  following
    abortion 639.6
    ectopic or molar pregnancy 639.6
    infusion, perfusion, or transfusion
      air 999.1
      thrombus 999.2
  heart (fatty) (*see also* Infarct, myocardium)
      410.9 ☑
  hepatic (vein) 453.0
  iliac (artery) 444.81
  iliofemoral 444.81
  in pregnancy, childbirth, or puerperium (pul-
      monary) — *see* Embolism, obstetrical
  intestine (artery) (vein) (with gangrene) 557.0
  intracranial (*see also* Embolism, brain) 434.1 ☑
    venous sinus (any) 325
      late effect — *see* category 326
      nonpyogenic 437.6
        in pregnancy or puerperium
            671.5 ☑
  kidney (artery) 593.81
  lateral sinus (venous) — *see* Embolism, intracra-
      nial venous sinus
  longitudinal sinus (venous) — *see* Embolism,
      intracranial venous sinus
  lower extremity 444.22
  lung (massive) — *see* Embolism, pulmonary
  meninges (*see also* Embolism, brain) 434.1 ☑
  mesenteric (artery) (with gangrene) 557.0
  multiple NEC 444.9
  obstetrical (pulmonary) 673.2 ☑
    air 673.0 ☑
    amniotic fluid (pulmonary) 673.1 ☑
    blood-clot 673.2 ☑
    cardiac 674.8 ☑
    fat 673.8 ☑
    heart 674.8 ☑
    pyemic 673.3 ☑
    septic 673.3 ☑
    specified NEC 674.8 ☑
  ophthalmic (*see also* Occlusion, retina) 362.30
  paradoxical NEC 444.9
  penis 607.82
  peripheral arteries NEC 444.22
    lower 444.22
    upper 444.21
  pituitary 253.8
  popliteal (artery) 444.22
  portal (vein) 452
  postoperative NEC 997.2
    cerebral 997.02
    mesenteric artery 997.71
    other vessels 997.79
    peripheral vascular 997.2
    pulmonary 415.11
      septic 415.11
    renal artery 997.72
  precerebral artery (*see also* Occlusion, artery,
      precerebral) 433.9 ☑
  puerperal — *see* Embolism, obstetrical
  pulmonary ▶(acute)◀ (artery) (vein) 415.19
    with
      abortion — *see* Abortion, by type, with
          embolism
      ectopic pregnancy (*see also* categories
          633.0–633.9) 639.6
      molar pregnancy (*see also* categories
          630–632) 639.6
    chronic 416.2   ●
    following
      abortion 639.6
      ectopic or molar pregnancy 639.6
    healed or old V12.51   ●
    iatrogenic 415.11
    in pregnancy, childbirth, or puerperium —
        see Embolism, obstetrical
    personal history of V12.51   ●
    postoperative 415.11
    septic 415.12
  pyemic (multiple) (*see also* Septicemia) 415.12
    with
      abortion — *see* Abortion, by type, with
          embolism
      ectopic pregnancy (*see also* categories
          633.0–633.9) 639.6

Embolism — *continued*
  pyemic (*see also* Septicemia) — *continued*
    with — *continued*
      molar pregnancy (*see also* categories
          630–632) 639.6
    Aerobacter aerogenes 415.12
    enteric gram-negative bacilli 415.12
    Enterobacter aerogenes 415.12
    Escherichia coli 415.12
    following
      abortion 639.6
      ectopic or molar pregnancy 639.6
    Hemophilus influenzae 415.12
    pneumococcal 415.12
    Proteus vulgaris 415.12
    Pseudomonas (aeruginosa) 415.12
    puerperal, postpartum, childbirth (any or-
        ganism) 673.3 ☑
    Serratia 415.12
    specified organism NEC 415.12
    staphylococcal 415.12
      aureus 415.12
      specified organism NEC 415.12
    streptococcal 415.12
  renal (artery) 593.81
    vein 453.3
  retina, retinal (*see also* Occlusion, retina) 362.30
  saddle (aorta) 444.0
  septic 415.12
    arterial 449
  septicemic — *see* Embolism, pyemic
  sinus — *see* Embolism, intracranial venous si-
      nus
  soap
    with
      abortion — *see* Abortion, by type, with
          embolism
      ectopic pregnancy (*see also* categories
          633.0–633.9) 639.6
      molar pregnancy (*see also* categories
          630–632) 639.6
    following
      abortion 639.6
      ectopic or molar pregnancy 639.6
  spinal cord (nonpyogenic) 336.1
    in pregnancy or puerperium 671.5 ☑
    pyogenic origin 324.1
      late effect — *see* category 326
  spleen, splenic (artery) 444.89
  thrombus (thromboembolism) following infu-
      sion, perfusion, or transfusion 999.2
  upper extremity 444.21
  vein 453.9
    with inflammation or phlebitis — *see*
        Thrombophlebitis
    antecubital   ●
      acute 453.81   ●
      chronic 453.71   ●
    axillary   ●
      acute 453.84   ●
      chronic 453.74   ●
    basilic   ●
      acute 453.81   ●
      chronic 453.71   ●
    brachial   ●
      acute 453.82   ●
      chronic 453.72   ●
    brachiocephalic (innominate)   ●
      acute 453.87   ●
      chronic 453.77   ●
    cephalic   ●
      acute 453.81   ●
      chronic 453.71   ●
    cerebral (*see also* Embolism, brain)
        434.1 ☑
    coronary (*see also* Infarct, myocardium)
        410.9 ☑
      without myocardial infarction 411.81
    hepatic 453.0
    internal jugular   ●
      acute 453.86   ●
      chronic 453.76   ●
    lower extremity ▶(superficial)◀
        453.6   ▲
      deep 453.40
        acute 453.40   ●

Embolism — *continued*
  vein — *continued*
    lower extremity — *continued*
      deep — *continued*
        acute — *continued*
          calf 453.42   ●
          distal (lower leg) 453.42   ●
          femoral 453.41   ●
          iliac 453.41   ●
          lower leg 453.42   ●
          peroneal 453.42   ●
          popliteal 453.41   ●
          proximal (upper leg) 453.41   ●
          thigh 453.41   ●
          tibial 453.42   ●
        chronic 453.50   ●
          calf 453.52   ●
          disal (lower leg) 453.52   ●
          femoral 453.51   ●
          iliac 453.51   ●
          lower leg 453.52   ●
          peroneal 453.52   ●
          popliteal 453.51   ●
          proximal (upper leg) 453.51   ●
          thigh 453.51   ●
          tibial 453.52   ●
      saphenous (greater) (lesser) 453.6   ●
      superficial 453.6   ●
    mesenteric (with gangrene) 557.0
    portal 452
    pulmonary — *see* Embolism, pulmonary
    radial   ●
      acute 453.82   ●
      chronic 453.72   ●
    renal 453.3
    saphenous (greater) (lesser) 453.6   ●
    specified NEC ▶(acute)◀ 453.89   ▲
      with inflammation or phlebitis — *see*
          Thrombophlebitis
      chronic 453.79   ●
    subclavian   ●
      acute 453.85   ●
      chronic 453.75   ●
    superior vena cava   ●
      acute 453.87   ●
      chronic 453.77   ●
    thoracic   ●
      acute 453.87   ●
      chronic 453.77   ●
    ulnar   ●
      acute 453.82   ●
      chronic 453.72   ●
    upper extremity 453.83   ●
      acute 453.83   ●
        deep 453.82   ●
        superficial 453.81   ●
      chronic 453.73   ●
        deep 453.72   ●
        superficial 453.71   ●
    vena cava   ●
      inferior 453.2   ●
      superior   ●
        acute 453.87   ●
        chronic 453.77   ●
    vessels of brain (*see also* Embolism, brain)
        434.1 ☑
Embolization — *see* Embolism
Embolus — *see* Embolism
Embryoma (M9080/1) — *see also* Neoplasm,
    by site, uncertain behavior
  benign (M9080/0) — *see* Neoplasm, by site,
      benign
  kidney (M8960/3) 189.0
  liver (M8970/3) 155.0
  malignant (M9080/3) (*see also* Neoplasm, by
      site, malignant)
    kidney (M8960/3) 189.0
    liver (M8970/3) 155.0
    testis (M9070/3) 186.9
      undescended 186.0
  testis (M9070/3) 186.9
    undescended 186.0
Embryonic
  circulation 747.9
  heart 747.9
  vas deferens 752.89

☑ Additional Digit Required — Refer to the Tabular List for Digit Selection

ⓦ Subterms under main terms may continue to next column or page

▶◀ Revised Text   ● New Line   ▲ Revised Code

Embryopathia NEC 759.9
Embryotomy, fetal 763.89
Embryotoxon 743.43
   interfering with vision 743.42
Emesis — *see also* Vomiting
   bilious 787.04 ●
   gravidarum — *see* Hyperemesis, gravidarum
Emissions, nocturnal (semen) 608.89
Emotional
   crisis — *see* Crisis, emotional
   disorder (*see also* Disorder, mental) 300.9
   instability (excessive) 301.3
   lability 799.24 ●
   overlay — *see* Reaction, adjustment
   upset 300.9
Emotionality, pathological 301.3
Emotogenic disease — *see also* Disorder, psychogenic 306.9
Emphysema (atrophic) (centriacinar) (centrilobular) (chronic) (diffuse) (essential) (hypertrophic) (interlobular) (lung) (obstructive) (panlobular) (paracicatricial) (paracinar) (postural) (pulmonary) (senile) (subpleural) (traction) (unilateral) (unilobular) (vesicular) 492.8
   with bronchitis
      chronic 491.20
         with
            acute bronchitis 491.22
            exacerbation (acute) 491.21
   bullous (giant) 492.0
   cellular tissue 958.7
      surgical 998.81
   compensatory 518.2
   congenital 770.2
   conjunctiva 372.89
   connective tissue 958.7
      surgical 998.81
   due to fumes or vapors 506.4
   eye 376.89
   eyelid 374.85
      surgical 998.81
      traumatic 958.7
   fetus or newborn (interstitial) (mediastinal) (unilobular) 770.2
   heart 416.9
   interstitial 518.1
      congenital 770.2
      fetus or newborn 770.2
   laminated tissue 958.7
      surgical 998.81
   mediastinal 518.1
      fetus or newborn 770.2
   newborn (interstitial) (mediastinal) (unilobular) 770.2
   obstructive diffuse with fibrosis 492.8
   orbit 376.89
   subcutaneous 958.7
      due to trauma 958.7
      nontraumatic 518.1
      surgical 998.81
   surgical 998.81
   thymus (gland) (congenital) 254.8
   traumatic 958.7
   tuberculous (*see also* Tuberculosis, pulmonary) 011.9 ☑
Employment examination (certification) V70.5
Empty sella (turcica) syndrome 253.8
Empyema (chest) (diaphragmatic) (double) (encapsulated) (general) (interlobar) (lung) (medial) (necessitatis) (perforating chest wall) (pleura) (pneumococcal) (residual) (sacculated) (streptococcal) (supradiaphragmatic) 510.9
   with fistula 510.0
   accessory sinus (chronic) (*see also* Sinusitis) 473.9
   acute 510.9
      with fistula 510.0
   antrum (chronic) (*see also* Sinusitis, maxillary) 473.0
   brain (any part) (*see also* Abscess, brain) 324.0
   ethmoidal (sinus) (chronic) (*see also* Sinusitis, ethmoidal) 473.2
   extradural (*see also* Abscess, extradural) 324.9

Empyema — *continued*
   frontal (sinus) (chronic) (*see also* Sinusitis, frontal) 473.1
   gallbladder (*see also* Cholecystitis, acute) 575.0
   mastoid (process) (acute) (*see also* Mastoiditis, acute) 383.00
   maxilla, maxillary 526.4
      sinus (chronic) (*see also* Sinusitis, maxillary) 473.0
   nasal sinus (chronic) (*see also* Sinusitis) 473.9
   sinus (accessory) (nasal) (*see also* Sinusitis) 473.9
   sphenoidal (chronic) (sinus) (*see also* Sinusitis, sphenoidal) 473.3
   subarachnoid (*see also* Abscess, extradural) 324.9
   subdural (*see also* Abscess, extradural) 324.9
   tuberculous (*see also* Tuberculosis, pleura) 012.0 ☑
   ureter (*see also* Ureteritis) 593.89
   ventricular (*see also* Abscess, brain) 324.0
Enameloma 520.2
Encephalitis (bacterial) (chronic) (hemorrhagic) (idiopathic) (nonepidemic) (spurious) (subacute) 323.9
   acute (*see also* Encephalitis, viral)
      disseminated (postinfectious) NEC 136.9 *[323.61]*
         postimmunization or postvaccination 323.51
      inclusional 049.8
      inclusion body 049.8
      necrotizing 049.8
   arboviral, arbovirus NEC 064
   arthropod-borne (*see also* Encephalitis, viral, arthropod-borne) 064
   Australian X 062.4
   Bwamba fever 066.3
   California (virus) 062.5
   Central European 063.2
   Czechoslovakian 063.2
   Dawson's (inclusion body) 046.2
   diffuse sclerosing 046.2
   due to
      actinomycosis 039.8 *[323.41]*
      cat-scratch disease 078.3 *[323.01]*
      human herpesvirus NEC 058.29
      human herpesvirus 6 058.21
      human herpesvirus 7 058.29
      infection classified elsewhere 136.9 *[323.41]*
      infectious mononucleosis 075 *[323.01]*
      malaria (*see also* Malaria) 084.6 *[323.2]*
      Negishi virus 064
      ornithosis 073.7 *[323.01]*
      prophylactic inoculation against smallpox 323.51
      rickettsiosis (*see also* Rickettsiosis) 083.9 *[323.1]*
      rubella 056.01
      toxoplasmosis (acquired) 130.0
         congenital (active) 771.2 *[323.41]*
      typhus (fever) (*see also* Typhus) 081.9 *[323.1]*
      vaccination (smallpox) 323.51
   Eastern equine 062.2
   endemic 049.8
   epidemic 049.8
   equine (acute) (infectious) (viral) 062.9
      Eastern 062.2
      Venezuelan 066.2
      Western 062.1
   Far Eastern 063.0
   following vaccination or other immunization procedure 323.51
   herpes 054.3
   human herpesvirus NEC 058.29
   human herpesvirus 6 058.21
   human herpesvirus 7 058.29
   Ilheus (virus) 062.8
   inclusion body 046.2
   infectious (acute) (virus) NEC 049.8
   influenzal 487.8 *[323.41]*
      lethargic 049.8
   Japanese (B type) 062.0
   La Crosse 062.5

Encephalitis — *continued*
   Langat 063.8
   late effect — *see* Late, effect, encephalitis
   lead 984.9 *[323.71]*
   lethargic (acute) (infectious) (influenzal) 049.8
   lethargica 049.8
   louping ill 063.1
   lupus 710.0 *[323.81]*
   lymphatica 049.0
   Mengo 049.8
   meningococcal 036.1
   mumps 072.2
   Murray Valley 062.4
   myoclonic 049.8
   Negishi virus 064
   otitic NEC 382.4 *[323.41]*
   parasitic NEC 123.9 *[323.41]*
   periaxialis (concentrica) (diffusa) 341.1
   postchickenpox 052.0
   postexanthematous NEC 057.9 *[323.62]*
   postimmunization 323.51
   postinfectious NEC 136.9 *[323.62]*
   postmeasles 055.0
   posttraumatic 323.81
   postvaccinal (smallpox) 323.51
   postvaricella 052.0
   postviral NEC 079.99 *[323.62]*
      postexanthematous 057.9 *[323.62]*
      specified NEC 057.8 *[323.62]*
   Powassan 063.8
   progressive subcortical (Binswanger's) 290.12
   Rasmussen 323.81
   Rio Bravo 049.8
   rubella 056.01
   Russian
      autumnal 062.0
      spring-summer type (taiga) 063.0
   saturnine 984.9 *[323.71]*
   Semliki Forest 062.8
   serous 048
   slow-acting virus NEC 046.8
   specified cause NEC 323.81
   St. Louis type 062.3
   subacute sclerosing 046.2
   subcorticalis chronica 290.12
   summer 062.0
   suppurative 324.0
   syphilitic 094.81
      congenital 090.41
   tick-borne 063.9
   torula, torular 117.5 *[323.41]*
   toxic NEC 989.9 *[323.71]*
   toxoplasmic (acquired) 130.0
      congenital (active) 771.2 *[323.41]*
   trichinosis 124 *[323.41]*
   Trypanosomiasis (*see also* Trypanosomiasis) 086.9 *[323.2]*
   tuberculous (*see also* Tuberculosis) 013.6 ☑
   type B (Japanese) 062.0
   type C 062.3
   van Bogaert's 046.2
   Venezuelan 066.2
   Vienna type 049.8
   viral, virus 049.9
      arthropod-borne NEC 064
         mosquito-borne 062.9
            Australian X disease 062.4
            California virus 062.5
            Eastern equine 062.2
            Ilheus virus 062.8
            Japanese (B type) 062.0
            Murray Valley 062.4
            specified type NEC 062.8
            St. Louis 062.3
            type B 062.0
            type C 062.3
            Western equine 062.1
         tick-borne 063.9
            biundulant 063.2
            Central European 063.2
            Czechoslovakian 063.2
            diphasic meningoencephalitis 063.2
            Far Eastern 063.0
            Langat 063.8
            louping ill 063.1

Encephalitis — *continued*
   viral, virus — *continued*
      arthropod-borne — *continued*
         tick-borne — *continued*
            Powassan 063.8
            Russian spring-summer (taiga) 063.0
            specified type NEC 063.8
         vector unknown 064
         Western equine 062.1
      slow acting NEC 046.8
      specified type NEC 049.8
      vaccination, prophylactic (against) V05.0
      von Economo's 049.8
      Western equine 062.1
      West Nile type 066.41
Encephalocele 742.0
   orbit 376.81
Encephalocystocele 742.0
Encephalomalacia (brain) (cerebellar) (cerebral) (cerebrospinal) — *see also* Softening, brain 434.9 ☑
   due to
      hemorrhage (*see also* Hemorrhage, brain) 431
      recurrent spasm of artery 435.9
   embolic (cerebral) (*see also* Embolism, brain) 434.1 ☑
   subcorticalis chronicus arteriosclerotica 290.12
   thrombotic (*see also* Thrombosis, brain) 434.0 ☑
Encephalomeningitis — *see* Meningoencephalitis
Encephalomeningocele 742.0
Encephalomeningomyelitis — *see* Meningoencephalitis
Encephalomeningopathy — *see also* Meningoencephalitis 349.9
Encephalomyelitis (chronic) (granulomatous) (myalgic, benign) — *see also* Encephalitis 323.9
   abortive disseminated 049.8
   acute disseminated (ADEM) (postinfectious) 136.9 *[323.61]*
      infectious 136.9 *[323.61]*
      noninfectious 323.81
      postimmunization 323.51
   due to
      cat-scratch disease 078.3 *[323.01]*
      infectious mononucleosis 075 *[323.01]*
      ornithosis 073.7 *[323.01]*
      vaccination (any) 323.51
   equine (acute) (infectious) 062.9
      Eastern 062.2
      Venezuelan 066.2
      Western 062.1
   funicularis infectiosa 049.8
   late effect — *see* Late, effect, encephalitis
   Munch-Peterson's 049.8
   postchickenpox 052.0
   postimmunization 323.51
   postmeasles 055.0
   postvaccinal (smallpox) 323.51
   rubella 056.01
   specified cause NEC 323.81
   syphilitic 094.81
   West Nile 066.41
Encephalomyelocele 742.0
Encephalomyelomeningitis — *see* Meningoencephalitis
Encephalomyeloneuropathy 349.9
Encephalomyelopathy 349.9
   subacute necrotizing (infantile) 330.8
Encephalomyeloradiculitis (acute) 357.0
Encephalomyeloradiculoneuritis (acute) 357.0
Encephalomyeloradiculopathy 349.9
Encephalomyocarditis 074.23
Encephalopathia hyperbilirubinemica, newborn 774.7
   due to isoimmunization (conditions classifiable to 773.0–773.2) 773.4
Encephalopathy (acute) 348.30
   alcoholic 291.2
   anoxic — *see* Damage, brain, anoxic
   arteriosclerotic 437.0

☑ Additional Digit Required — Refer to the Tabular List for Digit Selection   ▿ Subterms under main terms may continue to next column or page

Encephalopathy — continued
- arteriosclerotic — continued
  - late effect — see Late effect(s) (of) cerebrovascular disease
- bilirubin, newborn 774.7
  - due to isoimmunization 773.4
- congenital 742.9
- demyelinating (callosal) 341.8
- due to
  - birth injury (intracranial) 767.8
  - dialysis 294.8
    - transient 293.9
  - drugs — (see also Table of Drugs and Chemicals) 348.39
  - hyperinsulinism — see Hyperinsulinism
  - influenza (virus) 487.8
  - lack of vitamin (see also Deficiency, vitamin) 269.2
  - nicotinic acid deficiency 291.2
  - serum (nontherapeutic) (therapeutic) 999.5
  - syphilis 094.81
  - trauma (postconcussional) 310.2
    - current (see also Concussion, brain) 850.9
      - with skull fracture — see Fracture, skull, by site, with intracranial injury
  - vaccination 323.51
- hepatic 572.2
- hyperbilirubinemic, newborn 774.7
  - due to isoimmunization (conditions classifiable to 773.0–773.2) 773.4
- hypertensive 437.2
- hypoglycemic 251.2
- hypoxic (see also Damage, brain, anoxic)
  - ischemic (HIE) 768.70 ▲
    - mild 768.71 ●
    - moderate 768.72 ●
    - severe 768.73 ●
- infantile cystic necrotizing (congenital) 341.8
- lead 984.9 [323.71]
- leukopolio 330.0
- metabolic (see also Delirium) 348.31
  - toxic 349.82
- necrotizing
  - hemorrhagic (acute) 323.61
  - subacute 330.8
- other specified type NEC 348.39
- pellagrous 265.2
- portal-systemic 572.2
- postcontusional 310.2
- posttraumatic 310.2
- saturnine 984.9 [323.71]
- septic 348.31
- spongioform, subacute (viral) 046.19
- subacute
  - necrotizing 330.8
  - spongioform 046.19
  - viral, spongioform 046.19
- subcortical progressive (Schilder) 341.1
  - chronic (Binswanger's) 290.12
- toxic 349.82
  - metabolic 349.82
- traumatic (postconcussional) 310.2
  - current (see also Concussion, brain) 850.9
    - with skull fracture — see Fracture, skull, by site, with intracranial injury
- vitamin B deficiency NEC 266.9
- Wernicke's (superior hemorrhagic polioencephalitis) 265.1

Encephalorrhagia — see also Hemorrhage, brain 432.9
- healed or old V12.54
- late effect — see Late effect(s) (of) cerebrovascular disease

Encephalosis, posttraumatic 310.2
Enchondroma (M9220/0) — see also Neoplasm, bone, benign
- multiple, congenital 756.4
Enchondromatosis (cartilaginous) (congenital) (multiple) 756.4
Enchondroses, multiple (cartilaginous) (congenital) 756.4
Encopresis — see also Incontinence, feces 787.6
- nonorganic origin 307.7
Encounter for — see also Admission for

Encounter for — see also Admission for — continued
- administrative purpose only V68.9
  - referral of patient without examination or treatment V68.81
  - specified purpose NEC V68.89
- chemotherapy, ▶(oral) (intravenous),◀ antineoplastic V58.11
- dialysis
  - extracorporeal (renal) V56.0
  - peritoneal V56.8
- disability examination V68.01
- end-of-life care V66.7
- hospice care V66.7
- immunizations (childhood) appropriate for age V20.2 ●
- immunotherapy, antineoplastic V58.12
- palliative care V66.7
- paternity testing V70.4
- radiotherapy V58.0
- respirator [ventilator] dependence
  - during
    - mechanical failure V46.14
    - power failure V46.12
  - for weaning V46.13
- routine infant and child vision and hearing testing V20.2 ●
- school examination V70.3
  - following surgery V67.09 ●
- screening mammogram NEC V76.12
  - for high-risk patient V76.11
- terminal care V66.7
- weaning from respirator [ventilator] V46.13
Encystment — see Cyst
Endamebiasis — see Amebiasis
Endamoeba — see Amebiasis
Endarteritis (bacterial, subacute) (infective) (septic) 447.6
- brain, cerebral or cerebrospinal 437.4
  - late effect — see Late effect(s) (of) cerebrovascular disease
- coronary (artery) — see Arteriosclerosis, coronary
- deformans — see Arteriosclerosis
- embolic (see also Embolism) 444.9
- obliterans (see also Arteriosclerosis)
  - pulmonary 417.8
- pulmonary 417.8
- retina 362.18
- senile — see Arteriosclerosis
- syphilitic 093.89
  - brain or cerebral 094.89
  - congenital 090.5
  - spinal 094.89
- tuberculous (see also Tuberculosis) 017.9 ☑
Endemic — see condition
Endocarditis (chronic) (indeterminate) (interstitial) (marantic) (nonbacterial thrombotic) (residual) (scleroric) (sclerous) (senile) (valvular) 424.90
- with
  - rheumatic fever (conditions classifiable to 390)
    - active — see Endocarditis, acute, rheumatic
    - inactive or quiescent (with chorea) 397.9
- acute or subacute 421.9
  - rheumatic (aortic) (mitral) (pulmonary) (tricuspid) 391.1
    - with chorea (acute) (rheumatic) (Sydenham's) 392.0
- aortic (heart) (nonrheumatic) (valve) 424.1
  - with
    - mitral (valve) disease 396.9
      - active or acute 391.1
        - with chorea (acute) (rheumatic) (Sydenham's) 392.0
      - bacterial 421.0
    - rheumatic fever (conditions classifiable to 390)
      - active — see Endocarditis, acute, rheumatic
      - inactive or quiescent (with chorea) 395.9
        - with mitral disease 396.9

Endocarditis — continued
- aortic — continued
  - acute or subacute 421.9
  - arteriosclerotic 424.1
  - congenital 746.89
  - hypertensive 424.1
  - rheumatic (chronic) (inactive) 395.9
    - with mitral (valve) disease 396.9
      - active or acute 391.1
        - with chorea (acute) (rheumatic) (Sydenham's) 392.0
    - active or acute 391.1
      - with chorea (acute) (rheumatic) (Sydenham's) 392.0
    - specified cause, except rheumatic 424.1
    - syphilitic 093.22
  - arteriosclerotic or due to arteriosclerosis 424.99
  - atypical verrucous (Libman-Sacks) 710.0 [424.91]
  - bacterial (acute) (any valve) (chronic) (subacute) 421.0
  - blastomycotic 116.0 [421.1]
  - candidal 112.81
  - congenital 425.3
  - constrictive 421.0
  - Coxsackie 074.22
  - due to
    - blastomycosis 116.0 [421.1]
    - candidiasis 112.81
    - Coxsackie (virus) 074.22
    - disseminated lupus erythematosus 710.0 [424.91]
    - histoplasmosis (see also Histoplasmosis) 115.94
    - hypertension (benign) 424.99
    - moniliasis 112.81
    - prosthetic cardiac valve 996.61
    - Q fever 083.0 [421.1]
    - serratia marcescens 421.0
    - typhoid (fever) 002.0 [421.1]
  - fetal 425.3
  - gonococcal 098.84
  - hypertensive 424.99
  - infectious or infective (acute) (any valve) (chronic) (subacute) 421.0
  - lenta (acute) (any valve) (chronic) (subacute) 421.0
  - Libman-Sacks 710.0 [424.91]
  - Loeffler's (parietal fibroplastic) 421.0
  - malignant (acute) (any valve) (chronic) (subacute) 421.0
  - meningococcal 036.42
  - mitral (chronic) (double) (fibroid) (heart) (inactive) (valve) (with chorea) 394.9
    - with
      - aortic (valve) disease 396.9
        - active or acute 391.1
          - with chorea (acute) (rheumatic) (Sydenham's) 392.0
        - rheumatic fever (conditions classifiable to 390)
          - active — see Endocarditis, acute, rheumatic
          - inactive or quiescent (with chorea) 394.9
            - with aortic valve disease 396.9
      - active or acute 391.1
        - with chorea (acute) (rheumatic) (Sydenham's) 392.0
          - bacterial 421.0
      - arteriosclerotic 424.0
      - congenital 746.89
      - hypertensive 424.0
      - nonrheumatic 424.0
        - acute or subacute 421.9
      - syphilitic 093.21
  - monilial 112.81
  - mycotic (acute) (any valve) (chronic) (subacute) 421.0
  - pneumococcic (acute) (any valve) (chronic) (subacute) 421.0
  - pulmonary (chronic) (heart) (valve) 424.3

Endocarditis — continued
- pulmonary — continued
  - with
    - rheumatic fever (conditions classifiable to 390)
      - active — see Endocarditis, acute, rheumatic
      - inactive or quiescent (with chorea) 397.1
  - acute or subacute 421.9
    - rheumatic 391.1
      - with chorea (acute) (rheumatic) (Sydenham's) 392.0
  - arteriosclerotic or due to arteriosclerosis 424.3
  - congenital 746.09
  - hypertensive or due to hypertension (benign) 424.3
  - rheumatic (chronic) (inactive) (with chorea) 397.1
    - active or acute 391.1
      - with chorea (acute) (rheumatic) (Sydenham's) 392.0
  - syphilitic 093.24
  - purulent (acute) (any valve) (chronic) (subacute) 421.0
  - rheumatic (chronic) (inactive) (with chorea) 397.9
    - active or acute (aortic) (mitral) (pulmonary) (tricuspid) 391.1
      - with chorea (acute) (rheumatic) (Sydenham's) 392.0
  - septic (acute) (any valve) (chronic) (subacute) 421.0
  - specified cause, except rheumatic 424.99
  - streptococcal (acute) (any valve) (chronic) (subacute) 421.0
  - subacute — see Endocarditis, acute
  - suppurative (any valve) (acute) (chronic) (subacute) 421.0
  - syphilitic NEC 093.20
  - toxic (see also Endocarditis, acute) 421.9
  - tricuspid (chronic) (heart) (inactive) (rheumatic) (valve) (with chorea) 397.0
    - with
      - rheumatic fever (conditions classifiable to 390)
        - active — see Endocarditis, acute, rheumatic
        - inactive or quiescent (with chorea) 397.0
    - active or acute 391.1
      - with chorea (acute) (rheumatic) (Sydenham's) 392.0
    - arteriosclerotic 424.2
    - congenital 746.89
    - hypertensive 424.2
    - nonrheumatic 424.2
      - acute or subacute 421.9
    - specified cause, except rheumatic 424.2
    - syphilitic 093.23
  - tuberculous (see also Tuberculosis) 017.9 ☑ [424.91]
  - typhoid 002.0 [421.1]
  - ulcerative (acute) (any valve) (chronic) (subacute) 421.0
  - vegetative (acute) (any valve) (chronic) (subacute) 421.0
  - verrucous (acute) (any valve) (chronic) (subacute) NEC 710.0 [424.91]
    - nonbacterial 710.0 [424.91]
    - nonrheumatic 710.0 [424.91]
Endocardium, endocardial — see also condition
- cushion defect 745.60
  - specified type NEC 745.69
Endocervicitis — see also Cervicitis 616.0
- due to
  - intrauterine (contraceptive) device 996.65
  - gonorrheal (acute) 098.15
    - chronic or duration of 2 months or over 098.35
- hyperplastic 616.0
- syphilitic 095.8
- trichomonal 131.09
- tuberculous (see also Tuberculosis) 016.7 ☑
Endocrine — see condition

☑ Additional Digit Required — Refer to the Tabular List for Digit Selection   ▽ Subterms under main terms may continue to next column or page

102 — Volume 2 · October 2009   ▶◀ Revised Text   ● New Line   ▲ Revised Code   2010 ICD-9-CM

Index

Enteritis — Epilepsy, epileptic

Enteritis — *continued*
- regional — *continued*
  - intestine — *continued*
    - large — *continued*
      - with small intestine 555.2
      - small (duodenum, ileum, or jejunum) 555.0
        - with large intestine 555.2
- Salmonella infection 003.0
- salmonellosis 003.0
- segmental (*see also* Enteritis, regional) 555.9
- septic (*see also* Enteritis, due to, by organism) 009.0
- Shigella 004.9
- simple 558.9
- spasmodic 564.9
- spastic 564.9
- staphylococcal 008.41
  - due to food 005.0
- streptococcal 008.49
  - anaerobic 008.46
- toxic 558.2
- Treponema (denticola) (macrodentium) 008.46
- trichomonal 007.3
- tuberculous (*see also* Tuberculosis) 014.8 ☑
- typhosa 002.0
- ulcerative (chronic) (*see also* Colitis, ulcerative) 556.9
- Veillonella 008.46
- viral 008.8
  - adenovirus 008.62
  - enterovirus 008.67
  - specified virus NEC 008.69
- Yersinia enterocolitica 008.44
- zymotic 009.0

Enteroarticular syndrome 099.3
Enterobiasis 127.4
Enterobius vermicularis 127.4
Enterocele — *see also* Hernia 553.9
- pelvis, pelvic (acquired) (congenital) 618.6
- vagina, vaginal (acquired) (congenital) 618.6

Enterocolitis — *see also* Enteritis
- fetus or newborn (*see also* Enterocolitis, necrotizing, newborn) 777.8
  - necrotizing 777.50
- fulminant 557.0
- granulomatous 555.2
- hemorrhagic (acute) 557.0
  - chronic 557.1
- necrotizing (acute) (membranous) 557.0
  - newborn 777.50
    - with
      - perforation 777.53
      - pneumatosis and perforation 777.53
      - pneumatosis without perforation 777.52
      - without pneumatosis, without perforation 777.51 ●
    - stage I 777.51
    - stage II 777.52
    - stage III 777.53
  - primary necrotizing (*see also* Enterocolitis, necrotizing, newborn) 777.50
- pseudomembranous 008.45
  - newborn 008.45 ●
- radiation 558.1
  - newborn (*see also* Enterocolitis, necrotizing, newborn) 777.50
- ulcerative 556.0

Enterocystoma 751.5
Enterogastritis — *see* Enteritis
Enterogenous cyanosis 289.7
Enterolith, enterolithiasis (impaction) 560.39
- with hernia (*see also* Hernia, by site, with obstruction)
  - gangrenous — *see* Hernia, by site, with gangrene

Enteropathy 569.9
- exudative (of Gordon) 579.8
- gluten 579.0
- hemorrhagic, terminal 557.0
- protein-losing 579.8

Enteroperitonitis — *see also* Peritonitis 567.9
Enteroptosis 569.89
Enterorrhagia 578.9

Enterospasm 564.9
- psychogenic 306.4
Enterostenosis — *see also* Obstruction, intestine 560.9
Enterostomy status V44.4
- with complication 569.60
Enthesopathy 726.90
- ankle and tarsus 726.70
- elbow region 726.30
  - specified NEC 726.39
- hip 726.5
- knee 726.60
- peripheral NEC 726.8
- shoulder region 726.10
  - adhesive 726.0
- spinal 720.1
- wrist and carpus 726.4
Entrance, air into vein — *see* Embolism, air
Entrapment, nerve — *see* Neuropathy, entrapment
Entropion (eyelid) 374.00
- cicatricial 374.04
- congenital 743.62
- late effect of trachoma (healed) 139.1
- mechanical 374.02
- paralytic 374.02
- senile 374.01
- spastic 374.03
Enucleation of eye (current) (traumatic) 871.3
Enuresis 788.30
- habit disturbance 307.6
- nocturnal 788.36
  - psychogenic 307.6
- nonorganic origin 307.6
- psychogenic 307.6
Enzymopathy 277.9
Eosinopenia 288.59
Eosinophilia 288.3
- allergic 288.3
- hereditary 288.3
- idiopathic 288.3
- infiltrative 518.3
- Loeffler's 518.3
- myalgia syndrome 710.5
- pulmonary (tropical) 518.3
- secondary 288.3
- tropical 518.3
Eosinophilic — *see also* condition
- fasciitis 728.89
- granuloma (bone) 277.89
- infiltration lung 518.3
Ependymitis (acute) (cerebral) (chronic) (granular) — *see also* Meningitis 322.9
Ependymoblastoma (M9392/3)
- specified site — *see* Neoplasm, by site, malignant
- unspecified site 191.9
Ependymoma (epithelial) (malignant) (M9391/3)
- anaplastic type (M9392/3)
  - specified site — *see* Neoplasm, by site, malignant
  - unspecified site 191.9
- benign (M9391/0)
  - specified site — *see* Neoplasm, by site, benign
  - unspecified site 225.0
- myxopapillary (M9394/1) 237.5
- papillary (M9393/1) 237.5
  - specified site — *see* Neoplasm, by site, malignant
  - unspecified site 191.9
Ependymopathy 349.2
- spinal cord 349.2
Ephelides, ephelis 709.09
Ephemeral fever — *see also* Pyrexia 780.60
Epiblepharon (congenital) 743.62
Epicanthus, epicanthic fold (congenital) (eyelid) 743.63
Epicondylitis (elbow) (lateral) 726.32
- medial 726.31
Epicystitis — *see also* Cystitis 595.9
Epidemic — *see* condition
Epidermidalization, cervix — *see* condition
Epidermidization, cervix — *see* condition
Epidermis, epidermal — *see* condition
Epidermization, cervix — *see* condition

Epidermodysplasia verruciformis 078.19
Epidermoid
- cholesteatoma — *see* Cholesteatoma
- inclusion (*see also* Cyst, skin) 706.2
Epidermolysis
- acuta (combustiformis) (toxica) 695.15
- bullosa 757.39
- necroticans combustiformis 695.15
  - due to drug
    - correct substance properly administered 695.15
    - overdose or wrong substance given or taken 977.9
      - specified drug — *see* Table of Drugs and Chemicals
Epidermophytid — *see* Dermatophytosis
Epidermophytosis (infected) — *see* Dermatophytosis
Epidermosis, ear (middle) — *see also* Cholesteatoma 385.30
Epididymis — *see* condition
Epididymitis (nonvenereal) 604.90
- with abscess 604.0
- acute 604.99
- blennorrhagic (acute) 098.0
  - chronic or duration of 2 months or over 098.2
- caseous (*see also* Tuberculosis) 016.4 ☑
- chlamydial 099.54
- diphtheritic 032.89 [604.91]
- filarial 125.9 [604.91]
- gonococcal (acute) 098.0
  - chronic or duration of 2 months or over 098.2
- recurrent 604.99
- residual 604.99
- syphilitic 095.8 [604.91]
- tuberculous (*see also* Tuberculosis) 016.4 ☑
Epididymo-orchitis — *see also* Epididymitis 604.90
- with abscess 604.0
- chlamydial 099.54
- gonococcal (acute) 098.13
  - chronic or duration of 2 months or over 098.33
Epidural — *see* condition
Epigastritis — *see also* Gastritis 535.5 ☑
Epigastrium, epigastric — *see* condition
Epigastrocele — *see also* Hernia, epigastric 553.29
Epiglottiditis (acute) 464.30
- with obstruction 464.31
- chronic 476.1
- viral 464.30
  - with obstruction 464.31
Epiglottis — *see* condition
Epiglottitis (acute) 464.30
- with obstruction 464.31
- chronic 476.1
- viral 464.30
  - with obstruction 464.31
Epignathus 759.4
Epilepsia
- partialis continua (*see also* Epilepsy) 345.7 ☑
- procursiva (*see also* Epilepsy) 345.8 ☑
Epilepsy, epileptic (idiopathic) 345.9 ☑

> *Note* — *Use the following fifth-digit subclassification with categories 345.0, 345.1, 345.4–345.9:*
>
> 0   *without mention of intractable epilepsy*
>
> 1   *with intractable epilepsy*
>
> ▶*pharmacoresistant (pharmacologically resistant)*
>
> *poorly controlled*
>
> *refractory (medically)*
>
> *treatment resistant*◀

- abdominal 345.5 ☑
- absence (attack) 345.0 ☑
- akinetic 345.0 ☑
  - psychomotor 345.4 ☑
- automatism 345.4 ☑
- autonomic diencephalic 345.5 ☑

Epilepsy, epileptic — *continued*
- brain 345.9 ☑
- Bravais-Jacksonian 345.5 ☑
- cerebral 345.9 ☑
- climacteric 345.9 ☑
- clonic 345.1 ☑
- clouded state 345.9 ☑
- coma 345.3
- communicating 345.4 ☑
- complicating pregnancy, childbirth, or the puerperium 649.4 ☑
- congenital 345.9 ☑
- convulsions 345.9 ☑
- cortical (focal) (motor) 345.5 ☑
- cursive (running) 345.8 ☑
- cysticercosis 123.1
- deterioration
  - with behavioral disturbance 345.9 [294.11]
  - without behavioral disturbance 345.9 [294.10]
- due to syphilis 094.89
- equivalent 345.5 ☑
- fit 345.9 ☑
- focal (motor) 345.5 ☑
- gelastic 345.8 ☑
- generalized 345.9 ☑
  - convulsive 345.1 ☑
  - flexion 345.1 ☑
  - nonconvulsive 345.0 ☑
- grand mal (idiopathic) 345.1 ☑
- Jacksonian (motor) (sensory) 345.5 ☑
- Kojevnikoff's, Kojevnikov's, Kojewnikoff's 345.7 ☑
- laryngeal 786.2
- limbic system 345.4 ☑
- localization related (focal) (partial) and epileptic syndromes
  - with
    - complex partial seizures 345.4 ☑
    - simple partial seizures 345.5 ☑
- major (motor) 345.1 ☑
- minor 345.0 ☑
- mixed (type) 345.9 ☑
- motor partial 345.5 ☑
- musicogenic 345.1 ☑
- myoclonus, myoclonic 345.1 ☑
  - progressive (familial) 345.1 ☑ ▲
- nonconvulsive, generalized 345.0 ☑
- parasitic NEC 123.9
- partial (focalized) 345.5 ☑
  - with
    - impairment of consciousness 345.4 ☑
    - memory and ideational disturbances 345.4 ☑
    - without impairment of consciousness 345.5 ☑
  - abdominal type 345.5 ☑
  - motor type 345.5 ☑
  - psychomotor type 345.4 ☑
  - psychosensory type 345.4 ☑
  - secondarily generalized 345.4 ☑
  - sensory type 345.5 ☑
  - somatomotor type 345.5 ☑
  - somatosensory type 345.5 ☑
  - temporal lobe type 345.4 ☑
  - visceral type 345.5 ☑
  - visual type 345.5 ☑
- peripheral 345.9 ☑
- petit mal 345.0 ☑
- photokinetic 345.8 ☑
- progressive myoclonic (familial) 345.1 ☑ ▲
- psychic equivalent 345.5 ☑
- psychomotor 345.4 ☑
- psychosensory 345.4 ☑
- reflex 345.1 ☑
- seizure 345.9 ☑
- senile 345.9 ☑
- sensory-induced 345.5 ☑
- sleep (*see also* Narcolepsy) 347.00
- somatomotor type 345.5 ☑
- somatosensory 345.5 ☑
- specified type NEC 345.8 ☑

☑ Additional Digit Required — Refer to the Tabular List for Digit Selection   ▽ Subterms under main terms may continue to next column or page

☑ Additional Digit Required — Refer to the Tabular List for Digit Selection   ▽ Subterms under main terms may continue to next column or page

2010 ICD-9-CM   ▶◀ Revised Text   ● New Line   ▲ Revised Code   October 2009 • Volume 2 — 105

Erythrocythemia — *see* Erythremia
Erythrocytopenia 285.9
Erythrocytosis (megalosplenic)
  familial 289.6
  oval, hereditary (*see also* Elliptocytosis) 282.1
  secondary 289.0
  stress 289.0
Erythroderma — *see also* Erythema 695.9
  desquamativa (in infants) 695.89
  exfoliative 695.89
  ichthyosiform, congenital 757.1
  infantum 695.89
  maculopapular 696.2
  neonatorum 778.8
  psoriaticum 696.1
  secondary 695.9
Erythrodysesthesia, palmar plantar (PPE)
  693.0
Erythrogenesis imperfecta 284.09
Erythroleukemia (M9840/3) 207.0 ☑
Erythromelalgia 443.82
Erythromelia 701.8
Erythropenia 285.9
Erythrophagocytosis 289.9
Erythrophobia 300.23
Erythroplakia
  oral mucosa 528.79
  tongue 528.79
Erythroplasia (Queyrat) (M8080/2)
  specified site — *see* Neoplasm, skin, in situ
  unspecified site 233.5
Erythropoiesis, idiopathic ineffective 285.0
Escaped beats, heart 427.60
  postoperative 997.1
Esoenteritis — *see* Enteritis
Esophagalgia 530.89
Esophagectasis 530.89
  due to cardiospasm 530.0
Esophagismus 530.5
Esophagitis (alkaline) (chemical) (chronic) (infec-
  tional) (necrotic) (peptic) (postoperative)
  (regurgitant) 530.10
  acute 530.12
  candidal 112.84
  eosinophilic 530.13
  reflux 530.11
  specified NEC 530.19
  tuberculous (*see also* Tuberculosis) 017.8 ☑
  ulcerative 530.19
Esophagocele 530.6
Esophagodynia 530.89
Esophagomalacia 530.89
Esophagoptosis 530.89
Esophagospasm 530.5
Esophagostenosis 530.3
Esophagostomiasis 127.7
Esophagostomy
  complication 530.87
    infection 530.86
    malfunctioning 530.87
    mechanical 530.87
Esophagotracheal — *see* condition
Esophagus — *see* condition
Esophoria 378.41
  convergence, excess 378.84
  divergence, insufficiency 378.85
Esotropia (nonaccommodative) 378.00
  accommodative 378.35
  alternating 378.05
    with
      A pattern 378.06
      specified noncomitancy NEC 378.08
      V pattern 378.07
      X pattern 378.08
      Y pattern 378.08
    intermittent 378.22
  intermittent 378.20
    alternating 378.22
    monocular 378.21
  monocular 378.01
    with
      A pattern 378.02
      specified noncomitancy NEC 378.04
      V pattern 378.03
      X pattern 378.04
      Y pattern 378.04

Esotropia — *continued*
  monocular — *continued*
    intermittent 378.21
Espundia 085.5
Essential — *see* condition
Esterapenia 289.89
Esthesioneuroblastoma (M9522/3) 160.0
Esthesioneurocytoma (M9521/3) 160.0
Esthesioneuroepithelioma (M9523/3) 160.0
Esthiomene 099.1
Estivo-autumnal
  fever 084.0
  malaria 084.0
Estrangement V61.09
Estriasis 134.0
Ethanolaminuria 270.8
Ethanolism — *see also* Alcoholism 303.9 ☑
Ether dependence, dependency — *see also*
  Dependence 304.6 ☑
Etherism — *see also* Dependence 304.6 ☑
Ethmoid, ethmoidal — *see* condition
Ethmoiditis (chronic) (nonpurulent) (purulent)
  — *see also* Sinusitis, ethmoidal 473.2
  influenzal 487.1
  Woakes' 471.1
Ethylism — *see also* Alcoholism 303.9 ☑
Eulenburg's disease (congenital paramyotonia)
  359.29
Eunuchism 257.2
Eunuchoidism 257.2
  hypogonadotropic 257.2
European blastomycosis 117.5
Eustachian — *see* condition
Euthyroidism 244.9
Euthyroid sick syndrome 790.94
Evaluation
  fetal lung maturity 659.8 ☑
  for suspected condition (*see also* Observation)
    V71.9
    abuse V71.81
    exposure
      anthrax V71.82
      biologic agent NEC V71.83
      SARS V71.83
    neglect V71.81
    newborn — *see* Observation, suspected,
      condition, newborn
    specified condition NEC V71.89
  mental health V70.2
    requested by authority V70.1
  nursing care V63.8
  social service V63.8
Evans' syndrome (thrombocytopenic purpura)
  287.32
Event, apparent life threatening in newborn ●
  and infant (ALTE) 799.82 ●
Eventration
  colon into chest — *see* Hernia, diaphragm
  diaphragm (congenital) 756.6
Eversion
  bladder 596.8
  cervix (uteri) 622.0
    with mention of cervicitis 616.0
  foot NEC 736.79
    congenital 755.67
  lacrimal punctum 375.51
  punctum lacrimale (postinfectional) (senile)
    375.51
  ureter (meatus) 593.89
  urethra (meatus) 599.84
  uterus 618.1
    complicating delivery 665.2 ☑
      affecting fetus or newborn 763.89
    puerperal, postpartum 674.8 ☑
Evidence
  of malignancy
    cytologic
      without histologic confirmation
        anus 796.76
        cervix 795.06
        vagina 795.16
Evisceration
  birth injury 767.8
  bowel (congenital) — *see* Hernia, ventral
  congenital (*see also* Hernia, ventral) 553.29
  operative wound 998.32

Evisceration — *continued*
  traumatic NEC 869.1
    eye 871.3
Evulsion — *see* Avulsion
Ewing's
  angioendothelioma (M9260/3) — *see* Neo-
    plasm, bone, malignant
  sarcoma (M9260/3) — *see* Neoplasm, bone,
    malignant
  tumor (M9260/3) — *see* Neoplasm, bone,
    malignant
Exaggerated lumbosacral angle (with imping-
  ing spine) 756.12
Examination (general) (routine) (of) (for) V70.9
  allergy V72.7
  annual V70.0
  cardiovascular preoperative V72.81
  cervical Papanicolaou smear V76.2
    as a part of routine gynecological examina-
      tion V72.31
    to confirm findings of recent normal smear
      following initial abnormal smear
      V72.32
  child care (routine) V20.2
  clinical research investigation (normal control
    patient) (participant) V70.7
  dental V72.2
  developmental testing (child) (infant) V20.2
  donor (potential) V70.8
  ear V72.19
  eye V72.0
  following
    accident (motor vehicle) V71.4
    alleged rape or seduction (victim or culprit)
      V71.5
    inflicted injury (victim or culprit) NEC V71.6
    rape or seduction, alleged (victim or cul-
      prit) V71.5
    treatment (for) V67.9
      combined V67.6
      fracture V67.4
      involving high-risk medication NEC
        V67.51
      mental disorder V67.3
      specified condition NEC V67.59
  follow-up (routine) (following) V67.9
    cancer chemotherapy V67.2
    chemotherapy V67.2
    disease NEC V67.59
    high-risk medication NEC V67.51
    injury NEC V67.59
    population survey V70.6
    postpartum V24.2
    psychiatric V67.3
    psychotherapy V67.3
    radiotherapy V67.1
    specified surgery NEC V67.09
    surgery V67.00
      vaginal pap smear V67.01
  gynecological V72.31
    for contraceptive maintenance V25.40
      intrauterine device V25.42
      pill V25.41
      specified method NEC V25.49
  health (of)
    armed forces personnel V70.5
    checkup V70.0
    child, routine V20.2
    defined subpopulation NEC V70.5
    inhabitants of institutions V70.5
    occupational V70.5
    pre-employment screening V70.5
    preschool children V70.5
      for admission to school V70.3
    prisoners V70.5
      for entrance into prison V70.3
    prostitutes V70.5
    refugees V70.5
    school children V70.5
    students V70.5
  hearing V72.19
    following failed hearing screening V72.11
  infant
    8 to 28 days old V20.32 ●
    over 28 days old, routine V20.2 ●
    under 8 days old V20.31 ●

Examination — *continued*
  laboratory V72.60 ▲
    ordered as part of a routine general ●
      medical examination V72.62 ●
    pre-operative V72.63 ●
    pre-procedural V72.63 ●
    specified NEC V72.69 ●
  lactating mother V24.1
  medical (for) (of) V70.9
    administrative purpose NEC V70.3
    admission to
      old age home V70.3
      prison V70.3
      school V70.3
    adoption V70.3
    armed forces personnel V70.5
    at health care facility V70.0
    camp V70.3
    child, routine V20.2
    clinical research (control) (normal compar-
      ison) (participant) V70.7
    defined subpopulation NEC V70.5
    donor (potential) V70.8
    driving license V70.3
    general V70.9
      routine V70.0
      specified reason NEC V70.8
    immigration V70.3
    inhabitants of institutions V70.5
    insurance certification V70.3
    marriage V70.3
    medicolegal reasons V70.4
    naturalization V70.3
    occupational V70.5
    population survey V70.6
    pre-employment V70.5
    preschool children V70.5
      for admission to school V70.3
    prison V70.3
    prisoners V70.5
      for entrance into prison V70.3
    prostitutes V70.5
    refugees V70.5
    school children V70.5
    specified reason NEC V70.8
    sport competition V70.3
    students V70.5
  medicolegal reason V70.4
  pelvic (annual) (periodic) V72.31
  periodic (annual) (routine) V70.0
  postpartum
    immediately after delivery V24.0
    routine follow-up V24.2
  pregnancy (unconfirmed) (possible) V72.40
    negative result V72.41
    positive result V72.42
  prenatal V22.1
    first pregnancy V22.0
    high-risk pregnancy V23.9
      specified problem NEC V23.89
  preoperative V72.84
    cardiovascular V72.81
    respiratory V72.82
    specified NEC V72.83
  preprocedural V72.84
    cardiovascular V72.81
    general physical V72.83
    respiratory V72.82
    specified NEC V72.83
  prior to chemotherapy V72.83 ●
  psychiatric V70.2
    follow-up not needing further care V67.3
    requested by authority V70.1
  radiological NEC V72.5
  respiratory preoperative V72.82
  screening — *see* Screening
  sensitization V72.7
  skin V72.7
    hypersensitivity V72.7
  special V72.9
  specified type or reason NEC V72.85
    preoperative V72.83
    specified NEC V72.83
  teeth V72.2
  vaginal Papanicolaou smear V76.47

☑ Additional Digit Required — Refer to the Tabular List for Digit Selection

🔅 Subterms under main terms may continue to next column or page

▶◀ Revised Text   ● New Line   ▲ Revised Code

Examination — *continued*
vaginal Papanicolaou smear — *continued*
following hysterectomy for malignant
condition V67.01
victim or culprit following
alleged rape or seduction V71.5
inflicted injury NEC V71.6
vision V72.0
well baby V20.2
Exanthem, exanthema — *see also* Rash 782.1
Boston 048
epidemic, with meningitis 048
lichenoid psoriasiform 696.2
subitum 058.10
due to
human herpesvirus 6 058.11
human herpesvirus 7 058.12
viral, virus NEC 057.9
specified type NEC 057.8
Excess, excessive, excessively
alcohol level in blood 790.3
carbohydrate tissue, localized 278.1
carotene (dietary) 278.3
cold 991.9
specified effect NEC 991.8
convergence 378.84
crying 780.95
of
adolescent 780.95
adult 780.95
baby 780.92
child 780.95
infant (baby) 780.92
newborn 780.92
development, breast 611.1
diaphoresis (*see also* Hyperhidrosis) 780.8
distance, interarch 524.28
divergence 378.85
drinking (alcohol) NEC (*see also* Abuse, drugs,
nondependent) 305.0 ☑
continual (*see also* Alcoholism) 303.9 ☑
habitual (*see also* Alcoholism) 303.9 ☑
eating 783.6
eyelid fold (congenital) 743.62
fat 278.02
in heart (*see also* Degeneration, myocardial) 429.1
tissue, localized 278.1
foreskin 605
gas 787.3
gastrin 251.5
glucagon 251.4
heat (*see also* Heat) 992.9
horizontal
overjet 524.26
overlap 524.26
interarch distance 524.28
intermaxillary vertical dimension 524.37
interocclusal distance of teeth 524.37
large
colon 564.7
congenital 751.3
fetus or infant 766.0
with obstructed labor 660.1 ☑
affecting management of pregnancy
656.6 ☑
causing disproportion 653.5 ☑
newborn (weight of 4500 grams or more)
766.0
organ or site, congenital NEC — *see*
Anomaly, specified type NEC
lid fold (congenital) 743.62
long
colon 751.5
organ or site, congenital NEC — *see*
Anomaly, specified type NEC
umbilical cord (entangled)
affecting fetus or newborn 762.5
in pregnancy or childbirth 663.3 ☑
with compression 663.2 ☑
menstruation 626.2
number of teeth 520.1
causing crowding 524.31
nutrients (dietary) NEC 783.6
potassium (K) 276.7
salivation (*see also* Ptyalism) 527.7

Excess, excessive, excessively — *continued*
secretion (*see also* Hypersecretion)
milk 676.6 ☑
sputum 786.4
sweat (*see also* Hyperhidrosis) 780.8
short
organ or site, congenital NEC — *see*
Anomaly, specified type NEC
umbilical cord
affecting fetus or newborn 762.6
in pregnancy or childbirth 663.4 ☑
skin NEC 701.9
eyelid 743.62
acquired 374.30
sodium (Na) 276.0
spacing of teeth 524.32
sputum 786.4
sweating (*see also* Hyperhidrosis) 780.8
tearing (ducts) (eye) (*see also* Epiphora) 375.20
thirst 783.5
due to deprivation of water 994.3
tissue in reconstructed breast 612.0
tuberosity 524.07
vitamin
A (dietary) 278.2
administered as drug (chronic) (prolonged excessive intake) 278.2
reaction to sudden overdose 963.5
D (dietary) 278.4
administered as drug (chronic) (prolonged excessive intake) 278.4
reaction to sudden overdose 963.5
weight 278.02
gain 783.1
of pregnancy 646.1 ☑
loss 783.21
Excitability, abnormal, under minor stress
309.29
Excitation
catatonic (*see also* Schizophrenia) 295.2 ☑
psychogenic 298.1
reactive (from emotional stress, psychological
trauma) 298.1
Excitement
manic (*see also* Psychosis, affective) 296.0 ☑
recurrent episode 296.1 ☑
single episode 296.0 ☑
mental, reactive (from emotional stress, psychological trauma) 298.1
state, reactive (from emotional stress, psychological trauma) 298.1
Excluded pupils 364.76
Excoriation (traumatic) — *see also* Injury, superficial, by site 919.8
neurotic 698.4
Excyclophoria 378.44
Excyclotropia 378.33
Exencephalus, exencephaly 742.0
Exercise
breathing V57.0
remedial NEC V57.1
therapeutic NEC V57.1
Exfoliation
skin
due to erythematous condition 695.50
involving (percent of body surface)
less than 10 percent 695.50
10-19 percent 695.51
20-29 percent 695.52
30-39 percent 695.53
40-49 percent 695.54
50-59 percent 695.55
60-69 percent 695.56
70-79 percent 695.57
80-89 percent 695.58
90 percent or more 695.59
teeth
due to systemic causes 525.0
Exfoliative — *see also* condition
dermatitis 695.89
Exhaustion, exhaustive (physical NEC) 780.79
battle (*see also* Reaction, stress, acute) 308.9
cardiac (*see also* Failure, heart) 428.9
delirium (*see also* Reaction, stress, acute) 308.9
due to
cold 991.8

Exhaustion, exhaustive — *continued*
due to — *continued*
excessive exertion 994.5
exposure 994.4
overexertion 994.5
fetus or newborn 779.89
heart (*see also* Failure, heart) 428.9
heat 992.5
due to
salt depletion 992.4
water depletion 992.3
manic (*see also* Psychosis, affective) 296.0 ☑
recurrent episode 296.1 ☑
single episode 296.0 ☑
maternal, complicating delivery 669.8 ☑
affecting fetus or newborn 763.89
mental 300.5
myocardium, myocardial (*see also* Failure,
heart) 428.9
nervous 300.5
old age 797
postinfectional NEC 780.79
psychogenic 300.5
psychosis (*see also* Reaction, stress, acute)
308.9
senile 797
dementia 290.0
Exhibitionism (sexual) 302.4
Exomphalos 756.72 ▲
Exophoria 378.42
convergence, insufficiency 378.83
divergence, excess 378.85
Exophthalmic
cachexia 242.0 ☑
goiter 242.0 ☑
ophthalmoplegia 242.0 ☑ [376.22]
Exophthalmos 376.30
congenital 743.66
constant 376.31
endocrine NEC 259.9 [376.22]
hyperthyroidism 242.0 ☑ [376.21]
intermittent NEC 376.34
malignant 242.0 ☑ [376.21]
pulsating 376.35
endocrine NEC 259.9 [376.22]
thyrotoxic 242.0 ☑ [376.21]
Exostosis 726.91
cartilaginous (M9210/0) — *see* Neoplasm,
bone, benign
congenital 756.4
ear canal, external 380.81
gonococcal 098.89
hip 726.5
intracranial 733.3
jaw (bone) 526.81
luxurians 728.11
multiple (cancellous) (congenital) (hereditary)
756.4
nasal bones 726.91
orbit, orbital 376.42
osteocartilaginous (M9210/0) — *see* Neoplasm, bone, benign
spine 721.8
with spondylosis — *see* Spondylosis
syphilitic 095.5
wrist 726.4
Exotropia 378.10
alternating 378.15
with
A pattern 378.16
specified noncomitancy NEC 378.18
V pattern 378.17
X pattern 378.18
Y pattern 378.18
intermittent 378.24
intermittent 378.20
alternating 378.24
monocular 378.23
monocular 378.11
with
A pattern 378.12
specified noncomitancy NEC 378.14
V pattern 378.13
X pattern 378.14
Y pattern 378.14
intermittent 378.23

Explanation of
investigation finding V65.4 ☑
medication V65.4 ☑
Exposure ▶(suspected)◀ 994.9
algae bloom V87.32
cold 991.9
specified effect NEC 991.8
effects of 994.9
exhaustion due to 994.4
to
AIDS virus V01.79
anthrax V01.81
aromatic
amines V87.11
dyes V87.19
arsenic V87.01
asbestos V15.84
benzene V87.12
body fluids (hazardous) V15.85
cholera V01.0
chromium compounds V87.09
communicable disease V01.9
specified type NEC V01.89
dyes V87.2
aromatic V87.19
Escherichia coli (E. coli) V01.83
German measles V01.4
gonorrhea V01.6
hazardous
aromatic compounds NEC V87.19
body fluids V15.85
chemicals NEC V87.2
metals V87.09
substances V87.39
HIV V01.79
human immunodeficiency virus V01.79
lead V15.86
meningococcus V01.84
mold V87.31
nickel dust V87.09
parasitic disease V01.89
poliomyelitis V01.2
polycyclic aromatic hydrocarbons V87.19
potentially hazardous body fluids V15.85
rabies V01.5
rubella V01.4
SARS-associated coronavirus V01.82
smallpox V01.3
syphilis V01.6
tuberculosis V01.1
varicella V01.71
venereal disease V01.6
viral disease NEC V01.79
varicella V01.71
Exsanguination, fetal 772.0
Exstrophy
abdominal content 751.8
bladder (urinary) 753.5
Extensive — *see* condition
Extra — *see also* Accessory
rib 756.3
cervical 756.2
Extraction
with hook 763.89
breech NEC 669.6 ☑
affecting fetus or newborn 763.0
cataract postsurgical V45.61
manual NEC 669.8 ☑
affecting fetus or newborn 763.89
Extrasystole 427.60
atrial 427.61
postoperative 997.1
ventricular 427.69
Extrauterine gestation or pregnancy — *see*
Pregnancy, ectopic
Extravasation
blood 459.0
lower extremity 459.0
chemotherapy, vesicant 999.81 ▲
chyle into mesentery 457.8
pelvicalyceal 593.4
pyelosinus 593.4
urine 788.8
from ureter 788.8
vesicant
agent NEC 999.82 ▲

☑ Additional Digit Required — Refer to the Tabular List for Digit Selection   ▽ Subterms under main terms may continue to next column or page

Extravasation — continued
vesicant — continued
chemotherapy 999.81
Extremity — see condition
Extrophy — see Exstrophy
Extroversion
bladder 753.5
uterus 618.1
complicating delivery 665.2 ☑
affecting fetus or newborn 763.89
postpartal (old) 618.1
Extruded tooth 524.34
Extrusion
alveolus and teeth 524.75
breast implant (prosthetic) 996.54
device, implant, or graft — see Complications, mechanical
eye implant (ball) (globe) 996.59
intervertebral disc — see Displacement, intervertebral disc
lacrimal gland 375.43
mesh (reinforcing) 996.59
ocular lens implant 996.53
prosthetic device NEC — see Complications, mechanical
vitreous 379.26
Exudate, pleura — see Effusion, pleura
Exudates, retina 362.82
Exudative — see condition
Eye, eyeball, eyelid — see condition
Eyestrain 368.13
Eyeworm disease of Africa 125.2

F

Faber's anemia or syndrome (achlorhydric anemia) 280.9
Fabry's disease (angiokeratoma corporis diffusum) 272.7
Face, facial — see condition
Facet of cornea 371.44
Faciocephalalgia, autonomic — see also Neuropathy, peripheral, autonomic 337.9
Facioscapulohumeral myopathy 359.1
Factitious disorder, illness — see Illness, factitious
Factor
deficiency — see Deficiency, factor
psychic, associated with diseases classified elsewhere 316
risk — see Problem
Fahr-Volhard disease (malignant nephrosclerosis) 403.00
Failure, failed
adenohypophyseal 253.2
attempted abortion (legal) (see also Abortion, failed) 638.9
bone marrow (anemia) 284.9
acquired (secondary) 284.89
congenital 284.09
idiopathic 284.9
cardiac (see also Failure, heart) 428.9
newborn 779.89
cardiorenal (chronic) 428.9
hypertensive (see also Hypertension, cardiorenal) 404.93
cardiorespiratory 799.1
specified during or due to a procedure 997.1
long-term effect of cardiac surgery 429.4
cardiovascular (chronic) 428.9
cerebrovascular 437.8
cervical dilatation in labor 661.0 ☑
affecting fetus or newborn 763.7
circulation, circulatory 799.89
fetus or newborn 779.89
peripheral 785.50
compensation — see Disease, heart
congestive (see also Failure, heart) 428.0
conscious sedation, during procedure 995.24 ●
coronary (see also Insufficiency, coronary) 411.89
dental implant 525.79
due to
infection 525.71
lack of attached gingiva 525.72

Failure, failed — continued
dental implant — continued
due to — continued
occlusal trauma (caused by poor prosthetic design) 525.72
parafunctional habits 525.72
periodontal infection (peri-implantitis) 525.72
poor oral hygiene 525.72
unintentional loading 525.71
endosseous NEC 525.79
mechanical 525.73
osseointegration 525.71
due to
complications of systemic disease 525.71
poor bone quality 525.71
premature loading 525.71
iatrogenic 525.71
prior to intentional prosthetic loading 525.71
post-osseointegration
biological 525.72
iatrogenic 525.72
due to complications of systemic disease 525.72
mechanical 525.73
pre-integration 525.71
pre-osseointegration 525.71
dental prosthesis causing loss of dental implant 525.73
dental restoration
marginal integrity 525.61
periodontal anatomical integrity 525.65
descent of head (at term) 652.5 ☑
affecting fetus or newborn 763.1
in labor 660.0 ☑
affecting fetus or newborn 763.1
device, implant, or graft — see Complications, mechanical
engagement of head NEC 652.5 ☑
in labor 660.0 ☑
extrarenal 788.99
fetal head to enter pelvic brim 652.5 ☑
affecting fetus or newborn 763.1
in labor 660.0 ☑
affecting fetus or newborn 763.1
forceps NEC 660.7 ☑
affecting fetus or newborn 763.1
fusion (joint) (spinal) 996.49
growth in childhood 783.43
heart (acute) (sudden) 428.9
with
abortion — see Abortion, by type, with specified complication NEC
acute pulmonary edema (see also Failure, ventricular, left) 428.1
with congestion (see also Failure, heart) 428.0
decompensation (see also Failure, heart) 428.0
dilation — see Disease, heart
ectopic pregnancy (see also categories 633.0–633.9) 639.8
molar pregnancy (see also categories 630–632) 639.8
arteriosclerotic 440.9
combined left-right sided 428.0
combined systolic and diastolic 428.40
acute 428.41
acute on chronic 428.43
chronic 428.42
compensated (see also Failure, heart) 428.0
complicating
abortion — see Abortion, by type, with specified complication NEC
delivery (cesarean) (instrumental) 669.4 ☑
ectopic pregnancy (see also categories 633.0–633.9) 639.8
molar pregnancy (see also categories 630–632) 639.8
obstetric anesthesia or sedation 668.1 ☑
surgery 997.1

Failure, failed — continued
heart — continued
congestive (compensated) (decompensated) (see also Failure, heart) 428.0
with rheumatic fever (conditions classifiable to 390)
active 391.8
inactive or quiescent (with chorea) 398.91
fetus or newborn 779.89
hypertensive (see also Hypertension, heart) 402.91
with renal disease (see also Hypertension, cardiorenal) 404.91
with renal failure 404.93
benign 402.11
malignant 402.01
rheumatic (chronic) (inactive) (with chorea) 398.91
active or acute 391.8
with chorea (Sydenham's) 392.0
decompensated (see also Failure, heart) 428.0
degenerative (see also Degeneration, myocardial) 429.1
diastolic 428.30
acute 428.31
acute on chronic 428.33
chronic 428.32
due to presence of (cardiac) prosthesis 429.4
fetus or newborn 779.89
following
abortion 639.8
cardiac surgery 429.4
ectopic or molar pregnancy 639.8
high output NEC 428.9
hypertensive (see also Hypertension, heart) 402.91
with renal disease (see also Hypertension, cardiorenal) 404.91
with renal failure 404.93
benign 402.11
malignant 402.01
left (ventricular) (see also Failure, ventricular, left) 428.1
with right-sided failure (see also Failure, heart) 428.0
low output (syndrome) NEC 428.9
organic — see Disease, heart
postoperative (immediate) 997.1
long term effect of cardiac surgery 429.4
rheumatic (chronic) (congestive) (inactive) 398.91
right (secondary to left heart failure, conditions classifiable to 428.1) (ventricular) (see also Failure, heart) 428.0
senile 797
specified during or due to a procedure 997.1
long-term effect of cardiac surgery 429.4
systolic 428.20
acute 428.21
acute on chronic 428.23
chronic 428.22
thyrotoxic (see also Thyrotoxicosis) 242.9 ☑ [425.7]
valvular — see Endocarditis
hepatic 572.8
acute 570
due to a procedure 997.4
hepatorenal 572.4
hypertensive heart (see also Hypertension, heart) 402.91
benign 402.11
malignant 402.01
induction (of labor) 659.1 ☑
abortion (legal) (see also Abortion, failed) 638.9
affecting fetus or newborn 763.89
by oxytocic drugs 659.1 ☑
instrumental 659.0 ☑
mechanical 659.0 ☑
medical 659.1 ☑

Failure, failed — continued
induction — continued
surgical 659.0 ☑
initial alveolar expansion, newborn 770.4
involution, thymus (gland) 254.8
kidney — see Failure, renal
lactation 676.4 ☑
Leydig's cell, adult 257.2
liver 572.8
acute 570
medullary 799.89
mitral — see Endocarditis, mitral
moderate sedation, during procedure 995.24 ●
myocardium, myocardial (see also Failure, heart) 428.9
chronic (see also Failure, heart) 428.0
congestive (see also Failure, heart) 428.0
ovarian (primary) 256.39
iatrogenic 256.2
postablative 256.2
postirradiation 256.2
postsurgical 256.2
ovulation 628.0
prerenal 788.99
renal ▶(kidney)◀ 586
with
abortion — see Abortion, by type, with renal failure
ectopic pregnancy (see also categories 633.0–633.9) 639.3
edema (see also Nephrosis) 581.9
hypertension (see also Hypertension, kidney) 403.91
hypertensive heart disease (conditions classifiable to 402) 404.92
with heart failure 404.93
benign 404.12
with heart failure 404.13
malignant 404.02
with heart failure 404.03
molar pregnancy (see also categories 630–632) 639.3
tubular necrosis (acute) 584.5
acute 584.9
with lesion of
necrosis
cortical (renal) 584.6
medullary (renal) (papillary) 584.7
tubular 584.5
specified pathology NEC 584.8
chronic 585.9
hypertensive or with hypertension (see also Hypertension, kidney) 403.91
due to a procedure 997.5
following
abortion 639.3
crushing 958.5
ectopic or molar pregnancy 639.3
labor and delivery (acute) 669.3 ☑
hypertensive (see also Hypertension, kidney) 403.91
puerperal, postpartum 669.3 ☑
respiration, respiratory 518.81
acute 518.81
acute and chronic 518.84
center 348.89
newborn 770.84
chronic 518.83
due to trauma, surgery or shock 518.5
newborn 770.84
rotation
cecum 751.4
colon 751.4
intestine 751.4
kidney 753.3
sedation, during procedure ●
conscious 995.24 ●
moderate 995.24 ●
segmentation (see also Fusion)
fingers (see also Syndactylism, fingers) 755.11
toes (see also Syndactylism, toes) 755.13
seminiferous tubule, adult 257.2
senile (general) 797

☑ Additional Digit Required — Refer to the Tabular List for Digit Selection

Ⓦ Subterms under main terms may continue to next column or page

Failure, failed — continued
senile — continued
with psychosis 290.20
testis, primary (seminal) 257.2
to progress 661.2 ☑
to thrive
adult 783.7
child 783.41
newborn 779.34 ●
transplant 996.80
bone marrow 996.85
organ (immune or nonimmune cause)
996.80
bone marrow 996.85
heart 996.83
intestines 996.87
kidney 996.81
liver 996.82
lung 996.84
pancreas 996.86
specified NEC 996.89
skin 996.52
artificial 996.55
decellularized allodermis 996.55
temporary allograft or pigskin graft —
omit code
trial of labor NEC 660.6 ☑
affecting fetus or newborn 763.1
tubal ligation 998.89
urinary 586
vacuum extraction
abortion — see Abortion, failed
delivery NEC 660.7 ☑
affecting fetus or newborn 763.1
vasectomy 998.89
ventouse NEC 660.7 ☑
affecting fetus or newborn 763.1
ventricular (see also Failure, heart) 428.9
left 428.1
with rheumatic fever (conditions classifiable to 390)
active 391.8
with chorea 392.0
inactive or quiescent (with chorea)
398.91
hypertensive (see also Hypertension,
heart) 402.91
benign 402.11
malignant 402.01
rheumatic (chronic) (inactive) (with
chorea) 398.91
active or acute 391.8
with chorea 392.0
right (see also Failure, heart) 428.0
vital centers, fetus or newborn 779.89
weight gain in childhood 783.41
Fainting (fit) (spell) 780.2
Falciform hymen 752.49
Fallen arches 734
Falling, any organ or part — see Prolapse
Fall, maternal, affecting fetus or newborn
760.5
Fallopian
insufflation
fertility testing V26.21
following sterilization reversal V26.22
tube — see condition
Fallot's
pentalogy 745.2
tetrad or tetralogy 745.2
triad or trilogy 746.09
Fallout, radioactive (adverse effect) NEC 990
False — see also condition
bundle branch block 426.50
bursa 727.89
croup 478.75
joint 733.82
labor (pains) 644.1 ☑
opening, urinary, male 752.69
passage, urethra (prostatic) 599.4
positive
serological test for syphilis 795.6
Wassermann reaction 795.6
pregnancy 300.11
Family, familial — see also condition

Family, familial — see also condition —
continued
affected by
family member
currently on deployment (military)
V61.01
returned from deployment (military)
(current or past conflict) V61.02
disruption (see also Disruption, family) V61.09
estrangement V61.09
hemophagocytic
lymphohistiocytosis 288.4
reticulosis 288.4
Li-Fraumeni (syndrome) V84.01
planning advice V25.09
natural
procreative V26.41
to avoid pregnancy V25.04
problem V61.9
specified circumstance NEC V61.8
retinoblastoma (syndrome) 190.5
Famine 994.2
edema 262
Fanconi's anemia (congenital pancytopenia)
284.09
Fanconi (-de Toni) (-Debré) syndrome (cystinosis) 270.0
Farber (-Uzman) syndrome or disease (disseminated lipogranulomatosis) 272.8
Farcin 024
Farcy 024
Farmers'
lung 495.0
skin 692.74
Farsightedness 367.0
Fascia — see condition
Fasciculation 781.0
Fasciculitis optica 377.32
Fasciitis 729.4
eosinophilic 728.89
necrotizing 728.86
nodular 728.79
perirenal 593.4
plantar 728.71
pseudosarcomatous 728.79
traumatic (old) NEC 728.79
current — see Sprain, by site
Fasciola hepatica infestation 121.3
Fascioliasis 121.3
Fasciolopsiasis (small intestine) 121.4
Fasciolopsis (small intestine) 121.4
Fast pulse 785.0
Fat
embolism (cerebral) (pulmonary) (systemic)
958.1
with
abortion — see Abortion, by type, with
embolism
ectopic pregnancy (see also categories
633.0–633.9) 639.6
molar pregnancy (see also categories
630–632) 639.6
complicating delivery or puerperium
673.8 ☑
following
abortion 639.6
ectopic or molar pregnancy 639.6
in pregnancy, childbirth, or the puerperium
673.8 ☑
excessive 278.02
in heart (see also Degeneration, myocardial) 429.1
general 278.02
hernia, herniation 729.30
eyelid 374.34
knee 729.31
orbit 374.34
retro-orbital 374.34
retropatellar 729.31
specified site NEC 729.39
indigestion 579.8
in stool 792.1
localized (pad) 278.1
heart (see also Degeneration, myocardial)
429.1
knee 729.31

Fat — continued
localized — continued
retropatellar 729.31
necrosis (see also Fatty, degeneration)
breast (aseptic) (segmental) 611.3
mesentery 567.82
omentum 567.82
peritoneum 567.82
pad 278.1
Fatal familial insomnia (FFI) 046.72
Fatal syncope 798.1
Fatigue 780.79
auditory deafness (see also Deafness) 389.9
chronic, syndrome 780.71
combat (see also Reaction, stress, acute) 308.9
during pregnancy 646.8 ☑
general 780.79
psychogenic 300.5
heat (transient) 992.6
muscle 729.89
myocardium (see also Failure, heart) 428.9
nervous 300.5
neurosis 300.5
operational 300.89
postural 729.89
posture 729.89
psychogenic (general) 300.5
senile 797
syndrome NEC 300.5
chronic 780.71
undue 780.79
voice 784.49
Fatness 278.02
Fatty — see also condition
apron 278.1
degeneration (diffuse) (general) NEC 272.8
localized — see Degeneration, by site, fatty
placenta — see Placenta, abnormal
heart (enlarged) (see also Degeneration, myocardial) 429.1
infiltration (diffuse) (general) (see also Degeneration, by site, fatty) 272.8
heart (enlarged) (see also Degeneration,
myocardial) 429.1
liver 571.8
alcoholic 571.0
necrosis — see Degeneration, fatty
phanerosis 272.8
Fauces — see condition
Fauchard's disease (periodontitis) 523.40
Faucitis 478.29
Faulty — see also condition
position of teeth 524.30
Favism (anemia) 282.2
Favre-Racouchot disease (elastoidosis cutanea
nodularis) 701.8
Favus 110.9
beard 110.0
capitis 110.0
corporis 110.5
eyelid 110.8
foot 110.4
hand 110.2
scalp 110.0
specified site NEC 110.8
Feared complaint unfounded V65.5
Fear, fearfulness (complex) (reaction) 300.20
child 313.0
of
animals 300.29
closed spaces 300.29
crowds 300.29
eating in public 300.23
heights 300.29
open spaces 300.22
with panic attacks 300.21
public speaking 300.23
streets 300.22
with panic attacks 300.21
travel 300.22
with panic attacks 300.21
washing in public 300.23
transient 308.0
Febricula (continued) (simple) — see also Pyrexia
780.60
Febrile — see also Pyrexia 780.60

Febrile — see also Pyrexia — continued
convulsion (simple) 780.31
complex 780.32
seizure (simple) 780.31
atypical 780.32
complex 780.32
complicated 780.32
Febris — see also Fever 780.60
aestiva (see also Fever, hay) 477.9
flava (see also Fever, yellow) 060.9
melitensis 023.0
pestis (see also Plague) 020.9
puerperalis 672.0 ☑
recurrens (see also Fever, relapsing) 087.9
pediculo vestimenti 087.0
rubra 034.1
typhoidea 002.0
typhosa 002.0
Fecal — see condition
Fecalith (impaction) 560.39
with hernia (see also Hernia, by site, with obstruction)
gangrenous — see Hernia, by site, with
gangrene
appendix 543.9
congenital 777.1
Fede's disease 529.0
Feeble-minded 317
Feeble rapid pulse due to shock following
injury 958.4
Feeding
faulty (elderly) (infant) 783.3
newborn 779.31 ▲
formula check V20.2
improper (elderly) (infant) 783.3
newborn 779.31 ▲
problem (elderly) (infant) 783.3
newborn 779.31 ▲
nonorganic origin 307.59
Feeling of foreign body in throat 784.99
Feer's disease 985.0
Feet — see condition
Feigned illness V65.2
Feil-Klippel syndrome (brevicollis) 756.16
Feinmesser's (hidrotic) ectodermal dysplasia
757.31
Felix's disease (juvenile osteochondrosis, hip)
732.1
Felon (any digit) (with lymphangitis) 681.01
herpetic 054.6
Felty's syndrome (rheumatoid arthritis with
splenomegaly and leukopenia) 714.1
Feminism in boys 302.6
Feminization, testicular 259.51
with pseudohermaphroditism, male 259.51
Femoral hernia — see Hernia, femoral
Femora vara 736.32
Femur, femoral — see condition
Fenestra placenta — see Placenta, abnormal
Fenestration, fenestrated — see also Imperfect,
closure
aorta-pulmonary 745.0
aorticopulmonary 745.0
aortopulmonary 745.0
cusps, heart valve NEC 746.89
pulmonary 746.09
hymen 752.49
pulmonic cusps 746.09
Fenwick's disease 537.89
Fermentation (gastric) (gastrointestinal) (stomach) 536.8
intestine 564.89
psychogenic 306.4
psychogenic 306.4
Fernell's disease (aortic aneurysm) 441.9
Fertile eunuch syndrome 257.2
Fertility, meaning multiparity — see Multiparity
Fetal
alcohol syndrome 760.71
anemia 678.0 ☑
thrombocytopenia 678.0 ☑
twin to twin transfusion 678.0 ☑
Fetalis uterus 752.3
Fetid
breath 784.99

☑ Additional Digit Required — Refer to the Tabular List for Digit Selection   ⓦ Subterms under main terms may continue to next column or page

2010 ICD-9-CM   ▶◀ Revised Text   ● New Line   ▲ Revised Code   October 2009 • Volume 2 — 109

Fever — *continued*
  sweating 078.2
  swine 003.8
  sylvatic yellow 060.0
  Tahyna 062.5
  tertian — *see* Malaria, tertian
  Thailand hemorrhagic 065.4
  thermic 992.0
  three day 066.0
    with Coxsackie exanthem 074.8
  tick
    American mountain 066.1
    Colorado 066.1
    Kemerovo 066.1
    Mediterranean 082.1
    mountain 066.1
    nonexanthematous 066.1
    Quaranfil 066.1
  tick-bite NEC 066.1
  tick-borne NEC 066.1
    hemorrhagic NEC 065.3
  transitory of newborn 778.4
  trench 083.1
  tsutsugamushi 081.2
  typhogastric 002.0
  typhoid (abortive) (ambulant) (any site)
      (hemorrhagic) (infection) (intermittent)
      (malignant) (rheumatic) 002.0
  typhomalarial (*see also* Malaria) 084.6
  typhus — *see* Typhus
  undulant (*see also* Brucellosis) 023.9
  unknown origin (*see also* Pyrexia) 780.60
  uremic — *see* Uremia
  uveoparotid 135
  valley (Coccidioidomycosis) 114.0
  Venezuelan equine 066.2
  Volhynian 083.1
  Wesselsbron (viral) 066.3
  West
    African 084.8
    Nile (viral) 066.40
      with
        cranial nerve disorders 066.42
        encephalitis 066.41
        optic neuritis 066.42
        other complications 066.49
        other neurologic manifestations
            066.42
        polyradiculitis 066.42
  Whitmore's 025
  Wolhynian 083.1
  worm 128.9
  Yaroslav hemorrhagic 078.6
  yellow 060.9
    jungle 060.0
    sylvatic 060.0
    urban 060.1
    vaccination, prophylactic (against) V04.4
  Zika (viral) 066.3
Fibrillation
  atrial (established) (paroxysmal) 427.31
  auricular (atrial) (established) 427.31
  cardiac (ventricular) 427.41
  coronary (*see also* Infarct, myocardium)
      410.9 ☑
  heart (ventricular) 427.41
  muscular 728.9
  postoperative 997.1
  ventricular 427.41
Fibrin
  ball or bodies, pleural (sac) 511.0
  chamber, anterior (eye) (gelatinous exudate)
      364.04
Fibrinogenolysis (hemorrhagic) — *see* Fibrinolysis
Fibrinogenopenia (congenital) (hereditary) —
      see also Defect, coagulation 286.3
  acquired 286.6
Fibrinolysis (acquired) (hemorrhagic) (pathologic) 286.6
  with
    abortion — *see* Abortion, by type, with
        hemorrhage, delayed or excessive
    ectopic pregnancy (*see also* categories
        633.0–633.9) 639.1

Fibrinolysis — *continued*
  with — *continued*
    molar pregnancy (*see also* categories
        630–632) 639.1
  antepartum or intrapartum 641.3 ☑
    affecting fetus or newborn 762.1
  following
    abortion 639.1
    ectopic or molar pregnancy 639.1
  newborn, transient 776.2
  postpartum 666.3 ☑
Fibrinopenia (hereditary) — *see also* Defect, coagulation 286.3
  acquired 286.6
Fibrinopurulent — *see* condition
Fibrinous — *see* condition
Fibroadenoma (M9010/0)
  cellular intracanalicular (M9020/0) 217
  giant (intracanalicular) (M9020/0) 217
  intracanalicular (M9011/0)
    cellular (M9020/0) 217
    giant (M9020/0) 217
    specified site — *see* Neoplasm, by site,
        benign
    unspecified site 217
  juvenile (M9030/0) 217
  pericanicular (M9012/0)
    specified site — *see* Neoplasm, by site,
        benign
    unspecified site 217
  phyllodes (M9020/0) 217
  prostate 600.20
    with
      other lower urinary tract symptoms
          (LUTS) 600.21
      urinary
        obstruction 600.21
        retention 600.21
  specified site — *see* Neoplasm, by site, benign
  unspecified site 217
Fibroadenosis, breast (chronic) (cystic) (diffuse)
      (periodic) (segmental) 610.2
Fibroangioma (M9160/0) — *see also* Neoplasm,
      by site, benign
  juvenile (M9160/0)
    specified site — *see* Neoplasm, by site,
        benign
    unspecified site 210.7
Fibrocellulitis progressiva ossificans 728.11
Fibrochondrosarcoma (M9220/3) — *see* Neoplasm, cartilage, malignant
Fibrocystic
  disease 277.00
    bone NEC 733.29
    breast 610.1
    jaw 526.2
    kidney (congenital) 753.19
    liver 751.62
    lung 518.89
      congenital 748.4
    pancreas 277.00
  kidney (congenital) 753.19
Fibrodysplasia ossificans multiplex (progressiva) 728.11
Fibroelastosis (cordis) (endocardial) (endomyocardial) 425.3
Fibroid (tumor) (M8890/0) — *see also* Neoplasm,
      connective tissue, benign
  disease, lung (chronic) (*see also* Fibrosis, lung)
      515
  heart (disease) (*see also* Myocarditis) 429.0
  induration, lung (chronic) (*see also* Fibrosis,
      lung) 515
  in pregnancy or childbirth 654.1 ☑
    affecting fetus or newborn 763.89
    causing obstructed labor 660.2 ☑
      affecting fetus or newborn 763.1
  liver — *see* Cirrhosis, liver
  lung (*see also* Fibrosis, lung) 515
  pneumonia (chronic) (*see also* Fibrosis, lung)
      515
  uterus (M8890/0) (*see also* Leiomyoma, uterus)
      218.9
Fibrolipoma (M8851/0) — *see* Lipoma, by
      site 214.9

Fibroliposarcoma (M8850/3) — *see* Neoplasm,
      connective tissue, malignant
Fibroma (M8810/0) — *see also* Neoplasm, connective tissue, benign
  ameloblastic (M9330/0) 213.1
    upper jaw (bone) 213.0
  bone (nonossifying) 733.99
    ossifying (M9262/0) — *see* Neoplasm,
        bone, benign
  cementifying (M9274/0) — *see* Neoplasm,
      bone, benign
  chondromyxoid (M9241/0) — *see* Neoplasm,
      bone, benign
  desmoplastic (M8823/1) — *see* Neoplasm,
      connective tissue, uncertain behavior
  facial (M8813/0) — *see* Neoplasm, connective
      tissue, benign
  invasive (M8821/1) — *see* Neoplasm, connective tissue, uncertain behavior
  molle (M8851/0) (*see also* Lipoma, by site)
      214.9
  myxoid (M8811/0) — *see* Neoplasm, connective tissue, benign
  nasopharynx, nasopharyngeal (juvenile)
      (M9160/0) 210.7
  nonosteogenic (nonossifying) — *see* Dysplasia,
      fibrous
  odontogenic (M9321/0) 213.1
    upper jaw (bone) 213.0
  ossifying (M9262/0) — *see* Neoplasm, bone,
      benign
  periosteal (M8812/0) — *see* Neoplasm, bone,
      benign
  prostate 600.20
    with
      other lower urinary tract symptoms
          (LUTS) 600.21
      urinary
        obstruction 600.21
        retention 600.21
  soft (M8851/0) (*see also* Lipoma, by site) 214.9
Fibromatosis 728.79
  abdominal (M8822/1) — *see* Neoplasm, connective tissue, uncertain behavior
  aggressive (M8821/1) — *see* Neoplasm, connective tissue, uncertain behavior
  congenital generalized (CGF) 759.89
  Dupuytren's 728.6
  gingival 523.8
  plantar fascia 728.71
  proliferative 728.79
  pseudosarcomatous (proliferative) (subcutaneous) 728.79
  subcutaneous pseudosarcomatous (proliferative) 728.79
Fibromyalgia 729.1
Fibromyoma (M8890/0) — *see also* Neoplasm,
      connective tissue, benign
  uterus (corpus) (*see also* Leiomyoma, uterus)
      218.9
    in pregnancy or childbirth 654.1 ☑
      affecting fetus or newborn 763.89
      causing obstructed labor 660.2 ☑
        affecting fetus or newborn 763.1
Fibromyositis — *see also* Myositis 729.1
  scapulohumeral 726.2
Fibromyxolipoma (M8852/0) — *see also* Lipoma,
      by site 214.9
Fibromyxoma (M8811/0) — *see* Neoplasm,
      connective tissue, benign
Fibromyxosarcoma (M8811/3) — *see* Neoplasm,
      connective tissue, malignant
Fibro-odontoma, ameloblastic (M9290/0) 213.1
    upper jaw (bone) 213.0
Fibro-osteoma (M9262/0) — *see* Neoplasm,
      bone, benign
Fibroplasia, retrolental (*see also* Retinopathy of
      prematurity) 362.21
Fibropurulent — *see* condition
Fibrosarcoma (M8810/3) — *see also* Neoplasm,
      connective tissue, malignant
  ameloblastic (M9330/3) 170.1
    upper jaw (bone) 170.0
  congenital (M8814/3) — *see* Neoplasm, connective tissue, malignant

Fibrosarcoma — *see also* Neoplasm, connective
      tissue, malignant — *continued*
  fascial (M8813/3) — *see* Neoplasm, connective
      tissue, malignant
  infantile (M8814/3) — *see* Neoplasm, connective tissue, malignant
  odontogenic (M9330/3) 170.1
    upper jaw (bone) 170.0
  periosteal (M8812/3) — *see* Neoplasm, bone,
      malignant
Fibrosclerosis
  breast 610.3
  corpora cavernosa (penis) 607.89
  familial multifocal NEC 710.8
  multifocal (idiopathic) NEC 710.8
  penis (corpora cavernosa) 607.89
Fibrosis, fibrotic
  adrenal (gland) 255.8
  alveolar (diffuse) 516.3
  amnion 658.8 ☑
  anal papillae 569.49
  anus 569.49
  appendix, appendiceal, noninflammatory
      543.9
  arteriocapillary — *see* Arteriosclerosis
  bauxite (of lung) 503
  biliary 576.8
    due to Clonorchis sinensis 121.1
  bladder 596.8
    interstitial 595.1
    localized submucosal 595.1
    panmural 595.1
  bone, diffuse 756.59
  breast 610.3
  capillary (*see also* Arteriosclerosis)
    lung (chronic) (*see also* Fibrosis, lung) 515
  cardiac (*see also* Myocarditis) 429.0
  cervix 622.8
  chorion 658.8 ☑
  corpus cavernosum 607.89
  cystic (of pancreas) 277.00
    with
      manifestations
        gastrointestinal 277.03
        pulmonary 277.02
        specified NEC 277.09
      meconium ileus 277.01
      pulmonary exacerbation 277.02
  due to (presence of) any device, implant, or
      graft — *see* Complications, due to
      (presence of) any device, implant, or
      graft classified to 996.0–996.5 NEC
  ejaculatory duct 608.89
  endocardium (*see also* Endocarditis) 424.90
  endomyocardial (African) 425.0
  epididymis 608.89
  eye muscle 378.62
  graphite (of lung) 503
  heart (*see also* Myocarditis) 429.0
  hepatic (*see also* Cirrhosis, liver)
    due to Clonorchis sinensis 121.1
  hepatolienal — *see* Cirrhosis, liver
  hepatosplenic — *see* Cirrhosis, liver
  infrapatellar fat pad 729.31
  interstitial pulmonary, newborn 770.7
  intrascrotal 608.89
  kidney (*see also* Sclerosis, renal) 587
  liver — *see* Cirrhosis, liver
  lung (atrophic) (capillary) (chronic) (confluent)
      (massive) (perialveolar) (peribronchial)
      515
    with
      anthracosilicosis (occupational) 500
      anthracosis (occupational) 500
      asbestosis (occupational) 501
      bagassosis (occupational) 495.1
      bauxite 503
      berylliosis (occupational) 503
      byssinosis (occupational) 504
      calcicosis (occupational) 502
      chalicosis (occupational) 502
      dust reticulation (occupational) 504
      farmers' lung 495.0
      gannister disease (occupational) 502
      graphite 503
      pneumoconiosis (occupational) 505

☑ Additional Digit Required — Refer to the Tabular List for Digit Selection   ▽ Subterms under main terms may continue to next column or page

2010 ICD-9-CM   ▶◀ Revised Text   ● New Line   ▲ Revised Code   **Volume 2 — 111**

Fibrosis, fibrotic — *continued*
lung — *continued*
  with — *continued*
    pneumosiderosis (occupational) 503
    siderosis (occupational) 503
    silicosis (occupational) 502
    tuberculosis (*see also* Tuberculosis)
      011.4 ☑
  diffuse (idiopathic) (interstitial) 516.3
  due to
    bauxite 503
    fumes or vapors (chemical) (inhalation)
      506.4
    graphite 503
  following radiation 508.1
  postinflammatory 515
  silicotic (massive) (occupational) 502
  tuberculous (*see also* Tuberculosis)
    011.4 ☑
lymphatic gland 289.3
median bar 600.90
  with
    other lower urinary tract symptoms
      (LUTS) 600.91
    urinary
      obstruction 600.91
      retention 600.91
mediastinum (idiopathic) 519.3
meninges 349.2
muscle NEC 728.2
  iatrogenic (from injection) 999.9
myocardium, myocardial (*see also* Myocarditis)
  429.0
oral submucous 528.8
ovary 620.8
oviduct 620.8
pancreas 577.8
  cystic 277.00
    with
      manifestations
        gastrointestinal 277.03
        pulmonary 277.02
        specified NEC 277.09
      meconium ileus 277.01
      pulmonary exacerbation 277.02
penis 607.89
periappendiceal 543.9
periarticular (*see also* Ankylosis) 718.5 ☑
pericardium 423.1
perineum, in pregnancy or childbirth 654.8 ☑
  affecting fetus or newborn 763.89
  causing obstructed labor 660.2 ☑
    affecting fetus or newborn 763.1
perineural NEC 355.9
  foot 355.6
periureteral 593.89
placenta — *see* Placenta, abnormal
pleura 511.0
popliteal fat pad 729.31
preretinal 362.56
prostate (chronic) 600.90
  with
    other lower urinary tract symptoms
      (LUTS) 600.91
    urinary
      obstruction 600.91
      retention 600.91
pulmonary (chronic) (*see also* Fibrosis, lung)
  515
  alveolar capillary block 516.3
  interstitial
    diffuse (idiopathic) 516.3
    newborn 770.7
radiation — *see* Effect, adverse, radiation
rectal sphincter 569.49
retroperitoneal, idiopathic 593.4
sclerosing mesenteric (idiopathic) 567.82
scrotum 608.89
seminal vesicle 608.89
senile 797
skin NEC 709.2
spermatic cord 608.89
spleen 289.59
  bilharzial (*see also* Schistosomiasis) 120.9
subepidermal nodular (M8832/0) — *see* Neoplasm, skin, benign

Fibrosis, fibrotic — *continued*
submucous NEC 709.2
  oral 528.8
  tongue 528.8
syncytium — *see* Placenta, abnormal
testis 608.89
  chronic, due to syphilis 095.8
thymus (gland) 254.8
tunica vaginalis 608.89
ureter 593.89
urethra 599.84
uterus (nonneoplastic) 621.8
  bilharzial (*see also* Schistosomiasis) 120.9
  neoplastic (*see also* Leiomyoma, uterus)
    218.9
vagina 623.8
valve, heart (*see also* Endocarditis) 424.90
vas deferens 608.89
vein 459.89
  lower extremities 459.89
vesical 595.1
Fibrositis (periarticular) (rheumatoid) 729.0
humeroscapular region 726.2
nodular, chronic
  Jaccoud's 714.4
  rheumatoid 714.4
ossificans 728.11
scapulohumeral 726.2
Fibrothorax 511.0
Fibrotic — *see* Fibrosis
Fibrous — *see* condition
Fibroxanthoma (M8831/0) — *see also* Neoplasm,
  connective tissue, benign
  atypical (M8831/1) — *see* Neoplasm, connec-
    tive tissue, uncertain behavior
  malignant (M8831/3) — *see* Neoplasm, con-
    nective tissue, malignant
Fibroxanthosarcoma (M8831/3) — *see* Neoplasm, connective tissue, malignant
Fiedler's
disease (leptospiral jaundice) 100.0
myocarditis or syndrome (acute isolated my-
  ocarditis) 422.91
Fiessinger-Leroy (-Reiter) syndrome 099.3
Fiessinger-Rendu syndrome (erythema muli-
  forme exudativum) 695.19
Fifth disease (eruptive) 057.0
venereal 099.1
Filaria, filarial — *see* Infestation, filarial
Filariasis — *see also* Infestation, filarial 125.9
bancroftian 125.0
Brug's 125.1
due to
  bancrofti 125.0
  Brugia (Wuchereria) (malayi) 125.1
  Loa loa 125.2
  malayi 125.1
  organism NEC 125.6
  Wuchereria (bancrofti) 125.0
    malayi 125.1
Malayan 125.1
ozzardi 125.5
specified type NEC 125.6
Filatoff's, Filatov's, Filatow's disease (infectious
  mononucleosis) 075
File-cutters' disease 984.9
specified type of lead — *see* Table of Drugs
  and Chemicals
Filling defect
biliary tract 793.3
bladder 793.5
duodenum 793.4
gallbladder 793.3
gastrointestinal tract 793.4
intestine 793.4
kidney 793.5
stomach 793.4
ureter 793.5
Filtering bleb, eye (postglaucoma) (status)
  V45.69
with complication or rupture 997.99
postcataract extraction (complication) 997.99
Fimbrial cyst (congenital) 752.11
Fimbriated hymen 752.49
Financial problem affecting care V60.2

Findings, (abnormal), without diagnosis (examination) (laboratory test) 796.4
17-ketosteroids, elevated 791.9
acetonuria 791.6
acid phosphatase 790.5
albumin-globulin ratio 790.99
albuminuria 791.0
alcohol in blood 790.3
alkaline phosphatase 790.5
amniotic fluid 792.3
amylase 790.5
anisocytosis 790.09
antenatal screening 796.5
anthrax, positive 795.31
antibody titers, elevated 795.79
anticardiolipin antibody 795.79
antigen-antibody reaction 795.79
antiphospholipid antibody 795.79
bacteriuria 791.9
ballistocardiogram 794.39
bicarbonate 276.9
bile in urine 791.4
bilirubin 277.4
bleeding time (prolonged) 790.92
blood culture, positive 790.7
blood gas level (arterial) 790.91
blood sugar level 790.29
  high 790.29
    fasting glucose 790.21
    glucose tolerance test 790.22
  low 251.2
calcium 275.40
cancer antigen 125 [CA 125] 795.82
carbonate 276.9
carcinoembryonic antigen [CEA] 795.81
casts, urine 791.7
catecholamines 791.9
cells, urine 791.7
cerebrospinal fluid (color) (content) (pressure)
  792.0
cervical
  high risk human papillomavirus (HPV) DNA
    test positive 795.05
  low risk human papillomavirus (HPV) DNA
    test positive 795.09
chloride 276.9
cholesterol 272.9
  high 272.0
    with high triglycerides 272.2
chromosome analysis 795.2
chyluria 791.1
circulation time 794.39
cloudy dialysis effluent 792.5
cloudy urine 791.9
coagulation study 790.92
cobalt, blood 790.6
color of urine (unusual) NEC 791.9
copper, blood 790.6
C-reactive protein (CRP) 790.95
creatinine clearance 794.4
crystals, urine 791.9
culture, positive NEC 795.39
  blood 790.7
  HIV V08
  human immunodeficiency virus V08
  nose 795.39
    Staphylococcus — *see* Carrier (suspect-
      ed) of, Staphylococcus
  skin lesion NEC 795.39
  spinal fluid 792.0
  sputum 795.39
  stool 792.1
  throat 795.39
  urine 791.9
  viral
    human immunodeficiency V08
  wound 795.39
cytology specified site NEC 796.9 ●
echocardiogram 793.2
echoencephalogram 794.01
echogram NEC — *see* Findings, abnormal,
  structure
electrocardiogram (ECG) (EKG) 794.31
electroencephalogram (EEG) 794.02
electrolyte level, urinary 791.9
electromyogram (EMG) 794.17

Findings, (abnormal), without diagnosis —
  continued
electromyogram — *continued*
  ocular 794.14
electro-oculogram (EOG) 794.12
electroretinogram (ERG) 794.11
enzymes, serum NEC 790.5
fibrinogen titer coagulation study 790.92
filling defect — *see* Filling defect
function study NEC 794.9
  auditory 794.15
  bladder 794.9
  brain 794.00
  cardiac 794.30
  endocrine NEC 794.6
    thyroid 794.5
  kidney 794.4
  liver 794.8
  nervous system
    central 794.00
    peripheral 794.19
  oculomotor 794.14
  pancreas 794.9
  placenta 794.9
  pulmonary 794.2
  retina 794.11
  special senses 794.19
  spleen 794.9
  vestibular 794.16
gallbladder, nonvisualization 793.3
glucose 790.29
  elevated
    fasting 790.21
    tolerance test 790.22
glycosuria 791.5
heart
  shadow 793.2
  sounds 785.3
hematinuria 791.2
hematocrit
  drop (precipitous) 790.01
  elevated 282.7
  low 285.9
hematologic NEC 790.99
hematuria 599.70
hemoglobin
  drop 790.01 ●
  elevated 282.7
  low 285.9
hemoglobinuria 791.2
histological NEC 795.4
hormones 259.9
immunoglobulins, elevated 795.79
indolacetic acid, elevated 791.9
iron 790.6
karyotype 795.2
ketonuria 791.6
lactic acid dehydrogenase (LDH) 790.4
lead 790.6
lipase 790.5
lipids NEC 272.9
lithium, blood 790.6
liver function test 790.6
lung field (coin lesion) (shadow) 793.1
magnesium, blood 790.6
mammogram 793.80
  calcification 793.89
  calculus 793.89
  dense breasts 793.82 ●
  inconclusive 793.82 ●
    due to dense breasts 793.82 ●
  microcalcification 793.81
mediastinal shift 793.2
melanin, urine 791.9
microbiologic NEC 795.39
mineral, blood NEC 790.6
myoglobinuria 791.3
nasal swab, anthrax 795.31
neonatal screening 796.6
nitrogen derivatives, blood 790.6
nonvisualization of gallbladder 793.3
nose culture, positive 795.39
odor of urine (unusual) NEC 791.9
oxygen saturation 790.91
Papanicolaou (smear) 796.9
  anus 796.70

Findings, (abnormal), without diagnosis —
continued
  Papanicolaou — *continued*
    anus — *continued*
      with
        atypical squamous cells
          cannot exclude high grade
            squamous intraepithelial
            lesion (ASC-H) 796.72
          of undetermined significance
            (ASC-US) 796.71
        cytologic evidence of malignancy
          796.76
        high grade squamous intraepithe-
          lial lesion (HGSIL) 796.74
        low grade squamous intraepithelial
          lesion (LGSIL) 796.73
      glandular 796.70
      specified finding NEC 796.79
    cervix 795.00
      with
        atypical squamous cells
          cannot exclude high grade
            squamous intraepithelial
            lesion (ASC-H) 795.02
          of undetermined significance
            (ASC-US) 795.01
        cytologic evidence of malignancy
          795.06
        high grade squamous intraepithe-
          lial lesion (HGSIL) 795.04
        low grade squamous intraepithelial
          lesion (LGSIL) 795.03
      dyskaryotic 795.09
      nonspecific finding NEC 795.09
    other site 796.9
    vagina 795.10
      with
        atypical squamous cells
          cannot exclude high grade
            squamous intraepithelial
            lesion (ASC-H) 795.12
          of undetermined significance
            (ASC-US) 795.11
        cytologic evidence of malignancy
          795.16
        high grade squamous intraepithe-
          lial lesion (HGSIL) 795.14
        low grade squamous intraepithelial
          lesion (LGSIL) 795.13
      glandular 795.10
      specified NEC 795.19
  peritoneal fluid 792.9
  phonocardiogram 794.39
  phosphorus 275.3
  pleural fluid 792.9
  pneumoencephalogram 793.0
  PO$_2$-oxygen ratio 790.91
  poikilocytosis 790.09
  potassium
    deficiency 276.8
    excess 276.7
  PPD 795.5
  prostate specific antigen (PSA) 790.93
  protein, serum NEC 790.99
  proteinuria 791.0
  prothrombin time (partial) (prolonged) (PT)
    (PTT) 790.92
  pyuria 791.9
  radiologic (x-ray) 793.99
    abdomen 793.6
    biliary tract 793.3
    breast 793.89
      abnormal mammogram NOS 793.80
      mammographic
        calcification 793.89
        calculus 793.89
        microcalcification 793.81
    gastrointestinal tract 793.4
    genitourinary organs 793.5
    head 793.0
    image test inconclusive due to excess body
      fat 793.91
    intrathoracic organs NEC 793.2
    lung 793.1
    musculoskeletal 793.7

Findings, (abnormal), without diagnosis —
continued
  radiologic — *continued*
    placenta 793.99
    retroperitoneum 793.6
    skin 793.99
    skull 793.0
    subcutaneous tissue 793.99
  red blood cell 790.09
    count 790.09
    morphology 790.09
    sickling 790.09
    volume 790.09
  saliva 792.4
  scan NEC 794.9
    bladder 794.9
    bone 794.9
    brain 794.09
    kidney 794.4
    liver 794.8
    lung 794.2
    pancreas 794.9
    placental 794.9
    spleen 794.9
    thyroid 794.5
  sedimentation rate, elevated 790.1
  semen 792.2
  serological (for)
    human immunodeficiency virus (HIV)
      inconclusive 795.71
      positive V08
    syphilis — *see* Findings, serology for
      syphilis
  serology for syphilis
    false positive 795.6
    positive 097.1
      false 795.6
      follow-up of latent syphilis — *see*
        Syphilis, latent
      only finding — *see* Syphilis, latent
  serum 790.99
    blood NEC 790.99
    enzymes NEC 790.5
    proteins 790.99
  SGOT 790.4
  SGPT 790.4
  sickling of red blood cells 790.09
  skin test, positive 795.79
    tuberculin (without active tuberculosis)
      795.5
  sodium 790.6
    deficiency 276.1
    excess 276.0
  specified NEC 796.9   ●
  spermatozoa 792.2
  spinal fluid 792.0
    culture, positive 792.0
  sputum culture, positive 795.39
    for acid-fast bacilli 795.39
  stool NEC 792.1
    bloody 578.1
    occult 792.1
    color 792.1
    culture, positive 792.1
    occult blood 792.1
  stress test 794.39
  structure, body (echogram) (thermogram)
    (ultrasound) (x-ray) NEC 793.99
    abdomen 793.6
    breast 793.89
      abnormal mammogram 793.80
      mammographic
        calcification 793.89
        calculus 793.89
        microcalcification 793.81
    gastrointestinal tract 793.4
    genitourinary organs 793.5
    head 793.0
      echogram (ultrasound) 794.01
    intrathoracic organs NEC 793.2
    lung 793.1
    musculoskeletal 793.7
    placenta 793.99
    retroperitoneum 793.6
    skin 793.99
    subcutaneous tissue NEC 793.99

Findings, (abnormal), without diagnosis —
continued
  synovial fluid 792.9
  thermogram — *see* Findings, abnormal,
    structure
  throat culture, positive 795.39
  thyroid (function) 794.5
    metabolism (rate) 794.5
    scan 794.5
    uptake 794.5
  total proteins 790.99
  toxicology (drugs) (heavy metals) 796.0
  transaminase (level) 790.4
  triglycerides 272.9
    high 272.1
      with high cholesterol 272.2
  tuberculin skin test (without active tuberculo-
    sis) 795.5
  tumor markers NEC 795.89
  ultrasound (*see also* Findings, abnormal,
    structure)
    cardiogram 793.2
  uric acid, blood 790.6
  urine, urinary constituents 791.9
    acetone 791.6
    albumin 791.0
    bacteria 791.9
    bile 791.4
    blood 599.70
    casts or cells 791.7
    chyle 791.1
    culture, positive 791.9
    glucose 791.5
    hemoglobin 791.2
    ketone 791.6
    protein 791.0
    pus 791.9
    sugar 791.5
  vaginal
    fluid 792.9
    high risk human papillomavirus (HPV) DNA
      test positive 795.15
    low risk human papillomavirus (HPV) DNA
      test positive 795.19
  vanillylmandelic acid, elevated 791.9
  vectorcardiogram (VCG) 794.39
  ventriculogram (cerebral) 793.0
  VMA, elevated 791.9
  Wassermann reaction
    false positive 795.6
    positive 097.1
      follow-up of latent syphilis — *see*
        Syphilis, latent
      only finding — *see* Syphilis, latent
  white blood cell 288.9
    count 288.9
      elevated 288.60
      low 288.50
    differential 288.9
    morphology 288.9
  wound culture 795.39
  xerography 793.89
  zinc, blood 790.6
Finger — *see* condition
Finnish type nephrosis (congenital) 759.89
Fire, St. Anthony's — *see also* Erysipelas 035
Fish
  hook stomach 537.89
  meal workers' lung 495.8
Fisher's syndrome 357.0
Fissure, fissured
  abdominal wall (congenital) 756.79
  anus, anal 565.0
    congenital 751.5
  buccal cavity 528.9
  clitoris (congenital) 752.49
  ear, lobule (congenital) 744.29
  epiglottis (congenital) 748.3
  larynx 478.79
    congenital 748.3
  lip 528.5
    congenital (*see also* Cleft, lip) 749.10
  nipple 611.2
    puerperal, postpartum 676.1 ☑
  palate (congenital) (*see also* Cleft, palate)
    749.00

Fissure, fissured — *continued*
  postanal 565.0
  rectum 565.0
  skin 709.8
    streptococcal 686.9
  spine (congenital) (*see also* Spina bifida)
    741.9 ☑
  sternum (congenital) 756.3
  tongue (acquired) 529.5
    congenital 750.13
Fistula (sinus) 686.9
  abdomen (wall) 569.81
    bladder 596.2
    intestine 569.81
    ureter 593.82
    uterus 619.2
  abdominorectal 569.81
  abdominosigmoidal 569.81
  abdominothoracic 510.0
  abdominouterine 619.2
    congenital 752.3
  abdominovesical 596.2
  accessory sinuses (*see also* Sinusitis) 473.9
  actinomycotic — *see* Actinomycosis
  alveolar
    antrum (*see also* Sinusitis, maxillary) 473.0
    process 522.7
  anorectal 565.1
  antrobuccal (*see also* Sinusitis, maxillary) 473.0
  antrum (*see also* Sinusitis, maxillary) 473.0
  anus, anal (infectional) (recurrent) 565.1
    congenital 751.5
    tuberculous (*see also* Tuberculosis)
      014.8 ☑
  aortic sinus 747.29
  aortoduodenal 447.2
  appendix, appendicular 543.9
  arteriovenous (acquired) 447.0
    brain 437.3
      congenital 747.81
      ruptured (*see also* Hemorrhage,
        subarachnoid) 430
      ruptured (*see also* Hemorrhage, sub-
        arachnoid) 430
    cerebral 437.3
      congenital 747.81
    congenital (peripheral) 747.60
      brain — *see* Fistula, arteriovenous,
        brain, congenital
      coronary 746.85
      gastrointestinal 747.61
      lower limb 747.64
      pulmonary 747.3
      renal 747.62
      specified site NEC 747.69
      upper limb 747.63
    coronary 414.19
      congenital 746.85
    heart 414.19
    pulmonary (vessels) 417.0
      congenital 747.3
    surgically created (for dialysis) V45.11
      complication NEC 996.73
        atherosclerosis — *see* Arterioscler-
          sis, extremities
        embolism 996.74
        infection or inflammation 996.62
        mechanical 996.1
        occlusion NEC 996.74
        thrombus 996.74
    traumatic — *see* Injury, blood vessel, by
      site
  artery 447.2
  aural 383.81
    congenital 744.49
  auricle 383.81
    congenital 744.49
  Bartholin's gland 619.8
  bile duct (*see also* Fistula, biliary) 576.4
  biliary (duct) (tract) 576.4
    congenital 751.69
  bladder (neck) (sphincter) 596.2
    into seminal vesicle 596.2
  bone 733.99
  brain 348.89   ▲

☑ Additional Digit Required — Refer to the Tabular List for Digit Selection   ▽ Subterms under main terms may continue to next column or page

2010 ICD-9-CM   ▶◀ Revised Text   ● New Line   ▲ Revised Code   October 2009 · Volume 2 — 113

Fistula — *continued*
brain — *continued*
  arteriovenous — *see* Fistula, arteriovenous,
    brain
branchial (cleft) 744.41
branchiogenous 744.41
breast 611.0
  puerperal, postpartum 675.1 ☑
bronchial 510.0
bronchocutaneous, bronchomediastinal,
  bronchopleural, bronchopleuromedi-
  astinal (infective) 510.0
  tuberculous (*see also* Tuberculosis)
    011.3 ☑
bronchoesophageal 530.89
  congenital 750.3
buccal cavity (infective) 528.3
canal, ear 380.89
carotid-cavernous
  congenital 747.81
    with hemorrhage 430
  traumatic 900.82
    with hemorrhage (*see also* Hemor-
      rhage, brain, traumatic)
      853.0 ☑
    late effect 908.3
cecosigmoidal 569.81
cecum 569.81
cerebrospinal (fluid) 349.81
cervical, lateral (congenital) 744.41
cervicoaural (congenital) 744.49
cervicosigmoidal 619.1
cervicovesical 619.0
cervix 619.8
chest (wall) 510.0
cholecystocolic (*see also* Fistula, gallbladder)
  575.5
cholecystocolonic (*see also* Fistula, gallbladder)
  575.5
cholecystoduodenal (*see also* Fistula, gallbladder) 575.5
cholecystoenteric (*see also* Fistula, gallbladder)
  575.5
cholecystogastric (*see also* Fistula, gallbladder)
  575.5
cholecystointestinal (*see also* Fistula, gallbladder) 575.5
choledochoduodenal 576.4
cholocolic (*see also* Fistula, gallbladder) 575.5
coccyx 685.1
  with abscess 685.0
colon 569.81
colostomy 569.69
colovaginal (acquired) 619.1
common duct (bile duct) 576.4
congenital, NEC — *see* Anomaly, specified
  type NEC
cornea, causing hypotony 360.32
coronary, arteriovenous 414.19
  congenital 746.85
costal region 510.0
cul-de-sac, Douglas' 619.8
cutaneous 686.9
cystic duct (*see also* Fistula, gallbladder) 575.5
  congenital 751.69
dental 522.7
diaphragm 510.0
  bronchovisceral 510.0
  pleuroperitoneal 510.0
  pulmonoperitoneal 510.0
duodenum 537.4
ear (canal) (external) 380.89
enterocolic 569.81
enterocutaneous 569.81
enteroenteric 569.81
entero-uterine 619.1
  congenital 752.3
enterovaginal 619.1
  congenital 752.49
enterovesical 596.1
epididymis 608.89
  tuberculous (*see also* Tuberculosis)
    016.4 ☑
esophagobronchial 530.89
  congenital 750.3
esophagocutaneous 530.89

Fistula — *continued*
esophagopleurocutaneous 530.89
esophagotracheal 530.84
  congenital 750.3
esophagus 530.89
  congenital 750.4
ethmoid (*see also* Sinusitis, ethmoidal) 473.2
eyeball (cornea) (sclera) 360.32
eyelid 373.11
fallopian tube (external) 619.2
fecal 569.81
  congenital 751.5
from periapical lesion 522.7
frontal sinus (*see also* Sinusitis, frontal) 473.1
gallbladder 575.5
  with calculus, cholelithiasis, stones (*see also*
    Cholelithiasis) 574.2 ☑
  congenital 751.69
gastric 537.4
gastrocolic 537.4
  congenital 750.7
  tuberculous (*see also* Tuberculosis)
    014.8 ☑
gastroenterocolic 537.4
gastroesophageal 537.4
gastrojejunal 537.4
gastrojejunocolic 537.4
genital
  organs
    female 619.9
      specified site NEC 619.8
    male 608.89
  tract-skin (female) 619.2
hepatopleural 510.0
hepatopulmonary 510.0
horseshoe 565.1
ileorectal 569.81
ileosigmoidal 569.81
ileostomy 569.69
ileovesical 596.1
ileum 569.81
in ano 565.1
  tuberculous (*see also* Tuberculosis)
    014.8 ☑
inner ear (*see also* Fistula, labyrinth) 386.40
intestine 569.81
intestinocolonic (abdominal) 569.81
intestinoureteral 593.82
intestinouterine 619.1
intestinovaginal 619.1
  congenital 752.49
intestinovesical 596.1
involving female genital tract 619.9
  digestive-genital 619.1
  genital tract-skin 619.2
  specified site NEC 619.8
  urinary-genital 619.0
ischiorectal (fossa) 566
jejunostomy 569.69
jejunum 569.81
joint 719.80
  ankle 719.87
  elbow 719.82
  foot 719.87
  hand 719.84
  hip 719.85
  knee 719.86
  multiple sites 719.89
  pelvic region 719.85
  shoulder (region) 719.81
  specified site NEC 719.88
  tuberculous — *see* Tuberculosis, joint
  wrist 719.83
kidney 593.89
labium (majus) (minus) 619.8
labyrinth, labyrinthine NEC 386.40
  combined sites 386.48
  multiple sites 386.48
  oval window 386.42
  round window 386.41
  semicircular canal 386.43
lacrimal, lachrymal (duct) (gland) (sac) 375.61
lacrimonasal duct 375.61
laryngotracheal 748.3
larynx 478.79
lip 528.5

Fistula — *continued*
lip — *continued*
  congenital 750.25
lumbar, tuberculous (*see also* Tuberculosis)
  015.0 ☑ *[730.8]* ☑
lung 510.0
lymphatic (node) (vessel) 457.8
mamillary 611.0
mammary (gland) 611.0
  puerperal, postpartum 675.1 ☑
mastoid (process) (region) 383.1
maxillary (*see also* Sinusitis, maxillary) 473.0
mediastinal 510.0
mediastinobronchial 510.0
mediastinocutaneous 510.0
middle ear 385.89
mouth 528.3
nasal 478.19
  sinus (*see also* Sinusitis) 473.9
nasopharynx 478.29
nipple — *see* Fistula, breast
nose 478.19
oral (cutaneous) 528.3
  maxillary (*see also* Sinusitis, maxillary) 473.0
  nasal (with cleft palate) (*see also* Cleft,
    palate) 749.00
orbit, orbital 376.10
oro-antral (*see also* Sinusitis, maxillary) 473.0
oval window (internal ear) 386.42
oviduct (external) 619.2
palate (hard) 526.89
  soft 528.9
pancreatic 577.8
pancreaticoduodenal 577.8
parotid (gland) 527.4
  region 528.3
pelvoabdominointestinal 569.81
penis 607.89
perianal 565.1
pericardium (pleura) (sac) (*see also* Pericarditis)
  423.8
pericecal 569.81
perineal — *see* Fistula, perineum
perineorectal 569.81
perineosigmoidal 569.81
perineo-urethroscrotal 608.89
perineum, perineal (with urethral involvement)
  NEC 599.1
  tuberculous (*see also* Tuberculosis)
    017.9 ☑
  ureter 593.82
perirectal 565.1
  tuberculous (*see also* Tuberculosis)
    014.8 ☑
peritoneum (*see also* Peritonitis) 567.22
periurethral 599.1
pharyngo-esophageal 478.29
pharynx 478.29
  branchial cleft (congenital) 744.41
pilonidal (infected) (rectum) 685.1
  with abscess 685.0
pleura, pleural, pleurocutaneous, pleuroperitoneal 510.0
  stomach 510.0
  tuberculous (*see also* Tuberculosis)
    012.0 ☑
pleuropericardial 423.8
postauricular 383.81
postoperative, persistent 998.6
preauricular (congenital) 744.46
prostate 602.8
pulmonary 510.0
  arteriovenous 417.0
    congenital 747.3
  tuberculous (*see also* Tuberculosis, pul-
    monary) 011.9 ☑
pulmonoperitoneal 510.0
rectolabial 619.1
rectosigmoid (intercommunicating) 569.81
rectoureteral 593.82
rectourethral 599.1
  congenital 753.8
rectouterine 619.1
  congenital 752.3
rectovaginal 619.1
  congenital 752.49

Fistula — *continued*
rectovaginal — *continued*
  old, postpartal 619.1
  tuberculous (*see also* Tuberculosis)
    014.8 ☑
rectovesical 596.1
  congenital 753.8
rectovesicovaginal 619.1
rectovulvar 619.1
  congenital 752.49
rectum (to skin) 565.1
  tuberculous (*see also* Tuberculosis)
    014.8 ☑
renal 593.89
retroauricular 383.81
round window (internal ear) 386.41
salivary duct or gland 527.4
  congenital 750.24
sclera 360.32
scrotum (urinary) 608.89
  tuberculous (*see also* Tuberculosis)
    016.5 ☑
semicircular canals (internal ear) 386.43
sigmoid 569.81
  vesicoabdominal 596.1
sigmoidovaginal 619.1
  congenital 752.49
skin 686.9
  ureter 593.82
  vagina 619.2
sphenoidal sinus (*see also* Sinusitis, sphenoidal)
  473.3
splenocolic 289.59
stercoral 569.81
stomach 537.4
sublingual gland 527.4
  congenital 750.24
submaxillary
  gland 527.4
    congenital 750.24
  region 528.3
thoracic 510.0
  duct 457.8
thoracicoabdominal 510.0
thoracicogastric 510.0
thoracicointestinal 510.0
thoracoabdominal 510.0
thoracogastric 510.0
thorax 510.0
thyroglossal duct 759.2
thyroid 246.8
trachea (congenital) (external) (internal) 748.3
tracheoesophageal 530.84
  congenital 750.3
  following tracheostomy 519.09
traumatic
  arteriovenous (*see also* Injury, blood vessel,
    by site) 904.9
  brain — *see* Injury, intracranial
tuberculous — *see* Tuberculosis, by site
typhoid 002.0
umbilical 759.89
umbilico-urinary 753.8
urachal, urachus 753.7
ureter (persistent) 593.82
ureteroabdominal 593.82
ureterocervical 593.82
ureterorectal 593.82
ureterosigmoido-abdominal 593.82
ureterovaginal 619.0
ureterovesical 596.2
urethra 599.1
  congenital 753.8
  tuberculous (*see also* Tuberculosis)
    016.3 ☑
urethroperineal 599.1
urethroperineovesical 596.2
urethrorectal 599.1
  congenital 753.8
urethroscrotal 608.89
urethrovaginal 619.0
urethrovesical 596.2
urethrovesicovaginal 619.0
urinary (persistent) (recurrent) 599.1
uteroabdominal (anterior wall) 619.2
  congenital 752.3

Index

Fistula — Fistula

Fistula — *continued*
uteroenteric 619.1
uterofecal 619.1
uterointestinal 619.1
  congenital 752.3
uterorectal 619.1
  congenital 752.3
uteroureteric 619.0
uterovaginal 619.8
uterovesical 619.0
  congenital 752.3
uterus 619.8
vagina (wall) 619.8
  postpartal, old 619.8
vaginocutaneous (postpartal) 619.2
vaginoileal (acquired) 619.1
vaginoperineal 619.2
vesical NEC 596.2
vesicoabdominal 596.2
vesicocervicovaginal 619.0
vesicocolic 596.1
vesicocutaneous 596.2
vesicoenteric 596.1
vesicointestinal 596.1
vesicometrorectal 619.1
vesicoperineal 596.2
vesicorectal 596.1
  congenital 753.8
vesicosigmoidal 596.1
vesicosigmoidovaginal 619.1
vesicoureteral 596.2
vesicoureterovaginal 619.0
vesicourethral 596.2
vesicourethrorectal 596.1
vesicouterine 619.0
  congenital 752.3
vesicovaginal 619.0
vulvorectal 619.1
  congenital 752.49
Fit 780.39
apoplectic (*see also* Disease, cerebrovascular,
  acute) 436
  late effect — *see* Late effect(s) (of) cere-
    brovascular disease
epileptic (*see also* Epilepsy) 345.9 ☑
fainting 780.2
hysterical 300.11
newborn 779.0
Fitting (of)
artificial
  arm (complete) (partial) V52.0
  breast V52.4
    implant exchange (different material)
      (different size) V52.4
  eye(s) V52.2
  leg (complete) (partial) V52.1
brain neuropacemaker V53.02
cardiac pacemaker V53.31
carotid sinus pacemaker V53.39
cerebral ventricle (communicating) shunt
  V53.01
colostomy belt V53.5 ☑
contact lenses V53.1
cystostomy device V53.6
defibrillator, automatic implantable cardiac
  V53.32
dentures V52.3
device, unspecified type V53.90
  abdominal V53.59 ▲
  cardiac
    defibrillator, automatic implantable
      V53.32
    pacemaker V53.31
    specified NEC V53.39
  cerebral ventricle (communicating) shunt
    V53.01
  gastrointestinal NEC V53.59 ●
  insulin pump V53.91
  intestinal V53.50 ●
  intrauterine contraceptive V25.1
  nervous system V53.09
  orthodontic V53.4
  orthoptic V53.1
  other device V53.99
  prosthetic V52.9
    breast V52.4

Fitting — *continued*
device, unspecified type — *continued*
  prosthetic — *continued*
    dental V52.3
    eye V52.2
    specified type NEC V52.8
  special senses V53.09
  substitution
    auditory V53.09
    nervous system V53.09
    visual V53.09
  urinary V53.6
diaphragm (contraceptive) V25.02
gastric lap band V53.51 ●
gastrointestinal appliance and device NEC ●
  V53.59
glasses (reading) V53.1
growth rod V54.02
hearing aid V53.2
ileostomy device V53.5 ☑
intestinal appliance ▶and◀ device
  V53.50 ▲
intestinal appliance or device NEC V53.5 ☑
intrauterine contraceptive device V25.1
neuropacemaker (brain) (peripheral nerve)
  (spinal cord) V53.02
orthodontic device V53.4
orthopedic (device) V53.7
  brace V53.7
  cast V53.7
  corset V53.7
  shoes V53.7
pacemaker (cardiac) V53.31
  brain V53.02
  carotid sinus V53.39
  peripheral nerve V53.02
  spinal cord V53.02
prosthesis V52.9
  arm (complete) (partial) V52.0
  breast V52.4
    implant exchange (different material)
      (different size) V52.4
  dental V52.3
  eye V52.2
  leg (complete) (partial) V52.1
  specified type NEC V52.8
spectacles V53.1
wheelchair V53.8
Fitz-Hugh and Curtis syndrome 098.86
due to
  Chlamydia trachomatis 099.56
  Neisseria gonorrhoeae (gonococcal peri-
    tonitis) 098.86
Fitz's syndrome (acute hemorrhagic pancreatitis)
  577.0
Fixation
joint — *see* Ankylosis
larynx 478.79
pupil 364.76
stapes 385.22
  deafness (*see also* Deafness, conductive)
    389.04
uterus (acquired) — *see* Malposition, uterus
vocal cord 478.5
Flaccid — *see also* condition
foot 736.79
forearm 736.09
palate, congenital 750.26
Flail
chest 807.4
  newborn 767.3
joint (paralytic) 718.80
  ankle 718.87
  elbow 718.82
  foot 718.87
  hand 718.84
  hip 718.85
  knee 718.86
  multiple sites 718.89
  pelvic region 718.85
  shoulder (region) 718.81
  specified site NEC 718.88
  wrist 718.83
Flajani (-Basedow) syndrome or disease (exophthalmic goiter) 242.0 ☑
Flap, liver 572.8

Flare, anterior chamber (aqueous) (eye) 364.04
Flashback phenomena (drug) (hallucinogenic)
  292.89
Flat
chamber (anterior) (eye) 360.34
chest, congenital 754.89
electroencephalogram (EEG) 348.89 ▲
foot (acquired) (fixed type) (painful) (postural)
  (spastic) 734
  congenital 754.61
    rocker bottom 754.61
    vertical talus 754.61
  rachitic 268.1
  rocker bottom (congenital) 754.61
  vertical talus, congenital 754.61
organ or site, congenital NEC — *see* Anomaly,
  specified type NEC
pelvis 738.6
  with disproportion (fetopelvic) 653.2 ☑
    affecting fetus or newborn 763.1
    causing obstructed labor 660.1 ☑
      affecting fetus or newborn 763.1
  congenital 755.69
Flatau-Schilder disease 341.1
Flattening
head, femur 736.39
hip 736.39
lip (congenital) 744.89
nose (congenital) 754.0
  acquired 738.0
Flatulence 787.3
Flatus 787.3
vaginalis 629.89
Flax dressers' disease 504
Flea bite — *see* Injury, superficial, by site
Fleischer (-Kayser) ring (corneal pigmentation)
  275.1 *[371.14]*
Fleischner's disease 732.3
Fleshy mole 631
Flexibilitas cerea — *see also* Catalepsy 300.11
Flexion
cervix — *see* Flexion, uterus
contracture, joint (*see also* Contraction, joint)
  718.4 ☑
deformity, joint (*see also* Contraction, joint)
  736.9
  hip, congenital (*see also* Subluxation, con-
    genital, hip) 754.32
uterus (*see also* Malposition, uterus) 621.6
Flexner's
bacillus 004.1
diarrhea (ulcerative) 004.1
dysentery 004.1
Flexner-Boyd dysentery 004.2
Flexure — *see* condition
Floater, vitreous 379.24
Floating
cartilage (joint) (*see also* Disorder, cartilage,
  articular) 718.0 ☑
  knee 717.6
gallbladder (congenital) 751.69
kidney 593.0
  congenital 753.3
liver (congenital) 751.69
rib 756.3
spleen 289.59
Flooding 626.2
Floor — *see* condition
Floppy
infant NEC 781.99
iris syndrome 364.81
valve syndrome (mitral) 424.0
Flu — *see also* Influenza
bird 488.0 ●
gastric NEC 008.8
swine 488.1 ●
Fluctuating blood pressure 796.4
Fluid
abdomen 789.59
chest (*see also* Pleurisy, with effusion) 511.9
heart (*see also* Failure, heart) 428.0
joint (*see also* Effusion, joint) 719.0 ☑
loss (acute) 276.50
  with
    hypernatremia 276.0
    hyponatremia 276.1

Fluid — *continued*
lung (*see also* Edema, lung)
  encysted 511.89
  peritoneal cavity 789.59
    malignant 789.51
  pleural cavity (*see also* Pleurisy, with effusion)
    511.9
  retention 276.6
Flukes NEC — *see also* Infestation, fluke 121.9
blood NEC (*see also* Infestation, Schistosoma)
  120.9
liver 121.3
Fluor (albus) (vaginalis) 623.5
trichomonal (Trichomonas vaginalis) 131.00
Fluorosis (dental) (chronic) 520.3
Flushing 782.62
menopausal 627.2
Flush syndrome 259.2
Flutter
atrial or auricular 427.32
heart (ventricular) 427.42
  atrial 427.32
  impure 427.32
  postoperative 997.1
  ventricular 427.42
Flux (bloody) (serosanguineous) 009.0
Focal — *see* condition
Fochier's abscess — *see* Abscess, by site
Focus, Assmann's — *see also* Tuberculosis
  011.0 ☑
Fogo selvagem 694.4
Foix-Alajouanine syndrome 336.1
Folds, anomalous — *see also* Anomaly, specified
  type NEC
Bowman's membrane 371.31
Descemet's membrane 371.32
epicanthic 743.63
heart 746.89
posterior segment of eye, congenital 743.54
Folie à deux 297.3
Follicle
cervix (nabothian) (ruptured) 616.0
graafian, ruptured, with hemorrhage 620.0
nabothian 616.0
Folliclis (primary) — *see also* Tuberculosis
  017.0 ☑
Follicular — *see also* condition
cyst (atretic) 620.0
Folliculitis 704.8
abscedens et suffodiens 704.8
decalvans 704.09
gonorrheal (acute) 098.0
  chronic or duration of 2 months or more
    098.2
keloid, keloidalis 706.1
pustular 704.8
ulerythematosa reticulata 701.8
Folliculosis, conjunctival 372.02
Følling's disease (phenylketonuria) 270.1
Follow-up (examination) (routine) (following)
  V67.9
cancer chemotherapy V67.2
chemotherapy V67.2
fracture V67.4
high-risk medication V67.51
injury NEC V67.59
postpartum
  immediately after delivery V24.0
  routine V24.2
psychiatric V67.3
psychotherapy V67.3
radiotherapy V67.1
specified condition NEC V67.59
specified surgery NEC V67.09
surgery V67.00
  vaginal pap smear V67.01
treatment V67.9
  combined NEC V67.6
  fracture V67.4
  involving high-risk medication NEC V67.51
  mental disorder V67.3
  specified NEC V67.59
Fong's syndrome (hereditary osteoonychodys-
  plasia) 756.89
Food
allergy 693.1

☑ Additional Digit Required — Refer to the Tabular List for Digit Selection   🗊 Subterms under main terms may continue to next column or page

2010 ICD-9-CM   ▶◀ Revised Text   ● New Line   ▲ Revised Code   **October 2009 · Volume 2 — 115**

Food — *continued*
  anaphylactic shock — *see* Anaphylactic shock, due to, food
  asphyxia (from aspiration or inhalation) (*see also* Asphyxia, food) 933.1
  choked on (*see also* Asphyxia, food) 933.1
  deprivation 994.2
    specified kind of food NEC 269.8
  intoxication (*see also* Poisoning, food) 005.9
  lack of 994.2
  poisoning (*see also* Poisoning, food) 005.9
  refusal or rejection NEC 307.59
  strangulation or suffocation (*see also* Asphyxia, food) 933.1
  toxemia (*see also* Poisoning, food) 005.9
Foot — *see also* condition
  and mouth disease 078.4
  process disease 581.3
Foramen ovale (nonclosure) (patent) (persistent) 745.5
Forbes-Albright syndrome (nonpuerperal amenorrhea and lactation associated with pituitary tumor) 253.1
Forbes' (glycogen storage) disease 271.0
Forced birth or delivery NEC 669.8 ☑
  affecting fetus or newborn NEC 763.89
Forceps
  delivery NEC 669.5 ☑
    affecting fetus or newborn 763.2
Fordyce's disease (ectopic sebaceous glands) (mouth) 750.26
Fordyce-Fox disease (apocrine miliaria) 705.82
Forearm — *see* condition
Foreign body

Note — For foreign body with open wound, or other injury, see Wound, open, or the type of injury specified.

  accidentally left during a procedure 998.4
  anterior chamber (eye) 871.6
    magnetic 871.5
      retained or old 360.51
    retained or old 360.61
  ciliary body (eye) 871.6
    magnetic 871.5
      retained or old 360.52
    retained or old 360.62
  entering through orifice (current) (old)
    accessory sinus 932
    air passage (upper) 933.0
      lower 934.8
    alimentary canal 938
    alveolar process 935.0
    antrum (Highmore) 932
    anus 937
    appendix 936
    asphyxia due to (*see also* Asphyxia, food) 933.1
    auditory canal 931
    auricle 931
    bladder 939.0
    bronchioles 934.8
    bronchus (main) 934.1
    buccal cavity 935.0
    canthus (inner) 930.1
    cecum 936
    cervix (canal) uterine 939.1
    coil, ileocecal 936
    colon 936
    conjunctiva 930.1
    conjunctival sac 930.1
    cornea 930.0
    digestive organ or tract NEC 938
    duodenum 936
    ear (external) 931
    esophagus 935.1
    eye (external) 930.9
      combined sites 930.8
      intraocular — *see* Foreign body, by site
      specified site NEC 930.8
    eyeball 930.8
      intraocular — *see* Foreign body, intraocular
    eyelid 930.1
      retained or old 374.86
    frontal sinus 932
    gastrointestinal tract 938

Foreign body — *continued*
  entering through orifice — *continued*
    genitourinary tract 939.9
    globe 930.8
      penetrating 871.6
        magnetic 871.5
          retained or old 360.50
        retained or old 360.60
    gum 935.0
    Highmore's antrum 932
    hypopharynx 933.0
    ileocecal coil 936
    ileum 936
    inspiration (of) 933.1
    intestine (large) (small) 936
    lacrimal apparatus, duct, gland, or sac 930.2
    larynx 933.1
    lung 934.8
    maxillary sinus 932
    mouth 935.0
    nasal sinus 932
    nasopharynx 933.0
    nose (passage) 932
    nostril 932
    oral cavity 935.0
    palate 935.0
    penis 939.3
    pharynx 933.0
    pyriform sinus 933.0
    rectosigmoid 937
      junction 937
    rectum 937
    respiratory tract 934.9
      specified part NEC 934.8
    sclera 930.1
    sinus 932
      accessory 932
      frontal 932
      maxillary 932
      nasal 932
      pyriform 933.0
    small intestine 936
    stomach (hairball) 935.2
    suffocation by (*see also* Asphyxia, food) 933.1
    swallowed 938
      tongue 933.0
    tear ducts or glands 930.2
    throat 933.0
    tongue 935.0
      swallowed 933.0
    tonsil, tonsillar 933.0
      fossa 933.0
    trachea 934.0
    ureter 939.0
    urethra 939.0
    uterus (any part) 939.1
    vagina 939.2
    vulva 939.2
    wind pipe 934.0
  feeling of, in throat 784.99
  granuloma (old) 728.82
    bone 733.99
    in operative wound (inadvertently left) 998.4
      due to surgical material intentionally left — *see* Complications, due to (presence of) any device, implant, or graft classified to 996.0–996.5 NEC
    muscle 728.82
    skin 709.4
    soft tissue 709.4
    subcutaneous tissue 709.4
  in
    bone (residual) 733.99
    open wound — *see* Wound, open, by site complicated
    soft tissue (residual) 729.6
  inadvertently left in operation wound (causing adhesions, obstruction, or perforation) 998.4
  ingestion, ingested NEC 938
  inhalation or inspiration (*see also* Asphyxia, food) 933.1

Foreign body — *continued*
  internal organ, not entering through an orifice — *see* Injury, internal, by site, with open wound
  intraocular (nonmagnetic) 871.6
    combined sites 871.6
      magnetic 871.5
        retained or old 360.59
      retained or old 360.69
    magnetic 871.5
      retained or old 360.50
      retained or old 360.60
    specified site NEC 871.6
      magnetic 871.5
        retained or old 360.59
      retained or old 360.69
  iris (nonmagnetic) 871.6
    magnetic 871.5
      retained or old 360.52
      retained or old 360.62
  lens (nonmagnetic) 871.6
    magnetic 871.5
      retained or old 360.53
      retained or old 360.63
  lid, eye 930.1
  ocular muscle 870.4
    retained or old 376.6
  old or residual
    bone 733.99
    eyelid 374.86
    middle ear 385.83
    muscle 729.6
      ocular 376.6
    retrobulbar 376.6
    skin 729.6
      with granuloma 709.4
    soft tissue 729.6
      with granuloma 709.4
    subcutaneous tissue 729.6
      with granuloma 709.4
  operation wound, left accidentally 998.4
  orbit 870.4
    retained or old 376.6
  posterior wall, eye 871.6
    magnetic 871.5
      retained or old 360.55
    retained or old 360.65
  respiratory tree 934.9
    specified site NEC 934.8
  retained (old) (nonmagnetic) (in)
    anterior chamber (eye) 360.61
      magnetic 360.51
    ciliary body 360.62
      magnetic 360.52
    eyelid 374.86
    globe 360.60
      magnetic 360.50
    intraocular 360.60
      magnetic 360.50
      specified site NEC 360.69
        magnetic 360.59
    iris 360.62
      magnetic 360.52
    lens 360.63
      magnetic 360.53
    muscle 729.6
    orbit 376.6
    posterior wall of globe 360.65
      magnetic 360.55
    retina 360.65
      magnetic 360.55
    retrobulbar 376.6
    skin 729.6
      with granuloma 709.4
    soft tissue 729.6
      with granuloma 709.4
    subcutaneous tissue 729.6
      with granuloma 709.4
    vitreous 360.64
      magnetic 360.54
  retina 871.6
    magnetic 871.5
      retained or old 360.55
    retained or old 360.65
  superficial, without major open wound (*see also* Injury, superficial, by site) 919.6

Foreign body — *continued*
  swallowed NEC 938
  throat, feeling of 784.99
  vitreous (humor) 871.6
    magnetic 871.5
      retained or old 360.54
    retained or old 360.64
Forking, aqueduct of Sylvius 742.3
  with spina bifida (*see also* Spina Bifida) 741.0 ☑
Formation
  bone in scar tissue (skin) 709.3
  connective tissue in vitreous 379.25
  Elschnig pearls (postcataract extraction) 366.51
  hyaline in cornea 371.49
  sequestrum in bone (due to infection) (*see also* Osteomyelitis) 730.1 ☑
  valve
    colon, congenital 751.5
    ureter (congenital) 753.29
Formication 782.0
Fort Bragg fever 100.89
Fossa — *see also* condition
  pyriform — *see* condition
Foster care (status) V60.81 •
Foster-Kennedy syndrome 377.04
Fothergill's
  disease, meaning scarlatina anginosa 034.1
  neuralgia (*see also* Neuralgia, trigeminal) 350.1
Foul breath 784.99
Found dead (cause unknown) 798.9
Foundling V20.0
Fournier's disease (idiopathic gangrene) 608.83
Fourth
  cranial nerve — *see* condition
  disease 057.8
  molar 520.1
Foville's syndrome 344.89
Fox's
  disease (apocrine miliaria) 705.82
  impetigo (contagiosa) 684
Fox-Fordyce disease (apocrine miliaria) 705.82
Fracture (abduction) (adduction) (avulsion) (compression) (crush) (dislocation) (oblique) (separation) (closed) 829.0

Note — For fracture of any of the following sites with fracture of other bones — see Fracture, multiple.

"Closed" includes the following descriptions of fractures, with or without delayed healing, unless they are specified as open or compound:

comminuted	linear
depressed	simple
elevated	slipped epiphysis
fissured	spiral
greenstick	unspecified
impacted	

"Open" includes the following descriptions of fractures, with or without delayed healing:

compound	puncture
infected	with foreign body
missile	

For late effect of fracture, see Late, effect, fracture, by site.

  with
    internal injuries in same region (conditions classifiable to 860–869) (*see also* Injury, internal, by site)
    pelvic region — *see* Fracture, pelvis
  acetabulum (with visceral injury) (closed) 808.0
    open 808.1
  acromion (process) (closed) 811.01
    open 811.11
  alveolus (closed) 802.8
    open 802.9
  ankle (malleolus) (closed) 824.8
    bimalleolar (Dupuytren's) (Pott's) 824.4
      open 824.5

☑ Additional Digit Required — Refer to the Tabular List for Digit Selection

116 — Volume 2 • October 2009

▶◀ Revised Text   ● New Line   ▲ Revised Code

▽ Subterms under main terms may continue to next column or page

2010 ICD-9-CM

Food — Fracture

Index

Food — Fracture

Fracture — *continued*
  ankle — *continued*
    bone 825.21
      open 825.31
    lateral malleolus only (fibular) 824.2
      open 824.3
    medial malleolus only (tibial) 824.0
      open 824.1
    open 824.9
    pathologic 733.16
    talus 825.21
      open 825.31
    trimalleolar 824.6
      open 824.7
  antrum — *see* Fracture, skull, base
  arm (closed) 818.0
    and leg(s) (any bones) 828.0
      open 828.1
    both (any bones) (with rib(s)) (with sternum) 819.0
      open 819.1
    lower 813.80
      open 813.90
    open 818.1
    upper — *see* Fracture, humerus
  astragalus (closed) 825.21
    open 825.31
  atlas — *see* Fracture, vertebra, cervical, first
  axis — *see* Fracture, vertebra, cervical, second
  back — *see* Fracture, vertebra, by site
  Barton's — *see* Fracture, radius, lower end
  basal (skull) — *see* Fracture, skull, base
  Bennett's (closed) 815.01
    open 815.11
  bimalleolar (closed) 824.4
    open 824.5
  bone (closed) NEC 829.0
    birth injury NEC 767.3
    open 829.1
    pathologic NEC (*see also* Fracture, pathologic) 733.10
    stress NEC (*see also* Fracture, stress) 733.95
  boot top — *see* Fracture, fibula
  boxers' — *see* Fracture, metacarpal bone(s)
  breast bone — *see* Fracture, sternum
  bucket handle (semilunar cartilage) — *see* Tear, meniscus
  buckle — *see* Fracture, torus   ●
  burst — *see* Fracture, traumatic, by site
  bursting — *see* Fracture, phalanx, hand, distal
  calcaneus (closed) 825.0
    open 825.1
  capitate (bone) (closed) 814.07
    open 814.17
  capitellum (humerus) (closed) 812.49
    open 812.59
  carpal bone(s) (wrist NEC) (closed) 814.00
    open 814.10
    specified site NEC 814.09
      open 814.19
  cartilage, knee (semilunar) — *see* Tear, meniscus
  cervical — *see* Fracture, vertebra, cervical
  chauffeur's — *see* Fracture, ulna, lower end
  chisel — *see* Fracture, radius, upper end
  chronic — *see* Fracture, pathologic   ●
  clavicle (interligamentous part) (closed) 810.00
    acromial end 810.03
      open 810.13
    due to birth trauma 767.2
    open 810.10
    shaft (middle third) 810.02
      open 810.12
    sternal end 810.01
      open 810.11
  clayshovelers' — *see* Fracture, vertebra, cervical
  coccyx (*see also* Fracture, vertebra, coccyx)
    complicating delivery 665.6 ☑
  collar bone — *see* Fracture, clavicle
  Colles' (reversed) (closed) 813.41
    open 813.51
  comminuted — *see* Fracture, by site
  compression (*see also* Fracture, by site)
    nontraumatic — *see* Fracture, pathologic
  congenital 756.9

Fracture — *continued*
  coracoid process (closed) 811.02
    open 811.12
  coronoid process (ulna) (closed) 813.02
    mandible (closed) 802.23
      open 802.33
    open 813.12
  corpus cavernosum penis 959.13
  costochondral junction — *see* Fracture, rib
  costosternal junction — *see* Fracture, rib
  cranium — *see* Fracture, skull, by site
  cricoid cartilage (closed) 807.5
    open 807.6
  cuboid (ankle) (closed) 825.23
    open 825.33
  cuneiform
    foot (closed) 825.24
      open 825.34
    wrist (closed) 814.03
      open 814.13
  dental implant 525.73
  dental restorative material
    with loss of material 525.64
    without loss of material 525.63
  due to
    birth injury — *see* Birth injury, fracture
    gunshot — *see* Fracture, by site, open
    neoplasm — *see* Fracture, pathologic
    osteoporosis — *see* Fracture, pathologic
  Dupuytren's (ankle) (fibula) (closed) 824.4
    open 824.5
    radius 813.42
      open 813.52
  Duverney's — *see* Fracture, ilium
  elbow (*see also* Fracture, humerus, lower end)
    olecranon (process) (closed) 813.01
      open 813.11
    supracondylar (closed) 812.41
      open 812.51
  ethmoid (bone) (sinus) — *see* Fracture, skull, base
  face bone(s) (closed) NEC 802.8
    with
      other bone(s) — *see* Fracture, multiple, skull
      skull (*see also* Fracture, skull)
        involving other bones — *see* Fracture, multiple, skull
    open 802.9
  fatigue — *see* Fracture, march
  femur, femoral (closed) 821.00
    cervicotrochanteric 820.03
      open 820.13
    condyles, epicondyles 821.21
      open 821.31
    distal end — *see* Fracture, femur, lower end
    epiphysis (separation)
      capital 820.01
        open 820.11
      head 820.01
        open 820.11
      lower 821.22
        open 821.32
      trochanteric 820.01
        open 820.11
      upper 820.01
        open 820.11
    head 820.09
      open 820.19
    lower end or extremity (distal end) (closed) 821.20
      condyles, epicondyles 821.21
        open 821.31
      epiphysis (separation) 821.22
        open 821.32
      multiple sites 821.29
        open 821.39
      open 821.30
      specified site NEC 821.29
        open 821.39
      supracondylar 821.23
        open 821.33
      T-shaped 821.21
        open 821.31
    neck (closed) 820.8

Fracture — *continued*
  femur, femoral — *continued*
    neck — *continued*
      base (cervicotrochanteric) 820.03
        open 820.13
      extracapsular 820.20
        open 820.30
      intertrochanteric (section) 820.21
        open 820.31
      intracapsular 820.00
        open 820.10
      intratrochanteric 820.21
        open 820.31
      midcervical 820.02
        open 820.12
      open 820.9
      pathologic 733.14
        specified part NEC 733.15
      specified site NEC 820.09
        open 820.19
      transcervical 820.02
        open 820.12
      transtrochanteric 820.20
        open 820.30
    open 821.10
    pathologic 733.14
      specified part NEC 733.15
    peritrochanteric (section) 820.20
      open 820.30
    shaft (lower third) (middle third) (upper third) 821.01
      open 821.11
    subcapital 820.09
      open 820.19
    subtrochanteric (region) (section) 820.22
      open 820.32
    supracondylar 821.23
      open 821.33
    transepiphyseal 820.01
      open 820.11
    trochanter (greater) (lesser) (*see also* Fracture, femur, neck, by site) 820.20
      open 820.30
    T-shaped, into knee joint 821.21
      open 821.31
    upper end 820.8
      open 820.9
  fibula (closed) 823.81
    with tibia 823.82
      open 823.92
    distal end 824.8
      open 824.9
    epiphysis
      lower 824.8
        open 824.9
      upper — *see* Fracture, fibula, upper end
    head — *see* Fracture, fibula, upper end
    involving ankle 824.2
      open 824.3
    lower end or extremity 824.8
      open 824.9
    malleolus (external) (lateral) 824.2
      open 824.3
    open NEC 823.91
    pathologic 733.16
    proximal end — *see* Fracture, fibula, upper end
    shaft 823.21
      with tibia 823.22
        open 823.32
      open 823.31
    stress 733.93
    torus 823.41
      with tibia 823.42
    upper end or extremity (epiphysis) (head) (proximal end) (styloid) 823.01
      with tibia 823.02
        open 823.12
      open 823.11
  finger(s), of one hand (closed) (*see also* Fracture, phalanx, hand) 816.00
    with
      metacarpal bone(s), of same hand 817.0
        open 817.1

Fracture — *continued*
  finger(s), of one hand (*see also* Fracture, phalanx, hand) — *continued*
    with — *continued*
      thumb of same hand 816.03
        open 816.13
    open 816.10
  foot, except toe(s) alone (closed) 825.20
    open 825.30
  forearm (closed) NEC 813.80
    lower end (distal end) (lower epiphysis) 813.40
      open 813.50
    open 813.90
    shaft 813.20
      open 813.30
    upper end (proximal end) (upper epiphysis) 813.00
      open 813.10
  fossa, anterior, middle, or posterior — *see* Fracture, skull, base
  Fracture (abduction) (adduction) (avulsion) (compression) (crush) (dislocation) (oblique) (separation) (closed) 829.0
  frontal (bone) (*see also* Fracture, skull, vault)
    sinus — *see* Fracture, skull, base
  Galeazzi's — *see* Fracture, radius, lower end
  glenoid (cavity) (fossa) (scapula) (closed) 811.03
    open 811.13
  Gosselin's — *see* Fracture, ankle
  greenstick — *see* Fracture, by site
  grenade-throwers' — *see* Fracture, humerus, shaft
  gutter — *see* Fracture, skull, vault
  hamate (closed) 814.08
    open 814.18
  hand, one (closed) 815.00
    carpals 814.00
      open 814.10
      specified site NEC 814.09
        open 814.19
    metacarpals 815.00
      open 815.10
    multiple, bones of one hand 817.0
      open 817.1
    open 815.10
    phalanges (*see also* Fracture, phalanx, hand) 816.00
      open 816.10
  healing
    aftercare (*see also* Aftercare, fracture) V54.89
    change of cast V54.89
    complications — *see* condition
    convalescence V66.4
    removal of
      cast V54.89
      fixation device
        external V54.89
        internal V54.01
  heel bone (closed) 825.0
    open 825.1
  Hill-Sachs 812.09
  hip (closed) (*see also* Fracture, femur, neck) 820.8
    open 820.9
    pathologic 733.14
  humerus (closed) 812.20
    anatomical neck 812.02
      open 812.12
    articular process (*see also* Fracture humerus, condyle(s)) 812.44
      open 812.54
    capitellum 812.49
      open 812.59
    condyle(s) 812.44
      lateral (external) 812.42
        open 812.52
      medial (internal epicondyle) 812.43
        open 812.53
      open 812.54
    distal end — *see* Fracture, humerus, lower end

☑ Additional Digit Required — Refer to the Tabular List for Digit Selection   ⁽ᴿᴱᵛ⁾ Subterms under main terms may continue to next column or page

2010 ICD-9-CM   ▶◀ Revised Text   ● New Line   ▲ Revised Code   October 2009 • Volume 2 — 117

Fracture — *continued*
humerus — *continued*
  epiphysis
    lower (*see also* Fracture, humerus, condyle(s)) 812.44
      open 812.54
    upper 812.09
      open 812.19
  external condyle 812.42
    open 812.52
  great tuberosity 812.03
    open 812.13
  head 812.09
    open 812.19
  internal epicondyle 812.43
    open 812.53
  lesser tuberosity 812.09
    open 812.19
  lower end or extremity (distal end) (*see also* Fracture, humerus, by site) 812.40
    multiple sites NEC 812.49
      open 812.59
    open 812.50
    specified site NEC 812.49
      open 812.59
  neck 812.01
    open 812.11
  open 812.30
  pathologic 733.11
  proximal end — *see* Fracture, humerus, upper end
  shaft 812.21
    open 812.31
  supracondylar 812.41
    open 812.51
  surgical neck 812.01
    open 812.11
  trochlea 812.49
    open 812.59
  T-shaped 812.44
    open 812.54
  tuberosity — *see* Fracture, humerus, upper end
  upper end or extremity (proximal end) (*see also* Fracture, humerus, by site) 812.00
    open 812.10
    specified site NEC 812.09
      open 812.19
hyoid bone (closed) 807.5
  open 807.6
hyperextension — *see* Fracture, radius, lower end
ilium (with visceral injury) (closed) 808.41
  open 808.51
impaction, impacted — *see* Fracture, by site
incus — *see* Fracture, skull, base
innominate bone (with visceral injury) (closed) 808.49
  open 808.59
instep, of one foot (closed) 825.20
  with toe(s) of same foot 827.0
    open 827.1
  open 825.30
insufficiency — *see* Fracture, pathologic, by site
internal
  ear — *see* Fracture, skull, base
  semilunar cartilage, knee — *see* Tear, meniscus, medial
intertrochanteric — *see* Fracture, femur, neck, intertrochanteric
ischium (with visceral injury) (closed) 808.42
  open 808.52
jaw (bone) (lower) (closed) (*see also* Fracture, mandible) 802.20
  angle 802.25
    open 802.35
  open 802.30
  upper — *see* Fracture, maxilla
knee
  cap (closed) 822.0
    open 822.1
  cartilage (semilunar) — *see* Tear, meniscus
labyrinth (osseous) — *see* Fracture, skull, base
larynx (closed) 807.5

Fracture — *continued*
larynx — *continued*
  open 807.6
late effect — *see* Late, effects (of), fracture
Le Fort's — *see* Fracture, maxilla
leg (closed) 827.0
  with rib(s) or sternum 828.0
    open 828.1
  both (any bones) 828.0
    open 828.1
  lower — *see* Fracture, tibia
    open 827.1
  upper — *see* Fracture, femur
limb
  lower (multiple) (closed) NEC 827.0
    open 827.1
  upper (multiple) (closed) NEC 818.0
    open 818.1
long bones, due to birth trauma — *see* Birth injury, fracture
lower end or extremity (anterior lip) (posterior) 824.8
  open 824.9
lumbar — *see* Fracture, vertebra, lumbar
lunate bone (closed) 814.02
  open 814.12
malar bone (closed) 802.4
  open 802.5
Malgaigne's (closed) 808.43
  open 808.53
malleolus (closed) 824.8
  bimalleolar 824.4
    open 824.5
  lateral 824.2
    and medial (*see also* Fracture, malleolus, bimalleolar)
      with lip of tibia — *see* Fracture, malleolus, trimalleolar
    open 824.3
  medial (closed) 824.0
    and lateral (*see also* Fracture, malleolus, bimalleolar)
      with lip of tibia — *see* Fracture, malleolus, trimalleolar
    open 824.1
  open 824.9
  trimalleolar (closed) 824.6
    open 824.7
malleus — *see* Fracture, skull, base
malunion 733.81
mandible (closed) 802.20
  angle 802.25
    open 802.35
  body 802.28
    alveolar border 802.27
      open 802.37
    open 802.38
    symphysis 802.26
      open 802.36
  condylar process 802.21
    open 802.31
  coronoid process 802.23
    open 802.33
  multiple sites 802.29
    open 802.39
  open 802.30
  ramus NEC 802.24
    open 802.34
  subcondylar 802.22
    open 802.32
manubrium — *see* Fracture, sternum
march 733.95
  fibula 733.93
  metatarsals 733.94
  tibia 733.93
maxilla, maxillary (superior) (upper jaw) (closed) 802.4
  inferior — *see* Fracture, mandible
  open 802.5
meniscus, knee — *see* Tear, meniscus
metacarpus, metacarpal (bone(s)), of one hand (closed) 815.00
  with phalanx, phalanges, hand (finger(s)) (thumb) of same hand 817.0
    open 817.1
  base 815.02

Fracture — *continued*
metacarpus, metacarpal(s), of one hand — *continued*
  base — *continued*
    first metacarpal 815.01
      open 815.11
    open 815.12
    thumb 815.01
      open 815.11
  multiple sites 815.09
    open 815.19
  neck 815.04
    open 815.14
  open 815.10
  shaft 815.03
    open 815.13
metatarsus, metatarsal (bone(s)), of one foot (closed) 825.25
  with tarsal bone(s) 825.29
    open 825.39
  open 825.35
Monteggia's (closed) 813.03
  open 813.13
Moore's — *see* Fracture, radius, lower end
multangular bone (closed)
  larger 814.05
    open 814.15
  smaller 814.06
    open 814.16
multiple (closed) 829.0

Note — Multiple fractures of sites classifiable to the same three- or four-digit category are coded to that category, except for sites classifiable to 810–818 or 820–827 in different limbs.

Multiple fractures of sites classifiable to different fourth-digit subdivisions within the same three–digit category should be dealt with according to coding rules.

Multiple fractures of sites classifiable to different three–digit categories (identifiable from the listing under "Fracture"), and of sites classifiable to 810–818 or 820–827 in different limbs should be coded according to the following list, which should be referred to in the following priority order: skull or face bones, pelvis or vertebral column, legs, arms.

  arm (multiple bones in same arm except in hand alone) (sites classifiable to 810–817 with sites classifiable to a different three–digit category in 810–817 in same arm) (closed) 818.0
    open 818.1
  arms, both or arm(s) with rib(s) or sternum (sites classifiable to 810–818 with sites classifiable to same range of categories in other limb or to 807) (closed) 819.0
    open 819.1
  bones of trunk NEC (closed) 809.0
    open 809.1
  hand, metacarpal bone(s) with phalanx or phalanges of same hand (sites classifiable to 815 with sites classifiable to 816 in same hand) (closed) 817.0
    open 817.1
  leg (multiple bones in same leg) (sites classifiable to 820–826 with sites classifiable to a different three–digit category in that range in same leg) (closed) 827.0
    open 827.1
  legs, both or leg(s) with arm(s), rib(s), or sternum (sites classifiable to 820–827 with sites classifiable to same range of categories in other leg or to 807 or 810–819) (closed) 828.0
    open 828.1
open 829.1

Fracture — *continued*
multiple — *continued*
  pelvis with other bones except skull or face bones (sites classifiable to 808 with sites classifiable to 805–807 or 810–829) (closed) 809.0
    open 809.1
  skull, specified or unspecified bones, or face bone(s) with any other bone(s) (sites classifiable to 800–803 with sites classifiable to 805–829) (closed) 804.0 ☑

Note — Use the following fifth-digit subclassification with categories 800, 801, 803, and 804:

0   unspecified state of consciousness

1   with no loss of consciousness

2   with brief [less than one hour] loss of consciousness

3   with moderate [1–24 hours] loss of consciousness

4   with prolonged [more than 24 hours] loss of consciousness and return to pre–existing conscious level

5   with prolonged [more than 24 hours] loss of consciousness, without return to pre–existing conscious level

Use fifth-digit 5 to designate when a patient is unconscious and dies before regaining consciousness, regardless of the duration of the loss of consciousness

6   with loss of consciousness of unspecified duration

9   with concussion, unspecified

  with
    contusion, cerebral 804.1 ☑
    epidural hemorrhage 804.2 ☑
    extradural hemorrhage 804.2 ☑
    hemorrhage (intracranial) NEC 804.3 ☑
    intracranial injury NEC 804.4 ☑
    laceration, cerebral 804.1 ☑
    subarachnoid hemorrhage 804.2 ☑
    subdural hemorrhage 804.2 ☑
  open 804.5 ☑
    with
      contusion, cerebral 804.6 ☑
      epidural hemorrhage 804.7 ☑
      extradural hemorrhage 804.7 ☑
      hemorrhage (intracranial) NEC 804.8 ☑
      intracranial injury NEC 804.9 ☑
      laceration, cerebral 804.6 ☑
      subarachnoid hemorrhage 804.7 ☑
      subdural hemorrhage 804.7 ☑
  vertebral column with other bones, except skull or face bones (sites classifiable to 805 or 806 with sites classifiable to 807–808 or 810–829) (closed) 809.0
    open 809.1
nasal (bone(s)) (closed) 802.0
  open 802.1
  sinus — *see* Fracture, skull, base
navicular
  carpal (wrist) (closed) 814.01
    open 814.11
  tarsal (ankle) (closed) 825.22
    open 825.32
neck — *see* Fracture, vertebra, cervical
neural arch — *see* Fracture, vertebra, by site
nonunion 733.82
nose, nasal, (bone) (septum) (closed) 802.0
  open 802.1
occiput — *see* Fracture, skull, base
odontoid process — *see* Fracture, vertebra, cervical
olecranon (process) (ulna) (closed) 813.01

☑ Additional Digit Required — Refer to the Tabular List for Digit Selection ⬧ Subterms under main terms may continue to next column or page

118 — Volume 2   ▶◀ Revised Text   ● New Line   ▲ Revised Code   2010 ICD-9-CM

Fracture — *continued*
  olecranon — *continued*
    open 813.11
  open 829.1
  orbit, orbital (bone) (region) (closed) 802.8
    floor (blow-out) 802.6
      open 802.7
    open 802.9
    roof — *see* Fracture, skull, base
    specified part NEC 802.8
      open 802.9
  os
    calcis (closed) 825.0
      open 825.1
    magnum (closed) 814.07
      open 814.17
    pubis (with visceral injury) (closed) 808.2
      open 808.3
    triquetrum (closed) 814.03
      open 814.13
  osseous
    auditory meatus — *see* Fracture, skull, base
    labyrinth — *see* Fracture, skull, base
    ossicles, auditory (incus) (malleus) (stapes) — *see* Fracture, skull, base
  osteoporotic — *see* Fracture, pathologic
  palate (closed) 802.8
    open 802.9
  paratrooper — *see* Fracture, tibia, lower end
  parietal bone — *see* Fracture, skull, vault
  parry — *see* Fracture, Monteggia's
  patella (closed) 822.0
    open 822.1
  pathologic (cause unknown) 733.10
    ankle 733.16
    femur (neck) 733.14
      specified NEC 733.15
    fibula 733.16
    hip 733.14
    humerus 733.11
    radius (distal) 733.12
    specified site NEC 733.19
    tibia 733.16
    ulna 733.12
    vertebrae (collapse) 733.13
    wrist 733.12
  pedicle (of vertebral arch) — *see* Fracture, vertebra, by site
  pelvis, pelvic (bone(s)) (with visceral injury) (closed) 808.8
    multiple (with disruption of pelvic circle) 808.43
      open 808.53
    open 808.9
    rim (closed) 808.49
      open 808.59
  peritrochanteric (closed) 820.20
    open 820.30
  phalanx, phalanges, of one
    foot (closed) 826.0
      with bone(s) of same lower limb 827.0
        open 827.1
      open 826.1
    hand (closed) 816.00
      with metacarpal bone(s) of same hand 817.0
        open 817.1
      distal 816.02
        open 816.12
      middle 816.01
        open 816.11
      multiple sites NEC 816.03
        open 816.13
      open 816.10
      proximal 816.01
        open 816.11
  pisiform (closed) 814.04
    open 814.14
  pond — *see* Fracture, skull, vault
  Pott's (closed) 824.4
    open 824.5
  prosthetic device, internal — *see* Complications, mechanical
  pubis (with visceral injury) (closed) 808.2
    open 808.3
  Quervain's (closed) 814.01

Fracture — *continued*
  Quervain's — *continued*
    open 814.11
  radius (alone) (closed) 813.81
    with ulna NEC 813.83
      open 813.93
    distal end — *see* Fracture, radius, lower end
    epiphysis
      lower — *see* Fracture, radius, lower end
      upper — *see* Fracture, radius, upper end
    head — *see* Fracture, radius, upper end
    lower end or extremity (distal end) (lower epiphysis) 813.42
      with ulna (lower end) 813.44
        open 813.54
      open 813.52
      torus 813.45
        with ulna 813.47 ●
    neck — *see* Fracture, radius, upper end
    open NEC 813.91
    pathologic 733.12
    proximal end — *see* Fracture, radius, upper end
    shaft (closed) 813.21
      with ulna (shaft) 813.23
        open 813.33
      open 813.31
    upper end 813.07
      with ulna (upper end) 813.08
        open 813.18
      epiphysis 813.05
        open 813.15
      head 813.05
        open 813.15
      multiple sites 813.07
        open 813.17
      neck 813.06
        open 813.16
        open 813.17
      specified site NEC 813.07
        open 813.17
  ramus
    inferior or superior (with visceral injury) (closed) 808.2
      open 808.3
    ischium — *see* Fracture, ischium
    mandible 802.24
      open 802.34
  rib(s) (closed) 807.0 ☑

Note — Use the following fifth-digit subclassification with categories 807.0–807.1:

0	rib(s), unspecified
1	one rib
2	two ribs
3	three ribs
4	four ribs
5	five ribs
6	six ribs
7	seven ribs
8	eight or more ribs
9	multiple ribs, unspecified

    with flail chest (open) 807.4
    open 807.1 ☑
  root, tooth 873.63
    complicated 873.73
  sacrum — *see* Fracture, vertebra, sacrum
  scaphoid
    ankle (closed) 825.22
      open 825.32
    wrist (closed) 814.01
      open 814.11
  scapula (closed) 811.00
    acromial, acromion (process) 811.01
      open 811.11
    body 811.09
      open 811.19
    coracoid process 811.02
      open 811.12
    glenoid (cavity) (fossa) 811.03

Fracture — *continued*
  scapula — *continued*
    glenoid — *continued*
      open 811.13
    neck 811.03
      open 811.13
      open 811.10
  semilunar
    bone, wrist (closed) 814.02
      open 814.12
    cartilage (interior) (knee) — *see* Tear, meniscus
  sesamoid bone — *see* Fracture, by site
  Shepherd's (closed) 825.21
    open 825.31
  shoulder (*see also* Fracture, humerus, upper end)
    blade — *see* Fracture, scapula
  silverfork — *see* Fracture, radius, lower end
  sinus (ethmoid) (frontal) (maxillary) (nasal) (sphenoidal) — *see* Fracture, skull, base
  Skillern's — *see* Fracture, radius, shaft
  skull (multiple NEC) (with face bones) (closed) 803.0 ☑

Note — Use the following fifth-digit subclassification with categories 800, 801, 803, and 804:

0	unspecified state of consciousness
1	with no loss of consciousness
2	with brief [less than one hour] loss of consciousness
3	with moderate [1-24 hours] loss of consciousness
4	with prolonged [more than 24 hours] loss of consciousness and return to pre-existing conscious level
5	with prolonged [more than 24 hours] loss of consciousness, without return to pre-existing conscious level

Use fifth-digit 5 to designate when a patient is unconscious and dies before regaining consciousness, regardless of the duration of the loss of consciousness

6	with loss of consciousness of unspecified duration
9	with concussion, unspecified

    with
      contusion, cerebral 803.1 ☑
      epidural hemorrhage 803.2 ☑
      extradural hemorrhage 803.2 ☑
      hemorrhage (intracranial) NEC 803.3 ☑
      intracranial injury NEC 803.4 ☑
      laceration, cerebral 803.1 ☑
      other bones — *see* Fracture, multiple, skull
      subarachnoid hemorrhage 803.2 ☑
      subdural hemorrhage 803.2 ☑
    base (antrum) (ethmoid bone) (fossa) (internal ear) (nasal sinus) (occiput) (sphenoid) (temporal bone) (closed) 801.0 ☑
      with
        contusion, cerebral 801.1 ☑
        epidural hemorrhage 801.2 ☑
        extradural hemorrhage 801.2 ☑
        hemorrhage (intracranial) NEC 801.3 ☑
        intracranial injury NEC 801.4 ☑
        laceration, cerebral 801.1 ☑
        subarachnoid hemorrhage 801.2 ☑
        subdural hemorrhage 801.2 ☑
      open 801.5 ☑
        with
          contusion, cerebral 801.6 ☑

Fracture — *continued*
  skull — *continued*
    base — *continued*
      open — *continued*
        with — *continued*
          epidural hemorrhage 801.7 ☑
          extradural hemorrhage 801.7 ☑
          hemorrhage (intracranial) NEC 801.8 ☑
          intracranial injury NEC 801.9 ☑
          laceration, cerebral 801.6 ☑
          subarachnoid hemorrhage 801.7 ☑
          subdural hemorrhage 801.7 ☑
    birth injury 767.3
    face bones — *see* Fracture, face bones
    open 803.5 ☑
      with
        contusion, cerebral 803.6 ☑
        epidural hemorrhage 803.7 ☑
        extradural hemorrhage 803.7 ☑
        hemorrhage (intracranial) NEC 803.8 ☑
        intracranial injury NEC 803.9 ☑
        laceration, cerebral 803.6 ☑
        subarachnoid hemorrhage 803.7 ☑
        subdural hemorrhage 803.7 ☑
    vault (frontal bone) (parietal bone) (vertex) (closed) 800.0 ☑
      with
        contusion, cerebral 800.1 ☑
        epidural hemorrhage 800.2 ☑
        extradural hemorrhage 800.2 ☑
        hemorrhage (intracranial) NEC 800.3 ☑
        intracranial injury NEC 800.4 ☑
        laceration, cerebral 800.1 ☑
        subarachnoid hemorrhage 800.2 ☑
        subdural hemorrhage 800.2 ☑
      open 800.5 ☑
        with
          contusion, cerebral 800.6 ☑
          epidural hemorrhage 800.7 ☑
          extradural hemorrhage 800.7 ☑
          hemorrhage (intracranial) NEC 800.8 ☑
          intracranial injury NEC 800.9 ☑
          laceration, cerebral 800.6 ☑
          subarachnoid hemorrhage 800.7 ☑
          subdural hemorrhage 800.7 ☑
  Smith's 813.41
    open 813.51
  sphenoid (bone) (sinus) — *see* Fracture, skull, base
  spine (*see also* Fracture, vertebra, by site due to birth trauma) 767.4
  spinous process — *see* Fracture, vertebra, by site
  spontaneous — *see* Fracture, pathologic
  sprinters' — *see* Fracture, ilium
  stapes — *see* Fracture, skull, base
  stave (*see also* Fracture, metacarpus, metacarpal bone(s))
    spine — *see* Fracture, tibia, upper end
  sternum (closed) 807.2
    with flail chest (open) 807.4
    open 807.3
  Stieda's — *see* Fracture, femur, lower end
  stress 733.95
    fibula 733.93
    metatarsals 733.94

☑ Additional Digit Required — Refer to the Tabular List for Digit Selection   ▥ Subterms under main terms may continue to next column or page

2010 ICD-9-CM   ▶◀ Revised Text   ● New Line   ▲ Revised Code   October 2009 • Volume 2 — 119

Fracture — Fracture

Fracture — *continued*
  stress — *continued*
    specified site NEC 733.95
    tibia 733.93
  styloid process
    metacarpal (closed) 815.02
      open 815.12
    radius — *see* Fracture, radius, lower end
    temporal bone — *see* Fracture, skull, base
    ulna — *see* Fracture, ulna, lower end
  supracondylar, elbow 812.41
    open 812.51
  symphysis pubis (with visceral injury) (closed) 808.2
    open 808.3
  talus (ankle bone) (closed) 825.21
    open 825.31
  tarsus, tarsal bone(s) (with metatarsus) of one foot (closed) NEC 825.29
    open 825.39
  temporal bone (styloid) — *see* Fracture, skull, base
  tendon — *see* Sprain, by site
  thigh — *see* Fracture, femur, shaft
  thumb (and finger(s)) of one hand (closed) (*see also* Fracture, phalanx, hand) 816.00
    with metacarpal bone(s) of same hand 817.0
      open 817.1
    metacarpal(s) — *see* Fracture, metacarpus
    open 816.10
  thyroid cartilage (closed) 807.5
    open 807.6
  tibia (closed) 823.80
    with fibula 823.82
      open 823.92
    condyles — *see* Fracture, tibia, upper end
    distal end 824.8
      open 824.9
    epiphysis
      lower 824.8
        open 824.9
      upper — *see* Fracture, tibia, upper end
    head (involving knee joint) — *see* Fracture, tibia, upper end
    intercondyloid eminence — *see* Fracture, tibia, upper end
    involving ankle 824.0
      open 824.9
    lower end or extremity (anterior lip) (posterior lip) 824.8
      open 824.9
    malleolus (internal) (medial) 824.0
      open 824.1
    open NEC 823.90
    pathologic 733.16
    proximal end — *see* Fracture, tibia, upper end
    shaft 823.20
      with fibula 823.22
        open 823.32
      open 823.30
    spine — *see* Fracture, tibia, upper end
    stress 733.93
    torus 823.40
      with fibula 823.42
    tuberosity — *see* Fracture, tibia, upper end
    upper end or extremity (condyle) (epiphysis) (head) (spine) (proximal end) (tuberosity) 823.00
      with fibula 823.02
        open 823.12
      open 823.10
  toe(s), of one foot (closed) 826.0
    with bone(s) of same lower limb 827.0
      open 827.1
    open 826.1
  tooth (root) 873.63
    complicated 873.73
  torus
    fibula 823.41
      with tibia 823.42
    humerus 812.49 ●
    radius ▶(alone)◀ 813.45 ●
      with ulna 813.47 ●

Fracture — *continued*
  torus — *continued*
    tibia 823.40
      with fibula 823.42
    ulna (alone) 813.46 ●
      with radius 813.47 ●
  trachea (closed) 807.5
    open 807.6
  transverse process — *see* Fracture, vertebra, by site
  trapezium (closed) 814.05
    open 814.15
  trapezoid bone (closed) 814.06
    open 814.16
  trimalleolar (closed) 824.6
    open 824.7
  triquetral (bone) (closed) 814.03
    open 814.13
  trochanter (greater) (lesser) (closed) (*see also* Fracture, femur, neck, by site) 820.20
    open 820.30
  trunk (bones) (closed) 809.0
    open 809.1
  tuberosity (external) — *see* Fracture, by site
  ulna (alone) (closed) 813.82
    with radius NEC 813.83
      open 813.93
    coronoid process (closed) 813.02
      open 813.12
    distal end — *see* Fracture, ulna, lower end
    epiphysis
      lower — *see* Fracture, ulna, lower end
      upper — *see* Fracture, ulna, upper end
    head — *see* Fracture, ulna, lower end
    lower end (distal end) (head) (lower epiphysis) (styloid process) 813.43
      with radius (lower end) 813.44
        open 813.54
      open 813.53
    olecranon process (closed) 813.01
      open 813.11
    open NEC 813.92
    pathologic 733.12
    proximal end — *see* Fracture, ulna, upper end
    shaft 813.22
      with radius (shaft) 813.23
        open 813.33
      open 813.32
    styloid process — *see* Fracture, ulna, lower end
    torus 813.46 ●
      with radius 813.47 ●
    transverse — *see* Fracture, ulna, by site
    upper end (epiphysis) 813.04
      with radius (upper end) 813.08
        open 813.18
      multiple sites 813.04
        open 813.14
      open 813.14
      specified site NEC 813.04
        open 813.14
  unciform (closed) 814.08
    open 814.18
  vertebra, vertebral (back) (body) (column) (neural arch) (pedicle) (spine) (spinous process) (transverse process) (closed) 805.8
    with
      hematomyelia — *see* Fracture, vertebra, by site, with spinal cord injury
      injury to
        cauda equina — *see* Fracture, vertebra, sacrum, with spinal cord injury
        nerve — *see* Fracture, vertebra, by site, with spinal cord injury
      paralysis — *see* Fracture, vertebra, by site, with spinal cord injury
      paraplegia — *see* Fracture, vertebra, by site, with spinal cord injury
      quadriplegia — *see* Fracture, vertebra, by site, with spinal cord injury

Fracture — *continued*
  vertebra, vertebral — *continued*
    with — *continued*
      spinal concussion — *see* Fracture, vertebra, by site, with spinal cord injury
      spinal cord injury (closed) NEC 806.8

> *Note* — Use the following fifth-digit subclassification with categories 806.0–806.3:
>
> C_1–C_4 or unspecified level and D_1–D_6 (T_1–T_6) or unspecified level with:
>
> 0 unspecified spinal cord injury
> 1 complete lesion of cord
> 2 anterior cord syndrome
> 3 central cord syndrome
> 4 specified injury NEC
>
> C_5–C_7 level and D_7–D_{12} level with:
>
> 5 unspecified spinal cord injury
> 6 complete lesion of cord
> 7 anterior cord syndrome
> 8 central cord syndrome
> 9 specified injury NEC

        cervical 806.0 ☑
          open 806.1 ☑
        dorsal, dorsolumbar 806.2 ☑
          open 806.3 ☑
        open 806.9
        thoracic, thoracolumbar 806.2 ☑
          open 806.3 ☑
    atlanto-axial — *see* Fracture, vertebra, cervical
    cervical (hangman) (teardrop) (closed) 805.00
      with spinal cord injury — *see* Fracture, vertebra, with spinal cord injury, cervical
      first (atlas) 805.01
        open 805.11
      second (axis) 805.02
        open 805.12
      third 805.03
        open 805.13
      fourth 805.04
        open 805.14
      fifth 805.05
        open 805.15
      sixth 805.06
        open 805.16
      seventh 805.07
        open 805.17
      multiple sites 805.08
        open 805.18
      open 805.10
    chronic 733.13
    coccyx (closed) 805.6
      with spinal cord injury (closed) 806.60
        cauda equina injury 806.62
        complete lesion 806.61
          open 806.71
          open 806.72
        open 806.70
        specified type NEC 806.69
          open 806.79
      open 805.7
    collapsed 733.13
    compression, not due to trauma 733.13
    dorsal (closed) 805.2
      with spinal cord injury — *see* Fracture, vertebra, with spinal cord injury, dorsal
      open 805.3
    dorsolumbar (closed) 805.2
      with spinal cord injury — *see* Fracture, vertebra, with spinal cord injury, dorsal
      open 805.3
    due to osteoporosis 733.13
    fetus or newborn 767.4
    lumbar (closed) 805.4

Fracture — *continued*
  vertebra, vertebral — *continued*
    lumbar — *continued*
      with spinal cord injury (closed) 806.4
        open 806.5
      open 805.5
      nontraumatic 733.13
      open NEC 805.9
      pathologic (any site) 733.13
      sacrum (closed) 805.6
        with spinal cord injury 806.60
          cauda equina injury 806.62
            complete lesion 806.61
              open 806.71
              open 806.72
            open 806.70
          specified type NEC 806.69
            open 806.79
        open 805.7
      site unspecified (closed) 805.8
        with spinal cord injury (closed) 806.8
          open 806.9
        open 805.9
      stress (any site) 733.95
      thoracic (closed) 805.2
        with spinal cord injury — *see* Fracture, vertebra, with spinal cord injury, thoracic
        open 805.3
    vertex — *see* Fracture, skull, vault
    vomer (bone) 802.0
      open 802.1
    Wagstaffe's — *see* Fracture, ankle
    wrist (closed) 814.00
      open 814.10
      pathologic 733.12
    xiphoid (process) — *see* Fracture, sternum
    zygoma (zygomatic arch) (closed) 802.4
      open 802.5

Fragile X syndrome 759.83
Fragilitas
  crinium 704.2
  hair 704.2
  ossium 756.51
    with blue sclera 756.51
  unguium 703.8
    congenital 757.5
Fragility
  bone 756.51
    with deafness and blue sclera 756.51
  capillary (hereditary) 287.8
  hair 704.2
  nails 703.8
Fragmentation — *see* Fracture, by site
Frailty 797
Frambesia, frambesial (tropica) — *see also* Yaws 102.9
  initial lesion or ulcer 102.0
  primary 102.0
Frambeside
  gummatous 102.4
  of early yaws 102.2
Frambesioma 102.1
Franceschetti's syndrome (mandibulofacial dysostosis) 756.0
Francis' disease — *see also* Tularemia 021.9
Franklin's disease (heavy chain) 273.2
Frank's essential thrombocytopenia — *see also* Purpura, thrombocytopenic 287.39
Fraser's syndrome 759.89
Freckle 709.09
  malignant melanoma in (M8742/3) — *see* Melanoma
  melanotic (of Hutchinson) (M8742/2) — *see* Neoplasm, skin, in situ
  retinal 239.81 ●
Freeman-Sheldon syndrome 759.89
Freezing 991.9
  specified effect NEC 991.8
Freiberg's
  disease (osteochondrosis, second metatarsal) 732.5
  infraction of metatarsal head 732.5
  osteochondrosis 732.5
Frei's disease (climatic bubo) 099.1
Fremitus, friction, cardiac 785.3

Frenulum linguae 750.0

Frenum
    external os 752.49
    tongue 750.0

Frequency (urinary) NEC 788.41
    micturition 788.41
    nocturnal 788.43
    polyuria 788.42
    psychogenic 306.53

Frey's syndrome (auriculotemporal syndrome) 705.22

Friction
    burn (see also Injury, superficial, by site) 919.0
    fremitus, cardiac 785.3
    precordial 785.3
    sounds, chest 786.7

Friderichsen-Waterhouse syndrome or disease 036.3

Friedländer's
    B (bacillus) NEC (see also condition) 041.3
        sepsis or septicemia 038.49
    disease (endarteritis obliterans) — see Arteriosclerosis

Friedreich's
    ataxia 334.0
    combined systemic disease 334.0
    disease 333.2
        combined systemic 334.0
    myoclonia 333.2
    sclerosis (spinal cord) 334.0

Friedrich-Erb-Arnold syndrome (acropachyderma) 757.39

Frigidity 302.72
    psychic or psychogenic 302.72

Fröhlich's disease or syndrome (adiposogenital dystrophy) 253.8

Froin's syndrome 336.8

Frommel-Chiari syndrome 676.6 ☑

Frommel's disease 676.6 ☑

Frontal — see also condition
    lobe syndrome 310.0

Frostbite 991.3
    face 991.0
    foot 991.2
    hand 991.1
    specified site NEC 991.3

Frotteurism 302.89

Frozen 991.9
    pelvis 620.8
    shoulder 726.0

Fructosemia 271.2

Fructosuria (benign) (essential) 271.2

Fuchs'
    black spot (myopic) 360.21
    corneal dystrophy (endothelial) 371.57
    heterochromic cyclitis 364.21

Fucosidosis 271.8

Fugue 780.99
    dissociative 300.13
    hysterical (dissociative) 300.13
    reaction to exceptional stress (transient) 308.1

Fukuhara syndrome 277.87

Fuller Albright's syndrome (osteitis fibrosa disseminata) 756.59

Fuller's earth disease 502

Fulminant, fulminating — see condition

Functional — see condition

Functioning
    borderline intellectual V62.89

Fundus — see also condition
    flavimaculatus 362.76

Fungemia 117.9

Fungus, fungous
    cerebral 348.89   ▲
    disease NEC 117.9
    infection — see Infection, fungus
    testis (see also Tuberculosis) 016.5 ☑ [608.81]

Funiculitis (acute) 608.4
    chronic 608.4
    endemic 608.4
    gonococcal (acute) 098.14
        chronic or duration of 2 months or over 098.34
    tuberculous (see also Tuberculosis) 016.5 ☑

Funnel
    breast (acquired) 738.3
        congenital 754.81
        late effect of rickets 268.1
    chest (acquired) 738.3
        congenital 754.81
        late effect of rickets 268.1
    pelvis (acquired) 738.6
        with disproportion (fetopelvic) 653.3 ☑
            affecting fetus or newborn 763.1
            causing obstructed labor 660.1 ☑
                affecting fetus or newborn 763.1
        congenital 755.69
        tuberculous (see also Tuberculosis) 016.9 ☑

FUO — see also Pyrexia 780.60

Furfur 690.18
    microsporon 111.0

Furor, paroxysmal (idiopathic) — see also Epilepsy 345.8 ☑

Furriers' lung 495.8

Furrowed tongue 529.5
    congenital 750.13

Furrowing nail(s) (transverse) 703.8
    congenital 757.5

Furuncle 680.9
    abdominal wall 680.2
    ankle 680.6
    anus 680.5
    arm (any part, above wrist) 680.3
    auditory canal, external 680.0
    axilla 680.3
    back (any part) 680.2
    breast 680.2
    buttock 680.5
    chest wall 680.2
    corpus cavernosum 607.2
    ear (any part) 680.0
    eyelid 373.13

Furuncle — continued
    face (any part, except eye) 680.0
    finger (any) 680.4
    flank 680.2
    foot (any part) 680.7
    forearm 680.3
    gluteal (region) 680.5
    groin 680.2
    hand (any part) 680.4
    head (any part, except face) 680.8
    heel 680.7
    hip 680.6
    kidney (see also Abscess, kidney) 590.2
    knee 680.6
    labium (majus) (minus) 616.4
    lacrimal
        gland (see also Dacryoadenitis) 375.00
        passages (duct) (sac) (see also Dacryocystitis) 375.30
    leg, any part except foot 680.6
    malignant 022.0
    multiple sites 680.9
    neck 680.1
    nose (external) (septum) 680.0
    orbit 376.01
    partes posteriores 680.5
    pectoral region 680.2
    penis 607.2
    perineum 680.2
    pinna 680.0
    scalp (any part) 680.8
    scrotum 608.4
    seminal vesicle 608.0
    shoulder 680.3
    skin NEC 680.9
    specified site NEC 680.8
    spermatic cord 608.4
    temple (region) 680.0
    testis 604.90
    thigh 680.6
    thumb 680.4
    toe (any) 680.7
    trunk 680.2
    tunica vaginalis 608.4
    umbilicus 680.2
    upper arm 680.3
    vas deferens 608.4
    vulva 616.4
    wrist 680.4

Furunculosis — see also Furuncle 680.9
    external auditory meatus 680.0 [380.13]

Fusarium (infection) 118

Fusion, fused (congenital)
    anal (with urogenital canal) 751.5
    aorta and pulmonary artery 745.0
    astragaloscaphoid 755.67
    atria 745.5
    atrium and ventricle 745.69
    auditory canal 744.02
    auricles, heart 745.5
    binocular, with defective stereopsis 368.33
    bone 756.9

Fusion, fused — continued
    cervical spine — see Fusion, spine
    choanal 748.0
    commissure, mitral valve 746.5
    cranial sutures, premature 756.0
    cusps, heart valve NEC 746.89
        mitral 746.5
        tricuspid 746.89
    ear ossicles 744.04
    fingers (see also Syndactylism, fingers) 755.11
    hymen 752.42
    hymeno-urethral 599.89
        causing obstructed labor 660.1 ☑
            affecting fetus or newborn 763.1
    joint (acquired) (see also Ankylosis)
        congenital 755.8
    kidneys (incomplete) 753.3
    labium (majus) (minus) 752.49
    larynx and trachea 748.3
    limb 755.8
        lower 755.69
        upper 755.59
    lobe, lung 748.5
    lumbosacral (acquired) 724.6
        congenital 756.15
        surgical V45.4
    nares (anterior) (posterior) 748.0
    nose, nasal 748.0
    nostril(s) 748.0
    organ or site NEC — see Anomaly, specified type NEC
    ossicles 756.9
        auditory 744.04
    pulmonary valve segment 746.02
    pulmonic cusps 746.02
    ribs 756.3
    sacroiliac (acquired) (joint) 724.6
        congenital 755.69
        surgical V45.4
    skull, imperfect 756.0
    spine (acquired) 724.9
        arthrodesis status V45.4
        congenital (vertebra) 756.15
        postoperative status V45.4
    sublingual duct with submaxillary duct at opening in mouth 750.26
    talonavicular (bar) 755.67
    teeth, tooth 520.2
    testes 752.89
    toes (see also Syndactylism, toes) 755.13
    trachea and esophagus 750.3
    twins 759.4
    urethral-hymenal 599.89
    vagina 752.49
    valve cusps — see Fusion, cusps, heart valve
    ventricles, heart 745.4
    vertebra (arch) — see Fusion, spine
    vulva 752.49

Fusospirillosis (mouth) (tongue) (tonsil) 101

Fussy infant (baby) 780.91

☑ Additional Digit Required — Refer to the Tabular List for Digit Selection   ▼ Subterms under main terms may continue to next column or page

2010 ICD-9-CM   ▶◀ Revised Text   ● New Line   ▲ Revised Code   October 2009 • Volume 2 — 121

G

Gafsa boil 085.1
Gain, weight (abnormal) (excessive) — *see also*
    Weight, gain 783.1
Gaisböck's disease or syndrome (polycythemia
    hypertonica) 289.0
Gait
    abnormality 781.2
      hysterical 300.11
    ataxic 781.2
      hysterical 300.11
    disturbance 781.2
      hysterical 300.11
    paralytic 781.2
    scissor 781.2
    spastic 781.2
    staggering 781.2
      hysterical 300.11
Galactocele (breast) (infected) 611.5
    puerperal, postpartum 676.8 ☑
Galactophoritis 611.0
    puerperal, postpartum 675.2 ☑
Galactorrhea 676.6 ☑
    not associated with childbirth 611.6
Galactosemia (classic) (congenital) 271.1
Galactosuria 271.1
Galacturia 791.1
    bilharziasis 120.0
Galen's vein — *see* condition
Gallbladder — *see also* condition
    acute (*see also* Disease, gallbladder) 575.0
Gall duct — *see* condition
Gallop rhythm 427.89
Gallstone (cholemic) (colic) (impacted) — *see*
    also Cholelithiasis
    causing intestinal obstruction 560.31
Gambling, pathological 312.31
Gammaloidosis 277.39
Gammopathy 273.9
    macroglobulinemia 273.3
    monoclonal (benign) (essential) (idiopathic)
      (with lymphoplasmacytic dyscrasia)
      273.1
Gamna's disease (siderotic splenomegaly) 289.51
Gampsodactylia (congenital) 754.71
Gamstorp's disease (adynamia episodica
    hereditaria) 359.3
Gandy-Nanta disease (siderotic splenomegaly)
    289.51
Gang activity, without manifest psychiatric
    disorder V71.09
    adolescent V71.02
    adult V71.01
    child V71.02
Gangliocytoma (M9490/0) — *see* Neoplasm,
    connective tissue, benign
Ganglioglioma (M9505/1) — *see* Neoplasm, by
    site, uncertain behavior
Ganglion 727.43
    joint 727.41
    of yaws (early) (late) 102.6
    periosteal (*see also* Periostitis) 730.3 ☑
    tendon sheath (compound) (diffuse) 727.42
    tuberculous (*see also* Tuberculosis) 015.9 ☑
Ganglioneuroblastoma (M9490/3) — *see* Neo-
    plasm, connective tissue, malignant
Ganglioneuroma (M9490/0) — *see also* Neo-
    plasm, connective tissue, benign
    malignant (M9490/3) — *see* Neoplasm, con-
      nective tissue, malignant
Ganglioneuromatosis (M9491/0) — *see* Neo-
    plasm, connective tissue, benign
Ganglionitis
    fifth nerve (*see also* Neuralgia, trigeminal) 350.1
    gasserian 350.1
    geniculate 351.1
      herpetic 053.11
      newborn 767.5
    herpes zoster 053.11
    herpetic geniculate (Hunt's syndrome) 053.11
Gangliosidosis 330.1
Gangosa 102.5

Gangrene, gangrenous (anemia) (artery) (celluli-
    tis) (dermatitis) (dry) (infective) (moist)
    (pemphigus) (septic) (skin) (stasis) (ulcer)
    785.4
    with
      arteriosclerosis (native artery) 440.24
        bypass graft 440.30
          autologous vein 440.31
          nonautologous biological 440.32
      diabetes (mellitus) 250.7 ☑ *[785.4]*
        due to secondary diabetes
          249.7 ☑ *[785.4]*
    abdomen (wall) 785.4
    adenitis 683
    alveolar 526.5
    angina 462
      diphtheritic 032.0
    anus 569.49
    appendices epiploicae — *see* Gangrene,
      mesentery
    appendix — *see* Appendicitis, acute
    arteriosclerotic — *see* Arteriosclerosis, with,
      gangrene
    auricle 785.4
    Bacillus welchii (*see also* Gangrene, gas) 040.0
    bile duct (*see also* Cholangitis) 576.8
    bladder 595.89
    bowel — *see* Gangrene, intestine
    cecum — *see* Gangrene, intestine
    Clostridium perfringens or welchii (*see also*
      Gangrene, gas) 040.0
    colon — *see* Gangrene, intestine
    connective tissue 785.4
    cornea 371.40
    corpora cavernosa (infective) 607.2
      noninfective 607.89
    cutaneous, spreading 785.4
    decubital (*see also* Ulcer, pressure)
      707.00 *[785.4]*
    diabetic (any site) 250.7 ☑ *[785.4]*
      due to secondary diabetes 249.7 ☑ *[785.4]*
    dropsical 785.4
    emphysematous (*see also* Gangrene, gas) 040.0
    epidemic (ergotized grain) 988.2
    epididymis (infectional) (*see also* Epididymitis)
      604.99
    erysipelas (*see also* Erysipelas) 035
    extremity (lower) (upper) 785.4
    gallbladder or duct (*see also* Cholecystitis,
      acute) 575.0
    gas (bacillus) 040.0
      with
        abortion — *see* Abortion, by type, with
          sepsis
        ectopic pregnancy (*see also* categories
          633.0–633.9) 639.0
        molar pregnancy (*see also* categories
          630–632) 639.0
      following
        abortion 639.0
        ectopic or molar pregnancy 639.0
      puerperal, postpartum, childbirth
        670.8 ☑   ▲
    glossitis 529.0
    gum 523.8
    hernia — *see* Hernia, by site, with gangrene
    hospital noma 528.1
    intestine, intestinal (acute) (hemorrhagic)
      (massive) 557.0
      with
        hernia — *see* Hernia, by site, with gan-
          grene
        mesenteric embolism or infarction
          557.0
        obstruction (*see also* Obstruction, intes-
          tine) 560.9
    laryngitis 464.00
      with obstruction 464.01
    liver 573.8
    lung 513.0
      spirochetal 104.8
    lymphangitis 457.2
    Meleney's (cutaneous) 686.09
    mesentery 557.0
      with
        embolism or infarction 557.0

Gangrene, gangrenous — *continued*
    mesentery — *continued*
      with — *continued*
        intestinal obstruction (*see also* Obstruc-
          tion, intestine) 560.9
    mouth 528.1
    noma 528.1
    orchitis 604.90
    ovary (*see also* Salpingo-oophoritis) 614.2
    pancreas 577.0
    penis (infectional) 607.2
      noninfective 607.89
    perineum 785.4
    pharynx 462
    pneumonia 513.0
    Pott's 440.24
    presenile 443.1
    pulmonary 513.0
    pulp, tooth 522.1
    quinsy 475
    Raynaud's (symmetric gangrene) 443.0 *[785.4]*
    rectum 569.49
    retropharyngeal 478.24
    rupture — *see* Hernia, by site, with gangrene
    scrotum 608.4
      noninfective 608.83
    senile 440.24
    septic 034.0
    septic 034.0
    sore throat 462
    spermatic cord 608.4
      noninfective 608.89
    spine 785.4
    spirochetal NEC 104.8
    spreading cutaneous 785.4
    stomach 537.89
    stomatitis 528.1
    symmetrical 443.0 *[785.4]*
    testis (infectional) (*see also* Orchitis) 604.99
      noninfective 608.89
    throat 462
      diphtheritic 032.0
    thyroid (gland) 246.8
    tonsillitis (acute) 463
    tooth (pulp) 522.1
    tuberculous NEC (*see also* Tuberculosis)
      011.9 ☑
    tunica vaginalis 608.4
      noninfective 608.89
    umbilicus 785.4
    uterus (*see also* Endometritis) 615.9
    uvulitis 528.3
    vas deferens 608.4
      noninfective 608.89
    vulva (*see also* Vulvitis) 616.10
Gannister disease (occupational) 502
    with tuberculosis — *see* Tuberculosis, pul-
      monary
Ganser's syndrome, hysterical 300.16
Gardner-Diamond syndrome (autoerythrocyte
    sensitization) 287.2
Gargoylism 277.5
Garré's
    disease (*see also* Osteomyelitis) 730.1 ☑
    osteitis (sclerosing) (*see also* Osteomyelitis)
      730.1 ☑
    osteomyelitis (*see also* Osteomyelitis) 730.1 ☑
Garrod's pads, knuckle 728.79
Gartner's duct
    cyst 752.41
    persistent 752.41
Gas 787.3
    asphyxia, asphyxiation, inhalation, poisoning,
      suffocation NEC 987.9
      specified gas — *see* Table of Drugs and
        Chemicals
    bacillus gangrene or infection — *see* Gas,
      gangrene
    cyst, mesentery 568.89
    excessive 787.3
    gangrene 040.0
      with
        abortion — *see* Abortion, by type, with
          sepsis
        ectopic pregnancy (*see also* categories
          633.0–633.9) 639.0

Gas — *continued*
    gangrene — *continued*
      with — *continued*
        molar pregnancy (*see also* categories
          630–632) 639.0
      following
        abortion 639.0
        ectopic or molar pregnancy 639.0
      puerperal, postpartum, childbirth
        670.8 ☑   ▲
    on stomach 787.3
    pains 787.3
Gastradenitis 535.0 ☑
Gastralgia 536.8
    psychogenic 307.89
Gastrectasis, gastrectasia 536.1
    psychogenic 306.4
Gastric — *see* condition
Gastrinoma (M8153/1)
    malignant (M8153/3)
      pancreas 157.4
      specified site NEC — *see* Neoplasm, by site,
        malignant
      unspecified site 157.4
    specified site — *see* Neoplasm, by site, uncer-
      tain behavior
    unspecified site 235.5
Gastritis 535.5 ☑

> *Note* — *Use the following fifth-digit subclas-*
> *sification for category 535:*
>
> *0*   *without mention of hemorrhage*
>
> *1*   *with hemorrhage*

    acute 535.0 ☑
    alcoholic 535.3 ☑
    allergic 535.4 ☑
    antral 535.4 ☑
    atrophic 535.1 ☑
    atrophic-hyperplastic 535.1 ☑
    bile-induced 535.4 ☑
    catarrhal 535.0 ☑
    chronic (atrophic) 535.1 ☑
    cirrhotic 535.4 ☑
    corrosive (acute) 535.4 ☑
    dietetic 535.4 ☑
    due to diet deficiency 269.9 *[535.4]* ☑
    eosinophilic 535.7 ☑
    erosive 535.4 ☑
    follicular 535.4 ☑
      chronic 535.1 ☑
    giant hypertrophic 535.2 ☑
    glandular 535.4 ☑
      chronic 535.1 ☑
    hypertrophic (mucosa) 535.2 ☑
      chronic giant 211.1
    irritant 535.4 ☑
    nervous 306.4
    phlegmonous 535.0 ☑
    psychogenic 306.4
    sclerotic 535.4 ☑
    spastic 536.8
    subacute 535.0 ☑
    superficial 535.4 ☑
    suppurative 535.0 ☑
    toxic 535.4 ☑
    tuberculous (*see also* Tuberculosis) 017.9 ☑
Gastrocarcinoma (M8010/3) 151.9
Gastrocolic — *see* condition
Gastrocolitis — *see* Enteritis
Gastrodisciasis 121.8
Gastroduodenitis — *see also* Gastritis 535.5 ☑
    catarrhal 535.0 ☑
    infectional 535.0 ☑
    virus, viral 008.8
      specified type NEC 008.69
Gastrodynia 536.8
Gastroenteritis (acute) (catarrhal) (congestive)
    (hemorrhagic) (noninfectious) — *see also*
    Enteritis 558.9
    aertrycke infection 003.0
    allergic 558.3
    chronic 558.9
      ulcerative (*see also* Colitis, ulcerative) 556.9
    dietetic 558.9

☑ Additional Digit Required — Refer to the Tabular List for Digit Selection   ▽ Subterms under main terms may continue to next column or page

Gastroenteritis — see also Enteritis — continued
 due to
  antineoplastic chemotherapy 558.9
  food poisoning (see also Poisoning, food) 005.9
  radiation 558.1
 eosinophilic 558.41
 epidemic 009.0
 functional 558.9
 infectious (see also Enteritis, due to, by organism) 009.0
  presumed 009.1
 salmonella 003.0
 septic (see also Enteritis, due to, by organism) 009.0
 toxic 558.2
 tuberculous (see also Tuberculosis) 014.8 ☑
 ulcerative (see also Colitis, ulcerative) 556.9
 viral NEC 008.8
  specified type NEC 008.69
 zymotic 009.0
Gastroenterocolitis — see Enteritis
Gastroenteropathy, protein-losing 579.8
Gastroenteroptosis 569.89
Gastroesophageal laceration-hemorrhage syndrome 530.7
Gastroesophagitis 530.19
Gastrohepatitis — see also Gastritis 535.5 ☑
Gastrointestinal — see condition
Gastrojejunal — see condition
Gastrojejunitis — see also Gastritis 535.5 ☑
Gastrojejunocolic — see condition
Gastroliths 537.89
Gastromalacia 537.89
Gastroparalysis 536.3
 diabetic 250.6 ☑ [536.3]
  due to secondary diabetes 249.6 ☑ [536.3]
Gastroparesis 536.3
 diabetic 250.6 ☑ [536.3]
  due to secondary diabetes 249.6 ☑ [536.3]
Gastropathy 537.9
 congestive portal 537.89
 erythematous 535.5 ☑
 exudative 579.8
 portal hypertensive 537.89
Gastroptosis 537.5
Gastrorrhagia 578.0
Gastrorrhea 536.8
 psychogenic 306.4
Gastroschisis (congenital) 756.73 ▲
 acquired 569.89
Gastrospasm (neurogenic) (reflex) 536.8
 neurotic 306.4
 psychogenic 306.4
Gastrostaxis 578.0
Gastrostenosis 537.89
Gastrostomy
 attention to V55.1
 complication 536.40
  specified type 536.49
 infection 536.41
 malfunctioning 536.42
 status V44.1
Gastrosuccorrhea (continuous) (intermittent) 536.8
 neurotic 306.4
 psychogenic 306.4
Gaucher's
 disease (adult) (cerebroside lipidosis) (infantile) 272.7
 hepatomegaly 272.7
 splenomegaly (cerebroside lipidosis) 272.7
GAVE (gastric antral vascular ectasia) 537.82
 with hemorrhage 537.83
 without hemorrhage 537.82
Gayet's disease (superior hemorrhagic polioencephalitis) 265.1
Gayet-Wernicke's syndrome (superior hemorrhagic polioencephalitis) 265.1
Gee (-Herter) (-Heubner) (-Thaysen) disease or syndrome (nontropical sprue) 579.0
Gélineau's syndrome — see also Narcolepsy 347.00
Gemination, teeth 520.2

Gemistocytoma (M9411/3)
 specified site — see Neoplasm, by site, malignant
 unspecified site 191.9
General, generalized — see condtion
Genetic
 susceptibility to
  MEN (multiple endocrine neoplasia) V84.81
  neoplasia
   multiple endocrine [MEN] V84.81
  neoplasm
   malignant, of
    breast V84.01
    endometrium V84.04
    other V84.09
    ovary V84.02
    prostate V84.03
  specified disease NEC V84.89
Genital — see condition
 warts 078.11
Genito-anorectal syndrome 099.1
Genitourinary system — see condition
Genu
 congenital 755.64
 extrorsum (acquired) 736.42
  congenital 755.64
  late effects of rickets 268.1
 introrsum (acquired) 736.41
  congenital 755.64
  late effects of rickets 268.1
 rachitic (old) 268.1
 recurvatum (acquired) 736.5
  congenital 754.40
   with dislocation of knee 754.41
  late effects of rickets 268.1
 valgum (acquired) (knock-knee) 736.41
  congenital 755.64
  late effects of rickets 268.1
 varum (acquired) (bowleg) 736.42
  congenital 755.64
  late effect of rickets 268.1
Geographic tongue 529.1
Geophagia 307.52
Geotrichosis 117.9
 intestine 117.9
 lung 117.9
 mouth 117.9
Gephyrophobia 300.29
Gerbode defect 745.4
GERD (gastroesophageal reflux disease) 530.81
Gerhardt's
 disease (erythromelalgia) 443.82
 syndrome (vocal cord paralysis) 478.30
Gerlier's disease (epidemic vertigo) 078.81
German measles 056.9
 exposure to V01.4
Germinoblastoma (diffuse) (M9614/3) 202.8 ☑
 follicular (M9692/3) 202.0 ☑
Germinoma (M9064/3) — see Neoplasm, by site, malignant
Gerontoxon 371.41
Gerstmann-Sträussler-Scheinker syndrome (GSS) 046.71
Gerstmann's syndrome (finger agnosia) 784.69
Gestation (period) — see also Pregnancy
 ectopic NEC (see also Pregnancy, ectopic) 633.90
  with intrauterine pregnancy 633.91
Gestational proteinuria 646.2 ☑
 with hypertension — see Toxemia, of pregnancy
Ghon tubercle primary infection — see also Tuberculosis 010.0 ☑
Ghost
 teeth 520.4
 vessels, cornea 370.64
Ghoul hand 102.3
Gianotti Crosti syndrome 057.8
 due to known virus — see Infection, virus
 due to unknown virus 057.8
Giant
 cell
  epulis 523.8
  peripheral (gingiva) 523.8
  tumor, tendon sheath 727.02
 colon (congenital) 751.3

Giant — continued
 esophagus (congenital) 750.4
 kidney 753.3
 urticaria 995.1
  hereditary 277.6
Giardia lamblia infestation 007.1
Giardiasis 007.1
Gibert's disease (pityriasis rosea) 696.3
Gibraltar fever — see Brucellosis
Giddiness 780.4
 hysterical 300.11
 psychogenic 306.9
Gierke's disease (glycogenosis I) 271.0
Gigantism (cerebral) (hypophyseal) (pituitary) 253.0
Gilbert's disease or cholemia (familial non-hemolytic jaundice) 277.4
Gilchrist's disease (North American blastomycosis) 116.0
Gilford (-Hutchinson) disease or syndrome (progeria) 259.8
Gilles de la Tourette's disease (motor-verbal tic) 307.23
Gillespie's syndrome (dysplasia oculodentodigitalis) 759.89
Gingivitis 523.10
 acute 523.00
  necrotizing 101
  non-plaque induced 523.01
  plaque induced 523.00
 catarrhal 523.00
 chronic 523.10
  non-plaque induced 523.11
 desquamative 523.10
 expulsiva 523.40
 hyperplastic 523.10
 marginal, simple 523.10
 necrotizing, acute 101
 non-plaque induced 523.11
 pellagrous 265.2
 plaque induced 523.10
 ulcerative 523.10
  acute necrotizing 101
 Vincent's 101
Gingivoglossitis 529.0
Gingivopericementitis 523.40
Gingivosis 523.10
Gingivostomatitis 523.10
 herpetic 054.2
Giovannini's disease 117.9
GISA (glycopeptide intermediate staphylococcus aureus) V09.8 ☑
Glanders 024
Gland, glandular — see condition
Glanzmann (-Naegeli) disease or thrombasthenia 287.1
Glassblowers' disease 527.1
Glaucoma (capsular) (inflammatory) (noninflammatory) (primary) 365.9
 with increased episcleral venous pressure 365.82
 absolute 360.42
 acute 365.22
  narrow angle 365.22
  secondary 365.60
 angle closure 365.20
  acute 365.22
  chronic 365.23
  intermittent 365.21
  interval 365.21
  residual stage 365.24
  subacute 365.21
 borderline 365.00
 chronic 365.11
  noncongestive 365.11
  open angle 365.11
  simple 365.11
 closed angle — see Glaucoma, angle closure
 congenital 743.20
  associated with other eye anomalies 743.22
  simple 743.21
 congestive — see Glaucoma, narrow angle
 corticosteroid-induced (glaucomatous stage) 365.31
  residual stage 365.32

Glaucoma — continued
 hemorrhagic 365.60
 hypersecretion 365.81
 infantile 365.14
  congenital 743.20
   associated with other eye anomalies 743.22
   simple 743.21
 in or with
  aniridia 365.42
  Axenfeld's anomaly 365.41
  congenital syndromes NEC 759.89 [365.44]
  disorder of lens NEC 365.59
  inflammation, ocular 365.62   ●
  iris
   anomalies NEC 365.42
   atrophy, essential 365.42
   bombé 365.61
  microcornea 365.43
  neurofibromatosis 237.71 [365.44]
  ocular
   cysts NEC 365.64
   disorders NEC 365.60
   trauma 365.65
   tumors NEC 365.64
  pupillary block or seclusion 365.61
  Rieger's anomaly or syndrome 365.41
  seclusion of pupil 365.61
  Sturge-Weber (-Dimitri) syndrome 759.6 [365.44]
  systemic syndrome NEC 365.44
  tumor of globe 365.64
  vascular disorders NEC 365.63
 juvenile 365.14
 low tension 365.12
 malignant 365.83
 narrow angle (primary) 365.20
  acute 365.22
  chronic 365.23
  intermittent 365.21
  interval 365.21
  residual stage 365.24
  subacute 365.21
 newborn 743.20
  associated with other eye anomalies 743.22
  simple 743.21
 noncongestive (chronic) 365.11
 nonobstructive (chronic) 365.11
 obstructive 365.60
  due to lens changes 365.59
 open angle 365.10
  with
   borderline intraocular pressure 365.01
   cupping of optic discs 365.01
  primary 365.11
  residual stage 365.15
 phacolytic 365.51
 pigmentary 365.13
 postinfectious 365.60
 pseudoexfoliation 365.52
 secondary NEC 365.60
 simple (chronic) 365.11
 simplex 365.11
 steroid responders 365.03
 suspect 365.00
 syphilitic 095.8
 traumatic NEC 365.65
  newborn 767.8
 wide angle (see also Glaucoma, open angle) 365.10
Glaucomatous flecks (subcapsular) 366.31
Glazed tongue 529.4
Gleet 098.2
Glénard's disease or syndrome (enteroptosis) 569.89
Glinski-Simmonds syndrome (pituitary cachexia) 253.2
Glioblastoma (multiforme) (M9440/3)
 with sarcomatous component (M9442/3)
  specified site — see Neoplasm, by site, malignant
  unspecified site 191.9
 giant cell (M9441/3)
  specified site — see Neoplasm, by site, malignant

☑ Additional Digit Required — Refer to the Tabular List for Digit Selection   🔚 Subterms under main terms may continue to next column or page

Glioblastoma — continued
  giant cell — continued
    unspecified site 191.9
  specified site — see Neoplasm, by site, malignant
  unspecified site 191.9
Glioma (malignant) (M9380/3)
  astrocytic (M9400/3)
    specified site — see Neoplasm, by site, malignant
    unspecified site 191.9
  mixed (M9382/3)
    specified site — see Neoplasm, by site, malignant
    unspecified site 191.9
  nose 748.1
  specified site NEC — see Neoplasm, by site, malignant
  subependymal (M9383/1) 237.5
  unspecified site 191.9
Gliomatosis cerebri (M9381/3) 191.0
Glioneuroma (M9505/1) — see Neoplasm, by site, uncertain behavior
Gliosarcoma (M9380/3)
  specified site — see Neoplasm, by site, malignant
  unspecified site 191.9
Gliosis (cerebral) 349.89
  spinal 336.0
Glisson's
  cirrhosis — see Cirrhosis, portal
  disease (see also Rickets) 268.0
Glissonitis 573.3
Globinuria 791.2
Globus 306.4
  hystericus 300.11
Glomangioma (M8712/0) — see also Hemangioma 228.00
Glomangiosarcoma (M8710/3) — see Neoplasm, connective tissue, malignant
Glomerular nephritis — see also Nephritis 583.9
Glomerulitis — see also Nephritis 583.9
Glomerulonephritis — see also Nephritis 583.9
  with
    edema (see also Nephrosis) 581.9
    lesion of
      exudative nephritis 583.89
      interstitial nephritis (diffuse) (focal) 583.89
      necrotizing glomerulitis 583.4
        acute 580.4
        chronic 582.4
      renal necrosis 583.9
        cortical 583.6
        medullary 583.7
      specified pathology NEC 583.89
        acute 580.89
        chronic 582.89
    necrosis, renal 583.9
      cortical 583.6
      medullary (papillary) 583.7
    specified pathology or lesion NEC 583.89
  acute 580.9
    with
      exudative nephritis 580.89
      interstitial nephritis (diffuse) (focal) 580.89
      necrotizing glomerulitis 580.4
      extracapillary with epithelial crescents 580.4
      poststreptococcal 580.0
      proliferative (diffuse) 580.0
      rapidly progressive 580.4
      specified pathology NEC 580.89
  arteriolar (see also Hypertension, kidney) 403.90
  arteriosclerotic (see also Hypertension, kidney) 403.90
  ascending (see also Pyelitis) 590.80
  basement membrane NEC 583.89
    with
      pulmonary hemorrhage (Goodpasture's syndrome) 446.21 [583.81]
  chronic 582.9

Glomerulonephritis — see also Nephritis — continued
  chronic — continued
    with
      exudative nephritis 582.89
      interstitial nephritis (diffuse) (focal) 582.89
      necrotizing glomerulitis 582.4
      specified pathology or lesion NEC 582.89
    endothelial 582.2
    extracapillary with epithelial crescents 582.4
    hypocomplementemic persistent 582.2
    lobular 582.2
    membranoproliferative 582.2
    membranous 582.1
      and proliferative (mixed) 582.2
      sclerosing 582.1
    mesangiocapillary 582.2
    mixed membranous and proliferative 582.2
    proliferative (diffuse) 582.0
    rapidly progressive 582.4
    sclerosing 582.1
  cirrhotic — see Sclerosis, renal
  desquamative — see Nephrosis
  due to or associated with
    amyloidosis 277.39 [583.81]
      with nephrotic syndrome 277.39 [581.81]
      chronic 277.39 [582.81]
    diabetes mellitus 250.4 ☑ [583.81]
      with nephrotic syndrome 250.4 ☑ [581.81]
      due to secondary diabetes 249.4 ☑ [581.81]
      due to secondary diabetes 249.4 ☑ [581.81]
    diphtheria 032.89 [580.81]
    gonococcal infection (acute) 098.19 [583.81]
      chronic or duration of 2 months or over 098.39 [583.81]
    infectious hepatitis 070.9 [580.81]
    malaria (with nephrotic syndrome) 084.9 [581.81]
    mumps 072.79 [580.81]
    polyarteritis (nodosa) (with nephrotic syndrome) 446.0 [581.81]
    specified pathology NEC 583.89
      acute 580.89
      chronic 582.89
    streptotrichosis 039.8 [583.81]
    subacute bacterial endocarditis 421.0 [580.81]
    syphilis (late) 095.4
      congenital 090.5 [583.81]
      early 091.69 [583.81]
    systemic lupus erythematosus 710.0 [583.81]
      with nephrotic syndrome 710.0 [581.81]
      chronic 710.0 [582.81]
    tuberculosis (see also Tuberculosis) 016.0 ☑ [583.81]
    typhoid fever 002.0 [580.81]
  extracapillary with epithelial crescents 583.4
    acute 580.4
    chronic 582.4
  exudative 583.89
    acute 580.89
    chronic 582.89
  focal (see also Nephritis) 583.9
    embolic 580.4
  granular 582.89
  granulomatous 582.89
  hydremic (see also Nephrosis) 581.9
  hypocomplementemic persistent 583.2
    with nephrotic syndrome 581.2
    chronic 582.2
  immune complex NEC 583.89
  infective (see also Pyelitis) 590.80
  interstitial (diffuse) (focal) 583.89
    with nephrotic syndrome 581.89
    acute 580.89
    chronic 582.89

Glomerulonephritis — see also Nephritis — continued
  latent or quiescent 582.9
  lobular 583.2
    with nephrotic syndrome 581.2
    chronic 582.2
  membranoproliferative 583.2
    with nephrotic syndrome 581.2
    chronic 582.2
  membranous 583.1
    with nephrotic syndrome 581.1
    and proliferative (mixed) 583.2
      with nephrotic syndrome 581.2
      chronic 582.2
    chronic 582.1
    sclerosing 582.1
      with nephrotic syndrome 581.1
  mesangiocapillary 583.2
    with nephrotic syndrome 581.2
    chronic 582.2
  minimal change 581.3
  mixed membranous and proliferative 583.2
    with nephrotic syndrome 581.2
    chronic 582.2
  necrotizing 583.4
    acute 580.4
    chronic 582.4
  nephrotic (see also Nephrosis) 581.9
  old — see Glomerulonephritis, chronic
  parenchymatous 581.89
  poststreptococcal 580.0
  proliferative (diffuse) 583.0
    with nephrotic syndrome 581.0
    acute 580.0
    chronic 582.0
  purulent (see also Pyelitis) 590.80
  quiescent — see Nephritis, chronic
  rapidly progressive 583.4
    acute 580.4
    chronic 582.4
  sclerosing membranous (chronic) 582.1
    with nephrotic syndrome 581.1
  septic (see also Pyelitis) 590.80
  specified pathology or lesion NEC 583.89
    with nephrotic syndrome 581.89
    acute 580.89
    chronic 582.89
  suppurative (acute) (disseminated) (see also Pyelitis) 590.80
  toxic — see Nephritis, acute
  tubal, tubular — see Nephrosis, tubular
  type II (Ellis) — see Nephrosis
  vascular — see Hypertension, kidney
Glomerulosclerosis — see also Sclerosis, renal 587
  focal 582.1
    with nephrotic syndrome 581.1
  intercapillary (nodular) (with diabetes) 250.4 ☑ [581.81]
    due to secondary diabetes 249.4 ☑ [581.81]
Glossagra 529.6
Glossalgia 529.6
Glossitis 529.0
  areata exfoliativa 529.1
  atrophic 529.4
  benign migratory 529.1
  gangrenous 529.0
  Hunter's 529.4
  median rhomboid 529.2
  Moeller's 529.4
  pellagrous 265.2
Glossocele 529.8
Glossodynia 529.6
  exfoliativa 529.4
Glossoncus 529.8
Glossophytia 529.3
Glossoplegia 529.8
Glossoptosis 529.8
Glossopyrosis 529.6
Glossotrichia 529.3
Glossy skin 701.9
Glottis — see condition
Glottitis — see Glossitis

Glucagonoma (M8152/0)
  malignant (M8152/3)
    pancreas 157.4
    specified site NEC — see Neoplasm, by site, malignant
    unspecified site 157.4
  pancreas 211.7
  specified site NEC — see Neoplasm, by site, benign
  unspecified site 211.7
Glucoglycinuria 270.7
Glue ear syndrome 381.20
Glue sniffing (airplane glue) — see also Dependence 304.6 ☑
Glycinemia (with methylmalonic acidemia) 270.7
Glycinuria (renal) (with ketosis) 270.0
Glycogen
  infiltration (see also Disease, glycogen storage) 271.0
  storage disease (see also Disease, glycogen storage) 271.0
Glycogenosis — see also Disease, glycogen storage 271.0
  cardiac 271.0 [425.7]
  Cori, types I–VII 271.0
  diabetic, secondary 250.8 ☑ [259.8]
    due to secondary diabetes 249.8 ☑ [259.8]
  diffuse (with hepatic cirrhosis) 271.0
  generalized 271.0
  glucose-6-phosphatase deficiency 271.0
  hepatophosphorylase deficiency 271.0
  hepatorenal 271.0
  myophosphorylase deficiency 271.0
Glycopenia 251.2
Glycopeptide
  intermediate staphylococcus aureus (GISA) V09.8 ☑
  resistant
    enterococcus V09.8 ☑
    staphylococcus aureus (GRSA) V09.8 ☑
Glycoprolinuria 270.8
Glycosuria 791.5
  renal 271.4
Gnathostoma (spinigerum) (infection) (infestation) 128.1
  wandering swellings from 128.1
Gnathostomiasis 128.1
Goiter (adolescent) (colloid) (diffuse) (dipping) (due to iodine deficiency) (endemic) (euthyroid) (heart) (hyperplastic) (internal) (intrathoracic) (juvenile) (mixed type) (nonendemic) (parenchymatous) (plunging) (sporadic) (subclavicular) (substernal) 240.9
  with
    hyperthyroidism (recurrent) (see also Goiter, toxic) 242.0 ☑
    thyrotoxicosis (see also Goiter, toxic) 242.0 ☑
  adenomatous (see also Goiter, nodular) 241.9
  cancerous (M8000/3) 193
  complicating pregnancy, childbirth, or puerperium 648.1 ☑
  congenital 246.1
  cystic (see also Goiter, nodular) 241.9
  due to enzyme defect in synthesis of thyroid hormone (butane-insoluble iodine) (coupling) (deiodinase) (iodide trapping or organification) (iodotyrosine dehalogenase) (peroxidase) 246.1
  dyshormonogenic 246.1
  exophthalmic (see also Goiter, toxic) 242.0 ☑
  familial (with deaf-mutism) 243
  fibrous 245.3
  lingual 759.2
  lymphadenoid 245.2
  malignant (M8000/3) 193
  multinodular (nontoxic) 241.1
    toxic or with hyperthyroidism (see also Goiter, toxic) 242.2 ☑
  nodular (nontoxic) 241.9
    with
      hyperthyroidism (see also Goiter, toxic) 242.3 ☑
      thyrotoxicosis (see also Goiter, toxic) 242.3 ☑

☑ Additional Digit Required — Refer to the Tabular List for Digit Selection   ◤ Subterms under main terms may continue to next column or page

2010 ICD-9-CM   ▶◀ Revised Text   ● New Line   ▲ Revised Code   **Volume 2 — 125**

Goiter — continued
  nodular — continued
    endemic 241.9
    exophthalmic (diffuse) (see also Goiter, toxic) 242.0 ☑
    multinodular (nontoxic) 241.1
    sporadic 241.9
    toxic (see also Goiter, toxic) 242.3 ☑
    uninodular (nontoxic) 241.0
  nontoxic (nodular) 241.9
    multinodular 241.1
    uninodular 241.0
  pulsating (see also Goiter, toxic) 242.0 ☑
  simple 240.0
  toxic 242.0 ☑

> Note — Use the following fifth-digit subclassification with category 242:
>
> 0   without mention of thyrotoxic crisis or storm
>
> 1   with mention of thyrotoxic crisis or storm

  adenomatous 242.3 ☑
    multinodular 242.2 ☑
    uninodular 242.1 ☑
  multinodular 242.2 ☑
  nodular 242.3 ☑
    multinodular 242.2 ☑
    uninodular 242.1 ☑
  uninodular 242.1 ☑
  uninodular (nontoxic) 241.0
    toxic or with hyperthyroidism (see also Goiter, toxic) 242.1 ☑
Goldberg (-Maxwell) (-Morris) syndrome (testicular feminization) 259.51
Goldblatt's
  hypertension 440.1
  kidney 440.1
Goldenhar's syndrome (oculoauriculovertebral dysplasia) 756.0
Goldflam-Erb disease or syndrome 358.00
Goldscheider's disease (epidermolysis bullosa) 757.39
Goldstein's disease (familial hemorrhagic telangiectasia) 448.0
Golfer's elbow 726.32
Goltz-Gorlin syndrome (dermal hypoplasia) 757.39
Gonadoblastoma (M9073/1)
  specified site — see Neoplasm, by site uncertain behavior
  unspecified site
    female 236.2
    male 236.4
Gonecystitis — see also Vesiculitis 608.0
Gongylonemiasis 125.6
  mouth 125.6
Goniosynechiae 364.73
Gonococcemia 098.89
Gonococcus, gonococcal (disease) (infection) — see also condition 098.0
  anus 098.7
  bursa 098.52
  chronic NEC 098.2
  complicating pregnancy, childbirth, or puerperium 647.1 ☑
    affecting fetus or newborn 760.2
  conjunctiva, conjunctivitis (neonatorum) 098.40
  dermatosis 098.89
  endocardium 098.84
  epididymo-orchitis 098.13
    chronic or duration of 2 months or over 098.33
  eye (newborn) 098.40
  fallopian tube (chronic) 098.37
    acute 098.17
  genitourinary (acute) (organ) (system) (tract) (see also Gonorrhea) 098.0
    lower 098.0
      chronic 098.2
    upper 098.10
      chronic 098.30
  heart NEC 098.85
  joint 098.50

Gonococcus, gonococcal — see also condition — continued
  keratoderma 098.81
  keratosis (blennorrhagica) 098.81
  lymphatic (gland) (node) 098.89
  meninges 098.82
  orchitis (acute) 098.13
    chronic or duration of 2 months or over 098.33
  pelvis (acute) 098.19
    chronic or duration of 2 months or over 098.39
  pericarditis 098.83
  peritonitis 098.86
  pharyngitis 098.6
  pharynx 098.6
  proctitis 098.7
  pyosalpinx (chronic) 098.37
    acute 098.17
  rectum 098.7
  septicemia 098.89
  skin 098.89
  specified site NEC 098.89
  synovitis 098.51
  tendon sheath 098.51
  throat 098.6
  urethra (acute) 098.0
    chronic or duration of 2 months or over 098.2
  vulva (acute) 098.0
    chronic or duration of 2 months or over 098.2
Gonocytoma (M9073/1)
  specified site — see Neoplasm, by site, uncertain behavior
  unspecified site
    female 236.2
    male 236.4
Gonorrhea 098.0
  acute 098.0
  Bartholin's gland (acute) 098.0
    chronic or duration of 2 months or over 098.2
  bladder (acute) 098.11
    chronic or duration of 2 months or over 098.31
  carrier (suspected of) V02.7
  cervix (acute) 098.15
    chronic or duration of 2 months or over 098.35
  chronic 098.2
  complicating pregnancy, childbirth, or puerperium 647.1 ☑
    affecting fetus or newborn 760.2
  conjunctiva, conjunctivitis (neonatorum) 098.40
  contact V01.6
  Cowper's gland (acute) 098.0
    chronic or duration of 2 months or over 098.2
  duration of two months or over 098.2
  exposure to V01.6
  fallopian tube (chronic) 098.37
    acute 098.17
  genitourinary (acute) (organ) (system) (tract) 098.0
    chronic 098.2
    duration of two months or over 098.2
  kidney (acute) 098.19
    chronic or duration of 2 months or over 098.39
  ovary (acute) 098.19
    chronic or duration of 2 months or over 098.39
  pelvis (acute) 098.19
    chronic or duration of 2 months or over 098.39
  penis (acute) 098.0
    chronic or duration of 2 months or over 098.2
  prostate (acute) 098.12
    chronic or duration of 2 months or over 098.32
  seminal vesicle (acute) 098.14
    chronic or duration of 2 months or over 098.34

Gonorrhea — continued
  specified site NEC — see Gonococcus
  spermatic cord (acute) 098.14
    chronic or duration of 2 months or over 098.34
  urethra (acute) 098.0
    chronic or duration of 2 months or over 098.2
  vagina (acute) 098.0
    chronic or duration of 2 months or over 098.2
  vas deferens (acute) 098.14
    chronic or duration of 2 months or over 098.34
  vulva (acute) 098.0
    chronic or duration of 2 months or over 098.2
Goodpasture's syndrome (pneumorenal) 446.21
Good's syndrome 279.06
Gopalan's syndrome (burning feet) 266.2
Gordon's disease (exudative enteropathy) 579.8
Gorlin-Chaudhry-Moss syndrome 759.89
Gougerot-Blum syndrome (pigmented purpuric lichenoid dermatitis) 709.1
Gougerot-Carteaud disease or syndrome (confluent reticulate papillomatosis) 701.8
Gougerot-Hailey-Hailey disease (benign familial chronic pemphigus) 757.39
Gougerot (-Houwer) -Sjögren syndrome (keratoconjunctivitis sicca) 710.2
Gougerot's syndrome (trisymptomatic) 709.1
Gouley's syndrome (constrictive pericarditis) 423.2
Goundou 102.6
Gout, gouty 274.9
  with
    specified manifestations NEC 274.89 ●
    tophi (tophus) 274.03 ●
  acute 274.01
  arthritis 274.00 ▲
    acute 274.01 ●
  arthropathy 274.00 ▲
    acute 274.01 ●
    chronic (without mention of tophus (tophi)) 274.02 ●
      with tophus (tophi) 274.03 ●
  attack 274.01 ●
  chronic 274.02 ●
    tophaceous 274.03 ●
  degeneration, heart 274.82
  diathesis 274.9
  eczema 274.89
  episcleritis 274.89 [379.09]
  external ear (tophus) 274.81
  flare 274.01 ●
  glomerulonephritis 274.10
  iritis 274.89 [364.11]
  joint 274.00 ▲
  kidney 274.10
  lead 984.9
    specified type of lead — see Table of Drugs and Chemicals
  nephritis 274.10
  neuritis 274.89 [357.4]
  phlebitis 274.89 [451.9]
  rheumatic 714.0
  saturnine 984.9
    specified type of lead — see Table of Drugs and Chemicals
  spondylitis 274.00 ▲
  synovitis 274.00 ▲
  syphilitic 095.8
  tophi 274.03 ▲
    ear 274.81
    heart 274.82
    specified site NEC 274.82
Gowers'
  muscular dystrophy 359.1
  syndrome (vasovagal attack) 780.2
Gowers-Paton-Kennedy syndrome 377.04
Gradenigo's syndrome 383.02
Graft-versus-host disease 279.50
  due to organ transplant NEC — see Complications, transplant, organ

Graham Steell's murmur (pulmonic regurgitation) — see also Endocarditis, pulmonary 424.3
Grain-handlers' disease or lung 495.8
Grain mite (itch) 133.8
Grand
  mal (idiopathic) (see also Epilepsy) 345.1 ☑
    hysteria of Charcôt 300.11
    nonrecurrent or isolated 780.39
  multipara
    affecting management of labor and delivery 659.4 ☑
    status only (not pregnant) V61.5
Granite workers' lung 502
Granular — see also condition
  inflammation, pharynx 472.1
  kidney (contracting) (see also Sclerosis, renal) 587
  liver — see Cirrhosis, liver
  nephritis — see Nephritis
Granulation tissue, abnormal — see also Granuloma
  abnormal or excessive 701.5
  postmastoidectomy cavity 383.33
  postoperative 701.5
  skin 701.5
Granulocytopenia, granulocytopenic (primary) 288.00
  malignant 288.09
Granuloma NEC 686.1
  abdomen (wall) 568.89
    skin (pyogenicum) 686.1
      from residual foreign body 709.4
  annulare 695.89
  anus 569.49
  apical 522.6
  appendix 543.9
  aural 380.23
  beryllium (skin) 709.4
    lung 503
  bone (see also Osteomyelitis) 730.1 ☑
    eosinophilic 277.89
    from residual foreign body 733.99
  canaliculus lacrimalis 375.81
  cerebral 348.89   ▲
  cholesterin, middle ear 385.82
  coccidioidal (progressive) 114.3
    lung 114.4
    meninges 114.2
    primary (lung) 114.0
  colon 569.89
  conjunctiva 372.61
  dental 522.6
  ear, middle (cholesterin) 385.82
    with otitis media — see Otitis media
  eosinophilic 277.89
    bone 277.89
    lung 277.89
    oral mucosa 528.9
  exuberant 701.5
  eyelid 374.89
  facial
    lethal midline 446.3
    malignant 446.3
  faciale 701.8
  fissuratum (gum) 523.8
  foot NEC 686.1
  foreign body (in soft tissue) NEC 728.82
    bone 733.99
    in operative wound 998.4
    muscle 728.82
    skin 709.4
    subcutaneous tissue 709.4
  fungoides 202.1 ☑
  gangraenescens 446.3
  giant cell (central) (jaw) (reparative) 526.3
    gingiva 523.8
    peripheral (gingiva) 523.8
  gland (lymph) 289.3
  Hodgkin's (M9661/3) 201.1 ☑
  ileum 569.89
  infectious NEC 136.9
  inguinale (Donovan) 099.2
    venereal 099.2
  intestine 569.89
  iridocyclitis 364.10

☑ Additional Digit Required — Refer to the Tabular List for Digit Selection   ▼ Subterms under main terms may continue to next column or page

Granuloma — *continued*
  jaw (bone) 526.3
    reparative giant cell 526.3
  kidney (*see also* Infection, kidney) 590.9
  lacrimal sac 375.81
  larynx 478.79
  lethal midline 446.3
  lipid 277.89
  lipoid 277.89
  liver 572.8
  lung (infectious) (*see also* Fibrosis, lung) 515
    coccidioidal 114.4
    eosinophilic 277.89
  lymph gland 289.3
  Majocchi's 110.6
  malignant, face 446.3
  mandible 526.3
  mediastinum 519.3
  midline 446.3
  monilial 112.3
  muscle 728.82
    from residual foreign body 728.82
  nasal sinus (*see also* Sinusitis) 473.9
  operation wound 998.59
    foreign body 998.4
    stitch (external) 998.89
      internal wound 998.89
    talc 998.7
  oral mucosa, eosinophilic or pyogenic 528.9
  orbit, orbital 376.11
  paracoccidioidal 116.1
  penis, venereal 099.2
  periapical 522.6
  peritoneum 568.89
    due to ova of helminths NEC (*see also* Helminthiasis) 128.9
  postmastoidectomy cavity 383.33
  postoperative — *see* Granuloma, operation wound
  prostate 601.8
  pudendi (ulcerating) 099.2
  pudendorum (ulcerative) 099.2
  pulp, internal (tooth) 521.49
  pyogenic, pyogenicum (skin) 686.1
    maxillary alveolar ridge 522.6
    oral mucosa 528.9
  rectum 569.49
  reticulohistiocytic 277.89
  rubrum nasi 705.89
  sarcoid 135
  Schistosoma 120.9
  septic (skin) 686.1
  silica (skin) 709.4
  sinus (accessory) (infectional) (nasal) (*see also* Sinusitis) 473.9
  skin (pyogenicum) 686.1
    from foreign body or material 709.4
  sperm 608.89
  spine
    syphilitic (epidural) 094.89
    tuberculous (*see also* Tuberculosis) 015.0 ☑ [730.88]
  stitch (postoperative) 998.89
    internal wound 998.89
  suppurative (skin) 686.1
  suture (postoperative) 998.89
    internal wound 998.89
  swimming pool 031.1
  talc 728.82
    in operation wound 998.7
  telangiectaticum (skin) 686.1
  tracheostomy 519.09
  trichophyticum 110.6
  tropicum 102.4
  umbilicus 686.1
    newborn 771.4
  urethra 599.84
  uveitis 364.10
  vagina 099.2
  venereum 099.2
  vocal cords 478.5
  Wegener's (necrotizing respiratory granulomatosis) 446.4
Granulomatosis NEC 686.1
  disciformis chronica et progressiva 709.3
  infantiseptica 771.2

Granulomatosis — *continued*
  lipoid 277.89
  lipophagic, intestinal 040.2
  miliary 027.0
  necrotizing, respiratory 446.4
  progressive, septic 288.1
  Wegener's (necrotizing respiratory) 446.4
Granulomatous tissue — *see* Granuloma
Granulosis rubra nasi 705.89
Graphite fibrosis (of lung) 503
Graphospasm 300.89
  organic 333.84
Grating scapula 733.99
Gravel (urinary) — *see also* Calculus 592.9
Graves' disease (exophthalmic goiter) — *see also* Goiter, toxic 242.0 ☑
Gravis — *see* condition
Grawitz's tumor (hypernephroma) (M8312/3) 189.0
Grayness, hair (premature) 704.3
  congenital 757.4
Gray or grey syndrome (chloramphenicol) (newborn) 779.4
Greenfield's disease 330.0
Green sickness 280.9
Greenstick fracture — *see* Fracture, by site
Greig's syndrome (hypertelorism) 756.0
Grief 309.0
Griesinger's disease — *see also* Ancylostomiasis 126.9
Grinders'
  asthma 502
  lung 502
  phthisis (*see also* Tuberculosis) 011.4 ☑
Grinding, teeth 306.8
Grip
  Dabney's 074.1
  devil's 074.1
Grippe, grippal — *see also* Influenza
  Balkan 083.0
  intestinal 487.8
  summer 074.8
Grippy cold 487.1
Grisel's disease 723.5
Groin — *see* condition
Grooved
  nails (transverse) 703.8
  tongue 529.5
    congenital 750.13
Ground itch 126.9
Growing pains, children 781.99
Growth (fungoid) (neoplastic) (new) (M8000/1) — *see also* Neoplasm, by site, unspecified nature
  adenoid (vegetative) 474.12
  benign (M8000/0) — *see* Neoplasm, by site, benign
  fetal, poor 764.9 ☑
    affecting management of pregnancy 656.5 ☑
  malignant (M8000/3) — *see* Neoplasm, by site, malignant
  rapid, childhood V21.0
  secondary (M8000/6) — *see* Neoplasm, by site, malignant, secondary
GRSA (glycopeptide resistant staphylococcus aureus) V09.8 ☑
Gruber's hernia — *see* Hernia, Gruber's
Gruby's disease (tinea tonsurans) 110.0
GSS (Gerstmann-Sträussler-Scheinker syndrome) 046.71
G-trisomy 758.0
Guama fever 066.3
Gubler (-Millard) paralysis or syndrome 344.89
Guérin-Stern syndrome (arthrogryposis multiplex congenita) 754.89
Guertin's disease (electric chorea) 049.8
Guillain-Barré disease or syndrome 357.0
Guinea worms (infection) (infestation) 125.7
Guinon's disease (motor-verbal tic) 307.23
Gull and Sutton's disease — *see* Hypertension, kidney
Gull's disease (thyroid atrophy with myxedema) 244.8
Gum — *see* condition
Gumboil 522.7

Gumma (syphilitic) 095.9
  artery 093.89
    cerebral or spinal 094.89
  bone 095.5
    of yaws (late) 102.6
  brain 094.89
  cauda equina 094.89
  central nervous system NEC 094.9
  ciliary body 095.8 [364.11]
  congenital 090.5
    testis 090.5
  eyelid 095.8 [373.5]
  heart 093.89
  intracranial 094.89
  iris 095.8 [364.11]
  kidney 095.4
  larynx 095.8
  leptomeninges 094.2
  liver 095.3
  meninges 094.2
  myocardium 093.82
  nasopharynx 095.8
  neurosyphilitic 094.9
  nose 095.8
  orbit 095.8
  palate (soft) 095.8
  penis 095.8
  pericardium 093.81
  pharynx 095.8
  pituitary 095.8
  scrofulous (see also Tuberculosis) 017.0 ☑
  skin 095.8
  specified site NEC 095.8
  spinal cord 094.89
  tongue 095.8
  tonsil 095.8
  trachea 095.8
  tuberculous (*see also* Tuberculosis) 017.0 ☑
  ulcerative due to yaws 102.4
  ureter 095.8
  yaws 102.4
    bone 102.6
Gunn's syndrome (jaw-winking syndrome) 742.8
Gunshot wound — *see also* Wound, open, by site
  fracture — *see* Fracture, by site, open
  internal organs (abdomen, chest, or pelvis) — *see* Injury, internal, by site, with open wound
  intracranial — *see* Laceration, brain, with open intracranial wound
Günther's disease or syndrome (congenital erythropoietic porphyria) 277.1
Gustatory hallucination 780.1
Gynandrism 752.7
Gynandroblastoma (M8632/1)
  specified site — *see* Neoplasm, by site, uncertain behavior
  unspecified site
    female 236.2
    male 236.4
Gynandromorphism 752.7
Gynatresia (congenital) 752.49
Gynecoid pelvis, male 738.6
Gynecological examination V72.31
  for contraceptive maintenance V25.40
Gynecomastia 611.1
Gynephobia 300.29
Gyrate scalp 757.39

H

Haas' disease (osteochondrosis head of humerus) 732.3
Habermann's disease (acute parapsoriasis varioliformis) 696.2
Habit, habituation
  chorea 307.22
  disturbance, child 307.9
  drug (*see also* Dependence) 304.9 ☑
  laxative (*see also* Abuse, drugs, nondependent) 305.9 ☑
  spasm 307.20
    chronic 307.22
    transient (of childhood) 307.21
  tic 307.20
    chronic 307.22

Habit, habituation — *continued*
  tic — *continued*
    transient (of childhood) 307.21
  use of
    nonprescribed drugs (*see also* Abuse, drugs, nondependent) 305.9 ☑
    patent medicines (*see also* Abuse, drugs, nondependent) 305.9 ☑
  vomiting 536.2
Hadfield-Clarke syndrome (pancreatic infantilism) 577.8
Haff disease 985.1
Hageman factor defect, deficiency, or disease — *see also* Defect, coagulation 286.3
Haglund's disease (osteochondrosis os tibiale externum) 732.5
Haglund-Läwen-Fründ syndrome 717.89
Hagner's disease (hypertrophic pulmonary osteoarthropathy) 731.2
Hag teeth, tooth 524.39
Hailey-Hailey disease (benign familial chronic pemphigus) 757.39
Hair — *see also* condition
  plucking 307.9
Hairball in stomach 935.2
Hairy black tongue 529.3
Half vertebra 756.14
Halitosis 784.99
Hallermann-Streiff syndrome 756.0
Hallervorden-Spatz disease or syndrome 333.0
Hallopeau's
  acrodermatitis (continua) 696.1
  disease (lichen sclerosis et atrophicus) 701.0
Hallucination (auditory) (gustatory) (olfactory) (tactile) 780.1
  alcohol-induced 291.3
  drug-induced 292.12
  visual 368.16
Hallucinosis 298.9
  alcohol-induced (acute) 291.3
  drug-induced 292.12
Hallus — *see* Hallux
Hallux 735.9
  limitus 735.8
  malleus (acquired) 735.3
  rigidus (acquired) 735.2
    congenital 755.66
    late effects of rickets 268.1
  valgus (acquired) 735.0
    congenital 755.66
  varus (acquired) 735.1
    congenital 755.66
Halo, visual 368.15
Hamartoblastoma 759.6
Hamartoma 759.6
  epithelial (gingival), odontogenic, central, or peripheral (M9321/0) 213.1
  upper jaw (bone) 213.0
  vascular 757.32
Hamartosis, hamartoses NEC 759.6
Hamman's disease or syndrome (spontaneous mediastinal emphysema) 518.1
Hamman-Rich syndrome (diffuse interstitial pulmonary fibrosis) 516.3
Hammer toe (acquired) 735.4
  congenital 755.66
  late effects of rickets 268.1
Hand — *see* condition
Hand-foot syndrome 693.0
Hand-Schüller-Christian disease or syndrome (chronic histiocytosis x) 277.89
Hanging (asphyxia) (strangulation) (suffocation) 994.7
Hangnail (finger) (with lymphangitis) 681.02
Hangover (alcohol) — *see also* Abuse, drugs, nondependent 305.0 ☑
Hanot-Chauffard (-Troisier) syndrome (bronze diabetes) 275.0
Hanot's cirrhosis or disease — *see* Cirrhosis, biliary
Hansen's disease (leprosy) 030.9
  benign form 030.1
  malignant form 030.0
Harada's disease or syndrome 363.22
Hard chancre 091.0

☑ Additional Digit Required — Refer to the Tabular List for Digit Selection   ▽ Subterms under main terms may continue to next column or page

2010 ICD-9-CM   ►◄ Revised Text   ● New Line   ▲ Revised Code   Volume 2 — 127

Hardening
  artery — see Arteriosclerosis
  brain 348.89 ▲
  liver 571.8
Hard firm prostate 600.10
  with
    urinary
      obstruction 600.11
      retention 600.11
Harelip — see also Cleft, lip 749.10
Hare's syndrome (M8010/3) (carcinoma, pul-
    monary apex) 162.3
Harkavy's syndrome 446.0
Harlequin (fetus) 757.1
  color change syndrome 779.89
Harley's disease (intermittent hemoglobinuria)
    283.2
Harris'
  lines 733.91
  syndrome (organic hyperinsulinism) 251.1
Hart's disease or syndrome (pellagra-cerebellar
    ataxia-renal aminoaciduria) 270.0
Hartmann's pouch (abnormal sacculation of
    gallbladder neck) 575.8
  of intestine V44.3
    attention to V55.3
Hartnup disease (pellagra-cerebellar ataxia-renal
    aminoaciduria) 270.0
Harvester lung 495.0
Hashimoto's disease or struma (struma lym-
    phomatosa) 245.2
Hassall-Henle bodies (corneal warts) 371.41
Haut mal — see also Epilepsy 345.1 ☑
Haverhill fever 026.1
Hawaiian wood rose dependence 304.5 ☑
Hawkins' keloid 701.4
Hay
  asthma (see also Asthma) 493.0 ☑
  fever (allergic) (with rhinitis) 477.9
    with asthma (bronchial) (see also Asthma)
      493.0 ☑
    allergic, due to grass, pollen, ragweed, or
      tree 477.0
    conjunctivitis 372.05
    due to
      dander, animal (cat) (dog) 477.2
      dust 477.8
      fowl 477.8
      hair, animal (cat) (dog) 477.2
      pollen 477.0
      specified allergen other than pollen
        477.8
Hayem-Faber syndrome (achlorhydric anemia)
    280.9
Hayem-Widal syndrome (acquired hemolytic
    jaundice) 283.9
Haygarth's nodosities 715.04
Hazard-Crile tumor (M8350/3) 193
Hb (abnormal)
  disease — see Disease, hemoglobin
  trait — see Trait
H disease 270.0
Head — see also condition
  banging 307.3
Headache 784.0
  allergic 339.00
  associated with sexual activity 339.82
  cluster 339.00
    chronic 339.02
    episodic 339.01
  daily
    chronic 784.0
    new persistent (NPDH) 339.42
  drug induced 339.3
  due to
    loss, spinal fluid 349.0
    lumbar puncture 349.0
    saddle block 349.0 .
  emotional 307.81
  histamine 339.00
  hypnic 339.81
  lumbar puncture 349.0
  medication overuse 339.3
  menopausal 627.2
  menstrual 346.4 ☑
  migraine 346.9 ☑

Headache — continued
  nasal septum 784.0
  nonorganic origin 307.81
  orgasmic 339.82
  postspinal 349.0
  post-traumatic 339.20
    acute 339.21
    chronic 339.22
  premenstrual 346.4 ☑
  preorgasmic 339.82
  primary
    cough 339.83
    exertional 339.84
    stabbing 339.85
    thunderclap 339.43
  psychogenic 307.81
  psychophysiologic 307.81
  rebound 339.3
  short lasting unilateral neuralgiform with
    conjunctival injection and tearing
    (SUNCT) 339.05
  sick 346.9 ☑
  spinal 349.0
    complicating labor and delivery 668.8 ☑
    postpartum 668.8 ☑
  spinal fluid loss 349.0
  syndrome
    cluster 339.00
    complicated NEC 339.44
    periodic in child or adolescent 346.2 ☑
    specified NEC 339.89
  tension 307.81
    type 339.10
      chronic 339.12
      episodic 339.11
  vascular 784.0
    migraine type 346.9 ☑
  vasomotor 346.9 ☑
Health
  advice V65.4 ☑
  audit V70.0
  checkup V70.0
  education V65.4 ☑
  hazard (see also History of) V15.9
    falling V15.88
    specified cause NEC V15.89
  instruction V65.4 ☑
  services provided because (of)
    boarding school residence V60.6
    holiday relief for person providing home
      care V60.5
    inadequate
      housing V60.1
      resources V60.2
    lack of housing V60.0
    no care available in home V60.4
    person living alone V60.3
    poverty V60.3
    residence in institution V60.6
    specified cause NEC V60.89 ▲
    vacation relief for person providing home
      care V60.5
Healthy
  donor (see also Donor) V59.9
  infant or child
    accompanying sick mother V65.0
    receiving care V20.1
  person
    accompanying sick relative V65.0
    admitted for sterilization V25.2
    receiving prophylactic inoculation or vac-
      cination (see also Vaccination, pro-
      phylactic) V05.9
Hearing
  conservation and treatment V72.12
  examination V72.19
    following failed hearing screening V72.11
Heart — see condition
Heartburn 787.1
  psychogenic 306.4
Heat (effects) 992.9
  apoplexy 992.0
  burn (see also Burn, by site)
    from sun (see also Sunburn) 692.71
  collapse 992.1
  cramps 992.2

Heat — continued
  dermatitis or eczema 692.89
  edema 992.7
  erythema — see Burn, by site
  excessive 992.9
    specified effect NEC 992.8
  exhaustion 992.5
    anhydrotic 992.3
    due to
      salt (and water) depletion 992.4
      water depletion 992.3
  fatigue (transient) 992.6
  fever 992.0
  hyperpyrexia 992.0
  prickly 705.1
  prostration — see Heat, exhaustion
  pyrexia 992.0
  rash 705.1
  specified effect NEC 992.8
  stroke 992.0
  sunburn (see also Sunburn) 692.71
  syncope 992.1
Heavy-chain disease 273.2
Heavy-for-dates (fetus or infant) 766.1
  4500 grams or more 766.0
  exceptionally 766.0
Hebephrenia, hebephrenic (acute) — see also
    Schizophrenia 295.1 ☑
  dementia (praecox) (see also Schizophrenia)
    295.1 ☑
  schizophrenia (see also Schizophrenia)
    295.1 ☑
Heberden's
  disease or nodes 715.04
  syndrome (angina pectoris) 413.9
Hebra's disease
  dermatitis exfoliativa 695.89
  erythema multiforme exudativum 695.19
  pityriasis 695.89
    maculata et circinata 696.3
    rubra 695.89
      pilaris 696.4
  prurigo 698.2
Hebra, nose 040.1
Hedinger's syndrome (malignant carcinoid)
    259.2
Heel — see condition
Heerfordt's disease or syndrome (uveoparotitis)
    135
Hegglin's anomaly or syndrome 288.2
Heidenhain's disease 290.10
  with dementia 290.10
Heilmeyer-Schöner disease (M9842/3) 207.1 ☑
Heine-Medin disease — see also Poliomyelitis
    045.9 ☑
Heinz-body anemia, congenital 282.7
Heller's disease or syndrome (infantile psy-
    chosis) — see also Psychosis, childhood
    299.1 ☑
H.E.L.L.P. 642.5 ☑
Helminthiasis — see also Infestation, by specific
    parasite 128.9
  Ancylostoma (see also Ancylostoma) 126.9
  intestinal 127.9
    mixed types (types classifiable to more
      than one of the categories
      120.0–127.7) 127.8
    specified type 127.7
  mixed types (intestinal) (types classifiable to
    more than one of the categories
    120.0–127.7) 127.8
  Necator americanus 126.1
  specified type NEC 128.8
  Trichinella 124
Heloma 700
Hemangioblastoma (M9161/1) — see also
    Neoplasm, connective tissue, uncertain
    behavior
  malignant (M9161/3) — see Neoplasm, con-
    nective tissue, malignant
Hemangioblastomatosis, cerebelloretinal
    759.6
Hemangioendothelioma (M9130/1) — see also
    Neoplasm, by site, uncertain behavior
  benign (M9130/0) 228.00

Hemangioendothelioma — see also Neoplasm,
    by site, uncertain behavior —
    continued
  bone (diffuse) (M9130/3) — see Neoplasm,
    bone, malignant
  malignant (M9130/3) — see Neoplasm, con-
    nective tissue, malignant
  nervous system (M9130/0) 228.09
Hemangioendotheliosarcoma (M9130/3) —
    see Neoplasm, connective tissue, malignant
Hemangiofibroma (M9160/0) — see Neoplasm,
    by site, benign
Hemangiolipoma (M8861/0) — see Lipoma
Hemangioma (M9120/0) 228.00
  arteriovenous (M9123/0) — see Hemangioma,
    by site
  brain 228.02
  capillary (M9131/0) — see Hemangioma, by
    site
  cavernous (M9121/0) — see Hemangioma, by
    site
  central nervous system NEC 228.09
  choroid 228.09
  heart 228.09
  infantile (M9131/0) — see Hemangioma, by
    site
  intra-abdominal structures 228.04
  intracranial structures 228.02
  intramuscular (M9132/0) — see Hemangioma,
    by site
  iris 228.09
  juvenile (M9131/0) — see Hemangioma, by
    site
  malignant (M9120/3) — see Neoplasm, con-
    nective tissue, malignant
  meninges 228.09
    brain 228.02
    spinal cord 228.09
  peritoneum 228.04
  placenta — see Placenta, abnormal
  plexiform (M9131/0) — see Hemangioma, by
    site
  racemose (M9123/0) — see Hemangioma, by
    site
  retina 228.03
  retroperitoneal tissue 228.04
  sclerosing (M8832/0) — see Neoplasm, skin,
    benign
  simplex (M9131/0) — see Hemangioma, by
    site
  skin and subcutaneous tissue 228.01
  specified site NEC 228.09
  spinal cord 228.09
  venous (M9122/0) — see Hemangioma, by
    site
  verrucous keratotic (M9142/0) — see Heman-
    gioma, by site
Hemangiomatosis (systemic) 757.32
  involving single site — see Hemangioma
Hemangiopericytoma (M9150/1) — see also
    Neoplasm, connective tissue, uncertain
    behavior
  benign (M9150/0) — see Neoplasm, connec-
    tive tissue, benign
  malignant (M9150/3) — see Neoplasm, con-
    nective tissue, malignant
Hemangiosarcoma (M9120/3) — see Neoplasm,
    connective tissue, malignant
Hemarthrosis (nontraumatic) 719.10
  ankle 719.17
  elbow 719.12
  foot 719.17
  hand 719.14
  hip 719.15
  knee 719.16
  multiple sites 719.19
  pelvic region 719.15
  shoulder (region) 719.11
  specified site NEC 719.18
  traumatic — see Sprain, by site
  wrist 719.13
Hematemesis 578.0
  with ulcer — see Ulcer, by site, with hemor-
    rhage
  due to S. japonicum 120.2

Hematemesis — *continued*
Goldstein's (familial hemorrhagic telangiectasia) 448.0
newborn 772.4
due to swallowed maternal blood 777.3
Hematidrosis 705.89
Hematinuria — *see also* Hemoglobinuria 791.2
malarial 084.8
paroxysmal 283.2
Hematite miners' lung 503
Hematobilia 576.8
Hematocele (congenital) (diffuse) (idiopathic) 608.83
broad ligament 620.7
canal of Nuck 629.0
cord, male 608.83
fallopian tube 620.8
female NEC 629.0
ischiorectal 569.89
male NEC 608.83
ovary 629.0
pelvis, pelvic
female 629.0
with ectopic pregnancy (*see also* Pregnancy, ectopic) 633.90
with intrauterine pregnancy 633.91
male 608.83
periuterine 629.0
retrouterine 629.0
scrotum 608.83
spermatic cord (diffuse) 608.83
testis 608.84
traumatic — *see* Injury, internal, pelvis
tunica vaginalis 608.83
uterine ligament 629.0
uterus 621.4
vagina 623.6
vulva 624.5
Hematocephalus 742.4
Hematochezia — *see also* Melena 578.1
Hematochyluria — *see also* Infestation, filarial 125.9
Hematocolpos 626.8
Hematocornea 371.12
Hematogenous — *see* condition
Hematoma (skin surface intact) (traumatic) — *see also* Contusion

Note — Hematomas are coded according to origin and the nature and site of the hematoma or the accompanying injury. Hematomas of unspecified origin are coded as injuries of the sites involved, except:

(a)	hematomas of genital organs which are coded as diseases of the organ involved unless they complicate pregnancy or delivery

(b)	hematomas of the eye which are coded as diseases of the eye.

For late effect of hematoma classifiable to 920–924 see Late, effect, contusion

with
crush injury — *see* Crush
fracture — *see* Fracture, by site
injury of internal organs (*see also* Injury, internal, by site)
kidney — *see* Hematoma, kidney traumatic
liver — *see* Hematoma, liver, traumatic
spleen — *see* Hematoma, spleen
nerve injury — *see* Injury, nerve
open wound — *see* Wound, open, by site
skin surface intact — *see* Contusion
abdomen (wall) — *see* Contusion, abdomen
amnion 658.8 ☑
aorta, dissecting 441.00
abdominal 441.02
thoracic 441.01
thoracoabdominal 441.03
arterial (complicating trauma) 904.9
specified site — *see* Injury, blood vessel, by site
auricle (ear) 380.31
birth injury 767.8
skull 767.19

Hematoma — *see also* Contusion — *continued*
brain (traumatic) 853.0 ☑

Note — Use the following fifth-digit subclassification with categories 851–854:

0	unspecified state of consciousness

1	with no loss of consciousness

2	with brief [less than one hour] loss of consciousness

3	with moderate [1–24 hours] loss of consciousness

4	with prolonged [more than 24 hours] loss of consciousness and return to pre–existing conscious level

5	with prolonged [more than 24 hours] loss of consciousness, without return to pre–existing conscious level

Use fifth-digit 5 to designate when a patient is unconscious and dies before regaining consciousness, regardless of the duration of the loss of consciousness

6	with loss of consciousness of unspecified duration

9	with concussion, unspecified

with
cerebral
contusion — *see* Contusion, brain
laceration — *see* Laceration, brain
open intracranial wound 853.1 ☑
skull fracture — *see* Fracture, skull, by site
extradural or epidural 852.4 ☑
with open intracranial wound 852.5 ☑
fetus or newborn 767.0
nontraumatic 432.0
fetus or newborn NEC 767.0
nontraumatic (*see also* Hemorrhage, brain) 431
epidural or extradural 432.0
newborn NEC 772.8
subarachnoid, arachnoid, or meningeal (*see also* Hemorrhage, subarachnoid) 430
subdural (*see also* Hemorrhage, subdural) 432.1
subarachnoid, arachnoid, or meningeal 852.0 ☑
with open intracranial wound 852.1 ☑
fetus or newborn 772.2
nontraumatic (*see also* Hemorrhage, subarachnoid) 430
subdural 852.2 ☑
with open intracranial wound 852.3 ☑
fetus or newborn (localized) 767.0
nontraumatic (*see also* Hemorrhage, subdural) 432.1
breast (nontraumatic) 611.89
broad ligament (nontraumatic) 620.7
complicating delivery 665.7 ☑
traumatic — *see* Injury, internal, broad ligament
calcified NEC 959.9
capitis 920
due to birth injury 767.19
newborn 767.19
cerebral — *see* Hematoma, brain
cesarean section wound 674.3 ☑
chorion — *see* Placenta, abnormal
complicating delivery (perineum) (vulva) 664.5 ☑
pelvic 665.7 ☑
vagina 665.7 ☑
corpus
cavernosum (nontraumatic) 607.82
luteum (nontraumatic) (ruptured) 620.1
dura (mater) — *see* Hematoma, brain, subdural
epididymis (nontraumatic) 608.83
epidural (traumatic) (*see also* Hematoma, brain, extradural)
spinal — *see* Injury, spinal, by site

Hematoma — *see also* Contusion — *continued*
episiotomy 674.3 ☑
external ear 380.31
extradural (*see also* Hematoma, brain, extradural)
fetus or newborn 767.0
nontraumatic 432.0
fetus or newborn 767.0
fallopian tube 620.8
genital organ (nontraumatic)
female NEC 629.89
male NEC 608.83
traumatic (external site) 922.4
internal — *see* Injury, internal, genital organ
graafian follicle (ruptured) 620.0
internal organs (abdomen, chest, or pelvis) (*see also* Injury, internal, by site)
kidney — *see* Hematoma, kidney, traumatic
liver — *see* Hematoma, liver, traumatic
spleen — *see* Hematoma, spleen
intracranial — *see* Hematoma, brain
kidney, cystic 593.81
traumatic 866.01
with open wound into cavity 866.11
labia (nontraumatic) 624.5
lingual (and other parts of neck, scalp, or face, except eye) 920
liver (subcapsular) 573.8
birth injury 767.8
fetus or newborn 767.8
traumatic NEC 864.01
with
laceration — *see* Laceration, liver
open wound into cavity 864.11
mediastinum — *see* Injury, internal, mediastinum
meninges, meningeal (brain) (*see also* Hematoma, brain, subarachnoid)
spinal — *see* Injury, spinal, by site
mesosalpinx (nontraumatic) 620.8
traumatic — *see* Injury, internal, pelvis
muscle (traumatic) — *see* Contusion, by site
nontraumatic 729.92
nasal (septum) (and other part(s) of neck, scalp, or face, except eye) 920
obstetrical surgical wound 674.3 ☑
orbit, orbital (nontraumatic) 376.32
traumatic 921.2
ovary (corpus luteum) (nontraumatic) 620.1
traumatic — *see* Injury, internal, ovary
pelvis (female) (nontraumatic) 629.89
complicating delivery 665.7 ☑
male 608.83
traumatic (*see also* Injury, internal, pelvis)
specified organ NEC (*see also* Injury, internal, pelvis) 867.6
penis (nontraumatic) 607.82
pericranial (and neck, or face any part, except eye) 920
due to injury at birth 767.19
perineal wound (obstetrical) 674.3 ☑
complicating delivery 664.5 ☑
perirenal, cystic 593.81
pinna 380.31
placenta — *see* Placenta, abnormal
postoperative 998.12
retroperitoneal (nontraumatic) 568.81
traumatic — *see* Injury, internal, retroperitoneum
retropubic, male 568.81
scalp (and neck, or face any part, except eye) 920
fetus or newborn 767.19
scrotum (nontraumatic) 608.83
traumatic 922.4
seminal vesicle (nontraumatic) 608.83
traumatic — *see* Injury, internal, seminal, vesicle
soft tissue 729.92
spermatic cord (*see also* Injury, internal, spermatic cord)
nontraumatic 608.83

Hematoma — *see also* Contusion — *continued*
spinal (cord) (meninges) (*see also* Injury, spinal, by site)
fetus or newborn 767.4
nontraumatic 336.1
spleen 865.01
with
laceration — *see* Laceration, spleen
open wound into cavity 865.11
sternocleidomastoid, birth injury 767.8
sternomastoid, birth injury 767.8
subarachnoid (*see also* Hematoma, brain, subarachnoid)
fetus or newborn 772.2
nontraumatic (*see also* Hemorrhage, subarachnoid) 430
newborn 772.2
subdural (*see also* Hematoma, brain, subdural)
fetus or newborn (localized) 767.0
nontraumatic (*see also* Hemorrhage, subdural) 432.1
subperiosteal (syndrome) 267
traumatic — *see* Hematoma, by site
superficial, fetus or newborn 772.6
syncytium — *see* Placenta, abnormal
testis (nontraumatic) 608.83
birth injury 767.8
traumatic 922.4
tunica vaginalis (nontraumatic) 608.83
umbilical cord 663.6 ☑
affecting fetus or newborn 762.6
uterine ligament (nontraumatic) 620.7
traumatic — *see* Injury, internal, pelvis
uterus 621.4
traumatic — *see* Injury, internal, pelvis
vagina (nontraumatic) (ruptured) 623.6
complicating delivery 665.7 ☑
traumatic 922.4
vas deferens (nontraumatic) 608.83
traumatic — *see* Injury, internal, vas deferens
vitreous 379.23
vocal cord 920
vulva (nontraumatic) 624.5
complicating delivery 664.5 ☑
fetus or newborn 767.8
traumatic 922.4
Hematometra 621.4
Hematomyelia 336.1
with fracture of vertebra (*see also* Fracture, vertebra, by site, with spinal cord injury) 806.8
fetus or newborn 767.4
Hematomyelitis 323.9
late effect — *see* category 326
Hematoperitoneum — *see also* Hemoperitoneum 568.81
Hematopneumothorax — *see also* Hemothorax 511.89
Hematopoiesis, cyclic 288.02
Hematoporphyria (acquired) (congenital) 277.1
Hematoporphyrinuria (acquired) (congenital) 277.1
Hematorachis, hematorrhachis 336.1
fetus or newborn 767.4
Hematosalpinx 620.8
with
ectopic pregnancy (*see also* categories 633.0–633.9) 639.2
infectional (*see also* Salpingo-oophoritis) 614.2
molar pregnancy (*see also* categories 630–632) 639.2
Hematospermia 608.82
Hematothorax — *see also* Hemothorax 511.89
Hematotympanum 381.03
Hematuria (benign) (essential) (idiopathic) 599.70
due to S. hematobium 120.0
endemic 120.0
gross 599.71
intermittent 599.70
malarial 084.8
microscopic 599.72
paroxysmal 599.70

Hematuria — *continued*
- sulfonamide
  - correct substance properly administered 599.70
  - overdose or wrong substance given or taken 961.0
- tropical (bilharziasis) 120.0
- tuberculous (*see also* Tuberculosis) 016.9 ☑

Hematuric bilious fever 084.8
Hemeralopia 368.10
Hemiabiotrophy 799.89
Hemi-akinesia 781.8
Hemianalgesia — *see also* Disturbance, sensation 782.0
Hemianencephaly 740.0
Hemianesthesia — *see also* Disturbance, sensation 782.0
Hemianopia, hemianopsia (altitudinal) (homonymous) 368.46
- binasal 368.47
- bitemporal 368.47
- heteronymous 368.47
- syphilitic 095.8
Hemiasomatognosia 307.9
Hemiathetosis 781.0
Hemiatrophy 799.89
- cerebellar 334.8
- face 349.89
  - progressive 349.89
- fascia 728.9
- leg 728.2
- tongue 529.8
Hemiballism (us) 333.5
Hemiblock (cardiac) (heart) (left) 426.2
Hemicardia 746.89
Hemicephalus, hemicephaly 740.0
Hemichorea 333.5
Hemicrania 346.9 ☑
- congenital malformation 740.0
- continua 339.41
- paroxysmal 339.03
  - chronic 339.04
  - episodic 339.03
Hemidystrophy — *see* Hemiatrophy
Hemiectromelia 755.4
Hemihypalgesia — *see also* Disturbance, sensation 782.0
Hemihypertrophy (congenital) 759.89
- cranial 756.0
Hemihypesthesia — *see also* Disturbance, sensation 782.0
Hemi-inattention 781.8
Hemimelia 755.4
- lower limb 755.30
  - paraxial (complete) (incomplete) (intercalary) (terminal) 755.32
    - fibula 755.37
    - tibia 755.36
  - transverse (complete) (partial) 755.31
- upper limb 755.20
  - paraxial (complete) (incomplete) (intercalary) (terminal) 755.22
    - radial 755.26
    - ulnar 755.27
  - transverse (complete) (partial) 755.21
Hemiparalysis — *see also* Hemiplegia 342.9 ☑
Hemiparesis — *see also* Hemiplegia 342.9 ☑
Hemiparesthesia — *see also* Disturbance, sensation 782.0
Hemiplegia 342.9 ☑
- acute (*see also* Disease, cerebrovascular, acute) 436
- alternans facialis 344.89
- apoplectic (*see also* Disease, cerebrovascular, acute) 436
  - late effect or residual
    - affecting
      - dominant side 438.21
      - nondominant side 438.22
      - unspecified side 438.20
- arteriosclerotic 437.0
  - late effect or residual
    - affecting
      - dominant side 438.21
      - nondominant side 438.22
      - unspecified side 438.20

Hemiplegia — *continued*
- ascending (spinal) NEC 344.89
- attack (*see also* Disease, cerebrovascular, acute) 436
- brain, cerebral (current episode) 437.8
  - congenital 343.1
- cerebral — *see* Hemiplegia, brain
- congenital (cerebral) (spastic) (spinal) 343.1
- conversion neurosis (hysterical) 300.11
- cortical — *see* Hemiplegia, brain
- due to
  - arteriosclerosis 437.0
    - late effect or residual
      - affecting
        - dominant side 438.21
        - nondominant side 438.22
        - unspecified side 438.20
  - cerebrovascular lesion (*see also* Disease, cerebrovascular, acute) 436
    - late effect
      - affecting
        - dominant side 438.21
        - nondominant side 438.22
        - unspecified side 438.20
- embolic (current) (*see also* Embolism, brain) 434.1 ☑
  - late effect
    - affecting
      - dominant side 438.21
      - nondominant side 438.22
      - unspecified side 438.20
- flaccid 342.0 ☑
- hypertensive (current episode) 437.8
- infantile (postnatal) 343.4
- late effect
  - birth injury, intracranial or spinal 343.4
  - cerebrovascular lesion — *see* Late effect(s) (of) cerebrovascular disease
  - viral encephalitis 139.0
- middle alternating NEC 344.89
- newborn NEC 767.0
- seizure (current episode) (*see also* Disease, cerebrovascular, acute) 436
- spastic 342.1 ☑
  - congenital or infantile 343.1
- specified NEC 342.8 ☑
- thrombotic (current) (*see also* Thrombosis, brain) 434.0 ☑
  - late effect — *see* Late effect(s) (of) cerebrovascular disease
Hemisection, spinal cord — *see* Fracture, vertebra, by site, with spinal cord injury
Hemispasm 781.0
- facial 781.0
Hemispatial neglect 781.8
Hemisporosis 117.9
Hemitremor 781.0
Hemivertebra 756.14
Hemobilia 576.8
Hemocholecyst 575.8
Hemochromatosis (acquired) (diabetic) (hereditary) (liver) (myocardium) (primary idiopathic) (secondary) 275.0
- with refractory anemia 238.72
Hemodialysis V56.0
Hemoglobin — *see also* condition
- abnormal (disease) — *see* Disease, hemoglobin
- AS genotype 282.5
- fetal, hereditary persistence 282.7
- high-oxygen-affinity 289.0
- low NEC 285.9
- S (Hb-S), heterozygous 282.5
Hemoglobinemia 283.2
- due to blood transfusion NEC 999.89
  - bone marrow 996.85
- paroxysmal 283.2
Hemoglobinopathy (mixed) — *see also* Disease, hemoglobin 282.7
- with thalassemia 282.49
- sickle-cell 282.60
  - with thalassemia (without crisis) 282.41
    - with
      - crisis 282.42
        - vaso-occlusive pain 282.42
Hemoglobinuria, hemoglobinuric 791.2

Hemoglobinuria, hemoglobinuric — *continued*
- with anemia, hemolytic, acquired (chronic) NEC 283.2
- cold (agglutinin) (paroxysmal) (with Raynaud's syndrome) 283.2
- due to
  - exertion 283.2
  - hemolysis (from external causes) NEC 283.2
- exercise 283.2
- fever (malaria) 084.8
- infantile 791.2
- intermittent 283.2
- malarial 084.8
- march 283.2
- nocturnal (paroxysmal) 283.2
- paroxysmal (cold) (nocturnal) 283.2
Hemolymphangioma (M9175/0) 228.1
Hemolysis
- fetal — *see* Jaundice, fetus or newborn
- intravascular (disseminated) NEC 286.6
  - with
    - abortion — *see* Abortion, by type, with hemorrhage, delayed or excessive
    - ectopic pregnancy (*see also* categories 633.0–633.9) 639.1
    - hemorrhage of pregnancy 641.3 ☑
      - affecting fetus or newborn 762.1
    - molar pregnancy (*see also* categories 630–632) 639.1
  - acute 283.2
  - following
    - abortion 639.1
    - ectopic or molar pregnancy 639.1
- neonatal — *see* Jaundice, fetus or newborn
- transfusion NEC 999.89
  - bone marrow 996.85
Hemolytic — *see also* condition
- anemia — *see* Anemia, hemolytic
- uremic syndrome 283.11
Hemometra 621.4
Hemopericardium (with effusion) 423.0
- newborn 772.8
- traumatic (*see also* Hemothorax, traumatic) 860.2
  - with open wound into thorax 860.3
Hemoperitoneum 568.81
- infectional (*see also* Peritonitis) 567.29
- traumatic — *see* Injury, internal, peritoneum
Hemophagocytic syndrome 288.4
- infection-associated 288.4
Hemophilia (familial) (hereditary) 286.0
- A 286.0
  - carrier (asymptomatic) V83.01
    - symptomatic V83.02
- acquired 286.5
- B (Leyden) 286.1
- C 286.2
- calcipriva (*see also* Fibrinolysis) 286.7
- classical 286.0
- nonfamilial 286.7
- secondary 286.5
- vascular 286.4
Hemophilus influenzae NEC 041.5
- arachnoiditis (basic) (brain) (spinal) 320.0
  - late effect — *see* category 326
- bronchopneumonia 482.2
- cerebral ventriculitis 320.0
  - late effect — *see* category 326
- cerebrospinal inflammation 320.0
  - late effect — *see* category 326
- infection NEC 041.5
- leptomeningitis 320.0
  - late effect — *see* category 326
- meningitis (cerebral) (cerebrospinal) (spinal) 320.0
  - late effect — *see* category 326
- meningomyelitis 320.0
  - late effect — *see* category 326
- pachymeningitis (adhesive) (fibrous) (hemorrhagic) (hypertrophic) (spinal) 320.0
  - late effect — *see* category 326
- pneumonia (broncho-) 482.2
Hemophthalmos 360.43

Hemopneumothorax — *see also* Hemothorax 511.89
- traumatic 860.4
  - with open wound into thorax 860.5
Hemoptysis 786.3
- due to Paragonimus (westermani) 121.2
- newborn 770.3
- tuberculous (*see also* Tuberculosis, pulmonary) 011.9 ☑
Hemorrhage, hemorrhagic (nontraumatic) 459.0
- abdomen 459.0
- accidental (antepartum) 641.2 ☑
  - affecting fetus or newborn 762.1
- adenoid 474.8
- adrenal (capsule) (gland) (medulla) 255.41
  - newborn 772.5
- after labor — *see* Hemorrhage, postpartum
- alveolar
  - lung, newborn 770.3
  - process 525.8
- alveolus 525.8
- amputation stump (surgical) 998.11
  - secondary, delayed 997.69
- anemia (chronic) 280.0
  - acute 285.1
- antepartum — *see* Hemorrhage, pregnancy
- anus (sphincter) 569.3
- apoplexy (stroke) 432.9
- arachnoid — *see* Hemorrhage, subarachnoid
- artery NEC 459.0
  - brain (*see also* Hemorrhage, brain) 431
  - middle meningeal — *see* Hemorrhage, subarachnoid
- basilar (ganglion) (*see also* Hemorrhage, brain) 431
- bladder 596.8
- blood dyscrasia 289.9
- bowel 578.9
  - newborn 772.4
- brain (miliary) (nontraumatic) 431
  - with
    - birth injury 767.0
    - arachnoid — *see* Hemorrhage, subarachnoid
  - due to
    - birth injury 767.0
    - rupture of aneurysm (congenital) (*see also* Hemorrhage, subarachnoid) 430
      - mycotic 431
    - syphilis 094.89
  - epidural or extradural — *see* Hemorrhage, extradural
  - fetus or newborn (anoxic) (hypoxic) (due to birth trauma) (nontraumatic) 767.0
    - intraventricular 772.10
      - grade I 772.11
      - grade II 772.12
      - grade III 772.13
      - grade IV 772.14
  - iatrogenic 997.02
  - postoperative 997.02
  - puerperal, postpartum, childbirth 674.0 ☑
  - stem 431
  - subarachnoid, arachnoid, or meningeal — *see* Hemorrhage, subarachnoid
  - subdural — *see* Hemorrhage, subdural

Hemorrhage, hemorrhagic — *continued*
  brain — *continued*
    traumatic NEC 853.0 ☑

> *Note* — Use the following fifth-digit sub-classification with categories 851–854:
>
> 0   unspecified state of consciousness
>
> 1   with no loss of consciousness
>
> 2   with brief [less than one hour] loss of consciousness
>
> 3   with moderate [1–24 hours] loss of consciousness
>
> 4   with prolonged [more than 24 hours] loss of consciousness and return to pre–existing conscious level
>
> 5   with prolonged [more than 24 hours] loss of consciousness, without return to pre–existing conscious level
>
> Use fifth-digit 5 to designate when a patient is unconscious and dies before regaining consciousness, regardless of the duration of the loss of consciousness
>
> 6   with loss of consciousness of unspecified duration
>
> 9   with concussion, unspecified

    with
      cerebral
        contusion — *see* Contusion, brain
        laceration — *see* Laceration, brain
        open intracranial wound 853.1 ☑
        skull fracture — *see* Fracture, skull, by site
      extradural or epidural 852.4 ☑
        with open intracranial wound 852.5 ☑
      subarachnoid 852.0 ☑
        with open intracranial wound 852.1 ☑
      subdural 852.2 ☑
        with open intracranial wound 852.3 ☑
  breast 611.79
  bronchial tube — *see* Hemorrhage, lung
  bronchopulmonary — *see* Hemorrhage, lung
  bronchus (cause unknown) (*see also* Hemorrhage, lung) 786.3
  bulbar (*see also* Hemorrhage, brain) 431
  bursa 727.89
  capillary 448.9
    primary 287.8
  capsular — *see* Hemorrhage, brain
  cardiovascular 429.89
  cecum 578.9
  cephalic (*see also* Hemorrhage, brain) 431
  cerebellar (*see also* Hemorrhage, brain) 431
  cerebellum (*see also* Hemorrhage, brain) 431
  cerebral (*see also* Hemorrhage, brain) 431
    fetus or newborn (anoxic) (traumatic) 767.0
  cerebromeningeal (*see also* Hemorrhage, brain) 431
  cerebrospinal (*see also* Hemorrhage, brain) 431
  cerebrovascular accident — *see* Hemorrhage, brain
  cerebrum (*see also* Hemorrhage, brain) 431
  cervix (stump) (uteri) 622.8
  cesarean section wound 674.3 ☑
  chamber, anterior (eye) 364.41
  childbirth — *see* Hemorrhage, complicating, delivery
  choroid 363.61
    expulsive 363.62
  ciliary body 364.41
  cochlea 386.8
  colon — *see* Hemorrhage, intestine
  complicating
    delivery 641.9 ☑
      affecting fetus or newborn 762.1
      associated with
        afibrinogenemia 641.3 ☑

Hemorrhage, hemorrhagic — *continued*
  complicating — *continued*
    delivery — *continued*
      associated with — *continued*
        afibrinogenemia — *continued*
          affecting fetus or newborn 763.89
        coagulation defect 641.3 ☑
          affecting fetus or newborn 763.89
        hyperfibrinolysis 641.3 ☑
          affecting fetus or newborn 763.89
        hypofibrinogenemia 641.3 ☑
          affecting fetus or newborn 763.89
      due to
        low-lying placenta 641.1 ☑
          affecting fetus or newborn 762.0
        placenta previa 641.1 ☑
          affecting fetus or newborn 762.0
        premature separation of placenta 641.2 ☑
          affecting fetus or newborn 762.1
      retained
        placenta 666.0 ☑
        secundines 666.2 ☑
      trauma 641.8 ☑
        affecting fetus or newborn 763.89
      uterine leiomyoma 641.8 ☑
        affecting fetus or newborn 763.89
    surgical procedure 998.11
  complication(s)
    of dental implant placement 525.71
  concealed NEC 459.0
  congenital 772.9
  conjunctiva 372.72
    newborn 772.8
  cord, newborn 772.0
    slipped ligature 772.3
    stump 772.3
  corpus luteum (ruptured) 620.1
  cortical (*see also* Hemorrhage, brain) 431
  cranial 432.9
  cutaneous 782.7
    newborn 772.6
  cystitis — *see* Cystitis
  cyst, pancreas 577.2
  delayed
    with
      abortion — *see* Abortion, by type, with hemorrhage, delayed or excessive
      ectopic pregnancy (*see also* categories 633.0–633.9) 639.1
      molar pregnancy (*see also* categories 630–632) 639.1
    following
      abortion 639.1
      ectopic or molar pregnancy 639.1
    postpartum 666.2 ☑
  diathesis (familial) 287.9
    newborn 776.0
  disease 287.9
    newborn 776.0
    specified type NEC 287.8
  disorder 287.9
    due to intrinsic circulating anticoagulants 286.5
    specified type NEC 287.8
  due to
    any device, implant or graft (presence of) classifiable to 996.0–996.5 — *see* Complications, due to (presence of) any device, implant, or graft classified to 996.0–996.5NEC
    intrinsic circulating anticoagulant 286.5
  duodenum, duodenal 537.89
    ulcer — *see* Ulcer, duodenum, with hemorrhage
  dura mater — *see* Hemorrhage, subdural

Hemorrhage, hemorrhagic — *continued*
  endotracheal — *see* Hemorrhage, lung
  epicranial subaponeurotic (massive) 767.11
  epidural — *see* Hemorrhage, extradural
  episiotomy 674.3 ☑
  esophagus 530.82
    varix (*see also* Varix, esophagus, bleeding) 456.0
  excessive
    with
      abortion — *see* Abortion, by type, with hemorrhage, delayed or excessive
      ectopic pregnancy (*see also* categories 633.0–633.9) 639.1
      molar pregnancy (*see also* categories 630–632) 639.1
    following
      abortion 639.1
      ectopic or molar pregnancy 639.1
  external 459.0
  extradural (traumatic) (*see also* Hemorrhage, brain, traumatic, extradural)
    birth injury 767.0
    fetus or newborn (anoxic) (traumatic) 767.0
    nontraumatic 432.0
  eye 360.43
    chamber (anterior) (aqueous) 364.41
    fundus 362.81
  eyelid 374.81
  fallopian tube 620.8
  fetomaternal 772.0
    affecting management of pregnancy or puerperium 656.0 ☑
  fetus, fetal, ►affecting newborn◄ 772.0
    from
      cut end of co-twin's cord 772.0
      placenta 772.0
      ruptured cord 772.0
      vasa previa 772.0
    into
      co-twin 772.0
      mother's circulation 772.0
        affecting management of pregnancy or puerperium 656.0 ☑
  fever (*see also* Fever, hemorrhagic) 065.9
    with renal syndrome 078.6
    arthropod-borne NEC 065.9
    Bangkok 065.4
    Crimean 065.0
    dengue virus 065.4
    epidemic 078.6
    Junin virus 078.7
    Korean 078.6
    Machupo virus 078.7
    mite-borne 065.8
    mosquito-borne 065.4
    Philippine 065.4
    Russian (Yaroslav) 078.6
    Singapore 065.4
    southeast Asia 065.4
    Thailand 065.4
    tick-borne NEC 065.3
  fibrinogenolysis (*see also* Fibrinolysis) 286.6
  fibrinolytic (acquired) (*see also* Fibrinolysis) 286.6
  fontanel 767.19
  from tracheostomy stoma 519.09
  fundus, eye 362.81
  funis
    affecting fetus or newborn 772.0
    complicating delivery 663.8 ☑
  gastric (*see also* Hemorrhage, stomach) 578.9
  gastroenteric 578.9
    newborn 772.4
  gastrointestinal (tract) 578.9
    newborn 772.4
  genitourinary (tract) NEC 599.89
  gingiva 523.8
  globe 360.43
  gravidarum — *see* Hemorrhage, pregnancy
  gum 523.8
  heart 429.89
  hypopharyngeal (throat) 784.8
  intermenstrual 626.6
    irregular 626.6

Hemorrhage, hemorrhagic — *continued*
  intermenstrual — *continued*
    regular 626.5
  internal (organs) 459.0
    capsule (*see also* Hemorrhage, brain) 431
    ear 386.8
    newborn 772.8
  intestine 578.9
    congenital 772.4
    newborn 772.4
  into
    bladder wall 596.7
    bursa 727.89
    corpus luysii (*see also* Hemorrhage, brain) 431
  intra-abdominal 459.0
    during or following surgery 998.11
  intra-alveolar, newborn (lung) 770.3
  intracerebral (*see also* Hemorrhage, brain) 431
  intracranial NEC 432.9
    puerperal, postpartum, childbirth 674.0 ☑
    traumatic — *see* Hemorrhage, brain, traumatic
  intramedullary NEC 336.1
  intraocular 360.43
  intraoperative 998.11
  intrapartum — *see* Hemorrhage, complicating, delivery
  intrapelvic
    female 629.89
    male 459.0
  intraperitoneal 459.0
  intrapontine (*see also* Hemorrhage, brain) 431
  intrauterine 621.4
    complicating delivery — *see* Hemorrhage, complicating, delivery
    in pregnancy or childbirth — *see* Hemorrhage, pregnancy
    postpartum (*see also* Hemorrhage, postpartum) 666.1 ☑
  intraventricular (*see also* Hemorrhage, brain) 431
    fetus or newborn (anoxic) (traumatic) 772.10
      grade I 772.11
      grade II 772.12
      grade III 772.13
      grade IV 772.14
  intravesical 596.7
  iris (postinfectional) (postinflammatory) (toxic) 364.41
  joint (nontraumatic) 719.10
    ankle 719.17
    elbow 719.12
    foot 719.17
    forearm 719.13
    hand 719.14
    hip 719.15
    knee 719.16
    lower leg 719.16
    multiple sites 719.19
    pelvic region 719.15
    shoulder (region) 719.11
    specified site NEC 719.18
    thigh 719.15
    upper arm 719.12
    wrist 719.13
  kidney 593.81
  knee (joint) 719.16
  labyrinth 386.8
  leg NEC 459.0
  lenticular striate artery (*see also* Hemorrhage, brain) 431
  ligature, vessel 998.11
  liver 573.8
  lower extremity NEC 459.0
  lung 786.3
    newborn 770.3
    tuberculous (*see also* Tuberculosis, pulmonary) 011.9 ☑
  malaria 084.8
  marginal sinus 641.2 ☑
  massive subaponeurotic, birth injury 767.11
  maternal, affecting fetus or newborn 762.1
  mediastinum 786.3
  medulla (*see also* Hemorrhage, brain) 431

☑ Additional Digit Required — Refer to the Tabular List for Digit Selection   W Subterms under main terms may continue to next column or page

Index

Hemorrhage, hemorrhagic — Hemothorax

Hemorrhage, hemorrhagic — *continued*
- membrane (brain) (*see also* Hemorrhage, subarachnoid) 430
  - spinal cord — *see* Hemorrhage, spinal cord
- meninges, meningeal (brain) (middle) (*see also* Hemorrhage, subarachnoid) 430
  - spinal cord — *see* Hemorrhage, spinal cord
- mesentery 568.81
- metritis 626.8
- midbrain (*see also* Hemorrhage, brain) 431
- mole 631
- mouth 528.9
- mucous membrane NEC 459.0
  - newborn 772.8
- muscle 728.89
- nail (subungual) 703.8
- nasal turbinate 784.7
  - newborn 772.8
- nasopharynx 478.29
- navel, newborn 772.3
- newborn 772.9
  - adrenal 772.5
  - alveolar (lung) 770.3
  - brain (anoxic) (hypoxic) (due to birth trauma) 767.0
  - cerebral (anoxic) (hypoxic) (due to birth trauma) 767.0
  - conjunctiva 772.8
  - cutaneous 772.6
  - diathesis 776.0
    - due to vitamin K deficiency 776.0
  - epicranial subaponeurotic (massive) 767.11
  - gastrointestinal 772.4
  - internal (organs) 772.8
  - intestines 772.4
  - intra-alveolar (lung) 770.3
  - intracranial (from any perinatal cause) 767.0
  - intraventricular (from any perinatal cause) 772.10
    - grade I 772.11
    - grade II 772.12
    - grade III 772.13
    - grade IV 772.14
  - lung 770.3
  - pulmonary (massive) 770.3
  - spinal cord, traumatic 767.4
  - stomach 772.4
  - subaponeurotic (massive) 767.11
  - subarachnoid (from any perinatal cause) 772.2
  - subconjunctival 772.8
  - subgaleal 767.11
  - umbilicus 772.0
    - slipped ligature 772.3
    - vasa previa 772.0
- nipple 611.79
- nose 784.7
  - newborn 772.8
- obstetrical surgical wound 674.3 ✓
- omentum 568.89
  - newborn 772.4
- optic nerve (sheath) 377.42
- orbit 376.32
- ovary 620.1
- oviduct 620.8
- pancreas 577.8
- parathyroid (gland) (spontaneous) 252.8
- parturition — *see* Hemorrhage, complicating, delivery
- penis 607.82
- pericardium, pericarditis 423.0
- perineal wound (obstetrical) 674.3 ✓
- peritoneum, peritoneal 459.0
- peritonsillar tissue 474.8
  - after operation on tonsils 998.11
  - due to infection 475
- petechial 782.7
- pituitary (gland) 253.8
- placenta NEC 641.9 ✓
  - affecting fetus or newborn 762.1
  - from surgical or instrumental damage 641.8 ✓
    - affecting fetus or newborn 762.1
  - previa 641.1 ✓
    - affecting fetus or newborn 762.0

Hemorrhage, hemorrhagic — *continued*
- pleura — *see* Hemorrhage, lung
- polioencephalitis, superior 265.1
- polymyositis — *see* Polymyositis
- pons (*see also* Hemorrhage, brain) 431
- pontine (*see also* Hemorrhage, brain) 431
- popliteal 459.0
- postcoital 626.7
- postextraction (dental) 998.11
- postmenopausal 627.1
- postnasal 784.7
- postoperative 998.11
- postpartum (atonic) (following delivery of placenta) 666.1 ✓
  - delayed or secondary (after 24 hours) 666.2 ✓
  - retained placenta 666.0 ✓
  - third stage 666.0 ✓
- pregnancy (concealed) 641.9 ✓
  - accidental 641.2 ✓
    - affecting fetus or newborn 762.1
  - affecting fetus or newborn 762.1
  - before 22 completed weeks gestation 640.9 ✓
    - affecting fetus or newborn 762.1
  - due to
    - abruptio placenta 641.2 ✓
      - affecting fetus or newborn 762.1
    - afibrinogenemia or other coagulation defect (conditions classifiable to 286.0–286.9) 641.3 ✓
      - affecting fetus or newborn 762.1
    - coagulation defect 641.3 ✓
      - affecting fetus or newborn 762.1
    - hyperfibrinolysis 641.3 ✓
      - affecting fetus or newborn 762.1
    - hypofibrinogenemia 641.3 ✓
      - affecting fetus or newborn 762.1
    - leiomyoma, uterus 641.8 ✓
      - affecting fetus or newborn 762.1
    - low-lying placenta 641.1 ✓
      - affecting fetus or newborn 762.1
    - marginal sinus (rupture) 641.2 ✓
      - affecting fetus or newborn 762.1
    - placenta previa 641.1 ✓
      - affecting fetus or newborn 762.0
    - premature separation of placenta (normally implanted) 641.2 ✓
      - affecting fetus or newborn 762.1
    - threatened abortion 640.0 ✓
      - affecting fetus or newborn 762.1
    - trauma 641.8 ✓
      - affecting fetus or newborn 762.1
  - early (before 22 completed weeks gestation) 640.9 ✓
    - affecting fetus or newborn 762.1
  - previous, affecting management of pregnancy or childbirth V23.49
  - unavoidable — *see* Hemorrhage, pregnancy, due to placenta previa
- prepartum (mother) — *see* Hemorrhage, pregnancy
- preretinal, cause unspecified 362.81
- prostate 602.1
- puerperal (*see also* Hemorrhage, postpartum) 666.1 ✓
- pulmonary (*see also* Hemorrhage, lung)
  - newborn (massive) 770.3
  - renal syndrome 446.21
- purpura (primary) (*see also* Purpura, thrombocytopenic) 287.39
- rectum (sphincter) 569.3
- recurring, following initial hemorrhage at time of injury 958.2
- renal 593.81
  - pulmonary syndrome 446.21
- respiratory tract (*see also* Hemorrhage, lung) 786.3
- retina, retinal (deep) (superficial) (vessels) 362.81
  - diabetic 250.5 ✓ [362.01]
    - due to secondary diabetes 249.5 ✓ [362.01]
  - due to birth injury 772.8
- retrobulbar 376.89

Hemorrhage, hemorrhagic — *continued*
- retroperitoneal 459.0
- retroplacental (*see also* Placenta, separation) 641.2 ✓
- scalp 459.0
  - due to injury at birth 767.19
- scrotum 608.83
- secondary (nontraumatic) 459.0
  - following initial hemorrhage at time of injury 958.2
- seminal vesicle 608.83
- skin 782.7
  - newborn 772.6
- spermatic cord 608.83
- spinal (cord) 336.1
  - aneurysm (ruptured) 336.1
    - syphilitic 094.89
  - due to birth injury 767.4
  - fetus or newborn 767.4
- spleen 289.59
- spontaneous NEC 459.0
  - petechial 782.7
- stomach 578.9
  - newborn 772.4
  - ulcer — *see* Ulcer, stomach, with hemorrhage
- subaponeurotic, newborn 767.11
  - massive (birth injury) 767.11
- subarachnoid (nontraumatic) 430
  - fetus or newborn (anoxic) (traumatic) 772.2
  - puerperal, postpartum, childbirth 674.0 ✓
  - traumatic — *see* Hemorrhage, brain, traumatic, subarachnoid
- subconjunctival 372.72
  - due to birth injury 772.8
  - newborn 772.8
- subcortical (*see also* Hemorrhage, brain) 431
- subcutaneous 782.7
- subdiaphragmatic 459.0
- subdural (nontraumatic) 432.1
  - due to birth injury 767.0
  - fetus or newborn (anoxic) (hypoxic) (due to birth trauma) 767.0
  - puerperal, postpartum, childbirth 674.0 ✓
  - spinal 336.1
  - traumatic — *see* Hemorrhage, brain, traumatic, subdural
- subgaleal 767.11
- subhyaloid 362.81
- subperiosteal 733.99
- subretinal 362.81
- subtentorial (*see also* Hemorrhage, subdural) 432.1
- subungual 703.8
  - due to blood dyscrasia 287.8
- suprarenal (capsule) (gland) 255.41
  - fetus or newborn 772.5
- tentorium (traumatic) (*see also* Hemorrhage, brain, traumatic)
  - fetus or newborn 767.0
  - nontraumatic — *see* Hemorrhage, subdural
- testis 608.83
- thigh 459.0
- third stage 666.0 ✓
- thorax — *see* Hemorrhage, lung
- throat 784.8
- thrombocythemia 238.71
- thymus (gland) 254.8
- thyroid (gland) 246.3
  - cyst 246.3
- tongue 529.8
- tonsil 474.8
  - postoperative 998.11
- tooth socket (postextraction) 998.11
- trachea — *see* Hemorrhage, lung
- traumatic (*see also* nature of injury)
  - brain — *see* Hemorrhage, brain, traumatic
  - recurring or secondary (following initial hemorrhage at time of injury) 958.2
- tuberculous NEC (*see also* Tuberculosis, pulmonary) 011.9 ✓
- tunica vaginalis 608.83
- ulcer — *see* Ulcer, by site, with hemorrhage
- umbilicus, umbilical cord 772.0
  - after birth, newborn 772.3

Hemorrhage, hemorrhagic — *continued*
- umbilicus, umbilical cord — *continued*
  - complicating delivery 663.8 ✓
    - affecting fetus or newborn 772.0
  - slipped ligature 772.3
  - stump 772.3
- unavoidable (due to placenta previa) 641.1 ✓
  - affecting fetus or newborn 762.0
- upper extremity 459.0
- urethra (idiopathic) 599.84
- uterus, uterine (abnormal) 626.9
  - climacteric 627.0
  - complicating delivery — *see* Hemorrhage, complicating, delivery
  - due to
    - intrauterine contraceptive device 996.76
      - perforating uterus 996.32
  - functional or dysfunctional 626.8
  - in pregnancy — *see* Hemorrhage, pregnancy
  - intermenstrual 626.6
    - irregular 626.6
    - regular 626.5
  - postmenopausal 627.1
  - postpartum (*see also* Hemorrhage, postpartum) 666.1 ✓
  - prepubertal 626.8
  - pubertal 626.3
  - puerperal (immediate) 666.1 ✓
- vagina 623.8
- vasa previa 663.5 ✓
  - affecting fetus or newborn 772.0
- vas deferens 608.83
- ventricular (*see also* Hemorrhage, brain) 431
- vesical 596.8
- viscera 459.0
  - newborn 772.8
- vitreous (humor) (intraocular) 379.23
- vocal cord 478.5
- vulva 624.8

Hemorrhoids (anus) (rectum) (without complication) 455.6
- bleeding, prolapsed, strangulated, or ulcerated NEC 455.8
  - external 455.5
  - internal 455.2
- complicated NEC 455.8
- complicating pregnancy and puerperium 671.8 ✓
- external 455.3
  - with complication NEC 455.5
    - bleeding, prolapsed, strangulated, or ulcerated 455.5
    - thrombosed 455.4
- internal 455.0
  - with complication NEC 455.2
    - bleeding, prolapsed, strangulated, or ulcerated 455.2
    - thrombosed 455.1
- residual skin tag 455.9
- sentinel pile 455.9
- thrombosed NEC 455.7
  - external 455.4
  - internal 455.1

Hemosalpinx 620.8

Hemosiderosis 275.0
- dietary 275.0
- pulmonary (idiopathic) 275.0 [516.1]
- transfusion NEC 999.89
  - bone marrow 996.85

Hemospermia 608.82

Hemothorax 511.89
- bacterial, nontuberculous 511.1
- newborn 772.8
- nontuberculous 511.89
  - bacterial 511.1
- pneumococcal 511.1
- postoperative 998.11
- staphylococcal 511.1
- streptococcal 511.1
- traumatic 860.2
  - with
    - open wound into thorax 860.3
    - pneumothorax 860.4
      - with open wound into thorax 860.5

✓ Additional Digit Required — Refer to the Tabular List for Digit Selection   ⬇ Subterms under main terms may continue to next column or page

Hemothorax — continued
  tuberculous (see also Tuberculosis, pleura)
    012.0 ☑
Hemotympanum 385.89
Hench-Rosenberg syndrome (palindromic
  arthritis) — see also Rheumatism, palin-
  dromic 719.3 ☑
Henle's warts 371.41
Henoch (-Schönlein)
  disease or syndrome (allergic purpura) 287.0
  purpura (allergic) 287.0
Henpue, henpuye 102.6
Heparin-induced thrombocytopenia (HIT)
  289.84
Heparitinuria 277.5
Hepar lobatum 095.3
Hepatalgia 573.8
Hepatic — see also condition
  flexure syndrome 569.89
Hepatitis 573.3
  acute (see also Necrosis, liver) 570
    alcoholic 571.1
    infective 070.1
      with hepatic coma 070.0
  alcoholic 571.1
  amebic — see Abscess, liver, amebic
  anicteric (acute) — see Hepatitis, viral
  antigen-associated (HAA) — see Hepatitis, vi-
    ral, type B
  Australian antigen (positive) — see Hepatitis,
    viral, type B
  autoimmune 571.42
  catarrhal (acute) 070.1
    with hepatic coma 070.0
    chronic 571.40
    newborn 070.1
      with hepatic coma 070.0
  chemical 573.3
  cholangiolitic 573.8
  cholestatic 573.8
  chronic 571.40
    active 571.49
      viral — see Hepatitis, viral
    aggressive 571.49
    persistent 571.41
    viral — see Hepatitis, viral
  cytomegalic inclusion virus 078.5 [573.1]
  diffuse 573.3
  "dirty needle" — see Hepatitis, viral
  drug-induced 573.3
  due to
    Coxsackie 074.8 [573.1]
    cytomegalic inclusion virus 078.5 [573.1]
    infectious mononucleosis 075 [573.1]
    malaria 084.9 [573.2]
    mumps 072.71
    secondary syphilis 091.62
    toxoplasmosis (acquired) 130.5
      congenital (active) 771.2
  epidemic — see Hepatitis, viral, type A
  fetus or newborn 774.4
  fibrous (chronic) 571.49
    acute 570
  from injection, inoculation, or transfusion
    (blood) (other substance) (plasma)
    (serum) (onset within 8 months after
    administration) — see Hepatitis, viral
  fulminant (viral) (see also Hepatitis, viral) 070.9
    with hepatic coma 070.6
    type A 070.1
      with hepatic coma 070.0
    type B — see Hepatitis, viral, type B
  giant cell (neonatal) 774.4
  hemorrhagic 573.8
  history of
    B V12.09
    C V12.09
  homologous serum — see Hepatitis, viral
  hypertrophic (chronic) 571.49
    acute 570
  infectious, infective (acute) (chronic) (suba-
    cute) 070.1
    with hepatic coma 070.0
  inoculation — see Hepatitis, viral
  interstitial (chronic) 571.49
    acute 570

Hepatitis — continued
  lupoid 571.49
  malarial 084.9 [573.2]
  malignant (see also Necrosis, liver) 570
  neonatal (toxic) 774.4
  newborn 774.4
  parenchymatous (acute) (see also Necrosis,
    liver) 570
  peliosis 573.3
  persistent, chronic 571.41
  plasma cell 571.49
  postimmunization — see Hepatitis, viral
  postnecrotic 571.49
  posttransfusion — see Hepatitis, viral
  recurrent 571.49
  septic 573.3
  serum — see Hepatitis, viral
    carrier (suspected of) V02.61
  subacute (see also Necrosis, liver) 570
  suppurative (diffuse) 572.0
  syphilitic (late) 095.3
    congenital (early) 090.0 [573.2]
      late 090.5 [573.2]
    secondary 091.62
  toxic (noninfectious) 573.3
    fetus or newborn 774.4
  tuberculous (see also Tuberculosis) 017.9 ☑
  viral (acute) (anicteric) (cholangiolitic)
    (cholestatic) (chronic) (subacute) 070.9
    with hepatic coma 070.6
    AU-SH type virus — see Hepatitis, viral,
      type B
    Australian antigen — see Hepatitis, viral,
      type B
    B-antigen — see Hepatitis, viral, type B
    Coxsackie 074.8 [573.1]
    cytomegalic inclusion 078.5 [573.1]
    IH (virus) — see Hepatitis, viral, type A
    infectious hepatitis virus — see Hepatitis,
      viral, type A
    serum hepatitis virus — see Hepatitis, viral,
      type B
    SH — see Hepatitis, viral, type B
    specified type NEC 070.59
      with hepatic coma 070.49
    type A 070.1
      with hepatic coma 070.0
    type B (acute) 070.30
      with
        hepatic coma 070.20
          with hepatitis delta 070.21
        hepatitis delta 070.31
          with hepatic coma 070.21
      carrier status V02.61
      chronic 070.32
        with
          hepatic coma 070.22
            with hepatitis delta 070.23
          hepatitis delta 070.33
            with hepatic coma 070.23
    type C
      acute 070.51
        with hepatic coma 070.41
      carrier status V02.62
      chronic 070.54
        with hepatic coma 070.44
      in remission 070.54
      unspecified 070.70
        with hepatic coma 070.71
    type delta (with hepatitis B carrier state)
      070.52
      with
        active hepatitis B disease — see
          Hepatitis, viral, type B
        hepatic coma 070.42
    type E 070.53
      with hepatic coma 070.43
    vaccination and inoculation (prophylactic)
      V05.3
    Waldenström's (lupoid hepatitis) 571.49
Hepatization, lung (acute) — see also Pneumo-
  nia, lobar
  chronic (see also Fibrosis, lung) 515
Hepatoblastoma (M8970/3) 155.0
Hepatocarcinoma (M8170/3) 155.0
Hepatocholangiocarcinoma (M8180/3) 155.0

Hepatocholangioma, benign (M8180/0) 211.5
Hepatocholangitis 573.8
Hepatocystitis — see also Cholecystitis 575.10
Hepatodystrophy 570
Hepatolenticular degeneration 275.1
Hepatolithiasis — see Choledocholithiasis
Hepatoma (malignant) (M8170/3) 155.0
  benign (M8170/0) 211.5
  congenital (M8970/3) 155.0
  embryonal (M8970/3) 155.0
Hepatomegalia glycogenica diffusa 271.0
Hepatomegaly — see also Hypertrophy, liver
  789.1
  congenital 751.69
    syphilitic 090.0
  due to Clonorchis sinensis 121.1
  Gaucher's 272.7
  syphilitic (congenital) 090.0
Hepatoptosis 573.8
Hepatorrhexis 573.8
Hepatosis, toxic 573.8
Hepatosplenomegaly 571.8
  due to S. japonicum 120.2
  hyperlipemic (Bürger-Grutz type) 272.3
Herald patch 696.3
Hereditary — see condition
Heredodegeneration 330.9
  macular 362.70
Heredopathia atactica polyneuritiformis 356.3
Heredosyphilis — see also Syphilis, congenital
  090.9
Hermaphroditism (true) 752.7
  with specified chromosomal anomaly — see
    Anomaly, chromosomes, sex
Hernia, hernial (acquired) (recurrent) 553.9
  with
    gangrene (obstructed) NEC 551.9
    obstruction NEC 552.9
      and gangrene 551.9
  abdomen (wall) — see Hernia, ventral
  abdominal, specified site NEC 553.8
    with
      gangrene (obstructed) 551.8
      obstruction 552.8
        and gangrene 551.8
  appendix 553.8
    with
      gangrene (obstructed) 551.8
      obstruction 552.8
        and gangrene 551.8
  bilateral (inguinal) — see Hernia, inguinal
  bladder (sphincter)
    congenital (female) (male) 756.71
    female (see also Cystocele, female) 618.01
    male 596.8
  brain 348.4
    congenital 742.0
  broad ligament 553.8
  cartilage, vertebral — see Displacement, inter-
    vertebral disc
  cerebral 348.4
    congenital 742.0
    endaural 742.0
  ciliary body 364.89
    traumatic 871.1
  colic 553.9
    with
      gangrene (obstructed) 551.9
      obstruction 552.9
        and gangrene 551.9
  colon 553.9
    with
      gangrene (obstructed) 551.9
      obstruction 552.9
        and gangrene 551.9
  colostomy (stoma) 569.69
  Cooper's (retroperitoneal) 553.8
    with
      gangrene (obstructed) 551.8
      obstruction 552.8
        and gangrene 551.8
  crural — see Hernia, femoral
  diaphragm, diaphragmatic 553.3
    with
      gangrene (obstructed) 551.3
      obstruction 552.3

Hernia, hernial — continued
  diaphragm, diaphragmatic — continued
    with — continued
      obstruction — continued
        and gangrene 551.3
    congenital 756.6
    due to gross defect of diaphragm 756.6
    traumatic 862.0
      with open wound into cavity 862.1
  direct (inguinal) — see Hernia, inguinal
  disc, intervertebral — see Displacement, inter-
    vertebral disc
  diverticulum, intestine 553.9
    with
      gangrene (obstructed) 551.9
      obstruction 552.9
        and gangrene 551.9
  double (inguinal) — see Hernia, inguinal
  due to adhesion with obstruction 560.81
  duodenojejunal 553.8
    with
      gangrene (obstructed) 551.8
      obstruction 552.8
        and gangrene 551.8
  en glissade — see Hernia, inguinal
  enterostomy (stoma) 569.69
  epigastric 553.29
    with
      gangrene (obstruction) 551.29
      obstruction 552.29
        and gangrene 551.29
    recurrent 553.21
      with
        gangrene (obstructed) 551.21
        obstruction 552.21
          and gangrene 551.21
  esophageal hiatus (sliding) 553.3
    with
      gangrene (obstructed) 551.3
      obstruction 552.3
        and gangrene 551.3
    congenital 750.6
  external (inguinal) — see Hernia, inguinal
  fallopian tube 620.4
  fascia 728.89
  fat 729.30
    eyelid 374.34
    orbital 374.34
    pad 729.30
      eye, eyelid 374.34
      knee 729.31
      orbit 374.34
      popliteal (space) 729.31
      specified site NEC 729.39
  femoral (unilateral) 553.00
    with
      gangrene (obstructed) 551.00
      obstruction 552.00
        with gangrene 551.00
    bilateral 553.02
      gangrenous (obstructed) 551.02
      obstructed 552.02
        with gangrene 551.02
      recurrent 553.03
        gangrenous (obstructed) 551.03
        obstructed 552.03
          with gangrene 551.03
    recurrent (unilateral) 553.01
      bilateral 553.03
        gangrenous (obstructed) 551.03
        obstructed 552.03
          with gangrene 551.01
      gangrenous (obstructed) 551.01
      obstructed 552.01
        with gangrene 551.01
  foramen
    Bochdalek 553.3
      with
        gangrene (obstructed) 551.3
        obstruction 552.3
          and gangrene 551.3
      congenital 756.6
    magnum 348.4
    Morgagni, Morgagnian 553.3
      with
        gangrene 551.3

Index

Hernia, hernial — Herpes, herpetic

Hernia, hernial — *continued*
  foramen — *continued*
    Morgagni, Morgagnian — *continued*
      with — *continued*
        obstruction 552.3
          and gangrene 551.3
      congenital 756.6
  funicular (umbilical) 553.1
    with
      gangrene (obstructed) 551.1
      obstruction 552.1
        and gangrene 551.1
    spermatic cord — *see* Hernia, inguinal
  gangrenous — *see* Hernia, by site, with gangrene
  gastrointestinal tract 553.9
    with
      gangrene (obstructed) 551.9
      obstruction 552.9
        and gangrene 551.9
  gluteal — *see* Hernia, femoral
  Gruber's (internal mesogastric) 553.8
    with
      gangrene (obstructed) 551.8
      obstruction 552.8
        and gangrene 551.8
  Hesselbach's 553.8
    with
      gangrene (obstructed) 551.8
      obstruction 552.8
        and gangrene 551.8
  hiatal (esophageal) (sliding) 553.3
    with
      gangrene (obstructed) 551.3
      obstruction 552.3
        and gangrene 551.3
    congenital 750.6
  incarcerated (*see also* Hernia, by site, with obstruction) 552.9
    gangrenous (*see also* Hernia, by site, with gangrene) 551.9
  incisional 553.21
    with
      gangrene (obstructed) 551.21
      obstruction 552.21
        and gangrene 551.21
    lumbar — *see* Hernia, lumbar
    recurrent 553.21
      with
        gangrene (obstructed) 551.21
        obstruction 552.21
          and gangrene 551.21
  indirect (inguinal) — *see* Hernia, inguinal
  infantile — *see* Hernia, inguinal
  infrapatellar fat pad 729.31
  inguinal (direct) (double) (encysted) (external) (funicular) (indirect) (infantile) (internal) (interstitial) (oblique) (scrotal) (sliding) 550.9 ☑

Note — *Use the following fifth-digit subclassification with category 550:*

0 *unilateral or unspecified (not specified as recurrent)*

1 *unilateral or unspecified, recurrent*

2 *bilateral (not specified as recurrent)*

3 *bilateral, recurrent*

    with
      gangrene (obstructed) 550.0 ☑
      obstruction 550.1 ☑
        and gangrene 550.0 ☑
  internal 553.8
    with
      gangrene (obstructed) 551.8
      obstruction 552.8
        and gangrene 551.8
    inguinal — *see* Hernia, inguinal
  interstitial 553.9
    with
      gangrene (obstructed) 551.9
      obstruction 552.9
        and gangrene 551.9
    inguinal — *see* Hernia, inguinal
  intervertebral cartilage or disc — *see* Displacement, intervertebral disc

Hernia, hernial — *continued*
  intestine, intestinal 553.9
    with
      gangrene (obstructed) 551.9
      obstruction 552.9
        and gangrene 551.9
  intra-abdominal 553.9
    with
      gangrene (obstructed) 551.9
      obstruction 552.9
        and gangrene 551.9
  intraparietal 553.9
    with
      gangrene (obstructed) 551.9
      obstruction 552.9
        and gangrene 551.9
  iris 364.89
    traumatic 871.1
  irreducible (*see also* Hernia, by site, with obstruction) 552.9
    gangrenous (*see also* Hernia, by site, with gangrene) 551.9
  ischiatic 553.8
    with
      gangrene (obstructed) 551.8
      obstruction 552.8
        and gangrene 551.8
  ischiorectal 553.8
    with
      gangrene (obstructed) 551.8
      obstruction 552.8
        and gangrene 551.8
  lens 379.32
    traumatic 871.1
  linea
    alba — *see* Hernia, epigastric
    semilunaris — *see* Hernia, spigelian
  Littre's (diverticular) 553.9
    with
      gangrene (obstructed) 551.9
      obstruction 552.9
        and gangrene 551.9
  lumbar 553.8
    with
      gangrene (obstructed) 551.8
      obstruction 552.8
        and gangrene 551.8
    intervertebral disc 722.10
  lung (subcutaneous) 518.89
    congenital 748.69
  mediastinum 519.3
  mesenteric (internal) 553.8
    with
      gangrene (obstructed) 551.8
      obstruction 552.8
        and gangrene 551.8
  mesocolon 553.8
    with
      gangrene (obstructed) 551.8
      obstruction 552.8
        and gangrene 551.8
  muscle (sheath) 728.89
  nucleus pulposus — *see* Displacement, intervertebral disc
  oblique (inguinal) — *see* Hernia, inguinal
  obstructive (*see also* Hernia, by site, with obstruction) 552.9
    gangrenous (*see also* Hernia, by site, with gangrene) 551.9
  obturator 553.8
    with
      gangrene (obstructed) 551.8
      obstruction 552.8
        and gangrene 551.8
  omental 553.8
    with
      gangrene (obstructed) 551.8
      obstruction 552.8
        and gangrene 551.8
  orbital fat (pad) 374.34
  ovary 620.4
  oviduct 620.4
  paracolostomy (stoma) 569.69
  paraduodenal 553.8

Hernia, hernial — *continued*
  paraduodenal — *continued*
    with
      gangrene (obstructed) 551.8
      obstruction 552.8
        and gangrene 551.8
  paraesophageal 553.3
    with
      gangrene (obstructed) 551.3
      obstruction 552.3
        and gangrene 551.3
    congenital 750.6
  parahiatal 553.3
    with
      gangrene (obstructed) 551.3
      obstruction 552.3
        and gangrene 551.3
  paraumbilical 553.1
    with
      gangrene (obstructed) 551.1
      obstruction 552.1
        and gangrene 551.1
  parietal 553.9
    with
      gangrene (obstructed) 551.9
      obstruction 552.9
        and gangrene 551.9
  perineal 553.8
    with
      gangrene (obstructed) 551.8
      obstruction 552.8
        and gangrene 551.8
  peritoneal sac, lesser 553.8
    with
      gangrene (obstructed) 551.8
      obstruction 552.8
        and gangrene 551.8
  popliteal fat pad 729.31
  postoperative 553.21
    with
      gangrene (obstructed) 551.21
      obstruction 552.21
        and gangrene 551.21
  pregnant uterus 654.4 ☑
  prevesical 596.8
  properitoneal 553.8
    with
      gangrene (obstructed) 551.8
      obstruction 552.8
        and gangrene 551.8
  pudendal 553.8
    with
      gangrene (obstructed) 551.8
      obstruction 552.8
        and gangrene 551.8
  rectovaginal 618.6
  retroperitoneal 553.8
    with
      gangrene (obstructed) 551.8
      obstruction 552.8
        and gangrene 551.8
  Richter's (parietal) 553.9
    with
      gangrene (obstructed) 551.9
      obstruction 552.9
        and gangrene 551.9
  Rieux's, Riex's (retrocecal) 553.8
    with
      gangrene (obstructed) 551.8
      obstruction 552.8
        and gangrene 551.8
  sciatic 553.8
    with
      gangrene (obstructed) 551.8
      obstruction 552.8
        and gangrene 551.8
  scrotum, scrotal — *see* Hernia, inguinal
  sliding (inguinal) (*see also* Hernia, inguinal)
    hiatus — *see* Hernia, hiatal
  spigelian 553.29
    with
      gangrene (obstructed) 551.29
      obstruction 552.29
        and gangrene 551.29
  spinal (*see also* Spina bifida) 741.9 ☑
    with hydrocephalus 741.0 ☑

Hernia, hernial — *continued*
  strangulated (*see also* Hernia, by site, with obstruction) 552.9
    gangrenous (with obstruction) (*see also* Hernia, by site, with gangrene) 551.9
  supraumbilicus (linea alba) — *see* Hernia, epigastric
  tendon 727.9
  testis (nontraumatic) 550.9 ☑
    meaning
      scrotal hernia 550.9 ☑
      symptomatic late syphilis 095.8
  Treitz's (fossa) 553.8
    with
      gangrene (obstructed) 551.8
      obstruction 552.8
        and gangrene 551.8
  tunica
    albuginea 608.89
    vaginalis 752.89
  umbilicus, umbilical 553.1
    with
      gangrene (obstructed) 551.1
      obstruction 552.1
        and gangrene 551.1
  ureter 593.89
    with obstruction 593.4
  uterus 621.8
    pregnant 654.4 ☑
  vaginal (posterior) 618.6
  Velpeau's (femoral) (*see also* Hernia, femoral) 553.00
  ventral 553.20
    with
      gangrene (obstructed) 551.20
      obstruction 552.20
        and gangrene 551.20
    incisional 553.21
    recurrent 553.21
      with
        gangrene (obstructed) 551.21
        obstruction 552.21
          and gangrene 551.21
  vesical
    congenital (female) (male) 756.71
    female (*see also* Cystocele, female) 618.01
    male 596.8
  vitreous (into anterior chamber) 379.21
    traumatic 871.1
Herniation — *see also* Hernia
  brain (stem) 348.4
  cerebral 348.4
  gastric mucosa (into duodenal bulb) 537.89
  mediastinum 519.3
  nucleus pulposus — *see* Displacement, intervertebral disc
Herpangina 074.0
Herpes, herpetic 054.9
  auricularis (zoster) 053.71
    simplex 054.73
  blepharitis (zoster) 053.20
    simplex 054.41
  circinate 110.5
  circinatus 110.5
    bullous 694.5
  conjunctiva (simplex) 054.43
    zoster 053.21
  cornea (simplex) 054.43
    disciform (simplex) 054.43
    zoster 053.21
  encephalitis 054.3
  eye (zoster) 053.29
    simplex 054.40
  eyelid (zoster) 053.20
    simplex 054.41
  febrilis 054.9
  fever 054.9
  geniculate ganglionitis 053.11
  genital, genitalis 054.10
    specified site NEC 054.19
  gestationis 646.8 ☑
  gingivostomatitis 054.2
  iridocyclitis (simplex) 054.44
    zoster 053.22
  iris (any site) 695.10

☑ Additional Digit Required — Refer to the Tabular List for Digit Selection

▽ Subterms under main terms may continue to next column or page

◄ Revised Text   ● New Line   ▲ Revised Code

Herpes, herpetic — *continued*
  iritis (simplex) 054.44
  keratitis (simplex) 054.43
    dendritic 054.42
    disciform 054.43
    interstitial 054.43
      zoster 053.21
  keratoconjunctivitis (simplex) 054.43
    zoster 053.21
  labialis 054.9
    meningococcal 036.89
  lip 054.9
  meningitis (simplex) 054.72
    zoster 053.0
  ophthalmicus (zoster) 053.20
    simplex 054.40
  otitis externa (zoster) 053.71
    simplex 054.73
  penis 054.13
  perianal 054.10
  pharyngitis 054.79
  progenitalis 054.10
  scrotum 054.19
  septicemia 054.5
  simplex 054.9
    complicated 054.8
      ophthalmic 054.40
        specified NEC 054.49
      specified NEC 054.79
    congenital 771.2
    external ear 054.73
    keratitis 054.43
      dendritic 054.42
    meningitis 054.72
    myelitis 054.74
    neuritis 054.79
    specified complication NEC 054.79
      ophthalmic 054.49
    visceral 054.71
  stomatitis 054.2
  tonsurans 110.0
    maculosus (of Hebra) 696.3
  visceral 054.71
  vulva 054.12
  vulvovaginitis 054.11
  whitlow 054.6
  zoster 053.9
    auricularis 053.71
    complicated 053.8
      specified NEC 053.79
    conjunctiva 053.21
    cornea 053.21
    ear 053.71
    eye 053.29
    geniculate 053.11
    keratitis 053.21
      interstitial 053.21
    myelitis 053.14
    neuritis 053.10
    ophthalmicus(a) 053.20
    oticus 053.71
    otitis externa 053.71
    specified complication NEC 053.79
    specified site NEC 053.9
  zosteriform, intermediate type 053.9
Herrick's
  anemia (hemoglobin S disease) 282.61
  syndrome (hemoglobin S disease) 282.61
Hers' disease (glycogenosis VI) 271.0
Herter (-Gee) disease or syndrome (nontropical sprue) 579.0
Herter's infantilism (nontropical sprue) 579.0
Herxheimer's disease (diffuse idiopathic cutaneous atrophy) 701.8
Herxheimer's reaction 995.0
Hesitancy, urinary 788.64
Hesselbach's hernia — *see* Hernia, Hesselbach's
Heterochromia (congenital) 743.46
  acquired 364.53
  cataract 366.33
  cyclitis 364.21
  hair 704.3
  iritis 364.21
  retained metallic foreign body 360.62
    magnetic 360.52
  uveitis 364.21

Heterophoria 378.40
  alternating 378.45
  vertical 378.43
Heterophyes, small intestine 121.6
Heterophyiasis 121.6
Heteropsia 368.8
Heterotopia, heterotopic — *see also* Malposition, congenital
  cerebralis 742.4
  pancreas, pancreatic 751.7
  spinalis 742.59
Heterotropia 378.30
  intermittent 378.20
    vertical 378.31
  vertical (constant) (intermittent) 378.31
Heubner's disease 094.89
Heubner-Herter disease or syndrome (nontropical sprue) 579.0
Hexadactylism 755.0 ☑
Heyd's syndrome (hepatorenal) 572.4
HGSIL (high grade squamous intraepithelial lesion) (cytologic finding) (Pap smear finding)
  anus 796.74
  cervix 795.04
    biopsy finding — code to CIN II or CIN III
  vagina 795.14
Hibernoma (M8880/0) — *see* Lipoma
Hiccough 786.8
  epidemic 078.89
  psychogenic 306.1
Hiccup — *see also* Hiccough 786.8
Hicks (-Braxton) contractures 644.1 ☑
Hidden penis 752.65
Hidradenitis (axillaris) (suppurative) 705.83
Hidradenoma (nodular) (M8400/0) — *see also* Neoplasm, skin, benign
  clear cell (M8402/0) — *see* Neoplasm, skin, benign
  papillary (M8405/0) — *see* Neoplasm, skin, benign
Hidrocystoma (M8404/0) — *see* Neoplasm, skin, benign
HIE (hypoxic-ischemic encephalopathy) 768.70   ▲
  mild 768.71   ●
  moderate 768.72   ●
  severe 768.73   ●
High
  A₂ anemia 282.49
  altitude effects 993.2
    anoxia 993.2
    on
      ears 993.0
      sinuses 993.1
    polycythemia 289.0
  arch
    foot 755.67
    palate 750.26
  artery (arterial) tension (*see also* Hypertension) 401.9
    without diagnosis of hypertension 796.2
  basal metabolic rate (BMR) 794.7
  blood pressure (*see also* Hypertension) 401.9
    incidental reading (isolated) (nonspecific), no diagnosis of hypertension 796.2
  cholesterol 272.0
    with high triglycerides 272.2
  compliance bladder 596.4
  diaphragm (congenital) 756.6
  frequency deafness (congenital) (regional) 389.8
  head at term 652.5 ☑
    affecting fetus or newborn 763.1
  output failure (cardiac) (*see also* Failure, heart) 428.9
  oxygen-affinity hemoglobin 289.0
  palate 750.26
  risk
    behavior — *see* Problem
    family situation V61.9
      specified circumstance NEC V61.8
    human papillomavirus (HPV) DNA test positive
      anal 796.75
      cervical 795.05

High — *continued*
  risk — *continued*
    human papillomavirus DNA test positive — *continued*
      vaginal 795.15
    individual NEC V62.89
    infant NEC V20.1
    patient taking drugs (prescribed) V67.51
      nonprescribed (*see also* Abuse, drugs, nondependent) 305.9 ☑
    pregnancy V23.9
      inadequate prenatal care V23.7
      specified problem NEC V23.89
  temperature (of unknown origin) (*see also* Pyrexia) 780.60
  thoracic rib 756.3
  triglycerides 272.1
    with high cholesterol 272.2
Hildenbrand's disease (typhus) 081.9
Hilger's syndrome 337.09
Hill diarrhea 579.1
Hilliard's lupus — *see also* Tuberculosis 017.0 ☑
Hilum — *see* condition
Hip — *see* condition
Hippel's disease (retinocerebral angiomatosis) 759.6
Hippus 379.49
Hirschfeld's disease (acute diabetes mellitus) — *see also* Diabetes 250.0 ☑
  due to secondary diabetes 249.0 ☑
Hirschsprung's disease or megacolon (congenital) 751.3
Hirsuties — *see also* Hypertrichosis 704.1
Hirsutism — *see also* Hypertrichosis 704.1
Hirudiniasis (external) (internal) 134.2
Hiss-Russell dysentery 004.1
Histamine cephalgia 339.00
Histidinemia 270.5
Histidinuria 270.5
Histiocytic syndromes 288.4
Histiocytoma (M8832/0) — *see also* Neoplasm, skin, benign
  fibrous (M8830/0) (*see also* Neoplasm, skin, benign)
    atypical (M8830/1) — *see* Neoplasm, connective tissue, uncertain behavior
    malignant (M8830/3) — *see* Neoplasm, connective tissue, malignant
Histiocytosis (acute) (chronic) (subacute) 277.89
  acute differentiated progressive (M9722/3) 202.5 ☑
  cholesterol 277.89
  essential 277.89
  lipid, lipoid (essential) 272.7
  lipochrome (familial) 288.1
  malignant (M9720/3) 202.3 ☑
  non-Langerhans cell 277.89   ●
  polyostotic sclerosing 277.89   ●
  X (chronic) 277.89
    acute (progressive) (M9722/3) 202.5 ☑
Histoplasmosis 115.90
  with
    endocarditis 115.94
    meningitis 115.91
    pericarditis 115.93
    pneumonia 115.95
    retinitis 115.92
    specified manifestation NEC 115.99
  African (due to Histoplasma duboisii) 115.10
    with
      endocarditis 115.14
      meningitis 115.11
      pericarditis 115.13
      pneumonia 115.15
      retinitis 115.12
      specified manifestation NEC 115.19
  American (due to Histoplasma capsulatum) 115.00
    with
      endocarditis 115.04
      meningitis 115.01
      pericarditis 115.03
      pneumonia 115.05
      retinitis 115.02
      specified manifestation NEC 115.09
  Darling's — *see* Histoplasmosis, American

Histoplasmosis — *continued*
  large form (*see also* Histoplasmosis, African) 115.10
  lung 115.05
  small form (*see also* Histoplasmosis, American) 115.00
History (personal) of
  abuse
    emotional V15.42
    neglect V15.42
    physical V15.41
    sexual V15.41
  affective psychosis V11.1
  alcoholism V11.3
    specified as drinking problem (*see also* Abuse, drugs, nondependent) 305.0 ☑
  allergy to
    analgesic agent NEC V14.6
    anesthetic NEC V14.4
    antibiotic agent NEC V14.1
      penicillin V14.0
    anti-infective agent NEC V14.3
    arachnid bite V15.06   ●
    diathesis V15.09
    drug V14.9
      specified type NEC V14.8
    eggs V15.03
    food additives V15.05
    insect bite V15.06
    latex V15.07
    medicinal agents V14.9
      specified type NEC V14.8
    milk products V15.02
    narcotic agent NEC V14.5
    nuts V15.05
      peanuts V15.01
    penicillin V14.0
    radiographic dye V15.08
    seafood V15.04
    serum V14.7
    specified food NEC V15.05
    specified nonmedicinal agents NEC V15.09
    spider bite V15.06
    sulfa V14.2
    sulfonamides V14.2
    therapeutic agent NEC V15.09
    vaccine V14.7
  anemia V12.3
  arrest, sudden cardiac V12.53
  arthritis V13.4
  attack, transient ischemic (TIA) V12.54
  benign neoplasm of brain V12.41
  blood disease V12.3
  calculi, urinary V13.01
  cardiovascular disease V12.50
    myocardial infarction 412
  chemotherapy, antineoplastic V87.41
  child abuse V15.41
  cigarette smoking V15.82
  circulatory system disease V12.50
    myocardial infarction 412
  congenital malformation V13.69
  contraception V15.7
  death, sudden, successfully resuscitated V12.53
  deficit
    prolonged reversible ischemic neurologic (PRIND) V12.54
    reversible ischemic neurologic (RIND) V12.54
  diathesis, allergic V15.09
  digestive system disease V12.70
    peptic ulcer V12.71
    polyps, colonic V12.72
    specified NEC V12.79
  disease (of) V13.9
    blood V12.3
    blood-forming organs V12.3
    cardiovascular system V12.50
    circulatory system V12.50
      specified NEC V12.59
    digestive system V12.70
      peptic ulcer V12.71
      polyps, colonic V12.72
      specified NEC V12.79
    infectious V12.00

2010 ICD-9-CM   ►◄ Revised Text   ● New Line   ▲ Revised Code   **October 2009 • Volume 2 — 135**

☑ Additional Digit Required — Refer to the Tabular List for Digit Selection   Subterms under main terms may continue to next column or page

History of — *continued*
  disease — *continued*
    infectious — *continued*
      malaria V12.03
      methicillin resistant Staphylococcus aureus (MRSA) V12.04
      MRSA (methicillin resistant Staphylococcus aureus) V12.04
      poliomyelitis V12.02
      specified NEC V12.09
      tuberculosis V12.01
    parasitic V12.00
      specified NEC V12.09
    respiratory system V12.60
      pneumonia V12.61
      specified NEC V12.69
    skin V13.3
    specified site NEC V13.8
    subcutaneous tissue V13.3
    trophoblastic V13.1
      affecting management of pregnancy V23.1
  disorder (of) V13.9
    endocrine V12.2
    genital system V13.29
    hematological V12.3
    immunity V12.2
    mental V11.9
      affective type V11.1
      manic-depressive V11.1
      neurosis V11.2
      schizophrenia V11.0
      specified type NEC V11.8
    metabolic V12.2
    musculoskeletal NEC V13.59
    nervous system V12.40
      specified type NEC V12.49
    obstetric V13.29
      affecting management of current pregnancy V23.49
        pre-term labor V23.41
      pre-term labor V13.21
    sense organs V12.40
      specified type NEC V12.49
    specified site NEC V13.8
    urinary system V13.00
      calculi V13.01
      infection V13.02
      nephrotic syndrome V13.03
      specified NEC V13.09
  drug use
    nonprescribed (*see also* Abuse, drugs, nondependent) 305.9 ☑
    patent (*see also* Abuse, drugs, non-dependent) 305.9 ☑
  dysplasia
    cervical (conditions classifiable to 622.10-622.12) V13.22
  effect NEC of external cause V15.89
  embolism (pulmonary) V12.51
  emotional abuse V15.42
  encephalitis V12.42
  endocrine disorder V12.2
  estrogen therapy V87.43 ●
  extracorporeal membrane oxygenation (EC-MO) V15.87
  failed ●
    conscious sedation V15.80 ●
    moderate sedation V15.80 ●
  falling V15.88
  family
    allergy V19.6
    anemia V18.2
    arteriosclerosis V17.49
    arthritis V17.7
    asthma V17.5
    blindness V19.0
    blood disorder NEC V18.3
    cardiovascular disease V17.49
    carrier, genetic disease V18.9
    cerebrovascular disease V17.1
    chronic respiratory condition NEC V17.6
    colonic polyps V18.51
    congenital anomalies V19.5
    consanguinity V19.7
    coronary artery disease V17.3

History of — *continued*
  family — *continued*
    cystic fibrosis V18.19
    deafness V19.2
    diabetes mellitus V18.0
    digestive disorders V18.59
    disease or disorder (of)
      allergic V19.6
      blood NEC V18.3
      cardiovascular NEC V17.49
      cerebrovascular V17.1
      colonic polyps V18.51
      coronary artery V17.3
      death, sudden cardiac (SCD) V17.41
      digestive V18.59
      ear NEC V19.3
      endocrine V18.19
        multiple neoplasia [MEN] syndrome V18.11
      eye NEC V19.1
      genitourinary NEC V18.7
      hypertensive V17.49
      infectious V18.8
      ischemic heart V17.3
      kidney V18.69
        polycystic V18.61
      mental V17.0
      metabolic V18.19
      musculoskeletal NEC V17.89
        osteoporosis V17.81
      neurological NEC V17.2
      parasitic V18.8
      psychiatric condition V17.0
      skin condition V19.4
    ear disorder NEC V19.3
    endocrine disease V18.19
      multiple neoplasia [MEN] syndrome V18.11
    epilepsy V17.2
    eye disorder NEC V19.1
    genetic disease carrier V18.9
    genitourinary disease NEC V18.7
    glomerulonephritis V18.69
    gout V18.19
    hay fever V17.6
    hearing loss V19.2
    hematopoietic neoplasia V16.7
    Hodgkin's disease V16.7
    Huntington's chorea V17.2
    hydrocephalus V19.5
    hypertension V17.49
    infarction, myocardial V17.3
    infectious disease V18.8
    ischemic heart disease V17.3
    kidney disease V18.69
      polycystic V18.61
    leukemia V16.6
    lymphatic malignant neoplasia NEC V16.7
    malignant neoplasm (of) NEC V16.9
      anorectal V16.0
      anus V16.0
      appendix V16.0
      bladder V16.52
      bone V16.8
      brain V16.8
      breast V16.3
        male V16.8
      bronchus V16.1
      cecum V16.0
      cervix V16.49
      colon V16.0
      duodenum V16.0
      esophagus V16.0
      eye V16.8
      gallbladder V16.0
      gastrointestinal tract V16.0
      genital organs V16.40
      hemopoietic NEC V16.7
      ileum V16.0
      ilium V16.8
      intestine V16.0
      intrathoracic organs NEC V16.2
      kidney V16.51
      larynx V16.2
      liver V16.0
      lung V16.1

History of — *continued*
  family — *continued*
    malignant neoplasm — *continued*
      lymphatic NEC V16.7
      ovary V16.41
      oviduct V16.41
      pancreas V16.0
      penis V16.49
      prostate V16.42
      rectum V16.0
      respiratory organs NEC V16.2
      skin V16.8
      specified site NEC V16.8
      stomach V16.0
      testis V16.43
      trachea V16.1
      ureter V16.59
      urethra V16.59
      urinary organs V16.59
      uterus V16.49
      vagina V16.49
      vulva V16.49
    MEN (multiple endocrine neoplasia syndrome) V18.11
    mental retardation V18.4
    metabolic disease NEC V18.19
    mongolism V19.5
    multiple
      endocrine neoplasia [MEN] syndrome V18.11
      myeloma V16.7
    musculoskeletal disease NEC V17.89
      osteoporosis V17.81
    myocardial infarction V17.3
    nephritis V18.69
    nephrosis V18.69
    osteoporosis V17.81
    parasitic disease V18.8
    polycystic kidney disease V18.61
    psychiatric disorder V17.0
    psychosis V17.0
    retardation, mental V18.4
    retinitis pigmentosa V19.1
    schizophrenia V17.0
    skin conditions V19.4
    specified condition NEC V19.8
    stroke (cerebrovascular) V17.1
    sudden cardiac death (SCD) V17.41
    visual loss V19.0
  fracture, healed
    pathologic V13.51
    stress V13.52
    traumatic V15.51
  genital system disorder V13.29
    pre-term labor V13.21
  health hazard V15.9
    falling V15.88
    specified cause NEC V15.89
  hepatitis
    B V12.09
    C V12.09
  Hodgkin's disease V10.72
  hypospadias V13.61
  immunity disorder V12.2
  immunosuppression therapy V87.46 ●
  infarction, cerebral, without residual deficits V12.54
  infection
    central nervous system V12.42
    urinary (tract) V13.02
  infectious disease V12.00
    malaria V12.03
    methicillin resistant Staphylococcus aureus (MRSA) V12.04
    MRSA (methicillin resistant Staphylococcus aureus) V12.04
    poliomyelitis V12.02
    specified NEC V12.09
    tuberculosis V12.01
  injury NEC V15.59
    traumatic brain V15.52 ●
  insufficient prenatal care V23.7
  in utero procedure
    during pregnancy V15.21
    while a fetus V15.22
  irradiation V15.3

History of — *continued*
  leukemia V10.60
    lymphoid V10.61
    monocytic V10.63
    myeloid V10.62
    specified type NEC V10.69
  little or no prenatal care V23.7
  low birth weight (*see also* Status, low birth weight) V21.30
  lymphosarcoma V10.71
  malaria V12.03
  malignant carcinoid tumor V10.91 ●
  malignant neoplasm (of) V10.90 ▲
    accessory sinus V10.22
    adrenal V10.88
    anus V10.06
    bile duct V10.09
    bladder V10.51
    bone V10.81
    brain V10.85
    breast V10.3
    bronchus V10.11
    cervix uteri V10.41
    colon V10.05
    connective tissue NEC V10.89
    corpus uteri V10.42
    digestive system V10.00
      specified part NEC V10.09
    duodenum V10.09
    endocrine gland NEC V10.88
    epididymis V10.48
    esophagus V10.03
    eye V10.84
    fallopian tube V10.44
    female genital organ V10.40
      specified site NEC V10.44
    gallbladder V10.09
    gastrointestinal tract V10.00
    gum V10.02
    hematopoietic NEC V10.79
    hypopharynx V10.02
    ileum V10.09
    intrathoracic organs NEC V10.20
    jejunum V10.09
    kidney V10.52
    large intestine V10.05
    larynx V10.21
    lip V10.02
    liver V10.07
    lung V10.11
    lymphatic NEC V10.79
    lymph glands or nodes NEC V10.79
    male genital organ V10.45
      specified site NEC V10.49
    mediastinum V10.29
    melanoma (of skin) V10.82
    middle ear V10.22
    mouth V10.02
      specified part NEC V10.02
    nasal cavities V10.22
    nasopharynx V10.02
    nervous system NEC V10.86
    nose V10.22
    oropharynx V10.02
    ovary V10.43
    pancreas V10.09
    parathyroid V10.88
    penis V10.49
    pharynx V10.02
    pineal V10.88
    pituitary V10.88
    placenta V10.44
    pleura V10.29
    prostate V10.46
    rectosigmoid junction V10.06
    rectum V10.06
    renal pelvis V10.53
    respiratory organs NEC V10.20
    salivary gland V10.02
    skin V10.83
      melanoma V10.82
    small intestine NEC V10.09
    soft tissue NEC V10.89
    specified site NEC V10.89
    stomach V10.04
    testis V10.47

☑ Additional Digit Required — Refer to the Tabular List for Digit Selection   Subterms under main terms may continue to next column or page

136 — Volume 2 • October 2009   ▶◀ Revised Text   ● New Line   ▲ Revised Code   2010 ICD-9-CM

History of — *continued*
　malignant neoplasm — *continued*
　　thymus V10.29
　　thyroid V10.87
　　tongue V10.01
　　trachea V10.12
　　ureter V10.59
　　urethra V10.59
　　urinary organ V10.50
　　uterine adnexa V10.44
　　uterus V10.42
　　vagina V10.44
　　vulva V10.44
　malignant neuroendocrine tumor V10.91 ●
　manic-depressive psychosis V11.1
　meningitis V12.42
　mental disorder V11.9
　　affective type V11.1
　　manic-depressive V11.1
　　neurosis V11.2
　　schizophrenia V11.0
　　specified type NEC V11.8
　Merkel cell carcinoma V10.91 ●
　metabolic disorder V12.2
　methicillin resistant Staphylococcus aureus (MRSA) V12.04
　MRSA (methicillin resistant Staphylococcus aureus) V12.04
　musculoskeletal disorder NEC V13.59
　myocardial infarction 412
　neglect (emotional) V15.42
　nephric syndrome V13.03
　nervous system disorder V12.40
　　specified type NEC V12.49
　neurosis V11.2
　noncompliance with medical treatment V15.81
　nutritional deficiency V12.1
　obstetric disorder V13.29
　　affecting management of current pregnancy V23.49
　　　pre-term labor V23.41
　　pre-term labor V13.21
　parasitic disease V12.00
　　specified NEC V12.09
　perinatal problems V13.7
　　low birth weight (*see also* Status, low birth weight) V21.30
　physical abuse V15.41
　poisoning V15.6
　poliomyelitis V12.02
　polyps, colonic V12.72
　poor obstetric V13.29
　　affecting management of current pregnancy V23.49
　　　pre-term labor V23.41
　　pre-term labor V13.21
　prolonged reversible ischemic neurologic deficit (PRIND) V12.54
　psychiatric disorder V11.9
　　affective type V11.1
　　manic-depressive V11.1
　　neurosis V11.2
　　schizophrenia V11.0
　　specified type NEC V11.8
　psychological trauma V15.49
　　emotional abuse V15.42
　　neglect V15.42
　　physical abuse V15.41
　　rape V15.41
　psychoneurosis V11.2
　radiation therapy V15.3
　rape V15.41
　respiratory system disease V12.60
　　pneumonia V12.61
　　specified NEC V12.69
　reticulosarcoma V10.71
　return from military deployment V62.22
　reversible ischemic neurologic deficit (RIND) V12.54
　schizophrenia V11.0
　skin disease V13.3
　smoking (tobacco) V15.82
　steroid therapy V87.45 ●
　　inhaled V87.44 ●
　　systemic V87.45 ●

History of — *continued*
　stroke without residual deficits V12.54
　subcutaneous tissue disease V13.3
　sudden
　　cardiac
　　　arrest V12.53
　　　death (successfully resuscitated) V12.53
　surgery to
　　great vessels V15.1
　　heart V15.1
　　in utero
　　　during pregnancy V15.21
　　　while a fetus V15.22
　　organs NEC V15.29
　syndrome, nephrotic V13.03
　therapy
　　antineoplastic drug V87.41
　　drug NEC V87.49
　　estrogen V87.43 ●
　　immunosuppression V87.46 ●
　　monoclonal drug V87.42
　　steroid V87.45 ●
　　　inhaled V87.44 ●
　　　systemic V87.45 ●
　thrombophlebitis V12.52
　thrombosis V12.51
　tobacco use V15.82
　trophoblastic disease V13.1
　　affecting management of pregnancy V23.1
　tuberculosis V12.01
　ulcer, peptic V12.71
　urinary system disorder V13.00
　　calculi V13.01
　　infection V13.02
　　nephrotic syndrome V13.03
　　specified NEC V13.09
His-Werner disease (trench fever) 083.1
HIT (heparin-induced thrombocytopenia) 289.84
Hives (bold) — *see also* Urticaria 708.9
HIV infection (disease) (illness) — *see* Human immunodeficiency virus (disease) (illness) (infection)
Hoarseness 784.42　　　　　　▲
Hobnail liver — *see* Cirrhosis, portal
Hobo, hoboism V60.0
Hodgkin's
　disease (M9650/3) 201.9 ☑
　　lymphocytic
　　　depletion (M9653/3) 201.7 ☑
　　　　diffuse fibrosis (M9654/3) 201.7 ☑
　　　　reticular type (M9655/3) 201.7 ☑
　　　predominance (M9651/3) 201.4 ☑
　　lymphocytic-histiocytic predominance (M9651/3) 201.4 ☑
　　mixed cellularity (M9652/3) 201.6 ☑
　　nodular sclerosis (M9656/3) 201.5 ☑
　　　cellular phase (M9657/3) 201.5 ☑
　granuloma (M9661/3) 201.1 ☑
　lymphogranulomatosis (M9650/3) 201.9 ☑
　lymphoma (M9650/3) 201.9 ☑
　lymphosarcoma (M9650/3) 201.9 ☑
　paragranuloma (M9660/3) 201.0 ☑
　sarcoma (M9662/3) 201.2 ☑
Hodgson's disease (aneurysmal dilatation of aorta) 441.9
　ruptured 441.5
Hodi-potsy 111.0
Hoffa (-Kastert) disease or syndrome (liposynovitis prepatellaris) 272.8
Hoffmann-Bouveret syndrome (paroxysmal tachycardia) 427.2
Hoffman's syndrome 244.9 [359.5]
Hole
　macula 362.54
　optic disc, crater-like 377.22
　retina (macula) 362.54
　　round 361.31
　　　with detachment 361.01
Holla disease — *see also* Spherocytosis 282.0
Holländer-Simons syndrome (progressive lipodystrophy) 272.6
Hollow foot (congenital) 754.71
　acquired 736.73
Holmes' syndrome (visual disorientation) 368.16
Holoprosencephaly 742.2

Holoprosencephaly — *continued*
　due to
　　trisomy 13 758.1
　　trisomy 18 758.2
Holthouse's hernia — *see* Hernia, inguinal
Homesickness 309.89
Homocystinemia 270.4
Homocystinuria 270.4
Homologous serum jaundice (prophylactic) (therapeutic) — *see* Hepatitis, viral
Homosexuality — omit code
　ego-dystonic 302.0
　pedophilic 302.2
　problems with 302.0
Homozygous Hb-S disease 282.61
Honeycomb lung 518.89
　congenital 748.4
Hong Kong ear 117.3
HOOD (hereditary osteo-onychodysplasia) 756.89 ●
Hooded
　clitoris 752.49
　penis 752.69
Hookworm (anemia) (disease) (infestation) — *see* Ancylostomiasis
Hoppe-Goldflam syndrome 358.00
Hordeolum (external) (eyelid) 373.11
　internal 373.12
Horn
　cutaneous 702.8
　　cheek 702.8
　　eyelid 702.8
　　penis 702.8
　iliac 756.89
　nail 703.8
　　congenital 757.5
　papillary 700
Horner's
　syndrome (*see also* Neuropathy, peripheral, autonomic) 337.9
　　traumatic 954.0
　teeth 520.4
Horseshoe kidney (congenital) 753.3
Horton's
　disease (temporal arteritis) 446.5
　headache or neuralgia 339.00
Hospice care V66.7
Hospitalism (in children) NEC 309.83
Hourglass contraction, contracture
　bladder 596.8
　gallbladder 575.2
　　congenital 751.69
　stomach 536.8
　　congenital 750.7
　　psychogenic 306.4
　uterus 661.4 ☑
　　affecting fetus or newborn 763.7
Household circumstance affecting care V60.9
　specified type NEC V60.89　　　▲
Housemaid's knee 727.2
Housing circumstance affecting care V60.9
　specified type NEC V60.89　　　▲
HTLV-I infection 079.51
HTLV-II infection 079.52
HTLV-III/LAV (disease) (illness) (infection) — *see* Human immunodeficiency virus (disease) (illness) (infection)
HTLV-III (disease) (illness) (infection) — *see* Human immunodeficiency virus (disease) (illness) (infection)
Huchard's disease (continued arterial hypertension) 401.9
Hudson-Stähli lines 371.11
Huguier's disease (uterine fibroma) 218.9
Human bite (open wound) — *see also* Wound, open, by site
　intact skin surface — *see* Contusion
Human immunodeficiency virus (disease) (illness) 042
　infection V08
　　with symptoms, symptomatic 042
Human immunodeficiency virus-2 infection 079.53
Human immunovirus (disease) (illness) (infection) — *see* Human immunodeficiency virus (disease) (illness) (infection)
Human papillomavirus 079.4

Human papillomavirus — *continued*
　high risk, DNA test positive
　　anal 796.75
　　cervical 795.05
　　vaginal 795.15
　low risk, DNA test positive
　　anal 796.79
　　cervical 795.09
　　vaginal 795.19
Human parvovirus 079.83
Human T-cell lymphotrophic virus-I infection 079.51
Human T-cell lymphotrophic virus-II infection 079.52
Human T-cell lymphotrophic virus-III (disease) (illness) (infection) — *see* Human immunodeficiency virus (disease) (illness) (infection)
Humpback (acquired) 737.9
　congenital 756.19
Hum, venous — omit code
Hunchback (acquired) 737.9
　congenital 756.19
Hunger 994.2
　air, psychogenic 306.1
　disease 251.1
Hungry bone syndrome 275.5
Hunner's ulcer — *see also* Cystitis 595.1
Hunt's
　neuralgia 053.11
　syndrome (herpetic geniculate ganglionitis) 053.11
　　dyssynergia cerebellaris myoclonica 334.2
Hunter's glossitis 529.4
Hunterian chancre 091.0
Hunter (-Hurler) syndrome (mucopolysaccharidosis II) 277.5
Huntington's
　chorea 333.4
　disease 333.4
Huppert's disease (multiple myeloma) (M9730/3) 203.0 ☑
Hurler (-Hunter) disease or syndrome (mucopolysaccharidosis II) 277.5
Hürthle cell
　adenocarcinoma (M8290/3) 193
　adenoma (M8290/0) 226
　carcinoma (M8290/3) 193
　tumor (M8290/0) 226
Hutchinson's
　disease meaning
　　angioma serpiginosum 709.1
　　cheiropompholyx 705.81
　　prurigo estivalis 692.72
　　summer eruption, or summer prurigo 692.72
　incisors 090.5
　melanotic freckle (M8742/2) (*see also* Neoplasm, skin, in situ)
　　malignant melanoma in (M8742/3) — *see* Melanoma
　teeth or incisors (congenital syphilis) 090.5
Hutchinson-Boeck disease or syndrome (sarcoidosis) 135
Hutchinson-Gilford disease or syndrome (progeria) 259.8
Hyaline
　degeneration (diffuse) (generalized) 728.9
　　localized — *see* Degeneration, by site
　membrane (disease) (lung) (newborn) 769
Hyalinosis cutis et mucosae 272.8
Hyalin plaque, sclera, senile 379.16
Hyalitis (asteroid) 379.22
　syphilitic 095.8
Hydatid
　cyst or tumor (*see also* Echinococcus)
　　fallopian tube 752.11
　mole — *see* Hydatidiform mole
　Morgagni (congenital) 752.89
　　fallopian tube 752.11
Hydatidiform mole (benign) (complicating pregnancy) (delivered) (undelivered) 630
　invasive (M9100/1) 236.1
　malignant (M9100/1) 236.1
　previous, affecting management of pregnancy V23.1

☑ Additional Digit Required — Refer to the Tabular List for Digit Selection　　　　　　　　　　ᴺᴱᵂ Subterms under main terms may continue to next column or page

2010 ICD-9-CM　　　▶◀ Revised Text　　　● New Line　　　▲ Revised Code　　　**October 2009 • Volume 2 — 137**

Hydatidosis — *see* Echinococcus
Hyde's disease (prurigo nodularis) 698.3
Hydradenitis 705.83
Hydradenoma (M8400/0) — *see* Hidradenoma
Hydralazine lupus or syndrome
  correct substance properly administered 695.4
  overdose or wrong substance given or taken 972.6
Hydramnios 657.0 ☑
  affecting fetus or newborn 761.3
Hydrancephaly 742.3
  with spina bifida (*see also* Spina bifida) 741.0 ☑
Hydranencephaly 742.3
  with spina bifida (*see also* Spina bifida) 741.0 ☑
Hydrargyrism NEC 985.0
Hydrarthrosis — *see also* Effusion, joint 719.0 ☑
  gonococcal 098.50
  intermittent (*see also* Rheumatism, palindromic) 719.3 ☑
  of yaws (early) (late) 102.6
  syphilitic 095.8
    congenital 090.5
Hydremia 285.9
Hydrencephalocele (congenital) 742.0
Hydrencephalomeningocele (congenital) 742.0
Hydroa 694.0
  aestivale 692.72
  gestationis 646.8 ☑
  herpetiformis 694.0
  pruriginosa 694.0
  vacciniforme 692.72
Hydroadenitis 705.83
Hydrocalycosis — *see also* Hydronephrosis 591
  congenital 753.29
Hydrocalyx — *see also* Hydronephrosis 591
Hydrocele (calcified) (chylous) (idiopathic) (infantile) (inguinal canal) (recurrent) (senile) (spermatic cord) (testis) (tunica vaginalis) 603.9
  canal of Nuck (female) 629.1
    male 603.9
  congenital 778.6
  encysted 603.0
    congenital 778.6
  female NEC 629.89
  infected 603.1
  round ligament 629.89
  specified type NEC 603.8
    congenital 778.6
  spinalis (*see also* Spina bifida) 741.9 ☑
  vulva 624.8
Hydrocephalic fetus
  affecting management or pregnancy 655.0 ☑
  causing disproportion 653.6 ☑
    with obstructed labor 660.1 ☑
      affecting fetus or newborn 763.1
Hydrocephalus (acquired) (external) (internal) (malignant) (noncommunicating) (obstructive) (recurrent) 331.4
  aqueduct of Sylvius stricture 742.3
    with spina bifida (*see also* Spina bifida) 741.0 ☑
  chronic 742.3
    with spina bifida (*see also* Spina bifida) 741.0 ☑
  communicating 331.3
  congenital (external) (internal) 742.3
    with spina bifida (*see also* Spina bifida) 741.0 ☑
  due to
    stricture of aqueduct of Sylvius 742.3
      with spina bifida (*see also* Spina bifida) 741.0 ☑
    toxoplasmosis (congenital) 771.2
  fetal affecting management of pregnancy 655.0 ☑
  foramen Magendie block (acquired) 331.3
    congenital 742.3
      with spina bifida (*see also* Spina bifida) 741.0 ☑
  newborn 742.3
    with spina bifida (*see also* Spina bifida) 741.0 ☑
  normal pressure 331.5

Hydrocephalus — *continued*
  normal pressure — *continued*
    idiopathic (INPH) 331.5
    secondary 331.3
  otitic 348.2
  syphilitic, congenital 090.49
  tuberculous (*see also* Tuberculosis) 013.8 ☑
Hydrocolpos (congenital) 623.8
Hydrocystoma (M8404/0) — *see* Neoplasm, skin, benign
Hydroencephalocele (congenital) 742.0
Hydroencephalomeningocele (congenital) 742.0
Hydrohematopneumothorax — *see also* Hemothorax 511.89
Hydromeningitis — *see* Meningitis
Hydromeningocele (spinal) — *see also* Spina bifida 741.9 ☑
  cranial 742.0
Hydrometra 621.8
Hydrometrocolpos 623.8
Hydromicrocephaly 742.1
Hydromphalus (congenital) (since birth) 757.39
Hydromyelia 742.53
Hydromyelocele — *see also* Spina bifida 741.9 ☑
Hydronephrosis 591
  atrophic 591
  congenital 753.29
  due to S. hematobium 120.0
  early 591
  functionless (infected) 591
  infected 591
  intermittent 591
  primary 591
  secondary 591
  tuberculous (*see also* Tuberculosis) 016.0 ☑
Hydropericarditis — *see also* Pericarditis 423.9
Hydropericardium — *see also* Pericarditis 423.9
Hydroperitoneum 789.59
Hydrophobia 071
Hydrophthalmos — *see also* Buphthalmia 743.20
Hydropneumohemothorax — *see also* Hemothorax 511.89
Hydropneumopericarditis — *see also* Pericarditis 423.9
Hydropneumopericardium — *see also* Pericarditis 423.9
Hydropneumothorax 511.89
  nontuberculous 511.89
    bacterial 511.1
    pneumococcal 511.1
    staphylococcal 511.1
    streptococcal 511.1
  traumatic 860.0
    with open wound into thorax 860.1
  tuberculous (*see also* Tuberculosis, pleura) 012.0 ☑
Hydrops 782.3
  abdominis 789.59
  amnii (complicating pregnancy) (*see also* Hydramnios) 657.0 ☑
  articulorum intermittens (*see also* Rheumatism, palindromic) 719.3 ☑
  cardiac (*see also* Failure, heart) 428.0
  congenital — *see* Hydrops, fetalis
  endolymphatic — *see also* Disease, Ménière's 386.00
  fetal(is) or newborn 778.0
    due to isoimmunization 773.3
    not due to isoimmunization 778.0
  gallbladder 575.3
  idiopathic (fetus or newborn) 778.0
  joint (see also Effusion, joint) 719.0 ☑
  labyrinth (*see also* Disease, Ménière's) 386.00
  meningeal NEC 331.4
  nutritional 262
  pericardium — *see* Pericarditis
  pleura (*see also* Hydrothorax) 511.89
  renal (*see also* Nephrosis) 581.9
  spermatic cord (*see also* Hydrocele) 603.9
Hydropyonephrosis — *see also* Pyelitis 590.80
  chronic 590.00
Hydrorachis 742.53
Hydrorrhea (nasal) 478.19
  gravidarum 658.1 ☑

Hydrorrhea — *continued*
  pregnancy 658.1 ☑
Hydrosadenitis 705.83
Hydrosalpinx (fallopian tube) (follicularis) 614.1
Hydrothorax (double) (pleural) 511.89
  chylous (nonfilarial) 457.8
    filaria (*see also* Infestation, filarial) 125.9
  nontuberculous 511.89
    bacterial 511.1
    pneumococcal 511.1
    staphylococcal 511.1
    streptococcal 511.1
  traumatic 862.29
    with open wound into thorax 862.39
  tuberculous (*see also* Tuberculosis, pleura) 012.0 ☑
Hydroureter 593.5
  congenital 753.22
Hydroureteronephrosis — *see also* Hydronephrosis 591
Hydrourethra 599.84
Hydroxykynureninuria 270.2
Hydroxyprolinemia 270.8
Hydroxyprolinuria 270.8
Hygroma (congenital) (cystic) (M9173/0) 228.1
  prepatellar 727.3
  subdural — *see* Hematoma, subdural
Hymen — *see* condition
Hymenolepiasis (diminuta) (infection) (infestation) (nana) 123.6
Hymenolepsis (diminuta) (infection) (infestation) (nana) 123.6
Hypalgesia — *see also* Disturbance, sensation 782.0
Hyperabduction syndrome 447.8
Hyperacidity, gastric 536.8
  psychogenic 306.4
Hyperactive, hyperactivity 314.01
  basal cell, uterine cervix 622.10
  bladder 596.51
  bowel (syndrome) 564.9
    sounds 787.5
  cervix epithelial (basal) 622.10
  child 314.01
  colon 564.9
  gastrointestinal 536.8
    psychogenic 306.4
  intestine 564.9
  labyrinth (unilateral) 386.51
    with loss of labyrinthine reactivity 386.58
    bilateral 386.52
  nasal mucous membrane 478.19
  stomach 536.8
  thyroid (gland) (*see also* Thyrotoxicosis) 242.9 ☑
Hyperacusis 388.42
Hyperadrenalism (cortical) 255.3
  medullary 255.6
Hyperadrenocorticism 255.3
  congenital 255.2
  iatrogenic
    correct substance properly administered 255.3
    overdose or wrong substance given or taken 962.0
Hyperaffectivity 301.11
Hyperaldosteronism (atypical) (hyperplastic) (normoaldosteronal) (normotensive) (primary) 255.10
  secondary 255.14
Hyperalgesia — *see also* Disturbance, sensation 782.0
Hyperalimentation 783.6
  carotene 278.3
  specified NEC 278.8
  vitamin A 278.2
  vitamin D 278.4
Hyperaminoaciduria 270.9
  arginine 270.6
  citrulline 270.6
  cystine 270.0
  glycine 270.0
  lysine 270.7
  ornithine 270.6
  renal (types I, II, III) 270.0
Hyperammonemia (congenital) 270.6

Hyperamnesia 780.99
Hyperamylasemia 790.5
Hyperaphia 782.0
Hyperazotemia 791.9
Hyperbetalipoproteinemia (acquired) (essential) (familial) (hereditary) (primary) (secondary) 272.2
  with prebetalipoproteinemia 272.2
Hyperbilirubinemia 782.4
  congenital 277.4
  constitutional 277.4
  neonatal (transient) (*see also* Jaundice, fetus or newborn) 774.6
  of prematurity 774.2
Hyperbilirubinemica encephalopathia, newborn 774.7
  due to isoimmunization 773.4
Hypercalcemia, hypercalcemic (idiopathic) 275.42
  nephropathy 588.89
Hypercalcinuria 275.40
Hypercapnia 786.09
  with mixed acid-based disorder 276.4
  fetal, affecting newborn 770.89
Hypercarotinemia 278.3
Hypercementosis 521.5
Hyperchloremia 276.9
Hyperchlorhydria 536.8
  neurotic 306.4
  psychogenic 306.4
Hypercholesterinemia — *see* Hypercholesterolemia
Hypercholesterolemia 272.0
  with hyperglyceridemia, endogenous 272.2
  essential 272.0
  familial 272.0
  hereditary 272.0
  primary 272.0
  pure 272.0
Hypercholesterolosis 272.0
Hyperchylia gastrica 536.8
  psychogenic 306.4
Hyperchylomicronemia (familial) (with hyperbetalipoproteinemia) 272.3
Hypercoagulation syndrome (primary) 289.81
  secondary 289.82
Hypercorticosteronism
  correct substance properly administered 255.3
  overdose or wrong substance given or taken 962.0
Hypercortisonism
  correct substance properly administered 255.3
  overdose or wrong substance given or taken 962.0
Hyperdynamic beta-adrenergic state or syndrome (circulatory) 429.82
Hyperekplexia 759.89
Hyperelectrolytemia 276.9
Hyperemesis 536.2
  arising during pregnancy — *see* Hyperemesis, gravidarum
  gravidarum (mild) (before 22 completed weeks gestation) 643.0 ☑
    with
      carbohydrate depletion 643.1 ☑
      dehydration 643.1 ☑
      electrolyte imbalance 643.1 ☑
      metabolic disturbance 643.1 ☑
    affecting fetus or newborn 761.8
    severe (with metabolic disturbance) 643.1 ☑
  psychogenic 306.4
Hyperemia (acute) 780.99
  anal mucosa 569.49
  bladder 596.7
  cerebral 437.8
  conjunctiva 372.71
  ear, internal, acute 386.30
  enteric 564.89
  eye 372.71
  eyelid (active) (passive) 374.82
  intestine 564.89
  iris 364.41
  kidney 593.81
  labyrinth 386.30
  liver (active) (passive) 573.8

Hyperemia — *continued*
  lung 514
  ovary 620.8
  passive 780.99
  pulmonary 514
  renal 593.81
  retina 362.89
  spleen 289.59
  stomach 537.89
Hyperesthesia (body surface) — *see also* Distur-
    bance, sensation 782.0
  larynx (reflex) 478.79
    hysterical 300.11
  pharynx (reflex) 478.29
Hyperestrinism 256.0
Hyperestrogenism 256.0
Hyperestrogenosis 256.0
Hyperexplexia 759.89
Hyperextension, joint 718.80
  ankle 718.87
  elbow 718.82
  foot 718.87
  hand 718.84
  hip 718.85
  knee 718.86
  multiple sites 718.89
  pelvic region 718.85
  shoulder (region) 718.81
  specified site NEC 718.88
  wrist 718.83
Hyperfibrinolysis — *see* Fibrinolysis
Hyperfolliculinism 256.0
Hyperfructosemia 271.2
Hyperfunction
  adrenal (cortex) 255.3
    androgenic, acquired benign 255.3
    medulla 255.6
    virilism 255.2
  corticoadrenal NEC 255.3
  labyrinth — *see* Hyperactive, labyrinth
  medulloadrenal 255.6
  ovary 256.1
    estrogen 256.0
  pancreas 577.8
  parathyroid (gland) 252.00
  pituitary (anterior) (gland) (lobe) 253.1
  testicular 257.0
Hypergammaglobulinemia 289.89
  monoclonal, benign (BMH) 273.1
  polyclonal 273.0
  Waldenström's 273.0
Hyperglobulinemia 273.8
Hyperglycemia 790.29
  maternal
    affecting fetus or newborn 775.0
    manifest diabetes in infant 775.1
  postpancreatectomy (complete) (partial) 251.3
Hyperglyceridemia 272.1
  endogenous 272.1
  essential 272.1
  familial 272.1
  hereditary 272.1
  mixed 272.3
  pure 272.1
Hyperglycinemia 270.7
Hypergonadism
  ovarian 256.1
  testicular (infantile) (primary) 257.0
Hyperheparinemia — *see also* Circulating anti-
    coagulants 286.5
Hyperhidrosis, hyperidrosis 705.21
  axilla 705.21
  face 705.21
  focal (localized) 705.21
    primary 705.21
      axilla 705.21
      face 705.21
      palms 705.21
      soles 705.21
    secondary 705.22
      axilla 705.22
      face 705.22
      palms 705.22
      soles 705.22
  generalized 780.8
  palms 705.21

Hyperhidrosis, hyperidrosis — *continued*
  psychogenic 306.3
  secondary 780.8
  soles 705.21
Hyperhistidinemia 270.5
Hyperinsulinism (ectopic) (functional) (organic)
    NEC 251.1
  iatrogenic 251.0
  reactive 251.2
  spontaneous 251.2
  therapeutic misadventure (from administration
    of insulin) 962.3
Hyperiodemia 276.9
Hyperirritability (cerebral), in newborn 779.1
Hyperkalemia 276.7
Hyperkeratosis — *see also* Keratosis 701.1
  cervix 622.2
  congenital 757.39
  cornea 371.89
  due to yaws (early) (late) (palmar or plantar)
    102.3
  eccentrica 757.39
  figurata centrifuga atrophica 757.39
  follicularis 757.39
    in cutem penetrans 701.1
  limbic (cornea) 371.89
  palmoplantaris climacterica 701.1
  pinta (carate) 103.1
  senile (with pruritus) 702.0
  tongue 528.79
  universalis congenita 757.1
  vagina 623.1
  vocal cord 478.5
  vulva 624.09
Hyperkinesia, hyperkinetic (disease) (reaction)
    (syndrome) 314.9
  with
    attention deficit — *see* Disorder, attention
      deficit
    conduct disorder 314.2
    developmental delay 314.1
    simple disturbance of activity and atten-
      tion 314.01
    specified manifestation NEC 314.8
  heart (disease) 429.82
  of childhood or adolescence NEC 314.9
Hyperlacrimation — *see also* Epiphora 375.20
Hyperlipemia — *see also* Hyperlipidemia 272.4
Hyperlipidemia 272.4
  carbohydrate-induced 272.1
  combined 272.2 ▲
  endogenous 272.1
  exogenous 272.3
  fat-induced 272.3
  group
    A 272.0
    B 272.1
    C 272.2
    D 272.3
  mixed 272.2
  specified type NEC 272.4
Hyperlipidosis 272.7
  hereditary 272.7
Hyperlipoproteinemia (acquired) (essential)
    (familial) (hereditary) (primary) (secondary)
    272.4
  Fredrickson type
    I 272.3
    IIa 272.0
    IIb 272.2
    III 272.2
    IV 272.1
    V 272.3
  low-density-lipoid-type (LDL) 272.0
  very-low-density-lipoid-type (VLDL) 272.1
Hyperlucent lung, unilateral 492.8
Hyperluteinization 256.1
Hyperlysinemia 270.7
Hypermagnesemia 275.2
  neonatal 775.5
Hypermaturity (fetus or newborn)
  post-term infant 766.21
  prolonged gestation infant 766.22
Hypermenorrhea 626.2
Hypermetabolism 794.7
Hypermethioninemia 270.4

Hypermetropia (congenital) 367.0
Hypermobility
  cecum 564.9
  coccyx 724.71
  colon 564.9
    psychogenic 306.4
  ileum 564.89
  joint (acquired) 718.80
    ankle 718.87
    elbow 718.82
    foot 718.87
    hand 718.84
    hip 718.85
    knee 718.86
    multiple sites 718.89
    pelvic region 718.85
    shoulder (region) 718.81
    specified site NEC 718.88
    wrist 718.83
  kidney, congenital 753.3
  meniscus (knee) 717.5
  scapula 718.81
  stomach 536.8
    psychogenic 306.4
  syndrome 728.5
  testis, congenital 752.52
  urethral 599.81
Hypermotility
  gastrointestinal 536.8
  intestine 564.9
    psychogenic 306.4
  stomach 536.8
Hypernasality 784.43   ▲
Hypernatremia 276.0
  with water depletion 276.0
Hypernephroma (M8312/3) 189.0
Hyperopia 367.0
Hyperorexia 783.6
Hyperornithinemia 270.6
Hyperosmia — *see also* Disturbance, sensation
    781.1
Hyperosmolality 276.0
Hyperosteogenesis 733.99
Hyperostosis 733.99
  calvarial 733.3
  cortical 733.3
    infantile 756.59
  frontal, internal of skull 733.3
  interna frontalis 733.3
  monomelic 733.99
  skull 733.3
    congenital 756.0
  vertebral 721.8
    with spondylosis — *see* Spondylosis
    ankylosing 721.6
Hyperovarianism 256.1
Hyperovarism, hyperovaria 256.1
Hyperoxaluria (primary) 271.8
Hyperoxia 987.8
Hyperparathyroidism 252.00
  ectopic 259.3
  other 252.08
  primary 252.01
  secondary (of renal origin) 588.81
    non-renal 252.02
  tertiary 252.08
Hyperpathia — *see also* Disturbance, sensation
    782.0
  psychogenic 307.80
Hyperperistalsis 787.4
  psychogenic 306.4
Hyperpermeability, capillary 448.9
Hyperphagia 783.6
Hyperphenylalaninemia 270.1
Hyperphoria 378.40
  alternating 378.45
Hyperphosphatemia 275.3
Hyperpiesia — *see also* Hypertension 401.9
Hyperpiesis — *see also* Hypertension 401.9
Hyperpigmentation — *see* Pigmentation
Hyperpinealism 259.8
Hyperpipecolatemia 270.7
Hyperpituitarism 253.1
Hyperplasia, hyperplastic
  adenoids (lymphoid tissue) 474.12
    and tonsils 474.10

Hyperplasia, hyperplastic — *continued*
  adrenal (capsule) (cortex) (gland) 255.8
    with
      sexual precocity (male) 255.2
      virilism, adrenal 255.2
      virilization (female) 255.2
    congenital 255.2
    due to excess ACTH (ectopic) (pituitary)
      255.0
    medulla 255.8
  alpha cells (pancreatic)
    with
      gastrin excess 251.5
      glucagon excess 251.4
  appendix (lymphoid) 543.0
  artery, fibromuscular NEC 447.8
    carotid 447.8
    renal 447.3
  bone 733.99
    marrow 289.9
  breast (*see also* Hypertrophy, breast) 611.1
    ductal 610.8   ●
      atypical 610.8   ●
  carotid artery 447.8
  cementation, cementum (teeth) (tooth) 521.5
  cervical gland 785.6
  cervix (uteri) 622.10
    basal cell 622.10
    congenital 752.49
    endometrium 622.10
    polypoid 622.10
  chin 524.05
  clitoris, congenital 752.49
  dentin 521.5
  endocervicitis 616.0
  endometrium, endometrial (adenomatous)
    (atypical) (cystic) (glandular) (polypoid)
    (uterus) 621.30
    with atypia 621.33
    without atypia
      complex 621.32
      simple 621.31
    benign 621.34   ●
    cervix 622.10
  epithelial 709.8
    focal, oral, including tongue 528.79
    mouth (focal) 528.79
    nipple 611.89
    skin 709.8
    tongue (focal) 528.79
    vaginal wall 623.0
  erythroid 289.9
  fascialis ossificans (progressiva) 728.11
  fibromuscular, artery NEC 447.8
    carotid 447.8
    renal 447.3
  genital
    female 629.89
    male 608.89
  gingiva 523.8
  glandularis
    cystica uteri 621.30
    endometrium (uterus) 621.30
    interstitialis uteri 621.30
  granulocytic 288.69
  gum 523.8
  hymen, congenital 752.49
  islands of Langerhans 251.1
  islet cell (pancreatic) 251.9
    alpha cells
      with excess
        gastrin 251.5
        glucagon 251.4
    beta cells 251.1
  juxtaglomerular (complex) (kidney) 593.89
  kidney (congenital) 753.3
  liver (congenital) 751.69
  lymph node (gland) 785.6
  lymphoid (diffuse) (nodular) 785.6
    appendix 543.0
    intestine 569.89
  mandibular 524.02
    alveolar 524.72
    unilateral condylar 526.89
  Marchand multiple nodular (liver) — *see* Cir-
    rhosis, postnecrotic

☑ Additional Digit Required — Refer to the Tabular List for Digit Selection   ▽ Subterms under main terms may continue to next column or page

2010 ICD-9-CM   ▶◀ Revised Text   ● New Line   ▲ Revised Code   **October 2009 • Volume 2 — 139**

Hyperplasia, hyperplastic — *continued*
    maxillary 524.01
        alveolar 524.71
    medulla, adrenal 255.8
    myometrium, myometrial 621.2
    nose (lymphoid) (polypoid) 478.19
    oral soft tissue (inflammatory) (irritative) (mucosa) NEC 528.9
        gingiva 523.8
        tongue 529.8
    organ or site, congenital NEC — *see* Anomaly, specified type NEC
    ovary 620.8
    palate, papillary 528.9
    pancreatic islet cells 251.9
        alpha
            with excess
                gastrin 251.5
                glucagon 251.4
        beta 251.1
    parathyroid (gland) 252.01
    persistent, vitreous (primary) 743.51
    pharynx (lymphoid) 478.29
    prostate 600.90
        with
            other lower urinary tract symptoms (LUTS) 600.91
            urinary
                obstruction 600.91
                retention 600.91
        adenofibromatous 600.20
            with
                other lower urinary tract symptoms (LUTS) 600.21
                urinary
                    obstruction 600.21
                    retention 600.21
        nodular 600.10
            with
                urinary
                    obstruction 600.11
                    retention 600.11

Hyperplasia, hyperplastic — *continued*
    renal artery (fibromuscular) 447.3
    reticuloendothelial (cell) 289.9
    salivary gland (any) 527.1
    Schimmelbusch's 610.1
    suprarenal (capsule) (gland) 255.8
    thymus (gland) (persistent) 254.0
    thyroid (*see also* Goiter) 240.9
        primary 242.0 ☑
        secondary 242.2 ☑
    tonsil (lymphoid tissue) 474.11
        and adenoids 474.10
    urethrovaginal 599.89
    uterus, uterine (myometrium) 621.2
        endometrium (*see also* Hyperplasia, endometrium) 621.30
    vitreous (humor), primary persistent 743.51
    vulva 624.3
    zygoma 738.11
Hyperpnea — *see also* Hyperventilation 786.01
Hyperpotassemia 276.7
Hyperprebetalipoproteinemia 272.1
    with chylomicronemia 272.3
    familial 272.1
Hyperprolactinemia 253.1
Hyperprolinemia 270.8
Hyperproteinemia 273.8
Hyperprothrombinemia 289.89
Hyperpselaphesia 782.0
Hyperpyrexia 780.60
    heat (effects of) 992.0
    malarial (*see also* Malaria) 084.6
    malignant, due to anesthetic 995.86
    rheumatic — *see* Fever, rheumatic
    unknown origin (*see also* Pyrexia) 780.60
Hyperreactor, vascular 780.2
Hyperreflexia 796.1
    bladder, autonomic 596.54
        with cauda equina 344.61
    detrusor 344.61
Hypersalivation — *see also* Ptyalism 527.7
Hypersarcosinemia 270.8

Hypersecretion
    ACTH 255.3
    androgens (ovarian) 256.1
    calcitonin 246.0
    corticoadrenal 255.3
    cortisol 255.0
    estrogen 256.0
    gastric 536.8
        psychogenic 306.4
    gastrin 251.5
    glucagon 251.4
    hormone
        ACTH 255.3
        anterior pituitary 253.1
        growth NEC 253.0
        ovarian androgen 256.1
        testicular 257.0
        thyroid stimulating 242.8 ☑
    insulin — *see* Hyperinsulinism
    lacrimal glands (*see also* Epiphora) 375.20
    medulloadrenal 255.6
    milk 676.6 ☑
    ovarian androgens 256.1
    pituitary (anterior) 253.1
    salivary gland (any) 527.7
    testicular hormones 257.0
    thyrocalcitonin 246.0
    upper respiratory 478.9
Hypersegmentation, hereditary 288.2
    eosinophils 288.2
    neutrophil nuclei 288.2
Hypersensitive, hypersensitiveness, hypersensitivity — *see also* Allergy
    angiitis 446.20
        specified NEC 446.29
    carotid sinus 337.01
    colon 564.9
        psychogenic 306.4
    DNA (deoxyribonucleic acid) NEC 287.2
    drug (*see also* Allergy, drug) 995.27
    esophagus 530.89
    insect bites — *see* Injury, superficial, by site

Hypersensitive, hypersensitiveness, hypersensitivity — *see also* Allergy — *continued*
    labyrinth 386.58
    pain (*see also* Disturbance, sensation) 782.0
    pneumonitis NEC 495.9
    reaction (*see also* Allergy) 995.3
        upper respiratory tract NEC 478.8
    stomach (allergic) (nonallergic) 536.8
        psychogenic 306.4
Hypersomatotropism (classic) 253.0
Hypersomnia, unspecified 780.54
    with sleep apnea, unspecified 780.53
    alcohol induced 291.82
    drug induced 292.85
    due to
        medical condition classified elsewhere 327.14
        mental disorder 327.15
    idiopathic
        with long sleep time 327.11
        without long sleep time 327.12
    menstrual related 327.13
    nonorganic origin 307.43
        persistent (primary) 307.44
        transient 307.43
    organic 327.10
        other 327.19
    primary 307.44
    recurrent 327.13
Hypersplenia 289.4
Hypersplenism 289.4
Hypersteatosis 706.3
Hyperstimulation, ovarian 256.1
Hypersuprarenalism 255.3
Hypersusceptibility — *see* Allergy
Hyper-TBG-nemia 246.8
Hypertelorism 756.0
    orbit, orbital 376.41

☑ Additional Digit Required — Refer to the Tabular List for Digit Selection   ▽ Subterms under main terms may continue to next column or page

140 — Volume 2   ▶◀ Revised Text   ● New Line   ▲ Revised Code   2010 ICD-9-CM

	Malignant	Benign	Unspecified
Hypertension, hypertensive (arterial) (arteriolar) (crisis) (degeneration) (disease) (essential) (fluctuating) (idiopathic) (intermittent) (labile) (low renin) (orthostatic) (paroxysmal) (primary) (systemic) (uncontrolled) (vascular)	401.0	401.1	401.9
with			
chronic kidney disease			
stage I through stage IV, or unspecified	403.00	403.10	403.90
stage V or end stage renal disese	403.01	403.11	403.91
heart involvement (conditions classifiable to 429.0–429.3, 429.8, 429.9 due to hypertension) (see also Hypertension, heart)	402.00	402.10	402.90
with kidney involvement — see Hypertension, cardiorenal			
renal ▶(kidney)◀ involvement (only conditions classifiable to 585) (excludes conditions classifiable to 584) (see also Hypertension, kidney)	403.00	403.10	403.90
with heart involvement — see Hypertension, cardiorenal			
failure (and sclerosis) (see also Hypertension, kidney)	403.01	403.11	403.91
sclerosis without failure (see also Hypertension, kidney)	403.00	403.10	403.90
accelerated (see also Hypertension, by type, malignant))	401.0	—	—
antepartum — see Hypertension, complicating pregnancy, childbirth, or the puerperium			
cardiorenal (disease)	404.00	404.10	404.90
with			
chronic kidney disease			
stage I through stage IV, or unspecified	404.00	404.10	404.90
and heart failure	404.01	404.11	404.91
stage V or end stage renal disease	404.02	404.12	404.92
and heart failure	404.03	404.13	404.93
heart failure	404.01	404.11	404.91
and chronic kidney disease	404.01	404.11	404.91
stage I through stage IV or unspecified	404.01	404.11	404.91
stave V or end stage renal disease	404.03	404.13	404.93
cardiovascular disease (arteriosclerotic) (sclerotic)	402.00	402.10	402.90
with			
heart failure	402.01	402.11	402.91
renal involvement (conditions classifiable to 403) (see also Hypertension, cardiorenal)	404.00	404.10	404.90
cardiovascular renal (disease) (sclerosis) (see also Hypertension, cardiorenal)	404.00	404.10	404.90
cerebrovascular disease NEC	437.2	437.2	437.2
complicating pregnancy, childbirth, or the puerperium	642.2 ☑	642.0 ☑	642.9 ☑
with			
albuminuria (and edema) (mild)	—	—	642.4 ☑
severe			642.5 ☑
chronic kidney disesae	642.2 ☑	642.2 ☑	642.2 ☑
and heart disease	642.2 ☑	642.2 ☑	642.2 ☑
edema (mild)	—	—	642.4 ☑
severe	—	—	642.5 ☑
heart disease	642.2 ☑	642.2 ☑	642.2 ☑
and chronic kidney disease	642.2 ☑	642.2 ☑	642.2 ☑
renal disease	642.2 ☑	642.2 ☑	642.2 ☑
and heart disease	642.2 ☑	642.2 ☑	642.2 ☑
chronic	642.2 ☑	642.0 ☑	642.0 ☑
with pre-eclampsia or eclampsia	642.7 ☑	642.7 ☑	642.7 ☑
fetus or newborn	760.0	760.0	760.0
essential	—	642.0 ☑	642.0 ☑
with pre-eclampsia or eclampsia	—	642.7 ☑	642.7 ☑
fetus or newborn	760.0	760.0	760.0
gestational	—	—	642.3 ☑
pre-existing	642.2 ☑	642.0 ☑	642.0 ☑
with pre-eclampsia or eclampsia	642.7 ☑	642.7 ☑	642.7 ☑
fetus or newborn	760.0	760.0	760.0
secondary to renal disease	642.1 ☑	642.1 ☑	642.1 ☑
with pre-eclampsia or eclampsia	642.7 ☑	642.7 ☑	642.7 ☑
fetus or newborn	760.0	760.0	760.0
transient	—	—	642.3 ☑
due to			
aldosteronism, primary	405.09	405.19	405.99
brain tumor	405.09	405.19	405.99
bulbar poliomyelitis	405.09	405.19	405.99
calculus			
kidney	405.09	405.19	405.99
ureter	405.09	405.19	405.99

	Malignant	Benign	Unspecified
Hypertension, hypertensive — continued			
due to — continued			
coarctation, aorta	405.09	405.19	405.99
Cushing's disease	405.09	405.19	405.99
glomerulosclerosis (see also Hypertension, kidney)	403.00	403.10	403.90
periarteritis nodosa	405.09	405.19	405.99
pheochromocytoma	405.09	405.19	405.99
polycystic kidney(s)	405.09	405.19	405.99
polycythemia	405.09	405.19	405.99
porphyria	405.09	405.19	405.99
pyelonephritis	405.09	405.19	405.99
renal (artery)			
aneurysm	405.01	405.11	405.91
anomaly	405.01	405.11	405.91
embolism	405.01	405.11	405.91
fibromuscular hyperplasia	405.01	405.11	405.91
occlusion	405.01	405.11	405.91
stenosis	405.01	405.11	405.91
thrombosis	405.01	405.11	405.91
encephalopathy	437.2	437.2	437.2
gestational (transient) NEC	—	—	642.3 ☑
Goldblatt's	440.1	440.1	440.1
heart (disease) (conditions classifiable to 429.0–429.3, 429.8, 429.9 due to hypertension)	402.00	402.10	402.90
with heart failure	402.01	402.11	402.91
hypertensive kidney disease (conditions classifiable to 403) (see also Hypertension, cardiorenal)	404.00	404.10	404.90
renal sclerosis (see also Hypertension, cardiorenal)	404.00	404.10	404.90
intracranial, benign	—	348.2	—
intraocular	—	—	365.04
kidney	403.00	403.10	403.90
with			
chronic kidney disease			
stage I through stage IV, or unspecified	403.00	403.10	403.90
stage V or end stage renal disease	403.01	403.11	403.91
heart involvement (conditions classifiable to 429.0–429.3, 429.8, 429.9 due to hypertension) (see also Hypertension, cardiorenal)	404.00	404.10	404.90
hypertensive heart (disease) (conditions classifiable to 402) (see also Hypertension, cardiorenal)	404.00	404.10	404.90
lesser circulation	—	—	416.0
necrotizing	401.0	—	—
ocular	—	—	365.04
pancreatic duct — code to underlying condition			
with			
chronic pancreatitis	—	—	577.1
portal (due to chronic liver disease)	—	—	572.3
postoperative	—	—	997.91
psychogenic	—	—	306.2
puerperal, postpartum — see Hypertension, complicating pregnancy, childbirth, or the puerperium			
pulmonary (artery)	—	—	416.8
with cor pulmonale (chronic)	—	—	416.8
acute	—	—	415.0
idiopathic	—	—	416.0
primary	—	—	416.0
of newborn	—	—	747.83
secondary	—	—	416.8
renal (disease) (see also Hypertension, kidney)	403.00	403.10	403.90
renovascular NEC	405.01	405.11	405.91
secondary NEC	405.09	405.19	405.99
due to			
aldosteronism, primary	405.09	405.19	405.99
brain tumor	405.09	405.19	405.99
bulbar poliomyelitis	405.09	405.19	405.99
calculus			
kidney	405.09	405.19	405.99
ureter	405.09	405.19	405.99
coarctation, aorta	405.09	405.19	405.99
Cushing's disease	405.09	405.19	405.99
glomerulosclerosis (see also Hypertension, kidney)	403.00	403.10	403.90
periarteritis nodosa	405.09	405.19	405.99
pheochromocytoma	405.09	405.19	405.99
polycystic kidney(s)	405.09	405.19	405.99
polycythemia	405.09	405.19	405.99
porphyria	405.09	405.19	405.99
pyelonephritis	405.09	405.19	405.99
renal (artery)			
aneurysm	405.01	405.11	405.91

☑ Additional Digit Required — Refer to the Tabular List for Digit Selection   ▽ Subterms under main terms may continue to next column or page

2010 ICD-9-CM   ▶◀ Revised Text   ● New Line   ▲ Revised Code   **October 2009 • Volume 2 — 141**

	Malignant	Benign	Unspecified
Hypertension, hypertensive — *continued*			
secondary — *continued*			
due to — *continued*			
renal — *continued*			
anomaly	405.01	405.11	405.91
embolism	405.01	405.11	405.91
fibromuscular hyperplasia	405.01	405.11	405.91
occlusion	405.01	405.11	405.91
stenosis	405.01	405.11	405.91
thrombosis	405.01	405.11	405.91
transient	—	—	796.2
of pregnancy	—	—	642.3 ☑
vascular degeneration	401.0	401.1	401.9
venous, chronic (asymptomatic) (idiopathic)	—	—	459.30
with			
complication, NEC	—	—	459.39
inflammation	—	—	459.32
with ulcer	—	—	459.33
ulcer	—	—	459.31
with inflammation	—	—	459.33
due to			
deep vein thrombosis (*see also* Syndrome, postphlebetic)	—	—	459.10

Hyperthecosis, ovary 256.8
Hyperthermia (of unknown origin) — *see also*
    Pyrexia 780.60
    malignant (due to anesthesia) 995.86
    newborn 778.4
Hyperthymergasia — *see also* Psychosis, affec-
    tive 296.0 ☑
    reactive (from emotional stress, psychological
      trauma) 298.1
    recurrent episode 296.1 ☑
    single episode 296.0 ☑
Hyperthymism 254.8
Hyperthyroid (recurrent) — *see* Hyperthyroidism
Hyperthyroidism (latent) (preadult) (recurrent)
    (without goiter) 242.9 ☑

> *Note* — *Use the following fifth-digit*
> *subclassification with category 242:*
>
> 0   *without mention of thyrotoxic crisis*
>   *or storm*
>
> 1   *with mention of thyrotoxic crisis or*
>   *storm*

    with
      goiter (diffuse) 242.0 ☑
        adenomatous 242.3 ☑
          multinodular 242.2 ☑
          uninodular 242.1 ☑
        nodular 242.3 ☑
          multinodular 242.2 ☑
          uninodular 242.1 ☑
        thyroid nodule 242.1 ☑
    complicating pregnancy, childbirth, or puer-
      perium 648.1 ☑
    neonatal (transient) 775.3
Hypertonia — *see* Hypertonicity
Hypertonicity
    bladder 596.51
    fetus or newborn 779.89
    gastrointestinal (tract) 536.8
    infancy 779.89
      due to electrolyte imbalance 779.89
    muscle 728.85
    stomach 536.8
      psychogenic 306.4
    uterus, uterine (contractions) 661.4 ☑
      affecting fetus or newborn 763.7
Hypertony — *see* Hypertonicity
Hypertransaminemia 790.4
Hypertrichosis 704.1
    congenital 757.4
    eyelid 374.54
    lanuginosa 757.4
      acquired 704.1
Hypertriglyceridemia, essential 272.1
Hypertrophy, hypertrophic
    adenoids (infectional) 474.12
      and tonsils (faucial) (infective) (lingual)
        (lymphoid) 474.10
    adrenal 255.8
    alveolar process or ridge 525.8
    anal papillae 569.49
    apocrine gland 705.82
    artery NEC 447.8
      carotid 447.8
      congenital (peripheral) NEC 747.60
        gastrointestinal 747.61
        lower limb 747.64
        renal 747.62
        specified NEC 747.69
        spinal 747.82
        upper limb 747.63
      renal 447.3
    arthritis (chronic) (*see also* Osteoarthrosis)
      715.9 ☑
      spine (*see also* Spondylosis) 721.90
    arytenoid 478.79
    asymmetrical (heart) 429.9
    auricular — *see* Hypertrophy, cardiac
    Bartholin's gland 624.8
    bile duct 576.8
    bladder (sphincter) (trigone) 596.8
    blind spot, visual field 368.42
    bone 733.99
    brain 348.89
    breast 611.1

Hypertrophy, hypertrophic — *continued*
    breast — *continued*
      cystic 610.1
      fetus or newborn 778.7
      fibrocystic 610.1
      massive pubertal 611.1
      puerperal, postpartum 676.3 ☑
      senile (parenchymatous) 611.1
    cardiac (chronic) (idiopathic) 429.3
      with
        rheumatic fever (conditions classifiable
          to 390)
          active 391.8
            with chorea 392.0
          inactive or quiescent (with chorea)
            398.99
      congenital NEC 746.89
      fatty (*see also* Degeneration, myocardial)
        429.1
      hypertensive (*see also* Hypertension, heart)
        402.90
      rheumatic (with chorea) 398.99
        active or acute 391.8
          with chorea 392.0
      valve (*see also* Endocarditis) 424.90
        congenital NEC 746.89
    cartilage 733.99
    cecum 569.89
    cervix (uteri) 622.6
      congenital 752.49
      elongation 622.6
    clitoris (cirrhotic) 624.2
      congenital 752.49
    colon 569.89
      congenital 751.3
    conjunctiva, lymphoid 372.73
    cornea 371.89
    corpora cavernosa 607.89
    duodenum 537.89
    endometrium (uterus) (*see also* Hyperplasia,
      endometrium) 621.30
      cervix 622.6
    epididymis 608.89
    esophageal hiatus (congenital) 756.6
      with hernia — *see* Hernia, diaphragm
    eyelid 374.30
    falx, skull 733.99
    fat pad 729.30
      infrapatellar 729.31
      knee 729.31
      orbital 374.34
      popliteal 729.31
      prepatellar 729.31
      retropatellar 729.31
      specified site NEC 729.39
    foot (congenital) 755.67
    frenum, frenulum (tongue) 529.8
      linguae 529.8
      lip 528.5
    gallbladder or cystic duct 575.8
    gastric mucosa 535.2 ☑
    gingiva 523.8
    gland, glandular (general) NEC 785.6
    gum (mucous membrane) 523.8
    heart (idiopathic) (*see also* Hypertrophy, car-
      diac)
      valve (*see also* Endocarditis)
        congenital NEC 746.89
    hemifacial 754.0
    hepatic — *see* Hypertrophy, liver
    hiatus (esophageal) 756.6
    hilus gland 785.6
    hymen, congenital 752.49
    ileum 569.89
    infrapatellar fat pad 729.31
    intestine 569.89
    jejunum 569.89
    kidney (compensatory) 593.1
      congenital 753.3
    labial frenulum 528.5
    labium (majus) (minus) 624.3
    lacrimal gland, chronic 375.03
    ligament 728.9
      spinal 724.8
    linguae frenulum 529.8
    lingual tonsil (infectional) 474.11

Hypertrophy, hypertrophic — *continued*
    lip (frenum) 528.5
      congenital 744.81
    liver 789.1
      acute 573.8
      cirrhotic — *see* Cirrhosis, liver
      congenital 751.69
      fatty — *see* Fatty, liver
    lymph gland 785.6
      tuberculous — *see* Tuberculosis, lymph
        gland
    mammary gland — *see* Hypertrophy, breast
    maxillary frenulum 528.5
    Meckel's diverticulum (congenital) 751.0
    medial meniscus, acquired 717.3
    median bar 600.90
      with
        other lower urinary tract symptoms
          (LUTS) 600.91
        urinary
          obstruction 600.91
          retention 600.91
    mediastinum 519.3
    meibomian gland 373.2
    meniscus, knee, congenital 755.64
    metatarsal head 733.99
    metatarsus 733.99
    mouth 528.9
    mucous membrane
      alveolar process 523.8
      nose 478.19
      turbinate (nasal) 478.0
    muscle 728.9
    muscular coat, artery NEC 447.8
      carotid 447.8
      renal 447.3
    myocardium (*see also* Hypertrophy, cardiac)
      429.3
      idiopathic 425.4
    myometrium 621.2
    nail 703.8
      congenital 757.5
    nasal 478.19
      alae 478.19
      bone 738.0
      cartilage 478.19
      mucous membrane (septum) 478.19
      sinus (*see also* Sinusitis) 473.9
      turbinate 478.0
    nasopharynx, lymphoid (infectional) (tissue)
      (wall) 478.29
    neck, uterus 622.6
    nipple 611.1
    normal aperture diaphragm (congenital) 756.6
    nose (*see also* Hypertrophy, nasal) 478.19
    orbit 376.46
    organ or site, congenital NEC — *see* Anomaly,
      specified type NEC
    osteoarthropathy (pulmonary) 731.2
    ovary 620.8
    palate (hard) 526.89
      soft 528.9
    pancreas (congenital) 751.7
    papillae
      anal 569.49
      tongue 529.3
    parathyroid (gland) 252.01
    parotid gland 527.1
    penis 607.89
    phallus 607.89
      female (clitoris) 624.2
    pharyngeal tonsil 474.12
    pharyngitis 472.1
    pharynx 478.29
      lymphoid (infectional) (tissue) (wall) 478.29
    pituitary (fossa) (gland) 253.8
    popliteal fat pad 729.31
    preauricular (lymph) gland (Hampstead) 785.6
    prepuce (congenital) 605
      female 624.2
    prostate (asymptomatic) (early) (recurrent)
      600.90
      with
        other lower urinary tract symptlms
          (LUTS) 600.91

Hypertrophy, hypertrophic — *continued*
    prostate — *continued*
      with — *continued*
        urinary
          obstruction 600.91
          retention 600.91
      adenofibromatous 600.20
        with
          other lower urinary tract symptoms
            (LUTS) 600.21
          urinary
            obstruction 600.21
            retention 600.21
      benign 600.00
        with
          other lower urinary tract symptoms
            (LUTS) 600.01
          urinary
            obstruction 600.01
            retention 600.01
      congenital 752.89
    pseudoedematous hypodermal 757.0
    pseudomuscular 359.1
    pylorus (muscle) (sphincter) 537.0
      congenital 750.5
      infantile 750.5
    rectal sphincter 569.49
    rectum 569.49
    renal 593.1
    rhinitis (turbinate) 472.0
    salivary duct or gland 527.1
      congenital 750.26
    scaphoid (tarsal) 733.99
    scar 701.4
    scrotum 608.89
    sella turcica 253.8
    seminal vesicle 608.89
    sigmoid 569.89
    skin condition NEC 701.9
    spermatic cord 608.89
    spinal ligament 724.8
    spleen — *see* Splenomegaly
    spondylitis (spine) (*see also* Spondylosis)
      721.90
    stomach 537.89
    subaortic stenosis (idiopathic) 425.1
    sublingual gland 527.1
      congenital 750.26
    submaxillary gland 527.1
    suprarenal (gland) 255.8
    tendon 727.9
    testis 608.89
      congenital 752.89
    thymic, thymus (congenital) (gland) 254.0
    thyroid (gland) (*see also* Goiter) 240.9
      primary 242.0 ☑
      secondary 242.2 ☑
    toe (congenital) 755.65
      acquired 735.8
    tongue 529.8
      congenital 750.15
      frenum 529.8
      papillae (foliate) 529.3
    tonsil (faucial) (infective) (lingual) (lymphoid)
      474.11
      with
        adenoiditis 474.01
        tonsillitis 474.00
          and adenoiditis 474.02
      and adenoids 474.10
    tunica vaginalis 608.89
    turbinate (mucous membrane) 478.0
    ureter 593.89
    urethra 599.84
    uterus 621.2
      puerperal, postpartum 674.8 ☑
    uvula 528.9
    vagina 623.8
    vas deferens 608.89
    vein 459.89
    ventricle, ventricular (heart) (left) (right) (*see*
      also Hypertrophy, cardiac)
      congenital 746.89
      due to hypertension (left) (right) (*see also*
        Hypertension, heart) 402.90
        benign 402.10

☑ Additional Digit Required — Refer to the Tabular List for Digit Selection   ▽ Subterms under main terms may continue to next column or page

2010 ICD-9-CM   ▶◀ Revised Text   ● New Line   ▲ Revised Code   October 2009 • Volume 2 — 143

Hypertrophy, hypertrophic — continued
  ventricle, ventricular (see also Hypertrophy, cardiac) — continued
    due to hypertension (see also Hypertension, heart) — continued
      malignant 402.00
      right with ventricular septal defect, pulmonary stenosis or atresia, and dextraposition of aorta 745.2
  verumontanum 599.89
  vesical 596.8
  vocal cord 478.5
  vulva 624.3
    stasis (nonfilarial) 624.3
Hypertropia (intermittent) (periodic) 378.31
Hypertyrosinemia 270.2
Hyperuricemia 790.6
Hypervalinemia 270.3
Hyperventilation (tetany) 786.01
  hysterical 300.11
  psychogenic 306.1
  syndrome 306.1
Hyperviscidosis 277.00
Hyperviscosity (of serum) (syndrome) NEC 273.3
  polycythemic 289.0
  sclerocythemic 282.8
Hypervitaminosis (dietary) NEC 278.8
  A (dietary) 278.2
  D (dietary) 278.4
  from excessive administration or use of vitamin preparations (chronic) 278.8
    reaction to sudden overdose 963.5
  vitamin A 278.2
    reaction to sudden overdose 963.5
  vitamin D 278.4
    reaction to sudden overdose 963.5
  vitamin K
    correct substance properly administered 278.8
    overdose or wrong substance given or taken 964.3
Hypervolemia 276.6
Hypesthesia — see also Disturbance, sensation 782.0
  cornea 371.81
Hyphema (anterior chamber) (ciliary body) (iris) 364.41
  traumatic 921.3
Hyphemia — see Hyphema
Hypoacidity, gastric 536.8
  psychogenic 306.4
Hypoactive labyrinth (function) — see Hypofunction, labyrinth
Hypoadrenalism 255.41
  tuberculous (see also Tuberculosis) 017.6 ☑
Hypoadrenocorticism 255.41
  pituitary 253.4
Hypoalbuminemia 273.8
Hypoaldosteronism 255.42
Hypoalphalipoproteinemia 272.5
Hypobarism 993.2
Hypobaropathy 993.2
Hypobetalipoproteinemia (familial) 272.5
Hypocalcemia 275.41
  cow's milk 775.4
  dietary 269.3
  neonatal 775.4
  phosphate-loading 775.4
Hypocalcification, teeth 520.4
Hypochloremia 276.9
Hypochlorhydria 536.8
  neurotic 306.4
  psychogenic 306.4
Hypocholesteremia 272.5
Hypochondria (reaction) 300.7
Hypochondriac 300.7
Hypochondriasis 300.7
Hypochromasia blood cells 280.9
Hypochromic anemia 280.9
  due to blood loss (chronic) 280.0
    acute 285.1
  microcytic 280.9
Hypocoagulability — see also Defect, coagulation 286.9
Hypocomplementemia 279.8
Hypocythemia (progressive) 284.9

Hypodontia — see also Anodontia 520.0
Hypoeosinophilia 288.59
Hypoesthesia — see also Disturbance, sensation 782.0
  cornea 371.81
  tactile 782.0
Hypoestrinism 256.39
Hypoestrogenism 256.39
Hypoferremia 280.9
  due to blood loss (chronic) 280.0
Hypofertility
  female 628.9
  male 606.1
Hypofibrinogenemia 286.3
  acquired 286.6
  congenital 286.3
Hypofunction
  adrenal (gland) 255.41
    cortex 255.41
    medulla 255.5
    specified NEC 255.5
  cerebral 331.9
  corticoadrenal NEC 255.41
  intestinal 564.89
  labyrinth (unilateral) 386.53
    with loss of labyrinthine reactivity 386.55
    bilateral 386.54
      with loss of labyrinthine reactivity 386.56
  Leydig cell 257.2
  ovary 256.39
    postablative 256.2
  pituitary (anterior) (gland) (lobe) 253.2
    posterior 253.5
  testicular 257.2
    iatrogenic 257.1
    postablative 257.1
    postirradiation 257.1
    postsurgical 257.1
Hypogammaglobulinemia 279.00
  acquired primary 279.06
  non-sex-linked, congenital 279.06
  sporadic 279.06
  transient of infancy 279.09
Hypogenitalism (congenital) (female) (male) 752.89
  penis 752.69
Hypoglycemia (spontaneous) 251.2
  coma 251.0
    diabetic 250.3 ☑
      due to secondary diabetes 249.3 ☑
  diabetic 250.8 ☑
    due to secondary diabetes 249.8 ☑
  due to insulin 251.0
    therapeutic misadventure 962.3
  familial (idiopathic) 251.2
  following gastrointestinal surgery 579.3
  infantile (idiopathic) 251.2
  in infant of diabetic mother 775.0
  leucine-induced 270.3
  neonatal 775.6
  reactive 251.2
  specified NEC 251.1
Hypoglycemic shock 251.0
  diabetic 250.8 ☑
    due to secondary diabetes 249.8 ☑
  due to insulin 251.0
  functional (syndrome) 251.1
Hypogonadism
  female 256.39
  gonadotropic (isolated) 253.4
  hypogonadotropic (isolated) (with anosmia) 253.4
  isolated 253.4
  male 257.2
    hereditary familial (Reifenstein's syndrome) 259.52
  ovarian (primary) 256.39
  pituitary (secondary) 253.4
  testicular (primary) (secondary) 257.2
Hypohidrosis 705.0
Hypohidrotic ectodermal dysplasia 757.31
Hypoidrosis 705.0
Hypoinsulinemia, postsurgical 251.3
  postpancreatectomy (complete) (partial) 251.3
Hypokalemia 276.8

Hypokinesia 780.99
Hypoleukia splenica 289.4
Hypoleukocytosis 288.50
Hypolipidemia 272.5
Hypolipoproteinemia 272.5
Hypomagnesemia 275.2
  neonatal 775.4
Hypomania, hypomanic reaction — see also Psychosis, affective 296.0 ☑
  recurrent episode 296.1 ☑
  single episode 296.0 ☑
Hypomastia (congenital) 611.82
Hypomenorrhea 626.1
Hypometabolism 783.9
Hypomotility
  gastrointestinal tract 536.8
    psychogenic 306.4
  intestine 564.89
    psychogenic 306.4
  stomach 536.8
    psychogenic 306.4
Hyponasality 784.44   ▲
Hyponatremia 276.1
Hypo-ovarianism 256.39
Hypo-ovarism 256.39
Hypoparathyroidism (idiopathic) (surgically-induced) 252.1
  neonatal 775.4
Hypopharyngitis 462
Hypophoria 378.40
Hypophosphatasia 275.3
Hypophosphatemia (acquired) (congenital) (familial) 275.3
  renal 275.3
Hypophyseal, hypophysis — see also condition
  dwarfism 253.3
  gigantism 253.0
  syndrome 253.8
Hypophyseothalamic syndrome 253.8
Hypopiesis — see Hypotension
Hypopigmentation 709.00
  eyelid 374.53
Hypopinealism 259.8
Hypopituitarism (juvenile) (syndrome) 253.2
  due to
    hormone therapy 253.7
    hypophysectomy 253.7
    radiotherapy 253.7
  postablative 253.7
  postpartum hemorrhage 253.2
Hypoplasia, hypoplasis 759.89
  adrenal (gland) 759.1
  alimentary tract 751.8
    lower 751.2
    upper 750.8
  anus, anal (canal) 751.2
  aorta 747.22
  aortic
    arch (tubular) 747.10
    orifice or valve with hypoplasia of ascending aorta and defective development of left ventricle (with mitral valve atresia) 746.7
  appendix 751.2
  areola 757.6
  arm (see also Absence, arm, congenital) 755.20
  artery (congenital) (peripheral) 747.60
    brain 747.81
    cerebral 747.81
    coronary 746.85
    gastrointestinal 747.61
    lower limb 747.64
    pulmonary 747.3
    renal 747.62
    retinal 743.58
    specified NEC 747.69
    spinal 747.82
    umbilical 747.5
    upper limb 747.63
  auditory canal 744.29
    causing impairment of hearing 744.02
  biliary duct (common) or passage 751.61
  bladder 753.8
  bone NEC 756.9
    face 756.0
    malar 756.0

Hypoplasia, hypoplasis — continued
  bone — continued
    mandible 524.04
      alveolar 524.74
    marrow 284.9
      acquired (secondary) 284.89
      congenital 284.09
      idiopathic 284.9
    maxilla 524.03
      alveolar 524.73
    skull (see also Hypoplasia, skull) 756.0
  brain 742.1
    gyri 742.2
    specified part 742.2
  breast (areola) 611.82
  bronchus (tree) 748.3
  cardiac 746.89
    valve — see Hypoplasia, heart, valve
    vein 746.89
  carpus (see also Absence, carpal, congenital) 755.28
  cartilaginous 756.9
  cecum 751.2
  cementum 520.4
    hereditary 520.5
  cephalic 742.1
  cerebellum 742.2
  cervix (uteri) 752.49
  chin 524.06
  clavicle 755.51
  coccyx 756.19
  colon 751.2
  corpus callosum 742.2
  cricoid cartilage 748.3
  dermal, focal (Goltz) 757.39
  digestive organ(s) or tract NEC 751.8
    lower 751.2
    upper 750.8
  ear 744.29
    auricle 744.23
    lobe 744.29
    middle, except ossicles 744.03
      ossicles 744.04
    ossicles 744.04
  enamel of teeth (neonatal) (postnatal) (prenatal) 520.4
    hereditary 520.5
  endocrine (gland) NEC 759.2
  endometrium 621.8
  epididymis 752.89
  epiglottis 748.3
  erythroid, congenital 284.01
  erythropoietic, chronic acquired 284.81
  esophagus 750.3
  Eustachian tube 744.24
  eye (see also Microphthalmos) 743.10
    lid 743.62
  face 744.89
    bone(s) 756.0
  fallopian tube 752.19
  femur (see also Absence, femur, congenital) 755.34
  fibula (see also Absence, fibula, congenital) 755.37
  finger (see also Absence, finger, congenital) 755.29
  focal dermal 757.39
  foot 755.31
  gallbladder 751.69
  genitalia, genital organ(s)
    female 752.89
      external 752.49
      internal NEC 752.89
    in adiposogenital dystrophy 253.8
    male 752.89
      penis 752.69
  glottis 748.3
  hair 757.4
  hand 755.21
  heart 746.89
    left (complex) (syndrome) 746.7
    valve NEC 746.89
      pulmonary 746.01
  humerus (see also Absence, humerus, congenital) 755.24
  hymen 752.49

☑ Additional Digit Required –– Refer to the Tabular List for Digit Selection   ▽ Subterms under main terms may continue to next column or page

Hypoplasia, hypoplasis — *continued*
  intestine (small) 751.1
    large 751.2
  iris 743.46
  jaw 524.09
  kidney(s) 753.0
  labium (majus) (minus) 752.49
  labyrinth, membranous 744.05
  lacrimal duct (apparatus) 743.65
  larynx 748.3
  leg (*see also* Absence, limb, congenital, lower) 755.30
  limb 755.4
    lower (*see also* Absence, limb, congenital, lower) 755.30
    upper (*see also* Absence, limb, congenital, upper) 755.20
  liver 751.69
  lung (lobe) 748.5
  mammary (areolar) 611.82
  mandibular 524.04
    alveolar 524.74
    unilateral condylar 526.89
  maxillary 524.03
    alveolar 524.73
  medullary 284.9
  megakaryocytic 287.30
  metacarpus (*see also* Absence, metacarpal, congenital) 755.28
  metatarsus (*see also* Absence, metatarsal, congenital) 755.38
  muscle 756.89
    eye 743.69
  myocardium (congenital) (Uhl's anomaly) 746.84
  nail(s) 757.5
  nasolacrimal duct 743.65
  nervous system NEC 742.8
  neural 742.8
  nose, nasal 748.1
  ophthalmic (*see also* Microphthalmos) 743.10
  optic nerve 377.43
  organ
    of Corti 744.05
    or site NEC — *see* Anomaly, by site
  osseous meatus (ear) 744.03
  ovary 752.0
  oviduct 752.19
  pancreas 751.7
  parathyroid (gland) 759.2
  parotid gland 750.26
  patella 755.64
  pelvis, pelvic girdle 755.69
  penis 752.69
  peripheral vascular system (congenital) NEC 747.60
    gastrointestinal 747.61
    lower limb 747.64
    renal 747.62
    specified NEC 747.69
    spinal 747.82
    upper limb 747.63
  pituitary (gland) 759.2
  pulmonary 748.5
    arteriovenous 747.3
    artery 747.3
    valve 746.01
  punctum lacrimale 743.65
  radioulnar (*see also* Absence, radius, congenital, with ulna) 755.25
  radius (*see also* Absence, radius, congenital) 755.26
  rectum 751.2

Hypoplasia, hypoplasis — *continued*
  respiratory system NEC 748.9
  rib 756.3
  sacrum 756.19
  scapula 755.59
  shoulder girdle 755.59
  skin 757.39
  skull (bone) 756.0
    with
      anencephalus 740.0
      encephalocele 742.0
      hydrocephalus 742.3
        with spina bifida (*see also* Spina bifida) 741.0 ☑
      microcephalus 742.1
  spinal (cord) (ventral horn cell) 742.59
    vessel 747.82
  spine 756.19
  spleen 759.0
  sternum 756.3
  tarsus (*see also* Absence, tarsal, congenital) 755.38
  testis, testicle 752.89
  thymus (gland) 279.11
  thyroid (gland) 243
    cartilage 748.3
  tibiofibular (*see also* Absence, tibia, congenital, with fibula) 755.35
  toe (*see also* Absence, toe, congenital) 755.39
  tongue 750.16
  trachea (cartilage) (rings) 748.3
  Turner's (tooth) 520.4
  ulna (*see also* Absence, ulna, congenital) 755.27
  umbilical artery 747.5
  ureter 753.29
  uterus 752.3
  vagina 752.49
  vascular (peripheral) NEC (*see also* Hypoplasia, peripheral vascular system) 747.60
    brain 747.81
  vein(s) (peripheral) NEC (*see also* Hypoplasia, peripheral vascular system) 747.60
    brain 747.81
    cardiac 746.89
    great 747.49
    portal 747.49
    pulmonary 747.49
    vena cava (inferior) (superior) 747.49
  vertebra 756.19
  vulva 752.49
  zonule (ciliary) 743.39
  zygoma 738.12
Hypopotassemia 276.8
Hypoproaccelerinemia — *see also* Defect, coagulation 286.3
Hypoproconvertinemia (congenital) — *see also* Defect, coagulation 286.3
Hypoproteinemia (essential) (hypermetabolic) (idiopathic) 273.8
Hypoproteinosis 260
Hypoprothrombinemia (congenital) (hereditary) (idiopathic) — *see also* Defect, coagulation 286.3
  acquired 286.7
  newborn 776.3
Hypopselaphesia 782.0
Hypopyon (anterior chamber) (eye) 364.05
  iritis 364.05
  ulcer (cornea) 370.04
Hypopyrexia 780.99
Hyporeflex 796.1
Hyporeninemia, extreme 790.99

Hyporeninemia, extreme — *continued*
  in primary aldosteronism 255.10
Hyporesponsive episode 780.09
Hyposecretion
  ACTH 253.4
  ovary 256.39
    postablative 256.2
  salivary gland (any) 527.7
Hyposegmentation of neutrophils, hereditary 288.2
Hyposiderinemia 280.9
Hyposmolality 276.1
  syndrome 276.1
Hyposomatotropism 253.3
Hyposomnia, unspecified — *see also* Insomnia 780.52
  with sleep apnea, unspecified 780.51
Hypospadias (male) 752.61
  female 753.8
Hypospermatogenesis 606.1
Hyposphagma 372.72
Hyposplenism 289.59
Hypostasis, pulmonary 514
Hypostatic — *see* condition
Hyposthenuria 593.89
Hyposuprarenalism 255.41
Hypo-TBG-nemia 246.8
Hypotension (arterial) (constitutional) 458.9
  chronic 458.1
  iatrogenic 458.29
  maternal, syndrome (following labor and delivery) 669.2 ☑
  of hemodialysis 458.21
  orthostatic (chronic) 458.0
    dysautonomic-dyskinetic syndrome 333.0
  permanent idiopathic 458.1
  postoperative 458.29
  postural 458.0
  specified type NEC 458.8
  transient 796.3
Hypothermia (accidental) 991.6
  anesthetic 995.89
  associated with low environmental temperature 991.6
  newborn NEC 778.3
  not associated with low environmental temperature 780.65
Hypothymergasia — *see also* Psychosis, affective 296.2 ☑
  recurrent episode 296.3 ☑
  single episode 296.2 ☑
Hypothyroidism (acquired) 244.9
  complicating pregnancy, childbirth, or puerperium 648.1 ☑
  congenital 243
  due to
    ablation 244.1
      radioactive iodine 244.1
      surgical 244.0
    iodine (administration) (ingestion) 244.2
      radioactive 244.1
    irradiation therapy 244.1
    p-aminosalicylic acid (PAS) 244.3
    phenylbutazone 244.3
    resorcinol 244.3
    specified cause NEC 244.8
    surgery 244.0
  goitrous (sporadic) 246.1
  iatrogenic NEC 244.3
  iodine 244.2
  pituitary 244.8
  postablative NEC 244.1

Hypothyroidism — *continued*
  postsurgical 244.0
  primary 244.9
  secondary NEC 244.8
  specified cause NEC 244.8
  sporadic goitrous 246.1
Hypotonia, hypotonicity, hypotony 781.3
  benign congenital 358.8
  bladder 596.4
  congenital 779.89
    benign 358.8
  eye 360.30
    due to
      fistula 360.32
      ocular disorder NEC 360.33
    following loss of aqueous or vitreous 360.33
    primary 360.31
  infantile muscular (benign) 359.0
  muscle 728.9
  uterus, uterine (contractions) — *see* Inertia, uterus
Hypotrichosis 704.09
  congenital 757.4
  lid (congenital) 757.4
    acquired 374.55
  postinfectional NEC 704.09
Hypotropia 378.32
Hypoventilation 786.09
  congenital central alveolar syndrome 327.25
  idiopathic sleep related nonobstructive alveolar 327.24
  sleep related, in conditions classifiable elsewhere 327.26
Hypovitaminosis — *see also* Deficiency, vitamin 269.2
Hypovolemia 276.52
  surgical shock 998.0
  traumatic (shock) 958.4
Hypoxemia — *see also* Anoxia 799.02
  sleep related, in conditions classifiable elsewhere 327.26
Hypoxia — *see also* Anoxia 799.02
  cerebral 348.1
    during or resulting from a procedure 997.01
    newborn 770.88
      mild or moderate 768.6
      severe 768.5
  fetal, affecting newborn 770.88
  intrauterine — *see* Distress, fetal
  myocardial (*see also* Insufficiency, coronary) 411.89
    arteriosclerotic — *see* Arteriosclerosis, coronary
  newborn 770.88
  sleep related 327.24
Hypoxic-ischemic encephalopathy (HIE) 768.70 ▲
  mild 768.71 ●
  moderate 768.72 ●
  severe 768.73 ●
Hypsarrhythmia — *see also* Epilepsy 345.6 ☑
Hysteralgia, pregnant uterus 646.8 ☑
Hysteria, hysterical 300.10
  anxiety 300.20
  Charcôt's gland 300.11
  conversion (any manifestation) 300.11
  dissociative type NEC 300.15
  psychosis, acute 298.1
Hysteroepilepsy 300.11
Hysterotomy, affecting fetus or newborn 763.89

☑ Additional Digit Required — Refer to the Tabular List for Digit Selection   ▽ Subterms under main terms may continue to next column or page

2010 ICD-9-CM   ►◄ Revised Text   ● New Line   ▲ Revised Code   **October 2009 · Volume 2 — 145**

I

Iatrogenic syndrome of excess cortisol 255.0
IBM (inclusion body myositis) 359.71 ●
Iceland disease (epidemic neuromyasthenia) 049.8
Ichthyosis (congenita) 757.1
  acquired 701.1
  fetalis gravior 757.1
  follicularis 757.1
  hystrix 757.39
  lamellar 757.1
  lingual 528.6
  palmaris and plantaris 757.39
  simplex 757.1
  vera 757.1
  vulgaris 757.1
Ichthyotoxism 988.0
  bacterial (see also Poisoning, food) 005.9
Icteroanemia, hemolytic (acquired) 283.9
  congenital (see also Spherocytosis) 282.0
Icterus — see also Jaundice 782.4
  catarrhal — see Icterus, infectious
  conjunctiva 782.4
    newborn 774.6
  epidemic — see Icterus, infectious
  febrilis — see Icterus, infectious
  fetus or newborn — see Jaundice, fetus or newborn
  gravis (see also Necrosis, liver) 570
    complicating pregnancy 646.7 ☑
      affecting fetus or newborn 760.8
    fetus or newborn NEC 773.0
    obstetrical 646.7 ☑
      affecting fetus or newborn 760.8
  hematogenous (acquired) 283.9
  hemolytic (acquired) 283.9
    congenital (see also Spherocytosis) 282.0
  hemorrhagic (acute) 100.0
    leptospiral 100.0
    newborn 776.0
    spirochetal 100.0
  infectious 070.1
    with hepatic coma 070.0
    leptospiral 100.0
    spirochetal 100.0
  intermittens juvenilis 277.4
  malignant (see also Necrosis, liver) 570
  neonatorum (see also Jaundice, fetus or newborn) 774.6
  pernicious (see also Necrosis, liver) 570
  spirochetal 100.0
Ictus solaris, solis 992.0
Ideation
  suicidal V62.84
Identity disorder 313.82
  dissociative 300.14
  gender role (child) 302.6
    adult 302.85
  psychosexual (child) 302.6
    adult 302.85
Idioglossia 307.9
Idiopathic — see condition
Idiosyncrasy — see also Allergy 995.3
  drug, medicinal substance, and biological — see Allergy, drug
Idiot, idiocy (congenital) 318.2
  amaurotic (Bielschowsky) (-Jansky) (family) (infantile) (late) (juvenile) (late) (Vogt-Spielmeyer) 330.1
  microcephalic 742.1
  Mongolian 758.0
  oxycephalic 756.0
Id reaction (due to bacteria) 692.89
IEED (involuntary emotional expression disorder) 310.8
IFIS (intraoperative floppy iris syndrome) 364.81
IgE asthma 493.0 ☑
Ileitis (chronic) — see also Enteritis 558.9
  infectious 009.0
  noninfectious 558.9
  regional (ulcerative) 555.0
    with large intestine 555.2
  segmental 555.0
    with large intestine 555.2
  terminal (ulcerative) 555.0

Ileitis — see also Enteritis — continued
  terminal — continued
    with large intestine 555.2
Ileocolitis — see also Enteritis 558.9
  infectious 009.0
  regional 555.2
  ulcerative 556.1
Ileostomy status V44.2
  with complication 569.60
Ileotyphus 002.0
Ileum — see condition
Ileus (adynamic) (bowel) (colon) (inhibitory) (intestine) (neurogenic) (paralytic) 560.1
  arteriomesenteric duodenal 537.2
  due to gallstone (in intestine) 560.31
  duodenal, chronic 537.2
  following gastrointestinal surgery 997.4
  gallstone 560.31
  mechanical (see also Obstruction, intestine) 560.9
  meconium 777.1
    due to cystic fibrosis 277.01
  myxedema 564.89
  postoperative 997.4
  transitory, newborn 777.4
Iliac — see condition
Iliotibial band friction syndrome 728.89
Illegitimacy V61.6
Ill, louping 063.1
Illness — see also Disease
  factitious 300.19
    with
      combined psychological and physical signs and symptoms 300.19
      predominantly
        physical signs and symptoms 300.19
        psychological symptoms 300.16
    chronic (with physical symptoms) 301.51
  heart — see Disease, heart
  manic-depressive (see also Psychosis, affective) 296.80
  mental (see also Disorder, mental) 300.9
Imbalance 781.2
  autonomic (see also Neuropathy, peripheral, autonomic) 337.9
  electrolyte 276.9
    with
      abortion — see Abortion, by type, with metabolic disorder
      ectopic pregnancy (see also categories 633.0–633.9) 639.4
      hyperemesis gravidarum (before 22 completed weeks gestation) 643.1 ☑
      molar pregnancy (see also categories 630–632) 639.4
    following
      abortion 639.4
      ectopic or molar pregnancy 639.4
    neonatal, transitory NEC 775.5
  endocrine 259.9
  eye muscle NEC 378.9
    heterophoria — see Heterophoria
  glomerulotubular NEC 593.89
  hormone 259.9
  hysterical (see also Hysteria) 300.10
  labyrinth NEC 386.50
  posture 729.90
  sympathetic (see also Neuropathy, peripheral, autonomic) 337.9
Imbecile, imbecility 318.0
  moral 301.7
  old age 290.9
  senile 290.9
  specified IQ — see IQ
  unspecified IQ 318.0
Imbedding, intrauterine device 996.32
Imbibition, cholesterol (gallbladder) 575.6
Imerslund (-Gräsbeck) syndrome (anemia due to familial selective vitamin B_{12} malabsorption) 281.1
Iminoacidopathy 270.8
Iminoglycinuria, familial 270.8
Immature — see also Immaturity
  personality 301.89

Immaturity 765.1 ☑
  extreme 765.0 ☑
  fetus or infant light-for-dates — see Light-for-dates
  lung, fetus or newborn 770.4
  organ or site NEC — see Hypoplasia
  pulmonary, fetus or newborn 770.4
  reaction 301.89
  sexual (female) (male) 259.0
Immersion 994.1
  foot 991.4
  hand 991.4
Immobile, immobility
  complete
    due to severe physical disability or frailty 780.72
  intestine 564.89
  joint — see Ankylosis
  syndrome (paraplegic) 728.3
Immunization
  ABO
    affecting management of pregnancy 656.2 ☑
    fetus or newborn 773.1
  complication — see Complications, vaccination
  Rh factor
    affecting management of pregnancy 656.1 ☑
    fetus or newborn 773.0
    from transfusion 999.7
Immunodeficiency 279.3
  with
    adenosine-deaminase deficiency 279.2
    defect, predominant
      B-cell 279.00
      T-cell 279.10
    hyperimmunoglobulinemia 279.2
    lymphopenia, hereditary 279.2
    thrombocytopenia and eczema 279.12
    thymic
      aplasia 279.2
      dysplasia 279.2
  autosomal recessive, Swiss-type 279.2
  common variable 279.06
  severe combined (SCID) 279.2
  to Rh factor
    affecting management of pregnancy 656.1 ☑
    fetus or newborn 773.0
  X-linked, with increased IgM 279.05
Immunotherapy, prophylactic V07.2
  antineoplastic V58.12
Impaction, impacted
  bowel, colon, rectum 560.30
    with hernia (see also Hernia, by site, with obstruction)
      gangrenous — see Hernia, by site, with gangrene
    by
      calculus 560.39
      gallstone 560.31
    fecal 560.39
    specified type NEC 560.39
  calculus — see Calculus
  cerumen (ear) (external) 380.4
  cuspid 520.6
  dental 520.6
  fecal, feces 560.39
    with hernia (see also Hernia, by site, with obstruction)
      gangrenous — see Hernia, by site, with gangrene
  fracture — see Fracture, by site
  gallbladder — see Cholelithiasis
  gallstone(s) — see Cholelithiasis
    in intestine (any part) 560.31
  intestine(s) 560.30
    with hernia (see also Hernia, by site, with obstruction)
      gangrenous — see Hernia, by site, with gangrene
    by
      calculus 560.39
      gallstone 560.31
    fecal 560.39

Impaction, impacted — continued
  intestine(s) — continued
    specified type NEC 560.39
  intrauterine device (IUD) 996.32
  molar 520.6
  shoulder 660.4 ☑
    affecting fetus or newborn 763.1
  tooth, teeth 520.6
  turbinate 733.99
Impaired, impairment (function)
  arm V49.1
    movement, involving
      musculoskeletal system V49.1
      nervous system V49.2
  auditory discrimination 388.43
  back V48.3
  body (entire) V49.89
  cognitive, mild, so stated 331.83
  combined visual hearing V49.85
  dual sensory V49.85
  glucose
    fasting 790.21
    tolerance test (oral) 790.22
  hearing (see also Deafness) 389.9
    combined with visual impairment V49.85
  heart — see Disease, heart
  kidney (see also Disease, renal) 593.9
    disorder resulting from 588.9
      specified NEC 588.89
  leg V49.1
    movement, involving
      musculoskeletal system V49.1
      nervous system V49.2
  limb V49.1
    movement, involving
      musculoskeletal system V49.1
      nervous system V49.2
  liver 573.8
  mastication 524.9
  mild cognitive, so stated 331.83
  mobility
    ear ossicles NEC 385.22
    incostapedial joint 385.22
    malleus 385.21
  myocardium, myocardial (see also Insufficiency, myocardial) 428.0
  neuromusculoskeletal NEC V49.89
    back V48.3
    head V48.2
    limb V49.2
    neck V48.3
    spine V48.3
    trunk V48.3
  rectal sphincter 787.99
  renal (see also Disease, renal) 593.9
    disorder resulting from 588.9
      specified NEC 588.89
  spine V48.3
  vision NEC 369.9
    both eyes NEC 369.3
    combined with hearing impairment V49.85
    moderate 369.74
      both eyes 369.25
        with impairment of lesser eye (specified as)
          blind, not further specified 369.15
          low vision, not further specified 369.23
          near-total 369.17
          profound 369.18
          severe 369.24
          total 369.16
      one eye 369.74
        with vision of other eye (specified as)
          near-normal 369.75
          normal 369.76
    near-total 369.64
      both eyes 369.04
        with impairment of lesser eye (specified as)
          blind, not further specified 369.02
          total 369.03
      one eye 369.64

Impaired, impairment — continued
vision — continued
near-total — continued
one eye — continued
with vision of other eye (specified as)
near normal 369.65
normal 369.66
one eye 369.60
with low vision of other eye 369.10
profound 369.67
both eyes 369.08
with impairment of lesser eye (specified as)
blind, not further specified 369.05
near-total 369.07
total 369.06
one eye 369.67
with vision of other eye (specified as)
near-normal 369.68
normal 369.69
severe 369.71
both eyes 369.22
with impairment of lesser eye (specified as)
blind, not further specified 369.11
low vision, not further specified 369.21
near-total 369.13
profound 369.14
total 369.12
one eye 369.71
with vision of other eye (specified as)
near-normal 369.72
normal 369.73
total
both eyes 369.01
one eye 369.61
with vision of other eye (specified as)
near-normal 369.62
normal 369.63

Impaludism — see Malaria
Impediment, speech NEC 784.59 ▲
psychogenic 307.9
secondary to organic lesion 784.59 ▲
Impending
cerebrovascular accident or attack 435.9
coronary syndrome 411.1
delirium tremens 291.0
myocardial infarction 411.1
Imperception, auditory (acquired) (congenital) 389.9
Imperfect
aeration, lung (newborn) 770.5
closure (congenital)
alimentary tract NEC 751.8
lower 751.5
upper 750.8
atrioventricular ostium 745.69
atrium (secundum) 745.5
primum 745.61
branchial cleft or sinus 744.41
choroid 743.59
cricoid cartilage 748.3
cusps, heart valve NEC 746.89
pulmonary 746.09
ductus
arteriosus 747.0
Botalli 747.0
ear drum 744.29
causing impairment of hearing 744.03
endocardial cushion 745.60
epiglottis 748.3
esophagus with communication to bronchus or trachea 750.3
Eustachian valve 746.89
eyelid 743.62
face, facial (see also Cleft, lip) 749.10
foramen
Botalli 745.5
ovale 745.5

Imperfect — continued
closure — continued
genitalia, genital organ(s) or system
female 752.89
external 752.49
internal NEC 752.89
uterus 752.3
male 752.89
penis 752.69
glottis 748.3
heart valve (cusps) NEC 746.89
interatrial ostium or septum 745.5
interauricular ostium or septum 745.5
interventricular ostium or septum 745.4
iris 743.46
kidney 753.3
larynx 748.3
lens 743.36
lip (see also Cleft, lip) 749.10
nasal septum or sinus 748.1
nose 748.1
omphalomesenteric duct 751.0
optic nerve entry 743.57
organ or site NEC — see Anomaly, specified type, by site
ostium
interatrial 745.5
interauricular 745.5
interventricular 745.4
palate (see also Cleft, palate) 749.00
preauricular sinus 744.46
retina 743.56
roof of orbit 742.0
sclera 743.47
septum
aortic 745.0
aorticopulmonary 745.0
atrial (secundum) 745.5
primum 745.61
between aorta and pulmonary artery 745.0
heart 745.9
interatrial (secundum) 745.5
primum 745.61
interauricular (secundum) 745.5
primum 745.61
interventricular 745.4
with pulmonary stenosis or atresia, dextraposition of aorta, and hypertrophy of right ventricle 745.2
in tetralogy of Fallot 745.2
nasal 748.1
ventricular 745.4
with pulmonary stenosis or atresia, dextraposition of aorta, and hypertrophy of right ventricle 745.2
in tetralogy of Fallot 745.2
skull 756.0
with
anencephalus 740.0
encephalocele 742.0
hydrocephalus 742.3
with spina bifida (see also Spina bifida) 741.0 ☑
microcephalus 742.1
spine (with meningocele) (see also Spina bifida) 741.90
thyroid cartilage 748.3
trachea 748.3
tympanic membrane 744.29
causing impairment of hearing 744.03
uterus (with communication to bladder, intestine, or rectum) 752.3
uvula 749.02
with cleft lip (see also Cleft, palate, with cleft lip) 749.20
vitelline duct 751.0
development — see Anomaly, by site
erection 607.84
fusion — see Imperfect, closure
inflation lung (newborn) 770.5
intestinal canal 751.5
poise 729.90
rotation — see Malrotation

Imperfect — continued
septum, ventricular 745.4
Imperfectly descended testis 752.51
Imperforate (congenital) — see also Atresia
anus 751.2
bile duct 751.61
cervix (uteri) 752.49
esophagus 750.3
hymen 752.42
intestine (small) 751.1
large 751.2
jejunum 751.1
pharynx 750.29
rectum 751.2
salivary duct 750.23
urethra 753.6
urinary meatus 753.6
vagina 752.49
Impervious (congenital) — see also Atresia
anus 751.2
bile duct 751.61
esophagus 750.3
intestine (small) 751.1
large 751.5
rectum 751.2
urethra 753.6
Impetiginization of other dermatoses 684
Impetigo (any organism) (any site) (bullous) (circinate) (contagiosa) (neonatorum) (simplex) 684
Bockhart's (superficial folliculitis) 704.8
external ear 684 [380.13]
eyelid 684 [373.5]
Fox's (contagiosa) 684
furfuracea 696.5
herpetiformis 694.3
nonobstetrical 694.3
staphylococcal infection 684
ulcerative 686.8
vulgaris 684
Impingement, soft tissue between teeth 524.89
anterior 524.81
posterior 524.82
Implantation
anomalous (see also Anomaly, specified type, by site)
ureter 753.4
cyst
external area or site (skin) NEC 709.8
iris 364.61
vagina 623.8
vulva 624.8
dermoid (cyst)
external area or site (skin) NEC 709.8
iris 364.61
vagina 623.8
vulva 624.8
placenta, low or marginal — see Placenta previa
Implant, endometrial 617.9
Impotence (sexual) 607.84
organic origin NEC 607.84
psychogenic 302.72
Impoverished blood 285.9
Impression, basilar 756.0
Imprisonment V62.5
Improper
development, infant 764.9 ☑
Improperly tied umbilical cord (causing hemorrhage) 772.3
Impulses, obsessional 300.3
Impulsive 799.23 ▲
neurosis 300.3 ●
Impulsiveness 799.23 ●
Inaction, kidney — see also Disease, renal 593.9
Inactive — see condition
Inadequate, inadequacy
aesthetics of dental restoration 525.67
biologic 301.6
cardiac and renal — see Hypertension, cardiorenal
constitutional 301.6
development
child 783.40
fetus 764.9 ☑

Inadequate, inadequacy — continued
development — continued
fetus — continued
affecting management of pregnancy 656.5 ☑
genitalia
after puberty NEC 259.0
congenital — see Hypoplasia, genitalia
lungs 748.5
organ or site NEC — see Hypoplasia, by site
dietary 269.9
distance, interarch 524.28
education V62.3
environment
economic problem V60.2
household condition NEC V60.1
poverty V60.2
unemployment V62.0
functional 301.6
household care, due to
family member
handicapped or ill V60.4
temporarily away from home V60.4
on vacation V60.5
technical defects in home V60.1
temporary absence from home of person rendering care V60.4
housing (heating) (space) V60.1
interarch distance 524.28
material resources V60.2
mental (see also Retardation, mental) 319
nervous system 799.29 ▲
personality 301.6
prenatal care in current pregnancy V23.7
pulmonary
function 786.09
newborn 770.89
ventilation, newborn 770.89
respiration 786.09
newborn 770.89
sample
cytology
anal 796.78
cervical 795.08
vaginal 795.18
social 301.6
Inanition 263.9
with edema 262
due to
deprivation of food 994.2
malnutrition 263.9
fever 780.60
Inappropriate secretion
ACTH 255.0
antidiuretic hormone (ADH) (excessive) 253.6
deficiency 253.5
ectopic hormone NEC 259.3
pituitary (posterior) 253.6
Inattention after or at birth 995.52
Inborn errors of metabolism — see Disorder, metabolism
Incarceration, incarcerated
bubonocele (see also Hernia, inguinal, with obstruction)
gangrenous — see Hernia, inguinal, with gangrene
colon (by hernia) (see also Hernia, by site with obstruction)
gangrenous — see Hernia, by site, with gangrene
enterocele 552.9
gangrenous 551.9
epigastrocele 552.29
gangrenous 551.29
epiplocele 552.9
gangrenous 551.9
exomphalos 552.1
gangrenous 551.1
fallopian tube 620.8
hernia (see also Hernia, by site, with obstruction)
gangrenous — see Hernia, by site, with gangrene
iris, in wound 871.1
lens, in wound 871.1

Incarceration, incarcerated — continued
  merocele (see also Hernia, femoral, with obstruction) 552.00
  omentum (by hernia) (see also Hernia, by site, with obstruction)
    gangrenous — see Hernia, by site, with gangrene
  omphalocele 756.72
  rupture (meaning hernia) (see also Hernia, by site, with obstruction) 552.9
    gangrenous (see also Hernia, by site, with gangrene) 551.9
  sarcoepiplocele 552.9
    gangrenous 551.9
  sarcoepiplomphalocele 552.1
    with gangrene 551.1
  uterus 621.8
    gravid 654.3 ☑
      causing obstructed labor 660.2 ☑
        affecting fetus or newborn 763.1

Incident, cerebrovascular — see also Disease, cerebrovascular, acute 436

Incineration (entire body) (from fire, conflagration, electricity, or lightning) — see Burn, multiple, specified sites

Incised wound
  external — see Wound, open, by site
  internal organs (abdomen, chest, or pelvis) — see Injury, internal, by site, with open wound

Incision, incisional
  hernia — see Hernia, incisional
  surgical, complication — see Complications, surgical procedures
  traumatic
    external — see Wound, open, by site
    internal organs (abdomen, chest, or pelvis) — see Injury, internal, by site, with open wound

Inclusion
  azurophilic leukocytic 288.2
  blennorrhea (neonatal) (newborn) 771.6
  cyst — see Cyst, skin
  gallbladder in liver (congenital) 751.69

Incompatibility
  ABO
    affecting management of pregnancy 656.2 ☑
    fetus or newborn 773.1
    infusion or transfusion reaction 999.6
  blood (group) (Duffy) (E) (K(ell)) (Kidd) (Lewis) (M) (N) (P) (S) NEC
    affecting management of pregnancy 656.2 ☑
    fetus or newborn 773.2
    infusion or transfusion reaction 999.89
  contour of existing restoration of tooth with oral health 525.65
  marital V61.10
    involving
      divorce V61.03
      estrangement V61.09
  Rh (blood group) (factor)
    affecting management of pregnancy 656.1 ☑
    fetus or newborn 773.0
    infusion or transfusion reaction 999.7
  Rhesus — see Incompatibility, Rh

Incompetency, incompetence, incompetent
  annular
    aortic (valve) (see also Insufficiency, aortic) 424.1
    mitral (valve) (see also Insufficiency, mitral) 424.0
    pulmonary valve (heart) (see also Endocarditis, pulmonary) 424.3
  aortic (valve) (see also Insufficiency, aortic) 424.1
    syphilitic 093.22
  cardiac (orifice) 530.0
    valve — see Endocarditis
  cervix, cervical (os) 622.5
    in pregnancy 654.5 ☑
      affecting fetus or newborn 761.0
  chronotropic 426.89

Incompetency, incompetence, incompetent — continued
  chronotropic — continued
    with
      autonomic dysfunction 337.9
      ischemic heart disease 414.9
      left ventricular dysfunction 429.89 ▲
      sinus node dysfunction 427.81
  esophagogastric (junction) (sphincter) 530.0
  heart valve, congenital 746.89
    mitral (valve) — see Insufficiency, mitral
  papillary muscle (heart) 429.81
  pelvic fundus
    pubocervical tissue 618.81
    rectovaginal tissue 618.82
  pulmonary valve (heart) (see also Endocarditis, pulmonary) 424.3
    congenital 746.09
  tricuspid (annular) (rheumatic) (valve) (see also Endocarditis, tricuspid) 397.0
  valvular — see Endocarditis
  vein, venous (saphenous) (varicose) (see also Varicose, vein) 454.9
  velopharyngeal (closure)
    acquired 528.9
    congenital 750.29

Incomplete — see also condition
  bladder emptying 788.21
  expansion lungs (newborn) 770.5
  gestation (liveborn) — see Immaturity
  rotation — see Malrotation

Inconclusive
  image test due to excess body fat 793.91 ●
  mammogram, mammography 793.82 ●
    due to dense breasts 793.82 ●

Incontinence 788.30
  without sensory awareness 788.34
  anal sphincter 787.6
  continuous leakage 788.37
  feces 787.6
    due to hysteria 300.11
    nonorganic origin 307.7
  hysterical 300.11
  mixed (male) (female) (urge and stress) 788.33
  overflow 788.38
  paradoxical 788.39
  rectal 787.6
  specified NEC 788.39
  stress (female) 625.6
    male NEC 788.32
  urethral sphincter 599.84
  urge 788.31
    and stress (male) (female) 788.33
  urine 788.30
    active 788.30
    due to
      cognitive impairment 788.91
      immobility 788.91
      severe physical disability 788.91
    functional 788.91
    male 788.30
      stress 788.32
        and urge 788.33
    neurogenic 788.39
    nonorganic origin 307.6
    stress (female) 625.6
      male NEC 788.32
    urge 788.31
      and stress 788.33

Incontinentia pigmenti 757.33

Incoordinate
  uterus (action) (contractions) 661.4 ☑
    affecting fetus or newborn 763.7

Incoordination
  esophageal-pharyngeal (newborn) 787.24
  muscular 781.3
  papillary muscle 429.81

Increase, increased
  abnormal, in development 783.9
  androgens (ovarian) 256.1
  anticoagulants (antithrombin) (anti-VIIIa) (anti-IXa) (anti-Xa) (anti-XIa) 286.5
    postpartum 666.3 ☑
  cold sense (see also Disturbance, sensation) 782.0

Increase, increased — continued
  estrogen 256.0
  function
    adrenal (cortex) 255.3
      medulla 255.6
    pituitary (anterior) (gland) (lobe) 253.1
      posterior 253.6
  heat sense (see also Disturbance, sensation) 782.0
  intracranial pressure 781.99
    injury at birth 767.8
  light reflex of retina 362.13
  permeability, capillary 448.9
  pressure
    intracranial 781.99
      injury at birth 767.8
    intraocular 365.00
  pulsations 785.9
  pulse pressure 785.9
  sphericity, lens 743.36
  splenic activity 289.4
  venous pressure 459.89
    portal 572.3

Incrustation, cornea, lead or zinc 930.0
Incyclophoria 378.44
Incyclotropia 378.33
Indeterminate sex 752.7
India rubber skin 756.83
Indicanuria 270.2
Indigestion (bilious) (functional) 536.8
  acid 536.8
  catarrhal 536.8
  due to decomposed food NEC 005.9
  fat 579.8
  nervous 306.4
  psychogenic 306.4
Indirect — see condition
Indolent bubo NEC 099.8
Induced
  abortion — see Abortion, induced
  birth, affecting fetus or newborn 763.89
  delivery — see Delivery
  labor — see Delivery
Induration, indurated
  brain 348.89 ▲
  breast (fibrous) 611.79
    puerperal, postpartum 676.3 ☑
  broad ligament 620.8
  chancre 091.0
    anus 091.1
    congenital 090.0
    extragenital NEC 091.2
  corpora cavernosa (penis) (plastic) 607.89
  liver (chronic) 573.8
    acute 573.8
  lung (black) (brown) (chronic) (fibroid) (see also Fibrosis, lung) 515
    essential brown 275.0 [516.1]
  penile 607.89
  phlebitic — see Phlebitis
  skin 782.8
  stomach 537.89
Induratio penis plastica 607.89
Industrial — see condition
Inebriety — see also Abuse, drugs, nondependent 305.0 ☑
Inefficiency
  kidney (see also Disease, renal) 593.9
  thyroid (acquired) (gland) 244.9
Inelasticity, skin 782.8
Inequality, leg (acquired) (length) 736.81
  congenital 755.30
Inertia
  bladder 596.4
    neurogenic 596.54
      with cauda equina syndrome 344.61
  stomach 536.8
    psychogenic 306.4
  uterus, uterine 661.2 ☑
    affecting fetus or newborn 763.7
    primary 661.0 ☑
    secondary 661.1 ☑
  vesical 596.4
    neurogenic 596.54
      with cauda equina 344.61
Infant — see also condition

Infant — see also condition — continued
  excessive crying of 780.92
  fussy (baby) 780.91
  held for adoption V68.89
  newborn — see Newborn
  post-term (gestation period over 40 completed weeks to 42 completed weeks) 766.21
  prolonged gestation of (period over 42 completed weeks) 766.22
  syndrome of diabetic mother 775.0
"Infant Hercules" syndrome 255.2
Infantile — see also condition
  genitalia, genitals 259.0
    in pregnancy or childbirth NEC 654.4 ☑
      affecting fetus or newborn 763.89
      causing obstructed labor 660.2 ☑
        affecting fetus or newborn 763.1
  heart 746.9
  kidney 753.3
  lack of care 995.52
  macula degeneration 362.75
  melanodontia 521.05
  os, uterus (see also Infantile, genitalia) 259.0
  pelvis 738.6
    with disproportion (fetopelvic) 653.1 ☑
      affecting fetus or newborn 763.1
      causing obstructed labor 660.1 ☑
        affecting fetus or newborn 763.1
  penis 259.0
  testis 257.2
  uterus (see also Infantile, genitalia) 259.0
  vulva 752.49
Infantilism 259.9
  with dwarfism (hypophyseal) 253.3
  Brissaud's (infantile myxedema) 244.9
  celiac 579.0
  Herter's (nontropical sprue) 579.0
  hypophyseal 253.3
  hypothalamic (with obesity) 253.8
  idiopathic 259.9
  intestinal 579.0
  pancreatic 577.8
  pituitary 253.3
  renal 588.0
  sexual (with obesity) 259.0
Infants, healthy liveborn — see Newborn
Infarct, infarction
  adrenal (capsule) (gland) 255.41
  amnion 658.8 ☑
  anterior (with contiguous portion of intraventricular septum) NEC (see also Infarct, myocardium) 410.1 ☑
  appendices epiploicae 557.0
  bowel 557.0
  brain (stem) 434.91
    embolic (see also Embolism, brain) 434.11
    healed or old without residuals V12.54
    iatrogenic 997.02
    lacunar 434.91
    late effect — see Late effect(s) (of) cerebrovascular disease
    postoperative 997.02
    puerperal, postpartum, childbirth 674.0 ☑
    thrombotic (see also Thrombosis, brain) 434.01
  breast 611.89
  Brewer's (kidney) 593.81
  cardiac (see also Infarct, myocardium) 410.9 ☑
  cerebellar (see also Infarct, brain) 434.91
    embolic (see also Embolism, brain) 434.11
  cerebral (see also Infarct, brain) 434.91
    aborted 434.91
    embolic (see also Embolism, brain) 434.11
    thrombotic (see also Infarct, brain) 434.01
  chorion 658.8 ☑
  colon (acute) (agnogenic) (embolic) (hemorrhagic) (nonocclusive) (nonthrombotic) (occlusive) (segmental) (thrombotic) (with gangrene) 557.0
  coronary artery (see also Infarct, myocardium) 410.9 ☑
  cortical 434.91
    embolic (see also Embolism) 444.9
  fallopian tube 620.8
  gallbladder 575.8

☑ Additional Digit Required — Refer to the Tabular List for Digit Selection   ᵂ Subterms under main terms may continue to next column or page

148 — Volume 2 • October 2009   ▶◀ Revised Text   ● New Line   ▲ Revised Code   2010 ICD-9-CM

Infarct, infarction — *continued*
  heart (*see also* Infarct, myocardium) 410.9 ☑
  hepatic 573.4
  hypophysis (anterior lobe) 253.8
  impending (myocardium) 411.1
  intestine (acute) (agnogenic) (embolic) (hemorrhagic) (nonocclusive) (nonthrombotic) (occlusive) (thrombotic) (with gangrene) 557.0
  kidney 593.81
  lacunar 434.91
  liver 573.4
  lung (embolic) (thrombotic) 415.19
    with
      abortion — *see* Abortion, by type, with, embolism
      ectopic pregnancy (*see also* categories 633.0–633.9) 639.6
      molar pregnancy (*see also* categories 630–632) 639.6
    following
      abortion 639.6
      ectopic or molar pregnancy 639.6
    iatrogenic 415.11
    in pregnancy, childbirth, or puerperium — *see* Embolism, obstetrical
    postoperative 415.11
    septic 415.12
  lymph node or vessel 457.8
  medullary (brain) — *see* Infarct, brain
  meibomian gland (eyelid) 374.85
  mesentery, mesenteric (embolic) (thrombotic) (with gangrene) 557.0
  midbrain — *see* Infarct, brain
  myocardium, myocardial (acute or with a stated duration of 8 weeks or less) (with hypertension) 410.9 ☑

> *Note — Use the following fifth-digit subclassification with category 410:*
> 0 *episode unspecified*
> 1 *initial episode*
> 2 *subsequent episode without recurrence*

    with symptoms after 8 weeks from date of infarction 414.8
    anterior (wall) (with contiguous portion of intraventricular septum) NEC 410.1 ☑
    anteroapical (with contiguous portion of intraventricular septum) 410.1 ☑
    anterolateral (wall) 410.0 ☑
    anteroseptal (with contiguous portion of intraventricular septum) 410.1 ☑
    apical-lateral 410.5 ☑
    atrial 410.8 ☑
    basal-lateral 410.5 ☑
    chronic (with symptoms after 8 weeks from date of infarction) 414.8
    diagnosed on ECG, but presenting no symptoms 412
    diaphragmatic wall (with contiguous portion of intraventricular septum) 410.4 ☑
    healed or old, currently presenting no symptoms 412
    high lateral 410.5 ☑
    impending 411.1
    inferior (wall) (with contiguous portion of intraventricular septum) 410.4 ☑
    inferolateral (wall) 410.2 ☑
    inferoposterior wall 410.3 ☑
    intraoperative 997.1
    lateral wall 410.5 ☑
    non-Q wave 410.7 ☑
    non-ST elevation (NSTEMI) 410.7 ☑
    nontransmural 410.7 ☑
    papillary muscle 410.8 ☑
    past (diagnosed on ECG or other special investigation, but currently presenting no symptoms) 412
      with symptoms NEC 414.8
    posterior (strictly) (true) (wall) 410.6 ☑
    posterobasal 410.6 ☑

Infarct, infarction — *continued*
  myocardium, myocardial — *continued*
    posteroinferior 410.3 ☑
    posterolateral 410.5 ☑
    postprocedural 997.1
    previous, currently presenting no symptoms 412
    Q wave (*see also* Infarct, myo-cardium, by site) 410.9 ☑
    septal 410.8 ☑
    specified site NEC 410.8 ☑
    ST elevation (STEMI) 410.9 ☑
      anterior (wall) 410.1 ☑
      anterolateral (wall) 410.0 ☑
      inferior (wall) 410.4 ☑
      inferolateral (wall) 410.2 ☑
      inferoposterior wall 410.3 ☑
      lateral wall 410.5 ☑
      posterior (strictly) (true) (wall) 410.6 ☑
      specified site NEC 410.8 ☑
    subendocardial 410.7 ☑
    syphilitic 093.82
    non-ST elevation myocardial infarction (NSTEMI) 410.7 ☑
  nontransmural 410.7 ☑
  omentum 557.0
  ovary 620.8
  pancreas 577.8
  papillary muscle (*see also* Infarct, myocardium) 410.8 ☑
  parathyroid gland 252.8
  pituitary (gland) 253.8
  placenta (complicating pregnancy) 656.7 ☑
    affecting fetus or newborn 762.2
  pontine — *see* Infarct, brain
  posterior NEC (*see also* Infarct, myocardium) 410.6 ☑
  prostate 602.8
  pulmonary (artery) (hemorrhagic) (vein) 415.19
    with
      abortion — *see* Abortion, by type, with embolism
      ectopic pregnancy (*see also* categories 633.0–633.9) 639.6
      molar pregnancy (*see also* categories 630–632) 639.6
    following
      abortion 639.6
      ectopic or molar pregnancy 639.6
    iatrogenic 415.11
    in pregnancy, childbirth, or puerperium — *see* Embolism, obstetrical
    postoperative 415.11
    septic 415.12
  renal 593.81
    embolic or thrombotic 593.81
  retina, retinal 362.84
    with occlusion — *see* Occlusion, retina
  spinal (acute) (cord) (embolic) (nonembolic) 336.1
  spleen 289.59
    embolic or thrombotic 444.89
  subchorionic — *see* Infarct, placenta
  subendocardial (*see also* Infarct, myocardium) 410.7 ☑
  suprarenal (capsule) (gland) 255.41
  syncytium — *see* Infarct, placenta
  testis 608.83
  thrombotic (*see also* Thrombosis) 453.9
    artery, arterial — *see* Embolism
  thyroid (gland) 246.3
  ventricle (heart) (*see also* Infarct, myocardium) 410.9 ☑

Infecting — *see* condition
Infection, infected, infective (opportunistic) 136.9
  with lymphangitis — *see* Lymphangitis
  abortion — *see* Abortion, by type, with, sepsis
  abscess (skin) — *see* Abscess, by site
  Absidia 117.7
  acanthamoeba 136.21
  Acanthocheilonema (perstans) 125.4
    streptocerca 125.6
  accessory sinus (chronic) (*see also* Sinusitis) 473.9
  Achorion — *see* Dermatophytosis

Infection, infected, infective — *continued*
  Acremonium falciforme 117.4
  acromioclavicular (joint) 711.91
  actinobacillus
    lignieresii 027.8
    mallei 024
    muris 026.1
  actinomadura — *see* Actinomycosis
  Actinomyces (israelii) (*see also* Actinomycosis)
    muris-ratti 026.1
  Actinomycetales (actinomadura) (Actinomyces) (Nocardia) (Streptomyces) — *see* Actinomycosis
  actinomycotic NEC (*see also* Actinomycosis) 039.9
  adenoid (chronic) 474.01
    acute 463
    and tonsil (chronic) 474.02
      acute or subacute 463
  adenovirus NEC 079.0
    in diseases classified elsewhere — *see* category 079 ☑
    unspecified nature or site 079.0
  Aerobacter aerogenes NEC 041.85
    enteritis 008.2
  aerogenes capsulatus (*see also* Gangrene, gas) 040.0
  aertrycke (*see also* Infection, Salmonella) 003.9
  ajellomyces dermatitidis 116.0
  alimentary canal NEC (*see also* Enteritis, due to, by organism) 009.0
  Allescheria boydii 117.6
  Alternaria 118
  alveolus, alveolar (process) (pulpal origin) 522.4
  ameba, amebic (histolytica) (*see also* Amebiasis) 006.9
    acute 006.0
    chronic 006.1
    free-living 136.29
    hartmanni 007.8
    specified
      site NEC 006.8
      type NEC 007.8
  amniotic fluid or cavity 658.4 ☑
    affecting fetus or newborn 762.7
  anaerobes (cocci) (gram-negative) (gram-positive) (mixed) NEC 041.84
  anal canal 569.49
  Ancylostoma braziliense 126.2
  Angiostrongylus cantonensis 128.8
  anisakiasis 127.1
  Anisakis larva 127.1
  anthrax (*see also* Anthrax) 022.9
  antrum (chronic) (*see also* Sinusitis, maxillary) 473.0
  anus (papillae) (sphincter) 569.49
  arbor virus NEC 066.9
  arbovirus NEC 066.9
  argentophil-rod 027.0
  Ascaris lumbricoides 127.0
  ascomycetes 117.4
  Aspergillus (flavus) (fumigatus) (terreus) 117.3
  atypical
    acid-fast (bacilli) (*see also* Mycobacterium, atypical) 031.9
    mycobacteria (*see also* Mycobacterium, atypical) 031.9
  auditory meatus (circumscribed) (diffuse) (external) (*see also* Otitis, externa) 380.10
  auricle (ear) (*see also* Otitis, externa) 380.10
  axillary gland 683
  Babesiasis 088.82
  Babesiosis 088.82
  Bacillus NEC 041.89
    abortus 023.1
    anthracis (*see also* Anthrax) 022.9
    cereus (food poisoning) 005.89
    coli — *see* Infection, Escherichia coli
    coliform NEC 041.85
    Ducrey's (any location) 099.0
    Flexner's 004.1
    Friedländer's NEC 041.3
    fusiformis 101
    gas (gangrene) (*see also* Gangrene, gas) 040.0

Infection, infected, infective — *continued*
  Bacillus — *continued*
    mallei 024
    melitensis 023.0
    paratyphoid, paratyphosus 002.9
      A 002.1
      B 002.2
      C 002.3
    Schmorl's 040.3
    Shiga 004.0
    suipestifer (*see also* Infection, Salmonella) 003.9
    swimming pool 031.1
    typhosa 002.0
    welchii (*see also* Gangrene, gas) 040.0
    Whitmore's 025
  bacterial NEC 041.9
    specified NEC 041.89
      anaerobic NEC 041.84
      gram-negative NEC 041.85
        anaerobic NEC 041.84
  Bacterium
    paratyphosum 002.9
      A 002.1
      B 002.2
      C 002.3
    typhosum 002.0
  Bacteroides (fragilis) (melaninogenicus) (oralis) NEC 041.82
  balantidium coli 007.0
  Bartholin's gland 616.89
  Basidiobolus 117.7
  Bedsonia 079.98
    specified NEC 079.88
  bile duct 576.1
  bladder (*see also* Cystitis) 595.9
  Blastomyces, blastomycotic 116.0
    brasiliensis 116.1
    dermatitidis 116.0
    European 117.5
    loboi 116.2
    North American 116.0
    South American 116.1
  bleb
    postprocedural 379.60
      stage 1 379.61
      stage 2 379.62
      stage 3 379.63
  blood stream — *see also* Septicemia
    catheter-related (CRBSI) 999.31
  bone 730.9 ☑
    specified — *see* Osteomyelitis
  Bordetella 033.9
    bronchiseptica 033.8
    parapertussis 033.1
    pertussis 033.0
  Borrelia
    bergdorfi 088.81
    vincentii (mouth) (pharynx) (tonsil) 101
  bovine stomatitis 059.11
  brain (*see also* Encephalitis) 323.9
    late effect — *see* category 326
    membranes (*see also* Meningitis) 322.9
    septic 324.0
      late effect — *see* category 326
      meninges (*see also* Meningitis) 320.9
  branchial cyst 744.42
  breast 611.0
    puerperal, postpartum 675.2 ☑
      with nipple 675.9 ☑
        specified type NEC 675.8 ☑
      nonpurulent 675.2 ☑
      purulent 675.1 ☑
  bronchus (*see also* Bronchitis) 490
    fungus NEC 117.9
  Brucella 023.9
    abortus 023.1
    canis 023.3
    melitensis 023.0
    mixed 023.8
    suis 023.2
  Brugia (Wuchereria) malayi 125.1
  bursa — *see* Bursitis
  buttocks (skin) 686.9
  Candida (albicans) (tropicalis) (*see also* Candidiasis) 112.9

☑ Additional Digit Required — Refer to the Tabular List for Digit Selection   Subterms under main terms may continue to next column or page

2010 ICD-9-CM   ▶◀ Revised Text   ● New Line   ▲ Revised Code   Volume 2 — 149

Infection, infected, infective — *continued*

Candida (*see also* Candidiasis) — *continued*
    congenital 771.7
Candiru 136.8
Capillaria
    hepatica 128.8
    philippinensis 127.5
cartilage 733.99
catheter-related bloodstream (CRBSI) 999.31
cat liver fluke 121.0
cellulitis — *see* Cellulitis, by site
Cephalosporum falciforme 117.4
Cercomonas hominis (intestinal) 007.3
cerebrospinal (*see also* Meningitis) 322.9
    late effect — *see* category 326
cervical gland 683
cervix (*see also* Cervicitis) 616.0
cesarean section wound 674.3 ☑
Chilomastix (intestinal) 007.8
Chlamydia 079.98
    specified NEC 079.88
cholera (*see also* Cholera) 001.9
chorionic plate 658.8 ☑
Cladosporium
    bantianum 117.8
    carrionii 117.2
    mansoni 111.1
    trichoides 117.8
    wernecki 111.1
Clonorchis (sinensis) (liver) 121.1
Clostridium (haemolyticum) (novyi) NEC 041.84
    botulinum 005.1
    histolyticum (*see also* Gangrene, gas) 040.0
    oedematiens (*see also* Gangrene, gas) 040.0
    perfringens 041.83
        due to food 005.2
    septicum (*see also* Gangrene, gas) 040.0
    sordellii (*see also* Gangrene, gas) 040.0
    welchii (*see also* Gangrene, gas) 040.0
        due to food 005.2
Coccidioides (immitis) (*see also* Coccidioidomycosis) 114.9
coccus NEC 041.89
colon (*see also* Enteritis, due to, by organism) 009.0
    bacillus — *see* Infection, Escherichia coli
colostomy or enterostomy 569.61
common duct 576.1
complicating pregnancy, childbirth, or puerperium NEC 647.9 ☑
    affecting fetus or newborn 760.2
Condiobolus 117.7
congenital NEC 771.89
    Candida albicans 771.7
    chronic 771.2
    cytomegalovirus 771.1
    hepatitis, viral 771.2
    herpes simplex 771.2
    listeriosis 771.2
    malaria 771.2
    poliomyelitis 771.2
    rubella 771.0
    toxoplasmosis 771.2
    tuberculosis 771.2
    urinary (tract) 771.82
    vaccinia 771.2
coronavirus 079.89
    SARS-associated 079.82
corpus luteum (*see also* Salpingo-oophoritis) 614.2
Corynebacterium diphtheriae — *see* Diphtheria
cotia virus 059.8
Coxsackie (*see also* Coxsackie) 079.2
    endocardium 074.22
    heart NEC 074.20
    in diseases classified elsewhere — *see* category 079 ☑
    meninges 047.0
    myocardium 074.23
    pericardium 074.21
    pharynx 074.0
    specified disease NEC 074.8
    unspecified nature or site 079.2

Infection, infected, infective — *continued*

Cryptococcus neoformans 117.5
Cryptosporidia 007.4
Cunninghamella 117.7
cyst — *see* Cyst
Cysticercus cellulosae 123.1
cytomegalovirus 078.5
    congenital 771.1
dental (pulpal origin) 522.4
deuteromycetes 117.4
Dicrocoelium dendriticum 121.8
Dipetalonema (perstans) 125.4
    streptocerca 125.6
diphtherial — *see* Diphtheria
Diphyllobothrium (adult) (latum) (pacificum) 123.4
    larval 123.5
Diplogonoporus (grandis) 123.8
Dipylidium (caninum) 123.8
Dirofilaria 125.6
dog tapeworm 123.8
Dracunculus medinensis 125.7
Dreschlera 118
    hawaiiensis 117.8
Ducrey's bacillus (any site) 099.0
due to or resulting from
    central venous catheter 999.31
    device, implant, or graft (any) (presence of) — *see* Complications, infection and inflammation, due to (presence of) any device, implant, or graft classified to 996.0–996.5 NEC
    injection, inoculation, infusion, transfusion, or vaccination (prophylactic) (therapeutic) 999.39
    injury NEC — *see* Wound, open, by site, complicated
    surgery 998.59
duodenum 535.6 ☑
ear (*see also* Otitis)
    external (*see also* Otitis, externa) 380.10
    inner (*see also* Labyrinthitis) 386.30
    middle — *see* Otitis, media
Eaton's agent NEC 041.81
Eberthella typhosa 002.0
Ebola 078.89
echinococcosis 122.9
Echinococcus (*see also* Echinococcus) 122.9
Echinostoma 121.8
ECHO virus 079.1
    in diseases classified elsewhere — *see* category 079 ☑
    unspecified nature or site 079.1
Ehrlichiosis 082.40
    chaffeensis 082.41
    specified type NEC 082.49
Endamoeba — *see* Infection, ameba
endocardium (*see also* Endocarditis) 421.0
endocervix (*see also* Cervicitis) 616.0
Entamoeba — *see* Infection, ameba
enteric (*see also* Enteritis, due to, by organism) 009.0
Enterobacter aerogenes NEC 041.85
Enterobacter sakazakii 041.85
Enterobius vermicularis 127.4
enterococcus NEC 041.04
enterovirus NEC 079.89
    central nervous system NEC 048
    enteritis 008.67
    meningitis 047.9
Entomophthora 117.7
Epidermophyton — *see* Dermatophytosis
epidermophytosis — *see* Dermatophytosis
episiotomy 674.3 ☑
Epstein-Barr virus 075
    chronic 780.79 [139.8]
erysipeloid 027.1
Erysipelothrix (insidiosa) (rhusiopathiae) 027.1
erythema infectiosum 057.0
Escherichia coli NEC 041.4
    enteritis — *see* Enteritis, E. coli
    generalized 038.42
    intestinal — *see* Enteritis, E. coli
esophagostomy 530.86
ethmoidal (chronic) (sinus) (*see also* Sinusitis, ethmoidal) 473.2

Infection, infected, infective — *continued*

Eubacterium 041.84
Eustachian tube (ear) 381.50
    acute 381.51
    chronic 381.52
exanthema subitum (*see also* Exanthem subitum) 058.10
external auditory canal (meatus) (*see also* Otitis, externa) 380.10
eye NEC 360.00
eyelid 373.9
    specified NEC 373.8
fallopian tube (*see also* Salpingo-oophoritis) 614.2
fascia 728.89
Fasciola
    gigantica 121.3
    hepatica 121.3
Fasciolopsis (buski) 121.4
fetus (intra-amniotic) — *see* Infection, congenital
filarial — *see* Infestation, filarial
finger (skin) 686.9
    abscess (with lymphangitis) 681.00
        pulp 681.01
    cellulitis (with lymphangitis) 681.00
    distal closed space (with lymphangitis) 681.00
    nail 681.02
        fungus 110.1
fish tapeworm 123.4
    larval 123.5
flagellate, intestinal 007.9
fluke — *see* Infestation, fluke
focal
    teeth (pulpal origin) 522.4
    tonsils 474.00
        and adenoids 474.02
Fonsecaea
    compactum 117.2
    pedrosoi 117.2
food (*see also* Poisoning, food) 005.9
foot (skin) 686.9
    fungus 110.4
Francisella tularensis (*see also* Tularemia) 021.9
frontal sinus (chronic) (*see also* Sinusitis, frontal) 473.1
fungus NEC 117.9
    beard 110.0
    body 110.5
    dermatiacious NEC 117.8
    foot 110.4
    groin 110.3
    hand 110.2
    nail 110.1
    pathogenic to compromised host only 118
    perianal (area) 110.3
    scalp 110.0
    scrotum 110.8
    skin 111.9
        foot 110.4
        hand 110.2
    toenails 110.1
    trachea 117.9
Fusarium 118
Fusobacterium 041.84
gallbladder (*see also* Cholecystitis, acute) 575.0
Gardnerella vaginalis 041.89
gas bacillus (*see also* Gas, gangrene) 040.0
gastric (*see also* Gastritis) 535.5 ☑
Gastrodiscoides hominis 121.8
gastroenteric (*see also* Enteritis, due to, by organism) 009.0
gastrointestinal (*see also* Enteritis, due to, by organism) 009.0
gastrostomy 536.41
generalized NEC (*see also* Septicemia) 038.9
genital organ or tract NEC
    female 614.9
        with
            abortion — *see* Abortion, by type, with sepsis
            ectopic pregnancy (*see also* categories 633.0–633.9) 639.0
            molar pregnancy (*see also* categories 630–632) 639.0

Infection, infected, infective — *continued*

genital organ or tract — *continued*
    female — *continued*
        complicating pregnancy 646.6 ☑
            affecting fetus or newborn 760.8
        following
            abortion 639.0
            ectopic or molar pregnancy 639.0
        puerperal, postpartum, childbirth 670.8 ☑ ▲
        minor or localized 646.6 ☑
            affecting fetus or newborn 760.8
    male 608.4
genitourinary tract NEC 599.0
Ghon tubercle, primary (*see also* Tuberculosis) 010.0 ☑
Giardia lamblia 007.1
gingival (chronic) 523.10
    acute 523.00
    Vincent's 101
glanders 024
Glenosporopsis amazonica 116.2
Gnathostoma spinigerum 128.1
Gongylonema 125.6
gonococcal NEC (*see also* Gonococcus) 098.0
gram-negative bacilli NEC 041.85
    anaerobic 041.84
guinea worm 125.7
gum (*see also* Infection, gingival) 523.10
Hantavirus 079.81
heart 429.89
Helicobacter pylori [H. pylori] 041.86
helminths NEC 128.9
    intestinal 127.9
        mixed (types classifiable to more than one category in 120.0–127.7) 127.8
        specified type NEC 127.7
    specified type NEC 128.8
Hemophilus influenzae NEC 041.5
    generalized 038.41
herpes (simplex) (*see also* Herpes, simplex) 054.9
    congenital 771.2
    zoster (*see also* Herpes, zoster) 053.9
        eye NEC 053.29
Heterophyes heterophyes 121.6
Histoplasma (*see also* Histoplasmosis) 115.90
    capsulatum (*see also* Histoplasmosis, American) 115.00
    duboisii (*see also* Histoplasmosis, African) 115.10
HIV V08
    with symptoms, symptomatic 042
hookworm (*see also* Ancylostomiasis) 126.9
human herpesvirus NEC 058.89
human herpesvirus 6 058.81
human herpesvirus 7 058.82
human herpesvirus 8 058.89
human immunodeficiency virus V08
    with symptoms, symptomatic 042
human papillomavirus 079.4
hydrocele 603.1
hydronephrosis 591
Hymenolepis 123.6
hypopharynx 478.29
inguinal glands 683
    due to soft chancre 099.0
intestine, intestinal (*see also* Enteritis, due to, by organism) 009.0
intrauterine (*see also* Endometritis) 615.9
    complicating delivery 646.6 ☑
isospora belli or hominis 007.2
Japanese B encephalitis 062.0
jaw (bone) (acute) (chronic) (lower) (subacute) (upper) 526.4
joint — *see* Arthritis, infectious or infective
Kaposi's sarcoma-associated herpesvirus 058.89
kidney (cortex) (hematogenous) 590.9
    with
        abortion — *see* Abortion, by type, with urinary tract infection
        calculus 592.0

Infection, infected, infective — *continued*
  kidney — *continued*
    with — *continued*
      ectopic pregnancy (*see also* categories 633.0–633.9) 639.8
      molar pregnancy (*see also* categories 630–632) 639.8
    complicating pregnancy or puerperium 646.6 ☑
      affecting fetus or newborn 760.1
    following
      abortion 639.8
      ectopic or molar pregnancy 639.8
    pelvis and ureter 590.3
  Klebsiella pneumoniae NEC 041.3
  knee (skin) NEC 686.9
    joint — *see* Arthritis, infectious
  Koch's (*see also* Tuberculosis, pulmonary) 011.9 ☑
  labia (majora) (minora) (*see also* Vulvitis) 616.10
  lacrimal
    gland (*see also* Dacryoadenitis) 375.00
    passages (duct) (sac) (*see also* Dacryocystitis) 375.30
  larynx NEC 478.79
  leg (skin) NEC 686.9
  Leishmania (*see also* Leishmaniasis) 085.9
    braziliensis 085.5
    donovani 085.0
    ethiopica 085.3
    furunculosa 085.1
    infantum 085.0
    mexicana 085.4
    tropica (minor) 085.1
      major 085.2
  Leptosphaeria senegalensis 117.4
  leptospira (*see also* Leptospirosis) 100.9
    Australis 100.89
    Bataviae 100.89
    pyrogenes 100.89
    specified type NEC 100.89
  leptospirochetal NEC (*see also* Leptospirosis) 100.9
  Leptothrix — *see* Actinomycosis
  Listeria monocytogenes (listeriosis) 027.0
    congenital 771.2
  liver fluke — *see* Infestation, fluke, liver
  Loa loa 125.2
    eyelid 125.2 *[373.6]*
  Loboa loboi 116.2
  local, skin (staphylococcal) (streptococcal) NEC 686.9
    abscess — *see* Abscess, by site
    cellulitis — *see* Cellulitis, by site
    ulcer (*see also* Ulcer, skin) 707.9
  Loefflerella
    mallei 024
    whitmori 025
  lung 518.89
    atypical Mycobacterium 031.0
      tuberculous (*see also* Tuberculosis, pulmonary) 011.9 ☑
    basilar 518.89
    chronic 518.89
    fungus NEC 117.9
    spirochetal 104.8
    virus — *see* Pneumonia, virus
  lymph gland (axillary) (cervical) (inguinal) 683
    mesenteric 289.2
  lymphoid tissue, base of tongue or posterior pharynx, NEC 474.00
  madurella
    grisea 117.4
    mycetomii 117.4
  major
    with
      abortion — *see* Abortion, by type, with sepsis
      ectopic pregnancy (*see also* categories 633.0–633.9) 639.0
      molar pregnancy (*see also* categories 630–632) 639.0
    following
      abortion 639.0
      ectopic or molar pregnancy 639.0

Infection, infected, infective — *continued*
  major — *continued*
    puerperal, postpartum, childbirth 670.0 ☑
  Malassezia furfur 111.0
  Malleomyces
    mallei 024
    pseudomallei 025
  mammary gland 611.0
    puerperal, postpartum 675.2 ☑
  Mansonella (ozzardi) 125.5
  mastoid (suppurative) — *see* Mastoiditis
  maxilla, maxillary 526.4
    sinus (chronic) (*see also* Sinusitis, maxillary) 473.0
  mediastinum 519.2
  medina 125.7
  meibomian
    cyst 373.12
    gland 373.12
  melioidosis 025
  meninges (*see also* Meningitis) 320.9
  meningococcal (*see also* condition) 036.9
    brain 036.1
    cerebrospinal 036.0
    endocardium 036.42
    generalized 036.2
    meninges 036.0
    meningococcemia 036.2
    specified site NEC 036.89
  mesenteric lymph nodes or glands NEC 289.2
  Metagonimus 121.5
  metatarsophalangeal 711.97
  methicillin
    resistant Staphylococcus aureus (MRSA) 041.12
    susceptible Staphylococcus aureus (MSSA) 041.11
  microorganism resistant to drugs — *see* Resistance (to), drugs by microorganisms
  Microsporidia 136.8
  microsporum, microsporic — *see* Dermatophytosis
  Mima polymorpha NEC 041.85
  mixed flora NEC 041.89
  Monilia (*see also* Candidiasis) 112.9
    neonatal 771.7
  monkeypox 059.01
  Monosporium apiospermum 117.6
  mouth (focus) NEC 528.9
    parasitic 136.9
  MRSA (methicillin resistant Staphylococcus aureus) 041.12
  MSSA (methicillin susceptible Staphylococcus aureus) 041.11
  Mucor 117.7
  muscle NEC 728.89
  mycelium NEC 117.9
  mycetoma
    actinomycotic NEC (*see also* Actinomycosis) 039.9
    mycotic NEC 117.4
  Mycobacterium, mycobacterial (*see also* Mycobacterium) 031.9
  Mycoplasma NEC 041.81
  mycotic NEC 117.9
    pathogenic to compromised host only 118
    skin NEC 111.9
    systemic 117.9
  myocardium NEC 422.90
  nail (chronic) (with lymphangitis) 681.9
    finger 681.02
      fungus 110.1
    ingrowing 703.0
    toe 681.11
      fungus 110.1
  nasal sinus (chronic) (*see also* Sinusitis) 473.9
  nasopharynx (chronic) 478.29
    acute 460
  navel 686.9
    newborn 771.4
  Neisserian — *see* Gonococcus
  Neotestudina rosatii 117.4
  newborn, generalized 771.89
  nipple 611.0
    puerperal, postpartum 675.0 ☑
      with breast 675.9 ☑

Infection, infected, infective — *continued*
  nipple — *continued*
    puerperal, postpartum — *continued*
      with breast — *continued*
        specified type NEC 675.8 ☑
  Nocardia — *see* Actinomycosis
  nose 478.19
  nostril 478.19
  obstetrical surgical wound 674.3 ☑
  Oesophagostomum (apiostomum) 127.7
  Oestrus ovis 134.0
  Oidium albicans (*see also* Candidiasis) 112.9
  Onchocerca (volvulus) 125.3
    eye 125.3 *[360.13]*
    eyelid 125.3 *[373.6]*
    operation wound 998.59
  Opisthorchis (felineus) (tenuicollis) (viverrini) 121.0
  orbit 376.00
    chronic 376.10
  orthopoxvirus 059.00
    specified NEC 059.09
  ovary (*see also* Salpingo-oophoritis) 614.2
  Oxyuris vermicularis 127.4
  pancreas 577.0
  Paracoccidioides brasiliensis 116.1
  Paragonimus (westermani) 121.2
  parainfluenza virus 079.89
  parameningococcus NEC 036.9
    with meningitis 036.0
  parapoxvirus 059.10
    specified NEC 059.19
  parasitic NEC 136.9
  paratyphoid 002.9
    type A 002.1
    type B 002.2
    type C 002.3
  paraurethral ducts 597.89
  parotid gland 527.2
  Pasteurella NEC 027.2
    multocida (cat-bite) (dog-bite) 027.2
    pestis (*see also* Plague) 020.9
    pseudotuberculosis 027.2
    septica (cat-bite) (dog-bite) 027.2
    tularensis (*see also* Tularemia) 021.9
  pelvic, female (*see also* Disease, pelvis, inflammatory) 614.9
  penis (glans) (retention) NEC 607.2
    herpetic 054.13
  Peptococcus 041.84
  Peptostreptococcus 041.84
  periapical (pulpal origin) 522.4
  peridental 523.30
  perineal wound (obstetrical) 674.3 ☑
  periodontal 523.31
  periorbital 376.00
    chronic 376.10
  perirectal 569.49
  perirenal (*see also* Infection, kidney) 590.9
  peritoneal (*see also* Peritonitis) 567.9
  periureteral 593.89
  periurethral 597.89
  Petriellidium boydii 117.6
  pharynx 478.29
    Coxsackie virus 074.0
    phlegmonous 462
    posterior, lymphoid 474.00
  Phialophora
    gougerotii 117.8
    jeanselmei 117.8
    verrucosa 117.2
  Piedraia hortai 111.3
  pinna, acute 380.11
  pinta 103.9
    intermediate 103.1
    late 103.2
    mixed 103.3
    primary 103.0
  pinworm 127.4
  pityrosporum furfur 111.0
  pleuropneumonia-like organisms NEC (PPLO) 041.81
  pneumococcal NEC 041.2
    generalized (purulent) 038.2
  Pneumococcus NEC 041.2
  postoperative wound 998.59

Infection, infected, infective — *continued*
  posttraumatic NEC 958.3
  postvaccinal 999.39
  poxvirus 059.9
    specified NEC 059.8
  prepuce NEC 607.1
  Proprionibacterium 041.84
  prostate (capsule) (*see also* Prostatitis) 601.9
  Proteus (mirabilis) (morganii) (vulgaris) NEC 041.6
    enteritis 008.3
  protozoal NEC 136.8
    intestinal NEC 007.9
  Pseudomonas NEC 041.7
    mallei 024
    pneumonia 482.1
    pseudomallei 025
  psittacosis 073.9
  puerperal, postpartum (major) 670.0 ☑
    minor 646.6 ☑
  pulmonary — *see* Infection, lung
  purulent — *see* Abscess
  putrid, generalized — *see* Septicemia
  pyemic — *see* Septicemia
  Pyrenochaeta romeroi 117.4
  Q fever 083.0
  rabies 071
  rectum (sphincter) 569.49
  renal (*see also* Infection, kidney) 590.9
    pelvis and ureter 590.3
  resistant to drugs — *see* Resistance (to), drugs by microorganisms
  respiratory 519.8
    chronic 519.8
    influenzal (acute) (upper) 487.1
    lung 518.89
    rhinovirus 460
    syncytial virus 079.6
    upper (acute) (infectious) NEC 465.9
      with flu, grippe, or influenza 487.1
      influenzal 487.1
      multiple sites NEC 465.8
      streptococcal 034.0
      viral NEC 465.9
  respiratory syncytial virus (RSV) 079.6
  resulting from presence of shunt or other internal prosthetic device — *see* Complications, infection and inflammation, due to (presence of) any device, implant, or graft classified to 996.0–996.5 NEC
  retroperitoneal 567.39
  retrovirus 079.50
    human immunodeficiency virus type 2 [HIV2] 079.53
    human T-cell lymphotrophic virus type I [HTLV-I] 079.51
    human T-cell lymphotrophic virus type II [HTLV-II] 079.52
    specified NEC 079.59
  Rhinocladium 117.1
  Rhinosporidium — *see* beri 117.0
  rhinovirus
    in diseases classified elsewhere — *see* category 079 ☑
    unspecified nature or site 079.3
  Rhizopus 117.7
  rickettsial 083.9
  rickettsialpox 083.2
  rubella (*see also* Rubella) 056.9
    congenital 771.0
  Saccharomyces (*see also* Candidiasis) 112.9
  Saksenaea 117.7
  salivary duct or gland (any) 527.2
  Salmonella (aertrycke) (callinarum) (choleraesuis) (enteritidis) (suipestifer) (typhimurium) 003.9
    with
      arthritis 003.23
      gastroenteritis 003.0
      localized infection 003.20
        specified type NEC 003.29
      meningitis 003.21
      osteomyelitis 003.24
      pneumonia 003.22
      septicemia 003.1

☑ Additional Digit Required — Refer to the Tabular List for Digit Selection   ᵂ Subterms under main terms may continue to next column or page

2010 ICD-9-CM   ▶◀ Revised Text   ● New Line   ▲ Revised Code   Volume 2 — 151

Infection, infected, infective — *continued*
Salmonella — *continued*
　with — *continued*
　　specified manifestation NEC 003.8
　　due to food (poisoning) (any serotype) (*see also* Poisoning, food, due to, Salmonella)
　hirschfeldii 002.3
　localized 003.20
　　specified type NEC 003.29
　paratyphi 002.9
　　A 002.1
　　B 002.2
　　C 002.3
　schottmuelleri 002.2
　specified type NEC 003.8
　typhi 002.0
　typhosa 002.0
saprophytic 136.8
Sarcocystis, lindemanni 136.5
SARS-associated coronavirus 079.82
scabies 133.0
Schistosoma — *see* Infestation, Schistosoma
Schmorl's bacillus 040.3
scratch or other superficial injury — *see* Injury, superficial, by site
scrotum (acute) NEC 608.4
sealpox 059.12
secondary, burn or open wound (dislocation) (fracture) 958.3
seminal vesicle (*see also* Vesiculitis) 608.0
septic
　generalized — *see* Septicemia
　localized, skin (*see also* Abscess) 682.9
septicemic — *see* Septicemia
seroma 998.51
Serratia (marcescens) 041.85
　generalized 038.44
sheep liver fluke 121.3
Shigella 004.9
　boydii 004.2
　dysenteriae 004.0
　flexneri 004.1
　group
　　A 004.0
　　B 004.1
　　C 004.2
　　D 004.3
　Schmitz (-Stutzer) 004.0
　schmitzii 004.0
　Shiga 004.0
　sonnei 004.3
　specified type NEC 004.8
Sin Nombre virus 079.81
sinus (*see also* Sinusitis) 473.9
　pilonidal 685.1
　　with abscess 685.0
　skin NEC 686.9
Skene's duct or gland (*see also* Urethritis) 597.89
skin (local) (staphylococcal) (streptococcal) NEC 686.9
　abscess — *see* Abscess, by site
　cellulitis — *see* Cellulitis, by site
　due to fungus 111.9
　　specified type NEC 111.8
　mycotic 111.9
　　specified type NEC 111.8
　ulcer (*see also* Ulcer, skin) 707.9
slow virus 046.9
　specified condition NEC 046.8
Sparganum (mansoni) (proliferum) 123.5
spermatic cord NEC 608.4
sphenoidal (chronic) (sinus) (*see also* Sinusitis, sphenoidal) 473.3
Spherophorus necrophorus 040.3
spinal cord NEC (*see also* Encephalitis) 323.9
　abscess 324.1
　　late effect — *see* category 326
　late effect — *see* category 326
　meninges — *see* Meningitis
　streptococcal 320.2
Spirillum
　minus or minor 026.0
　morsus muris 026.0
　obermeieri 087.0

Infection, infected, infective — *continued*
spirochetal NEC 104.9
　lung 104.8
　specified nature or site NEC 104.8
spleen 289.59
Sporothrix schenckii 117.1
Sporotrichum (schenckii) 117.1
Sporozoa 136.8
staphylococcal NEC 041.10
　aureus 041.11
　　methicillin
　　　resistant (MRSA) 041.12
　　　susceptible (MSSA) 041.11
　food poisoning 005.0
　generalized (purulent) 038.10
　　aureus 038.11
　　　methicillin
　　　　resistant 038.12
　　　　susceptible 038.11
　　specified organism NEC 038.19
　pneumonia 482.40
　　aureus 482.41
　　　methicillin
　　　　resistant (MRSA) 482.42
　　　　susceptible (MSSA) 482.41
　　MRSA (methicillin resistant Staphylococcus aureus) 482.42
　　MSSA (methicillin susceptible Staphylococcus aureus) 482.41
　　specified type NEC 482.49
　septicemia 038.10
　　aureus 038.11
　　　methicillin
　　　　resistant (MRSA) 038.12
　　　　susceptible (MSSA) 038.11
　　MRSA (methicillin resistant Staphylococcus aureus) 038.12
　　MSSA (methicillin susceptible Staphylococcus aureus) 038.11
　　specified organism NEC 038.19
　specified NEC 041.19
steatoma 706.2
Stellantchasmus falcatus 121.6
Streptobacillus moniliformis 026.1
streptococcal NEC 041.00
　generalized (purulent) 038.0
　Group
　　A 041.01
　　B 041.02
　　C 041.03
　　D [enterococcus] 041.04
　　G 041.05
　pneumonia — *see* Pneumonia, streptococcal
　septicemia 038.0
　sore throat 034.0
　specified NEC 041.09
Streptomyces — *see* Actinomycosis
streptotrichosis — *see* Actinomycosis
Strongyloides (stercoralis) 127.2
stump (amputation) (posttraumatic) (surgical) 997.62
　traumatic — *see* Amputation, traumatic, by site, complicated
subcutaneous tissue, local NEC 686.9
submaxillary region 528.9
suipestifer (*see also* Infection, Salmonella) 003.9
swimming pool bacillus 031.1
syphilitic — *see* Syphilis
systemic — *see* Septicemia
Taenia — *see* Infestation, Taenia
Taeniarhynchus saginatus 123.2
tanapox 059.21
tapeworm — *see* Infestation, tapeworm
tendon (sheath) 727.89
Ternidens diminutus 127.7
testis (*see also* Orchitis) 604.90
thigh (skin) 686.9
threadworm 127.4
throat 478.29
　pneumococcal 462
　staphylococcal 462
　streptococcal 034.0
　viral NEC (*see also* Pharyngitis) 462
thumb (skin) 686.9
　abscess (with lymphangitis) 681.00

Infection, infected, infective — *continued*
thumb — *continued*
　abscess — *continued*
　　pulp 681.01
　cellulitis (with lymphangitis) 681.00
　nail 681.02
thyroglossal duct 529.8
toe (skin) 686.9
　abscess (with lymphangitis) 681.10
　cellulitis (with lymphangitis) 681.10
　nail 681.11
　　fungus 110.1
tongue NEC 529.0
　parasitic 112.0
tonsil (faucial) (lingual) (pharyngeal) 474.00
　acute or subacute 463
　and adenoid 474.02
　tag 474.00
tooth, teeth 522.4
　periapical (pulpal origin) 522.4
　peridental 523.30
　periodontal 523.31
　pulp 522.0
　socket 526.5
TORCH — *see* Infection, congenital NEC without active infection 760.2
Torula histolytica 117.5
Toxocara (cani) (cati) (felis) 128.0
Toxoplasma gondii (*see also* Toxoplasmosis) 130.9
trachea, chronic 491.8
　fungus 117.9
traumatic NEC 958.3
trematode NEC 121.9
trench fever 083.1
Treponema
　denticola 041.84
　macrodenticum 041.84
　pallidum (*see also* Syphilis) 097.9
Trichinella (spiralis) 124
Trichomonas 131.9
　bladder 131.09
　cervix 131.09
　hominis 007.3
　intestine 007.3
　prostate 131.03
　specified site NEC 131.8
　urethra 131.02
　urogenitalis 131.00
　vagina 131.01
　vulva 131.01
Trichophyton, trichophytid — *see* Dermatophytosis
Trichosporon (beigelii) cutaneum 111.2
Trichostrongylus 127.6
Trichuris (trichiuria) 127.3
Trombicula (irritans) 133.8
Trypanosoma (*see also* Trypanosomiasis) 086.9
　cruzi 086.2
tubal (*see also* Salpingo-oophoritis) 614.2
tuberculous NEC (*see also* Tuberculosis) 011.9 ☑
tubo-ovarian (*see also* Salpingo-oophoritis) 614.2
tunica vaginalis 608.4
tympanic membrane — *see* Myringitis
typhoid (abortive) (ambulant) (bacillus) 002.0
typhus 081.9
　flea-borne (endemic) 081.0
　louse-borne (epidemic) 080
　mite-borne 081.2
　recrudescent 081.1
　tick-borne 082.9
　　African 082.1
　　North Asian 082.2
umbilicus (septic) 686.9
　newborn NEC 771.4
ureter 593.89
urethra (*see also* Urethritis) 597.80
urinary (tract) NEC 599.0
　with
　　abortion — *see* Abortion, by type, with urinary tract infection
　　ectopic pregnancy (*see also* categories 633–633.9) 639.8

Infection, infected, infective — *continued*
urinary — *continued*
　with — *continued*
　　molar pregnancy (*see also* categories 630–632) 639.8
　candidal 112.2
　complicating pregnancy, childbirth, or puerperium 646.6 ☑
　　affecting fetus or newborn 760.1
　　asymptomatic 646.5 ☑
　　　affecting fetus or newborn 760.1
　diplococcal (acute) 098.0
　　chronic 098.2
　due to Trichomonas (vaginalis) 131.00
　following
　　abortion 639.8
　　ectopic or molar pregnancy 639.8
　gonococcal (acute) 098.0
　　chronic or duration of 2 months or over 098.2
　newborn 771.82
　trichomonal 131.00
　tuberculous (*see also* Tuberculosis) 016.3 ☑
　uterus, uterine (*see also* Endometritis) 615.9
　utriculus masculinus NEC 597.89
　vaccination 999.39
　vagina (granulation tissue) (wall) (*see also* Vaginitis) 616.10
　varicella 052.9
　varicose veins — *see* Varicose, veins
　variola 050.9
　　major 050.0
　　minor 050.1
　vas deferens NEC 608.4
　Veillonella 041.84
　verumontanum 597.89
　vesical (*see also* Cystitis) 595.9
　Vibrio
　　cholerae 001.0
　　　El Tor 001.1
　　parahaemolyticus (food poisoning) 005.4
　　vulnificus 041.85
　Vincent's (gums) (mouth) (tonsil) 101
vaccination 999.39
virus, viral 079.99
　adenovirus
　　in diseases classified elsewhere — *see* category 079 ☑
　　unspecified nature or site 079.0
　central nervous system NEC 049.9
　　enterovirus 048
　　　meningitis 047.9
　　　　specified type NEC 047.8
　　slow virus 046.9
　　specified condition NEC 046.8
　chest 519.8
　conjunctivitis 077.99
　　specified type NEC 077.8
　coronavirus 079.89
　　SARS-associated 079.82
　Coxsackie (*see also* Infection, Coxsackie) 079.2
　Ebola 065.8
　ECHO
　　in diseases classified elsewhere — *see* category 079 ☑
　　unspecified nature or site 079.1
　encephalitis 049.9
　　arthropod-borne NEC 064
　　tick-borne 063.9
　　　specified type NEC 063.8
　enteritis NEC (*see also* Enteritis, viral) 008.8
　exanthem NEC 057.9
　Hantavirus 079.81
　human papilloma 079.4
　in diseases classified elsewhere — *see* category 079 ☑
　intestine (*see also* Enteritis, viral) 008.8
　lung — *see* Pneumonia, viral
　respiratory syncytial (RSV) 079.6
　retrovirus 079.50
　rhinovirus
　　in diseases classified elsewhere — *see* category 079 ☑

Subterms under main terms may continue to next column or page

Infestation — *continued*
  tapeworm — *continued*
    broad 123.4
      larval 123.5
    dog 123.8
    dwarf 123.6
    fish 123.4
      larval 123.5
    pork 123.0
    rat 123.6
  Ternidens diminutus 127.7
  Tetranychus molestissimus 133.8
  threadworm 127.4
  tongue 112.0
  Toxocara (cani) (cati) (felis) 128.0
  trematode(s) NEC 121.9
  Trichina spiralis 124
  Trichinella spiralis 124
  Trichocephalus 127.3
  Trichomonas 131.9
    bladder 131.09
    cervix 131.09
    intestine 007.3
    prostate 131.03
    specified site NEC 131.8
    urethra (female) (male) 131.02
    urogenital 131.00
    vagina 131.01
    vulva 131.01
  Trichophyton — *see* Dermatophytosis
  Trichostrongylus instabilis 127.6
  Trichuris (trichiuria) 127.3
  Trombicula (irritans) 133.8
  Trypanosoma — *see* Trypanosomiasis
  Tunga penetrans 134.1
  Uncinaria americana 126.1
  whipworm 127.3
  worms NEC 128.9
    intestinal 127.9
  Wuchereria 125.0
    bancrofti 125.0
    malayi 125.1

Infiltrate, infiltration
  with an iron compound 275.0
  amyloid (any site) (generalized) 277.39
  calcareous (muscle) NEC 275.49
    localized — *see* Degeneration, by site
  calcium salt (muscle) 275.49
  chemotherapy, vesicant 999.81 ▲
  corneal (*see also* Edema, cornea) 371.20
  eyelid 373.9
  fatty (diffuse) (generalized) 272.8
    localized — *see* Degeneration, by site, fatty
  glycogen, glycogenic (*see also* Disease, glycogen storage) 271.0
  heart, cardiac
    fatty (*see also* Degeneration, myocardial) 429.1
    glycogenic 271.0 *[425.7]*
  inflammatory in vitreous 379.29
  kidney (*see also* Disease, renal) 593.9
  leukemic (M9800/3) — *see* Leukemia
  liver 573.8
    fatty — *see* Fatty, liver
    glycogen (*see also* Disease, glycogen storage) 271.0
  lung (*see also* Infiltrate, pulmonary) 518.3
    eosinophilic 518.3
    x-ray finding only 793.1
  lymphatic (*see also* Leukemia, lymphatic) 204.9 ☑
    gland, pigmentary 289.3
  muscle, fatty 728.9
  myelogenous (*see also* Leukemia, myeloid) 205.9 ☑
  myocardium, myocardial
    fatty (*see also* Degeneration, myocardial) 429.1
    glycogenic 271.0 *[425.7]*
  pulmonary 518.3
    with
      eosinophilia 518.3
      pneumonia — *see* Pneumonia, by type
    x-ray finding only 793.1
  Ranke's primary (*see also* Tuberculosis) 010.0 ☑

Infiltrate, infiltration — *continued*
  skin, lymphocytic (benign) 709.8
  thymus (gland) (fatty) 254.8
  urine 788.8
  vesicant
    agent NEC 999.82 ▲
    chemotherapy 999.81 ▲
  vitreous humor 379.29

Infirmity 799.89
  senile 797

Inflammation, inflamed, inflammatory (with exudation)
  abducens (nerve) 378.54
  accessory sinus (chronic) (*see also* Sinusitis) 473.9
  adrenal (gland) 255.8
  alimentary canal — *see* Enteritis
  alveoli (teeth) 526.5
    scorbutic 267
  amnion — *see* Amnionitis
  anal canal 569.49
  antrum (chronic) (*see also* Sinusitis, maxillary) 473.0
  anus 569.49
  appendix (*see also* Appendicitis) 541
  arachnoid — *see* Meningitis
  areola 611.0
    puerperal, postpartum 675.0 ☑
  areolar tissue NEC 686.9
  artery — *see* Arteritis
  auditory meatus (external) (*see also* Otitis, externa) 380.10
  Bartholin's gland 616.89
  bile duct or passage 576.1
  bladder (*see also* Cystitis) 595.9
  bleb
    postprocedural 379.60
      stage 1 379.61
      stage 2 379.62
      stage 3 379.63
  bone — *see* Osteomyelitis
  bowel (*see also* Enteritis) 558.9
  brain (*see also* Encephalitis) 323.9
    late effect — *see* category 326
    membrane — *see* Meningitis
  breast 611.0
    puerperal, postpartum 675.2 ☑
  broad ligament (*see also* Disease, pelvis, inflammatory) 614.4
    acute 614.3
  bronchus — *see* Bronchitis
  bursa — *see* Bursitis
  capsule
    liver 573.3
    spleen 289.59
  catarrhal (*see also* Catarrh) 460
    vagina 616.10
  cecum (*see also* Appendicitis) 541
  cerebral (*see also* Encephalitis) 323.9
    late effect — *see* category 326
    membrane — *see* Meningitis
  cerebrospinal (*see also* Meningitis) 322.9
    late effect — *see* category 326
    meningococcal 036.0
    tuberculous (*see also* Tuberculosis) 013.6 ☑
  cervix (uteri) (*see also* Cervicitis) 616.0
  chest 519.9
  choroid NEC (*see also* Choroiditis) 363.20
  cicatrix (tissue) — *see* Cicatrix
  colon (*see also* Enteritis) 558.9
    granulomatous 555.1
    newborn 558.9
  connective tissue (diffuse) NEC 728.9
  cornea (*see also* Keratitis) 370.9
    with ulcer (*see also* Ulcer, cornea) 370.00
  corpora cavernosa (penis) 607.2
  cranial nerve — *see* Disorder, nerve, cranial
  diarrhea — *see* Diarrhea
  disc (intervertebral) (space) 722.90
    cervical, cervicothoracic 722.91
    lumbar, lumbosacral 722.93
    thoracic, thoracolumbar 722.92
  Douglas' cul-de-sac or pouch (chronic) (*see also* Disease, pelvis, inflammatory) 614.4

Inflammation, inflamed, inflammatory — *continued*
  Douglas' cul-de-sac or pouch (*see also* Disease, pelvis, inflammatory) — *continued*
    acute 614.3
  due to (presence of) any device, implant, or graft classifiable to 996.0–996.5 — *see* Complications, infection and inflammation, due to (presence of) any device, implant, or graft classified to 996.0–996.5 NEC
  duodenum 535.6 ☑
  dura mater — *see* Meningitis
  ear (*see also* Otitis)
    external (*see also* Otitis, externa) 380.10
    inner (*see also* Labyrinthitis) 386.30
    middle — *see* Otitis media
  esophagus 530.10
  ethmoidal (chronic) (sinus) (*see also* Sinusitis, ethmoidal) 473.2
  Eustachian tube (catarrhal) 381.50
    acute 381.51
    chronic 381.52
  extrarectal 569.49
  eye 379.99
  eyelid 373.9
    specified NEC 373.8
  fallopian tube (*see also* Salpingo-oophoritis) 614.2
  fascia 728.9
  fetal membranes (acute) 658.4 ☑
    affecting fetus or newborn 762.7
  follicular, pharynx 472.1
  frontal (chronic) (sinus) (*see also* Sinusitis, frontal) 473.1
  gallbladder (*see also* Cholecystitis, acute) 575.0
  gall duct (*see also* Cholecystitis) 575.10
  gastrointestinal (*see also* Enteritis) 558.9
  genital organ (diffuse) (internal)
    female 614.9
      with
        abortion — *see* Abortion, by type, with sepsis
        ectopic pregnancy (*see also* categories 633.0–633.9) 639.0
        molar pregnancy (*see also* categories 630–632) 639.0
      complicating pregnancy, childbirth, or puerperium 646.6 ☑
        affecting fetus or newborn 760.8
      following
        abortion 639.0
        ectopic or molar pregnancy 639.0
    male 608.4
  gland (lymph) (*see also* Lymphadenitis) 289.3
  glottis (*see also* Laryngitis) 464.00
    with obstruction 464.01
  granular, pharynx 472.1
  gum 523.10
  heart (*see also* Carditis) 429.89
  hepatic duct 576.8
  hernial sac — *see* Hernia, by site
  ileum (*see also* Enteritis) 558.9
    terminal or regional 555.0
      with large intestine 555.2
  intervertebral disc 722.90
    cervical, cervicothoracic 722.91
    lumbar, lumbosacral 722.93
    thoracic, thoracolumbar 722.92
  intestine (*see also* Enteritis) 558.9
  jaw (acute) (bone) (chronic) (lower) (suppurative) (upper) 526.4
  jejunum — *see* Enteritis
  joint NEC (*see also* Arthritis) 716.9 ☑
    sacroiliac 720.2
  kidney (*see also* Nephritis) 583.9
  knee (joint) 716.66
    tuberculous (active) (*see also* Tuberculosis) 015.2 ☑
  labium (majus) (minus) (*see also* Vulvitis) 616.10
  lacrimal
    gland (*see also* Dacryoadenitis) 375.00
    passages (duct) (sac) (*see also* Dacryocystitis) 375.30
  larynx (*see also* Laryngitis) 464.00

Inflammation, inflamed, inflammatory — *continued*
  larynx (*see also* Laryngitis) — *continued*
    with obstruction 464.01
    diphtheritic 032.3
  leg NEC 686.9
  lip 528.5
  liver (capsule) (*see also* Hepatitis) 573.3
    acute 570
    chronic 571.40
    suppurative 572.0
  lung (acute) (*see also* Pneumonia) 486
    chronic (interstitial) 518.89
  lymphatic vessel (*see also* Lymphangitis) 457.2
  lymph node or gland (*see also* Lymphadenitis) 289.3
  mammary gland 611.0
    puerperal, postpartum 675.2 ☑
  maxilla, maxillary 526.4
    sinus (chronic) (*see also* Sinusitis, maxillary) 473.0
  membranes of brain or spinal cord — *see* Meningitis
  meninges — *see* Meningitis
  mouth 528.00
  muscle 728.9
  myocardium (*see also* Myocarditis) 429.0
  nasal sinus (chronic) (*see also* Sinusitis) 473.9
  nasopharynx — *see* Nasopharyngitis
  navel 686.9
    newborn NEC 771.4
  nerve NEC 729.2
  nipple 611.0
    puerperal, postpartum 675.0 ☑
  nose 478.19
    suppurative 472.0
  oculomotor nerve 378.51
  optic nerve 377.30
  orbit (chronic) 376.10
    acute 376.00
    chronic 376.10
  ovary (*see also* Salpingo-oophoritis) 614.2
  oviduct (*see also* Salpingo-oophoritis) 614.2
  pancreas — *see* Pancreatitis
  parametrium (chronic) (*see also* Disease, pelvis, inflammatory) 614.4
    acute 614.3
  parotid region 686.9
    gland 527.2
  pelvis, female (*see also* Disease, pelvis, inflammatory) 614.9
  penis (corpora cavernosa) 607.2
  perianal 569.49
  pericardium (*see also* Pericarditis) 423.9
  perineum (female) (male) 686.9
  perirectal 569.49
  peritoneum (*see also* Peritonitis) 567.9
  periuterine (*see also* Disease, pelvis, inflammatory) 614.9
  perivesical (*see also* Cystitis) 595.9
  petrous bone (*see also* Petrositis) 383.20
  pharynx (*see also* Pharyngitis) 462
    follicular 472.1
    granular 472.1
  pia mater — *see* Meningitis
  pleura — *see* Pleurisy
  postmastoidectomy cavity 383.30
    chronic 383.33
  pouch, internal ileoanal 569.71 ●
  prostate (*see also* Prostatitis) 601.9
  rectosigmoid — *see* Rectosigmoiditis
  rectum (*see also* Proctitis) 569.49
  respiratory, upper (*see also* Infection, respiratory, upper) 465.9
    chronic, due to external agent — *see* Condition, respiratory, chronic, due to, external agent
    due to
      fumes or vapors (chemical) (inhalation) 506.2
      radiation 508.1
  retina (*see also* Retinitis) 363.20
  retrocecal (*see also* Appendicitis) 541
  retroperitoneal (*see also* Peritonitis) 567.9
  salivary duct or gland (any) (suppurative) 527.2
  scorbutic, alveoli, teeth 267

Inflammation, inflamed, inflammatory — *continued*
scrotum 608.4
sigmoid — *see* Enteritis
sinus (*see also* Sinusitis) 473.9
Skene's duct or gland (*see also* Urethritis) 597.89
skin 686.9
spermatic cord 608.4
sphenoidal (sinus) (*see also* Sinusitis, sphenoidal) 473.3
spinal
  cord (*see also* Encephalitis) 323.9
    late effect — *see* category 326
  membrane — *see* Meningitis
  nerve — *see* Disorder, nerve
spine (*see also* Spondylitis) 720.9
spleen (capsule) 289.59
stomach — *see* Gastritis
stricture, rectum 569.49
subcutaneous tissue NEC 686.9
suprarenal (gland) 255.8
synovial (fringe) (membrane) — *see* Bursitis
tendon (sheath) NEC 726.90
testis (*see also* Orchitis) 604.90
thigh 686.9
throat (*see also* Sore throat) 462
thymus (gland) 254.8
thyroid (gland) (*see also* Thyroiditis) 245.9
tongue 529.0
tonsil — *see* Tonsillitis
trachea — *see* Tracheitis
trochlear nerve 378.53
tubal (*see also* Salpingo-oophoritis) 614.2
tuberculous NEC (*see also* Tuberculosis) 011.9 ☑
tubo-ovarian (*see also* Salpingo-oophoritis) 614.2
tunica vaginalis 608.4
tympanic membrane — *see* Myringitis
umbilicus, umbilical 686.9
  newborn NEC 771.4
uterine ligament (*see also* Disease, pelvis, inflammatory) 614.4
  acute 614.3
uterus (catarrhal) (*see also* Endometritis) 615.9
uveal tract (anterior) (*see also* Iridocyclitis) 364.3
  posterior — *see* Chorioretinitis
  sympathetic 360.11
vagina (*see also* Vaginitis) 616.10
vas deferens 608.4
vein (*see also* Phlebitis) 451.9
  thrombotic 451.9
    cerebral (*see also* Thrombosis, brain) 434.0 ☑
    leg 451.2
      deep (vessels) NEC 451.19
      superficial (vessels) 451.0
    lower extremity 451.2
      deep (vessels) NEC 451.19
      superficial (vessels) 451.0
vocal cord 478.5
vulva (*see also* Vulvitis) 616.10
Inflation, lung imperfect (newborn) 770.5
Influenza, influenzal 487.1
with
  bronchitis 487.1
  bronchopneumonia 487.0
  cold (any type) 487.1
  digestive manifestations 487.8
  hemoptysis 487.1
  involvement of
    gastrointestinal tract 487.8
    nervous system 487.8
  laryngitis 487.1
  manifestations NEC 487.8
    respiratory 487.1
      pneumonia 487.0
  pharyngitis 487.1
  pneumonia (any form classifiable to 480–483, 485–486) 487.0
  respiratory manifestations NEC 487.1
  sinusitis 487.1
  sore throat 487.1
  tonsillitis 487.1

Influenza, influenzal — *continued*
with — *continued*
  tracheitis 487.1
  upper respiratory infection (acute) 487.1
abdominal 487.8
A/H5N1 488.0 ●
Asian 487.1
avian 488.0 ●
bronchial 487.1
bronchopneumonia 487.0
catarrhal 487.1
due to identified
  avian influenza virus 488.0 ●
  novel H1N1 influenza virus 488.1 ●
epidemic 487.1
gastric 487.8
intestinal 487.8
laryngitis 487.1
maternal affecting fetus or newborn 760.2
  manifest influenza in infant 771.2
novel A/H1N1 488.1 ●
novel (2009) H1N1 488.1 ●
pharyngitis 487.1
pneumonia (any form) 487.0
respiratory (upper) 487.1
specified NEC 487.1 ●
stomach 487.8
vaccination, prophylactic (against) V04.81
Influenza-like disease 487.1
Infraction, Freiberg's (metatarsal head) 732.5
Infraeruption, teeth 524.34
Infusion complication, misadventure, or reaction — *see* Complication, infusion
Ingestion
chemical — *see* Table of Drugs and Chemicals
drug or medicinal substance
  overdose or wrong substance given or taken 977.9
    specified drug — *see* Table of Drugs and Chemicals
foreign body NEC (*see also* Foreign body) 938
Ingrowing
hair 704.8
nail (finger) (toe) (infected) 703.0
Inguinal — *see also* condition
testis 752.51
Inhalation
carbon monoxide 986
flame
  lung 947.1
  mouth 947.0
food or foreign body (*see also* Asphyxia, food or foreign body) 933.1
gas, fumes, or vapor (noxious) 987.9
  specified agent — *see* Table of Drugs and Chemicals
liquid or vomitus (*see also* Asphyxia, food or foreign body) 933.1
lower respiratory tract NEC 934.9
meconium (fetus or newborn) 770.11
  with respiratory symptoms 770.12
mucus (*see also* Asphyxia, mucus) 933.1
oil (causing suffocation) (*see also* Asphyxia, food or foreign body) 933.1
pneumonia — *see* Pneumonia, aspiration
smoke 987.9
steam 987.9
stomach contents or secretions (*see also* Asphyxia, food or foreign body) 933.1
  in labor and delivery 668.0 ☑
Inhibition, inhibited
academic as adjustment reaction 309.23
orgasm
  female 302.73
  male 302.74
sexual
  desire 302.71
  excitement 302.72
work as adjustment reaction 309.23
Inhibitor, systemic lupus erythematosus (presence of) 286.5
Iniencephalus, iniencephaly 740.2
Injected eye 372.74

Injury 959.9

> *Note* — For abrasion, insect bite (nonvenomous), blister, or scratch, see Injury, superficial.
>
> For laceration, traumatic rupture, tear, or penetrating wound of internal organs, such as heart, lung, liver, kidney, pelvic organs, whether or not accompanied by open wound in the same region, see Injury, internal.
>
> For nerve injury, see Injury, nerve.
>
> For late effect of injuries classifiable to 850–854, 860–869, 900–919, 950–959, see Late, effect, injury, by type.

abdomen, abdominal (viscera) (*see also* Injury, internal, abdomen)
  muscle or wall 959.12
acoustic, resulting in deafness 951.5
adenoid 959.09
adrenal (gland) — *see* Injury, internal, adrenal
alveolar (process) 959.09
ankle (and foot) (and knee) (and leg, except thigh) 959.7
anterior chamber, eye 921.3
anus 959.19
aorta (thoracic) 901.0
  abdominal 902.0
appendix — *see* Injury, internal, appendix
arm, upper (and shoulder) 959.2
artery (complicating trauma) (*see also* Injury, blood vessel, by site) 904.9
  cerebral or meningeal (*see also* Hemorrhage, brain, traumatic, subarachnoid) 852.0 ☑
auditory canal (external) (meatus) 959.09
auricle, auris, ear 959.09
axilla 959.2
back 959.19
bile duct — *see* Injury, internal, bile duct
birth (*see also* Birth, injury)
  canal NEC, complicating delivery 665.9 ☑
bladder (sphincter) — *see* Injury, internal, bladder
blast (air) (hydraulic) (immersion) (underwater) NEC 869.0
  with open wound into cavity NEC 869.1
  abdomen or thorax — *see* Injury, internal, by site
  brain — *see* Concussion, brain
  ear (acoustic nerve trauma) 951.5
    with perforation of tympanic membrane — *see* Wound, open, ear, drum
blood vessel NEC 904.9
  abdomen 902.9
    multiple 902.87
    specified NEC 902.89
  aorta (thoracic) 901.0
    abdominal 902.0
  arm NEC 903.9
  axillary 903.00
    artery 903.01
    vein 903.02
  azygos vein 901.89
  basilic vein 903.1
  brachial (artery) (vein) 903.1
  bronchial 901.89
  carotid artery 900.00
    common 900.01
    external 900.02
    internal 900.03
  celiac artery 902.20
    specified branch NEC 902.24
  cephalic vein (arm) 903.1
  colica dextra 902.26
  cystic
    artery 902.24
    vein 902.39
  deep plantar 904.6
  digital (artery) (vein) 903.5
  due to accidental puncture or laceration during procedure 998.2
  extremity
    lower 904.8
      multiple 904.7

Injury — *continued*
blood vessel — *continued*
  extremity — *continued*
    lower — *continued*
      specified NEC 904.7
    upper 903.9
      multiple 903.8
      specified NEC 903.8
  femoral
    artery (superficial) 904.1
      above profunda origin 904.0
      common 904.0
    vein 904.2
  gastric
    artery 902.21
    vein 902.39
  head 900.9
    intracranial — *see* Injury, intracranial
    multiple 900.82
    specified NEC 900.89
  hemiazygos vein 901.89
  hepatic
    artery 902.22
    vein 902.11
  hypogastric 902.59
    artery 902.51
    vein 902.52
  ileocolic
    artery 902.26
    vein 902.31
  iliac 902.50
    artery 902.53
    specified branch NEC 902.59
    vein 902.54
  innominate
    artery 901.1
    vein 901.3
  intercostal (artery) (vein) 901.81
  jugular vein (external) 900.81
    internal 900.1
  leg NEC 904.8
  mammary (artery) (vein) 901.82
  mesenteric
    artery 902.20
      inferior 902.27
      specified branch NEC 902.29
      superior (trunk) 902.25
        branches, primary 902.26
    vein 902.39
      inferior 902.32
      superior (and primary subdivisions) 902.31
  neck 900.9
    multiple 900.82
    specified NEC 900.89
  ovarian 902.89
    artery 902.81
    vein 902.82
  palmar artery 903.4
  pelvis 902.9
    multiple 902.87
    specified NEC 902.89
  plantar (deep) (artery) (vein) 904.6
  popliteal 904.40
    artery 904.41
    vein 904.42
  portal 902.33
  pulmonary 901.40
    artery 901.41
    vein 901.42
  radial (artery) (vein) 903.2
  renal 902.40
    artery 902.41
    specified NEC 902.49
    vein 902.42
  saphenous
    artery 904.7
    vein (greater) (lesser) 904.3
  splenic
    artery 902.23
    vein 902.34
  subclavian
    artery 901.1
    vein 901.3
  suprarenal 902.49
  thoracic 901.9

Index

Injury — Injury

Injury — *continued*
  blood vessel — *continued*
    thoracic — *continued*
      multiple 901.83
      specified NEC 901.89
    tibial 904.50
      artery 904.50
        anterior 904.51
        posterior 904.53
      vein 904.50
        anterior 904.52
        posterior 904.54
    ulnar (artery) (vein) 903.3
    uterine 902.59
      artery 902.55
      vein 902.56
    vena cava
      inferior 902.10
        specified branches NEC 902.19
      superior 901.2
  brachial plexus 953.4
    newborn 767.6
  brain ►(traumatic)◄ NEC (*see also* Injury, intracranial) 854.0 ☑
    due to fracture of skull — *see* Fracture, ●
      skull, by site   ●
  breast 959.19
  broad ligament — *see* Injury, internal, broad ligament
  bronchus, bronchi — *see* Injury, internal, bronchus
  brow 959.09
  buttock 959.19
  canthus, eye 921.1
  cathode ray 990
  cauda equina 952.4
    with fracture, vertebra — *see* Fracture, vertebra, sacrum
  cavernous sinus (*see also* Injury, intracranial) 854.0 ☑
  cecum — *see* Injury, internal, cecum
  celiac ganglion or plexus 954.1
  cerebellum (*see also* Injury, intracranial) 854.0 ☑
  cervix (uteri) — *see* Injury, internal, cervix
  cheek 959.09
  chest (*see also* Injury, internal, chest)
    wall 959.11
  childbirth (*see also* Birth, injury)
    maternal NEC 665.9 ☑
  chin 959.09
  choroid (eye) 921.3
  clitoris 959.14
  coccyx 959.19
    complicating delivery 665.6 ☑
  colon — *see* Injury, internal, colon
  common duct — *see* Injury, internal, common duct
  conjunctiva 921.1
    superficial 918.2
  cord
    spermatic — *see* Injury, internal, spermatic cord
    spinal — *see* Injury, spinal, by site
  cornea 921.3
    abrasion 918.1
    due to contact lens 371.82
    penetrating — *see* Injury, eyeball, penetrating
    superficial 918.1
      due to contact lens 371.82
  cortex (cerebral) (*see also* Injury, intracranial) 854.0 ☑
    visual 950.3
  costal region 959.11
  costochondral 959.11
  cranial
    bones — *see* Fracture, skull, by site
    cavity (*see also* Injury, intracranial) 854.0 ☑
    nerve — *see* Injury, nerve, cranial
  crushing — *see* Crush
  cutaneous sensory nerve
    lower limb 956.4
    upper limb 955.5
  deep tissue — *see* Contusion, by site
    meaning pressure ulcer 707.25

Injury — *continued*
  delivery (*see also* Birth, injury)
    maternal NEC 665.9 ☑
  Descemet's membrane — *see* Injury, eyeball, penetrating
  diaphragm — *see* Injury, internal, diaphragm
  diffuse axonal — *see* Injury, intracranial
  duodenum — *see* Injury, internal, duodenum
  ear (auricle) (canal) (drum) (external) 959.09
  elbow (and forearm) (and wrist) 959.3
  epididymis 959.14
  epigastric region 959.12
  epiglottis 959.09
  epiphyseal, current — *see* Fracture, by site
  esophagus — *see* Injury, internal, esophagus
  Eustachian tube 959.09
  extremity (lower) (upper) NEC 959.8
  eye 921.9
    penetrating eyeball — *see* Injury, eyeball, penetrating
    superficial 918.9
  eyeball 921.3
    penetrating 871.7
      with
        partial loss (of intraocular tissue) 871.2
        prolapse or exposure (of intraocular tissue) 871.1
      without prolapse 871.0
      foreign body (nonmagnetic) 871.6
        magnetic 871.5
    superficial 918.9
  eyebrow 959.09
  eyelid(s) 921.1
    laceration — *see* Laceration, eyelid
    superficial 918.0
  face (and neck) 959.09
  fallopian tube — *see* Injury, internal, fallopian tube
  finger(s) (nail) 959.5
  flank 959.19
  foot (and ankle) (and knee) (and leg, except thigh) 959.7
  forceps NEC 767.9
    scalp 767.19
  forearm (and elbow) (and wrist) 959.3
  forehead 959.09
  gallbladder — *see* Injury, internal, gallbladder
  gasserian ganglion 951.2
  gastrointestinal tract — *see* Injury, internal, gastrointestinal tract
  genital organ(s)
    with
      abortion — *see* Abortion, by type, with, damage to pelvic organs
      ectopic pregnancy (*see also* categories 633.0–633.9) 639.2
      molar pregnancy (*see also* categories 630–632) 639.2
    external 959.14
      fracture of corpus cavernosum penis 959.13
    following
      abortion 639.2
      ectopic or molar pregnancy 639.2
    internal — *see* Injury, internal, genital organs
    obstetrical trauma NEC 665.9 ☑
      affecting fetus or newborn 763.89
  gland
    lacrimal 921.1
      laceration 870.8
    parathyroid 959.09
    salivary 959.09
    thyroid 959.09
  globe (eye) (*see also* Injury, eyeball) 921.3
  grease gun — *see* Wound, open, by site, complicated
  groin 959.19
  gum 959.09
  hand(s) (except fingers) 959.4
  head NEC 959.01
    with
      loss of consciousness 850.5
      skull fracture — *see* Fracture, skull, by site

Injury — *continued*
  heart — *see* Injury, internal, heart
  heel 959.7
  hip (and thigh) 959.6
  hymen 959.14
  hyperextension (cervical) (vertebra) 847.0
  ileum — *see* Injury, internal, ileum
  iliac region 959.19
  infrared rays NEC 990
  instrumental (during surgery) 998.2
    birth injury — *see* Birth, injury
    nonsurgical (*see also* Injury, by site) 959.9
    obstetrical 665.9 ☑
      affecting fetus or newborn 763.89
      bladder 665.5 ☑
      cervix 665.3 ☑
      high vaginal 665.4 ☑
      perineal NEC 664.9 ☑
      urethra 665.5 ☑
      uterus 665.5 ☑
  internal 869.0

> Note — For injury of internal organ(s) by foreign body entering through a natural orifice (e.g., inhaled, ingested, or swallowed) — *see* Foreign body, entering through orifice.
>
> For internal injury of any of the following sites with internal injury of any other of the sites — *see* Injury, internal, multiple.

    with
      fracture
        pelvis — *see* Fracture, pelvis
        specified site, except pelvis — *see* Injury, internal, by site
      open wound into cavity 869.1
    abdomen, abdominal (viscera) NEC 868.00
      with
        fracture, pelvis — *see* Fracture, pelvis
        open wound into cavity 868.10
      specified site NEC 868.09
        with open wound into cavity 868.19
    adrenal (gland) 868.01
      with open wound into cavity 868.11
    aorta (thoracic) 901.0
      abdominal 902.0
    appendix 863.85
      with open wound into cavity 863.95
    bile duct 868.02
      with open wound into cavity 868.12
    bladder (sphincter) 867.0
      with
        abortion — *see* Abortion, by type, with damage to pelvic organs
        ectopic pregnancy (*see also* categories 633.0–633.9) 639.2
        molar pregnancy (*see also* categories 630–632) 639.2
        open wound into cavity 867.1
      following
        abortion 639.2
        ectopic or molar pregnancy 639.2
      obstetrical trauma 665.5 ☑
        affecting fetus or newborn 763.89
    blood vessel — *see* Injury, blood vessel, by site
    broad ligament 867.6
      with open wound into cavity 867.7
    bronchus, bronchi 862.21
      with open wound into cavity 862.31
    cecum 863.89
      with open wound into cavity 863.99
    cervix (uteri) 867.4
      with
        abortion — *see* Abortion, by type, with damage to pelvic organs
        ectopic pregnancy (*see also* categories 633.0–633.9) 639.2
        molar pregnancy (*see also* categories 630–632) 639.2
        open wound into cavity 867.5

Injury — *continued*
  internal — *continued*
    cervix — *continued*
      following
        abortion 639.2
        ectopic or molar pregnancy 639.2
      obstetrical trauma 665.3 ☑
        affecting fetus or newborn 763.89
    chest (*see also* Injury, internal, intrathoracic organs) 862.8
      with open wound into cavity 862.9
    colon 863.40
      with
        open wound into cavity 863.50
        rectum 863.46
          with open wound into cavity 863.56
      ascending (right) 863.41
        with open wound into cavity 863.51
      descending (left) 863.43
        with open wound into cavity 863.53
      multiple sites 863.46
        with open wound into cavity 863.56
      sigmoid 863.44
        with open wound into cavity 863.54
      specified site NEC 863.49
        with open wound into cavity 863.59
      transverse 863.42
        with open wound into cavity 863.52
    common duct 868.02
      with open wound into cavity 868.12
    complicating delivery 665.9 ☑
      affecting fetus or newborn 763.89
    diaphragm 862.0
      with open wound into cavity 862.1
    duodenum 863.21
      with open wound into cavity 863.31
    esophagus (intrathoracic) 862.22
      with open wound into cavity 862.32
      cervical region 874.4
        complicated 874.5
    fallopian tube 867.6
      with open wound into cavity 867.7
    gallbladder 868.02
      with open wound into cavity 868.12
    gastrointestinal tract NEC 863.80
      with open wound into cavity 863.90
    genital organ NEC 867.6
      with open wound into cavity 867.7
    heart 861.00
      with open wound into thorax 861.10
    ileum 863.29
      with open wound into cavity 863.39
    intestine NEC 863.89
      with open wound into cavity 863.99
    large NEC 863.40
      with open wound into cavity 863.50
    small NEC 863.20
      with open wound into cavity 863.30
    intra-abdominal (organ) 868.00
      with open wound into cavity 868.10
      multiple sites 868.09
        with open wound into cavity 868.19
      specified site NEC 868.09
        with open wound into cavity 868.19
    intrathoracic organs (multiple) 862.8
      with open wound into cavity 862.9
      diaphragm (only) — *see* Injury, internal, diaphragm
      heart (only) — *see* Injury, internal, heart
      lung (only) — *see* Injury, internal, lung
      specified site NEC 862.29
        with open wound into cavity 862.39
    intrauterine (*see also* Injury, internal, uterus) 867.4

☑ Additional Digit Required — Refer to the Tabular List for Digit Selection   ▼ Subterms under main terms may continue to next column or page

156 — Volume 2 • October 2009   ►◄ Revised Text   ● New Line   ▲ Revised Code   2010 ICD-9-CM

Injury — *continued*
  internal — *continued*
    intrauterine (*see also* Injury, internal, uterine) — *continued*
      with open wound into cavity 867.5
    jejunum 863.29
      with open wound into cavity 863.39
    kidney (subcapsular) 866.00
      with
        disruption of parenchyma (complete) 866.03
          with open wound into cavity 866.13
        hematoma (without rupture of capsule) 866.01
          with open wound into cavity 866.11
        laceration 866.02
          with open wound into cavity 866.12
        open wound into cavity 866.10
    liver 864.00
      with
        contusion 864.01
          with open wound into cavity 864.11
        hematoma 864.01
          with open wound into cavity 864.11
        laceration 864.05
          with open wound into cavity 864.15
          major (disruption of hepatic parenchyma) 864.04
            with open wound into cavity 864.14
          minor (capsule only) 864.02
            with open wound into cavity 864.12
          moderate (involving parenchyma) 864.03
            with open wound into cavity 864.13
          multiple 864.04
          stellate 864.04
            with open wound into cavity 864.14
        open wound into cavity 864.10
    lung 861.20
      with open wound into thorax 861.30
      hemopneumothorax — *see* Hemopneumothorax, traumatic
      hemothorax — *see* Hemothorax, traumatic
      pneumohemothorax — *see* Pneumohemothorax, traumatic
      pneumothorax — *see* Pneumothorax, traumatic
      transfusion related, acute (TRALI) 518.7
    mediastinum 862.29
      with open wound into cavity 862.39
    mesentery 863.89
      with open wound into cavity 863.99
    mesosalpinx 867.6
      with open wound into cavity 867.7
    multiple 869.0

> *Note — Multiple internal injuries of sites classifiable to the same three- or four-digit category should be classified to that category.*
>
> *Multiple injuries classifiable to different fourth-digit subdivisions of 861 (heart and lung injuries) should be dealt with according to coding rules.*

      internal
        with open wound into cavity 869.1
        intra–abdominal organ (sites classifiable to 863–868)
          with
            intrathoracic organ(s) (sites classifiable to 861–862) 869.0
              with open wound into cavity 869.1

Injury — *continued*
  internal — *continued*
    multiple — *continued*
      intra–abdominal organ — *continued*
        with — *continued*
          other intra–abdominal organ(s) (sites classifiable to 863–868, except where classifiable to the same three–digit category) 868.09
            with open wound into cavity 868.19
        intrathoracic organ (sites classifiable to 861–862)
          with
            intra–abdominal organ(s) (sites classifiable to 863–868) 869.0
              with open wound into cavity 869.1
            other intrathoracic organ(s) (sites classifiable to 861–862, except where classifiable to the same three–digit category) 862.8
              with open wound into cavity 862.9
    myocardium — *see* Injury, internal, heart
    ovary 867.6
      with open wound into cavity 867.7
    pancreas (multiple sites) 863.84
      with open wound into cavity 863.94
      body 863.82
        with open wound into cavity 863.92
      head 863.81
        with open wound into cavity 863.91
      tail 863.83
        with open wound into cavity 863.93
    pelvis, pelvic (organs) (viscera) 867.8
      with
        fracture, pelvis — *see* Fracture, pelvis
        open wound into cavity 867.9
      specified site NEC 867.6
        with open wound into cavity 867.7
    peritoneum 868.03
      with open wound into cavity 868.13
    pleura 862.29
      with open wound into cavity 862.39
    prostate 867.6
      with open wound into cavity 867.7
    rectum 863.45
      with
        colon 863.46
          with open wound into cavity 863.56
        open wound into cavity 863.55
    retroperitoneum 868.04
      with open wound into cavity 868.14
    round ligament 867.6
      with open wound into cavity 867.7
    seminal vesicle 867.6
      with open wound into cavity 867.7
    spermatic cord 867.6
      with open wound into cavity 867.7
    scrotal — *see* Wound, open, spermatic cord
    spleen 865.00
      with
        disruption of parenchyma (massive) 865.04
          with open wound into cavity 865.14
        hematoma (without rupture of capsule) 865.01
          with open wound into cavity 865.11
        open wound into cavity 865.10
        tear, capsular 865.02

Injury — *continued*
  internal — *continued*
    spleen — *continued*
      with — *continued*
        tear, capsular — *continued*
          with open wound into cavity 865.12
          extending into parenchyma 865.03
            with open wound into cavity 865.13
    stomach 863.0
      with open wound into cavity 863.1
    suprarenal gland (multiple) 868.01
      with open wound into cavity 868.11
    thorax, thoracic (cavity) (organs) (multiple) (*see also* Injury, internal, intrathoracic organs) 862.8
      with open wound into cavity 862.9
    thymus (gland) 862.29
      with open wound into cavity 862.39
    trachea (intrathoracic) 862.29
      with open wound into cavity 862.39
      cervical region (*see also* Wound, open, trachea) 874.02
    ureter 867.2
      with open wound into cavity 867.3
    urethra (sphincter) 867.0
      with
        abortion — *see* Abortion, by type, with damage to pelvic organs
        ectopic pregnancy (*see also* categories 633.0–633.9) 639.2
        molar pregnancy (*see also* categories 630–632) 639.2
        open wound into cavity 867.1
      following
        abortion 639.2
        ectopic or molar pregnancy 639.2
      obstetrical trauma 665.5 ☑
        affecting fetus or newborn 763.89
    uterus 867.4
      with
        abortion — *see* Abortion, by type, with damage to pelvic organs
        ectopic pregnancy (*see also* categories 633.0–633.9) 639.2
        molar pregnancy (*see also* categories 630–632) 639.2
        open wound into cavity 867.5
      following
        abortion 639.2
        ectopic or molar pregnancy 639.2
      obstetrical trauma NEC 665.5 ☑
        affecting fetus or newborn 763.89
    vas deferens 867.6
      with open wound into cavity 867.7
    vesical (sphincter) 867.0
      with open wound into cavity 867.1
    viscera (abdominal) (*see also* Injury, internal, multiple) 868.00
      with
        fracture, pelvis — *see* Fracture, pelvis
        open wound into cavity 868.10
      thoracic NEC (*see also* Injury, internal, intrathoracic organs) 862.8
        with open wound into cavity 862.9
  interscapular region 959.19
  intervertebral disc 959.19
  intestine — *see* Injury, internal, intestine
  intra-abdominal (organs) NEC — *see* Injury, internal, intra-abdominal

---

Injury — *continued*
  intracranial ►(traumatic)◄ 854.0 ☑

> *Note — Use the following fifth-digit subclassification with categories 851–854:*
>
> 0   *unspecified state of consciousness*
>
> 1   *with no loss of consciousness*
>
> 2   *with brief [less than one hour] loss of consciousness*
>
> 3   *with moderate [1–24 hours] loss of consciousness*
>
> 4   *with prolonged [more than 24 hours] loss of consciousness and return to pre–existing conscious level*
>
> 5   *with prolonged [more than 24 hours] loss of consciousness, without return to pre–existing conscious level*
>
> *Use fifth-digit 5 to designate when a patient is unconscious and dies before regaining consciousness, regardless of the duration of the loss of consciousness*
>
> 6   *with loss of consciousness of unspecified duration*
>
> 9   *with concussion, unspecified*

    with
      open intracranial wound 854.1 ☑
      skull fracture — *see* Fracture, skull, by site
    contusion 851.8 ☑
      with open intracranial wound 851.9 ☑
      brain stem 851.4 ☑
        with open intracranial wound 851.5 ☑
      cerebellum 851.4 ☑
        with open intracranial wound 851.5 ☑
      cortex (cerebral) 851.0 ☑
        with open intracranial wound 851.2 ☑
    hematoma — *see* Injury, intracranial, hemorrhage
    hemorrhage 853.0 ☑
      with
        laceration — *see* Injury, intracranial, laceration
        open intracranial wound 853.1 ☑
      extradural 852.4 ☑
        with open intracranial wound 852.5 ☑
      subarachnoid 852.0 ☑
        with open intracranial wound 852.1 ☑
      subdural 852.2 ☑
        with open intracranial wound 852.3 ☑
    laceration 851.8 ☑
      with open intracranial wound 851.9 ☑
      brain stem 851.6 ☑
        with open intracranial wound 851.7 ☑
      cerebellum 851.6 ☑
        with open intracranial wound 851.7 ☑
      cortex (cerebral) 851.2 ☑
        with open intracranial wound 851.3 ☑
  intraocular — *see* Injury, eyeball, penetrating
  intrathoracic organs (multiple) — *see* Injury, internal, intrathoracic organs
  intrauterine — *see* Injury, internal, intrauterine
  iris 921.3
    penetrating — *see* Injury, eyeball, penetrating
  jaw 959.09
  jejunum — *see* Injury, internal, jejunum
  joint NEC 959.9
    old or residual 718.80
      ankle 718.87
      elbow 718.82
      foot 718.87
      hand 718.84

☑ Additional Digit Required — Refer to the Tabular List for Digit Selection   ▽ Subterms under main terms may continue to next column or page

2010 ICD-9-CM   ►◄ Revised Text   ● New Line   ▲ Revised Code   October 2009 • Volume 2 — 157

Injury — *continued*
  joint — *continued*
    old or residual — *continued*
      hip 718.85
      knee 718.86
      multiple sites 718.89
      pelvic region 718.85
      shoulder (region) 718.81
      specified site NEC 718.88
      wrist 718.83
  kidney — *see* Injury, internal, kidney
    acute (nontraumatic) 584.9
  knee (and ankle) (and foot) (and leg, except thigh) 959.7
  labium (majus) (minus) 959.14
  labyrinth, ear 959.09
  lacrimal apparatus, gland, or sac 921.1
    laceration 870.8
  larynx 959.09
  late effect — *see* Late, effects (of), injury
  leg, except thigh (and ankle) (and foot) (and knee) 959.7
    upper or thigh 959.6
  lens, eye 921.3
    penetrating — *see* Injury, eyeball, penetrating
  lid, eye — *see* Injury, eyelid
  lip 959.09
  liver — *see* Injury, internal, liver
  lobe, parietal — *see* Injury, intracranial
  lumbar (region) 959.19
    plexus 953.5
  lumbosacral (region) 959.19
    plexus 953.5
  lung — *see* Injury, internal, lung
  malar region 959.09
  mastoid region 959.09
  maternal, during pregnancy, affecting fetus or newborn 760.5
  maxilla 959.09
  mediastinum — *see* Injury, internal, mediastinum
  membrane
    brain (*see also* Injury, intracranial) 854.0 ☑
    tympanic 959.09
  meningeal artery — *see* Hemorrhage, brain, traumatic, subarachnoid
  meninges (cerebral) — *see* Injury, intracranial
  mesenteric
    artery — *see* Injury, blood vessel, mesenteric, artery
    plexus, inferior 954.1
    vein — *see* Injury, blood vessel, mesenteric, vein
  mesentery — *see* Injury, internal, mesentery
  mesosalpinx — *see* Injury, internal, mesosalpinx
  middle ear 959.09
  midthoracic region 959.11
  mouth 959.09
  multiple (sites not classifiable to the same four–digit category in 959.0–959.7) 959.8
    internal 869.0
      with open wound into cavity 869.1
  musculocutaneous nerve 955.4
  nail
    finger 959.5
    toe 959.7
  nasal (septum) (sinus) 959.09
  nasopharynx 959.09
  neck (and face) 959.09
  nerve 957.9
    abducens 951.3
    abducent 951.3
    accessory 951.6
    acoustic 951.5
    ankle and foot 956.9
    anterior crural, femoral 956.1
    arm (*see also* Injury, nerve, upper limb) 955.9
    auditory 951.5
    axillary 955.0
    brachial plexus 953.4
    cervical sympathetic 954.0
    cranial 951.9

Injury — *continued*
  nerve — *continued*
    cranial — *continued*
      first or olfactory 951.8
      second or optic 950.0
      third or oculomotor 951.0
      fourth or trochlear 951.1
      fifth or trigeminal 951.2
      sixth or abducens 951.3
      seventh or facial 951.4
      eighth, acoustic, or auditory 951.5
      ninth or glossopharyngeal 951.8
      tenth, pneumogastric, or vagus 951.8
      eleventh or accessory 951.6
      twelfth or hypoglossal 951.7
      newborn 767.7
    cutaneous sensory
      lower limb 956.4
      upper limb 955.5
    digital (finger) 955.6
      toe 956.5
    facial 951.4
      newborn 767.5
    femoral 956.1
    finger 955.9
    foot and ankle 956.9
    forearm 955.9
    glossopharyngeal 951.8
    hand and wrist 955.9
    head and neck, superficial 957.0
    hypoglossal 951.7
    involving several parts of body 957.8
    leg (*see also* Injury, nerve, lower limb) 956.9
    lower limb 956.9
      multiple 956.8
      specified site NEC 956.5
    lumbar plexus 953.5
    lumbosacral plexus 953.5
    median 955.1
      forearm 955.1
      wrist and hand 955.1
    multiple (in several parts of body) (sites not classifiable to the same three-digit category) 957.8
    musculocutaneous 955.4
    musculospiral 955.3
      upper arm 955.3
    oculomotor 951.0
    olfactory 951.8
    optic 950.0
    pelvic girdle 956.9
      multiple sites 956.8
      specified site NEC 956.5
    peripheral 957.9
      multiple (in several regions) (sites not classifiable to the same three-digit category) 957.8
      specified site NEC 957.1
    peroneal 956.3
      ankle and foot 956.3
      lower leg 956.3
    plantar 956.5
    plexus 957.9
      celiac 954.1
      mesenteric, inferior 954.1
      spinal 953.9
        brachial 953.4
        lumbosacral 953.5
        multiple sites 953.8
      sympathetic NEC 954.1
    pneumogastric 951.8
    radial 955.3
      wrist and hand 955.3
    sacral plexus 953.5
    sciatic 956.0
      thigh 956.0
    shoulder girdle 955.9
      multiple 955.8
      specified site NEC 955.7
    specified site NEC 957.1
    spinal 953.9
      plexus — *see* Injury, nerve, plexus, spinal
      root 953.9
        cervical 953.0
        dorsal 953.1

Injury — *continued*
  nerve — *continued*
    spinal — *continued*
      root — *continued*
        lumbar 953.2
        multiple sites 953.8
        sacral 953.3
    splanchnic 954.1
    sympathetic NEC 954.1
      cervical 954.0
    thigh 956.9
    tibial 956.5
      ankle and foot 956.2
      lower leg 956.5
      posterior 956.2
      toe 956.9
    trigeminal 951.2
    trochlear 951.1
    trunk, excluding shoulder and pelvic girdles 954.9
      specified site NEC 954.8
      sympathetic NEC 954.1
    ulnar 955.2
      forearm 955.2
      wrist (and hand) 955.2
    upper limb 955.9
      multiple 955.8
      specified site NEC 955.7
    vagus 951.8
    wrist and hand 955.9
  nervous system, diffuse 957.8
  nose (septum) 959.09
  obstetrical NEC 665.9 ☑
    affecting fetus or newborn 763.89
  occipital (region) (scalp) 959.09
    lobe (*see also* Injury, intracranial) 854.0 ☑
  optic 950.9
    chiasm 950.1
    cortex 950.3
    nerve 950.0
    pathways 950.2
  orbit, orbital (region) 921.2
    penetrating 870.3
      with foreign body 870.4
  ovary — *see* Injury, internal, ovary
  paint-gun — *see* Wound, open, by site, complicated
  palate (soft) 959.09
  pancreas — *see* Injury, internal, pancreas
  parathyroid (gland) 959.09
  parietal (region) (scalp) 959.09
    lobe — *see* Injury, intracranial
  pelvic
    floor 959.19
      complicating delivery 664.1 ☑
        affecting fetus or newborn 763.89
    joint or ligament, complicating delivery 665.6 ☑
      affecting fetus or newborn 763.89
    organs (*see also* Injury, internal, pelvis)
      with
        abortion — *see* Abortion, by type, with damage to pelvic organs
        ectopic pregnancy (*see also* categories 633.0–633.9) 639.2
        molar pregnancy (*see also* categories 633.0–633.9) 639.2
      following
        abortion 639.2
        ectopic or molar pregnancy 639.2
      obstetrical trauma 665.5 ☑
        affecting fetus or newborn 763.89
  pelvis 959.19
  penis 959.14
    fracture of corpus cavernosum 959.13
  perineum 959.14
  peritoneum — *see* Injury, internal, peritoneum
  periurethral tissue
    with
      abortion — *see* Abortion, by type, with damage to pelvic organs
      ectopic pregnancy (*see also* categories 633.0–633.9) 639.2
      molar pregnancy (*see also* categories 630–632) 639.2

Injury — *continued*
  periurethral tissue — *continued*
    complicating delivery 665.5 ☑
      affecting fetus or newborn 763-9
    following
      abortion 639.2
      ectopic or molar pregnancy 639.2
  phalanges
    foot 959.7
    hand 959.5
  pharynx 959.09
  pleura — *see* Injury, internal, pleura
  popliteal space 959.7
  post-cardiac surgery (syndrome) 429.4
  prepuce 959.14
  prostate — *see* Injury, internal, prostate
  pubic region 959.19
  pudenda 959.14
  radiation NEC 990
  radioactive substance or radium NEC 990
  rectovaginal septum 959.14
  rectum — *see* Injury, internal, rectum
  retina 921.3
    penetrating — *see* Injury, eyeball, penetrating
  retroperitoneal — *see* Injury, internal, retroperitoneum
  roentgen rays NEC 990
  round ligament — *see* Injury, internal, round ligament
  sacral (region) 959.19
    plexus 953.5
  sacroiliac ligament NEC 959.19
  sacrum 959.19
  salivary ducts or glands 959.09
  scalp 959.09
    due to birth trauma 767.19
    fetus or newborn 767.19
  scapular region 959.2
  sclera 921.3
    penetrating — *see* Injury, eyeball, penetrating
    superficial 918.2
  scrotum 959.14
  seminal vesicle — *see* Injury, internal, seminal vesicle
  shoulder (and upper arm) 959.2
  sinus
    cavernous (*see also* Injury, intracranial) 854.0 ☑
    nasal 959.09
  skeleton NEC, birth injury 767.3
  skin NEC 959.9
  skull — *see* Fracture, skull, by site
  soft tissue (of external sites) (severe) — *see* Wound, open, by site
  specified site NEC 959.8
  spermatic cord — *see* Injury, internal, spermatic cord
  spinal (cord) 952.9
    with fracture, vertebra — *see* Fracture, vertebra, by site, with spinal cord injury
    cervical (C_1-C_4) 952.00
      with
        anterior cord syndrome 952.02
        central cord syndrome 952.03
        complete lesion of cord 952.01
        incomplete lesion NEC 952.04
        posterior cord syndrome 952.04
      C_5-C_7 level 952.05
        with
          anterior cord syndrome 952.07
          central cord syndrome 952.08
          complete lesion of cord 952.06
          incomplete lesion NEC 952.09
          posterior cord syndrome 952.09
        specified type NEC 952.09
      specified type NEC 952.04
    dorsal (D_1-D_6) (T_1-T_6) (thoracic) 952.10
      with
        anterior cord syndrome 952.12
        central cord syndrome 952.13
        complete lesion of cord 952.11
        incomplete lesion NEC 952.14
        posterior cord syndrome 952.14

Injury — *continued*
  spinal — *continued*
    dorsal — *continued*
      D$_7$-D$_{12}$ level (T$_7$-T$_{12}$) 952.15
        with
          anterior cord syndrome 952.17
          central cord syndrome 952.18
          complete lesion of cord 952.16
          incomplete lesion NEC 952.19
          posterior cord syndrome 952.19
        specified type NEC 952.19
      specified type NEC 952.14
    lumbar 952.2
    multiple sites 952.8
    nerve (root) NEC — *see* Injury, nerve, spinal, root
    plexus 953.9
      brachial 953.4
      lumbosacral 953.5
      multiple sites 953.8
    sacral 952.3
    thoracic (*see also* Injury, spinal, dorsal) 952.10
  spleen — *see* Injury, internal, spleen
  stellate ganglion 954.1
  sternal region 959.11
  stomach — *see* Injury, internal, stomach
  subconjunctival 921.1
  subcutaneous 959.9
  subdural — *see* Injury, intracranial
  submaxillary region 959.09
  submental region 959.09
  subungual
    fingers 959.5
    toes 959.7
  superficial 919 ☑

Note — Use the following fourth-digit subdivisions with categories 910–919:

0   *Abrasion or friction burn without mention of infection*

1   *Abrasion or friction burn, infected*

2   *Blister without mention of infection*

3   *Blister, infected*

4   *Insect bite, nonvenomous, without mention of infection*

5   *Insect bite, nonvenomous, infected*

6   *Superficial foreign body (splinter) without major open wound and without mention of infection*

7   *Superficial foreign body (splinter) without major open wound, infected*

8   *Other and unspecified superficial injury without mention of infection*

9   *Other and unspecified superficial injury, infected*

For late effects of superficial injury, see category 906.2.

---

    abdomen, abdominal (muscle) (wall) (and other part(s) of trunk) 911 ☑
    ankle (and hip, knee, leg, or thigh) 916 ☑
    anus (and other part(s) of trunk) 911 ☑
    arm 913 ☑
      upper (and shoulder) 912 ☑
    auditory canal (external) (meatus) (and other part(s) of face, neck, or scalp, except eye) 910 ☑
    axilla (and upper arm) 912 ☑
    back (and other part(s) of trunk) 911 ☑
    breast (and other part(s) of trunk) 911 ☑
    brow (and other part(s) of face, neck, or scalp, except eye) 910 ☑
    buttock (and other part(s) of trunk) 911 ☑
    canthus, eye 918.0
    cheek(s) (and other part(s) of face, neck, or scalp, except eye) 910 ☑
    chest wall (and other part(s) of trunk) 911 ☑
    chin (and other part(s) of face, neck, or scalp, except eye) 910 ☑
    clitoris (and other part(s) of trunk) 911 ☑

Injury — *continued*
  superficial — *continued*
    conjunctiva 918.2
    cornea 918.1
      due to contact lens 371.82
    costal region (and other part(s) of trunk) 911 ☑
    ear(s) (auricle) (canal) (drum) (external) (and other part(s) of face, neck, or scalp, except eye) 910 ☑
    elbow (and forearm) (and wrist) 913 ☑
    epididymis (and other part(s) of trunk) 911 ☑
    epigastric region (and other part(s) of trunk) 911 ☑
    epiglottis (and other part(s) of face, neck, or scalp, except eye) 910 ☑
    eye(s) (and adnexa) NEC 918.9
    eyelid(s) (and periocular area) 918.0
    face (any part(s), except eye) (and neck or scalp) 910 ☑
    finger(s) (nail) (any) 915 ☑
    flank (and other part(s) of trunk) 911 ☑
    foot (phalanges) (and toe(s)) 917 ☑
    forearm (and elbow) (and wrist) 913 ☑
    forehead (and other part(s) of face, neck, or scalp, except eye) 910 ☑
    globe (eye) 918.9
    groin (and other part(s) of trunk) 911 ☑
    gum(s) (and other part(s) of face, neck, or scalp, except eye) 910 ☑
    hand(s) (except fingers alone) 914 ☑
    head (and other part(s) of face, neck, or scalp, except eye) 910 ☑
    heel (and foot or toe) 917 ☑
    hip (and ankle, knee, leg, or thigh) 916 ☑
    iliac region (and other part(s) of trunk) 911 ☑
    interscapular region (and other part(s) of trunk) 911 ☑
    iris 918.9
    knee (and ankle, hip, leg, or thigh) 916 ☑
    labium (majus) (minus) (and other part(s) of trunk) 911 ☑
    lacrimal (apparatus) (gland) (sac) 918.0
    leg (lower) (upper) (and ankle, hip, knee, or thigh) 916 ☑
    lip(s) (and other part(s) of face, neck, or scalp, except eye) 910 ☑
    lower extremity (except foot) 916 ☑
    lumbar region (and other part(s) of trunk) 911 ☑
    malar region (and other part(s) of face, neck, or scalp, except eye) 910 ☑
    mastoid region (and other part(s) of face, neck, or scalp, except eye) 910 ☑
    midthoracic region (and other part(s) of trunk) 911 ☑
    mouth (and other part(s) of face, neck, or scalp, except eye) 910 ☑
    multiple sites (not classifiable to the same three-digit category) 919 ☑
    nasal (septum) (and other part(s) of face, neck, or scalp, except eye) 910 ☑
    neck (and face or scalp, any part(s), except eye) 910 ☑
    nose (septum) (and other part(s) of face, neck, or scalp, except eye) 910 ☑
    occipital region (and other part(s) of face, neck, or scalp, except eye) 910 ☑
    orbital region 918.0
    palate (soft) (and other part(s) of face, neck, or scalp, except eye) 910 ☑
    parietal region (and other part(s) of face, neck, or scalp, except eye) 910 ☑
    penis (and other part(s) of trunk) 911 ☑
    perineum (and other part(s) of trunk) 911 ☑
    periocular area 918.0
    pharynx (and other part(s) of face, neck, or scalp, except eye) 910 ☑
    popliteal space (and ankle, hip, leg, or thigh) 916 ☑
    prepuce (and other part(s) of trunk) 911 ☑

Injury — *continued*
  superficial — *continued*
    pubic region (and other part(s) of trunk) 911 ☑
    pudenda (and other part(s) of trunk) 911 ☑
    sacral region (and other part(s) of trunk) 911 ☑
    salivary (ducts) (glands) (and other part(s) of face, neck, or scalp, except eye) 910 ☑
    scalp (and other part(s) of face or neck, except eye) 910 ☑
    scapular region (and upper arm) 912 ☑
    sclera 918.2
    scrotum (and other part(s) of trunk) 911 ☑
    shoulder (and upper arm) 912 ☑
    skin NEC 919 ☑
    specified site(s) NEC 919 ☑
    sternal region (and other part(s) of trunk) 911 ☑
    subconjunctival 918.2
    subcutaneous NEC 919 ☑
    submaxillary region (and other part(s) of face, neck, or scalp, except eye) 910 ☑
    submental region (and other part(s) of face, neck, or scalp, except eye) 910 ☑
    supraclavicular fossa (and other part(s) of face, neck, or scalp, except eye) 910 ☑
    supraorbital 918.0
    temple (and other part(s) of face, neck, or scalp, except eye) 910 ☑
    temporal region (and other part(s) of face, neck, or scalp, except eye) 910 ☑
    testis (and other part(s) of trunk) 911 ☑
    thigh (and ankle, hip, knee, or leg) 916 ☑
    thorax, thoracic (external) (and other part(s) of trunk) 911 ☑
    throat (and other part(s) of face, neck, or scalp, except eye) 910 ☑
    thumb(s) (nail) 915 ☑
    toe(s) (nail) (subungual) (and foot) 917 ☑
    tongue (and other part(s) of face, neck, or scalp, except eye) 910 ☑
    tooth, teeth (*see also* Abrasion, dental) 521.20
    trunk (any part(s)) 911 ☑
    tunica vaginalis 959.14
    tympanum, tympanic membrane (and other part(s) of face, neck, or scalp, except eye) 910 ☑
    upper extremity NEC 913 ☑
    uvula (and other part(s) of face, neck, or scalp, except eye) 910 ☑
    vagina (and other part(s) of trunk) 911 ☑
    vulva (and other part(s) of trunk) 911 ☑
    wrist (and elbow) (and forearm) 913 ☑
  supraclavicular fossa 959.19
  supraorbital 959.09
  surgical complication (external or internal site) 998.2
  symphysis pubis 959.19
    complicating delivery 665.6 ☑
      affecting fetus or newborn 763.89
  temple 959.09
  temporal region 959.09
  testis 959.14
  thigh (and hip) 959.6
  thorax, thoracic (external) 959.11
    cavity — *see* Injury, internal, thorax
    internal — *see* Injury, internal, intrathoracic organs
  throat 959.09
  thumb(s) (nail) 959.5
  thymus — *see* Injury, internal, thymus
  thyroid (gland) 959.09
  toe (nail) (any) 959.7
  tongue 959.09
  tonsil 959.09
  tooth NEC 873.63
    complicated 873.73
  trachea — *see* Injury, internal, trachea

Injury — *continued*
  trunk 959.19
  tunica vaginalis 959.14
  tympanum, tympanic membrane 959.09
  ultraviolet rays NEC 990
  ureter — *see* Injury, internal, ureter
  urethra (sphincter) — *see* Injury, internal, urethra
  uterus — *see* Injury, internal, uterus
  uvula 959.09
  vagina 959.14
  vascular — *see* Injury, blood vessel
  vas deferens — *see* Injury, internal, vas deferens
  vein (*see also* Injury, blood vessel, by site) 904.9
  vena cava
    inferior 902.10
    superior 901.2
  vesical (sphincter) — *see* Injury, internal, vesical
  viscera (abdominal) — *see* Injury, internal, viscera
    with fracture, pelvis — *see* Fracture, pelvis
  visual 950.9
    cortex 950.3
  vitreous (humor) 871.2
  vulva 959.14
  whiplash (cervical spine) 847.0
  wringer — *see* Crush, by site
  wrist (and elbow) (and forearm) 959.3
  x-ray NEC 990
Inoculation — *see also* Vaccination
  complication or reaction — *see* Complication, vaccination
INPH (idiopathic normal pressure hydrocephalus) 331.5
Insanity, insane — *see also* Psychosis 298.9
  adolescent (*see also* Schizophrenia) 295.9 ☑
  alternating (*see also* Psychosis, affective, circular) 296.7
  confusional 298.9
    acute 293.0
    subacute 293.1
  delusional 298.9
  paralysis, general 094.1
    progressive 094.1
  paresis, general 094.1
  senile 290.20
Insect
  bite — *see* Injury, superficial, by site
  venomous, poisoning by 989.5
Insemination, artificial V26.1
Insensitivity
  adrenocorticotropin hormone (ACTH) 255.41
  androgen 259.50
    complete 259.51
    partial 259.52
Insertion
  cord (umbilical) lateral or velamentous 663.8 ☑
    affecting fetus or newborn 762.6
  intrauterine contraceptive device V25.1
  placenta, vicious — *see* Placenta, previa
  subdermal implantable contraceptive V25.5
  velamentous, umbilical cord 663.8 ☑
    affecting fetus or newborn 762.6
Insolation 992.0
  meaning sunstroke 992.0
Insomnia, unspecified 780.52
  with sleep apnea, unspecified 780.51
  adjustment 307.41
  alcohol induced 291.82
  behavioral, of childhood V69.5
  drug induced 292.85
  due to
    medical condition classified elsewhere 327.01
    mental disorder 327.02
  fatal familial (FFI) 046.72
  idiopathic 307.42
  nonorganic origin 307.41
    persistent (primary) 307.42
    transient 307.41
  organic 327.00
    other 327.09
  paradoxical 307.42

☑ Additional Digit Required — Refer to the Tabular List for Digit Selection   ▽ Subterms under main terms may continue to next column or page

2010 ICD-9-CM   ▶◀ Revised Text   ● New Line   ▲ Revised Code   **Volume 2 — 159**

☑ Additional Digit Required — Refer to the Tabular List for Digit Selection   🔖 Subterms under main terms may continue to next column or page

160 — Volume 2   ▶◀ Revised Text   ● New Line   ▲ Revised Code   2010 ICD-9-CM

Index

Insomnia, unspecified — Intoxication

Intoxication — *continued*
acute
  alcoholic 305.0 ☑
    with alcoholism 303.0 ☑
    hangover effects 305.0 ☑
  caffeine 305.9 ☑
  hallucinogenic (*see also* Abuse, drugs,
    nondependent) 305.3 ☑
alcohol (acute) 305.0 ☑
  with alcoholism 303.0 ☑
  hangover effects 305.0 ☑
  idiosyncratic 291.4
  pathological 291.4
alimentary canal 558.2
ammonia (hepatic) 572.2
caffeine 305.9 ☑
chemical (*see also* Table of Drugs and Chemicals)
  via placenta or breast milk 760.70
    alcohol 760.71
    anticonvulsants
    antifungals
    anti-infective agents 760.74
    antimetabolics
    cocaine 760.75
    "crack" 760.75
    hallucinogenic agents NEC 760.73
    medicinal agents NEC 760.79
    narcotics 760.72
    obstetric anesthetic or analgesic drug
      763.5
    specified agent NEC 760.79
    suspected, affecting management of
      pregnancy 655.5 ☑
cocaine, through placenta or breast milk
  760.75
delirium
  alcohol 291.0
  drug 292.81
drug 292.89
  with delirium 292.81
  correct substance properly administered
    (*see also* Allergy, drug) 995.27
  newborn 779.4
  obstetric anesthetic or sedation 668.9 ☑
    affecting fetus or newborn 763.5
  overdose or wrong substance given or
    taken — *see* Table of Drugs and
    Chemicals
  pathologic 292.2
  specific to newborn 779.4
  via placenta or breast milk 760.70
    alcohol 760.71
    anticonvulsants 760.77
    antifungals 760.74
    anti-infective agents 760.74
    antimetabolics 760.78
    cocaine 760.75
    "crack" 760.75
    hallucinogenic agents 760.73
    medicinal agents NEC 760.79
    narcotics 760.72
    obstetric anesthetic or analgesic drug
      763.5
    specified agent NEC 760.79
    suspected, affecting management of
      pregnancy 655.5 ☑
enteric — *see* Intoxication, intestinal
fetus or newborn, via placenta or breast milk
  760.70
  alcohol 760.71
  anticonvulsants 760.77
  antifungals 760.74
  anti-infective agents 760.74
  antimetabolics 760.78
  cocaine 760.75
  "crack" 760.75
  hallucinogenic agents 760.73
  medicinal agents NEC 760.79
  narcotics 760.72
  obstetric anesthetic or analgesic drug
    763.5
  specified agent NEC 760.79
  suspected, affecting management of
    pregnancy 655.5 ☑
food — *see* Poisoning, food

Intoxication — *continued*
gastrointestinal 558.2
hallucinogenic (acute) 305.3 ☑
hepatocerebral 572.2
idiosyncratic alcohol 291.4
intestinal 569.89
  due to putrefaction of food 005.9
methyl alcohol (*see also* Alcoholism) 305.0 ☑
  with alcoholism 303.0 ☑
non-foodborne due to toxins of Clostridium
  botulinum [C. botulinum] — *see* Botulism
pathologic 291.4
  drug 292.2
potassium (K) 276.7
septic
  with
    abortion — *see* Abortion, by type, with
      sepsis
    ectopic pregnancy (*see also* categories
      633.0–633.9) 639.0
    molar pregnancy (*see also* categories
      630–632) 639.0
  during labor 659.3 ☑
  following
    abortion 639.0
    ectopic or molar pregnancy 639.0
  generalized — *see* Septicemia
  puerperal, postpartum, childbirth
    670.2 ☑   ▲
serum (prophylactic) (therapeutic) 999.5
uremic — *see* Uremia
water 276.6
Intracranial — *see* condition
Intrahepatic gallbladder 751.69
Intraligamentous — *see also* condition
  pregnancy — *see* Pregnancy, cornual
Intraocular — *see also* condition
  sepsis 360.00
Intrathoracic — *see also* condition
  kidney 753.3
  stomach — *see* Hernia, diaphragm
Intrauterine contraceptive device
  checking V25.42
  insertion V25.1
  in situ V45.51
  management V25.42
  prescription V25.02
    repeat V25.42
  reinsertion V25.42
  removal V25.42
Intraventricular — *see* condition
Intrinsic deformity — *see* Deformity
Intruded tooth 524.34
Intrusion, repetitive, of sleep (due to environmental disturbances) (with atypical
  polysomnographic features) 307.48
Intumescent, lens (eye) NEC 366.9
  senile 366.12
Intussusception (colon) (enteric) (intestine)
  (rectum) 560.0
  appendix 543.9
  congenital 751.5
  fallopian tube 620.8
  ileocecal 560.0
  ileocolic 560.0
  ureter (with obstruction) 593.4
Invagination
  basilar 756.0
  colon or intestine 560.0
Invalid (since birth) 799.89
Invalidism (chronic) 799.89
Inversion
  albumin-globulin (A-G) ratio 273.8
  bladder 596.8
  cecum (*see also* Intussusception) 560.0
  cervix 622.8
  nipple 611.79
    congenital 757.6
    puerperal, postpartum 676.3 ☑
  optic papilla 743.57
  organ or site, congenital NEC — *see* Anomaly,
    specified type NEC
  sleep rhythm 327.39
    nonorganic origin 307.45
  testis (congenital) 752.51

Inversion — *continued*
  uterus (postinfectional) (postpartal, old) 621.7
    chronic 621.7
    complicating delivery 665.2 ☑
      affecting fetus or newborn 763.89
  vagina — *see* Prolapse, vagina
Investigation
  allergens V72.7
  clinical research (control) (normal comparison)
    (participant) V70.7
Inviability — *see* Immaturity
Involuntary movement, abnormal 781.0
Involution, involutional — *see also* condition
  breast, cystic or fibrocystic 610.1
  depression (*see also* Psychosis, affective)
    296.2 ☑
    recurrent episode 296.3 ☑
    single episode 296.2 ☑
  melancholia (*see also* Psychosis, affective)
    296.2 ☑
    recurrent episode 296.3 ☑
    single episode 296.2 ☑
  ovary, senile 620.3
  paranoid state (reaction) 297.2
  paraphrenia (climacteric) (menopause) 297.2
  psychosis 298.8
  thymus failure 254.8
IQ
  under 20 318.2
  20-34 318.1
  35-49 318.0
  50-70 317
IRDS 769
Irideremia 743.45
Iridis rubeosis 364.42
  diabetic 250.5 ☑ *[364.42]*
    due to secondary diabetes
      249.5 ☑ *[364.42]*
Iridochoroiditis (panuveitis) 360.12
Iridocyclitis NEC 364.3
  acute 364.00
    primary 364.01
    recurrent 364.02
  chronic 364.10
    in
      lepromatous leprosy 030.0 *[364.11]*
      sarcoidosis 135 *[364.11]*
      tuberculosis (*see also* Tuberculosis)
        017.3 ☑ *[364.11]*
  due to allergy 364.04
  endogenous 364.01
  gonococcal 098.41
  granulomatous 364.10
  herpetic (simplex) 054.44
    zoster 053.22
  hypopyon 364.05
  lens induced 364.23
  nongranulomatous 364.00
  primary 364.01
  recurrent 364.02
  rheumatic 364.10
  secondary 364.04
    infectious 364.03
    noninfectious 364.04
  subacute 364.00
    primary 364.01
    recurrent 364.02
  sympathetic 360.11
  syphilitic (secondary) 091.52
  tuberculous (chronic) (*see also* Tuberculosis)
    017.3 ☑ *[364.11]*
Iridocyclochoroiditis (panuveitis) 360.12
Iridodialysis 364.76
Iridodonesis 364.89
Iridoplegia (complete) (partial) (reflex) 379.49
Iridoschisis 364.52
Iris — *see* condition
Iritis 364.3
  acute 364.00
    primary 364.01
    recurrent 364.02
  chronic 364.10
    in
      sarcoidosis 135 *[364.11]*
      tuberculosis (*see also* Tuberculosis)
        017.3 ☑ *[364.11]*

Iritis — *continued*
  diabetic 250.5 ☑ *[364.42]*
    due to secondary diabetes
      249.5 ☑ *[364.42]*
  due to
    allergy 364.04
    herpes simplex 054.44
    leprosy 030.0 *[364.11]*
  endogenous 364.01
  gonococcal 098.41
  gouty 274.89 *[364.11]*
  granulomatous 364.10
  hypopyon 364.05
  lens induced 364.23
  nongranulomatous 364.00
  papulosa 095.8 *[364.11]*
  primary 364.01
  recurrent 364.02
  rheumatic 364.10
  secondary 364.04
    infectious 364.03
    noninfectious 364.04
  subacute 364.00
    primary 364.01
    recurrent 364.02
  sympathetic 360.11
  syphilitic (secondary) 091.52
    congenital 090.0 *[364.11]*
    late 095.8 *[364.11]*
  tuberculous (*see also* Tuberculosis)
    017.3 ☑ *[364.11]*
  uratic 274.89 *[364.11]*
Iron
  deficiency anemia 280.9
  metabolism disease 275.0
  storage disease 275.0
Iron-miners' lung 503
Irradiated enamel (tooth, teeth) 521.89
Irradiation
  burn — *see* Burn, by site
  effects, adverse 990
Irreducible, irreducibility — *see* condition
Irregular, irregularity
  action, heart 427.9
  alveolar process 525.8
  bleeding NEC 626.4
  breathing 786.09
  colon 569.89
  contour
    acquired 371.70
      of cornea 743.41
        acquired 371.70
    reconstructed breast 612.0
  dentin in pulp 522.3
  eye movements NEC 379.59
  menstruation (cause unknown) 626.4
  periods 626.4
  prostate 602.9
  pupil 364.75
  respiratory 786.09
  septum (nasal) 470
  shape, organ or site, congenital NEC — *see*
    Distortion
  sleep-wake rhythm (non-24-hour) 327.39
    nonorganic origin 307.45
  vertebra 733.99
Irritability 799.22   ▲
  bladder 596.8
    neurogenic 596.54
      with cauda equina syndrome 344.61
  bowel (syndrome) 564.1
  bronchial (*see also* Bronchitis) 490
  cerebral, newborn 779.1
  colon 564.1
    psychogenic 306.4
  duodenum 564.89
  heart (psychogenic) 306.2
  ileum 564.89
  jejunum 564.89
  myocardium 306.2
  nervousness 799.21
  rectum 564.89
  stomach 536.9
    psychogenic 306.4
  sympathetic (nervous system) (*see also* Neu-
    ropathy, peripheral, autonomic) 337.9

☑ Additional Digit Required — Refer to the Tabular List for Digit Selection   ▼ Subterms under main terms may continue to next column or page

2010 ICD-9-CM   ▶◀ Revised Text   ● New Line   ▲ Revised Code   October 2009 • Volume 2 — 161

Irritability — *continued*
  urethra 599.84
  ventricular (heart) (psychogenic) 306.2
Irritable — ▶*see also* Irritability◀ 799.22
Irritation
  anus 569.49
  axillary nerve 353.0
  bladder 596.8
  brachial plexus 353.0
  brain (traumatic) (*see also* Injury, intracranial)
      854.0 ☑
    nontraumatic — *see* Encephalitis
  bronchial (*see also* Bronchitis) 490
  cerebral (traumatic) (*see also* Injury, intracra-
      nial) 854.0 ☑
    nontraumatic — *see* Encephalitis
  cervical plexus 353.2
  cervix (*see also* Cervicitis) 616.0
  choroid, sympathetic 360.11
  cranial nerve — *see* Disorder, nerve, cranial
  digestive tract 536.9
    psychogenic 306.4
  gastric 536.9
    psychogenic 306.4
  gastrointestinal (tract) 536.9
    functional 536.9
    psychogenic 306.4
  globe, sympathetic 360.11
  intestinal (bowel) 564.9
  labyrinth 386.50
  lumbosacral plexus 353.1
  meninges (traumatic) (*see also* Injury, intracra-
      nial) 854.0 ☑
    nontraumatic — *see* Meningitis
  myocardium 306.2
  nerve — *see* Disorder, nerve
  nervous 799.21   ▲
  nose 478.19
  penis 607.89
  perineum 709.9
  peripheral
    autonomic nervous system (*see also* Neu-
        ropathy, peripheral, autonomic)
        337.9
    nerve — *see* Disorder, nerve
  peritoneum (*see also* Peritonitis) 567.9
  pharynx 478.29
  plantar nerve 355.6
  spinal (cord) (traumatic) (*see also* Injury, spinal,
      by site)
    nerve (*see also* Disorder, nerve)
      root NEC 724.9
      traumatic — *see* Injury, nerve, spinal
    nontraumatic — *see* Myelitis

Irritation — *continued*
  stomach 536.9
    psychogenic 306.4
  sympathetic nerve NEC (*see also* Neuropathy,
      peripheral, autonomic) 337.9
  ulnar nerve 354.2
  vagina 623.9
Isambert's disease 012.3 ☑
Ischemia, ischemic 459.9
  basilar artery (with transient neurologic deficit)
      435.0
  bone NEC 733.40
  bowel (transient) 557.9
    acute 557.0
    chronic 557.1
    due to mesenteric artery insufficiency
        557.1
  brain (*see also* Ischemia, cerebral)
    recurrent focal 435.9
  cardiac (*see also* Ischemia, heart) 414.9
  cardiomyopathy 414.8
  carotid artery (with transient neurologic
      deficit) 435.8
  cerebral (chronic) (generalized) 437.1
    arteriosclerotic 437.0
    intermittent (with transient neurologic
        deficit) 435.9
    newborn 779.2
    puerperal, postpartum, childbirth 674.0 ☑
    recurrent focal (with transient neurologic
        deficit) 435.9
    transient (with transient neurologic deficit)
        435.9
  colon 557.9
    acute 557.0
    chronic 557.1
    due to mesenteric artery insufficiency
        557.1
  coronary (chronic) (*see also* Ischemia, heart)
      414.9
  heart (chronic or with a stated duration of over
      8 weeks) 414.9
    acute or with a stated duration of 8 weeks
        or less (*see also* Infarct, myocardi-
        um) 410.9 ☑
      without myocardial infarction 411.89
        with coronary (artery) occlusion
            411.81
    subacute 411.89
  intestine (transient) 557.9
    acute 557.0
    chronic 557.1
    due to mesenteric artery insufficiency
        557.1

Ischemia, ischemic — *continued*
  kidney 593.81
  labyrinth 386.50
  muscles, leg 728.89
  myocardium, myocardial (chronic or with a
      stated duration of over 8 weeks) 414.8
    acute (*see also* Infarct, myocardium)
        410.9 ☑
      without myocardial infarction 411.89
        with coronary (artery) occlusion
            411.81
  renal 593.81
  retina, retinal 362.84
  small bowel 557.9
    acute 557.0
    chronic 557.1
    due to mesenteric artery insufficiency
        557.1
  spinal cord 336.1
  subendocardial (*see also* Insufficiency, coro-
      nary) 411.89
  vertebral artery (with transient neurologic
      deficit) 435.1
Ischialgia — *see also* Sciatica 724.3
Ischiopagus 759.4
Ischium, ischial — *see* condition
Ischomenia 626.8
Ischuria 788.5
Iselin's disease or osteochondrosis 732.5
Islands of
  parotid tissue in
    lymph nodes 750.26
    neck structures 750.26
  submaxillary glands in
    fascia 750.26
    lymph nodes 750.26
    neck muscles 750.26
Islet cell tumor, pancreas (M8150/0) 211.7
Isoimmunization NEC — *see also* Incompatibility
      656.2 ☑
  anti-E 656.2 ☑
  fetus or newborn 773.2
    ABO blood groups 773.1
    Rhesus (Rh) factor 773.0
Isolation V07.0
  social V62.4
Isosporosis 007.2
Issue
  medical certificate NEC V68.09
    cause of death V68.09
    disability examination V68.01
    fitness V68.09
    incapacity V68.09
  repeat prescription NEC V68.1

Issue — *continued*
  repeat prescription — *continued*
    appliance V68.1
    contraceptive V25.40
      device NEC V25.49
        intrauterine V25.42
        specified type NEC V25.49
      pill V25.41
    glasses V68.1
    medicinal substance V68.1
Itch — *see also* Pruritus 698.9
  bakers' 692.89
  barbers' 110.0
  bricklayers' 692.89
  cheese 133.8
  clam diggers' 120.3
  coolie 126.9
  copra 133.8
  Cuban 050.1
  dew 126.9
  dhobie 110.3
  eye 379.99
  filarial (*see also* Infestation, filarial) 125.9
  grain 133.8
  grocers' 133.8
  ground 126.9
  harvest 133.8
  jock 110.3
  Malabar 110.9
    beard 110.0
    foot 110.4
    scalp 110.0
  meaning scabies 133.0
  Norwegian 133.0
  perianal 698.0
  poultrymen's 133.8
  sarcoptic 133.0
  scrub 134.1
  seven year V61.10
    meaning scabies 133.0
  straw 133.8
  swimmers' 120.3
  washerwoman's 692.4
  water 120.3
  winter 698.8
Itsenko-Cushing syndrome (pituitary ba-
      sophilism) 255.0
Ivemark's syndrome (asplenia with congenital
      heart disease) 759.0
Ivory bones 756.52
Ixodes 134.8
Ixodiasis 134.8

☑ Additional Digit Required — Refer to the Tabular List for Digit Selection   ▽ Subterms under main terms may continue to next column or page

J

Jaccoud's nodular fibrositis, chronic (Jaccoud's syndrome) 714.4

Jackson's
  membrane 751.4
  paralysis or syndrome 344.89
  veil 751.4

Jacksonian
  epilepsy (see also Epilepsy) 345.5 ☑
  seizures (focal) (see also Epilepsy) 345.5 ☑

Jacob's ulcer (M8090/3) — see Neoplasm, skin, malignant, by site

Jacquet's dermatitis (diaper dermatitis) 691.0

Jadassohn's
  blue nevus (M8780/0) — see Neoplasm, skin, benign
  disease (maculopapular erythroderma) 696.2
  intraepidermal epithelioma (M8096/0) — see Neoplasm, skin, benign

Jadassohn-Lewandowski syndrome (pachyonychia congenita) 757.5

Jadassohn-Pellizari's disease (anetoderma) 701.3

Jadassohn-Tièche nevus (M8780/0) — see Neoplasm, skin, benign

Jaffe-Lichtenstein (-Uehlinger) syndrome 252.01

Jahnke's syndrome (encephalocutaneous angiomatosis) 759.6

Jakob-Creutzfeldt disease (CJD) (syndrome) 046.19
  with dementia
    with behavioral disturbance 046.19 [294.11]
    without behavioral disturbance 046.19 [294.10]
  familial 046.19
  iatrogenic 046.19
  specified NEC 046.19
  sporadic 046.19
  variant (vCJD) 046.11
    with dementia
      with behavioral disturbance 046.11 [294.11]
      without behavioral disturbance 046.11 [294.10]

Jaksch (-Luzet) disease or syndrome (pseudoleukemia infantum) 285.8

Jamaican
  neuropathy 349.82
  paraplegic tropical ataxic-spastic syndrome 349.82

Janet's disease (psychasthenia) 300.89

Janiceps 759.4

Jansky-Bielschowsky amaurotic familial idiocy 330.1

Japanese
  B type encephalitis 062.0
  river fever 081.2
  seven-day fever 100.89

Jaundice (yellow) 782.4
  acholuric (familial) (splenomegalic) (see also Spherocytosis) 282.0
    acquired 283.9
  breast milk 774.39
  catarrhal (acute) 070.1
    with hepatic coma 070.0
    chronic 571.9
    epidemic — see Jaundice, epidemic
  cholestatic (benign) 782.4
  chronic idiopathic 277.4
  epidemic (catarrhal) 070.1
    with hepatic coma 070.0
    leptospiral 100.0
    spirochetal 100.0
  febrile (acute) 070.1
    with hepatic coma 070.0
    leptospiral 100.0
    spirochetal 100.0
  fetus or newborn 774.6
    due to or associated with
      ABO
        absence or deficiency of enzyme system for bilirubin conjugation (congenital) 774.39
        antibodies 773.1

Jaundice — continued
  fetus or newborn — continued
    due to or associated with — continued
      blood group incompatibility NEC 773.2
      breast milk inhibitors to conjugation 774.39
        associated with preterm delivery 774.2
      bruising 774.1
      Crigler-Najjar syndrome 277.4 [774.31]
      delayed conjugation 774.30
        associated with preterm delivery 774.2
        development 774.39
      drugs or toxins transmitted from mother 774.1
      G-6-PD deficiency 282.2 [774.0]
      galactosemia 271.1 [774.5]
      Gilbert's syndrome 277.4 [774.31]
      hepatocellular damage 774.4
      hereditary hemolytic anemia (see also Anemia, hemolytic) 282.9 [774.0]
      hypothyroidism, congenital 243 [774.31]
      incompatibility, maternal/fetal NEC 773.2
      incompatibility, maternal/fetal 773.1
      infection 774.1
      inspissated bile syndrome 774.4
      isoimmunization NEC 773.2
      isoimmunization 773.1
      mucoviscidosis 277.01 [774.5]
      obliteration of bile duct, congenital 751.61 [774.5]
      polycythemia 774.1
      preterm delivery 774.2
      red cell defect 282.9 [774.0]
      Rh
        antibodies 773.0
        incompatibility, maternal/fetal 773.0
        isoimmunization 773.0
      spherocytosis (congenital) 282.0 [774.0]
      swallowed maternal blood 774.1
    physiological NEC 774.6
  from injection, inoculation, infusion, or transfusion (blood) (plasma) (serum) (other substance) (onset within 8 months after administration) — see Hepatitis, viral
  Gilbert's (familial nonhemolytic) 277.4
  hematogenous 283.9
  hemolytic (acquired) 283.9
    congenital (see also Spherocytosis) 282.0
  hemorrhagic (acute) 100.0
    leptospiral 100.0
    newborn 776.0
    spirochetal 100.0
  hepatocellular 573.8
  homologous (serum) — see Hepatitis, viral
  idiopathic, chronic 277.4
  infectious (acute) (subacute) 070.1
    with hepatic coma 070.0
    leptospiral 100.0
    spirochetal 100.0
  leptospiral 100.0
  malignant (see also Necrosis, liver) 570
  newborn (physiological) (see also Jaundice, fetus or newborn) 774.6
  nonhemolytic, congenital familial (Gilbert's) 277.4
  nuclear, newborn (see also Kernicterus of newborn) 774.7
  obstructive NEC (see also Obstruction, biliary) 576.8
  postimmunization — see Hepatitis, viral
  posttransfusion — see Hepatitis, viral
  regurgitation (see also Obstruction, biliary) 576.8
  serum (homologous) (prophylactic) (therapeutic) — see Hepatitis, viral
  spirochetal (hemorrhagic) 100.0
  symptomatic 782.4
    newborn 774.6

Jaw — see condition

Jaw-blinking 374.43
  congenital 742.8

Jaw-winking phenomenon or syndrome 742.8

Jealousy
  alcoholic 291.5
  childhood 313.3
  sibling 313.3

Jejunitis — see also Enteritis 558.9

Jejunostomy status V44.4

Jejunum, jejunal — see condition

Jensen's disease 363.05

Jericho boil 085.1

Jerks, myoclonic 333.2

Jervell-Lange-Nielsen syndrome 426.82

Jeune's disease or syndrome (asphyxiating thoracic dystrophy) 756.4

Jigger disease 134.1

Job's syndrome (chronic granulomatous disease) 288.1

Jod-Basedow phenomenon 242.8 ☑

Johnson-Stevens disease (erythema multiforme exudativum) 695.13

Joint — see also condition
  Charcôt's 094.0 [713.5]
  false 733.82
  flail — see Flail, joint
  mice — see Loose, body, joint, by site
  sinus to bone 730.9 ☑
  von Gies' 095.8

Jordan's anomaly or syndrome 288.2

Josephs-Diamond-Blackfan anemia (congenital hypoplastic) 284.01

Joubert syndrome 759.89

Jumpers' knee 727.2

Jungle yellow fever 060.0

Jüngling's disease (sarcoidosis) 135

Junin virus hemorrhagic fever 078.7

Juvenile — see also condition
  delinquent 312.9
    group (see also Disturbance, conduct) 312.2 ☑
  neurotic 312.4

K

Kabuki syndrome 759.89

Kahler (-Bozzolo) disease (multiple myeloma) (M9730/3) 203.0 ☑

Kakergasia 300.9

Kakke 265.0

Kala-azar (Indian) (infantile) (Mediterranean) (Sudanese) 085.0

Kalischer's syndrome (encephalocutaneous angiomatosis) 759.6

Kallmann's syndrome (hypogonadotropic hypogonadism with anosmia) 253.4

Kanner's syndrome (autism) — see also Psychosis, childhood 299.0 ☑

Kaolinosis 502

Kaposi's
  disease 757.33
    lichen ruber 696.4
      acuminatus 696.4
      moniliformis 697.8
    xeroderma pigmentosum 757.33
  sarcoma (M9140/3) 176.9
    adipose tissue 176.1
    aponeurosis 176.1
    artery 176.1
    associated herpesvirus infection 058.89
    blood vessel 176.1
    bursa 176.1
    connective tissue 176.1
    external genitalia 176.8
    fascia 176.1
    fatty tissue 176.1
    fibrous tissue 176.1
    gastrointestinal tract NEC 176.3
    ligament 176.1
    lung 176.4
    lymph
      gland(s) 176.5
      node(s) 176.5
    lymphatic(s) NEC 176.1
    muscle (skeletal) 176.1
    oral cavity NEC 176.8
    palate 176.2

Kaposi's — continued
  sarcoma — continued
    scrotum 176.8
    skin 176.0
    soft tissue 176.1
    specified site NEC 176.8
    subcutaneous tissue 176.1
    synovia 176.1
    tendon (sheath) 176.1
    vein 176.1
    vessel 176.1
    viscera NEC 176.9
    vulva 176.8
  varicelliform eruption 054.0
    vaccinia 999.0

Kartagener's syndrome or triad (sinusitis, bronchiectasis, situs inversus) 759.3

Kasabach-Merritt syndrome (capillary hemangioma associated with thrombocytopenic purpura) 287.39

Kaschin-Beck disease (endemic polyarthritis) — see Disease, Kaschin-Beck

Kast's syndrome (dyschondroplasia with hemangiomas) 756.4

Katatonia — see Catatonia

Katayama disease or fever 120.2

Kathisophobia 781.0

Kawasaki disease 446.1

Kayser-Fleischer ring (cornea) (pseudosclerosis) 275.1 [371.14]

Kaznelson's syndrome (congenital hypoplastic anemia) 284.01

Kearns-Sayre syndrome 277.87

Kedani fever 081.2

Kelis 701.4

Kelly (-Patterson) syndrome (sideropenic dysphagia) 280.8

Keloid, cheloid 701.4
  Addison's (morphea) 701.0
  cornea 371.00
  Hawkins' 701.4
  scar 701.4

Keloma 701.4

Kenya fever 082.1

Keratectasia 371.71
  congenital 743.41

Keratinization NEC
  alveolar ridge mucosa
    excessive 528.72
    minimal 528.71

Keratitis (nodular) (nonulcerative) (simple) (zonular) NEC 370.9
  with ulceration (see also Ulcer, cornea) 370.00
  actinic 370.24
  arborescens 054.42
  areolar 370.22
  bullosa 370.8
  deep — see Keratitis, interstitial
  dendritic(a) 054.42
  desiccation 370.34
  diffuse interstitial 370.52
  disciform(is) 054.43
    varicella 052.7 [370.44]
  epithelialis vernalis 372.13 [370.32]
  exposure 370.34
  filamentary 370.23
  gonococcal (congenital) (prenatal) 098.43
  herpes, herpetic (simplex) NEC 054.43
    zoster 053.21
  hypopyon 370.04
  in
    chickenpox 052.7 [370.44]
    exanthema (see also Exanthem) 057.9 [370.44]
    paravaccinia (see also Paravaccinia) 051.9 [370.44]
    smallpox (see also Smallpox) 050.9 [370.44]
    vernal conjunctivitis 372.13 [370.32]
  interstitial (nonsyphilitic) 370.50
    with ulcer (see also Ulcer, cornea) 370.00
    diffuse 370.52
    herpes, herpetic (simplex) 054.43
      zoster 053.21
    syphilitic (congenital) (hereditary) 090.3
    tuberculous (see also Tuberculosis) 017.3 ☑ [370.59]

☑ Additional Digit Required — Refer to the Tabular List for Digit Selection   ▽ Subterms under main terms may continue to next column or page

2010 ICD-9-CM   ▶◀ Revised Text   ● New Line   ▲ Revised Code   Volume 2 — 163

Jaccoud's nodular fibrositis, chronic — Keratitis

☑ Additional Digit Required — Refer to the Tabular List for Digit Selection   ▼ Subterms under main terms may continue to next column or page

164 — Volume 2   ▶◀ Revised Text   ● New Line   ▲ Revised Code   2010 ICD-9-CM

Kyrle's disease (hyperkeratosis follicularis in cutem penetrans) 701.1

L

Labia, labium — *see* condition
Labiated hymen 752.49
Labile
   blood pressure 796.2
   emotions, emotionality 301.3
   vasomotor system 443.9
Lability, emotional 799.24   ●
Labioglossal paralysis 335.22
Labium leporinum — *see also* Cleft, lip 749.10
Labor — *see also* Delivery
   with complications — *see* Delivery, complicated
   abnormal NEC 661.9 ☑
      affecting fetus or newborn 763.7
   arrested active phase 661.1 ☑
      affecting fetus or newborn 763.7
   desultory 661.2 ☑
      affecting fetus or newborn 763.7
   dyscoordinate 661.4 ☑
      affecting fetus or newborn 763.7
   early onset (22-36 weeks gestation) 644.2 ☑
   failed
      induction 659.1 ☑
         mechanical 659.0 ☑
         medical 659.1 ☑
         surgical 659.0 ☑
         trial (vaginal delivery) 660.6 ☑
   false 644.1 ☑
   forced or induced, affecting fetus or newborn 763.89
   hypertonic 661.4 ☑
      affecting fetus or newborn 763.7
   hypotonic 661.2 ☑
      affecting fetus or newborn 763.7
      primary 661.0 ☑
         affecting fetus or newborn 763.7
      secondary 661.1 ☑
         affecting fetus or newborn 763.7
   incoordinate 661.4 ☑
      affecting fetus or newborn 763.7
   irregular 661.2 ☑
      affecting fetus or newborn 763.7
   long — *see* Labor, prolonged
   missed (at or near term) 656.4 ☑
   obstructed NEC 660.9 ☑
      affecting fetus or newborn 763.1
      due to female genital mutilation 660.8 ☑
      specified cause NEC 660.8 ☑
         affecting fetus or newborn 763.1
   pains, spurious 644.1 ☑
   precipitate 661.3 ☑
      affecting fetus or newborn 763.6
   premature 644.2 ☑
      threatened 644.0 ☑
   prolonged or protracted 662.1 ☑
      first stage 662.0 ☑
         affecting fetus or newborn 763.89
      second stage 662.2 ☑
         affecting fetus or newborn 763.89
      affecting fetus or newborn 763.89
   threatened NEC 644.1 ☑
   undelivered 644.1 ☑
Labored breathing — *see also* Hyperventilation 786.09
Labyrinthitis (inner ear) (destructive) (latent) 386.30
   circumscribed 386.32
   diffuse 386.31
   focal 386.32
   purulent 386.33
   serous 386.31
   suppurative 386.33
   syphilitic 095.8
   toxic 386.34
   viral 386.35
Laceration — *see also* Wound, open, by site
   accidental, complicating surgery 998.2
   Achilles tendon 845.09
      with open wound 892.2
   anus (sphincter) 879.6

Laceration — *see also* Wound, open, by site — *continued*
   anus — *continued*
      with
         abortion — *see* Abortion, by type, with damage to pelvic organs
         ectopic pregnancy (*see also* categories 633.0–633.9) 639.2
         molar pregnancy (*see also* categories 630–632) 639.2
      complicated 879.7
      complicating delivery (healed) (old) 654.8 ☑
         with laceration of anal or rectal mucosa 664.3 ☑
         not associated with third-degree perineal laceration 664.6 ☑
      following
         abortion 639.2
         ectopic or molar pregnancy 639.2
      nontraumatic, nonpuerperal (healed) (old) 569.43
   bladder (urinary)
      with
         abortion — *see* Abortion, by type, with damage to pelvic organs
         ectopic pregnancy (*see also* categories 633.0–633.9) 639.2
         molar pregnancy (*see also* categories 630–632) 639.2
      following
         abortion 639.2
         ectopic or molar pregnancy 639.2
      obstetrical trauma 665.5 ☑
   blood vessel — *see* Injury, blood vessel, by site
   bowel
      with
         abortion — *see* Abortion, by type, with damage to pelvic organs
         ectopic pregnancy (*see also* categories 633.0–633.9) 639.2
         molar pregnancy (*see also* categories 630–632) 639.2
      following
         abortion 639.2
         ectopic or molar pregnancy 639.2
      obstetrical trauma 665.5 ☑
   brain (cerebral) (membrane) (with hemorrhage) 851.8 ☑

> *Note* — Use the following fifth-digit subclassification with categories 851–854:
>
> 0   *unspecified state of consciousness*
>
> 1   *with no loss of consciousness*
>
> 2   *with brief [less than one hour] loss of consciousness*
>
> 3   *with moderate [1–24 hours] loss of consciousness*
>
> 4   *with prolonged [more than 24 hours] loss of consciousness and return to pre–existing conscious level*
>
> 5   *with prolonged [more than 24 hours] loss of consciousness, without return to pre–existing conscious level*
>
> *Use fifth-digit 5 to designate when a patient is unconscious and dies before regaining consciousness, regardless of the duration of the loss of consciousness*
>
> 6   *with loss of consciousness of unspecified duration*
>
> 9   *with concussion, unspecified*

      with
         open intracranial wound 851.9 ☑
         skull fracture — *see* Fracture, skull, by site
      cerebellum 851.6 ☑
         with open intracranial wound 851.7 ☑
      cortex 851.2 ☑
         with open intracranial wound 851.3 ☑
      during birth 767.0
      stem 851.6 ☑
         with open intracranial wound 851.7 ☑

Laceration — *see also* Wound, open, by site — *continued*
   broad ligament
      with
         abortion — *see* Abortion, by type, with damage to pelvic organs
         ectopic pregnancy (*see also* categories 633.0–633.9) 639.2
         molar pregnancy (*see also* categories 630–632) 639.2
      following
         abortion 639.2
         ectopic or molar pregnancy 639.2
      nontraumatic 620.6
      obstetrical trauma 665.6 ☑
      syndrome (nontraumatic) 620.6
   capsule, joint — *see* Sprain, by site
   cardiac — *see* Laceration, heart
   causing eversion of cervix uteri (old) 622.0
   central, complicating delivery 664.4 ☑
   cerebellum — *see* Laceration, brain, cerebellum
   cerebral (*see also* Laceration, brain)
      during birth 767.0
   cervix (uteri)
      with
         abortion — *see* Abortion, by type, with damage to pelvic organs
         ectopic pregnancy (*see also* categories 633.0–633.9) 639.2
         molar pregnancy (*see also* categories 630–632) 639.2
      following
         abortion 639.2
         ectopic or molar pregnancy 639.2
      nonpuerperal, nontraumatic 622.3
      obstetrical trauma (current) 665.3 ☑
      old (postpartal) 622.3
      traumatic — *see* Injury, internal, cervix
   chordae heart 429.5
   complicated 879.9
   cornea — *see* Laceration, eyeball
      superficial 918.1
   cortex (cerebral) — *see* Laceration, brain, cortex
   esophagus 530.89
   eye(s) — *see* Laceration, ocular
   eyeball NEC 871.4
      with prolapse or exposure of intraocular tissue 871.1
      penetrating — *see* Penetrating wound, eyeball
      specified as without prolapse of intraocular tissue 871.0
   eyelid NEC 870.8
      full thickness 870.1
         involving lacrimal passages 870.2
      skin (and periocular area) 870.0
         penetrating — *see* Penetrating wound, orbit
   fourchette
      with
         abortion — *see* Abortion, by type, with damage to pelvic organs
         ectopic pregnancy (*see also* categories 633.0–633.9) 639.2
         molar pregnancy (*see also* categories 630–632) 639.2
      complicating delivery 664.0 ☑
      following
         abortion 639.2
         ectopic or molar pregnancy 639.2
   heart (without penetration of heart chambers) 861.02
      with
         open wound into thorax 861.12
         penetration of heart chambers 861.03
            with open wound into thorax 861.13
   hernial sac — *see* Hernia, by site
   internal organ (abdomen) (chest) (pelvis) NEC — *see* Injury, internal, by site
      NEC — *see* Injury, internal, by site
   kidney (parenchyma) 866.02

Laceration — *see also* Wound, open, by site — *continued*
   kidney — *continued*
      with
         complete disruption of parenchyma (rupture) 866.03
            with open wound into cavity 866.13
         open wound into cavity 866.12
   labia
      complicating delivery 664.0 ☑
   ligament (*see also* Sprain, by site)
      with open wound — *see* Wound, open, by site
   liver 864.05
      with open wound into cavity 864.15
      major (disruption of hepatic parenchyma) 864.04
         with open wound into cavity 864.14
      minor (capsule only) 864.02
         with open wound into cavity 864.12
      moderate (involving parenchyma without major disruption) 864.03
         with open wound into cavity 864.13
      multiple 864.04
         with open wound into cavity 864.14
      stellate 864.04
         with open wound into cavity 864.14
   lung 861.22
      with open wound into thorax 861.32
   meninges — *see* Laceration, brain
   meniscus (knee) (*see also* Tear, meniscus) 836.2
      old 717.5
      site other than knee (*see also* Sprain, by site)
         old NEC (*see also* Disorder, cartilage, articular) 718.0 ☑
   muscle (*see also* Sprain, by site)
      with open wound — *see* Wound, open, by site
   myocardium — *see* Laceration, heart
   nerve — *see* Injury, nerve, by site
   ocular NEC (*see also* Laceration, eyeball) 871.4
      adnexa NEC 870.8
      penetrating 870.3
         with foreign body 870.4
   orbit (eye) 870.8
      penetrating 870.3
         with foreign body 870.4
   pelvic
      floor (muscles)
         with
            abortion — *see* Abortion, by type, with damage to pelvic organs
            ectopic pregnancy (*see also* categories 633.0–633.9) 639.2
            molar pregnancy (*see also* categories 630–632) 639.2
         complicating delivery 664.1 ☑
         following
            abortion 639.2
            ectopic or molar pregnancy 639.2
         nonpuerperal 618.7
         old (postpartal) 618.7
      organ NEC
         with
            abortion — *see* Abortion, by type, with damage to pelvic organs
            ectopic pregnancy (*see also* categories 633.0–633.9) 639.2
            molar pregnancy (*see also* categories 630–632) 639.2
         complicating delivery 665.5 ☑
           affecting fetus or newborn 763.89
         following
            abortion 639.2
            ectopic or molar pregnancy 639.2
         obstetrical trauma 665.5 ☑
   perineum, perineal (old) (postpartal) 618.7
      with
         abortion — *see* Abortion, by type, with damage to pelvic floor

☑ Additional Digit Required — Refer to the Tabular List for Digit Selection   ▽ Subterms under main terms may continue to next column or page

2010 ICD-9-CM   ▶◀ Revised Text   ● New Line   ▲ Revised Code   October 2009 • Volume 2 — 165

Kyrle's disease — Laceration

Laryngitis — continued
  catarrhal 476.0
  chronic 476.0
    with tracheitis (chronic) 476.1
    due to external agent — see Condition, respiratory, chronic, due to
  diphtheritic (membranous) 032.3
  due to external agent — see Inflammation, respiratory, upper, due to
  Hemophilus influenzae 464.00
    with obstruction 464.01
  H. influenzae 464.00
    with obstruction 464.01
  hypertrophic 476.0
  influenzal 487.1
  pachydermic 478.79
  sicca 476.0
  spasmodic 478.75
    acute 464.00
      with obstruction 464.01
  streptococcal 034.0
  stridulous 478.75
  syphilitic 095.8
    congenital 090.5
  tuberculous (see also Tuberculosis, larynx) 012.3 ☑
  Vincent's 101
Laryngocele (congenital) (ventricular) 748.3
Laryngofissure 478.79
  congenital 748.3
Laryngomalacia (congenital) 748.3
Laryngopharyngitis (acute) 465.0
  chronic 478.9
    due to external agent — see Condition, respiratory, chronic, due to
  due to external agent — see Inflammation, respiratory, upper, due to
  septic 034.0
Laryngoplegia — see also Paralysis, vocal cord 478.30
Laryngoptosis 478.79
Laryngospasm 478.75
  due to external agent — see Condition, respiratory, acute, due to
Laryngostenosis 478.74
  congenital 748.3
Laryngotracheitis (acute) (infectional) (viral) — see also Laryngitis 464.20
  with obstruction 464.21
  atrophic 476.1
  Borrelia vincenti 101
  catarrhal 476.1
  chronic 476.1
    due to external agent — see Condition, respiratory, chronic, due to
  diphtheritic (membranous) 032.3
  due to external agent — see Inflammation, respiratory, upper, due to
  H. influenzae 464.20
    with obstruction 464.21
  hypertrophic 476.1
  influenzal 487.1
  pachydermic 478.75
  sicca 476.1
  spasmodic 478.75
    acute 464.20
      with obstruction 464.21
  streptococcal 034.0
  stridulous 478.75
  syphilitic 095.8
    congenital 090.5
  tuberculous (see also Tuberculosis, larynx) 012.3 ☑
  Vincent's 101
Laryngotracheobronchitis — see also Bronchitis 490
  acute 466.0
  chronic 491.8
  viral 466.0
Laryngotracheobronchopneumonitis — see Pneumonia, broncho-
Larynx, laryngeal — see condition
Lasègue's disease (persecution mania) 297.9
Lassa fever 078.89
Lassitude — see also Weakness 780.79
Late — see also condition

Late — see also condition — continued
  effect(s) (of) (see also condition)
    abscess
      intracranial or intraspinal (conditions classifiable to 324) — see category 326
    adverse effect of drug, medicinal or biological substance 909.5
    allergic reaction 909.9
    amputation
      postoperative (late) 997.60
      traumatic (injury classifiable to 885–887 and 895–897) 905.9
    burn (injury classifiable to 948–949) 906.9
      extremities NEC (injury classifiable to 943 or 945) 906.7
      hand or wrist (injury classifiable to 944) 906.6
      eye (injury classifiable to 940) 906.5
      face, head, and neck (injury classifiable to 941) 906.5
      specified site NEC (injury classifiable to 942 and 946–947) 906.8
    cerebrovascular disease (conditions classifiable to 430–437) 438.9
    with
      alterations of sensations 438.6
      aphasia 438.11
      apraxia 438.81
      ataxia 438.84
      cognitive deficits 438.0
      disturbances of vision 438.7
      dysarthria 438.13 ●
      dysphagia 438.82
      dysphasia 438.12
      facial droop 438.83
      facial weakness 438.83
      fluency disorder 438.14 ●
      hemiplegia/hemiparesis
        affecting
          dominant side 438.21
          nondominant side 438.22
          unspecified side 438.20
      monoplegia of lower limb
        affecting
          dominant side 438.41
          nondominant side 438.42
          unspecified side 438.40
      monoplegia of upper limb
        affecting
          dominant side 438.31
          nondominant side 438.32
          unspecified side 438.30
      paralytic syndrome NEC
        affecting
          bilateral 438.53
          dominant side 438.51
          nondominant side 438.52
          unspecified side 438.50
      speech and language deficit 438.10
        specified type NEC 438.19
      stuttering 438.14 ●
      vertigo 438.85
      specified type NEC 438.89
    childbirth complication(s) 677
    complication(s) of
      childbirth 677
      delivery 677
      pregnancy 677
      puerperium 677
      surgical and medical care (conditions classifiable to 996–999) 909.3
      trauma (conditions classifiable to 958) 908.6
    contusion (injury classifiable to 920–924) 906.3
    crushing (injury classifiable to 925–929) 906.4
    delivery complication(s) 677
    dislocation (injury classifiable to 830–839) 905.6
    encephalitis or encephalomyelitis (conditions classifiable to 323) — see category 326
      in infectious diseases 139.8

Late — see also condition — continued
  effect(s) (see also condition) — continued
    encephalitis or encephalomyelitis — see category — continued
      in infectious diseases — continued
        viral (conditions classifiable to 049.8, 049.9, 062–064) 139.0
    external cause NEC (conditions classifiable to 995) 909.9
    certain conditions classifiable to categories 991–994 909.4
    foreign body in orifice (injury classifiable to 930–939) 908.5
    fracture (multiple) (injury classifiable to 828–829) 905.5
    extremity
      lower (injury classifiable to 821–827) 905.4
        neck of femur (injury classifiable to 820) 905.3
      upper (injury classifiable to 810–819) 905.2
    face and skull (injury classifiable to 800–804) 905.0
    skull and face (injury classifiable to 800–804) 905.0
    spine and trunk (injury classifiable to 805 and 807–809) 905.1
      with spinal cord lesion (injury classifiable to 806) 907.2
    infection
      pyogenic, intracranial — see category 326
    infectious diseases (conditions classifiable to 001–136) NEC 139.8
    injury (injury classifiable to 959) 908.9
      blood vessel 908.3
        abdomen and pelvis (injury classifiable to 902) 908.4
        extremity (injury classifiable to 903–904) 908.3
        head and neck (injury classifiable to 900) 908.3
        intracranial (injury classifiable to 850–854) 907.0
          with skull fracture 905.0
        thorax (injury classifiable to 901) 908.4
      internal organ NEC (injury classifiable to 867 and 869) 908.2
        abdomen (injury classifiable to 863–866 and 868) 908.1
        thorax (injury classifiable to 860–862) 908.0
      intracranial (injury classifiable to 850–854) 907.0
        with skull fracture (injury classifiable to 800–801 and 803–804) 905.0
      nerve NEC (injury classifiable to 957) 907.9
        cranial (injury classifiable to 950–951) 907.1
        peripheral NEC (injury classifiable to 957) 907.9
        lower limb and pelvic girdle (injury classifiable to 956) 907.5
        upper limb and shoulder girdle (injury classifiable to 955) 907.4
        roots and plexus(es), spinal (injury classifiable to 953) 907.3
        trunk (injury classifiable to 954) 907.3
      spinal
        cord (injury classifiable to 806 and 952) 907.2
        nerve root(s) and plexus(es) (injury classifiable to 953) 907.3
      superficial (injury classifiable to 910–919) 906.2
      tendon (tendon injury classifiable to 840–848, 880–884 with .2, and 890–894 with .2) 905.8

Late — see also condition — continued
  effect(s) (see also condition) — continued
    meningitis
      bacterial (conditions classifiable to 320) — see category 326
      unspecified cause (conditions classifiable to 322) — see category 326
    myelitis (see also Late, effect(s) (of), encephalitis) — see category 326
    parasitic diseases (conditions classifiable to 001–136 NEC) 139.8
    phlebitis or thrombophlebitis of intracranial venous sinuses (conditions classifiable to 325) — see category 326
    poisoning due to drug, medicinal or biological substance (conditions classifiable to 960–979) 909.0
    poliomyelitis, acute (conditions classifiable to 045) 138
    pregnancy complication(s) 677
    puerperal complication(s) 677
    radiation (conditions classifiable to 990) 909.2
    rickets 268.1
    sprain and strain without mention of tendon injury (injury classifiable to 840–848, except tendon injury) 905.7
      tendon involvement 905.8
    toxic effect of
      drug, medicinal or biological substance (conditions classifiable to 960–979) 909.0
      nonmedical substance (conditions classifiable to 980–989) 909.1
    trachoma (conditions classifiable to 076) 139.1
    tuberculosis 137.0
      bones and joints (conditions classifiable to 015) 137.3
      central nervous system (conditions classifiable to 013) 137.1
      genitourinary (conditions classifiable to 016) 137.2
      pulmonary (conditions classifiable to 010–012) 137.0
      specified organs NEC (conditions classifiable to 014, 017–018) 137.4
    viral encephalitis (conditions classifiable to 049.8, 049.9, 062–064) 139.0
    wound, open
      extremity (injury classifiable to 880–884 and 890–894, except .2) 906.1
      tendon (injury classifiable to 880–884 with .2 and 890–894 with .2) 905.8
      head, neck, and trunk (injury classifiable to 870–879) 906.0
    infant
      post-term (gestation period over 40 completed weeks to 42 completed weeks) 766.21
      prolonged gestation (period over 42 completed weeks) 766.22
Latent — see condition
Lateral — see condition
Laterocession — see Lateroversion
Lateroflexion — see Lateroversion
Lateroversion
  cervix — see Lateroversion, uterus
  uterus, uterine (cervix) (postinfectional) (postpartal, old) 621.6
    congenital 752.3
    in pregnancy or childbirth 654.4 ☑
      affecting fetus or newborn 763.89
Lathyrism 988.2
Launois-Bensaude's lipomatosis 272.8
Launois-Cléret syndrome (adiposogenital dystrophy) 253.8
Launois' syndrome (pituitary gigantism) 253.0
Laurence-Moon-Biedl syndrome (obesity, polydactyly, and mental retardation) 759.89

☑ Additional Digit Required — Refer to the Tabular List for Digit Selection   ▽ Subterms under main terms may continue to next column or page

2010 ICD-9-CM   ►◄ Revised Text   ● New Line   ▲ Revised Code   October 2009 · Volume 2 — 167

Laryngitis — Laurence-Moon-Biedl syndrome

LAV (disease) (illness) (infection) — *see* Human immunodeficiency virus (disease) (illness) (infection)

LAV/HTLV-III (disease) (illness) (infection) — *see* Human immunodeficiency virus (disease) (illness) (infection)

Lawford's syndrome (encephalocutaneous angiomatosis) 759.6

Laxative habit — *see also* Abuse, drugs, nondependent 305.9 ☑

Lax, laxity — *see also* Relaxation
    ligament 728.4
    skin (acquired) 701.8
       congenital 756.83

Lazy leukocyte syndrome 288.09

LCAD (long chain/very long chain acyl CoA dehydrogenase deficiency, VLCAD) 277.85

LCHAD (long chain 3-hydroxyacyl CoA dehydrogenase deficiency) 277.85

Lead — *see also* condition
    exposure ▶(suspected)◀ to V15.86
    incrustation of cornea 371.15
    poisoning 984.9
       specified type of lead — *see* Table of Drugs and Chemicals

Lead miners' lung 503

Leakage
    amniotic fluid 658.1 ☑
       with delayed delivery 658.2 ☑
       affecting fetus or newborn 761.1
    bile from drainage tube (T tube) 997.4
    blood (microscopic), fetal, into maternal circulation 656.0 ☑
       affecting management of pregnancy or puerperium 656.0 ☑
    device, implant, or graft — *see* Complications, mechanical
    spinal fluid at lumbar puncture site 997.09
    urine, continuous 788.37

Leaky heart — *see* Endocarditis

Learning defect, specific NEC (strephosymbolia) 315.2

Leather bottle stomach (M8142/3) 151.9

Leber's
    congenital amaurosis 362.76
    optic atrophy (hereditary) 377.16

Lederer's anemia or disease (acquired infectious hemolytic anemia) 283.19

Lederer-Brill syndrome (acquired infectious hemolytic anemia) 283.19

Leeches (aquatic) (land) 134.2

Left-sided neglect 781.8

Leg — *see* condition

Legal investigation V62.5

Legg (-Calvé) -Perthes disease or syndrome (osteochondrosis, femoral capital) 732.1

Legionnaires' disease 482.84

Leigh's disease 330.8

Leiner's disease (exfoliative dermatitis) 695.89

Leiofibromyoma (M8890/0) — *see also* Leiomyoma
    uterus (cervix) (corpus) (*see also* Leiomyoma, uterus) 218.9

Leiomyoblastoma (M8891/1) — *see* Neoplasm, connective tissue, uncertain behavior

Leiomyofibroma (M8890/0) — *see also* Neoplasm, connective tissue, benign
    uterus (cervix) (corpus) (*see also* Leiomyoma, uterus) 218.9

Leiomyoma (M8890/0) — *see also* Neoplasm, connective tissue, benign
    bizarre (M8893/0) — *see* Neoplasm, connective tissue, benign
    cellular (M8892/1) — *see* Neoplasm, connective tissue, uncertain behavior
    epithelioid (M8891/1) — *see* Neoplasm, connective tissue, uncertain behavior
    prostate (polypoid) 600.20
       with
          other lower urinary tract symptoms (LUTS) 600.21
          urinary
             obstruction 600.21
             retention 600.21
    uterus (cervix) (corpus) 218.9
       interstitial 218.1

Leiomyoma — *see also* Neoplasm, connective tissue, benign — *continued*
    uterus — *continued*
       intramural 218.1
       submucous 218.0
       subperitoneal 218.2
       subserous 218.2
       vascular (M8894/0) — *see* Neoplasm, connective tissue, benign

Leiomyomatosis (intravascular) (M8890/1) — *see* Neoplasm, connective tissue, uncertain behavior

Leiomyosarcoma (M8890/3) — *see also* Neoplasm, connective tissue, malignant
    epithelioid (M8891/3) — *see* Neoplasm, connective tissue, malignant

Leishmaniasis 085.9
    American 085.5
       cutaneous 085.4
       mucocutaneous 085.5
    Asian desert 085.2
    Brazilian 085.5
    cutaneous 085.9
       acute necrotizing 085.2
       American 085.4
       Asian desert 085.2
       diffuse 085.3
       dry form 085.1
       Ethiopian 085.3
       eyelid 085.5 *[373.6]*
       late 085.1
       lepromatous 085.3
       recurrent 085.1
       rural 085.2
       ulcerating 085.1
       urban 085.1
       wet form 085.2
       zoonotic form 085.2
    dermal (*see also* Leishmaniasis, cutaneous)
       post kala-azar 085.0
    eyelid 085.5 *[373.6]*
    infantile 085.0
    Mediterranean 085.0
    mucocutaneous (American) 085.5
    naso-oral 085.5
    nasopharyngeal 085.5
    Old World 085.1
    tegumentaria diffusa 085.4
    vaccination, prophylactic (against) V05.2
    visceral (Indian) 085.0

Leishmanoid, dermal — *see also* Leishmaniasis, cutaneous
    post kala-azar 085.0

Leloir's disease 695.4

Lemiere syndrome 451.89

Lengthening, leg 736.81

Lennox-Gastaut syndrome 345.0 ☑
    with tonic seizures 345.1 ☑

Lennox's syndrome — *see also* Epilepsy 345.0 ☑

Lens — *see* condition

Lenticonus (anterior) (posterior) (congenital) 743.36

Lenticular degeneration, progressive 275.1

Lentiglobus (posterior) (congenital) 743.36

Lentigo (congenital) 709.09
    juvenile 709.09
    Maligna (M8742/2) (*see also* Neoplasm, skin, in situ)
       melanoma (M8742/3) — *see* Melanoma
    senile 709.09

Leonine leprosy 030.0

Leontiasis
    ossium 733.3
    syphilitic 095.8
       congenital 090.5

Léopold-Lévi's syndrome (paroxysmal thyroid instability) 242.9 ☑

Lepore hemoglobin syndrome 282.49

Lepothrix 039.0

Lepra 030.9
    Willan's 696.1

Leprechaunism 259.8

Lepromatous leprosy 030.0

Leprosy 030.9

Leprosy — *continued*
    anesthetic 030.1
    beriberi 030.1
    borderline (group B) (infiltrated) (neuritic) 030.3
    cornea (*see also* Leprosy, by type) 030.9 *[371.89]*
    dimorphous (group B) (infiltrated) (lepromatous) (neuritic) (tuberculoid) 030.3
    eyelid 030.0 *[373.4]*
    indeterminate (group I) (macular) (neuritic) (uncharacteristic) 030.2
    leonine 030.0
    lepromatous (diffuse) (infiltrated) (macular) (neuritic) (nodular) (type L) 030.0
    macular (early) (neuritic) (simple) 030.2
    maculoanesthetic 030.1
    mixed 030.0
    neuro 030.1
    nodular 030.0
    primary neuritic 030.3
    specified type or group NEC 030.8
    tubercular 030.1
    tuberculoid (macular) (maculoanesthetic) (major) (minor) (neuritic) (type T) 030.1

Leptocytosis, hereditary 282.49

Leptomeningitis (chronic) (circumscribed) (hemorrhagic) (nonsuppurative) — *see also* Meningitis 322.9
    aseptic 047.9
       adenovirus 049.1
       Coxsackie virus 047.0
       ECHO virus 047.1
       enterovirus 047.9
       lymphocytic choriomeningitis 049.0
    epidemic 036.0
    late effect — *see* category 326
    meningococcal 036.0
    pneumococcal 320.1
    syphilitic 094.2
    tuberculous (*see also* Tuberculosis, meninges) 013.0 ☑

Leptomeningopathy — *see also* Meningitis 322.9

Leptospiral — *see* condition

Leptospirochetal — *see* condition

Leptospirosis 100.9
    autumnalis 100.89
    canicula 100.89
    grippotyphosa 100.89
    hebdomidis 100.89
    icterohemorrhagica 100.0
    nanukayami 100.89
    pomona 100.89
    Weil's disease 100.0

Leptothricosis — *see* Actinomycosis

Leptothrix infestation — *see* Actinomycosis

Leptotricosis — *see* Actinomycosis

Leptus dermatitis 133.8

Leriche's syndrome (aortic bifurcation occlusion) 444.0

Léris pleonosteosis 756.89

Léri-Weill syndrome 756.59

Lermoyez's syndrome — *see also* Disease, Ménière's 386.00

Lesbianism — *omit code*
    ego-dystonic 302.0
    problems with 302.0

Lesch-Nyhan syndrome (hypoxanthineguanine-phosphoribosyltransferase deficiency) 277.2

Lesion(s)
    abducens nerve 378.54
    alveolar process 525.8
    anorectal 569.49
    aortic (valve) — *see* Endocarditis, aortic
    auditory nerve 388.5
    basal ganglion 333.90
    bile duct (*see also* Disease, biliary) 576.8
    bladder 596.9
    bone 733.90
    brachial plexus 353.0
    brain 348.89 ▲
       congenital 742.9
       vascular (*see also* Lesion, cerebrovascular) 437.9

Lesion(s) — *continued*
    brain — *continued*
       vascular (*see also* Lesion, cerebrovascular) — *continued*
          degenerative 437.1
          healed or old without residuals V12.54
          hypertensive 437.2
          late effect — *see* Late effect(s) (of) cerebrovascular disease
    buccal 528.9
    calcified — *see* Calcification
    canthus 373.9
    carate — *see* Pinta, lesions
    cardia 537.89
    cardiac — *see also* Disease, heart
       congenital 746.9
       valvular — *see* Endocarditis
    cauda equina 344.60
       with neurogenic bladder 344.61
    cecum 569.89
    cerebral — *see* Lesion, brain
    cerebrovascular (*see also* Disease, cerebrovascular NEC) 437.9
       degenerative 437.1
       healed or old without residuals V12.54
       hypertensive 437.2
       specified type NEC 437.8
    cervical root (nerve) NEC 353.2
    chiasmal 377.54
       associated with
          inflammatory disorders 377.54
          neoplasm NEC 377.52
          pituitary 377.51
          pituitary disorders 377.51
          vascular disorders 377.53
    chorda tympani 351.8
    coin, lung 793.1
    colon 569.89
    congenital — *see* Anomaly
    conjunctiva 372.9
    coronary artery (*see also* Ischemia, heart) 414.9
    cranial nerve 352.9
       first 352.0
       second 377.49
       third
          partial 378.51
          total 378.52
       fourth 378.53
       fifth 350.9
       sixth 378.54
       seventh 351.9
       eighth 388.5
       ninth 352.2
       tenth 352.3
       eleventh 352.4
       twelfth 352.5
    cystic — *see* Cyst
    degenerative — *see* Degeneration
    dermal (skin) 709.9
    Dieulafoy (hemorrhagic)
       of
          duodenum 537.84
          intestine 569.86
          stomach 537.84
    duodenum 537.89
       with obstruction 537.3
    eyelid 373.9
    gasserian ganglion 350.8
    gastric 537.89
    gastroduodenal 537.89
    gastrointestinal 569.89
    glossopharyngeal nerve 352.2
    heart (organic) (*see also* Disease, heart)
       vascular — *see* Disease, cardiovascular
    helix (ear) 709.9
    high grade myelodysplastic syndrome 238.73
    hyperchromic, due to pinta (carate) 103.1
    hyperkeratotic (*see also* Hyperkeratosis) 701.1
    hypoglossal nerve 352.5
    hypopharynx 478.29
    hypothalamic 253.9
    ileocecal coil 569.89
    ileum 569.89
    iliohypogastric nerve 355.79
    ilioinguinal nerve 355.79
    in continuity — *see* Injury, nerve, by site

☑ Additional Digit Required — Refer to the Tabular List for Digit Selection   ▶◀ Revised Text   ● New Line   ▲ Revised Code   ▼ Subterms under main terms may continue to next column or page

168 — Volume 2 • October 2009   2010 ICD-9-CM

Lesion(s) — *continued*
  inflammatory — *see* Inflammation
  intestine 569.89
  intracerebral — *see* Lesion, brain
  intrachiasmal (optic) (*see also* Lesion, chiasmal)
    377.54
  intracranial, space-occupying NEC 784.2
  joint 719.90
    ankle 719.97
    elbow 719.92
    foot 719.97
    hand 719.94
    hip 719.95
    knee 719.96
    multiple sites·719.99
    pelvic region 719.95
    sacroiliac (old) 724.6
    shoulder (region) 719.91
    specified site NEC 719.98
    wrist 719.93
  keratotic (*see also* Keratosis) 701.1
  kidney (*see also* Disease, renal) 593.9
  laryngeal nerve (recurrent) 352.3
  leonine 030.0
  lip 528.5
  liver 573.8
  low grade myelodysplastic syndrome 238.72
  lumbosacral
    plexus 353.1
    root (nerve) NEC 353.4
  lung 518.89
    coin 793.1
  maxillary sinus 473.0
  mitral — *see* Endocarditis, mitral
  Morel Lavallée — *see* Hematoma, by site ●
  motor cortex 348.89 ▲
  nerve (*see also* Disorder, nerve) 355.9
  nervous system 349.9
    congenital 742.9
  nonallopathic NEC 739.9
    in region (of)
      abdomen 739.9
      acromioclavicular 739.7
      cervical, cervicothoracic 739.1
      costochondral 739.8
      costovertebral 739.8
      extremity
        lower 739.6
        upper 739.7
      head 739.0
      hip 739.5
      lower extremity 739.6
      lumbar, lumbosacral 739.3
      occipitocervical 739.0
      pelvic 739.5
      pubic 739.5
      rib cage 739.8
      sacral, sacrococcygeal, sacroiliac 739.4
      sternochondral 739.8
      sternoclavicular 739.7
      thoracic, thoracolumbar 739.2
      upper extremity 739.7
  nose (internal) 478.19
  obstructive — *see* Obstruction
  obturator nerve 355.79
  occlusive
    artery — *see* Embolism, artery
  organ or site NEC — *see* Disease, by site
  osteolytic 733.90
  paramacular, of retina 363.32
  peptic 537.89
  periodontal, due to traumatic occlusion 523.8
  perirectal 569.49
  peritoneum (granulomatous) 568.89
  pigmented (skin) 709.00
  pinta — *see* Pinta, lesions
  polypoid — *see* Polyp
  prechiasmal (optic) (*see also* Lesion, chiasmal)
    377.54
  primary (*see also* Syphilis, primary)
    carate 103.0
    pinta 103.0
    yaws 102.0
  pulmonary 518.89
    valve (*see also* Endocarditis, pulmonary)
      424.3

Lesion(s) — *continued*
  pylorus 537.89
  radiation NEC 990
  radium NEC 990
  rectosigmoid 569.89
  retina, retinal (*see also* Retinopathy)
    vascular 362.17
  retroperitoneal 568.89
  romanus 720.1
  sacroiliac (joint) 724.6
  salivary gland 527.8
    benign lymphoepithelial 527.8
  saphenous nerve 355.79
  secondary — *see* Syphilis, secondary
  sigmoid 569.89
  sinus (accessory) (nasal) (*see also* Sinusitis)
    473.9
  skin 709.9
    suppurative 686.00
  SLAP (superior glenoid labrum) 840.7
  space-occupying, intracranial NEC 784.2
  spinal cord 336.9
    congenital 742.9
    traumatic (complete) (incomplete) (trans-
      verse) (*see also* Injury, spinal, by
      site)
      with
        broken
          back — *see* Fracture, vertebra,
            by site, with spinal cord
            injury
          neck — *see* Fracture, vertebra,
            cervical, with spinal cord
            injury
        fracture, vertebra — *see* Fracture,
          vertebra, by site, with spinal
          cord injury
  spleen 289.50
  stomach 537.89
  superior glenoid labrum (SLAP) 840.7
  syphilitic — *see* Syphilis
  tertiary — *see* Syphilis, tertiary
  thoracic root (nerve) 353.3
  tonsillar fossa 474.9
  tooth, teeth 525.8
    white spot 521.01
  traumatic NEC (*see also* nature and site of in-
    jury) 959.9
  tricuspid (valve) — *see* Endocarditis, tricuspid
  trigeminal nerve 350.9
  ulcerated or ulcerative — *see* Ulcer
  uterus NEC 621.9
  vagina 623.8
  vagus nerve 352.3
  valvular — *see* Endocarditis
  vascular 459.9
    affecting central nervous system (*see also*
      Lesion, cerebrovascular) 437.9
    following trauma (*see also* Injury, blood
      vessel, by site) 904.9
    retina 362.17
    traumatic — *see* Injury, blood vessel, by
      site
    umbilical cord 663.6 ☑
      affecting fetus or newborn 762.6
  visual
    cortex NEC (*see also* Disorder, visual, cortex)
      377.73
    pathway NEC (*see also* Disorder, visual,
      pathway) 377.63
  warty — *see* Verruca
  white spot, on teeth 521.01
  x-ray NEC 990
Lethargic — *see* condition
Lethargy 780.79
Letterer-Siwe disease (acute histiocytosis X)
    (M9722/3) 202.5 ☑
Leucinosis 270.3
Leucocoria 360.44
Leucosarcoma (M9850/3) 207.8 ☑
Leukasmus 270.2

Leukemia, leukemic (congenital) (M9800/3)
    208.9 ☑

*Note – Use the following fifth-digit subclas-
sification for categories 203–208:*

0	*without mention of having*
	achieved remission
	failed remission
1	*with remission*
2	*in relapse*

  acute NEC (M9801/3) 208.0 ☑
  aleukemic NEC (M9804/3) 208.8 ☑
    granulocytic (M9864/3) 205.8 ☑
  basophilic (M9870/3) 205.1 ☑
  blast (cell) (M9801/3) 208.0 ☑
  blastic (M9801/3) 208.0 ☑
    granulocytic (M9861/3) 205.0 ☑
  chronic NEC (M9803/3) 208.1 ☑
  compound (M9810/3) 207.8 ☑
  eosinophilic (M9880/3) 205.1 ☑
  giant cell (M9910/3) 207.2 ☑
  granulocytic (M9860/3) 205.9 ☑
    acute (M9861/3) 205.0 ☑
    aleukemic (M9864/3) 205.8 ☑
    blastic (M9861/3) 205.0 ☑
    chronic (M9863/3) 205.1 ☑
    subacute (M9862/3) 205.2 ☑
    subleukemic (M9864/3) 205.8 ☑
  hairy cell (M9940/3) 202.4 ☑
  hemoblastic (M9801/3) 208.0 ☑
  histiocytic (M9890/3) 206.9 ☑
  lymphatic (M9820/3) 204.9 ☑
    acute (M9821/3) 204.0 ☑
    aleukemic (M9824/3) 204.8 ☑
    chronic (M9823/3) 204.1 ☑
    subacute (M9822/3) 204.2 ☑
    subleukemic (M9824/3) 204.8 ☑
  lymphoblastic (M9821/3) 204.0 ☑
  lymphocytic (M9820/3) 204.9 ☑
    acute (M9821/3) 204.0 ☑
    aleukemic (M9824/3) 204.8 ☑
    chronic (M9823/3) 204.1 ☑
    granular   ●
      large T-cell 204.8 ☑   ●
    subacute (M9822/3) 204.2 ☑
    subleukemic (M9824/3) 204.8 ☑
  lymphogenous (M9820/3) — *see* Leukemia,
    lymphoid
  lymphoid (M9820/3) 204.9 ☑
    acute (M9821/3) 204.0 ☑
    aleukemic (M9824/3) 204.8 ☑
    blastic (M9821/3) 204.0 ☑
    chronic (M9823/3) 204.1 ☑
    subacute (M9822/3) 204.2 ☑
    subleukemic (M9824/3) 204.8 ☑
  lymphosarcoma cell (M9850/3) 207.8 ☑
  mast cell (M9900/3) 207.8 ☑
  megakaryocytic (M9910/3) 207.2 ☑
  megakaryocytoid (M9910/3) 207.2 ☑
  mixed (cell) (M9810/3) 207.8 ☑
  monoblastic (M9891/3) 206.0 ☑
  monocytic (Schilling-type) (M9890/3) 206.9 ☑
    acute (M9891/3) 206.0 ☑
    aleukemic (M9894/3) 206.8 ☑
    chronic (M9893/3) 206.1 ☑
    Naegeli-type (M9863/3) 205.1 ☑
    subacute (M9892/3) 206.2 ☑
    subleukemic (M9894/3) 206.8 ☑
  monocytoid (M9890/3) 206.9 ☑
    acute (M9891/3) 206.0 ☑
    aleukemic (M9894/3) 206.8 ☑
    chronic (M9893/3) 206.1 ☑
    myelogenous (M9863/3) 205.1 ☑
    subacute (M9892/3) 206.2 ☑
    subleukemic (M9894/3) 206.8 ☑
  monomyelocytic (M9860/3) — *see* Leukemia,
    myelomonocytic
  myeloblastic (M9861/3) 205.0 ☑
  myelocytic (M9863/3) 205.1 ☑
    acute (M9861/3) 205.0 ☑
  myelogenous (M9860/3) 205.9 ☑
    acute (M9861/3) 205.0 ☑

Leukemia, leukemic — *continued*
  myelogenous — *continued*
    aleukemic (M9864/3) 205.8 ☑
    chronic (M9863/3) 205.1 ☑
    monocytoid (M9863/3) 205.1 ☑
    subacute (M9862/3) 205.2 ☑
    subleukemic (M9864) 205.8 ☑
  myeloid (M9860/3) 205.9 ☑
    acute (M9861/3) 205.0 ☑
    aleukemic (M9864/3) 205.8 ☑
    chronic (M9863/3) 205.1 ☑
    subacute (M9862/3) 205.2 ☑
    subleukemic (M9864/3) 205.8 ☑
  myelomonocytic (M9860/3) 205.9 ☑
    acute (M9861/3) 205.0 ☑
    chronic (M9863/3) 205.1 ☑
  Naegeli-type monocytic (M9863/3) 205.1 ☑
  neutrophilic (M9865/3) 205.1 ☑
  plasma cell (M9830/3) 203.1 ☑
  plasmacytic (M9830/3) 203.1 ☑
  prolymphocytic (M9825/3) — *see* Leukemia,
    lymphoid
  promyelocytic, acute (M9866/3) 205.0 ☑
  Schilling-type monocytic (M9890/3) — *see*
    Leukemia, monocytic
  stem cell (M9801/3) 208.0 ☑
  subacute NEC (M9802/3) 208.2 ☑
  subleukemic NEC (M9804/3) 208.8 ☑
  thrombocytic (M9910/3) 207.2 ☑
  undifferentiated (M9801/3) 208.0 ☑
Leukemoid reaction (basophilic) (lymphocytic)
    (monocytic) (myelocytic) (neutrophilic)
    288.62
Leukoaraiosis (hypertensive) 437.1   ●
Leukoariosis — *see* Leukoaraiosis   ●
Leukoclastic vasculitis 446.29
Leukocoria 360.44
Leukocythemia — *see* Leukemia
Leukocytopenia 288.50
Leukocytosis 288.60
  basophilic 288.8
  eosinophilic 288.3
  lymphocytic 288.8
  monocytic 288.8
  neutrophilic 288.8
Leukoderma 709.09
  syphilitic 091.3
    late 095.8
Leukodermia — *see also* Leukoderma 709.09
Leukodystrophy (cerebral) (globoid cell)
    (metachromatic) (progressive) (su-
    danophilic) 330.0
Leukoedema, mouth or tongue 528.79
Leukoencephalitis
  acute hemorrhagic (postinfectious) NEC
    136.9 [323.61]
    postimmunization or postvaccinal 323.51
  subacute sclerosing 046.2
    van Bogaert's 046.2
    van Bogaert's (sclerosing) 046.2
Leukoencephalopathy — *see also* Encephalitis
    323.9
  acute necrotizing hemorrhagic (postinfectious)
    136.9 [323.61]
    postimmunization or postvaccinal 323.51
  Binswanger's 290.12   ●
  metachromatic 330.0
  multifocal (progressive) 046.3
  progressive multifocal 046.3
  reversible, posterior 348.5
Leukoerythroblastosis 289.9
Leukoerythrosis 289.0
Leukokeratosis — *see also* Leukoplakia 702.8
  mouth 528.6
  nicotina palati 528.79
  tongue 528.6
Leukokoria 360.44
Leukokraurosis vulva, vulvae 624.09
Leukolymphosarcoma (M9850/3) 207.8 ☑
Leukoma (cornea) (interfering with central vision)
    371.03
  adherent 371.04
Leukomalacia, periventricular 779.7
Leukomelanopathy, hereditary 288.2
Leukonychia (punctata) (striata) 703.8

Lesion(s) — Leukonychia

☑ Additional Digit Required — Refer to the Tabular List for Digit Selection   ▽ Subterms under main terms may continue to next column or page

2010 ICD-9-CM   ▶◀ Revised Text   ● New Line   ▲ Revised Code   **October 2009 • Volume 2 — 169**

Leukonychia — continued
congenital 757.5
Leukopathia
unguium 703.8
congenital 757.5
Leukopenia 288.50
basophilic 288.59
cyclic 288.02
eosinophilic 288.59
familial 288.59
malignant (see also Agranulocytosis) 288.09
periodic 288.02
transitory neonatal 776.7
Leukopenic — see condition
Leukoplakia 702.8
anus 569.49
bladder (postinfectional) 596.8
buccal 528.6
cervix (uteri) 622.2
esophagus 530.83
gingiva 528.6
kidney (pelvis) 593.89
larynx 478.79
lip 528.6
mouth 528.6
oral soft tissue (including tongue) (mucosa) 528.6
palate 528.6
pelvis (kidney) 593.89
penis (infectional) 607.0
rectum 569.49
syphilitic 095.8
tongue 528.6
tonsil 478.29
ureter (postinfectional) 593.89
urethra (postinfectional) 599.84
uterus 621.8
vagina 623.1
vesical 596.8
vocal cords 478.5
vulva 624.09
Leukopolioencephalopathy 330.0
Leukorrhea (vagina) 623.5
due to trichomonas (vaginalis) 131.00
trichomonal (Trichomonas vaginalis) 131.00
Leukosarcoma (M9850/3) 207.8 ☑
Leukosis (M9800/3) — see Leukemia
Lev's disease or syndrome (acquired complete heart block) 426.0
Levi's syndrome (pituitary dwarfism) 253.3
Levocardia (isolated) 746.87
with situs inversus 759.3
Levulosuria 271.2
Lewandowski's disease (primary) — see also Tuberculosis 017.0 ☑
Lewandowski-Lutz disease (epidermodysplasia verruciformis) 078.19
Lewy body dementia 331.82
Lewy body disease 331.82
Leyden's disease (periodic vomiting) 536.2
Leyden-Möbius dystrophy 359.1
Leydig cell
carcinoma (M8650/3)
specified site — see Neoplasm, by site, malignant
unspecified site
female 183.0
male 186.9
tumor (M8650/1)
benign (M8650/0)
specified site — see Neoplasm, by site, benign
unspecified site
female 220
male 222.0
malignant (M8650/3)
specified site — see Neoplasm, by site, malignant
unspecified site
female 183.0
male 186.9
specified site — see Neoplasm, by site, uncertain behavior
unspecified site
female 236.2
male 236.4

Leydig-Sertoli cell tumor (M8631/0)
specified site — see Neoplasm, by site, benign
unspecified site
female 220
male 222.0
LGSIL (low grade squamous intraepithelial lesion)
anus 796.73
cervix 795.03
vagina 795.13
Liar, pathologic 301.7
Libman-Sacks disease or syndrome 710.0 [424.91]
Lice (infestation) 132.9
body (pediculus corporis) 132.1
crab 132.2
head (pediculus capitis) 132.0
mixed (classifiable to more than one of the categories 132.0–132.2) 132.3
pubic (pediculus pubis) 132.2
Lichen 697.9
albus 701.0
annularis 695.89
atrophicus 701.0
corneus obtusus 698.3
myxedematous 701.8
nitidus 697.1
pilaris 757.39
acquired 701.1
planopilaris 697.0
planus (acute) (chronicus) (hypertrophic) (verrucous) 697.0
morphoeicus 701.0
sclerosus (et atrophicus) 701.0
ruber 696.4
acuminatus 696.4
moniliformis 697.8
obtusus corneus 698.3
of Wilson 697.0
planus 697.0
sclerosus (et atrophicus) 701.0
scrofulosus (primary) (see also Tuberculosis) 017.0 ☑
simplex (Vidal's) 698.3
chronicus 698.3
circumscriptus 698.3
spinulosus 757.39
mycotic 117.9
striata 697.8
urticatus 698.2
Lichenification 698.3
nodular 698.3
Lichenoides tuberculosis (primary) — see also Tuberculosis 017.0 ☑
Lichtheim's disease or syndrome (subacute combined sclerosis with pernicious anemia) 281.0 [336.2]
Lien migrans 289.59
Lientery — see also Diarrhea 787.91
infectious 009.2
Life circumstance problem NEC V62.89
Li-Fraumeni cancer syndrome V84.01
Ligament — see condition
Light-for-dates (infant) 764.0 ☑
with signs of fetal malnutrition 764.1 ☑
affecting management of pregnancy 656.5 ☑
Light-headedness 780.4
Lightning (effects) (shock) (stroke) (struck by) 994.0
burn — see Burn, by site
foot 266.2
Lightwood's disease or syndrome (renal tubular acidosis) 588.89
Lignac's disease (cystinosis) 270.0
Lignac (-Fanconi) syndrome (cystinosis) 270.0
Lignac (-de Toni) (-Fanconi) (-Debré) syndrome (cystinosis) 270.0
Ligneous thyroiditis 245.3
Likoff's syndrome (angina in menopausal women) 413.9
Limb — see condition
Limitation of joint motion — see also Stiffness, joint 719.5 ☑
sacroiliac 724.6
Limit dextrinosis 271.0
Limited
cardiac reserve — see Disease, heart

Limited — continued
duction, eye NEC 378.63
mandibular range of motion 524.52
Lindau (-von Hippel) disease (angiomatosis retinocerebellosa) 759.6
Lindau's disease (retinocerebral angiomatosis) 759.6
Linea corneae senilis 371.41
Lines
Beau's (transverse furrows on fingernails) 703.8
Harris' 733.91
Hudson-Stähli 371.11
Stähli's 371.11
Lingua
geographical 529.1
nigra (villosa) 529.3
plicata 529.5
congenital 750.13
tylosis 528.6
Lingual (tongue) — see also condition
thyroid 759.2
Linitis (gastric) 535.4 ☑
plastica (M8142/3) 151.9
Lioderma essentialis (cum melanosis et telangiectasia) 757.33
Lip — see also condition
biting 528.9
Lipalgia 272.8
Lipedema — see Edema
Lipemia — see also Hyperlipidemia 272.4
retina, retinalis 272.3
Lipidosis 272.7
cephalin 272.7
cerebral (infantile) (juvenile) (late) 330.1
cerebroretinal 330.1 [362.71]
cerebroside 272.7
cerebrospinal 272.7
chemically-induced 272.7
cholesterol 272.7
diabetic 250.8 ☑ [272.7]
due to secondary diabetes 249.8 ☑ [272.7]
dystopic (hereditary) 272.7
glycolipid 272.7
hepatosplenomegalic 272.3
hereditary, dystopic 272.7
sulfatide 330.0
Lipoadenoma (M8324/0) — see Neoplasm, by site, benign
Lipoblastoma (M8881/0) — see Lipoma, by site
Lipoblastomatosis (M8881/0) — see Lipoma, by site
Lipochondrodystrophy 277.5
Lipochrome histiocytosis (familial) 288.1
Lipodystrophia progressiva 272.6
Lipodystrophy (progressive) 272.6
insulin 272.6
intestinal 040.2
mesenteric 567.82
Lipofibroma (M8851/0) — see Lipoma, by site
Lipoglycoproteinosis 272.8
Lipogranuloma, sclerosing 709.8
Lipogranulomatosis (disseminated) 272.8
kidney 272.8
Lipoid — see also condition
histiocytosis 272.7
essential 272.7
nephrosis (see also Nephrosis) 581.3
proteinosis of Urbach 272.8
Lipoidemia — see also Hyperlipidemia 272.4
Lipoidosis — see also Lipidosis 272.7
Lipoma (M8850/0) 214.9
breast (skin) 214.1
face 214.0
fetal (M8881/0) (see also Lipoma, by site)
fat cell (M8880/0) — see Lipoma, by site
infiltrating (M8856/0) — see Lipoma, by site
intra-abdominal 214.3
intramuscular (M8856/0) — see Lipoma, by site
intrathoracic 214.2
kidney 214.3
mediastinum 214.2
muscle 214.8
peritoneum 214.3
retroperitoneum 214.3
skin 214.1

Lipoma — continued
skin — continued
face 214.0
spermatic cord 214.4
spindle cell (M8857/0) — see Lipoma, by site
stomach 214.3
subcutaneous tissue 214.1
face 214.0
thymus 214.2
thyroid gland 214.2
Lipomatosis (dolorosa) 272.8
epidural 214.8
fetal (M8881/0) — see Lipoma, by site
Launois-Bensaude's 272.8
Lipomyohemangioma (M8860/0)
specified site — see Neoplasm, connective tissue, benign
unspecified site 223.0
Lipomyoma (M8860/0)
specified site — see Neoplasm, connective tissue, benign
unspecified site 223.0
Lipomyxoma (M8852/0) — see Lipoma, by site
Lipomyxosarcoma (M8852/3) — see Neoplasm, connective tissue, malignant
Lipophagocytosis 289.89
Lipoproteinemia (alpha) 272.4
broad-beta 272.2
floating-beta 272.2
hyper-pre-beta 272.1
Lipoproteinosis (Rössle-Urbach-Wiethe) 272.8
Liposarcoma (M8850/3) — see also Neoplasm, connective tissue, malignant
differentiated type (M8851/3) — see Neoplasm, connective tissue, malignant
embryonal (M8852/3) — see Neoplasm, connective tissue, malignant
mixed type (M8855/3) — see Neoplasm, connective tissue, malignant
myxoid (M8852/3) — see Neoplasm, connective tissue, malignant
pleomorphic (M8854/3) — see Neoplasm, connective tissue, malignant
round cell (M8853/3) — see Neoplasm, connective tissue, malignant
well differentiated type (M8851/3) — see Neoplasm, connective tissue, malignant
Liposynovitis prepatellaris 272.8
Lipping
cervix 622.0
spine (see also Spondylosis) 721.90
vertebra (see also Spondylosis) 721.90
Lip pits (mucus), congenital 750.25
Lipschütz disease or ulcer 616.50
Lipuria 791.1
bilharziasis 120.0
Liquefaction, vitreous humor 379.21
Lisping 307.9
Lissauer's paralysis 094.1
Lissencephalia, lissencephaly 742.2
Listerellose 027.0
Listeriose 027.0
Listeriosis 027.0
congenital 771.2
fetal 771.2
suspected fetal damage affecting management of pregnancy 655.4 ☑
Listlessness 780.79
Lithemia 790.6
Lithiasis — see also Calculus
hepatic (duct) — see Choledocholithiasis
urinary 592.9
Lithopedion 779.9
affecting management of pregnancy 656.8 ☑
Lithosis (occupational) 502
with tuberculosis — see Tuberculosis, pulmonary
Lithuria 791.9
Litigation V62.5
Little
league elbow 718.82
stroke syndrome 435.9
Little's disease — see Palsy, cerebral
Littre's
gland — see condition

☑ Additional Digit Required — Refer to the Tabular List for Digit Selection   ᵂ Subterms under main terms may continue to next column or page

170 — Volume 2   ▶◀ Revised Text   ● New Line   ▲ Revised Code   2010 ICD-9-CM

Littre's — *continued*
hernia — *see* Hernia, Littre's
Littritis — *see also* Urethritis 597.89
Livedo 782.61
annularis 782.61
racemose 782.61
reticularis 782.61
Live flesh 781.0
Liver — *see also* condition
donor V59.6
Livida, asphyxia
newborn 768.6
Living
alone V60.3
with handicapped person V60.4
Lloyd's syndrome 258.1
Loa loa 125.2
Loasis 125.2
Lobe, lobar — *see* condition
Lobo's disease or blastomycosis 116.2
Lobomycosis 116.2
Lobotomy syndrome 310.0
Lobstein's disease (brittle bones and blue sclera) 756.51
Lobster-claw hand 755.58
Lobulation (congenital) — *see also* Anomaly, specified type NEC, by site
kidney, fetal 753.3
liver, abnormal 751.69
spleen 759.0
Lobule, lobular — *see* condition
Local, localized — *see* condition
Locked bowel or intestine — *see also* Obstruction, intestine 560.9
Locked-in state 344.81
Locked twins 660.5 ☑
affecting fetus or newborn 763.1
Locking
joint (*see also* Derangement, joint) 718.90
knee 717.9
Lockjaw — *see also* Tetanus 037
Locomotor ataxia (progressive) 094.0
Löffler's
endocarditis 421.0
eosinophilia or syndrome 518.3
pneumonia 518.3
syndrome (eosinophilic pneumonitis) 518.3
Löfgren's syndrome (sarcoidosis) 135
Loiasis 125.2
eyelid 125.2 [373.6]
Loneliness V62.89
Lone star fever 082.8
Longitudinal stripes or grooves, nails 703.8
congenital 757.5
Long labor 662.1 ☑
affecting fetus or newborn 763.89
first stage 662.0 ☑
second stage 662.2 ☑
Long-term (current) **drug use** V58.69
antibiotics V58.62
anticoagulants V58.61
anti-inflammatories, non-steroidal (NSAID) V58.64
antiplatelets/antithrombotics V58.63
aspirin V58.66
high-risk medications NEC V58.69
insulin V58.67
methadone V58.69
opiate analgesic V58.69
pain killers V58.69
anti-inflammatories, non-steroidal (NSAID) V58.64
aspirin V58.66
steroids V58.65
tamoxifen V07.51   ▲
Loop
intestine (*see also* Volvulus) 560.2
intrascleral nerve 379.29
vascular on papilla (optic) 743.57
Loose — *see also* condition
body
in tendon sheath 727.82
joint 718.10
ankle 718.17
elbow 718.12
foot 718.17

Loose — *see also* condition — *continued*
body — *continued*
joint — *continued*
hand 718.14
hip 718.15
knee 717.6
multiple sites 718.19
pelvic region 718.15
prosthetic implant — *see* Complications, mechanical
shoulder (region) 718.11
specified site NEC 718.18
wrist 718.13
cartilage (joint) (*see also* Loose, body, joint) 718.1 ☑
knee 717.6
facet (vertebral) 724.9
prosthetic implant — *see* Complications, mechanical
sesamoid, joint (*see also* Loose, body, joint) 718.1 ☑
tooth, teeth 525.8
Loosening epiphysis 732.9
Looser (-Debray) -Milkman syndrome (osteomalacia with pseudofractures) 268.2
Lop ear (deformity) 744.29
Lorain's disease or syndrome (pituitary dwarfism) 253.3
Lorain-Levi syndrome (pituitary dwarfism) 253.3
Lordosis (acquired) (postural) 737.20
congenital 754.2
due to or associated with
Charcôt-Marie-Tooth disease 356.1 [737.42]
mucopolysaccharidosis 277.5 [737.42]
neurofibromatosis 237.71 [737.42]
osteitis
deformans 731.0 [737.42]
fibrosa cystica 252.01 [737.42]
osteoporosis (*see also* Osteoporosis) 733.00 [737.42]
poliomyelitis (*see also* Poliomyelitis) 138 [737.42]
tuberculosis (*see also* Tuberculosis) 015.0 ☑ [737.42]
late effect of rickets 268.1 [737.42]
postlaminectomy 737.21
postsurgical NEC 737.22
rachitic 268.1 [737.42]
specified NEC 737.29
tuberculous (*see also* Tuberculosis) 015.0 ☑ [737.42]
Loss
appetite 783.0
hysterical 300.11
nonorganic origin 307.59
psychogenic 307.59
blood — *see* Hemorrhage
central vision 368.41
consciousness 780.09
transient 780.2
control, sphincter, rectum 787.6
nonorganic origin 307.7
ear ossicle, partial 385.24
elasticity, skin 782.8
extremity or member, traumatic, current — *see* Amputation, traumatic
fluid (acute) 276.50
with
hypernatremia 276.0
hyponatremia 276.1
fetus or newborn 775.5
hair 704.00
hearing (*see also* Deafness)
central 389.14
conductive (air) 389.00
with sensorineural hearing loss 389.20
bilateral 389.22
unilateral 389.21
bilateral 389.06
combined types 389.08
external ear 389.01
inner ear 389.04
middle ear 389.03
multiple types 389.08
tympanic membrane 389.02
unilateral 389.05

Loss — *continued*
hearing (*see also* Deafness) — *continued*
mixed conductive and sensorineural 389.20
bilateral 389.22
unilateral 389.21
mixed type 389.20
bilateral 389.22
unilateral 389.21
nerve
bilateral 389.12
unilateral 389.13
neural
bilateral 389.12
unilateral 389.13
noise-induced 388.12
perceptive NEC (*see also* Loss, hearing, sensorineural) 389.10
sensorineural 389.10
with conductive hearing loss 389.20
bilateral 389.22
unilateral 389.21
asymmetrical 389.16
bilateral 389.18
central 389.14
neural 389.12
bilateral 389.12
unilateral 389.13
sensory
bilateral 389.11
unilateral 389.17
unilateral 389.15
sensory
bilateral 389.11
unilateral 389.17
specified type NEC 389.8
sudden NEC 388.2
height 781.91
labyrinthine reactivity (unilateral) 386.55
bilateral 386.56
memory (*see also* Amnesia) 780.93
mild, following organic brain damage 310.8   ▲
mind (*see also* Psychosis) 298.9
occlusal vertical dimension 524.37
organ or part — *see* Absence, by site, acquired
sensation 782.0
sense of
smell (*see also* Disturbance, sensation) 781.1
taste (*see also* Disturbance, sensation) 781.1
touch (*see also* Disturbance, sensation) 781.1
sight (acquired) (complete) (congenital) — *see* Blindness
spinal fluid
headache 349.0
substance of
bone (*see also* Osteoporosis) 733.00
cartilage 733.99
ear 380.32
vitreous (humor) 379.26
tooth, teeth
acquired 525.10
due to
caries 525.13
extraction 525.10
periodontal disease 525.12
specified NEC 525.19
trauma 525.11
vision, visual (*see also* Blindness) 369.9
both eyes (*see also* Blindness, both eyes) 369.3
complete (*see also* Blindness, both eyes) 369.00
one eye 369.8
sudden 368.11
transient 368.12
vitreous 379.26
voice (*see also* Aphonia) 784.41
weight (cause unknown) 783.21
Lou Gehrig's disease 335.20
Louis-Bar syndrome (ataxia-telangiectasia) 334.8
Louping ill 063.1
Lousiness — *see* Lice

Low
back syndrome 724.2
basal metabolic rate (BMR) 794.7
birthweight 765.1 ☑
extreme (less than 1000 grams) 765.0 ☑
for gestational age 764.0 ☑
status (*see also* Status, low birth weight) V21.30
bladder compliance 596.52
blood pressure (*see also* Hypotension) 458.9
reading (incidental) (isolated) (nonspecific) 796.3
cardiac reserve — *see* Disease, heart
compliance bladder 596.52
frequency deafness — *see* Disorder, hearing
function (*see also* Hypofunction)
kidney (*see also* Disease, renal) 593.9
liver 573.9
hemoglobin 285.9
implantation, placenta — *see* Placenta, previa
insertion, placenta — *see* Placenta, previa
lying
kidney 593.0
organ or site, congenital — *see* Malposition, congenital
placenta — *see* Placenta, previa
output syndrome (cardiac) (*see also* Failure, heart) 428.9
platelets (blood) (*see also* Thrombocytopenia) 287.5
reserve, kidney (*see also* Disease, renal) 593.9
risk
human papillomavirus (HPA) DNA test positive
anal 796.79
cervical 795.09
vaginal 795.19
salt syndrome 593.9
tension glaucoma 365.12
vision 369.9
both eyes 369.20
one eye 369.70
Lower extremity — *see* condition
Lowe (-Terrey-MacLachlan) syndrome (oculocerebrorenal dystrophy) 270.8
Lown (-Ganong) -Levine syndrome (short P-R interval, normal QRS complex, and paroxysmal supraventricular tachycardia) 426.81
LSD reaction — *see also* Abuse, drugs, nondependent 305.3 ☑
L-shaped kidney 753.3
Lucas-Championnière disease (fibrinous bronchitis) 466.0
Lucey-Driscoll syndrome (jaundice due to delayed conjugation) 774.30
Ludwig's
angina 528.3
disease (submaxillary cellulitis) 528.3
Lues (venerea), **luetic** — *see* Syphilis
Luetscher's syndrome (dehydration) 276.51
Lumbago 724.2
due to displacement, intervertebral disc 722.10
Lumbalgia 724.2
due to displacement, intervertebral disc 722.10
Lumbar — *see* condition
Lumbarization, vertebra 756.15
Lumbermen's itch 133.8
Lump — *see also* Mass
abdominal 789.3 ☑
breast 611.72
chest 786.6
epigastric 789.3 ☑
head 784.2
kidney 753.3
liver 789.1
lung 786.6
mediastinal 786.6
neck 784.2
nose or sinus 784.2
pelvic 789.3 ☑
skin 782.2
substernal 786.6
throat 784.2
umbilicus 789.3 ☑
Lunacy — *see also* Psychosis 298.9
Lunatomalacia 732.3

☑ Additional Digit Required — Refer to the Tabular List for Digit Selection   ▧ Subterms under main terms may continue to next column or page

2010 ICD-9-CM   ▶◀ Revised Text   ● New Line   ▲ Revised Code   **October 2009 • Volume 2 — 171**

Lung — see also condition
- donor V59.8
- drug addict's 417.8
- mainliners' 417.8
- vanishing 492.0

Lupoid (miliary) **of Boeck** 135

Lupus 710.0
- anticoagulant 289.81
- Cazenave's (erythematosus) 695.4
- discoid (local) 695.4
- disseminated 710.0
- erythematodes (discoid) (local) 695.4
- erythematosus (discoid) (local) 695.4
    - disseminated 710.0
    - eyelid 373.34
    - systemic 710.0
        - with
            - encephalitis 710.0 [323.81]
            - lung involvement 710.0 [517.8]
        - inhibitor (presence of) 286.5
- exedens 017.0 ☑
- eyelid (see also Tuberculosis) 017.0 ☑ [373.4]
- Hilliard's 017.0 ☑
- hydralazine
    - correct substance properly administered 695.4
    - overdose or wrong substance given or taken 972.6
- miliaris disseminatus faciei 017.0 ☑
- nephritis 710.0 [583.81]
    - acute 710.0 [580.81]
    - chronic 710.0 [582.81]
- nontuberculous, not disseminated 695.4
- pernio (Besnier) 135
- tuberculous (see also Tuberculosis) 017.0 ☑
    - eyelid (see also Tuberculosis) 017.0 ☑ [373.4]
- vulgaris 017.0 ☑

Luschka's joint disease 721.90

Luteinoma (M8610/0) 220

Lutembacher's disease or syndrome (atrial septal defect with mitral stenosis) 745.5

Luteoma (M8610/0) 220

Lutz-Miescher disease (elastosis perforans serpiginosa) 701.1

Lutz-Splendore-de Almeida disease (Brazilian blastomycosis) 116.1

Luxatio
- bulbi due to birth injury 767.8
- coxae congenita (see also Dislocation, hip, congenital) 754.30
- erecta — see Dislocation, shoulder
- imperfecta — see Sprain, by site
- perinealis — see Dislocation, hip

Luxation — see also Dislocation, by site
- eyeball 360.81
    - due to birth injury 767.8
    - lateral 376.36
- genital organs (external) NEC — see Wound, open, genital organs
- globe (eye) 360.81
    - lateral 376.36
- lacrimal gland (postinfectional) 375.16
- lens (old) (partial) 379.32
    - congenital 743.37
        - syphilitic 090.49 [379.32]
    - Marfan's disease 090.49
    - spontaneous 379.32
- penis — see Wound, open, penis
- scrotum — see Wound, open, scrotum
- testis — see Wound, open, testis

L-xyloketosuria 271.8

Lycanthropy — see also Psychosis 298.9

Lyell's disease or syndrome (toxic epidermal necrolysis) 695.15
- due to drug
    - correct substance properly administered 695.15
    - overdose or wrong substance given or taken 977.9
        - specified drug — see Table of Drugs and Chemicals

Lyme disease 088.81

Lymph
- gland or node — see condition
- scrotum (see also Infestation, filarial) 125.9

Lymphadenitis 289.3
- with
    - abortion — see Abortion, by type, with sepsis
    - ectopic pregnancy (see also categories 633.0–633.9) 639.0
    - molar pregnancy (see also categories 630–632) 639.0
- acute 683
    - mesenteric 289.2
- any site, except mesenteric 289.3
    - acute 683
    - chronic 289.1
    - mesenteric (acute) (chronic) (nonspecific) (subacute) 289.2
    - subacute 289.1
        - mesenteric 289.2
- breast, puerperal, postpartum 675.2 ☑
- chancroidal (congenital) 099.0
- chronic 289.1
    - mesenteric 289.2
- dermatopathic 695.89
- due to
    - anthracosis (occupational) 500
    - Brugia (Wuchereria) malayi 125.1
    - diphtheria (toxin) 032.89
    - lymphogranuloma venereum 099.1
    - Wuchereria bancrofti 125.0
- following
    - abortion 639.0
    - ectopic or molar pregnancy 639.0
- generalized 289.3
- gonorrheal 098.89
- granulomatous 289.1
- infectional 683
- mesenteric (acute) (chronic) (nonspecific) (subacute) 289.2
    - due to Bacillus typhi 002.0
    - tuberculous (see also Tuberculosis) 014.8 ☑
- mycobacterial 031.8
- purulent 683
- pyogenic 683
- regional 078.3
- septic 683
- streptococcal 683
- subacute, unspecified site 289.1
- suppurative 683
- syphilitic (early) (secondary) 091.4
    - late 095.8
- tuberculous — see Tuberculosis, lymph gland
- venereal 099.1

Lymphadenoid goiter 245.2

Lymphadenopathy (general) 785.6
- due to toxoplasmosis (acquired) 130.7
    - congenital (active) 771.2

Lymphadenopathy-associated virus (disease) (illness) (infection) — see Human immunodeficiency virus (disease) (illness) (infection)

Lymphadenosis 785.6
- acute 075

Lymphangiectasis 457.1
- conjunctiva 372.89
- postinfectional 457.1
- scrotum 457.1

Lymphangiectatic elephantiasis, nonfilarial 457.1

Lymphangioendothelioma (M9170/0) 228.1
- malignant (M9170/3) — see Neoplasm, connective tissue, malignant

Lymphangioma (M9170/0) 228.1
- capillary (M9171/0) 228.1
- cavernous (M9172/0) 228.1
- cystic (M9173/0) 228.1
- malignant (M9170/3) — see Neoplasm, connective tissue, malignant

Lymphangiomyoma (M9174/0) 228.1

Lymphangiomyomatosis (M9174/1) — see Neoplasm, connective tissue, uncertain behavior

Lymphangiosarcoma (M9170/3) — see Neoplasm, connective tissue, malignant

Lymphangitis 457.2

Lymphangitis — continued
- with
    - abortion — see Abortion, by type, with sepsis
    - abscess — see Abscess, by site
    - cellulitis — see Abscess, by site
    - ectopic pregnancy (see also categories 633.0–633.9) 639.0
    - molar pregnancy (see also categories 630–632) 639.0
- acute (with abscess or cellulitis) 682.9
    - specified site — see Abscess, by site
- breast, puerperal, postpartum 675.2 ☑
- chancroidal 099.0
- chronic (any site) 457.2
- due to
    - Brugia (Wuchereria) malayi 125.1
    - Wuchereria bancrofti 125.0
- following
    - abortion 639.0
    - ectopic or molar pregnancy 639.0
- gangrenous 457.2
- penis
    - acute 607.2
    - gonococcal (acute) 098.0
        - chronic or duration of 2 months or more 098.2
- puerperal, postpartum, childbirth 670.8 ☑ ▲
- strumous, tuberculous (see also Tuberculosis) 017.2 ☑
- subacute (any site) 457.2
- tuberculous — see Tuberculosis, lymph gland

Lymphatic (vessel) — see condition

Lymphatism 254.8
- scrofulous (see also Tuberculosis) 017.2 ☑

Lymphectasia 457.1

Lymphedema — see also Elephantiasis 457.1
- acquired (chronic) 457.1
- chronic hereditary 757.0
- congenital 757.0
- idiopathic hereditary 757.0
- praecox 457.1
- secondary 457.1
- surgical NEC 997.99
    - postmastectomy (syndrome) 457.0

Lymph-hemangioma (M9120/0) — see Hemangioma, by site

Lymphoblastic — see condition

Lymphoblastoma (diffuse) (M9630/3) 200.1 ☑
- giant follicular (M9690/3) 202.0 ☑
- macrofollicular (M9690/3) 202.0 ☑

Lymphoblastosis, acute benign 075

Lymphocele 457.8

Lymphocythemia 288.51

Lymphocytic — see also condition
- chorioencephalitis (acute) (serous) 049.0
- choriomeningitis (acute) (serous) 049.0

Lymphocytoma (diffuse) (malignant) (M9620/3) 200.1 ☑

Lymphocytomatosis (M9620/3) 200.1 ☑

Lymphocytopenia 288.51

Lymphocytosis (symptomatic) 288.61
- infectious (acute) 078.89

Lymphoepithelioma (M8082/3) — see Neoplasm, by site, malignant

Lymphogranuloma (malignant) (M9650/3) 201.9 ☑
- inguinale 099.1
- venereal (any site) 099.1
    - with stricture of rectum 099.1
- venereum 099.1

Lymphogranulomatosis (malignant) (M9650/3) 201.9 ☑
- benign (Boeck's sarcoid) (Schaumann's) 135
- Hodgkin's (M9650/3) 201.9 ☑

Lymphohistiocytosis, familial hemophagocytic 288.4

Lymphoid — see condition

Lympholeukoblastoma (M9850/3) 207.8 ☑

Lympholeukosarcoma (M9850/3) 207.8 ☑

Lymphoma (malignant) (M9590/3) 202.8 ☑

> Note — Use the following fifth-digit subclassification with categories 200–202:
>
> 0   unspecified site, extranodal and solid organ sites
>
> 1   lymph nodes of head, face, and neck
>
> 2   intrathoracic lymph nodes
>
> 3   intra–abdominal lymph nodes
>
> 4   lymph nodes of axilla and upper limb
>
> 5   lymph nodes of inguinal region and lower limb
>
> 6   intrapelvic lymph nodes
>
> 7   spleen
>
> 8   lymph nodes of multiple sites

- benign (M9590/0) — see Neoplasm, by site, benign
- Burkitt's type (lymphoblastic) (undifferentiated) (M9750/3) 200.2 ☑
- Castleman's (mediastinal lymph node hyperplasia) 785.6
- centroblastic-centrocytic
    - diffuse (M9614/3) 202.8 ☑
    - follicular (M9692/3) 202.0 ☑
- centroblastic type (diffuse) (M9632/3) 202.8 ☑
    - follicular (M9697/3) 202.0 ☑
- centrocytic (M9622/3) 202.8 ☑
- compound (M9613/3) 200.8 ☑
- convoluted cell type (lymphoblastic) (M9602/3) 202.8 ☑
- diffuse NEC (M9590/3) 202.8 ☑
    - large B cell 202.8 ☑
- follicular (giant) (M9690/3) 202.0 ☑
    - center cell (diffuse) (M9615/3) 202.8 ☑
        - cleaved (diffuse) (M9623/3) 202.8 ☑
            - follicular (M9695/3) 202.0 ☑
        - non-cleaved (diffuse) (M9633/3) 202.8 ☑
            - follicular (M9698/3) 202.0 ☑
    - centroblastic-centrocytic (M9692/3) 202.0 ☑
    - centroblastic type (M9697/3) 202.0 ☑
    - large cell 202.0 ☑ ●
    - lymphocytic
        - intermediate differentiation (M9694/3) 202.0 ☑
        - poorly differentiated (M9696/3) 202.0 ☑
    - mixed (cell type) (lymphocytic-histiocytic) (small cell and large cell) (M9691/3) 202.0 ☑
- germinocytic (M9622/3) 202.8 ☑
- giant, follicular or follicle (M9690/3) 202.0 ☑
- histiocytic (diffuse) (M9640/3) 200.0 ☑
    - nodular (M9642/3) 200.0 ☑
    - pleomorphic cell type (M9641/3) 200.0 ☑
- Hodgkin's (M9650/3) (see also Disease, Hodgkin's) 201.9 ☑
- immunoblastic (type) (M9612/3) 200.8 ☑
- large cell (M9640/3) 200.7 ☑
    - anaplastic 200.6 ☑
    - nodular (M9642/3) 202.0 ☑ ▲
    - pleomorphic cell type (M9641/3) 200.0 ☑
- lymphoblastic (diffuse) (M9630/3) 200.1 ☑
    - Burkitt's type (M9750/3) 200.2 ☑
    - convoluted cell type (M9602/3) 202.8 ☑
- lymphocytic (cell type) (diffuse) (M9620/3) 200.1 ☑
    - with plasmacytoid differentiation, diffuse (M9611/3) 200.8 ☑
    - intermediate differentiation (diffuse) (M9621/3) 200.1 ☑
        - follicular (M9694/3) 202.0 ☑
        - nodular (M9694/3) 202.0 ☑
    - nodular (M9690/3) 202.0 ☑
    - poorly differentiated (diffuse) (M9630/3) 200.1 ☑
        - follicular (M9696/3) 202.0 ☑
        - nodular (M9696/3) 202.0 ☑

☑ Additional Digit Required — Refer to the Tabular List for Digit Selection   ▽ Subterms under main terms may continue to next column or page

172 — Volume 2 · October 2009   ►◄ Revised Text   ● New Line   ▲ Revised Code   2010 ICD-9-CM

Lymphoma — *continued*
  lymphocytic — *continued*
    well differentiated (diffuse) (M9620/3)
      200.1 ✓
      follicular (M9693/3) 202.0 ✓
      nodular (M9693/3) 202.0 ✓
    lymphocytic-histiocytic, mixed (diffuse)
      (M9613/3) 200.8 ✓
      follicular (M9691/3) 202.0 ✓
      nodular (M9691/3) 202.0 ✓
    lymphoplasmacytoid type (M9611/3) 200.8 ✓
    lymphosarcoma type (M9610/3) 200.1 ✓
    macrofollicular (M9690/3) 202.0 ✓
    mantle cell 200.4 ✓
    marginal zone 200.3 ✓
      extranodal B-cell 200.3 ✓
      nodal B-cell 200.3 ✓
      splenic B-cell 200.3 ✓
    mixed cell type (diffuse) (M9613/3) 200.8 ✓
      follicular (M9691/3) 202.0 ✓
      nodular (M9691/3) 202.0 ✓
    nodular (M9690/3) 202.0 ✓
      histiocytic (M9642/3) 200.0 ✓
      lymphocytic (M9690/3) 202.0 ✓
        intermediate differentiation (M9694/3)
          202.0 ✓
        poorly differentiated (M9696/3)
          202.0 ✓
      mixed (cell type) (lymphocytic-histiocytic)
        (small cell and large cell) (M9691/3)
        202.0 ✓
    non-Hodgkin's type NEC (M9591/3) 202.8 ✓
    peripheral T-cell 202.7 ✓
    primary central nervous system 200.5 ✓
    reticulum cell (type) (M9640/3) 200.0 ✓
    small cell and large cell, mixed (diffuse)
      (M9613/3) 200.8 ✓
      follicular (M9691/3) 202.0 ✓
      nodular (9691/3) 202.0 ✓
    stem cell (type) (M9601/3) 202.8 ✓
    T-cell 202.1 ✓
      peripheral 202.7 ✓
    undifferentiated (cell type) (non-Burkitt's)
      (M9600/3) 202.8 ✓
      Burkitt's type (M9750/3) 200.2 ✓
Lymphomatosis (M9590/3) — *see also* Lymphoma
  granulomatous 099.1
Lymphopathia
  venereum 099.1
  veneris 099.1
Lymphopenia 288.51
  familial 279.2
Lymphoreticulosis, benign (of inoculation) 078.3
Lymphorrhea 457.8
Lymphosarcoma (M9610/3) 200.1 ✓
  diffuse (M9610/3) 200.1 ✓
    with plasmacytoid differentiation
      (M9611/3) 200.8 ✓
    lymphoplasmacytic (M9611/3) 200.8 ✓
  follicular (giant) (M9690/3) 202.0 ✓
    lymphoblastic (M9696/3) 202.0 ✓
    lymphocytic, intermediate differentiation
      (M9694/3) 202.0 ✓
    mixed cell type (M9691/3) 202.0 ✓
  giant follicular (M9690/3) 202.0 ✓
  Hodgkin's (M9650/3) 201.9 ✓
  immunoblastic (M9612/3) 200.8 ✓
  lymphoblastic (diffuse) (M9630/3) 200.1 ✓
    follicular (M9696/3) 202.0 ✓
    nodular (M9696/3) 202.0 ✓
  lymphocytic (diffuse) (M9620/3) 200.1 ✓
    intermediate differentiation (diffuse)
      (M9621/3) 200.1 ✓
      follicular (M9694/3) 202.0 ✓
      nodular (M9694/3) 202.0 ✓
  mixed cell type (diffuse) (M9613/3) 200.8 ✓
    follicular (M9691/3) 202.0 ✓
    nodular (M9691/3) 202.0 ✓
  nodular (M9690/3) 202.0 ✓
    lymphoblastic (M9696/3) 202.0 ✓
    lymphocytic, intermediate differentiation
      (M9694/3) 202.0 ✓

Lymphosarcoma — *continued*
  nodular — *continued*
    mixed cell type (M9691/3) 202.0 ✓
    prolymphocytic (M9631/3) 200.1 ✓
    reticulum cell (M9640/3) 200.0 ✓
Lymphostasis 457.8
Lypemania — *see also* Melancholia 296.2 ✓
Lyssa 071

M

Macacus ear 744.29
Maceration
  fetus (cause not stated) 779.9
  wet feet, tropical (syndrome) 991.4
Machado-Joseph disease 334.8
Machupo virus hemorrhagic fever 078.7
Macleod's syndrome (abnormal transradiancy, one lung) 492.8
Macrocephalia, macrocephaly 756.0
Macrocheilia (congenital) 744.81
Macrochilia (congenital) 744.81
Macrocolon (congenital) 751.3
Macrocornea 743.41
  associated with buphthalmos 743.22
Macrocytic — *see* condition
Macrocytosis 289.89
Macrodactylia, macrodactylism (fingers) (thumbs) 755.57
  toes 755.65
Macrodontia 520.2
Macroencephaly 742.4
Macrogenia 524.05
Macrogenitosomia (female) (male) (praecox) 255.2
Macrogingivae 523.8
Macroglobulinemia (essential) (idiopathic) (monoclonal) (primary) (syndrome) (Waldenström's) 273.3
Macroglossia (congenital) 750.15
  acquired 529.8
Macrognathia, macrognathism (congenital) 524.00
  mandibular 524.02
    alveolar 524.72
  maxillary 524.01
    alveolar 524.71
Macrogyria 742.4
Macrohydrocephalus — *see also* Hydrocephalus 331.4
Macromastia — *see also* Hypertrophy, breast 611.1
Macrophage activation syndrome 288.4
Macropsia 368.14
Macrosigmoid 564.7
  congenital 751.3
Macrospondylitis, acromegalic 253.0
Macrostomia (congenital) 744.83
Macrotia (external ear) (congenital) 744.22
Macula
  cornea, corneal
    congenital 743.43
      interfering with vision 743.42
    interfering with central vision 371.03
    not interfering with central vision 371.02
  degeneration (*see also* Degeneration, macula) 362.50
    hereditary (*see also* Dystrophy, retina) 362.70
  edema, cystoid 362.53
Maculae ceruleae 132.1
Macules and papules 709.8
Maculopathy, toxic 362.55
Madarosis 374.55
Madelung's
  deformity (radius) 755.54
  disease (lipomatosis) 272.8
  lipomatosis 272.8
Madness — *see also* Psychosis 298.9
  myxedema (acute) 293.0
    subacute 293.1
Madura
  disease (actinomycotic) 039.9
    mycotic 117.4
  foot (actinomycotic) 039.4
    mycotic 117.4
Maduromycosis (actinomycotic) 039.9

Maduromycosis — *continued*
  mycotic 117.4
Maffucci's syndrome (dyschondroplasia with hemangiomas) 756.4
Magenblase syndrome 306.4
Main en griffe (acquired) 736.06
  congenital 755.59
Maintenance
  chemotherapy regimen or treatment V58.11
  dialysis regimen or treatment
    extracorporeal (renal) V56.0
    peritoneal V56.8
    renal V56.0
  drug therapy or regimen
    chemotherapy, antineoplastic V58.11
    immunotherapy, antineoplastic V58.12
  external fixation NEC V54.89
  radiotherapy V58.0
  traction NEC V54.89
Majocchi's
  disease (purpura annularis telangiectodes) 709.1
  granuloma 110.6
Major — *see* condition
Mal
  cerebral (idiopathic) (*see also* Epilepsy) 345.9 ✓
  comital (*see also* Epilepsy) 345.9 ✓
  de los pintos (*see also* Pinta) 103.9
  de Meleda 757.39
  de mer 994.6
  lie — *see* Presentation, fetal
  perforant (*see also* Ulcer, lower extremity) 707.15
Malabar itch 110.9
  beard 110.0
  foot 110.4
  scalp 110.0
Malabsorption 579.9
  calcium 579.8
  carbohydrate 579.8
  disaccharide 271.3
  drug-induced 579.8
  due to bacterial overgrowth 579.8
  fat 579.8
  folate, congenital 281.2
  galactose 271.1
  glucose-galactose (congenital) 271.3
  intestinal 579.9
  isomaltose 271.3
  lactose (hereditary) 271.3
  methionine 270.4
  monosaccharide 271.8
  postgastrectomy 579.3
  postsurgical 579.3
  protein 579.8
  sucrose (-isomaltose) (congenital) 271.3
  syndrome 579.9
    postgastrectomy 579.3
    postsurgical 579.3
Malacia, bone 268.2
  juvenile (*see also* Rickets) 268.0
  Kienböck's (juvenile) (lunate) (wrist) 732.3
    adult 732.8
Malacoplakia
  bladder 596.8
  colon 569.89
  pelvis (kidney) 593.89
  ureter 593.89
  urethra 599.84
Malacosteon 268.2
  juvenile (*see also* Rickets) 268.0
Maladaptation — *see* Maladjustment
Maladie de Roger 745.4
Maladjustment
  conjugal V61.10
    involving
      divorce V61.03
      estrangement V61.09
  educational V62.3
  family V61.9
    specified circumstance NEC V61.8
  marital V61.10
    involving
      divorce V61.03
      estrangement V61.09

Maladjustment — *continued*
  occupational V62.29
    current military deployment status V62.21
  simple, adult (*see also* Reaction, adjustment) 309.9
  situational acute (*see also* Reaction, adjustment) 309.9
  social V62.4
Malaise 780.79
Malakoplakia — *see* Malacoplakia
Malaria, malarial (fever) 084.6
  algid 084.9
  any type, with
    algid malaria 084.9
    blackwater fever 084.8
    fever
      blackwater 084.8
      hemoglobinuric (bilious) 084.8
    hemoglobinuria, malarial 084.8
    hepatitis 084.9 [573.2]
    nephrosis 084.9 [581.81]
    pernicious complication NEC 084.9
      cardiac 084.9
      cerebral 084.9
  cardiac 084.9
  carrier (suspected) of V02.9
  cerebral 084.9
  complicating pregnancy, childbirth, or puerperium 647.4 ✓
  congenital 771.2
  congestion, congestive 084.6
    brain 084.9
  continued 084.0
  estivo-autumnal 084.0
  falciparum (malignant tertian) 084.0
  hematinuria 084.8
  hematuria 084.8
  hemoglobinuria 084.8
  hemorrhagic 084.6
  induced (therapeutically) 084.7
    accidental — *see* Malaria, by type
  liver 084.9 [573.2]
  malariae (quartan) 084.2
  malignant (tertian) 084.0
  mixed infections 084.5
  monkey 084.4
  ovale 084.3
  pernicious, acute 084.0
  Plasmodium, P.
    falciparum 084.0
    malariae 084.2
    ovale 084.3
    vivax 084.1
  quartan 084.2
  quotidian 084.0
  recurrent 084.6
    induced (therapeutically) 084.7
    accidental — *see* Malaria, by type
  remittent 084.6
  specified types NEC 084.4
  spleen 084.6
  subtertian 084.0
  tertian (benign) 084.1
    malignant 084.0
  tropical 084.0
  typhoid 084.6
  vivax (benign tertian) 084.1
Malassez's disease (testicular cyst) 608.89
Malassimilation 579.9
Maldescent, testis 752.51
Maldevelopment — *see also* Anomaly, by site
  brain 742.9
  colon 751.5
  hip (joint) 755.63
    congenital dislocation (*see also* Dislocation, hip, congenital) 754.30
  mastoid process 756.0
  middle ear, except ossicles 744.03
    ossicles 744.04
  newborn (not malformation) 764.9 ✓
  ossicles, ear 744.04
  spine 756.10
  toe 755.66
Male type pelvis 755.69
  with disproportion (fetopelvic) 653.2 ✓
    affecting fetus or newborn 763.1

✓ Additional Digit Required — Refer to the Tabular List for Digit Selection

▽ Subterms under main terms may continue to next column or page

2010 ICD-9-CM

▶◀ Revised Text

● New Line

▲ Revised Code

Volume 2 — 173

Male type pelvis — continued
  with disproportion — continued
    causing obstructed labor 660.1 ☑
      affecting fetus or newborn 763.1
Malformation (congenital) — see also Anomaly
  bone 756.9
  bursa 756.9
  Chiari
    type I 348.4
    type II (see also Spina bifida) 741.0 ☑
    type III 742.0
    type IV 742.2
  circulatory system NEC 747.9
    specified type NEC 747.89
  cochlea 744.05
  digestive system NEC 751.9
    lower 751.5
    specified type NEC 751.8
    upper 750.9
  eye 743.9
  gum 750.9
  heart NEC 746.9
    specified type NEC 746.89
    valve 746.9
  internal ear 744.05
  joint NEC 755.9
    specified type NEC 755.8
  Mondini's (congenital) (malformation, cochlea) 744.05
  muscle 756.9
  nervous system (central) 742.9
  pelvic organs or tissues
    in pregnancy or childbirth 654.9 ☑
      affecting fetus or newborn 763.89
      causing obstructed labor 660.2 ☑
        affecting fetus or newborn 763.1
  placenta (see also Placenta, abnormal) 656.7 ☑
  respiratory organs 748.9
    specified type NEC 748.8
  Rieger's 743.44
  sense organs NEC 742.9
    specified type NEC 742.8
  skin 757.9
    specified type NEC 757.8
  spinal cord 742.9
  teeth, tooth NEC 520.9
  tendon 756.9
  throat 750.9
  umbilical cord (complicating delivery) 663.9 ☑
    affecting fetus or newborn 762.6
  umbilicus 759.9
  urinary system NEC 753.9
    specified type NEC 753.8
  venous — see Anomaly, vein
Malfunction — see also Dysfunction
  arterial graft 996.1
  cardiac pacemaker 996.01
  catheter device — see Complications, mechanical, catheter
  colostomy 569.62
    valve 569.62
  cystostomy 997.5
  device, implant, or graft NEC — see Complications, mechanical
  enteric stoma 569.62
  enterostomy 569.62
  esophagostomy 530.87
  gastroenteric 536.8
  gastrostomy 536.42
  ileostomy
    valve 569.62
  nephrostomy 997.5
  pacemaker — see Complications, mechanical, pacemaker
  prosthetic device, internal — see Complications, mechanical
  tracheostomy 519.02
  valve
    colostomy 569.62
    ileostomy 569.62
  vascular graft or shunt 996.1
Malgaigne's fracture (closed) 808.43
  open 808.53

Malherbe's
  calcifying epithelioma (M8110/0) — see Neoplasm, skin, benign
  tumor (M8110/0) — see Neoplasm, skin, benign
Malibu disease 919.8
  infected 919.9
Malignancy (M8000/3) — see Neoplasm, by site, malignant
Malignant — see condition
Malingerer, malingering V65.2
Mallet, finger (acquired) 736.1
  congenital 755.59
  late effect of rickets 268.1
Malleus 024
Mallory's bodies 034.1
Mallory-Weiss syndrome 530.7
Malnutrition (calorie) 263.9
  complicating pregnancy 648.9 ☑
  degree
    first 263.1
    second 263.0
    third 262
    mild 263.1
    moderate 263.0
    severe 261
      protein-calorie 262
  fetus 764.2 ☑
    "light-for-dates" 764.1 ☑
  following gastrointestinal surgery 579.3
  intrauterine or fetal 764.2 ☑
    fetus or infant "light-for-dates" 764.1 ☑
  lack of care, or neglect (child) (infant) 995.52
    adult 995.84
  malignant 260
  mild 263.1
  moderate 263.0
  protein 260
  protein-calorie 263.9
    severe 262
    specified type NEC 263.8
  severe 261
    protein-calorie NEC 262
Malocclusion (teeth) 524.4
  angle's class I 524.21
  angle's class II 524.22
  angle's class III 524.23
  due to
    abnormal swallowing 524.59
    accessory teeth (causing crowding) 524.31
    dentofacial abnormality NEC 524.89
    impacted teeth (causing crowding) 520.6
    missing teeth 524.30
    mouth breathing 524.59
    sleep postures 524.59
    supernumerary teeth (causing crowding) 524.31
    thumb sucking 524.59
    tongue, lip, or finger habits 524.59
  temporomandibular (joint) 524.69
Malposition
  cardiac apex (congenital) 746.87
  cervix — see Malposition, uterus
  congenital
    adrenal (gland) 759.1
    alimentary tract 751.8
      lower 751.5
      upper 750.8
    aorta 747.21
    appendix 751.5
    arterial trunk 747.29
    artery (peripheral) NEC (see also Malposition, congenital, peripheral vascular system) 747.60
      coronary 746.85
      pulmonary 747.3
    auditory canal 744.29
      causing impairment of hearing 744.02
    auricle (ear) 744.29
      causing impairment of hearing 744.02
      cervical 744.43
    biliary duct or passage 751.69
    bladder (mucosa) 753.8
      exteriorized or extroverted 753.5
    brachial plexus 742.8
    brain tissue 742.4

Malposition — continued
  congenital — continued
    breast 757.6
    bronchus 748.3
    cardiac apex 746.87
    cecum 751.5
    clavicle 755.51
    colon 751.5
    digestive organ or tract NEC 751.8
      lower 751.5
      upper 750.8
    ear (auricle) (external) 744.29
      ossicles 744.04
    endocrine (gland) NEC 759.2
    epiglottis 748.3
    Eustachian tube 744.24
    eye 743.8
    facial features 744.89
    fallopian tube 752.19
    finger(s) 755.59
      supernumerary 755.01
    foot 755.67
    gallbladder 751.69
    gastrointestinal tract 751.8
    genitalia, genital organ(s) or tract
      female 752.89
        external 752.49
        internal NEC 752.89
      male 752.89
        penis 752.69
        scrotal transposition 752.81
    glottis 748.3
    hand 755.59
    heart 746.87
      dextrocardia 746.87
        with complete transposition of viscera 759.3
    hepatic duct 751.69
    hip (joint) (see also Dislocation, hip, congenital) 754.30
    intestine (large) (small) 751.5
      with anomalous adhesions, fixation, or malrotation 751.4
    joint NEC 755.8
    kidney 753.3
    larynx 748.3
    limb 755.8
      lower 755.69
      upper 755.59
    liver 751.69
    lung (lobe) 748.69
    nail(s) 757.5
    nerve 742.8
    nervous system NEC 742.8
    nose, nasal (septum) 748.1
    organ or site NEC — see Anomaly, specified type NEC, by site
    ovary 752.0
    pancreas 751.7
    parathyroid (gland) 759.2
    patella 755.64
    peripheral vascular system 747.60
      gastrointestinal 747.61
      lower limb 747.64
      renal 747.62
      specified NEC 747.69
      spinal 747.82
      upper limb 747.63
    pituitary (gland) 759.2
    respiratory organ or system NEC 748.9
    rib (cage) 756.3
      supernumerary in cervical region 756.2
    scapula 755.59
    shoulder 755.59
    spinal cord 742.59
    spine 756.19
    spleen 759.0
    sternum 756.3
    stomach 750.7
    symphysis pubis 755.69
    testis (undescended) 752.51
    thymus (gland) 759.2
    thyroid (gland) (tissue) 759.2
      cartilage 748.3
    toe(s) 755.66
      supernumerary 755.02

Malposition — continued
  congenital — continued
    tongue 750.19
    trachea 748.3
    uterus 752.3
    vein(s) (peripheral) NEC (see also Malposition, congenital, peripheral vascular system) 747.60
      great 747.49
      portal 747.49
      pulmonary 747.49
      vena cava (inferior) (superior) 747.49
  device, implant, or graft — see Complications, mechanical
  fetus NEC (see also Presentation, fetal) 652.9 ☑
    with successful version 652.1 ☑
      affecting fetus or newborn 763.1
    before labor, affecting fetus or newborn 761.7
    causing obstructed labor 660.0 ☑
    in multiple gestation (one fetus or more) 652.6 ☑
      with locking 660.5 ☑
      causing obstructed labor 660.0 ☑
  gallbladder (see also Disease, gallbladder) 575.8
  gastrointestinal tract 569.89
    congenital 751.8
  heart (see also Malposition, congenital, heart) 746.87
  intestine 569.89
    congenital 751.5
  pelvic organs or tissues
    in pregnancy or childbirth 654.4 ☑
      affecting fetus or newborn 763.89
      causing obstructed labor 660.2 ☑
        affecting fetus or newborn 763.1
  placenta — see Placenta, previa
  stomach 537.89
    congenital 750.7
  tooth, teeth 524.30
    with impaction 520.6
  uterus (acquired) (acute) (adherent) (any degree) (asymptomatic) (postinfectional) (postpartal, old) 621.6
    anteflexion or anteversion (see also Anteversion, uterus) 621.6
    congenital 752.3
    flexion 621.6
      lateral (see also Lateroversion, uterus) 621.6
    in pregnancy or childbirth 654.4 ☑
      affecting fetus or newborn 763.89
      causing obstructed labor 660.2 ☑
        affecting fetus or newborn 763.1
    inversion 621.6
    lateral (flexion) (version) (see also Lateroversion, uterus) 621.6
    lateroflexion (see also Lateroversion, uterus) 621.6
    lateroversion (see also Lateroversion, uterus) 621.6
    retroflexion or retroversion (see also Retroversion, uterus) 621.6
Malposture 729.90
Malpresentation, fetus — see also Presentation, fetal 652.9 ☑
Malrotation
  cecum 751.4
  colon 751.4
  intestine 751.4
  kidney 753.3
MALT (mucosa associated lymphoid tissue) 200.3 ☑
Malta fever — see also Brucellosis 023.9
Maltosuria 271.3
Maltreatment (of)
  adult 995.80
    emotional 995.82
    multiple forms 995.85
    neglect (nutritional) 995.84
    physical 995.81
    psychological 995.82
    sexual 995.83
  child 995.50
    emotional 995.51

Maltreatment — *continued*
- child — *continued*
  - multiple forms 995.59
  - neglect (nutritional) 995.52
  - physical 995.54
    - shaken infant syndrome 995.55
  - psychological 995.51
  - sexual 995.53
  - spouse (*see also* Maltreatment, adult) 995.80

Malt workers' lung 495.4

Malum coxae senilis 715.25

Malunion, fracture 733.81

Mammillitis — *see also* Mastitis 611.0
- puerperal, postpartum 675.2 ☑

Mammitis — *see also* Mastitis 611.0
- puerperal, postpartum 675.2 ☑

Mammographic
- calcification 793.89
- calculus 793.89
- microcalcification 793.81

Mammoplasia 611.1

Management
- contraceptive V25.9
  - specified type NEC V25.8
- procreative V26.9
  - specified type NEC V26.89

Mangled NEC — *see also* nature and site of injury 959.9

Mania (monopolar) — *see also* Psychosis, affective 296.0 ☑
- alcoholic (acute) (chronic) 291.9
- Bell's — *see* Mania, chronic
- chronic 296.0 ☑
  - recurrent episode 296.1 ☑
  - single episode 296.0 ☑
- compulsive 300.3
- delirious (acute) 296.0 ☑
  - recurrent episode 296.1 ☑
  - single episode 296.0 ☑
- epileptic (*see also* Epilepsy) 345.4 ☑
- hysterical 300.10
- inhibited 296.89
- puerperal (after delivery) 296.0 ☑
  - recurrent episode 296.1 ☑
  - single episode 296.0 ☑
- recurrent episode 296.1 ☑
- senile 290.8
- single episode 296.0 ☑
- stupor 296.89
- stuporous 296.89
- unproductive 296.89

Manic-depressive insanity, psychosis, reaction, or syndrome — *see also* Psychosis, affective 296.80
- circular (alternating) 296.7
  - currently
    - depressed 296.5 ☑
    - episode unspecified 296.7
    - hypomanic, previously depressed 296.4 ☑
    - manic 296.4 ☑
    - mixed 296.6 ☑
- depressed (type), depressive 296.2 ☑
  - atypical 296.82
  - recurrent episode 296.3 ☑
  - single episode 296.2 ☑
- hypomanic 296.0 ☑
  - recurrent episode 296.1 ☑
  - single episode 296.0 ☑
- manic 296.0 ☑
  - atypical 296.81
  - recurrent episode 296.1 ☑
  - single episode 296.0 ☑
- mixed NEC 296.89
- perplexed 296.89
- stuporous 296.89

Manifestations, rheumatoid
- lungs 714.81
- pannus — *see* Arthritis, rheumatoid
- subcutaneous nodules — *see* Arthritis, rheumatoid

Mankowsky's syndrome (familial dysplastic osteopathy) 731.2

Mannoheptulosuria 271.8

Mannosidosis 271.8

Manson's
- disease (schistosomiasis) 120.1
- pyosis (pemphigus contagiosus) 684
- schistosomiasis 120.1

Mansonellosis 125.5

Manual — *see* condition

Maple bark disease 495.6

Maple bark-strippers' lung 495.6

Maple syrup (urine) disease or syndrome 270.3

Marable's syndrome (celiac artery compression) 447.4

Marasmus 261
- brain 331.9
- due to malnutrition 261
- intestinal 569.89
- nutritional 261
- senile 797
- tuberculous NEC (*see also* Tuberculosis) 011.9 ☑

Marble
- bones 756.52
- skin 782.61

Marburg disease (virus) 078.89

March
- foot 733.94
- hemoglobinuria 283.2

Marchand multiple nodular hyperplasia (liver) 571.5

Marchesani (-Weill) syndrome (brachymorphism and ectopia lentis) 759.89

Marchiafava (-Bignami) disease or syndrome 341.8

Marchiafava-Micheli syndrome (paroxysmal nocturnal hemoglobinuria) 283.2

Marcus Gunn's syndrome (jaw-winking syndrome) 742.8

Marfan's
- congenital syphilis 090.49
- disease 090.49
- syndrome (arachnodactyly) 759.82
  - meaning congenital syphilis 090.49
  - with luxation of lens 090.49 [379.32]

Marginal
- implantation, placenta — *see* Placenta, previa
- placenta — *see* Placenta, previa
- sinus (hemorrhage) (rupture) 641.2 ☑
  - affecting fetus or newborn 762.1

Marie's
- cerebellar ataxia 334.2
- syndrome (acromegaly) 253.0

Marie-Bamberger disease or syndrome (hypertrophic) (pulmonary) (secondary) 731.2
- idiopathic (acropachyderma) 757.39
- primary (acropachyderma) 757.39

Marie-Charcôt-Tooth neuropathic atrophy, muscle 356.1

Marie-Strümpell arthritis or disease (ankylosing spondylitis) 720.0

Marihuana, marijuana
- abuse (*see also* Abuse, drugs, nondependent) 305.2 ☑
- dependence (*see also* Dependence) 304.3 ☑

Marion's disease (bladder neck obstruction) 596.0

Marital conflict V61.10

Mark
- port wine 757.32
- raspberry 757.32
- strawberry 757.32
- stretch 701.3
- tattoo 709.09

Maroteaux-Lamy syndrome (mucopolysaccharidosis VI) 277.5

Marriage license examination V70.3

Marrow (bone)
- arrest 284.9
- megakaryocytic 287.30
- poor function 289.9

Marseilles fever 082.1

Marshall's (hidrotic) **ectodermal dysplasia** 757.31

Marsh's disease (exophthalmic goiter) 242.0 ☑

Marsh fever — *see also* Malaria 084.6

Martin-Albright syndrome (pseudohypoparathyroidism) 275.49

Martin's disease 715.27

Martorell-Fabre syndrome (pulseless disease) 446.7

Masculinization, female, with adrenal hyperplasia 255.2

Masculinovoblastoma (M8670/0) 220

Masochism 302.83

Masons' lung 502

Mass
- abdominal 789.3 ☑
- anus 787.99
- bone 733.90
- breast 611.72
- cheek 784.2
- chest 786.6
- cystic — *see* Cyst
- ear 388.8
- epigastric 789.3 ☑
- eye 379.92
- female genital organ 625.8
- gum 784.2
- head 784.2
- intracranial 784.2
- joint 719.60
  - ankle 719.67
  - elbow 719.62
  - foot 719.67
  - hand 719.64
  - hip 719.65
  - knee 719.66
  - multiple sites 719.69
  - pelvic region 719.65
  - shoulder (region) 719.61
  - specified site NEC 719.68
  - wrist 719.63
- kidney (*see also* Disease, kidney) 593.9
- lung 786.6
- lymph node 785.6
- malignant (M8000/3) — *see* Neoplasm, by site, malignant
- mediastinal 786.6
- mouth 784.2
- muscle (limb) 729.89
- neck 784.2
- nose or sinus 784.2
- palate 784.2
- pelvis, pelvic 789.3 ☑
- penis 607.89
- perineum 625.8
- rectum 787.99
- scrotum 608.89
- skin 782.2
- specified organ NEC — *see* Disease of specified organ or site
- splenic 789.2
- substernal 786.6
  - thyroid (*see also* Goiter) 240.9
- superficial (localized) 782.2
- testes 608.89
- throat 784.2
- tongue 784.2
- umbilicus 789.3 ☑
- uterus 625.8
- vagina 625.8
- vulva 625.8

Massive — *see* condition

Mastalgia 611.71
- psychogenic 307.89

Mast cell
- disease 757.33
  - systemic (M9741/3) 202.6 ☑
- leukemia (M9900/3) 207.8 ☑
- sarcoma (M9742/3) 202.6 ☑
- tumor (M9740/1) 238.5
  - malignant (M9740/3) 202.6 ☑

Masters-Allen syndrome 620.6

Mastitis (acute) (adolescent) (diffuse) (interstitial) (lobular) (nonpuerperal) (nonsuppurative) (parenchymatous) (phlegmonous) (simple) (subacute) (suppurative) 611.0
- chronic (cystic) (fibrocystic) 610.1
- cystic 610.1
  - Schimmelbusch's type 610.1
- fibrocystic 610.1
- infective 611.0
- lactational 675.2 ☑
- lymphangitis 611.0

Mastitis — *continued*
- neonatal (noninfective) 778.7
  - infective 771.5
- periductal 610.4
- plasma cell 610.4
- puerperalis 675.2 ☑
- puerperal, postpartum, (interstitial) (nonpurulent) (parenchymatous) 675.2 ☑
  - purulent 675.1 ☑
  - stagnation 676.2 ☑
- retromammary 611.0
  - puerperal, postpartum 675.1 ☑
- submammary 611.0
  - puerperal, postpartum 675.1 ☑

Mastocytoma (M9740/1) 238.5
- malignant (M9740/3) 202.6 ☑

Mastocytosis 757.33
- malignant (M9741/3) 202.6 ☑
- systemic (M9741/3) 202.6 ☑

Mastodynia 611.71
- psychogenic 307.89

Mastoid — *see* condition

Mastoidalgia — *see also* Otalgia 388.70

Mastoiditis (coalescent) (hemorrhagic) (pneumococcal) (streptococcal) (suppurative) 383.9
- acute or subacute 383.00
  - with
    - Gradenigo's syndrome 383.02
    - petrositis 383.02
    - specified complication NEC 383.02
    - subperiosteal abscess 383.01
- chronic (necrotic) (recurrent) 383.1
- tuberculous (*see also* Tuberculosis) 015.6 ☑

Mastopathy, mastopathia 611.9
- chronica cystica 610.1
- diffuse cystic 610.1
- estrogenic 611.89
- ovarian origin 611.89

Mastoplasia 611.1

Masturbation 307.9

Maternal condition, affecting fetus or newborn
- acute yellow atrophy of liver 760.8
- albuminuria 760.1
- anesthesia or analgesia 763.5
- blood loss 762.1
- chorioamnionitis 762.7
- circulatory disease, chronic (conditions classifiable to 390–459, 745–747) 760.3
- congenital heart disease (conditions classifiable to 745–746) 760.3
- cortical necrosis of kidney 760.1
- death 761.6
- diabetes mellitus 775.0
  - manifest diabetes in the infant 775.1
- disease NEC 760.9
  - circulatory system, chronic (conditions classifiable to 390–459, 745–747) 760.3
  - genitourinary system (conditions classifiable to 580–599) 760.1
  - respiratory (conditions classifiable to 490–519, 748) 760.3
- eclampsia 760.0
- hemorrhage NEC 762.1
- hepatitis acute, malignant, or subacute 760.8
- hyperemesis (gravidarum) 761.8
- hypertension (arising during pregnancy) (conditions classifiable to 642) 760.0
- infection
  - disease classifiable to 001-136 ☑, 760.2
  - genital tract NEC 760.8
  - urinary tract 760.1
- influenza 760.2
  - manifest influenza in the infant 771.2
- injury (conditions classifiable to 800–996) 760.5
- malaria 760.2
  - manifest malaria in infant or fetus 771.2
- malnutrition 760.4
- necrosis of liver 760.8
- nephritis (conditions classifiable to 580–583) 760.1
- nephrosis (conditions classifiable to 581) 760.1
- noxious substance transmitted via breast milk or placenta 760.70

☑ Additional Digit Required — Refer to the Tabular List for Digit Selection   ▼ᵐⁱⁿ Subterms under main terms may continue to next column or page

2010 ICD-9-CM   ▶◀ Revised Text   ● New Line   ▲ Revised Code   Volume 2 — 175

Maternal condition, affecting fetus or newborn — *continued*
  noxious substance transmitted via breast milk or placenta — *continued*
    alcohol 760.71
    anticonvulsants 760.77
    antifungals 760.74
    anti-infective agents 760.74
    antimetabolics 760.78
    cocaine 760.75
    "crack" 760.75
    diethylstilbestrol [DES] 760.76
    hallucinogenic agents 760.73
    medicinal agents NEC 760.79
    narcotics 760.72
    obstetric anesthetic or analgesic drug 760.72
    specified agent NEC 760.79
  nutritional disorder (conditions classifiable to 260–269) 760.4
  operation unrelated to current delivery (*see also* Newborn, affected by) 760.64
  pre-eclampsia 760.0
  pyelitis or pyelonephritis, arising during pregnancy (conditions classifiable to 590) 760.1
  renal disease or failure 760.1
  respiratory disease, chronic (conditions classifiable to 490–519, 748) 760.3
  rheumatic heart disease (chronic) (conditions classifiable to 393–398) 760.3
  rubella (conditions classifiable to 056) 760.2
    manifest rubella in the infant or fetus 771.0
  surgery unrelated to current delivery (*see also* Newborn, affected by) 760.64
    to uterus or pelvic organs 760.64
  syphilis (conditions classifiable to 090–097) 760.2
    manifest syphilis in the infant or fetus 090.0
  thrombophlebitis 760.3
  toxemia (of pregnancy) 760.0
    pre-eclamptic 760.0
  toxoplasmosis (conditions classifiable to 130) 760.2
    manifest toxoplasmosis in the infant or fetus 771.2
  transmission of chemical substance through the placenta 760.70
    alcohol 760.71
    anticonvulsants 760.77
    antifungals 760.74
    anti-infective 760.74
    antimetabolics 760.78
    cocaine 760.75
    "crack" 760.75
    diethylstilbestrol [DES] 760.76
    hallucinogenic agents 760.73
    narcotics 760.72
    specified substance NEC 760.79
  uremia 760.1
  urinary tract conditions (conditions classifiable to 580–599) 760.1
  vomiting (pernicious) (persistent) (vicious) 761.8
Maternity — *see* Delivery
Matheiu's disease (leptospiral jaundice) 100.0
Mauclaire's disease or osteochondrosis 732.3
Maxcy's disease 081.0
Maxilla, maxillary — *see* condition
May (-Hegglin) anomaly or syndrome 288.2
Mayaro fever 066.3
Mazoplasia 610.8
MBD (minimal brain dysfunction), child — *see also* Hyperkinesia 314.9
MCAD (medium chain acyl CoA dehydrogenase deficiency) 277.85
McArdle (-Schmid-Pearson) disease or syndrome (glycogenosis V) 271.0
McCune-Albright syndrome (osteitis fibrosa disseminata) 756.59
MCLS (mucocutaneous lymph node syndrome) 446.1
McQuarrie's syndrome (idiopathic familial hypoglycemia) 251.2
Measles (black) (hemorrhagic) (suppressed) 055.9

Measles — *continued*
  with
    encephalitis 055.0
    keratitis 055.71
    keratoconjunctivitis 055.71
    otitis media 055.2
    pneumonia 055.1
  complication 055.8
    specified type NEC 055.79
  encephalitis 055.0
  French 056.9
  German 056.9
  keratitis 055.71
  keratoconjunctivitis 055.71
  liberty 056.9
  otitis media 055.2
  pneumonia 055.1
  specified complications NEC 055.79
  vaccination, prophylactic (against) V04.2
Meatitis, urethral — *see also* Urethritis 597.89
Meat poisoning — *see* Poisoning, food
Meatus, meatal — *see* condition
Meat-wrappers' asthma 506.9
Meckel's
  diverticulitis 751.0
  diverticulum (displaced) (hypertrophic) 751.0
Meconium
  aspiration 770.11
    with
      pneumonia 770.12
      pneumonitis 770.12
      respiratory symptoms 770.12
    below vocal cords 770.11
      with respiratory symptoms 770.12
    syndrome 770.12
  delayed passage in newborn 777.1
  ileus 777.1
    due to cystic fibrosis 277.01
  in liquor 792.3
    noted during delivery 656.8 ☑
  insufflation 770.11
    with respiratory symptoms 770.12
  obstruction
    fetus or newborn 777.1
      in mucoviscidosis 277.01
  passage of 792.3
    noted during delivery 763.84
  peritonitis 777.6
  plug syndrome (newborn) NEC 777.1
  staining 779.84
Median — *see also* condition
  arcuate ligament syndrome 447.4
  bar (prostate) 600.90
    with
      other lower urinary tract symptoms (LUTS) 600.91
      urinary
        obstruction 600.91
        retention 600.91
  rhomboid glossitis 529.2
  vesical orifice 600.90
    with
      other lower urinary tract symptoms (LUTS) 600.91
      urinary
        obstruction 600.91
        retention 600.91
Mediastinal shift 793.2
Mediastinitis (acute) (chronic) 519.2
  actinomycotic 039.8
  syphilitic 095.8
  tuberculous (*see also* Tuberculosis) 012.8 ☑
Mediastinopericarditis — *see also* Pericarditis 423.9
  acute 420.90
  chronic 423.8
    rheumatic 393
  rheumatic, chronic 393
Mediastinum, mediastinal — *see* condition
Medical services provided for — *see* Health, services provided because of)
Medicine poisoning (by overdose) (wrong substance given or taken in error) 977.9
  specified drug or substance — *see* Table of Drugs and Chemicals
Medin's disease (poliomyelitis) 045.9 ☑

Mediterranean
  anemia (with other hemoglobinopathy) 282.49
  disease or syndrome (hemipathic) 282.49
  fever (*see also* Brucellosis) 023.9
    familial 277.31
  kala-azar 085.0
  leishmaniasis 085.0
  tick fever 082.1
Medulla — *see* condition
Medullary
  cystic kidney 753.16
  sponge kidney 753.17
Medullated fibers
  optic (nerve) 743.57
  retina 362.85
Medulloblastoma (M9470/3)
  desmoplastic (M9471/3) 191.6
  specified site — *see* Neoplasm, by site, malignant
  unspecified site 191.6
Medulloepithelioma (M9501/3) — *see also* Neoplasm, by site, malignant
  teratoid (M9502/3) — *see* Neoplasm, by site, malignant
Medullomyoblastoma (M9472/3)
  specified site — *see* Neoplasm, by site, malignant
  unspecified site 191.6
Meekeren-Ehlers-Danlos syndrome 756.83
Megacaryocytic — *see* condition
Megacolon (acquired) (functional) (not Hirschsprung's disease) 564.7
  aganglionic 751.3
  congenital, congenitum 751.3
  Hirschsprung's (disease) 751.3
  psychogenic 306.4
  toxic (*see also* Colitis, ulcerative) 556.9
Megaduodenum 537.3
Megaesophagus (functional) 530.0
  congenital 750.4
Megakaryocytic — *see* condition
Megalencephaly 742.4
Megalerythema (epidermicum) (infectiosum) 057.0
Megalia, cutis et ossium 757.39
Megaloappendix 751.5
Megalocephalus, megalocephaly NEC 756.0
Megalocornea 743.41
  associated with buphthalmos 743.22
Megalocytic anemia 281.9
Megalodactylia (fingers) (thumbs) 755.57
  toes 755.65
Megaloduodenum 751.5
Megaloesophagus (functional) 530.0
  congenital 750.4
Megalogastria (congenital) 750.7
Megalomania 307.9
Megalophthalmos 743.8
Megalopsia 368.14
Megalosplenia — *see also* Splenomegaly 789.2
Megaloureter 593.89
  congenital 753.22
Megarectum 569.49
Megasigmoid 564.7
  congenital 751.3
Megaureter 593.89
  congenital 753.22
Megrim 346.9 ☑
Meibomian
  cyst 373.2
    infected 373.12
  gland — *see* condition
  infarct (eyelid) 374.85
  stye 373.11
Meibomitis 373.12
Meige
  -Milroy disease (chronic hereditary edema) 757.0
  syndrome (blepharospasm-oromandibular dystonia) 333.82
Melalgia, nutritional 266.2
Melancholia — *see also* Psychosis, affective 296.90
  climacteric 296.2 ☑
    recurrent episode 296.3 ☑
    single episode 296.2 ☑

Melancholia — *see also* Psychosis, affective — *continued*
  hypochondriac 300.7
  intermittent 296.2 ☑
    recurrent episode 296.3 ☑
    single episode 296.2 ☑
  involutional 296.2 ☑
    recurrent episode 296.3 ☑
    single episode 296.2 ☑
  menopausal 296.2 ☑
    recurrent episode 296.3 ☑
    single episode 296.2 ☑
  puerperal 296.2 ☑
  reactive (from emotional stress, psychological trauma) 298.0
  recurrent 296.3 ☑
  senile 290.21
  stuporous 296.2 ☑
    recurrent episode 296.3 ☑
    single episode 296.2 ☑
Melanemia 275.0
Melanoameloblastoma (M9363/0) — *see* Neoplasm, bone, benign
Melanoblastoma (M8720/3) — *see* Melanoma
Melanoblastosis
  Block-Sulzberger 757.33
  cutis linearis sive systematisata 757.33
Melanocarcinoma (M8720/3) — *see* Melanoma
Melanocytoma, eyeball (M8726/0) 224.0
Melanoderma, melanodermia 709.09
  Addison's (primary adrenal insufficiency) 255.41
Melanodontia, infantile 521.05
Melanodontoclasia 521.05
Melanoepithelioma (M8720/3) — *see* Melanoma
Melanoma (malignant) (M8720/3) 172.9

> Note — Except where otherwise indicated, the morphological varieties of melanoma in the list below should be coded by site as for "Melanoma (malignant)". Internal sites should be coded to malignant neoplasm of those sites.

  abdominal wall 172.5
  ala nasi 172.3
  amelanotic (M8730/3) — *see* Melanoma, by site
  ankle 172.7
  anus, anal 154.3
    canal 154.2
  arm 172.6
  auditory canal (external) 172.2
  auricle (ear) 172.2
  auricular canal (external) 172.2
  axilla 172.5
  axillary fold 172.5
  back 172.5
  balloon cell (M8722/3) — *see* Melanoma, by site
  benign (M8720/0) — *see* Neoplasm, skin, benign
  breast (female) (male) 172.5
  brow 172.3
  buttock 172.5
  canthus (eye) 172.1
  cheek (external) 172.3
  chest wall 172.5
  chin 172.3
  choroid 190.6
  conjunctiva 190.3
  ear (external) 172.2
  epithelioid cell (M8771/3) (*see also* Melanoma, by site)
    and spindle cell, mixed (M8775/3) — *see* Melanoma, by site
  external meatus (ear) 172.2
  eye 190.9
  eyebrow 172.3
  eyelid (lower) (upper) 172.1
  face NEC 172.3
  female genital organ (external) NEC 184.4
  finger 172.6
  flank 172.5
  foot 172.7
  forearm 172.6

☑ Additional Digit Required — Refer to the Tabular List for Digit Selection   ▿ Subterms under main terms may continue to next column or page

Melanoma — continued
  forehead 172.3
  foreskin 187.1
  gluteal region 172.5
  groin 172.5
  hand 172.6
  heel 172.7
  helix 172.2
  hip 172.7
  in
    giant pigmented nevus (M8761/3) — see Melanoma, by site
    Hutchinson's melanotic freckle (M8742/3) — see Melanoma, by site
    junctional nevus (M8740/3) — see Melanoma, by site
    precancerous melanosis (M8741/3) — see Melanoma, by site
  in situ — see Melanoma, by site
    skin 172.9
  interscapular region 172.5
  iris 190.0
  jaw 172.3
  juvenile (M8770/0) — see Neoplasm, skin, benign
  knee 172.7
  labium
    majus 184.1
    minus 184.2
  lacrimal gland 190.2
  leg 172.7
  lip (lower) (upper) 172.0
  liver 197.7
  lower limb NEC 172.7
  male genital organ (external) NEC 187.9
  meatus, acoustic (external) 172.2
  meibomian gland 172.1
  metastatic
    of or from specified site — see Melanoma, by site
    site not of skin — see Neoplasm, by site, malignant, secondary
    to specified site — see Neoplasm, by site, malignant, secondary
    unspecified site 172.9
  nail 172.9
    finger 172.6
    toe 172.7
  neck 172.4
  nodular (M8721/3) — see Melanoma, by site
  nose, external 172.3
  orbit 190.1
  penis 187.4
  perianal skin 172.5
  perineum 172.5
  pinna 172.2
  popliteal (fossa) (space) 172.7
  prepuce 187.1
  pubes 172.5
  pudendum 184.4
  retina 190.5
  scalp 172.4
  scrotum 187.7
  septum nasal (skin) 172.3
  shoulder 172.6
  skin NEC 172.8
    in situ 172.9
  spindle cell (M8772/3) (see also Melanoma, by site)
    type A (M8773/3) 190.0
    type B (M8774/3) 190.0
  submammary fold 172.5
  superficial spreading (M8743/3) — see Melanoma, by site
  temple 172.3
  thigh 172.7
  toe 172.7
  trunk NEC 172.5
  umbilicus 172.5
  upper limb NEC 172.6
  vagina vault 184.0
  vulva 184.4
Melanoplakia 528.9
Melanosarcoma (M8720/3) — see also Melanoma
  epithelioid cell (M8771/3) — see Melanoma

Melanosis 709.09
  addisonian (primary adrenal insufficiency) 255.41
    tuberculous (see also Tuberculosis) 017.6 ☑
  adrenal 255.41
  colon 569.89
  conjunctiva 372.55
    congenital 743.49
  corii degenerativa 757.33
  cornea (presenile) (senile) 371.12
    congenital 743.43
      interfering with vision 743.42
  eye 372.55
    congenital 743.49
  jute spinners' 709.09
  lenticularis progressiva 757.33
  liver 573.8
  precancerous (M8741/2) (see also Neoplasm, skin, in situ)
    malignant melanoma in (M8741/3) — see Melanoma
  prenatal 743.43
    interfering with vision 743.42
  Riehl's 709.09
  sclera 379.19
    congenital 743.47
  suprarenal 255.41
  tar 709.09
  toxic 709.09
Melanuria 791.9
Melasma 709.09
  adrenal (gland) 255.41
  suprarenal (gland) 255.41
MELAS syndrome (mitochondrial encephalopathy, lactic acidosis and stroke-like episodes) 277.87
Melena 578.1
  due to
    swallowed maternal blood 777.3
    ulcer — see Ulcer, by site, with hemorrhage
  newborn 772.4
    due to swallowed maternal blood 777.3
Meleney's
  gangrene (cutaneous) 686.09
  ulcer (chronic undermining) 686.09
Melioidosis 025
Melitensis, febris 023.0
Melitococcosis 023.0
Melkersson (-Rosenthal) syndrome 351.8
Mellitus, diabetes — see Diabetes
Melorheostosis (bone) (leri) 733.99
Meloschisis 744.83
Melotia 744.29
Membrana
  capsularis lentis posterior 743.39
  epipapillaris 743.57
Membranacea placenta — see Placenta, abnormal
Membranaceous uterus 621.8
Membrane, membranous — see also condition
  folds, congenital — see Web
  Jackson's 751.4
  over face (causing asphyxia), fetus or newborn 768.9
  premature rupture — see Rupture, membranes, premature
  pupillary 364.74
    persistent 743.46
  retained (complicating delivery) (with hemorrhage) 666.2 ☑
    without hemorrhage 667.1 ☑
  secondary (eye) 366.50
  unruptured (causing asphyxia) 768.9
  vitreous humor 379.25
Membranitis, fetal 658.4 ☑
  affecting fetus or newborn 762.7
Memory disturbance, loss or lack — see also Amnesia 780.93
  mild, following organic brain damage 310.8 ▲
MEN (multiple endocrine neoplasia) (syndromes)
  type I 258.01
  type IIA 258.02
  type IIB 258.03

Menadione (vitamin K) **deficiency** 269.0
Menarche, precocious 259.1
Mendacity, pathologic 301.7
Mendelson's syndrome (resulting from a procedure) 997.39
  obstetric 668.0 ☑
Mende's syndrome (ptosis-epicanthus) 270.2
Ménétrier's disease or syndrome (hypertrophic gastritis) 535.2 ☑
Ménière's disease, syndrome, or vertigo 386.00
  cochlear 386.02
  cochleovestibular 386.01
  inactive 386.04
  in remission 386.04
  vestibular 386.03
Meninges, meningeal — see condition
Meningioma (M9530/0) — see also Neoplasm, meninges, benign
  angioblastic (M9535/0) — see Neoplasm, meninges, benign
  angiomatous (M9534/0) — see Neoplasm, meninges, benign
  endotheliomatous (M9531/0) — see Neoplasm, meninges, benign
  fibroblastic (M9532/0) — see Neoplasm, meninges, benign
  fibrous (M9532/0) — see Neoplasm, meninges, benign
  hemangioblastic (M9535/0) — see Neoplasm, meninges, benign
  hemangiopericytic (M9536/0) — see Neoplasm, meninges, benign
  malignant (M9530/3) — see Neoplasm, meninges, malignant
  meningiothelial (M9531/0) — see Neoplasm, meninges, benign
  meningotheliomatous (M9531/0) — see Neoplasm, meninges, benign
  mixed (M9537/0) — see Neoplasm, meninges, benign
  multiple (M9530/1) 237.6
  papillary (M9538/1) 237.6
  psammomatous (M9533/0) — see Neoplasm, meninges, benign
  syncytial (M9531/0) — see Neoplasm, meninges, benign
  transitional (M9537/0) — see Neoplasm, meninges, benign
Meningiomatosis (diffuse) (M9530/1) 237.6
Meningism — see also Meningismus 781.6
Meningismus (infectional) (pneumococcal) 781.6
  due to serum or vaccine 997.09 [321.8]
  influenzal NEC 487.8
Meningitis (basal) (basic) (basilar) (brain) (cerebral) (cervical) (congestive) (diffuse) (hemorrhagic) (infantile) (membranous) (metastatic) (nonspecific) (pontine) (progressive) (simple) (spinal) (subacute) (sympathetica) (toxic) 322.9
  abacterial NEC (see also Meningitis, aseptic) 047.9
  actinomycotic 039.8 [320.7]
  adenoviral 049.1
  Aerobacter aerogenes 320.82
  anaerobes (cocci) (gram-negative) (gram-positive) (mixed) (NEC) 320.81
  arbovirus NEC 066.9 [321.2]
    specified type NEC 066.8 [321.2]
  aseptic (acute) NEC 047.9
    adenovirus 049.1
    Coxsackie virus 047.0
    due to
      adenovirus 049.1
      Coxsackie virus 047.0
      ECHO virus 047.1
      enterovirus 047.9
      mumps 072.1
      poliovirus (see also Poliomyelitis) 045.2 ☑ [321.2]
    ECHO virus 047.1
    herpes (simplex) virus 054.72
      zoster 053.0
    leptospiral 100.81
    lymphocytic choriomeningitis 049.0
    noninfective 322.0

Meningitis — continued
  Bacillus pyocyaneus 320.89
  bacterial NEC 320.9
    anaerobic 320.81
      gram-negative 320.82
        anaerobic 320.81
  Bacteroides (fragilis) (oralis) (melaninogenicus) 320.81
  cancerous (M8000/6) 198.4
  candidal 112.83
  carcinomatous (M8010/6) 198.4
  caseous (see also Tuberculosis, meninges) 013.0 ☑
  cerebrospinal (acute) (chronic) (diplococcal) (endemic) (epidemic) (fulminant) (infectious) (malignant) (meningococcal) (sporadic) 036.0
    carrier (suspected) of V02.59
  chronic NEC 322.2
  clear cerebrospinal fluid NEC 322.0
  Clostridium (haemolyticum) (novyi) NEC 320.81
  coccidioidomycosis 114.2
  Coxsackie virus 047.0
  cryptococcal 117.5 [321.0]
  diplococcal 036.0
    gram-negative 036.0
    gram-positive 320.1
  Diplococcus pneumoniae 320.1
  due to
    actinomycosis 039.8 [320.7]
    adenovirus 049.1
    coccidiomycosis 114.2
    enterovirus 047.9
      specified NEC 047.8
    histoplasmosis (see also Histoplasmosis) 115.91
    Listerosis 027.0 [320.7]
    Lyme disease 088.81 [320.7]
    moniliasis 112.83
    mumps 072.1
    neurosyphilis 094.2
    nonbacterial organisms NEC 321.8
    oidiomycosis 112.83
    poliovirus (see also Poliomyelitis) 045.2 ☑ [321.2]
    preventive immunization, inoculation, or vaccination 997.09 [321.8]
    sarcoidosis 135 [321.4]
    sporotrichosis 117.1 [321.1]
    syphilis 094.2
      acute 091.81
      congenital 090.42
      secondary 091.81
    trypanosomiasis (see also Trypanosomiasis) 086.9 [321.3]
    whooping cough 033.9 [320.7]
  ECHO virus 047.1
  E. coli 320.82
  endothelial-leukocytic, benign, recurrent 047.9
  Enterobacter aerogenes 320.82
  enteroviral 047.9
    specified type NEC 047.8
  enterovirus 047.9
    specified NEC 047.8
  eosinophilic 322.1
  epidemic NEC 036.0
  Escherichia coli (E. coli) 320.82
  Eubacterium 320.81
  fibrinopurulent NEC 320.9
    specified type NEC 320.89
  Friedländer (bacillus) 320.82
  fungal NEC 117.9 [321.1]
  Fusobacterium 320.81
  gonococcal 098.82
  gram-negative bacteria NEC 320.82
    anaerobic 320.81
    cocci 036.0
      specified NEC 320.82
  gram-negative cocci NEC 036.0
    specified NEC 320.82
  gram-positive cocci NEC 320.9
  herpes (simplex) virus 054.72
    zoster 053.0
  H. influenzae 320.0
  infectious NEC 320.9

☑ Additional Digit Required — Refer to the Tabular List for Digit Selection

▽ Subterms under main terms may continue to next column or page

Index

Meningitis — Merycism

Meningitis — continued
  influenzal 320.0
  Klebsiella pneumoniae 320.82
  late effect — see Late, effect, meningitis
  leptospiral (aseptic) 100.81
  Listerella (monocytogenes) 027.0 [320.7]
  Listeria monocytogenes 027.0 [320.7]
  lymphocytic (acute) (benign) (serous) 049.0
    choriomeningitis virus 049.0
  meningococcal (chronic) 036.0
  Mima polymorpha 320.82
  Mollaret's 047.9
  monilial 112.83
  mumps (virus) 072.1
  mycotic NEC 117.9 [321.1]
  Neisseria 036.0
  neurosyphilis 094.2
  nonbacterial NEC (see also Meningitis, aseptic)
    047.9
  nonpyogenic NEC 322.0
  oidiomycosis 112.83
  ossificans 349.2
  Peptococcus 320.81
  Peptostreptococcus 320.81
  pneumococcal 320.1
  poliovirus (see also Poliomyelitis)
    045.2 ✓ [321.2]
  Proprionibacterium 320.81
  Proteus morganii 320.82
  Pseudomonas (aeruginosa) (pyocyaneus)
    320.82
  purulent NEC 320.9
    specified organism NEC 320.89
  pyogenic NEC 320.9
    specified organism NEC 320.89
  Salmonella 003.21
  septic NEC 320.9
    specified organism NEC 320.89
  serosa circumscripta NEC 322.0
  serous NEC (see also Meningitis, aseptic) 047.9
    lymphocytic 049.0
    syndrome 348.2
  Serratia (marcescens) 320.82
  specified organism NEC 320.89
  sporadic cerebrospinal 036.0
  sporotrichosis 117.1 [321.1]
  staphylococcal 320.3
  sterile 997.09
  streptococcal (acute) 320.2
  suppurative 320.9
    specified organism NEC 320.89
  syphilitic 094.2
    acute 091.81
    congenital 090.42
    secondary 091.81
  torula 117.5 [321.0]
  traumatic (complication of injury) 958.8
  Treponema (denticola) (macrodenticum)
    320.81
  trypanosomiasis 086.1 [321.3]
  tuberculous (see also Tuberculosis, meninges)
    013.0 ✓
  typhoid 002.0 [320.7]
  Veillonella 320.81
  Vibrio vulnificus 320.82
  viral, virus NEC (see also Meningitis, aseptic)
    047.9
  Wallgren's (see also Meningitis, aseptic) 047.9
Meningocele (congenital) (spinal) — see also
    Spina bifida 741.9 ✓
  acquired (traumatic) 349.2
  cerebral 742.0
  cranial 742.0
Meningocerebritis — see Meningoencephalitis
Meningococcemia (acute) (chronic) 036.2
Meningococcus, meningococcal — see also
    condition 036.9
  adrenalitis, hemorrhagic 036.3
  carditis 036.40
  carrier (suspected) of V02.59
  cerebrospinal fever 036.0
  encephalitis 036.1
  endocarditis 036.42
  exposure to V01.84
  infection NEC 036.9
  meningitis (cerebrospinal) 036.0

Meningococcus, meningococcal — see also
    condition — continued
  myocarditis 036.43
  optic neuritis 036.81
  pericarditis 036.41
  septicemia (chronic) 036.2
Meningoencephalitis — see also Encephalitis
    323.9
  acute NEC 048
  bacterial, purulent, pyogenic, or septic — see
    Meningitis
  chronic NEC 094.1
  diffuse NEC 094.1
  diphasic 063.2
  due to
    actinomycosis 039.8 [320.7]
    blastomycosis NEC (see also Blastomycosis)
      116.0 [323.41]
    free-living amebae 136.29
    Listeria monocytogenes 027.0 [320.7]
    Lyme disease 088.81 [320.7]
    mumps 072.2
    Naegleria (amebae) (gruberi) (organisms)
      136.29
    rubella 056.01
    sporotrichosis 117.1 [321.1]
    toxoplasmosis (acquired) 130.0
      congenital (active) 771.2 [323.41]
    Trypanosoma 086.1 [323.2]
  epidemic 036.0
  herpes 054.3
  herpetic 054.3
  H. influenzae 320.0
  infectious (acute) 048
  influenzal 320.0
  late effect — see category 326
  Listeria monocytogenes 027.0 [320.7]
  lymphocytic (serous) 049.0
  mumps 072.2
  parasitic NEC 123.9 [323.41]
  pneumococcal 320.1
  primary amebic 136.29
  rubella 056.01
  serous 048
    lymphocytic 049.0
  specific 094.2
  staphylococcal 320.3
  streptococcal 320.2
  syphilitic 094.2
  toxic NEC 989.9 [323.71]
    due to
      carbon tetrachloride (vapor)
        987.8 [323.71]
      hydroxyquinoline derivatives poisoning
        961.3 [323.71]
      lead 984.9 [323.71]
      mercury 985.0 [323.71]
      thallium 985.8 [323.71]
  toxoplasmosis (acquired) 130.0
  trypanosomic 086.1 [323.2]
  tuberculous (see also Tuberculosis, meninges)
    013.0 ✓
  virus NEC 048
Meningoencephalocele 742.0
  syphilitic 094.89
  congenital 090.49
Meningoencephalomyelitis — see also Menin-
    goencephalitis 323.9
  acute NEC 048
    disseminated (postinfectious)
      136.9 [323.61]
      postimmunization or postvaccination
        323.51
    due to
      actinomycosis 039.8 [320.7]
      torula 117.5 [323.41]
      toxoplasma or toxoplasmosis (acquired)
        130.0
        congenital (active) 771.2 [323.41]
  late effect — see category 326
Meningoencephalomyelopathy — see also
    Meningoencephalomyelitis 349.9
Meningoencephalopathy — see also Menin-
    goencephalitis 348.39
Meningoencephalopoliomyelitis — see also
    Poliomyelitis, bulbar 045.0 ✓

Meningoencephalopoliomyelitis — see also
    Poliomyelitis, bulbar — continued
  late effect 138
Meningomyelitis — see also Meningoencephali-
    tis 323.9
  blastomycotic NEC (see also Blastomycosis)
    116.0 [323.41]
  due to
    actinomycosis 039.8 [320.7]
    blastomycosis (see also Blastomycosis)
      116.0 [323.41]
    Meningococcus 036.0
    sporotrichosis 117.1 [323.41]
    torula 117.5 [323.41]
  late effect — see category 326
  lethargic 049.8
  meningococcal 036.0
  syphilitic 094.2
  tuberculous (see also Tuberculosis, meninges)
    013.0 ✓
Meningomyelocele — see also Spina bifida
    741.9 ✓
  syphilitic 094.89
Meningomyeloneuritis — see Meningoen-
    cephalitis
Meningoradiculitis — see Meningitis
Meningovascular — see condition
Meniscocytosis 282.60
Menkes' syndrome — see Syndrome, Menkes'
Menolipsis 626.0
Menometrorrhagia 626.2
Menopause, menopausal (symptoms) (syn-
    drome) 627.2
  arthritis (any site) NEC 716.3 ✓
  artificial 627.4
  bleeding 627.0
  crisis 627.2
  depression (see also Psychosis, affective)
    296.2 ✓
    agitated 296.2 ✓
      recurrent episode 296.3 ✓
      single episode 296.2 ✓
    psychotic 296.2 ✓
      recurrent episode 296.3 ✓
      single episode 296.2 ✓
    recurrent episode 296.3 ✓
    single episode 296.2 ✓
  melancholia (see also Psychosis, affective)
    296.2 ✓
    recurrent episode 296.3 ✓
    single episode 296.2 ✓
  paranoid state 297.2
  paraphrenia 297.2
  postsurgical 627.4
  premature 256.31
    postirradiation 256.2
    postsurgical 256.2
  psychoneurosis 627.2
  psychosis NEC 298.8
  surgical 627.4
  toxic polyarthritis NEC 716.39
Menorrhagia (primary) 626.2
  climacteric 627.0
  menopausal 627.0
  postclimacteric 627.1
  postmenopausal 627.1
  preclimacteric 627.0
  premenopausal 627.0
  puberty (menses retained) 626.3
Menorrhalgia 625.3
Menoschesis 626.8
Menostaxis 626.2
Menses, retention 626.8
Menstrual — see also Menstruation
  cycle, irregular 626.4
  disorders NEC 626.9
  extraction V25.3
  fluid, retained 626.8
  molimen 625.4
  period, normal V65.5
  regulation V25.3
Menstruation
  absent 626.0
  anovulatory 628.0
  delayed 626.8
  difficult 625.3

Menstruation — continued
  disorder 626.9
    psychogenic 306.52
    specified NEC 626.8
  during pregnancy 640.8 ✓
  excessive 626.2
  frequent 626.2
  infrequent 626.1
  irregular 626.4
  latent 626.8
  membranous 626.8
  painful (primary) (secondary) 625.3
    psychogenic 306.52
  passage of clots 626.2
  precocious 626.8
  protracted 626.8
  retained 626.8
  retrograde 626.8
  scanty 626.1
  suppression 626.8
  vicarious (nasal) 625.8
Mentagra — see also Sycosis 704.8
Mental — see also condition
  deficiency (see also Retardation, mental) 319
  deterioration (see also Psychosis) 298.9
  disorder (see also Disorder, mental) 300.9
  exhaustion 300.5
  insufficiency (congenital) (see also Retardation,
    mental) 319
  observation without need for further medical
    care NEC V71.09
  retardation (see also Retardation, mental) 319
  subnormality (see also Retardation, mental)
    319
    mild 317
    moderate 318.0
    profound 318.2
    severe 318.1
  upset (see also Disorder, mental) 300.9
Meralgia paresthetica 355.1
Mercurial — see condition
Mercurialism NEC 985.0
Merergasia 300.9
Merkel cell tumor — see ▶Carcinoma, Merkel
    cell◀
Merocele — see also Hernia, femoral 553.00
Meromelia 755.4
  lower limb 755.30
    intercalary 755.32
      femur 755.34
        tibiofibular (complete) (incomplete)
          755.33
      fibula 755.37
      metatarsal(s) 755.38
      tarsal(s) 755.38
      tibia 755.36
      tibiofibular 755.35
    terminal (complete) (partial) (transverse)
      755.31
      longitudinal 755.32
        metatarsal(s) 755.38
        phalange(s) 755.39
        tarsal(s) 755.38
      transverse 755.31
  upper limb 755.20
    intercalary 755.22
      carpal(s) 755.28
      humeral 755.24
        radioulnar (complete) (incomplete)
          755.23
      metacarpal(s) 755.28
      phalange(s) 755.29
      radial 755.26
      radioulnar 755.25
      ulnar 755.27
    terminal (complete) (partial) (transverse)
      755.21
      longitudinal 755.22
        carpal(s) 755.28
        metacarpal(s) 755.28
        phalange(s) 755.29
      transverse 755.21
Merosmia 781.1
MERRF syndrome (myoclonus with epilepsy and
    with ragged red fibers) 277.87
Merycism — see also Vomiting

✓ Additional Digit Required — Refer to the Tabular List for Digit Selection
178 — Volume 2 • October 2009   ▶◀ Revised Text   ● New Line   ▲ Revised Code   ▽ Subterms under main terms may continue to next column or page
2010 ICD-9-CM

Merycism — see also Vomiting — continued
  psychogenic 307.53
Merzbacher-Pelizaeus disease 330.0
Mesaortitis — see Aortitis
Mesarteritis — see Arteritis
Mesencephalitis — see also Encephalitis 323.9
  late effect — see category 326
Mesenchymoma (M8990/1) — see also Neo-
  plasm, connective tissue, uncertain behav-
  ior
  benign (M8990/0) — see Neoplasm, connec-
    tive tissue, benign
  malignant (M8990/3) — see Neoplasm, con-
    nective tissue, malignant
Mesenteritis
  retractile 567.82
  sclerosing 567.82
Mesentery, mesenteric — see condition
Mesiodens, mesiodentes 520.1
  causing crowding 524.31
Mesio-occlusion 524.23
Mesocardia (with asplenia) 746.87
Mesocolon — see condition
Mesonephroma (malignant) (M9110/3) — see
  also Neoplasm, by site, malignant
  benign (M9110/0) — see Neoplasm, by site,
    benign
Mesophlebitis — see Phlebitis
Mesostromal dysgenesis 743.51
Mesothelioma (malignant) (M9050/3) — see also
  Neoplasm, by site, malignant
  benign (M9050/0) — see Neoplasm, by site,
    benign
  biphasic type (M9053/3) (see also Neoplasm,
    by site, malignant)
    benign (M9053/0) — see Neoplasm, by
      site, benign
  epithelioid (M9052/3) (see also Neoplasm, by
    site, malignant)
    benign (M9052/0) — see Neoplasm, by
      site, benign
  fibrous (M9051/3) (see also Neoplasm, by site,
    malignant)
    benign (M9051/0) — see Neoplasm, by
      site, benign
Metabolic syndrome 277.7
Metabolism disorder 277.9
  specified type NEC 277.89
Metagonimiasis 121.5
Metagonimus infestation (small intestine) 121.5
Metal
  pigmentation (skin) 709.00
  polishers' disease 502
Metalliferous miners' lung 503
Metamorphopsia 368.14
Metaplasia
  bone, in skin 709.3
  breast 611.89
  cervix — omit code
  endometrium (squamous) 621.8
  esophagus 530.85
  intestinal, of gastric mucosa 537.89
  kidney (pelvis) (squamous) (see also Disease,
    renal) 593.89
  myelogenous 289.89
  myeloid 289.89
    agnogenic 238.76
    megakaryocytic 238.76
  spleen 289.59
  squamous cell
    amnion 658.8 ☑
    bladder 596.8
    cervix — see condition
    trachea 519.19
    tracheobronchial tree 519.19
    uterus 621.8
      cervix — see condition
Metastasis, metastatic
  abscess — see Abscess
  calcification 275.40
  cancer, neoplasm, or disease
    from specified site (M8000/3) — see Neo-
      plasm, by site, malignant
    to specified site (M8000/6) — see Neo-
      plasm, by site, secondary

Metastasis, metastatic — continued
  deposits (in) (M8000/6) — see Neoplasm, by
    site, secondary
  mesentery, of neuroendocrine tumor 209.71 ●
  pneumonia 038.8 [484.8]
  spread (to) (M8000/6) — see Neoplasm, by
    site, secondary
Metatarsalgia 726.70
  anterior 355.6
  due to Freiberg's disease 732.5
  Morton's 355.6
Metatarsus, metatarsal — see also condition
  abductus valgus (congenital) 754.60
  adductus varus (congenital) 754.53
  primus varus 754.52
  valgus (adductus) (congenital) 754.60
  varus (abductus) (congenital) 754.53
    primus 754.52
Methadone use 304.00
Methemoglobinemia 289.7
  acquired (with sulfhemoglobinemia) 289.7
  congenital 289.7
  enzymatic 289.7
  Hb-M disease 289.7
  hereditary 289.7
  toxic 289.7
Methemoglobinuria — see also Hemoglobinuria
  791.2
Methicillin
  resistant staphyloccocus aureus (MRSA) 041.12
    colonization V02.54
    personal history of V12.04
  susceptible staphylococcus aureus (MSSA)
    041.11
    colonization V02.53
Methioninemia 270.4
Metritis (catarrhal) (septic) (suppurative) — see
  also Endometritis 615.9
  blennorrhagic 098.16
    chronic or duration of 2 months or over
      098.36
  cervical (see also Cervicitis) 616.0
  gonococcal 098.16
    chronic or duration of 2 months or over
      098.36
  hemorrhagic 626.8
  puerperal, postpartum, childbirth
    670.1 ☑ ▲
    septic 670.2 ☑
  tuberculous (see also Tuberculosis) 016.7 ☑
Metropathia hemorrhagica 626.8
Metroperitonitis — see also Peritonitis, pelvic,
  female 614.5
Metrorrhagia 626.6
  arising during pregnancy — see Hemorrhage,
    pregnancy
  postpartum NEC 666.2 ☑
  primary 626.6
  psychogenic 306.59
  puerperal 666.2 ☑
Metrorrhexis — see Rupture, uterus
Metrosalpingitis — see also Salpingo-oophoritis
  614.2
Metrostaxis 626.6
Metrovaginitis — see also Endometritis 615.9
  gonococcal (acute) 098.16
    chronic or duration of 2 months or over
      098.36
Mexican fever — see Typhus, Mexican
Meyenburg-Altherr-Uehlinger syndrome
  733.99
Meyer-Schwickerath and Weyers syndrome
  (dysplasia oculodentodigitalis) 759.89
Meynert's amentia (nonalcoholic) 294.0
  alcoholic 291.1
Mibelli's disease 757.39
Mice, joint — see also Loose, body, joint 718.1 ☑
  knee 717.6
Micheli-Rietti syndrome (thalassemia minor)
  282.49
Michotte's syndrome 721.5
Micrencephalon, micrencephaly 742.1
Microalbuminuria 791.0
Microaneurysm, retina 362.14
  diabetic 250.5 ☑ [362.01]

Microaneurysm, retina — continued
  diabetic — continued
    due to secondary diabetes
      249.5 ☑ [362.01]
Microangiopathy 443.9
  diabetic (peripheral) 250.7 ☑ [443.81]
    due to secondary diabetes
      249.7 ☑ [443.81]
    retinal 250.5 ☑ [362.01]
      due to secondary diabetes
        249.5 ☑ [362.01]
  peripheral 443.9
    diabetic 250.7 ☑ [443.81]
      due to secondary diabetes
        249.7 ☑ [443.81]
  retinal 362.18
    diabetic 250.5 ☑ [362.01]
      due to secondary diabetes
        249.5 ☑ [362.01]
  thrombotic 446.6
    Moschcowitz's (thrombotic thrombocy-
      topenic purpura) 446.6
Microcalcification, mammographic 793.81
Microcephalus, microcephalic, microcephaly
  742.1
  due to toxoplasmosis (congenital) 771.2
Microcheilia 744.82
Microcolon (congenital) 751.5
Microcornea (congenital) 743.41
Microcytic — see condition
Microdeletions NEC 758.33
Microdontia 520.2
Microdrepanocytosis (thalassemia-Hb-S disease)
  282.49
Microembolism
  atherothrombotic — see Atheroembolism
  retina 362.33
Microencephalon 742.1
Microfilaria streptocerca infestation 125.3
Microgastria (congenital) 750.7
Microgenia 524.06
Microgenitalia (congenital) 752.89
  penis 752.64
Microglioma (M9710/3)
  specified site — see Neoplasm, by site, malig-
    nant
  unspecified site 191.9
Microglossia (congenital) 750.16
Micrognathia, micrognathism (congenital)
  524.00
  mandibular 524.04
    alveolar 524.74
  maxillary 524.03
    alveolar 524.73
Microgyria (congenital) 742.2
Microinfarct, heart — see also Insufficiency,
  coronary 411.89
Microlithiasis, alveolar, pulmonary 516.2
Micromastia 611.82
Micromyelia (congenital) 742.59
Micropenis 752.64
Microphakia (congenital) 743.36
Microphthalmia (congenital) — see also Microph-
  thalmos 743.10
Microphthalmos (congenital) 743.10
  associated with eye and adnexal anomalies
    NEC 743.12
  due to toxoplasmosis (congenital) 771.2
  isolated 743.11
  simple 743.11
  syndrome 759.89
Micropsia 368.14
Microsporidiosis 136.8
Microsporon furfur infestation 111.0
Microsporosis — see also Dermatophytosis 110.9
  nigra 111.1
Microstomia (congenital) 744.84
Microthelia 757.6
Microthromboembolism — see Embolism
Microtia (congenital) (external ear) 744.23
Microtropia 378.34
Micturition
  disorder NEC 788.69
    psychogenic 306.53
  frequency 788.41
    psychogenic 306.53

Micturition — continued
  nocturnal 788.43
  painful 788.1
    psychogenic 306.53
Middle
  ear — see condition
  lobe (right) syndrome 518.0
Midplane — see condition
Miescher's disease 709.3
  cheilitis 351.8
  granulomatosis disciformis 709.3
Miescher-Leder syndrome or granulomatosis
  709.3
Mieten's syndrome 759.89
Migraine (idiopathic) 346.9 ☑

> Note — The following fifth digit subclassifi-
> cation is for use with category 346:
>
> 0 without mention of intractable mi-
>   graine without mention of status mi-
>   grainosus
>
> 1 with intractable migraine, so stated,
>   without mention of status migrain-
>   osus
>
> 2 without mention of intractable mi-
>   graine with status migrainosus
>
> 3 with intractable migraine, so stated,
>   with status migrainosus

  with aura (acute-onset) (without headache)
    (prolonged) (typical) 346.0 ☑
  without aura 346.1 ☑
    chronic 346.7 ☑
    transformed 346.7 ☑
  abdominal (syndrome) 346.2 ☑
  allergic (histamine) 346.2 ☑
  atypical 346.8 ☑
  basilar 346.0 ☑
  chronic without aura 346.7 ☑
  classic(al) 346.0 ☑
  common 346.1 ☑
  hemiplegic 346.3 ☑
    familial 346.3 ☑
    sporadic 346.3 ☑
  lower-half 339.00
  menstrual 346.4 ☑
  menstrually related 346.4 ☑
  ophthalmic 346.8 ☑
  ophthalmoplegic 346.2 ☑
  premenstrual 346.4 ☑
  pure menstrual 346.4 ☑
  retinal 346.0 ☑
  specified form NEC 346.8 ☑
  transformed without aura 346.7 ☑
  variant 346.2 ☑
Migrant, social V60.0
Migratory, migrating — see also condition
  person V60.0
  testis, congenital 752.52
Mikulicz's disease or syndrome (dryness of
  mouth, absent or decreased lacrimation)
  527.1
Milian atrophia blanche 701.3
Miliaria (crystallina) (rubra) (tropicalis) 705.1
  apocrine 705.82
Miliary — see condition
Milium — see also Cyst, sebaceous 706.2
  colloid 709.3
  eyelid 374.84
Milk
  crust 690.11
  excess secretion 676.6 ☑
  fever, female 672.0 ☑
  poisoning 988.8
  retention 676.2 ☑
  sickness 988.8
  spots 423.1
Milkers' nodes 051.1
Milk-leg (deep vessels) 671.4 ☑
  complicating pregnancy 671.3 ☑
  nonpuerperal 451.19
  puerperal, postpartum, childbirth 671.4 ☑
Milkman (-Looser) disease or syndrome (osteomalacia with pseudofractures) 268.2

Milky urine — *see also* Chyluria 791.1
Millar's asthma (laryngismus stridulus) 478.75
Millard-Gubler-Foville paralysis 344.89
Millard-Gubler paralysis or syndrome 344.89
Miller-Dieker syndrome 758.33
Miller's disease (osteomalacia) 268.2
Miller Fisher's syndrome 357.0
Milles' syndrome (encephalocutaneous angiomatosis) 759.6
Mills' disease 335.29
Millstone makers' asthma or lung 502
Milroy's disease (chronic hereditary edema) 757.0
Miners' — *see also* condition
   asthma 500
   elbow 727.2
   knee 727.2
   lung 500
   nystagmus 300.89
   phthisis (*see also* Tuberculosis) 011.4 ☑
   tuberculosis (see also Tuberculosis) 011.4 ☑
Minkowski-Chauffard syndrome — *see also* Spherocytosis 282.0
Minor — *see* condition
Minor's disease 336.1
Minot's disease (hemorrhagic disease, newborn) 776.0
Minot-von Willebrand (-Jürgens) disease or syndrome (angiohemophilia) 286.4
Minus (and plus) hand (intrinsic) 736.09
Miosis (persistent) (pupil) 379.42
Mirizzi's syndrome (hepatic duct stenosis) — *see also* Obstruction, biliary 576.2
   with calculus, cholelithiasis, or stones — *see* Choledocholithiasis
Mirror writing 315.09
   secondary to organic lesion 784.69
Misadventure (prophylactic) (therapeutic) — *see also* Complications 999.9
   administration of insulin 962.3
   infusion — *see* Complications, infusion
   local applications (of fomentations, plasters, etc.) 999.9
      burn or scald — *see* Burn, by site
   medical care (early) (late) NEC 999.9
      adverse effect of drugs or chemicals — *see* Table of Drugs and Chemicals
      burn or scald — *see* Burn, by site
   radiation NEC 990
   radiotherapy NEC 990
   surgical procedure (early) (late) — *see* Complications, surgical procedure
   transfusion — *see* Complications, transfusion
   vaccination or other immunological procedure — *see* Complications, vaccination
Misanthropy 301.7
Miscarriage — *see* Abortion, spontaneous
Mischief, malicious, child — *see also* Disturbance, conduct 312.0 ☑
Misdirection
   aqueous 365.83
Mismanagement, feeding 783.3
Misplaced, misplacement
   kidney (*see also* Disease, renal) 593.0
      congenital 753.3
   organ or site, congenital NEC — *see* Malposition, congenital
Missed
   abortion 632
   delivery (at or near term) 656.4 ☑
   labor (at or near term) 656.4 ☑
Misshapen reconstructed breast 612.0
Missing — *see also* Absence
   teeth (acquired) 525.10
      congenital (see also Anodontia) 520.0
      due to
         caries 525.13
         extraction 525.10
         periodontal disease 525.12
         specified NEC 525.19
         trauma 525.11
      vertebrae (congenital) 756.13
Misuse of drugs NEC — *see also* Abuse, drug, nondependent 305.9 ☑
Mitchell's disease (erythromelalgia) 443.82

Mite(s)
   diarrhea 133.8
   grain (itch) 133.8
   hair follicle (itch) 133.8
   in sputum 133.8
Mitochondrial encephalopathy, lactic acidosis and stroke-like episodes (MELAS syndrome) 277.87
Mitochondrial neurogastrointestinal encephalopathy syndrome (MNGIE) 277.87
Mitral — *see* condition
Mittelschmerz 625.2
Mixed — *see* condition
Mljet disease (mal de Meleda) 757.39
Mobile, mobility
   cecum 751.4
   coccyx 733.99
   excessive — *see* Hypermobility
   gallbladder 751.69
   kidney 593.0
      congenital 753.3
   organ or site, congenital NEC — *see* Malposition, congenital
   spleen 289.59
Mobitz heart block (atrioventricular) 426.10
   type I (Wenckebach's) 426.13
   type II 426.12
Möbius'
   disease 346.2 ☑
   syndrome
      congenital oculofacial paralysis 352.6
      ophthalmoplegic migraine 346.2 ☑
Moeller(-Barlow) disease (infantile scurvy) 267
   glossitis 529.4
Mohr's syndrome (types I and II) 759.89
Mola destruens (M9100/1) 236.1
Molarization, premolars 520.2
Molar pregnancy 631
   hydatidiform (delivered) (undelivered) 630
Molding, head (during birth) — *omit code*
Mold(s) in vitreous 117.9
Mole (pigmented) (M8720/0) — *see also* Neoplasm, skin, benign
   blood 631
   Breus' 631
   cancerous (M8720/3) — *see* Melanoma
   carneous 631
   destructive (M9100/1) 236.1
   ectopic — *see* Pregnancy, ectopic
   fleshy 631
   hemorrhagic 631
   hydatid, hydatidiform (benign) (complicating pregnancy) (delivered) (undelivered) (*see also* Hydatidiform mole) 630
      invasive (M9100/1) 236.1
      malignant (M9100/1) 236.1
      previous, affecting management of pregnancy V23.1
   invasive (hydatidiform) (M9100/1) 236.1
   malignant
      meaning
         malignant hydatidiform mole (9100/1) 236.1
         melanoma (M8720/3) — *see* Melanoma
   nonpigmented (M8730/0) — *see* Neoplasm, skin, benign
   pregnancy NEC 631
   skin (M8720/0) — *see* Neoplasm, skin, benign
   tubal — *see* Pregnancy, tubal
   vesicular (*see also* Hydatidiform mole) 630
Molimen, molimina (menstrual) 625.4
Mollaret's meningitis 047.9
Mollities (cerebellar) (cerebral) 437.8
   ossium 268.2
Molluscum
   contagiosum 078.0
   epitheliale 078.0
   fibrosum (M8851/0) — *see* Lipoma, by site
   pendulum (M8851/0) — *see* Lipoma, by site
Mönckeberg's arteriosclerosis, degeneration, disease, or sclerosis — *see also* Arteriosclerosis, extremities 440.20
Monday fever 504
Monday morning dyspnea or asthma 504
Mondini's malformation (cochlea) 744.05

Mondor's disease (thrombophlebitis of breast) 451.89
Mongolian, mongolianism, mongolism, mongoloid 758.0
   spot 757.33
Monilethrix (congenital) 757.4
Monilia infestation — *see* Candidiasis
Moniliasis — *see also* Candidiasis
   neonatal 771.7
   vulvovaginitis 112.1
Monkeypox 059.01
Monoarthritis 716.60
   ankle 716.67
   arm 716.62
      lower (and wrist) 716.63
      upper (and elbow) 716.62
   foot (and ankle) 716.67
   forearm (and wrist) 716.63
   hand 716.64
   leg 716.66
      lower 716.66
      upper 716.65
   pelvic region (hip) (thigh) 716.65
   shoulder (region) 716.61
   specified site NEC 716.68
Monoblastic — *see* condition
Monochromatism (cone) (rod) 368.54
Monocytic — *see* condition
Monocytopenia 288.59
Monocytosis (symptomatic) 288.63
Monofixation syndrome 378.34
Monomania — *see also* Psychosis 298.9
Mononeuritis 355.9
   cranial nerve — *see* Disorder, nerve, cranial
   femoral nerve 355.2
   lateral
      cutaneous nerve of thigh 355.1
      popliteal nerve 355.3
   lower limb 355.8
      specified nerve NEC 355.79
   medial popliteal nerve 355.4
   median nerve 354.1
   multiplex 354.5
   plantar nerve 355.6
   posterior tibial nerve 355.5
   radial nerve 354.3
   sciatic nerve 355.0
   ulnar nerve 354.2
   upper limb 354.9
      specified nerve NEC 354.8
   vestibular 388.5
Mononeuropathy — *see also* Mononeuritis 355.9
   diabetic NEC 250.6 ☑ *[355.9]*
      due to secondary diabetes 249.6 ☑ *[355.9]*
      lower limb 250.6 ☑ *[355.8]*
         due to secondary diabetes 249.6 ☑ *[355.8]*
      upper limb 250.6 ☑ *[354.9]*
         due to secondary diabetes 249.6 ☑ *[354.9]*
   iliohypogastric nerve 355.79
   ilioinguinal nerve 355.79
   obturator nerve 355.79
   saphenous nerve 355.79
Mononucleosis, infectious 075
   with hepatitis 075 *[573.1]*
Monoplegia 344.5
   brain (current episode) (*see also* Paralysis, brain) 437.8
      fetus or newborn 767.8
   cerebral (current episode) (*see also* Paralysis, brain) 437.8
   congenital or infantile (cerebral) (spastic) (spinal) 343.3
   embolic (current) (*see also* Embolism, brain) 434.1 ☑
      late effect — *see* Late effect(s) (of) cerebrovascular disease
   infantile (cerebral) (spastic) (spinal) 343.3
   lower limb 344.30
      affecting
         dominant side 344.31
         nondominant side 344.32
      due to late effect of cerebrovascular accident — *see* Late effect(s) (of) cerebrovascular accident

Monoplegia — *continued*
   newborn 767.8
   psychogenic 306.0
      specified as conversion reaction 300.11
   thrombotic (current) (*see also* Thrombosis, brain) 434.0 ☑
      late effect — *see* Late effect(s) (of) cerebrovascular disease
   transient 781.4
   upper limb 344.40
      affecting
         dominant side 344.41
         nondominant side 344.42
      due to late effect of cerebrovascular accident — *see* Late effect(s) (of) cerebrovascular accident
Monorchism, monorchidism 752.89
Monteggia's fracture (closed) 813.03
   open 813.13
Mood swings
   brief compensatory 296.99
   rebound 296.99
Mooren's ulcer (cornea) 370.07
Moore's syndrome — *see also* Epilepsy 345.5 ☑
Mooser bodies 081.0
Mooser-Neill reaction 081.0
Moral
   deficiency 301.7
   imbecility 301.7
Morax-Axenfeld conjunctivitis 372.03
Morbilli — *see also* Measles 055.9
Morbus
   anglicus, anglorum 268.0
   Beigel 111.2
   caducus (*see also* Epilepsy) 345.9 ☑
   caeruleus 746.89
   celiacus 579.0
   comitialis (see also Epilepsy) 345.9 ☑
   cordis (*see also* Disease, heart)
      valvulorum — *see* Endocarditis
   coxae 719.95
      tuberculous (*see also* Tuberculosis) 015.1 ☑
   hemorrhagicus neonatorum 776.0
   maculosus neonatorum 772.6
   renum 593.0
   senilis (*see also* Osteoarthrosis) 715.9 ☑
Morel-Kraepelin disease — *see also* Schizophrenia 295.9 ☑
Morel-Moore syndrome (hyperostosis frontalis interna) 733.3
Morel-Morgagni syndrome (hyperostosis frontalis interna) 733.3
Morgagni
   cyst, organ, hydatid, or appendage 752.89
      fallopian tube 752.11
   disease or syndrome (hyperostosis frontalis interna) 733.3
Morgagni-Adams-Stokes syndrome (syncope with heart block) 426.9
Morgagni-Stewart-Morel syndrome (hyperostosis frontalis interna) 733.3
Moria — *see also* Psychosis 298.9
Morning sickness 643.0 ☑
Moron 317
Morphea (guttate) (linear) 701.0
Morphine dependence — *see also* Dependence 304.0 ☑
Morphinism — *see also* Dependence 304.0 ☑
Morphinomania — *see also* Dependence 304.0 ☑
Morphoea 701.0
Morquio (-Brailsford) (-Ullrich) disease or syndrome (mucopolysaccharidosis IV) 277.5
   kyphosis 277.5
Morris syndrome (testicular feminization) 259.51
Morsus humanus (open wound) — *see also* Wound, open, by site
   skin surface intact — *see* Contusion
Mortification (dry) (moist) — *see also* Gangrene 785.4
Morton's
   disease 355.6
   foot 355.6
   metatarsalgia (syndrome) 355.6

☑ Additional Digit Required — Refer to the Tabular List for Digit Selection

▽ Subterms under main terms may continue to next column or page

▶◀ Revised Text   ● New Line   ▲ Revised Code

Morton's — *continued*
  neuralgia 355.6
  neuroma 355.6
  syndrome (metatarsalgia) (neuralgia) 355.6
  toe 355.6
Morvan's disease 336.0
Mosaicism, mosaic (chromosomal) 758.9
  autosomal 758.5
  sex 758.81
Moschcowitz's syndrome (thrombotic thrombo-cytopenic purpura) 446.6
Mother yaw 102.0
Motion sickness (from travel, any vehicle) (from roundabouts or swings) 994.6
Mottled teeth (enamel) (endemic) (nonendemic) 520.3
Mottling enamel (endemic) (nonendemic) (teeth) 520.3
Mouchet's disease 732.5
Mould(s) (in vitreous) 117.9
Moulders'
  bronchitis 502
  tuberculosis (*see also* Tuberculosis) 011.4 ☑
Mounier-Kuhn syndrome 748.3
  with
    acute exacerbation 494.1
    bronchiectasis 494.0
      with (acute) exacerbation 494.1
    acquired 519.19
      with bronchiectasis 494.0
        with (acute) exacerbation 494.1
Mountain
  fever — *see* Fever, mountain
  sickness 993.2
    with polycythemia, acquired 289.0
    acute 289.0
  tick fever 066.1
Mouse, joint — *see also* Loose, body, joint 718.1 ☑
  knee 717.6
Mouth — *see* condition
Movable
  coccyx 724.71
  kidney (*see also* Disease, renal) 593.0
    congenital 753.3
  organ or site, congenital NEC — *see* Malposition, congenital
  spleen 289.59
Movement
  abnormal (dystonic) (involuntary) 781.0
  decreased fetal 655.7 ☑
  paradoxical facial 374.43
Moya Moya disease 437.5
Mozart's ear 744.29
MRSA (methicillin-resistant staphylococcus aureus) 041.12
  colonization V02.54
  personal history of V12.04
MSSA (methicillin susceptible staphylococcus aureus) 041.11
  colonization V02.53
Mucha's disease (acute parapsoriasis varioliformis) 696.2
Mucha-Haberman syndrome (acute parapsoriasis varioliformis) 696.2
Mu-chain disease 273.2
Mucinosis (cutaneous) (papular) 701.8
Mucocele
  appendix 543.9
  buccal cavity 528.9
  gallbladder (*see also* Disease, gallbladder) 575.3
  lacrimal sac 375.43
  orbit (eye) 376.81
  salivary gland (any) 527.6
  sinus (accessory) (nasal) 478.19
  turbinate (bone) (middle) (nasal) 478.19
  uterus 621.8
Mucocutaneous lymph node syndrome (acute) (febrile) (infantile) 446.1
Mucoenteritis 564.9
Mucolipidosis I, II, III 272.7
Mucopolysaccharidosis (types 1-6) 277.5
  cardiopathy 277.5 *[425.7]*
Mucormycosis (lung) 117.7

Mucosa associated lymphoid tissue (MALT) 200.3 ☑
Mucositis — *see also* Inflammation, by site 528.00
  cervix (ulcerative) 616.81
  due to
    antineoplastic therapy (ulcerative) 528.01
    other drugs (ulcerative) 528.02
    specified NEC 528.09
  gastrointestinal (ulcerative) 538
  nasal (ulcerative) 478.11
  necroticans agranulocytica (*see also* Agranulocytosis) 288.09
  ulcerative 528.00
  vagina (ulcerative) 616.81
  vulva (ulcerative) 616.81
Mucous — *see also* condition
  patches (syphilitic) 091.3
    congenital 090.0
Mucoviscidosis 277.00
  with meconium obstruction 277.01
Mucus
  asphyxia or suffocation (*see also* Asphyxia, mucus) 933.1
    newborn 770.18
  in stool 792.1
  plug (*see also* Asphyxia, mucus) 933.1
    aspiration, of newborn 770.17
    tracheobronchial 519.19
      newborn 770.18
Muguet 112.0
Mulberry molars 090.5
Müllerian mixed tumor (M8950/3) — *see* Neoplasm, by site, malignant
Multicystic kidney 753.19
Multilobed placenta — *see* Placenta, abnormal
Multinodular prostate 600.10
  with
    urinary
      obstruction 600.11
      retention 600.11
Multiparity V61.5
  affecting
    fetus or newborn 763.89
    management of
      labor and delivery 659.4 ☑
      pregnancy V23.3
  requiring contraceptive management (*see also* Contraception) V25.9
Multipartita placenta — *see* Placenta, abnormal
Multiple, multiplex — *see also* condition
  birth
    affecting fetus or newborn 761.5
    healthy liveborn — *see* Newborn, multiple
  digits (congenital) 755.00
    fingers 755.01
    toes 755.02
  organ or site NEC — *see* Accessory
  personality 300.14
  renal arteries 747.62
Mumps 072.9
  with complication 072.8
    specified type NEC 072.79
  encephalitis 072.2
  hepatitis 072.71
  meningitis (aseptic) 072.1
  meningoencephalitis 072.2
  oophoritis 072.79
  orchitis 072.0
  pancreatitis 072.3
  polyneuropathy 072.72
  vaccination, prophylactic (against) V04.6
Mumu — *see also* Infestation, filarial 125.9
Münchausen syndrome 301.51
Münchmeyer's disease or syndrome (exostosis luxurians) 728.11
Mural — *see* condition
Murmur (cardiac) (heart) (nonorganic) (organic) 785.2
  abdominal 787.5
  aortic (valve) (*see also* Endocarditis, aortic) 424.1
  benign — *omit code*
  cardiorespiratory 785.2
  diastolic — *see* condition
  Flint (*see also* Endocarditis, aortic) 424.1

Murmur — *continued*
  functional — *omit code*
  Graham Steell (pulmonic regurgitation) (*see also* Endocarditis, pulmonary) 424.3
  innocent — *omit code*
  insignificant — *omit code*
  midsystolic 785.2
  mitral (valve) — *see* Stenosis, mitral
  physiologic — *see* condition
  presystolic, mitral — *see* Insufficiency, mitral
  pulmonic (valve) (*see also* Endocarditis, pulmonary) 424.3
  Still's (vibratory) — *omit code*
  systolic (valvular) — *see* condition
  tricuspid (valve) — *see* Endocarditis, tricuspid
  undiagnosed 785.2
  valvular — *see* condition
  vibratory — *omit code*
Murri's disease (intermittent hemoglobinuria) 283.2
Muscae volitantes 379.24
Muscle, muscular — *see* condition
Musculoneuralgia 729.1
Mushrooming hip 718.95
Mushroom workers' (pickers') lung 495.5
Mutation
  factor V leiden 289.81
  prothrombin gene 289.81
Mutism — *see also* Aphasia 784.3
  akinetic 784.3
  deaf (acquired) (congenital) 389.7
  hysterical 300.11
  selective (elective) 313.23
    adjustment reaction 309.83
Myà's disease (congenital dilation, colon) 751.3
Myalgia (intercostal) 729.1
  eosinophilia syndrome 710.5
  epidemic 074.1
    cervical 078.89
  psychogenic 307.89
  traumatic NEC 959.9
Myasthenia 358.00
  cordis — *see* Failure, heart
  gravis 358.00
    with exacerbation (acute) 358.01
    in crisis 358.01
    neonatal 775.2
    pseudoparalytica 358.00
  stomach 536.8
    psychogenic 306.4
  syndrome
    in
      botulism 005.1 *[358.1]*
      diabetes mellitus 250.6 ☑ *[358.1]*
        due to secondary diabetes 249.6 ☑ *[358.1]*
      hypothyroidism (*see also* Hypothyroidism) 244.9 *[358.1]*
      malignant neoplasm NEC 199.1 *[358.1]*
      pernicious anemia 281.0 *[358.1]*
      thyrotoxicosis (*see also* Thyrotoxicosis) 242.9 ☑ *[358.1]*
Myasthenic 728.87
Mycelium infection NEC 117.9
Mycetismus 988.1
Mycetoma (actinomycotic) 039.9
  bone 039.8
    mycotic 117.4
  foot 039.4
    mycotic 117.4
  madurae 039.9
    mycotic 117.4
  maduromycotic 039.9
    mycotic 117.4
  mycotic 117.4
  nocardial 039.9
Mycobacteriosis — *see* Mycobacterium
Mycobacterium, mycobacterial (infection) 031.9
  acid-fast (bacilli) 031.9
  anonymous (*see also* Mycobacterium, atypical) 031.9
  atypical (acid-fast bacilli) 031.9
    cutaneous 031.1
    pulmonary 031.0

Mycobacterium, mycobacterial — *continued*
  atypical — *continued*
    pulmonary — *continued*
      tuberculous (*see also* Tuberculosis, pulmonary) 011.9 ☑
    specified site NEC 031.8
  avium 031.0
    intracellulare complex bacteremia (MAC) 031.2
  balnei 031.1
  Battey 031.0
  cutaneous 031.1
  disseminated 031.2
    avium-intracellulare complex (DMAC) 031.2
  fortuitum 031.0
  intracellulare (battey bacillus) 031.0
  kakerifu 031.8
  kansasii 031.0
  kasongo 031.8
  leprae — *see* Leprosy
  luciflavum 031.0
  marinum 031.1
  pulmonary 031.0
    tuberculous (*see also* Tuberculosis, pulmonary) 011.9 ☑
  scrofulaceum 031.1
  tuberculosis (human, bovine) (*see also* Tuberculosis)
    avian type 031.0
  ulcerans 031.1
  xenopi 031.0
Mycosis, mycotic 117.9
  cutaneous NEC 111.9
  ear 111.8 *[380.15]*
  fungoides (M9700/3) 202.1 ☑
  mouth 112.0
  pharynx 117.9
  skin NEC 111.9
  stomatitis 112.0
  systemic NEC 117.9
  tonsil 117.9
  vagina, vaginitis 112.1
Mydriasis (persistent) (pupil) 379.43
Myelatelia 742.59
Myelinoclasis, perivascular, acute (postinfectious) NEC 136.9 *[323.61]*
  postimmunization or postvaccinal 323.51
Myelinosis, central pontine 341.8
Myelitis (ascending) (cerebellar) (childhood) (chronic) (descending) (diffuse) (disseminated) (pressure) (progressive) (spinal cord) (subacute) — *see also* Encephalitis 323.9
  acute (transverse) 341.20
    idiopathic 341.22
    in conditions classified elsewhere 341.21
  due to
    infection classified elsewhere 136.9 *[323.42]*
    specified cause NEC 323.82
    vaccination (any) 323.52
    viral diseases classified elsewhere 323.02
  herpes simplex 054.74
  herpes zoster 053.14
  late effect — *see* category 326
  optic neuritis in 341.0
  postchickenpox 052.2
  postimmunization 323.52
  postinfectious 136.9 *[323.63]*
  postvaccinal 323.52
  postvaricella 052.2
  syphilitic (transverse) 094.89
  toxic 989.9 *[323.72]*
  transverse 323.82
    acute 341.20
      idiopathic 341.22
      in conditions classified elsewhere 341.21
    idiopathic 341.22
  tuberculous (*see also* Tuberculosis) 013.6 ☑
  virus 049.9
Myeloblastic — *see* condition
Myelocele — *see also* Spina bifida 741.9 ☑
  with hydrocephalus 741.0 ☑
Myelocystocele — *see also* Spina bifida 741.9 ☑

☑ Additional Digit Required — Refer to the Tabular List for Digit Selection   ⓦ Subterms under main terms may continue to next column or page

2010 ICD-9-CM   ▶◀ Revised Text   ● New Line   ▲ Revised Code   **Volume 2 — 181**

Myelocytic — see condition
Myelocytoma 205.1 ☑
Myelodysplasia (spinal cord) 742.59
    meaning myelodysplastic syndrome — see
      Syndrome, myelodysplastic
Myeloencephalitis — see Encephalitis
Myelofibrosis 289.83
    with myeloid metaplasia 238.76
    idiopathic (chronic) 238.76
    megakaryocytic 238.79
    primary 238.76
    secondary 289.83
Myelogenous — see condition
Myeloid — see condition
Myelokathexis 288.09
Myeloleukodystrophy 330.0
Myelolipoma (M8870/0) — see Neoplasm, by
    site, benign
Myeloma (multiple) (plasma cell) (plasmacytic)
    (M9730/3) 203.0 ☑
    monostotic (M9731/1) 238.6
    solitary (M9731/1) 238.6
Myelomalacia 336.8
Myeloma, multiple (M9730/3) 203.0 ☑
Myelomatosis (M9730/3) 203.0 ☑
Myelomeningitis — see Meningoencephalitis
Myelomeningocele (spinal cord) — see also
    Spina bifida 741.9 ☑
    fetal, causing fetopelvic disproportion
      653.7 ☑
Myelo-osteo-musculodysplasia hereditaria
    756.89
Myelopathic — see condition
Myelopathy (spinal cord) 336.9
    cervical 721.1
    diabetic 250.6 ☑ *[336.3]*
      due to secondary diabetes 249.6 ☑ *[336.3]*
    drug-induced 336.8
    due to or with
      carbon tetrachloride 987.8 *[323.72]*
      degeneration or displacement, interverte-
        bral disc 722.70
        cervical, cervicothoracic 722.71
        lumbar, lumbosacral 722.73
        thoracic, thoracolumbar 722.72
      hydroxyquinoline derivatives 961.3 *[323.72]*
      infection — see Encephalitis
      intervertebral disc disorder 722.70
        cervical, cervicothoracic 722.71
        lumbar, lumbosacral 722.73
        thoracic, thoracolumbar 722.72
      lead 984.9 *[323.72]*
      mercury 985.0 *[323.72]*
      neoplastic disease (see also Neoplasm, by
        site) 239.9 *[336.3]*
      pernicious anemia 281.0 *[336.3]*
      spondylosis 721.91
        cervical 721.1
        lumbar, lumbosacral 721.42
        thoracic 721.41
      thallium 985.8 *[323.72]*
    lumbar, lumbosacral 721.42
    necrotic (subacute) 336.1
    radiation-induced 336.8
    spondylogenic NEC 721.91
      cervical 721.1
      lumbar, lumbosacral 721.42
      thoracic 721.41
    thoracic 721.41
    toxic NEC 989.9 *[323.72]*
    transverse (see also Myelitis) 323.82
    vascular 336.1
Myelophthisis 284.2
Myeloproliferative disease (M9960/1) 238.79
Myeloradiculitis — see also Polyneuropathy
    357.0
Myeloradiculodysplasia (spinal) 742.59
Myelosarcoma (M9930/3) 205.3 ☑
Myelosclerosis 289.89
    with myeloid metaplasia (M9961/1) 238.76
    disseminated, of nervous system 340
    megakaryocytic (M9961/1) 238.79
Myelosis (M9860/3) — see also Leukemia,
    myeloid 205.9 ☑
    acute (M9861/3) 205.0 ☑
    aleukemic (M9864/3) 205.8 ☑

Myelosis — see also Leukemia, myeloid —
    continued
    chronic (M9863/3) 205.1 ☑
    erythremic (M9840/3) 207.0 ☑
      acute (M9841/3) 207.0 ☑
    megakaryocytic (M9920/3) 207.2 ☑
    nonleukemic (chronic) 288.8
    subacute (M9862/3) 205.2 ☑
Myesthenia — see Myasthenia
Myiasis (cavernous) 134.0
    orbit 134.0 *[376.13]*
Myoadenoma, prostate 600.20
    with
        other lower urinary tract symptoms (LUTS)
        600.21
      urinary
        obstruction 600.21
        retention 600.21
Myoblastoma
    granular cell (M9580/0) (see also Neoplasm,
      connective tissue, benign)
      malignant (M9580/3) — see Neoplasm,
        connective tissue, malignant
    tongue (M9580/0) 210.1
Myocardial — see condition
Myocardiopathy (congestive) (constrictive) (fa-
    milial) (hypertrophic nonobstructive) (idio-
    pathic) (infiltrative) (obstructive) (primary)
    (restrictive) (sporadic) 425.4
    alcoholic 425.5
    amyloid 277.39 *[425.7]*
    beriberi 265.0 *[425.7]*
    cobalt-beer 425.5
    due to
      amyloidosis 277.39 *[425.7]*
      beriberi 265.0 *[425.7]*
      cardiac glycogenosis 271.0 *[425.7]*
      Chagas' disease 086.0
      Friedreich's ataxia 334.0 *[425.8]*
      influenza 487.8 *[425.8]*
      mucopolysaccharidosis 277.5 *[425.7]*
      myotonia atrophica 359.21 *[425.8]*
      progressive muscular dystrophy
        359.1 *[425.8]*
      sarcoidosis 135 *[425.8]*
    glycogen storage 271.0 *[425.7]*
    hypertrophic obstructive 425.1
    metabolic NEC 277.9 *[425.7]*
    nutritional 269.9 *[425.7]*
    obscure (African) 425.2
    peripartum 674.5 ☑
    postpartum 674.5 ☑
    secondary 425.9
    thyrotoxic (see also Thyrotoxicosis)
      242.9 ☑ *[425.7]*
    toxic NEC 425.9
Myocarditis (fibroid) (interstitial) (old) (progres-
    sive) (senile) (with arteriosclerosis) 429.0
    with
      rheumatic fever (conditions classifiable to
        390) 398.0
        active (see also Myocarditis, acute,
          rheumatic) 391.2
        inactive or quiescent (with chorea)
          398.0
    active (nonrheumatic) 422.90
      rheumatic 391.2
        with chorea (acute) (rheumatic)
          (Sydenham's) 392.0
    acute or subacute (interstitial) 422.90
      due to Streptococcus (beta-hemolytic)
        391.2
      idiopathic 422.91
      rheumatic 391.2
        with chorea (acute) (rheumatic)
          (Sydenham's) 392.0
      specified type NEC 422.99
    aseptic of newborn 074.23
    bacterial (acute) 422.92
    chagasic 086.0
    chronic (interstitial) 429.0
    congenital 746.89
    constrictive 425.4
    Coxsackie (virus) 074.23
    diphtheritic 032.82

Myocarditis — continued
    due to or in
      Coxsackie (virus) 074.23
      diphtheria 032.82
      epidemic louse-borne typhus 080 *[422.0]*
      influenza 487.8 *[422.0]*
      Lyme disease 088.81 *[422.0]*
      scarlet fever 034.1 *[422.0]*
      toxoplasmosis (acquired) 130.3
      tuberculosis (see also Tuberculosis)
        017.9 ☑ *[422.0]*
      typhoid 002.0 *[422.0]*
      typhus NEC 081.9 *[422.0]*
    eosinophilic 422.91
    epidemic of newborn 074.23
    Fiedler's (acute) (isolated) (subacute) 422.91
    giant cell (acute) (subacute) 422.91
    gonococcal 098.85
    granulomatous (idiopathic) (isolated) (nonspe-
      cific) 422.91
    hypertensive (see also Hypertension, heart)
      402.90
    idiopathic 422.91
      granulomatous 422.91
    infective 422.92
    influenzal 487.8 *[422.0]*
    isolated (diffuse) (granulomatous) 422.91
    malignant 422.99
    meningococcal 036.43
    nonrheumatic, active 422.90
    parenchymatous 422.90
    pneumococcal (acute) (subacute) 422.92
    rheumatic (chronic) (inactive) (with chorea)
      398.0
      active or acute 391.2
        with chorea (acute) (rheumatic)
          (Sydenham's) 392.0
    septic 422.92
    specific (giant cell) (productive) 422.91
    staphylococcal (acute) (subacute) 422.92
    suppurative 422.92
    syphilitic (chronic) 093.82
    toxic 422.93
      rheumatic (see also Myocarditis, acute
        rheumatic) 391.2
    tuberculous (see also Tuberculosis)
      017.9 ☑ *[422.0]*
    typhoid 002.0 *[422.0]*
    valvular — see Endocarditis
    viral, except Coxsackie 422.91
      Coxsackie 074.23
      of newborn (Coxsackie) 074.23
Myocardium, myocardial — see condition
Myocardosis — see also Cardiomyopathy 425.4
Myoclonia (essential) 333.2
    epileptica 345.1 ☑ ▲
    Friedrich's 333.2
    massive 333.2
Myoclonic
    epilepsy, familial (progressive) 345.1 ☑ ▲
    jerks 333.2
Myoclonus (familial essential) (multifocal) (sim-
    plex) 333.2
    with epilepsy and with ragged red fibers
      (MERRF syndrome) 277.87
    facial 351.8
    massive (infantile) 333.2
    palatal 333.2 ●
    pharyngeal 333.2 ▲
Myocytolysis 429.1 ●
Myodiastasis 728.84
Myoendocarditis — see also Endocarditis
    acute or subacute 421.9
Myoepithelioma (M8982/0) — see Neoplasm,
    by site, benign
Myofascitis (acute) 729.1
    low back 724.2
Myofibroma (M8890/0) — see also Neoplasm,
    connective tissue, benign
    uterus (cervix) (corpus) (see also Leiomyoma)
      218.9
Myofibromatosis
    infantile 759.89
Myofibrosis 728.2
    heart (see also Myocarditis) 429.0
    humeroscapular region 726.2

Myofibrosis — continued
    scapulohumeral 726.2
Myofibrositis — see also Myositis 729.1
    scapulohumeral 726.2
Myogelosis (occupational) 728.89
Myoglobinuria 791.3
Myoglobinuria, primary 791.3
Myokymia — see also Myoclonus
    facial 351.8
Myolipoma (M8860/0)
    specified site — see Neoplasm, connective
      tissue, benign
    unspecified site 223.0
Myoma (M8895/0) — see also Neoplasm, connec-
    tive tissue, benign
    cervix (stump) (uterus) (see also Leiomyoma)
      218.9
    malignant (M8895/3) — see Neoplasm, con-
      nective tissue, malignant
    prostate 600.20
      with
        other lower urinary tract symptoms
        (LUTS) 600.21
        urinary
          obstruction 600.21
          retention 600.21
    uterus (cervix) (corpus) (see also Leiomyoma)
      218.9
      in pregnancy or childbirth 654.1 ☑
        affecting fetus or newborn 763.89
        causing obstructed labor 660.2 ☑
          affecting fetus or newborn 763.1
Myomalacia 728.9
    cordis, heart (see also Degeneration, myocar-
      dial) 429.1
Myometritis — see also Endometritis 615.9
Myometrium — see condition
Myonecrosis, clostridial 040.0
Myopathy 359.9
    alcoholic 359.4
    amyloid 277.39 *[359.6]*
    benign, congenital 359.0
    central core 359.0
    centronuclear 359.0
    congenital (benign) 359.0
    critical illness 359.81
    distal 359.1
    due to drugs 359.4
    endocrine 259.9 *[359.5]*
      specified type NEC 259.8 *[359.5]*
    extraocular muscles 376.82
    facioscapulohumeral 359.1
    in
      Addison's disease 255.41 *[359.5]*
      amyloidosis 277.39 *[359.6]*
      cretinism 243 *[359.5]*
      Cushing's syndrome 255.0 *[359.5]*
      disseminated lupus erythematosus
        710.0 *[359.6]*
      giant cell arteritis 446.5 *[359.6]*
      hyperadrenocorticism NEC 255.3 *[359.5]*
      hyperparathyroidism 252.01 *[359.5]*
      hypopituitarism 253.2 *[359.5]*
      hypothyroidism (see also Hypothyroidism)
        244.9 *[359.5]*
      malignant neoplasm NEC (M8000/3) 199.1
        [359.6]
      myxedema (see also Myxedema)
        244.9 *[359.5]*
      polyarteritis nodosa 446.0 *[359.6]*
      rheumatoid arthritis 714.0 *[359.6]*
      sarcoidosis 135 *[359.6]*
      scleroderma 710.1 *[359.6]*
      Sjögren's disease 710.2 *[359.6]*
      thyrotoxicosis (see also Thyrotoxicosis)
        242.9 ☑ *[359.5]*
    inflammatory 359.79 ▲
      immune NEC 359.79 ●
      specified NEC 359.79 ●
    intensive care (ICU) 359.81
    limb-girdle 359.1
    myotubular 359.0
    necrotizing, acute 359.81
    nemaline 359.0
    ocular 359.1
    oculopharyngeal 359.1

Myopathy — *continued*
　of critical illness 359.81
　primary 359.89
　progressive NEC 359.89
　proximal myotonic (PROMM) 359.21
　quadriplegic, acute 359.81
　rod body 359.0
　scapulohumeral 359.1
　specified type NEC 359.89
　toxic 359.4
Myopericarditis — *see also* Pericarditis 423.9
Myopia (axial) (congenital) (increased curvature
　　or refraction, nucleus of lens) 367.1
　degenerative, malignant 360.21
　malignant 360.21
　progressive high (degenerative) 360.21
Myosarcoma (M8895/3) — *see* Neoplasm, con-
　　nective tissue, malignant
Myosis (persistent) 379.42
　stromal (endolymphatic) (M8931/1) 236.0
Myositis 729.1
　clostridial 040.0
　due to posture 729.1
　epidemic 074.1
　fibrosa or fibrous (chronic) 728.2
　　Volkmann's (complicating trauma) 958.6
　inclusion body (IBM) 359.71
　infective 728.0
　interstitial 728.81
　multiple — *see* Polymyositis
　occupational 729.1
　orbital, chronic 376.12
　ossificans 728.12
　　circumscribed 728.12
　　progressive 728.11
　　traumatic 728.12
　progressive fibrosing 728.11
　purulent 728.0
　rheumatic 729.1
　rheumatoid 729.1
　suppurative 728.0
　syphilitic 095.6
　traumatic (old) 729.1
Myospasia impulsiva 307.23
Myotonia (acquisita) (intermittens) 728.85
　atrophica 359.21
　congenita 359.22
　　acetazolamide responsive 359.22
　　dominant form 359.22
　　recessive form 359.22
　drug-induced 359.24
　dystrophica 359.21
　fluctuans 359.29
　levior 359.22
　permanens 359.29
Myotonic pupil 379.46
Myriapodiasis 134.1
Myringitis
　with otitis media — *see* Otitis media
　acute 384.00
　　specified type NEC 384.09
　bullosa hemorrhagica 384.01
　bullous 384.01
　chronic 384.1
Mysophobia 300.29
Mytilotoxism 988.0
Myxadenitis labialis 528.5
Myxedema (adult) (idiocy) (infantile) (juvenile)
　　(thyroid gland) — *see also* Hypothyroidism
　　244.9
　circumscribed 242.9 ☑
　congenital 243
　cutis 701.8
　localized (pretibial) 242.9 ☑
　madness (acute) 293.0
　　subacute 293.1
　papular 701.8
　pituitary 244.8
　postpartum 674.8 ☑
　pretibial 242.9 ☑
　primary 244.9
Myxochondrosarcoma (M9220/3) — *see* Neo-
　　plasm, cartilage, malignant
Myxofibroma (M8811/0) — *see also* Neoplasm,
　　connective tissue, benign
　odontogenic (M9320/0) 213.1

Myxofibroma — *see also* Neoplasm, connective
　　tissue, benign — *continued*
　odontogenic — *continued*
　　upper jaw (bone) 213.0
Myxofibrosarcoma (M8811/3) — *see* Neoplasm,
　　connective tissue, malignant
Myxolipoma (M8852/0) — *see also* Lipoma, by
　　site 214.9
Myxoliposarcoma (M8852/3) — *see* Neoplasm,
　　connective tissue, malignant
Myxoma (M8840/0) — *see also* Neoplasm, con-
　　nective tissue, benign
　odontogenic (M9320/0) 213.1
　　upper jaw (bone) 213.0
Myxosarcoma (M8840/3) — *see* Neoplasm,
　　connective tissue, malignant

N

Naegeli's
　disease (hereditary hemorrhagic thrombasthe-
　　nia) 287.1
　leukemia, monocytic (M9863/3) 205.1 ☑
　syndrome (incontinentia pigmenti) 757.33
Naffziger's syndrome 353.0
Naga sore — *see also* Ulcer, skin 707.9
Nägele's pelvis 738.6
　with disproportion (fetopelvic) 653.0 ☑
　　affecting fetus or newborn 763.1
　　causing obstructed labor 660.1 ☑
　　　affecting fetus or newborn 763.1
Nager-de Reynier syndrome (dysostosis
　　mandibularis) 756.0
Nail — *see also* condition
　biting 307.9
　patella syndrome (hereditary osteoonychodys-
　　plasia) 756.89
Nanism, nanosomia — *see also* Dwarfism 259.4
　hypophyseal 253.3
　pituitary 253.3
　renis, renalis 588.0
Nanukayami 100.89
Napkin rash 691.0
Narcissism 301.81
Narcolepsy 347.00
　with cataplexy 347.01
　in conditions classified elsewhere 347.10
　　with cataplexy 347.11
Narcosis
　carbon dioxide (respiratory) 786.09
　due to drug
　　correct substance properly administered
　　　780.09
　　overdose or wrong substance given or
　　　taken 977.9
　　　specified drug — *see* Table of Drugs
　　　　and Chemicals
Narcotism (chronic) — *see also* Dependence
　　304.9 ☑
　acute
　　correct substance properly administered
　　　349.82
　　overdose or wrong substance given or
　　　taken 967.8
　　　specified drug — *see* Table of Drugs
　　　　and Chemicals
NARP (ataxia and retinitis pigmentosa) 277.87
Narrow
　anterior chamber angle 365.02
　pelvis (inlet) (outlet) — *see* Contraction, pelvis
Narrowing
　artery NEC 447.1
　　auditory, internal 433.8 ☑
　　basilar 433.0 ☑
　　　with other precerebral artery 433.3 ☑
　　　bilateral 433.3 ☑
　　carotid 433.1 ☑
　　　with other precerebral artery 433.3 ☑
　　　bilateral 433.3 ☑
　　cerebellar 433.8 ☑
　　choroidal 433.8 ☑
　　communicating posterior 433.8 ☑
　　coronary (*see also* Arteriosclerosis, coro-
　　　nary)
　　　congenital 746.85
　　　due to syphilis 090.5

Narrowing — *continued*
　artery — *continued*
　　hypophyseal 433.8 ☑
　　pontine 433.8 ☑
　　precerebral NEC 433.9 ☑
　　　multiple or bilateral 433.3 ☑
　　　specified NEC 433.8 ☑
　　vertebral 433.2 ☑
　　　with other precerebral artery 433.3 ☑
　　　bilateral 433.3 ☑
　auditory canal (external) (*see also* Stricture, ear
　　canal, acquired) 380.50
　cerebral arteries 437.0
　cicatricial — *see* Cicatrix
　congenital — *see* Anomaly, congenital
　coronary artery — *see* Narrowing, artery,
　　coronary
　ear, middle 385.22
　Eustachian tube (*see also* Obstruction, Eustachi-
　　an tube) 381.60
　eyelid 374.46
　　congenital 743.62
　intervertebral disc or space NEC — *see* Degen-
　　eration, intervertebral disc
　joint space, hip 719.85
　larynx 478.74
　lids 374.46
　　congenital 743.62
　mesenteric artery (with gangrene) 557.0
　palate 524.89
　palpebral fissure 374.46
　retinal artery 362.13
　ureter 593.3
　urethra (*see also* Stricture, urethra) 598.9
Narrowness, abnormal, eyelid 743.62
Nasal — *see* condition
Nasolacrimal — *see* condition
Nasopharyngeal — *see also* condition
　bursa 478.29
　pituitary gland 759.2
　torticollis 723.5
Nasopharyngitis (acute) (infective) (subacute)
　　460
　chronic 472.2
　　due to external agent — *see* Condition,
　　　respiratory, chronic, due to
　due to external agent — *see* Condition, respi-
　　ratory, due to
　septic 034.0
　streptococcal 034.0
　suppurative (chronic) 472.2
　ulcerative (chronic) 472.2
Nasopharynx, nasopharyngeal — *see* condition
Natal tooth, teeth 520.6
Nausea — *see also* Vomiting 787.02
　with vomiting 787.01
　epidemic 078.82
　gravidarum — *see* Hyperemesis, gravidarum
　marina 994.6
Navel — *see* condition
Neapolitan fever — *see also* Brucellosis 023.9
Near drowning 994.1
Nearsightedness 367.1
Near-syncope 780.2
Nebécourt's syndrome 253.3
Nebula, cornea (eye) 371.01
　congenital 743.43
　interfering with vision 743.42
Necator americanus infestation 126.1
Necatoriasis 126.1
Neck — *see* condition
Necrencephalus — *see also* Softening, brain
　　437.8
Necrobacillosis 040.3
Necrobiosis 799.89
　brain or cerebral (*see also* Softening, brain)
　　437.8
　lipoidica 709.3
　　diabeticorum 250.8 ☑ [709.3]
　　　due to secondary diabetes
　　　　249.8 ☑ [709.3]
Necrodermolysis 695.15
Necrolysis, toxic epidermal 695.15
　due to drug
　　correct substance properly administered
　　　695.15

Necrolysis, toxic epidermal — *continued*
　due to drug — *continued*
　　overdose or wrong substance given or
　　　taken 977.9
　　　specified drug — *see* Table of Drugs
　　　　and Chemicals
　Stevens-Johnson syndrome overlap (SJS-TEN
　　overlap syndrome) 695.14
Necrophilia 302.89
Necrosis, necrotic
　adrenal (capsule) (gland) 255.8
　antrum, nasal sinus 478.19
　aorta (hyaline) (*see also* Aneurysm, aorta) 441.9
　　cystic medial 441.00
　　　abdominal 441.02
　　　thoracic 441.01
　　　thoracoabdominal 441.03
　　ruptured 441.5
　arteritis 446.0
　artery 447.5
　aseptic, bone 733.40
　　femur (head) (neck) 733.42
　　　medial condyle 733.43
　　humoral head 733.41
　　jaw 733.45
　　medial femoral condyle 733.43
　　specific site NEC 733.49
　　talus 733.44
　avascular, bone NEC (*see also* Necrosis, aseptic,
　　bone) 733.40
　bladder (aseptic) (sphincter) 596.8
　bone (*see also* Osteomyelitis) 730.1 ☑
　　acute 730.0 ☑
　　aseptic or avascular 733.40
　　　femur (head) (neck) 733.42
　　　　medial condyle 733.43
　　　humoral head 733.41
　　　jaw 733.45
　　　medial femoral condyle 733.43
　　　specified site NEC 733.49
　　　talus 733.44
　　ethmoid 478.19
　　ischemic 733.40
　　jaw 526.4
　　　aseptic 733.45
　　marrow 289.89
　　Paget's (osteitis deformans) 731.0
　　tuberculous — *see* Tuberculosis, bone
　brain (softening) (*see also* Softening, brain)
　　437.8
　breast (aseptic) (fat) (segmental) 611.3
　bronchus, bronchi 519.19
　central nervous system NEC (*see also* Soften-
　　ing, brain) 437.8
　cerebellar (*see also* Softening, brain) 437.8
　cerebral (softening) (*see also* Softening, brain)
　　437.8
　cerebrospinal (softening) (*see also* Softening,
　　brain) 437.8
　colon 557.0
　cornea (*see also* Keratitis) 371.40
　cortical, kidney 583.6
　cystic medial (aorta) 441.00
　　abdominal 441.02
　　thoracic 441.01
　　thoracoabdominal 441.03
　dental 521.09
　　pulp 522.1
　due to swallowing corrosive substance — *see*
　　Burn, by site
　ear (ossicle) 385.24
　esophagus 530.89
　ethmoid (bone) 478.19
　eyelid 374.50
　fat, fatty (generalized) (*see also* Degeneration,
　　fatty) 272.8
　　abdominal wall 567.82
　　breast (aseptic) (segmental) 611.3
　　intestine 569.89
　　localized — *see* Degeneration, by site, fatty
　　mesentery 567.82
　　omentum 567.82
　　pancreas 577.8
　　peritoneum 567.82
　　skin (subcutaneous) 709.3
　　　newborn 778.1

Necrosis, necrotic — *continued*
  femur (aseptic) (avascular) 733.42
    head 733.42
    medial condyle 733.43
    neck 733.42
  gallbladder (*see also* Cholecystitis, acute) 575.0
  gangrenous 785.4
  gastric 537.89
  glottis 478.79
  heart (myocardium) — *see* Infarct, myocardium
  hepatic (*see also* Necrosis, liver) 570
  hip (aseptic) (avascular) 733.42
  intestine (acute) (hemorrhagic) (massive) 557.0
  ischemic 785.4
  jaw 526.4
    aseptic 733.45
  kidney (bilateral) 583.9
    acute 584.9
    cortical 583.6
      acute 584.6
        with
          abortion — *see* Abortion, by type, with renal failure
          ectopic pregnancy (*see also* categories 633.0–633.9) 639.3
          molar pregnancy (*see also* categories 630–632) 639.3
        complicating pregnancy 646.2 ☑
          affecting fetus or newborn 760.1
        following labor and delivery 669.3 ☑
    medullary (papillary) (*see also* Pyelitis) 590.80
      in
        acute renal failure 584.7
        nephritis, nephropathy 583.7
    papillary (*see also* Pyelitis) 590.80
      in
        acute renal failure 584.7
        nephritis, nephropathy 583.7
    tubular 584.5
      with
        abortion — *see* Abortion, by type, with renal failure
        ectopic pregnancy (*see also* categories 633.0–633.9) 639.3

Necrosis, necrotic — *continued*
  kidney — *continued*
    tubular — *continued*
      with — *continued*
        molar pregnancy (*see also* categories 630–632) 639.3
      complicating
        abortion 639.3
        ectopic or molar pregnancy 639.3
        pregnancy 646.2 ☑
          affecting fetus or newborn 760.1
      following labor and delivery 669.3 ☑
      traumatic 958.5
  larynx 478.79
  liver (acute) (congenital) (diffuse) (massive) (subacute) 570
    with
      abortion — *see* Abortion, by type, with specified complication NEC
      ectopic pregnancy (*see also* categories 633.0–633.9) 639.8
      molar pregnancy (*see also* categories 630–632) 639.8
    complicating pregnancy 646.7 ☑
      affecting fetus or newborn 760.8
    following
      abortion 639.8
      ectopic or molar pregnancy 639.8
    obstetrical 646.7 ☑
    postabortal 639.8
    puerperal, postpartum 674.8 ☑
    toxic 573.3
  lung 513.0
  lymphatic gland 683
  mammary gland 611.3
  mastoid (chronic) 383.1
  mesentery 557.0
    fat 567.82
  mitral valve — *see* Insufficiency, mitral
  myocardium, myocardial — *see* Infarct, myocardium
  nose (septum) 478.19
  omentum 557.0
    with mesenteric infarction 557.0
    fat 567.82
  orbit, orbital 376.10
  ossicles, ear (aseptic) 385.24
  ovary (*see also* Salpingo-oophoritis) 614.2

Necrosis, necrotic — *continued*
  pancreas (aseptic) (duct) (fat) 577.8
    acute 577.0
    infective 577.0
  papillary, kidney (*see also* Pyelitis) 590.80
  perineum 624.8
  peritoneum 557.0
    with mesenteric infarction 557.0
    fat 567.82
  pharynx 462
    in granulocytopenia 288.09
  phosphorus 983.9
  pituitary (gland) (postpartum) (Sheehan) 253.2
  placenta (*see also* Placenta, abnormal) 656.7 ☑
  pneumonia 513.0
  pulmonary 513.0
  pulp (dental) 522.1
  pylorus 537.89
  radiation — *see* Necrosis, by site
  radium — *see* Necrosis, by site
  renal — *see* Necrosis, kidney
  sclera 379.19
  scrotum 608.89
  skin or subcutaneous tissue 709.8
    due to burn — see Burn, by site
    gangrenous 785.4
  spine, spinal (column) 730.18
    acute 730.18
    cord 336.1
  spleen 289.59
  stomach 537.89
  stomatitis 528.1
  subcutaneous fat 709.3
    fetus or newborn 778.1
  subendocardial — *see* Infarct, myocardium
  suprarenal (capsule) (gland) 255.8
  teeth, tooth 521.09
  testis 608.89
  thymus (gland) 254.8
  tonsil 474.8
  trachea 519.19
  tuberculous NEC — *see* Tuberculosis
  tubular (acute) (anoxic) (toxic) 584.5
    due to a procedure 997.5
  umbilical cord, affecting fetus or newborn 762.6
  vagina 623.8
  vertebra (lumbar) 730.18

Necrosis, necrotic — *continued*
  vertebra — *continued*
    acute 730.18
    tuberculous (*see also* Tuberculosis) 015.0 ☑ *[730.8]* ☑
  vesical (aseptic) (bladder) 596.8
  vulva 624.8
  x-ray — *see* Necrosis, by site
Necrospermia 606.0
Necrotizing angiitis 446.0
Negativism 301.7
Neglect (child) (newborn) NEC 995.52
  adult 995.84
  after or at birth 995.52
  hemispatial 781.8
  left-sided 781.8
  sensory 781.8
  visuospatial 781.8
Negri bodies 071
Neill-Dingwall syndrome (microcephaly and dwarfism) 759.89
Neisserian infection NEC — *see* Gonococcus
Nematodiasis NEC — *see also* Infestation, Nematode 127.9
  ancylostoma (*see also* Ancylostomiasis) 126.9
Neoformans cryptococcus infection 117.5
Neonatal — *see also* condition
  abstinence syndrome 779.5   ●
  adrenoleukodystrophy 277.86
  teeth, tooth 520.6
Neonatorum — *see* condition
Neoplasia
  anal intraepithelial I [AIN I] (histologically confirmed) 569.44
  anal intraepithelial II [AIN II] (histologically confirmed) 569.44
  anal intraepithelial III [AIN III] 230.6
    anal canal 230.5
  endometrial intraepithelial [EIN] 621.35   ●
  multiple endocrine [MEN]
    type I 258.01
    type IIA 258.02
    type IIB 258.03
  vaginal intraepithelial I [VAIN I] 623.0
  vaginal intraepithelial II [VAIN II] 623.0
  vaginal intraepithelial III [VAIN III] 233.31
  vulvular intraepithelial I [VIN I] 624.01
  vulvular intraepithelial II [VIN II] 624.02
  vulvular intraepithelial III [VIN III] 233.32

☑ Additional Digit Required — Refer to the Tabular List for Digit Selection   Subterms under main terms may continue to next column or page

184 — Volume 2 • October 2009   ▶◀ Revised Text   ● New Line   ▲ Revised Code   2010 ICD-9-CM

	Malignant			Benign	Uncertain Behavior	Unspecified
	Primary	Secondary	Ca in situ			
Neoplasm, neoplastic	199.1	199.1	234.9	229.9	238.9	239.9

Notes — 1. The list below gives the code numbers for neoplasms by anatomical site. For each site there are six possible code numbers according to whether the neoplasm in question is malignant, benign, in situ, of uncertain behavior, or of unspecified nature. The description of the neoplasm will often indicate which of the six columns is appropriate; e.g., malignant melanoma of skin, benign fibroadenoma of breast, carcinoma in situ of cervix uteri.

Where such descriptors are not present, the remainder of the Index should be consulted where guidance is given to the appropriate column for each morphological (histological) variety listed; e.g., Mesonephroma — see Neoplasm, malignant; Embryoma — see also Neoplasm, uncertain behavior; Disease, Bowen's — see Neoplasm, skin, in situ. However, the guidance in the Index can be overridden if one of the descriptors mentioned above is present; e.g., malignant adenoma of colon is coded to 153.9 and not to 211.3 as the adjective "malignant" overrides the Index entry "Adenoma — see also Neoplasm, benign."

2. Sites marked with the sign * (e.g., face NEC*) should be classified to malignant neoplasm of skin of these sites if the variety of neoplasm is a squamous cell carcinoma or an epidermoid carcinoma, and to benign neoplasm of skin of these sites if the variety of neoplasm is a papilloma (any type).

	Malignant			Benign	Uncertain Behavior	Unspecified
	Primary	Secondary	Ca in situ			
abdomen, abdominal	195.2	198.89	234.8	229.8	238.8	239.89 ▲
cavity	195.2	198.89	234.8	229.8	238.8	239.89 ▲
organ	195.2	198.89	234.8	229.8	238.8	239.89 ▲
viscera	195.2	198.89	234.8	229.8	238.8	239.89 ▲
wall	173.5	198.2	232.5	216.5	238.2	239.2
connective tissue	171.5	198.89	—	215.5	238.1	239.2
abdominopelvic	195.8	198.89	234.8	229.8	238.8	239.89 ▲
accessory sinus — see Neoplasm, sinus						
acoustic nerve	192.0	198.4	—	225.1	237.9	239.7
acromion (process)	170.4	198.5	—	213.4	238.0	239.2
adenoid (pharynx) (tissue)	147.1	198.89	230.0	210.7	235.1	239.0
adipose tissue (see also Neoplasm, connective tissue)	171.9	198.89	—	215.9	238.1	239.2
adnexa (uterine)	183.9	198.82	233.39	221.8	236.3	239.5
adrenal (cortex) (gland) (medulla)	194.0	198.7	234.8	227.0	237.2	239.7
ala nasi (external)	173.3	198.2	232.3	216.3	238.2	239.2
alimentary canal or tract NEC	159.9	197.8	230.9	211.9	235.5	239.0
alveolar	143.9	198.89	230.0	210.4	235.1	239.0
mucosa	143.9	198.89	230.0	210.4	235.1	239.0
lower	143.1	198.89	230.0	210.4	235.1	239.0
upper	143.0	198.89	230.0	210.4	235.1	239.0
ridge or process	170.1	198.5	—	213.1	238.0	239.2
carcinoma	143.9	—	—	—	—	—
lower	143.1	—	—	—	—	—
upper	143.0	—	—	—	—	—
lower	170.1	198.5	—	213.1	238.0	239.2
mucosa	143.9	198.89	230.0	210.4	235.1	239.0
lower	143.1	198.89	230.0	210.4	235.1	239.0
upper	143.0	198.89	230.0	210.4	235.1	239.0
upper	170.0	198.5	—	213.0	238.0	239.2
sulcus	145.1	198.89	230.0	210.4	235.1	239.0
alveolus	143.9	198.89	230.0	210.4	235.1	239.0
lower	143.1	198.89	230.0	210.4	235.1	239.0
upper	143.0	198.89	230.0	210.4	235.1	239.0
ampulla of Vater	156.2	197.8	230.8	211.5	235.3	239.0
ankle NEC*	195.5	198.89	232.7	229.8	238.8	239.89 ▲
anorectum, anorectal (junction)	154.8	197.5	230.7	211.4	235.2	239.0
antecubital fossa or space*	195.4	198.89	232.6	229.8	238.8	239.89 ▲
antrum (Highmore) (maxillary)	160.2	197.3	231.8	212.0	235.9	239.1
pyloric	151.2	197.8	230.2	211.1	235.2	239.0
tympanicum	160.1	197.3	231.8	212.0	235.9	239.1
anus, anal	154.3	197.5	230.6	211.4	235.5	239.0
canal	154.2	197.5	230.5	211.4	235.5	239.0
contiguous sites with rectosigmoid	154.8	—	—	—	—	—

	Malignant			Benign	Uncertain Behavior	Unspecified
	Primary	Secondary	Ca in situ			
Neoplasm, neoplastic — continued						
anus, anal — continued						
contiguous sites with rectosigmoid junction or rectum — continued						
junction or rectum						
margin	173.5	198.2	232.5	216.5	238.2	239.2
skin	173.5	198.2	232.5	216.5	238.2	239.2
sphincter	154.2	197.5	230.5	211.4	235.5	239.0
aorta (thoracic)	171.4	198.89	—	215.4	238.1	239.2
abdominal	171.5	198.89	—	215.5	238.1	239.2
aortic body	194.6	198.89	—	227.6	237.3	239.7
aponeurosis	171.9	198.89	—	215.9	238.1	239.2
palmar	171.2	198.89	—	215.2	238.1	239.2
plantar	171.3	198.89	—	215.3	238.1	239.2
appendix	153.5	197.5	230.3	211.3	235.2	239.0
arachnoid (cerebral)	192.1	198.4	—	225.2	237.6	239.7
spinal	192.3	198.4	—	225.4	237.6	239.7
areola (female)	174.0	198.81	233.0	217	238.3	239.3
male	175.0	198.81	233.0	217	238.3	239.3
arm NEC*	195.4	198.89	232.6	229.8	238.8	239.89 ▲
artery — see Neoplasm, connective tissue						
aryepiglottic fold	148.2	198.89	230.0	210.8	235.1	239.0
hypopharyngeal aspect	148.2	198.89	230.0	210.8	235.1	239.0
laryngeal aspect	161.1	197.3	231.0	212.1	235.6	239.1
marginal zone	148.2	198.89	230.0	210.8	235.1	239.0
arytenoid (cartilage)	161.3	197.3	231.0	212.1	235.6	239.1
fold — see Neoplasm, aryepiglottic						
associated with transplanted organ	199.2	—	—	—	—	—
atlas	170.2	198.5	—	213.2	238.0	239.2
atrium, cardiac	164.1	198.89	—	212.7	238.8	239.89 ▲
auditory canal (external) (skin)	173.2	198.2	232.2	216.2	238.2	239.2
internal	160.1	197.3	231.8	212.0	235.9	239.1
nerve	192.0	198.4	—	225.1	237.9	239.7
tube	160.1	197.3	231.8	212.0	235.9	239.1
Eustachian	160.1	197.3	231.8	212.0	235.9	239.1
opening	147.2	198.89	230.0	210.7	235.1	239.0
auricle, ear	173.2	198.2	232.2	216.2	238.2	239.2
cartilage	171.0	198.89	—	215.0	238.1	239.2
auricular canal (external)	173.2	198.2	232.2	216.2	238.2	239.2
internal	160.1	197.3	231.8	212.0	235.9	239.1
autonomic nerve or nervous system NEC	171.9	198.89	—	215.9	238.1	239.2
axilla, axillary	195.1	198.89	234.8	229.8	238.8	239.89 ▲
fold	173.5	198.2	232.5	216.5	238.2	239.2
back NEC*	195.8	198.89	232.5	229.8	238.8	239.89 ▲
Bartholin's gland	184.1	198.82	233.32	221.2	236.3	239.5
basal ganglia	191.0	198.3	—	225.0	237.5	239.6
basis pedunculi	191.7	198.3	—	225.0	237.5	239.6
bile or biliary (tract)	156.9	197.8	230.8	211.5	235.3	239.0
canaliculi (biliferi) (intrahepatic)	155.1	197.8	230.8	211.5	235.3	239.0
canals, interlobular	155.1	197.8	230.8	211.5	235.3	239.0
contiguous sites	156.8	—	—	—	—	—
duct or passage (common) (cystic) (extrahepatic)	156.1	197.8	230.8	211.5	235.3	239.0
contiguous sites with gallbladder	156.8	—	—	—	—	—
interlobular	155.1	197.8	230.8	211.5	235.3	239.0
intrahepatic	155.1	197.8	230.8	211.5	235.3	239.0

☑ Additional Digit Required — Refer to the Tabular List for Digit Selection

▽ Subterms under main terms may continue to next column or page

Neoplasm, neoplastic — continued

	Malignant			Benign	Uncertain Behavior	Unspecified
	Primary	Secondary	Ca in situ			
bile or biliary — continued						
duct or passage — continued						
intrahepatic — continued						
and						
extrahepatic	156.9	197.8	230.8	211.5	235.3	239.0
bladder (urinary)	188.9	198.1	233.7	223.3	236.7	239.4
contiguous sites	188.8	—	—	—	—	—
dome	188.1	198.1	233.7	223.3	236.7	239.4
neck	188.5	198.1	233.7	223.3	236.7	239.4
orifice	188.9	198.1	233.7	223.3	236.7	239.4
ureteric	188.6	198.1	233.7	223.3	236.7	239.4
urethral	188.5	198.1	233.7	223.3	236.7	239.4
sphincter	188.8	198.1	233.7	223.3	236.7	239.4
trigone	188.0	198.1	233.7	223.3	236.7	239.4
urachus	188.7	—	233.7	223.3	236.7	239.4
wall	188.9	198.1	233.7	223.3	236.7	239.4
anterior	188.3	198.1	233.7	223.3	236.7	239.4
lateral	188.2	198.1	233.7	223.3	236.7	239.4
posterior	188.4	198.1	233.7	223.3	236.7	239.4
blood vessel — see Neoplasm, connective tissue						
bone (periosteum)	170.9	198.5	—	213.9	238.0	239.2

Note — Carcinomas and adenocarcinomas, of any type other than intraosseous or odontogenic, of the sites listed under "Neoplasm, bone" should be considered as constituting metastatic spread from an unspecified primary site and coded to 198.5 for morbidity coding.

	Malignant			Benign	Uncertain Behavior	Unspecified
	Primary	Secondary	Ca in situ			
acetabulum	170.6	198.5	—	213.6	238.0	239.2
acromion (process)	170.4	198.5	—	213.4	238.0	239.2
ankle	170.8	198.5	—	213.8	238.0	239.2
arm NEC	170.4	198.5	—	213.4	238.0	239.2
astragalus	170.8	198.5	—	213.8	238.0	239.2
atlas	170.2	198.5	—	213.2	238.0	239.2
axis	170.2	198.5	—	213.2	238.0	239.2
back NEC	170.2	198.5	—	213.2	238.0	239.2
calcaneus	170.8	198.5	—	213.8	238.0	239.2
calvarium	170.0	198.5	—	213.0	238.0	239.2
carpus (any)	170.5	198.5	—	213.5	238.0	239.2
cartilage NEC	170.9	198.5	—	213.9	238.0	239.2
clavicle	170.3	198.5	—	213.3	238.0	239.2
clivus	170.0	198.5	—	213.0	238.0	239.2
coccygeal vertebra	170.6	198.5	—	213.6	238.0	239.2
coccyx	170.6	198.5	—	213.6	238.0	239.2
costal cartilage	170.3	198.5	—	213.3	238.0	239.2
costovertebral joint	170.3	198.5	—	213.3	238.0	239.2
cranial	170.0	198.5	—	213.0	238.0	239.2
cuboid	170.8	198.5	—	213.8	238.0	239.2
cuneiform	170.9	198.5	—	213.9	238.0	239.2
ankle	170.8	198.5	—	213.8	238.0	239.2
wrist	170.5	198.5	—	213.5	238.0	239.2
digital	170.9	198.5	—	213.9	238.0	239.2
finger	170.5	198.5	—	213.5	238.0	239.2
toe	170.8	198.5	—	213.8	238.0	239.2
elbow	170.4	198.5	—	213.4	238.0	239.2
ethmoid (labyrinth)	170.0	198.5	—	213.0	238.0	239.2
face	170.0	198.5	—	213.0	238.0	239.2
lower jaw	170.1	198.5	—	213.1	238.0	239.2
femur (any part)	170.7	198.5	—	213.7	238.0	239.2
fibula (any part)	170.7	198.5	—	213.7	238.0	239.2
finger (any)	170.5	198.5	—	213.5	238.0	239.2
foot	170.8	198.5	—	213.8	238.0	239.2
forearm	170.4	198.5	—	213.4	238.0	239.2
frontal	170.0	198.5	—	213.0	238.0	239.2
hand	170.5	198.5	—	213.5	238.0	239.2
heel	170.8	198.5	—	213.8	238.0	239.2
hip	170.6	198.5	—	213.6	238.0	239.2

Neoplasm, neoplastic — continued

	Malignant			Benign	Uncertain Behavior	Unspecified
	Primary	Secondary	Ca in situ			
bone — continued						
humerus (any part)	170.4	198.5	—	213.4	238.0	239.2
hyoid	170.0	198.5	—	213.0	238.0	239.2
ilium	170.6	198.5	—	213.6	238.0	239.2
innominate	170.6	198.5	—	213.6	238.0	239.2
intervertebral cartilage or disc	170.2	198.5	—	213.2	238.0	239.2
ischium	170.6	198.5	—	213.6	238.0	239.2
jaw (lower)	170.1	198.5	—	213.1	238.0	239.2
upper	170.0	198.5	—	213.0	238.0	239.2
knee	170.7	198.5	—	213.7	238.0	239.2
leg NEC	170.7	198.5	—	213.7	238.0	239.2
limb NEC	170.9	198.5	—	213.9	238.0	239.2
lower (long bones)	170.7	198.5	—	213.7	238.0	239.2
short bones	170.8	198.5	—	213.8	238.0	239.2
upper (long bones)	170.4	198.5	—	213.4	238.0	239.2
short bones	170.5	198.5	—	213.5	238.0	239.2
long	170.9	198.5	—	213.9	238.0	239.2
lower limbs NEC	170.7	198.5	—	213.7	238.0	239.2
upper limbs NEC	170.4	198.5	—	213.4	238.0	239.2
malar	170.0	198.5	—	213.0	238.0	239.2
mandible	170.1	198.5	—	213.1	238.0	239.2
marrow NEC	202.9 ☑	198.5	—	—	—	238.79
mastoid	170.0	198.5	—	213.0	238.0	239.2
maxilla, maxillary (superior)	170.0	198.5	—	213.0	238.0	239.2
inferior	170.1	198.5	—	213.1	238.0	239.2
metacarpus (any)	170.5	198.5	—	213.5	238.0	239.2
metatarsus (any)	170.8	198.5	—	213.8	238.0	239.2
navicular (ankle)	170.8	198.5	—	213.8	238.0	239.2
hand	170.5	198.5	—	213.5	238.0	239.2
nose, nasal	170.0	198.5	—	213.0	238.0	239.2
occipital	170.0	198.5	—	213.0	238.0	239.2
orbit	170.0	198.5	—	213.0	238.0	239.2
parietal	170.0	198.5	—	213.0	238.0	239.2
patella	170.8	198.5	—	213.8	238.0	239.2
pelvic	170.6	198.5	—	213.6	238.0	239.2
phalanges	170.9	198.5	—	213.9	238.0	239.2
foot	170.8	198.5	—	213.8	238.0	239.2
hand	170.5	198.5	—	213.5	238.0	239.2
pubic	170.6	198.5	—	213.6	238.0	239.2
radius (any part)	170.4	198.5	—	213.4	238.0	239.2
rib	170.3	198.5	—	213.3	238.0	239.2
sacral vertebra	170.6	198.5	—	213.6	238.0	239.2
sacrum	170.6	198.5	—	213.6	238.0	239.2
scaphoid (of hand)	170.5	198.5	—	213.5	238.0	239.2
of ankle	170.8	198.5	—	213.8	238.0	239.2
scapula (any part)	170.4	198.5	—	213.4	238.0	239.2
sella turcica	170.0	198.5	—	213.0	238.0	239.2
short	170.9	198.5	—	213.9	238.0	239.2
lower limb	170.8	198.5	—	213.8	238.0	239.2
upper limb	170.5	198.5	—	213.5	238.0	239.2
shoulder	170.4	198.5	—	213.4	238.0	239.2
skeleton, skeletal NEC	170.9	198.5	—	213.9	238.0	239.2
skull	170.0	198.5	—	213.0	238.0	239.2
sphenoid	170.0	198.5	—	213.0	238.0	239.2
spine, spinal (column)	170.2	198.5	—	213.2	238.0	239.2
coccyx	170.6	198.5	—	213.6	238.0	239.2
sacrum	170.6	198.5	—	213.6	238.0	239.2
sternum	170.3	198.5	—	213.3	238.0	239.2
tarsus (any)	170.8	198.5	—	213.8	238.0	239.2
temporal	170.0	198.5	—	213.0	238.0	239.2
thumb	170.5	198.5	—	213.5	238.0	239.2
tibia (any part)	170.7	198.5	—	213.7	238.0	239.2
toe (any)	170.8	198.5	—	213.8	238.0	239.2
trapezium	170.5	198.5	—	213.5	238.0	239.2

Neoplasm, neoplastic — continued	Malignant			Benign	Uncertain Behavior	Unspecified
	Primary	Secondary	Ca in situ			
bone — *continued*						
trapezoid	170.5	198.5	—	213.5	238.0	239.2
turbinate	170.0	198.5	—	213.0	238.0	239.2
ulna (any part)	170.4	198.5	—	213.4	238.0	239.2
unciform	170.5	198.5	—	213.5	238.0	239.2
vertebra (column)	170.2	198.5	—	213.2	238.0	239.2
coccyx	170.6	198.5	—	213.6	238.0	239.2
sacrum	170.6	198.5	—	213.6	238.0	239.2
vomer	170.0	198.5	—	213.0	238.0	239.2
wrist	170.5	198.5	—	213.5	238.0	239.2
xiphoid process	170.3	198.5	—	213.3	238.0	239.2
zygomatic	170.0	198.5	—	213.0	238.0	239.2
book-leaf (mouth)	145.8	198.89	230.0	210.4	235.1	239.0
bowel — *see* Neoplasm, intestine						
brachial plexus	171.2	198.89	—	215.2	238.1	239.2
brain NEC	191.9	198.3	—	225.0	237.5	239.6
basal ganglia	191.0	198.3	—	225.0	237.5	239.6
cerebellopontine angle	191.6	198.3	—	225.0	237.5	239.6
cerebellum NOS	191.6	198.3	—	225.0	237.5	239.6
cerebrum	191.0	198.3	—	225.0	237.5	239.6
choroid plexus	191.5	198.3	—	225.0	237.5	239.6
contiguous sites	191.8	—	—	—	—	—
corpus callosum	191.8	198.3	—	225.0	237.5	239.6
corpus striatum	191.0	198.3	—	225.0	237.5	239.6
cortex (cerebral)	191.0	198.3	—	225.0	237.5	239.6
frontal lobe	191.1	198.3	—	225.0	237.5	239.6
globus pallidus	191.0	198.3	—	225.0	237.5	239.6
hippocampus	191.2	198.3	—	225.0	237.5	239.6
hypothalamus	191.0	198.3	—	225.0	237.5	239.6
internal capsule	191.0	198.3	—	225.0	237.5	239.6
medulla oblongata	191.7	198.3	—	225.0	237.5	239.6
meninges	192.1	198.4	—	225.2	237.6	239.7
midbrain	191.7	198.3	—	225.0	237.5	239.6
occipital lobe	191.4	198.3	—	225.0	237.5	239.6
parietal lobe	191.3	198.3	—	225.0	237.5	239.6
peduncle	191.7	198.3	—	225.0	237.5	239.6
pons	191.7	198.3	—	225.0	237.5	239.6
stem	191.7	198.3	—	225.0	237.5	239.6
tapetum	191.8	198.3	—	225.0	237.5	239.6
temporal lobe	191.2	198.3	—	225.0	237.5	239.6
thalamus	191.0	198.3	—	225.0	237.5	239.6
uncus	191.2	198.3	—	225.0	237.5	239.6
ventricle (floor)	191.5	198.3	—	225.0	237.5	239.6
branchial (cleft) (vestiges)	146.8	198.89	230.0	210.6	235.1	239.0
breast (connective tissue) (female) (glandular tissue) (soft parts)	174.9	198.81	233.0	217	238.3	239.3
areola	174.0	198.81	233.0	217	238.3	239.3
male	175.0	198.81	233.0	217	238.3	239.3
axillary tail	174.6	198.81	233.0	217	238.3	239.3
central portion	174.1	198.81	233.0	217	238.3	239.3
contiguous sites	174.8	—	—	—	—	—
ectopic sites	174.8	198.81	233.0	217	238.3	239.3
inner	174.8	198.81	233.0	217	238.3	239.3
lower	174.8	198.81	233.0	217	238.3	239.3
lower-inner quadrant	174.3	198.81	233.0	217	238.3	239.3
lower-outer quadrant	174.5	198.81	233.0	217	238.3	239.3
male	175.9	198.81	233.0	217	238.3	239.3
areola	175.0	198.81	233.0	217	238.3	239.3
ectopic tissue	175.9	198.81	233.0	217	238.3	239.3
nipple	175.0	198.81	233.0	217	238.3	239.3
mastectomy site (skin)	173.5	198.2	—	—	—	—
specified as breast tissue	174.8	198.81	—	—	—	—
midline	174.8	198.81	233.0	217	238.3	239.3

Neoplasm, neoplastic — continued	Malignant			Benign	Uncertain Behavior	Unspecified
	Primary	Secondary	Ca in situ			
breast — *continued*						
nipple	174.0	198.81	233.0	217	238.3	239.3
male	175.0	198.81	233.0	217	238.3	239.3
outer	174.8	198.81	233.0	217	238.3	239.3
skin	173.5	198.2	232.5	216.5	238.2	239.2
tail (axillary)	174.6	198.81	233.0	217	238.3	239.3
upper	174.8	198.81	233.0	217	238.3	239.3
upper-inner quadrant	174.2	198.81	233.0	217	238.3	239.3
upper-outer quadrant	174.4	198.81	233.0	217	238.3	239.3
broad ligament	183.3	198.82	233.39	221.0	236.3	239.5
bronchiogenic, bronchogenic (lung)	162.9	197.0	231.2	212.3	235.7	239.1
bronchiole	162.9	197.0	231.2	212.3	235.7	239.1
bronchus	162.9	197.0	231.2	212.3	235.7	239.1
carina	162.2	197.0	231.2	212.3	235.7	239.1
contiguous sites with lung or trachea	162.8	—	—	—	—	—
lower lobe of lung	162.5	197.0	231.2	212.3	235.7	239.1
main	162.2	197.0	231.2	212.3	235.7	239.1
middle lobe of lung	162.4	197.0	231.2	212.3	235.7	239.1
upper lobe of lung	162.3	197.0	231.2	212.3	235.7	239.1
brow	173.3	198.2	232.3	216.3	238.2	239.2
buccal (cavity)	145.9	198.89	230.0	210.4	235.1	239.0
commissure	145.0	198.89	230.0	210.4	235.1	239.0
groove (lower) (upper)	145.1	198.89	230.0	210.4	235.1	239.0
mucosa	145.0	198.89	230.0	210.4	235.1	239.0
sulcus (lower) (upper)	145.1	198.89	230.0	210.4	235.1	239.0
bulbourethral gland	189.3	198.1	233.9	223.81	236.99	239.5
bursa — *see* Neoplasm, connective tissue						
buttock NEC*	195.3	198.89	232.5	229.8	238.8	239.89 ▲
calf*	195.5	198.89	232.7	229.8	238.8	239.89 ▲
calvarium	170.0	198.5	—	213.0	238.0	239.2
calyx, renal	189.1	198.0	233.9	223.1	236.91	239.5
canal						
anal	154.2	197.5	230.5	211.4	235.5	239.0
auditory (external)	173.2	198.2	232.2	216.2	238.2	239.2
auricular (external)	173.2	198.2	232.2	216.2	238.2	239.2
canaliculi, biliary (biliferi) (intrahepatic)	155.1	197.8	230.8	211.5	235.3	239.0
canthus (eye) (inner) (outer)	173.1	198.2	232.1	216.1	238.2	239.2
capillary — *see* Neoplasm, connective tissue						
caput coli	153.4	197.5	230.3	211.3	235.2	239.0
cardia (gastric)	151.0	197.8	230.2	211.1	235.2	239.0
cardiac orifice (stomach)	151.0	197.8	230.2	211.1	235.2	239.0
cardio-esophageal junction	151.0	197.8	230.2	211.1	235.2	239.0
cardio-esophagus	151.0	197.8	230.2	211.1	235.2	239.0
carina (bronchus)	162.2	197.0	231.2	212.3	235.7	239.1
carotid (artery)	171.0	198.89	—	215.0	238.1	239.2
body	194.5	198.89	—	227.5	237.3	239.7
carpus (any bone)	170.5	198.5	—	213.5	238.0	239.2
cartilage (articular) (joint) NEC (*see also* Neoplasm, bone)	170.9	198.5	—	213.9	238.0	239.2
arytenoid	161.3	197.3	231.0	212.1	235.6	239.1
auricular	171.0	198.89	—	215.0	238.1	239.2
bronchi	162.2	197.3	—	212.3	235.7	239.1

☑ Additional Digit Required — Refer to the Tabular List for Digit Selection　　　　　　　　Subterms under main terms may continue to next column or page

Neoplasm, neoplastic — continued

	Malignant Primary	Malignant Secondary	Malignant Ca in situ	Benign	Uncertain Behavior	Unspecified
cartilage (see also Neoplasm, bone) — continued						
connective tissue — see Neoplasm, connective tissue						
costal	170.3	198.5	—	213.3	238.0	239.2
cricoid	161.3	197.3	231.0	212.1	235.6	239.1
cuneiform	161.3	197.3	231.0	212.1	235.6	239.1
ear (external)	171.0	198.89	—	215.0	238.1	239.2
ensiform	170.3	198.5	—	213.3	238.0	239.2
epiglottis	161.1	197.3	231.0	212.1	235.6	239.1
anterior surface	146.4	198.89	230.0	210.6	235.1	239.0
eyelid	171.0	198.89	—	215.0	238.1	239.2
intervertebral	170.2	198.5	—	213.2	238.0	239.2
larynx, laryngeal	161.3	197.3	231.0	212.1	235.6	239.1
nose, nasal	160.0	197.3	231.8	212.0	235.9	239.1
pinna	171.0	198.89	—	215.0	238.1	239.2
rib	170.3	198.5	—	213.3	238.0	239.2
semilunar (knee)	170.7	198.5	—	213.7	238.0	239.2
thyroid	161.3	197.3	231.0	212.1	235.6	239.1
trachea	162.0	197.3	231.1	212.2	235.7	239.1
cauda equina	192.2	198.3	—	225.3	237.5	239.7
cavity						
buccal	145.9	198.89	230.0	210.4	235.1	239.0
nasal	160.0	197.3	231.8	212.0	235.9	239.1
oral	145.9	198.89	230.0	210.4	235.1	239.0
peritoneal	158.9	197.6	—	211.8	235.4	239.0
tympanic	160.1	197.3	231.8	212.0	235.9	239.1
cecum	153.4	197.5	230.3	211.3	235.2	239.0
central nervous system — see Neoplasm, nervous system						
white matter	191.0	198.3	—	225.0	237.5	239.6
cerebellopontine (angle)	191.6	198.3	—	225.0	237.5	239.6
cerebellum, cerebellar	191.6	198.3	—	225.0	237.5	239.6
cerebrum, cerebral (cortex) (hemisphere) (white matter)	191.0	198.3	—	225.0	237.5	239.6
meninges	192.1	198.4	—	225.2	237.6	239.7
peduncle	191.7	198.3	—	225.0	237.5	239.6
ventricle (any)	191.5	198.3	—	225.0	237.5	239.6
cervical region	195.0	198.89	234.8	229.8	238.8	239.89 ▲
cervix (cervical) (uteri) (uterus)	180.9	198.82	233.1	219.0	236.0	239.5
canal	180.0	198.82	233.1	219.0	236.0	239.5
contiguous sites	180.8	—	—	—	—	—
endocervix (canal) (gland)	180.0	198.82	233.1	219.0	236.0	239.5
exocervix	180.1	198.82	233.1	219.0	236.0	239.5
external os	180.1	198.82	233.1	219.0	236.0	239.5
internal os	180.0	198.82	233.1	219.0	236.0	239.5
nabothian gland	180.0	198.82	233.1	219.0	236.0	239.5
squamocolumnar junction	180.8	198.82	233.1	219.0	236.0	239.5
stump	180.8	198.82	233.1	219.0	236.0	239.5
cheek	195.0	198.89	234.8	229.8	238.8	239.89 ▲
external	173.3	198.2	232.3	216.3	238.2	239.2
inner aspect	145.0	198.89	230.0	210.4	235.1	239.0
internal	145.0	198.89	230.0	210.4	235.1	239.0
mucosa	145.0	198.89	230.0	210.4	235.1	239.0
chest (wall) NEC	195.1	198.89	234.8	229.8	238.8	239.89 ▲
chiasma opticum	192.0	198.4	—	225.1	237.9	239.7
chin	173.3	198.2	232.3	216.3	238.2	239.2
choana	147.3	198.89	230.0	210.7	235.1	239.0
cholangiole	155.1	197.8	230.8	211.5	235.3	239.0
choledochal duct	156.1	197.8	230.8	211.5	235.3	239.0
choroid	190.6	198.4	234.0	224.6	238.8	239.81 ▲
plexus	191.5	198.3	—	225.0	237.5	239.6
ciliary body	190.0	198.4	234.0	224.0	238.8	239.89 ▲
clavicle	170.3	198.5	—	213.3	238.0	239.2
clitoris	184.3	198.82	233.32	221.2	236.3	239.5
clivus	170.0	198.5	—	213.0	238.0	239.2
cloacogenic zone	154.8	197.5	230.7	211.4	235.5	239.0
coccygeal						
body or glomus	194.6	198.89	—	227.6	237.3	239.7
vertebra	170.6	198.5	—	213.6	238.0	239.2
coccyx	170.6	198.5	—	213.6	238.0	239.2
colon (see also Neoplasm, intestine, large) and rectum	154.0	197.5	230.4	211.4	235.2	239.0
columnella	173.3	198.2	232.3	216.3	238.2	239.2
column, spinal — see Neoplasm, spine						
commissure						
labial, lip	140.6	198.89	230.0	210.4	235.1	239.0
laryngeal	161.0	197.3	231.0	212.1	235.6	239.1
common (bile) duct	156.1	197.8	230.8	211.5	235.3	239.0
concha	173.2	198.2	232.2	216.2	238.2	239.2
nose	160.0	197.3	231.8	212.0	235.9	239.1
conjunctiva	190.3	198.4	234.0	224.3	238.8	239.89 ▲
connective tissue NEC	171.9	198.89	—	215.9	238.1	239.2

> Note — For neoplasms of connective tissue (blood vessel, bursa, fascia, ligament, muscle, peripheral nerves, sympathetic and parasympathetic nerves and ganglia, synovia, tendon, etc.) or of morphological types that indicate connective tissue, code according to the list under "Neoplasm, connective tissue"; for sites that do not appear in this list, code to neoplasm of that site; e.g.,
>
> liposarcoma, shoulder 171.2
>
> leiomyosarcoma, stomach 151.9
>
> neurofibroma, chest wall 215.4
>
> Morphological types that indicate connective tissue appear in the proper place in the alphabetic index with the instruction "see Neoplasm, connective tissue…"

	Malignant Primary	Malignant Secondary	Malignant Ca in situ	Benign	Uncertain Behavior	Unspecified
abdomen	171.5	198.89	—	215.5	238.1	239.2
abdominal wall	171.5	198.89	—	215.5	238.1	239.2
ankle	171.3	198.89	—	215.3	238.1	239.2
antecubital fossa or space	171.2	198.89	—	215.2	238.1	239.2
arm	171.2	198.89	—	215.2	238.1	239.2
auricle (ear)	171.0	198.89	—	215.0	238.1	239.2
axilla	171.4	198.89	—	215.4	238.1	239.2
back	171.7	198.89	—	215.7	238.1	239.2
breast (female) (see also Neoplasm, breast)	174.9	198.81	233.0	217	238.3	239.3
male	175.9	198.81	233.0	217	238.3	239.3
buttock	171.6	198.89	—	215.6	238.1	239.2
calf	171.3	198.89	—	215.3	238.1	239.2
cervical region	171.0	198.89	—	215.0	238.1	239.2
cheek	171.0	198.89	—	215.0	238.1	239.2
chest (wall)	171.4	198.89	—	215.4	238.1	239.2
chin	171.0	198.89	—	215.0	238.1	239.2
contiguous sites	171.8	—	—	—	—	—
diaphragm	171.4	198.89	—	215.4	238.1	239.2
ear (external)	171.0	198.89	—	215.0	238.1	239.2
elbow	171.2	198.89	—	215.2	238.1	239.2
extrarectal	171.6	198.89	—	215.6	238.1	239.2
extremity	171.8	198.89	—	215.8	238.1	239.2
lower	171.3	198.89	—	215.3	238.1	239.2
upper	171.2	198.89	—	215.2	238.1	239.2
eyelid	171.0	198.89	—	215.0	238.1	239.2
face	171.0	198.89	—	215.0	238.1	239.2
finger	171.2	198.89	—	215.2	238.1	239.2
flank	171.7	198.89	—	215.7	238.1	239.2
foot	171.3	198.89	—	215.3	238.1	239.2
forearm	171.2	198.89	—	215.2	238.1	239.2
forehead	171.0	198.89	—	215.0	238.1	239.2
gastric	171.5	198.89	—	215.5	238.1	—
gastrointestinal	171.5	198.89	—	215.5	238.1	—
gluteal region	171.6	198.89	—	215.6	238.1	239.2
great vessels NEC	171.4	198.89	—	215.4	238.1	239.2
groin	171.6	198.89	—	215.6	238.1	239.2

☑ Additional Digit Required — Refer to the Tabular List for Digit Selection   ▽ Subterms under main terms may continue to next column or page

188 — Volume 2 • October 2009   ►◄ Revised Text   ● New Line   ▲ Revised Code   2010 ICD-9-CM

	Malignant					
	Primary	Secondary	Ca in situ	Benign	Uncertain Behavior	Unspecified

Neoplasm, neoplastic — *continued*
connective tissue — *continued*

	Primary	Secondary	Ca in situ	Benign	Uncertain Behavior	Unspecified
hand	171.2	198.89	—	215.2	238.1	239.2
head	171.0	198.89	—	215.0	238.1	239.2
heel	171.3	198.89	—	215.3	238.1	239.2
hip	171.3	198.89	—	215.3	238.1	239.2
hypochondrium	171.5	198.89	—	215.5	238.1	239.2
iliopsoas muscle	171.6	198.89	—	215.5	238.1	239.2
infraclavicular region	171.4	198.89	—	215.4	238.1	239.2
inguinal (canal) (region)	171.6	198.89	—	215.6	238.1	239.2
intestine	171.5	198.89	—	215.5	238.1	—
intrathoracic	171.4	198.89	—	215.4	238.1	239.2
ischorectal fossa	171.6	198.89	—	215.6	238.1	239.2
jaw	143.9	198.89	230.0	210.4	235.1	239.0
knee	171.3	198.89	—	215.3	238.1	239.2
leg	171.3	198.89	—	215.3	238.1	239.2
limb NEC	171.9	198.89	—	215.8	238.1	239.2
lower	171.3	198.89	—	215.3	238.1	239.2
upper	171.2	198.89	—	215.2	238.1	239.2
nates	171.6	198.89	—	215.6	238.1	239.2
neck	171.0	198.89	—	215.0	238.1	239.2
orbit	190.1	198.4	234.0	224.1	238.8	239.89 ▲
pararectal	171.6	198.89	—	215.6	238.1	239.2
para-urethral	171.6	198.89	—	215.6	238.1	239.2
paravaginal	171.6	198.89	—	215.6	238.1	239.2
pelvis (floor)	171.6	198.89	—	215.6	238.1	239.2
pelvo-abdominal	171.8	198.89	—	215.8	238.1	239.2
perineum	171.6	198.89	—	215.6	238.1	239.2
perirectal (tissue)	171.6	198.89	—	215.6	238.1	239.2
periurethral (tissue)	171.6	198.89	—	215.6	238.1	239.2
popliteal fossa or space	171.3	198.89	—	215.3	238.1	239.2
presacral	171.6	198.89	—	215.6	238.1	239.2
psoas muscle	171.5	198.89	—	215.5	238.1	239.2
pterygoid fossa	171.0	198.89	—	215.0	238.1	239.2
rectovaginal septum or wall	171.6	198.89	—	215.6	238.1	239.2
rectovesical	171.6	198.89	—	215.6	238.1	239.2
retroperitoneum	158.0	197.6	—	211.8	235.4	239.0
sacrococcygeal region	171.6	198.89	—	215.6	238.1	239.2
scalp	171.0	198.89	—	215.0	238.1	239.2
scapular region	171.4	198.89	—	215.4	238.1	239.2
shoulder	171.2	198.89	—	215.2	238.1	239.2
skin (dermis) NEC	173.9	198.2	232.9	216.9	238.2	239.2
stomach	171.5	198.89	—	215.5	238.1	—
submental	171.0	198.89	—	215.0	238.1	239.2
supraclavicular region	171.0	198.89	—	215.0	238.1	239.2
temple	171.0	198.89	—	215.0	238.1	239.2
temporal region	171.0	198.89	—	215.0	238.1	239.2
thigh	171.3	198.89	—	215.3	238.1	239.2
thoracic (duct) (wall)	171.4	198.89	—	215.4	238.1	239.2
thorax	171.4	198.89	—	215.4	238.1	239.2
thumb	171.2	198.89	—	215.2	238.1	239.2
toe	171.3	198.89	—	215.3	238.1	239.2
trunk	171.7	198.89	—	215.7	238.1	239.2
umbilicus	171.5	198.89	—	215.5	238.1	239.2
vesicorectal	171.6	198.89	—	215.6	238.1	239.2
wrist	171.2	198.89	—	215.2	238.1	239.2
conus medullaris	192.2	198.3	—	225.3	237.5	239.7
cord (true) (vocal)	161.0	197.3	231.0	212.1	235.6	239.1
false	161.1	197.3	231.0	212.1	235.6	239.1
spermatic	187.6	198.82	233.6	222.8	236.6	239.5
spinal (cervical) (lumbar) (thoracic)	192.2	198.3	—	225.3	237.5	239.7
cornea (limbus)	190.4	198.4	234.0	224.4	238.8	239.89 ▲
corpus						
albicans	183.0	198.6	233.39	220	236.2	239.5

Neoplasm, neoplastic — *continued*
corpus — *continued*

	Primary	Secondary	Ca in situ	Benign	Uncertain Behavior	Unspecified
callosum, brain	191.8	198.3	—	225.0	237.5	239.6
cavernosum	187.3	198.82	233.5	222.1	236.6	239.5
gastric	151.4	197.8	230.2	211.1	235.2	239.0
penis	187.3	198.82	233.5	222.1	236.6	239.5
striatum, cerebrum	191.0	198.3	—	225.0	237.5	239.6
uteri	182.0	198.82	233.2	219.1	236.0	239.5
isthmus	182.1	198.82	233.2	219.1	236.0	239.5
cortex						
adrenal	194.0	198.7	234.8	227.0	237.2	239.7
cerebral	191.0	198.3	—	225.0	237.5	239.6
costal cartilage	170.3	198.5	—	213.3	238.0	239.2
costovertebral joint	170.3	198.5	—	213.3	238.0	239.2
Cowper's gland	189.3	198.1	233.9	223.81	236.99	239.5
cranial (fossa, any)	191.9	198.3	—	225.0	237.5	239.6
meninges	192.1	198.4	—	225.2	237.6	239.7
nerve (any)	192.0	198.4	—	225.1	237.9	239.7
craniobuccal pouch	194.3	198.89	234.8	227.3	237.0	239.7
craniopharyngeal (duct) (pouch)	194.3	198.89	234.8	227.3	237.0	239.7
cricoid	148.0	198.89	230.0	210.8	235.1	239.0
cartilage	161.3	197.3	231.0	212.1	235.6	239.1
cricopharynx	148.0	198.89	230.0	210.8	235.1	239.0
crypt of Morgagni	154.8	197.5	230.7	211.4	235.2	239.0
crystalline lens	190.0	198.4	234.0	224.0	238.8	239.89 ▲
cul-de-sac (Douglas')	158.8	197.6	—	211.8	235.4	239.0
cuneiform cartilage	161.3	197.3	231.0	212.1	235.6	239.1
cutaneous — *see* Neoplasm, skin						
cutis — *see* Neoplasm, skin						
cystic (bile) duct (common)	156.1	197.8	230.8	211.5	235.3	239.0
dermis — *see* Neoplasm, skin						
diaphragm	171.4	198.89	—	215.4	238.1	239.2
digestive organs, system, tube, or tract NEC	159.9	197.8	230.9	211.9	235.5	239.0
contiguous sites with peritoneum	159.8	—	—	—	—	—
disc, intervertebral	170.2	198.5	—	213.2	238.0	239.2
disease, generalized	199.0	199.0	234.9	229.9	238.9	199.0
disseminated	199.0	199.0	234.9	229.9	238.9	199.0
Douglas' cul-de-sac or pouch	158.8	197.6	—	211.8	235.4	239.0
duodenojejunal junction	152.8	197.4	230.7	211.2	235.2	239.0
duodenum	152.0	197.4	230.7	211.2	235.2	239.0
dura (cranial) (mater)	192.1	198.4	—	225.2	237.6	239.7
cerebral	192.1	198.4	—	225.2	237.6	239.7
spinal	192.3	198.4	—	225.4	237.6	239.7
ear (external)	173.2	198.2	232.2	216.2	238.2	239.2
auricle or auris	173.2	198.2	232.2	216.2	238.2	239.2
canal, external	173.2	198.2	232.2	216.2	238.2	239.2
cartilage	171.0	198.89	—	215.0	238.1	239.2
external meatus	173.2	198.2	232.2	216.2	238.2	239.2
inner	160.1	197.3	231.8	212.0	235.9	239.89 ▲
lobule	173.2	198.2	232.2	216.2	238.2	239.2
middle	160.1	197.3	231.8	212.0	235.9	239.89 ▲
contiguous sites with accessory sinuses or nasal cavities	160.8	—	—	—	—	—
skin	173.2	198.2	232.2	216.2	238.2	239.2
earlobe	173.2	198.2	232.2	216.2	238.2	239.2
ejaculatory duct	187.8	198.82	233.6	222.8	236.6	239.5
elbow NEC*	195.4	198.89	232.6	229.8	238.8	239.89 ▲
endocardium	164.1	198.89	—	212.7	238.8	239.89 ▲
endocervix (canal) (gland)	180.0	198.82	233.1	219.0	236.0	239.5

☑ Additional Digit Required — Refer to the Tabular List for Digit Selection   ▽ Subterms under main terms may continue to next column or page

2010 ICD-9-CM   ▶◀ Revised Text   ● New Line   ▲ Revised Code   **October 2009 · Volume 2 — 189**

Index

Neoplasm, endocrine gland — Neoplasm, genital organ or tract

	Malignant					
	Primary	Secondary	Ca in situ	Benign	Uncertain Behavior	Unspecified
Neoplasm, neoplastic — *continued*						
endocrine gland						
NEC	194.9	198.89	—	227.9	237.4	239.7
pluriglandular						
NEC	194.8	198.89	234.8	227.8	237.4	239.7
endometrium (gland) (stroma)	182.0	198.82	233.2	219.1	236.0	239.5
ensiform cartilage	170.3	198.5	—	213.3	238.0	239.2
enteric — *see* Neoplasm, intestine						
ependyma (brain)	191.5	198.3	—	225.0	237.5	239.6
epicardium	164.1	198.89	—	212.7	238.8	239.89 ▲
epididymis	187.5	198.82	233.6	222.3	236.6	239.5
epidural	192.9	198.4	—	225.9	237.9	239.7
epiglottis	161.1	197.3	231.0	212.1	235.6	239.1
anterior aspect or surface	146.4	198.89	230.0	210.6	235.1	239.0
cartilage	161.3	197.3	231.0	212.1	235.6	239.1
free border (margin)	146.4	198.89	230.0	210.6	235.1	239.0
junctional region	146.5	198.89	230.0	210.6	235.1	239.0
posterior (laryngeal) surface	161.1	197.3	231.0	212.1	235.6	239.1
suprahyoid portion	161.1	197.3	231.0	212.1	235.6	239.1
esophagogastric junction	151.0	197.8	230.2	211.1	235.2	239.0
esophagus	150.9	197.8	230.1	211.0	235.5	239.0
abdominal	150.2	197.8	230.1	211.0	235.5	239.0
cervical	150.0	197.8	230.1	211.0	235.5	239.0
contiguous sites	150.8	—	—	—	—	—
distal (third)	150.5	197.8	230.1	211.0	235.5	239.0
lower (third)	150.5	197.8	230.1	211.0	235.5	239.0
middle (third)	150.4	197.8	230.1	211.0	235.5	239.0
proximal (third)	150.3	197.8	230.1	211.0	235.5	239.0
specified part NEC	150.8	197.8	230.1	211.0	235.5	239.0
thoracic	150.1	197.8	230.1	211.0	235.5	239.0
upper (third)	150.3	197.8	230.1	211.0	235.5	239.0
ethmoid (sinus)	160.3	197.3	231.8	212.0	235.9	239.1
bone or labyrinth	170.0	198.5	—	213.0	238.0	239.2
Eustachian tube	160.1	197.3	231.8	212.0	235.9	239.1
exocervix	180.1	198.82	233.1	219.0	236.0	239.5
external						
meatus (ear)	173.2	198.2	232.2	216.2	238.2	239.2
os, cervix uteri	180.1	198.82	233.1	219.0	236.0	239.5
extradural	192.9	198.4	—	225.9	237.9	239.7
extrahepatic (bile) duct	156.1	197.8	230.8	211.5	235.3	239.0
contiguous sites with gallbladder	156.8	—	—	—	—	—
extraocular muscle	190.1	198.4	234.0	224.1	238.8	239.89 ▲
extrarectal	195.3	198.89	234.8	229.8	238.8	239.89 ▲
extremity*	195.8	198.89	232.8	229.8	238.8	239.89 ▲
lower*	195.5	198.89	232.7	229.8	238.8	239.89 ▲
upper*	195.4	198.89	232.6	229.8	238.8	239.89 ▲
eye NEC	190.9	198.4	234.0	224.9	238.8	239.89 ▲
contiguous sites	190.8	—	—	—	—	—
specified sites NEC	190.8	198.4	234.0	224.8	238.8	239.89 ▲
eyeball	190.0	198.4	234.0	224.0	238.8	239.89 ▲
eyebrow	173.3	198.2	232.3	216.3	238.2	239.2
eyelid (lower) (skin) (upper)	173.1	198.2	232.1	216.1	238.2	239.2
cartilage	171.0	198.89	—	215.0	238.1	239.2
face NEC*	195.0	198.89	232.3	229.8	238.8	239.89 ▲
fallopian tube (accessory)	183.2	198.82	233.39	221.0	236.3	239.5
falx (cerebelli) (cerebri)	192.1	198.4	—	225.2	237.6	239.7
fascia (*see also* Neoplasm, connective tissue)						
palmar	171.2	198.89	—	215.2	238.1	239.2
plantar	171.3	198.89	—	215.3	238.1	239.2

	Malignant					
	Primary	Secondary	Ca in situ	Benign	Uncertain Behavior	Unspecified
Neoplasm, neoplastic — *continued*						
fatty tissue — *see* Neoplasm, connective tissue						
fauces, faucial NEC	146.9	198.89	230.0	210.6	235.1	239.0
pillars	146.2	198.89	230.0	210.6	235.1	239.0
tonsil	146.0	198.89	230.0	210.5	235.1	239.0
femur (any part)	170.7	198.5	—	213.7	238.0	239.2
fetal membrane	181	198.82	233.2	219.8	236.1	239.5
fibrous tissue — *see* Neoplasm, connective tissue						
fibula (any part)	170.7	198.5	—	213.7	238.0	239.2
filum terminale	192.2	198.3	—	225.3	237.5	239.7
finger NEC*	195.4	198.89	232.6	229.8	238.8	239.89 ▲
flank NEC*	195.8	198.89	232.5	229.8	238.8	239.89 ▲
follicle, nabothian	180.0	198.82	233.1	219.0	236.0	239.5
foot NEC*	195.5	198.89	232.7	229.8	238.8	239.89 ▲
forearm NEC*	195.4	198.89	232.6	229.8	238.8	239.89 ▲
forehead (skin)	173.3	198.2	232.3	216.3	238.2	239.2
foreskin	187.1	198.82	233.5	222.1	236.6	239.5
fornix						
pharyngeal	147.3	198.89	230.0	210.7	235.1	239.0
vagina	184.0	198.82	233.31	221.1	236.3	239.5
fossa (of)						
anterior (cranial)	191.9	198.3	—	225.0	237.5	239.6
cranial	191.9	198.3	—	225.0	237.5	239.6
ischiorectal	195.3	198.89	234.8	229.8	238.8	239.89 ▲
middle (cranial)	191.9	198.3	—	225.0	237.5	239.6
pituitary	194.3	198.89	234.8	227.3	237.0	239.7
posterior (cranial)	191.9	198.3	—	225.0	237.5	239.6
pterygoid	171.0	198.89	—	215.0	238.1	239.2
pyriform	148.1	198.89	230.0	210.8	235.1	239.0
Rosenmüller	147.2	198.89	230.0	210.7	235.1	239.0
tonsillar	146.1	198.89	230.0	210.6	235.1	239.0
fourchette	184.4	198.82	233.32	221.2	236.3	239.5
frenulum						
labii — *see* Neoplasm, lip, internal						
linguae	141.3	198.89	230.0	210.1	235.1	239.0
frontal						
bone	170.0	198.5	—	213.0	238.0	239.2
lobe, brain	191.1	198.3	—	225.0	237.5	239.6
meninges	192.1	198.4	—	225.2	237.6	239.7
pole	191.1	198.3	—	225.0	237.5	239.6
sinus	160.4	197.3	231.8	212.0	235.9	239.1
fundus						
stomach	151.3	197.8	230.2	211.1	235.2	239.0
uterus	182.0	198.82	233.2	219.1	236.0	239.5
gallbladder	156.0	197.8	230.8	211.5	235.3	239.0
contiguous sites with extrahepatic bile ducts	156.8	—	—	—	—	—
gall duct (extrahepatic)	156.1	197.8	230.8	211.5	235.3	239.0
intrahepatic	155.1	197.8	230.8	211.5	235.3	239.0
ganglia (*see also* Neoplasm, connective tissue)	171.9	198.89	—	215.9	238.1	239.2
basal	191.0	198.3	—	225.0	237.5	239.6
ganglion (*see also* Neoplasm, connective tissue)	171.9	198.89	—	215.9	238.1	239.2
cranial nerve	192.0	198.4	—	225.1	237.9	239.7
Gartner's duct	184.0	198.82	233.31	221.1	236.3	239.5
gastric — *see* Neoplasm, stomach						
gastrocolic	159.8	197.8	230.9	211.9	235.5	239.0
gastroesophageal junction	151.0	197.8	230.2	211.1	235.2	239.0
gastrointestinal (tract) NEC	159.9	197.8	230.9	211.9	235.5	239.0
generalized	199.0	199.0	234.9	229.9	238.9	199.0
genital organ or tract						

Neoplasm, neoplastic — continued

Site	Malignant — Primary	Malignant — Secondary	Malignant — Ca in situ	Benign	Uncertain Behavior	Unspecified
genital organ or tract — *continued*						
female NEC	184.9	198.82	233.39	221.9	236.3	239.5
contiguous sites	184.8	—	—	—	—	—
specified site NEC	184.8	198.82	233.39	221.8	236.3	239.5
male NEC	187.9	198.82	233.6	222.9	236.6	239.5
contiguous sites	187.8	—	—	—	—	—
specified site NEC	187.8	198.82	233.6	222.8	236.6	239.5
genitourinary tract						
female	184.9	198.82	233.39	221.9	236.3	239.5
male	187.9	198.82	233.6	222.9	236.6	239.5
gingiva (alveolar) (marginal)	143.9	198.89	230.0	210.4	235.1	239.0
lower	143.1	198.89	230.0	210.4	235.1	239.0
mandibular	143.1	198.89	230.0	210.4	235.1	239.0
maxillary	143.0	198.89	230.0	210.4	235.1	239.0
upper	143.0	198.89	230.0	210.4	235.1	239.0
gland, glandular (lymphatic) (system) (see also Neoplasm, lymph gland)						
endocrine NEC	194.9	198.89	—	227.9	237.4	239.7
salivary — see Neoplasm, salivary, gland						
glans penis	187.2	198.82	233.5	222.1	236.6	239.5
globus pallidus	191.0	198.3	—	225.0	237.5	239.6
glomus						
coccygeal	194.6	198.89	—	227.6	237.3	239.7
jugularis	194.6	198.89	—	227.6	237.3	239.7
glosso-epiglottic fold(s)	146.4	198.89	230.0	210.6	235.1	239.0
glossopalatine fold	146.2	198.89	230.0	210.6	235.1	239.0
glossopharyngeal sulcus	146.1	198.89	230.0	210.6	235.1	239.0
glottis	161.0	197.3	231.0	212.1	235.6	239.1
gluteal region*	195.3	198.89	232.5	229.8	238.8	239.89 ▲
great vessels NEC	171.4	198.89	—	215.4	238.1	239.2
groin NEC	195.3	198.89	232.5	229.8	238.8	239.89 ▲
gum	143.9	198.89	230.0	210.4	235.1	239.0
contiguous sites	143.8	—	—	—	—	—
lower	143.1	198.89	230.0	210.4	235.1	239.0
upper	143.0	198.89	230.0	210.4	235.1	239.0
hand NEC*	195.4	198.89	232.6	229.8	238.8	239.89 ▲
head NEC*	195.0	198.89	232.4	229.8	238.8	239.89 ▲
heart	164.1	198.89	—	212.7	238.8	239.89 ▲
contiguous sites with mediastinum or thymus	164.8	—	—	—	—	—
heel NEC*	195.5	198.89	232.7	229.8	238.8	239.89 ▲
helix	173.2	198.2	232.2	216.2	238.2	239.2
hematopoietic, hemopoietic tissue NEC	202.8 ☑	198.89	—	—	—	238.79
hemisphere, cerebral	191.0	198.3	—	225.0	237.5	239.6
hemorrhoidal zone	154.2	197.5	230.5	211.4	235.5	239.0
hepatic	155.2	197.7	230.8	211.5	235.3	239.0
duct (bile)	156.1	197.8	230.8	211.5	235.3	239.0
flexure (colon)	153.0	197.5	230.3	211.3	235.2	239.0
primary	155.0	—	—	—	—	—
hilus of lung	162.2	197.0	231.2	212.3	235.7	239.1
hip NEC*	195.5	198.89	232.7	229.8	238.8	239.89 ▲
hippocampus, brain	191.2	198.3	—	225.0	237.5	239.6
humerus (any part)	170.4	198.5	—	213.4	238.0	239.2
hymen	184.0	198.82	233.31	221.1	236.3	239.5
hypopharynx, hypopharyngeal NEC	148.9	198.89	230.0	210.8	235.1	239.0
contiguous sites	148.8	—	—	—	—	—

Neoplasm, neoplastic — continued

Site	Malignant — Primary	Malignant — Secondary	Malignant — Ca in situ	Benign	Uncertain Behavior	Unspecified
hypopharynx, hypopharyngeal — *continued*						
postcricoid region	148.0	198.89	230.0	210.8	235.1	239.0
posterior wall	148.3	198.89	230.0	210.8	235.1	239.0
pyriform fossa (sinus)	148.1	198.89	230.0	210.8	235.1	239.0
specified site NEC	148.8	198.89	230.0	210.8	235.1	239.0
wall	148.9	198.89	230.0	210.8	235.1	239.0
posterior	148.3	198.89	230.0	210.8	235.1	239.0
hypophysis	194.3	198.89	234.8	227.3	237.0	239.7
hypothalamus	191.0	198.3	—	225.0	237.5	239.6
ileocecum, ileocecal (coil) (junction) (valve)	153.4	197.5	230.3	211.3	235.2	239.0
ileum	152.2	197.4	230.7	211.2	235.2	239.0
ilium	170.6	198.5	—	213.6	238.0	239.2
immunoproliferative NEC	203.8 ☑	—		—		—
infraclavicular (region)*	195.1	198.89	232.5	229.8	238.8	239.89 ▲
inguinal (region)*	195.3	198.89	232.5	229.8	238.8	239.89 ▲
insula	191.0	198.3	—	225.0	237.5	239.6
insular tissue (pancreas)	157.4	197.8	230.9	211.7	235.5	239.0
brain	191.0	198.3	—	225.0	237.5	239.6
interarytenoid fold	148.2	198.89	230.0	210.8	235.1	239.0
hypopharyngeal aspect	148.2	198.89	230.0	210.8	235.1	239.0
laryngeal aspect	161.1	197.3	231.0	212.1	235.6	239.1
marginal zone	148.2	198.89	230.0	210.8	235.1	239.0
interdental papillae	143.9	198.89	230.0	210.4	235.1	239.0
lower	143.1	198.89	230.0	210.4	235.1	239.0
upper	143.0	198.89	230.0	210.4	235.1	239.0
internal						
capsule	191.0	198.3	—	225.0	237.5	239.6
os (cervix)	180.0	198.82	233.1	219.0	236.0	239.5
intervertebral cartilage or disc	170.2	198.5	—	213.2	238.0	239.2
intestine, intestinal	159.0	197.8	230.7	211.9	235.2	239.0
large	153.9	197.5	230.3	211.3	235.2	239.0
appendix	153.5	197.5	230.3	211.3	235.2	239.0
caput coli	153.4	197.5	230.3	211.3	235.2	239.0
cecum	153.4	197.5	230.3	211.3	235.2	239.0
colon	153.9	197.5	230.3	211.3	235.2	239.0
and rectum	154.0	197.5	230.4	211.4	235.2	239.0
ascending	153.6	197.5	230.3	211.3	235.2	239.0
caput	153.4	197.5	230.3	211.3	235.2	239.0
contiguous sites	153.8	—	—	—	—	—
descending	153.2	197.5	230.3	211.3	235.2	239.0
distal	153.2	197.5	230.3	211.3	235.2	239.0
left	153.2	197.5	230.3	211.3	235.2	239.0
pelvic	153.3	197.5	230.3	211.3	235.2	239.0
right	153.6	197.5	230.3	211.3	235.2	239.0
sigmoid (flexure)	153.3	197.5	230.3	211.3	235.2	239.0
transverse	153.1	197.5	230.3	211.3	235.2	239.0
contiguous sites	153.8	—	—	—	—	—
hepatic flexure	153.0	197.5	230.3	211.3	235.2	239.0
ileocecum, ileocecal (coil) (valve)	153.4	197.5	230.3	211.3	235.2	239.0
sigmoid flexure (lower) (upper)	153.3	197.5	230.3	211.3	235.2	239.0
splenic flexure	153.7	197.5	230.3	211.3	235.2	239.0
small	152.9	197.4	230.7	211.2	235.2	239.0
contiguous sites	152.8	—	—	—	—	—
duodenum	152.0	197.4	230.7	211.2	235.2	239.0
ileum	152.2	197.4	230.7	211.2	235.2	239.0
jejunum	152.1	197.4	230.7	211.2	235.2	239.0

Neoplasm, neoplastic — continued

	Malignant			Benign	Uncertain Behavior	Unspecified
	Primary	Secondary	Ca in situ			
intestine, intestinal — *continued*						
tract NEC	159.0	197.8	230.7	211.9	235.2	239.0
intra-abdominal	195.2	198.89	234.8	229.8	238.8	239.89 ▲
intracranial NEC	191.9	198.3	—	225.0	237.5	239.6
intrahepatic (bile) duct	155.1	197.8	230.8	211.5	235.3	239.0
intraocular	190.0	198.4	234.0	224.0	238.8	239.89 ▲
intraorbital	190.1	198.4	234.0	224.1	238.8	239.89 ▲
intrasellar	194.3	198.89	234.8	227.3	237.0	239.7
intrathoracic (cavity) (organs NEC)	195.1	198.89	234.8	229.8	238.8	239.89 ▲
contiguous sites with respiratory organs	165.8	—	—	—	—	—
iris	190.	198.4	234.0	224.0	238.8	239.89 ▲
ischiorectal (fossa)	195.3	198.89	234.8	229.8	238.8	239.89 ▲
ischium	170.6	198.5	—	213.6	238.0	239.2
island of Reil	191.0	198.3	—	225.0	237.5	239.6
islands or islets of Langerhans	157.4	197.8	230.9	211.7	235.5	239.0
isthmus uteri	182.1	198.82	233.2	219.1	236.0	239.5
jaw	195.0	198.89	234.8	229.8	238.8	239.89 ▲
bone	170.1	198.5	—	213.1	238.0	239.2
carcinoma	143.9	—	—	—	—	—
lower	143.1	—	—	—	—	—
upper	143.0	—	—	—	—	—
lower	170.1	198.5	—	213.1	238.0	239.2
upper	170.0	198.5	—	213.0	238.0	239.2
carcinoma (any type) (lower) (upper)	195.0	—	—	—	—	—
skin	173.3	198.2	232.3	216.3	238.2	239.2
soft tissues	143.9	198.89	230.0	210.4	235.1	239.0
lower	143.1	198.89	230.0	210.4	235.1	239.0
upper	143.0	198.89	230.0	210.4	235.1	239.0
jejunum	152.1	197.4	230.7	211.2	235.2	239.0
joint NEC (*see also* Neoplasm, bone)	170.9	198.5	—	213.9	238.0	239.2
acromioclavicular	170.4	198.5	—	213.4	238.0	239.2
bursa or synovial membrane — *see* Neoplasm, connective tissue						
costovertebral	170.3	198.5	—	213.3	238.0	239.2
sternocostal	170.3	198.5	—	213.3	238.0	239.2
temporomandibular	170.1	198.5	—	213.1	238.0	239.2
junction						
anorectal	154.8	197.5	230.7	211.4	235.5	239.0
cardioesophageal	151.0	197.8	230.2	211.1	235.2	239.0
esophagogastric	151.0	197.8	230.2	211.1	235.2	239.0
gastroesophageal	151.0	197.8	230.2	211.1	235.2	239.0
hard and soft palate	145.5	198.89	230.0	210.4	235.1	239.0
ileocecal	153.4	197.5	230.3	211.3	235.2	239.0
pelvirectal	154.0	197.5	230.4	211.4	235.2	239.0
pelviureteric	189.1	198.0	233.9	223.1	236.91	239.5
rectosigmoid	154.0	197.5	230.4	211.4	235.2	239.0
squamocolumnar, of cervix	180.8	198.82	233.1	219.0	236.0	239.5
kidney (parenchyma)	189.0	198.0	233.9	223.0	236.91	239.5
calyx	189.1	198.0	233.9	223.1	236.91	239.5
hilus	189.1	198.0	233.9	223.1	236.91	239.5
pelvis	189.1	198.0	233.9	223.1	236.91	239.5
knee NEC*	195.5	198.89	232.7	229.8	238.8	239.89 ▲
labia (skin)	184.4	198.82	233.32	221.2	236.3	239.5
majora	184.1	198.82	233.32	221.2	236.3	239.5
minora	184.2	198.82	233.32	221.2	236.3	239.5
labial (*see also* Neoplasm, lip)						
sulcus (lower) (upper)	145.1	198.89	230.0	210.4	235.1	239.0
labium (skin)	184.4	198.82	233.32	221.2	236.3	239.5

Neoplasm, neoplastic — continued

	Malignant			Benign	Uncertain Behavior	Unspecified
	Primary	Secondary	Ca in situ			
labium — *continued*						
majus	184.1	198.82	233.32	221.2	236.3	239.5
minus	184.2	198.82	233.32	221.2	236.3	239.5
lacrimal						
canaliculi	190.7	198.4	234.0	224.7	238.8	239.89 ▲
duct (nasal)	190.7	198.4	234.0	224.7	238.8	239.89 ▲
gland	190.2	198.4	234.0	224.2	238.8	239.89 ▲
punctum	190.7	198.4	234.0	224.7	238.8	239.89 ▲
sac	190.7	198.4	234.0	224.7	238.8	239.89 ▲
Langerhans, islands or islets	157.4	197.8	230.9	211.7	235.5	239.0
laryngopharynx	148.9	198.89	230.0	210.8	235.1	239.0
larynx, laryngeal NEC	161.9	197.3	231.0	212.1	235.6	239.1
aryepiglottic fold	161.1	197.3	231.0	212.1	235.6	239.1
cartilage (arytenoid) (cricoid) (cuneiform) (thyroid)	161.3	197.3	231.0	212.1	235.6	239.1
commissure (anterior) (posterior)	161.0	197.3	231.0	212.1	235.6	239.1
contiguous sites	161.8	—	—	—	—	—
extrinsic NEC	161.1	197.3	231.0	212.1	235.6	239.1
meaning hypopharynx	148.9	198.89	230.0	210.8	235.1	239.0
interarytenoid fold	161.1	197.3	231.0	212.1	235.6	239.1
intrinsic	161.0	197.3	231.0	212.1	235.6	239.1
ventricular band	161.1	197.3	231.0	212.1	235.6	239.1
leg NEC*	195.5	198.89	232.7	229.8	238.8	239.89 ▲
lens, crystalline	190.0	198.4	234.0	224.0	238.8	239.89 ▲
lid (lower) (upper)	173.1	198.2	232.1	216.1	238.2	239.2
ligament (*see also* Neoplasm, connective tissue)						
broad	183.3	198.82	233.39	221.0	236.3	239.5
Mackenrodt's	183.8	198.82	233.39	221.8	236.3	239.5
non-uterine — *see* Neoplasm, connective tissue						
round	183.5	198.82	—	221.0	236.3	239.5
sacro-uterine	183.4	198.82	—	221.0	236.3	239.5
uterine	183.4	198.82	—	221.0	236.3	239.5
utero-ovarian	183.8	198.82	233.39	221.8	236.3	239.5
uterosacral	183.4	198.82	—	221.0	236.3	239.5
limb*	195.8	198.89	232.8	229.8	238.8	239.89 ▲
lower*	195.5	198.89	232.7	229.8	238.8	239.89 ▲
upper*	195.4	198.89	232.6	229.8	238.8	239.89 ▲
limbus of cornea	190.4	198.4	234.0	224.4	238.8	239.89 ▲
lingual NEC (*see also* Neoplasm, tongue)	141.9	198.89	230.0	210.1	235.1	239.0
lingula, lung	162.3	197.0	231.2	212.3	235.7	239.1
lip (external) (lipstick area) (vermillion border)	140.9	198.89	230.0	210.0	235.1	239.0
buccal aspect — *see* Neoplasm, lip, internal						
commissure	140.6	198.89	230.0	210.4	235.1	239.0
contiguous sites	140.8	—	—	—	—	—
with oral cavity or pharynx	149.8	—	—	—	—	—
frenulum — *see* Neoplasm, lip, internal						
inner aspect — *see* Neoplasm, lip, internal						
internal (buccal) (frenulum) (mucosa) (oral)	140.5	198.89	230.0	210.0	235.1	239.0
lower	140.4	198.89	230.0	210.0	235.1	239.0
upper	140.3	198.89	230.0	210.0	235.1	239.0

☑ Additional Digit Required — Refer to the Tabular List for Digit Selection   ▽ Subterms under main terms may continue to next column or page

192 — Volume 2 • October 2009   ►◄ Revised Text   ● New Line   ▲ Revised Code   2010 ICD-9-CM

Neoplasm, neoplastic — *continued*

	Malignant					
	Primary	Secondary	Ca in situ	Benign	Uncertain Behavior	Unspecified
lip — *continued*						
lower	140.1	198.89	230.0	210.0	235.1	239.0
internal (buccal) (frenulum) (mucosa) (oral)	140.4	198.89	230.0	210.0	235.1	239.0
mucosa — *see* Neoplasm, lip, internal						
oral aspect — *see* Neoplasm, lip, internal						
skin (commissure) (lower) (upper)	173.0	198.2	232.0	216.0	238.2	239.2
upper	140.0	198.89	230.0	210.0	235.1	239.0
internal (buccal) (frenulum) (mucosa) (oral)	140.3	198.89	230.0	210.0	235.1	239.0
liver	155.2	197.7	230.8	211.5	235.3	239.0
primary	155.0	—	—	—	—	—
lobe						
azygos	162.3	197.0	231.2	212.3	235.7	239.1
frontal	191.1	198.3	—	225.0	237.5	239.6
lower	162.5	197.0	231.2	212.3	235.7	239.1
middle	162.4	197.0	231.2	212.3	235.7	239.1
occipital	191.4	198.3	—	225.0	237.5	239.6
parietal	191.3	198.3	—	225.0	237.5	239.6
temporal	191.2	198.3	—	225.0	237.5	239.6
upper	162.3	197.0	231.2	212.3	235.7	239.1
lumbosacral plexus	171.6	198.4	—	215.6	238.1	239.2
lung	162.9	197.0	231.2	212.3	235.7	239.1
azygos lobe	162.3	197.0	231.2	212.3	235.7	239.1
carina	162.2	197.0	231.2	212.3	235.7	239.1
contiguous sites with bronchus or trachea	162.8	—	—	—	—	—
hilus	162.2	197.0	231.2	212.3	235.7	239.1
lingula	162.3	197.0	231.2	212.3	235.7	239.1
lobe NEC	162.9	197.0	231.2	212.3	235.7	239.1
lower lobe	162.5	197.0	231.2	212.3	235.7	239.1
main bronchus	162.2	197.0	231.2	212.3	235.7	239.1
middle lobe	162.4	197.0	231.2	212.3	235.7	239.1
upper lobe	162.3	197.0	231.2	212.3	235.7	239.1
lymph, lymphatic channel NEC (*see also* Neoplasm, connective tissue)	171.9	198.89	—	215.9	238.1	239.2
gland (secondary)	—	196.9	—	229.0	238.8	239.89 ▲
abdominal	—	196.2	—	229.0	238.8	239.89 ▲
aortic	—	196.2	—	229.0	238.8	239.89 ▲
arm	—	196.3	—	229.0	238.8	239.89 ▲
auricular (anterior) (posterior)	—	196.0	—	229.0	238.8	239.89 ▲
axilla, axillary	—	196.3	—	229.0	238.8	239.89 ▲
brachial	—	196.3	—	229.0	238.8	239.89 ▲
bronchial	—	196.1	—	229.0	238.8	239.89 ▲
bronchopulmonary	—	196.1	—	229.0	238.8	239.89 ▲
celiac	—	196.2	—	229.0	238.8	239.89 ▲
cervical	—	196.0	—	229.0	238.8	239.89 ▲
cervicofacial	—	196.0	—	229.0	238.8	239.89 ▲
Cloquet	—	196.5	—	229.0	238.8	239.89 ▲
colic	—	196.2	—	229.0	238.8	239.89 ▲
common duct	—	196.2	—	229.0	238.8	239.89 ▲
cubital	—	196.3	—	229.0	238.8	239.89 ▲
diaphragmatic	—	196.1	—	229.0	238.8	239.89 ▲
epigastric, inferior	—	196.6	—	229.0	238.8	239.89 ▲
epitrochlear	—	196.3	—	229.0	238.8	239.89 ▲
esophageal	—	196.1	—	229.0	238.8	239.89 ▲
face	—	196.0	—	229.0	238.8	239.89 ▲
femoral	—	196.5	—	229.0	238.8	239.89 ▲
gastric	—	196.2	—	229.0	238.8	239.89 ▲

Neoplasm, neoplastic — *continued*

	Malignant					
	Primary	Secondary	Ca in situ	Benign	Uncertain Behavior	Unspecified
lymph, lymphatic — *continued*						
gland — *continued*						
groin	—	196.5	—	229.0	238.8	239.89 ▲
head	—	196.0	—	229.0	238.8	239.89 ▲
hepatic	—	196.2	—	229.0	238.8	239.89 ▲
hilar (pulmonary)	—	196.1	—	229.0	238.8	239.89 ▲
splenic	—	196.2	—	229.0	238.8	239.89 ▲
hypogastric	—	196.6	—	229.0	238.8	239.89 ▲
ileocolic	—	196.2	—	229.0	238.8	239.89 ▲
iliac	—	196.6	—	229.0	238.8	239.89 ▲
infraclavicular	—	196.3	—	229.0	238.8	239.89 ▲
inguina, inguinal	—	196.5	—	229.0	238.8	239.89 ▲
innominate	—	196.1	—	229.0	238.8	239.89 ▲
intercostal	—	196.1	—	229.0	238.8	239.89 ▲
intestinal	—	196.2	—	229.0	238.8	239.89 ▲
intra-abdominal	—	196.2	—	229.0	238.8	239.89 ▲
intrapelvic	—	196.6	—	229.0	238.8	239.89 ▲
intrathoracic	—	196.1	—	229.0	238.8	239.9
jugular	—	196.0	—	229.0	238.8	239.89 ▲
leg	—	196.5	—	229.0	238.8	239.89 ▲
limb						
lower	—	196.5	—	229.0	238.8	239.89 ▲
upper	—	196.3	—	229.0	238.8	239.89 ▲
lower limb	—	196.5	—	229.0	238.8	239.89 ▲
lumbar	—	196.2	—	229.0	238.8	239.89 ▲
mandibular	—	196.0	—	229.0	238.8	239.89 ▲
mediastinal	—	196.1	—	229.0	238.8	239.89 ▲
mesenteric (inferior) (superior)	—	196.2	—	229.0	238.8	239.89 ▲
midcolic	—	196.2	—	229.0	238.8	239.89 ▲
multiple sites in categories 196.0–196.6	—	196.8	—	229.0	238.8	239.89 ▲
neck	—	196.0	—	229.0	238.8	239.89 ▲
obturator	—	196.6	—	229.0	238.8	239.89 ▲
occipital	—	196.0	—	229.0	238.8	239.89 ▲
pancreatic	—	196.2	—	229.0	238.8	239.89 ▲
para-aortic	—	196.2	—	229.0	238.8	239.89 ▲
paracervical	—	196.6	—	229.0	238.8	239.89 ▲
parametrial	—	196.6	—	229.0	238.8	239.89 ▲
parasternal	—	196.1	—	229.0	238.8	239.89 ▲
parotid	—	196.0	—	229.0	238.8	239.89 ▲
pectoral	—	196.3	—	229.0	238.8	239.89 ▲
pelvic	—	196.6	—	229.0	238.8	239.89 ▲
peri-aortic	—	196.2	—	229.0	238.8	239.89 ▲
peripancreatic	—	196.2	—	229.0	238.8	239.89 ▲
popliteal	—	196.5	—	229.0	238.8	239.89 ▲
porta hepatis	—	196.2	—	229.0	238.8	239.89 ▲
portal	—	196.2	—	229.0	238.8	239.89 ▲
preauricular	—	196.0	—	229.0	238.8	239.89 ▲
prelaryngeal	—	196.0	—	229.0	238.8	239.89 ▲
presymphysial	—	196.6	—	229.0	238.8	239.89 ▲
pretracheal	—	196.0	—	229.0	238.8	239.89 ▲
primary (any site) NEC	202.9 ☑	—	—	—	—	—
pulmonary (hiler)	—	196.1	—	229.0	238.8	239.89 ▲
pyloric	—	196.2	—	229.0	238.8	239.89 ▲
retroperitoneal	—	196.2	—	229.0	238.8	239.89 ▲
retropharyngeal	—	196.0	—	229.0	238.8	239.89 ▲
Rosenmüller's	—	196.5	—	229.0	238.8	239.89 ▲
sacral	—	196.6	—	229.0	238.8	239.89 ▲
scalene	—	196.0	—	229.0	238.8	239.89 ▲
site NEC	—	196.9	—	229.0	238.8	239.89 ▲
splenic (hilar)	—	196.2	—	229.0	238.8	239.89 ▲
subclavicular	—	196.3	—	229.0	238.8	239.89 ▲
subinguinal	—	196.5	—	229.0	238.8	239.89 ▲
sublingual	—	196.0	—	229.0	238.8	239.89 ▲
submandibular	—	196.0	—	229.0	238.8	239.89 ▲
submaxillary	—	196.0	—	229.0	238.8	239.89 ▲
submental	—	196.0	—	229.0	238.8	239.89 ▲

☑ Additional Digit Required — Refer to the Tabular List for Digit Selection

▽ Subterms under main terms may continue to next column or page

	Malignant			Benign	Uncertain Behavior	Unspecified
	Primary	Secondary	Ca in situ			
Neoplasm, neoplastic — *continued*						
lymph, lymphatic — *continued*						
gland — *continued*						
subscapular	—	196.3	—	229.0	238.8	239.89 ▲
supraclavicular	—	196.0	—	229.0	238.8	239.89 ▲
thoracic	—	196.1	—	229.0	238.8	239.89 ▲
tibial	—	196.5	—	229.0	238.8	239.89 ▲
tracheal	—	196.1	—	229.0	238.8	239.89 ▲
tracheobronchial	—	196.1	—	229.0	238.8	239.89 ▲
upper limb	—	196.3	—	229.0	238.8	239.89 ▲
Virchow's	—	196.0	—	229.0	238.8	239.89 ▲
node (*see also* Neoplasm, lymph gland)						
primary NEC	202.9 ☑	—	—	—	—	—
vessel (*see also* Neoplasm, connective tissue)	171.9	198.89	—	215.9	238.1	239.2
Mackenrodt's ligament	183.8	198.82	233.39	221.8	236.3	239.5
malar	170.0	198.5	—	213.0	238.0	239.2
region — *see* Neoplasm, cheek						
mammary gland — *see* Neoplasm, breast						
mandible	170.1	198.5	—	213.1	238.0	239.2
alveolar						
mucosa	143.1	198.89	230.0	210.4	235.1	239.0
mucose	143.1	198.89	230.0	210.4	235.1	239.0
ridge or process	170.1	198.5	—	213.1	238.0	239.2
carcinoma	143.1	—	—	—	—	—
carcinoma	143.1	—	—	—	—	—
marrow (bone) NEC	202.9 ☑	198.5	—	—	—	238.79
mastectomy site (skin)	173.5	198.2	—	—	—	—
specified as breast tissue	174.8	198.81				
mastoid (air cells) (antrum) (cavity)	160.1	197.3	231.8	212.0	235.9	239.1
bone or process	170.0	198.5	—	213.0	238.0	239.2
maxilla, maxillary (superior)	170.0	198.5	—	213.0	238.0	239.2
alveolar						
mucosa	143.0	198.89	230.0	210.4	235.1	239.0
ridge or process	170.0	198.5	—	213.0	238.0	239.2
carcinoma	143.0	—	—	—	—	—
antrum	160.2	197.3	231.8	212.0	235.9	239.1
carcinoma	143.0	—	—	—	—	—
inferior — *see* Neoplasm, mandible						
sinus	160.2	197.3	231.8	212.0	235.9	239.1
meatus						
external (ear)	173.2	198.2	232.2	216.2	238.2	239.2
Meckel's diverticulum	152.3	197.4	230.7	211.2	235.2	239.0
mediastinum, mediastinal	164.9	197.1	—	212.5	235.8	239.89 ▲
anterior	164.2	197.1	—	212.5	235.8	239.89 ▲
contiguous sites with heart and thymus	164.8	—	—	—	—	—
posterior	164.3	197.1	—	212.5	235.8	239.89 ▲
medulla						
adrenal	194.0	198.7	234.8	227.0	237.2	239.7
oblongata	191.7	198.3	—	225.0	237.5	239.6
meibomian gland	173.1	198.2	232.1	216.1	238.2	239.2
meninges (brain) (cerebral) (cranial) (intracranial)	192.1	198.4	—	225.2	237.6	239.7
spinal (cord)	192.3	198.4	—	225.4	237.6	239.7

	Malignant			Benign	Uncertain Behavior	Unspecified
	Primary	Secondary	Ca in situ			
Neoplasm, neoplastic — *continued*						
meniscus, knee joint (lateral) (medial)	170.7	198.5	—	213.7	238.0	239.2
mesentery, mesenteric	158.8	197.6	—	211.8	235.4	239.0
mesoappendix	158.8	197.6	—	211.8	235.4	239.0
mesocolon	158.8	197.6	—	211.8	235.4	239.0
mesopharynx — *see* Neoplasm, oropharynx						
mesosalpinx	183.3	198.82	233.39	221.0	236.3	239.5
mesovarium	183.3	198.82	233.39	221.0	236.3	239.5
metacarpus (any bone)	170.5	198.5	—	213.5	238.0	239.2
metastatic NEC (*see also* Neoplasm, by site, secondary)	—	199.1	—	—	—	—
metatarsus (any bone)	170.8	198.5	—	213.8	238.0	239.2
midbrain	191.7	198.3	—	225.0	237.5	239.6
milk duct — *see* Neoplasm, breast						
mons						
pubis	184.4	198.82	233.32	221.2	236.3	239.5
veneris	184.4	198.82	233.32	221.2	236.3	239.5
motor tract	192.9	198.4	—	225.9	237.9	239.7
brain	191.9	198.3	—	225.0	237.5	239.6
spinal	192.2	198.3	—	225.3	237.5	239.7
mouth	145.9	198.89	230.0	210.4	235.1	239.0
contiguous sites	145.8	—	—	—	—	—
floor	144.9	198.89	230.0	210.3	235.1	239.0
anterior portion	144.0	198.89	230.0	210.3	235.1	239.0
contiguous sites	144.8	—	—	—	—	—
lateral portion	144.1	198.89	230.0	210.3	235.1	239.0
roof	145.5	198.89	230.0	210.4	235.1	239.0
specified part NEC	145.8	198.89	230.0	210.4	235.1	239.0
vestibule	145.1	198.89	230.0	210.4	235.1	239.0
mucosa						
alveolar (ridge or process)	143.9	198.89	230.0	210.4	235.1	239.0
lower	143.1	198.89	230.0	210.4	235.1	239.0
upper	143.0	198.89	230.0	210.4	235.1	239.0
buccal	145.0	198.89	230.0	210.4	235.1	239.0
cheek	145.0	198.89	230.0	210.4	235.1	239.0
lip — *see* Neoplasm, lip, internal						
nasal	160.0	197.3	231.8	212.0	235.9	239.1
oral	145.0	198.89	230.0	210.4	235.1	239.0
Müllerian duct						
female	184.8	198.82	233.39	221.8	236.3	239.5
male	187.8	198.82	233.6	222.8	236.6	239.5
multiple sites NEC	199.0	199.0	234.9	229.9	238.9	199.0
muscle (*see also* Neoplasm, connective tissue)						
extraocular	190.1	198.4	234.0	224.1	238.8	239.89 ▲
myocardium	164.1	198.89	—	212.7	238.8	239.89 ▲
myometrium	182.0	198.82	233.2	219.1	236.0	239.5
myopericardium	164.1	198.89	—	212.7	238.8	239.89 ▲
nabothian gland (follicle)	180.0	198.82	233.1	219.0	236.0	239.5
nail	173.9	198.2	232.9	216.9	238.2	239.2
finger	173.6	198.2	232.6	216.6	238.2	239.2
toe	173.7	198.2	232.7	216.7	238.2	239.2
nares, naris (anterior) (posterior)	160.0	197.3	231.8	212.0	235.9	239.1
nasal — *see* Neoplasm, nose						
nasolabial groove	173.3	198.2	232.3	216.3	238.2	239.2
nasolacrimal duct	190.7	198.4	234.0	224.7	238.8	239.89 ▲
nasopharynx, nasopharyngeal	147.9	198.89	230.0	210.7	235.1	239.0
contiguous sites	147.8	—	—	—	—	—

☑ Additional Digit Required — Refer to the Tabular List for Digit Selection ▽ Subterms under main terms may continue to next column or page

194 — Volume 2 · October 2009   ▶◀ Revised Text   ● New Line   ▲ Revised Code   2010 ICD-9-CM

	Malignant					
	Primary	Secondary	Ca in situ	Benign	Uncertain Behavior	Unspecified
Neoplasm, neoplastic — *continued*						
nasopharynx, nasopharyngeal — *continued*						
floor	147.3	198.89	230.0	210.7	235.1	239.0
roof	147.0	198.89	230.0	210.7	235.1	239.0
specified site NEC	147.8	198.89	230.0	210.7	235.1	239.0
wall	147.9	198.89	230.0	210.7	235.1	239.0
anterior	147.3	198.89	230.0	210.7	235.1	239.0
lateral	147.2	198.89	230.0	210.7	235.1	239.0
posterior	147.1	198.89	230.0	210.7	235.1	239.0
superior	147.0	198.89	230.0	210.7	235.1	239.0
nates	173.5	198.2	232.5	216.5	238.2	239.2
neck NEC*	195.0	198.89	234.8	229.8	238.8	239.89 ▲
nerve (autonomic) (ganglion) (parasympathetic) (peripheral) (sympathetic) (*see also* Neoplasm, connective tissue)						
abducens	192.0	198.4	—	225.1	237.9	239.7
accessory (spinal)	192.0	198.4	—	225.1	237.9	239.7
acoustic	192.0	198.4	—	225.1	237.9	239.7
auditory	192.0	198.4	—	225.1	237.9	239.7
brachial	171.2	198.89	—	215.2	238.1	239.2
cranial (any)	192.0	198.4	—	225.1	237.9	239.7
facial	192.0	198.4	—	225.1	237.9	239.7
femoral	171.3	198.89	—	215.3	238.1	239.2
glossopharyngeal	192.0	198.4	—	225.1	237.9	239.7
hypoglossal	192.0	198.4	—	225.1	237.9	239.7
intercostal	171.4	198.89	—	215.4	238.1	239.2
lumbar	171.7	198.89	—	215.7	238.1	239.2
median	171.2	198.89	—	215.2	238.1	239.2
obturator	171.3	198.89	—	215.3	238.1	239.2
oculomotor	192.0	198.4	—	225.1	237.9	239.7
olfactory	192.0	198.4	—	225.1	237.9	239.7
optic	192.0	198.4	—	225.1	237.9	239.7
peripheral NEC	171.9	198.89	—	215.9	238.1	239.2
radial	171.2	198.89	—	215.2	238.1	239.2
sacral	171.6	198.89	—	215.6	238.1	239.2
sciatic	171.3	198.89	—	215.3	238.1	239.2
spinal NEC	171.9	198.89	—	215.9	238.1	239.2
trigeminal	192.0	198.4	—	225.1	237.9	239.7
trochlear	192.0	198.4	—	225.1	237.9	239.7
ulnar	171.2	198.89	—	215.2	238.1	239.2
vagus	192.0	198.4	—	225.1	237.9	239.7
nervous system (central)						
NEC	192.9	198.4	—	225.9	237.9	239.7
autonomic NEC	171.9	198.89	—	215.9	238.1	239.2
brain (*see also* Neoplasm, brain)						
membrane or meninges	192.1	198.4	—	225.2	237.6	239.7
contiguous sites	192.8	—	—	—	—	—
parasympathetic NEC	171.9	198.89	—	215.9	238.1	239.2
sympathetic NEC	171.9	198.89	—	215.9	238.1	239.2
nipple (female)	174.0	198.81	233.0	217	238.3	239.3
male	175.0	198.81	233.0	217	238.3	239.3
nose, nasal	195.0	198.89	234.8	229.8	238.8	239.89 ▲
ala (external)	173.3	198.2	232.3	216.3	238.2	239.2
bone	170.0	198.5	—	213.0	238.0	239.2
cartilage	160.0	197.3	231.8	212.0	235.9	239.1
cavity	160.0	197.3	231.8	212.0	235.9	239.1
contiguous sites with accessory sinuses or middle ear	160.8	—	—	—	—	—
choana	147.3	198.89	230.0	210.7	235.1	239.0
external (skin)	173.3	198.2	232.3	216.3	238.2	239.2
fossa	160.0	197.3	231.8	212.0	235.9	239.1
internal	160.0	197.3	231.8	212.0	235.9	239.1
mucosa	160.0	197.3	231.8	212.0	235.9	239.1
septum	160.0	197.3	231.8	212.0	235.9	239.1
Neoplasm, neoplastic — *continued*						
nose, nasal — *continued*						
septum — *continued*						
posterior margin	147.3	198.89	230.0	210.7	235.1	239.0
sinus — *see* Neoplasm, sinus						
skin	173.3	198.2	232.3	216.3	238.2	239.2
turbinate (mucosa)	160.0	197.3	231.8	212.0	235.9	239.1
bone	170.0	198.5	—	213.0	238.0	239.2
vestibule	160.0	197.3	231.8	212.0	235.9	239.1
nostril	160.0	197.3	231.8	212.0	235.9	239.1
nucleus pulposus	170.2	198.5	—	213.2	238.0	239.2
occipital						
bone	170.0	198.5	—	213.0	238.0	239.2
lobe or pole, brain	191.4	198.3	—	225.0	237.5	239.6
odontogenic — *see* Neoplasm, jaw bone						
oesophagus — *see* Neoplasm, esophagus						
olfactory nerve or bulb	192.0	198.4	—	225.1	237.9	239.7
olive (brain)	191.7	198.3	—	225.0	237.5	239.6
omentum	158.8	197.6	—	211.8	235.4	239.0
operculum (brain)	191.0	198.3	—	225.0	237.5	239.6
optic nerve, chiasm, or tract	192.0	198.4	—	225.1	237.9	239.7
oral (cavity)	145.9	198.89	230.0	210.4	235.1	239.0
contiguous sites with lip or pharynx	149.8	—	—	—	—	—
ill-defined	149.9	198.89	230.0	210.4	235.1	239.0
mucosa	145.9	198.89	230.0	210.4	235.1	239.0
orbit	190.1	198.4	234.0	224.1	238.8	239.89 ▲
bone	170.0	198.5	—	213.0	238.0	239.2
eye	190.1	198.4	234.0	224.1	238.8	239.89 ▲
soft parts	190.1	198.4	234.0	224.1	238.8	239.89 ▲
organ of Zuckerkandl	194.6	198.89	—	227.6	237.3	239.7
oropharynx	146.9	198.89	230.0	210.6	235.1	239.0
branchial cleft (vestige)	146.8	198.89	230.0	210.6	235.1	239.0
contiguous sites	146.8	—	—	—	—	—
junctional region	146.5	198.89	230.0	210.6	235.1	239.0
lateral wall	146.6	198.89	230.0	210.6	235.1	239.0
pillars of fauces	146.2	198.89	230.0	210.6	235.1	239.0
posterior wall	146.7	198.89	230.0	210.6	235.1	239.0
specified part NEC	146.8	198.89	230.0	210.6	235.1	239.0
vallecula	146.3	198.89	230.0	210.6	235.1	239.0
os						
external	180.1	198.82	233.1	219.0	236.0	239.5
internal	180.0	198.82	233.1	219.0	236.0	239.5
ovary	183.0	198.6	233.39	220	236.2	239.5
oviduct	183.2	198.82	233.39	221.0	236.3	239.5
palate	145.5	198.89	230.0	210.4	235.1	239.0
hard	145.2	198.89	230.0	210.4	235.1	239.0
junction of hard and soft palate	145.5	198.89	230.0	210.4	235.1	239.0
soft	145.3	198.89	230.0	210.4	235.1	239.0
nasopharyngeal surface	147.3	198.89	230.0	210.7	235.1	239.0
posterior surface	147.3	198.89	230.0	210.7	235.1	239.0
superior surface	147.3	198.89	230.0	210.7	235.1	239.0
palatoglossal arch	146.2	198.89	230.0	210.6	235.1	239.0
palatopharyngeal arch	146.2	198.89	230.0	210.6	235.1	239.0
pallium	191.0	198.3	—	225.0	237.5	239.6
palpebra	173.1	198.2	232.1	216.1	238.2	239.2
pancreas	157.9	197.8	230.9	211.6	235.5	239.0
body	157.1	197.8	230.9	211.6	235.5	239.0
contiguous sites	157.8	—	—	—	—	—

☑ Additional Digit Required — Refer to the Tabular List for Digit Selection

▽ Subterms under main terms may continue to next column or page

	Malignant			Benign	Uncertain Behavior	Unspecified
	Primary	Secondary	Ca in situ			
Neoplasm, neoplastic —						
continued						
pancreas — *continued*						
duct (of Santorini) (of						
Wirsung)	157.3	197.8	230.9	211.6	235.5	239.0
ectopic tissue	157.8	197.8	230.9	211.6	235.5	239.0
head	157.0	197.8	230.9	211.6	235.5	239.0
islet cells	157.4	197.8	230.9	211.7	235.5	239.0
neck	157.8	197.8	230.9	211.6	235.5	239.0
tail	157.2	197.8	230.9	211.6	235.5	239.0
para-aortic body	194.6	198.89	—	227.6	237.3	239.7
paraganglion NEC	194.6	198.89	—	227.6	237.3	239.7
parametrium	183.4	198.82	—	221.0	236.3	239.5
paranephric	158.0	197.6	—	211.8	235.4	239.0
pararectal	195.3	198.89	—	229.8	238.8	239.89 ▲
parasagittal						
(region)	195.0	198.89	234.8	229.8	238.8	239.89 ▲
parasellar	192.9	198.4	—	225.9	237.9	239.7
parathyroid (gland)	194.1	198.89	234.8	227.1	237.4	239.7
paraurethral	195.3	198.89	—	229.8	238.8	239.89 ▲
gland	189.4	198.1	233.9	223.89	236.99	239.5
paravaginal	195.3	198.89	—	229.8	238.8	239.89 ▲
parenchyma,						
kidney	189.0	198.0	233.9	223.0	236.91	239.5
parietal						
bone	170.0	198.5	—	213.0	238.0	239.2
lobe, brain	191.3	198.3	—	225.0	237.5	239.6
paroophoron	183.3	198.82	233.39	221.0	236.3	239.5
parotid (duct)						
(gland)	142.0	198.89	230.0	210.2	235.0	239.0
parovarium	183.3	198.82	233.39	221.0	236.3	239.5
patella	170.8	198.5	—	213.8	238.0	239.2
peduncle, cerebral	191.7	198.3	—	225.0	237.5	239.6
pelvirectal junction	154.0	197.5	230.4	211.4	235.2	239.0
pelvis, pelvic	195.3	198.89	234.8	229.8	238.8	239.89 ▲
bone	170.6	198.5	—	213.6	238.0	239.2
floor	195.3	198.89	234.8	229.8	238.8	239.89 ▲
renal	189.1	198.0	233.9	223.1	236.91	239.5
viscera	195.3	198.89	234.8	229.8	238.8	239.89 ▲
wall	195.3	198.89	234.8	229.8	238.8	239.89 ▲
pelvo-abdominal	195.8	198.89	234.8	229.8	238.8	239.89 ▲
penis	187.4	198.82	233.5	222.1	236.6	239.5
body	187.3	198.82	233.5	222.1	236.6	239.5
corpus						
(cavernosum)	187.3	198.82	233.5	222.1	236.6	239.5
glans	187.2	198.82	233.5	222.1	236.6	239.5
skin NEC	187.4	198.82	233.5	222.1	236.6	239.5
periadrenal (tissue)	158.0	197.6	—	211.8	235.4	239.0
perianal (skin)	173.5	198.2	232.5	216.5	238.2	239.2
pericardium	164.1	198.89	—	212.7	238.8	239.89 ▲
perinephric	158.0	197.6	—	211.8	235.4	239.0
perineum	195.3	198.89	234.8	229.8	238.8	239.89 ▲
periodontal tissue						
NEC	143.9	198.89	230.0	210.4	235.1	239.0
periosteum — *see*						
Neoplasm, bone						
peripancreatic	158.0	197.6	—	211.8	235.4	239.0
peripheral nerve						
NEC	171.9	198.89	—	215.9	238.1	239.2
perirectal (tissue)	195.3	198.89	—	229.8	238.8	239.89 ▲
perirenal (tissue)	158.0	197.6	—	211.8	235.4	239.0
peritoneum, peritoneal						
(cavity)	158.9	197.6	—	211.8	235.4	239.0
contiguous sites	158.8	—	—	—	—	—
with digestive						
organs	159.8	—	—	—	—	—
parietal	158.8	197.6	—	211.8	235.4	239.0
pelvic	158.8	197.6	—	211.8	235.4	239.0
specified part						
NEC	158.8	197.6	—	211.8	235.4	239.0
peritonsillar (tissue)	195.0	198.89	234.8	229.8	238.8	239.89 ▲
periurethral tissue	195.3	198.89	—	229.8	238.8	239.89 ▲
phalanges	170.9	198.5	—	213.9	238.0	239.2
foot	170.8	198.5	—	213.8	238.0	239.2
hand	170.5	198.5	—	213.5	238.0	239.2

	Malignant			Benign	Uncertain Behavior	Unspecified
	Primary	Secondary	Ca in situ			
Neoplasm, neoplastic —						
continued						
pharynx,						
pharyngeal	149.0	198.89	230.0	210.9	235.1	239.0
bursa	147.1	198.89	230.0	210.7	235.1	239.0
fornix	147.3	198.89	230.0	210.7	235.1	239.0
recess	147.2	198.89	230.0	210.7	235.1	239.0
region	149.0	198.89	230.0	210.9	235.1	239.0
tonsil	147.1	198.89	230.0	210.7	235.1	239.0
wall (lateral)						
(posterior)	149.0	198.89	230.0	210.9	235.1	239.0
pia mater (cerebral)						
(cranial)	192.1	198.4	—	225.2	237.6	239.7
spinal	192.3	198.4	—	225.4	237.6	239.7
pillars of fauces	146.2	198.89	230.0	210.6	235.1	239.0
pineal (body)						
(gland)	194.4	198.89	234.8	227.4	237.1	239.7
pinna (ear) NEC	173.2	198.2	232.2	216.2	238.2	239.2
cartilage	171.0	198.89	—	215.0	238.1	239.2
piriform fossa or						
sinus	148.1	198.89	230.0	210.8	235.1	239.0
pituitary (body) (fossa)						
(gland) (lobe)	194.3	198.89	234.8	227.3	237.0	239.7
placenta	181	198.82	233.2	219.8	236.1	239.5
pleura, pleural						
(cavity)	163.9	197.2	—	212.4	235.8	239.1
contiguous sites	163.8	—	—	—	—	—
parietal	163.0	197.2	—	212.4	235.8	239.1
visceral	163.1	197.2	—	212.4	235.8	239.1
plexus						
brachial	171.2	198.89	—	215.2	238.1	239.2
cervical	171.0	198.89	—	215.0	238.1	239.2
choroid	191.5	198.3	—	225.0	237.5	239.6
lumbosacral	171.6	198.89	—	215.6	238.1	239.2
sacral	171.6	198.89	—	215.6	238.1	239.2
pluri-endocrine	194.8	198.89	234.8	227.8	237.4	239.7
pole						
frontal	191.1	198.3	—	225.0	237.5	239.6
occipital	191.4	198.3	—	225.0	237.5	239.6
pons (varolii)	191.7	198.3	—	225.0	237.5	239.6
popliteal fossa or						
space*	195.5	198.89	234.8	229.8	238.8	239.89 ▲
postcricoid (region)	148.0	198.89	230.0	210.8	235.1	239.0
posterior fossa						
(cranial)	191.9	198.3	—	225.0	237.5	239.6
postnasal space	147.9	198.89	230.0	210.7	235.1	239.0
prepuce	187.1	198.82	233.5	222.1	236.6	239.5
prepylorus	151.1	197.8	230.2	211.1	235.2	239.0
presacral (region)	195.3	198.89	—	229.8	238.8	239.89 ▲
prostate (gland)	185	198.82	233.4	222.2	236.5	239.5
utricle	189.3	198.1	233.9	223.81	236.99	239.5
pterygoid fossa	171.0	198.89	—	215.0	238.1	239.2
pubic bone	170.6	198.5	—	213.6	238.0	239.2
pudenda, pudendum						
(female)	184.4	198.82	233.32	221.2	236.3	239.5
pulmonary	162.9	197.0	231.2	212.3	235.7	239.1
putamen	191.0	198.3	—	225.0	237.5	239.6
pyloric						
antrum	151.2	197.8	230.2	211.1	235.2	239.0
canal	151.1	197.8	230.2	211.1	235.2	239.0
pylorus	151.1	197.8	230.2	211.1	235.2	239.0
pyramid (brain)	191.7	198.3	—	225.0	237.5	239.6
pyriform fossa or						
sinus	148.1	198.89	230.0	210.8	235.1	239.0
radius (any part)	170.4	198.5	—	213.4	238.0	239.2
Rathke's pouch	194.3	198.89	234.8	227.3	237.0	239.7
rectosigmoid (colon)						
(junction)	154.0	197.5	230.4	211.4	235.2	239.0
contiguous sites with						
anus or						
rectum	154.8	—	—	—	—	—
rectouterine pouch	158.8	197.6	—	211.8	235.4	239.0
rectovaginal septum or						
wall	195.3	198.89	234.8	229.8	238.8	239.89 ▲
rectovesical septum	195.3	198.89	234.8	229.8	238.8	239.89 ▲
rectum (ampulla)	154.1	197.5	230.4	211.4	235.2	239.0
and colon	154.0	197.5	230.4	211.4	235.2	239.0

☑ Additional Digit Required — Refer to the Tabular List for Digit Selection　　　　　　　　　　　　　　🖐 Subterms under main terms may continue to next column or page

196 — Volume 2 · October 2009　　　▶◀ Revised Text　　　● New Line　　　▲ Revised Code　　　2010 ICD-9-CM

	Malignant					
	Primary	Secondary	Ca in situ	Benign	Uncertain Behavior	Unspecified
Neoplasm, neoplastic — *continued*						
rectum — *continued*						
contiguous sites with anus or rectosigmoid junction	154.8	—	—	—	—	—
renal	189.0	198.0	233.9	223.0	236.91	239.5
calyx	189.1	198.0	233.9	223.1	236.91	239.5
hilus	189.1	198.0	233.9	223.1	236.91	239.5
parenchyma	189.0	198.0	233.9	223.0	236.91	239.5
pelvis	189.1	198.0	233.9	223.1	236.91	239.5
respiratory						
organs or system NEC	165.9	197.3	231.9	212.9	235.9	239.1
contiguous sites with intrathoracic organs	165.8	—	—	—	—	—
specified sites NEC	165.8	197.3	231.8	212.8	235.9	239.1
tract NEC	165.9	197.3	231.9	212.9	235.9	239.1
upper	165.0	197.3	231.9	212.9	235.9	239.1
retina	190.5	198.4	234.0	224.5	238.8	239.81 ▲
retrobulbar	190.1	198.4	—	224.1	238.8	239.89 ▲
retrocecal	158.0	197.6	—	211.8	235.4	239.0
retromolar (area) (triangle) (trigone)	145.6	198.89	230.0	210.4	235.1	239.0
retro-orbital	195.0	198.89	234.8	229.8	238.8	239.89 ▲
retroperitoneal (space) (tissue)	158.0	197.6	—	211.8	235.4	239.0
contiguous sites	158.8	—	—	—	—	—
retroperitoneum	158.0	197.6	—	211.8	235.4	239.0
contiguous sites	158.8	—	—	—	—	—
retropharyngeal	149.0	198.89	230.0	210.9	235.1	239.0
retrovesical (septum)	195.3	198.89	234.8	229.8	238.8	239.89 ▲
rhinencephalon	191.0	198.3	—	225.0	237.5	239.6
rib	170.3	198.5	—	213.3	238.0	239.2
Rosenmüller's fossa	147.2	198.89	230.0	210.7	235.1	239.0
round ligament	183.5	198.82	—	221.0	236.3	239.5
sacrococcyx, sacrococcygeal	170.6	198.5	—	213.6	238.0	239.2
region	195.3	198.89	234.8	229.8	238.8	239.89 ▲
sacrouterine ligament	183.4	198.82	—	221.0	236.3	239.5
sacrum, sacral (vertebra)	170.6	198.5	—	213.6	238.0	239.2
salivary gland or duct (major)	142.9	198.89	230.0	210.2	235.0	239.0
contiguous sites	142.8	—	—	—	—	—
minor NEC	145.9	198.89	230.0	210.4	235.1	239.0
parotid	142.0	198.89	230.0	210.2	235.0	239.0
pluriglandular	142.8	198.89	—	210.2	235.0	239.0
sublingual	142.2	198.89	230.0	210.2	235.0	239.0
submandibular	142.1	198.89	230.0	210.2	235.0	239.0
submaxillary	142.1	198.89	230.0	210.2	235.0	239.0
salpinx (uterine)	183.2	198.82	233.39	221.0	236.3	239.5
Santorini's duct	157.3	197.8	230.9	211.6	235.5	239.0
scalp	173.4	198.2	232.4	216.4	238.2	239.2
scapula (any part)	170.4	198.5	—	213.4	238.0	239.2
scapular region	195.1	198.89	234.8	229.8	238.8	239.89 ▲
scar NEC (*see also* Neoplasm, skin)	173.9	198.2	232.9	216.9	238.2	239.2
sciatic nerve	171.3	198.89	—	215.3	238.1	239.2
sclera	190.0	198.4	234.0	224.0	238.8	239.89 ▲
scrotum (skin)	187.7	198.82	—	222.4	236.6	239.5
sebaceous gland — *see* Neoplasm, skin						
sella turcica	194.3	198.89	234.8	227.3	237.0	239.7
bone	170.0	198.5	—	213.0	238.0	239.2
semilunar cartilage (knee)	170.7	198.5	—	213.7	238.0	239.2
seminal vesicle	187.8	198.82	233.6	222.8	236.6	239.5
septum						
nasal	160.0	197.3	231.8	212.0	235.9	239.1

	Malignant					
	Primary	Secondary	Ca in situ	Benign	Uncertain Behavior	Unspecified
Neoplasm, neoplastic — *continued*						
septum — *continued*						
nasal — *continued*						
posterior margin	147.3	198.89	230.0	210.7	235.1	239.0
rectovaginal	195.3	198.89	234.8	229.8	238.8	239.89 ▲
rectovesical	195.3	198.89	234.8	229.8	238.8	239.89 ▲
urethrovaginal	184.9	198.82	233.39	221.9	236.3	239.5
vesicovaginal	184.9	198.82	233.39	221.9	236.3	239.5
shoulder NEC*	195.4	198.89	232.6	229.8	238.8	239.89 ▲
sigmoid flexure (lower) (upper)	153.3	197.5	230.3	211.3	235.2	239.0
sinus (accessory)	160.9	197.3	231.8	212.0	235.9	239.1
bone (any)	170.0	198.5	—	213.0	238.0	239.2
contiguous sites with middle ear or nasal cavities	160.8	—	—	—	—	—
ethmoidal	160.3	197.3	231.8	212.0	235.9	239.1
frontal	160.4	197.3	231.8	212.0	235.9	239.1
maxillary	160.2	197.3	231.8	212.0	235.9	239.1
nasal, paranasal NEC	160.9	197.3	231.8	212.0	235.9	239.1
pyriform	148.1	198.89	230.0	210.8	235.1	239.0
sphenoidal	160.5	197.3	231.8	212.0	235.9	239.1
skeleton, skeletal NEC	170.9	198.5	—	213.9	238.0	239.2
Skene's gland	189.4	198.1	233.9	223.89	236.99	239.5
skin NEC	173.9	198.2	232.9	216.9	238.2	239.2
abdominal wall	173.5	198.2	232.5	216.5	238.2	239.2
ala nasi	173.3	198.2	232.3	216.3	238.2	239.2
ankle	173.7	198.2	232.7	216.7	238.2	239.2
antecubital space	173.6	198.2	232.6	216.6	238.2	239.2
anus	173.5	198.2	232.5	216.5	238.2	239.2
arm	173.6	198.2	232.6	216.6	238.2	239.2
auditory canal (external)	173.2	198.2	232.2	216.2	238.2	239.2
auricle (ear)	173.2	198.2	232.2	216.2	238.2	239.2
auricular canal (external)	173.2	198.2	232.2	216.2	238.2	239.2
axilla, axillary fold	173.5	198.2	232.5	216.5	238.2	239.2
back	173.5	198.2	232.5	216.5	238.2	239.2
breast	173.5	198.2	232.5	216.5	238.2	239.2
brow	173.3	198.2	232.3	216.3	238.2	239.2
buttock	173.5	198.2	232.5	216.5	238.2	239.2
calf	173.7	198.2	232.7	216.7	238.2	239.2
canthus (eye) (inner) (outer)	173.1	198.2	232.1	216.1	238.2	239.2
cervical region	173.4	198.2	232.4	216.4	238.2	239.2
cheek (external)	173.3	198.2	232.3	216.3	238.2	239.2
chest (wall)	173.5	198.2	232.5	216.5	238.2	239.2
chin	173.3	198.2	232.3	216.3	238.2	239.2
clavicular area	173.5	198.2	232.5	216.5	238.2	239.2
clitoris	184.3	198.82	233.32	221.2	236.3	239.5
columnella	173.3	198.2	232.3	216.3	238.2	239.2
concha	173.2	198.2	232.2	216.2	238.2	239.2
contiguous sites	173.8	—	—	—	—	—
ear (external)	173.2	198.2	232.2	216.2	238.2	239.2
elbow	173.6	198.2	232.6	216.6	238.2	239.2
eyebrow	173.3	198.2	232.3	216.3	238.2	239.2
eyelid	173.1	198.2	232.1	—	238.2	239.2
face NEC	173.3	198.2	232.3	216.3	238.2	239.2
female genital organs (external)	184.4	198.82	233.30	221.2	236.3	239.5
clitoris	184.3	198.82	233.32	221.2	236.3	239.5
labium NEC	184.4	198.82	233.32	221.2	236.3	239.5
majus	184.1	198.82	233.32	221.2	236.3	239.5
minus	184.2	198.82	233.32	221.2	236.3	239.5
pudendum	184.4	198.82	233.32	221.2	236.3	239.5
vulva	184.4	198.82	233.32	221.2	236.3	239.5
finger	173.6	198.2	232.6	216.6	238.2	239.2
flank	173.5	198.2	232.5	216.5	238.2	239.2
foot	173.7	198.2	232.7	216.7	238.2	239.2
forearm	173.6	198.2	232.6	216.6	238.2	239.2
forehead	173.3	198.2	232.3	216.3	238.2	239.2
glabella	173.3	198.2	232.3	216.3	238.2	239.2

☑ Additional Digit Required — Refer to the Tabular List for Digit Selection   ⒲ Subterms under main terms may continue to next column or page

2010 ICD-9-CM   ►◄ Revised Text   ● New Line   ▲ Revised Code   October 2009 · Volume 2 — 197

Neoplasm, sudoriferous, sudoriparous gland, site unspecified — Neoplasm, skin

Neoplasm, neoplastic —	Malignant			Benign	Uncertain Behavior	Unspecified
	Primary	Secondary	Ca in situ			
continued						
skin — *continued*						
gluteal region	173.5	198.2	232.5	216.5	238.2	239.2
groin	173.5	198.2	232.5	216.5	238.2	239.2
hand	173.6	198.2	232.6	216.6	238.2	239.2
head NEC	173.4	198.2	232.4	216.4	238.2	239.2
heel	173.7	198.2	232.7	216.7	238.2	239.2
helix	173.2	198.2	—	216.2	238.2	239.2
hip	173.7	198.2	232.7	216.7	238.2	239.2
infraclavicular						
region	173.5	198.2	232.5	216.5	238.2	239.2
inguinal region	173.5	198.2	232.5	216.5	238.2	239.2
jaw	173.3	198.2	232.3	216.3	238.2	239.2
knee	173.7	198.2	232.7	216.7	238.2	239.2
labia						
majora	184.1	198.82	233.32	221.2	236.3	239.5
minora	184.2	198.82	233.32	221.2	236.3	239.5
leg	173.7	198.2	232.7	216.7	238.2	239.2
lid (lower)						
(upper)	—	198.2	232.1	216.1	238.2	239.2
limb NEC	173.9	198.2	232.9	216.9	238.2	239.5
lower	173.7	198.2	232.7	216.7	238.2	239.2
upper	173.6	198.2	232.6	216.6	238.2	239.2
lip (lower)						
(upper)	173.0	198.2	232.0	216.0	238.2	239.2
male genital						
organs	187.9	198.82	233.6	222.9	236.6	239.5
penis	187.4	198.82	233.5	222.1	236.6	239.5
prepuce	187.1	198.82	233.5	222.1	236.6	239.5
scrotum	187.7	198.82	233.6	222.4	236.6	239.5
mastectomy site	173.5	198.2	—	—	—	—
specified as breast						
tissue	174.8	198.81	—	—	—	—
meatus, acoustic						
(external)	173.2	198.2	232.2	216.2	238.2	239.2
nates	173.5	198.2	232.5	216.5	238.2	239.0
neck	173.4	198.2	232.4	216.4	238.2	239.2
nose (external)	173.3	198.2	232.3	216.3	238.2	239.2
palm	173.6	198.2	232.6	216.6	238.2	239.2
palpebra	173.1	198.2	232.1	216.1	238.2	239.2
penis NEC	187.4	198.82	233.5	222.1	236.6	239.5
perianal	173.5	198.2	232.5	216.5	238.2	239.2
perineum	173.5	198.2	232.5	216.5	238.2	239.2
pinna	173.2	198.2	232.2	216.2	238.2	239.2
plantar	173.7	198.2	232.7	216.7	238.2	239.2
popliteal fossa or						
space	173.7	198.2	232.7	216.7	238.2	239.2
prepuce	187.1	198.82	233.5	222.1	236.6	239.5
pubes	173.5	198.2	232.5	216.5	238.2	239.2
sacrococcygeal						
region	173.5	198.2	232.5	216.5	238.2	239.2
scalp	173.4	198.2	232.4	216.4	238.2	239.2
scapular region	173.5	198.2	232.5	216.5	238.2	239.2
scrotum	187.7	198.82	233.6	222.4	236.6	239.5
shoulder	173.6	198.2	232.6	216.6	238.2	239.2
sole (foot)	173.7	198.2	232.7	216.7	238.2	239.2
specified sites						
NEC	173.8	198.2	232.8	216.8	232.8	239.2
submammary						
fold	173.5	198.2	232.5	216.5	238.2	239.2
supraclavicular						
region	173.4	198.2	232.4	216.4	238.2	239.2
temple	173.3	198.2	232.3	216.3	238.2	239.2
thigh	173.7	198.2	232.7	216.7	238.2	239.2
thoracic wall	173.5	198.2	232.5	216.5	238.2	239.2
thumb	173.6	198.2	232.6	216.6	238.2	239.2
toe	173.7	198.2	232.7	216.7	238.2	239.2
tragus	173.2	198.2	232.2	216.2	238.2	239.2
trunk	173.5	198.2	232.5	216.5	238.2	239.2
umbilicus	173.5	198.2	232.5	216.5	238.2	239.2
vulva	184.4	198.82	233.32	221.2	236.3	239.5
wrist	173.6	198.2	232.6	216.6	238.2	239.2
skull	170.0	198.5	—	213.0	238.0	239.2

Neoplasm, neoplastic —	Malignant			Benign	Uncertain Behavior	Unspecified
	Primary	Secondary	Ca in situ			
continued						
soft parts or tissues —						
see Neoplasm,						
connective tissue						
specified site NEC	195.8	198.89	234.8	229.8	238.8	239.89 ▲
specified site — *see*						
Neoplasm, skin						
spermatic cord	187.6	198.82	233.6	222.8	236.6	239.5
sphenoid	160.5	197.3	231.8	212.0	235.9	239.1
bone	170.0	198.5	—	213.0	238.0	239.2
sinus	160.5	197.3	231.8	212.0	235.9	239.1
sphincter						
anal	154.2	197.5	230.5	211.4	235.5	239.0
of Oddi	156.1	197.8	230.8	211.5	235.3	239.0
spine, spinal						
(column)	170.2	198.5	—	213.2	238.0	239.2
bulb	191.7	198.3	—	225.0	237.5	239.6
coccyx	170.6	198.5	—	213.6	238.0	239.2
cord (cervical) (lumbar)						
(sacral)						
(thoracic)	192.2	198.3	—	225.3	237.5	239.7
dura mater	192.3	198.4	—	225.4	237.6	239.7
lumbosacral	170.2	198.5	—	213.2	238.0	239.2
membrane	192.3	198.4	—	225.4	237.6	239.7
meninges	192.3	198.4	—	225.4	237.6	239.7
nerve (root)	171.9	198.89	—	215.9	238.1	239.2
pia mater	192.3	198.4	—	225.4	237.6	239.7
root	171.9	198.89	—	215.9	238.1	239.2
sacrum	170.6	198.5	—	213.6	238.0	239.2
spleen, splenic NEC	159.1	197.8	230.9	211.9	235.5	239.0
flexure (colon)	153.7	197.5	230.3	211.3	235.2	239.0
stem, brain	191.7	198.3	—	225.0	237.5	239.6
Stensen's duct	142.0	198.89	230.0	210.2	235.0	239.0
sternum	170.3	198.5	—	213.3	238.0	239.2
stomach	151.9	197.8	230.2	211.1	235.2	239.0
antrum (pyloric)	151.2	197.8	230.2	211.1	235.2	239.0
body	151.4	197.8	230.2	211.1	235.2	239.0
cardia	151.0	197.8	230.2	211.1	235.2	239.0
cardiac orifice	151.0	197.8	230.2	211.1	235.2	239.0
contiguous sites	151.8	—	—	—	—	—
corpus	151.4	197.8	230.2	211.1	235.2	239.0
fundus	151.3	197.8	230.2	211.1	235.2	239.0
greater curvature						
NEC	151.6	197.8	230.2	211.1	235.2	239.0
lesser curvature						
NEC	151.5	197.8	230.2	211.1	235.2	239.0
prepylorus	151.1	197.8	230.2	211.1	235.2	239.0
pylorus	151.1	197.8	230.2	211.1	235.2	239.0
wall NEC	151.9	197.8	230.2	211.1	235.2	239.0
anterior NEC	151.8	197.8	230.2	211.1	235.2	239.0
posterior NEC	151.8	197.8	230.2	211.1	235.2	239.0
stroma,						
endometrial	182.0	198.82	233.2	219.1	236.0	239.5
stump, cervical	180.8	198.82	233.1	219.0	236.0	239.5
subcutaneous (nodule)						
(tissue) NEC — *see*						
Neoplasm,						
connective tissue						
subdural	192.1	198.4	—	225.2	237.6	239.7
subglottis,						
subglottic	161.2	197.3	231.0	212.1	235.6	239.1
sublingual	144.9	198.89	230.0	210.3	235.1	239.0
gland or duct	142.2	198.89	230.0	210.2	235.0	239.0
submandibular						
gland	142.1	198.89	230.0	210.2	235.0	239.0
submaxillary gland or						
duct	142.1	198.89	230.0	210.2	235.0	239.0
submental	195.0	198.89	234.8	229.8	238.8	239.89 ▲
subpleural	162.9	197.0	—	212.3	235.7	239.1
substernal	164.2	197.1	—	212.5	235.8	239.89 ▲
sudoriferous,						
sudoriparous gland,						
site unspecified	173.9	198.2	232.9	216.9	238.2	239.2
specified site — *see*						
Neoplasm, skin						

Neoplasm, neoplastic— *continued*	Primary	Secondary	Ca in situ	Benign	Uncertain Behavior	Unspecified
supraclavicular region	195.0	198.89	234.8	229.8	238.8	239.89 ▲
supraglottis	161.1	197.3	231.0	212.1	235.6	239.1
suprarenal (capsule) (cortex) (gland) (medulla)	194.0	198.7	234.8	227.0	237.2	239.7
suprasellar (region)	191.9	198.3	—	225.0	237.5	239.6
sweat gland (apocrine) (eccrine), site unspecified	173.9	198.2	232.9	216.9	238.2	239.2
sympathetic nerve or nervous system NEC	171.9	198.89	—	215.9	238.1	239.2
symphysis pubis	170.6	198.5	—	213.6	238.0	239.2
synovial membrane — *see* Neoplasm, connective tissue						
tapetum, brain	191.8	198.3	—	225.0	237.5	239.6
tarsus (any bone)	170.8	198.5	—	213.8	238.0	239.2
temple (skin)	173.3	198.2	232.3	216.3	238.2	239.2
temporal						
bone	170.0	198.5	—	213.0	238.0	239.2
lobe or pole	191.2	198.3	—	225.0	237.5	239.6
region	195.0	198.89	234.8	229.8	238.8	239.89 ▲
skin	173.3	198.2	232.3	216.3	238.2	239.2
tendon (sheath) — *see* Neoplasm, connective tissue						
tentorium (cerebelli)	192.1	198.4	—	225.2	237.6	239.7
testis, testes (descended) (scrotal)	186.9	198.82	233.6	222.0	236.4	239.5
ectopic	186.0	198.82	233.6	222.0	236.4	239.5
retained	186.0	198.82	233.6	222.0	236.4	239.5
undescended	186.0	198.82	233.6	222.0	236.4	239.5
thalamus	191.0	198.3	—	225.0	237.5	239.6
thigh NEC*	195.5	198.89	234.8	229.8	238.8	239.89 ▲
thorax, thoracic (cavity) (organs NEC)	195.1	198.89	234.8	229.8	238.8	239.89 ▲
duct	171.4	198.89	—	215.4	238.1	239.2
wall NEC	195.1	198.89	234.8	229.8	238.8	239.89 ▲
throat	149.0	198.89	230.0	210.9	235.1	239.0
thumb NEC*	195.4	198.89	232.6	229.8	238.8	239.89 ▲
thymus (gland)	164.0	198.89	—	212.6	235.8	239.89 ▲
contiguous sites with heart and mediastinum	164.8	—	—	—	—	—
thyroglossal duct	193	198.89	234.8	226	237.4	239.7
thyroid (gland)	193	198.89	234.8	226	237.4	239.7
cartilage	161.3	197.3	231.0	212.1	235.6	239.1
tibia (any part)	170.7	198.5	—	213.7	238.0	239.2
toe NEC*	195.5	198.89	232.7	229.8	238.8	239.89 ▲
tongue	141.9	198.89	230.0	210.1	235.1	239.0
anterior (two-thirds) NEC	141.4	198.89	230.0	210.1	235.1	239.0
dorsal surface	141.1	198.89	230.0	210.1	235.1	239.0
ventral surface	141.3	198.89	230.0	210.1	235.1	239.0
base (dorsal surface)	141.0	198.89	230.0	210.1	235.1	239.0
border (lateral)	141.2	198.89	230.0	210.1	235.1	239.0
contiguous sites	141.8	—	—	—	—	—
dorsal surface NEC	141.1	198.89	230.0	210.1	235.1	239.0
fixed part NEC	141.0	198.89	230.0	210.1	235.1	239.0
foreamen cecum	141.1	198.89	230.0	210.1	235.1	239.0
frenulum linguae	141.3	198.89	230.0	210.1	235.1	239.0
junctional zone	141.5	198.89	230.0	210.1	235.1	239.0
margin (lateral)	141.2	198.89	230.0	210.1	235.1	239.0
midline NEC	141.1	198.89	230.0	210.1	235.1	239.0
mobile part NEC	141.4	198.89	230.0	210.1	235.1	239.0
posterior (third)	141.0	198.89	230.0	210.1	235.1	239.0
root	141.0	198.89	230.0	210.1	235.1	239.0
surface (dorsal)	141.1	198.89	230.0	210.1	235.1	239.0
base	141.0	198.89	230.0	210.1	235.1	239.0
ventral	141.3	198.89	230.0	210.1	235.1	239.0

Neoplasm, neoplastic— *continued*	Primary	Secondary	Ca in situ	Benign	Uncertain Behavior	Unspecified
tongue — *continued*						
tip	141.2	198.89	230.0	210.1	235.1	239.0
tonsil	141.6	198.89	230.0	210.1	235.1	239.0
tonsil	146.0	198.89	230.0	210.5	235.1	239.0
fauces, faucial	146.0	198.89	230.0	210.5	235.1	239.0
lingual	141.6	198.89	230.0	210.1	235.1	239.0
palatine	146.0	198.89	230.0	210.5	235.1	239.0
pharyngeal	147.1	198.89	230.0	210.7	235.1	239.0
pillar (anterior) (posterior)	146.2	198.89	230.0	210.6	235.1	239.0
tonsillar fossa	146.1	198.89	230.0	210.6	235.1	239.0
tooth socket NEC	143.9	198.89	230.0	210.4	235.1	239.0
trachea (cartilage) (mucosa)	162.0	197.3	231.1	212.2	235.7	239.1
contiguous sites with bronchus or lung	162.8	—	—	—	—	—
tracheobronchial	162.8	197.3	231.1	212.2	235.7	239.1
contiguous sites with lung	162.8	—	—	—	—	—
tragus	173.2	198.2	232.2	216.2	238.2	239.2
trunk NEC*	195.8	198.89	232.5	229.8	238.8	239.89 ▲
tubo-ovarian	183.8	198.82	233.39	221.8	236.3	239.5
tunica vaginalis	187.8	198.82	233.6	222.8	236.6	239.5
turbinate (bone)	170.0	198.5	—	213.0	238.0	239.2
nasal	160.0	197.3	231.8	212.0	235.9	239.1
tympanic cavity	160.1	197.3	231.8	212.0	235.9	239.1
ulna (any part)	170.4	198.5	—	213.4	238.0	239.2
umbilicus, umbilical	173.5	198.2	232.5	216.5	238.2	239.2
uncus, brain	191.2	198.3	—	225.0	237.5	239.6
unknown site or unspecified	199.1	199.1	234.9	229.9	238.9	239.9
urachus	188.7	198.1	233.7	223.3	236.7	239.4
ureter-bladder (junction)	188.6	198.1	233.7	223.3	236.7	239.4
ureter, ureteral	189.2	198.1	233.9	223.2	236.91	239.5
orifice (bladder)	188.6	198.1	233.7	223.3	236.7	239.4
urethra, urethral (gland)	189.3	198.1	233.9	223.81	236.99	239.5
orifice, internal	188.5	198.1	233.7	223.3	236.7	239.4
urethrovaginal (septum)	184.9	198.82	233.39	221.9	236.3	239.5
urinary organ or system NEC	189.9	198.1	233.9	223.9	236.99	239.5
bladder — *see* Neoplasm, bladder						
contiguous sites	189.8	—	—	—	—	—
specified sites NEC	189.8	198.1	233.9	223.89	236.99	239.5
utero-ovarian	183.8	198.82	233.39	221.8	236.3	239.5
ligament	183.3	198.82	—	221.0	236.3	239.5
uterosacral ligament	183.4	198.82	—	221.0	236.3	239.5
uterus, uteri, uterine	179	198.82	233.2	219.9	236.0	239.5
adnexa NEC	183.9	198.82	233.39	221.8	236.3	239.5
contiguous sites	183.8	—	—	—	—	—
body	182.0	198.82	233.2	219.1	236.0	239.5
contiguous sites	182.8	—	—	—	—	—
cervix	180.9	198.82	233.1	219.0	236.0	239.5
cornu	182.0	198.82	233.2	219.1	236.0	239.5
corpus	182.0	198.82	233.2	219.1	236.0	239.5
endocervix (canal) (gland)	180.0	198.82	233.1	219.0	236.0	239.5
endometrium	182.0	198.82	233.2	219.1	236.0	239.5
exocervix	180.1	198.82	233.1	219.0	236.0	239.5
external os	180.1	198.82	233.1	219.0	236.0	239.5
fundus	182.0	198.82	233.2	219.1	236.0	239.5
internal os	180.0	198.82	233.1	219.0	236.0	239.5
isthmus	182.1	198.82	233.2	219.1	236.0	239.5
ligament	183.4	198.82	—	221.0	236.3	239.5
broad	183.3	198.82	233.39	221.0	236.3	239.5

Index

Neoplasm, uterus, uteri, uterine — Neoplasm, Zuckerkandl's organ

	Malignant			Benign	Uncertain Behavior	Unspecified
	Primary	Secondary	Ca in situ			
Neoplasm, neoplastic —						
continued						
uterus, uteri, uterine —						
continued						
ligament — *continued*						
round	183.5	198.82	—	221.0	236.3	239.5
lower segment	182.1	198.82	233.2	219.1	236.0	239.5
myometrium	182.0	198.82	233.2	219.1	236.0	239.5
squamocolumnar						
junction	180.8	198.82	233.1	219.0	236.0	239.5
tube	183.2	198.82	233.39	221.0	236.3	239.5
utricle, prostatic	189.3	198.1	233.9	223.81	236.99	239.5
uveal tract	190.0	198.4	234.0	224.0	238.8	239.89 ▲
uvula	145.4	198.89	230.0	210.4	235.1	239.0
vagina, vaginal (fornix)						
(vault) (wall)	184.0	198.82	233.31	221.1	236.3	239.5
vaginovesical	184.9	198.82	233.39	221.9	236.3	239.5
septum	184.9	198.82	233.39	221.9	236.3	239.5
vallecula (epiglottis)	146.3	198.89	230.0	210.6	235.1	239.0
vascular — *see*						
Neoplasm,						
connective tissue						
vas deferens	187.6	198.82	233.6	222.8	236.6	239.5
Vater's ampulla	156.2	197.8	230.8	211.5	235.3	239.0
vein, venous — *see*						
Neoplasm,						
connective tissue						
vena cava (abdominal)						
(inferior)	171.5	198.89	—	215.5	238.1	239.2
superior	171.4	198.89	—	215.4	238.1	239.2
ventricle (cerebral) (floor)						
(fourth) (lateral)						
(third)	191.5	198.3	—	225.0	237.5	239.6
cardiac (left)						
(right)	164.1	198.89	—	212.7	238.8	239.89 ▲
ventricular band of						
larynx	161.1	197.3	231.0	212.1	235.6	239.1
ventriculus — see						
Neoplasm, stomach						
vermillion border — *see*						
Neoplasm, lip						
vermis, cerebellum	191.6	198.3	—	225.0	237.5	239.6
vertebra (column)	170.2	198.5	—	213.2	238.0	239.2
coccyx	170.6	198.5	—	213.6	238.0	239.2
sacrum	170.6	198.5	—	213.6	238.0	239.2
vesical — *see* Neoplasm,						
bladder						
vesicle, seminal	187.8	198.82	233.6	222.8	236.6	239.5
vesicocervical tissue	184.9	198.82	233.39	221.9	236.3	239.5
vesicorectal	195.3	198.89	234.8	229.8	238.8	239.89 ▲
vesicovaginal	184.9	198.82	233.39	221.9	236.3	239.5
septum	184.9	198.82	233.39	221.9	236.3	239.5
vessel (blood) — *see*						
Neoplasm,						
connective tissue						
vestibular gland,						
greater	184.1	198.82	233.32	221.2	236.3	239.5
vestibule						
mouth	145.1	198.89	230.0	210.4	235.1	239.0
nose	160.0	197.3	231.8	212.0	235.9	239.1
Virchow's gland	—	196.0	—	229.0	238.8	239.89 ▲
viscera NEC	195.8	198.89	234.8	229.8	238.8	239.89 ▲
vocal cords (true)	161.0	197.3	231.0	212.1	235.6	239.1
false	161.1	197.3	231.0	212.1	235.6	239.1
vomer	170.0	198.5	—	213.0	238.0	239.2
vulva	184.4	198.82	233.32	221.2	236.3	239.5
vulvovaginal gland	184.4	198.82	233.32	221.2	236.3	239.5
Waldeyer's ring	149.1	198.89	230.0	210.9	235.1	239.0
Wharton's duct	142.1	198.89	230.0	210.2	235.0	239.0
white matter (central)						
(cerebral)	191.0	198.3	—	225.0	237.5	239.6
windpipe	162.0	197.3	231.1	212.2	235.7	239.1
Wirsung's duct	157.3	197.8	230.9	211.6	235.5	239.0
wolffian (body) (duct)						
female	184.8	198.82	233.39	221.8	236.3	239.5
male	187.8	198.82	233.6	222.8	236.6	239.5

	Malignant			Benign	Uncertain Behavior	Unspecified
	Primary	Secondary	Ca in situ			
Neoplasm, neoplastic —						
continued						
womb — *see* Neoplasm,						
uterus						
wrist NEC*	195.4	198.89	232.6	229.8	238.8	239.89 ▲
xiphoid process	170.3	198.5	—	213.3	238.0	239.2
Zuckerkandl's						
organ	194.6	198.89	—	227.6	237.3	239.7

Neovascularization
- choroid 362.16
- ciliary body 364.42
- cornea 370.60
  - deep 370.63
  - localized 370.61
- iris 364.42
- retina 362.16
- subretinal 362.16

Nephralgia 788.0

Nephritis, nephritic (albuminuric) (azotemic) (congenital) (degenerative) (diffuse) (disseminated) (epithelial) (familial) (focal) (granulomatous) (hemorrhagic) (infantile) (nonsuppurative, excretory) (uremic) 583.9
- with
  - edema — see Nephrosis
  - lesion of
    - glomerulonephritis
      - hypocomplementemic persistent 583.2
        - with nephrotic syndrome 581.2
        - chronic 582.2
      - lobular 583.2
        - with nephrotic syndrome 581.2
        - chronic 582.2
      - membranoproliferative 583.2
        - with nephrotic syndrome 581.2
        - chronic 582.2
      - membranous 583.1
        - with nephrotic syndrome 581.1
        - chronic 582.1
      - mesangiocapillary 583.2
        - with nephrotic syndrome 581.2
        - chronic 582.2
      - mixed membranous and proliferative 583.2
        - with nephrotic syndrome 581.2
        - chronic 582.2
      - proliferative (diffuse) 583.0
        - with nephrotic syndrome 581.0
        - acute 580.0
        - chronic 582.0
      - rapidly progressive 583.4
        - acute 580.4
        - chronic 582.4
    - interstitial nephritis (diffuse) (focal) 583.89
      - with nephrotic syndrome 581.89
      - acute 580.89
      - chronic 582.89
    - necrotizing glomerulitis 583.4
      - acute 580.4
      - chronic 582.4
    - renal necrosis 583.9
      - cortical 583.6
      - medullary 583.7
    - specified pathology NEC 583.89
      - with nephrotic syndrome 581.89
      - acute 580.89
      - chronic 582.89
- necrosis, renal 583.9
  - cortical 583.6
  - medullary (papillary) 583.7
- nephrotic syndrome (see also Nephrosis) 581.9
- papillary necrosis 583.7
- specified pathology NEC 583.89
- acute 580.9
  - extracapillary with epithelial crescents 580.4
  - hypertensive (see also Hypertension, kidney) 403.90
  - necrotizing 580.4
  - poststreptococcal 580.0
  - proliferative (diffuse) 580.0
  - rapidly progressive 580.4
  - specified pathology NEC 580.89
- amyloid 277.39 [583.81]
  - chronic 277.39 [582.81]
- arteriolar (see also Hypertension, kidney) 403.90
- arteriosclerotic (see also Hypertension, kidney) 403.90
- ascending (see also Pyelitis) 590.80
- atrophic 582.9

Nephritis, nephritic — continued
- basement membrane NEC 583.89
  - with
    - pulmonary hemorrhage (Goodpasture's syndrome) 446.21 [583.81]
- calculous, calculus 592.0
- cardiac (see also Hypertension, kidney) 403.90
- cardiovascular (see also Hypertension, kidney) 403.90
- chronic 582.9
  - arteriosclerotic (see also Hypertension, kidney) 403.90
  - hypertensive (see also Hypertension, kidney) 403.90
- cirrhotic (see also Sclerosis, renal) 587
- complicating pregnancy, childbirth, or puerperium 646.2 ☑
  - with hypertension 642.1 ☑
    - affecting fetus or newborn 760.0
    - affecting fetus or newborn 760.1
- croupous 580.9
- desquamative — see Nephrosis
- due to
  - amyloidosis 277.39 [583.81]
    - chronic 277.39 [582.81]
  - arteriosclerosis (see also Hypertension, kidney) 403.90
  - diabetes mellitus 250.4 ☑ [583.81]
    - with nephrotic syndrome 250.4 ☑ [581.81]
      - due to secondary diabetes 249.4 ☑ [581.81]   ▲
    - due to secondary diabetes 249.4 ☑ [583.81]   ▲
  - diphtheria 032.89 [580.81]
  - gonococcal infection (acute) 098.19 [583.81]
    - chronic or duration of 2 months or over 098.39 [583.81]
  - gout 274.10
  - infectious hepatitis 070.9 [580.81]
  - mumps 072.79 [580.81]
  - specified kidney pathology NEC 583.89
    - acute 580.89
    - chronic 582.89
  - streptotrichosis 039.8 [583.81]
  - subacute bacterial endocarditis 421.0 [580.81]
  - systemic lupus erythematosus 710.0 [583.81]
    - chronic 710.0 [582.81]
  - typhoid fever 002.0 [580.81]
- endothelial 582.2
- end stage (chronic) (terminal) NEC 585.6
- epimembranous 581.1
- exudative 583.89
  - with nephrotic syndrome 581.89
  - acute 580.89
  - chronic 582.89
- gonococcal (acute) 098.19 [583.81]
  - chronic or duration of 2 months or over 098.39 [583.81]
- gouty 274.10
- hereditary (Alport's syndrome) 759.89
- hydremic — see Nephrosis
- hypertensive (see also Hypertension, kidney) 403.90
- hypocomplementemic persistent 583.2
  - with nephrotic syndrome 581.2
  - chronic 582.2
- immune complex NEC 583.89
- infective (see also Pyelitis) 590.80
- interstitial (diffuse) (focal) 583.89
  - with nephrotic syndrome 581.89
  - acute 580.89
  - chronic 582.89
- latent or quiescent — see Nephritis, chronic
- lead 984.9
  - specified type of lead — see Table of Drugs and Chemicals
- lobular 583.2
  - with nephrotic syndrome 581.2
  - chronic 582.2
- lupus 710.0 [583.81]
  - acute 710.0 [580.81]

Nephritis, nephritic — continued
- lupus — continued
  - chronic 710.0 [582.81]
- membranoproliferative 583.2
  - with nephrotic syndrome 581.2
  - chronic 582.2
- membranous 583.1
  - with nephrotic syndrome 581.1
  - chronic 582.1
- mesangiocapillary 583.2
  - with nephrotic syndrome 581.2
  - chronic 582.2
- minimal change 581.3
- mixed membranous and proliferative 583.2
  - with nephrotic syndrome 581.2
  - chronic 582.2
- necrotic, necrotizing 583.4
  - acute 580.4
  - chronic 582.4
- nephrotic — see Nephrosis
- old — see Nephritis, chronic
- parenchymatous 581.89
- polycystic 753.12
  - adult type (APKD) 753.13
  - autosomal dominant 753.13
  - autosomal recessive 753.14
  - childhood type (CPKD) 753.14
  - infantile type 753.14
- poststreptococcal 580.0
- pregnancy — see Nephritis, complicating pregnancy
- proliferative 583.0
  - with nephrotic syndrome 581.0
  - acute 580.0
  - chronic 582.0
- purulent (see also Pyelitis) 590.80
- rapidly progressive 583.4
  - acute 580.4
  - chronic 582.4
- salt-losing or salt-wasting (see also Disease, renal) 593.9
- saturnine 984.9
  - specified type of lead — see Table of Drugs and Chemicals
- septic (see also Pyelitis) 590.80
- specified pathology NEC 583.89
  - acute 580.89
  - chronic 582.89
- staphylococcal (see also Pyelitis) 590.80
- streptotrichosis 039.8 [583.81]
- subacute (see also Nephrosis) 581.9
- suppurative (see also Pyelitis) 590.80
- syphilitic (late) 095.4
  - congenital 090.5 [583.81]
  - early 091.69 [583.81]
- terminal (chronic) (end-stage) NEC 585.6
- toxic — see Nephritis, acute
- tubal, tubular — see Nephrosis, tubular
- tuberculous (see also Tuberculosis) 016.0 ☑ [583.81]
- type II (Ellis) — see Nephrosis
- vascular — see Hypertension, kidney
- war 580.9

Nephroblastoma (M8960/3) 189.0
- epithelial (M8961/3) 189.0
- mesenchymal (M8962/3) 189.0

Nephrocalcinosis 275.49

Nephrocystitis, pustular — see also Pyelitis 590.80

Nephrolithiasis (congenital) (pelvis) (recurrent) 592.0
- uric acid 274.11

Nephroma (M8960/3) 189.0
- mesoblastic (M8960/1) 236.9 ☑

Nephronephritis — see also Nephrosis 581.9

Nephronopthisis 753.16

Nephropathy — see also Nephritis 583.9
- with
  - exudative nephritis 583.89
  - interstitial nephritis (diffuse) (focal) 583.89
  - medullary necrosis 583.7
  - necrosis 583.9
    - cortical 583.6
    - medullary or papillary 583.7
  - papillary necrosis 583.7
  - specified lesion or cause NEC 583.89

Nephropathy — see also Nephritis — continued
- analgesic 583.89
  - with medullary necrosis, acute 584.7
- arteriolar (see also Hypertension, kidney) 403.90
- arteriosclerotic (see also Hypertension, kidney) 403.90
- complicating pregnancy 646.2 ☑
- diabetic 250.4 ☑ [583.81]
  - due to secondary diabetes 249.4 ☑ [583.81]
- gouty 274.10
  - specified type NEC 274.19
- hereditary amyloid 277.31
- hypercalcemic 588.89
- hypertensive (see also Hypertension, kidney) 403.90
- hypokalemic (vacuolar) 588.89
- IgA 583.9
- obstructive 593.89
  - congenital 753.20
- phenacetin 584.7
- phosphate-losing 588.0
- potassium depletion 588.89
- proliferative (see also Nephritis, proliferative) 583.0
- protein-losing 588.89
- salt-losing or salt-wasting (see also Disease, renal) 593.9
- sickle-cell (see also Disease, sickle-cell) 282.60 [583.81]
- toxic 584.5
- vasomotor 584.5
- water-losing 588.89

Nephroptosis — see also Disease, renal 593.0
- congenital (displaced) 753.3

Nephropyosis — see also Abscess, kidney 590.2

Nephrorrhagia 593.81

Nephrosclerosis (arteriolar) (arteriosclerotic) (chronic) (hyaline) — see also Hypertension, kidney 403.90
- gouty 274.10
- hyperplastic (arteriolar) (see also Hypertension, kidney) 403.90
- senile (see also Sclerosis, renal) 587

Nephrosis, nephrotic (Epstein's) (syndrome) 581.9
- with
  - lesion of
    - focal glomerulosclerosis 581.1
    - glomerulonephritis
      - endothelial 581.2
      - hypocomplementemic persistent 581.2
      - lobular 581.2
      - membranoproliferative 581.2
      - membranous 581.1
      - mesangiocapillary 581.2
      - minimal change 581.3
      - mixed membranous and proliferative 581.2
      - proliferative 581.0
    - segmental hyalinosis 581.1
    - specified pathology NEC 581.89
- acute — see Nephrosis, tubular
- anoxic — see Nephrosis, tubular
- arteriosclerotic (see also Hypertension, kidney) 403.90
- chemical — see Nephrosis, tubular
- cholemic 572.4
- complicating pregnancy, childbirth, or puerperium — see Nephritis, complicating pregnancy
- diabetic 250.4 ☑ [581.81]
  - due to secondary diabetes 249.4 ☑ [581.81]
- Finnish type (congenital) 759.89
- hemoglobinuric — see Nephrosis, tubular
- in
  - amyloidosis 277.39 [581.81]
  - diabetes mellitus 250.4 ☑ [581.81]
    - due to secondary diabetes 249.4 ☑ [581.81]
  - epidemic hemorrhagic fever 078.6
  - malaria 084.9 [581.81]

☑ Additional Digit Required — Refer to the Tabular List for Digit Selection
             Subterms under main terms may continue to next column or page

202 — Volume 2 • October 2009   ▶◀ Revised Text   ● New Line   ▲ Revised Code   **2010 ICD-9-CM**

Neuroma — *see also* Neoplasm, connective tissue, benign — *continued*
  amputation (traumatic) (*see also* Injury, nerve, by site)
    surgical complication (late) 997.61
  appendix 211.3
  auditory nerve 225.1
  digital 355.6
    toe 355.6
  interdigital (toe) 355.6
  intermetatarsal 355.6
  Morton's 355.6
  multiple 237.70
    type 1 237.71
    type 2 237.72
  nonneoplastic 355.9
    arm NEC 354.9
    leg NEC 355.8
    lower extremity NEC 355.8
    specified site NEC — *see* Mononeuritis, by site
    upper extremity NEC 354.9
  optic (nerve) 225.1
  plantar 355.6
  plexiform (M9550/0) — *see* Neoplasm, connective tissue, benign
  surgical (nonneoplastic) 355.9
    arm NEC 354.9
    leg NEC 355.8
    lower extremity NEC 355.8
    upper extremity NEC 354.9
  traumatic (*see also* Injury, nerve, by site)
    old — *see* Neuroma, nonneoplastic
Neuromyalgia 729.1
Neuromyasthenia (epidemic) 049.8
Neuromyelitis 341.8
  ascending 357.0
  optica 341.0
Neuromyopathy NEC 358.9
Neuromyositis 729.1
Neuronevus (M8725/0) — *see* Neoplasm, skin, benign
Neuronitis 357.0
  ascending (acute) 355.2
  vestibular 386.12
Neuroparalytic — *see* condition
Neuropathy, neuropathic — *see also* Disorder, nerve 355.9
  acute motor 357.82
  alcoholic 357.5
    with psychosis 291.1
  arm NEC 354.9
  ataxia and retinitis pigmentosa (NARP syndrome) 277.87
  autonomic (peripheral) — *see* Neuropathy, peripheral, autonomic
  axillary nerve 353.0
  brachial plexus 353.0
  cervical plexus 353.2
  chronic
    progressive segmentally demyelinating 357.89
    relapsing demyelinating 357.89
  congenital sensory 356.2
  Déjérine-Sottas 356.0
  diabetic 250.6 ☑ *[357.2]*
    autonomic (peripheral) 250.6 ☑ *[337.1]* ●
    due to secondary diabetes 249.6 ☑ *[357.2]*
      autonomic (peripheral) ●
        249.6 ☑ *[337.1]* ●
  entrapment 355.9
    iliohypogastric nerve 355.79
    ilioinguinal nerve 355.79
    lateral cutaneous nerve of thigh 355.1
    median nerve 354.0
    obturator nerve 355.79
    peroneal nerve 355.3
    posterior tibial nerve 355.5
    saphenous nerve 355.79
    ulnar nerve 354.2
  facial nerve 351.9
  hereditary 356.9
    peripheral 356.0
    sensory (radicular) 356.2
  hypertrophic
    Charcôt-Marie-Tooth 356.1

Neuropathy, neuropathic — *see also* Disorder, nerve — *continued*
  hypertrophic — *continued*
    Déjérine-Sottas 356.0
    interstitial 356.9
    Refsum 356.3
  intercostal nerve 354.8
  ischemic — *see* Disorder, nerve
  Jamaican (ginger) 357.7
  leg NEC 355.8
  lower extremity NEC 355.8
  lumbar plexus 353.1
  median nerve 354.1
  motor
    acute 357.82
  multiple (acute) (chronic) (*see also* Polyneuropathy) 356.9
  optic 377.39
    ischemic 377.41
    nutritional 377.33
    toxic 377.34
  peripheral (nerve) (*see also* Polyneuropathy) 356.9
    arm NEC 354.9
    autonomic 337.9
      amyloid 277.39 *[337.1]*
      idiopathic 337.00
      in
        amyloidosis 277.39 *[337.1]*
        diabetes (mellitus) 250.6 ☑ *[337.1]*
          due to secondary diabetes 249.6 ☑ *[337.1]*
        diseases classified elsewhere 337.1
        gout 274.89 *[337.1]*
        hyperthyroidism 242.9 ☑ *[337.1]*
      due to
        antitetanus serum 357.6
        arsenic 357.7
        drugs 357.6
        lead 357.7
        organophosphate compounds 357.7
        toxic agent NEC 357.7
      hereditary 356.0
      idiopathic 356.9
        progressive 356.4
        specified type NEC 356.8
      in diseases classified elsewhere — *see* Polyneuropathy, in
    leg NEC 355.8
    lower extremity NEC 355.8
    upper extremity NEC 354.9
  plantar nerves 355.6
  progressive
    hypertrophic interstitial 356.9 ●
    inflammatory 357.89 ●
  radicular NEC 729.2
    brachial 723.4
    cervical NEC 723.4
    hereditary sensory 356.2
    lumbar 724.4
    lumbosacral 724.4
    thoracic NEC 724.4
  sacral plexus 353.1
  sciatic 355.0
  spinal nerve NEC 355.9
    root (*see also* Radiculitis) 729.2
  toxic 357.7
  trigeminal sensory 350.8
  ulnar nerve 354.2
  upper extremity NEC 354.9
  uremic 585.9 *[357.4]*
  vitamin B$_{12}$ 266.2 *[357.4]*
    with anemia (pernicious) 281.0 *[357.4]*
      due to dietary deficiency 281.1 *[357.4]*
Neurophthisis — *see also* Disorder, nerve
  diabetic 250.6 ☑ *[357.2]*
    due to secondary diabetes 249.6 ☑ *[357.2]*
  peripheral 356.9
Neuropraxia — *see* Injury, nerve
Neuroretinitis 363.05
  syphilitic 094.85
Neurosarcoma (M9540/3) — *see* Neoplasm, connective tissue, malignant
Neurosclerosis — *see* Disorder, nerve
Neurosis, neurotic 300.9
  accident 300.16

Neurosis, neurotic — *continued*
  anancastic, anankastic 300.3
  anxiety (state) 300.00
    generalized 300.02
    panic type 300.01
  asthenic 300.5
  bladder 306.53
  cardiac (reflex) 306.2
  cardiovascular 306.2
  climacteric, unspecified type 627.2
  colon 306.4
  compensation 300.16
  compulsive, compulsion 300.3
  conversion 300.11
  craft 300.89
  cutaneous 306.3
  depersonalization 300.6
  depressive (reaction) (type) 300.4
  endocrine 306.6
  environmental 300.89
  fatigue 300.5
  functional (*see also* Disorder, psychosomatic) 306.9
  gastric 306.4
  gastrointestinal 306.4
  genitourinary 306.50
  heart 306.2
  hypochondriacal 300.7
  hysterical 300.10
    conversion type 300.11
    dissociative type 300.15
  impulsive 300.3
  incoordination 306.0
    larynx 306.1
    vocal cord 306.1
  intestine 306.4
  larynx 306.1
    hysterical 300.11
    sensory 306.1
  menopause, unspecified type 627.2
  mixed NEC 300.89
  musculoskeletal 306.0
  obsessional 300.3
    phobia 300.3
  obsessive-compulsive 300.3
  occupational 300.89
  ocular 306.7
  oral 307.0
  organ (*see also* Disorder, psychosomatic) 306.9
  pharynx 306.1
  phobic 300.20
  posttraumatic (acute) (situational) 309.81
    chronic 309.81
  psychasthenic (type) 300.89
  railroad 300.16
  rectum 306.4
  respiratory 306.1
  rumination 306.4
  senile 300.89
  sexual 302.70
  situational 300.89
  specified type NEC 300.89
  state 300.9
    with depersonalization episode 300.6
  stomach 306.4
  vasomotor 306.2
  visceral 306.4
  war 300.16
Neurospongioblastosis diffusa 759.5
Neurosyphilis (arrested) (early) (inactive) (late) (latent) (recurrent) 094.9
  with ataxia (cerebellar) (locomotor) (spastic) (spinal) 094.0
  acute meningitis 094.2
  aneurysm 094.89
  arachnoid (adhesive) 094.2
  arteritis (any artery) 094.89
  asymptomatic 094.3
  congenital 090.40
  dura (mater) 094.89
  general paresis 094.1
  gumma 094.9
  hemorrhagic 094.9
  juvenile (asymptomatic) (meningeal) 090.40
  leptomeninges (aseptic) 094.2
  meningeal 094.2

Neurosyphilis — *continued*
  meninges (adhesive) 094.2
  meningovascular (diffuse) 094.2
  optic atrophy 094.84
  parenchymatous (degenerative) 094.1
  paresis (*see also* Paresis, general) 094.1
  paretic (*see also* Paresis, general) 094.1
  relapse 094.9
  remission in (sustained) 094.9
  serological 094.3
  specified nature or site NEC 094.89
  tabes (dorsalis) 094.0
    juvenile 090.40
  tabetic 094.0
    juvenile 090.40
  taboparesis 094.1
    juvenile 090.40
  thrombosis 094.89
  vascular 094.89
Neurotic — *see also* Neurosis 300.9
  excoriation 698.4
  psychogenic 306.3
Neurotmesis — *see* Injury, nerve, by site
Neurotoxemia — *see* Toxemia
Neutro-occlusion 524.21
Neutropenia, neutropenic (idiopathic) (pernicious) (primary) 288.00
  chronic 288.09
    hypoplastic 288.09
  congenital (nontransient) 288.01
  cyclic 288.02
  drug induced 288.03
  due to infection 288.04
  fever 288.00
  genetic 288.01
  immune 288.09
  infantile 288.01
  malignant 288.09
  neonatal, transitory (isoimmune) (maternal transfer) 776.7
  periodic 288.02
  splenic 289.53
  splenomegaly 289.53
  toxic 288.09
Neutrophilia, hereditary giant 288.2
Nevocarcinoma (M8720/3) — *see* Melanoma
Nevus (M8720/0) — *see also* Neoplasm, skin, benign

> *Note* — Except where otherwise indicated, varieties of nevus in the list below that are followed by a morphology code number (M-----/0) should be coded by site as for "Neoplasm, skin, benign."

  acanthotic 702.8
  achromic (M8730/0)
  amelanotic (M8730/0)
  anemic, anemicus 709.09
  angiomatous (M9120/0) (*see also* Hemangioma) 228.00
  araneus 448.1
  avasculosus 709.09
  balloon cell (M8722/0)
  bathing trunk (M8761/1) 238.2
  blue (M8780/0)
    cellular (M8790/0)
    giant (M8790/0)
    Jadassohn's (M8780/0)
    malignant (M8780/3) — *see* Melanoma
  capillary (M9131/0) (*see also* Hemangioma) 228.00
  cavernous (M9121/0) (*see also* Hemangioma) 228.00
  cellular (M8720/0)
    blue (M8790/0)
  comedonicus 757.33
  compound (M8760/0)
  conjunctiva (M8720/0) 224.3
  dermal (M8750/0)
    and epidermal (M8760/0)
  epithelioid cell (and spindle cell) (M8770/0)
  flammeus 757.32
    osteohypertrophic 759.89
  hairy (M8720/0)
  halo (M8723/0)
  hemangiomatous (M9120/0) (*see also* Hemangioma) 228.00

☑ Additional Digit Required — Refer to the Tabular List for Digit Selection   ⬢ Subterms under main terms may continue to next column or page

Nevus — see also Neoplasm, skin, benign — continued
 intradermal (M8750/0)
 intraepidermal (M8740/0)
 involuting (M8724/0)
 Jadassohn's (blue) (M8780/0)
 junction, junctional (M8740/0)
  malignant melanoma in (M8740/3) — see Melanoma
 juvenile (M8770/0)
 lymphatic (M9170/0) 228.1
 magnocellular (M8726/0)
  specified site — see Neoplasm, by site, benign
  unspecified site 224.0
 malignant (M8720/3) — see Melanoma
 meaning hemangioma (M9120/0) (see also Hemangioma) 228.00
 melanotic (pigmented) (M8720/0)
 multiplex 759.5
 nonneoplastic 448.1
 nonpigmented (M8730/0)
 nonvascular (M8720/0)
 oral mucosa, white sponge 750.26
 osteohypertrophic, flammeus 759.89
 papillaris (M8720/0)
 papillomatosus (M8720/0)
 pigmented (M8720/0)
  giant (M8761/1) (see also Neoplasm, skin, uncertain behavior)
   malignant melanoma in (M8761/3) — see Melanoma
  systematicus 757.33
 pilosus (M8720/0)
 port wine 757.32
 sanguineous 757.32
 sebaceous (senile) 702.8
 senile 448.1
 spider 448.1
 spindle cell (and epithelioid cell) (M8770/0)
 stellar 448.1
 strawberry 757.32
 syringocystadenomatous papilliferous (M8406/0)
 unius lateris 757.33
 Unna's 757.32
 vascular 757.32
 verrucous 757.33
 white sponge (oral mucosa) 750.26
Newborn (infant) (liveborn)
 abstinence syndrome 779.5 ●
 affected by
  amniocentesis 760.61
  maternal abuse of drugs (gestational) (via placenta) (via breast milk) (see also Noxious, substances transmitted through placenta or breast milk (affecting fetus or newborn)) 760.70
   methamphetamine(s) 760.72
  procedure
   amniocentesis 760.61
   in utero NEC 760.62
   surgical on mother
    during pregnancy NEC 760.63
    previous not associated with pregnancy 760.64
 apnea 770.81
  obstructive 770.82
  specified NEC 770.82
 breast buds 779.89
 cardiomyopathy 425.4
  congenital 425.3
 convulsion 779.0
 electrolyte imbalance NEC (transitory) 775.5
 fever (environmentally-induced) 778.4
 gestation
  24 completed weeks 765.22
  25-26 completed weeks 765.23
  27-28 completed weeks 765.24
  29-30 completed weeks 765.25
  31-32 completed weeks 765.26
  33-34 completed weeks 765.27
  35-36 completed weeks 765.28
  37 or more completed weeks 765.29
  less than 24 completed weeks 765.21
  unspecified completed weeks 765.20

Newborn — continued
 infection 771.89
  candida 771.7
  mastitis 771.5
  specified NEC 771.89
  urinary tract 771.82
 mastitis 771.5
 multiple NEC
  born in hospital (without mention of cesarean delivery or section) V37.00
   with cesarean delivery or section V37.01
  born outside hospital
   hospitalized V37.1
   not hospitalized V37.2
  mates all liveborn
   born in hospital (without mention of cesarean delivery or section) V34.00
    with cesarean delivery or section V34.01
   born outside hospital
    hospitalized V34.1
    not hospitalized V34.2
  mates all stillborn
   born in hospital (without mention of cesarean delivery or section) V35.00
    with cesarean delivery or section V35.01
   born outside hospital
    hospitalized V35.1
    not hospitalized V35.2
  mates liveborn and stillborn
   born in hospital (without mention of cesarean delivery or section) V36.00
    with cesarean delivery or section V36.01
   born outside hospital
    hospitalized V36.1
    not hospitalized V36.2
 omphalitis 771.4
 seizure 779.0
 sepsis 771.81
 single
  born in hospital (without mention of cesarean delivery or section) V30.00
   with cesarean delivery or section V30.01
  born outside hospital
   hospitalized V30.1
   not hospitalized V30.2
 specified condition NEC 779.89
 twin NEC
  born in hospital (without mention of cesarean delivery or section) V33.00
   with cesarean delivery or section V33.01
  born outside hospital
   hospitalized V33.1
   not hospitalized V33.2
  mate liveborn
   born in hospital V31.0 ☑
   born outside hospital
    hospitalized V31.1
    not hospitalized V31.2
  mate stillborn
   born in hospital V32.0 ☑
   born outside hospital
    hospitalized V32.1
    not hospitalized V32.2
 unspecified as to single or multiple birth
  born in hospital (without mention of cesarean delivery or section) V39.00
   with cesarean delivery or section V39.01
  born outside hospital
   hospitalized V39.1
   not hospitalized V39.2
 weight check V20.32 ●
Newcastle's conjunctivitis or disease 077.8
Nezelof's syndrome (pure alymphocytosis) 279.13
Niacin (amide) **deficiency** 265.2

Nicolas-Durand-Favre disease (climatic bubo) 099.1
Nicolas-Favre disease (climatic bubo) 099.1
Nicotinic acid (amide) **deficiency** 265.2
Niemann-Pick disease (lipid histiocytosis) (splenomegaly) 272.7
Night
 blindness (see also Blindness, night) 368.60
  congenital 368.61
  vitamin A deficiency 264.5
 cramps 729.82
 sweats 780.8
 terrors, child 307.46
Nightmare 307.47
 REM-sleep type 307.47
Nipple — see condition
Nisbet's chancre 099.0
Nishimoto (-Takeuchi) disease 437.5
Nitritoid crisis or reaction — see Crisis, nitritoid
Nitrogen retention, extrarenal 788.99
Nitrosohemoglobinemia 289.89
Njovera 104.0
No
 diagnosis 799.9
 disease (found) V71.9
 room at the inn V65.0
Nocardiasis — see Nocardiosis
Nocardiosis 039.9
 with pneumonia 039.1
 lung 039.1
 specified type NEC 039.8
Nocturia 788.43
 psychogenic 306.53
Nocturnal — see also condition
 dyspnea (paroxysmal) 786.09
 emissions 608.89
 enuresis 788.36
  psychogenic 307.6
 frequency (micturition) 788.43
  psychogenic 306.53
Nodal rhythm disorder 427.89
Nodding of head 781.0
Node(s) — see also Nodule(s)
 Heberden's 715.04
 larynx 478.79
 lymph — see condition
 milkers' 051.1
 Osler's 421.0
 rheumatic 729.89
 Schmorl's 722.30
  lumbar, lumbosacral 722.32
  specified region NEC 722.39
  thoracic, thoracolumbar 722.31
 singers' 478.5
 skin NEC 782.2
 tuberculous — see Tuberculosis, lymph gland
 vocal cords 478.5
Nodosities, Haygarth's 715.04
Nodule(s), nodular
 actinomycotic (see also Actinomycosis) 039.9
 arthritic — see Arthritis, nodosa
 breast 793.89
 cutaneous 782.2
 Haygarth's 715.04
 inflammatory — see Inflammation
 juxta-articular 102.7
  syphilitic 095.7
  yaws 102.7
 larynx 478.79
 lung, solitary 518.89
  emphysematous 492.8
 milkers' 051.1
 prostate 600.10
  with
   urinary
    obstruction 600.11
    retention 600.11
 retrocardiac 785.9
 rheumatic 729.89
 rheumatoid — see Arthritis, rheumatoid
 scrotum (inflammatory) 608.4
 singers' 478.5
 skin NEC 782.2
 solitary, lung 518.89
  emphysematous 492.8
 subcutaneous 782.2

Nodule(s), nodular — continued
 thyroid (gland) (nontoxic) (uninodular) 241.0
  with
   hyperthyroidism 242.1 ☑
   thyrotoxicosis 242.1 ☑
  toxic or with hyperthyroidism 242.1 ☑
  vocal cords 478.5
Noma (gangrenous) (hospital) (infective) 528.1
 auricle (see also Gangrene) 785.4
 mouth 528.1
 pudendi (see also Vulvitis) 616.10
 vulvae (see also Vulvitis) 616.10
Nomadism V60.0
Non-adherence
 artificial skin graft 996.55
 decellularized allodermis graft 996.55
Non-autoimmune hemolytic anemia NEC 283.10
Nonclosure — see also Imperfect, closure
 ductus
  arteriosus 747.0
  Botalli 747.0
 Eustachian valve 746.89
 foramen
  Botalli 745.5
  ovale 745.5
Noncompliance with medical treatment V15.81
 renal dialysis V45.12
Nondescent (congenital) — see also Malposition, congenital
 cecum 751.4
 colon 751.4
 testis 752.51
Nondevelopment
 brain 742.1
  specified part 742.2
 heart 746.89
 organ or site, congenital NEC — see Hypoplasia
Nonengagement
 head NEC 652.5 ☑
  in labor 660.1 ☑
   affecting fetus or newborn 763.1
Nonexanthematous tick fever 066.1
Nonexpansion, lung (newborn) NEC 770.4
Nonfunctioning
 cystic duct (see also Disease, gallbladder) 575.8
 gallbladder (see also Disease, gallbladder) 575.8
 kidney (see also Disease, renal) 593.9
 labyrinth 386.58
Nonhealing
 stump (surgical) 997.69
 wound, surgical 998.83
Nonimplantation of ovum, causing infertility 628.3
Noninsufflation, fallopian tube 628.2
Nonne-Milroy-Meige syndrome (chronic hereditary edema) 757.0
Nonovulation 628.0
Nonpatent fallopian tube 628.2
Nonpneumatization, lung NEC 770.4
Nonreflex bladder 596.54
 with cauda equina 344.61
Nonretention of food — see Vomiting
Nonrotation — see Malrotation
Nonsecretion, urine — see also Anuria 788.5
 newborn 753.3
Nonunion
 fracture 733.82
 organ or site, congenital NEC — see Imperfect, closure
 symphysis pubis, congenital 755.69
 top sacrum, congenital 756.19
Nonviability 765.0 ☑
Nonvisualization, gallbladder 793.3
Nonvitalized tooth 522.9
Non-working side interference 524.56
Normal
 delivery — see category 650
 menses V65.5
 state (feared complaint unfounded) V65.5
Normoblastosis 289.89
Normocytic anemia (infectional) 285.9
 due to blood loss (chronic) 280.0

Normocytic anemia — *continued*
  due to blood loss — *continued*
    acute 285.1
Norrie's disease (congenital) (progressive ocu-
  loacousticocerebral degeneration) 743.8
North American blastomycosis 116.0
Norwegian itch 133.0
Nosebleed 784.7
Nose, nasal — *see* condition
Nosomania 298.9
Nosophobia 300.29
Nostalgia 309.89
Notched lip, congenital — *see also* Cleft, lip
  749.10
Notching nose, congenital (tip) 748.1
Notch of iris 743.46
Nothnagel's
  syndrome 378.52
  vasomotor acroparesthesia 443.89
Novy's relapsing fever (American) 087.1
Noxious
  foodstuffs, poisoning by
    fish 988.0
    fungi 988.1
    mushrooms 988.1
    plants (food) 988.2
    shellfish 988.0
    specified type NEC 988.8
    toadstool 988.1
  substances transmitted through placenta or
    breast milk (affecting fetus or newborn)
    760.70

Noxious — *continued*
  substances transmitted through placenta or
    breast milk — *continued*
    acetretin 760.78
    alcohol 760.71
    aminopterin 760.78
    antiandrogens 760.79
    anticonvulsant 760.77
    antifungal 760.74
    anti-infective agents 760.74
    antimetabolic 760.78
    atorvastatin 760.78
    carbamazepine 760.77
    cocaine 760.75
    "crack" 760.75
    diethylstilbestrol (DES) 760.76
    divalproex sodium 760.77
    endocrine disrupting chemicals 760.79
    estrogens 760.79
    etretinate 760.78
    fluconazole 760.74
    fluvastatin 760.78
    hallucinogenic agents NEC 760.73
    hormones 760.79
    lithium 760.79
    lovastatin 760.78
    medicinal agents NEC 760.79
    methotrexate 760.78
    misoprostil 760.79
    narcotics 760.72
    obstetric anesthetic or analgesic 763.5
    phenobarbital 760.77

Noxious — *continued*
  substances transmitted through placenta or
    breast milk — *continued*
    phenytoin 760.77
    pravastatin 760.78
    progestins 760.79
    retinoic acid 760.78
    simvastatin 760.78
    solvents 760.79
    specified agent NEC 760.79
    statins 760.78
    suspected, affecting management of
      pregnancy 655.5 ☑
    tetracycline 760.74
    thalidomide 760.79
    trimethadione 760.77
    valproate 760.77
    valproic acid 760.77
    vitamin A 760.78
NPDH (new persistent daily headache) 339.42
Nuchal hitch (arm) 652.8 ☑
Nucleus pulposus — *see* condition
Numbness 782.0
Nuns' knee 727.2
Nursemaid's
  elbow 832.2   ▲
  shoulder 831.0 ☑

Nutmeg liver 573.8
Nutrition, deficient or insufficient (particular
  kind of food) 269.9
  due to
    insufficient food 994.2
    lack of
      care (child) (infant) 995.52
        adult 995.84
      food 994.2
Nyctalopia — *see also* Blindness, night 368.60
  vitamin A deficiency 264.5
Nycturia 788.43
  psychogenic 306.53
Nymphomania 302.89
Nystagmus 379.50
  associated with vestibular system disorders
    379.54
  benign paroxysmal positional 386.11
  central positional 386.2
  congenital 379.51
  deprivation 379.53
  dissociated 379.55
  latent 379.52
  miners' 300.89
  positional
    benign paroxysmal 386.11
    central 386.2
  specified NEC 379.56
  vestibular 379.54
  visual deprivation 379.53

☑ Additional Digit Required — Refer to the Tabular List for Digit Selection   ▽ Subterms under main terms may continue to next column or page

2010 ICD-9-CM   ►◄ Revised Text   ● New Line   ▲ Revised Code   October 2009 · Volume 2 — 205

O

Oasthouse urine disease 270.2
Obermeyer's relapsing fever (European) 087.0
Obesity (constitutional) (exogenous) (familial) (nutritional) (simple) 278.00
  adrenal 255.8
  complicating pregnancy, childbirth, or puerperium 649.1 ☑
  due to hyperalimentation 278.00
  endocrine NEC 259.9
  endogenous 259.9
  Fröhlich's (adiposogenital dystrophy) 253.8
  glandular NEC 259.9
  hypothyroid (see also Hypothyroidism) 244.9
  morbid 278.01
  of pregnancy 649.1 ☑
  pituitary 253.8
  severe 278.01
  thyroid (see also Hypothyroidism) 244.9
Oblique — see also condition
  lie before labor, affecting fetus or newborn 761.7
Obliquity, pelvis 738.6
Obliteration
  abdominal aorta 446.7
  appendix (lumen) 543.9
  artery 447.1
  ascending aorta 446.7
  bile ducts 576.8
    with calculus, choledocholithiasis, or stones — see Choledocholithiasis
    congenital 751.61
      jaundice from 751.61 [774.5]
  common duct 576.8
    with calculus, choledocholithiasis, or stones — see Choledocholithiasis
    congenital 751.61
  cystic duct 575.8
    with calculus, choledocholithiasis, or stones — see Choledocholithiasis
  disease, arteriolar 447.1
  endometrium 621.8
  eye, anterior chamber 360.34
  fallopian tube 628.2
  lymphatic vessel 457.1
    postmastectomy 457.0
  organ or site, congenital NEC — see Atresia
  placental blood vessels — see Placenta, abnormal
  supra-aortic branches 446.7
  ureter 593.89
  urethra 599.84
  vein 459.9
  vestibule (oral) 525.8
Observation (for) V71.9
  without need for further medical care V71.9
  accident NEC V71.4
    at work V71.3
  criminal assault V71.6
  deleterious agent ingestion V71.89
  disease V71.9
    cardiovascular V71.7
    heart V71.7
    mental V71.09
    specified condition NEC V71.89
  foreign body ingestion V71.89
  growth and development variations V21.8
  injuries (accidental) V71.4
    inflicted NEC V71.6
      during alleged rape or seduction V71.5
  malignant neoplasm, suspected V71.1
  postpartum
    immediately after delivery V24.0
    routine follow-up V24.2
  pregnancy
    high-risk V23.9
      specified problem NEC V23.89
    normal (without complication) V22.1
      with nonobstetric complication V22.2
      first V22.0
  rape or seduction, alleged V71.5
    injury during V71.5
  suicide attempt, alleged V71.89
  suspected (undiagnosed) (unproven)
    abuse V71.81
    cardiovascular disease V71.7

Observation — continued
  suspected — continued
    child or wife battering victim V71.6
    concussion (cerebral) V71.6
    condition NEC V71.89
      infant — see Observation, suspected, condition, newborn
    maternal and fetal
      amniotic cavity and membrane problem V89.01
      cervical shortening V89.05
      fetal anomaly V89.03
      fetal growth problem V89.04
      oligohydramnios V89.01
      other specified problem NEC V89.09
      placental problem V89.02
      polyhydramnios V89.01
    newborn V29.9
      cardiovascular disease V29.8
      congenital anomaly V29.8
      genetic V29.3
      infectious V29.8
      ingestion foreign object V29.8
      injury V29.8
      metabolic V29.3
      neoplasm V29.8
      neurological V29.1
      poison, poisoning V29.8
      respiratory V29.2
      specified NEC V29.8
    exposure
      anthrax V71.82
      biologic agent NEC V71.83
      SARS V71.83
    infectious disease not requiring isolation V71.89
    malignant neoplasm V71.1
    mental disorder V71.09
    neglect V71.81
    neoplasm
      benign V71.89
      malignant V71.1
    specified condition NEC V71.89
    tuberculosis V71.2
  tuberculosis, suspected V71.2
Obsession, obsessional 300.3
  ideas and mental images 300.3
  impulses 300.3
  neurosis 300.3
  phobia 300.3
  psychasthenia 300.3
  ruminations 300.3
  state 300.3
  syndrome 300.3
Obsessive-compulsive 300.3
  neurosis 300.3
  personality 301.4
  reaction 300.3
Obstetrical trauma NEC (complicating delivery) 665.9 ☑
  with
    abortion — see Abortion, by type, with damage to pelvic organs
    ectopic pregnancy (see also categories 633.0–633.9) 639.2
    molar pregnancy (see also categories 630–632) 639.2
  affecting fetus or newborn 763.89
  following
    abortion 639.2
    ectopic or molar pregnancy 639.2
Obstipation — see also Constipation 564.00
  psychogenic 306.4
Obstruction, obstructed, obstructive
  airway NEC 519.8
    with
      allergic alveolitis NEC 495.9
      asthma NEC (see also Asthma) 493.9 ☑
      bronchiectasis 494.0
        with acute exacerbation 494.1
      bronchitis (chronic) (see also Bronchitis, with, obstruction) 491.20
      emphysema NEC 492.8
    chronic 496

Obstruction, obstructed, obstructive — continued
  airway — continued
    chronic — continued
      with
        allergic alveolitis NEC 495.5
        asthma NEC (see also Asthma) 493.2 ☑
        bronchiectasis 494.0
          with acute exacerbation 494.1
        bronchitis (chronic) (see also Bronchitis, with, obstruction) 491.20
        emphysema NEC 492.8
      due to
        bronchospasm 519.11
        foreign body 934.9
        inhalation of fumes or vapors 506.9
        laryngospasm 478.75
    alimentary canal (see also Obstruction, intestine) 560.9
    ampulla of Vater 576.2
      with calculus, cholelithiasis, or stones — see Choledocholithiasis
    aortic (heart) (valve) (see also Stenosis, aortic) 424.1
      rheumatic (see also Stenosis, aortic, rheumatic) 395.0
    aortoiliac 444.0
    aqueduct of Sylvius 331.4
      congenital 742.3
        with spina bifida (see also Spina bifida) 741.0 ☑
    Arnold-Chiari (see also Spina bifida) 741.0 ☑
    artery (see also Embolism, artery) 444.9
      basilar (complete) (partial) (see also Occlusion, artery, basilar) 433.0 ☑
      carotid (complete) (partial) (see also Occlusion, artery, carotid) 433.1 ☑
      precerebral — see Occlusion, artery, precerebral NEC
      retinal (central) (see also Occlusion, retina) 362.30
      vertebral (complete) (partial) (see also Occlusion, artery, vertebral) 433.2 ☑
    asthma (chronic) (with obstructive pulmonary disease) 493.2 ☑
    band (intestinal) 560.81
    bile duct or passage (see also Obstruction, biliary) 576.2
      congenital 751.61
        jaundice from 751.61 [774.5]
    biliary (duct) (tract) 576.2
      with calculus 574.51
        with cholecystitis (chronic) 574.41
          acute 574.31
      congenital 751.61
        jaundice from 751.61 [774.5]
      gallbladder 575.2
        with calculus 574.21
          with cholecystitis (chronic) 574.11
            acute 574.01
    bladder neck (acquired) 596.0
      congenital 753.6
    bowel (see also Obstruction, intestine) 560.9
    bronchus 519.19
    canal, ear (see also Stricture, ear canal, acquired) 380.50
    cardia 537.89
    caval veins (inferior) (superior) 459.2
    cecum (see also Obstruction, intestine) 560.9
    circulatory 459.9
    colon (see also Obstruction, intestine) 560.9
      sympathicotonic 560.89
    common duct (see also Obstruction, biliary) 576.2
      congenital 751.61
    coronary (artery) (heart) (see also Arteriosclerosis, coronary)
      acute (see also Infarct, myocardium) 410.9 ☑
        without myocardial infarction 411.81
    cystic duct (see also Obstruction, gallbladder) 575.2
      congenital 751.61

Obstruction, obstructed, obstructive — continued
  device, implant, or graft — see Complications, due to (presence of) any device, implant, or graft classified to 996.0–996.5 NEC
  due to foreign body accidentally left in operation wound 998.4
  duodenum 537.3
    congenital 751.1
    due to
      compression NEC 537.3
      cyst 537.3
      intrinsic lesion or disease NEC 537.3
      scarring 537.3
      torsion 537.3
      ulcer 532.91
      volvulus 537.3
  ejaculatory duct 608.89
  endocardium 424.90
    arteriosclerotic 424.99
    specified cause, except rheumatic 424.99
  esophagus 530.3
  eustachian tube (complete) (partial) 381.60
    cartilaginous
      extrinsic 381.63
      intrinsic 381.62
    due to
      cholesteatoma 381.61
      osseous lesion NEC 381.61
      polyp 381.61
    osseous 381.61
  fallopian tube (bilateral) 628.2
  fecal 560.39
    with hernia (see also Hernia, by site, with obstruction)
      gangrenous — see Hernia, by site, with gangrene
  foramen of Monro (congenital) 742.3
    with spina bifida (see also Spina bifida) 741.0 ☑
  foreign body — see Foreign body
  gallbladder 575.2
    with calculus, cholelithiasis, or stones 574.21
      with cholecystitis (chronic) 574.11
        acute 574.01
    congenital 751.69
      jaundice from 751.69 [774.5]
  gastric outlet 537.0
  gastrointestinal (see also Obstruction, intestine) 560.9
  glottis 478.79
  hepatic 573.8
    duct (see also Obstruction, biliary) 576.2
      congenital 751.61
  icterus (see also Obstruction, biliary) 576.8
    congenital 751.61
  ileocecal coil (see also Obstruction, intestine) 560.9
  ileum (see also Obstruction, intestine) 560.9
  iliofemoral (artery) 444.81
  internal anastomosis — see Complications, mechanical, graft
  intestine (mechanical) (neurogenic) (paroxysmal) (postinfectional) (reflex) 560.9
    with
      adhesions (intestinal) (peritoneal) 560.81
      hernia (see also Hernia, by site, with obstruction)
        gangrenous — see Hernia, by site, with gangrene
    adynamic (see also Ileus) 560.1
    by gallstone 560.31
    congenital or infantile (small) 751.1
      large 751.2
    due to
      Ascaris lumbricoides 127.0
      mural thickening 560.89
      procedure 997.4
        involving urinary tract 997.5
    impaction 560.39
    infantile — see Obstruction, intestine, congenital

☑ Additional Digit Required — Refer to the Tabular List for Digit Selection

Subterms under main terms may continue to next column or page

2010 ICD-9-CM

◄► Revised Text
● New Line
▲ Revised Code

Volume 2 — 207

Obstruction, obstructed, obstructive — *continued*

intestine — *continued*
  newborn
    due to
      fecaliths 777.1
      inspissated milk 777.2
      meconium (plug) 777.1
        in mucoviscidosis 277.01
      transitory 777.4
    specified cause NEC 560.89
    transitory, newborn 777.4
    volvulus 560.2
  intracardiac ball valve prosthesis 996.02
  jaundice (*see also* Obstruction, biliary) 576.8
    congenital 751.61
  jejunum (*see also* Obstruction, intestine) 560.9
  kidney 593.89
  labor 660.9 ☑
    affecting fetus or newborn 763.1
    by
      bony pelvis (conditions classifiable to 653.0–653.9) 660.1 ☑
      deep transverse arrest 660.3 ☑
      impacted shoulder 660.4 ☑
      locked twins 660.5 ☑
      malposition (fetus) (conditions classifiable to 652.0–652.9) 660.0 ☑
        head during labor 660.3 ☑
      persistent occipitoposterior position 660.3 ☑
      soft tissue, pelvic (conditions classifiable to 654.0–654.9) 660.2 ☑
lacrimal
  canaliculi 375.53
    congenital 743.65
    punctum 375.52
    sac 375.54
  lacrimonasal duct 375.56
    congenital 743.65
    neonatal 375.55
lacteal, with steatorrhea 579.2
laryngitis (*see also* Laryngitis) 464.01
larynx 478.79
  congenital 748.3
liver 573.8
  cirrhotic (*see also* Cirrhosis, liver) 571.5
lung 518.89
  with
    asthma — *see* Asthma
    bronchitis (chronic) 491.20
    emphysema NEC 492.8
  airway, chronic 496
  chronic NEC 496
    with
      asthma (chronic) (obstructive) 493.2 ☑
  disease, chronic 496
    with
      asthma (chronic) (obstructive) 493.2 ☑
  emphysematous 492.8
lymphatic 457.1
meconium
  fetus or newborn 777.1
    in mucoviscidosis 277.01
  newborn due to fecaliths 777.1
mediastinum 519.3
mitral (rheumatic) — *see* Stenosis, mitral
nasal 478.19
  duct 375.56
    neonatal 375.55
  sinus — *see* Sinusitis
nasolacrimal duct 375.56
  congenital 743.65
  neonatal 375.55
nasopharynx 478.29
nose 478.19
organ or site, congenital NEC — *see* Atresia
pancreatic duct 577.8
parotid gland 527.8
pelviureteral junction (*see also* Obstruction, ureter) 593.4
pharynx 478.29
portal (circulation) (vein) 452
prostate 600.90

Obstruction, obstructed, obstructive — *continued*

prostate — *continued*
  with
    other lower urinary tract symptoms (LUTS) 600.91
    urinary
      obstruction 600.91
      retention 600.91
  valve (urinary) 596.0
pulmonary
  valve (heart) (*see also* Endocarditis, pulmonary) 424.3
  vein, isolated 747.49
pyemic — *see* Septicemia
pylorus (acquired) 537.0
  congenital 750.5
  infantile 750.5
rectosigmoid (*see also* Obstruction, intestine) 560.9
rectum 569.49
renal 593.89
respiratory 519.8
  chronic 496
retinal (artery) (vein) (central) (*see also* Occlusion, retina) 362.30
salivary duct (any) 527.8
  with calculus 527.5
sigmoid (*see also* Obstruction, intestine) 560.9
sinus (accessory) (nasal) (*see also* Sinusitis) 473.9
Stensen's duct 527.8
stomach 537.89
  acute 536.1
  congenital 750.7
submaxillary gland 527.8
  with calculus 527.5
thoracic duct 457.1
thrombotic — *see* Thrombosis
tooth eruption 520.6
trachea 519.19
tracheostomy airway 519.09
tricuspid — *see* Endocarditis, tricuspid
upper respiratory, congenital 748.8
ureter (functional) 593.4
  congenital 753.20
  due to calculus 592.1
ureteropelvic junction, congenital 753.21
ureterovesical junction, congenital 753.22
urethra 599.60
  congenital 753.6
urinary (moderate) 599.60
  organ or tract (lower) 599.60
    due to
      benign prostatic hypertrophy (BPH) - see category 600
    specified NEC 599.69
      due to
        benign prostatic hypertrophy (BPH) — see category 600
  prostatic valve 596.0
uropathy 599.60
uterus 621.8
vagina 623.2
valvular — *see* Endocarditis
vascular graft or shunt 996.1
  atherosclerosis — *see* Arteriosclerosis, coronary
  embolism 996.74
  occlusion NEC 996.74
  thrombus 996.74
vein, venous 459.2
  caval (inferior) (superior) 459.2
  thrombotic — *see* Thrombosis
vena cava (inferior) (superior) 459.2
ventricular shunt 996.2
vesical 596.0
vesicourethral orifice 596.0
vessel NEC 459.9
Obturator — *see* condition
Occlusal
  plane deviation 524.76
  wear, teeth 521.10
Occlusion
  anus 569.49

Occlusion — *continued*

anus — *continued*
  congenital 751.2
  infantile 751.2
aortoiliac (chronic) 444.0
aqueduct of Sylvius 331.4
  congenital 742.3
    with spina bifida (*see also* Spina bifida) 741.0 ☑
arteries of extremities, lower 444.22
  without thrombus or embolus (*see also* Arteriosclerosis, extremities) 440.20
  due to stricture or stenosis 447.1
  upper 444.21
    without thrombus or embolus (*see also* Arteriosclerosis, extremities) 440.20
    due to stricture or stenosis 447.1
artery NEC (*see also* Embolism, artery) 444.9
  auditory, internal 433.8 ☑
  basilar 433.0 ☑
    with other precerebral artery 433.3 ☑
    bilateral 433.3 ☑
  brain or cerebral (*see also* Infarct, brain) 434.9 ☑
  carotid 433.1 ☑
    with other precerebral artery 433.3 ☑
    bilateral 433.3 ☑
  cerebellar (anterior inferior) (posterior inferior) (superior) 433.8 ☑
  cerebral (*see also* Infarct, brain) 434.9 ☑
  choroidal (anterior) 433.8 ☑
  chronic total
    coronary 414.2
    extremity(ies) 440.4
  communicating posterior 433.8 ☑
  complete
    coronary 414.2
    extremity(ies) 440.4
  coronary (thrombotic) (*see also* Infarct, myocardium) 410.9 ☑
    acute 410.9 ☑
      without myocardial infarction 411.81
    chronic total 414.2
    complete 414.2
    healed or old 412
    total 414.2
  extremity(ies)
    chronic total 440.4
    complete 440.4
    total 440.4
  hypophyseal 433.8 ☑
  iliac (artery) 444.81
  mesenteric (embolic) (thrombotic) (with gangrene) 557.0
  pontine 433.8 ☑
  precerebral NEC 433.9 ☑
    late effect — *see* Late effect(s) (of) cerebrovascular disease
    multiple or bilateral 433.3 ☑
    puerperal, postpartum, childbirth 674.0 ☑
    specified NEC 433.8 ☑
  renal 593.81
  retinal — *see* Occlusion, retina, artery
  spinal 433.8 ☑
  vertebral 433.2 ☑
    with other precerebral artery 433.3 ☑
    bilateral 433.3 ☑
basilar (artery) — *see* Occlusion, artery, basilar
bile duct (any) (*see also* Obstruction, biliary) 576.2
bowel (*see also* Obstruction, intestine) 560.9
brain (artery) (vascular) (*see also* Infarct, brain) 434.9 ☑
breast (duct) 611.89
carotid (artery) (common) (internal) — *see* Occlusion, artery, carotid
cerebellar (anterior inferior) (artery) (posterior inferior) (superior) 433.8 ☑
cerebral (artery) (*see also* Infarct, brain) 434.9 ☑
cerebrovascular (*see also* Infarct, brain) 434.9 ☑

Occlusion — *continued*

cerebrovascular (*see also* Infarct, brain) — *continued*
  diffuse 437.0
cervical canal (*see also* Stricture, cervix) 622.4
  by falciparum malaria 084.0
cervix (uteri) (*see also* Stricture, cervix) 622.4
choanal 748.0
choroidal (artery) 433.8 ☑
colon (*see also* Obstruction, intestine) 560.9
communicating posterior artery 433.8 ☑
coronary (artery) (thrombotic) (*see also* Infarct, myocardium) 410.9 ☑
  without myocardial infarction 411.81
  acute 410.9 ☑
    without myocardial infarction 411.81
  healed or old 412
cystic duct (*see also* Obstruction, gallbladder) 575.2
  congenital 751.69
disto
  division I 524.22
  division II 524.22
embolic — *see* Embolism
fallopian tube 628.2
  congenital 752.19
gallbladder (*see also* Obstruction, gallbladder) 575.2
  congenital 751.69
    jaundice from 751.69 [774.5]
gingiva, traumatic 523.8
hymen 623.3
  congenital 752.42
hypophyseal (artery) 433.8 ☑
iliac artery 444.81
intestine (*see also* Obstruction, intestine) 560.9
kidney 593.89
lacrimal apparatus — *see* Stenosis, lacrimal
lung 518.89
lymph or lymphatic channel 457.1
mammary duct 611.89
mesenteric artery (embolic) (thrombotic) (with gangrene) 557.0
nose 478.1 ☑
  congenital 748.0
organ or site, congenital NEC — *see* Atresia
oviduct 628.2
  congenital 752.19
periodontal, traumatic 523.8
peripheral arteries (lower extremity) 444.22
  without thrombus or embolus (*see also* Arteriosclerosis, extremities) 440.20
  due to stricture or stenosis 447.1
  upper extremity 444.21
    without thrombus or embolus (*see also* Arteriosclerosis, extremities) 440.20
    due to stricture or stenosis 447.1
pontine (artery) 433.8 ☑
posterior lingual, of mandibular teeth 524.29
precerebral artery — *see* Occlusion, artery, precerebral NEC
puncta lacrimalia 375.52
pupil 364.74
pylorus (*see also* Stricture, pylorus) 537.0
renal artery 593.81
retina, retinal (vascular) 362.30
  artery, arterial 362.30
    branch 362.32
    central (total) 362.31
    partial 362.33
    transient 362.34
    tributary 362.32
  vein 362.30
    branch 362.36
    central (total) 362.35
    incipient 362.37
    partial 362.37
    tributary 362.36
spinal artery 433.8 ☑
stent
  coronary 996.72
teeth (mandibular) (posterior lingual) 524.29
thoracic duct 457.1
tubal 628.2
ureter (complete) (partial) 593.4

Occlusion — *continued*
  ureter — *continued*
    congenital 753.29
  urethra (*see also* Stricture, urethra) 598.9
    congenital 753.6
  uterus 621.8
  vagina 623.2
  vascular NEC 459.9
  vein — *see* Thrombosis
  vena cava
    inferior 453.2   ●
    superior   ●
      acute 453.87   ●
      chronic 453.77   ●
  ventricle (brain) NEC 331.4
  vertebral (artery) — *see* Occlusion, artery, vertebral
  vessel (blood) NEC 459.9
  vulva 624.8
Occlusio pupillae 364.74
Occupational
  problems NEC V62.29
  therapy V57.21
Ochlophobia 300.29
Ochronosis (alkaptonuric) (congenital) (endogenous) 270.2
  with chloasma of eyelid 270.2
Ocular muscle — *see also* condition
  myopathy 359.1
  torticollis 781.93
Oculoauriculovertebral dysplasia 756.0
Oculogyric
  crisis or disturbance 378.87
    psychogenic 306.7
Oculomotor syndrome 378.81
Oddi's sphincter spasm 576.5
Odelberg's disease (juvenile osteochondrosis) 732.1
Odontalgia 525.9
Odontoameloblastoma (M9311/0) 213.1
  upper jaw (bone) 213.0
Odontoclasia 521.05
Odontoclasis 873.63
  complicated 873.73
Odontodysplasia, regional 520.4
Odontogenesis imperfecta 520.5
Odontoma (M9280/0) 213.1
  ameloblastic (M9311/0) 213.1
    upper jaw (bone) 213.0
  calcified (M9280/0) 213.1
    upper jaw (bone) 213.0
  complex (M9282/0) 213.1
    upper jaw (bone) 213.0
  compound (M9281/0) 213.1
    upper jaw (bone) 213.0
  fibroameloblastic (M9290/0) 213.1
    upper jaw (bone) 213.0
  follicular 526.0
  upper jaw (bone) 213.0
Odontomyelitis (closed) (open) 522.0
Odontonecrosis 521.09
Odontorrhagia 525.8
Odontosarcoma, ameloblastic (M9290/3) 170.1
  upper jaw (bone) 170.0
Odynophagia 787.20
Oesophagostomiasis 127.7
Oesophagostomum infestation 127.7
Oestriasis 134.0
Ogilvie's syndrome (sympathicotonic colon obstruction) 560.89
Oguchi's disease (retina) 368.61
Ohara's disease — *see also* Tularemia 021.9
Oidiomycosis — *see also* Candidiasis 112.9
Oidiomycotic meningitis 112.83
Oidium albicans infection — *see also* Candidiasis 112.9
Old age 797
  dementia (of) 290.0
Olfactory — *see* condition
Oligemia 285.9
Oligergasia — *see also* Retardation, mental 319
Oligoamnios 658.0 ☑
  affecting fetus or newborn 761.2
Oligoastrocytoma, mixed (M9382/3)
  specified site — *see* Neoplasm, by site, malignant

Oligoastrocytoma, mixed — *continued*
  unspecified site 191.9
Oligocythemia 285.9
Oligodendroblastoma (M9460/3)
  specified site — *see* Neoplasm, by site, malignant
  unspecified site 191.9
Oligodendroglioma (M9450/3)
  anaplastic type (M9451/3)
    specified site — *see* Neoplasm, by site, malignant
    unspecified site 191.9
  specified site — *see* Neoplasm, by site, malignant
  unspecified site 191.9
Oligodendroma — *see* Oligodendroglioma
Oligodontia — *see also* Anodontia 520.0
Oligoencephalon 742.1
Oligohydramnios 658.0 ☑
  affecting fetus or newborn 761.2
  due to premature rupture of membranes 658.1 ☑
    affecting fetus or newborn 761.2
Oligohydrosis 705.0
Oligomenorrhea 626.1
Oligophrenia — *see also* Retardation, mental 319
  phenylpyruvic 270.1
Oligospermia 606.1
Oligotrichia 704.09
  congenita 757.4
Oliguria 788.5
  with
    abortion — *see* Abortion, by type, with renal failure
    ectopic pregnancy (*see also* categories 633.0–633.9) 639.3
    molar pregnancy (*see also* categories 630–632) 639.3
  complicating
    abortion 639.3
    ectopic or molar pregnancy 639.3
    pregnancy 646.2 ☑
      with hypertension — *see* Toxemia, of pregnancy
    due to a procedure 997.5
    following labor and delivery 669.3 ☑
    heart or cardiac — *see* Failure, heart
    puerperal, postpartum 669.3 ☑
    specified due to a procedure 997.5
Ollier's disease (chondrodysplasia) 756.4
Omentitis — *see also* Peritonitis 567.9
Omentocele — *see also* Hernia, omental 553.8
Omentum, omental — *see* condition
Omphalitis (congenital) (newborn) 771.4
  not of newborn 686.9
  tetanus 771.3
Omphalocele 756.72   ▲
Omphalomesenteric duct, persistent 751.0
Omphalorrhagia, newborn 772.3
Omsk hemorrhagic fever 065.1
Onanism 307.9
Onchocerciasis 125.3
  eye 125.3 [360.13]
Onchocercosis 125.3
Oncocytoma (M8290/0) — *see* Neoplasm, by site, benign
Ondine's curse 348.89   ▲
Oneirophrenia — *see also* Schizophrenia 295.4 ☑
Onychauxis 703.8
  congenital 757.5
Onychia (with lymphangitis) 681.9
  dermatophytic 110.1
  finger 681.02
  toe 681.11
Onychitis (with lymphangitis) 681.9
  finger 681.02
  toe 681.11
Onychocryptosis 703.0
Onychodystrophy 703.8
  congenital 757.5
Onychogryphosis 703.8
Onychogryposis 703.8
Onycholysis 703.8
Onychomadesis 703.8
Onychomalacia 703.8

Onychomycosis 110.1
  finger 110.1
  toe 110.1
Onycho-osteodysplasia 756.89
Onychophagy 307.9
Onychoptosis 703.8
Onychorrhexis 703.8
  congenital 757.5
Onychoschizia 703.8
Onychotrophia — *see also* Atrophy, nail 703.8
O'nyong-nyong fever 066.3
Onyxis (finger) (toe) 703.0
Onyxitis (with lymphangitis) 681.9
  finger 681.02
  toe 681.11
Oocyte (egg) (ovum)
  donor V59.70
    over age 35 V59.73
      anonymous recipient V59.73
      designated recipient V59.74
    under age 35 V59.71
      anonymous recipient V59.71
      designated recipient V59.72
Oophoritis (cystic) (infectional) (interstitial) — *see also* Salpingo-oophoritis 614.2
  complicating pregnancy 646.6 ☑
  fetal (acute) 752.0
  gonococcal (acute) 098.19
    chronic or duration of 2 months or over 098.39
  tuberculous (*see also* Tuberculosis) 016.6 ☑
Opacity, opacities
  cornea 371.00
    central 371.03
    congenital 743.43
      interfering with vision 743.42
    degenerative (*see also* Degeneration, cornea) 371.40
    hereditary (*see also* Dystrophy, cornea) 371.50
    inflammatory (*see also* Keratitis) 370.9
    late effect of trachoma (healed) 139.1
    minor 371.01
    peripheral 371.02
  enamel (fluoride) (nonfluoride) (teeth) 520.3
  lens (*see also* Cataract) 366.9
  snowball 379.22
  vitreous (humor) 379.24
    congenital 743.51
Opalescent dentin (hereditary) 520.5
Open, opening
  abnormal, organ or site, congenital — *see* Imperfect, closure
  angle with
    borderline intraocular pressure 365.01
    cupping of discs 365.01
  bite
    anterior 524.24
    posterior 524.25
  false — *see* Imperfect, closure
  margin on tooth restoration 525.61
  restoration margins 525.61
  wound — *see* Wound, open, by site
Operation
  causing mutilation of fetus 763.89
  destructive, on live fetus, to facilitate birth 763.89
  for delivery, fetus or newborn 763.89
  maternal, unrelated to current delivery, affecting fetus or newborn (*see also* Newborn, affected by) 760.64
Operational fatigue 300.89
Operative — *see* condition
Operculitis (chronic) 523.40
  acute 523.30
Operculum, retina 361.32
  with detachment 361.01
Ophiasis 704.01
Ophthalmia — *see also* Conjunctivitis 372.30
  actinic rays 370.24
  allergic (acute) 372.05
    chronic 372.14
  blennorrhagic (neonatorum) 098.40
  catarrhal 372.03
  diphtheritic 032.81
  Egyptian 076.1

Ophthalmia — *see also* Conjunctivitis — *continued*
  electric, electrica 370.24
  gonococcal (neonatorum) 098.40
  metastatic 360.11
  migraine 346.8 ☑
  neonatorum, newborn 771.6
    gonococcal 098.40
  nodosa 360.14
  phlyctenular 370.31
    with ulcer (*see also* Ulcer, cornea) 370.00
  sympathetic 360.11
Ophthalmitis — *see* Ophthalmia
Ophthalmocele (congenital) 743.66
Ophthalmoneuromyelitis 341.0
Ophthalmopathy, infiltrative with thyrotoxicosis 242.0 ☑
Ophthalmoplegia — *see also* Strabismus 378.9
  anterior internuclear 378.86
  ataxia-areflexia syndrome 357.0
  bilateral 378.9
  diabetic 250.5 ☑ [378.86]
    due to secondary diabetes 249.5 ☑ [378.86]
  exophthalmic 242.0 ☑ [376.22]
  external 378.55
    progressive 378.72
    total 378.56
  internal (complete) (total) 367.52
  internuclear 378.86
  migraine 346.2 ☑
  painful 378.55
  Parinaud's 378.81
  progressive external 378.72
  supranuclear, progressive 333.0
  total (external) 378.56
    internal 367.52
  unilateral 378.9
Opisthognathism 524.00
Opisthorchiasis (felineus) (tenuicollis) (viverrini) 121.0
Opisthotonos, opisthotonus 781.0
Opitz's disease (congestive splenomegaly) 289.51
Opiumism — *see also* Dependence 304.0 ☑
Oppenheim's disease 358.8
Oppenheim-Urbach disease or syndrome (necrobiosis lipoidica diabeticorum) 250.8 ☑ [709.3]
  due to secondary diabetes 249.8 ☑ [709.3]
Opsoclonia 379.59
Optic nerve — *see* condition
Orbit — *see* condition
Orchioblastoma (M9071/3) 186.9
Orchitis (nonspecific) (septic) 604.90
  with abscess 604.0
  blennorrhagic (acute) 098.13
    chronic or duration of 2 months or over 098.33
  diphtheritic 032.89 [604.91]
  filarial 125.9 [604.91]
  gangrenous 604.99
  gonococcal (acute) 098.13
    chronic or duration of 2 months or over 098.33
  mumps 072.0
  parotidea 072.0
  suppurative 604.99
  syphilitic 095.8 [604.91]
  tuberculous (*see also* Tuberculosis) 016.5 ☑ [608.81]
Orf 051.2
Organic — *see also* condition
  heart — *see* Disease, heart
  insufficiency 799.89
Oriental
  bilharziasis 120.2
  schistosomiasis 120.2
  sore 085.1
Orientation
  ego-dystonic sexual 302.0
Orifice — *see* condition
Origin, both great vessels from right ventricle 745.11
Ormond's disease or syndrome 593.4
Ornithosis 073.9

☑ Additional Digit Required — Refer to the Tabular List for Digit Selection   ⓘ Subterms under main terms may continue to next column or page

2010 ICD-9-CM   ►◄ Revised Text   ● New Line   ▲ Revised Code   October 2009 • Volume 2 — 209

Ornithosis — *continued*
  with
    complication 073.8
      specified NEC 073.7
    pneumonia 073.0
    pneumonitis (lobular) 073.0
Orodigitofacial dysostosis 759.89
Oropouche fever 066.3
Orotaciduria, oroticaciduria (congenital)
  (hereditary) (pyrimidine deficiency) 281.4
Oroya fever 088.0
Orthodontics V58.5
  adjustment V53.4
  aftercare V58.5
  fitting V53.4
Orthopnea 786.02
Orthoptic training V57.4
Osgood-Schlatter
  disease 732.4
  osteochondrosis 732.4
Osler's
  disease (M9950/1) (polycythemia vera) 238.4
  nodes 421.0
Osler-Rendu disease (familial hemorrhagic
  telangiectasia) 448.0
Osler-Vaquez disease (M9950/1) (polycythemia
  vera) 238.4
Osler-Weber-Rendu syndrome (familial hemorrhagic telangiectasia) 448.0
Osmidrosis 705.89
Osseous — *see* condition
Ossification
  artery — *see* Arteriosclerosis
  auricle (ear) 380.39
  bronchus 519.19
  cardiac (*see also* Degeneration, myocardial)
    429.1
  cartilage (senile) 733.99
  coronary (artery) — *see* Arteriosclerosis, coro-
    nary
  diaphragm 728.10
  ear 380.39
    middle (*see also* Otosclerosis) 387.9
  falx cerebri 349.2
  fascia 728.10
  fontanel
    defective or delayed 756.0
    premature 756.0
  heart (*see also* Degeneration, myocardial) 429.1
    valve — *see* Endocarditis
  larynx 478.79
  ligament
    posterior longitudinal 724.8
      cervical 723.7
  meninges (cerebral) 349.2
    spinal 336.8
  multiple, eccentric centers 733.99
  muscle 728.10
    heterotopic, postoperative 728.13
  myocardium, myocardial (*see also* Degenera-
    tion, myocardial) 429.1
  penis 607.81
  periarticular 728.89
  sclera 379.16
  tendon 727.82
  trachea 519.19
  tympanic membrane (*see also* Tympanosclero-
    sis) 385.00
  vitreous (humor) 360.44
Osteitis — *see also* Osteomyelitis 730.2 ☑
  acute 730.0 ☑
  alveolar 526.5
  chronic 730.1 ☑
  condensans (ilii) 733.5
  deformans (Paget's) 731.0
    due to or associated with malignant neo-
      plasm (*see also* Neoplasm, bone,
      malignant) 170.9 *[731.1]*
  due to yaws 102.6
  fibrosa NEC 733.29
    cystica (generalisata) 252.01
    disseminata 756.59
    osteoplastica 252.01
  fragilitans 756.51
  Garré's (sclerosing) 730.1 ☑
  infectious (acute) (subacute) 730.0 ☑

Osteitis — *see also* Osteomyelitis —
  continued
  infectious — *continued*
    chronic or old 730.1 ☑
    jaw (acute) (chronic) (lower) (neonatal) (sup-
      purative) (upper) 526.4
  parathyroid 252.01
  petrous bone (*see also* Petrositis) 383.20
  pubis 733.5
  sclerotic, nonsuppurative 730.1 ☑
  syphilitic 095.5
  tuberculosa
    cystica (of Jüngling) 135
    multiplex cystoides 135
Osteoarthritica spondylitis (spine) — *see also*
  Spondylosis 721.90
Osteoarthritis — *see also* Osteoarthrosis 715.9 ☑
  distal interphalangeal 715.9 ☑
  hyperplastic 731.2
  interspinalis (*see also* Spondylosis) 721.90
  spine, spinal NEC (*see also* Spondylosis) 721.90
Osteoarthropathy — *see also* Osteoarthrosis
  715.9 ☑
  chronic idiopathic hypertrophic 757.39
  familial idiopathic 757.39
  hypertrophic pulmonary 731.2
    secondary 731.2
  idiopathic hypertrophic 757.39
  primary hypertrophic 731.2
  pulmonary hypertrophic 731.2
  secondary hypertrophic 731.2
Osteoarthrosis (degenerative) (hypertrophic)
  (rheumatoid) 715.9 ☑

> *Note* — *Use the following fifth-digit*
> *subclassification with category 715:*
>
> 0   *site unspecified*
> 1   *shoulder region*
> 2   *upper arm*
> 3   *forearm*
> 4   *hand*
> 5   *pelvic region and thigh*
> 6   *lower leg*
> 7   *ankle and foot*
> 8   *other specified sites except spine*
> 9   *multiple sites*

  Deformans alkaptonurica 270.2
  generalized 715.09
  juvenilis (Köhler's) 732.5
  localized 715.3 ☑
    idiopathic 715.1 ☑
    primary 715.1 ☑
    secondary 715.2 ☑
  multiple sites, not specified as generalized
    715.89
  polyarticular 715.09
  spine (*see also* Spondylosis) 721.90
  temporomandibular joint 524.69
Osteoblastoma (M9200/0) — *see* Neoplasm,
  bone, benign
Osteochondritis — *see also* Osteochondrosis
  732.9
  dissecans 732.7
  hip 732.7
  ischiopubica 732.1
  multiple 756.59
  syphilitic (congenital) 090.0
Osteochondrodermodysplasia 756.59
Osteochondrodystrophy 277.5
  deformans 277.5
  familial 277.5
  fetalis 756.4
Osteochondrolysis 732.7
Osteochondroma (M9210/0) — *see also* Neoplasm, bone, benign
  multiple, congenital 756.4
Osteochondromatosis (M9210/1) 238.0
  synovial 727.82
Osteochondromyxosarcoma (M9180/3) — *see*
  Neoplasm, bone, malignant
Osteochondropathy NEC 732.9

Osteochondrosarcoma (M9180/3) — *see* Neoplasm, bone, malignant
Osteochondrosis 732.9
  acetabulum 732.1
  adult spine 732.8
  astragalus 732.5
  Blount's 732.4
  Buchanan's (juvenile osteochondrosis of iliac
    crest) 732.1
  Buchman's (juvenile osteochondrosis) 732.1
  Burns' 732.3
  calcaneus 732.5
  capitular epiphysis (femur) 732.1
  carpal
    lunate (wrist) 732.3
    scaphoid 732.3
  coxae juvenilis 732.1
  deformans juvenilis (coxae) (hip) 732.1
    Scheuermann's 732.0
    spine 732.0
    tibia 732.4
    vertebra 732.0
  Diaz's (astragalus) 732.5
  dissecans (knee) (shoulder) 732.7
  femoral capital epiphysis 732.1
  femur (head) (juvenile) 732.1
  foot (juvenile) 732.5
  Freiberg's (disease) (second metatarsal) 732.5
  Haas' 732.3
  Haglund's (os tibiale externum) 732.5
  hand (juvenile) 732.3
  head of
    femur 732.1
    humerus (juvenile) 732.3
  hip (juvenile) 732.1
  humerus (juvenile) 732.3
  iliac crest (juvenile) 732.1
  ilium (juvenile) 732.1
  ischiopubic synchondrosis 732.1
  Iselin's (osteochondrosis fifth metatarsal) 732.5
  juvenile, juvenilis 732.6
    arm 732.3
    capital femoral epiphysis 732.1
    capitellum humeri 732.3
    capitular epiphysis 732.1
    carpal scaphoid 732.3
    clavicle, sternal epiphysis 732.6
    coxae 732.1
    deformans 732.1
    foot 732.5
    hand 732.3
    hip and pelvis 732.1
    lower extremity, except foot 732.4
    lunate, wrist 732.3
    medial cuneiform bone 732.5
    metatarsal (head) 732.5
    metatarsophalangeal 732.5
    navicular, ankle 732.5
    patella 732.4
    primary patellar center (of Köhler) 732.4
    specified site NEC 732.6
    spine 732.0
    tarsal scaphoid 732.5
    tibia (epiphysis) (tuberosity) 732.4
    upper extremity 732.3
    vertebra (body) (Calvé) 732.0
      epiphyseal plates (of Scheuermann)
      732.0
  Kienböck's (disease) 732.3
  Köhler's (disease) (navicular, ankle) 732.5
    patellar 732.4
    tarsal navicular 732.5
  Legg-Calvé-Perthes (disease) 732.1
  lower extremity (juvenile) 732.4
  lunate bone 732.3
  Mauclaire's 732.3
  metacarpal heads (of Mauclaire) 732.3
  metatarsal (fifth) (head) (second) 732.5
  navicular, ankle 732.5
  os calcis 732.5
  Osgood-Schlatter 732.4
  os tibiale externum 732.5
  Panner's 732.3
  patella (juvenile) 732.4
  patellar center
    primary (of Köhler) 732.4

Osteochondrosis — *continued*
  patellar center — *continued*
    secondary (of Sinding-Larsen) 732.4
  pelvis (juvenile) 732.1
  Pierson's 732.1
  radial head (juvenile) 732.3
  Scheuermann's 732.0
  Sever's (calcaneum) 732.5
  Sinding-Larsen (secondary patellar center)
    732.4
  spine (juvenile) 732.0
    adult 732.8
  symphysis pubis (of Pierson) (juvenile) 732.1
  syphilitic (congenital) 090.0
  tarsal (navicular) (scaphoid) 732.5
  tibia (proximal) (tubercle) 732.4
  tuberculous — *see* Tuberculosis, bone
  ulna 732.3
  upper extremity (juvenile) 732.3
  van Neck's (juvenile osteochondrosis) 732.1
  vertebral (juvenile) 732.0
    adult 732.8
Osteoclastoma (M9250/1) 238.0
  malignant (M9250/3) — *see* Neoplasm, bone,
    malignant
Osteocopic pain 733.90
Osteodynia 733.90
Osteodystrophy
  azotemic 588.0
  chronica deformans hypertrophica 731.0
  congenital 756.50
    specified type NEC 756.59
  deformans 731.0
  fibrosa localisata 731.0
  parathyroid 252.01
  renal 588.0
Osteofibroma (M9262/0) — *see* Neoplasm, bone,
  benign
Osteofibrosarcoma (M9182/3) — *see* Neoplasm,
  bone, malignant
Osteogenesis imperfecta 756.51
Osteogenic — *see* condition
Osteoma (M9180/0) — *see also* Neoplasm, bone,
  benign
  osteoid (M9191/0) (*see also* Neoplasm, bone,
    benign)
    giant (M9200/0) — *see* Neoplasm, bone,
      benign
Osteomalacia 268.2
  chronica deformans hypertrophica 731.0
  due to vitamin D deficiency 268.2
  infantile (*see also* Rickets) 268.0
  juvenile (*see also* Rickets) 268.0
  pelvis 268.2
  vitamin D-resistant 275.3
Osteomalacic bone 268.2
Osteomalacosis 268.2
Osteomyelitis (general) (infective) (localized)
  (neonatal) (purulent) (pyogenic) (septic)
  (staphylococcal) (streptococcal) (suppurative) (with periostitis) 730.2 ☑

> *Note* — *Use the following fifth-digit*
> *subclassification with category 730:*
>
> 0   *site unspecified*
> 1   *shoulder region*
> 2   *upper arm*
> 3   *forearm*
> 4   *hand*
> 5   *pelvic region and thigh*
> 6   *lower leg*
> 7   *ankle and foot*
> 8   *other specified sites*
> 9   *multiple sites*

  acute or subacute 730.0 ☑
  chronic or old 730.1 ☑
  due to or associated with
    diabetes mellitus 250.8 ☑ *[731.8]*
      due to secondary diabetes
        249.8 ☑ *[731.8]*
    tuberculosis (*see also* Tuberculosis, bone)
      015.9 ☑ *[730.8]* ☑

☑ Additional Digit Required — Refer to the Tabular List for Digit Selection   ▿ Subterms under main terms may continue to next column or page

210 — Volume 2   ▶◀ Revised Text   ● New Line   ▲ Revised Code   **2010 ICD-9-CM**

Osteomyelitis — continued
  due to or associated with — continued
    tuberculosis (see also Tuberculosis, bone)
      — continued
      limb bones 015.5 ☑ [730.8] ☑
      specified bones NEC
        015.7 ☑ [730.8] ☑
      spine 015.0 ☑ [730.8] ☑
      typhoid 002.0 [730.8] ☑
    Garré's 730.1 ☑
    jaw (acute) (chronic) (lower) (neonatal) (suppurative) (upper) 526.4
    nonsuppurating 730.1 ☑
    orbital 376.03
    petrous bone (see also Petrositis) 383.20
    Salmonella 003.24
    sclerosing, nonsuppurative 730.1 ☑
    sicca 730.1 ☑
    syphilitic 095.5
      congenital 090.0 [730.8] ☑
    tuberculous — see Tuberculosis, bone
    typhoid 002.0 [730.8] ☑
Osteomyelofibrosis 289.89
Osteomyelosclerosis 289.89
Osteonecrosis 733.40
  meaning osteomyelitis 730.1 ☑
Osteo-onycho-arthro dysplasia 756.89
Osteo-onychodysplasia, hereditary 756.89
Osteopathia
  condensans disseminata 756.53
  hyperostotica multiplex infantilis 756.59
  hypertrophica toxica 731.2
  striata 756.4
Osteopathy resulting from poliomyelitis —
  see also Poliomyelitis 045.9 ☑ [730.7] ☑
  familial dysplastic 731.2
Osteopecilia 756.53
Osteopenia 733.90
  borderline 733.90
Osteoperiostitis — see also Osteomyelitis
  730.2 ☑
  ossificans toxica 731.2
  toxica ossificans 731.2
Osteopetrosis (familial) 756.52
Osteophyte — see Exostosis
Osteophytosis — see Exostosis
Osteopoikilosis 756.53
Osteoporosis (generalized) 733.00
  circumscripta 731.0
  disuse 733.03
  drug-induced 733.09
  idiopathic 733.02
  postmenopausal 733.01
  posttraumatic 733.7
  screening V82.81
  senile 733.01
  specified type NEC 733.09
Osteoporosis-osteomalacia syndrome 268.2
Osteopsathyrosis 756.51
Osteoradionecrosis, jaw 526.89
Osteosarcoma (M9180/3) — see also Neoplasm, bone, malignant
  chondroblastic (M9181/3) — see Neoplasm, bone, malignant
  fibroblastic (M9182/3) — see Neoplasm, bone, malignant
  in Paget's disease of bone (M9184/3) — see Neoplasm, bone, malignant
  juxtacortical (M9190/3) — see Neoplasm, bone, malignant
  parosteal (M9190/3) — see Neoplasm, bone, malignant
  telangiectatic (M9183/3) — see Neoplasm, bone, malignant
Osteosclerosis 756.52
  fragilis (generalisata) 756.52
Osteosclerotic anemia 289.89
Osteosis
  acromegaloid 757.39
  cutis 709.3
  parathyroid 252.01
  renal fibrocystic 588.0
Österreicher-Turner syndrome 756.89
Ostium
  atrioventriculare commune 745.69

Ostium — continued
  primum (arteriosum) (defect) (persistent) 745.61
  secundum (arteriosum) (defect) (patent) (persistent) 745.5
Ostrum-Furst syndrome 756.59
Os, uterus — see condition
Otalgia 388.70
  otogenic 388.71
  referred 388.72
Othematoma 380.31
Otitic hydrocephalus 348.2
Otitis 382.9
  with effusion 381.4
    purulent 382.4
    secretory 381.4
    serous 381.4
    suppurative 382.4
  acute 382.9
  adhesive (see also Adhesions, middle ear) 385.10
  chronic 382.9
    with effusion 381.3
    mucoid, mucous (simple) 381.20
    purulent 382.3
    secretory 381.3
    serous 381.10
    suppurative 382.3
  diffuse parasitic 136.8
  externa (acute) (diffuse) (hemorrhagica) 380.10
    actinic 380.22
    candidal 112.82
    chemical 380.22
    chronic 380.23
      mycotic — see Otitis, externa, mycotic
      specified type NEC 380.23
    circumscribed 380.10
    contact 380.22
    due to
      erysipelas 035 [380.13]
      impetigo 684 [380.13]
      seborrheic dermatitis 690.10 [380.13]
    eczematoid 380.22
    furuncular 680.0 [380.13]
    infective 380.10
      chronic 380.16
    malignant 380.14
    mycotic (chronic) 380.15
      due to
        aspergillosis 117.3 [380.15]
        moniliasis 112.82
        otomycosis 111.8 [380.15]
    reactive 380.22
    specified type NEC 380.22
    tropical 111.8 [380.15]
  insidiosa (see also Otosclerosis) 387.9
  interna (see also Labyrinthitis) 386.30
  media (hemorrhagic) (staphylococcal) (streptococcal) 382.9
    acute 382.9
      with effusion 381.00
      allergic 381.04
        mucoid 381.05
        sanguineous 381.06
        serous 381.04
      catarrhal 381.00
      exudative 381.00
      mucoid 381.02
        allergic 381.05
      necrotizing 382.00
        with spontaneous rupture of ear drum 382.01
        in
          influenza 487.8 [382.02]
          measles 055.2
          scarlet fever 034.1 [382.02]
      nonsuppurative 381.00
      purulent 382.00
        with spontaneous rupture of ear drum 382.01
      sanguineous 381.03
        allergic 381.06
      secretory 381.01
      seromucinous 381.02
      serous 381.01
        allergic 381.04

Otitis — continued
  media — continued
    acute — continued
      suppurative 382.00
        with spontaneous rupture of ear drum 382.01
        due to
          influenza 487.8 [382.02]
          scarlet fever 034.1 [382.02]
      transudative 381.00
    adhesive (see also Adhesions, middle ear) 385.10
    allergic 381.4
      acute 381.04
        mucoid 381.05
        sanguineous 381.06
        serous 381.04
      chronic 381.3
    catarrhal 381.4
      acute 381.00
      chronic (simple) 381.10
    chronic 382.9
      with effusion 381.3
      adhesive (see also Adhesions, middle ear) 385.10
      allergic 381.3
      atticoantral, suppurative (with posterior or superior marginal perforation of ear drum) 382.2
      benign suppurative (with anterior perforation of ear drum) 382.1
      catarrhal 381.10
      exudative 381.3
      mucinous 381.20
      mucoid, mucous (simple) 381.20
      mucosanguineous 381.29
      nonsuppurative 381.3
      purulent 382.3
      secretory 381.3
      seromucinous 381.3
      serosanguineous 381.19
      serous (simple) 381.10
      suppurative 382.3
        atticoantral (with posterior or superior marginal perforation of ear drum) 382.2
        benign (with anterior perforation of ear drum) 382.1
        tuberculous (see also Tuberculosis) 017.4 ☑
        tubotympanic 382.1
      transudative 381.3
    exudative 381.4
      acute 381.00
      chronic 381.3
    fibrotic (see also Adhesions, middle ear) 385.10
    mucoid, mucous 381.4
      acute 381.02
      chronic (simple) 381.20
    mucosanguineous, chronic 381.29
    nonsuppurative 381.4
      acute 381.00
      chronic 381.3
    postmeasles 055.2
    purulent 382.4
      acute 382.00
        with spontaneous rupture of ear drum 382.01
      chronic 382.3
    sanguineous, acute 381.03
      allergic 381.06
    secretory 381.4
      acute or subacute 381.01
      chronic 381.3
    seromucinous 381.4
      acute or subacute 381.02
      chronic 381.3
    serosanguineous, chronic 381.19
    serous 381.4
      acute or subacute 381.01
      chronic (simple) 381.10
    subacute — see Otitis, media, acute
    suppurative 382.4
      acute 382.00

Otitis — continued
  media — continued
    suppurative — continued
      acute — continued
        with spontaneous rupture of ear drum 382.01
      chronic 382.3
        atticoantral 382.2
        benign 382.1
        tuberculous (see also Tuberculosis) 017.4 ☑
        tubotympanic 382.1
    transudative 381.4
      acute 381.00
      chronic 381.3
    tuberculous (see also Tuberculosis) 017.4 ☑
    postmeasles 055.2
Otoconia 386.8
Otolith syndrome 386.19
Otomycosis 111.8 [380.15]
  in
    aspergillosis 117.3 [380.15]
    moniliasis 112.82
Otopathy 388.9
Otoporosis — see also Otosclerosis 387.9
Otorrhagia 388.69
  traumatic — see nature of injury
Otorrhea 388.60
  blood 388.69
  cerebrospinal (fluid) 388.61
Otosclerosis (general) 387.9
  cochlear (endosteal) 387.2
  involving
    otic capsule 387.2
    oval window
      nonobliterative 387.0
      obliterative 387.1
    round window 387.2
  nonobliterative 387.0
  obliterative 387.1
  specified type NEC 387.8
Otospongiosis — see also Otosclerosis 387.9
Otto's disease or pelvis 715.35
Outburst, aggressive — see also Disturbance, conduct 312.0 ☑
  in children or adolescents 313.9
Outcome of delivery
  multiple birth NEC V27.9
    all liveborn V27.5
    all stillborn V27.7
    some liveborn V27.6
    unspecified V27.9
  single V27.9
    liveborn V27.0
    stillborn V27.1
  twins V27.9
    both liveborn V27.2
    both stillborn V27.4
    one liveborn, one stillborn V27.3
Outlet — see also condition
  syndrome (thoracic) 353.0
Outstanding ears (bilateral) 744.29
Ovalocytosis (congenital) (hereditary) — see also Elliptocytosis 282.1
Ovarian — see also condition
  pregnancy — see Pregnancy, ovarian
  remnant syndrome 620.8
  vein syndrome 593.4
Ovaritis (cystic) — see also Salpingo-oophoritis 614.2
Ovary, ovarian — see condition
Overactive — see also Hyperfunction
  bladder 596.51
  eye muscle (see also Strabismus) 378.9
  hypothalamus 253.8
  thyroid (see also Thyrotoxicosis) 242.9 ☑
Overactivity, child 314.01
Overbite (deep) (excessive) (horizontal) (vertical) 524.29
Overbreathing — see also Hyperventilation 786.01
Overconscientious personality 301.4
Overdevelopment — see also Hypertrophy
  breast (female) (male) 611.1
  nasal bones 738.0

Overdevelopment — *see also* Hypertrophy — *continued*
  prostate, congenital 752.89
Overdistention — *see* Distention
Overdose overdosage (drug) 977.9
  specified drug or substance — *see* Table of Drugs and Chemicals
Overeating 783.6
  nonorganic origin 307.51
Overexertion (effects) (exhaustion) 994.5
Overexposure (effects) 994.9
  exhaustion 994.4
Overfeeding — *see also* Overeating 783.6
Overfill, endodontic 526.62
Overgrowth, bone NEC 733.99
Overhanging
  tooth restoration 525.62
  unrepairable, dental restorative materials 525.62
Overheated (effects) (places) — *see* Heat
Overinhibited child 313.0
Overjet 524.29
  excessive horizontal 524.26
Overlaid, overlying (suffocation) 994.7
Overlap
  excessive horizontal 524.26
Overlapping toe (acquired) 735.8
  congenital (fifth toe) 755.66
Overload
  fluid 276.6
  potassium (K) 276.7
  sodium (Na) 276.0
Overnutrition — *see also* Hyperalimentation 783.6
Overproduction — *see also* Hypersecretion
  ACTH 255.3
  cortisol 255.0
  growth hormone 253.0
  thyroid-stimulating hormone (TSH) 242.8 ☑
Overriding
  aorta 747.21
  finger (acquired) 736.29
    congenital 755.59
  toe (acquired) 735.8
    congenital 755.66
Oversize
  fetus (weight of 4500 grams or more) 766.0
    affecting management of pregnancy 656.6 ☑
    causing disproportion 653.5 ☑
      with obstructed labor 660.1 ☑
        affecting fetus or newborn 763.1
Overstimulation, ovarian 256.1
Overstrained 780.79
  heart — *see* Hypertrophy, cardiac
Overweight — *see also* Obesity 278.02
Overwork 780.79
Oviduct — *see* condition
Ovotestis 752.7
Ovulation (cycle)
  failure or lack of 628.0
  pain 625.2
Ovum
  blighted 631
  donor V59.70
    over age 35 V59.73
      anonymous recipient V59.73
      designated recipient V59.74
    under age 35 V59.71
      anonymous recipient V59.71
      designated recipient V59.72
  dropsical 631
  pathologic 631
Owren's disease or syndrome (parahemophilia) — *see also* Defect, coagulation 286.3
Oxalosis 271.8
Oxaluria 271.8
Ox heart — *see* Hypertrophy, cardiac
OX syndrome 758.6
Oxycephaly, oxycephalic 756.0
  syphilitic, congenital 090.0
Oxyuriasis 127.4
Oxyuris vermicularis (infestation) 127.4
Ozena 472.0

P

Pacemaker syndrome 429.4
Pachyderma, pachydermia 701.8
  laryngis 478.5
  laryngitis 478.79
  larynx (verrucosa) 478.79
Pachydermatitis 701.8
Pachydermatocele (congenital) 757.39
  acquired 701.8
Pachydermatosis 701.8
Pachydermoperiostitis
  secondary 731.2
Pachydermoperiostosis
  primary idiopathic 757.39
  secondary 731.2
Pachymeningitis (adhesive) (basal) (brain) (cerebral) (cervical) (chronic) (circumscribed) (external) (fibrous) (hemorrhagic) (hypertrophic) (internal) (purulent) (spinal) (suppurative) — *see also* Meningitis 322.9
  gonococcal 098.82
Pachyonychia (congenital) 757.5
  acquired 703.8
Pachyperiosteodermia
  primary or idiopathic 757.39
  secondary 731.2
Pachyperiostosis
  primary or idiopathic 757.39
  secondary 731.2
Pacinian tumor (M9507/0) — *see* Neoplasm, skin, benign
Pads, knuckle or Garrod's 728.79
Paget's disease (osteitis deformans) 731.0
  with infiltrating duct carcinoma of the breast (M8541/3) — *see* Neoplasm, breast, malignant
  bone 731.0
    osteosarcoma in (M9184/3) — *see* Neoplasm, bone, malignant
  breast (M8540/3) 174.0
  extramammary (M8542/3) (*see also* Neoplasm, skin, malignant)
    anus 154.3
    skin 173.5
  malignant (M8540/3)
    breast 174.0
    specified site NEC (M8542/3) — *see* Neoplasm, skin, malignant
    unspecified site 174.0
  mammary (M8540/3) 174.0
  necrosis of bone 731.0
  nipple (M8540/3) 174.0
  osteitis deformans 731.0
Paget-Schroetter syndrome (intermittent venous claudication) 453.89 ▲
Pain(s) (*see also* Painful) 780.96
  abdominal 789.0 ☑
  acute 338.19
    due to trauma 338.11
    postoperative 338.18
      post-thoracotomy 338.12
  adnexa (uteri) 625.9
  alimentary, due to vascular insufficiency 557.9
  anginoid (*see also* Pain, precordial) 786.51
  anus 569.42
  arch 729.5
  arm 729.5
  axillary 729.5
  back (postural) 724.5
    low 724.2
    psychogenic 307.89
  bile duct 576.9
  bladder 788.99
  bone 733.90
  breast 611.71
    psychogenic 307.89
  broad ligament 625.9
  cancer associated 338.3
  cartilage NEC 733.90
  cecum 789.0 ☑
  cervicobrachial 723.3
  chest (central) 786.50
    atypical 786.59
    midsternal 786.51
    musculoskeletal 786.59
    noncardiac 786.59

Pain(s) (*see also* Painful) — *continued*
  chest — *continued*
    substernal 786.51
    wall (anterior) 786.52
  chronic 338.29
    associated with significant psychosocial dysfunction 338.4
    due to trauma 338.21
    postoperative 338.28
      post-thoracotomy 338.22
    syndrome 338.4
  coccyx 724.79
  colon 789.0 ☑
  common duct 576.9
  coronary — *see* Angina
  costochondral 786.52
  diaphragm 786.52
  due to (presence of) any device, implant, or graft classifiable to 996.0–996.5 — *see* Complications, due to (presence of) any device, implant, or graft classified to 996.0–996.5 NEC
  malignancy (primary) (secondary) 338.3
  ear (*see also* Otalgia) 388.70
  epigastric, epigastrium 789.06
  extremity (lower) (upper) 729.5
  eye 379.91
  face, facial 784.0
    atypical 350.2
    nerve 351.8
  false (labor) 644.1 ☑
  female genital organ NEC 625.9
    psychogenic 307.89
  finger 729.5
  flank 789.0 ☑
  foot 729.5
  gallbladder 575.9
  gas (intestinal) 787.3
  gastric 536.8
  generalized 780.96
  genital organ
    female 625.9
    male 608.9
    psychogenic 307.89
  groin 789.0 ☑
  growing 781.99
  hand 729.5
  head (*see also* Headache) 784.0
  heart (see also Pain, precordial) 786.51
  infraorbital (*see also* Neuralgia, trigeminal) 350.1
  intermenstrual 625.2
  jaw 526.9
  joint 719.40
    ankle 719.47
    elbow 719.42
    foot 719.47
    hand 719.44
    hip 719.45
    knee 719.46
    multiple sites 719.49
    pelvic region 719.45
    psychogenic 307.89
    shoulder (region) 719.41
    specified site NEC 719.48
    wrist 719.43
  kidney 788.0
  labor, false or spurious 644.1 ☑
  laryngeal 784.1
  leg 729.5
  limb 729.5
  low back 724.2
  lumbar region 724.2
  mastoid (*see also* Otalgia) 388.70
  maxilla 526.9
  menstrual 625.3
  metacarpophalangeal (joint) 719.44
  metatarsophalangeal (joint) 719.47
  mouth 528.9
  muscle 729.1
    intercostal 786.59
  musculoskeletal (see also Pain, by site) 729.1
  nasal 478.19
  nasopharynx 478.29
  neck NEC 723.1
    psychogenic 307.89

Pain(s) (*see also* Painful) — *continued*
  neoplasm related (acute) (chronic) 338.3
  nerve NEC 729.2
  neuromuscular 729.1
  nose 478.19
  ocular 379.91
  ophthalmic 379.91
  orbital region 379.91
  osteocopic 733.90
  ovary 625.9
    psychogenic 307.89
  over heart (*see also* Pain, precordial) 786.51
  ovulation 625.2
  pelvic (female) 625.9
    male NEC 789.0 ☑
      psychogenic 307.89
    psychogenic 307.89
  penis 607.9
    psychogenic 307.89
  pericardial (*see also* Pain, precordial) 786.51
  perineum
    female 625.9
    male 608.9
  pharynx 478.29
  pleura, pleural, pleuritic 786.52
  postoperative 338.18
    acute 338.18
    chronic 338.28
  post-thoracotomy 338.12
    acute 338.12
    chronic 338.22
  preauricular 388.70
  precordial (region) 786.51
    psychogenic 307.89
  premenstrual 625.4
  psychogenic 307.80
    cardiovascular system 307.89
    gastrointestinal system 307.89
    genitourinary system 307.89
    heart 307.89
    musculoskeletal system 307.89
    respiratory system 307.89
    skin 306.3
  radicular (spinal) (*see also* Radiculitis) 729.2
  rectum 569.42
  respiration 786.52
  retrosternal 786.51
  rheumatic NEC 729.0
    muscular 729.1
  rib 786.50
  root (spinal) (*see also* Radiculitis) 729.2
  round ligament (stretch) 625.9
  sacroiliac 724.6
  sciatic 724.3
  scrotum 608.9
    psychogenic 307.89
  seminal vesicle 608.9
  sinus 478.19
  skin 782.0
  spermatic cord 608.9
  spinal root (*see also* Radiculitis) 729.2
  stomach 536.8
    psychogenic 307.89
  substernal 786.51
  temporomandibular (joint) 524.62
  temporomaxillary joint 524.62
  testis 608.9
    psychogenic 307.89
  thoracic spine 724.1
    with radicular and visceral pain 724.4
  throat 784.1
  tibia 733.90
  toe 729.5
  tongue 529.6
  tooth 525.9
  total hip replacement 996.77
  total knee replacement 996.77
  trigeminal (*see also* Neuralgia, trigeminal) 350.1
  tumor associated 338.3
  umbilicus 789.05
  ureter 788.0
  urinary (organ) (system) 788.0
  uterus 625.9
    psychogenic 307.89
  vagina 625.9
  vertebrogenic (syndrome) 724.5

Pain(s) (see also Painful) — continued
vesical 788.99
vulva 625.9
xiphoid 733.90
Painful — see also Pain
arc syndrome 726.19
coitus
female 625.0
male 608.89
psychogenic 302.76
ejaculation (semen) 608.89
psychogenic 302.79
erection 607.3
feet syndrome 266.2
menstruation 625.3
psychogenic 306.52
micturition 788.1
ophthalmoplegia 378.55
respiration 786.52
scar NEC 709.2
urination 788.1
wire sutures 998.89
Painters' colic 984.9
specified type of lead — see Table of Drugs
and Chemicals
Palate — see condition
Palatoplegia 528.9
Palatoschisis — see also Cleft, palate 749.00
Palilalia 784.69
Palindromic arthritis — see also Rheumatism,
palindromic 719.3 ☑
Palliative care V66.7
Pallor 782.61
temporal, optic disc 377.15
Palmar — see also condition
fascia — see condition
Palpable
cecum 569.89
kidney 593.89
liver 573.9
lymph nodes 785.6
ovary 620.8
prostate 602.9
spleen (see also Splenomegaly) 789.2
uterus 625.8
Palpitation (heart) 785.1
psychogenic 306.2
Palsy — see also Paralysis 344.9
atrophic diffuse 335.20
Bell's 351.0
newborn 767.5
birth 767.7
brachial plexus 353.0
fetus or newborn 767.6
brain (see also Palsy, cerebral)
noncongenital or noninfantile 344.89
late effect — see Late effect(s) (of)
cerebrovascular disease
syphilitic 094.89
congenital 090.49
bulbar (chronic) (progressive) 335.22
pseudo NEC 335.23
supranuclear NEC 344.8 ☑
cerebral (congenital) (infantile) (spastic) 343.9
athetoid 333.71
diplegic 343.0
late effect — see Late effect(s) (of)
cerebrovascular disease
hemiplegic 343.1
monoplegic 343.3
noncongenital or noninfantile 437.8
late effect — see Late effect(s) (of)
cerebrovascular disease
paraplegic 343.0
quadriplegic 343.2
spastic, not congenital or infantile 344.89
syphilitic 094.89
congenital 090.49
tetraplegic 343.2
cranial nerve (see also Disorder, nerve, cranial)
multiple 352.6
creeping 335.21
divers' 993.3
Erb's (birth injury) 767.6
facial 351.0
newborn 767.5

Palsy — see also Paralysis — continued
glossopharyngeal 352.2
Klumpke (-Déjérine) 767.6
lead 984.9
specified type of lead — see Table of Drugs
and Chemicals
median nerve (tardy) 354.0
peroneal nerve (acute) (tardy) 355.3
progressive supranuclear 333.0
pseudobulbar NEC 335.23
radial nerve (acute) 354.3
seventh nerve 351.0
newborn 767.5
shaking (see also Parkinsonism) 332.0
spastic (cerebral) (spinal) 343.9
hemiplegic 343.1
specified nerve NEC — see Disorder, nerve
supranuclear NEC 356.8
progressive 333.0
ulnar nerve (tardy) 354.2
wasting 335.21
Paltauf-Sternberg disease 201.9 ☑
Paludism — see Malaria
Panama fever 084.0
Panaris (with lymphangitis) 681.9
finger 681.02
toe 681.11
Panaritium (with lymphangitis) 681.9
finger 681.02
toe 681.11
Panarteritis (nodosa) 446.0
brain or cerebral 437.4
Pancake heart 793.2
with cor pulmonale (chronic) 416.9
Pancarditis (acute) (chronic) 429.89
with
rheumatic
fever (active) (acute) (chronic) (subacute) 391.8
inactive or quiescent 398.99
rheumatic, acute 391.8
chronic or inactive 398.99
Pancoast's syndrome or tumor (carcinoma,
pulmonary apex) (M8010/3) 162.3
Pancoast-Tobias syndrome (M8010/3) (carcinoma, pulmonary apex) 162.3
Pancolitis 556.6
Pancreas, pancreatic — see condition
Pancreatitis 577.0
acute (edematous) (hemorrhagic) (recurrent)
577.0
annular 577.0
apoplectic 577.0
calcerceous 577.0
chronic (infectious) 577.1
recurrent 577.1
cystic 577.2
fibrous 577.8
gangrenous 577.0
hemorrhagic (acute) 577.0
interstitial (chronic) 577.1
acute 577.0
malignant 577.0
mumps 072.3
painless 577.1
recurrent 577.1
relapsing 577.1
subacute 577.0
suppurative 577.0
syphilitic 095.8
Pancreatolithiasis 577.8
Pancytolysis 289.9
Pancytopenia (acquired) 284.1
with malformations 284.09
congenital 284.09
Panencephalitis — see also Encephalitis
subacute, sclerosing 046.2
Panhematopenia 284.81
congenital 284.09
constitutional 284.09
splenic, primary 289.4
Panhemocytopenia 284.81
congenital 284.09
constitutional 284.09
Panhypogonadism 257.2
Panhypopituitarism 253.2

Panhypopituitarism — continued
prepubertal 253.3
Panic (attack) (state) 300.01
reaction to exceptional stress (transient) 308.0
Panmyelopathy, familial constitutional 284.09
Panmyelophthisis 284.2
acquired (secondary) 284.81
congenital 284.2
idiopathic 284.9
Panmyelosis (acute) (M9951/1) 238.79
Panner's disease 732.3
capitellum humeri 732.3
head of humerus 732.3
tarsal navicular (bone) (osteochondrosis) 732.5
Panneuritis endemica 265.0 [357.4]
Panniculitis 729.30
back 724.8
knee 729.31
mesenteric 567.82
neck 723.6
nodular, nonsuppurative 729.30
sacral 724.8
specified site NEC 729.39
Panniculus adiposus (abdominal) 278.1
Pannus (corneal) 370.62
abdominal (symptomatic) 278.1
allergic eczematous 370.62
degenerativus 370.62
keratic 370.62
rheumatoid — see Arthritis, rheumatoid
trachomatosus, trachomatous (active)
076.1 [370.62]
late effect 139.1
Panophthalmitis 360.02
Panotitis — see Otitis media
Pansinusitis (chronic) (hyperplastic) (nonpurulent) (purulent) 473.8
acute 461.8
due to fungus NEC 117.9
tuberculous (see also Tuberculosis) 012.8 ☑
Panuveitis 360.12
sympathetic 360.11
Panvalvular disease — see Endocarditis, mitral
Papageienkrankheit 073.9
Papanicolaou smear
anus 796.70
with
atypical squamous cells
cannot exclude high grade squamous intraepithelial lesion
(ASC-H) 796.72
of undetermined significance (ASC-
US) 796.71
cytologic evidence of malignancy
796.76
high grade squamous intraepithelial
lesion (HGSIL) 796.74
low grade squamous intraepithelial lesion (LGSIL) 796.73
glandular 796.70
specified finding NEC 796.79
unsatisfactory cytology 796.78
cervix (screening test) V76.2
as part of gynecological examination
V72.31
for suspected malignant neoplasm V76.2
no disease found V71.1
inadequate cytology sample 795.08
nonspecific abnormal finding 795.00
with
atypical squamous cells
cannot exclude high grade
squamous intraepithelial
lesion (ASC-H) 795.02
of undetermined significance
(ASC-US) 795.01
cytologic evidence of malignancy
795.06
high grade squamous intraepithelial lesion (HGSIL) 795.04
low grade squamous intraepithelial
lesion (LGSIL) 795.03
nonspecific finding NEC 795.09
to confirm findings of recent normal
smear following initial abnormal smear V72.32

Papanicolaou smear — continued
cervix — continued
satisfactory smear but lacking transformation zone 795.07
unsatisfactory cervical cytology 795.08
other specified site (see also Screening, malignant neoplasm)
for suspected malignant neoplasm (see also Screening, malignant neoplasm)
no disease found V71.1
nonspecific abnormal finding 796.9
vagina V76.47
with
atypical squamous cells
cannot exclude high grade squamous intraepithelial lesion
(ASC-H) 795.12
of undetermined significance (ASC-
US) 795.11
cytologic evidence of malignancy
795.16
high grade squamous intraepithelial
lesion (HGSIL) 795.14
low grade squamous intraepithelial lesion (LGSIL) 795.13
abnormal NEC 795.19
following hysterectomy for malignant
condition V67.01
inadequate cytology sample 795.18
unsatisfactory cytology 795.18
Papilledema 377.00
associated with
decreased ocular pressure 377.02
increased intracranial pressure 377.01
retinal disorder 377.03
choked disc 377.00
infectional 377.00
Papillitis 377.31
anus 569.49
chronic lingual 529.4
necrotizing, kidney 584.7
optic 377.31
rectum 569.49
renal, necrotizing 584.7
tongue 529.0
Papilloma (M8050/0) — see also Neoplasm, by
site, benign

> Note — Except where otherwise indicated,
> the morphological varieties of papilloma in
> the list below should be coded by site as for
> "Neoplasm, benign."

acuminatum (female) (male) 078.11
bladder (urinary) (transitional cell) (M8120/1)
236.7
benign (M8120/0) 223.3
choroid plexus (M9390/0) 225.0
anaplastic type (M9390/3) 191.5
malignant (M9390/3) 191.5
ductal (M8503/0)
dyskeratotic (M8052/0)
epidermoid (M8052/0)
hyperkeratotic (M8052/0)
intracystic (M8504/0)
intraductal (M8503/0)
inverted (M8053/0)
keratotic (M8052/0)
parakeratotic (M8052/0)
pinta (primary) 103.0
renal pelvis (transitional cell) (M8120/1) 236.99
benign (M8120/0) 223.1
Schneiderian (M8121/0)
specified site — see Neoplasm, by site,
benign
unspecified site 212.0
serous surface (M8461/0)
borderline malignancy (M8461/1)
specified site — see Neoplasm, by site,
uncertain behavior
unspecified site 236.2
specified site — see Neoplasm, by site,
benign
unspecified site 220
squamous (cell) (M8052/0)
transitional (cell) (M8120/0)
bladder (urinary) (M8120/1) 236.7

Index

Papilloma — Paralysis, paralytic

Papilloma — *see also* Neoplasm, by site, benign
— *continued*
  transitional — *continued*
    inverted type (M8121/1) — *see* Neoplasm, by site, uncertain behavior
    renal pelvis (M8120/1) 236.91
    ureter (M8120/1) 236.91
    ureter (transitional cell) (M8120/1) 236.91
      benign (M8120/0) 223.2
    urothelial (M8120/1) — *see* Neoplasm, by site, uncertain behavior
    verrucous (M8051/0)
    villous (M8261/1) — *see* Neoplasm, by site, uncertain behavior
    yaws, plantar or palmar 102.1
Papillomata, multiple, of yaws 102.1
Papillomatosis (M8060/0) — *see also* Neoplasm, by site, benign
  confluent and reticulate 701.8
  cutaneous 701.8
  ductal, breast 610.1
  Gougerot-Carteaud (confluent reticulate) 701.8
  intraductal (diffuse) (M8505/0) — *see* Neoplasm, by site, benign
  subareolar duct (M8506/0) 217
Papillon-Léage and Psaume syndrome (orodigitofacial dysostosis) 759.89
Papule 709.8
  carate (primary) 103.0
  fibrous, of nose (M8724/0) 216.3
  pinta (primary) 103.0
Papulosis, malignant 447.8
Papyraceous fetus 779.89
  complicating pregnancy 646.0 ☑
Paracephalus 759.7
Parachute mitral valve 746.5
Paracoccidioidomycosis 116.1
  mucocutaneous-lymphangitic 116.1
  pulmonary 116.1
  visceral 116.1
Paracoccidiomycosis — *see* Paracoccidioidomycosis
Paracusis 388.40
Paradentosis 523.5
Paradoxical facial movements 374.43
Paraffinoma 999.9
Paraganglioma (M8680/1)
  adrenal (M8700/0) 227.0
    malignant (M8700/3) 194.0
  aortic body (M8691/1) 237.3
    malignant (M8691/3) 194.6
  carotid body (M8692/1) 237.3
    malignant (M8692/3) 194.5
  chromaffin (M8700/0) (*see also* Neoplasm, by site, benign)
    malignant (M8700/3) — *see* Neoplasm, by site, malignant
  extra-adrenal (M8693/1)
    malignant (M8693/3)
      specified site — *see* Neoplasm, by site, malignant
      unspecified site 194.6
    specified site — *see* Neoplasm, by site, uncertain behavior
    unspecified site 237.3
  glomus jugulare (M8690/1) 237.3
    malignant (M8690/3) 194.6
  jugular (M8690/1) 237.3
    malignant (M8680/3)
      specified site — *see* Neoplasm, by site, malignant
      unspecified site 194.6
  nonchromaffin (M8693/1)
    malignant (M8693/3)
      specified site — *see* Neoplasm, by site, malignant
      unspecified site 194.6
    specified site — *see* Neoplasm, by site, uncertain behavior
    unspecified site 237.3
  parasympathetic (M8682/1)
    specified site — *see* Neoplasm, by site, uncertain behavior
    unspecified site 237.3
  specified site — *see* Neoplasm, by site, uncertain behavior

Paraganglioma — *continued*
  sympathetic (M8681/1)
    specified site — *see* Neoplasm, by site, uncertain behavior
    unspecified site 237.3
  unspecified site 237.3
Parageusia 781.1
  psychogenic 306.7
Paragonimiasis 121.2
Paragranuloma, Hodgkin's (M9660/3) 201.0 ☑
Parahemophilia — *see also* Defect, coagulation 286.3
Parakeratosis 690.8
  psoriasiformis 696.2
  variegata 696.2
Paralysis, paralytic (complete) (incomplete) 344.9
  with
    broken
      back — *see* Fracture, vertebra, by site, with spinal cord injury
      neck — *see* Fracture, vertebra, cervical, with spinal cord injury
    fracture, vertebra — *see* Fracture, vertebra, by site, with spinal cord injury
  syphilis 094.89
  abdomen and back muscles 355.9
  abdominal muscles 355.9
  abducens (nerve) 378.54
  abductor 355.9
    lower extremity 355.8
    upper extremity 354.9
  accessory nerve 352.4
  accommodation 367.51
    hysterical 300.11
  acoustic nerve 388.5
  agitans 332.0
    arteriosclerotic 332.0
  alternating 344.89
    oculomotor 344.89
  amyotrophic 335.20
  ankle 355.8
  anterior serratus 355.9
  anus (sphincter) 569.49
  apoplectic (current episode) (*see also* Disease, cerebrovascular, acute) 436
    late effect — *see* Late effect(s) (of) cerebrovascular disease
  arm 344.40
    affecting
      dominant side 344.41
      nondominant side 344.42
    both 344.2
    hysterical 300.11
    late effect — *see* Late effect(s) (of) cerebrovascular disease
    psychogenic 306.0
    transient 781.4
    traumatic NEC (*see also* Injury, nerve, upper limb) 955.9
  arteriosclerotic (current episode) 437.0
    late effect — *see* Late effect(s) (of) cerebrovascular disease
  ascending (spinal), acute 357.0
  associated, nuclear 344.89
  asthenic bulbar 358.00
  ataxic NEC 334.9
    general 094.1
  athetoid 333.71
  atrophic 356.9
    infantile, acute (*see also* Poliomyelitis, with paralysis) 045.1 ☑
    muscle NEC 355.9
    progressive 335.21
    spinal (acute) (*see also* Poliomyelitis, with paralysis) 045.1 ☑
  attack (*see also* Disease, cerebrovascular, acute) 436
  axillary 353.0
  Babinski-Nageotte's 344.89
  Bell's 351.0
    newborn 767.5
  Benedikt's 344.89
  birth (injury) 767.7
    brain 767.0
    intracranial 767.0

Paralysis, paralytic — *continued*
  birth — *continued*
    spinal cord 767.4
  bladder (sphincter) 596.53
    neurogenic 596.54
      with cauda equina syndrome 344.61
    puerperal, postpartum, childbirth 665.5 ☑
    sensory 596.54
      with cauda equina 344.61
    spastic 596.54
      with cauda equina 344.61
  bowel, colon, or intestine (*see also* Ileus) 560.1
  brachial plexus 353.0
    due to birth injury 767.6
    newborn 767.6
  brain
    congenital — *see* Palsy, cerebral
    current episode 437.8
    diplegia 344.2
    hemiplegia 342.9 ☑
      late effect — *see* Late effect(s) (of) cerebrovascular disease
    infantile — *see* Palsy, cerebral
    late effect — *see* Late effect(s) (of) cerebrovascular disease
    monoplegia (*see also* Monoplegia)
      late effect — *see* Late effect(s) (of) cerebrovascular disease
    paraplegia 344.1
    quadriplegia — *see* Quadriplegia
    syphilitic, congenital 090.49
    triplegia 344.89
  bronchi 519.19
  Brown-Séquard's 344.89
  bulbar (chronic) (progressive) 335.22
    infantile (*see also* Poliomyelitis, bulbar) 045.0 ☑
    poliomyelitic (*see also* Poliomyelitis, bulbar) 045.0 ☑
    pseudo 335.23
    supranuclear 344.89
  bulbospinal 358.00
  cardiac (*see also* Failure, heart) 428.9
  cerebral
    current episode 437.8
    spastic, infantile — *see* Palsy, cerebral
  cerebrocerebellar 437.8
    diplegic infantile 343.0
  cervical
    plexus 353.2
    sympathetic NEC 337.09
  Céstan-Chenais 344.89
  Charcôt-Marie-Tooth type 356.1
  childhood — *see* Palsy, cerebral
  Clark's 343.9
  colon (*see also* Ileus) 560.1
  compressed air 993.3
  compression
    arm NEC 354.9
    cerebral — *see* Paralysis, brain
    leg NEC 355.8
    lower extremity NEC 355.8
    upper extremity NEC 354.9
  congenital (cerebral) (spastic) (spinal) — *see* Palsy, cerebral
  conjugate movement (of eye) 378.81
    cortical (nuclear) (supranuclear) 378.81
  convergence 378.83
  cordis (*see also* Failure, heart) 428.9
  cortical (*see also* Paralysis, brain) 437.8
  cranial or cerebral nerve (*see also* Disorder, nerve, cranial) 352.9
  creeping 335.21
  crossed leg 344.89
  crutch 953.4
  deglutition 784.99
    hysterical 300.11
  dementia 094.1
  descending (spinal) NEC 335.9
  diaphragm (flaccid) 519.4
    due to accidental section of phrenic nerve during procedure 998.2
  digestive organs NEC 564.89
  diplegic — *see* Diplegia
  divergence (nuclear) 378.85
  divers' 993.3

Paralysis, paralytic — *continued*
  Duchenne's 335.22
  due to intracranial or spinal birth injury — *see* Palsy, cerebral
  embolic (current episode) (*see also* Embolism, brain) 434.1 ☑
    late effect — *see* Late effect(s) (of) cerebrovascular disease
  enteric (*see also* Ileus) 560.1
    with hernia — *see* Hernia, by site, with obstruction
  Erb (-Duchenne) (birth) (newborn) 767.6
  Erb's syphilitic spastic spinal 094.89
  esophagus 530.89
  essential, infancy (*see also* Poliomyelitis) 045.9 ☑
  extremity
    lower — *see* Paralysis, leg
    spastic (hereditary) 343.3
      noncongenital or noninfantile 344.1
    transient (cause unknown) 781.4
    upper — *see* Paralysis, arm
  eye muscle (extrinsic) 378.55
    intrinsic 367.51
  facial (nerve) 351.0
    birth injury 767.5
    congenital 767.5
    following operation NEC 998.2
    newborn 767.5
  familial 359.3
    periodic 359.3
    spastic 334.1
  fauces 478.29
  finger NEC 354.9
  foot NEC 355.8
  gait 781.2
  gastric nerve 352.3
  gaze 378.81
  general 094.1
    ataxic 094.1
    insane 094.1
    juvenile 090.40
    progressive 094.1
    tabetic 094.1
  glossopharyngeal (nerve) 352.2
  glottis (*see also* Paralysis, vocal cord) 478.30
  gluteal 353.4
  Gubler (-Millard) 344.89
  hand 354.9
    hysterical 300.11
    psychogenic 306.0
  heart (*see also* Failure, heart) 428.9
  hemifacial, progressive 349.89
  hemiplegic — *see* Hemiplegia
  hyperkalemic periodic (familial) 359.3
  hypertensive (current episode) 437.8
  hypoglossal (nerve) 352.5
  hypokalemic periodic 359.3
  Hyrtl's sphincter (rectum) 569.49
  hysterical 300.11
  ileus (*see also* Ileus) 560.1
  infantile (*see also* Poliomyelitis) 045.9 ☑
    atrophic acute 045.1 ☑
    bulbar 045.0 ☑
    cerebral — *see* Palsy, cerebral
    paralytic 045.1 ☑
    progressive acute 045.9 ☑
    spastic — *see* Palsy, cerebral
    spinal 045.9 ☑
  infective (*see also* Poliomyelitis) 045.9 ☑
  inferior nuclear 344.9
  insane, general or progressive 094.1
  internuclear 378.86
  interosseous 355.9
  intestine (*see also* Ileus) 560.1
  intracranial (current episode) (*see also* Paralysis, brain) 437.8
    due to birth injury 767.0
  iris 379.49
    due to diphtheria (toxin) 032.81 *[379.49]*
  ischemic, Volkmann's (complicating trauma) 958.6
  isolated sleep, recurrent
  Jackson's 344.89
  jake 357.7
  Jamaica ginger (jake) 357.7

Paralysis, paralytic — *continued*
juvenile general 090.40
Klumpke (-Déjérine) (birth) (newborn) 767.6
labioglossal (laryngeal) (pharyngeal) 335.22
Landry's 357.0
laryngeal nerve (recurrent) (superior) (*see also* Paralysis, vocal cord) 478.30
larynx (*see also* Paralysis, vocal cord) 478.30
due to diphtheria (toxin) 032.3
late effect
due to
birth injury, brain or spinal (cord) — *see* Palsy, cerebral
edema, brain or cerebral — *see* Paralysis, brain
lesion
late effect — *see* Late effect(s) (of) cerebrovascular disease
spinal (cord) — *see* Paralysis, spinal
lateral 335.24
lead 984.9
specified type of lead — *see* Table of Drugs and Chemicals
left side — *see* Hemiplegia
leg 344.30
affecting
dominant side 344.31
nondominant side 344.32
both (*see also* Paraplegia) 344.1
crossed 344.89
hysterical 300.11
psychogenic 306.0
transient or transitory 781.4
traumatic NEC (*see also* Injury, nerve, lower limb) 956.9
levator palpebrae superioris 374.31
limb NEC 344.5
all four — *see* Quadriplegia
quadriplegia — *see* Quadriplegia
lip 528.5
Lissauer's 094.1
local 355.9
lower limb (*see also* Paralysis, leg)
both (*see also* Paraplegia) 344.1
lung 518.89
newborn 770.89
median nerve 354.1
medullary (tegmental) 344.89
mesencephalic NEC 344.89
tegmental 344.89
middle alternating 344.89
Millard-Gubler-Foville 344.89
monoplegic — *see* Monoplegia
motor NEC 344.9
cerebral — *see* Paralysis, brain
spinal — *see* Paralysis, spinal
multiple
cerebral — *see* Paralysis, brain
spinal — *see* Paralysis, spinal
muscle (flaccid) 359.9
due to nerve lesion NEC 355.9
eye (extrinsic) 378.55
intrinsic 367.51
oblique 378.51
iris sphincter 364.89
ischemic (complicating trauma) (Volkmann's) 958.6
pseudohypertrophic 359.1
muscular (atrophic) 359.9
progressive 335.21
musculocutaneous nerve 354.9
musculospiral 354.9
nerve (*see also* Disorder, nerve)
third or oculomotor (partial) 378.51
total 378.52
fourth or trochlear 378.53
sixth or abducens 378.54
seventh or facial 351.0
birth injury 767.5
due to
injection NEC 999.9
operation NEC 997.09
newborn 767.5
accessory 352.4
auditory 388.5
birth injury 767.7

Paralysis, paralytic — *continued*
nerve (*see also* Disorder, nerve) — *continued*
cranial or cerebral (*see also* Disorder, nerve, cranial) 352.9
facial 351.0
birth injury 767.5
newborn 767.5
laryngeal (*see also* Paralysis, vocal cord) 478.30
newborn 767.7
phrenic 354.8
newborn 767.7
radial 354.3
birth injury 767.6
newborn 767.6
syphilitic 094.89
traumatic NEC (*see also* Injury, nerve, by site) 957.9
trigeminal 350.9
ulnar 354.2
newborn NEC 767.0
normokalemic periodic 359.3
obstetrical, newborn 767.7
ocular 378.9
oculofacial, congenital 352.6
oculomotor (nerve) (partial) 378.51
alternating 344.89
external bilateral 378.55
total 378.52
olfactory nerve 352.0
palate 528.9
palatopharyngolaryngeal 352.6
paratrigeminal 350.9
periodic (familial) (hyperkalemic) (hypokalemic) (normokalemic) (potassium sensitive) (secondary) 359.3
peripheral
autonomic nervous system — *see* Neuropathy, peripheral, autonomic
nerve NEC 355.9
peroneal (nerve) 355.3
pharynx 478.29
phrenic nerve 354.8
plantar nerves 355.6
pneumogastric nerve 352.3
poliomyelitis (current) (*see also* Poliomyelitis, with paralysis) 045.1 ☑
bulbar 045.0 ☑
popliteal nerve 355.3
pressure (*see also* Neuropathy, entrapment) 355.9
progressive 335.21
atrophic 335.21
bulbar 335.22
general 094.1
hemifacial 349.89
infantile, acute (*see also* Poliomyelitis) 045.9 ☑
multiple 335.20
pseudobulbar 335.23
pseudohypertrophic 359.1
muscle 359.1
psychogenic 306.0
pupil, pupillary 379.49
quadriceps 355.8
quadriplegic (*see also* Quadriplegia) 344.0 ☑
radial nerve 354.3
birth injury 767.6
rectum (sphincter) 569.49
rectus muscle (eye) 378.55
recurrent
isolated sleep 327.43
laryngeal nerve (*see also* Paralysis, vocal cord) 478.30
respiratory (muscle) (system) (tract) 786.09
center NEC 344.89
fetus or newborn 770.87
congenital 768.9
newborn 768.9
right side — *see* Hemiplegia
Saturday night 354.3
saturnine 984.9
specified type of lead — *see* Table of Drugs and Chemicals
sciatic nerve 355.0

Paralysis, paralytic — *continued*
secondary — *see* Paralysis, late effect
seizure (cerebral) (current episode) (*see also* Disease, cerebrovascular, acute) 436
late effect — *see* Late effect(s) (of) cerebrovascular disease
senile NEC 344.9
serratus magnus 355.9
shaking (*see also* Parkinsonism) 332.0
shock (*see also* Disease, cerebrovascular, acute) 436
late effect — *see* Late effect(s) (of) cerebrovascular disease
shoulder 354.9
soft palate 528.9
spasmodic — *see* Paralysis, spastic
spastic 344.9
cerebral infantile — *see* Palsy, cerebral
congenital (cerebral) — *see* Palsy, cerebral
familial 334.1
hereditary 334.1
infantile 343.9
noncongenital or noninfantile, cerebral 344.9
syphilitic 094.0
spinal 094.89
sphincter, bladder (*see also* Paralysis, bladder) 596.53
spinal (cord) NEC 344.1
accessory nerve 352.4
acute (*see also* Poliomyelitis) 045.9 ☑
ascending acute 357.0
atrophic (acute) (*see also* Poliomyelitis, with paralysis) 045.1 ☑
spastic, syphilitic 094.89
congenital NEC 343.9
hemiplegic — *see* Hemiplegia
hereditary 336.8
infantile (*see also* Poliomyelitis) 045.9 ☑
late effect NEC 344.89
monoplegic — *see* Monoplegia
nerve 355.9
progressive 335.10
quadriplegic — *see* Quadriplegia
spastic NEC 343.9
traumatic — *see* Injury, spinal, by site
sternomastoid 352.4
stomach 536.3
diabetic 250.6 ☑ *[536.3]*
due to secondary diabetes 249.6 ☑ *[536.3]*
nerve (nondiabetic) 352.3
stroke (current episode) — *see* Infarct, brain
late effect — *see* Late effect(s) (of) cerebrovascular disease
subscapularis 354.8
superior nuclear NEC 334.9
supranuclear 356.8
sympathetic
cervical NEC 337.09
nerve NEC (*see also* Neuropathy, peripheral, autonomic) 337.9
nervous system — *see* Neuropathy, peripheral, autonomic
syndrome 344.9
specified NEC 344.89
syphilitic spastic spinal (Erb's) 094.89
tabetic general 094.1
thigh 355.8
throat 478.29
diphtheritic 032.0
muscle 478.29
thrombotic (current episode) (*see also* Thrombosis, brain) 434.0 ☑
late effect — *see* Late effect(s) (of) cerebrovascular disease
thumb NEC 354.9
tick (-bite) 989.5
Todd's (postepileptic transitory paralysis) 344.89
toe 355.6
tongue 529.8
transient
arm or leg NEC 781.4
traumatic NEC (*see also* Injury, nerve, by site) 957.9

Paralysis, paralytic — *continued*
trapezius 352.4
traumatic, transient NEC (*see also* Injury, nerve, by site) 957.9
trembling (*see also* Parkinsonism) 332.0
triceps brachii 354.9
trigeminal nerve 350.9
trochlear nerve 378.53
ulnar nerve 354.2
upper limb (*see also* Paralysis, arm)
both (*see also* Diplegia) 344.2
uremic — *see* Uremia
uveoparotitic 135
uvula 528.9
hysterical 300.11
postdiphtheritic 032.0
vagus nerve 352.3
vasomotor NEC 337.9
velum palati 528.9
vesical (*see also* Paralysis, bladder) 596.53
vestibular nerve 388.5
visual field, psychic 368.16
vocal cord 478.30
bilateral (partial) 478.33
complete 478.34
complete (bilateral) 478.34
unilateral (partial) 478.31
complete 478.32
Volkmann's (complicating trauma) 958.6
wasting 335.21
Weber's 344.89
wrist NEC 354.9
Paramedial orifice, urethrovesical 753.8
Paramenia 626.9
Parametritis (chronic) — *see also* Disease, pelvis, inflammatory 614.4
acute 614.3
puerperal, postpartum, childbirth 670.8 ☑ ▲
Parametrium, parametric — *see* condition
Paramnesia — *see also* Amnesia 780.93
Paramolar 520.1
causing crowding 524.31
Paramyloidosis 277.30
Paramyoclonus multiplex 333.2
Paramyotonia 359.29
congenita (of von Eulenburg) 359.29
Paraneoplastic syndrome — *see* condition
Parangi — *see also* Yaws 102.9
Paranoia 297.1
alcoholic 291.5
querulans 297.8
senile 290.20
Paranoid
dementia (*see also* Schizophrenia) 295.3 ☑
praecox (acute) 295.3 ☑
senile 290.20
personality 301.0
psychosis 297.9
alcoholic 291.5
climacteric 297.2
drug-induced 292.11
involutional 297.2
menopausal 297.2
protracted reactive 298.4
psychogenic 298.4
acute 298.3
senile 290.20
reaction (chronic) 297.9
acute 298.3
schizophrenia (acute) (*see also* Schizophrenia) 295.3 ☑
state 297.9
alcohol-induced 291.5
climacteric 297.2
drug-induced 292.11
due to or associated with
arteriosclerosis (cerebrovascular) 290.42
presenile brain disease 290.12
senile brain disease 290.20
involutional 297.2
menopausal 297.2
senile 290.20
simple 297.0
specified type NEC 297.8

☑ Additional Digit Required — Refer to the Tabular List for Digit Selection

Subterms under main terms may continue to next column or page

Index

Paranoid — Pelviperitonitis

Paranoid — *continued*
 tendencies 301.0
 traits 301.0
 trends 301.0
 type, psychopathic personality 301.0
Paraparesis — *see also* Paraplegia 344.1
Paraphasia 784.3
Paraphilia — *see also* Deviation, sexual 302.9
Paraphimosis (congenital) 605
 chancroidal 099.0
Paraphrenia, paraphrenic (late) 297.2
 climacteric 297.2
 dementia (*see also* Schizophrenia) 295.3 ☑
 involutional 297.2
 menopausal 297.2
 schizophrenia (acute) (*see also* Schizophrenia)
  295.3 ☑
Paraplegia 344.1
 with
  broken back — *see* Fracture, vertebra, by
   site, with spinal cord injury
  fracture, vertebra — *see* Fracture, vertebra,
   by site, with spinal cord injury
 ataxic — *see* Degeneration, combined, spinal
  cord
 brain (current episode) (*see also* Paralysis,
  brain) 437.8
 cerebral (current episode) (*see also* Paralysis,
  brain) 437.8
 congenital or infantile (cerebral) (spastic)
  (spinal) 343.0
 cortical — *see* Paralysis, brain
 familial spastic 334.1
 functional (hysterical) 300.11
 hysterical 300.11
 infantile 343.0
 late effect 344.1
 Pott's (*see also* Tuberculosis) 015.0 ☑ *[730.88]*
 psychogenic 306.0
 spastic
  Erb's spinal 094.89
  hereditary 334.1
  not infantile or congenital 344.1
 spinal (cord)
  traumatic NEC — *see* Injury, spinal, by site
 syphilitic (spastic) 094.89
 traumatic NEC — *see* Injury, spinal, by site
Paraproteinemia 273.2
 benign (familial) 273.1
 monoclonal 273.1
 secondary to malignant or inflammatory disease 273.1
Parapsoriasis 696.2
 en plaques 696.2
 guttata 696.2
 lichenoides chronica 696.2
 retiformis 696.2
 varioliformis (acuta) 696.2
Parascarlatina 057.8
Parasitic — *see also* condition
 disease NEC (*see also* Infestation, parasitic)
  136.9
  contact V01.89
  exposure to V01.89
  intestinal NEC 129
  skin NEC 134.9
 stomatitis 112.0
 sycosis 110.0
  beard 110.0
  scalp 110.0
 twin 759.4
Parasitism NEC 136.9
 intestinal NEC 129
 skin NEC 134.9
 specified — *see* Infestation
Parasitophobia 300.29
Parasomnia 307.47
 alcohol induced 291.82
 drug induced 292.85
 nonorganic origin 307.47
 organic 327.40
  in conditions classified elsewhere 327.44
 other 327.49
Paraspadias 752.69
Paraspasm facialis 351.8
Parathyroid gland — *see* condition

Parathyroiditis (autoimmune) 252.1
Parathyroprival tetany 252.1
Paratrachoma 077.0
Paratyphilitis — *see also* Appendicitis 541
Paratyphoid (fever) — *see* Fever, paratyphoid
Paratyphus — *see* Fever, paratyphoid
Paraurethral duct 753.8
Para-urethritis 597.89
 gonococcal (acute) 098.0
  chronic or duration of 2 months or over
   098.2
Paravaccinia NEC 051.9
 milkers' node 051.1
Paravaginitis — *see also* Vaginitis 616.10
Parencephalitis — *see also* Encephalitis 323.9
 late effect — *see* category 326
Parergasia 298.9
Paresis — *see also* Paralysis 344.9
 accommodation 367.51
 bladder (spastic) (sphincter) (*see also* Paralysis,
  bladder) 596.53
  tabetic 094.0
 bowel, colon, or intestine (*see also* Ileus) 560.1
 brain or cerebral — *see* Paralysis, brain
 extrinsic muscle, eye 378.55
 general 094.1
  arrested 094.1
  brain 094.1
  cerebral 094.1
  insane 094.1
  juvenile 090.40
   remission 090.49
  progressive 094.1
  remission (sustained) 094.1
  tabetic 094.1
 heart (*see also* Failure, heart) 428.9
 infantile (*see also* Poliomyelitis) 045.9 ☑
 insane 094.1
 juvenile 090.40
 late effect — *see* Paralysis, late effect
 luetic (general) 094.1
 peripheral progressive 356.9
 pseudohypertrophic 359.1
 senile NEC 344.9
 stomach 536.3
  diabetic 250.6 ☑ *[536.3]*
   due to secondary diabetes
    249.6 ☑ *[536.3]*
 syphilitic (general) 094.1
  congenital 090.40
 transient, limb 781.4
 vesical (sphincter) NEC 596.53
Paresthesia — *see also* Disturbance, sensation
  782.0
 Berger's (paresthesia of lower limb) 782.0
 Bernhardt 355.1
 Magnan's 782.0
Paretic — *see* condition
Parinaud's
 conjunctivitis 372.02
 oculoglandular syndrome 372.02
 ophthalmoplegia 378.81
 syndrome (paralysis of conjugate upward
  gaze) 378.81
Parkes Weber and Dimitri syndrome (encephalocutaneous angiomatosis) 759.6
Parkinson's disease, syndrome, or tremor —
  see Parkinsonism
Parkinsonism (arteriosclerotic) (idiopathic) (primary) 332.0
 associated with orthostatic hypotension (idiopathic) (symptomatic) 333.0
 due to drugs 332.1
 neuroleptic-induced 332.1
 secondary 332.1
 syphilitic 094.82
Parodontitis 523.40
Parodontosis 523.5
Paronychia (with lymphangitis) 681.9
 candidal (chronic) 112.3
 chronic 681.9
  candidal 112.3
  finger 681.02
  toe 681.11
 finger 681.02
 toe 681.11

Paronychia — *continued*
 tuberculous (primary) (*see also* Tuberculosis)
  017.0 ☑
Parorexia NEC 307.52
 hysterical 300.11
Parosmia 781.1
 psychogenic 306.7
Parotid gland — *see* condition
Parotiditis — *see also* Parotitis 527.2
 epidemic 072.9
 infectious 072.9
Parotitis 527.2
 allergic 527.2
 chronic 527.2
 epidemic (*see also* Mumps) 072.9
 infectious (*see also* Mumps) 072.9
 noninfectious 527.2
 nonspecific toxic 527.2
 not mumps 527.2
 postoperative 527.2
 purulent 527.2
 septic 527.2
 suppurative (acute) 527.2
 surgical 527.2
 toxic 527.2
Paroxysmal — *see also* condition
 dyspnea (nocturnal) 786.09
Parrot's disease (syphilitic osteochondritis) 090.0
Parrot fever 073.9
Parry's disease or syndrome (exophthalmic
  goiter) 242.0 ☑
Parry-Romberg syndrome 349.89
Parsonage-Aldren-Turner syndrome 353.5
Parsonage-Turner syndrome 353.5
Parson's disease (exophthalmic goiter) 242.0 ☑
Pars planitis 363.21
Particolored infant 757.39
Parturition — *see* Delivery
Parvovirus 079.83
 B19 079.83
 human 079.83
Passage
 false, urethra 599.4
 meconium noted during delivery 763.84
 of sounds or bougies (*see also* Attention to ar-
  tificial opening) V55.9
Passive — *see* condition
Pasteurella septica 027.2
Pasteurellosis — *see also* Infection, Pasteurella
  027.2
PAT (paroxysmal atrial tachycardia) 427.0
Patau's syndrome (trisomy D1) 758.1
Patch
 herald 696.3
Patches
 mucous (syphilitic) 091.3
  congenital 090.0
 smokers' (mouth) 528.6
Patellar — *see* condition
Patellofemoral syndrome 719.46
Patent — *see also* Imperfect closure
 atrioventricular ostium 745.69
 canal of Nuck 752.41
 cervix 622.5
  complicating pregnancy 654.5 ☑
  affecting fetus or newborn 761.0
 ductus arteriosus or Botalli 747.0
 Eustachian
  tube 381.7
  valve 746.89
 foramen
  Botalli 745.5
  ovale 745.5
 interauricular septum 745.5
 interventricular septum 745.4
 omphalomesenteric duct 751.0
 os (uteri) — *see* Patent, cervix
 ostium secundum 745.5
 urachus 753.7
 vitelline duct 751.0
Paternity testing V70.4
Paterson-Kelly syndrome or web (sideropenic
  dysphagia) 280.8
Paterson (-Brown) (-Kelly) syndrome
  (sideropenic dysphagia) 280.8

Paterson's syndrome (sideropenic dysphagia)
  280.8
Pathologic, pathological — *see also* condition
 asphyxia 799.01
 drunkenness 291.4
 emotionality 301.3
 fracture — *see* Fracture, pathologic
 liar 301.7
 personality 301.9
 resorption, tooth 521.40
  external 521.42
  internal 521.41
  specified NEC 521.49
 sexuality (*see also* Deviation, sexual) 302.9
Pathology (of) — *see also* Disease
 periradicular, associated with previous endodontic treatment 526.69
Patterned motor discharge, idiopathic — *see*
  also Epilepsy 345.5 ☑
Patulous — *see also* Patent
 anus 569.49
 Eustachian tube 381.7
Pause, sinoatrial 427.81
Pavor nocturnus 307.46
Pavy's disease 593.6
Paxton's disease (white piedra) 111.2
Payr's disease or syndrome (splenic flexure
  syndrome) 569.89
PBA (pseudobulbar affect) 310.8
Pearls
 Elschnig 366.51
 enamel 520.2
Pearl-workers' disease (chronic osteomyelitis)
  — *see also* Osteomyelitis 730.1 ☑
Pectenitis 569.49
Pectenosis 569.49
Pectoral — *see* condition
Pectus
 carinatum (congenital) 754.82
  acquired 738.3
  rachitic (*see also* Rickets) 268.0
 excavatum (congenital) 754.81
  acquired 738.3
  rachitic (*see also* Rickets) 268.0
 recurvatum (congenital) 754.81
  acquired 738.3
Pedatrophia 261
Pederosis 302.2
Pediculosis (infestation) 132.9
 capitis (head louse) (any site) 132.0
 corporis (body louse) (any site) 132.1
 eyelid 132.0 *[373.6]*
 mixed (classifiable to more than one category
  in 132.0–132.2) 132.3
 pubis (pubic louse) (any site) 132.2
 vestimenti 132.1
 vulvae 132.2
Pediculus (infestation) — *see* Pediculosis
Pedophilia 302.2
Peg-shaped teeth 520.2
Pelade 704.01
Pel's crisis 094.0
Pel-Ebstein disease — *see* Disease, Hodgkin's
Pelger-Huët anomaly or syndrome (hereditary
  hyposegmentation) 288.2
Peliosis (rheumatica) 287.0
Pelizaeus-Merzbacher
 disease 330.0
 sclerosis, diffuse cerebral 330.0
Pellagra (alcoholic or with alcoholism) 265.2
 with polyneuropathy 265.2 *[357.4]*
Pellagra-cerebellar-ataxia-renal
  aminoaciduria syndrome 270.0
Pellegrini's disease (calcification, knee joint)
  726.62
Pellegrini (-Stieda) disease or syndrome (cal-
  cification, knee joint) 726.62
Pellizzi's syndrome (pineal) 259.8
Pelvic — *see also* condition
 congestion-fibrosis syndrome 625.5
 kidney 753.3
Pelvioectasis 591
Pelviolithiasis 592.0
Pelviperitonitis
 female (*see also* Peritonitis, pelvic, female)
  614.5

☑ Additional Digit Required — Refer to the Tabular List for Digit Selection   ▽ Subterms under main terms may continue to next column or page

216 — Volume 2   ▶◀ Revised Text   ● New Line   ▲ Revised Code   **2010 ICD-9-CM**

Pelviperitonitis — *continued*
  male (*see also* Peritonitis) 567.21
Pelvis, pelvic — *see also* condition or type
  infantile 738.6
  Nägele's 738.6
  obliquity 738.6
  Robert's 755.69
Pemphigoid 694.5
  benign, mucous membrane 694.60
    with ocular involvement 694.61
  bullous 694.5
  cicatricial 694.60
    with ocular involvement 694.61
  juvenile 694.2
Pemphigus 694.4
  benign 694.5
    chronic familial 757.39
  Brazilian 694.4
  circinatus 694.0
  congenital, traumatic 757.39
  conjunctiva 694.61
  contagiosus 684
  erythematodes 694.4
  erythematosus 694.4
  foliaceus 694.4
  frambesiodes 694.4
  gangrenous (*see also* Gangrene) 785.4
  malignant 694.4
  neonatorum, newborn 684
  ocular 694.61
  papillaris 694.4
  seborrheic 694.4
  South American 694.4
  syphilitic (congenital) 090.0
  vegetans 694.4
  vulgaris 694.4
  wildfire 694.4
Pendred's syndrome (familial goiter with deaf-mutism) 243
Pendulous
  abdomen 701.9
    in pregnancy or childbirth 654.4 ☑
      affecting fetus or newborn 763.89
  breast 611.89
Penetrating wound — *see also* Wound, open, by site
  with internal injury — *see* Injury, internal, by site, with open wound
  eyeball 871.7
    with foreign body (nonmagnetic) 871.6
      magnetic 871.5
  ocular (*see also* Penetrating wound, eyeball) 871.7
    adnexa 870.3
      with foreign body 870.4
    orbit 870.3
      with foreign body 870.4
Penetration, pregnant uterus by instrument
  with
    abortion — *see* Abortion, by type, with damage to pelvic organs
    ectopic pregnancy (*see also* categories 633.0–633.9) 639.2
    molar pregnancy (*see also* categories 630–632) 639.2
  complication of delivery 665.1 ☑
    affecting fetus or newborn 763.89
  following
    abortion 639.2
    ectopic or molar pregnancy 639.2
Penfield's syndrome — *see also* Epilepsy 345.5 ☑
Penicilliosis of lung 117.3
Penis — *see* condition
Penitis 607.2
Pentalogy (of Fallot) 745.2
Penta X syndrome 758.81
Pentosuria (benign) (essential) 271.8
Peptic acid disease 536.8
Peregrinating patient V65.2
Perforated — *see* Perforation
Perforation, perforative (nontraumatic)
  antrum (*see also* Sinusitis, maxillary) 473.0
  appendix 540.0
    with peritoneal abscess 540.1
  atrial septum, multiple 745.5

Perforation, perforative — *continued*
  attic, ear 384.22
    healed 384.81
  bile duct, except cystic (*see also* Disease, biliary) 576.3
    cystic 575.4
  bladder (urinary) 596.6
    with
      abortion — *see* Abortion, by type, with damage to pelvic organs
      ectopic pregnancy (*see also* categories 633.0–633.9) 639.2
      molar pregnancy (*see also* categories 630–632) 639.2
    following
      abortion 639.2
      ectopic or molar pregnancy 639.2
    obstetrical trauma 665.5 ☑
  bowel 569.83
    with
      abortion — *see* Abortion, by type, with damage to pelvic organs
      ectopic pregnancy (*see also* categories 633.0–633.9) 639.2
      molar pregnancy (*see also* categories 630–632) 639.2
    fetus or newborn 777.6
    following
      abortion 639.2
      ectopic or molar pregnancy 639.2
    obstetrical trauma 665.5 ☑
  broad ligament
    with
      abortion — *see* Abortion, by type, with damage to pelvic organs
      ectopic pregnancy (*see also* categories 633.0–633.9) 639.2
      molar pregnancy (*see also* categories 630–632) 639.2
    following
      abortion 639.2
      ectopic or molar pregnancy 639.2
    obstetrical trauma 665.6 ☑
  by
    device, implant, or graft — *see* Complications, mechanical
    foreign body left accidentally in operation wound 998.4
    instrument (any) during a procedure, accidental 998.2
  cecum 540.0
    with peritoneal abscess 540.1
  cervix (uteri) (*see also* Injury, internal, cervix)
    with
      abortion — *see* Abortion, by type, with damage to pelvic organs
      ectopic pregnancy (*see also* categories 633.0–633.9) 639.2
      molar pregnancy (*see also* categories 630–632) 639.2
    following
      abortion 639.2
      ectopic or molar pregnancy 639.2
    obstetrical trauma 665.3 ☑
  colon 569.83
  common duct (bile) 576.3
  cornea (*see also* Ulcer, cornea) 370.00
    due to ulceration 370.06
  cystic duct 575.4
  diverticulum (*see also* Diverticula) 562.10
    small intestine 562.00
  duodenum, duodenal (ulcer) — *see* Ulcer, duodenum, with perforation
  ear drum — *see* Perforation, tympanum
  enteritis — *see* Enteritis
  esophagus 530.4
  ethmoidal sinus (*see also* Sinusitis, ethmoidal) 473.2
  foreign body (external site) (*see also* Wound, open, by site, complicated)
    internal site, by ingested object — *see* Foreign body
  frontal sinus (*see also* Sinusitis, frontal) 473.1
  gallbladder or duct (*see also* Disease, gallbladder) 575.4

Perforation, perforative — *continued*
  gastric (ulcer) — *see* Ulcer, stomach, with perforation
  heart valve — *see* Endocarditis
  ileum (*see also* Perforation, intestine) 569.83
  instrumental
    external — *see* Wound, open, by site
    pregnant uterus, complicating delivery 665.9 ☑
    surgical (accidental) (blood vessel) (nerve) (organ) 998.2
  intestine 569.83
    with
      abortion — *see* Abortion, by type, with damage to pelvic organs
      ectopic pregnancy (*see also* categories 633.0–633.9) 639.2
      molar pregnancy (*see also* categories 630–632) 639.2
    fetus or newborn 777.6
    obstetrical trauma 665.5 ☑
    ulcerative NEC 569.83
  jejunum, jejunal 569.83
    ulcer — *see* Ulcer, gastrojejunal, with perforation
  mastoid (antrum) (cell) 383.89
  maxillary sinus (*see also* Sinusitis, maxillary) 473.0
  membrana tympani — *see* Perforation, tympanum
  nasal
    septum 478.19
      congenital 748.1
      syphilitic 095.8
    sinus (*see also* Sinusitis) 473.9
      congenital 748.1
  palate (hard) 526.89
    soft 528.9
      syphilitic 095.8
        syphilitic 095.8
  palatine vault 526.89
    syphilitic 095.8
      congenital 090.5
  pelvic
    floor
      with
        abortion — *see* Abortion, by type, with damage to pelvic organs
        ectopic pregnancy (*see also* categories 633.0–633.9) 639.2
        molar pregnancy (*see also* categories 630–632) 639.2
      obstetrical trauma 664.1 ☑
    organ
      with
        abortion — *see* Abortion, by type, with damage to pelvic organs
        ectopic pregnancy (*see also* categories 633.0–633.9) 639.2
        molar pregnancy (*see also* categories 630–632) 639.2
      following
        abortion 639.2
        ectopic or molar pregnancy 639.2
      obstetrical trauma 665.5 ☑
  perineum — *see* Laceration, perineum
  periurethral tissue
    with
      abortion — *see* Abortion, by type, with damage to pelvic organs
      ectopic pregnancy (*see also* categories 633.0–633.9) 639.2
      molar pregnancy (*see also* categories 630–632) 639.2
  pharynx 478.29
  pylorus, pyloric (ulcer) — *see* Ulcer, stomach, with perforation
  rectum 569.49
  root canal space 526.61
  sigmoid 569.83
  sinus (accessory) (chronic) (nasal) (*see also* Sinusitis) 473.9
  sphenoidal sinus (*see also* Sinusitis, sphenoidal) 473.3

Perforation, perforative — *continued*
  stomach (due to ulcer) — *see* Ulcer, stomach, with perforation
  surgical (accidental) (by instrument) (blood vessel) (nerve) (organ) 998.2
  traumatic
    external — *see* Wound, open, by site
    eye (*see also* Penetrating wound, ocular) 871.7
    internal organ — *see* Injury, internal, by site
    tympanum (membrane) (persistent posttraumatic) (postinflammatory) 384.20
      with
        otitis media — *see* Otitis media
      attic 384.22
      central 384.21
      healed 384.81
      marginal NEC 384.23
      multiple 384.24
      pars flaccida 384.22
      total 384.25
      traumatic — *see* Wound, open, ear, drum
    typhoid, gastrointestinal 002.0
    ulcer — *see* Ulcer, by site, with perforation
  ureter 593.89
  urethra
    with
      abortion — *see* Abortion, by type, with damage to pelvic organs
      ectopic pregnancy (*see also* categories 633.0–633.9) 639.2
      molar pregnancy (*see also* categories 630–632) 639.2
    following
      abortion 639.2
      ectopic or molar pregnancy 639.2
    obstetrical trauma 665.5 ☑
  uterus (*see also* Injury, internal, uterus)
    with
      abortion — *see* Abortion, by type, with damage to pelvic organs
      ectopic pregnancy (*see also* categories 633.0–633.9) 639.2
      molar pregnancy (*see also* categories 630–632) 639.2
    by intrauterine contraceptive device 996.32
    following
      abortion 639.2
      ectopic or molar pregnancy 639.2
    obstetrical trauma — *see* Injury, internal, uterus, obstetrical trauma
  uvula 528.9
    syphilitic 095.8
  vagina — *see* Laceration, vagina
  viscus NEC 799.89
    traumatic 868.00
      with open wound into cavity 868.10
Periadenitis mucosa necrotica recurrens 528.2
Periangiitis 446.0
Periantritis 535.4 ☑
Periappendicitis (acute) — *see also* Appendicitis 541
Periarteritis (disseminated) (infectious) (necrotizing) (nodosa) 446.0
Periarthritis (joint) 726.90
  Duplay's 726.2
  gonococcal 098.50
  humeroscapularis 726.2
  scapulohumeral 726.2
  shoulder 726.2
  wrist 726.4
Periarthrosis (angioneural) — *see* Periarthritis
Peribronchitis 491.9
  tuberculous (*see also* Tuberculosis) 011.3 ☑
Pericapsulitis, adhesive (shoulder) 726.0
Pericarditis (granular) (with decompensation) (with effusion) 423.9
  with
    rheumatic fever (conditions classifiable to 390)
      active (*see also* Pericarditis, rheumatic) 391.0
      inactive or quiescent 393
  actinomycotic 039.8 *[420.0]*
  acute (nonrheumatic) 420.90

☑ Additional Digit Required — Refer to the Tabular List for Digit Selection   ▽ Subterms under main terms may continue to next column or page

2010 ICD-9-CM   ▶◀ Revised Text   ● New Line   ▲ Revised Code   **Volume 2 — 217**

Pericarditis — continued
  acute — continued
    with chorea (acute) (rheumatic) (Syden-
      ham's) 392.0
    bacterial 420.99
    benign 420.91
    hemorrhagic 420.90
    idiopathic 420.91
    infective 420.90
    nonspecific 420.91
    rheumatic 391.0
      with chorea (acute) (rheumatic)
        (Sydenham's) 392.0
    sicca 420.90
    viral 420.91
  adhesive or adherent (external) (internal) 423.1
    acute — see Pericarditis, acute
    rheumatic (external) (internal) 393
  amebic 006.8 [420.0]
  bacterial (acute) (subacute) (with serous or
    seropurulent effusion) 420.99
  calcareous 423.2
  cholesterol (chronic) 423.8
    acute 420.90
  chronic (nonrheumatic) 423.8
    rheumatic 393
  constrictive 423.2
  Coxsackie 074.21
  due to
    actinomycosis 039.8 [420.0]
    amebiasis 006.8 [420.0]
    Coxsackie (virus) 074.21
    histoplasmosis (see also Histoplasmosis)
      115.93
    nocardiosis 039.8 [420.0]
    tuberculosis (see also Tuberculosis)
      017.9 ☑ [420.0]
  fibrinocaseous (see also Tuberculosis)
    017.9 ☑ [420.0]
  fibrinopurulent 420.99
  fibrinous — see Pericarditis, rheumatic
  fibropurulent 420.99
  fibrous 423.1
  gonococcal 098.83
  hemorrhagic 423.0
  idiopathic (acute) 420.91
  infective (acute) 420.90
  meningococcal 036.41
  neoplastic (chronic) 423.8
    acute 420.90
  nonspecific 420.91
  obliterans, obliterating 423.1
  plastic 423.1
  pneumococcal (acute) 420.99
  postinfarction 411.0
  purulent (acute) 420.99
  rheumatic (active) (acute) (with effusion) (with
    pneumonia) 391.0
    with chorea (acute) (rheumatic) (Syden-
      ham's) 392.0
    chronic or inactive (with chorea) 393
  septic (acute) 420.99
  serofibrinous — see Pericarditis, rheumatic
  staphylococcal (acute) 420.99
  streptococcal (acute) 420.99
  suppurative (acute) 420.99
  syphilitic 093.81
  tuberculous (acute) (chronic) (see also Tuber-
    culosis) 017.9 ☑ [420.0]
  uremic 585.9 [420.0]
  viral (acute) 420.91
Pericardium, pericardial — see condition
Pericellulitis — see also Cellulitis 682.9
Pericementitis 523.40
  acute 523.30
  chronic (suppurative) 523.40
Pericholecystitis — see also Cholecystitis 575.10
Perichondritis
  auricle 380.00
    acute 380.01
    chronic 380.02
  bronchus 491.9
  ear (external) 380.00
    acute 380.01
    chronic 380.02
  larynx 478.71

Perichondritis — continued
  larynx — continued
    syphilitic 095.8
    typhoid 002.0 [478.71]
  nose 478.19
  pinna 380.00
    acute 380.01
    chronic 380.02
  trachea 478.9
Periclasia 523.5
Pericolitis 569.89
Pericoronitis (chronic) 523.40
  acute 523.33
Pericystitis — see also Cystitis 595.9
Pericytoma (M9150/1) — see Neoplasm,
  connective tissue, uncertain behavior
  benign (M9150/0) — see Neoplasm, connec-
    tive tissue, benign
  malignant (M9150/3) — see Neoplasm, con-
    nective tissue, malignant
Peridacryocystitis, acute 375.32
Peridiverticulitis — see also Diverticulitis 562.11
Periduodenitis 535.6 ☑
Periendocarditis — see also Endocarditis 424.90
  acute or subacute 421.9
Periepididymitis — see also Epididymitis 604.90
Perifolliculitis (abscedens) 704.8
  capitis, abscedens et suffodiens 704.8
  dissecting, scalp 704.8
  scalp 704.8
  superficial pustular 704.8
Perigastritis (acute) 535.0 ☑
Perigastrojejunitis (acute) 535.0 ☑
Perihepatitis (acute) 573.3
  chlamydial 099.56
  gonococcal 098.86
Peri-ileitis (subacute) 569.89
Perilabyrinthitis (acute) — see Labyrinthitis
Perimeningitis — see Meningitis
Perimetritis — see also Endometritis 615.9
Perimetrosalpingitis — see also Salpingo-
  oophoritis 614.2
Perineocele 618.05
Perinephric — see condition
Perinephritic — see condition
Perinephritis — see also Infection, kidney 590.9
  purulent (see also Abscess, kidney) 590.2
Perineum, perineal — see condition
Perineuritis NEC 729.2
Periodic — see also condition
  disease (familial) 277.31
  edema 995.1
    hereditary 277.6
  fever 277.31
  headache syndromes in child or adolescent
    346.2 ☑
  limb movement disorder 327.51
  paralysis (familial) 359.3
  peritonitis 277.31
  polyserositis 277.31
  somnolence (see also Narcolepsy) 347.00
Periodontal
  cyst 522.8
  pocket 523.8
Periodontitis (chronic) (complex) (compound)
  (simplex) 523.40
  acute 523.33
  aggressive 523.30
    generalized 523.32
    localized 523.31
  apical 523.40
    acute (pulpal origin) 522.4
    generalized 523.42
    localized 523.41
Periodontoclasia 523.5
Periodontosis 523.5
Periods — see also Menstruation
  heavy 626.2
  irregular 626.4
Perionychia (with lymphangitis) 681.9
  finger 681.02
  toe 681.11
Perioophoritis — see also Salpingo-oophoritis
  614.2
Periorchitis — see also Orchitis 604.90
Periosteum, periosteal — see condition

Periostitis (circumscribed) (diffuse) (infective)
  730.3 ☑

| Note — Use the following fifth-digit subclas- |
| sification with category 730: |

0	site unspecified
1	shoulder region
2	upper arm
3	forearm
4	hand
5	pelvic region and thigh
6	lower leg
7	ankle and foot
8	other specified sites
9	multiple sites

  with osteomyelitis (see also Osteomyelitis)
    730.2 ☑
    acute or subacute 730.0 ☑
    chronic or old 730.1 ☑
  albuminosa, albuminosus 730.3 ☑
  alveolar 526.5
  alveolodental 526.5
  dental 526.5
  gonorrheal 098.89
  hyperplastica, generalized 731.2
  jaw (lower) (upper) 526.4
  monomelic 733.99
  orbital 376.02
  syphilitic 095.5
    congenital 090.0 [730.8] ☑
    secondary 091.61
  tuberculous (see also Tuberculosis, bone)
    015.9 ☑ [730.8] ☑
  yaws (early) (hypertrophic) (late) 102.6
Periostosis — see also Periostitis 730.3 ☑
  with osteomyelitis (see also Osteomyelitis)
    730.2 ☑
    acute or subacute 730.0 ☑
    chronic or old 730.1 ☑
  hyperplastic 756.59
Peripartum cardiomyopathy 674.5 ☑
Periphlebitis — see also Phlebitis 451.9
  lower extremity 451.2
    deep (vessels) 451.19
    superficial (vessels) 451.0
  portal 572.1
  retina 362.18
  superficial (vessels) 451.0
  tuberculous (see also Tuberculosis) 017.9 ☑
    retina 017.3 ☑ [362.18]
Peripneumonia — see Pneumonia
Periproctitis 569.49
Periprostatitis — see also Prostatitis 601.9
Perirectal — see condition
Perirenal — see condition
Perisalpingitis — see also Salpingo-oophoritis
  614.2
Perisigmoiditis 569.89
Perisplenitis (infectional) 289.59
Perispondylitis — see Spondylitis
Peristalsis reversed or visible 787.4
Peritendinitis — see also Tenosynovitis 726.90
  adhesive (shoulder) 726.0
Perithelioma (M9150/1) — see Pericytoma
Peritoneum, peritoneal — see also condition
  equilibration test V56.32
Peritonitis (acute) (adhesive) (fibrinous) (hemor-
  rhagic) (idiopathic) (localized) (perforative)
  (primary) (with adhesions) (with effusion)
  567.9
  with or following
    abortion — see Abortion, by type, with
      sepsis
    abscess 567.21
    appendicitis 540.0
      with peritoneal abscess 540.1
    ectopic pregnancy (see also categories
      633.0–633.9) 639.0
    molar pregnancy (see also categories
      630–632) 639.0
  aseptic 998.7

Peritonitis — continued
  bacterial 567.29
    spontaneous 567.23
  bile, biliary 567.81
  chemical 998.7
  chlamydial 099.56
  chronic proliferative 567.89
  congenital NEC 777.6
  diaphragmatic 567.22
  diffuse NEC 567.29
  diphtheritic 032.83
  disseminated NEC 567.29
  due to
    bile 567.81
    foreign
      body or object accidentally left during
        a procedure (instrument)
        (sponge) (swab) 998.4
      substance accidentally left during a
        procedure (chemical) (powder)
        (talc) 998.7
    talc 998.7
    urine 567.89
  fibrinopurulent 567.29
  fibrinous 567.29
  fibrocaseous (see also Tuberculosis) 014.0 ☑
  fibropurulent 567.29
  general, generalized (acute) 567.21
  gonococcal 098.86
  in infective disease NEC 136.9 [567.0]
  meconium (newborn) 777.6
  pancreatic 577.8
  paroxysmal, benign 277.31
  pelvic
    female (acute) 614.5
      chronic NEC 614.7
        with adhesions 614.6
      puerperal, postpartum, childbirth
        670.8 ☑   ▲
    male (acute) 567.21
  periodic (familial) 277.31
  phlegmonous 567.29
  pneumococcal 567.1
  postabortal 639.0
  proliferative, chronic 567.89
  puerperal, postpartum, childbirth
    670.8 ☑   ▲
  purulent 567.29
  septic 567.29
  spontaneous bacterial 567.23
  staphylococcal 567.29
  streptococcal 567.29
  subdiaphragmatic 567.29
  subphrenic 567.29
  suppurative 567.29
  syphilitic 095.2
    congenital 090.0 [567.0]
  talc 998.7
  tuberculous (see also Tuberculosis) 014.0 ☑
  urine 567.89
Peritonsillar — see condition
Peritonsillitis 475
Perityphlitis — see also Appendicitis 541
Periureteritis 593.89
Periurethral — see condition
Periurethritis (gangrenous) 597.89
Periuterine — see condition
Perivaginitis — see also Vaginitis 616.10
Perivasculitis, retinal 362.18
Perivasitis (chronic) 608.4
Periventricular leukomalacia 779.7
Perivesiculitis (seminal) — see also Vesiculitis
  608.0
Perlèche 686.8
  due to
    moniliasis 112.0
    riboflavin deficiency 266.0
Pernicious — see condition
Pernio, perniosis 991.5
Persecution
  delusion 297.9
  social V62.4
Perseveration (tonic) 784.69
Persistence, persistent (congenital) 759.89
  anal membrane 751.2
  arteria stapedia 744.04

☑ Additional Digit Required — Refer to the Tabular List for Digit Selection   ⃝ᵂ Subterms under main terms may continue to next column or page

Persistence, persistent — *continued*
  atrioventricular canal 745.69
  bloody ejaculate 792.2
  branchial cleft 744.41
  bulbus cordis in left ventricle 745.8
  canal of Cloquet 743.51
  capsule (opaque) 743.51
  cilioretinal artery or vein 743.51
  cloaca 751.5
  communication — *see* Fistula, congenital
  convolutions
    aortic arch 747.21
    fallopian tube 752.19
    oviduct 752.19
    uterine tube 752.19
  double aortic arch 747.21
  ductus
    arteriosus 747.0
    Botalli 747.0
  fetal
    circulation 747.83
    form of cervix (uteri) 752.49
    hemoglobin (hereditary) ("Swiss variety") 282.7
    pulmonary hypertension 747.83
  foramen
    Botalli 745.5
    ovale 745.5
  Gartner's duct 752.41
  hemoglobin, fetal (hereditary) (HPFH) 282.7
  hyaloid
    artery (generally incomplete) 743.51
    system 743.51
  hymen (tag)
    in pregnancy or childbirth 654.8 ☑
      causing obstructed labor 660.2 ☑
  lanugo 757.4
  left
    posterior cardinal vein 747.49
    root with right arch of aorta 747.21
    superior vena cava 747.49
  Meckel's diverticulum 751.0
  mesonephric duct 752.89
    fallopian tube 752.11
  mucosal disease (middle ear) (with posterior or superior marginal perforation of ear drum) 382.2
  nail(s), anomalous 757.5
  occiput, anterior or posterior 660.3 ☑
    fetus or newborn 763.1
  omphalomesenteric duct 751.0
  organ or site NEC — *see* Anomaly, specified type NEC
  ostium
    atrioventriculare commune 745.69
    primum 745.61
    secundum 745.5
  ovarian rests in fallopian tube 752.19
  pancreatic tissue in intestinal tract 751.5
  primary (deciduous)
    teeth 520.6
    vitreous hyperplasia 743.51
  pulmonary hypertension 747.83
  pupillary membrane 743.46
    iris 743.46
  Rhesus (Rh) titer 999.7
  right aortic arch 747.21
  sinus
    urogenitalis 752.89
    venosus with imperfect incorporation in right auricle 747.49
  thymus (gland) 254.8
    hyperplasia 254.0
  thyroglossal duct 759.2
  thyrolingual duct 759.2
  truncus arteriosus or communis 745.0
  tunica vasculosa lentis 743.39
  umbilical sinus 753.7
  urachus 753.7
  vegetative state 780.03
  vitelline duct 751.0
  wolffian duct 752.89
Person (with)
  admitted for clinical research, as participant or control subject V70.7

Person — *continued*
  affected by
    family member
      currently on deployment (military) V61.01
      returned from deployment (military) (current or past conflict) V61.02
  awaiting admission to adequate facility elsewhere V63.2
  undergoing social agency investigation V63.8
  concern (normal) about sick person in family V61.49
  consulting on behalf of another V65.19
    pediatric
      pre-adoption visit for adoptive parents V65.11 ●
      pre-birth visit for expectant parents V65.11 ●
  currently deployed in theater or in support of military war, peacekeeping and humanitarian operations V62.21
  feared
    complaint in whom no diagnosis was made V65.5
    condition not demonstrated V65.5
  feigning illness V65.2
  healthy, accompanying sick person V65.0
  history of military war, peacekeeping and humanitarian deployment (current or past conflict) V62.22
  living (in)
    without
      adequate
        financial resources V60.2
        housing (heating) (space) V60.1
      housing (permanent) (temporary) V60.0
      material resources V60.2
      person able to render necessary care V60.4
      shelter V60.0
    alone V60.3
    boarding school V60.6
    residence remote from hospital or medical care facility V63.0
    residential institution V60.6
  medical services in home not available V63.1
  on waiting list V63.2
    undergoing social agency investigation V63.8
  sick or handicapped in family V61.49
  "worried well" V65.5
Personality
  affective 301.10
  aggressive 301.3
  amoral 301.7
  anancastic, anankastic 301.4
  antisocial 301.7
  asocial 301.7
  asthenic 301.6
  avoidant 301.82
  borderline 301.83
  change 310.1
  compulsive 301.4
  cycloid 301.13
  cyclothymic 301.13
  dependent 301.6
  depressive (chronic) 301.12
  disorder, disturbance NEC 301.9
    with
      antisocial disturbance 301.7
      pattern disturbance NEC 301.9
      sociopathic disturbance 301.7
      trait disturbance 301.9
  dual 300.14
  dyssocial 301.7
  eccentric 301.89
    "haltlose" type 301.89
  emotionally unstable 301.59
  epileptoid 301.3
  explosive 301.3
  fanatic 301.0
  histrionic 301.50
  hyperthymic 301.11
  hypomanic 301.11

Personality — *continued*
  hypothymic 301.12
  hysterical 301.50
  immature 301.89
  inadequate 301.6
  labile 301.59
  masochistic 301.89
  morally defective 301.7
  multiple 300.14
  narcissistic 301.81
  obsessional 301.4
  obsessive-compulsive 301.4
  overconscientious 301.4
  paranoid 301.0
  passive (-dependent) 301.6
  passive-aggressive 301.84
  pathologic NEC 301.9
  pattern defect or disturbance 301.9
  pseudosocial 301.7
  psychoinfantile 301.59
  psychoneurotic NEC 301.89
  psychopathic 301.9
    with
      amoral trend 301.7
      antisocial trend 301.7
      asocial trend 301.7
      pathologic sexuality (*see also* Deviation, sexual) 302.9
    mixed types 301.9
  schizoid 301.20
  type A 301.4
  unstable (emotional) 301.59
Perthes' disease (capital femoral osteochondrosis) 732.1
Pertussis — *see also* Whooping cough 033.9
  vaccination, prophylactic (against) V03.6
Peruvian wart 088.0
Perversion, perverted
  appetite 307.52
    hysterical 300.11
  function
    pineal gland 259.8
    pituitary gland 253.9
      anterior lobe
        deficient 253.2
        excessive 253.1
      posterior lobe 253.6
    placenta — *see* Placenta, abnormal
  sense of smell or taste 781.1
    psychogenic 306.7
  sexual (*see also* Deviation, sexual) 302.9
Pervious, congenital — *see also* Imperfect, closure
  ductus arteriosus 747.0
Pes (congenital) — *see also* Talipes 754.70
  abductus (congenital) 754.60
    acquired 736.79
  acquired NEC 736.79
    planus 734
  adductus (congenital) 754.79
    acquired 736.79
  cavus 754.71
    acquired 736.73
  planovalgus (congenital) 754.69
    acquired 736.79
  planus (acquired) (any degree) 734
    congenital 754.61
    rachitic 268.1
  valgus (congenital) 754.61
    acquired 736.79
  varus (congenital) 754.50
    acquired 736.79
Pest — *see also* Plague 020.9
Pestis — *see also* Plague 020.9
  bubonica 020.0
  fulminans 020.0
  minor 020.8
  pneumonica — *see* Plague, pneumonic
Petechial
  fever 036.0
  typhus 081.9
Petechia, petechiae 782.7
  fetus or newborn 772.6
Petges-Cléjat or Petges-Clégat syndrome (poikilodermatomyositis) 710.3

Petit's
  disease (*see also* Hernia, lumbar) 553.8
Petit mal (idiopathic) — *see also* Epilepsy 345.0 ☑
  status 345.2
Petrellidosis 117.6
Petrositis 383.20
  acute 383.21
  chronic 383.22
Peutz-Jeghers disease or syndrome 759.6
Peyronie's disease 607.85
Pfeiffer's disease 075
Phacentocele 379.32
  traumatic 921.3
Phacoanaphylaxis 360.19
Phacocele (old) 379.32
  traumatic 921.3
Phaehyphomycosis 117.8
Phagedena (dry) (moist) — *see also* Gangrene 785.4
  arteriosclerotic 440.24
  geometric 686.09
  penis 607.89
  senile 440.2 ☑ [785.4]
  sloughing 785.4
  tropical (*see also* Ulcer, skin) 707.9
  vulva 616.50
Phagedenic — *see also* condition
  abscess (*see also* Abscess)
    chancroid 099.0
  bubo NEC 099.8
  chancre 099.0
  ulcer (tropical) (*see also* Ulcer, skin) 707.9
Phagomania 307.52
Phakoma 362.89
Phantom limb (syndrome) 353.6
Pharyngeal — *see also* condition
  arch remnant 744.41
  pouch syndrome 279.11
Pharyngitis (acute) (catarrhal) (gangrenous) (infective) (malignant) (membranous) (phlegmonous) (pneumococcal) (pseudomembranous) (simple) (staphylococcal) (subacute) (suppurative) (ulcerative) (viral) 462
  with influenza, flu, or grippe 487.1
  aphthous 074.0
  atrophic 472.1
  chlamydial 099.51
  chronic 472.1
  Coxsackie virus 074.0
  diphtheritic (membranous) 032.0
  follicular 472.1
  fusospirochetal 101
  gonococcal 098.6
  granular (chronic) 472.1
  herpetic 054.79
  hypertrophic 472.1
  infectional, chronic 472.1
  influenzal 487.1
  lymphonodular, acute 074.8
  septic 034.0
  streptococcal 034.0
  tuberculous (*see also* Tuberculosis) 012.8 ☑
  vesicular 074.0
Pharyngoconjunctival fever 077.2
Pharyngoconjunctivitis, viral 077.2
Pharyngolaryngitis (acute) 465.0
  chronic 478.9
  septic 034.0
Pharyngoplegia 478.29
Pharyngotonsillitis 465.8
  tuberculous 012.8 ☑
Pharyngotracheitis (acute) 465.8
  chronic 478.9
Pharynx, pharyngeal — *see* condition
Phase of life problem NEC V62.89
Phenomenon
  Arthus' 995.21
  flashback (drug) 292.89
  jaw-winking 742.8
  Jod-Basedow 242.8 ☑
  L. E. cell 710.0
  lupus erythematosus cell 710.0
  Pelger-Huët (hereditary hyposegmentation) 288.2

☑ Additional Digit Required — Refer to the Tabular List for Digit Selection   🔽 Subterms under main terms may continue to next column or page

2010 ICD-9-CM   ▶◀ Revised Text   ● New Line   ▲ Revised Code   October 2009 • Volume 2 — 219

Phenomenon — *continued*
  Raynaud's (paroxysmal digital cyanosis) (secondary) 443.0
  Reilly's (*see also* Neuropathy, peripheral, autonomic) 337.9
  vasomotor 780.2
  vasospastic 443.9
  vasovagal 780.2
  Wenckebach's, heart block (second degree) 426.13
Phenylketonuria (PKU) 270.1
Phenylpyruvicaciduria 270.1
Pheochromoblastoma (M8700/3)
  specified site — *see* Neoplasm, by site, malignant
  unspecified site 194.0
Pheochromocytoma (M8700/0)
  malignant (M8700/3)
    specified site — *see* Neoplasm, by site, malignant
    unspecified site 194.0
  specified site — *see* Neoplasm, by site, benign
  unspecified site 227.0
Phimosis (congenital) 605
  chancroidal 099.0
  due to infection 605
Phlebectasia — *see also* Varicose, vein 454.9
  congenital NEC 747.60
  esophagus (*see also* Varix, esophagus) 456.1
    with hemorrhage (*see also* Varix, esophagus, bleeding) 456.0
Phlebitis (infective) (pyemic) (septic) (suppurative) 451.9
  antecubital vein 451.82
  arm NEC 451.84
    axillary vein 451.89
    basilic vein 451.82
    deep 451.83
    superficial 451.82
  axillary vein 451.89
  basilic vein 451.82
  blue 451.9
  brachial vein 451.83
  breast, superficial 451.89
  cavernous (venous) sinus — *see* Phlebitis, intracranial sinus
  cephalic vein 451.82
  cerebral (venous) sinus — *see* Phlebitis, intracranial sinus
  chest wall, superficial 451.89
  complicating pregnancy or puerperium 671.2 ☑ ▲
    affecting fetus or newborn 760.3
  cranial (venous) sinus — *see* Phlebitis, intracranial sinus
  deep (vessels) 451.19
    femoral vein 451.11
    specified vessel NEC 451.19
  due to implanted device — *see* Complications, due to (presence of) any device, implant, or graft classified to 996.0–996.5 NEC
  during or resulting from a procedure 997.2
  femoral vein (deep) (superficial) 451.11
  femoropopliteal 451.19
  following infusion, perfusion, or transfusion 999.2
  gouty 274.89 *[451.9]*
  hepatic veins 451.89
  iliac vein 451.81
  iliofemoral 451.11
  intracranial sinus (any) (venous) 325
    late effect — *see* category 326
    nonpyogenic 437.6
      in pregnancy or puerperium 671.5 ☑
  jugular vein 451.89
  lateral (venous) sinus — *see* Phlebitis, intracranial sinus
  leg 451.2
    deep (vessels) 451.19
      femoral vein 451.11
      specified vessel NEC 451.19
    superficial (vessels) 451.0
      femoral vein 451.11
    longitudinal sinus — *see* Phlebitis, intracranial sinus

Phlebitis — *continued*
  lower extremity 451.2
    deep (vessels) 451.19
      femoral vein 451.11
      specified vessel NEC 451.19
    migrans, migrating (superficial) 453.1
    superficial (vessels) 451.0
      femoral vein 451.11
  pelvic
    with
      abortion — *see* Abortion, by type, with sepsis
      ectopic pregnancy (*see also* categories 633.0–633.9) 639.0
      molar pregnancy (*see also* categories 630–632) 639.0
    following
      abortion 639.0
      ectopic or molar pregnancy 639.0
    puerperal, postpartum 671.4 ☑
  popliteal vein 451.19
  portal (vein) 572.1
  postoperative 997.2
  pregnancy 671.2 ☑ ▲
    deep 671.3 ☑
    specified type NEC 671.5 ☑
    superficial 671.2 ☑
  puerperal, postpartum, childbirth 671.2 ☑ ▲
    deep 671.4 ☑
    lower extremities 671.2 ☑
    pelvis 671.4 ☑
    specified site NEC 671.5 ☑
    superficial 671.2 ☑
  radial vein 451.83
  retina 362.18
  saphenous (great) (long) 451.0
    accessory or small 451.0
  sinus (meninges) — *see* Phlebitis, intracranial sinus
  specified site NEC 451.89
  subclavian vein 451.89
  syphilitic 093.89
  tibial vein 451.19
  ulcer, ulcerative 451.9
    leg 451.2
      deep (vessels) 451.19
        femoral vein 451.11
        specified vessel NEC 451.19
      superficial (vessels) 451.0
        femoral vein 451.11
    lower extremity 451.2
      deep (vessels) 451.19
        femoral vein 451.11
        specified vessel NEC 451.19
      superficial (vessels) 451.0
  ulnar vein 451.83
  umbilicus 451.89
  upper extremity (*see also* Phlebitis, arm)
    deep (veins) 451.83
      brachial vein 451.83
      radial vein 451.83
      ulnar vein 451.83
    superficial (veins) 451.82
      antecubital vein 451.82
      basilica vein 451.82
      cephalic vein 451.82
  uterus (septic) (*see also* Endometritis) 615.9
  varicose (leg) (lower extremity) (*see also* Varicose, vein) 454.1
Phlebofibrosis 459.89
Phleboliths 459.89
Phlebosclerosis 459.89
Phlebothrombosis — *see* Thrombosis
Phlebotomus fever 066.0
Phlegmasia
  alba dolens (deep vessels) 451.19
    complicating pregnancy 671.3 ☑
    nonpuerperal 451.19
    puerperal, postpartum, childbirth 671.4 ☑
  cerulea dolens 451.19
Phlegm, choked on 933.1
Phlegmon — *see also* Abscess 682.9
  erysipelatous (*see also* Erysipelas) 035
  iliac 682.2
    fossa 540.1

Phlegmon — *see also* Abscess — *continued*
  throat 478.29
Phlegmonous — *see* condition
Phlyctenulosis (allergic) (keratoconjunctivitis) (nontuberculous) 370.31
  cornea 370.31
    with ulcer (*see also* Ulcer, cornea) 370.00
  tuberculous (*see also* Tuberculosis) 017.3 ☑ *[370.31]*
Phobia, phobic (reaction) 300.20
  animal 300.29
  isolated NEC 300.29
  obsessional 300.3
  simple NEC 300.29
  social 300.23
  specified NEC 300.29
  state 300.20
Phocas' disease 610.1
Phocomelia 755.4
  lower limb 755.32
    complete 755.33
    distal 755.35
    proximal 755.34
  upper limb 755.22
    complete 755.23
    distal 755.25
    proximal 755.24
Phoria — *see also* Heterophoria 378.40
Phosphate-losing tubular disorder 588.0
Phosphatemia 275.3
Phosphaturia 275.3
Photoallergic response 692.72
Photocoproporphyria 277.1
Photodermatitis (sun) 692.72
  light other than sun 692.82
Photokeratitis 370.24
Photo-ophthalmia 370.24
Photophobia 368.13
Photopsia 368.15
Photoretinitis 363.31
Photoretinopathy 363.31
Photosensitiveness (sun) 692.72
  light other than sun 692.82
Photosensitization (skin) (sun) 692.72
  light other than sun 692.82
Phototoxic response 692.72
Phrenitis 323.9
Phrynoderma 264.8
Phthiriasis (pubis) (any site) 132.2
  with any infestation classifiable to 132.0, 132.1, 132.3
Phthirus infestation — *see* Phthiriasis
Phthisis — *see also* Tuberculosis 011.9 ☑
  bulbi (infectional) 360.41
  colliers' 011.4 ☑
  cornea 371.05
  eyeball (due to infection) 360.41
  millstone makers' 011.4 ☑
  miners' 011.4 ☑
  potters' 011.4 ☑
  sandblasters' 011.4 ☑
  stonemasons' 011.4 ☑
Phycomycosis 117.7
Physalopteriasis 127.7
Physical therapy NEC V57.1
  breathing exercises V57.0
Physiological cup, optic papilla
  borderline, glaucoma suspect 365.00
  enlarged 377.14
  glaucomatous 377.14
Phytobezoar 938
  intestine 936
  stomach 935.2
Pian — *see also* Yaws 102.9
Pianoma 102.1
Piarhemia, piarrhemia — *see also* Hyperlipemia 272.4
  bilharziasis 120.9
Pica 307.52
  hysterical 300.11
Pick's
  cerebral atrophy 331.11
    with dementia
      with behavioral disturbance 331.11 *[294.11]*

Pick's — *continued*
  cerebral atrophy — *continued*
    with dementia — *continued*
      without behavioral disturbance 331.11 *[294.10]*
  disease
    brain 331.11
      dementia in
        with behavioral disturbance 331.11 *[294.11]*
        without behavioral disturbance 331.11 *[294.10]*
    lipid histiocytosis 272.7
    liver (pericardial pseudocirrhosis of liver) 423.2
    pericardium (pericardial pseudocirrhosis of liver) 423.2
    polyserositis (pericardial pseudocirrhosis of liver) 423.2
    syndrome
      heart (pericardial pseudocirrhosis of liver) 423.2
      liver (pericardial pseudocirrhosis of liver) 423.2
  tubular adenoma (M8640/0)
    specified site — *see* Neoplasm, by site, benign
    unspecified site
      female 220
      male 222.0
Pick-Herxheimer syndrome (diffuse idiopathic cutaneous atrophy) 701.8
Pick-Niemann disease (lipid histiocytosis) 272.7
Pickwickian syndrome (cardiopulmonary obesity) 278.8
Piebaldism, classic 709.09
Piedra 111.2
  beard 111.2
    black 111.3
    white 111.2
  black 111.3
  scalp 111.3
    black 111.3
    white 111.2
  white 111.2
Pierre Marie-Bamberger syndrome (hypertrophic pulmonary osteoarthropathy) 731.2
Pierre Marie's syndrome (pulmonary hypertrophic osteoarthropathy) 731.2
Pierre Mauriac's syndrome (diabetes-dwarfism-obesity) 258.1
Pierre Robin deformity or syndrome (congenital) 756.0
Pierson's disease or osteochondrosis 732.1
Pigeon
  breast or chest (acquired) 738.3
    congenital 754.82
    rachitic (*see also* Rickets) 268.0
  breeders' disease or lung 495.2
  fanciers' disease or lung 495.2
  toe 735.8
Pigmentation (abnormal) 709.00
  anomaly 709.00
    congenital 757.33
    specified NEC 709.09
  conjunctiva 372.55
  cornea 371.10
    anterior 371.11
    posterior 371.13
    stromal 371.12
  lids (congenital) 757.33
    acquired 374.52
  limbus corneae 371.10
  metals 709.00
  optic papilla, congenital 743.57
  retina (congenital) (grouped) (nevoid) 743.53
    acquired 362.74
  scrotum, congenital 757.33
Piles — *see* Hemorrhoids
Pili
  annulati or torti (congenital) 757.4
  incarnati 704.8
Pill roller hand (intrinsic) 736.09
Pilomatrixoma (M8110/0) — *see* Neoplasm, skin, benign
Pilonidal — *see* condition

Pimple 709.8
PIN I (prostatic intraepithelial neoplasia I) 602.3
PIN II (prostatic intraepithelial neoplasia II) 602.3
PIN III (prostatic intraepithelial neoplasia III) 233.4
Pinched nerve — *see* Neuropathy, entrapment
Pineal body or gland — *see* condition
Pinealoblastoma (M9362/3) 194.4
Pinealoma (M9360/1) 237.1
   malignant (M9360/3) 194.4
Pineoblastoma (M9362/3) 194.4
Pineocytoma (M9361/1) 237.1
Pinguecula 372.51
Pingueculitis 372.34
Pinhole meatus — *see also* Stricture, urethra 598.9
Pink
   disease 985.0
   eye 372.03
   puffer 492.8
Pinkus' disease (lichen nitidus) 697.1
Pinpoint
   meatus (*see also* Stricture, urethra) 598.9
   os uteri (*see also* Stricture, cervix) 622.4
Pinselhaare (congenital) 757.4
Pinta 103.9
   cardiovascular lesions 103.2
   chancre (primary) 103.0
   erythematous plaques 103.1
   hyperchromic lesions 103.1
   hyperkeratosis 103.1
   lesions 103.9
      cardiovascular 103.2
      hyperchromic 103.1
      intermediate 103.1
      late 103.2
      mixed 103.3
      primary 103.0
      skin (achromic) (cicatricial) (dyschromic) 103.2
         hyperchromic 103.1
         mixed (achromic and hyperchromic) 103.3
   papule (primary) 103.0
   skin lesions (achromic) (cicatricial) (dyschromic) 103.2
      hyperchromic 103.1
      mixed (achromic and hyperchromic) 103.3
   vitiligo 103.2
Pintid 103.0
Pinworms (disease) (infection) (infestation) 127.4
Piry fever 066.8
Pistol wound — *see* Gunshot wound
Pitchers' elbow 718.82
Pithecoid pelvis 755.69
   with disproportion (fetopelvic) 653.2 ☑
      affecting fetus or newborn 763.1
      causing obstructed labor 660.1 ☑
Pithiatism 300.11
Pit, lip (mucus), **congenital** 750.25
Pitted — *see also* Pitting
   teeth 520.4
Pitting (edema) — *see also* Edema 782.3
   lip 782.3
   nail 703.8
      congenital 757.5
Pituitary gland — *see* condition
Pituitary snuff-takers' disease 495.8
Pityriasis 696.5
   alba 696.5
   capitis 690.11
   circinata (et maculata) 696.3
   Hebra's (exfoliative dermatitis) 695.89
   lichenoides et varioliformis 696.2
   maculata (et circinata) 696.3
   nigra 111.1
   pilaris 757.39
      acquired 701.1
      Hebra's 696.4
   rosea 696.3
   rotunda 696.3
   rubra (Hebra) 695.89
      pilaris 696.4
   sicca 690.18
   simplex 690.18
   specified type NEC 696.5
   streptogenes 696.5

Pityriasis — *continued*
   versicolor 111.0
      scrotal 111.0
Placenta, placental
   ablatio 641.2 ☑
      affecting fetus or newborn 762.1
   abnormal, abnormality 656.7 ☑
      with hemorrhage 641.8 ☑
         affecting fetus or newborn 762.1
      affecting fetus or newborn 762.2
   abruptio 641.2 ☑
      affecting fetus or newborn 762.1
   accessory lobe — *see* Placenta, abnormal
   accreta (without hemorrhage) 667.0 ☑
      with hemorrhage 666.0 ☑
   adherent (without hemorrhage) 667.0 ☑
      with hemorrhage 666.0 ☑
   apoplexy — *see* Placenta, separation
   battledore — *see* Placenta, abnormal
   bilobate — *see* Placenta, abnormal
   bipartita — *see* Placenta, abnormal
   carneous mole 631
   centralis — *see* Placenta, previa
   circumvallata — *see* Placenta, abnormal
   cyst (amniotic) — *see* Placenta, abnormal
   deficiency — *see* Placenta, insufficiency
   degeneration — *see* Placenta, insufficiency
   detachment (partial) (premature) (with hemorrhage) 641.2 ☑
      affecting fetus or newborn 762.1
   dimidiata — *see* Placenta, abnormal
   disease 656.7 ☑
      affecting fetus or newborn 762.2
   duplex — *see* Placenta, abnormal
   dysfunction — *see* Placenta, insufficiency
   fenestrata — *see* Placenta, abnormal
   fibrosis — *see* Placenta, abnormal
   fleshy mole 631
   hematoma — *see* Placenta, abnormal
   hemorrhage NEC — *see* Placenta, separation
   hormone disturbance or malfunction — *see* Placenta, abnormal
   hyperplasia — *see* Placenta, abnormal
   increta (without hemorrhage) 667.0 ☑
      with hemorrhage 666.0 ☑
   infarction 656.7 ☑
      affecting fetus or newborn 762.2
   insertion, vicious — *see* Placenta, previa
   insufficiency
      affecting
         fetus or newborn 762.2
         management of pregnancy 656.5 ☑
   lateral — *see* Placenta, previa
   low implantation or insertion — *see* Placenta, previa
   low-lying — *see* Placenta, previa
   malformation — *see* Placenta, abnormal
   malposition — *see* Placenta, previa
   marginalis, marginata — *see* Placenta, previa
   marginal sinus (hemorrhage) (rupture) 641.2 ☑
      affecting fetus or newborn 762.1
   membranacea — *see* Placenta, abnormal
   multilobed — *see* Placenta, abnormal
   multipartita — *see* Placenta, abnormal
   necrosis — *see* Placenta, abnormal
   percreta (without hemorrhage) 667.0 ☑
      with hemorrhage 666.0 ☑
   polyp 674.4 ☑
   previa (central) (centralis) (complete) (lateral) (marginal) (marginalis) (partial) (partialis) (total) (with hemorrhage) 641.1 ☑
      without hemorrhage (before labor and delivery) (during pregnancy) 641.0 ☑
      affecting fetus or newborn 762.0
      noted
         before labor, without hemorrhage (with cesarean delivery) 641.0 ☑
         during pregnancy (without hemorrhage) 641.0 ☑
   retention (with hemorrhage) 666.0 ☑
      without hemorrhage 667.0 ☑

Placenta, placental — *continued*
   retention — *continued*
      fragments, complicating puerperium (delayed hemorrhage) 666.2 ☑
         without hemorrhage 667.1 ☑
      postpartum, puerperal 666.2 ☑
   separation (normally implanted) (partial) (premature) (with hemorrhage) 641.2 ☑
      affecting fetus or newborn 762.1
   septuplex — *see* Placenta, abnormal
   small — *see* Placenta, insufficiency
   softening (premature) — *see* Placenta, abnormal
   spuria — *see* Placenta, abnormal
   succenturiata — *see* Placenta, abnormal
   syphilitic 095.8
   transfusion syndromes 762.3
   transmission of chemical substance — *see* Absorption, chemical, through placenta
   trapped (with hemorrhage) 666.0 ☑
      without hemorrhage 667.0 ☑
   trilobate — *see* Placenta, abnormal
   tripartita — *see* Placenta, abnormal
   triplex — *see* Placenta, abnormal
   varicose vessel — *see* Placenta, abnormal
   vicious insertion — *see* Placenta, previa
Placentitis
   affecting fetus or newborn 762.7
   complicating pregnancy 658.4 ☑
Plagiocephaly (skull) 754.0
Plague 020.9
   abortive 020.8
   ambulatory 020.8
   bubonic 020.0
   cellulocutaneous 020.1
   lymphatic gland 020.0
   pneumonic 020.5
      primary 020.3
      secondary 020.4
   pulmonary — *see* Plague, pneumonic
   pulmonic — *see* Plague, pneumonic
   septicemic 020.2
   tonsillar 020.9
      septicemic 020.2
   vaccination, prophylactic (against) V03.3
Planning, family V25.09
   contraception V25.9
   natural
      procreative V26.41
      to avoid pregnancy V25.04
   procreation V26.49
      natural V26.41
Plaque
   artery, arterial — *see* Arteriosclerosis
   calcareous — *see* Calcification
   Hollenhorst's (retinal) 362.33
   tongue 528.6
Plasma cell myeloma 203.0 ☑
Plasmacytoma, plasmocytoma (solitary) (M9731/1) 238.6
   benign (M9731/0) — *see* Neoplasm, by site, benign
   malignant (M9731/3) 203.8 ☑
Plasmacytopenia 288.59
Plasmacytosis 288.64
Plaster ulcer — *see also* Ulcer, pressure 707.00
Plateau iris syndrome 364.82
Platybasia 756.0
Platyonychia (congenital) 757.5
   acquired 703.8
Platypelloid pelvis 738.6
   with disproportion (fetopelvic) 653.2 ☑
      affecting fetus or newborn 763.1
      causing obstructed labor 660.1 ☑
         affecting fetus or newborn 763.1
   congenital 755.69
Platyspondylia 756.19
Plethora 782.62
   newborn 776.4
Pleuralgia 786.52
Pleura, pleural — *see* condition

Pleurisy (acute) (adhesive) (chronic) (costal) (diaphragmatic) (double) (dry) (fetid) (fibrinous) (fibrous) (interlobar) (latent) (lung) (old) (plastic) (primary) (residual) (sicca) (sterile) (subacute) (unresolved) (with adherent pleura) 511.0
   with
      effusion (without mention of cause) 511.9
         bacterial, nontuberculous 511.1
         nontuberculous NEC 511.9
            bacterial 511.1
            pneumococcal 511.1
            specified type NEC 511.89
            staphylococcal 511.1
            streptococcal 511.1
         tuberculous (*see also* Tuberculosis, pleura) 012.0 ☑
            primary, progressive 010.1 ☑
      influenza, flu, or grippe 487.1
      tuberculosis — *see* Pleurisy, tuberculous
   encysted 511.89
   exudative (*see also* Pleurisy, with effusion) 511.9
      bacterial, nontuberculous 511.1
   fibrinopurulent 510.9
      with fistula 510.0
   fibropurulent 510.9
      with fistula 510.0
   hemorrhagic 511.89
   influenzal 487.1
   pneumococcal 511.0
      with effusion 511.1
   purulent 510.9
      with fistula 510.0
   septic 510.9
      with fistula 510.0
   serofibrinous (*see also* Pleurisy, with effusion) 511.9
      bacterial, nontuberculous 511.1
   seropurulent 510.9
      with fistula 510.0
   serous (*see also* Pleurisy, with effusion) 511.9
      bacterial, nontuberculous 511.1
   staphylococcal 511.0
      with effusion 511.1
   streptococcal 511.0
      with effusion 511.1
   suppurative 510.9
      with fistula 510.0
   traumatic (post) (current) 862.29
      with open wound into cavity 862.39
   tuberculous (with effusion) (*see also* Tuberculosis, pleura) 012.0 ☑
      primary, progressive 010.1 ☑
Pleuritis sicca — *see* Pleurisy
Pleurobronchopneumonia — *see also* Pneumonia, broncho- 485
Pleurodynia 786.52
   epidemic 074.1
   viral 074.1
Pleurohepatitis 573.8
Pleuropericarditis — *see also* Pericarditis 423.9
   acute 420.90
Pleuropneumonia (acute) (bilateral) (double) (septic) — *see also* Pneumonia 486
   chronic (*see also* Fibrosis, lung) 515
Pleurorrhea — *see also* Hydrothorax 511.89
Plexitis, brachial 353.0
Plica
   knee 727.83
   polonica 132.0
   syndrome 727.83
   tonsil 474.8
Plicae dysphonia ventricularis 784.49
Plicated tongue 529.5
   congenital 750.13
Plug
   bronchus NEC 519.19
   meconium (newborn) NEC 777.1
   mucus — *see* Mucus, plug
Plumbism 984.9
   specified type of lead — *see* Table of Drugs and Chemicals
Plummer's disease (toxic nodular goiter) 242.3 ☑

Index

Plummer-Vinson syndrome — Pneumonia

Plummer-Vinson syndrome (sideropenic dysphagia) 280.8
Pluricarential syndrome of infancy 260
Plurideficiency syndrome of infancy 260
Plus (and minus) hand (intrinsic) 736.09
PMDD (premenstrual dysphoric disorder) 625.4
PMS 625.4
Pneumathemia — see Air, embolism, by type
Pneumatic drill or hammer disease 994.9
Pneumatocele (lung) 518.89
   intracranial 348.89 ▲
   tension 492.0
Pneumatosis
   cystoides intestinalis 569.89
   peritonei 568.89
   pulmonum 492.8
Pneumaturia 599.84
Pneumoblastoma (M8981/3) — **see** Neoplasm, lung, malignant
Pneumocephalus 348.89 ▲
Pneumococcemia 038.2
Pneumococcus, pneumococcal — **see** condition
Pneumoconiosis (due to) (inhalation of) 505
   aluminum 503
   asbestos 501
   bagasse 495.1
   bauxite 503
   beryllium 503
   carbon electrode makers' 503
   coal
      miners' (simple) 500
      workers' (simple) 500
   cotton dust 504
   diatomite fibrosis 502
   dust NEC 504
      inorganic 503
      lime 502
      marble 502
      organic NEC 504
   fumes or vapors (from silo) 506.9
   graphite 503
   hard metal 503
   mica 502
   moldy hay 495.0
   rheumatoid 714.81
   silica NEC 502
      and carbon 500
   silicate NEC 502
   talc 502
Pneumocystis carinii pneumonia 136.3
Pneumocystis jiroveci pneumonia 136.3
Pneumocystosis 136.3
   with pneumonia 136.3
Pneumoenteritis 025
Pneumohemopericardium — **see also** Pericarditis 423.9
Pneumohemothorax — **see also** Hemothorax 511.89
   traumatic 860.4
      with open wound into thorax 860.5
Pneumohydropericardium — **see also** Pericarditis 423.9
Pneumohydrothorax — **see also** Hydrothorax 511.89
Pneumomediastinum 518.1
   congenital 770.2
   fetus or newborn 770.2
Pneumomycosis 117.9
Pneumonia (acute) (Alpenstich) (benign) (bilateral) (brain) (cerebral) (circumscribed) (congestive) (creeping) (delayed resolution) (double) (epidemic) (fever) (flash) (fulminant) (fungoid) (granulomatous) (hemorrhagic) (incipient) (infantile) (infectious) (infiltration) (insular) (intermittent) (latent) (lobe) (migratory) (newborn) (organized) (overwhelming) (primary) (progressive) (pseudolobar) (purulent) (resolved) (secondary) (senile) (septic) (suppurative) (terminal) (true) (unresolved) (vesicular) 486
   with influenza, flu, or grippe 487.0
   adenoviral 480.0
   adynamic 514
   alba 090.0
   allergic 518.3

Pneumonia — *continued*
   alveolar — *see* Pneumonia, lobar
   anaerobes 482.81
   anthrax 022.1 *[484.5]*
   apex, apical — *see* Pneumonia, lobar
   ascaris 127.0 *[484.8]*
   aspiration 507.0
      due to
         aspiration of microorganisms
            bacterial 482.9
               specified type NEC 482.89
            specified organism NEC 483.8
               bacterial NEC 482.89
            viral 480.9
               specified type NEC 480.8
         food (regurgitated) 507.0
         gastric secretions 507.0
         milk 507.0
         oils, essences 507.1
         solids, liquids NEC 507.8
         vomitus 507.0
      fetal 770.18
         due to
            blood 770.16
            clear amniotic fluid 770.14
            meconium 770.12
            postnatal stomach contents 770.86
      newborn 770.18
         due to
            blood 770.16
            clear amniotic fluid 770.14
            meconium 770.12
            postnatal stomach contents 770.86
   asthenic 514
   atypical (disseminated) (focal) (primary) 486
      with influenza 487.0
   bacillus 482.9
      specified type NEC 482.89
   bacterial 482.9
      specified type NEC 482.89
   Bacteroides (fragilis) (oralis) (melaninogenicus) 482.81
   basal, basic, basilar — *see* Pneumonia, lobar
   bronchiolitis obliterans organized (BOOP) 516.8
   broncho-, bronchial (confluent) (croupous) (diffuse) (disseminated) (hemorrhagic) (involving lobes) (lobar) (terminal) 485
      with influenza 487.0
      allergic 518.3
      aspiration (*see also* Pneumonia, aspiration) 507.0
      bacterial 482.9
         specified type NEC 482.89
      capillary 466.19
         with bronchospasm or obstruction 466.19
      chronic (*see also* Fibrosis, lung) 515
      congenital (infective) 770.0
      diplococcal 481
      Eaton's agent 483.0
      Escherichia coli (E. coli) 482.82
      Friedländer's bacillus 482.0
      Hemophilus influenzae 482.2
      hiberno-vernal 083.0 *[484.8]*
      hypostatic 514
      influenzal 487.0
      inhalation (*see also* Pneumonia, aspiration) 507.0
         due to fumes or vapors (chemical) 506.0
      Klebsiella 482.0
      lipid 507.1
         endogenous 516.8
      Mycoplasma (pneumoniae) 483.0
      ornithosis 073.0
      pleuropneumonia-like organisms (PPLO) 483.0
      pneumococcal 481
      Proteus 482.83
      Pseudomonas 482.1
      specified organism NEC 483.8
         bacterial NEC 482.89
      staphylococcal 482.40
         aureus 482.41

Pneumonia — *continued*
   broncho-, bronchial — *continued*
      staphylococcal — *continued*
         aureus — *continued*
            methicillin
               resistant (MRSA) 482.42
               susceptible (MSSA) 482.41
            specified type NEC 482.49
      streptococcal — *see* Pneumonia, streptococcal
      typhoid 002.0 *[484.8]*
      viral, virus (*see also* Pneumonia, viral) 480.9
   Butyrivibrio (fibriosolvens) 482.81
   Candida 112.4
   capillary 466.19
      with bronchospasm or obstruction 466.19
   caseous (*see also* Tuberculosis) 011.6 ☑
   catarrhal — *see* Pneumonia, broncho-
   central — *see* Pneumonia, lobar
   Chlamydia, chlamydial 483.1
      pneumoniae 483.1
      psittaci 073.0
      specified type NEC 483.1
      trachomatis 483.1
   cholesterol 516.8
   chronic (*see also* Fibrosis, lung) 515
   cirrhotic (chronic) (*see also* Fibrosis, lung) 515
   Clostridium (haemolyticum) (novyi) NEC 482.81
   confluent — *see* Pneumonia, broncho-
   congenital (infective) 770.0
      aspiration 770.18
   croupous — *see* Pneumonia, lobar
   cytomegalic inclusion 078.5 *[484.1]*
   deglutition (*see also* Pneumonia, aspiration) 507.0
   desquamative interstitial 516.8
   diffuse — *see* Pneumonia, broncho-
   diplococcal, diplococcus (broncho-) (lobar) 481
   disseminated (focal) — *see* Pneumonia, broncho-
   due to
      adenovirus 480.0
      anaerobes 482.81
      Bacterium anitratum 482.83
      Chlamydia, chlamydial 483.1
         pneumoniae 483.1
         psittaci 073.0
         specified type NEC 483.1
         trachomatis 483.1
      coccidioidomycosis 114.0
      Diplococcus (pneumoniae) 481
      Eaton's agent 483.0
      Escherichia coli (E. coli) 482.82
      Friedländer's bacillus 482.0
      fumes or vapors (chemical) (inhalation) 506.0
      fungus NEC 117.9 *[484.7]*
         coccidioidomycosis 114.0
      Hemophilus influenzae (H. influenzae) 482.2
      Herellea 482.83
      influenza 487.0
      Klebsiella pneumoniae 482.0
      Mycoplasma (pneumoniae) 483.0
      parainfluenza virus 480.2
      pleuropneumonia-like organism (PPLO) 483.0
      Pneumococcus 481
      Pneumocystis carinii 136.3
      Pneumocystis jiroveci 136.3
      Proteus 482.83
      Pseudomonas 482.1
      respiratory syncytial virus 480.1
      rickettsia 083.9 *[484.8]*
      SARS-associated coronavirus 480.3
      specified
         bacteria NEC 482.89
         organism NEC 483.8
         virus NEC 480.8
      Staphylococcus 482.40
         aureus 482.41
            methicillin
               resistant (MRSA) 482.42
               susceptible (MSSA) 482.41

Pneumonia — *continued*
   due to — *continued*
      Staphylococcus — *continued*
         specified type NEC 482.49
      Streptococcus (*see also* Pneumonia, streptococcal) pneumoniae 481
      virus (*see also* Pneumonia, viral) 480.9
      SARS-associated coronavirus 480.3
   Eaton's agent 483.0
   embolic, embolism — (*see* Embolism, pulmonary)
   eosinophilic 518.3
   Escherichia coli (E. coli) 482.82
   Eubacterium 482.81
   fibrinous — *see* Pneumonia, lobar
   fibroid (chronic) (*see also* Fibrosis, lung) 515
   fibrous (*see also* Fibrosis, lung) 515
   Friedländer's bacillus 482.0
   Fusobacterium (nucleatum) 482.81
   gangrenous 513.0
   giant cell (*see also* Pneumonia, viral) 480.9
   gram-negative bacteria NEC 482.83
      anaerobic 482.81
   grippal 487.0
   Hemophilus influenzae (bronchial) (lobar) 482.2
   hypostatic (broncho-) (lobar) 514
   in
      actinomycosis 039.1
      anthrax 022.1 *[484.5]*
      aspergillosis 117.3 *[484.6]*
      candidiasis 112.4
      coccidioidomycosis 114.0
      cytomegalic inclusion disease 078.5 *[484.1]*
      histoplasmosis (*see also* Histoplasmosis) 115.95
      infectious disease NEC 136.9 *[484.8]*
      measles 055.1
      mycosis, systemic NEC 117.9 *[484.7]*
      nocardiasis, nocardiosis 039.1
      ornithosis 073.0
      pneumocystosis 136.3
      psittacosis 073.0
      Q fever 083.0 *[484.8]*
      salmonellosis 003.22
      toxoplasmosis 130.4
      tularemia 021.2
      typhoid (fever) 002.0 *[484.8]*
      varicella 052.1
      whooping cough (*see also* Whooping cough) 033.9 *[484.3]*
   infective, acquired prenatally 770.0
   influenzal (broncho) (lobar) (virus) 487.0
   inhalation (*see also* Pneumonia, aspiration) 507.0
      fumes or vapors (chemical) 506.0
   interstitial 516.8
      with influenzal 487.0
      acute 136.3
      chronic (*see also* Fibrosis, lung) 515
      desquamative 516.8
      hypostatic 514
      lipoid 507.1
      lymphoid 516.8
      plasma cell 136.3
      Pseudomonas 482.1
   intrauterine (infective) 770.0
      aspiration 770.18
         blood 770.16
         clear amniotic fluid 770.14
         meconium 770.12
         postnatal stomach contents 770.86
   Klebsiella pneumoniae 482.0
   Legionnaires' 482.84
   lipid, lipoid (exogenous) (interstitial) 507.1
      endogenous 516.8
   lobar (diplococcal) (disseminated) (double) (interstitial) (pneumococcal, any type) 481
      with influenza 487.0
      bacterial 482.9
         specified type NEC 482.89
      chronic (*see also* Fibrosis, lung) 515
      Escherichia coli (E. coli) 482.82
      Friedländer's bacillus 482.0

☑ Additional Digit Required — Refer to the Tabular List for Digit Selection

ᴺᴱᶜ Subterms under main terms may continue to next column or page

►◄ Revised Text   ● New Line   ▲ Revised Code

Pneumonia — *continued*
  lobar — *continued*
    Hemophilus influenzae (H. influenzae) 482.2
    hypostatic 514
    influenzal 487.0
    Klebsiella 482.0
    ornithosis 073.0
    Proteus 482.83
    Pseudomonas 482.1
    psittacosis 073.0
    specified organism NEC 483.8
      bacterial NEC 482.89
    staphylococcal 482.40
      aureus 482.41
        methicillin
          resistant (MRSA) 482.42
          susceptible (MSSA) 482.41
      specified type NEC 482.49
    streptococcal — *see* Pneumonia, streptococcal
    viral, virus (*see also* Pneumonia, viral) 480.9
  lobular (confluent) — *see* Pneumonia, broncho-
  Löffler's 518.3
  massive — *see* Pneumonia, lobar
  meconium aspiration 770.12
  metastatic NEC 038.8 *[484.8]*
  methicillin resistant Staphylococcus aureus (MRSA) 482.42
  methicillin susceptible Staphylococcus aureus (MSSA) 482.41
  MRSA (methicillin resistant Staphylococcus aureus) 482.42
  MSSA (methicillin susceptible Staphylococcus aureus) 482.41
  Mycoplasma (pneumoniae) 483.0
  necrotic 513.0
  nitrogen dioxide 506.9
  orthostatic 514
  parainfluenza virus 480.2
  parenchymatous (*see also* Fibrosis, lung) 515
  passive 514
  patchy — *see* Pneumonia, broncho-
  Peptococcus 482.81
  Peptostreptococcus 482.81
  plasma cell 136.3
  pleurolobar — see Pneumonia, lobar
  pleuropneumonia-like organism (PPLO) 483.0
  pneumococcal (broncho) (lobar) 481
  Pneumocystis (carinii) (jiroveci) 136.3
  postinfectional NEC 136.9 *[484.8]*
  postmeasles 055.1
  postoperative 997.39
  primary atypical 486
  Proprionibacterium 482.81
  Proteus 482.83
  Pseudomonas 482.1
  psittacosis 073.0
  radiation 508.0
  respiratory syncytial virus 480.1
  resulting from a procedure 997.39
  rheumatic 390 *[517.1]*
  Salmonella 003.22
  SARS-associated coronavirus 480.3
  segmented, segmental — *see* Pneumonia, broncho-
  Serratia (marcescens) 482.83
  specified
    bacteria NEC 482.89
    organism NEC 483.8
    virus NEC 480.8
  spirochetal 104.8 *[484.8]*
  staphylococcal (broncho) (lobar) 482.40
    aureus 482.41
      methicillin
        resistant 482.42
        susceptible (MSSA) 482.41
    specified type NEC 482.49
  static, stasis 514
  streptococcal (broncho) (lobar) NEC 482.30
    Group
      A 482.31
      B 482.32
    specified NEC 482.39
    pneumoniae 481

Pneumonia — *continued*
  streptococcal — *continued*
    specified type NEC 482.39
    Streptococcus pneumoniae 481
  traumatic (complication) (early) (secondary) 958.8
  tuberculous (any) (*see also* Tuberculosis) 011.6 ☑
  tularemic 021.2
  TWAR agent 483.1
  varicella 052.1
  Veillonella 482.81
  ventilator associated 997.31
  viral, virus (broncho) (interstitial) (lobar) 480.9
    with influenza, flu, or grippe 487.0
    adenoviral 480.0
    parainfluenza 480.2
    respiratory syncytial 480.1
    SARS-associated coronavirus 480.3
    specified type NEC 480.8
  white (congenital) 090.0
Pneumonic — *see* condition
Pneumonitis (acute) (primary) — *see also* Pneumonia 486
  allergic 495.9
    specified type NEC 495.8
  aspiration 507.0
    due to fumes or gases 506.0
    fetal 770.18
      due to
        blood 770.16
        clear amniotic fluid 770.14
        meconium 770.12
        postnatal stomach contents 770.86
    newborn 770.18
      due to
        blood 770.16
        clear amniotic fluid 770.14
        meconium 770.12
        postnatal stomach contents 770.86
    obstetric 668.0 ☑
  chemical 506.0
    due to fumes or gases 506.0
  cholesterol 516.8
  chronic (*see also* Fibrosis, lung) 515
  congenital rubella 771.0
  crack 506.0
  due to
    crack (cocaine) 506.0
    fumes or vapors 506.0
    inhalation
      food (regurgitated), milk, vomitus 507.0
      oils, essences 507.1
      saliva 507.0
      solids, liquids NEC 507.8
    toxoplasmosis (acquired) 130.4
      congenital (active) 771.2 *[484.8]*
  eosinophilic 518.3
  fetal aspiration 770.18
    due to
      blood 770.16
      clear amniotic fluid 770.14
      meconium 770.12
      postnatal stomach contents 770.86
  hypersensitivity 495.9
  interstitial (chronic) (*see also* Fibrosis, lung) 515
    lymphoid 516.8
  lymphoid, interstitial 516.8
  meconium aspiration 770.12
  postanesthetic
    correct substance properly administered 507.0
    obstetric 668.0 ☑
    overdose or wrong substance given 968.4
      specified anesthetic — *see* Table of Drugs and Chemicals
  postoperative 997.3 ☑
    obstetric 668.0 ☑
  radiation 508.0
  rubella, congenital 771.0
  "ventilation" 495.7
  ventilator associated 997.31 ●
  wood-dust 495.8
Pneumonoconiosis — *see* Pneumoconiosis
Pneumoparotid 527.8
Pneumopathy NEC 518.89

Pneumopathy — *continued*
  alveolar 516.9
    specified NEC 516.8
  due to dust NEC 504
  parietoalveolar 516.9
    specified condition NEC 516.8
Pneumopericarditis — *see* Pericarditis 423.9
  acute 420.90
Pneumopericardium — *see also* Pericarditis
  congenital 770.2
  fetus or newborn 770.2
  traumatic (post) (*see also* Pneumothorax, traumatic) 860.0
    with open wound into thorax 860.1
Pneumoperitoneum 568.89
  fetus or newborn 770.2
Pneumophagia (psychogenic) 306.4
Pneumopleurisy, pneumopleuritis — *see also* Pneumonia 486
Pneumopyopericardium 420.99
Pneumopyothorax — *see also* Pyopneumothorax 510.9
  with fistula 510.0
Pneumorrhagia 786.3
  newborn 770.3
  tuberculous (*see also* Tuberculosis, pulmonary) 011.9 ☑
Pneumosiderosis (occupational) 503
Pneumothorax (acute) (chronic) 512.8
  congenital 770.2
  due to operative injury of chest wall or lung 512.1
    accidental puncture or laceration 512.1
  fetus or newborn 770.2
  iatrogenic 512.1
  postoperative 512.1
  spontaneous 512.8
    fetus or newborn 770.2
    tension 512.0
  sucking 512.8
    iatrogenic 512.1
    postoperative 512.1
  tense valvular, infectional 512.0
  tension 512.0
    iatrogenic 512.1
    postoperative 512.1
    spontaneous 512.0
  traumatic 860.0
    with
      hemothorax 860.4
        with open wound into thorax 860.5
      open wound into thorax 860.1
  tuberculous (*see also* Tuberculosis) 011.7 ☑
Pocket(s)
  endocardial (*see also* Endocarditis) 424.90
  periodontal 523.8
Podagra 274.01 ▲
Podencephalus 759.89
Poikilocytosis 790.09
Poikiloderma 709.09
  Civatte's 709.09
  congenital 757.33
  vasculare atrophicans 696.2
Poikilodermatomyositis 710.3
Pointed ear 744.29
Poise imperfect 729.90
Poisoned — *see* Poisoning
Poisoning (acute) — *see also* Table of Drugs and Chemicals
  Bacillus, B.
    aertrycke (*see also* Infection, Salmonella) 003.9
    botulinus 005.1
    cholerae (suis) (*see also* Infection, Salmonella) 003.9
    paratyphosus (*see also* Infection, Salmonella) 003.9
    suipestifer (*see also* Infection, Salmonella) 003.9
  bacterial toxins NEC 005.9
  berries, noxious 988.2
  blood (general) — *see* Septicemia
  botulism 005.1
  bread, moldy, mouldy — *see* Poisoning, food
  Ciguatera 988.0
  damaged meat — *see* Poisoning, food

Poisoning — *see also* Table of Drugs and Chemicals — *continued*
  death-cap (Amanita phalloides) (Amanita verna) 988.1
  decomposed food — *see* Poisoning, food
  diseased food — *see* Poisoning, food
  drug — *see* Table of Drugs and Chemicals
  epidemic, fish, meat, or other food — *see* Poisoning, food
  fava bean 282.2
  fish (bacterial) (*see also* Poisoning, food)
    noxious 988.0
  food (acute) (bacterial) (diseased) (infected) NEC 005.9
    due to
      bacillus
        aertrycke (*see also* Poisoning, food, due to Salmonella) 003.9
        botulinus 005.1
        cereus 005.89
        choleraesuis (*see also* Poisoning, food, due to Salmonella) 003.9
        paratyphosus (*see also* Poisoning, food, due to Salmonella) 003.9
        suipestifer (*see also* Poisoning, food, due to Salmonella) 003.9
      Clostridium 005.3
        botulinum 005.1
        perfringens 005.2
        welchii 005.2
      Salmonella (aertrycke) (callinarum) (choleraesuis) (enteritidis) (paratyphi) (suipestifer) 003.9
        with
          gastroenteritis 003.0
          localized infection(s) (*see also* Infection, Salmonella) 003.20
          septicemia 003.1
          specified manifestation NEC 003.8
      specified bacterium NEC 005.89
      Staphylococcus 005.0
      Streptococcus 005.89
      Vibrio parahaemolyticus 005.4
      Vibrio vulnificus 005.81
    noxious or naturally toxic 988.0
      berries 988.2
      fish 988.0
      mushroom 988.1
      plants NEC 988.2
  ice cream — *see* Poisoning, food
  ichthyotoxism (bacterial) 005.9
  kreotoxism, food 005.9
  malarial — *see* Malaria
  meat — *see* Poisoning, food
  mushroom (noxious) 988.1
  mussel (*see also* Poisoning, food)
    noxious 988.0
  noxious foodstuffs (*see also* Poisoning, food, noxious) 988.9
    specified type NEC 988.8
  plants, noxious 988.2
  pork (*see also* Poisoning, food)
    specified NEC 988.8
    Trichinosis 124
  ptomaine — *see* Poisoning, food
  putrefaction, food — *see* Poisoning, food
  radiation 508.0
  Salmonella (*see also* Infection, Salmonella) 003.9
  sausage (*see also* Poisoning, food)
    Trichinosis 124
  saxitoxin 988.0
  shellfish (*see also* Poisoning, food)
    noxious (amnesic) (azaspiracid) (diarrheic) (neurotoxic) (paralytic) 988.0
  Staphylococcus, food 005.0
  toxic, from disease NEC 799.89
  truffles — *see* Poisoning, food
  uremic — *see* Uremia
  uric acid 274.9
  water 276.6

Poison ivy, oak, sumac or other plant dermati-tis 692.6
Poker spine 720.0
Policeman's disease 729.2
Polioencephalitis (acute) (bulbar) — *see also*
  Poliomyelitis, bulbar 045.0 ☑
  inferior 335.22
  influenzal 487.8
  superior hemorrhagic (acute) (Wernicke's)
    265.1
  Wernicke's (superior hemorrhagic) 265.1
Polioencephalomyelitis (acute) (anterior) (bul-bar) — *see also* Polioencephalitis 045.0 ☑
Polioencephalopathy, superior hemorrhagic
  265.1
  with
    beriberi 265.0
    pellagra 265.2
Poliomeningoencephalitis — *see* Meningoen-cephalitis
Poliomyelitis (acute) (anterior) (epidemic)
  045.9 ☑

  Note — Use the following fifth-digit subclassification with category 045:

  0 poliovirus, unspecified type

  1 poliovirus, type I

  2 poliovirus, type II

  3 poliovirus, type III

  with
    paralysis 045.1 ☑
      bulbar 045.0 ☑
    abortive 045.2 ☑
    ascending 045.9 ☑
      progressive 045.9 ☑
    bulbar 045.0 ☑
    cerebral 045.0 ☑
    chronic 335.21
    congenital 771.2
    contact V01.2
    deformities 138
    exposure to V01.2
    late effect 138
    nonepidemic 045.9 ☑
    nonparalytic 045.2 ☑
    old with deformity 138
    posterior, acute 053.19
    residual 138
    sequelae 138
    spinal, acute 045.9 ☑
    syphilitic (chronic) 094.89
    vaccination, prophylactic (against) V04.0
Poliosis (eyebrow) (eyelashes) 704.3
  circumscripta (congenital) 757.4
    acquired 704.3
    congenital 757.4
Pollakiuria 788.41
  psychogenic 306.53
Pollinosis 477.0
Pollitzer's disease (hidradenitis suppurativa)
  705.83
Polyadenitis — *see also* Adenitis 289.3
  malignant 020.0
Polyalgia 729.99   ▲
Polyangiitis (essential) 446.0
Polyarteritis (nodosa) (renal) 446.0
Polyarthralgia 719.49
  psychogenic 306.0
Polyarthritis, polyarthropathy NEC 716.59
  due to or associated with other specified
    conditions — *see* Arthritis, due to or
    associated with
  endemic (*see also* Disease, Kaschin-Beck)
    716.0 ☑
  inflammatory 714.9
    specified type NEC 714.89
  juvenile (chronic) 714.30
    acute 714.31
  migratory — *see* Fever, rheumatic
  rheumatic 714.0
    fever (acute) — *see* Fever, rheumatic
Polycarential syndrome of infancy 260
Polychondritis (atrophic) (chronic) (relapsing)
  733.99

Polycoria 743.46
Polycystic (congenital) (disease) 759.89
  degeneration, kidney — *see* Polycystic, kidney
  kidney (congenital) 753.12
    adult type (APKD) 753.13
    autosomal dominant 753.13
    autosomal recessive 753.14
    childhood type (CPKD) 753.14
    infantile type 753.14
  liver 751.62
  lung 518.89
    congenital 748.4
  ovary, ovaries 256.4
  spleen 759.0
Polycythemia (primary) (rubra) (vera) (M9950/1)
  238.4
  acquired 289.0
  benign 289.0
    familial 289.6
  due to
    donor twin 776.4
    fall in plasma volume 289.0
    high altitude 289.0
    maternal-fetal transfusion 776.4
    stress 289.0
  emotional 289.0
  erythropoietin 289.0
  familial (benign) 289.6
  Gaisböck's (hypertonica) 289.0
  high altitude 289.0
  hypertonica 289.0
  hypoxemic 289.0
  neonatorum 776.4
  nephrogenous 289.0
  relative 289.0
  secondary 289.0
  spurious 289.0
  stress 289.0
Polycytosis cryptogenica 289.0
Polydactylism, polydactyly 755.00
  fingers 755.01
  toes 755.02
Polydipsia 783.5
Polydystrophic oligophrenia 277.5
Polyembryoma (M9072/3) — *see* Neoplasm, by
  site, malignant
Polygalactia 676.6 ☑
Polyglandular
  deficiency 258.9
  dyscrasia 258.9
  dysfunction 258.9
  syndrome 258.8
Polyhydramnios — *see also* Hydramnios
  657.0 ☑
Polymastia 757.6
Polymenorrhea 626.2
Polymicrogyria 742.2
Polymyalgia 725
  arteritica 446.5
  rheumatica 725
Polymyositis (acute) (chronic) (hemorrhagic)
  710.4
  with involvement of
    lung 710.4 *[517.8]*
    skin 710.3
  ossificans (generalisata) (progressiva) 728.19
  Wagner's (dermatomyositis) 710.3
Polyneuritis, polyneuritic — *see also* Polyneu-ropathy 356.9
  alcoholic 357.5
    with psychosis 291.1
  cranialis 352.6
  demyelinating, chronic inflammatory (CIDP)
    357.81
  diabetic 250.6 ☑ *[357.2]*
    due to secondary diabetes 249.6 ☑ *[357.2]*
  due to lack of vitamin NEC 269.2 *[357.4]*
  endemic 265.0 *[357.4]*
  erythredema 985.0
  febrile 357.0
  hereditary ataxic 356.3
  idiopathic, acute 357.0
  infective (acute) 357.0
  nutritional 269.9 *[357.4]*
  postinfectious 357.0
Polyneuropathy (peripheral) 356.9

Polyneuropathy — *continued*
  alcoholic 357.5
  amyloid 277.39 *[357.4]*
  arsenical 357.7
  critical illness 357.82
  demyelinating, chronic inflammatory (CIDP)
    357.81
  diabetic 250.6 ☑ *[357.2]*
    due to secondary diabetes 249.6 ☑ *[357.2]*
  due to
    antitetanus serum 357.6
    arsenic 357.7
    drug or medicinal substance 357.6
      correct substance properly adminis-tered 357.6
      overdose or wrong substance given or
        taken 977.9
      specified drug — *see* Table of
        Drugs and Chemicals
    lack of vitamin NEC 269.2 *[357.4]*
    lead 357.7
    organophosphate compounds 357.7
    pellagra 265.2 *[357.4]*
    porphyria 277.1 *[357.4]*
    serum 357.6
    toxic agent NEC 357.7
  hereditary 356.0
  idiopathic 356.9
    progressive 356.4
  in
    amyloidosis 277.39 *[357.4]*
    avitaminosis 269.2 *[357.4]*
      specified NEC 269.1 *[357.4]*
    beriberi 265.0 *[357.4]*
    collagen vascular disease NEC 710.9 *[357.1]*
    deficiency
      B-complex NEC 266.2 *[357.4]*
      vitamin B 266.1 *[357.4]*
      vitamin B6 266.9 *[357.4]*
    diabetes 250.6 ☑ *[357.2]*
      due to secondary diabetes
        249.6 ☑ *[357.2]*
    diphtheria (*see also* Diphtheria)
      032.89 *[357.4]*
    disseminated lupus erythematosus
      710.0 *[357.1]*
    herpes zoster 053.13
    hypoglycemia 251.2 *[357.4]*
    malignant neoplasm (M8000/3) NEC 199.1
      [357.3]
    mumps 072.72
    pellagra 265.2 *[357.4]*
    polyarteritis nodosa 446.0 *[357.1]*
    porphyria 277.1 *[357.4]*
    rheumatoid arthritis 714.0 *[357.1]*
    sarcoidosis 135 *[357.4]*
    uremia 585.9 *[357.4]*
  lead 357.7
  nutritional 269.9 *[357.4]*
    specified NEC 269.8 *[357.4]*
  postherpetic 053.13
  progressive 356.4
  sensory (hereditary) 356.2
  specified NEC 356.8
Polyonychia 757.5
Polyopia 368.2
  refractive 368.15
Polyorchism, polyorchidism (three testes)
  752.89
Polyorrhymenitis (peritoneal) — *see also* Poly-serositis 568.82
  pericardial 423.2
Polyostotic fibrous dysplasia 756.54
Polyotia 744.1
Polyphagia 783.6
Polypoid — *see* condition
Polyposis — *see also* Polyp
  coli (adenomatous) (M8220/0) 211.3
    adenocarcinoma in (M8220/3) 153.9
    carcinoma in (M8220/3) 153.9
  familial (M8220/0) 211.3
  intestinal (adenomatous) (M8220/0) 211.3
  multiple (M8221/0) — *see* Neoplasm, by site,
    benign

Polyp, polypus

  *Note — Polyps of organs or sites that do not
  appear in the list below should be coded to
  the residual category for diseases of the organ or site concerned.*

  accessory sinus 471.8
  adenoid tissue 471.0
  adenomatous (M8210/0) (*see also* Neoplasm,
    by site, benign)
    adenocarcinoma in (M8210/3) — *see*
      Neoplasm, by site, malignant
    carcinoma in (M8210/3) — *see* Neoplasm,
      by site, malignant
    multiple (M8221/0) — *see* Neoplasm, by
      site, benign
  antrum 471.8
  anus, anal (canal) (nonadenomatous) 569.0
    adenomatous 211.4
  Bartholin's gland 624.6
  bladder (M8120/1) 236.7
  broad ligament 620.8
  cervix (uteri) 622.7
    adenomatous 219.0
    in pregnancy or childbirth 654.6 ☑
      affecting fetus or newborn 763.89
      causing obstructed labor 660.2 ☑
    mucous 622.7
    nonneoplastic 622.7
  choanal 471.0
  cholesterol 575.6
  clitoris 624.6
  colon (M8210/0) (*see also* Polyp, adenoma-tous) 211.3
  corpus uteri 621.0
  dental 522.0
  ear (middle) 385.30
  endometrium 621.0
  ethmoidal (sinus) 471.8
  fallopian tube 620.8
  female genital organs NEC 624.8
  frontal (sinus) 471.8
  gallbladder 575.6
  gingiva 523.8
  gum 523.8
  labia 624.6
  larynx (mucous) 478.4
  malignant (M8000/3) — *see* Neoplasm, by
    site, malignant
  maxillary (sinus) 471.8
  middle ear 385.30
  myometrium 621.0
  nares
    anterior 471.9
    posterior 471.0
  nasal (mucous) 471.9
    cavity 471.0
    septum 471.9
  nasopharyngeal 471.0
  neoplastic (M8210/0) — *see* Neoplasm, by
    site, benign
  nose (mucous) 471.9
  oviduct 620.8
  paratubal 620.8
  pharynx 478.29
    congenital 750.29
  placenta, placental 674.4 ☑
  prostate 600.20
    with
      other lower urinary tract symptoms
        (LUTS) 600.21
      urinary
        obstruction 600.21
        retention 600.21
  pudenda 624.6
  pulp (dental) 522.0
  rectosigmoid 211.4
  rectum (nonadenomatous) 569.0
    adenomatous 211.4
  septum (nasal) 471.9
  sinus (accessory) (ethmoidal) (frontal) (maxil-lary) (sphenoidal) 471.8
  sphenoidal 471.8
  stomach (M8210/0) 211.1
  tube, fallopian 620.8
  turbinate, mucous membrane 471.8
  ureter 593.89

Polyp, polypus — *continued*
  urethra 599.3
  uterine
    ligament 620.8
    tube 620.8
  uterus (body) (corpus) (mucous) 621.0
    in pregnancy or childbirth 654.1 ☑
      affecting fetus or newborn 763.89
      causing obstructed labor 660.2 ☑
  vagina 623.7
  vocal cord (mucous) 478.4
  vulva 624.6
Polyradiculitis (acute) 357.0
Polyradiculoneuropathy (acute) (segmentally demyelinating) 357.0
Polysarcia 278.00
Polyserositis (peritoneal) 568.82
  due to pericarditis 423.2
  paroxysmal (familial) 277.31
  pericardial 423.2
  periodic (familial) 277.31
  pleural — *see* Pleurisy
  recurrent 277.31
  tuberculous (*see also* Tuberculosis, polyserositis) 018.9 ☑
Polysialia 527.7
Polysplenia syndrome 759.0
Polythelia 757.6
Polytrichia — *see also* Hypertrichosis 704.1
Polyunguia (congenital) 757.5
  acquired 703.8
Polyuria 788.42
Pompe's disease (glycogenosis II) 271.0
Pompholyx 705.81
Poncet's disease (tuberculous rheumatism) — *see also* Tuberculosis 015.9 ☑
Pond fracture — *see* Fracture, skull, vault
Ponos 085.0
Pons, pontine — *see* condition
Poor
  aesthetics of existing restoration of tooth 525.67
  contractions, labor 661.2 ☑
    affecting fetus or newborn 763.7
  fetal growth NEC 764.9 ☑
    affecting management of pregnancy 656.5 ☑
  incorporation
    artificial skin graft 996.55
    decellularized allodermis graft 996.55
  obstetrical history V13.29
    affecting management of current pregnancy V23.49
      pre-term labor V23.41
    pre-term labor V13.21
  sucking reflex (newborn) 796.1
  vision NEC 369.9
Poradenitis, nostras 099.1
Porencephaly (congenital) (developmental) (true) 742.4
  acquired 348.0
  nondevelopmental 348.0
  traumatic (post) 310.2
Porocephaliasis 134.1
Porokeratosis 757.39
  disseminated superficial actinic (DSAP) 692.75
Poroma, eccrine (M8402/0) — *see* Neoplasm, skin, benign
Porphyria (acute) (congenital) (constitutional) (erythropoietic) (familial) (hepatica) (idiopathic) (idiosyncratic) (intermittent) (latent) (mixed hepatic) (photosensitive) (South African genetic) (Swedish) 277.1
  acquired 277.1
  cutaneatarda
    hereditaria 277.1
    symptomatica 277.1
  due to drugs
    correct substance properly administered 277.1
    overdose or wrong substance given or taken 977.9
      specified drug — *see* Table of Drugs and Chemicals
  secondary 277.1
  toxic NEC 277.1

Porphyria — *continued*
  variegata 277.1
Porphyrinuria (acquired) (congenital) (secondary) 277.1
Porphyruria (acquired) (congenital) 277.1
Portal — *see* condition
Port wine nevus or mark 757.32
Posadas-Wernicke disease 114.9
Position
  fetus, abnormal (*see also* Presentation, fetal) 652.9 ☑
  teeth, faulty (*see also* Anomaly, position tooth) 524.30
Positive
  culture (nonspecific) 795.39
    AIDS virus V08
    blood 790.7
    HIV V08
    human immunodeficiency virus V08
    nose 795.39
      Staphylococcus — *see* Carrier (suspected) of, Staphylococcus
    skin lesion NEC 795.39
    spinal fluid 792.0
    sputum 795.39
    stool 792.1
    throat 795.39
    urine 791.9
    wound 795.39
  findings, anthrax 795.31
  HIV V08
  human immunodeficiency virus (HIV) V08
  PPD 795.5
  serology
    AIDS virus V08
      inconclusive 795.71
    HIV V08
      inconclusive 795.71
    human immunodeficiency virus (HIV) V08
      inconclusive 795.71
    syphilis 097.1
      with signs or symptoms — *see* Syphilis, by site and stage
      false 795.6
  skin test 795.7 ☑
    tuberculin (without active tuberculosis) 795.5
  VDRL 097.1
    with signs or symptoms — *see* Syphilis, by site and stage
    false 795.6
  Wassermann reaction 097.1
    false 795.6
Postcardiotomy syndrome 429.4
Postcaval ureter 753.4
Postcholecystectomy syndrome 576.0
Postclimacteric bleeding 627.1
Postcommissurotomy syndrome 429.4
Postconcussional syndrome 310.2
Postcontusional syndrome 310.2
Postcricoid region — *see* condition
Post-dates (pregnancy) — *see* Pregnancy
Postencephalitic — *see also* condition
  syndrome 310.8
Posterior — *see* condition
Posterolateral sclerosis (spinal cord) — *see* Degeneration, combined
Postexanthematous — *see* condition
Postfebrile — *see* condition
Postgastrectomy dumping syndrome 564.2
Posthemiplegic chorea 344.89
Posthemorrhagic anemia (chronic) 280.0
  acute 285.1
  newborn 776.5
Posthepatitis syndrome 780.79
Postherpetic neuralgia (intercostal) (syndrome) (zoster) 053.19
  geniculate ganglion 053.11
  ophthalmica 053.19
  trigeminal 053.12
Posthitis 607.1
Postimmunization complication or reaction — *see* Complications, vaccination
Postinfectious — *see* condition
Postinfluenzal syndrome 780.79
Postlaminectomy syndrome 722.80

Postlaminectomy syndrome — *continued*
  cervical, cervicothoracic 722.81
  kyphosis 737.12
  lumbar, lumbosacral 722.83
  thoracic, thoracolumbar 722.82
Postleukotomy syndrome 310.0
Postlobectomy syndrome 310.0
Postmastectomy lymphedema (syndrome) 457.0
Postmaturity, postmature (fetus or newborn) (gestation period over 42 completed weeks) 766.22
  affecting management of pregnancy
    post-term pregnancy 645.1 ☑
    prolonged pregnancy 645.2 ☑
  syndrome 766.22
Postmeasles — *see also* condition
  complication 055.8
    specified NEC 055.79
Postmenopausal
  endometrium (atrophic) 627.8
    suppurative (see also Endometritis) 615.9
  hormone replacement therapy V07.4
  status (age related) (natural) V49.81
Postnasal drip 784.91
Postnatal — *see* condition
Postoperative — *see also* condition
  confusion state 293.9
  psychosis 293.9
  status NEC (*see also* Status (post)) V45.89
Postpancreatectomy hyperglycemia 251.3
Postpartum — *see also* condition
  anemia 648.2 ☑
  cardiomyopathy 674.5 ☑
  observation
    immediately after delivery V24.0
    routine follow-up V24.2
Postperfusion syndrome NEC 999.89
  bone marrow 996.85
Postpoliomyelitic — *see* condition
Postsurgery status NEC — *see also* Status (post) V45.89
Post-term (pregnancy) 645.1 ☑
  infant (gestation period over 40 completed weeks to 42 completed weeks) 766.21
Post-transplant lymphoproliferative disorder (PTLD) 238.77
Posttraumatic — *see* condition
Posttraumatic brain syndrome, nonpsychotic 310.2
Post-traumatic stress disorder (PTSD) 309.81
Post-typhoid abscess 002.0
Postures, hysterical 300.11
Postvaccinal reaction or complication — *see* Complications, vaccination
Postvagotomy syndrome 564.2
Postvalvulotomy syndrome 429.4
Postvasectomy sperm count V25.8
Potain's disease (pulmonary edema) 514
Potain's syndrome (gastrectasis with dyspepsia) 536.1
Pott's
  curvature (spinal) (*see also* Tuberculosis) 015.0 ☑ *[737.43]*
  disease or paraplegia (*see also* Tuberculosis) 015.0 ☑ *[730.88]*
  fracture (closed) 824.4
    open 824.5
  gangrene 440.24
  osteomyelitis (*see also* Tuberculosis) 015.0 ☑ *[730.88]*
  spinal curvature (*see also* Tuberculosis) 015.0 ☑ *[737.43]*
  tumor, puffy (*see also* Osteomyelitis) 730.2 ☑
Potter's
  asthma 502
  disease 753.0
  facies 754.0
  lung 502
  syndrome (with renal agenesis) 753.0
Pouch
  bronchus 748.3
  Douglas' — *see* condition
  esophagus, esophageal (congenital) 750.4
    acquired 530.6
  gastric 537.1

Pouch — *continued*
  Hartmann's (abnormal sacculation of gallbladder neck) 575.8
    of intestine V44.3
      attention to V55.3
  pharynx, pharyngeal (congenital) 750.27
Pouchitis 569.71
Poulet's disease 714.2
Poultrymen's itch 133.8
Poverty V60.2
PPE (palmar plantar erythrodysesthesia) 693.0
Prader-Labhart-Willi-Fanconi syndrome (hypogenital dystrophy with diabetic tendency) 759.81
Prader-Willi syndrome (hypogenital dystrophy with diabetic tendency) 759.81
Preachers' voice 784.49
Pre-AIDS — *see* Human immunodeficiency virus (disease) (illness) (infection)
Preauricular appendage 744.1
Prebetalipoproteinemia (acquired) (essential) (familial) (hereditary) (primary) (secondary) 272.1
  with chylomicronemia 272.3
Precipitate labor 661.3 ☑
  affecting fetus or newborn 763.6
Preclimacteric bleeding 627.0
  menorrhagia 627.0
Precocious
  adrenarche 259.1
  menarche 259.1
  menstruation 626.8
  pubarche 259.1
  puberty NEC 259.1
  sexual development NEC 259.1
  thelarche 259.1
Precocity, sexual (constitutional) (cryptogenic) (female) (idiopathic) (male) NEC 259.1
  with adrenal hyperplasia 255.2
Precordial pain 786.51
  psychogenic 307.89
Predeciduous teeth 520.2
Prediabetes, prediabetic 790.29
  complicating pregnancy, childbirth, or puerperium 648.8 ☑
  fetus or newborn 775.89
Predislocation status of hip, at birth — *see also* Subluxation, congenital, hip 754.32
Preeclampsia (mild) 642.4 ☑
  with pre-existing hypertension 642.7 ☑
  affecting fetus or newborn 760.0
  severe 642.5 ☑
  superimposed on pre-existing hypertensive disease 642.7 ☑
Preeruptive color change, teeth, tooth 520.8
Preexcitation 426.7
  atrioventricular conduction 426.7
  ventricular 426.7
Preglaucoma 365.00
Pregnancy (single) (uterine) (without sickness) V22.2

Note — Use the following fifth-digit subclassification with categories 640–649, 651–▶679◀:

0   *unspecified as to episode of care*

1   *delivered, with or without mention of antepartum condition*

2   *delivered, with mention of postpartum complication*

3   *antepartum condition or complication*

4   *postpartum condition or complication*

  abdominal (ectopic) 633.00
    with intrauterine pregnancy 633.01
    affecting fetus or newborn 761.4
  abnormal NEC 646.9 ☑
  ampular — *see* Pregnancy, tubal
  broad ligament — *see* Pregnancy, cornual
  cervical — *see* Pregnancy, cornual
  chemical 631
  combined (extrauterine and intrauterine) — *see* Pregnancy, cornual

---

☑ Additional Digit Required — Refer to the Tabular List for Digit Selection   ☝ Subterms under main terms may continue to next column or page

☑ Additional Digit Required — Refer to the Tabular List for Digit Selection   ⵤ Subterms under main terms may continue to next column or page

Pregnancy — *continued*
 complicated — *continued*
  placenta, placental — *continued*
    separation (premature) (undelivered) 641.2 ☑
  placentitis 658.4 ☑
  polyhydramnios 657.0 ☑
  postmaturity
    post-term 645.1 ☑
    prolonged 645.2 ☑
  prediabetes 648.8 ☑
  pre-eclampsia (mild) 642.4 ☑
    severe 642.5 ☑
    superimposed on pre-existing hypertensive disease 642.7 ☑
  premature rupture of membranes 658.1 ☑
    with delayed delivery 658.2 ☑
  previous
    infertility V23.0
    in utero procedure during previous pregnancy V23.86
    nonobstetric condition V23.89
    poor obstetrical history V23.49
    premature delivery V23.41
    trophoblastic disease (conditions classifiable to 630) V23.1
  prolapse, uterus 654.4 ☑
  proteinuria (gestational) 646.2 ☑
    with hypertension — *see* Toxemia, of pregnancy
  pruritus (neurogenic) 646.8 ☑
  psychosis or psychoneurosis 648.4 ☑
  ptyalism 646.8 ☑
  pyelitis (conditions classifiable to 590.0–590.9) 646.6 ☑
  renal disease or failure NEC 646.2 ☑
    with secondary hypertension 642.1 ☑
    hypertensive 642.2 ☑
  retention, retained dead ovum 631
  retroversion, uterus 654.3 ☑
  Rh immunization, incompatibility, or sensitization 656.1 ☑
  rubella (conditions classifiable to 056) 647.5 ☑
  rupture
    amnion (premature) 658.1 ☑
      with delayed delivery 658.2 ☑
    marginal sinus (hemorrhage) 641.2 ☑
    membranes (premature) 658.1 ☑
      with delayed delivery 658.2 ☑
    uterus (before onset of labor) 665.0 ☑
  salivation (excessive) 646.8 ☑
  salpingo-oophoritis (conditions classifiable to 614.0–614.2) 646.6 ☑
  septicemia (conditions classifiable to 038.0–038.9) 647.8 ☑
    postpartum 670.2 ☑ ▲
    puerperal 670.2 ☑ ▲
  smoking 649.0 ☑
  spasms, uterus (abnormal) 646.8 ☑
  specified condition NEC 646.8 ☑
  spotting 649.5 ☑
  spurious labor pains 644.1 ☑
  status post
    bariatric surgery 649.2 ☑
    gastric banding 649.2 ☑
    gastric bypass for obesity 649.2 ☑
    obesity surgery 649.2 ☑
  superfecundation 651.9 ☑
  superfetation 651.9 ☑
  syphilis (conditions classifiable to 090–097) 647.0 ☑
  threatened
    abortion 640.0 ☑
    premature delivery 644.2 ☑
    premature labor 644.0 ☑
  thrombophlebitis (superficial) 671.2 ☑
    deep 671.3 ☑
    septic 670.3 ☑ ●
  thrombosis 671.2 ☑ ▲
    venous (superficial) 671.2 ☑
    deep 671.3 ☑
  thyroid dysfunction (conditions classifiable to 240–246) 648.1 ☑

Pregnancy — *continued*
 complicated — *continued*
  thyroiditis 648.1 ☑
  thyrotoxicosis 648.1 ☑
  tobacco use disorder 649.0 ☑
  torsion of uterus 654.4 ☑
  toxemia — *see* Toxemia, of pregnancy
  transverse lie or presentation 652.3 ☑
    with successful version 652.1 ☑
  trauma 648.9 ☑
    obstetrical 665.9 ☑
  tuberculosis (conditions classifiable to 010–018) 647.3 ☑
  tumor
    cervix 654.6 ☑
    ovary 654.4 ☑
    pelvic organs or tissue NEC 654.4 ☑
    uterus (body) 654.1 ☑
      cervix 654.6 ☑
    vagina 654.7 ☑
    vulva 654.8 ☑
  unstable lie 652.0 ☑
  uremia — *see* Pregnancy, complicated, renal disease
  urethritis 646.6 ☑
  vaginitis or vulvitis (conditions classifiable to 616.1) 646.6 ☑
  varicose
    placental vessels 656.7 ☑
    veins (legs) 671.0 ☑
      perineum 671.1 ☑
      vulva 671.1 ☑
  varicosity, labia or vulva 671.1 ☑
  venereal disease NEC (conditions classifiable to 099) 647.2 ☑
  venous complication 671.9 ☑ ●
  viral disease NEC (conditions classifiable to 042, 050–055, 057–079, 795.05, 795.15, 796.75) 647.6 ☑
  vomiting (incoercible) (pernicious) (persistent) (uncontrollable) (vicious) 643.9 ☑
    due to organic disease or other cause 643.8 ☑
    early — *see* Hyperemesis, gravidarum
    late (after 22 completed weeks gestation) 643.2 ☑
  young maternal age 659.8 ☑
 complications NEC 646.9 ☑
 cornual 633.80
   with intrauterine pregnancy 633.81
     affecting fetus or newborn 761.4
 death, maternal NEC 646.9 ☑
 delivered — *see* Delivery
 ectopic (ruptured) NEC 633.90
   with intrauterine pregnancy 633.91
   abdominal — *see* Pregnancy, abdominal
     affecting fetus or newborn 761.4
   combined (extrauterine and intrauterine) — *see* Pregnancy, cornual
   ovarian — *see* Pregnancy, ovarian
   specified type NEC 633.80
     with intrauterine pregnancy 633.81
       affecting fetus or newborn 761.4
   tubal — *see* Pregnancy, tubal
 examination, pregnancy
   negative result V72.41
   not confirmed V72.40
   positive result V72.42
 extrauterine — *see* Pregnancy, ectopic
 fallopian — *see* Pregnancy, tubal
 false 300.11
   labor (pains) 644.1 ☑
 fatigue 646.8 ☑
 illegitimate V61.6
 incidental finding V22.2
 in double uterus 654.0 ☑
 interstitial — *see* Pregnancy, cornual
 intraligamentous — *see* Pregnancy, cornual
 intramural — *see* Pregnancy, cornual
 intraperitoneal — *see* Pregnancy, abdominal
 isthmian — *see* Pregnancy, tubal
 management affected by
   abnormal, abnormality
     fetus (suspected) 655.9 ☑

Pregnancy — *continued*
 management affected by — *continued*
  abnormal, abnormality — *continued*
    fetus — *continued*
      specified NEC 655.8 ☑
    placenta 656.7 ☑
  advanced maternal age NEC 659.6 ☑
    multigravida 659.6 ☑
    primigravida 659.5 ☑
  antibodies (maternal)
    anti-c 656.1 ☑
    anti-d 656.1 ☑
    anti-e 656.1 ☑
    blood group (ABO) 656.2 ☑
      Rh(esus) 656.1 ☑
  appendicitis 648.9 ☑
  bariatric surgery status 649.2 ☑
  coagulation defect 649.3 ☑
  elderly multigravida 659.6 ☑
  elderly primigravida 659.5 ☑
  epilepsy 649.4 ☑
  fetal (suspected)
    abnormality 655.9 ☑
      abdominal 655.8 ☑
      acid-base balance 656.8 ☑
      cardiovascular 655.8 ☑
      facial 655.8 ☑
      gastrointestinal 655.8 ☑
      genitourinary 655.8 ☑
      heart rate or rhythm 659.7 ☑
      limb 655.8 ☑
      specified NEC 655.8 ☑
    acidemia 656.3 ☑
    anencephaly 655.0 ☑
    aneuploidy 655.1 ☑
    bradycardia 659.7 ☑
    central nervous system malformation 655.0 ☑
    chromosomal abnormalities (conditions classifiable to 758.0–758.9) 655.1 ☑
    damage from
      drugs 655.5 ☑
        obstetric, anesthetic, or sedative 655.5 ☑
      environmental toxins 655.8 ☑
      intrauterine contraceptive device 655.8 ☑
      maternal
        alcohol addiction 655.4 ☑
        disease NEC 655.4 ☑
        drug use 655.5 ☑
        listeriosis 655.4 ☑
        rubella 655.3 ☑
        toxoplasmosis 655.4 ☑
        viral infection 655.3 ☑
      radiation 655.6 ☑
    death (near term) 656.4 ☑
      early (before 22 completed weeks' gestation) 632
    distress 656.8 ☑
    excessive growth 656.6 ☑
    fetal-maternal hemorrhage 656.0 ☑
    growth retardation 656.5 ☑
    hereditary disease 655.2 ☑
    hereditary disease in family (possibly) affecting fetus 655.2 ☑
    hydrocephalus 655.0 ☑
    incompatibility, blood groups (ABO) 656.2 ☑
    intrauterine death 656.4 ☑
    poor growth 656.5 ☑
    Rh(esus) 656.1 ☑
    spina bifida (with myelomeningocele) 655.0 ☑
  gastric banding status 649.2 ☑
  gastric bypass status for obesity 649.2 ☑
  insufficient prenatal care V23.7
  intrauterine death 656.4 ☑
  isoimmunization (ABO) 656.2 ☑
    Rh(esus) 656.1 ☑
  large-for-dates fetus 656.6 ☑
  light-for-dates fetus 656.5 ☑
  meconium in liquor 656.8 ☑

Pregnancy — *continued*
 management affected by — *continued*
  mental disorder (conditions classifiable to 290–303, 305.0, 305.2–305.9, 306–316, 317–319) 648.4 ☑
  multiparity (grand) 659.4 ☑
  obesity 649.1 ☑
    surgery status 649.2 ☑
  poor obstetric history V23.49
    pre-term labor V23.41
  postmaturity
    post-term 645.1 ☑
    prolonged 645.2 ☑
  post-term pregnancy 645.1 ☑
  previous
    abortion V23.2
      habitual 646.3 ☑
    cesarean delivery 654.2 ☑
    difficult delivery V23.49
    forceps delivery V23.49
    habitual abortions 646.3 ☑
    hemorrhage, antepartum or postpartum V23.49
    hydatidiform mole V23.1
    infertility V23.0
    in utero procedure during previous pregnancy V23.86
    malignancy NEC V23.89
    nonobstetrical conditions V23.8 ☑
    premature delivery V23.41
    trophoblastic disease (conditions in 630) V23.1
    vesicular mole V23.1
  prolonged pregnancy 645.2 ☑
  small-for-dates fetus 656.5 ☑
  smoking 649.0 ☑
  spotting 649.5 ☑
  suspected conditions not found
    amniotic cavity and membrane problem V89.01
    cervical shortening V89.05
    fetal anomaly V89.03
    fetal growth problem V89.04
    oligohydramnios V89.01
    other specified problem NEC V89.09
    placental problem V89.02
    polyhydramnios V89.01
  tobacco use disorder 649.0 ☑
  venous complication 671.9 ☑ ●
  young maternal age 659.8 ☑
 maternal death NEC 646.9 ☑
 mesometric (mural) — *see* Pregnancy, cornual
 molar 631
   hydatidiform (*see also* Hydatidiform mole) 630
     previous, affecting management of pregnancy V23.1
     previous, affecting management of pregnancy V23.49
 multiple NEC 651.9 ☑
   with fetal loss and retention of one or more fetus(es) 651.6 ☑
   affecting fetus or newborn 761.5
   following (elective) fetal reduction 651.7 ☑
   specified type NEC 651.8 ☑
     with fetal loss and retention of one or more fetus(es) 651.6 ☑
     following (elective) fetal reduction 651.7 ☑
 mural — *see* Pregnancy, cornual
 observation NEC V22.1
   first pregnancy V22.0
   high-risk V23.9
     specified problem NEC V23.89
 ovarian 633.20
   with intrauterine pregnancy 633.21
     affecting fetus or newborn 761.4
 possible, not (yet) confirmed V72.40
 postmature
   post-term 645.1 ☑
   prolonged 645.2 ☑
 post-term 645.1 ☑
 prenatal care only V22.1
   first pregnancy V22.0

Pregnancy — continued
 prenatal care only — continued
  high-risk V23.9
   specified problem NEC V23.89
 prolonged 645.2 ☑
 quadruplet NEC 651.2 ☑
  with fetal loss and retention of one or more
    fetus(es) 651.5 ☑
  affecting fetus or newborn 761.5
  following (elective) fetal reduction
    651.7 ☑
 quintuplet NEC 651.8 ☑
  with fetal loss and retention of one or more
    fetus(es) 651.6 ☑
  affecting fetus or newborn 761.5
  following (elective) fetal reduction
    651.7 ☑
 resulting from
  assisted reproductive technology V23.85
  in vitro fertilization V23.85
 sextuplet NEC 651.8 ☑
  with fetal loss and retention of one or more
    fetus(es) 651.6 ☑
  affecting fetus or newborn 761.5
  following (elective) fetal reduction
    651.7 ☑
 spurious 300.11
 superfecundation NEC 651.9 ☑
  with fetal loss and retention of one or more
    fetus(es) 651.6 ☑
  following (elective) fetal reduction
    651.7 ☑
 superfetation NEC 651.9 ☑
  with fetal loss and retention of one or more
    fetus(es) 651.6 ☑
  following (elective) fetal reduction
    651.7 ☑
 supervision (of) (for) (see also Pregnancy,
    management affected by)
  elderly
   multigravida V23.82
   primigravida V23.81
  high-risk V23.9
   insufficient prenatal care V23.7
   specified problem NEC V23.89
  multiparity V23.3
  normal NEC V22.1
   first V22.0
  poor
   obstetric history V23.49
    pre-term labor V23.41
   reproductive history V23.5
  previous
   abortion V23.2
   hydatidiform mole V23.1
   infertility V23.0
   neonatal death V23.5
   stillbirth V23.5
   trophoblastic disease V23.1
   vesicular mole V23.1
  specified problem NEC V23.89
  young
   multigravida V23.84
   primigravida V23.83
 triplet NEC 651.1 ☑
  with fetal loss and retention of one or more
    fetus(es) 651.4 ☑
  affecting fetus or newborn 761.5
  following (elective) fetal reduction
    651.7 ☑
 tubal (with rupture) 633.10
  with intrauterine pregnancy 633.11
  affecting fetus or newborn 761.4
 twin NEC 651.0 ☑
  with fetal loss and retention of one fetus
    651.3 ☑
  affecting fetus or newborn 761.5
  conjoined 678.1 ☑
  following (elective) fetal reduction
    651.7 ☑
 unconfirmed V72.40
 undelivered (no other diagnosis) V22.2
  with false labor 644.1 ☑
  high-risk V23.9
   specified problem NEC V23.89

Pregnancy — continued
 unwanted NEC V61.7
Pregnant uterus — see condition
Preiser's disease (osteoporosis) 733.09
Prekwashiorkor 260
Preleukemia 238.75
Preluxation of hip, congenital — see also Sub-
    luxation, congenital, hip 754.32
Premature — see also condition
 beats (nodal) 427.60
  atrial 427.61
  auricular 427.61
  postoperative 997.1
  specified type NEC 427.69
  supraventricular 427.61
  ventricular 427.69
 birth NEC 765.1 ☑
 closure
  cranial suture 756.0
  fontanel 756.0
  foramen ovale 745.8
 contractions 427.60
  atrial 427.61
  auricular 427.61
  auriculoventricular 427.61
  heart (extrasystole) 427.60
  junctional 427.60
  nodal 427.60
  postoperative 997.1
  ventricular 427.69
 ejaculation 302.75
 infant NEC 765.1 ☑
  excessive 765.0 ☑
  light-for-dates — see Light-for-dates
 labor 644.2 ☑
  threatened 644.0 ☑
 lungs 770.4
 menopause 256.31
 puberty 259.1
 rupture of membranes or amnion 658.1 ☑
  affecting fetus or newborn 761.1
  delayed delivery following 658.2 ☑
 senility (syndrome) 259.8
 separation, placenta (partial) — see Placenta,
    separation
 ventricular systole 427.69
Prematurity NEC 765.1 ☑
 extreme 765.0 ☑
Premenstrual syndrome 625.4
Premenstrual tension 625.4
Premolarization, cuspids 520.2
Premyeloma 273.1
Prenatal
 care, normal pregnancy V22.1
  first V22.0
 death, cause unknown — see Death, fetus
 screening — see Antenatal, screening
 teeth 520.6
Prepartum — see condition
Preponderance, left or right ventricular 429.3
Prepuce — see condition
PRES (posterior reversible encephalopathy syn-
    drome) 348.39
Presbycardia 797
 hypertensive (see also Hypertension, heart)
    402.90
Presbycusis 388.01
Presbyesophagus 530.89
Presbyophrenia 310.1
Presbyopia 367.4
Prescription of contraceptives NEC V25.02
 diaphragm V25.02
 oral (pill) V25.01
  emergency V25.03
  postcoital V25.03
  repeat V25.41
 repeat V25.40
  oral (pill) V25.41
Presenile — see also condition
 aging 259.8
 dementia (see also Dementia, presenile) 290.10
Presenility 259.8
Presentation, fetal
 abnormal 652.9 ☑
  with successful version 652.1 ☑

Presentation, fetal — continued
 abnormal — continued
  before labor, affecting fetus or newborn
    761.7
  causing obstructed labor 660.0 ☑
   affecting fetus or newborn, any, except
    breech 763.1
  in multiple gestation (one or more)
    652.6 ☑
  specified NEC 652.8 ☑
 arm 652.7 ☑
  causing obstructed labor 660.0 ☑
 breech (buttocks) (complete) (frank) 652.2 ☑
  with successful version 652.1 ☑
   before labor, affecting fetus or new-
    born 761.7
  before labor, affecting fetus or newborn
    761.7
 brow 652.4 ☑
  causing obstructed labor 660.0 ☑
 buttocks 652.2 ☑
 chin 652.4 ☑
 complete 652.2 ☑
 compound 652.8 ☑
 cord 663.0 ☑
 extended head 652.4 ☑
 face 652.4 ☑
  to pubes 652.8 ☑
 footling 652.8 ☑
 frank 652.2 ☑
 hand, leg, or foot NEC 652.8 ☑
 incomplete 652.8 ☑
 mentum 652.4 ☑
 multiple gestation (one fetus or more)
    652.6 ☑
 oblique 652.3 ☑
  with successful version 652.1 ☑
 shoulder 652.8 ☑
  affecting fetus or newborn 763.1
 transverse 652.3 ☑
  with successful version 652.1 ☑
 umbilical cord 663.0 ☑
 unstable 652.0 ☑
Prespondylolisthesis (congenital) (lumbosacral)
    756.11
Pressure
 area, skin ulcer (see also Ulcer, pressure) 707.00
 atrophy, spine 733.99
 birth, fetus or newborn NEC 767.9
 brachial plexus 353.0
 brain 348.4
  injury at birth 767.0
 cerebral — see Pressure, brain
 chest 786.59
 cone, tentorial 348.4
  injury at birth 767.0
 funis — see Compression, umbilical cord
 hyposystolic (see also Hypotension) 458.9
 increased
  intracranial 781.99
   due to
    benign intracranial hypertension
    348.2
    hydrocephalus — see hydro-
    cephalus
    injury at birth 767.8
  intraocular 365.00
 lumbosacral plexus 353.1
 mediastinum 519.3
 necrosis (chronic) (skin) (see also Decubitus)
    707.00
 nerve — see Compression, nerve
 paralysis (see also Neuropathy, entrapment)
    355.9
 pre-ulcer skin changes limited to persistent
    focal erythema (see also Ulcer, pressure)
    707.21
 sore (chronic) (see also Ulcer, pressure) 707.00
 spinal cord 336.9
 ulcer (chronic) (see also Ulcer, pressure) 707.00
 umbilical cord — see Compression, umbilical
    cord
 venous, increased 459.89
Pre-syncope 780.2
Preterm infant NEC 765.1 ☑

Preterm infant — continued
 extreme 765.0 ☑
Priapism (penis) 607.3
Prickling sensation — see also Disturbance,
    sensation 782.0
Prickly heat 705.1
Primary — see condition
Primigravida, elderly
 affecting
  fetus or newborn 763.89
  management of pregnancy, labor, and
    delivery 659.5 ☑
Primipara, old
 affecting
  fetus or newborn 763.89
  management of pregnancy, labor, and
    delivery 659.5 ☑
Primula dermatitis 692.6
Primus varus (bilateral) (metatarsus) 754.52
PRIND (prolonged reversible ischemic neurologic
    deficit) 434.91
 history of (personal) V12.54
Pringle's disease (tuberous sclerosis) 759.5
Prinzmetal's angina 413.1
Prinzmetal-Massumi syndrome (anterior chest
    wall) 786.52
Prizefighter ear 738.7
Problem (with) V49.9
 academic V62.3
 acculturation V62.4
 adopted child V61.24   ▲
 aged
  in-law V61.3
  parent V61.3
  person NEC V61.8
 alcoholism in family V61.41
 anger reaction (see also Disturbance, conduct)
    312.0
 behavioral V40.9
  specified NEC V40.3
 behavior, child 312.9
 betting V69.3
 biological child V61.23   ●
 cardiorespiratory NEC V47.2
 career choice V62.29
 care of sick or handicapped person in family
    or household V61.49
 communication V40.1
 conscience regarding medical care V62.6
 delinquency (juvenile) 312.9
 diet, inappropriate V69.1
 digestive NEC V47.3
 ear NEC V41.3
 eating habits, inappropriate V69.1
 economic V60.2
  affecting care V60.9
   specified type NEC V60.89   ▲
 educational V62.3
 enuresis, child 307.6
 exercise, lack of V69.0
 eye NEC V41.1
 family V61.9
  specified circumstance NEC V61.8
 fear reaction, child 313.0
 feeding (elderly) (infant) 783.3
  newborn 779.31   ▲
  nonorganic 307.59
 fetal, affecting management of pregnancy
    656.9 ☑
  specified type NEC 656.8 ☑
 financial V60.2
 foster child V61.25   ▲
 functional V41.9
  specified type NEC V41.8
 gambling V69.3
 genital NEC V47.5
 head V48.9
  deficiency V48.0
  disfigurement V48.6
  mechanical V48.2
  motor V48.2
  movement of V48.2
  sensory V48.4
  specified condition NEC V48.8
 hearing V41.2
 high-risk sexual behavior V69.2

Problem — *continued*
  identity 313.82
  influencing health status NEC V49.89
  internal organ NEC V47.9
    deficiency V47.0
    mechanical or motor V47.1
  interpersonal NEC V62.81
  jealousy, child 313.3
  learning V40.0
  legal V62.5
  life circumstance NEC V62.89
  lifestyle V69.9
    specified NEC V69.8
  limb V49.9
    deficiency V49.0
    disfigurement V49.4
    mechanical V49.1
    motor V49.2
    movement, involving
      musculoskeletal system V49.1
      nervous system V49.2
    sensory V49.3
    specified condition NEC V49.5
  litigation V62.5
  living alone V60.3
  loneliness NEC V62.89
  marital V61.10
    involving
      divorce V61.03
      estrangement V61.09
      psychosexual disorder 302.9
      sexual function V41.7
    relationship V61.10
  mastication V41.6
  medical care, within family V61.49
  mental V40.9
    specified NEC V40.2
  mental hygiene, adult V40.9
  multiparity V61.5
  nail biting, child 307.9
  neck V48.9
    deficiency V48.1
    disfigurement V48.7
    mechanical V48.3
    motor V48.3
    movement V48.3
    sensory V48.5
    specified condition NEC V48.8
  neurological NEC 781.99
  none (feared complaint unfounded) V65.5
  occupational V62.29
  parent-child V61.20
    adopted child V61.24 ●
    biological child V61.23 ●
    foster child V61.25 ●
    relationship V61.20
  partner V61.10
    relationship V61.10
  personal NEC V62.89
    interpersonal conflict NEC V62.81
  personality (*see also* Disorder, personality) 301.9
  phase of life V62.89
  placenta, affecting management of pregnancy 656.9 ☑
    specified type NEC 656.8 ☑
  poverty V60.2
  presence of sick or handicapped person in family or household V61.49
  psychiatric 300.9
  psychosocial V62.9
    specified type NEC V62.89
  relational NEC V62.81
  relationship, childhood 313.3
  religious or spiritual belief
    other than medical care V62.89
    regarding medical care V62.6
  self-damaging behavior V69.8
  sexual
    behavior, high-risk V69.2
    function NEC V41.7
  sibling
    relational V61.8
    relationship V61.8
  sight V41.0
  sleep disorder, child 307.40

Problem — *continued*
  sleep, lack of V69.4
  smell V41.5
  speech V40.1
  spite reaction, child (*see also* Disturbance, conduct) 312.0 ☑
  spoiled child reaction (*see also* Disturbance, conduct) 312.1 ☑
  substance abuse in family V61.42 ●
  swallowing V41.6
  tantrum, child (*see also* Disturbance, conduct) 312.1 ☑
  taste V41.5
  thumb sucking, child 307.9
  tic (child) 307.21
  trunk V48.9
    deficiency V48.1
    disfigurement V48.7
    mechanical V48.3
    motor V48.3
    movement V48.3
    sensory V48.5
    specified condition NEC V48.8
  unemployment V62.0
  urinary NEC V47.4
  voice production V41.4
Procedure (surgical) **not done** NEC V64.3
  because of
    contraindication V64.1
    patient's decision V64.2
      for reasons of conscience or religion V62.6
    specified reason NEC V64.3
Procidentia
  anus (sphincter) 569.1
  rectum (sphincter) 569.1
  stomach 537.89
  uteri 618.1
Proctalgia 569.42
  fugax 564.6
  spasmodic 564.6
    psychogenic 307.89
Proctitis 569.49
  amebic 006.8
  chlamydial 099.52
  gonococcal 098.7
  granulomatous 555.1
  idiopathic 556.2
    with ulcerative sigmoiditis 556.3
  tuberculous (*see also* Tuberculosis) 014.8 ☑
  ulcerative (chronic) (nonspecific) 556.2
    with ulcerative sigmoiditis 556.3
Proctocele
  female (without uterine prolapse) 618.04
    with uterine prolapse 618.4
      complete 618.3
      incomplete 618.2
  male 569.49
Proctocolitis, idiopathic 556.2
  with ulcerative sigmoiditis 556.3
Proctoptosis 569.1
Proctosigmoiditis 569.89
  ulcerative (chronic) 556.3
Proctospasm 564.6
  psychogenic 306.4
Prodromal-AIDS — *see* Human immunodeficiency virus (disease) (illness) (infection)
Profichet's disease or syndrome 729.90
Progeria (adultorum) (syndrome) 259.8
Prognathism (mandibular) (maxillary) 524.00
Progonoma (melanotic) (M9363/0) — *see* Neoplasm, by site, benign
Progressive — *see* condition
Prolapse, prolapsed
  anus, anal (canal) (sphincter) 569.1
  arm or hand, complicating delivery 652.7 ☑
    causing obstructed labor 660.0 ☑
      affecting fetus or newborn 763.1
    fetus or newborn 763.1
  bladder (acquired) (mucosa) (sphincter)
    congenital (female) (male) 756.71
    female (*see also* Cystocele, female) 618.01
    male 596.8
  breast implant (prosthetic) 996.54
  cecostomy 569.69
  cecum 569.89

Prolapse, prolapsed — *continued*
  cervix, cervical (hypertrophied) 618.1
    anterior lip, obstructing labor 660.2 ☑
      affecting fetus or newborn 763.1
    congenital 752.49
    postpartal (old) 618.1
    stump 618.84
  ciliary body 871.1
  colon (pedunculated) 569.89
  colostomy 569.69
  conjunctiva 372.73
  cord — *see* Prolapse, umbilical cord
  disc (intervertebral) — *see* Displacement, intervertebral disc
  duodenum 537.89
  eye implant (orbital) 996.59
    lens (ocular) 996.53
  fallopian tube 620.4
  fetal extremity, complicating delivery 652.8 ☑
    causing obstructed labor 660.0 ☑
    fetus or newborn 763.1
  funis — *see* Prolapse, umbilical cord
  gastric (mucosa) 537.89
  genital, female 618.9
    specified NEC 618.89
  globe 360.81
  ileostomy bud 569.69
  intervertebral disc — *see* Displacement, intervertebral disc
  intestine (small) 569.89
  iris 364.89
    traumatic 871.1
  kidney (*see also* Disease, renal) 593.0
    congenital 753.3
  laryngeal muscles or ventricle 478.79
  leg, complicating delivery 652.8 ☑
    causing obstructed labor 660.0 ☑
    fetus or newborn 763.1
  liver 573.8
  meatus urinarius 599.5
  mitral valve 424.0
  ocular lens implant 996.53
  organ or site, congenital NEC — *see* Malposition, congenital
  ovary 620.4
  pelvic (floor), female 618.89
  perineum, female 618.89
  pregnant uterus 654.4 ☑
  rectum (mucosa) (sphincter) 569.1
    due to Trichuris trichiuria 127.3
  spleen 289.59
  stomach 537.89
  umbilical cord
    affecting fetus or newborn 762.4
    complicating delivery 663.0 ☑
  ureter 593.89
    with obstruction 593.4
  ureterovesical orifice 593.89
  urethra (acquired) (infected) (mucosa) 599.5
    congenital 753.8
  uterovaginal 618.4
    complete 618.3
    incomplete 618.2
    specified NEC 618.89
  uterus (first degree) (second degree) (third degree) (complete) (without vaginal wall prolapse) 618.1
    with mention of vaginal wall prolapse — *see* Prolapse, uterovaginal
    congenital 752.3
    in pregnancy or childbirth 654.4 ☑
      affecting fetus or newborn 763.1
      causing obstructed labor 660.2 ☑
        affecting fetus or newborn 763.1
    postpartal (old) 618.1
  uveal 871.1
  vagina (anterior) (posterior) (vault) (wall) (without uterine prolapse) 618.00
    with uterine prolapse 618.4
      complete 618.3
      incomplete 618.2
    paravaginal 618.02
    posthysterectomy 618.5
    specified NEC 618.09
  vitreous (humor) 379.26
    traumatic 871.1

Prolapse, prolapsed — *continued*
  womb — *see* Prolapse, uterus
Prolapsus, female 618.9
Proliferative — *see* condition
Prolinemia 270.8
Prolinuria 270.8
Prolonged, prolongation
  bleeding time (*see also* Defect, coagulation) 790.92
    "idiopathic" (in von Willebrand's disease) 286.4
  coagulation time (*see also* Defect, coagulation) 790.92
  gestation syndrome 766.22
  labor 662.1 ☑
    affecting fetus or newborn 763.89
    first stage 662.0 ☑
    second stage 662.2 ☑
  pregnancy 645.2 ☑
  PR interval 426.11
  prothrombin time (*see also* Defect, coagulation) 790.92
  QT interval 794.31
    syndrome 426.82
  rupture of membranes (24 hours or more prior to onset of labor) 658.2 ☑
  uterine contractions in labor 661.4 ☑
    affecting fetus or newborn 763.7
Prominauris 744.29
Prominence
  auricle (ear) (congenital) 744.29
    acquired 380.32
  ischial spine or sacral promontory
    with disproportion (fetopelvic) 653.3 ☑
      affecting fetus or newborn 763.1
      causing obstructed labor 660.1 ☑
        affecting fetus or newborn 763.1
  nose (congenital) 748.1
    acquired 738.0
PROMM (proximal myotonic myotonia) 359.21
Pronation
  ankle 736.79
  foot 736.79
    congenital 755.67
Prophylactic
  administration of
    agents affecting estrogen receptors and estrogen levels NEC V07.59
    anastrozole (Arimidex) V07.52
    antibiotics V58.62
    antitoxin, any V07.2
    antivenin V07.2
    aromatase inhibitors V07.52
    chemotherapeutic agent NEC V07.39
      fluoride V07.31
    diphtheria antitoxin V07.2
    drug V07.39
    estrogen receptor downregulators V07.59
    exemestane (Aromasin) V07.52 ●
    exemestar (Aromasin) V07.52
    fulvestrant (Faslodex) V07.59
    gamma globulin V07.2
    gonadotropin-releasing hormone (GnRH) agonist V07.59
    goserelin acetate (Zoladex) V07.59
    immune sera (gamma globulin) V07.2
    letrozole (Femara) V07.52
    leuprolide acetate (leuprorelin) (Lupron) V07.59
    megestrol acetate (Megace) V07.59
    raloxifene (Evista) V07.51
    RhoGAM V07.2
    selective estrogen receptor modulators (SERMs) V07.51
    tamoxifen (Nolvadex) V07.51
    tetanus antitoxin V07.2
    toremifene (Fareston) V07.51
  chemotherapy NEC V07.39
    fluoride V07.31
  hormone replacement (postmenopausal) V07.4
  immunotherapy V07.2
  measure V07.9
    specified type NEC V07.8
  medication V07.39
  postmenopausal hormone replacement V07.4

☑ Additional Digit Required — Refer to the Tabular List for Digit Selection   ▽ Subterms under main terms may continue to next column or page

2010 ICD-9-CM   ▶◀ Revised Text   ● New Line   ▲ Revised Code   October 2009 · Volume 2 — 229

Prophylactic — continued
sterilization V25.2
Proptosis (ocular) — see also Exophthalmos
376.30
thyroid 242.0 ☑
Propulsion
eyeball 360.81
Prosecution, anxiety concerning V62.5
Prosopagnosia 368.16
Prostate, prostatic — see condition
Prostatism 600.90
with
other lower urinary tract symptoms (LUTS)
600.91
urinary
obstruction 600.91
retention 600.91
Prostatitis (congestive) (suppurative) 601.9
acute 601.0
cavitary 601.8
chlamydial 099.54
chronic 601.1
diverticular 601.8
due to Trichomonas (vaginalis) 131.03
fibrous 600.90
with
other lower urinary tract symptoms
(LUTS) 600.91
urinary
obstruction 600.91
retention 600.91
gonococcal (acute) 098.12
chronic or duration of 2 months or over
098.32
granulomatous 601.8
hypertrophic 600.00
with
other lower urinary tract symptoms
(LUTS) 600.01
urinary
obstruction 600.01
retention 600.01
specified type NEC 601.8
subacute 601.1
trichomonal 131.03
tuberculous (see also Tuberculosis)
016.5 ☑ [601.4]
Prostatocystitis 601.3
Prostatorrhea 602.8
Prostatoseminovesiculitis, trichomonal 131.03
Prostration 780.79
heat 992.5
anhydrotic 992.3
due to
salt (and water) depletion 992.4
water depletion 992.3
nervous 300.5
newborn 779.89
senile 797
Protanomaly 368.51
Protanopia (anomalous trichromat) (complete)
(incomplete) 368.51
Protection (against) (from) — see Prophylactic
Protein
deficiency 260
malnutrition 260
sickness (prophylactic) (therapeutic) 999.5
Proteinemia 790.99
Proteinosis
alveolar, lung or pulmonary 516.0
lipid 272.8
lipoid (of Urbach) 272.8
Proteinuria — see also Albuminuria 791.0
Bence-Jones NEC 791.0
gestational 646.2 ☑
with hypertension — see Toxemia, of
pregnancy
orthostatic 593.6
postural 593.6
Proteolysis, pathologic 286.6
Protocoproporphyria 277.1
Protoporphyria (erythepatic) (erythropoietic)
277.1
Protrusio acetabuli 718.65
Protrusion
acetabulum (into pelvis) 718.65

Protrusion — continued
device, implant, or graft — see Complications,
mechanical
ear, congenital 744.29
intervertebral disc — see Displacement, intervertebral disc
nucleus pulposus — see Displacement, intervertebral disc
Proud flesh 701.5
Prune belly (syndrome) 756.71
Prurigo (ferox) (gravis) (Hebra's) (hebrae) (mitis)
(simplex) 698.2
agria 698.3
asthma syndrome 691.8
Besnier's (atopic dermatitis) (infantile eczema)
691.8
eczematodes allergicum 691.8
estivalis (Hutchinson's) 692.72
Hutchinson's 692.72
nodularis 698.3
psychogenic 306.3
Pruritus, pruritic 698.9
ani 698.0
psychogenic 306.3
conditions NEC 698.9
psychogenic 306.3
due to Onchocerca volvulus 125.3
ear 698.9
essential 698.9
genital organ(s) 698.1
psychogenic 306.3
gravidarum 646.8 ☑
hiemalis 698.8
neurogenic (any site) 306.3
perianal 698.0
psychogenic (any site) 306.3
scrotum 698.1
psychogenic 306.3
senile, senilis 698.8
Trichomonas 131.9
vulva, vulvae 698.1
psychogenic 306.3
Psammocarcinoma (M8140/3) — see Neoplasm,
by site, malignant
Pseudarthrosis, pseudoarthrosis (bone) 733.82
joint following fusion V45.4
Pseudoacanthosis
nigricans 701.8
Pseudoaneurysm — see Aneurysm
Pseudoangina (pectoris) — see Angina
Pseudoangioma 452
Pseudo-Argyll-Robertson pupil 379.45
Pseudoarteriosus 747.89
Pseudoarthrosis — see Pseudarthrosis
Pseudoataxia 799.89
Pseudobulbar affect (PBA) 310.8
Pseudobursa 727.89
Pseudocholera 025
Pseudochromidrosis 705.89
Pseudocirrhosis, liver, pericardial 423.2
Pseudocoarctation 747.21
Pseudocowpox 051.1
Pseudocoxalgia 732.1
Pseudocroup 478.75
Pseudocyesis 300.11
Pseudocyst
lung 518.89
pancreas 577.2
retina 361.19
Pseudodementia 300.16
Pseudoelephantiasis neuroarthritica 757.0
Pseudoemphysema 518.89
Pseudoencephalitis
superior (acute) hemorrhagic 265.1
Pseudoerosion cervix, congenital 752.49
Pseudoexfoliation, lens capsule 366.11
Pseudofracture (idiopathic) (multiple) (sponta-
neous) (symmetrical) 268.2
Pseudoglanders 025
Pseudoglioma 360.44
Pseudogout — see Chondrocalcinosis
Pseudohallucination 780.1
Pseudohemianesthesia 782.0
Pseudohemophilia (Bernuth's) (hereditary)
(typeB) 286.4
type A 287.8

Pseudohemophilia — continued
vascular 287.8
Pseudohermaphroditism 752.7
with chromosomal anomaly — see Anomaly,
chromosomal
adrenal 255.2
female (without adrenocortical disorder) 752.7
with adrenocortical disorder 255.2
adrenal 255.2
male (without gonadal disorder) 752.7
with
adrenocortical disorder 255.2
cleft scrotum 752.7
feminizing testis 259.51
gonadal disorder 257.9
adrenal 255.2
Pseudohole, macula 362.54
Pseudo-Hurler's disease (mucolipidosis III) 272.7
Pseudohydrocephalus 348.2
Pseudohypertrophic muscular dystrophy
(Erb's) 359.1
Pseudohypertrophy, muscle 359.1
Pseudohypoparathyroidism 275.49
Pseudoinfluenza 487.1
Pseudoinsomnia 307.49
Pseudoleukemia 288.8
infantile 285.8
Pseudomembranous — see condition
Pseudomeningocele (cerebral) (infective) 349.2
postprocedural 997.01
spinal 349.2
Pseudomenstruation 626.8
Pseudomucinous
cyst (ovary) (M8470/0) 220
peritoneum 568.89
Pseudomyeloma 273.1
Pseudomyxoma peritonei (M8480/6) 197.6
Pseudoneuritis optic (nerve) 377.24
papilla 377.24
congenital 743.57
Pseudoneuroma — see Injury, nerve, by site
Pseudo-obstruction
intestine (chronic) (idiopathic) (intermittent
secondary) (primary) 564.89
acute 560.89
Pseudopapilledema 377.24
Pseudoparalysis
arm or leg 781.4
atonic, congenital 358.8
Pseudopelade 704.09
Pseudophakia V43.1
Pseudopolycythemia 289.0
Pseudopolyposis, colon 556.4
Pseudoporencephaly 348.0
Pseudopseudohypoparathyroidism 275.49
Pseudopsychosis 300.16
Pseudopterygium 372.52
Pseudoptosis (eyelid) 374.34
Pseudorabies 078.89
Pseudoretinitis, pigmentosa 362.65
Pseudorickets 588.0
senile (Pozzi's) 731.0
Pseudorubella 057.8
Pseudoscarlatina 057.8
Pseudosclerema 778.1
Pseudosclerosis (brain)
Jakob's 046.19
of Westphal (-Strümpell) (hepatolenticular
degeneration) 275.1
spastic 046.19
with dementia
with behavioral disturbance
046.19 [294.11]
without behavioral disturbance
046.19 [294.10]
Pseudoseizure 780.39
non-psychiatric 780.39
psychiatric 300.11
Pseudotabes 799.89
diabetic 250.6 ☑ [337.1]
due to secondary diabetes 249.6 ☑ [337.1]
Pseudotetanus — see also Convulsions 780.39
Pseudotetany 781.7
hysterical 300.11
Pseudothalassemia 285.0
Pseudotrichinosis 710.3

Pseudotruncus arteriosus 747.29
Pseudotuberculosis, pasteurella (infection)
027.2
Pseudotumor
cerebri 348.2
orbit (inflammatory) 376.11
Pseudo-Turner's syndrome 759.89
Pseudoxanthoma elasticum 757.39
Psilosis (sprue) (tropical) 579.1
Monilia 112.89
nontropical 579.0
not sprue 704.00
Psittacosis 073.9
Psoitis 728.89
Psora NEC 696.1
Psoriasis 696.1
any type, except arthropathic 696.1
arthritic, arthropathic 696.0
buccal 528.6
flexural 696.1
follicularis 696.1
guttate 696.1
inverse 696.1
mouth 528.6
nummularis 696.1
psychogenic 316 [696.1]
punctata 696.1
pustular 696.1
rupioides 696.1
vulgaris 696.1
Psorospermiasis 136.4
Psorospermosis 136.4
follicularis (vegetans) 757.39
Psychalgia 307.80
Psychasthenia 300.89
compulsive 300.3
mixed compulsive states 300.3
obsession 300.3
Psychiatric disorder or problem NEC 300.9
Psychogenic — see also condition
factors associated with physical conditions 316
Psychoneurosis, psychoneurotic — see also
Neurosis 300.9
anxiety (state) 300.00
climacteric 627.2
compensation 300.16
compulsion 300.3
conversion hysteria 300.11
depersonalization 300.6
depressive type 300.4
dissociative hysteria 300.15
hypochondriacal 300.7
hysteria 300.10
conversion type 300.11
dissociative type 300.15
mixed NEC 300.89
neurasthenic 300.5
obsessional 300.3
obsessive-compulsive 300.3
occupational 300.89
personality NEC 301.89
phobia 300.20
senile NEC 300.89
Psychopathic — see also condition
constitution, posttraumatic 310.2
with psychosis 293.9
personality 301.9
amoral trends 301.7
antisocial trends 301.7
asocial trends 301.7
mixed types 301.7
state 301.9
Psychopathy, sexual — see also Deviation, sexual 302.9
Psychophysiologic, psychophysiological
condition — see Reaction, psychophysiologic
Psychose passionelle 297.8
Psychosexual identity disorder 302.6
adult-life 302.85
childhood 302.6
Psychosis 298.9
acute hysterical 298.1
affecting management of pregnancy, childbirth, or puerperium 648.4 ☑

Psychosis — *continued*
affective (*see also* Disorder, mood) 296.90

> *Note* — *Use the following fifth-digit sub-classification with categories 296.0–296.6:*
>
> 0   unspecified
>
> 1   mild
>
> 2   moderate
>
> 3   severe, without mention of psychotic behavior
>
> 4   severe, specified as with psychotic behavior
>
> 5   in partial or unspecified remission
>
> 6   in full remission

drug-induced 292.84
due to or associated with physical condition 293.83
involutional 293.83
recurrent episode 296.3 ☑
single episode 296.2 ☑
manic-depressive 296.80
circular (alternating) 296.7
currently depressed 296.5 ☑
currently manic 296.4 ☑
depressed type 296.2 ☑
atypical 296.82
recurrent episode 296.3 ☑
single episode 296.2 ☑
manic 296.0 ☑
atypical 296.81
recurrent episode 296.1 ☑
single episode 296.0 ☑
mixed type NEC 296.89
specified type NEC 296.89
senile 290.21
specified type NEC 296.99
alcoholic 291.9
with
anxiety 291.89
delirium tremens 291.0
delusions 291.5
dementia 291.2
hallucinosis 291.3
jealousy 291.5
mood disturbance 291.89
paranoia 291.5
persisting amnesia 291.1
sexual dysfunction 291.89
sleep disturbance 291.89
amnestic confabulatory 291.1
delirium tremens 291.0
hallucinosis 291.3
Korsakoff's, Korsakov's, Korsakow's 291.1
paranoid type 291.5
pathological intoxication 291.4
polyneuritic 291.1
specified type NEC 291.89
alternating (*see also* Psychosis, manic-depressive, circular) 296.7
anergastic (*see also* Psychosis, organic) 294.9
arteriosclerotic 290.40
with
acute confusional state 290.41
delirium 290.41
delusions 290.42
depressed mood 290.43
depressed type 290.43
paranoid type 290.42
simple type 290.40
uncomplicated 290.40
atypical 298.9
depressive 296.82
manic 296.81
borderline (schizophrenia) (*see also* Schizophrenia) 295.5 ☑
of childhood (*see also* Psychosis, childhood) 299.8 ☑
prepubertal 299.8 ☑
brief reactive 298.8

Psychosis — *continued*
childhood, with origin specific to 299.9 ☑

> *Note* — *Use the following fifth-digit sub-classification with category 299:*
>
> 0   current or active state
>
> 1   residual state

atypical 299.8 ☑
specified type NEC 299.8 ☑
circular (*see also* Psychosis, manic-depressive, circular) 296.7
climacteric (*see also* Psychosis, involutional) 298.8
confusional 298.9
acute 293.0
reactive 298.2
subacute 293.1
depressive (*see also* Psychosis, affective) 296.2 ☑
atypical 296.82
involutional 296.2 ☑
with hypomania (bipolar II) 296.89
recurrent episode 296.3 ☑
single episode 296.2 ☑
psychogenic 298.0
reactive (emotional stress) (psychological trauma) 298.0
recurrent episode 296.3 ☑
with hypomania (bipolar II) 296.89
single episode 296.2 ☑
disintegrative, childhood (*see also* Psychosis, childhood) 299.1 ☑
drug 292.9
with
affective syndrome 292.84
amnestic syndrome 292.83
anxiety 292.89
delirium 292.81
withdrawal 292.0
delusions 292.11
dementia 292.82
depressive state 292.84
hallucinations 292.12
hallucinosis 292.12
mood disorder 292.84
mood disturbance 292.84
organic personality syndrome NEC 292.89
sexual dysfunction 292.89
sleep disturbance 292.89
withdrawal syndrome (and delirium) 292.0
affective syndrome 292.84
delusions 292.11
hallucinatory state 292.12
hallucinosis 292.12
paranoid state 292.11
specified type NEC 292.89
withdrawal syndrome (and delirium) 292.0
due to or associated with physical condition (*see also* Psychosis, organic) 293.9
epileptic NEC 294.8
excitation (psychogenic) (reactive) 298.1
exhaustive (*see also* Reaction, stress, acute) 308.9
hypomanic (*see also* Psychosis, affective) 296.0 ☑
recurrent episode 296.1 ☑
single episode 296.0 ☑
hysterical 298.8
acute 298.1
in
conditions classified elsewhere
with
delusions 293.81
hallucinations 293.82
pregnancy, childbirth, or puerperium 648.4 ☑
incipient 298.8
schizophrenic (*see also* Schizophrenia) 295.5 ☑
induced 297.3
infantile (*see also* Psychosis, childhood) 299.0 ☑
infective 293.9

Psychosis — *continued*
infective — *continued*
acute 293.0
subacute 293.1
interactional (childhood) (*see also* Psychosis, childhood) 299.1 ☑
involutional 298.8
depressive (*see also* Psychosis, affective) 296.2 ☑
recurrent episode 296.3 ☑
single episode 296.2 ☑
melancholic 296.2 ☑
recurrent episode 296.3 ☑
single episode 296.2 ☑
paranoid state 297.2
paraphrenia 297.2
Korsakoff's, Korakov's, Korsakow's (nonalcoholic) 294.0
alcoholic 291.1
mania (phase) (*see also* Psychosis, affective) 296.0 ☑
recurrent episode 296.1 ☑
single episode 296.0 ☑
manic (*see also* Psychosis, affective) 296.0 ☑
atypical 296.81
recurrent episode 296.1 ☑
single episode 296.0 ☑
manic-depressive 296.80
circular 296.7
currently
depressed 296.5 ☑
manic 296.4 ☑
mixed 296.6 ☑
depressive 296.2 ☑
recurrent episode 296.3 ☑
with hypomania (bipolar II) 296.89
single episode 296.2 ☑
hypomanic 296.0 ☑
recurrent episode 296.1 ☑
single episode 296.0 ☑
manic 296.0 ☑
atypical 296.81
recurrent episode 296.1 ☑
single episode 296.0 ☑
mixed NEC 296.89
perplexed 296.89
stuporous 296.89
menopausal (*see also* Psychosis, involutional) 298.8
mixed schizophrenic and affective (*see also* Schizophrenia) 295.7 ☑
multi-infarct (cerebrovascular) (*see also* Psychosis, arteriosclerotic) 290.40
organic NEC 294.9
due to or associated with
addiction
alcohol (*see also* Psychosis, alcoholic) 291.9
drug (*see also* Psychosis, drug) 292.9
alcohol intoxication, acute (*see also* Psychosis, alcoholic) 291.9
alcoholism (*see also* Psychosis, alcoholic) 291.9
arteriosclerosis (cerebral) (*see also* Psychosis, arteriosclerotic) 290.40
cerebrovascular disease
acute (psychosis) 293.0
arteriosclerotic (*see also* Psychosis, arteriosclerotic) 290.40
childbirth — *see* Psychosis, puerperal
dependence
alcohol (*see also* Psychosis, alcoholic) 291.9
drug 292.9
disease
alcoholic liver (*see also* Psychosis, alcoholic) 291.9
brain
arteriosclerotic (*see also* Psychosis, arteriosclerotic) 290.40
cerebrovascular
acute (psychosis) 293.0

Psychosis — *continued*
organic — *continued*
due to or associated with — *continued*
disease — *continued*
cerebrovascular — *continued*
arteriosclerotic (*see also* Psychosis, arteriosclerotic) 290.40
endocrine or metabolic 293.9
acute (psychosis) 293.0
subacute (psychosis) 293.1
Jakob-Creutzfeldt 046.19
with behavioral disturbance 046.19 *[294.11]*
without behavioral disturbance 046.19 *[294.10]*
familial 046.19
iatrogenic 046.19
specified NEC 046.19
sporadic 046.19
variant 046.11
with dementia
with behavioral disturbance 046.11 *[294.11]*
without behavioral disturbance 046.11 *[294.10]*
liver, alcoholic (*see also* Psychosis, alcoholic) 291.9
disorder
cerebrovascular
acute (psychosis) 293.0
endocrine or metabolic 293.9
acute (psychosis) 293.0
subacute (psychosis) 293.1
epilepsy
with behavioral disturbance 345.9 ☑ *[294.11]*
without behavioral disturbance 345.9 ☑ *[294.10]*
transient (acute) 293.0
Huntington's chorea
with behavioral disturbance 333.4 *[294.11]*
without behavioral disturbance 333.4 *[294.10]*
infection
brain 293.9
acute (psychosis) 293.0
chronic 294.8
subacute (psychosis) 293.1
intracranial NEC 293.9
acute (psychosis) 293.0
chronic 294.8
subacute (psychosis) 293.1
intoxication
alcoholic (acute) (*see also* Psychosis, alcoholic) 291.9
pathological 291.4
drug (*see also* Psychosis, drug) 292.2
ischemia
cerebrovascular (generalized) (*see also* Psychosis, arteriosclerotic) 290.40
Jakob-Creutzfeldt disease (syndrome) 046.19
with behavioral disturbance 046.19 *[294.11]*
without behavioral disturbance 046.19 *[294.10]*
variant 046.11
with dementia
with behavioral disturbance 046.11 *[294.11]*
without behavioral disturbance 046.11 *[294.10]*
multiple sclerosis
with behavioral disturbance 340 *[294.11]*
without behavioral disturbance 340 *[294.10]*
physical condition NEC 293.9

☑ Additional Digit Required — Refer to the Tabular List for Digit Selection   🔺 Subterms under main terms may continue to next column or page

2010 ICD-9-CM   ▶◀ Revised Text   ● New Line   ▲ Revised Code   **Volume 2 — 231**

Puerperal — continued
- hemorrhage — continued
  - pontine 674.0 ☑
  - subarachnoid 674.0 ☑
  - subcortical 674.0 ☑
  - subdural 674.0 ☑
  - uterine, delayed 666.2 ☑
  - ventricular 674.0 ☑
- hemorrhoids 671.8 ☑
- hepatorenal syndrome 674.8 ☑
- hypertrophy
  - breast 676.3 ☑
  - mammary gland 676.3 ☑
- induration breast (fibrous) 676.3 ☑
- infarction
  - lung — see Puerperal, embolism
  - pulmonary — see Puerperal, embolism
- infection
  - Bartholin's gland 646.6 ☑
  - breast 675.2 ☑
    - with nipple 675.9 ☑
      - specified type NEC 675.8 ☑
  - cervix 646.6 ☑
  - endocervix 646.6 ☑
  - fallopian tube 670.8 ☑ ▲
  - generalized 670.0 ☑
  - genital tract (major) 670.0 ☑
    - minor or localized 646.6 ☑
  - kidney (bacillus coli) 646.6 ☑
  - mammary gland 675.2 ☑
    - with nipple 675.9 ☑
      - specified type NEC 675.8 ☑
  - nipple 675.0 ☑
    - with breast 675.9 ☑
      - specified type NEC 675.8 ☑
  - ovary 670.8 ☑ ▲
  - pelvic 670.8 ☑ ▲
  - peritoneum 670.8 ☑ ▲
  - renal 646.6 ☑
  - tubo-ovarian 670.8 ☑ ▲
  - urinary (tract) NEC 646.6 ☑
    - asymptomatic 646.5 ☑
  - uterus, uterine 670.8 ☑ ▲
  - vagina 646.6 ☑
- inflammation (see also Puerperal, infection)
  - areola 675.1 ☑
  - Bartholin's gland 646.6 ☑
  - breast 675.2 ☑
  - broad ligament 670.8 ☑ ▲
  - cervix (uteri) 646.6 ☑
  - fallopian tube 670.8 ☑ ▲
  - genital organs 670.8 ☑ ▲
    - localized 646.6 ☑
  - mammary gland 675.2 ☑
  - nipple 675.0 ☑
  - ovary 670.8 ☑ ▲
  - oviduct 670.8 ☑ ▲
  - pelvis 670.8 ☑ ▲
  - periuterine 670.8 ☑ ▲
  - tubal 670.8 ☑ ▲
  - vagina 646.6 ☑
  - vein — see Puerperal, phlebitis
- inversion, nipple 676.3 ☑
- ischemia, cerebral 674.0 ☑
- lymphangitis 670.8 ☑
  - breast 675.2 ☑
- malaria (conditions classifiable to 084) 647.4 ☑
- malnutrition 648.9 ☑
- mammillitis 675.0 ☑
- mammitis 675.2 ☑
- mania 296.0 ☑
  - recurrent episode 296.1 ☑
  - single episode 296.0 ☑
- mastitis 675.2 ☑
  - purulent 675.1 ☑
  - retromammary 675.1 ☑
  - submammary 675.1 ☑
- melancholia 296.2 ☑
  - recurrent episode 296.3 ☑
  - single episode 296.2 ☑

Puerperal — continued
- mental disorder (conditions classifiable to 290–303, 305.0, 305.2–305.9, 306–316, 317–319) 648.4 ☑
- metritis (suppurative) 670.1 ☑ ▲
  - septic 670.2 ☑ ●
- metroperitonitis 670.8 ☑ ▲
- metrorrhagia 666.2 ☑
- metrosalpingitis 670.8 ☑ ▲
- metrovaginitis 670.8 ☑ ▲
- milk leg 671.4 ☑
- monoplegia, cerebral 674.0 ☑
- necrosis
  - kidney, tubular 669.3 ☑
  - liver (acute) (subacute) (conditions classifiable to 570) 674.8 ☑
  - ovary 670.8 ☑
  - renal cortex 669.3 ☑
- nephritis or nephrosis (conditions classifiable to 580–589) 646.2 ☑
  - with hypertension 642.1 ☑
- nutritional deficiency (conditions classifiable to 260–269) 648.9 ☑
- occlusion, precerebral artery 674.0 ☑
- oliguria 669.3 ☑
- oophoritis 670.8 ☑ ▲
- ovaritis 670.8 ☑ ▲
- paralysis
  - bladder (sphincter) 665.5 ☑
  - cerebral 674.0 ☑
- paralytic stroke 674.0 ☑
- parametritis 670.8 ☑ ▲
- paravaginitis 646.6 ☑
- pelviperitonitis 670.8 ☑ ▲
- perimetritis 670.8 ☑ ▲
- perimetrosalpingitis 670.8 ☑ ▲
- perinephritis 646.6 ☑
- perioophoritis 670.8 ☑ ▲
- periphlebitis — see Puerperal, phlebitis
- perisalpingitis 670.8 ☑ ▲
- peritoneal infection 670.8 ☑ ▲
- peritonitis (pelvic) 670.8 ☑ ▲
- perivaginitis 646.6 ☑
- phlebitis 671.2 ☑ ▲
  - deep 671.4 ☑
  - intracranial sinus (venous) 671.5 ☑
  - pelvic 671.4 ☑
  - specified site NEC 671.5 ☑
  - superficial 671.2 ☑
- phlegmasia alba dolens 671.4 ☑
- placental polyp 674.4 ☑
- pneumonia, embolic — see Puerperal, embolism
- prediabetes 648.8 ☑
- pre-eclampsia (mild) 642.4 ☑
  - with pre-existing hypertension 642.7 ☑
  - severe 642.5 ☑
- psychosis, unspecified (see also Psychosis, puerperal) 293.89
- pyelitis 646.6 ☑
- pyelocystitis 646.6 ☑
- pyelohydronephrosis 646.6 ☑
- pyelonephritis 646.6 ☑
- pyelonephrosis 646.6 ☑
- pyemia 670.2 ☑ ▲
- pyocystitis 646.6 ☑
- pyohemia 670.2 ☑ ▲
- pyometra 670.8 ☑ ▲
- pyonephritis 646.6 ☑
- pyonephrosis 646.6 ☑
- pyo-oophoritis 670.8 ☑ ▲
- pyosalpingitis 670.8 ☑ ▲
- pyosalpinx 670.8 ☑ ▲
- pyrexia (of unknown origin) 672.0 ☑
- renal
  - disease NEC 646.2 ☑
  - failure, acute 669.3 ☑
- retention
  - decidua (fragments) (with delayed hemorrhage) 666.2 ☑
    - without hemorrhage 667.1 ☑
  - placenta (fragments) (with delayed hemorrhage) 666.2 ☑
    - without hemorrhage 667.1 ☑

Puerperal — continued
- retention — continued
  - secundines (fragments) (with delayed hemorrhage) 666.2 ☑
    - without hemorrhage 667.1 ☑
- retracted nipple 676.0 ☑
- rubella (conditions classifiable to 056) 647.5 ☑
- salpingitis 670.8 ☑ ▲
- salpingo-oophoritis 670.8 ☑ ▲
- salpingo-ovaritis 670.8 ☑ ▲
- salpingoperitonitis 670.8 ☑ ▲
- sapremia 670.2 ☑ ▲
- secondary perineal tear 674.2 ☑ ▲
- sepsis (pelvic) 670.2 ☑ ▲
- septicemia 670.2 ☑ ▲
- subinvolution (uterus) 674.8 ☑
- sudden death (cause unknown) 674.9 ☑
- suppuration — see Puerperal, abscess
- syphilis (conditions classifiable to 090–097) 647.0 ☑
- tetanus 670.2 ☑ ▲
- thelitis 675.0 ☑
- thrombocytopenia 666.3 ☑
- thrombophlebitis (superficial) 671.2 ☑
  - deep 671.4 ☑
  - pelvic 671.4 ☑
  - septic 670.3 ☑ ●
  - specified site NEC 671.5 ☑
- thrombosis (venous) — see Thrombosis, puerperal
- thyroid dysfunction (conditions classifiable to 240–246) 648.1 ☑
- toxemia (see also Toxemia, of pregnancy) 642.4 ☑
  - eclamptic 642.6 ☑
    - with pre-existing hypertension 642.7 ☑
  - pre-eclamptic (mild) 642.4 ☑
    - with
      - convulsions 642.6 ☑
      - pre-existing hypertension 642.7 ☑
    - severe 642.5 ☑
- tuberculosis (conditions classifiable to 010–018) 647.3 ☑
- uremia 669.3 ☑
- vaginitis (conditions classifiable to 616.1) 646.6 ☑
- varicose veins (legs) 671.0 ☑
  - vulva or perineum 671.1 ☑
- venous complication 671.9 ☑ ●
- vulvitis (conditions classifiable to 616.1) 646.6 ☑
- vulvovaginitis (conditions classifiable to 616.1) 646.6 ☑
- white leg 671.4 ☑

Pulled muscle — see Sprain, by site
Pulmolithiasis 518.89
Pulmonary — see condition
Pulmonitis (unknown etiology) 486
Pulpitis (acute) (anachoretic) (chronic) (hyperplastic) (putrescent) (suppurative) (ulcerative) 522.0
Pulpless tooth 522.9
Pulse
- alternating 427.89
  - psychogenic 306.2
- bigeminal 427.89
- fast 785.0
- feeble, rapid, due to shock following injury 958.4
- rapid 785.0
- slow 427.89
- strong 785.9
- trigeminal 427.89
- water-hammer (see also Insufficiency, aortic) 424.1
- weak 785.9

Pulseless disease 446.7
Pulsus
- alternans or trigeminy 427.89
  - psychogenic 306.2

Punch drunk 310.2
Puncta lacrimalia occlusion 375.52
Punctiform hymen 752.49

Puncture (traumatic) — see also Wound, open, by site
- accidental, complicating surgery 998.2
- bladder, nontraumatic 596.6
- by
  - device, implant, or graft — see Complications, mechanical
  - foreign body
    - internal organs (see also Injury, internal, by site)
      - by ingested object — see Foreign body
    - left accidentally in operation wound 998.4
  - instrument (any) during a procedure, accidental 998.2
- internal organs, abdomen, chest, or pelvis — see Injury, internal, by site
- kidney, nontraumatic 593.89
Pupil — see condition
Pupillary membrane 364.74
- persistent 743.46
Pupillotonia 379.46
- pseudotabetic 379.46
Purpura 287.2
- abdominal 287.0
- allergic 287.0
- anaphylactoid 287.0
- annularis telangiectodes 709.1
- arthritic 287.0
- autoerythrocyte sensitization 287.2
- autoimmune 287.0
- bacterial 287.0
- Bateman's (senile) 287.2
- capillary fragility (hereditary) (idiopathic) 287.8
- cryoglobulinemic 273.2
- devil's pinches 287.2
- fibrinolytic (see also Fibrinolysis) 286.6
- fulminans, fulminous 286.6
- gangrenous 287.0
- hemorrhagic (see also Purpura, thrombocytopenic) 287.39
  - nodular 272.7
  - nonthrombocytopenic 287.0
  - thrombocytopenic 287.39
- Henoch's (purpura nervosa) 287.0
- Henoch-Schönlein (allergic) 287.0
- hypergammaglobulinemic (benign primary) (Waldenström's) 273.0
- idiopathic 287.31
  - nonthrombocytopenic 287.0
  - thrombocytopenic 287.31
- immune thrombocytopenic 287.31
- infectious 287.0
- malignant 287.0
- neonatorum 772.6
- nervosa 287.0
- newborn NEC 772.6
- nonthrombocytopenic 287.2
  - hemorrhagic 287.0
  - idiopathic 287.0
- nonthrombopenic 287.2
- peliosis rheumatica 287.0
- pigmentaria, progressiva 709.09
- posttransfusion 287.4
- primary 287.0
- primitive 287.0
- red cell membrane sensitivity 287.2
- rheumatica 287.0
- Schönlein (-Henoch) (allergic) 287.0
- scorbutic 267
- senile 287.2
- simplex 287.2
- symptomatica 287.0
- telangiectasia annularis 709.1
- thrombocytopenic (see also Thrombocytopenia) 287.30
  - congenital 287.33
  - essential 287.30
  - hereditary 287.31
  - idiopathic 287.31
  - immune 287.31
  - neonatal, transitory (see also Thrombocytopenia, neonatal transitory) 776.1
  - primary 287.30
  - puerperal, postpartum 666.3 ☑

☑ Additional Digit Required — Refer to the Tabular List for Digit Selection   ▷◁ Subterms under main terms may continue to next column or page

2010 ICD-9-CM   ▶◀ Revised Text   ● New Line   ▲ Revised Code   October 2009 • Volume 2 — 233

Purpura — continued
  thrombocytopenic (see also Thrombocytopenia) — continued
    thrombotic 446.6
  thrombohemolytic (see also Fibrinolysis) 286.6
  thrombopenic (see also Thrombocytopenia) 287.30
    congenital 287.33
    essential 287.30
    thrombotic 446.6
      thrombocytic 446.6
      thrombocytopenic 446.6
  toxic 287.0
  variolosa 050.0
  vascular 287.0
  visceral symptoms 287.0
  Werlhof's (see also Purpura, thrombocytopenic) 287.39
Purpuric spots 782.7
Purulent — see condition
Pus
  absorption, general — see Septicemia
  in
    stool 792.1
    urine 791.9
  tube (rupture) (see also Salpingo-oophoritis) 614.2
Pustular rash 782.1
Pustule 686.9
  malignant 022.0
  nonmalignant 686.9
Putnam-Dana syndrome (subacute combined sclerosis with pernicious anemia) 281.0 [336.2]
Putnam's disease (subacute combined sclerosis with pernicious anemia) 281.0 [336.2]
Putrefaction, intestinal 569.89
Putrescent pulp (dental) 522.1
Pyarthritis — see Pyarthrosis
Pyarthrosis — see also Arthritis, pyogenic 711.0 ☑
  tuberculous — see Tuberculosis, joint
Pycnoepilepsy, pycnolepsy (idiopathic) — see also Epilepsy 345.0 ☑
Pyelectasia 593.89
Pyelectasis 593.89
Pyelitis (congenital) (uremic) 590.80
  with
    abortion — see Abortion, by type, with specified complication NEC
    contracted kidney 590.00
    ectopic pregnancy (see also categories 633.0–633.9) 639.8
    molar pregnancy (see also categories 630–632) 639.8
  acute 590.10
    with renal medullary necrosis 590.11
  chronic 590.00
    with
      renal medullary necrosis 590.01
  complicating pregnancy, childbirth, or puerperium 646.6 ☑
    affecting fetus or newborn 760.1
  cystica 590.3
  following
    abortion 639.8
    ectopic or molar pregnancy 639.8
  gonococcal 098.19
    chronic or duration of 2 months or over 098.39
  tuberculous (see also Tuberculosis) 016.0 ☑ [590.81]
Pyelocaliectasis 593.89
Pyelocystitis — see also Pyelitis 590.80
Pyelohydronephrosis 591
Pyelonephritis — see also Pyelitis 590.80
  acute 590.10
    with renal medullary necrosis 590.11
  chronic 590.00
  syphilitic (late) 095.4
  tuberculous (see also Tuberculosis) 016.0 ☑ [590.81]
Pyelophlebitis — see also Pyelitis 590.80
  chronic 590.00
Pyelophlebitis 451.89
Pyelo-ureteric cystica 590.3

Pyemia, pyemic (purulent) — see also Septicemia 038.9
  abscess — see Abscess
  arthritis (see also Arthritis, pyogenic) 711.0 ☑
  Bacillus coli 038.42
  embolism (see also Septicemia) 415.12
  fever 038.9
  infection 038.9
  joint (see also Arthritis, pyogenic) 711.0 ☑
  liver 572.1
  meningococcal 036.2
  newborn 771.81
  phlebitis — see Phlebitis
  pneumococcal 038.2
  portal 572.1
  postvaccinal 999.39
  puerperal 670.2 ☑
  specified organism NEC 038.8
  staphylococcal 038.10
    aureus 038.11
      methicillin
        resistant 038.12
        susceptible 038.11
    specified organism NEC 038.19
  streptococcal 038.0
  tuberculous — see Tuberculosis, miliary
Pygopagus 759.4
Pykno-epilepsy, pyknolepsy (idiopathic) — see also Epilepsy 345.0 ☑
Pyle (-Cohn) disease (craniometaphyseal dysplasia) 756.89
Pylephlebitis (suppurative) 572.1
Pylethrombophlebitis 572.1
Pylethrombosis 572.1
Pyloritis — see also Gastritis 535.5 ☑
Pylorospasm (reflex) 537.81
  congenital or infantile 750.5
  neurotic 306.4
  newborn 750.5
  psychogenic 306.4
Pylorus, pyloric — see condition
Pyoarthrosis — see Pyarthrosis
Pyocele
  mastoid 383.00
  sinus (accessory) (nasal) (see also Sinusitis) 473.9
  turbinate (bone) 473.9
  urethra (see also Urethritis) 597.0
Pyococcal dermatitis 686.00
Pyococcide, skin 686.00
Pyocolpos — see also Vaginitis 616.10
Pyocyaneus dermatitis 686.09
Pyocystitis — see Cystitis 595.9
Pyoderma, pyodermia 686.00
  gangrenosum 686.01
  specified type NEC 686.09
  vegetans 686.8
Pyodermatitis 686.00
  vegetans 686.8
Pyogenic — see condition
Pyohemia — see Septicemia
Pyohydronephrosis — see also Pyelitis 590.80
Pyometra 615.9
Pyometritis — see also Endometritis 615.9
Pyometrium — see also Endometritis 615.9
Pyomyositis 728.0
  ossificans 728.19
  tropical (bungpagga) 040.81
Pyonephritis — see also Pyelitis 590.80
  chronic 590.00
Pyonephrosis (congenital) — see also Pyelitis 590.80
  acute 590.10
Pyo-oophoritis — see also Salpingo-oophoritis 614.2
Pyo-ovarium — see also Salpingo-oophoritis 614.2
Pyopericarditis 420.99
Pyopericardium 420.99
Pyophlebitis — see Phlebitis
Pyopneumopericardium 420.99
Pyopneumothorax (infectional) 510.9
  with fistula 510.0
  subdiaphragmatic (see also Peritonitis) 567.29
  subphrenic (see also Peritonitis) 567.29

Pyopneumothorax — continued
  tuberculous (see also Tuberculosis, pleura) 012.0 ☑
Pyorrhea (alveolar) (alveolaris) 523.40
  degenerative 523.5
Pyosalpingitis — see also Salpingo-oophoritis 614.2
Pyosalpinx — see also Salpingo-oophoritis 614.2
Pyosepticemia — see Septicemia
Pyosis
  Corlett's (impetigo) 684
  Manson's (pemphigus contagiosus) 684
Pyothorax 510.9
  with fistula 510.0
  tuberculous (see also Tuberculosis, pleura) 012.0 ☑
● **Pyoureter** 593.89
  tuberculous (see also Tuberculosis) 016.2 ☑
Pyramidopallidonigral syndrome 332.0
Pyrexia (of unknown origin) (P.U.O.) 780.60
  atmospheric 992.0
  during labor 659.2 ☑
  environmentally-induced newborn 778.4
  heat 992.0
  newborn, environmentally-induced 778.4
  puerperal 672.0 ☑
Pyroglobulinemia 273.8
Pyromania 312.33
Pyrosis 787.1
Pyrroloporphyria 277.1
Pyuria (bacterial) 791.9

Q

Q fever 083.0
  with pneumonia 083.0 [484.8]
Quadricuspid aortic valve 746.89
Quadrilateral fever 083.0
Quadriparesis — see Quadriplegia
  meaning muscle weakness 728.87
Quadriplegia 344.00
  with fracture, vertebra (process) — see Fracture, vertebra, cervical, with spinal cord injury
  brain (current episode) 437.8
  C1-C4
    complete 344.01
    incomplete 344.02
  C5-C7
    complete 344.03
    incomplete 344.04
  cerebral (current episode) 437.8
  congenital or infantile (cerebral) (spastic) (spinal) 343.2
  cortical 437.8
  embolic (current episode) (see also Embolism, brain) 434.1 ☑
  functional 780.72
  infantile (cerebral) (spastic) (spinal) 343.2
  newborn NEC 767.0
  specified NEC 344.09
  thrombotic (current episode) (see also Thrombosis, brain) 434.0 ☑
  traumatic — see Injury, spinal, cervical
Quadruplet
  affected by maternal complications of pregnancy 761.5
  healthy liveborn — see Newborn, multiple
  pregnancy (complicating delivery) NEC 651.8 ☑
    with fetal loss and retention of one or more fetus(es) 651.5 ☑
    following (elective) fetal reduction 651.7 ☑
Quarrelsomeness 301.3
Quartan
  fever 084.2
  malaria (fever) 084.2
Queensland fever 083.0
  coastal 083.0
  seven-day 100.89
Quervain's disease 727.04
  thyroid (subacute granulomatous thyroiditis) 245.1
Queyrat's erythroplasia (M8080/2)
  specified site — see Neoplasm, skin, in situ

Queyrat's erythroplasia — continued
  unspecified site 233.5
Quincke's disease or edema — see Edema, angioneurotic
Quinquaud's disease (acne decalvans) 704.09
Quinsy (gangrenous) 475
Quintan fever 083.1
Quintuplet
  affected by maternal complications of pregnancy 761.5
  healthy liveborn — see Newborn, multiple
  pregnancy (complicating delivery) NEC 651.2 ☑
    with fetal loss and retention of one or more fetus(es) 651.6 ☑
    following (elective) fetal reduction 651.7 ☑
Quotidian
  fever 084.0
  malaria (fever) 084.0

R

Rabbia 071
Rabbit fever — see also Tularemia 021.9
Rabies 071
  contact V01.5
  exposure to V01.5
  inoculation V04.5
    reaction — see Complications, vaccination
  vaccination, prophylactic (against) V04.5
Rachischisis — see also Spina bifida 741.9 ☑
Rachitic — see also condition
  deformities of spine 268.1
  pelvis 268.1
    with disproportion (fetopelvic) 653.2 ☑
      affecting fetus or newborn 763.1
      causing obstructed labor 660.1 ☑
        affecting fetus or newborn 763.1
Rachitis, rachitism — see also Rickets
  acute 268.0
  fetalis 756.4
  renalis 588.0
  tarda 268.0
Racket nail 757.5
Radial nerve — see condition
Radiation effects or sickness — see also Effect, adverse, radiation
  cataract 366.46
  dermatitis 692.82
    sunburn (see also Sunburn) 692.71
Radiculitis (pressure) (vertebrogenic) 729.2
  accessory nerve 723.4
  anterior crural 724.4
  arm 723.4
  brachial 723.4
  cervical NEC 723.4
  due to displacement of intervertebral disc — see Neuritis, due to, displacement intervertebral disc
  leg 724.4
  lumbar NEC 724.4
  lumbosacral 724.4
  rheumatic 729.2
  syphilitic 094.89
  thoracic (with visceral pain) 724.4
Radiculomyelitis 357.0
  toxic, due to
    Clostridium tetani 037
    Corynebacterium diphtheriae 032.89
Radiculopathy — see also Radiculitis 729.2
Radioactive substances, adverse effect — see Effect, adverse, radioactive substance
Radiodermal burns (acute) (chronic) (occupational) — see Burn, by site
Radiodermatitis 692.82
Radionecrosis — see Effect, adverse, radiation
Radiotherapy session V58.0
Radium, adverse effect — see Effect, adverse, radioactive substance
Raeder-Harbitz syndrome (pulseless disease) 446.7
Rage — see also Disturbance, conduct 312.0 ☑
  meaning rabies 071
Rag sorters' disease 022.1
Raillietiniasis 123.8
Railroad neurosis 300.16

Railway spine 300.16
Raised — *see* Elevation
Raiva 071
Rake teeth, tooth 524.39
Rales 786.7
Ramifying renal pelvis 753.3
Ramsay Hunt syndrome (herpetic geniculate
    ganglionitis) 053.11
    meaning dyssynergia cerebellaris myoclonica
       334.2
Ranke's primary infiltration — *see also* Tuber-
    culosis 010.0 ☑
Ranula 527.6
    congenital 750.26
Rape
    adult 995.83
    alleged, observation or examination V71.5
    child 995.53
Rapid
    feeble pulse, due to shock, following injury
       958.4
    heart (beat) 785.0
       psychogenic 306.2
    respiration 786.06
       psychogenic 306.1
    second stage (delivery) 661.3 ☑
       affecting fetus or newborn 763.6
    time-zone change syndrome 327.35
Rarefaction, bone 733.99
Rash 782.1
    canker 034.1
    diaper 691.0
    drug (internal use) 693.0
       contact 692.3
    ECHO 9 virus 078.89
    enema 692.89
    food (*see also* Allergy, food) 693.1
    heat 705.1
    napkin 691.0
    nettle 708.8
    pustular 782.1
    rose 782.1
       epidemic 056.9
       of infants 057.8
    scarlet 034.1
    serum (prophylactic) (therapeutic) 999.5
    toxic 782.1
    wandering tongue 529.1
Rasmussen's aneurysm — *see also* Tuberculosis
    011.2 ☑
Rat-bite fever 026.9
    due to Streptobacillus moniliformis 026.1
    spirochetal (morsus muris) 026.0
Rathke's pouch tumor (M9350/1) 237.0
Raymond (-Céstan) syndrome 433.8 ☑
Raynaud's
    disease or syndrome (paroxysmal digital
       cyanosis) 443.0
    gangrene (symmetric) 443.0 [785.4]
    phenomenon (paroxysmal digital cyanosis)
       (secondary) 443.0
RDS 769
Reaction
    acute situational maladjustment (*see also* Re-
       action, adjustment) 309.9
    adaptation (*see also* Reaction, adjustment)
       309.9
    adjustment 309.9
       with
          anxious mood 309.24
             with depressed mood 309.28
          conduct disturbance 309.3
             combined with disturbance of
                emotions 309.4
          depressed mood 309.0
             brief 309.0
                with anxious mood 309.28
             prolonged 309.1
          elective mutism 309.83
          mixed emotions and conduct 309.4
          mutism, elective 309.83
          physical symptoms 309.82
          predominant disturbance (of)
             conduct 309.3
             emotions NEC 309.29
                mixed 309.28

Reaction — *continued*
    adjustment — *continued*
       with — *continued*
          predominant disturbance — *contin-*
             ued
             mixed, emotions and conduct
                309.4
             specified type NEC 309.89
          specific academic or work inhibition
             309.23
          withdrawal 309.83
       depressive 309.0
          with conduct disturbance 309.4
          brief 309.0
          prolonged 309.1
       specified type NEC 309.89
    adverse food NEC 995.7
    affective (*see also* Psychosis, affective) 296.90
       specified type NEC 296.99
    aggressive 301.3
       unsocialized (*see also* Disturbance, con-
          duct) 312.0 ☑
    allergic (*see also* Allergy) 995.3
       drug, medicinal substance, and biological
          — *see* Allergy, drug
       food — *see* Allergy, food
       serum 999.5
    anaphylactic — *see* Shock, anaphylactic
    anesthesia — *see* Anesthesia, complication
    anger 312.0 ☑
    antisocial 301.7
    antitoxin (prophylactic) (therapeutic) — *see*
       Complications, vaccination
    anxiety 300.00
    Arthus 995.21
    asthenic 300.5
    compulsive 300.3
    conversion (anesthetic) (autonomic) (hyperki-
       netic) (mixed paralytic) (paresthetic)
       300.11
    deoxyribonuclease (DNA) (DNase) hypersensi-
       tivity NEC 287.2
    depressive 300.4
       acute 309.0
       affective (*see also* Psychosis, affective)
          296.2 ☑
          recurrent episode 296.3 ☑
          single episode 296.2 ☑
       brief 309.0
       manic (*see also* Psychosis, affective) 296.80
       neurotic 300.4
       psychoneurotic 300.4
       psychotic 298.0
    dissociative 300.15
    drug NEC (*see also* Table of Drugs and Chemi-
       cals) 995.20
       allergic (*see also* Allergy, drug) 995.27
       correct substance properly administered
          995.20
       obstetric anesthetic or analgesic NEC
          668.9 ☑
          affecting fetus or newborn 763.5
          specified drug — *see* Table of Drugs
             and Chemicals
       overdose or poisoning 977.9
          specified drug — *see* Table of Drugs
             and Chemicals
       specific to newborn 779.4
       transmitted via placenta or breast milk —
          see Absorption, drug, through pla-
          centa
       withdrawal NEC 292.0
          infant of dependent mother 779.5
       wrong substance given or taken in error
          977.9
          specified drug — *see* Table of Drugs
             and Chemicals
    dyssocial 301.7
    dystonic, acute, due to drugs 333.72
    erysipeloid 027.1
    fear 300.20
       child 313.0
    fluid loss, cerebrospinal 349.0
    food (*see also* Allergy, food)
       adverse NEC 995.7

Reaction — *continued*
    food (*see also* Allergy, food) — *continued*
       anaphylactic shock — *see* Anaphylactic
          shock, due to, food
    foreign
       body NEC 728.82
          in operative wound (inadvertently left)
             998.4
             due to surgical material intentional-
                ly left — *see* Complications,
                due to (presence of) any
                device, implant, or graft
                classified to 996.0–996.5
                NEC
          substance accidentally left during a proce-
             dure (chemical) (powder) (talc)
             998.7
             body or object (instrument) (sponge)
                (swab) 998.4
    graft-versus-host (GVH) 279.50
    grief (acute) (brief) 309.0
       prolonged 309.1
    gross stress (*see also* Reaction, stress, acute)
       308.9
    group delinquent (*see also* Disturbance, con-
       duct) 312.2 ☑
    Herxheimer's 995.0
    hyperkinetic (*see also* Hyperkinesia) 314.9
    hypochondriacal 300.7
    hypoglycemic, due to insulin 251.0
       therapeutic misadventure 962.3
    hypomanic (*see also* Psychosis, affective)
       296.0 ☑
       recurrent episode 296.1 ☑
       single episode 296.0 ☑
    hysterical 300.10
       conversion type 300.11
       dissociative 300.15
    id (bacterial cause) 692.89
    immaturity NEC 301.89
       aggressive 301.3
       emotional instability 301.59
    immunization — *see* Complications, vaccina-
       tion
    incompatibility
       blood group
          ABO 999.6   ●
          minor blood group 999.89   ●
          Rh (factor) (infusion) (transfusion) 999.7
    inflammatory — *see* Infection
    infusion — *see* Complications, infusion
    inoculation (immune serum) — *see* Complica-
       tions, vaccination
    insulin 995.23
    involutional
       paranoid 297.2
       psychotic (*see also* Psychosis, affective,
          depressive) 296.2 ☑
    leukemoid (basophilic) (lymphocytic) (mono-
       cytic) (myelocytic) (neutrophilic) 288.62
    LSD (*see also* Abuse, drugs, nondependent)
       305.3 ☑
    lumbar puncture 349.0
    manic-depressive (*see also* Psychosis, affective)
       296.80
       depressed 296.2 ☑
          recurrent episode 296.3 ☑
          single episode 296.2 ☑
       hypomanic 296.0 ☑
    neurasthenic 300.5
    neurogenic (*see also* Neurosis) 300.9
    neurotic NEC 300.9
    neurotic-depressive 300.4
    nitritoid — *see* Crisis, nitritoid
    obsessive compulsive 300.3
    organic 293.9
       acute 293.0
       subacute 293.1
    overanxious, child or adolescent 313.0
    paranoid (chronic) 297.9
       acute 298.3
       climacteric 297.2
       involutional 297.2
       menopausal 297.2
       senile 290.20
       simple 297.0

Reaction — *continued*
    passive
       aggressive 301.84
       dependency 301.6
    personality (*see also* Disorder, personality)
       301.9
    phobic 300.20
    postradiation — *see* Effect, adverse, radiation
    psychogenic NEC 300.9
    psychoneurotic (*see also* Neurosis) 300.9
       anxiety 300.00
       compulsive 300.3
       conversion 300.11
       depersonalization 300.6
       depressive 300.4
       dissociative 300.15
       hypochondriacal 300.7
       hysterical 300.10
          conversion type 300.11
          dissociative type 300.15
       neurasthenic 300.5
       obsessive 300.3
       obsessive-compulsive 300.3
       phobic 300.20
       tension state 300.9
    psychophysiologic NEC (*see also* Disorder,
       psychosomatic) 306.9
       cardiovascular 306.2
       digestive 306.4
       endocrine 306.6
       gastrointestinal 306.4
       genitourinary 306.50
       heart 306.2
       hemic 306.8
       intestinal (large) (small) 306.4
       laryngeal 306.1
       lymphatic 306.8
       musculoskeletal 306.0
       pharyngeal 306.1
       respiratory 306.1
       skin 306.3
       special sense organs 306.7
    psychosomatic (*see also* Disorder, psychoso-
       matic) 306.9
    psychotic (*see also* Psychosis) 298.9
       depressive 298.0
       due to or associated with physical condi-
          tion (*see also* Psychosis, organic)
          293.9
       involutional (*see also* Psychosis, affective)
          296.2 ☑
          recurrent episode 296.3 ☑
          single episode 296.2 ☑
    pupillary (myotonic) (tonic) 379.46
    radiation — *see* Effect, adverse, radiation
    runaway (*see also* Disturbance, conduct)
       socialized 312.2 ☑
       undersocialized, unsocialized 312.1 ☑
    scarlet fever toxin — *see* Complications, vacci-
       nation
    schizophrenic (*see also* Schizophrenia)
       295.9 ☑
       latent 295.5 ☑
    serological for syphilis — *see* Serology for
       syphilis
    serum (prophylactic) (therapeutic) 999.5
       immediate 999.4
    situational (*see also* Reaction, adjustment)
       309.9
       acute, to stress 308.3
       adjustment (*see also* Reaction, adjustment)
          309.9
    somatization (*see also* Disorder, psychosomat-
       ic) 306.9
    spinal puncture 349.0
    spite, child (*see also* Disturbance, conduct)
       312.0 ☑
    stress, acute 308.9
       with predominant disturbance (of)
          consciousness 308.1
          emotions 308.0
          mixed 308.4
          psychomotor 308.2
          specified type NEC 308.3
       bone or cartilage — *see* Fracture, stress

☑ Additional Digit Required — Refer to the Tabular List for Digit Selection   Ⓦ Subterms under main terms may continue to next column or page

2010 ICD-9-CM   ▶◀ Revised Text   ● New Line   ▲ Revised Code   October 2009 • Volume 2 — 235

Reaction — *continued*
  surgical procedure — *see* Complications, surgical procedure
  tetanus antitoxin — *see* Complications, vaccination
  toxin-antitoxin — *see* Complications, vaccination
  transfusion (blood) (bone marrow) (lymphocytes) (allergic) — *see* Complications, transfusion
  tuberculin skin test, nonspecific (without active tuberculosis) 795.5
    positive (without active tuberculosis) 795.5
  ultraviolet — *see* Effect, adverse, ultraviolet
  undersocialized, unsocialized (*see also* Disturbance, conduct)
    aggressive (type) 312.0 ☑
    unaggressive (type) 312.1 ☑
  vaccination (any) — *see* Complications, vaccination
  white graft (skin) 996.52
  withdrawing, child or adolescent 313.22
  x-ray — *see* Effect, adverse, x-rays
Reactive depression — *see also* Reaction, depressive 300.4
  neurotic 300.4
  psychoneurotic 300.4
  psychotic 298.0
Rebound tenderness 789.6 ☑
Recalcitrant patient V15.81
Recanalization, thrombus — *see* Thrombosis
Recession, receding
  chamber angle (eye) 364.77
  chin 524.06
  gingival (postinfective) (postoperative) 523.20
    generalized 523.25
    localized 523.24
    minimal 523.21
    moderate 523.22
    severe 523.23
Recklinghausen-Applebaum disease (hemochromatosis) 275.0
Recklinghausen's disease (M9540/1) 237.71
  bones (osteitis fibrosa cystica) 252.01
Reclus' disease (cystic) 610.1
Recrudescent typhus (fever) 081.1
Recruitment, auditory 388.44
Rectalgia 569.42
Rectitis 569.49
Rectocele
  female (without uterine prolapse) 618.04
    with uterine prolapse 618.4
      complete 618.3
      incomplete 618.2
  in pregnancy or childbirth 654.4 ☑
    causing obstructed labor 660.2 ☑
      affecting fetus or newborn 763.1
  male 569.49
  vagina, vaginal (outlet) 618.04
Rectosigmoiditis 569.89
  ulcerative (chronic) 556.3
Rectosigmoid junction — *see* condition
Rectourethral — *see* condition
Rectovaginal — *see* condition
Rectovesical — *see* condition
Rectum, rectal — *see* condition
Recurrent — *see* condition
Red bugs 133.8
Red cedar asthma 495.8
Redness
  conjunctiva 379.93
  eye 379.93
  nose 478.19
Reduced ventilatory or vital capacity 794.2
Reduction
  function
    kidney (*see also* Disease, renal) 593.9
    liver 573.8
  ventilatory capacity 794.2
  vital capacity 794.2
Redundant, redundancy
  abdomen 701.9
  anus 751.5
  cardia 537.89
  clitoris 624.2
  colon (congenital) 751.5

Redundant, redundancy — *continued*
  foreskin (congenital) 605
  intestine 751.5
  labia 624.3
  organ or site, congenital NEC — *see* Accessory
  panniculus (abdominal) 278.1
  prepuce (congenital) 605
  pylorus 537.89
  rectum 751.5
  scrotum 608.89
  sigmoid 751.5
  skin (of face) 701.9
    eyelids 374.30
  stomach 537.89
  uvula 528.9
  vagina 623.8
Reduplication — *see* Duplication
Referral
  adoption (agency) V68.89
  nursing care V63.8
  patient without examination or treatment V68.81
  social services V63.8
Reflex — *see also* condition
  blink, deficient 374.45
  hyperactive gag 478.29
  neurogenic bladder NEC 596.54
    atonic 596.54
      with cauda equina syndrome 344.61
  vasoconstriction 443.9
  vasovagal 780.2
Reflux 530.81
  acid 530.81
  esophageal 530.81
    with esophagitis 530.11
  esophagitis 530.11
  gastroesophageal 530.81
  mitral — *see* Insufficiency, mitral
  ureteral — *see* Reflux, vesicoureteral
  vesicoureteral 593.70
    with
      reflux nephropathy 593.73
        bilateral 593.72
        unilateral 593.71
Reformed gallbladder 576.0
Reforming, artificial openings — *see also* Attention to, artificial, opening V55.9
Refractive error — *see also* Error, refractive 367.9
Refsum's disease or syndrome (heredopathia atactica polyneuritiformis) 356.3
Refusal of
  food 307.59
    hysterical 300.11
  treatment because of, due to
    patient's decision NEC V64.2
    reason of conscience or religion V62.6
Regaud
  tumor (M8082/3) — *see* Neoplasm, nasopharynx, malignant
  type carcinoma (M8082/3) — *see* Neoplasm, nasopharynx, malignant
Regional — *see* condition
Regulation feeding (elderly) (infant) 783.3
  newborn 779.31 ▲
Regurgitated
  food, choked on 933.1
  stomach contents, choked on 933.1
Regurgitation 787.03
  aortic (valve) (*see also* Insufficiency, aortic) 424.1
    congenital 746.4
    syphilitic 093.22
  food (*see also* Vomiting)
    with reswallowing — *see* Rumination
    newborn 779.33 ▲
  gastric contents — *see* Vomiting
  heart — *see* Endocarditis
  mitral (valve) (*see also* Insufficiency, mitral)
    congenital 746.6
  myocardial — *see* Endocarditis
  pulmonary (heart) (valve) (*see also* Endocarditis, pulmonary) 424.3
  stomach — *see* Vomiting
  tricuspid — *see* Endocarditis, tricuspid
  valve, valvular — *see* Endocarditis
  vesicoureteral — *see* Reflux, vesicoureteral

Rehabilitation V57.9
  multiple types V57.89
  occupational V57.21
  specified type NEC V57.89
  speech ►(-language)◄ V57.3
  vocational V57.22
Reichmann's disease or syndrome (gastrosuccorrhea) 536.8
Reifenstein's syndrome (hereditary familial hypogonadism, male) 259.52
Reilly's syndrome or phenomenon — *see also* Neuropathy, peripheral, autonomic 337.9
Reimann's periodic disease 277.31
Reinsertion, contraceptive device V25.42
Reiter's disease, syndrome, or urethritis 099.3 *[711.1]* ☑
Rejection
  food, hysterical 300.11
  transplant 996.80
    bone marrow 996.85
    corneal 996.51
    organ (immune or nonimmune cause) 996.80
      bone marrow 996.85
      heart 996.83
      intestines 996.87
      kidney 996.81
      liver 996.82
      lung 996.84
      pancreas 996.86
      specified NEC 996.89
    skin 996.52
      artificial 996.55
      decellularized allodermis 996.55
Relapsing fever 087.9
  Carter's (Asiatic) 087.0
  Dutton's (West African) 087.1
  Koch's 087.9
  louse-borne (epidemic) 087.0
  Novy's (American) 087.1
  Obermeyer's (European) 087.0
  Spirillum 087.9
  tick-borne (endemic) 087.1
Relaxation
  anus (sphincter) 569.49
    due to hysteria 300.11
  arch (foot) 734
    congenital 754.61
  back ligaments 728.4
  bladder (sphincter) 596.59
  cardio-esophageal 530.89
  cervix (*see also* Incompetency, cervix) 622.5
  diaphragm 519.4
  inguinal rings — *see* Hernia, inguinal
  joint (capsule) (ligament) (paralytic) (*see also* Derangement, joint) 718.90
    congenital 755.8
  lumbosacral joint 724.6
  pelvic floor 618.89
  pelvis 618.89
  perineum 618.89
  posture 729.90
  rectum (sphincter) 569.49
  sacroiliac (joint) 724.6
  scrotum 608.89
  urethra (sphincter) 599.84
  uterus (outlet) 618.89
  vagina (outlet) 618.89
  vesical 596.59
Remains
  canal of Cloquet 743.51
  capsule (opaque) 743.51
Remittent fever (malarial) 084.6
Remnant
  canal of Cloquet 743.51
  capsule (opaque) 743.51
  cervix, cervical stump (acquired) (postoperative) 622.8
  cystic duct, postcholecystectomy 576.0
  fingernail 703.8
    congenital 757.5
  meniscus, knee 717.5
  thyroglossal duct 759.2
  tonsil 474.8
    infected 474.00
  urachus 753.7

Remote effect of cancer — *see* condition
Removal (of)
  catheter (urinary) (indwelling) V53.6
    from artificial opening — *see* Attention to, artificial, opening
    non-vascular V58.82
    vascular V58.81
  cerebral ventricle (communicating) shunt V53.01
  device (*see also* Fitting (of))
    contraceptive V25.42
    fixation
      external V54.89
      internal V54.01
    traction V54.89
  drains V58.49
  dressing
    wound V58.30
      nonsurgical V58.30
      surgical V58.31
  ileostomy V55.2
  Kirschner wire V54.89
  nonvascular catheter V58.82
  pin V54.01
  plaster cast V54.89
  plate (fracture) V54.01
  rod V54.01
  screw V54.01
  splint, external V54.89
  staples V58.32
  subdermal implantable contraceptive V25.43
  sutures V58.32
  traction device, external V54.89
  vascular catheter V58.81
  wound packing V58.30
    nonsurgical V58.30
    surgical V58.31
Ren
  arcuatus 753.3
  mobile, mobilis (*see also* Disease, renal) 593.0
    congenital 753.3
  unguliformis 753.3
Renal — *see also* condition
  glomerulohyalinosis-diabetic syndrome 250.4 ☑ *[581.81]*
    due to secondary diabetes 249.4 ☑ *[581.81]*
Rendu-Osler-Weber disease or syndrome (familial hemorrhagic telangiectasia) 448.0
Reninoma (M8361/1) 236.91
Rénon-Delille syndrome 253.8
Repair
  pelvic floor, previous, in pregnancy or childbirth 654.4 ☑
    affecting fetus or newborn 763.89
  scarred tissue V51.8
Replacement by artificial or mechanical device or prosthesis of — *see also* Fitting (of
  artificial skin V43.83
  bladder V43.5
  blood vessel V43.4
  breast V43.82
  eye globe V43.0
  heart
    with
      assist device V43.21
      fully implantable artificial heart V43.22
    valve V43.3
  intestine V43.89
  joint V43.60
    ankle V43.66
    elbow V43.62
    finger V43.69
    hip (partial) (total) V43.64
    knee V43.65
    shoulder V43.61
    specified NEC V43.69
    wrist V43.63
  kidney V43.89
  larynx V43.81
  lens V43.1
  limb(s) V43.7
  liver V43.89
  lung V43.89
  organ NEC V43.89

☑ Additional Digit Required — Refer to the Tabular List for Digit Selection

⮟ Subterms under main terms may continue to next column or page

►◄ Revised Text   ● New Line   ▲ Revised Code

Replacement by artificial or mechanical device or prosthesis of — *see also* Fitting (of — *continued*
  continued
  pancreas V43.89
  skin (artificial) V43.83
  tissue NEC V43.89
Reprogramming
  cardiac pacemaker V53.31
Request for expert evidence V68.2
Reserve, decreased or low
  cardiac — *see* Disease, heart
  kidney (*see also* Disease, renal) 593.9
Residual — *see also* condition
  bladder 596.8
  foreign body — *see* Retention, foreign body
  state, schizophrenic (*see also* Schizophrenia) 295.6 ☑
  urine 788.69
Resistance, resistant (to)
  activated protein C 289.81

> *Note — use the following subclassification for categories V09.5, V09.7, V09.8, V09.9:*
>
> 0 *without mention of resistance to multiple drugs*
>
> 1 *with resistance to multiple drugs*
>
>   *V09.5 quinolones and fluoro-quinolones*
>
>   *V09.7 antimycobacterial agents*
>
>   *V09.8 specified drugs NEC*
>
>   *V09.9 unspecified drugs*

  drugs by microorganisms V09.9 ☑
    Amikacin V09.4
    aminoglycosides V09.4
    Amodiaquine V09.5 ☑
    Amoxicillin V09.0
    Ampicillin V09.0
    antimycobacterial agents V09.7 ☑
    Azithromycin V09.2
    Azlocillin V09.0
    Aztreonam V09.1
    Bacampicillin V09.0
    Bacitracin V09.8 ☑
    Benznidazole V09.8 ☑
    B-lactam antibiotics V09.1
    Capreomycin V09.7 ☑
    Carbenicillin V09.0
    Cefaclor V09.1
    Cefadroxil V09.1
    Cefamandole V09.1
    Cefatetan V09.1
    Cefazolin V09.1
    Cefixime V09.1
    Cefonicid V09.1
    Cefoperazone V09.1
    Ceforanide V09.1
    Cefotaxime V09.1
    Cefoxitin V09.1
    Ceftazidime V09.1
    Ceftizoxime V09.1
    Ceftriaxone V09.1
    Cefuroxime V09.1
    Cephalexin V09.1
    Cephaloglycin V09.1
    Cephaloridine V09.1
    Cephalosporins V09.1
    Cephalothin V09.1
    Cephapirin V09.1
    Cephradine V09.1
    Chloramphenicol V09.8 ☑
    Chloraquine V09.5 ☑
    Chlorguanide V09.8 ☑
    Chlorproguanil V09.8 ☑
    Chlortetracycline V09.3
    Cinoxacin V09.5 ☑
    Ciprofloxacin V09.5 ☑
    Clarithromycin V09.2
    Clindamycin V09.8 ☑
    Clioquinol V09.5 ☑
    Clofazimine V09.7 ☑
    Cloxacillin V09.0
    Cyclacillin V09.0
    Cycloserine V09.7 ☑

Resistance, resistant — *continued*
  drugs by microorganisms — *continued*
    Dapsone [DZ] V09.7 ☑
    Demeclocycline V09.3
    Dicloxacillin V09.0
    Doxycycline V09.3
    Enoxacin V09.5 ☑
    Erythromycin V09.2
    Ethambutol [EMB] V09.7 ☑
    Ethionamide [ETA] V09.7 ☑
    fluoroquinolones V09.5 ☑
    Gentamicin V09.4
    Halofantrine V09.8 ☑
    Imipenem V09.1
    Iodoquinol V09.5 ☑
    Isoniazid [INH] V09.7 ☑
    Kanamycin V09.4
    macrolides V09.2
    Mafenide V09.6
    MDRO (multiple drug resistant organisms) NOS V09.91
    Mefloquine V09.8 ☑
    Melasoprol V09.8 ☑
    Methacycline V09.3
    Methenamine V09.8 ☑
    Methicillin — *see* Infection, Methicillin V09.0
    Metronidazole V09.8 ☑
    Mezlocillin V09.0
    Minocycline V09.3
    multiple drug resistant organisms NOS V09.91
    Nafcillin V09.0
    Nalidixic acid V09.5 ☑
    Natamycin V09.2
    Neomycin V09.4
    Netilmicin V09.4
    Nimorazole V09.8 ☑
    Nitrofurantoin V09.8 ☑
    Nitrofurtimox V09.8 ☑
    Norfloxacin V09.5 ☑
    Nystatin V09.2
    Ofloxacin V09.5 ☑
    Oleandomycin V09.2
    Oxacillin V09.0
    Oxytetracycline V09.3
    Para-amino salicylic acid [PAS] V09.7 ☑
    Paromomycin V09.4
    Penicillin (G) (V) (VK) V09.0
    penicillins V09.0
    Pentamidine V09.8 ☑
    Piperacillin V09.0
    Primaquine V09.5 ☑
    Proguanil V09.8 ☑
    Pyrazinamide [PZA] V09.7 ☑
    Pyrimethamine/Sulfalene V09.8 ☑
    Pyrimethamine/Sulfodoxine V09.8 ☑
    Quinacrine V09.5 ☑
    Quinidine V09.8 ☑
    Quinine V09.8 ☑
    quinolones V09.5 ☑
    Rifabutin V09.7 ☑
    Rifampin [RIF] V09.7 ☑
    Rifamycin V09.7 ☑
    Rolitetracycline V09.3
    specified drugs NEC V09.8 ☑
    Spectinomycin V09.8 ☑
    Spiramycin V09.2
    Streptomycin [SM] V09.4
    Sulfacetamide V09.6
    Sulfacytine V09.6
    Sulfadiazine V09.6
    Sulfadoxine V09.6
    Sulfamethoxazole V09.6
    Sulfapyridine V09.6
    Sulfasalizine V09.6
    Sulfasoxazole V09.6
    sulfonamides V09.6
    Sulfoxone V09.7 ☑
    tetracycline V09.3
    tetracyclines V09.3
    Thiamphenicol V09.8 ☑
    Ticarcillin V09.0
    Tinidazole V09.8 ☑
    Tobramycin V09.4

Resistance, resistant — *continued*
  drugs by microorganisms — *continued*
    Triamphenicol V09.8 ☑
    Trimethoprim V09.8 ☑
    Vancomycin V09.8 ☑
  insulin 277.7
  thyroid hormone 246.8
Resorption
  biliary 576.8
    purulent or putrid (*see also* Cholecystitis) 576.8
  dental (roots) 521.40
    alveoli 525.8
    pathological
      external 521.42
      internal 521.41
      specified NEC 521.49
  septic — *see* Septicemia
  teeth (roots) 521.40
    pathological
      external 521.42
      internal 521.41
      specified NEC 521.49
Respiration
  asymmetrical 786.09
  bronchial 786.09
  Cheyne-Stokes (periodic respiration) 786.04
  decreased, due to shock following injury 958.4
  disorder of 786.00
    psychogenic 306.1
    specified NEC 786.09
  failure 518.81
    acute 518.81
    acute and chronic 518.84
    chronic 518.83
    newborn 770.84
  insufficiency 786.09
    acute 518.82
    newborn NEC 770.89
  Kussmaul (air hunger) 786.09
  painful 786.52
  periodic 786.09
    high altitude 327.22
  poor 786.09
    newborn NEC 770.89
  sighing 786.7
    psychogenic 306.1
  wheezing 786.07
Respiratory — *see also* condition
  distress 786.09
    acute 518.82
    fetus or newborn NEC 770.89
    syndrome (newborn) 769
      adult (following shock, surgery, or trauma) 518.5
      specified NEC 518.82
  failure 518.81
    acute 518.81
    acute and chronic 518.84
    chronic 518.83
Respiratory syncytial virus (RSV) 079.6
  bronchiolitis 466.11
  pneumonia 480.1
  vaccination, prophylactic (against) V04.82
Response
  photoallergic 692.72
  phototoxic 692.72
Restless legs syndrome (RLS) 333.94
Restlessness 799.29   ▲
Restoration of organ continuity from previous sterilization (tuboplasty) (vasoplasty) V26.0
Rest, rests
  mesonephric duct 752.89
    fallopian tube 752.11
  ovarian, in fallopian tubes 752.19
  wolffian duct 752.89
Restriction of housing space V60.1
Restzustand, schizophrenic — *see also* Schizophrenia 295.6 ☑
Retained — *see* Retention
Retardation
  development, developmental, specific (*see also* Disorder, development, specific) 315.9
    learning, specific 315.2
      arithmetical 315.1

Retardation — *continued*
  development, developmental, specific (*see also* Disorder, development, specific) — *continued*
    learning, specific — *continued*
      language (skills) 315.31
        expressive 315.31
        mixed receptive-expressive 315.32
      mathematics 315.1
      reading 315.00
        phonological 315.39
      written expression 315.2
    motor 315.4
  endochondral bone growth 733.91
  growth (physical) in childhood 783.43
    due to malnutrition 263.2
    fetal (intrauterine) 764.9 ☑
      affecting management of pregnancy 656.5 ☑
  intrauterine growth 764.9 ☑
    affecting management of pregnancy 656.5 ☑
  mental 319
    borderline V62.89
    mild, IQ 50-70 317
    moderate, IQ 35-49 318.0
    profound, IQ under 20 318.2
    severe, IQ 20-34 318.1
  motor, specific 315.4
  physical 783.43
    child 783.43
    due to malnutrition 263.2
    fetus (intrauterine) 764.9 ☑
      affecting management of pregnancy 656.5 ☑
  psychomotor NEC 307.9
  reading 315.00
Retching — *see* Vomiting
Retention, retained
  bladder (*see also* Retention, urine) 788.20
    psychogenic 306.53
  carbon dioxide 276.2
  cholelithiasis 997.4
  cyst — *see* Cyst
  dead
    fetus (after 22 completed weeks gestation) 656.4 ☑
      early fetal death (before 22 completed weeks gestation) 632
    ovum 631
  decidua (following delivery) (fragments) (with hemorrhage) 666.2 ☑
    without hemorrhage 667.1 ☑
  deciduous tooth 520.6
  dental root 525.3
  fecal (*see also* Constipation) 564.00
  fluid 276.6
  foreign body (*see also* Foreign body, retained)
    bone 733.99
    current trauma — *see* Foreign body, by site or type
    middle ear 385.83
    muscle 729.6
    soft tissue NEC 729.6
  gallstones 997.4
  gastric 536.8
  membranes (following delivery) (with hemorrhage) 666.2 ☑
    with abortion — *see* Abortion, by type
    without hemorrhage 667.1 ☑
  menses 626.8
  milk (puerperal) 676.2 ☑
  nitrogen, extrarenal 788.99
  placenta (total) (with hemorrhage) 666.0 ☑
    with abortion — *see* Abortion, by type
    without hemorrhage 667.0 ☑
    portions or fragments 666.2 ☑
      without hemorrhage 667.1 ☑
  products of conception
    early pregnancy (fetal death before 22 completed weeks gestation) 632
    following
      abortion — *see* Abortion, by type
      delivery 666.2 ☑
        with hemorrhage 666.2 ☑
        without hemorrhage 667.1 ☑

Retention, retained — continued
- secundines (following delivery) (with hemorrhage) 666.2 ☑
  - with abortion — see Abortion, by type
  - without hemorrhage 667.1 ☑
  - complicating puerperium (delayed hemorrhage) 666.2 ☑
- smegma, clitoris 624.8
- urine NEC 788.20
  - bladder, incomplete emptying 788.21
    - due to
      - benign prostatic hypertrophy (BPH) — see category 600
  - due to
    - benign prostatic hypertrophy (BPH) — see category 600
  - psychogenic 306.53
  - specified NEC 788.29
- water (in tissue) (see also Edema) 782.3

Reticulation, dust (occupational) 504
Reticulocytosis NEC 790.99
Reticuloendotheliosis
- acute infantile (M9722/3) 202.5 ☑
- leukemic (M9940/3) 202.4 ☑
- malignant (M9720/3) 202.3 ☑
- nonlipid (M9722/3) 202.5 ☑

Reticulohistiocytoma (giant cell) 277.89
Reticulohistiocytosis, multicentric 272.8
Reticulolymphosarcoma (diffuse) (M9613/3) 200.8 ☑
- follicular (M9691/3) 202.0 ☑
- nodular (M9691/3) 202.0 ☑

Reticulosarcoma (M9640/3) 200.0 ☑
- nodular (M9642/3) 200.0 ☑
- pleomorphic cell type (M9641/3) 200.0 ☑

Reticulosis (skin)
- acute of infancy (M9722/3) 202.5 ☑
- familial hemophagocytic 288.4
- histiocytic medullary (M9721/3) 202.3 ☑
- lipomelanotic 695.89
- malignant (M9720/3) 202.3 ☑
- Sézary's (M9701/3) 202.2 ☑

Retina, retinal — see condition
Retinitis — see also Chorioretinitis 363.20
- albuminurica 585.9 [363.10]
- arteriosclerotic 440.8 [362.13]
- central angiospastic 362.41
- Coat's 362.12
- diabetic 250.5 ☑ [362.01]
  - due to secondary diabetes 249.5 ☑ [362.01]
- disciformis 362.52
- disseminated 363.10
  - metastatic 363.14
  - neurosyphilitic 094.83
  - pigment epitheliopathy 363.15
- exudative 362.12
- focal 363.00
  - in histoplasmosis 115.92
    - capsulatum 115.02
    - duboisii 115.12
  - juxtapapillary 363.05
  - macular 363.06
  - paramacular 363.06
  - peripheral 363.08
  - posterior pole NEC 363.07
- gravidarum 646.8 ☑
- hemorrhagica externa 362.12
- juxtapapillary (Jensen's) 363.05
- luetic — see Retinitis, syphilitic
- metastatic 363.14
- pigmentosa 362.74
- proliferans 362.29
- proliferating 362.29
- punctata albescens 362.76
- renal 585.9 [363.13]
- syphilitic (secondary) 091.51
  - congenital 090.0 [363.13]
  - early 091.51
  - late 095.8 [363.13]
- syphilitica, central, recurrent 095.8 [363.13]
- tuberculous (see also Tuberculous) 017.3 ☑ [363.13]

Retinoblastoma (M9510/3) 190.5
- differentiated type (M9511/3) 190.5
- undifferentiated type (M9512/3) 190.5

Retinochoroiditis — see also Chorioretinitis 363.20
- central angiospastic 362.41
- disseminated 363.10
  - metastatic 363.14
  - neurosyphilitic 094.83
  - pigment epitheliopathy 363.15
  - syphilitic 094.83
- due to toxoplasmosis (acquired) (focal) 130.2
- focal 363.00
  - in histoplasmosis 115.92
    - capsulatum 115.02
    - duboisii 115.12
  - juxtapapillary (Jensen's) 363.05
  - macular 363.06
  - paramacular 363.06
  - peripheral 363.08
  - posterior pole NEC 363.07
- juxtapapillaris 363.05
- syphilitic (disseminated) 094.83

Retinopathy (background) 362.10
- arteriosclerotic 440.8 [362.13]
- atherosclerotic 440.8 [362.13]
- central serous 362.41
- circinate 362.10
- Coat's 362.12
- diabetic 250.5 ☑ [362.01]
  - due to secondary diabetes 249.5 ☑ [362.01]
  - nonproliferative 250.5 ☑ [362.03]
    - due to secondary diabetes 249.5 ☑ [362.03]
    - mild 250.5 ☑ [362.04]
      - due to secondary diabetes 249.5 ☑ [362.04]
    - moderate 250.5 ☑ [362.05]
      - due to secondary diabetes 249.5 ☑ [362.05]
    - severe 250.5 ☑ [362.06]
      - due to secondary diabetes 249.5 ☑ [362.06]
  - proliferative 250.5 ☑ [362.02]
    - due to secondary diabetes 249.5 ☑ [362.02]
- exudative 362.12
- hypertensive 362.11
- nonproliferative
  - diabetic 250.5 ☑ [362.03]
    - due to secondary diabetes 249.5 ☑ [362.03]
    - mild 250.5 ☑ [362.04]
      - due to secondary diabetes 249.5 ☑ [362.04]
    - moderate 250.5 ☑ [362.05]
      - due to secondary diabetes 249.5 ☑ [362.05]
    - severe 250.5 ☑ [362.06]
      - due to secondary diabetes 249.5 ☑ [362.06]
- of prematurity 362.20
  - cicatricial 362.21
  - stage
    - 0 362.22
    - 1 362.23
    - 2 362.24
    - 3 362.25
    - 4 362.26
    - 5 362.27
- pigmentary, congenital 362.74
- proliferative 362.29
  - diabetic 250.5 ☑ [362.02]
    - due to secondary diabetes 249.5 ☑ [362.02]
  - sickle-cell 282.60 [362.29]
- solar 363.31

Retinoschisis 361.10
- bullous 361.12
- congenital 743.56
- flat 361.11
- juvenile 362.73

Retractile testis 752.52
Retraction
- cervix — see Retraction, uterus
- drum (membrane) 384.82
- eyelid 374.41
- finger 736.29

Retraction — continued
- head 781.0
- lid 374.41
- lung 518.89
- mediastinum 519.3
- nipple 611.79
  - congenital 757.6
  - puerperal, postpartum 676.0 ☑
- palmar fascia 728.6
- pleura (see also Pleurisy) 511.0
- ring, uterus (Bandl's) (pathological) 661.4 ☑
  - affecting fetus or newborn 763.7
- sternum (congenital) 756.3
  - acquired 738.3
  - during respiration 786.9
- substernal 738.3
- supraclavicular 738.8
- syndrome (Duane's) 378.71
- uterus 621.6
- valve (heart) — see Endocarditis

Retrobulbar — see condition
Retrocaval ureter 753.4
Retrocecal — see also condition
- appendix (congenital) 751.5
Retrocession — see Retroversion
Retrodisplacement — see Retroversion
Retroflection, retroflexion — see Retroversion
Retrognathia, retrognathism (mandibular) (maxillary) 524.10
Retrograde
- ejaculation 608.87
- menstruation 626.8
Retroiliac ureter 753.4
Retroperineal — see condition
Retroperitoneal — see condition
Retroperitonitis 567.39
Retropharyngeal — see condition
Retroplacental — see condition
Retroposition — see Retroversion
Retrosternal thyroid (congenital) 759.2
Retroversion, retroverted
- cervix — see Retroversion, uterus
- female NEC (see also Retroversion, uterus) 621.6
- iris 364.70
- testis (congenital) 752.51
- uterus, uterine (acquired) (acute) (adherent) (any degree) (asymptomatic) (cervix) (postinfectional) (postpartal, old) 621.6
  - congenital 752.3
  - in pregnancy or childbirth 654.3 ☑
    - affecting fetus or newborn 763.89
    - causing obstructed labor 660.2 ☑
      - affecting fetus or newborn 763.1
Retrusion, premaxilla (developmental) 524.04
Rett's syndrome 330.8
Reverse, reversed
- peristalsis 787.4
Reye-Sheehan syndrome (postpartum pituitary necrosis) 253.2
Reye's syndrome 331.81
Rh (factor)
- hemolytic disease 773.0
- incompatibility, immunization, or sensitization
  - affecting management of pregnancy 656.1 ☑
  - fetus or newborn 773.0
  - transfusion reaction 999.7
- negative mother, affecting fetus or newborn 773.0
- titer elevated 999.7
- transfusion reaction 999.7
Rhabdomyolysis (idiopathic) 728.88
Rhabdomyoma (M8900/0) — see also Neoplasm, connective tissue, benign
- adult (M8904/0) — see Neoplasm, connective tissue, benign
- fetal (M8903/0) — see Neoplasm, connective tissue, benign
- glycogenic (M8904/0) — see Neoplasm, connective tissue, benign
Rhabdomyosarcoma (M8900/3) — see also Neoplasm, connective tissue, malignant
- alveolar (M8920/3) — see Neoplasm, connective tissue, malignant

Rhabdomyosarcoma — see also Neoplasm, connective tissue, malignant — continued
- embryonal (M8910/3) — see Neoplasm, connective tissue, malignant
- mixed type (M8902/3) — see Neoplasm, connective tissue, malignant
- pleomorphic (M8901/3) — see Neoplasm, connective tissue, malignant
Rhabdosarcoma (M8900/3) — see Rhabdomyosarcoma
Rhesus (factor) (Rh) incompatibility — see Rh, incompatibility
Rheumaticosis — see Rheumatism
Rheumatism, rheumatic (acute NEC) 729.0
- adherent pericardium 393
- arthritis
  - acute or subacute — see Fever, rheumatic
  - chronic 714.0
  - spine 720.0
- articular (chronic) NEC (see also Arthritis) 716.9 ☑
  - acute or subacute — see Fever, rheumatic
- back 724.9
- blennorrhagic 098.59
- carditis — see Disease, heart, rheumatic
- cerebral — see Fever, rheumatic
- chorea (acute) — see Chorea, rheumatic
- chronic NEC 729.0
- coronary arteritis 391.9
  - chronic 398.99
- degeneration, myocardium (see also Degeneration, myocardium, with rheumatic fever) 398.0
- desert 114.0
- febrile — see Fever, rheumatic
- fever — see Fever, rheumatic
- gonococcal 098.59
- gout 274.00 ▲
- heart
  - disease (see also Disease, heart, rheumatic) 398.90
  - failure (chronic) (congestive) (inactive) 398.91
- hemopericardium — see Rheumatic, pericarditis
- hydropericardium — see Rheumatic, pericarditis
- inflammatory (acute) (chronic) (subacute) — see Fever, rheumatic
- intercostal 729.0
  - meaning Tietze's disease 733.6
- joint (chronic) NEC (see also Arthritis) 716.9 ☑
  - acute — see Fever, rheumatic
- mediastinopericarditis — see Rheumatic, pericarditis
- muscular 729.0
- myocardial degeneration (see also Degeneration, myocardium, with rheumatic fever) 398.0
- myocarditis (chronic) (inactive) (with chorea) 398.0
  - active or acute 391.2
    - with chorea (acute) (rheumatic) (Sydenham's) 392.0
- myositis 729.1
- neck 724.9
- neuralgic 729.0
- neuritis (acute) (chronic) 729.2
- neuromuscular 729.0
- nodose — see Arthritis, nodosa
- nonarticular 729.0
- palindromic 719.30
  - ankle 719.37
  - elbow 719.32
  - foot 719.37
  - hand 719.34
  - hip 719.35
  - knee 719.36
  - multiple sites 719.39
  - pelvic region 719.35
  - shoulder (region) 719.31
  - specified site NEC 719.38
  - wrist 719.33
- pancarditis, acute 391.8

☑ Additional Digit Required — Refer to the Tabular List for Digit Selection

🔱 Subterms under main terms may continue to next column or page

---

☑ Additional Digit Required — Refer to the Tabular List for Digit Selection   ▼ Subterms under main terms may continue to next column or page

Rubella — continued
  complication — continued
    neurological — continued
      specified type NEC 056.09
      specified type NEC 056.79
    congenital 771.0
  contact V01.4
  exposure to V01.4
  maternal
    with suspected fetal damage affecting
      management of pregnancy
      655.3 ☑
    affecting fetus or newborn 760.2
      manifest rubella in infant 771.0
  specified complications NEC 056.79
  vaccination, prophylactic (against) V04.3
Rubeola (measles) — see also Measles 055.9
  complicated 055.8
  meaning rubella (see also Rubella) 056.9
  scarlatinosis 057.8
Rubeosis iridis 364.42
  diabetica 250.5 ☑ [364.42]
  due to secondary diabetes
    249.5 ☑ [364.42]
Rubinstein-Taybi's syndrome (brachydactylia,
  short stature and mental retardation)
  759.89
Rudimentary (congenital) — see also Agenesis
  arm 755.22
  bone 756.9
  cervix uteri 752.49
  eye (see also Microphthalmos) 743.10
  fallopian tube 752.19
  leg 755.32
  lobule of ear 744.21
  patella 755.64
  respiratory organs in thoracopagus 759.4
  tracheal bronchus 748.3
  uterine horn 752.3
  uterus 752.3
    in male 752.7
    solid or with cavity 752.3
  vagina 752.49
Rud's syndrome (mental deficiency, epilepsy,
  and infantilism) 759.89
Ruiter-Pompen (-Wyers) syndrome (angiokeratoma corporis diffusum) 272.7
Ruled out condition — see also Observation,
  suspected V71.9
Rumination — see also Vomiting
  disorder 307.53
  neurotic 300.3
  obsessional 300.3
  psychogenic 307.53
Runaway reaction — see also Disturbance,
  conduct
  socialized 312.2 ☑
  undersocialized, unsocialized 312.1 ☑
Runeberg's disease (progressive pernicious
  anemia) 281.0
Runge's syndrome (postmaturity) 766.22
Runny nose 784.99
Rupia 091.3
  congenital 090.0
  tertiary 095.9
Rupture, ruptured 553.9
  abdominal viscera NEC 799.89
    obstetrical trauma 665.5 ☑
  abscess (spontaneous) — see Abscess, by site
  amnion — see Rupture, membranes
  aneurysm — see Aneurysm
  anus (sphincter) — see Laceration, anus
  aorta, aortic 441.5
    abdominal 441.3
    arch 441.1
    ascending 441.1
    descending 441.5
      abdominal 441.3
      thoracic 441.1
    syphilitic 093.0
    thoracoabdominal 441.6
    thorax, thoracic 441.1
    transverse 441.1
    traumatic (thoracic) 901.0
      abdominal 902.0

Rupture, ruptured — continued
  aorta, aortic — continued
    valve or cusp (see also Endocarditis, aortic)
      424.1
  appendix (with peritonitis) 540.0
    with peritoneal abscess 540.1
    traumatic — see Injury, internal, gastroin-
      testinal tract
  arteriovenous fistula, brain (congenital) 430
  artery 447.2
    brain (see also Hemorrhage, brain) 431
    coronary (see also Infarct, myocardium)
      410.9 ☑
    heart (see also Infarct, myocardium)
      410.9 ☑
    pulmonary 417.8
    traumatic (complication) (see also Injury,
      blood vessel, by site) 904.9
  bile duct, except cystic (see also Disease, bil-
    iary) 576.3
    cystic 575.4
    traumatic — see Injury, internal, intra-ab-
      dominal
  bladder (sphincter) 596.6
    with
      abortion — see Abortion, by type, with
        damage to pelvic organs
      ectopic pregnancy (see also categories
        633.0–633.9) 639.2
      molar pregnancy (see also categories
        630–632) 639.2
    following
      abortion 639.2
      ectopic or molar pregnancy 639.2
    nontraumatic 596.6
    obstetrical trauma 665.5 ☑
    spontaneous 596.6
    traumatic — see Injury, internal, bladder
  blood vessel (see also Hemorrhage) 459.0
    brain (see also Hemorrhage, brain) 431
    heart (see also Infarct, myocardium)
      410.9 ☑
    traumatic (complication) (see also Injury,
      blood vessel, by site) 904.9
  bone — see Fracture, by site
  bowel 569.89
    traumatic — see Injury, internal, intestine
  Bowman's membrane 371.31
  brain
    aneurysm (congenital) (see also Hemor-
      rhage, subarachnoid) 430
      late effect — see Late effect(s) (of)
        cerebrovascular disease
      syphilitic 094.87
    hemorrhagic (see also Hemorrhage, brain)
      431
    injury at birth 767.0
    syphilitic 094.89
  capillaries 448.9
  cardiac (see also Infarct, myocardium) 410.9 ☑
  cartilage (articular) (current) (see also Sprain,
    by site)
    knee — see Tear, meniscus
    semilunar — see Tear, meniscus
  cecum (with peritonitis) 540.0
    with peritoneal abscess 540.1
    traumatic 863.89
      with open wound into cavity 863.99
  cerebral aneurysm (congenital) (see also
    Hemorrhage, subarachnoid) 430
    late effect — see Late effect(s) (of) cere-
      brovascular disease
  cervix (uteri)
    with
      abortion — see Abortion, by type, with
        damage to pelvic organs
      ectopic pregnancy (see also categories
        633.0–633.9) 639.2
      molar pregnancy (see also categories
        630–632) 639.2
    following
      abortion 639.2
      ectopic or molar pregnancy 639.2
    obstetrical trauma 665.3 ☑
    traumatic — see Injury, internal, cervix
  chordae tendineae 429.5

Rupture, ruptured — continued
  choroid (direct) (indirect) (traumatic) 363.63
  circle of Willis (see also Hemorrhage, subarach-
    noid) 430
    late effect — see Late effect(s) (of) cere-
      brovascular disease
  colon 569.89
    traumatic — see Injury, internal, colon
  cornea (traumatic) (see also Rupture, eye)
    due to ulcer 370.00
  coronary (artery) (thrombotic) (see also Infarct,
    myocardium) 410.9 ☑
  corpus luteum (infected) (ovary) 620.1
  cyst — see Cyst
  cystic duct (see also Disease, gallbladder) 575.4
  Descemet's membrane 371.33
    traumatic — see Rupture, eye
  diaphragm (see also Hernia, diaphragm)
    traumatic — see Injury, internal, di-
      aphragm
  diverticulum
    bladder 596.3
    intestine (large) (see also Diverticula)
      562.10
      small 562.00
  duodenal stump 537.89
  duodenum (ulcer) — see Ulcer, duodenum,
    with perforation
  ear drum (see also Perforation, tympanum)
    384.20
    with otitis media — see Otitis media
    traumatic — see Wound, open, ear
  esophagus 530.4
    traumatic 862.22
      with open wound into cavity 862.32
      cervical region — see Wound, open,
        esophagus
  eye (without prolapse of intraocular tissue)
    871.0
    with
      exposure of intraocular tissue 871.1
      partial loss of intraocular tissue 871.2
      prolapse of intraocular tissue 871.1
    due to burn 940.5
  fallopian tube 620.8
    due to pregnancy — see Pregnancy, tubal
    traumatic — see Injury, internal, fallopian
      tube
  fontanel 767.3
  free wall (ventricle) (see also Infarct, myocardi-
    um) 410.9 ☑
  gallbladder or duct (see also Disease, gallblad-
    der) 575.4
    traumatic — see Injury, internal, gallblad-
      der
  gastric (see also Rupture, stomach) 537.89
    vessel 459.0
  globe (eye) (traumatic) — see Rupture, eye
  graafian follicle (hematoma) 620.0
  heart (auricle) (ventricle) (see also Infarct, my-
    ocardium) 410.9 ☑
    infectional 422.90
    traumatic — see Rupture, myocardium,
      traumatic
  hymen 623.8
  internal
    organ, traumatic (see also Injury, internal,
      by site)
      heart — see Rupture, myocardium,
        traumatic
      kidney — see Rupture, kidney
      liver — see Rupture, liver
      spleen — see Rupture, spleen, traumat-
        ic
    semilunar cartilage — see Tear, meniscus
  intervertebral disc — see Displacement, inter-
    vertebral disc
    traumatic (current) — see Dislocation,
      vertebra
  intestine 569.89
    traumatic — see Injury, internal, intestine
  intracranial, birth injury 767.0
  iris 364.76
    traumatic — see Rupture, eye
  joint capsule — see Sprain, by site
  kidney (traumatic) 866.03

Rupture, ruptured — continued
  kidney — continued
    with open wound into cavity 866.13
    due to birth injury 767.8
    nontraumatic 593.89
  lacrimal apparatus (traumatic) 870.2
  lens (traumatic) 366.20
  ligament (see also Sprain, by site)
    with open wound — see Wound, open,
      by site
    old (see also Disorder, cartilage, articular)
      718.0 ☑
  liver (traumatic) 864.04
    with open wound into cavity 864.14
    due to birth injury 767.8
    nontraumatic 573.8
  lymphatic (node) (vessel) 457.8
  marginal sinus (placental) (with hemorrhage)
    641.2 ☑
    affecting fetus or newborn 762.1
  meaning hernia — see Hernia
  membrana tympani (see also Perforation,
    tympanum) 384.20
    with otitis media — see Otitis media
    traumatic — see Wound, open, ear
  membranes (spontaneous)
    artificial
      delayed delivery following 658.3 ☑
        affecting fetus or newborn 761.1
        fetus or newborn 761.1
    delayed delivery following 658.2 ☑
      affecting fetus or newborn 761.1
    premature (less than 24 hours prior to on-
      set of labor) 658.1 ☑
      affecting fetus or newborn 761.1
      delayed delivery following 658.2 ☑
        affecting fetus or newborn 761.1
  meningeal artery (see also Hemorrhage, sub-
    arachnoid) 430
    late effect — see Late effect(s) (of) cere-
      brovascular disease
  meniscus (knee) (see also Tear, meniscus)
    old (see also Derangement, meniscus)
      717.5
      site other than knee — see Disorder,
        cartilage, articular
    site other than knee — see Sprain, by site
  mesentery 568.89
    traumatic — see Injury, internal, mesentery
  mitral — see Insufficiency, mitral
  muscle (traumatic) NEC (see also Sprain, by
    site)
    with open wound — see Wound, open,
      by site
    nontraumatic 728.83
  musculotendinous cuff (nontraumatic)
    (shoulder) 840.4
  mycotic aneurysm, causing cerebral hemor-
    rhage (see also Hemorrhage, subarach-
    noid) 430
    late effect — see Late effect(s) (of) cere-
      brovascular disease
  myocardium, myocardial (see also Infarct, my-
    ocardium) 410.9 ☑
    traumatic 861.03
      with open wound into thorax 861.13
  nontraumatic (meaning hernia) (see also Her-
    nia, by site) 553.9
  obstructed (see also Hernia, by site, with ob-
    struction) 552.9
    gangrenous (see also Hernia, by site, with
      gangrene) 551.9
  operation wound (see also Dehiscence) 998.32
    internal 998.31
  ovary, ovarian 620.8
    corpus luteum 620.1
    follicle (graafian) 620.0
  oviduct 620.8
    due to pregnancy — see Pregnancy, tubal
  pancreas 577.8
    traumatic — see Injury, internal, pancreas
  papillary muscle (ventricular) 429.6
  pelvic
    floor, complicating delivery 664.1 ☑
    organ NEC — see Injury, pelvic, organs
  penis (traumatic) — see Wound, open, penis

☑ Additional Digit Required — Refer to the Tabular List for Digit Selection

▽ Subterms under main terms may continue to next column or page

Rupture, ruptured — *continued*
perineum 624.8
during delivery (*see also* Laceration, perineum, complicating delivery)
664.4 ☑
pharynx (nontraumatic) (spontaneous) 478.29
pregnant uterus (before onset of labor)
665.0 ☑
prostate (traumatic) — *see* Injury, internal, prostate
pulmonary
artery 417.8
valve (heart) (*see also* Endocarditis, pulmonary) 424.3
vein 417.8
vessel 417.8
pupil, sphincter 364.75
pus tube (*see also* Salpingo-oophoritis) 614.2
pyosalpinx (*see also* Salpingo-oophoritis) 614.2
rectum 569.49
traumatic — *see* Injury, internal, rectum
retina, retinal (traumatic) (without detachment) 361.30
with detachment (*see also* Detachment, retina, with retinal defect) 361.00
rotator cuff (capsule) (traumatic) 840.4
nontraumatic, complete 727.61
sclera 871.0
semilunar cartilage, knee (*see also* Tear, meniscus) 836.2
old (*see also* Derangement, meniscus)
717.5
septum (cardiac) 410.8 ☑
sigmoid 569.89
traumatic — *see* Injury, internal, colon, sigmoid
sinus of Valsalva 747.29
spinal cord (*see also* Injury, spinal, by site)
due to injury at birth 767.4
fetus or newborn 767.4
syphilitic 094.89
traumatic (*see also* Injury, spinal, by site)
with fracture — *see* Fracture, vertebra, by site, with spinal cord injury
spleen 289.59
congenital 767.8
due to injury at birth 767.8
malarial 084.9
nontraumatic 289.59
spontaneous 289.59
traumatic 865.04

Rupture, ruptured — *continued*
spleen — *continued*
traumatic — *continued*
with open wound into cavity 865.14
splenic vein 459.0
stomach 537.89
due to injury at birth 767.8
traumatic — *see* Injury, internal, stomach
ulcer — *see* Ulcer, stomach, with perforation
synovium 727.50
specified site NEC 727.59
tendon (traumatic) (*see also* Sprain, by site)
with open wound — *see* Wound, open, by site
Achilles 845.09
nontraumatic 727.67
ankle 845.09
nontraumatic 727.68
biceps (long head) 840.8
nontraumatic 727.62
foot 845.10
interphalangeal (joint) 845.13
metatarsophalangeal (joint) 845.12
nontraumatic 727.68
specified site NEC 845.19
tarsometatarsal (joint) 845.11
hand 842.10
carpometacarpal (joint) 842.11
interphalangeal (joint) 842.13
metacarpophalangeal (joint) 842.12
nontraumatic 727.63
extensors 727.63
flexors 727.64
specified site NEC 842.19
nontraumatic 727.60
specified site NEC 727.69
patellar 844.8
nontraumatic 727.66
quadriceps 844.8
nontraumatic 727.65
rotator cuff (capsule) 840.4
nontraumatic, complete 727.61
wrist 842.00
carpal (joint) 842.01
nontraumatic 727.63
extensors 727.63
flexors 727.64
radiocarpal (joint) (ligament) 842.02
radioulnar (joint), distal 842.09
specified site NEC 842.09

Rupture, ruptured — *continued*
testis (traumatic) 878.2
complicated 878.3
due to syphilis 095.8
thoracic duct 457.8
tonsil 474.8
traumatic
with open wound — *see* Wound, open, by site
aorta — *see* Rupture, aorta, traumatic
ear drum — *see* Wound, open, ear, drum
external site — *see* Wound, open, by site
eye 871.2
globe (eye) — *see* Wound, open, eyeball
internal organ (abdomen, chest, or pelvis)
(*see also* Injury, internal, by site)
heart — *see* Rupture, myocardium, traumatic
kidney — *see* Rupture, kidney
liver — *see* Rupture, liver
spleen — *see* Rupture, spleen, traumatic
ligament, muscle, or tendon (*see also* Sprain, by site)
with open wound — *see* Wound, open, by site
meaning hernia — *see* Hernia
tricuspid (heart) (valve) — *see* Endocarditis, tricuspid
tube, tubal 620.8
abscess (*see also* Salpingo-oophoritis) 614.2
due to pregnancy — *see* Pregnancy, tubal
tympanum, tympanic (membrane) (*see also* Perforation, tympanum) 384.20
with otitis media — *see* Otitis media
traumatic — *see* Wound, open, ear, drum
umbilical cord 663.8 ☑
fetus or newborn 772.0
ureter (traumatic) (*see also* Injury, internal, ureter) 867.2
nontraumatic 593.89
urethra 599.84
with
abortion — *see* Abortion, by type, with damage to pelvic organs
ectopic pregnancy (*see also* categories 633.0–633.9) 639.2
molar pregnancy (*see also* categories 630–632) 639.2
following
abortion 639.2

Rupture, ruptured — *continued*
urethra — *continued*
following — *continued*
ectopic or molar pregnancy 639.2
obstetrical trauma 665.5 ☑
traumatic — *see* Injury, internal urethra
uterosacral ligament 620.8
uterus (traumatic) (*see also* Injury, internal uterus)
affecting fetus or newborn 763.89
during labor 665.1 ☑
nonpuerperal, nontraumatic 621.8
nontraumatic 621.8
pregnant (during labor) 665.1 ☑
before labor 665.0 ☑
vagina 878.6
complicated 878.7
complicating delivery — *see* Laceration, vagina, complicating delivery
valve, valvular (heart) — *see* Endocarditis
varicose vein — *see* Varicose, vein
varix — *see* Varix
vena cava 459.0
ventricle (free wall) (left) (*see also* Infarct, myocardium) 410.9 ☑
vesical (urinary) 596.6
traumatic — *see* Injury, internal, bladder
vessel (blood) 459.0
pulmonary 417.8
viscus 799.89
vulva 878.4
complicated 878.5
complicating delivery 664.0 ☑
Russell's dwarf (uterine dwarfism and craniofacial dysostosis) 759.89
Russell's dysentery 004.8
Russell (-Silver) syndrome (congenital hemihypertrophy and short stature) 759.89
Russian spring-summer type encephalitis
063.0
Rust's disease (tuberculous spondylitis)
015.0 ☑ *[720.81]*
Rustitskii's disease (multiple myeloma)
(M9730/3) 203.0 ☑
Ruysch's disease (Hirschsprung's disease) 751.3
Rytand-Lipsitch syndrome (complete atrioventricular block) 426.0

☑ Additional Digit Required — Refer to the Tabular List for Digit Selection   ▽ Subterms under main terms may continue to next column or page

2010 ICD-9-CM   ▶◀ Revised Text   ● New Line   ▲ Revised Code   **Volume 2 — 241**

S

Saber
- shin 090.5
- tibia 090.5

Saccharomyces infection — *see also* Candidiasis 112.9

Saccharopinuria 270.7

Saccular — *see* condition

Sacculation
- aorta (nonsyphilitic) (*see also* Aneurysm, aorta) 441.9
  - ruptured 441.5
  - syphilitic 093.0
- bladder 596.3
- colon 569.89
- intralaryngeal (congenital) (ventricular) 748.3
- larynx (congenital) (ventricular) 748.3
- organ or site, congenital — *see* Distortion
- pregnant uterus, complicating delivery 654.4 ☑
  - affecting fetus or newborn 763.1
  - causing obstructed labor 660.2 ☑
    - affecting fetus or newborn 763.1
- rectosigmoid 569.89
- sigmoid 569.89
- ureter 593.89
- urethra 599.2
- vesical 596.3

Sachs (-Tay) disease (amaurotic familial idiocy) 330.1

Sacks-Libman disease 710.0 *[424.91]*

Sac, lacrimal — *see* condition

Sacralgia 724.6

Sacralization
- fifth lumbar vertebra 756.15
- incomplete (vertebra) 756.15

Sacrodynia 724.6

Sacroiliac joint — *see* condition

Sacroiliitis NEC 720.2

Sacrum — *see* condition

Saddle
- back 737.8
- embolus, aorta 444.0
- nose 738.0
  - congenital 754.0
  - due to syphilis 090.5

Sadism (sexual) 302.84

Saemisch's ulcer 370.04

Saenger's syndrome 379.46

Sago spleen 277.39

Sailors' skin 692.74

Saint
- Anthony's fire (*see also* Erysipelas) 035
- Guy's dance — *see* Chorea
- Louis-type encephalitis 062.3
- triad (*see also* Hernia, diaphragm) 553.3
- Vitus' dance — *see* Chorea

Salicylism
- correct substance properly administered 535.4 ☑
- overdose or wrong substance given or taken 965.1

Salivary duct or gland — *see also* condition
- virus disease 078.5

Salivation (excessive) — *see also* Ptyalism 527.7

Salmonella (aertrycke) (choleraesuis) (enteritidis) (gallinarum) (suipestifer) (typhimurium) — *see also* Infection, Salmonella 003.9
- arthritis 003.23
- carrier (suspected) of V02.3
- meningitis 003.21
- osteomyelitis 003.24
- pneumonia 003.22
- septicemia 003.1
- typhosa 002.0
  - carrier (suspected) of V02.1

Salmonellosis 003.0
- with pneumonia 003.22

Salpingitis (catarrhal) (fallopian tube) (nodular) (pseudofollicular) (purulent) (septic) — *see also* Salpingo-oophoritis 614.2
- ear 381.50
  - acute 381.51
  - chronic 381.52
  - Eustachian (tube) 381.50

Salpingitis — *see also* Salpingo-oophoritis — *continued*
- Eustachian — *continued*
  - acute 381.51
  - chronic 381.52
- follicularis 614.1
- gonococcal (chronic) 098.37
  - acute 098.17
- interstitial, chronic 614.1
- isthmica nodosa 614.1
- old — *see* Salpingo-oophoritis, chronic
- puerperal, postpartum, childbirth 670.8 ☑ ▲
- specific (chronic) 098.37
  - acute 098.17
- tuberculous (acute) (chronic) (*see also* Tuberculosis) 016.6 ☑
- venereal (chronic) 098.37
  - acute 098.17

Salpingocele 620.4

Salpingo-oophoritis (catarrhal) (purulent) (ruptured) (septic) (suppurative) 614.2
- acute 614.0
  - with
    - abortion — *see* Abortion, by type, with sepsis
    - ectopic pregnancy (*see also* categories 633.0–633.9) 639.0
    - molar pregnancy (*see also* categories 630–632) 639.0
  - following
    - abortion 639.0
    - ectopic or molar pregnancy 639.0
  - gonococcal 098.17
  - puerperal, postpartum, childbirth 670.8 ☑ ▲
  - tuberculous (*see also* Tuberculosis) 016.6 ☑
- chronic 614.1
  - gonococcal 098.37
  - tuberculous (see also Tuberculosis) 016.6 ☑
- complicating pregnancy 646.6 ☑
  - affecting fetus or newborn 760.8
- gonococcal (chronic) 098.37
  - acute 098.17
- old — *see* Salpingo-oophoritis, chronic
- puerperal 670.8 ☑ ▲
- specific — *see* Salpingo-oophoritis, gonococcal
- subacute (*see also* Salpingo-oophoritis, acute) 614.0
- tuberculous (acute) (chronic) (*see also* Tuberculosis) 016.6 ☑
- venereal — *see* Salpingo-oophoritis, gonococcal

Salpingo-ovaritis — *see also* Salpingo-oophoritis 614.2

Salpingoperitonitis — *see also* Salpingo-oophoritis 614.2

Salt-losing
- nephritis (*see also* Disease, renal) 593.9
- syndrome (*see also* Disease, renal) 593.9

Salt-rheum — *see also* Eczema 692.9

Salzmann's nodular dystrophy 371.46

Sampling
- chorionic villus V28.89

Sampson's cyst or tumor 617.1

Sandblasters'
- asthma 502
- lung 502

Sander's disease (paranoia) 297.1

Sandfly fever 066.0

Sandhoff's disease 330.1

Sanfilippo's syndrome (mucopolysaccharidosis III) 277.5

Sanger-Brown's ataxia 334.2

San Joaquin Valley fever 114.0

Sao Paulo fever or typhus 082.0

Saponification, mesenteric 567.89

Sapremia — *see* Septicemia

Sarcocele (benign)
- syphilitic 095.8
- congenital 090.5

Sarcoepiplocele — *see also* Hernia 553.9

Sarcoepiplomphalocele — *see also* Hernia, umbilicus 553.1

Sarcoid (any site) 135
- with lung involvement 135 *[517.8]*
- Boeck's 135
- Darier-Roussy 135
- Spiegler-Fendt 686.8

Sarcoidosis 135
- cardiac 135 *[425.8]*
- lung 135 *[517.8]*

Sarcoma (M8800/3) — *see also* Neoplasm, connective tissue, malignant
- alveolar soft part (M9581/3) — *see* Neoplasm, connective tissue, malignant
- ameloblastic (M9330/3) 170.1
  - upper jaw (bone) 170.0
- botryoid (M8910/3) — *see* Neoplasm, connective tissue, malignant
- botryoides (M8910/3) — *see* Neoplasm, connective tissue, malignant
- cerebellar (M9480/3) 191.6
  - circumscribed (arachnoidal) (M9471/3) 191.6
- circumscribed (arachnoidal) cerebellar (M9471/3) 191.6
- clear cell, of tendons and aponeuroses (M9044/3) — *see* Neoplasm, connective tissue, malignant
- embryonal (M8991/3) — *see* Neoplasm, connective tissue, malignant
- endometrial (stromal) (M8930/3) 182.0
  - isthmus 182.1
- endothelial (M9130/3) (*see also* Neoplasm, connective tissue, malignant)
  - bone (M9260/3) — *see* Neoplasm, bone, malignant
- epithelioid cell (M8804/3) — *see* Neoplasm, connective tissue, malignant
- Ewing's (M9260/3) — *see* Neoplasm, bone, malignant
- follicular dendritic cell 202.9 ☑
- germinoblastic (diffuse) (M9632/3) 202.8 ☑
  - follicular (M9697/3) 202.0 ☑
- giant cell (M8802/3) (*see also* Neoplasm, connective tissue, malignant)
  - bone (M9250/3) — *see* Neoplasm, bone, malignant
- glomoid (M8710/3) — *see* Neoplasm, connective tissue, malignant
- granulocytic (M9930/3) 205.3 ☑
- hemangioendothelial (M9130/3) — *see* Neoplasm, connective tissue, malignant
- hemorrhagic, multiple (M9140/3) — *see* Kaposi's, sarcoma
- Hodgkin's (M9662/3) 201.2 ☑
- immunoblastic (M9612/3) 200.8 ☑
- interdigitating dendritic cell 202.9 ☑
- Kaposi's (M9140/3) — *see* Kaposi's, sarcoma
- Kupffer cell (M9124/3) 155.0
- Langerhans cell 202.9 ☑
- leptomeningeal (M9530/3) — *see* Neoplasm, meninges, malignant
- lymphangioendothelial (M9170/3) — *see* Neoplasm, connective tissue, malignant
- lymphoblastic (M9630/3) 200.1 ☑
- lymphocytic (M9620/3) 200.1 ☑
- mast cell (M9740/3) 202.6 ☑
- melanotic (M8720/3) — *see* Melanoma
- meningeal (M9530/3) — *see* Neoplasm, meninges, malignant
- meningothelial (M9530/3) — *see* Neoplasm, meninges, malignant
- mesenchymal (M8800/3) (*see also* Neoplasm, connective tissue, malignant)
  - mixed (M8990/3) — *see* Neoplasm, connective tissue, malignant
- mesothelial (M9050/3) — *see* Neoplasm, by site, malignant
- monstrocellular (M9481/3)
  - specified site — *see* Neoplasm, by site, malignant
  - unspecified site 191.9
- myeloid (M9930/3) 205.3 ☑
- neurogenic (M9540/3) — *see* Neoplasm, connective tissue, malignant

Sarcoma — *see also* Neoplasm, connective tissue, malignant — *continued*
- odontogenic (M9270/3) 170.1
  - upper jaw (bone) 170.0
- osteoblastic (M9180/3) — *see* Neoplasm, bone, malignant
- osteogenic (M9180/3) (*see also* Neoplasm, bone, malignant)
  - juxtacortical (M9190/3) — *see* Neoplasm, bone, malignant
  - periosteal (M9190/3) — *see* Neoplasm, bone, malignant
- periosteal (M8812/3) (*see also* Neoplasm, bone, malignant)
  - osteogenic (M9190/3) — *see* Neoplasm, bone, malignant
- plasma cell (M9731/3) 203.8 ☑
- pleomorphic cell (M8802/3) — *see* Neoplasm, connective tissue, malignant
- reticuloendothelial (M9720/3) 202.3 ☑
- reticulum cell (M9640/3) 200.0 ☑
  - nodular (M9642/3) 200.0 ☑
  - pleomorphic cell type (M9641/3) 200.0 ☑
- round cell (M8803/3) — *see* Neoplasm, connective tissue, malignant
- small cell (M8803/3) — *see* Neoplasm, connective tissue, malignant
- spindle cell (M8801/3) — *see* Neoplasm, connective tissue, malignant
- stromal (endometrial) (M8930/3) 182.0
  - isthmus 182.1
- synovial (M9040/3) (*see also* Neoplasm, connective tissue, malignant)
  - biphasic type (M9043/3) — *see* Neoplasm, connective tissue, malignant
  - epithelioid cell type (M9042/3) — *see* Neoplasm, connective tissue, malignant
  - spindle cell type (M9041/3) — *see* Neoplasm, connective tissue, malignant

Sarcomatosis
- meningeal (M9539/3) — *see* Neoplasm, meninges, malignant
- specified site NEC (M8800/3) — *see* Neoplasm, connective tissue, malignant
- unspecified site (M8800/6) 171.9

Sarcosinemia 270.8

Sarcosporidiosis 136.5

Satiety, early 780.94

Satisfactory smear but lacking transformation zone
- anal 796.77
- cervical 795.07

Saturnine — *see* condition

Saturnism 984.9
- specified type of lead — *see* Table of Drugs and Chemicals

Satyriasis 302.89

Sauriasis — *see* Ichthyosis

Sauriderma 757.39

Sauriosis — *see* Ichthyosis

Savill's disease (epidemic exfoliative dermatitis) 695.89

SBE (subacute bacterial endocarditis) 421.0

Scabies (any site) 133.0

Scabs 782.8

Scaglietti-Dagnini syndrome (acromegalic macrospondylitis) 253.0

Scald, scalded — *see also* Burn, by site
- skin syndrome 695.81

Scalenus anticus (anterior) syndrome 353.0

Scales 782.8

Scalp — *see* condition

Scaphocephaly 756.0

Scaphoiditis, tarsal 732.5

Scapulalgia 733.90

Scapulohumeral myopathy 359.1

Scarabiasis 134.1

Scarlatina 034.1
- anginosa 034.1
- maligna 034.1
- myocarditis, acute 034.1 *[422.0]*
  - old (*see also* Myocarditis) 429.0
- otitis media 034.1 *[382.02]*
- ulcerosa 034.1

Scarlatinella 057.8

☑ Additional Digit Required — Refer to the Tabular List for Digit Selection   ▽ Subterms under main terms may continue to next column or page

2010 ICD-9-CM   ▶◀ Revised Text   ● New Line   ▲ Revised Code   October 2009 • Volume 2 — 243

Scarlet fever (albuminuria) (angina) (convulsions) (lesions of lid) (rash) 034.1
Scar, scarring — *see also* Cicatrix 709.2
  adherent 709.2
  atrophic 709.2
  cervix
    in pregnancy or childbirth 654.6 ☑
      affecting fetus or newborn 763.89
      causing obstructed labor 660.2 ☑
        affecting fetus or newborn 763.1
  cheloid 701.4
  chorioretinal 363.30
    disseminated 363.35
    macular 363.32
    peripheral 363.34
    posterior pole NEC 363.33
  choroid (*see also* Scar, chorioretinal) 363.30
  compression, pericardial 423.9
  congenital 757.39
  conjunctiva 372.64
  cornea 371.00
    xerophthalmic 264.6
  due to previous cesarean delivery, complicating pregnancy or childbirth 654.2 ☑
    affecting fetus or newborn 763.89
  duodenal (bulb) (cap) 537.3
  hypertrophic 701.4
  keloid 701.4
  labia 624.4
  lung (base) 518.89
  macula 363.32
    disseminated 363.35
    peripheral 363.34
  muscle 728.89
  myocardium, myocardial 412
  painful 709.2
  papillary muscle 429.81
  posterior pole NEC 363.33
    macular — *see* Scar, macula
  postnecrotic (hepatic) (liver) 571.9
  psychic V15.49
  retina (*see also* Scar, chorioretinal) 363.30
  trachea 478.9
  uterus 621.8
    in pregnancy or childbirth NEC 654.9 ☑
      affecting fetus or newborn 763.89
      due to previous cesarean delivery 654.2 ☑
  vulva 624.4
Schamberg's disease, dermatitis, or dermatosis (progressive pigmentary dermatosis) 709.09
Schatzki's ring (esophagus) (lower) (congenital) 750.3
  acquired 530.3
Schaufenster krankheit 413.9
Schaumann's
  benign lymphogranulomatosis 135
  disease (sarcoidosis) 135
  syndrome (sarcoidosis) 135
Scheie's syndrome (mucopolysaccharidosis IS) 277.5
Schenck's disease (sporotrichosis) 117.1
Scheuermann's disease or osteochondrosis 732.0
Scheuthauer-Marie-Sainton syndrome (cleidocranialis dysostosis) 755.59
Schilder (-Flatau) disease 341.1
Schilling-type monocytic leukemia (M9890/3) 206.9 ☑
Schimmelbusch's disease, cystic mastitis, or hyperplasia 610.1
Schirmer's syndrome (encephalocutaneous angiomatosis) 759.6
Schistocelia 756.79
Schistoglossia 750.13
Schistosoma infestation — *see* Infestation, Schistosoma
Schistosomiasis 120.9
  Asiatic 120.2
  bladder 120.0
  chestermani 120.8
  colon 120.1
  cutaneous 120.3
  due to
    S. hematobium 120.0

Schistosomiasis — *continued*
  due to — *continued*
    S. japonicum 120.2
    S. mansoni 120.1
    S. mattheii 120.8
  eastern 120.2
  genitourinary tract 120.0
  intestinal 120.1
  lung 120.2
  Manson's (intestinal) 120.1
  Oriental 120.2
  pulmonary 120.2
  specified type NEC 120.8
  vesical 120.0
Schizencephaly 742.4
Schizo-affective psychosis — *see also* Schizophrenia 295.7 ☑
Schizodontia 520.2
Schizoid personality 301.20
  introverted 301.21
  schizotypal 301.22
Schizophrenia, schizophrenic (reaction) 295.9 ☑

> *Note — Use the following fifth-digit subclassification with category 295:*
> 0 *unspecified*
> 1 *subchronic*
> 2 *chronic*
> 3 *subchronic with acute exacerbation*
> 4 *chronic with acute exacerbation*
> 5 *in remission*

  acute (attack) NEC 295.8 ☑
    episode 295.4 ☑
  atypical form 295.8 ☑
  borderline 295.5 ☑
  catalepsy 295.2 ☑
  catatonic (type) (acute) (excited) (withdrawn) 295.2 ☑
  childhood (type) (*see also* Psychosis, childhood) 299.9 ☑
  chronic NEC 295.6 ☑
  coenesthesiopathic 295.8 ☑
  cyclic (type) 295.7 ☑
  disorganized (type) 295.1 ☑
  flexibilitas cerea 295.2 ☑
  hebephrenic (type) (acute) 295.1 ☑
  incipient 295.5 ☑
  latent 295.5 ☑
  paranoid (type) (acute) 295.3 ☑
  paraphrenic (acute) 295.3 ☑
  prepsychotic 295.5 ☑
  primary (acute) 295.0 ☑
  prodromal 295.5 ☑
  pseudoneurotic 295.5 ☑
  pseudopsychopathic 295.5 ☑
  reaction 295.9 ☑
  residual type (state) 295.6 ☑
  restzustand 295.6 ☑
  schizo-affective (type) (depressed) (excited) 295.7 ☑
  schizophreniform type 295.4 ☑
  simple (type) (acute) 295.0 ☑
  simplex (acute) 295.0 ☑
  specified type NEC 295.8 ☑
  syndrome of childhood NEC (*see also* Psychosis, childhood) 299.9 ☑
  undifferentiated type 295.9 ☑
    acute 295.8 ☑
    chronic 295.6 ☑
Schizothymia 301.20
  introverted 301.21
  schizotypal 301.22
Schlafkrankheit 086.5
Schlatter-Osgood disease (osteochondrosis, tibial tubercle) 732.4
Schlatter's tibia (osteochondrosis) 732.4
Schloffer's tumor — *see also* Peritonitis 567.29
Schmidt's syndrome
  sphallo-pharyngo-laryngeal hemiplegia 352.6
  thyroid-adrenocortical insufficiency 258.1
  vagoaccessory 352.6

Schmincke
  carcinoma (M8082/3) — *see* Neoplasm, nasopharynx, malignant
  tumor (M8082/3) — *see* Neoplasm, nasopharynx, malignant
Schmitz (-Stutzer) dysentery 004.0
Schmorl's disease or nodes 722.30
  lumbar, lumbosacral 722.32
  specified region NEC 722.39
  thoracic, thoracolumbar 722.31
Schneiderian
  carcinoma (M8121/3)
    specified site — *see* Neoplasm, by site, malignant
    unspecified site 160.0
  papilloma (M8121/0)
    specified site — *see* Neoplasm, by site, benign
    unspecified site 212.0
Schneider's syndrome 047.9
Schnitzler syndrome 273.1
Schoffer's tumor — *see also* Peritonitis 567.29
Scholte's syndrome (malignant carcinoid) 259.2
Scholz's disease 330.0
Scholz (-Bielschowsky-Henneberg) syndrome 330.0
Schönlein (-Henoch) disease (primary) (purpura) (rheumatic) 287.0
School examination V70.3
  following surgery V67.09 ●
Schottmüller's disease — *see also* Fever, paratyphoid 002.9
Schroeder's syndrome (endocrine-hypertensive) 255.3
Schüller-Christian disease or syndrome (chronic histiocytosis X) 277.89
Schultz's disease or syndrome (agranulocytosis) 288.09
Schultze's acroparesthesia, simple 443.89
Schwalbe-Ziehen-Oppenheimer disease 333.6
Schwannoma (M9560/0) — *see also* Neoplasm, connective tissue, benign
  malignant (M9560/3) — *see* Neoplasm, connective tissue, malignant
Schwartz-Bartter syndrome (inappropriate secretion of antidiuretic hormone) 253.6
Schwartz (-Jampel) syndrome 359.23
Schweninger-Buzzi disease (macular atrophy) 701.3
Sciatic — *see* condition
Sciatica (infectional) 724.3
  due to
    displacement of intervertebral disc 722.10
    herniation, nucleus pulposus 722.10
  wallet 724.3
Scimitar syndrome (anomalous venous drainage, right lung to inferior vena cava) 747.49
Sclera — *see* condition
Sclerectasia 379.11
Scleredema
  adultorum 710.1
  Buschke's 710.1
  newborn 778.1
Sclerema
  adiposum (newborn) 778.1
  adultorum 710.1
  edematosum (newborn) 778.1
  neonatorum 778.1
  newborn 778.1
Scleriasis — *see* Scleroderma
Scleritis 379.00
  with corneal involvement 379.05
  anterior (annular) (localized) 379.03
  brawny 379.06
  granulomatous 379.09
  posterior 379.07
  specified NEC 379.09
  suppurative 379.09
  syphilitic 095.0
  tuberculous (nodular) (*see also* Tuberculosis) 017.3 ☑ *[379.09]*
Sclerochoroiditis — *see also* Scleritis 379.00
Scleroconjunctivitis — *see also* Scleritis 379.00
Sclerocystic ovary (syndrome) 256.4
Sclerodactylia 701.0

Scleroderma, sclerodermia (acrosclerotic) (diffuse) (generalized) (progressive) (pulmonary) 710.1
  circumscribed 701.0
  linear 701.0
  localized (linear) 701.0
  newborn 778.1
Sclerokeratitis 379.05
  meaning sclerosing keratitis 370.54
  tuberculous (*see also* Tuberculosis) 017.3 ☑ *[379.09]*
Scleromalacia
  multiple 731.0
  perforans 379.04
Scleroma, trachea 040.1
Scleromyxedema 701.8
Scleroperikeratitis 379.05
Sclerose en plaques 340
Sclerosis, sclerotic
  adrenal (gland) 255.8
  Alzheimer's 331.0
    with dementia — *see* Alzheimer's, dementia
  amyotrophic (lateral) 335.20
  annularis fibrosi
    aortic 424.1
    mitral 424.0
  aorta, aortic 440.0
    valve (*see also* Endocarditis, aortic) 424.1
  artery, arterial, arteriolar, arteriovascular — *see* Arteriosclerosis
  ascending multiple 340
  Baló's (concentric) 341.1
  basilar — *see* Sclerosis, brain
  bone (localized) NEC 733.99
  brain (general) (lobular) 348.89 ▲
    Alzheimer's — *see* Alzheimer's, dementia
    artery, arterial 437.0
    atrophic lobar 331.0
      with dementia
        with behavioral disturbance 331.0 *[294.11]*
        without behavioral disturbance 331.0 *[294.10]*
    diffuse 341.1
      familial (chronic) (infantile) 330.0
      infantile (chronic) (familial) 330.0
      Pelizaeus-Merzbacher type 330.0
    disseminated 340
    hereditary 334.2
    hippocampal 348.81 ●
    infantile (degenerative) (diffuse) 330.0
    insular 340
    Krabbe's 330.0
    mesial temporal 348.81 ●
    miliary 340
    multiple 340
    Pelizaeus-Merzbacher 330.0
    progressive familial 330.0
    senile 437.0
    temporal 348.81 ●
      mesial 348.81 ●
    tuberous 759.5
  bulbar, progressive 340
  bundle of His 426.50
    left 426.3
    right 426.4
  cardiac — *see* Arteriosclerosis, coronary
  cardiorenal (*see also* Hypertension, cardiorenal) 404.90
  cardiovascular (*see also* Disease, cardiovascular) 429.2
    renal (*see also* Hypertension, cardiorenal) 404.90
  centrolobar, familial 330.0
  cerebellar — *see* Sclerosis, brain
  cerebral — *see* Sclerosis, brain
  cerebrospinal 340
    disseminated 340
    multiple 340
  cerebrovascular 437.0
  choroid 363.40
    diffuse 363.56
  combined (spinal cord) (*see also* Degeneration, combined)
    multiple 340

Sclerosis, sclerotic — *continued*
  concentric, Baló's 341.1
  cornea 370.54
  coronary (artery) — *see* Arteriosclerosis, coronary
  corpus cavernosum
    female 624.8
    male 607.89
  Dewitzky's
    aortic 424.1
    mitral 424.0
  diffuse NEC 341.1
  disease, heart — *see* Arteriosclerosis, coronary
  disseminated 340
  dorsal 340
  dorsolateral (spinal cord) — *see* Degeneration, combined
  endometrium 621.8
  extrapyramidal 333.90
  eye, nuclear (senile) 366.16
  Friedreich's (spinal cord) 334.0
  funicular (spermatic cord) 608.89
  gastritis 535.4 ☑
  general (vascular) — *see* Arteriosclerosis
  gland (lymphatic) 457.8
  hepatic 571.9
  hereditary
    cerebellar 334.2
    spinal 334.0
  hippocampal 348.81   ●
  idiopathic cortical (Garré's) (*see also* Osteomyelitis) 730.1 ☑
  ilium, piriform 733.5
  insular 340
    pancreas 251.8
  Islands of Langerhans 251.8
  kidney — *see* Sclerosis, renal
  larynx 478.79
  lateral 335.24
    amyotrophic 335.20
    descending 335.24
    primary 335.24
    spinal 335.24
  liver 571.9
  lobar, atrophic (of brain) 331.0
    with dementia
      with behavioral disturbance 331.0 [294.11]
      without behavioral disturbance 331.0 [294.10]
  lung (*see also* Fibrosis, lung) 515
  mastoid 383.1
  mesial temporal 348.81   ●
  mitral — *see* Endocarditis, mitral
  Mönckeberg's (medial) (*see also* Arteriosclerosis, extremities) 440.20
  multiple (brain stem) (cerebral) (generalized) (spinal cord) 340
  myocardium, myocardial — *see* Arteriosclerosis, coronary
  nuclear (senile), eye 366.16
  ovary 620.8
  pancreas 577.8
  penis 607.89
  peripheral arteries (*see also* Arteriosclerosis, extremities) 440.20
  plaques 340
  pluriglandular 258.8
  polyglandular 258.8
  posterior (spinal cord) (syphilitic) 094.0
  posterolateral (spinal cord) — *see* Degeneration, combined
  prepuce 607.89
  primary lateral 335.24
  progressive systemic 710.1
  pulmonary (*see also* Fibrosis, lung) 515
    artery 416.0
    valve (heart) (*see also* Endocarditis, pulmonary) 424.3
  renal 587
    with
      cystine storage disease 270.0
      hypertension (*see also* Hypertension, kidney) 403.90

Sclerosis, sclerotic — *continued*
  renal — *continued*
    with — *continued*
      hypertensive heart disease (conditions classifiable to 402) (*see also* Hypertension, cardiorenal) 404.90
      arteriolar (hyaline) (*see also* Hypertension, kidney) 403.90
      hyperplastic (*see also* Hypertension, kidney) 403.90
    retina (senile) (vascular) 362.17
  rheumatic
    aortic valve 395.9
    mitral valve 394.9
  Schilder's 341.1
  senile — *see* Arteriosclerosis
  spinal (cord) (general) (progressive) (transverse) 336.8
    ascending 357.0
    combined (*see also* Degeneration, combined)
      multiple 340
      syphilitic 094.89
    disseminated 340
    dorsolateral — *see* Degeneration, combined
    hereditary (Friedreich's) (mixed form) 334.0
    lateral (amyotrophic) 335.24
    multiple 340
    posterior (syphilitic) 094.0
  stomach 537.89
  subendocardial, congenital 425.3
  systemic (progressive) 710.1
    with lung involvement 710.1 [517.2]
  temporal 348.81   ●
    mesial 348.81   ●
  tricuspid (heart) (valve) — *see* Endocarditis, tricuspid
  tuberous (brain) 759.5
  tympanic membrane (*see also* Tympanosclerosis) 385.00
  valve, valvular (heart) — *see* Endocarditis
  vascular — *see* Arteriosclerosis
  vein 459.89
Sclerotenonitis 379.07
Sclerotitis — *see also* Scleritis 379.00
  syphilitic 095.0
  tuberculous (*see also* Tuberculosis) 017.3 ☑ [379.09]
Scoliosis (acquired) (postural) 737.30
  congenital 754.2
  due to or associated with
    Charcôt-Marie-Tooth disease 356.1 [737.43]
    mucopolysaccharidosis 277.5 [737.43]
    neurofibromatosis 237.71 [737.43]
    osteitis
      deformans 731.0 [737.43]
      fibrosa cystica 252.01 [737.43]
    osteoporosis (*see also* Osteoporosis) 733.00 [737.43]
    poliomyelitis 138 [737.43]
    radiation 737.33
    tuberculosis (*see also* Tuberculosis) 015.0 ☑ [737.43]
  idiopathic 737.30
    infantile
      progressive 737.32
      resolving 737.31
  paralytic 737.39
  rachitic 268.1
  sciatic 724.3
  specified NEC 737.39
  thoracogenic 737.34
  tuberculous (*see also* Tuberculosis) 015.0 ☑ [737.43]
Scoliotic pelvis 738.6
  with disproportion (fetopelvic) 653.0 ☑
    affecting fetus or newborn 763.1
    causing obstructed labor 660.1 ☑
      affecting fetus or newborn 763.1
Scorbutus, scorbutic 267
  anemia 281.8
Scotoma (ring) 368.44
  arcuate 368.43
  Bjerrum 368.43
  blind spot area 368.42

Scotoma — *continued*
  central 368.41
  centrocecal 368.41
  paracecal 368.42
  paracentral 368.41
  scintillating 368.12
  Seidel 368.43
Scratch — *see* Injury, superficial, by site
Scratchy throat 784.99
Screening (for) V82.9
  alcoholism V79.1
  anemia, deficiency NEC V78.1
    iron V78.0
  anomaly, congenital V82.89
  antenatal, of mother V28.9
    alphafetoprotein levels, raised V28.1
    based on amniocentesis V28.2
      chromosomal anomalies V28.0
      raised alphafetoprotein levels V28.1
    fetal growth retardation using ultrasonics V28.4
      ultrasonics V28.4
    genomic V28.89
    isoimmunization V28.5
    malformations using ultrasonics V28.3
    proteomic V28.89
    raised alphafetoprotein levels V28.1
    risk
      pre-term labor V28.82
    specified condition NEC V28.89
    Streptococcus B V28.6
  arterial hypertension V81.1
  arthropod-borne viral disease NEC V73.5
  asymptomatic bacteriuria V81.5
  bacterial
    and spirochetal sexually transmitted diseases V74.5
    conjunctivitis V74.4
    disease V74.9
      sexually transmitted V74.5
      specified condition NEC V74.8
  bacteriuria, asymptomatic V81.5
  blood disorder NEC V78.9
    specified type NEC V78.8
  bronchitis, chronic V81.3
  brucellosis V74.8
  cancer — *see* Screening, malignant neoplasm
  cardiovascular disease NEC V81.2
  cataract V80.2
  Chagas' disease V75.3
  chemical poisoning V82.5
  cholera V74.0
  cholesterol level V77.91
  chromosomal
    anomalies
      by amniocentesis, antenatal V28.0
      maternal postnatal V82.4
    athletes V70.3
  condition
    cardiovascular NEC V81.2
    eye NEC V80.2
    genitourinary NEC V81.6
    neurological ►NEC◄ V80.09   ▲
    respiratory NEC V81.4
    skin V82.0
    specified NEC V82.89
  congenital
    anomaly V82.89
      eye V80.2
    dislocation of hip V82.3
    eye condition or disease V80.2
  conjunctivitis, bacterial V74.4
  contamination NEC (*see also* Poisoning) V82.5
  coronary artery disease V81.0
  cystic fibrosis V77.6
  deficiency anemia NEC V78.1
    iron V78.0
  dengue fever V73.5
  depression V79.0
  developmental handicap V79.9
    in early childhood V79.3
    specified type NEC V79.8
  diabetes mellitus V77.1
  diphtheria V74.3
  disease or disorder V82.9
    bacterial V74.9

Screening — *continued*
  disease or disorder — *continued*
    bacterial — *continued*
      specified NEC V74.8
    blood V78.9
      specified type NEC V78.8
    blood-forming organ V78.9
      specified type NEC V78.8
    cardiovascular NEC V81.2
      hypertensive V81.1
      ischemic V81.0
    Chagas' V75.3
    chlamydial V73.98
      specified NEC V73.88
    ear NEC V80.3
    endocrine NEC V77.99
    eye NEC V80.2
    genitourinary NEC V81.6
    heart NEC V81.2
      hypertensive V81.1
      ischemic V81.0
    HPV (human papillomavirus) V73.81
    human papillomavirus V73.81
    immunity NEC V77.99
    infectious NEC V75.9
    lipoid NEC V77.91
    mental V79.9
      specified type NEC V79.8
    metabolic NEC V77.99
      inborn NEC V77.7
    neurological ►NEC◄ V80.09   ▲
    nutritional NEC V77.99
    rheumatic NEC V82.2
    rickettsial V75.0
    sexually transmitted V74.5
      bacterial V74.5
      spirochetal V74.5
    sickle-cell V78.2
      trait V78.2
    specified type NEC V82.89
    thyroid V77.0
    vascular NEC V81.2
      ischemic V81.0
    venereal V74.5
    viral V73.99
      arthropod-borne NEC V73.5
      specified type NEC V73.89
  dislocation of hip, congenital V82.3
  drugs in athletes V70.3
  elevated titer V82.9
  emphysema (chronic) V81.3
  encephalitis, viral (mosquito or tick borne) V73.5
  endocrine disorder NEC V77.99
  eye disorder NEC V80.2
    congenital V80.2
  fever
    dengue V73.5
    hemorrhagic V73.5
    yellow V73.4
  filariasis V75.6
  galactosemia V77.4
  genetic V82.79
    disease carrier status V82.71
  genitourinary condition NEC V81.6
  glaucoma V80.1
  gonorrhea V74.5
  gout V77.5
  Hansen's disease V74.2
  heart disease NEC V81.2
    hypertensive V81.1
    ischemic V81.0
  heavy metal poisoning V82.5
  helminthiasis, intestinal V75.7
  hematopoietic malignancy V76.89
  hemoglobinopathies NEC V78.3
  hemorrhagic fever V73.5
  Hodgkin's disease V76.89
  hormones in athletes V70.3
  HPV (human papillomavirus) V73.81
  human papillomavirus (HPV) V73.81
  hypercholesterolemia V77.91
  hyperlipidemia V77.91
  hypertension V81.1
  immunity disorder NEC V77.99
  inborn errors of metabolism NEC V77.7

☑ Additional Digit Required — Refer to the Tabular List for Digit Selection   ⊽ Subterms under main terms may continue to next column or page

2010 ICD-9-CM   ►◄ Revised Text   ● New Line   ▲ Revised Code   October 2009 • Volume 2 — 245

Screening — continued
  infection
    bacterial V74.9
      specified type NEC V74.8
    mycotic V75.4
    parasitic NEC V75.8
  infectious disease V75.9
    specified type NEC V75.8
  ingestion of radioactive substance V82.5
  intestinal helminthiasis V75.7
  iron deficiency anemia V78.0
  ischemic heart disease V81.0
  lead poisoning V82.5
  leishmaniasis V75.2
  leprosy V74.2
  leptospirosis V74.8
  leukemia V76.89
  lipoid disorder NEC V77.91
  lymphoma V76.89
  malaria V75.1
  malignant neoplasm (of) V76.9
    bladder V76.3
    blood V76.89
    breast V76.10
      mammogram NEC V76.12
        for high-risk patient V76.11
      specified type NEC V76.19
    cervix V76.2
    colon V76.51
    colorectal V76.51
    hematopoietic system V76.89
    intestine V76.50
      colon V76.51
      small V76.52
    lung V76.0
    lymph (glands) V76.89
    nervous system V76.81
    oral cavity V76.42
    other specified neoplasm NEC V76.89
    ovary V76.46
    prostate V76.44
    rectum V76.41
    respiratory organs V76.0
    skin V76.43
    specified sites NEC V76.49
    testis V76.45
    vagina V76.47
      following hysterectomy for malignant
        condition V67.01
  malnutrition V77.2
  mammogram NEC V76.12
    for high-risk patient V76.11
  maternal postnatal chromosomal anomalies
    V82.4
  measles V73.2
  mental
    disorder V79.9
      specified type NEC V79.8
    retardation V79.2
  metabolic disorder NEC V77.99
  metabolic errors, inborn V77.7
  mucoviscidosis V77.6
  multiphasic V82.6
  mycosis V75.4
  mycotic infection V75.4
  nephropathy V81.5
  neurological condition ▶NEC◀ V80.09   ▲
  nutritional disorder V77.99
  obesity V77.8
  osteoporosis V82.81
  parasitic infection NEC V75.8
  phenylketonuria V77.3
  plague V74.8
  poisoning
    chemical NEC V82.5
    contaminated water supply V82.5
    heavy metal V82.5
  poliomyelitis V73.0
  postnatal chromosomal anomalies, maternal
    V82.4
  prenatal — see Screening, antenatal
  pulmonary tuberculosis V74.1
  radiation exposure V82.5
  renal disease V81.5
  respiratory condition NEC V81.4
  rheumatic disorder NEC V82.2

Screening — continued
  rheumatoid arthritis V82.1
  rickettsial disease V75.0
  rubella V73.3
  schistosomiasis V75.5
  senile macular lesions of eye V80.2
  sexually transmitted diseases V74.5
    bacterial V74.5
    spirochetal V74.5
  sickle-cell anemia, disease, or trait V78.2
  skin condition V82.0
  sleeping sickness V75.3
  smallpox V73.1
  special V82.9
    specified condition NEC V82.89
  specified type NEC V82.89
  spirochetal disease V74.9
    sexually transmitted V74.5
    specified type NEC V74.8
  stimulants in athletes V70.3
  syphilis V74.5
  tetanus V74.8
  thyroid disorder V77.0
  trachoma V73.6
  traumatic brain injury V80.01   ●
  trypanosomiasis V75.3
  tuberculosis, pulmonary V74.1
  venereal disease V74.5
  viral encephalitis
    mosquito-borne V73.5
    tick-borne V73.5
  whooping cough V74.8
  worms, intestinal V75.7
  yaws V74.6
  yellow fever V73.4
Scrofula — see also Tuberculosis 017.2 ☑
Scrofulide (primary) — see also Tuberculosis
  017.0 ☑
Scrofuloderma, scrofulodermia (any site) (primary) — see also Tuberculosis 017.0 ☑
Scrofulosis (universal) — see also Tuberculosis
  017.2 ☑
Scrofulosis lichen (primary) — see also Tubercu-
  losis 017.0 ☑
Scrofulous — see condition
Scrotal tongue 529.5
  congenital 750.13
Scrotum — see condition
Scurvy (gum) (infantile) (rickets) (scorbutic) 267
Sea-blue histiocyte syndrome 272.7
Seabright-Bantam syndrome (pseudohypoparathyroidism) 275.49
Sealpox 059.12
Seasickness 994.6
Seatworm 127.4
Sebaceous
  cyst (see also Cyst, sebaceous) 706.2
  gland disease NEC 706.9
Sebocystomatosis 706.2
Seborrhea, seborrheic 706.3
  adiposa 706.3
  capitis 690.11
  congestiva 695.4
  corporis 706.3
  dermatitis 690.10
    infantile 690.12
  diathesis in infants 695.89
  eczema 690.18
    infantile 690.12
  keratosis 702.19
    inflamed 702.11
  nigricans 705.89
  sicca 690.18
  wart 702.19
    inflamed 702.11
Seckel's syndrome 759.89
Seclusion pupil 364.74
Seclusiveness, child 313.22
Secondary — see also condition
  neoplasm — see Neoplasm, by site, malignant,
    secondary
Secretan's disease or syndrome (posttraumatic
  edema) 782.3
Secretion
  antidiuretic hormone, inappropriate (syn-
    drome) 253.6

Secretion — continued
  catecholamine, by pheochromocytoma 255.6
  hormone
    antidiuretic, inappropriate (syndrome)
      253.6
    by
      carcinoid tumor 259.2
      pheochromocytoma 255.6
    ectopic NEC 259.3
  urinary
    excessive 788.42
    suppression 788.5
Section
  cesarean
    affecting fetus or newborn 763.4
    post mortem, affecting fetus or newborn
      761.6
    previous, in pregnancy or childbirth
      654.2 ☑
      affecting fetus or newborn 763.89
  nerve, traumatic — see Injury, nerve, by site
Seeligmann's syndrome (ichthyosis congenita)
  757.1
Segmentation, incomplete (congenital) — see
  also Fusion
  bone NEC 756.9
  lumbosacral (joint) 756.15
  vertebra 756.15
    lumbosacral 756.15
Seizure(s) 780.39
  akinetic (idiopathic) (see also Epilepsy)
    345.0 ☑
    psychomotor 345.4 ☑
  apoplexy, apoplectic (see also Disease, cere-
    brovascular, acute) 436
  atonic (see also Epilepsy) 345.0 ☑
  autonomic 300.11
  brain or cerebral (see also Disease, cerebrovas-
    cular, acute) 436
  convulsive (see also Convulsions) 780.39
  cortical (focal) (motor) (see also Epilepsy)
    345.5 ☑
  disorder (see also Epilepsy) 345.9 ☑   ●
  due to stroke 438.89
  epilepsy, epileptic (cryptogenic) (see also
    Epilepsy) 345.9 ☑
  epileptiform, epileptoid 780.39
    focal (see also Epilepsy) 345.5 ☑
  febrile (simple) 780.31
    with status epilepticus 345.3
    atypical 780.32
    complex 780.32
    complicated 780.32
  heart — see Disease, heart
  hysterical 300.11
  Jacksonian (focal) (see also Epilepsy) 345.5 ☑
    motor type 345.5 ☑
    sensory type 345.5 ☑
  migraine triggered 346.0 ☑
  newborn 779.0
  paralysis (see also Disease, cerebrovascular,
    acute) 436
  recurrent 345.9 ☑
    epileptic — see Epilepsy
  repetitive 780.39
    epileptic — see Epilepsy
  salaam (see also Epilepsy) 345.6 ☑
  uncinate (see also Epilepsy) 345.4 ☑
Self-mutilation 300.9
Semicoma 780.09
Semiconsciousness 780.09
Seminal
  vesicle — see condition
  vesiculitis (see also Vesiculitis) 608.0
Seminoma (M9061/3)
  anaplastic type (M9062/3)
    specified site — see Neoplasm, by site,
      malignant
    unspecified site 186.9
  specified site — see Neoplasm, by site, malig-
    nant
  spermatocytic (M9063/3)
    specified site — see Neoplasm, by site,
      malignant
    unspecified site 186.9
  unspecified site 186.9

Semliki Forest encephalitis 062.8
Senear-Usher disease or syndrome (pemphigus
  erythematosus) 694.4
Senecio jacobae dermatitis 692.6
Senectus 797
Senescence 797
Senile — see also condition 797
  cervix (atrophic) 622.8
  degenerative atrophy, skin 701.3
  endometrium (atrophic) 621.8
  fallopian tube (atrophic) 620.3
  heart (failure) 797
  lung 492.8
  ovary (atrophic) 620.3
  syndrome 259.8
  vagina, vaginitis (atrophic) 627.3
  wart 702.0
Senility 797
  with
    acute confusional state 290.3
    delirium 290.3
    mental changes 290.9
    psychosis NEC (see also Psychosis, senile)
      290.20
  premature (syndrome) 259.8
Sensation
  burning (see also Disturbance, sensation) 782.0
    tongue 529.6
  choking 784.99
  loss of (see also Disturbance, sensation) 782.0
  prickling (see also Disturbance, sensation)
    782.0
  tingling (see also Disturbance, sensation) 782.0
Sense loss (touch) — see also Disturbance, sensation 782.0
  smell 781.1
  taste 781.1
Sensibility disturbance NEC (cortical) (deep)
  (vibratory) — see also Disturbance, sensation 782.0
Sensitive dentine 521.89
Sensitiver Beziehungswahn 297.8
Sensitivity, sensitization — see also Allergy
  autoerythrocyte 287.2
  carotid sinus 337.01
  child (excessive) 313.21
  cold, autoimmune 283.0
  methemoglobin 289.7
  suxamethonium 289.89
  tuberculin, without clinical or radiological
    symptoms 795.5
Sensory
  extinction 781.8
  neglect 781.8
Separation
  acromioclavicular — see Dislocation,
    acromioclavicular
  anxiety, abnormal 309.21
  apophysis, traumatic — see Fracture, by site
  choroid 363.70
    hemorrhagic 363.72
    serous 363.71
  costochondral (simple) (traumatic) — see
    Dislocation, costochondral
  delayed
    umbilical cord 779.83
  epiphysis, epiphyseal
    nontraumatic 732.9
      upper femoral 732.2
    traumatic — see Fracture, by site
  fracture — see Fracture, by site
  infundibulum cardiac from right ventricle by
    a partition 746.83
  joint (current) (traumatic) — see Dislocation,
    by site
  placenta (normally implanted) — see Placenta,
    separation
  pubic bone, obstetrical trauma 665.6 ☑
  retina, retinal (see also Detachment, retina)
    361.9
    layers 362.40
      sensory (see also Retinoschisis) 361.10
    pigment epithelium (exudative) 362.42
      hemorrhagic 362.43
  sternoclavicular (traumatic) — see Dislocation,
    sternoclavicular

☑ Additional Digit Required — Refer to the Tabular List for Digit Selection   ☷ Subterms under main terms may continue to next column or page

Separation — continued
symphysis pubis, obstetrical trauma 665.6 ☑
tracheal ring, incomplete (congenital) 748.3
Sepsis (generalized) 995.91
with
abortion — see Abortion, by type, with sepsis
acute organ dysfunction 995.92
ectopic pregnancy (see also categories 633.0–633.9) 639.0
molar pregnancy (see also categories 630–632) 639.0
multiple organ dysfunction (MOD) 995.92
buccal 528.3
complicating labor 659.3 ☑
dental (pulpal origin) 522.4
female genital organ NEC 614.9
fetus (intrauterine) 771.81
following
abortion 639.0
ectopic or molar pregnancy 639.0
infusion, perfusion, or transfusion 999.39
Friedländer's 038.49
intraocular 360.00
localized
in operation wound 998.59
skin (see also Abscess) 682.9
malleus 024
nadir 038.9
newborn (organism unspecified) NEC 771.81
oral 528.3
puerperal, postpartum, childbirth (pelvic) 670.2 ☑ ▲
resulting from infusion, injection, transfusion, or vaccination 999.39
severe 995.92
skin, localized (see also Abscess) 682.9
umbilical (newborn) (organism unspecified) 771.89
tetanus 771.3
urinary 599.0
meaning sepsis 995.91
meaning urinary tract infection 599.0
Septate — see also Septum
Septic — see also condition
adenoids 474.01
and tonsils 474.02
arm (with lymphangitis) 682.3
embolus — see Embolism
finger (with lymphangitis) 681.00
foot (with lymphangitis) 682.7
gallbladder (see also Cholecystitis) 575.8
hand (with lymphangitis) 682.4
joint (see also Arthritis, septic) 711.0 ☑
kidney (see also Infection, kidney) 590.9
leg (with lymphangitis) 682.6
mouth 528.3
nail 681.9
finger 681.02
toe 681.11
shock (endotoxic) 785.52
sore (see also Abscess) 682.9
throat 034.0
milk-borne 034.0
streptococcal 034.0
spleen (acute) 289.59
teeth (pulpal origin) 522.4
throat 034.0
thrombus — see Thrombosis
toe (with lymphangitis) 681.10
tonsils 474.00
and adenoids 474.02
umbilical cord (newborn) (organism unspecified) 771.89
uterus (see also Endometritis) 615.9
Septicemia, septicemic (generalized) (suppurative) 038.9
with
abortion — see Abortion, by type, with sepsis
ectopic pregnancy (see also categories 633.0–633.9) 639.0
molar pregnancy (see also categories 630–632) 639.0
Aerobacter aerogenes 038.49
anaerobic 038.3

Septicemia, septicemic — continued
anthrax 022.3
Bacillus coli 038.42
Bacteroides 038.3
Clostridium 038.3
complicating labor 659.3 ☑
cryptogenic 038.9
enteric gram-negative bacilli 038.40
Enterobacter aerogenes 038.49
Erysipelothrix (insidiosa) (rhusiopathiae) 027.1
Escherichia coli 038.42
following
abortion 639.0
ectopic or molar pregnancy 639.0
infusion, injection, transfusion, or vaccination 999.39
Friedländer's (bacillus) 038.49
gangrenous 038.9
gonococcal 098.89
gram-negative (organism) 038.40
anaerobic 038.3
Hemophilus influenzae 038.41
herpes (simplex) 054.5
herpetic 054.5
Listeria monocytogenes 027.0
meningeal — see Meningitis
meningococcal (chronic) (fulminating) 036.2
methicillin
resistant Staphylococcus aureus (MRSA) 038.12
susceptible Staphylococcus aureus (MSSA) 038.11
MRSA (methicillin resistant Staphylococcus aureus) 038.12
MSSA (methicillin susceptible Staphylococcus aureus) 038.11
navel, newborn (organism unspecified) 771.89
newborn (organism unspecified) 771.81
plague 020.2
pneumococcal 038.2
postabortal 639.0
postoperative 998.59
Proteus vulgaris 038.49
Pseudomonas (aeruginosa) 038.43
puerperal, postpartum 670.2 ☑ ▲
Salmonella (aertrycke) (callinarum) (choleraesuis) (enteritidis) (suipestifer) 003.1
Serratia 038.44
Shigella (see also Dysentery, bacillary) 004.9
specified organism NEC 038.8
staphylococcal 038.10
aureus 038.11
methicillin
resistant (MRSA) 038.12
susceptible (MSSA) 038.11
specified organism NEC 038.19
streptococcal (anaerobic) 038.0
Streptococcus pneumoniae 038.2
suipestifer 003.1
umbilicus, newborn (organism unspecified) 771.89
viral 079.99
Yersinia enterocolitica 038.49
Septum, septate (congenital) — see also Anomaly, specified type NEC
anal 751.2
aqueduct of Sylvius 742.3
with spina bifida (see also Spina bifida) 741.0 ☑
hymen 752.49
uterus (see also Double, uterus) 752.2
vagina 752.49
in pregnancy or childbirth 654.7 ☑
affecting fetus or newborn 763.89
causing obstructed labor 660.2 ☑
affecting fetus or newborn 763.1
Sequestration
lung (congenital) (extralobar) (intralobar) 748.5
orbit 376.10
pulmonary artery (congenital) 747.3
splenic 289.52
Sequestrum
bone (see also Osteomyelitis) 730.1 ☑
jaw 526.4
dental 525.8
jaw bone 526.4

Sequestrum — continued
sinus (accessory) (nasal) (see also Sinusitis) 473.9
maxillary 473.0
Sequoiosis asthma 495.8
Serology for syphilis
doubtful
with signs or symptoms — see Syphilis, by site and stage
follow-up of latent syphilis — see Syphilis, latent
false positive 795.6
negative, with signs or symptoms — see Syphilis, by site and stage
positive 097.1
with signs or symptoms — see Syphilis, by site and stage
false 795.6
follow-up of latent syphilis — see Syphilis, latent
only finding — see Syphilis, latent
reactivated 097.1
Seroma (postoperative) (non-infected) 998.13
infected 998.51
post-traumatic 729.91
Seropurulent — see condition
Serositis, multiple 569.89
pericardial 423.2
peritoneal 568.82
pleural — see Pleurisy
Serotonin syndrome 333.99
Serous — see condition
Sertoli cell
adenoma (M8640/0)
specified site — see Neoplasm, by site, benign
unspecified site
female 220
male 222.0
carcinoma (M8640/3)
specified site — see Neoplasm, by site, malignant
unspecified site 186.9
syndrome (germinal aplasia) 606.0
tumor (M8640/0)
with lipid storage (M8641/0)
specified site — see Neoplasm, by site, benign
unspecified site
female 220
male 222.0
specified site — see Neoplasm, by site, benign
unspecified site
female 220
male 222.0
Sertoli-Leydig cell tumor (M8631/0)
specified site — see Neoplasm, by site, benign
unspecified site
female 220
male 222.0
Serum
allergy, allergic reaction 999.5
shock 999.4
arthritis 999.5 [713.6]
complication or reaction NEC 999.5
disease NEC 999.5
hepatitis 070.3 ☑
intoxication 999.5
jaundice (homologous) — see Hepatitis, viral, type B
neuritis 999.5
poisoning NEC 999.5
rash NEC 999.5
reaction NEC 999.5
sickness NEC 999.5
Sesamoiditis 733.99
Seven-day fever 061
of
Japan 100.89
Queensland 100.89
Sever's disease or osteochondrosis (calcaneum) 732.5
Sex chromosome mosaics 758.81
Sex reassignment surgery status (see also Trans-sexualism) 302.50

Sextuplet
affected by maternal complications of pregnancy 761.5
healthy liveborn — see Newborn, multiple
pregnancy (complicating delivery) NEC 651.8 ☑
with fetal loss and retention of one or more fetus(es) 651.6 ☑
following (elective) fetal reduction 651.7 ☑
Sexual
anesthesia 302.72
deviation (see also Deviation, sexual) 302.9
disorder (see also Deviation, sexual) 302.9
frigidity (female) 302.72
function, disorder of (psychogenic) 302.70
specified type NEC 302.79
immaturity (female) (male) 259.0
impotence 607.84
organic origin NEC 607.84
psychogenic 302.72
precocity (constitutional) (cryptogenic) (female) (idiopathic) (male) NEC 259.1
with adrenal hyperplasia 255.2
sadism 302.84
Sexuality, pathological — see also Deviation, sexual 302.9
Sézary's disease, reticulosis, or syndrome (M9701/3) 202.2 ☑
Shadow, lung 793.1
Shaken infant syndrome 995.55
Shaking
head (tremor) 781.0
palsy or paralysis (see also Parkinsonism) 332.0
Shallowness, acetabulum 736.39
Shaver's disease or syndrome (bauxite pneumoconiosis) 503
Shearing
artificial skin graft 996.55
decellularized allodermis graft 996.55
Sheath (tendon) — see condition
Shedding
nail 703.8
teeth, premature, primary (deciduous) 520.6
Sheehan's disease or syndrome (postpartum pituitary necrosis) 253.2
Shelf, rectal 569.49
Shell
shock (current) (see also Reaction, stress, acute) 308.9
lasting state 300.16
teeth 520.5
Shield kidney 753.3
Shifting
pacemaker 427.89
sleep-work schedule (affecting sleep) 327.36
Shift, mediastinal 793.2
Shiga's
bacillus 004.0
dysentery 004.0
Shigella (dysentery) — see also Dysentery, bacillary 004.9
carrier (suspected) of V02.3
Shigellosis — see also Dysentery, bacillary 004.9
Shingles — see also Herpes, zoster 053.9
eye NEC 053.29
Shin splints 844.9
Shipyard eye or disease 077.1
Shirodkar suture, in pregnancy 654.5 ☑
Shock 785.50
with
abortion — see Abortion, by type, with shock
ectopic pregnancy (see also categories 633.0–633.9) 639.5
molar pregnancy (see also categories 630–632) 639.5
allergic — see Shock, anaphylactic
anaclitic 309.21
anaphylactic 995.0
chemical — see Table of Drugs and Chemicals
correct medicinal substance properly administered 995.0

☑ Additional Digit Required — Refer to the Tabular List for Digit Selection

⬛ Subterms under main terms may continue to next column or page

2010 ICD-9-CM
▶◀ Revised Text
● New Line
▲ Revised Code
October 2009 • Volume 2 — 247

Shock — *continued*
  anaphylactic — *continued*
    drug or medicinal substance
      correct substance properly administered 995.0
      overdose or wrong substance given or taken 977.9
      specified drug — *see* Table of Drugs and Chemicals
    following sting(s) 989.5
    food — *see* Anaphylactic shock, due to, food
    immunization 999.4
    serum 999.4
  anaphylactoid — *see* Shock, anaphylactic
  anesthetic
    correct substance properly administered 995.0
    overdose or wrong substance given 968.4
      specified anesthetic — *see* Table of Drugs and Chemicals
  birth, fetus or newborn NEC 779.89
  cardiogenic 785.51
  chemical substance — *see* Table of Drugs and Chemicals
  circulatory 785.59
  complicating
    abortion — *see* Abortion, by type, with shock
    ectopic pregnancy (*see also* categories 633.0–633.9) 639.5
    labor and delivery 669.1 ☑
    molar pregnancy (*see also* categories 630–632) 639.5
  culture 309.29
  due to
    drug 995.0
      correct substance properly administered 995.0
      overdose or wrong substance given or taken 977.9
      specified drug — *see* Table of Drugs and Chemicals
    food — *see* Anaphylactic shock, due to, food
  during labor and delivery 669.1 ☑
  electric 994.8
    from electroshock gun (taser) 994.8
  endotoxic 785.52
    due to surgical procedure 998.0
  following
    abortion 639.5
    ectopic or molar pregnancy 639.5
    injury (immediate) (delayed) 958.4
    labor and delivery 669.1 ☑
  gram-negative 785.52
  hematogenic 785.59
  hemorrhagic
    due to
      disease 785.59
      surgery (intraoperative) (postoperative) 998.0
      trauma 958.4
  hypovolemic NEC 785.59
    surgical 998.0
    traumatic 958.4
  insulin 251.0
    therapeutic misadventure 962.3
  kidney 584.5
    traumatic (following crushing) 958.5
  lightning 994.0
  lung 518.5
  nervous (*see also* Reaction, stress, acute) 308.9
  obstetric 669.1 ☑
    with
      abortion — *see* Abortion, by type, with shock
      ectopic pregnancy (*see also* categories 633.0–633.9) 639.5
      molar pregnancy (*see also* categories 630–632) 639.5
    following
      abortion 639.5
      ectopic or molar pregnancy 639.5
  paralysis, paralytic (*see also* Disease, cerebrovascular, acute) 436

Shock — *continued*
  paralysis, paralytic (*see also* Disease, cerebrovascular, acute) — *continued*
    late effect — *see* Late effect(s) (of) cerebrovascular disease
  pleural (surgical) 998.0
    due to trauma 958.4
  postoperative 998.0
    with
      abortion — *see* Abortion, by type, with shock
      ectopic pregnancy (*see also* categories 633.0–633.9) 639.5
      molar pregnancy (*see also* categories 630–632) 639.5
    following
      abortion 639.5
      ectopic or molar pregnancy 639.5
  psychic (*see also* Reaction, stress, acute) 308.9
    past history (of) V15.49
  psychogenic (*see also* Reaction, stress, acute) 308.9
  septic 785.52
    with
      abortion — *see* Abortion, by type, with shock
      ectopic pregnancy (*see also* categories 633.0–633.9) 639.5
      molar pregnancy (*see also* categories 630–632) 639.5
    due to
      surgical procedure 998.0
      transfusion NEC 999.89 ▲
        bone marrow 996.85
    following
      abortion 639.5
      ectopic or molar pregnancy 639.5
      surgical procedure 998.0
      transfusion NEC 999.89 ▲
        bone marrow 996.85
  spinal (*see also* Injury, spinal, by site)
    with spinal bone injury — *see* Fracture, vertebra, by site, with spinal cord injury
  surgical 998.0
  therapeutic misadventure NEC (*see also* Complications) 998.89
  thyroxin 962.7
  toxic 040.82
  transfusion — *see* Complications, transfusion
  traumatic (immediate) (delayed) 958.4
Shoemakers' chest 738.3
Short, shortening, shortness
  Achilles tendon (acquired) 727.81
  arm 736.89
    congenital 755.20
  back 737.9
  bowel syndrome 579.3
  breath 786.05
  cervical, cervix 649.7 ☑
    gravid uterus 649.7 ☑
    non-gravid uterus 622.5
      acquired 622.5
      congenital 752.49
  chain acyl CoA dehydrogenase deficiency (SCAD) 277.85
  common bile duct, congenital 751.69
  cord (umbilical) 663.4 ☑
    affecting fetus or newborn 762.6
  cystic duct, congenital 751.69
  esophagus (congenital) 750.4
  femur (acquired) 736.81
    congenital 755.34
  frenulum linguae 750.0
  frenum, lingual 750.0
  hamstrings 727.81
  hip (acquired) 736.39
    congenital 755.63
  leg (acquired) 736.81
    congenital 755.30
  metatarsus (congenital) 754.79
    acquired 736.79
  organ or site, congenital NEC — *see* Distortion
  palate (congenital) 750.26
  P-R interval syndrome 426.81
  radius (acquired) 736.09

Short, shortening, shortness — *continued*
  radius — *continued*
    congenital 755.26
  round ligament 629.89
  sleeper 307.49
  stature, constitutional (hereditary) (idiopathic) 783.43
  tendon 727.81
    Achilles (acquired) 727.81
      congenital 754.79
    congenital 756.89
  thigh (acquired) 736.81
    congenital 755.34
  tibialis anticus 727.81
  umbilical cord 663.4 ☑
    affecting fetus or newborn 762.6
  urethra 599.84
  uvula (congenital) 750.26
  vagina 623.8
Shortsightedness 367.1
Shoshin (acute fulminating beriberi) 265.0
Shoulder — *see* condition
Shovel-shaped incisors 520.2
Shower, thromboembolic — *see* Embolism
Shunt (status)
  aortocoronary bypass V45.81
  arterial-venous (dialysis) V45.11
  arteriovenous, pulmonary (acquired) 417.0
    congenital 747.3
    traumatic (complication) 901.40
  cerebral ventricle (communicating) in situ V45.2
  coronary artery bypass V45.81
  surgical, prosthetic, with complications — *see* Complications, shunt
  vascular NEC V45.89
Shutdown
  renal 586
    with
      abortion — *see* Abortion, by type, with renal failure
      ectopic pregnancy (*see also* categories 633.0–633.9) 639.3
      molar pregnancy (*see also* categories 630–632) 639.3
    complicating
      abortion 639.3
      ectopic or molar pregnancy 639.3
    following labor and delivery 669.3 ☑
Shwachman's syndrome 288.02
Shy-Drager syndrome (orthostatic hypotension with multisystem degeneration) 333.0
Sialadenitis (any gland) (chronic) (suppurative) 527.2
  epidemic — *see* Mumps
Sialadenosis, periodic 527.2
Sialaporia 527.7
Sialectasia 527.8
Sialitis 527.2
Sialoadenitis — *see also* Sialadenitis 527.2
Sialoangitis 527.2
Sialodochitis (fibrinosa) 527.2
Sialodocholithiasis 527.5
Sialolithiasis 527.5
Sialorrhea — *see also* Ptyalism 527.7
  periodic 527.2
Sialosis 527.8
  rheumatic 710.2
Siamese twin 759.4
  complicating pregnancy 678.1 ☑
Sicard's syndrome 352.6
Sicca syndrome (keratoconjunctivitis) 710.2
Sick 799.9
  cilia syndrome 759.89
  or handicapped person in family V61.49
Sickle-cell
  anemia (see also Disease, sickle-cell) 282.60
  disease (see also Disease, sickle-cell) 282.60
  hemoglobin
    C disease (without crisis) 282.63
      with
        crisis 282.64
        vaso-occlusive pain 282.64
    D disease (without crisis) 282.68
      with crisis 282.69
    E disease (without crisis) 282.68

Sickle-cell — *continued*
  hemoglobin — *continued*
    E disease — *continued*
      with crisis 282.69
    thalassemia (without crisis) 282.41
      with
        crisis 282.42
        vaso-occlusive pain 282.42
    trait 282.5
Sicklemia — *see also* Disease, sickle-cell 282.60
  trait 282.5
Sickness
  air (travel) 994.6
  airplane 994.6
  alpine 993.2
  altitude 993.2
  Andes 993.2
  aviators' 993.2
  balloon 993.2
  car 994.6
  compressed air 993.3
  decompression 993.3
  green 280.9
  harvest 100.89
  milk 988.8
  morning 643.0 ☑
  motion 994.6
  mountain 993.2
    acute 289.0
  protein (*see also* Complications, vaccination) 999.5
  radiation NEC 990
  roundabout (motion) 994.6
  sea 994.6
  serum NEC 999.5
  sleeping (African) 086.5
    by Trypanosoma 086.5
      gambiense 086.3
      rhodesiense 086.4
    Gambian 086.3
    late effect 139.8
    Rhodesian 086.4
  sweating 078.2
  swing (motion) 994.6
  train (railway) (travel) 994.6
  travel (any vehicle) 994.6
Sick sinus syndrome 427.81
Sideropenia — *see also* Anemia, iron deficiency 280.9
Siderosis (lung) (occupational) 503
  cornea 371.15
  eye (bulbi) (vitreous) 360.23
  lens 360.23
Siegal-Cattan-Mamou disease (periodic) 277.31
Siemens' syndrome
  ectodermal dysplasia 757.31
  keratosis follicularis spinulosa (decalvans) 757.39
Sighing respiration 786.7
Sigmoid
  flexure — *see* condition
  kidney 753.3
Sigmoiditis — *see* Enteritis
Silfverskiöld's syndrome 756.50
Silicosis, silicotic (complicated) (occupational) (simple) 502
  fibrosis, lung (confluent) (massive) (occupational) 502
  non-nodular 503
  pulmonum 502
Silicotuberculosis — *see also* Tuberculosis 011.4 ☑
Silo fillers' disease 506.9
Silver's syndrome (congenital hemihypertrophy and short stature) 759.89
Silver wire arteries, retina 362.13
Silvestroni-Bianco syndrome (thalassemia minima) 282.49
Simian crease 757.2
Simmonds' cachexia or disease (pituitary cachexia) 253.2
Simons' disease or syndrome (progressive lipodystrophy) 272.6
Simple, simplex — *see* condition
Sinding-Larsen disease (juvenile osteopathia patellae) 732.4

Singapore hemorrhagic fever 065.4
Singers' node or nodule 478.5
Single
  atrium 745.69
  coronary artery 746.85
  umbilical artery 747.5
  ventricle 745.3
Singultus 786.8
  epidemicus 078.89
Sinus — see also Fistula
  abdominal 569.81
  arrest 426.6
  arrhythmia 427.89
  bradycardia 427.89
    chronic 427.81
  branchial cleft (external) (internal) 744.41
  coccygeal (infected) 685.1
    with abscess 685.0
  dental 522.7
  dermal (congenital) 685.1
    with abscess 685.0
  draining — see Fistula
  infected, skin NEC 686.9
  marginal, ruptured or bleeding 641.2 ☑
    affecting fetus or newborn 762.1
  pause 426.6
  pericranii 742.0
  pilonidal (infected) (rectum) 685.1
    with abscess 685.0
  preauricular 744.46
  rectovaginal 619.1
  sacrococcygeal (dermoid) (infected) 685.1
    with abscess 685.0
  skin
    infected NEC 686.9
    noninfected — see Ulcer, skin
  tachycardia 427.89
  tarsi syndrome 726.79
  testis 608.89
  tract (postinfectional) — see Fistula
  urachus 753.7
Sinuses, Rokitansky-Aschoff — see also Disease, gallbladder 575.8
Sinusitis (accessory) (nasal) (hyperplastic) (non-purulent) (purulent) (chronic) 473.9
  with influenza, flu, or grippe 487.1
  acute 461.9
    ethmoidal 461.2
    frontal 461.1
    maxillary 461.0
    specified type NEC 461.8
    sphenoidal 461.3
  allergic (see also Fever, hay) 477.9
  antrum — see Sinusitis, maxillary
  due to
    fungus, any sinus 117.9
    high altitude 993.1
  ethmoidal 473.2
    acute 461.2
  frontal 473.1
    acute 461.1
  influenzal 487.1
  maxillary 473.0
    acute 461.0
  specified site NEC 473.8
  sphenoidal 473.3
    acute 461.3
  syphilitic, any sinus 095.8
  tuberculous, any sinus (see also Tuberculosis) 012.8 ☑
Sinusitis-bronchiectasis-situs inversus (syndrome) (triad) 759.3
Sioloangitis 527.2
Sipple's syndrome (medullary thyroid carcinoma-pheochromocytoma) 258.02
Sirenomelia 759.89
Siriasis 992.0
Sirkari's disease 085.0
SIRS (systemic inflammatory response syndrome) 995.90
  due to
    infectious process 995.91
      with acute organ dysfunction 995.92
    non-infectious process 995.93
      with acute organ dysfunction 995.94
Siti 104.0

Sitophobia 300.29
Situational
  disturbance (transient) (see also Reaction, adjustment) 309.9
    acute 308.3
  maladjustment, acute (see also Reaction, adjustment) 309.9
  reaction (see also Reaction, adjustment) 309.9
    acute 308.3
Situation, psychiatric 300.9
Situs inversus or transversus 759.3
  abdominalis 759.3
  thoracis 759.3
Sixth disease
  due to
    human herpesvirus 6 058.11
    human herpesvirus 7 058.12
Sjögren-Larsson syndrome (ichthyosis congenita) 757.1
Sjögren (-Gougerot) syndrome or disease (keratoconjunctivitis sicca) 710.2
  with lung involvement 710.2 [517.8]
SJS-TEN (Stevens-Johnson syndrome - toxic epidermal necrolysis overlap syndrome) 695.14
Skeletal — see condition
Skene's gland — see condition
Skenitis — see also Urethritis 597.89
  gonorrheal (acute) 098.0
    chronic or duration of 2 months or over 098.2
Skerljevo 104.0
Skevas-Zerfus disease 989.5
Skin — see also condition
  donor V59.1
  hidebound 710.9
SLAP lesion (superior glenoid labrum) 840.7
Slate-dressers' lung 502
Slate-miners' lung 502
Sleep
  deprivation V69.4
  disorder 780.50
    with apnea — see Apnea, sleep
    child 307.40
      movement, unspecified 780.58
    nonorganic origin 307.40
      specified type NEC 307.49
  disturbance 780.50
    with apnea — see Apnea, sleep
    nonorganic origin 307.40
      specified type NEC 307.49
  drunkenness 307.47
  movement disorder, unspecified 780.58
  paroxysmal (see also Narcolepsy) 347.00
  related movement disorder, unspecified 780.58
  rhythm inversion 327.39
    nonorganic origin 307.45
  walking 307.46
    hysterical 300.13
Sleeping sickness 086.5
  late effect 139.8
Sleeplessness — see also Insomnia 780.52
  menopausal 627.2
  nonorganic origin 307.41
Slipped, slipping
  epiphysis (postinfectional) 732.9
    traumatic (old) 732.9
      current — see Fracture, by site
      upper femoral (nontraumatic) 732.2
  intervertebral disc — see Displacement, intervertebral disc
  ligature, umbilical 772.3
  patella 717.89
  rib 733.99
  sacroiliac joint 724.6
  tendon 727.9
  ulnar nerve, nontraumatic 354.2
  vertebra NEC (see also Spondylolisthesis) 756.12
Slocumb's syndrome 255.3
Sloughing (multiple) (skin) 686.9
  abscess — see Abscess, by site
  appendix 543.9
  bladder 596.8
  fascia 728.9

Sloughing — continued
  graft — see Complications, graft
  phagedena (see also Gangrene) 785.4
  reattached extremity (see also Complications, reattached extremity) 996.90
  rectum 569.49
  scrotum 608.89
  tendon 727.9
  transplanted organ (see also Rejection, transplant, organ, by site) 996.80
  ulcer (see also Ulcer, skin) 707.9
Slow
  feeding newborn 779.31
  fetal, growth NEC 764.9 ☑
    affecting management of pregnancy 656.5 ☑
Slowing
  heart 427.89
  urinary stream 788.62
Sluder's neuralgia or syndrome 337.09
Slurred, slurring, speech 784.59 ▲
Small-for-dates — see also Light-for-dates 764.0 ☑
  affecting management of pregnancy 656.5 ☑
Smallpox 050.9
  contact V01.3
  exposure to V01.3
  hemorrhagic (pustular) 050.0
  malignant 050.0
  modified 050.2
  vaccination
    complications — see Complications, vaccination
    prophylactic (against) V04.1
Small, smallness
  cardiac reserve — see Disease, heart
  for dates
    fetus or newborn 764.0 ☑
      with malnutrition 764.1 ☑
      affecting management of pregnancy 656.5 ☑
    infant, term 764.0 ☑
      with malnutrition 764.1 ☑
      affecting management of pregnancy 656.5 ☑
  introitus, vagina 623.3
  kidney, unknown cause 589.9
    bilateral 589.1
    unilateral 589.0
  ovary 620.8
  pelvis
    with disproportion (fetopelvic) 653.1 ☑
      affecting fetus or newborn 763.1
      causing obstructed labor 660.1 ☑
        affecting fetus or newborn 763.1
  placenta — see Placenta, insufficiency
  uterus 621.8
  white kidney 582.9
Smith's fracture (separation) (closed) 813.41
  open 813.51
Smith-Lemli Opitz syndrome (cerebrohepatorenal syndrome) 759.89
Smith-Magenis syndrome 758.33
Smith-Strang disease (oasthouse urine) 270.2
Smokers'
  bronchitis 491.0
  cough 491.0
  syndrome (see also Abuse, drugs, nondependent) 305.1
  throat 472.1
  tongue 528.6
Smoking complicating pregnancy, childbirth, or the puerperium 649.0 ☑
Smothering spells 786.09
Snaggle teeth, tooth 524.39
Snapping
  finger 727.05
  hip 719.65
  jaw 524.69
    temporomandibular joint sounds on opening or closing 524.64
  knee 717.9
  thumb 727.05
Sneddon-Wilkinson disease or syndrome (subcorneal pustular dermatosis) 694.1
Sneezing 784.99

Sneezing — continued
  intractable 478.19
Sniffing
  cocaine (see also Dependence) 304.2 ☑
  ether (see also Dependence) 304.6 ☑
  glue (airplane) (see also Dependence) 304.6 ☑
Snoring 786.09
Snow blindness 370.24
Snuffles (nonsyphilitic) 460
  syphilitic (infant) 090.0
Social migrant V60.0
Sodoku 026.0
Soemmering's ring 366.51
Soft — see also condition
  enlarged prostate 600.00
    with
      other lower urinary tract symptoms (LUTS) 600.01
      urinary
        obstruction 600.01
        retention 600.01
  nails 703.8
Softening
  bone 268.2
  brain (necrotic) (progressive) 434.9 ☑
    arteriosclerotic 437.0
    congenital 742.4
    embolic (see also Embolism, brain) 434.1 ☑
    hemorrhagic (see also Hemorrhage, brain) 431
    occlusive 434.9 ☑
    thrombotic (see also Thrombosis, brain) 434.0 ☑
  cartilage 733.92
  cerebellar — see Softening, brain
  cerebral — see Softening, brain
  cerebrospinal — see Softening, brain
  myocardial, heart (see also Degeneration, myocardial) 429.1
  nails 703.8
  spinal cord 336.8
  stomach 537.89
Solar fever 061
Soldier's
  heart 306.2
  patches 423.1
Solitary
  cyst
    bone 733.21
    kidney 593.2
  kidney (congenital) 753.0
  tubercle, brain (see also Tuberculosis, brain) 013.2 ☑
  ulcer, bladder 596.8
Somatization reaction, somatic reaction — see also Disorder, psychosomatic 306.9
  disorder 300.81
Somatoform disorder 300.82
  atypical 300.82
  severe 300.81
  undifferentiated 300.82
Somnambulism 307.46
  hysterical 300.13
Somnolence 780.09
  nonorganic origin 307.43
  periodic 349.89
Sonne dysentery 004.3
Soor 112.0
Sore
  Delhi 085.1
  desert (see also Ulcer, skin) 707.9
  eye 379.99
  Lahore 085.1
  mouth 528.9
    canker 528.2
    due to dentures 528.9
  muscle 729.1
  Naga (see also Ulcer, skin) 707.9
  oriental 085.1
  pressure (see also Ulcer, pressure) 707.00
    with gangrene (see also Ulcer, pressure) 707.00 [785.4]
  skin NEC 709.9
  soft 099.0
  throat 462

☑ Additional Digit Required — Refer to the Tabular List for Digit Selection
▽ Subterms under main terms may continue to next column or page

2010 ICD-9-CM
▶◀ Revised Text   ● New Line   ▲ Revised Code
October 2009 • Volume 2 — 249

Sore — continued
 throat — continued
  with influenza, flu, or grippe 487.1
  acute 462
  chronic 472.1
  clergyman's 784.49
  coxsackie (virus) 074.0
  diphtheritic 032.0
  epidemic 034.0
  gangrenous 462
  herpetic 054.79
  influenzal 487.1
  malignant 462
  purulent 462
  putrid 462
  septic 034.0
  streptococcal (ulcerative) 034.0
  ulcerated 462
  viral NEC 462
   Coxsackie 074.0
  tropical (see also Ulcer, skin) 707.9
  veldt (see also Ulcer, skin) 707.9
Sotos' syndrome (cerebral gigantism) 253.0
Sounds
 friction, pleural 786.7
 succussion, chest 786.7
 temporomandibular joint
  on opening or closing 524.64
South African cardiomyopathy syndrome 425.2
South American
 blastomycosis 116.1
 trypanosomiasis — see Trypanosomiasis
Southeast Asian hemorrhagic fever 065.4
Spacing, teeth, abnormal 524.30
 excessive 524.32
Spade-like hand (congenital) 754.89
Spading nail 703.8
 congenital 757.5
Spanemia 285.9
Spanish collar 605
Sparganosis 123.5
Spasmodic — see condition
Spasmophilia — see also Tetany 781.7
Spasm, spastic, spasticity — see also condition 781.0
 accommodation 367.53
 ampulla of Vater (see also Disease, gallbladder) 576.8
 anus, ani (sphincter) (reflex) 564.6
  psychogenic 306.4
 artery NEC 443.9
  basilar 435.0
  carotid 435.8
  cerebral 435.9
   specified artery NEC 435.8
  retinal (see also Occlusion, retinal, artery) 362.30
  vertebral 435.1
  vertebrobasilar 435.3
 Bell's 351.0
 bladder (sphincter, external or internal) 596.8
 bowel 564.9
  psychogenic 306.4
 bronchus, bronchiole 519.11
 cardia 530.0
 cardiac — see Angina
 carpopedal (see also Tetany) 781.7
 cecum 564.9
  psychogenic 306.4
 cerebral (arteries) (vascular) 435.9
  specified artery NEC 435.8
 cerebrovascular 435.9
 cervix, complicating delivery 661.4 ☑
  affecting fetus or newborn 763.7
 ciliary body (of accommodation) 367.53
 colon 564.1
  psychogenic 306.4
 common duct (see also Disease, biliary) 576.8
 compulsive 307.22
 conjugate 378.82
 convergence 378.84
 coronary (artery) — see Angina
 diaphragm (reflex) 786.8
  psychogenic 306.1
 duodenum, duodenal (bulb) 564.89

Spasm, spastic, spasticity — see also condition — continued
 esophagus (diffuse) 530.5
  psychogenic 306.4
 facial 351.8
 fallopian tube 620.8
 gait 781.2
 gastrointestinal (tract) 536.8
  psychogenic 306.4
 glottis 478.75
  hysterical 300.11
  psychogenic 306.1
   specified as conversion reaction 300.11
  reflex through recurrent laryngeal nerve 478.75
 habit 307.20
  chronic 307.22
  transient (of childhood) 307.21
 heart — see Angina
 hourglass — see Contraction, hourglass
 hysterical 300.11
 infantile (see also Epilepsy) 345.6 ☑
 internal oblique, eye 378.51
 intestinal 564.9
  psychogenic 306.4
 larynx, laryngeal 478.75
  hysterical 300.11
  psychogenic 306.1
   specified as conversion reaction 300.11
 levator palpebrae superioris 333.81
 lightning (see also Epilepsy) 345.6 ☑
 mobile 781.0
 muscle 728.85
  back 724.8
  psychogenic 306.0
 nerve, trigeminal 350.1
 nervous 306.0
 nodding 307.3
  infantile (see also Epilepsy) 345.6 ☑
 occupational 300.89
 oculogyric 378.87
 ophthalmic artery 362.30
 orbicularis 781.0
 perineal 625.8
 peroneo-extensor (see also Flat, foot) 734
 pharynx (reflex) 478.29
  hysterical 300.11
  psychogenic 306.1
   specified as conversion reaction 300.11
 pregnant uterus, complicating delivery 661.4 ☑
 psychogenic 306.0
 pylorus 537.81
  adult hypertrophic 537.0
  congenital or infantile 750.5
  psychogenic 306.4
 rectum (sphincter) 564.6
  psychogenic 306.4
 retinal artery NEC (see also Occlusion, retina, artery) 362.30
 sacroiliac 724.6
 salaam (infantile) (see also Epilepsy) 345.6 ☑
 saltatory 781.0
 sigmoid 564.9
  psychogenic 306.4
 sphincter of Oddi (see also Disease, gallbladder) 576.5
 stomach 536.8
  neurotic 306.4
 throat 478.29
  hysterical 300.11
  psychogenic 306.1
   specified as conversion reaction 300.11
 tic 307.20
  chronic 307.22
  transient (of childhood) 307.21
 tongue 529.8
 torsion 333.6
 trigeminal nerve 350.1
  postherpetic 053.12
 ureter 593.89
 urethra (sphincter) 599.84
 uterus 625.8
  complicating labor 661.4 ☑
   affecting fetus or newborn 763.7
 vagina 625.1

Spasm, spastic, spasticity — see also condition — continued
 vagina — continued
  psychogenic 306.51
 vascular NEC 443.9
 vasomotor NEC 443.9
 vein NEC 459.89
 vesical (sphincter, external or internal) 596.8
 viscera 789.0 ☑
Spasmus nutans 307.3
Spastic — see also Spasm
 child 343.9
Spasticity — see also Spasm
 cerebral, child 343.9
Speakers' throat 784.49
Specific, specified — see condition
Speech
 defect, disorder, disturbance, impediment NEC 784.59 ▲
  psychogenic 307.9
 ▶(language)◀ therapy V57.3
Spells 780.39
 breath-holding 786.9
Spencer's disease (epidemic vomiting) 078.82
Spens' syndrome (syncope with heart block) 426.9
Spermatic cord — see condition
Spermatocele 608.1
 congenital 752.89
Spermatocystitis 608.4
Spermatocytoma (M9063/3)
 specified site — see Neoplasm, by site, malignant
 unspecified site 186.9
Spermatorrhea 608.89
Sperm counts
 fertility testing V26.21
 following sterilization reversal V26.22
 postvasectomy V25.8
Sphacelus — see also Gangrene 785.4
Sphenoidal — see condition
Sphenoiditis (chronic) — see also Sinusitis, sphenoidal 473.3
Sphenopalatine ganglion neuralgia 337.09
Sphericity, increased, lens 743.36
Spherocytosis (congenital) (familial) (hereditary) 282.0
 hemoglobin disease 282.7
 sickle-cell (disease) 282.60
Spherophakia 743.36
Sphincter — see condition
Sphincteritis, sphincter of Oddi — see also Cholecystitis 576.8
Sphingolipidosis 272.7
Sphingolipodystrophy 272.7
Sphingomyelinosis 272.7
Spicule tooth 520.2
Spider
 finger 755.59
 nevus 448.1
 vascular 448.1
Spiegler-Fendt sarcoid 686.8
Spielmeyer-Stock disease 330.1
Spielmeyer-Vogt disease 330.1
Spina bifida (aperta) 741.9 ☑

Note — Use the following fifth-digit subclassification with category 741:

0	unspecified region
1	cervical region
2	dorsal [thoracic} region
3	lumbar region

 with hydrocephalus 741.0 ☑
  fetal (suspected), affecting management of pregnancy 655.0 ☑
 occulta 756.17
Spindle, Krukenberg's 371.13
Spine, spinal — see condition
Spiradenoma (eccrine) (M8403/0) — see Neoplasm, skin, benign
Spirillosis NEC — see also Fever, relapsing 087.9
Spirillum minus 026.0
Spirillum obermeieri infection 087.0
Spirochetal — see condition
Spirochetosis 104.9

Spirochetosis — continued
 arthritic, arthritica 104.9 [711.8] ☑
 bronchopulmonary 104.8
 icterohemorrhagica 100.0
 lung 104.8
Spitting blood — see also Hemoptysis 786.3
Splanchnomegaly 569.89
Splanchnoptosis 569.89
Spleen, splenic — see also condition
 agenesis 759.0
 flexure syndrome 569.89
 neutropenia syndrome 289.53
 sequestration syndrome 289.52
Splenectasis — see also Splenomegaly 789.2
Splenitis (interstitial) (malignant) (nonspecific) 289.59
 malarial (see also Malaria) 084.6
 tuberculous (see also Tuberculosis) 017.7 ☑
Splenocele 289.59
Splenomegalia — see Splenomegaly
Splenomegalic — see condition
Splenomegaly 789.2
 Bengal 789.2
 cirrhotic 289.51
 congenital 759.0
 congestive, chronic 289.51
 cryptogenic 789.2
 Egyptian 120.1
 Gaucher's (cerebroside lipidosis) 272.7
 idiopathic 789.2
 malarial (see also Malaria) 084.6
 neutropenic 289.53
 Niemann-Pick (lipid histiocytosis) 272.7
 siderotic 289.51
 syphilitic 095.8
  congenital 090.0
 tropical (Bengal) (idiopathic) 789.2
Splenopathy 289.50
Splenopneumonia — see Pneumonia
Splenoptosis 289.59
Splinter — see Injury, superficial, by site
Split, splitting
 heart sounds 427.89
 lip, congenital (see also Cleft, lip) 749.10
 nails 703.8
 urinary stream 788.61
Spoiled child reaction — see also Disturbance, conduct 312.1 ☑
Spondylarthritis — see also Spondylosis 721.90
Spondylarthrosis — see also Spondylosis 721.90
Spondylitis 720.9
 ankylopoietica 720.0
 ankylosing (chronic) 720.0
 atrophic 720.9
  ligamentous 720.9
 chronic (traumatic) (see also Spondylosis) 721.90
 deformans (chronic) (see also Spondylosis) 721.90
 gonococcal 098.53
 gouty 274.00 ▲
 hypertrophic (see also Spondylosis) 721.90
 infectious NEC 720.9
 juvenile (adolescent) 720.0
 Kümmell's 721.7
 Marie-Strümpell (ankylosing) 720.0
 muscularis 720.9
 ossificans ligamentosa 721.6
 osteoarthritica (see also Spondylosis) 721.90
 posttraumatic 721.7
 proliferative 720.0
 rheumatoid 720.0
 rhizomelica 720.0
 sacroiliac NEC 720.2
 senescent (see also Spondylosis) 721.90
 senile (see also Spondylosis) 721.90
 static (see also Spondylosis) 721.90
 traumatic (chronic) (see also Spondylosis) 721.90
 tuberculous (see also Tuberculosis) 015.0 ☑ [720.81]
 typhosa 002.0 [720.81]
Spondyloarthrosis — see also Spondylosis 721.90
Spondylolisthesis (congenital) (lumbosacral) 756.12

Spondylolisthesis — *continued*
  with disproportion (fetopelvic) 653.3 ☑
    affecting fetus or newborn 763.1
    causing obstructed labor 660.1 ☑
      affecting fetus or newborn 763.1
  acquired 738.4
  degenerative 738.4
  traumatic 738.4
    acute (lumbar) — *see* Fracture, vertebra, lumbar
    site other than lumbosacral — *see* Fracture, vertebra, by site
Spondylolysis (congenital) 756.11
  acquired 738.4
  cervical 756.19
  lumbosacral region 756.11
    with disproportion (fetopelvic) 653.3 ☑
      affecting fetus or newborn 763.1
      causing obstructed labor 660.1 ☑
        affecting fetus or newborn 763.1
Spondylopathy
  inflammatory 720.9
    specified type NEC 720.89
  traumatic 721.7
Spondylose rhizomelique 720.0
Spondylosis 721.90
  with
    disproportion 653.3 ☑
      affecting fetus or newborn 763.1
      causing obstructed labor 660.1 ☑
        affecting fetus or newborn 763.1
    myelopathy NEC 721.91
  cervical, cervicodorsal 721.0
    with myelopathy 721.1
  inflammatory 720.9
  lumbar, lumbosacral 721.3
    with myelopathy 721.42
  sacral 721.3
    with myelopathy 721.42
  thoracic 721.2
    with myelopathy 721.41
  traumatic 721.7
Sponge
  divers' disease 989.5
  inadvertently left in operation wound 998.4
  kidney (medullary) 753.17
Spongioblastoma (M9422/3)
  multiforme (M9440/3)
    specified site — *see* Neoplasm, by site, malignant
    unspecified site 191.9
  polare (M9423/3)
    specified site — *see* Neoplasm, by site, malignant
    unspecified site 191.9
  primitive polar (M9443/3)
    specified site — *see* Neoplasm, by site, malignant
    unspecified site 191.9
  specified site — *see* Neoplasm, by site, malignant
  unspecified site 191.9
Spongiocytoma (M9400/3)
  specified site — *see* Neoplasm, by site, malignant
  unspecified site 191.9
Spongioneuroblastoma (M9504/3) — *see* Neoplasm, by site, malignant
Spontaneous — *see also* condition
  fracture — *see* Fracture, pathologic
Spoon nail 703.8
  congenital 757.5
Sporadic — *see* condition
Sporotrichosis (bones) (cutaneous) (disseminated) (epidermal) (lymphatic) (lymphocutaneous) (mucous membranes) (pulmonary) (skeletal) (visceral) 117.1
Sporotrichum schenckii infection 117.1
Spots, spotting
  atrophic (skin) 701.3
  Bitôt's (in the young child) 264.1
  café au lait 709.09
  cayenne pepper 448.1
  complicating pregnancy 649.5 ☑
  cotton wool (retina) 362.83
  de Morgan's (senile angiomas) 448.1

Spots, spotting — *continued*
  Fúchs' black (myopic) 360.21
  intermenstrual
    irregular 626.6
    regular 626.5
  interpalpebral 372.53
  Koplik's 055.9
  liver 709.09
  Mongolian (pigmented) 757.33
  of pregnancy 649.5 ☑
  purpuric 782.7
  ruby 448.1
Spotted fever — *see* Fever, spotted
Sprain, strain (joint) (ligament) (muscle) (tendon) 848.9
  abdominal wall (muscle) 848.8
  Achilles tendon 845.09
  acromioclavicular 840.0
  ankle 845.00
    and foot 845.00
  anterior longitudinal, cervical 847.0
  arm 840.9
    upper 840.9
      and shoulder 840.9
  astragalus 845.00
  atlanto-axial 847.0
  atlanto-occipital 847.0
  atlas 847.0
  axis 847.0
  back (*see also* Sprain, spine) 847.9
  breast bone 848.40
  broad ligament — *see* Injury, internal, broad ligament
  calcaneofibular 845.02
  carpal 842.01
  carpometacarpal 842.11
  cartilage
    costal, without mention of injury to sternum 848.3
      involving sternum 848.42
    ear 848.8
    knee 844.9
      with current tear (*see also* Tear, meniscus) 836.2
    semilunar (knee) 844.8
      with current tear (*see also* Tear, meniscus) 836.2
    septal, nose 848.0
    thyroid region 848.2
    xiphoid 848.49
  cervical, cervicodorsal, cervicothoracic 847.0
  chondrocostal, without mention of injury to sternum 848.3
    involving sternum 848.42
  chondrosternal 848.42
  chronic (joint) — *see* Derangement, joint
  clavicle 840.9
  coccyx 847.4
  collar bone 840.9
  collateral, knee (medial) (tibial) 844.1
    lateral (fibular) 844.0
    recurrent or old 717.89
      lateral 717.81
      medial 717.82
  coracoacromial 840.8
  coracoclavicular 840.1
  coracohumeral 840.2
  coracoid (process) 840.9
  coronary, knee 844.8
  costal cartilage, without mention of injury to sternum 848.3
    involving sternum 848.42
  cricoarytenoid articulation 848.2
  cricothyroid articulation 848.2
  cruciate
    knee 844.2
    old 717.89
      anterior 717.83
      posterior 717.84
  deltoid
    ankle 845.01
    shoulder 840.8
  dorsal (spine) 847.1
  ear cartilage 848.8
  elbow 841.9
    and forearm 841.9

Sprain, strain — *continued*
  elbow — *continued*
    specified site NEC 841.8
  femur (proximal end) 843.9
    distal end 844.9
  fibula (proximal end) 844.9
    distal end 845.00
  fibulocalcaneal 845.02
  finger(s) 842.10
  foot 845.10
    and ankle 845.00
  forearm 841.9
    and elbow 841.9
    specified site NEC 841.8
  glenoid (shoulder) (*see also* SLAP lesion) 840.8
  hand 842.10
  hip 843.9
    and thigh 843.9
  humerus (proximal end) 840.9
    distal end 841.9
  iliofemoral 843.0
  infraspinatus 840.3
  innominate
    acetabulum 843.9
    pubic junction 848.5
    sacral junction 846.1
  internal
    collateral, ankle 845.01
    semilunar cartilage 844.8
      with current tear (*see also* Tear, meniscus) 836.2
      old 717.5
  interphalangeal
    finger 842.13
    toe 845.13
  ischiocapsular 843.1
  jaw (cartilage) (meniscus) 848.1
    old 524.69
  knee 844.9
    and leg 844.9
    old 717.5
      collateral
        lateral 717.81
        medial 717.82
      cruciate
        anterior 717.83
        posterior 717.84
  late effect — *see* Late, effects (of), sprain
  lateral collateral, knee 844.0
    old 717.81
  leg 844.9
    and knee 844.9
  ligamentum teres femoris 843.8
  low back 846.9
  lumbar (spine) 847.2
  lumbosacral 846.0
    chronic or old 724.6
  mandible 848.1
    old 524.69
  maxilla 848.1
  medial collateral, knee 844.1
    old 717.82
  meniscus
    jaw 848.1
      old 524.69
    knee 844.8
      with current tear (*see also* Tear, meniscus) 836.2
      old 717.5
    mandible 848.1
      old 524.69
    specified site NEC 848.8
  metacarpal 842.10
    distal 842.12
    proximal 842.11
  metacarpophalangeal 842.12
  metatarsal 845.10
  metatarsophalangeal 845.12
  midcarpal 842.19
  midtarsal 845.19
  multiple sites, except fingers alone or toes alone 848.8
  neck 847.0
  nose (septal cartilage) 848.0
  occiput from atlas 847.0
  old — *see* Derangement, joint

Sprain, strain — *continued*
  orbicular, hip 843.8
  patella(r) 844.8
    old 717.89
  pelvis 848.5
  phalanx
    finger 842.10
    toe 845.10
  radiocarpal 842.02
  radiohumeral 841.2
  radioulnar 841.9
    distal 842.09
  radius, radial (proximal end) 841.9
    and ulna 841.9
      distal 842.09
    collateral 841.0
    distal end 842.00
  recurrent — *see* Sprain, by site
  rib (cage), without mention of injury to sternum 848.3
    involving sternum 848.42
  rotator cuff (capsule) 840.4
  round ligament (*see also* Injury, internal, round ligament)
    femur 843.8
  sacral (spine) 847.3
  sacrococcygeal 847.3
  sacroiliac (region) 846.9
    chronic or old 724.6
    ligament 846.1
    specified site NEC 846.8
  sacrospinatus 846.2
  sacrospinous 846.2
  sacrotuberous 846.3
  scaphoid bone, ankle 845.00
  scapula(r) 840.9
  semilunar cartilage (knee) 844.8
    with current tear (*see also* Tear, meniscus) 836.2
    old 717.5
  septal cartilage (nose) 848.0
  shoulder 840.9
    and arm, upper 840.9
    blade 840.9
  specified site NEC 848.8
  spine 847.9
    cervical 847.0
    coccyx 847.4
    dorsal 847.1
    lumbar 847.2
    lumbosacral 846.0
      chronic or old 724.6
    sacral 847.3
    sacroiliac (*see also* Sprain, sacroiliac) 846.9
      chronic or old 724.6
    thoracic 847.1
  sternoclavicular 848.41
  sternum 848.40
  subglenoid (*see also* SLAP lesion) 840.8
  subscapularis 840.5
  supraspinatus 840.6
  symphysis
    jaw 848.1
      old 524.69
    mandibular 848.1
      old 524.69
    pubis 848.5
  talofibular 845.09
  tarsal 845.10
  tarsometatarsal 845.11
  temporomandibular 848.1
    old 524.69
  teres
    ligamentum femoris 843.8
    major or minor 840.8
  thigh (proximal end) 843.9
    and hip 843.9
    distal end 844.9
  thoracic (spine) 847.1
  thorax 848.8
  thumb 842.10
  thyroid cartilage or region 848.2
  tibia (proximal end) 844.9
    distal end 845.00
  tibiofibular
    distal 845.03

Sprain, strain — *continued*
  tibiofibular — *continued*
      superior 844.3
  toe(s) 845.10
  trachea 848.8
  trapezoid 840.8
  ulna, ulnar (proximal end) 841.9
      collateral 841.1
      distal end 842.00
  ulnohumeral 841.3
  vertebrae (*see also* Sprain, spine) 847.9
      cervical, cervicodorsal, cervicothoracic 847.0
  wrist (cuneiform) (scaphoid) (semilunar) 842.00
  xiphoid cartilage 848.49
Sprengel's deformity (congenital) 755.52
Spring fever 309.23
Sprue 579.1
  celiac 579.0
  idiopathic 579.0
  meaning thrush 112.0
  nontropical 579.0
  tropical 579.1
Spur — *see also* Exostosis
  bone 726.91
      calcaneal 726.73
  calcaneal 726.73
  iliac crest 726.5
  nose (septum) 478.19
      bone 726.91
  septal 478.19
Spuria placenta — *see* Placenta, abnormal
Spurway's syndrome (brittle bones and blue sclera) 756.51
Sputum, abnormal (amount) (color) (excessive) (odor) (purulent) 786.4
  bloody 786.3
Squamous — *see also* condition
  cell metaplasia
      bladder 596.8
      cervix — *see* condition
  epithelium in
      cervical canal (congenital) 752.49
      uterine mucosa (congenital) 752.3
  metaplasia
      bladder 596.8
      cervix — *see* condition
Squashed nose 738.0
  congenital 754.0
Squeeze, divers' 993.3
Squint — *see also* Strabismus 378.9
  accommodative (*see also* Esotropia) 378.00
  concomitant (*see also* Heterotropia) 378.30
Stab — *see also* Wound, open, by site
  internal organs — *see* Injury, internal, by site, with open wound
Staggering gait 781.2
  hysterical 300.11
Staghorn calculus 592.0
Stain, staining
  meconium 779.84
  port wine 757.32
  tooth, teeth (hard tissues) 521.7
      due to
          accretions 523.6
          deposits (betel) (black) (green) (materia alba) (orange) (tobacco) 523.6
          metals (copper) (silver) 521.7
          nicotine 523.6
          pulpal bleeding 521.7
          tobacco 523.6
Stälh's
  ear 744.29
  pigment line (cornea) 371.11
Stälhi's pigment lines (cornea) 371.11
Stammering 307.0
Standstill
  atrial 426.6
  auricular 426.6
  cardiac (*see also* Arrest, cardiac) 427.5
  sinoatrial 426.6
  sinus 426.6
  ventricular (*see also* Arrest, cardiac) 427.5
Stannosis 503
Stanton's disease (melioidosis) 025

Staphylitis (acute) (catarrhal) (chronic) (gangrenous) (membranous) (suppurative) (ulcerative) 528.3
Staphylococcemia 038.10
  aureus 038.11
  specified organism NEC 038.19
Staphylococcus, staphylococcal — *see* condition
Staphyloderma (skin) 686.00
Staphyloma 379.11
  anterior, localized 379.14
  ciliary 379.11
  cornea 371.73
  equatorial 379.13
  posterior 379.12
  posticum 379.12
  ring 379.15
  sclera NEC 379.11
Starch eating 307.52
Stargardt's disease 362.75
Starvation (inanition) (due to lack of food) 994.2
  edema 262
  voluntary NEC 307.1
Stasis
  bile (duct) (*see also* Disease, biliary) 576.8
  bronchus (*see also* Bronchitis) 490
  cardiac (*see also* Failure, heart) 428.0
  cecum 564.89
  colon 564.89
  dermatitis (*see also* Varix, with stasis dermatitis) 454.1
  duodenal 536.8
  eczema (*see also* Varix, with stasis dermatitis) 454.1
  edema (*see also* Hypertension, venous) 459.30
  foot 991.4
  gastric 536.3
  ileocecal coil 564.89
  ileum 564.89
  intestinal 564.89
  jejunum 564.89
  kidney 586
  liver 571.9
      cirrhotic — *see* Cirrhosis, liver
  lymphatic 457.8
  pneumonia 514
  portal 571.9
  pulmonary 514
  rectal 564.89
  renal 586
      tubular 584.5
  stomach 536.3
  ulcer
      with varicose veins 454.0
      without varicose veins 459.81
  urine NEC (*see also* Retention, urine) 788.20
  venous 459.81
State
  affective and paranoid, mixed, organic psychotic 294.8
  agitated 307.9
      acute reaction to stress 308.2
  anxiety (neurotic) (*see also* Anxiety) 300.00
      specified type NEC 300.09
  apprehension (*see also* Anxiety) 300.00
      specified type NEC 300.09
  climacteric, female 627.2
      following induced menopause 627.4
  clouded
      epileptic (*see also* Epilepsy) 345.9 ☑
      paroxysmal (idiopathic) (*see also* Epilepsy) 345.9 ☑
  compulsive (mixed) (with obsession) 300.3
  confusional 298.9
      acute 293.0
          with
              arteriosclerotic dementia 290.41
              presenile brain disease 290.11
              senility 290.3
          alcoholic 291.0
          drug-induced 292.81
      epileptic 293.0
      postoperative 293.9
      reactive (emotional stress) (psychological trauma) 298.2
      subacute 293.1

State — *continued*
  constitutional psychopathic 301.9
  convulsive (*see also* Convulsions) 780.39
  depressive NEC 311
      induced by drug 292.84
      neurotic 300.4
  dissociative 300.15
  hallucinatory 780.1
      induced by drug 292.12
  hypercoagulable (primary) 289.81
      secondary 289.82
  hyperdynamic beta-adrenergic circulatory 429.82
  locked-in 344.81
  menopausal 627.2
      artificial 627.4
      following induced menopause 627.4
  neurotic NEC 300.9
      with depersonalization episode 300.6
  obsessional 300.3
  oneiroid (*see also* Schizophrenia) 295.4 ☑
  panic 300.01
  paranoid 297.9
      alcohol-induced 291.5
      arteriosclerotic 290.42
      climacteric 297.2
      drug-induced 292.11
      in
          presenile brain disease 290.12
          senile brain disease 290.20
      involutional 297.2
      menopausal 297.2
      senile 290.20
      simple 297.0
  postleukotomy 310.0
  pregnant (*see also* Pregnancy) V22.2
  psychogenic, twilight 298.2
  psychotic, organic (*see also* Psychosis, organic) 294.9
      mixed paranoid and affective 294.8
      senile or presenile NEC 290.9
      transient NEC 293.9
          with
              anxiety 293.84
              delusions 293.81
              depression 293.83
              hallucinations 293.82
  residual schizophrenic (*see also* Schizophrenia) 295.6 ☑
  tension (*see also* Anxiety) 300.9
  transient organic psychotic 293.9
      anxiety type 293.84
      depressive type 293.83
      hallucinatory type 293.83
      paranoid type 293.81
      specified type NEC 293.89
  twilight
      epileptic 293.0
      psychogenic 298.2
  vegetative (persistent) 780.03
Status (post)
  absence
      epileptic (*see also* Epilepsy) 345.2
      of organ, acquired (postsurgical) — *see* Absence, by site, acquired
  administration of tPA (rtPA) in a different institution within the last 24 hours prior to admission to facility V45.88
  anastomosis of intestine (for bypass) V45.3
  anginosus 413.9
  angioplasty, percutaneous transluminal coronary V45.82
  ankle prosthesis V43.66
  aortocoronary bypass or shunt V45.81
  arthrodesis V45.4
  artificially induced condition NEC V45.89
  artificial opening (of) V44.9
      gastrointestinal tract NEC V44.4
      specified site NEC V44.8
      urinary tract NEC V44.6
      vagina V44.7
  aspirator V46.0
  asthmaticus (*see also* Asthma) 493.9 ☑
  awaiting organ transplant V49.83
  bariatric surgery V45.86

Status — *continued*
  bariatric surgery — *continued*
      complicating pregnancy, childbirth, or the puerperium 649.2 ☑
  bed confinement V49.84
  breast
      correction V43.82
      implant removal V45.83
      reconstruction V43.82
  cardiac
      device (in situ) V45.00
          carotid sinus V45.09
              fitting or adjustment V53.39
          defibrillator, automatic implantable V45.02
          pacemaker V45.01
              fitting or adjustment V53.31
  carotid sinus stimulator V45.09
  cataract extraction V45.61
  chemotherapy V66.2
      current V58.69
  circumcision, female 629.20
  clitorectomy (female genital mutilation type I) 629.21
      with excision of labia minora (female genital mutilation type II) 629.22
  colonization — *see* Carrier (suspected) of
  colostomy V44.3
  contraceptive device V45.59
      intrauterine V45.51
      subdermal V45.52
  convulsivus idiopathicus (*see also* Epilepsy) 345.3
  coronary artery bypass or shunt V45.81
  cutting
      female genital 629.20
          specified NEC 629.29
          type I 629.21
          type II 629.22
          type III 629.23
          type IV 629.29
  cystostomy V44.50
      appendico-vesicostomy V44.52
      cutaneous-vesicostomy V44.51
      specified type NEC V44.59
  defibrillator, automatic implantable cardiac V45.02
  delinquent immunization V15.83 ●
  dental crowns V45.84
  dental fillings V45.84
  dental restoration V45.84
  dental sealant V49.82
  dialysis (hemo) (peritoneal) V45.11
  donor V59.9
  drug therapy or regimen V67.59
      high-risk medication NEC V67.51
  elbow prosthesis V43.62
  enterostomy V44.4
  epileptic, epilepticus (absence) (grand mal) (*see also* Epilepsy) 345.3
      focal motor 345.7 ☑
      partial 345.7 ☑
      petit mal 345.2
      psychomotor 345.7 ☑
      temporal lobe 345.7 ☑
  estrogen receptor
      negative [ER-] V86.1
      positive [ER+] V86.0
  eye (adnexa) surgery V45.69
  female genital
      cutting 629.20
          specified NEC 629.29
          type I 629.21
          type II 629.22
          type III 629.23
          type IV 629.29
      mutilation 629.20
          type I 629.21
          type II 629.22
          type III 629.23
          type IV 629.29
  filtering bleb (eye) (postglaucoma) V45.69
      with rupture or complication 997.99
      postcataract extraction (complication) 997.99
  finger joint prosthesis V43.69

☑ Additional Digit Required — Refer to the Tabular List for Digit Selection

Subterms under main terms may continue to next column or page

2010 ICD-9-CM

▶◀ Revised Text　　　● New Line　　　▲ Revised Code

October 2009 • Volume 2 — 253

Status — Stenosis

Index

Stenosis — Strabismus

Stenosis — *see also* Stricture — *continued*
lacrimal
canaliculi 375.53
duct 375.56
congenital 743.65
punctum 375.52
congenital 743.65
sac 375.54
congenital 743.65
lacrimonasal duct 375.56
congenital 743.65
neonatal 375.55
larynx 478.74
congenital 748.3
syphilitic 095.8
congenital 090.5
mitral (valve) (chronic) (inactive) 394.0
with
aortic (valve)
disease (insufficiency) 396.1
insufficiency or incompetence 396.1
stenosis or obstruction 396.0
incompetency, insufficiency or regurgitation 394.2
with aortic valve disease 396.8
active or acute 391.1
with chorea (acute) (rheumatic) (Sydenham's) 392.0
congenital 746.5
specified cause, except rheumatic 424.0
syphilitic 093.21
myocardium, myocardial (*see also* Degeneration, myocardial) 429.1
hypertrophic subaortic (idiopathic) 425.1
nares (anterior) (posterior) 478.19
congenital 748.0
nasal duct 375.56
congenital 743.65
nasolacrimal duct 375.56
congenital 743.65
neonatal 375.55
organ or site, congenital NEC — *see* Atresia
papilla of Vater 576.2
with calculus, cholelithiasis, or stones —
see Choledocholithiasis
pulmonary (artery) (congenital) 747.3
with ventricular septal defect, dextraposition of aorta and hypertrophy of right ventricle 745.2
acquired 417.8
infundibular 746.83
in tetralogy of Fallot 745.2
subvalvular 746.83
valve (*see also* Endocarditis, pulmonary) 424.3
congenital 746.02
vein 747.49
acquired 417.8
vessel NEC 417.8
pulmonic (congenital) 746.02
infundibular 746.83
subvalvular 746.83
pylorus (hypertrophic) 537.0
adult 537.0
congenital 750.5
infantile 750.5
rectum (sphincter) (*see also* Stricture, rectum) 569.2
renal artery 440.1
salivary duct (any) 527.8
sphincter of Oddi (*see also* Obstruction, biliary) 576.2
spinal 724.00
cervical 723.0
lumbar, lumbosacral 724.02
nerve (root) NEC 724.9
specified region NEC 724.09
thoracic, thoracolumbar 724.01
stomach, hourglass 537.6
subaortic 746.81
hypertrophic (idiopathic) 425.1
supra (valvular)-aortic 747.22
trachea 519.19
congenital 748.3
syphilitic 095.8

Stenosis — *see also* Stricture — *continued*
trachea — *continued*
tuberculous (*see also* Tuberculosis) 012.8 ☑
tracheostomy 519.02
tricuspid (valve) (*see also* Endocarditis, tricuspid) 397.0
congenital 746.1
nonrheumatic 424.2
tubal 628.2
ureter (*see also* Stricture, ureter) 593.3
congenital 753.29
urethra (*see also* Stricture, urethra) 598.9
vagina 623.2
congenital 752.49
in pregnancy or childbirth 654.7 ☑
affecting fetus or newborn 763.89
causing obstructed labor 660.2 ☑
affecting fetus or newborn 763.1
valve (cardiac) (heart) (*see also* Endocarditis) 424.90
congenital NEC 746.89
aortic 746.3
mitral 746.5
pulmonary 746.02
tricuspid 746.1
urethra 753.6
valvular (*see also* Endocarditis) 424.90
congenital NEC 746.89
urethra 753.6
vascular graft or shunt 996.1
atherosclerosis — *see* Arteriosclerosis, extremities
embolism 996.74
occlusion NEC 996.74
thrombus 996.74
vena cava (inferior) (superior) 459.2
congenital 747.49
ventricular shunt 996.2
vulva 624.8
Stercolith — *see also* Fecalith 560.39
appendix 543.9
Stercoraceous, stercoral ulcer 569.82
anus or rectum 569.41
Stereopsis, defective
with fusion 368.33
without fusion 368.32
Stereotypes NEC 307.3
Sterility
female — *see* Infertility, female
male (*see also* Infertility, male) 606.9
Sterilization, admission for V25.2
status
tubal ligation V26.51
vasectomy V26.52
Sternalgia — *see also* Angina 413.9
Sternopagus 759.4
Sternum bifidum 756.3
Sternutation 784.99
Steroid
effects (adverse) (iatrogenic)
cushingoid
correct substance properly administered 255.0
overdose or wrong substance given or taken 962.0
diabetes — *see* Diabetes, secondary
correct substance properly administered 251.8
overdose or wrong substance given or taken 962.0
due to
correct substance properly administered 255.8
overdose or wrong substance given or taken 962.0
fever
correct substance properly administered 780.60
overdose or wrong substance given or taken 962.0
withdrawal
correct substance properly administered 255.41
overdose or wrong substance given or taken 962.0

Steroid — *continued*
responder 365.03
Stevens-Johnson disease or syndrome (erythema multiforme exudativum) 695.13
toxic epidermal necrolysis overlap (SJS-TEN overlap syndrome) 695.14
Stewart-Morel syndrome (hyperostosis frontalis interna) 733.3
Sticker's disease (erythema infectiosum) 057.0
Stickler syndrome 759.89
Sticky eye 372.03
Stieda's disease (calcification, knee joint) 726.62
Stiff
back 724.8
neck (*see also* Torticollis) 723.5
Stiff-baby 759.89
Stiff-man syndrome 333.91
Stiffness, joint NEC 719.50
ankle 719.57
back 724.8
elbow 719.52
finger 719.54
hip 719.55
knee 719.56
multiple sites 719.59
sacroiliac 724.6
shoulder 719.51
specified site NEC 719.58
spine 724.9
surgical fusion V45.4
wrist 719.53
Stigmata, congenital syphilis 090.5
Stillbirth, stillborn NEC 779.9
Still's disease or syndrome 714.30
adult onset 714.2
Stiller's disease (asthenia) 780.79
Still-Felty syndrome (rheumatoid arthritis with splenomegaly and leukopenia) 714.1
Stilling-Türk-Duane syndrome (ocular retraction syndrome) 378.71
Stimulation, ovary 256.1
Sting (animal) (bee) (fish) (insect) (jellyfish) (Portuguese man-o-war) (wasp) (venomous) 989.5
anaphylactic shock or reaction 989.5
plant 692.6
Stippled epiphyses 756.59
Stitch
abscess 998.59
burst (in external operation wound) (*see also* Dehiscence) 998.32
internal 998.31
in back 724.5
Stojano's (subcostal) **syndrome** 098.86
Stokes-Adams syndrome (syncope with heart block) 426.9
Stokes' disease (exophthalmic goiter) 242.0 ☑
Stokvis' (-Talma) disease (enterogenous cyanosis) 289.7
Stomach — *see* condition
Stoma malfunction
colostomy 569.62
cystostomy 997.5
enterostomy 569.62
esophagostomy 530.87
gastrostomy 536.42
ileostomy 569.62
nephrostomy 997.5
tracheostomy 519.02
ureterostomy 997.5
Stomatitis 528.00
angular 528.5
due to dietary or vitamin deficiency 266.0
aphthous 528.2
bovine 059.11
candidal 112.0
catarrhal 528.00
denture 528.9
diphtheritic (membranous) 032.0
due to
dietary deficiency 266.0
thrush 112.0
vitamin deficiency 266.0
epidemic 078.4
epizootic 078.4
follicular 528.00

Stomatitis — *continued*
gangrenous 528.1
herpetic 054.2
herpetiformis 528.2
malignant 528.00
membranous acute 528.00
monilial 112.0
mycotic 112.0
necrotic 528.1
ulcerative 101
necrotizing ulcerative 101
parasitic 112.0
septic 528.00
specified NEC 528.09
spirochetal 101
suppurative (acute) 528.00
ulcerative 528.00
necrotizing 101
ulceromembranous 101
vesicular 528.00
with exanthem 074.3
Vincent's 101
Stomatocytosis 282.8
Stomatomycosis 112.0
Stomatorrhagia 528.9
Stone(s) — *see also* Calculus
bladder 594.1
diverticulum 594.0
cystine 270.0
heart syndrome (*see also* Failure, ventricular, left) 428.1
kidney 592.0
prostate 602.0
pulp (dental) 522.2
renal 592.0
salivary duct or gland (any) 527.5
ureter 592.1
urethra (impacted) 594.2
urinary (duct) (impacted) (passage) 592.9
bladder 594.1
diverticulum 594.0
lower tract NEC 594.9
specified site 594.8
xanthine 277.2
Stonecutters' lung 502
tuberculous (*see also* Tuberculosis) 011.4 ☑
Stonemasons'
asthma, disease, or lung 502
tuberculous (*see also* Tuberculosis) 011.4 ☑
phthisis (*see also* Tuberculosis) 011.4 ☑
Stoppage
bowel (*see also* Obstruction, intestine) 560.9
heart (*see also* Arrest, cardiac) 427.5
intestine (*see also* Obstruction, intestine) 560.9
urine NEC (*see also* Retention, urine) 788.20
Storm, thyroid (apathetic) — *see also* Thyrotoxicosis 242.9 ☑
Strabismus (alternating) (congenital) (nonparalytic) 378.9
concomitant (*see also* Heterotropia) 378.30
convergent (*see also* Esotropia) 378.00
divergent (*see also* Exotropia) 378.10
convergent (*see also* Esotropia) 378.00
divergent (*see also* Exotropia) 378.10
due to adhesions, scars — *see* Strabismus, mechanical
in neuromuscular disorder NEC 378.73
intermittent 378.20
vertical 378.31
latent 378.40
convergent (esophoria) 378.41
divergent (exophoria) 378.42
vertical 378.43
mechanical 378.60
due to
Brown's tendon sheath syndrome 378.61
specified musculofascial disorder NEC 378.62
paralytic 378.50
third or oculomotor nerve (partial) 378.51
total 378.52
fourth or trochlear nerve 378.53
sixth or abducens nerve 378.54
specified type NEC 378.73

☑ Additional Digit Required — Refer to the Tabular List for Digit Selection

🐾 Subterms under main terms may continue to next column or page

Strabismus — *continued*
  vertical (hypertropia) 378.31
Strain — *see also* Sprain, by site
  eye NEC 368.13
  heart — *see* Disease, heart
  meaning gonorrhea — *see* Gonorrhea
  on urination 788.65
  physical NEC V62.89
  postural 729.90
  psychological NEC V62.89
Strands
  conjunctiva 372.62
  vitreous humor 379.25
Strangulation, strangulated 994.7
  appendix 543.9
  asphyxiation or suffocation by 994.7
  bladder neck 596.0
  bowel — *see* Strangulation, intestine
  colon — *see* Strangulation, intestine
  cord (umbilical) — *see* Compression, umbilical cord
  due to birth injury 767.8
  food or foreign body (*see also* Asphyxia, food) 933.1
  hemorrhoids 455.8
    external 455.5
    internal 455.2
  hernia (*see also* Hernia, by site, with obstruction)
    gangrenous — *see* Hernia, by site, with gangrene
  intestine (large) (small) 560.2
    with hernia (*see also* Hernia, by site, with obstruction)
      gangrenous — *see* Hernia, by site, with gangrene
    congenital (small) 751.1
      large 751.2
  mesentery 560.2
  mucus (*see also* Asphyxia, mucus) 933.1
    newborn 770.18
  omentum 560.2
  organ or site, congenital NEC — *see* Atresia
  ovary 620.8
    due to hernia 620.4
  penis 607.89
    foreign body 939.3
  rupture (*see also* Hernia, by site, with obstruction) 552.9
    gangrenous (*see also* Hernia, by site, with gangrene) 551.9
  stomach, due to hernia (*see also* Hernia, by site, with obstruction) 552.9
    with gangrene (*see also* Hernia, by site, with gangrene) 551.9
  umbilical cord — *see* Compression, umbilical cord
  vesicourethral orifice 596.0
Strangury 788.1
Strawberry
  gallbladder (*see also* Disease, gallbladder) 575.6
  mark 757.32
  tongue (red) (white) 529.3
Straw itch 133.8
Streak, ovarian 752.0
Strephosymbolia 315.01
  secondary to organic lesion 784.69
Streptobacillary fever 026.1
Streptobacillus moniliformis 026.1
Streptococcemia 038.0
Streptococcicosis — *see* Infection, streptococcal
Streptococcus, streptococcal — *see* condition
Streptoderma 686.00
Streptomycosis — *see* Actinomycosis
Streptothricosis — *see* Actinomycosis
Streptothrix — *see* Actinomycosis
Streptotrichosis — *see* Actinomycosis
Stress 308.9
  fracture — *see* Fracture, stress
  polycythemia 289.0
  reaction (gross) (*see also* Reaction, stress, acute) 308.9
Stretching, nerve — *see* Injury, nerve, by site
Striae (albicantes) (atrophicae) (cutis distensae) (distensae) 701.3

Striations of nails 703.8
Stricture — *see also* Stenosis 799.89
  ampulla of Vater 576.2
    with calculus, cholelithiasis, or stones — *see* Choledocholithiasis
  anus (sphincter) 569.2
    congenital 751.2
    infantile 751.2
  aorta (ascending) 747.22
    arch 747.10
    arteriosclerotic 440.0
    calcified 440.0
  aortic (valve) (*see also* Stenosis, aortic) 424.1
    congenital 746.3
  aqueduct of Sylvius (congenital) 742.3
    with spina bifida (*see also* Spina bifida) 741.0 ☑
    acquired 331.4
  artery 447.1
    basilar — *see* Narrowing, artery, basilar
    carotid (common) (internal) — *see* Narrowing, artery, carotid
    celiac 447.4
    cerebral 437.0
      congenital 747.81
      due to
        embolism (*see also* Embolism, brain) 434.1 ☑
        thrombus (*see also* Thrombosis, brain) 434.0 ☑
    congenital (peripheral) 747.60
      cerebral 747.81
      coronary 746.85
      gastrointestinal 747.61
      lower limb 747.64
      renal 747.62
      retinal 743.58
      specified NEC 747.69
      spinal 747.82
      umbilical 747.5
      upper limb 747.63
    coronary — *see* Arteriosclerosis, coronary
      congenital 746.85
    precerebral — *see* Narrowing, artery, precerebral NEC
    pulmonary (congenital) 747.3
      acquired 417.8
    renal 440.1
    vertebral — *see* Narrowing, artery, vertebral
  auditory canal (congenital) (external) 744.02
    acquired (*see also* Stricture, ear canal, acquired) 380.50
  bile duct or passage (any) (postoperative) (*see also* Obstruction, biliary) 576.2
    congenital 751.61
  bladder 596.8
    congenital 753.6
    neck 596.0
      congenital 753.6
  bowel (*see also* Obstruction, intestine) 560.9
  brain 348.89   ▲
  bronchus 519.19
    syphilitic 095.8
  cardia (stomach) 537.89
    congenital 750.7
  cardiac (*see also* Disease, heart)
    orifice (stomach) 537.89
  cardiovascular (*see also* Disease, cardiovascular) 429.2
  carotid artery — *see* Narrowing, artery, carotid
  cecum (*see also* Obstruction, intestine) 560.9
  cervix, cervical (canal) 622.4
    congenital 752.49
    in pregnancy or childbirth 654.6 ☑
      affecting fetus or newborn 763.89
      causing obstructed labor 660.2 ☑
        affecting fetus or newborn 763.1
  colon (*see also* Obstruction, intestine) 560.9
    congenital 751.2
  colostomy 569.62
  common bile duct (*see also* Obstruction, biliary) 576.2
    congenital 751.61
  coronary (artery) — *see* Arteriosclerosis, coronary

Stricture — *see also* Stenosis — *continued*
  coronary — *see* Arteriosclerosis, coronary — *continued*
    congenital 746.85
  cystic duct (*see also* Obstruction, gallbladder) 575.2
    congenital 751.61
  cystostomy 997.5
  digestive organs NEC, congenital 751.8
  duodenum 537.3
    congenital 751.1
  ear canal (external) (congenital) 744.02
    acquired 380.50
      secondary to
        inflammation 380.53
        surgery 380.52
        trauma 380.51
  ejaculatory duct 608.85
  enterostomy 569.62
  esophagostomy 530.87
  esophagus (corrosive) (peptic) 530.3
    congenital 750.3
    syphilitic 095.8
      congenital 090.5
  eustachian tube (*see also* Obstruction, Eustachian tube) 381.60
    congenital 744.24
  fallopian tube 628.2
    gonococcal (chronic) 098.37
      acute 098.17
    tuberculous (*see also* Tuberculosis) 016.6 ☑
  gallbladder (*see also* Obstruction, gallbladder) 575.2
    congenital 751.69
  glottis 478.74
  heart (*see also* Disease, heart)
    congenital NEC 746.89
    valve (*see also* Endocarditis)
      congenital NEC 746.89
        aortic 746.3
        mitral 746.5
        pulmonary 746.02
        tricuspid 746.1
  hepatic duct (*see also* Obstruction, biliary) 576.2
  hourglass, of stomach 537.6
  hymen 623.3
  hypopharynx 478.29
  intestine (*see also* Obstruction, intestine) 560.9
    congenital (small) 751.1
      large 751.2
    ischemic 557.1
  lacrimal
    canaliculi 375.53
      congenital 743.65
    punctum 375.52
      congenital 743.65
    sac 375.54
      congenital 743.65
  lacrimonasal duct 375.56
    congenital 743.65
    neonatal 375.55
  larynx 478.79
    congenital 748.3
    syphilitic 095.8
      congenital 090.5
  lung 518.89
  meatus
    ear (congenital) 744.02
      acquired (*see also* Stricture, ear canal, acquired) 380.50
      osseous (congenital) (ear) 744.03
        acquired (*see also* Stricture, ear canal, acquired) 380.50
    urinarius (*see also* Stricture, urethra) 598.9
      congenital 753.6
  mitral (valve) (*see also* Stenosis, mitral) 394.0
    congenital 746.5
    specified cause, except rheumatic 424.0
  myocardium, myocardial (*see also* Degeneration, myocardial) 429.1
    hypertrophic subaortic (idiopathic) 425.1
  nares (anterior) (posterior) 478.19
    congenital 748.0
  nasal duct 375.56

Stricture — *see also* Stenosis — *continued*
  nasal duct — *continued*
    congenital 743.65
    neonatal 375.55
  nasolacrimal duct 375.56
    congenital 743.65
    neonatal 375.55
  nasopharynx 478.29
    syphilitic 095.8
  nephrostomy 997.5
  nose 478.19
    congenital 748.0
  nostril (anterior) (posterior) 478.19
    congenital 748.0
  organ or site, congenital NEC — *see* Atresia
  osseous meatus (congenital) (ear) 744.03
    acquired (*see also* Stricture, ear canal, acquired) 380.50
  os uteri (*see also* Stricture, cervix) 622.4
  oviduct — *see* Stricture, fallopian tube
  pelviureteric junction 593.3
  pharynx (dilation) 478.29
  prostate 602.8
  pulmonary, pulmonic
    artery (congenital) 747.3
      acquired 417.8
      noncongenital 417.8
    infundibulum (congenital) 746.83
    valve (*see also* Endocarditis, pulmonary) 424.3
      congenital 746.02
    vein (congenital) 747.49
      acquired 417.8
    vessel NEC 417.8
  punctum lacrimale 375.52
    congenital 743.65
  pylorus (hypertrophic) 537.0
    adult 537.0
    congenital 750.5
    infantile 750.5
  rectosigmoid 569.89
  rectum (sphincter) 569.2
    congenital 751.2
    due to
      chemical burn 947.3
      irradiation 569.2
      lymphogranuloma venereum 099.1
    gonococcal 098.7
    inflammatory 099.1
    syphilitic 095.8
    tuberculous (*see also* Tuberculosis) 014.8 ☑
  renal artery 440.1
  salivary duct or gland (any) 527.8
  sigmoid (flexure) (*see also* Obstruction, intestine) 560.9
  spermatic cord 608.85
  stoma (following) (of)
    colostomy 569.62
    cystostomy 997.5
    enterostomy 569.62
    esophagostomy 530.87
    gastrostomy 536.42
    ileostomy 569.62
    nephrostomy 997.5
    tracheostomy 519.02
    ureterostomy 997.5
  stomach 537.89
    congenital 750.7
    hourglass 537.6
  subaortic 746.81
    hypertrophic (acquired) (idiopathic) 425.1
  subglottic 478.74
    syphilitic NEC 095.8
  tendon (sheath) 727.81
  trachea 519.19
    congenital 748.3
    syphilitic 095.8
    tuberculous (*see also* Tuberculosis) 012.8 ☑
  tracheostomy 519.02
  tricuspid (valve) (*see also* Endocarditis, tricuspid) 397.0
    congenital 746.1
    nonrheumatic 424.2
  tunica vaginalis 608.85

☑ Additional Digit Required — Refer to the Tabular List for Digit Selection   ▽ Subterms under main terms may continue to next column or page

2010 ICD-9-CM   ▶◀ Revised Text   ● New Line   ▲ Revised Code   **October 2009 • Volume 2 — 255**

Stricture — *see also* Stenosis — *continued*
ureter (postoperative) 593.3
  congenital 753.29
  tuberculous (*see also* Tuberculosis)
   016.2 ☑
ureteropelvic junction 593.3
  congenital 753.21
ureterovesical orifice 593.3
  congenital 753.22
urethra (anterior) (meatal) (organic) (posterior)
  (spasmodic) 598.9
  associated with schistosomiasis (*see also*
   Schistosomiasis) 120.9 [598.01]
  congenital (valvular) 753.6
  due to
   infection 598.00
    syphilis 095.8 [598.01]
   trauma 598.1
  gonococcal 098.2 [598.01]
  gonorrheal 098.2 [598.01]
  infective 598.00
  late effect of injury 598.1
  postcatheterization 598.2
  postobstetric 598.1
  postoperative 598.2
  specified cause NEC 598.8
  syphilitic 095.8 [598.01]
  traumatic 598.1
  valvular, congenital 753.6
urinary meatus (*see also* Stricture, urethra)
  598.9
  congenital 753.6
uterus, uterine 621.5
  os (external) (internal) — *see* Stricture,
   cervix
vagina (outlet) 623.2
  congenital 752.49
valve (cardiac) (heart) (*see also* Endocarditis)
  424.90
  congenital (cardiac) (heart) NEC 746.89
   aortic 746.3
   mitral 746.5
   pulmonary 746.02
   tricuspid 746.1
   urethra 753.6
valvular (*see also* Endocarditis) 424.90
vascular graft or shunt 996.1
  atherosclerosis — *see* Arteriosclerosis, extremities
  embolism 996.74
  occlusion NEC 996.74
  thrombus 996.74
vas deferens 608.85
  congenital 752.89
vein 459.2
vena cava (inferior) (superior) NEC 459.2
  congenital 747.49
ventricular shunt 996.2
vesicourethral orifice 596.0
  congenital 753.6
vulva (acquired) 624.8
Stridor 786.1
congenital (larynx) 748.3
Stridulous — *see* condition
Strippling of nails 703.8
Stroke 434.91
apoplectic (*see also* Disease, cerebrovascular,
  acute) 436
brain — *see* Infarct, brain
embolic 434.11
epileptic — *see* Epilepsy
healed or old V12.54
heart — *see* Disease, heart
heat 992.0
hemorrhagic — *see* Hemorrhage, brain
iatrogenic 997.02
in evolution 434.91
ischemic 434.91
late effect — *see* Late effect(s) (of) cerebrovascular disease
lightning 994.0
paralytic — *see* Infarct, brain
postoperative 997.02
progressive 435.9
thrombotic 434.01
Stromatosis, endometrial (M8931/1) 236.0

Strong pulse 785.9
Strongyloides stercoralis infestation 127.2
Strongyloidiasis 127.2
Strongyloidosis 127.2
Strongylus (gibsoni) infestation 127.7
Strophulus (newborn) 779.89
pruriginosus 698.2
Struck by lightning 994.0
Struma — *see also* Goiter 240.9
fibrosa 245.3
Hashimoto (struma lymphomatosa) 245.2
lymphomatosa 245.2
nodosa (simplex) 241.9
  endemic 241.9
   multinodular 241.1
  sporadic 241.9
  toxic or with hyperthyroidism 242.3 ☑
   multinodular 242.2 ☑
   uninodular 242.1 ☑
  toxicosa 242.3 ☑
   multinodular 242.2 ☑
   uninodular 242.1 ☑
  uninodular 241.0
ovarii (M9090/0) 220
  and carcinoid (M9091/1) 236.2
  malignant (M9090/3) 183.0
Riedel's (ligneous thyroiditis) 245.3
scrofulous (*see also* Tuberculosis) 017.2 ☑
tuberculous (*see also* Tuberculosis) 017.2 ☑
  abscess 017.2 ☑
  adenitis 017.2 ☑
  lymphangitis 017.2 ☑
  ulcer 017.2 ☑
Strumipriva cachexia — *see also* Hypothyroidism 244.9
Strümpell-Marie disease or spine (ankylosing
  spondylitis) 720.0
Strümpell-Westphal pseudosclerosis (hepatolenticular degeneration) 275.1
Stuart's disease (congenital factor X deficiency)
  — *see also* Defect, coagulation 286.3
Stuart-Prower factor deficiency (congenital
  factor X deficiency) — *see also* Defect, coagulation 286.3
Students' elbow 727.2
Stuffy nose 478.19
Stump — *see also* Amputation
cervix, cervical (healed) 622.8
Stupor 780.09
catatonic (*see also* Schizophrenia) 295.2 ☑
circular (*see also* Psychosis, manic-depressive,
  circular) 296.7
manic 296.89
manic-depressive (*see also* Psychosis, affective)
  296.89
mental (anergic) (delusional) 298.9
psychogenic 298.8
reaction to exceptional stress (transient) 308.2
traumatic NEC (*see also* Injury, intracranial)
  with spinal (cord)
   lesion — *see* Injury, spinal, by site
   shock — *see* Injury, spinal, by site
Sturge (-Weber) (-Dimitri) disease or syn-
  drome (encephalocutaneous angiomatosis) 759.6
Sturge-Kalischer-Weber syndrome (encephalocutaneous angiomatosis) 759.6
Stuttering 307.0
due to late effect of cerebrovascular disease ●
  (*see also* Late effect(s) (of) cerebrovas- ●
  cular disease) 438.14 ●
Sty, stye 373.11
external 373.11
internal 373.12
meibomian 373.12
Subacidity, gastric 536.8
psychogenic 306.4
Subacute — *see* condition
Subarachnoid — *see* condition
Subclavian steal syndrome 435.2
Subcortical — *see* condition
Subcostal syndrome 098.86
nerve compression 354.8
Subcutaneous, subcuticular — *see* condition
Subdelirium 293.1
Subdural — *see* condition

Subendocardium — *see* condition
Subependymoma (M9383/1) 237.5
Suberosis 495.3
Subglossitis — *see* Glossitis
Subhemophilia 286.0
Subinvolution (uterus) 621.1
breast (postlactational) (postpartum) 611.89
chronic 621.1
puerperal, postpartum 674.8 ☑
Sublingual — *see* condition
Sublinguitis 527.2
Subluxation — *see also* Dislocation, by site
congenital NEC (*see also* Malposition, congenital)
  hip (unilateral) 754.32
   with dislocation of other hip 754.35
   bilateral 754.33
  joint
   lower limb 755.69
   shoulder 755.59
   upper limb 755.59
  lower limb (joint) 755.69
  shoulder (joint) 755.59
  upper limb (joint) 755.59
lens 379.32
  anterior 379.33
  posterior 379.34
radial head 832.2 ●
rotary, cervical region of spine — *see* Fracture,
  vertebra, cervical
Submaxillary — *see* condition
Submersion (fatal) (nonfatal) 994.1
Submissiveness (undue), in child 313.0
Submucous — *see* condition
Subnormal, subnormality
accommodation (*see also* Disorder, accommodation) 367.9
mental (*see also* Retardation, mental) 319
  mild 317
  moderate 318.0
  profound 318.2
  severe 318.1
temperature (accidental) 991.6
  not associated with low environmental
   temperature 780.99
Subphrenic — *see* condition
Subscapular nerve — *see* condition
Subseptus uterus 752.3
Subsiding appendicitis 542
Substance abuse in family V61.42 ●
Substernal thyroid — *see also* Goiter 240.9
congenital 759.2
Substitution disorder 300.11
Subtentorial — *see* condition
Subtertian
fever 084.0
malaria (fever) 084.0
Subthyroidism (acquired) — *see also* Hypothyroidism 244.9
congenital 243
Succenturiata placenta — *see* Placenta, abnor-
  mal
Succussion sounds, chest 786.7
Sucking thumb, child 307.9
Sudamen 705.1
Sudamina 705.1
Sudanese kala-azar 085.0
Sudden
death, cause unknown (less than 24 hours)
  798.1
  cardiac (SCD)
   family history of V17.41
   personal history of, successfully resusci-
    tated V12.53
  during childbirth 669.9 ☑
  infant 798.0
  puerperal, postpartum 674.9 ☑
hearing loss NEC 388.2
heart failure (*see also* Failure, heart) 428.9
infant death syndrome 798.0
Sudeck's atrophy, disease, or syndrome 733.7
SUDS (sudden unexplained death) 798.2
Suffocation — *see also* Asphyxia 799.01
by
  bed clothes 994.7
  bunny bag 994.7

Suffocation — *see also* Asphyxia —
  continued
by — *continued*
  cave-in 994.7
  constriction 994.7
  drowning 994.1
  inhalation
   food or foreign body (*see also* Asphyxia,
    food or foreign body) 933.1
   oil or gasoline (*see also* Asphyxia, food
    or foreign body) 933.1
  overlying 994.7
  plastic bag 994.7
  pressure 994.7
  strangulation 994.7
during birth 768.1
mechanical 994.7
Sugar
blood
  high 790.29
  low 251.2
in urine 791.5
Suicide, suicidal (attempted)
by poisoning — *see* Table of Drugs and
  Chemicals
ideation V62.84
risk 300.9
tendencies 300.9
trauma NEC (*see also* nature and site of injury)
  959.9
Suipestifer infection — *see also* Infection,
  Salmonella 003.9
Sulfatidosis 330.0
Sulfhemoglobinemia, sulphemoglobinemia
  (acquired) (congenital) 289.7
Sumatran mite fever 081.2
Summer — *see* condition
Sunburn 692.71
first degree 692.71
second degree 692.76
third degree 692.77
dermatitis 692.71
due to
  other ultraviolet radiation 692.82
  tanning bed 692.82
SUNCT (short lasting unilateral neuralgiform
  headache with conjunctival injection and
  tearing) 339.05
Sunken
acetabulum 718.85
fontanels 756.0
Sunstroke 992.0
Superfecundation 651.9 ☑
with fetal loss and retention of one or more
  fetus(es) 651.6 ☑
following (elective) fetal reduction 651.7 ☑
Superfetation 651.9 ☑
with fetal loss and retention of one or more
  fetus(es) 651.6 ☑
following (elective) fetal reduction 651.7 ☑
Superinvolution uterus 621.8
Supernumerary (congenital)
aortic cusps 746.89
auditory ossicles 744.04
bone 756.9
breast 757.6
carpal bones 755.56
cusps, heart valve NEC 746.89
  mitral 746.5
  pulmonary 746.09
digit(s) 755.00
  finger 755.01
  toe 755.02
ear (lobule) 744.1
fallopian tube 752.19
finger 755.01
hymen 752.49
kidney 753.3
lacrimal glands 743.64
lacrimonasal duct 743.65
lobule (ear) 744.1
mitral cusps 746.5
muscle 756.82
nipples 757.6
organ or site NEC — *see* Accessory
ossicles, auditory 744.04

☑ Additional Digit Required — Refer to the Tabular List for Digit Selection   ▽ Subterms under main terms may continue to next column or page

256 — Volume 2 • October 2009   ▶◀ Revised Text   ● New Line   ▲ Revised Code   2010 ICD-9-CM

Supernumerary — *continued*
- ovary 752.0
- oviduct 752.19
- pulmonic cusps 746.09
- rib 756.3
  - cervical or first 756.2
    - syndrome 756.2
- roots (of teeth) 520.2
- spinal vertebra 756.19
- spleen 759.0
- tarsal bones 755.67
- teeth 520.1
  - causing crowding 524.31
- testis 752.89
- thumb 755.01
- toe 755.02
- uterus 752.2
- vagina 752.49
- vertebra 756.19

Supervision (of)
- contraceptive method previously prescribed V25.40
  - intrauterine device V25.42
  - oral contraceptive (pill) V25.41
  - specified type NEC V25.49
  - subdermal implantable contraceptive V25.43
- dietary (for) V65.3
  - allergy (food) V65.3
  - colitis V65.3
  - diabetes mellitus V65.3
  - food allergy intolerance V65.3
  - gastritis V65.3
  - hypercholesterolemia V65.3
  - hypoglycemia V65.3
  - intolerance (food) V65.3
  - obesity V65.3
  - specified NEC V65.3
- lactation V24.1
- newborn health ●
  - 8 to 28 days old V20.32 ●
  - under 8 days old V20.31 ●
- pregnancy — *see* Pregnancy, supervision of

Supplemental teeth 520.1
- causing crowding 524.31

Suppression
- binocular vision 368.31
- lactation 676.5 ☑
- menstruation 626.8
- ovarian secretion 256.39
- renal 586
- urinary secretion 788.5
- urine 788.5

Suppuration, suppurative — *see also* condition
- accessory sinus (chronic) (*see also* Sinusitis) 473.9
- adrenal gland 255.8
- antrum (chronic) (*see also* Sinusitis, maxillary) 473.0
- bladder (*see also* Cystitis) 595.89
- bowel 569.89
- brain 324.0
  - late effect 326
- breast 611.0
  - puerperal, postpartum 675.1 ☑
- dental periosteum 526.5
- diffuse (skin) 686.00
- ear (middle) (*see also* Otitis media) 382.4
  - external (*see also* Otitis, externa) 380.10
  - internal 386.33
- ethmoidal (sinus) (chronic) (*see also* Sinusitis, ethmoidal) 473.2
- fallopian tube (*see also* Salpingo-oophoritis) 614.2
- frontal (sinus) (chronic) (*see also* Sinusitis, frontal) 473.1
- gallbladder (*see also* Cholecystitis, acute) 575.0
- gum 523.30
- hernial sac — *see* Hernia, by site
- intestine 569.89
- joint (*see also* Arthritis, suppurative) 711.0 ☑
- labyrinthine 386.33
- lung 513.0
- mammary gland 611.0
  - puerperal, postpartum 675.1 ☑
- maxilla, maxillary 526.4

Suppuration, suppurative — *see also* condition — *continued*
- maxilla, maxillary — *continued*
  - sinus (chronic) (*see also* Sinusitis, maxillary) 473.0
- muscle 728.0
- nasal sinus (chronic) (*see also* Sinusitis) 473.9
- pancreas 577.0
- parotid gland 527.2
- pelvis, pelvic
  - female (*see also* Disease, pelvis, inflammatory) 614.4
    - acute 614.3
  - male (*see also* Peritonitis) 567.21
- pericranial (*see also* Osteomyelitis) 730.2 ☑
- salivary duct or gland (any) 527.2
- sinus (nasal) (*see also* Sinusitis) 473.9
- sphenoidal (sinus) (chronic) (*see also* Sinusitis, sphenoidal) 473.3
- thymus (gland) 254.1
- thyroid (gland) 245.0
- tonsil 474.8
- uterus (*see also* Endometritis) 615.9
- vagina 616.10
- wound (*see also* Wound, open, by site, complicated)
  - dislocation — *see* Dislocation, by site, compound
  - fracture — *see* Fracture, by site, open
  - scratch or other superficial injury — *see* Injury, superficial, by site

Supraeruption, teeth 524.34
Supraglottitis 464.50
- with obstruction 464.51
Suprapubic drainage 596.8
Suprarenal (gland) — *see* condition
Suprascapular nerve — *see* condition
Suprasellar — *see* condition
Supraspinatus syndrome 726.10
Surfer knots 919.8 ●
- infected 919.9 ●
Surgery
- cosmetic NEC V50.1
  - breast reconstruction following mastectomy V51.0
  - following healed injury or operation V51.8
  - hair transplant V50.0
- elective V50.9
  - breast
    - augmentation or reduction V50.1
    - reconstruction following mastectomy V51.0
  - circumcision, ritual or routine (in absence of medical indication) V50.2
  - cosmetic NEC V50.1
  - ear piercing V50.3
  - face-lift V50.1
  - following healed injury or operation V51.8
  - hair transplant V50.0
- not done because of
  - contraindication V64.1
  - patient's decision V64.2
  - specified reason NEC V64.3
- plastic
  - breast
    - augmentation or reduction V50.1
    - reconstruction following mastectomy V51.0
  - cosmetic V50.1
  - face-lift V50.1
  - following healed injury or operation V51.8
  - repair of scarred tissue (following healed injury or operation) V51.8
  - specified type NEC V50.8
- previous, in pregnancy or childbirth
  - cervix 654.6 ☑
    - affecting fetus or newborn (*see also* Newborn, affected by) 760.63
    - causing obstructed labor 660.2 ☑
      - affecting fetus or newborn 763.1
  - pelvic soft tissues NEC 654.9 ☑
    - affecting fetus or newborn (*see also* Newborn, affected by) 760.63
    - causing obstructed labor 660.2 ☑
      - affecting fetus or newborn 763.1
  - perineum or vulva 654.8 ☑

Surgery — *continued*
- previous, in pregnancy or childbirth — *continued*
  - uterus NEC 654.9 ☑
    - affecting fetus or newborn (*see also* Newborn, affected by) 760.63
    - causing obstructed labor 660.2 ☑
      - affecting fetus or newborn 763.1
    - due to previous cesarean delivery 654.2 ☑
  - vagina 654.7 ☑
Surgical
- abortion — *see* Abortion, legal
- emphysema 998.81
- kidney (*see also* Pyelitis) 590.80
- operation NEC 799.9
- procedures, complication or misadventure — *see* Complications, surgical procedure
- shock 998.0
Survey
- fetal anatomic V28.81
Susceptibility
- genetic
  - to
    - MEN (multiple endocrine neoplasia) V84.81
    - neoplasia
      - multiple endocrine [MEN] V84.81
    - neoplasm
      - malignant, of
        - breast V84.01
        - endometrium V84.04
        - other V84.09
        - ovary V84.02
        - prostate V84.03
      - specified disease V84.89
Suspected condition, ruled out — *see also* Observation, suspected V71.9
- specified condition NEC V71.89
Suspended uterus, in pregnancy or childbirth 654.4 ☑
- affecting fetus or newborn 763.89
- causing obstructed labor 660.2 ☑
  - affecting fetus or newborn 763.1
Sutton and Gull's disease (arteriolar nephrosclerosis) — *see also* Hypertension, kidney 403.90
Sutton's disease 709.09
Suture
- burst (in external operation wound) (*see also* Dehiscence) 998.32
  - internal 998.31
- inadvertently left in operation wound 998.4
- removal V58.32
- Shirodkar, in pregnancy (with or without cervical incompetence) 654.5 ☑
Swab inadvertently left in operation wound 998.4
Swallowed, swallowing
- difficulty (*see also* Dysphagia) 787.20
- foreign body NEC (*see also* Foreign body) 938
Swamp fever 100.89
Swan neck hand (intrinsic) 736.09
Sweat(s), sweating
- disease or sickness 078.2
- excessive (*see also* Hyperhidrosis) 780.8
- fetid 705.89
- fever 078.2
- gland disease 705.9
  - specified type NEC 705.89
- miliary 078.2
- night 780.8
Sweeley-Klionsky disease (angiokeratoma corporis diffusum) 272.7
Sweet's syndrome (acute febrile neutrophilic dermatosis) 695.89
Swelling 782.3
- abdominal (not referable to specific organ) 789.3 ☑
- adrenal gland, cloudy 255.8
- ankle 719.07
- anus 787.99
- arm 729.81
- breast 611.72
- Calabar 125.2
- cervical gland 785.6

Swelling — *continued*
- cheek 784.2
- chest 786.6
- ear 388.8
- epigastric 789.3 ☑
- extremity (lower) (upper) 729.81
- eye 379.92
- female genital organ 625.8
- finger 729.81
- foot 729.81
- glands 785.6
- gum 784.2
- hand 729.81
- head 784.2
- inflammatory — *see* Inflammation
- joint (*see also* Effusion, joint) 719.0 ☑
  - tuberculous — *see* Tuberculosis, joint
- kidney, cloudy 593.89
- leg 729.81
- limb 729.81
- liver 573.8
- lung 786.6
- lymph nodes 785.6
- mediastinal 786.6
- mouth 784.2
- muscle (limb) 729.81
- neck 784.2
- nose or sinus 784.2
- palate 784.2
- pelvis 789.3 ☑
- penis 607.83
- perineum 625.8
- rectum 787.99
- scrotum 608.86
- skin 782.2
- splenic (*see also* Splenomegaly) 789.2
- substernal 786.6
- superficial, localized (skin) 782.2
- testicle 608.86
- throat 784.2
- toe 729.81
- tongue 784.2
- tubular (*see also* Disease, renal) 593.9
- umbilicus 789.3 ☑
- uterus 625.8
- vagina 625.8
- vulva 625.8
- wandering, due to Gnathostoma (spinigerum) 128.1
- white — *see* Tuberculosis, arthritis

Swift's disease 985.0
Swimmers'
- ear (acute) 380.12
- itch 120.3
Swimming in the head 780.4
Swollen — *see also* Swelling
- glands 785.6
Swyer-James syndrome (unilateral hyperlucent lung) 492.8
Swyer's syndrome (XY pure gonadal dysgenesis) 752.7
Sycosis 704.8
- barbae (not parasitic) 704.8
- contagiosa 110.0
- lupoid 704.8
- mycotic 110.0
- parasitic 110.0
- vulgaris 704.8
Sydenham's chorea — *see* Chorea, Sydenham's
Sylvatic yellow fever 060.0
Sylvest's disease (epidemic pleurodynia) 074.1
Symblepharon 372.63
- congenital 743.62
Symonds' syndrome 348.2
Sympathetic — *see* condition
Sympatheticotonia — *see also* Neuropathy, peripheral, autonomic 337.9
Sympathicoblastoma (M9500/3)
- specified site — *see* Neoplasm, by site, malignant
- unspecified site 194.0
Sympathicogonioma (M9500/3) — *see* Sympathicoblastoma
Sympathoblastoma (M9500/3) — *see* Sympathicoblastoma

☑ Additional Digit Required — Refer to the Tabular List for Digit Selection   ▽ Subterms under main terms may continue to next column or page

Sympathogonioma (M9500/3) — see Sympathicoblastoma
Symphalangy — see also Syndactylism 755.10
Symptoms, specified (general) NEC 780.99
  abdomen NEC 789.9
  bone NEC 733.90
  breast NEC 611.79
  cardiac NEC 785.9
  cardiovascular NEC 785.9
  chest NEC 786.9
  development NEC 783.9
  digestive system NEC 787.99
  emotional state NEC 799.29   ●
  eye NEC 379.99
  gastrointestinal tract NEC 787.99
  genital organs NEC
    female 625.9
    male 608.9
  head and neck NEC 784.99
  heart NEC 785.9
  joint NEC 719.60
    ankle 719.67
    elbow 719.62
    foot 719.67
    hand 719.64
    hip 719.65
    knee 719.66
    multiple sites 719.69
    pelvic region 719.65
    shoulder (region) 719.61
    specified site NEC 719.68
    wrist 719.63
  larynx NEC 784.99
  limbs NEC 729.89
  lymphatic system NEC 785.9
  menopausal 627.2
  metabolism NEC 783.9
  mouth NEC 528.9
  muscle NEC 728.9
  musculoskeletal NEC 781.99
    limbs NEC 729.89
  nervous system NEC 781.99
  neurotic NEC 300.9
  nutrition, metabolism, and development NEC
    783.9
  pelvis NEC 789.9
    female 625.9
  peritoneum NEC 789.9
  respiratory system NEC 786.9
  skin and integument NEC 782.9
  subcutaneous tissue NEC 782.9
  throat NEC 784.99
  tonsil NEC 784.99
  urinary system NEC 788.99
  vascular NEC 785.9
Sympus 759.89
Synarthrosis 719.80
  ankle 719.87
  elbow 719.82
  foot 719.87
  hand 719.84
  hip 719.85
  knee 719.86
  multiple sites 719.89
  pelvic region 719.85
  shoulder (region) 719.81
  specified site NEC 719.88
  wrist 719.83
Syncephalus 759.4
Synchondrosis 756.9
  abnormal (congenital) 756.9
  ischiopubic (van Neck's) 732.1
Synchysis (senile) (vitreous humor) 379.21
  scintillans 379.22
Syncope (near) (pre-) 780.2
  anginosa 413.9
  bradycardia 427.89
  cardiac 780.2
  carotid sinus 337.01
  complicating delivery 669.2 ☑
  due to lumbar puncture 349.0
  fatal 798.1
  heart 780.2
  heat 992.1
  laryngeal 786.2
  tussive 786.2

Syncope — continued
  vasoconstriction 780.2
  vasodepressor 780.2
  vasomotor 780.2
  vasovagal 780.2
Syncytial infarct — see Placenta, abnormal
Syndactylism, syndactyly (multiple sites) 755.10
  fingers (without fusion of bone) 755.11
    with fusion of bone 755.12
  toes (without fusion of bone) 755.13
    with fusion of bone 755.14
Syndrome — see also Disease
  with 5q deletion 238.74
  5q minus 238.74
  abdominal
    acute 789.0 ☑
    migraine 346.2 ☑
    muscle deficiency 756.79
  Abercrombie's (amyloid degeneration) 277.39
  abnormal innervation 374.43
  abstinence
    alcohol 291.81
    drug 292.0
    neonatal 779.5   ●
  Abt-Letterer-Siwe (acute histiocytosis X)
    (M9722/3) 202.5 ☑
  Achard-Thiers (adrenogenital) 255.2
  acid pulmonary aspiration 997.39
    obstetric (Mendelson's) 668.0 ☑
  acquired immune deficiency 042
  acquired immunodeficiency 042
  acrocephalosyndactylism 755.55
  acute abdominal 789.0 ☑
  acute chest 517.3
  acute coronary 411.1
  Adair-Dighton (brittle bones and blue sclera,
    deafness) 756.51
  Adams-Stokes (-Morgagni) (syncope with
    heart block) 426.9
  Addisonian 255.41
  Adie (-Holmes) (pupil) 379.46
  adiposogenital 253.8
  adrenal
    hemorrhage 036.3
    meningococcic 036.3
  adrenocortical 255.3
  adrenogenital (acquired) (congenital) 255.2
    feminizing 255.2
    iatrogenic 760.79
    virilism (acquired) (congenital) 255.2
  affective organic NEC 293.89
    drug-induced 292.84
  afferent loop NEC 537.89
  African macroglobulinemia 273.3
  Ahumada-Del Castillo (nonpuerperal galactor-
    rhea and amenorrhea) 253.1
  air blast concussion — see Injury, internal, by
    site
  Alagille 759.89
  Albright (-Martin) (pseudohypoparathy-
    roidism) 275.49
  Albright-McCune-Sternberg (osteitis fibrosa
    disseminata) 756.59
  alcohol withdrawal 291.81
  Alder's (leukocyte granulation anomaly) 288.2
  Aldrich (-Wiskott) (eczema-thrombocytopenia)
    279.12
  Alibert-Bazin (mycosis fungoides) (M9700/3)
    202.1 ☑
  Alice in Wonderland 293.89
  alien hand 781.8
  Allen-Masters 620.6
  Alligator baby (ichthyosis congenita) 757.1
  Alport's (hereditary hematuria-nephropathy-
    deafness) 759.89
  Alvarez (transient cerebral ischemia) 435.9
  alveolar capillary block 516.3
  Alzheimer's 331.0
    with dementia — see Alzheimer's, demen-
      tia
  amnestic (confabulatory) 294.0
    alcohol-induced persisting 291.1
    drug-induced 292.83
    posttraumatic 294.0
  amotivational 292.89
  amyostatic 275.1

Syndrome — see also Disease — continued
  amyotrophic lateral sclerosis 335.20
  androgen insensitivity 259.51
    partial 259.52
  Angelman 759.89
  angina (see also Angina) 413.9
  ankyloglossia superior 750.0
  anterior
    chest wall 786.52
    compartment (tibial) 958.8
    spinal artery 433.8 ☑
      compression 721.1
    tibial (compartment) 958.8
  antibody deficiency 279.00
    agammaglobulinemic 279.00
    congenital 279.04
    hypogammaglobulinemic 279.00
  anticardiolipin antibody 289.81
  antimongolism 758.39
  antiphospholipid antibody 289.81
  Anton (-Babinski) (hemiasomatognosia) 307.9
  anxiety (see also Anxiety) 300.00
    organic 293.84
  aortic
    arch 446.7
    bifurcation (occlusion) 444.0
    ring 747.21
  Apert's (acrocephalosyndactyly) 755.55
  Apert-Gallais (adrenogenital) 255.2
  aphasia-apraxia-alexia 784.69
  apical ballooning 429.83
  "approximate answers" 300.16
  arcuate ligament (-celiac axis) 447.4
  arcus aortae 446.7
  arc welders' 370.24
  argentaffin, argintaffinoma 259.2
  Argonz-Del Castillo (nonpuerperal galactor-
    rhea and amenorrhea) 253.1
  Argyll Robertson's (syphilitic) 094.89
    nonsyphilitic 379.45
  Armenian 277.31
  arm-shoulder (see also Neuropathy, peripheral,
    autonomic) 337.9
  Arnold-Chiari (see also Spina bifida) 741.0 ☑
    type I 348.4
    type II 741.0 ☑
    type III 742.0
    type IV 742.2
  Arrillaga-Ayerza (pulmonary artery sclerosis
    with pulmonary hypertension) 416.0
  arteriomesenteric duodenum occlusion 537.89
  arteriovenous steal 996.73
  arteritis, young female (obliterative brachio-
    cephalic) 446.7
  aseptic meningitis — see Meningitis, aseptic
  Asherman's 621.5
  Asperger's 299.8 ☑
  asphyctic (see also Anxiety) 300.00
  aspiration, of newborn (massive) 770.18
    meconium 770.12
  ataxia-telangiectasia 334.8
  Audry's (acropachyderma) 757.39
  auriculotemporal 350.8
  autoimmune lymphoproliferative (ALPS) ●
    279.41   ●
  autosomal (see also Abnormal, autosomes
    NEC)
    deletion 758.39
      5p 758.31
      22q11.2 758.32
  Avellis' 344.89
  Axenfeld's 743.44
  Ayerza (-Arrillaga) (pulmonary artery sclerosis
    with pulmonary hypertension) 416.0
  Baader's (erythema multiforme exudativum)
    695.19
  Baastrup's 721.5
  Babinski (-Vaquez) (cardiovascular syphilis)
    093.89
  Babinski-Fröhlich (adiposogenital dystrophy)
    253.8
  Babinski-Nageotte 344.89
  Bagratuni's (temporal arteritis) 446.5
  Bakwin-Krida (craniometaphyseal dysplasia)
    756.89

Syndrome — see also Disease — continued
  Balint's (psychic paralysis of visual disorienta-
    tion) 368.16
  Ballantyne (-Runge) (postmaturity) 766.22
  ballooning posterior leaflet 424.0
  Banti's — see Cirrhosis, liver
  Bardet-Biedl (obesity, polydactyly, and mental
    retardation) 759.89
  Bard-Pic's (carcinoma, head of pancreas) 157.0
  Barlow (-Möller) (infantile scurvy) 267
  Barlow's (mitral valve prolapse) 424.0
  Baron Munchausen's 301.51
  Barré-Guillain 357.0
  Barré-Liéou (posterior cervical sympathetic)
    723.2
  Barrett's (chronic peptic ulcer of esophagus)
    530.85
  Bársony-Polgár (corkscrew esophagus) 530.5
  Bársony-Teschendorf (corkscrew esophagus)
    530.5
  Barth 759.89
  Bartter's (secondary hyperaldosteronism with
    juxtaglomerular hyperplasia) 255.13
  basal cell nevus 759.89   ●
  Basedow's (exophthalmic goiter) 242.0 ☑
  basilar artery 435.0
  basofrontal 377.04
  Bassen-Kornzweig (abetalipoproteinemia)
    272.5
  Batten-Steinert 359.21
  battered
    adult 995.81
    baby or child 995.54
    spouse 995.81
  Baumgarten-Cruveilhier (cirrhosis of liver)
    571.5
  Beals 759.82
  Bearn-Kunkel (-Slater) (lupoid hepatitis) 571.49
  Beau's (see also Degeneration, myocardial)
    429.1
  Bechterew-Strümpell-Marie (ankylosing
    spondylitis) 720.0
  Beck's (anterior spinal artery occlusion)
    433.8 ☑
  Beckwith (-Wiedemann) 759.89
  Behçet's 136.1
  Bekhterev-Strümpell-Marie (ankylosing
    spondylitis) 720.0
  Benedikt's 344.89
  Béquez César (-Steinbrinck-Chédiak-Higashi)
    (congenital gigantism of peroxidase
    granules) 288.2
  Bernard-Horner (see also Neuropathy, periph-
    eral, autonomic) 337.9
  Bernard-Sergent (acute adrenocortical insuffi-
    ciency) 255.41
  Bernhardt-Roth 355.1
  Bernheim's (see also Failure, heart) 428.0
  Bertolotti's (sacralization of fifth lumbar verte-
    bra) 756.15
  Besnier-Boeck-Schaumann (sarcoidosis) 135
  Bianchi's (aphasia-apraxia-alexia syndrome)
    784.69
  Biedl-Bardet (obesity, polydactyly, and mental
    retardation) 759.89
  Biemond's (obesity, polydactyly, and mental
    retardation) 759.89
  big spleen 289.4
  bilateral polycystic ovarian 256.4
  Bing-Horton's 339.00
  Biörck (-Thorson) (malignant carcinoid) 259.2
  Birt-Hogg-Dube 759.89
  Blackfan-Diamond (congenital hypoplastic
    anemia) 284.01
  black lung 500
  black widow spider bite 989.5
  bladder neck (see also Incontinence, urine)
    788.30
  blast (concussion) — see Blast, injury
  blind loop (postoperative) 579.2
  Bloch-Siemens (incontinentia pigmenti) 757.33
  Bloch-Sulzberger (incontinentia pigmenti)
    757.33
  Bloom (-Machacek) (-Torre) 757.39
  Blount-Barber (tibia vara) 732.4

☑ Additional Digit Required — Refer to the Tabular List for Digit Selection   ^{NEW} Subterms under main terms may continue to next column or page

Syndrome — *see also* Disease — *continued*
blue
  bloater 491.20
    with
      acute bronchitis 491.22
      exacerbation (acute) 491.21
  diaper 270.0
  drum 381.02
  sclera 756.51
  toe 445.02
Boder-Sedgwick (ataxia-telangiectasia) 334.8
Boerhaave's (spontaneous esophageal rupture) 530.4
Bonnevie-Ullrich 758.6
Bonnier's 386.19
Borjeson-Forssman-Lehmann 759.89
Bouillaud's (rheumatic heart disease) 391.9
Bourneville (-Pringle) (tuberous sclerosis) 759.5
Bouveret (-Hoffmann) (paroxysmal tachycardia) 427.2
brachial plexus 353.0
Brachman-de Lange (Amsterdam dwarf, mental retardation, and brachycephaly) 759.89
bradycardia-tachycardia 427.81
Brailsford-Morquio (dystrophy) (mucopolysaccharidosis IV) 277.5
brain (acute) (chronic) (nonpsychotic) (organic) (with behavioral reaction) (with neurotic reaction) 310.9
  with
    presenile brain disease (*see also* Dementia, presenile) 290.10
    psychosis, psychotic reaction (*see also* Psychosis, organic) 294.9
  chronic alcoholic 291.2
  congenital (*see also* Retardation, mental) 319
  postcontusional 310.2
  posttraumatic
    nonpsychotic 310.2
    psychotic 293.9
      acute 293.0
      chronic (*see also* Psychosis, organic) 294.8
      subacute 293.1
  psycho-organic (*see also* Syndrome, psycho-organic) 310.9
  psychotic (*see also* Psychosis, organic) 294.9
  senile (*see also* Dementia, senile) 290.0
branchial arch 744.41
Brandt's (acrodermatitis enteropathica) 686.8
Brennemann's 289.2
Briquet's 300.81
Brissaud-Meige (infantile myxedema) 244.9
broad ligament laceration 620.6
Brock's (atelectasis due to enlarged lymph nodes) 518.0
broken heart 429.83
Brown-Séquard 344.89
brown spot 756.59
Brown's tendon sheath 378.61
Brugada 746.89
Brugsch's (acropachyderma) 757.39
bubbly lung 770.7
Buchem's (hyperostosis corticalis) 733.3
Budd-Chiari (hepatic vein thrombosis) 453.0
Büdinger-Ludloff-Läwen 717.89
bulbar 335.22
  lateral (*see also* Disease, cerebrovascular, acute) 436
Bullis fever 082.8
bundle of Kent (anomalous atrioventricular excitation) 426.7
Bürger-Grütz (essential familial hyperlipemia) 272.3
Burke's (pancreatic insufficiency and chronic neutropenia) 577.8
Burnett's (milk-alkali) 275.42
Burnier's (hypophyseal dwarfism) 253.3
burning feet 266.2
Bywaters' 958.5
Caffey's (infantile cortical hyperostosis) 756.59
Calvé-Legg-Perthes (osteochondrosis, femoral capital) 732.1

Syndrome — *see also* Disease — *continued*
Caplan (-Colinet) syndrome 714.81
capsular thrombosis (*see also* Thrombosis, brain) 434.0 ☑
carbohydrate-deficient glycoprotein (CDGS) 271.8
carcinogenic thrombophlebitis 453.1
carcinoid 259.2
cardiac asthma (*see also* Failure, ventricular, left) 428.1
cardiacos negros 416.0
cardiofaciocutaneous 759.89 ●
cardiopulmonary obesity 278.8
cardiorenal (*see also* Hypertension, cardiorenal) 404.90
cardiorespiratory distress (idiopathic), newborn 769
cardiovascular renal (*see also* Hypertension, cardiorenal) 404.90
cardiovasorenal 272.7
Carini's (ichthyosis congenita) 757.1
carotid
  artery (internal) 435.8
  body or sinus 337.01
carpal tunnel 354.0
Carpenter's 759.89
Cassidy (-Scholte) (malignant carcinoid) 259.2
cat-cry 758.31
cauda equina 344.60
causalgia 355.9
  lower limb 355.71
  upper limb 354.4
cavernous sinus 437.6
celiac 579.0
  artery compression 447.4
  axis 447.4
central pain 338.0
cerebellomedullary malformation (*see also* Spina bifida) 741.0 ☑
cerebral gigantism 253.0
cerebrohepatorenal 759.89
cervical (root) (spine) NEC 723.8
  disc 722.71
  posterior, sympathetic 723.2
  rib 353.0
  sympathetic paralysis 337.09
  traumatic (acute) NEC 847.0
cervicobrachial (diffuse) 723.3
cervicocranial 723.2
cervicodorsal outlet 353.2
Céstan (-Raymond) 433.8 ☑
Céstan's 344.89
Céstan-Chenais 344.89
chancriform 114.1
Charcôt's (intermittent claudication) 443.9
  angina cruris 443.9
  due to atherosclerosis 440.21
Charcôt-Marie-Tooth 356.1
Charcôt-Weiss-Baker 337.01
CHARGE association 759.89
Cheadle (-Möller) (-Barlow) (infantile scurvy) 267
Chédiak-Higashi (-Steinbrinck) (congenital gigantism of peroxidase granules) 288.2
chest wall 786.52
Chiari's (hepatic vein thrombosis) 453.0
Chiari-Frommel 676.6 ☑
chiasmatic 368.41
Chilaiditi's (subphrenic displacement, colon) 751.4
chondroectodermal dysplasia 756.55
chorea-athetosis-agitans 275.1
Christian's (chronic histiocytosis X) 277.89
chromosome 4 short arm deletion 758.39
chronic pain 338.4
Churg-Strauss 446.4
Clarke-Hadfield (pancreatic infantilism) 577.8
Claude's 352.6
Claude Bernard-Horner (*see also* Neuropathy, peripheral, autonomic) 337.9
Clérambault's
  automatism 348.89 ▲
  erotomania 297.8
Clifford's (postmaturity) 766.22
climacteric 627.2

Syndrome — *see also* Disease — *continued*
Clouston's (hidrotic ectodermal dysplasia) 757.31
clumsiness 315.4
Cockayne's (microencephaly and dwarfism) 759.89
Cockayne-Weber (epidermolysis bullosa) 757.39
Coffin-Lowry 759.89
Cogan's (nonsyphilitic interstitial keratitis) 370.52
cold injury (newborn) 778.2
Collet (-Sicard) 352.6
combined immunity deficiency 279.2
compartment(al) (anterior) (deep) (posterior) 958.8
  nontraumatic
    abdomen 729.73
    arm 729.71
    buttock 729.72
    fingers 729.71
    foot 729.72
    forearm 729.71
    hand 729.71
    hip 729.72
    leg 729.72
    lower extremity 729.72
    shoulder 729.71
    specified site NEC 729.79
    thigh 729.72
    toes 729.72
    upper extremity 729.71
    wrist 729.71
  post-surgical (*see also* Syndrome, compartment, non-traumatic) 998.89
  traumatic 958.90
    adomen 958.93
    arm 958.91
    buttock 958.92
    fingers 958.91
    foot 958.92
    forearm 958.91
    hand 958.91
    hip 958.92
    leg 958.92
    lower extremity 958.92
    shoulder 958.91
    specified site NEC 958.99
    thigh 958.92
    tibial 958.92
    toes 958.92
    upper extremity 958.91
    wrist 958.91
complex regional pain — *see also* Dystrophy, sympathetic
  type I — *see* Dystrophy, sympathetic (posttraumatic) (reflex)
  type II — *see* Causalgia
compression 958.5
  cauda equina 344.60
    with neurogenic bladder 344.61
concussion 310.2
congenital
  affecting more than one system 759.7
    specified type NEC 759.89
  congenital central alveolar hypoventilation 327.25
  facial diplegia 352.6
  muscular hypertrophy-cerebral 759.89
congestion-fibrosis (pelvic) 625.5
conjunctivourethrosynovial 099.3
Conn (-Louis) (primary aldosteronism) 255.12
Conradi (-Hünermann) (chondrodysplasia calcificans congenita) 756.59
conus medullaris 336.8
Cooke-Apert-Gallais (adrenogenital) 255.2
Cornelia de Lange's (Amsterdam dwarf, mental retardation, and brachycephaly) 759.8 ☑
coronary insufficiency or intermediate 411.1
cor pulmonale 416.9
corticosexual 255.2
Costen's (complex) 524.60
costochondral junction 733.6
costoclavicular 353.0
costovertebral 253.0

Syndrome — *see also* Disease — *continued*
Cotard's (paranoia) 297.1
Cowden 759.6
craniovertebral 723.2
Creutzfeldt-Jakob 046.19
  with dementia
    with behavioral disturbance 046.19 *[294.11]*
    without behavioral disturbance 046.19 *[294.10]*
  variant 046.11
    with dementia
      with behavioral disturbance 046.11 *[294.11]*
      without behavioral disturbance 046.11 *[294.10]*
crib death 798.0
cricopharyngeal 787.20
cri-du-chat 758.31
Crigler-Najjar (congenital hyperbilirubinemia) 277.4
crocodile tears 351.8
Cronkhite-Canada 211.3
croup 464.4
CRST (cutaneous systemic sclerosis) 710.1
crush 958.5
crushed lung (*see also* Injury, internal, lung) 861.20
Cruveilhier-Baumgarten (cirrhosis of liver) 571.5
cubital tunnel 354.2
Cuiffini-Pancoast (M8010/3) (carcinoma, pulmonary apex) 162.3
Curschmann (-Batten) (-Steinert) 359.21
Cushing's (iatrogenic) (idiopathic) (pituitary basophilism) (pituitary-dependent) 255.0
  overdose or wrong substance given or taken 962.0
Cyriax's (slipping rib) 733.99
cystic duct stump 576.0
Da Costa's (neurocirculatory asthenia) 306.2
Dameshek's (erythroblastic anemia) 282.49
Dana-Putnam (subacute combined sclerosis with pernicious anemia) 281.0 *[336.2]*
Danbolt (-Closs) (acrodermatitis enteropathica) 686.8
Dandy-Walker (atresia, foramen of Magendie) 742.3
  with spina bifida (*see also* Spina bifida) 741.0 ☑
Danlos' 756.83
Davies-Colley (slipping rib) 733.99
dead fetus 641.3 ☑
defeminization 255.2
defibrination (*see also* Fibrinolysis) 286.6
Degos' 447.8
Deiters' nucleus 386.19
Déjérine-Roussy 338.0
Déjérine-Thomas 333.0
de Lange's (Amsterdam dwarf, mental retardation, and brachycephaly) (Cornelia) 759.89
Del Castillo's (germinal aplasia) 606.0
deletion chromosomes 758.39
delusional
  induced by drug 292.11
dementia-aphonia, of childhood (*see also* Psychosis, childhood) 299.1 ☑
demyelinating NEC 341.9
denial visual hallucination 307.9
depersonalization 300.6
de Quervain's 259.51
Dercum's (adiposis dolorosa) 272.8
de Toni-Fanconi (-Debré) (cystinosis) 270.0
diabetes-dwarfism-obesity (juvenile) 258.1
diabetes mellitus-hypertension-nephrosis 250.4 ☑ *[581.81]*
  due to secondary diabetes 249.4 ☑ *[581.81]*
diabetes mellitus in newborn infant 775.1
diabetes-nephrosis 250.4 ☑ *[581.81]*
  due to secondary diabetes 249.4 ☑ *[581.81]*
diabetic amyotrophy 250.6 ☑ *[353.5]*
  due to secondary diabetes 249.6 ☑ *[353.5]*

☑ Additional Digit Required — Refer to the Tabular List for Digit Selection   ᴺᴱᶜ Subterms under main terms may continue to next column or page

2010 ICD-9-CM   ▶◀ Revised Text   ● New Line   ▲ Revised Code   **October 2009 · Volume 2 — 259**

Syndrome — see also Disease — continued

Diamond-Blackfan (congenital hypoplastic anemia) 284.01

Diamond-Gardener (autoerythrocyte sensitization) 287.2

DIC (diffuse or disseminated intravascular coagulopathy) (see also Fibrinolysis) 286.6

diencephalohypophyseal NEC 253.8

diffuse cervicobrachial 723.3

diffuse obstructive pulmonary 496

DiGeorge's (thymic hypoplasia) 279.11

Dighton's 756.51

Di Guglielmo's (erythremic myelosis) (M9841/3) 207.0 ☑

disequilibrium 276.9

disseminated platelet thrombosis 446.6

Ditthomska 307.81

Doan-Wisemann (primary splenic neutropenia) 289.53

Döhle body-panmyelopathic 288.2

Donohue's (leprechaunism) 259.8

dorsolateral medullary (see also Disease, cerebrovascular, acute) 436

double athetosis 333.71

double whammy 360.81

Down's (mongolism) 758.0

Dresbach's (elliptocytosis) 282.1

Dressler's (postmyocardial infarction) 411.0

hemoglobinuria 283.2

postcardiotomy 429.4

drug withdrawal, infant, of dependent mother 779.5

dry skin 701.1

eye 375.15

DSAP (disseminated superficial actinic porokeratosis) 692.75

Duane's (retraction) 378.71

Duane-Stilling-Türk (ocular retraction syndrome) 378.71

Dubin-Johnson (constitutional hyperbilirubinemia) 277.4

Dubin-Sprinz (constitutional hyperbilirubinemia) 277.4

Duchenne's 335.22

due to abnormality

autosomal NEC (see also Abnormal, autosomes NEC) 758.5

13 758.1

18 758.2

21 or 22 758.0

D1 758.1

E3 758.2

G 758.0

chromosomal 758.89

sex 758.81

dumping 564.2

nonsurgical 536.8

Duplay's 726.2

Dupré's (meningism) 781.6

Dyke-Young (acquired macrocytic hemolytic anemia) 283.9

dyspraxia 315.4

dystocia, dystrophia 654.9 ☑

Eagle-Barret 756.71

Eales' 362.18

Eaton-Lambert (see also Neoplasm, by site, malignant) 199.1 [358.1]

Ebstein's (downward displacement, tricuspid valve into right ventricle) 746.2

ectopic ACTH secretion 255.0

eczema-thrombocytopenia 279.12

Eddowes' (brittle bones and blue sclera) 756.51

Edwards' 758.2

efferent loop 537.89

effort (aviators') (psychogenic) 306.2

Ehlers-Danlos 756.83

Eisenmenger's (ventricular septal defect) 745.4

Ekbom's (restless legs) 333.94

Ekman's (brittle bones and blue sclera) 756.51

electric feet 266.2

Elephant man 237.71

Ellison-Zollinger (gastric hypersecretion with pancreatic islet cell tumor) 251.5

Ellis-van Creveld (chondroectodermal dysplasia) 756.55

Syndrome — see also Disease — continued

embryonic fixation 270.2

empty sella (turcica) 253.8

endocrine-hypertensive 255.3

Engel-von Recklinghausen (osteitis fibrosa cystica) 252.01

enteroarticular 099.3

entrapment — see Neuropathy, entrapment

eosinophilia myalgia 710.5

epidemic vomiting 078.82

Epstein's — see Nephrosis

Erb (-Oppenheim)-Goldflam 358.00

Erdheim's (acromegalic macrospondylitis) 253.0

Erdheim-Chester 277.89 ●

Erlacher-Blount (tibia vara) 732.4

erythrocyte fragmentation 283.19

euthyroid sick 790.94

Evans' (thrombocytopenic purpura) 287.32

excess cortisol, iatrogenic 255.0

exhaustion 300.5

extrapyramidal 333.90

eyelid-malar-mandible 756.0

eye retraction 378.71

Faber's (achlorhydric anemia) 280.9

Fabry (-Anderson) (angiokeratoma corporis diffusum) 272.7

facet 724.8

Fallot's 745.2

falx (see also Hemorrhage, brain) 431

familial eczema-thrombocytopenia 279.12

Fanconi (-de Toni) (-Debré) (cystinosis) 270.0

Fanconi's (anemia) (congenital pancytopenia) 284.09

Farber (-Uzman) (disseminated lipogranulomatosis) 272.8

fatigue NEC 300.5

chronic 780.71

faulty bowel habit (idiopathic megacolon) 564.7

FDH (focal dermal hypoplasia) 757.39

fecal reservoir 560.39

Feil-Klippel (brevicollis) 756.16

Felty's (rheumatoid arthritis with splenomegaly and leukopenia) 714.1

fertile eunuch 257.2

fetal alcohol 760.71

late effect 760.71

fibrillation-flutter 427.32

fibrositis (periarticular) 729.0

Fiedler's (acute isolated myocarditis) 422.91

Fiessinger-Leroy (-Reiter) 099.3

Fiessinger-Rendu (erythema multiforme exudativum) 695.19

first arch 756.0

Fisher's 357.0

fish odor 270.8

Fitz's (acute hemorrhagic pancreatitis) 577.0

Fitz-Hugh and Curtis 098.86

due to

Chlamydia trachomatis 099.56

Neisseria gonorrhoeae (gonococcal peritonitis) 098.86

Flajani (-Basedow) (exophthalmic goiter) 242.0 ☑

flat back

acquired 737.29

postprocedural 738.5

floppy

infant 781.99

iris 364.81

valve (mitral) 424.0

flush 259.2

Foix-Alajouanine 336.1

Fong's (hereditary osteo-onychodysplasia) 756.89

foramen magnum 348.4

Forbes-Albright (nonpuerperal amenorrhea and lactation associated with pituitary tumor) 253.1

Foster-Kennedy 377.04

Foville's (peduncular) 344.89

fragile X 759.83

Franceschetti's (mandibulofacial dysostosis) 756.0

Fraser's 759.89

Syndrome — see also Disease — continued

Freeman-Sheldon 759.89

Frey's (auriculotemporal) 705.22

Friderichsen-Waterhouse 036.3

Friedrich-Erb-Arnold (acropachyderma) 757.39

Fröhlich's (adiposogenital dystrophy) 253.8

Froin's 336.8

Frommel-Chiari 676.6 ☑

frontal lobe 310.0

Fukuhara 277.87

Fuller Albright's (osteitis fibrosa disseminata) 756.59

functional

bowel 564.9

prepubertal castrate 752.89

Gaisböck's (polycythemia hypertonica) 289.0

ganglion (basal, brain) 333.90

geniculi 351.1

Ganser's, hysterical 300.16

Gardner-Diamond (autoerythrocyte sensitization) 287.2

gastroesophageal junction 530.0

gastroesophageal laceration-hemorrhage 530.7

gastrojejunal loop obstruction 537.89

Gayet-Wernicke's (superior hemorrhagic polioencephalitis) 265.1

Gee-Herter-Heubner (nontropical sprue) 579.0

Gélineau's (see also Narcolepsy) 347.00

genito-anorectal 099.1

Gerhardt's (vocal cord paralysis) 478.30

Gerstmann's (finger agnosia) 784.69

Gerstmann-Sträussler-Scheinker (GSS) 046.71

Gianotti Crosti 057.8

due to known virus — see Infection, virus

due to unknown virus 057.8

Gilbert's 277.4

Gilford (-Hutchinson) (progeria) 259.8

Gilles de la Tourette's 307.23

Gillespie's (dysplasia oculodentodigitalis) 759.89

Glénard's (enteroptosis) 569.89

Glinski-Simmonds (pituitary cachexia) 253.2

glucuronyl transferase 277.4

glue ear 381.20

Goldberg (-Maxwell) (-Morris) (testicular feminization) 259.51

Goldenhar's (oculoauriculovertebral dysplasia) 756.0

Goldflam-Erb 358.00

Goltz-Gorlin (dermal hypoplasia) 757.39

Good's 279.06

Goodpasture's (pneumorenal) 446.21

Gopalan's (burning feet) 266.2

Gorlin's 759.89 ●

Gorlin-Chaudhry-Moss 759.89

Gougerot-Blum (pigmented purpuric lichenoid dermatitis) 709.1

Gougerot-Carteaud (confluent reticulate papillomatosis) 701.8

Gougerot (-Houwer)-Sjögren (keratoconjunctivitis sicca) 710.2

Gouley's (constrictive pericarditis) 423.2

Gowers' (vasovagal attack) 780.2

Gowers-Paton-Kennedy 377.04

Gradenigo's 383.02

gray or grey (chloramphenicol) (newborn) 779.4

Greig's (hypertelorism) 756.0

GSS (Gerstmann-Sträussler-Scheinker) 046.71

Gubler-Millard 344.89

Guérin-Stern (arthrogryposis multiplex congenita) 754.89

Guillain-Barré (-Strohl) 357.0

Gunn's (jaw-winking syndrome) 742.8

Günther's (congenital erythropoietic porphyria) 277.1

gustatory sweating 350.8

H₃O 759.81

Hadfield-Clarke (pancreatic infantilism) 577.8

Haglund-Läwen-Fründ 717.89

hairless women 257.8

hair tourniquet (see also Injury, superficial, by site)

finger 915.8

infected 915.9

Syndrome — see also Disease — continued

hair tourniquet (see also Injury, superficial, by site) — continued

penis 911.8

infected 911.9

toe 917.8

infected 917.9

Hallermann-Streiff 756.0

Hallervorden-Spatz 333.0

Hamman's (spontaneous mediastinal emphysema) 518.1

Hamman-Rich (diffuse interstitial pulmonary fibrosis) 516.3

hand-foot 693.0

Hand-Schüller-Christian (chronic histiocytosis X) 277.89

Hanot-Chauffard (-Troisier) (bronze diabetes) 275.0

Harada's 363.22

Hare's (M8010/3) (carcinoma, pulmonary apex) 162.3

Harkavy's 446.0

harlequin color change 779.89

Harris' (organic hyperinsulinism) 251.1

Hart's (pellagra-cerebellar ataxia-renal aminoaciduria) 270.0

Hayem-Faber (achlorhydric anemia) 280.9

Hayem-Widal (acquired hemolytic jaundice) 283.9

headache — see Headache, syndrome

Heberden's (angina pectoris) 413.9

Hedinger's (malignant carcinoid) 259.2

Hegglin's 288.2

Heller's (infantile psychosis) (see also Psychosis, childhood) 299.1 ☑

H.E.L.L.P 642.5 ☑

hemolytic-uremic (adult) (child) 283.11

hemophagocytic 288.4

infection-associated 288.4

Hench-Rosenberg (palindromic arthritis) (see also Rheumatism, palindromic) 719.3 ☑

Henoch-Schönlein (allergic purpura) 287.0

hepatic flexure 569.89

hepatorenal 572.4

due to a procedure 997.4

following delivery 674.8 ☑

hepatourologic 572.4

Herrick's (hemoglobin S disease) 282.61

Herter (-Gee) (nontropical sprue) 579.0

Heubner-Herter (nontropical sprue) 579.0

Heyd's (hepatorenal) 572.4

HHHO 759.81

high grade myelodysplastic 238.73

with 5q deletion 238.73

Hilger's 337.09

histiocytic 288.4

Hoffa (-Kastert) (liposynovitis prepatellaris) 272.8

Hoffmann's 244.9 [359.5]

Hoffmann-Bouveret (paroxysmal tachycardia) 427.2

Hoffmann-Werdnig 335.0

Holländer-Simons (progressive lipodystrophy) 272.6

Holmes' (visual disorientation) 368.16

Holmes-Adie 379.46

Hoppe-Goldflam 358.00

Horner's (see also Neuropathy, peripheral, autonomic) 337.9

traumatic — see Injury, nerve, cervical sympathetic

hospital addiction 301.51

hungry bone 275.5

Hunt's (herpetic geniculate ganglionitis) 053.11

dyssynergia cerebellaris myoclonica 334.2

Hunter (-Hurler) (mucopolysaccharidosis II) 277.5

hunterian glossitis 529.4

Hurler (-Hunter) (mucopolysaccharidosis II) 277.5

Hutchinson-Boeck (sarcoidosis) 135

Hutchinson-Gilford (progeria) 259.8

Hutchinson's incisors or teeth 090.5

☑ Additional Digit Required — Refer to the Tabular List for Digit Selection

▼ Subterms under main terms may continue to next column or page

Syndrome — *see also* Disease — *continued*
hydralazine
  correct substance properly administered 695.4
  overdose or wrong substance given or taken 972.6
hydraulic concussion (abdomen) (*see also* Injury, internal, abdomen) 868.00
hyperabduction 447.8
hyperactive bowel 564.9
hyperaldosteronism with hypokalemic alkalosis (Bartter's) 255.13
hypercalcemic 275.42
hypercoagulation NEC 289.89
hypereosinophilic (idiopathic) 288.3
hyperkalemic 276.7
hyperkinetic (*see also* Hyperkinesia)
  heart 429.82
hyperlipemia-hemolytic anemia-icterus 571.1
hypermobility 728.5
hypernatremia 276.0
hyperosmolarity 276.0
hyperperfusion 997.01
hypersomnia-bulimia 349.89
hypersplenic 289.4
hypersympathetic (*see also* Neuropathy, peripheral, autonomic) 337.9
hypertransfusion, newborn 776.4
hyperventilation, psychogenic 306.1
hyperviscosity (of serum) NEC 273.3
  polycythemic 289.0
  sclerothymic 282.8
hypoglycemic (familial) (neonatal) 251.2
  functional 251.1
hypokalemic 276.8
hypophyseal 253.8
hypophyseothalamic 253.8
hypopituitarism 253.2
hypoplastic left heart 746.7
hypopotassemia 276.8
hyposmolality 276.1
hypotension, maternal 669.2 ☑
hypothenar hammer 443.89
hypotonia-hypomentia-hypogonadism-obesity 759.81
ICF (intravascular coagulation-fibrinolysis) (*see also* Fibrinolysis) 286.6
idiopathic cardiorespiratory distress, newborn 769
idiopathic nephrotic (infantile) 581.9
iliotibial band 728.89
Imerslund (-Gräsbeck) (anemia due to familial selective vitamin B$_{12}$ malabsorption) 281.1
immobility (paraplegic) 728.3
immunity deficiency, combined 279.2
impending coronary 411.1
impingement
  shoulder 726.2
  vertebral bodies 724.4
inappropriate secretion of antidiuretic hormone (ADH) 253.6
incomplete
  mandibulofacial 756.0
infant
  death, sudden (SIDS) 798.0
  Hercules 255.2
  of diabetic mother 775.0
  shaken 995.55
infantilism 253.3
inferior vena cava 459.2
influenza-like 487.1
inspissated bile, newborn 774.4
insufficient sleep 307.44
intermediate coronary (artery) 411.1
internal carotid artery (*see also* Occlusion, artery, carotid) 433.1 ☑
interspinous ligament 724.8
intestinal
  carcinoid 259.2
  gas 787.3
  knot 560.2
intraoperative floppy iris (IFIS) 364.81
intravascular
  coagulation-fibrinolysis (ICF) (*see also* Fibrinolysis) 286.6

Syndrome — *see also* Disease — *continued*
intravascular — *continued*
  coagulopathy (*see also* Fibrinolysis) 286.6
inverted Marfan's 759.89
IRDS (idiopathic respiratory distress, newborn) 769
irritable
  bowel 564.1
  heart 306.2
  weakness 300.5
ischemic bowel (transient) 557.9
  chronic 557.1
  due to mesenteric artery insufficiency 557.1
Itsenko-Cushing (pituitary basophilism) 255.0
IVC (intravascular coagulopathy) (*see also* Fibrinolysis) 286.6
Ivemark's (asplenia with congenital heart disease) 759.0
Jaccoud's 714.4
Jackson's 344.89
Jadassohn-Lewandowski (pachyonchia congenita) 757.5
Jaffe-Lichtenstein (-Uehlinger) 252.01
Jahnke's (encephalocutaneous angiomatosis) 759.6
Jakob-Creutzfeldt 046.19
  with dementia
    with behavioral disturbance 046.19 *[294.11]*
    without behavioral disturbance 046.19 *[294.10]*
  variant 046.11
    with dementia
      with behavioral disturbance 046.11 *[294.11]*
      without behavioral disturbance 046.11 *[294.10]*
Jaksch's (pseudoleukemia infantum) 285.8
Jaksch-Hayem (-Luzet) (pseudoleukemia infantum) 285.8
jaw-winking 742.8
jejunal 564.2
Jervell-Lange-Nielsen 426.82
jet lag 327.35
Jeune's (asphyxiating thoracic dystrophy of newborn) 756.4
Job's (chronic granulomatous disease) 288.1
Jordan's 288.2
Joseph-Diamond-Blackfan (congenital hypoplastic anemia) 284.01
Joubert 759.89
jugular foramen 352.6
Kabuki 759.89
Kahler's (multiple myeloma) (M9730/3) 203.0 ☑
Kalischer's (encephalocutaneous angiomatosis) 759.6
Kallmann's (hypogonadotropic hypogonadism with anosmia) 253.4
Kanner's (autism) (*see also* Psychosis, childhood) 299.0 ☑
Kartagener's (sinusitis, bronchiectasis, situs inversus) 759.3
Kasabach-Merritt (capillary hemangioma associated with thrombocytopenic purpura) 287.39
Kast's (dyschondroplasia with hemangiomas) 756.4
Kaznelson's (congenital hypoplastic anemia) 284.01
Kearns-Sayre 277.87
Kelly's (sideropenic dysphagia) 280.8
Kimmelstiel-Wilson (intercapillary glomerulosclerosis) 250.4 ☑ *[581.81]*
  due to secondary diabetes 249.4 ☑ *[581.81]*
Klauder's (erythema multiforme exudativum) 695.19
Kleine-Levin 327.13
Klein-Waardenburg (ptosis-epicanthus) 270.2
Klinefelter's 758.7
Klippel-Feil (brevicollis) 756.16
Klippel-Trenaunay 759.89
Klumpke (-Déjérine) (injury to brachial plexus at birth) 767.6

Syndrome — *see also* Disease — *continued*
Klüver-Bucy (-Terzian) 310.0
Köhler-Pellegrini-Stieda (calcification, knee joint) 726.62
König's 564.89
Korsakoff (-Wernicke) (nonalcoholic) 294.0
Korsakoff's (nonalcoholic) 294.0
  alcoholic 291.1
  alcoholic 291.1
Kostmann's (infantile genetic agranulocytosis) 288.01
Krabbe's
  congenital muscle hypoplasia 756.89
  cutaneocerebral angioma 759.6
Kunkel (lupoid hepatitis) 571.49
labyrinthine 386.50
laceration, broad ligament 620.6
Landau-Kleffner 345.8 ☑
Langdon Down (mongolism) 758.0
Larsen's (flattened facies and multiple congenital dislocations) 755.8
lateral
  cutaneous nerve of thigh 355.1
  medullary (*see also* Disease, cerebrovascular acute) 436
Launois' (pituitary gigantism) 253.0
Launois-Cléret (adiposogenital dystrophy) 253.8
Laurence-Moon (-Bardet)-Biedl (obesity, polydactyly, and mental retardation) 759.89
Lawford's (encephalocutaneous angiomatosis) 759.6
lazy
  leukocyte 288.09
  posture 728.3
Lederer-Brill (acquired infectious hemolytic anemia) 283.19
Legg-Calvé-Perthes (osteochondrosis capital femoral) 732.1
Lemiere 451.89
Lennox's (*see also* Epilepsy) 345.0 ☑
Lennox-Gastaut syndrome 345.0 ☑
  with tonic seizures 345.1 ☑
lenticular 275.1
Léopold-Lévi's (paroxysmal thyroid instability) 242.9 ☑
Lepore hemoglobin 282.49
Leriche's (aortic bifurcation occlusion) 444.0
Léri-Weill 756.59
Lermoyez's (*see also* Disease, Ménière's) 386.00
Lesch-Nyhan (hypoxanthine-guanine-phosphoribosyltransferase deficiency) 277.2
leukoencephalopathy, reversible, posterior 348.5
Lev's (acquired complete heart block) 426.0
Levi's (pituitary dwarfism) 253.3
Lévy-Roussy 334.3
Lichtheim's (subacute combined sclerosis with pernicious anemia) 281.0 *[336.2]*
Li-Fraumeni V84.01
Lightwood's (renal tubular acidosis) 588.89
Lignac (-de Toni) (-Fanconi) (-Debré) (cystinosis) 270.0
Likoff's (angina in menopausal women) 413.9
liver-kidney 572.4
Lloyd's 258.1
lobotomy 310.0
Löffler's (eosinophilic pneumonitis) 518.3
Löfgren's (sarcoidosis) 135
long arm 18 or 21 deletion 758.39
Looser (-Debray)-Milkman (osteomalacia with pseudofractures) 268.2
Lorain-Levi (pituitary dwarfism) 253.3
Louis-Bar (ataxia-telangiectasia) 334.8
low
  atmospheric pressure 993.2
  back 724.2
    psychogenic 306.0
  output (cardiac) (*see also* Failure, heart) 428.9
Lowe's (oculocerebrorenal dystrophy) 270.8
lower radicular, newborn 767.4
Lowe-Terrey-MacLachlan (oculocerebrorenal dystrophy) 270.8

Syndrome — *see also* Disease — *continued*
Lown (-Ganong)-Levine (short P-R interval, normal QRS complex, and supraventricular tachycardia) 426.81
Lucey-Driscoll (jaundice due to delayed conjugation) 774.30
Luetscher's (dehydration) 276.51
lumbar vertebral 724.4
Lutembacher's (atrial septal defect with mitral stenosis) 745.5
Lyell's (toxic epidermal necrolysis) 695.15
  due to drug
    correct substance properly administered 695.15
    overdose or wrong substance given or taken 977.9
    specified drug — *see* Table of Drugs and Chemicals
MacLeod's 492.8
macrogenitosomia praecox 259.8
macroglobulinemia 273.3
macrophage activation 288.4
Maffucci's (dyschondroplasia with hemangiomas) 756.4
Magenblase 306.4
magnesium-deficiency 781.7
malabsorption 579.9
  postsurgical 579.3
  spinal fluid 331.3
Mal de Debarquement 780.4
malignant carcinoid 259.2
Mallory-Weiss 530.7
mandibulofacial dysostosis 756.0
manic-depressive (*see also* Psychosis, affective) 296.80
Mankowsky's (familial dysplastic osteopathy) 731.2
maple syrup (urine) 270.3
Marable's (celiac artery compression) 447.4
Marchesani (-Weill) (brachymorphism and ectopia lentis) 759.89
Marchiafava-Bignami 341.8
Marchiafava-Micheli (paroxysmal nocturnal hemoglobinuria) 283.2
Marcus Gunn's (jaw-winking syndrome) 742.8
Marfan's (arachnodactyly) 759.82
  meaning congenital syphilis 090.49
  with luxation of lens 090.49 *[379.32]*
Marie's (acromegaly) 253.0
  primary or idiopathic (acropachyderma) 757.39
  secondary (hypertrophic pulmonary osteoarthropathy) 731.2
Markus-Adie 379.46
Maroteaux-Lamy (mucopolysaccharidosis VI) 277.5
Martin's 715.27
Martin-Albright (pseudohypoparathyroidism) 275.49
Martorell-Fabré (pulseless disease) 446.7
massive aspiration of newborn 770.18
Masters-Allen 620.6
mastocytosis 757.33
maternal hypotension 669.2 ☑
maternal obesity 646.1 ☑
May (-Hegglin) 288.2
McArdle (-Schmid) (-Pearson) (glycogenosis V) 271.0
McCune-Albright (osteitis fibrosa disseminata) 756.59
McQuarrie's (idiopathic familial hypoglycemia) 251.2
meconium
  aspiration 770.12
  plug (newborn) NEC 777.1
median arcuate ligament 447.4
mediastinal fibrosis 519.3
Meekeren-Ehlers-Danlos 756.83
Meige (blepharospasm-oromandibular dystonia) 333.82
  -Milroy (chronic hereditary edema) 757.0
MELAS (mitochondrial encephalopathy, lactic acidosis and stroke-like episodes) 277.87
Melkersson (-Rosenthal) 351.8

☑ Additional Digit Required — Refer to the Tabular List for Digit Selection   ꝥ Subterms under main terms may continue to next column or page

2010 ICD-9-CM   ▶◀ Revised Text   ● New Line   ▲ Revised Code   **Volume 2 — 261**

☑ Additional Digit Required — Refer to the Tabular List for Digit Selection   ▽ Subterms under main terms may continue to next column or page

262 — Volume 2 • October 2009   ▶◀ Revised Text   ● New Line   ▲ Revised Code   **2010 ICD-9-CM**

Syndrome — Syndrome

☑ Additional Digit Required — Refer to the Tabular List for Digit Selection   ⏷ Subterms under main terms may continue to next column or page

2010 ICD-9-CM   ▶◀ Revised Text   ● New Line   ▲ Revised Code   **Volume 2 — 263**

Syndrome — *see also* Disease — *continued*

superior
cerebellar artery (*see also* Disease, cerebrovascular, acute) 436
mesenteric artery 557.1
pulmonary sulcus (tumor) (M8010/3) 162.3
vena cava 459.2
suprarenal cortical 255.3
supraspinatus 726.10
Susac 348.39
swallowed blood 777.3
sweat retention 705.1
Sweet's (acute febrile neutrophilic dermatosis) 695.89
Swyer's (XY pure gonadal dysgenesis) 752.7
Swyer-James (unilateral hyperlucent lung) 492.8
Symonds' 348.2
sympathetic
cervical paralysis 337.09
pelvic 625.5
syndactylic oxycephaly 755.55
syphilitic-cardiovascular 093.89
systemic
fibrosclerosing 710.8
inflammatory response (SIRS) 995.90
due to
infectious process 995.91
with acute organ dysfunction 995.92
non-infectious process 995.93
with acute organ dysfunction 995.94
systolic click (-murmur) 785.2
Tabagism 305.1
tachycardia-bradycardia 427.81
Takayasu (-Onishi) (pulseless disease) 446.7
Takotsubo 429.83
Tapia's 352.6
tarsal tunnel 355.5
Taussig-Bing (transposition, aorta and overriding pulmonary artery) 745.11
Taybi's (otopalatodigital) 759.89
Taylor's 625.5
teething 520.7
tegmental 344.89
telangiectasis-pigmentation-cataract 757.33
temporal 383.02
lobectomy behavior 310.0
temporomandibular joint-pain-dysfunction [TMJ] NEC 524.60
specified NEC 524.69
Terry's (*see also* Retinopathy of prematurity) 362.21
testicular feminization 259.51
testis, nonvirilizing 257.8
tethered (spinal) cord 742.59
thalamic 338.0
Thibierge-Weissenbach (cutaneous systemic sclerosis) 710.1
Thiele 724.6
thoracic outlet (compression) 353.0
thoracogenous rheumatic (hypertrophic pulmonary osteoarthropathy) 731.2
Thorn's (*see also* Disease, renal) 593.9
Thorson-Biörck (malignant carcinoid) 259.2
thrombopenia-hemangioma 287.39
thyroid-adrenocortical insufficiency 258.1
Tietze's 733.6
time-zone (rapid) 327.35
Tobias' (carcinoma, pulmonary apex) (M8010/3) 162.3
toilet seat 926.0
Tolosa-Hunt 378.55
Toni-Fanconi (cystinosis) 270.0
Touraine's (hereditary osteo-onychodysplasia) 756.89
Touraine-Solente-Golé (acropachyderma) 757.39
toxic
oil 710.5
shock 040.82
transfusion
fetal-maternal 772.0
twin
donor (infant) 772.0

Syndrome — *see also* Disease — *continued*

transfusion — *continued*
twin — *continued*
recipient (infant) 776.4
transient left ventricular apical ballooning 429.83
Treacher Collins' (incomplete mandibulofacial dysostosis) 756.0
trigeminal plate 259.8
triple X female 758.81
trisomy NEC 758.5
13 or D$_1$ 758.1
16-18 or E 758.2
18 or E$_3$ 758.2
20 758.5
21 or G (mongolism) 758.0
22 or G (mongolism) 758.0
G 758.0
Troisier-Hanot-Chauffard (bronze diabetes) 275.0
tropical wet feet 991.4
Trousseau's (thrombophlebitis migrans visceral cancer) 453.1
tumor lysis (following antineoplastic drug therapy) (spontaneous) 277.88 ●
Türk's (ocular retraction syndrome) 378.71
Turner's 758.6
Turner-Varny 758.6
Twiddler's (due to)
automatic implantable defibrillator 996.04
pacemaker 996.01
twin-to-twin transfusion 762.3
recipient twin 776.4
Uehlinger's (acropachyderma) 757.39
Ullrich (-Bonnevie) (-Turner) 758.6
Ullrich-Feichtiger 759.89
underwater blast injury (abdominal) (*see also* Injury, internal, abdomen) 868.00
universal joint, cervix 620.6
Unverricht (-Lundborg) 345.1 ☑ ▲
Unverricht-Wagner (dermatomyositis) 710.3
upward gaze 378.81
Urbach-Oppenheim (necrobiosis lipoidica diabeticorum) 250.8 ☑ [709.3]
due to secondary diabetes 249.8 ☑ [709.3]
Urbach-Wiethe (lipoid proteinosis) 272.8
uremia, chronic 585.9
urethral 597.81
urethro-oculoarticular 099.3
urethro-oculosynovial 099.3
urohepatic 572.4
uveocutaneous 364.24
uveomeningeal, uveomeningitis 363.22
vagohypoglossal 352.6
vagovagal 780.2
van Buchem's (hyperostosis corticalis) 733.3
van der Hoeve's (brittle bones and blue sclera, deafness) 756.51
van der Hoeve-Halbertsma-Waardenburg (ptosis-epicanthus) 270.2
van der Hoeve-Waardenburg-Gualdi (ptosis-epicanthus) 270.2
vanishing twin 651.33
van Neck-Odelberg (juvenile osteochondrosis) 732.1
vascular splanchnic 557.0
vasomotor 443.9
vasovagal 780.2
VATER 759.89
Velo-cardio-facial 758.32
vena cava (inferior) (superior) (obstruction) 459.2
Verbiest's (claudicatio intermittens spinalis) 435.1
Vernet's 352.6
vertebral
artery 435.1
compression 721.1
lumbar 724.4
steal 435.1
vertebrogenic (pain) 724.5
vertiginous NEC 386.9
video display tube 723.8
Villaret's 352.6
Vinson-Plummer (sideropenic dysphagia) 280.8

Syndrome — *see also* Disease — *continued*

virilizing adrenocortical hyperplasia, congenital 255.2
virus, viral 079.99
visceral larval migrans 128.0
visual disorientation 368.16
vitamin B$_6$ deficiency 266.1
vitreous touch 997.99
Vogt's (corpus striatum) 333.71
Vogt-Koyanagi 364.24
Volkmann's 958.6
von Bechterew-Strümpell (ankylosing spondylitis) 720.0
von Graefe's 378.72
von Hippel-Lindau (angiomatosis retinocerebellosa) 759.6
von Schroetter's (intermittent venous claudication) 453.89 ▲
von Willebrand (-Jürgens) (angiohemophilia) 286.4
Waardenburg-Klein (ptosis epicanthus) 270.2
Wagner (-Unverricht) (dermatomyositis) 710.3
Waldenström's (macroglobulinemia) 273.3
Waldenström-Kjellberg (sideropenic dysphagia) 280.8
Wallenberg's (posterior inferior cerebellar artery) (*see also* Disease, cerebrovascular, acute) 436
Waterhouse (-Friderichsen) 036.3
water retention 276.6
Weber's 344.89
Weber-Christian (nodular nonsuppurative panniculitis) 729.30
Weber-Cockayne (epidermolysis bullosa) 757.39
Weber-Dimitri (encephalocutaneous angiomatosis) 759.6
Weber-Gubler 344.89
Weber-Leyden 344.89
Weber-Osler (familial hemorrhagic telangiectasia) 448.0
Wegener's (necrotizing respiratory granulomatosis) 446.4
Weill-Marchesani (brachymorphism and ectopia lentis) 759.89
Weingarten's (tropical eosinophilia) 518.3
Weiss-Baker (carotid sinus syncope) 337.01
Weissenbach-Thibierge (cutaneous systemic sclerosis) 710.1
Werdnig-Hoffman 335.0
Werlhof-Wichmann (*see also* Purpura, thrombocytopenic) 287.39
Wermer's (polyendocrine adenomatosis) 258.01
Werner's (progeria adultorum) 259.8
Wernicke's (nonalcoholic) (superior hemorrhagic polioencephalitis) 265.1
Wernicke-Korsakoff (nonalcoholic) 294.0
alcoholic 291.1
Westphal-Strümpell (hepatolenticular degeneration) 275.1
wet
brain (alcoholic) 303.9 ☑
feet (maceration) (tropical) 991.4
lung
adult 518.5
newborn 770.6
whiplash 847.0
Whipple's (intestinal lipodystrophy) 040.2
"whistling face" (craniocarpotarsal dystrophy) 759.89
Widal (-Abrami) (acquired hemolytic jaundice) 283.9
Wilkie's 557.1
Wilkinson-Sneddon (subcorneal pustular dermatosis) 694.1
Willan-Plumbe (psoriasis) 696.1
Willebrand (-Jürgens) (angiohemophilia) 286.4
Willi-Prader (hypogenital dystrophy with diabetic tendency) 759.81
Wilson's (hepatolenticular degeneration) 275.1
Wilson-Mikity 770.7
Wiskott-Aldrich (eczema-thrombocytopenia) 279.12
withdrawal
alcohol 291.81

Syndrome — *see also* Disease — *continued*

withdrawal — *continued*
drug 292.0
infant of dependent mother 779.5
Woakes' (ethmoiditis) 471.1
Wolff-Parkinson-White (anomalous atrioventricular excitation) 426.7
Wright's (hyperabduction) 447.8
X
cardiac 413.9
dysmetabolic 277.7
xiphoidalgia 733.99
XO 758.6
XXX 758.81
XXXXY 758.81
XXY 758.7
yellow vernix (placental dysfunction) 762.2
Zahorsky's 074.0
Zellweger 277.86
Zieve's (jaundice, hyperlipemia and hemolytic anemia) 571.1
Zollinger-Ellison (gastric hypersecretion with pancreatic islet cell tumor) 251.5
Zuelzer-Ogden (nutritional megaloblastic anemia) 281.2

Synechia (iris) (pupil) 364.70
anterior 364.72
peripheral 364.73
intrauterine (traumatic) 621.5
posterior 364.71
vulvae, congenital 752.49

Synesthesia — *see also* Disturbance, sensation 782.0

Synodontia 520.2

Synophthalmus 759.89

Synorchidism 752.89

Synorchism 752.89

Synostosis (congenital) 756.59
astragaloscaphoid 755.67
radioulnar 755.53
talonavicular (bar) 755.67
tarsal 755.67

Synovial — *see* condition

Synovioma (M9040/3) — *see also* Neoplasm, connective tissue, malignant
benign (M9040/0) — *see* Neoplasm, connective tissue, benign

Synoviosarcoma (M9040/3) — *see* Neoplasm, connective tissue, malignant

Synovitis (*see also* Tenosynovitis) 727.00
chronic crepitant, wrist 727.2
due to crystals — *see* Arthritis, due to crystals
gonococcal 098.51
gouty 274.00 ▲
specified NEC 727.09
syphilitic 095.7
congenital 090.0
traumatic, current — *see* Sprain, by site
tuberculous — *see* Tuberculosis, synovitis
villonodular 719.20
ankle 719.27
elbow 719.22
foot 719.27
hand 719.24
hip 719.25
knee 719.26
multiple sites 719.29
pelvic region 719.25
shoulder (region) 719.21
specified site NEC 719.28
wrist 719.23

Syphilide 091.3
congenital 090.0
newborn 090.0
tubercular 095.8
congenital 090.0

Syphilis, syphilitic (acquired) 097.9
with lung involvement 095.1
abdomen (late) 095.2
acoustic nerve 094.86
adenopathy (secondary) 091.4
adrenal (gland) 095.8
with cortical hypofunction 095.8
age under 2 years NEC (*see also* Syphilis, congenital) 090.9
acquired 097.9

☑ Additional Digit Required — Refer to the Tabular List for Digit Selection

⩗ Subterms under main terms may continue to next column or page

▶◀ Revised Text   ● New Line   ▲ Revised Code

Syphilis, syphilitic — *continued*
  alopecia (secondary) 091.82
  anemia 095.8
  aneurysm (artery) (ruptured) 093.89
    aorta 093.0
    central nervous system 094.89
    congenital 090.5
  anus 095.8
    primary 091.1
    secondary 091.3
  aorta, aortic (arch) (abdominal) (insufficiency) (pulmonary) (regurgitation) (stenosis) (thoracic) 093.89
    aneurysm 093.0
  arachnoid (adhesive) 094.2
  artery 093.89
    cerebral 094.89
    spinal 094.89
  arthropathy (neurogenic) (tabetic) 094.0 *[713.5]*
  asymptomatic — *see* Syphilis, latent
  ataxia, locomotor (progressive) 094.0
  atrophoderma maculatum 091.3
  auricular fibrillation 093.89
  Bell's palsy 094.89
  bladder 095.8
  bone 095.5
    secondary 091.61
  brain 094.89
  breast 095.8
  bronchus 095.8
  bubo 091.0
  bulbar palsy 094.89
  bursa (late) 095.7
  cardiac decompensation 093.89
  cardiovascular (early) (late) (primary) (secondary) (tertiary) 093.9
    specified type and site NEC 093.89
  causing death under 2 years of age (*see also* Syphilis, congenital) 090.9
    stated to be acquired NEC 097.9
  central nervous system (any site) (early) (late) (latent) (primary) (recurrent) (relapse) (secondary) (tertiary) 094.9
    with
      ataxia 094.0
      paralysis, general 094.1
        juvenile 090.40
      paresis (general) 094.1
        juvenile 090.40
      tabes (dorsalis) 094.0
        juvenile 090.40
      taboparesis 094.1
        juvenile 090.40
    aneurysm (ruptured) 094.87
    congenital 090.40
    juvenile 090.40
    remission in (sustained) 094.9
    serology doubtful, negative, or positive 094.9
    specified nature or site NEC 094.89
    vascular 094.89
  cerebral 094.89
    meningovascular 094.2
    nerves 094.89
    sclerosis 094.89
    thrombosis 094.89
  cerebrospinal 094.89
    tabetic 094.0
  cerebrovascular 094.89
  cervix 095.8
  chancre (multiple) 091.0
    extragenital 091.2
    Rollet's 091.2
  Charcôt's joint 094.0 *[713.5]*
  choked disc 094.89 *[377.00]*
  chorioretinitis 091.51
    congenital 090.0 *[363.13]*
    late 094.83
  choroiditis 091.51
    congenital 090.0 *[363.13]*
    late 094.83
    prenatal 090.0 *[363.13]*
  choroidoretinitis (secondary) 091.51
    congenital 090.0 *[363.13]*
    late 094.83

Syphilis, syphilitic — *continued*
  ciliary body (secondary) 091.52
    late 095.8 *[364.11]*
  colon (late) 095.8
  combined sclerosis 094.89
  complicating pregnancy, childbirth or puerperium 647.0 ☑
    affecting fetus or newborn 760.2
  condyloma (latum) 091.3
  congenital 090.9
    with
      encephalitis 090.41
      paresis (general) 090.40
      tabes (dorsalis) 090.40
      taboparesis 090.40
    chorioretinitis, choroiditis 090.0 *[363.13]*
    early or less than 2 years after birth NEC 090.2
      with manifestations 090.0
      latent (without manifestations) 090.1
        negative spinal fluid test 090.1
        serology, positive 090.1
      symptomatic 090.0
    interstitial keratitis 090.3
    juvenile neurosyphilis 090.40
    late or 2 years or more after birth NEC 090.7
      chorioretinitis, choroiditis 090.5 *[363.13]*
      interstitial keratitis 090.3
      juvenile neurosyphilis NEC 090.40
      latent (without manifestations) 090.6
        negative spinal fluid test 090.6
        serology, positive 090.6
      symptomatic or with manifestations NEC 090.5
        interstitial keratitis 090.3
  conjugal 097.9
    tabes 094.0
  conjunctiva 095.8 *[372.10]*
  contact V01.6
  cord, bladder 094.0
  cornea, late 095.8 *[370.59]*
  coronary (artery) 093.89
    sclerosis 093.89
  coryza 095.8
    congenital 090.0
  cranial nerve 094.89
  cutaneous — *see* Syphilis, skin
  dacryocystitis 095.8
  degeneration, spinal cord 094.89
  d'emblée 095.8
  dementia 094.1
    paralytica 094.1
      juvenilis 090.40
  destruction of bone 095.5
  dilatation, aorta 093.0
  due to blood transfusion 097.9
  dura mater 094.89
  ear 095.8
    inner 095.8
      nerve (eighth) 094.86
      neurorecurrence 094.86
  early NEC 091.0
    cardiovascular 093.9
    central nervous system 094.9
      paresis 094.1
      tabes 094.0
    latent (without manifestations) (less than 2 years after infection) 092.9
      negative spinal fluid test 092.9
      serological relapse following treatment 092.0
      serology positive 092.9
    paresis 094.1
    relapse (treated, untreated) 091.7
    skin 091.3
    symptomatic NEC 091.89
      extragenital chancre 091.2
      primary, except extragenital chancre 091.0
      secondary (*see also* Syphilis, secondary) 091.3
        relapse (treated, untreated) 091.7
      tabes 094.0
      ulcer 091.3
  eighth nerve 094.86

Syphilis, syphilitic — *continued*
  endemic, nonvenereal 104.0
  endocarditis 093.20
    aortic 093.22
    mitral 093.21
    pulmonary 093.24
    tricuspid 093.23
  epididymis (late) 095.8
  epiglottis 095.8
  epiphysitis (congenital) 090.0
  esophagus 095.8
  Eustachian tube 095.8
  exposure to V01.6
  eye 095.8 *[363.13]*
    neuromuscular mechanism 094.85
  eyelid 095.8 *[373.5]*
    with gumma 095.8 *[373.5]*
    ptosis 094.89
  fallopian tube 095.8
  fracture 095.5
  gallbladder (late) 095.8
  gastric 095.8
    crisis 094.0
    polyposis 095.8
  general 097.9
    paralysis 094.1
      juvenile 090.40
  genital (primary) 091.0
  glaucoma 095.8
  gumma (late) NEC 095.9
    cardiovascular system 093.9
    central nervous system 094.9
    congenital 090.5
    heart or artery 093.89
  heart 093.89
    block 093.89
    decompensation 093.89
    disease 093.89
    failure 093.89
    valve (*see also* Syphilis, endocarditis) 093.20
  hemianesthesia 094.89
  hemianopsia 095.8
  hemiparesis 094.89
  hemiplegia 094.89
  hepatic artery 093.89
  hepatitis 095.3
  hepatomegaly 095.3
    congenital 090.0
  hereditaria tarda (*see also* Syphilis, congenital, late) 090.7
  hereditary (*see also* Syphilis, congenital) 090.9
    interstitial keratitis 090.3
  Hutchinson's teeth 090.5
  hyalitis 095.8
  inactive — *see* Syphilis, latent
  infantum NEC (*see also* Syphilis, congenital) 090.9
  inherited — *see* Syphilis, congenital
  internal ear 095.8
  intestine (late) 095.8
  iris, iritis (secondary) 091.52
    late 095.8 *[364.11]*
  joint (late) 095.8
  keratitis (congenital) (early) (interstitial) (late) (parenchymatous) (punctata profunda) 090.3
  kidney 095.4
  lacrimal apparatus 095.8
  laryngeal paralysis 095.8
  larynx 095.8
  late 097.0
    cardiovascular 093.9
    central nervous system 094.9
      latent or 2 years or more after infection (without manifestations) 096
        negative spinal fluid test 096
        serology positive 096
    paresis 094.1
    specified site NEC 095.8
    symptomatic or with symptoms 095.9
    tabes 094.0
  latent 097.1
    central nervous system 094.9
    date of infection unspecified 097.1
    early or less than 2 years after infection 092.9

Syphilis, syphilitic — *continued*
  latent — *continued*
    late or 2 years or more after infection 096
    serology
      doubtful
        follow-up of latent syphilis 097.1
          central nervous system 094.9
          date of infection unspecified 097.1
          early or less than 2 years after infection 092.9
          late or 2 years or more after infection 096
        positive, only finding 097.1
          date of infection unspecified 097.1
          early or less than 2 years after infection 097.1
          late or 2 years or more after infection 097.1
  lens 095.8
  leukoderma 091.3
    late 095.8
  lienis 095.8
  lip 091.3
    chancre 091.2
    late 095.8
    primary 091.2
  Lissauer's paralysis 094.1
  liver 095.3
    secondary 091.62
  locomotor ataxia 094.0
  lung 095.1
  lymphadenitis (secondary) 091.4
  lymph gland (early) (secondary) 091.4
    late 095.8
  macular atrophy of skin 091.3
    striated 095.8
  maternal, affecting fetus or newborn 760.2
    manifest syphilis in newborn — *see* Syphilis, congenital
  mediastinum (late) 095.8
  meninges (adhesive) (basilar) (brain) (spinal cord) 094.2
  meningitis 094.2
    acute 091.81
    congenital 090.42
  meningoencephalitis 094.2
  meningovascular 094.2
    congenital 090.49
  mesarteritis 093.89
    brain 094.89
    spine 094.89
  middle ear 095.8
  mitral stenosis 093.21
  monoplegia 094.89
  mouth (secondary) 091.3
    late 095.8
  mucocutaneous 091.3
    late 095.8
  mucous
    membrane 091.3
      late 095.8
    patches 091.3
      congenital 090.0
  mulberry molars 090.5
  muscle 095.6
  myocardium 093.82
  myositis 095.6
  nasal sinus 095.8
  neonatorum NEC (*see also* Syphilis, congenital) 090.9
  nerve palsy (any cranial nerve) 094.89
  nervous system, central 094.9
  neuritis 095.8
    acoustic nerve 094.86
  neurorecidive of retina 094.83
  neuroretinitis 094.85
  newborn (*see also* Syphilis, congenital) 090.9
  nodular superficial 095.8
  nonvenereal, endemic 104.0
  nose 095.8
    saddle back deformity 090.5
    septum 095.8
      perforated 095.8
  occlusive arterial disease 093.89
  ophthalmic 095.8 *[363.13]*

Syphilis, syphilitic — *continued*
ophthalmoplegia 094.89
optic nerve (atrophy) (neuritis) (papilla) 094.84
orbit (late) 095.8
orchitis 095.8
organic 097.9
osseous (late) 095.5
osteochondritis (congenital) 090.0
osteoporosis 095.5
ovary 095.8
oviduct 095.8
palate 095.8
  gumma 095.8
  perforated 090.5
pancreas (late) 095.8
pancreatitis 095.8
paralysis 094.89
  general 094.1
  juvenile 090.40
paraplegia 094.89
paresis (general) 094.1
  juvenile 090.40
paresthesia 094.89
Parkinson's disease or syndrome 094.82
paroxysmal tachycardia 093.89
pemphigus (congenital) 090.0
penis 091.0
  chancre 091.0
  late 095.8
pericardium 093.81
perichondritis, larynx 095.8
periosteum 095.5
  congenital 090.0
  early 091.61
  secondary 091.61
peripheral nerve 095.8
petrous bone (late) 095.5
pharynx 095.8
  secondary 091.3
pituitary (gland) 095.8
placenta 095.8
pleura (late) 095.8
pneumonia, white 090.0
pontine (lesion) 094.89
portal vein 093.89
primary NEC 091.2
  anal 091.1
  and secondary (*see also* Syphilis, secondary) 091.9
  cardiovascular 093.9
  central nervous system 094.9
  extragenital chancre NEC 091.2
  fingers 091.2
  genital 091.0
  lip 091.2
  specified site NEC 091.2
  tonsils 091.2
prostate 095.8
psychosis (intracranial gumma) 094.89
ptosis (eyelid) 094.89
pulmonary (late) 095.1
  artery 093.89
pulmonum 095.1
pyelonephritis 095.4
recently acquired, symptomatic NEC 091.89
rectum 095.8
respiratory tract 095.8
retina
  late 094.83
  neurorecidive 094.83
retrobulbar neuritis 094.85
salpingitis 095.8
sclera (late) 095.0
sclerosis
  cerebral 094.89
  coronary 093.89
  multiple 094.89
  subacute 094.89
scotoma (central) 095.8
scrotum 095.8
secondary (and primary) 091.9
  adenopathy 091.4
  anus 091.3
  bone 091.61
  cardiovascular 093.9
  central nervous system 094.9

Syphilis, syphilitic — *continued*
secondary — *continued*
  chorioretinitis, choroiditis 091.51
  hepatitis 091.62
  liver 091.62
  lymphadenitis 091.4
  meningitis, acute 091.81
  mouth 091.3
  mucous membranes 091.3
  periosteum 091.61
  periostitis 091.61
  pharynx 091.3
  relapse (treated) (untreated) 091.7
  skin 091.3
  specified form NEC 091.89
  tonsil 091.3
  ulcer 091.3
  viscera 091.69
  vulva 091.3
seminal vesicle (late) 095.8
seronegative
  with signs or symptoms — *see* Syphilis, by site or stage
seropositive
  with signs or symptoms — *see* Syphilis, by site and stage
  follow-up of latent syphilis — *see* Syphilis, latent
  only finding — *see* Syphilis, latent
seventh nerve (paralysis) 094.89
sinus 095.8
sinusitis 095.8
skeletal system 095.5
skin (early) (secondary) (with ulceration) 091.3
  late or tertiary 095.8
small intestine 095.8
spastic spinal paralysis 094.0
spermatic cord (late) 095.8
spinal (cord) 094.89
  with
    paresis 094.1
    tabes 094.0
spleen 095.8
splenomegaly 095.8
spondylitis 095.5
staphyloma 095.8
stigmata (congenital) 090.5
stomach 095.8
synovium (late) 095.7
tabes dorsalis (early) (late) 094.0
  juvenile 090.40
tabetic type 094.0
  juvenile 090.40
taboparesis 094.1
  juvenile 090.40
tachycardia 093.89
tendon (late) 095.7
tertiary 097.0
  with symptoms 095.8
  cardiovascular 093.9
  central nervous system 094.9
  multiple NEC 095.8
  specified site NEC 095.8
testis 095.8
thorax 095.8
throat 095.8
thymus (gland) 095.8
thyroid (late) 095.8
tongue 095.8
tonsil (lingual) 095.8
  primary 091.2
  secondary 091.3
trachea 095.8
tricuspid valve 093.23
tumor, brain 094.89
tunica vaginalis (late) 095.8
ulcer (any site) (early) (secondary) 091.3
  late 095.9
  perforating 095.9
    foot 094.0
urethra (stricture) 095.8
urogenital 095.8
uterus 095.8
uveal tract (secondary) 091.50
  late 095.8 *[363.13]*
uveitis (secondary) 091.50

Syphilis, syphilitic — *continued*
uveitis — *continued*
  late 095.8 *[363.13]*
uvula (late) 095.8
  perforated 095.8
vagina 091.0
  late 095.8
valvulitis NEC 093.20
vascular 093.89
  brain or cerebral 094.89
  vein 093.89
    cerebral 094.89
ventriculi 095.8
vesicae urinariae 095.8
viscera (abdominal) 095.2
  secondary 091.69
vitreous (hemorrhage) (opacities) 095.8
vulva 091.0
  late 095.8
  secondary 091.3
Syphiloma 095.9
  cardiovascular system 093.9
  central nervous system 094.9
  circulatory system 093.9
  congenital 090.5
Syphilophobia 300.29
Syringadenoma (M8400/0) — *see also* Neoplasm, skin, benign
  papillary (M8406/0) — *see* Neoplasm, skin, benign
Syringobulbia 336.0
Syringocarcinoma (M8400/3) — *see* Neoplasm, skin, malignant
Syringocystadenoma (M8400/0) — *see also* Neoplasm, skin, benign
  papillary (M8406/0) — *see* Neoplasm, skin, benign
Syringocystoma (M8407/0) — *see* Neoplasm, skin, benign
Syringoma (M8407/0) — *see also* Neoplasm, skin, benign
  chondroid (M8940/0) — *see* Neoplasm, by site, benign
Syringomyelia 336.0
Syringomyelitis 323.9
  late effect — *see* category 326
Syringomyelocele — *see also* Spina bifida 741.9 ☑
Syringopontia 336.0
  disease, combined — *see* Degeneration, combined
  fibrosclerosing syndrome 710.8
  inflammatory response syndrome (SIRS) 995.90
    due to
      infectious process 995.91
        with organ dysfunction 995.92
      non-infectious process 995.93
        with organ dysfunction 995.94
  lupus erythematosus 710.0
    inhibitor 286.5
System, systemic — *see also* condition
  disease, combined — *see* Degeneration, combined
  fibrosclerosing syndrome 710.8
  inflammatory response syndrome (SIRS) 995.90
    due to
      infectious process 995.91
        with acute organ dysfunction 995.92
      non-infectious process 995.93
        with acute organ dysfunction 995.94
  lupus erythematosus 710.0
    inhibitor 286.5

■ **T** ■

Tab — *see* Tag
Tabacism 989.84
Tabacosis 989.84
Tabardillo 080
  flea-borne 081.0
  louse-borne 080
Tabes, tabetic
  with
    central nervous system syphilis 094.0
    Charcôt's joint 094.0 *[713.5]*

Tabes, tabetic — *continued*
with — *continued*
  cord bladder 094.0
  crisis, viscera (any) 094.0
  paralysis, general 094.1
  paresis (general) 094.1
  perforating ulcer 094.0
arthropathy 094.0 *[713.5]*
bladder 094.0
bone 094.0
cerebrospinal 094.0
congenital 090.40
conjugal 094.0
dorsalis 094.0
  neurosyphilis 094.0
early 094.0
juvenile 090.40
latent 094.0
mesenterica (*see also* Tuberculosis) 014.8 ☑
paralysis insane, general 094.1
peripheral (nonsyphilitic) 799.89
spasmodic 094.0
  not dorsal or dorsalis 343.9
syphilis (cerebrospinal) 094.0
Taboparalysis 094.1
Taboparesis (remission) 094.1
  with
    Charcôt's joint 094.1 *[713.5]*
    cord bladder 094.1
    perforating ulcer 094.1
  juvenile 090.40
Tache noir 923.20
Tachyalimentation 579.3
Tachyarrhythmia, tachyrhythmia — *see also* Tachycardia
  paroxysmal with sinus bradycardia 427.81
Tachycardia 785.0
atrial 427.89
auricular 427.89
AV nodal re-entry (re-entrant) 427.89
junctional ectopic 427.0
newborn 779.82
nodal 427.89
  nonparoxysmal atrioventricular 426.89
nonparoxysmal atrioventricular (nodal) 426.89
nonsustained 427.2
paroxysmal 427.2
  with sinus bradycardia 427.81
  atrial (PAT) 427.0
    psychogenic 316 *[427.0]*
  atrioventricular (AV) 427.0
    psychogenic 316 *[427.0]*
  essential 427.2
  junctional 427.0
  nodal 427.0
  psychogenic 316 *[427.2]*
    atrial 316 *[427.0]*
    supraventricular 316 *[427.0]*
    ventricular 316 *[427.1]*
  supraventricular 427.0
    psychogenic 316 *[427.0]*
  ventricular 427.1
    psychogenic 316 *[427.1]*
postoperative 997.1
psychogenic 306.2
sick sinus 427.81
sinoauricular 427.89
sinus 427.89
supraventricular 427.89
sustained 427.2
  supraventricular 427.0
  ventricular 427.1
ventricular (paroxysmal) 427.1
  psychogenic 316 *[427.1]*
Tachygastria 536.8
Tachypnea 786.06
hysterical 300.11
newborn (idiopathic) (transitory) 770.6
psychogenic 306.1
transitory, of newborn 770.6
Taenia (infection) (infestation) — *see also* Infestation, taenia 123.3
diminuta 123.6
echinococcal infestation (*see also* Echinococcus) 122.9
nana 123.6

☑ Additional Digit Required — Refer to the Tabular List for Digit Selection   ▽ Subterms under main terms may continue to next column or page

266 — Volume 2   ►◄ Revised Text   ● New Line   ▲ Revised Code   2010 ICD-9-CM

☑ Additional Digit Required — Refer to the Tabular List for Digit Selection   ▥ Subterms under main terms may continue to next column or page

2010 ICD-9-CM   ▶◀ Revised Text   ● New Line   ▲ Revised Code   October 2009 • Volume 2 — 267

Temper tantrum (childhood) — see also Disturbance, conduct 312.1 ☑
Temple — see condition
Temporal — see also condition
    lobe syndrome 310.0
Temporomandibular joint-pain-dysfunction syndrome 524.60
Temporosphenoidal — see condition
Tendency
    bleeding (see also Defect, coagulation) 286.9
    homosexual, ego-dystonic 302.0
    paranoid 301.0
    suicide 300.9
Tenderness
    abdominal (generalized) (localized) 789.6 ☑
        rebound 789.6 ☑
    skin 782.0
Tendinitis, tendonitis — see also Tenosynovitis 726.90
    Achilles 726.71
    adhesive 726.90
        shoulder 726.0
    calcific 727.82
        shoulder 726.11
    gluteal 726.5
    patellar 726.64
    peroneal 726.79
    pes anserinus 726.61
    psoas 726.5
    tibialis (anterior) (posterior) 726.72
    trochanteric 726.5
Tendon — see condition
Tendosynovitis — see Tenosynovitis
Tendovaginitis — see Tenosynovitis
Tenesmus 787.99
    rectal 787.99
    vesical 788.99
Tenia — see Taenia
Teniasis — see Taeniasis
Tennis elbow 726.32
Tenonitis — see also Tenosynovitis
    eye (capsule) 376.04
Tenontosynovitis — see Tenosynovitis
Tenontothecitis — see Tenosynovitis
Tenophyte 727.9
Tenosynovitis (see also Synovitis) 727.00
    adhesive 726.90
        shoulder 726.0
    ankle 727.06
    bicipital (calcifying) 726.12
    buttock 727.09
    due to crystals — see Arthritis, due to crystals
    elbow 727.09
    finger 727.05
    foot 727.06
    gonococcal 098.51
    hand 727.05
    hip 727.09
    knee 727.09
    radial styloid 727.04
    shoulder 726.10
        adhesive 726.0
    specified NEC 727.09
    spine 720.1
    supraspinatus 726.10
    toe 727.06
    tuberculous — see Tuberculosis, tenosynovitis
    wrist 727.05
Tenovaginitis — see Tenosynovitis
Tension
    arterial, high (see also Hypertension) 401.9
        without diagnosis of hypertension 796.2
    headache 307.81
    intraocular (elevated) 365.00
    nervous 799.21 ▲
    ocular (elevated) 365.00
    pneumothorax 512.0
        iatrogenic 512.1
        postoperative 512.1
        spontaneous 512.0
    premenstrual 625.4
    state 300.9
Tentorium — see condition
Teratencephalus 759.89
Teratism 759.7

Teratoblastoma (malignant) (M9080/3) — see Neoplasm, by site, malignant
Teratocarcinoma (M9081/3) — see also Neoplasm, by site, malignant
    liver 155.0
Teratoma (solid) (M9080/1) — see also Neoplasm, by site, uncertain behavior
    adult (cystic) (M9080/0) — see Neoplasm, by site, benign
    and embryonal carcinoma, mixed (M9081/3) — see Neoplasm, by site, malignant
    benign (M9080/0) — see Neoplasm, by site, benign
    combined with choriocarcinoma (M9101/3) — see Neoplasm, by site, malignant
    cystic (adult) (M9080/0) — see Neoplasm, by site, benign
    differentiated type (M9080/0) — see Neoplasm, by site, benign
    embryonal (M9080/3) (see also Neoplasm, by site, malignant)
        liver 155.0
    fetal
        sacral, causing fetopelvic disproportion 653.7 ☑
    immature (M9080/3) — see Neoplasm, by site, malignant
    liver (M9080/3) 155.0
        adult, benign, cystic, differentiated type or mature (M9080/0) 211.5
    malignant (M9080/3) (see also Neoplasm, by site, malignant)
        anaplastic type (M9082/3) — see Neoplasm, by site, malignant
        intermediate type (M9083/3) — see Neoplasm, by site, malignant
        liver (M9080/3) 155.0
        trophoblastic (M9102/3)
            specified site — see Neoplasm, by site, malignant
            unspecified site 186.9
        undifferentiated type (M9082/3) — see Neoplasm, by site, malignant
    mature (M9080/0) — see Neoplasm, by site, benign
        malignant (M9080/3) — see Neoplasm, by site, malignant
    ovary (M9080/0) 220
        embryonal, immature, or malignant (M9080/3) 183.0
    suprasellar (M9080/3) — see Neoplasm, by site, malignant
    testis (M9080/3) 186.9
        adult, benign, cystic, differentiated type or mature (M9080/0) 222.0
        undescended 186.0
Terminal care V66.7
Termination
    anomalous (see also Malposition, congenital)
        portal vein 747.49
        right pulmonary vein 747.42
    pregnancy (legal) (therapeutic) — see Abortion, legal 635.9 ☑
        fetus NEC 779.6
        illegal (see also Abortion, illegal) 636.9 ☑
Ternidens diminutus infestation 127.7
Terrors, night (child) 307.46
Terry's syndrome (see also Retinopathy of prematurity) 362.21
Tertiary — see condition
Tessellated fundus, retina (tigroid) 362.89
Test(s)
    adequacy
        hemodialysis V56.31
        peritoneal dialysis V56.32
    AIDS virus V72.69 ▲
    allergen V72.7
    bacterial disease NEC (see also Screening, by name of disease) V74.9
    basal metabolic rate V72.69 ▲
    blood
        alcohol V70.4 ●
        drug V70.4 ●
            for therapeutic drug monitoring V58.83 ●

Test(s) — continued
    blood — continued
        for routine general physical examination ●
            V72.62 ●
        prior to treatment or procedure V72.63 ●
        typing V72.86 ●
            Rh typing V72.86 ●
    developmental, infant or child V20.2
    Dick V74.8
    fertility V26.21
    genetic
        female V26.32
        for genetic disease carrier status
            female V26.31
            male V26.34
        male V26.39
    hearing V72.19
        following failed hearing screening V72.11
        routine, for infant and child V20.2 ●
    HIV V72.69
    human immunodeficiency virus V72.69 ▲
    immunity status V72.61 ●
    Kveim V82.89
    laboratory V72.60 ▲
        for medicolegal reason V70.4
        ordered as part of a routine general medical examination V72.62 ●
        pre-operative V72.63 ●
        pre-procedural V72.63 ●
        specified NEC V72.69 ●
    male partner of habitual aborter V26.35
    Mantoux (for tuberculosis) V74.1
    mycotic organism V75.4
    nuchal translucency V28.89
    parasitic agent NEC V75.8
    paternity V70.4
    peritoneal equilibration V56.32
    pregnancy
        negative result V72.41
        positive result V72.42
            first pregnancy V72.42
        unconfirmed V72.40
    preoperative V72.84
        cardiovascular V72.81
        respiratory V72.82
        specified NEC V72.83
    procreative management NEC V26.29
        genetic disease carrier status
            female V26.31
            male V26.34
    Rh typing V72.86
    sarcoidosis V82.89
    Schick V74.3
    Schultz-Charlton V74.8
    skin, diagnostic
        allergy V72.7
        bacterial agent NEC (see also Screening, by name of disease) V74.9
        Dick V74.8
        hypersensitivity V72.7
        Kveim V82.89
        Mantoux V74.1
        mycotic organism V75.4
        parasitic agent NEC V75.8
        sarcoidosis V82.89
        Schick V74.3
        Schultz-Charlton V74.8
        tuberculin V74.1
    specified type NEC V72.85
    tuberculin V74.1
    vision V72.0
        routine, for infant and child V20.2 ●
    Wassermann
        positive (see also Serology for syphilis, positive) 097.1
        false 795.6
Testicle, testicular, testis — see also condition
    feminization (syndrome) 259.51
Tetanus, tetanic (cephalic) (convulsions) 037
    with
        abortion — see Abortion, by type, with sepsis
        ectopic pregnancy (see also categories 633.0–633.9) 639.0
        molar pregnancy — see categories 630–632 639.0

Tetanus, tetanic — continued
    following
        abortion 639.0
        ectopic or molar pregnancy 639.0
    inoculation V03.7
        reaction (due to serum) — see Complications, vaccination
    neonatorum 771.3
    puerperal, postpartum, childbirth 670.8 ☑ ▲
Tetany, tetanic 781.7
    alkalosis 276.3
    associated with rickets 268.0
    convulsions 781.7
        hysterical 300.11
    functional (hysterical) 300.11
    hyperkinetic 781.7
        hysterical 300.11
    hyperpnea 786.01
        hysterical 300.11
        psychogenic 306.1
    hyperventilation 786.01
        hysterical 300.11
        psychogenic 306.1
    hypocalcemic, neonatal 775.4
    hysterical 300.11
    neonatal 775.4
    parathyroid (gland) 252.1
    parathyroprival 252.1
    postoperative 252.1
    postthyroidectomy 252.1
    pseudotetany 781.7
        hysterical 300.11
    psychogenic 306.1
        specified as conversion reaction 300.11
Tetralogy of Fallot 745.2
Tetraplegia — see Quadriplegia
Thailand hemorrhagic fever 065.4
Thalassanemia 282.49
Thalassemia (alpha) (beta) (disease) (Hb-C) (Hb-D) (Hb-E) (Hb-H) (Hb-I) (high fetal gene) (high fetal hemoglobin) (intermedia) (major) (minima) (minor) (mixed) (trait) (with other hemoglobinopathy) 282.49
    Hb-S (without crisis) 282.41
        with
            crisis 282.42
            vaso-occlusive pain 282.42
    sickle-cell (without crisis) 282.41
        with
            crisis 282.42
            vaso-occlusive pain 282.42
Thalassemic variants 282.49
Thaysen-Gee disease (nontropical sprue) 579.0
Thecoma (M8600/0) 220
    malignant (M8600/3) 183.0
Thelarche, precocious 259.1
Thelitis 611.0
    puerperal, postpartum 675.0 ☑
Therapeutic — see condition
Therapy V57.9
    blood transfusion, without reported diagnosis V58.2
    breathing V57.0
    chemotherapy, antineoplastic V58.11
        fluoride V07.31
        prophylactic NEC V07.39
    dialysis (intermittent) (treatment)
        extracorporeal V56.0
        peritoneal V56.8
        renal V56.0
        specified type NEC V56.8
    exercise NEC V57.1
        breathing V57.0
    extracorporeal dialysis (renal) V56.0
    fluoride prophylaxis V07.31
    hemodialysis V56.0
    hormone replacement (postmenopausal) V07.4
    immunotherapy antineoplastic V58.12
    long term oxygen therapy V46.2
    occupational V57.21
    orthoptic V57.4
    orthotic V57.81
    peritoneal dialysis V56.8
    physical NEC V57.1

Therapy — *continued*
  postmenopausal hormone replacement V07.4
  radiation V58.0
  speech ▶(-language)◀ V57.3
  vocational V57.22
Thermalgesia 782.0
Thermalgia 782.0
Thermanalgesia 782.0
Thermanesthesia 782.0
Thermic — *see condition*
Thermography (abnormal) 793.99
  breast 793.89
Thermoplegia 992.0
Thesaurismosis
  amyloid 277.39
  bilirubin 277.4
  calcium 275.40
  cystine 270.0
  glycogen (*see also* Disease, glycogen storage) 271.0
  kerasin 272.7
  lipoid 272.7
  melanin 255.41
  phosphatide 272.7
  urate 274.9
Thiaminic deficiency 265.1
  with beriberi 265.0
Thibierge-Weissenbach syndrome (cutaneous systemic sclerosis) 710.1
Thickened endometrium 793.5
Thickening
  bone 733.99
    extremity 733.99
  breast 611.79
  hymen 623.3
  larynx 478.79
  nail 703.8
    congenital 757.5
  periosteal 733.99
  pleura (*see also* Pleurisy) 511.0
  skin 782.8
  subepiglottic 478.79
  tongue 529.8
  valve, heart — *see* Endocarditis
Thiele syndrome 724.6
Thigh — *see condition*
Thinning vertebra — *see also* Osteoporosis 733.00
Thirst, excessive 783.5
  due to deprivation of water 994.3
Thomsen's disease 359.22
Thomson's disease (congenital poikiloderma) 757.33
Thoracic — *see also* condition
  kidney 753.3
  outlet syndrome 353.0
  stomach — *see* Hernia, diaphragm
Thoracogastroschisis (congenital) 759.89
Thoracopagus 759.4
Thoracoschisis 756.3
Thoracoscopic surgical procedure converted to open procedure V64.42
Thorax — *see* condition
Thorn's syndrome — *see also* Disease, renal 593.9
Thornwaldt's, Tornwaldt's
  bursitis (pharyngeal) 478.29
  cyst 478.26
  disease (pharyngeal bursitis) 478.29
Thorson-Biörck syndrome (malignant carcinoid) 259.2
Threadworm (infection) (infestation) 127.4
Threatened
  abortion or miscarriage 640.0 ☑
    with subsequent abortion (*see also* Abortion, spontaneous) 634.9 ☑
    affecting fetus 762.1
    labor 644.1 ☑
      affecting fetus or newborn 761.8
      premature 644.0 ☑
    miscarriage 640.0 ☑
      affecting fetus 762.1
  premature
    delivery 644.2 ☑
      affecting fetus or newborn 761.8
    labor 644.0 ☑

Threatened — *continued*
  premature — *continued*
    labor — *continued*
      before 22 completed weeks gestation 640.0 ☑
Three-day fever 066.0
Threshers' lung 495.0
Thrix annulata (congenital) 757.4
Throat — *see* condition
Thrombasthenia (Glanzmann's) (hemorrhagic) (hereditary) 287.1
Thromboangiitis 443.1
  obliterans (general) 443.1
    cerebral 437.1
    vessels
      brain 437.1
      spinal cord 437.1
Thromboarteritis — *see* Arteritis
Thromboasthenia (Glanzmann's) (hemorrhagic) (hereditary) 287.1
Thrombocytasthenia (Glanzmann's) 287.1
Thrombocythemia (primary) (M9962/1) 238.71
  essential 238.71
  hemorrhagic 238.71
  idiopathic (hemorrhagic) (M9962/1) 238.71
Thrombocytopathy (dystrophic) (granulopenic) 287.1
Thrombocytopenia, thrombocytopenic 287.5
  with
    absent radii (TAR) syndrome
    giant hemangioma
  amegakaryocytic, congenital 287.33
  congenital 287.33
  cyclic 287.39
  dilutional 287.4
  due to
    drugs 287.4
    extracorporeal circulation of blood 287.4
    massive blood transfusion 287.4
    platelet alloimmunization 287.4
  essential 287.30
  fetal 678.0 ☑
  heparin-induced (HIT) 289.84
  hereditary 287.33
  Kasabach-Merritt 287.39
  neonatal, transitory 776.1
    due to
      exchange transfusion 776.1
      idiopathic maternal thrombocytopenia 776.1
      isoimmunization 776.1
  primary 287.30
  puerperal, postpartum 666.3 ☑
  purpura (*see also* Purpura, thrombocytopenic) 287.30
    thrombotic 446.6
  secondary 287.4
  sex-linked 287.39
Thrombocytosis 238.71
  essential 238.71
  primary 238.71
Thromboembolism — *see* Embolism
Thrombopathy (Bernard-Soulier) 287.1
  constitutional 286.4
  Willebrand-Jürgens (angiohemophilia) 286.4
Thrombopenia — *see also* Thrombocytopenia 287.5
Thrombophlebitis 451.9
  antecubital vein 451.82
  antepartum (superficial) 671.2 ☑
    affecting fetus or newborn 760.3
    deep 671.3 ☑
  arm 451.89
    deep 451.83
    superficial 451.82
  breast, superficial 451.89
  cavernous (venous) sinus — *see* Thrombophlebitis, intracranial venous sinus
  cephalic vein 451.82
  cerebral (sinus) (vein) 325
    late effect — *see* category 326
    nonpyogenic 437.6
      in pregnancy or puerperium 671.5 ☑
      late effect — *see* Late effect(s) (of) cerebrovascular disease

Thrombophlebitis — *continued*
  due to implanted device — *see* Complications, due to (presence of) any device, implant or graft classified to 996.0–996.5 NEC
  during or resulting from a procedure NEC 997.2
  femoral 451.11
  femoropopliteal 451.19
  following infusion, perfusion, or transfusion 999.2
  hepatic (vein) 451.89
  idiopathic, recurrent 453.1
  iliac vein 451.81
  iliofemoral 451.11
  intracranial venous sinus (any) 325
    late effect — *see* category 326
    nonpyogenic 437.6
      in pregnancy or puerperium 671.5 ☑
      late effect — *see* Late effect(s) (of) cerebrovascular disease
  jugular vein 451.89
  lateral (venous) sinus — *see* Thrombophlebitis, intracranial venous sinus
  leg 451.2
    deep (vessels) 451.19
      femoral vein 451.11
      specified vessel NEC 451.19
    superficial (vessels) 451.0
      femoral vein 451.11
  longitudinal (venous) sinus — *see* Thrombophlebitis, intracranial venous sinus
  lower extremity 451.2
    deep (vessels) 451.19
      femoral vein 451.11
      specified vessel NEC 451.19
    superficial (vessels) 451.0
  migrans, migrating 453.1
  pelvic
    with
      abortion — *see* Abortion, by type, with sepsis
      ectopic pregnancy (*see also* categories 633.0–633.9) 639.0
      molar pregnancy (*see also* categories 630–632) 639.0
    following
      abortion 639.0
      ectopic or molar pregnancy 639.0
    puerperal 671.4 ☑
  popliteal vein 451.19
  portal (vein) 572.1
  postoperative 997.2
  pregnancy (superficial) 671.2 ☑
    affecting fetus or newborn 760.3
    deep 671.3 ☑
  puerperal, postpartum, childbirth (extremities) (superficial) 671.2 ☑
    deep 671.4 ☑
    pelvic 671.4 ☑
    septic 670.3 ☑   ●
    specified site NEC 671.5 ☑
  radial vein 451.83
  saphenous (greater) (lesser) 451.0
  sinus (intracranial) — *see* Thrombophlebitis, intracranial venous sinus
  specified site NEC 451.89
  tibial vein 451.19
Thrombosis, thrombotic (marantic) (multiple) (progressive) (vein) (vessel) 453.9
  with childbirth or during the puerperium — *see* Thrombosis, puerperal, postpartum
  antepartum — *see* Thrombosis, pregnancy
  aorta, aortic 444.1
    abdominal 444.0
    bifurcation 444.0
    saddle 444.0
    terminal 444.0
    thoracic 444.1
    valve — *see* Endocarditis, aortic
  apoplexy (*see also* Thrombosis, brain) 434.0 ☑
    late effect — *see* Late effect(s) (of) cerebrovascular disease
  appendix, septic — *see* Appendicitis, acute
  arteriolar-capillary platelet, disseminated 446.6
  artery, arteries (postinfectional) 444.9

Thrombosis, thrombotic — *continued*
  artery, arteries — *continued*
    auditory, internal 433.8 ☑
    basilar (*see also* Occlusion, artery, basilar) 433.0 ☑
    carotid (common) (internal) (*see also* Occlusion, artery, carotid) 433.1 ☑
      with other precerebral artery 433.3 ☑
    cerebellar (anterior inferior) (posterior inferior) (superior) 433.8 ☑
    cerebral (*see also* Thrombosis, brain) 434.0 ☑
    choroidal (anterior) 433.8 ☑
    communicating posterior 433.8 ☑
    coronary (*see also* Infarct, myocardium) 410.9 ☑
      without myocardial infarction 411.81
      due to syphilis 093.89
      healed or specified as old 412
    extremities 444.22
      lower 444.22
      upper 444.21
    femoral 444.22
    hepatic 444.89
    hypophyseal 433.8 ☑
    meningeal, anterior or posterior 433.8 ☑
    mesenteric (with gangrene) 557.0
    ophthalmic (*see also* Occlusion, retina) 362.30
    pontine 433.8 ☑
    popliteal 444.22
    precerebral — *see* Occlusion, artery, precerebral NEC
    pulmonary 415.19
      iatrogenic 415.11
      personal history of V12.51   ●
      postoperative 415.11
      septic 415.12
    renal 593.81
    retinal (*see also* Occlusion, retina) 362.30
    specified site NEC 444.89
    spinal, anterior or posterior 433.8 ☑
    traumatic (complication) (early) (*see also* Injury, blood vessel, by site) 904.9
    vertebral (*see also* Occlusion, artery, vertebral) 433.2 ☑
      with other precerebral artery 433.3 ☑
  atrial (endocardial) 424.90
    without endocarditis 429.89
    due to syphilis 093.89
  auricular (*see also* Infarct, myocardium) 410.9 ☑
  axillary ▶(acute)◀ (vein) 453.84   ▲
    chronic 453.74   ●
    personal history of V12.51   ●
  basilar (artery) (*see also* Occlusion, artery, basilar) 433.0 ☑
  bland NEC 453.9
  brain (artery) (stem) 434.0 ☑
    due to syphilis 094.89
    iatrogenic 997.02
    late effect — *see* Late effect(s) (of) cerebrovascular disease
    postoperative 997.02
    puerperal, postpartum, childbirth 674.0 ☑
    sinus (*see also* Thrombosis, intracranial venous sinus) 325
  capillary 448.9
    arteriolar, generalized 446.6
  cardiac (*see also* Infarct, myocardium) 410.9 ☑
    due to syphilis 093.89
    healed or specified as old 412
    valve — *see* Endocarditis
  carotid (artery) (common) (internal) (*see also* Occlusion, artery, carotid) 433.1 ☑
    with other precerebral artery 433.3 ☑
  cavernous sinus (venous) — *see* Thrombosis, intracranial venous sinus
  cerebellar artery (anterior inferior) (posterior inferior) (superior) 433.8 ☑
    late effect — *see* Late effect(s) (of) cerebrovascular disease
  cerebral (arteries) (*see also* Thrombosis, brain) 434.0 ☑

☑ Additional Digit Required — Refer to the Tabular List for Digit Selection   ▽ Subterms under main terms may continue to next column or page

Index | **Thrombosis, thrombotic — Thyrotoxic**

Thrombosis, thrombotic — *continued*
- cerebral (*see also* Thrombosis, brain) — *continued*
  - late effect — *see* Late effect(s) (of) cerebrovascular disese
- coronary (artery) (*see also* Infarct, myocardium) 410.9 ☑
  - without myocardial infarction 411.81
  - due to syphilis 093.89
  - healed or specified as old 412
- corpus cavernosum 607.82
- cortical (*see also* Thrombosis, brain) 434.0 ☑
- due to (presence of) any device, implant, or graft classifiable to 996.0–996.5 — *see* Complications, due to (presence of) any device, implant, or graft classified to 996.0–996.5 NEC
- effort 453.89 ▲
- endocardial — *see* Infarct, myocardium
- eye (*see also* Occlusion, retina) 362.30
- femoral (vein) 453.6
  - with inflammation or phlebitis 451.11
  - artery 444.22
  - deep 453.41
  - personal history of V12.51 ●
- genital organ, male 608.83
- heart (chamber) (*see also* Infarct, myocardium) 410.9 ☑
- hepatic (vein) 453.0
  - artery 444.89
  - infectional or septic 572.1
- iliac (vein) 453.89 ▲
  - with inflammation or phlebitis 451.81
  - artery (common) (external) (internal) 444.81
  - personal history of V12.51 ●
- inflammation, vein — *see* Thrombophlebitis
- internal carotid artery (*see also* Occlusion, artery, carotid) 433.1 ☑
  - with other precerebral artery 433.3 ☑
- intestine (with gangrene) 557.0
- intracranial (*see also* Thrombosis, brain) 434.0 ☑
  - venous sinus (any) 325
    - nonpyogenic origin 437.6
      - in pregnancy or puerperium 671.5 ☑
- intramural (*see also* Infarct, myocardium) 410.9 ☑
  - without
    - cardiac condition 429.89
    - coronary artery disease 429.89
    - myocardial infarction 429.89
  - healed or specified as old 412
- jugular (bulb)
  - external ●
    - acute 453.89 ●
    - chronic 453.79 ●
  - internal ●
    - acute 453.86 ●
    - chronic 453.76 ●
- kidney 593.81
  - artery 593.81
- lateral sinus (venous) — *see* Thrombosis, intracranial venous sinus
- leg ▶(*see also* Thrombosis, lower extremity)◀ 453.6 ▲
  - with inflammation or phlebitis — *see* Thrombophlebitis
  - deep (vessels) 453.40
    - acute 453.40 ●
      - lower distal 453.42 ●
      - upper (proximal) 453.41 ●
    - chronic 453.50 ●
      - lower (distal) 453.52 ●
      - upper (proximal) 453.51 ●
    - lower (distal) 453.42
    - upper (proximal) 453.41
  - personal history of V12.51 ●
  - superficial (vessels) 453.6 ▲
- liver (venous) 453.0
  - artery 444.89
  - infectional or septic 572.1
  - portal vein 452
- longitudinal sinus (venous) — *see* Thrombosis, intracranial venous sinus

Thrombosis, thrombotic — *continued*
- lower extremity ▶(superficial)◀ 453.6 ▲
  - deep vessels 453.40
    - acute 453.40 ●
      - calf 453.42 ●
      - distal (lower leg) 453.42 ●
      - femoral 453.41 ●
      - iliac 453.41 ●
      - lower leg 453.42 ●
      - peroneal 453.42 ●
      - popliteal 453.41 ●
      - proximal (upper leg) 453.41 ●
      - thigh 453.41 ●
      - tibial 453.42 ●
    - chronic 453.50 ●
      - calf 453.52 ●
      - distal (lower leg) 453.52 ●
      - femoral 453.51 ●
      - iliac 453.51 ●
      - lower leg 453.52 ●
      - peroneal 453.52 ●
      - popliteal 453.51 ●
      - proximal (upper leg) 453.51 ●
      - thigh 453.51 ●
      - tibial 453.52 ●
    - personal history of V12.51 ●
  - saphenous (greater) (lesser) 453.6 ●
  - superficial 453.6 ●
- lung 415.19
  - iatrogenic 415.11
  - personal history of V12.51 ●
  - postoperative 415.11
  - septic 415.12
- marantic, dural sinus 437.6
- meninges (brain) (*see also* Thrombosis, brain) 434.0 ☑
- mesenteric (artery) (with gangrene) 557.0
  - vein (inferior) (superior) 557.0
- mitral — *see* Insufficiency, mitral
- mural (heart chamber) (*see also* Infarct, myocardium) 410.9 ☑
  - without
    - cardiac condition 429.89
    - coronary artery disease 429.89
    - myocardial infarction 429.89
  - due to syphilis 093.89
  - following myocardial infarction 429.79
  - healed or specified as old 412
- omentum (with gangrene) 557.0
- ophthalmic (artery) (*see also* Occlusion, retina) 362.30
- pampiniform plexus (male) 608.83
  - female 620.8
- parietal (*see also* Infarct, myocardium) 410.9 ☑
- penis, penile 607.82
- peripheral arteries 444.22
  - lower 444.22
  - upper 444.21
- platelet 446.6
- portal 452
  - due to syphilis 093.89
  - infectional or septic 572.1
- precerebral artery (*see also* Occlusion, artery, precerebral NEC)
- pregnancy 671.2 ☑ ▲
  - deep (vein) 671.3 ☑
  - superficial (vein) 671.2 ☑
- puerperal, postpartum, childbirth 671.2 ☑ ▲
  - brain (artery) 674.0 ☑
    - venous 671.5 ☑
  - cardiac 674.8 ☑
  - cerebral (artery) 674.0 ☑
    - venous 671.5 ☑
  - deep (vein) 671.4 ☑
  - intracranial sinus (nonpyogenic) (venous) 671.5 ☑
  - pelvic 671.4 ☑
  - pulmonary (artery) 673.2 ☑
  - specified site NEC 671.5 ☑
  - superficial 671.2 ☑
- pulmonary (artery) (vein) 415.19
  - iatrogenic 415.11
  - personal history of V12.51 ●
  - postoperative 415.11
  - septic 415.12

Thrombosis, thrombotic — *continued*
- renal (artery) 593.81
  - vein 453.3
- resulting from presence of shunt or other internal prosthetic device — *see* Complications, due to (presence of) any device, implant, or graft classified to 996.0–996.5 NEC
- retina, retinal (artery) 362.30
  - arterial branch 362.32
  - central 362.31
  - partial 362.33
  - vein
    - central 362.35
    - tributary (branch) 362.36
- saphenous vein (greater) (lesser) 453.6 ●
- scrotum 608.83
- seminal vesicle 608.83
- sigmoid (venous) sinus — *see* Thrombosis, intracranial venous sinus 325
- silent NEC 453.9
- sinus, intracranial (venous) (any) (*see also* Thrombosis, intracranial venous sinus) 325
- softening, brain (*see also* Thrombosis, brain) 434.0 ☑
- specified site NEC ▶(acute)◀ 453.89 ▲
  - chronic 453.79 ●
- spermatic cord 608.83
- spinal cord 336.1
  - due to syphilis 094.89
  - in pregnancy or puerperium 671.5 ☑
  - pyogenic origin 324.1
    - late effect — *see* category 326
- spleen, splenic 289.59
  - artery 444.89
- testis 608.83
- traumatic (complication) (early) (*see also* Injury, blood vessel, by site) 904.9
- tricuspid — *see* Endocarditis, tricuspid
- tumor — *see* Neoplasm, by site
- tunica vaginalis 608.83
- umbilical cord (vessels) 663.6 ☑
  - affecting fetus or newborn 762.6
- upper extremity 453.83 ●
  - acute 453.83 ●
    - deep 453.82 ●
    - superficial 453.81 ●
  - chronic 453.73 ●
    - deep 453.72 ●
    - superficial 453.71 ●
- vas deferens 608.83
- vein
  - antecubital
    - acute 453.81 ●
    - chronic 453.71 ●
  - axillary
    - acute 453.84 ●
    - chronic 453.74 ●
  - basilic
    - acute 453.81 ●
    - chronic 453.71 ●
  - brachial
    - acute 453.82 ●
    - chronic 453.72 ●
  - brachiocephalic (innominate)
    - acute 453.87 ●
    - chronic 453.77 ●
  - cephalic
    - acute 453.81 ●
    - chronic 453.71 ●
  - deep 453.40
    - personal history of V12.51 ●
  - internal jugular
    - acute 453.86 ●
    - chronic 453.76 ●
  - lower extremity — *see* Thrombosis, lower extremity
  - personal history of V12.51 ●
  - radial
    - acute 453.82 ●
    - chronic 453.72 ●
  - saphenous (greater) (lesser) 453.6 ●
  - specified site NEC
    - acute 453.89 ●
    - chronic 453.79 ●

Thrombosis, thrombotic — *continued*
- vein — *continued*
  - subclavian ●
    - acute 453.85 ●
    - chronic 453.75 ●
  - superior vena cava
    - acute 453.87 ●
    - chronic 453.77 ●
  - thoracic
    - acute 453.87 ●
    - chronic 453.77 ●
  - ulnar
    - acute 453.82 ●
    - chronic 453.72 ●
  - upper extremity — *see* Thrombosis, upper extremity ●
  - vena cava
    - inferior 453.2 ●
      - personal history of V12.51 ●
    - superior
      - acute 453.87 ●
      - chronic 453.77 ●

Thrombus — *see* Thrombosis
Thrush 112.0
- newborn 771.7
Thumb — *see also* condition
- gamekeeper's 842.12
- sucking (child problem) 307.9
Thygeson's superficial punctate keratitis 370.21
Thymergasia — *see also* Psychosis, affective 296.80
Thymitis 254.8
Thymoma (benign) (M8580/0) 212.6
- malignant (M8580/3) 164.0
Thymus, thymic (gland) — *see* condition
Thyrocele — *see also* Goiter 240.9
Thyroglossal — *see also* condition
- cyst 759.2
- duct, persistent 759.2
Thyroid (body) (gland) — *see also* condition
- hormone resistance 246.8
- lingual 759.2
Thyroiditis 245.9
- acute (pyogenic) (suppurative) 245.0
  - nonsuppurative 245.0
- autoimmune 245.2
- chronic (nonspecific) (sclerosing) 245.8
  - fibrous 245.3
  - lymphadenoid 245.2
  - lymphocytic 245.2
  - lymphoid 245.2
- complicating pregnancy, childbirth, or puerperium 648.1 ☑
- de Quervain's (subacute granulomatous) 245.1
- fibrous (chronic) 245.3
- giant (cell) (follicular) 245.1
- granulomatous (de Quervain's) (subacute) 245.1
- Hashimoto's (struma lymphomatosa) 245.2
- iatrogenic 245.4
- invasive (fibrous) 245.3
- ligneous 245.3
- lymphocytic (chronic) 245.2
- lymphoid 245.2
- lymphomatous 245.2
- pseudotuberculous 245.1
- pyogenic 245.0
- radiation 245.4
- Riedel's (ligneous) 245.3
- subacute 245.1
- suppurative 245.0
- tuberculous (*see also* Tuberculosis) 017.5 ☑
- viral 245.1
- woody 245.3
Thyrolingual duct, persistent 759.2
Thyromegaly 240.9
Thyrotoxic
- crisis or storm (*see also* Thyrotoxicosis) 242.9 ☑
- heart failure (*see also* Thyrotoxicosis) 242.9 ☑ [425.7]

☑ Additional Digit Required — Refer to the Tabular List for Digit Selection   🔄 Subterms under main terms may continue to next column or page

270 — Volume 2 • October 2009   ▶◀ Revised Text   ● New Line   ▲ Revised Code   2010 ICD-9-CM

Thyrotoxicosis 242.9 ☑

Note — Use the following fifth-digit subclassification with category 242:

0   without mention of thyrotoxic crisis or storm

1   with mention of thyrotoxic crisis or storm

with
- goiter (diffuse) 242.0 ☑
  - adenomatous 242.3 ☑
    - multinodular 242.2 ☑
    - uninodular 242.1 ☑
  - nodular 242.3 ☑
    - multinodular 242.2 ☑
    - uninodular 242.1 ☑
- infiltrative
  - dermopathy 242.0 ☑
  - ophthalmopathy 242.0 ☑
- thyroid acropachy 242.0 ☑
- complicating pregnancy, childbirth, or puerperium 648.1 ☑

due to
- ectopic thyroid nodule 242.4 ☑
- ingestion of (excessive) thyroid material 242.8 ☑
- specified cause NEC 242.8 ☑

factitia 242.8 ☑

heart 242.9 ☑ [425.7]

neonatal (transient) 775.3

TIA (transient ischemic attack) 435.9

with transient neurologic deficit 435.9

late effect — see Late effect(s) (of) cerebrovascular disease

Tibia vara 732.4

Tic 307.20
- breathing 307.20
- child problem 307.21
- compulsive 307.22
- convulsive 307.20
- degenerative (generalized) (localized) 333.3
  - facial 351.8
- douloureux (see also Neuralgia, trigeminal) 350.1
  - atypical 350.2
- habit 307.20
  - chronic (motor or vocal) 307.22
  - transient (of childhood) 307.21
- lid 307.20
  - transient (of childhood) 307.21
- motor-verbal 307.23
- occupational 300.89
- orbicularis 307.20
  - transient (of childhood) 307.21
- organic origin 333.3
- postchoreic — see Chorea
- psychogenic 307.20
  - compulsive 307.22
- salaam 781.0
- spasm 307.20
  - chronic (motor or vocal) 307.22
  - transient (of childhood) 307.21

Tick-bite fever NEC 066.1
- African 087.1
- Colorado (virus) 066.1
- Rocky Mountain 082.0

Tick (-borne) fever NEC 066.1
- American mountain 066.1
- Colorado 066.1
- hemorrhagic NEC 065.3
  - Crimean 065.0
  - Kyasanur Forest 065.2
  - Omsk 065.1
- mountain 066.1
- nonexanthematous 066.1

Tick paralysis 989.5

Tics and spasms, compulsive 307.22

Tietze's disease or syndrome 733.6

Tight, tightness
- anus 564.89
- chest 786.59
- fascia (lata) 728.9
- foreskin (congenital) 605
- hymen 623.3
- introitus (acquired) (congenital) 623.3

Tight, tightness — continued
- rectal sphincter 564.89
- tendon 727.81
  - Achilles (heel) 727.81
- urethral sphincter 598.9

Tilting vertebra 737.9

Timidity, child 313.21

Tinea (intersecta) (tarsi) 110.9
- amiantacea 110.0
- asbestina 110.0
- barbae 110.0
- beard 110.0
- black dot 110.0
- blanca 111.2
- capitis 110.0
- corporis 110.5
- cruris 110.3
- decalvans 704.09
- flava 111.0
- foot 110.4
- furfuracea 111.0
- imbricata (Tokelau) 110.5
- lepothrix 039.0
- manuum 110.2
- microsporic (see also Dermatophytosis) 110.9
- nigra 111.1
- nodosa 111.2
- pedis 110.4
- scalp 110.0
- specified site NEC 110.8
- sycosis 110.0
- tonsurans 110.0
- trichophytic (see also Dermatophytosis) 110.9
- unguium 110.1
- versicolor 111.0

Tingling sensation — see also Disturbance, sensation 782.0

Tin-miners' lung 503

Tinnitus (aurium) 388.30
- audible 388.32
- objective 388.32
- subjective 388.31

Tipped, teeth 524.33

Tipping
- pelvis 738.6
  - with disproportion (fetopelvic) 653.0 ☑
    - affecting fetus or newborn 763.1
    - causing obstructed labor 660.1 ☑
      - affecting fetus or newborn 763.1
- teeth 524.33

Tiredness 780.79

Tissue — see condition

Tobacco
- abuse (affecting health) NEC (see also Abuse, drugs, nondependent) 305.1
- heart 989.84
- use disorder complicating pregnancy, childbirth, or the puerperium 649.0 ☑

Tobias' syndrome (carcinoma, pulmonary apex) (M8010/3) 162.3

Tocopherol deficiency 269.1

Todd's
- cirrhosis — see Cirrhosis, biliary
- paralysis (postepileptic transitory paralysis) 344.89

Toe — see condition

Toilet, artificial opening — see also Attention to, artificial, opening V55.9

Tokelau ringworm 110.5

Tollwut 071

Tolosa-Hunt syndrome 378.55

Tommaselli's disease
- correct substance properly administered 599.70
- overdose or wrong substance given or taken 961.4

Tongue — see also condition
- worms 134.1

Tongue tie 750.0

Tonic pupil 379.46

Toni-Fanconi syndrome (cystinosis) 270.0

Tonsil — see condition

Tonsillitis (acute) (catarrhal) (croupous) (follicular) (gangrenous) (infective) (lacunar) (lingual) (malignant) (membranous) (phlegmonous) (pneumococcal) (pseudomembranous) (purulent) (septic) (staphylococcal) (subacute) (suppurative) (toxic) (ulcerative) (vesicular) (viral) 463
- with influenza, flu, or grippe 487.1
- chronic 474.00
- diphtheritic (membranous) 032.0
- hypertrophic 474.00
- influenzal 487.1
- parenchymatous 475
- streptococcal 034.0
- tuberculous (see also Tuberculosis) 012.8 ☑
- Vincent's 101

Tonsillopharyngitis 465.8

Toothache 525.9

Tooth, teeth — see condition

Topagnosis 782.0

Tophi (gouty) 274.03   ▲
- ear 274.81
- heart 274.82
- specified site NEC 274.82

TORCH infection — see also Infection, congenital 760.2

Torn — see Tear, torn

Tornwaldt's bursitis (disease) (pharyngeal bursitis) 478.29
- cyst 478.26

Torpid liver 573.9

Torsion
- accessory tube 620.5
- adnexa (female) 620.5
- aorta (congenital) 747.29
  - acquired 447.1
- appendix
  - epididymis 608.24
  - testis 608.23
- bile duct 576.8
  - with calculus, choledocholithiasis or stones — see Choledocholithiasis
  - congenital 751.69
- bowel, colon, or intestine 560.2
- cervix — see Malposition, uterus
- duodenum 537.3
- dystonia — see Dystonia, torsion
- epididymis 608.24
  - appendix 608.24
- fallopian tube 620.5
- gallbladder (see also Disease, gallbladder) 575.8
  - congenital 751.69
- gastric 537.89
- hydatid of Morgagni (female) 620.5
- kidney (pedicle) 593.89
- Meckel's diverticulum (congenital) 751.0
- mesentery 560.2
- omentum 560.2
- organ or site, congenital NEC — see Anomaly, specified type NEC
- ovary (pedicle) 620.5
  - congenital 752.0
- oviduct 620.5
- penis 607.89
  - congenital 752.69
- renal 593.89
- spasm — see Dystonia, torsion
- spermatic cord 608.22
  - extravaginal 608.21
  - intravaginal 608.22
- spleen 289.59
- testicle, testis 608.20
  - appendix 608.23
- tibia 736.89
- umbilical cord — see Compression, umbilical cord
- uterus (see also Malposition, uterus) 621.6

Torticollis (intermittent) (spastic) 723.5
- congenital 754.1
  - sternomastoid 754.1
- due to birth injury 767.8
- hysterical 300.11
- ocular 781.93
- psychogenic 306.0
  - specified as conversion reaction 300.11

Torticollis — continued
- rheumatic 723.5
- rheumatoid 714.0
- spasmodic 333.83
- traumatic, current NEC 847.0

Tortuous
- artery 447.1
- fallopian tube 752.19
- organ or site, congenital NEC — see Distortion
- renal vessel (congenital) 747.62
- retina vessel (congenital) 743.58
  - acquired 362.17
- ureter 593.4
- urethra 599.84
- vein — see Varicose, vein

Torula, torular (infection) 117.5
- histolytica 117.5
- lung 117.5

Torulosis 117.5

Torus
- fracture
  - fibula 823.41
    - with tibia 823.42
  - humerus 812.49   ●
  - radius ▶(alone)◀ 813.45   ●
    - with ulna 813.47   ●
  - tibia 823.40
    - with fibula 823.42
  - ulna (alone) 813.46   ●
    - with radius 813.47   ●
- mandibularis 526.81
- palatinus 526.81

Touch, vitreous 997.99

Touraine-Solente-Golé syndrome (acropachyderma) 757.39

Touraine's syndrome (hereditary osteo-onychodysplasia) 756.89

Tourette's disease (motor-verbal tic) 307.23

Tower skull 756.0
- with exophthalmos 756.0

Toxemia 799.89
- with
  - abortion — see Abortion, by type, with toxemia
- bacterial — see Septicemia
- biliary (see also Disease, biliary) 576.8
- burn — see Burn, by site
- congenital NEC 779.89
- eclamptic 642.6 ☑
  - with pre-existing hypertension 642.7 ☑
- erysipelatous (see also Erysipelas) 035
- fatigue 799.89
- fetus or newborn NEC 779.89
- food (see also Poisoning, food) 005.9
- gastric 537.89
- gastrointestinal 558.2
- intestinal 558.2
- kidney (see also Disease, renal) 593.9
- lung 518.89
- malarial NEC (see also Malaria) 084.6
- maternal (of pregnancy), affecting fetus or newborn 760.0
- myocardial — see Myocarditis, toxic
- of pregnancy (mild) (pre-eclamptic) 642.4 ☑
  - with
    - convulsions 642.6 ☑
    - pre-existing hypertension 642.7 ☑
  - affecting fetus or newborn 760.0
  - severe 642.5 ☑
- pre-eclamptic — see Toxemia, of pregnancy
- puerperal, postpartum — see Toxemia, of pregnancy
- pulmonary 518.89
- renal (see also Disease, renal) 593.9
- septic (see also Septicemia) 038.9
- small intestine 558.2
- staphylococcal 038.10
  - aureus 038.11
  - due to food 005.0
  - specified organism NEC 038.19
- stasis 799.89
- stomach 537.89
- uremic (see also Uremia) 586
- urinary 586

Toxemica cerebropathia psychica (nonalcoholic) 294.0

☑ Additional Digit Required — Refer to the Tabular List for Digit Selection

Subterms under main terms may continue to next column or page

Toxemica cerebropathia psychica — *continued*
  alcoholic 291.1
Toxic (poisoning) — *see also* condition
  from drug or poison — *see* Table of Drugs and Chemicals
  oil syndrome 710.5
  shock syndrome 040.82
  thyroid (gland) (*see also* Thyrotoxicosis) 242.9 ☑
Toxicemia — *see* Toxemia
Toxicity
  dilantin
    asymptomatic 796.0
    symptomatic — *see* Table of Drugs and Chemicals
  drug
    asymptomatic 796.0
    symptomatic — *see* Table of Drugs and Chemicals
  fava bean 282.2
  from drug or poison
    asymptomatic 796.0
    symptomatic — *see* Table of Drugs and Chemicals
Toxicosis — *see also* Toxemia 799.89
  capillary, hemorrhagic 287.0
Toxinfection 799.89
  gastrointestinal 558.2
Toxocariasis 128.0
Toxoplasma infection, generalized 130.9
Toxoplasmosis (acquired) 130.9
  with pneumonia 130.4
  congenital, active 771.2
  disseminated (multisystemic) 130.8
  maternal
    with suspected damage to fetus affecting management of pregnancy 655.4 ☑
    affecting fetus or newborn 760.2
      manifest toxoplasmosis in fetus or newborn 771.2
  multiple sites 130.8
  multisystemic disseminated 130.8
  specified site NEC 130.7
Trabeculation, bladder 596.8
Trachea — *see* condition
Tracheitis (acute) (catarrhal) (infantile) (membranous) (plastic) (pneumococcal) (septic) (suppurative) (viral) 464.10
  with
    bronchitis 490
      acute or subacute 466.0
      chronic 491.8
      tuberculosis — *see* Tuberculosis, pulmonary
    laryngitis (acute) 464.20
      with obstruction 464.21
      chronic 476.1
      tuberculous (*see also* Tuberculosis, larynx) 012.3 ☑
    obstruction 464.11
  chronic 491.8
    with
      bronchitis (chronic) 491.8
      laryngitis (chronic) 476.1
    due to external agent — *see* Condition, respiratory, chronic, due to
  diphtheritic (membranous) 032.3
    due to external agent — *see* Inflammation, respiratory, upper, due to
  edematous 464.11
  influenzal 487.1
  streptococcal 034.0
  syphilitic 095.8
  tuberculous (*see also* Tuberculosis) 012.8 ☑
Trachelitis (nonvenereal) — *see also* Cervicitis 616.0
  trichomonal 131.09
Tracheobronchial — *see* condition
Tracheobronchitis — *see also* Bronchitis 490
  acute or subacute 466.0
    with bronchospasm or obstruction 466.0
  chronic 491.8
  influenzal 487.1
  senile 491.8

Tracheobronchomegaly (congenital) 748.3
  with bronchiectasis 494.0
    with (acute) exacerbation 494.1
  acquired 519.19
    with bronchiectasis 494.0
      with (acute) exacerbation 494.1
Tracheobronchopneumonitis — *see* Pneumonia, broncho
Tracheocele (external) (internal) 519.19
  congenital 748.3
Tracheomalacia 519.19
  congenital 748.3
Tracheopharyngitis (acute) 465.8
  chronic 478.9
    due to external agent — *see* Condition, respiratory, chronic, due to
    due to external agent — *see* Inflammation, respiratory, upper, due to
Tracheostenosis 519.19
  congenital 748.3
Tracheostomy
  attention to V55.0
  complication 519.00
  granuloma 519.09
  hemorrhage 519.09
  infection 519.01
  malfunctioning 519.02
  obstruction 519.09
  sepsis 519.01
  status V44.0
  stenosis 519.02
Trachoma, trachomatous 076.9
  active (stage) 076.1
  contraction of conjunctiva 076.1
  dubium 076.0
  healed or late effect 139.1
  initial (stage) 076.0
  Türck's (chronic catarrhal laryngitis) 476.0
Trachyphonia 784.49
Training
  insulin pump V65.46
  orthoptic V57.4
  orthotic V57.81
Train sickness 994.6
Trait
  hemoglobin
    abnormal NEC 282.7
      with thalassemia 282.49
    C (*see also* Disease, hemoglobin, C) 282.7
      with elliptocytosis 282.7
    S (Hb-S) 282.5
    Lepore 282.49
    with other abnormal hemoglobin NEC 282.49
  paranoid 301.0
  sickle-cell 282.5
    with
      elliptocytosis 282.5
      spherocytosis 282.5
Traits, paranoid 301.0
Tramp V60.0
Trance 780.09
  hysterical 300.13
Transaminasemia 790.4
Transfusion, blood
  without reported diagnosis V58.2
  donor V59.01
    stem cells V59.02
  fetal twin to twin 678.0 ☑
  incompatible
    ABO 999.6 ●
    minor blood group 999.89 ●
  reaction or complication — *see* Complications, transfusion
  related acute lung injury (TRALI) 518.7
  syndrome
    fetomaternal 772.0
    twin-to-twin
      blood loss (donor twin) 772.0
      recipient twin 776.4
  twin to twin fetal 678.0 ☑
Transient — *see also* condition
  alteration of awareness 780.02
  blindness 368.12
  deafness (ischemic) 388.02
  global amnesia 437.7

Transient — *see also* condition — *continued*
  hyperglycemia (post-procedural) 790.29 ●
  hypoglycemia (post-procedural) 251.2 ●
  person (homeless) NEC V60.0
Transitional, lumbosacral joint of vertebra 756.19
Translocation
  autosomes NEC 758.5
    13-15 758.1
    16-18 758.2
    21 or 22 758.0
    balanced in normal individual 758.4
    D₁ 758.1
    E₃ 758.2
    G 758.0
  balanced autosomal in normal individual 758.4
  chromosomes NEC 758.89
  Down's syndrome 758.0
Translucency, iris 364.53
Transmission of chemical substances through the placenta (affecting fetus or newborn) 760.70
  alcohol 760.71
  anticonvulsants 760.77
  antifungals 760.74
  anti-infective agents 760.74
  antimetabolics 760.78
  cocaine 760.75
  "crack" 760.75
  diethylstilbestrol [DES] 760.76
  hallucinogenic agents 760.73
  medicinal agents NEC 760.79
  narcotics 760.72
  obstetric anesthetic or analgesic drug 763.5
  specified agent NEC 760.79
  suspected, affecting management of pregnancy 655.5 ☑
Transplant(ed)
  bone V42.4
    marrow V42.81
  complication (*see also* Complications, due to (presence of) any device, implant, or graft classified to 996.0–996.5 NEC)
    bone marrow 996.85
    corneal graft NEC 996.79
      infection or inflammation 996.69
      reaction 996.51
      rejection 996.51
    organ (failure) (immune or nonimmune cause) (infection) (rejection) 996.80
      bone marrow 996.85
      heart 996.83
      intestines 996.87
      kidney 996.81
      liver 996.82
      lung 996.84
      pancreas 996.86
      specified NEC 996.89
    previously removed due to complication, failure, rejection or infection V45.87
    removal status V45.87
    skin NEC 996.79
      infection or inflammation 996.69
      rejection 996.52
        artificial 996.55
        decellularized allodermis 996.55
  cornea V42.5
  hair V50.0
  heart V42.1
    valve V42.2
  intestine V42.84
  kidney V42.0
  liver V42.7
  lung V42.6
  organ V42.9
    specified NEC V42.89
  pancreas V42.83
  peripheral stem cells V42.82
  skin V42.3
  stem cells, peripheral V42.82
  tissue V42.9
    specified NEC V42.89
Transplants, ovarian, endometrial 617.1
Transposed — *see* Transposition
Transposition (congenital) — *see also* Malposition, congenital

Transposition — *see also* Malposition, congenital — *continued*
  abdominal viscera 759.3
  aorta (dextra) 745.11
  appendix 751.5
  arterial trunk 745.10
  colon 751.5
  great vessels (complete) 745.10
    both originating from right ventricle 745.11
    corrected 745.12
    double outlet right ventricle 745.11
    incomplete 745.11
    partial 745.11
    specified type NEC 745.19
  heart 746.87
    with complete transposition of viscera 759.3
  intestine (large) (small) 751.5
  pulmonary veins 747.49
  reversed jejunal (for bypass) (status) V45.3
  scrotal 752.81
  stomach 750.7
    with general transposition of viscera 759.3
  teeth, tooth 524.30
  vessels (complete) 745.10
    partial 745.11
  viscera (abdominal) (thoracic) 759.3
Trans-sexualism 302.50
  with
    asexual history 302.51
    heterosexual history 302.53
    homosexual history 302.52
Transverse — *see also* condition
  arrest (deep), in labor 660.3 ☑
    affecting fetus or newborn 763.1
  lie 652.3 ☑
    before labor, affecting fetus or newborn 761.7
    causing obstructed labor 660.0 ☑
      affecting fetus or newborn 763.1
    during labor, affecting fetus or newborn 763.1
Transvestism, transvestitism (transvestic fetishism) 302.3
Trapped placenta (with hemorrhage) 666.0 ☑
  without hemorrhage 667.0 ☑
Traumatic — *see* ▶*also*◄ condition
  brain injury (TBI) (*see also* Injury, intracranial) ● 854.0 ●
    with skull fracture — *see* Fracture, skull, ● by site ●
Trauma, traumatism — *see also* Injury, by site 959.9
  birth — *see* Birth, injury NEC
  causing hemorrhage of pregnancy or delivery 641.8 ☑
  complicating
    abortion — *see* Abortion, by type, with damage to pelvic organs
    ectopic pregnancy (*see also* categories 633.0–633.9) 639.2
    molar pregnancy (*see also* categories 630–632) 639.2
  during delivery NEC 665.9 ☑
  following
    abortion 639.2
    ectopic or molar pregnancy 639.2
  maternal, during pregnancy, affecting fetus or newborn 760.5
  neuroma — *see* Injury, nerve, by site
  previous major, affecting management of pregnancy, childbirth, or puerperium V23.89
  psychic (current) (*see also* Reaction, adjustment)
    previous (history) V15.49
  psychologic, previous (affecting health) V15.49
  transient paralysis — *see* Injury, nerve, by site
Treacher Collins' syndrome (incomplete facial dysostosis) 756.0
Treitz's hernia — *see* Hernia, Treitz's
Trematode infestation NEC 121.9
Trematodiasis NEC 121.9
Trembles 988.8
Trembling paralysis — *see also* Parkinsonism 332.0

☑ Additional Digit Required — Refer to the Tabular List for Digit Selection　　　　　　　　　　　　　◥ Subterms under main terms may continue to next column or page

Tremor 781.0
- essential (benign) 333.1
- familial 333.1
- flapping (liver) 572.8
- hereditary 333.1
- hysterical 300.11
- intention 333.1
- medication-induced postural 333.1
- mercurial 985.0
- muscle 728.85
- Parkinson's (see also Parkinsonism) 332.0
- psychogenic 306.0
  - specified as conversion reaction 300.11
- senilis 797
- specified type NEC 333.1

Trench
- fever 083.1
- foot 991.4
- mouth 101
- nephritis — see Nephritis, acute

Treponema pallidum infection — see also Syphilis 097.9

Treponematosis 102.9
- due to
  - T. pallidum — see Syphilis
  - T. pertenue (yaws) (see also Yaws) 102.9

Triad
- Kartagener's 759.3
- Reiter's (complete) (incomplete) 099.3
- Saint's (see also Hernia, diaphragm) 553.3

Trichiasis 704.2
- cicatricial 704.2
- eyelid 374.05
  - with entropion (see also Entropion) 374.00

Trichinella spiralis (infection) (infestation) 124

Trichinelliasis 124

Trichinellosis 124

Trichiniasis 124

Trichinosis 124

Trichobezoar 938
- intestine 936
- stomach 935.2

Trichocephaliasis 127.3

Trichocephalosis 127.3

Trichocephalus infestation 127.3

Trichoclasis 704.2

Trichoepithelioma (M8100/0) — see also Neoplasm, skin, benign
- breast 217
- genital organ NEC — see Neoplasm, by site, benign
- malignant (M8100/3) — see Neoplasm, skin, malignant

Trichofolliculoma (M8101/0) — see Neoplasm, skin, benign

Tricholemmoma (M8102/0) — see Neoplasm, skin, benign

Trichomatosis 704.2

Trichomoniasis 131.9
- bladder 131.09
- cervix 131.09
- intestinal 007.3
- prostate 131.03
- seminal vesicle 131.09
- specified site NEC 131.8
- urethra 131.02
- urogenitalis 131.00
- vagina 131.01
- vulva 131.01
- vulvovaginal 131.01

Trichomycosis 039.0
- axillaris 039.0
- nodosa 111.2
- nodularis 111.2
- rubra 039.0

Trichonocardiosis (axillaris) (palmellina) 039.0

Trichonodosis 704.2

Trichophytide — see Dermatophytosis

Trichophytid, trichophyton infection — see also Dermatophytosis 110.9

Trichophytobezoar 938
- intestine 936
- stomach 935.2

Trichophytosis — see Dermatophytosis

Trichoptilosis 704.2

Trichorrhexis (nodosa) 704.2

Trichosporosis nodosa 111.2

Trichostasis spinulosa (congenital) 757.4

Trichostrongyliasis (small intestine) 127.6

Trichostrongylosis 127.6

Trichostrongylus (instabilis) infection 127.6

Trichotillomania 312.39

Trichromat, anomalous (congenital) 368.59

Trichromatopsia, anomalous (congenital) 368.59

Trichuriasis 127.3

Trichuris trichiuria (any site) (infection) (infestation) 127.3

Tricuspid (valve) — see condition

Trifid — see also Accessory
- kidney (pelvis) 753.3
- tongue 750.13

Trigeminal neuralgia — see also Neuralgia, trigeminal 350.1

Trigeminoencephaloangiomatosis 759.6

Trigeminy 427.89
- postoperative 997.1

Trigger finger (acquired) 727.03
- congenital 756.89

Trigonitis (bladder) (chronic) (pseudomembranous) 595.3
- tuberculous (see also Tuberculosis) 016.1 ☑

Trigonocephaly 756.0

Trihexosidosis 272.7

Trilobate placenta — see Placenta, abnormal

Trilocular heart 745.8

Trimethylaminuria 270.8

Tripartita placenta — see Placenta, abnormal

Triple — see also Accessory
- kidneys 753.3
- uteri 752.2
- X female 758.81

Triplegia 344.89
- congenital or infantile 343.8

Triplet
- affected by maternal complications of pregnancy 761.5
- healthy liveborn — see Newborn, multiple
- pregnancy (complicating delivery) NEC 651.1 ☑
  - with fetal loss and retention of one or more fetus(es) 651.4 ☑
  - following (elective) fetal reduction 651.7 ☑

Triplex placenta — see Placenta, abnormal

Triplication — see Accessory

Trismus 781.0
- neonatorum 771.3
- newborn 771.3

Trisomy (syndrome) NEC 758.5
- 13 (partial) 758.1
- 16-18 758.2
- 18 (partial) 758.2
- 21 (partial) 758.0
- 22 758.0
- autosomes NEC 758.5
- D₁ 758.1
- E₃ 758.2
- G (group) 758.0
- group D₁ 758.1
- group E 758.2
- group G 758.0

Tritanomaly 368.53

Tritanopia 368.53

Troisier-Hanot-Chauffard syndrome (bronze diabetes) 275.0

Trombidiosis 133.8

Trophedema (hereditary) 757.0
- congenital 757.0

Trophoblastic disease — see also Hydatidiform mole 630
- previous, affecting management of pregnancy V23.1

Tropholymphedema 757.0

Trophoneurosis NEC 356.9
- arm NEC 354.9
- disseminated 710.1
- facial 349.89
- leg NEC 355.8
- lower extremity NEC 355.8
- upper extremity NEC 354.9

Tropical — see also condition

Tropical — see also condition — continued
- maceration feet (syndrome) 991.4
- wet foot (syndrome) 991.4

Trouble — see also Disease
- bowel 569.9
- heart — see Disease, heart
- intestine 569.9
- kidney (see also Disease, renal) 593.9
- nervous 799.21
- sinus (see also Sinusitis) 473.9

Trousseau's syndrome (thrombophlebitis migrans) 453.1

Truancy, childhood — see also Disturbance, conduct
- socialized 312.2 ☑
- undersocialized, unsocialized 312.1 ☑

Truncus
- arteriosus (persistent) 745.0
- common 745.0
- communis 745.0

Trunk — see condition

Trychophytide — see Dermatophytosis

Trypanosoma infestation — see Trypanosomiasis

Trypanosomiasis 086.9
- with meningoencephalitis 086.9 [323.2]
- African 086.5
  - due to Trypanosoma 086.5
    - gambiense 086.3
    - rhodesiense 086.4
- American 086.2
  - with
    - heart involvement 086.0
    - other organ involvement 086.1
    - without mention of organ involvement 086.2
- Brazilian — see Trypanosomiasis, American
- Chagas' — see Trypanosomiasis, American
- due to Trypanosoma
  - cruzi — see Trypanosomiasis, American
  - gambiense 086.3
  - rhodesiense 086.4
- gambiensis, Gambian 086.3
- North American — see Trypanosomiasis, American
- rhodesiensis, Rhodesian 086.4
- South American — see Trypanosomiasis, American

T-shaped incisors 520.2

Tsutsugamushi fever 081.2

Tubercle — see also Tuberculosis
- brain, solitary 013.2 ☑
- Darwin's 744.29
- epithelioid noncaseating 135
- Ghon, primary infection 010.0 ☑

Tuberculid, tuberculide (indurating) (lichenoid) (miliary) (papulonecrotic) (primary) (skin) (subcutaneous) 017.0 ☑ — see also Tuberculosis

Tuberculoma — see also Tuberculosis
- brain (any part) 013.2 ☑
- meninges (cerebral) (spinal) 013.1 ☑
- spinal cord 013.4 ☑

Tuberculosis, tubercular, tuberculous (calcification) (calcified) (caseous) (chromogenic acid-fast bacilli) (congenital) (degeneration) (disease) (fibrocaseous) (fistula) (gangrene) (interstitial) (isolated circumscribed lesions) (necrosis) (parenchymatous) (ulcerative) 011.9 ☑

> Note — Use the following fifth-digit subclassification with categories 010–018:
>
> 0   unspecified
>
> 1   bacteriological or histological examination not done
>
> 2   bacteriological or histological examination unknown (at present)
>
> 3   tubercle bacilli found (in sputum) by microscopy
>
> 4   tubercle bacilli not found (in sputum) by microscopy, but found by bacterial culture
>
> 5   tubercle bacilli not found by bacteriological exam–ination, but tuberculosis confirmed histologically
>
> 6   tubercle bacilli not found by bacteriological or histological examination, but tuberculosis confirmed by other methods [inoculation of animals]
>
> For tuberculous conditions specified as late effects or sequelae, see category 137.

- abdomen 014.8 ☑
  - lymph gland 014.8 ☑
- abscess 011.9 ☑
  - arm 017.9 ☑
  - bone (see also Osteomyelitis, due to, tuberculosis) 015.9 ☑ [730.8] ☑
    - hip 015.1 ☑ [730.85]
    - knee 015.2 ☑ [730.86]
    - sacrum 015.0 ☑ [730.88]
    - specified site NEC 015.7 ☑ [730.88]
    - spinal 015.0 ☑ [730.88]
    - vertebra 015.0 ☑ [730.88]
  - brain 013.3 ☑
  - breast 017.9 ☑
  - Cowper's gland 016.5 ☑
  - dura (mater) 013.8 ☑
    - brain 013.3 ☑
    - spinal cord 013.5 ☑
  - epidural 013.8 ☑
    - brain 013.3 ☑
    - spinal cord 013.5 ☑
  - frontal sinus — see Tuberculosis, sinus
  - genital organs NEC 016.9 ☑
    - female 016.7 ☑
    - male 016.5 ☑
  - genitourinary NEC 016.9 ☑
  - gland (lymphatic) — see Tuberculosis, lymph gland
  - hip 015.1 ☑
  - iliopsoas 015.0 ☑ [730.88]
  - intestine 014.8 ☑
  - ischiorectal 014.8 ☑
  - joint 015.9 ☑
    - hip 015.1 ☑
    - knee 015.2 ☑
    - specified joint NEC 015.8 ☑
    - vertebral 015.0 ☑ [730.88]
  - kidney 016.0 ☑ [590.81]
  - knee 015.2 ☑
  - lumbar 015.0 ☑ [730.88]
  - lung 011.2 ☑
    - primary, progressive 010.8 ☑
  - meninges (cerebral) (spinal) 013.0 ☑
  - pelvic 016.9 ☑
    - female 016.7 ☑
    - male 016.5 ☑
  - perianal 014.8 ☑
    - fistula 014.8 ☑
  - perinephritic 016.0 ☑ [590.81]
  - perineum 017.9 ☑
  - perirectal 014.8 ☑
  - psoas 015.0 ☑ [730.88]

☑ Additional Digit Required — Refer to the Tabular List for Digit Selection

Subterms under main terms may continue to next column or page

Index

Tuberculosis, tubercular, tuberculous — Tuberculosis, tubercular, tuberculous

Tuberculosis, tubercular, tuberculous — *continued*

abscess — *continued*
  rectum 014.8 ✓
  retropharyngeal 012.8 ✓
  sacrum 015.0 ✓ *[730.88]*
  scrofulous 017.2 ✓
  scrotum 016.5 ✓
  skin 017.0 ✓
    primary 017.0 ✓
  spinal cord 013.5 ✓
  spine or vertebra (column)
    015.0 ✓ *[730.88]*
  strumous 017.2 ✓
  subdiaphragmatic 014.8 ✓
  testis 016.5 ✓
  thigh 017.9 ✓
  urinary 016.3 ✓
    kidney 016.0 ✓ *[590.81]*
    uterus 016.7 ✓
accessory sinus — *see* Tuberculosis, sinus
Addison's disease 017.6 ✓
adenitis (*see also* Tuberculosis, lymph gland)
  017.2 ✓
adenoids 012.8 ✓
adenopathy (*see also* Tuberculosis, lymph
  gland) 017.2 ✓
  tracheobronchial 012.1 ✓
    primary progressive 010.8 ✓
adherent pericardium 017.9 ✓ *[420.0]*
adnexa (uteri) 016.7 ✓
adrenal (capsule) (gland) 017.6 ✓
air passage NEC 012.8 ✓
alimentary canal 014.8 ✓
anemia 017.9 ✓
ankle (joint) 015.8 ✓
  bone 015.5 ✓ *[730.87]*
anus 014.8 ✓
apex (*see also* Tuberculosis, pulmonary)
  011.9 ✓
apical (*see also* Tuberculosis, pulmonary)
  011.9 ✓
appendicitis 014.8 ✓
appendix 014.8 ✓
arachnoid 013.0 ✓
artery 017.9 ✓
arthritis (chronic) (synovial) 015.9 ✓ *[711.40]*
  ankle 015.8 ✓ *[730.87]*
  hip 015.1 ✓ *[711.45]*
  knee 015.2 ✓ *[711.46]*
  specified site NEC 015.8 ✓ *[711.48]*
  spine or vertebra (column)
    015.0 ✓ *[720.81]*
  wrist 015.8 ✓ *[730.83]*
articular — *see* Tuberculosis, joint
ascites 014.0 ✓
asthma (*see also* Tuberculosis, pulmonary)
  011.9 ✓
axilla, axillary 017.2 ✓
  gland 017.2 ✓
bilateral (*see also* Tuberculosis, pulmonary)
  011.9 ✓
bladder 016.1 ✓
bone (*see also* Osteomyelitis, due to, tuberculosis) 015.9 ✓ *[730.8]*
  hip 015.1 ✓ *[730.85]*
  knee 015.2 ✓ *[730.86]*
  limb NEC 015.5 ✓ *[730.88]*
  sacrum 015.0 ✓ *[730.88]*
  specified site NEC 015.7 ✓ *[730.88]*
  spinal or vertebral column
    015.0 ✓ *[730.88]*
bowel 014.8 ✓
  miliary 018.9 ✓
brain 013.2 ✓
breast 017.9 ✓
broad ligament 016.7 ✓
bronchi, bronchial, bronchus 011.3 ✓
  ectasia, ectasis 011.5 ✓
  fistula 011.3 ✓
    primary, progressive 010.8 ✓
  gland 012.1 ✓
    primary, progressive 010.8 ✓

Tuberculosis, tubercular, tuberculous — *continued*

bronchi, bronchial, bronchus — *continued*
  isolated 012.2 ✓
  lymph gland or node 012.1 ✓
    primary, progressive 010.8 ✓
bronchiectasis 011.5 ✓
bronchitis 011.3 ✓
bronchopleural 012.0 ✓
bronchopneumonia, bronchopneumonic
  011.6 ✓
bronchorrhagia 011.3 ✓
bronchotracheal 011.3 ✓
  isolated 012.2 ✓
bronchus — *see* Tuberculosis, bronchi
bronze disease (Addison's) 017.6 ✓
buccal cavity 017.9 ✓
bulbourethral gland 016.5 ✓
bursa (*see also* Tuberculosis, joint) 015.9 ✓
cachexia NEC (*see also* Tuberculosis, pulmonary) 011.9 ✓
cardiomyopathy 017.9 ✓ *[425.8]*
caries (*see also* Tuberculosis, bone)
  015.9 ✓ *[730.8]*
cartilage (*see also* Tuberculosis, bone)
  015.9 ✓ *[730.8]*
  intervertebral 015.0 ✓ *[730.88]*
catarrhal (*see also* Tuberculosis, pulmonary)
  011.9 ✓
cecum 014.8 ✓
cellular tissue (primary) 017.0 ✓
cellulitis (primary) 017.0 ✓
central nervous system 013.9 ✓
  specified site NEC 013.8 ✓
cerebellum (current) 013.2 ✓
cerebral (current) 013.2 ✓
  meninges 013.0 ✓
cerebrospinal 013.6 ✓
  meninges 013.0 ✓
cerebrum (current) 013.2 ✓
cervical 017.2 ✓
  gland 017.2 ✓
  lymph nodes 017.2 ✓
cervicitis (uteri) 016.7 ✓
cervix 016.7 ✓
chest (*see also* Tuberculosis, pulmonary)
  011.9 ✓
childhood type or first infection 010.0 ✓
choroid 017.3 ✓ *[363.13]*
choroiditis 017.3 ✓ *[363.13]*
ciliary body 017.3 ✓ *[364.11]*
colitis 014.8 ✓
colliers' 011.4 ✓
colliquativa (primary) 017.0 ✓
colon 014.8 ✓
  ulceration 014.8 ✓
complex, primary 010.0 ✓
complicating pregnancy, childbirth, or puerperium 647.3 ✓
  affecting fetus or newborn 760.2
congenital 771.2
conjunctiva 017.3 ✓ *[370.31]*
connective tissue 017.9 ✓
  bone — *see* Tuberculosis, bone
contact V01.1
converter (tuberculin skin test) (without disease) 795.5
cornea (ulcer) 017.3 ✓ *[370.31]*
Cowper's gland 016.5 ✓
coxae 015.1 ✓ *[730.85]*
coxalgia 015.1 ✓ *[730.85]*
cul-de-sac of Douglas 014.8 ✓
curvature, spine 015.0 ✓ *[737.40]*
cutis (colliquativa) (primary) 017.0 ✓
cystitis 016.1 ✓
cyst, ovary 016.6 ✓
dacryocystitis 017.3 ✓ *[375.32]*
dactylitis 015.5 ✓
diarrhea 014.8 ✓
diffuse (*see also* Tuberculosis, miliary) 018.9 ✓
  lung — *see* Tuberculosis, pulmonary
  meninges 013.0 ✓
digestive tract 014.8 ✓

Tuberculosis, tubercular, tuberculous — *continued*

disseminated (*see also* Tuberculosis, miliary)
  018.9 ✓
  meninges 013.0 ✓
duodenum 014.8 ✓
dura (mater) 013.9 ✓
  abscess 013.8 ✓
    cerebral 013.3 ✓
    spinal 013.5 ✓
dysentery 014.8 ✓
ear (inner) (middle) 017.4 ✓
  bone 015.6 ✓
  external (primary) 017.0 ✓
  skin (primary) 017.0 ✓
elbow 015.8 ✓
emphysema — *see* Tuberculosis, pulmonary
empyema 012.0 ✓
encephalitis 013.6 ✓
endarteritis 017.9 ✓
endocarditis (any valve) 017.9 ✓ *[424.91]*
endocardium (any valve) 017.9 ✓ *[424.91]*
endocrine glands NEC 017.9 ✓
endometrium 016.7 ✓
enteric, enterica 014.8 ✓
enteritis 014.8 ✓
enterocolitis 014.8 ✓
epididymis 016.4 ✓
epididymitis 016.4 ✓
epidural abscess 013.8 ✓
  brain 013.3 ✓
  spinal cord 013.5 ✓
epiglottis 012.3 ✓
episcleritis 017.3 ✓ *[379.00]*
erythema (induratum) (nodosum) (primary)
  017.1 ✓
esophagus 017.8 ✓
Eustachian tube 017.4 ✓
exposure to V01.1
exudative 012.0 ✓
  primary, progressive 010.1 ✓
eye 017.3 ✓
eyelid (primary) 017.0 ✓
  lupus 017.0 ✓ *[373.4]*
fallopian tube 016.6 ✓
fascia 017.9 ✓
fauces 012.8 ✓
finger 017.9 ✓
first infection 010.0 ✓
fistula, perirectal 014.8 ✓
Florida 011.6 ✓
foot 017.9 ✓
funnel pelvis 137.3
gallbladder 017.9 ✓
galloping (*see also* Tuberculosis, pulmonary)
  011.9 ✓
ganglionic 015.9 ✓
gastritis 017.9 ✓
gastrocolic fistula 014.8 ✓
gastroenteritis 014.8 ✓
gastrointestinal tract 014.8 ✓
general, generalized 018.9 ✓
  acute 018.0 ✓
  chronic 018.8 ✓
genital organs NEC 016.9 ✓
  female 016.7 ✓
  male 016.5 ✓
genitourinary NEC 016.9 ✓
genu 015.2 ✓
glandulae suprarenalis 017.6 ✓
glandular, general 017.2 ✓
glottis 012.3 ✓
grinders' 011.4 ✓
groin 017.2 ✓
gum 017.9 ✓
hand 017.9 ✓
heart 017.9 ✓ *[425.8]*
hematogenous — *see* Tuberculosis, miliary
hemoptysis (*see also* Tuberculosis, pulmonary)
  011.9 ✓
hemorrhage NEC (*see also* Tuberculosis, pulmonary) 011.9 ✓
hemothorax 012.0 ✓

Tuberculosis, tubercular, tuberculous — *continued*

hepatitis 017.9 ✓
hilar lymph nodes 012.1 ✓
  primary, progressive 010.8 ✓
hip (disease) (joint) 015.1 ✓
  bone 015.1 ✓ *[730.85]*
hydrocephalus 013.8 ✓
hydropneumothorax 012.0 ✓
hydrothorax 012.0 ✓
hypoadrenalism 017.6 ✓
hypopharynx 012.8 ✓
ileocecal (hyperplastic) 014.8 ✓
ileocolitis 014.8 ✓
ileum 014.8 ✓
iliac spine (superior) 015.0 ✓ *[730.88]*
incipient NEC (*see also* Tuberculosis, pulmonary) 011.9 ✓
indurativa (primary) 017.1 ✓
infantile 010.0 ✓
infection NEC 011.9 ✓
  without clinical manifestation 010.0 ✓
infraclavicular gland 017.2 ✓
inguinal gland 017.2 ✓
inguinalis 017.2 ✓
intestine (any part) 014.8 ✓
iris 017.3 ✓ *[364.11]*
iritis 017.3 ✓ *[364.11]*
ischiorectal 014.8 ✓
jaw 015.7 ✓ *[730.88]*
jejunum 014.8 ✓
joint 015.9 ✓
  hip 015.1 ✓
  knee 015.2 ✓
  specified site NEC 015.8 ✓
  vertebral 015.0 ✓ *[730.88]*
keratitis 017.3 ✓ *[370.31]*
  interstitial 017.3 ✓ *[370.59]*
keratoconjunctivitis 017.3 ✓ *[370.31]*
kidney 016.0 ✓
knee (joint) 015.2 ✓
kyphoscoliosis 015.0 ✓ *[737.43]*
kyphosis 015.0 ✓ *[737.41]*
lacrimal apparatus, gland 017.3 ✓
laryngitis 012.3 ✓
larynx 012.3 ✓
leptomeninges, leptomeningitis (cerebral)
  (spinal) 013.0 ✓
lichenoides (primary) 017.0 ✓
linguae 017.9 ✓
lip 017.9 ✓
liver 017.9 ✓
lordosis 015.0 ✓ *[737.42]*
lung — *see* Tuberculosis, pulmonary
luposa 017.0 ✓
  eyelid 017.0 ✓ *[373.4]*
lymphadenitis — *see* Tuberculosis, lymph
  gland
lymphangitis — *see* Tuberculosis, lymph gland
lymphatic (gland) (vessel) — *see* Tuberculosis,
  lymph gland
lymph gland or node (peripheral) 017.2 ✓
  abdomen 014.8 ✓
  bronchial 012.1 ✓
    primary, progressive 010.8 ✓
  cervical 017.2 ✓
  hilar 012.1 ✓
    primary, progressive 010.8 ✓
  intrathoracic 012.1 ✓
    primary, progressive 010.8 ✓
  mediastinal 012.1 ✓
    primary, progressive 010.8 ✓
  mesenteric 014.8 ✓
  peripheral 017.2 ✓
  retroperitoneal 014.8 ✓
  tracheobronchial 012.1 ✓
    primary, progressive 010.8 ✓
malignant NEC (*see also* Tuberculosis, pulmonary) 011.9 ✓
mammary gland 017.9 ✓
marasmus NEC (*see also* Tuberculosis, pulmonary) 011.9 ✓
mastoiditis 015.6 ✓

✓ Additional Digit Required — Refer to the Tabular List for Digit Selection

Subterms under main terms may continue to next column or page

Tuberculosis, tubercular, tuberculous — *continued*
  maternal, affecting fetus or newborn 760.2
  mediastinal (lymph) gland or node 012.1 ☑
    primary, progressive 010.8 ☑
  mediastinitis 012.8 ☑
    primary, progressive 010.8 ☑
  mediastinopericarditis 017.9 *[420.0]*
  mediastinum 012.8 ☑
    primary, progressive 010.8 ☑
  medulla 013.9 ☑
    brain 013.2 ☑
    spinal cord 013.4 ☑
  melanosis, Addisonian 017.6 ☑
  membrane, brain 013.0 ☑
  meninges (cerebral) (spinal) 013.0 ☑
  meningitis (basilar) (brain) (cerebral) (cerebrospinal) (spinal) 013.0 ☑
  meningoencephalitis 013.0 ☑
  mesentery, mesenteric 014.8 ☑
    lymph gland or node 014.8 ☑
  miliary (any site) 018.9 ☑
    acute 018.0 ☑
    chronic 018.8 ☑
    specified type NEC 018.8 ☑
  millstone makers' 011.4 ☑
  miners' 011.4 ☑
  moulders' 011.4 ☑
  mouth 017.9 ☑
  multiple 018.9 ☑
    acute 018.0 ☑
    chronic 018.8 ☑
  muscle 017.9 ☑
  myelitis 013.6 ☑
  myocarditis 017.9 ☑ *[422.0]*
  myocardium 017.9 ☑ *[422.0]*
  nasal (passage) (sinus) 012.8 ☑
  nasopharynx 012.8 ☑
  neck gland 017.2 ☑
  nephritis 016.0 ☑ *[583.81]*
  nerve 017.9 ☑
  nose (septum) 012.8 ☑
  ocular 017.3 ☑
  old NEC 137.0
    without residuals V12.01
  omentum 014.8 ☑
  oophoritis (acute) (chronic) 016.6 ☑
  optic 017.3 ☑ *[377.39]*
    nerve trunk 017.3 ☑ *[377.39]*
    papilla, papillae 017.3 ☑ *[377.39]*
  orbit 017.3 ☑
  orchitis 016.5 ☑ *[608.81]*
  organ, specified NEC 017.9 ☑
  orificialis (primary) 017.0 ☑
  osseous (*see also* Tuberculosis, bone) 015.9 ☑ *[730.8]*
  osteitis (*see also* Tuberculosis, bone) 015.9 ☑ *[730.8]*
  osteomyelitis (*see also* Tuberculosis, bone) 015.9 ☑ *[730.8]*
  otitis (media) 017.4 ☑
  ovaritis (acute) (chronic) 016.6 ☑
  ovary (acute) (chronic) 016.6 ☑
  oviducts (acute) (chronic) 016.6 ☑
  pachymeningitis 013.0 ☑
  palate (soft) 017.9 ☑
  pancreas 017.9 ☑
  papulonecrotic (primary) 017.0 ☑
  parathyroid glands 017.9 ☑
  paronychia (primary) 017.0 ☑
  parotid gland and region 017.9 ☑
  pelvic organ NEC 016.9 ☑
    female 016.7 ☑
    male 016.5 ☑
  pelvis (bony) 015.7 ☑ *[730.85]*
  penis 016.5 ☑
  peribronchitis 011.3 ☑
  pericarditis 017.9 ☑ *[420.0]*
  pericardium 017.9 ☑ *[420.0]*
  perichondritis, larynx 012.3 ☑
  perineum 017.9 ☑
  periostitis (*see also* Tuberculosis, bone) 015.9 ☑ *[730.8]*

Tuberculosis, tubercular, tuberculous — *continued*
  periphlebitis 017.9 ☑
    eye vessel 017.3 ☑ *[362.18]*
    retina 017.3 ☑ *[362.18]*
  perirectal fistula 014.8 ☑
  peritoneal gland 014.8 ☑
  peritoneum 014.0 ☑
  peritonitis 014.0 ☑
  pernicious NEC (*see also* Tuberculosis, pulmonary) 011.9 ☑
  pharyngitis 012.8 ☑
  pharynx 012.8 ☑
  phlyctenulosis (conjunctiva) 017.3 ☑ *[370.31]*
  phthisis NEC (*see also* Tuberculosis, pulmonary) 011.9 ☑
  pituitary gland 017.9 ☑
  placenta 016.7 ☑
  pleura, pleural, pleurisy, pleuritis (fibrinous) (obliterative) (purulent) (simple plastic) (with effusion) 012.0 ☑
    primary, progressive 010.1 ☑
  pneumonia, pneumonic 011.6 ☑
  pneumothorax 011.7 ☑
  polyserositis 018.9 ☑
    acute 018.0 ☑
    chronic 018.8 ☑
  potters' 011.4 ☑
  prepuce 016.5 ☑
  primary 010.9 ☑
    complex 010.0 ☑
    complicated 010.8 ☑
      with pleurisy or effusion 010.1 ☑
    progressive 010.8 ☑
      with pleurisy or effusion 010.1 ☑
    skin 017.0 ☑
  proctitis 014.8 ☑
  prostate 016.5 ☑ *[601.4]*
  prostatitis 016.5 ☑ *[601.4]*
  pulmonaris (*see also* Tuberculosis, pulmonary) 011.9 ☑
  pulmonary (artery) (incipient) (malignant) (multiple round foci) (pernicious) (reinfection stage) 011.9 ☑
    cavitated or with cavitation 011.2 ☑
      primary, progressive 010.8 ☑
    childhood type or first infection 010.0 ☑
    chromogenic acid-fast bacilli 795.39
    fibrosis or fibrotic 011.4 ☑
    infiltrative 011.0 ☑
      primary, progressive 010.9 ☑
    nodular 011.1 ☑
    specified NEC 011.8 ☑
    sputum positive only 795.39
    status following surgical collapse of lung NEC 011.9 ☑
  pyelitis 016.0 ☑ *[590.81]*
  pyelonephritis 016.0 ☑ *[590.81]*
  pyemia — *see* Tuberculosis, miliary
  pyonephrosis 016.0 ☑
  pyopneumothorax 012.0 ☑
  pyothorax 012.0 ☑
  rectum (with abscess) 014.8 ☑
    fistula 014.8 ☑
  reinfection stage (*see also* Tuberculosis, pulmonary) 011.9 ☑
  renal 016.0 ☑
  renis 016.0 ☑
  reproductive organ 016.7 ☑
  respiratory NEC (*see also* Tuberculosis, pulmonary) 011.9 ☑
    specified site NEC 012.8 ☑
  retina 017.3 ☑ *[363.13]*
  retroperitoneal (lymph gland or node) 014.8 ☑
    gland 014.8 ☑
  retropharyngeal abscess 012.8 ☑
  rheumatism 015.9 ☑
  rhinitis 012.8 ☑
  sacroiliac (joint) 015.8 ☑
  sacrum 015.0 ☑ *[730.88]*
  salivary gland 017.9 ☑
  salpingitis (acute) (chronic) 016.6 ☑
  sandblasters' 011.4 ☑

Tuberculosis, tubercular, tuberculous — *continued*
  sclera 017.3 ☑ *[379.09]*
  scoliosis 015.0 ☑ *[737.43]*
  scrofulous 017.2 ☑
  scrotum 016.5 ☑
  seminal tract or vesicle 016.5 ☑ *[608.81]*
  senile NEC (*see also* Tuberculosis, pulmonary) 011.9 ☑
  septic NEC (*see also* Tuberculosis, miliary) 018.9 ☑
  shoulder 015.8 ☑
    blade 015.7 ☑ *[730.8]*
  sigmoid 014.8 ☑
  sinus (accessory) (nasal) 012.8 ☑
    bone 015.7 ☑ *[730.88]*
    epididymis 016.4 ☑
  skeletal NEC (*see also* Osteomyelitis, due to tuberculosis) 015.9 ☑ *[730.8]*
  skin (any site) (primary) 017.0 ☑
  small intestine 014.8 ☑
  soft palate 017.9 ☑
  spermatic cord 016.5 ☑
  spinal
    column 015.0 ☑ *[730.88]*
    cord 013.4 ☑
    disease 015.0 ☑ *[730.88]*
    medulla 013.4 ☑
    membrane 013.0 ☑
    meninges 013.0 ☑
  spine 015.0 ☑ *[730.88]*
  spleen 017.7 ☑
  splenitis 017.7 ☑
  spondylitis 015.0 ☑ *[720.81]*
  spontaneous pneumothorax — *see* Tuberculosis, pulmonary
  sternoclavicular joint 015.8 ☑
  stomach 017.9 ☑
  stonemasons' 011.4 ☑
  struma 017.2 ☑
  subcutaneous tissue (cellular) (primary) 017.0 ☑
  subcutis (primary) 017.0 ☑
  subdeltoid bursa 017.9 ☑
  submaxillary 017.9 ☑
    region 017.9 ☑
  supraclavicular gland 017.2 ☑
  suprarenal (capsule) (gland) 017.6 ☑
  swelling, joint (*see also* Tuberculosis, joint) 015.9 ☑
  symphysis pubis 015.7 ☑ *[730.88]*
  synovitis 015.9 ☑ *[727.01]*
    hip 015.1 ☑ *[727.01]*
    knee 015.2 ☑ *[727.01]*
    specified site NEC 015.8 ☑ *[727.01]*
    spine or vertebra 015.0 ☑ *[727.01]*
  systemic — *see* Tuberculosis, miliary
  tarsitis (eyelid) 017.0 ☑ *[373.4]*
    ankle (bone) 015.5 ☑ *[730.87]*
  tendon (sheath) — *see* Tuberculosis, tenosynovitis
  tenosynovitis 015.9 ☑ *[727.01]*
    hip 015.1 ☑ *[727.01]*
    knee 015.2 ☑ *[727.01]*
    specified site NEC 015.8 ☑ *[727.01]*
    spine or vertebra 015.0 ☑ *[727.01]*
  testis 016.5 ☑ *[608.81]*
  throat 012.8 ☑
  thymus gland 017.9 ☑
  thyroid gland 017.5 ☑
  toe 017.9 ☑
  tongue 017.9 ☑
  tonsil (lingual) 012.8 ☑
  tonsillitis 012.8 ☑
  trachea, tracheal 012.8 ☑
    gland 012.1 ☑
      primary, progressive 010.8 ☑
    isolated 012.2 ☑
  tracheobronchial 011.3 ☑
    glandular 012.1 ☑
      primary, progressive 010.8 ☑
    isolated 012.2 ☑
    lymph gland or node 012.1 ☑

Tuberculosis, tubercular, tuberculous — *continued*
  tracheobronchial — *continued*
    lymph gland or node — *continued*
      primary, progressive 010.8 ☑
  tubal 016.6 ☑
  tunica vaginalis 016.5 ☑
  typhlitis 014.8 ☑
  ulcer (primary) (skin) 017.0 ☑
    bowel or intestine 014.8 ☑
    specified site NEC — *see* Tuberculosis, by site
    unspecified site — *see* Tuberculosis, pulmonary
  ureter 016.2 ☑
  urethra, urethral 016.3 ☑
  urinary organ or tract 016.3 ☑
    kidney 016.0 ☑
  uterus 016.7 ☑
  uveal tract 017.3 ☑ *[363.13]*
  uvula 017.9 ☑
  vaccination, prophylactic (against) V03.2
  vagina 016.7 ☑
  vas deferens 016.5 ☑
  vein 017.9 ☑
  verruca (primary) 017.0 ☑
  verrucosa (cutis) (primary) 017.0 ☑
  vertebra (column) 015.0 ☑ *[730.88]*
  vesiculitis 016.5 ☑ *[608.81]*
  viscera NEC 014.8 ☑
  vulva 016.7 ☑ *[616.51]*
  wrist (joint) 015.8 ☑
    bone 015.5 ☑ *[730.83]*

Tuberculum
  auriculae 744.29
  occlusal 520.2
  paramolare 520.2

Tuberosity
  jaw, excessive 524.07
  maxillary, entire 524.07

Tuberous sclerosis (brain) 759.5

Tube, tubal, tubular — *see also* condition
  ligation, admission for V25.2

Tubo-ovarian — *see* condition

Tuboplasty, after previous sterilization V26.0

Tubotympanitis 381.10

Tularemia 021.9
  with
    conjunctivitis 021.3
    pneumonia 021.2
  bronchopneumonic 021.2
  conjunctivitis 021.3
  cryptogenic 021.1
  disseminated 021.8
  enteric 021.1
  generalized 021.8
  glandular 021.8
  intestinal 021.1
  oculoglandular 021.3
  ophthalmic 021.3
  pneumonia 021.2
  pulmonary 021.2
  specified NEC 021.8
  typhoidal 021.1
  ulceroglandular 021.0
  vaccination, prophylactic (against) V03.4

Tularensis conjunctivitis 021.3

Tumefaction — *see also* Swelling
  liver (*see also* Hypertrophy, liver) 789.1

Tumor (M8000/1) — *see also* Neoplasm, by site, unspecified nature
  Abrikossov's (M9580/0) (*see also* Neoplasm, connective tissue, benign)
    malignant (M9580/3) — *see* Neoplasm, connective tissue, malignant
  acinar cell (M8550/1) — *see* Neoplasm, by site, uncertain behavior
  acinic cell (M8550/1) — *see* Neoplasm, by site, uncertain behavior
  adenomatoid (M9054/0) (*see also* Neoplasm, by site, benign)
    odontogenic (M9300/0) 213.1
      upper jaw (bone) 213.0
  adnexal (skin) (M8390/0) — *see* Neoplasm, skin, benign

Index

Tumor — Tumor

Tumor — *see also* Neoplasm, by site, unspecified nature — *continued*
adrenal
  cortical (benign) (M8370/0) 227.0
    malignant (M8370/3) 194.0
  rest (M8671/0) — *see* Neoplasm, by site, benign
alpha cell (M8152/0)
  malignant (M8152/3)
    pancreas 157.4
    specified site NEC — *see* Neoplasm, by site, malignant
    unspecified site 157.4
  pancreas 211.7
  specified site NEC — *see* Neoplasm, by site, benign
  unspecified site 211.7
aneurysmal (*see also* Aneurysm) 442.9
aortic body (M8691/1) 237.3
  malignant (M8691/3) 194.6
argentaffin (M8241/1) — *see* Neoplasm, by site, uncertain behavior
basal cell (M8090/1) (*see also* Neoplasm, skin, uncertain behavior)
benign (M8000/0) — *see* Neoplasm, by site, benign
beta cell (M8151/0)
  malignant (M8151/3)
    pancreas 157.4
    specified site — *see* Neoplasm, by site, malignant
    unspecified site 157.4
  pancreas 211.7
  specified site NEC — *see* Neoplasm, by site, benign
  unspecified site 211.7
blood — *see* Hematoma
Brenner (M9000/0) 220
  borderline malignancy (M9000/1) 236.2
  malignant (M9000/3) 183.0
  proliferating (M9000/1) 236.2
Brooke's (M8100/0) — *see* Neoplasm, skin, benign
brown fat (M8880/0) — *see* Lipoma, by site
Burkitt's (M9750/3) 200.2 ☑
calcifying epithelial odontogenic (M9340/0) 213.1
  upper jaw (bone) 213.0
carcinoid (M8240/1) 209.60
  benign 209.60
    appendix 209.51
    ascending colon 209.53
    bronchus 209.61
    cecum 209.52
    colon 209.50
    descending colon 209.55
    duodenum 209.41
    foregut 209.65
    hindgut 209.67
    ileum 209.43
    jejunum 209.42
    kidney 209.64
    large intestine 209.50
    lung 209.61
    midgut 209.66
    rectum 209.57
    sigmoid colon 209.56
    small intestine 209.40
    specified NEC 209.69
    stomach 209.63
    thymus 209.62
    transverse colon 209.54
  malignant (of) 209.20
    appendix 209.11
    ascending colon 209.13
    bronchus 209.21
    cecum 209.12
    colon 209.10
    descending colon 209.15
    duodenum 209.01
    foregut 209.25
    hindgut 209.27
    ileum 209.03
    jejunum 209.02
    kidney 209.24
    large intestine 209.10

Tumor — *see also* Neoplasm, by site, unspecified nature — *continued*
carcinoid — *continued*
  malignant — *continued*
    lung 209.21
    midgut 209.26
    rectum 209.17
    sigmoid colon 209.16
    small intestine 209.00
    specified NEC 209.29
    stomach 209.23
    thymus 209.22
    transverse colon 209.14
  secondary — *see* Tumor, neuroendocrine, secondary ●
carotid body (M8692/1) 237.3
  malignant (M8692/3) 194.5
Castleman's (mediastinal lymph node hyperplasia) 785.6
cells (M8001/1) (*see also* Neoplasm, by site, unspecified nature)
  benign (M8001/0) — *see* Neoplasm, by site, benign
  malignant (M8001/3) — *see* Neoplasm, by site, malignant
  uncertain whether benign or malignant (M8001/1) — *see* Neoplasm, by site, uncertain nature
cervix
  in pregnancy or childbirth 654.6 ☑
    affecting fetus or newborn 763.89
    causing obstructed labor 660.2 ☑
      affecting fetus or newborn 763.1
chondromatous giant cell (M9230/0) — *see* Neoplasm, bone, benign
chromaffin (M8700/0) (*see also* Neoplasm, by site, benign)
  malignant (M8700/3) — *see* Neoplasm, by site, malignant
Cock's peculiar 706.2
Codman's (benign chondroblastoma) (M9230/0) — *see* Neoplasm, bone, benign
dentigerous, mixed (M9282/0) 213.1
  upper jaw (bone) 213.0
dermoid (M9084/0) — *see* Neoplasm, by site, benign
  with malignant transformation (M9084/3) 183.0
desmoid (extra-abdominal) (M8821/1) (*see also* Neoplasm, connective tissue, uncertain behavior)
  abdominal (M8822/1) — *see* Neoplasm, connective tissue, uncertain behavior
embryonal (mixed) (M9080/1) (*see also* Neoplasm, by site, uncertain behavior)
  liver (M9080/3) 155.0
endodermal sinus (M9071/3)
  specified site — *see* Neoplasm, by site, malignant
  unspecified site
    female 183.0
    male 186.9
epithelial
  benign (M8010/0) — *see* Neoplasm, by site, benign
  malignant (M8010/3) — *see* Neoplasm, by site, malignant
Ewing's (M9260/3) — *see* Neoplasm, bone, malignant
fatty — *see* Lipoma
fetal, causing disproportion 653.7 ☑
  causing obstructed labor 660.1 ☑
fibroid (M8890/0) — *see* Leiomyoma
G cell (M8153/1)
  malignant (M8153/3)
    pancreas 157.4
    specified site NEC — *see* Neoplasm, by site, malignant
    unspecified site 157.4
  specified site — *see* Neoplasm, by site, uncertain behavior
  unspecified site 235.5
giant cell (type) (M8003/1) (*see also* Neoplasm, by site, unspecified nature)

Tumor — *see also* Neoplasm, by site, unspecified nature — *continued*
giant cell (*see also* Neoplasm, by site, unspecified nature) — *continued*
  bone (M9250/1) 238.0
    malignant (M9250/3) — *see* Neoplasm, bone, malignant
  chondromatous (M9230/0) — *see* Neoplasm, bone, benign
  malignant (M8003/3) — *see* Neoplasm, by site, malignant
  peripheral (gingiva) 523.8
  soft parts (M9251/1) (*see also* Neoplasm, connective tissue, uncertain behavior)
    malignant (M9251/3) — *see* Neoplasm, connective tissue, malignant
  tendon sheath 727.02
glomus (M8711/0) (*see also* Hemangioma, by site)
  jugulare (M8690/1) 237.3
    malignant (M8690/3) 194.6
gonadal stromal (M8590/1) — *see* Neoplasm, by site, uncertain behavior
granular cell (M9580/0) (*see also* Neoplasm, connective tissue, benign)
  malignant (M9580/3) — *see* Neoplasm, connective tissue, malignant
granulosa cell (M8620/1) 236.2
  malignant (M8620/3) 183.0
granulosa cell-theca cell (M8621/1) 236.2
  malignant (M8621/3) 183.0
Grawitz's (hypernephroma) (M8312/3) 189.0
hazard-crile (M8350/3) 193
hemorrhoidal — *see* Hemorrhoids
hilar cell (M8660/0) 220
Hürthle cell (benign) (M8290/0) 226
  malignant (M8290/3) 193
hydatid (*see also* Echinococcus) 122.9
hypernephroid (M8311/1) (*see also* Neoplasm, by site, uncertain behavior)
interstitial cell (M8650/1) (*see also* Neoplasm, by site, uncertain behavior)
  benign (M8650/0) — *see* Neoplasm, by site, benign
  malignant (M8650/3) — *see* Neoplasm, by site, malignant
islet cell (M8150/0)
  malignant (M8150/3)
    pancreas 157.4
    specified site — *see* Neoplasm, by site, malignant
    unspecified site 157.4
  pancreas 211.7
  specified site NEC — *see* Neoplasm, by site, benign
  unspecified site 211.7
juxtaglomerular (M8361/1) 236.91
Krukenberg's (M8490/6) 198.6
Leydig cell (M8650/1)
  benign (M8650/0)
    specified site — *see* Neoplasm, by site, benign
    unspecified site
      female 220
      male 222.0
  malignant (M8650/3)
    specified site — *see* Neoplasm, by site, malignant
    unspecified site
      female 183.0
      male 186.9
  specified site — *see* Neoplasm, by site, uncertain behavior
  unspecified site
    female 236.2
    male 236.4
lipid cell, ovary (M8670/0) 220
lipoid cell, ovary (M8670/0) 220
lymphomatous, benign (M9590/0) (*see also* Neoplasm, by site, benign)
lysis syndrome (following antineoplastic drug therapy) (spontaneous) 277.88 ●
Malherbe's (M8110/0) — *see* Neoplasm, skin, benign

Tumor — *see also* Neoplasm, by site, unspecified nature — *continued*
malignant (M8000/3) (*see also* Neoplasm, by site, malignant)
  fusiform cell (type) (M8004/3) — *see* Neoplasm, by site, malignant
  giant cell (type) (M8003/3) — *see* Neoplasm, by site, malignant
  mixed NEC (M8940/3) — *see* Neoplasm, by site, malignant
  small cell (type) (M8002/3) — *see* Neoplasm, by site, malignant
  spindle cell (type) (M8004/3) — *see* Neoplasm, by site, malignant
mast cell (M9740/1) 238.5
  malignant (M9740/3) 202.6 ☑
melanotic, neuroectodermal (M9363/0) — *see* Neoplasm, by site, benign
Merkel cell — *see* ▶Carcinoma, Merkel cell◀
mesenchymal
  malignant (M8800/3) — *see* Neoplasm, connective tissue, malignant
  mixed (M8990/1) — *see* Neoplasm, connective tissue, uncertain behavior
mesodermal, mixed (M8951/3) (*see also* Neoplasm, by site, malignant)
  liver 155.0
mesonephric (M9110/1) (*see also* Neoplasm, by site, uncertain behavior)
  malignant (M9110/3) — *see* Neoplasm, by site, malignant
metastatic
  from specified site (M8000/3) — *see* Neoplasm, by site, malignant
  to specified site (M8000/6) — *see* Neoplasm, by site, malignant, secondary
mixed NEC (M8940/0) (*see also* Neoplasm, by site, benign)
  malignant (M8940/3) — *see* Neoplasm, by site, malignant
mucocarcinoid, malignant (M8243/3) — *see* Neoplasm, by site, malignant
mucoepidermoid (M8430/1) — *see* Neoplasm, by site, uncertain behavior
Müllerian, mixed (M8950/3) — *see* Neoplasm, by site, malignant
myoepithelial (M8982/0) — *see* Neoplasm, by site, benign
neuroendocrine 209.60 ●
  malignant poorly differentiated 209.30 ●
  secondary 209.70 ●
    bone 209.73 ●
    distant lymph nodes 209.71 ●
    liver 209.72 ●
    peritoneum 209.74 ●
    site specified NEC 209.79 ●
neurogenic olfactory (M9520/3) 160.0
nonencapsulated sclerosing (M8350/3) 193
odontogenic (M9270/1) 238.0
  adenomatoid (M9300/0) 213.1
    upper jaw (bone) 213.0
  benign (M9270/0) 213.1
    upper jaw (bone) 213.0
  calcifying epithelial (M9340/0) 213.1
    upper jaw (bone) 213.0
  malignant (M9270/3) 170.1
    upper jaw (bone) 170.0
  squamous (M9312/0) 213.1
    upper jaw (bone) 213.0
ovarian stromal (M8590/1) 236.2
ovary
  in pregnancy or childbirth 654.4 ☑
    affecting fetus or newborn 763.89
    causing obstructed labor 660.2 ☑
      affecting fetus or newborn 763.1
pacinian (M9507/0) — *see* Neoplasm, skin, benign
Pancoast's (M8010/3) 162.3
papillary — *see* Papilloma
pelvic, in pregnancy or childbirth 654.9 ☑
  affecting fetus or newborn 763.89
  causing obstructed labor 660.2 ☑
    affecting fetus or newborn 763.1
phantom 300.11
plasma cell (M9731/1) 238.6

Tumor — *see also* Neoplasm, by site, unspecified nature — *continued*
  plasma cell — *continued*
    benign (M9731/0) — *see* Neoplasm, by site, benign
    malignant (M9731/3) 203.8 ☑
  polyvesicular vitelline (M9071/3)
    specified site — *see* Neoplasm, by site, malignant
    unspecified site
      female 183.0
      male 186.9
  Pott's puffy (*see also* Osteomyelitis) 730.2 ☑
  Rathke's pouch (M9350/1) 237.0
  regaud's (M8082/3) — *see* Neoplasm, nasopharynx, malignant
  rete cell (M8140/0) 222.0
  retinal anlage (M9363/0) — *see* Neoplasm, by site, benign
  Rokitansky's 620.2
  salivary gland type, mixed (M8940/0) (*see also* Neoplasm, by site, benign)
    malignant (M8940/3) — *see* Neoplasm, by site, malignant
  Sampson's 617.1
  Schloffer's (*see also* Peritonitis) 567.29
  Schmincke (M8082/3) — *see* Neoplasm, nasopharynx, malignant
  sebaceous (*see also* Cyst, sebaceous) 706.2
  secondary (M8000/6) — *see* Neoplasm, by site, secondary
    carcinoid — *see* Tumor, neuroendocrine, ●
      secondary ●
    neuroendocrine — *see* Tumor, neuroen- ●
      docrine, secondary ●
  Sertoli cell (M8640/0)
    with lipid storage (M8641/0)
      specified site — *see* Neoplasm, by site, benign
      unspecified site
        female 220
        male 222.0
    specified site — *see* Neoplasm, by site, benign
    unspecified site
      female 220
      male 222.0
  Sertoli-Leydig cell (M8631/0)
    specified site, — *see* Neoplasm, by site, benign
    unspecified site
      female 220
      male 222.0
  sex cord (-stromal) (M8590/1) — *see* Neoplasm, by site, uncertain behavior
  skin appendage (M8390/0) — *see* Neoplasm, skin, benign
  soft tissue
    benign (M8800/0) — *see* Neoplasm, connective tissue, benign
    malignant (M8800/3) — *see* Neoplasm, connective tissue, malignant
  sternomastoid 754.1
  stromal
    abdomen
      benign 215.5
      malignant NEC 171.5
      uncertain behavior 238.1
    digestive system 238.1
      benign 215.5
      malignant NEC 171.5
      uncertain behavior 238.1
    gastric 238.1
      benign 215.5
      malignant 151.9
      uncertain behavior 238.1
    gastrointestinal 238.1
      benign 215.5
      malignant NEC 171.5
      uncertain behavior 238.1
    intestine (small) 238.1
      benign 215.5
      malignant 152.9
      uncertain behavior 238.1
    stomach 238.1
      benign 215.5

Tumor — *see also* Neoplasm, by site, unspecified nature — *continued*
  stromal — *continued*
    stomach — *continued*
      malignant 151.9
      uncertain behavior 238.1
  superior sulcus (lung) (pulmonary) (syndrome) (M8010/3) 162.3
  suprasulcus (M8010/3) 162.3
  sweat gland (M8400/1) (*see also* Neoplasm, skin, uncertain behavior)
    benign (M8400/0) — *see* Neoplasm, skin, benign
    malignant (M8400/3) — *see* Neoplasm, skin, malignant
  syphilitic brain 094.89
    congenital 090.49
  testicular stromal (M8590/1) 236.4
  theca cell (M8600/0) 220
  theca cell-granulosa cell (M8621/1) 236.2
  theca-lutein (M8610/0) 220
  turban (M8200/0) 216.4
  uterus
    in pregnancy or childbirth 654.1 ☑
      affecting fetus or newborn 763.89
      causing obstructed labor 660.2 ☑
        affecting fetus or newborn 763.1
  vagina
    in pregnancy or childbirth 654.7 ☑
      affecting fetus or newborn 763.89
      causing obstructed labor 660.2 ☑
        affecting fetus or newborn 763.1
  varicose (*see also* Varicose, vein) 454.9
  von Recklinghausen's (M9540/1) 237.71
  vulva
    in pregnancy or childbirth 654.8 ☑
      affecting fetus or newborn 763.89
      causing obstructed labor 660.2 ☑
        affecting fetus or newborn 763.1
  Warthin's (salivary gland) (M8561/0) 210.2
  white (*see also* Tuberculosis, arthritis)
  White-Darier 757.39
  Wilms' (nephroblastoma) (M8960/3) 189.0
  yolk sac (M9071/3)
    specified site — *see* Neoplasm, by site, malignant
    unspecified site
      female 183.0
      male 186.9
Tumorlet (M8040/1) — *see* Neoplasm, by site, uncertain behavior
Tungiasis 134.1
Tunica vasculosa lentis 743.39
Tunnel vision 368.45
Turban tumor (M8200/0) 216.4
Türck's trachoma (chronic catarrhal laryngitis) 476.0
Türk's syndrome (ocular retraction syndrome) 378.71
Turner's
  hypoplasia (tooth) 520.4
  syndrome 758.6
  tooth 520.4
Turner-Kieser syndrome (hereditary osteo-onychodysplasia) 756.89
Turner-Varny syndrome 758.6
Turricephaly 756.0
Tussis convulsiva — *see also* Whooping cough 033.9
Twiddler's syndrome (due to)
  automatic implantable defibrillator 996.04
  pacemaker 996.01
Twin
  affected by maternal complications of pregnancy 761.5
  conjoined 759.4
    fetal 678.1 ☑
  healthy liveborn — *see* Newborn, twin
  pregnancy (complicating delivery) NEC 651.0 ☑
    with fetal loss and retention of one fetus 651.3 ☑
    conjoined 678.1 ☑
    following (elective) fetal reduction
Twinning, teeth 520.2

Twist, twisted
  bowel, colon, or intestine 560.2
  hair (congenital) 757.4
  mesentery 560.2
  omentum 560.2
  organ or site, congenital NEC — *see* Anomaly, specified type NEC
  ovarian pedicle 620.5
    congenital 752.0
  umbilical cord — *see* Compression, umbilical cord
Twitch 781.0
Tylosis 700
  buccalis 528.6
  gingiva 523.8
  linguae 528.6
  palmaris et plantaris 757.39
Tympanism 787.3
Tympanites (abdominal) (intestine) 787.3
Tympanitis — *see* Myringitis
Tympanosclerosis 385.00
  involving
    combined sites NEC 385.09
      with tympanic membrane 385.03
    tympanic membrane 385.01
      with ossicles 385.02
        and middle ear 385.03
Tympanum — *see* condition
Tympany
  abdomen 787.3
  chest 786.7
Typhlitis — *see also* Appendicitis 541
Typhoenteritis 002.0
Typhogastric fever 002.0
Typhoid (abortive) (ambulant) (any site) (fever) (hemorrhagic) (infection) (intermittent) (malignant) (rheumatic) 002.0
  with pneumonia 002.0 [484.8]
  abdominal 002.0
  carrier (suspected) of V02.1
  cholecystitis (current) 002.0
  clinical (Widal and blood test negative) 002.0
  endocarditis 002.0 [421.1]
  inoculation reaction — *see* Complications, vaccination
  meningitis 002.0 [320.7]
  mesenteric lymph nodes 002.0
  myocarditis 002.0 [422.0]
  osteomyelitis (*see also* Osteomyelitis, due to, typhoid) 002.0 [730.8] ☑
  perichondritis, larynx 002.0 [478.71]
  pneumonia 002.0 [484.8]
  spine 002.0 [720.81]
  ulcer (perforating) 002.0
  vaccination, prophylactic (against) V03.1
  Widal negative 002.0
Typhomalaria (fever) — *see also* Malaria 084.6
Typhomania 002.0
Typhoperitonitis 002.0
Typhus (fever) 081.9
  abdominal, abdominalis 002.0
  African tick 082.1
  amarillic (*see also* Fever, Yellow) 060.9
  brain 081.9
  cerebral 081.9
  classical 080
  endemic (flea-borne) 081.0
  epidemic (louse-borne) 080
  exanthematic NEC 080
  exanthematicus SAI 080
    brillii SAI 081.1
    Mexicanus SAI 081.0
    pediculo vestimenti causa 080
    typhus murinus 081.0
  flea-borne 081.0
  Indian tick 082.1
  Kenya tick 082.1
  louse-borne 080
  Mexican 081.0
    flea-borne 081.0
    louse-borne 080
    tabardillo 080
  mite-borne 081.2
  murine 081.0
  North Asian tick-borne 082.2
  petechial 081.9

Typhus — *continued*
  Queensland tick 082.3
  rat 081.0
  recrudescent 081.1
  recurrent (*see also* Fever, relapsing) 087.9
  São Paulo 082.0
  scrub (China) (India) (Malaya) (New Guinea) 081.2
  shop (of Malaya) 081.0
  Siberian tick 082.2
  tick-borne NEC 082.9
  tropical 081.2
  vaccination, prophylactic (against) V05.8
Tyrosinemia 270.2
  neonatal 775.89
Tyrosinosis (Medes) (Sakai) 270.2
Tyrosinuria 270.2
Tyrosyluria 270.2

U

Uehlinger's syndrome (acropachyderma) 757.39
Uhl's anomaly or disease (hypoplasia of myocardium, right ventricle) 746.84
Ulcerosa scarlatina 034.1
Ulcer, ulcerated, ulcerating, ulceration, ulcerative 707.9
  with gangrene 707.9 [785.4]
  abdomen (wall) (*see also* Ulcer, skin) 707.8
  ala, nose 478.19
  alveolar process 526.5
  amebic (intestine) 006.9
    skin 006.6
  anastomotic — *see* Ulcer, gastrojejunal
  anorectal 569.41
  antral — *see* Ulcer, stomach
  anus (sphincter) (solitary) 569.41
    varicose — *see* Varicose, ulcer, anus
  aorta — *see* Aneuysm
  aphthous (oral) (recurrent) 528.2
    genital organ(s)
      female 616.50
      male 608.89
    mouth 528.2
  arm (*see also* Ulcer, skin) 707.8
  arteriosclerotic plaque — *see* Arteriosclerosis, by site
  artery NEC 447.2
    without rupture 447.8
  atrophic NEC — *see* Ulcer, skin
  Barrett's (chronic peptic ulcer of esophagus) 530.85
  bile duct 576.8
  bladder (solitary) (sphincter) 596.8
    bilharzial (*see also* Schistosomiasis) 120.9 [595.4]
    submucosal (*see also* Cystitis) 595.1
    tuberculous (*see also* Tuberculosis) 016.1 ☑
  bleeding NEC — *see* Ulcer, peptic, with hemorrhage
  bone 730.9 ☑
  bowel (*see also* Ulcer, intestine) 569.82
  breast 611.0
  bronchitis 491.8
  bronchus 519.19
  buccal (cavity) (traumatic) 528.9
  burn (acute) — *see* Ulcer, duodenum
  Buruli 031.1
  buttock (*see also* Ulcer, skin) 707.8
    decubitus (*see also* Ulcer, pressure) 707.00
  cancerous (M8000/3) — *see* Neoplasm, by site, malignant
  cardia — *see* Ulcer, stomach
  cardio-esophageal (peptic) 530.20
    with bleeding 530.21
  cecum (*see also* Ulcer, intestine) 569.82
  cervix (uteri) (trophic) 622.0
    with mention of cervicitis 616.0
  chancroidal 099.0
  chest (wall) (*see also* Ulcer, skin) 707.8
  Chiclero 085.4
  chin (pyogenic) (*see also* Ulcer, skin) 707.8
  chronic (cause unknown) (*see also* Ulcer, skin)
    penis 607.89
  Cochin-China 085.1
  colitis — *see* Colitis, ulcerative

Index

Ulcer, ulcerated, ulcerating — Ulcer, ulcerated, ulcerating

Ulcer, ulcerated, ulcerating, ulceration, ulcerative — *continued*
  colon (*see also* Ulcer, intestine) 569.82
  conjunctiva (acute) (postinfectional) 372.00
  cornea (infectional) 370.00
    with perforation 370.06
    annular 370.02
    catarrhal 370.01
    central 370.03
    dendritic 054.42
    marginal 370.01
    mycotic 370.05
    phlyctenular, tuberculous (*see also* Tuberculosis) 017.3 ☑ *[370.31]*
    ring 370.02
    rodent 370.07
    serpent, serpiginous 370.04
    superficial marginal 370.01
    tuberculous (*see also* Tuberculosis)
      017.3 ☑ *[370.31]*
  corpus cavernosum (chronic) 607.89
  crural — *see* Ulcer, lower extremity
  Curling's — *see* Ulcer, duodenum
  Cushing's — *see* Ulcer, peptic
  cystitis (interstitial) 595.1
  decubitus (unspecified site) (*see also* Ulcer, pressure) 707.00
    with gangrene 707.00 *[785.4]*
    ankle 707.06
    back
      lower 707.03
      upper 707.02
    buttock 707.05
    coccyx 707.03
    elbow 707.01
    head 707.09
    heel 707.07
    hip 707.04
    other site 707.09
    sacrum 707.03
    shoulder blades 707.02
  dendritic 054.42
  diabetes, diabetic (mellitus) 250.8 ☑ *[707.9]*
    due to secondary diabetes 249.8 ☑ *[707.9]*
    lower limb 250.8 ☑ *[707.10]*
      ankle 250.8 ☑ *[707.13]*
        due to secondary diabetes
          249.8 ☑ *[707.13]*
      calf 250.8 ☑ *[707.12]*
        due to secondary diabetes
          249.8 ☑ *[707.12]*
      due to secondary diabetes
        249.8 ☑ *[707.10]*
      foot 250.8 ☑ *[707.15]*
        due to secondary diabetes
          249.8 ☑ *[707.15]*
      heel 250.8 ☑ *[707.14]*
        due to secondary diabetes
          249.8 ☑ *[707.14]*
      knee 250.8 ☑ *[707.19]*
        due to secondary diabetes
          249.8 ☑ *[707.19]*
      specified site NEC 250.8 ☑ *[707.19]*
        due to secondary diabetes
          249.8 ☑ *[707.19]*
      thigh 250.8 ☑ *[707.11]*
        due to secondary diabetes
          249.8 ☑ *[707.11]*
      toes 250.8 ☑ *[707.15]*
        due to secondary diabetes
          249.8 ☑ *[707.15]*
    specified site NEC 250.8 ☑ *[707.8]*
      due to secondary diabetes
        249.8 ☑ *[707.8]*
  Dieulafoy — *see* Lesion, Dieulafoy
  due to
    infection NEC — *see* Ulcer, skin
    radiation, radium — *see* Ulcer, by site
    trophic disturbance (any region) — *see* Ulcer, skin
    x-ray — *see* Ulcer, by site

Ulcer, ulcerated, ulcerating, ulceration, ulcerative — *continued*
  duodenum, duodenal (eroded) (peptic)
    532.9 ☑

  Note — *Use the following fifth-digit subclassification with categories 531–534:*
  0   *without mention of obstruction*
  1   *with obstruction*

    with
      hemorrhage (chronic) 532.4 ☑
        and perforation 532.6 ☑
      perforation (chronic) 532.5 ☑
        and hemorrhage 532.6 ☑
    acute 532.3 ☑
      with
        hemorrhage 532.0 ☑
          and perforation 532.2 ☑
        perforation 532.1 ☑
          and hemorrhage 532.2 ☑
      bleeding (recurrent) — *see* Ulcer, duodenum, with hemorrhage
    chronic 532.7 ☑
      with
        hemorrhage 532.4 ☑
          and perforation 532.6 ☑
        perforation 532.5 ☑
          and hemorrhage 532.6 ☑
    penetrating — *see* Ulcer, duodenum, with perforation
    perforating — *see* Ulcer, duodenum, with perforation
  dysenteric NEC 009.0
  elusive 595.1
  endocarditis (any valve) (acute) (chronic) (subacute) 421.0
  enteritis — *see* Colitis, ulcerative
  enterocolitis 556.0
  epiglottis 478.79
  esophagus (peptic) 530.20
    with bleeding 530.21
    due to ingestion
      aspirin 530.20
      chemicals 530.20
      medicinal agents 530.20
    fungal 530.20
    infectional 530.20
    varicose (*see also* Varix, esophagus) 456.1
      bleeding (*see also* Varix, esophagus, bleeding) 456.0
  eye NEC 360.00
    dendritic 054.42
  eyelid (region) 373.01
  face (*see also* Ulcer, skin) 707.8
  fauces 478.29
  Fenwick (-Hunner) (solitary) (*see also* Cystitis) 595.1
  fistulous NEC — *see* Ulcer, skin
  foot (indolent) (*see also* Ulcer, lower extremity) 707.15
    perforating 707.15
      leprous 030.1
      syphilitic 094.0
    trophic 707.15
    varicose 454.0
      inflamed or infected 454.2
  frambesial, initial or primary 102.0
  gallbladder or duct 575.8
  gall duct 576.8
  gangrenous (*see also* Gangrene) 785.4
  gastric — *see* Ulcer, stomach
  gastrocolic — *see* Ulcer, gastrojejunal
  gastroduodenal — *see* Ulcer, peptic
  gastroesophageal — *see* Ulcer, stomach
  gastrohepatic — *see* Ulcer, stomach
  gastrointestinal — *see* Ulcer, gastrojejunal
  gastrojejunal (eroded) (peptic) 534.9 ☑

  Note — *Use the following fifth-digit subclassification with categories 531–534:*
  0   *without mention of obstruction*
  1   *with obstruction*

    with
      hemorrhage (chronic) 534.4 ☑

Ulcer, ulcerated, ulcerating, ulceration, ulcerative — *continued*
  gastrojejunal — *continued*
    with — *continued*
      hemorrhage — *continued*
        and perforation 534.6 ☑
      perforation 534.5 ☑
        and hemorrhage 534.6 ☑
    acute 534.3 ☑
      with
        hemorrhage 534.0 ☑
          and perforation 534.2 ☑
        perforation 534.1 ☑
          and hemorrhage 534.2 ☑
      bleeding (recurrent) — *see* Ulcer, gastrojejunal, with hemorrhage
    chronic 534.7 ☑
      with
        hemorrhage 534.4 ☑
          and perforation 534.6 ☑
        perforation 534.5 ☑
          and hemorrhage 534.6 ☑
    penetrating — *see* Ulcer, gastrojejunal, with perforation
    perforating — *see* Ulcer, gastrojejunal, with perforation
  gastrojejunocolic — *see* Ulcer, gastrojejunal
  genital organ
    female 629.89
    male 608.89
  gingiva 523.8
  gingivitis 523.10
  glottis 478.79
  granuloma of pudenda 099.2
  groin (*see also* Ulcer, skin) 707.8
  gum 523.8
  gumma, due to yaws 102.4
  hand (*see also* Ulcer, skin) 707.8
  hard palate 528.9
  heel (*see also* Ulcer, lower extremity) 707.14
    decubitus (*see also* Ulcer, pressure) 707.07
  hemorrhoids 455.8
    external 455.5
    internal 455.2
  hip (*see also* Ulcer, skin) 707.8
    decubitus (*see also* Ulcer, pressure) 707.04
  Hunner's 595.1
  hypopharynx 478.29
  hypopyon (chronic) (subacute) 370.04
  hypostaticum — *see* Ulcer, varicose
  ileocolitis 556.1
  ileum (*see also* Ulcer, intestine) 569.82
  intestine, intestinal 569.82
    with perforation 569.83
    amebic 006.9
    duodenal — *see* Ulcer, duodenum
    granulocytopenic (with hemorrhage) 288.09
    marginal 569.82
    perforating 569.83
    small, primary 569.82
    stercoraceous 569.82
    stercoral 569.82
    tuberculous (*see also* Tuberculosis) 014.8 ☑
    typhoid (fever) 002.0
    varicose 456.8
  ischemic 707.9
    lower extremity (*see also* Ulcer, lower extremity) 707.10
      ankle 707.13
      calf 707.12
      foot 707.15
      heel 707.14
      knee 707.19
      specified site NEC 707.19
      thigh 707.11
      toes 707.15
  jejunum, jejunal — *see* Ulcer, gastrojejunal
  keratitis (*see also* Ulcer, cornea) 370.00
  knee — *see* Ulcer, lower extremity
  labium (majus) (minus) 616.50
  laryngitis (*see also* Laryngitis) 464.00
    with obstruction 464.01
  larynx (aphthous) (contact) 478.79
    diphtheritic 032.3

Ulcer, ulcerated, ulcerating, ulceration, ulcerative — *continued*
  leg — *see* Ulcer, lower extremity
  lip 528.5
  Lipschütz's 616.50
  lower extremity (atrophic) (chronic) (neurogenic) (perforating) (pyogenic) (trophic) (tropical) 707.10
    with gangrene (*see also* Ulcer, lower extremity) 707.10 *[785.4]*
      arteriosclerotic 440.24
    ankle 707.13
    arteriosclerotic 440.23
      with gangrene 440.24
    calf 707.12
    decubitus (*see also* Ulcer, pressure) 707.00
      with gangrene 707.00 *[785.4]*
      ankle 707.06
      buttock 707.05
      heel 707.07
      hip 707.04
    foot 707.15
    heel 707.14
    knee 707.19
    specified site NEC 707.19
    thigh 707.11
    toes 707.15
    varicose 454.0
      inflamed or infected 454.2
  luetic — *see* Ulcer, syphilitic
  lung 518.89
    tuberculous (*see also* Tuberculosis) 011.2 ☑
  malignant (M8000/3) — *see* Neoplasm, by site, malignant
  marginal NEC — *see* Ulcer, gastrojejunal
  meatus (urinarius) 597.89
  Meckel's diverticulum 751.0
  Meleney's (chronic undermining) 686.09
  Mooren's (cornea) 370.07
  mouth (traumatic) 528.9
  mycobacterial (skin) 031.1
  nasopharynx 478.29
  navel cord (newborn) 771.4
  neck (*see also* Ulcer, skin) 707.8
    uterus 622.0
  neurogenic NEC — *see* Ulcer, skin
  nose, nasal (infectional) (passage) 478.19
    septum 478.19
      varicose 456.8
    skin — *see* Ulcer, skin
    spirochetal NEC 104.8
  oral mucosa (traumatic) 528.9
  palate (soft) 528.9
  penetrating NEC — *see* Ulcer, peptic, with perforation
  penis (chronic) 607.89
  peptic (site unspecified) 533.9 ☑

  Note — *Use the following fifth-digit subclassification with categories 531–534:*
  0   *without mention of obstruction*
  1   *with obstruction*

    with
      hemorrhage 533.4 ☑
        and perforation 533.6 ☑
      perforation (chronic) 533.5 ☑
        and hemorrhage 533.6 ☑
    acute 533.3 ☑
      with
        hemorrhage 533.0 ☑
          and perforation 533.2 ☑
        perforation 533.1 ☑
          and hemorrhage 533.2 ☑
      bleeding (recurrent) — *see* Ulcer, peptic, with hemorrhage
    chronic 533.7 ☑
      with
        hemorrhage 533.4 ☑
          and perforation 533.6 ☑
        perforation 533.5 ☑
          and hemorrhage 533.6 ☑
    penetrating — *see* Ulcer, peptic, with perforation

☑ Additional Digit Required — Refer to the Tabular List for Digit Selection

Subterms under main terms may continue to next column or page

Ulcer, ulcerated, ulcerating, ulceration, ulcerative — *continued*

perforating NEC (*see also* Ulcer, peptic, with perforation) 533.5 ☑
  skin 707.9
perineum (*see also* Ulcer, skin) 707.8
peritonsillar 474.8
phagedenic (tropical) NEC — *see* Ulcer, skin
pharynx 478.29
phlebitis — *see* Phlebitis
plaster (*see also* Ulcer, pressure) 707.00
popliteal space — *see* Ulcer, lower extremity
postpyloric — *see* Ulcer, duodenum
prepuce 607.89
prepyloric — *see* Ulcer, stomach
pressure 707.00
  with
    abrasion, blister, partial thickness skin loss involving epidermis and/or dermis 707.22
    full thickness skin loss involving damage or necrosis of subcutaneous tissue 707.23
    gangrene 707.00 *[785.4]*
    necrosis of soft tissue through to underlying muscle, tendon, or bone 707.24
  ankle 707.06
  back
    lower 707.03
    upper 707.02
  buttock 707.05
  coccyx 707.03
  elbow 707.01
  head 707.09
  healed — omit code
  healing — code to Ulcer, pressure, by stage
  heel 707.07
  hip 707.04
  other site 707.09
  sacrum 707.03
  shoulder blades 707.02
  stage
    I (healing) 707.21
    II (healing) 707.22
    III (healing) 707.23
    IV (healing) 707.24
    unspecified (healing) 707.20
  unstageable 707.25
primary of intestine 569.82
  with perforation 569.83
proctitis 556.2
  with ulcerative sigmoiditis 556.3
prostate 601.8
pseudopeptic — *see* Ulcer, peptic
pyloric — *see* Ulcer, stomach
rectosigmoid 569.82
  with perforation 569.83
rectum (sphincter) (solitary) 569.41
  stercoraceous, stercoral 569.41
  varicose — *see* Varicose, ulcer, anus
retina (*see also* Chorioretinitis) 363.20
rodent (M8090/3) (*see also* Neoplasm, skin, malignant)
  cornea 370.07
round — *see* Ulcer, stomach
sacrum (region) (*see also* Ulcer, skin) 707.8
Saemisch's 370.04
scalp (*see also* Ulcer, skin) 707.8
sclera 379.09
scrofulous (*see also* Tuberculosis) 017.2 ☑
scrotum 608.89
  tuberculous (*see also* Tuberculosis) 016.5 ☑
  varicose 456.4
seminal vesicle 608.89
sigmoid 569.82
  with perforation 569.83
skin (atrophic) (chronic) (neurogenic) (non-healing) (perforating) (pyogenic) (trophic) 707.9
  with gangrene 707.9 *[785.4]*
    amebic 006.6
  decubitus (*see also* Ulcer, pressure) 707.00
    with gangrene 707.00 *[785.4]*

Ulcer, ulcerated, ulcerating, ulceration, ulcerative — *continued*

skin — *continued*
  in granulocytopenia 288.09
  lower extremity (*see also* Ulcer, lower extremity) 707.10
    with gangrene 707.10 *[785.4]*
      arteriosclerotic 440.24
    ankle 707.13
    arteriosclerotic 440.23
      with gangrene 440.24
    calf 707.12
    foot 707.15
    heel 707.14
    knee 707.19
    specified site NEC 707.19
    thigh 707.11
    toes 707.15
  mycobacterial 031.1
  syphilitic (early) (secondary) 091.3
  tuberculous (primary) (*see also* Tuberculosis) 017.0 ☑
  varicose — *see* Ulcer, varicose
sloughing NEC — *see* Ulcer, skin
soft palate 528.9
solitary, anus or rectum (sphincter) 569.41
sore throat 462
  streptococcal 034.0
spermatic cord 608.89
spine (tuberculous) 015.0 ☑ *[730.88]*
stasis (leg) (venous) 454.0
  with varicose veins 454.0
  without varicose veins 459.81
  inflamed or infected 454.2
stercoral, stercoraceous 569.82
  with perforation 569.83
  anus or rectum 569.41
stomach (eroded) (peptic) (round) 531.9 ☑

Note — Use the following fifth-digit subclassification with categories 531–534:

0   without mention of obstruction

1   with obstruction

  with
    hemorrhage 531.4 ☑
      and perforation 531.6 ☑
    perforation (chronic) 531.5 ☑
      and hemorrhage 531.6 ☑
  acute 531.3 ☑
    with
      hemorrhage 531.0 ☑
        and perforation 531.2 ☑
      perforation 531.1 ☑
        and hemorrhage 531.2 ☑
  bleeding (recurrent) — *see* Ulcer, stomach, with hemorrhage
  chronic 531.7 ☑
    with
      hemorrhage 531.4 ☑
        and perforation 531.6 ☑
      perforation 531.5 ☑
        and hemorrhage 531.6 ☑
  penetrating — *see* Ulcer, stomach, with perforation
  perforating — *see* Ulcer, stomach, with perforation
stoma, stomal — *see* Ulcer, gastrojejunal
stomatitis 528.00
stress — *see* Ulcer, peptic
strumous (tuberculous) (*see also* Tuberculosis) 017.2 ☑
submental (*see also* Ulcer, skin) 707.8
submucosal, bladder 595.1
syphilitic (any site) (early) (secondary) 091.3
  late 095.9
  perforating 095.9
    foot 094.0
testis 608.89
thigh — *see* Ulcer, lower extremity
throat 478.29
  diphtheritic 032.0
toe — *see* Ulcer, lower extremity
tongue (traumatic) 529.0
tonsil 474.8
  diphtheritic 032.0

Ulcer, ulcerated, ulcerating, ulceration, ulcerative — *continued*

trachea 519.19
trophic — *see* Ulcer, skin
tropical NEC (*see also* Ulcer, skin) 707.9
tuberculous — *see* Tuberculosis, ulcer
tunica vaginalis 608.89
turbinate 730.9 ☑
typhoid (fever) 002.0
  perforating 002.0
umbilicus (newborn) 771.4
unspecified site NEC — *see* Ulcer, skin
urethra (meatus) (*see also* Urethritis) 597.89
uterus 621.8
  cervix 622.0
    with mention of cervicitis 616.0
  neck 622.0
    with mention of cervicitis 616.0
vagina 616.89
valve, heart 421.0
varicose (lower extremity, any part) 454.0
  anus — *see* Varicose, ulcer, anus
  broad ligament 456.5
  esophagus (*see also* Varix, esophagus) 456.1
    bleeding (*see also* Varix, esophagus, bleeding) 456.0
  inflamed or infected 454.2
  nasal septum 456.8
  perineum 456.6
  rectum — *see* Varicose, ulcer, anus
  scrotum 456.4
  specified site NEC 456.8
  sublingual 456.3
  vulva 456.6
vas deferens 608.89
vesical (*see also* Ulcer, bladder) 596.8
vulva (acute) (infectional) 616.50
  Behçet's syndrome 136.1 *[616.51]*
  herpetic 054.12
  tuberculous 016.7 ☑ *[616.51]*
vulvobuccal, recurring 616.50
x-ray — *see* Ulcer, by site
yaws 102.4
Ulcus — *see also* Ulcer
cutis tuberculosum (*see also* Tuberculosis) 017.0 ☑
duodeni — *see* Ulcer, duodenum
durum 091.0
  extragenital 091.2
gastrojejunale — *see* Ulcer, gastrojejunal
hypostaticum — *see* Ulcer, varicose
molle (cutis) (skin) 099.0
serpens corneae (pneumococcal) 370.04
ventriculi — *see* Ulcer, stomach
Ulegyria 742.4
Ulerythema
acneiforma 701.8
centrifugum 695.4
ophryogenes 757.4
Ullrich-Feichtiger syndrome 759.89
Ullrich (-Bonnevie) (-Turner) syndrome 758.6
Ulnar — *see* condition
Ulorrhagia 523.8
Ulorrhea 523.8
Umbilicus, umbilical — *see also* condition
cord necrosis, affecting fetus or newborn 762.6
Unacceptable
existing dental restoration
  contours 525.65
  morphology 525.65
Unavailability of medical facilities (at) V63.9
due to
  investigation by social service agency V63.8
  lack of services at home V63.1
  remoteness from facility V63.0
  waiting list V63.2
    home V63.1
  outpatient clinic V63.0
  specified reason NEC V63.8
Uncinaria americana infestation 126.1
Uncinariasis — *see also* Ancylostomiasis 126.9
Unconscious, unconsciousness 780.09
Underdevelopment — *see also* Undeveloped
sexual 259.0

Underfill, endodontic 526.63
Undernourishment 269.9
Undernutrition 269.9
Under observation — *see* Observation
Underweight 783.22
for gestational age — *see* Light-for-dates
Underwood's disease (sclerema neonatorum) 778.1
Undescended — *see also* Malposition, congenital
cecum 751.4
colon 751.4
testis 752.51
Undetermined diagnosis or cause 799.9
Undeveloped, undevelopment — *see also* Hypoplasia
brain (congenital) 742.1
cerebral (congenital) 742.1
fetus or newborn 764.9 ☑
heart 746.89
lung 748.5
testis 257.2
uterus 259.0
Undiagnosed (disease) 799.9
Undulant fever — *see also* Brucellosis 023.9
Unemployment, anxiety concerning V62.0
Unequal leg (acquired) (length) 736.81
congenital 755.30
Unerupted teeth, tooth 520.6
Unextracted dental root 525.3
Unguis incarnatus 703.0
Unicornis uterus 752.3
Unicorporeus uterus 752.3
Uniformis uterus 752.3
Unilateral — *see also* condition
development, breast 611.89
organ or site, congenital NEC — *see* Agenesis
vagina 752.49
Unilateralis uterus 752.3
Unilocular heart 745.8
Uninhibited bladder 596.54
with cauda equina syndrome 344.61
neurogenic — *see also* Neurogenic, bladder 596.54
Union, abnormal — *see also* Fusion
divided tendon 727.89
larynx and trachea 748.3
Universal
joint, cervix 620.6
mesentery 751.4
Unknown
cause of death 799.9
diagnosis 799.9
Unna's disease (seborrheic dermatitis) 690.10
Unresponsiveness, adrenocorticotropin (ACTH) 255.41
Unsatisfactory
cytology smear
  anal 796.78
  cervical 795.08
  vaginal 795.18
restoration, tooth (existing) 525.60
  specified NEC 525.69
Unsoundness of mind — *see also* Psychosis 298.9
Unspecified cause of death 799.9
Unstable
back NEC 724.9
colon 569.89
joint — *see* Instability, joint
lie 652.0 ☑
  affecting fetus or newborn (before labor) 761.7
  causing obstructed labor 660.0 ☑
    affecting fetus or newborn 763.1
lumbosacral joint (congenital) 756.19
  acquired 724.6
sacroiliac 724.6
spine NEC 724.9
Untruthfulness, child problem — *see also* Disturbance, conduct 312.0 ☑
Unverricht (-Lundborg) disease, syndrome, or epilepsy 345.1 ☑ ▲
Unverricht-Wagner syndrome (dermatomyositis) 710.3
Upper respiratory — *see* condition

☑ Additional Digit Required — Refer to the Tabular List for Digit Selection

▶◀ Revised Text   ● New Line   ▲ Revised Code

Subterms under main terms may continue to next column or page

2010 ICD-9-CM

October 2009 • Volume 2 — 279

Ulcer, ulcerated, ulcerating — Upper respiratory

Index

Upset — Uvulitis

Upset
- gastric 536.8
  - psychogenic 306.4
- gastrointestinal 536.8
  - psychogenic 306.4
  - virus (see also Enteritis, viral) 008.8
- intestinal (large) (small) 564.9
  - psychogenic 306.4
- menstruation 626.9
- mental 300.9
- stomach 536.8
  - psychogenic 306.4

Urachus — see also condition
- patent 753.7
- persistent 753.7

Uratic arthritis 274.00 ▲

Urbach's lipoid proteinosis 272.8

Urbach-Oppenheim disease or syndrome (necrobiosis lipoidica diabeticorum) 250.8 ☑ [709.3]
- due to secondary diabetes 249.8 ☑ [709.3]

Urbach-Wiethe disease or syndrome (lipoid proteinosis) 272.8

Urban yellow fever 060.1

Urea, blood, high — see Uremia

Uremia, uremic (absorption) (amaurosis) (amblyopia) (aphasia) (apoplexy) (coma) (delirium) (dementia) (dropsy) (dyspnea) (fever) (intoxication) (mania) (paralysis) (poisoning) (toxemia) (vomiting) 586
- with
  - abortion — see Abortion, by type, with renal failure
  - ectopic pregnancy (see also categories 633.0–633.9) 639.3
  - hypertension (see also Hypertension, kidney) 403.91
  - molar pregnancy (see also categories 630–632) 639.3
- chronic 585.9
- complicating
  - abortion 639.3
  - ectopic or molar pregnancy 639.3
  - hypertension (see also Hypertension, kidney) 403.91
  - labor and delivery 669.3 ☑
- congenital 779.89
- extrarenal 788.99
- hypertensive (chronic) (see also Hypertension, kidney) 403.91
- maternal NEC, affecting fetus or newborn 760.1
- neuropathy 585.9 [357.4]
- pericarditis 585.9 [420.0]
- prerenal 788.99
- pyelitic (see also Pyelitis) 590.80

Ureteralgia 788.0

Ureterectasis 593.89

Ureteritis 593.89
- cystica 590.3
- due to calculus 592.1
- gonococcal (acute) 098.19
  - chronic or duration of 2 months or over 098.39
- nonspecific 593.89

Ureterocele (acquired) 593.89
- congenital 753.23

Ureterolith 592.1

Ureterolithiasis 592.1

Ureterostomy status V44.6
- with complication 997.5

Ureter, ureteral — see condition

Urethralgia 788.99

Urethra, urethral — see condition

Urethritis (abacterial) (acute) (allergic) (anterior) (chronic) (nonvenereal) (posterior) (recurrent) (simple) (subacute) (ulcerative) (undifferentiated) 597.80
- diplococcal (acute) 098.0
  - chronic or duration of 2 months or over 098.2
- due to Trichomonas (vaginalis) 131.02
- gonococcal (acute) 098.0
  - chronic or duration of 2 months or over 098.2
- nongonococcal (sexually transmitted) 099.40
  - Chlamydia trachomatis 099.41
  - Reiter's 099.3
  - specified organism NEC 099.49
- nonspecific (sexually transmitted) (see also Urethritis, nongonococcal) 099.40
- not sexually transmitted 597.80
- Reiter's 099.3
- trichomonal or due to Trichomonas (vaginalis) 131.02
- tuberculous (see also Tuberculosis) 016.3 ☑
- venereal NEC (see also Urethritis, nongonococcal) 099.40

Urethrocele
- female 618.03
  - with uterine prolapse 618.4
    - complete 618.3
    - incomplete 618.2
- male 599.5

Urethrolithiasis 594.2

Urethro-oculoarticular syndrome 099.3

Urethro-oculosynovial syndrome 099.3

Urethrorectal — see condition

Urethrorrhagia 599.84

Urethrorrhea 788.7

Urethrostomy status V44.6
- with complication 997.5

Urethrotrigonitis 595.3

Urethrovaginal — see condition

Urhidrosis, uridrosis 705.89

Uric acid
- diathesis 274.9
- in blood 790.6

Uricacidemia 790.6

Uricemia 790.6

Uricosuria 791.9

Urination
- frequent 788.41
- painful 788.1
- urgency 788.63

Urinemia — see Uremia

Urine, urinary — see also condition
- abnormality NEC 788.69
- blood in (see also Hematuria) 599.70
- discharge, excessive 788.42
- enuresis 788.30
  - nonorganic origin 307.6
- extravasation 788.8
- frequency 788.41
- hesitancy 788.64
- incontinence 788.30
  - active 788.30
  - female 788.30
    - stress 625.6
      - and urge 788.33
  - male 788.30
    - stress 788.32

Urine, urinary — see also condition — continued
- incontinence — continued
  - male — continued
    - stress — continued
      - and urge 788.33
    - mixed (stress and urge) 788.33
    - neurogenic 788.39
    - nonorganic origin 307.6
    - overflow 788.38
    - stress (female) 625.6
      - male NEC 788.32
  - intermittent stream 788.61
  - pus in 791.9
  - retention or stasis NEC 788.20
    - bladder, incomplete emptying 788.21
    - psychogenic 306.53
    - specified NEC 788.29
  - secretion
    - deficient 788.5
    - excessive 788.42
    - frequency 788.41
  - strain 788.65
  - stream
    - intermittent 788.61
    - slowing 788.62
    - splitting 788.61
    - weak 788.62
  - urgency 788.63

Urinoma NEC 599.9
- bladder 596.8
- kidney 593.89
- renal 593.89
- ureter 593.89
- urethra 599.84

Uroarthritis, infectious 099.3

Urodialysis 788.5

Urolithiasis 592.9

Uronephrosis 593.89

Uropathy 599.9
- obstructive 599.60

Urosepsis 599.0
- meaning sepsis 995.91
- meaning urinary tract infection 599.0

Urticaria 708.9
- with angioneurotic edema 995.1
  - hereditary 277.6
- allergic 708.0
- cholinergic 708.5
- chronic 708.8
- cold, familial 708.2
- dermatographic 708.3
- due to
  - cold or heat 708.2
  - drugs 708.0
  - food 708.0
  - inhalants 708.0
  - plants 708.8
  - serum 999.5
- factitial 708.3
- giant 995.1
  - hereditary 277.6
- gigantea 995.1
  - hereditary 277.6
- idiopathic 708.1
- larynx 995.1
  - hereditary 277.6
- neonatorum 778.8
- nonallergic 708.1
- papulosa (Hebra) 698.2
- perstans hemorrhagica 757.39

Urticaria — continued
- pigmentosa 757.33
- recurrent periodic 708.8
- serum 999.5
- solare 692.72
- specified type NEC 708.8
- thermal (cold) (heat) 708.2
- vibratory 708.4

Urticarioides acarodermatitis 133.9

Use of
- methadone 304.00
- nonprescribed drugs (see also Abuse, drugs, nondependent) 305.9 ☑
- patent medicines (see also Abuse, drugs, nondependent) 305.9 ☑

Usher-Senear disease (pemphigus erythematosus) 694.4

Uta 085.5

Uterine size-date discrepancy 649.6 ☑

Uteromegaly 621.2

Uterovaginal — see condition

Uterovesical — see condition

Uterus — see condition

Utriculitis (utriculus prostaticus) 597.89

Uveal — see condition

Uveitis (anterior) — see also Iridocyclitis 364.3
- acute or subacute 364.00
  - due to or associated with
    - gonococcal infection 098.41
    - herpes (simplex) 054.44
      - zoster 053.22
  - primary 364.01
  - recurrent 364.02
  - secondary (noninfectious) 364.04
    - infectious 364.03
- allergic 360.11
- chronic 364.10
  - due to or associated with
    - sarcoidosis 135 [364.11]
    - tuberculosis (see also Tuberculosis) 017.3 ☑ [364.11]
- due to
  - operation 360.11
  - toxoplasmosis (acquired) 130.2
    - congenital (active) 771.2
- granulomatous 364.10
- heterochromic 364.21
- lens-induced 364.23
- nongranulomatous 364.00
- posterior 363.20
  - disseminated — see Chorioretinitis, disseminated
  - focal — see Chorioretinitis, focal
- recurrent 364.02
- sympathetic 360.11
- syphilitic (secondary) 091.50
  - congenital 090.0 [363.13]
  - late 095.8 [363.13]
- tuberculous (see also Tuberculosis) 017.3 ☑ [364.11]

Uveoencephalitis 363.22

Uveokeratitis — see Iridocyclitis 364.3

Uveoparotid fever 135

Uveoparotitis 135

Uvula — see condition

Uvulitis (acute) (catarrhal) (chronic) (gangrenous) (membranous) (suppurative) (ulcerative) 528.3

☑ Additional Digit Required — Refer to the Tabular List for Digit Selection

▽ Subterms under main terms may continue to next column or page

▶◀ Revised Text   ● New Line   ▲ Revised Code

V

Vaccination

complication or reaction — see Complications, vaccination

delayed V64.00

not carried out V64.00

because of

acute illness V64.01

allergy to vaccine or component V64.04

caregiver refusal V64.05

chronic illness V64.02

guardian refusal V64.05

immune compromised state V64.03

parent refusal V64.05

patient had disease being vaccinated against V64.08

patient refusal V64.06

reason NEC V64.09

religious reasons V64.07

prophylactic (against) V05.9

arthropod-borne viral

disease NEC V05.1

encephalitis V05.0

chickenpox V05.4

cholera (alone) V03.0

with typhoid-paratyphoid (cholera + TAB) V06.0

common cold V04.7

diphtheria (alone) V03.5

with

poliomyelitis (DTP+ polio) V06.3

tetanus V06.5

pertussis combined (DTP) (DTaP) V06.1

typhoid-paratyphoid (DTP + TAB) V06.2

disease (single) NEC V05.9

bacterial NEC V03.9

specified type NEC V03.89

combination NEC V06.9

specified type NEC V06.8

specified type NEC V05.8

encephalitis, viral, arthropod-borne V05.0

Hemophilus influenzae, type B [Hib] V03.81

hepatitis, viral V05.3

influenza V04.81

with

Streptococcus pneumoniae [pneumococcus] V06.6

leishmaniasis V05.2

measles (alone) V04.2

with mumps-rubella (MMR) V06.4

mumps (alone) V04.6

with measles and rubella (MMR) V06.4

pertussis alone V03.6

plague V03.3

poliomyelitis V04.0

with diphtheria-tetanus-pertussis (DTP + polio) V06.3

rabies V04.5

respiratory syncytial virus (RSV) V04.82

rubella (alone) V04.3

with measles and mumps (MMR) V06.4

smallpox V04.1

Streptococcus pneumoniae [pneumococcus] V03.82

with

influenza V06.6

tetanus toxoid (alone) V03.7

with diphtheria [Td] [DT] V06.5

with

pertussis (DTP) (DTaP) V06.1

with poliomyelitis (DTP+polio) V06.3

tuberculosis (BCG) V03.2

tularemia V03.4

typhoid-paratyphoid (TAB) (alone) V03.1

with diphtheria-tetanus-pertussis (TAB + DTP) V06.2

varicella V05.4

viral

disease NEC V04.89

encephalitis, arthropod-borne V05.0

hepatitis V05.3

yellow fever V04.4

Vaccinia (generalized) 999.0

without vaccination 051.02

congenital 771.2

conjunctiva 999.39

eyelids 999.0 [373.5]

localized 999.39

nose 999.39

not from vaccination 051.02

eyelid 051.02 [373.5]

sine vaccinatione 051.02

Vacuum

extraction of fetus or newborn 763.3

in sinus (accessory) (nasal) (see also Sinusitis) 473.9

Vagabond V60.0

Vagabondage V60.0

Vagabonds' disease 132.1

Vaginalitis (tunica) 608.4

Vagina, vaginal — see also condition

high risk human papillomavirus (HPV) DNA test positive 795.15

low risk human papillomavirus (HPV) DNA test positive 795.19

Vaginismus (reflex) 625.1

functional 306.51

hysterical 300.11

psychogenic 306.51

Vaginitis (acute) (chronic) (circumscribed) (diffuse) (emphysematous) (Hemophilus vaginalis) (nonspecific) (nonvenereal) (ulcerative) 616.10

with

abortion — see Abortion, by type, with sepsis

ectopic pregnancy (see also categories 633.0–633.9) 639.0

molar pregnancy (see also categories 630–632) 639.0

adhesive, congenital 752.49

atrophic, postmenopausal 627.3

bacterial 616.10

blennorrhagic (acute) 098.0

chronic or duration of 2 months or over 098.2

candidal 112.1

chlamydial 099.53

complicating pregnancy or puerperium 646.6 ✓

affecting fetus or newborn 760.8

congenital (adhesive) 752.49

due to

C. albicans 112.1

Trichomonas (vaginalis) 131.01

following

abortion 639.0

ectopic or molar pregnancy 639.0

gonococcal (acute) 098.0

chronic or duration of 2 months or over 098.2

granuloma 099.2

Monilia 112.1

mycotic 112.1

pinworm 127.4 [616.11]

postirradiation 616.10

postmenopausal atrophic 627.3

senile (atrophic) 627.3

syphilitic (early) 091.0

late 095.8

trichomonal 131.01

tuberculous (see also Tuberculosis) 016.7 ✓

venereal NEC 099.8

Vaginosis — see Vaginitis

Vagotonia 352.3

Vagrancy V60.0

VAIN I (vaginal intraepithelial neoplasia I) 623.0

VAIN II (vaginal intraepithelial neoplasia II) 623.0

VAIN III (vaginal intraepithelial neoplasia III) 233.31

Vallecula — see condition

Valley fever 114.0

Valsuani's disease (progressive pernicious anemia, puerperal) 648.2 ✓

Valve, valvular (formation) — see also condition

cerebral ventricle (communicating) in situ V45.2

cervix, internal os 752.49

Valve, valvular — see also condition — continued

colon 751.5

congenital NEC — see Atresia

formation, congenital NEC — see Atresia

heart defect — see Anomaly, heart, valve

ureter 753.29

pelvic junction 753.21

vesical orifice 753.22

urethra 753.6

Valvulitis (chronic) — see also Endocarditis 424.90

rheumatic (chronic) (inactive) (with chorea) 397.9

active or acute (aortic) (mitral) (pulmonary) (tricuspid) 391.1

syphilitic NEC 093.20

aortic 093.22

mitral 093.21

pulmonary 093.24

tricuspid 093.23

Valvulopathy — see Endocarditis

van Bogaert-Nijssen (-Peiffer) disease 330.0

van Bogaert's leukoencephalitis (sclerosing) (subacute) 046.2

van Buchem's syndrome (hyperostosis corticalis) 733.3

Vancomycin (glycopeptide)

intermediate staphylococcus aureus (VISA/GISA) V09.8 ✓

resistant

enterococcus (VRE) V09.8 ✓

staphylococcus aureus (VRSA/GRSA) V09.8 ✓

van Creveld-von Gierke disease (glycogenosis I) 271.0

van den Bergh's disease (enterogenous cyanosis) 289.7

van der Hoeve-Halbertsma-Waardenburg syndrome (ptosis-epicanthus) 270.2

van der Hoeve-Waardenburg-Gualdi syndrome (ptosis epicanthus) 270.2

van der Hoeve's syndrome (brittle bones and blue sclera, deafness) 756.51

Vanillism 692.89

Vanishing lung 492.0

Vanishing twin 651.33

van Neck (-Odelberg) disease or syndrome (juvenile osteochondrosis) 732.1

Vapor asphyxia or suffocation NEC 987.9

specified agent — see Table of Drugs and Chemicals

Vaquez's disease (M9950/1) 238.4

Vaquez-Osler disease (polycythemia vera) (M9950/1) 238.4

Variance, lethal ball, prosthetic heart valve 996.02

Variants, thalassemic 282.49

Variations in hair color 704.3

Varicella 052.9

with

complication 052.8

specified NEC 052.7

pneumonia 052.1

vaccination and inoculation (prophylactic) V05.4

exposure to V01.71

vaccination and inoculation (against) (prophylactic) V05.4

Varices — see Varix

Varicocele (scrotum) (thrombosed) 456.4

ovary 456.5

perineum 456.6

spermatic cord (ulcerated) 456.4

Varicose

aneurysm (ruptured) (see also Aneurysm) 442.9

dermatitis (lower extremity) — see Varicose, vein, inflamed or infected

eczema — see Varicose, vein

phlebitis — see Varicose, vein, inflamed or infected

placental vessel — see Placenta, abnormal

tumor — see Varicose, vein

ulcer (lower extremity, any part) 454.0

anus 455.8

external 455.5

Varicose — continued

ulcer — continued

anus — continued

internal 455.2

esophagus (see also Varix, esophagus) 456.1

bleeding (see also Varix, esophagus, bleeding) 456.0

inflamed or infected 454.2

nasal septum 456.8

perineum 456.6

rectum — see Varicose, ulcer, anus

scrotum 456.4

specified site NEC 456.8

vein (lower extremity) (ruptured) (see also Varix) 454.9

with

complications NEC 454.8

edema 454.8

inflammation or infection 454.1

ulcerated 454.2

pain 454.8

stasis dermatitis 454.1

with ulcer 454.2

swelling 454.8

ulcer 454.0

inflamed or infected 454.2

anus — see Hemorrhoids

broad ligament 456.5

congenital (peripheral) 747.60

gastrointestinal 747.61

lower limb 747.64

renal 747.62

specified NEC 747.69

upper limb 747.63

esophagus (ulcerated) (see also Varix, esophagus) 456.1

bleeding (see also Varix, esophagus, bleeding) 456.0

inflamed or infected 454.1

with ulcer 454.2

in pregnancy or puerperium 671.0 ✓

vulva or perineum 671.1 ✓

nasal septum (with ulcer) 456.8

pelvis 456.5

perineum 456.6

in pregnancy, childbirth, or puerperium 671.1 ✓

rectum — see Hemorrhoids

scrotum (ulcerated) 456.4

specified site NEC 456.8

sublingual 456.3

ulcerated 454.0

inflamed or infected 454.2

umbilical cord, affecting fetus or newborn 762.6

urethra 456.8

vulva 456.6

in pregnancy, childbirth, or puerperium 671.1 ✓

vessel (see also Varix)

placenta — see Placenta, abnormal

Varicosis, varicosities, varicosity — see also Varix 454.9

Variola 050.9

hemorrhagic (pustular) 050.0

major 050.0

minor 050.1

modified 050.2

Varioloid 050.2

Variolosa, purpura 050.0

Varix (lower extremity) (ruptured) 454.9

with

complications NEC 454.8

edema 454.8

inflammation or infection 454.1

with ulcer 454.2

pain 454.8

stasis dermatitis 454.1

with ulcer 454.2

swelling 454.8

ulcer 454.0

with inflammation or infection 454.2

aneurysmal (see also Aneurysm) 442.9

anus — see Hemorrhoids

✓ Additional Digit Required — Refer to the Tabular List for Digit Selection

▽ Subterms under main terms may continue to next column or page

2010 ICD-9-CM

◄► Revised Text ● New Line ▲ Revised Code

Volume 2 — 281

Vaccination — Varix

Varix — continued
  arteriovenous (congenital) (peripheral) NEC
      747.60
    gastrointestinal 747.61
    lower limb 747.64
    renal 747.62
    specified NEC 747.69
    spinal 747.82
    upper limb 747.63
  bladder 456.5
  broad ligament 456.5
  congenital (peripheral) 747.60
  esophagus (ulcerated) 456.1
    bleeding 456.0
      in
          cirrhosis of liver 571.5 *[456.20]*
          portal hypertension 572.3 *[456.20]*
      congenital 747.69
        in
            cirrhosis of liver 571.5 *[456.21]*
              with bleeding 571.5 *[456.20]*
            portal hypertension 572.3 *[456.21]*
              with bleeding 572.3 *[456.20]*
  gastric 456.8
  inflamed or infected 454.1
    ulcerated 454.2
  in pregnancy or puerperium 671.0 ☑
    perineum 671.1 ☑
    vulva 671.1 ☑
  labia (majora) 456.6
  orbit 456.8
    congenital 747.69
  ovary 456.5
  papillary 448.1
  pelvis 456.5
  perineum 456.6
    in pregnancy or puerperium 671.1 ☑
  pharynx 456.8
  placenta — see Placenta, abnormal
  prostate 456.8
  rectum — see Hemorrhoids
  renal papilla 456.8
  retina 362.17
  scrotum (ulcerated) 456.4
  sigmoid colon 456.8
  specified site NEC 456.8
  spinal (cord) (vessels) 456.8
  spleen, splenic (vein) (with phlebolith) 456.8
  sublingual 456.3
  ulcerated 454.0
    inflamed or infected 454.2
  umbilical cord, affecting fetus or newborn
      762.6
  uterine ligament 456.5
  vocal cord 456.8
  vulva 456.6
    in pregnancy, childbirth, or puerperium
        671.1 ☑
Vasa previa 663.5 ☑
  affecting fetus or newborn 762.6
  hemorrhage from, affecting fetus or newborn
      772.0
Vascular — see also condition
  loop on papilla (optic) 743.57
  sheathing, retina 362.13
  spasm 443.9
  spider 448.1
Vascularity, pulmonary, congenital 747.3
Vascularization
  choroid 362.16
  cornea 370.60
    deep 370.63
    localized 370.61
  retina 362.16
  subretinal 362.16
Vasculitis 447.6
  allergic 287.0
  cryoglobulinemic 273.2
  disseminated 447.6
  kidney 447.8
  leukocytoclastic 446.29
  nodular 695.2
  retinal 362.18
  rheumatic — see Fever, rheumatic
Vasculopathy
  cardiac allograft 996.83

Vas deferens — see condition
Vas deferentitis 608.4
Vasectomy, admission for V25.2
Vasitis 608.4
  nodosa 608.4
  scrotum 608.4
  spermatic cord 608.4
  testis 608.4
  tuberculous (see also Tuberculosis) 016.5 ☑
  tunica vaginalis 608.4
  vas deferens 608.4
Vasodilation 443.9
Vasomotor — see condition
Vasoplasty, after previous sterilization V26.0
Vasoplegia, splanchnic — see also Neuropathy,
      peripheral, autonomic 337.9
Vasospasm 443.9
  cerebral (artery) 435.9
    with transient neurologic deficit 435.9
  coronary 413.1
  nerve
    arm NEC 354.9
    autonomic 337.9
    brachial plexus 353.0
    cervical plexus 353.2
    leg NEC 355.8
    lower extremity NEC 355.8
    peripheral NEC 355.9
    spinal NEC 355.9
    sympathetic 337.9
    upper extremity NEC 354.9
  peripheral NEC 443.9
  retina (artery) (see also Occlusion, retinal,
      artery) 362.30
Vasospastic — see condition
Vasovagal attack (paroxysmal) 780.2
  psychogenic 306.2
Vater's ampulla — see condition
VATER syndrome 759.89
vCJD (variant Creutzfeldt-Jakob disease) 046.11
Vegetation, vegetative
  adenoid (nasal fossa) 474.2
  consciousness (persistent) 780.03
  endocarditis (acute) (any valve) (chronic)
      (subacute) 421.0
  heart (mycotic) (valve) 421.0
  state (persistent) 780.03
Veil
  Jackson's 751.4
  over face (causing asphyxia) 768.9
Vein, venous — see condition
Veldt sore — see also Ulcer, skin 707.9
Velo-cardio-facial syndrome 758.32
Velpeau's hernia — see Hernia, femoral
Venereal
  balanitis NEC 099.8
  bubo 099.1
  disease 099.9
    specified nature or type NEC 099.8
  granuloma inguinale 099.2
  lymphogranuloma (Durand-Nicolas-Favre),
      any site 099.1
  salpingitis 098.37
  urethritis (see also Urethritis, nongonococcal)
      099.40
  vaginitis NEC 099.8
  warts 078.11
Vengefulness, in child — see also Disturbance,
      conduct 312.0 ☑
Venofibrosis 459.89
Venom, venomous
  bite or sting (animal or insect) 989.5
  poisoning 989.5
Venous — see condition
Ventouse delivery NEC 669.5 ☑
  affecting fetus or newborn 763.3
Ventral — see condition
Ventricle, ventricular — see also condition
  escape 427.69
  standstill (see also Arrest, cardiac) 427.5
Ventriculitis, cerebral — see also Meningitis
      322.9
Ventriculostomy status V45.2
Verbiest's syndrome (claudicatio intermittens
      spinalis) 435.1
Vernet's syndrome 352.6

Verneuil's disease (syphilitic bursitis) 095.7
Verruca (filiformis) 078.10
  acuminata (any site) 078.11
  necrogenica (primary) (see also Tuberculosis)
      017.0 ☑
  peruana 088.0
  peruviana 088.0
  plana (juvenilis) 078.19
  plantaris 078.12
  seborrheica 702.19
    inflamed 702.11
  senilis 702.0
  tuberculosa (primary) (see also Tuberculosis)
      017.0 ☑
  venereal 078.11
  viral 078.10
    specified NEC 078.19
  vulgaris 078.10
Verrucosities — see also Verruca 078.10
Verrucous endocarditis (acute) (any valve)
      (chronic) (subacute) 710.0 *[424.91]*
  nonbacterial 710.0 *[424.91]*
Verruga
  peruana 088.0
  peruviana 088.0
Verse's disease (calcinosis intervertebralis)
      275.49 *[722.90]*
Version
  before labor, affecting fetus or newborn 761.7
  cephalic (correcting previous malposition)
      652.1 ☑
    affecting fetus or newborn 763.1
  cervix — see Version, uterus
  uterus (postinfectional) (postpartal, old) (see
      also Malposition, uterus) 621.6
    forward — see Anteversion, uterus
    lateral — see Lateroversion, uterus
Vertebra, vertebral — see condition
Vertigo 780.4
  auditory 386.19
  aural 386.19
  benign paroxysmal positional 386.11
  central origin 386.2
  cerebral 386.2
  Dix and Hallpike (epidemic) 386.12
  endemic paralytic 078.81
  epidemic 078.81
    Dix and Hallpike 386.12
    Gerlier's 078.81
    Pedersen's 386.12
    vestibular neuronitis 386.12
  epileptic — see Epilepsy
  Gerlier's (epidemic) 078.81
  hysterical 300.11
  labyrinthine 386.10
  laryngeal 786.2
  malignant positional 386.2
  Ménière's (see also Disease, Ménière's) 386.00
  menopausal 627.2
  otogenic 386.19
  paralytic 078.81
  paroxysmal positional, benign 386.11
  Pedersen's (epidemic) 386.12
  peripheral 386.10
    specified type NEC 386.19
  positional
    benign paroxysmal 386.11
    malignant 386.2
Verumontanitis (chronic) — see also Urethritis
      597.89
Vesania — see also Psychosis 298.9
Vesical — see condition
Vesicle
  cutaneous 709.8
  seminal — see condition
  skin 709.8
Vesicocolic — see condition
Vesicoperineal — see condition
Vesicorectal — see condition
Vesicourethrorectal — see condition
Vesicovaginal — see condition
Vesicular — see condition
Vesiculitis (seminal) 608.0
  amebic 006.8
  gonorrheal (acute) 098.14

Vesiculitis — continued
  gonorrheal — continued
    chronic or duration of 2 months or over
        098.34
  trichomonal 131.09
  tuberculous (see also Tuberculosis)
      016.5 ☑ *[608.81]*
Vestibulitis (ear) — see also Labyrinthitis 386.30
  nose (external) 478.19
  vulvar 625.71
Vestibulopathy, acute peripheral (recurrent)
      386.12
Vestige, vestigial — see also Persistence
  branchial 744.41
  structures in vitreous 743.51
Vibriosis NEC 027.9
Vidal's disease (lichen simplex chronicus) 698.3
Video display tube syndrome 723.8
Vienna-type encephalitis 049.8
Villaret's syndrome 352.6
Villous — see condition
VIN I (vulvar intraepithelial neoplasia I) 624.01
VIN II (vulvar intraepithelial neoplasia II) 624.02
VIN III (vulvar intraepithelial neoplasia III) 233.32
Vincent's
  angina 101
  bronchitis 101
  disease 101
  gingivitis 101
  infection (any site) 101
  laryngitis 101
  stomatitis 101
  tonsillitis 101
Vinson-Plummer syndrome (sideropenic dys-
      phagia) 280.8
Viosterol deficiency — see also Deficiency, cal-
      ciferol 268.9
Virchow's disease 733.99
Viremia 790.8
Virilism (adrenal) (female) NEC 255.2
  with
    3-beta-hydroxysteroid dehydrogenase
        defect 255.2
    11-hydroxylase defect 255.2
    21-hydroxylase defect 255.2
  adrenal
    hyperplasia 255.2
    insufficiency (congenital) 255.2
    cortical hyperfunction 255.2
Virilization (female) (suprarenal) — see also Viril-
      ism 255.2
  isosexual 256.4
Virulent bubo 099.0
Virus, viral — see also condition
  infection NEC (see also Infection, viral) 079.99
  septicemia 079.99
  yaba monkey tumor 059.22
VISA (vancomycin intermediate staphylococcus
      aureus) V09.8 ☑
Viscera, visceral — see condition
Visceroptosis 569.89
Visible peristalsis 787.4
Vision, visual
  binocular, suppression 368.31
  blurred, blurring 368.8
    hysterical 300.11
  defect, defective (see also Impaired, vision)
      369.9
  disorientation (syndrome) 368.16
  disturbance NEC (see also Disturbance, vision)
      368.9
    hysterical 300.11
  examination V72.0
  field, limitation 368.40
  fusion, with defective stereopsis 368.33
  hallucinations 368.16
  halos 368.16
  loss 369.9
    both eyes (see also Blindness, both eyes)
        369.3
    complete (see also Blindness, both eyes)
        369.00
    one eye 369.8
    sudden 368.16
  low (both eyes) 369.20

☑ Additional Digit Required — Refer to the Tabular List for Digit Selection   ▼ Subterms under main terms may continue to next column or page

282 — Volume 2   ▶◀ Revised Text   ● New Line   ▲ Revised Code   2010 ICD-9-CM

Vision, visual — *continued*
  low — *continued*
    one eye (other eye normal) (*see also* Impaired, vision) 369.70
      blindness, other eye 369.10
    perception, simultaneous without fusion 368.32
    tunnel 368.45

Vitality, lack or want of 780.79
  newborn 779.89

Vitamin deficiency NEC — *see also* Deficiency, vitamin 269.2

Vitelline duct, persistent 751.0

Vitiligo 709.01
  due to pinta (carate) 103.2
  eyelid 374.53
  vulva 624.8

Vitium cordis — *see* Disease, heart

Vitreous — *see also* condition
  touch syndrome 997.99

VLCAD (long chain/very long chain acyl CoA dehydrogenase deficiency, LCAD) 277.85

Vocal cord — *see* condition

Vocational rehabilitation V57.22

Vogt's (Cecile) disease or syndrome 333.7 ☑

Vogt-Koyanagi syndrome 364.24

Vogt-Spielmeyer disease (amaurotic familial idiocy) 330.1

Voice
  change (*see also* Dysphonia) 784.49 ▲
  loss (*see also* Aphonia) 784.41

Volhard-Fahr disease (malignant nephrosclerosis) 403.00

Volhynian fever 083.1

Volkmann's ischemic contracture or paralysis (complicating trauma) 958.6

Voluntary starvation 307.1

Volvulus (bowel) (colon) (intestine) 560.2
  with
    hernia (*see also* Hernia, by site, with obstruction)
      gangrenous — *see* Hernia, by site, with gangrene
    perforation 560.2
  congenital 751.5
  duodenum 537.3
  fallopian tube 620.5
  oviduct 620.5
  stomach (due to absence of gastrocolic ligament) 537.89

Vomiting 787.03
  with nausea 787.01
  allergic 535.4 ☑
  asphyxia 933.1
  bilious (cause unknown) 787.04 ▲
    following gastrointestinal surgery 564.3
    newborn 779.32 ●
  blood (*see also* Hematemesis) 578.0
  causing asphyxia, choking, or suffocation (*see also* Asphyxia, food) 933.1
  cyclical 536.2
    associated with migraine 346.2 ☑
    psychogenic 306.4
  epidemic 078.82
  fecal matter 569.87 ▲
  following gastrointestinal surgery 564.3
  functional 536.8
    psychogenic 306.4
  habit 536.2
  hysterical 300.11
  nervous 306.4
  neurotic 306.4
  newborn 779.33 ▲
    bilious 779.32 ●
  of or complicating pregnancy 643.9 ☑
    due to
      organic disease 643.8 ☑
      specific cause NEC 643.8 ☑
    early — *see* Hyperemesis, gravidarum
    late (after 22 completed weeks of gestation) 643.2 ☑
  pernicious or persistent 536.2
    complicating pregnancy — *see* Hyperemesis, gravidarum
  psychogenic 306.4
  physiological 787.03 ▲

Vomiting — *continued*
  physiological — *continued*
    bilious 787.04 ●
  psychic 306.4
  psychogenic 307.54
  stercoral 569.89
  uncontrollable 536.2
    psychogenic 306.4
  uremic — *see* Uremia
  winter 078.82

von Bechterew (-Strumpell) disease or syndrome (ankylosing spondylitis) 720.0

von Bezold's abscess 383.01

von Economo's disease (encephalitis lethargica) 049.8

von Eulenburg's disease (congenital paramyotonia) 359.29

von Gierke's disease (glycogenosis I) 271.0

von Gies' joint 095.8

von Graefe's disease or syndrome 378.72

von Hippel (-Lindau) disease or syndrome (retinocerebral angiomatosis) 759.6

von Jaksch's anemia or disease (pseudoleukemia infantum) 285.8

von Recklinghausen-Applebaum disease (hemochromatosis) 275.0

von Recklinghausen's
  disease or syndrome (nerves) (skin) (M9540/1) 237.71
    bones (osteitis fibrosa cystica) 252.01
    tumor (M9540/1) 237.71

von Schroetter's syndrome (intermittent venous claudication) 453.89 ▲

von Willebrand (-Jürgens) (-Minot) disease or syndrome (angiohemophilia) 286.4

von Zambusch's disease (lichen sclerosus et atrophicus) 701.0

Voorhoeve's disease or dyschondroplasia 756.4

Vossius' ring 921.3
  late effect 366.21

Voyeurism 302.82

VRE (vancomycin resistant enterococcus) V09.8 ☑

Vrolik's disease (osteogenesis imperfecta) 756.51

VRSA (vancomycin resistant staphylococcus aureus) V09.8 ☑

Vulva — *see* condition

Vulvismus 625.1

Vulvitis (acute) (allergic) (chronic) (gangrenous) (hypertrophic) (intertriginous) 616.10
  with
    abortion — *see* Abortion, by type, with sepsis
    ectopic pregnancy (*see also* categories 633.0–633.9) 639.0
    molar pregnancy (*see also* categories 630–632) 639.0
  adhesive, congenital 752.49
  blennorrhagic (acute) 098.0
    chronic or duration of 2 months or over 098.2
  chlamydial 099.53
  complicating pregnancy or puerperium 646.6 ☑
  due to Ducrey's bacillus 099.0
  following
    abortion 639.0
    ectopic or molar pregnancy 639.0
  gonococcal (acute) 098.0
    chronic or duration of 2 months or over 098.2
  herpetic 054.11
  leukoplakic 624.09
  monilial 112.1
  puerperal, postpartum, childbirth 646.6 ☑
  syphilitic (early) 091.0
    late 095.8
  trichomonal 131.01

Vulvodynia 625.70
  specified NEC 625.79

Vulvorectal — *see* condition

Vulvovaginitis — *see also* Vulvitis 616.10
  amebic 006.8
  chlamydial 099.53
  gonococcal (acute) 098.0

Vulvovaginitis — *see also* Vulvitis — *continued*
  gonococcal — *continued*
    chronic or duration of 2 months or over 098.2
  herpetic 054.11
  monilial 112.1
  trichomonal (Trichomonas vaginalis) 131.01

W

Waardenburg-Klein syndrome (ptosis-epicanthus) 270.2

Waardenburg's syndrome 756.89
  meaning ptosis-epicanthus 270.2

Wagner's disease (colloid milium) 709.3

Wagner (-Unverricht) syndrome (dermatomyositis) 710.3

Waiting list, person on V63.2
  undergoing social agency investigation V63.8

Wakefulness disorder — *see also* Hypersomnia 780.54
  nonorganic origin 307.43

Waldenström's
  disease (osteochondrosis, capital femoral) 732.1
  hepatitis (lupoid hepatitis) 571.49
  hypergammaglobulinemia 273.0
  macroglobulinemia 273.3
  purpura, hypergammaglobulinemic 273.0
  syndrome (macroglobulinemia) 273.3

Waldenström-Kjellberg syndrome (sideropenic dysphagia) 280.8

Walking
  difficulty 719.7
    psychogenic 307.9
  sleep 307.46
    hysterical 300.13

Wall, abdominal — *see* condition

Wallenberg's syndrome (posterior inferior cerebellar artery) — *see also* Disease, cerebrovascular, acute 436

Wallgren's
  disease (obstruction of splenic vein with collateral circulation) 459.89
  meningitis (*see also* Meningitis, aseptic) 047.9

Wandering
  acetabulum 736.39
  gallbladder 751.69
  kidney, congenital 753.3
  organ or site, congenital NEC — *see* Malposition, congenital
  pacemaker (atrial) (heart) 427.89
  spleen 289.59

Wardrop's disease (with lymphangitis) 681.9
  finger 681.02
  toe 681.11

War neurosis 300.16

Wart (digitate) (filiform) (infectious) (viral) 078.10
  common 078.19
  external genital organs (venereal) 078.11
  fig 078.19
  flat 078.19
  genital 078.11
  Hassall-Henle's (of cornea) 371.41
  Henle's (of cornea) 371.41
  juvenile 078.19
  moist 078.10
  Peruvian 088.0
  plantar 078.12
  prosector (*see also* Tuberculosis) 017.0 ☑
  seborrheic 702.19
    inflamed 702.11
  senile 702.0
  specified NEC 078.19
  syphilitic 091.3
  tuberculous (*see also* Tuberculosis) 017.0 ☑
  venereal (female) (male) 078.11

Warthin's tumor (salivary gland) (M8561/0) 210.2

Washerwoman's itch 692.4

Wassilieff's disease (leptospiral jaundice) 100.0

Wasting
  disease 799.4
    due to malnutrition 261
  extreme (due to malnutrition) 261
  muscular NEC 728.2
  palsy, paralysis 335.21

Wasting — *continued*
  pelvic muscle 618.83

Water
  clefts 366.12
  deprivation of 994.3
  in joint (*see also* Effusion, joint) 719.0 ☑
  intoxication 276.6
  itch 120.3
  lack of 994.3
  loading 276.6
  on
    brain — *see* Hydrocephalus
    chest 511.89
  poisoning 276.6

Waterbrash 787.1

Water-hammer pulse — *see also* Insufficiency, aortic 424.1

Waterhouse (-Friderichsen) disease or syndrome 036.3

Water-losing nephritis 588.89

Watermelon stomach 537.82
  with hemorrhage 537.83
  without hemorrhage 537.82

Wax in ear 380.4

Waxy
  degeneration, any site 277.39
  disease 277.39
  kidney 277.39 [583.81]
  liver (large) 277.39
  spleen 277.39

Weak, weakness (generalized) 780.79
  arches (acquired) 734
    congenital 754.61
  bladder sphincter 596.59
  congenital 779.89
  eye muscle — *see* Strabismus
  facial 781.94
  foot (double) — *see* Weak, arches
  heart, cardiac (*see also* Failure, heart) 428.9
    congenital 746.9
  mind 317
  muscle (generalized) 728.87
  myocardium (*see also* Failure, heart) 428.9
  newborn 779.89
  pelvic fundus
    pubocervical tissue 618.81
    rectovaginal tissue 618.82
  pulse 785.9
  senile 797
  urinary stream 788.62
  valvular — *see* Endocarditis

Wear, worn, tooth, teeth (approximal) (hard tissues) (interproximal) (occlusal) — *see also* Attrition, teeth 521.10

Weather, weathered
  effects of
    cold NEC 991.9
      specified effect NEC 991.8
    hot (*see also* Heat) 992.9
    skin 692.74

Weber-Christian disease or syndrome (nodular nonsuppurative panniculitis) 729.30

Weber-Cockayne syndrome (epidermolysis bullosa) 757.39

Weber-Dimitri syndrome 759.6

Weber-Gubler syndrome 344.89

Weber-Leyden syndrome 344.89

Weber-Osler syndrome (familial hemorrhagic telangiectasia) 448.0

Weber's paralysis or syndrome 344.89

Web, webbed (congenital) — *see also* Anomaly, specified type NEC
  canthus 743.63
  digits (*see also* Syndactylism) 755.10
  duodenal 751.5
  esophagus 750.3
  fingers (*see also* Syndactylism, fingers) 755.11
  larynx (glottic) (subglottic) 748.2
  neck (pterygium colli) 744.5
  Paterson-Kelly (sideropenic dysphagia) 280.8
  popliteal syndrome 756.89
  toes (*see also* Syndactylism, toes) 755.13

Wedge-shaped or wedging vertebra — *see also* Osteoporosis 733.00

Wegener's granulomatosis or syndrome 446.4

Index

Wegner's disease — Wound, open

Wegner's disease (syphilitic osteochondritis) 090.0

Weight
gain (abnormal) (excessive) 783.1
during pregnancy 646.1 ☑
insufficient 646.8 ☑
less than 1000 grams at birth 765.0 ☑
loss (cause unknown) 783.21

Weightlessness 994.9

Weil's disease (leptospiral jaundice) 100.0

Weill-Marchesani syndrome (brachymorphism and ectopia lentis) 759.89

Weingarten's syndrome (tropical eosinophilia) 518.3

Weir Mitchell's disease (erythromelalgia) 443.82

Weiss-Baker syndrome (carotid sinus syncope) 337.01

Weissenbach-Thibierge syndrome (cutaneous systemic sclerosis) 710.1

Wen — see also Cyst, sebaceous 706.2

Wenckebach's phenomenon, heart block (second degree) 426.13

Werdnig-Hoffmann syndrome (muscular atrophy) 335.0

Werlhof-Wichmann syndrome — see also Purpura, thrombocytopenic 287.39

Werlhof's disease — see also Purpura, thrombocytopenic 287.39

Wermer's syndrome or disease (polyendocrine adenomatosis) 258.01

Werner's disease or syndrome (progeria adultorum) 259.8

Werner-His disease (trench fever) 083.1

Werner-Schultz disease (agranulocytosis) 288.09

Wernicke's encephalopathy, disease, or syndrome (superior hemorrhagic polioencephalitis) 265.1

Wernicke-Korsakoff syndrome or psychosis (nonalcoholic) 294.0
alcoholic 291.1

Wernicke-Posadas disease — see also Coccidioidomycosis 114.9

Wesselsbron fever 066.3

West African fever 084.8

West Nile
encephalitis 066.41
encephalomyelitis 066.41
fever 066.40
with
cranial nerve disorders 066.42
encephalitis 066.41
optic neuritis 066.42
other complications 066.49
other neurologic manifestations 066.42
polyradiculitis 066.42
virus 066.40

Westphal-Strümpell syndrome (hepatolenticular degeneration) 275.1

Wet
brain (alcoholic) (see also Alcoholism) 303.9 ☑
feet, tropical (syndrome) (maceration) 991.4
lung (syndrome)
adult 518.5
newborn 770.6

Wharton's duct — see condition

Wheal 709.8

Wheelchair confinement status V46.3

Wheezing 786.07

Whiplash injury or syndrome 847.0

Whipple's disease or syndrome (intestinal lipodystrophy) 040.2

Whipworm 127.3

"Whistling face" syndrome (craniocarpotarsal dystrophy) 759.89

White — see also condition
kidney
large — see Nephrosis
small 582.9
leg, puerperal, postpartum, childbirth 671.4 ☑
nonpuerperal 451.19
mouth 112.0
patches of mouth 528.6
sponge nevus of oral mucosa 750.26
spot lesions, teeth 521.01

White's disease (congenital) (keratosis follicularis) 757.39

Whitehead 706.2

Whitlow (with lymphangitis) 681.01
herpetic 054.6

Whitmore's disease or fever (melioidosis) 025

Whooping cough 033.9
with pneumonia 033.9 [484.3]
due to
Bordetella
bronchoseptica 033.8
with pneumonia 033.8 [484.3]
parapertussis 033.1
with pneumonia 033.1 [484.3]
pertussis 033.0
with pneumonia 033.0 [484.3]
specified organism NEC 033.8
with pneumonia 033.8 [484.3]
vaccination, prophylactic (against) V03.6

Wichmann's asthma (laryngismus stridulus) 478.75

Widal (-Abrami) syndrome (acquired hemolytic jaundice) 283.9

Widening aorta — see also Aneurysm, aorta 441.9
ruptured 441.5

Wilkie's disease or syndrome 557.1

Wilkinson-Sneddon disease or syndrome (subcorneal pustular dermatosis) 694.1

Willan's lepra 696.1

Willan-Plumbe syndrome (psoriasis) 696.1

Willebrand (-Jürgens) syndrome or thrombopathy (angiohemophilia) 286.4

Willi-Prader syndrome (hypogenital dystrophy with diabetic tendency) 759.81

Willis' disease (diabetes mellitus) — see also Diabetes 250.0 ☑
due to secondary diabetes 249.0 ☑

Wilms' tumor or neoplasm (nephroblastoma) (M8960/3) 189.0

Wilson's
disease or syndrome (hepatolenticular degeneration) 275.1
hepatolenticular degeneration 275.1
lichen ruber 697.0

Wilson-Brocq disease (dermatitis exfoliativa) 695.89

Wilson-Mikity syndrome 770.7

Window — see also Imperfect, closure aorticopulmonary 745.0

Winged scapula 736.89

Winter — see also condition
vomiting disease 078.82

Wise's disease 696.2

Wiskott-Aldrich syndrome (eczema-thrombocytopenia) 279.12

Withdrawal symptoms, syndrome
alcohol 291.81
delirium (acute) 291.0
chronic 291.1
newborn 760.71
drug or narcotic 292.0
newborn, infant of dependent mother 779.5
steroid NEC
correct substance properly administered 255.41
overdose or wrong substance given or taken 962.0

Withdrawing reaction, child or adolescent 313.22

Witts' anemia (achlorhydric anemia) 280.9

Witzelsucht 301.9

Woakes' syndrome (ethmoiditis) 471.1

Wohlfart-Kugelberg-Welander disease 335.11

Woillez's disease (acute idiopathic pulmonary congestion) 518.5

Wolff-Parkinson-White syndrome (anomalous atrioventricular excitation) 426.7

Wolhynian fever 083.1

Wolman's disease (primary familial xanthomatosis) 272.7

Wood asthma 495.8

Woolly, wooly hair (congenital) (nevus) 757.4

Wool-sorters' disease 022.1

Word
blindness (congenital) (developmental) 315.01
secondary to organic lesion 784.61
deafness (secondary to organic lesion) 784.69

Word — continued
deafness — continued
developmental 315.31

Worm(s) (colic) (fever) (infection) (infestation) — see also Infestation 128.9
guinea 125.7
in intestine NEC 127.9

Worm-eaten soles 102.3

Worn out — see also Exhaustion 780.79
artificial heart valve 996.02 ●
cardiac defibrillator V53.32 ●
cardiac pacemaker lead or battery V53.31 ●
joint prosthesis (see also Complications, mechanical, device NEC, prosthetic NEC, joint) 996.46

"Worried well" V65.5

Wound, open (by cutting or piercing instrument) (by firearms) (cut) (dissection) (incised) (laceration) (penetration) (perforating) (puncture) (with initial hemorrhage, not internal) 879.8

Note — For fracture with open wound, see Fracture.

For laceration, traumatic rupture, tear or penetrating wound of internal organs, such as heart, lung, liver, kidney, pelvic organs, etc., whether or not accompanied by open wound or fracture in the same region, see Injury, internal.

For contused wound, see Contusion. For crush injury, see Crush. For abrasion, insect bite (nonvenomous), blister, or scratch, see Injury, superficial.

Complicated includes wounds with:
    delayed healing
    delayed treatment
    foreign body
    primary infection

For late effect of open wound, see Late, effect, wound, open, by site.

---

abdomen, abdominal (external) (muscle) 879.2
complicated 879.3
wall (anterior) 879.2
complicated 879.3
lateral 879.4
complicated 879.5
alveolar (process) 873.62
complicated 873.72
ankle 891.0
with tendon involvement 891.2
complicated 891.1
anterior chamber, eye (see also Wound, open, intraocular) 871.9
anus 879.6
complicated 879.7
arm 884.0
with tendon involvement 884.2
complicated 884.1
forearm 881.00
with tendon involvement 881.20
complicated 881.10
multiple sites — see Wound, open, multiple, upper limb
upper 880.03
with tendon involvement 880.23
complicated 880.13
multiple sites (with axillary or shoulder regions) 880.09
with tendon involvement 880.29
complicated 880.19
artery — see Injury, blood vessel, by site
auditory
canal (external) (meatus) 872.02
complicated 872.12
ossicles (incus) (malleus) (stapes) 872.62
complicated 872.72
auricle, ear 872.01
complicated 872.11
axilla 880.02
with tendon involvement 880.22
complicated 880.12
with tendon involvement 880.29

Wound, open — continued
axilla — continued
involving other sites of upper arm 880.09
complicated 880.19
back 876.0
complicated 876.1
bladder — see Injury, internal, bladder
blood vessel — see Injury, blood vessel, by site
brain — see Injury, intracranial, with open intracranial wound
breast 879.0
complicated 879.1
brow 873.42
complicated 873.52
buccal mucosa 873.61
complicated 873.71
buttock 877.0
complicated 877.1
calf 891.0
with tendon involvement 891.2
complicated 891.1
canaliculus lacrimalis 870.8
with laceration of eyelid 870.2
canthus, eye 870.8
laceration — see Laceration, eyelid
cavernous sinus — see Injury, intracranial
cerebellum — see Injury, intracranial
cervical esophagus 874.4
complicated 874.5
cervix — see Injury, internal, cervix
cheek(s) (external) 873.41
complicated 873.51
internal 873.61
complicated 873.71
chest (wall) (external) 875.0
complicated 875.1
chin 873.44
complicated 873.54
choroid 363.63
ciliary body (eye) (see also Wound, open, intraocular) 871.9
clitoris 878.8
complicated 878.9
cochlea 872.64
complicated 872.74
complicated 879.9
conjunctiva — see Wound, open, intraocular
cornea (nonpenetrating) (see also Wound, open, intraocular) 871.9
costal region 875.0
complicated 875.1
Descemet's membrane (see also Wound, open, intraocular) 871.9
digit(s)
foot 893.0
with tendon involvement 893.2
complicated 893.1
hand 883.0
with tendon involvement 883.2
complicated 883.1
drumhead, ear 872.61
complicated 872.71
ear 872.8
canal 872.02
complicated 872.12
complicated 872.9
drum 872.61
complicated 872.71
external 872.00
complicated 872.10
multiple sites 872.69
complicated 872.79
ossicles (incus) (malleus) (stapes) 872.62
complicated 872.72
specified part NEC 872.69
complicated 872.79
elbow 881.01
with tendon involvement 881.21
complicated 881.11
epididymis 878.2
complicated 878.3
epigastric region 879.2
complicated 879.3
epiglottis 874.01
complicated 874.11
esophagus (cervical) 874.4

☑ Additional Digit Required — Refer to the Tabular List for Digit Selection   ⬇ Subterms under main terms may continue to next column or page

284 — Volume 2 • October 2009   ▶◀ Revised Text   ● New Line   ▲ Revised Code   2010 ICD-9-CM

Wound, open — *continued*
esophagus — *continued*
  complicated 874.5
    thoracic — *see* Injury, internal, esophagus
  Eustachian tube 872.63
    complicated 872.73
  extremity
    lower (multiple) NEC 894.0
      with tendon involvement 894.2
      complicated 894.1
    upper (multiple) NEC 884.0
      with tendon involvement 884.2
      complicated 884.1
  eye(s) (globe) — *see* Wound, open, intraocular
  eyeball NEC 871.9
    laceration (*see also* Laceration, eyeball) 871.4
    penetrating (*see also* Penetrating wound, eyeball) 871.7
  eyebrow 873.42
    complicated 873.52
  eyelid NEC 870.8
    laceration — *see* Laceration, eyelid
  face 873.40
    complicated 873.50
    multiple sites 873.49
      complicated 873.59
    specified part NEC 873.49
      complicated 873.59
  fallopian tube — *see* Injury, internal, fallopian tube
  finger(s) (nail) (subungual) 883.0
    with tendon involvement 883.2
    complicated 883.1
  flank 879.4
    complicated 879.5
  foot (any part except toe(s) alone) 892.0
    with tendon involvement 892.2
    complicated 892.1
  forearm 881.00
    with tendon involvement 881.20
    complicated 881.10
  forehead 873.42
    complicated 873.52
  genital organs (external) NEC 878.8
    complicated 878.9
    internal — *see* Injury, internal, by site
  globe (eye) (*see also* Wound, open, eyeball) 871.9
  groin 879.4
    complicated 879.5
  gum(s) 873.62
    complicated 873.72
  hand (except finger(s) alone) 882.0
    with tendon involvement 882.2
    complicated 882.1
  head NEC 873.8
    with intracranial injury — *see* Injury, intracranial
      due to or associated with skull fracture — *see* Fracture, skull
    complicated 873.9
    scalp — *see* Wound, open, scalp
  heel 892.0
    with tendon involvement 892.2
    complicated 892.1
  high-velocity (grease gun) — *see* Wound, open, complicated, by site
  hip 890.0
    with tendon involvement 890.2
    complicated 890.1
  hymen 878.6
    complicated 878.7
  hypochondrium 879.4
    complicated 879.5
  hypogastric region 879.2
    complicated 879.3
  iliac (region) 879.4
    complicated 879.5
  incidental to
    dislocation — *see* Dislocation, open, by site
    fracture — *see* Fracture, open, by site
    intracranial injury — *see* Injury, intracranial, with open intracranial wound
    nerve injury — *see* Injury, nerve, by site

Wound, open — *continued*
inguinal region 879.4
  complicated 879.5
instep 892.0
  with tendon involvement 892.2
  complicated 892.1
interscapular region 876.0
  complicated 876.1
intracranial — *see* Injury, intracranial, with open intracranial wound
intraocular 871.9
  with
    partial loss (of intraocular tissue) 871.2
    prolapse or exposure (of intraocular tissue) 871.1
    without prolapse (of intraocular tissue) 871.0
  laceration (*see also* Laceration, eyeball) 871.4
  penetrating 871.7
    with foreign body (nonmagnetic) 871.6
      magnetic 871.5
  iris (*see also* Wound, open, eyeball) 871.9
jaw (fracture not involved) 873.44
  with fracture — *see* Fracture, jaw
  complicated 873.54
knee 891.0
  with tendon involvement 891.2
  complicated 891.1
labium (majus) (minus) 878.4
  complicated 878.5
lacrimal apparatus, gland, or sac 870.8
  with laceration of eyelid 870.2
larynx 874.01
  with trachea 874.00
    complicated 874.10
  complicated 874.11
leg (multiple) 891.0
  with tendon involvement 891.2
  complicated 891.1
  lower 891.0
    with tendon involvement 891.2
    complicated 891.1
  thigh 890.0
    with tendon involvement 890.2
    complicated 890.1
  upper 890.0
    with tendon involvement 890.2
    complicated 890.1
lens (eye) (alone) (*see also* Cataract, traumatic) 366.20
  with involvement of other eye structures — *see* Wound, open, eyeball
limb
  lower (multiple) NEC 894.0
    with tendon involvement 894.2
    complicated 894.1
  upper (multiple) NEC 884.0
    with tendon involvement 884.2
    complicated 884.1
lip 873.43
  complicated 873.53
loin 876.0
  complicated 876.1
lumbar region 876.0
  complicated 876.1
malar region 873.41
  complicated 873.51
mastoid region 873.49
  complicated 873.59
mediastinum — *see* Injury, internal, mediastinum
midthoracic region 875.0
  complicated 875.1
mouth 873.60
  complicated 873.70
  floor 873.64
    complicated 873.74
  multiple sites 873.69
    complicated 873.79
  specified site NEC 873.69
    complicated 873.79

Wound, open — *continued*
multiple, unspecified site(s) 879.8

> *Note* — Multiple open wounds of sites classifiable to the same four-digit category should be classified to that category unless they are in different limbs.
>
> Multiple open wounds of sites classifiable to different four-digit categories, or to different limbs, should be coded separately.

  complicated 879.9
  lower limb(s) (one or both) (sites classifiable to more than one three-digit category in 890 to 893) 894.0
    with tendon involvement 894.2
    complicated 894.1
  upper limb(s) (one or both) (sites classifiable to more than one three-digit category in 880 to 883) 884.0
    with tendon involvement 884.2
    complicated 884.1
muscle — *see* Sprain, by site
nail
  finger(s) 883.0
    complicated 883.1
  thumb 883.0
    complicated 883.1
  toe(s) 893.0
    complicated 893.1
nape (neck) 874.8
  complicated 874.9
  specified part NEC 874.8
    complicated 874.9
nasal (*see also* Wound, open, nose)
  cavity 873.22
    complicated 873.32
  septum 873.21
    complicated 873.31
  sinuses 873.23
    complicated 873.33
nasopharynx 873.22
  complicated 873.32
neck 874.8
  complicated 874.9
  nape 874.8
    complicated 874.9
  specified part NEC 874.8
    complicated 874.9
nerve — *see* Injury, nerve, by site
non-healing surgical 998.83
nose 873.20
  complicated 873.30
  multiple sites 873.29
    complicated 873.39
  septum 873.21
    complicated 873.31
  sinuses 873.23
    complicated 873.33
occipital region — *see* Wound, open, scalp
ocular NEC 871.9
  adnexa 870.9
    specified region NEC 870.8
  laceration (*see also* Laceration, ocular) 871.4
  muscle (extraocular) 870.3
    with foreign body 870.4
    eyelid 870.1
    intraocular — *see* Wound, open, eyeball
  penetrating (*see also* Penetrating wound, ocular) 871.7
orbit 870.8
  penetrating 870.3
    with foreign body 870.4
orbital region 870.9
ovary — *see* Injury, internal, pelvic organs
palate 873.65
  complicated 873.75
palm 882.0
  with tendon involvement 882.2
  complicated 882.1
parathyroid (gland) 874.2
  complicated 874.3
parietal region — *see* Wound, open, scalp
pelvic floor or region 879.6
  complicated 879.7

Wound, open — *continued*
penis 878.0
  complicated 878.1
perineum 879.6
  complicated 879.7
periocular area 870.8
  laceration of skin 870.0
pharynx 874.4
  complicated 874.5
pinna 872.01
  complicated 872.11
popliteal space 891.0
  with tendon involvement 891.2
  complicated 891.1
prepuce 878.0
  complicated 878.1
pubic region 879.2
  complicated 879.3
pudenda 878.8
  complicated 878.9
rectovaginal septum 878.8
  complicated 878.9
sacral region 877.0
  complicated 877.1
sacroiliac region 877.0
  complicated 877.1
salivary (ducts) (glands) 873.69
  complicated 873.79
scalp 873.0
  complicated 873.1
scalpel, fetus or newborn 767.8
scapular region 880.01
  with tendon involvement 880.21
  complicated 880.11
  involving other sites of upper arm 880.09
    with tendon involvement 880.29
    complicated 880.19
sclera (*see also* Wound, open, intraocular) 871.9
scrotum 878.2
  complicated 878.3
seminal vesicle — *see* Injury, internal, pelvic organs
shin 891.0
  with tendon involvement 891.2
  complicated 891.1
shoulder 880.00
  with tendon involvement 880.20
  complicated 880.10
  involving other sites of upper arm 880.09
    with tendon involvement 880.29
    complicated 880.19
skin NEC 879.8
  complicated 879.9
skull (*see also* Injury, intracranial, with open intracranial wound)
  with skull fracture — *see* Fracture, skull
spermatic cord (scrotal) 878.2
  complicated 878.3
  pelvic region — *see* Injury, internal, spermatic cord
spinal cord — *see* Injury, spinal
sternal region 875.0
  complicated 875.1
subconjunctival — *see* Wound, open, intraocular
subcutaneous NEC 879.8
  complicated 879.9
submaxillary region 873.44
  complicated 873.54
submental region 873.44
  complicated 873.54
subungual
  finger(s) (thumb) — *see* Wound, open, finger
  toe(s) — *see* Wound, open, toe
supraclavicular region 874.8
  complicated 874.9
supraorbital 873.42
  complicated 873.52
surgical, non-healing 998.83
temple 873.49
  complicated 873.59
temporal region 873.49
  complicated 873.59
testis 878.2
  complicated 878.3

☑ Additional Digit Required — Refer to the Tabular List for Digit Selection   ⩗ Subterms under main terms may continue to next column or page

2010 ICD-9-CM   ▶◀ Revised Text   ● New Line   ▲ Revised Code   **Volume 2 — 285**

Wound, open — *continued*
- thigh 890.0
  - with tendon involvement 890.2
  - complicated 890.1
- thorax, thoracic (external) 875.0
  - complicated 875.1
- throat 874.8
  - complicated 874.9
- thumb (nail) (subungual) 883.0
  - with tendon involvement 883.2
  - complicated 883.1
- thyroid (gland) 874.2
  - complicated 874.3
- toe(s) (nail) (subungual) 893.0
  - with tendon involvement 893.2
  - complicated 893.1
- tongue 873.64
  - complicated 873.74
- tonsil — *see* Wound, open, neck
- trachea (cervical region) 874.02
  - with larynx 874.00
    - complicated 874.10
  - complicated 874.12
  - intrathoracic — *see* Injury, internal, trachea
- trunk (multiple) NEC 879.6
  - complicated 879.7
  - specified site NEC 879.6
    - complicated 879.7
- tunica vaginalis 878.2
  - complicated 878.3
- tympanic membrane 872.61
  - complicated 872.71
- tympanum 872.61
  - complicated 872.71
- umbilical region 879.2
  - complicated 879.3
- ureter — *see* Injury, internal, ureter
- urethra — *see* Injury, internal, urethra
- uterus — *see* Injury, internal, uterus
- uvula 873.69
  - complicated 873.79
- vagina 878.6
  - complicated 878.7
- vas deferens — *see* Injury, internal, vas deferens
- vitreous (humor) 871.2
- vulva 878.4
  - complicated 878.5
- wrist 881.02
  - with tendon involvement 881.22
  - complicated 881.12

Wright's syndrome (hyperabduction) 447.8
- pneumonia 390 *[517.1]*

Wringer injury — *see* Crush injury, by site

Wrinkling of skin 701.8

Wrist — *see also* condition
- drop (acquired) 736.05

Wrong drug (given in error) NEC 977.9
- specified drug or substance — *see* Table of Drugs and Chemicals

Wry neck — *see also* Torticollis
- congenital 754.1

Wuchereria infestation 125.0
- bancrofti 125.0
- Brugia malayi 125.1
- malayi 125.1

Wuchereriasis 125.0

Wuchereriosis 125.0

Wuchernde struma langhans (M8332/3) 193

X

Xanthelasma 272.2
- eyelid 272.2 *[374.51]*
- palpebrarum 272.2 *[374.51]*

Xanthelasmatosis (essential) 272.2

Xanthelasmoidea 757.33

Xanthine stones 277.2

Xanthinuria 277.2

Xanthofibroma (M8831/0) — *see* Neoplasm, connective tissue, benign

Xanthoma(s), xanthomatosis 272.2
- with
  - hyperlipoproteinemia
    - type I 272.3
    - type III 272.2
    - type IV 272.1
    - type V 272.3
- bone 272.7
- craniohypophyseal 277.89
- cutaneotendinous 272.7
- diabeticorum 250.8 ☑ *[272.2]*
  - due to secondary diabetes 249.8 ☑ *[272.2]*
- disseminatum 272.7
- eruptive 272.2
- eyelid 272.2 *[374.51]*
- familial 272.7
- hereditary 272.7
- hypercholesterinemic 272.0
- hypercholesterolemic 272.0
- hyperlipemic 272.4
- hyperlipidemic 272.4
- infantile 272.7
- joint 272.7
- juvenile 272.7
- multiple 272.7
- multiplex 272.7
- primary familial 272.7
- tendon (sheath) 272.7
- tuberosum 272.2
- tuberous 272.2
- tubo-eruptive 272.2

Xanthosis 709.09
- surgical 998.81

Xenophobia 300.29

Xeroderma (congenital) 757.39
- acquired 701.1
  - eyelid 373.33
- eyelid 373.33

Xeroderma — *continued*
- pigmentosum 757.33
- vitamin A deficiency 264.8

Xerophthalmia 372.53
- vitamin A deficiency 264.7

Xerosis
- conjunctiva 372.53
  - with Bitôt's spot 372.53
    - vitamin A deficiency 264.1
  - vitamin A deficiency 264.0
- cornea 371.40
  - with corneal ulceration 370.00
    - vitamin A deficiency 264.3
  - vitamin A deficiency 264.2
- cutis 706.8
- skin 706.8

Xerostomia 527.7

Xiphodynia 733.90

Xiphoidalgia 733.90

Xiphoiditis 733.99

Xiphopagus 759.4

XO syndrome 758.6

X-ray
- effects, adverse, NEC 990
- of chest
  - for suspected tuberculosis V71.2
  - routine V72.5

XXX syndrome 758.81

XXXXY syndrome 758.81

XXY syndrome 758.7

Xyloketosuria 271.8

Xylosuria 271.8

Xylulosuria 271.8

XYY syndrome 758.81

Y

Yaba monkey tumor virus 059.22

Yawning 786.09
- psychogenic 306.1

Yaws 102.9
- bone or joint lesions 102.6
- butter 102.1
- chancre 102.0
- cutaneous, less than five years after infection 102.2
- early (cutaneous) (macular) (maculopapular) (micropapular) (papular) 102.2
  - frambeside 102.2
  - skin lesions NEC 102.2
- eyelid 102.9 *[373.4]*
- ganglion 102.6
- gangosis, gangosa 102.5
- gumma, gummata 102.4
  - bone 102.6
- gummatous
  - frambeside 102.4
  - osteitis 102.6
  - periostitis 102.6
- hydrarthrosis 102.6

Yaws — *continued*
- hyperkeratosis (early) (late) (palmar) (plantar) 102.3
- initial lesions 102.0
- joint lesions 102.6
- juxta-articular nodules 102.7
- late nodular (ulcerated) 102.4
- latent (without clinical manifestations) (with positive serology) 102.8
- mother 102.0
- mucosal 102.7
- multiple papillomata 102.1
- nodular, late (ulcerated) 102.4
- osteitis 102.6
- papilloma, papillomata (palmar) (plantar) 102.1
- periostitis (hypertrophic) 102.6
- ulcers 102.4
- wet crab 102.1

Yeast infection — *see also* Candidiasis 112.9

Yellow
- atrophy (liver) 570
  - chronic 571.8
  - resulting from administration of blood, plasma, serum, or other biological substance (within 8 months of administration) — *see* Hepatitis, viral
- fever — *see* Fever, yellow
- jack (*see also* Fever, yellow) 060.9
- jaundice (*see also* Jaundice) 782.4
- vernix syndrome 762.2

Yersinia septica 027.8

Z

Zagari's disease (xerostomia) 527.7

Zahorsky's disease (exanthema subitum) (*see also* Exanthem subitum) 058.10
- syndrome (herpangina) 074.0

Zellweger syndrome 277.86

Zenker's diverticulum (esophagus) 530.6

Ziehen-Oppenheim disease 333.6

Zieve's syndrome (jaundice, hyperlipemia, and hemolytic anemia) 571.1

Zika fever 066.3

Zollinger-Ellison syndrome (gastric hypersecretion with pancreatic islet cell tumor) 251.5

Zona — *see also* Herpes, zoster 053.9

Zoophilia (erotica) 302.1

Zoophobia 300.29

Zoster (herpes) — *see also* Herpes, zoster 053.9

Zuelzer (-Ogden) anemia or syndrome (nutritional megaloblastic anemia) 281.2

Zygodactyly — *see also* Syndactylism 755.10

Zygomycosis 117.7

Zymotic — *see* condition

☑ Additional Digit Required — Refer to the Tabular List for Digit Selection

▽ Subterms under main terms may continue to next column or page

SECTION 2

Alphabetic Index to Poisoning and External Causes of Adverse Effects of Drugs and Other Chemical Substances

TABLE OF DRUGS AND CHEMICALS

This table contains a classification of drugs and other chemical substances to identify poisoning states and external causes of adverse effects.

Each of the listed substances in the table is assigned a code according to the poisoning classification (960-989). These codes are used when there is a statement of poisoning, overdose, wrong substance given or taken, or intoxication.

The table also contains a listing of external causes of adverse effects. An adverse effect is a pathologic manifestation due to ingestion or exposure to drugs or other chemical substances (e.g., dermatitis, hypersensitivity reaction, aspirin gastritis). The adverse effect is to be identified by the appropriate code found in Section 1, Index to Diseases and Injuries. An external cause code can then be used to identify the circumstances involved. The table headings pertaining to external causes are defined below:

Accidental poisoning (E850-E869) — accidental overdose of drug, wrong substance given or taken, drug taken inadvertently, accidents in the usage of drugs and biologicals in medical and surgical procedures, and to show external causes of poisonings classifiable to 980-989.

Therapeutic use (E930-E949) — a correct substance properly administered in therapeutic or prophylactic dosage as the external cause of adverse effects.

Suicide attempt (E950-E952) — instances in which self-inflicted injuries or poisonings are involved.

Assault (E961-E962) — injury or poisoning inflicted by another person with the intent to injure or kill.

Undetermined (E980-E982) — to be used when the intent of the poisoning or injury cannot be determined whether it was intentional or accidental.

The American Hospital Formulary Service list numbers are included in the table to help classify new drugs not identified in the table by name. The AHFS list numbers are keyed to the continually revised American Hospital Formulary Service (AHFS).* These listings are found in the table under the main term **Drug**.

Excluded from the table are radium and other radioactive substances. The classification of adverse effects and complications pertaining to these substances will be found in Section 1, Index to Diseases and Injuries, and Section 3, Index to External Causes of Injuries.

Although certain substances are indexed with one or more subentries, the majority are listed according to one use or state. It is recognized that many substances may be used in various ways, in medicine and in industry, and may cause adverse effects whatever the state of the agent (solid, liquid, or fumes arising from a liquid). In cases in which the reported data indicates a use or state not in the table, or which is clearly different from the one listed, an attempt should be made to classify the substance in the form which most nearly expresses the reported facts.

*American Hospital Formulary Service, 2 vol. (Washington, D.C.: American Society of Hospital Pharmacists, 1959-)

☑ Additional Digit Required — Refer to the Tabular List for Digit Selection   ▽ Subterms under main terms may continue to next column or page

2010 ICD-9-CM   ▶◀ Revised Text   ● New Line   ▲ Revised Code   Volume 2 — 287

	Poisoning	Accident	Therapeutic Use	Suicide Attempt	Assault	Undetermined
			External Cause (E-Code)			
1-propanol	980.3	E860.4	—	E950.9	E962.1	E980.9
2-propanol	980.2	E860.3	—	E950.9	E962.1	E980.9
2, 4-D (dichlorophenoxyacetic acid)	989.4	E863.5	—	E950.6	E962.1	E980.7
2, 4-toluene diisocyanate	983.0	E864.0	—	E950.7	E962.1	E980.6
2, 4, 5-T (trichlorophenoxyacetic acid)	989.2	E863.5	—	E950.6	E962.1	E980.7
14-hydroxydihydromorphinone	965.09	E850.2	E935.2	E950.0	E962.0	E980.0
ABOB	961.7	E857	E931.7	E950.4	E962.0	E980.4
Abrus (seed)	988.2	E865.3	—	E950.9	E962.1	E980.9
Absinthe	980.0	E860.1	—	E950.9	E962.1	E980.9
beverage	980.0	E860.0	—	E950.9	E962.1	E980.9
Acenocoumarin, acenocoumarol	964.2	E858.2	E934.2	E950.4	E962.0	E980.4
Acepromazine	969.1	E853.0	E939.1	E950.3	E962.0	E980.3
Acetal	982.8	E862.4	—	E950.9	E962.1	E980.9
Acetaldehyde (vapor)	987.8	E869.8	—	E952.8	E962.2	E982.8
liquid	989.89	E866.8	—	E950.9	E962.1	E980.9
Acetaminophen	965.4	E850.4	E935.4	E950.0	E962.0	E980.0
Acetaminosalol	965.1	E850.3	E935.3	E950.0	E962.0	E980.0
Acetanilid(e)	965.4	E850.4	E935.4	E950.0	E962.0	E980.0
Acetarsol, acetarsone	961.1	E857	E931.1	E950.4	E962.0	E980.4
Acetazolamide	974.2	E858.5	E944.2	E950.4	E962.0	E980.4
Acetic						
acid	983.1	E864.1	—	E950.7	E962.1	E980.6
with sodium acetate (ointment)	976.3	E858.7	E946.3	E950.4	E962.0	E980.4
irrigating solution	974.5	E858.5	E944.5	E950.4	E962.0	E980.4
lotion	976.2	E858.7	E946.2	E950.4	E962.0	E980.4
anhydride	983.1	E864.1	—	E950.7	E962.1	E980.6
ether (vapor)	982.8	E862.4	—	E950.9	E962.1	E980.9
Acetohexamide	962.3	E858.0	E932.3	E950.4	E962.0	E980.4
Acetomenaphthone	964.3	E858.2	E934.3	E950.4	E962.0	E980.4
Acetomorphine	965.01	E850.0	E935.0	E950.0	E962.0	E980.0
Acetone (oils) (vapor)	982.8	E862.4	—	E950.9	E962.1	E980.9
Acetophenazine (maleate)	969.1	E853.0	E939.1	E950.3	E962.0	E980.3
Acetophenetidin	965.4	E850.4	E935.4	E950.0	E962.0	E980.0
Acetophenone	982.0	E862.4	—	E950.9	E962.1	E980.9
Acetorphine	965.09	E850.2	E935.2	E950.0	E962.0	E980.0
Acetosulfone (sodium)	961.8	E857	E931.8	E950.4	E962.0	E980.4
Acetrizoate (sodium)	977.8	E858.8	E947.8	E950.4	E962.0	E980.4
Acetylcarbromal	967.3	E852.2	E937.3	E950.2	E962.0	E980.2
Acetylcholine (chloride)	971.0	E855.3	E941.0	E950.4	E962.0	E980.4
Acetylcysteine	975.5	E858.6	E945.5	E950.4	E962.0	E980.4
Acetyldigitoxin	972.1	E858.3	E942.1	E950.4	E962.0	E980.4
Acetyldihydrocodeine	965.09	E850.2	E935.2	E950.0	E962.0	E980.0
Acetyldihydrocodeinone	965.09	E850.2	E935.2	E950.0	E962.0	E980.0
Acetylene (gas) (industrial)	987.1	E868.1	—	E951.8	E962.2	E981.8
incomplete combustion of — see Carbon monoxide, fuel, utility						
tetrachloride (vapor)	982.3	E862.4	—	E950.9	E962.1	E980.9
Acetyliodosalicylic acid	965.1	E850.3	E935.3	E950.0	E962.0	E980.0
Acetylphenylhydrazine	965.8	E850.8	E935.8	E950.0	E962.0	E980.0
Acetylsalicylic acid	965.1	E850.3	E935.3	E950.0	E962.0	E980.0
Achromycin	960.4	E856	E930.4	E950.4	E962.0	E980.4
ophthalmic preparation	976.5	E858.7	E946.5	E950.4	E962.0	E980.4
topical NEC	976.0	E858.7	E946.0	E950.4	E962.0	E980.4
Acidifying agents	963.2	E858.1	E933.2	E950.4	E962.0	E980.4
Acids (corrosive) NEC	983.1	E864.1	—	E950.7	E962.1	E980.6
Aconite (wild)	988.2	E865.4	—	E950.9	E962.1	E980.9
Aconitine (liniment)	976.8	E858.7	E946.8	E950.4	E962.0	E980.4
Aconitum ferox	988.2	E865.4	—	E950.9	E962.1	E980.9
Acridine	983.0	E864.0	—	E950.7	E962.1	E980.6
vapor	987.8	E869.8	—	E952.8	E962.2	E982.8
Acriflavine	961.9	E857	E931.9	E950.4	E962.0	E980.4
Acrisorcin	976.0	E858.7	E946.0	E950.4	E962.0	E980.4
Acrolein (gas)	987.8	E869.8	—	E952.8	E962.2	E982.8
liquid	989.89	E866.8	—	E950.9	E962.1	E980.9
Actaea spicata	988.2	E865.4	—	E950.9	E962.1	E980.9
Acterol	961.5	E857	E931.5	E950.4	E962.0	E980.4
ACTH	962.4	E858.0	E932.4	E950.4	E962.0	E980.4
Acthar	962.4	E858.0	E932.4	E950.4	E962.0	E980.4
Actinomycin (C) (D)	960.7	E856	E930.7	E950.4	E962.0	E980.4
Adalin (acetyl)	967.3	E852.2	E937.3	E950.2	E962.0	E980.2
Adenosine (phosphate)	977.8	E858.8	E947.8	E950.4	E962.0	E980.4
ADH	962.5	E858.0	E932.5	E950.4	E962.0	E980.4
Adhesives	989.89	E866.6	—	E950.9	E962.1	E980.9
Adicillin	960.0	E856	E930.0	E950.4	E962.0	E980.4
Adiphenine	975.1	E855.6	E945.1	E950.4	E962.0	E980.4
Adjunct, pharmaceutical	977.4	E858.8	E947.4	E950.4	E962.0	E980.4

	Poisoning	Accident	Therapeutic Use	Suicide Attempt	Assault	Undetermined
			External Cause (E-Code)			
Adrenal (extract, cortex or medulla) (glucocorticoids) (hormones) (mineralocorticoids)	962.0	E858.0	E932.0	E950.4	E962.0	E980.4
ENT agent	976.6	E858.7	E946.6	E950.4	E962.0	E980.4
ophthalmic preparation	976.5	E858.7	E946.5	E950.4	E962.0	E980.4
topical NEC	976.0	E858.7	E946.0	E950.4	E962.0	E980.4
Adrenalin	971.2	E855.5	E941.2	E950.4	E962.0	E980.4
Adrenergic blocking agents	971.3	E855.6	E941.3	E950.4	E962.0	E980.4
Adrenergics	971.2	E855.5	E941.2	E950.4	E962.0	E980.4
Adrenochrome (derivatives)	972.8	E858.3	E942.8	E950.4	E962.0	E980.4
Adrenocorticotropic hormone	962.4	E858.0	E932.4	E950.4	E962.0	E980.4
Adrenocorticotropin	962.4	E858.0	E932.4	E950.4	E962.0	E980.4
Adriamycin	960.7	E856	E930.7	E950.4	E962.0	E980.4
Aerosol spray — see Sprays						
Aerosporin	960.8	E856	E930.8	E950.4	E962.0	E980.4
ENT agent	976.6	E858.7	E946.6	E950.4	E962.0	E980.4
ophthalmic preparation	976.5	E858.7	E946.5	E950.4	E962.0	E980.4
topical NEC	976.0	E858.7	E946.0	E950.4	E962.0	E980.4
Aethusa cynapium	988.2	E865.4	—	E950.9	E962.1	E980.9
Afghanistan black	969.6	E854.1	E939.6	E950.3	E962.0	E980.3
Aflatoxin	989.7	E865.9	—	E950.9	E962.1	E980.9
African boxwood	988.2	E865.4	—	E950.9	E962.1	E980.9
Agar (-agar)	973.3	E858.4	E943.3	E950.4	E962.0	E980.4
Agricultural agent NEC	989.89	E863.9	—	E950.6	E962.1	E980.7
Agrypnal	967.0	E851	E937.0	E950.1	E962.0	—
Air contaminant(s), source or type not specified	987.9	E869.9	—	E952.9	E962.2	E982.9
specified type — see specific substance						
Akee	988.2	E865.4	—	E950.9	E962.1	E980.9
Akrinol	976.0	E858.7	E946.0	E950.4	E962.0	E980.4
Alantolactone	961.6	E857	E931.6	E950.4	E962.0	E980.4
Albamycin	960.8	E856	E930.8	E950.4	E962.0	E980.4
Albumin (normal human serum)	964.7	E858.2	E934.7	E950.4	E962.0	E980.4
Albuterol	975.7	E858.6	E945.7	E950.4	E962.0	E980.4
Alcohol	980.9	E860.9	—	E950.9	E962.1	E980.9
absolute	980.0	E860.1	—	E950.9	E962.1	E980.9
beverage	980.0	E860.0	E947.8	E950.9	E962.1	E980.9
amyl	980.3	E860.4	—	E950.9	E962.1	E980.9
antifreeze	980.1	E860.2	—	E950.9	E962.1	E980.9
butyl	980.3	E860.4	—	E950.9	E962.1	E980.9
dehydrated	980.0	E860.1	—	E950.9	E962.1	E980.9
beverage	980.0	E860.0	E947.8	E950.9	E962.1	E980.9
denatured	980.0	E860.1	—	E950.9	E962.1	E980.9
deterrents	977.3	E858.8	E947.3	E950.4	E962.0	E980.4
diagnostic (gastric function)	977.8	E858.8	E947.8	E950.4	E962.0	E980.4
ethyl	980.0	E860.1	—	E950.9	E962.1	E980.9
beverage	980.0	E860.0	E947.8	E950.9	E962.1	E980.9
grain	980.0	E860.1	—	E950.9	E962.1	E980.9
beverage	980.0	E860.0	E947.8	E950.9	E962.1	E980.9
industrial	980.9	E860.9	—	E950.9	E962.1	E980.9
isopropyl	980.2	E860.3	—	E950.9	E962.1	E980.9
methyl	980.1	E860.2	—	E950.9	E962.1	E980.9
preparation for consumption	980.0	E860.0	E947.8	E950.9	E962.1	E980.9
propyl	980.3	E860.4	—	E950.9	E962.1	E980.9
secondary	980.2	E860.3	—	E950.9	E962.1	E980.9
radiator	980.1	E860.2	—	E950.9	E962.1	E980.9
rubbing	980.2	E860.3	—	E950.9	E962.1	E980.9
specified type NEC	980.8	E860.8	—	E950.9	E962.1	E980.9
surgical	980.9	E860.9	—	E950.9	E962.1	E980.9
vapor (from any type of alcohol)	987.8	E869.8	—	E952.8	E962.2	E982.8
wood	980.1	E860.2	—	E950.9	E962.1	E980.9
Alcuronium chloride	975.2	E858.6	E945.2	E950.4	E962.0	E980.4
Aldactone	974.4	E858.5	E944.4	E950.4	E962.0	E980.4
Aldicarb	989.3	E863.2	—	E950.6	E962.1	E980.7
Aldomet	972.6	E858.3	E942.6	E950.4	E962.0	E980.4
Aldosterone	962.0	E858.0	E932.0	E950.4	E962.0	E980.4
Aldrin (dust)	989.2	E863.0	—	E950.6	E962.1	E980.7
Algeldrate	973.0	E858.4	E943.0	E950.4	E962.0	E980.4
Alidase	963.4	E858.1	E933.4	E950.4	E962.0	E980.4
Aliphatic thiocyanates	989.0	E866.8	—	E950.9	E962.1	E980.9
Alkaline antiseptic solution (aromatic)	976.6	E858.7	E946.6	E950.4	E962.0	E980.4

    Nontherapeutic use substance

▽ Subterms under main terms may continue to next column or page

	Poisoning	Accident	Therapeutic Use	Suicide Attempt	Assault	Undetermined
Alkalinizing agents						
(medicinal)	963.3	E858.1	E933.3	E950.4	E962.0	E980.4
Alkalis, caustic	983.2	E864.2	—	E950.7	E962.1	E980.6
Alkalizing agents						
(medicinal)	963.3	E858.1	E933.3	E950.4	E962.0	E980.4
Alka-seltzer	965.1	E850.3	E935.3	E950.0	E962.0	E980.0
Alkavervir	972.6	E858.3	E942.6	E950.4	E962.0	E980.4
Allegron	969.05 ▲	E854.0	E939.0	E950.3	E962.0	E980.3
Alleve — Naproxen						
Allobarbital,						
allobarbitone	967.0	E851	E937.0	E950.1	E962.0	E980.1
Allopurinol	974.7	E858.5	E944.7	E950.4	E962.0	E980.4
Allylestrenol	962.2	E858.0	E932.2	E950.4	E962.0	E980.4
Allylisopropylacetylurea	967.8	E852.8	E937.8	E950.2	E962.0	E980.2
Allylisopropylmalonylurea	967.0	E851	E937.0	E950.1	E962.0	E980.1
Allyltribromide	967.3	E852.2	E937.3	E950.2	E962.0	E980.2
Aloe, aloes, aloin	973.1	E858.4	E943.1	E950.4	E962.0	E980.4
Alosetron	973.8	E858.4	E943.8	E950.4	E962.0	E980.4
Aloxidone	966.0	E855.0	E936.0	E950.4	E962.0	E980.4
Aloxiprin	965.1	E850.3	E935.3	E950.0	E962.0	E980.0
Alpha-1 blockers	971.3	E855.6	E941.3	E950.4	E962.0	E980.4
Alpha amylase	963.4	E858.1	E933.4	E950.4	E962.0	E980.4
Alphaprodine						
(hydrochloride)	965.09	E850.2	E935.2	E950.0	E962.0	E980.0
Alpha tocopherol	963.5	E858.1	E933.5	E950.4	E962.0	E980.4
Alseroxylon	972.6	E858.3	E942.6	E950.4	E962.0	E980.4
Alum (ammonium)						
(potassium)	983.2	E864.2	—	E950.7	E962.1	E980.6
medicinal (astringent)						
NEC	976.2	E858.7	E946.2	E950.4	E962.0	E980.4
Aluminium, aluminum (gel)						
(hydroxide)	973.0	E858.4	E943.0	E950.4	E962.0	E980.4
acetate solution	976.2	E858.7	E946.2	E950.4	E962.0	E980.4
aspirin	965.1	E850.3	E935.3	E950.0	E962.0	E980.0
carbonate	973.0	E858.4	E943.0	E950.4	E962.0	E980.4
glycinate	973.0	E858.4	E943.0	E950.4	E962.0	E980.4
nicotinate	972.2	E858.3	E942.2	E950.4	E962.0	E980.4
ointment (surgical)						
(topical)	976.3	E858.7	E946.3	E950.4	E962.0	E980.4
phosphate	973.0	E858.4	E943.0	E950.4	E962.0	E980.4
subacetate	976.2	E858.7	E946.2	E950.4	E962.0	E980.4
topical NEC	976.3	E858.7	E946.3	E950.4	E962.0	E980.4
Alurate	967.0	E851	E937.0	E950.1	E962.0	E980.1
Alverine (citrate)	975.1	E858.6	E945.1	E950.4	E962.0	E980.4
Alvodine	965.09	E850.2	E935.2	E950.0	E962.0	E980.0
Amanita phalloides	988.1	E865.5	—	E950.9	E962.1	E980.9
Amantadine						
(hydrochloride)	966.4	E855.0	E936.4	E950.4	E962.0	E980.4
Ambazone	961.9	E857	E931.9	E950.4	E962.0	E980.4
Ambenonium	971.0	E855.3	E941.0	E950.4	E962.0	E980.4
Ambutonium bromide	971.1	E855.4	E941.1	E950.4	E962.0	E980.4
Ametazole	977.8	E858.8	E947.8	E950.4	E962.0	E980.4
Amethocaine (infiltration)						
(topical)	968.5	E855.2	E938.5	E950.4	E962.0	E980.4
nerve block (peripheral)						
(plexus)	968.6	E855.2	E938.6	E950.4	E962.0	E980.4
spinal	968.7	E855.2	E938.7	E950.4	E962.0	E980.4
Amethopterin	963.1	E858.1	E933.1	E950.4	E962.0	E980.4
Amfepramone	977.0	E858.8	E947.0	E950.4	E962.0	E980.4
Amidon	965.02	E850.1	E935.1	E950.0	E962.0	E980.0
Amidopyrine	965.5	E850.5	E935.5	E950.0	E962.0	E980.0
Aminacrine	976.0	E858.7	E946.0	E950.4	E962.0	E980.4
Aminitrozole	961.5	E857	E931.5	E950.4	E962.0	E980.4
Aminoacetic acid	974.5	E858.5	E944.5	E950.4	E962.0	E980.4
Amino acids	974.5	E858.5	E944.5	E950.4	E962.0	E980.4
Aminocaproic acid	964.4	E858.2	E934.4	E950.4	E962.0	E980.4
Aminoethylisothiourium	963.8	E858.1	E933.8	E950.4	E962.0	E980.4
Aminoglutethimide	966.3	E855.0	E936.3	E950.4	E962.0	E980.4
Aminometradine	974.3	E858.5	E944.3	E950.4	E962.0	E980.4
Aminopentamide	971.1	E855.4	E941.1	E950.4	E962.0	E980.4
Aminophenazone	965.5	E850.5	E935.5	E950.0	E962.0	E980.0
Aminophenol	983.0	E864.0	—	E950.7	E962.1	E980.6
Aminophenylpyridone	969.5	E853.8	E939.5	E950.3	E962.0	E980.3
Aminophyllin	975.7	E858.6	E945.7	E950.4	E962.0	E980.4
Aminopterin	963.1	E858.1	E933.1	E950.4	E962.0	E980.4
Aminopyrine	965.5	E850.5	E935.5	E950.0	E962.0	E980.0
Aminosalicylic acid	961.8	E857	E931.8	E950.4	E962.0	E980.4
Amiphenazole	970.1	E854.3	E940.1	E950.4	E962.0	E980.4
Amiquinsin	972.6	E858.3	E942.6	E950.4	E962.0	E980.4
Amisometradine	974.3	E858.5	E944.3	E950.4	E962.0	E980.4
Amitriptyline	969.05 ▲	E854.0	E939.0	E950.3	E962.0	E980.3

	Poisoning	Accident	Therapeutic Use	Suicide Attempt	Assault	Undetermined
Ammonia (fumes) (gas)						
(vapor)	987.8	E869.8	—	E952.8	E962.2	E982.8
liquid (household) NEC	983.2	E861.4	—	E950.7	E962.1	E980.6
spirit, aromatic	970.8	E854.3	E940.8	E950.4	E962.0	E980.4
Ammoniated mercury	976.0	E858.7	E946.0	E950.4	E962.0	E980.4
Ammonium						
carbonate	983.2	E864.2	—	E950.7	E962.1	E980.6
chloride (acidifying agent)	963.2	E858.1	E933.2	E950.4	E962.0	E980.4
expectorant	975.5	E858.6	E945.5	E950.4	E962.0	E980.4
compounds (household)						
NEC	983.2	E861.4	—	E950.7	E962.1	E980.6
fumes (any usage)	987.8	E869.8	—	E952.8	E962.2	E982.8
industrial	983.2	E864.2	—	E950.7	E962.1	E980.6
ichthyosulfonate	976.4	E858.7	E946.4	E950.4	E962.0	E980.4
mandelate	961.9	E857	E931.9	E950.4	E962.0	E980.4
Amobarbital	967.0	E851	E937.0	E950.1	E962.0	E980.1
Amodiaquin(e)	961.4	E857	E931.4	E950.4	E962.0	E980.4
Amopyroquin(e)	961.4	E857	E931.4	E950.4	E962.0	E980.4
Amphenidone	969.5	E853.8	E939.5	E950.3	E962.0	E980.3
Amphetamine	969.72 ▲	E854.2	E939.7	E950.3	E962.0	E980.3
Amphomycin	960.8	E856	E930.8	E950.4	E962.0	E980.4
Amphotericin B	960.1	E856	E930.1	E950.4	E962.0	E980.4
topical	976.0	E858.7	E946.0	E950.4	E962.0	E980.4
Ampicillin	960.0	E856	E930.0	E950.4	E962.0	E980.4
Amprotropine	971.1	E855.4	E941.1	E950.4	E962.0	E980.4
Amygdalin	977.8	E858.8	E947.8	E950.4	E962.0	E980.4
Amyl						
acetate (vapor)	982.8	E862.4	—	E950.9	E962.1	E980.9
alcohol	980.3	E860.4	—	E950.9	E962.1	E980.9
nitrite (medicinal)	972.4	E858.3	E942.4	E950.4	E962.0	E980.4
Amylase (alpha)	963.4	E858.1	E933.4	E950.4	E962.0	E980.4
Amylene hydrate	980.8	E860.8	—	E950.9	E962.1	E980.9
Amylobarbitone	967.0	E851	E937.0	E950.1	E962.0	E980.1
Amylocaine	968.9	E855.2	E938.9	E950.4	E962.0	E980.4
infiltration (subcutaneous)	968.5	E855.2	E938.5	E950.4	E962.0	E980.4
nerve block (peripheral)						
(plexus)	968.6	E855.2	E938.6	E950.4	E962.0	E980.4
spinal	968.7	E855.2	E938.7	E950.4	E962.0	E980.4
topical (surface)	968.5	E855.2	E938.5	E950.4	E962.0	E980.4
Amytal (sodium)	967.0	E851	E937.0	E950.1	E962.0	E980.1
Analeptics	970.0	E854.3	E940.0	E950.4	E962.0	E980.4
Analgesics	965.9	E850.9	E935.9	E950.0	E962.0	E980.0
aromatic NEC	965.4	E850.4	E935.4	E950.0	E962.0	E980.0
non-narcotic NEC	965.7	E850.7	E935.7	E950.0	E962.0	E980.0
specified NEC	965.8	E850.8	E935.8	E950.0	E962.0	E980.0
Anamirta cocculus	988.2	E865.3	—	E950.9	E962.1	E980.9
Ancillin	960.0	E856	E930.0	E950.4	E962.0	E980.4
Androgens (anabolic						
congeners)	962.1	E858.0	E932.1	E950.4	E962.0	E980.4
Androstalone	962.1	E858.0	E932.1	E950.4	E962.0	E980.4
Androsterone	962.1	E858.0	E932.1	E950.4	E962.0	E980.4
Anemone pulsatilla	988.2	E865.4	—	E950.9	E962.1	E980.9
Anesthesia, anesthetic						
(general) NEC	968.4	E855.1	E938.4	E950.4	E962.0	E980.4
block (nerve) (plexus)	968.6	E855.2	E938.6	E950.4	E962.0	E980.4
gaseous NEC	968.2	E855.1	E938.2	E950.4	E962.0	E980.4
halogenated hydrocarbon						
derivatives NEC	968.2	E855.1	E938.2	E950.4	E962.0	E980.4
infiltration (intradermal)						
(subcutaneous)						
(submucosal)	968.5	E855.2	E938.5	E950.4	E962.0	E980.4
intravenous	968.3	E855.1	E938.3	E950.4	E962.0	E980.4
local NEC	968.9	E855.2	E938.9	E950.4	E962.0	E980.4
nerve blocking (peripheral)						
(plexus)	968.6	E855.2	E938.6	E950.4	E962.0	E980.4
rectal NEC	968.3	E855.1	E938.3	E950.4	E962.0	E980.4
spinal	968.7	E855.2	E938.7	E950.4	E962.0	E980.4
surface	968.5	E855.2	E938.5	E950.4	E962.0	E980.4
topical	968.5	E855.2	E938.5	E950.4	E962.0	E980.4
Aneurine	963.5	E858.1	E933.5	E950.4	E962.0	E980.4
Anginine — *see* Glyceryl trinitrate						
Angio-Conray	977.8	E858.8	E947.8	E950.4	E962.0	E980.4
Angiotensin	971.2	E855.5	E941.2	E950.4	E962.0	E980.4
Anhydrohydroxyprogesterone	962.2	E858.0	E932.2	E950.4	E962.0	E980.4
Anhydron	974.3	E858.5	E944.3	E950.4	E962.0	E980.4
Anileridine	965.09	E850.2	E935.2	E950.0	E962.0	E980.0
Aniline (dye) (liquid)	983.0	E864.0	—	E950.7	E962.1	E980.6
analgesic	965.4	E850.4	E935.4	E950.0	E962.0	E980.0
derivatives, therapeutic						
NEC	965.4	E850.4	E935.4	E950.0	E962.0	E980.0
vapor	987.8	E869.8	—	E952.8	E962.2	E982.8

Nontherapeutic use substance

▼ Subterms under main terms may continue to next column or page

		External Cause (E-Code)			
Poisoning	**Accident**	**Therapeutic Use**	**Suicide Attempt**	**Assault**	**Undetermined**
Aniscoropine — 971.1	E855.4	E941.1	E950.4	E962.0	E980.4
Anisindione — 964.2	E858.2	E934.2	E950.4	E962.0	E980.4
Anorexic agents — 977.0	E858.8	E947.0	E950.4	E962.0	E980.4
Ant (bite) (sting) — —	E905.5	—	E950.9	E962.1	E980.9
Antabuse — 977.3	E858.8	E947.3	E950.4	E962.0	E980.4
Antacids — 973.0	E858.4	E943.0	E950.4	E962.0	E980.4
Antazoline — 963.0	E858.1	E933.0	E950.4	E962.0	E980.4
Anthralin — 976.4	E858.7	E946.4	E950.4	E962.0	E980.4
Anthramycin — 960.7	E856	E930.7	E950.4	E962.0	E980.4
Antiadrenergics — 971.3	E855.6	E941.3	E950.4	E962.0	E980.4
Antiallergic agents — 963.0	E858.1	E933.0	E950.4	E962.0	E980.4
Antianemic agents NEC — 964.1	E858.2	E934.1	E950.4	E962.0	E980.4
Antiaris toxicaria — 988.2	E865.4	—	E950.9	E962.1	E980.9
Antiarteriosclerotic agents — 972.2	E858.3	E942.2	E950.4	E962.0	E980.4
Antiasthmatics — 975.7	E858.6	E945.7	E950.4	E962.0	E980.4
Antibiotics — 960.9	E856	E930.9	E950.4	E962.0	E980.4
antifungal — 960.1	E856	E930.1	E950.4	E962.0	E980.4
antimycobacterial — 960.6	E856	E930.6	E950.4	E962.0	E980.4
antineoplastic — 960.7	E856	E930.7	E950.4	E962.0	E980.4
cephalosporin (group) — 960.5	E856	E930.5	E950.4	E962.0	E980.4
chloramphenicol (group) — 960.2	E856	E930.2	E950.4	E962.0	E980.4
macrolides — 960.3	E856	E930.3	E950.4	E962.0	E980.4
specified NEC — 960.8	E856	E930.8	E950.4	E962.0	E980.4
tetracycline (group) — 960.4	E856	E930.4	E950.4	E962.0	E980.4
Anticancer agents NEC — 963.1	E858.1	E933.1	E950.4	E962.0	E980.4
antibiotics — 960.7	E856	E930.7	E950.4	E962.0	E980.4
Anticholinergics — 971.1	E855.4	E941.1	E950.4	E962.0	E980.4
Anticholinesterase (organophosphorus) (reversible) — 971.0	E855.3	E941.0	E950.4	E962.0	E980.4
Anticoagulants — 964.2	E858.2	E934.2	E950.4	E962.0	E980.4
antagonists — 964.5	E858.2	E934.5	E950.4	E962.0	E980.4
Anti-common cold agents NEC — 975.6	E858.6	E945.6	E950.4	E962.0	E980.4
Anticonvulsants NEC — 966.3	E855.0	E936.3	E950.4	E962.0	E980.4
Antidepressants — 969.00 ▲	E854.0	E939.0	E950.3	E962.0	E980.3
monoamine oxidase inhibitors (MAOI) ● — 969.01	E854.0	E939.0	E950.3	E962.0	E980.3
specified type NEC ● — 969.09	E854.0	E939.0	E950.3	E962.0	E980.3
SSNRI (selective serotonin and norepinephrine reuptake inhibitors) ● — 969.02	E854.0	E939.0	E950.3	E962.0	E980.3
SSRI (selective serotonin reuptake inhibitors) ● — 969.03	E854.0	E939.0	E950.3	E962.0	E980.3
tetracyclic ● — 969.04	E854.0	E939.0	E950.3	E962.0	E980.3
tricyclic ● — 969.05	E854.0	E939.0	E950.3	E962.0	E980.3
Antidiabetic agents — 962.3	E858.0	E932.3	E950.4	E962.0	E980.4
Antidiarrheal agents — 973.5	E858.4	E943.5	E950.4	E962.0	E980.4
Antidiuretic hormone — 962.5	E858.0	E932.5	E950.4	E962.0	E980.4
Antidotes NEC — 977.2	E858.8	E947.2	E950.4	E962.0	E980.4
Antiemetic agents — 963.0	E858.1	E933.0	E950.4	E962.0	E980.4
Antiepilepsy agent NEC — 966.3	E855.0	E936.3	E950.4	E962.0	E980.4
Antifertility pills — 962.2	E858.0	E932.2	E950.4	E962.0	E980.4
Antiflatulents — 973.8	E858.4	E943.8	E950.4	E962.0	E980.4
Antifreeze — 989.89	E866.8	—	E950.9	E962.1	E980.9
alcohol — 980.1	E860.2	—	E950.9	E962.1	E980.9
ethylene glycol — 982.8	E862.4	—	E950.9	E962.1	E980.9
Antifungals (nonmedicinal) (sprays) — 989.4	E863.6	—	E950.6	E962.1	E980.7
medicinal NEC — 961.9	E857	E931.9	E950.4	E962.0	E980.4
antibiotic — 960.1	E856	E930.1	E950.4	E962.0	E980.4
topical — 976.0	E858.7	E946.0	E950.4	E962.0	E980.4
Antigastric secretion agents — 973.0	E858.4	E943.0	E950.4	E962.0	E980.4
Antihelmintics — 961.6	E857	E931.6	E950.4	E962.0	E980.4
Antihemophilic factor (human) — 964.7	E858.2	E934.7	E950.4	E962.0	E980.4
Antihistamine — 963.0	E858.1	E933.0	E950.4	E962.0	E980.4
Antihypertensive agents NEC — 972.6	E858.3	E942.6	E950.4	E962.0	E980.4
Anti-infectives NEC — 961.9	E857	E931.9	E950.4	E962.0	E980.4
antibiotics — 960.9	E856	E930.9	E950.4	E962.0	E980.4
specified NEC — 960.8	E856	E930.8	E950.4	E962.0	E980.4
antihelmintic — 961.6	E857	E931.6	E950.4	E962.0	E980.4
antimalarial — 961.4	E857	E931.4	E950.4	E962.0	E980.4
antimycobacterial NEC — 961.8	E857	E931.8	E950.4	E962.0	E980.4
antibiotics — 960.6	E856	E930.6	E950.4	E962.0	E980.4
antiprotozoal NEC — 961.5	E857	E931.5	E950.4	E962.0	—
blood — 961.4	E857	E931.4	E950.4	E962.0	E980.4
antiviral — 961.7	E857	E931.7	E950.4	E962.0	E980.4
arsenical — 961.1	E857	E931.1	E950.4	E962.0	E980.4

		External Cause (E-Code)			
Poisoning	**Accident**	**Therapeutic Use**	**Suicide Attempt**	**Assault**	**Undetermined**
Anti-infectives — *continued*					
ENT agents — 976.6	E858.7	E946.6	E950.4	E962.0	E980.4
heavy metals NEC — 961.2	E857	E931.2	E950.4	E962.0	E980.4
local — 976.0	E858.7	E946.0	E950.4	E962.0	E980.4
ophthalmic preparation — 976.5	E858.7	E946.5	E950.4	E962.0	E980.4
topical NEC — 976.0	E858.7	E946.0	E950.4	E962.0	E980.4
Anti-inflammatory agents					
(topical) — 976.0	E858.7	E946.0	E950.4	E962.0	E980.4
Antiknock (tetraethyl lead) — 984.1	E862.1	—	E950.9	—	E980.9
Antilipemics — 972.2	E858.3	E942.2	E950.4	E962.0	E980.4
Antimalarials — 961.4	E857	E931.4	E950.4	E962.0	E980.4
Antimony (compounds) (vapor) NEC — 985.4	E866.2	—	E950.9	E962.1	E980.9
anti-infectives — 961.2	E857	E931.2	E950.4	E962.0	E980.4
pesticides (vapor) — 985.4	E863.4	—	E950.6	E962.2	E980.7
potassium tartrate — 961.2	E857	E931.2	E950.4	E962.0	E980.4
tartrated — 961.2	E857	E931.2	E950.4	E962.0	E980.4
Antimuscarinic agents — 971.1	E855.4	E941.1	E950.4	E962.0	E980.4
Antimycobacterials NEC — 961.8	E857	E931.8	E950.4	E962.0	E980.4
antibiotics — 960.6	E856	E930.6	E950.4	E962.0	E980.4
Antineoplastic agents — 963.1	E858.1	E933.1	E950.4	E962.0	E980.4
antibiotics — 960.7	E856	E930.7	E950.4	E962.0	E980.4
Anti-Parkinsonism agents — 966.4	E855.0	E936.4	E950.4	E962.0	E980.4
Antiphlogistics — 965.69	E850.6	E935.6	E950.0	E962.0	E980.0
Antiprotozoals NEC — 961.5	E857	E931.5	E950.4	E962.0	E980.4
blood — 961.4	E857	E931.4	E950.4	E962.0	E980.4
Antipruritics (local) — 976.1	E858.7	E946.1	E950.4	E962.0	E980.4
Antipsychotic agents NEC — 969.3	E853.8	E939.3	E950.3	E962.0	E980.3
Antipyretics — 965.9	E850.9	E935.9	E950.0	E962.0	E980.0
specified NEC — 965.8	E850.8	E935.8	E950.0	E962.0	E980.0
Antipyrine — 965.5	E850.5	E935.5	E950.0	E962.0	E980.0
Antirabies serum (equine) — 979.9	E858.8	E949.9	E950.4	E962.0	E980.4
Antirheumatics — 965.69	E850.6	E935.6	E950.0	E962.0	E980.0
Antiseborrheics — 976.4	E858.7	E946.4	E950.4	E962.0	E980.4
Antiseptics (external) (medicinal) — 976.0	E858.7	E946.0	E950.4	E962.0	E980.4
Antistine — 963.0	E858.1	E933.0	E950.4	E962.0	E980.4
Antithyroid agents — 962.8	E858.0	E932.8	E950.4	E962.0	E980.4
Antitoxin, any — 979.9	E858.8	E949.9	E950.4	E962.0	E980.4
Antituberculars — 961.8	E857	E931.8	E950.4	E962.0	E980.4
antibiotics — 960.6	E856	E930.6	E950.4	E962.0	E980.4
Antitussives — 975.4	E858.6	E945.4	E950.4	E962.0	E980.4
Antivaricose agents (sclerosing) — 972.7	E858.3	E942.7	E950.4	E962.0	E980.4
Antivenin (crotaline) (spider-bite) — 979.9	E858.8	E949.9	E950.4	E962.0	E980.4
Antivert — 963.0	E858.1	E933.0	E950.4	E962.0	E980.4
Antivirals NEC — 961.7	E857	E931.7	E950.4	E962.0	E980.4
Ant poisons — *see* Pesticides					
Antrol — 989.4	E863.4	—	E950.6	E962.1	E980.7
fungicide — 989.4	E863.6	—	E950.6	E962.1	E980.7
Apomorphine hydrochloride (emetic) — 973.6	E858.4	E943.6	E950.4	E962.0	E980.4
Appetite depressants, central — 977.0	E858.8	E947.0	E950.4	E962.0	E980.4
Apresoline — 972.6	E858.3	E942.6	E950.4	E962.0	E980.4
Aprobarbital, aprobarbitone — 967.0	E851	E937.0	E950.1	E962.0	E980.1
Apronalide — 967.8	E852.8	E937.8	E950.2	E962.0	E980.2
Aqua fortis — 983.1	E864.1	—	E950.7	E962.1	E980.6
Arachis oil (topical) — 976.3	E858.7	E946.3	E950.4	E962.0	E980.4
cathartic — 973.2	E858.4	E943.2	E950.4	E962.0	E980.4
Aralen — 961.4	E857	E931.4	E950.4	E962.0	E980.4
Arginine salts — 974.5	E858.5	E944.5	E950.4	E962.0	E980.4
Argyrol — 976.0	E858.7	E946.0	E950.4	E962.0	E980.4
ENT agent — 976.6	E858.7	E946.6	E950.4	E962.0	E980.4
ophthalmic preparation — 976.5	E858.7	E946.5	E950.4	E962.0	E980.4
Aristocort — 962.0	E858.0	E932.0	E950.4	E962.0	E980.4
ENT agent — 976.6	E858.7	E946.6	E950.4	E962.0	E980.4
ophthalmic preparation — 976.5	E858.7	E946.5	E950.4	E962.0	E980.4
topical NEC — 976.0	E858.7	E946.0	E950.4	E962.0	E980.4
Aromatics, corrosive — 983.0	E864.0	—	E950.7	E962.1	E980.6
disinfectants — 983.0	E861.4	—	E950.7	E962.1	E980.6
Arsenate of lead					
(insecticide) — 985.1	E863.4	—	E950.8	E962.1	E980.8
herbicide — 985.1	E863.5	—	E950.8	E962.1	E980.8
Arsenic, arsenicals (compounds) (dust) (fumes) (vapor) NEC — 985.1	E866.3	—	E950.8	E962.1	E980.8
anti-infectives — 961.1	E857	E931.1	E950.4	E962.0	E980.4
pesticide (dust) (fumes) — 985.1	E863.4	—	E950.8	E962.1	E980.8

▽ Subterms under main terms may continue to next column or page

	External Cause (E-Code)					
	Poisoning	Accident	Therapeutic Use	Suicide Attempt	Assault	Undetermined
Arsine (gas)	985.1	E866.3	—	E950.8	E962.1	E980.8
Arsphenamine (silver)	961.1	E857	E931.1	E950.4	E962.0	E980.4
Arsthinol	961.1	E857	E931.1	E950.4	E962.0	E980.4
Artane	971.1	E855.4	E941.1	E950.4	E962.0	E980.4
Arthropod (venomous)						
NEC	989.5	E905.5	—	E950.9	E962.1	E980.9
Asbestos	989.81	E866.8	—	E950.9	E962.1	E980.9
Ascaridole	961.6	E857	E931.6	E950.4	E962.0	E980.4
Ascorbic acid	963.5	E858.1	E933.5	E950.4	E962.0	E980.4
Asiaticoside	976.0	E858.7	E946.0	E950.4	E962.0	E980.4
Aspidium (oleoresin)	961.6	E857	E931.6	E950.4	E962.0	E980.4
Aspirin	965.1	E850.3	E935.3	E950.0	E962.0	E980.0
Astringents (local)	976.2	E858.7	E946.2	E950.4	E962.0	E980.4
Atabrine	961.3	E857	E931.3	E950.4	E962.0	E980.4
Ataractics	969.5	E853.8	E939.5	E950.3	E962.0	E980.3
Atonia drug, intestinal	973.3	E858.4	E943.3	E950.4	E962.0	E980.4
Atophan	974.7	E858.5	E944.7	E950.4	E962.0	E980.4
Atropine	971.1	E855.4	E941.1	E950.4	E962.0	E980.4
Attapulgite	973.5	E858.4	E943.5	E950.4	E962.0	E980.4
Attenuvax	979.4	E858.8	E949.4	E950.4	E962.0	E980.4
Aureomycin	960.4	E856	E930.4	E950.4	E962.0	E980.4
ophthalmic preparation	976.5	E858.7	E946.5	E950.4	E962.0	E980.4
topical NEC	976.0	E858.7	E946.0	E950.4	E962.0	E980.4
Aurothioglucose	965.69	E850.6	E935.6	E950.0	E962.0	E980.0
Aurothioglycanide	965.69	E850.6	E935.6	E950.0	E962.0	E980.0
Aurothiomalate	965.69	E850.6	E935.6	E950.0	E962.0	E980.0
Automobile fuel	981	E862.1	—	E950.9	E962.1	E980.9
Autonomic nervous system						
agents NEC	971.9	E855.9	E941.9	E950.4	E962.0	E980.4
Avlosulfon	961.8	E857	E931.8	E950.4	E962.0	E980.4
Avomine	967.8	E852.8	E937.8	E950.2	E962.0	E980.2
Azacyclonol	969.5	E853.8	E939.5	E950.3	E962.0	E980.3
Azapetine	971.3	E855.6	E941.3	E950.4	E962.0	E980.4
Azaribine	963.1	E858.1	E933.1	E950.4	E962.0	E980.4
Azaserine	960.7	E856	E930.7	E950.4	E962.0	E980.4
Azathioprine	963.1	E858.1	E933.1	E950.4	E962.0	E980.4
Azosulfamide	961.0	E857	E931.0	E950.4	E962.0	E980.4
Azulfidine	961.0	E857	E931.0	E950.4	E962.0	E980.4
Azuresin	977.8	E858.8	E947.8	E950.4	E962.0	E980.4
Bacimycin	976.0	E858.7	E946.0	E950.4	E962.0	E980.4
ophthalmic preparation	976.5	E858.7	E946.5	E950.4	E962.0	E980.4
Bacitracin	960.8	E856	E930.8	E950.4	E962.0	E980.4
ENT agent	976.6	E858.7	E946.6	E950.4	E962.0	E980.4
ophthalmic preparation	976.5	E858.7	E946.5	E950.4	E962.0	E980.4
topical NEC	976.0	E858.7	E946.0	E950.4	E962.0	E980.4
Baking soda	963.3	E858.1	E933.3	E950.4	E962.0	E980.4
BAL	963.8	E858.1	E933.8	E950.4	E962.0	E980.4
Bamethan (sulfate)	972.5	E858.3	E942.5	E950.4	E962.0	E980.4
Bamipine	963.0	E858.1	E933.0	E950.4	E962.0	E980.4
Baneberry	988.2	E865.4	—	E950.9	E962.1	E980.9
Banewort	988.2	E865.4	—	E950.9	E962.1	E980.9
Barbenyl	967.0	E851	E937.0	E950.1	E962.0	E980.1
Barbital, barbitone	967.0	E851	E937.0	E950.1	E962.0	E980.1
Barbiturates, barbituric						
acid	967.0	E851	E937.0	E950.1	E962.0	E980.1
anesthetic (intravenous)	968.3	E855.1	E938.3	E950.4	E962.0	E980.4
Barium (carbonate) (chloride)						
(sulfate)	985.8	E866.4	—	E950.9	E962.1	E980.9
diagnostic agent	977.8	E858.8	E947.8	E950.4	E962.0	E980.4
pesticide	985.8	E863.4	—	E950.6	E962.1	E980.7
rodenticide	985.8	E863.7	—	E950.6	E962.1	E980.7
Barrier cream	976.3	E858.7	E946.3	E950.4	E962.0	E980.4
Battery acid or fluid	983.1	E864.1	—	E950.7	E962.1	E980.6
Bay rum	980.8	E860.8	—	E950.9	E962.1	E980.9
BCG vaccine	978.0	E858.8	E948.0	E950.4	E962.0	E980.4
Bearsfoot	988.2	E865.4	—	E950.9	E962.1	E980.9
Beclamide	966.3	E855.0	E936.3	E950.4	E962.0	E980.4
Bee (sting) (venom)	989.5	E905.3	—	E950.9	E962.1	E980.9
Belladonna (alkaloids)	971.1	E855.4	E941.1	E950.4	E962.0	E980.4
Bemegride	970.0	E854.3	E940.0	E950.4	E962.0	E980.4
Benactyzine	969.8	E855.8	E939.8	E950.3	E962.0	E980.3
Benadryl	963.0	E858.1	E933.0	E950.4	E962.0	E980.4
Bendrofluazide	974.3	E858.5	E944.3	E950.4	E962.0	E980.4
Bendroflumethiazide	974.3	E858.5	E944.3	E950.4	E962.0	E980.4
Benemid	974.7	E858.5	E944.7	E950.4	E962.0	E980.4
Benethamine penicillin G	960.0	E856	E930.0	E950.4	E962.0	E980.4
Benisone	976.0	E858.7	E946.0	E950.4	E962.0	E980.4
Benoquin	976.8	E858.7	E946.8	E950.4	E962.0	E980.4
Benoxinate	968.5	E855.2	E938.5	E950.4	E962.0	E980.4
Bentonite	976.3	E858.7	E946.3	E950.4	E962.0	E980.4
Benzalkonium (chloride)	976.0	E858.7	E946.0	E950.4	E962.0	E980.4
ophthalmic preparation	976.5	E858.7	E946.5	E950.4	E962.0	E980.4
Benzamidosalicylate						
(calcium)	961.8	E857	E931.8	E950.4	E962.0	E980.4
Benzathine penicillin	960.0	E856	E930.0	E950.4	E962.0	E980.4
Benzcarbimine	963.1	E858.1	E933.1	E950.4	E962.0	E980.4
Benzedrex	971.2	E855.5	E941.2	E950.4	E962.0	E980.4
Benzedrine						
(amphetamine)	969.72 ▲	E854.2	E939.7	E950.3	E962.0	E980.3
Benzene (acetyl) (dimethyl)						
(methyl) (solvent) (vapor)	982.0	E862.4	—	E950.9	E962.1	E980.9
hexachloride (gamma)						
(insecticide) (vapor)	989.2	E863.0	—	E950.6	E962.1	E980.7
Benzethonium	976.0	E858.7	E946.0	E950.4	E962.0	E980.4
Benzhexol (chloride)	966.4	E855.0	E936.4	E950.4	E962.0	E980.4
Benzilonium	971.1	E855.4	E941.1	E950.4	E962.0	E980.4
Benzin(e) — see Ligroin						
Benziodarone	972.4	E858.3	E942.4	E950.4	E962.0	E980.4
Benzocaine	968.5	E855.2	E938.5	E950.4	E962.0	E980.4
Benzodiapin	969.4	E853.2	E939.4	E950.3	E962.0	E980.3
Benzodiazepines						
(tranquilizers) NEC	969.4	E853.2	E939.4	E950.3	E962.0	E980.3
Benzoic acid (with salicylic acid)						
(anti-infective)	976.0	E858.7	E946.0	E950.4	E962.0	E980.4
Benzoin	976.3	E858.7	E946.3	E950.4	E962.0	E980.4
Benzol (vapor)	982.0	E862.4	—	E950.9	E962.1	E980.9
Benzomorphan	965.09	E850.2	E935.2	E950.0	E962.0	E980.0
Benzonatate	975.4	E858.6	E945.4	E950.4	E962.0	E980.4
Benzothiadiazides	974.3	E858.5	E944.3	E950.4	E962.0	E980.4
Benzoylpas	961.8	E857	E931.8	E950.4	E962.0	E980.4
Benzperidol	969.5	E853.8	E939.5	E950.3	E962.0	E980.3
Benzphetamine	977.0	E858.8	E947.0	E950.4	E962.0	E980.4
Benzpyrinium	971.0	E855.3	E941.0	E950.4	E962.0	E980.4
Benzquinamide	963.0	E858.1	E933.0	E950.4	E962.0	E980.4
Benzthiazide	974.3	E858.5	E944.3	E950.4	E962.0	E980.4
Benztropine	971.1	E855.4	E941.1	E950.4	E962.0	E980.4
Benzyl						
acetate	982.8	E862.4	—	E950.9	E962.1	E980.9
benzoate (anti-infective)	976.0	E858.7	E946.0	E950.4	E962.0	E980.4
morphine	965.09	E850.2	E935.2	E950.0	E962.0	E980.0
penicillin	960.0	E856	E930.0	E950.4	E962.0	E980.4
Bephenium						
hydroxynapthoate	961.6	E857	E931.6	E950.4	E962.0	E980.4
Bergamot oil	989.89	E866.8	—	E950.9	E962.1	E980.9
Berries, poisonous	988.2	E865.3	—	E950.9	E962.1	E980.9
Beryllium (compounds)						
(fumes)	985.3	E866.4	—	E950.9	E962.1	E980.9
Beta-carotene	976.3	E858.7	E946.3	E950.4	E962.0	E980.4
Beta-Chlor	967.1	E852.0	E937.1	E950.2	E962.0	E980.2
Betamethasone	962.0	E858.0	E932.0	E950.4	E962.0	E980.4
topical	976.0	E858.7	E946.0	E950.4	E962.0	E980.4
Betazole	977.8	E858.8	E947.8	E950.4	E962.0	E980.4
Bethanechol	971.0	E855.3	E941.0	E950.4	E962.0	E980.4
Bethanidine	972.6	E858.3	E942.6	E950.4	E962.0	E980.4
Betula oil	976.3	E858.7	E946.3	E950.4	E962.0	E980.4
Bhang	969.6	E854.1	E939.6	E950.3	E962.0	E980.3
Bialamicol	961.5	E857	E931.5	E950.4	E962.0	E980.4
Bichloride of mercury — see Mercury, chloride						
Bichromates (calcium) (crystals)						
(potassium) (sodium)	983.9	E864.3	—	E950.7	E962.1	E980.6
fumes	987.8	E869.8	—	E952.8	E962.2	E982.8
Biguanide derivatives,						
oral	962.3	E858.0	E932.3	E950.4	E962.0	E980.4
Biligrafin	977.8	E858.8	E947.8	E950.4	E962.0	E980.4
Bilopaque	977.8	E858.8	E947.8	E950.4	E962.0	E980.4
Bioflavonoids	972.8	E858.3	E942.8	E950.4	E962.0	E980.4
Biological substance NEC	979.9	E858.8	E949.9	E950.4	E962.0	E980.4
Biperiden	966.4	E855.0	E936.4	E950.4	E962.0	E980.4
Bisacodyl	973.1	E858.4	E943.1	E950.4	E962.0	E980.4
Bishydroxycoumarin	964.2	E858.2	E934.2	E950.4	E962.0	E980.4
Bismarsen	961.1	E857	E931.1	E950.4	E962.0	E980.4
Bismuth (compounds)						
NEC	985.8	E866.4	—	E950.9	E962.1	E980.9
anti-infectives	961.2	E857	E931.2	E950.4	E962.0	E980.4
subcarbonate	973.5	E858.4	E943.5	E950.4	E962.0	E980.4
sulfarsphenamine	961.1	E857	E931.1	E950.4	E962.0	E980.4
Bisphosphonates						
intravenous	963.1	E858.1	E933.7	E950.4	E962.0	E980.4
oral	963.1	E858.1	E933.6	E950.4	E962.0	E980.4
Bithionol	961.6	E857	E931.6	E950.4	E962.0	E980.4
Bitter almond oil	989.0	E866.8	—	E950.9	E962.1	E980.9
Bittersweet	988.2	E865.4	—	E950.9	E962.1	E930.9
Black						

Subterms under main terms may continue to next column or page

			External Cause (E-Code)			
	Poisoning	Accident	Therapeutic Use	Suicide Attempt	Assault	Undetermined
Black — continued						
flag	989.4	E863.4	—	E950.6	E962.1	E980.7
henbane	988.2	E865.4	—	E950.9	E962.1	E980.9
leaf (40)	989.4	E863.4	—	E950.6	E962.1	E980.7
widow spider (bite)	989.5	E905.1	—	E950.9	E962.1	E980.9
antivenin	979.9	E858.8	E949.9	E950.4	E962.0	E980.4
Blast furnace gas (carbon monoxide from)	986	E868.8	—	E952.1	E962.2	E981.2
Bleach NEC	983.9	E864.3	—	E950.7	E962.1	E980.6
Bleaching solutions	983.9	E864.3	—	E950.7	E962.1	E980.6
Bleomycin (sulfate)	960.7	E856	E930.7	E950.4	E962.0	E980.4
Blockain	968.9	E855.2	E938.9	E950.4	E962.0	E980.4
infiltration (subcutaneous)	968.5	E855.2	E938.5	E950.4	E962.0	E980.4
nerve block (peripheral) (plexus)	968.6	E855.2	E938.6	E950.4	E962.0	E980.4
topical (surface)	968.5	E855.2	E938.5	E950.4	E962.0	E980.4
Blood (derivatives) (natural) (plasma) (whole)	964.7	E858.2	E934.7	E950.4	E962.0	E980.4
affecting agent	964.9	E858.2	E934.9	E950.4	E962.0	E980.4
specified NEC	964.8	E858.2	E934.8	E950.4	E962.0	E980.4
substitute (macromolecular)	964.8	E858.2	E934.8	E950.4	E962.0	E980.4
Blue velvet	965.09	E850.2	E935.2	E950.0	E962.0	E980.0
Bone meal	989.89	E866.5	—	E950.9	E962.1	E980.9
Bonine	963.0	E858.1	E933.0	E950.4	E962.0	E980.4
Boracic acid	976.0	E858.7	E946.0	E950.4	E962.0	E980.4
ENT agent	976.6	E858.7	E946.6	E950.4	E962.0	E980.4
ophthalmic preparation	976.5	E858.7	E946.5	E950.4	E962.0	E980.4
Borate (cleanser) (sodium)	989.6	E861.3	—	E950.9	E962.1	E980.9
Borax (cleanser)	989.6	E861.3	—	E950.9	E962.1	E980.9
Boric acid	976.0	E858.7	E946.0	E950.4	E962.0	E980.4
ENT agent	976.6	E858.7	E946.6	E950.4	E962.0	E980.4
ophthalmic preparation	976.5	E858.7	E946.5	E950.4	E962.0	E980.4
Boron hydride NEC	989.89	E866.8	—	E950.9	E962.1	E980.9
fumes or gas	987.8	E869.8	—	E952.8	E962.2	E982.8
Botox	975.3	E858.6	E945.3	E950.4	E962.0	E980.4
Brake fluid vapor	987.8	E869.8	—	E952.8	E962.2	E982.8
Brass (compounds) (fumes)	985.8	E866.4	—	E950.9	E962.1	E980.9
Brasso	981	E861.3	—	E950.9	E962.1	E980.9
Bretylium (tosylate)	972.6	E858.3	E942.6	E950.4	E962.0	E980.4
Brevital (sodium)	968.3	E855.1	E938.3	E950.4	E962.0	E980.4
British antilewisite	963.8	E858.1	E933.8	E950.4	E962.0	E980.4
Bromal (hydrate)	967.3	E852.2	E937.3	E950.2	E962.0	E980.2
Bromelains	963.4	E858.1	E933.4	E950.4	E962.0	E980.4
Bromides NEC	967.3	E852.2	E937.3	E950.2	E962.0	E980.2
Bromine (vapor)	987.8	E869.8	—	E952.8	E962.2	E982.8
compounds (medicinal)	967.3	E852.2	E937.3	E950.2	E962.0	E980.2
Bromisovalum	967.3	E852.2	E937.3	E950.2	E962.0	E980.2
Bromobenzyl cyanide	987.5	E869.3	—	E952.8	E962.2	E982.8
Bromodiphenhydramine	963.0	E858.1	E933.0	E950.4	E962.0	E980.4
Bromoform	967.3	E852.2	E937.3	E950.2	E962.0	E980.2
Bromophenol blue reagent	977.8	E858.8	E947.8	E950.4	E962.0	E980.4
Bromosalicylhydroxamic acid	961.8	E857	E931.8	E950.4	E962.0	E980.4
Bromo-seltzer	965.4	E850.4	E935.4	E950.0	E962.0	E980.0
Brompheniramine	963.0	E858.1	E933.0	E950.4	E962.0	E980.4
Bromural	967.3	E852.2	E937.3	E950.2	E962.0	E980.2
Brown spider (bite) (venom)	989.5	E905.1	—	E950.9	E962.1	E980.9
Brucia	988.2	E865.3	—	E950.9	E962.1	E980.9
Brucine	989.1	E863.7	—	E950.6	E962.1	E980.7
Brunswick green — see Copper						
Bruten — see Ibuprofen						
Bryonia (alba) (dioica)	988.2	E865.4	—	E950.9	E962.1	E980.9
Buclizine	969.5	E853.8	E939.5	E950.3	E962.0	E980.3
Bufferin	965.1	E850.3	E935.3	E950.0	E962.0	E980.0
Bufotenine	969.6	E854.1	E939.6	E950.3	E962.0	E980.3
Buphenine	971.2	E855.5	E941.2	E950.4	E962.0	E980.4
Bupivacaine	968.9	E855.2	E938.9	E950.4	E962.0	E980.4
infiltration (subcutaneous)	968.5	E855.2	E938.5	E950.4	E962.0	E980.4
nerve block (peripheral) (plexus)	968.6	E855.2	E938.6	E950.4	E962.0	E980.4
Busulfan	963.1	E858.1	E933.1	E950.4	E962.0	E980.4
Butabarbital (sodium)	967.0	E851	E937.0	E950.1	E962.0	E980.1
Butabarbitone	967.0	E851	E937.0	E950.1	E962.0	E980.1
Butabarpal	967.0	E851	E937.0	E950.1	E962.0	E980.1
Butacaine	968.5	E855.2	E938.5	E950.4	E962.0	E980.4
Butallylonal	967.0	E851	E937.0	E950.1	E962.0	E980.1
Butane (distributed in mobile container)	987.0	E868.0	—	E951.1	E962.2	E981.1
Butane — continued						
distributed through pipes	987.0	E867	—	E951.0	E962.2	E981.0
incomplete combustion of — see Carbon monoxide, butane						
Butanol	980.3	E860.4	—	E950.9	E962.1	E980.9
Butanone	982.8	E862.4	—	E950.9	E962.1	E980.9
Butaperazine	969.1	E853.0	E939.1	E950.3	E962.0	E980.3
Butazolidin	965.5	E850.5	E935.5	E950.0	E962.0	E980.0
Butethal	967.0	E851	E937.0	E950.1	E962.0	E980.1
Butethamate	971.1	E855.4	E941.1	E950.4	E962.0	E980.4
Buthalitone (sodium)	968.3	E855.1	E938.3	E950.4	E962.0	E980.4
Butisol (sodium)	967.0	E851	E937.0	E950.1	E962.0	E980.1
Butobarbital, butobarbitone	967.0	E851	E937.0	E950.1	E962.0	E980.1
Butriptyline	969.05 ▲	E854.0	E939.0	E950.3	E962.0	E980.3
Buttercups	988.2	E865.4	—	E950.9	E962.1	E980.9
Butter of antimony — see Antimony						
Butyl						
acetate (secondary)	982.8	E862.4	—	E950.9	E962.1	E980.9
alcohol	980.3	E860.4	—	E950.9	E962.1	E980.9
carbinol	980.8	E860.8	—	E950.9	E962.1	E980.9
carbitol	982.8	E862.4	—	E950.9	E962.1	E980.9
cellosolve	982.8	E862.4	—	E950.9	E962.1	E980.9
chloral (hydrate)	967.1	E852.0	E937.1	E950.2	E962.0	E980.2
formate	982.8	E862.4	—	E950.9	E962.1	E980.9
scopolammonium bromide	971.1	E855.4	E941.1	E950.4	E962.0	E980.4
Butyn	968.5	E855.2	E938.5	E950.4	E962.0	E980.4
Butyrophenone (-based tranquilizers)	969.2	E853.1	E939.2	E950.3	E962.0	E980.3
Cacodyl, cacodylic acid — see Arsenic						
Cactinomycin	960.7	E856	E930.7	E950.4	E962.0	E980.4
Cade oil	976.4	E858.7	E946.4	E950.4	E962.0	E980.4
Cadmium (chloride) (compounds) (dust) (fumes) (oxide)	985.5	E866.4	—	E950.9	E962.1	E980.9
sulfide (medicinal) NEC	976.4	E858.7	E946.4	E950.4	E962.0	E980.4
Caffeine	969.71 ▲	E854.2	E939.7	E950.3	E962.0	E980.3
Calabar bean	988.2	E865.4	—	E950.9	E962.1	E980.9
Caladium seguinium	988.2	E865.4	—	E950.9	E962.1	E980.9
Calamine (liniment) (lotion)	976.3	E858.7	E946.3	E950.4	E962.0	E980.4
Calciferol	963.5	E858.1	E933.5	E950.4	E962.0	E980.4
Calcium (salts) NEC	974.5	E858.5	E944.5	E950.4	E962.0	E980.4
acetylsalicylate	965.1	E850.3	E935.3	E950.0	E962.0	E980.0
benzamidosalicylate	961.8	E857	E931.8	E950.4	E962.0	E980.4
carbaspirin	965.1	E850.3	E935.3	E950.0	E962.0	E980.0
carbimide (citrated)	977.3	E858.8	E947.3	E950.4	E962.0	E980.4
carbonate (antacid)	973.0	E858.4	E943.0	E950.4	E962.0	E980.4
cyanide (citrated)	977.3	E858.8	E947.3	E950.4	E962.0	E980.4
dioctyl sulfosuccinate	973.2	E858.4	E943.2	E950.4	E962.0	E980.4
disodium edathamil	963.8	E858.1	E933.8	E950.4	E962.0	E980.4
disodium edetate	963.8	E858.1	E933.8	E950.4	E962.0	E980.4
EDTA	963.8	E858.1	E933.8	E950.4	E962.0	E980.4
hydrate, hydroxide	983.2	E864.2	—	E950.7	E962.1	E980.6
mandelate	961.9	E857	E931.9	E950.4	E962.0	E980.4
oxide	983.2	E864.2	—	E950.7	E962.1	E980.6
Calomel — see Mercury, chloride						
Caloric agents NEC	974.5	E858.5	E944.5	E950.4	E962.0	E980.4
Calusterone	963.1	E858.1	E933.1	E950.4	E962.0	E980.4
Camoquin	961.4	E857	E931.4	E950.4	E962.0	E980.4
Camphor (oil)	976.1	E858.7	E946.1	E950.4	E962.0	E980.4
Candeptin	976.0	E858.7	E946.0	E950.4	E962.0	E980.4
Candicidin	976.0	E858.7	E946.0	E950.4	E962.0	E980.4
Cannabinols	969.6	E854.1	E939.6	E950.3	E962.0	E980.3
Cannabis (derivatives) (indica) (sativa)	969.6	E854.1	E939.6	E950.3	E962.0	E980.3
Canned heat	980.1	E860.2	—	E950.9	E962.1	E980.9
Cantharides, cantharidin, cantharis	976.8	E858.7	E946.8	E950.4	E962.0	E980.4
Capillary agents	972.8	E858.3	E942.8	E950.4	E962.0	E980.4
Capreomycin	960.6	E856	E930.6	E950.4	E962.0	E980.4
Captodiame, captodiamine	969.5	E853.8	E939.5	E950.3	E962.0	E980.3
Caramiphen (hydrochloride)	971.1	E855.4	E941.1	E950.4	E962.0	E980.4
Carbachol	971.0	E855.3	E941.0	E950.4	E962.0	E980.4
Carbacrylamine resins	974.5	E858.5	E944.5	E950.4	E962.0	E980.4

Nontherapeutic use substance

▼ Subterms under main terms may continue to next column or page

		External Cause (E-Code)				
	Poisoning	Accident	Therapeutic Use	Suicide Attempt	Assault	Undetermined
Carbamate (sedative)	967.8	E852.8	E937.8	E950.2	E962.0	E980.2
herbicide	989.3	E863.5	—	E950.6	E962.1	E980.7
insecticide	989.3	E863.2	—	E950.6	E962.1	E980.7
Carbamazepine	966.3	E855.0	E936.3	E950.4	E962.0	E980.4
Carbamic esters	967.8	E852.8	E937.8	E950.2	E962.0	E980.2
Carbamide	974.4	E858.5	E944.4	E950.4	E962.0	E980.4
topical	976.8	E858.7	E946.8	E950.4	E962.0	E980.4
Carbamylcholine chloride	971.0	E855.3	E941.0	E950.4	E962.0	E980.4
Carbarsone	961.1	E857	E931.1	E950.4	E962.0	E980.4
Carbaryl	989.3	E863.2	—	E950.6	E962.1	E980.7
Carbaspirin	965.1	E850.3	E935.3	E950.0	E962.0	E980.0
Carbazochrome	972.8	E858.3	E942.8	E950.4	E962.0	E980.4
Carbenicillin	960.0	E856	E930.0	E950.4	E962.0	E980.4
Carbenoxolone	973.8	E858.4	E943.8	E950.4	E962.0	E980.4
Carbetapentane	975.4	E858.6	E945.4	E950.4	E962.0	E980.4
Carbimazole	962.8	E858.0	E932.8	E950.4	E962.0	E980.4
Carbinol	980.1	E860.2	—	E950.9	E962.1	E980.9
Carbinoxamine	963.0	E858.1	E933.0	E950.4	E962.0	E980.4
Carbitol	982.8	E862.4	—	E950.9	E962.1	E980.9
Carbocaine	968.9	E855.2	E938.9	E950.4	E962.0	E980.4
infiltration (subcutaneous)	968.5	E855.2	E938.5	E950.4	E962.0	E980.4
nerve block (peripheral) (plexus)	968.6	E855.2	E938.6	E950.4	E962.0	E980.4
topical (surface)	968.5	E855.2	E938.5	E950.4	E962.0	E980.4
Carbol-fuchsin solution	976.0	E858.7	E946.0	E950.4	E962.0	E980.4
Carbolic acid — see also Phenol	983.0	E864.0	—	E950.7	E962.1	E980.6
Carbomycin	960.8	E856	E930.8	E950.4	E962.0	E980.4
Carbon						
bisulfide (liquid) (vapor)	982.2	E862.4	—	E950.9	E962.1	E980.9
dioxide (gas)	987.8	E869.8	—	E952.8	E962.2	E982.8
disulfide (liquid) (vapor)	982.2	E862.4	—	E950.9	E962.1	E980.9
monoxide (from incomplete combustion of) (in) NEC	986	E868.9	—	E952.1	E962.2	E981.1
blast furnace gas	986	E868.8	—	E952.1	E962.2	E981.1
butane (distributed in mobile container)	986	E868.0	—	E951.1	E962.2	E981.1
distributed through pipes	986	E867	—	E951.0	E962.2	E981.0
charcoal fumes	986	E868.3	—	E952.1	E962.2	E981.1
coal						
gas (piped)	986	E867	—	E951.0	E962.2	E981.0
solid (in domestic stoves, fireplaces)	986	E868.3	—	E952.1	E962.2	E981.1
coke (in domestic stoves, fireplaces)	986	E868.3	—	E952.1	E962.2	E981.1
exhaust gas (motor) not in transit	986	E868.2	—	E952.0	E962.2	E982.0
combustion engine, any not in watercraft	986	E868.2	—	E952.0	E962.2	E982.0
farm tractor, not in transit	986	E868.2	—	E952.0	E962.2	E982.0
gas engine	986	E868.2	—	E952.0	E962.2	E982.0
motor pump	986	E868.2	—	E952.0	E962.2	E982.0
motor vehicle, not in transit	986	E868.2	—	E952.0	E962.2	E982.0
fuel (in domestic use)	986	E868.3	—	E952.1	E962.2	E981.1
gas (piped)	986	E867	—	E951.0	E962.2	E981.0
in mobile container	986	E868.0	—	E951.1	E962.2	E981.1
utility	986	E868.1	—	E951.8	E962.2	E981.1
in mobile container	986	E868.0	—	E951.1	E962.2	E981.1
piped (natural)	986	E867	—	E951.0	E962.2	E981.0
illuminating gas	986	E868.1	—	E951.8	E962.2	E981.8
industrial fuels or gases, any	986	E868.8	—	E952.1	E962.2	E982.1
kerosene (in domestic stoves, fireplaces)	986	E868.3	—	E952.1	E962.2	E982.1
kiln gas or vapor	986	E868.8	—	E952.1	E962.2	E982.1
motor exhaust gas, not in transit	986	E868.2	—	E952.0	E962.2	E982.0
piped gas (manufactured) (natural)	986	E867	—	E951.0	E962.2	E981.0
producer gas	986	E868.8	—	E952.1	E962.2	E982.1
propane (distributed in mobile container)	986	E868.0	—	E951.1	E962.2	E981.1
distributed through pipes	986	E867	—	E951.0	E962.2	E981.0
specified source NEC	986	E868.8	—	E952.1	E962.2	E982.1
stove gas	986	E868.1	—	E951.8	E962.2	E981.8
piped	986	E867	—	E951.0	E962.2	E981.0
utility gas	986	E868.1	—	E951.8	E962.2	E981.8
piped	986	E867	—	E951.0	E962.2	E981.0

		External Cause (E-Code)				
	Poisoning	Accident	Therapeutic Use	Suicide Attempt	Assault	Undetermined
Carbon — continued						
monoxide — continued						
water gas	986	E868.1	—	E951.8	E962.2	E981.8
wood (in domestic stoves, fireplaces)	986	E868.3	—	E952.1	E962.2	E982.1
tetrachloride (vapor) NEC	987.8	E869.8	—	E952.8	E962.2	E982.8
liquid (cleansing agent) NEC	982.1	E861.3	—	E950.9	E962.1	E980.9
solvent	982.1	E862.4	—	E950.9	E962.1	E980.9
Carbonic acid (gas)	987.8	E869.8	—	E952.8	E962.2	E982.8
anhydrase inhibitors	974.2	E858.5	E944.2	E950.4	E962.0	E980.4
Carbowax	976.3	E858.7	E946.3	E950.4	E962.0	E980.4
Carbrital	967.0	E851	E937.0	E950.1	E962.0	E980.1
Carbromal (derivatives)	967.3	E852.2	E937.3	E950.2	E962.0	E980.2
Cardiac						
depressants	972.0	E858.3	E942.0	E950.4	E962.0	E980.4
rhythm regulators	972.0	E858.3	E942.0	E950.4	E962.0	E980.4
Cardiografin	977.8	E858.8	E947.8	E950.4	E962.0	E980.4
Cardio-green	977.8	E858.8	E947.8	E950.4	E962.0	E980.4
Cardiotonic glycosides	972.1	E858.3	E942.1	E950.4	E962.0	E980.4
Cardiovascular agents NEC	972.9	E858.3	E942.9	E950.4	E962.0	E980.4
Cardrase	974.2	E858.5	E944.2	E950.4	E962.0	E980.4
Carfusin	976.0	E858.7	E946.0	E950.4	E962.0	E980.4
Carisoprodol	968.0	E855.1	E938.0	E950.4	E962.0	E980.4
Carmustine	963.1	E858.1	E933.1	E950.4	E962.0	E980.4
Carotene	963.5	E858.1	E933.5	E950.4	E962.0	E980.4
Carphenazine (maleate)	969.1	E853.0	E939.1	E950.3	E962.0	E980.3
Carter's Little Pills	973.1	E858.4	E943.1	E950.4	E962.0	E980.4
Cascara (sagrada)	973.1	E858.4	E943.1	E950.4	E962.0	E980.4
Cassava	988.2	E865.4	—	E950.9	E962.1	E980.9
Castellani's paint	976.0	E858.7	E946.0	E950.4	E962.0	E980.4
Castor						
bean	988.2	E865.3	—	E950.9	E962.1	E980.9
oil	973.1	E858.4	E943.1	E950.4	E962.0	E980.4
Caterpillar (sting)	989.5	E905.5	—	E950.9	E962.1	E980.9
Catha (edulis)	970.8	E854.3	E940.8	E950.4	E962.0	E980.4
Cathartics NEC	973.3	E858.4	E943.3	E950.4	E962.0	E980.4
contact	973.1	E858.4	E943.1	E950.4	E962.0	E980.4
emollient	973.2	E858.4	E943.2	E950.4	E962.0	E980.4
intestinal irritants	973.1	E858.4	E943.1	E950.4	E962.0	E980.4
saline	973.3	E858.4	E943.3	E950.4	E962.0	E980.4
Cathomycin	960.8	E856	E930.8	E950.4	E962.0	E980.4
Caustic(s)	983.9	E864.4	—	E950.7	E962.1	E980.6
alkali	983.2	E864.2	—	E950.7	E962.1	E980.6
hydroxide	983.2	E864.2	—	E950.7	E962.1	E980.6
potash	983.2	E864.2	—	E950.7	E962.1	E980.6
soda	983.2	E864.2	—	E950.7	E962.1	E980.6
specified NEC	983.9	E864.3	—	E950.7	E962.1	E980.6
Ceepryn	976.0	E858.7	E946.0	E950.4	E962.0	E980.4
ENT agent	976.6	E858.7	E946.6	E950.4	E962.0	E980.4
lozenges	976.6	E858.7	E946.6	E950.4	E962.0	E980.4
Celestone	962.0	E858.0	E932.0	E950.4	E962.0	E980.4
topical	976.0	E858.7	E946.0	E950.4	E962.0	E980.4
Cellosolve	982.8	E862.4	—	E950.9	E962.1	E980.9
Cell stimulants and proliferants	976.8	E858.7	E946.8	E950.4	E962.0	E980.4
Cellulose derivatives, cathartic	973.3	E858.4	E943.3	E950.4	E962.0	E980.4
nitrates (topical)	976.3	E858.7	E946.3	E950.4	E962.0	E980.4
Centipede (bite)	989.5	E905.4	—	E950.9	E962.1	E980.9
Central nervous system						
depressants	968.4	E855.1	E938.4	E950.4	E962.0	E980.4
anesthetic (general) NEC	968.4	E855.1	E938.4	E950.4	E962.0	E980.4
gases NEC	968.2	E855.1	E938.2	E950.4	E962.0	E980.4
intravenous	968.3	E855.1	E938.3	E950.4	E962.0	E980.4
barbiturates	967.0	E851	E937.0	E950.1	E962.0	E980.1
bromides	967.3	E852.2	E937.3	E950.2	E962.0	E980.2
cannabis sativa	969.6	E854.1	E939.6	E950.3	E962.0	E980.3
chloral hydrate	967.1	E852.0	E937.1	E950.2	E962.0	E980.2
hallucinogenics	969.6	E854.1	E939.6	E950.3	E962.0	E980.3
hypnotics	967.9	E852.9	E937.9	E950.2	E962.0	E980.2
specified NEC	967.8	E852.8	E937.8	E950.2	E962.0	E980.2
muscle relaxants	968.0	E855.1	E938.0	E950.4	E962.0	E980.4
paraldehyde	967.2	E852.1	E937.2	E950.2	E962.0	E980.2
sedatives	967.9	E852.9	E937.9	E950.2	E962.0	E980.2
mixed NEC	967.6	E852.5	E937.6	E950.2	E962.0	E980.2
specified NEC	967.8	E852.8	E937.8	E950.2	E962.0	E980.2
muscle-tone depressants	—			—	—	E980.4
stimulants	970.9	E854.3	E940.9	E950.4	E962.0	E980.4
amphetamines	969.72 ▲	E854.2	E939.7	E950.3	E962.0	E980.3
analeptics	970.0	E854.3	E940.0	E950.4	E962.0	E980.4

Nontherapeutic use substance

▶◀ Revised Text   ● New Line   ▲ Revised Code

▽ Subterms under main terms may continue to next column or page

		External Cause (E-Code)				
	Poisoning	Accident	Therapeutic Use	Suicide Attempt	Assault	Undeter-mined
Central nervous system — *continued*						
stimulants — continued						
antidepressants	969.00 ▲	E854.0	E939.0	E950.3	E962.0	E980.3
opiate antagonists	970.1	E854.3	E940.0	E950.4	E962.0	E980.4
specified NEC	970.8	E854.3	E940.8	E950.4	E962.0	E980.4
Cephalexin	960.5	E856	E930.5	E950.4	E962.0	E980.4
Cephaloglycin	960.5	E856	E930.5	E950.4	E962.0	E980.4
Cephaloridine	960.5	E856	E930.5	E950.4	E962.0	E980.4
Cephalosporins NEC	960.5	E856	E930.5	E950.4	E962.0	E980.4
N (adicillin)	960.0	E856	E930.0	E950.4	E962.0	E980.4
Cephalothin (sodium)	960.5	E856	E930.5	E950.4	E962.0	E980.4
Cerbera (odallam)	988.2	E865.4	—	E950.9	E962.1	E980.9
Cerberin	972.1	E858.3	E942.1	E950.4	E962.0	E980.4
Cerebral stimulants	970.9	E854.3	E940.9	E950.4	E962.0	E980.4
psychotherapeutic	969.79 ▲	E854.2	E939.7	E950.3	E962.0	E980.3
specified NEC	970.8	E854.3	E940.8	E950.4	E962.0	E980.4
Cetalkonium (chloride)	976.0	E858.7	E946.0	E950.4	E962.0	E980.4
Cetoxime	963.0	E858.1	E933.0	E950.4	E962.0	E980.4
Cetrimide	976.2	E858.7	E946.2	E950.4	E962.0	E980.4
Cetylpyridinium	976.0	E858.7	E946.0	E950.4	E962.0	E980.4
ENT agent	976.6	E858.7	E946.6	E950.4	E962.0	E980.4
lozenges	976.6	E858.7	E946.6	E950.4	E962.0	E980.4
Cevadilla — *see* Sabadilla						
Cevitamic acid	963.5	E858.1	E933.5	E950.4	E962.0	E980.4
Chalk, precipitated	973.0	E858.4	E943.0	E950.4	E962.0	E980.4
Charcoal						
fumes (carbon monoxide)	986	E868.3	—	E952.1	E962.2	E982.1
industrial	986	E868.8	—	E952.1	E962.2	E982.1
medicinal (activated)	973.0	E858.4	E943.0	E950.4	E962.0	E980.4
Chelating agents NEC	977.2	E858.8	E947.2	E950.4	E962.0	E980.4
Chelidonium majus	988.2	E865.4	—	E950.9	E962.1	E980.9
Chemical substance	989.9	E866.9	—	E950.9	E962.1	E980.9
specified NEC	989.89	E866.8	—	E950.9	E962.1	E980.9
Chemotherapy, antineoplastic	963.1	E858.1	E933.1	E950.4	E962.0	E980.4
Chenopodium (oil)	961.6	E857	E931.6	E950.4	E962.0	E980.4
Cherry laurel	988.2	E865.4	—	E950.9	E962.1	E980.9
Chiniofon	961.3	E857	E931.3	E950.4	E962.0	E980.4
Chlophedianol	975.4	E858.6	E945.4	E950.4	E962.0	E980.4
Chloral (betaine) (formamide) (hydrate)	967.1	E852.0	E937.1	E950.2	E962.0	E980.2
Chloralamide	967.1	E852.0	E937.1	E950.2	E962.0	E980.2
Chlorambucil	963.1	E858.1	E933.1	E950.4	E962.0	E980.4
Chloramphenicol	960.2	E856	E930.2	E950.4	E962.0	E980.4
ENT agent	976.6	E858.7	E946.6	E950.4	E962.0	E980.4
ophthalmic preparation	976.5	E858.7	E946.5	E950.4	E962.0	E980.4
topical NEC	976.0	E858.7	E946.0	E950.4	E962.0	E980.4
Chlorate(s) (potassium) (sodium)						
NEC	983.9	E864.3	—	E950.7	E962.1	E980.6
herbicides	989.4	E863.5	—	E950.6	E962.1	E980.7
Chlorcyclizine	963.0	E858.1	E933.0	E950.4	E962.0	E980.4
Chlordan(e) (dust)	989.2	E863.0	—	E950.6	E962.1	E980.7
Chlordantoin	976.0	E858.7	E946.0	E950.4	E962.0	E980.4
Chlordiazepoxide	969.4	E853.2	E939.4	E950.3	E962.0	E980.3
Chloresium	976.8	E858.7	E946.8	E950.4	E962.0	E980.4
Chlorethiazol	967.1	E852.0	E937.1	E950.2	E962.0	E980.2
Chlorethyl — *see* Ethyl, chloride						
Chloretone	967.1	E852.0	E937.1	E950.2	E962.0	E980.2
Chlorex	982.3	E862.4	—	E950.9	E962.1	E980.9
Chlorhexadol	967.1	E852.0	E937.1	E950.2	E962.0	E980.2
Chlorhexidine (hydrochloride)	976.0	E858.7	E946.0	E950.4	E962.0	E980.4
Chlorhydroxyquinolin	976.0	E858.7	E946.0	E950.4	E962.0	E980.4
Chloride of lime (bleach)	983.9	E864.3	—	E950.7	E962.1	E980.6
Chlorinated						
camphene	989.2	E863.0	—	E950.6	E962.1	E980.7
diphenyl	989.89	E866.8	—	E950.9	E962.1	E980.9
hydrocarbons NEC	989.2	E863.0	—	E950.6	E962.1	E980.7
solvent	982.3	E862.4	—	E950.9	E962.1	E980.9
lime (bleach)	983.9	E864.3	—	E950.7	E962.1	E980.6
naphthalene — *see* Naphthalene						
pesticides NEC	989.2	E863.0	—	E950.6	E962.1	E980.7
soda — *see* Sodium, hypochlorite						
Chlorine (fumes) (gas)	987.6	E869.8	—	E952.8	E962.2	E982.8
bleach	983.9	E864.3	—	E950.7	E962.1	E980.6
compounds NEC	983.9	E864.3	—	E950.7	E962.1	E980.6
disinfectant	983.9	E861.4	—	E950.7	E962.1	E980.6
releasing agents NEC	983.9	E864.3	—	E950.7	E962.1	E980.6

		External Cause (E-Code)				
	Poisoning	Accident	Therapeutic Use	Suicide Attempt	Assault	Undeter-mined
Chlorisondamine	972.3	E858.3	E942.3	E950.4	E962.0	E980.4
Chlormadinone	962.2	E858.0	E932.2	E950.4	E962.0	E980.4
Chlormerodrin	974.0	E858.5	E944.0	E950.4	E962.0	E980.4
Chlormethiazole	967.1	E852.0	E937.1	E950.2	E962.0	E980.2
Chlormethylenecycline	960.4	E856	E930.4	E950.4	E962.0	E980.4
Chlormezanone	969.5	E853.8	E939.5	E950.3	E962.0	E980.3
Chloroacetophenone	987.5	E869.3	—	E952.8	E962.2	E982.8
Chloroaniline	983.0	E864.0	—	E950.7	E962.1	E980.6
Chlorobenzene, chlorobenzol	982.0	E862.4	—	E950.9	E962.1	E980.9
Chlorobutanol	967.1	E852.0	E937.1	E950.2	E962.0	E980.2
Chlorodinitrobenzene	983.0	E864.0	—	E950.7	E962.1	E980.6
dust or vapor	987.8	E869.8	—	E952.8	E962.2	E982.8
Chloroethane — *see* Ethyl, chloride						
Chloroform (fumes) (vapor)	987.8	E869.8	—	E952.8	E962.2	E982.8
anesthetic (gas)	968.2	E855.1	E938.2	E950.4	E962.0	E980.4
liquid NEC	968.4	E855.1	E938.4	E950.4	E962.0	E980.4
solvent	982.3	E862.4	—	E950.9	E962.1	E980.9
Chloroguanide	961.4	E857	E931.4	E950.4	E962.0	E980.4
Chloromycetin	960.2	E856	E930.2	E950.4	E962.0	E980.4
ENT agent	976.6	E858.7	E946.6	E950.4	E962.0	E980.4
ophthalmic preparation	976.5	E858.7	E946.5	E950.4	E962.0	E980.4
otic solution	976.6	E858.7	E946.6	E950.4	E962.0	E980.4
topical NEC	976.0	E858.7	E946.0	E950.4	E962.0	E980.4
Chloronitrobenzene	983.0	E864.0	—	E950.7	E962.1	E980.6
dust or vapor	987.8	E869.8	—	E952.8	E962.2	E982.8
Chlorophenol	983.0	E864.0	—	E950.7	E962.1	E980.6
Chlorophenothane	989.2	E863.0	—	E950.6	E962.1	E980.7
Chlorophyll (derivatives)	976.8	E858.7	E946.8	E950.4	E962.0	E980.4
Chloropicrin (fumes)	987.8	E869.8	—	E952.8	E962.2	E982.8
fumigant	989.4	E863.8	—	E950.6	E962.1	E980.7
fungicide	989.4	E863.6	—	E950.6	E962.1	E980.7
pesticide (fumes)	989.4	E863.4	—	E950.6	E962.1	E980.7
Chloroprocaine	968.9	E855.2	E938.9	E950.4	E962.0	E980.4
infiltration (subcutaneous)	968.5	E855.2	E938.5	E950.4	E962.0	E980.4
nerve block (peripheral) (plexus)	968.6	E855.2	E938.6	E950.4	E962.0	E980.4
Chloroptic	976.5	E858.7	E946.5	E950.4	E962.0	E980.4
Chloropurine	963.1	E858.1	E933.1	E950.4	E962.0	E980.4
Chloroquine (hydrochloride) (phosphate)	961.4	E857	E931.4	E950.4	E962.0	E980.4
Chlorothen	963.0	E858.1	E933.0	E950.4	E962.0	E980.4
Chlorothiazide	974.3	E858.5	E944.3	E950.4	E962.0	E980.4
Chlorotrianisene	962.2	E858.0	E932.2	E950.4	E962.0	E980.4
Chlorovinyldichloroarsine	985.1	E866.3	—	E950.8	E962.1	E980.8
Chloroxylenol	976.0	E858.7	E946.0	E950.4	E962.0	E980.4
Chlorphenesin (carbamate)	968.0	E855.1	E938.0	E950.4	E962.0	E980.4
topical (antifungal)	976.0	E858.7	E946.0	E950.4	E962.0	E980.4
Chlorpheniramine	963.0	E858.1	E933.0	E950.4	E962.0	E980.4
Chlorphenoxamine	966.4	E855.0	E936.4	E950.4	E962.0	E980.4
Chlorphentermine	977.0	E858.8	E947.0	E950.4	E962.0	E980.4
Chlorproguanil	961.4	E857	E931.4	E950.4	E962.0	E980.4
Chlorpromazine	969.1	E853.0	E939.1	E950.3	E962.0	E980.3
Chlorpropamide	962.3	E858.0	E932.3	E950.4	E962.0	E980.4
Chlorprothixene	969.3	E853.8	E939.3	E950.3	E962.0	E980.3
Chlorquinaldol	976.0	E858.7	E946.0	E950.4	E962.0	E980.4
Chlortetracycline	960.4	E856	E930.4	E950.4	E962.0	E980.4
Chlorthalidone	974.4	E858.5	E944.4	E950.4	E962.0	E980.4
Chlortrianisene	962.2	E858.0	E932.2	E950.4	E962.0	E980.4
Chlor-Trimeton	963.0	E858.1	E933.0	E950.4	E962.0	E980.4
Chlorzoxazone	968.0	E855.1	E938.0	E950.4	E962.0	E980.4
Choke damp	987.8	E869.8	—	E952.8	E962.2	E982.8
Cholebrine	977.8	E858.8	E947.8	E950.4	E962.0	E980.4
Cholera vaccine	978.2	E858.8	E948.2	E950.4	E962.0	E980.4
Cholesterol-lowering agents	972.2	E858.3	E942.2	E950.4	E962.0	E980.4
Cholestyramine (resin)	972.2	E858.3	E942.2	E950.4	E962.0	E980.4
Cholic acid	973.4	E858.4	E943.4	E950.4	E962.0	E980.4
Choline						
dihydrogen citrate	977.1	E858.8	E947.1	E950.4	E962.0	E980.4
salicylate	965.1	E850.3	E935.3	E950.0	E962.0	E980.0
theophyllinate	974.1	E858.5	E944.1	E950.4	E962.0	E980.4
Cholinergics	971.0	E855.3	E941.0	E950.4	E962.0	E980.4
Cholografin	977.8	E858.8	E947.8	E950.4	E962.0	E980.4
Chorionic gonadotropin	962.4	E858.0	E932.4	E950.4	E962.0	E980.4
Chromates	983.9	E864.3	—	E950.7	E962.1	E980.6
dust or mist	987.8	E869.8	—	E952.8	E962.2	E982.8
lead	984.0	E866.0	—	E950.9	E962.1	E980.9
paint	984.0	E861.5	—	E950.9	E962.1	E980.9

Nontherapeutic use substance

☞ Subterms under main terms may continue to next column or page

	Poisoning	Accident	Therapeutic Use	Suicide Attempt	Assault	Undeter-mined
External Cause (E-Code)						
Chromic acid	983.9	E864.3	—	E950.7	E962.1	E980.6
dust or mist	987.8	E869.8	—	E952.8	E962.2	E982.8
Chromium	985.6	E866.4		E950.9	E962.1	E980.9
compounds — see Chromates						
Chromonar	972.4	E858.3	E942.4	E950.4	E962.0	E980.4
Chromyl chloride	983.9	E864.3	—	E950.7	E962.1	E980.6
Chrysarobin (ointment)	976.4	E858.7	E946.4	E950.4	E962.0	E980.4
Chrysazin	973.1	E858.4	E943.1	E950.4	E962.0	E980.4
Chymar	963.4	E858.1	E933.4	E950.4	E962.0	E980.4
ophthalmic preparation	976.5	E858.7	E946.5	E950.4	E962.0	E980.4
Chymotrypsin	963.4	E858.1	E933.4	E950.4	E962.0	E980.4
ophthalmic preparation	976.5	E858.7	E946.5	E950.4	E962.0	E980.4
Cicuta maculata or virosa	988.2	E865.4	—	E950.9	E962.1	E980.9
Cigarette lighter fluid	981	E862.1	—	E950.9	E962.1	E980.9
Cinchocaine (spinal)	968.7	E855.2	E938.7	E950.4	E962.0	E980.4
topical (surface)	968.5	E855.2	E938.5	E950.4	E962.0	E980.4
Cinchona	961.4	E857	E931.4	E950.4	E962.0	E980.4
Cinchonine alkaloids	961.4	E857	E931.4	E950.4	E962.0	E980.4
Cinchophen	974.7	E858.5	E944.7	E950.4	E962.0	E980.4
Cinnarizine	963.0	E858.1	E933.0	E950.4	E962.0	E980.4
Citanest	968.9	E855.2	E938.9	E950.4	E962.0	E980.4
infiltration (subcutaneous)	968.5	E855.2	E938.5	E950.4	E962.0	E980.4
nerve block (peripheral)						
(plexus)	968.6	E855.2	E938.6	E950.4	E962.0	E980.4
Citric acid	989.89	E866.8	—	E950.9	E962.1	E980.9
Citrovorum factor	964.1	E858.2	E934.1	E950.4	E962.0	E980.4
Claviceps purpurea	988.2	E865.4	—	E950.9	E962.1	E980.9
Cleaner, cleansing agent						
NEC	989.89	E861.3	—	E950.9	E962.1	E980.9
of paint or varnish	982.8	E862.9	—	E950.9	E962.1	E980.9
Clematis vitalba	988.2	E865.4	—	E950.9	E962.1	E980.9
Clemizole	963.0	E858.1	E933.0	E950.4	E962.0	E980.4
penicillin	960.0	E856	E930.0	E950.4	E962.0	E980.4
Clidinium	971.1	E855.4	E941.1	E950.4	E962.0	E980.4
Clindamycin	960.8	E856	E930.8	E950.4	E962.0	E980.4
Cliradon	965.09	E850.2	E935.2	E950.0	E962.0	E980.0
Clocortolone	962.0	E858.0	E932.0	E950.4	E962.0	E980.4
Clofedanol	975.4	E858.6	E945.4	E950.4	E962.0	E980.4
Clofibrate	972.2	E858.3	E942.2	E950.4	E962.0	E980.4
Clomethiazole	967.1	E852.0	E937.1	E950.2	E962.0	E980.2
Clomiphene	977.8	E858.8	E947.8	E950.4	E962.0	E980.4
Clonazepam	969.4	E853.2	E939.4	E950.3	E962.0	E980.3
Clonidine	972.6	E858.3	E942.6	E950.4	E962.0	E980.4
Clopamide	974.3	E858.5	E944.3	E950.4	E962.0	E980.4
Clorazepate	969.4	E853.2	E939.4	E950.3	E962.0	E980.3
Clorexolone	974.4	E858.5	E944.4	E950.4	E962.0	E980.4
Clorox (bleach)	983.9	E864.3		E950.7	E962.1	E980.6
Clortermine	977.0	E858.8	E947.0	E950.4	E962.0	E980.4
Clotrimazole	976.0	E858.7	E946.0	E950.4	E962.0	E980.4
Cloxacillin	960.0	E856	E930.0	E950.4	E962.0	E980.4
Coagulants NEC	964.5	E858.2	E934.5	E950.4	E962.0	E980.4
Coal (carbon monoxide from) —						
see also Carbon, monoxide,						
coal						
oil — see Kerosene						
tar NEC	983.0	E864.0	—	E950.7	E962.1	E980.6
fumes	987.8	E869.8	—	E952.8	E962.2	E982.8
medicinal (ointment)	976.4	E858.7	E946.4	E950.4	E962.0	E980.4
analgesics NEC	965.5	E850.5	E935.5	E950.0	E962.0	E980.0
naphtha (solvent)	981	E862.0	—	E950.9	E962.1	E980.9
Cobalt (fumes) (industrial)	985.8	E866.4	—	E950.9	E962.1	E980.9
Cobra (venom)	989.5	E905.0	—	E950.9	E962.1	E980.9
Coca (leaf)	970.8	E854.3	E940.8	E950.4	E962.0	E980.4
Cocaine (hydrochloride)						
(salt)	970.8	E854.3	E940.8	E950.4	E962.0	E980.4
topical anesthetic	968.5	E855.2	E938.5	E950.4	E962.0	E980.4
Coccidioidin	977.8	E858.8	E947.8	E950.4	E962.0	E980.4
Cocculus indicus	988.2	E865.3	—	E950.9	E962.1	E980.9
Cochineal	989.89	E866.8	—	E950.9	E962.1	E980.9
medicinal products	977.4	E858.8	E947.4	E950.4	E962.0	E980.4
Codeine	965.09	E850.2	E935.2	E950.0	E962.0	E980.0
Coffee	989.89	E866.8		E950.9	E962.1	E980.9
Cogentin	971.1	E855.4	E941.1	E950.4	E962.0	E980.4
Coke fumes or gas (carbon						
monoxide)	986	E868.3	—	E952.1	E962.2	E982.1
industrial use	986	E868.8	—	E952.1	E962.2	E982.1
Colace	973.2	E858.4	E943.2	E950.4	E962.0	E980.4
Colchicine	974.7	E858.5	E944.7	E950.4	E962.0	E980.4
Colchicum	988.2	E865.3	—	E950.9	E962.1	E980.9
Cold cream	976.3	E858.7	E946.3	E950.4	E962.0	E980.4
Colestipol	972.2	E858.3	E942.2	E950.4	E962.0	E980.4
Colistimethate	960.8	E856	E930.8	E950.4	E962.0	E980.4

	Poisoning	Accident	Therapeutic Use	Suicide Attempt	Assault	Undeter-mined
External Cause (E-Code)						
Colistin	960.8	E856	E930.8	E950.4	E962.0	E980.4
Collagen	977.8	E866.8	E947.8	E950.9	E962.1	E980.9
Collagenase	976.8	E858.7	E946.8	E950.4	E962.0	E980.4
Collodion (flexible)	976.3	E858.7	E946.3	E950.4	E962.0	E980.4
Colocynth	973.1	E858.4	E943.1	E950.4	E962.0	E980.4
Coloring matter — see Dye(s)						
Combustion gas — see Carbon,						
monoxide						
Compazine	969.1	E853.0	E939.1	E950.3	E962.0	E980.3
Compound						
42 (warfarin)	989.4	E863.7	—	E950.6	E962.1	E980.7
269 (endrin)	989.2	E863.0	—	E950.6	E962.1	E980.7
497 (dieldrin)	989.2	E863.0	—	E950.6	E962.1	E980.7
1080 (sodium						
fluoroacetate)	989.4	E863.7	—	E950.6	E962.1	E980.7
3422 (parathion)	989.3	E863.1	—	E950.6	E962.1	E980.7
3911 (phorate)	989.3	E863.1	—	E950.6	E962.1	E980.7
3956 (toxaphene)	989.2	E863.0	—	E950.6	E962.1	E980.7
4049 (malathion)	989.3	E863.1	—	E950.6	E962.1	E980.7
4124 (dicapthon)	989.4	E863.4	—	E950.6	E962.1	E980.7
E (cortisone)	962.0	E858.0	E932.0	E950.4	E962.0	E980.4
F (hydrocortisone)	962.0	E858.0	E932.0	E950.4	E962.0	E980.4
Congo red	977.8	E858.8	E947.8	E950.4	E962.0	E980.4
Coniine, conine	965.7	E850.7	E935.7	E950.0	E962.0	E980.0
Conium (maculatum)	988.2	E865.4	—	E950.9	E962.1	E980.9
Conjugated estrogens						
(equine)	962.2	E858.0	E932.2	E950.4	E962.0	E980.4
Contac	975.6	E858.6	E945.6	E950.4	E962.0	E980.4
Contact lens solution	976.5	E858.7	E946.5	E950.4	E962.0	E980.4
Contraceptives (oral)	962.2	E858.0	E932.2	E950.4	E962.0	E980.4
vaginal	976.8	E858.7	E946.8	E950.4	E962.0	E980.4
Contrast media						
(roentgenographic)	977.8	E858.8	E947.8	E950.4	E962.0	E980.4
Convallaria majalis	988.2	E865.4	—	E950.9	E962.1	E980.9
Copper (dust) (fumes) (salts)						
NEC	985.8	E866.4	—	E950.9	E962.1	E980.9
arsenate, arsenite	985.1	E866.3	—	E950.8	E962.1	E980.8
insecticide	985.1	E863.4	—	E950.8	E962.1	E980.8
emetic	973.6	E858.4	E943.6	E950.4	E962.0	E980.4
fungicide	985.8	E863.6	—	E950.6	E962.1	E980.7
insecticide	985.8	E863.4	—	E950.6	E962.1	E980.7
oleate	976.0	E858.7	E946.0	E950.4	E962.0	E980.4
sulfate	983.9	E864.3	—	E950.7	E962.1	E980.6
cupric	973.6	E858.4	E943.6	E950.4	E962.0	E980.4
cuprous	983.9	E864.3	—	E950.7	E962.1	E980.6
fungicide	983.9	E863.6	—	E950.7	E962.1	E980.6
Copperhead snake (bite)						
(venom)	989.5	E905.0	—	E950.9	E962.1	E980.9
Coral (sting)	989.5	E905.6	—	E950.9	E962.1	E980.9
snake (bite) (venom)	989.5	E905.0	—	E950.9	E962.1	E980.9
Cordran	976.0	E858.7	E946.0	E950.4	E962.0	E980.4
Corn cures	976.4	E858.7	E946.4	E950.4	E962.0	E980.4
Cornhusker's lotion	976.3	E858.7	E946.3	E950.4	E962.0	E980.4
Corn starch	976.3	E858.7	E946.3	E950.4	E962.0	E980.4
Corrosive	983.9	E864.4	—	E950.7	E962.1	E980.6
acids NEC	983.1	E864.1	—	E950.7	E962.1	E980.6
aromatics	983.0	E864.0	—	E950.7	E962.1	E980.6
disinfectant	983.0	E861.4	—	E950.7	E962.1	E980.6
fumes NEC	987.9	E869.9	—	E952.9	E962.2	E982.9
specified NEC	983.9	E864.3	—	E950.7	E962.1	E980.6
sublimate — see Mercury,						
chloride						
Cortate	962.0	E858.0	E932.0	E950.4	E962.0	E980.4
Cort-Dome	962.0	E858.0	E932.0	E950.4	E962.0	E980.4
ENT agent	976.6	E858.7	E946.6	E950.4	E962.0	E980.4
ophthalmic preparation	976.5	E858.7	E946.5	E950.4	E962.0	E980.4
topical NEC	976.0	E858.7	E946.0	E950.4	E962.0	E980.4
Cortef	962.0	E858.0	E932.0	E950.4	E962.0	E980.4
ENT agent	976.6	E858.7	E946.6	E950.4	E962.0	E980.4
ophthalmic preparation	976.5	E858.7	E946.5	E950.4	E962.0	E980.4
topical NEC	976.0	E858.7	E946.0	E950.4	E962.0	E980.4
Corticosteroids						
(fluorinated)	962.0	E858.0	E932.0	E950.4	E962.0	E980.4
ENT agent	976.6	E858.7	E946.6	E950.4	E962.0	E980.4
ophthalmic preparation	976.5	E858.7	E946.5	E950.4	E962.0	E980.4
topical NEC	976.0	E858.7	E946.0	E950.4	E962.0	E980.4
Corticotropin	962.4	E858.0	E932.4	E950.4	E962.0	E980.4
Cortisol	962.0	E858.0	E932.0	E950.4	E962.0	E980.4
ENT agent	976.6	E858.7	E946.6	E950.4	E962.0	E980.4
ophthalmic preparation	976.5	E858.7	E946.5	E950.4	E962.0	E980.4
topical NEC	976.0	E858.7	E946.0	E950.4	E962.0	E980.4

Nontherapeutic use substance

▽ Subterms under main terms may continue to next column or page

	Poisoning	Accident	Therapeutic Use	Suicide Attempt	Assault	Undetermined
Cortisone derivatives						
(acetate)	962.0	E858.0	E932.0	E950.4	E962.0	E980.4
ENT agent	976.6	E858.7	E946.6	E950.4	E962.0	E980.4
ophthalmic preparation	976.5	E858.7	E946.5	E950.4	E962.0	E980.4
topical NEC	976.0	E858.7	E946.0	E950.4	E962.0	E980.4
Cortogen	962.0	E858.0	E932.0	E950.4	E962.0	E980.4
ENT agent	976.6	E858.7	E946.6	E950.4	E962.0	E980.4
ophthalmic preparation	976.5	E858.7	E946.5	E950.4	E962.0	E980.4
Cortone	962.0	E858.0	E932.0	E950.4	E962.0	E980.4
ENT agent	976.6	E858.7	E946.6	E950.4	E962.0	E980.4
ophthalmic preparation	976.5	E858.7	E946.5	E950.4	E962.0	E980.4
Cortril	962.0	E858.0	E932.0	E950.4	E962.0	E980.4
ENT agent	976.6	E858.7	E946.6	E950.4	E962.0	E980.4
ophthalmic preparation	976.5	E858.7	E946.5	E950.4	E962.0	E980.4
topical NEC	976.0	E858.7	E946.0	E950.4	E962.0	E980.4
Cosmetics	989.89	E866.7	—	E950.9	E962.1	E980.9
Cosyntropin	977.8	E858.8	E947.8	E950.4	E962.0	E980.4
Cotarnine	964.5	E858.2	E934.5	E950.4	E962.0	E980.4
Cottonseed oil	976.3	E858.7	E946.3	E950.4	E962.0	E980.4
Cough mixtures						
(antitussives)	975.4	E858.6	E945.4	E950.4	E962.0	E980.4
containing opiates	965.09	E850.2	E935.2	E950.0	E962.0	E980.0
expectorants	975.5	E858.6	E945.5	E950.4	E962.0	E980.4
Coumadin	964.2	E858.2	E934.2	E950.4	E962.0	E980.4
rodenticide	989.4	E863.7	—	E950.6	E962.1	E980.7
Coumarin	964.2	E858.2	E934.2	E950.4	E962.0	E980.4
Coumetarol	964.2	E858.2	E934.2	E950.4	E962.0	E980.4
Cowbane	988.2	E865.4	—	E950.9	E962.1	E980.9
Cozyme	963.5	E858.1	E933.5	E950.4	E962.0	E980.4
Crack	970.8	E854.3	E940.8	E950.4	E962.0	E980.4
Creolin	983.0	E864.0	—	E950.7	E962.1	E980.6
disinfectant	983.0	E861.4	—	E950.7	E962.1	E980.6
Creosol (compound)	983.0	E864.0	—	E950.7	E962.1	E980.6
Creosote (beechwood) (coal tar)	983.0	E864.0	—	E950.7	E962.1	E980.6
medicinal (expectorant)	975.5	E858.6	E945.5	E950.4	E962.0	E980.4
syrup	975.5	E858.6	E945.5	E950.4	E962.0	E980.4
Cresol	983.0	E864.0	—	E950.7	E962.1	E980.6
disinfectant	983.0	E861.4	—	E950.7	E962.1	E980.6
Cresylic acid	983.0	E864.0	—	E950.7	E962.1	E980.6
Cropropamide	965.7	E850.7	E935.7	E950.0	E962.0	E980.0
with crotethamide	970.0	E854.3	E940.0	E950.4	E962.0	E980.4
Crotamiton	976.0	E858.7	E946.0	E950.4	E962.0	E980.4
Crotethamide	965.7	E850.7	E935.7	E950.0	E962.0	E980.0
with cropropamide	970.0	E854.3	E940.0	E950.4	E962.0	E980.4
Croton (oil)	973.1	E858.4	E943.1	E950.4	E962.0	E980.4
chloral	967.1	E852.0	E937.1	E950.2	E962.0	E980.2
Crude oil	981	E862.1	—	E950.9	E962.1	E980.9
Cryogenine	965.8	E850.8	E935.8	E950.0	E962.0	E980.0
Cryolite (pesticide)	989.4	E863.4	—	E950.6	E962.1	E980.7
Cryptenamine	972.6	E858.3	E942.6	E950.4	E962.0	E980.4
Crystal violet	976.0	E858.7	E946.0	E950.4	E962.0	E980.4
Cuckoopint	988.2	E865.4	—	E950.9	E962.1	E980.9
Cumetharol	964.2	E858.2	E934.2	E950.4	E962.0	E980.4
Cupric sulfate	973.6	E858.4	E943.6	E950.4	E962.0	E980.4
Cuprous sulfate	983.9	E864.3	—	E950.7	E962.1	E980.6
Curare, curarine	975.2	E858.6	E945.2	E950.4	E962.0	E980.4
Cyanic acid — see Cyanide(s)						
Cyanide(s) (compounds) (hydrogen) (potassium) (sodium) NEC	989.0	E866.8	—	E950.9	E962.1	E980.9
dust or gas (inhalation) NEC	987.7	E869.8	—	E952.8	E962.2	E982.8
fumigant	989.0	E863.8	—	E950.6	E962.1	E980.7
mercuric — see Mercury						
pesticide (dust) (fumes)	989.0	E863.4	—	E950.6	E962.1	E980.7
Cyanocobalamin	964.1	E858.2	E934.1	E950.4	E962.0	E980.4
Cyanogen (chloride) (gas) NEC	987.8	E869.8	—	E952.8	E962.2	E982.8
Cyclaine	968.5	E855.2	E938.5	E950.4	E962.0	E980.4
Cyclamen europaeum	988.2	E865.4	—	E950.9	E962.1	E980.9
Cyclandelate	972.5	E858.3	E942.5	E950.4	E962.0	E980.4
Cyclazocine	965.09	E850.2	E935.2	E950.0	E962.0	E980.0
Cyclizine	963.0	E858.1	E933.0	E950.4	E962.0	E980.4
Cyclobarbital, cyclobarbitone	967.0	E851	E937.0	E950.1	E962.0	E980.1
Cycloguanil	961.4	E857	E931.4	E950.4	E962.0	E980.4
Cyclohexane	982.0	E862.4	—	E950.9	E962.1	E980.9
Cyclohexanol	980.8	E860.8	—	E950.9	E962.1	E980.9
Cyclohexanone	982.8	E862.4	—	E950.9	E962.1	E980.9
Cyclomethycaine	968.5	E855.2	E938.5	E950.4	E962.0	E980.4
Cyclopentamine	971.2	E855.5	E941.2	E950.4	E962.0	E980.4
Cyclopenthiazide	974.3	E858.5	E944.3	E950.4	E962.0	E980.4
Cyclopentolate	971.1	E855.4	E941.1	E950.4	E962.0	E980.4
Cyclophosphamide	963.1	E858.1	E933.1	E950.4	E962.0	E980.4
Cyclopropane	968.2	E855.1	E938.2	E950.4	E962.0	E980.4
Cycloserine	960.6	E856	E930.6	E950.4	E962.0	E980.4
Cyclothiazide	974.3	E858.5	E944.3	E950.4	E962.0	E980.4
Cycrimine	966.4	E855.0	E936.4	E950.4	E962.0	E980.4
Cymarin	972.1	E858.3	E942.1	E950.4	E962.0	E980.4
Cyproheptadine	963.0	E858.1	E933.0	E950.4	E962.0	E980.4
Cyprolidol ▲	969.09 ▲	E854.0	E939.0	E950.3	E962.0	E980.3
Cytarabine	963.1	E858.1	E933.1	E950.4	E962.0	E980.4
Cytisus						
laburnum	988.2	E865.4	—	E950.9	E962.1	E980.9
scoparius	988.2	E865.4	—	E950.9	E962.1	E980.9
Cytomel	962.7	E858.0	E932.7	E950.4	E962.0	E980.4
Cytosine (antineoplastic)	963.1	E858.1	E933.1	E950.4	E962.0	E980.4
Cytoxan	963.1	E858.1	E933.1	E950.4	E962.0	E980.4
Dacarbazine	963.1	E858.1	E933.1	E950.4	E962.0	E980.4
Dactinomycin	960.7	E856	E930.7	E950.4	E962.0	E980.4
DADPS	961.8	E857	E931.8	E950.4	E962.0	E980.4
Dakin's solution (external)	976.0	E858.7	E946.0	E950.4	E962.0	E980.4
Dalmane	969.4	E853.2	E939.4	E950.3	E962.0	E980.3
DAM	977.2	E858.8	E947.2	E950.4	E962.0	E980.4
Danilone	964.2	E858.2	E934.2	E950.4	E962.0	E980.4
Danthron	973.1	E858.4	E943.1	E950.4	E962.0	E980.4
Dantrolene	975.2	E858.6	E945.2	E950.4	E962.0	E980.4
Daphne (gnidium) (mezereum)	988.2	E865.4	—	E950.9	E962.1	E980.9
berry	988.2	E865.3	—	E950.9	E962.1	E980.9
Dapsone	961.8	E857	E931.8	E950.4	E962.0	E980.4
Daraprim	961.4	E857	E931.4	E950.4	E962.0	E980.4
Darnel	988.2	E865.3	—	E950.9	E962.1	E980.9
Darvon	965.8	E850.8	E935.8	E950.0	E962.0	E980.0
Daunorubicin	960.7	E856	E930.7	E950.4	E962.0	E980.4
DBI	962.3	E858.0	E932.3	E950.4	E962.0	E980.4
D-Con (rodenticide)	989.4	E863.7	—	E950.6	E962.1	E980.7
DDS	961.8	E857	E931.8	E950.4	E962.0	E980.4
DDT	989.2	E863.0	—	E950.6	E962.1	E980.7
Deadly nightshade	988.2	E865.4	—	E950.9	E962.1	E980.9
berry	988.2	E865.3	—	E950.9	E962.1	E980.9
Deanol ▲	969.79 ▲	E854.2	E939.7	E950.3	E962.0	E980.3
Debrisoquine	972.6	E858.3	E942.6	E950.4	E962.0	E980.4
Decaborane	989.89	E866.8	—	E950.9	E962.1	E980.9
fumes	987.8	E869.8	—	E952.8	E962.2	E982.8
Decadron	962.0	E858.0	E932.0	E950.4	E962.0	E980.4
ENT agent	976.6	E858.7	E946.6	E950.4	E962.0	E980.4
ophthalmic preparation	976.5	E858.7	E946.5	E950.4	E962.0	E980.4
topical NEC	976.0	E858.7	E946.0	E950.4	E962.0	E980.4
Decahydronaphthalene	982.0	E862.4	—	E950.9	E962.1	E980.9
Decalin	982.0	E862.4	—	E950.9	E962.1	E980.9
Decamethonium	975.2	E858.6	E945.2	E950.4	E962.0	E980.4
Decholin	973.4	E858.4	E943.4	E950.4	E962.0	E980.4
sodium (diagnostic)	977.8	E858.8	E947.8	E950.4	E962.0	E980.4
Declomycin	960.4	E856	E930.4	E950.4	E962.0	E980.4
Deferoxamine	963.8	E858.1	E933.8	E950.4	E962.0	E980.4
Dehydrocholic acid	973.4	E858.4	E943.4	E950.4	E962.0	E980.4
DeKalin	982.0	E862.4	—	E950.9	E962.1	E980.9
Delalutin	962.2	E858.0	E932.2	E950.4	E962.0	E980.4
Delphinium	988.2	E865.3	—	E950.9	E962.1	E980.9
Deltasone	962.0	E858.0	E932.0	E950.4	E962.0	E980.4
Deltra	962.0	E858.0	E932.0	E950.4	E962.0	E980.4
Delvinal	967.0	E851	E937.0	E950.1	E962.0	E980.1
Demecarium (bromide)	971.0	E855.3	E941.0	E950.4	E962.0	E980.4
Demeclocycline	960.4	E856	E930.4	E950.4	E962.0	E980.4
Demecolcine	963.1	E858.1	E933.1	E950.4	E962.0	E980.4
Demelanizing agents	976.8	E858.7	E946.8	E950.4	E962.0	E980.4
Demerol	965.09	E850.2	E935.2	E950.0	E962.0	E980.0
Demethylchlortetracycline	960.4	E856	E930.4	E950.4	E962.0	E980.4
Demethyltetracycline	960.4	E856	E930.4	E950.4	E962.0	E980.4
Demeton	989.3	E863.1	—	E950.6	E962.1	E980.7
Demulcents	976.3	E858.7	E946.3	E950.4	E962.0	E980.4
Demulen	962.2	E858.0	E932.2	E950.4	E962.0	E980.4
Denatured alcohol	980.0	E860.1	—	E950.9	E962.1	E980.9
Dendrid	976.5	E858.7	E946.5	E950.4	E962.0	E980.4
Dental agents, topical	976.7	E858.7	E946.7	E950.4	E962.0	E980.4
Deodorant spray (feminine hygiene)	976.8	E858.7	E946.8	E950.4	E962.0	E980.4
Deoxyribonuclease	963.4	E858.1	E933.4	E950.4	E962.0	E980.4
Depressants						
appetite, central	977.0	E858.8	E947.0	E950.4	E962.0	E980.4
cardiac	972.0	E858.3	E942.0	E950.4	E962.0	E980.4

▼ Subterms under main terms may continue to next column or page

▶◀ Revised Text   ● New Line   ▲ Revised Code

	Poisoning	Accident	Therapeutic Use	Suicide Attempt	Assault	Undetermined
Depressants — *continued*						
central nervous system						
(anesthetic)	968.4	E855.1	E938.4	E950.4	E962.0	E980.4
psychotherapeutic	969.5	E853.9	E939.5	E950.3	E962.0	E980.3
Dequalinium	976.0	E858.7	E946.0	E950.4	E962.0	E980.4
Dermolate	976.2	E858.7	E946.2	E950.4	E962.0	E980.4
DES	962.2	E858.0	E932.2	E950.4	E962.0	E980.4
Desenex	976.0	E858.7	E946.0	E950.4	E962.0	E980.4
Deserpidine	972.6	E858.3	E942.6	E950.4	E962.0	E980.4
Desipramine	969.05 ▲	E854.0	E939.0	E950.3	E962.0	E980.3
Deslanoside	972.1	E858.3	E942.1	E950.4	E962.0	E980.4
Desocodeine	965.09	E850.2	E935.2	E950.0	E962.0	E980.0
Desomorphine	965.09	E850.2	E935.2	E950.0	E962.0	E980.0
Desonide	976.0	E858.7	E946.0	E950.4	E962.0	E980.4
Desoxycorticosterone						
derivatives	962.0	E858.0	E932.0	E950.4	E962.0	E980.4
Desoxyephedrine	969.72 ▲	E854.2	E939.7	E950.3	E962.0	E980.3
DET	969.6	E854.1	E939.6	E950.3	E962.0	E980.3
Detergents (ingested)						
(synthetic)	989.6	E861.0	—	E950.9	E962.1	E980.9
ENT agent	976.6	E858.7	E946.6	E950.4	E962.0	E980.4
external medication	976.2	E858.7	E946.2	E950.4	E962.0	E980.4
ophthalmic preparation	976.5	E858.7	E946.5	E950.4	E962.0	E980.4
topical NEC	976.0	E858.7	E946.0	E950.4	E962.0	E980.4
Deterrent, alcohol	977.3	E858.8	E947.3	E950.4	E962.0	E980.4
Detrothyronine	962.7	E858.0	E932.7	E950.4	E962.0	E980.4
Dettol (external						
medication)	976.0	E858.7	E946.0	E950.4	E962.0	E980.4
Dexamethasone	962.0	E858.0	E932.0	E950.4	E962.0	E980.4
Dexamphetamine	969.72 ▲	E854.2	E939.7	E950.3	E962.0	E980.3
Dexedrine	969.72 ▲	E854.2	E939.7	E950.3	E962.0	E980.3
Dexpanthenol	963.5	E858.1	E933.5	E950.4	E962.0	E980.4
Dextran	964.8	E858.2	E934.8	E950.4	E962.0	E980.4
Dextriferron	964.0	E858.2	E934.0	E950.4	E962.0	E980.4
Dextroamphetamine	969.72 ▲	E854.2	E939.7	E950.3	E962.0	E980.3
Dextro calcium						
pantothenate	963.5	E858.1	E933.5	E950.4	E962.0	E980.4
Dextromethorphan	975.4	E858.6	E945.4	E950.4	E962.0	E980.4
Dextromoramide	965.09	E850.2	E935.2	E950.0	E962.0	E980.0
Dextro pantothenyl						
alcohol	963.5	E858.1	E933.5	E950.4	E962.0	E980.4
topical	976.8	E858.7	E946.8	E950.4	E962.0	E980.4
Dextropropoxyphene						
(hydrochloride)	965.8	E850.8	E935.8	E950.0	E962.0	E980.0
Dextrorphan	965.09	E850.2	E935.2	E950.0	E962.0	E980.0
Dextrose NEC	974.5	E858.5	E944.5	E950.4	E962.0	E980.4
Dextrothyroxin	962.7	E858.0	E932.7	E950.4	E962.0	E980.4
DFP	971.0	E855.3	E941.0	E950.4	E962.0	E980.4
DHE-45	972.9	E858.3	E942.9	E950.4	E962.0	E980.4
Diabinese	962.3	E858.0	E932.3	E950.4	E962.0	E980.4
Diacetyl monoxime	977.2	E858.8	E947.2	E950.4	E962.0	E980.4
Diacetylmorphine	965.01	E850.0	E935.0	E950.0	E962.0	E980.0
Diagnostic agents	977.8	E858.8	E947.8	E950.4	E962.0	E980.4
Dial (soap)	976.2	E858.7	E946.2	E950.4	E962.0	E980.4
sedative	967.0	E851	E937.0	E950.1	E962.0	E980.1
Diallylbarbituric acid	967.0	E851	E937.0	E950.1	E962.0	E980.1
Diaminodiphenylsulfone	961.8	E857	E931.8	E950.4	E962.0	E980.4
Diamorphine	965.01	E850.0	E935.0	E950.0	E962.0	E980.0
Diamox	974.2	E858.5	E944.2	E950.4	E962.0	E980.4
Diamthazole	976.0	E858.7	E946.0	E950.4	E962.0	E980.4
Diaphenylsulfone	961.8	E857	E931.8	E950.4	E962.0	E980.4
Diasone (sodium)	961.8	E857	E931.8	E950.4	E962.0	E980.4
Diazepam	969.4	E853.2	E939.4	E950.3	E962.0	E980.3
Diazinon	989.3	E863.1	—	E950.6	E962.1	E980.7
Diazomethane (gas)	987.8	E869.8	—	E952.8	E962.2	E982.8
Diazoxide	972.5	E858.3	E942.5	E950.4	E962.0	E980.4
Dibenamine	971.3	E855.6	E941.3	E950.4	E962.0	E980.4
Dibenzheptropine	963.0	E858.1	E933.0	E950.4	E962.0	E980.4
Dibenzyline	971.3	E855.6	E941.3	E950.4	E962.0	E980.4
Diborane (gas)	987.8	E869.8	—	E952.8	E962.2	E982.8
Dibromomannitol	963.1	E858.1	E933.1	E950.4	E962.0	E980.4
Dibucaine (spinal)	968.7	E855.2	E938.7	E950.4	E962.0	E980.4
topical (surface)	968.5	E855.2	E938.5	E950.4	E962.0	E980.4
Dibunate sodium	975.4	E858.6	E945.4	E950.4	E962.0	E980.4
Dibutoline	971.1	E855.4	E941.1	E950.4	E962.0	E980.4
Dicapthon	989.4	E863.4	—	E950.6	E962.1	E980.7
Dichloralphenazone	967.1	E852.0	E937.1	E950.2	E962.0	E980.2
Dichlorodifluoromethane	987.4	E869.2	—	E952.8	E962.2	E982.8
Dichloroethane	982.3	E862.4	—	E950.9	E962.1	E980.9
Dichloroethylene	982.3	E862.4	—	E950.9	E962.1	E980.9
Dichloroethyl sulfide	987.8	E869.8	—	E952.8	E962.2	E982.8
Dichlorohydrin	982.3	E862.4	—	E950.9	E962.1	E980.9

	Poisoning	Accident	Therapeutic Use	Suicide Attempt	Assault	Undetermined
Dichloromethane (solvent)						
(vapor)	982.3	E862.4	—	E950.9	E962.1	E980.9
Dichlorophen(e)	961.6	E857	E931.6	E950.4	E962.0	E980.4
Dichlorphenamide	974.2	E858.5	E944.2	E950.4	E962.0	E980.4
Dichlorvos	989.3	E863.1	—	E950.6	E962.1	E980.7
Diclofenac sodium	965.69	E850.6	E935.6	E950.0	E962.0	E980.0
Dicoumarin, dicumarol	964.2	E858.2	E934.2	E950.4	E962.0	E980.4
Dicyanogen (gas)	987.8	E869.8	—	E952.8	E962.2	E982.8
Dicyclomine	971.1	E855.4	E941.1	E950.4	E962.0	E980.4
Dieldrin (vapor)	989.2	E863.0	—	E950.6	E962.1	E980.7
Dienestrol	962.2	E858.0	E932.2	E950.4	E962.0	E980.4
Dietetics	977.0	E858.8	E947.0	E950.4	E962.0	E980.4
Diethazine	966.4	E855.0	E936.4	E950.4	E962.0	E980.4
Diethyl						
barbituric acid	967.0	E851	E937.0	E950.1	E962.0	E980.1
carbamazine	961.6	E857	E931.6	E950.4	E962.0	E980.4
carbinol	980.8	E860.8	—	E950.9	E962.1	E980.9
carbonate	982.8	E862.4	—	E950.9	E962.1	E980.9
dioxide	982.8	E862.4	—	E950.9	E962.1	E980.9
ether (vapor) — see ther(s)						
glycol (monoacetate)						
(monoethyl ether)	982.8	E862.4	—	E950.9	E962.1	E980.9
propion	977.0	E858.8	E947.0	E950.4	E962.0	E980.4
stilbestrol	962.2	E858.0	E932.2	E950.4	E962.0	E980.4
Diethylene						
Diethylsulfone-diethylmethane	967.8	E852.8	E937.8	E950.2	E962.0	E980.2
Difencloxazine	965.09	E850.2	E935.2	E950.0	E962.0	E980.0
Diffusin	963.4	E858.1	E933.4	E950.4	E962.0	E980.4
Diflos	971.0	E855.3	E941.0	E950.4	E962.0	E980.4
Digestants	973.4	E858.4	E943.4	E950.4	E962.0	E980.4
Digitalin(e)	972.1	E858.3	E942.1	E950.4	E962.0	E980.4
Digitalis glycosides	972.1	E858.3	E942.1	E950.4	E962.0	E980.4
Digitoxin	972.1	E858.3	E942.1	E950.4	E962.0	E980.4
Digoxin	972.1	E858.3	E942.1	E950.4	E962.0	E980.4
Dihydrocodeine	965.09	E850.2	E935.2	E950.0	E962.0	E980.0
Dihydrocodeinone	965.09	E850.2	E935.2	E950.0	E962.0	E980.0
Dihydroergocristine	972.9	E858.3	E942.9	E950.4	E962.0	E980.4
Dihydroergotamine	972.9	E858.3	E942.9	E950.4	E962.0	E980.4
Dihydroergotoxine	972.9	E858.3	E942.9	E950.4	E962.0	E980.4
Dihydrohydroxycodeinone	965.09	E850.2	E935.2	E950.0	E962.0	E980.0
Dihydrohydroxymorphinone	965.09	E850.2	E935.2	E950.0	E962.0	E980.0
Dihydroisocodeine	965.09	E850.2	E935.2	E950.0	E962.0	E980.0
Dihydromorphine	965.09	E850.2	E935.2	E950.0	E962.0	E980.0
Dihydromorphinone	965.09	E850.2	E935.2	E950.0	E962.0	E980.0
Dihydrostreptomycin	960.6	E856	E930.6	E950.4	E962.0	E980.4
Dihydrotachysterol	962.6	E858.0	E932.6	E950.4	E962.0	E980.4
Dihydroxyanthraquinone	973.1	E858.4	E943.1	E950.4	E962.0	E980.4
Dihydroxycodeinone	965.09	E850.2	E935.2	E950.0	E962.0	E980.0
Diiodohydroxyquin	961.3	E857	E931.3	E950.4	E962.0	E980.4
topical	976.0	E858.7	E946.0	E950.4	E962.0	E980.4
Diiodohydroxyquinoline	961.3	E857	E931.3	E950.4	E962.0	E980.4
Dilantin	966.1	E855.0	E936.1	E950.4	E962.0	E980.4
Dilaudid	965.09	E850.2	E935.2	E950.0	E962.0	E980.0
Diloxanide	961.5	E857	E931.5	E950.4	E962.0	E980.4
Dimefline	970.0	E854.3	E940.0	E950.4	E962.0	E980.4
Dimenhydrinate	963.0	E858.1	E933.0	E950.4	E962.0	E980.4
Dimercaprol	963.8	E858.1	E933.8	E950.4	E962.0	E980.4
Dimercaptopropanol	963.8	E858.1	E933.8	E950.4	E962.0	E980.4
Dimetane	963.0	E858.1	E933.0	E950.4	E962.0	E980.4
Dimethicone	976.3	E858.7	E946.3	E950.4	E962.0	E980.4
Dimethindene	963.0	E858.1	E933.0	E950.4	E962.0	E980.4
Dimethisoquin	968.5	E855.2	E938.5	E950.4	E962.0	E980.4
Dimethisterone	962.2	E858.0	E932.2	E950.4	E962.0	E980.4
Dimethoxanate	975.4	E858.6	E945.4	E950.4	E962.0	E980.4
Dimethyl						
arsine, arsinic acid — see Arsenic						
carbinol	980.2	E860.3	—	E950.9	E962.1	E980.9
diguanide	962.3	E858.0	E932.3	E950.4	E962.0	E980.4
ketone	982.8	E862.4	—	E950.9	E962.1	E980.9
vapor	987.8	E869.8	—	E952.8	E962.2	E982.8
meperidine	965.09	E850.2	E935.2	E950.0	E962.0	E980.0
parathion	989.3	E863.1	—	E950.6	E962.1	E980.7
polysiloxane	973.8	E858.4	E943.8	E950.4	E962.0	E980.4
sulfate (fumes)	987.8	E869.8	—	E952.8	E962.2	E982.8
liquid	983.9	E864.3	—	E950.7	E962.1	E980.6
sulfoxide NEC	982.8	E862.4	—	E950.9	E962.1	E980.9
medicinal	976.4	E858.7	E946.4	E950.4	E962.0	E980.4
triptamine	969.6	E854.1	E939.6	E950.3	E962.0	E980.3
tubocurarine	975.2	E858.6	E945.2	E950.4	E962.0	E980.4
Dindevan	964.2	E858.2	E934.2	E950.4	E962.0	E980.4
Dinitrobenzene	983.0	E864.0	—	E950.7	E962.1	E980.6

Nontherapeutic use substance

▽ Subterms under main terms may continue to next column or page

		External Cause (E-Code)			
	Poisoning	Accident	Therapeutic Use	Suicide Attempt	Assault	Undetermined

	Poisoning	Accident	Therapeutic Use	Suicide Attempt	Assault	Undetermined
Dinitrobenzene — *continued*						
vapor	987.8	E869.8	—	E952.8	E962.2	E982.8
Dinitro (-ortho-) cresol						
(herbicide) (spray)	989.4	E863.5		E950.6	E962.1	E980.7
insecticide	989.4	E863.4		E950.6	E962.1	E980.7
Dinitro-orthocresol						
(herbicide)	989.4	E863.5		E950.6	E962.1	E980.7
insecticide	989.4	E863.4		E950.6	E962.1	E980.7
Dinitrophenol (herbicide)						
(spray)	989.4	E863.5		E950.6	E962.1	E980.7
insecticide	989.4	E863.4		E950.6	E962.1	E980.7
Dinoprost	975.0	E858.6	E945.0	E950.4	E962.0	E980.4
Dioctyl sulfosuccinate (calcium)						
(sodium)	973.2	E858.4	E943.2	E950.4	E962.0	E980.4
Diodoquin	961.3	E857	E931.3	E950.4	E962.0	E980.4
Dione derivatives NEC	966.3	E855.0	E936.3	E950.4	E962.0	E980.4
Dionin	965.09	E850.2	E935.2	E950.0	E962.0	E980.0
Dioxane	982.8	E862.4	—	E950.9	E962.1	E980.9
Dioxin — *see* Herbicide						
Dioxyline	972.5	E858.3	E942.5	E950.4	E962.0	E980.4
Dipentene	982.8	E862.4	—	E950.9	E962.1	E980.9
Diphemanil	971.1	E855.4	E941.1	E950.4	E962.0	E980.4
Diphenadione	964.2	E858.2	E934.2	E950.4	E962.0	E980.4
Diphenhydramine	963.0	E858.1	E933.0	E950.4	E962.0	E980.4
Diphenidol	963.0	E858.1	E933.0	E950.4	E962.0	E980.4
Diphenoxylate	973.5	E858.4	E943.5	E950.4	E962.0	E980.4
Diphenylchloroarsine	985.1	E866.3	—	E950.8	E962.1	E980.8
Diphenylhydantoin						
(sodium)	966.1	E855.0	E936.1	E950.4	E962.0	E980.4
Diphenylpyraline	963.0	E858.1	E933.0	E950.4	E962.0	E980.4
Diphtheria						
antitoxin	979.9	E858.8	E949.9	E950.4	E962.0	E980.4
toxoid	978.5	E858.8	E948.5	E950.4	E962.0	E980.4
with tetanus toxoid	978.9	E858.8	E948.9	E950.4	E962.0	E980.4
with pertussis component	978.6	E858.8	E948.6	E950.4	E962.0	E980.4
vaccine	978.5	E858.8	E948.5	E950.4	E962.0	E980.4
Dipipanone	965.09	E850.2	E935.2	E950.0	E962.0	E980.0
Diplovax	979.5	E858.8	E949.5	E950.4	E962.0	E980.4
Diprophylline	975.1	E858.6	E945.1	E950.4	E962.0	E980.4
Dipyridamole	972.4	E858.3	E942.4	E950.4	E962.0	E980.4
Dipyrone	965.5	E850.5	E935.5	E950.0	E962.0	E980.0
Diquat	989.4	E863.5		E950.6	E962.1	E980.7
Disinfectant NEC	983.9	E861.4	—	E950.7	E962.1	E980.6
alkaline	983.2	E861.4	—	E950.7	E962.1	E980.6
aromatic	983.0	E861.4	—	E950.7	E962.1	E980.6
Disipal	966.4	E855.0	E936.4	E950.4	E962.0	E980.4
Disodium edetate	963.8	E858.1	E933.8	E950.4	E962.0	E980.4
Disulfamide	974.4	E858.5	E944.4	E950.4	E962.0	E980.4
Disulfanilamide	961.0	E857	E931.0	E950.4	E962.0	E980.4
Disulfiram	977.3	E858.8	E947.3	E950.4	E962.0	E980.4
Dithiazanine	961.6	E857	E931.6	E950.4	E962.0	E980.4
Dithioglycerol	963.8	E858.1	E933.8	E950.4	E962.0	E980.4
Dithranol	976.4	E858.7	E946.4	E950.4	E962.0	E980.4
Diucardin	974.3	E858.5	E944.3	E950.4	E962.0	E980.4
Diupres	974.3	E858.5	E944.3	E950.4	E962.0	E980.4
Diuretics NEC	974.4	E858.5	E944.4	E950.4	E962.0	E980.4
carbonic acid anhydrase inhibitors	974.2	E858.5	E944.2	E950.4	E962.0	E980.4
mercurial	974.0	E858.5	E944.0	E950.4	E962.0	E980.4
osmotic	974.4	E858.5	E944.4	E950.4	E962.0	E980.4
purine derivatives	974.1	E858.5	E944.1	E950.4	E962.0	E980.4
saluretic	974.3	E858.5	E944.3	E950.4	E962.0	E980.4
Diuril	974.3	E858.5	E944.3	E950.4	E962.0	E980.4
Divinyl ether	968.2	E855.1	E938.2	E950.4	E962.0	E980.4
D-lysergic acid diethylamide	969.6	E854.1	E939.6	E950.3	E962.0	E980.3
DMCT	960.4	E856	E930.4	E950.4	E962.0	E980.4
DMSO	982.8	E862.4	—	E950.9	E962.1	E980.9
DMT	969.6	E854.1	E939.6	E950.3	E962.0	E980.3
DNOC	989.4	E863.5	—	E950.6	E962.1	E980.7
DOCA	962.0	E858.0	E932.0	E950.4	E962.0	E980.4
Dolophine	965.02	E850.1	E935.1	E950.0	E962.0	E980.0
Doloxene	965.8	E850.8	E935.8	E950.0	E962.0	E980.0
DOM	969.6	E854.1	E939.6	E950.3	E962.0	E980.3
Domestic gas — *see* Gas, utility						
Domiphen (bromide)						
(lozenges)	976.6	E858.7	E946.6	E950.4	E962.0	E980.4
Dopa (levo)	966.4	E855.0	E936.4	E950.4	E962.0	E980.4
Dopamine	971.2	E855.5	E941.2	E950.4	E962.0	E980.4
Doriden	967.5	E852.4	E937.5	E950.2	E962.0	E980.2
Dormiral	967.0	E851	E937.0	E950.1	E962.0	E980.1

	Poisoning	Accident	Therapeutic Use	Suicide Attempt	Assault	Undetermined
Dormison	967.8	E852.8	E937.8	E950.2	E962.0	E980.2
Dornase	963.4	E858.1	E933.4	E950.4	E962.0	E980.4
Dorsacaine	968.5	E855.2	E938.5	E950.4	E962.0	E980.4
Dothiepin hydrochloride	969.05 ▲	E854.0	E939.0	E950.3	E962.0	E980.3
Doxapram	970.0	E854.3	E940.0	E950.4	E962.0	E980.4
Doxepin	969.05 ▲	E854.0	E939.0	E950.3	E962.0	E980.3
Doxorubicin	960.7	E856	E930.7	E950.4	E962.0	E980.4
Doxycycline	960.4	E856	E930.4	E950.4	E962.0	E980.4
Doxylamine	963.0	E858.1	E933.0	E950.4	E962.0	E980.4
Dramamine	963.0	E858.1	E933.0	E950.4	E962.0	E980.4
Drano (drain cleaner)	983.2	E864.2	—	E950.7	E962.1	E980.6
Dromoran	965.09	E850.2	E935.2	E950.0	E962.0	E980.0
Dromostanolone	962.1	E858.0	E932.1	E950.4	E962.0	E980.4
Droperidol	969.2	E853.1	E939.2	E950.3	E962.0	E980.3
Drotrecogin alfa	964.2	E858.2	E934.2	E950.4	E962.0	E980.4
Drug	977.9	E858.9	E947.9	E950.5	E962.0	E980.5
AHFS List						
4:00 antihistamine drugs	963.0	E858.1	E933.0	E950.4	E962.0	E980.4
8:04 amebacides	961.5	E857	E931.5	E950.4	E962.0	E980.4
arsenical anti-infectives	961.1	E857	E931.1	E950.4	E962.0	E980.4
quinoline derivatives	961.3	E857	E931.3	E950.4	E962.0	E980.4
8:08 anthelmintics	961.6	E857	E931.6	E950.4	E962.0	E980.4
quinoline derivatives	961.3	E857	E931.3	E950.4	E962.0	E980.4
8:12.04 antifungal antibiotics	960.1	E856	E930.1	E950.4	E962.0	E980.4
8:12.06 cephalosporins	960.5	E856	E930.5	E950.4	E962.0	E980.4
8:12.08 chloramphenicol	960.2	E856	E930.2	E950.4	E962.0	E980.4
8:12.12 erythromycins	960.3	E856	E930.3	E950.4	E962.0	E980.4
8:12.16 penicillins	960.0	E856	E930.0	E950.4	E962.0	E980.4
8:12.20 streptomycins	960.6	E856	E930.6	E950.4	E962.0	E980.4
8:12.24 tetracyclines	960.4	E856	E930.4	E950.4	E962.0	E980.4
8:12.28 other antibiotics	960.8	E856	E930.8	E950.4	E962.0	E980.4
antimycobacterial	960.6	E856	E930.6	E950.4	E962.0	E980.4
macrolides	960.3	E856	E930.3	E950.4	E962.0	E980.4
8:16 antituberculars	961.8	E857	E931.8	E950.4	E962.0	E980.4
antibiotics	960.6	E856	E930.6	E950.4	E962.0	E980.4
8:18 antivirals	961.7	E857	E931.7	E950.4	E962.0	E980.4
8:20 plasmodicides (antimalarials)	961.4	E857	E931.4	E950.4	E962.0	E980.4
8:24 sulfonamides	961.0	E857	E931.0	E950.4	E962.0	E980.4
8:26 sulfones	961.8	E857	E931.8	E950.4	E962.0	E980.4
8:28 treponemicides	961.2	E857	E931.2	E950.4	E962.0	E980.4
8:32 trichomonacides	961.5	E857	E931.5	E950.4	E962.0	E980.4
nitrofuran derivatives	961.9	E857	E931.9	E950.4	E962.0	E980.4
quinoline derivatives	961.3	E857	E931.3	E950.4	E962.0	E980.4
8:36 urinary germicides	961.9	E857	E931.9	E950.4	E962.0	E980.4
quinoline derivatives	961.3	E857	E931.3	E950.4	E962.0	E980.4
8:40 other anti-infectives	961.9	E857	E931.9	E950.4	E962.0	E980.4
10:00 antineoplastic agents	963.1	E858.1	E933.1	E950.4	E962.0	E980.4
antibiotics	960.7	E856	E930.7	E950.4	E962.0	E980.4
progestogens	962.2	E858.0	E932.2	E950.4	E962.0	E980.4
12:04 parasympathomimetic (cholinergic) agents	971.0	E855.3	E941.0	E950.4	E962.0	E980.4
12:08 parasympatholytic (cholinergic-blocking) agents	971.1	E855.4	E941.1	E950.4	E962.0	E980.4
12:12 Sympathomimetic (adrenergic) agents	971.2	E855.5	E941.2	E950.4	E962.0	E980.4
12:16 sympatholytic (adrenergic-blocking) agents	971.3	E855.6	E941.3	E950.4	E962.0	E980.4
12:20 skeletal muscle relaxants central nervous system muscle-tone depressants	968.0	E855.1	E938.0	E950.4	E962.0	E980.4
myoneural blocking agents	975.2	E858.6	E945.2	E950.4	E962.0	E980.4
16:00 blood derivatives	964.7	E858.2	E934.7	E950.4	E962.0	E980.4
20:04.04 iron preparations	964.0	E858.2	E934.0	E950.4	E962.0	E980.4
20:04.08 liver and stomach preparations	964.1	E858.2	E934.1	E950.4	E962.0	E980.4
20:04 antianemia drugs	964.1	E858.2	E934.1	E950.4	E962.0	E980.4
20:12.04 anticoagulants	964.2	E858.2	E934.2	E950.4	E962.0	E980.4
20:12.08 antiheparin agents	964.5	E858.2	E934.5	E950.4	E962.0	E980.4
20:12.12 coagulants	964.5	E858.2	E934.5	E950.4	E962.0	E980.4
20:12.16 hemostatics NEC	964.5	E858.2	E934.5	E950.4	E962.0	E980.4
capillary active drugs	972.8	E858.3	E942.8	E950.4	E962.0	E980.4
24:04 cardiac drugs	972.9	E858.3	E942.9	E950.4	E962.0	E980.4
cardiotonic agents	972.1	E858.3	E942.1	E950.4	E962.0	E980.4
rhythm regulators	972.0	E858.3	E942.0	E950.4	E962.0	E980.4

Nontherapeutic use substance

Subterms under main terms may continue to next column or page

Drug — continued	Poisoning	Accident	Therapeutic Use	Suicide Attempt	Assault	Undetermined
24:06 antilipemic agents	972.2	E858.3	E942.2	E950.4	E962.0	E980.4
thyroid derivatives	962.7	E858.0	E932.7	E950.4	E962.0	E980.4
24:08 hypotensive agents	972.6	E858.3	E942.6	E950.4	E962.0	E980.4
adrenergic blocking agents	971.3	E855.6	E941.3	E950.4	E962.0	E980.4
ganglion blocking agents	972.3	E858.3	E942.3	E950.4	E962.0	E980.4
vasodilators	972.5	E858.3	E942.5	E950.4	E962.0	E980.4
24:12 vasodilating agents NEC	972.5	E858.3	E942.5	E950.4	E962.0	E980.4
coronary	972.4	E858.3	E942.4	E950.4	E962.0	E980.4
nicotinic acid derivatives	972.2	E858.3	E942.2	E950.4	E962.0	E980.4
24:16 sclerosing agents	972.7	E858.3	E942.7	E950.4	E962.0	E980.4
28:04 general anesthetics	968.4	E855.1	E938.4	E950.4	E962.0	E980.4
gaseous anesthetics	968.2	E855.1	E938.2	E950.4	E962.0	E980.4
halothane	968.1	E855.1	E938.1	E950.4	E962.0	E980.4
intravenous anesthetics	968.3	E855.1	E938.3	E950.4	E962.0	E980.4
28:08 analgesics and antipyretics	965.9	E850.9	E935.9	E950.0	E962.0	E980.0
antirheumatics	965.69	E850.6	E935.6	E950.0	E962.0	E980.0
aromatic analgesics	965.4	E850.4	E935.4	E950.0	E962.0	E980.0
non-narcotic NEC	965.7	E850.7	E935.7	E950.0	E962.0	E980.0
opium alkaloids	965.00	E850.2	E935.2	E950.0	E962.0	E980.0
heroin	965.01	E850.0	E935.0	E950.0	E962.0	E980.0
methadone	965.02	E850.1	E935.1	E950.0	E962.0	E980.0
specified type NEC	965.09	E850.2	E935.2	E950.0	E962.0	E980.0
pyrazole derivatives	965.5	E850.5	E935.5	E950.0	E962.0	E980.0
salicylates	965.1	E850.3	E935.3	E950.0	E962.0	E980.0
specified NEC	965.8	E850.8	E935.8	E950.0	E962.0	E980.0
28:10 narcotic antagonists	970.1	E854.3	E940.1	E950.4	E962.0	E980.4
28:12 anticonvulsants	966.3	E855.0	E936.3	E950.4	E962.0	E980.4
barbiturates	967.0	E851	E937.0	E950.1	E962.0	E980.1
benzodiazepine-based tranquilizers	969.4	E853.2	E939.4	E950.3	E962.0	E980.3
bromides	967.3	E852.2	E937.3	E950.2	E962.0	E980.2
hydantoin derivatives	966.1	E855.0	E936.1	E950.4	E962.0	E980.4
oxazolidine (derivatives)	966.0	E855.0	E936.0	E950.4	E962.0	E980.4
succinimides	966.2	E855.0	E936.2	E950.4	E962.0	E980.4
28:16.04 antidepressants	969.00 ▲	E854.0	E939.0	E950.3	E962.0	E980.3
28:16.08 tranquilizers	969.5	E853.9	E939.5	E950.3	E962.0	E980.3
benzodiazepine-based	969.4	E853.2	E939.4	E950.3	E962.0	E980.3
butyrophenone-based	969.2	E853.1	E939.2	E950.3	E962.0	E980.3
major NEC	969.3	E853.8	E939.3	E950.3	E962.0	E980.3
phenothiazine-based	969.1	E853.0	E939.1	E950.3	E962.0	E980.3
28:16.12 other psychotherapeutic agents	969.8	E855.8	E939.8	E950.3	E962.0	E980.3
28:20 respiratory and cerebral stimulants	970.9	E854.3	E940.9	E950.4	E962.0	E980.4
analeptics	970.0	E854.3	E940.0	E950.4	E962.0	E980.4
anorexigenic agents	977.0	E858.8	E947.0	E950.4	E962.0	E980.4
psychostimulants	969.70 ▲	E854.2	E939.7	E950.3	E962.0	E980.3
specified NEC	970.8	E854.3	E940.8	E950.4	E962.0	E980.4
28:24 sedatives and hypnotics	967.9	E852.9	E937.9	E950.2	E962.0	E980.2
barbiturates	967.0	E851	E937.0	E950.1	E962.0	E980.1
benzodiazepine-based tranquilizers	969.4	E853.2	E939.4	E950.3	E962.0	E980.3
chloral hydrate (group)	967.1	E852.0	E937.1	E950.2	E962.0	E980.2
glutethamide group	967.5	E852.4	E937.5	E950.2	E962.0	E980.2
intravenous anesthetics	968.3	E855.1	E938.3	E950.4	E962.0	E980.4
methaqualone (compounds)	967.4	E852.3	E937.4	E950.2	E962.0	E980.2
paraldehyde	967.2	E852.1	E937.2	E950.2	E962.0	E980.2
phenothiazine-based tranquilizers	969.1	E853.0	E939.1	E950.3	E962.0	E980.3
specified NEC	967.8	E852.8	E937.8	E950.2	E962.0	E980.2
thiobarbiturates	968.3	E855.1	E938.3	E950.4	E962.0	E980.4
tranquilizer NEC	969.5	E853.9	E939.5	E950.3	E962.0	E980.3
36:04 to 36:88 diagnostic agents	977.8	E858.8	E947.8	E950.4	E962.0	E980.4
40:00 electrolyte, caloric, and water balance agents NEC	974.5	E858.5	E944.5	E950.4	E962.0	E980.4
40:04 acidifying agents	963.2	E858.1	E933.2	E950.4	E962.0	E980.4
40:08 alkalinizing agents	963.3	E858.1	E933.3	E950.4	E962.0	E980.4
40:10 ammonia detoxicants	974.5	E858.5	E944.5	E950.4	E962.0	E980.4
40:12 replacement solutions	974.5	E858.5	E944.5	E950.4	E962.0	E980.4
plasma expanders	964.8	E858.2	E934.8	E950.4	E962.0	E980.4

Drug — continued	Poisoning	Accident	Therapeutic Use	Suicide Attempt	Assault	Undetermined
40:16 sodium-removing resins	974.5	E858.5	E944.5	E950.4	E962.0	E980.4
40:18 potassium-removing resins	974.5	E858.5	E944.5	E950.4	E962.0	E980.4
40:20 caloric agents	974.5	E858.5	E944.5	E950.4	E962.0	E980.4
40:24 salt and sugar substitutes	974.5	E858.5	E944.5	E950.4	E962.0	E980.4
40:28 diuretics NEC	974.4	E858.5	E944.4	E950.4	E962.0	E980.4
carbonic acid anhydrase inhibitors	974.2	E858.5	E944.2	E950.4	E962.0	E980.4
mercurials	974.0	E858.5	E944.0	E950.4	E962.0	E980.4
purine derivatives	974.1	E858.5	E944.1	E950.4	E962.0	E980.4
saluretics	974.3	E858.5	E944.3	E950.4	E962.0	E980.4
thiazides	974.3	E858.5	E944.3	E950.4	E962.0	E980.4
40:36 irrigating solutions	974.5	E858.5	E944.5	E950.4	E962.0	E980.4
40:40 uricosuric agents	974.7	E858.5	E944.7	E950.4	E962.0	E980.4
44:00 enzymes	963.4	E858.1	E933.4	E950.4	E962.0	E980.4
fibrinolysis-affecting agents	964.4	E858.2	E934.4	E950.4	E962.0	E980.4
gastric agents	973.4	E858.4	E943.4	E950.4	E962.0	E980.4
48:00 expectorants and cough preparations						
antihistamine agents	963.0	E858.1	E933.0	E950.4	E962.0	E980.4
antitussives	975.4	E858.6	E945.4	E950.4	E962.0	E980.4
codeine derivatives	965.09	E850.2	E935.2	E950.0	E962.0	E980.0
expectorants	975.5	E858.6	E945.5	E950.4	E962.0	E980.4
narcotic agents NEC	965.09	E850.2	E935.2	E950.0	E962.0	E980.0
52:04.04 antibiotics (EENT)						
ENT agent	976.6	E858.7	E946.6	E950.4	E962.0	E980.4
ophthalmic preparation	976.5	E858.7	E946.5	E950.4	E962.0	E980.4
52:04.06 antivirals (EENT)						
ENT agent	976.6	E858.7	E946.6	E950.4	E962.0	E980.4
ophthalmic preparation	976.5	E858.7	E946.5	E950.4	E962.0	E980.4
52:04.08 sulfonamides (EENT)						
ENT agent	976.6	E858.7	E946.6	E950.4	E962.0	E980.4
ophthalmic preparation	976.5	E858.7	E946.5	E950.4	E962.0	E980.4
52:04.12 miscellaneous anti-infectives (EENT)						
ENT agent	976.6	E858.7	E946.6	E950.4	E962.0	E980.4
ophthalmic preparation	976.5	E858.7	E946.5	E950.4	E962.0	E980.4
52:04 anti-infectives (EENT)						
ENT agent	976.6	E858.7	E946.6	E950.4	E962.0	E980.4
ophthalmic preparation	976.5	E858.7	E946.5	E950.4	E962.0	E980.4
52:08 anti-inflammatory agents (EENT)						
ENT agent	976.6	E858.7	E946.6	E950.4	E962.0	E980.4
ophthalmic preparation	976.5	E858.7	E946.5	E950.4	E962.0	E980.4
52:10 carbonic anhydrase inhibitors	974.2	E858.5	E944.2	E950.4	E962.0	E980.4
52:12 contact lens solutions	976.5	E858.7	E946.5	E950.4	E962.0	E980.4
52:16 local anesthetics (EENT)	968.5	E855.2	E938.5	E950.4	E962.0	E980.4
52:20 miotics	971.0	E855.3	E941.0	E950.4	E962.0	E980.4
52:24 mydriatics						
adrenergics	971.2	E855.5	E941.2	E950.4	E962.0	E980.4
anticholinergics	971.1	E855.4	E941.1	E950.4	E962.0	E980.4
antimuscarinics	971.1	E855.4	E941.1	E950.4	E962.0	E980.4
parasympatholytics	971.1	E855.4	E941.1	E950.4	E962.0	E980.4
spasmolytics	971.1	E855.4	E941.1	E950.4	E962.0	E980.4
sympathomimetics	971.2	E855.5	E941.2	E950.4	E962.0	E980.4
52:28 mouth washes and gargles	976.6	E858.7	E946.6	E950.4	E962.0	E980.4
52:32 vasoconstrictors (EENT)	971.2	E855.5	E941.2	E950.4	E962.0	E980.4
52:36 unclassified agents (EENT)						
ENT agent	976.6	E858.7	E946.6	E950.4	E962.0	E980.4
ophthalmic preparation	976.5	E858.7	E946.5	E950.4	E962.0	E980.4
56:04 antacids and adsorbents	973.0	E858.4	E943.0	E950.4	E962.0	E980.4
56:08 antidiarrhea agents	973.5	E858.4	E943.5	E950.4	E962.0	E980.4
56:10 antiflatulents	973.8	E858.4	E943.8	E950.4	E962.0	E980.4
56:12 cathartics NEC	973.3	E858.4	E943.3	E950.4	E962.0	E980.4
emollients	973.2	E858.4	E943.2	E950.4	E962.0	E980.4
irritants	973.1	E858.4	E943.1	E950.4	E962.0	E980.4
56:16 digestants	973.4	E858.4	E943.4	E950.4	E962.0	E980.4
56:20 emetics and antiemetics						
antiemetics	963.0	E858.1	E933.0	E950.4	E962.0	E980.4
emetics	973.6	E858.4	E943.6	E950.4	E962.0	E980.4
56:24 lipotropic agents	977.1	E858.8	E947.1	E950.4	E962.0	E980.4

▨ Nontherapeutic use substance   ▽ Subterms under main terms may continue to next column or page

Drug — continued	Poisoning	Accident	Therapeutic Use	Suicide Attempt	Assault	Undetermined
56:40 miscellaneous G.I. drugs	973.8	E858.4	E943.8	E950.4	E962.0	E980.4
60:00 gold compounds	965.69	E850.6	E935.6	E950.0	E962.0	E980.0
64:00 heavy metal antagonists	963.8	E858.1	E933.8	E950.4	E962.0	E980.4
68:04 adrenals	962.0	E858.0	E932.0	E950.4	E962.0	E980.4
68:08 androgens	962.1	E858.0	E932.1	E950.4	E962.0	E980.4
68:12 contraceptives, oral	962.2	E858.0	E932.2	E950.4	E962.0	E980.4
68:16 estrogens	962.2	E858.0	E932.2	E950.4	E962.0	E980.4
68:18 gonadotropins	962.4	E858.0	E932.4	E950.4	E962.0	E980.4
68:20.08 insulins	962.3	E858.0	E932.3	E950.4	E962.0	E980.4
68:20 insulins and antidiabetic agents	962.3	E858.0	E932.3	E950.4	E962.0	E980.4
68:24 parathyroid	962.6	E858.0	E932.6	E950.4	E962.0	E980.4
68:28 pituitary (posterior)	962.5	E858.0	E932.5	E950.4	E962.0	E980.4
anterior	962.4	E858.0	E932.4	E950.4	E962.0	E980.4
68:32 progestogens	962.2	E858.0	E932.2	E950.4	E962.0	E980.4
68:34 other corpus luteum hormones NEC	962.2	E858.0	E932.2	E950.4	E962.0	E980.4
68:36 thyroid and antithyroid antithyroid	962.8	E858.0	E932.8	E950.4	E962.0	E980.4
thyroid (derivatives)	962.7	E858.0	E932.7	E950.4	E962.0	E980.4
72:00 local anesthetics NEC	968.9	E855.2	E938.9	E950.4	E962.0	E980.4
infiltration (intradermal) (subcutaneous) (submucosal)	968.5	E855.2	E938.5	E950.4	E962.0	E980.4
nerve blocking (peripheral) (plexus) (regional)	968.6	E855.2	E938.6	E950.4	E962.0	E980.4
spinal	968.7	E855.2	E938.7	E950.4	E962.0	E980.4
topical (surface)	968.5	E855.2	E938.5	E950.4	E962.0	E980.4
76:00 oxytocics	975.0	E858.6	E945.0	E950.4	E962.0	E980.4
78:00 radioactive agents	990	—	—	—	—	—
80:04 serums NEC	979.9	E858.8	E949.9	E950.4	E962.0	E980.4
immune gamma globulin (human)	964.6	E858.2	E934.6	E950.4	E962.0	E980.4
80:08 toxoids NEC	978.8	E858.8	E948.8	E950.4	E962.0	E980.4
diphtheria	978.5	E858.8	E948.5	E950.4	E962.0	E980.4
and diphtheria	978.9	E858.8	E948.9	E950.4	E962.0	E980.4
with pertussis component	978.6	E858.8	E948.6	E950.4	E962.0	E980.4
and tetanus	978.9	E858.8	E948.9	E950.4	E962.0	E980.4
with pertussis component	978.6	E858.8	E948.6	E950.4	E962.0	E980.4
tetanus	978.4	E858.8	E948.4	E950.4	E962.0	E980.4
80:12 vaccines	979.9	E858.8	E949.9	E950.4	E962.0	E980.4
bacterial NEC	978.8	E858.8	E948.8	E950.4	E962.0	E980.4
with other bacterial components	978.9	E858.8	E948.9	E950.4	E962.0	E980.4
pertussis component	978.6	E858.8	E948.6	E950.4	E962.0	E980.4
viral and rickettsial components	979.7	E858.8	E949.7	E950.4	E962.0	E980.4
rickettsial NEC	979.6	E858.8	E949.6	E950.4	E962.0	E980.4
with bacterial component	979.7	E858.8	E949.7	E950.4	E962.0	E980.4
pertussis component	978.6	E858.8	E948.6	E950.4	E962.0	E980.4
viral component	979.7	E858.8	E949.7	E950.4	E962.0	E980.4
viral NEC	979.6	E858.8	E949.6	E950.4	E962.0	E980.4
with bacterial component	979.7	E858.8	E949.7	E950.4	E962.0	E980.4
pertussis component	978.6	E858.8	E948.6	E950.4	E962.0	E980.4
rickettsial component	979.7	E858.8	E949.7	E950.4	E962.0	E980.4
84:04.04 antibiotics (skin and mucous membrane)	976.0	E858.7	E946.0	E950.4	E962.0	E980.4
84:04.08 fungicides (skin and mucous membrane)	976.0	E858.7	E946.0	E950.4	E962.0	E980.4
84:04.12 scabicides and pediculicides (skin and mucous membrane)	976.0	E858.7	E946.0	E950.4	E962.0	E980.4
84:04.16 miscellaneous local anti-infectives (skin and mucous membrane)	976.0	E858.7	E946.0	E950.4	E962.0	E980.4
84:06 anti-inflammatory agents (skin and mucous membrane)	976.0	E858.7	E946.0	E950.4	E962.0	E980.4
84:08 antipruritics and local anesthetics antipruritics	976.1	E858.7	E946.1	E950.4	E962.0	E980.4
local anesthetics	968.5	E855.2	E938.5	E950.4	E962.0	E980.4

Drug — continued	Poisoning	Accident	Therapeutic Use	Suicide Attempt	Assault	Undetermined
84:12 astringents	976.2	E858.7	E946.2	E950.4	E962.0	E980.4
84:16 cell stimulants and proliferants	976.8	E858.7	E946.8	E950.4	E962.0	E980.4
84:20 detergents	976.2	E858.7	E946.2	E950.4	E962.0	E980.4
84:24 emollients, demulcents, and protectants	976.3	E858.7	E946.3	E950.4	E962.0	E980.4
84:28 keratolytic agents	976.4	E858.7	E946.4	E950.4	E962.0	E980.4
84:32 keratoplastic agents	976.4	E858.7	E946.4	E950.4	E962.0	E980.4
84:36 miscellaneous agents (skin and mucous membrane)	976.8	E858.7	E946.8	E950.4	E962.0	E980.4
86:00 spasmolytic agents	975.1	E858.6	E945.1	E950.4	E962.0	E980.4
antiasthmatics	975.7	E858.6	E945.7	E950.4	E962.0	E980.4
papaverine	972.5	E858.3	E942.5	E950.4	E962.0	E980.4
theophylline	974.1	E858.5	E944.1	E950.4	E962.0	E980.4
88:04 vitamin A	963.5	E858.1	E933.5	E950.4	E962.0	E980.4
88:08 vitamin B complex	963.5	E858.1	E933.5	E950.4	E962.0	E980.4
hematopoietic vitamin	964.1	E858.2	E934.1	E950.4	E962.0	E980.4
nicotinic acid derivatives	972.2	E858.3	E942.2	E950.4	E962.0	E980.4
88:12 vitamin C	963.5	E858.1	E933.5	E950.4	E962.0	E980.4
88:16 vitamin D	963.5	E858.1	E933.5	E950.4	E962.0	E980.4
88:20 vitamin E	963.5	E858.1	E933.5	E950.4	E962.0	E980.4
88:24 vitamin K activity	964.3	E858.2	E934.3	E950.4	E962.0	E980.4
88:28 multivitamin preparations	963.5	E858.1	E933.5	E950.4	E962.0	E980.4
92:00 unclassified therapeutic agents	977.8	E858.8	E947.8	E950.4	E962.0	E980.4
specified NEC	977.8	E858.8	E947.8	E950.4	E962.0	E980.4
Duboisine	971.1	E855.4	E941.1	E950.4	E962.0	E980.4
Dulcolax	973.1	E858.4	E943.1	E950.4	E962.0	E980.4
Duponol (C) (EP)	976.2	E858.7	E946.2	E950.4	E962.0	E980.4
Durabolin	962.1	E858.0	E932.1	E950.4	E962.0	E980.4
Dyclone	968.5	E855.2	E938.5	E950.4	E962.0	E980.4
Dyclonine	968.5	E855.2	E938.5	E950.4	E962.0	E980.4
Dydrogesterone	962.2	E858.0	E932.2	E950.4	E962.0	E980.4
Dyes NEC	989.89	E866.8	—	E950.9	E962.1	E980.9
diagnostic agents	977.8	E858.8	E947.8	E950.4	E962.0	E980.4
pharmaceutical NEC	977.4	E858.8	E947.4	E950.4	E962.0	E980.4
Dyfols	971.0	E855.3	E941.0	E950.4	E962.0	E980.4
Dymelor	962.3	E858.0	E932.3	E950.4	E962.0	E980.4
Dynamite	989.89	E866.8	—	E950.9	E962.1	E980.9
fumes	987.8	E869.8	—	E952.8	E962.2	E982.8
Dyphylline	975.1	E858.6	E945.1	E950.4	E962.0	E980.4
Ear preparations	976.6	E858.7	E946.6	E950.4	E962.0	E980.4
Echothiophate, ecothiopate	971.0	E855.3	E941.0	E950.4	E962.0	E980.4
Ecstasy	969.72 ▲	E854.2	E939.7	E950.3	E962.0	E980.3
Ectylurea	967.8	E852.8	E937.8	E950.2	E962.0	E980.2
Edathamil disodium	963.8	E858.1	E933.8	E950.4	E962.0	E980.4
Edecrin	974.4	E858.5	E944.4	E950.4	E962.0	E980.4
Edetate, disodium (calcium)	963.8	E858.1	E933.8	E950.4	E962.0	E980.4
Edrophonium	971.0	E855.3	E941.0	E950.4	E962.0	E980.4
Elase	976.8	E858.7	E946.8	E950.4	E962.0	E980.4
Elaterium	973.1	E858.4	E943.1	E950.4	E962.0	E980.4
Elder	988.2	E865.4	—	E950.9	E962.1	E980.9
berry (unripe)	988.2	E865.3	—	E950.9	E962.1	E980.9
Electrolytes NEC	974.5	E858.5	E944.5	E950.4	E962.0	E980.4
Electrolytic agent NEC	974.5	E858.5	E944.5	E950.4	E962.0	E980.4
Embramine	963.0	E858.1	E933.0	E950.4	E962.0	E980.4
Emetics	973.6	E858.4	E943.6	E950.4	E962.0	E980.4
Emetine (hydrochloride)	961.5	E857	E931.5	E950.4	E962.0	E980.4
Emollients	976.3	E858.7	E946.3	E950.4	E962.0	E980.4
Emylcamate	969.5	E853.8	E939.5	E950.3	E962.0	E980.3
Encyprate	969.09 ▲	E854.0	E939.0	E950.3	E962.0	E980.3
Endocaine	968.5	E855.2	E938.5	E950.4	E962.0	E980.4
Endrin	989.2	E863.0	—	E950.6	E962.1	E980.7
Enflurane	968.2	E855.1	E938.2	E950.4	E962.0	E980.4
Enovid	962.2	E858.0	E932.2	E950.4	E962.0	E980.4
ENT preparations (anti-infectives)	976.6	E858.7	E946.6	E950.4	E962.0	E980.4
Enzodase	963.4	E858.1	E933.4	E950.4	E962.0	E980.4
Enzymes NEC	963.4	E858.1	E933.4	E950.4	E962.0	E980.4
Epanutin	966.1	E855.0	E936.1	E950.4	E962.0	E980.4
Ephedra (tincture)	971.2	E855.5	E941.2	E950.4	E962.0	E980.4
Ephedrine	971.2	E855.5	E941.2	E950.4	E962.0	E980.4
Epiestriol	962.2	E858.0	E932.2	E950.4	E962.0	E980.4
Epilim — see Sodium valproate						
Epinephrine	971.2	E855.5	E941.2	E950.4	E962.0	E980.4
Epsom salt	973.3	E858.4	E943.3	E950.4	E962.0	E980.4
Equanil	969.5	E853.8	E939.5	E950.3	E962.0	E980.3

Nontherapeutic use substance

▽ Subterms under main terms may continue to next column or page

▶◀ Revised Text   ● New Line   ▲ Revised Code

	Poisoning	Accident	Therapeutic Use	Suicide Attempt	Assault	Undetermined
Equisetum (diuretic)	974.4	E858.5	E944.4	E950.4	E962.0	E980.4
Ergometrine	975.0	E858.6	E945.0	E950.4	E962.0	E980.4
Ergonovine	975.0	E858.6	E945.0	E950.4	E962.0	E980.4
Ergot NEC	988.2	E865.4	—	E950.9	E962.1	E980.9
medicinal (alkaloids)	975.0	E858.6	E945.0	E950.4	E962.0	E980.4
Ergotamine (tartrate) (for						
migraine) NEC	972.9	E858.3	E942.9	E950.4	E962.0	E980.4
Ergotrate	975.0	E858.6	E945.0	E950.4	E962.0	E980.4
Erythrityl tetranitrate	972.4	E858.3	E942.4	E950.4	E962.0	E980.4
Erythrol tetranitrate	972.4	E858.3	E942.4	E950.4	E962.0	E980.4
Erythromycin	960.3	E856	E930.3	E950.4	E962.0	E980.4
ophthalmic preparation	976.5	E858.7	E946.5	E950.4	E962.0	E980.4
topical NEC	976.0	E858.7	E946.0	E950.4	E962.0	E980.4
Eserine	971.0	E855.3	E941.0	E950.4	E962.0	E980.4
Eskabarb	967.0	E851	E937.0	E950.1	E962.0	E980.1
Eskalith	969.8	E855.8	E939.8	E950.3	E962.0	E980.3
Estradiol (cypionate)						
(dipropionate) (valerate)	962.2	E858.0	E932.2	E950.4	E962.0	E980.4
Estriol	962.2	E858.0	E932.2	E950.4	E962.0	E980.4
Estrogens (with						
progestogens)	962.2	E858.0	E932.2	E950.4	E962.0	E980.4
Estrone	962.2	E858.0	E932.2	E950.4	E962.0	E980.4
Etafedrine	971.2	E855.5	E941.2	E950.4	E962.0	E980.4
Ethacrynate sodium	974.4	E858.5	E944.4	E950.4	E962.0	E980.4
Ethacrynic acid	974.4	E858.5	E944.4	E950.4	E962.0	E980.4
Ethambutol	961.8	E857	E931.8	E950.4	E962.0	E980.4
Ethamide	974.2	E858.5	E944.2	E950.4	E962.0	E980.4
Ethamivan	970.0	E854.3	E940.0	E950.4	E962.0	E980.4
Ethamsylate	964.5	E858.2	E934.5	E950.4	E962.0	E980.4
Ethanol	980.0	E860.1	—	E950.9	E962.1	E980.9
beverage	980.0	E860.0	—	E950.9	E962.1	E980.9
Ethchlorvynol	967.8	E852.8	E937.8	E950.2	E962.0	E980.2
Ethebenecid	974.7	E858.5	E944.7	E950.4	E962.0	E980.4
Ether(s) (diethyl) (ethyl)						
(vapor)	987.8	E869.8	—	E952.8	E962.2	E982.8
anesthetic	968.2	E855.1	E938.2	E950.4	E962.0	E980.4
petroleum — see Ligroin						
solvent	982.8	E862.4	—	E950.9	E962.1	E980.9
Ethidine chloride (vapor)	987.8	E869.8	—	E952.8	E962.2	E982.8
liquid (solvent)	982.3	E862.4	—	E950.9	E962.1	E980.9
Ethinamate	967.8	E852.8	E937.8	E950.2	E962.0	E980.2
Ethinylestradiol	962.2	E858.0	E932.2	E950.4	E962.0	E980.4
Ethionamide	961.8	E857	E931.8	E950.4	E962.0	E980.4
Ethisterone	962.2	E858.0	E932.2	E950.4	E962.0	E980.4
Ethobral	967.0	E851	E937.0	E950.1	E962.0	E980.1
Ethocaine (infiltration)						
(topical)	968.5	E855.2	E938.5	E950.4	E962.0	E980.4
nerve block (peripheral)						
(plexus)	968.6	E855.2	E938.6	E950.4	E962.0	E980.4
spinal	968.7	E855.2	E938.7	E950.4	E962.0	E980.4
Ethoheptazine (citrate)	965.7	E850.7	E935.7	E950.0	E962.0	E980.0
Ethopropazine	966.4	E855.0	E936.4	E950.4	E962.0	E980.4
Ethosuximide	966.2	E855.0	E936.2	E950.4	E962.0	E980.4
Ethotoin	966.1	E855.0	E936.1	E950.4	E962.0	E980.4
Ethoxazene	961.9	E857	E931.9	E950.4	E962.0	E980.4
Ethoxzolamide	974.2	E858.5	E944.2	E950.4	E962.0	E980.4
Ethyl						
acetate (vapor)	982.8	E862.4	—	E950.9	E962.1	E980.9
alcohol	980.0	E860.1	—	E950.9	E962.1	E980.9
beverage	980.0	E860.0	—	E950.9	E962.1	E980.9
aldehyde (vapor)	987.8	E869.8	—	E952.8	E962.2	E982.8
liquid	989.89	E866.8	—	E950.9	E962.1	E980.9
aminobenzoate	968.5	E855.2	E938.5	E950.4	E962.0	E980.4
biscoumacetate	964.2	E858.2	E934.2	E950.4	E962.0	E980.4
bromide (anesthetic)	968.2	E855.1	E938.2	E950.4	E962.0	E980.4
carbamate						
(antineoplastic)	963.1	E858.1	E933.1	E950.4	E962.0	E980.4
carbinol	980.3	E860.4	—	E950.9	E962.1	E980.9
chaulmoograte	961.8	E857	E931.8	E950.4	E962.0	E980.4
chloride (vapor)	987.8	E869.8	—	E952.8	E962.2	E982.8
anesthetic (local)	968.5	E855.2	E938.5	E950.4	E962.0	E980.4
inhaled	968.2	E855.1	E938.2	E950.4	E962.0	E980.4
solvent	982.3	E862.4	—	E950.9	E962.1	E980.9
estranol	962.1	E858.0	E932.1	E950.4	E962.0	E980.4
ether — see Ether(s)						
formate (solvent) NEC	982.8	E862.4	—	E950.9	E962.1	E980.9
iodoacetate	987.5	E869.3	—	E952.8	E962.2	E982.8
lactate (solvent) NEC	982.8	E862.4	—	E950.9	E962.1	E980.9
methylcarbinol	980.8	E860.8	—	E950.9	E962.1	E980.9
morphine	965.09	E850.2	E935.2	E950.0	E962.0	E980.0
Ethylene (gas)	987.1	E869.8	—	E952.8	E962.2	E982.8
anesthetic (general)	968.2	E855.1	E938.2	E950.4	E962.0	E980.4

	Poisoning	Accident	Therapeutic Use	Suicide Attempt	Assault	Undetermined
Ethylene — continued						
chlorohydrin (vapor)	982.3	E862.4	—	E950.9	E962.1	E980.9
dichloride (vapor)	982.3	E862.4	—	E950.9	E962.1	E980.9
glycol(s) (any) (vapor)	982.8	E862.4	—	E950.9	E962.1	E980.9
Ethylidene						
chloride NEC	982.3	E862.4	—	E950.9	E962.1	E980.9
diethyl ether	982.8	E862.4	—	E950.9	E962.1	E980.9
Ethynodiol	962.2	E858.0	E932.2	E950.4	E962.0	E980.4
Etidocaine	968.9	E855.2	E938.9	E950.4	E962.0	E980.4
infiltration (subcutaneous)	968.5	E855.2	E938.5	E950.4	E962.0	E980.4
nerve (peripheral) (plexus)	968.6	E855.2	E938.6	E950.4	E962.0	E980.4
Etilfen	967.0	E851	E937.0	E950.1	E962.0	E980.1
Etomide	965.7	E850.7	E935.7	E950.0	E962.0	E980.0
Etorphine	965.09	E850.2	E935.2	E950.0	E962.0	E980.0
Etoval	967.0	E851	E937.0	E950.1	E962.0	E980.1
Etryptamine	969.01 ▲	E854.0	E939.0	E950.3	E962.0	E980.3
Eucaine	968.5	E855.2	E938.5	E950.4	E962.0	E980.4
Eucalyptus (oil) NEC	975.5	E858.6	E945.5	E950.4	E962.0	E980.4
Eucatropine	971.1	E855.4	E941.1	E950.4	E962.0	E980.4
Eucodal	965.09	E850.2	E935.2	E950.0	E962.0	E980.0
Euneryl	967.0	E851	E937.0	E950.1	E962.0	E980.1
Euphthalmine	971.1	E855.4	E941.1	E950.4	E962.0	E980.4
Eurax	976.0	E858.7	E946.0	E950.4	E962.0	E980.4
Euresol	976.4	E858.7	E946.4	E950.4	E962.0	E980.4
Euthroid	962.7	E858.0	E932.7	E950.4	E962.0	E980.4
Evans blue	977.8	E858.8	E947.8	E950.4	E962.0	E980.4
Evipal	967.0	E851	E937.0	E950.1	E962.0	E980.1
sodium	968.3	E855.1	E938.3	E950.4	E962.0	E980.4
Evipan	967.0	E851	E937.0	E950.1	E962.0	E980.1
sodium	968.3	E855.1	E938.3	E950.4	E962.0	E980.4
Exalgin	965.4	E850.4	E935.4	E950.0	E962.0	E980.0
Excipients,						
pharmaceutical	977.4	E858.8	E947.4	E950.4	E962.0	E980.4
Exhaust gas — see Carbon,						
monoxide						
Ex-Lax (phenolphthalein)	973.1	E858.4	E943.1	E950.4	E962.0	E980.4
Expectorants	975.5	E858.6	E945.5	E950.4	E962.0	E980.4
External medications (skin)						
(mucous membrane)	976.9	E858.7	E946.9	E950.4	E962.0	E980.4
dental agent	976.7	E858.7	E946.7	E950.4	E962.0	E980.4
ENT agent	976.6	E858.7	E946.6	E950.4	E962.0	E980.4
ophthalmic preparation	976.5	E858.7	E946.5	E950.4	E962.0	E980.4
specified NEC	976.8	E858.7	E946.8	E950.4	E962.0	E980.4
Eye agents (anti-infective)	976.5	E858.7	E946.5	E950.4	E962.0	E980.4
Factor IX complex						
(human)	964.5	E858.2	E934.5	E950.4	E962.0	E980.4
Fecal softeners	973.2	E858.4	E943.2	E950.4	E962.0	E980.4
Fenbutrazate	977.0	E858.8	E947.0	E950.4	E962.0	E980.4
Fencamfamin	970.8	E854.3	E940.8	E950.4	E962.0	E980.4
Fenfluramine	977.0	E858.8	E947.0	E950.4	E962.0	E980.4
Fenoprofen	965.61	E850.6	E935.6	E950.0	E962.0	E980.0
Fentanyl	965.09	E850.2	E935.2	E950.0	E962.0	E980.0
Fentazin	969.1	E853.0	E939.1	E950.3	E962.0	E980.3
Fenticlor, fentichlor	976.0	E858.7	E946.0	E950.4	E962.0	E980.4
Fer de lance (bite) (venom)	989.5	E905.0	—	E950.9	E962.1	E980.9
Ferric — see Iron						
Ferrocholinate	964.0	E858.2	E934.0	E950.4	E962.0	E980.4
Ferrous fumerate, gluconate,						
lactate, salt NEC, sulfate						
(medicinal)	964.0	E858.2	E934.0	E950.4	E962.0	E980.4
Ferrum — see Iron						
Fertilizers NEC	989.89	E866.5	—	E950.9	E962.1	E980.4
with herbicide mixture	989.4	E863.5	—	E950.6	E962.1	E980.7
Fibrinogen (human)	964.7	E858.2	E934.7	E950.4	E962.0	E980.4
Fibrinolysin (human)	964.4	E858.2	E934.4	E950.4	E962.0	E980.4
Fibrinolysis-affecting						
agents	964.4	E858.2	E934.4	E950.4	E962.0	E980.4
Filix mas	961.6	E857	E931.6	E950.4	E962.0	E980.4
Fiorinal	965.1	E850.3	E935.3	E950.0	E962.0	E980.0
Fire damp	987.1	E869.8	—	E952.8	E962.2	E982.8
Fish, nonbacterial or						
noxious	988.0	E865.2	—	E950.9	E962.1	E980.9
shell	988.0	E865.1	—	E950.9	E962.1	E980.9
Flagyl	961.5	E857	E931.5	E950.4	E962.0	E980.4
Flavoxate	975.1	E858.6	E945.1	E950.4	E962.0	E980.4
Flaxedil	975.2	E858.6	E945.2	E950.4	E962.0	E980.4
Flaxseed (medicinal)	976.3	E858.7	E946.3	E950.4	E962.0	E980.4
Flomax	971.3	E855.6	E941.3	E950.4	E962.0	E980.4
Florantyrone	973.4	E858.4	E943.4	E950.4	E962.0	E980.4
Floraquin	961.3	E857	E931.3	E950.4	E962.0	E980.4
Florinef	962.0	E858.0	E932.0	E950.4	E962.0	E980.4
ENT agent	976.6	E858.7	E946.6	E950.4	E962.0	E980.4

Nontherapeutic use substance

▽ Subterms under main terms may continue to next column or page

	Poisoning	Accident	Therapeutic Use	Suicide Attempt	Assault	Undetermined
Florinef — continued						
ophthalmic preparation	976.5	E858.7	E946.5	E950.4	E962.0	E980.4
topical NEC	976.0	E858.7	E946.0	E950.4	E962.0	E980.4
Flowers of sulfur	976.4	E858.7	E946.4	E950.4	E962.0	E980.4
Floxuridine	963.1	E858.1	E933.1	E950.4	E962.0	E980.4
Flucytosine	961.9	E857	E931.9	E950.4	E962.0	E980.4
Fludrocortisone	962.0	E858.0	E932.0	E950.4	E962.0	E980.4
ENT agent	976.6	E858.7	E946.6	E950.4	E962.0	E980.4
ophthalmic preparation	976.5	E858.7	E946.5	E950.4	E962.0	E980.4
topical NEC	976.0	E858.7	E946.0	E950.4	E962.0	E980.4
Flumethasone	976.0	E858.7	E946.0	E950.4	E962.0	E980.4
Flumethiazide	974.3	E858.5	E944.3	E950.4	E962.0	E980.4
Flumidin	961.7	E857	E931.7	E950.4	E962.0	E980.4
Flunitrazepam	969.4	E853.2	E939.4	E950.3	E962.0	E980.3
Fluocinolone	976.0	E858.7	E946.0	E950.4	E962.0	E980.4
Fluocortolone	962.0	E858.0	E932.0	E950.4	E962.0	E980.4
Fluohydrocortisone	962.0	E858.0	E932.0	E950.4	E962.0	E980.4
ENT agent	976.6	E858.7	E946.6	E950.4	E962.0	E980.4
ophthalmic preparation	976.5	E858.7	E946.5	E950.4	E962.0	E980.4
topical NEC	976.0	E858.7	E946.0	E950.4	E962.0	E980.4
Fluonid	976.0	E858.7	E946.0	E950.4	E962.0	E980.4
Fluopromazine	969.1	E853.0	E939.1	E950.3	E962.0	E980.3
Fluoracetate	989.4	E863.7	—	E950.6	E962.1	E980.7
Fluorescein (sodium)	977.8	E858.8	E947.8	E950.4	E962.0	E980.4
Fluoride(s) (pesticides) (sodium) NEC	989.4	E863.4	—	E950.6	E962.1	E980.7
hydrogen — see Hydrofluoric acid						
medicinal	976.7	E858.7	E946.7	E950.4	E962.0	E980.4
not pesticide NEC	983.9	E864.4	—	E950.7	E962.1	E980.6
stannous	976.7	E858.7	E946.7	E950.4	E962.0	E980.4
Fluorinated corticosteroids	962.0	E858.0	E932.0	E950.4	E962.0	E980.4
Fluorine (compounds) (gas)	987.8	E869.8	—	E952.8	E962.2	E982.8
salt — see Fluoride(s)						
Fluoristan	976.7	E858.7	E946.7	E950.4	E962.0	E980.4
Fluoroacetate	989.4	E863.7	—	E950.6	E962.1	E980.7
Fluorodeoxyuridine	963.1	E858.1	E933.1	E950.4	E962.0	E980.4
Fluorometholone (topical) NEC	976.0	E858.7	E946.0	E950.4	E962.0	E980.4
ophthalmic preparation	976.5	E858.7	E946.5	E950.4	E962.0	E980.4
Fluorouracil	963.1	E858.1	E933.1	E950.4	E962.0	E980.4
Fluothane	968.1	E855.1	E938.1	E950.4	E962.0	E980.4
Fluoxetine hydrochloride	969.03 ▲	E854.0	E939.0	E950.3	E962.0	E980.3
Fluoxymesterone	962.1	E858.0	E932.1	E950.4	E962.0	E980.4
Fluphenazine	969.1	E853.0	E939.1	E950.3	E962.0	E980.3
Fluprednisolone	962.0	E858.0	E932.0	E950.4	E962.0	E980.4
Flurandrenolide	976.0	E858.7	E946.0	E950.4	E962.0	E980.4
Flurazepam (hydrochloride)	969.4	E853.2	E939.4	E950.3	E962.0	E980.3
Flurbiprofen	965.61	E850.6	E935.6	E950.0	E962.0	E980.0
Flurobate	976.0	E858.7	E946.0	E950.4	E962.0	E980.4
Flurothyl	969.8	E855.8	E939.8	E950.3	E962.0	E980.3
Fluroxene	968.2	E855.1	E938.2	E950.4	E962.0	E980.4
Folacin	964.1	E858.2	E934.1	E950.4	E962.0	E980.4
Folic acid	964.1	E858.2	E934.1	E950.4	E962.0	E980.4
Follicle stimulating hormone	962.4	E858.0	E932.4	E950.4	E962.0	E980.4
Food, foodstuffs, nonbacterial or noxious	988.9	E865.9	—	E950.9	E962.1	E980.9
berries, seeds	988.2	E865.3	—	E950.9	E962.1	E980.9
fish	988.0	E865.2	—	E950.9	E962.1	E980.9
mushrooms	988.1	E865.5	—	E950.9	E962.1	E980.9
plants	988.2	E865.9	—	E950.9	E962.1	E980.9
specified type NEC	988.2	E865.4	—	E950.9	E962.1	E980.9
shellfish	988.0	E865.1	—	E950.9	E962.1	E980.9
specified NEC	988.8	E865.8	—	E950.9	E962.1	E980.9
Fool's parsley	988.2	E865.4	—	E950.9	E962.1	E980.9
Formaldehyde (solution)	989.89	E861.4	—	E950.9	E962.1	E980.9
fungicide	989.4	E863.6	—	E950.6	E962.1	E980.7
gas or vapor	987.8	E869.8	—	E952.8	E962.2	E982.8
Formalin	989.89	E861.4	—	E950.9	E962.1	E980.9
fungicide	989.4	E863.6	—	E950.6	E962.1	E980.7
vapor	987.8	E869.8	—	E952.8	E962.2	E982.8
Formic acid	983.1	E864.1	—	E950.7	E962.1	E980.6
automobile	981	E862.1	—	E950.9	E962.1	E980.9
exhaust gas, not in transit	986	E868.2	—	E952.0	E962.2	E982.0
vapor NEC	987.1	E869.8	—	E952.8	E962.2	E982.8
gas (domestic use) (see also Carbon, monoxide, fuel)						

	Poisoning	Accident	Therapeutic Use	Suicide Attempt	Assault	Undetermined
Formic acid — continued						
gas (see also Carbon, monoxide, fuel) — continued						
utility	987.1	E868.1	—	E951.8	E962.2	E981.8
incomplete combustion of — see Carbon, monoxide, fuel, utility						
in mobile container	987.0	E868.0	—	E951.1	E962.2	E981.1
piped (natural)	987.1	E867	—	E951.0	E962.2	E981.0
industrial, incomplete combustion	986	E868.3	—	E952.1	E962.2	E982.1
vapor	987.8	E869.8	—	E952.8	E962.2	E982.8
Fowler's solution	985.1	E866.3	—	E950.8	E962.1	E980.8
Foxglove	988.2	E865.4	—	E950.9	E962.1	E980.9
Fox green	977.8	E858.8	E947.8	E950.4	E962.0	E980.4
Framycetin	960.8	E856	E930.8	E950.4	E962.0	E980.4
Frangula (extract)	973.1	E858.4	E943.1	E950.4	E962.0	E980.4
Frei antigen	977.8	E858.8	E947.8	E950.4	E962.0	E980.4
Freons	987.4	E869.2	—	E952.8	E962.2	E982.8
Fructose	974.5	E858.5	E944.5	E950.4	E962.0	E980.4
Frusemide	974.4	E858.5	E944.4	E950.4	E962.0	E980.4
FSH	962.4	E858.0	E932.4	E950.4	E962.0	E980.4
Fuel						
Fugillin	960.8	E856	E930.8	E950.4	E962.0	E980.4
Fulminate of mercury	985.0	E866.1	—	E950.9	E962.1	E980.9
Fulvicin	960.1	E856	E930.1	E950.4	E962.0	E980.4
Fumadil	960.8	E856	E930.8	E950.4	E962.0	E980.4
Fumagillin	960.8	E856	E930.8	E950.4	E962.0	E980.4
Fumes (from)	987.9	E869.9	—	E952.9	E962.2	E982.9
carbon monoxide — see Carbon, monoxide						
charcoal (domestic use)	986	E868.3	—	E952.1	E962.2	E982.1
chloroform — see Chloroform						
coke (in domestic stoves, fireplaces)	986	E868.3	—	E952.1	E962.2	E982.1
corrosive NEC	987.8	E869.8	—	E952.8	E962.2	E982.8
ether — see Ether(s)						
freons	987.4	E869.2	—	E952.8	E962.2	E982.8
hydrocarbons	987.1	E869.8	—	E952.8	E962.2	E982.8
petroleum (liquefied)	987.0	E868.0	—	E951.1	E962.2	E981.1
distributed through pipes (pure or mixed with air)	987.0	E867	—	E951.0	E962.2	E981.0
lead — see Lead						
metals — see specified metal						
nitrogen dioxide	987.2	E869.0	—	E952.8	E962.2	E982.8
pesticides — see Pesticides						
petroleum (liquefied)	987.0	E868.0	—	E951.1	E962.2	E981.1
distributed through pipes (pure or mixed with air)	987.0	E867	—	E951.0	E962.2	E981.0
polyester	987.8	E869.8	—	E952.8	E962.2	E982.8
specified, source other (see also substance specified)	987.8	E869.8	—	E952.8	E962.2	E982.8
sulfur dioxide	987.3	E869.1	—	E952.8	E962.2	E982.8
Fumigants	989.4	E863.8	—	E950.6	E962.1	E980.7
Fungicides — see also Antifungals	989.4	E863.6	—	E950.6	E962.1	E980.7
Fungi, noxious, used as food	988.1	E865.5	—	E950.9	E962.1	E980.9
Fungizone	960.1	E856	E930.1	E950.4	E962.0	E980.4
topical	976.0	E858.7	E946.0	E950.4	E962.0	E980.4
Furacin	976.0	E858.7	E946.0	E950.4	E962.0	E980.4
Furadantin	961.9	E857	E931.9	E950.4	E962.0	E980.4
Furazolidone	961.9	E857	E931.9	E950.4	E962.0	E980.4
Furnace (coal burning) (domestic), gas from	986	E868.3	—	E952.1	E962.2	E982.1
industrial	986	E868.8	—	E952.1	E962.2	E982.1
Furniture polish	989.89	E861.2	—	E950.9	E962.1	E980.9
Furosemide	974.4	E858.5	E944.4	E950.4	E962.0	E980.4
Furoxone	961.9	E857	E931.9	E950.4	E962.0	E980.4
Fusel oil (amyl) (butyl) (propyl)	980.3	E860.4	—	E950.9	E962.1	E980.9
Fusidic acid	960.8	E856	E930.8	E950.4	E962.0	E980.4
Gallamine	975.2	E858.6	E945.2	E950.4	E962.0	E980.4
Gallotannic acid	976.2	E858.7	E946.2	E950.4	E962.0	E980.4
Gamboge	973.1	E858.4	E943.1	E950.4	E962.0	E980.4
Gamimune	964.6	E858.2	E934.6	E950.4	E962.0	E980.4
Gamma-benzene hexachloride (vapor)	989.2	E863.0	—	E950.6	E962.1	E980.7
Gamma globulin	964.6	E858.2	E934.6	E950.4	E962.0	E980.4

Nontherapeutic use substance

302 — Volume 2 • October 2009   ▶◀ Revised Text   ● New Line   ▲ Revised Code   ⬇ Subterms under main terms may continue to next column or page   2010 ICD-9-CM

	External Cause (E-Code)					
	Poisoning	Accident	Therapeutic Use	Suicide Attempt	Assault	Undetermined
Gamma hydroxy butyrate (GHB)	968.4	E855.1	E938.4	E950.4	E962.0	E980.4
Gamulin	964.6	E858.2	E934.6	E950.4	E962.0	E980.4
Ganglionic blocking agents	972.3	E858.3	E942.3	E950.4	E962.0	E980.4
Ganja	969.6	E854.1	E939.6	E950.3	E962.0	E980.3
Garamycin	960.8	E856	E930.8	E950.4	E962.0	E980.4
ophthalmic preparation	976.5	E858.7	E946.5	E950.4	E962.0	E980.4
topical NEC	976.0	E858.7	E946.0	E950.4	E962.0	E980.4
Gardenal	967.0	E851	E937.0	E950.1	E962.0	E980.1
Gardepanyl	967.0	E851	E937.0	E950.1	E962.0	E980.1
Gas	987.9	E869.9	—	E952.9	E962.2	E982.9
acetylene	987.1	E868.1	—	E951.8	E962.2	E981.8
incomplete combustion of — see Carbon, monoxide, fuel, utility						
air contaminants, source or type not specified	987.9	E869.9	—	E952.9	E962.2	E982.9
anesthetic (general) NEC	968.2	E855.1	E938.2	E950.4	E962.0	E980.4
blast furnace	986	E868.8	—	E952.1	E962.2	E982.1
butane — see Butane						
carbon monoxide — see Carbon, monoxide						
chlorine	987.6	E869.8	—	E952.8	E962.2	E982.8
coal — see Carbon, monoxide, coal						
cyanide	987.7	E869.8	—	E952.8	E962.2	E982.8
dicyanogen	987.8	E869.8	—	E952.8	E962.2	E982.8
domestic — see Gas, utility						
exhaust — see Carbon, monoxide, exhaust gas						
from wood- or coal-burning stove or fireplace	986	E868.3	—	E952.1	E962.2	E982.1
fuel (domestic use) (see also Carbon, monoxide, fuel)						
industrial use	986	E868.8	—	E952.1	E962.2	E982.1
utility	987.1	E868.1	—	E951.8	E962.2	E981.8
incomplete combustion of — see Carbon, monoxide, fuel, utility						
in mobile container	987.0	E868.0	—	E951.1	E962.2	E981.1
piped (natural)	987.1	E867	—	E951.0	E962.2	E981.0
garage	986	E868.2	—	E952.0	E962.2	E982.0
hydrocarbon NEC	987.1	E869.8	—	E952.8	E962.2	E982.8
incomplete combustion of — see Carbon, monoxide, fuel, utility						
liquefied (mobile container)	987.0	E868.0	—	E951.1	E962.2	E981.1
piped	987.0	E867	—	E951.0	E962.2	E981.0
hydrocyanic acid	987.7	E869.8	—	E952.8	E962.2	E982.8
illuminating — see Gas, utility						
incomplete combustion, any — see Carbon, monoxide						
kiln	986	E868.8	—	E952.1	E962.2	E982.1
lacrimogenic	987.5	E869.3	—	E952.8	E962.2	E982.8
marsh	987.1	E869.8	—	E952.8	E962.2	E982.8
motor exhaust, not in transit	986	E868.8	—	E952.1	E962.2	E982.1
mustard — see Mustard, gas						
natural	987.1	E867	—	E951.0	E962.2	E981.0
nerve (war)	987.9	E869.9	—	E952.9	E962.2	E982.9
oils	981	E862.1	—	E950.9	E962.1	E980.9
petroleum (liquefied) (distributed in mobile containers)	987.0	E868.0	—	E951.1	E962.2	E981.1
piped (pure or mixed with air)	987.0	E867	—	E951.1	E962.2	E981.1
piped (manufactured) (natural) NEC	987.1	E867	—	E951.0	E962.2	E981.0
producer	986	E868.8	—	E952.1	E962.2	E982.1
propane — see Propane						
refrigerant (freon)	987.4	E869.2	—	E952.8	E962.2	E982.8
not freon	987.9	E869.9	—	E952.9	E962.2	E982.9
sewer	987.8	E869.8	—	E952.8	E962.2	E982.8
specified source NEC (see also substance specified)	987.8	E869.8	—	E952.8	E962.2	E982.8
stove — see Gas, utility						
tear	987.5	E869.3	—	E952.8	E962.2	E982.8
utility (for cooking, heating, or lighting) (piped) NEC	987.1	E868.1	—	E951.8	E962.2	E981.8

	External Cause (E-Code)					
	Poisoning	Accident	Therapeutic Use	Suicide Attempt	Assault	Undetermined
Gas — continued						
utility — continued						
incomplete combustion of — see Carbon, monoxide, fuel, utilty						
in mobile container	987.0	E868.0	—	E951.1	E962.2	E981.1
piped (natural)	987.1	E867	—	E951.0	E962.2	E981.0
water	987.1	E868.1	—	E951.8	E962.2	E981.8
incomplete combustion of — see Carbon, monoxide, fuel, utility						
Gaseous substance — see Gas						
Gasoline, gasolene	981	E862.1	—	E950.9	E962.1	E980.9
vapor	987.1	E869.8	—	E952.8	E962.2	E982.8
Gastric enzymes	973.4	E858.4	E943.4	E950.4	E962.0	E980.4
Gastrografin	977.8	E858.8	E947.8	E950.4	E962.0	E980.4
Gastrointestinal agents	973.9	E858.4	E943.9	E950.4	E962.0	E980.4
specified NEC	973.8	E858.4	E943.8	E950.4	E962.0	E980.4
Gaultheria procumbens	988.2	E865.4	—	E950.9	E962.1	E980.9
Gelatin (intravenous)	964.8	E858.2	E934.8	E950.4	E962.0	E980.4
absorbable (sponge)	964.5	E858.2	E934.5	E950.4	E962.0	E980.4
Gelfilm	976.8	E858.7	E946.8	E950.4	E962.0	E980.4
Gelfoam	964.5	E858.2	E934.5	E950.4	E962.0	E980.4
Gelsemine	970.8	E854.3	E940.8	E950.4	E962.0	E980.4
Gelsemium (sempervirens)	988.2	E865.4	—	E950.9	E962.1	E980.9
Gemonil	967.0	E851	E937.0	E950.1	E962.0	E980.1
Gentamicin	960.8	E856	E930.8	E950.4	E962.0	E980.4
ophthalmic preparation	976.5	E858.7	E946.5	E950.4	E962.0	E980.4
topical NEC	976.0	E858.7	E946.0	E950.4	E962.0	E980.4
Gentian violet	976.0	E858.7	E946.0	E950.4	E962.0	E980.4
Gexane	976.0	E858.7	E946.0	E950.4	E962.0	E980.4
Gila monster (venom)	989.5	E905.0	—	E950.9	E962.1	E980.9
Ginger, Jamaica	989.89	E866.8	—	E950.9	E962.1	E980.9
Gitalin	972.1	E858.3	E942.1	E950.4	E962.0	E980.4
Gitoxin	972.1	E858.3	E942.1	E950.4	E962.0	E980.4
Glandular extract (medicinal) NEC	977.9	E858.9	E947.9	E950.5	E962.0	E980.5
Glaucarubin	961.5	E857	E931.5	E950.4	E962.0	E980.4
Globin zinc insulin	962.3	E858.0	E932.3	E950.4	E962.0	E980.4
Glucagon	962.3	E858.0	E932.3	E950.4	E962.0	E980.4
Glucochloral	967.1	E852.0	E937.1	E950.2	E962.0	E980.2
Glucocorticoids	962.0	E858.0	E932.0	E950.4	E962.0	E980.4
Glucose	974.5	E858.5	E944.5	E950.4	E962.0	E980.4
oxidase reagent	977.8	E858.8	E947.8	E950.4	E962.0	E980.4
Glucosulfone sodium	961.8	E857	E931.8	E950.4	E962.0	E980.4
Glue(s)	989.89	E866.6	—	E950.9	E962.1	E980.9
Glutamic acid (hydrochloride)	973.4	E858.4	E943.4	E950.4	E962.0	E980.4
Glutaraldehyde	989.89	E861.4	—	E950.9	E962.1	E980.9
Glutathione	963.8	E858.1	E933.8	E950.4	E962.0	E980.4
Glutethimide (group)	967.5	E852.4	E937.5	E950.2	E962.0	E980.2
Glycerin (lotion)	976.3	E858.7	E946.3	E950.4	E962.0	E980.4
Glycerol (topical)	976.3	E858.7	E946.3	E950.4	E962.0	E980.4
Glyceryl						
guaiacolate	975.5	E858.6	E945.5	E950.4	E962.0	E980.4
triacetate (topical)	976.0	E858.7	E946.0	E950.4	E962.0	E980.4
trinitrate	972.4	E858.3	E942.4	E950.4	E962.0	E980.4
Glycine	974.5	E858.5	E944.5	E950.4	E962.0	E980.4
Glycobiarsol	961.1	E857	E931.1	E950.4	E962.0	E980.4
Glycols (ether)	982.8	E862.4	—	E950.9	E962.1	E980.9
Glycopyrrolate	971.1	E855.4	E941.1	E950.4	E962.0	E980.4
Glymidine	962.3	E858.0	E932.3	E950.4	E962.0	E980.4
Gold (compounds) (salts)	965.69	E850.6	E935.6	E950.0	E962.0	E980.0
Golden sulfide of antimony	985.4	E866.2	—	E950.9	E962.1	E980.9
Goldylocks	988.2	E865.4	—	E950.9	E962.1	E980.9
Gonadal tissue extract	962.9	E858.0	E932.9	E950.4	E962.0	E980.4
beverage	980.0	E860.0	—	E950.9	E962.1	E980.9
female	962.2	E858.0	E932.2	E950.4	E962.0	E980.4
male	962.1	E858.0	E932.1	E950.4	E962.0	E980.4
Gonadotropin	962.4	E858.0	E932.4	E950.4	E962.0	E980.4
Grain alcohol	980.0	E860.1	—	E950.9	E962.1	E980.9
Gramicidin	960.8	E856	E930.8	E950.4	E962.0	E980.4
Gratiola officinalis	988.2	E865.4	—	E950.9	E962.1	E980.9
Grease	989.89	E866.8	—	E950.9	E962.1	E980.9
Green hellebore	988.2	E865.4	—	E950.9	E962.1	E980.9
Green soap	976.2	E858.7	E946.2	E950.4	E962.0	E980.4
Grifulvin	960.1	E856	E930.1	E950.4	E962.0	E980.4
Griseofulvin	960.1	E856	E930.1	E950.4	E962.0	E980.4
Growth hormone	962.4	E858.0	E932.4	E950.4	E962.0	E980.4
Guaiacol	975.5	E858.6	E945.5	E950.4	E962.0	E980.4
Guaiac reagent	977.8	E858.8	E947.8	E950.4	E962.0	E980.4

Nontherapeutic use substance

Subterms under main terms may continue to next column or page

Index

Guaifenesin — Hydroxyquinoline derivatives

	Poisoning	Accident	Therapeutic Use	Suicide Attempt	Assault	Undetermined
Guaifenesin	975.5	E858.6	E945.5	E950.4	E962.0	E980.4
Guaiphenesin	975.5	E858.6	E945.5	E950.4	E962.0	E980.4
Guanatol	961.4	E857	E931.4	E950.4	E962.0	E980.4
Guanethidine	972.6	E858.3	E942.6	E950.4	E962.0	E980.4
Guano	989.89	E866.5	—	E950.9	E962.1	E980.9
Guanochlor	972.6	E858.3	E942.6	E950.4	E962.0	E980.4
Guanoctine	972.6	E858.3	E942.6	E950.4	E962.0	E980.4
Guanoxan	972.6	E858.3	E942.6	E950.4	E962.0	E980.4
Hair treatment agent NEC	976.4	E858.7	E946.4	E950.4	E962.0	E980.4
Halcinonide	976.0	E858.7	E946.0	E950.4	E962.0	E980.4
Halethazole	976.0	E858.7	E946.0	E950.4	E962.0	E980.4
Hallucinogens	969.6	E854.1	E939.6	E950.3	E962.0	E980.3
Haloperidol	969.2	E853.1	E939.2	E950.3	E962.0	E980.3
Haloprogin	976.0	E858.7	E946.0	E950.4	E962.0	E980.4
Halotex	976.0	E858.7	E946.0	E950.4	E962.0	E980.4
Halothane	968.1	E855.1	E938.1	E950.4	E962.0	E980.4
Halquinols	976.0	E858.7	E946.0	E950.4	E962.0	E980.4
Hand sanitizer	976.0	E858.7	E946.0	E950.4	E962.0	E980.4
Harmonyl	972.6	E858.3	E942.6	E950.4	E962.0	E980.4
Hartmann's solution	974.5	E858.5	E944.5	E950.4	E962.0	E980.4
Hashish	969.6	E854.1	E939.6	E950.3	E962.0	E980.3
Hawaiian wood rose seeds	969.6	E854.1	E939.6	E950.3	E962.0	E980.3
Headache cures, drugs, powders NEC	977.9	E858.9	E947.9	E950.5	E962.0	E980.9
Heavenly Blue (morning glory)	969.6	E854.1	E939.6	E950.3	E962.0	E980.3
Heavy metal antagonists	963.8	E858.1	E933.8	E950.4	E962.0	E980.4
anti-infectives	961.2	E857	E931.2	E950.4	E962.0	E980.4
Hedaquinium	976.0	E858.7	E946.0	E950.4	E962.0	E980.4
Hedge hyssop	988.2	E865.4	—	E950.9	E962.1	E980.9
Heet	976.8	E858.7	E946.8	E950.4	E962.0	E980.4
Helenin	961.6	E857	E931.6	E950.4	E962.0	E980.4
Hellebore (black) (green) (white)	988.2	E865.4	—	E950.9	E962.1	E980.9
Hemlock	988.2	E865.4	—	E950.9	E962.1	E980.9
Hemostatics	964.5	E858.2	E934.5	E950.4	E962.0	E980.4
capillary active drugs	972.8	E858.3	E942.8	E950.4	E962.0	E980.4
Henbane	988.2	E865.4	—	E950.9	E962.1	E980.9
Heparin (sodium)	964.2	E858.2	E934.2	E950.4	E962.0	E980.4
Heptabarbital, heptabarbitone	967.0	E851	E937.0	E950.1	E962.0	E980.1
Heptachlor	989.2	E863.0	—	E950.6	E962.1	E980.7
Heptalgin	965.09	E850.2	E935.2	E950.0	E962.0	E980.0
Herbicides	989.4	E863.5	—	E950.6	E962.1	E980.7
Heroin	965.01	E850.0	E935.0	E950.0	E962.0	E980.0
Herplex	976.5	E858.7	E946.5	E950.4	E962.0	E980.4
HES	964.8	E858.2	E934.8	E950.4	E962.0	E980.4
Hetastarch	964.8	E858.2	E934.8	E950.4	E962.0	E980.4
Hexachlorocyclohexane	989.2	E863.0	—	E950.6	E962.1	E980.7
Hexachlorophene	976.2	E858.7	E946.2	E950.4	E962.0	E980.4
Hexadimethrine (bromide)	964.5	E858.2	E934.5	E950.4	E962.0	E980.4
Hexafluorenium	975.2	E858.6	E945.2	E950.4	E962.0	E980.4
Hexa-germ	976.2	E858.7	E946.2	E950.4	E962.0	E980.4
Hexahydrophenol	980.8	E860.8	—	E950.9	E962.1	E980.9
Hexalin	980.8	E860.8	—	E950.9	E962.1	E980.9
Hexamethonium	972.3	E858.3	E942.3	E950.4	E962.0	E980.4
Hexamethyleneamine	961.9	E857	E931.9	E950.4	E962.0	E980.4
Hexamine	961.9	E857	E931.9	E950.4	E962.0	E980.4
Hexanone	982.8	E862.4	—	E950.9	E962.1	E980.9
Hexapropymate	967.8	E852.8	E937.8	E950.2	E962.0	E980.2
Hexestrol	962.2	E858.0	E932.2	E950.4	E962.0	E980.4
Hexethal (sodium)	967.0	E851	E937.0	E950.1	E962.0	E980.1
Hexetidine	976.0	E858.7	E946.0	E950.4	E962.0	E980.4
Hexobarbital, hexobarbitone	967.0	E851	E937.0	E950.1	E962.0	E980.1
sodium (anesthetic)	968.3	E855.1	E938.3	E950.4	E962.0	E980.4
soluble	968.3	E855.1	E938.3	E950.4	E962.0	E980.4
Hexocyclium	971.1	E855.4	E941.1	E950.4	E962.0	E980.4
Hexoestrol	962.2	E858.0	E932.2	E950.4	E962.0	E980.4
Hexone	982.8	E862.4	—	E950.9	E962.1	E980.9
Hexylcaine	968.5	E855.2	E938.5	E950.4	E962.0	E980.4
Hexylresorcinol	961.6	E857	E931.6	E950.4	E962.0	E980.4
Hinkle's pills	973.1	E858.4	E943.1	E950.4	E962.0	E980.4
Histalog	977.8	E858.8	E947.8	E950.4	E962.0	E980.4
Histamine (phosphate)	972.5	E858.3	E942.5	E950.4	E962.0	E980.4
Histoplasmin	977.8	E858.8	E947.8	E950.4	E962.0	E980.4
Holly berries	988.2	E865.3	—	E950.9	E962.1	E980.9
Homatropine	971.1	E855.4	E941.1	E950.4	E962.0	E980.4
Homo-tet	964.6	E858.2	E934.6	E950.4	E962.0	E980.4

	Poisoning	Accident	Therapeutic Use	Suicide Attempt	Assault	Undetermined
Hormones (synthetic substitute)						
NEC	962.9	E858.0	E932.9	E950.4	E962.0	E980.4
adrenal cortical steroids	962.0	E858.0	E932.0	E950.4	E962.0	E980.4
antidiabetic agents	962.3	E858.0	E932.3	E950.4	E962.0	E980.4
follicle stimulating	962.4	E858.0	E932.4	E950.4	E962.0	E980.4
gonadotropic	962.4	E858.0	E932.4	E950.4	E962.0	E980.4
growth	962.4	E858.0	E932.4	E950.4	E962.0	E980.4
ovarian (substitutes)	962.2	E858.0	E932.2	E950.4	E962.0	E980.4
parathyroid (derivatives)	962.6	E858.0	E932.6	E950.4	E962.0	E980.4
pituitary (posterior)	962.5	E858.0	E932.5	E950.4	E962.0	E980.4
anterior	962.4	E858.0	E932.4	E950.4	E962.0	E980.4
thyroid (derivative)	962.7	E858.0	E932.7	E950.4	E962.0	E980.4
Hornet (sting)	989.5	E905.3	—	E950.9	E962.1	E980.9
Horticulture agent NEC	989.4	E863.9	—	E950.6	E962.1	E980.7
Hyaluronidase	963.4	E858.1	E933.4	E950.4	E962.0	E980.4
Hyazyme	963.4	E858.1	E933.4	E950.4	E962.0	E980.4
Hycodan	965.09	E850.2	E935.2	E950.0	E962.0	E980.0
Hydantoin derivatives	966.1	E855.0	E936.1	E950.4	E962.0	E980.4
Hydeltra	962.0	E858.0	E932.0	E950.4	E962.0	E980.4
Hydergine	971.3	E855.6	E941.3	E950.4	E962.0	E980.4
Hydrabamine penicillin	960.0	E856	E930.0	E950.4	E962.0	E980.4
Hydralazine, hydrallazine	972.6	E858.3	E942.6	E950.4	E962.0	E980.4
Hydrargaphen	976.0	E858.7	E946.0	E950.4	E962.0	E980.4
Hydrazine	983.9	E864.3	—	E950.7	E962.1	E980.6
Hydriodic acid	975.5	E858.6	E945.5	E950.4	E962.0	E980.4
Hydrocarbon gas	987.1	E869.8	—	E952.8	E962.2	E982.8
incomplete combustion of — see Carbon, monoxide, fuel, utility						
liquefied (mobile container)	987.0	E868.0	—	E951.1	E962.2	E981.1
piped (natural)	987.0	E867	—	E951.0	E962.2	E981.0
Hydrochloric acid (liquid)	983.1	E864.1	—	E950.7	E962.1	E980.6
medicinal	973.4	E858.4	E943.4	E950.4	E962.0	E980.4
vapor	987.8	E869.8	—	E952.8	E962.2	E982.8
Hydrochlorothiazide	974.3	E858.5	E944.3	E950.4	E962.0	E980.4
Hydrocodone	965.09	E850.2	E935.2	E950.0	E962.0	E980.0
Hydrocortisone	962.0	E858.0	E932.0	E950.4	E962.0	E980.4
ENT agent	976.6	E858.7	E946.6	E950.4	E962.0	E980.4
ophthalmic preparation	976.5	E858.7	E946.5	E950.4	E962.0	E980.4
topical NEC	976.0	E858.7	E946.0	E950.4	E962.0	E980.4
Hydrocortone	962.0	E858.0	E932.0	E950.4	E962.0	E980.4
ENT agent	976.6	E858.7	E946.6	E950.4	E962.0	E980.4
ophthalmic preparation	976.5	E858.7	E946.5	E950.4	E962.0	E980.4
topical NEC	976.0	E858.7	E946.0	E950.4	E962.0	E980.4
Hydrocyanic acid — see Cyanide(s)						
Hydroflumethiazide	974.3	E858.5	E944.3	E950.4	E962.0	E980.4
Hydrofluoric acid (liquid)	983.1	E864.1	—	E950.7	E962.1	E980.6
vapor	987.8	E869.8	—	E952.8	E962.2	E982.8
Hydrogen	987.8	E869.8	—	E952.8	E962.2	E982.8
arsenide	985.1	E866.3	—	E950.8	E962.1	E980.8
arseniureted	985.1	E866.3	—	E950.8	E962.1	E980.8
cyanide (salts)	989.0	E866.8	—	E950.9	E962.1	E980.9
gas	987.7	E869.8	—	E952.8	E962.2	E982.8
fluoride (liquid)	983.1	E864.1	—	E950.7	E962.1	E980.6
vapor	987.8	E869.8	—	E952.8	E962.2	E982.8
peroxide (solution)	976.6	E858.7	E946.6	E950.4	E962.0	E980.4
phosphureted	987.8	E869.8	—	E952.8	E962.2	E982.8
sulfide (gas)	987.8	E869.8	—	E952.8	E962.2	E982.8
arseniureted	985.1	E866.3	—	E950.8	E962.1	E980.8
sulfureted	987.8	E869.8	—	E952.8	E962.2	E982.8
Hydromorphinol	965.09	E850.2	E935.2	E950.0	E962.0	E980.0
Hydromorphinone	965.09	E850.2	E935.2	E950.0	E962.0	E980.0
Hydromorphone	965.09	E850.2	E935.2	E950.0	E962.0	E980.0
Hydromox	974.3	E858.5	E944.3	E950.4	E962.0	E980.4
Hydrophilic lotion	976.3	E858.7	E946.3	E950.4	E962.0	E980.4
Hydroquinone	983.0	E864.0	—	E950.7	E962.1	E980.6
vapor	987.8	E869.8	—	E952.8	E962.2	E982.8
Hydrosulfuric acid (gas)	987.8	E869.8	—	E952.8	E962.2	E982.8
Hydrous wool fat (lotion)	976.3	E858.7	E946.3	E950.4	E962.0	E980.4
Hydroxide, caustic	983.2	E864.2	—	E950.7	E962.1	E980.6
Hydroxocobalamin	964.1	E858.2	E934.1	E950.4	E962.0	E980.4
Hydroxyamphetamine	971.2	E855.5	E941.2	E950.4	E962.0	E980.4
Hydroxychloroquine	961.4	E857	E931.4	E950.4	E962.0	E980.4
Hydroxydihydrocodeinone	965.09	E850.2	E935.2	E950.0	E962.0	E980.0
Hydroxyethyl starch	964.8	E858.2	E934.8	E950.4	E962.0	E980.4
Hydroxyphenamate	969.5	E853.8	E939.5	E950.3	E962.0	E980.3
Hydroxyphenylbutazone	965.5	E850.5	E935.5	E950.0	E962.0	E980.0
Hydroxyprogesterone	962.2	E858.0	E932.2	E950.4	E962.0	E980.4
Hydroxyquinoline derivatives	961.3	E857	E931.3	E950.4	E962.0	E980.4

Nontherapeutic use substance

⬇ Subterms under main terms may continue to next column or page

▶◀ Revised Text　　● New Line　　▲ Revised Code

2010 ICD-9-CM

	Poisoning	Accident	Therapeutic Use	Suicide Attempt	Assault	Undetermined
Hydroxystilbamidine	961.5	E857	E931.5	E950.4	E962.0	E980.4
Hydroxyurea	963.1	E858.1	E933.1	E950.4	E962.0	E980.4
Hydroxyzine	969.5	E853.8	E939.5	E950.3	E962.0	E980.3
Hyoscine (hydrobromide)	971.1	E855.4	E941.1	E950.4	E962.0	E980.4
Hyoscyamine	971.1	E855.4	E941.1	E950.4	E962.0	E980.4
Hyoscyamus (albus) (niger)	988.2	E865.4	—	E950.9	E962.1	E980.9
Hypaque	977.8	E858.8	E947.8	E950.4	E962.0	E980.4
Hypertussis	964.6	E858.2	E934.6	E950.4	E962.0	E980.4
Hypnotics NEC	967.9	E852.9	E937.9	E950.2	E962.0	E980.2
Hypochlorites — see Sodium, hypochlorite						
Hypotensive agents NEC	972.6	E858.3	E942.6	E950.4	E962.0	E980.4
Ibufenac	965.69	E850.6	E935.6	E950.0	E962.0	E980.0
Ibuprofen	965.61	E850.6	E935.6	E950.0	E962.0	E980.0
ICG	977.8	E858.8	E947.8	E950.4	E962.0	E980.4
Ichthammol	976.4	E858.7	E946.4	E950.4	E962.0	E980.4
Ichthyol	976.4	E858.7	E946.4	E950.4	E962.0	E980.4
Idoxuridine	976.5	E858.7	E946.5	E950.4	E962.0	E980.4
IDU	976.5	E858.7	E946.5	E950.4	E962.0	E980.4
Iletin	962.3	E858.0	E932.3	E950.4	E962.0	E980.4
Ilex	988.2	E865.4	—	E950.9	E962.1	E980.9
Illuminating gas — see Gas, utility						
Ilopan	963.5	E858.1	E933.5	E950.4	E962.0	E980.4
Ilotycin	960.3	E856	E930.3	E950.4	E962.0	E980.4
ophthalmic preparation	976.5	E858.7	E946.5	E950.4	E962.0	E980.4
topical NEC	976.0	E858.7	E946.0	E950.4	E962.0	E980.4
Imipramine	969.05 ▲	E854.0	E939.0	E950.3	E962.0	E980.3
Immu-G	964.6	E858.2	E934.6	E950.4	E962.0	E980.4
Immuglobin	964.6	E858.2	E934.6	E950.4	E962.0	E980.4
Immune serum globulin	964.6	E858.2	E934.6	E950.4	E962.0	E980.4
Immunosuppressive agents	963.1	E858.1	E933.1	E950.4	E962.0	E980.4
Immu-tetanus	964.6	E858.2	E934.6	E950.4	E962.0	E980.4
Indandione (derivatives)	964.2	E858.2	E934.2	E950.4	E962.0	E980.4
Inderal	972.0	E858.3	E942.0	E950.4	E962.0	E980.4
Indian						
hemp	969.6	E854.1	E939.6	E950.3	E962.0	E980.3
tobacco	988.2	E865.4	—	E950.9	E962.1	E980.9
Indigo carmine	977.8	E858.8	E947.8	E950.4	E962.0	E980.4
Indocin	965.69	E850.6	E935.6	E950.0	E962.0	E980.0
Indocyanine green	977.8	E858.8	E947.8	E950.4	E962.0	E980.4
Indomethacin	965.69	E850.6	E935.6	E950.0	E962.0	E980.0
Industrial						
alcohol	980.9	E860.9	—	E950.9	E962.1	E980.9
fumes	987.8	E869.8	—	E952.8	E962.2	E982.8
solvents (fumes) (vapors)	982.8	E862.9	—	E950.9	E962.1	E980.9
Influenza vaccine	979.6	E858.8	E949.6	E950.4	E962.0	E982.8
Ingested substances NEC	989.9	E866.9	—	E950.9	E962.1	E980.9
INH (isoniazid)	961.8	E857	E931.8	E950.4	E962.0	E980.4
Inhalation, gas (noxious) — see Gas						
Ink	989.89	E866.8	—	E950.9	E962.1	E980.9
Innovar	967.6	E852.5	E937.6	E950.2	E962.0	E980.2
Inositol niacinate	972.2	E858.3	E942.2	E950.4	E962.0	E980.4
Inproquone	963.1	E858.1	E933.1	E950.4	E962.0	E980.4
Insecticides — see also						
Pesticides	989.4	E863.4	—	E950.6	E962.1	E980.7
chlorinated	989.2	E863.0	—	E950.6	E962.1	E980.7
mixtures	989.4	E863.3	—	E950.6	E962.1	E980.7
organochlorine (compounds)	989.2	E863.0	—	E950.6	E962.1	E980.7
organophosphorus (compounds)	989.3	E863.1	—	E950.6	E962.1	E980.7
Insect (sting), venomous	989.5	E905.5	—	E950.9	E962.1	E980.9
Insular tissue extract	962.3	E858.0	E932.3	E950.4	E962.0	E980.4
Insulin (amorphous) (globin) (isophane) (Lente) (NPH) (protamine) (Semilente) (Ultralente) (zinc)	962.3	E858.0	E932.3	E950.4	E962.0	E980.4
Intranarcon	968.3	E855.1	E938.3	E950.4	E962.0	E980.4
Inulin	977.8	E858.8	E947.8	E950.4	E962.0	E980.4
Invert sugar	974.5	E858.5	E944.5	E950.4	E962.0	E980.4
Inza — see Naproxen						
Iodide NEC — see also						
Iodine	976.0	E858.7	E946.0	E950.4	E962.0	E980.4
mercury (ointment)	976.0	E858.7	E946.0	E950.4	E962.0	E980.4
methylate	976.0	E858.7	E946.0	E950.4	E962.0	E980.4
potassium (expectorant) NEC	975.5	E858.6	E945.5	E950.4	E962.0	E980.4
Iodinated glycerol	975.5	E858.6	E945.5	E950.4	E962.0	E980.4

	Poisoning	Accident	Therapeutic Use	Suicide Attempt	Assault	Undetermined
Iodine (antiseptic, external) (tincture) NEC	976.0	E858.7	E946.0	E950.4	E962.0	E980.4
diagnostic	977.8	E858.8	E947.8	E950.4	E962.0	E980.4
for thyroid conditions (antithyroid)	962.8	E858.0	E932.8	E950.4	E962.0	E980.4
vapor	987.8	E869.8	—	E952.8	E962.2	E982.8
Iodized oil	977.8	E858.8	E947.8	E950.4	E962.0	E980.4
Iodobismitol	961.2	E857	E931.2	E950.4	E962.0	E980.4
Iodochlorhydroxyquin	961.3	E857	E931.3	E950.4	E962.0	E980.4
topical	976.0	E858.7	E946.0	E950.4	E962.0	E980.4
Iodoform	976.0	E858.7	E946.0	E950.4	E962.0	E980.4
Iodopanoic acid	977.8	E858.8	E947.8	E950.4	E962.0	E980.4
Iodophthalein	977.8	E858.8	E947.8	E950.4	E962.0	E980.4
Ion exchange resins	974.5	E858.5	E944.5	E950.4	E962.0	E980.4
Iopanoic acid	977.8	E858.8	E947.8	E950.4	E962.0	E980.4
Iophendylate	977.8	E858.8	E947.8	E950.4	E962.0	E980.4
Iothiouracil	962.8	E858.0	E932.8	E950.4	E962.0	E980.4
Ipecac	973.6	E858.4	E943.6	E950.4	E962.0	E980.4
Ipecacuanha	973.6	E858.4	E943.6	E950.4	E962.0	E980.4
Ipodate	977.8	E858.8	E947.8	E950.4	E962.0	E980.4
Ipral	967.0	E851	E937.0	E950.1	E962.0	E980.1
Ipratropium	975.1	E858.6	E945.1	E950.4	E962.0	E980.4
Iproniazid	969.01 ▲	E854.0	E939.0	E950.3	E962.0	E980.3
Iron (compounds) (medicinal) (preparations)	964.0	E858.2	E934.0	E950.4	E962.0	E980.4
dextran	964.0	E858.2	E934.0	E950.4	E962.0	E980.4
nonmedicinal (dust) (fumes) NEC	985.8	E866.4	—	E950.9	E962.1	E980.9
Irritant drug	977.9	E858.9	E947.9	E950.5	E962.0	E980.5
Ismelin	972.6	E858.3	E942.6	E950.4	E962.0	E980.4
Isoamyl nitrite	972.4	E858.3	E942.4	E950.4	E962.0	E980.4
Isobutyl acetate	982.8	E862.4	—	E950.9	E962.1	E980.9
Isocarboxazid	969.01 ▲	E854.0	E939.0	E950.3	E962.0	E980.3
Isoephedrine	971.2	E855.5	E941.2	E950.4	E962.0	E980.4
Isoetharine	971.2	E855.5	E941.2	E950.4	E962.0	E980.4
Isofluorophate	971.0	E855.3	E941.0	E950.4	E962.0	E980.4
Isoniazid (INH)	961.8	E857	E931.8	E950.4	E962.0	E980.4
Isopentaquine	961.4	E857	E931.4	E950.4	E962.0	E980.4
Isophane insulin	962.3	E858.0	E932.3	E950.4	E962.0	E980.4
Isopregnenone	962.2	E858.0	E932.2	E950.4	E962.0	E980.4
Isoprenaline	971.2	E855.5	E941.2	E950.4	E962.0	E980.4
Isopropamide	971.1	E855.4	E941.1	E950.4	E962.0	E980.4
Isopropanol	980.2	E860.3	—	E950.9	E962.1	E980.9
topical (germicide)	976.0	E858.7	E946.0	E950.4	E962.0	E980.4
Isopropyl						
acetate	982.8	E862.4	—	E950.9	E962.1	E980.9
alcohol	980.2	E860.3	—	E950.9	E962.1	E980.9
topical (germicide)	976.0	E858.7	E946.0	E950.4	E962.0	E980.4
ether	982.8	E862.4	—	E950.9	E962.1	E980.9
Isoproterenol	971.2	E855.5	E941.2	E950.4	E962.0	E980.4
Isosorbide dinitrate	972.4	E858.3	E942.4	E950.4	E962.0	E980.4
Isothipendyl	963.0	E858.1	E933.0	E950.4	E962.0	E980.4
Isoxazolyl penicillin	960.0	E856	E930.0	E950.4	E962.0	E980.4
Isoxsuprine hydrochloride	972.5	E858.3	E942.5	E950.4	E962.0	E980.4
l-thyroxine sodium	962.7	E858.0	E932.7	E950.4	E962.0	E980.4
Jaborandi (pilocarpus) (extract)	971.0	E855.3	E941.0	E950.4	E962.0	E980.4
Jalap	973.1	E858.4	E943.1	E950.4	E962.0	E980.4
Jamaica						
dogwood (bark)	965.7	E850.7	E935.7	E950.0	E962.0	E980.0
ginger	989.89	E866.8	—	E950.9	E962.1	E980.9
Jatropha	988.2	E865.4	—	E950.9	E962.1	E980.9
curcas	988.2	E865.3	—	E950.9	E962.1	E980.9
Jectofer	964.0	E858.2	E934.0	E950.4	E962.0	E980.4
Jellyfish (sting)	989.5	E905.6	—	E950.9	E962.1	E980.9
Jequirity (bean)	988.2	E865.3	—	E950.9	E962.1	E980.9
Jimson weed	988.2	E865.4	—	E950.9	E962.1	E980.9
seeds	988.2	E865.3	—	E950.9	E962.1	E980.9
Juniper tar (oil) (ointment)	976.4	E858.7	E946.4	E950.4	E962.0	E980.4
Kallikrein	972.5	E858.3	E942.5	E950.4	E962.0	E980.4
Kanamycin	960.6	E856	E930.6	E950.4	E962.0	E980.4
Kantrex	960.6	E856	E930.6	E950.4	E962.0	E980.4
Kaolin	973.5	E858.4	E943.5	E950.4	E962.0	E980.4
Karaya (gum)	973.3	E858.4	E943.3	E950.4	E962.0	E980.4
Kemithal	968.3	E855.1	E938.3	E950.4	E962.0	E980.4
Kenacort	962.0	E858.0	E932.0	E950.4	E962.0	E980.4
Keratolytics	976.4	E858.7	E946.4	E950.4	E962.0	E980.4
Keratoplastics	976.4	E858.7	E946.4	E950.4	E962.0	E980.4
Kerosene, kerosine (fuel) (solvent) NEC	981	E862.1	—	E950.9	E962.1	E980.9
insecticide	981	E863.4	—	E950.6	E962.1	E980.7

Nontherapeutic use substance

External Cause (E-Code)

Substance	Poisoning	Accident	Therapeutic Use	Suicide Attempt	Assault	Undetermined
Kerosene, kerosine (fuel) (solvent) — *continued*						
vapor	987.1	E869.8	—	E952.8	E962.2	E982.8
Ketamine	968.3	E855.1	E938.3	E950.4	E962.0	E980.4
Ketobemidone	965.09	E850.2	E935.2	E950.0	E962.0	E980.0
Ketols	982.8	E862.4	—	E950.9	E962.1	E980.9
Ketone oils	982.8	E862.4	—	E950.9	E962.1	E980.9
Ketoprofen	965.61	E850.6	E935.6	E950.0	E962.0	E980.0
Kiln gas or vapor (carbon monoxide)	986	E868.8	—	E952.1	E962.2	E982.1
Konsyl	973.3	E858.4	E943.3	E950.4	E962.0	E980.4
Kosam seed	988.2	E865.3		E950.9	E962.1	E980.9
Krait (venom)	989.5	E905.0	—	E950.9	E962.1	E980.9
Kwell (insecticide)	989.2	E863.0		E950.6	E962.1	E980.7
anti-infective (topical)	976.0	E858.7	E946.0	E950.4	E962.0	E980.4
Laburnum (flowers)						
(seeds)	988.2	E865.3		E950.9	E962.1	E980.9
leaves	988.2	E865.4		E950.9	E962.1	E980.9
Lacquers	989.89	E861.6		E950.9	E962.1	E980.9
Lacrimogenic gas	987.5	E869.3	—	E952.8	E962.2	E982.8
Lactic acid	983.1	E864.1		E950.7	E962.1	E980.6
Lactobacillus acidophilus	973.5	E858.4	E943.5	E950.4	E962.0	E980.4
Lactoflavin	963.5	E858.1	E933.5	E950.4	E962.0	E980.4
Lactuca (virosa) (extract)	967.8	E852.8	E937.8	E950.2	E962.0	E980.2
Lactucarium	967.8	E852.8	E937.8	E950.2	E962.0	E980.2
Laevulose	974.5	E858.5	E944.5	E950.4	E962.0	E980.4
Lanatoside (C)	972.1	E858.3	E942.1	E950.4	E962.0	E980.4
Lanolin (lotion)	976.3	E858.7	E946.3	E950.4	E962.0	E980.4
Largactil	969.1	E853.0	E939.1	E950.3	E962.0	E980.3
Larkspur	988.2	E865.3		E950.9	E962.1	E980.9
Laroxyl	969.05 ▲	E854.0	E939.0	E950.3	E962.0	E980.3
Lasix	974.4	E858.5	E944.4	E950.4	E962.0	E980.4
Latex	989.82	E866.8		E950.9	E962.1	E980.9
Lathyrus (seed)	988.2	E865.3		E950.9	E962.1	E980.9
Laudanum	965.09	E850.2	E935.2	E950.0	E962.0	E980.0
Laudexium	975.2	E858.6	E945.2	E950.4	E962.0	E980.4
Laurel, black or cherry	988.2	E865.4	—	E950.9	E962.1	E980.9
Laurolinium	976.0	E858.7	E946.0	E950.4	E962.0	E980.4
Lauryl sulfoacetate	976.2	E858.7	E946.2	E950.4	E962.0	E980.4
Laxatives NEC	973.3	E858.4	E943.3	E950.4	E962.0	E980.4
emollient	973.2	E858.4	E943.2	E950.4	E962.0	E980.4
L-dopa	966.4	E855.0	E936.4	E950.4	E962.0	E980.4
Lead (dust) (fumes) (vapor)						
NEC	984.9	E866.0	—	E950.9	E962.1	E980.9
acetate (dust)	984.1	E866.0	—	E950.9	E962.1	E980.9
anti-infectives	961.2	E857	E931.2	E950.4	E962.0	E980.4
antiknock compound (tetraethyl)	984.1	E862.1	—	E950.9	E962.1	E980.9
arsenate, arsenite (dust) (insecticide) (vapor)	985.1	E863.4	—	E950.8	E962.1	E980.8
herbicide	985.1	E863.5	—	E950.8	E962.1	E980.8
carbonate	984.0	E866.0	—	E950.9	E962.1	E980.9
paint	984.0	E861.5	—	E950.9	E962.1	E980.9
chromate	984.0	E866.0	—	E950.9	E962.1	E980.9
paint	984.0	E861.5	—	E950.9	E962.1	E980.9
dioxide	984.0	E866.0	—	E950.9	E962.1	E980.9
inorganic (compound)	984.0	E866.0	—	E950.9	E962.1	E980.9
paint	984.0	E861.5	—	E950.9	E962.1	E980.9
iodide	984.0	E866.0	—	E950.9	E962.1	E980.9
pigment (paint)	984.0	E861.5	—	E950.9	E962.1	E980.9
monoxide (dust)	984.0	E866.0	—	E950.9	E962.1	E980.9
paint	984.0	E861.5	—	E950.9	E962.1	E980.9
organic	984.1	E866.0	—	E950.9	E962.1	E980.9
oxide	984.0	E866.0	—	E950.9	E962.1	E980.9
paint	984.0	E861.5	—	E950.9	E962.1	E980.9
paint	984.0	E861.5	—	E950.9	E962.1	E980.9
salts	984.0	E866.0	—	E950.9	E962.1	E980.9
specified compound NEC	984.8	E866.0	—	E950.9	E962.1	E980.9
tetra-ethyl	984.1	E862.1	—	E950.9	E962.1	E980.9
Lebanese red	969.6	E854.1	E939.6	E950.3	E962.0	E980.3
Lente Iletin (insulin)	962.3	E858.0	E932.3	E950.4	E962.0	E980.4
Leptazol	970.0	E854.3	E940.0	E950.4	E962.0	E980.4
Leritine	965.09	E850.2	E935.2	E950.0	E962.0	E980.0
Letter	962.7	E858.0	E932.7	E950.4	E962.0	E980.4
Lettuce opium	967.8	E852.8	E937.8	E950.2	E962.0	E980.2
Leucovorin (factor)	964.1	E858.2	E934.1	E950.4	E962.0	E980.4
Leukeran	963.1	E858.1	E933.1	E950.4	E962.0	E980.4
Levalbuterol	975.7	E858.6	E945.7	E950.4	E962.0	E980.4
Levallorphan	970.1	E854.3	E940.1	E950.4	E962.0	E980.4
Levanil	967.8	E852.8	E937.8	E950.2	E962.0	E980.2
Levarterenol	971.2	E855.5	E941.2	E950.4	E962.0	E980.4
Levodopa	966.4	E855.0	E936.4	E950.4	E962.0	E980.4

External Cause (E-Code)

Substance	Poisoning	Accident	Therapeutic Use	Suicide Attempt	Assault	Undetermined
Levo-dromoran	965.09	E850.2	E935.2	E950.0	E962.0	E980.0
Levoid	962.7	E858.0	E932.7	E950.4	E962.0	E980.4
Levo-iso-methadone	965.02	E850.1	E935.1	E950.0	E962.0	E980.0
Levomepromazine	967.8	E852.8	E937.8	E950.2	E962.0	E980.2
Levoprome	967.8	E852.8	E937.8	E950.2	E962.0	E980.2
Levopropoxyphene	975.4	E858.6	E945.4	E950.4	E962.0	E980.4
Levorphan, levophanol	965.09	E850.2	E935.2	E950.0	E962.0	E980.0
Levothyroxine (sodium)	962.7	E858.0	E932.7	E950.4	E962.0	E980.4
Levsin	971.1	E855.4	E941.1	E950.4	E962.0	E980.4
Levulose	974.5	E858.5	E944.5	E950.4	E962.0	E980.4
Lewisite (gas)	985.1	E866.3	—	E950.8	E962.1	E980.8
Librium	969.4	E853.2	E939.4	E950.3	E962.0	E980.3
Lidex	976.0	E858.7	E946.0	E950.4	E962.0	E980.4
Lidocaine (infiltration) (topical)	968.5	E855.2	E938.5	E950.4	E962.0	E980.4
nerve block (peripheral) (plexus)	968.6	E855.2	E938.6	E950.4	E962.0	E980.4
spinal	968.7	E855.2	E938.7	E950.4	E962.0	E980.4
Lighter fluid	981	E862.1	—	E950.9	E962.1	E980.9
Lignocaine (infiltration) (topical)	968.5	E855.2	E938.5	E950.4	E962.0	E980.4
nerve block (peripheral) (plexus)	968.6	E855.2	E938.6	E950.4	E962.0	E980.4
spinal	968.7	E855.2	E938.7	E950.4	E962.0	E980.4
Ligroin(e) (solvent)	981	E862.0	—	E950.9	E962.1	E980.9
vapor	987.1	E869.8	—	E952.8	E962.2	E982.8
Ligustrum vulgare	988.2	E865.3	—	E950.9	E962.1	E980.9
Lily of the valley	988.2	E865.4	—	E950.9	E962.1	E980.9
Lime (chloride)	983.2	E864.2	—	E950.7	E962.1	E980.6
solution, sulfated	976.4	E858.7	E946.4	E950.4	E962.0	E980.4
Limonene	982.8	E862.4	—	E950.9	E962.1	E980.9
Lincomycin	960.8	E856	E930.8	E950.4	E962.0	E980.4
Lindane (insecticide) (vapor)	989.2	E863.0	—	E950.6	E962.1	E980.7
anti-infective (topical)	976.0	E858.7	E946.0	E950.4	E962.0	E980.4
Liniments NEC	976.9	E858.7	E946.9	E950.4	E962.0	E980.4
Linoleic acid	972.2	E858.3	E942.2	E950.4	E962.0	E980.4
Liothyronine	962.7	E858.0	E932.7	E950.4	E962.0	E980.4
Liotrix	962.7	E858.0	E932.7	E950.4	E962.0	E980.4
Lipancreatin	973.4	E858.4	E943.4	E950.4	E962.0	E980.4
Lipo-Lutin	962.2	E858.0	E932.2	E950.4	E962.0	E980.4
Lipotropic agents	977.1	E858.8	E947.1	E950.4	E962.0	E980.4
Liquefied petroleum gases	987.0	E868.0	—	E951.1	E962.2	E981.1
piped (pure or mixed with air)	987.0	E867	—	E951.0	E962.2	E981.0
Liquid petrolatum	973.2	E858.4	E943.2	E950.4	E962.0	E980.4
substance	989.9	E866.9	—	E950.9	E962.1	E980.9
specified NEC	989.89	E866.8	—	E950.9	E962.1	E980.9
Lirugen	979.4	E858.8	E949.4	E950.4	E962.0	E980.4
Lithane	969.8	E855.8	E939.8	E950.3	E962.0	E980.3
Lithium	985.8	E866.4	—	E950.9	E962.1	E980.9
carbonate	969.8	E855.8	E939.8	E950.3	E962.0	E980.3
Lithonate	969.8	E855.8	E939.8	E950.3	E962.0	E980.3
Liver (extract) (injection) (preparations)	964.1	E858.2	E934.1	E950.4	E962.0	E980.4
Lizard (bite) (venom)	989.5	E905.0	—	E950.9	E962.1	E980.9
LMD	964.8	E858.2	E934.8	E950.4	E962.0	E980.4
Lobelia	988.2	E865.4	—	E950.9	E962.1	E980.9
Lobeline	970.0	E854.3	E940.0	E950.4	E962.0	E980.4
Locorten	976.0	E858.7	E946.0	E950.4	E962.0	E980.4
Lolium temulentum	988.2	E865.3	—	E950.9	E962.1	E980.9
Lomotil	973.5	E858.4	E943.5	E950.4	E962.0	E980.4
Lomustine	963.1	E858.1	E933.1	E950.4	E962.0	E980.4
Lophophora williamsii	969.6	E854.1	E939.6	E950.3	E962.0	E980.3
Lorazepam	969.4	E853.2	E939.4	E950.3	E962.0	E980.3
Lotions NEC	976.9	E858.7	E946.9	E950.4	E962.0	E980.4
Lotronex	973.8	E858.4	E943.8	E950.4	E962.0	E980.4
Lotusate	967.0	E851	E937.0	E950.1	E962.0	E980.1
Lowila	976.2	E858.7	E946.2	E950.4	E962.0	E980.4
Loxapine	969.3	E853.8	E939.3	E950.3	E962.0	E980.3
Lozenges (throat)	976.6	E858.7	E946.6	E950.4	E962.0	E980.4
LSD (25)	969.6	E854.1	E939.6	E950.3	E962.0	E980.3
L-Tryptophan — *see* amino acid						
Lubricating oil NEC	981	E862.2	—	E950.9	E962.1	E980.9
Lucanthone	961.6	E857	E931.6	E950.4	E962.0	E980.4
Luminal	967.0	E851	E937.0	E950.1	E962.0	E980.1
Lung irritant (gas) NEC	987.9	E869.9	—	E952.9	E962.2	E982.9
Lutocylol	962.2	E858.0	E932.2	E950.4	E962.0	E980.4
Lutromone	962.2	E858.0	E932.2	E950.4	E962.0	E980.4
Lututrin	975.0	E858.6	E945.0	E950.4	E962.0	E980.4

Nontherapeutic use substance

▼ Subterms under main terms may continue to next column or page

▶◀ Revised Text   ● New Line   ▲ Revised Code

	Poisoning	Accident	Therapeutic Use	Suicide Attempt	Assault	Undetermined
Lye (concentrated)	983.2	E864.2	—	E950.7	E962.1	E980.6
Lygranum (skin test)	977.8	E858.8	E947.8	E950.4	E962.0	E980.4
Lymecycline	960.4	E856	E930.4	E950.4	E962.0	E980.4
Lymphogranuloma venereum antigen	977.8	E858.8	E947.8	E950.4	E962.0	E980.4
Lynestrenol	962.2	E858.0	E932.2	E950.4	E962.0	E980.4
Lyovac Sodium Edecrin	974.4	E858.5	E944.4	E950.4	E962.0	E980.4
Lypressin	962.5	E858.0	E932.5	E950.4	E962.0	E980.4
Lysergic acid (amide) (diethylamide)	969.6	E854.1	E939.6	E950.3	E962.0	E980.3
Lysergide	969.6	E854.1	E939.6	E950.3	E962.0	E980.3
Lysine vasopressin	962.5	E858.0	E932.5	E950.4	E962.0	E980.4
Lysol	983.0	E864.0	—	E950.7	E962.1	E980.6
Lytta (vitatta)	976.8	E858.7	E946.8	E950.4	E962.0	E980.4
Mace	987.5	E869.3	—	E952.8	E962.2	E982.8
Macrolides (antibiotics)	960.3	E856	E930.3	E950.4	E962.0	E980.4
Mafenide	976.0	E858.7	E946.0	E950.4	E962.0	E980.4
Magaldrate	973.0	E858.4	E943.0	E950.4	E962.0	E980.4
Magic mushroom	969.6	E854.1	E939.6	E950.3	E962.0	E980.3
Magnamycin	960.8	E856	E930.8	E950.4	E962.0	E980.4
Magnesia magma	973.0	E858.4	E943.0	E950.4	E962.0	E980.4
Magnesium (compounds) (fumes) NEC	985.8	E866.4	—	E950.9	E962.1	E980.9
antacid	973.0	E858.4	E943.0	E950.4	E962.0	E980.4
carbonate	973.0	E858.4	E943.0	E950.4	E962.0	E980.4
cathartic	973.3	E858.4	E943.3	E950.4	E962.0	E980.4
citrate	973.3	E858.4	E943.3	E950.4	E962.0	E980.4
hydroxide	973.0	E858.4	E943.0	E950.4	E962.0	E980.4
oxide	973.0	E858.4	E943.0	E950.4	E962.0	E980.4
sulfate (oral)	973.3	E858.4	E943.3	E950.4	E962.0	E980.4
intravenous	966.3	E855.0	E936.3	E950.4	E962.0	E980.4
trisilicate	973.0	E858.4	E943.0	E950.4	E962.0	E980.4
Malathion (insecticide)	989.3	E863.1	—	E950.6	E962.1	E980.7
Male fern (oleoresin)	961.6	E857	E931.6	E950.4	E962.0	E980.4
Mandelic acid	961.9	E857	E931.9	E950.4	E962.0	E980.4
Manganese compounds (fumes) NEC	985.2	E866.4	—	E950.9	E962.1	E980.9
Mannitol (diuretic) (medicinal) NEC	974.4	E858.5	E944.4	E950.4	E962.0	E980.4
hexanitrate	972.4	E858.3	E942.4	E950.4	E962.0	E980.4
mustard	963.1	E858.1	E933.1	E950.4	E962.0	E980.4
Mannomustine	963.1	E858.1	E933.1	E950.4	E962.0	E980.4
MAO inhibitors	969.01 ▲	E854.0	E939.0	E950.3	E962.0	E980.3
Mapharsen	961.1	E857	E931.1	E950.4	E962.0	E980.4
Marcaine	968.9	E855.2	E938.9	E950.4	E962.0	E980.4
infiltration (subcutaneous)	968.5	E855.2	E938.5	E950.4	E962.0	E980.4
nerve block (peripheral) (plexus)	968.6	E855.2	E938.6	E950.4	E962.0	E980.4
Marezine	963.0	E858.1	E933.0	E950.4	E962.0	E980.4
Marihuana, marijuana (derivatives)	969.6	E854.1	E939.6	E950.3	E962.0	E980.3
Marine animals or plants (sting)	989.5	E905.6	—	E950.9	E962.1	E980.9
Marplan	969.01 ▲	E854.0	E939.0	E950.3	E962.0	E980.3
Marsh gas	987.1	E869.8	—	E952.8	E962.2	E982.8
Marsilid	969.01 ▲	E854.0	E939.0	E950.3	E962.0	E980.3
Matulane	963.1	E858.1	E933.1	E950.4	E962.0	E980.4
Mazindol	977.0	E858.8	E947.0	E950.4	E962.0	E980.4
MDMA	969.72 ▲	E854.2	E939.7	E950.3	E962.0	E980.3
Meadow saffron	988.2	E865.3	—	E950.9	E962.1	E980.9
Measles vaccine	979.4	E858.8	E949.4	E950.4	E962.0	E980.4
Meat, noxious or nonbacterial	988.8	E865.0	—	E950.9	E962.1	E980.9
Mebanazine	969.01 ▲	E854.0	E939.0	E950.3	E962.0	E980.3
Mebaral	967.0	E851	E937.0	E950.1	E962.0	E980.1
Mebendazole	961.6	E857	E931.6	E950.4	E962.0	E980.4
Mebeverine	975.1	E858.6	E945.1	E950.4	E962.0	E980.4
Mebhydroline	963.0	E858.1	E933.0	E950.4	E962.0	E980.4
Mebrophenhydramine	963.0	E858.1	E933.0	E950.4	E962.0	E980.4
Mebutamate	969.5	E853.8	E939.5	E950.3	E962.0	E980.3
Mecamylamine (chloride)	972.3	E858.3	E942.3	E950.4	E962.0	E980.4
Mechlorethamine hydrochloride	963.1	E858.1	E933.1	E950.4	E962.0	E980.4
Meclizene (hydrochloride)	963.0	E858.1	E933.0	E950.4	E962.0	E980.4
Meclofenoxate	970.0	E854.3	E940.0	E950.4	E962.0	E980.4
Meclozine (hydrochloride)	963.0	E858.1	E933.0	E950.4	E962.0	E980.4
Medazepam	969.4	E853.2	E939.4	E950.3	E962.0	E980.3
Medicine, medicinal substance	977.9	E858.9	E947.9	E950.5	E962.0	E980.5
specified NEC	977.8	E858.8	E947.8	E950.4	E962.0	E980.4
Medinal	967.0	E851	E937.0	E950.1	E962.0	E980.1
Medomin	967.0	E851	E937.0	E950.1	E962.0	E980.1

	Poisoning	Accident	Therapeutic Use	Suicide Attempt	Assault	Undetermined
Medroxyprogesterone	962.2	E858.0	E932.2	E950.4	E962.0	E980.4
Medrysone	976.5	E858.7	E946.5	E950.4	E962.0	E980.4
Mefenamic acid	965.7	E850.7	E935.7	E950.0	E962.0	E980.0
Megahallucinogen	969.6	E854.1	E939.6	E950.3	E962.0	E980.3
Megestrol	962.2	E858.0	E932.2	E950.4	E962.0	E980.4
Meglumine	977.8	E858.8	E947.8	E950.4	E962.0	E980.4
Meladinin	976.3	E858.7	E946.3	E950.4	E962.0	E980.4
Melanizing agents	976.3	E858.7	E946.3	E950.4	E962.0	E980.4
Melarsoprol	961.1	E857	E931.1	E950.4	E962.0	E980.4
Melia azedarach	988.2	E865.3	—	E950.9	E962.1	E980.9
Mellaril	969.1	E853.0	E939.1	E950.3	E962.0	E980.3
Meloxine	976.3	E858.7	E946.3	E950.4	E962.0	E980.4
Melphalan	963.1	E858.1	E933.1	E950.4	E962.0	E980.4
Menadiol sodium diphosphate	964.3	E858.2	E934.3	E950.4	E962.0	E980.4
Menadione (sodium bisulfite)	964.3	E858.2	E934.3	E950.4	E962.0	E980.4
Menaphthone	964.3	E858.2	E934.3	E950.4	E962.0	E980.4
Meningococcal vaccine	978.8	E858.8	E948.8	E950.4	E962.0	E980.4
Menningovax-C	978.8	E858.8	E948.8	E950.4	E962.0	E980.4
Menotropins	962.4	E858.0	E932.4	E950.4	E962.0	E980.4
Menthol NEC	976.1	E858.7	E946.1	E950.4	E962.0	E980.4
Mepacrine	961.3	E857	E931.3	E950.4	E962.0	E980.4
Meparfynol	967.8	E852.8	E937.8	E950.2	E962.0	E980.2
Mepazine	969.1	E853.0	E939.1	E950.3	E962.0	E980.3
Mepenzolate	971.1	E855.4	E941.1	E950.4	E962.0	E980.4
Meperidine	965.09	E850.2	E935.2	E950.0	E962.0	E980.0
Mephenamin(e)	966.4	E855.0	E936.4	E950.4	E962.0	E980.4
Mephenesin (carbamate)	968.0	E855.1	E938.0	E950.4	E962.0	E980.4
Mephenoxalone	969.5	E853.8	E939.5	E950.3	E962.0	E980.3
Mephentermine	971.2	E855.5	E941.2	E950.4	E962.0	E980.4
Mephenytoin	966.1	E855.0	E936.1	E950.4	E962.0	E980.4
Mephobarbital	967.0	E851	E937.0	E950.1	E962.0	E980.1
Mepiperphenidol	971.1	E855.4	E941.1	E950.4	E962.0	E980.4
Mepivacaine	968.9	E855.2	E938.9	E950.4	E962.0	E980.4
infiltration (subcutaneous)	968.5	E855.2	E938.5	E950.4	E962.0	E980.4
nerve block (peripheral) (plexus)	968.6	E855.2	E938.6	E950.4	E962.0	E980.4
topical (surface)	968.5	E855.2	E938.5	E950.4	E962.0	E980.4
Meprednisone	962.0	E858.0	E932.0	E950.4	E962.0	E980.4
Meprobam	969.5	E853.8	E939.5	E950.3	E962.0	E980.3
Meprobamate	969.5	E853.8	E939.5	E950.3	E962.0	E980.3
Mepyramine (maleate)	963.0	E858.1	E933.0	E950.4	E962.0	E980.4
Meralluride	974.0	E858.5	E944.0	E950.4	E962.0	E980.4
Merbaphen	974.0	E858.5	E944.0	E950.4	E962.0	E980.4
Merbromin	976.0	E858.7	E946.0	E950.4	E962.0	E980.4
Mercaptomerin	974.0	E858.5	E944.0	E950.4	E962.0	E980.4
Mercaptopurine	963.1	E858.1	E933.1	E950.4	E962.0	E980.4
Mercumatilin	974.0	E858.5	E944.0	E950.4	E962.0	E980.4
Mercuramide	974.0	E858.5	E944.0	E950.4	E962.0	E980.4
Mercuranin	976.0	E858.7	E946.0	E950.4	E962.0	E980.4
Mercurochrome	976.0	E858.7	E946.0	E950.4	E962.0	E980.4
Mercury, mercuric, mercurous (compounds) (cyanide) (fumes) (nonmedicinal) (vapor) NEC	985.0	E866.1	—	E950.9	E962.1	E980.9
ammoniated	976.0	E858.7	E946.0	E950.4	E962.0	E980.4
anti-infective	961.2	E857	E931.2	E950.4	E962.0	E980.4
topical	976.0	E858.7	E946.0	E950.4	E962.0	E980.4
chloride (antiseptic) NEC	976.0	E858.7	E946.0	E950.4	E962.0	E980.4
fungicide	985.0	E863.6	—	E950.6	E962.1	E980.7
diuretic compounds	974.0	E858.5	E944.0	E950.4	E962.0	E980.4
fungicide	985.0	E863.6	—	E950.6	E962.1	E980.7
organic (fungicide)	985.0	E863.6	—	E950.6	E962.1	E980.7
Merethoxylline	974.0	E858.5	E944.0	E950.4	E962.0	E980.4
Mersalyl	974.0	E858.5	E944.0	E950.4	E962.0	E980.4
Merthiolate (topical)	976.0	E858.7	E946.0	E950.4	E962.0	E980.4
ophthalmic preparation	976.5	E858.7	E946.5	E950.4	E962.0	E980.4
Meruvax	979.4	E858.8	E949.4	E950.4	E962.0	E980.4
Mescal buttons	969.6	E854.1	E939.6	E950.3	E962.0	E980.3
Mescaline (salts)	969.6	E854.1	E939.6	E950.3	E962.0	E980.3
Mesoridazine besylate	969.1	E853.0	E939.1	E950.3	E962.0	E980.3
Mestanolone	962.1	E858.0	E932.1	E950.4	E962.0	E980.4
Mestranol	962.2	E858.0	E932.2	E950.4	E962.0	E980.4
Metacresylacetate	976.0	E858.7	E946.0	E950.4	E962.0	E980.4
Metaldehyde (snail killer) NEC	989.4	E863.4	—	E950.6	E962.1	E980.7
Metals (heavy) (nonmedicinal) NEC	985.9	E866.4	—	E950.9	E962.1	E980.9
dust, fumes, or vapor NEC	985.9	E866.4	—	E950.9	E962.1	E980.9
light NEC	985.9	E866.4	—	E950.9	E962.1	E980.9

Nontherapeutic use substance

🚾 Subterms under main terms may continue to next column or page

	Poisoning	Accident	Therapeutic Use	Suicide Attempt	Assault	Undetermined
External Cause (E-Code)						

Metals (heavy) (nonmedicinal)
— continued
light — continued

	Poisoning	Accident	Therapeutic Use	Suicide Attempt	Assault	Undetermined
dust, fumes, or vapor NEC	985.9	E866.4	—	E950.9	E962.1	E980.9
pesticides (dust) (vapor)	985.9	E863.4	—	E950.6	E962.1	E980.7
Metamucil	973.3	E858.4	E943.3	E950.4	E962.0	E980.4
Metaphen	976.0	E858.7	E946.0	E950.4	E962.0	E980.4
Metaproterenol	975.1	E858.6	E945.1	E950.4	E962.0	E980.4
Metaraminol	972.8	E858.3	E942.8	E950.4	E962.0	E980.4
Metaxalone	968.0	E855.1	E938.0	E950.4	E962.0	E980.4
Metformin	962.3	E858.0	E932.3	E950.4	E962.0	E980.4
Methacycline	960.4	E856	E930.4	E950.4	E962.0	E980.4
Methadone	965.02	E850.1	E935.1	E950.0	E962.0	E980.0
Methallenestril	962.2	E858.0	E932.2	E950.4	E962.0	E980.4
Methamphetamine	969.72 ▲	E854.2	E939.7	E950.3	E962.0	E980.3
Methandienone	962.1	E858.0	E932.1	E950.4	E962.0	E980.4
Methandriol	962.1	E858.0	E932.1	E950.4	E962.0	E980.4
Methandrostenolone	962.1	E858.0	E932.1	E950.4	E962.0	E980.4
Methane gas	987.1	E869.8	—	E952.8	E962.2	E982.8
Methanol	980.1	E860.2	—	E950.9	E962.1	E980.9
vapor	987.8	E869.8	—	E952.8	E962.2	E982.8
Methantheline	971.1	E855.4	E941.1	E950.4	E962.0	E980.4
Methaphenilene	963.0	E858.1	E933.0	E950.4	E962.0	E980.4
Methapyrilene	963.0	E858.1	E933.0	E950.4	E962.0	E980.4
Methaqualone (compounds)	967.4	E852.3	E937.4	E950.2	E962.0	E980.2
Metharbital, metharbitone	967.0	E851	E937.0	E950.1	E962.0	E980.1
Methazolamide	974.2	E858.5	E944.2	E950.4	E962.0	E980.4
Methdilazine	963.0	E858.1	E933.0	E950.4	E962.0	E980.4
Methedrine	969.72 ▲	E854.2	E939.7	E950.3	E962.0	E980.3
Methenamine (mandelate)	961.9	E857	E931.9	E950.4	E962.0	E980.4
Methenolone	962.1	E858.0	E932.1	E950.4	E962.0	E980.4
Methergine	975.0	E858.6	E945.0	E950.4	E962.0	E980.4
Methiacil	962.8	E858.0	E932.8	E950.4	E962.0	E980.4
Methicillin (sodium)	960.0	E856	E930.0	E950.4	E962.0	E980.4
Methimazole	962.8	E858.0	E932.8	E950.4	E962.0	E980.4
Methionine	977.1	E858.8	E947.1	E950.4	E962.0	E980.4
Methisazone	961.7	E857	E931.7	E950.4	E962.0	E980.4
Methitural	967.0	E851	E937.0	E950.1	E962.0	E980.1
Methixene	971.1	E855.4	E941.1	E950.4	E962.0	E980.4
Methobarbital, methobarbitone	967.0	E851	E937.0	E950.1	E962.0	E980.1
Methocarbamol	968.0	E855.1	E938.0	E950.4	E962.0	E980.4
Methohexital, methohexitone (sodium)	968.3	E855.1	E938.3	E950.4	E962.0	E980.4
Methoin	966.1	E855.0	E936.1	E950.4	E962.0	E980.4
Methopholine	965.7	E850.7	E935.7	E950.0	E962.0	E980.0
Methorate	975.4	E858.6	E945.4	E950.4	E962.0	E980.4
Methoserpidine	972.6	E858.3	E942.6	E950.4	E962.0	E980.4
Methotrexate	963.1	E858.1	E933.1	E950.4	E962.0	E980.4
Methotrimeprazine	967.8	E852.8	E937.8	E950.2	E962.0	E980.2
Methoxa-Dome	976.3	E858.7	E946.3	E950.4	E962.0	E980.4
Methoxamine	971.2	E855.5	E941.2	E950.4	E962.0	E980.4
Methoxsalen	976.3	E858.7	E946.3	E950.4	E962.0	E980.4
Methoxybenzyl penicillin	960.0	E856	E930.0	E950.4	E962.0	E980.4
Methoxychlor	989.2	E863.0	—	E950.6	E962.1	E980.7
Methoxyflurane	968.2	E855.1	E938.2	E950.4	E962.0	E980.4
Methoxyphenamine	971.2	E855.5	E941.2	E950.4	E962.0	E980.4
Methoxypromazine	969.1	E853.0	E939.1	E950.3	E962.0	E980.3
Methoxypsoralen	976.3	E858.7	E946.3	E950.4	E962.0	E980.4
Methscopolamine (bromide)	971.1	E855.4	E941.1	E950.4	E962.0	E980.4
Methsuximide	966.2	E855.0	E936.2	E950.4	E962.0	E980.4
Methyclothiazide	974.3	E858.5	E944.3	E950.4	E962.0	E980.4
Methyl						
acetate	982.8	E862.4	—	E950.9	E962.1	E980.9
acetone	982.8	E862.4	—	E950.9	E962.1	E980.9
alcohol	980.1	E860.2	—	E950.9	E962.1	E980.9
amphetamine	969.72 ▲	E854.2	E939.7	E950.3	E962.0	E980.3
androstanolone	962.1	E858.0	E932.1	E950.4	E962.0	E980.4
atropine	971.1	E855.4	E941.1	E950.4	E962.0	E980.4
benzene	982.0	E862.4	—	E950.9	E962.1	E980.9
bromide (gas)	987.8	E869.8	—	E952.8	E962.2	E982.8
fumigant	987.8	E863.8	—	E950.6	E962.2	E980.7
butanol	980.8	E860.8	—	E950.9	E962.1	E980.9
carbinol	980.1	E860.2	—	E950.9	E962.1	E980.9
cellosolve	982.8	E862.4	—	E950.9	E962.1	E980.9
cellulose	973.3	E858.4	E943.3	E950.4	E962.0	E980.4
chloride (gas)	987.8	E869.8	—	E952.8	E962.2	E982.8
cyclohexane	982.8	E862.4	—	E950.9	E962.1	E980.9

	Poisoning	Accident	Therapeutic Use	Suicide Attempt	Assault	Undetermined
External Cause (E-Code)						

Methyl — continued

	Poisoning	Accident	Therapeutic Use	Suicide Attempt	Assault	Undetermined
cyclohexanone	982.8	E862.4	—	E950.9	E962.1	E980.9
dihydromorphinone	965.09	E850.2	E935.2	E950.0	E962.0	E980.0
ergometrine	975.0	E858.6	E945.0	E950.4	E962.0	E980.4
ergonovine	975.0	E858.6	E945.0	E950.4	E962.0	E980.4
ethyl ketone	982.8	E862.4	—	E950.9	E962.1	E980.9
hydrazine	983.9	E864.3	—	E950.7	E962.1	E980.6
isobutyl ketone	982.8	E862.4	—	E950.9	E962.1	E980.9
morphine NEC	965.09	E850.2	E935.2	E950.0	E962.0	E980.0
parafynol	967.8	E852.8	E937.8	E950.2	E962.0	E980.2
parathion	989.3	E863.1	—	E950.6	E962.1	E980.7
pentynol NEC	967.8	E852.8	E937.8	E950.2	E962.0	E980.2
peridol	969.2	E853.1	E939.2	E950.3	E962.0	E980.3
phenidate	969.73 ▲	E854.2	E939.7	E950.3	E962.0	E980.3
prednisolone	962.0	E858.0	E932.0	E950.4	E962.0	E980.4
ENT agent	976.6	E858.7	E946.6	E950.4	E962.0	E980.4
ophthalmic preparation	976.5	E858.7	E946.5	E950.4	E962.0	E980.4
topical NEC	976.0	E858.7	E946.0	E950.4	E962.0	E980.4
propylcarbinol	980.8	E860.8	—	E950.9	E962.1	E980.9
rosaniline NEC	976.0	E858.7	E946.0	E950.4	E962.0	E980.4
salicylate NEC	976.3	E858.7	E946.3	E950.4	E962.0	E980.4
sulfate (fumes)	987.8	E869.8	—	E952.8	E962.2	E982.8
liquid	983.9	E864.3	—	E950.7	E962.1	E980.6
sulfonal	967.8	E852.8	E937.8	E950.2	E962.0	E980.2
testosterone	962.1	E858.0	E932.1	E950.4	E962.0	E980.4
thiouracil	962.8	E858.0	E932.8	E950.4	E962.0	E980.4
Methylated spirit	980.0	E860.1	—	E950.9	E962.1	E980.9
Methyldopa	972.6	E858.3	E942.6	E950.4	E962.0	E980.4
Methylene						
blue	961.9	E857	E931.9	E950.4	E962.0	E980.4
chloride or dichloride (solvent) NEC	982.3	E862.4	—	E950.9	E962.1	E980.9
Methylhexabital	967.0	E851	E937.0	E950.1	E962.0	E980.1
Methylparaben (ophthalmic)	976.5	E858.7	E946.5	E950.4	E962.0	E980.4
Methyprylon	967.5	E852.4	E937.5	E950.2	E962.0	E980.2
Methysergide	971.3	E855.6	E941.3	E950.4	E962.0	E980.4
Metoclopramide	963.0	E858.1	E933.0	E950.4	E962.0	E980.4
Metofoline	965.7	E850.7	E935.7	E950.0	E962.0	E980.0
Metopon	965.09	E850.2	E935.2	E950.0	E962.0	E980.0
Metronidazole	961.5	E857	E931.5	E950.4	E962.0	E980.4
Metycaine	968.9	E855.2	E938.9	E950.4	E962.0	E980.4
infiltration (subcutaneous)	968.5	E855.2	E938.5	E950.4	E962.0	E980.4
nerve block (peripheral) (plexus)	968.6	E855.2	E938.6	E950.4	E962.0	E980.4
topical (surface)	968.5	E855.2	E938.5	E950.4	E962.0	E980.4
Metyrapone	977.8	E858.8	E947.8	E950.4	E962.0	E980.4
Mevinphos	989.3	E863.1	—	E950.6	E962.1	E980.7
Mezereon (berries)	988.2	E865.3	—	E950.9	E962.1	E980.9
Micatin	976.0	E858.7	E946.0	E950.4	E962.0	E980.4
Miconazole	976.0	E858.7	E946.0	E950.4	E962.0	E980.4
Midol	965.1	E850.3	E935.3	E950.0	E962.0	E980.0
Mifepristone	962.9	E858.0	E932.9	E950.4	E962.0	E980.4
Milk of magnesia	973.0	E858.4	E943.0	E950.4	E962.0	E980.4
Millipede (tropical) (venomous)	989.5	E905.4	—	E950.9	E962.1	E980.9
Miltown	969.5	E853.8	E939.5	E950.3	E962.0	E980.3
Mineral						
oil (medicinal)	973.2	E858.4	E943.2	E950.4	E962.0	E980.4
nonmedicinal	981	E862.1	—	E950.9	E962.1	E980.9
topical	976.3	E858.7	E946.3	E950.4	E962.0	E980.4
salts NEC	974.6	E858.5	E944.6	E950.4	E962.0	E980.4
spirits	981	E862.0	—	E950.9	E962.1	E980.9
Minocycline	960.4	E856	E930.4	E950.4	E962.0	E980.4
Mithramycin (antineoplastic)	960.7	E856	E930.7	E950.4	E962.0	E980.4
Mitobronitol	963.1	E858.1	E933.1	E950.4	E962.0	E980.4
Mitomycin (antineoplastic)	960.7	E856	E930.7	E950.4	E962.0	E980.4
Mitotane	963.1	E858.1	E933.1	E950.4	E962.0	E980.4
Moderil	972.6	E858.3	E942.6	E950.4	E962.0	E980.4
Mogadon — see Nitrazepam						
Molindone	969.3	E853.8	E939.3	E950.3	E962.0	E980.3
Monistat	976.0	E858.7	E946.0	E950.4	E962.0	E980.4
Monkshood	988.2	E865.4	—	E950.9	E962.1	E980.9
Monoamine oxidase inhibitors	969.01 ▲	E854.0	E939.0	E950.3	E962.0	E980.3
Monochlorobenzene	982.0	E862.4	—	E950.9	E962.1	E980.9
Monosodium glutamate	989.89	E866.8	—	E950.9	E962.1	E980.9
Monoxide, carbon — see Carbon, monoxide						
Moperone	969.2	E853.1	E939.2	E950.3	E962.0	E980.3
Morning glory seeds	969.6	E854.1	E939.6	E950.3	E962.0	E980.3

Nontherapeutic use substance

▽ Subterms under main terms may continue to next column or page

▶◀ Revised Text   ● New Line   ▲ Revised Code

	Poisoning	Accident	Therapeutic Use	Suicide Attempt	Assault	Undetermined
Moroxydine						
(hydrochloride)	961.7	E857	E931.7	E950.4	E962.0	E980.4
Morphazinamide	961.8	E857	E931.8	E950.4	E962.0	E980.4
Morphinans	965.09	E850.2	E935.2	E950.0	E962.0	E980.0
Morphine NEC	965.09	E850.2	E935.2	E950.0	E962.0	E980.0
antagonists	970.1	E854.3	E940.1	E950.4	E962.0	E980.4
Morpholinylethylmorphine	965.09	E850.2	E935.2	E950.0	E962.0	E980.0
Morrhuate sodium	972.7	E858.3	E942.7	E950.4	E962.0	E980.4
Moth balls — *see also*						
Pesticides	989.4	E863.4	—	E950.6	E962.1	E980.7
naphthalene	983.0	E863.4	—	E950.7	E962.1	E980.6
Motor exhaust gas — *see*						
Carbon, monoxide, exhaust gas						
Mouth wash	976.6	E858.7	E946.6	E950.4	E962.0	E980.4
Mucolytic agent	975.5	E858.6	E945.5	E950.4	E962.0	E980.4
Mucomyst	975.5	E858.6	E945.5	E950.4	E962.0	E980.4
Mucous membrane agents						
(external)	976.9	E858.7	E946.9	E950.4	E962.0	E980.4
specified NEC	976.8	E858.7	E946.8	E950.4	E962.0	E980.4
Mumps						
immune globulin (human)	964.6	E858.2	E934.6	E950.4	E962.0	E980.4
skin test antigen	977.8	E858.8	E947.8	E950.4	E962.0	E980.4
vaccine	979.6	E858.8	E949.6	E950.4	E962.0	E980.4
Mumpsvax	979.6	E858.8	E949.6	E950.4	E962.0	E980.4
Muriatic acid — *see*						
Hydrochloric acid						
Muscarine	971.0	E855.3	E941.0	E950.4	E962.0	E980.4
Muscle affecting agents						
NEC	975.3	E858.6	E945.3	E950.4	E962.0	E980.4
oxytocic	975.0	E858.6	E945.0	E950.4	E962.0	E980.4
relaxants	975.3	E858.6	E945.3	E950.4	E962.0	E980.4
central nervous system	968.0	E855.1	E938.0	E950.4	E962.0	E980.4
skeletal	975.2	E858.6	E945.2	E950.4	E962.0	E980.4
smooth	975.1	E858.6	E945.1	E950.4	E962.0	E980.4
Mushrooms, noxious	988.1	E865.5	—	E950.9	E962.1	E980.9
Mussel, noxious	988.0	E865.1	—	E950.9	E962.1	E980.9
Mustard (emetic)	973.6	E858.4	E943.6	E950.4	E962.0	E980.4
gas	987.8	E869.8	—	E952.8	E962.2	E982.8
nitrogen	963.1	E858.1	E933.1	E950.4	E962.0	E980.4
Mustine	963.1	E858.1	E933.1	E950.4	E962.0	E980.4
M-vac	979.4	E858.8	E949.4	E950.4	E962.0	E980.4
Mycifradin	960.8	E856	E930.8	E950.4	E962.0	E980.4
topical	976.0	E858.7	E946.0	E950.4	E962.0	E980.4
Mycitracin	960.8	E856	E930.8	E950.4	E962.0	E980.4
ophthalmic preparation	976.5	E858.7	E946.5	E950.4	E962.0	E980.4
Mycostatin	960.1	E856	E930.1	E950.4	E962.0	E980.4
topical	976.0	E858.7	E946.0	E950.4	E962.0	E980.4
Mydriacyl	971.1	E855.4	E941.1	E950.4	E962.0	E980.4
Myelobromal	963.1	E858.1	E933.1	E950.4	E962.0	E980.4
Myleran	963.1	E858.1	E933.1	E950.4	E962.0	E980.4
Myochrysin(e)	965.69	E850.6	E935.6	E950.0	E962.0	E980.0
Myoneural blocking						
agents	975.2	E858.6	E945.2	E950.4	E962.0	E980.4
Myristica fragrans	988.2	E865.3	—	E950.9	E962.1	E980.9
Myristicin	988.2	E865.3	—	E950.9	E962.1	E980.9
Mysoline	966.3	E855.0	E936.3	E950.4	E962.0	E980.4
Nafcillin (sodium)	960.0	E856	E930.0	E950.4	E962.0	E980.4
Nail polish remover	982.8	E862.4	—	E950.9	E962.1	E908.9
Nalidixic acid	961.9	E857	E931.9	E950.4	E962.0	E980.4
Nalorphine	970.1	E854.3	E940.1	E950.4	E962.0	E980.4
Naloxone	970.1	E854.3	E940.1	E950.4	E962.0	E980.4
Nandrolone (decanoate)						
(phenproprioate)	962.1	E858.0	E932.1	E950.4	E962.0	E980.4
Naphazoline	971.2	E855.5	E941.2	E950.4	E962.0	E980.4
Naphtha (painter's)						
(petroleum)	981	E862.0	—	E950.9	E962.1	E980.9
solvent	981	E862.0	—	E950.9	E962.1	E980.9
vapor	987.1	E869.8	—	E952.8	E962.2	E982.8
Naphthalene (chlorinated)	983.0	E864.0	—	E950.7	E962.1	E980.6
insecticide or moth						
repellent	983.0	E863.4	—	E950.7	E962.1	E980.6
vapor	987.8	E869.8	—	E952.8	E962.2	E982.8
Naphthol	983.0	E864.0	—	E950.7	E962.1	E980.6
Naphthylamine	983.0	E864.0	—	E950.7	E962.1	E980.6
Naprosyn — *see* Naproxen						
Naproxen	965.61	E850.6	E935.6	E950.0	E962.0	E980.0
Narcotic (drug)	967.9	E852.9	E937.9	E950.2	E962.0	E980.2
analgesic NEC	965.8	E850.8	E935.8	E950.0	E962.0	E980.0
antagonist	970.1	E854.3	E940.1	E950.4	E962.0	E980.4
specified NEC	967.8	E852.8	E937.8	E950.2	E962.0	E980.2
Narcotine	975.4	E858.6	E945.4	E950.4	E962.0	E980.4
Nardil	969.01 ▲	E854.0	E939.0	E950.3	E962.0	E980.3
Natrium cyanide — *see*						
Cyanide(s)						
Natural						
blood (product)	964.7	E858.2	E934.7	E950.4	E962.0	E980.4
gas (piped)	987.1	E867	—	E951.0	E962.2	E981.0
incomplete combustion	986	E867	—	E951.0	E962.2	E981.0
Nealbarbital,						
nealbarbitone	967.0	E851	E937.0	E950.1	E962.0	E980.1
Nectadon	975.4	E858.6	E945.4	E950.4	E962.0	E980.4
Nematocyst (sting)	989.5	E905.6	—	E950.9	E962.1	E980.9
Nembutal	967.0	E851	E937.0	E950.1	E962.0	E980.1
Neoarsphenamine	961.1	E857	E931.1	E950.4	E962.0	E980.4
Neocinchophen	974.7	E858.5	E944.7	E950.4	E962.0	E980.4
Neomycin	960.8	E856	E930.8	E950.4	E962.0	E980.4
ENT agent	976.6	E858.7	E946.6	E950.4	E962.0	E980.4
ophthalmic preparation	976.5	E858.7	E946.5	E950.4	E962.0	E980.4
topical NEC	976.0	E858.7	E946.0	E950.4	E962.0	E980.4
Neonal	967.0	E851	E937.0	E950.1	E962.0	E980.1
Neoprontosil	961.0	E857	E931.0	E950.4	E962.0	E980.4
Neosalvarsan	961.1	E857	E931.1	E950.4	E962.0	E980.4
Neosilversalvarsan	961.1	E857	E931.1	E950.4	E962.0	E980.4
Neosporin	960.8	E856	E930.8	E950.4	E962.0	E980.4
ENT agent	976.6	E858.7	E946.6	E950.4	E962.0	E980.4
opthalmic preparation	976.5	E858.7	E946.5	E950.4	E962.0	E980.4
topical NEC	976.0	E858.7	E946.0	E950.4	E962.0	E980.4
Neostigmine	971.0	E855.3	E941.0	E950.4	E962.0	E980.4
Neraval	967.0	E851	E937.0	E950.1	E962.0	E980.1
Neravan	967.0	E851	E937.0	E950.1	E962.0	E980.1
Nerium oleander	988.2	E865.4	—	E950.9	E962.1	E980.9
Nerve gases (war)	987.9	E869.9	—	E952.9	E962.2	E982.9
Nesacaine	968.9	E855.2	E938.9	E950.4	E962.0	E980.4
infiltration (subcutaneous)	968.5	E855.2	E938.5	E950.4	E962.0	E980.4
nerve block (peripheral)						
(plexus)	968.6	E855.2	E938.6	E950.4	E962.0	E980.4
Neurobarb	967.0	E851	E937.0	E950.1	E962.0	E980.1
Neuroleptics NEC	969.3	E853.8	E939.3	E950.3	E962.0	E980.3
Neuroprotective agent	977.8	E858.8	E947.8	E950.4	E962.0	E980.4
Neutral spirits	980.0	E860.1	—	E950.9	E962.1	E980.9
beverage	980.0	E860.0	—	E950.9	E962.1	E980.9
Niacin, niacinamide	972.2	E858.3	E942.2	E950.4	E962.0	E980.4
Nialamide	969.01 ▲	E854.0	E939.0	E950.3	E962.0	E980.3
Nickle (carbonyl) (compounds)						
(fumes) (tetracarbonyl)						
(vapor)	985.8	E866.4	—	E950.9	E962.1	E980.9
Niclosamide	961.6	E857	E931.6	E950.4	E962.0	E980.4
Nicomorphine	965.09	E850.2	E935.2	E950.0	E962.0	E980.0
Nicotinamide	972.2	E858.3	E942.2	E950.4	E962.0	E980.4
Nicotine (insecticide) (spray)						
(sulfate) NEC	989.4	E863.4	—	E950.6	E962.1	E980.7
not insecticide	989.89	E866.8	—	E950.9	E962.1	E980.9
Nicotinic acid (derivatives)	972.2	E858.3	E942.2	E950.4	E962.0	E980.4
Nicotinyl alcohol	972.2	E858.3	E942.2	E950.4	E962.0	E980.4
Nicoumalone	964.2	E858.2	E934.2	E950.4	E962.0	E980.4
Nifenazone	965.5	E850.5	E935.5	E950.0	E962.0	E980.0
Nifuraldezone	961.9	E857	E931.9	E950.4	E962.0	E980.4
Nightshade (deadly)	988.2	E865.4	—	E950.9	E962.1	E980.9
Nikethamide	970.0	E854.3	E940.0	E950.4	E962.0	E980.4
Nilstat	960.1	E856	E930.1	E950.4	E962.0	E980.4
topical	976.0	E858.7	E946.0	E950.4	E962.0	E980.4
Nimodipine	977.8	E858.8	E947.8	E950.4	E962.0	E980.4
Niridazole	961.6	E857	E931.6	E950.4	E962.0	E980.4
Nisentil	965.09	E850.2	E935.2	E950.0	E962.0	E980.0
Nitrates	972.4	E858.3	E942.4	E950.4	E962.0	E980.4
Nitrazepam	969.4	E853.2	E939.4	E950.3	E962.0	E980.3
Nitric						
acid (liquid)	983.1	E864.1	—	E950.7	E962.1	E980.6
vapor	987.8	E869.8	—	E952.8	E962.2	E982.8
oxide (gas)	987.2	E869.0	—	E952.8	E962.2	E982.8
Nitrite, amyl (medicinal)						
(vapor)	972.4	E858.3	E942.4	E950.4	E962.0	E980.4
Nitroaniline	983.0	E864.0	—	E950.7	E962.1	E980.6
vapor	987.8	E869.8	—	E952.8	E962.2	E982.8
Nitrobenzene,						
nitrobenzol	983.0	E864.0	—	E950.7	E962.1	E980.6
vapor	987.8	E869.8	—	E952.8	E962.2	E982.8
Nitrocellulose	976.3	E858.7	E946.3	E950.4	E962.0	E980.4
Nitrofuran derivatives	961.9	E857	E931.9	E950.4	E962.0	E980.4
Nitrofurantoin	961.9	E857	E931.9	E950.4	E962.0	E980.4
Nitrofurazone	976.0	E858.7	E946.0	E950.4	E962.0	E980.4
Nitrogen (dioxide) (gas)						
(oxide)	987.2	E869.0	—	E952.8	E962.2	E982.8
mustard (antineoplastic)	963.1	E858.1	E933.1	E950.4	E962.0	E980.4

Nontherapeutic use substance

	Poisoning	Accident	Therapeutic Use	Suicide Attempt	Assault	Undetermined
Nitrogen — *continued*						
nonmedicinal	989.89	E866.8	—	E950.9	E962.1	E980.9
fumes	987.8	E869.8	—	E952.8	E962.2	E982.8
Nitroglycerin, nitroglycerol						
(medicinal)	972.4	E858.3	E942.4	E950.4	E962.0	E980.4
Nitrohydrochloric acid	983.1	E864.1	—	E950.7	E962.1	E980.6
Nitromersol	976.0	E858.7	E946.0	E950.4	E962.0	E980.4
Nitronaphthalene	983.0	E864.0	—	E950.7	E962.2	E980.6
Nitrophenol	983.0	E864.0	—	E950.7	E962.2	E980.6
Nitrothiazol	961.6	E857	E931.6	E950.4	E962.0	E980.4
Nitrotoluene, nitrotoluol	983.0	E864.0	—	E950.7	E962.1	E980.6
vapor	987.8	E869.8	—	E952.8	E962.2	E982.8
Nitrous	968.2	E855.1	E938.2	E950.4	E962.0	E980.4
acid (liquid)	983.1	E864.1	—	E950.7	E962.1	E980.6
fumes	987.2	E869.0	—	E952.8	E962.2	E982.8
oxide (anesthetic) NEC	968.2	E855.1	E938.2	E950.4	E962.0	E980.4
Nitrozone	976.0	E858.7	E946.0	E950.4	E962.0	E980.4
Noctec	967.1	E852.0	E937.1	E950.2	E962.0	E980.2
Noludar	967.5	E852.4	E937.5	E950.2	E962.0	E980.2
Noptil	967.0	E851	E937.0	E950.1	E962.0	E980.1
Noradrenalin	971.2	E855.5	E941.2	E950.4	E962.0	E980.4
Noramidopyrine	965.5	E850.5	E935.5	E950.0	E962.0	E980.0
Norepinephrine	971.2	E855.5	E941.2	E950.4	E962.0	E980.4
Norethandrolone	962.1	E858.0	E932.1	E950.4	E962.0	E980.4
Norethindrone	962.2	E858.0	E932.2	E950.4	E962.0	E980.4
Norethisterone	962.2	E858.0	E932.2	E950.4	E962.0	E980.4
Norethynodrel	962.2	E858.0	E932.2	E950.4	E962.0	E980.4
Norlestrin	962.2	E858.0	E932.2	E950.4	E962.0	E980.4
Norlutin	962.2	E858.0	E932.2	E950.4	E962.0	E980.4
Normison — *see* Benzodiazepines						
Normorphine	965.09	E850.2	E935.2	E950.0	E962.0	E980.0
Nortriptyline •	969.05 ▲	E854.0	E939.0	E950.3	E962.0	E980.3
Noscapine	975.4	E858.6	E945.4	E950.4	E962.0	E980.4
Nose preparations	976.6	E858.7	E946.6	E950.4	E962.0	E980.4
Novobiocin	960.8	E856	E930.8	E950.4	E962.0	E980.4
Novocain (infiltration)						
(topical)	968.5	E855.2	E938.5	E950.4	E962.0	E980.4
nerve block (peripheral) (plexus)	968.6	E855.2	E938.6	E950.4	E962.0	E980.4
spinal	968.7	E855.2	E938.7	E950.4	E962.0	E980.4
Noxythiolin	961.9	E857	E931.9	E950.4	E962.0	E980.4
NPH Iletin (insulin)	962.3	E858.0	E932.3	E950.4	E962.0	E980.4
Numorphan	965.09	E850.2	E935.2	E950.0	E962.0	E980.0
Nunol	967.0	E851	E937.0	E950.1	E962.0	E980.1
Nupercaine (spinal						
anesthetic)	968.7	E855.2	E938.7	E950.4	E962.0	E980.4
topical (surface)	968.5	E855.2	E938.5	E950.4	E962.0	E980.4
Nutmeg oil (liniment)	976.3	E858.7	E946.3	E950.4	E962.0	E980.4
Nux vomica	989.1	E863.7	—	E950.6	E962.1	E980.7
Nydrazid	961.8	E857	E931.8	E950.4	E962.0	E980.4
Nylidrin	971.2	E855.5	E941.2	E950.4	E962.0	E980.4
Nystatin	960.1	E856	E930.1	E950.4	E962.0	E980.4
topical	976.0	E858.7	E946.0	E950.4	E962.0	E980.4
Nytol	963.0	E858.1	E933.0	E950.4	E962.0	E980.4
Oblivion	967.8	E852.8	E937.8	E950.2	E962.0	E980.2
Octyl nitrite	972.4	E858.3	E942.4	E950.4	E962.0	E980.4
Oestradiol (cypionate)						
(dipropionate) (valerate)	962.2	E858.0	E932.2	E950.4	E962.0	E980.4
Oestriol	962.2	E858.0	E932.2	E950.4	E962.0	E980.4
Oestrone	962.2	E858.0	E932.2	E950.4	E962.0	E980.4
Oil (of) NEC	989.89	E866.8	—	E950.9	E962.1	E980.9
bitter almond	989.0	E866.8	—	E950.9	E962.1	E980.9
camphor	976.1	E858.7	E946.1	E950.4	E962.0	E980.4
colors	989.89	E861.6	—	E950.9	E962.1	E980.9
fumes	987.8	E869.8	—	E952.8	E962.2	E982.8
lubricating	981	E862.2	—	E950.9	E962.1	E980.9
specified source, other — *see substance specified*						
vitriol (liquid)	983.1	E864.1	—	E950.7	E962.1	E980.6
fumes	987.8	E869.8	—	E952.8	E962.2	E982.8
wintergreen (bitter) NEC	976.3	E858.7	E946.3	E950.4	E962.0	E980.4
Ointments NEC	976.9	E858.7	E946.9	E950.4	E962.0	E980.4
Oleander	988.2	E865.4	—	E950.9	E962.1	E980.9
Oleandomycin	960.3	E856	E930.3	E950.4	E962.0	E980.4
Oleovitamin A	963.5	E858.1	E933.5	E950.4	E962.0	E980.4
Oleum ricini	973.1	E858.4	E943.1	E950.4	E962.0	E980.4
Olive oil (medicinal) NEC	973.2	E858.4	E943.2	E950.4	E962.0	E980.4
OMPA	989.3	E863.1	—	E950.6	E962.1	E980.7
Oncovin	963.1	E858.1	E933.1	E950.4	E962.0	E980.4
Ophthaine	968.5	E855.2	E938.5	E950.4	E962.0	E980.4
Ophthetic	968.5	E855.2	E938.5	E950.4	E962.0	E980.4

	Poisoning	Accident	Therapeutic Use	Suicide Attempt	Assault	Undetermined
Opiates, opioids, opium						
NEC	965.00	E850.2	E935.2	E950.0	E962.0	E980.0
antagonists	970.1	E854.3	E940.1	E950.4	E962.0	E980.4
Oracon	962.2	E858.0	E932.2	E950.4	E962.0	E980.4
Oragrafin	977.8	E858.8	E947.8	E950.4	E962.0	E980.4
Oral contraceptives	962.2	E858.0	E932.2	E950.4	E962.0	E980.4
Orciprenaline	975.1	E858.6	E945.1	E950.4	E962.0	E980.4
Organidin	975.5	E858.6	E945.5	E950.4	E962.0	E980.4
Organophosphates	989.3	E863.1	—	E950.6	E962.1	E980.7
Orimune	979.5	E858.8	E949.5	E950.4	E962.0	E980.4
Orinase	962.3	E858.0	E932.3	E950.4	E962.0	E980.4
Orphenadrine	966.4	E855.0	E936.4	E950.4	E962.0	E980.4
Ortal (sodium)	967.0	E851	E937.0	E950.1	E962.0	E980.1
Orthoboric acid	976.0	E858.7	E946.0	E950.4	E962.0	E980.4
ENT agent	976.6	E858.7	E946.6	E950.4	E962.0	E980.4
ophthalmic preparation	976.5	E858.7	E946.5	E950.4	E962.0	E980.4
Orthocaine	968.5	E855.2	E938.5	E950.4	E962.0	E980.4
Ortho-Novum	962.2	E858.0	E932.2	E950.4	E962.0	E980.4
Orthotolidine (reagent)	977.8	E858.8	E947.8	E950.4	E962.0	E980.4
Osmic acid (liquid)	983.1	E864.1	—	E950.7	E962.1	E980.6
fumes	987.8	E869.8	—	E952.8	E962.2	E982.8
Osmotic diuretics	974.4	E858.5	E944.4	E950.4	E962.0	E980.4
Ouabain	972.1	E858.3	E942.1	E950.4	E962.0	E980.4
Ovarian hormones (synthetic substitutes)	962.2	E858.0	E932.2	E950.4	E962.0	E980.4
Ovral	962.2	E858.0	E932.2	E950.4	E962.0	E980.4
Ovulation suppressants	962.2	E858.0	E932.2	E950.4	E962.0	E980.4
Ovulen	962.2	E858.0	E932.2	E950.4	E962.0	E980.4
Oxacillin (sodium)	960.0	E856	E930.0	E950.4	E962.0	E980.4
Oxalic acid	983.1	E864.1	—	E950.7	E962.1	E980.6
Oxanamide	969.5	E853.8	E939.5	E950.3	E962.0	E980.3
Oxandrolone	962.1	E858.0	E932.1	E950.4	E962.0	E980.4
Oxaprozin	965.61	E850.6	E935.6	E950.0	E962.0	E980.0
Oxazepam	969.4	E853.2	E939.4	E950.3	E962.0	E980.3
Oxazolidine derivatives	966.0	E855.0	E936.0	E950.4	E962.0	E980.4
Ox bile extract	973.4	E858.4	E943.4	E950.4	E962.0	E980.4
Oxedrine	971.2	E855.5	E941.2	E950.4	E962.0	E980.4
Oxeladin	975.4	E858.6	E945.4	E950.4	E962.0	E980.4
Oxethazaine NEC	968.5	E855.2	E938.5	E950.4	E962.0	E980.4
Oxidizing agents NEC	983.9	E864.3	—	E950.7	E962.1	E980.6
Oxolinic acid	961.3	E857	E931.3	E950.4	E962.0	E980.4
Oxophenarsine	961.1	E857	E931.1	E950.4	E962.0	E980.4
Oxsoralen	976.3	E858.7	E946.3	E950.4	E962.0	E980.4
Oxtriphylline	975.7	E858.6	E945.7	E950.4	E962.0	E980.4
Oxybuprocaine	968.5	E855.2	E938.5	E950.4	E962.0	E980.4
Oxybutynin	975.1	E858.6	E945.1	E950.4	E962.0	E980.4
Oxycodone	965.09	E850.2	E935.2	E950.0	E962.0	E980.0
Oxygen	987.8	E869.8	—	E952.8	E962.2	E982.8
Oxylone	976.0	E858.7	E946.0	E950.4	E962.0	E980.4
ophthalmic preparation	976.5	E858.7	E946.5	E950.4	E962.0	E980.4
Oxymesterone	962.1	E858.0	E932.1	E950.4	E962.0	E980.4
Oxymetazoline	971.2	E855.5	E941.2	E950.4	E962.0	E980.4
Oxymetholone	962.1	E858.0	E932.1	E950.4	E962.0	E980.4
Oxymorphone	965.09	E850.2	E935.2	E950.0	E962.0	E980.0
Oxypertine •	969.09 ▲	E854.0	E939.0	E950.3	E962.0	E980.3
Oxyphenbutazone	965.5	E850.5	E935.5	E950.0	E962.0	E980.0
Oxyphencyclimine	971.1	E855.4	E941.1	E950.4	E962.0	E980.4
Oxyphenisatin	973.1	E858.4	E943.1	E950.4	E962.0	E980.4
Oxyphenonium	971.1	E855.4	E941.1	E950.4	E962.0	E980.4
Oxyquinoline	961.3	E857	E931.3	E950.4	E962.0	E980.4
Oxytetracycline	960.4	E856	E930.4	E950.4	E962.0	E980.4
Oxytocics	975.0	E858.6	E945.0	E950.4	E962.0	E980.4
Oxytocin	975.0	E858.6	E945.0	E950.4	E962.0	E980.4
Ozone	987.8	E869.8	—	E952.8	E962.2	E982.8
PABA	976.3	E858.7	E946.3	E950.4	E962.0	E980.4
Packed red cells	964.7	E858.2	E934.7	E950.4	E962.0	E980.4
Paint NEC	989.89	E861.6	—	E950.9	E962.1	E980.9
cleaner	982.8	E862.9	—	E950.9	E962.1	E980.9
fumes NEC	987.8	E869.8	—	E952.8	E962.1	E982.8
lead (fumes)	984.0	E861.5	—	E950.9	E962.1	E980.9
solvent NEC	982.8	E862.9	—	E950.9	E962.1	E980.9
stripper	982.8	E862.9	—	E950.9	E962.1	E980.9
Palfium	965.09	E850.2	E935.2	E950.0	E962.0	E980.0
Palivizumab	979.9	E858.8	E949.6	E950.4	E962.0	E980.4
Paludrine	961.4	E857	E931.4	E950.4	E962.0	E980.4
PAM	977.2	E855.8	E947.2	E950.4	E962.0	E980.4
Pamaquine (naphthoate)	961.4	E857	E931.4	E950.4	E962.0	E980.4
Pamprin	965.1	E850.3	E935.3	E950.0	E962.0	E980.0
Panadol	965.4	E850.4	E935.4	E950.0	E962.0	E980.0
Pancreatic dornase (mucolytic)	963.4	E858.1	E933.4	E950.4	E962.0	E980.4
Pancreatin	973.4	E858.4	E943.4	E950.4	E962.0	E980.4

	Poisoning	Accident	Therapeutic Use	Suicide Attempt	Assault	Undetermined
Pancrelipase	973.4	E858.4	E943.4	E950.4	E962.0	E980.4
Pangamic acid	963.5	E858.1	E933.5	E950.4	E962.0	E980.4
Panthenol	963.5	E858.1	E933.5	E950.4	E962.0	E980.4
topical	976.8	E858.7	E946.8	E950.4	E962.0	E980.4
Pantopaque	977.8	E858.8	E947.8	E950.4	E962.0	E980.4
Pantopon	965.00	E850.2	E935.2	E950.0	E962.0	E980.0
Pantothenic acid	963.5	E858.1	E933.5	E950.4	E962.0	E980.4
Panwarfin	964.2	E858.2	E934.2	E950.4	E962.0	E980.4
Papain	973.4	E858.4	E943.4	E950.4	E962.0	E980.4
Papaverine	972.5	E858.3	E942.5	E950.4	E962.0	E980.4
Para-aminobenzoic acid	976.3	E858.7	E946.3	E950.4	E962.0	E980.4
Para-aminophenol derivatives	965.4	E850.4	E935.4	E950.0	E962.0	E980.0
Para-aminosalicylic acid (derivatives)	961.8	E857	E931.8	E950.4	E962.0	E980.4
Paracetaldehyde (medicinal)	967.2	E852.1	E937.2	E950.2	E962.0	E980.2
Paracetamol	965.4	E850.4	E935.4	E950.0	E962.0	E980.0
Paracodin	965.09	E850.2	E935.2	E950.0	E962.0	E980.0
Paradione	966.0	E855.0	E936.0	E950.4	E962.0	E980.4
Paraffin(s) (wax)	981	E862.3	—	E950.9	E962.1	E980.9
liquid (medicinal)	973.2	E858.4	E943.2	E950.4	E962.0	E980.4
nonmedicinal (oil)	981	E962.1		E950.9	E962.1	E980.9
Paraldehyde (medicinal)	967.2	E852.1	E937.2	E950.2	E962.0	E980.2
Paramethadione	966.0	E855.0	E936.0	E950.4	E962.0	E980.4
Paramethasone	962.0	E858.0	E932.0	E950.4	E962.0	E980.4
Paraquat	989.4	E863.5		E950.6	E962.1	E980.7
Parasympatholytics	971.1	E855.4	E941.1	E950.4	E962.0	E980.4
Parasympathomimetics	971.0	E855.3	E941.0	E950.4	E962.0	E980.4
Parathion	989.3	E863.1	—	E950.6	E962.1	E980.7
Parathormone	962.6	E858.0	E932.6	E950.4	E962.0	E980.4
Parathyroid (derivatives)	962.6	E858.0	E932.6	E950.4	E962.0	E980.4
Paratyphoid vaccine	978.1	E858.8	E948.1	E950.4	E962.0	E980.4
Paredrine	971.2	E855.5	E941.2	E950.4	E962.0	E980.4
Paregoric	965.00	E850.2	E935.2	E950.0	E962.0	E980.0
Pargyline	972.3	E858.3	E942.3	E950.4	E962.0	E980.4
Paris green	985.1	E866.3	—	E950.8	E962.1	E980.8
insecticide	985.1	E863.4		E950.8	E962.1	E980.8
Parnate	969.01 ▲	E854.0	E939.0	E950.3	E962.0	E980.3
Paromomycin	960.8	E856	E930.8	E950.4	E962.0	E980.4
Paroxypropione	963.1	E858.1	E933.1	E950.4	E962.0	E980.4
Parzone	965.09	E850.2	E935.2	E950.0	E962.0	E980.0
PAS	961.8	E857	E931.8	E950.4	E962.0	E980.4
PCBs	981	E862.3	—	E950.9	E962.1	E980.9
PCP (pentachlorophenol)	989.4	E863.6	—	E950.6	E962.1	E980.7
herbicide	989.4	E863.5	—	E950.6	E962.1	E980.7
insecticide	989.4	E863.4	—	E950.6	E962.1	E980.7
phencyclidine	968.3	E855.1	E938.3	E950.4	E962.0	E980.4
Peach kernel oil (emulsion)	973.2	E858.4	E943.2	E950.4	E962.0	E980.4
Peanut oil (emulsion) NEC	973.2	E858.4	E943.2	E950.4	E962.0	E980.4
topical	976.3	E858.7	E946.3	E950.4	E962.0	E980.4
Pearly Gates (morning glory seeds)	969.6	E854.1	E939.6	E950.3	E962.0	E980.3
Pecazine	969.1	E853.0	E939.1	E950.3	E962.0	E980.3
Pecilocin	960.1	E856	E930.1	E950.4	E962.0	E980.4
Pectin (with kaolin) NEC	973.5	E858.4	E943.5	E950.4	E962.0	E980.4
Pelletierine tannate	961.6	E857	E931.6	E950.4	E962.0	E980.4
Pemoline	969.79 ▲	E854.2	E939.7	E950.3	E962.0	E980.3
Pempidine	972.3	E858.3	E942.3	E950.4	E962.0	E980.4
Penamecillin	960.0	E856	E930.0	E950.4	E962.0	E980.4
Penethamate hydriodide	960.0	E856	E930.0	E950.4	E962.0	E980.4
Penicillamine	963.8	E858.1	E933.8	E950.4	E962.0	E980.4
Penicillin (any type)	960.0	E856	E930.0	E950.4	E962.0	E980.4
Penicillinase	963.4	E858.1	E933.4	E950.4	E962.0	E980.4
Pentachlorophenol (fungicide)	989.4	E863.6	—	E950.6	E962.1	E980.7
herbicide	989.4	E863.5	—	E950.6	E962.1	E980.7
insecticide	989.4	E863.4	—	E950.6	E962.1	E980.7
Pentaerythritol	972.4	E858.3	E942.4	E950.4	E962.0	E980.4
chloral	967.1	E852.0	E937.1	E950.2	E962.0	E980.2
tetranitrate NEC	972.4	E858.3	E942.4	E950.4	E962.0	E980.4
Pentagastrin	977.8	E858.8	E947.8	E950.4	E962.0	E980.4
Pentalin	982.3	E862.4	—	E950.9	E962.1	E980.9
Pentamethonium (bromide)	972.3	E858.3	E942.3	E950.4	E962.0	E980.4
Pentamidine	961.5	E857	E931.5	E950.4	E962.0	E980.4
Pentanol	980.8	E860.8	—	E950.9	E962.1	E980.9
Pentaquine	961.4	E857	E931.4	E950.4	E962.0	E980.4
Pentazocine	965.8	E850.8	E935.8	E950.0	E962.0	E980.0
Penthienate	971.1	E855.4	E941.1	E950.4	E962.0	E980.4
Pentobarbital, pentobarbitone (sodium)	967.0	E851	E937.0	E950.1	E962.0	E980.1
Pentolinium (tartrate)	972.3	E858.3	E942.3	E950.4	E962.0	E980.4
Pentothal	968.3	E855.1	E938.3	E950.4	E962.0	E980.4
Pentylenetetrazol	970.0	E854.3	E940.0	E950.4	E962.0	E980.4
Pentylsalicylamide	961.8	E857	E931.8	E950.4	E962.0	E980.4
Pepsin	973.4	E858.4	E943.4	E950.4	E962.0	E980.4
Peptavlon	977.8	E858.8	E947.8	E950.4	E962.0	E980.4
Percaine (spinal)	968.7	E855.2	E938.7	E950.4	E962.0	E980.4
topical (surface)	968.5	E855.2	E938.5	E950.4	E962.0	E980.4
Perchloroethylene (vapor)	982.3	E862.4	—	E950.9	E962.1	E980.9
medicinal	961.6	E857	E931.6	E950.4	E962.0	E980.4
Percodan	965.09	E850.2	E935.2	E950.0	E962.0	E980.0
Percogesic	965.09	E850.2	E935.2	E950.0	E962.0	E980.0
Percorten	962.0	E858.0	E932.0	E950.4	E962.0	E980.4
Pergonal	962.4	E858.0	E932.4	E950.4	E962.0	E980.4
Perhexiline	972.4	E858.3	E942.4	E950.4	E962.0	E980.4
Periactin	963.0	E858.1	E933.0	E950.4	E962.0	E980.4
Periclor	967.1	E852.0	E937.1	E950.2	E962.0	E980.2
Pericyazine	969.1	E853.0	E939.1	E950.3	E962.0	E980.3
Peritrate	972.4	E858.3	E942.4	E950.4	E962.0	E980.4
Permanganates NEC	983.9	E864.3		E950.7	E962.1	E980.6
potassium (topical)	976.0	E858.7	E946.0	E950.4	E962.0	E980.4
Pernocton	967.0	E851	E937.0	E950.1	E962.0	E980.1
Pernoston	967.0	E851	E937.0	E950.1	E962.0	E980.1
Peronin(e)	965.09	E850.2	E935.2	E950.0	E962.0	E980.0
Perphenazine	969.1	E853.0	E939.1	E950.3	E962.0	E980.3
Pertofrane	969.05 ▲	E854.0	E939.0	E950.3	E962.0	E980.3
Pertussis immune serum (human)	964.6	E858.2	E934.6	E950.4	E962.0	E980.4
vaccine (with diphtheria toxoid) (with tetanus toxoid)	978.6	E858.8	E948.6	E950.4	E962.0	E980.4
Peruvian balsam	976.8	E858.7	E946.8	E950.4	E962.0	E980.4
Pesticides (dust) (fumes) (vapor)	989.4	E863.4	—	E950.6	E962.1	E980.7
arsenic	985.1	E863.4	—	E950.8	E962.1	E980.8
chlorinated	989.2	E863.0	—	E950.6	E962.1	E980.7
cyanide	989.0	E863.4	—	E950.6	E962.1	E980.7
kerosene	981	E863.4	—	E950.6	E962.1	E980.7
mixture (of compounds)	989.4	E863.3	—	E950.6	E962.1	E980.7
naphthalene	983.0	E863.4	—	E950.7	E962.1	E980.6
organochlorine (compounds)	989.2	E863.0		E950.6	E962.1	E980.7
petroleum (distillate) (products) NEC	981	E863.4	—	E950.6	E962.1	E980.7
specified ingredient NEC	989.4	E863.4	—	E950.6	E962.1	E980.7
strychnine	989.1	E863.4	—	E950.6	E962.1	E980.7
thallium	985.8	E863.7	—	E950.6	E962.1	E980.7
Pethidine (hydrochloride)	965.09	E850.2	E935.2	E950.0	E962.0	E980.0
Petrichloral	967.1	E852.0	E937.1	E950.2	E962.0	E980.2
Petrol	981	E862.1		E950.9	E962.1	E980.9
vapor	987.1	E869.8		E952.8	E962.2	E982.8
Petrolatum (jelly) (ointment)	976.3	E858.7	E946.3	E950.4	E962.0	E980.4
hydrophilic	976.3	E858.7	E946.3	E950.4	E962.0	E980.4
liquid	973.2	E858.4	E943.2	E950.4	E962.0	E980.4
topical	976.3	E858.7	E946.3	E950.4	E962.0	E980.4
nonmedicinal	981	E862.1	—	E950.9	E962.1	E980.9
Petroleum (cleaners) (fuels) (products) NEC	981	E862.1		E950.9	E962.1	E980.9
benzin(e) — see Ligroin						
ether — see Ligroin						
jelly — see Petrolatum						
naphtha — see Ligroin						
pesticide	981	E863.4	—	E950.6	E962.1	E980.7
solids	981	E862.3	—	E950.9	E962.1	E980.9
solvents	981	E862.0	—	E950.9	E962.1	E980.9
vapor	987.1	E869.8	—	E952.8	E962.2	E982.8
Peyote	969.6	E854.1	E939.6	E950.3	E962.0	E980.3
Phanodorm, phanodorn	967.0	E851	E937.0	E950.1	E962.0	E980.1
Phanquinone, phanquone	961.5	E857	E931.5	E950.4	E962.0	E980.4
Pharmaceutical excipient or adjunct	977.4	E858.8	E947.4	E950.4	E962.0	E980.4
Phenacemide	966.3	E855.0	E936.3	E950.4	E962.0	E980.4
Phenacetin	965.4	E850.4	E935.4	E950.0	E962.0	E980.0
Phenadoxone	965.09	E850.2	E935.2	E950.0	E962.0	E980.0
Phenaglycodol	969.5	E853.8	E939.5	E950.3	E962.0	E980.3
Phenantoin	966.1	E855.0	E936.1	E950.4	E962.0	E980.4
Phenaphthazine reagent	977.8	E858.8	E947.8	E950.4	E962.0	E980.4
Phenazocine	965.09	E850.2	E935.2	E950.0	E962.0	E980.0
Phenazone	965.5	E850.5	E935.5	E950.0	E962.0	E980.0

▽ Subterms under main terms may continue to next column or page

Substance	Poisoning	Accident	Therapeutic Use	Suicide Attempt	Assault	Undetermined
Phenazopyridine	976.1	E858.7	E946.1	E950.4	E962.0	E980.4
Phenbenicillin	960.0	E856	E930.0	E950.4	E962.0	E980.4
Phenbutrazate	977.0	E858.8	E947.0	E950.4	E962.0	E980.4
Phencyclidine	968.3	E855.1	E938.3	E950.4	E962.0	E980.4
Phendimetrazine	977.0	E858.8	E947.0	E950.4	E962.0	E980.4
Phenelzine	969.01▲	E854.0	E939.0	E950.3	E962.0	E980.3
Phenergan	967.8	E852.8	E937.8	E950.2	E962.0	E980.2
Phenethicillin (potassium)	960.0	E856	E930.0	E950.4	E962.0	E980.4
Phenetsal	965.1	E850.3	E935.3	E950.4	E962.0	E980.0
Pheneturide	966.3	E855.0	E936.3	E950.4	E962.0	E980.4
Phenformin	962.3	E858.0	E932.3	E950.4	E962.0	E980.4
Phenglutarimide	971.1	E855.4	E941.1	E950.4	E962.0	E980.4
Phenicarbazide	965.8	E850.8	E935.8	E950.4	E962.0	E980.0
Phenindamine (tartrate)	963.0	E858.1	E933.0	E950.4	E962.0	E980.4
Phenindione	964.2	E858.2	E934.2	E950.4	E962.0	E980.4
Pheniprazine	969.01▲	E854.0	E939.0	E950.3	E962.0	E980.3
Pheniramine (maleate)	963.0	E858.1	E933.0	E950.4	E962.0	E980.4
Phenmetrazine	977.0	E858.8	E947.0	E950.4	E962.0	E980.4
Phenobal	967.0	E851	E937.0	E950.1	E962.0	E980.1
Phenobarbital	967.0	E851	E937.0	E950.1	E962.0	E980.1
Phenobarbitone	967.0	E851	E937.0	E950.1	E962.0	E980.1
Phenoctide	976.0	E858.7	E946.0	E950.4	E962.0	E980.4
Phenol (derivatives) NEC	983.0	E864.0	—	E950.7	E962.1	E980.6
disinfectant	983.0	E864.0	—	E950.7	E962.1	E980.6
pesticide	989.4	E863.4	—	E950.6	E962.1	E980.7
red	977.8	E858.8	E947.8	E950.4	E962.0	E980.4
Phenolphthalein	973.1	E858.4	E943.1	E950.4	E962.0	E980.4
Phenolsulfonphthalein	977.8	E858.8	E947.8	E950.4	E962.0	E980.4
Phenomorphan	965.09	E850.2	E935.2	E950.0	E962.0	E980.0
Phenonyl	967.0	E851	E937.0	E950.1	E962.0	E980.1
Phenoperidine	965.09	E850.2	E935.2	E950.0	E962.0	E980.0
Phenoquin	974.7	E858.5	E944.7	E950.4	E962.0	E980.4
Phenothiazines (tranquilizers)						
NEC	969.1	E853.0	E939.1	E950.3	E962.0	E980.3
insecticide	989.3	E863.4	—	E950.6	E962.1	E980.7
Phenoxybenzamine	971.3	E855.6	E941.3	E950.4	E962.0	E980.4
Phenoxymethyl penicillin	960.0	E856	E930.0	E950.4	E962.0	E980.4
Phenprocoumon	964.2	E858.2	E934.2	E950.4	E962.0	E980.4
Phensuximide	966.2	E855.0	E936.2	E950.4	E962.0	E980.4
Phentermine	977.0	E858.8	E947.0	E950.4	E962.0	E980.4
Phentolamine	971.3	E855.6	E941.3	E950.4	E962.0	E980.4
Phenyl						
butazone	965.5	E850.5	E935.5	E950.0	E962.0	E980.0
enediamine	983.0	E864.0	—	E950.7	E962.1	E980.6
hydrazine	983.0	E864.0	—	E950.7	E962.1	E980.6
antineoplastic	963.1	E858.1	E933.1	E950.4	E962.0	E980.4
mercuric compounds — see Mercury						
salicylate	976.3	E858.7	E946.3	E950.4	E962.0	E980.4
Phenylephrin	971.2	E855.5	E941.2	E950.4	E962.0	E980.4
Phenylethylbiguanide	962.3	E858.0	E932.3	E950.4	E962.0	E980.4
Phenylpropanolamine	971.2	E855.5	E941.2	E950.4	E962.0	E980.4
Phenylsulfthion	989.3	E863.1	—	E950.6	E962.1	E980.7
Phenyramidol, phenyramidon	965.7	E850.7	E935.7	E950.0	E962.0	E980.0
Phenytoin	966.1	E855.0	E936.1	E950.4	E962.0	E980.4
pHisoHex	976.2	E858.7	E946.2	E950.4	E962.0	E980.4
Pholcodine	965.09	E850.2	E935.2	E950.0	E962.0	E980.0
Phorate	989.3	E863.1	—	E950.6	E962.1	E980.7
Phosdrin	989.3	E863.1	—	E950.6	E962.1	E980.7
Phosgene (gas)	987.8	E869.8	—	E952.8	E962.2	E982.8
Phosphate (tricresyl)	989.89	E866.8	—	E950.9	E962.1	E980.9
organic	989.3	E863.1	—	E950.6	E962.1	E980.7
solvent	982.8	E862.4	—	E950.9	E926.1	E980.9
Phosphine	987.8	E869.8	—	E952.8	E962.2	E982.8
fumigant	987.8	E863.8	—	E950.6	E962.2	E980.7
Phospholine	971.0	E855.3	E941.0	E950.4	E962.0	E980.4
Phosphoric acid	983.1	E864.1	—	E950.7	E962.1	E980.6
Phosphorus (compounds) NEC	983.9	E864.3	—	E950.7	E962.1	E980.6
rodenticide	983.9	E863.7	—	E950.7	E962.1	E980.6
Phthalimidoglutarimide	967.8	E852.8	E937.8	E950.2	E962.0	E980.2
Phthalylsulfathiazole	961.0	E857	E931.0	E950.4	E962.0	E980.4
Phylloquinone	964.3	E858.2	E934.3	E950.4	E962.0	E980.4
Physeptone	965.02	E850.1	E935.1	E950.0	E962.0	E980.0
Physostigma venenosum	988.2	E865.4	—	E950.9	E962.1	E980.9
Physostigmine	971.0	E855.3	E941.0	E950.4	E962.0	E980.4
Phytolacca decandra	988.2	E865.4	—	E950.9	E962.1	E980.9
Phytomenadione	964.3	E858.2	E934.3	E950.4	E962.0	E980.4
Phytonadione	964.3	E858.2	E934.3	E950.4	E962.0	E980.4
Picric (acid)	983.0	E864.0	—	E950.7	E962.1	E980.6
Picrotoxin	970.0	E854.3	E940.0	E950.4	E962.0	E980.4
Pilocarpine	971.0	E855.3	E941.0	E950.4	E962.0	E980.4
Pilocarpus (jaborandi) extract	971.0	E855.3	E941.0	E950.4	E962.0	E980.4
Pimaricin	960.1	E856	E930.1	E950.4	E962.0	E980.4
Piminodine	965.09	E850.2	E935.2	E950.0	E962.0	E980.0
Pine oil, pinesol (disinfectant)	983.9	E861.4	—	E950.7	E962.1	E980.6
Pinkroot	961.6	E857	E931.6	E950.4	E962.0	E980.4
Pipadone	965.09	E850.2	E935.2	E950.0	E962.0	E980.0
Pipamazine	963.0	E858.1	E933.0	E950.4	E962.0	E980.4
Pipazethate	975.4	E858.6	E945.4	E950.4	E962.0	E980.4
Pipenzolate	971.1	E855.4	E941.1	E950.4	E962.0	E980.4
Piperacetazine	969.1	E853.0	E939.1	E950.3	E962.0	E980.3
Piperazine NEC	961.6	E857	E931.6	E950.4	E962.0	E980.4
estrone sulfate	962.2	E858.0	E932.2	E950.4	E962.0	E980.4
Piper cubeba	988.2	E865.4	—	E950.9	E962.1	E980.9
Piperidione	975.4	E858.6	E945.4	E950.4	E962.0	E980.4
Piperidolate	971.1	E855.4	E941.1	E950.4	E962.0	E980.4
Piperocaine	968.9	E855.2	E938.9	E950.4	E962.0	E980.4
infiltration (subcutaneous)	968.5	E855.2	E938.5	E950.4	E962.0	E980.4
nerve block (peripheral) (plexus)	968.6	E855.2	E938.6	E950.4	E962.0	E980.4
topical (surface)	968.5	E855.2	E938.5	E950.4	E962.0	E980.4
Pipobroman	963.1	E858.1	E933.1	E950.4	E962.0	E980.4
Pipradrol	970.8	E854.3	E940.8	E950.4	E962.0	E980.4
Piscidia (bark) (erythrina)	965.7	E850.7	E935.7	E950.0	E962.0	E980.0
Pitch	983.0	E864.0	—	E950.7	E962.1	E980.6
Pitkin's solution	968.7	E855.2	E938.7	E950.4	E962.0	E980.4
Pitocin	975.0	E858.6	E945.0	E950.4	E962.0	E980.4
Pitressin (tannate)	962.5	E858.0	E932.5	E950.4	E962.0	E980.4
Pituitary extracts (posterior)	962.5	E858.0	E932.5	E950.4	E962.0	E980.4
anterior	962.4	E858.0	E932.4	E950.4	E962.0	E980.4
Pituitrin	962.5	E858.0	E932.5	E950.4	E962.0	E980.4
Placental extract	962.9	E858.0	E932.9	E950.4	E962.0	E980.4
Placidyl	967.8	E852.8	E937.8	E950.2	E962.0	E980.2
Plague vaccine	978.3	E858.8	E948.3	E950.4	E962.0	E980.4
Plant foods or fertilizers NEC	989.89	E866.5	—	E950.9	E962.1	E980.9
mixed with herbicides	989.4	E863.5	—	E950.6	E962.1	E980.7
Plants, noxious, used as food	988.2	E865.9	—	E950.9	E962.1	E980.9
berries and seeds	988.2	E865.3	—	E950.9	E962.1	E980.9
specified type NEC	988.2	E865.4	—	E950.9	E962.1	E980.9
Plasma (blood)	964.7	E858.2	E934.7	E950.4	E962.0	E980.4
expanders	964.8	E858.2	E934.8	E950.4	E962.0	E980.4
Plasmanate	964.7	E858.2	E934.7	E950.4	E962.0	E980.4
Plegicil	969.1	E853.0	E939.1	E950.3	E962.0	E980.3
Podophyllin	976.4	E858.7	E946.4	E950.4	E962.0	E980.4
Podophyllum resin	976.4	E858.7	E946.4	E950.4	E962.0	E980.4
Poison NEC	989.9	E866.9	—	E950.9	E962.1	E980.9
Poisonous berries	988.2	E865.3	—	E950.9	E962.1	E980.9
Pokeweed (any part)	988.2	E865.4	—	E950.9	E962.1	E980.9
Poldine	971.1	E855.4	E941.1	E950.4	E962.0	E980.4
Poliomyelitis vaccine	979.5	E858.8	E949.5	E950.4	E962.0	E980.4
Poliovirus vaccine	979.5	E858.8	E949.5	E950.4	E962.0	E980.4
Polish (car) (floor) (furniture) (metal) (silver)	989.89	E861.2	—	E950.9	E962.1	E980.9
abrasive	989.89	E861.3	—	E950.9	E962.1	E980.9
porcelain	989.89	E861.3	—	E950.9	E962.1	E980.9
Poloxalkol	973.2	E858.4	E943.2	E950.4	E962.0	E980.4
Polyaminostyrene resins	974.5	E858.5	E944.5	E950.4	E962.0	E980.4
Polychlorinated biphenyl — see PCBs						
Polycycline	960.4	E856	E930.4	E950.4	E962.0	E980.4
Polyester resin hardener	982.8	E862.4	—	E950.9	E962.1	E980.9
fumes	987.8	E869.8	—	E952.8	E962.2	E982.8
Polyestradiol (phosphate)	962.2	E858.0	E932.2	E950.4	E962.0	E980.4
Polyethanolamine alkyl sulfate	976.2	E858.7	E946.2	E950.4	E962.0	E980.4
Polyethylene glycol	976.3	E858.7	E946.3	E950.4	E962.0	E980.4
Polyferose	964.0	E858.2	E934.0	E950.4	E962.0	E980.4
Polymyxin B	960.8	E856	E930.8	E950.4	E962.0	E980.4
ENT agent	976.6	E858.7	E946.6	E950.4	E962.0	E980.4
ophthalmic preparation	976.5	E858.7	E946.5	E950.4	E962.0	E980.4
topical NEC	976.0	E858.7	E946.0	E950.4	E962.0	E980.4
Polynoxylin(e)	976.0	E858.7	E946.0	E950.4	E962.0	E980.4
Polyoxymethyleneurea	976.0	E858.7	E946.0	E950.4	E962.0	E980.4
Polytetrafluoroethylene (inhaled)	987.8	E869.8	—	E952.8	E962.2	E982.8
Polythiazide	974.3	E858.5	E944.3	E950.4	E962.0	E980.4
Polyvinylpyrrolidone	964.8	E858.2	E934.8	E950.4	E962.0	E980.4

Nontherapeutic use substance

Ⓥ Subterms under main terms may continue to next column or page

	Poisoning	Accident	Therapeutic Use	Suicide Attempt	Assault	Undetermined
Pontocaine (hydrochloride)						
(infiltration) (topical)	968.5	E855.2	E938.5	E950.4	E962.0	E980.4
nerve block (peripheral)						
(plexus)	968.6	E855.2	E938.6	E950.4	E962.0	E980.4
spinal	968.7	E855.2	E938.7	E950.4	E962.0	E980.4
Pot	969.6	E854.1	E939.6	E950.3	E962.0	E980.3
Potash (caustic)	983.2	E864.2	—	E950.7	E962.1	E980.6
Potassic saline injection						
(lactated)	974.5	E858.5	E944.5	E950.4	E962.0	E980.4
Potassium (salts) NEC	974.5	E858.5	E944.5	E950.4	E962.0	E980.4
aminosalicylate	961.8	E857	E931.8	E950.4	E962.0	E980.4
arsenite (solution)	985.1	E866.3	—	E950.8	E962.1	E980.8
bichromate	983.9	E864.3	—	E950.7	E962.1	E980.6
bisulfate	983.9	E864.3	—	E950.7	E962.1	E980.6
bromide (medicinal) NEC	967.3	E852.2	E937.3	E950.2	E962.0	E980.2
carbonate	983.2	E864.2	—	E950.7	E962.1	E980.6
chlorate NEC	983.9	E864.3	—	E950.7	E962.1	E980.6
cyanide — see Cyanide						
hydroxide	983.2	E864.2	—	E950.7	E962.1	E980.6
iodide (expectorant) NEC	975.5	E858.6	E945.5	E950.4	E962.0	E980.4
nitrate	989.89	E866.8	—	E950.9	E962.1	E980.6
oxalate	983.9	E864.3	—	E950.7	E962.1	E980.6
perchlorate NEC	977.8	E858.8	E947.8	E950.4	E962.0	E980.4
antithyroid	962.8	E858.0	E932.8	E950.4	E962.0	E980.4
permanganate	976.0	E858.7	E946.0	E950.4	E962.0	E980.4
nonmedicinal	983.9	E864.3	—	E950.7	E962.1	E980.6
Povidone-iodine (anti-infective)						
NEC	976.0	E858.7	E946.0	E950.4	E962.0	E980.4
Practolol	972.0	E858.3	E942.0	E950.4	E962.0	E980.4
Pralidoxime (chloride)	977.2	E858.8	E947.2	E950.4	E962.0	E980.4
Pramoxine	968.5	E855.2	E938.5	E950.4	E962.0	E980.4
Prazosin	972.6	E858.3	E942.6	E950.4	E962.0	E980.4
Prednisolone	962.0	E858.0	E932.0	E950.4	E962.0	E980.4
ENT agent	976.6	E858.7	E946.6	E950.4	E962.0	E980.4
ophthalmic preparation	976.5	E858.7	E946.5	E950.4	E962.0	E980.4
topical NEC	976.0	E858.7	E946.0	E950.4	E962.0	E980.4
Prednisone	962.0	E858.0	E932.0	E950.4	E962.0	E980.4
Pregnanediol	962.2	E858.0	E932.2	E950.4	E962.0	E980.4
Pregneninolone	962.2	E858.0	E932.2	E950.4	E962.0	E980.4
Preludin	977.0	E858.8	E947.0	E950.4	E962.0	E980.4
Premarin	962.2	E858.0	E932.2	E950.4	E962.0	E980.4
Prenylamine	972.4	E858.3	E942.4	E950.4	E962.0	E980.4
Preparation H	976.8	E858.7	E946.8	E950.4	E962.0	E980.4
Preservatives	989.89	E866.8	—	E950.9	E962.1	E980.9
Pride of China	988.2	E865.3	—	E950.9	E962.1	E980.9
Prilocaine	968.9	E855.2	E938.9	E950.4	E962.0	E980.4
infiltration (subcutaneous)	968.5	E855.2	E938.5	E950.4	E962.0	E980.4
nerve block (peripheral)						
(plexus)	968.6	E855.2	E938.6	E950.4	E962.0	E980.4
Primaquine	961.4	E857	E931.4	E950.4	E962.0	E980.4
Primidone	966.3	E855.0	E936.3	E950.4	E962.0	E980.4
Primula (veris)	988.2	E865.4	—	E950.9	E962.1	E980.9
Prinadol	965.09	E850.2	E935.2	E950.0	E962.0	E980.0
Priscol, Priscoline	971.3	E855.6	E941.3	E950.4	E962.0	E980.4
Privet	988.2	E865.4	—	E950.9	E962.1	E980.9
Privine	971.2	E855.5	E941.2	E950.4	E962.0	E980.4
Pro-Banthine	971.1	E855.4	E941.1	E950.4	E962.0	E980.4
Probarbital	967.0	E851	E937.0	E950.1	E962.0	E980.1
Probenecid	974.7	E858.5	E944.7	E950.4	E962.0	E980.4
Procainamide						
(hydrochloride)	972.0	E858.3	E942.0	E950.4	E962.0	E980.4
Procaine (hydrochloride)						
(infiltration) (topical)	968.5	E855.2	E938.5	E950.4	E962.0	E980.4
nerve block (peripheral)						
(plexus)	968.6	E855.2	E938.6	E950.4	E962.0	E980.4
penicillin G	960.0	E856	E930.0	E950.4	E962.0	E980.4
spinal	968.7	E855.2	E938.7	E950.4	E962.0	E980.4
Procalmidol	969.5	E853.8	E939.5	E950.3	E962.0	E980.3
Procarbazine	963.1	E858.1	E933.1	E950.4	E962.0	E980.4
Prochlorperazine	969.1	E853.0	E939.1	E950.3	E962.0	E980.3
Procyclidine	966.4	E855.0	E936.4	E950.4	E962.0	E980.4
Producer gas	986	E868.8	—	E952.1	E962.2	E982.1
Profenamine	966.4	E855.0	E936.4	E950.4	E962.0	E980.4
Profenil	975.1	E858.6	E945.1	E950.4	E962.0	E980.4
Progesterones	962.2	E858.0	E932.2	E950.4	E962.0	E980.4
Progestin	962.2	E858.0	E932.2	E950.4	E962.0	E980.4
Progestogens (with						
estrogens)	962.2	E858.0	E932.2	E950.4	E962.0	E980.4
Progestone	962.2	E858.0	E932.2	E950.4	E962.0	E980.4
Proguanil	961.4	E857	E931.4	E950.4	E962.0	E980.4
Prolactin	962.4	E858.0	E932.4	E950.4	E962.0	E980.4
Proloid	962.7	E858.0	E932.7	E950.4	E962.0	E980.4
Proluton	962.2	E858.0	E932.2	E950.4	E962.0	E980.4
Promacetin	961.8	E857	E931.8	E950.4	E962.0	E980.4
Promazine	969.1	E853.0	E939.1	E950.3	E962.0	E980.3
Promedol	965.09	E850.2	E935.2	E950.0	E962.0	E980.0
Promethazine	967.8	E852.8	E937.8	E950.2	E962.0	E980.2
Promin	961.8	E857	E931.8	E950.4	E962.0	E980.4
Pronestyl (hydrochloride)	972.0	E858.3	E942.0	E950.4	E962.0	E980.4
Pronetalol, pronethalol	972.0	E858.3	E942.0	E950.4	E962.0	E980.4
Prontosil	961.0	E857	E931.0	E950.4	E962.0	E980.4
Propamidine isethionate	961.5	E857	E931.5	E950.4	E962.0	E980.4
Propanal (medicinal)	967.8	E852.8	E937.8	E950.2	E962.0	E980.2
Propane (gas) (distributed in						
mobile container)	987.0	E868.0	—	E951.1	E962.2	E981.1
distributed through pipes	987.0	E867	—	E951.0	E962.2	E981.0
incomplete combustion of —						
see Carbon monoxide,						
Propane						
Propanidid	968.3	E855.1	E938.3	E950.4	E962.0	E980.4
Propanol	980.3	E860.4	—	E950.9	E962.1	E980.9
Propantheline	971.1	E855.4	E941.1	E950.4	E962.0	E980.4
Proparacaine	968.5	E855.2	E938.5	E950.4	E962.0	E980.4
Propatyl nitrate	972.4	E858.3	E942.4	E950.4	E962.0	E980.4
Propicillin	960.0	E856	E930.0	E950.4	E962.0	E980.4
Propiolactone (vapor)	987.8	E869.8	—	E952.8	E962.2	E982.8
Propiomazine	967.8	E852.8	E937.8	E950.2	E962.0	E980.2
Propionaldehyde						
(medicinal)	967.8	E852.8	E937.8	E950.2	E962.0	E980.2
Propionate compound	976.0	E858.7	E946.0	E950.4	E962.0	E980.4
Propion gel	976.0	E858.7	E946.0	E950.4	E962.0	E980.4
Propitocaine	968.9	E855.2	E938.9	E950.4	E962.0	E980.4
infiltration (subcutaneous)	968.5	E855.2	E938.5	E950.4	E962.0	E980.4
nerve block (peripheral)						
(plexus)	968.6	E855.2	E938.6	E950.4	E962.0	E980.4
Propoxur	989.3	E863.2	—	E950.6	E962.1	E980.7
Propoxycaine	968.9	E855.2	E938.9	E950.4	E962.0	E980.4
infiltration (subcutaneous)	968.5	E855.2	E938.5	E950.4	E962.0	E980.4
nerve block (peripheral)						
(plexus)	968.6	E855.2	E938.6	E950.4	E962.0	E980.4
topical (surface)	968.5	E855.2	E938.5	E950.4	E962.0	E980.4
Propoxyphene						
(hydrochloride)	965.8	E850.8	E935.8	E950.0	E962.0	E980.0
Propranolol	972.0	E858.3	E942.0	E950.4	E962.0	E980.4
Propyl						
alcohol	980.3	E860.4	—	E950.9	E962.1	E980.9
carbinol	980.3	E860.4	—	E950.9	E962.1	E980.9
hexadrine	971.2	E855.5	E941.2	E950.4	E962.0	E980.4
iodone	977.8	E858.8	E947.8	E950.4	E962.0	E980.4
thiouracil	962.8	E858.0	E932.8	E950.4	E962.0	E980.4
Propylene	987.1	E869.8	—	E952.8	E962.2	E982.8
Propylparaben						
(ophthalmic)	976.5	E858.7	E946.5	E950.4	E962.0	E980.4
Proscillaridin	972.1	E858.3	E942.1	E950.4	E962.0	E980.4
Prostaglandins	975.0	E858.6	E945.0	E950.4	E962.0	E980.4
Prostigmin	971.0	E855.3	E941.0	E950.4	E962.0	E980.4
Protamine (sulfate)	964.5	E858.2	E934.5	E950.4	E962.0	E980.4
zinc insulin	962.3	E858.0	E932.3	E950.4	E962.0	E980.4
Protectants (topical)	976.3	E858.7	E946.3	E950.4	E962.0	E980.4
Protein hydrolysate	974.5	E858.5	E944.5	E950.4	E962.0	E980.4
Prothiaden — see Dothiepin						
hydrochloride						
Prothionamide	961.8	E857	E931.8	E950.4	E962.0	E980.4
Prothipendyl	969.5	E853.8	E939.5	E950.3	E962.0	E980.3
Protokylol	971.2	E855.5	E941.2	E950.4	E962.0	E980.4
Protopam	977.2	E858.8	E947.2	E950.4	E962.0	E980.4
Protoveratrine(s) (A) (B)	972.6	E858.3	E942.6	E950.4	E962.0	E980.4
Protriptyline	969.05 ▲	E854.0	E939.0	E950.3	E962.0	E980.3
Provera	962.2	E858.0	E932.2	E950.4	E962.0	E980.4
Provitamin A	963.5	E858.1	E933.5	E950.4	E962.0	E980.4
Proxymetacaine	968.5	E855.2	E938.5	E950.4	E962.0	E980.4
Proxyphylline	975.1	E858.6	E945.1	E950.4	E962.0	E980.4
Prozac — see Fluoxetine						
hydrochloride						
Prunus						
laurocerasus	988.2	E865.4	—	E950.9	E962.1	E980.9
virginiana	988.2	E865.4	—	E950.9	E962.1	E980.9
Prussic acid	989.0	E866.8	—	E950.9	E962.1	E980.9
vapor	987.7	E869.8	—	E952.8	E962.2	E982.8
Pseudoephedrine	971.2	E855.5	E941.2	E950.4	E962.0	E980.4
Psilocin	969.6	E854.1	E939.6	E950.3	E962.0	E980.3
Psilocybin	969.6	E854.1	E939.6	E950.3	E962.0	E980.3
PSP	977.8	E858.8	E947.8	E950.4	E962.0	E980.4
Psychedelic agents	969.6	E854.1	E939.6	E950.3	E962.0	E980.3

	Poisoning	Accident	Therapeutic Use	Suicide Attempt	Assault	Undetermined
			External Cause (E-Code)			
Psychodysleptics	969.6	E854.1	E939.6	E950.3	E962.0	E980.3
Psychostimulants	969.70 ▲	E854.2	E939.7	E950.3	E962.0	E980.3
Psychotherapeutic agents	969.9	E855.9	E939.9	E950.3	E962.0	E980.3
antidepressants	969.00 ▲	E854.0	E939.0	E950.3	E962.0	E980.3
specified NEC	969.8	E855.8	E939.8	E950.3	E962.0	E980.3
tranquilizers NEC	969.5	E853.9	E939.5	E950.3	E962.0	E980.3
Psychotomimetic agents	969.6	E854.1	E939.6	E950.3	E962.0	E980.3
Psychotropic agents	969.9	E854.8	E939.9	E950.3	E962.0	E980.3
specified NEC	969.8	E854.8	E939.8	E950.3	E962.0	E980.3
Psyllium	973.3	E858.4	E943.3	E950.4	E962.0	E980.4
Pteroylglutamic acid	964.1	E858.2	E934.1	E950.4	E962.0	E980.4
Pteroyltriglutamate	963.1	E858.1	E933.1	E950.4	E962.0	E980.4
PTFE	987.8	E869.8	—	E952.8	E962.2	E982.8
Pulsatilla	988.2	E865.4	—	E950.9	E962.1	E980.9
Purex (bleach)	983.9	E864.3	—	E950.7	E962.1	E980.6
Purine diuretics	974.1	E858.5	E944.1	E950.4	E962.0	E980.4
Purinethol	963.1	E858.1	E933.1	E950.4	E962.0	E980.4
PVP	964.8	E858.2	E934.8	E950.4	E962.0	E980.4
Pyrabital	965.7	E850.7	E935.7	E950.0	E962.0	E980.0
Pyramidon	965.5	E850.5	E935.5	E950.0	E962.0	E980.0
Pyrantel (pamoate)	961.6	E857	E931.6	E950.4	E962.0	E980.4
Pyrathiazine	963.0	E858.1	E933.0	E950.4	E962.0	E980.4
Pyrazinamide	961.8	E857	E931.8	E950.4	E962.0	E980.4
Pyrazinoic acid (amide)	961.8	E857	E931.8	E950.4	E962.0	E980.4
Pyrazole (derivatives)	965.5	E850.5	E935.5	E950.0	E962.0	E980.0
Pyrazolone (analgesics)	965.5	E850.5	E935.5	E950.0	E962.0	E980.0
Pyrethrins, pyrethrum	989.4	E863.4	—	E950.6	E962.1	E980.7
Pyribenzamine	963.0	E858.1	E933.0	E950.4	E962.0	E980.4
Pyridine (liquid) (vapor)	982.0	E862.4	—	E950.9	E962.1	E980.9
aldoxime chloride	977.2	E858.8	E947.2	E950.4	E962.0	E980.4
Pyridium	976.1	E858.7	E946.1	E950.4	E962.0	E980.4
Pyridostigmine	971.0	E855.3	E941.0	E950.4	E962.0	E980.4
Pyridoxine	963.5	E858.1	E933.5	E950.4	E962.0	E980.4
Pyrilamine	963.0	E858.1	E933.0	E950.4	E962.0	E980.4
Pyrimethamine	961.4	E857	E931.4	E950.4	E962.0	E980.4
Pyrogallic acid	983.0	E864.0	—	E950.7	E962.1	E980.6
Pyroxylin	976.3	E858.7	E946.3	E950.4	E962.0	E980.4
Pyrrobutamine	963.0	E858.1	E933.0	E950.4	E962.0	E980.4
Pyrrocitine	968.5	E855.2	E938.5	E950.4	E962.0	E980.4
Pyrvinium (pamoate)	961.6	E857	E931.6	E950.4	E962.0	E980.4
PZI	962.3	E858.0	E932.3	E950.4	E962.0	E980.4
Quaalude	967.4	E852.3	E937.4	E950.2	E962.0	E980.2
Quaternary ammonium derivatives	971.1	E855.4	E941.1	E950.4	E962.0	E980.4
Quicklime	983.2	E864.2	—	E950.7	E962.1	E980.6
Quinacrine	961.3	E857	E931.3	E950.4	E962.0	E980.4
Quinaglute	972.0	E858.3	E942.0	E950.4	E962.0	E980.4
Quinalbarbitone	967.0	E851	E937.0	E950.1	E962.0	E980.1
Quinestradiol	962.2	E858.0	E932.2	E950.4	E962.0	E980.4
Quinethazone	974.3	E858.5	E944.3	E950.4	E962.0	E980.4
Quinidine (gluconate) (polygalacturonate) (salts) (sulfate)	972.0	E858.3	E942.0	E950.4	E962.0	E980.4
Quinine	961.4	E857	E931.4	E950.4	E962.0	E980.4
Quiniobine	961.3	E857	E931.3	E950.4	E962.0	E980.4
Quinolines	961.3	E857	E931.3	E950.4	E962.0	E980.4
Quotane	968.5	E855.2	E938.5	E950.4	E962.0	E980.4
Rabies						
immune globulin (human)	964.6	E858.2	E934.6	E950.4	E962.0	E980.4
vaccine	979.1	E858.8	E949.1	E950.4	E962.0	E980.4
Racemoramide	965.09	E850.2	E935.2	E950.0	E962.0	E980.0
Racemorphan	965.09	E850.2	E935.2	E950.0	E962.0	E980.0
Radiator alcohol	980.1	E860.2	—	E950.9	E962.1	E980.9
Radio-opaque (drugs) (materials)	977.8	E858.8	E947.8	E950.4	E962.0	E980.4
Ranunculus	988.2	E865.4	—	E950.9	E962.1	E980.9
Rat poison	989.4	E863.7	—	E950.6	E962.1	E980.7
Rattlesnake (venom)	989.5	E905.0	—	E950.9	E962.1	E980.9
Raudixin	972.6	E858.3	E942.6	E950.4	E962.0	E980.4
Rautensin	972.6	E858.3	E942.6	E950.4	E962.0	E980.4
Rautina	972.6	E858.3	E942.6	E950.4	E962.0	E980.4
Rautotal	972.6	E858.3	E942.6	E950.4	E962.0	E980.4
Rauwiloid	972.6	E858.3	E942.6	E950.4	E962.0	E980.4
Rauwoldin	972.6	E858.3	E942.6	E950.4	E962.0	E980.4
Rauwolfia (alkaloids)	972.6	E858.3	E942.6	E950.4	E962.0	E980.4
Realgar	985.1	E866.3	—	E950.8	E962.1	E980.8
Red cells, packed	964.7	E858.2	E934.7	E950.4	E962.0	E980.4
Reducing agents, industrial NEC	983.9	E864.3	—	E950.7	E962.1	E980.6
Refrigerant gas (freon)	987.4	E869.2	—	E952.8	E962.2	E982.8
central nervous system	968.0	E855.1	E938.0	E950.4	E962.0	E980.4

	Poisoning	Accident	Therapeutic Use	Suicide Attempt	Assault	Undetermined
			External Cause (E-Code)			
Refrigerant gas — *continued*						
not freon	987.9	E869.9	—	E952.9	E962.2	E982.9
Regroton	974.4	E858.5	E944.4	E950.4	E962.0	E980.4
Rela	968.0	E855.1	E938.0	E950.4	E962.0	E980.4
Relaxants, skeletal muscle (autonomic)	975.2	E858.6	E945.2	E950.4	E962.0	E980.4
Renese	974.3	E858.5	E944.3	E950.4	E962.0	E980.4
Renografin	977.8	E858.8	E947.8	E950.4	E962.0	E980.4
Replacement solutions	974.5	E858.5	E944.5	E950.4	E962.0	E980.4
Rescinnamine	972.6	E858.3	E942.6	E950.4	E962.0	E980.4
Reserpine	972.6	E858.3	E942.6	E950.4	E962.0	E980.4
Resorcin, resorcinol	976.4	E858.7	E946.4	E950.4	E962.0	E980.4
Respaire	975.5	E858.6	E945.5	E950.4	E962.0	E980.4
Respiratory agents NEC	975.8	E858.6	E945.8	E950.4	E962.0	E980.4
Retinoic acid	976.8	E858.7	E946.8	E950.4	E962.0	E980.4
Retinol	963.5	E858.1	E933.5	E950.4	E962.0	E980.4
Rh (D) immune globulin (human)	964.6	E858.2	E934.6	E950.4	E962.0	E980.4
Rhodine	965.1	E850.3	E935.3	E950.0	E962.0	E980.0
RhoGAM	964.6	E858.2	E934.6	E950.4	E962.0	E980.4
Riboflavin	963.5	E858.1	E933.5	E950.4	E962.0	E980.4
Ricin	989.89	E866.8	—	E950.9	E962.1	E980.9
Ricinus communis	988.2	E865.3	—	E950.9	E962.1	E980.9
Rickettsial vaccine NEC	979.6	E858.8	E949.6	E950.4	E962.0	E980.4
with viral and bacterial vaccine	979.7	E858.8	E949.7	E950.4	E962.0	E980.4
Rifampin	960.6	E856	E930.6	E950.4	E962.0	E980.4
Rimifon	961.8	E857	E931.8	E950.4	E962.0	E980.4
Ringer's injection (lactated)	974.5	E858.5	E944.5	E950.4	E962.0	E980.4
Ristocetin	960.8	E856	E930.8	E950.4	E962.0	E980.4
Ritalin	969.73 ▲	E854.2	E939.7	E950.3	E962.0	E980.3
Roach killers — *see* Pesticides						
Rocky Mountain spotted fever vaccine	979.6	E858.8	E949.6	E950.4	E962.0	E980.4
Rodenticides	989.4	E863.7	—	E950.6	E962.1	E980.7
Rohypnol	969.4	E853.2	E939.4	E950.3	E962.0	E980.3
Rolaids	973.0	E858.4	E943.0	E950.4	E962.0	E980.4
Rolitetracycline	960.4	E856	E930.4	E950.4	E962.0	E980.4
Romilar	975.4	E858.6	E945.4	E950.4	E962.0	E980.4
Rose water ointment	976.3	E858.7	E946.3	E950.4	E962.0	E980.4
Rosuvastatin calcium	972.1	E858.3	E942.2	E950.4	E962.0	E980.4
Rotenone	989.4	E863.7	—	E950.6	E962.1	E980.7
Rotoxamine	963.0	E858.1	E933.0	E950.4	E962.0	E980.4
Rough-on-rats	989.4	E863.7	—	E950.6	E962.1	E980.7
RU486	962.9	E858.0	E932.9	E950.4	E962.0	E980.4
Rubbing alcohol	980.2	E860.3	—	E950.9	E962.1	E980.9
Rubella virus vaccine	979.4	E858.8	E949.4	E950.4	E962.0	E980.4
Rubelogen	979.4	E858.8	E949.4	E950.4	E962.0	E980.4
Rubeovax	979.4	E858.8	E949.4	E950.4	E962.0	E980.4
Rubidomycin	960.7	E856	E930.7	E950.4	E962.0	E980.4
Rue	988.2	E865.4	—	E950.9	E962.1	E980.9
Ruta	988.2	E865.4	—	E950.9	E962.1	E980.9
Sabadilla (medicinal)	976.0	E858.7	E946.0	E950.4	E962.0	E980.4
pesticide	989.4	E863.4	—	E950.6	E962.1	E980.7
Sabin oral vaccine	979.5	E858.8	E949.5	E950.4	E962.0	E980.4
Saccharated iron oxide	964.0	E858.2	E934.0	E950.4	E962.0	E980.4
Saccharin	974.5	E858.5	E944.5	E950.4	E962.0	E980.4
Safflower oil	972.2	E858.3	E942.2	E950.4	E962.0	E980.4
Salbutamol sulfate	975.7	E858.6	E945.7	E950.4	E962.0	E980.4
Salicylamide	965.1	E850.3	E935.3	E950.0	E962.0	E980.0
Salicylate(s)	965.1	E850.3	E935.3	E950.0	E962.0	E980.0
methyl	976.3	E858.7	E946.3	E950.4	E962.0	E980.4
theobromine calcium	974.1	E858.5	E944.1	E950.4	E962.0	E980.4
Salicylazosulfapyridine	961.0	E857	E931.0	E950.4	E962.0	E980.4
Salicylhydroxamic acid	976.0	E858.7	E946.0	E950.4	E962.0	E980.4
Salicylic acid (keratolytic) NEC	976.4	E858.7	E946.4	E950.4	E962.0	E980.4
congeners	965.1	E850.3	E935.3	E950.0	E962.0	E980.0
salts	965.1	E850.3	E935.3	E950.0	E962.0	E980.0
Saliniazid	961.8	E857	E931.8	E950.4	E962.0	E980.4
Salol	976.3	E858.7	E946.3	E950.4	E962.0	E980.4
Salt (substitute) NEC	974.5	E858.5	E944.5	E950.4	E962.0	E980.4
Saluretics	974.3	E858.5	E944.3	E950.4	E962.0	E980.4
Saluron	974.3	E858.5	E944.3	E950.4	E962.0	E980.4
Salvarsan 606 (neosilver) (silver)	961.1	E857	E931.1	E950.4	E962.0	E980.4
Sambucus canadensis	988.2	E865.4	—	E950.9	E962.1	E980.9
berry	988.2	E865.3	—	E950.9	E962.1	E980.9
Sandril	972.6	E858.3	E942.6	E950.4	E962.0	E980.4
Sanguinaria canadensis	988.2	E865.4	—	E950.9	E962.1	E980.9
Saniflush (cleaner)	983.9	E861.3	—	E950.7	E962.1	E980.6

	Poisoning	Accident	Therapeutic Use	Suicide Attempt	Assault	Undetermined
Santonin	961.6	E857	E931.6	E950.4	E962.0	E980.4
Santyl	976.8	E858.7	E946.8	E950.4	E962.0	E980.4
Sarkomycin	960.7	E856	E930.7	E950.4	E962.0	E980.4
Saroten	969.05 ▲	E854.0	E939.0	E950.3	E962.0	E980.3
Saturnine — see Lead						
Savin (oil)	976.4	E858.7	E946.4	E950.4	E962.0	E980.4
Scammony	973.1	E858.4	E943.1	E950.4	E962.0	E980.4
Scarlet red	976.8	E858.7	E946.8	E950.4	E962.0	E980.4
Scheele's green	985.1	E866.3	—	E950.8	E962.1	E980.8
insecticide	985.1	E863.4	—	E950.8	E962.1	E980.8
Schradan	989.3	E863.1	—	E950.6	E962.1	E980.7
Schweinfurt(h) green	985.1	E866.3	—	E950.8	E962.1	E980.8
insecticide	985.1	E863.4	—	E950.8	E962.1	E980.8
Scilla — see Squill						
Sclerosing agents	972.7	E858.3	E942.7	E950.4	E962.0	E980.4
Scopolamine	971.1	E855.4	E941.1	E950.4	E962.0	E980.4
Scouring powder	989.89	E861.3	—	E950.9	E962.1	E980.9
Sea						
anemone (sting)	989.5	E905.6	—	E950.9	E962.1	E980.9
cucumber (sting)	989.5	E905.6	—	E950.9	E962.1	E980.9
snake (bite) (venom)	989.5	E905.0	—	E950.9	E962.1	E980.9
urchin spine (puncture)	989.5	E905.6	—	E950.9	E962.1	E980.9
Secbutabarbital	967.0	E851	E937.0	E950.1	E962.0	E980.1
Secbutabarbitone	967.0	E851	E937.0	E950.1	E962.0	E980.1
Secobarbital	967.0	E851	E937.0	E950.1	E962.0	E980.1
Seconal	967.0	E851	E937.0	E950.1	E962.0	E980.1
Secretin	977.8	E858.8	E947.8	E950.4	E962.0	E980.4
Sedatives, nonbarbiturate	967.9	E852.9	E937.9	E950.2	E962.0	E980.2
specified NEC	967.8	E852.8	E937.8	E950.2	E962.0	E980.2
Sedormid	967.8	E852.8	E937.8	E950.2	E962.0	E980.2
Seed (plant)	988.2	E865.3	—	E950.9	E962.1	E980.9
disinfectant or dressing	989.89	E866.5	—	E950.9	E962.1	E980.9
Selective serotonin and norepinephrine reuptake inhibitors (SSNRI) ●	969.02	E854.0	E939.0	E950.3	E962.0	E980.3
Selective serotonin reuptake inhibitors (SSRI) ●	969.03	E854.0	E939.0	E950.3	E962.0	E980.3
Selenium (fumes) NEC	985.8	E866.4	—	E950.9	E962.1	E980.9
disulfide or sulfide	976.4	E858.7	E946.4	E950.4	E962.0	E980.4
Selsun	976.4	E858.7	E946.4	E950.4	E962.0	E980.4
Senna	973.1	E858.4	E943.1	E950.4	E962.0	E980.4
Septisol	976.2	E858.7	E946.2	E950.4	E962.0	E980.4
Serax	969.4	E853.2	E939.4	E950.3	E962.0	E980.3
Serenesil	967.8	E852.8	E937.8	E950.2	E962.0	E980.2
Serenium (hydrochloride)	961.9	E857	E931.9	E950.4	E962.0	E980.4
Serepax — see Oxazepam						
Sernyl	968.3	E855.1	E938.3	E950.4	E962.0	E980.4
Serotonin	977.8	E858.8	E947.8	E950.4	E962.0	E980.4
Serpasil	972.6	E858.3	E942.6	E950.4	E962.0	E980.4
Sewer gas	987.8	E869.8	—	E952.8	E962.2	E982.8
Shampoo	989.6	E861.0	—	E950.9	E962.1	E980.9
Shellfish, nonbacterial or noxious	988.0	E865.1	—	E950.9	E962.1	E980.9
Silicones NEC	989.83	E866.8	E947.8	E950.9	E962.1	E980.9
Silvadene	976.0	E858.7	E946.0	E950.4	E962.0	E980.4
Silver (compound) (medicinal) NEC	976.0	E858.7	E946.0	E950.4	E962.0	E980.4
anti-infectives	976.0	E858.7	E946.0	E950.4	E962.0	E980.4
arsphenamine	961.1	E857	E931.1	E950.4	E962.0	E980.4
nitrate	976.0	E858.7	E946.0	E950.4	E962.0	E980.4
ophthalmic preparation	976.5	E858.7	E946.5	E950.4	E962.0	E980.4
toughened (keratolytic)	976.4	E858.7	E946.4	E950.4	E962.0	E980.4
nonmedicinal (dust)	985.8	E866.4	—	E950.9	E962.1	E980.9
protein (mild) (strong)	976.0	E858.7	E946.0	E950.4	E962.0	E980.4
salvarsan	961.1	E857	E931.1	E950.4	E962.0	E980.4
Simethicone	973.8	E858.4	E943.8	E950.4	E962.0	E980.4
Sinequan	969.05 ▲	E854.0	E939.0	E950.3	E962.0	E980.3
Singoserp	972.6	E858.3	E942.6	E950.4	E962.0	E980.4
Sintrom	964.2	E858.2	E934.2	E950.4	E962.0	E980.4
Sitosterols	972.2	E858.3	E942.2	E950.4	E962.0	E980.4
Skeletal muscle relaxants	975.2	E858.6	E945.2	E950.4	E962.0	E980.4
Skin						
agents (external)	976.9	E858.7	E946.9	E950.4	E962.0	E980.4
specified NEC	976.8	E858.7	E946.8	E950.4	E962.0	E980.4
test antigen	977.8	E858.8	E947.8	E950.4	E962.0	E980.4
Sleep-eze	963.0	E858.1	E933.0	E950.4	E962.0	E980.4
Sleeping draught (drug) (pill) (tablet)	967.9	E852.9	E937.9	E950.2	E962.0	E980.2
Smallpox vaccine	979.0	E858.8	E949.0	E950.4	E962.0	E980.4
Smelter fumes NEC	985.9	E866.4	—	E950.9	E962.1	E980.9
Smog	987.3	E869.1	—	E952.8	E962.2	E982.8
Smoke NEC	987.9	E869.9	—	E952.9	E962.2	E982.9
Smooth muscle relaxant	975.1	E858.6	E945.1	E950.4	E962.0	E980.4
Snail killer	989.4	E863.4	—	E950.6	E962.1	E980.7
Snake (bite) (venom)	989.5	E905.0	—	E950.9	E962.1	E980.9
Snuff	989.89	E866.8	—	E950.9	E962.1	E980.9
Soap (powder) (product)	989.6	E861.1	—	E950.9	E962.1	E980.9
bicarb	963.3	E858.1	E933.3	E950.4	E962.0	E980.4
chlorinated — see Sodium, hypochlorite						
medicinal, soft	976.2	E858.7	E946.2	E950.4	E962.0	E980.4
Soda (caustic)	983.2	E864.2	—	E950.7	E962.1	E980.6
Sodium						
acetosulfone	961.8	E857	E931.8	E950.4	E962.0	E980.4
acetrizoate	977.8	E858.8	E947.8	E950.4	E962.0	E980.4
amytal	967.0	E851	E937.0	E950.1	E962.0	E980.1
arsenate — see Arsenic						
bicarbonate	963.3	E858.1	E933.3	E950.4	E962.0	E980.4
bichromate	983.9	E864.3	—	E950.7	E962.1	E980.6
biphosphate	963.2	E858.1	E933.2	E950.4	E962.0	E980.4
bisulfate	983.9	E864.3	—	E950.7	E962.1	E980.6
borate (cleanser)	989.6	E861.3	—	E950.9	E962.1	E980.9
bromide NEC	967.3	E852.2	E937.3	E950.2	E962.0	E980.2
cacodylate (nonmedicinal) NEC	978.8	E858.8	E948.8	E950.4	E962.0	E980.4
anti-infective	961.1	E857	E931.1	E950.4	E962.0	E980.4
herbicide	989.4	E863.5	—	E950.6	E962.1	E980.7
calcium edetate	963.8	E858.1	E933.8	E950.4	E962.0	E980.4
carbonate NEC	983.2	E864.2	—	E950.7	E962.1	E980.6
chlorate NEC	983.9	E864.3	—	E950.7	E962.1	E980.6
herbicide	983.9	E863.5	—	E950.7	E962.1	E980.6
chloride NEC	974.5	E858.5	E944.5	E950.4	E962.0	E980.4
chromate	983.9	E864.3	—	E950.7	E962.1	E980.6
citrate	963.3	E858.1	E933.3	E950.4	E962.0	E980.4
cyanide — see Cyanide(s)						
cyclamate	974.5	E858.5	E944.5	E950.4	E962.0	E980.4
diatrizoate	977.8	E858.8	E947.8	E950.4	E962.0	E980.4
dibunate	975.4	E858.6	E945.4	E950.4	E962.0	E980.4
dioctyl sulfosuccinate	973.2	E858.4	E943.2	E950.4	E962.0	E980.4
edetate	963.8	E858.1	E933.8	E950.4	E962.0	E980.4
ethacrynate	974.4	E858.5	E944.4	E950.4	E962.0	E980.4
fluoroacetate (dust) (rodenticide)	989.4	E863.7	—	E950.6	E962.1	E980.7
fluoride — see Fluoride(s)						
free salt	974.5	E858.5	E944.5	E950.4	E962.0	E980.4
glucosulfone	961.8	E857	E931.8	E950.4	E962.0	E980.4
hydroxide	983.2	E864.2	—	E950.7	E962.1	E980.6
hypochlorite (bleach) NEC	983.9	E864.3	—	E950.7	E962.1	E980.6
disinfectant	983.9	E861.4	—	E950.7	E962.1	E980.6
medicinal (anti-infective) (external)	976.0	E858.7	E946.0	E950.4	E962.0	E980.4
vapor	987.8	E869.8	—	E952.8	E962.2	E982.8
hyposulfite	976.0	E858.7	E946.0	E950.4	E962.0	E980.4
indigotindisulfonate	977.8	E858.8	E947.8	E950.4	E962.0	E980.4
iodide	977.8	E858.8	E947.8	E950.4	E962.0	E980.4
iothalamate	977.8	E858.8	E947.8	E950.4	E962.0	E980.4
iron edetate	964.0	E858.2	E934.0	E950.4	E962.0	E980.4
lactate	963.3	E858.1	E933.3	E950.4	E962.0	E980.4
lauryl sulfate	976.2	E858.7	E946.2	E950.4	E962.0	E980.4
L-triiodothyronine	962.7	E858.0	E932.7	E950.4	E962.0	E980.4
metrizoate	977.8	E858.8	E947.8	E950.4	E962.0	E980.4
monofluoracetate (dust) (rodenticide)	989.4	E863.7	—	E950.6	E962.1	E980.7
morrhuate	972.7	E858.3	E942.7	E950.4	E962.0	E980.4
nafcillin	960.0	E856	E930.0	E950.4	E962.0	E980.4
nitrate (oxidizing agent)	983.9	E864.3	—	E950.7	E962.1	E980.6
nitrite (medicinal)	972.4	E858.3	E942.4	E950.4	E962.0	E980.4
nitroferricyanide	972.6	E858.3	E942.6	E950.4	E962.0	E980.4
nitroprusside	972.6	E858.3	E942.6	E950.4	E962.0	E980.4
para-aminohippurate	977.8	E858.8	E947.8	E950.4	E962.0	E980.4
perborate (nonmedicinal) NEC	989.89	E866.8	—	E950.9	E962.1	E980.9
medicinal	976.6	E858.7	E946.6	E950.4	E962.0	E980.4
soap	989.6	E861.1	—	E950.9	E962.1	E980.9
percarbonate — see Sodium, perborate						
phosphate	973.3	E858.4	E943.3	E950.4	E962.0	E980.4
polystyrene sulfonate	974.5	E858.5	E944.5	E950.4	E962.0	E980.4
propionate	976.0	E858.7	E946.0	E950.4	E962.0	E980.4
psylliate	972.7	E858.3	E942.7	E950.4	E962.0	E980.4
removing resins	974.5	E858.5	E944.5	E950.4	E962.0	E980.4
salicylate	965.1	E850.3	E935.3	E950.0	E962.0	E980.0
sulfate	973.3	E858.4	E943.3	E950.4	E962.0	E980.4

		External Cause (E-Code)				
	Poisoning	Accident	Therapeutic Use	Suicide Attempt	Assault	Undetermined
Sodium — *continued*						
sulfoxone	961.8	E857	E931.8	E950.4	E962.0	E980.4
tetradecyl sulfate	972.7	E858.3	E942.7	E950.4	E962.0	E980.4
thiopental	968.3	E855.1	E938.3	E950.4	E962.0	E980.4
thiosalicylate	965.1	E850.3	E935.3	E950.0	E962.0	E980.0
thiosulfate	976.0	E858.7	E946.0	E950.4	E962.0	E980.4
tolbutamide	977.8	E858.8	E947.8	E950.4	E962.0	E980.4
tyropanoate	977.8	E858.8	E947.8	E950.4	E962.0	E980.4
valproate	966.3	E855.0	E936.3	E950.4	E962.0	E980.4
Solanine	977.8	E858.8	E947.8	E950.4	E962.0	E980.4
Solanum dulcamara	988.2	E865.4	—	E950.9	E962.1	E980.9
Solapsone	961.8	E857	E931.8	E950.4	E962.0	E980.4
Solasulfone	961.8	E857	E931.8	E950.4	E962.0	E980.4
Soldering fluid	983.1	E864.1	—	E950.7	E962.1	E980.6
Solid substance	989.9	E866.9	—	E950.9	E962.1	E980.9
specified NEC	989.9	E866.8	—	E950.9	E962.1	E980.9
Solvents, industrial	982.8	E862.9	—	E950.9	E962.1	E980.9
naphtha	981	E862.0	—	E950.9	E962.1	E980.9
petroleum	981	E862.0	—	E950.9	E962.1	E980.9
specified NEC	982.8	E862.4	—	E950.9	E962.1	E980.9
Soma	968.0	E855.1	E938.0	E950.4	E962.0	E980.4
Somatotropin	962.4	E858.0	E932.4	E950.4	E962.0	E980.4
Sominex	963.0	E858.1	E933.0	E950.4	E962.0	E980.4
Somnos	967.1	E852.0	E937.1	E950.2	E962.0	E980.2
Somonal	967.0	E851	E937.0	E950.1	E962.0	E980.1
Soneryl	967.0	E851	E937.0	E950.1	E962.0	E980.1
Soothing syrup	977.9	E858.9	E947.9	E950.5	E962.0	E980.5
Sopor	967.4	E852.3	E937.4	E950.2	E962.0	E980.2
Soporific drug	967.9	E852.9	E937.9	E950.2	E962.0	E980.2
specified type NEC	967.8	E852.8	E937.8	E950.2	E962.0	E980.2
Sorbitol NEC	977.4	E858.8	E947.4	E950.4	E962.0	E980.4
Sotradecol	972.7	E858.3	E942.7	E950.4	E962.0	E980.4
Spacoline	975.1	E858.6	E945.1	E950.4	E962.0	E980.4
Spanish fly	976.8	E858.7	E946.8	E950.4	E962.0	E980.4
Sparine	969.1	E853.0	E939.1	E950.3	E962.0	E980.3
Sparteine	975.0	E858.6	E945.0	E950.4	E962.0	E980.4
Spasmolytics	975.1	E858.6	E945.1	E950.4	E962.0	E980.4
anticholinergics	971.1	E855.4	E941.1	E950.4	E962.0	E980.4
Spectinomycin	960.8	E856	E930.8	E950.4	E962.0	E980.4
Speed	969.72 ▲	E854.2	E939.7	E950.3	E962.0	E980.3
Spermicides	976.8	E858.7	E946.8	E950.4	E962.0	E980.4
Spider (bite) (venom)	989.5	E905.1	—	E950.9	E962.1	E980.9
antivenin	979.9	E858.8	E949.9	E950.4	E962.0	E980.4
Spigelia (root)	961.6	E857	E931.6	E950.4	E962.0	E980.4
Spiperone	969.2	E853.1	E939.2	E950.3	E962.0	E980.3
Spiramycin	960.3	E856	E930.3	E950.4	E962.0	E980.4
Spirilene	969.5	E853.8	E939.5	E950.3	E962.0	E980.3
Spirit(s) (neutral) NEC	980.0	E860.1	—	E950.9	E962.1	E980.9
beverage	980.0	E860.0	—	E950.9	E962.1	E980.9
industrial	980.9	E860.9	—	E950.9	E962.1	E980.9
mineral	981	E862.0	—	E950.9	E962.1	E980.9
of salt — see Hydrochloric acid						
surgical	980.9	E860.9	—	E950.9	E962.1	E980.9
Spironolactone	974.4	E858.5	E944.4	E950.4	E962.0	E980.4
Sponge, absorbable						
(gelatin)	964.5	E858.2	E934.5	E950.4	E962.0	E980.4
Sporostacin	976.0	E858.7	E946.0	E950.4	E962.0	E980.4
Sprays (aerosol)	989.89	E866.8	—	E950.9	E962.1	E980.9
cosmetic	989.89	E866.7	—	E950.9	E962.1	E980.9
medicinal NEC	977.9	E858.9	E947.9	E950.5	E962.0	E980.5
pesticides — see Pesticides						
specified content — see substance specified						
Spurge flax	988.2	E865.4	—	E950.9	E962.1	E980.9
Spurges	988.2	E865.4	—	E950.9	E962.1	E980.9
Squill (expectorant) NEC	975.5	E858.6	E945.5	E950.4	E962.0	E980.4
rat poison	989.4	E863.7	—	E950.6	E962.1	E980.7
Squirting cucumber						
(cathartic)	973.1	E858.4	E943.1	E950.4	E962.0	E980.4
SSNRI (selective serotonin and norepinephrine reuptake inhibitors) ●	969.02	E854.0	E939.0	E950.3	E962.0	E980.3
SSRI (selective serotonin reuptake inhibitors) ●	969.03	E854.0	E939.0	E950.3	E962.0	E980.3
Stains	989.89	E866.8	—	E950.9	E962.1	E980.9
Stannous — *see also* Tin						
fluoride	976.7	E858.7	E946.7	E950.4	E962.0	E980.4
Stanolone	962.1	E858.0	E932.1	E950.4	E962.0	E980.4
Stanozolol	962.1	E858.0	E932.1	E950.4	E962.0	E980.4
Staphisagria or stavesacre						
(pediculicide)	976.0	E858.7	E946.0	E950.4	E962.0	E980.4
Stelazine	969.1	E853.0	E939.1	E950.3	E962.0	E980.3
Stemetil	969.1	E853.0	E939.1	E950.3	E962.0	E980.3
Sterculia (cathartic) (gum)	973.3	E858.4	E943.3	E950.4	E962.0	E980.4
Sternutator gas	987.8	E869.8	—	E952.8	E962.2	E982.8
Steroids NEC	962.0	E858.0	E932.0	E950.4	E962.0	E980.4
ENT agent	976.6	E858.7	E946.6	E950.4	E962.0	E980.4
ophthalmic preparation	976.5	E858.7	E946.5	E950.4	E962.0	E980.4
topical NEC	976.0	E858.7	E946.0	E950.4	E962.0	E980.4
Stibine	985.8	E866.4	—	E950.9	E962.1	E980.9
Stibophen	961.2	E857	E931.2	E950.4	E962.0	E980.4
Stilbamide, stilbamidine	961.5	E857	E931.5	E950.4	E962.0	E980.4
Stilbestrol	962.2	E858.0	E932.2	E950.4	E962.0	E980.4
Stimulants (central nervous system)	970.9	E854.3	E940.9	E950.4	E962.0	E980.4
analeptics	970.0	E854.3	E940.0	E950.4	E962.0	E980.4
opiate antagonist	970.1	E854.3	E940.1	E950.4	E962.0	E980.4
psychotherapeutic NEC	969.09 ▲	E854.0	E939.0	E950.3	E962.0	E980.3
specified NEC	970.8	E854.3	E940.8	E950.4	E962.0	E980.4
Storage batteries (acid) (cells)	983.1	E864.1	—	E950.7	E962.1	E980.6
Stovaine	968.9	E855.2	E938.9	E950.4	E962.0	E980.4
infiltration (subcutaneous)	968.5	E855.2	E938.5	E950.4	E962.0	E980.4
nerve block (peripheral) (plexus)	968.6	E855.2	E938.6	E950.4	E962.0	E980.4
spinal	968.7	E855.2	E938.7	E950.4	E962.0	E980.4
topical (surface)	968.5	E855.2	E938.5	E950.4	E962.0	E980.4
Stovarsal	961.1	E857	E931.1	E950.4	E962.0	E980.4
Stove gas — *see* Gas, utility						
Stoxil	976.5	E858.7	E946.5	E950.4	E962.0	E980.4
STP	969.6	E854.1	E939.6	E950.3	E962.0	E980.3
Stramonium (medicinal) NEC	971.1	E855.4	E941.1	E950.4	E962.0	E980.4
natural state	988.2	E865.4	—	E950.9	E962.1	E980.9
Streptodornase	964.4	E858.2	E934.4	E950.4	E962.0	E980.4
Streptoduocin	960.6	E856	E930.6	E950.4	E962.0	E980.4
Streptokinase	964.4	E858.2	E934.4	E950.4	E962.0	E980.4
Streptomycin	960.6	E856	E930.6	E950.4	E962.0	E980.4
Streptozocin	960.7	E856	E930.7	E950.4	E962.0	E980.4
Stripper (paint) (solvent)	982.8	E862.9	—	E950.9	E962.1	E980.9
Strobane	989.2	E863.0	—	E950.6	E962.1	E980.7
Strophanthin	972.1	E858.3	E942.1	E950.4	E962.0	E980.4
Strophanthus hispidus or kombe	988.2	E865.4	—	E950.9	E962.1	E980.9
Strychnine (rodenticide) (salts)	989.1	E863.7	—	E950.6	E962.1	E980.7
medicinal NEC	970.8	E854.3	E940.8	E950.4	E962.0	E980.4
Strychnos (ignatii) — *see* Strychnine						
Styramate	968.0	E855.1	E938.0	E950.4	E962.0	E980.4
Styrene	983.0	E864.0	—	E950.7	E962.1	E980.6
Succinimide (anticonvulsant)	966.2	E855.0	E936.2	E950.4	E962.0	E980.4
mercuric — *see* Mercury						
Succinylcholine	975.2	E858.6	E945.2	E950.4	E962.0	E980.4
Succinylsulfathiazole	961.0	E857	E931.0	E950.4	E962.0	E980.4
Sucrose	974.5	E858.5	E944.5	E950.4	E962.0	E980.4
Sulfacetamide	961.0	E857	E931.0	E950.4	E962.0	E980.4
ophthalmic preparation	976.5	E858.7	E946.5	E950.4	E962.0	E980.4
Sulfachlorpyridazine	961.0	E857	E931.0	E950.4	E962.0	E980.4
Sulfacytine	961.0	E857	E931.0	E950.4	E962.0	E980.4
Sulfadiazine	961.0	E857	E931.0	E950.4	E962.0	E980.4
silver (topical)	976.0	E858.7	E946.0	E950.4	E962.0	E980.4
Sulfadimethoxine	961.0	E857	E931.0	E950.4	E962.0	E980.4
Sulfadimidine	961.0	E857	E931.0	E950.4	E962.0	E980.4
Sulfaethidole	961.0	E857	E931.0	E950.4	E962.0	E980.4
Sulfafurazole	961.0	E857	E931.0	E950.4	E962.0	E980.4
Sulfaguanidine	961.0	E857	E931.0	E950.4	E962.0	E980.4
Sulfamerazine	961.0	E857	E931.0	E950.4	E962.0	E980.4
Sulfameter	961.0	E857	E931.0	E950.4	E962.0	E980.4
Sulfamethizole	961.0	E857	E931.0	E950.4	E962.0	E980.4
Sulfamethoxazole	961.0	E857	E931.0	E950.4	E962.0	E980.4
Sulfamethoxydiazine	961.0	E857	E931.0	E950.4	E962.0	E980.4
Sulfamethoxypyridazine	961.0	E857	E931.0	E950.4	E962.0	E980.4
Sulfamethylthiazole	961.0	E857	E931.0	E950.4	E962.0	E980.4
Sulfamylon	976.0	E858.7	E946.0	E950.4	E962.0	E980.4
Sulfan blue (diagnostic dye)	977.8	E858.8	E947.8	E950.4	E962.0	E980.4
Sulfanilamide	961.0	E857	E931.0	E950.4	E962.0	E980.4
Sulfanilylguanidine	961.0	E857	E931.0	E950.4	E962.0	E980.4
Sulfaphenazole	961.0	E857	E931.0	E950.4	E962.0	E980.4
Sulfaphenylthiazole	961.0	E857	E931.0	E950.4	E962.0	E980.4
Sulfaproxyline	961.0	E857	E931.0	E950.4	E962.0	E980.4
Sulfapyridine	961.0	E857	E931.0	E950.4	E962.0	E980.4

Nontherapeutic use substance

▽ Subterms under main terms may continue to next column or page

    ▶◀ Revised Text   ● New Line   ▲ Revised Code

	Poisoning	Accident	Therapeutic Use	Suicide Attempt	Assault	Undetermined
Sulfapyrimidine	961.0	E857	E931.0	E950.4	E962.0	E980.4
Sulfarsphenamine	961.1	E857	E931.1	E950.4	E962.0	E980.4
Sulfasalazine	961.0	E857	E931.0	E950.4	E962.0	E980.4
Sulfasomizole	961.0	E857	E931.0	E950.4	E962.0	E980.4
Sulfasuxidine	961.0	E857	E931.0	E950.4	E962.0	E980.4
Sulfinpyrazone	974.7	E858.5	E944.7	E950.4	E962.0	E980.4
Sulfisoxazole	961.0	E857	E931.0	E950.4	E962.0	E980.4
ophthalmic preparation	976.5	E858.7	E946.5	E950.4	E962.0	E980.4
Sulfomyxin	960.8	E856	E930.8	E950.4	E962.0	E980.4
Sulfonal	967.8	E852.8	E937.8	E950.2	E962.0	E980.2
Sulfonamides (mixtures)	961.0	E857	E931.0	E950.4	E962.0	E980.4
Sulfones	961.8	E857	E931.8	E950.4	E962.0	E980.4
Sulfonethylmethane	967.8	E852.8	E937.8	E950.2	E962.0	E980.2
Sulfonmethane	967.8	E852.8	E937.8	E950.2	E962.0	E980.2
Sulfonphthal, sulfonphthol	977.8	E858.8	E947.8	E950.4	E962.0	E980.4
Sulfonylurea derivatives, oral	962.3	E858.0	E932.3	E950.4	E962.0	E980.4
Sulfoxone	961.8	E857	E931.8	E950.4	E962.0	E980.4
Sulfur, sulfureted, sulfuric, sulfurous, sulfuryl (compounds) NEC	989.89	E866.8	—	E950.9	E962.1	E980.9
acid	983.1	E864.1	—	E950.7	E962.1	E980.6
dioxide	987.3	E869.1	—	E952.8	E962.2	E982.8
ether — see Ether(s)						
hydrogen	987.8	E869.8	—	E952.8	E962.2	E982.8
medicinal (keratolytic) (ointment) NEC	976.4	E858.7	E946.4	E950.4	E962.0	E980.4
pesticide (vapor)	989.4	E863.4	—	E950.6	E962.1	E980.7
vapor NEC	987.8	E869.8	—	E952.8	E962.2	E982.8
Sulkowitch's reagent	977.8	E858.8	E947.8	E950.4	E962.0	E980.4
Sulphadione	961.8	E857	E931.8	E950.4	E962.0	E980.4
Sulph — see also Sulf-						
Sulthiame, sultiame	966.3	E855.0	E936.3	E950.4	E962.0	E980.4
Superinone	975.5	E858.6	E945.5	E950.4	E962.0	E980.4
Suramin	961.5	E857	E931.5	E950.4	E962.0	E980.4
Surfacaine	968.5	E855.2	E938.5	E950.4	E962.0	E980.4
Surital	968.3	E855.1	E938.3	E950.4	E962.0	E980.4
Sutilains	976.8	E858.7	E946.8	E950.4	E962.0	E980.4
Suxamethonium (bromide) (chloride) (iodide)	975.2	E858.6	E945.2	E950.4	E962.0	E980.4
Suxethonium (bromide)	975.2	E858.6	E945.2	E950.4	E962.0	E980.4
Sweet oil (birch)	976.3	E858.7	E946.3	E950.4	E962.0	E980.4
Sym-dichloroethyl ether	982.3	E862.4	—	E950.9	E962.1	E980.9
Sympatholytics	971.3	E855.6	E941.3	E950.4	E962.0	E980.4
Sympathomimetics	971.2	E855.5	E941.2	E950.4	E962.0	E980.4
Synagis	979.6	E858.8	E949.6	E950.4	E962.0	E980.4
Synalar	976.0	E858.7	E946.0	E950.4	E962.0	E980.4
Synthroid	962.7	E858.0	E932.7	E950.4	E962.0	E980.4
Syntocinon	975.0	E858.6	E945.0	E950.4	E962.0	E980.4
Syrosingopine	972.6	E858.3	E942.6	E950.4	E962.0	E980.4
Systemic agents (primarily)	963.9	E858.1	E933.9	E950.4	E962.0	E980.4
specified NEC	963.8	E858.1	E933.8	E950.4	E962.0	E980.4
Tablets — see also specified substance	977.9	E858.9	E947.9	E950.5	E962.0	E980.5
Tace	962.2	E858.0	E932.2	E950.4	E962.0	E980.4
Tacrine	971.0	E855.3	E941.0	E950.4	E962.0	E980.4
Talbutal	967.0	E851	E937.0	E950.1	E962.0	E980.1
Talc	976.3	E858.7	E946.3	E950.4	E962.0	E980.4
Talcum	976.3	E858.7	E946.3	E950.4	E962.0	E980.4
Tamsulosin	971.3	E855.6	E941.3	E950.4	E962.0	E980.4
Tandearil, tanderil	965.5	E850.5	E935.5	E950.0	E962.0	E980.0
Tannic acid	983.1	E864.1	—	E950.7	E962.1	E980.6
medicinal (astringent)	976.2	E858.7	E946.2	E950.4	E962.0	E980.4
Tannin — see Tannic acid						
Tansy	988.2	E865.4	—	E950.9	E962.1	E980.9
TAO	960.3	E856	E930.3	E950.4	E962.0	E980.4
Tapazole	962.8	E858.0	E932.8	E950.4	E962.0	E980.4
Tar NEC	983.0	E864.0	—	E950.7	E962.1	E980.6
camphor — see Naphthalene						
fumes	987.8	E869.8	—	E952.8	E962.2	E982.8
Taractan	969.3	E853.8	E939.3	E950.3	E962.0	E980.3
Tarantula (venomous)	989.5	E905.1	—	E950.9	E962.1	E980.9
Tartar emetic (anti-infective)	961.2	E857	E931.2	E950.4	E962.0	E980.4
Tartaric acid	983.1	E864.1	—	E950.7	E962.1	E980.6
Tartrated antimony (anti-infective)	961.2	E857	E931.2	E950.4	E962.0	E980.4
TCA — see Trichloroacetic acid						
TDI	983.0	E864.0	—	E950.7	E962.1	E980.6
vapor	987.8	E869.8	—	E952.8	E962.2	E982.8
Tear gas	987.5	E869.3	—	E952.8	E962.2	E982.8
Teclothiazide	974.3	E858.5	E944.3	E950.4	E962.0	E980.4
Tegretol	966.3	E855.0	E936.3	E950.4	E962.0	E980.4
Telepaque	977.8	E858.8	E947.8	E950.4	E962.0	E980.4
Tellurium	985.8	E866.4	—	E950.9	E962.1	E980.9
fumes	985.8	E866.4	—	E950.9	E962.1	E980.9
TEM	963.1	E858.1	E933.1	E950.4	E962.0	E980.4
Temazepan — see Benzodiazepines						
TEPA	963.1	E858.1	E933.1	E950.4	E962.0	E980.4
TEPP	989.3	E863.1	—	E950.6	E962.1	E980.7
Terbutaline	971.2	E855.5	E941.2	E950.4	E962.0	E980.4
Teroxalene	961.6	E857	E931.6	E950.4	E962.0	E980.4
Terpin hydrate	975.5	E858.6	E945.5	E950.4	E962.0	E980.4
Terramycin	960.4	E856	E930.4	E950.4	E962.0	E980.4
Tessalon	975.4	E858.6	E945.4	E950.4	E962.0	E980.4
Testosterone	962.1	E858.0	E932.1	E950.4	E962.0	E980.4
Tetanus (vaccine)	978.4	E858.8	E948.4	E950.4	E962.0	E980.4
antitoxin	979.9	E858.8	E949.9	E950.4	E962.0	E980.4
immune globulin (human)	964.6	E858.2	E934.6	E950.4	E962.0	E980.4
toxoid	978.4	E858.8	E948.4	E950.4	E962.0	E980.4
with diphtheria toxoid	978.9	E858.8	E948.9	E950.4	E962.0	E980.4
with pertussis	978.6	E858.8	E948.6	E950.4	E962.0	E980.4
Tetrabenazine	969.5	E853.8	E939.5	E950.3	E962.0	E980.3
Tetracaine (infiltration) (topical)	968.5	E855.2	E938.5	E950.4	E962.0	E980.4
nerve block (peripheral) (plexus)	968.6	E855.2	E938.6	E950.4	E962.0	E980.4
spinal	968.7	E855.2	E938.7	E950.4	E962.0	E980.4
Tetrachlorethylene — see Tetrachloroethylene						
Tetrachlormethiazide	974.3	E858.5	E944.3	E950.4	E962.0	E980.4
Tetrachloroethane (liquid) (vapor)	982.3	E862.4	—	E950.9	E962.1	E980.9
paint or varnish	982.3	E861.6	—	E950.9	E962.1	E980.9
Tetrachloroethylene (liquid) (vapor)	982.3	E862.4	—	E950.9	E962.1	E980.9
medicinal	961.6	E857	E931.6	E950.4	E962.0	E980.4
Tetrachloromethane — see Carbon, tetrachloride						
Tetracycline	960.4	E856	E930.4	E950.4	E962.0	E980.4
ophthalmic preparation	976.5	E858.7	E946.5	E950.4	E962.0	E980.4
topical NEC	976.0	E858.7	E946.0	E950.4	E962.0	E980.4
Tetraethylammonium chloride	972.3	E858.3	E942.3	E950.4	E962.0	E980.4
Tetraethyl lead (antiknock compound)	984.1	E862.1	—	E950.9	E962.1	E980.9
Tetraethyl pyrophosphate	989.3	E863.1	—	E950.6	E962.1	E980.7
Tetraethylthiuram disulfide	977.3	E858.8	E947.3	E950.4	E962.0	E980.4
Tetrahydroaminoacridine	971.0	E855.3	E941.0	E950.4	E962.0	E980.4
Tetrahydrocannabinol	969.6	E854.1	E939.6	E950.3	E962.0	E980.3
Tetrahydronaphthalene	982.0	E862.4	—	E950.9	E962.1	E980.9
Tetrahydrozoline	971.2	E855.5	E941.2	E950.4	E962.0	E980.4
Tetralin	982.0	E862.4	—	E950.9	E962.1	E980.9
Tetramethylthiuram (disulfide) NEC	989.4	E863.6	—	E950.6	E962.1	E980.7
medicinal	976.2	E858.7	E946.2	E950.4	E962.0	E980.4
Tetronal	967.8	E852.8	E937.8	E950.2	E962.0	E980.2
Tetryl	983.0	E864.0	—	E950.7	E962.1	E980.6
Thalidomide	967.8	E852.8	E937.8	E950.2	E962.0	E980.2
Thallium (compounds) (dust) NEC	985.8	E866.4	—	E950.9	E962.1	E980.9
pesticide (rodenticide)	985.8	E863.7	—	E950.6	E962.1	E980.7
THC	969.6	E854.1	E939.6	E950.3	E962.0	E980.3
Thebacon	965.09	E850.2	E935.2	E950.0	E962.0	E980.0
Thebaine	965.09	E850.2	E935.2	E950.0	E962.0	E980.0
Theobromine (calcium salicylate)	974.1	E858.5	E944.1	E950.4	E962.0	E980.4
Theophylline (diuretic)	974.1	E858.5	E944.1	E950.4	E962.0	E980.4
ethylenediamine	975.7	E858.6	E945.7	E950.4	E962.0	E980.4
Thiabendazole	961.6	E857	E931.6	E950.4	E962.0	E980.4
Thialbarbital, thialbarbitone	968.3	E855.1	E938.3	E950.4	E962.0	E980.4
Thiamine	963.5	E858.1	E933.5	E950.4	E962.0	E980.4
Thiamylal (sodium)	968.3	E855.1	E938.3	E950.4	E962.0	E980.4
Thiazesim	969.09 ▲	E854.0	E939.0	E950.3	E962.0	E980.3
Thiazides (diuretics)	974.3	E858.5	E944.3	E950.4	E962.0	E980.4
Thiethylperazine	963.0	E858.1	E933.0	E950.4	E962.0	E980.4
Thimerosal (topical)	976.0	E858.7	E946.0	E950.4	E962.0	E980.4
ophthalmic preparation	976.5	E858.7	E946.5	E950.4	E962.0	E980.4

Nontherapeutic use substance

▽ Subterms under main terms may continue to next column or page

	Poisoning	Accident	Therapeutic Use	Suicide Attempt	Assault	Undetermined
Thioacetazone	961.8	E857	E931.8	E950.4	E962.0	E980.3
Thiobarbiturates	968.3	E855.1	E938.3	E950.4	E962.0	E980.4
Thiobismol	961.2	E857	E931.2	E950.4	E962.0	E980.4
Thiocarbamide	962.8	E858.0	E932.8	E950.4	E962.0	E980.4
Thiocarbarsone	961.1	E857	E931.1	E950.4	E962.0	E980.4
Thiocarlide	961.8	E857	E931.8	E950.4	E962.0	E980.4
Thioguanine	963.1	E858.1	E933.1	E950.4	E962.0	E980.4
Thiomercaptomerin	974.0	E858.5	E944.0	E950.4	E962.0	E980.4
Thiomerin	974.0	E858.5	E944.0	E950.4	E962.0	E980.4
Thiopental, thiopentone (sodium)	968.3	E855.1	E938.3	E950.4	E962.0	E980.4
Thiopropazate	969.1	E853.0	E939.1	E950.3	E962.0	E980.3
Thioproperazine	969.1	E853.0	E939.1	E950.3	E962.0	E980.3
Thioridazine	969.1	E853.0	E939.1	E950.3	E962.0	E980.3
Thio-TEPA, thiotepa	963.1	E858.1	E933.1	E950.4	E962.0	E980.4
Thiothixene	969.3	E853.8	E939.3	E950.4	E962.0	E980.3
Thiouracil	962.8	E858.0	E932.8	E950.4	E962.0	E980.4
Thiourea	962.8	E858.0	E932.8	E950.4	E962.0	E980.4
Thiphenamil	971.1	E855.4	E941.1	E950.4	E962.0	E980.4
Thiram NEC	989.4	E863.6	—	E950.6	E962.1	E980.7
medicinal	976.2	E858.7	E946.2	E950.4	E962.0	E980.4
Thonzylamine	963.0	E858.1	E933.0	E950.4	E962.0	E980.4
Thorazine	969.1	E853.0	E939.1	E950.3	E962.0	E980.3
Thornapple	988.2	E865.4	—	E950.9	E962.1	E980.9
Throat preparation (lozenges) NEC	976.6	E858.7	E946.6	E950.4	E962.0	E980.4
Thrombin	964.5	E858.2	E934.5	E950.4	E962.0	E980.4
Thrombolysin	964.4	E858.2	E934.4	E950.4	E962.0	E980.4
Thymol	983.0	E864.0	—	E950.7	E962.1	E980.6
Thymus extract	962.9	E858.0	E932.9	E950.4	E962.0	E980.4
Thyroglobulin	962.7	E858.0	E932.7	E950.4	E962.0	E980.4
Thyroid (derivatives) (extract)	962.7	E858.0	E932.7	E950.4	E962.0	E980.4
Thyrolar	962.7	E858.0	E932.7	E950.4	E962.0	E980.4
Thyrothrophin, thyrotropin	977.8	E858.8	E947.8	E950.4	E962.0	E980.4
Thyroxin(e)	962.7	E858.0	E932.7	E950.4	E962.0	E980.4
Tigan	963.0	E858.1	E933.0	E950.4	E962.0	E980.4
Tigloidine	968.0	E855.1	E938.0	E950.4	E962.0	E980.4
Tin (chloride) (dust) (oxide) NEC	985.8	E866.4	—	E950.9	E962.1	E980.9
anti-infectives	961.2	E857	E931.2	E950.4	E962.0	E980.4
Tinactin	976.0	E858.7	E946.0	E950.4	E962.0	E980.4
Tincture, iodine — see Iodine						
Tindal	969.1	E853.0	E939.1	E950.3	E962.0	E980.3
Titanium (compounds) (vapor)	985.8	E866.4	—	E950.9	E962.1	E980.9
ointment	976.3	E858.7	E946.3	E950.4	E962.0	E980.4
Titroid	962.7	E858.0	E932.7	E950.4	E962.0	E980.4
TMTD — see Tetramethylthiuram disulfide						
TNT	989.89	E866.8	—	E950.9	E962.1	E980.9
fumes	987.8	E869.8	—	E952.8	E962.2	E982.8
Toadstool	988.1	E865.5	—	E950.9	E962.1	E980.9
Tobacco NEC	989.84	E866.8	—	E950.9	E962.1	E980.9
Indian	988.2	E865.4	—	E950.9	E962.1	E980.9
smoke, second-hand	987.8	E869.4	—	—	—	—
Tocopherol	963.5	E858.1	E933.5	E950.4	E962.0	E980.4
Tocosamine	975.0	E858.6	E945.0	E950.4	E962.0	E980.4
Tofranil	969.05 ▲	E854.0	E939.0	E950.3	E962.0	E980.3
Toilet deodorizer	989.89	E866.8	—	E950.9	E962.1	E980.9
Tolazamide	962.3	E858.0	E932.3	E950.4	E962.0	E980.4
Tolazoline	971.3	E855.6	E941.3	E950.4	E962.0	E980.4
Tolbutamide	962.3	E858.0	E932.3	E950.4	E962.0	E980.4
sodium	977.8	E858.8	E947.8	E950.4	E962.0	E980.4
Tolmetin	965.69	E850.6	E935.6	E950.0	E962.0	E980.0
Tolnaftate	976.0	E858.7	E946.0	E950.4	E962.0	E980.4
Tolpropamine	976.1	E858.7	E946.1	E950.4	E962.0	E980.4
Tolserol	968.0	E855.1	E938.0	E950.4	E962.0	E980.4
Toluene (liquid) (vapor)	982.0	E862.4	—	E950.9	E962.1	E980.9
diisocyanate	983.0	E864.0	—	E950.7	E962.1	E980.6
Toluidine	983.0	E864.0	—	E950.7	E962.1	E980.6
vapor	987.8	E869.8	—	E952.8	E962.2	E982.8
Toluol (liquid) (vapor)	982.0	E862.4	—	E950.9	E962.1	E980.9
Tolylene-2, 4-diisocyanate	983.0	E864.0	—	E950.7	E962.1	E980.6
Tonics, cardiac	972.1	E858.3	E942.1	E950.4	E962.0	E980.4
Toxaphene (dust) (spray)	989.2	E863.0	—	E950.6	E962.1	E980.7
Toxoids NEC	978.8	E858.8	E948.8	E950.4	E962.0	E980.4
Tractor fuel NEC	981	E862.1	—	E950.9	E962.1	E980.9
Tragacanth	973.3	E858.4	E943.3	E950.4	E962.0	E980.4
Tramazoline	971.2	E855.5	E941.2	E950.4	E962.0	E980.4
Tranquilizers	969.5	E853.9	E939.5	E950.3	E962.0	E980.3
benzodiazepine-based	969.4	E853.2	E939.4	E950.3	E962.0	E980.3
butyrophenone-based	969.2	E853.1	E939.2	E950.3	E962.0	E980.3
major NEC	969.3	E853.8	E939.3	E950.3	E962.0	E980.3
phenothiazine-based	969.1	E853.0	E939.1	E950.3	E962.0	E980.3
specified NEC	969.5	E853.8	E939.5	E950.3	E962.0	E980.3
Trantoin	961.9	E857	E931.9	E950.4	E962.0	E980.4
Tranxene	969.4	E853.2	E939.4	E950.3	E962.0	E980.3
Tranylcypromine (sulfate)	969.01 ▲	E854.0	E939.0	E950.3	E962.0	E980.3
Trasentine	975.1	E858.6	E945.1	E950.4	E962.0	E980.4
Travert	974.5	E858.5	E944.5	E950.4	E962.0	E980.4
Trecator	961.8	E857	E931.8	E950.4	E962.0	E980.4
Tretinoin	976.8	E858.7	E946.8	E950.4	E962.0	E980.4
Triacetin	976.0	E858.7	E946.0	E950.4	E962.0	E980.4
Triacetyloleandomycin	960.3	E856	E930.3	E950.4	E962.0	E980.4
Triamcinolone	962.0	E858.0	E932.0	E950.4	E962.0	E980.4
ENT agent	976.6	E858.7	E946.6	E950.4	E962.0	E980.4
medicinal (keratolytic)	976.4	E858.7	E946.4	E950.4	E962.0	E980.4
ophthalmic preparation	976.5	E858.7	E946.5	E950.4	E962.0	E980.4
topical NEC	976.0	E858.7	E946.0	E950.4	E962.0	E980.4
Triamterene	974.4	E858.5	E944.4	E950.4	E962.0	E980.4
Triaziquone	963.1	E858.1	E933.1	E950.4	E962.0	E980.4
Tribromacetaldehyde	967.3	E852.2	E937.3	E950.2	E962.0	E980.2
Tribromoethanol	968.2	E855.1	E938.2	E950.4	E962.0	E980.4
Tribromomethane	967.3	E852.2	E937.3	E950.2	E962.0	E980.2
Trichlorethane	982.3	E862.4	—	E950.9	E962.1	E980.9
Trichlormethiazide	974.3	E858.5	E944.3	E950.4	E962.0	E980.4
Trichloroacetic acid	983.1	E864.1	—	E950.7	E962.1	E980.6
Trichloroethanol	967.1	E852.0	E937.1	E950.2	E962.0	E980.2
Trichloroethylene (liquid) (vapor)	982.3	E862.4	—	E950.9	E962.1	E980.9
anesthetic (gas)	968.2	E855.1	E938.2	E950.4	E962.0	E980.4
Trichloroethyl phosphate	967.1	E852.0	E937.1	E950.2	E962.0	E980.2
Trichlorofluoromethane NEC	987.4	E869.2	—	E952.8	E962.2	E982.8
Trichlorotriethylamine	963.1	E858.1	E933.1	E950.4	E962.0	E980.4
Trichomonacides NEC	961.5	E857	E931.5	E950.4	E962.0	E980.4
Trichomycin	960.1	E856	E930.1	E950.4	E962.0	E980.4
Triclofos	967.1	E852.0	E937.1	E950.2	E962.0	E980.2
Tricresyl phosphate	989.89	E866.8	—	E950.9	E962.1	E980.9
solvent	982.8	E862.4	—	E950.9	E962.1	E980.9
Tricyclamol	966.4	E855.0	E936.4	E950.4	E962.0	E980.4
Tridesilon	976.0	E858.7	E946.0	E950.4	E962.0	E980.4
Tridihexethyl	971.1	E855.4	E941.1	E950.4	E962.0	E980.4
Tridione	966.0	E855.0	E936.0	E950.4	E962.0	E980.4
Triethanolamine NEC	983.2	E864.2	—	E950.7	E962.1	E980.6
detergent	983.2	E861.0	—	E950.7	E962.1	E980.6
trinitrate	972.4	E858.3	E942.4	E950.4	E962.0	E980.4
Triethanomelamine	963.1	E858.1	E933.1	E950.4	E962.0	E980.4
Triethylene melamine	963.1	E858.1	E933.1	E950.4	E962.0	E980.4
Triethylenephosphoramide	963.1	E858.1	E933.1	E950.4	E962.0	E980.4
Triethylenethiophosphoramide	963.1	E858.1	E933.1	E950.4	E962.0	E980.4
Trifluoperazine	969.1	E853.0	E939.1	E950.3	E962.0	E980.3
Trifluperidol	969.2	E853.1	E939.2	E950.3	E962.0	E980.3
Triflupromazine	969.1	E853.0	E939.1	E950.3	E962.0	E980.3
Trihexyphenidyl	971.1	E855.4	E941.1	E950.4	E962.0	E980.4
Triiodothyronine	962.7	E858.0	E932.7	E950.4	E962.0	E980.4
Trilene	968.2	E855.1	E938.2	E950.4	E962.0	E980.4
Trimeprazine	963.0	E858.1	E933.0	E950.4	E962.0	E980.4
Trimetazidine	972.4	E858.3	E942.4	E950.4	E962.0	E980.4
Trimethadione	966.0	E855.0	E936.0	E950.4	E962.0	E980.4
Trimethaphan	972.3	E858.3	E942.3	E950.4	E962.0	E980.4
Trimethidinium	972.3	E858.3	E942.3	E950.4	E962.0	E980.4
Trimethobenzamide	963.0	E858.1	E933.0	E950.4	E962.0	E980.4
Trimethylcarbinol	980.8	E860.8	—	E950.9	E962.1	E980.9
Trimethylpsoralen	976.3	E858.7	E946.3	E950.4	E962.0	E980.4
Trimeton	963.0	E858.1	E933.0	E950.4	E962.0	E980.4
Trimipramine	969.05 ▲	E854.0	E939.0	E950.3	E962.0	E980.3
Trimustine	963.1	E858.1	E933.1	E950.4	E962.0	E980.4
Trinitrin	972.4	E858.3	E942.4	E950.4	E962.0	E980.4
Trinitrophenol	983.0	E864.0	—	E950.7	E962.1	E980.6
Trinitrotoluene	989.89	E866.8	—	E950.9	E962.1	E980.9
fumes	987.8	E869.8	—	E952.8	E962.2	E982.8
Trional	967.8	E852.8	E937.8	E950.2	E962.0	E980.2
Trioxide of arsenic — see Arsenic						
Trioxsalen	976.3	E858.7	E946.3	E950.4	E962.0	E980.4
Tripelennamine	963.0	E858.1	E933.0	E950.4	E962.0	E980.4
Triperidol	969.2	E853.1	E939.2	E950.3	E962.0	E980.3
Triprolidine	963.0	E858.1	E933.0	E950.4	E962.0	E980.4
Trisoralen	976.3	E858.7	E946.3	E950.4	E962.0	E980.4
Troleandomycin	960.3	E856	E930.3	E950.4	E962.0	E980.4

Nontherapeutic use substance

Subterms under main terms may continue to next column or page

	Poisoning	Accident	Therapeutic Use	Suicide Attempt	Assault	Undetermined
Trolnitrate (phosphate)	972.4	E858.3	E942.4	E950.4	E962.0	E980.4
Trometamol	963.3	E858.1	E933.3	E950.4	E962.0	E980.4
Tromethamine	963.3	E858.1	E933.3	E950.4	E962.0	E980.4
Tronothane	968.5	E855.2	E938.5	E950.4	E962.0	E980.4
Tropicamide	971.1	E855.4	E941.1	E950.4	E962.0	E980.4
Troxidone	966.0	E855.0	E936.0	E950.4	E962.0	E980.4
Tryparsamide	961.1	E857	E931.1	E950.4	E962.0	E980.4
Trypsin	963.4	E858.1	E933.4	E950.4	E962.0	E980.4
Tryptizol	969.05 ▲	E854.0	E939.0	E950.3	E962.0	E980.3
Tuaminoheptane	971.2	E855.5	E941.2	E950.4	E962.0	E980.4
Tuberculin (old)	977.8	E858.8	E947.8	E950.4	E962.0	E980.4
Tubocurare	975.2	E858.6	E945.2	E950.4	E962.0	E980.4
Tubocurarine	975.2	E858.6	E945.2	E950.4	E962.0	E980.4
Turkish green	969.6	E854.1	E939.6	E950.3	E962.0	E980.3
Turpentine (spirits of) (liquid)						
(vapor)	982.8	E862.4	—	E950.9	E962.1	E980.9
Tybamate	969.5	E853.8	E939.5	E950.3	E962.0	E980.3
Tyloxapol	975.5	E858.6	E945.5	E950.4	E962.0	E980.4
Tymazoline	971.2	E855.5	E941.2	E950.4	E962.0	E980.4
Typhoid vaccine	978.1	E858.8	E948.1	E950.4	E962.0	E980.4
Typhus vaccine	979.2	E858.8	E949.2	E950.4	E962.0	E980.4
Tyrothricin	976.0	E858.7	E946.0	E950.4	E962.0	E980.4
ENT agent	976.6	E858.7	E946.6	E950.4	E962.0	E980.4
ophthalmic preparation	976.5	E858.7	E946.5	E950.4	E962.0	E980.4
Undecenoic acid	976.0	E858.7	E946.0	E950.4	E962.0	E980.4
Undecylenic acid	976.0	E858.7	E946.0	E950.4	E962.0	E980.4
Unna's boot	976.3	E858.7	E946.3	E950.4	E962.0	E980.4
Uracil mustard	963.1	E858.1	E933.1	E950.4	E962.0	E980.4
Uramustine	963.1	E858.1	E933.1	E950.4	E962.0	E980.4
Urari	975.2	E858.6	E945.2	E950.4	E962.0	E980.4
Urea	974.4	E858.5	E944.4	E950.4	E962.0	E980.4
topical	976.8	E858.7	E946.8	E950.4	E962.0	E980.4
Urethan(e)						
(antineoplastic)	963.1	E858.1	E933.1	E950.4	E962.0	E980.4
Urginea (maritima) (scilla) — see Squill						
Uric acid metabolism agents NEC	974.7	E858.5	E944.7	E950.4	E962.0	E980.4
Urokinase	964.4	E858.2	E934.4	E950.4	E962.0	E980.4
Urokon	977.8	E858.8	E947.8	E950.4	E962.0	E980.4
Urotropin	961.9	E857	E931.9	E950.4	E962.0	E980.4
Urtica	988.2	E865.4	—	E950.9	E962.1	E980.9
Utility gas — see Gas, utility						
Vaccine NEC	979.9	E858.8	E949.9	E950.4	E962.0	E980.4
bacterial NEC	978.8	E858.8	E948.8	E950.4	E962.0	E980.4
with						
other bacterial component	978.9	E858.8	E948.9	E950.4	E962.0	E980.4
pertussis component	978.6	E858.8	E948.6	E950.4	E962.0	E980.4
viral-rickettsial component	979.7	E858.8	E949.7	E950.4	E962.0	E980.4
mixed NEC	978.9	E858.8	E948.9	E950.4	E962.0	E980.4
BCG	978.0	E858.8	E948.0	E950.4	E962.0	E980.4
cholera	978.2	E858.8	E948.2	E950.4	E962.0	E980.4
diphtheria	978.5	E858.8	E948.5	E950.4	E962.0	E980.4
influenza	979.6	E858.8	E949.6	E950.4	E962.0	E980.4
measles	979.4	E858.8	E949.4	E950.4	E962.0	E980.4
meningococcal	978.8	E858.8	E948.8	E950.4	E962.0	E980.4
mumps	979.6	E858.8	E949.6	E950.4	E962.0	E980.4
paratyphoid	978.1	E858.8	E948.1	E950.4	E962.0	E980.4
pertussis (with diphtheria toxoid) (with tetanus toxoid)	978.6	E858.8	E948.6	E950.4	E962.0	E980.4
plague	978.3	E858.8	E948.3	E950.4	E962.0	E980.4
poliomyelitis	979.5	E858.8	E949.5	E950.4	E962.0	E980.4
poliovirus	979.5	E858.8	E949.5	E950.4	E962.0	E980.4
rabies	979.1	E858.8	E949.1	E950.4	E962.0	E980.4
respiratory syncytial virus	979.6	E858.8	E949.6	E950.4	E962.0	E980.4
rickettsial NEC	979.6	E858.8	E949.6	E950.4	E962.0	E980.4
with						
bacterial component	979.7	E858.8	E949.7	E950.4	E962.0	E980.4
pertussis component	978.6	E858.8	E948.6	E950.4	E962.0	E980.4
viral component	979.7	E858.8	E949.7	E950.4	E962.0	E980.4
Rocky mountain spotted fever	979.6	E858.8	E949.6	E950.4	E962.0	E980.4
rotavirus	979.6	E858.8	E949.6	E950.4	E962.0	E980.4
rubella virus	979.4	E858.8	E949.4	E950.4	E962.0	E980.4
sabin oral	979.5	E858.8	E949.5	E950.4	E962.0	E980.4
smallpox	979.0	E858.8	E949.0	E950.4	E962.0	E980.4
tetanus	978.4	E858.8	E948.4	E950.4	E962.0	E980.4
typhoid	978.1	E858.8	E948.1	E950.4	E962.0	E980.4
typhus	979.2	E858.8	E949.2	E950.4	E962.0	E980.4
Vaccine — continued						
viral NEC	979.6	E858.8	E949.6	E950.4	E962.0	E980.4
with						
bacterial component	979.7	E858.8	E949.7	E950.4	E962.0	E980.4
pertussis component	978.6	E858.8	E948.6	E950.4	E962.0	E980.4
rickettsial component	979.7	E858.8	E949.7	E950.4	E962.0	E980.4
yellow fever	979.3	E858.8	E949.3	E950.4	E962.0	E980.4
Vaccinia immune globulin (human)	964.6	E858.2	E934.6	E950.4	E962.0	E980.4
Vaginal contraceptives	976.8	E858.7	E946.8	E950.4	E962.0	E980.4
Valethamate	971.1	E855.4	E941.1	E950.4	E962.0	E980.4
Valisone	976.0	E858.7	E946.0	E950.4	E962.0	E980.4
Valium	969.4	E853.2	E939.4	E950.3	E962.0	E980.3
Valmid	967.8	E852.8	E937.8	E950.2	E962.0	E980.2
Vanadium	985.8	E866.4	—	E950.9	E962.1	E980.9
Vancomycin	960.8	E856	E930.8	E950.4	E962.0	E980.4
Vapor — see also Gas	987.9	E869.9	—	E952.9	E962.2	E982.9
kiln (carbon monoxide)	986	E868.8	—	E952.1	E962.2	E982.1
lead — see Lead						
specified source NEC (see also specific substance)	987.8	E869.8	—	E952.8	E962.2	E982.8
Varidase	964.4	E858.2	E934.4	E950.4	E962.0	E980.4
Varnish	989.89	E861.6	—	E950.9	E962.1	E980.9
cleaner	982.8	E862.9	—	E950.9	E962.1	E980.9
Vaseline	976.3	E858.7	E946.3	E950.4	E962.0	E980.4
Vasodilan	972.5	E858.3	E942.5	E950.4	E962.0	E980.4
Vasodilators NEC	972.5	E858.3	E942.5	E950.4	E962.0	E980.4
coronary	972.4	E858.3	E942.4	E950.4	E962.0	E980.4
Vasopressin	962.5	E858.0	E932.5	E950.4	E962.0	E980.4
Vasopressor drugs	962.5	E858.0	E932.5	E950.4	E962.0	E980.4
Venom, venomous (bite) (sting)	989.5	E905.9	—	E950.9	E962.1	E980.9
arthropod NEC	989.5	E905.5	—	E950.9	E962.1	E980.9
bee	989.5	E905.3	—	E950.9	E962.1	E980.9
centipede	989.5	E905.4	—	E950.9	E962.1	E980.9
hornet	989.5	E905.3	—	E950.9	E962.1	E980.9
lizard	989.5	E905.0	—	E950.9	E962.1	E980.9
marine animals or plants	989.5	E905.6	—	E950.9	E962.1	E980.9
millipede (tropical)	989.5	E905.4	—	E950.9	E962.1	E980.9
plant NEC	989.5	E905.7	—	E950.9	E962.1	E980.9
marine	989.5	E905.6	—	E950.9	E962.1	E980.9
scorpion	989.5	E905.2	—	E950.9	E962.1	E980.9
snake	989.5	E905.0	—	E950.9	E962.1	E980.9
specified NEC	989.5	E905.8	—	E950.9	E962.1	E980.9
spider	989.5	E905.1	—	E950.9	E962.1	E980.9
wasp	989.5	E905.3	—	E950.9	E962.1	E980.9
Ventolin — see Salbutamol sulfate						
Veramon	967.0	E851	E937.0	E950.1	E962.0	E980.1
Veratrum						
album	988.2	E865.4	—	E950.9	E962.1	E980.9
alkaloids	972.6	E858.3	E942.6	E950.4	E962.0	E980.4
viride	988.2	E865.4	—	E950.9	E962.1	E980.9
Verdigris — see also Copper	985.8	E866.4	—	E950.9	E962.1	E980.9
Veronal	967.0	E851	E937.0	E950.1	E962.0	E980.1
Veroxil	961.6	E857	E931.6	E950.4	E962.0	E980.4
Versidyne	965.7	E850.7	E935.7	E950.0	E962.0	E980.0
Viagra	972.5	E858.3	E942.5	E950.4	E962.0	E980.4
Vienna						
green	985.1	E866.3	—	E950.8	E962.1	E980.8
insecticide	985.1	E863.4	—	E950.6	E962.1	E980.7
red	989.89	E866.8	—	E950.9	E962.1	E980.9
pharmaceutical dye	977.4	E858.8	E947.4	E950.4	E962.0	E980.4
Vinbarbital, vinbarbitone	967.0	E851	E937.0	E950.1	E962.0	E980.1
Vinblastine	963.1	E858.1	E933.1	E950.4	E962.0	E980.4
Vincristine	963.1	E858.1	E933.1	E950.4	E962.0	E980.4
Vinesthene, vinethene	968.2	E855.1	E938.2	E950.4	E962.0	E980.4
Vinyl						
bital	967.0	E851	E937.0	E950.1	E962.0	E980.1
ether	968.2	E855.1	E938.2	E950.4	E962.0	E980.4
Vioform	961.3	E857	E931.3	E950.4	E962.0	E980.4
topical	976.0	E858.7	E946.0	E950.4	E962.0	E980.4
Viomycin	960.6	E856	E930.6	E950.4	E962.0	E980.4
Viosterol	963.5	E858.1	E933.5	E950.4	E962.0	E980.4
Viper (venom)	989.5	E905.0	—	E950.9	E962.1	E980.9
Viprynium (embonate)	961.6	E857	E931.6	E950.4	E962.0	E980.4
Virugon	961.7	E857	E931.7	E950.4	E962.0	E980.4
Visine	976.5	E858.7	E946.5	E950.4	E962.0	E980.4
Vitamins NEC	963.5	E858.1	E933.5	E950.4	E962.0	E980.4
B_{12}	964.1	E858.2	E934.1	E950.4	E962.0	E980.4
hematopoietic	964.1	E858.2	E934.1	E950.4	E962.0	E980.4

Nontherapeutic use substance

▽ Subterms under main terms may continue to next column or page

		External Cause (E-Code)				
	Poisoning	Accident	Therapeutic Use	Suicide Attempt	Assault	Undeter-mined
Vitamins — *continued*						
K	964.3	E858.2	E934.3	E950.4	E962.0	E980.4
Vleminckx's solution	976.4	E858.7	E946.4	E950.4	E962.0	E980.4
Voltaren — *see* Diclofenac sodium						
Warfarin (potassium)						
(sodium)	964.2	E858.2	E934.2	E950.4	E962.0	E980.4
rodenticide	989.4	E863.7	—	E950.6	E962.1	E980.7
Wasp (sting)	989.5	E905.3	—	E950.9	E962.1	E980.9
Water						
balance agents NEC	974.5	E858.5	E944.5	E950.4	E962.0	E980.4
gas	987.1	E868.1	—	E951.8	E962.2	E981.8
incomplete combustion of — see Carbon, monoxide, fuel, utility						
hemlock	988.2	E865.4	—	E950.9	E962.1	E980.9
moccasin (venom)	989.5	E905.0	—	E950.9	E962.1	E980.9
Wax (paraffin) (petroleum)	981	E862.3	—	E950.9	E962.1	E980.9
automobile	989.89	E861.2	—	E950.9	E962.1	E980.9
floor	981	E862.0	—	E950.9	E962.1	E980.9
Weed killers NEC	989.4	E863.5	—	E950.6	E962.1	E980.7
Welldorm	967.1	E852.0	E937.1	E950.2	E962.0	E980.2
White						
arsenic — *see* Arsenic						
hellebore	988.2	E865.4	—	E950.9	E962.1	E980.9
lotion (keratolytic)	976.4	E858.7	E946.4	E950.4	E962.0	E980.4
spirit	981	E862.0	—	E950.9	E962.1	E980.9
Whitewashes	989.89	E861.6	—	E950.9	E962.1	E980.9
Whole blood	964.7	E858.2	E934.7	E950.4	E962.0	E980.4
Wild						
black cherry	988.2	E865.4	—	E950.9	E962.1	E980.9
poisonous plants NEC	988.2	E865.4	—	E950.9	E962.1	E980.9
Window cleaning fluid	989.89	E861.3	—	E950.9	E962.1	E980.9
Wintergreen (oil)	976.3	E858.7	E946.3	E950.4	E962.0	E980.4
Witch hazel	976.2	E858.7	E946.2	E950.4	E962.0	E980.4
Wood						
alcohol	980.1	E860.2	—	E950.9	E962.1	E980.9
spirit	980.1	E860.2	—	E950.9	E962.1	E980.9
Woorali	975.2	E858.6	E945.2	E950.4	E962.0	E980.4
Wormseed, American	961.6	E857	E931.6	E950.4	E962.0	E980.4
Xanthine diuretics	974.1	E858.5	E944.1	E950.4	E962.0	E980.4
Xanthocillin	960.0	E856	E930.0	E950.4	E962.0	E980.4
Xanthotoxin	976.3	E858.7	E946.3	E950.4	E962.0	E980.4
Xigris	964.2	E858.2	E934.2	E950.4	E962.0	E980.4
Xylene (liquid) (vapor)	982.0	E862.4	—	E950.9	E962.1	E980.9
Xylocaine (infiltration)						
(topical)	968.5	E855.2	E938.5	E950.4	E962.0	E980.4
nerve block (peripheral)						
(plexus)	968.6	E855.2	E938.6	E950.4	E962.0	E980.4
spinal	968.7	E855.2	E938.7	E950.4	E962.0	E980.4
Xylol (liquid) (vapor)	982.0	E862.4	—	E950.9	E962.1	E980.9
Xylometazoline	971.2	E855.5	E941.2	E950.4	E962.0	E980.4
Yellow						
fever vaccine	979.3	E858.8	E949.3	E950.4	E962.0	E980.4
jasmine	988.2	E865.4	—	E950.9	E962.1	E980.9
Yew	988.2	E865.4	—	E950.9	E962.1	E980.9
Zactane	965.7	E850.7	E935.7	E950.0	E962.0	E980.0
Zaroxolyn	974.3	E858.5	E944.3	E950.4	E962.0	E980.4
Zephiran (topical)	976.0	E858.7	E946.0	E950.4	E962.0	E980.4
ophthalmic preparation	976.5	E858.7	E946.5	E950.4	E962.0	E980.4
Zerone	980.1	E860.2	—	E950.9	E962.1	E980.9
Zinc (compounds) (fumes) (salts) (vapor) NEC	985.8	E866.4	—	E950.9	E962.1	E980.9
anti-infectives	976.0	E858.7	E946.0	E950.4	E962.0	E980.4
antivaricose	972.7	E858.3	E942.7	E950.4	E962.0	E980.4
bacitracin	976.0	E858.7	E946.0	E950.4	E962.0	E980.4
chloride	976.2	E858.7	E946.2	E950.4	E962.0	E980.4
gelatin	976.3	E858.7	E946.3	E950.4	E962.0	E980.4
oxide	976.3	E858.7	E946.3	E950.4	E962.0	E980.4
peroxide	976.0	E858.7	E946.0	E950.4	E962.0	E980.4
pesticides	985.8	E863.4	—	E950.6	E962.1	E980.7
phosphide (rodenticide)	985.8	E863.7	—	E950.6	E962.1	E980.7
stearate	976.3	E858.7	E946.3	E950.4	E962.0	E980.4
sulfate (antivaricose)	972.7	E858.3	E942.7	E950.4	E962.0	E980.4
ENT agent	976.6	E858.7	E946.6	E950.4	E962.0	E980.4
ophthalmic solution	976.5	E858.7	E946.5	E950.4	E962.0	E980.4
topical NEC	976.0	E858.7	E946.0	E950.4	E962.0	E980.4
undecylenate	976.0	E858.7	E946.0	E950.4	E962.0	E980.4
Zovant	964.2	E858.2	E934.2	E950.4	E962.0	E980.4
Zoxazolamine	968.0	E855.1	E938.0	E950.4	E962.0	E980.4
Zygadenus (venenosus)	988.2	E865.4	—	E950.9	E962.1	E980.9

Nontherapeutic use substance

Subterms under main terms may continue to next column or page

►◄ Revised Text   ● New Line   ▲ Revised Code

SECTION 3

Alphabetic Index to External Causes of Injury and Poisoning (E Code)

This section contains the index to the codes which classify environmental events, circumstances, and other conditions as the cause of injury and other adverse effects. Where a code from the section Supplementary Classification of External Causes of Injury and Poisoning (E800-E999) is applicable, it is intended that the E code shall be used in addition to a code from the main body of the classification, Chapters 1 to 17.

The alphabetic index to the E codes is organized by main terms which describe the accident, circumstance, event, or specific agent which caused the injury or other adverse effect.

Note — Transport accidents (E800-E848) include accidents involving:

> *aircraft and spacecraft (E840-E845)*
>
> *watercraft (E830-E838)*
>
> *motor vehicle (E810-E825)*
>
> *railway (E800-E807)*
>
> *other road vehicles (E826-E829)*

For definitions and examples related to transport accidents — see Volume 1 code categories E800-E848.

The fourth-digit subdivisions for use with categories E800-E848 to identify the injured person are found at the end of this section.

For identifying the place in which an accident or poisoning occurred (circumstances classifiable to categories E850-E869 and E880-E928) — see the listing in this section under "Accident, occurring."

See the Table of Drugs and Chemicals (Section 2 of this volume) for identifying the specific agent involved in drug overdose or a wrong substance given or taken in error, and for intoxication or poisoning by a drug or other chemical substance.

The specific adverse effect, reaction, or localized toxic effect to a correct drug or substance properly administered in therapeutic or prophylactic dosage should be classified according to the nature of the adverse effect (e.g., allergy, dermatitis, tachycardia) listed in Section 1 of this volume.

A

Abandonment
- causing exposure to weather conditions — *see* Exposure
- child, with intent to injure or kill E968.4
- helpless person, infant, newborn E904.0
  - with intent to injure or kill E968.4

Abortion, criminal, injury to child E968.8

Abuse (alleged) (suspected)
- adult
  - by
    - child E967.4
    - ex-partner E967.3
    - ex-spouse E967.3
    - father E967.0
    - grandchild E967.7
    - grandparent E967.6
    - mother E967.2
    - non-related caregiver E967.8
    - other relative E967.7
    - other specified person E967.1
    - partner E967.3
    - sibling E967.5
    - spouse E967.3
    - stepfather E967.0
    - stepmother E967.2
    - unspecified person E967.9
- child
  - by
    - boyfriend of parent or guardian E967.0
    - child E967.4
    - father E967.0
    - female partner of parent or guardian E967.2
    - girlfriend of parent or guardian E967.2
    - grandchild E967.7
    - grandparent E967.6
    - male partner of parent or guardian E967.2
    - mother E967.2
    - non-related caregiver E967.8
    - other relative E967.7
    - other specified person(s) E967.1
    - sibling E967.5
    - stepfather E967.0
    - stepmother E967.2
    - unspecified person E967.9

Accident (to) E928.9
- aircraft (in transit) (powered) E841 ☑
  - at landing, take-off E840 ☑
  - due to, caused by cataclysm — *see* categories E908 ☑, E909 ☑
  - late effect of E929.1
  - unpowered (*see also* Collision, aircraft, unpowered) E842 ☑
  - while alighting, boarding E843 ☑
- amphibious vehicle
  - on
    - land — *see* Accident, motor vehicle
    - water — *see* Accident, watercraft
- animal-drawn vehicle NEC E827 ☑
- animal, ridden NEC E828 ☑
- balloon (*see also* Collision, aircraft, unpowered) E842 ☑
- caused by, due to
  - abrasive wheel (metalworking) E919.3
  - animal NEC E906.9
    - being ridden (in sport or transport) E828 ☑
  - avalanche NEC E909.2
  - band saw E919.4
  - bench saw E919.4
  - bore, earth-drilling or mining (land) (seabed) E919.1
  - bulldozer E919.7
  - cataclysmic
    - earth surface movement or eruption E909.9
    - storm E908.9
  - chain
    - hoist E919.2
      - agricultural operations E919.0
      - mining operations E919.1
    - saw E920.1
    - circular saw E919.4

Accident (to) — *continued*
- caused by, due to — *continued*
  - cold (excessive) (*see also* Cold, exposure to) E901.9
  - combine E919.0
  - conflagration — *see* Conflagration
  - corrosive liquid, substance NEC E924.1
  - cotton gin E919.8
  - crane E919.2
    - agricultural operations E919.0
    - mining operations E919.1
  - cutting or piercing instrument (*see also* Cut) E920.9
  - dairy equipment E919.8
  - derrick E919.2
    - agricultural operations E919.0
    - mining operations E919.1
  - drill E920.1
    - earth (land) (seabed) E919.1
    - hand (powered) E920.1
      - not powered E920.4
    - metalworking E919.3
    - woodworking E919.4
  - earth(-)
    - drilling machine E919.1
    - moving machine E919.7
    - scraping machine E919.7
  - electric
    - current (*see also* Electric shock) E925.9
    - motor (*see also* Accident, machine, by type of machine)
      - current (of) — *see* Electric shock
  - elevator (building) (grain) E919.2
    - agricultural operations E919.0
    - mining operations E919.1
  - environmental factors NEC E928.9
  - excavating machine E919.7
  - explosive material (*see also* Explosion) E923.9
  - farm machine E919.0
  - firearm missile — *see* Shooting
  - fire, flames (*see also* Fire)
    - conflagration — *see* Conflagration
  - forging (metalworking) machine E919.3
  - forklift (truck) E919.2
    - agricultural operations E919.0
    - mining operations E919.1
  - gas turbine E919.5
  - harvester E919.0
  - hay derrick, mower, or rake E919.0
  - heat (excessive) (*see also* Heat) E900.9
  - hoist (*see also* Accident, caused by, due to, lift) E919.2
    - chain — *see* Accident, caused by, due to, chain
    - shaft E919.1
  - hot
    - liquid E924.0
      - caustic or corrosive E924.1
    - object (not producing fire or flames) E924.8
    - substance E924.9
      - caustic or corrosive E924.1
      - liquid (metal) NEC E924.0
      - specified type NEC E924.8
  - human bite E928.3
  - ignition — *see* Ignition
  - internal combustion engine E919.5
  - landslide NEC E909.2
  - lathe (metalworking) E919.3
    - turnings E920.8
    - woodworking E919.4
  - lift, lifting (appliances) E919.2
    - agricultural operations E919.0
    - mining operations E919.1
    - shaft E919.1
  - lightning NEC E907
  - machine, machinery (*see also* Accident, machine)
    - drilling, metal E919.3
    - manufacturing, for manufacture of
      - beverages E919.8
      - clothing E919.8
      - foodstuffs E919.8
      - paper E919.8
      - textiles E919.8

Accident (to) — *continued*
- caused by, due to — *continued*
  - machine, machinery (*see also* Accident, machine) — *continued*
    - milling, metal E919.3
    - moulding E919.4
    - power press, metal E919.3
    - printing E919.8
    - rolling mill, metal E919.3
    - sawing, metal E919.3
    - specified type NEC E919.8
    - spinning E919.8
    - weaving E919.8
  - natural factor NEC E928.9
  - overhead plane E919.4
  - plane E920.4
    - overhead E919.4
  - powered
    - hand tool NEC E920.1
    - saw E919.4
      - hand E920.1
  - printing machine E919.8
  - pulley (block) E919.2
    - agricultural operations E919.0
    - mining operations E919.1
    - transmission E919.6
  - radial saw E919.4
  - radiation — *see* Radiation
  - reaper E919.0
  - road scraper E919.7
    - when in transport under its own power — *see* categories E810-E825 ☑
  - roller coaster E919.8
  - sander E919.4
  - saw E920.4
    - band E919.4
    - bench E919.4
    - chain E920.1
    - circular E919.4
    - hand E920.4
      - powered E920.1
    - powered, except hand E919.4
    - radial E919.4
  - sawing machine, metal E919.3
  - shaft
    - hoist E919.1
    - lift E919.1
    - transmission E919.6
  - shears E920.4
    - hand E920.4
      - powered E920.1
    - mechanical E919.3
  - shovel E920.4
    - steam E919.7
  - spinning machine E919.8
  - steam (*see also* Burning, steam)
    - engine E919.5
    - shovel E919.7
  - thresher E919.0
  - thunderbolt NEC E907
  - tractor E919.0
    - when in transport under its own power — *see* categories E810-E825 ☑
  - transmission belt, cable, chain, gear, pinion, pulley, shaft E919.6
  - turbine (gas) (water driven) E919.5
  - under-cutter E919.1
  - weaving machine E919.8
  - winch E919.2
    - agricultural operations E919.0
    - mining operations E919.1
- diving E883.0
  - with insufficient air supply E913.2
- glider (hang) (*see also* Collision, aircraft, unpowered) E842 ☑
- hovercraft
  - on
    - land — *see* Accident, motor vehicle
    - water — *see* Accident, watercraft
- ice yacht (*see also* Accident, vehicle NEC) E848
- in
  - medical, surgical procedure
    - as, or due to misadventure — *see* Misadventure

Accident (to) — *continued*
- in — *continued*
  - medical, surgical procedure — *continued*
    - causing an abnormal reaction or later complication without mention of misadventure — *see* Reaction, abnormal
- kite carrying a person (*see also* Collision, involving aircraft, unpowered) E842 ☑
- land yacht (*see also* Accident, vehicle NEC) E848
- late effect of — *see* Late effect
- launching pad E845 ☑
- machine, machinery (*see also* Accident, caused by, due to, by specific type of machine) E919.9
  - agricultural including animal-powered E919.0
  - earth-drilling E919.1
  - earth moving or scraping E919.7
  - excavating E919.7
  - involving transport under own power on highway or transport vehicle — *see* categories E810-E825 ☑, E840-E845 ☑
  - lifting (appliances) E919.2
  - metalworking E919.3
  - mining E919.1
  - prime movers, except electric motors E919.5
    - electric motors — *see* Accident, machine, by specific type of machine
  - recreational E919.8
  - specified type NEC E919.8
  - transmission E919.6
  - watercraft (deck) (engine room) (galley) (laundry) (loading) E836 ☑
  - woodworking or forming E919.4
- motor vehicle (on public highway) (traffic) E819 ☑
  - due to cataclysm — *see* categories E908 ☑, E909 ☑
  - involving
    - collision (*see also* Collision, motor vehicle) E812 ☑
    - nontraffic, not on public highway — *see* categories E820-E825 ☑
    - not involving collision — *see* categories E816-E819 ☑
- nonmotor vehicle NEC E829 ☑
  - nonroad — *see* Accident, vehicle NEC
  - road, except pedal cycle, animal-drawn vehicle, or animal being ridden E829 ☑
- nonroad vehicle NEC — *see* Accident, vehicle NEC
- not elsewhere classifiable involving
  - cable car (not on rails) E847
    - on rails E829 ☑
  - coal car in mine E846
  - hand truck — *see* Accident, vehicle NEC
  - logging car E846
  - sled(ge), meaning snow or ice vehicle E848
  - tram, mine or quarry E846
  - truck
    - mine or quarry E846
    - self-propelled, industrial E846
    - station baggage E846
  - tub, mine or quarry E846
  - vehicle NEC E848
    - snow and ice E848
    - used only on industrial premises E846
  - wheelbarrow E848
- occurring (at) (in)
  - apartment E849.0
  - baseball field, diamond E849.4
  - construction site, any E849.3
  - dock E849.8
    - yard E849.3
  - dormitory E849.7
  - factory (building) (premises) E849.3
  - farm E849.1
    - buildings E849.1
    - house E849.0

☑ Additional Digit Required — Refer to the Tabular List for Digit Selection

⬬ Subterms under main terms may continue to next column or page

Accident (to) — *continued*
  occurring — *continued*
    football field E849.4
    forest E849.8
    garage (place of work) E849.3
      private (home) E849.0
    gravel pit E849.2
    gymnasium E849.4
    highway E849.5
    home (private) (residential) E849.0
      institutional E849.7
    hospital E849.7
    hotel E849.6
    house (private) (residential) E849.0
      movie E849.6
      public E849.6
    institution, residential E849.7
    jail E849.7
    mine E849.2
    motel E849.6
    movie house E849.6
    office (building) E849.6
    orphanage E849.7
    park (public) E849.4
      mobile home E849.8
      trailer E849.8
    parking lot or place E849.8
    place
      industrial NEC E849.3
      parking E849.8
      public E849.8
        specified place NEC E849.5
      recreational NEC E849.4
      sport NEC E849.4
    playground (park) (school) E849.4
    prison E849.6
    public building NEC E849.6
    quarry E849.2
    railway
      line NEC E849.8
      yard E849.3
    residence
      home (private) E849.0
    resort (beach) (lake) (mountain) (seashore)
        (vacation) E849.4
    restaurant E849.6
    sand pit E849.2
    school (building) (private) (public) (state)
        E849.6
      reform E849.7
      riding E849.4
    seashore E849.8
      resort E849.4
    shop (place of work) E849.3
      commercial E849.6
    skating rink E849.4
    sports palace E849.4
    stadium E849.4
    store E849.6
    street E849.5
    swimming pool (public) E849.4
      private home or garden E849.0
    tennis court, public E849.4
    theatre, theater E849.6
    trailer court E849.8
    tunnel E849.2
      under construction E849.2
    warehouse E849.3
    yard
      dock E849.3
      industrial E849.3
      private (home) E849.0
      railway E849.3
  off-road type motor vehicle (not on public
      highway) NEC E821 ☑
    on public highway — *see* categories
        E810-E819 ☑
  pedal cycle E826 ☑
  railway E807 ☑
    due to cataclysm — *see* categories
        E908 ☑, E909 ☑
    involving
      avalanche E909.2
      burning by engine, locomotive, train
          (*see also* Explosion, railway en-
          gine) E803 ☑

Accident (to) — *continued*
  railway — *continued*
    involving — *continued*
      collision (*see also* Collision, railway)
          E800 ☑
      derailment (*see also* Derailment, rail-
          way) E802 ☑
      explosion (*see also* Explosion, railway
          engine) E803 ☑
      fall (*see also* Fall, from, railway rolling
          stock) E804 ☑
      fire (*see also* Explosion, railway engine)
          E803 ☑
      hitting by, being struck by
        object falling in, on, from, rolling
            stock, train, vehicle E806 ☑
        rolling stock, train, vehicle E805 ☑
      overturning, railway rolling stock, train,
          vehicle (*see also* Derailment,
          railway) E802 ☑
      running off rails, railway (*see also* Derail-
          ment, railway) E802 ☑
      specified circumstances NEC E806 ☑
      train or vehicle hit by
        avalanche E909.2
        falling object (earth, rock, tree)
            E806 ☑
          due to cataclysm — *see* cate-
              gories E908 ☑, E909 ☑
        landslide E909.2
  roller skate E885.1
  scooter (nonmotorized) E885.0
  skateboard E885.2
  ski(ing) E885.3
    jump E884.9
    lift or tow (with chair or gondola) E847
  snowboard E885.4
  snow vehicle, motor driven (not on public
      highway) E820 ☑
    on public highway — *see* categories
        E810-E819 ☑
  spacecraft E845 ☑
  specified cause NEC E928.8
  street car E829 ☑
  traffic NEC E819 ☑
  vehicle NEC (with pedestrian) E848
    battery powered
      airport passenger vehicle E846
      truck (baggage) (mail) E846
    powered commercial or industrial (with
        other vehicle or object within
        commercial or industrial premises)
        E846
  watercraft E838 ☑
    with
      drowning or submersion resulting from
          accident other than to watercraft
          E832 ☑
      accident to watercraft E830 ☑
      injury, except drowning or submersion,
          resulting from
        accident other than to watercraft
            — *see* categories
            E833-E838 ☑
        accident to watercraft E831 ☑
    due to, caused by cataclysm — *see* cate-
        gories E908 ☑, E909 ☑
    machinery E836 ☑
Acid throwing E961
Acosta syndrome E902.0
Activity (involving) E030 ●
  aerobic and step exercise (class) E009.2 ●
  alpine skiing E003.2 ●
  animal care NEC E019.9 ●
  arts and handcrafts NEC E012.9 ●
  athletics NEC E008.9 ●
    played
      as a team or group NEC E007.9 ●
      individually NEC E006.9 ●
  baking E015.2 ●
  ballet E005.0 ●
  barbells E010.2 ●
  baseball E007.3 ●
  BASE (Building, Antenna, Span, Earth) ●
    jumping E004.2 ●

Activity — *continued*
  basketball E007.6 ●
  bathing (personal) E013.0 ●
  beach volleyball E007.7 ●
  bike riding E006.4 ●
  boogie boarding E002.7 ●
  bowling E006.3 ●
  boxing E008.0 ●
  brass instrument playing E018.3 ●
  building and construction E016.2 ●
  bungee jumping E004.3 ●
  calisthenics E009.1 ●
  canoeing (in calm and turbulent water) ●
      E002.5
  capture the flag E007.8 ●
  cardiorespiratory exercise NEC E009.9 ●
  caregiving (providing) NEC E014.9 ●
    bathing E014.0 ●
    lifting E014.1 ●
  cellular
    communication device E011.1 ●
    telephone E011.1 ●
  challenge course E009.4 ●
  cheerleading E005.4 ●
  circuit training E009.3 ●
  cleaning
    floor E013.4 ●
  climbing NEC E004.9 ●
    mountain E004.0 ●
    rock E004.0 ●
    wall climbing E004.0 ●
  combatives E008.4 ●
  computer
    keyboarding E011.0 ●
    technology NEC E011.9 ●
  confidence course E009.4 ●
  construction (building) E016.2 ●
  cooking and baking E015.2 ●
  cooking and grilling NEC E015.9 ●
  cool down exercises E009.1 ●
  cricket E007.9 ●
  crocheting E012.0 ●
  cross country skiing E003.3 ●
  dancing (all types) E005.0 ●
  digging
    dirt E016.0 ●
  dirt digging E016.0 ●
  dishwashing E015.0 ●
  diving (platform) (springboard) E002.1 ●
    underwater E002.4 ●
  dodge ball E007.8 ●
  downhill skiing E003.2 ●
  drum playing E018.1 ●
  dumbbells E010.2 ●
  electronic
    devices NEC E011.9 ●
      hand held interactive E011.1 ●
    game playing (using) (with) ●
      interactive device E011.1 ●
      keyboard or other stationary device ●
          E011.0
  elliptical machine E009.0 ●
  exercise(s)
    machines (primarily for) ●
      cardiorespiratory conditioning E009.0 ●
      muscle strengthening E010.0 ●
    muscle strengthening (non-machine) ●
        NEC E010.9
  external motion NEC E017.9 ●
    rollercoaster E017.0 ●
  field hockey E007.4 ●
  figure skating (pairs) (singles) E003.0 ●
  flag football E007.1 ●
  floor mopping and cleaning E013.4 ●
  food preparation and clean up E015.0 ●
  football (American) NOS E007.0 ●
    flag E007.1 ●
    tackle E007.0 ●
    touch E007.1 ●
  four square E007.8 ●
  free weights E010.2 ●
  frisbee (ultimate) E008.3 ●
  furniture
    building E012.2 ●
    finishing E012.2 ●
    repair E012.2 ●

Activity — *continued*
  game playing (electronic) ●
    using
      interactive device E011.1 ●
      keyboard or other stationary device ●
          E011.0
  gardening E016.1 ●
  golf E006.2 ●
  grass drills E009.5 ●
  grilling and smoking food E015.1 ●
  grooming and shearing an animal E019.2 ●
  guerilla drills E009.5 ●
  gymnastics (rhythmic) E005.2 ●
  handball E008.2 ●
  handcrafts NEC E012.9 ●
  hand held interactive electronic device ●
      E011.1
  hang gliding E004.4 ●
  hiking (on level or elevated terrain) E001.0 ●
  hockey (ice) E003.1 ●
    field E007.4 ●
  horseback riding E006.1 ●
  household maintenance NEC E013.9 ●
  ice NEC E003.9 ●
    dancing E003.0 ●
    hockey E003.1 ●
    skating E003.0 ●
  inline roller skating E006.0 ●
  ironing E013.3 ●
  judo E008.4 ●
  jumping (off) NEC E004.9 ●
    BASE (Building, Antenna, Span, Earth) ●
        E004.2
    bungee E004.3 ●
    jacks E009.1 ●
    rope E006.5 ●
  jumping jacks E009.1 ●
  jumping rope E006.5 ●
  karate E008.4 ●
  kayaking (in calm and turbulent water) ●
      E002.5
  keyboarding (computer) E011.0 ●
  kickball E007.8 ●
  knitting E012.0 ●
  lacrosse E007.4 ●
  land maintenance NEC E016.9 ●
  landscaping E016.1 ●
  laundry E013.1 ●
  machines (exercise) primarily for cardiores- ●
      piratory conditioning E009.0
  maintenance
    building E016.9 ●
    household NEC E013.9 ●
    land E016.9 ●
    property E016.9 ●
  marching (on level or elevated terrain) ●
      E001.0
  martial arts E008.4 ●
  microwave oven E015.2 ●
  milking an animal E019.1 ●
  mopping (floor) E013.4 ●
  mountain climbing E004.0 ●
  muscle strengthening
    exercises (non-machine) NEC E010.9 ●
    machines E010.0 ●
  musical keyboard (electronic) playing E018.0 ●
  nordic skiing E003.3 ●
  obstacle course E009.4 ●
  oven (microwave) E015.2 ●
  packing up and unpacking in moving to a ●
      new residence E013.5
  parasailing E002.9 ●
  percussion instrument playing NEC E018.1 ●
  personal
    bathing and showering E013.0 ●
    hygiene NEC E013.8 ●
    showering E013.0 ●
  physical
    games generally associated with school ●
        recess, summer camp and chil-
        dren E007.8
    training NEC E009.9 ●
  piano playing E018.0 ●
  pilates E010.3 ●
  platform diving E002.1 ●

Accident (to) — Activity

☑ Additional Digit Required — Refer to the Tabular List for Digit Selection   ▽ Subterms under main terms may continue to next column or page

2010 ICD-9-CM   ▶◀ Revised Text   ● New Line   ▲ Revised Code   October 2009 • Volume 2 — 323

Activity — *continued*
- playing musical instrument
  - brass instrument E018.3
  - drum E018.1
  - musical keyboard (electronic) E018.0
  - percussion instrument NEC E018.1
  - piano E018.0
  - string instrument E018.2
  - wind instrument E018.3
- property maintenance NEC E016.9
- pruning (garden and lawn) E016.1
- pull-ups E010.1
- push-ups E010.1
- racquetball E008.2
- rafting (in calm and turbulent water) E002.5
- raking (leaves) E016.0
- rappelling E004.1
- refereeing a sports activity E029.0
- residential relocation E013.5
- rhythmic
  - gymnastics E005.2
  - movement NEC E005.9
- riding
  - horseback E006.1
  - rollercoaster E017.0
- rock climbing E004.0
- rollercoaster riding E017.0
- roller skating (inline) E006.0
- rough housing and horseplay E029.2
- rowing (in calm and turbulent water) E002.5
- rugby E007.2
- running E001.1
- SCUBA diving E002.4
- sewing E012.1
- shoveling E016.0
  - dirt E016.0
  - snow E016.0
- showering (personal) E013.0
- sit-ups E010.1
- skateboarding E006.0
- skating (ice) E003.0
  - roller E006.0
- skiing (alpine) (downhill) E003.2
  - cross country E003.3
  - nordic E003.3
- sledding (snow) E003.2
- smoking and grilling food E015.1
- snorkeling E002.4
- snow NEC E003.9
  - boarding E003.2
  - shoveling E016.0
  - sledding E003.2
  - tubing E003.2
- soccer E007.5
- softball E007.3
- specified NEC E029.9
- spectator at an event E029.1
- sports NEC E008.9
- sports played as a team or group NEC E007.9
- sports played individually NEC E006.9
- springboard diving E002.1
- squash E008.2
- stationary bike E009.0
- step (stepping) exercise (class) E009.2
- stepper machine E009.0
- stove E015.2
- string instrument playing E018.2
- surfing E002.7
- swimming E002.0
- tackle football E007.0
- tap dancing E005.0
- tennis E008.2
- tobogganing E003.2
- touch football E007.1
- track and field events (non-running) E006.6
  - running E001.1
- trampoline E005.3
- treadmill E009.0
- trimming shrubs E016.1
- tubing (in calm and turbulent water) E002.5
  - snow E003.2
- ultimate frisbee E008.3
- underwater diving E002.4
- unpacking in moving to a new residence E013.5

Activity — *continued*
- use of stove, oven and microwave oven E015.2
- vacuuming E013.2
- volleyball (beach) (court) E007.7
- wake boarding E002.6
- walking (on level or elevated terrain) E001.0
  - an animal E019.0
- walking an animal E019.0
- wall climbing E004.0
- warm up and cool down exercises E009.1
- water NEC E002.9
  - aerobics E002.3
  - craft NEC E002.9
  - exercise E002.3
  - polo E002.2
  - skiing E002.6
  - sliding E002.8
  - survival training and testing E002.9
- weeding (garden and lawn) E016.1
- wind instrument playing E018.3
- windsurfing E002.7
- wrestling E008.1
- yoga E005.1

Activity status E000.9
- civilian
  - done for
    - financial or other compensation E000.0
    - pay or income E000.0
  - for income E000.0
  - hobby or leisure E000.8
- military E000.1
  - off duty E000.8
- off duty military E000.8
- recreation E000.8
- specified NEC E000.8
- sport not for income E000.8
- student E000.8
- volunteer E000.8

Aeroneurosis E902.1
Aero-otitis media — *see* Effects of, air pressure
Aerosinusitis — *see* Effects of, air pressure
After-effect, late — *see* Late effect
Air
- blast
  - in
    - terrorism E979.2
    - war operations E993.9 ▲
- embolism (traumatic) NEC E928.9
  - in
    - infusion or transfusion E874.1
    - perfusion E874.2
- sickness E903
Alpine sickness E902.0
Altitude sickness — *see* Effects of, air pressure
Anaphylactic shock, anaphylaxis — *see also* Table of Drugs and Chemicals E947.9
- due to bite or sting (venomous) — *see* Bite, venomous
Andes disease E902.0
Apoplexy
- heat — *see* Heat
Arachnidism E905.1
Arson E968.0
Asphyxia, asphyxiation
- by
  - chemical
    - in
      - terrorism E979.7
      - war operations E997.2
  - explosion — *see* Explosion
  - food (bone) (regurgitated food) (seed) E911
  - foreign object, except food E912
  - fumes
    - in
      - terrorism (chemical weapons) E979.7
      - war operations E997.2
  - gas (*see also* Table of Drugs and Chemicals)
    - in
      - terrorism E979.7
      - war operations E997.2
    - legal
      - execution E978

Asphyxia, asphyxiation — *continued*
- by — *continued*
  - gas (*see also* Table of Drugs and Chemicals) — *continued*
    - legal — *continued*
      - intervention (tear) E972
      - tear E972
  - mechanical means (*see also* Suffocation) E913.9
- from
  - conflagration — *see* Conflagration
  - fire (*see also* Fire) E899
    - in
      - terrorism E979.3
      - war operations E990.9
  - ignition — *see* Ignition
Aspiration
- foreign body — *see* Foreign body, aspiration
- mucus, not of newborn (with asphyxia, obstruction respiratory passage, suffocation) E912
- phlegm (with asphyxia, obstruction respiratory passage, suffocation) E912
- vomitus (with asphyxia, obstruction respiratory passage, suffocation) (*see also* Foreign body, aspiration, food) E911
Assassination (attempt) — *see also* Assault E968.9
Assault (homicidal) (by) (in) E968.9
- acid E961
  - swallowed E962.1
- air gun E968.6
- BB gun E968.6
- bite NEC E968.8
  - of human being E968.7
- bomb ((placed in) car or house) E965.8
  - antipersonnel E965.5
  - letter E965.7
  - petrol E965.6
- brawl (hand) (fists) (foot) E960.0
- burning, burns (by fire) E968.0
  - acid E961
    - swallowed E962.1
  - caustic, corrosive substance E961
    - swallowed E962.1
  - chemical from swallowing caustic, corrosive substance NEC E962.1
  - hot liquid E968.3
  - scalding E968.3
  - vitriol E961
    - swallowed E962.1
- caustic, corrosive substance E961
  - swallowed E962.1
- cut, any part of body E966
- dagger E966
- drowning E964
- explosive(s) E965.9
  - bomb (*see also* Assault, bomb) E965.8
  - dynamite E965.8
- fight (hand) (fists) (foot) E960.0
  - with weapon E968.9
    - blunt or thrown E968.2
    - cutting or piercing E966
    - firearm — *see* Shooting, homicide
- fire E968.0
- firearm(s) — *see* Shooting, homicide
- garrotting E963
- gunshot (wound) — *see* Shooting, homicide
- hanging E963
- injury NEC E968.9
- knife E966
- late effect of E969
- ligature E963
- poisoning E962.9
  - drugs or medicinals E962.0
  - gas(es) or vapors, except drugs and medicinals E962.2
  - solid or liquid substances, except drugs and medicinals E962.1
- puncture, any part of body E966
- pushing
  - before moving object, train, vehicle E968.5
  - from high place E968.1
- rape E960.1
- scalding E968.3
- shooting — *see* Shooting, homicide

Assault — *continued*
- sodomy E960.1
- stab, any part of body E966
- strangulation E963
- submersion E964
- suffocation E963
- transport vehicle E968.5
- violence NEC E968.9
- vitriol E961
  - swallowed E962.1
- weapon E968.9
  - blunt or thrown E968.2
  - cutting or piercing E966
  - firearm — *see* Shooting, homicide
- wound E968.9
  - cutting E966
  - gunshot — *see* Shooting, homicide
  - knife E966
  - piercing E966
  - puncture E966
  - stab E966
Attack by animal NEC E906.9
Avalanche E909.2
- falling on or hitting
  - motor vehicle (in motion) (on public highway) E909.2
  - railway train E909.2
Aviators' disease E902.1

B

Barotitis, barodontalgia, barosinusitis, barotrauma (otitic) (sinus) — *see* Effects of, air pressure
Battered
- baby or child (syndrome) — *see* Abuse, child; category E967 ☑
- person other than baby or child — *see* Assault
Bayonet wound — *see also* Cut, by bayonet E920.3
- in
  - legal intervention E974
  - terrorism E979.8
  - war operations E995.2 ▲
Bean in nose E912
Bed set on fire NEC E898.0
Beheading (by guillotine)
- homicide E966
- legal execution E978
Bending, injury in E927.8
Bends E902.0
Bite
- animal NEC E906.5
  - other specified (except arthropod) E906.3
  - venomous NEC E905.9
- arthropod (nonvenomous) NEC E906.4
  - venomous — *see* Sting
- black widow spider E905.1
- cat E906.3
- centipede E905.4
- cobra E905.0
- copperhead snake E905.0
- coral snake E905.0
- dog E906.0
- fer de lance E905.0
- gila monster E905.0
- human being
  - accidental E928.3
  - assault E968.7
- insect (nonvenomous) E906.4
  - venomous — *see* Sting
- krait E905.0
- late effect of — *see* Late effect
- lizard E906.2
  - venomous E905.0
- mamba E905.0
- marine animal
  - nonvenomous E906.3
    - snake E906.2
  - venomous E905.6
    - snake E905.0
- millipede E906.4
  - venomous E905.4
- moray eel E906.3
- rat E906.1
- rattlesnake E905.0
- rodent, except rat E906.3

☑ Additional Digit Required — Refer to the Tabular List for Digit Selection   ☜ Subterms under main terms may continue to next column or page

324 — Volume 2 • October 2009   ▶◀ Revised Text   ● New Line   ▲ Revised Code   2010 ICD-9-CM

Bite — *continued*
  serpent — *see* Bite, snake
  shark E906.3
  snake (venomous) E905.0
    nonvenomous E906.2
    sea E905.0
  spider E905.1
    nonvenomous E906.4
  tarantula (venomous) E905.1
  venomous NEC E905.9
    by specific animal — *see category* E905 ☑
  viper E905.0
  water moccasin E905.0
Blast (air)
  from nuclear explosion E996 ☑
  in
    terrorism E979.2
      from nuclear explosion E979.5
      underwater E979.0
    war operations E993.9 ▲
      from nuclear explosion ▶(*see also* War operations, injury due to, nuclear weapons)◀ E996.0 ▲
      underwater E992.9 ▲
Blizzard E908.3
Blow E928.9
  by law-enforcing agent, police (on duty) E975
    with blunt object (baton) (nightstick) (stave) (truncheon) E973
Blowing up — *see also* Explosion E923.9
Brawl (hand) (fists) (foot) E960.0
Breakage (accidental)
  cable of cable car not on rails E847
  ladder (causing fall) E881.0
  part (any) of
    animal-drawn vehicle E827 ☑
    ladder (causing fall) E881.0
    motor vehicle
      in motion (on public highway) E818 ☑
        not on public highway E825 ☑
    nonmotor road vehicle, except animal-drawn vehicle or pedal cycle E829 ☑
    off-road type motor vehicle (not on public highway) NEC E821 ☑
      on public highway E818 ☑
    pedal cycle E826 ☑
    scaffolding (causing fall) E881.1
    snow vehicle, motor-driven (not on public highway) E820 ☑
      on public highway E818 ☑
    vehicle NEC — *see* Accident, vehicle
Broken
  glass
    fall on E888.0
    injury by E920.8
  power line (causing electric shock) E925.1
Bumping against, into (accidentally)
  object (moving) E917.9
    caused by crowd E917.1
      with subsequent fall E917.6
    furniture E917.3
      with subsequent fall E917.7
    in
      running water E917.2
      sports E917.0
        with subsequent fall E917.5
    stationary E917.4
      with subsequent fall E917.8
  person(s) E917.9
    with fall E886.9
      in sports E886.0
    as, or caused by, a crowd E917.1
      with subsequent fall E917.6
    in sports E917.0
      with fall E886.0
Burning, burns (accidental) (by) (from) (on) E899
  acid (any kind) E924.1
    swallowed — *see* Table of Drugs and Chemicals
  airgun E928.7 ●
  bedclothes (*see also* Fire, specified NEC) E898.0
  blowlamp (*see also* Fire, specified NEC) E898.1
  blowtorch (*see also* Fire, specified NEC) E898.1
  boat, ship, watercraft — *see* categories E830 ☑, E831 ☑, E837 ☑

Burning, burns — *continued*
  bonfire (controlled) E897
    uncontrolled E892
  candle (*see also* Fire, specified NEC) E898.1
  caustic liquid, substance E924.1
    swallowed — *see* Table of Drugs and Chemicals
  chemical E924.1
    from swallowing caustic, corrosive substance — *see* Table of Drugs and Chemicals
    in
      terrorism E979.7
      war operations E997.2
  cigar(s) or cigarette(s) (*see also* Fire, specified NEC) E898.1
  clothes, clothing, nightdress — *see* Ignition, clothes
    with conflagration — *see* Conflagration
  conflagration — *see* Conflagration
  corrosive liquid, substance E924.1
    swallowed — *see* Table of Drugs and Chemicals
  electric current (*see also* Electric shock) E925.9
  firearm E928.7 ●
  fire, flames (*see also* Fire) E899
  flare, Verey pistol E922.8
  heat
    from appliance (electrical) E924.8
    in local application, or packing during medical or surgical procedure E873.5
  homicide (attempt) (*see also* Assault, burning) E968.0
  hot
    liquid E924.0
      caustic or corrosive E924.1
    object (not producing fire or flames) E924.8
    substance E924.9
      caustic or corrosive E924.1
      liquid (metal) NEC E924.0
      specified type NEC E924.8
    tap water E924.2
  ignition (*see also* Ignition)
    clothes, clothing, nightdress (*see also* Ignition, clothes)
      with conflagration — *see* Conflagration
    highly inflammable material (benzine) (fat) (gasoline) (kerosene) (paraffin) (petrol) E894
  in
    terrorism E979.3
      from nuclear explosion E979.5
      petrol bomb E979.3
    war operations (from fire-producing device or conventional weapon) E990.9
      from nuclear explosion ▶(*see also* War operations, injury due to, nuclear weapons)◀ E996.2 ▲
      incendiary bomb E990.0 ●
      petrol bomb E990.0
  inflicted by other person
    stated as
      homicidal, intentional (*see also* Assault, burning) E968.0
      undetermined whether accidental or intentional (*see also* Burn, stated as undetermined whether accidental or intentional) E988.1
  internal, from swallowed caustic, corrosive liquid, substance — *see* Table of Drugs and Chemicals
  lamp (*see also* Fire, specified NEC) E898.1
  late effect of NEC E929.4
  lighter (cigar) (cigarette) (*see also* Fire, specified NEC) E898.1
  lightning E907
  liquid (boiling) (hot) (molten) E924.0
    caustic, corrosive (external) E924.1
      swallowed — *see* Table of Drugs and Chemicals
  local application of externally applied substance in medical or surgical care E873.5
  machinery — *see* Accident, machine
  matches (*see also* Fire, specified NEC) E898.1

Burning, burns — *continued*
  medicament, externally applied E873.5
  metal, molten E924.0
  object (hot) E924.8
    producing fire or flames — *see* Fire
  oven (electric) (gas) E924.8
  pipe (smoking) (*see also* Fire, specified NEC) E898.1
  radiation — *see* Radiation
  railway engine, locomotive, train (*see also* Explosion, railway engine) E803 ☑
  self-inflicted (unspecified whether accidental or intentional) E988.1
    caustic or corrosive substance NEC E988.7
    stated as intentional, purposeful E958.1
      caustic or corrosive substance NEC E958.7
    stated as undetermined whether accidental or intentional E988.1
      caustic or corrosive substance NEC E988.7
  steam E924.0
    pipe E924.8
  substance (hot) E924.9
    boiling or molten E924.0
    caustic, corrosive (external) E924.1
      swallowed — *see* Table of Drugs and Chemicals
  suicidal (attempt) NEC E958.1
    caustic substance E958.7
    late effect of E959
  tanning bed E926.2
  therapeutic misadventure
    overdose of radiation E873.2
  torch, welding (*see also* Fire, specified NEC) E898.1
  trash fire (*see also* Burning, bonfire) E897
  vapor E924.0
  vitriol E924.1
  x-rays E926.3
    in medical, surgical procedure — *see* Misadventure, failure, in dosage, radiation
Butted by animal E906.8

C

Cachexia, lead or saturnine E866.0
  from pesticide NEC (*see also* Table of Drugs and Chemicals) E863.4
Caisson disease E902.2
Capital punishment (any means) E978
Car sickness E903
Casualty (not due to war) NEC E928.9
  terrorism E979.8
  war (*see also* War operations) E995.9 ▲
Cat
  bite E906.3
  scratch E906.8
Cataclysmic (any injury)
  earth surface movement or eruption E909.9
    specified type NEC E909.8
  storm or flood resulting from storm E908.9
    specified type NEC E909.8
Catching fire — *see* Ignition
Caught
  between
    objects (moving) (stationary and moving) E918
    and machinery — *see* Accident, machine
  by cable car, not on rails E847
  in
    machinery (moving parts of) — *see*, Accident, machine
    object E918
Cave-in (causing asphyxia, suffocation (by pressure)) — *see also* Suffocation, due to, cave-in E913.3
  with injury other than asphyxia or suffocation E916
    with asphyxia or suffocation (*see also* Suffocation, due to, cave-in) E913.3
  struck or crushed by E916
    with asphyxia or suffocation (*see also* Suffocation, due to, cave-in) E913.3
Change(s) in air pressure — *see also* Effects of, air pressure

Change(s) in air pressure — *see also* Effects of, air pressure
  sudden, in aircraft (ascent) (descent) (causing aeroneurosis or aviators' disease) E902.1
Chilblains E901.0
  due to manmade conditions E901.1
Choking (on) (any object except food or vomitus) E912
  apple E911 — *continued*
  bone E911
  food, any type (regurgitated) E911
  mucus or phlegm E912
  seed E911
Civil insurrection — *see* War operations
Cloudburst E908.8
Cold, exposure to (accidental) (excessive) (extreme) (place) E901.9
  causing chilblains or immersion foot E901.0
  due to
    manmade conditions E901.1
    specified cause NEC E901.8
    weather (conditions) E901.0
  late effect of NEC E929.5
  self-inflicted (undetermined whether accidental or intentional) E988.3
    suicidal E958.3
  suicide E958.3
Colic, lead, painter's, or saturnine — *see* category E866 ☑
Collapse
  building E916
    burning (uncontrolled fire) E891.8
      in terrorism E979.3
      private E890.8
  dam E909.3
  due to heat — *see* Heat
  machinery — *see* Accident, machine or vehicle
  man-made structure E909.3
  postoperative NEC E878.9
  structure
    burning (uncontrolled fire) NEC E891.8
      in terrorism E979.3
Collision (accidental)

> **Note** — In the case of collisions between different types of vehicles, persons and objects, priority in classification is in the following order:
>
>   *Aircraft*
>
>   *Watercraft*
>
>   *Motor vehicle*
>
>   *Railway vehicle*
>
>   *Pedal cycle*
>
>   *Animal-drawn vehicle*
>
>   *Animal being ridden*
>
>   *Streetcar or other nonmotor road vehicle*
>
>   *Other vehicle*
>
>   *Pedestrian or person using pedestrian conveyance*
>
>   *Object (except where falling from or set in motion by vehicle etc. listed above)*
>
> *In the listing below, the combinations are listed only under the vehicle etc. having priority. For definitions, see Supplementary Classification of External Causes of Injury and Poisoning (E800-E999).*

  aircraft (with object or vehicle) (fixed) (movable) (moving) E841 ☑
    with
      person (while landing, taking off) (without accident to aircraft) E844 ☑
      powered (in transit) (with unpowered aircraft) E841 ☑
        while landing, taking off E840 ☑
      unpowered E842 ☑
        while landing, taking off E840 ☑

☑ Additional Digit Required — Refer to the Tabular List for Digit Selection   ▽ Subterms under main terms may continue to next column or page

Index

Collision — Conflagration

Collision — *continued*
- animal being ridden (in sport or transport) E828 ☑
  - and
    - animal (being ridden) (herded) (unattended) E828 ☑
    - nonmotor road vehicle, except pedal cycle or animal-drawn vehicle E828 ☑
    - object (fallen) (fixed) (movable) (moving) not falling from or set in motion by vehicle of higher priority E828 ☑
    - pedestrian (conveyance or vehicle) E828 ☑
- animal-drawn vehicle E827 ☑
  - and
    - animal (being ridden) (herded) (unattended) E827 ☑
    - nonmotor road vehicle, except pedal cycle E827 ☑
    - object (fallen) (fixed) (movable) (moving) not falling from or set in motion by vehicle of higher priority E827 ☑
    - pedestrian (conveyance or vehicle) E827 ☑
    - streetcar E827 ☑
- motor vehicle (on public highway) (traffic accident) E812 ☑
  - after leaving, running off, public highway (without antecedent collision) (without re-entry) E816 ☑
  - with antecedent collision on public highway — *see* categories E810-E815 ☑
    - with re-entrance collision with another motor vehicle E811 ☑
  - and
    - abutment (bridge) (overpass) E815 ☑
    - animal (herded) (unattended) E815 ☑
      - carrying person, property E813 ☑
    - animal-drawn vehicle E813 ☑
    - another motor vehicle (abandoned) (disabled) (parked) (stalled) (stopped) E812 ☑
      - with, involving re-entrance (on same roadway) (across median strip) E811 ☑
    - any object, person, or vehicle off the public highway resulting from a noncollision motor vehicle nontraffic accident E816 ☑
    - avalanche, fallen or not moving E815 ☑
      - falling E909.2
    - boundary fence E815 ☑
    - culvert E815 ☑
    - fallen
      - stone E815 ☑
      - tree E815 ☑
    - guard post or guard rail E815 ☑
    - inter-highway divider E815 ☑
    - landslide, fallen or not moving E815 ☑
      - moving E909
    - machinery (road) E815 ☑
    - nonmotor road vehicle NEC E813 ☑
    - object (any object, person, or vehicle off the public highway resulting from a noncollision motor vehicle nontraffic accident) E815 ☑
      - off, normally not on, public highway resulting from a noncollision motor vehicle traffic accident E816 ☑
    - pedal cycle E813 ☑
    - pedestrian (conveyance) E814 ☑
    - person (using pedestrian conveyance) E814 ☑
    - post or pole (lamp) (light) (signal) (telephone) (utility) E815 ☑
    - railway rolling stock, train, vehicle E810 ☑
    - safety island E815 ☑
    - street car E813 ☑

Collision — *continued*
- motor vehicle — *continued*
  - and — *continued*
    - traffic signal, sign, or marker (temporary) E815 ☑
    - tree E815 ☑
    - tricycle E813 ☑
    - wall of cut made for road E815 ☑
  - due to cataclysm — *see* categories E908 ☑, E909 ☑
  - not on public highway, nontraffic accident E822 ☑
  - and
    - animal (carrying person, property) (herded) (unattended) E822 ☑
    - animal-drawn vehicle E822 ☑
    - another motor vehicle (moving), except off-road motor vehicle E822 ☑
      - stationary E823 ☑
    - avalanche, fallen, not moving E823 ☑
      - moving E909.2
    - landslide, fallen, not moving E823 ☑
      - moving E909.2
    - nonmotor vehicle (moving) E822 ☑
      - stationary E823 ☑
    - object (fallen) (normally) (fixed) (movable but not in motion) (stationary) E823 ☑
      - moving, except when falling from, set in motion by, aircraft or cataclysm E822 ☑
    - pedal cycle (moving) E822 ☑
      - stationary E823 ☑
    - pedestrian (conveyance) E822 ☑
    - person (using pedestrian conveyance) E822 ☑
    - railway rolling stock, train, vehicle (moving) E822 ☑
      - stationary E823 ☑
    - road vehicle (any) (moving) E822 ☑
      - stationary E823 ☑
    - tricycle (moving) E822 ☑
      - stationary E823 ☑
  - off-road type motor vehicle (not on public highway) E821 ☑
  - and
    - animal (being ridden) (-drawn vehicle) E821 ☑
    - another off-road motor vehicle, except snow vehicle E821 ☑
    - other motor vehicle, not on public highway E821 ☑
    - other object or vehicle NEC, fixed or movable, not set in motion by aircraft, motor vehicle on highway, or snow vehicle, motor driven E821 ☑
    - pedal cycle E821 ☑
    - pedestrian (conveyance) E821 ☑
    - railway train E821 ☑
  - on public highway — *see* Collision, motor vehicle
- pedal cycle E826 ☑
  - and
    - animal (carrying person, property) (herded) (unherded) E826 ☑
    - animal-drawn vehicle E826 ☑
    - another pedal cycle E826 ☑
    - nonmotor road vehicle E826 ☑
    - object (fallen) (fixed) (movable) (moving) not falling from or set in motion by aircraft, motor vehicle, or railway train NEC E826 ☑
    - pedestrian (conveyance) E826 ☑
    - person (using pedestrian conveyance) E826 ☑
    - street car E826 ☑

Collision — *continued*
- pedestrian(s) (conveyance) E917.9
  - with fall E886.9
    - in sports E886.0
  - and
    - crowd, human stampede E917.1
      - with subsequent fall E917.6
    - furniture E917.3
      - with subsequent fall E917.7
    - machinery — *see* Accident, machine
    - object (fallen) (moving) not falling from NEC, fixed or set in motion by any vehicle classifiable to E800-E848 ☑, E917.9
      - with subsequent fall E917.6
      - caused by a crowd E917.1
        - with subsequent fall E917.6
      - furniture E917.3
        - with subsequent fall E917.7
      - in
        - running water E917.2
          - with drowning or submersion — *see* Submersion
        - sports E917.0
          - with subsequent fall E917.5
        - stationary E917.4
          - with subsequent fall E917.8
    - vehicle, nonmotor, nonroad E848
  - in
    - running water E917.2
      - with drowning or submersion — *see* Submersion
    - sports E917.0
      - with fall E886.0
- person(s) (using pedestrian conveyance) (*see also* Collision, pedestrian) E917.9
- railway (rolling stock) (train) (vehicle) (with (subsequent) derailment, explosion, fall or fire) E800 ☑
  - with antecedent derailment E802 ☑
  - and
    - animal (carrying person) (herded) (unattended) E801 ☑
    - another railway train or vehicle E800 ☑
    - buffers E801 ☑
    - fallen tree on railway E801 ☑
    - farm machinery, nonmotor (in transport) (stationary) E801 ☑
    - gates E801 ☑
    - nonmotor vehicle E801 ☑
    - object (fallen) (fixed) (movable) (moving) not falling from, set in motion by, aircraft or motor vehicle NEC E801 ☑
    - pedal cycle E801 ☑
    - pedestrian (conveyance) E805 ☑
    - person (using pedestrian conveyance) E805 ☑
    - platform E801 ☑
    - rock on railway E801 ☑
    - street car E801 ☑
- snow vehicle, motor-driven (not on public highway) E820 ☑
  - and
    - animal (being ridden) (-drawn vehicle) E820 ☑
    - another off-road motor vehicle E820 ☑
    - other motor vehicle, not on public highway E820 ☑
    - other object or vehicle NEC, fixed or movable, not set in motion by aircraft or motor vehicle on highway E820 ☑
    - pedal cycle E820 ☑
    - pedestrian (conveyance) E820 ☑
    - railway train E820 ☑
  - on public highway — *see* Collision, motor vehicle
- street car(s) E829 ☑
  - and
    - animal, herded, not being ridden, unattended E829 ☑

Collision — *continued*
- street car(s) — *continued*
  - and — *continued*
    - nonmotor road vehicle NEC E829 ☑
    - object (fallen) (fixed) (movable) (moving) not falling from or set in motion by aircraft, animal-drawn vehicle, animal being ridden, motor vehicle, pedal cycle, or railway train E829 ☑
    - pedestrian (conveyance) E829 ☑
    - person (using pedestrian conveyance) E829 ☑
- vehicle
  - animal-drawn — *see* Collision, animal-drawn vehicle
  - motor — *see* Collision, motor vehicle
  - nonmotor
    - nonroad E848
    - and
      - another nonmotor, nonroad vehicle E848
      - object (fallen) (fixed) (movable) (moving) not falling from or set in motion by aircraft, animal-drawn vehicle, animal being ridden, motor vehicle, nonmotor road vehicle, pedal cycle, railway train, or streetcar E848
    - road, except animal being ridden, animal-drawn vehicle, or pedal cycle E829 ☑
    - and
      - animal, herded, not being ridden, unattended E829 ☑
      - another nonmotor road vehicle, except animal being ridden, animal-drawn vehicle, or pedal cycle E829 ☑
      - object (fallen) (fixed) (movable) (moving) not falling from or set in motion by, aircraft, animal-drawn vehicle, animal being ridden, motor vehicle, pedal cycle, or railway train E829 ☑
      - pedestrian (conveyance) E829 ☑
      - person (using pedestrian conveyance) E829 ☑
      - vehicle, nonmotor, nonroad E829 ☑
- watercraft E838 ☑
  - and
    - person swimming or water skiing E838 ☑
  - causing
    - drowning, submersion E830 ☑
    - injury except drowning, submersion E831 ☑
Combustion, spontaneous — *see* Ignition
Complication of medical or surgical procedure or treatment
- as an abnormal reaction — *see* Reaction, abnormal
- delayed, without mention of misadventure — *see* Reaction, abnormal
- due to misadventure — *see* Misadventure
Compression
- divers' squeeze E902.2
- trachea by
  - food E911
  - foreign body, except food E912
Conflagration
- building or structure, except private dwelling (barn) (church) (convalescent or residential home) (factory) (farm outbuilding) (hospital) (hotel) (institution) (educational) (domitory) (residential) (school) (shop) (store) (theater) E891.9

☑   Additional Digit Required — Refer to the Tabular List for Digit Selection   ▽ Subterms under main terms may continue to next column or page

Conflagration — *continued*
  building or structure, except private dwelling
    — *continued*
    with or causing (injury due to)
      accident or injury NEC E891.9
        specified circumstance NEC E891.8
      burns, burning E891.3
      carbon monoxide E891.2
      fumes E891.2
        polyvinylchloride (PVC) or similar
          material E891.1
      smoke E891.2
      causing explosion E891.0
    in terrorism E979.3
  not in building or structure E892
  private dwelling (apartment) (boarding house)
    (camping place) (caravan) (farmhouse)
    (home (private)) (house) (lodging
    house) (private garage) (rooming
    house) (tenement) E890.9
    with or causing (injury due to)
      accident or injury NEC E890.9
        specified circumstance NEC E890.8
      burns, burning E890.3
      carbon monoxide E890.2
      fumes E890.2
        polyvinylchloride (PVC) or similar
          material E890.1
      smoke E890.2
      causing explosion E890.0
Constriction, external
  caused by
    hair E928.4
    other object E928.5
Contact with
  dry ice E901.1
  liquid air, hydrogen, nitrogen E901.1
Cramp(s)
  Heat — *see* Heat
  swimmers (*see also* category E910) E910.2
    not in recreation or sport E910.3
Cranking (car) (truck) (bus) (engine), injury by
  E917.9
Crash
  aircraft (in transit) (powered) E841 ☑
    at landing, take-off E840 ☑
    in
      terrorism E979.1
      war operations E994.9   ▲
    on runway NEC E840 ☑
    stated as
      homicidal E968.8
      suicidal E958.6
      undetermined whether accidental or
        intentional E988.6
    unpowered E842 ☑
  glider E842 ☑
  motor vehicle (*see also* Accident, motor vehi-
    cle)
    homicidal E968.5
    suicidal E958.5
    undetermined whether accidental or inten-
      tional E988.5
Crushed (accidentally) E928.9
  between
    boat(s), ship(s), watercraft (and dock or
      pier) (without accident to water-
      craft) E838 ☑
      after accident to, or collision, watercraft
        E831 ☑
    objects (moving) (stationary and moving)
      E918
  by
    avalanche NEC E909.2
    boat, ship, watercraft after accident to,
      collision, watercraft E831 ☑
    cave-in E916
      with asphyxiation or suffocation (*see*
        also Suffocation, due to, cave-
        in) E913.3
    crowd, human stampede E917.1
    falling
      aircraft (*see also* Accident, aircraft)
        E841 ☑
        in
          terrorism E979.1

Crushed — *continued*
  by — *continued*
    falling — *continued*
      aircraft (*see also* Accident, aircraft) —
        continued
        in — *continued*
          war operations E994.8   ▲
      earth, material E916
        with asphyxiation or suffocation
          (*see also* Suffocation, due to,
          cave-in) E913.3
      object E916
        on ship, watercraft E838 ☑
        while loading, unloading watercraft
          E838 ☑
    firearm E928.7   ●
    landslide NEC E909.2
    lifeboat after abandoning ship E831 ☑
    machinery — *see* Accident, machine
    railway rolling stock, train, vehicle (part of)
      E805 ☑
    slide trigger mechanism, scope or other ●
      part of gun E928.7   ●
    street car E829 ☑
    vehicle NEC — *see* Accident, vehicle NEC
  in
    machinery — *see* Accident, machine
    object E918
    transport accident — *see* categories
      E800-E848 ☑
  late effect of NEC E929.9
Cut, cutting (any part of body) (accidental) E920.9
  by
    arrow E920.8
    axe E920.4
    bayonet (*see also* Bayonet wound) E920.3
      in war operations E995.2   ●
    blender E920.2
    broken glass E920.8
      following fall E888.0
    can opener E920.4
      powered E920.2
    chisel E920.4
    circular saw E919.4
    cutting or piercing instrument (*see also*
      category) E920 ☑
      following fall E888.0
      late effect of E929.8
    dagger E920.3
    dart E920.8
    drill — *see* Accident, caused by drill
    edge of stiff paper E920.8
    electric
      beater E920.2
      fan E920.2
      knife E920.2
      mixer E920.2
    firearm component E928.7   ●
    fork E920.4
    garden fork E920.4
    hand saw or tool (not powered) E920.4
      powered E920.1
    hedge clipper E920.4
      powered E920.1
    hoe E920.4
    ice pick E920.4
    knife E920.3
      electric E920.2
      in war operations E995.2   ●
    lathe turnings E920.8
    lawn mower E920.4
      powered E920.0
      riding E919.8
    machine — *see* Accident, machine
    meat
      grinder E919.8
      slicer E919.8
    nails E920.8
    needle E920.4
      hypodermic E920.5
    object, edged, pointed, sharp — *see* cate-
      gory E920 ☑
      following fall E888.0
    paper cutter E920.4
    piercing instrument (*see also* category)
      E920 ☑

Cut, cutting — *continued*
  by — *continued*
    piercing instrument (*see also* category) —
      continued
      late effect of E929.8
    pitchfork E920.4
    powered
      can opener E920.2
      garden cultivator E920.1
        riding E919.8
      hand saw E920.1
      hand tool NEC E920.1
      hedge clipper E920.1
      household appliance or implement
        E920.2
      lawn mower (hand) E920.0
        riding E919.8
      rivet gun E920.1
      staple gun E920.1
    rake E920.4
    saw
      circular E919.4
      hand E920.4
    scissors E920.4
    screwdriver E920.4
    sewing machine (electric) (powered)
      E920.2
      not powered E920.4
    shears E920.4
    shovel E920.4
    slide trigger mechanism, scope or other ●
      part of gun E928.7   ●
    spade E920.4
    splinters E920.8
    sword E920.3
      in war operations E995.2   ●
    tin can lid E920.8
    wood slivers E920.8
  homicide (attempt) E966
  inflicted by other person
    stated as
      intentional, homicidal E966
      undetermined whether accidental or
        intentional E986
  late effect of NEC E929.8
  legal
    execution E978
    intervention E974
  self-inflicted (unspecified whether accidental
    or intentional) E986
    stated as intentional, purposeful E956
  stated as undetermined whether accidental
    or intentional E986
  suicidal (attempt) E956
  terrorism E979.8
  war operations E995.2   ▲
Cyclone E908.1

D

**Death due to injury occurring one year or
  more previous** — *see* Late effect
Decapitation (accidental circumstances) NEC
  E928.9
  homicidal E966
  legal execution (by guillotine) E978
Deprivation — *see also* Privation
  homicidal intent E968.4
Derailment (accidental)
  railway (rolling stock) (train) (vehicle) (with
    subsequent collision) E802 ☑
    with
      collision (antecedent) (*see also* Colli-
        sion, railway) E800 ☑
      explosion (subsequent) (without an-
        tecedent collision) E802 ☑
        antecedent collision E803 ☑
      fall (without collision (antecedent))
        E802 ☑
      fire (without collision (antecedent))
        E802 ☑
    street car E829 ☑
Descent
  parachute (voluntary) (without accident to
    aircraft) E844 ☑

Descent — *continued*
  parachute — *continued*
    due to accident to aircraft — *see* cate-
      gories E840-E842 ☑
Desertion
  child, with intent to injure or kill E968.4
  helpless person, infant, newborn E904.0
    with intent to injure or kill E968.4
Destitution — *see* Privation
Dirty bomb (*see also* War operations, injury due ●
  to, nuclear weapons) E996.9
Disability, late effect or sequela of injury —
  see Late effect
Disease
  Andes E902.0
  aviators' E902.1
  caisson E902.2
  range E902.0
Divers' disease, palsy, paralysis, squeeze
  E902.2
Dog bite E906.0
Dragged by
  cable car (not on rails) E847
    on rails E829 ☑
  motor vehicle (on highway) E814 ☑
    not on highway, nontraffic accident
      E825 ☑
  street car E829 ☑
Drinking poison (accidental) — *see* Table of
  Drugs and Chemicals
Drowning — *see* Submersion
Dust in eye E914

E

Earth falling (on) (with asphyxia or suffocation
  (by pressure)) — *see also* Suffocation, due
  to, cave-in E913.3
  as, or due to, a cataclysm (involving any
    transport vehicle) — *see* categories
    E908 ☑, E909 ☑
  not due to cataclysmic action E913.3
    motor vehicle (in motion) (on public
      highway) E813 ☑
      not on public highway E825 ☑
    nonmotor road vehicle NEC E829 ☑
    pedal cycle E826 ☑
    railway rolling stock, train, vehicle E806 ☑
    street car E829 ☑
    struck or crushed by E916
      with asphyxiation or suffocation E913.3
      with injury other than asphyxia, suffo-
        cation E916
Earthquake (any injury) E909.0
Effect(s) (adverse) of
  air pressure E902.9
    at high altitude E902.9
      in aircraft E902.1
      residence or prolonged visit (causing
        conditions classifiable to
        E902.0) E902.0
    due to
      diving E902.2
      specified cause NEC E902.8
    in aircraft E902.1
  cold, excessive (exposure to) (*see also* Cold,
    exposure to) E901.9
  heat (excessive) (*see also* Heat) E900.9
  hot
    place — *see* Heat
    weather E900.0
  insulation — *see* Heat
  late — *see* Late effect of
  motion E903
  nuclear explosion or weapon
    in
      terrorism E979.5
      war operations ►(*see also* War opera-
        tions, injury due to, nuclear
        weapons)◄ E996.9   ▲
  radiation — *see* Radiation
  terrorism, secondary E979.9
  travel E903

☑ Additional Digit Required — Refer to the Tabular List for Digit Selection   ▽ Subterms under main terms may continue to next column or page

2010 ICD-9-CM   ►◄ Revised Text   ● New Line   ▲ Revised Code   **October 2009 · Volume 2 — 327**

Index

Electric shock, electrocution — Fall, falling

Electric shock, electrocution (accidental) (from
    exposed wire, faulty appliance, high volt-
    age cable, live rail, open socket) (by) (in)
    E925.9
    appliance or wiring
        domestic E925.0
        factory E925.2
        farm (building) E925.8
            house E925.0
        home E925.0
        industrial (conductor) (control apparatus)
            (transformer) E925.2
        outdoors E925.8
        public building E925.8
        residential institution E925.8
        school E925.8
        specified place NEC E925.8
    caused by other person
        stated as
            intentional, homicidal E968.8
            undetermined whether accidental or
                intentional E988.4
    electric power generating plant, distribution
        station E925.1
    electroshock gun (taser) (stun gun) E925.8
        caused by other person E968.8
        legal intervention E975
        stated as accidental E925.8
        stated as intentional E968.8
        due to legal intervention E975
        stated as intentional self-harm (suicidal
            attempt) E958.4
        stated as undetermined whether acciden-
            tal or intentional E988.4
        suicide (attempt) E958.4
    homicide (attempt) E968.8
    legal execution E978
    lightning E907
    machinery E925.9
        domestic E925.0
        factory E925.2
        farm E925.8
        home E925.0
    misadventure in medical or surgical procedure
        in electroshock therapy E873.4
    self-inflicted (undetermined whether acciden-
        tal or intentional) E988.4
    stated as intentional E958.4
    stated as undetermined whether accidental
        or intentional E988.4
    suicidal (attempt) E958.4
    transmission line E925.1

Electrocution — *see* Electric shock

Embolism
    air (traumatic) NEC — *see* Air, embolism

Encephalitis
    lead or saturnine E866.0
        from pesticide NEC E863.4

Entanglement
    in
        bedclothes, causing suffocation E913.0
        wheel of pedal cycle E826 ☑

Entry of foreign body, material, any — *see*
    Foreign body

Execution, legal (any method) E978

Exertion, excessive physical, from prolonged
    activity E927.2

Exhaustion
    cold — *see* Cold, exposure to
    due to excessive exertion E927.8
    heat — *see* Heat

Explosion (accidental) (in) (of) (on) E923.9
    acetylene E923.2
    aerosol can E921.8
    aircraft (in transit) (powered) E841 ☑
        at landing, take-off E840 ☑
        in
            terrorism E979.1
            war operations
                from   ●
                    enemy fire or explosive(s) ●
                      (device placed on air- ●
                      craft) E994.0
                  own onboard explosives ●
                    E994.1
    unpowered E842 ☑

Explosion — *continued*
    air tank (compressed) (in machinery) E921.1
    anesthetic gas in operating theatre E923.2
    automobile tire NEC E921.8
        causing transport accident — *see* cate-
            gories E810-E825 ☑
    blasting (cap) (materials) E923.1
    boiler (machinery), not on transport vehicle
        E921.0
        steamship — *see* Explosion, watercraft
    bomb E923.8
        in
            terrorism E979.2
            war operations E993.8
                after cessation of hostilities
                    E998.1   ▲
                atom, hydrogen or nuclear ▶(*see*
                    also War operations, injury
                    due to, nuclear weapons)◀
                    E996.9
                injury by fragments from E991.9
                    antipersonnel bomb E991.3
    butane E923.2
    caused by
        other person
            stated as
                intentional, homicidal — *see* As-
                  sault, explosive
                undetermined whether accidental
                  or homicidal E985.5
    coal gas E923.2
    detonator E923.1
    dynamite E923.1
    explosive (material) NEC E923.9
        gas(es) E923.2
        missile E923.8
        in
            terrorism E979.2
            war operations E993.1   ▲
                injury by fragments from E991.9
                  antipersonnel bomb E991.3
        used in blasting operations E923.1
    fire-damp E923.2
    fireworks E923.0
    gas E923.2
        cylinder (in machinery) E921.1
        pressure tank (in machinery) E921.1
    gasoline (fumes) (tank) not in moving motor
        vehicle E923.2
    grain store (military) (munitions) E923.8
    grenade E923.8
        in
            terrorism E979.2
            war operations E993.8   ▲
                injury by fragments from
                  E991.4   ▲
    homicide (attempt) — *see* Assault, explosive
    hot water heater, tank (in machinery) E921.0
    in mine (of explosive gases) NEC E923.2
    late effect of NEC E929.8
    machinery (*see also* Accident, machine)
        pressure vessel — *see* Explosion, pressure
            vessel
    methane E923.2
    missile E923.8
        in
            terrorism E979.2
            war operations E993.1   ▲
                injury by fragments from E991.4
    motor vehicle (part of)
        in motion (on public highway) E818 ☑
        not on public highway E825 ☑
    munitions (dump) (factory) E923.8
        in
            terrorism E979.2
            war operations E993.9   ▲
    of mine E923.8
        in
            terrorism
                at sea or in harbor E979.0
                land E979.2
                marine E979.0
            war operations
                after cessation of hostilities
                    E998.0   ▲
                at sea or in harbor E992.2   ▲

Explosion — *continued*
    of mine — *continued*
        in — *continued*
            war operations — *continued*
                land E993.8   ▲
                  after cessation of hostilities
                    E998.0   ▲
                  injury by fragments from
                    E991.4   ▲
                marine E992.2   ▲
    own weapons
        in
            terrorism (*see also* Suicide) E979.2
            war operations E993.7   ▲
                injury by fragments from E991.9
                  antipersonnel bomb E991.3
    pressure
        cooker E921.8
        gas tank (in machinery) E921.1
        vessel (in machinery) E921.9
            on transport vehicle — *see* categories
                E800-E848 ☑
            specified type NEC E921.8
    propane E923.2
    railway engine, locomotive, train (boiler) (with
        subsequent collision, derailment, fall)
        E803 ☑
        with
            collision (antecedent) (*see also* Colli-
                sion, railway) E800 ☑
            derailment (antecedent) E802 ☑
            fire (without antecedent collision or
                derailment) E803 ☑
    secondary fire resulting from — *see* Fire
    self-inflicted (unspecified whether accidental
        or intentional) E985.5
        stated as intentional, purposeful E955.5
    shell (artillery) E923.8
        in
            terrorism E979.2
            war operations E993.2   ▲
                injury by fragments from
                  E991.4   ▲
    stated as undetermined whether caused acci-
        dentally or purposely inflicted E985.5
    steam or water lines (in machinery) E921.0
    suicide (attempted) E955.5
    terrorism — *see* Terrorism, explosion
    torpedo E923.8
        in
            terrorism E979.0
            war operations E992.0   ▲
    transport accident — *see* categories
        E800-E848 ☑
    war operations — *see* War operations, explo-
        sion
    watercraft (boiler) E837 ☑
        causing drowning, submersion (after
            jumping from watercraft) E830 ☑

Exposure (weather) (conditions) (rain) (wind)
    E904.3
    with homicidal intent E968.4
    environmental
        to
            algae bloom E928.6
            blue-green algae bloom E928.6
            brown tide E928.6
            cyanobacteria bloom E928.6
            Florida red tide E928.6
            harmful alage
                and toxins E928.6
                bloom E928.6
            pfiesteria piscicida E928.6
            red tide E928.6
    excessive E904.3
        cold (*see also* Cold, exposure to) E901.9
            self-inflicted — *see* Cold, exposure to,
                self-inflicted
        heat (*see also* Heat) E900.9
    helpless person, infant, newborn due to
        abandonment or neglect E904.0
    noise E928.1
    prolonged in deep-freeze unit or refrigerator
        E901.1
    radiation — *see* Radiation

Exposure — *continued*
    resulting from transport accident — *see* cate-
        gories E800-E848 ☑
    smoke from, due to
        fire — *see* Fire
        tobacco, second-hand E869.4
    vibration E928.2

External cause status E000.9   ●
    civilian   ●
        done for   ●
            financial or other compensation
                E000.0   ●
            pay or income E000.0   ●
    for income E000.0   ●
    hobby or leisure E000.8   ●
    military E000.1   ●
        off duty E000.8   ●
    off duty military E000.8   ●
    recreation E000.8   ●
    specified NEC E000.8   ●
    sport not for income E000.8   ●
    student E000.8   ●
    volunteer E000.8   ●

F

Fallen on by
    animal (horse) (not being ridden) E906.8
        being ridden (in sport or transport)
            E828 ☑

Fall, falling (accidental) E888.9
    building E916
        burning E891.8
            private E890.8
    down
        escalator E880.0
        ladder E881.0
            in boat, ship, watercraft E833 ☑
        staircase E880.9
        stairs, steps — *see* Fall, from, stairs
    earth (with asphyxia or suffocation (by pres-
        sure)) (*see also* Earth, falling) E913.3
    from, off
        aircraft (at landing, take-off) (in-transit)
            (while alighting, boarding) E843 ☑
            resulting from accident to aircraft —
                see categories E840-E842 ☑
        animal (in sport or transport) E828 ☑
        animal-drawn vehicle E827 ☑
        balcony E882
        bed E884.4 ☑
        bicycle E826 ☑
        boat, ship, watercraft (into water) E832 ☑
            after accident to, collision, fire on
                E830 ☑
                and subsequently struck by (part
                  of) boat E831 ☑
            and subsequently struck by (part of)
                while alighting, boat E831 ☑
            burning, crushed, sinking E830 ☑
                and subsequently struck by (part
                  of) boat E831 ☑
        bridge E882
        building E882
            burning (uncontrolled fire) E891.8
                in terrorism E979.3
            private E890.8
        bunk in boat, ship, watercraft E834 ☑
            due to accident to watercraft E831 ☑
        cable car (not on rails) E847
            on rails E829 ☑
        car — *see* Fall from motor vehicle
        chair E884.2
        cliff E884.1
        commode E884.6
        curb (sidewalk) E880.1
        elevation aboard ship E834 ☑
            due to accident to ship E831 ☑
        embankment E884.9
        escalator E880.0
        fire escape E882
        flagpole E882
        furniture NEC E884.5
        gangplank (into water) (*see also* Fall, from,
            boat) E832 ☑
            to deck, dock E834 ☑

☑ Additional Digit Required — Refer to the Tabular List for Digit Selection   🅦 Subterms under main terms may continue to next column or page

328 — Volume 2 • October 2009   ▶◀ Revised Text   ● New Line   ▲ Revised Code   **2010 ICD-9-CM**

Fall, falling — *continued*
from, off — *continued*
  hammock on ship E834 ☑
    due to accident to watercraft E831 ☑
  haystack E884.9
  heelies E885.1
  high place NEC E884.9
    stated as undetermined whether accidental or intentional — *see* Jumping, from, high place
  horse (in sport or transport) E828 ☑
  in-line skates E885.1
  ladder E881.0
    in boat, ship, watercraft E833 ☑
      due to accident to watercraft E831 ☑
  machinery (*see also* Accident, machine)
    not in operation E884.9
  motor vehicle (in motion) (on public highway) E818 ☑
    not on public highway E825 ☑
      stationary, except while alighting, boarding, entering, leaving E884.9
      while alighting, boarding, entering, leaving E824 ☑
    stationary, except while alighting, boarding, entering, leaving E884.9
    while alighting, boarding, entering, leaving, except off-road type motor vehicle E817 ☑
    off-road type — *see* Fall, from, off-road type motor vehicle
  nonmotor road vehicle (while alighting, boarding) NEC E829 ☑
    stationary, except while alighting, boarding, entering, leaving E884.9
  off road type motor vehicle (not on public highway) NEC E821 ☑
    on public highway E818 ☑
      while alighting, boarding, entering, leaving E817 ☑
  snow vehicle — *see* Fall from snow vehicle, motor-driven
  one
    deck to another on ship E834 ☑
      due to accident to ship E831 ☑
    level to another NEC E884.9
      boat, ship, or watercraft E834 ☑
        due to accident to watercraft E831 ☑
  pedal cycle E826 ☑
  playground equipment E884.0
  railway rolling stock, train, vehicle (while alighting, boarding) E804 ☑
  with
    collision (*see also* Collision, railway) E800 ☑
    derailment (*see also* Derailment, railway) E802 ☑
    explosion (*see also* Explosion, railway engine) E803 ☑
  rigging (aboard ship) E834 ☑
    due to accident to watercraft E831 ☑
  roller skates E885.1
  scaffolding E881.1
  scooter (nonmotorized) E885.0
  sidewalk (curb) E880.1
    moving E885.9
  skateboard E885.2
  skis E885.3
  snowboard E885.4
  snow vehicle, motor-driven (not on public highway) E820 ☑
    on public highway E818 ☑
      while alighting, boarding, entering, leaving E817 ☑
  stairs, steps E880.9
    boat, ship, watercraft E833 ☑
      due to accident to watercraft E831 ☑

Fall, falling — *continued*
from, off — *continued*
  stairs, steps — *continued*
    motor bus, motor vehicle — *see* Fall, from, motor vehicle, while alighting, boarding
    street car E829 ☑
  stationary vehicle NEC E884.9
  stepladder E881.0
  street car (while boarding, alighting) E829 ☑
    stationary, except while boarding or alighting E884.9
  structure NEC E882
    burning (uncontrolled fire) E891.8
      in terrorism E979.3
  table E884.9
  toilet E884.6
  tower E882
  tree E884.9
  turret E882
  vehicle NEC (*see also* Accident, vehicle NEC)
    stationary E884.9
  viaduct E882
  wall E882
  wheelchair E884.3
  wheelies E885.1
  window E882
in, on
  aircraft (at landing, take-off) (in-transit) E843 ☑
    resulting from accident to aircraft — *see* categories E840-E842 ☑
  boat, ship, watercraft E835 ☑
    due to accident to watercraft E831 ☑
    one level to another NEC E834 ☑
    on ladder, stairs E833 ☑
  cutting or piercing instrument or machine E888.0
  deck (of boat, ship, watercraft) E835 ☑
    due to accident to watercraft E831 ☑
  escalator E880.0
  gangplank E835 ☑
  glass, broken E888.0
  knife E888.0
  ladder E881.0
    in boat, ship, watercraft E833 ☑
      due to accident to watercraft E831 ☑
  object
    edged, pointed or sharp E888.0
    other E888.1
  pitchfork E888.0
  railway rolling stock, train, vehicle (while alighting, boarding) E804 ☑
  with
    collision (*see also* Collision, railway) E800 ☑
    derailment (*see also* Derailment, railway) E802 ☑
    explosion (see also Explosion, railway engine) E803 ☑
  scaffolding E881.1
  scissors E888.0
  staircase, stairs, steps (*see also* Fall, from, stairs) E880.9
  street car E829 ☑
  water transport (*see also* Fall, in, boat) E835 ☑
into
  cavity E883.9
  dock E883.9
    from boat, ship, watercraft (*see also* Fall, from, boat) E832 ☑
  hold (of ship) E834 ☑
    due to accident to watercraft E831 ☑
  hole E883.9
  manhole E883.2
  moving part of machinery — *see* Accident, machine
  opening in surface NEC E883.9
  pit E883.9
  quarry E883.9
  shaft E883.9
  storm drain E883.2

Fall, falling — *continued*
into — *continued*
  tank E883.9
  water (with drowning or submersion) E910.9
  well E883.1
late effect of NEC E929.3
object (*see also* Hit by, object, falling) E916
other E888.8
over
  animal E885.9
  cliff E884.1
  embankment E884.9
  small object E885.9
overboard (*see also* Fall, from, boat) E832 ☑
resulting in striking against object E888.1
  sharp E888.0
rock E916
same level NEC E888.9
  aircraft (any kind) E843 ☑
    resulting from accident to aircraft — *see* categories E840-E842 ☑
  boat, ship, watercraft E835 ☑
    due to accident to, collision, watercraft E831 ☑
  from
    collision, pushing, shoving, by or with other person(s) E886.9
      as, or caused by, a crowd E917.6
      in sports E886.0
    in-line skates E885.1
    roller skates E885.1
    scooter (nonmotorized) E885.0
    skateboard E885.2
    slipping stumbling, tripping E885 ☑
    snowboard E885.4
  snowslide E916
    as avalanche E909.2
  stone E916
  through
    hatch (on ship) E834 ☑
      due to accident to watercraft E831 ☑
    roof E882
    window E882
  timber E916
  while alighting from, boarding, entering, leaving
    aircraft (any kind) E843 ☑
    motor bus, motor vehicle — *see* Fall, from, motor vehicle, while alighting, boarding
    nonmotor road vehicle NEC E829 ☑
    railway train E804 ☑
    street car E829 ☑

Fell or jumped from high place, so stated — *see* Jumping, from, high place
Felo-de-se — *see also* Suicide E958.9
Fever
  heat — *see* Heat
  thermic — *see* Heat
Fight (hand) (fist) (foot) — *see also* Assault, fight E960.0
Fire (accidental) (caused by great heat from appliance (electrical), hot object or hot substance) (secondary, resulting from explosion) E899
  conflagration — *see* Conflagration
  controlled, normal (in brazier, fireplace, furnace, or stove) (charcoal) (coal) (coke) (electric) (gas) (wood)
    bonfire E897
    brazier, not in building or structure E897
    in building or structure, except private dwelling (barn) (church) (convalescent or residential home) (factory) (farm outbuilding) (hospital) (hotel) (institution (educational) (dormitory) (residential) (private garage) (school) (shop) (store) (theatre) E896
    in private dwelling (apartment) (boarding house) (camping place) (caravan) (farmhouse) (home (private)) (house) (lodging house) (rooming house) (tenement) E895
    not in building or structure E897

Fire, hot object or hot substance — *continued*
controlled, normal — *continued*
  trash E897
  forest (uncontrolled) E892
  grass (uncontrolled) E892
  hay (uncontrolled) E892
  homicide (attempt) E968.0
    late effect of E969
  in, of, on, starting in E892
    aircraft (in transit) (powered) E841 ☑
      at landing, take-off E840 ☑
      stationary E892
      unpowered (balloon) (glider) E842 ☑
    balloon E842 ☑
    boat, ship, watercraft — *see* categories E830 ☑, E831 ☑, E837 ☑
    building or structure, except private dwelling (barn) (church) (convalescent or residential home) (factory) (farm outbuilding) (hospital) (hotel) (institution (educational) (dormitory) (residential) (school) (shop) (store) (theatre) (*see also* Conflagration, building or structure, except private dwelling) E891.9
    forest (uncontrolled) E892
    glider E842 ☑
    grass (uncontrolled) E892
    hay (uncontrolled) E892
    lumber (uncontrolled) E892
    machinery — *see* Accident, machine
    mine (uncontrolled) E892
    motor vehicle (in motion) (on public highway) E818 ☑
      not on public highway E825 ☑
      stationary E892
    prairie (uncontrolled) E892
    private dwelling (apartment) (boarding house) (camping place) (caravan) (farmhouse) (home (private)) (house) (lodging house) (private garage) (rooming house) (tenement) (*see also* Conflagration, private dwelling) E890.9
    railway rolling stock, train, vehicle (*see also* Explosion, railway engine) E803 ☑
      stationary E892
    room NEC E898.1
    street car (in motion) E829 ☑
      stationary E892
    terrorism (by fire-producing device) E979.3
      fittings or furniture (burning building) (uncontrolled fire) E979.3
      from nuclear explosion E979.5
    transport vehicle, stationary NEC E892
    tunnel (uncontrolled) E892
    war operations (by fire-producing device or conventional weapon) E990.9
      from nuclear explosion ▶(*see also* War operations, injury due to, nuclear weapons)◀ E996.2 ▲
      incendiary bomb E990.0 ●
      petrol bomb E990.0
  late effect of NEC E929.4
  lumber (uncontrolled) E892
  mine (uncontrolled) E892
  prairie (uncontrolled) E892
  self-inflicted (unspecified whether accidental or intentional) E988.1
    stated as intentional, purposeful E958.1
  specified NEC E898.1
  with
    conflagration — *see* Conflagration
    ignition (of)
      clothing — *see* Ignition, clothes
      highly inflammable material (benzine) (fat) (gasoline) (kerosene) (paraffin) (petrol) E894
  started by other person
    stated as
      with intent to injure or kill E968.0
      undetermined whether or not with intent to injure or kill E988.1
  suicide (attempted) E958.1
    late effect of E959

☑ Additional Digit Required — Refer to the Tabular List for Digit Selection   ▽ Subterms under main terms may continue to next column or page

Fire, hot object or hot substance — *continued*
    tunnel (uncontrolled) E892
Fireball effects from nuclear explosion
    in
        terrorism E979.5
        war operations ▶(*see also* War operations,
            injury due to, nuclear weapons)◀
            E996.2   ▲
Fireworks (explosion) E923.0
Flash burns from explosion — *see also* Explosion E923.9
Flood (any injury) (resulting from storm) E908.2
    caused by collapse of dam or manmade
        structure E909.3
Forced landing (aircraft) E840 ☑
Foreign body, object or material (entrance into)
        (accidental)
    air passage (causing injury) E915
        with asphyxia, obstruction, suffocation
            E912
            food or vomitus E911
        nose (with asphyxia, obstruction, suffoca-
            tion) E912
            causing injury without asphyxia, ob-
                struction, suffocation E915
    alimentary canal (causing injury) (with obstruc-
        tion) E915
        with asphyxia, obstruction respiratory
            passage, suffocation E912
            food E911
        mouth E915
            with asphyxia, obstruction, suffocation
                E912
                food E911
        pharynx E915
            with asphyxia, obstruction, suffocation
                E912
                food E911
    aspiration (with asphyxia, obstruction respira-
        tory passage, suffocation) E912
        causing injury without asphyxia, obstruc-
            tion respiratory passage, suffoca-
            tion E915
        food (regurgitated) (vomited) E911
            causing injury without asphyxia, ob-
                struction respiratory passage,
                suffocation E915
    mucus (not of newborn) E912
    phlegm E912
    bladder (causing injury or obstruction) E915
    bronchus, bronchi — *see* Foreign body, air
        passages
    conjunctival sac E914
    digestive system — *see* Foreign body, alimen-
        tary canal
    ear (causing injury or obstruction) E915
    esophagus (causing injury or obstruction) (*see
        also* Foreign body, alimentary canal)
        E915
    eye (any part) E914
    eyelid E914
    hairball (stomach) (with obstruction) E915
    ingestion — *see* Foreign body, alimentary
        canal
    inhalation — *see* Foreign body, aspiration
    intestine (causing injury or obstruction) E915
    iris E914
    lacrimal apparatus E914
    larynx — *see* Foreign body, air passage
    late effect of NEC E929.8
    lung — *see* Foreign body, air passage
    mouth — *see* Foreign body, alimentary canal,
        mouth
    nasal passage — *see* Foreign body, air pas-
        sage, nose
    nose — *see* Foreign body, air passage, nose
    ocular muscle E914
    operation wound (left in) — *see* Misadventure,
        foreign object
    orbit E914
    pharynx — *see* Foreign body, alimentary canal,
        pharynx
    rectum (causing injury or obstruction) E915
    stomach (hairball) (causing injury or obstruc-
        tion) E915
    tear ducts or glands E914

Foreign body, object or material —
        continued
    trachea — *see* Foreign body, air passage
    urethra (causing injury or obstruction) E915
    vagina (causing injury or obstruction) E915
Found dead, injured
    from exposure (to) — *see* Exposure
    on
        public highway E819 ☑
        railway right of way E807 ☑
Fracture (circumstances unknown or unspecified)
        E887
    due to specified external means — *see* man-
        ner of accident
    late effect of NEC E929.3
    occurring in water transport NEC E835 ☑
Freezing — *see* Cold, exposure to
Frostbite E901.0
    due to manmade conditions E901.1
Frozen — *see* Cold, exposure to

G

Garrotting, homicidal (attempted) E963
Gored E906.8
Gunshot wound — *see also* Shooting E922.9

H

Hailstones, injury by E904.3
Hairball (stomach) (with obstruction) E915
Hanged himself — *see also* Hanging, self-inflict-
        ed E983.0
Hang gliding E842 ☑
Hanging (accidental) E913.8
    caused by other person
        in accidental circumstances E913.8
        stated as
            intentional, homicidal E963
            undetermined whether accidental or
                intentional E983.0
    homicide (attempt) E963
    in bed or cradle E913.0
    legal execution E978
    self-inflicted (unspecified whether accidental
        or intentional) E983.0
        in accidental circumstances E913.8
        stated as intentional, purposeful E953.0
    stated as undetermined whether accidental
        or intentional E983.0
    suicidal (attempt) E953.0
Heat (apoplexy) (collapse) (cramps) (effects of)
        (excessive) (exhaustion) (fever) (prostra-
        tion) (stroke) E900.9
    due to
        manmade conditions (as listed in E900.1,
            except boat, ship, watercraft)
            E900.1
        weather (conditions) E900.0
    from
        electric heating appartus causing burning
            E924.8
        nuclear explosion
            in
                terrorism E979.5
                war operations ▶(*see also* War op-
                    erations, injury due to, nucle-
                    ar weapons)◀ E996.2   ▲
    generated in, boiler, engine, evaporator, fire
        room of boat, ship, watercraft E838 ☑
    inappropriate in local application or packing
        in medical or surgical procedure E873.5
    late effect of NEC E989
Hemorrhage
    delayed following medical or surgical treat-
        ment without mention of misadven-
        ture — *see* Reaction, abnormal
    during medical or surgical treatment as misad-
        venture — *see* Misadventure, cut
High
    altitude, effects E902.9
    level of radioactivity, effects — *see* Radiation
    pressure effects (*see also* Effects of, air pressure)
        from rapid descent in water (causing cais-
            son or divers' disease, palsy, or
            paralysis) E902.2
    temperature, effects — *see* Heat

Hit, hitting (accidental) by
    aircraft (propeller) (without accident to aircraft)
        E844 ☑
        unpowered E842 ☑
    avalanche E909.2
    being thrown against object in or part of
        motor vehicle (in motion) (on public
            highway) E818 ☑
        not on public highway E825 ☑
        nonmotor road vehicle NEC E829 ☑
        street car E829 ☑
    boat, ship, watercraft
        after fall from watercraft E838 ☑
            damaged, involved in accident E831 ☑
        while swimming, water skiing E838 ☑
    bullet (*see also* Shooting) E922.9
        from air gun E922.4
        in
            terrorism E979.4
            war operations E991.2
                rubber E991.0
    flare, Verey pistol (*see also* Shooting) E922.8
    hailstones E904.3
    landslide E909.2
    law-enforcing agent (on duty) E975
        with blunt object (baton) (night stick)
            (stave) (truncheon) E973
    machine — *see* Accident, machine
    missile
        firearm (*see also* Shooting) E922.9
        in
            terrorism — *see* Terrorism, missile
            war operations — *see* War operations,
                missile
    motor vehicle (on public highway) (traffic ac-
        cident) E814 ☑
        not on public highway, nontraffic accident
            E822 ☑
    nonmotor road vehicle NEC E829 ☑
    object
        falling E916
            from, in, on
                aircraft E844 ☑
                    due to accident to aircraft —
                        see categories
                        E840-E842 ☑
                    unpowered E842 ☑
                boat, ship, watercraft E838 ☑
                    due to accident to watercraft
                        E831 ☑
                building E916
                    burning (uncontrolled fire)
                        E891.8
                        in terrorism E979.3
                        private E890.8
                cataclysmic
                    earth surface movement or
                        eruption E909.9
                    storm E908.9
                cave-in E916
                    with asphyxiation or suffocation
                        (*see also* Suffocation,
                        due to, cave-in) E913.3
                earthquake E909.0
                motor vehicle (in motion) (on pub-
                    lic highway) E818 ☑
                    not on public highway E825 ☑
                    stationary E916
                nonmotor road vehicle NEC
                    E829 ☑
                pedal cycle E826 ☑
                railway rolling stock, train, vehicle
                    E806 ☑
                street car E829 ☑
                structure, burning NEC E891.8
                vehicle, stationary E916
        moving NEC — *see* Striking against, object
        projected NEC — *see* Striking against, ob-
            ject
        set in motion by
            compressed air or gas, spring, striking,
                throwing — *see* Striking
                against, object
            explosion — *see* Explosion

Hit, hitting by — *continued*
    object — *continued*
        thrown into, on, or towards
            motor vehicle (in motion) (on public
                highway) E818 ☑
            not on public highway E825 ☑
            nonmotor road vehicle NEC E829 ☑
            pedal cycle E826 ☑
            street car E829 ☑
        off-road type motor vehicle (not on public
            highway) E821 ☑
            on public highway E814 ☑
        other person(s) E917.9
            with blunt or thrown object E917.9
                in sports E917.0
                    with subsequent fall E917.5
            intentionally, homicidal E968.2
            as, or caused by, a crowd E917.1
                with subsequent fall E917.6
            in sports E917.0
        pedal cycle E826 ☑
        police (on duty) E975
            with blunt object (baton) (nightstick)
                (stave) (truncheon) E973
        railway, rolling stock, train, vehicle (part of)
            E805 ☑
        shot — *see* Shooting
        snow vehicle, motor-driven (not on public
            highway) E820 ☑
            on public highway E814 ☑
        street car E829 ☑
        vehicle NEC — *see* Accident, vehicle NEC
Homicide, homicidal (attempt) (justifiable) —
        see also Assault E968.9
Hot
    liquid, object, substance, accident caused by
        (*see also* Accident, caused by, hot, by
        type of substance)
    late effect of E929.8
    place, effects — *see* Heat
    weather, effects E900.0
Humidity, causing problem E904.3
Hunger E904.1
    resulting from
        abandonment or neglect E904.0
        transport accident — *see* categories
            E800-E848 ☑
Hurricane (any injury) E908.0
Hypobarism, hypobaropathy — *see* Effects of,
        air pressure
Hypothermia — *see* Cold, exposure to

I

Ictus
    caloris — *see* Heat
    solaris E900.0
Ignition (accidental)
    anesthetic gas in operating theatre E923.2
    bedclothes
        with
            conflagration — *see* Conflagration
            ignition (of)
                clothing — *see* Ignition, clothes
                highly inflammable material (ben-
                    zine) (fat) (gasoline)
                    (kerosene) (paraffin) (petrol)
                    E894
    benzine E894
    clothes, clothing (from controlled fire) (in
        building) E893.9
        with conflagration — *see* Conflagration
        from
            bonfire E893.2
            highly inflammable material E894
            sources or material as listed in E893.8
            trash fire E893.2
            uncontrolled fire — *see* Conflagration
        in
            private dwelling E893.0
            specified building or structure, except
                private dwelling E893.1
            not in building or structure E893.2
    explosive material — *see* Explosion
    fat E894
    gasoline E894

Ignition — *continued*
kerosene E894
material
explosive — *see* Explosion
highly inflammable E894
with conflagration — *see* Conflagration
with explosion E923.2
nightdress — *see* Ignition, clothes
paraffin E894
petrol E894
Immersion — *see* Submersion
Implantation of quills of porcupine E906.8
Inanition (from) E904.9
hunger — *see* Lack of, food
resulting from homicidal intent E968.4
thirst — *see* Lack of, water
Inattention after, at birth E904.0
homicidal, infanticidal intent E968.4
Infanticide — *see also* Assault
Ingestion
foreign body (causing injury) (with obstruction) — *see* Foreign body, alimentary canal
poisonous substance NEC — *see* Table of Drugs and Chemicals
Inhalation
excessively cold substance, manmade E901.1
foreign body — *see* Foreign body, aspiration
liquid air, hydrogen, nitrogen E901.1
mucus, not of newborn (with asphyxia, obstruction respiratory passage, suffocation) E912
phlegm (with asphyxia, obstruction respiratory passage, suffocation) E912
poisonous gas — *see* Table of Drugs and Chemicals
smoke from, due to
fire — *see* Fire
tobacco, second-hand E869.4
vomitus (with asphyxia, obstruction respiratory passage, suffocation) E911
Injury, injured (accidental(ly)) NEC E928.9
by, caused by, from
air rifle (BB gun) E922.4
animal (not being ridden) NEC E906.9
being ridden (in sport or transport) E828 ☑
assault (*see also* Assault) E968.9
avalanche E909.2
bayonet (*see also* Bayonet wound) E920.3
being thrown against some part of, or object in
motor vehicle (in motion) (on public highway) E818 ☑
not on public highway E825 ☑
nonmotor road vehicle NEC E829 ☑
off-road motor vehicle NEC E821 ☑
railway train E806 ☑
snow vehicle, motor-driven E820 ☑
street car E829 ☑
bending E927.8
bite, human E928.3
broken glass E920.8
bullet — *see* Shooting
cave-in (*see also* Suffocation, due to, cave-in) E913.3
without asphyxiation or suffocation E916
earth surface movement or eruption E909.9
storm E908.9
cloudburst E908.8
component of firearm or air gun E928.7 ●
cutting or piercing instrument (*see also* Cut) E920.9
cyclone E908.1
earthquake E909.0
earth surface movement or eruption E909.9
electric current (*see also* Electric shock) E925.9
explosion (*see also* Explosion) E923.9
of gun part E928.7 ●
fire — *see* Fire
flare, Verey pistol E922.8
flood E908.2

Injury, injured — *continued*
by, caused by, from — *continued*
foreign body — *see* Foreign body
gun recoil E928.7 ●
hailstones E904.3
hurricane E908.0
landslide E909.2
law-enforcing agent, police, in course of legal intervention — *see* Legal intervention
lightning E907
live rail or live wire — *see* Electric shock
machinery (*see also* Accident, machine)
aircraft, without accident to aircraft E844 ☑
boat, ship, watercraft (deck) (engine room) (galley) (laundry) (loading) E836 ☑
mechanism of firearm or air gun E928.7 ●
missile
explosive E923.8
firearm — *see* Shooting
in
terrorism — *see* Terrorism, missile
war operations — *see* War operations, missile
moving part of motor vehicle (in motion) (on public highway) E818 ☑
not on public highway, nontraffic accident E825 ☑
while alighting, boarding, entering, leaving — *see* Fall, from, motor vehicle, while alighting, boarding
nail E920.8
needle (sewing) E920.4
hypodermic E920.5
noise E928.1
object
fallen on
motor vehicle (in motion) (on public highway) E818 ☑
not on public highway E825 ☑
falling — *see* Hit by, object, falling
paintball gun E922.5
radiation — *see* Radiation
railway rolling stock, train, vehicle (part of) E805 ☑
door or window E806 ☑
recoil of firearm E928.7 ●
rotating propeller, aircraft E844 ☑
rough landing of off-road type motor vehicle (after leaving ground or rough terrain) E821 ☑
snow vehicle E820 ☑
saber (*see also* Wound, saber) E920.3
shot — *see* Shooting
sound waves E928.1
splinter or sliver, wood E920.8
straining E927.8
street car (door) E829 ☑
suicide (attempt) E958.9
sword E920.3
terrorism — *see* Terrorism
third rail — *see* Electric shock
thunderbolt E907
tidal wave E909.4
caused by storm E908.0
tornado E908.1
torrential rain E908.2
twisting E927.8
vehicle NEC — *see* Accident, vehicle NEC
vibration E928.2
volcanic eruption E909.1
weapon burst, in war operations E993.9 ▲
weightlessness (in spacecraft, real or simulated) E928.0
wood splinter or sliver E920.8
due to
civil insurrection — *see* War operations
occurring after cessation of hostilities E998.9 ▲
terrorism — *see* Terrorism
war operations — *see* War operations

Injury, injured — *continued*
due to — *continued*
war operations — *see* War operations — *continued*
occurring after cessation of hostilities E998.9 ▲
weapon of mass destruction [WMD] E997.3 ●
homicidal (*see also* Assault) E968.9
inflicted (by)
in course of arrest (attempted), suppression of disturbance, maintenance of order, by law enforcing agents — *see* Legal intervention
law-enforcing agent (on duty) — *see* Legal intervention
other person
stated as
accidental E928.9
homicidal, intentional — *see* Assault
undetermined whether accidental or intentional — *see* Injury, stated as undetermined
police (on duty) — *see* Legal intervention
in, on
civil insurrection — *see* War operations
fight E960.0
parachute descent (voluntary) (without accident to aircraft) E844 ☑
with accident to aircraft — *see* categories E840-E842 ☑
public highway E819 ☑
railway right of way E807 ☑
terrorism — *see* Terrorism
war operations — *see* War operations
late effect of E929.9
purposely (inflicted) by other person(s) — *see* Assault
self-inflicted (unspecified whether accidental or intentional) E988.9
stated as
accidental E928.9
intentionally, purposely E958.9
specified cause NEC E928.8
stated as
hanging E983.0
knife E986
late effect of E989
puncture (any part of body) E986
shooting — *see* Shooting, stated as undetermined whether accidental or intentional
specified means NEC E988.8
stab (any part of body) E986
strangulation — *see* Suffocation, stated as undetermined whether accidental or intentional
submersion E984
suffocation — *see* Suffocation, stated as undetermined whether accidental or intentional
undetermined whether accidentally or purposely inflicted (by) E988.9
cut (any part of body) E986
cutting or piercing instrument (classifiable to E920) E986
drowning E984
explosive(s) (missile) E985.5
falling from high place E987.9
manmade structure, except residential E987.1
natural site E987.2
residential premises E987.0
to child due to criminal abortion E968.8
Insufficient nourishment — *see also* Lack of, food
homicidal intent E968.4
Insulation, effects — *see* Heat
Interruption of respiration by
food lodged in esophagus E911
foreign body, except food, in esophagus E912
Intervention, legal — *see* Legal intervention
Intoxication, drug or poison — *see* Table of Drugs and Chemicals
Irradiation — *see* Radiation

J

Jammed (accidentally)
between objects (moving) (stationary and moving) E918
in object E918
Jumped or fell from high place, so stated — *see* Jumping, from, high place, stated as in undetermined circumstances
Jumping
before train, vehicle or other moving object (unspecified whether accidental or intentional) E988.0
stated as
intentional, purposeful E958.0
suicidal (attempt) E958.0
from
aircraft
by parachute (voluntarily) (without accident to aircraft) E844 ☑
due to accident to aircraft — *see* categories E840-E842 ☑
boat, ship, watercraft (into water)
after accident to, fire on, watercraft E830 ☑
and subsequently struck by (part of) boat E831 ☑
burning, crushed, sinking E830 ☑
and subsequently struck by (part of) boat E831 ☑
voluntarily, without accident (to boat) with injury other than drowning or submersion E883.0
building (*see also* Jumping, from, high place)
burning (uncontrolled fire) E891.8
in terrorism E979.3
private E890.8
cable car (not on rails) E847
on rails E829 ☑
high place
in accidental circumstances or in sport — *see* categories E880-E884
stated as
with intent to injure self E957.9
man-made structures NEC E957.1
natural sites E957.2
residential premises E957.0
in undetermined circumstances E987.9
man-made structures NEC E987.1
natural sites E987.2
residential premises E987.0
suicidal (attempt) E957.9
man-made structures NEC E957.1
natural sites E957.1
residential premises E957.0
motor vehicle (in motion) (on public highway) — *see* Fall, from, motor vehicle
nonmotor road vehicle NEC E829 ☑
street car E829 ☑
structure (*see also* Jumping, from, high place)
burning NEC (uncontrolled fire) E891.8
in terrorism E979.3
into water
with injury other than drowning or submersion E883.0
drowning or submersion — *see* Submersion
from, off, watercraft — *see* Jumping, from, boat
Justifiable homicide — *see* Assault

K

Kicked by
animal E906.8
person(s) (accidentally) E917.9
with intent to injure or kill E960.0
as, or caused by a crowd E917.1
with subsequent fall E917.6
in fight E960.0

☑ Additional Digit Required — Refer to the Tabular List for Digit Selection   ᵛᵒˡ Subterms under main terms may continue to next column or page

2010 ICD-9-CM   ▶◀ Revised Text   ● New Line   ▲ Revised Code   October 2009 • Volume 2 — 331

Kicked by — *continued*
　person(s) — *continued*
　　in sports E917.0
　　　with subsequent fall E917.5
Kicking against
　object (moving) E917.9
　　in sports E917.0
　　　with subsequent fall E917.5
　　stationary E917.4
　　　with subsequent fall E917.8
　person — *see* Striking against, person
Killed, killing (accidentally) NEC — *see also* Injury
　　E928.9
　in
　　action — *see* War operations
　　brawl, fight (hand) (fists) (foot) E960.0
　　　by weapon (*see also* Assault)
　　　　cutting, piercing E966
　　　　firearm — *see* Shooting, homicide
　self
　　stated as
　　　accident E928.9
　　　suicide — *see* Suicide
　　unspecified whether accidental or suicidal
　　　E988.9
Knocked down (accidentally) (by) NEC E928.9
　animal (not being ridden) E906.8
　　being ridden (in sport or transport)
　　　E828 ☑
　blast from explosion (*see also* Explosion) E923.9
　crowd, human stampede E917.6
　late effect of — *see* Late effect
　person (accidentally) E917.9
　　in brawl, fight E960.0
　　in sports E917.5
　transport vehicle — *see* vehicle involved under
　　Hit by
　while boxing E917.5

L

Laceration NEC E928.9
Lack of
　air (refrigerator or closed place), suffocation
　　by E913.2
　care (helpless person) (infant) (newborn)
　　E904.0
　　homicidal intent E968.4
　food except as result of transport accident
　　E904.1
　　helpless person, infant, newborn due to
　　　abandonment or neglect E904.0
　water except as result of transport accident
　　E904.2
　　helpless person, infant, newborn due to
　　　abandonment or neglect E904.0
Landslide E909.2
　falling on, hitting
　　motor vehicle (any) (in motion) (on or off
　　　public highway) E909.2
　　railway rolling stock, train, vehicle E909.2
Late effect of
　accident NEC (accident classifiable to E928.9)
　　E929.9
　　specified NEC (accident classifiable to
　　　E910–E928.8) E929.8
　assault E969
　fall, accidental (accident classifiable to
　　E880–E888) E929.3
　fire, accident caused by (accident classifiable
　　to E890–E899) E929.4
　homicide, attempt (any means) E969
　injury due to terrorism E999.1
　injury undetermined whether accidentally or
　　purposely inflicted (injury classifiable
　　to E980–E988) E989
　legal intervention (injury classifiable to
　　E970–E976) E977
　medical or surgical procedure, test or therapy
　　as, or resulting in, or from
　　　abnormal or delayed reaction or compli-
　　　　cation — *see* Reaction, abnor-
　　　　mal
　　　misadventure — *see* Misadventure
　motor vehicle accident (accident classifiable
　　to E810–E825) E929.0

Late effect of — *continued*
　natural or environmental factor, accident due
　　to (accident classifiable to E900–E909)
　　E929.5
　poisoning, accidental (accident classifiable to
　　E850–E858, E860–E869) E929.2
　suicide, attempt (any means) E959
　transport accident NEC (accident classifiable
　　to E800–E807, E826–E838, E840–E848)
　　E929.1
　war operations, injury due to (injury classifiable
　　to E990–E998) E999.0
Launching pad accident E845 ☑
Legal
　execution, any method E978
　intervention (by) (injury from) E976
　　baton E973
　　bayonet E974
　　blow E975
　　blunt object (baton) (nightstick) (stave)
　　　(truncheon) E973
　　cutting or piercing instrument E974
　　dynamite E971
　　execution, any method E973
　　explosive(s) (shell) E971
　　firearm(s) E970
　　gas (asphyxiation) (poisoning) (tear) E972
　　grenade E971
　　late effect of E977
　　machine gun E970
　　manhandling E975
　　mortar bomb E971
　　nightstick E973
　　revolver E970
　　rifle E970
　　specified means NEC E975
　　stabbing E974
　　stave E973
　　truncheon E973
Lifting, injury in E927.8
Lightning (shock) (stroke) (struck by) E907
Liquid (noncorrosive) in eye E914
　corrosive E924.1
Loss of control
　motor vehicle (on public highway) (without
　　antecedent collision) E816 ☑
　　with
　　　antecedent collision on public highway
　　　　— *see* Collision, motor vehicle
　　　involving any object, person or ve-
　　　　hicle not on public highway
　　　　E816 ☑
　　　not on public highway, nontraffic
　　　　accident E825 ☑
　　　　with antecedent collision — *see*
　　　　　Collision, motor vehicle,
　　　　　not on public highway
　　　on public highway — *see* Collision,
　　　　motor vehicle
　　off-road type motor vehicle (not on public
　　　highway) E821 ☑
　　　on public highway — *see* Loss of control,
　　　　motor vehicle
　　snow vehicle, motor-driven (not on public
　　　highway) E820 ☑
　　　on public highway — *see* Loss of control,
　　　　motor vehicle
Lost at sea E832 ☑
　with accident to watercraft E830 ☑
　in war operations E995.8　　　　　　　　▲
Low
　pressure, effects — *see* Effects of, air pressure
　temperature, effects — *see* Cold, exposure to
**Lying before train, vehicle or other moving
　object** (unspecified whether accidental or
　intentional) E988.0
　stated as intentional, purposeful, suicidal (at-
　　tempt) E958.0
Lynching — *see also* Assault E968.9

M

**Malfunction, atomic power plant in water
　transport** E838 ☑
Mangled (accidentally) NEC E928.9
Manhandling (in brawl, fight) E960.0

Manhandling — *continued*
　legal intervention E975
Manslaughter (nonaccidental) — *see* Assault
Marble in nose E912
Mauled by animal E906.8
Medical procedure, complication of
　delayed or as an abnormal reaction
　　without mention of misadventure — *see*
　　　Reaction, abnormal
　　due to or as a result of misadventure — *see*
　　　Misadventure
Melting of fittings and furniture in burning
　in terrorism E979.3
Minamata disease E865.2
**Misadventure(s) to patient(s) during surgical
　or medical care** E876.9
　contaminated blood, fluid, drug or biological
　　substance (presence of agents and
　　toxins as listed in E875) E875.9
　　administered (by) NEC E875.9
　　　infusion E875.0
　　　injection E875.1
　　　specified means NEC E875.2
　　　transfusion E875.0
　　　vaccination E875.1
　cut, cutting, puncture, perforation or hemor-
　　rhage (accidental) (inadvertent) (inap-
　　propriate) (during) E870.9
　　aspiration of fluid or tissue (by puncture
　　　or catheterization, except heart)
　　　E870.5
　　biopsy E870.8
　　　needle (aspirating) E870.5
　　blood sampling E870.5
　　catheterization E870.5
　　　heart E870.6
　　dialysis (kidney) E870.2
　　endoscopic examination E870.4
　　enema E870.7
　　infusion E870.1
　　injection E870.3
　　lumbar puncture E870.5
　　needle biopsy E870.5
　　paracentesis, abdominal E870.5
　　perfusion E870.2
　　specified procedure NEC E870.8
　　surgical operation E870.0
　　thoracentesis E870.5
　　transfusion E870.1
　　vaccination E870.3
　excessive amount of blood or other fluid dur-
　　ing transfusion or infusion E873.0
　failure
　　in dosage E873.9
　　　electroshock therapy E873.4
　　　inappropriate temperature (too hot or
　　　　too cold) in local application
　　　　and packing E873.5
　　　infusion
　　　　excessive amount of fluid E873.0
　　　　incorrect dilution of fluid E873.1
　　　insulin-shock therapy E873.4
　　　nonadministration of necessary drug
　　　　or medicinal E873.6
　　　overdose (*see also* Overdose)
　　　　radiation, in therapy E873.2
　　　radiation
　　　　inadvertent exposure of patient
　　　　　(receiving radiation for test
　　　　　or therapy) E873.3
　　　　not receiving radiation for test
　　　　　or therapy — *see* Radia-
　　　　　tion
　　　overdose E873.2
　　specified procedure NEC E873.8
　　transfusion
　　　excessive amount of blood E873.0
　　mechanical, of instrument or apparatus
　　　(during procedure) E874.9
　　　aspiration of fluid or tissue (by punc-
　　　　ture or catheterization, except
　　　　of heart) E874.4
　　　biopsy E874.8
　　　　needle (aspirating) E874.4
　　　blood sampling E874.4
　　　catheterization E874.4

**Misadventure(s) to patient(s) during surgical
　or medical care** — *continued*
　failure — *continued*
　　mechanical, of instrument or apparatus —
　　　continued
　　　catheterization — *continued*
　　　　heart E874.5
　　　dialysis (kidney) E874.2
　　　endoscopic examination E874.3
　　　enema E874.8
　　　infusion E874.1
　　　injection E874.8
　　　lumbar puncture E874.4
　　　needle biopsy E874.4
　　　paracentesis, abdominal E874.4
　　　perfusion E874.2
　　　specified procedure NEC E874.8
　　　surgical operation E874.0
　　　thoracentesis E874.4
　　　transfusion E874.1
　　　vaccination E874.8
　　sterile precautions (during procedure)
　　　E872.9
　　　aspiration of fluid or tissue (by punc-
　　　　ture or catheterization, except
　　　　heart) E872.5
　　　biopsy E872.8
　　　　needle (aspirating) E872.5
　　　blood sampling E872.5
　　　catheterization E872.5
　　　　heart E872.6
　　　dialysis (kidney) E872.2
　　　endoscopic examination E872.4
　　　enema E872.8
　　　infusion E872.1
　　　injection E872.3
　　　lumbar puncture E872.5
　　　needle biopsy E872.5
　　　paracentesis, abdominal E872.5
　　　perfusion E872.2
　　　removal of catheter or packing E872.8
　　　specified procedure NEC E872.8
　　　surgical operation E872.0
　　　thoracentesis E872.5
　　　transfusion E872.1
　　　vaccination E872.3
　　suture or ligature during surgical proce-
　　　dure E876.2
　　to introduce or to remove tube or instru-
　　　ment E876.4
　　　foreign object left in body — *see* Mis-
　　　　adventure, foreign object
　foreign object left in body (during procedure)
　　E871.9
　　aspiration of fluid or tissue (by puncture
　　　or catheterization, except heart)
　　　E871.5
　　biopsy E871.8
　　　needle (aspirating) E871.5
　　blood sampling E871.5
　　catheterization E871.5
　　　heart E871.6
　　dialysis (kidney) E871.2
　　endoscopic examination E871.4
　　enema E871.8
　　infusion E871.1
　　injection E871.3
　　lumbar puncture E871.5
　　needle biopsy E871.5
　　paracentesis, abdominal E871.5
　　perfusion E871.2
　　removal of catheter or packing E871.7
　　specified procedure NEC E871.8
　　surgical operation E871.0
　　thoracentesis E871.5
　　transfusion E871.1
　　vaccination E871.3
　hemorrhage — *see* Misadventure, cut
　inadvertent exposure of patient to radiation
　　(being received for test or therapy)
　　E873.3
　inappropriate
　　temperature (too hot or too cold) in local
　　　application or packing E873.5
　infusion (*see also* Misadventure, by specific
　　type, infusion)

☑ Additional Digit Required — Refer to the Tabular List for Digit Selection　　　　　　　🔻 Subterms under main terms may continue to next column or page

332 — Volume 2 • October 2009　　　▶◀ Revised Text　　　● New Line　　　▲ Revised Code　　　**2010 ICD-9-CM**

Misadventure(s) to patient(s) during surgical or medical care — *continued*
infusion (*see also* Misadventure, by specific type, infusion) — *continued*
excessive amount of fluid E873.0
incorrect dilution of fluid E873.1
wrong fluid E876.1
mismatched blood in transfusion E876.0
nonadministration of necessary drug or medicinal E873.6
overdose (*see also* Overdose)
radiation, in therapy E873.2
perforation — *see* Misadventure, cut
performance of correct operation (procedure) on wrong ●
body part E876.7 ●
side E876.7 ●
site E876.7 ●
performance of operation (procedure)
intended for another patient E876.6
on patient not scheduled for surgery E876.6
on wrong patient E876.6
performance of ►wrong◄ operation ►on correct patient◄ E876.5
puncture — *see* Misadventure, cut
specified type NEC E876.8
failure
suture or ligature during surgical operation E876.2
to introduce or to remove tube or instrument E876.4
foreign object left in body E871.9
infusion of wrong fluid E876.1
performance of inappropriate operation E876.5
transfusion of mismatched blood E876.0
wrong
fluid in infusion E876.1
placement of endotracheal tube during anesthetic procedure E876.3
transfusion (*see also* Misadventure, by specific type, transfusion)
excessive amount of blood E873.0
mismatched blood E876.0
wrong
device implanted into correct surgical ● site E876.5
drug given in error — *see* Table of Drugs and Chemicals
fluid in infusion E876.1
placement of endotracheal tube during anesthetic procedure E876.3
procedure (operation) performed on the ● correct patient E876.5 ●
Motion (effects) E903
sickness E903
Mountain sickness E902.0
Mucus aspiration or inhalation, not of newborn (with asphyxia, obstruction respiratory passage, suffocation) E912
Mudslide of cataclysmic nature E909.2
Murder (attempt) — *see also* Assault E968.9

N

Nail, injury by E920.8
Needlestick (sewing needle) E920.4
hypodermic E920.5
Neglect — *see also* Privation
criminal E968.4
homicidal intent E968.4
Noise (causing injury) (pollution) E928.1
Nuclear weapon — *see also* War operations, injury due to, nuclear weapons E996.9 ●

O

Object
falling
from, in, on, hitting
aircraft E844 ☑
due to accident to aircraft — *see* categories E840-E842 ☑
machinery (*see also* Accident, machine)
not in operation E916

Object — *continued*
falling
from, in, on, hitting — *continued*
motor vehicle (in motion) (on public highway) E818 ☑
not on public highway E825 ☑
stationary E916
nonmotor road vehicle NEC E829 ☑
pedal cycle E826 ☑
person E916
railway rolling stock, train, vehicle E806 ☑
street car E829 ☑
watercraft E838 ☑
due to accident to watercraft E831 ☑
set in motion by
accidental explosion of pressure vessel — *see* category E921 ☑
firearm — *see* category E922 ☑
machine(ry) — *see* Accident, machine
transport vehicle — *see* categories E800-E848 ☑
thrown from, in, on, towards
aircraft E844 ☑
cable car (not on rails) E847
on rails E829 ☑
motor vehicle (in motion) (on public highway) E818 ☑
not on public highway E825 ☑
nonmotor road vehicle NEC E829 ☑
pedal cycle E826 ☑
street car E829 ☑
vehicle NEC — *see* Accident, vehicle NEC
Obstruction
air passages, larynx, respiratory passages
by
external means NEC — *see* Suffocation
food, any type (regurgitated) (vomited) E911
material or object, except food E912
mucus E912
phlegm E912
vomitus E911
digestive tract, except mouth or pharynx
by
food, any type E915
foreign body (any) E915
esophagus
without asphyxia or obstruction of respiratory passage E915
food E911
foreign body, except food E912
mouth or pharynx
by
food, any type E911
material or object, except food E912
respiration — *see* Obstruction, air passages
Oil in eye E914
Overdose
anesthetic (drug) — *see* Table of Drugs and Chemicals
drug — *see* Table of Drugs and Chemicals
Overexertion E927.9
from
lifting E927.8
maintaining prolonged positions E927.1
holding E927.1
sitting E927.1
standing E927.1
prolonged static position E927.1
pulling E927.8
pushing E927.8
sudden strenuous movement E927.0
Overexposure (accidental) (to)
cold (*see also* Cold, exposure to) E901.9
due to manmade conditions E901.1
heat (*see also* Heat) E900.9
radiation — *see* Radiation
radioactivity — *see* Radiation
sun, except sunburn E900.0
weather — *see* Exposure
wind — *see* Exposure
Overheated — *see also* Heat E900.9
Overlaid E913.0

Overturning (accidental)
animal-drawn vehicle E827 ☑
boat, ship, watercraft
causing
drowning, submersion E830 ☑
injury except drowning, submersion E831 ☑
machinery — *see* Accident, machine
motor vehicle (*see also* Loss of control, motor vehicle) E816 ☑
with antecedent collision on public highway — *see* Collision, motor vehicle
not on public highway, nontraffic accident E825 ☑
with antecedent collision — *see* Collision, motor vehicle, not on public highway
nonmotor road vehicle NEC E829 ☑
off-road type motor vehicle — *see* Loss of control, off-road type motor vehicle
pedal cycle E826 ☑
railway rolling stock, train, vehicle (*see also* Derailment, railway) E802 ☑
street car E829 ☑
vehicle NEC — *see* Accident, vehicle NEC

P

Palsy, divers' E902.2
Parachuting (voluntary) (without accident to aircraft) E844 ☑
due to accident to aircraft — *see* categories E840-E842 ☑
Paralysis
divers' E902.2
lead or saturnine E866.0
from pesticide NEC E863.4
Pecked by bird E906.8
Performance of correct operation (procedure) ●
on wrong ●
body part E876.7 ●
side E876.7 ●
site E876.7 ●
Performance of operation (procedure)
intended for another patient E876.6 ●
on patient not scheduled for surgery E876.6 ●
on wrong patient E876.6 ●
Performance of wrong operation on correct ●
patient E876.5 ●
Phlegm aspiration or inhalation (with asphyxia, obstruction respiratory passage, suffocation) E912
Piercing — *see also* Cut E920.9
by slide trigger mechanism, scope or other ● part of gun E928.7 ●
Pinched
between objects (moving) (stationary and moving) E918
by slide trigger mechanism, scope or other ● part of gun E928.7 ●
in object E918
Pinned under
machine(ry) — *see* Accident, machine
Place of occurrence of accident — *see* Accident (to), occurring (at) (in)
Plumbism E866.0
from insecticide NEC E863.4
Poisoning (accidental) (by) — *see also* Table of Drugs and Chemicals
carbon monoxide
generated by
aircraft in transit E844 ☑
motor vehicle
in motion (on public highway) E818 ☑
not on public highway E825 ☑
watercraft (in transit) (not in transit) E838 ☑
caused by injection of poisons or toxins into or through skin by plant thorns, spines, or other mechanism E905.7
marine or sea plants E905.6
fumes or smoke due to
conflagration — *see* Conflagration
explosion or fire — *see* Fire
ignition — *see* Ignition

Poisoning — *see also* Table of Drugs and Chemicals — *continued*
gas
in legal intervention E972
legal execution, by E978
on watercraft E838
used as anesthetic — *see* Table of Drugs and Chemicals
in
terrorism (chemical weapons) E979.7
war operations E997.2
execution E978
intervention
by gas E972
late effect of — *see* Late effect
legal
Pressure, external, causing asphyxia, suffocation — *see also* Suffocation E913.9
Privation E904.9
food (*see also* Lack of, food) E904.1
helpless person, infant, newborn due to abandonment or neglect E904.0
late effect of NEC E929.5
resulting from transport accident — *see* categories E800-E848 ☑
water (*see also* Lack of, water) E904.2
Projected objects, striking against or struck by — *see* Striking against, object
Prolonged stay in
high altitude (causing conditions as listed in E902.0) E902.0
weightless environment E928.0
Prostration
heat — *see* Heat
Pulling, injury in E927.8
Puncture, puncturing — *see also* Cut E920.9
by
plant thorns or spines E920.8
toxic reaction E905.7
marine or sea plants E905.6
sea-urchin spine E905.6
● **Pushing** (injury in) (overexertion) E927.8
by other person(s) (accidental) E917.9
with fall E886.9
in sports E886.0
as, or caused by, a crowd, human stampede E917.1
with subsequent fall E917.6
before moving vehicle or object
stated as
intentional, homicidal E968.5
undetermined whether accidental or intentional E988.8
from
high place
in accidental circum-stances — *see* categories E880-E884 ☑
stated as
intentional, homicidal E968.1
undetermined whether accidental or intentional E987.9
man-made structure, except residential E987.1
natural site E987.2
residential E987.0
motor vehicle (*see also* Fall, from, motor vehicle) E818 ☑
stated as
intentional, homicidal E968.5
undetermined whether accidental or intentional E988.8
in sports E917.0
with fall E886.0

R

Radiation (exposure to) E926.9
abnormal reaction to medical test or therapy E879.2
arc lamps E926.2
atomic power plant (malfunction) NEC E926.9
in water transport E838 ☑
electromagnetic, ionizing E926.3
gamma rays E926.3
in
terrorism (from or following nuclear explosion) (direct) (secondary) E979.5

☑ Additional Digit Required — Refer to the Tabular List for Digit Selection   ⟨ᵂᴮ⟩ Subterms under main terms may continue to next column or page

Radiation — continued

in — continued

terrorism — continued

laser E979.8

war operations ▶(see also War operations, injury due to, nuclear weapons)◀ E996.3 ▲

laser(s) E997.0

water transport E838 ☑

inadvertent exposure of patient (receiving test or therapy) E873.3

infrared (heaters and lamps) E926.1

excessive heat E900.1

ionized, ionizing (particles, artificially accelerated) E926.8

electromagnetic E926.3

isotopes, radioactive — see Radiation, radioactive isotopes

laser(s) E926.4

in

terrorism E979.8

war operations E997.0

misadventure in medical care — see Misadventure, failure, in dosage, radiation

late effect of NEC E929.8

excessive heat from — see Heat

light sources (visible) (ultraviolet) E926.2

misadventure in medical or surgical procedure — see Misadventure, failure, in dosage, radiation

overdose (in medical or surgical procedure) E873.2

radar E926.0

radioactive isotopes E926.5

atomic power plant malfunction E926.5

in water transport E838 ☑

misadventure in medical or surgical treatment — see Misadventure, failure, in dosage, radiation

radiobiologicals — see Radiation, radioactive isotopes

radiofrequency E926.0

radiopharmaceuticals — see Radiation, radioactive isotopes

radium NEC E926.9

sun E926.2

excessive heat from E900.0

tanning bed E926.2

welding arc or torch E926.2

excessive heat from E900.1

x-rays (hard) (soft) E926.3

misadventure in medical or surgical treatment — see Misadventure, failure, in dosage, radiation

Rape E960.1

Reaction, abnormal to or following (medical or surgical procedure) E879.9

amputation (of limbs) E878.5

anastomosis (arteriovenous) (blood vessel) (gastrojejunal) (skin) (tendon) (natural, artificial material, tissue) E878.2

external stoma, creation of E878.3

aspiration (of fluid) E879.4

tissue E879.8

biopsy E879.8

blood

sampling E879.7

transfusion

procedure E879.8

bypass — see Reaction, abnormal, anastomosis

catheterization

cardiac E879.0

urinary E879.6

colostomy E878.3

cystostomy E878.3

dialysis (kidney) E879.1

drugs or biologicals — see Table of Drugs and Chemicals

duodenostomy E878.3

electroshock therapy E879.3

formation of external stoma E878.3

gastrostomy E878.3

graft — see Reaction, abnormal, anastomosis

hypothermia E879.8

Reaction, abnormal to or following — continued

implant, implantation (of)

artificial

internal device (cardiac pacemaker) (electrodes in brain) (heart valve prosthesis) (orthopedic) E878.1

material or tissue (for anastomosis or bypass) E878.2

with creation of external stoma E878.3

natural tissues (for anastomosis or bypass) E878.2

with creation of external stoma E878.3

as transplantion — see Reaction, abnormal, transplant

infusion

procedure E879.8

injection

procedure E879.8

specific type of procedure E879.9

insertion of gastric or duodenal sound E879.5

insulin-shock therapy E879.3

lumbar puncture E879.4

perfusion E879.1

procedures other than surgical operation (see also Reaction, abnormal, by)

specified procedure E879.9

radiological procedure or therapy E879.2

removal of organ (partial) (total) NEC E878.6

with

anastomosis, bypass or graft E878.2

formation of external stoma E878.3

implant of artificial internal device E878.1

transplant(ation)

partial organ E878.4

whole organ E878.0

sampling

blood E879.7

fluid NEC E879.4

tissue E879.8

shock therapy E879.3

surgical operation (see also Reaction, abnormal, by specified type of operation) E878.9

restorative NEC E878.4

with

anastomosis, bypass or graft E878.2

fomation of external stoma E878.3

implant(ation) — see Reaction, abnormal, implant

transplant(ation) — see Reaction, abnormal, transplant

specified operation NEC E878.8

thoracentesis E879.4

transfusion

procedure E879.8

transplant, transplantation (heart) (kidney) (liver) E878.0

partial organ E878.4

ureterostomy E878.3

vaccination E879.8

Reduction in

atmospheric pressure (see also Effects of, air pressure)

while surfacing from

deep water diving causing caisson or divers' disease, palsy or paralysis E902.2

underground E902.8

Residual (effect) — see Late effect

Rock falling on or hitting (accidentally)

motor vehicle (in motion) (on public highway) E818 ☑

not on public highway E825 ☑

nonmotor road vehicle NEC E829 ☑

pedal cycle E826 ☑

person E916

railway rolling stock, train, vehicle E806 ☑

Running off, away

animal (being ridden) (in sport or transport) E828 ☑

not being ridden E906.8

animal-drawn vehicle E827 ☑

rails, railway (see also Derailment) E802 ☑

Running off, away — continued

roadway

motor vehicle (without antecedent collision) E816 ☑

with

antecedent collision — see Collision motor vehicle

subsequent collision

involving any object, person or vehicle not on public highway E816 ☑

on public highway E811 ☑

nontraffic accident E825 ☑

with antecedent collision — see Collision, motor vehicle, not on public highway

nonmotor road vehicle NEC E829 ☑

pedal cycle E826 ☑

Run over (accidentally) (by)

animal (not being ridden) E906.8

being ridden (in sport or transport) E828 ☑

animal-drawn vehicle E827 ☑

machinery — see Accident, machine

motor vehicle (on public highway) — see Hit by, motor vehicle

nonmotor road vehicle NEC E829 ☑

railway train E805 ☑

street car E829 ☑

vehicle NEC E848

S

Saturnism E866.0

from insecticide NEC E863.4

Scald, scalding (accidental) (by) (from) (in) E924.0

acid — see Scald, caustic

boiling tap water E924.2

caustic or corrosive liquid, substance E924.1

swallowed — see Table of Drugs and Chemicals

homicide (attempt) — see Assault, burning

inflicted by other person

stated as

intentional or homicidal E968.3

undetermined whether accidental or intentional E988.2

late effect of NEC E929.8

liquid (boiling) (hot) E924.0

local application of externally applied substance in medical or surgical care E873.5

molten metal E924.0

self-inflicted (unspecified whether accidental or intentional) E988.2

stated as intentional, purposeful E958.2

stated as undetermined whether accidental or intentional E988.2

steam E924.0

tap water (boiling) E924.2

transport accident — see categories E800-E848 ☑

vapor E924.0

Scratch, cat E906.8

Sea

sickness E903

Self-mutilation — see Suicide

Sequelae (of)

in

terrorism E999.1

war operations E999.0

Shock

anaphylactic (see also Table of Drugs and Chemicals) E947.9

due to

bite (venomous) — see Bite, venomous NEC

sting — see Sting

electric (see also Electric shock) E925.9

from electric appliance or current (see also Electric shock) E925.9

Shooting, shot (accidental(ly)) E922.9

air gun E922.4

BB gun E922.4

hand gun (pistol) (revolver) E922.0

himself (see also Shooting, self-inflicted) E985.4

Shooting, shot — continued

himself (see also Shooting, self-inflicted) — continued

hand gun (pistol) (revolver) E985.0

military firearm, except hand gun E985.3

hand gun (pistol) (revolver) E985.0

rifle (hunting) E985.2

military E985.3

shotgun (automatic) E985.1

specified firearm NEC E985.4

Verey pistol E985.4

homicide (attempt) E965.4

air gun E968.6

BB gun E968.6

hand gun (pistol) (revolver) E965.0

military firearm, except hand gun E965.3

hand gun (pistol) (revolver) E965.0

paintball gun E965.4

rifle (hunting) E965.2

military E965.3

shotgun (automatic) E965.1

specified firearm NEC E965.4

Verey pistol E965.4

in

terrorism — see Terrorism, shooting

war operations — see War operations, shooting

inflicted by other person

in accidental circumstances E922.9

hand gun (pistol) (revolver) E922.0

military firearm, except hand gun E922.3

hand gun (pistol) (revolver) E922.0

rifle (hunting) E922.2

military E922.3

shotgun (automatic) E922.1

specified firearm NEC E922.8

Verey pistol E922.8

stated as

intentional, homicidal E965.4

hand gun (pistol) (revolver) E965.0

military firearm, except hand gun E965.3

hand gun (pistol) (revolver) E965.0

paintball gun E965.4

rifle (hunting) E965.2

military E965.3

shotgun (automatic) E965.1

specified firearm E965.4

Verey pistol E965.4

undetermined whether accidental or intentional E985.4

air gun E985.6

BB gun E985.6

hand gun (pistol) (revolver) E985.0

military firearm, except hand gun E985.3

hand gun (pistol) (revolver) E985.0

paintball gun E985.7

rifle (hunting) E985.2

shotgun (automatic) E985.1

specified firearm NEC E985.4

Verey pistol E985.4

legal

execution E978

intervention E970

military firearm, except hand gun E922.3

hand gun (pistol) (revolver) E922.0

paintball gun E922.5

rifle (hunting) E922.2

military E922.3

self-inflicted (unspecified whether accidental or intentional) E985.4

air gun E985.6

BB gun E985.6

hand gun (pistol) (revolver) E985.0

military firearm, except hand gun E985.3

hand gun (pistol) (revolver) E985.0

paintball gun E985.7

rifle (hunting) E985.2

military E985.3

shotgun (automatic) E985.1

specified firearm NEC E985.4

Shooting, shot — *continued*
  self-inflicted — *continued*
    stated as
      accidental E922.9
        hand gun (pistol) (revolver) E922.0
        military firearm, except hand gun E922.3
          hand gun (pistol) (revolver) E922.0
        paintball gun E922.5
        rifle (hunting) E922.2
        military E922.3
        shotgun (automatic) E922.1
        specified firearm NEC E922.8
        Verey pistol E922.8
      intentional, purposeful E955.4
        hand gun (pistol) (revolver) E955.0
        military firearm, except hand gun E955.3
          hand gun (pistol) (revolver) E955.0
        paintball gun E955.7
        rifle (hunting) E955.2
        military E955.3
        shotgun (automatic) E955.1
        specified firearm NEC E955.4
        Verey pistol E955.4
  shotgun (automatic) E922.1
  specified firearm NEC E922.8
  stated as undetermined whether accidental or intentional E985.4
    hand gun (pistol) (revolver) E985.0
    military firearm, except hand gun E985.3
      hand gun (pistol) (revolver) E985.0
    paintball gun E985.7
    rifle (hunting) E985.2
    military E985.3
    shotgun (automatic) E985.1
    specified firearm NEC E985.4
    Verey pistol E985.4
  suicidal (attempt) E955.4
    air gun E955.6
    BB gun E955.6
    hand gun (pistol) (revolver) E955.0
    military firearm, except hand gun E955.3
      hand gun (pistol) (revolver) E955.0
    paintball gun E955.7
    rifle (hunting) E955.2
    military E955.3
    shotgun (automatic) E955.1
    specified firearm NEC E955.4
    Verey pistol E955.4
  Verey pistol E922.8
Shoving (accidentally) by other person — *see also* Pushing by other person E917.9
Sickness
  air E903
  alpine E902.0
  car E903
  motion E903
  mountain E902.0
  sea E903
  travel E903
Sinking (accidental)
  boat, ship, watercraft (causing drowning, submersion) E830 ☑
    causing injury except drowning, submersion E831 ☑
Siriasis E900.0
Skydiving E844 ☑
Slashed wrists — *see also* Cut, self-inflicted E986
Slipping (accidental)
  on
    deck (of boat, ship, watercraft) (icy) (oily) (wet) E835 ☑
    ice E885.9
    ladder of ship E833 ☑
      due to accident to watercraft E831 ☑
    mud E885.9
    oil E885.9
    snow E885.9
    stairs of ship E833 ☑
      due to accident to watercraft E831 ☑
    surface
      slippery E885 ☑
      wet E885 ☑

Sliver, wood, injury by E920.8
Smothering, smothered — *see also* Suffocation E913.9
Smouldering building or structure in terrorism E979.3
Sodomy (assault) E960.1
Solid substance in eye (any part) or adnexa E914
Sound waves (causing injury) E928.1
Splinter, injury by E920.8
Stab, stabbing E966
  accidental — *see* Cut
Starvation E904.1
  helpless person, infant, newborn — *see* Lack of Food
  homicidal intent E968.4
  late effect of NEC E929.5
  resulting from accident connected with transport — *see* categories E800-E848 ☑
Stepped on
  by
    animal (not being ridden) E906.8
      being ridden (in sport or transport) E828 ☑
    crowd E917.1
    person E917.9
      in sports E917.0
  in sports E917.0
Stepping on
  object (moving) E917.9
    in sports E917.0
      with subsequent fall E917.5
    stationary E917.4
      with subsequent fall E917.8
  person E917.9
    as, or caused by a crowd E917.1
      with subsequent fall E917.6
    in sports E917.0
Sting E905.9
  ant E905.5
  bee E905.3
  caterpillar E905.5
  coral E905.6
  hornet E905.3
  insect NEC E905.5
  jellyfish E905.6
  marine animal or plant E905.6
  nematocysts E905.6
  scorpion E905.2
  sea anemone E905.6
  sea cucumber E905.6
  wasp E905.3
  yellow jacket E905.3
Storm E908.9
  specified type NEC E908.8
Straining, injury in E927.8
Strangling — *see* Suffocation
Strangulation — *see* Suffocation
Strenuous movements (in recreational or other activities) E927.8
Striking against
  bottom (when jumping or diving into water) E883.0
  object (moving) E917.9
    caused by crowd E917.1
      with subsequent fall E917.6
    furniture E917.3
      with subsequent fall E917.7
    in
      running water E917.2
        with drowning or submersion — *see* Submersion
      sports E917.0
        with subsequent fall E917.5
    stationary E917.4
      with subsequent fall E917.8
  person(s) E917.9
    with fall E886.9
      in sports E886.0
    as, or caused by, a crowd E917.1
      with subsequent fall E917.6
    in sports E917.0
      with fall E886.0
Stroke
  heat — *see* Heat

Stroke — *continued*
  lightning E907
Struck by — *see also* Hit by
  bullet
    in
      terrorism E979.4
      war operations E991.2
        rubber E991.0
  lightning E907
  missile
    in terrorism — *see* Terrorism, missile
  object
    falling
      from, in, on
        building
          burning (uncontrolled fire)
            in terrorism E979.3
  thunderbolt E907
Stumbling over animal, carpet, curb, rug or (small) object (with fall) E885.9
  without fall — *see* Striking against, object
Submersion (accidental) E910.8
  boat, ship, watercraft (causing drowning, submersion) E830 ☑
    causing injury except drowning, submersion E831 ☑
  by other person
    in accidental circumstances — *see* category E910 ☑
    intentional, homicidal E964
    stated as undetermined whether accidental or intentional E984
  due to
    accident
      machinery — *see* Accident, machine
      to boat, ship, watercraft E830 ☑
      transport — *see* categories E800-E848 ☑
    avalanche E909.2
    cataclysmic
      earth surface movement or eruption E909.9
      storm E908.9
    cloudburst E908.8
    cyclone E908.1
    fall
      from
        boat, ship, watercraft (not involved in accident) E832 ☑
          burning, crushed E830 ☑
          involved in accident, collision E830 ☑
        gangplank (into water) E832 ☑
        overboard NEC E832 ☑
    flood E908.2
    hurricane E908.0
    jumping into water E910.8
      from boat, ship, watercraft
        burning, crushed, sinking E830 ☑
        involved in accident, collision E830 ☑
        not involved in accident, for swim E910.2
      in recreational activity (without diving equipment) E910.2
        with or using diving equipment E910.1
      to rescue another person E910.3
  homicide (attempt) E964
  in
    bathtub E910.4
    specified activity, not sport, transport or recreational E910.3
    sport or recreational activity (without diving equipment) E910.2
      with or using diving equipment E910.1
      water skiing E910.0
    swimming pool NEC E910.8
    terrorism E979.8
    war operations E995.4   ▲
      intentional E995.3   ●
    water transport E832 ☑
      due to accident to boat, ship, watercraft E830 ☑
  landslide E909.2
    overturning boat, ship, watercraft E909.2

Submersion (accidental) — *continued*
  landslide — *continued*
    sinking boat, ship, watercraft E909.2
    submersion boat, ship, watercraft E909.2
    tidal wave E909.4
      caused by storm E908.0
    torrential rain E908.2
  late effect of NEC E929.8
  quenching tank E910.8
  self-inflicted (unspecified whether accidental or intentional) E984
    in accidental circumstances — *see* category E910 ☑
    stated as intentional, purposeful E954
  stated as undetermined whether accidental or intentional E984
  suicidal (attempted) E954
  while
    attempting rescue of another person E910.3
    engaged in
      marine salvage E910.3
      underwater construction or repairs E910.3
    fishing, not from boat E910.2
    hunting, not from boat E910.2
    ice skating E910.2
    pearl diving E910.3
    placing fishing nets E910.3
    playing in water E910.2
    scuba diving E910.1
      nonrecreational E910.3
    skin diving E910.1
    snorkel diving E910.2
    spear fishing underwater E910.1
    surfboarding E910.2
    swimming (swimming pool) E910.2
    wading (in water) E910.2
    water skiing E910.0
Sucked
  into
    jet (aircraft) E844 ☑
Suffocation (accidental) (by external means) (by pressure) (mechanical) E913.9
  caused by other person
    in accidental circumstances — *see* category E913 ☑
    stated as
      intentional, homicidal E963
      undetermined whether accidental or intentional E983.9
        by, in
          hanging E983.0
          plastic bag E983.1
          specified means NEC E983.8
  due to, by
    avalanche E909.2
    bedclothes E913.0
    bib E913.0
    blanket E913.0
    cave-in E913.3
      caused by cataclysmic earth surface movement or eruption E909.9
    conflagration — *see* Conflagration
    explosion — *see* Explosion
    falling earth, other substance E913.3
    fire — *see* Fire
    food, any type (ingestion) (inhalation) (regurgitated) (vomited) E911
    foreign body, except food (ingestion) (inhalation) E912
    ignition — *see* Ignition
    landslide E909.2
    machine(ry) — *see* Accident, machine
    material, object except food entering by nose or mouth, ingested, inhaled E912
    mucus (aspiration) (inhalation), not of newborn E912
    phlegm (aspiration) (inhalation) E912
    pillow E913.0
    plastic bag — *see* Suffocation, in, plastic bag
    sheet (plastic) E913.0
    specified means NEC E913.8
    vomitus (aspiration) (inhalation) E911

☑ Additional Digit Required — Refer to the Tabular List for Digit Selection   ▽ Subterms under main terms may continue to next column or page

Index

Suffocation — War operations

Suffocation — *continued*
homicidal (attempt) E963
in war operations E995.3 ●
in
airtight enclosed place E913.2
baby carriage E913.0
bed E913.0
closed place E913.2
cot, cradle E913.0
perambulator E913.0
plastic bag (in accidental circumstances) E913.1
homicidal, purposely inflicted by other person E963
self-inflicted (unspecified whether accidental or intentional) E983.1
in accidental circumstances E913.1
intentional, suicidal E953.1
stated as undetermined whether accidentally or purposely inflicted E983.1
suicidal, purposely self-inflicted E953.1
refrigerator E913.2
war operations E995.3 ●
self-inflicted (*see also* Suffocation, stated as undetermined whether accidental or intentional) E953.9
in accidental circumstances — *see* category E913 ☑
stated as intentional, purposeful — *see* Suicide, suffocation
stated as undetermined whether accidental or intentional E983.9
by, in
hanging E983.0
plastic bag E983.1
specified means NEC E983.8
suicidal — *see* Suicide, suffocation
Suicide, suicidal (attempted) (by) E958.9
burning, burns E958.1
caustic substance E958.7
poisoning E950.7
swallowed E950.7
cold, extreme E958.3
cut (any part of body) E956
cutting or piercing instrument (classifiable to E920) E956
drowning E954
electrocution E958.4
explosive(s) (classifiable to E923) E955.5
fire E958.1
firearm (classifiable to E922) — *see* Shooting, suicidal
hanging E953.0
jumping
before moving object, train, vehicle E958.0
from high place — *see* Jumping, from, high place, stated as, suicidal
knife E956
late effect of E959
motor vehicle, crashing of E958.5
poisoning — *see* Table of Drugs and Chemicals
puncture (any part of body) E956
scald E958.2
shooting — *see* Shooting, suicidal
specified means NEC E958.8
stab (any part of body) E956
strangulation — *see* Suicide, suffocation
submersion E954
suffocation E953.9
by, in
hanging E953.0
plastic bag E953.1
specified means NEC E953.8
wound NEC E958.9
Sunburn E926.2
Sunstroke E900.0
Supersonic waves (causing injury) E928.1
Surgical procedure, complication of
delayed or as an abnormal reaction without mention of misadventure — *see* Reaction, abnormal
due to or as a result of misadventure — *see* Misadventure

Swallowed, swallowing
foreign body — *see* Foreign body, alimentary canal
poison — *see* Table of Drugs and Chemicals
substance
caustic — *see* Table of Drugs and Chemicals
corrosive — *see* Table of Drugs and Chemicals
poisonous — *see* Table of Drugs and Chemicals
Swimmers cramp — *see also* category E910
E910.2
not in recreation or sport E910.3
Syndrome, battered
baby or child — *see* Abuse, child
wife — *see* Assault

T

Tackle in sport E886.0
Terrorism (injury) (by) (in) E979.8
air blast E979.2
aircraft burned, destroyed, exploded, shot down E979.1
used as a weapon E979.1
anthrax E979.6
asphyxia from
chemical (weapons) E979.7
fire, conflagration (caused by fire-producing device) E979.3
from nuclear explosion E979.5
gas or fumes E979.7
bayonet E979.8
biological agents E979.6
blast (air) (effects) E979.2
from nuclear explosion E979.5
underwater E979.0
bomb (antipersonnel) (mortar) (explosion) (fragments) E979.2
bullet(s) (from carbine, machine gun, pistol, rifle, shotgun) E979.4
burn from
chemical E979.7
fire, conflagration (caused by fire-producing device) E979.3
from nuclear explosion E979.5
gas E979.7
burning aircraft E979.1
chemical E979.7
cholera E979.6
conflagration E979.3
crushed by falling aircraft E979.1
depth-charge E979.0
destruction of aircraft E979.1
disability, as sequelae one year or more after injury E999.1
drowning E979.8
effect
of nuclear weapon (direct) (secondary) E979.5
secondary NEC E979.9
sequelae E999.1
explosion (artillery shell) (breech-block) (cannon block) E979.2
aircraft E979.1
bomb (antipersonnel) (mortar) E979.2
nuclear (atom) (hydrogen) E979.5
depth-charge E979.0
grenade E979.2
injury by fragments from E979.2
land-mine E979.2
marine weapon E979.0
mine (land) E979.2
at sea or in harbor E979.0
marine E979.0
missile (explosive) NEC E979.2
munitions (dump) (factory) E979.2
nuclear (weapon) E979.5
other direct and secondary effects of E979.5
sea-based artillery shell E979.0
torpedo E979.0
exposure to ionizing radiation from nuclear explosion E979.5
falling aircraft E979.1
firearms E979.4

Terrorism — *continued*
fireball effects from nuclear explosion E979.5
fire or fire-producing device E979.3
fragments from artillery shell, bomb NEC, grenade, guided missile, land-mine, rocket, shell, shrapnel E979.2
gas or fumes E979.7
grenade (explosion) (fragments) E979.2
guided missile (explosion) (fragments) E979.2
nuclear E979.5
heat from nuclear explosion E979.5
hot substances E979.3
hydrogen cyanide E979.7
land-mine (explosion) (fragments) E979.2
laser(s) E979.8
late effect of E999.1
lewisite E979.7
lung irritant (chemical) (fumes) (gas) E979.7
marine mine E979.0
mine
at sea E979.0
in harbor E979.0
land (explosion) (fragments) E979.2
marine E979.0
missile (explosion) (fragments) (guided) E979.2
marine E979.0
nuclear weapons E979.5
mortar bomb (explosion) (fragments) E979.2
mustard gas E979.7
nerve gas E979.7
nuclear weapons E979.5
pellets (shotgun) E979.4
petrol bomb E979.3
phosgene E979.7
piercing object E979.8
poisoning (chemical) (fumes) (gas) E979.7
radiation, ionizing from nuclear explosion E979.5
rocket (explosion) (fragments) E979.2
saber, sabre E979.8
sarin E979.7
screening smoke E979.7
sequelae effect (of) E999.1
shell (aircraft) (artillery) (cannon) (land-based) (explosion) (fragments) E979.2
sea-based E979.0
shooting E979.4
bullet(s) E979.4
pellet(s) (rifle) (shotgun) E979.4
shrapnel E979.2
smallpox E979.7
stabbing object(s) E979.8
submersion E979.8
torpedo E979.0
underwater blast E979.0
vesicant (chemical) (fumes) (gas) E979.7
weapon burst E979.2
Thermic fever E900.9
Thermoplegia E900.9
Thirst — *see also* Lack of water
resulting from accident connected with transport — *see* categories E800-E848 ☑
Thrown (accidentally)
against object in or part of vehicle
by motion of vehicle
aircraft E844 ☑
boat, ship, watercraft E838 ☑
motor vehicle (on public highway) E818 ☑
not on public highway E825 ☑
off-road type (not on public highway) E821 ☑
on public highway E818 ☑
snow vehicle E820 ☑
on public highway E818 ☑
nonmotor road vehicle NEC E829 ☑
railway rolling stock, train, vehicle E806 ☑
street car E829 ☑
from
animal (being ridden) (in sport or transport) E828 ☑
high place, homicide (attempt) E968.1
machinery — *see* Accident, machine
vehicle NEC — *see* Accident, vehicle NEC
off — *see* Thrown, from

Thrown — *continued*
overboard (by motion of boat, ship, watercraft) E832 ☑
by accident to boat, ship, watercraft E830 ☑
Thunderbolt NEC E907
Tidal wave (any injury) E909.4
caused by storm E908.0
Took
overdose of drug — *see* Table of Drugs and Chemicals
poison — *see* Table of Drugs and Chemicals
Tornado (any injury) E908.1
Torrential rain (any injury) E908.2
Traffic accident NEC E819 ☑
Trampled by animal E906.8
being ridden (in sport or transport) E828 ☑
Trapped (accidently)
between
objects (moving) (stationary and moving) E918
by
door of
elevator E918
motor vehicle (on public highway) (while alighting, boarding) — *see* Fall, from, motor vehicle, while alighting
railway train (underground) E806 ☑
street car E829 ☑
subway train E806 ☑
in object E918
Trauma
cumulative
from
repetitive
impact E927.4
motion or movements E927.3
sudden from strenuous movement E927.0
Travel (effects) E903
sickness E903
Tree
falling on or hitting E916
motor vehicle (in motion) (on public highway) E818 ☑
not on public highway E825 ☑
nonmotor road vehicle NEC E829 ☑
pedal cycle E826 ☑
person E916
railway rolling stock, train, vehicle E806 ☑
street car E829 ☑
Trench foot E901.0
Tripping over animal, carpet, curb, rug, or small object (with fall) E885 ☑
without fall — *see* Striking against, object
Tsunami E909.4
Twisting, injury in E927.8

V

Violence, nonaccidental — *see also* Assault E968.9
Volcanic eruption (any injury) E909.1
Vomitus in air passages (with asphyxia, obstruction or suffocation) E911

W

War operations (during hostilities) (injury) (by) (in) E995.9 ▲
after cessation of hostilities, injury due to E998.9 ▲
air blast E993.9 ▲
aircraft burned, destroyed, exploded, shot down E994 ☑
asphyxia from
chemical E997.2
fire, conflagration (caused by fire producing device or conventional weapon) E990.9
from nuclear explosion ▶(*see also* War operations, injury due to, nuclear weapons)◀ E996.8 ▲
incendiary bomb E990.0 ●
petrol bomb E990.0 ●
fumes E997.2
gas E997.2

☑ Additional Digit Required — Refer to the Tabular List for Digit Selection ▶◀ Revised Text ● New Line ▲ Revised Code ☝ Subterms under main terms may continue to next column or page

War operations — continued

baton (nightstick) E995.1 ●
battle wound NEC E995.8 ●
bayonet E995.2 ▲
biological warfare agents E997.1
blast (air) (effects) E993.9 ▲
  from nuclear explosion ►(see also War operations, injury due to, nuclear weapons)◄ E996.1 ▲
  underwater E992.9 ▲
bomb (mortar) (explosion) E993.2 ▲
  after cessation of hostilities E998.1 ▲
  fragments, injury by E991.4 ▲
    antipersonnel E991.3
bullet(s) (from carbine, machine gun, pistol, rifle, shotgun) E991.2
  rubber E991.0
burn from
  chemical E997.2
  fire, conflagration (caused by fire-producing device or conventional weapon) E990.9
    from
      conventional weapon E990.3
      flamethrower E990.1 ●
      incendiary bomb E990.0 ●
      incendiary bullet E990.2 ●
      nuclear explosion E996.2
      petrol bomb E990.0
  gas E997.2
burning aircraft E994.3 ▲
chemical E997.2
chlorine E997.2
conventional warfare, specified form NEC E995.8 ▲
crushing by falling aircraft E994.8 ▲
depth charge E992.1 ▲
destruction of aircraft E994.9 ▲
detonation of own munitions (ammunition) ● (artillery) (mortars), unintentional ● E993.6
disability as sequela one year or more after injury E999.0
discharge of own munitions launch device ● (autocannons) (automatic grenade ● launchers) (missile launchers) (small ● arms), unintentional E993.7 ●
drowning E995.4 ▲
effect nuclear weapon ►(see also War operations, injury due to, nuclear weapons)◄ E996.9 ▲
explosion (breech block) (cannon shell) E993.9 ▲
  after cessation of hostilities
    bomb placed in war E998.1 ●
    mine placed in war E998.0 ●
  aircraft E994.1 ▲
    due to
      enemy fire or explosives E994.0 ●
      own onboard explosives E994.1 ●
  artillery shell E993.2 ▲
  bomb (mortar) E993.2 ▲
    aerial E993.0 ●
    atom ►(see also War operations, injury due to, nuclear weapons)◄ E996.9 ▲
    hydrogen ►(see also War operations, injury due to, nuclear weapons)◄ E996.9 ▲
    injury by fragments from E991.4 ▲
      antipersonnel E991.3
    nuclear ►(see also War operations, injury due to, nuclear weapons)◄ E996.9 ▲
  depth charge E992.1 ▲
  injury by fragments from E991.4 ▲
    antipersonnel E991.3
  marine weapon ►NEC◄ E992.8 ▲
  mine
    at sea or in harbor E992.2 ▲
    land E993.8 ▲
      injury by fragments from E991.4 ▲
    marine E992.2 ▲
  missile, guided E993.1 ●
  mortar E993.2 ●

War operations — continued

explosion — continued
  munitions (accidental) (being used in war) (dump) (factory) E993.9 ▲
    own E993.7 ●
      ammunition (artillery) (mortars) ● E993.6
      launch device (autocannons) ● (automatic grenade launchers) (missile launchers) (small arms) E993.7 ●
  nuclear (weapon) ►(see also War operations, injury due to, nuclear weapons)◄ E996.9 ▲
  own weapons (accidental) E993.7 ▲
    injury by fragments from E991.9 ●
      antipersonnel E991.3
  sea-based artillery shell E992.3 ▲
  specified NEC E993.8 ●
  torpedo E992.0 ▲
exposure to ionizing radiation from nuclear explosion ►(see also War operations, injury due to, nuclear weapons)◄ E996.3 ▲
falling aircraft E994.8 ▲
fireball effects from nuclear explosion E996.2 ▲
fire or fire-producing device E990.9
  flamethrower E990.1 ●
  incendiary bomb E990.0 ●
  incendiary bullet E990.2 ●
  indirectly caused from conventional weapon E990.3 ●
  petrol bomb E990.0
fragments from
  antipersonnel bomb E991.3
  artillery shell E991.4 ▲
  bomb NEC E991.4 ●
  grenade E991.4 ●
  guided missile E991.4 ●
  land mine E991.4 ●
  rocket E991.4 ●
  shell E991.4 ●
  shrapnel E991.9 ●
fumes E997.2
gas E997.2
grenade (explosion) E993.8 ▲
  fragments, injury by E991.4 ▲
guided missile (explosion) E993.1 ▲
  fragments, injury by E991.4 ▲
  nuclear ►(see also War operations, injury due to, nuclear weapons)◄ E996.9 ▲
heat from nuclear explosion E996.2 ▲
injury due to
  aerial bomb E993.0 ●
  air blast E993.9 ●
  aircraft shot down E994.0 ●
  artillery shell E993.2 ●
  blast E993.9 ●
    wave E993.9 ●
    wind E993.9 ●
  bomb E993.8 ●
  but occurring after cessation of hostilities ●
    explosion of bombs E998.1 ●
    explosion of mines E998.0 ●
    specified NEC E998.8 ●
  conventional warfare E995.9 ●
    specified form NEC E995.8 ●
  depth charge E992.1 ●
  destruction of aircraft E994.9 ●
    due to
      air to air missile E994.0 ●
      collision with other aircraft E994.2 ●
      enemy fire or explosives E994.0 ●
      on board explosion (explosives) E994.1 ●
      on board fire E994.3 ●
      rocket propelled grenade [RPG] E994.0 ●
      small arms fire E994.0 ●
      surface to air missile E994.0 ●
    specified NEC E994.8 ●

War operations — continued

injury due to — continued
  dirty bomb (see also War operations, injury due to, nuclear weapons) ●
    E996.9 ●
  drowning E995.4 ●
  explosion (direct pressure) (indirect pressure) (due to) E993.9 ●
    depth charge E992.1 ●
    improvised explosive device [IED] ●
      person borne E993.3 ●
      roadside E993.5 ●
      specified NEC E993.5 ●
      transport vehicle (air) (land) (water) borne E993.4 ●
      vehicle (air) (land) (water) borne ● E993.4 ●
    marine mines (in harbor) (at sea) E992.2 ●
    marine weapons E992.9 ●
      specified NEC E992.8 ●
    sea based artillery shell E992.3 ●
    specified NEC E993.8 ●
    torpedo E992.0 ●
    unintentional (of own)
      autocannons E993.7 ●
      automatic grenade launchers E993.7 ●
      launch device discharge E993.7 ●
      missile launchers E993.7 ●
      munitions detonation (ammuni- ● tion) (artillery) (mortars) E993.6 ●
      small arms E993.7 ●
  fragments (from) E991.9 ●
    artillery E991.8 ●
    artillery shells E991.4 ●
    autocannons E991.8 ●
    automatic grenade launchers [AGL] E991.8 ●
    bombs E991.4 ●
      antipersonnel E991.3 ●
    detonation of unexploded ordnance ● [UXO] E991.4 ●
    grenade E991.4 ●
    guided missile E991.4 ●
    improvised explosive device [IED] ●
      person borne E991.5 ●
      roadside E991.7 ●
      specified NEC E991.7 ●
      transport vehicle (air) (land) (wa- ● ter) borne E991.6 ●
      vehicle (air) (land) (water) borne ● E991.6 ●
    land mine E991.4 ●
    missile launchers E991.8 ●
    mortars E991.8 ●
    munitions (artillery shells) (bombs) ● (grenades) (rockets) (shells) ● E991.4 ●
    rockets E991.4 ●
    shells E991.4 ●
    small arms E991.8 ●
    specified NEC E991.9 ●
    weapons (artillery) (autocannons) ● (mortars) (small arms) E991.8 ●
  grenade E993.8 ●
  guided missile E993.1 ●
  hand to hand combat, unarmed E995.0 ●
  improvised explosive device [IED]
    person borne E993.3 ●
    roadside E993.5 ●
    specified NEC E993.5 ●
    transport vehicle (air) (land) (water) borne E993.4 ●
    vehicle (air) (land) (water) borne E993.4 ●
  inability to surface or obtain air E995.4 ●
  land mine E993.8 ●
  marine mines (in harbor) (at sea) E992.2 ●
  marine weapons E992.9 ●
    specified NEC E992.8 ●
  mortar E993.2 ●
  nuclear weapons E996.9 ●
    beta burns E996.3 ●
    blast debris E996.1 ●

War operations — continued

injury due to — continued
  nuclear weapons — continued
    blast pressure E996.0 ●
    burns due to thermal radiation E996.2 ●
    direct blast effect E996.0 ●
    fallout exposure E996.3 ●
    fireball effect E996.2 ●
    flash burns E996.2 ●
    heat effect E996.2 ●
    indirect blast effect E996.1 ●
    nuclear radiation effects E996.3 ●
    radiation exposure (acute) E996.3 ●
    radiation sickness E996.3 ●
    secondary effects E996.3 ●
    specified effects NEC E996.8 ●
    thermal radiation effect E996.2 ●
  piercing object E995.2 ●
  restriction of airway, intentional E995.3 ●
  sea based artillery shell E992.3 ●
  shrapnel E991.9 ●
  stave E995.1 ●
  strangulation E995.3 ●
  strike by blunt object (baton) (nightstick) ● (stave) E995.1 ●
  submersion (accidental) (unintentional) E995.4 ●
    intentional E995.3 ●
  suffocation E995.3 ●
    accidental E995.4 ●
  torpedo E992.0 ●
  underwater blast E992.9 ●
  weapon of mass destruction [WMD] E997.3 ●
knife E995.2 ●
lacrimator (gas) (chemical) E997.2
land mine (explosion) E993.8 ▲
  after cessation of hostilities E998.0 ▲
  fragments, injury by E991.4 ▲
laser(s) E997.0
late effect of E999.0
lewisite E997.2
lung irritant (chemical) (fumes) (gas) E997.2
marine mine E992.2 ▲
mine
  after cessation of hostilities E998.0 ▲
  at sea E992.2 ▲
  in harbor E992.2 ▲
  land (explosion) E993.8 ▲
    fragments, injury by E991.4 ▲
  marine E992.2 ▲
missile (guided) (explosion) E993.1 ▲
  fragments, injury by E991.4 ▲
  marine E992.8 ▲
  nuclear ►(see also War operations, injury due to, nuclear weapons)◄ E996.9 ▲
mortar bomb (explosion) E993.2 ▲
  fragments, injury by E991.4 ▲
mustard gas E997.2
nerve gas E997.2
phosgene E997.2
piercing object E995.2 ●
poisoning (chemical) (fumes) (gas) E997.2
radiation, ionizing from nuclear explosion ►(see also War operations, injury due to, nuclear weapons)◄ E996.3 ▲
rocket (explosion) E993.8 ▲
  fragments, injury by E991.4 ▲
saber, sabre E995.2 ▲
screening smoke E997.8
shell (aircraft) (artillery) (cannon) (land based) (explosion) E993.2 ▲
  fragments, injury by E991.4 ▲
  sea-based E992.3 ▲
shooting E991.2
  after cessation of hostilities E998.8 ▲
  bullet(s) E991.2
    rubber E991.0
  pellet(s) (rifle) E991.1
  shrapnel E991.9
  submersion E995 ☑
  torpedo E992 ☑
stave E995.2

War operations — *continued*
   strike by blunt object (baton) (nightstick) ●
      (stave) E995.1
   submersion E995.4   ▲
      intentional E995.3   ●
   sword E995.2   ●
   torpedo E992.0   ▲
   unconventional warfare, except by nuclear
      weapon E997.9
      biological (warfare) E997.1
      gas, fumes, chemicals E997.2
      laser(s) E997.0
      specified type NEC E997.8

War operations — *continued*
   underwater blast E992.9   ▲
   vesicant (chemical) (fumes) (gas) E997.2
   weapon burst E993.9   ▲
Washed
   away by flood — *see* Flood
   away by tidal wave — *see* Tidal wave
   off road by storm (transport vehicle) E908.9
   overboard E832 ☑
Weapon of mass destruction [WMD] E997.3 ●
Weather exposure — *see also* Exposure
   cold E901.0
   hot E900.0

Weightlessness (causing injury) (effects of) (in
   spacecraft, real or simulated) E928.0
Wound (accidental) NEC — *see also* Injury E928.9
   battle (*see also* War operations) E995.9   ▲
   bayonet E920.3
      in
         legal intervention E974
         war operations E995.2   ▲
   gunshot — *see* Shooting
   incised — *see* Cut
   saber, sabre E920.3
      in war operations E995.2   ▲

Wrong   ●
   body part, performance of correct operation ●
      (procedure) on E876.7
   device implanted into correct surgical site ●
      E876.5
   patient, performance of operation (proce- ●
      dure) on E876.6
   procedure (operation) performed on correct ●
      patient E876.5
   side, performance of correct operation ●
      (procedure) on E876.7
   site, performance of correct operation (pro- ●
      cedure) on E876.7

☑ Additional Digit Required — Refer to the Tabular List for Digit Selection   ▽ Subterms under main terms may continue to next column or page

Railway Accidents (E800-E807)

The following fourth-digit subdivisions are for use with categories E800-E807 to identify the injured person:

.0 Railway employee
Any person who by virtue of his employment in connection with a railway, whether by the railway company or not, is at increased risk of involvement in a railway accident, such as:
catering staff on train
postal staff on train
driver
railway fireman
guard
shunter
porter
sleeping car attendant

.1 Passenger on railway
Any authorized person traveling on a train, except a railway employee
EXCLUDES intending passenger waiting at station (.8)
unauthorized rider on railway vehicle (.8)

.2 Pedestrian See definition (r), E-Codes-2

.3 Pedal cyclist See definition (p), E-Codes-2

.8 Other specified person Intending passenger waiting at station
Unauthorized rider on railway vehicle

.9 Unspecified person

Motor Vehicle Traffic and Nontraffic Accidents (E810-E825)

The following fourth-digit subdivisions are for use with categories E810-E819 and E820-E825 to identify the injured person:

.0 Driver of motor vehicle other than motorcycle See definition (1), E-Codes-2

.1 Passenger in motor vehicle other than motorcycle See definition (1), E-Codes-2

.2 Motorcyclist See definition (1), E-Codes-2

.3 Passenger on motorcycle See definition (1), E-Codes-2

.4 Occupant of streetcar

.5 Rider of animal; occupant of animal-drawn vehicle

.6 Pedal cyclist See definition (p), E-Codes-2

.7 Pedestrian See definition (r), E-Codes-2

.8 Other specified person
Occupant of vehicle other than above
Person in railway train involved in accident
Unauthorized rider of motor vehicle

.9 Unspecified person

Other Road Vehicle Accidents (E826-E829)
(animal-drawn vehicle, streetcar, pedal cycle, and other nonmotor road vehicle accidents)

The following fourth-digit subdivisions are for use with categories E826-E829 to identify the injured person:

.0 Pedestrian See definition (r), E-Codes-2

.1 Pedal cyclist (does not apply to codes E827, E828, E829) See definition (p), E-Codes-2

.2 Rider of animal (does not apply to code E829)

.3 Occupant of animal-drawn vehicle (does not apply to codes E828, E829)

.4 Occupant of streetcar

.8 Other specified person

.9 Unspecified person

Water Transport Accidents (E830-E838)

The following fourth-digit subdivisions are for use with categories E830-E838 to identify the injured person:

.0 Occupant of small boat, unpowered

.1 Occupant of small boat, powered See definition (t), E-Codes-2
EXCLUDES water skier (.4)

.2 Occupant of other watercraft — crew
Persons:
engaged in operation of watercraft
providing passenger services [cabin attendants, ship's physician, catering personnel]
working on ship during voyage in other capacity [musician in band, operators of shops and beauty parlors]

.3 Occupant of other watercraft — other than crew
Passenger
Occupant of lifeboat, other than crew, after abandoning ship

.4 Water skier

.5 Swimmer

.6 Dockers, stevedores
Longshoreman employed on the dock in loading and unloading ships

.8 Other specified person
Immigration and custom officials on board ship
Persons:
accompanying passenger or member of crew visiting boat
Pilot (guiding ship into port)

.9 Unspecified person

Air and Space Transport Accidents (E840-E845)

The following fourth-digit subdivisions are for use with categories E840-E845 to identify the injured person:

.0 Occupant of spacecraft
Crew
Passenger (civilian)
(military)   in military aircraft [air force]
Troops   [army] [national guard] [navy]

.1 Occupant of military aircraft, any
EXCLUDES occupants of aircraft operated under jurisdiction of police departments (.5) parachutist (.7)

.2 Crew of commercial aircraft (powered) in surface to surface transport

.3 Other occupant of commercial aircraft (powered) in surface to surface transport
Flight personnel:
not part of crew
on familiarization flight Passenger on aircraft

.4 Occupant of commercial aircraft (powered) in surface to air transport
Occupant [crew] [passenger] of aircraft (powered) engaged in activities, such as:
air drops of emergency supplies
air drops of parachutists, except from military craft
crop dusting
lowering of construction material [bridge or telephone pole]
sky writing

.5 Occupant of other powered aircraft
Occupant [crew] [passenger] of aircraft (powered) engaged in activities, such as:
aerial spraying (crops)(fire retardants)
aerobatic flying
aircraft racing
rescue operation
storm surveillance
traffic surveillance
Occupant of private plane NOS

.6 Occupant of unpowered aircraft, except parachutist
Occupant of aircraft classifiable to E842

.7 Parachutist (military)(other)
Person making voluntary descent
person making descent after accident to aircraft (.1-.6)

.8 Ground crew, airline employee
Persons employed at airfields (civil)(military) or launching pads, not occupants of aircraft

.9 Other person

☑ Additional Digit Required — Refer to the Tabular List for Digit Selection
▽ Subterms under main terms may continue to next column or page
2010 ICD-9-CM   ▶◀ Revised Text   ● New Line   ▲ Revised Code   Volume 2 — 339

1. INFECTIOUS AND PARASITIC DISEASES (001-139)

Note: Categories for "late effects" of infectious and parasitic diseases are to be found at 137-139.

INCLUDES   diseases generally recognized as communicable or transmissible as well as a few diseases of unknown but possibly infectious origin

EXCLUDES   *acute respiratory infections (460-466)*
carrier or suspected carrier of infectious organism (V02.0-V02.9)
certain localized infections
influenza ▶*(487.0-487.8, 488.0-488.1)*◀

INTESTINAL INFECTIOUS DISEASES (001-009)

EXCLUDES   *helminthiases (120.0-129)*

✓4ᵗʰ 001 Cholera
DEF: An acute infectious enteritis caused by a potent enterotoxin produced by *Vibrio cholerae*; changes the permeability of the mucosa of the intestines leads to diarrhea and dehydration.

001.0 Due to Vibrio cholerae

001.1 Due to Vibrio cholerae el tor

001.9 Cholera, unspecified

✓4ᵗʰ 002 Typhoid and paratyphoid fevers
DEF: Typhoid fever: an acute generalized illness caused by *Salmonella typhi;* clinical features are fever, headache, abdominal pain, cough, toxemia, leukopenia, abnormal pulse, rose spots on the skin, bacteremia, hyperplasia of intestinal lymph nodes, mesenteric lymphadenopathy, and Peyer's patches in the intestines.

DEF: Paratyphoid fever: a prolonged febrile illness, caused by salmonella serotypes other than *S. typhi*, especially *S. enteritidis* serotypes paratyphi A and B and *S. choleraesuis*.

002.0 Typhoid fever
Typhoid (fever) (infection) [any site]

002.1 Paratyphoid fever A

002.2 Paratyphoid fever B

002.3 Paratyphoid fever C

002.9 Paratyphoid fever, unspecified

✓4ᵗʰ 003 Other salmonella infections
INCLUDES   infection or food poisoning by Salmonella [any serotype]

DEF: Infections caused by a genus of gram-negative, anaerobic bacteria of the family *Enterobacteriaceae;* major symptoms are enteric fevers, acute gastroenteritis and septicemia.

003.0 Salmonella gastroenteritis
Salmonellosis

003.1 Salmonella septicemia

✓5ᵗʰ 003.2 Localized salmonella infections
003.20 Localized salmonella infection, unspecified

003.21 Salmonella meningitis

003.22 Salmonella pneumonia

003.23 Salmonella arthritis

003.24 Salmonella osteomyelitis

003.29 Other

003.8 Other specified salmonella infections

003.9 Salmonella infection, unspecified

✓4ᵗʰ 004 Shigellosis
INCLUDES   bacillary dysentery

DEF: Acute infectious dysentery caused by the genus *Shigella,* of the family *Enterobacteriaceae;* affecting the colon causing blood- stained stools, tenesmus, abdominal cramps and fever.

004.0 Shigella dysenteriae
Infection by group A Shigella (Schmitz) (Shiga)

004.1 Shigella flexneri
Infection by group B Shigella

004.2 Shigella boydii
Infection by group C Shigella

004.3 Shigella sonnei
Infection by group D Shigella

004.8 Other specified Shigella infections

004.9 Shigellosis, unspecified

✓4ᵗʰ 005 Other food poisoning (bacterial)
EXCLUDES   *salmonella infections (003.0-003.9)*
toxic effect of:
food contaminants (989.7)
noxious foodstuffs (988.0-988.9)

DEF: Enteritis caused by ingesting contaminated foods and characterized by diarrhea, abdominal pain, vomiting; symptoms may be mild or life threatening.

005.0 Staphylococcal food poisoning
Staphylococcal toxemia specified as due to food

005.1 Botulism food poisoning
Botulism NOS
Food poisoning due to Clostridium botulinum
EXCLUDES   *infant botulism (040.41)*
wound botulism (040.42)

005.2 Food poisoning due to Clostridium perfringens [C. welchii]
Enteritis necroticans

005.3 Food poisoning due to other Clostridia

005.4 Food poisoning due to Vibrio parahaemolyticus

✓5ᵗʰ 005.8 Other bacterial food poisoning
EXCLUDES   *salmonella food poisoning (003.0-003.9)*

005.81 Food poisoning due to Vibrio vulnificus

005.89 Other bacterial food poisoning
Food poisoning due to Bacillus cereus

005.9 Food poisoning, unspecified

✓4ᵗʰ 006 Amebiasis
INCLUDES   infection due to Entamoeba histolytica

EXCLUDES   *amebiasis due to organisms other than Entamoeba histolytica (007.8)*

DEF: Infection of the large intestine caused by *Entamoeba histolytica;* usually asymptomatic but symptoms may range from mild diarrhea to profound life-threatening dysentery. Extraintestinal complications include hepatic abscess, which may rupture, causing life-threatening infections.

006.0 Acute amebic dysentery without mention of abscess
Acute amebiasis
DEF: Sudden, severe *Entamoeba histolytica* infection causing bloody stools.

006.1 Chronic intestinal amebiasis without mention of abscess
Chronic:
amebiasis
amebic dysentery

006.2 Amebic nondysenteric colitis
DEF: *Entamoeba histolytica* infection with inflamed colon but no dysentery.

006.3 Amebic liver abscess
Hepatic amebiasis

006.4 Amebic lung abscess
Amebic abscess of lung (and liver)

006.5 Amebic brain abscess
Amebic abscess of brain (and liver) (and lung)

006.6 Amebic skin ulceration
Cutaneous amebiasis

006.8 Amebic infection of other sites
Amebic: Ameboma
appendicitis
balanitis
EXCLUDES   *specific infections by free-living amebae (136.21-136.29)*

006.9 Amebiasis, unspecified
Amebiasis NOS

✓4ᵗʰ
✓5ᵗʰ   Additional Digit Required   Unspecified Code   Other Specified Code   Manifestation Code   ▶◀ Revised Text   ● New Code   ▲ Revised Code Title

2010 ICD-9-CM   **October 2009 · Volume 1 – 1**

Infectious and Parasitic Diseases

007–009.0

√4th **007 Other protozoal intestinal diseases**

INCLUDES protozoal:
  colitis
  diarrhea
  dysentery

007.0 Balantidiasis
  Infection by Balantidium coli

007.1 Giardiasis
  Infection by Giardia lamblia
  Lambliasis

007.2 Coccidiosis
  Infection by Isospora belli and Isospora hominis
  Isosporiasis

007.3 Intestinal trichomoniasis
  DEF: Colitis, diarrhea, or dysentery caused by the protozoa *Trichomonas.*

007.4 Cryptosporidiosis
  DEF: An intestinal infection by protozoan parasites causing intractable diarrhea in patients with AIDS and other immunosuppressed individuals.
  AHA: 4Q, '97, 30

007.5 Cyclosporiasis
  DEF: An infection of the small intestine by the protozoal organism, *Cyclospora caytenanesis*, spread to humans though ingestion of contaminated water or food. Symptoms include watery diarrhea, loss of appetite, increased gas, stomach cramps, nausea, vomiting, muscle aches, low grade fever, and fatigue.
  AHA: 4Q, '00, 38

007.8 Other specified protozoal intestinal diseases
  Amebiasis due to organisms other than Entamoeba histolytica

007.9 Unspecified protozoal intestinal disease
  Flagellate diarrhea
  Protozoal dysentery NOS

√4th **008 Intestinal infections due to other organisms**

INCLUDES any condition classifiable to 009.0-009.3 with mention of the responsible organisms

EXCLUDES *food poisoning by these organisms (005.0-005.9)*

√5th **008.0 Escherichia coli [E. coli]**
  AHA: 4Q, '92, 17

  008.00 E. coli, unspecified
    E. coli enteritis NOS

  008.01 Enteropathogenic E. coli
    DEF: *E. coli* causing inflammation of intestines.

  008.02 Enterotoxigenic E. coli
    DEF: A toxic reaction to *E. coli* of the intestinal mucosa, causing voluminous watery secretions.

  008.03 Enteroinvasive E. coli
    DEF: *E. coli* infection penetrating intestinal mucosa.

  008.04 Enterohemorrhagic E. coli
    DEF: E. coli infection penetrating the intestinal mucosa, producing microscopic ulceration and bleeding.

  008.09 Other intestinal E. coli infections

008.1 Arizona group of paracolon bacilli

008.2 Aerobacter aerogenes
  Enterobacter aeogenes

008.3 Proteus (mirabilis) (morganii)

√5th **008.4 Other specified bacteria**
  AHA: 4Q, '92, 18

  008.41 Staphylococcus
    Staphylococcal enterocolitis

  008.42 Pseudomonas
    AHA: 2Q, '89, 10

  008.43 Campylobacter

  008.44 Yersinia enterocolitica

  008.45 Clostridium difficile
    Pseudomembranous colitis
    DEF: An overgrowth of a species of bacterium that is a part of the normal colon flora in human infants and sometimes in adults; produces a toxin that causes pseudomembranous enterocolitis.; typically is seen in patients undergoing antibiotic therapy.
    A04.7 Enterocolitis due to clostridium difficile I-10

  008.46 Other anaerobes
    Anaerobic enteritis NOS
    Bacteroides (fragilis)
    Gram-negative anaerobes

  008.47 Other gram-negative bacteria
    Gram-negative enteritis NOS
    EXCLUDES *gram-negative anaerobes (008.46)*

  008.49 Other
    AHA: 2Q, '89, 10; 1Q, '88, 6

008.5 Bacterial enteritis, unspecified

√5th **008.6 Enteritis due to specified virus**
  AHA: 4Q, '92, 18

  008.61 Rotavirus

  008.62 Adenovirus

  008.63 Norwalk virus
    ▶Norovirus◀
    Norwalk-like agent

  008.64 Other small round viruses [SRVs]
    Small round virus NOS

  008.65 Calicivirus
    DEF: Enteritis due to a subgroup of *Picornaviruses.*

  008.66 Astrovirus

  008.67 Enterovirus NEC
    Coxsackie virus
    Echovirus
    EXCLUDES *poliovirus (045.0-045.9)*

  008.69 Other viral enteritis
    Torovirus
    AHA: 1Q, '03, 10

008.8 Other organism, not elsewhere classified
  Viral:
    enteritis NOS
    gastroenteritis
  EXCLUDES *influenza with involvement of gastrointestinal tract (487.8)*
  A08.4 Viral intestinal infection unspecified I-10

√4th **009 Ill-defined intestinal infections**
  EXCLUDES *diarrheal disease or intestinal infection due to specified organism (001.0-008.8)*
    diarrhea following gastrointestinal surgery (564.4)
    intestinal malabsorption (579.0-579.9)
    ischemic enteritis (557.0-557.9)
    other noninfectious gastroenteritis and colitis (558.1-558.9)
    regional enteritis (555.0-555.9)
    ulcerative colitis (556)

009.0 Infectious colitis, enteritis, and gastroenteritis
  Colitis
  Enteritis } septic
  Gastroenteritis
  Dysentery:
    NOS
    catarrhal
    hemorrhagic
  DEF: Colitis: An inflammation of mucous membranes of the colon.
  DEF: Enteritis: An inflammation of mucous membranes of the small intestine.
  DEF: Gastroenteritis: An inflammation of mucous membranes of stomach and intestines.
  AHA: 3Q, '99, 4
  A09 Infectious gastroenteritis and colitis unspec I-10

Infectious and Parasitic Diseases

009.1 Colitis, enteritis, and gastroenteritis of presumed infectious origin
> EXCLUDES colitis NOS (558.9)
> enteritis NOS (558.9)
> gastroenteritis NOS (558.9)
>
> AHA: 3Q, '99, 6

009.2 Infectious diarrhea
> Diarrhea:
> dysenteric
> epidemic
> Infectious diarrheal disease NOS

009.3 Diarrhea of presumed infectious origin
> EXCLUDES diarrhea NOS (787.91)
>
> AHA: N-D, '87, 7

TUBERCULOSIS (010–018)

INCLUDES infection by Mycobacterium tuberculosis (human) (bovine)

EXCLUDES congenital tuberculosis (771.2)
late effects of tuberculosis (137.0-137.4)

The following fifth digit subclassification is for use with categories 010-018:

0 unspecified
1 bacteriological or histological examination not done
2 bacteriological or histological examination unknown (at present)
3 tubercle bacilli found (in sputum) by microscopy
4 tubercle bacilli not found (in sputum) by microscopy, but found by bacterial culture
5 tubercle bacilli not found by bacteriological examination, but tuberculosis confirmed histologically
6 tubercle bacilli not found by bacteriological or histological examination but tuberculosis confirmed by other methods [inoculation of animals]

DEF: An infection by Mycobacterium tuberculosis causing the formation of small, rounded nodules, called tubercles, that can disseminate throughout the body via lymph and blood vessels. Localized tuberculosis is most often seen in the lungs.

√4ᵗʰ **010 Primary tuberculous infection**
> DEF: Tuberculosis of the lungs occurring when the patient is first infected.

§ √5ᵗʰ **010.0 Primary tuberculous infection**
[0-6]
> EXCLUDES nonspecific reaction to tuberculin skin test without active tuberculosis (795.5)
> positive PPD (795.5)
> positive tuberculin skin test without active tuberculosis (795.5)
>
> DEF: Hilar or paratracheal lymph node enlargement in pulmonary tuberculosis.

§ √5ᵗʰ **010.1 Tuberculous pleurisy in primary progressive tuberculosis**
[0-6]
> DEF: Inflammation and exudation in the lining of the tubercular lung.

§ √5ᵗʰ **010.8 Other primary progressive tuberculosis**
[0-6]
> EXCLUDES tuberculous erythema nodosum (017.1)

§ √5ᵗʰ **010.9 Primary tuberculous infection, unspecified**
[0-6]

√4ᵗʰ **011 Pulmonary tuberculosis**
> Use additional code to identify any associated silicosis (502)

§ √5ᵗʰ **011.0 Tuberculosis of lung, infiltrative**
[0-6]

§ √5ᵗʰ **011.1 Tuberculosis of lung, nodular**
[0-6]

§ √5ᵗʰ **011.2 Tuberculosis of lung with cavitation**
[0-6]

§ √5ᵗʰ **011.3 Tuberculosis of bronchus**
[0-6]
> EXCLUDES isolated bronchial tuberculosis (012.2)

§ √5ᵗʰ **011.4 Tuberculous fibrosis of lung**
[0-6]

§ √5ᵗʰ **011.5 Tuberculous bronchiectasis**
[0-6]

§ √5ᵗʰ **011.6 Tuberculous pneumonia [any form]**
[0-6]
> DEF: Inflammatory pulmonary reaction to tuberculous cells.

§ √5ᵗʰ **011.7 Tuberculous pneumothorax**
[0-6]
> DEF: Spontaneous rupture of damaged tuberculous pulmonary tissue.

§ √5ᵗʰ **011.8 Other specified pulmonary tuberculosis**
[0-6]

§ √5ᵗʰ **011.9 Pulmonary tuberculosis, unspecified**
[0-6]
> Respiratory tuberculosis NOS
> Tuberculosis of lung NOS

√4ᵗʰ **012 Other respiratory tuberculosis**
> EXCLUDES respiratory tuberculosis, unspecified (011.9)

§ √5ᵗʰ **012.0 Tuberculous pleurisy**
[0-6]
> Tuberculosis of pleura
> Tuberculous empyema
> Tuberculous hydrothorax
> EXCLUDES pleurisy with effusion without mention of cause (511.9)
> tuberculous pleurisy in primary progressive tuberculosis (010.1)
>
> DEF: Inflammation and exudation in the lining of the tubercular lung.

§ √5ᵗʰ **012.1 Tuberculosis of intrathoracic lymph nodes**
[0-6]
> Tuberculosis of lymph nodes:
> hilar
> mediastinal
> tracheobronchial
> Tuberculous tracheobronchial adenopathy
> EXCLUDES that specified as primary (010.0-010.9)

§ √5ᵗʰ **012.2 Isolated tracheal or bronchial tuberculosis**
[0-6]

§ √5ᵗʰ **012.3 Tuberculous laryngitis**
[0-6]
> Tuberculosis of glottis

§ √5ᵗʰ **012.8 Other specified respiratory tuberculosis**
[0-6]
> Tuberculosis of:
> mediastinum
> nasopharynx
> nose (septum)
> sinus [any nasal]

√4ᵗʰ **013 Tuberculosis of meninges and central nervous system**

§ √5ᵗʰ **013.0 Tuberculous meningitis**
[0-6]
> Tuberculosis of meninges (cerebral) (spinal)
> Tuberculous:
> leptomeningitis
> meningoencephalitis
> EXCLUDES tuberculoma of meninges (013.1)

§ √5ᵗʰ **013.1 Tuberculoma of meninges**
[0-6]

§ √5ᵗʰ **013.2 Tuberculoma of brain**
[0-6]
> Tuberculosis of brain (current disease)

§ √5ᵗʰ **013.3 Tuberculous abscess of brain**
[0-6]

§ √5ᵗʰ **013.4 Tuberculoma of spinal cord**
[0-6]

§ √5ᵗʰ **013.5 Tuberculous abscess of spinal cord**
[0-6]

§ √5ᵗʰ **013.6 Tuberculous encephalitis or myelitis**
[0-6]

§ √5ᵗʰ **013.8 Other specified tuberculosis of central nervous system**
[0-6]

§ √5ᵗʰ **013.9 Unspecified tuberculosis of central nervous system**
[0-6]
> Tuberculosis of central nervous system NOS

§ Requires fifth digit. Valid digits are in [brackets] under each code. See beginning of section 010-018 for codes and definitions.

§ ✓5ᵗʰ **016.7 Other female genital organs** ♀
[0-6]   Tuberculous:
cervicitis
endometritis

§ ✓5ᵗʰ **016.9 Genitourinary tuberculosis, unspecified**
[0-6]

✓4ᵗʰ **017 Tuberculosis of other organs**

§ ✓5ᵗʰ **017.0 Skin and subcutaneous cellular tissue**
[0-6]   Lupus: Tuberculosis:
exedens   colliquativa
vulgaris   cutis
Scrofuloderma   lichenoides
papulonecrotica
verrucosa cutis

EXCLUDES *lupus erythematosus (695.4)*
disseminated (710.0)
lupus NOS (710.0)
nonspecific reaction to tuberculin skin test
without active tuberculosis (795.5)
positive PPD (795.5)
positive tuberculin skin test without active
tuberculosis (795.5)

§ ✓5ᵗʰ **017.1 Erythema nodosum with hypersensitivity**
[0-6]   **reaction in tuberculosis**
Bazin's disease
Erythema:
induratum
nodosum, tuberculous
Tuberculosis indurativa
EXCLUDES *erythema nodosum NOS (695.2)*
DEF: Tender, inflammatory, bilateral nodules appearing on the
shins and thought to be an allergic reaction to tuberculotoxin.

§ ✓5ᵗʰ **017.2 Peripheral lymph nodes**
[0-6]   Scrofula
Scrofulous abscess
Tuberculous adenitis
EXCLUDES *tuberculosis of lymph nodes:*
bronchial and mediastinal (012.1)
mesenteric and retroperitoneal (014.8)
tuberculous tracheobronchial adenopathy
(012.1)
DEF: Scrofula: Old name for tuberculous cervical
lymphadenitis.

§ ✓5ᵗʰ **017.3 Eye**
[0-6]   Use additional code to identify manifestation, as:
tuberculous:
chorioretinitis, disseminated (363.13)
episcleritis (379.09)
interstitial keratitis (370.59)
iridocyclitis, chronic (364.11)
keratoconjunctivitis (phlyctenular) (370.31)

§ ✓5ᵗʰ **017.4 Ear**
[0-6]   Tuberculosis of ear
Tuberculous otitis media
EXCLUDES *tuberculous mastoiditis (015.6)*

§ ✓5ᵗʰ **017.5 Thyroid gland**
[0-6]

§ ✓5ᵗʰ **017.6 Adrenal glands**
[0-6]   Addison's disease, tuberculous

§ ✓5ᵗʰ **017.7 Spleen**
[0-6]

§ ✓5ᵗʰ **017.8 Esophagus**
[0-6]

§ ✓5ᵗʰ **017.9 Other specified organs**
[0-6]   Use additional code to identify manifestation, as:
tuberculosis of:
endocardium [any valve] (424.91)
myocardium (422.0)
pericardium (420.0)

✓4ᵗʰ **014 Tuberculosis of intestines, peritoneum, and mesenteric**
glands

§ ✓5ᵗʰ **014.0 Tuberculous peritonitis**
[0-6]   Tuberculous ascites
DEF: Tuberculous inflammation of the membrane lining the
abdomen.

§ ✓5ᵗʰ **014.8 Other**
[0-6]   Tuberculosis (of):
anus
intestine (large) (small)
mesenteric glands
rectum
retroperitoneal (lymph nodes)
Tuberculous enteritis

✓4ᵗʰ **015 Tuberculosis of bones and joints**
Use additional code to identify manifestation, as:
tuberculous:
arthropathy (711.4)
necrosis of bone (730.8)
osteitis (730.8)
osteomyelitis (730.8)
synovitis (727.01)
tenosynovitis (727.01)

§ ✓5ᵗʰ **015.0 Vertebral column**
[0-6]   Pott's disease
Use additional code to identify manifestation, as:
curvature of spine [Pott's] (737.4)
kyphosis (737.4)
spondylitis (720.81)

§ ✓5ᵗʰ **015.1 Hip**
[0-6]

§ ✓5ᵗʰ **015.2 Knee**
[0-6]

§ ✓5ᵗʰ **015.5 Limb bones**
[0-6]   Tuberculous dactylitis

§ ✓5ᵗʰ **015.6 Mastoid**
[0-6]   Tuberculous mastoiditis

§ ✓5ᵗʰ **015.7 Other specified bone**
[0-6]

§ ✓5ᵗʰ **015.8 Other specified joint**
[0-6]

§ ✓5ᵗʰ **015.9 Tuberculosis of unspecified bones and joints**
[0-6]

✓4ᵗʰ **016 Tuberculosis of genitourinary system**

§ ✓5ᵗʰ **016.0 Kidney**
[0-6]   Renal tuberculosis
Use additional code to identify manifestation, as:
tuberculous:
nephropathy (583.81)
pyelitis (590.81)
pyelonephritis (590.81)

§ ✓5ᵗʰ **016.1 Bladder**
[0-6]

§ ✓5ᵗʰ **016.2 Ureter**
[0-6]

§ ✓5ᵗʰ **016.3 Other urinary organs**
[0-6]

§ ✓5ᵗʰ **016.4 Epididymis** ♂
[0-6]

§ ✓5ᵗʰ **016.5 Other male genital organs** ♂
[0-6]   Use additional code to identify manifestation, as:
tuberculosis of:
prostate (601.4)
seminal vesicle (608.81)
testis (608.81)

§ ✓5ᵗʰ **016.6 Tuberculous oophoritis and salpingitis** ♀
[0-6]

---

§   Requires fifth digit. Valid digits are in [brackets] under each code. See beginning of section 010-018 for codes and definitions.

N Newborn Age: 0   P Pediatric Age: 0-17   M Maternity Age: 12-55   A Adult Age: 15-124

✓4th **018 Miliary tuberculosis**

> INCLUDES   tuberculosis:
>> disseminated
>> generalized
>> miliary, whether of a single specified site, multiple sites, or unspecified site
>> polyserositis
>
> **DEF:** A form of tuberculosis caused by caseous material carried through the bloodstream planting seedlike tubercles in various body organs.

§ ✓5th **018.0 Acute miliary tuberculosis**
> [0-6]

§ ✓5th **018.8 Other specified miliary tuberculosis**
> [0-6]

§ ✓5th **018.9 Miliary tuberculosis, unspecified**
> [0-6]

ZOONOTIC BACTERIAL DISEASES (020-027)

✓4th **020 Plague**

> INCLUDES   infection by Yersinia [Pasteurella] pestis

> **020.0 Bubonic**
>> **DEF:** Most common acute and severe form of plague characterized by lymphadenopathy (buboes), chills, fever and headache.

> **020.1 Cellulocutaneous**
>> **DEF:** Plague characterized by inflammation and necrosis of skin.

> **020.2 Septicemic**
>> **DEF:** Plague characterized by massive infection in the bloodstream.

> **020.3 Primary pneumonic**
>> **DEF:** Plague characterized by massive pulmonary infection.

> **020.4 Secondary pneumonic**
>> **DEF:** Lung infection as a secondary complication of plague.

> **020.5 Pneumonic, unspecified**

> **020.8 Other specified types of plague**
>> Abortive plague
>> Ambulatory plague
>> Pestis minor

> **020.9 Plague, unspecified**

✓4th **021 Tularemia**

> INCLUDES   deerfly fever
>> infection by Francisella [Pasteurella] tularensis
>> rabbit fever
>
> **DEF:** A febrile disease transmitted by the bites of deer flies, fleas and ticks, by inhalations of aerosolized *F. tularensis* or by ingestion of contaminated food or water; patients quickly develop fever, chills, weakness, headache, backache and malaise.

> **021.0 Ulceroglandular tularemia**
>> **DEF:** Lesions occur at the site *Francisella tularensis* organism enters body, usually the fingers or hands.

> **021.1 Enteric tularemia**
>> Tularemia:
>>> cryptogenic
>>> intestinal
>>> typhoidal

> **021.2 Pulmonary tularemia**
>> Bronchopneumonic tularemia

> **021.3 Oculoglandular tularemia**
>> **DEF:** Painful conjunctival infection by *Francisella tularensis* organism with possible corneal, preauricular lymph, or lacrimal involvement.

> **021.8 Other specified tularemia**
>> Tularemia:
>>> generalized or disseminated
>>> glandular

> **021.9 Unspecified tularemia**

✓4th **022 Anthrax**

> **DEF:** An bacterial disease usually transmitted by contact with infected animals or their discharges; primary routes of inoculation are cutaneous, gastrointestinal and by inhalation.
> **AHA:** 4Q '02, 70

> **022.0 Cutaneous anthrax**
>> Malignant pustule

> **022.1 Pulmonary anthrax**
>> Respiratory anthrax
>> Wool-sorters' disease

> **022.2 Gastrointestinal anthrax**

> **022.3 Anthrax septicemia**

> **022.8 Other specified manifestations of anthrax**

> **022.9 Anthrax, unspecified**

✓4th **023 Brucellosis**

> INCLUDES   fever:
>> Malta
>> Mediterranean
>> undulant
>
> **DEF:** An infectious disease caused by gram-negative, aerobic coccobacilli organisms; transmitted to humans through contact with infected tissue or dairy products; fever, sweating, weakness and aching are symptoms of the disease.

> **023.0 Brucella melitensis**
>> **DEF:** Infection from direct or indirect contact with infected sheep or goats.

> **023.1 Brucella abortus**
>> **DEF:** Infection from direct or indirect contact with infected cattle.

> **023.2 Brucella suis**
>> **DEF:** Infection from direct or indirect contact with infected swine.

> **023.3 Brucella canis**
>> **DEF:** Infection from direct or indirect contact with infected dogs.

> **023.8 Other brucellosis**
>> Infection by more than one organism

> **023.9 Brucellosis, unspecified**

024 Glanders

> Infection by:
>> Actinobacillus mallei
>> Malleomyces mallei
>> Pseudomonas mallei
> Farcy
> Malleus
> **DEF:** Equine infection causing mucosal inflammation and skin ulcers in humans.

025 Melioidosis

> Infection by:
>> Malleomyces pseudomallei
>> Pseudomonas pseudomallei
>> Whitmore's bacillus
> Pseudoglanders
> **DEF:** Rare infection caused by *Pseudomonas pseudomallei;* clinical symptoms range from localized infection to fatal septicemia.

✓4th **026 Rat-bite fever**

> **026.0 Spirillary fever**
>> Rat-bite fever due to Spirillum minor [S. minus]
>> Sodoku

> **026.1 Streptobacillary fever**
>> Epidemic arthritic erythema
>> Haverhill fever
>> Rat-bite fever due to Streptobacillus moniliformis

> **026.9 Unspecified rat-bite fever**

---

§   Requires fifth digit. Valid digits are in [brackets] under each code. See beginning of section 010-018 for codes and definitions.

| ✓4th ✓5th Additional Digit Required | Unspecified Code | Other Specified Code | Manifestation Code | ▶◀ Revised Text | ● New Code | ▲ Revised Code Title |

√4ᵗʰ **027 Other zoonotic bacterial diseases**

027.0 Listeriosis
Infection
Septicemia } by Listeria monocytogenes

Use additional code to identify manifestation, as meningitis (320.7)

EXCLUDES *congenital listeriosis (771.2)*

027.1 Erysipelothrix infection
Erysipeloid (of Rosenbach)
Infection
Septicemia } by Erysipelothrix insidiosa [E. rhusiopathiae]

DEF: Usually associated with handling of fish, meat, or poultry; symptoms range from localized inflammation to septicemia.

027.2 Pasteurellosis
Pasteurella pseudotuberculosis infection
Mesenteric adenitis
Septic infection (cat bite) (dog bite) } by Pasteurella multocida [P. septica]

EXCLUDES *infection by:*
Francisella [Pasteurella] tularensis (021.0-021.9)
Yersinia [Pasteurella] pestis (020.0-020.9)

DEF: Swelling, abscesses, or septicemia from *Pasteurella multocida*, commonly transmitted to humans by a dog or cat scratch.

027.8 Other specified zoonotic bacterial diseases

027.9 Unspecified zoonotic bacterial disease

OTHER BACTERIAL DISEASES (030-041)

EXCLUDES *bacterial venereal diseases (098.0-099.9)*
bartonellosis (088.0)

√4ᵗʰ **030 Leprosy**

INCLUDES Hansen's disease
infection by Mycobacterium leprae

030.0 Lepromatous [type L]
Lepromatous leprosy (macular) (diffuse) (infiltrated) (nodular) (neuritic)

DEF: Infectious, disseminated leprosy bacilli with lesions and deformities.

030.1 Tuberculoid [type T]
Tuberculoid leprosy (macular) (maculoanesthetic) (major) (minor) (neuritic)

DEF: Relatively benign, self-limiting leprosy with neuralgia and scales.

030.2 Indeterminate [group I]
Indeterminate [uncharacteristic] leprosy (macular) (neuritic)

DEF: Uncharacteristic leprosy, frequently an early manifestation.

030.3 Borderline [group B]
Borderline or dimorphous leprosy (infiltrated) (neuritic)

DEF: Transitional form of leprosy, neither lepromatous nor tuberculoid.

030.8 Other specified leprosy

030.9 Leprosy, unspecified

√4ᵗʰ **031 Diseases due to other mycobacteria**

031.0 Pulmonary
Battey disease
Infection by Mycobacterium:
avium
intracellulare [Battey bacillus]
kansasii

031.1 Cutaneous
Buruli ulcer
Infection by Mycobacterium:
marinum [M. balnei]
ulcerans

031.2 Disseminated
Disseminated mycobacterium avium-intracellulare complex (DMAC)
Mycobacterium avium-intracellulare complex (MAC) bacteremia

DEF: Disseminated mycobacterium avium-intracellulare complex (DMAC): A serious systemic form of MAC commonly observed in patients in the late course of AIDS.
DEF: Mycobacterium avium-intracellulare complex (MAC) bacterium: Human pulmonary disease, lymphadenitis in children and systemic disease in immunocompromised individuals caused by a slow growing, gram-positive, aerobic organism.
AHA: 4Q, '97, 31

031.8 Other specified mycobacterial diseases

031.9 Unspecified diseases due to mycobacteria
Atypical mycobacterium infection NOS

√4ᵗʰ **032 Diphtheria**

INCLUDES infection by Corynebacterium diphtheriae

032.0 Faucial diphtheria
Membranous angina, diphtheritic
DEF: Diphtheria of the throat.

032.1 Nasopharyngeal diphtheria

032.2 Anterior nasal diphtheria

032.3 Laryngeal diphtheria
Laryngotracheitis, diphtheritic

√5ᵗʰ **032.8 Other specified diphtheria**

032.81 Conjunctival diphtheria
Pseudomembranous diphtheritic conjunctivitis

032.82 Diphtheritic myocarditis

032.83 Diphtheritic peritonitis

032.84 Diphtheritic cystitis

032.85 Cutaneous diphtheria

032.89 Other

032.9 Diphtheria, unspecified

√4ᵗʰ **033 Whooping cough**

INCLUDES pertussis

Use additional code to identify any associated pneumonia (484.3)
DEF: An acute, highly contagious respiratory tract infection caused by *Bordetella pertussis* and *B. bronchiseptica*; characteristic paroxysmal cough.

033.0 Bordetella pertussis [B. pertussis]

033.1 Bordetella parapertussis [B. parapertussis]

033.8 Whooping cough due to other specified organism
Bordetella bronchiseptica [B. bronchiseptica]

033.9 Whooping cough, unspecified organism

√4ᵗʰ **034 Streptococcal sore throat and scarlet fever**

034.0 Streptococcal sore throat
Septic:
angina
sore throat
Streptococcal:
angina
Streptococcal:
laryngitis
pharyngitis
tonsillitis

J02.0 Streptococcal pharyngitis I-10

034.1 Scarlet fever
Scarlatina
EXCLUDES *parascarlatina (057.8)*
DEF: Streptococcal infection and fever with red rash spreading from trunk.

035 Erysipelas
EXCLUDES *postpartum or puerperal erysipelas ▶(670.8)◀*
DEF: An acute superficial cellulitis involving the dermal lymphatics; it is often caused by group A streptococci.

✓4ᵗʰ 036 Meningococcal infection

036.0 Meningococcal meningitis
Cerebrospinal fever (meningococcal)
Meningitis:
    cerebrospinal
    epidemic

036.1 Meningococcal encephalitis

036.2 Meningococcemia
Meningococcal septicemia

036.3 Waterhouse-Friderichsen syndrome, meningococcal
Meningococcal hemorrhagic adrenalitis
Meningococcic adrenal syndrome
Waterhouse-Friderichsen syndrome NOS

✓5ᵗʰ 036.4 Meningococcal carditis

    036.40 Meningococcal carditis, unspecified

    036.41 Meningococcal pericarditis
      DEF: Meningococcal infection of the outer membrane of the heart.

    036.42 Meningococcal endocarditis
      DEF: Meningococcal infection of the membranes lining the cavities of the heart.

    036.43 Meningococcal myocarditis
      DEF: Meningococcal infection of the muscle of the heart.

✓5ᵗʰ 036.8 Other specified meningococcal infections

    036.81 Meningococcal optic neuritis

    036.82 Meningococcal arthropathy

    036.89 Other

036.9 Meningococcal infection, unspecified
Meningococcal infection NOS

037 Tetanus
    EXCLUDES   *tetanus:*
        complicating:
          abortion (634-638 with .0, 639.0)
          ectopic or molar pregnancy (639.0)
        neonatorum (771.3)
        puerperal ▶(670.8)◀

DEF: An acute, often fatal, infectious disease caused by the anaerobic, spore-forming bacillus *Clostridium tetani;* the bacillus enters the body through a contaminated wound, burns, surgical wounds, or cutaneous ulcers. Symptoms: lockjaw, spasms, seizures, and paralysis.

✓4ᵗʰ 038 Septicemia
Use additional code for systemic inflammatory response syndrome (SIRS) (995.91-995.92)
    EXCLUDES   *bacteremia (790.7)*
        during labor (659.3)
        following ectopic or molar pregnancy (639.0)
        following infusion, injection, transfusion, or vaccination (999.3)
        postpartum, puerperal (670)
        septicemia (sepsis) of newborn (771.81)
        that complicating abortion (634-638 with .0, 639.0)

DEF: A systemic disease associated with the presence and persistence of pathogenic microorganisms or their toxins in the blood.
AHA: 2Q, '04, 16; 4Q, '88, 10; 3Q, '88, 12
TIP: Sequence any underlying cause (e.g., due to device or injury) first, before septicemia code.

038.0 Streptococcal septicemia
    AHA: 4Q, '03, 79; 2Q, '96, 5

✓5ᵗʰ 038.1 Staphylococcal septicemia
    AHA: 4Q, '97, 32

    038.10 Staphylococcal septicemia, unspecified

    038.11 Methicillin susceptible Staphylococcus aureus septicemia
      MSSA septicemia
      Staphylococcus aureus septicemia NOS
      AHA: 4Q, '08, 69-70; 1Q, '05, 7; 2Q, '00, 5; 4Q, '98, 42
      A41.0 Sepsis due to Staphylococcus aureus   **I-10**

038.12 Methicillin resistant Staphylococcus aureus septicemia
    AHA: 4Q, '08, 69-73

038.19 Other staphylococcal septicemia
    AHA: 2Q, '00, 5
    A41.1 Sepsis due to other spec Staphylococcus **I-10**

038.2 Pneumococcal septicemia [Streptococcus pneumoniae septicemia]
    AHA: 2Q, '96, 5; 1Q, '91, 13

038.3 Septicemia due to anaerobes
Septicemia due to bacteroides
    EXCLUDES   *gas gangrene (040.0)*
        that due to anaerobic streptococci (038.0)
DEF: Infection of blood by microorganisms categorized as gram-negative by Gram's method of staining for identification of bacteria.

✓5ᵗʰ 038.4 Septicemia due to other gram-negative organisms
DEF: Infection of blood by microorganisms categorized as gram-negative by Gram's method of staining for identification of bacteria.

    038.40 Gram-negative organism, unspecified
      Gram-negative septicemia NOS

    038.41 Hemophilus influenzae [H. influenzae]

    038.42 Escherichia coli [E. coli]
      AHA: 4Q, '03, 73
      A41.51 Sepsis due to Escherichia coli [E coli] **I-10**

    038.43 Pseudomonas

    038.44 Serratia

    038.49 Other
      A41.59 Other Gram-negative sepsis   **I-10**

038.8 Other specified septicemias
    EXCLUDES   *septicemia (due to):*
        anthrax (022.3)
        gonococcal (098.89)
        herpetic (054.5)
        meningococcal (036.2)
        septicemic plague (020.2)

038.9 Unspecified septicemia
Septicemia NOS
    EXCLUDES   *bacteremia NOS (790.7)*
AHA: 4Q, '07, 97; 2Q, '05, 18-19; 2Q, '04, 16; 4Q, '03, 79; 2Q, '00, 3; 3Q, '99, 5, 9; 1Q, '98, 5; 3Q, '96, 16; 2Q, '96, 6
TIP: Ensure that documentation includes clinical evidence of systemic infection; do not code if documentation indicates "urosepsis" only.
A41.9 Sepsis unspecified   **I-10**

✓4ᵗʰ 039 Actinomycotic infections
    INCLUDES   actinomycotic mycetoma
      infection by Actinomycetales, such as species of Actinomyces, Actinomadura, Nocardia, Streptomyces
      maduromycosis (actinomycotic)
      schizomycetoma (actinomycotic)
DEF: Inflammatory lesions and abscesses at site of infection by *Actinomyces israelii.*

039.0 Cutaneous
Erythrasma
Trichomycosis axillaris

039.1 Pulmonary
Thoracic actinomycosis

039.2 Abdominal

039.3 Cervicofacial

039.4 Madura foot
    EXCLUDES   *madura foot due to mycotic infection (117.4)*

039.8 Of other specified sites

039.9 Of unspecified site
Actinomycosis NOS
Maduromycosis NOS
Nocardiosis NOS

✓4th 040 Other bacterial diseases

EXCLUDES bacteremia NOS (790.7)
bacterial infection NOS (041.9)

040.0 Gas gangrene
Gas bacillus infection or gangrene
Infection by Clostridium:
histolyticum
oedematiens
perfringens [welchii]
septicum
sordellii
Malignant edema
Myonecrosis, clostridial
Myositis, clostridial
AHA: 1Q, '95, 11

040.1 Rhinoscleroma
DEF: Growths on the nose and nasopharynx caused by Klebsiella rhinoscleromatis.

040.2 Whipple's disease
Intestinal lipodystrophy

040.3 Necrobacillosis
DEF: Infection with Fusobacterium necrophorum causing abscess or necrosis.
AHA: 4Q, '07, 85

✓5th 040.4 Other specified botulism
Non-foodborne intoxication due to toxins of Clostridium botulinum [C. botulinum]
EXCLUDES botulism NOS (005.1)
food poisoning due to toxins of Clostridium botulinum (005.1)

040.41 Infant botulism ▣P
DEF: Colonization of Clostridium botulinum spores in the large intestine; release of neurotoxins results in constipation; may progress to neuromuscular paralysis; affects infants of less than six months.
AHA: 4Q, '07, 60

040.42 Wound botulism
Non-foodborne botulism NOS
Use additional code to identify complicated open wound
AHA: 4Q, '07, 60

✓5th 040.8 Other specified bacterial diseases

040.81 Tropical pyomyositis

040.82 Toxic shock syndrome
Use additional code to identify the organism
DEF: Syndrome caused by staphylococcal exotoxin that may rapidly progress to severe and intractable shock; symptoms include sunburn-like rash with peeling of skin on palms and soles, sudden onset high fever, vomiting, diarrhea, myalgia, and hypotension.
AHA: 4Q, '02, 44

040.89 Other
AHA: N-D, '86, 7

✓4th 041 Bacterial infection in conditions classified elsewhere and of unspecified site
Note: This category is provided to be used as an additional code to identify the bacterial agent in diseases classified elsewhere. This category will also be used to classify bacterial infections of unspecified nature or site.
EXCLUDES septicemia (038.0-038.9)
AHA: 2Q, '01, 12; J-A, '84, 19

✓5th 041.0 Streptococcus

041.00 Streptococcus, unspecified

041.01 Group A
AHA: 1Q, '02, 3

041.02 Group B
B95.1 Streptococcus group B cause of dz class elsewhere ▣I-10

041.03 Group C

041.04 Group D [Enterococcus]
B95.2 Enterococcus as the cause of dz class elsewhere ▣I-10

041.05 Group G

041.09 Other Streptococcus
B95.4 Oth streptococcus cause of dz class elsewhere ▣I-10

✓5th 041.1 Staphylococcus

041.10 Staphylococcus, unspecified
AHA: 2Q, '06, 15

041.11 Methicillin susceptible Staphylococcus aureus
MSSA
Staphylococcus aureus NOS
AHA: 4Q, '08, 69-70; 2Q, '06, 16; 4Q, '03, 104, 106; 2Q, '01, 11; 4Q, '98, 42, 54; 4Q, '97, 32
B95.6 Staphylococcus aureus cause of dz class elsewhere ▣I-10

041.12 Methicillin resistant Staphylococcus aureus
Methicillin-resistant staphylococcus aureus (MRSA)
AHA: 4Q, '08, 69-70, 73
TIP: Do not assign if combination code (with localized infection) available, or if only colonization or carrier status documented.

041.19 Other Staphylococcus
AHA: 2Q, '08, 3
B95.7 Other staphylococcus cause of dz class elsewhere ▣I-10

041.2 Pneumococcus

041.3 Klebsiella pneumoniae
AHA: 4Q, '08, 149

041.4 Escherichia coli [E. coli]
B96.2 Escherichia coli cause of dz class elsewhere ▣I-10

041.5 Hemophilus influenzae [H. influenzae]

041.6 Proteus (mirabilis) (morganii)

041.7 Pseudomonas
AHA: 4Q, '02, 45
B96.5 Pseudomonas as the cause of dz class elsewhere ▣I-10

✓5th 041.8 Other specified bacterial infections

041.81 Mycoplasma
Eaton's agent
Pleuropneumonia-like organisms [PPLO]

041.82 Bacteroides fragilis
DEF: Anaerobic gram-negative bacilli of the gastrointestinal tract; frequently implicated in intra-abdominal infection; commonly resistant to antibiotics.

041.83 Clostridium perfringens

041.84 Other anaerobes
Gram-negative anaerobes
EXCLUDES Helicobacter pylori (041.86)

041.85 Other gram-negative organisms
Aerobacter aerogenes
Gram-negative bacteria NOS
Mima polymorpha
Serratia
EXCLUDES gram-negative anaerobes (041.84)
AHA: 1Q, '95, 18

041.86 Helicobacter pylori [H. pylori]
AHA: 4Q, '95, 60
B96.81 Helicobacter pylori cause of dz class elsewhere ▣I-10

041.89 Other specified bacteria
AHA: 2Q, '06, 7; 2Q, '03, 7
A49.8 Other bacterial infections of unspec site ▣I-10

041.9 Bacterial infection, unspecified
AHA: 2Q, '91, 9

N Newborn Age: 0   P Pediatric Age: 0-17   M Maternity Age: 12-55   A Adult Age: 15-124

HUMAN IMMUNODEFICIENCY VIRUS (HIV) INFECTION (042)

042 Human immunodeficiency virus [HIV] disease

Acquired immune deficiency syndrome
Acquired immunodeficiency syndrome
AIDS
AIDS-like syndrome
AIDS-related complex
ARC
HIV infection, symptomatic

Use additional code(s) to identify all manifestations of HIV
Use additional code to identify HIV-2 infection (079.53)

EXCLUDES   *asymptomatic HIV infection status (V08)*
exposure to HIV virus (V01.79)
nonspecific serologic evidence of HIV (795.71)

AHA: 4Q, '07, 63; 3Q, '06, 15; 1Q, '05, 7; 2Q, '04, 11; 1Q, '04, 5; 1Q, '03, 15;
1Q, '99, 14; 4Q, '97, 30, 31; 1Q, '93, 21; 2Q, '92, 11; 3Q, '90, 17; J-A, '87, 8

TIP: Code only confirmed cases of HIV infection/illness; may be coded
from provider's diagnostic statement.

B20 Human immunodeficiency virus [HIV] disease   **I-10**

POLIOMYELITIS AND OTHER NON-ARTHROPOD-BORNE VIRAL DISEASES AND PRION DISEASES OF CENTRAL NERVOUS SYSTEM (045-049)

✓4ᵗʰ 045 Acute poliomyelitis

EXCLUDES   *late effects of acute poliomyelitis (138)*

The following fifth-digit subclassification is for use with category 045:

   0 **poliovirus, unspecified type**
   1 **poliovirus type I**
   2 **poliovirus type II**
   3 **poliovirus type III**

§ **✓5ᵗʰ 045.0 Acute paralytic poliomyelitis specified as bulbar**
[0-3]
    Infantile paralysis (acute) } specified as bulbar
    Poliomyelitis (acute) (anterior) }
    Polioencephalitis (acute) (bulbar)
    Polioencephalomyelitis (acute) (anterior) (bulbar)

    DEF: Acute paralytic infection occurring where the brain
    merges with the spinal cord; affecting breathing, swallowing,
    and heart rate.

§ **✓5ᵗʰ 045.1 Acute poliomyelitis with other paralysis**
[0-3]
    Paralysis:
      acute atrophic, spinal
      infantile, paralytic
    Poliomyelitis (acute)
      anterior } with paralysis except bulbar
      epidemic

    DEF: Paralytic infection affecting peripheral or spinal nerves.

§ **✓5ᵗʰ 045.2 Acute nonparalytic poliomyelitis**
[0-3]
    Poliomyelitis (acute)
      anterior } specified as nonparalytic
      epidemic

    DEF: Nonparalytic infection causing pain, stiffness, and
    paresthesias.

§ **✓5ᵗʰ 045.9 Acute poliomyelitis, unspecified**
[0-3]
    Infantile paralysis
    Poliomyelitis (acute) } unspecified whether paralytic
      anterior } or nonparalytic
      epidemic

✓4ᵗʰ 046 Slow virus infections and prion diseases of central nervous system

046.0 Kuru
    DEF: A chronic, progressive, fatal nervous system disorder;
    clinical symptoms include cerebellar ataxia, trembling,
    spasticity and progressive dementia.

✓5ᵗʰ 046.1 Jakob-Creutzfeldt disease
    ▶Use additional code to identify dementia:
      with behavioral disturbance (294.11)
      without behavioral disturbance (294.10)◀

    046.11 Variant Creutzfeldt-Jakob disease
      vCJD
      AHA: 4Q, '08, 73-75

046.19 Other and unspecified Creutzfeldt-Jacob disease
    CJD
    Familial Creutzfeldt-Jakob disease
    Iatrogenic Creutzfeldt-Jakob disease
    Jakob-Creutzfeldt disease, unspecified
    Sporadic Creutzfeldt-Jakob disease
    Subacute spongiform encephalopathy

    EXCLUDES   *variant Creutzfeldt-Jakob disease*
      (vCJD) (046.11)

    DEF: Communicable, progressive spongiform
    encephalopathy thought to be caused by an
    infectious particle known as a "prion"
    (proteinaceous infection particle); a progressive,
    fatal disease manifested principally by mental
    deterioration.
    AHA: 4Q, '08, 73-75

046.2 Subacute sclerosing panencephalitis
    Dawson's inclusion body encephalitis
    Van Bogaert's sclerosing leukoencephalitis
    DEF: Progressive viral infection causing cerebral dysfunction,
    blindness, dementia, and death (SSPE).

046.3 Progressive multifocal leukoencephalopathy
    Multifocal leukoencephalopathy NOS
    DEF: Infection affecting cerebral cortex in patients with
    weakened immune systems.

✓5ᵗʰ 046.7 Other specified prion diseases of central nervous system
    EXCLUDES   *Creutzfeldt-Jakob disease (046.11-046.19)*
      Jakob-Creutzfeldt disease (046.11-046.19)
      kuru (046.0)
      variant Creutzfeldt-Jakob disease (vCJD)
      (046.11)

    046.71 Gerstmann-Sträussler-Scheinker syndrome
      GSS syndrome
      AHA: 4Q, '08, 73-75

    046.72 Fatal familial insomnia
      FFI
      AHA: 4Q, '08, 73-75

    046.79 Other and unspecified prion disease of central nervous system

046.8 Other specified slow virus infection of central nervous system

046.9 Unspecified slow virus infection of central nervous system

✓4ᵗʰ 047 Meningitis due to enterovirus

    INCLUDES   meningitis:
      abacterial
      aseptic
      viral

    EXCLUDES   *meningitis due to:*
      adenovirus (049.1)
      arthropod-borne virus (060.0-066.9)
      leptospira (100.81)
      virus of:
        herpes simplex (054.72)
        herpes zoster (053.0)
        lymphocytic choriomeningitis (049.0)
        mumps (072.1)
        poliomyelitis (045.0-045.9)
      any other infection specifically classified elsewhere

    AHA: J-F, '87, 6

047.0 Coxsackie virus

047.1 ECHO virus
    Meningo-eruptive syndrome

047.8 Other specified viral meningitis

047.9 Unspecified viral meningitis
    Viral meningitis NOS
    A87.9 Viral meningitis unspecified   **I-10**

---

§   Requires fifth digit. Valid digits are in [brackets] under each code. See category 045 for codes and definitions.

✓4ᵗʰ ✓5ᵗʰ Additional Digit Required   Unspecified Code   Other Specified Code   Manifestation Code   ▶◀ Revised Text   ● New Code   ▲ Revised Code Title

2010 ICD-9-CM   **October 2009 · Volume 1 – 9**

Infectious and Parasitic Diseases

048–054.10

048 Other enterovirus diseases of central nervous system
Boston exanthem

✓4th 049 Other non-arthropod-borne viral diseases of central nervous system
EXCLUDES late effects of viral encephalitis (139.0)

049.0 Lymphocytic choriomeningitis
Lymphocytic:
meningitis (serous) (benign)
meningoencephalitis (serous) (benign)

049.1 Meningitis due to adenovirus
DEF: Inflammation of lining of brain caused by Arenaviruses and usually occurring in adults in fall and winter months.

049.8 Other specified non-arthropod-borne viral diseases of central nervous system
Encephalitis: Encephalitis:
acute: lethargica
inclusion body   Rio Bravo
necrotizing   von Economo's disease
epidemic
EXCLUDES human herpesvirus 6 encephalitis (058.21)
other human herpesvirus encephalitis (058.29)

049.9 Unspecified non-arthropod-borne viral diseases of central nervous system
Viral encephalitis NOS

VIRAL DISEASES ▶GENERALLY◀ ACCOMPANIED BY EXANTHEM (050-059)
EXCLUDES arthropod-borne viral diseases (060.0-066.9)
Boston exanthem (048)

✓4th 050 Smallpox

050.0 Variola major
Hemorrhagic (pustular) smallpox
Malignant smallpox
Purpura variolosa
DEF: Form of smallpox known for its high mortality; exists only in laboratories.

050.1 Alastrim
Variola minor
DEF: Mild form of smallpox known for its low mortality rate.

050.2 Modified smallpox
Varioloid
DEF: Mild form occurring in patients with history of infection or vaccination.

050.9 Smallpox, unspecified

✓4th 051 Cowpox and paravaccinia

✓5th 051.0 Cowpox and vaccinia not from vaccination

051.01 Cowpox
DEF: A disease contracted by milking infected cows; vesicles usually appear on the fingers, hands and adjacent areas and usually disappear without scarring; other symptoms local edema, lymphangitis, and regional lymphadenitis with or without fever.
AHA: 4Q, '08, 76-77

051.02 Vaccinia not from vaccination
EXCLUDES vaccinia (generalized) (from vaccination) (999.0)
AHA: 4Q, '08, 76-77

051.1 Pseudocowpox
Milkers' node
DEF: Hand lesions and mild fever in dairy workers caused by exposure to paravaccinia.

051.2 Contagious pustular dermatitis
Ecthyma contagiosum
Orf
DEF: Skin eruptions caused by exposure to poxvirus-infected sheep or goats.

051.9 Paravaccinia, unspecified

✓4th 052 Chickenpox
DEF: Contagious infection by Varicella-zoster virus causing rash with pustules and fever.

052.0 Postvaricella encephalitis
Postchickenpox encephalitis

052.1 Varicella (hemorrhagic) pneumonitis

052.2 Postvaricella myelitis
Postchickenpox myelitis
AHA: 4Q, '06, 58-63

052.7 With other specified complications
AHA: 1Q, '02, 3

052.8 With unspecified complication

052.9 Varicella without mention of complication
Chickenpox NOS   Varicella NOS

✓4th 053 Herpes zoster
INCLUDES shingles
zona
DEF: Self-limiting infection by varicella-zoster virus causing unilateral eruptions and neuralgia along affected nerves.

053.0 With meningitis
DEF: Varicella-zoster virus infection causing inflammation of the lining of the brain and/or spinal cord.

✓5th 053.1 With other nervous system complications

053.10 With unspecified nervous system complication

053.11 Geniculate herpes zoster
Herpetic geniculate ganglionitis
DEF: Unilateral eruptions and neuralgia along the facial nerve geniculum affecting face and outer and middle ear.

053.12 Postherpetic trigeminal neuralgia
DEF: Severe oral or nasal pain following a herpes zoster infection.

053.13 Postherpetic polyneuropathy
DEF: Multiple areas of pain following a herpes zoster infection.

053.14 Herpes zoster myelitis
AHA: 4Q, '06, 58-63

053.19 Other

✓5th 053.2 With ophthalmic complications

053.20 Herpes zoster dermatitis of eyelid
Herpes zoster ophthalmicus

053.21 Herpes zoster keratoconjunctivitis

053.22 Herpes zoster iridocyclitis

053.29 Other

✓5th 053.7 With other specified complications

053.71 Otitis externa due to herpes zoster

053.79 Other

053.8 With unspecified complication

053.9 Herpes zoster without mention of complication
Herpes zoster NOS
B02.9 Zoster without complications [I-10]

✓4th 054 Herpes simplex
EXCLUDES congenital herpes simplex (771.2)

054.0 Eczema herpeticum
Kaposi's varicelliform eruption
DEF: Herpes simplex virus invading site of preexisting skin inflammation.

✓5th 054.1 Genital herpes
AHA: J-F, '87, 15, 16

054.10 Genital herpes, unspecified
Herpes progenitalis
A60.00 Herpesviral infection urogenital system [I-10] unspec

N Newborn Age: 0   P Pediatric Age: 0-17   M Maternity Age: 12-55   A Adult Age: 15-124

054.11   **Herpetic vulvovaginitis** ♀

054.12   **Herpetic ulceration of vulva** ♀

054.13   **Herpetic infection of penis** ♂

054.19   **Other**

054.2   **Herpetic gingivostomatitis**

054.3   **Herpetic meningoencephalitis**
Herpes encephalitis   Simian B disease

> **EXCLUDES**   *human herpesvirus 6 encephalitis (058.21)*
> *other human herpesvirus encephalitis (058.29)*

DEF: Inflammation of the brain and its lining, caused by infection of herpes simplex 1 in adults and simplex 2 in newborns.

√5ᵗʰ 054.4   **With ophthalmic complications**

054.40   With unspecified ophthalmic complication

054.41   **Herpes simplex dermatitis of eyelid**

054.42   **Dendritic keratitis**

054.43   **Herpes simplex disciform keratitis**

054.44   **Herpes simplex iridocyclitis**

054.49   Other

054.5   **Herpetic septicemia**
AHA: 2Q, '00, 5

054.6   **Herpetic whitlow**
Herpetic felon
DEF: A primary infection of the terminal segment of a finger by herpes simplex; intense itching and pain start the disease, vesicles form, and tissue ultimately is destroyed.

√5ᵗʰ 054.7   **With other specified complications**

054.71   **Visceral herpes simplex**

054.72   **Herpes simplex meningitis**

054.73   **Herpes simplex otitis externa**

054.74   **Herpes simplex myelitis**
AHA: 4Q, '06, 58-63

054.79   Other

054.8   With unspecified complication

054.9   **Herpes simplex without mention of complication**
B00.9 Herpesviral infection unspecified   I-10

√4ᵗʰ **055 Measles**

> **INCLUDES**   morbilli
> rubeola

055.0   **Postmeasles encephalitis**

055.1   **Postmeasles pneumonia**

055.2   **Postmeasles otitis media**

√5ᵗʰ 055.7   **With other specified complications**

055.71   **Measles keratoconjunctivitis**
Measles keratitis

055.79   Other

055.8   With unspecified complication

055.9   **Measles without mention of complication**

√4ᵗʰ **056 Rubella**

> **INCLUDES**   German measles
> **EXCLUDES**   *congenital rubella (771.0)*

DEF: Acute but usually benign togavirus infection causing fever, sore throat, and rash; associated with complications to fetus as a result of maternal infection.

√5ᵗʰ 056.0   **With neurological complications**

056.00   With unspecified neurological complication

056.01   **Encephalomyelitis due to rubella**
Encephalitis
Meningoencephalitis } due to rubella

056.09   Other

√5ᵗʰ 056.7   **With other specified complications**

056.71   **Arthritis due to rubella**

056.79   Other

056.8   With unspecified complications

056.9   **Rubella without mention of complication**

√4ᵗʰ **057 Other viral exanthemata**

DEF: Skin eruptions or rashes and fever caused by viruses, including poxviruses.

057.0   **Erythema infectiosum [fifth disease]**
DEF: A moderately contagious, benign, epidemic disease, usually seen in children, of probable viral etiology; a red macular rash appears on face and may spread to the limbs and trunk.

057.8   Other specified viral exanthemata
Dukes (-Filatow) disease
Fourth disease
Parascarlatina
Pseudoscarlatina

> **EXCLUDES**   *exanthema subitum [sixth disease]*
> *(058.10-058.12)*
> *roseola infantum (058.10-058.12)*

057.9   Viral exanthem, unspecified

√4ᵗʰ **058 Other human herpesvirus**

> **EXCLUDES**   *congenital herpes (771.2)*
> *cytomegalovirus (078.5)*
> *Epstein-Barr virus (075)*
> *herpes NOS (054.0-054.9)*
> *herpes simplex (054.0-054.9)*
> *herpes zoster (053.0-053.9)*
> *human herpesvirus NOS (054.0-054.9)*
> *human herpesvirus 1 (054.0-054.9)*
> *human herpesvirus 2 (054.0-054.9)*
> *human herpesvirus 3 (052.0-053.9)*
> *human herpesvirus 4 (075)*
> *human herpesvirus 5 (078.5)*
> *varicella (052.0-052.9)*
> *varicella-zoster virus (052.0-053.9)*

AHA: 4Q, '07, 61

√5ᵗʰ 058.1   **Roseola infantum**
Exanthema subitum [sixth disease]

058.10   Roseola infantum, unspecified   P
Exanthema subitum [sixth disease], unspecified
AHA: 4Q, '07, 63

058.11   **Roseola infantum due to human herpesvirus 6**   P
Exanthema subitum [sixth disease] due to human herpesvirus 6

058.12   **Roseola infantum due to human herpesvirus 7**   P
Exanthema subitum [sixth disease] due to human herpesvirus 7

√5ᵗʰ 058.2   **Other human herpesvirus encephalitis**

> **EXCLUDES**   *herpes encephalitis NOS (054.3)*
> *herpes simplex encephalitis (054.3)*
> *human herpesvirus encephalitis NOS (054.3)*
> *simian B herpesvirus encephalitis (054.3)*

058.21   **Human herpesvirus 6 encephalitis**

058.29   Other human herpesvirus encephalitis
Human herpesvirus 7 encephalitis

√5ᵗʰ 058.8   **Other human herpesvirus infections**

058.81   **Human herpesvirus 6 infection**

058.82   **Human herpesvirus 7 infection**

058.89   Other human herpesvirus infection
Human herpesvirus 8 infection
Kaposi's sarcoma-associated herpesvirus infection
AHA: 4Q, '07, 63

√4ᵗʰ √5ᵗʰ   Additional Digit Required   **Unspecified Code**   **Other Specified Code**   **Manifestation Code**   ▶◀ Revised Text   ● New Code   ▲ Revised Code Title

2010 ICD-9-CM   **Volume 1 – 11**

✓4th **059 Other poxvirus infections**

EXCLUDES contagious pustular dermatitis (051.2)
cowpox (051.01)
ecthyma contagiosum (051.2)
milker's nodule (051.1)
orf (051.2)
paravaccinia NOS (051.9)
pseudocowpox (051.1)
smallpox (050.0-050.9)
vaccinia (generalized) (from vaccination) (999.0)
vaccinia not from vaccination (051.02)

AHA: ▶4Q, '08, 76-78◀

✓5th **059.0 Other orthopoxvirus infections**

059.00 Orthopoxvirus infection, unspecified
059.01 Monkeypox
059.09 Other orthopoxvirus infection

✓5th **059.1 Other parapoxvirus infections**

059.10 Parapoxvirus infection, unspecified
059.11 Bovine stomatitis
059.12 Sealpox
059.19 Other parapoxvirus infections

✓5th **059.2 Yatapoxvirus infections**

059.20 Yatapoxvirus infection, unspecified
059.21 Tanapox
059.22 Yaba monkey tumor virus

059.8 Other poxvirus infections

059.9 Poxvirus infections, unspecified

ARTHROPOD-BORNE VIRAL DISEASES (060-066)

Use additional code to identify any associated meningitis (321.2)

EXCLUDES late effects of viral encephalitis (139.0)

✓4th **060 Yellow fever**

DEF: Fever and jaundice from infection by mosquito-borne virus of genus *Flavivirus*.

060.0 Sylvatic

Yellow fever: Yellow fever:
jungle sylvan

DEF: Yellow fever transmitted from animal to man, via mosquito.

060.1 Urban

DEF: Yellow fever transmitted from man to man, via mosquito.

060.9 Yellow fever, unspecified

061 Dengue

Breakbone fever

EXCLUDES hemorrhagic fever caused by dengue virus (065.4)

DEF: Acute, self-limiting infection by mosquito-borne virus characterized by fever and generalized aches.

✓4th **062 Mosquito-borne viral encephalitis**

062.0 Japanese encephalitis

Japanese B encephalitis

DEF: Flavivirus causing inflammation of the brain, with a wide range of clinical manifestations.

062.1 Western equine encephalitis

DEF: Alphavirus WEE infection causing inflammation of the brain, found in areas west of the Mississippi; transmitted horse to mosquito to man.

062.2 Eastern equine encephalitis

EXCLUDES Venezuelan equine encephalitis (066.2)

DEF: Alphavirus EEE causing inflammation of the brain and spinal cord, found from Canada to South America and Mexico; transmitted horse to mosquito to man.

062.3 St. Louis encephalitis

DEF: Epidemic form caused by Flavivirus and transmitted by mosquito, and characterized by fever, difficulty in speech, and headache.

062.4 Australian encephalitis

Australian arboencephalitis
Australian X disease
Murray Valley encephalitis

DEF: Flavivirus causing inflammation of the brain, occurring in Australia and New Guinea.

062.5 California virus encephalitis

Encephalitis: Tahyna fever
California
La Crosse

DEF: Bunyamwere virus causing inflammation of the brain.

062.8 Other specified mosquito-borne viral encephalitis

Encephalitis by Ilheus virus

EXCLUDES West Nile virus (066.40-066.49)

062.9 Mosquito-borne viral encephalitis, unspecified

✓4th **063 Tick-borne viral encephalitis**

INCLUDES diphasic meningoencephalitis

063.0 Russian spring-summer [taiga] encephalitis

063.1 Louping ill

DEF: Inflammation of brain caused by virus transmitted sheep to tick to man; incidence usually limited to British Isles.

063.2 Central European encephalitis

DEF: Inflammation of brain caused by virus transmitted by tick; limited to central Europe and presenting with two distinct phases.

063.8 Other specified tick-borne viral encephalitis

Langat encephalitis Powassan encephalitis

063.9 Tick-borne viral encephalitis, unspecified

064 Viral encephalitis transmitted by other and unspecified arthropods

Arthropod-borne viral encephalitis, vector unknown
Negishi virus encephalitis

EXCLUDES viral encephalitis NOS (049.9)

✓4th **065 Arthropod-borne hemorrhagic fever**

065.0 Crimean hemorrhagic fever [CHF Congo virus]

Central Asian hemorrhagic fever

065.1 Omsk hemorrhagic fever

065.2 Kyasanur Forest disease

065.3 Other tick-borne hemorrhagic fever

065.4 Mosquito-borne hemorrhagic fever

Chikungunya hemorrhagic fever
Dengue hemorrhagic fever

EXCLUDES Chikungunya fever (066.3)
dengue (061)
yellow fever (060.0-060.9)

065.8 Other specified arthropod-borne hemorrhagic fever

Mite-borne hemorrhagic fever

065.9 Arthropod-borne hemorrhagic fever, unspecified

Arbovirus hemorrhagic fever NOS

✓4th **066 Other arthropod-borne viral diseases**

066.0 Phlebotomus fever

Changuinola fever Sandfly fever

DEF: Sandfly-borne viral infection occurring in Asia, Mideast and South America.

066.1 Tick-borne fever

Nairobi sheep disease Tick fever:
Tick fever: Kemerovo
American mountain Quaranfil
Colorado

066.2 Venezuelan equine fever

Venezuelan equine encephalitis

DEF: Alphavirus VEE infection causing inflammation of the brain, usually limited to South America, Mexico, and Florida; transmitted horse to mosquito to man.

066.3 **Other mosquito-borne fever**

Fever (viral):	Fever (viral):
Bunyamwera	Oropouche
Bwamba	Pixuna
Chikungunya	Rift valley
Guama	Ross river
Mayaro	Wesselsbron
Mucambo	Zika
O'Nyong-Nyong	

　　　EXCLUDES　dengue (061)
　　　　　　　　　yellow fever (060.0-060.9)

√5ᵗʰ **066.4** **West Nile fever**

　　AHA: 4Q, '02, 44

　　DEF: Mosquito-borne fever causing fatal inflammation of the brain, the lining of the brain, or of the lining of the brain and spinal cord.

066.40 **West Nile fever, unspecified**
　　West Nile fever NOS
　　West Nile fever without complications
　　West Nile virus NOS

066.41 **West Nile fever with encephalitis**
　　West Nile encephalitis
　　West Nile encephalomyelitis
　　AHA: 4Q, '04, 51

066.42 **West Nile fever with other neurologic manifestation**
　　Use additional code to specify the neurologic manifestation
　　AHA: 4Q, '04, 51

066.49 **West Nile fever with other complications**
　　Use additional code to specify the other conditions

066.8 **Other specified arthropod-borne viral diseases**
　　Chandipura fever
　　Piry fever

066.9 **Arthropod-borne viral disease, unspecified**
　　Arbovirus infection NOS

OTHER DISEASES DUE TO VIRUSES AND CHLAMYDIAE (070-079)

√4ᵗʰ **070** **Viral hepatitis**

　　INCLUDES　viral hepatitis (acute) (chronic)
　　EXCLUDES　cytomegalic inclusion virus hepatitis (078.5)

　　The following fifth-digit subclassification is for use with categories 070.2 and 070.3:
　　0 acute or unspecified, without mention of hepatitis delta
　　1 acute or unspecified, with hepatitis delta
　　2 chronic, without mention of hepatitis delta
　　3 chronic, with hepatitis delta

　　DEF: Hepatitis A : HAV infection is self-limiting with flulike symptoms; transmission, fecal-oral.
　　DEF: Hepatitis B: HBV infection can be chronic and systemic; transmission, bodily fluids.
　　DEF: Hepatitis C: HCV infection can be chronic and systemic; transmission, blood transfusion and unidentified agents.
　　DEF: Hepatitis D (delta): HDV occurs only in the presence of hepatitis B virus.
　　DEF: Hepatitis E: HEV is epidemic form; transmission and nature under investigation.
　　AHA: 2Q, '07, 5

070.0 **Viral hepatitis A with hepatic coma**

070.1 **Viral hepatitis A without mention of hepatic coma**
　　Infectious hepatitis

§ √5ᵗʰ **070.2** **Viral hepatitis B with hepatic coma**
　　[0-3]　AHA: 4Q, '91, 28; For code 070.20: 2Q, '07, 6

§ √5ᵗʰ **070.3** **Viral hepatitis B without mention of hepatic coma**
　　[0-3]　Serum hepatitis
　　　　AHA: 1Q, '93, 28; 4Q, '91, 28
　　　　B16.9 Acute hep B w/o delta-agent & w/o hepatic coma　I-10

√5ᵗʰ **070.4** **Other specified viral hepatitis with hepatic coma**

　　AHA: 4Q, '91, 28

070.41 **Acute hepatitis C with hepatic coma**

070.42 **Hepatitis delta without mention of active hepatitis B disease with hepatic coma**
　　Hepatitis delta with hepatitis B carrier state

070.43 **Hepatitis E with hepatic coma**

070.44 **Chronic hepatitis C with hepatic coma**
　　AHA: 2Q, '07, 5

070.49 **Other specified viral hepatitis with hepatic coma**

√5ᵗʰ **070.5** **Other specified viral hepatitis without mention of hepatic coma**

　　AHA: 4Q, '91, 28

070.51 **Acute hepatitis C without mention of hepatic coma**

070.52 **Hepatitis delta without mention of active hepatititis B disease or hepatic coma**

070.53 **Hepatitis E without mention of hepatic coma**

070.54 **Chronic hepatitis C without mention of hepatic coma**
　　AHA: ▶4Q, '08, 120;◀ 3Q, '07, 7; 2Q, '06, 13
　　B18.2 Chronic viral hepatitis C　I-10

070.59 **Other specified viral hepatitis without mention of hepatic coma**

070.6 **Unspecified viral hepatitis with hepatic coma**
　　EXCLUDES　unspecified viral hepatitis C with hepatic coma (070.71)

√5ᵗʰ **070.7** **Unspecified viral hepatitis C**

070.70 **Unspecified viral hepatitis C without hepatic coma**
　　Unspecified viral hepatitis C NOS
　　AHA: 4Q, '04, 52
　　B19.20 Unspecified viral hepatits C w/o hepatic coma　I-10

070.71 **Unspecified viral hepatitis C with hepatic coma**
　　AHA: 4Q, '04, 52

070.9 **Unspecified viral hepatitis without mention of hepatic coma**
　　Viral hepatitis NOS
　　EXCLUDES　unspecified viral hepatitis C without hepatic coma (070.70)

071 **Rabies**
　　Hydrophobia
　　Lyssa
　　DEF: Acute infectious disease of the CNS caused by a rhabdovirus; usually spread by bites by infected animals; progresses from fever, restlessness, and extreme excitability, to hydrophobia, seizures, confusion and death.

√4ᵗʰ **072** **Mumps**
　　DEF: Acute infectious disease caused by paramyxovirus; usually seen in children less than 15 years of age; salivary glands are typically enlarged, involves other organs, such as testes, pancreas and meninges.

072.0 **Mumps orchitis**　　　　♂

072.1 **Mumps meningitis**

072.2 **Mumps encephalitis**
　　Mumps meningoencephalitis

072.3 **Mumps pancreatitis**

√5ᵗʰ **072.7** **Mumps with other specified complications**

072.71 **Mumps hepatitis**

072.72 **Mumps polyneuropathy**

072.79 **Other**

072.8 **Mumps with unspecified complication**

---

§　Requires fifth digit. Valid digits are in [brackets] under each code. See category 070 for codes and definitions.

√4ᵗʰ √5ᵗʰ Additional Digit Required	Unspecified Code	Other Specified Code	Manifestation Code	▶◀ Revised Text	● New Code	▲ Revised Code Title

Infectious and Parasitic Diseases

072.9–078.3

072.9 Mumps without mention of complication
Epidemic parotitis
Infectious parotitis

✓4ᵗʰ **073 Ornithosis**

INCLUDES parrot fever
psittacosis

DEF: *Chlamydia psittaci* infection often transmitted from birds to humans.

073.0 With pneumonia
Lobular pneumonitis due to ornithosis

073.7 With other specified complications

073.8 With unspecified complication

073.9 Ornithosis, unspecified

✓4ᵗʰ **074 Specific diseases due to Coxsackie virus**

EXCLUDES *Coxsackie virus:*
infection NOS (079.2)
meningitis (047.0)

074.0 Herpangina
Vesicular pharyngitis

DEF: Acute infectious coxsackie virus infection causing throat lesions, fever, and vomiting; generally affects children in summer.

074.1 Epidemic pleurodynia
Bornholm disease
Devil's grip
Epidemic:
myalgia
myositis

DEF: Paroxysmal pain in chest, accompanied by fever and usually limited to children and young adults; caused by coxsackie virus.

✓5ᵗʰ **074.2 Coxsackie carditis**

074.20 Coxsackie carditis, unspecified

074.21 Coxsackie pericarditis
DEF: Coxsackie infection of the outer lining of the heart.

074.22 Coxsackie endocarditis
DEF: Coxsackie infection within the heart's cavities.

074.23 Coxsackie myocarditis
Aseptic myocarditis of newborn
DEF: Coxsackie infection of the muscle of the heart.

074.3 Hand, foot, and mouth disease
Vesicular stomatitis and exanthem
DEF: Mild coxsackie infection causing lesions on hands, feet and oral mucosa, most commonly seen in preschool children.

074.8 Other specified diseases due to Coxsackie virus
Acute lymphonodular pharyngitis

075 Infectious mononucleosis
Glandular fever
Monocytic angina
Pfeiffer's disease

DEF: Acute infection by Epstein-Barr virus causing fever, sore throat, enlarged lymph glands and spleen, and fatigue; usually seen in teens and young adults.

AHA: 3Q, '01, 13; M-A, '87, 8

✓4ᵗʰ **076 Trachoma**

EXCLUDES *late effect of trachoma (139.1)*

DEF: A chronic infectious disease of the cornea and conjunctiva caused by a strain of the bacteria *Chlamydia trachomatis;* the infection can cause photophobia, pain, excessive tearing and sometimes blindness.

076.0 Initial stage
Trachoma dubium

076.1 Active stage
Granular conjunctivitis (trachomatous)
Trachomatous:
follicular conjunctivitis
pannus

076.9 Trachoma, unspecified
Trachoma NOS

✓4ᵗʰ **077 Other diseases of conjunctiva due to viruses and Chlamydiae**

EXCLUDES *ophthalmic complications of viral diseases classified elsewhere*

077.0 Inclusion conjunctivitis
Paratrachoma
Swimming pool conjunctivitis
EXCLUDES *inclusion blennorrhea (neonatal) (771.6)*
DEF: Pus in conjunctiva caused by *Chlamydiae trachomatis.*

077.1 Epidemic keratoconjunctivitis
Shipyard eye
DEF: Highly contagious corneal or conjunctival infection caused by adenovirus type 8; symptoms include inflammation and corneal infiltrates.

077.2 Pharyngoconjunctival fever
Viral pharyngoconjunctivitis

077.3 Other adenoviral conjunctivitis
Acute adenoviral follicular conjunctivitis

077.4 Epidemic hemorrhagic conjunctivitis
Apollo:
conjunctivitis
disease
Conjunctivitis due to enterovirus type 70
Hemorrhagic conjunctivitis (acute) (epidemic)

077.8 Other viral conjunctivitis
Newcastle conjunctivitis

✓5ᵗʰ **077.9 Unspecified diseases of conjunctiva due to viruses and Chlamydiae**

077.98 Due to Chlamydiae

077.99 Due to viruses
Viral conjunctivitis NOS

✓4ᵗʰ **078 Other diseases due to viruses and Chlamydiae**

EXCLUDES *viral infection NOS (079.0-079.9)*
viremia NOS (790.8)

078.0 Molluscum contagiosum
DEF: Benign poxvirus infection causing small bumps on the skin or conjunctiva; transmitted by close contact.

✓5ᵗʰ **078.1 Viral warts**
Viral warts due to human papilloma virus
DEF: A keratotic papilloma of the epidermis caused by the human papilloma virus; the superficial vegetative lesions last for varying durations and eventually regress spontaneously.
AHA: 2Q, '97, 9; 4Q, '93, 22

078.10 Viral warts, unspecified
Verruca:
Vulgaris
Warts (infectious)

078.11 Condyloma acuminatum
Condyloma NOS
Genital warts NOS
DEF: Clusters of mucosa or epidermal lesions on external genitalia; viral infection is sexually transmitted.

078.12 Plantar wart
Verruca plantaris
AHA: ▶4Q, '08, 78-79◀

078.19 Other specified viral warts
Common wart
Flat wart
Verruca plana

078.2 Sweating fever
Miliary fever
Sweating disease
DEF: A viral infection characterized by profuse sweating; various papular, vesicular and other eruptions cause the blockage of sweat glands.

078.3 Cat-scratch disease
Benign lymphoreticulosis (of inoculation)
Cat-scratch fever

Ⓝ Newborn Age: 0   Ⓟ Pediatric Age: 0-17   Ⓜ Maternity Age: 12-55   Ⓐ Adult Age: 15-124

078.4 Foot and mouth disease
Aphthous fever
Epizootic:
aphthae
stomatitis
DEF: Ulcers on oral mucosa, legs, and feet after exposure to infected animal.

078.5 Cytomegaloviral disease
Cytomegalic inclusion disease
Salivary gland virus disease
Use additional code to identify manifestation, as:
cytomegalic inclusion virus:
hepatitis (573.1)
pneumonia (484.1)
EXCLUDES   congenital cytomegalovirus infection (771.1)
DEF: A herpesvirus associated with serious disease morbidity including fever, leukopenia, pneumonia, retinitis, hepatitis and organ transplant; often leads to hepatomegaly, splenomegaly and thrombocytopenia; a common post-transplant complication.
AHA: 1Q, '03, 10; 3Q, '98, 4; 2Q, '93, 11; 1Q, '89, 9

078.6 Hemorrhagic nephrosonephritis
Hemorrhagic fever:
epidemic
Korean
Russian
with renal syndrome
DEF: Viral infection causing kidney dysfunction and bleeding disorders.

078.7 Arenaviral hemorrhagic fever
Hemorrhagic fever: Hemorrhagic fever:
Argentine   Junin virus
Bolivian   Machupo virus

✓5ᵗʰ 078.8 Other specified diseases due to viruses and Chlamydiae
EXCLUDES   epidemic diarrhea (009.2)
lymphogranuloma venereum (099.1)

078.81 Epidemic vertigo

078.82 Epidemic vomiting syndrome
Winter vomiting disease

078.88 Other specified diseases due to Chlamydiae
AHA: 4Q, '96, 22

078.89 Other specified diseases due to viruses
Epidemic cervical myalgia
Marburg disease

✓4ᵗʰ 079 Viral and chlamydial infection in conditions classified elsewhere and of unspecified site
Note: This category is provided to be used as an additional code to identify the viral agent in diseases classifiable elsewhere. This category will also be used to classify virus infection of unspecified nature or site.

079.0 Adenovirus

079.1 ECHO virus
DEF: An "orphan" enteric RNA virus, certain serotypes of which are associated with human disease, especially aseptic meningitis.

079.2 Coxsackie virus
DEF: A heterogenous group of viruses associated with aseptic meningitis, myocarditis, pericarditis, and acute onset juvenile diabetes.

079.3 Rhinovirus
DEF: Rhinoviruses affect primarily the upper respiratory tract. Over 100 distinct types infect humans.

079.4 Human papillomavirus
DEF: Viral infection caused by the genus *Papillomavirus* causing cutaneous and genital warts, including verruca vulgaris and condyloma acuminatum; certain types are associated with cervical dysplasia, cancer and other genital malignancies.
AHA: 2Q, '97, 9; 4Q, '93, 22
TIP: Do not assign for viral warts; see instead subcategory 078.1.

✓5ᵗʰ 079.5 Retrovirus
EXCLUDES   human immunodeficiency virus, type 1 [HIV-1] (042)
human T-cell lymphotrophic virus, type III [HTLV-III] (042)
lymphadenopathy-associated virus [LAV] (042)
DEF: A large group of RNA viruses that carry reverse transcriptase and include the leukoviruses and lentiviruses.
AHA: 4Q, '93, 22, 23

079.50 Retrovirus, unspecified

079.51 Human T-cell lymphotrophic virus, type I [HTLV-I]

079.52 Human T-cell lymphotrophic virus, type II [HTLV-II]

079.53 Human immunodeficiency virus, type 2 [HIV-2]

079.59 Other specified retrovirus

079.6 Respiratory syncytial virus [RSV]
DEF: The major respiratory pathogen of young children, causing severe bronchitis and bronchopneumonia, and minor infection in adults.
AHA: 4Q, '96, 27, 28

✓5ᵗʰ 079.8 Other specified viral and chlamydial infections
AHA: 1Q, '88, 12

079.81 Hantavirus
DEF: An infection caused by the Muerto Canyon virus whose primary rodent reservoir is the deer mouse Peromyscus maniculatus; commonly characterized by fever, myalgias, headache, cough.
AHA: 4Q, '95, 60

079.82 SARS-associated coronavirus
DEF: A life-threatening respiratory disease, severe acute respiratory syndrome (SARS); etiology coronavirus; presenting symptoms may range from mild to severe forms of flu-like conditions; fever, chills, cough, headache, myalgia; diagnosis of SARS is based upon clinical, laboratory, and epidemiological criteria.
AHA: 4Q, '03, 46

079.83 Parvovirus B19
Human parvovirus
Parvovirus NOS
EXCLUDES   erythema infectiosum [fifth disease] (057.0)
DEF: The only known parvovirus to cause disease in humans; manifestation is erythema infectiosum; also associated with polyarthropathy, chronic anemia, red cell aplasia, and fetal hydrops.
AHA: 4Q, '07, 64

079.88 Other specified chlamydial infection

079.89 Other specified viral infection

✓5ᵗʰ 079.9 Unspecified viral and chlamydial infections
EXCLUDES   viremia NOS (790.8)

079.98 Unspecified chlamydial infection
Chlamydial infections NOS

079.99 Unspecified viral infection
Viral infections NOS
B97.8 Other viral agents cause of dz class   I-10
elsewhere

Infectious and Parasitic Diseases

080–085.0

RICKETTSIOSES AND OTHER ARTHROPOD-BORNE DISEASES (080-088)

> *EXCLUDES* arthropod-borne viral diseases (060.0-066.9)

080 Louse-borne [epidemic] typhus
Typhus (fever):
classical
epidemic
exanthematic NOS
louse-borne
DEF: *Rickettsia prowazekii;* causes severe headache, rash, high fever.

✓4ᵗʰ **081 Other typhus**

081.0 Murine [endemic] typhus
Typhus (fever):
endemic
flea-borne
DEF: Milder typhus caused by *Rickettsia typhi (mooseri);* transmitted by rat flea.

081.1 Brill's disease
Brill-Zinsser disease
Recrudescent typhus (fever)

081.2 Scrub typhus
Japanese river fever
Kedani fever
Mite-borne typhus
Tsutsugamushi
DEF: Typhus caused by *Rickettsia tsutsugamushi* transmitted by chigger.

081.9 Typhus, unspecified
Typhus (fever) NOS

✓4ᵗʰ **082 Tick-borne rickettsioses**

082.0 Spotted fevers
Rocky mountain spotted fever
Sao Paulo fever

082.1 Boutonneuse fever
African tick typhus
India tick typhus
Kenya tick typhus
Marseilles fever
Mediterranean tick fever

082.2 North Asian tick fever
Siberian tick typhus

082.3 Queensland tick typhus

✓5ᵗʰ **082.4 Ehrlichiosis**
AHA: 3Q, '06, 11; 4Q, '00, 38

082.40 Ehrlichiosis, unspecified

082.40 Ehrlichiosis chaffeensis [E. chaffeensis]
DEF: A febrile illness caused by bacterial infection, also called human monocytic ehrlichiosis (HME). Causal organism is *Ehrlichia chaffeensis,* transmitted by the Lone Star tick. Symptoms include fever, chills, myalgia, nausea, vomiting, diarrhea, confusion, and severe headache occurring one week after a tick bite. Clinical findings are lymphadenopathy, rash, thrombocytopenia, leukopenia, and abnormal liver function tests.

082.49 Other ehrlichiosis

082.8 Other specified tick-borne rickettsioses
Lone star fever
AHA: 4Q, '99, 19

082.9 Tick-borne rickettsiosis, unspecified
Tick-borne typhus NOS

✓4ᵗʰ **083 Other rickettsioses**

083.0 Q fever
DEF: Infection of *Coxiella burnettii* usually acquired through airborne organisms.

083.1 Trench fever
Quintan fever
Wolhynian fever

083.2 Rickettsialpox
Vesicular rickettsiosis
DEF: Infection of *Rickettsia akari* usually acquired through a mite bite.

083.8 Other specified rickettsioses

083.9 Rickettsiosis, unspecified

✓4ᵗʰ **084 Malaria**
Note: Subcategories 084.0-084.6 exclude the listed conditions with mention of pernicious complications (084.8-084.9).
> *EXCLUDES* congenital malaria (771.2)

DEF: Mosquito-borne disease causing high fever and prostration and cataloged by species of *Plasmodium: P. falciparum, P. malariae, P. ovale, and P. vivax.*

084.0 Falciparum malaria [malignant tertian]
Malaria (fever):
by Plasmodium falciparum
subtertian

084.1 Vivax malaria [benign tertian]
Malaria (fever) by Plasmodium vivax

084.2 Quartan malaria
Malaria (fever) by Plasmodium malariae
Malariae malaria

084.3 Ovale malaria
Malaria (fever) by Plasmodium ovale

084.4 Other malaria
Monkey malaria

084.5 Mixed malaria
Malaria (fever) by more than one parasite

084.6 Malaria, unspecified
Malaria (fever) NOS

084.7 Induced malaria
Therapeutically induced malaria
> *EXCLUDES* accidental infection from syringe, blood transfusion, etc. (084.0-084.6, above, according to parasite species) transmission from mother to child during delivery (771.2)

084.8 Blackwater fever
Hemoglobinuric:
fever (bilious)
malaria
Malarial hemoglobinuria
DEF: Severe hemic and renal complication of *Plasmodium falciparum* infection.

084.9 Other pernicious complications of malaria
Algid malaria
Cerebral malaria
Use additional code to identify complication, as:
malarial:
hepatitis (573.2)
nephrosis (581.81)

✓4ᵗʰ **085 Leishmaniasis**

085.0 Visceral [kala-azar]
Dumdum fever
Infection by Leishmania:
donovani
infantum
Leishmaniasis:
dermal, post-kala-azar
Mediterranean
visceral (Indian)

Ⓝ Newborn Age: 0   Ⓟ Pediatric Age: 0-17   Ⓜ Maternity Age: 12-55   Ⓐ Adult Age: 15-124

085.1 Cutaneous, urban
Aleppo boil
Baghdad boil
Delhi boil
Infection by Leishmania tropica (minor)
Leishmaniasis, cutaneous:
  dry form
  late
  recurrent
  ulcerating
Oriental sore

085.2 Cutaneous, Asian desert
Infection by Leishmania tropica major
Leishmaniasis, cutaneous:
  acute necrotizing
  rural
  wet form
  zoonotic form

085.3 Cutaneous, Ethiopian
Infection by Leishmania ethiopica
Leishmaniasis, cutaneous:
  diffuse
  lepromatous

085.4 Cutaneous, American
Chiclero ulcer
Infection by Leishmania mexicana
Leishmaniasis tegumentaria diffusa

085.5 Mucocutaneous (American)
Espundia
Infection by Leishmania braziliensis
Uta

085.9 Leishmaniasis, unspecified

✓4th **086 Trypanosomiasis**
Use additional code to identify manifestations, as:
trypanosomiasis:
  encephalitis (323.2)
  meningitis (321.3)

086.0 Chagas' disease with heart involvement
American trypanosomiasis   } with heart
Infection by Trypanosoma cruzi   involvement
Any condition classifiable to 086.2 with heart
  involvement

086.1 Chagas' disease with other organ involvement
American trypanosomiasis   } with involvement of organ
Infection by Trypanosoma   other than heart
cruzi
Any condition classifiable to 086.2 with involvement of
  organ other than heart

086.2 Chagas' disease without mention of organ involvement
American trypanosomiasis
Infection by Trypanosoma cruzi

086.3 Gambian trypanosomiasis
Gambian sleeping sickness
Infection by Trypanosoma gambiense

086.4 Rhodesian trypanosomiasis
Infection by Trypanosoma rhodesiense
Rhodesian sleeping sickness

086.5 African trypanosomiasis, unspecified
Sleeping sickness NOS

086.9 Trypanosomiasis, unspecified

✓4th **087 Relapsing fever**
INCLUDES   recurrent fever
DEF: Infection of *Borrelia;* symptoms are episodic and include fever and
arthralgia.

087.0 Louse-borne

087.1 Tick-borne

087.9 Relapsing fever, unspecified

✓4th **088 Other arthropod-borne diseases**

088.0 Bartonellosis
Carrión's disease   Verruga peruana
Oroya fever

✓5th **088.8 Other specified arthropod-borne diseases**

088.81 Lyme disease
Erythema chronicum migrans
DEF: A recurrent multisystem disorder caused by the
spirochete *Borrelia burgdorferi* with the carrier being
the tick; begins with lesions of erythema chronicum
migrans; it is followed by arthritis of the large joints,
myalgia, malaise, and neurological and cardiac
manifestations.
AHA: 4Q, '91, 15; 3Q, '90, 14; 2Q, '89, 10
TIP: Do not assign if patient has been cured of Lyme
disease but has residual chronic condition; refer
instead to late-effect code 139.8.

088.82 Babesiosis
Babesiasis
DEF: A tick-borne disease caused by infection of
Babesia, characterized by fever, malaise, listlessness,
severe anemia and hemoglobinuria.
AHA: 4Q, '93, 23

088.89 Other

088.9 Arthropod-borne disease, unspecified

SYPHILIS AND OTHER VENEREAL DISEASES (090-099)

EXCLUDES   nonvenereal endemic syphilis (104.0)
urogenital trichomoniasis (131.0)

✓4th **090 Congenital syphilis**
DEF: Infection by spirochete *Treponema pallidum* acquired in utero from
the infected mother.

090.0 Early congenital syphilis, symptomatic
Congenital syphilitic: Congenital syphilitic:
  choroiditis   splenomegaly
  coryza (chronic)   Syphilitic (congenital):
  hepatomegaly   epiphysitis
  mucous patches   osteochondritis
  periostitis   pemphigus
Any congenital syphilitic condition specified as early or
  manifest less than two years after birth

090.1 Early congenital syphilis, latent
Congenital syphilis without clinical manifestations, with
  positive serological reaction and negative spinal
  fluid test, less than two years after birth

090.2 Early congenital syphilis, unspecified
Congenital syphilis NOS, less than two years after birth

090.3 Syphilitic interstitial keratitis
Syphilitic keratitis:
  parenchymatous
  punctata profunda
EXCLUDES   interstitial keratitis NOS (370.50)

✓5th **090.4 Juvenile neurosyphilis**
Use additional code to identify any associated mental
  disorder
DEF: *Treponema pallidum* infection involving the nervous
system.

090.40 Juvenile neurosyphilis, unspecified
Congenital neurosyphilis
Dementia paralytica juvenilis
Juvenile:
  general paresis
  tabes
  taboparesis

090.41 Congenital syphilitic encephalitis
DEF: Congenital *Treponema pallidum* infection
involving the brain.

090.42 Congenital syphilitic meningitis
DEF: Congenital *Treponema pallidum* infection
involving the lining of the brain and/or spinal cord.

090.49 Other

090.5 Other late congenital syphilis, symptomatic
Gumma due to congenital syphilis
Hutchinson's teeth
Syphilitic saddle nose

Any congenital syphilitic condition specified as late or manifest two years or more after birth

090.6 Late congenital syphilis, latent
Congenital syphilis without clinical manifestations, with positive serological reaction and negative spinal fluid test, two years or more after birth

090.7 Late congenital syphilis, unspecified
Congenital syphilis NOS, two years or more after birth

090.9 Congenital syphilis, unspecified

✓4ᵗʰ **091 Early syphilis, symptomatic**
EXCLUDES early cardiovascular syphilis (093.0-093.9)
early neurosyphilis (094.0-094.9)

091.0 Genital syphilis (primary)
Genital chancre
DEF: Genital lesion at the site of initial infection by *Treponema pallidum.*

091.1 Primary anal syphilis
DEF: Anal lesion at the site of initial infection by *Treponema pallidum.*

091.2 Other primary syphilis
Primary syphilis of: Primary syphilis of:
  breast   lip
  fingers   tonsils
DEF: Lesion at the site of initial infection by *Treponema pallidum.*

091.3 Secondary syphilis of skin or mucous membranes
Condyloma latum   Secondary syphilis of:
Secondary syphilis of: skin
  anus   tonsils
  mouth   vulva
  pharynx
DEF: Transitory or chronic lesions following initial syphilis infection.

091.4 Adenopathy due to secondary syphilis
Syphilitic adenopathy (secondary)
Syphilitic lymphadenitis (secondary)

✓5ᵗʰ **091.5 Uveitis due to secondary syphilis**

091.50 Syphilitic uveitis, unspecified

091.51 Syphilitic chorioretinitis (secondary)
DEF: Inflammation of choroid and retina as a secondary infection.

091.52 Syphilitic iridocyclitis (secondary)
DEF: Inflammation of iris and ciliary body as a secondary infection.

✓5ᵗʰ **091.6 Secondary syphilis of viscera and bone**

091.61 Secondary syphilitic periostitis
DEF: Inflammation of outer layers of bone as a secondary infection.

091.62 Secondary syphilitic hepatitis
Secondary syphilis of liver

091.69 Other viscera

091.7 Secondary syphilis, relapse
Secondary syphilis, relapse (treated) (untreated)
DEF: Return of symptoms of syphilis following asymptomatic period.

✓5ᵗʰ **091.8 Other forms of secondary syphilis**

091.81 Acute syphilitic meningitis (secondary)
DEF: Sudden, severe inflammation of the lining of the brain and/or spinal cord as a secondary infection.

091.82 Syphilitic alopecia
DEF: Hair loss following initial syphilis infection.

091.89 Other

091.9 Unspecified secondary syphilis

✓4ᵗʰ **092 Early syphilis, latent**
INCLUDES syphilis (acquired) without clinical manifestations, with positive serological reaction and negative spinal fluid test, less than two years after infection

092.0 Early syphilis, latent, serological relapse after treatment

092.9 Early syphilis, latent, unspecified

✓4ᵗʰ **093 Cardiovascular syphilis**

093.0 Aneurysm of aorta, specified as syphilitic
Dilatation of aorta, specified as syphilitic

093.1 Syphilitic aortitis
DEF: Inflammation of the aorta – the main artery leading from the heart.

✓5ᵗʰ **093.2 Syphilitic endocarditis**
DEF: Inflammation of the tissues lining the cavities of the heart.

093.20 Valve, unspecified
Syphilitic ostial coronary disease

093.21 Mitral valve

093.22 Aortic valve
Syphilitic aortic incompetence or stenosis

093.23 Tricuspid valve

093.24 Pulmonary valve

✓5ᵗʰ **093.8 Other specified cardiovascular syphilis**

093.81 Syphilitic pericarditis
DEF: Inflammation of the outer lining of the heart.

093.82 Syphilitic myocarditis
DEF: Inflammation of the muscle of the heart.

093.89 Other

093.9 Cardiovascular syphilis, unspecified

✓4ᵗʰ **094 Neurosyphilis**
Use additional code to identify any associated mental disorder

094.0 Tabes dorsalis
Locomotor ataxia (progressive)
Posterior spinal sclerosis (syphilitic)
Tabetic neurosyphilis

Use additional code to identify manifestation, as:
neurogenic arthropathy [Charcot's joint disease] (713.5)

DEF: Progressive degeneration of nerves associated with long-term syphilis; causing pain, wasting away, incontinence, and ataxia.

094.1 General paresis
Dementia paralytica
General paralysis (of the insane) (progressive)
Paretic neurosyphilis
Taboparesis

DEF: Degeneration of brain associated with long-term syphilis, causing loss of brain function, progressive dementia, and paralysis.

094.2 Syphilitic meningitis
Meningovascular syphilis
EXCLUDES acute syphilitic meningitis (secondary) (091.81)
DEF: Inflammation of the lining of the brain and/or spinal cord.

094.3 Asymptomatic neurosyphilis

✓5ᵗʰ **094.8 Other specified neurosyphilis**

094.81 Syphilitic encephalitis

094.82 Syphilitic Parkinsonism
DEF: Decreased motor function, tremors, and muscular rigidity.

094.83 Syphilitic disseminated retinochoroiditis
DEF: Inflammation of retina and choroid due to neurosyphilis.

N Newborn Age: 0   P Pediatric Age: 0-17   M Maternity Age: 12-55   A Adult Age: 15-124

094.84 Syphilitic optic atrophy
DEF: Degeneration of the eye and its nerves due to neurosyphilis.

094.85 Syphilitic retrobulbar neuritis
DEF: Inflammation of the posterior optic nerve to neurosyphilis.

094.86 Syphilitic acoustic neuritis
DEF: Inflammation of acoustic nerve due to neurosyphilis.

094.87 Syphilitic ruptured cerebral aneurysm

094.89 Other

094.9 Neurosyphilis, unspecified
Gumma (syphilitic)
Syphilis (early) (late)　　} of central nervous system
Syphiloma　　　　　　　　　　NOS

095 Other forms of late syphilis, with symptoms
INCLUDES　gumma (syphilitic)
syphilis, late, tertiary, or unspecified stage

095.0 Syphilitic episcleritis

095.1 Syphilis of lung

095.2 Syphilitic peritonitis

095.3 Syphilis of liver

095.4 Syphilis of kidney

095.5 Syphilis of bone

095.6 Syphilis of muscle
Syphilitic myositis

095.7 Syphilis of synovium, tendon, and bursa
Syphilitic:
bursitis
synovitis

095.8 Other specified forms of late symptomatic syphilis
EXCLUDES　cardiovascular syphilis (093.0-093.9)
neurosyphilis (094.0-094.9)

095.9 Late symptomatic syphilis, unspecified

096 Late syphilis, latent
Syphilis (acquired) without clinical manifestations, with positive serological reaction and negative spinal fluid test, two years or more after infection

✓4th 097 Other and unspecified syphilis

097.0 Late syphilis, unspecified

097.1 Latent syphilis, unspecified
Positive serological reaction for syphilis

097.9 Syphilis, unspecified
Syphilis (acquired) NOS
EXCLUDES　syphilis NOS causing death under two years of age (090.9)

✓4th 098 Gonococcal infections
DEF: *Neisseria gonorrhoeae* infection generally acquired in utero or in sexual congress.

098.0 Acute, of lower genitourinary tract
Gonococcal:
Bartholinitis (acute)
urethritis (acute)
vulvovaginitis (acute)
Gonorrhea (acute):
NOS
genitourinary (tract) NOS

✓5th 098.1 Acute, of upper genitourinary tract

098.10 Gonococcal infection (acute) of upper genitourinary tract, site unspecified

098.11 Gonococcal cystitis (acute) upper
Gonorrhea (acute) of bladder

098.12 Gonococcal prostatitis (acute)　　♂

098.13 Gonococcal epididymo-orchitis (acute)　　♂
Gonococcal orchitis (acute)
DEF: Acute inflammation of the testes.

098.14 Gonococcal seminal vesiculitis (acute)　　♂
Gonorrhea (acute) of seminal vesicle

098.15 Gonococcal cervicitis (acute)　　♀
Gonorrhea (acute) of cervix

098.16 Gonococcal endometritis (acute)　　♀
Gonorrhea (acute) of uterus

098.17 Gonococcal salpingitis, specified as acute　　♀
DEF: Acute inflammation of the fallopian tubes.

098.19 Other

098.2 Chronic, of lower genitourinary tract
Gonoccocal:
Bartholinitis
urethritis　　　　　} specified as chronic or
vulvovaginitis　　　　with duration of
Gonorrhea:　　　　　　two months or
NOS　　　　　　　　　　more
genitourinary (tract)
Any condition classifiable to 098.0 specified as chronic or with duration of two months or more

✓5th 098.3 Chronic, of upper genitourinary tract
INCLUDES　any condition classifiable to 098.1 stated as chronic or with a duration of two months or more

098.30 Chronic gonococcal infection of upper genitourinary tract, site unspecified

098.31 Gonococcal cystitis, chronic
Gonorrhea of bladder, chronic
Any condition classifiable to 098.11, specified as chronic

098.32 Gonococcal prostatitis, chronic　　♂
Any condition classifiable to 098.12, specified as chronic

098.33 Gonococcal epididymo-orchitis, chronic　　♂
Chronic gonococcal orchitis
Any condition classifiable to 098.13, specified as chronic
DEF: Chronic inflammation of the testes.

098.34 Gonococcal seminal vesiculitis, chronic　　♂
Gonorrhea of seminal vesicle, chronic
Any condition classifiable to 098.14, specified as chronic

098.35 Gonococcal cervicitis, chronic　　♀
Gonorrhea of cervix, chronic
Any condition classifiable to 098.15, specified as chronic

098.36 Gonococcal endometritis, chronic　　♀
Any condition classifiable to 098.16, specified as chronic
DEF: Chronic inflammation of the uterus.

098.37 Gonococcal salpingitis (chronic)　　♀
DEF: Chronic inflammation of the fallopian tubes.

098.39 Other

✓5th 098.4 Gonococcal infection of eye

098.40 Gonococcal conjunctivitis (neonatorum)
Gonococcal ophthalmia (neonatorum)
DEF: Infection of conjunctiva present at birth.

098.41 Gonococcal iridocyclitis
DEF: Inflammation and infection of iris and ciliary body.

098.42 Gonococcal endophthalmia
DEF: Inflammation and infection of contents of eyeball.

098.43 Gonococcal keratitis
DEF: Inflammation and infection of the cornea.

098.49 Other

✓4th					
✓5th Additional Digit Required	Unspecified Code	Other Specified Code	Manifestation Code	▶◀ Revised Text	● New Code	▲ Revised Code Title

✓5th **098.5 Gonococcal infection of joint**

098.50 Gonococcal arthritis
Gonococcal infection of joint NOS

098.51 Gonococcal synovitis and tenosynovitis

098.52 Gonococcal bursitis
DEF: Inflammation of the sac-like cavities in a joint.

098.53 Gonococcal spondylitis

098.59 Other
Gonococcal rheumatism

098.6 Gonococcal infection of pharynx

098.7 Gonococcal infection of anus and rectum
Gonococcal proctitis

✓5th **098.8 Gonococcal infection of other specified sites**

098.81 Gonococcal keratosis (blennorrhagica)
DEF: Pustular skin lesions caused by *Neisseria gonorrhoeae.*

098.82 Gonococcal meningitis
DEF: Inflammation of lining of brain and/or spinal cord.

098.83 Gonococcal pericarditis
DEF: Inflammation of the outer lining of the heart.

098.84 Gonococcal endocarditis
DEF: Inflammation of tissues lining the cavities of heart.

098.85 Other gonococcal heart disease

098.86 Gonococcal peritonitis
DEF: Inflammation of the membrane lining the abdomen.

098.89 Other
Gonococcemia

✓4th **099 Other venereal diseases**

099.0 Chancroid
Bubo (inguinal):
chancroidal
due to Hemophilus ducreyi
Chancre:
Ducrey's
simple
soft
Ulcus molle (cutis)(skin)
DEF: A sexually transmitted disease caused by *Haemophilus ducreyi;* identified by a painful primary ulcer at the site of inoculation (usually external genitalia) with related lymphadenitis.

099.1 Lymphogranuloma venereum
Climatic or tropical bubo
(Durand-) Nicolas-Favre disease
Esthiomene
Lymphogranuloma inguinale
DEF: Sexually transmitted infection of *Chlamydia trachomatis* causing skin lesions.

099.2 Granuloma inguinale
Donovanosis
Granuloma pudendi (ulcerating)
Granuloma venereum
Pudendal ulcer
DEF: Chronic, sexually transmitted infection of *Calymmatobacterium granulomatis* causing progressive, anogenital skin ulcers.

099.3 Reiter's disease
Reiter's syndrome
Use additional code for associated:
arthropathy (711.1)
conjunctivitis (372.33)
DEF: A symptom complex of unknown etiology consisting of urethritis, conjunctivitis, arthritis and myocutaneous lesions. occurs most commonly in young men and patients with HIV. Also a form of reactive arthritis.

✓5th **099.4 Other nongonococcal urethritis [NGU]**

099.40 Unspecified
Nonspecific urethritis

099.41 Chlamydia trachomatis

099.49 Other specified organism

✓5th **099.5 Other venereal diseases due to Chlamydia trachomatis**
EXCLUDES *Chlamydia trachomatis infection of conjunctiva (076.0-076.9, 077.0, 077.9)*
Lymphogranuloma venereum (099.1)
DEF: Venereal diseases caused by *Chlamydia trachomatis* at other sites besides the urethra (e.g., pharynx, anus and rectum, conjunctiva and peritoneum).

099.50 Unspecified site

099.51 Pharynx

099.52 Anus and rectum

099.53 Lower genitourinary sites
Use additional code to specify site of infection, such as:
bladder (595.4)
cervix (616.0)
vagina and vulva (616.11)
EXCLUDES *urethra (099.41)*

099.54 Other genitourinary sites
Use additional code to specify site of infection, such as:
pelvic inflammatory disease NOS (614.9)
testis and epididymis (604.91)

099.55 Unspecified genitourinary site

099.56 Peritoneum
Perihepatitis

099.59 Other specified site

099.8 Other specified venereal diseases

099.9 Venereal disease, unspecified

OTHER SPIROCHETAL DISEASES (100-104)

✓4th **100 Leptospirosis**
DEF: A blood infection of any spirochete of the genus Leptospire; transmitted to humans by exposure to contaminated animal tissues or water. Patients present with flulike symptoms: characteristic muscle aches involving the thighs and low back..

100.0 Leptospirosis icterohemorrhagica
Leptospiral or spirochetal jaundice (hemorrhagic)
Weil's disease

✓5th **100.8 Other specified leptospiral infections**

100.81 Leptospiral meningitis (aseptic)

100.89 Other
Fever:
Fort Bragg
pretibial
swamp
Infection by Leptospira:
australis
bataviae
pyrogenes

100.9 Leptospirosis, unspecified

101 Vincent's angina
Acute necrotizing ulcerative:
gingivitis
stomatitis
Fusospirochetal pharyngitis
Spirochetal stomatitis
Trench mouth
Vincent's:
gingivitis
infection [any site]
DEF: Painful ulceration with edema and hypermic patches of the oropharyngeal and throat membranes; it is caused by spreading of acute ulcerative gingivitis.

N Newborn Age: 0   P Pediatric Age: 0-17   M Maternity Age: 12-55   A Adult Age: 15-124

✓4ᵗʰ **102 Yaws**

> **INCLUDES** frambesia
> pian
>
> **DEF:** An infectious, endemic, tropical disease caused by *Treponema pertenue;* usually affects persons 15 years old or younger; a primary cutaneous lesion develops, then a granulomatous skin eruption, and occasionally lesions that destroy skin and bone.

102.0 Initial lesions
Chancre of yaws
Frambesia, initial or primary
Initial frambesial ulcer
Mother yaw

102.1 Multiple papillomata and wet crab yaws
Butter yaws
Frambesioma
Pianoma
Plantar or palmar papilloma of yaws

102.2 Other early skin lesions
Cutaneous yaws, less than five years after infection
Early yaws (cutaneous) (macular) (papular) (maculopapular) (micropapular)
Frambeside of early yaws

102.3 Hyperkeratosis
Ghoul hand
Hyperkeratosis, palmar or plantar (early) (late) due to yaws
Worm-eaten soles

> **DEF:** Overgrowth of skin of palm of bottoms of feet, due to yaws.

102.4 Gummata and ulcers
Gummatous frambeside
Nodular late yaws (ulcerated)

> **DEF:** Rubbery lesions and areas of dead skin caused by yaws.

102.5 Gangosa
Rhinopharyngitis mutilans

> **DEF:** Massive, mutilating lesions of the nose and oral cavity caused by yaws.

102.6 Bone and joint lesions
Goundou
Gumma, bone } of yaws (late)
Gummatous osteitis or periostitis

Hydrarthrosis
Osteitis } of yaws (early) (late)
Periostitis (hypertrophic)

102.7 Other manifestations
Juxta-articular nodules of yaws
Mucosal yaws

102.8 Latent yaws
Yaws without clinical manifestations, with positive serology

102.9 Yaws, unspecified

✓4ᵗʰ **103 Pinta**

> **DEF:** A chronic form of treponematosis, endemic in areas of tropical America; it is identified by the presence of red, violet, blue, coffee-colored or white spots on the skin.

103.0 Primary lesions
Chancre (primary)
Papule (primary) } of pinta [carate]
Pintid

103.1 Intermediate lesions
Erythematous plaques
Hyperchronic lesions } of pinta [carate]
Hyperkeratosis

103.2 Late lesions
Cardiovascular lesions
Skin lesions:
  achromic
  cicatricial } of pinta [carate]
  dyschromic
Vitiligo

103.3 Mixed lesions
Achromic and hyperchromic skin lesions of pinta [carate]

103.9 Pinta, unspecified

✓4ᵗʰ **104 Other spirochetal infection**

104.0 Nonvenereal endemic syphilis
Bejel
Njovera

> **DEF:** *Treponema pallidum, T. pertenue,* or *T. caroteum* infection transmitted non-sexually, causing lesions on mucosa and skin.

104.8 Other specified spirochetal infections

> **EXCLUDES** relapsing fever (087.0-087.9)
> syphilis (090.0-097.9)

104.9 Spirochetal infection, unspecified

MYCOSES (110-118)

Use additional code to identify manifestation as:
arthropathy (711.6)
meningitis (321.0-321.1)
otitis externa (380.15)

> **EXCLUDES** infection by Actinomycetales, such as species of Actinomyces, Actinomadura, Nocardia, Streptomyces (039.0-039.9)

✓4ᵗʰ **110 Dermatophytosis**

> **INCLUDES** infection by species of Epidermophyton, Microsporum, and Trichophyton
> tinea, any type except those in 111
>
> **DEF:** Superficial infection of the skin caused by a parasitic fungus.

110.0 Of scalp and beard
Kerion
Sycosis, mycotic
Trichophytic tinea [black dot tinea], scalp

110.1 Of nail
Dermatophytic onychia
Onychomycosis
Tinea unguium
  B35.1 Tinea unguium   **I-10**

110.2 Of hand
Tinea manuum

110.3 Of groin and perianal area
Dhobie itch
Eczema marginatum
Tinea cruris

110.4 Of foot
Athlete's foot
Tinea pedis

110.5 Of the body
Herpes circinatus
Tinea imbricata [Tokelau]

110.6 Deep seated dermatophytosis
Granuloma trichophyticum
Majocchi's granuloma

110.8 Of other specified sites

110.9 Of unspecified site
Favus NOS
Microsporic tinea NOS
Ringworm NOS

✓4ᵗʰ **111 Dermatomycosis, other and unspecified**

111.0 Pityriasis versicolor
Infection by Malassezia [Pityrosporum] furfur
Tinea flava
Tinea versicolor

111.1 Tinea nigra
Infection by Cladosporium species
Keratomycosis nigricans
Microsporosis nigra
Pityriasis nigra
Tinea palmaris nigra

✓4ᵗʰ ✓5ᵗʰ **Additional Digit Required**   **Unspecified Code**   **Other Specified Code**   **Manifestation Code**   ▶◀ Revised Text   ● New Code   ▲ Revised Code Title

2010 ICD-9-CM   **Volume 1 – 21**

111.2 Tinea blanca
Infection by Trichosporon (beigelii) cutaneum
White piedra

111.3 Black piedra
Infection by Piedraia hortai

111.8 Other specified dermatomycoses

111.9 Dermatomycosis, unspecified

✓4th **112 Candidiasis**

INCLUDES infection by Candida species
moniliasis

EXCLUDES neonatal monilial infection (771.7)

DEF: Fungal infection caused by *Candida*; usually seen in mucous membranes or skin.

112.0 Of mouth
Thrush (oral)
B37.0 Candidal stomatitis   I-10

112.1 Of vulva and vagina   ♀
Candidal vulvovaginitis
Monilial vulvovaginitis
B37.3 Candidiasis of vulva and vagina   I-10

112.2 Of other urogenital sites
Candidal balanitis
AHA: 4Q, '03, 105; 4Q, '96, 33

112.3 Of skin and nails
Candidal intertrigo
Candidal onychia
Candidal perionyxis [paronychia]
B37.2 Candidiasis of skin and nail   I-10

112.4 Of lung
Candidal pneumonia
AHA: 2Q, '98, 7

112.5 Disseminated
Systemic candidiasis
AHA: 2Q, '00, 5; 2Q, '89, 10

✓5th **112.8 Of other specified sites**

112.81 Candidal endocarditis

112.82 Candidal otitis externa
Otomycosis in moniliasis

112.83 Candidal meningitis

112.84 Candidal esophagitis
AHA: 4Q, '92, 19
B37.81 Candidal esophagitis   I-10

112.85 Candidal enteritis
AHA: 4Q, '92, 19

112.89 Other
AHA: 1Q, '92, 17; 3Q, '91, 20

112.9 Of unspecified site

✓4th **114 Coccidioidomycosis**

INCLUDES infection by Coccidioides (immitis)
Posada-Wernicke disease

DEF: A fungal disease caused by inhalation of dust particles containing arthrospores of *Coccidiodes immitis*; a self-limited respiratory infection; the primary form is known as San Joaquin fever, desert fever or valley fever.

AHA: 4Q, '93, 23

114.0 Primary coccidioidomycosis (pulmonary)
Acute pulmonary coccidioidomycosis
Coccidioidomycotic pneumonitis
Desert rheumatism
Pulmonary coccidioidomycosis
San Joaquin Valley fever

DEF: Acute, self-limiting *Coccidioides immitis* infection of the lung.

B38.0 Acute pulmonary coccidioidomycosis   I-10

114.1 Primary extrapulmonary coccidioidomycosis
Chancriform syndrome
Primary cutaneous coccidioidomycosis

DEF: Acute, self-limiting *Coccidioides immitis* infection in nonpulmonary site.

114.2 Coccidioidal meningitis

DEF: *Coccidioides immitis* infection of the lining of the brain and/or spinal cord.

114.3 Other forms of progressive coccidioidomycosis
Coccidioidal granuloma
Disseminated coccidioidomycosis

114.4 Chronic pulmonary coccidioidomycosis

114.5 Pulmonary coccidioidomycosis, unspecified

114.9 Coccidioidomycosis, unspecified

✓4th **115 Histoplasmosis**

The following fifth-digit subclassification is for use with category 115:
0 **without mention of manifestation**
1 **meningitis**
2 **retinitis**
3 **pericarditis**
4 **endocarditis**
5 **pneumonia**
9 **other**

§ ✓5th **115.0 Infection by Histoplasma capsulatum**
[0-5, 9]   American histoplasmosis
Darling's disease
Reticuloendothelial cytomycosis
Small form histoplasmosis

DEF: Infection resulting from inhalation of fungal spores, causing acute pneumonia, an influenza-like illness, or a disseminated disease of the reticuloendothelial system. In immunocompromised patients it can reactivate, affecting lungs, meninges, heart, peritoneum and adrenals.

§ ✓5th **115.1 Infection by Histoplasma duboisii**
[0-5, 9]   African histoplasmosis
Large form histoplasmosis

§ ✓5th **115.9 Histoplasmosis, unspecified**
[0-5, 9]   Histoplasmosis NOS

✓4th **116 Blastomycotic infection**

116.0 Blastomycosis
Blastomycotic dermatitis
Chicago disease
Cutaneous blastomycosis
Disseminated blastomycosis
Gilchrist's disease
Infection by Blastomyces [Ajellomyces] dermatitidis
North American blastomycosis
Primary pulmonary blastomycosis

116.1 Paracoccidioidomycosis
Brazilian blastomycosis
Infection by Paracoccidioides [Blastomyces] brasiliensis
Lutz-Splendore-Almeida disease
Mucocutaneous-lymphangitic paracoccidioidomycosis
Pulmonary paracoccidioidomycosis
South American blastomycosis
Visceral paracoccidioidomycosis

116.2 Lobomycosis
Infections by Loboa [Blastomyces] loboi
Keloidal blastomycosis
Lobo's disease

✓4th **117 Other mycoses**

117.0 Rhinosporidiosis
Infection by Rhinosporidium seeberi

117.1 Sporotrichosis
Cutaneous sporotrichosis
Disseminated sporotrichosis
Infection by Sporothrix [Sporotrichum] schenckii
Lymphocutaneous sporotrichosis
Pulmonary sporotrichosis
Sporotrichosis of the bones

§ Requires fifth digit. Valid digits are in [brackets] under each code. See category 115 for codes and definitions.

N Newborn Age: 0   P Pediatric Age: 0-17   M Maternity Age: 12-55   A Adult Age: 15-124

117.2 Chromoblastomycosis
Chromomycosis
Infection by Cladosporidium carrionii, Fonsecaea compactum, Fonsecaea pedrosoi, Phialophora verrucosa

117.3 Aspergillosis
Infection by Aspergillus species, mainly A. fumigatus, A. flavus group, A. terreus group
AHA: 4Q, '97, 40

117.4 Mycotic mycetomas
Infection by various genera and species of Ascomycetes and Deuteromycetes, such as Acremonium [Cephalosporium] falciforme, Neotestudina rosatii, Madurella grisea, Madurella mycetomii, Pyrenochaeta romeroi, Zopfia [Leptosphaeria] senegalensis
Madura foot, mycotic
Maduromycosis, mycotic
EXCLUDES actinomycotic mycetomas (039.0-039.9)

117.5 Cryptococcosis
Busse-Buschke's disease
European cryptococcosis
Infection by Cryptococcus neoformans
Pulmonary cryptococcosis
Systemic cryptococcosis
Torula

117.6 Allescheriosis [Petriellidosis]
Infections by Allescheria [Petriellidium] boydii [Monosporium apiospermum]
EXCLUDES mycotic mycetoma (117.4)

117.7 Zygomycosis [Phycomycosis or Mucormycosis]
Infection by species of Absidia, Basidiobolus, Conidiobolus, Cunninghamella, Entomophthora, Mucor, Rhizopus, Saksenaea

117.8 Infection by dematiacious fungi, [Phaehyphomycosis]
Infection by dematiacious fungi, such as Cladosporium trichoides [bantianum], Dreschlera hawaiiensis, Phialophora gougerotii, Phialophora jeanselmi

117.9 Other and unspecified mycoses

118 Opportunistic mycoses
Infection of skin, subcutaneous tissues, and/or organs by a wide variety of fungi generally considered to be pathogenic to compromised hosts only (e.g., infection by species of Alternaria, Dreschlera, Fusarium)
Use additional code to identify manifestation, such as:
keratitis (370.8)

HELMINTHIASES (120-129)

✓4th 120 Schistosomiasis [bilharziasis]
DEF: Infection caused by Schistosoma, a genus of flukes or trematode parasites.

120.0 Schistosoma haematobium
Vesical schistosomiasis NOS

120.1 Schistosoma mansoni
Intestinal schistosomiasis NOS

120.2 Schistosoma japonicum
Asiatic schistosomiasis NOS
Katayama disease or fever

120.3 Cutaneous
Cercarial dermatitis
Infection by cercariae of Schistosoma
Schistosome dermatitis
Swimmers' itch

120.8 Other specified schistosomiasis
Infection by Schistosoma:
bovis
intercalatum
mattheii
spindale
Schistosomiasis chestermani

120.9 Schistosomiasis, unspecified
Blood flukes NOS
Hemic distomiasis

✓4th 121 Other trematode infections

121.0 Opisthorchiasis
Infection by:
cat liver fluke
Opisthorchis (felineus) (tenuicollis) (viverrini)

121.1 Clonorchiasis
Biliary cirrhosis due to clonorchiasis
Chinese liver fluke disease
Hepatic distomiasis due to Clonorchis sinensis
Oriental liver fluke disease

121.2 Paragonimiasis
Infection by Paragonimus
Lung fluke disease (oriental)
Pulmonary distomiasis

121.3 Fascioliasis
Infection by Fasciola:
gigantica
hepatica
Liver flukes NOS
Sheep liver fluke infection

121.4 Fasciolopsiasis
Infection by Fasciolopsis (buski)
Intestinal distomiasis

121.5 Metagonimiasis
Infection by Metagonimus yokogawai

121.6 Heterophyiasis
Infection by:
Heterophyes heterophyes
Stellantchasmus falcatus

121.8 Other specified trematode infections
Infection by:
Dicrocoelium dendriticum
Echinostoma ilocanum
Gastrodiscoides hominis

121.9 Trematode infection, unspecified
Distomiasis NOS
Fluke disease NOS

✓4th 122 Echinococcosis
INCLUDES echinococciasis
hydatid disease
hydatidosis
DEF: Infection caused by larval forms of tapeworms of the genus Echinococcus.

122.0 Echinococcus granulosus infection of liver

122.1 Echinococcus granulosus infection of lung

122.2 Echinococcus granulosus infection of thyroid

122.3 Echinococcus granulosus infection, other

122.4 Echinococcus granulosus infection, unspecified

122.5 Echinococcus multilocularis infection of liver

122.6 Echinococcus multilocularis infection, other

122.7 Echinococcus multilocularis infection, unspecified

122.8 Echinococcosis, unspecified, of liver

122.9 Echinococcosis, other and unspecified

✓4th 123 Other cestode infection

123.0 Taenia solium infection, intestinal form
Pork tapeworm (adult) (infection)

123.1 Cysticercosis
Cysticerciasis
Infection by Cysticercus cellulosae [larval form of Taenia solium]
AHA: 2Q, '97, 8

123.2 Taenia saginata infection
Beef tapeworm (infection)
Infection by Taeniarhynchus saginatus

123.3 Taeniasis, unspecified

Infectious and Parasitic Diseases

123.4–130.2

123.4 Diphyllobothriasis, intestinal
Diphyllobothrium (adult) (latum) (pacificum) infection
Fish tapeworm (infection)

123.5 Sparganosis [larval diphyllobothriasis]
Infection by:
  Diphyllobothrium larvae
  Sparganum (mansoni) (proliferum)
  Spirometra larvae

123.6 Hymenolepiasis
Dwarf tapeworm (infection)
Hymenolepis (diminuta) (nana) infection
Rat tapeworm (infection)

123.8 Other specified cestode infection
Diplogonoporus (grandis) ⎫
Dipylidium (caninum)   ⎬ infection
Dog tapeworm (infection) ⎭

123.9 Cestode infection, unspecified
Tapeworm (infection) NOS

124 Trichinosis
Trichinella spiralis infection
Trichinellosis
Trichiniasis
DEF: Infection by *Trichinella spiralis*, the smallest of the parasitic nematodes.

√4ᵗʰ 125 Filarial infection and dracontiasis

125.0 Bancroftian filariasis
Chyluria   ⎫
Elephantiasis   ⎪
Infection   ⎬ due to Wuchereria bancrofti
Lymphadenitis   ⎪
Lymphangitis   ⎭
Wuchereriasis

125.1 Malayan filariasis
Brugia filariasis ⎫
Chyluria   ⎪
Elephantiasis   ⎬ due to Brugia [Wuchereria]
Infection   ⎪   malayi
Lymphadenitis   ⎪
Lymphangitis   ⎭

125.2 Loiasis
Eyeworm disease of Africa
Loa loa infection

125.3 Onchocerciasis
Onchocerca volvulus infection
Onchocercosis

125.4 Dipetalonemiasis
Infection by:
  Acanthocheilonema perstans
  Dipetalonema perstans

125.5 Mansonella ozzardi infection
Filariasis ozzardi

125.6 Other specified filariasis
Dirofilaria infection
Infection by:
  Acanthocheilonema streptocerca
  Dipetalonema streptocerca

125.7 Dracontiasis
Guinea-worm infection
Infection by Dracunculus medinensis

125.9 Unspecified filariasis

√4ᵗʰ 126 Ancylostomiasis and necatoriasis
INCLUDES cutaneous larva migrans due to Ancylostoma
hookworm (disease) (infection)
uncinariasis

126.0 Ancylostoma duodenale

126.1 Necator americanus

126.2 Ancylostoma braziliense

126.3 Ancylostoma ceylanicum

126.8 Other specified Ancylostoma

126.9 Ancylostomiasis and necatoriasis, unspecified
Creeping eruption NOS
Cutaneous larva migrans NOS

√4ᵗʰ 127 Other intestinal helminthiases

127.0 Ascariasis
Ascaridiasis
Infection by Ascaris lumbricoides
Roundworm infection

127.1 Anisakiasis
Infection by Anisakis larva

127.2 Strongyloidiasis
Infection by Strongyloides stercoralis
EXCLUDES trichostrongyliasis (127.6)

127.3 Trichuriasis
Infection by Trichuris trichiuria
Trichocephaliasis
Whipworm (disease) (infection)

127.4 Enterobiasis
Infection by Enterobius vermicularis
Oxyuriasis
Oxyuris vermicularis infection
Pinworm (disease) (infection)
Threadworm infection

127.5 Capillariasis
Infection by Capillaria philippinensis
EXCLUDES infection by Capillaria hepatica (128.8)

127.6 Trichostrongyliasis
Infection by Trichostrongylus species

127.7 Other specified intestinal helminthiasis
Infection by:
  Oesophagostomum apiostomum and related species
  Ternidens diminutus
  other specified intestinal helminth
Physalopteriasis

127.8 Mixed intestinal helminthiasis
Infection by intestinal helminths classified to more than
  one of the categories 120.0-127.7
Mixed helminthiasis NOS

127.9 Intestinal helminthiasis, unspecified

√4ᵗʰ 128 Other and unspecified helminthiases

128.0 Toxocariasis
Larva migrans visceralis
Toxocara (canis) (cati) infection
Visceral larva migrans syndrome

128.1 Gnathostomiasis
Infection by Gnathostoma spinigerum and related species

128.8 Other specified helminthiasis
Infection by:
  Angiostrongylus cantonensis
  Capillaria hepatica
  other specified helminth

128.9 Helminth infection, unspecified
Helminthiasis NOS
Worms NOS

129 Intestinal parasitism, unspecified

OTHER INFECTIOUS AND PARASITIC DISEASES (130–136)

√4ᵗʰ 130 Toxoplasmosis
INCLUDES infection by toxoplasma gondii
toxoplasmosis (acquired)
EXCLUDES congenital toxoplasmosis (771.2)

130.0 Meningoencephalitis due to toxoplasmosis
Encephalitis due to acquired toxoplasmosis

130.1 Conjunctivitis due to toxoplasmosis

130.2 Chorioretinitis due to toxoplasmosis
Focal retinochoroiditis due to acquired toxoplasmosis

130.3 **Myocarditis due to toxoplasmosis**

130.4 **Pneumonitis due to toxoplasmosis**

130.5 **Hepatitis due to toxoplasmosis**

130.7 **Toxoplasmosis of other specified sites**

130.8 **Multisystemic disseminated toxoplasmosis**
Toxoplasmosis of multiple sites

130.9 **Toxoplasmosis, unspecified**

131 Trichomoniasis

> INCLUDES infection due to Trichomonas (vaginalis)

√5th **131.0 Urogenital trichomoniasis**

131.00 **Urogenital trichomoniasis, unspecified**
Fluor (vaginalis) ⎫ trichomonal or due to
Leukorrhea   ⎬ Trichomonas
(vaginalis) ⎭ (vaginalis)

DEF: *Trichomonas vaginalis* infection of reproductive and urinary organs, transmitted through coitus.

131.01 **Trichomonal vulvovaginitis**   ♀
Vaginitis, trichomonal or due to Trichomonas (vaginalis)

DEF: *Trichomonas vaginalis* infection of vulva and vagina; often asymptomatic, transmitted through coitus.

131.02 **Trichomonal urethritis**
DEF: *Trichomonas vaginalis* infection of the urethra.

131.03 **Trichomonal prostatitis**   ♂
DEF: *Trichomonas vaginalis* infection of the prostate.

131.09 **Other**

131.8 **Other specified sites**
> EXCLUDES intestinal (007.3)

131.9 **Trichomoniasis, unspecified**

√4th **132 Pediculosis and phthirus infestation**

132.0 **Pediculus capitis [head louse]**

132.1 **Pediculus corporis [body louse]**

132.2 **Phthirus pubis [pubic louse]**
Pediculus pubis

132.3 **Mixed infestation**
Infestation classifiable to more than one of the categories 132.0-132.2

132.9 **Pediculosis, unspecified**

√4th **133 Acariasis**

133.0 **Scabies**
Infestation by Sarcoptes scabiei
Norwegian scabies
Sarcoptic itch

133.8 **Other acariasis**
Chiggers
Infestation by:
Demodex folliculorum
Trombicula

133.9 **Acariasis, unspecified**
Infestation by mites NOS

√4th **134 Other infestation**

134.0 **Myiasis**
Infestation by:
Dermatobia (hominis)
fly larvae
Gasterophilus (intestinalis)
maggots
Oestrus ovis

134.1 **Other arthropod infestation**
Infestation by: Jigger disease
chigoe   Scarabiasis
sand flea   Tungiasis
Tunga penetrans

134.2 **Hirudiniasis**
Hirudiniasis (external) (internal)
Leeches (aquatic) (land)

134.8 **Other specified infestations**

134.9 **Infestation, unspecified**
Infestation (skin) NOS   Skin parasites NOS

135 Sarcoidosis
Besnier-Boeck-Schaumann disease
Lupoid (miliary) of Boeck
Lupus pernio (Besnier)
Lymphogranulomatosis, benign (Schaumann's)
Sarcoid (any site):
NOS
Boeck
Darier-Roussy
Uveoparotid fever

DEF: A chronic, granulomatous reticulosis (abnormal increase in cells), affecting any organ or tissue; acute form has high rate of remission; chronic form is progressive.

D86.9 Sarcoidosis unspecified   I-10

√4th **136 Other and unspecified infectious and parasitic diseases**

136.0 **Ainhum**
Dactylolysis spontanea

DEF: A disease affecting the toes, especially the fifth digit, and the fingers, mostly seen in black adult males; characterized by a linear constriction around the affected digit leading to spontaneous amputation of the distal part of the digit.

136.1 **Behçet's syndrome**
DEF: A chronic inflammatory disorder of unknown etiology involving the small blood vessels; characterized by recurrent aphthous ulceration of the oral and pharyngeal mucous membranes and the genitalia, skin lesions, severe uvetis, retinal vascularitis and optic atrophy.

√5th **136.2 Specific infections by free-living amebae**
AHA: ▶4Q, '08, 79-81◀

136.21 **Specific infection due to acanthamoeba**
Use additional code to identify manifestation, such as:
keratitis (370.8)
AHA: ▶4Q, '08, 81◀

136.29 **Other specific infections by free-living amebae**
Meningoencephalitis due to Naegleria

136.3 **Pneumocystosis**
Pneumonia due to Pneumocystis carinii
Pneumonia due to Pneumocystis jiroveci
AHA: 1Q, '05, 7; 1Q, '03, 15; N-D, '87, 5-6
DEF: *Pneumocystis carinii* fungus causing pneumonia in immunocompromised patients; a leading cause of death among AIDS patients.

136.4 **Psorospermiasis**

136.5 **Sarcosporidiosis**
Infection by Sarcocystis lindemanni
DEF: *Sarcocystis* infection causing muscle cysts of intestinal inflammation.

136.8 **Other specified infectious and parasitic diseases**
Candiru infestation

136.9 **Unspecified infectious and parasitic diseases**
Infectious disease NOS
Parasitic disease NOS
AHA: 2Q, '91, 8

LATE EFFECTS OF INFECTIOUS AND PARASITIC DISEASES (137-139)

√4th **137 Late effects of tuberculosis**
Note: This category is to be used to indicate conditions classifiable to 010-018 as the cause of late effects, which are themselves classified elsewhere. The "late effects" include those specified as such, as sequelae, or as due to old or inactive tuberculosis, without evidence of active disease.

137.0 **Late effects of respiratory or unspecified tuberculosis**

√4th Additional Digit Required █ Unspecified Code █ Other Specified Code █ Manifestation Code ▶◀ Revised Text ● New Code ▲ Revised Code Title
√5th

Infectious and Parasitic Diseases

137.1   Late effects of central nervous system tuberculosis

137.2   Late effects of genitourinary tuberculosis

137.3   Late effects of tuberculosis of bones and joints

137.4   Late effects of tuberculosis of other specified organs

138   Late effects of acute poliomyelitis

Note: This category is to be used to indicate conditions classifiable to 045 as the cause of late effects, which are themselves classified elsewhere. The "late effects" include conditions specified as such, or as sequelae, or as due to old or inactive poliomyelitis, without evidence of active disease.

B91 Sequelae of poliomyelitis   I-10

 139   Late effects of other infectious and parasitic diseases

Note: This category is to be used to indicate conditions classifiable to categories 001-009, 020-041, 046-136 as the cause of late effects, which are themselves classified elsewhere. The "late effects" include conditions specified as such; they also include sequela of diseases classifiable to the above categories if there is evidence that the disease itself is no longer present.

139.0   **Late effects of viral encephalitis**
Late effects of conditions classifiable to 049.8-049.9, 062-064

139.1   **Late effects of trachoma**
Late effects of conditions classifiable to 076

139.8   **Late effects of other and unspecified infectious and parasitic diseases**
AHA: 2Q, '06, 17; 4Q, '91, 15; 3Q, '90, 14; M-A, '87, 8

2. NEOPLASMS (140-239)

Notes:

1. Content

This chapter contains the following broad groups:

140-195	Malignant neoplasms, stated or presumed to be primary, of specified sites, except of lymphatic and hematopoietic tissue
196-198	Malignant neoplasms, stated or presumed to be secondary, of specified sites
199	Malignant neoplasms, without specification of site
200-208	Malignant neoplasms, stated or presumed to be primary, of lymphatic and hematopoietic tissue
209	Neuroendocrine tumors
210-229	Benign neoplasms
230-234	Carcinoma in situ
235-238	Neoplasms of uncertain behavior [see Note, above category 235]
239	Neoplasms of unspecified nature

2. Functional activity

All neoplasms are classified in this chapter, whether or not functionally active. An additional code from Chapter 3 may be used to identify such functional activity associated with any neoplasm, e.g.:

catecholamine-producing malignant pheochromocytoma of adrenal:

code 194.0, additional code 255.6

basophil adenoma of pituitary with Cushing's syndrome:

code 227.3, additional code 255.0

3. Morphology [Histology]

For those wishing to identify the histological type of neoplasms, a comprehensive coded nomenclature, which comprises the morphology rubrics of the ICD-Oncology, is given in Appendix A.

4. Malignant neoplasms overlapping site boundaries

Categories 140-195 are for the classification of primary malignant neoplasms according to their point of origin. A malignant neoplasm that overlaps two or more subcategories within a three-digit rubric and whose point of origin cannot be determined should be classified to the subcategory .8 "Other."

For example, "carcinoma involving tip and ventral surface of tongue" should be assigned to 141.8. On the other hand, "carcinoma of tip of tongue, extending to involve the ventral surface" should be coded to 141.2, as the point of origin, the tip, is known. Three subcategories (149.8, 159.8, 165.8) have been provided for malignant neoplasms that overlap the boundaries of three-digit rubrics within certain systems.

Overlapping malignant neoplasms that cannot be classified as indicated above should be assigned to the appropriate subdivision of category 195 (Malignant neoplasm of other and ill-defined sites).

> **DEF:** An abnormal growth; morphology determines behavior, i.e., whether it will remain intact (benign) or spread to adjacent tissue (malignant). The term mass is not synonymous with neoplasm, as it is often used to describe cysts and thickenings such as those occurring with hematoma or infection.
> **AHA:** 2Q, '90, 7

MALIGNANT NEOPLASM OF LIP, ORAL CAVITY, AND PHARYNX (140-149)

EXCLUDES carcinoma in situ (230.0)

✓4ᵗʰ 140 Malignant neoplasm of lip
EXCLUDES skin of lip (173.0)

140.0 Upper lip, vermilion border
Upper lip:
NOS
external
lipstick area

140.1 Lower lip, vermilion border
Lower lip:
NOS
external
lipstick area

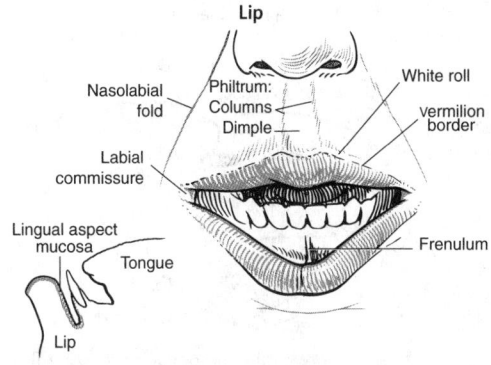

Lip

140.3 Upper lip, inner aspect
Upper lip:
buccal aspect
frenulum
mucosa
oral aspect

140.4 Lower lip, inner aspect
Lower lip:
buccal aspect
frenulum
mucosa
oral aspect

140.5 Lip, unspecified, inner aspect
Lip, not specified whether upper or lower:
buccal aspect
frenulum
mucosa
oral aspect

140.6 Commissure of lip
Labial commissure

140.8 Other sites of lip
Malignant neoplasm of contiguous or overlapping sites of lip whose point of origin cannot be determined

140.9 Lip, unspecified, vermilion border
Lip, not specified as upper or lower:
NOS
external
lipstick area

✓4ᵗʰ 141 Malignant neoplasm of tongue

141.0 Base of tongue
Dorsal surface of base of tongue
Fixed part of tongue NOS
AHA: 4Q, '06, 90

141.1 Dorsal surface of tongue
Anterior two-thirds of tongue, dorsal surface
Dorsal tongue NOS
Midline of tongue
EXCLUDES dorsal surface of base of tongue (141.0)

141.2 Tip and lateral border of tongue

141.3 Ventral surface of tongue
Anterior two-thirds of tongue, ventral surface
Frenulum linguae

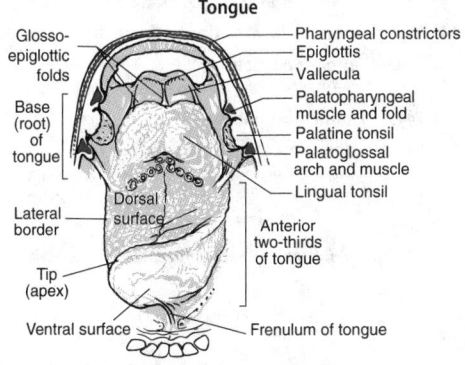

Tongue

✓4ᵗʰ / ✓5ᵗʰ Additional Digit Required   **Unspecified Code**   **Other Specified Code**   **Manifestation Code**   ▶◀ Revised Text   ● New Code   ▲ Revised Code Title

2010 ICD-9-CM   **Volume 1 – 27**

Neoplasms

141.4–146.1

Main Salivary Glands

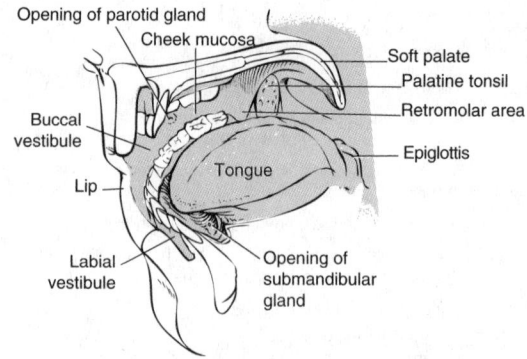

Mouth

141.4 Anterior two-thirds of tongue, part unspecified
Mobile part of tongue NOS

141.5 Junctional zone
Border of tongue at junction of fixed and mobile parts at insertion of anterior tonsillar pillar

141.6 Lingual tonsil

141.8 Other sites of tongue
Malignant neoplasm of contiguous or overlapping sites of tongue whose point of origin cannot be determined

141.9 Tongue, unspecified
Tongue NOS

✓4ᵗʰ **142 Malignant neoplasm of major salivary glands**

INCLUDES salivary ducts

EXCLUDES malignant neoplasm of minor salivary glands:
NOS (145.9)
buccal mucosa (145.0)
soft palate (145.3)
tongue (141.0-141.9)
tonsil, palatine (146.0)

142.0 Parotid gland

142.1 Submandibular gland
Submaxillary gland

142.2 Sublingual gland

142.8 Other major salivary glands
Malignant neoplasm of contiguous or overlapping sites of salivary glands and ducts whose point of origin cannot be determined

142.9 Salivary gland, unspecified
Salivary gland (major) NOS

✓4ᵗʰ **143 Malignant neoplasm of gum**

INCLUDES alveolar (ridge) mucosa
gingiva (alveolar) (marginal)
interdental papillae

EXCLUDES malignant odontogenic neoplasms (170.0-170.1)

143.0 Upper gum

143.1 Lower gum

143.8 Other sites of gum
Malignant neoplasm of contiguous or overlapping sites of gum whose point of origin cannot be determined

143.9 Gum, unspecified

✓4ᵗʰ **144 Malignant neoplasm of floor of mouth**

144.0 Anterior portion
Anterior to the premolar-canine junction

144.1 Lateral portion

144.8 Other sites of floor of mouth
Malignant neoplasm of contiguous or overlapping sites of floor of mouth whose point of origin cannot be determined

144.9 Floor of mouth, part unspecified

Oropharynx

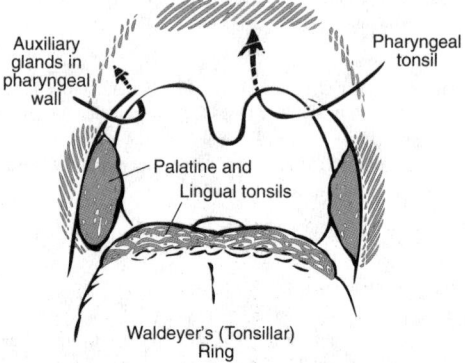

✓4ᵗʰ **145 Malignant neoplasm of other and unspecified parts of mouth**

EXCLUDES mucosa of lips (140.0-140.9)

145.0 Cheek mucosa
Buccal mucosa
Cheek, inner aspect

145.1 Vestibule of mouth
Buccal sulcus (upper) (lower)
Labial sulcus (upper) (lower)

145.2 Hard palate

145.3 Soft palate
EXCLUDES nasopharyngeal [posterior] [superior] surface of soft palate (147.3)

145.4 Uvula

145.5 Palate, unspecified
Junction of hard and soft palate
Roof of mouth

145.6 Retromolar area

145.8 Other specified parts of mouth
Malignant neoplasm of contiguous or overlapping sites of mouth whose point of origin cannot be determined

145.9 Mouth, unspecified
Buccal cavity NOS
Minor salivary gland, unspecified site
Oral cavity NOS

✓4ᵗʰ **146 Malignant neoplasm of oropharynx**

146.0 Tonsil
Tonsil:
NOS
faucial
palatine
EXCLUDES lingual tonsil (141.6)
pharyngeal tonsil (147.1)
AHA: S-O, '87, 8

146.1 Tonsillar fossa

N Newborn Age: 0   P Pediatric Age: 0-17   M Maternity Age: 12-55   A Adult Age: 15-124

Nasopharynx

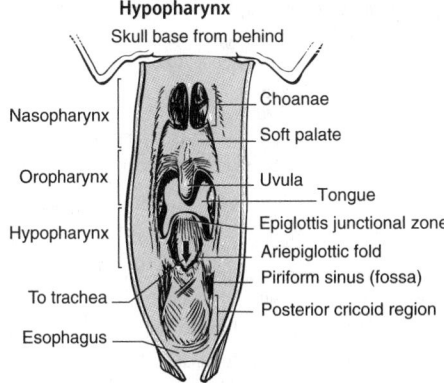

Hypopharynx

146.2   Tonsillar pillars (anterior) (posterior)
Faucial pillar
Glossopalatine fold
Palatoglossal arch
Palatopharyngeal arch

146.3   Vallecula
Anterior and medial surface of the pharyngoepiglottic
fold

146.4   Anterior aspect of epiglottis
Epiglottis, free border [margin]
Glossoepiglottic fold(s)
EXCLUDES   epiglottis:
NOS (161.1)
suprahyoid portion (161.1)

146.5   Junctional region
Junction of the free margin of the epiglottis, the
aryepiglottic fold, and the pharyngoepiglottic fold

146.6   Lateral wall of oropharynx

146.7   Posterior wall of oropharynx

146.8   Other specified sites of oropharynx
Branchial cleft
Malignant neoplasm of contiguous or overlapping sites of
oropharynx whose point of origin cannot be
determined

146.9   Oropharynx, unspecified
AHA: 2Q, '02, 6

✓4ᵗʰ 147   Malignant neoplasm of nasopharynx

147.0   Superior wall
Roof of nasopharynx

147.1   Posterior wall
Adenoid
Pharyngeal tonsil

147.2   Lateral wall
Fossa of Rosenmüller
Opening of auditory tube
Pharyngeal recess

147.3   Anterior wall
Floor of nasopharynx
Nasopharyngeal [posterior] [superior] surface of soft
palate
Posterior margin of nasal septum and choanae

147.8   Other specified sites of nasopharynx
Malignant neoplasm of contiguous or overlapping sites of
nasopharynx whose point of origin cannot be
determined

147.9   Nasopharynx, unspecified
Nasopharyngeal wall NOS

✓4ᵗʰ 148   Malignant neoplasm of hypopharynx

148.0   Postcricoid region

148.1   Pyriform sinus
Pyriform fossa

148.2   Aryepiglottic fold, hypopharyngeal aspect
Aryepiglottic fold or interarytenoid fold:
NOS
marginal zone
EXCLUDES   aryepiglottic fold or interarytenoid fold,
laryngeal aspect (161.1)

148.3   Posterior hypopharyngeal wall

148.8   Other specified sites of hypopharynx
Malignant neoplasm of contiguous or overlapping sites of
hypopharynx whose point of origin cannot be
determined

148.9   Hypopharynx, unspecified
Hypopharyngeal wall NOS
Hypopharynx NOS

**✓4ᵗʰ 149   Malignant neoplasm of other and ill-defined sites within
the lip, oral cavity, and pharynx**

149.0   Pharynx, unspecified

149.1   Waldeyer's ring

149.8   Other
Malignant neoplasms of lip, oral cavity, and pharynx
whose point of origin cannot be assigned to any
one of the categories 140-148
EXCLUDES   "book leaf" neoplasm [ventral surface of
tongue and floor of mouth] (145.8)

149.9   Ill-defined

MALIGNANT NEOPLASM OF DIGESTIVE ORGANS AND PERITONEUM (150-159)
EXCLUDES   carcinoma in situ (230.1-230.9)

✓4ᵗʰ 150   Malignant neoplasm of esophagus

150.0   Cervical esophagus

150.1   Thoracic esophagus

150.2   Abdominal esophagus
EXCLUDES   adenocarcinoma (151.0)
cardio-esophageal junction (151.0)

150.3   Upper third of esophagus
Proximal third of esophagus

150.4   Middle third of esophagus

150.5   Lower third of esophagus
Distal third of esophagus
EXCLUDES   adenocarcinoma (151.0)
cardio-esophageal junction (151.0)

150.8   Other specified part
Malignant neoplasm of contiguous or overlapping sites of
esophagus whose point of origin cannot be
determined

150.9   Esophagus, unspecified

146.2–150.9

✓4ᵗʰ ✓5ᵗʰ Additional Digit Required   **Unspecified Code**   **Other Specified Code**   **Manifestation Code**   ▶◀ Revised Text   ● New Code   ▲ Revised Code Title

2010 ICD-9-CM   **Volume 1 – 29**

Neoplasms

√4ᵗʰ 151 Malignant neoplasm of stomach

> **EXCLUDES** *benign carcinoid tumor of stomach (209.63)*
> *malignant carcinoid tumor of stomach (209.23)*

151.0 Cardia
Cardiac orifice
Cardio-esophageal junction
> **EXCLUDES** *squamous cell carcinoma (150.2, 150.5)*

151.1 Pylorus
Prepylorus
Pyloric canal

151.2 Pyloric antrum
Antrum of stomach NOS

151.3 Fundus of stomach

151.4 Body of stomach

151.5 Lesser curvature, unspecified
Lesser curvature, not classifiable to 151.1-151.4

151.6 Greater curvature, unspecified
Greater curvature, not classifiable to 151.0-151.4

151.8 Other specified sites of stomach
Anterior wall, not classifiable to 151.0-151.4
Posterior wall, not classifiable to 151.0-151.4
Malignant neoplasm of contiguous or overlapping sites of stomach whose point of origin cannot be determined

151.9 Stomach, unspecified
Carcinoma ventriculi
Gastric cancer
AHA: 2Q, '01, 17

√4ᵗʰ 152 Malignant neoplasm of small intestine, including duodenum

> **EXCLUDES** *benign carcinoid tumor of small intestine and duodenum (209.40-209.43)*
> *malignant carcinoid tumor of small intestine and duodenum (209.00-209.03)*

152.0 Duodenum

152.1 Jejunum

152.2 Ileum
> **EXCLUDES** *ileocecal valve (153.4)*

152.3 Meckel's diverticulum

152.8 Other specified sites of small intestine
Duodenojejunal junction
Malignant neoplasm of contiguous or overlapping sites of small intestine whose point of origin cannot be determined

152.9 Small intestine, unspecified

√4ᵗʰ 153 Malignant neoplasm of colon

> **EXCLUDES** *benign carcinoid tumor of colon (209.50-209.56)*
> *malignant carcinoid tumor of colon (209.10-209.16)*

153.0 Hepatic flexure

153.1 Transverse colon

153.2 Descending colon
Left colon

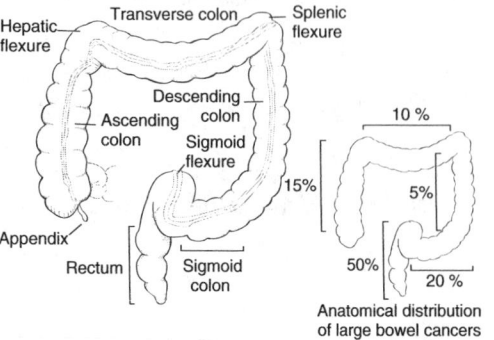

Colon

153.3 Sigmoid colon
Sigmoid (flexure)
> **EXCLUDES** *rectosigmoid junction (154.0)*

153.4 Cecum
Ileocecal valve
C18.0 Malignant neoplasm of cecum   I-10

153.5 Appendix

153.6 Ascending colon
Right colon
C18.2 Malignant neoplasm of ascending colon   I-10

153.7 Splenic flexure

153.8 Other specified sites of large intestine
Malignant neoplasm of contiguous or overlapping sites of colon whose point of origin cannot be determined
> **EXCLUDES** *ileocecal valve (153.4)*
> *rectosigmoid junction (154.0)*

153.9 Colon, unspecified
Large intestine NOS
C18.9 Malignant neoplasm of colon unspecified   I-10

√4ᵗʰ 154 Malignant neoplasm of rectum, rectosigmoid junction, and anus

> **EXCLUDES** *benign carcinoid tumor of rectum (209.57)*
> *malignant carcinoid tumor of rectum (209.17)*

154.0 Rectosigmoid junction
Colon with rectum
Rectosigmoid (colon)

154.1 Rectum
Rectal ampulla
C20 Malignant neoplasm of rectum   I-10

154.2 Anal canal
Anal sphincter
> **EXCLUDES** *skin of anus (172.5, 173.5)*
AHA: 1Q, '01, 8

154.3 Anus, unspecified
> **EXCLUDES** *anus:*
> *margin (172.5, 173.5)*
> *skin (172.5, 173.5)*
> *perianal skin (172.5, 173.5)*

154.8 Other
Anorectum
Cloacogenic zone
Malignant neoplasm of contiguous or overlapping sites of rectum, rectosigmoid junction, and anus whose point of origin cannot be determined

√4ᵗʰ 155 Malignant neoplasm of liver and intrahepatic bile ducts

155.0 Liver, primary
Carcinoma:
hepatocellular
liver cell
liver, specified as primary
Hepatoblastoma
AHA: ▶4Q, '08, 82◀
C22.0 Liver cell carcinoma   I-10

155.1 Intrahepatic bile ducts
Canaliculi biliferi
Interlobular:
bile ducts
biliary canals
Intrahepatic:
biliary passages
canaliculi
gall duct
> **EXCLUDES** *hepatic duct (156.1)*

155.2 Liver, not specified as primary or secondary

N Newborn Age: 0   P Pediatric Age: 0-17   M Maternity Age: 12-55   A Adult Age: 15-124

✓4th 156 Malignant neoplasm of gallbladder and extrahepatic bile ducts

156.0 Gallbladder

156.1 Extrahepatic bile ducts
Biliary duct or passage NOS
Common bile duct
Cystic duct
Hepatic duct
Sphincter of Oddi

156.2 Ampulla of Vater
DEF: Malignant neoplasm in the area of dilation at the juncture of the common bile and pancreatic ducts near the opening into the lumen of the duodenum.

156.8 Other specified sites of gallbladder and extrahepatic bile ducts
Malignant neoplasm of contiguous or overlapping sites of gallbladder and extrahepatic bile ducts whose point of origin cannot be determined

156.9 Biliary tract, part unspecified
Malignant neoplasm involving both intrahepatic and extrahepatic bile ducts

✓4th 157 Malignant neoplasm of pancreas
AHA: 4Q, '07, 72

157.0 Head of pancreas
AHA: 2Q, '05, 9; 4Q, '00, 40

157.1 Body of pancreas

157.2 Tail of pancreas

157.3 Pancreatic duct
Duct of:
Santorini
Wirsung

157.4 Islets of Langerhans
Islets of Langerhans, any part of pancreas
Use additional code to identify any functional activity
DEF: Malignant neoplasm within the structures of the pancreas that produce insulin, somatostatin and glucagon.

157.8 Other specified sites of pancreas
Ectopic pancreatic tissue
Malignant neoplasm of contiguous or overlapping sites of pancreas whose point of origin cannot be determined

157.9 Pancreas, part unspecified
AHA: 4Q, '89, 11
C25.9 Malignant neoplasm of pancreas unspecified   [I-10]

✓4th 158 Malignant neoplasm of retroperitoneum and peritoneum

158.0 Retroperitoneum
Periadrenal tissue
Perinephric tissue
Perirenal tissue
Retrocecal tissue

158.8 Specified parts of peritoneum
Cul-de-sac (of Douglas)
Malignant neoplasm of contiguous or overlapping sites of retroperitoneum and peritoneum whose point of origin cannot be determined
Mesentery
Mesocolon
Omentum
Peritoneum:
parietal
pelvic
Rectouterine pouch

158.9 Peritoneum, unspecified

✓4th 159 Malignant neoplasm of other and ill-defined sites within the digestive organs and peritoneum

159.0 Intestinal tract, part unspecified
Intestine NOS

Retroperitoneum and Peritoneum

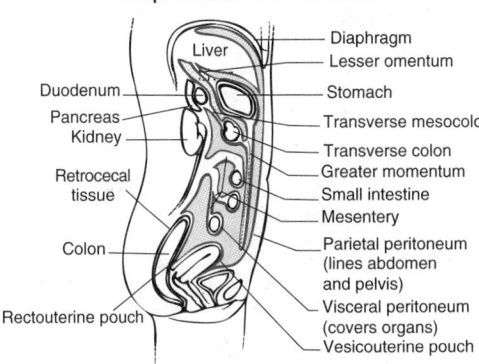

159.1 Spleen, not elsewhere classified
Angiosarcoma } of spleen
Fibrosarcoma }
EXCLUDES *Hodgkin's disease (201.0-201.9)*
lymphosarcoma (200.1)
reticulosarcoma (200.0)

159.8 Other sites of digestive system and intra-abdominal organs
Malignant neoplasm of digestive organs and peritoneum whose point of origin cannot be assigned to any one of the categories 150-158
EXCLUDES *anus and rectum (154.8)*
cardio-esophageal junction (151.0)
colon and rectum (154.0)

159.9 Ill-defined
Alimentary canal or tract NOS
Gastrointestinal tract NOS
EXCLUDES *abdominal NOS (195.2)*
intra-abdominal NOS (195.2)

NEOPLASM OF RESPIRATORY AND INTRATHORACIC ORGANS (160-165)
EXCLUDES *carcinoma in situ (231.0-231.9)*

✓4th 160 Malignant neoplasm of nasal cavities, middle ear, and accessory sinuses

160.0 Nasal cavities
Cartilage of nose   Septum of nose
Conchae, nasal   Vestibule of nose
Internal nose
EXCLUDES *nasal bone (170.0)*
nose NOS (195.0)
olfactory bulb (192.0)
posterior margin of septum and choanae (147.3)
skin of nose (172.3, 173.3)
turbinates (170.0)

160.1 Auditory tube, middle ear, and mastoid air cells
Antrum tympanicum
Eustachian tube
Tympanic cavity
EXCLUDES *auditory canal (external) (172.2, 173.2)*
bone of ear (meatus) (170.0)
cartilage of ear (171.0)
ear (external) (skin) (172.2, 173.2)

160.2 Maxillary sinus
Antrum (Highmore) (maxillary)

160.3 Ethmoidal sinus

160.4 Frontal sinus

160.5 Sphenoidal sinus

160.8 Other
Malignant neoplasm of contiguous or overlapping sites of nasal cavities, middle ear, and accessory sinuses whose point of origin cannot be determined

160.9 Accessory sinus, unspecified

Neoplasms

161–170.2

✓4ᵗʰ **161 Malignant neoplasm of larynx**

161.0 Glottis
Intrinsic larynx
Laryngeal commissure (anterior) (posterior)
True vocal cord
Vocal cord NOS

161.1 Supraglottis
Aryepiglottic fold or interarytenoid fold, laryngeal aspect
Epiglottis (suprahyoid portion) NOS
Extrinsic larynx
False vocal cords
Posterior (laryngeal) surface of epiglottis
Ventricular bands

> **EXCLUDES** *anterior aspect of epiglottis (146.4)*
> *aryepiglottic fold or interarytenoid fold:*
> *NOS (148.2)*
> *hypopharyngeal aspect (148.2)*
> *marginal zone (148.2)*

161.2 Subglottis

161.3 Laryngeal cartilages
Cartilage:
  arytenoid
  cricoid
Cartilage:
  cuneiform
  thyroid

161.8 Other specified sites of larynx
Malignant neoplasm of contiguous or overlapping sites of larynx whose point of origin cannot be determined

AHA: 3Q, '07, 7

161.9 Larynx, unspecified

✓4ᵗʰ **162 Malignant neoplasm of trachea, bronchus, and lung**

> **EXCLUDES** *benign carcinoid tumor of bronchus (209.61)*
> *malignant carcinoid tumor of bronchus (209.21)*

162.0 Trachea
Cartilage
Mucosa
} of trachea

162.2 Main bronchus
Carina
Hilus of lung

162.3 Upper lobe, bronchus or lung

AHA: 1Q, '04, 4

C34.10 Malig neoplasm upper lobe bronchus/lung uns side I-10

162.4 Middle lobe, bronchus or lung

162.5 Lower lobe, bronchus or lung

162.8 Other parts of bronchus or lung
Malignant neoplasm of contiguous or overlapping sites of bronchus or lung whose point of origin cannot be determined

AHA: 3Q, '06, 7

TIP: Assign when two separate tumors classifiable to category 162 are present, overlapping and no point of origin is determined.

162.9 Bronchus and lung, unspecified

AHA: 3Q, '06, 14-15; 2Q, '97, 3; 4Q, '96, 48

C34.90 Malig neoplas bronchus/lung unspec, unspec side I-10

✓4ᵗʰ **163 Malignant neoplasm of pleura**

163.0 Parietal pleura

163.1 Visceral pleura

163.8 Other specified sites of pleura
Malignant neoplasm of contiguous or overlapping sites of pleura whose point of origin cannot be determined

163.9 Pleura, unspecified

✓4ᵗʰ **164 Malignant neoplasm of thymus, heart, and mediastinum**

164.0 Thymus

> **EXCLUDES** *benign carcinoid tumor of the thymus (209.62)*
> *malignant carcinoid tumor of the thymus (209.22)*

164.1 Heart
Endocardium
Epicardium
Myocardium
Pericardium

> **EXCLUDES** *great vessels (171.4)*

164.2 Anterior mediastinum

164.3 Posterior mediastinum

164.8 Other
Malignant neoplasm of contiguous or overlapping sites of thymus, heart, and mediastinum whose point of origin cannot be determined

164.9 Mediastinum, part unspecified

✓4ᵗʰ **165 Malignant neoplasm of other and ill-defined sites within the respiratory system and intrathoracic organs**

165.0 Upper respiratory tract, part unspecified

165.8 Other
Malignant neoplasm of respiratory and intrathoracic organs whose point of origin cannot be assigned to any one of the categories 160-164

165.9 Ill-defined sites within the respiratory system
Respiratory tract NOS

> **EXCLUDES** *intrathoracic NOS (195.1)*
> *thoracic NOS (195.1)*

MALIGNANT NEOPLASM OF BONE, CONNECTIVE TISSUE, SKIN, AND BREAST (170-176)

> **EXCLUDES** *carcinoma in situ:*
> *breast (233.0)*
> *skin (232.0-232.9)*

✓4ᵗʰ **170 Malignant neoplasm of bone and articular cartilage**

> **INCLUDES** cartilage (articular) (joint)
> periosteum

> **EXCLUDES** *bone marrow NOS (202.9)*
> *cartilage:*
> *ear (171.0)*
> *eyelid (171.0)*
> *larynx (161.3)*
> *nose (160.0)*
> *synovia (171.0-171.9)*

AHA: 4Q, '06, 103

TIP: Do not assign for bone metastasis; see instead code 198.5.

170.0 Bones of skull and face, except mandible
Bone:
  ethmoid
  frontal
  malar
  nasal
  occipital
  orbital
  parietal
Bone:
  sphenoid
  temporal
  zygomatic
  Maxilla (superior)
  Turbinate
  Upper jaw bone
  Vomer

> **EXCLUDES** *carcinoma, any type except intraosseous or odontogenic:*
> *maxilla, maxillary (sinus) (160.2)*
> *upper jaw bone (143.0)*
> *jaw bone (lower) (170.1)*

170.1 Mandible
Inferior maxilla
Jaw bone NOS
Lower jaw bone

> **EXCLUDES** *carcinoma, any type except intraosseous or odontogenic:*
> *jaw bone NOS (143.9)*
> *lower (143.1)*
> *upper jaw bone (170.0)*

170.2 Vertebral column, excluding sacrum and coccyx
Spinal column
Spine
Vertebra

> **EXCLUDES** *sacrum and coccyx (170.6)*

N Newborn Age: 0   **P** Pediatric Age: 0-17   **M** Maternity Age: 12-55   **A** Adult Age: 15-124

Skull

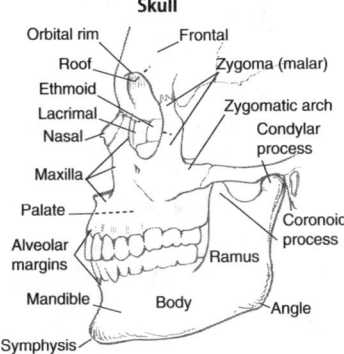

170.3 Ribs, sternum, and clavicle
Costal cartilage
Costovertebral joint
Xiphoid process

170.4 Scapula and long bones of upper limb
Acromion
Bones NOS of upper limb
Humerus
Radius
Ulna
AHA: 2Q, '99, 9

170.5 Short bones of upper limb
Carpal	Scaphoid (of hand)
Cuneiform, wrist	Semilunar or lunate
Metacarpal	Trapezium
Navicular, of hand	Trapezoid
Phalanges of hand	Unciform
Pisiform	

170.6 Pelvic bones, sacrum, and coccyx
Coccygeal vertebra
Ilium
Ischium
Pubic bone
Sacral vertebra

170.7 Long bones of lower limb
Bones NOS of lower limb
Femur
Fibula
Tibia

170.8 Short bones of lower limb
Astragalus [talus]	Navicular (of ankle)
Calcaneus	Patella
Cuboid	Phalanges of foot
Cuneiform, ankle	Tarsal
Metatarsal	

170.9 Bone and articular cartilage, site unspecified

√4th **171 Malignant neoplasm of connective and other soft tissue**

INCLUDES blood vessel
bursa
fascia
fat
ligament, except uterine
muscle
peripheral, sympathetic, and parasympathetic nerves
and ganglia
synovia
tendon (sheath)

EXCLUDES cartilage (of):
articular (170.0-170.9)
larynx (161.3)
nose (160.0)
connective tissue:
breast (174.0-175.9)
internal organs–code to malignant neoplasm of the
site [e.g., leiomyosarcoma of stomach, 151.9]
heart (164.1)
uterine ligament (183.4)

171.0 Head, face, and neck
Cartilage of:
ear
eyelid
AHA: 2Q, '99, 6

171.2 Upper limb, including shoulder
Arm
Finger
Forearm
Hand

171.3 Lower limb, including hip
Foot
Leg
Popliteal space
Thigh
Toe

171.4 Thorax
Axilla
Diaphragm
Great vessels
EXCLUDES heart (164.1)
mediastinum (164.2-164.9)
thymus (164.0)

171.5 Abdomen
Abdominal wall
Hypochondrium
EXCLUDES peritoneum (158.8)
retroperitoneum (158.0)

171.6 Pelvis
Buttock
Groin
Inguinal region
Perineum
EXCLUDES pelvic peritoneum (158.8)
retroperitoneum (158.0)
uterine ligament, any (183.3-183.5)

171.7 Trunk, unspecified
Back NOS
Flank NOS

**171.8 Other specified sites of connective and other soft
tissue**
Malignant neoplasm of contiguous or overlapping sites of
connective tissue whose point of origin cannot be
determined

171.9 Connective and other soft tissue, site unspecified

√4th **172 Malignant melanoma of skin**

INCLUDES melanocarcinoma
melanoma (skin) NOS
melanoma in situ of skin

EXCLUDES skin of genital organs (184.0-184.9, 187.1-187.9)
sites other than skin–code to malignant neoplasm of the
site

DEF: Malignant neoplasm of melanocytes; most common in skin, may
involve oral cavity, esophagus, anal canal, vagina, leptomeninges, or
conjunctiva.

172.0 Lip
EXCLUDES vermilion border of lip (140.0-140.1, 140.9)

172.1 Eyelid, including canthus

172.2 Ear and external auditory canal
Auricle (ear)
Auricular canal, external
External [acoustic] meatus
Pinna

172.3 Other and unspecified parts of face
Cheek (external)
Chin
Eyebrow
Forehead
Nose, external
Temple

172.4 Scalp and neck

√4th √5th **Additional Digit Required**   **Unspecified Code**   **Other Specified Code**   **Manifestation Code**   ▶◄ Revised Text   ● New Code   ▲ Revised Code Title

2010 ICD-9-CM   **Volume 1 – 33**

172.5 Trunk, except scrotum
Axilla	Perianal skin
Breast	Perineum
Buttock	Umbilicus
Groin	

> **EXCLUDES** *anal canal (154.2)*
> *anus NOS (154.3)*
> *scrotum (187.7)*

172.6 Upper limb, including shoulder
Arm	Forearm
Finger	Hand

172.7 Lower limb, including hip
Ankle	Leg
Foot	Popliteal area
Heel	Thigh
Knee	Toe

172.8 Other specified sites of skin
Malignant melanoma of contiguous or overlapping sites of skin whose point of origin cannot be determined

172.9 Melanoma of skin, site unspecified

✓4ᵗʰ **173 Other malignant neoplasm of skin**

> **INCLUDES** malignant neoplasm of:
> sebaceous glands
> sudoriferous, sudoriparous glands
> sweat glands

> **EXCLUDES** *Kaposi's sarcoma (176.0-176.9)*
> *malignant melanoma of skin (172.0-172.9)*
> *skin of genital organs (184.0-184.9, 187.1-187.9)*

AHA: 1Q, '00, 18; 2Q, '96, 12

TIP: Do not assign for malignant neoplasm of skin documented as melanoma; see instead category 172.

173.0 Skin of lip
> **EXCLUDES** *vermilion border of lip (140.0-140.1, 140.9)*

173.1 Eyelid, including canthus
> **EXCLUDES** *cartilage of eyelid (171.0)*

173.2 Skin of ear and external auditory canal
Auricle (ear)
Auricular canal, external
External meatus
Pinna
> **EXCLUDES** *cartilage of ear (171.0)*

173.3 Skin of other and unspecified parts of face
Cheek, external	Forehead
Chin	Nose, external
Eyebrow	Temple

AHA: 1Q, '00, 3

173.4 Scalp and skin of neck

173.5 Skin of trunk, except scrotum
Axillary fold
Perianal skin
Skin of:
  abdominal wall
  anus
  back
  breast
  buttock
  chest wall
  groin
  perineum
Umbilicus
> **EXCLUDES** *anal canal (154.2)*
> *anus NOS (154.3)*
> *skin of scrotum (187.7)*

AHA: 1Q, '01, 8

173.6 Skin of upper limb, including shoulder
Arm	Forearm
Finger	Hand

173.7 Skin of lower limb, including hip
Ankle	Leg
Foot	Popliteal area
Heel	Thigh
Knee	Toe

173.8 Other specified sites of skin
Malignant neoplasm of contiguous or overlapping sites of skin whose point of origin cannot be determined

173.9 Skin, site unspecified

✓4ᵗʰ **174 Malignant neoplasm of female breast**

Use additional code to identify estrogen receptor status (V86.0, V86.1)

> **INCLUDES** breast (female)
> connective tissue
> soft parts
> Paget's disease of:
> breast
> nipple

> **EXCLUDES** *skin of breast (172.5, 173.5)*

AHA: 3Q, '97, 8; 4Q, '89, 11

TIP: For bilateral breast malignancy, do not assign two codes unless documentation indicates separate sites (i.e., different fourth digits).

174.0 Nipple and areola ♀

174.1 Central portion ♀

174.2 Upper-inner quadrant ♀

174.3 Lower-inner quadrant ♀

174.4 Upper-outer quadrant ♀
AHA: ▶4Q, '08, 155;◀ 1Q, '04, 3; 3Q, '97, 8

174.5 Lower-outer quadrant ♀

174.6 Axillary tail ♀

174.8 Other specified sites of female breast ♀
Ectopic sites
Inner breast
Lower breast
Midline of breast
Outer breast
Upper breast
Malignant neoplasm of contiguous or overlapping sites of breast whose point of origin cannot be determined

174.9 Breast (female), unspecified ♀
AHA: 3Q, '05, 11; 2Q, '94, 10; 4Q, '89, 11
C50.911 Malig neoplasm of uns site of rt female breast `I-10`

✓4ᵗʰ **175 Malignant neoplasm of male breast**

Use additional code to identify estrogen receptor status (V86.0, V86.1)

> **EXCLUDES** *skin of breast (172.5, 173.5)*

175.0 Nipple and areola ♂

175.9 Other and unspecified sites of male breast ♂
Ectopic breast tissue, male

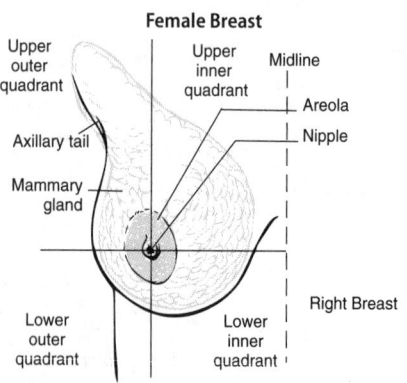

Female Breast

Ⓝ Newborn Age: 0	Ⓟ Pediatric Age: 0-17	Ⓜ Maternity Age: 12-55	Ⓐ Adult Age: 15-124

✓4ᵗʰ **176 Kaposi's sarcoma**
AHA: 4Q, '91, 24

176.0 Skin
AHA: 4Q, '07, 63; 4Q, '94, 29; 4Q, '91, 24

176.1 Soft tissue
Blood vessel	Ligament
Connective tissue	Lymphatic(s) NEC
Fascia	Muscle

EXCLUDES   *lymph glands and nodes (176.5)*

176.2 Palate

176.3 Gastrointestinal sites

176.4 Lung

176.5 Lymph nodes

176.8 Other specified sites
Oral cavity NEC

176.9 Unspecified
Viscera NOS

MALIGNANT NEOPLASM OF GENITOURINARY ORGANS (179-189)

EXCLUDES   *carcinoma in situ (233.1-233.9)*

179 Malignant neoplasm of uterus, part unspecified   ♀

✓4ᵗʰ **180 Malignant neoplasm of cervix uteri**
INCLUDES   invasive malignancy [carcinoma]
EXCLUDES   *carcinoma in situ (233.1)*

180.0 Endocervix   ♀
Cervical canal NOS
Endocervical canal
Endocervical gland

180.1 Exocervix   ♀

180.8 Other specified sites of cervix   ♀
Cervical stump
Squamocolumnar junction of cervix
Malignant neoplasm of contiguous or overlapping sites of cervix uteri whose point of origin cannot be determined

180.9 Cervix uteri, unspecified   ♀

181 Malignant neoplasm of placenta   ♀
Choriocarcinoma NOS
Chorioepithelioma NOS
EXCLUDES   *chorioadenoma (destruens) (236.1)*
hydatidiform mole (630)
malignant (236.1)
invasive mole (236.1)
male choriocarcinoma NOS (186.0-186.9)

✓4ᵗʰ **182 Malignant neoplasm of body of uterus**
EXCLUDES   *carcinoma in situ (233.2)*

182.0 Corpus uteri, except isthmus   ♀
Cornu	Fundus
Endometrium	Myometrium

C54.9 Malignant neoplasm of corpus uteri unspecified   I-10

182.1 Isthmus   ♀
Lower uterine segment

182.8 Other specified sites of body of uterus   ♀
Malignant neoplasm of contiguous or overlapping sites of body of uterus whose point of origin cannot be determined
EXCLUDES   *uterus NOS (179)*

✓4ᵗʰ **183 Malignant neoplasm of ovary and other uterine adnexa**
EXCLUDES   *Douglas' cul-de-sac (158.8)*

183.0 Ovary   ♀
Use additional code to identify any functional activity
AHA: 4Q, '07, 96
C56.9 Malignant neoplasm of ovary unspecified side   I-10

183.2 Fallopian tube   ♀
Oviduct
Uterine tube

183.3 Broad ligament   ♀
Mesovarium
Parovarian region

183.4 Parametrium   ♀
Uterine ligament NOS
Uterosacral ligament

183.5 Round ligament   ♀
AHA: 3Q, '99, 5

183.8 Other specified sites of uterine adnexa   ♀
Tubo-ovarian
Utero-ovarian
Malignant neoplasm of contiguous or overlapping sites of ovary and other uterine adnexa whose point of origin cannot be determined

183.9 Uterine adnexa, unspecified   ♀

✓4ᵗʰ **184 Malignant neoplasm of other and unspecified female genital organs**
EXCLUDES   *carcinoma in situ (233.30-233.39)*

184.0 Vagina   ♀
Gartner's duct
Vaginal vault

184.1 Labia majora   ♀
Greater vestibular [Bartholin's] gland

184.2 Labia minora   ♀

184.3 Clitoris   ♀

184.4 Vulva, unspecified   ♀
External female genitalia NOS
Pudendum

184.8 Other specified sites of female genital organs   ♀
Malignant neoplasm of contiguous or overlapping sites of female genital organs whose point of origin cannot be determined

184.9 Female genital organ, site unspecified   ♀
Female genitourinary tract NOS

185 Malignant neoplasm of prostate   ♂
EXCLUDES   *seminal vesicles (187.8)*
AHA: 3Q, '03, 13; 3Q, '99, 5; 3Q, '92, 7
TIP: Assign as a secondary diagnosis if patient treated for BPH and incidental finding of carcinoma of the prostate is made.
C61 Malignant neoplasm of prostate   I-10

✓4ᵗʰ **186 Malignant neoplasm of testis**
Use additional code to identify any functional activity

186.0 Undescended testis   ♂
Ectopic testis
Retained testis

186.9 Other and unspecified testis   ♂
Testis:
NOS
descended
scrotal

✓4ᵗʰ **187 Malignant neoplasm of penis and other male genital organs**

187.1 Prepuce   ♂
Foreskin

187.2 Glans penis   ♂

187.3 Body of penis   ♂
Corpus cavernosum

187.4 Penis, part unspecified   ♂
Skin of penis NOS

187.5 Epididymis   ♂

187.6 Spermatic cord   ♂
Vas deferens

187.7 Scrotum   ♂
Skin of scrotum

✓4ᵗʰ ✓5ᵗʰ Additional Digit Required   Unspecified Code   Other Specified Code   Manifestation Code   ▶◀ Revised Text   ● New Code   ▲ Revised Code Title

2010 ICD-9-CM   **Volume 1 – 35**

187.8 **Other specified sites of male genital organs** ♂
Seminal vesicle
Tunica vaginalis
Malignant neoplasm of contiguous or overlapping sites of penis and other male genital organs whose point of origin cannot be determined

187.9 **Male genital organ, site unspecified** ♂
Male genital organ or tract NOS

✓4th **188 Malignant neoplasm of bladder**
EXCLUDES carcinoma in situ (233.7)

188.0 **Trigone of urinary bladder**

188.1 **Dome of urinary bladder**

188.2 **Lateral wall of urinary bladder**

188.3 **Anterior wall of urinary bladder**

188.4 **Posterior wall of urinary bladder**

188.5 **Bladder neck**
Internal urethral orifice

188.6 **Ureteric orifice**

188.7 **Urachus**

188.8 **Other specified sites of bladder**
Malignant neoplasm of contiguous or overlapping sites of bladder whose point of origin cannot be determined

188.9 **Bladder, part unspecified**
Bladder wall NOS
AHA: 1Q, '00, 5
C67.9 Malignant neoplasm of bladder unspecified **I-10**

✓4th **189 Malignant neoplasm of kidney and other and unspecified urinary organs**
EXCLUDES benign carcinoid tumor of kidney (209.64)
malignant carcinoid tumor of kidney (209.24)

189.0 **Kidney, except pelvis**
Kidney NOS
Kidney parenchyma
AHA: 2Q, '05, 4; 2Q, '04, 4
C64.9 Malig neoplasm kidney no renal pelvis uns side **I-10**

189.1 **Renal pelvis**
Renal calyces
Ureteropelvic junction

189.2 **Ureter**
EXCLUDES ureteric orifice of bladder (188.6)

189.3 **Urethra**
EXCLUDES urethral orifice of bladder (188.5)

189.4 **Paraurethral glands**

189.8 **Other specified sites of urinary organs**
Malignant neoplasm of contiguous or overlapping sites of kidney and other urinary organs whose point of origin cannot be determined

189.9 **Urinary organ, site unspecified**
Urinary system NOS

MALIGNANT NEOPLASM OF OTHER AND UNSPECIFIED SITES (190-199)
EXCLUDES carcinoma in situ (234.0-234.9)

✓4th **190 Malignant neoplasm of eye**
EXCLUDES carcinoma in situ (234.0)
▶dark area on retina and choroid (239.81)◄
eyelid (skin) (172.1, 173.1)
cartilage (171.0)
optic nerve (192.0)
orbital bone (170.0)
▶retinal freckle (239.81)◄

190.0 **Eyeball, except conjunctiva, cornea, retina, and choroid**
Ciliary body   Sclera
Crystalline lens   Uveal tract
Iris

190.1 **Orbit**
Connective tissue of orbit
Extraocular muscle
Retrobulbar
EXCLUDES bone of orbit (170.0)

190.2 **Lacrimal gland**

190.3 **Conjunctiva**

190.4 **Cornea**

190.5 **Retina**

190.6 **Choroid**

190.7 **Lacrimal duct**
Lacrimal sac
Nasolacrimal duct

190.8 **Other specified sites of eye**
Malignant neoplasm of contiguous or overlapping sites of eye whose point of origin cannot be determined

190.9 **Eye, part unspecified**

✓4th **191 Malignant neoplasm of brain**
EXCLUDES cranial nerves (192.0)
retrobulbar area (190.1)
AHA: 4Q, '07, 104

191.0 **Cerebrum, except lobes and ventricles**
Basal ganglia   Globus pallidus
Cerebral cortex   Hypothalamus
Corpus striatum   Thalamus

191.1 **Frontal lobe**
AHA: 4Q, '05, 118

191.2 **Temporal lobe**
Hippocampus
Uncus
AHA: 4Q, '06, 123

191.3 **Parietal lobe**

191.4 **Occipital lobe**

191.5 **Ventricles**
Choroid plexus
Floor of ventricle

191.6 **Cerebellum NOS**
Cerebellopontine angle

191.7 **Brain stem**
Cerebral peduncle
Medulla oblongata
Midbrain
Pons

191.8 **Other parts of brain**
Corpus callosum
Tapetum
Malignant neoplasm of contiguous or overlapping sites of brain whose point of origin cannot be determined

191.9 **Brain, unspecified**
Cranial fossa NOS

Brain and Meninges

Fourth ventricle
Cerebrum
Corpus callosum
Thalamus
Hypothalamus
Hypophysis
Pons
Cerebellum
Medulla oblongata
Midsagittal Section (between hemispheres)

☑4ᵗʰ **192 Malignant neoplasm of other and unspecified parts of nervous system**

> **EXCLUDES** *peripheral, sympathetic, and parasympathetic nerves and ganglia (171.0-171.9)*

192.0 Cranial nerves
Olfactory bulb

192.1 Cerebral meninges
Dura (mater)   Meninges NOS
Falx (cerebelli) (cerebri)   Tentorium

192.2 Spinal cord
Cauda equina

192.3 Spinal meninges

192.8 Other specified sites of nervous system
Malignant neoplasm of contiguous or overlapping sites of other parts of nervous system whose point of origin cannot be determined

192.9 Nervous system, part unspecified
Nervous system (central) NOS
> **EXCLUDES** *meninges NOS (192.1)*

193 Malignant neoplasm of thyroid gland
Thyroglossal duct
Use additional code to identify any functional activity

C73 Malignant neoplasm of thyroid gland   I-10

☑4ᵗʰ **194 Malignant neoplasm of other endocrine glands and related structures**
> **EXCLUDES** *islets of Langerhans (157.4)*
> *neuroendocrine tumors (209.00-209.69)*
> *ovary (183.0)*
> *testis (186.0-186.9)*
> *thymus (164.0)*

194.0 Adrenal gland
Adrenal cortex   Suprarenal gland
Adrenal medulla

194.1 Parathyroid gland

194.3 Pituitary gland and craniopharyngeal duct
Craniobuccal pouch   Rathke's pouch
Hypophysis   Sella turcica
AHA: J-A, '85, 9

194.4 Pineal gland

194.5 Carotid body

194.6 Aortic body and other paraganglia
Coccygeal body
Glomus jugulare
Para-aortic body

194.8 Other
Pluriglandular involvement NOS
Note: If the sites of multiple involvements are known, they should be coded separately.

194.9 Endocrine gland, site unspecified

☑4ᵗʰ **195 Malignant neoplasm of other and ill-defined sites**
> **INCLUDES** *malignant neoplasms of contiguous sites, not elsewhere classified, whose point of origin cannot be determined*
> **EXCLUDES** *malignant neoplasm:*
> *lymphatic and hematopoietic tissue (200.0-208.9)*
> *secondary sites (196.0-198.8)*
> *unspecified site (199.0-199.1)*

195.0 Head, face, and neck
Cheek NOS   Nose NOS
Jaw NOS   Supraclavicular region NOS
AHA: 4Q, '03, 107

195.1 Thorax
Axilla
Chest (wall) NOS
Intrathoracic NOS

195.2 Abdomen
Intra-abdominal NOS
AHA: 2Q, '97, 3

195.3 Pelvis
Groin
Inguinal region NOS
Presacral region
Sacrococcygeal region
Sites overlapping systems within pelvis, as:
rectovaginal (septum)
rectovesical (septum)

195.4 Upper limb

195.5 Lower limb

195.8 Other specified sites
Back NOS
Flank NOS
Trunk NOS

☑4ᵗʰ **196 Secondary and unspecified malignant neoplasm of lymph nodes**
> **EXCLUDES** *any malignant neoplasm of lymph nodes, specified as primary (200.0-202.9)*
> *Hodgkin's disease (201.0-201.9)*
> *lymphosarcoma (200.1)*
> *other forms of lymphoma (202.0-202.9)*
> *reticulosarcoma (200.0)*
> ▶*secondary neuroendocrine tumor of (distant) lymph nodes (209.71)*◀

AHA: 2Q, '92, 3; M-J, '85, 3

196.0 Lymph nodes of head, face, and neck
Cervical   Scalene
Cervicofacial   Supraclavicular
AHA: 3Q, '07, 7

C77.0 Sec & uns malig neo lymph nodes head face & neck   I-10

196.1 Intrathoracic lymph nodes
Bronchopulmonary   Mediastinal
Intercostal   Tracheobronchial
AHA: 3Q, '06, 7

196.2 Intra-abdominal lymph nodes
Intestinal
Mesenteric
Retroperitoneal
AHA: 4Q, '03, 111

C77.2 Sec & uns malig neoplasm intra-abd lymph nodes   I-10

196.3 Lymph nodes of axilla and upper limb
Brachial   Infraclavicular
Epitrochlear   Pectoral

196.5 Lymph nodes of inguinal region and lower limb
Femoral
Groin
Popliteal
Tibial

196.6 Intrapelvic lymph nodes
Hypogastric   Obturator
Iliac   Parametrial

196.8 Lymph nodes of multiple sites

196.9 Site unspecified
Lymph nodes NOS

Lymph Nodes

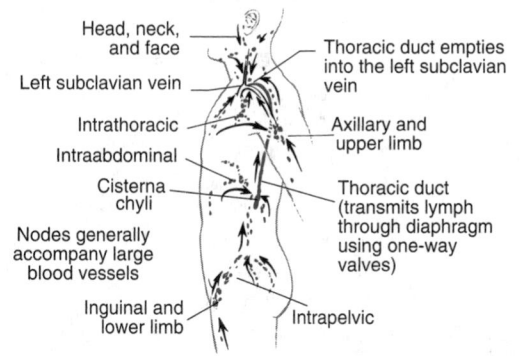

Head, neck, and face
Left subclavian vein
Intrathoracic
Intraabdominal
Cisterna chyli
Nodes generally accompany large blood vessels
Inguinal and lower limb
Thoracic duct empties into the left subclavian vein
Axillary and upper limb
Thoracic duct (transmits lymph through diaphragm using one-way valves)
Intrapelvic

☑4ᵗʰ ☑5ᵗʰ Additional Digit Required   Unspecified Code   Other Specified Code   Manifestation Code   ▶◀ Revised Text   ● New Code   ▲ Revised Code Title

2010 ICD-9-CM   **October 2009 · Volume 1 – 37**

Neoplasms

197–200.0

✓4th **197 Secondary malignant neoplasm of respiratory and digestive systems**

> EXCLUDES   *lymph node metastasis (196.0-196.9)*
> ▶*secondary neuroendocrine tumor of liver (209.72)*
> *secondary neuroendocrine tumor of respiratory organs (209.79)*◀
>
> AHA: M-J, '85, 3

197.0 Lung
Bronchus
AHA: 1Q, '06, 4; 2Q, '99, 9
C78.00 Secondary malig neoplasm of lung unspec side I-10

197.1 Mediastinum
AHA: 3Q, '06, 7

197.2 Pleura
AHA: 1Q, '08, 16; 3Q, '07, 3; 4Q, '03, 110; 4Q, '89, 11
TIP: Do not assign for malignant pleural effusion; see instead code 511.81.
C78.2 Secondary malignant neoplasm of pleura I-10

197.3 Other respiratory organs
Trachea

197.4 Small intestine, including duodenum

197.5 Large intestine and rectum

197.6 Retroperitoneum and peritoneum
AHA: 2Q, '04, 4; 4Q, '89, 11
C78.6 Sec malignant neoplasm of retroperiton & periton I-10

197.7 Liver, specified as secondary
AHA: 1Q, '06, 4; 2Q, '05, 9
C78.7 Secondary malignant neoplasm of liver I-10

197.8 Other digestive organs and spleen
AHA: 2Q, '97, 3; 2Q, '92, 3

✓4th **198 Secondary malignant neoplasm of other specified sites**

> EXCLUDES   *lymph node metastasis (196.0-196.9)*
> ▶*secondary neuroendocrine tumor of other specified sites (209.79)*◀
>
> AHA: M-J, '85, 3

198.0 Kidney

198.1 Other urinary organs

198.2 Skin
Skin of breast

198.3 Brain and spinal cord
AHA: 3Q, '07, 4; 3Q, '99, 7
C79.31 Secondary malignant neoplasm of brain I-10

198.4 Other parts of nervous system
Meninges (cerebral) (spinal)
AHA: J-F, '87, 7

198.5 Bone and bone marrow
AHA: 1Q, '07, 6; 4Q, '03, 110; 3Q, '99, 5; 2Q, '92, 3; 1Q, '91, 16; 4Q, '89, 10
C79.51 Secondary malignant neoplasm of bone I-10

198.6 Ovary ♀

198.7 Adrenal gland
Suprarenal gland
C79.70 Sec malignant neoplasm of adrenal gland uns side I-10

✓5th **198.8 Other specified sites**

198.81 Breast
> EXCLUDES   *skin of breast (198.2)*

198.82 Genital organs

198.89 Other
> EXCLUDES   *retroperitoneal lymph nodes (196.2)*
> AHA: 2Q, '05, 4; 2Q, '97, 4
> TIP: Assign for intra-abdominal metastasis when no further specificity of site is documented.
> **C79.89** Secondary malignant neoplasm of other I-10 spec sites

✓4th **199 Malignant neoplasm without specification of site**

> EXCLUDES   *malignant carcinoid tumor of unknown primary site (209.20)*
> ▶*malignant (poorly differentiated) neuroendocrine carcinoma, any site (209.30)*◀
> *malignant* ▶*(poorly differentiated)*◀ *neuroendocrine tumor, any site (209.30)*
> *neuroendocrine carcinoma* ▶*(high grade),*◀ *any site (209.30)*

199.0 Disseminated
Carcinomatosis
Generalized: ⎫
cancer ⎪ unspecified site (primary)
malignancy ⎬ (secondary)
Multiple cancer ⎭
AHA: 4Q, '89, 10

199.1 Other
Cancer ⎫
Carcinoma ⎬ unspecified site (primary)
Malignancy ⎭ (secondary)
AHA: 3Q, '06, 14-15; 1Q, '06, 4
TIP: Assign if patient is assessed for a metastatic tumor but primary site is unknown.
C80.1 Malignant neoplasm unspecified I-10

199.2 Malignant neoplasm associated with transplanted organ
Code first complication of transplanted organ (996.80-996.89)
▶Use additional code for specific malignancy◀
AHA: 4Q, '08, 82-83
TIP: Assign first the appropriate code from subcategory 996.8, Complications of transplanted organ; use additional code for the specific malignancy.

MALIGNANT NEOPLASM OF LYMPHATIC AND HEMATOPOIETIC TISSUE (200-208)

> EXCLUDES   ▶*autoimmune lymphoproliferative syndrome (279.41)*◀
> *secondary neoplasm of:*
> *bone marrow (198.5)*
> *spleen (197.8)*
> *secondary and unspecified neoplasm of lymph nodes (196.0-196.9)*

The following fifth-digit subclassification is for use with categories 200-202:

0 unspecified site, extranodal and solid organ sites
1 lymph nodes of head, face, and neck
2 intrathoracic lymph nodes
3 intra-abdominal lymph nodes
4 lymph nodes of axilla and upper limb
5 lymph nodes of inguinal region and lower limb
6 intrapelvic lymph nodes
7 spleen
8 lymph nodes of multiple sites

✓4th **200 Lymphosarcoma and reticulosarcoma and other specified malignant tumors of lymphatic tissue**
AHA: 4Q, '07, 65; 2Q, '92, 3; N-D, '86, 5

§ ✓5th **200.0 Reticulosarcoma**
[0-8]   Lymphoma (malignant):
histiocytic (diffuse):
nodular
pleomorphic cell type
reticulum cell type
Reticulum cell sarcoma:
NOS
pleomorphic cell type
DEF: Malignant lymphoma of primarily histolytic cells; commonly originates in reticuloendothelium of lymph nodes.
AHA: For Code 200.03: 3Q, '01, 12

§ Requires fifth digit. Valid digits are in [brackets] under each code. See beginning of section 200-208 for codes and definitions.

N Newborn Age: 0   P Pediatric Age: 0-17   M Maternity Age: 12-55   A Adult Age: 15-124

§ ✓5th **200.1 Lymphosarcoma**
[0-8]　　Lymphoblastoma (diffuse)　Lymphosarcoma:
　　　　Lymphoma (malignant):　　　　NOS
　　　　　lymphoblastic (diffuse)　　diffuse NOS
　　　　　lymphocytic (cell type)　　lymphoblastic (diffuse)
　　　　　　(diffuse)　　　　　　　lymphocytic (diffuse)
　　　　　lymphosarcoma type　　　prolymphocytic

　　　　EXCLUDES　*lymphosarcoma:*
　　　　　　　　　　　follicular or nodular (202.0)
　　　　　　　　　　　mixed cell type (200.8)
　　　　　　　　　lymphosarcoma cell leukemia (207.8)

　　　　DEF: Malignant lymphoma created from anaplastic lymphoid
　　　　cells resembling lymphocytes or lymphoblasts.

§ ✓5th **200.2 Burkitt's tumor or lymphoma**
[0-8]　　Malignant lymphoma, Burkitt's type

　　　　DEF: Large osteolytic lesion most common in jaw or as
　　　　abdominal mass; usually found in central Africa but reported
　　　　elsewhere.

§ ✓5th **200.3 Marginal zone lymphoma**
[0-8]　　Extranodal marginal zone B-cell lymphoma
　　　　Mucosa associated lymphoid tissue [MALT]
　　　　Nodal marginal zone B-cell lymphoma
　　　　Splenic marginal zone B-cell lymphoma
　　　　AHA: 4Q, '07, 65

§ ✓5th **200.4 Mantle cell lymphoma**
[0-8]　　**AHA:** 4Q, '07, 65

§ ✓5th **200.5 Primary central nervous system lymphoma**
[0-8]　　**AHA:** 4Q, '07, 66

§ ✓5th **200.6 Anaplastic large cell lymphoma**
[0-8]　　**AHA:** 4Q, '07, 66

§ ✓5th **200.7 Large cell lymphoma**
[0-8]　　**AHA:** 4Q, '07, 66

§ ✓5th **200.8 Other named variants**
[0-8]　　Lymphoma (malignant):
　　　　　lymphoplasmacytoid type
　　　　　mixed lymphocytic-histiocytic (diffuse)
　　　　Lymphosarcoma, mixed cell type (diffuse)
　　　　Reticulolymphosarcoma (diffuse)

✓4th **201 Hodgkin's disease**
　　　　DEF: Painless, progressive enlargement of lymph nodes, spleen and
　　　　general lymph tissue; symptoms include anorexia, lassitude, weight
　　　　loss, fever, pruritis, night sweats, anemia.
　　　　AHA: 2Q, '92, 3; N-D, '86, 5

§ ✓5th **201.0 Hodgkin's paragranuloma**
[0-8]

§ ✓5th **201.1 Hodgkin's granuloma**
[0-8]　　**AHA:** 2Q, '99, 7

§ ✓5th **201.2 Hodgkin's sarcoma**
[0-8]

§ ✓5th **201.4 Lymphocytic-histiocytic predominance**
[0-8]

§ ✓5th **201.5 Nodular sclerosis**
[0-8]　　Hodgkin's disease, nodular sclerosis:
　　　　　NOS
　　　　　cellular phase

§ ✓5th **201.6 Mixed cellularity**
[0-8]

§ ✓5th **201.7 Lymphocytic depletion**
[0-8]　　Hodgkin's disease, lymphocytic depletion:
　　　　　NOS
　　　　　diffuse fibrosis
　　　　　reticular type

§ ✓5th **201.9 Hodgkin's disease, unspecified**
[0-8]　　Hodgkin's:　　　　　Malignant:
　　　　　disease NOS　　　　lymphogranuloma
　　　　　lymphoma NOS　　　lymphogranulomatosis

✓4th **202 Other malignant neoplasms of lymphoid and histiocytic
tissue**
　　　　AHA: 2Q, '92, 3; N-D, '86, 5

§ ✓5th **202.0 Nodular lymphoma**
[0-8]　　Brill-Symmers disease
　　　　Lymphoma:
　　　　　follicular (giant) ▶(large cell)◀
　　　　　lymphocytic, nodular
　　　　Lymphosarcoma:
　　　　　follicular (giant)
　　　　　nodular

　　　　DEF: Lymphomatous cells clustered into nodules within the
　　　　lymph node; usually occurs in older adults and may involve all
　　　　nodes and possibly extranodal sites.

§ ✓5th **202.1 Mycosis fungoides**
[0-8]　　**EXCLUDES** ▶*peripheral T-cell lymphoma (202.7)*◀

　　　　DEF: Type of cutaneous T-cell lymphoma; may evolve into
　　　　generalized lymphoma; formerly thought to be of fungoid
　　　　origin.
　　　　AHA: 2Q, '92, 4

§ ✓5th **202.2 Sézary's disease**
[0-8]　　**DEF:** Type of cutaneous T-cell lymphoma with erythroderma,
　　　　intense pruritus, peripheral lymphadenopathy, abnormal
　　　　hyperchromatic mononuclear cells in skin, lymph nodes and
　　　　peripheral blood.
　　　　AHA: 2Q, '99, 7

§ ✓5th **202.3 Malignant histiocytosis**
[0-8]　　Histiocytic medullary reticulosis
　　　　Malignant:
　　　　　reticuloendotheliosis
　　　　　reticulosis

§ ✓5th **202.4 Leukemic reticuloendotheliosis**
[0-8]　　Hairy-cell leukemia

　　　　DEF: Chronic leukemia with large, mononuclear cells with
　　　　"hairy" appearance in marrow, spleen, liver, blood.

§ ✓5th **202.5 Letterer-Siwe disease**
[0-8]　　Acute:
　　　　　differentiated progressive histiocytosis
　　　　　histiocytosis X (progressive)
　　　　　infantile reticuloendotheliosis
　　　　　reticulosis of infancy

　　　　EXCLUDES　*Hand-Schüller-Christian disease (277.89)*
　　　　　　　　　　histiocytosis (acute) (chronic) (277.89)
　　　　　　　　　　histiocytosis X (chronic) (277.89)

　　　　DEF: A recessive reticuloendotheliosis of early childhood, with
　　　　a hemorrhagic tendency, eczema-like skin eruption,
　　　　hepatosplenomegaly, lymph node enlargement, and
　　　　progressive anemia; often a fatal disease with no established
　　　　cause.

§ ✓5th **202.6 Malignant mast cell tumors**
[0-8]　　Malignant:　　　　　Mast cell sarcoma
　　　　　mastocytoma　　　Systemic tissue mast
　　　　　mastocytosis　　　　cell disease

　　　　EXCLUDES　*mast cell leukemia (207.8)*

§ ✓5th **202.7 Peripheral T-cell lymphoma**
[0-8]　　**AHA:** 4Q, '07, 66

§ ✓5th **202.8 Other lymphomas**
[0-8]　　Lymphoma (malignant):
　　　　　NOS
　　　　　diffuse

　　　　EXCLUDES　*benign lymphoma (229.0)*

　　　　AHA: 4Q, '06, 135; 2Q, '06, 20-21; 2Q, '92, 4; **For code 202.80:**
　　　　4Q, '08, 83; 1Q, '08, 16; 3Q, '07, 3

　　　　C85.70 Oth spec types non-Hodgkins lymphoma unspec I-10
　　　　site

§ ✓5th **202.9 Other and unspecified malignant neoplasms of
lymphoid and histiocytic tissue**
[0-8]　　Follicular dendritic cell sarcoma
　　　　Interdigitating dendritic cell sarcoma
　　　　Langerhans cell sarcoma
　　　　Malignant neoplasm of bone marrow NOS

§　Requires fifth digit. Valid digits are in [brackets] under each code. See beginning of section 200-208 for codes and definitions.

✓4ᵗʰ **203 Multiple myeloma and immunoproliferative neoplasms**
  AHA: ▶4Q, '08, 83-84;◀4Q, '91, 26

  The following fifth-digit subclassification is for use with category 203:
    0 without mention of having achieved remission
      Failed remission
    1 in remission
    2 in relapse

§ ✓5ᵗʰ **203.0 Multiple myeloma**
  [0-2]   Kahler's disease   Myelomatosis
    EXCLUDES solitary myeloma (238.6)
    AHA: 1Q, '96, 16; 4Q, '89, 10; For code 203.00: 2Q, '07, 8
    For code 203.01: ▶4Q, '08, 91◀
    C90.00 Multiple myeloma not in remission   I-10

§ ✓5ᵗʰ **203.1 Plasma cell leukemia**
  [0-2]   Plasmacytic leukemia
    AHA: 4Q, '91, 26; S-O, '86, 12

§ ✓5ᵗʰ **203.8 Other immunoproliferative neoplasms**
  [0-2]   AHA: 4Q, '90, 26; S-O, '86, 12

✓4ᵗʰ **204 Lymphoid leukemia**
  INCLUDES leukemia:
      lymphatic
      lymphoblastic
      lymphocytic
      lymphogenous
  AHA: ▶4Q, '08, 83-84;◀ 3Q, '93, 4

  The following fifth-digit subclassification is for use with category 204:
    0 without mention of having achieved remission
      Failed remission
    1 in remission
    2 in relapse

§ ✓5ᵗʰ **204.0 Acute**
  [0-2]   **EXCLUDES** acute exacerbation of chronic lymphoid
          leukemia (204.1)
    AHA: 3Q, '99, 6

§ ✓5ᵗʰ **204.1 Chronic**
  [0-2]   C91.10 Chronic lymphocytic leukemia not in remission   I-10

§ ✓5ᵗʰ **204.2 Subacute**
  [0-2]

§ ✓5ᵗʰ **204.8 Other lymphoid leukemia**
  [0-2]   Aleukemic leukemia: Aleukemic leukemia:
      lymphatic   lymphoid
      lymphocytic

§ ✓5ᵗʰ **204.9 Unspecified lymphoid leukemia**
  [0-2]

✓4ᵗʰ **205 Myeloid leukemia**
  INCLUDES leukemia:
      granulocytic
      myeloblastic
      myelocytic
      myelogenous
      myelomonocytic
      myelosclerotic
      myelosis
  AHA: ▶4Q, '08, 83-84;◀ 3Q, '93, 3; 4Q, '91, 26; 4Q, '90, 3; M-J, '85, 18

  The following fifth-digit subclassification is for use with category 205:
    0 without mention of having achieved remission
      Failed remission
    1 in remission
    2 in relapse

§ ✓5ᵗʰ **205.0 Acute**
  [0-2]   Acute promyelocytic leukemia
    EXCLUDES acute exacerbation of chronic myeloid
          leukemia (205.1)
    AHA: 2Q, '06, 20-21
    C92.00 Acute myeloid leukemia not in remission   I-10

§ ✓5ᵗʰ **205.1 Chronic**
  [0-2]   Eosinophilic leukemia
      Neutrophilic leukemia
    AHA: 1Q, '00, 6; J-A, '85, 13 ; For code 205.10: ▶4Q, '08, 142◀

§ ✓5ᵗʰ **205.2 Subacute**
  [0-2]

§ ✓5ᵗʰ **205.3 Myeloid sarcoma**
  [0-2]   Chloroma
      Granulocytic sarcoma

§ ✓5ᵗʰ **205.8 Other myeloid leukemia**
  [0-2]   Aleukemic leukemia: Aleukemic leukemia:
      granulocytic   myeloid
      myelogenous   Aleukemic myelosis

§ ✓5ᵗʰ **205.9 Unspecified myeloid leukemia**
  [0-2]

✓4ᵗʰ **206 Monocytic leukemia**
  INCLUDES leukemia:
      histiocytic
      monoblastic
      monocytoid
  AHA: ▶4Q, '08, 83-84◀

  The following fifth-digit subclassification is for use with category 206:
    0 without mention of having achieved remission
      Failed remission
    1 in remission
    2 in relapse

§ ✓5ᵗʰ **206.0 Acute**
  [0-2]   **EXCLUDES** acute exacerbation of chronic monocytic
          leukemia (206.1)

§ ✓5ᵗʰ **206.1 Chronic**
  [0-2]

§ ✓5ᵗʰ **206.2 Subacute**
  [0-2]

§ ✓5ᵗʰ **206.8 Other monocytic leukemia**
  [0-2]   Aleukemic:
        monocytic leukemia
        monocytoid leukemia

§ ✓5ᵗʰ **206.9 Unspecified monocytic leukemia**
  [0-2]

✓4ᵗʰ **207 Other specified leukemia**
  EXCLUDES leukemic reticuloendotheliosis (202.4)
        plasma cell leukemia (203.1)
  AHA: ▶4Q, '08, 83-85◀

  The following fifth-digit subclassification is for use with category 207:
    0 without mention of having achieved remission
      Failed remission
    1 in remission
    2 in relapse

§ ✓5ᵗʰ **207.0 Acute erythremia and erythroleukemia**
  [0-2]   Acute erythremic myelosis
      Di Guglielmo's disease
      Erythremic myelosis
    DEF: Erythremia: polycythemia vera.
    DEF: Erythroleukemia: a malignant blood dyscrasia (a
      myeloproliferative disorder).

§ ✓5ᵗʰ **207.1 Chronic erythremia**
  [0-2]   Heilmeyer-Schöner disease

§ ✓5ᵗʰ **207.2 Megakaryocytic leukemia**
  [0-2]   Megakaryocytic myelosis
      Thrombocytic leukemia

§ ✓5ᵗʰ **207.8 Other specified leukemia**
  [0-2]   Lymphosarcoma cell leukemia

---

§   Requires fifth digit. Valid digits are in [brackets] under each code. See appropriate category for codes and definitions.

N Newborn Age: 0   P Pediatric Age: 0-17   M Maternity Age: 12-55   A Adult Age: 15-124

√4ᵗʰ **208 Leukemia of unspecified cell type**

> AHA: 4Q, '08, 83-85

> The following fifth-digit subclassification is for use with category 208:
> 0 **without mention of having achieved remission**
>   Failed remission
> 1 **in remission**
> 2 **in relapse**

§ √5ᵗʰ **208.0 Acute**
[0-2]
  Acute leukemia NOS   Stem cell leukemia
  Blast cell leukemia
  EXCLUDES *acute exacerbation of chronic unspecified leukemia (208.1)*

§ √5ᵗʰ **208.1 Chronic**
[0-2]
  Chronic leukemia NOS

§ √5ᵗʰ **208.2 Subacute**
[0-2]
  Subacute leukemia NOS

§ √5ᵗʰ **208.8 Other leukemia of unspecified cell type**
[0-2]

§ √5ᵗʰ **208.9 Unspecified leukemia**
[0-2]
  Leukemia NOS

NEUROENDOCRINE TUMORS (209)

√4ᵗʰ **209 Neuroendocrine tumors**

> Code first any associated multiple endocrine neoplasia syndrome (258.01-258.03)
> Use additional code to identify associated endocrine syndrome, such as:
> carcinoid syndrome (259.2)
> **EXCLUDES** ▶*benign pancreatic islet cell tumors (211.7)*◀
> ▶*malignant*◀ *pancreatic islet cell tumors (157.4)*
> AHA: 4Q, '08, 85-89

√5ᵗʰ **209.0 Malignant carcinoid tumors of the small intestine**

209.00 Malignant carcinoid tumor of the small intestine, unspecified portion

209.01 Malignant carcinoid tumor of the duodenum

209.02 Malignant carcinoid tumor of the jejunum

209.03 Malignant carcinoid tumor of the ileum

√5ᵗʰ **209.1 Malignant carcinoid tumors of the appendix, large intestine, and rectum**

209.10 Malignant carcinoid tumor of the large intestine, unspecified portion
  Malignant carcinoid tumor of the colon NOS

209.11 Malignant carcinoid tumor of the appendix

209.12 Malignant carcinoid tumor of the cecum

209.13 Malignant carcinoid tumor of the ascending colon

209.14 Malignant carcinoid tumor of the transverse colon

209.15 Malignant carcinoid tumor of the descending colon

209.16 Malignant carcinoid tumor of the sigmoid colon

209.17 Malignant carcinoid tumor of the rectum

√5ᵗʰ **209.2 Malignant carcinoid tumors of other and unspecified sites**

209.20 Malignant carcinoid tumor of unknown primary site

209.21 Malignant carcinoid tumor of the bronchus and lung

209.22 Malignant carcinoid tumor of the thymus

209.23 Malignant carcinoid tumor of the stomach
  AHA: 4Q, '08, 89

209.24 Malignant carcinoid tumor of the kidney

209.25 Malignant carcinoid tumor of the foregut NOS

209.26 Malignant carcinoid tumor of the midgut NOS

209.27 Malignant carcinoid tumor of the hindgut NOS

209.29 Malignant carcinoid tumors of other sites

√5ᵗʰ **209.3 Malignant poorly differentiated neuroendocrine tumors**

209.30 Malignant poorly differentiated neuroendocrine carcinoma, any site
  High grade neuroendocrine carcinoma, any site
  Malignant poorly differentiated neuroendocrine tumor NOS
  EXCLUDES ▶ *Merkel cell carcinoma (209.31-209.36)*◀

● **209.31 Merkel cell carcinoma of the face**
  Merkel cell carcinoma of the ear
  Merkel cell carcinoma of the eyelid, including canthus
  Merkel cell carcinoma of the lip

● **209.32 Merkel cell carcinoma of the scalp and neck**

● **209.33 Merkel cell carcinoma of the upper limb**

● **209.34 Merkel cell carcinoma of the lower limb**

● **209.35 Merkel cell carcinoma of the trunk**

● **209.36 Merkel cell carcinoma of other sites**
  Merkel cell carcinoma of the buttock
  Merkel cell carcinoma of the genitals
  Merkel cell carcinoma NOS

√5ᵗʰ **209.4 Benign carcinoid tumors of the small intestine**

209.40 Benign carcinoid tumor of the small intestine, unspecified portion

209.41 Benign carcinoid tumor of the duodenum

209.42 Benign carcinoid tumor of the jejunum

209.43 Benign carcinoid tumor of the ileum

√5ᵗʰ **209.5 Benign carcinoid tumors of the appendix, large intestine, and rectum**

209.50 Benign carcinoid tumor of the large intestine, unspecified portion
  Benign carcinoid tumor of the colon NOS

209.51 Benign carcinoid tumor of the appendix

209.52 Benign carcinoid tumor of the cecum

209.53 Benign carcinoid tumor of the ascending colon

209.54 Benign carcinoid tumor of the transverse colon

209.55 Benign carcinoid tumor of the descending colon

209.56 Benign carcinoid tumor of the sigmoid colon

209.57 Benign carcinoid tumor of the rectum

√5ᵗʰ **209.6 Benign carcinoid tumors of other and unspecified sites**

209.60 Benign carcinoid tumor of unknown primary site
  Carcinoid tumor NOS
  Neuroendocrine tumor NOS

209.61 Benign carcinoid tumor of the bronchus and lung

209.62 Benign carcinoid tumor of the thymus

209.63 Benign carcinoid tumor of the stomach

209.64 Benign carcinoid tumor of the kidney

209.65 Benign carcinoid tumor of the foregut NOS

209.66 Benign carcinoid tumor of the midgut NOS

209.67 Benign carcinoid tumor of the hindgut NOS

209.69 Benign carcinoid tumors of other sites

● √5ᵗʰ **209.7 Secondary neuroendocrine tumors**
  Secondary carcinoid tumors

● **209.70 Secondary neuroendocrine tumor, unspecified site**

● **209.71 Secondary neuroendocrine tumor of distant lymph nodes**
  Mesentery metastasis of neuroendocrine tumor

√4ᵗʰ / √5ᵗʰ **Additional Digit Required**   Unspecified Code   Other Specified Code   Manifestation Code   ▶◀ Revised Text   ● New Code   ▲ Revised Code Title

2010 ICD-9-CM   **October 2009 • Volume 1 – 41**

208–209.71

- **209.72** Secondary neuroendocrine tumor of liver
- **209.73** Secondary neuroendocrine tumor of bone
- **209.74** Secondary neuroendocrine tumor of peritoneum
- **209.75** Secondary Merkel cell carcinoma
  - Merkel cell carcinoma nodal presentation
  - Merkel cell carcinoma visceral metastatic presentation
  - Secondary Merkel cell carcinoma, any site
- **209.79** Secondary neuroendocrine tumor of other sites

BENIGN NEOPLASMS (210-229)

✓4ᵗʰ **210 Benign neoplasm of lip, oral cavity, and pharynx**

> **EXCLUDES** cyst (of):
> jaw (526.0-526.2, 526.89)
> oral soft tissue (528.4)
> radicular (522.8)

210.0 Lip
Frenulum labii
Lip (inner aspect) (mucosa) (vermilion border)
> **EXCLUDES** labial commissure (210.4)
> skin of lip (216.0)

210.1 Tongue
Lingual tonsil

210.2 Major salivary glands
Gland: Gland:
  parotid   submandibular
  sublingual
> **EXCLUDES** benign neoplasms of minor salivary glands:
> NOS (210.4)
> buccal mucosa (210.4)
> lips (210.0)
> palate (hard) (soft) (210.4)
> tongue (210.1)
> tonsil, palatine (210.5)

210.3 Floor of mouth

210.4 Other and unspecified parts of mouth
Gingiva
Gum (upper) (lower)
Labial commissure
Oral cavity NOS
Oral mucosa
Palate (hard) (soft)
Uvula
> **EXCLUDES** benign odontogenic neoplasms of bone
> (213.0-213.1)
> developmental odontogenic cysts (526.0)
> mucosa of lips (210.0)
> nasopharyngeal [posterior] [superior] surface
> of soft palate (210.7)

210.5 Tonsil
Tonsil (faucial) (palatine)
> **EXCLUDES** lingual tonsil (210.1)
> pharyngeal tonsil (210.7)
> tonsillar:
> fossa (210.6)
> pillars (210.6)

210.6 Other parts of oropharynx
Branchial cleft or vestiges
Epiglottis, anterior aspect
Fauces NOS
Mesopharynx NOS
Tonsillar:
  fossa
  pillars
Vallecula
> **EXCLUDES** epiglottis:
> NOS (212.1)
> suprahyoid portion (212.1)

210.7 Nasopharynx
Adenoid tissue   Pharyngeal tonsil
Lymphadenoid tissue   Posterior nasal septum

210.8 Hypopharynx
Arytenoid fold   Postcricoid region
Laryngopharynx   Pyriform fossa

210.9 Pharynx, unspecified
Throat NOS

✓4ᵗʰ **211 Benign neoplasm of other parts of digestive system**
> **EXCLUDES** benign stromal tumors of digestive system (215.5)

211.0 Esophagus

211.1 Stomach
Body ⎫
Cardia ⎬ of stomach
Fundus ⎭
Cardiac orifice
Pylorus
> **EXCLUDES** benign carcinoid tumors of the stomach
> (209.63)

D13.1 Benign neoplasm of stomach   **I-10**

211.2 Duodenum, jejunum, and ileum
Small intestine NOS
> **EXCLUDES** ampulla of Vater (211.5)
> benign carcinoid tumors of the small intestine
> (209.40-209.43)
> ileocecal valve (211.3)

211.3 Colon
Appendix
Cecum
Ileocecal valve
Large intestine NOS
> **EXCLUDES** benign carcinoid tumors of the large intestine
> (209.50-209.56)
> rectosigmoid junction (211.4)

AHA: 3Q, '05, 17; 2Q, '05, 16; 4Q, '01, 56

D12.6 Benign neoplasm of colon unspecified   **I-10**

211.4 Rectum and anal canal
Anal canal or sphincter
Anus NOS
Rectosigmoid junction
> **EXCLUDES** anus:
> margin (216.5)
> skin (216.5)
> benign carcinoid tumors of the rectum (209.57)
> perianal skin (216.5)

211.5 Liver and biliary passages
Ampulla of Vater
Common bile duct
Cystic duct
Gallbladder
Hepatic duct
Sphincter of Oddi

211.6 Pancreas, except islets of Langerhans

211.7 Islets of Langerhans
Islet cell tumor
Use additional code to identify any functional activity

211.8 Retroperitoneum and peritoneum
Mesentery
Mesocolon
Omentum
Retroperitoneal tissue

211.9 Other and unspecified site
Alimentary tract NOS
Digestive system NOS
Gastrointestinal tract NOS
Intestinal tract NOS
Intestine NOS
Spleen, not elsewhere classified

✓4ᵗʰ 212 Benign neoplasm of respiratory and intrathoracic organs

212.0 Nasal cavities, middle ear, and accessory sinuses
Cartilage of nose
Eustachian tube
Nares
Septum of nose
Sinus:
ethmoidal
frontal
maxillary
sphenoidal

EXCLUDES *auditory canal (external) (216.2)*
bone of:
ear (213.0)
nose [turbinates] (213.0)
cartilage of ear (215.0)
ear (external) (skin) (216.2)
nose NOS (229.8)
skin (216.3)
olfactory bulb (225.1)
polyp of:
accessory sinus (471.8)
ear (385.30-385.35)
nasal cavity (471.0)
posterior margin of septum and choanae
(210.7)

212.1 Larynx
Cartilage:
arytenoid
cricoid
cuneiform
thyroid
Epiglottis (suprahyoid portion) NOS
Glottis
Vocal cords (false)(true)

EXCLUDES *epiglottis, anterior aspect (210.6)*
polyp of vocal cord or larynx (478.4)

212.2 Trachea

212.3 Bronchus and lung
Carina
Hilus of lung

EXCLUDES *benign carcinoid tumors of bronchus and lung*
(209.61)

212.4 Pleura

212.5 Mediastinum

212.6 Thymus

EXCLUDES *benign carcinoid tumors of thymus (209.62)*

212.7 Heart

EXCLUDES *great vessels (215.4)*

212.8 Other specified sites

212.9 Site unspecified
Respiratory organ NOS
Upper respiratory tract NOS

EXCLUDES *intrathoracic NOS (229.8)*
thoracic NOS (229.8)

✓4ᵗʰ 213 Benign neoplasm of bone and articular cartilage

INCLUDES cartilage (articular) (joint)
periosteum

EXCLUDES *cartilage of:*
ear (215.0)
eyelid (215.0))
larynx (212.1)
nose (212.0)
exostosis NOS (726.91)
synovia (215.0-215.9)

213.0 Bones of skull and face

EXCLUDES *lower jaw bone (213.1)*

213.1 Lower jaw bone

213.2 Vertebral column, excluding sacrum and coccyx

213.3 Ribs, sternum, and clavicle

213.4 Scapula and long bones of upper limb

213.5 Short bones of upper limb

213.6 Pelvic bones, sacrum, and coccyx

213.7 Long bones of lower limb

213.8 Short bones of lower limb

213.9 Bone and articular cartilage, site unspecified

✓4ᵗʰ 214 Lipoma

INCLUDES angiolipoma
fibrolipoma
hibernoma
lipoma (fetal) (infiltrating) (intramuscular)
myelolipoma
myxolipoma

DEF: Benign tumor frequently composed of mature fat cells; may occasionally be composed of fetal fat cells.

214.0 Skin and subcutaneous tissue of face

214.1 Other skin and subcutaneous tissue

214.2 Intrathoracic organs

214.3 Intra-abdominal organs

214.4 Spermatic cord   ♂

214.8 Other specified sites
AHA: 3Q, '94, 7

214.9 Lipoma, unspecified site

✓4ᵗʰ 215 Other benign neoplasm of connective and other soft tissue

INCLUDES blood vessel
bursa
fascia
ligament
muscle
peripheral, sympathetic, and parasympathetic nerves
and ganglia
synovia
tendon (sheath)

EXCLUDES *cartilage:*
articular (213.0-213.9)
larynx (212.1)
nose (212.0)
connective tissue of:
breast (217)
internal organ, except lipoma and
hemangioma–code to benign neoplasm of the
site
lipoma (214.0-214.9)

215.0 Head, face, and neck

215.2 Upper limb, including shoulder

215.3 Lower limb, including hip

215.4 Thorax

EXCLUDES *heart (212.7)*
mediastinum (212.5)
thymus (212.6)

215.5 Abdomen
Abdominal wall
Benign stromal tumors of abdomen
Hypochondrium

215.6 Pelvis
Buttock
Groin
Inguinal region
Perineum

EXCLUDES *uterine:*
leiomyoma (218.0-218.9)
ligament, any (221.0)

215.7 Trunk, unspecified
Back NOS
Flank NOS

215.8 Other specified sites

215.9 Site unspecified

Neoplasms

216–222.1

✓4th **216 Benign neoplasm of skin**

INCLUDES   blue nevus
dermatofibroma
hydrocystoma
pigmented nevus
syringoadenoma
syringoma

EXCLUDES   skin of genital organs (221.0-222.9)

AHA: 1Q, '00, 21

216.0 Skin of lip

EXCLUDES   vermilion border of lip (210.0)

216.1 Eyelid, including canthus

EXCLUDES   cartilage of eyelid (215.0)

216.2 Ear and external auditory canal
Auricle (ear)
Auricular canal, external
External meatus
Pinna

EXCLUDES   cartilage of ear (215.0)

216.3 Skin of other and unspecified parts of face
Cheek, external
Eyebrow
Nose, external
Temple

216.4 Scalp and skin of neck

AHA: 3Q, '91, 12

216.5 Skin of trunk, except scrotum
Axillary fold   Skin of:
Perianal skin   buttock
Skin of: chest wall
  abdominal wall   groin
  anus   perineum
  back   Umbilicus
  breast

EXCLUDES   anal canal (211.4)
anus NOS (211.4)
skin of scrotum (222.4)

216.6 Skin of upper limb, including shoulder

216.7 Skin of lower limb, including hip

216.8 Other specified sites of skin

216.9 Skin, site unspecified

217 Benign neoplasm of breast
Breast (male) (female):
  connective tissue
  glandular tissue
  soft parts

EXCLUDES   adenofibrosis (610.2)
benign cyst of breast (610.0)
fibrocystic disease (610.1)
skin of breast (216.5)

AHA: 1Q, '00, 4

✓4th **218 Uterine leiomyoma**

INCLUDES   fibroid (bleeding) (uterine)
uterine:
  fibromyoma
  myoma

DEF: Benign tumor primarily derived from uterine smooth muscle
tissue; may contain fibrous, fatty, or epithelial tissue; also called uterine
fibroid or myoma.

218.0 Submucous leiomyoma of uterus   ♀

218.1 Intramural leiomyoma of uterus   ♀
Interstitial leiomyoma of uterus

D25.1 Intramural leiomyoma of uterus   I-10

218.2 Subserous leiomyoma of uterus   ♀

218.9 Leiomyoma of uterus, unspecified   ♀

AHA: 1Q, '03, 4

D25.9 Leiomyoma of uterus unspecified   I-10

Types of Uterine Fibroids

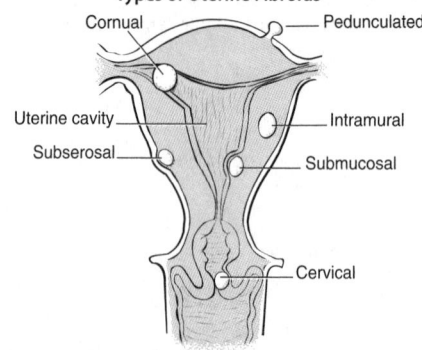

✓4th **219 Other benign neoplasm of uterus**

219.0 Cervix uteri   ♀

219.1 Corpus uteri   ♀
Endometrium
Fundus
Myometrium

219.8 Other specified parts of uterus   ♀

219.9 Uterus, part unspecified   ♀

220 Benign neoplasm of ovary   ♀
Use additional code to identify any functional activity (256.0-256.1)

EXCLUDES   cyst:
corpus albicans (620.2)
corpus luteum (620.1)
endometrial (617.1)
follicular (atretic) (620.0)
graafian follicle (620.0)
ovarian NOS (620.2)
retention (620.2)

D27.9 Benign neoplasm of ovary unspecified side   I-10

✓4th **221 Benign neoplasm of other female genital organs**

INCLUDES   adenomatous polyp
benign teratoma

EXCLUDES   cyst:
epoophoron (752.11)
fimbrial (752.11)
Gartner's duct (752.11)
parovarian (752.11)

221.0 Fallopian tube and uterine ligaments   ♀
Oviduct
Parametruim
Uterine ligament (broad) (round) (uterosacral)
Uterine tube

221.1 Vagina   ♀

221.2 Vulva   ♀
Clitoris
External female genitalia NOS
Greater vestibular [Bartholin's] gland
Labia (majora) (minora)
Pudendum

EXCLUDES   Bartholin's (duct) (gland) cyst (616.2)

221.8 Other specified sites of female genital organs   ♀

221.9 Female genital organ, site unspecified   ♀
Female genitourinary tract NOS

✓4th **222 Benign neoplasm of male genital organs**

222.0 Testis   ♂
Use additional code to identify any functional activity

222.1 Penis   ♂
Corpus cavernosum
Glans penis
Prepuce

N Newborn Age: 0   P Pediatric Age: 0-17   M Maternity Age: 12-55   A Adult Age: 15-124

222.2 Prostate ♂

> EXCLUDES adenomatous hyperplasia of prostate
> (600.20-600.21)
> prostatic:
> adenoma (600.20-600.21)
> enlargement (600.00-600.01)
> hypertrophy (600.00-600.01)

222.3 Epididymis ♂

222.4 Scrotum ♂
Skin of scrotum

222.8 Other specified sites of male genital organs ♂
Seminal vesicle
Spermatic cord

222.9 Male genital organ, site unspecified ♂
Male genitourinary tract NOS

√4ᵗʰ **223 Benign neoplasm of kidney and other urinary organs**

223.0 Kidney, except pelvis
Kidney NOS

> EXCLUDES benign carcinoid tumors of kidney (209.64)
> renal:
> calyces (223.1)
> pelvis (223.1)

223.1 Renal pelvis

223.2 Ureter

> EXCLUDES ureteric orifice of bladder (223.3)

223.3 Bladder

√5ᵗʰ **223.8 Other specified sites of urinary organs**

223.81 Urethra

> EXCLUDES urethral orifice of bladder (223.3)

223.89 Other
Paraurethral glands

223.9 Urinary organ, site unspecified
Urinary system NOS

√4ᵗʰ **224 Benign neoplasm of eye**

> EXCLUDES cartilage of eyelid (215.0)
> eyelid (skin) (216.1)
> optic nerve (225.1)
> orbital bone (213.0)

224.0 Eyeball, except conjunctiva, cornea, retina, and choroid
Ciliary body
Iris
Sclera
Uveal tract

224.1 Orbit

> EXCLUDES bone of orbit (213.0)

224.2 Lacrimal gland

224.3 Conjunctiva

224.4 Cornea

224.5 Retina

> EXCLUDES hemangioma of retina (228.03)

224.6 Choroid

Eyeball

Posterior segment
Vitreous
Optic nerve
Optic disc
Choroid
Sclera
Retina
Conjunctiva
Sclera
Lens
Cornea
Iris
Anterior chamber
Pars plana

224.7 Lacrimal duct
Lacrimal sac
Nasolacrimal duct

224.8 Other specified parts of eye

224.9 Eye, part unspecified

√4ᵗʰ **225 Benign neoplasm of brain and other parts of nervous system**

> EXCLUDES hemangioma (228.02)
> neurofibromatosis (237.7)
> peripheral, sympathetic, and parasympathetic nerves
> and ganglia (215.0-215.9)
> retrobulbar (224.1)

225.0 Brain

225.1 Cranial nerves
Acoustic neuroma
AHA: 4Q, '04, 113

225.2 Cerebral meninges
Meninges NOS
Meningioma (cerebral)
D32.9 Benign neoplasm of meninges unspecified I-10

225.3 Spinal cord
Cauda equina

225.4 Spinal meninges
Spinal meningioma

225.8 Other specified sites of nervous system

225.9 Nervous system, part unspecified
Nervous system (central) NOS

> EXCLUDES meninges NOS (225.2)

226 Benign neoplasm of thyroid glands
Use additional code to identify any functional activity

√4ᵗʰ **227 Benign neoplasm of other endocrine glands and related structures**
Use additional code to identify any functional activity

> EXCLUDES ovary (220)
> pancreas (211.6)
> testis (222.0)

227.0 Adrenal gland
Suprarenal gland

227.1 Parathyroid gland

227.3 Pituitary gland and craniopharyngeal duct (pouch)
Craniobuccal pouch
Hypophysis
Rathke's pouch
Sella turcica

227.4 Pineal gland
Pineal body

227.5 Carotid body

227.6 Aortic body and other paraganglia
Coccygeal body
Glomus jugulare
Para-aortic body
AHA: N-D, '84, 17

227.8 Other

227.9 Endocrine gland, site unspecified

√4ᵗʰ √5ᵗʰ Additional Digit Required   Unspecified Code   Other Specified Code   Manifestation Code   ▶◀ Revised Text   ● New Code   ▲ Revised Code Title

2010 ICD-9-CM **Volume 1 – 45**

222.2–227.9

Neoplasms

228–232.2

√4th **228 Hemangioma and lymphangioma, any site**

INCLUDES   angioma (benign) (cavernous) (congenital) NOS
cavernous nevus
glomus tumor
hemangioma (benign) (congenital)

EXCLUDES   *benign neoplasm of spleen, except hemangioma and
lymphangioma (211.9)*
glomus jugulare (227.6)
nevus:
NOS (216.0-216.9)
blue or pigmented (216.0-216.9)
vascular (757.32)

AHA: 1Q, '00, 21

√5th **228.0 Hemangioma, any site**

AHA: J-F, '85, 19

DEF: A common benign tumor usually occurring in infancy;
composed of newly formed blood vessels due to
malformation of angioblastic tissue.

228.00 Of unspecified site

228.01 Of skin and subcutaneous tissue

228.02 Of intracranial structures

228.03 Of retina

228.04 Of intra-abdominal structures
Peritoneum
Retroperitoneal tissue

228.09 Of other sites
Systemic angiomatosis
AHA: 3Q, '91, 20

228.1 Lymphangioma, any site
Congenital lymphangioma
Lymphatic nevus

√4th **229 Benign neoplasm of other and unspecified sites**

229.0 Lymph nodes
EXCLUDES   *lymphangioma (228.1)*

229.8 Other specified sites
Intrathoracic NOS
Thoracic NOS

229.9 Site unspecified

CARCINOMA IN SITU (230-234)

INCLUDES   Bowen's disease
erythroplasia
Queyrat's erythroplasia

EXCLUDES   *leukoplakia–see Alphabetic Index*

DEF: A neoplastic type; with tumor cells confined to epithelium of
origin; without further invasion.

√4th **230 Carcinoma in situ of digestive organs**

230.0 Lip, oral cavity, and pharynx
Gingiva
Hypopharynx
Mouth [any part]
Nasopharynx
Oropharynx
Salivary gland or duct
Tongue
EXCLUDES   *aryepiglottic fold or interarytenoid fold,*
laryngeal aspect (231.0)
epiglottis:
NOS (231.0)
suprahyoid portion (231.0)
skin of lip (232.0)

230.1 Esophagus

230.2 Stomach
Body ⎫
Cardia ⎬ of stomach
Fundus ⎭
Cardiac orifice
Pylorus

230.3 Colon
Appendix
Cecum
Ileocecal valve
Large intestine NOS
EXCLUDES   *rectosigmoid junction (230.4)*

230.4 Rectum
Rectosigmoid junction

230.5 Anal canal
Anal sphincter

230.6 Anus, unspecified
EXCLUDES   *anus:*
margin (232.5)
skin (232.5)
perianal skin (232.5)

230.7 Other and unspecified | parts of intestine
Duodenum
Ileum
Jejunum
Small intestine NOS
EXCLUDES   *ampulla of Vater (230.8)*

230.8 Liver and biliary system
Ampulla of Vater
Common bile duct
Cystic duct
Gallbladder
Hepatic duct
Sphincter of Oddi

230.9 Other and unspecified | digestive organs
Digestive organ NOS
Gastrointestinal tract NOS
Pancreas
Spleen

√4th **231 Carcinoma in situ of respiratory system**

231.0 Larynx
Cartilage:
arytenoid
cricoid
cuneiform
thyroid
Epiglottis:
NOS
posterior surface
suprahyoid portion
Vocal cords (false)(true)
EXCLUDES   *aryepiglottic fold or interarytenoid fold:*
NOS (230.0)
hypopharyngeal aspect (230.0)
marginal zone (230.0)

231.1 Trachea

231.2 Bronchus and lung
Carina
Hilus of lung

231.8 Other specified parts of respiratory system
Accessory sinuses
Middle ear
Nasal cavities
Pleura
EXCLUDES   *ear (external) (skin) (232.2)*
nose NOS (234.8)
skin (232.3)

231.9 Respiratory system, part unspecified
Respiratory organ NOS

√4th **232 Carcinoma in situ of skin**

INCLUDES   pigment cells
EXCLUDES   *melanoma in situ of skin (172.0-172.9)*

232.0 Skin of lip
EXCLUDES   *vermilion border of lip (230.0)*

232.1 Eyelid, including canthus

232.2 Ear and external auditory canal

N Newborn Age: 0   P Pediatric Age: 0-17   M Maternity Age: 12-55   A Adult Age: 15-124

232.3 Skin of other and unspecified parts of face

232.4 Scalp and skin of neck

232.5 Skin of trunk, except scrotum
Anus, margin
Axillary fold
Perianal skin
Skin of:
abdominal wall
anus
back
Skin of:
breast
buttock
chest wall
groin
perineum
Umbilicus

> EXCLUDES   anal canal (230.5)
> anus NOS (230.6)
> skin of genital organs (233.30-233.39,
> 233.5-233.6)

232.6 Skin of upper limb, including shoulder

232.7 Skin of lower limb, including hip

232.8 Other specified sites of skin

232.9 Skin, site unspecified

✓4th **233** Carcinoma in situ of breast and genitourinary system
TIP: For patients with carcinoma in situ found incidentally when admitted for treatment of another condition, sequence the 233 code as a secondary condition.

233.0 Breast
> EXCLUDES   Paget's disease (174.0-174.9)
> skin of breast (232.5)

TIP: Assign for tumors specified as intraductal carcinoma.

233.1 Cervix uteri ♀
Adenocarcinoma in situ of cervix
Cervical intraepithelial glandular neoplasia, grade III
Cervical intraepithelial neoplasia III [CIN III]
Severe dysplasia of cervix
> EXCLUDES   cervical intraepithelial neoplasia II [CIN II]
> (622.12)
> cytologic evidence of malignancy without
> histologic confirmation (795.06)
> high grade squamous intraepithelial lesion
> (HGSIL) (795.04)
> moderate dysplasia of cervix (622.12)

AHA: 3Q, '92, 7; 3Q, '92, 8; 1Q, '91, 11

233.2 Other and unspecified parts of uterus ♀

✓5th **233.3** Other and unspecified female genital organs
AHA: 4Q, '07, 67

233.30 Unspecified female genital organ ♀

233.31 Vagina ♀
Severe dysplasia of vagina
Vaginal intraepithelial neoplasia III [VAIN III]

233.32 Vulva ♀
Severe dysplasia of vulva
Vulvar intraepithelial neoplasia III [VIN III]

233.39 Other female genital organ ♀

233.4 Prostate ♂

233.5 Penis ♂

233.6 Other and unspecified male genital organs ♂

233.7 Bladder

233.9 Other and unspecified urinary organs

✓4th **234** Carcinoma in situ of other and unspecified sites

234.0 Eye
> EXCLUDES   cartilage of eyelid (234.8)
> eyelid (skin) (232.1)
> optic nerve (234.8)
> orbital bone (234.8)

234.8 Other specified sites
Endocrine gland [any]

234.9 Site unspecified
Carcinoma in situ NOS

NEOPLASMS OF UNCERTAIN BEHAVIOR (235-238)

Note: Categories 235–238 classify by site certain histomorphologically well-defined neoplasms, the subsequent behavior of which cannot be predicted from the present appearance.

TIP: Typically assigned for cases in which the tumor is in transition and may be undergoing malignant transformation, but continued study is required for accurate classification.

✓4th **235** Neoplasm of uncertain behavior of digestive and respiratory systems
> EXCLUDES   stromal tumors of uncertain behavior of digestive system
> (238.1)

235.0 Major salivary glands
Gland:
parotid
sublingual
submandibular
> EXCLUDES   minor salivary glands (235.1)

235.1 Lip, oral cavity, and pharynx
Gingiva
Hypopharynx
Minor salivary glands
Mouth
Nasopharynx
Oropharynx
Tongue
> EXCLUDES   aryepiglottic fold or interarytenoid fold,
> laryngeal aspect (235.6)
> epiglottis:
> NOS (235.6)
> suprahyoid portion (235.6)
> skin of lip (238.2)

235.2 Stomach, intestines, and rectum

235.3 Liver and biliary passages
Ampulla of Vater
Bile ducts [any]
Gallbladder
Liver

235.4 Retroperitoneum and peritoneum

235.5 Other and unspecified digestive organs
Anal:
canal
sphincter
Anus NOS
Esophagus
Pancreas
Spleen
> EXCLUDES   anus:
> margin (238.2)
> skin (238.2)
> perianal skin (238.2)

235.6 Larynx
> EXCLUDES   aryepiglottic fold or interarytenoid fold:
> NOS (235.1)
> hypopharyngeal aspect (235.1)
> marginal zone (235.1)

235.7 Trachea, bronchus, and lung

235.8 Pleura, thymus, and mediastinum

235.9 Other and unspecified respiratory organs
Accessory sinuses
Middle ear
Nasal cavities
Respiratory organ NOS
> EXCLUDES   ear (external) (skin) (238.2)
> nose (238.8)
> skin (238.2)

✓4th **236** Neoplasm of uncertain behavior of genitourinary organs

236.0 Uterus ♀

236.1 Placenta ♀
Chorioadenoma (destruens)
Invasive mole
Malignant hydatid(iform) mole

236.2 Ovary ♀
Use additional code to identify any functional activity

✓4th
✓5th Additional Digit Required | Unspecified Code | Other Specified Code | Manifestation Code | ▶◀ Revised Text | ● New Code | ▲ Revised Code Title

2010 ICD-9-CM | **Volume 1 – 47**

236.3 Other and unspecified female genital organs   ♀

236.4 Testis   ♂

    Use additional code to identify any functional activity

236.5 Prostate   ♂

236.6 Other and unspecified male genital organs   ♂

236.7 Bladder

√5th **236.9** Other and unspecified urinary organs

    236.90 Urinary organ, unspecified

    236.91 Kidney and ureter

    236.99 Other

√4th **237** Neoplasm of uncertain behavior of endocrine glands and nervous system

237.0 Pituitary gland and craniopharyngeal duct

    Use additional code to identify any functional activity

237.1 Pineal gland

237.2 Adrenal gland

    Suprarenal gland

    Use additional code to identify any functional activity

237.3 Paraganglia

    Aortic body   Coccygeal body

    Carotid body   Glomus jugulare

    AHA: N-D, '84, 17

237.4 Other and unspecified endocrine glands

    Parathyroid gland

    Thyroid gland

237.5 Brain and spinal cord

237.6 Meninges

    Meninges:

      NOS

      cerebral

      spinal

√5th **237.7** Neurofibromatosis

    von Recklinghausen's disease

    DEF: An inherited condition with developmental changes in the nervous system, muscles, bones and skin; multiple soft tumors (neurofibromas) distributed over the entire body.

    237.70 Neurofibromatosis, unspecified

    237.71 Neurofibromatosis, type 1 [von Recklinghausen's disease]

    237.72 Neurofibromatosis, type 2 [acoustic neurofibromatosis]

      DEF: Inherited condition with cutaneous lesions, benign tumors of peripheral nerves and bilateral 8th nerve masses.

237.9 Other and unspecified parts of nervous system

    Cranial nerves

    EXCLUDES   *peripheral, sympathetic, and parasympathetic nerves and ganglia (238.1)*

√4th **238** Neoplasm of uncertain behavior of other and unspecified sites and tissues

238.0 Bone and articular cartilage

    EXCLUDES   *cartilage:*

        ear (238.1)

        eyelid (238.1)

        larynx (235.6)

        nose (235.9)

        synovia (238.1)

    AHA: 4Q, '04, 128

238.1 Connective and other soft tissue

    Peripheral, sympathetic, and parasympathetic nerves and ganglia

    Stromal tumors of digestive system

    EXCLUDES   *cartilage (of):*

        articular (238.0)

        larynx (235.6)

        nose (235.9)

        connective tissue of breast (238.3)

238.2 Skin

    EXCLUDES   *anus NOS (235.5)*

        skin of genital organs (236.3, 236.6)

        vermilion border of lip (235.1)

    TIP: Assign when documentation indicates keratocanthoma only.

238.3 Breast

    EXCLUDES   *skin of breast (238.2)*

238.4 Polycythemia vera

    DEF: Abnormal proliferation of all bone marrow elements, increased red cell mass and total blood volume; unknown etiology, frequently associated with splenomegaly, leukocytosis, and thrombocythemia.

    D45 Polycythemia vera   `I-10`

238.5 Histiocytic and mast cells

    Mast cell tumor NOS

    Mastocytoma NOS

238.6 Plasma cells

    Plasmacytoma NOS

    Solitary myeloma

√5th **238.7** Other lymphatic and hematopoietic tissues

    EXCLUDES   *acute myelogenous leukemia (205.0)*

        chronic myelomonocytic leukemia (205.1)

        myelosclerosis NOS (289.89)

        myelosis:

          NOS (205.9)

          megakaryocytic (207.2)

    AHA: 3Q, '01, 13; 1Q, '97, 5; 2Q, '89, 8

    238.71 Essential thrombocythemia

      Essential hemorrhagic thrombocythemia

      Essential thrombocytosis

      Idiopathic (hemorrhagic) thrombocythemia

      Primary thrombocytosis

      AHA: 4Q, '06, 63-66

      D47.3 Essential (hemorrhagic) thrombocythemia   `I-10`

    238.72 Low grade myelodysplastic syndrome lesions

      Refractory anemia (RA)

      ▶Refractory anemia with excess blasts-1 (RAEB-1)◀

      Refractory anemia with ringed sideroblasts (RARS)

      Refractory cytopenia with multilineage dysplasia (RCMD)

      Refractory cytopenia with multilineage dysplasia and ringed sideroblasts (RCMD-RS)

      DEF: Refractory anemia (RA): Form of bone marrow disorder (myelodysplastic syndrome) that interferes with red blood cell production in the bone marrow; unresponsive to hematinics; characteristic normal or hypercellular marrow with abnormal erythrocyte development and reticulocytopenia.

      AHA: 4Q, '06, 63-66

    238.73 High grade myelodysplastic syndrome lesions

      Refractory anemia with excess blasts-2 (RAEB-2)

      AHA: 4Q, '06, 63-66

    238.74 Myelodysplastic syndrome with 5q deletion

      5q minus syndrome NOS

      EXCLUDES   *constitutional 5q deletion (758.39)*

        high grade myelodysplastic syndrome with 5q deletion (238.73)

      AHA: 4Q, '06, 63-66

    238.75 Myelodysplastic syndrome, unspecified

      AHA: 4Q, '06, 63-66

      D46.9 Myelodysplastic syndrome unspecified   `I-10`

N Newborn Age: 0   P Pediatric Age: 0-17   M Maternity Age: 12-55   A Adult Age: 15-124

238.76 Myelofibrosis with myeloid metaplasia
Agnogenic myeloid metaplasia
Idiopathic myelofibrosis (chronic)
Myelosclerosis with myeloid metaplasia
Primary myelofibrosis

> **EXCLUDES** myelofibrosis NOS (289.83)
> myelophthisic anemia (284.2)
> myelophthisis (284.2)
> secondary myelofibrosis (289.83)

AHA: 4Q, '06, 63-66

238.77 Post-transplant lymphoproliferative disorder [PTLD]
Code first complications of transplant (996.80-996.89)

> **DEF:** Excessive proliferation of B-cell lymphocytes following Epstein-Barr virus infection in organ transplant patients; may progress to non-Hodgkins lymphoma.

AHA: 4Q, '08, 90-91

238.79 Other lymphatic and hematopoietic tissues
Lymphoproliferative disease (chronic) NOS
Megakaryocytic myelosclerosis
Myeloproliferative disease (chronic) NOS
Panmyelosis (acute)

AHA: 4Q, '06, 63-66

238.8 Other specified sites
Eye   Heart

> **EXCLUDES** eyelid (skin) (238.2)
> cartilage (238.1)

238.9 Site unspecified

NEOPLASMS OF UNSPECIFIED NATURE (239)

√4ᵗʰ **239 Neoplasms of unspecified nature**
Note: Category 239 classifies by site neoplasms of unspecified morphology and behavior. The term "mass," unless otherwise stated, is not to be regarded as a neoplastic growth.

> **INCLUDES** "growth" NOS
> neoplasm NOS
> new growth NOS
> tumor NOS

TIP: Do not assign for inpatient cases; more information should be available.

239.0 Digestive system

> **EXCLUDES** anus:
> margin (239.2)
> skin (239.2)
> perianal skin (239.2)

239.1 Respiratory system

239.2 Bone, soft tissue, and skin

> **EXCLUDES** anal canal (239.0)
> anus NOS (239.0)
> bone marrow (202.9)
> cartilage:
> larynx (239.1)
> nose (239.1)
> connective tissue of breast (239.3)
> skin of genital organs (239.5)
> vermilion border of lip (239.0)

239.3 Breast

> **EXCLUDES** skin of breast (239.2)

239.4 Bladder

239.5 Other genitourinary organs

239.6 Brain

> **EXCLUDES** cerebral meninges (239.7)
> cranial nerves (239.7)

239.7 Endocrine glands and other parts of nervous system

> **EXCLUDES** peripheral, sympathetic, and parasympathetic nerves and ganglia (239.2)

√5ᵗʰ **239.8 Other specified sites**

> **EXCLUDES** eyelid (skin) (239.2)
> cartilage (239.2)
> great vessels (239.2)
> optic nerve (239.7)

● **239.81 Retina and choroid**
Dark area on retina
Retinal freckle

● **239.89 Other specified sites**

239.9 Site unspecified

√4ᵗʰ / √5ᵗʰ Additional Digit Required   Unspecified Code   Other Specified Code   Manifestation Code   ►◄ Revised Text   ● New Code   ▲ Revised Code Title

2010 ICD-9-CM   **October 2009 • Volume 1 – 49**

238.76–239.9

3. ENDOCRINE, NUTRITIONAL AND METABOLIC DISEASES, AND IMMUNITY DISORDERS (240-279)

EXCLUDES *endocrine and metabolic disturbances specific to the fetus and newborn (775.0-775.9)*

Note: All neoplasms, whether functionally active or not, are classified in Chapter 2. Codes in Chapter 3 (i.e., 242.8, 246.0, 251-253, 255-259) may be used to identify such functional activity associated with any neoplasm, or by ectopic endocrine tissue.

DISORDERS OF THYROID GLAND (240-246)

√4th **240 Simple and unspecified goiter**

> **DEF:** An enlarged thyroid gland often caused by an inadequate dietary intake of iodine.

240.0 Goiter, specified as simple

> Any condition classifiable to 240.9, specified as simple

240.9 Goiter, unspecified

> Enlargement of thyroid
> Goiter or struma:
> NOS
> diffuse colloid
> endemic
> hyperplastic
> nontoxic (diffuse)
> parenchymatous
> sporadic
> **EXCLUDES** *congenital (dyshormonogenic) goiter (246.1)*

√4th **241 Nontoxic nodular goiter**

> **EXCLUDES** *adenoma of thyroid (226)*
> *cystadenoma of thyroid (226)*

241.0 Nontoxic uninodular goiter

> Thyroid nodule
> Uninodular goiter (nontoxic)
> **DEF:** Enlarged thyroid, commonly due to decreased thyroid production, with single nodule; no clinical hypothyroidism.
> E04.1 Nontoxic single thyroid nodule [I-10]

241.1 Nontoxic multinodular goiter

> Multinodular goiter (nontoxic)
> **DEF:** Enlarged thyroid, commonly due to decreased thyroid production with multiple nodules; no clinical hypothyroidism.

241.9 Unspecified nontoxic nodular goiter

> Adenomatous goiter
> Nodular goiter (nontoxic) NOS
> Struma nodosa (simplex)

√4th **242 Thyrotoxicosis with or without goiter**

> **EXCLUDES** *neonatal thyrotoxicosis (775.3)*
> **DEF:** A condition caused by excess quantities of thyroid hormones being introduced into the tissues

> The following fifth-digit subclassification is for use with categories 242:
> **0 without mention of thyrotoxic crisis or storm**
> **1 with mention of thyrotoxic crisis or storm**

§ √5th **242.0 Toxic diffuse goiter**
[0-1]
> Basedow's disease
> Exophthalmic or toxic goiter NOS
> Graves' disease
> Primary thyroid hyperplasia
> **DEF:** Diffuse thyroid enlargement accompanied by hyperthyroidism, bulging eyes, and dermopathy.

§ √5th **242.1 Toxic uninodular goiter**
[0-1]
> Thyroid nodule ⎫ toxic or with hyperthyroidism
> Uninodular goiter ⎭
> **DEF:** Symptomatic hyperthyroidism with a single nodule on the enlarged thyroid gland. Abrupt onset of symptoms; including extreme nervousness, insomnia, weight loss, tremors, and psychosis or coma.

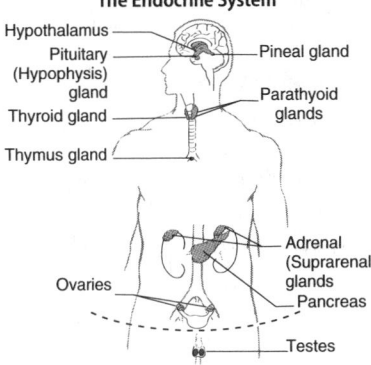

The Endocrine System

§ √5th **242.2 Toxic multinodular goiter**
[0-1]
> Secondary thyroid hyperplasia
> **DEF:** Symptomatic hyperthyroidism with multiple nodules on the enlarged thyroid gland. Abrupt onset of symptoms; including extreme nervousness, insomnia, weight loss, tremors, and psychosis or coma.

§ √5th **242.3 Toxic nodular goiter, unspecified**
[0-1]
> Adenomatous goiter ⎫
> Nodular goiter ⎬ toxic or with hyperthyroidism
> Struma nodosa ⎭
> Any condition classifiable to 241.9 specified as toxic or with hyperthyroidism

§ √5th **242.4 Thyrotoxicosis from ectopic thyroid nodule**
[0-1]

§ √5th **242.8 Thyrotoxicosis of other specified origin**
[0-1]
> Overproduction of thyroid-stimulating hormone [TSH]
> Thyrotoxicosis:
> factitia from ingestion of excessive thyroid material
> Use additional E code to identify cause, if drug-induced

§ √5th **242.9 Thyrotoxicosis without mention of goiter or other cause**
[0-1]
> Hyperthyroidism NOS
> Thyrotoxicosis NOS
> E05.90 Thyrotoxicosis uns w/o thyrotoxic crisis or storm [I-10]

243 Congenital hypothyroidism

> Congenital thyroid insufficiency
> Cretinism (athyrotic) (endemic)
> Use additional code to identify associated mental retardation
> **EXCLUDES** *congenital (dyshormonogenic) goiter (246.1)*
> **DEF:** Underproduction of thyroid hormone present from birth.

√4th **244 Acquired hypothyroidism**

> **INCLUDES** athyroidism (acquired)
> hypothyroidism (acquired)
> myxedema (adult) (juvenile)
> thyroid (gland) insufficiency (acquired)

244.0 Postsurgical hypothyroidism

> **DEF:** Underproduction of thyroid hormone due to surgical removal of all or part of the thyroid gland.
> E89.0 Postprocedural hypothyroidism [I-10]

244.1 Other postablative hypothyroidism

> Hypothyroidism following therapy, such as irradiation

244.2 Iodine hypothyroidism

> Hypothyroidism resulting from administration or ingestion of iodide
> Use additional E code to identify drug

244.3 Other iatrogenic hypothyroidism

> Hypothyroidism resulting from:
> P-aminosalicylic acid [PAS]
> Phenylbutazone
> Resorcinol
> Iatrogenic hypothyroidism NOS
> Use additional E code to identify drug

---

§ Requires fifth digit. Valid digits are in [brackets] under each code. See category 242 for codes and definitions.

√4th Additional Digit Required   Unspecified Code   Other Specified Code   Manifestation Code   ►◄ Revised Text   ● New Code   ▲ Revised Code Title

244.8 Other specified acquired hypothyroidism
Secondary hypothyroidism NEC
AHA: J-A, '85, 9

244.9 Unspecified hypothyroidism
Hypothyroidism
Myxedema } primary or NOS
AHA: 3Q, '99, 19; 4Q, '96, 29
E03.9 Hypothyroidism unspecified   I-10

✓4ᵗʰ 245 Thyroiditis

245.0 Acute thyroiditis
Abscess of thyroid
Thyroiditis:
nonsuppurative, acute
pyogenic
suppurative
Use additional code to identify organism
DEF: Inflamed thyroid caused by infection, with abscess and liquid puris.

245.1 Subacute thyroiditis
Thyroiditis: Thyroiditis:
de Quervain's   granulomatous
giant cell   viral
DEF: Inflammation of the thyroid, characterized by fever and painful enlargement of the thyroid gland, with granulomas in the gland.

245.2 Chronic lymphocytic thyroiditis
Hashimoto's disease   Thyroiditis:
Struma lymphomatosa   autoimmune
lymphocytic (chronic)
DEF: Autoimmune disease of thyroid; lymphocytes infiltrate the gland and thyroid antibodies are produced; women more often affected.

245.3 Chronic fibrous thyroiditis
Struma fibrosa
Thyroiditis:
invasive (fibrous)
ligneous
Riedel's
DEF: Persistent fibrosing inflammation of thyroid with adhesions to nearby structures; rare condition.

245.4 Iatrogenic thyroiditis
Use additional code to identify cause
DEF: Thyroiditis resulting from treatment or intervention by physician or in a patient intervention setting.

245.8 Other and unspecified chronic thyroiditis
Chronic thyroiditis: Chronicthyroiditis:
NOS   nonspecific

245.9 Thyroiditis, unspecified
Thyroiditis NOS

✓4ᵗʰ 246 Other disorders of thyroid

246.0 Disorders of thyrocalcitonin secretion
Hypersecretion of calcitonin or thyrocalcitonin

246.1 Dyshormonogenic goiter
Congenital (dyshormonogenic) goiter
Goiter due to enzyme defect in synthesis of thyroid hormone
Goitrous cretinism (sporadic)

246.2 Cyst of thyroid
EXCLUDES cystadenoma of thyroid (226)

246.3 Hemorrhage and infarction of thyroid

246.8 Other specified disorders of thyroid
Abnormality of thyroid-binding globulin
Atrophy of thyroid
Hyper-TBG-nemia
Hypo-TBG-nemia
AHA: 2Q, '06, 5

246.9 Unspecified disorder of thyroid
E07.9 Disorder of thyroid unspecified   I-10

DISEASES OF OTHER ENDOCRINE GLANDS (249-259)

✓4ᵗʰ 249 Secondary diabetes mellitus
INCLUDES diabetes mellitus (due to) (in) (secondary) (with):
drug-induced or chemical induced infection
Use additional code to identify any associated insulin use (V58.67)

EXCLUDES gestational diabetes (648.8)
hyperglycemia NOS (790.29)
neonatal diabetes mellitus (775.1)
nonclinical diabetes (790.29)
Type I diabetes–see category 250
Type II diabetes–see category 250

The following fifth-digit subclassification is for use with category 249:
0 not stated as uncontrolled, or unspecified
1 uncontrolled

AHA: ▶4Q, '08, 91-95◄

TIP: Do not assign a code from category 249 if the secondary DM is due to pancreatectomy; assign instead 251.3 Postsurgical hypoinsulinemia.

§ ✓5ᵗʰ 249.0 Secondary diabetes mellitus without mention
[0-1] of complication
Secondary diabetes mellitus without mention of complication or manifestation classifiable to 249.1-249.9
Secondary diabetes mellitus NOS
E09.9 Drug/chemical induced diabetes mellitus w/o   I-10
comp

§ ✓5ᵗʰ 249.1 Secondary diabetes mellitus with ketoacidosis
[0-1] Secondary diabetes mellitus with diabetic acidosis without mention of coma
Secondary diabetes mellitus with diabetic ketosis without mention of coma

§ ✓5ᵗʰ 249.2 Secondary diabetes mellitus with hyperosmolarity
[0-1] Secondary diabetes mellitus with hyperosmolar (nonketotic) coma

§ ✓5ᵗʰ 249.3 Secondary diabetes mellitus with other coma
[0-1] Secondary diabetes mellitus with diabetic coma (with ketoacidosis)
Secondary diabetes mellitus with diabetic hypoglycemic coma
Secondary diabetes mellitus with insulin coma NOS
EXCLUDES secondary diabetes mellitus with hyperosmolar coma (249.2)

§ ✓5ᵗʰ 249.4 Secondary diabetes mellitus with renal manifestations
[0-1] Use additional code to identify manifestation, as:
chronic kidney disease (585.1-585.9)
diabetic nephropathy NOS (583.81)
diabetic nephrosis (581.81)
intercapillary glomerulosclerosis (581.81)
Kimmelstiel-Wilson syndrome (581.81)

§ ✓5ᵗʰ 249.5 Secondary diabetes mellitus with ophthalmic
[0-1] manifestations
Use additional code to identify manifestation, as:
diabetic blindness (369.00-369.9)
diabetic cataract (366.41)
diabetic glaucoma (365.44)
diabetic macular edema (362.07)
diabetic retinal edema (362.07)
diabetic retinopathy (362.01-362.07)

§ ✓5ᵗʰ 249.6 Secondary diabetes mellitus with neurological
[0-1] manifestations
Use additional code to identify manifestation, as:
diabetic amyotrophy (353.5)
diabetic gastroparalysis (536.3)
diabetic gastroparesis (536.3)
diabetic mononeuropathy (354.0-355.9)
diabetic neurogenic arthropathy (713.5)
diabetic peripheral autonomic neuropathy (337.1)
diabetic polyneuropathy (357.2)
AHA: For code 249.60: 4Q, '08, 94

---

§ Requires fifth digit. Valid digits are in [brackets] under each code. See category 249 for codes and definitions.

N Newborn Age: 0   P Pediatric Age: 0-17   M Maternity Age: 12-55   A Adult Age: 15-124

§ √5th **249.7 Secondary diabetes mellitus with peripheral**
[0-1]   **circulatory disorders**
           Use additional code to identify manifestation, as:
              diabetic gangrene (785.4)
              diabetic peripheral angiopathy (443.81)

§ √5th **249.8 Secondary diabetes mellitus with other**
[0-1]   **specified manifestations**
           Secondary diabetic hypoglycemia in diabetes mellitus
           Secondary hypoglycemic shock in diabetes mellitus
           Use additional code to identify manifestation, as:
              any associated ulceration (707.10-707.9)
              diabetic bone changes (731.8)

§ √5th **249.9 Secondary diabetes mellitus with unspecified**
[0-1]   **complication**

√4th **250 Diabetes mellitus**
       EXCLUDES *gestational diabetes (648.8)*
                 hyperglycemia NOS (790.29)
                 neonatal diabetes mellitus (775.1)
                 nonclinical diabetes (790.29)
                 secondary diabetes (249.0-249.9)

       The following fifth-digit subclassification is for use with category 250:
       0 type II or unspecified type, not state as uncontrolled
          Fifth-digit 0 is for use for type II patients, even if the patient
          requires insulin
          Use additional code, if applicable, for associated long-term
          (current) insulin use V58.67
       1 type I [juvenile type], not stated as uncontrolled
       2 type II or unspecified type, uncontrolled
          Fifth-digit 2 is for use for type II patients, even if the patient
          requires insulin
          Use additional code, if applicable, for associated long-term
          (current) insulin use V58.67
       3 type I [juvenile type], uncontrolled

       DEF: Diabetes mellitus: Inability to metabolize carbohydrates, proteins,
       and fats due to insufficient secretion of insulin. Symptoms may be
       unremarkable, with long-term compli- cations, involving kidneys,
       nerves, blood vessels, and eyes.
       DEF: Uncontrolled diabetes: A nonspecific term indicating that the cur-
       rent treatment regimen does not keep the blood sugar level of a
       patient within acceptable levels.
       AHA: 4Q, '04, 56; 2Q, '04, 17; 2Q, '02, 13; 2Q,'01, 16; 2Q,'98, 15; 4Q, '97, 32;
       2Q, '97, 14; 3Q, '96, 5; 4Q, '93, 19; 2Q, '92, 5; 3Q, '91, 3; 2Q, '90, 22; N-D,
       '85, 11
       TIP: Use of insulin does not ensure type I DM; if patient is on routine
       insulin, assign also V58.67 Long-term (current) use of insulin.

§ √5th **250.0 Diabetes mellitus without mention of complication**
[0-3]   Diabetes mellitus without mention of complication or
              manifestation classifiable to 250.1-250.9
           Diabetes (mellitus) NOS
           AHA: 1Q, '06, 14; 4Q, '97, 32; 3Q, '91, 3, 12; N-D, '85, 11; **For code
           250.00:** 1Q, '05, 15; 4Q, '04, 55; 4Q, '03, 105, 108; 2Q, '03, 16; 1Q,
           '02, 7, 11; **For code 250.01:** 4Q, '04, 55; 4Q, '03, 110; 2Q, '03, 6; **For
           code 250.02:** 1Q, '03, 5
           E11.9 Type 2 diabetes mellitus w/o complications   I-10

§ √5th **250.1 Diabetes with ketoacidosis**
[0-3]   Diabetic:
              acidosis }
              ketosis   } without mention of coma
           DEF: Diabetic hyperglycemic crisis causing ketone presence in
           body fluids.
           AHA: 3Q, '91, 6; **For code 250.11:** 4Q, '03, 82; **For code 250.13:** 2Q,
           '06, 19-20
           E10.10 Type 1 diabetes mellitus w/ketoacidosis w/o   I-10
           coma

§ √5th **250.2 Diabetes with hyperosmolarity**
[0-3]   Hyperosmolar (nonketotic) coma
           AHA: 4Q, '93, 19; 3Q, '91, 7

§ √5th **250.3 Diabetes with other coma**
[0-3]   Diabetic coma (with ketoacidosis)
           Diabetic hypoglycemic coma
           Insulin coma NOS
           EXCLUDES *diabetes with hyperosmolar coma (250.2)*
           DEF: Coma (not hyperosmolar) caused by hyperglycemia or
           hypoglycemia as complication of diabetes.
           AHA: 3Q, '91, 7, 12

§ √5th **250.4 Diabetes with renal manifestations**
[0-3]   Use additional code to identify manifestation, as:
              chronic kidney disease (585.1-585.9)
              diabetic:
                 nephropathy NOS (583.81)
                 nephrosis (581.81)
              intercapillary glomerulosclerosis (581.81)
              Kimmelstiel-Wilson syndrome (581.81)
           AHA: 3Q, '91, 8, 12; S-O, '87, 9; S-O, '84, 3; **For code 250.40:** 1Q,
           '03, 20
           E11.22 Type 2 diabetes mellitus w/diabetic CKD   I-10

§ √5th **250.5 Diabetes with ophthalmic manifestations**
[0-3]   Use additional code to identify manifestation, as:
              diabetic:
                 blindness (369.00-369.9)
                 cataract (366.41)
                 glaucoma (365.44)
                 macular edema (362.07)
                 retinal edema (362.07)
                 retinopathy (362.01-362.07)
           AHA: 4Q, '05, 65; 3Q, '91, 8; S-O, '85, 11; **For code 250.50:**
           4Q, '05, 67
           E10.36 Type 1 diabetes mellitus with diabetic cataract   I-10

§ √5th **250.6 Diabetes with neurological manifestations**
[0-3]   Use additional code to identify manifestation, as:
              diabetic:
                 amyotrophy (353.5)
                 gastroparalysis (536.3)
                 gastroparesis (536.3)
                 mononeuropathy (354.0-355.9)
                 neurogenic arthropathy (713.5)
                 peripheral autonomic neuropathy (337.1)
                 polyneuropathy (357.2)
           AHA: ▶2Q, '09, 13, 15;◀3Q, '08, 5; 2Q, '93, 6; 2Q, '92, 15; 3Q, '91,
           9; N-D, '84, 9; **For code 250.60:** 4Q, '03, 105; **For code 250.61:** 2Q,
           '04, 7
           E11.40 Type 2 diabetes mellitus w/diab neuropathy uns   I-10

§ √5th **250.7 Diabetes with peripheral circulatory disorders**
[0-3]   Use additional code to identify manifestation, as:
              diabetic:
                 gangrene (785.4)
                 peripheral angiopathy (443.81)
           DEF: Blood vessel damage or disease, usually in the feet, legs,
           or hands, as a complication of diabetes.
           AHA: 1Q, '96, 10; 3Q, '94, 5; 2Q, '94, 17; 3Q, '91, 10, 12; 3Q, '90,
           15; **For code 250.70:** 1Q, '04, 14
           E10.51 Type 1 DM w/diab periph angiopathy w/o   I-10
           gangrene

§ √5th **250.8 Diabetes with other specified manifestations**
[0-3]   Diabetic hypoglycemia NOS
           Hypoglycemic shock NOS
           Use additional code to identify manifestation, as:
              any associated ulceration (707.10-707.9)
              diabetic bone changes (731.8)
           AHA: 4Q, '00, 44; 4Q, '97, 43; 2Q, '97, 16; 4Q, '93, 20; 3Q, '91, 10;
           For code 250.80: 1Q, '04, 14
           TIP: Assign for diabetic osteomyelitis, along with code 731.8
           and the appropriate code from category 730.
           E11.610 Type 2 DM with diabetic neuropathic   I-10
           arthropathy

§ √5th **250.9 Diabetes with unspecified complication**
[0-3]   **AHA:** 2Q, '92, 15; 3Q, '91, 7, 12
           TIP: Do not assign with any other code in category 250.
           E10.8 Type 1 diabetes mellitus with unspecified comp   I-10

√4th **251 Other disorders of pancreatic internal secretion**

     251.0 Hypoglycemic coma
           Iatrogenic hyperinsulinism
           Non-diabetic insulin coma
           Use additional E code to identify cause, if drug-induced
           EXCLUDES *hypoglycemic coma in diabetes mellitus*
                     (249.3, 250.3)
           DEF: Coma induced by low blood sugar in non-diabetic
           patient.
           AHA: M-A, '85, 8

§ Requires fifth digit. Valid digits are in [brackets] under each code. See appropriate category for codes and definitions.

251.1 Other specified hypoglycemia

Hyperinsulinism: Hyperplasia of pancreatic
NOS islet beta cells NOS
ectopic
functional

Use additional E code to identify cause, if drug-induced

> **EXCLUDES** *hypoglycemia:*
> *in diabetes mellitus (249.8, 250.8)*
> *in infant of diabetic mother (775.0)*
> *hypoglycemic coma (251.0)*
> *neonatal hypoglycemia (775.6)*

DEF: Excessive production of insulin by the pancreas; associated with obesity and insulin-producing tumors.

AHA: 1Q, '03, 10

251.2 Hypoglycemia, unspecified

Hypoglycemia: Hypoglycemia:
NOS spontaneous
reactive

> **EXCLUDES** *hypoglycemia:*
> *with coma (251.0)*
> *in diabetes mellitus (249.8, 250.8)*
> *leucine-induced (270.3)*

AHA: M-A, '85, 8

E16.2 Hypoglycemia unspecified   I-10

251.3 Postsurgical hypoinsulinemia

Hypoinsulinemia following complete or partial
pancreatectomy
Postpancreatectomy hyperglycemia

▶Use additional code to identify (any associated):
acquired absence of pancreas (V45.79)
insulin use (V58.67)
secondary diabetes mellitus (249.00-249.91)◀

> **EXCLUDES** ▶*transient hyperglycemia post procedure (790.29)*
> *transient hypoglycemia post procedure (251.2)*◀

AHA: 3Q, '91, 6

251.4 Abnormality of secretion of glucagon

Hyperplasia of pancreatic islet alpha cells with glucagon excess

DEF: Production malfunction of a pancreatic hormone secreted by cells of the islets of Langerhans.

251.5 Abnormality of secretion of gastrin

Hyperplasia of pancreatic alpha cells with gastrin excess
Zollinger-Ellison syndrome

251.8 Other specified disorders of pancreatic internal secretion

AHA: 2Q, '98, 15; 3Q, '91, 6

E16.8 Oth spec d/o of pancreatic internal secretion   I-10

251.9 Unspecified disorder of pancreatic internal secretion

Islet cell hyperplasia NOS

√4ᵗʰ **252 Disorders of parathyroid gland**

> **EXCLUDES** *hungry bone syndrome (275.5)*

√5ᵗʰ **252.0 Hyperparathyroidism**

> **EXCLUDES** *ectopic hyperparathyroidism (259.3)*

DEF: Abnormally high secretion of parathyroid hormones causing bone deterioration, reduced renal function, kidney stones.

252.00 Hyperparathyroidism, unspecified

E21.3 Hyperparathyroidism unspecified   I-10

Dorsal View of Parathyroid Glands

Pharynx

Thyroid gland

Parathyroid glands

Trachea

Esophagus

Parathyroid glands

Parathyroid hormone (PTH)

Calcium in bones ───────────→ Calcium in blood

252.01 Primary hyperparathyroidism

Hyperplasia of parathyroid

DEF: Parathyroid dysfunction commonly caused by hyperplasia of two or more glands; characteristic hypercalcemia and increased parathyroid hormone levels.

252.02 Secondary hyperparathyroidism, non-renal

> **EXCLUDES** *secondary hyperparathyroidism (of renal origin) (588.81)*

DEF: Underlying disease of nonrenal origin decreases blood levels of calcium causing the parathyroid to release increased levels of parathyroid hormone; parathyroid hormone levels return to normal once underlying condition is treated and blood calcium levels are normal.

AHA: 4Q, '04, 57-59

252.08 Other hyperparathyroidism

Tertiary hyperparathyroidism

DEF: Tertiary hyperparathyroidism: chronic secondary hyperparathyroidism with adenomatous parathyroid causing irreversible abnormal production of parathyroid hormone (PTH); PTH remains high after the serum calcium levels are brought under control.

252.1 Hypoparathyroidism

Parathyroiditis (autoimmune) Tetany:
Tetany: parathyroprival
parathyroid

> **EXCLUDES** *pseudohypoparathyroidism (275.4)*
> *pseudopseudohypoparathyroidism (275.4)*
> *tetany NOS (781.7)*
> *transitory neonatal hypoparathyroidism (775.4)*

DEF: Abnormally low secretion of parathyroid hormones which causes decreased calcium and increased phosphorus in the blood. Resulting in muscle cramps, tetany, urinary frequency and cataracts.

252.8 Other specified disorders of parathyroid gland

Cyst } of parathyroid
Hemorrhage

252.9 Unspecified disorder of parathyroid gland

√4ᵗʰ **253 Disorders of the pituitary gland and its hypothalamic control**

> **INCLUDES** the listed conditions whether the disorder is in the pituitary or the hypothalamus

> **EXCLUDES** *Cushing's syndrome (255.0)*

253.0 Acromegaly and gigantism

Overproduction of growth hormone

DEF: Acromegaly: chronic, middle age condition; caused by hypersecretion of the pituitary growth hormone; enlarged parts of skeleton, especially the nose, ears, jaws, fingers and toes.

DEF: Gigantism: pituitary gigantism caused by excess growth of short flat bones; men may grow 78 to 80 inches tall.

N Newborn Age: 0   P Pediatric Age: 0-17   M Maternity Age: 12-55   A Adult Age: 15-124

253.1   Other and unspecified anterior pituitary hyperfunction
Forbes-Albright syndrome
EXCLUDES   overproduction of:
ACTH (255.3)
thyroid-stimulating hormone [TSH] (242.8)
DEF: Spontaneous galactorrhea-amenorrhea syndrome unrelated to pregnancy; usually related to presence of pituitary tumor.
AHA: J-A, '85, 9

253.2   Panhypopituitarism
Cachexia, pituitary
Necrosis of pituitary (postpartum)
Pituitary insufficiency NOS
Sheehan's syndrome
Simmonds' disease
EXCLUDES   iatrogenic hypopituitarism (253.7)
DEF: Damage to or absence of pituitary gland leading to impaired sexual function, weight loss, fatigue, bradycardia, hypotension, pallor, depression, and impaired growth in children; called Simmonds' disease if cachexia is prominent.

253.3   Pituitary dwarfism
Isolated deficiency of (human) growth hormone [HGH]
Lorain-Levi dwarfism
DEF: Dwarfism with infantile physical characteristics due to abnormally low secretion of growth hormone and gonadotropin deficiency.

253.4   Other anterior pituitary disorders
Isolated or partial deficiency of an anterior pituitary hormone, other than growth hormone
Prolactin deficiency
AHA: J-A, '85, 9

253.5   Diabetes insipidus
Vasopressin deficiency
EXCLUDES   nephrogenic diabetes insipidus (588.1)
DEF: Metabolic disorder causing insufficient antidiuretic hormone release; symptoms include frequent urination, thirst, ravenous hunger, loss of weight, fatigue.

253.6   Other disorders of neurohypophysis
Syndrome of inappropriate secretion of antidiuretic hormone [ADH]
EXCLUDES   ectopic antidiuretic hormone secretion (259.3)
E22.2 Synd inappropriate secrectn antiduretic hormone   **I-10**

253.7   Iatrogenic pituitary disorders
Hypopituitarism:
hormone-induced
hypophysectomy-induced
postablative
radiotherapy-induced
Use additional E code to identify cause
DEF: Pituitary dysfunction that results from drug therapy, radiation therapy, or surgery, causing mild to severe symptoms.

253.8   Other disorders of the pituitary and other syndromes of diencephalohypophyseal origin
Abscess of pituitary   Cyst of Rathke's pouch
Adiposogenital dystrophy   Fröhlich's syndrome
EXCLUDES   craniopharyngioma (237.0)

253.9   Unspecified
Dyspituitarism

✓4th **254   Diseases of thymus gland**
EXCLUDES   aplasia or dysplasia with immunodeficiency (279.2)
hypoplasia with immunodeficiency (279.2)
myasthenia gravis (358.00-358.01)

254.0   Persistent hyperplasia of thymus
Hypertrophy of thymus
DEF: Continued abnormal growth of the twin lymphoid lobes that produce T lymphocytes.

254.1   Abscess of thymus

254.8   Other specified diseases of thymus gland
Astrophy
Cyst   } of thymus
EXCLUDES   thymoma (212.6)

254.9   Unspecified disease of thymus gland

✓4th **255   Disorders of adrenal glands**
INCLUDES   the listed conditions whether the basic disorder is in the adrenals or is pituitary-induced

255.0   Cushing's syndrome
Adrenal hyperplasia due to excess ACTH
Cushing's syndrome:
NOS
iatrogenic
idiopathic
pituitary-dependent
Ectopic ACTH syndrome
Iatrogenic syndrome of excess cortisol
Overproduction of cortisol
Use additional E code to identify cause, if drug-induced
EXCLUDES   congenital adrenal hyperplasia (255.2)
DEF: Due to adrenal cortisol oversecretion or glucocorticoid medications; may cause excess fatty tissue of the face, neck and body; osteoporosis and curvature of spine, hypertension, diabetes mellitus, female genitourinary problems, male impotence, degeneration of muscle tissues, weakness.

✓5th **255.1   Hyperaldosteronism**
DEF: Oversecretion of aldosterone causing fluid retention, hypertension.
AHA: 4Q, '03, 48

255.10   Hyperaldosteronism, unspecified
Aldosteronism NOS
Primary aldosteronism, unspecified
EXCLUDES   Conn's syndrome (255.12)

255.11   Glucocorticoid-remediable aldosteronism
Familial aldosteronism type I
EXCLUDES   Conn's syndrome (255.12)
DEF: Rare autosomal dominant familial form of primary aldosteronism in which the secretion of aldosterone is under the influence of adrenocortiotrophic hormone (ACTH) rather than the renin-angiotensin mechanism; moderate hypersecretion of aldosterone and suppressed plasma renin activity rapidly reversed by administration of glucosteroids; symptoms include hypertension and mild hypokalemia.

255.12   Conn's syndrome
DEF: A type of primary aldosteronism caused by an adenoma of the glomerulosa cells in the adrenal cortex; presence of hypertension.

255.13   Bartter's syndrome
DEF: A cluster of symptoms caused by a defect in the ability of the kidney to reabsorb potassium; signs include alkalosis (hypokalemic alkalosis), increased aldosterone, increased plasma renin, and normal blood pressure; symptoms include muscle cramping, weakness, constipation, frequency of urination, and failure to grow; also known as urinary potassium wasting or juxtaglomerular cell hyperplasia.

255.14   Other secondary aldosteronism
AHA: 3Q, '06, 24

255.2 Adrenogenital disorders
Achard-Thiers syndrome
Adrenogenital syndromes, virilizing or feminizing, whether acquired or associated with congenital adrenal hyperplasia consequent on inborn enzyme defects in hormone synthesis
Congenital adrenal hyperplasia
Female adrenal pseudohermaphroditism
Male:
  macrogenitosomia praecox
  sexual precocity with adrenal hyperplasia
Virilization (female) (suprarenal)
EXCLUDES adrenal hyperplasia due to excess ACTH (255.0)
  isosexual virilization (256.4)

255.3 Other corticoadrenal overactivity
Acquired benign adrenal androgenic overactivity
Overproduction of ACTH

√5ᵗʰ **255.4 Corticoadrenal insufficiency**
EXCLUDES tuberculous Addison's disease (017.6)
DEF: Underproduction of adrenal hormones causing low blood pressure.
AHA: 4Q, '07, 68; 3Q, '06, 24

255.41 Glucocorticoid deficiency
Addisonian crisis
Addison's disease NOS
Adrenal atrophy (autoimmune)
Adrenal calcification
Adrenal crisis
Adrenal hemorrhage
Adrenal infarction
Adrenal insufficiency NOS
Combined glucocorticoid and mineralocorticoid deficiency
Corticoadrenal insufficiency NOS
DEF: Decreased function of the adrenal cortex resulting in insufficient production of glucocorticoid, the hormone regulating carbohydrate, fat, and protein metabolism; manifestations: hyponatremia, hyperpigmentation, orthostatic hypotension, anemia, loss of appetite, and malaise.
AHA: 4Q, '07, 68, 69
E27.1 Primary adrenocortical insufficiency I-10

255.42 Mineralocorticoid deficiency
Hypoaldosteronism
EXCLUDES combined glucocorticoid and mineralocorticoid deficiency (255.41)
DEF: Decreased function of the adrenal cortex resulting in insufficient production of mineralocorticoid, which regulates electrolyte and water balance; manifestations: hyponatremia, hyperkalemia, and mild acidosis.

255.5 Other adrenal hypofunction
Adrenal medullary insufficiency
EXCLUDES Waterhouse-Friderichsen syndrome (meningococcal) (036.3)

255.6 Medulloadrenal hyperfunction
Catecholamine secretion by pheochromocytoma

255.8 Other specified disorders of adrenal glands
Abnormality of cortisol-binding globulin

255.9 Unspecified disorder of adrenal glands

√4ᵗʰ **256 Ovarian dysfunction**
AHA: 4Q, '00, 51

256.0 Hyperestrogenism   ♀
DEF: Excess secretion of estrogen by the ovaries; characterized by ovaries containing multiple follicular cysts filled with serous fluid.

256.1 Other ovarian hyperfunction   ♀
Hypersecretion of ovarian androgens
AHA: 3Q, '95, 15

256.2 Postablative ovarian failure   ♀
Ovarian failure:
  iatrogenic
  postirradiation
  postsurgical
Use additional code for states associated with artificial menopause (627.4)
EXCLUDES acquired absence of ovary (V45.77)
  asymptomatic age-related (natural) postmenopausal status (V49.81)
DEF: Failed ovarian function after medical or surgical intervention.
AHA: 2Q, '02, 12

√5ᵗʰ **256.3 Other ovarian failure**
Use additional code for states associated with natural menopause (627.2)
EXCLUDES asymptomatic age-related (natural) postmenopausal status (V49.81)
AHA: 4Q, '01, 41

256.31 Premature menopause   A ♀
DEF: Permanent cessation of ovarian function before the age of 40 occuring naturally of unknown cause.

256.39 Other ovarian failure   ♀
Delayed menarche
Ovarian hypofunction
Primary ovarian failure NOS

256.4 Polycystic ovaries   ♀
Isosexual virilization
Stein-Leventhal syndrome
DEF: Multiple serous filled cysts of ovary; symptoms of infertility, hirsutism, oligomenorrhea or amenorrhea.
E28.2 Polycystic ovarian syndrome I-10

256.8 Other ovarian dysfunction   ♀

256.9 Unspecified ovarian dysfunction   ♀

√4ᵗʰ **257 Testicular dysfunction**

257.0 Testicular hyperfunction   ♂
Hypersecretion of testicular hormones

257.1 Postablative testicular hypofunction   ♂
Testicular hypofunction:
  iatrogenic
  postirradiation
  postsurgical

257.2 Other testicular hypofunction
Defective biosynthesis of testicular androgen
Eunuchoidism:
  NOS
  hypogonadotropic
Failure:
  Leydig's cell, adult
  seminiferous tubule, adult
Testicular hypogonadism
EXCLUDES azoospermia (606.0)

257.8 Other testicular dysfunction
EXCLUDES androgen insensitivity syndromes (259.50-259.52)

257.9 Unspecified testicular dysfunction   ♂

√4ᵗʰ **258 Polyglandular dysfunction and related disorders**

√5ᵗʰ **258.0 Polyglandular activity in multiple endocrine adenomatosis**
Multiple endocrine neoplasia [MEN] syndromes
Use additional codes to identify any malignancies and other conditions associated with the syndromes
AHA: 4Q, '07, 70

258.01 Multiple endocrine neoplasia [MEN] type I
Wermer's syndrome
DEF: Wermer's syndrome: A rare hereditary condition characterized by the presence of adenomas or hyperplasia in more than one endocrine gland causing premature aging.
AHA: ▶4Q, '08, 86, 89;◀ 4Q, '07, 70, 72

N Newborn Age: 0   P Pediatric Age: 0-17   M Maternity Age: 12-55   A Adult Age: 15-124

258.02　Multiple endocrine neoplasia [MEN] type IIA
Sipple's syndrome
DEF: Sipple's syndrome: A hereditary disorder caused by a defect in the RET gene causing overactivity of the thyroid, adrenal, and parathyroid glands, resulting in adrenal pheochromocytoma and thyroid medullary carcinoma.

258.03　Multiple endocrine neoplasia [MEN] type IIB

258.1　Other combinations of endocrine dysfunction
Lloyd's syndrome
Schmidt's syndrome

258.8　Other specified polyglandular dysfunction

258.9　Polyglandular dysfunction, unspecified

√4th **259　Other endocrine disorders**

259.0　Delay in sexual development and puberty, not elsewhere classified
Delayed puberty

259.1　Precocious sexual development and puberty, not elsewhere classified　　　P
Sexual precocity:
NOS
constitutional
cryptogenic
idiopathic

259.2　Carcinoid syndrome
Hormone secretion by carcinoid tumors
DEF: Presence of carcinoid tumors that spread to liver; characterized by cyanotic flushing of skin, diarrhea, bronchospasm, acquired tricuspid and pulmonary stenosis, sudden drops in blood pressure, edema, ascites.
AHA: ▶4Q, '08, 85-86, 89◀

259.3　Ectopic hormone secretion, not elsewhere classified
Ectopic:
antidiuretic hormone secretion [ADH]
hyperparathyroidism
EXCLUDES　ectopic ACTH syndrome (255.0)
AHA: N-D, '85, 4

259.4　Dwarfism, not elsewhere classified
Dwarfism:
NOS
constitutional
EXCLUDES　dwarfism:
achondroplastic (756.4)
intrauterine (759.7)
nutritional (263.2)
pituitary (253.3)
renal (588.0)
progeria (259.8)

√5th **259.5　Androgen insensitivity syndrome**
DEF: X chromosome abnormality that prohibits the body from recognizing androgen; XY genotype with ambiguous genitalia.
AHA: ▶4Q, '08, 95-96;◀ 4Q, '05, 53

259.50　Androgen insensitivity, unspecified

259.51　Androgen insensitivity syndrome
Complete androgen insensitivity
de Quervain's syndrome
Goldberg-Maxwell Syndrome

259.52　Partial androgen insensitivity
Partial androgen insensitivity syndrome
Reifenstein syndrome

259.8　Other specified endocrine disorders
Pineal gland dysfunction
Progeria
Werner's syndrome

259.9　Unspecified endocrine disorder
Disturbance:
endocrine NOS
hormone NOS
Infantilism NOS

NUTRITIONAL DEFICIENCIES (260-269)
EXCLUDES　deficiency anemias (280.0-281.9)
TIP: Assign first a code for the underlying condition (e.g., anorexia nervosa) if specified.

260　Kwashiorkor
Nutritional edema with dyspigmentation of skin and hair
DEF: Syndrome, particularly of children; excessive carbohydrate with inadequate protein intake, inhibited growth potential, anomalies in skin and hair pigmentation, edema and liver disease.
E40 Kwashiorkor　　　I-10

261　Nutritional marasmus
Nutritional atrophy
Severe calorie deficiency
Severe malnutrition NOS
DEF: Protein-calorie malabsorption or malnutrition in children; characterized by tissue wasting, dehydration, and subcutaneous fat depletion; may occur with infectious disease; also called infantile atrophy.
AHA: 4Q, '07, 97; 3Q, '06, 14; 2Q, '06, 12
E41 Nutritional marasmus　　　I-10

262　Other severe, protein-calorie malnutrition
Nutritional edema without mention of dyspigmentation of skin and hair
AHA: 4Q, '92, 24; J-A, '85, 12

√4th **263　Other and unspecified protein-calorie malnutrition**
AHA: 4Q, '92, 24

263.0　Malnutrition of moderate degree
DEF: Malnutrition characterized by biochemical changes in electrolytes, lipids, blood plasma.
AHA: J-A, '85, 1

263.1　Malnutrition of mild degree
AHA: J-A, '85, 1

263.2　Arrested development following protein-calorie malnutrition
Nutritional dwarfism
Physical retardation due to malnutrition

263.8　Other protein-calorie malnutrition

263.9　Unspecified protein-calorie malnutrition
Dystrophy due to malnutrition
Malnutrition (calorie) NOS
EXCLUDES　nutritional deficiency NOS (269.9)
AHA: 4Q, '03, 109; N-D, '84, 19
E46 Unspecified protein-calorie malnutrition　　　I-10

√4th **264　Vitamin A deficiency**

264.0　With conjunctival xerosis
DEF: Vitamin A deficiency with conjunctival dryness.

264.1　With conjunctival xerosis and Bitot's spot
Bitot's spot in the young child
DEF: Vitamin A deficiency with conjunctival dryness, superficial spots of keratinized epithelium.

264.2　With corneal xerosis
DEF: Vitamin A deficiency with corneal dryness.

264.3　With corneal ulceration and xerosis
DEF: Vitamin A deficiency with corneal dryness, epithelial ulceration.

264.4　With keratomalacia
DEF: Vitamin A deficiency creating corneal dryness; progresses to corneal insensitivity, softness, necrosis; usually bilateral.

264.5　With night blindness
DEF: Vitamin A deficiency causing vision failure in dim light.

264.6　With xerophthalmic scars of cornea
DEF: Vitamin A deficiency with corneal scars from dryness.

264.7　Other ocular manifestations of vitamin A deficiency
Xerophthalmia due to vitamin A deficiency

264.8　Other manifestations of vitamin A deficiency
Follicular keratosis ⎫
Xeroderma　　　⎬ due to vitamin A deficiency

264.9　Unspecified vitamin A deficiency
Hypovitaminosis A NOS

√4th **265 Thiamine and niacin deficiency states**

265.0 Beriberi

DEF: Inadequate vitamin B$_1$ (thiamine) intake, affects heart and peripheral nerves; individual may become edematous and develop cardiac disease due to the excess fluid; affects alcoholic.

265.1 Other and unspecified manifestations of thiamine deficiency

Other vitamin B$_1$ deficiency states

265.2 Pellagra

Deficiency:
niacin (-tryptophan)
nicotinamide
nicotinic acid
vitamin PP
Pellagra (alcoholic)

DEF: Niacin deficiency causing dermatitis, inflammation of mucous membranes, diarrhea, and psychic disturbances.

√4th **266 Deficiency of B-complex components**

266.0 Ariboflavinosis

Riboflavin [vitamin B$_2$] deficiency

DEF: Vitamin B$_2$ (riboflavin) deficiency marked by swollen lips and tongue fissures, corneal vascularization, scaling lesions, and anemia.

AHA: S-O, '86, 10

266.1 Vitamin B$_6$ deficiency

Deficiency:
pyridoxal
pyridoxamine
pyridoxine
Vitamin B$_6$ deficiency syndrome

EXCLUDES *vitamin B$_6$-responsive sideroblastic anemia (285.0)*

DEF: Vitamin B$_6$ deficiency causing skin, lip, and tongue disturbances, peripheral neuropathy; and convulsions in infants.

266.2 Other B-complex deficiencies

Deficiency:
cyanocobalamin
folic acid
vitamin B$_{12}$

EXCLUDES *combined system disease with anemia (281.0-281.1)*
deficiency anemias (281.0-281.9)
subacute degeneration of spinal cord with anemia (281.0-281.1)

E53.8 Deficiency of other specified B group vitamins `I-10`

266.9 Unspecified vitamin B deficiency

267 Ascorbic acid deficiency

Deficiency of vitamin C
Scurvy

EXCLUDES *scorbutic anemia (281.8)*

DEF: Vitamin C deficiency causing swollen gums, myalgia, weight loss, and weakness.

√4th **268 Vitamin D deficiency**

EXCLUDES *vitamin D-resistant:*
osteomalacia (275.3)
rickets (275.3)

268.0 Rickets, active

EXCLUDES *celiac rickets (579.0)*
renal rickets (588.0)

DEF: Inadequate vitamin D intake, usually in pediatrics, that affects bones most involved with muscular action; may cause nodules on ends and sides of bones; delayed closure of fontanels in infants; symptoms may include muscle soreness, and profuse sweating.

268.1 Rickets, late effect

Any condition specified as due to rickets and stated to be a late effect or sequela of rickets

Code first the nature of late effect

DEF: Distorted or demineralized bones as a result of vitamin D deficiency.

268.2 Osteomalacia, unspecified

DEF: Softening of bones due to decrease in calcium; marked by pain, tenderness, muscular weakness, anorexia, and weight loss.

268.9 Unspecified vitamin D deficiency

Avitaminosis D

√4th **269 Other nutritional deficiencies**

269.0 Deficiency of vitamin K

EXCLUDES *deficiency of coagulation factor due to vitamin K deficiency (286.7)*
vitamin K deficiency of newborn (776.0)

269.1 Deficiency of other vitamins

Deficiency:
vitamin E
vitamin P

269.2 Unspecified vitamin deficiency

Multiple vitamin deficiency NOS

269.3 Mineral deficiency, not elsewhere classified

Deficiency:
calcium, dietary
iodine

EXCLUDES *deficiency:*
calcium NOS (275.4)
potassium (276.8)
sodium (276.1)

269.8 Other nutritional deficiency

EXCLUDES *adult failure to thrive (783.7)*
failure to thrive in childhood (783.41)
feeding problems (783.3)
newborn ▶(779.31-779.34)◀

269.9 Unspecified nutritional deficiency

OTHER METABOLIC AND IMMUNITY DISORDERS (270-279)

Use additional code to identify any associated mental retardation

√4th **270 Disorders of amino-acid transport and metabolism**

EXCLUDES *abnormal findings without manifest disease (790.0-796.9)*
disorders of purine and pyrimidine metabolism (277.1-277.2)
gout ▶(274.00-274.9)◀

270.0 Disturbances of amino-acid transport

Cystinosis
Cystinuria
Fanconi (-de Toni) (-Debré) syndrome
Glycinuria (renal)
Hartnup disease

270.1 Phenylketonuria [PKU]

Hyperphenylalaninemia

DEF: Inherited metabolic condition causing excess phenylpyruvic and other acids in urine; results in mental retardation, neurological manifestations, including spasticity and tremors, light pigmentation, eczema, and mousy odor.

270.2 Other disturbances of aromatic amino-acid metabolism

Albinism
Alkaptonuria
Alkaptonuric ochronosis
Disturbances of metabolism of tyrosine and tryptophan
Homogentisic acid defects
Hydroxykynureninuria
Hypertyrosinemia
Indicanuria
Kynureninase defects
Oasthouse urine disease
Ochronosis
Tyrosinosis
Tyrosinuria
Waardenburg syndrome

EXCLUDES *vitamin B$_6$-deficiency syndrome (266.1)*

AHA: 3Q, '99, 20

270.3 Disturbances of branched-chain amino-acid metabolism
Disturbances of metabolism of leucine, isoleucine, and valine
Hypervalinemia
Intermittent branched-chain ketonuria
Leucine-induced hypoglycemia
Leucinosis
Maple syrup urine disease
AHA: 3Q, '00, 8

270.4 Disturbances of sulphur-bearing amino-acid metabolism
Cystathioninemia
Cystathioninuria
Disturbances of metabolism of methionine, homocystine, and cystathionine
Homocystinuria
Hypermethioninemia
Methioninemia
AHA: 2Q, '07, 7;1Q, '04, 6

270.5 Disturbances of histidine metabolism
Carnosinemia
Histidinemia
Hyperhistidinemia
Imidazole aminoaciduria

270.6 Disorders of urea cycle metabolism
Argininosuccinic aciduria
Citrullinemia
Disorders of metabolism of ornithine, citrulline, argininosuccinic acid, arginine, and ammonia
Hyperammonemia
Hyperomithinemia

270.7 Other disturbances of straight-chain amino-acid metabolism
Glucoglycinuria
Glycinemia (with methyl-malonic acidemia)
Hyperglycinemia
Hyperlysinemia
Other disturbances of metabolism of glycine, threonine, serine, glutamine, and lysine
Pipecolic acidemia
Saccharopinuria
AHA: 3Q, '00, 8

270.8 Other specified disorders of amino-acid metabolism
Alaninemia   Iminoacidopathy
Ethanolaminuria   Prolinemia
Glycoprolinuria   Prolinuria
Hydroxyprolinemia   Sarcosinemia
Hyperprolinemia

270.9 Unspecified disorder of amino-acid metabolism

√4ᵗʰ **271 Disorders of carbohydrate transport and metabolism**
EXCLUDES abnormality of secretion of glucagon (251.4)
diabetes mellitus (249.0-249.9, 250.0-250.9)
hypoglycemia NOS (251.2)
mucopolysaccharidosis (277.5)

271.0 Glycogenosis
Amylopectinosis
Glucose-6-phosphatase deficiency
Glycogen storage disease
McArdle's disease
Pompe's disease
von Gierke's disease
DEF: Excess glycogen storage; rare inherited trait affects liver, kidneys; causes various symptoms depending on type, though often weakness and muscle cramps.
AHA: 1Q, '98, 5

271.1 Galactosemia
Galactose-1-phosphate uridyl transferase deficiency
Galactosuria
DEF: Any of three genetic disorders due to defective galactose metabolism; symptoms include failure to thrive in infancy, jaundice, liver and spleen damage, cataracts, and mental retardation.

271.2 Hereditary fructose intolerance
Essential benign fructosuria
Fructosemia
DEF: Chromosome recessive disorder of carbohydrate metabolism; in infants, occurs after dietary sugar introduced; characterized by enlarged spleen, yellowish cast to skin, and progressive inability to thrive.

271.3 Intestinal disaccharidase deficiencies and disaccharide malabsorption
Intolerance or malabsorption (congenital) (of):
glucose-galactose
lactose
sucrose-isomaltose
E73.9 Lactose intolerance unspecified   I-10

271.4 Renal glycosuria
Renal diabetes
DEF: Persistent abnormal levels of glucose in urine, with normal blood glucose levels; caused by failure of the renal tubules to reabsorb glucose.

271.8 Other specified disorders of carbohydrate transport and metabolism
Essential benign pentosuria   Mannosidosis
Fucosidosis   Oxalosis
Glycolic aciduria   Xylosuria
Hyperoxaluria (primary)   Xylulosuria

271.9 Unspecified disorder of carbohydrate transport and metabolism

√4ᵗʰ **272 Disorders of lipoid metabolism**
EXCLUDES localized cerebral lipidoses (330.1)

272.0 Pure hypercholesterolemia
Familial hypercholesterolemia
Fredrickson Type IIa hyperlipoproteinemia
Hyperbetalipoproteinemia
Hyperlipidemia, Group A
Low-density-lipoid-type [LDL] hyperlipoproteinemia
AHA: 4Q, '05, 71
E78.0 Pure hypercholesterolemia   I-10

272.1 Pure hyperglyceridemia
Endogenous hyperglyceridemia
Fredrickson Type IV hyperlipoproteinemia
Hyperlipidemia, Group B
Hyperprebetalipoproteinemia
Hypertriglyceridemia, essential
Very-low-density-lipoid-type [VLDL] hyperlipoproteinemia

272.2 Mixed hyperlipidemia
Broad- or floating-betalipoproteinemia
►Combined hyperlipidemia
Elevated cholesterol with elevated triglycerides NEC◄
Fredrickson Type IIb or III hyperlipoproteinemia
Hypercholesterolemia with endogenous hyperglyceridemia
Hyperbetalipoproteinemia with prebetalipoproteinemia
Tubo-eruptive xanthoma
Xanthoma tuberosum
DEF: Elevated levels of lipoprotein, a complex of fats and proteins, in blood due to inherited metabolic disorder.

Lipid Metabolism

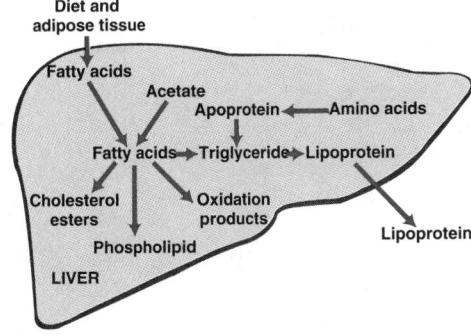

Diet and adipose tissue — Fatty acids — Acetate — Apoprotein ← Amino acids — Fatty acids → Triglyceride → Lipoprotein — Cholesterol esters — Oxidation products — Phospholipid — Lipoprotein — LIVER

272.3 Hyperchylomicronemia
Bürger-Grütz syndrome
Fredrickson type I or V hyperlipoproteinemia
Hyperlipidemia, Group D
Mixed hyperglyceridemia

272.4 Other and unspecified hyperlipidemia
Alpha-lipoproteinemia   Hyperlipoproteinemia NOS
Hyperlipidemia NOS
DEF: Hyperlipoproteinemia: elevated levels of transient chylomicrons in the blood which are a form of lipoproteins that transport dietary cholesterol and triglycerides from the small intestine to the blood.
AHA: 1Q, '05, 17
E78.4 Other hyperlipidemia   `I-10`

272.5 Lipoprotein deficiencies
Abetalipoproteinemia
Bassen-Kornzweig syndrome
High-density lipoid deficiency
Hypoalphalipoproteinemia
Hypobetalipoproteinemia (familial)
DEF: Abnormally low levels of lipoprotein, a complex of fats and protein, in the blood.

272.6 Lipodystrophy
Barraquer-Simons disease   Progressive lipodystrophy
Use additional E code to identify cause, if iatrogenic
EXCLUDES *intestinal lipodystrophy (040.2)*
DEF: Disturbance of fat metabolism resulting in loss of fatty tissue in some areas of the body.

272.7 Lipidoses
Chemically-induced lipidosis
Disease:
    Anderson's
    Fabry's
    Gaucher's
    I cell [mucolipidosis I]
    lipoid storage NOS
    Niemann-Pick
    pseudo-Hurler's or mucolipdosis III
    triglyceride storage, Type I or II
    Wolman's or triglyceride storage, Type III
Mucolipidosis II
Primary familial xanthomatosis
EXCLUDES *cerebral lipidoses (330.1)*
          Tay-Sachs disease (330.1)
DEF: Lysosomal storage diseases marked by an abnormal amount of lipids in reticuloendothelial cells.

272.8 Other disorders of lipoid metabolism
Hoffa's disease or liposynovitis prepatellaris
Launois-Bensaude's lipomatosis
Lipoid dermatoarthritis

272.9 Unspecified disorder of lipoid metabolism

✓4ᵗʰ **273 Disorders of plasma protein metabolism**
EXCLUDES *agammaglobulinemia and hypogammaglobulinemia*
          (279.0-279.2)
          coagulation defects (286.0-286.9)
          hereditary hemolytic anemias (282.0-282.9)

273.0 Polyclonal hypergammaglobulinemia
Hypergammaglobulinemic purpura:
    benign primary
    Waldenström's
DEF: Elevated blood levels of gamma globulins, frequently found in patients with chronic infectious diseases.

273.1 Monoclonal paraproteinemia
Benign monoclonal hypergammaglobulinemia [BMH]
Monoclonal gammopathy:
    NOS
    associated with lymphoplasmacytic dyscrasias
    benign
Paraproteinemia:
    benign (familial)
    secondary to malignant or inflammatory disease
DEF: Elevated blood levels of macroglobulins (plasma globulins of high weight); characterized by malignant neoplasms of bone marrow, spleen, liver, or lymph nodes; symptoms include weakness, fatigue, bleeding disorders, and vision problems.

273.2 Other paraproteinemias
Cryoglobulinemic:
    purpura
    vasculitis
Mixed cryoglobulinemia
AHA: 2Q, '08, 17

273.3 Macroglobulinemia
Macroglobulinemia (idiopathic) (primary)
Waldenström's macroglobulinemia

273.4 Alpha-1-antitrypsin deficiency
AAT deficiency
DEF: Disorder of plasma protein metabolism that results in a deficiency of Alpha-1-antitrypsin, an acute-phase reactive protein, released into the blood in response to infection or injury to protect tissue against the harmful effect of enzymes.

273.8 Other disorders of plasma protein metabolism
Abnormality of transport protein
Bisalbuminemia
AHA: 2Q, '98, 11
E88.09 Oth disorders of plasma-protein metablolis NEC   `I-10`

273.9 Unspecified disorder of plasma protein metabolism

✓4ᵗʰ **274 Gout**
EXCLUDES *lead gout (984.0-984.9)*
DEF: Purine and pyrimidine metabolic disorders; manifested by hyperuricemia and recurrent acute inflammatory arthritis; monosodium urate or monohydrate crystals may be deposited in and around the joints, leading to joint destruction, and severe crippling.
AHA: 2Q, '95, 4

✓5ᵗʰ **274.0 Gouty arthropathy**
●   **274.00 Gouty arthropathy, unspecified**
          M10.00 Idiopathic gout unspecified site   `I-10`
●   **274.01 Acute gouty arthropathy**
          Acute gout
          Gout attack
          Gout flare
          Podagra
●   **274.02 Chronic gouty arthropathy without mention of tophus (tophi)**
          Chronic gout
●   **274.03 Chronic gouty arthropathy with tophus (tophi)**
          Chronic tophaceous gout
          Gout with tophi NOS

✓5ᵗʰ **274.1 Gouty nephropathy**
    274.10 Gouty nephropathy, unspecified
          AHA: N-D, '85, 15
    274.11 Uric acid nephrolithiasis
          DEF: Sodium urate stones in the kidney.
    274.19 Other

✓5ᵗʰ **274.8 Gout with other specified manifestations**
    274.81 Gouty tophi of ear
          DEF: Chalky sodium urate deposit in the ear due to gout; produces chronic inflammation of external ear.

274.82 Gouty tophi of other sites
Gouty tophi of heart
> **EXCLUDES** ▶gout with tophi NOS (274.03)
> gouty arthropathy with tophi
> (274.03)◀

274.89 Other
Use additional code to identify manifestations,
as:
gouty:
iritis (364.11)
neuritis (357.4)

274.9 Gout, unspecified
M10.9 Gout unspecified   I-10

✓4th **275 Disorders of mineral metabolism**
> **EXCLUDES** abnormal findings without manifest disease
> (790.0-796.9)

275.0 Disorders of iron metabolism
Bronzed diabetes   Pigmentary cirrhosis
Hemochromatosis   (of liver)
> **EXCLUDES** anemia:
> iron deficiency (280.0-280.9)
> sideroblastic (285.0)

AHA: 2Q, '97, 11
E83.10 Disorder of iron metablolism unspecified   I-10

275.1 Disorders of copper metabolism
Hepatolenticular degeneration
Wilson's disease

275.2 Disorders of magnesium metabolism
Hypermagnesemia   Hypomagnesemia
E83.40 Disorders of magnesium metabolism unspec   I-10

275.3 Disorders of phosphorus metabolism
Familial hypophosphatemia
Hypophosphatasia
Vitamin D-resistant:
osteomalacia
rickets

✓5th **275.4 Disorders of calcium metabolism**
> **EXCLUDES** hungry bone syndrome (275.5)
> parathyroid disorders (252.00-252.9)
> vitamin D deficiency (268.0-268.9)

AHA: 4Q, '97, 33

275.40 Unspecified disorder of calcium metabolism

275.41 Hypocalcemia
DEF: Abnormally decreased blood calcium level;
symptoms include hyperactive deep tendon
reflexes, muscle, abdominal cramps, and
carpopedal spasm.
AHA: 3Q, '07, 5
E83.51 Hypocalcemia   I-10

275.42 Hypercalcemia
DEF: Abnormally increased blood calcium level;
symptoms include muscle weakness, fatigue,
nausea, depression, and constipation.
AHA: 4Q, '03, 110

275.49 Other disorders of calcium metabolism
Nephrocalcinosis
Pseudohypoparathyroidism
Pseudopseudohypoparathyroidism
DEF: Nephrocalcinosis: calcium phosphate deposits
in the tubules of the kidney with resultant renal
insufficiency.
DEF: Pseudohypoparathyroidism: inherited
hypoparathyroidismdisorder; caused by inadequate
response to parathyroid hormone, not hormonal
deficiency; includes muscle cramps, tetany, urinary
frequency, blurred vision due to cataracts, and dry
scaly skin.
DEF: Pseudopseudohypoparathyroidism: clinical
manifestations of hypoparathyroidism without
affecting blood calcium levels.

275.5 Hungry bone syndrome
DEF: Marked and prolonged hypocalcemia; usually involves an
extended history of elevated levels of parathyroid hormone,
related bone demineralization causing the bone to sequester
calcium.
AHA: 4Q, 08, 96-97

275.8 Other specified disorders of mineral metabolism

275.9 Unspecified disorder of mineral metabolism

✓4th **276 Disorders of fluid, electrolyte, and acid-base balance**
> **EXCLUDES** diabetes insipidus (253.5)
> familial periodic paralysis (359.3)

276.0 Hyperosmolality and/or hypernatremia
Sodium [Na] excess   Sodium [Na] overload

276.1 Hyposmolality and/or hyponatremia
Sodium [Na] deficiency
E87.1 Hypo-osmolality and hyponatremia   I-10

276.2 Acidosis
Acidosis: Acidosis:
NOS   metabolic
lactic   respiratory
> **EXCLUDES** diabetic acidosis (249.1, 250.1)

DEF: Disorder involves decrease of pH (hydrogen ion)
concentration in blood and cellular tissues; caused by
increase in acid and decrease in bicarbonate.
AHA: J-F, '87, 15
E87.2 Acidosis   I-10

276.3 Alkalosis
Alkalosis: Alkalosis:
NOS   respiratory
metabolic
DEF: Increased blood alkalinity (base) without relative loss of
base in body fluids; caused by increased arterial plasma
bicarbonate concentration or loss of carbon dioxide due to
hyperventilation.

276.4 Mixed acid-base balance disorder
Hypercapnia with mixed acid-base disorder

✓5th **276.5 Volume depletion**
> **EXCLUDES** hypovolemic shock:
> postoperative (998.0)
> traumatic (958.4)

AHA: 4Q, '05, 54; 2Q, '05, 9; 1Q, '03, 5, 22; 3Q, '02, 21; 4Q, '97,
30; 2Q, '88, 9

276.50 Volume depletion, unspecified
DEF: Depletion of total body water (dehydration)
and/or contraction of total intravascular plasma
(hypovolemia).
E86.9 Volume depletion unspecified   I-10

276.51 Dehydration
DEF: Depletion of total body water; blood volume
may be normal while fluid is pulled from other
tissues.
AHA: 1Q, '08, 10
E86.0 Dehydration   I-10

276.52 Hypovolemia
Depletion of volume of plasma
DEF: Depletion of volume plasma; depletion of total
blood volume.

276.6 Fluid overload
Fluid retention
> **EXCLUDES** ascites (789.51-789.59)
> localized edema (782.3)

AHA: 3Q, '07, 9; 4Q, '06, 136

276.7 Hyperpotassemia
Hyperkalemia   Potassium [K]:
Potassium [K]:   intoxication
excess   overload
DEF: Elevated blood levels of potassium; symptoms include
abnormal EKG readings, weakness; related to defective renal
excretion.
AHA: 1Q, '05, 9; 2Q,'01, 12
E87.5 Hyperkalemia   I-10

✓4th ✓5th   Additional Digit Required   Unspecified Code   Other Specified Code   Manifestation Code   ▶◀ Revised Text   ● New Code   ▲ Revised Code Title

2010 ICD-9-CM   **October 2009 • Volume 1 – 61**

276.8 Hypopotassemia
Hypokalemia
Potassium [K] deficiency

DEF: Decreased blood levels of potassium; symptoms include neuromuscular disorders.

E87.6 Hypokalemia   `I-10`

276.9 Electrolyte and fluid disorders not elsewhere classified
Electrolyte imbalance
Hyperchloremia
Hypochloremia

EXCLUDES   *electrolyte imbalance:*
     associated with hyperemesis gravidarum (643.1)
     complicating labor and delivery (669.0)
     following abortion and ectopic or molar pregnancy (634-638 with .4, 639.4)

AHA: J-F, '87, 15

E87.8 Oth disorders of electrolyte & fluid balance NEC   `I-10`

√4ᵗʰ **277 Other and unspecified disorders of metabolism**

√5ᵗʰ **277.0 Cystic fibrosis**
Fibrocystic disease of the pancreas
Mucoviscidosis

DEF: Genetic disorder of infants, children, and young adults marked by exocrine gland dysfunction; characterized by chronic pulmonary disease with excess mucus production, pancreatic deficiency, and high levels of electrolytes in the sweat.

AHA: 4Q, '90, 16; 3Q, '90, 18

TIP: Sequencing of CF is determined by circumstances of admission. If a patient is admitted for CF, sequence the CF first. If admitted for a complication of CF (e.g., pneumothorax, acute bronchitis, or acute cor pulmonale), sequence the complication first.

277.00 Without mention of meconium ileus
Cystic fibrosis NOS

AHA: 2Q, '03, 12

E84.9 Cystic fibrosis unspecified   `I-10`

277.01 With meconium ileus   `N`
Meconium:
     ileus (of newborn)
     obstruction of intestine in mucoviscidosis

277.02 With pulmonary manifestations
Cystic fibrosis with pulmonary exacerbation

Use additional code to identify any infectious organism present, such as:
     pseudomonas (041.7)

277.03 With gastrointestinal manifestations

EXCLUDES   *with meconium ileus (277.01)*

AHA: 4Q, '02, 45

277.09 With other manifestations

277.1 Disorders of porphyrin metabolism
Hematoporphyria
Hematoporphyrinuria
Hereditary coproporphyria
Porphyria
Porphyrinuria
Protocoproporphyria
Protoporphyria
Pyrroloporphyria

277.2 Other disorders of purine and pyrimidine metabolism
Hypoxanthine-guanine-phosphoribosyltransferase deficiency [HG-PRT deficiency]
Lesch-Nyhan syndrome
Xanthinuria

EXCLUDES   *gout ▶(274.00-274.9)◀*
     orotic aciduric anemia (281.4)

√5ᵗʰ **277.3 Amyloidosis**

DEF: Conditions of diverse etiologies characterized by the accumulation of insoluble fibrillar proteins (amyloid) in various organs and tissues of the body, compromising vital functions.

AHA: 1Q, '96, 16

277.30 Amyloidosis, unspecified
Amyloidosis NOS

AHA: 4Q, '06, 66

277.31 Familial Mediterranean fever
Benign paroxysmal peritonitis
Hereditary amyloid nephropathy
Periodic familial polyserositis
Recurrent polyserositis

DEF: Early-life onset of recurrent attacks characterized by high fevers with pain and inflammation of chest and abdominal cavities, skin and joints, also rash or vasculitis. Etiology unknown, possibly genetic, but may be precipitated by stress, trauma or exertion.

AHA: 4Q, '06, 66

277.39 Other amyloidosis
Hereditary cardiac amyloidosis
Inherited systemic amyloidosis
Neuropathic (Portuguese) (Swiss) amyloidosis
Secondary amyloidosis

AHA: ▶1Q, '09, 9;◀ 2Q, '08, 8; 4Q, '06, 66

277.4 Disorders of bilirubin excretion
Hyperbilirubinemia:
     congenital
     constitutional
Syndrome:
     Crigler-Najjar
     Dubin-Johnson
     Gilbert's
     Rotor's

EXCLUDES   *hyperbilirubinemias specific to the perinatal period (774.0-774.7)*

277.5 Mucopolysaccharidosis
Gargoylism
Hunter's syndrome
Hurler's syndrome
Lipochondrodystrophy
Maroteaux-Lamy syndrome
Morquio-Brailsford disease
Osteochondrodystrophy
Sanfilippo's syndrome
Scheie's syndrome

DEF: Metabolic disorders evidenced by excretion of various mucopolysaccharides in urine and infiltration of these substances into connective tissue, with resulting defects of bone, cartilage and connective tissue.

277.6 Other deficiencies of circulating enzymes
Hereditary angioedema

277.7 Dysmetabolic syndrome X

Use additional code for associated manifestation, such as:
     cardiovascular disease (414.00-414.07)
     obesity (278.00-278.01)

DEF: A specific group of metabolic disorders that are related to the state of insulin resistance (decreased cellular response to insulin) without elevated blood sugars; often related to elevated cholesterol and triglycerides, obesity, cardiovascular disease, and high blood pressure.

AHA: 4Q, '01, 42

√5ᵗʰ **277.8 Other specified disorders of metabolism**

AHA: 4Q, '03, 50; 2Q, '01, 18; S-O, '87, 9

277.81 Primary carnitine deficiency

277.82 Carnitine deficiency due to inborn errors of metabolism

277.83 Iatrogenic carnitine deficiency
Carnitine deficiency due to:
     hemodialysis
     valproic acid therapy

`N` Newborn Age: 0   `P` Pediatric Age: 0-17   `M` Maternity Age: 12-55   `A` Adult Age: 15-124

277.84 Other secondary carnitine deficiency

277.85 Disorders of fatty acid oxidation
Carnitine palmitoyltransferase deficiencies (CPT1, CPT2)
Glutaric aciduria type II (type IIA, IIB, IIC)
Long chain 3-hydroxyacyl CoA dehydrogenase deficiency (LCHAD)
Long chain/very long chain acyl CoA dehydrogenase deficiency (LCAD, VLCAD)
Medium chain acyl CoA dehydrogenase deficiency (MCAD)
Short chain acyl CoA dehydrogenase deficiency (SCAD)

> **EXCLUDES**   *primary carnitine deficiency (277.81)*

277.86 Peroxisomal disorders
Adrenomyeloneuropathy
Neonatal adrenoleukodystrophy
Rhizomelic chrondrodysplasia punctata
X-linked adrenoleukodystrophy
Zellweger syndrome

> **EXCLUDES**   *infantile Refsum disease (356.3)*

277.87 Disorders of mitochondrial metabolism
Kearns-Sayre syndrome
Mitochondrial Encephalopathy, Lactic Acidosis and Stroke-like episodes (MELAS syndrome)
Mitochondrial Neurogastrointestinal Encephalopathy syndrome (MNGIE)
Myoclonus with Epilepsy and with Ragged Red Fibers (MERRF syndrome)
Neuropathy, Ataxia and Retinitis Pigmentosa (NARP syndrome)

Use additional code for associated conditions

> **EXCLUDES**   *disorders of pyruvate metabolism (271.8)*
> *Leber's optic atrophy (377.16)*
> *Leigh's subacute necrotizing encephalopathy (330.8)*
> *Reye's syndrome (331.81)*

AHA: 4Q, '04, 62

● **277.88 Tumor lysis syndrome**
Spontaneous tumor lysis syndrome
Tumor lysis syndrome following antineoplastic drug therapy

Use additional E code to identify cause, if drug-induced

277.89 Other specified disorders of metabolism
Hand-Schüller-Christian disease
Histiocytosis (acute) (chronic)
Histiocytosis X (chronic)

> **EXCLUDES**   *histiocytosis:*
> *acute differentiated progressive (202.5)*
> *X, acute (progressive) (202.5)*

277.9 Unspecified disorder of metabolism
Enzymopathy NOS

√4th **278 Overweight, obesity and other hyperalimentation**

> **EXCLUDES**   *hyperalimentation NOS (783.6)*
> *poisoning by vitamins NOS (963.5)*
> *polyphagia (783.6)*

√5th **278.0 Overweight and obesity**
Use additional code to identify Body Mass Index (BMI), if known (V85.0-V85.54)

> **EXCLUDES**   *adiposogenital dystrophy (253.8)*
> *obesity of endocrine origin NOS (259.9)*

AHA: 4Q, '05, 97

278.00 Obesity, unspecified
Obesity NOS
DEF: BMI (body mass index) between 30.0 and 38.9.
AHA: 4Q, '01, 42; 1Q, '99, 5, 6

278.01 Morbid obesity
Severe obesity
DEF: BMI (body mass index) greater than 39.
AHA: ▶2Q, '09, 11;◀2Q, '06, 5-6; 3Q, '03, 6-8
E66.01 Morbid (severe) obesity due to excess calories   I-10

278.02 Overweight
DEF: BMI (body mass index) between 25 and 29.9.
AHA: 4Q, '05, 55
E66.3 Overweight   I-10

278.1 Localized adiposity
Fat pad
AHA: 2Q, '06, 10

278.2 Hypervitaminosis A

278.3 Hypercarotinemia
DEF: Elevated blood carotene level due to ingesting excess carotenoids or the inability to convert carotenoids to vitamin A.

278.4 Hypervitaminosis D
DEF: Weakness, fatigue, loss of weight, and other symptoms resulting from ingesting excessive amounts of vitamin D.

278.8 Other hyperalimentation
AHA: ▶2Q, '09, 11◀

√4th **279 Disorders involving the immune mechanism**

√5th **279.0 Deficiency of humoral immunity**
DEF: Inadequate immune response to bacterial infections with potential reinfection by viruses due to lack of circulating immunoglobulins (acquired antibodies).

279.00 Hypogammaglobulinemia, unspecified
Agammaglobulinemia NOS

279.01 Selective IgA immunodeficiency

279.02 Selective IgM immunodeficiency

279.03 Other selective immunoglobulin deficiencies
Selective deficiency of IgG

279.04 Congenital hypogammaglobulinemia
Agammaglobulinemia:
Bruton's type
X-linked

279.05 Immunodeficiency with increased IgM
Immunodeficiency with hyper-IgM:
autosomal recessive
X-linked

279.06 Common variable immunodeficiency
Dysgammaglobulinemia (acquired) (congenital) (primary)
Hypogammaglobulinemia:
acquired primary
congenital non-sex-linked
sporadic

279.09 Other
Transient hypogammaglobulinemia of infancy

√5th **279.1 Deficiency of cell-mediated immunity**

279.10 Immunodeficiency with predominant T-cell defect, unspecified
AHA: S-O, '87, 10

279.11 DiGeorge's syndrome
Pharyngeal pouch syndrome
Thymic hypoplasia
DEF: Congenital hypoplasia or aplasia of the thymus, parathyroid glands; related heart defects, anomalies of the great vessels, esophageal atresia, and abnormalities of facial structures.

279.12 Wiskott-Aldrich syndrome
DEF: A disease characterized by chronic conditions, such as eczema, suppurative otitis media and anemia; results from an X-linked recessive gene and is classified as an immune deficiency syndrome.

279.13 Nezelof's syndrome

Cellular immunodeficiency with abnormal immunoglobulin deficiency

DEF: Immune system disorder characterized by a pathological deficiency in cellular immunity and humoral antibodies resulting in inability to fight infectious diseases.

279.19 Other

EXCLUDES   *ataxia-telangiectasia (334.8)*

279.2 Combined immunity deficiency

Agammaglobulinemia:
    autosomal recessive
    Swiss-type
    x-linked recessive
Severe combined immunodeficiency [SCID]
Thymic:
    alymophoplasia
    aplasia or dysplasia with immunodeficiency

EXCLUDES   *thymic hypoplasia (279.11)*

DEF: Agammaglobulinemia: No immunoglobulins in the blood.

DEF: Thymic alymphoplasia: Severe combined immunodeficiency; result of failed lymphoid tissue development.

279.3 Unspecified immunity deficiency

√5th **279.4 Autoimmune disease, not elsewhere classified**

EXCLUDES   *transplant failure or rejection (996.80-996.89)*

AHA: 3Q, 08, 5

●   **279.41 Autoimmune lymphoproliferative syndrome**
       ALPS

●   **279.49 Autoimmune disease, not elsewhere classified**

Autoimmune disease NOS

√5th **279.5 Graft-versus-host disease**

Code first underlying cause, such as:
    complication of blood transfusion ▶(999.89)◀
    complication of transplanted organ (996.80-996.89)

Use additional code to identify associated manifestations, such as:
    desquamative dermatitis (695.89)
    diarrhea (787.91)
    elevated bilirubin (782.4)
    hair loss (704.09)

DEF: A complication of transplantation, most commonly bone marrow; may involve skin, GI tract, liver and cause increased susceptibility to infection; results when donor cells responsible for immune response attack the cells of the transplant recipient.

AHA: 4Q, 08, 97-99, 154

279.50 Graft-versus-host disease, unspecified

AHA: 4Q, 08, 99

279.51 Acute graft-versus-host disease

AHA: 4Q, 08, 99

279.52 Chronic graft-versus-host disease

279.53 Acute on chronic graft-versus-host disease

279.8 Other specified disorders involving the immune mechanism

Single complement [C_1-C_9] deficiency or dysfunction

279.9 Unspecified disorder of immune mechanism

AHA: 3Q, '92, 13

N Newborn Age: 0   P Pediatric Age: 0-17   M Maternity Age: 12-55   A Adult Age: 15-124

4. DISEASES OF THE BLOOD AND BLOOD-FORMING ORGANS (280-289)

> EXCLUDES   anemia complicating pregnancy or the puerperium (648.2)

✓4th 280 Iron deficiency anemias

> INCLUDES   anemia:
> asiderotic
> hypochromic-microcytic
> sideropenic
>
> EXCLUDES   familial microcytic anemia (282.49)

280.0 Secondary to blood loss (chronic)
Normocytic anemia due to blood loss
> EXCLUDES   acute posthemorrhagic anemia (285.1)

AHA: 4Q, '93, 34

280.1 Secondary to inadequate dietary iron intake

280.8 Other specified iron deficiency anemias
Paterson-Kelly syndrome
Plummer-Vinson syndrome
Sideropenic dysphagia

280.9 Iron deficiency anemia, unspecified
Anemia:
achlorhydric
chlorotic
idiopathic hypochromic
iron [Fe] deficiency NOS

✓4th 281 Other deficiency anemias

281.0 Pernicious anemia
Anemia:
Addison's
Biermer's
congenital pernicious
Congenital intrinsic factor [Castle's] deficiency
> EXCLUDES   combined system disease without mention of anemia (266.2)
> subacute degeneration of spinal cord without mention of anemia (266.2)

DEF: Chronic progressive anemia due to Vitamin B12 malabsorption; caused by lack of a secretion of intrinsic factor, which is produced by the gastric mucosa of the stomach.

AHA: N-D, '84, 1; S-O, '84, 16

281.1 Other vitamin B$_{12}$ deficiency anemia
Anemia:
vegan's
vitamin B$_{12}$ deficiency (dietary)
due to selective vitamin B$_{12}$ malabsorption with proteinuria
Syndrome:
Imerslund's
Imerslund-Gräsbeck
> EXCLUDES   combined system disease without mention of anemia (266.2)
> subacute degeneration of spinal cord without mention of anemia (266.2)

281.2 Folate-deficiency anemia
Congenital folate malabsorption
Folate or folic acid deficiency anemia:
NOS
dietary
drug-induced
Goat's milk anemia
Nutritional megaloblastic anemia (of infancy)
Use additional E code to identify drug

DEF: Macrocytic anemia resembles pernicious anemia but without absence of hydrochloric acid secretions; responsive to folic acid therapy.

281.3 Other specified megaloblastic anemias not elsewhere classified
Combined B$_{12}$ and folate-deficiency anemia
Refractory megaloblastic anemia

DEF: Megaloblasts predominant in bone marrow with few normoblasts; rare familial type associated with proteinuria and genitourinary tract anomalies.

281.4 Protein-deficiency anemia
Amino-acid-deficiency anemia

281.8 Anemia associated with other specified nutritional deficiency
Scorbutic anemia

281.9 Unspecified deficiency anemia
Anemia:
dimorphic
macrocytic
megaloblastic NOS
nutritional NOS
simple chronic

✓4th 282 Hereditary hemolytic anemias

DEF: Escalated rate of erythrocyte destruction; similar to all anemias, occurs when imbalance exists between blood loss and blood production.

282.0 Hereditary spherocytosis
Acholuric (familial) jaundice
Congenital hemolytic anemia (spherocytic)
Congenital spherocytosis
Minkowski-Chauffard syndrome
Spherocytosis (familial)
> EXCLUDES   hemolytic anemia of newborn (773.0-773.5)

DEF: Hereditary, chronic illness marked by abnormal red blood cell membrane; symptoms include enlarged spleen, jaundice; and anemia in severe cases.

282.1 Hereditary elliptocytosis
Elliptocytosis (congenital)
Ovalocytosis (congenital) (hereditary)

DEF: Genetic hemolytic anemia characterized by malformed, elliptical erythrocytes; there is increased destruction of red cells with resulting anemia.

282.2 Anemias due to disorders of glutathione metabolism
Anemia:
6-phosphogluconic dehydrogenase deficiency
enzyme deficiency, drug-induced
erythrocytic glutathione deficiency
glucose-6-phosphate dehydrogenase [G-6-PD] deficiency
glutathione-reductase deficiency
hemolytic nonspherocytic (hereditary), type I
Disorder of pentose phosphate pathway
Favism

282.3 Other hemolytic anemias due to enzyme deficiency
Anemia:
hemolytic nonspherocytic (hereditary), type II
hexokinase deficiency
pyruvate kinase [PK] deficiency
triosephosphate isomerase deficiency

✓5th 282.4 Thalassemias
> EXCLUDES   sickle-cell:
> disease (282.60-282.69)
> trait (282.5)

DEF: Inherited hemolytic disorders characterized by decreased production of at least one polypeptide globin chain results in defective hemoglobin synthesis; symptoms include severe anemia, expanded marrow spaces, transfusional and absorptive iron overload, impaired growth rate, thickened cranial bones, and pathologic fractures.

AHA: 4Q, '03, 51

282.41 Sickle-cell thalassemia without crisis
Sickle-cell thalassemia NOS
Thalassemia Hb-S disease without crisis

282.42 Sickle-cell thalassemia with crisis
Sickle-cell thalassemia with vaso-occlusive pain
Thalassemia Hb-S disease with crisis
Use additional code for type of crisis, such as:
acute chest syndrome (517.3)
splenic sequestration (289.52)

✓4th ✓5th   Additional Digit Required   Unspecified Code   Other Specified Code   Manifestation Code   ►◄ Revised Text   ● New Code   ▲ Revised Code Title

2010 ICD-9-CM   **Volume 1 – 65**

Blood and Blood-Forming Organs

282.49–283.9

282.49 Other thalassemia
Cooley's anemia
Hb-Bart's disease
Hereditary leptocytosis
Mediterranean anemia (with other
    hemoglobinopathy)
Microdrepanocytosis
Thalassemia (alpha) (beta) (intermedia) (major)
    (minima) (minor) (mixed) (trait) (with
    other hemoglobinopathy)
Thalassemia NOS

282.5 Sickle-cell trait
Hb-AS genotype
Hemoglobin S [Hb-S] trait
Heterozygous:
    hemoglobin S
    Hb-S

> **EXCLUDES** *that with other hemoglobinopathy*
> *(282.60-282.69)*
> *that with thalassemia (282.49)*

DEF: Heterozygous genetic makeup characterized by one gene for normal hemoglobin and one for sickle-cell hemoglobin; clinical disease rarely present.

TIP: Do not assign along with another code for sickle-cell disease or thalassemia.

√5th **282.6 Sickle-cell disease**
Sickle-cell anemia

> **EXCLUDES** *sickle-cell thalassemia (282.41-282.42)*
> *sickle-cell trait (282.5)*

DEF: Inherited blood disorder; sickle-shaped red blood cells are hard and pointed, clogging blood flow; anemia characterized by, periodic episodes of pain, acute abdominal discomfort, skin ulcerations of the legs, increased infections.

282.60 Sickle-cell disease, unspecified
Sickle-cell anemia NOS
AHA: 2Q, '97, 11

282.61 Hb-SS disease without crisis

282.62 Hb-SS disease with crisis
Hb-SS disease with vaso-occlusive pain
Sickle-cell crisis NOS
Use additional code for type of crisis, such as:
    acute chest syndrome (517.3)
    splenic sequestration (289.52)
AHA: 4Q, '03, 56; 2Q, '98, 8; 2Q, '91, 15

282.63 Sickle-cell/Hb-C disease without crisis
Hb-S/Hb-C disease without crisis

282.64 Sickle-cell/Hb-C disease with crisis
Hb-S/Hb-C disease with crisis
Sickle-cell/Hb-C disease with vaso-occlusive
    pain
Use additional code for type of crisis, such as:
    acute chest syndrome (517.3)
    splenic sequestration (289.52)
AHA: 4Q, '03, 51

282.68 Other sickle-cell disease without crisis
Hb-S/Hb-D
Hb-S/Hb-E   } diseases without
Sickle-cell/Hb-D   crisis
Sickle-cell/Hb-E
AHA: 4Q, '03, 51

282.69 Other sickle-cell disease with crisis
Hb-S/Hb-D
Hb-S/Hb-E   } diseases with crisis
Sickle-cell/Hb-D
Sickle-cell/Hb-E
Other sickle-cell disease with vaso-occlusive
    pain
Use additional code for type of crisis, such as:
    acute chest syndrome (517.3)
    splenic sequestration (289.52)

282.7 Other hemoglobinopathies
Abnormal hemoglobin NOS
Congenital Heinz-body anemia
Disease:
    hemoglobin C [Hb-C]
    hemoglobin D [Hb-D]
    hemoglobin E [Hb-E]
    hemoglobin Zurich [Hb-Zurich]
Hemoglobinopathy NOS
Hereditary persistence of fetal hemoglobin [HPFH]
Unstable hemoglobin hemolytic disease

> **EXCLUDES** *familial polycythemia (289.6)*
> *hemoglobin M [Hb-M] disease (289.7)*
> *high-oxygen-affinity hemoglobin (289.0)*

DEF: Any disorder of hemoglobin due to alteration of molecular structure; may include overt anemia.

282.8 Other specified hereditary hemolytic anemias
Stomatocytosis

282.9 Hereditary hemolytic anemia, unspecified
Hereditary hemolytic anemia NOS

√4th **283 Acquired hemolytic anemias**
DEF: Non-heriditary anemia characterized by premature destruction of red blood cells; caused by infectious organisms, poisons, and physical agents
AHA: N-D, '84, 1

283.0 Autoimmune hemolytic anemias
Autoimmune hemolytic disease (cold type) (warm type)
Chronic cold hemagglutinin disease
Cold agglutinin disease or hemoglobinuria
Hemolytic anemia:
    cold type (secondary) (symptomatic)
    drug-induced
    warm type (secondary) (symptomatic)
Use additional E code to identify cause, if drug-induced

> **EXCLUDES** *Evans' syndrome (287.32)*
> *hemolytic disease of newborn (773.0-773.5)*

AHA: ▶3Q, '08, 5◀

√5th **283.1 Non-autoimmune hemolytic anemias**
Use additional E code to identify cause
DEF: Hemolytic anemia and thrombocytopenia with acute renal failure; relatively rare condition; 50 percent of patients require renal dialysis.
AHA: 4Q, '93, 25

283.10 Non-autoimmune hemolytic anemia, unspecified

283.11 Hemolytic-uremic syndrome

283.19 Other non-autoimmune hemolytic anemias
Hemolytic anemia:
    mechanical
    microangiopathic
    toxic

283.2 Hemoglobinuria due to hemolysis from external causes
Acute intravascular hemolysis
Hemoglobinuria:
    from exertion
    march
    paroxysmal (cold) (nocturnal)
    due to other hemolysis
Marchiafava-Micheli syndrome
Use additional E code to identify cause

283.9 Acquired hemolytic anemia, unspecified
Acquired hemolytic anemia NOS
Chronic idiopathic hemolytic anemia

N Newborn Age: 0   P Pediatric Age: 0-17   M Maternity Age: 12-55   A Adult Age: 15-124

✓4th **284 Aplastic anemia and other bone marrow failure syndromes**

> **DEF:** Bone marrow failure to produce the normal amount of blood components; generally non-responsive to usual therapy.
> **AHA:** 1Q, '91, 14; N-D, '84, 1; S-0, '84, 16

✓5th **284.0 Constitutional aplastic anemia**

> **AHA:** 1Q, '91, 14

> **284.01 Constitutional red blood cell aplasia**
> Aplasia, (pure) red cell:
> congenital
> of infants
> primary
> Blackfan-Diamond syndrome
> Familial hypoplastic anemia
> **AHA:** 4Q, '06, 67-69

> **284.09 Other constitutional aplastic anemia**
> Fanconi's anemia
> Pancytopenia with malformations
> **AHA:** 4Q, '06, 67-69

284.1 Pancytopenia

> **EXCLUDES** *pancytopenia (due to) (with):*
> *aplastic anemia NOS (284.9)*
> *bone marrow infiltration (284.2)*
> *constitutional red blood cell aplasia (284.01)*
> *drug induced (284.89)*
> *hairy cell leukemia (202.4)*
> *human immunodeficiency virus disease (042)*
> *leukoerythroblastic anemia (284.2)*
> *malformations (284.09)*
> *myelodysplastic syndromes (238.72-238.75)*
> *myeloproliferative disease (238.79)*
> *other constitutional aplastic anemia (284.09)*

> **AHA:** 4Q, '06, 67-69

284.2 Myelophthisis

> Leukoerythroblastic anemia
> Myelophthisic anemia

> *Code first the underlying disorder, such as:*
> malignant neoplasm of breast (174.0-174.9, 175.0-175.9)
> tuberculosis (015.0-015.9)

> **EXCLUDES** *idiopathic myelofibrosis (238.76)*
> *myelofibrosis NOS (289.83)*
> *myelofibrosis with myeloid metaplasia (238.76)*
> *primary myelofibrosis (238.76)*
> *secondary myelofibrosis (289.83)*

> **DEF:** A secondary disease process involving replacement of normal hematopoeitic tissue in the bone marrow with abnormal tissue, such as fibrous tissue or tumors. Occurs with advanced-stage neoplasms, granulomatous diseases such as miliary tuberculosis, and other inflammatory.
> **AHA:** 4Q, '06, 67-69

✓5th **284.8 Other specified aplastic anemias**

> **AHA:** 4Q, '07, 72; 3Q, '05, 11; 1Q, '97, 5; 1Q, '92, 15; 1Q, '91, 14

> **284.81 Red cell aplasia (acquired) (adult) (with thymoma)**
> Red cell aplasia NOS

> **284.89 Other specified aplastic anemias**
> Aplastic anemia (due to):
> chronic systemic disease
> drugs
> infection
> radiation
> toxic (paralytic)
> Use additional E code to identify cause
> **AHA:** ▶1Q, '09, 20;◀ 2Q, '08, 6

284.9 Aplastic anemia, unspecified

> Anemia: Anemia:
> aplastic (idiopathic) NOS   nonregenerative
> aregenerative   Medullary hypoplasia
> hypoplastic NOS
> **EXCLUDES** *refractory anemia (238.72)*

✓4th **285 Other and unspecified anemias**

> **AHA:** 1Q, '91, 14; N-D, '84, 1

285.0 Sideroblastic anemia

> Anemia:
> hypochromic with iron loading
> sideroachrestic
> sideroblastic:
> acquired
> congenital
> hereditary
> primary
> secondary (drug-induced) (due to disease)
> sex-linked hypochromic
> vitamin B6-responsive
> Pyridoxine-responsive (hypochromic) anemia

> Use additional E code to identify cause, if drug induced
> **EXCLUDES** *refractory sideroblastic anemia (238.72)*

> **DEF:** Characterized by a disruption of final heme synthesis; results in iron overload of reticuloendothelial tissues.

285.1 Acute posthemorrhagic anemia

> Anemia due to acute blood loss
> **EXCLUDES** *anemia due to chronic blood loss (280.0)*
> *blood loss anemia NOS (280.0)*
> **AHA:** 1Q, '07, 19; 2Q, '92, 15

✓5th **285.2 Anemia of chronic disease**

> Anemia in ▶(due to) (with)◀ chronic illness
> **AHA:** 4Q, '00, 39

> **285.21 Anemia in chronic kidney disease**
> Anemia in end stage renal disease
> Erythropoietin-resistant anemia (EPO resistant anemia)
> **TIP:** Assign also a code for the chronic kidney disease (585.X).

> **285.22 Anemia in neoplastic disease**
> **EXCLUDES** ▶ *anemia due to antineoplastic chemotherapy (285.3)*◀
> **TIP:** Assign also a code for the neoplasm causing the anemia. Do not assign if anemia is caused by chemotherapy drugs, which is reported as an adverse effect.

> **285.29 Anemia of other chronic disease**
> Anemia in other chronic illness

285.3 Antineoplastic chemotherapy induced anemia

> Anemia due to antineoplastic chemotherapy
> **EXCLUDES** *anemia due to drug NEC–code to type of anemia*
> *anemia in neoplastic disease (285.22)*
> *aplastic anemia due to antineoplastic chemotherapy (284.89)*

285.8 Other specified anemias

> Anemia:
> dyserythropoietic (congenital)
> dyshematopoietic (congenital)
> von Jaksch's
> Infantile pseudoleukemia
> **AHA:** 1Q, '91, 16

285.9 Anemia, unspecified

> Anemia: Anemia:
> NOS   profound
> essential   progressive
> normocytic, not due   secondary
> to blood loss   Oligocythemia
> **EXCLUDES** *anemia (due to):*
> *blood loss:*
> *acute (285.1)*
> *chronic or unspecified (280.0)*
> *iron deficiency (280.0-280.9)*
> **AHA:** ▶1Q, '09, 17, 20;◀ 1Q, '07, 19; 1Q, '02, 14; 2Q, '92, 16; M-A, '85, 13; N-D, '84, 1
> **TIP:** Assign for "postoperative anemia" if there is no mention of blood loss.

Blood and Blood-Forming Organs

286–287.0

✓4ᵗʰ **286　Coagulation defects**

> AHA: 2Q, '06, 17

286.0　Congenital factor VIII disorder

Antihemophilic globulin [AHG] deficiency
Factor VIII (functional) deficiency
Hemophilia:
　NOS
　A
　classical
　familial
　hereditary
Subhemophilia

> EXCLUDES　*factor VIII deficiency with vascular defect*
> 　　　　　　*(286.4)*

> DEF: Hereditary, sex-linked, results in missing antihemophilic globulin (AHG) (factor VIII); causes abnormal coagulation characterized by increased bleeding, large bruises of skin, bleeding in mouth, nose, gastrointestinal tract; hemorrhages into joints, resulting in swelling and impaired function.

286.1　Congenital factor IX disorder

Christmas disease
Deficiency:
　factor IX (functional)
　plasma thromboplastin component [PTC]
Hemophilia B

> DEF: Deficiency of plasma thromboplastin component (PTC) (factor IX) and plasma thromboplastin antecedent (PTA); PTC deficiency clinically indistinguishable from classical hemophilia.

286.2　Congenital factor XI deficiency

Hemophilia C
Plasma thromboplastin antecedent [PTA] deficiency
Rosenthal's disease

286.3　Congenital deficiency of other clotting factors

Congenital afibrinogenemia
Deficiency:
　AC globulin factor:
　　I [fibrinogen]
　　II [prothrombin]
　　V [labile]
　　VII [stable]
　　X [Stuart-Prower]
　　XII [Hageman]
　　XIII [fibrin stabilizing]
　Laki-Lorand factor
　proaccelerin
Disease
　Owren's
　Stuart-Prower
Dysfibrinogenemia (congenital)
Dysprothrombinemia (constitutional)
Hypoproconvertinemia
Hypoprothrombinemia (hereditary)
Parahemophilia

286.4　von Willebrand's disease

Angiohemophilia (A) (B)
Constitutional thrombopathy
Factor VIII deficiency with vascular defect
Pseudohemophilia type B
Vascular hemophilia
von Willebrand's (-Jürgens') disease

> EXCLUDES　*factor VIII deficiency:*
> 　　　　　　*NOS (286.0)*
> 　　　　　　*with functional defect (286.0)*
> 　　　　　　*hereditary capillary fragility (287.8)*

> DEF: Abnormal blood coagulation caused by deficient blood Factor VII; congenital; symptoms include excess or prolonged bleeding.

286.5　Hemorrhagic disorder due to intrinsic circulating anticoagulants

Antithrombinemia　　　　　Increase in:
Antithromboplastinemia　　　anti-XIa
Antithromboplastino-　　　　antithrombin
　-genemia　　　　　　　　Secondary hemophilia
Hyperheparinemia　　　　　Systemic lupus erythema-
Increase in:　　　　　　　　　tosus [SLE] inhibitor
　anti-VIIIa
　anti-IXa
　anti-Xa

> AHA: 3Q, '04, 7; No.5, '93, 16; 3Q, '92, 15; 3Q, '90, 14

> TIP: Do not assign for Coumadin/warfarin toxicity, poisoning or adverse effect. Follow coding guidelines for poisoning and adverse reactions.

286.6　Defibrination syndrome

Afibrinogenemia, acquired
Consumption coagulopathy
Diffuse or disseminated intravascular coagulation [DIC syndrome]
Fibrinolytic hemorrhage, acquired
Hemorrhagic fibrinogenolysis
Pathologic fibrinolysis
Purpura:
　fibrinolytic
　fulminans

> EXCLUDES　*that complicating:*
> 　　　　　　*abortion (634-638 with .1, 639.1)*
> 　　　　　　*pregnancy or the puerperium (641.3, 666.3)*
> 　　　　　　*disseminated intravascular coagulation in*
> 　　　　　　*newborn (776.2)*

> DEF: Characterized by destruction of circulating fibrinogen; often precipitated by other conditions, such as injury, causing release of thromboplastic particles in blood stream.

> AHA: 4Q, '93, 29

286.7　Acquired coagulation factor deficiency

Deficiency of coagulation factor due to:
　liver disease
　vitamin K deficiency
Hypoprothrombinemia, acquired

Use additional E code to identify cause, if drug induced

> EXCLUDES　*vitamin K deficiency of newborn (776.0)*

> AHA: 4Q, '93, 29

286.9　Other and unspecified coagulation defects

Defective coagulation NOS
Deficiency, coagulation factor NOS
Delay, coagulation
Disorder:
　coagulation
　hemostasis

> EXCLUDES　*abnormal coagulation profile (790.92)*
> 　　　　　　*hemorrhagic disease of newborn (776.0)*
> 　　　　　　*that complicating:*
> 　　　　　　*abortion (634-638 with .1, 639.1)*
> 　　　　　　*pregnancy or the puerperium (641.3, 666.3)*

> AHA: 4Q, '99, 22; 4Q, '93, 29

✓4ᵗʰ **287　Purpura and other hemorrhagic conditions**

> EXCLUDES　*hemorrhagic thrombocythemia (238.79)*
> 　　　　　　*purpura fulminans (286.6)*

> AHA: 1Q, '91, 14

287.0　Allergic purpura

Peliosis rheumatica　　　　Purpura:
Purpura:　　　　　　　　　rheumatica
　anaphylactoid　　　　　Schönlein-Henoch
　autoimmune　　　　　　vascular
　Henoch's　　　　　　　Vasculitis, allergic
　nonthrombocytopenic:
　　hemorrhagic
　　idiopathic

> EXCLUDES　*hemorrhagic purpura (287.39)*
> 　　　　　　*purpura annularis telangiectodes (709.1)*

> DEF: Any hemorrhagic condition, thrombocytic or nonthrombocytopenic in origin, caused by a presumed allergic reaction.

287.1   Qualitative platelet defects
Thrombasthenia (hemorrhagic) (hereditary)
Thrombocytasthenia
Thrombocytopathy (dystrophic)
Thrombopathy (Bernard-Soulier)
> **EXCLUDES**   von Willebrand's disease (286.4)

287.2   Other nonthrombocytopenic purpuras
Purpura:
NOS
senile
simplex

√5ᵗʰ **287.3   Primary thrombocytopenia**
> **EXCLUDES**   thrombotic thrombocytopenic purpura (446.6)
> transient thrombocytopenia of newborn
> (776.1)

DEF: Decrease in number of blood platelets in circulating
blood and purpural skin hemorrhages.
AHA: 4Q, '05, 56

287.30   Primary thrombocytopenia, unspecified
Megakaryocytic hypoplasia

287.31   Immune thrombocytopenic purpura
Idiopathic thrombocytopenic purpura
Tidal platelet dysgenesis

DEF: Tidal platelet dysgenesis: Platelet counts
fluctuate from normal to very low within periods of
20 to 40 days and may involve autoimmune platelet
destruction.
AHA: 4Q, '05, 57

287.32   Evans' syndrome
DEF: Combination of immunohemolytic anemia and
autoimmune hemolytic anemia, sometimes with
neutropenia.

**287.33   Congenital and hereditary thrombocytopenic
purpura**
Congenital and hereditary thrombocytopenia
Thrombocytopenia with absent radii (TAR)
syndrome
> **EXCLUDES**   Wiskott-Aldrich syndrome (279.12)

DEF: Thrombocytopenia with absent radii (TAR)
syndrome: autosomal recessive syndrome
characterized by thrombocytopenia and bilateral
radial aplasia; manifestations include skeletal,
gastrointestinal, hematologic, and cardiac system
abnormalities.

287.39   Other primary thrombocytopenia

287.4   Secondary thrombocytopenia
Posttransfusion purpura
Thrombocytopenia (due to):
dilutional
drugs
extracorporeal circulation of blood
massive blood transfusion
platelet alloimmunization
Use additional E code to identify cause
> **EXCLUDES**   heparin-induced thrombocytopenia (HIT)
> (289.84)
> transient thrombocytopenia of newborn
> (776.1)

DEF: Reduced number of platelets in circulating blood as
consequence of an underlying disease or condition.
AHA: 4Q, '99, 22; 4Q '93, 29

287.5   Thrombocytopenia, unspecified

287.8   Other specified hemorrhagic conditions
Capillary fragility (hereditary)
Vascular pseudohemophilia

287.9   Unspecified hemorrhagic conditions
Hemorrhagic diathesis (familial)

√4ᵗʰ **288   Diseases of white blood cells**
> **EXCLUDES**   leukemia (204.0-208.9)

AHA: 4Q, '06, 69; 1Q, '91, 14

√5ᵗʰ **288.0   Neutropenia**
Decreased absolute neutrophil count [ANC]
Use additional code for any associated:
fever (780.61)
mucositis (478.11, 528.00-528.09, 538, 616.81)
> **EXCLUDES**   neutropenic splenomegaly (289.53)
> transitory neonatal neutropenia (776.7)

DEF: Sudden, severe condition characterized by reduced
number of white blood cells; results in sores in the throat,
stomach or skin; symptoms include chills, fever.
AHA: 4Q, '06, 69-73; 3Q, '05, 11; 3Q, '99, 6; 2Q, '99, 9; 3Q, '96, 16;
2Q, '96, 6

288.00   Neutropenia, unspecified
AHA: 4Q, '06, 69-73

288.01   Congenital neutropenia
Congenital agranulocytosis
Infantile genetic agranulocytosis
Kostmann's syndrome
AHA: 4Q, '06, 69-73

288.02   Cyclic neutropenia
Cyclic hematopoiesis
Periodic neutropenia
AHA: 4Q, '06, 69-73

288.03   Drug induced neutropenia
Use additional E code to identify drug
AHA: 4Q, '06, 69-73
TIP: Assign for neutropenic fever due to chemother-
apy drugs, along with codes for the fever, adverse
effect, and the underlying malignancy.

288.04   Neutropenia due to infection
AHA: 4Q, '06, 69-73

288.09   Other neutropenia
Agranulocytosis
Neutropenia:
immune
toxic
AHA: 4Q, '06, 69-73

**288.1   Functional disorders of polymorphonuclear
neutrophils**
Chronic (childhood) granulomatous disease
Congenital dysphagocytosis
Job's syndrome
Lipochrome histiocytosis (familial)
Progressive septic granulomatosis

288.2   Genetic anomalies of leukocytes
Anomaly (granulation) (gran ulocyte) or syndrome:
Alder's (-Reilly)
Chédiak-Steinbrinck (-Higashi)
Jordan's
May-Hegglin
Pelger-Huet
Hereditary:
hypersegmentation
hyposegmentation
leukomelanopathy

288.3   Eosinophilia
Eosinophilia:
allergic
hereditary
idiopathic
secondary
Eosinophilic leukocytosis
> **EXCLUDES**   Löffler's syndrome (518.3)
> pulmonary eosinophilia (518.3)

DEF: Elevated number of eosinophils in the blood;
characteristic of allergic states and various parasitic infections.
AHA: 3Q, '00, 11

288.4   Hemophagocytic syndromes
Familial hemophagocytic lymphohistiocytosis
Familial hemophagocytic reticulosis
Hemophagocytic syndrome, infection-associated
Histiocytic syndromes
Macrophage activation syndrome
AHA: 4Q, '06, 69-73

√5ᵗʰ **288.5   Decreased white blood cell count**
EXCLUDES   neutropenia (288.01-288.09)

288.50   Leukocytopenia, unspecified
Decreased leukocytes, unspecified
Decreased white blood cell count, unspecified
Leukopenia NOS
AHA: 4Q, '06, 69-73

288.51   Lymphocytopenia
Decreased lymphocytes
AHA: 4Q, '06, 69-73

288.59   Other decreased white blood cell count
Basophilic leukopenia
Eosinophilic leukopenia
Monocytopenia
Plasmacytopenia
AHA: 4Q, '06, 69-73

√5ᵗʰ **288.6   Elevated white blood cell count**
EXCLUDES   eosinophilia (288.3)

288.60   Leukocytosis, unspecified
Elevated leukocytes, unspecified
Elevated white blood cell count, unspecified
AHA: 4Q, '06, 69-73

288.61   Lymphocytosis (symptomatic)
Elevated lymphocytes
AHA: 4Q, '06, 69-73

288.62   Leukemoid reaction
Basophilic leukemoid reaction
Lymphocytic leukemoid reaction
Monocytic leukemoid reaction
Myelocytic leukemoid reaction
Neutrophilic leukemoid reaction
AHA: 4Q, '06, 69-73

288.63   Monocytosis (symptomatic)
EXCLUDES   infectious mononucleosis (075)
AHA: 4Q, '06, 69-73

288.64   Plasmacytosis
AHA: 4Q, '06, 69-73

288.65   Basophilia
AHA: 4Q, '06, 69-73

288.66   Bandemia
Bandemia without diagnosis of specific infection
EXCLUDES   confirmed infection–code to
infection
leukemia (204.00-208.9)
DEF: Increase in early neutrophil cells, called band cells; may indicate infection.
AHA: 4Q, '07, 73
TIP: Do not assign based on lab values alone; physician must substantiate bandemia without evidence of corresponding infection.

288.69   Other elevated white blood cell count
AHA: 4Q, '06, 69-73

288.8   Other specified disease of white blood cells
EXCLUDES   decreased white blood cell counts
(288.50-288.59)
elevated white blood cell counts
(288.60-288.69)
immunity disorders (279.0-279.9)
AHA: M-A, '87, 12

288.9   Unspecified disease of white blood cells

√4ᵗʰ **289   Other diseases of blood and blood-forming organs**

289.0   Polycythemia, secondary
High-oxygen-affinity hemoglobin
Polycythemia:
acquired
benign
due to:
fall in plasma volume
high altitude
emotional
erythropoietin
hypoxemic
nephrogenous
relative
spurious
stress
EXCLUDES   polycythemia:
neonatal (776.4)
primary (238.4)
vera (238.4)
DEF: Elevated number of red blood cells in circulating blood as result of reduced oxygen supply to the tissues.
D75.1 Secondary polycythemia   I-10

289.1   Chronic lymphadenitis
Chronic:
adenitis   } any lymph node, except
lymphadenitis }   mesenteric
EXCLUDES   acute lymphadenitis (683)
mesenteric (289.2)
enlarged glands NOS (785.6)
DEF: Persistent inflammation of lymph node tissue; origin of infection is usually elsewhere.
I88.1 Chronic lymphadenitis except mesenteric   I-10

289.2   Nonspecific mesenteric lymphadenitis
Mesenteric lymphadenitis (acute) (chronic)
DEF: Inflammation of the lymph nodes in peritoneal fold that encases abdominal organs; disease resembles acute appendicitis; unknown etiology.
I88.0 Nonspecific mesenteric lymphadenitis   I-10

289.3   Lymphadenitis, unspecified, except mesenteric
AHA: 2Q, '92, 8
I88.9 Nonspecific lymphadenitis unspecified   I-10

289.4   Hypersplenism
"Big spleen" syndrome
Dyssplenism
Hypersplenia
EXCLUDES   primary splenic neutropenia (289.53)
DEF: An overactive spleen; causing a deficiency of the peripheral blood components, an increase in bone marrow cells and sometimes a notable increase in the size of the spleen.
D73.1 Hypersplenism   I-10

√5ᵗʰ **289.5   Other diseases of spleen**

289.50   Disease of spleen, unspecified
D73.9 Disease of spleen unspecified   I-10

289.51   Chronic congestive splenomegaly
D73.2 Chronic congestive splenomegaly   I-10

289.52   Splenic sequestration
Code first sickle-cell disease in crisis (282.42,
282.62, 282.64, 282.69)
DEF: Blood is entrapped in the spleen due to vessel occlusion; most often associated with sickle-cell disease; spleen becomes enlarged and there is a sharp drop in hemoglobin.
AHA: 4Q, '03, 51

289.53   Neutropenic splenomegaly
AHA: 4Q, '06, 73
D73.81 Neutropenic splenomegaly   I-10

N Newborn Age: 0   P Pediatric Age: 0-17   M Maternity Age: 12-55   A Adult Age: 15-124

289.59 Other
Lien migrans
Perisplenitis
Splenic:
    abscess
    atrophy
    cyst
Splenic:
    fibrosis
    infarction
    rupture, nontraumatic
Splenitis
Wandering spleen

EXCLUDES *bilharzial splenic fibrosis*
(120.0-120.9)
hepatolienal fibrosis (571.5)
splenomegaly NOS (789.2)

D73.89 Other diseases of spleen

289.6 Familial polycythemia
Familial:
    benign polycythemia
    erythrocytosis
DEF: Elevated number of red blood cells.

289.7 Methemoglobinemia
Congenital NADH [DPNH]-methemoglobin- reductase
    deficiency
Hemoglobin M [Hb-M] disease
Methemoglobinemia:
    NOS
    acquired (with sulfhemoglobinemia)
    hereditary
    toxic
Stokvis' disease
Sulfhemoglobinemia
Use additional E code to identify cause
DEF: Presence of blood methemoglobin, a chemically altered form of hemoglobin; causes cyanosis, headache, ataxia, dyspnea, tachycardia, nausea, stupor, and coma.
D74.0 Congenital methemoglobinemia

√5ᵗʰ 289.8 Other specified diseases of blood and blood-forming organs
DEF: Hypercoagulable states: a group of inherited or acquired abnormalities of specific proteins and anticoagulant factors; also called thromboembolic states or thrombotic disorders, result in abnormal development of blood clots.
AHA: 4Q, '03, 56; 1Q, '02, 16; 2Q, '89, 8; M-A, '87, 12

289.81 Primary hypercoagulable state
Activated protein C resistance
Antithrombin III deficiency
Factor V Leiden mutation
Lupus anticoagulant
Protein C deficiency
Protein S deficiency
Prothrombin gene mutation
DEF: Activated protein C resistance: decreased effectiveness of protein C to degrade factor V, necessary to inhibit clotting cascade; also called Factor V Leiden mutation.
DEF: Antithrombin III deficiency: deficiency in plasma antithrombin III one of six naturally occurring antithrombins that limit coagulation.
DEF: Factor V Leiden mutation: also called activated protein C resistance.
DEF: Lupus anticoagulant: deficiency in a circulating anticoagulant that inhibits the conversion of prothrombin into thrombin; also called anti-phospholipid syndrome.
DEF: Protein C deficiency: deficiency of activated protein C which functions to bring the blood-clotting process into balance; same outcome as factor V Leiden mutation.
DEF: Protein S deficiency: similar to protein C deficiency; protein S is a vitamin K dependent cofactor in the activation of protein C.
DEF: Prothrombin gene mutation: increased levels of prothrombin, or factor II, a plasma protein that is converted to thrombin, which acts upon fibrinogen to form the fibrin.
D68.59 Other primary thrombophilia

289.82 Secondary hypercoagulable state
EXCLUDES *heparin-induced thrombocytopenia*
(HIT) (289.84)
D68.69 Other thrombophilia

289.83 Myelofibrosis
Myelofibrosis NOS
Secondary myelofibrosis
Code first the underlying disorder, such as:
    malignant neoplasm of breast (174.0-174.9,
    175.0-175.9)
Use additional code for associated therapy-related myelodysplastic syndrome, if applicable (238.72, 238.73)
Use additional external cause code if due to anti-neoplastic chemotherapy (E933.1)

EXCLUDES *idiopathic myelofibrosis (238.76)*
leukoerythroblastic anemia (284.2)
myelofibrosis with myeloid
    metaplasia (238.76)
myelophthisic anemia (284.2)
myelophthisis (284.2)
primary myelofibrosis (238.76)

DEF: A progressive bone marrow disease characterized by the replacement of bone marrow with the overgrowth of neoplastic stem cells and fibrotic tissue, also progressive anemia and enlarged spleen.
AHA: 4Q, '06, 73
D75.81 Myelofibrosis

289.84 Heparin-induced thrombocytopenia [HIT]
DEF: ▶Immune-mediated reaction to heparin therapy causing an abrupt fall in platelet count and serious complications such as pulmonary embolism, stroke, AMI or DVT◀
AHA: ▶4Q, '08, 100-101◀

289.89 Other specified diseases of blood and blood-forming organs
Hypergammaglobulinemia
Pseudocholinesterase deficiency
D75.89 Oth specified dz of blood & blood-forming organs

289.9 Unspecified diseases of blood and blood-forming organs
Blood dyscrasia NOS
Erythroid hyperplasia
AHA: M-A, '85, 14
D75.9 Disease of blood and blood-forming organs unspec

5. MENTAL DISORDERS (290-319)

PSYCHOSES (290-299)

EXCLUDES mental retardation (317-319)

ORGANIC PSYCHOTIC CONDITIONS (290-294)

INCLUDES psychotic organic brain syndrome

EXCLUDES nonpsychotic syndromes of organic etiology
(310.0-310.9)
psychoses classifiable to 295-298 and without
impairment of orientation, comprehension,
calculation, learning capacity, and judgment, but
associated with physical disease, injury, or
condition affecting the brain [eg., following
childbirth] (295.0-298.8)

√4ᵗʰ **290 Dementias**
Code first the associated neurological condition

EXCLUDES dementia due to alcohol (291.0-291.2)
dementia due to drugs (292.82)
dementia not classified as senile, presenile, or
arteriosclerotic (294.10-294.11)
psychoses classifiable to 295-298 occurring in the
senium without dementia or delirium
(295.0-298.8)
senility with mental changes of nonpsychotic severity
(310.1)
transient organic psychotic conditions (293.0-293.9)

290.0 Senile dementia, uncomplicated Ⓐ
Senile dementia:
NOS
simple type
EXCLUDES mild memory disturbances, not amounting to
dementia, associated with senile brain
disease ▶(310.8)◀
senile dementia with:
delirium or confusion (290.3)
delusional [paranoid] features (290.20)
depressive features (290.21)
AHA: 4Q, '99, 4
F03 Unspecified dementia   I-10

√5ᵗʰ **290.1 Presenile dementia**
Brain syndrome with presenile brain disease
EXCLUDES arteriosclerotic dementia (290.40-290.43)
dementia associated with other cerebral
conditions (294.10-294.11)
AHA: N-D, '84, 20

290.10 Presenile dementia, uncomplicated Ⓐ
Presenile dementia:
NOS
simple type

290.11 Presenile dementia with delirium Ⓐ
Presenile dementia with acute confusional state
AHA: 1Q, '88, 3

290.12 Presenile dementia with delusional features Ⓐ
Presenile dementia, paranoid type

290.13 Presenile dementia with depressive Ⓐ
features
Presenile dementia, depressed type

√5ᵗʰ **290.2 Senile dementia with delusional or depressive features**
EXCLUDES senile dementia:
NOS (290.0)
with delirium and/or confusion (290.3)

290.20 Senile dementia with delusional features Ⓐ
Senile dementia, paranoid type
Senile psychosis NOS

290.21 Senile dementia with depressive features Ⓐ

290.3 Senile dementia with delirium Ⓐ
Senile dementia with acute confusional state
EXCLUDES senile:
dementia NOS (290.0)
psychosis NOS (290.20)

√5ᵗʰ **290.4 Vascular dementia**
Multi-infarct dementia or psychosis
Use additional code to identify cerebral atherosclerosis
(437.0)
EXCLUDES suspected cases with no clear evidence of
arteriosclerosis (290.9)
AHA: 1Q, '88, 3

290.40 Vascular dementia, uncomplicated Ⓐ
Arteriosclerotic dementia:
NOS
simple type
F01.50 Vascular dementia without behavioral   I-10
disturbance

290.41 Vascular dementia with delirium Ⓐ
Arteriosclerotic dementia with acute
confusional state

290.42 Vascular dementia with delusions Ⓐ
Arteriosclerotic dementia, paranoid type

290.43 Vascular dementia with depressed mood Ⓐ
Arteriosclerotic dementia, depressed type

290.8 Other specified senile psychotic conditions
Presbyophrenic psychosis

290.9 Unspecified senile psychotic condition Ⓐ

√4ᵗʰ **291 Alcohol induced mental disorders**
EXCLUDES alcoholism without psychosis (303.0-303.9)
AHA: 1Q, '88, 3; S-O, '86, 3

291.0 Alcohol withdrawal delirium
Alcoholic delirium
Delirium tremens
EXCLUDES alcohol withdrawal (291.81)
AHA: 2Q, '91, 11
F10.921 Alcohol use unspecified w/intoxication delirium   I-10

291.1 Alcohol induced persisting amnestic disorder
Alcoholic polyneuritic psychosis
Korsakoff's psychosis, alcoholic
Wernicke-Korsakoff syndrome (alcoholic)
DEF: Prominent and lasting reduced memory span, disordered
time appreciation and confabulation, occurring in alcoholics,
as sequel to acute alcoholic psychosis.
AHA: 1Q, '88, 3

291.2 Alcohol induced persisting dementia
Alcoholic dementia NOS
Alcoholism associated with dementia NOS
Chronic alcoholic brain syndrome
F10.27 Alcohol depend alcohol-induced persist dementia   I-10

291.3 Alcohol induced psychotic disorder with hallucinations
Alcoholic:
hallucinosis (acute)
psychosis with hallucinosis
EXCLUDES alcohol withdrawal with delirium (291.0)
schizophrenia (295.0-295.9) and paranoid
states (297.0-297.9) taking the form of
chronic hallucinosis with clear
consciousness in an alcoholic
DEF: Psychosis lasting less than six months with slight or no
clouding of consciousness in which auditory hallucinations
predominate.
AHA: 2Q, '91, 11

291.4 Idiosyncratic alcohol intoxication
Pathologic:
alcohol intoxication
drunkenness
EXCLUDES acute alcohol intoxication (305.0)
in alcoholism (303.0)
simple drunkenness (305.0)
DEF: Unique behavioral patterns, like belligerence, after intake
of relatively small amounts of alcohol; behavior not due to
excess consumption.

√4ᵗʰ
√5ᵗʰ Additional Digit Required   Unspecified Code   Other Specified Code   Manifestation Code   ▶◀ Revised Text   ● New Code   ▲ Revised Code Title
2010 ICD-9-CM   **October 2009 • Volume 1 – 73**

290–291.4

Mental Disorders

291.5 Alcohol induced psychotic disorder with delusions
Alcoholic: Alcoholic:
paranoia   psychosis, paranoid type
> **EXCLUDES** nonalcoholic paranoid states (297.0-297.9)
> schizophrenia, paranoid type (295.3)

✓5th **291.8 Other specified alcohol induced mental disorders**
AHA: 3Q, '94, 13; J-A, '85, 10

291.81 Alcohol withdrawal
Alcohol:
abstinence syndrome or symptoms
withdrawal syndrome or symptoms
> **EXCLUDES** alcohol withdrawal:
> delirium (291.0)
> hallucinosis (291.3)
> delirium tremens (291.0)

AHA: 4Q, '96, 28; 2Q, '91, 11

F10.239 Alcohol dependence with withdrawal I-10
unspecified

291.82 Alcohol induced sleep disorders
Alcohol induced circadian rhythm sleep
disorders
Alcohol induced hypersomnia
Alcohol induced insomnia
Alcohol induced parasomnia

291.89 Other
Alcohol induced anxiety disorder
Alcohol induced mood disorder
Alcohol induced sexual dysfunction

291.9 Unspecified alcohol induced mental disorders
Alcoholic:
mania NOS
psychosis NOS
Alcoholism (chronic) with psychosis
Alcohol related disorder NOS

✓4th **292 Drug induced mental disorders**
> **INCLUDES** organic brain syndrome associated with consumption
> of drugs

Use additional code for any associated drug dependence
(304.0-304.9)
Use additional E code to identify drug
AHA: 3Q, '04, 8; 2Q, '91, 11; S-O, '86, 3

292.0 Drug withdrawal
Drug:
abstinence syndrome or symptoms
withdrawal syndrome or symptoms
AHA: 1Q, '97, 12; 1Q, '88, 3
TIP: Assign only for patients who suffer mental or behavioral
disturbances due to drug withdrawal, regardless of the circumstances.
F19.939 Oth psychoactive sbstnc use uns w/withdraw uns I-10

✓5th **292.1 Drug induced psychotic disorders**

**292.11 Drug induced psychotic disorder with
delusions**
Paranoid state induced by drugs

**292.12 Drug induced psychotic disorder with
hallucinations**
Hallucinatory state induced by drugs
> **EXCLUDES** states following LSD or other
> hallucinogens, lasting only a
> few days or less ["bad trips"]
> (305.3)

292.2 Pathological drug intoxication
Drug reaction:
NOS   } resulting in brief psychotic
idiosyncratic   states
pathologic
> **EXCLUDES** expected brief psychotic reactions to
> hallucinogens ["bad trips"] (305.3)
> physiological side-effects of drugs (e.g.,
> dystonias)

✓5th **292.8 Other specified drug induced mental disorders**

292.81 Drug induced delirium
AHA: 1Q, '88, 3
F19.921 Oth psychoactv sbstnc use uns I-10
intoxcat delirium

292.82 Drug induced persisting dementia

292.83 Drug induced persisting amnestic disorder

292.84 Drug induced mood disorder
Depressive state induced by drugs

292.85 Drug induced sleep disorders
Drug induced circadian rhythm sleep disorder
Drug induced hypersomnia
Drug induced insomnia
Drug induced parasomnia

292.89 Other
Drug induced anxiety disorder
Drug induced organic personality syndrome
Drug induced sexual dysfunction
Drug intoxication

292.9 Unspecified drug induced mental disorder
Drug related disorder NOS
Organic psychosis NOS due to or associated with drugs

✓4th **293 Transient mental disorders due to conditions classified
elsewhere**
> **INCLUDES** transient organic mental disorders not associated with
> alcohol or drugs

Code first the associated physical or neurological condition
> **EXCLUDES** confusional state or delirium superimposed on senile
> dementia (290.3)
> dementia due to:
> alcohol (291.0-291.9)
> arteriosclerosis (290.40-290.43)
> drugs (292.82)
> senility (290.0)

293.0 Delirium due to conditions classified elsewhere
Acute:
confusional state
infective psychosis
organic reaction
posttraumatic organic psychosis
psycho-organic syndrome
Acute psychosis associated with endocrine, metabolic, or
cerebrovascular disorder
Epileptic:
confusional state
twilight state
AHA: 1Q, '88, 3
F05 Delirium due to known physiological condition I-10

293.1 Subacute delirium
Subacute:
confusional state
infective psychosis
organic reaction
posttraumatic organic psychosis
psycho-organic syndrome
psychosis associated with endocrine or metabolic
disorder

✓5th **293.8 Other specified transient mental disorders due to
conditions classified elsewhere**

**293.81 Psychotic disorder with delusions in
conditions classified elsewhere**
Transient organic psychotic condition, paranoid
type

**293.82 Psychotic disorder with hallucinations in
conditions classified elsewhere**
Transient organic psychotic condition,
hallucinatory type

**293.83 Mood disorder in conditions classified
elsewhere**
Transient organic psychotic condition,
depressive type

N Newborn Age: 0   P Pediatric Age: 0-17   M Maternity Age: 12-55   A Adult Age: 15-124

293.84   Anxiety disorder in conditions classified elsewhere
AHA: 4Q, '96, 29

293.89   Other
Catatonic disorder in conditions classified elsewhere

293.9   Unspecified transient mental disorder in conditions classified elsewhere
Organic psychosis:
   infective NOS
   posttraumatic NOS
   transient NOS
Psycho-organic syndrome

✓4th **294   Persistent mental disorders due to conditions classified elsewhere**
INCLUDES   organic psychotic brain syndromes (chronic), not elsewhere classified

AHA: M-A, '85, 12

294.0   Amnestic disorder in conditions classified elsewhere
Korsakoff's psychosis or syndrome (nonalcoholic)
Code first underlying condition
EXCLUDES   alcoholic:
   amnestic syndrome (291.1)
   Korsakoff's psychosis (291.1)

✓5th **294.1   Dementia in conditions classified elsewhere**
Dementia of the Alzheimer's type
Code first any underlying physical condition, as:
dementia in:
   Alzheimer's disease (331.0)
   cerebral lipidoses (330.1)
   dementia with Lewy bodies (331.82)
   dementia with Parkinsonism (331.82)
   epilepsy (345.0-345.9)
   frontal dementia (331.19)
   frontotemporal dementia (331.19)
   general paresis [syphilis] (094.1)
   hepatolenticular degeneration (275.1)
   Huntington's chorea (333.4)
   Jakob-Creutzfeldt disease ▶(046.11-046.19)◀
   multiple sclerosis (340)
   Pick's disease of the brain (331.11)
   polyarteritis nodosa (446.0)
   syphilis (094.1)
EXCLUDES   dementia:
   arteriosclerotic (290.40-290.43)
   presenile (290.10-290.13)
   senile (290.0)
   epileptic psychosis NOS (294.8)

AHA: 4Q, '00, 40; 1Q, '99, 14; N-D, '85, 5

294.10   Dementia in conditions classified elsewhere without behavioral disturbance
Dementia in conditions classified elsewhere NOS
F02.80 Dementia in oth dz class elsw w/o behavrl disturb   I-10

294.11   Dementia in conditions classified elsewhere with behavioral disturbance
Aggressive behavior
Combative behavior
Violent behavior
Wandering off
AHA: 4Q, '00, 41
TIP: Review entire medical record for documentation of behavioral disturbance (aggressive, combative, violent behavior, wandering off); requires physician substantiation.

294.8   Other persistent mental disorders due to conditions classified elsewhere
Amnestic disorder NOS
Dementia NOS
Epileptic psychosis NOS
Mixed paranoid and affective organic psychotic states
Use additional code for associated epilepsy (345.0-345.9)
EXCLUDES   mild memory disturbances, not amounting to dementia ▶(310.8)◀

AHA: 3Q, '03, 14; 1Q, '88, 5
F06.8 Oth spec mental disord d/t known physiol cond   I-10

294.9   Unspecified persistent mental disorders due to conditions classified elsewhere
Cognitive disorder NOS
Organic psychosis (chronic)
AHA: 2Q, '07, 4

OTHER PSYCHOSES (295-299)
Use additional code to identify any associated physical disease, injury, or condition affecting the brain with psychoses classifiable to 295-298

✓4th **295   Schizophrenic disorders**
INCLUDES   schizophrenia of the types described in 295.0-295.9 occurring in children
EXCLUDES   childhood type schizophrenia (299.9)
   infantile autism (299.0)

The following fifth-digit subclassification is for use with category 295:
   0   unspecified
   1   subchronic
   2   chronic
   3   subchronic with acute exacerbation
   4   chronic with acute exacerbation
   5   in remission

DEF: Group of disorders with disturbances in thought (delusions, hallucinations), mood (blunted, flattened, inappropriate affect), sense of self; also bizarre, purposeless behavior, repetitious activity, or inactivity.

§ ✓5th **295.0   Simple type**
[0-5]   Schizophrenia simplex
EXCLUDES   latent schizophrenia (295.5)

§ ✓5th **295.1   Disorganized type**
[0-5]   Hebephrenia
Hebephrenic type schizophrenia
DEF: Inappropriate behavior; results in extreme incoherence and disorganization of time, place and sense of social appropriateness; withdrawal from routine social interaction may occur.

§ ✓5th **295.2   Catatonic type**
[0-5]   Catatonic (schizophrenia):
   agitation
   excitation
   excited type
   stupor
   withdrawn type
Schizophrenic:
   catalepsy
   catatonia
   flexibilitas cerea
DEF: Extreme changes in motor activity; one extreme is decreased response or reaction to the environment and the other is spontaneous activity.

§ ✓5th **295.3   Paranoid type**
[0-5]   Paraphrenic schizophrenia
EXCLUDES   involutional paranoid state (297.2)
   paranoia (297.1)
   paraphrenia (297.2)
DEF: Preoccupied with delusional suspicions and auditory hallucinations related to single theme; usually hostile, grandiose, overly religious, occasionally hypochondriacal.
F20.0 Paranoid schizophrenia   I-10

§   Requires fifth digit. Valid digits are in [brackets] under each code. See category 295 for codes and definitions.

Mental Disorders

295.4–296.7

§ ✓5ᵗʰ **295.4 Schizophreniform disorder**
[0-5]   Oneirophrenia
Schizophreniform:
    attack
    psychosis, confusional type

> **EXCLUDES** *acute forms of schizophrenia of:*
>   *catatonic type (295.2)*
>   *hebephrenic type (295.1)*
>   *paranoid type (295.3)*
>   *simple type (295.0)*
>   *undifferentiated type (295.8)*

§ ✓5ᵗʰ **295.5 Latent schizophrenia**
[0-5]   Latent schizophrenic reaction
Schizophrenia:
    borderline
    incipient
    prepsychotic
    prodromal
    pseudoneurotic
    pseudopsychopathic

> **EXCLUDES** *schizoid personality (301.20-301.22)*

AHA: For code 295.50: 1Q, '06, 10

§ ✓5ᵗʰ **295.6 Residual type**
[0-5]   Chronic undifferentiated schizophrenia
Restzustand (schizophrenic)
Schizophrenic residual state

AHA: For code 295.62: 4Q, '06, 78

§ ✓5ᵗʰ **295.7 Schizoaffective disorder**
[0-5]   Cyclic schizophrenia
Mixed schizophrenic and affective psychosis
Schizo-affective psychosis
Schizophreniform psychosis, affective type

F25.9 Schizoaffective disorder unspecified   I-10

§ ✓5ᵗʰ **295.8 Other specified types of schizophrenia**
[0-5]   Acute (undifferentiated) schizophrenia
Atypical schizophrenia
Cenesthopathic schizophrenia

> **EXCLUDES** *infantile autism (299.0)*

§ ✓5ᵗʰ **295.9 Unspecified schizophrenia**
[0-5]   Schizophrenia:
    NOS
    mixed NOS
    undifferentiated NOS
    undifferentiated type
Schizophrenic reaction NOS
Schizophreniform psychosis NOS

AHA: 3Q, '95, 6

F20.9 Schizophrenia unspecified   I-10

✓4ᵗʰ **296 Episodic mood disorders**

> **INCLUDES** *episodic affective disorders*

> **EXCLUDES** *neurotic depression (300.4)*
> *reactive depressive psychosis (298.0)*
> *reactive excitation (298.1)*

The following fifth-digit subclassification is for use with categories 296.0-296.6:

   0 unspecified
   1 mild
   2 moderate
   3 severe, without mention of psychotic behavior
   4 severe, specified as with psychotic behavior
   5 in partial or unspecified remission
   6 in full remission

AHA: M-A, '85, 14

§ ✓5ᵗʰ **296.0 Bipolar I disorder, single manic episode**
[0-6]   Hypomania (mild) NOS
Hypomanic psychosis
Mania (momopolar) NOS
Manic-depressive psychosis or reaction: } single episode or unspecified
    hypomanic
    manic

> **EXCLUDES** *circular type, if there was a previous attack of depression (296.4)*

DEF: Mood disorder identified by hyperactivity; may show extreme agitation or exaggerated excitability; speech and thought processes may be accelerated.

§ ✓5ᵗʰ **296.1 Manic disorder, recurrent episode**
[0-6]   Any condition classifiable to 296.0, stated to be recurrent

> **EXCLUDES** *circular type, if there was a previous attack of depression (296.4)*

§ ✓5ᵗʰ **296.2 Major depressive disorder, single episode**
[0-6]   Depressive psychosis
Endogenous depression
Involutional melancholia
Manic-depressive psychosis or reaction, depressed type   } single episode or unspecified
Monopolar depression
Psychotic depression

> **EXCLUDES** *circular type, if previous attack was of manic type (296.5)*
> *depression NOS (311)*
> *reactive depression (neurotic) (300.4)*
> *psychotic (298.0)*

DEF: Mood disorder that produces depression; may exhibit as sadness, low self-esteem, or guilt feelings; other manifestations may be withdrawal from friends and family; interrupted sleep.

F32.9 Major depressive disorder single episode uns   I-10

§ ✓5ᵗʰ **296.3 Major depressive disorder, recurrent episode**
[0-6]   Any condition classifiable to 296.2, stated to be recurrent

> **EXCLUDES** *circular type, if previous attack was of manic type (296.5)*
> *depression NOS (311)*
> *reactive depression (neurotic) (300.4)*
> *psychotic (298.0)*

F33.2 Maj dprsv disord recur sev w/o psychot features   I-10

§ ✓5ᵗʰ **296.4 Bipolar I disorder, most recent episode (or current) manic**
[0-6]   Bipolar disorder, now manic
Manic-depressive psychosis, circular type but currently manic

> **EXCLUDES** *brief compensatory or rebound mood swings (296.99)*

F31.2 Bipolar d/o currnt epis mnic sev w/psychotc ftur   I-10

§ ✓5ᵗʰ **296.5 Bipolar I disorder, most recent episode (or current) depressed**
[0-6]   Bipolar disorder, now depressed
Manic-depressive psychosis, circular type but currently depressed

> **EXCLUDES** *brief compensatory or rebound mood swings (296.99)*

F31.30 Bipol disord currnt epis dprsd mild/mod sev uns   I-10

§ ✓5ᵗʰ **296.6 Bipolar I disorder, most recent episode (or current) mixed**
[0-6]   Manic-depressive psychosis, circular type, mixed

296.7 Bipolar I disorder, most recent episode (or current) unspecified
    Atypical bipolar affective disorder NOS
Manic-depressive psychosis, circular type, current condition not specified as either manic or depressive

DEF: Manic-depressive disorder referred to as bipolar because of the mood range from manic to depressive.

---

§   Requires fifth digit. Valid digits are in [brackets] under each code. See appropriate category for codes and definitions.

   N Newborn Age: 0   P Pediatric Age: 0-17   M Maternity Age: 12-55   A Adult Age: 15-124

✓5ᵗʰ **296.8 Other and unspecified bipolar disorders**

296.80 Bipolar disorder, unspecified
Bipolar disorder NOS
Manic-depressive:
reaction NOS
syndrome NOS
F31.9 Bipolar disorder unspecified [I-10]

296.81 Atypical manic disorder

296.82 Atypical depressive disorder

296.89 Other
Bipolar II disorder
Manic-depressive psychosis, mixed type
F31.81 Bipolar II disorder [I-10]

✓5ᵗʰ **296.9 Other and unspecified episodic mood disorder**
EXCLUDES psychogenic affective psychoses (298.0-298.8)

296.90 Unspecified episodic mood disorder
Affective psychosis NOS
Melancholia NOS
Mood disorder NOS
AHA: M-A, '85, 14
F39 Unspecified mood [affective] disorder [I-10]

296.99 Other specified episodic mood disorder
Mood swings:
brief compensatory
rebound

✓4ᵗʰ **297 Delusional disorders**
INCLUDES paranoid disorders
EXCLUDES acute paranoid reaction (298.3)
alcoholic jealousy or paranoid state (291.5)
paranoid schizophrenia (295.3)

297.0 Paranoid state, simple

297.1 Delusional disorder
Chronic paranoid psychosis
Sander's disease
Systematized delusions
EXCLUDES paranoid personality disorder (301.0)
F22 Delusional disorders [I-10]

297.2 Paraphrenia
Involutional paranoid state
Late paraphrenia
Paraphrenia (involutional)
DEF: Paranoid schizophrenic disorder that persists over a prolonged period but does not distort personality despite persistent delusions.

297.3 Shared psychotic disorder
Folie à deux
Induced psychosis or paranoid disorder
DEF: Mental disorder two people share; first person with the delusional disorder convinces second person because of a close relationship and shared experiences to accept the delusions.

297.8 Other specified paranoid states
Paranoia querulans
Sensitiver Beziehungswahn
EXCLUDES acute paranoid reaction or state (298.3)
senile paranoid state (290.20)

297.9 Unspecified paranoid state
Paranoid:
disorder NOS
psychosis NOS
reaction NOS
state NOS
AHA: J-A, '85, 9

✓4ᵗʰ **298 Other nonorganic psychoses**
INCLUDES psychotic conditions due to or provoked by:
emotional stress
environmental factors as major part of etiology

298.0 Depressive type psychosis
Psychogenic depressive psychosis
Psychotic reactive depression
Reactive depressive psychosis
EXCLUDES manic-depressive psychosis, depressed type (296.2-296.3)
neurotic depression (300.4)
reactive depression NOS (300.4)

298.1 Excitative type psychosis
Acute hysterical psychosis
Psychogenic excitation
Reactive excitation
EXCLUDES manic-depressive psychosis, manic type (296.0-296.1)
DEF: Affective disorder similar to manic-depressive psychosis, in the manic phase, seemingly brought on by stress.

298.2 Reactive confusion
Psychogenic confusion
Psychogenic twilight state
EXCLUDES acute confusional state (293.0)
DEF: Confusion, disorientation, cloudiness in consciousness; brought on by severe emotional upheaval.

298.3 Acute paranoid reaction
Acute psychogenic paranoid psychosis
Bouffée délirante
EXCLUDES paranoid states (297.0-297.9)

298.4 Psychogenic paranoid psychosis
Protracted reactive paranoid psychosis

298.8 Other and unspecified reactive psychosis
Brief psychotic disorder
Brief reactive psychosis NOS
Hysterical psychosis
Psychogenic psychosis NOS
Psychogenic stupor
EXCLUDES acute hysterical psychosis (298.1)

298.9 Unspecified psychosis
Atypical psychosis
Psychosis NOS
Psychotic disorder NOS
AHA: 3Q, '06, 22
F28 Oth psych d/o not d/t sbstnc/knwn physiolog cond [I-10]

✓4ᵗʰ **299 Pervasive developmental disorders**
EXCLUDES adult type psychoses occurring in childhood, as:
affective disorders (296.0-296.9)
manic-depressive disorders (296.0-296.9)
schizophrenia (295.0-295.9)

The following fifth-digit subclassification is for use with category 299:
0 current or active state
1 residual state

§ ✓5ᵗʰ **299.0 Autistic disorder**
[0-1] Childhood autism
Infantile psychosis
Kanner's syndrome
EXCLUDES disintegrative psychosis (299.1)
Heller's syndrome (299.1)
schizophrenic syndrome of childhood (299.9)
DEF: Severe mental disorder of children, results in impaired social behavior; abnormal development of communicative skills, appears to be unaware of the need for emotional support and little emotional response to family members.

§ Requires fifth digit. Valid digits are in [brackets] under each code. See category 299 for codes and definitions.

✓4ᵗʰ ✓5ᵗʰ **Additional Digit Required**   **Unspecified Code**   **Other Specified Code**   **Manifestation Code**   ▶◀ Revised Text   ● New Code   ▲ Revised Code Title

Mental Disorders

299.1–300.29

§ ✓5th **299.1** **Childhood disintegrative disorder**
[0-1]   Heller's syndrome

       Use additional code to identify any associated neurological disorder

       EXCLUDES   *infantile autism (299.0)*
                        schizophrenic syndrome of childhood (299.9)

       DEF: Mental disease of children identified by impaired development of reciprocal social skills, verbal and nonverbal communication skills, imaginative play.

§ ✓5th **299.8** **Other specified pervasive developmental disorders**
[0-1]   Asperger's disorder
       Atypical childhood psychosis
       Borderline psychosis of childhood

       EXCLUDES   *simple stereotypes without psychotic disturbance (307.3)*

§ ✓5th **299.9** **Unspecified pervasive developmental disorder**
[0-1]   Child psychosis NOS
       Pervasive developmental disorder NOS
       Schizophrenia, childhood type NOS
       Schizophrenic syndrome of childhood NOS

       EXCLUDES   *schizophrenia of adult type occurring in childhood (295.0-295.9)*

NEUROTIC DISORDERS, PERSONALITY DISORDERS, AND OTHER NONPSYCHOTIC MENTAL DISORDERS (300-316)

✓4th **300** **Anxiety, dissociative and somatoform disorders**

✓5th **300.0** **Anxiety states**

       EXCLUDES   *anxiety in:*
                        acute stress reaction (308.0)
                        transient adjustment reaction (309.24)
                neurasthenia (300.5)
                psychophysiological disorders (306.0-306.9)
                separation anxiety (309.21)

       DEF: Mental disorder characterized by anxiety and avoidance behavior not particularly related to any specific situation or stimulus; symptoms include emotional instability, apprehension, fatigue.

       300.00 **Anxiety state, unspecified**
            Anxiety:
                neurosis
                reaction
                state (neurotic)
            Atypical anxiety disorder

            AHA: 1Q, '02, 6

            TIP: For chest pain due to anxiety, assign chest pain code first, because chest pain is not integral to the diagnosis of anxiety.

            F41.9 Anxiety disorder unspecified   **I-10**

       300.01 **Panic disorder without agoraphobia**
            Panic:
                attack
                state

            EXCLUDES   *panic disorder with agoraphobia (300.21)*

            DEF: Neurotic disorder characterized by recurrent panic or anxiety, apprehension, fear or terror; symptoms include shortness of breath, palpitations, dizziness, shakiness; fear of dying may persis.

            F41.0 Panic d/o [epis paroxysmal anxiety] w/o   **I-10**
            agoraphobia

       300.02 **Generalized anxiety disorder**

       300.09 **Other**

✓5th **300.1** **Dissociative, conversion and factitious disorders**

       EXCLUDES   *adjustment reaction (309.0-309.9)*
                        anorexia nervosa (307.1)
                        gross stress reaction (308.0-308.9)
                        hysterical personality (301.50-301.59)
                        psychophysiologic disorders (306.0-306.9)

       300.10 **Hysteria, unspecified**

300.11 **Conversion disorder**
       Astasia-abasia, hysterical
       Conversion hysteria or reaction
       Hysterical:
            blindness
            deafness
            paralysis

       DEF: Mental disorder that impairs physical functions with no physiological basis; sensory motor symptoms include seizures, paralysis, temporary blindness; increase in stress or avoidance of unpleasant responsibilities may precipitate.

       AHA: N-D, '85, 15

300.12 **Dissociative amnesia**
       Hysterical amnesia

300.13 **Dissociative fugue**
       Hysterical fugue

       DEF: Dissociative hysteria; identified by loss of memory, flight from familiar surroundings; conscious activity is not associated with perception of surroundings, no later memory of episode.

300.14 **Dissociative identity disorder**

300.15 **Dissociative disorder or reaction, unspecified**

       DEF: Hysterical neurotic episode; sudden but temporary changes in perceived identity, memory, consciousness, segregated memory patterns exist separate from dominant personality.

300.16 **Factitious disorder with predominantly psychological signs and symptoms**
       Compensation neurosis
       Ganser's syndrome, hysterical

       DEF: A disorder characterized by the purposeful assumption of mental illness symptoms; which are acted out more often when another person is present.

300.19 **Other and unspecified factitious illness**
       Factitious disorder (with combined psychological and physical signs and symptoms) (with predominantly physical signs and symptoms) NOS

       EXCLUDES   *multiple operations or hospital addiction syndrome (301.51)*

✓5th **300.2** **Phobic disorders**

       EXCLUDES   *anxiety state not associated with a specific situation or object (300.00-300.09)*
                        obsessional phobias (300.3)

300.20 **Phobia, unspecified**
       Anxiety-hysteria NOS
       Phobia NOS

300.21 **Agoraphobia with panic disorder**
       Fear of:
            open spaces
            streets   } with panic attacks
            travel
       Panic disorder with agoraphobia

       EXCLUDES   *agoraphobia without panic disorder (300.22)*
                        panic disorder without agoraphobia (300.01)

300.22 **Agoraphobia without mention of panic attacks**
       Any condition classifiable to 300.21 without mention of panic attacks

300.23 **Social phobia**
       Fear of:
            eating in public
            public speaking
            washing in public

300.29 **Other isolated or specific phobias**
       Acrophobia   Claustrophobia
       Animal phobias   Fear of crowds

---

§   Requires fifth digit. Valid digits are in [brackets] under each code. See category 299 for codes and definitions.

N Newborn Age: 0   **P** Pediatric Age: 0-17   **M** Maternity Age: 12-55   **A** Adult Age: 15-124

300.3 Obsessive-compulsive disorders
Anancastic neurosis
Compulsive neurosis
Obsessional phobia [any]

> EXCLUDES *obsessive-compulsive symptoms occurring in:*
> *endogenous depression (296.2-296.3)*
> *organic states (eg., encephalitis)*
> *schizophrenia (295.0-295.9)*

300.4 Dysthymic disorder
Anxiety depression
Depression with anxiety
Depressive reaction
Neurotic depressive state
Reactive depression

> EXCLUDES *adjustment reaction with depressive*
> *symptoms (309.0-309.1)*
> *depression NOS (311)*
> *manic-depressive psychosis, depressed type*
> *(296.2-296.3)*
> *reactive depressive psychosis (298.0)*

DEF: Depression without psychosis; less severe depression related to personal change or unexpected circumstances; also referred to as "reactional depression."

F34.1 Dysthymic disorder   [I-10]

300.5 Neurasthenia
Fatigue neurosis
Nervous debility
Psychogenic:
asthenia
general fatigue
Use additional code to identify any associated physical disorder

> EXCLUDES *anxiety state (300.00-300.09)*
> *neurotic depression (300.4)*
> *psychophysiological disorders (306.0-306.9)*
> *specific nonpsychotic mental disorders*
> *following organic brain damage*
> *(310.0-310.9)*

DEF: Physical and mental symptoms caused primarily by what is known as mental exhaustion; symptoms include chronic weakness, fatigue.

300.6 Depersonalization disorder
Derealization (neurotic)
Neurotic state with depersonalization episode

> EXCLUDES *depersonalization associated with:*
> *anxiety (300.00-300.09)*
> *depression (300.4)*
> *manic-depressive disorder or psychosis*
> *(296.0-296.9)*
> *schizophrenia (295.0-295.9)*

DEF: Dissociative disorder characterized by feelings of strangeness about self or body image; symptoms include dizziness, anxiety, fear of insanity, loss of reality of surroundings.

300.7 Hypochondriasis
Body dysmorphic disorder

> EXCLUDES *hypochondriasis in:*
> *hysteria (300.10-300.19)*
> *manic-depressive psychosis, depressed type*
> *(296.2-296.3)*
> *neurasthenia (300.5)*
> *obsessional disorder (300.3)*
> *schizophrenia (295.0-295.9)*

√5ᵗʰ 300.8 Somatoform disorders

300.81 Somatization disorder
Briquet's disorder
Severe somatoform disorder

300.82 Undifferentiated somatoform disorder
Atypical somatoform disorder
Somatoform disorder NOS

DEF: Disorders in which patients have symptoms that suggest an organic disease but no evidence of physical disorder after repeated testing.

AHA: 4Q, '96, 29

300.89 Other somatoform disorders
Occupational neurosis, including writers' cramp
Psychasthenia
Psychasthenic neurosis

300.9 Unspecified nonpsychotic mental disorder
Psychoneurosis NOS

√4ᵗʰ 301 Personality disorders

> INCLUDES character neurosis

Use additional code to identify any associated neurosis or psychosis, or physical condition

> EXCLUDES *nonpsychotic personality disorder associated with*
> *organic brain syndromes (310.0-310.9)*

301.0 Paranoid personality disorder
Fanatic personality
Paranoid personality (disorder)
Paranoid traits

> EXCLUDES *acute paranoid reaction (298.3)*
> *alcoholic paranoia (291.5)*
> *paranoid schizophrenia (295.3)*
> *paranoid states (297.0-297.9)*

AHA: J-A, '85, 9

√5ᵗʰ 301.1 Affective personality disorder

> EXCLUDES *affective psychotic disorders (296.0-296.9)*
> *neurasthenia (300.5)*
> *neurotic depression (300.4)*

301.10 Affective personality disorder, unspecified

301.11 Chronic hypomanic personality disorder
Chronic hypomanic disorder
Hypomanic personality

301.12 Chronic depressive personality disorder
Chronic depressive disorder
Depressive character or personality

301.13 Cyclothymic disorder
Cycloid personality
Cyclothymia
Cyclothymic personality

√5ᵗʰ 301.2 Schizoid personality disorder

> EXCLUDES *schizophrenia (295.0-295.9)*

301.20 Schizoid personality disorder, unspecified

301.21 Introverted personality

301.22 Schizotypal personality disorder

301.3 Explosive personality disorder
Aggressive:
personality
reaction
Aggressiveness
Emotional instability (excessive)
Pathological emotionality
Quarrelsomeness

> EXCLUDES *dyssocial personality (301.7)*
> *hysterical neurosis (300.10-300.19)*

301.4 Obsessive-compulsive personality disorder
Anancastic personality
Obsessional personality

> EXCLUDES *obsessive-compulsive disorder (300.3)*
> *phobic state (300.20-300.29)*

√5ᵗʰ 301.5 Histrionic personality disorder

> EXCLUDES *hysterical neurosis (300.10-300.19)*

DEF: Extreme emotional behavior, often theatrical; often concerned about own appeal; may demand attention, exhibit seductive behavior.

301.50 Histrionic personality disorder, unspecified
Hysterical personality NOS

301.51 Chronic factitious illness with physical symptoms
Hospital addiction syndrome
Multiple operations syndrome
Munchausen syndrome

 Additional Digit Required   Unspecified Code   Other Specified Code   Manifestation Code   ►◄ Revised Text   ● New Code   ▲ Revised Code Title

2010 ICD-9-CM   Volume 1 – 79

301.59 Other histrionic personality disorder
Personality:
emotionally unstable
labile
psychoinfantile

301.6 Dependent personality disorder
Asthenic personality
Inadequate personality
Passive personality
EXCLUDES neurasthenia (300.5)
passive-aggressive personality (301.84)
DEF: Overwhelming feeling of helplessness; fears of
abandonment may persist; difficulty in making personal
decisions without confirmation by others; low self-esteem
due to irrational sensitivity to criticism.

301.7 Antisocial personality disorder
Amoral personality
Asocial personality
Dyssocial personality
Personality disorder with predominantly sociopathic or
asocial manifestation
EXCLUDES disturbance of conduct without specifiable
personality disorder (312.0-312.9)
explosive personality (301.3)
DEF: Continuous antisocial behavior that violates rights of
others; social traits include extreme aggression, total
disregard for traditional social rules.
AHA: S-O, '84, 16

✓5ᵗʰ **301.8 Other personality disorders**

301.81 Narcissistic personality disorder
DEF: Grandiose fantasy or behavior, lack of social
empathy, hypersensitive to the lack of others'
judgment, exploits others; need for continual
admiration.

301.82 Avoidant personality disorder
DEF: Personality disorder marked by feelings of
social inferiority; sensitivity to criticism, emotionally
restrained due to fear of rejection.

301.83 Borderline personality disorder
DEF: Personality disorder characterized by unstable
moods, self-image, and interpersonal relationships;
uncontrolled anger, impulsive and self-destructive
acts, fears of abandonment, feelings of emptiness
and boredom, recurrent suicide threats or
self-mutilation.
F60.3 Borderline personality disorder   I-10

301.84 Passive-aggressive personality
DEF: Pattern of procrastination and refusal to meet
standards; introduce own obstacles to success and
exploit failure.

301.89 Other
Personality: Personality:
eccentric   masochistic
"haltlose" type   psychoneurotic
immature
EXCLUDES psychoinfantile personality (301.59)

301.9 Unspecified personality disorder
Pathological personality NOS
Personality disorder NOS
Psychopathic:
constitutional state
personality (disorder)

✓4ᵗʰ **302 Sexual and gender identity disorders**
EXCLUDES sexual disorder manifest in:
organic brain syndrome (290.0-294.9, 310.0-310.9)
psychosis (295.0-298.9)

302.0 Ego-dystonic sexual orientation
Ego-dystonic lesbianism
Sexual orientation conflict disorder
EXCLUDES homosexual pedophilia (302.2)

302.1 Zoophilia
Bestiality
DEF: A sociodeviant disorder marked by engaging in sexual
intercourse with animals.

302.2 Pedophilia
DEF: A sociodeviant condition of adults characterized by
sexual activity with children.

302.3 Transvestic fetishism
EXCLUDES trans-sexualism (302.5)
DEF: The desire to dress in clothing of opposite sex.

302.4 Exhibitionism
DEF: Sexual deviant behavior; exposure of genitals to
strangers; behavior prompted by intense sexual urges and
fantasies.

✓5ᵗʰ **302.5 Trans-sexualism**
Sex reassignment surgery status
EXCLUDES transvestism (302.3)
DEF: Gender identity disturbance; overwhelming desire to
change anatomic sex, due to belief that individual is a
member of the opposite sex.

302.50 With unspecified sexual history

302.51 With asexual history

302.52 With homosexual history

302.53 With heterosexual history

302.6 Gender identity disorder in children
Feminism in boys
Gender identity disorder NOS
EXCLUDES gender identity disorder in adult (302.85)
trans-sexualism (302.50-302.53)
transvestism (302.3)

✓5ᵗʰ **302.7 Psychosexual dysfunction**
EXCLUDES impotence of organic origin (607.84)
normal transient symptoms from ruptured
hymen
transient or occasional failures of erection due
to fatigue, anxiety, alcohol, or drugs

302.70 Psychosexual dysfunction, unspecified
Sexual dysfunction NOS

302.71 Hypoactive sexual desire disorder
EXCLUDES decreased sexual desire NOS (799.81)

302.72 With inhibited sexual excitement
Female sexual arousal disorder
Frigidity
Impotence
Male erectile disorder

302.73 Female orgasmic disorder   ♀

302.74 Male orgasmic disorder   ♂

302.75 Premature ejaculation   ♂

302.76 Dyspareunia, psychogenic   ♀
DEF: Difficult or painful sex due to psychosomatic
state.

**302.79 With other specified psychosexual
dysfunctions**
Sexual aversion disorder

✓5ᵗʰ **302.8 Other specified psychosexual disorders**

302.81 Fetishism
DEF: Psychosexual disorder noted for intense sexual
urges and arousal precipitated by fantasies; use of
inanimate objects, such as clothing, to stimulate
sexual arousal, orgasm.

302.82 Voyeurism
DEF: Psychosexual disorder characterized by
uncontrollable impulse to observe others, without
their knowledge, who are nude or engaged in
sexual activity.

302.83 Sexual masochism

> **DEF:** Psychosexual disorder noted for need to achieve sexual gratification through humiliating or hurtful acts inflicted on self.

302.84 Sexual sadism

> **DEF:** Psychosexual disorder noted for need to achieve sexual gratification through humiliating or hurtful acts inflicted on someone else.

302.85 Gender identity disorder in adolescents or adults

> Use additional code to identify sex reassignment surgery status (302.5)
>
> **EXCLUDES**   gender identity disorder NOS (302.6)
> gender identity disorder in children (302.6)

302.89 Other

> Frotteurism
> Nymphomania
> Satyriasis

302.9 Unspecified psychosexual disorder

> Paraphilia NOS   Sexual deviation NOS
> Pathologic sexuality NOS   Sexual disorder NOS

✓4ᵗʰ 303 Alcohol dependence syndrome

> Use additional code to identify any associated condition, as:
> alcoholic psychoses (291.0-291.9)
> drug dependence (304.0-304.9)
> physical complications of alcohol, such as:
> cerebral degeneration (331.7)
> cirrhosis of liver (571.2)
> epilepsy (345.0-345.9)
> gastritis (535.3)
> hepatitis (571.1)
> liver damage NOS (571.3)
>
> **EXCLUDES**   drunkenness NOS (305.0)

> The following fifth-digit subclassification is for use with category 303:
>
> 0 unspecified
> 1 continuous
> 2 episodic
> 3 in remission

AHA: 3Q, '95, 6; 2Q, '91, 9; 4Q, '88, 8; S-O, '86, 3

TIP: The patient has become physically addicted to alcohol and often experiences withdrawal symptoms when not drinking. Do not assign both 303.0X and 303.9X on the same encounter.

§ ✓5ᵗʰ 303.0 Acute alcoholic intoxication
[0-3]
> Acute drunkenness in alcoholism

§ ✓5ᵗʰ 303.9 Other and unspecified alcohol dependence
[0-3]
> Chronic alcoholism
> Dipsomania
>
> **AHA:** 2Q, '02, 4; 2Q, '89, 9 ; **For code 303.90:** 2Q, '07, 6
>
> **F10.20** Alcohol dependence uncomplicated   **I-10**
> **F10.21** Alcohol dependence in remission   **I-10**

✓4ᵗʰ 304 Drug dependence

> **EXCLUDES**   nondependent abuse of drugs (305.1-305.9)

> The following fifth-digit subclassification is for use with category 304:
>
> 0 unspecified
> 1 continuous
> 2 episodic
> 3 in remission

AHA: 2Q, '91, 10; 4Q, '88, 8; S-O, '86, 3

§ ✓5ᵗʰ 304.0 Opioid type dependence
[0-3]
> Heroin
> Meperidine
> Methadone
> Morphine
> Opium
> Opium alkaloids and their derivatives
> Synthetics with morphine-like effects
>
> **AHA:** 2Q, '06, 7

§ ✓5ᵗʰ 304.1 Sedative, hypnotic or anxiolytic dependence
[0-3]
> Barbiturates
> Nonbarbiturate sedatives and tranquilizers with a similar effect:
> chlordiazepoxide
> diazepam
> glutethimide
> meprobamate
> methaqualone

§ ✓5ᵗʰ 304.2 Cocaine dependence
[0-3]
> Coca leaves and derivatives
>
> **F14.20** Cocaine dependence uncomplicated   **I-10**

§ ✓5ᵗʰ 304.3 Cannabis dependence
[0-3]
> Hashish
> Hemp
> Marihuana

§ ✓5ᵗʰ 304.4 Amphetamine and other psychostimulant dependence
[0-3]
> Methylphenidate
> Phenmetrazine

§ ✓5ᵗʰ 304.5 Hallucinogen dependence
[0-3]
> Dimethyltryptamine [DMT]
> Lysergic acid diethylamide [LSD] and derivatives
> Mescaline
> Psilocybin

§ ✓5ᵗʰ 304.6 Other specified drug dependence
[0-3]
> Absinthe addiction
> Glue sniffing
> Inhalant dependence
> Phencyclidine dependence
>
> **EXCLUDES**   tobacco dependence (305.1)

§ ✓5ᵗʰ 304.7 Combinations of opioid type drug with any other
[0-3]
> **AHA:** M-A, '86, 12

§ ✓5ᵗʰ 304.8 Combinations of drug dependence excluding opioid type drug
[0-3]
> **AHA:** M-A, '86, 12

§ ✓5ᵗʰ 304.9 Unspecified drug dependence
[0-3]
> Drug addiction NOS
> Drug dependence NOS
>
> **AHA: For code 304.90:** 4Q, '03, 103

✓4ᵗʰ 305 Nondependent abuse of drugs

> Note: Includes cases where a person, for whom no other diagnosis is possible, has come under medical care because of the maladaptive effect of a drug on which he is not dependent and that he has taken on his own initiative to the detriment of his health or social functioning.
>
> **EXCLUDES**   alcohol dependence syndrome (303.0-303.9)
> drug dependence (304.0-304.9)
> drug withdrawal syndrome (292.0)
> poisoning by drugs or medicinal substances (960.0-979.9)

> The following fifth-digit subclassification is for use with codes 305.0, 305.2-305.9:
>
> 0 unspecified
> 1 continuous
> 2 episodic
> 3 in remission

AHA: 2Q, '91, 10; 4Q, '88, 8; S-O, '86, 3

§ ✓5ᵗʰ 305.0 Alcohol abuse
[0-3]
> Drunkenness NOS
> Excessive drinking of alcohol NOS
> "Hangover" (alcohol)
> Inebriety NOS
>
> **EXCLUDES**   acute alcohol intoxication in alcoholism (303.0)
> alcoholic psychoses (291.0-291.9)
>
> **AHA:** 3Q, '96, 16
>
> **F10.10** Alcohol abuse uncomplicated   **I-10**

---

§   Requires fifth digit. Valid digits are in [brackets] under each code. See appropriate category for codes and definitions.

✓4ᵗʰ / ✓5ᵗʰ   Additional Digit Required   Unspecified Code   Other Specified Code   Manifestation Code   ►◄ Revised Text   ● New Code   ▲ Revised Code Title

2010 ICD-9-CM   **Volume 1 – 81**

305.1 **Tobacco use disorder**
Tobacco dependence

EXCLUDES *history of tobacco use (V15.82)*
smoking complicating pregnancy (649.0)
tobacco use disorder complicating pregnancy (649.0)

AHA: ▶1Q, '09, 16;◀ 2Q, '96, 10; N-D, '84, 12

F17.210 Nicotine dependence cigarettes uncomplicated   I-10

§ ✓5ᵗʰ **305.2** **Cannabis abuse**
[0-3]   **F12.10** Cannabis abuse uncomplicated   I-10

§ ✓5ᵗʰ **305.3** **Hallucinogen abuse**
[0-3]   Acute intoxication from hallucinogens ["bad trips"]
LSD reaction

§ ✓5ᵗʰ **305.4** **Sedative, hypnotic or anxiolytic abuse**
[0-3]

§ ✓5ᵗʰ **305.5** **Opioid abuse**
[0-3]

§ ✓5ᵗʰ **305.6** **Cocaine abuse**
[0-3]   **AHA:** 1Q, '93, 25; **For code 305.60:** 1Q, '05, 6

F14.10 Cocaine abuse uncomplicated   I-10

§ ✓5ᵗʰ **305.7** **Amphetamine or related acting sympathomimetic**
[0-3]   **abuse**

AHA: For code 305.70: 2Q, '03, 10-11

§ ✓5ᵗʰ **305.8** **Antidepressant type abuse**
[0-3]

§ ✓5ᵗʰ **305.9** **Other, mixed, or** unspecified drug abuse
[0-3]   Caffeine intoxication
Inhalant abuse
"Laxative habit"
Misuse of drugs NOS
Nonprescribed use of drugs or patent medicinals
Phencyclidine abuse

AHA: 3Q, '99, 20

✓4ᵗʰ **306** **Physiological malfunction arising from mental factors**

INCLUDES psychogenic:
physical symptoms ⎫
physiological ⎬ not involving tissue
manifestations ⎭ damage

EXCLUDES *hysteria (300.11-300.19)*
physical symptoms secondary to a psychiatric disorder classified elsewhere
psychic factors associated with physical conditions involving tissue damage classified elsewhere (316)
specific nonpsychotic mental disorders following organic brain damage (310.0-310.9)

DEF: Functional disturbances or interruptions due to mental or psychological causes; no tissue damage sustained in these conditions.

306.0 **Musculoskeletal**
Psychogenic paralysis
Psychogenic torticollis

EXCLUDES *Gilles de la Tourette's syndrome (307.23)*
paralysis as hysterical or conversion reaction (300.11)
tics (307.20-307.22)

306.1 **Respiratory**
Psychogenic:
air hunger
cough
hiccough
hyperventilation
yawning

EXCLUDES *psychogenic asthma (316 and 493.9)*

306.2 **Cardiovascular**
Cardiac neurosis
Cardiovascular neurosis
Neurocirculatory asthenia
Psychogenic cardiovascular disorder

EXCLUDES *psychogenic paroxysmal tachycardia (316 and 427.2)*

DEF: Neurocirculatory asthenia: functional nervous and circulatory irregularities with palpitations, dyspnea, fatigue, rapid pulse, precordial pain, fear of effort, discomfort during exercise, anxiety; also called DaCosta's syndrome, Effort syndrome, Irritable or Soldier's Heart.

AHA: J-A, '85, 14

306.3 **Skin**
Psychogenic pruritus

EXCLUDES *psychogenic:*
alopecia (316 and 704.00)
dermatitis (316 and 692.9)
eczema (316 and 691.8 or 692.9)
urticaria (316 and 708.0-708.9)

306.4 **Gastrointestinal**
Aerophagy
Cyclical vomiting, psychogenic
Diarrhea, psychogenic
Nervous gastritis
Psychogenic dyspepsia

EXCLUDES *cyclical vomiting NOS (536.2)*
associated with migraine (346.2)
globus hystericus (300.11)
mucous colitis (316 and 564.9)
psychogenic:
cardiospasm (316 and 530.0)
duodenal ulcer (316 and 532.0-532.9)
gastric ulcer (316 and 531.0-531.9)
peptic ulcer NOS (316 and 533.0-533.9)
vomiting NOS (307.54)

DEF: Aerophagy: excess swallowing of air, usually unconscious; related to anxiety; results in distended abdomen or belching, often interpreted by the patient as a physical disorder.

AHA: 2Q, '89, 11

✓5ᵗʰ **306.5** **Genitourinary**

EXCLUDES *enuresis, psychogenic (307.6)*
frigidity (302.72)
impotence (302.72)
psychogenic dyspareunia (302.76)

306.50 **Psychogenic genitourinary malfunction, unspecified**

306.51 **Psychogenic vaginismus**   ♀
Functional vaginismus

DEF: Psychogenic response resulting in painful contractions of vaginal canal muscles; can be severe enough to prevent sexual intercourse.

306.52 **Psychogenic dysmenorrhea**   ♀

306.53 **Psychogenic dysuria**

306.59 **Other**

AHA: M-A, '87, 11

306.6 **Endocrine**

306.7 **Organs of special sense**

EXCLUDES *hysterical blindness or deafness (300.11)*
psychophysical visual disturbances (368.16)

306.8 **Other specified psychophysiological malfunction**
Bruxism
Teeth grinding

306.9 **Unspecified psychophysiological malfunction**
Psychophysiologic disorder NOS
Psychosomatic disorder NOS

---

§   Requires fifth digit. Valid digits are in [brackets] under each code. See category 305 for codes and definitions.

N Newborn Age: 0   P Pediatric Age: 0-17   M Maternity Age: 12-55   A Adult Age: 15-124

✓4ᵗʰ 307 Special symptoms or syndromes, not elsewhere classified

Note: This category is intended for use if the psychopathology is manifested by a single specific symptom or group of symptoms which is not part of an organic illness or other mental disorder classifiable elsewhere.

> **EXCLUDES** those due to mental disorders classified elsewhere
> those of organic origin

307.0 Stuttering

> **EXCLUDES** dysphasia ▶(784.59)◀
> lisping or lalling (307.9)
> retarded development of speech (315.31-315.39)
> ▶stuttering (fluency disorder) due to late effect of cerebrovascular accident (438.14)◀

307.1 Anorexia nervosa

> **EXCLUDES** eating disturbance NOS (307.50)
> feeding problem (783.3)
> of nonorganic origin (307.59)
> loss of appetite (783.0)
> of nonorganic origin (307.59)

> **AHA:** 2Q, '06, 12; 4Q, '89, 11

> **TIP:** Assign an additional code for any associated malnutrition.

✓5ᵗʰ 307.2 Tics

> **EXCLUDES** nail-biting or thumb-sucking (307.9)
> stereotypes occurring in isolation (307.3)
> tics of organic origin (333.3)

> **DEF:** Involuntary muscle response usually confined to the face, shoulders.

307.20 Tic disorder, unspecified
Tic disorder NOS

307.21 Transient tic disorder

307.22 Chronic motor or vocal tic disorder

307.23 Tourette's disorder
Motor-verbal tic disorder

> **DEF:** Syndrome of facial and vocal tics in childhood; progresses to spontaneous or involuntary jerking, obscene utterances, other uncontrollable actions considered inappropriate.

307.3 Stereotypic movement disorder
Body-rocking
Head banging
Spasmus nutans
Stereotypes NOS

> **EXCLUDES** tics (307.20-307.23)
> of organic origin (333.3)

✓5ᵗʰ 307.4 Specific disorders of sleep of nonorganic origin

> **EXCLUDES** narcolepsy (347.00-347.11)
> organic hypersomnia (327.10-327.19)
> organic insomnia (327.00-327.09)
> those of unspecified cause (780.50-780.59)

307.40 Nonorganic sleep disorder, unspecified

307.41 Transient disorder of initiating or maintaining sleep
Adjustment insomnia
Hyposomnia ⎱ associated with intermittent
Insomnia ⎰ emotional reactions or
Sleeplessness ⎰ conflicts

307.42 Persistent disorder of initiating or maintaining sleep
Hyposomnia, insomnia, or sleeplessness associated with:
anxiety
conditioned arousal
depression (major) (minor)
psychosis
Idiopathic insomnia
Paradoxical insomnia
Primary insomnia
Psychophysiological insomnia

307.43 Transient disorder of initiating or maintaining wakefulness
Hypersomnia associated with acute or intermittent emotional reactions or conflicts

307.44 Persistent disorder of initiating or maintaining wakefulness
Hypersomnia associated with depression (major) (minor)
Insufficient sleep syndrome
Primary hypersomnia

> **EXCLUDES** sleep deprivation (V69.4)

307.45 Circadian rhythm sleep disorder of nonorganic origin

307.46 Sleep arousal disorder
Night terror disorder
Night terrors
Sleep terror disorder
Sleepwalking
Somnambulism

> **DEF:** Sleepwalking marked by extreme terror, panic, screaming, confusion; no recall of event upon arousal; term may refer to simply the act of sleepwalking.

307.47 Other dysfunctions of sleep stages or arousal from sleep
Nightmare disorder
Nightmares:
NOS
REM-sleep type
Sleep drunkenness

307.48 Repetitive intrusions of sleep
Repetitive intrusion of sleep with:
atypical polysomnographic features
environmental disturbances
repeated REM-sleep interruptions

307.49 Other
"Short-sleeper"
Subjective insomnia complaint

✓5ᵗʰ 307.5 Other and unspecified disorders of eating

> **EXCLUDES** anorexia:
> nervosa (307.1)
> of unspecified cause (783.0)
> overeating, of unspecified cause (783.6)
> vomiting:
> NOS (787.03)
> cyclical (536.2)
> associated with migraine (346.2)
> psychogenic (306.4)

307.50 Eating disorder, unspecified
Eating disorder NOS

307.51 Bulimia nervosa
Overeating of nonorganic origin

> **DEF:** Mental disorder commonly characterized by binge eating followed by self-induced vomiting; perceptions of being fat; and fear the inability to stop eating voluntarily.

307.52 Pica
Perverted appetite of nonorganic origin

> **DEF:** Compulsive eating disorder characterized by craving for substances, other than food; such as paint chips or dirt.

307.53 Rumination disorder
Regurgitation, of nonorganic origin, of food with reswallowing

> **EXCLUDES** obsessional rumination (300.3)

307.54 Psychogenic vomiting

307.59 Other
Feeding disorder of infancy or early childhood of nonorganic origin
Infantile feeding ⎱ of nonorganic
disturbances ⎰ origin
Loss of appetite ⎰

✓4ᵗʰ Additional Digit Required   **Unspecified Code**   **Other Specified Code**   **Manifestation Code**   ▶◀ Revised Text   ● New Code   ▲ Revised Code Title

2010 ICD-9-CM

October 2009 • Volume 1 – 83

Mental Disorders

307.6–309.82

307.6 Enuresis
Enuresis (primary) (secondary) of nonorganic origin
EXCLUDES *enuresis of unspecified cause (788.3)*
DEF: Involuntary urination past age of normal control; also called bedwetting; no trace to biological problem; focus on psychological issues.

307.7 Encopresis
Encopresis (continuous) (discontinuous) of nonorganic origin
EXCLUDES *encopresis of unspecified cause (787.6)*
DEF: Inability to control bowel movements; cause traced to psychological, not biological, problems.

√5ᵗʰ **307.8 Pain disorders related to psychological factors**

307.80 Psychogenic pain, site unspecified

307.81 Tension headache
EXCLUDES *headache:*
NOS (784.0)
migraine (346.0-346.9)
syndromes (339.00-339.89)
tension type (339.10-339.12)
AHA: ▶4Q, '08, 103;◀ N-D, '85, 16

307.89 Other
Code first to type or site of pain
EXCLUDES *pain disorder exclusively attributed to psychological factors (307.80)*
psychogenic pain (307.80)

307.9 Other and unspecified special symptoms or syndromes, not elsewhere classified
Communication disorder NOS
Hair plucking
Lalling
Lisping
Masturbation
Nail-biting
Thumb-sucking

√4ᵗʰ **308 Acute reaction to stress**
INCLUDES catastrophic stress
combat fatigue
gross stress reaction (acute)
transient disorders in response to exceptional physical or mental stress which usually subside within hours or days
EXCLUDES *adjustment reaction or disorder (309.0-309.9)*
chronic stress reaction (309.1-309.9)

308.0 Predominant disturbance of emotions
Anxiety
Emotional crisis   } as acute reaction to exceptional [gross] stress
Panic state

308.1 Predominant disturbance of consciousness
Fugues as acute reaction to exceptional [gross] stress

308.2 Predominant psychomotor disturbance
Agitation states   } as acute reaction to exceptional
Stupor   [gross] stress

308.3 Other acute reactions to stress
Acute situational disturbance
Acute stress disorder
EXCLUDES *prolonged posttraumatic emotional disturbance (309.81)*

308.4 Mixed disorders as reaction to stress

308.9 Unspecified acute reaction to stress

√4ᵗʰ **309 Adjustment reaction**
INCLUDES adjustment disorders
reaction (adjustment) to chronic stress
EXCLUDES *acute reaction to major stress (308.0-308.9)*
neurotic disorders (300.0-300.9)

309.0 Adjustment disorder with depressed mood
Grief reaction
EXCLUDES *affective psychoses (296.0-296.9)*
neurotic depression (300.4)
prolonged depressive reaction (309.1)
psychogenic depressive psychosis (298.0)
F43.21 Adjustment disorder with depressed mood   I-10

309.1 Prolonged depressive reaction
EXCLUDES *affective psychoses (296.0-296.9)*
brief depressive reaction (309.0)
neurotic depression (300.4)
psychogenic depressive psychosis (298.0)

√5ᵗʰ **309.2 With predominant disturbance of other emotions**

309.21 Separation anxiety disorder
DEF: Abnormal apprehension by a child when physically separated from support environment; byproduct of abnormal symbiotic child-parent relationship.

309.22 Emancipation disorder of adolescence and early adult life
DEF: Adjustment reaction of late adolescence; conflict over independence from parental supervision; symptoms include difficulty in making decisions, increased reliance on parental advice, deliberate adoption of values in opposition of parents.

309.23 Specific academic or work inhibition

309.24 Adjustment disorder with anxiety

309.28 Adjustment disorder with mixed anxiety and depressed mood
Adjustment reaction with anxiety and depression
F43.23 Adjustment d/o w/mixed anxiety & depressed mood   I-10

309.29 Other
Culture shock

309.3 Adjustment disorder with disturbance of conduct
Conduct disturbance
Destructiveness   } as adjustment reaction
EXCLUDES *destructiveness in child (312.9)*
disturbance of conduct NOS (312.9)
dyssocial behavior without manifest psychiatric disorder (V71.01-V71.02)
personality disorder with predominantly sociopathic or asocial manifestations (301.7)

309.4 Adjustment disorder with mixed disturbance of emotions and conduct

√5ᵗʰ **309.8 Other specified adjustment reactions**

309.81 Posttraumatic stress disorder
Chronic posttraumatic stress disorder
Concentration camp syndrome
Posttraumatic stress disorder NOS
Post-traumatic stress disorder (PTSD)
EXCLUDES *acute stress disorder (308.3)*
posttraumatic brain syndrome:
nonpsychotic (310.2)
psychotic (293.0-293.9)
DEF: Preoccupation with traumatic events beyond normal experience; i.e., rape, personal assault, etc;; also recurring flashbacks of trauma; symptoms include difficulty remembering, sleeping, or concentrating, and guilt feelings for surviving.

309.82 Adjustment reaction with physical symptoms

Ⓝ Newborn Age: 0   Ⓟ Pediatric Age: 0-17   Ⓜ Maternity Age: 12-55   Ⓐ Adult Age: 15-124

309.83　Adjustment reaction with withdrawal
　　　　Elective mutism as adjustment reaction
　　　　Hospitalism (in children) NOS

309.89　Other

309.9　Unspecified adjustment reaction
　　　Adaptation reaction NOS
　　　Adjustment reaction NOS

✓4ᵗʰ **310　Specific nonpsychotic mental disorders due to brain damage**
　　EXCLUDES　neuroses, personality disorders, or other nonpsychotic conditions occurring in a form similar to that seen with functional disorders but in association with a physical condition (300.0-300.9, 301.0-301.9)

310.0　Frontal lobe syndrome
　　　Lobotomy syndrome
　　　Postleucotomy syndrome [state]
　　　EXCLUDES　postcontusion syndrome (310.2)

310.1　Personality change due to conditions classified elsewhere
　　　Cognitive or personality change of other type, of nonpsychotic severity
　　　Organic psychosyndrome of nonpsychotic severity
　　　Presbyophrenia NOS
　　　Senility with mental changes of nonpsychotic severity
　　　EXCLUDES ▶ mild cognitive impairment (331.83)
　　　　　postconcussion syndrome (310.2)
　　　　　signs and symptoms involving emotional state (799.21-799.29)◀
　　　DEF: Personality disorder caused by organic factors, such as brain lesions, head trauma, or cerebrovascular accident (CVA).
　　　AHA: 2Q, '05, 6

310.2　Postconcussion syndrome
　　　Postcontusion syndrome or encephalopathy
　　　Posttraumatic brain syndrome, nonpsychotic
　　　Status postcommotio cerebri
　　　Use additional code to identify associated post-traumatic headache, if applicable (339.20-339.22)
　　　EXCLUDES　frontal lobe syndrome (310.0)
　　　　　postencephalitic syndrome (310.8)
　　　　　any organic psychotic conditions following head injury (293.0-294.0)
　　　DEF: Nonpsychotic disorder due to brain trauma, causes symptoms unrelated to any disease process; symptoms include amnesia, serial headaches, rapid heartbeat, fatigue, disrupted sleep patterns, inability to concentrate.
　　　AHA: 4Q, '90, 24
　　　TIP: For treatment within 24 to 48 hours of the concussion, clarify with physician whether the concussion is still in the acute phase; if so, assign instead a code from 850.X subcategory.

310.8　Other specified nonpsychotic mental disorders following organic brain damage
　　　Mild memory disturbance
　　　Postencephalitic syndrome
　　　Other focal (partial) organic psychosyndromes
　　　EXCLUDES ▶ memory loss of unknown cause (780.93)◀

310.9　Unspecified nonpsychotic mental disorder following organic brain damage
　　　AHA: 4Q, '03, 103

311　Depressive disorder, not elsewhere classified
　　　Depressive disorder NOS
　　　Depressive state NOS
　　　Depression NOS
　　　EXCLUDES　acute reaction to major stress with depressive symptoms (308.0)
　　　　　affective personality disorder (301.10-301.13)
　　　　　affective psychoses (296.0-296.9)
　　　　　brief depressive reaction (309.0)
　　　　　depressive states associated with stressful events (309.0-309.1)
　　　　　disturbance of emotions specific to childhood and adolescence, with misery and unhappiness (313.1)
　　　　　mixed adjustment reaction with depressive symptoms (309.4)
　　　　　neurotic depression (300.4)
　　　　　prolonged depressive adjustment reaction (309.1)
　　　　　psychogenic depressive psychosis (298.0)
　　　AHA: 4Q, '03, 75

✓4ᵗʰ **312　Disturbance of conduct, not elsewhere classified**
　　　EXCLUDES　adjustment reaction with disturbance of conduct (309.3)
　　　　　drug dependence (304.0-304.9)
　　　　　dyssocial behavior without manifest psychiatric disorder (V71.01-V71.02)
　　　　　personality disorder with predominantly sociopathic or asocial manifestations (301.7)
　　　　　sexual deviations (302.0-302.9)

　　　The following fifth-digit subclassification is for use with categories 312.0-312.2
　　　　0　unspecified
　　　　1　mild
　　　　2　moderate
　　　　3　severe

§ ✓5ᵗʰ **312.0　Undersocialized conduct disorder, aggressive type**
[0-3]　　　Aggressive outburst
　　　Anger reaction
　　　Unsocialized aggressive disorder
　　　DEF: Mental condition identified by behaviors disrespectful of others' rights and of age-appropriate social norms or rules; symptoms include bullying, vandalism, verbal and physical abusiveness, lying, stealing, defiance.

§ ✓5ᵗʰ **312.1　Undersocialized conduct disorder, unaggressive type**
[0-3]　　　Childhood truancy, unsocialized
　　　Solitary stealing
　　　Tantrums

§ ✓5ᵗʰ **312.2　Socialized conduct disorder**
[0-3]　　　Childhood truancy, socialized
　　　Group delinquency
　　　EXCLUDES　gang activity without manifest psychiatric disorder (V71.01)

✓5ᵗʰ **312.3　Disorders of impulse control, not elsewhere classified**
　　312.30　Impulse control disorder, unspecified
　　312.31　Pathological gambling
　　312.32　Kleptomania
　　312.33　Pyromania
　　312.34　Intermittent explosive disorder
　　312.35　Isolated explosive disorder
　　312.39　Other
　　　　Trichotillomania

312.4　Mixed disturbance of conduct and emotions
　　　Neurotic delinquency
　　　EXCLUDES　compulsive conduct disorder (312.3)

✓5ᵗʰ **312.8　Other specified disturbances of conduct, not elsewhere classified**
　　312.81　Conduct disorder, childhood onset type
　　312.82　Conduct disorder, adolescent onset type
　　312.89　Other conduct disorder
　　　　Conduct disorder of unspecified onset

§　Requires fifth digit. Valid digits are in [brackets] under each code. See category 312 for codes and definitions.

✓4ᵗʰ ✓5ᵗʰ　Additional Digit Required　　Unspecified Code　　Other Specified Code　　Manifestation Code　　▶◀ Revised Text　　● New Code　　▲ Revised Code Title
2010 ICD-9-CM　　　　　　　　　　　　　　　　　　　　　　　**October 2009 • Volume 1 – 85**

312.9 **Unspecified disturbance of conduct**
Delinquency (juvenile)
Disruptive behavior disorder NOS

✓4ᵗʰ **313** **Disturbance of emotions specific to childhood and adolescence**
EXCLUDES *adjustment reaction (309.0-309.9)*
emotional disorder of neurotic type (300.0-300.9)
masturbation, nail-biting, thumbsucking, and other isolated symptoms (307.0-307.9)

313.0 **Overanxious disorder**
Anxiety and fearfulness } of childhood and
Overanxious disorder } adolescence
EXCLUDES *abnormal separation anxiety (309.21)*
anxiety states (300.00-300.09)
hospitalism in children (309.83)
phobic state (300.20-300.29)

313.1 **Misery and unhappiness disorder**
EXCLUDES *depressive neurosis (300.4)*

✓5ᵗʰ **313.2** **Sensitivity, shyness, and social withdrawal disorder**
EXCLUDES *infantile autism (299.0)*
schizoid personality (301.20-301.22)
schizophrenia (295.0-295.9)

313.21 **Shyness disorder of childhood**
Sensitivity reaction of childhood or adolescence

313.22 **Introverted disorder of childhood**
Social withdrawal } of childhood and
Withdrawal reaction } adolescence

313.23 **Selective mutism**
EXCLUDES *elective mutism as adjustment reaction (309.83)*

313.3 **Relationship problems**
Sibling jealousy
EXCLUDES *relationship problems associated with aggression, destruction, or other forms of conduct disturbance (312.0-312.9)*

✓5ᵗʰ **313.8** **Other or mixed emotional disturbances of childhood or adolescence**

313.81 **Oppositional defiant disorder**
DEF: Mental disorder of children noted for pervasive opposition, defiance of authority.

313.82 **Identity disorder**
Identity problem
DEF: Distress of adolescents caused by inability to form acceptable self-identity; uncertainty about career choice, sexual orientation, moral values.

313.83 **Academic underachievement disorder**

313.89 **Other** P
Reactive attachment disorder of infancy or early childhood

313.9 **Unspecified emotional disturbance of childhood or adolescence** P
Mental disorder of infancy, childhood or adolescence NOS

✓4ᵗʰ **314** **Hyperkinetic syndrome of childhood**
EXCLUDES *hyperkinesis as symptom of underlying disorder–code the underlying disorder*
DEF: A behavioral disorder usually diagnosed at an early age; characterized by the inability to focus attention for a normal period of time.

✓5ᵗʰ **314.0** **Attention deficit disorder**
Adult
Child
TIP: These codes may be assigned for patients of any age.

314.00 **Without mention of hyperactivity**
Predominantly inattentive type
AHA: 1Q, '97, 8

314.01 **With hyperactivity**
Combined type
Overactivity NOS
Predominantly hyperactive/impulsive type
Simple disturbance of attention with overactivity
AHA: 1Q, '97, 8
F90.1 ADHD predominantly hyperactive type I-10

314.1 **Hyperkinesis with developmental delay**
Developmental disorder of hyperkinesis
Use additional code to identify any associated neurological disorder

314.2 **Hyperkinetic conduct disorder**
Hyperkinetic conduct disorder without developmental delay
EXCLUDES *hyperkinesis with significant delays in specific skills (314.1)*

314.8 **Other specified manifestations of hyperkinetic syndrome**

314.9 **Unspecified hyperkinetic syndrome**
Hyperkinetic reaction of childhood or adolescence NOS
Hyperkinetic syndrome NOS

✓4ᵗʰ **315** **Specific delays in development**
EXCLUDES *that due to a neurological disorder (320.0-389.9)*

✓5ᵗʰ **315.0** **Specific reading disorder**

315.00 **Reading disorder, unspecified**

315.01 **Alexia**
DEF: Lack of ability to understand written language; manifestation of aphasia.

315.02 **Developmental dyslexia**
DEF: Serious impairment of reading skills unexplained in relation to general intelligence and teaching processes.

315.09 **Other**
Specific spelling difficulty

315.1 **Mathematics disorder**
Dyscalculia

315.2 **Other specific learning difficulties**
Disorder of written expression
EXCLUDES *specific arithmetical disorder (315.1)*
specific reading disorder (315.00-315.09)

✓5ᵗʰ **315.3** **Developmental speech or language disorder**

315.31 **Expressive language disorder**
Developmental aphasia
Word deafness
EXCLUDES *acquired aphasia (784.3)*
elective mutism (309.83, 313.0, 313.23)

315.32 **Mixed receptive-expressive language disorder**
Central auditory processing disorder
EXCLUDES *acquired auditory processing disorder (388.45)*

315.34 **Speech and language developmental delay due to hearing loss**
AHA: 4Q, '07, 80, 81

315.39 **Other**
Developmental articulation disorder
Dyslalia
Phonological disorder
EXCLUDES *lisping and lalling (307.9)*
stammering and stuttering (307.0)
AHA: 3Q, '07, 7

315.4 **Developmental coordination disorder**
Clumsiness syndrome
Dyspraxia syndrome
Specific motor development disorder

N Newborn Age: 0   P Pediatric Age: 0-17   M Maternity Age: 12-55   A Adult Age: 15-124

315.5 Mixed development disorder
AHA: 2Q, '02, 11

315.8 Other specified delays in development
F88 Other disorders of psychological development   I-10

315.9 Unspecified delay in development
Developmental disorder NOS
Learning disorder NOS

316 Psychic factors associated with diseases classified elsewhere
Psychologic factors in physical conditions classified elsewhere
Use additional code to identify the associated physical condition, as:
psychogenic:
asthma (493.9)
dermatitis (692.9)
duodenal ulcer (532.0-532.9)
eczema (691.8, 692.9)
gastric ulcer (531.0-531.9)
mucous colitis (564.9)
paroxysmal tachycardia (427.2)
ulcerative colitis (556)
urticaria (708.0-708.9)
psychosocial dwarfism (259.4)

EXCLUDES *physical symptoms and physiological malfunctions, not involving tissue damage, of mental origin (306.0-306.9)*

MENTAL RETARDATION (317-319)
Use additional code(s) to identify any associated psychiatric or physical condition(s)

317 Mild mental retardation
High-grade defect
IQ 50-70
Mild mental subnormality
F70 Mild mental retardation   I-10

√4ᵗʰ **318 Other specified mental retardation**

318.0 Moderate mental retardation
IQ 35-49
Moderate mental subnormality

318.1 Severe mental retardation
IQ 20-34
Severe mental subnormality

318.2 Profound mental retardation
IQ under 20
Profound mental subnormality

319 Unspecified mental retardation
Mental deficiency NOS
Mental subnormality NOS
F79 Unspecified mental reatardation   I-10

6. DISEASES OF THE NERVOUS SYSTEM AND SENSE ORGANS (320-389)

INFLAMMATORY DISEASES OF THE CENTRAL NERVOUS SYSTEM (320-326)

✓4ᵗʰ **320 Bacterial meningitis**

INCLUDES   arachnoiditis
leptomeningitis
meningitis } bacterial
meningoencephalitis
meningomyelitis
pachymeningitis

DEF: Bacterial infection causing inflammation of the lining of the brain and/or spinal cord.
AHA: J-F, '87, 6

320.0 Hemophilus meningitis
Meningitis due to Hemophilus influenzae [H. influenzae]

320.1 Pneumococcal meningitis

320.2 Streptococcal meningitis

320.3 Staphylococcal meningitis

320.7   *Meningitis in other bacterial diseases classified elsewhere*

Code first underlying disease, as:
actinomycosis (039.8)
listeriosis (027.0)
typhoid fever (002.0)
whooping cough (033.0-033.9)

EXCLUDES   meningitis (in):
epidemic (036.0)
gonococcal (098.82)
meningococcal (036.0)
salmonellosis (003.21)
syphilis:
NOS (094.2)
congenital (090.42)
meningovascular (094.2)
secondary (091.81)
tuberculous (013.0)

✓5ᵗʰ **320.8 Meningitis due to other specified bacteria**

320.81 Anaerobic meningitis
Bacteroides (fragilis)
Gram-negative anaerobes

320.82 Meningitis due to gram-negative bacteria, not elsewhere classified
Aerobacter aerogenes   Klebsiella
pneumoniae   Proteus morganii
Escherichia coli [E. coli]   Pseudomonas
Friedländer bacillus

EXCLUDES   gram-negative anaerobes (320.81)

320.89 Meningitis due to other specified bacteria
Bacillus pyocyaneus

320.9 Meningitis due to unspecified bacterium
Meningitis: Meningitis:
bacterial NOS   pyogenic NOS
purulent NOS   suppurative NOS

✓4ᵗʰ **321 Meningitis due to other organisms**

INCLUDES   arachnoiditis
leptomeningitis } due to organisms other
meningitis   than bacterial
pachymeningitis

DEF: Infection causing inflammation of the lining of the brain and/or spinal cord, due to organisms other than bacteria.
AHA: J-F, '87, 6

321.0   *Cryptococcal meningitis*
Code first underlying disease (117.5)

321.1   *Meningitis in other fungal diseases*
Code first underlying disease (110.0-118)

EXCLUDES   meningitis in:
candidiasis (112.83)
coccidioidomycosis (114.2)
histoplasmosis (115.01, 115.11, 115.91)

321.2   *Meningitis due to viruses not elsewhere classified*
Code first underlying disease, as:
meningitis due to arbovirus (060.0-066.9)

EXCLUDES   meningitis (due to):
abacterial (047.0-047.9)
adenovirus (049.1)
aseptic NOS (047.9)
Coxsackie (virus)(047.0)
ECHO virus (047.1)
enterovirus (047.0-047.9)
herpes simplex virus (054.72)
herpes zoster virus (053.0)
lymphocytic choriomeningitis virus (049.0)
mumps (072.1)
viral NOS (047.9)
meningo-eruptive syndrome (047.1)

AHA: 4Q, '04, 51

321.3   *Meningitis due to trypanosomiasis*
Code first underlying disease (086.0-086.9)

321.4   *Meningitis in sarcoidosis*
Code first underlying disease (135)

321.8   *Meningitis due to other nonbacterial organisms classified elsewhere*
Code first underlying disease
EXCLUDES   leptospiral meningitis (100.81)

✓4ᵗʰ **322 Meningitis of unspecified cause**

INCLUDES   arachnoiditis
leptomeningitis } with no organism specified
meningitis   as cause
pachymeningitis

DEF: Infection causing inflammation of the lining of the brain and/or spinal cord, due to unspecified cause.
AHA: J-F, '87, 6

322.0 Nonpyogenic meningitis
Meningitis with clear cerebrospinal fluid

322.1 Eosinophilic meningitis

322.2 Chronic meningitis

322.9 Meningitis, unspecified

✓4ᵗʰ **323 Encephalitis, myelitis, and encephalomyelitis**

INCLUDES   acute disseminated encephalomyelitis
meningoencephalitis, except bacterial
meningomyelitis, except bacterial
myelitis:
ascending
transverse

EXCLUDES   acute transverse myelitis NOS (341.20)
acute transverse myelitis in conditions classified elsewhere (341.21)
bacterial:
meningoencephalitis (320.0-320.9)
meningomyelitis (320.0-320.9)
idiopathic transverse myelitis (341.22)

DEF: Encephalitis: inflammation of brain tissues.
DEF: Myelitis: inflammation of the spinal cord.
DEF: Encephalomyelitis: inflammation of brain and spinal cord.

✓5ᵗʰ **323.0 Encephalitis, myelitis, and encephalomyelitis in viral diseases classified elsewhere**
Code first underlying disease, as:
cat-scratch disease (078.3)
infectious mononucleosis (075)
ornithosis (073.7)

✓4ᵗʰ Additional Digit Required   Unspecified Code   Other Specified Code   Manifestation Code   ▶◀ Revised Text   ● New Code   ▲ Revised Code Title
✓5ᵗʰ
2010 ICD-9-CM   **Volume 1 – 89**

Nervous System and Sense Organs

323.01–324.9

323.01   *Encephalitis and encephalomyelitis in viral diseases classified elsewhere*

EXCLUDES   encephalitis (in):
arthropod-borne viral (062.0-064)
herpes simplex (054.3)
mumps (072.2)
other viral diseases of central nervous system (049.8-049.9)
poliomyelitis (045.0-045.9)
rubella (056.01)
slow virus infections of central nervous system (046.0-046.9)
viral NOS (049.9)
West Nile (066.41)

AHA: 4Q, '06, 58-63

323.02   *Myelitis in viral diseases classified elsewhere*

EXCLUDES   myelitis (in):
herpes simplex (054.74)
herpes zoster (053.14)
poliomyelitis (045.0-045.9)
rubella (056.01)
other viral diseases of central nervous system (049.8-049.9)

AHA: 4Q, '06, 58-63

323.1   *Encephalitis, myelitis, and encephalomyelitis in rickettsial diseases classified elsewhere*

Code first underlying disease (080-083.9)
DEF: Inflammation of the brain caused by rickettsial disease carried by louse, tick, or mite.

323.2   *Encephalitis, myelitis, and encephalomyelitis in protozoal diseases classified elsewhere*

Code first underlying disease, as:
malaria (084.0-084.9)
trypanosomiasis (086.0-086.9)
DEF: Inflammation of the brain caused by protozoal disease carried by mosquitoes and flies.

√5th 323.4   Other encephalitis, myelitis, and encephalomyelitis due to infection classified elsewhere

Code first underlying disease

323.41   *Other encephalitis and encephalomyelitis due to infection classified elsewhere*

EXCLUDES   encephalitis (in):
meningococcal (036.1)
syphilis:
NOS (094.81)
congenital (090.41)
toxoplasmosis (130.0)
tuberculosis (013.6)
meningoencephalitis due to free-living ameba [Naegleria] (136.29)

AHA: 4Q, '06, 58-63

323.42   *Other myelitis due to infection classified elsewhere*

EXCLUDES   myelitis (in):
syphilis (094.89)
tuberculosis (013.6)

AHA: 4Q, '06, 58-63

√5th 323.5   Encephalitis, myelitis, and encephalomyelitis following immunization procedures

Use additional E code to identify vaccine

323.51   Encephalitis and encephalomyelitis following immunization procedures

Encephalitis postimmunization or postvaccinal
Encephalomyelitis postimmunization or postvaccinal
AHA: 4Q, '06, 58-63

323.52   Myelitis following immunization procedures

Myelitis postimmunization or postvaccinal
AHA: 4Q, '06, 58-63

√5th 323.6   Postinfectious encephalitis, myelitis, and encephalomyelitis

Code first underlying disease
DEF: Infection, inflammation of brain several weeks following the outbreak of a systemic infection.

323.61   *Infectious acute disseminated encephalomyelitis [ADEM]*

Acute necrotizing hemorrhagic encephalopathy

EXCLUDES   noninfectious acute disseminated encephalo- myelitis (ADEM) (323.81)

AHA: 4Q, '06, 58-63

323.62   *Other postinfectious encephalitis and encephalomyelitis*

EXCLUDES   encephalitis:
postchickenpox (052.0)
postmeasles (055.0)

AHA: 4Q, '06, 58-63

323.63   *Postinfectious myelitis*

EXCLUDES   postchickenpox myelitis (052.2)
herpes simplex myelitis (054.74)
herpes zoster myelitis (053.14)

AHA: 4Q, '06, 58-63

√5th 323.7   Toxic encephalitis, myelitis, and encephalomyelitis

Code first underlying cause, as:
carbon tetrachloride (982.1)
hydroxyquinoline derivatives (961.3)
lead (984.0-984.9)
mercury (985.0)
thallium (985.8)

AHA: 2Q, '97, 8

323.71   *Toxic encephalitis and encephalomyelitis*

AHA: 4Q, '06, 58-63

323.72   *Toxic myelitis*

AHA: 4Q, '06, 58-63

√5th 323.8   Other causes of encephalitis, myelitis, and encephalomyelitis

323.81   Other causes of encephalitis and encephalomyelitis

Noninfectious acute disseminated encephalomyelitis (ADEM)
AHA: 4Q, '06, 58-63

323.82   Other causes of myelitis

Transverse myelitis NOS
AHA: 4Q, '06, 58-63

323.9   Unspecified cause of encephalitis, myelitis, and encephalomyelitis

√4th 324   Intracranial and intraspinal abscess

324.0   Intracranial abscess

Abscess (embolic):
cerebellar
cerebral
Abscess (embolic) of brain [any part]:
epidural
extradural
otogenic
subdural

EXCLUDES   tuberculous (013.3)

324.1   Intraspinal abscess

Abscess (embolic) of spinal cord [any part]:
epidural
extradural
subdural

EXCLUDES   tuberculous (013.5)

324.9   Of unspecified site

Extradural or subdural abscess NOS

N Newborn Age: 0   P Pediatric Age: 0-17   M Maternity Age: 12-55   A Adult Age: 15-124

325 Phlebitis and thrombophlebitis of intracranial venous sinuses

Embolism
Endophlebitis
Phlebitis, septic or suppurative   } of cavernous, lateral or other intracranial or unspecified intracranial venous sinus
Thrombophlebitis
Thrombosis

EXCLUDES *that specified as:*
   complicating pregnancy, childbirth, or the puerperium (671.5)
   of nonpyogenic origin (437.6)

DEF: Inflammation and formation of blood clot in a vein within the brain or its lining.

326 Late effects of intracranial abscess or pyogenic infection

Note: This category is to be used to indicate conditions whose primary classification is to 320-325 [excluding 320.7, 321.0-321.8, 323.01-323.42, 323.6-323.7] as the cause of late effects, themselves classifiable elsewhere. The "late effects" include conditions specified as such, or as sequelae, which may occur at any time after the resolution of the causal condition.

Use additional code to identify condition, as:
   hydrocephalus (331.4)
   paralysis (342.0-342.9, 344.0-344.9)

ORGANIC SLEEP DISORDERS (327)

TIP: If the sleep disorder is not documented with the etiology related to an organic disease process, see instead subcategory 307.4.

√4ᵗʰ 327 Organic sleep disorders
AHA: 4Q, '05, 59-64

√5ᵗʰ 327.0 Organic disorders of initiating and maintaining sleep [Organic insomnia]
   EXCLUDES *insomnia NOS (780.52)*
   insomnia not due to a substance or known physiological condition (307.41-307.42)
   insomnia with sleep apnea NOS (780.51)

327.00 Organic insomnia, unspecified

327.01 Insomnia due to medical condition classified elsewhere
   Code first underlying condition
   EXCLUDES *insomnia due to mental disorder (327.02)*

327.02 Insomnia due to mental disorder
   Code first mental disorder
   EXCLUDES *alcohol induced insomnia (291.82)*
   drug induced insomnia (292.85)

327.09 Other organic insomnia

√5ᵗʰ 327.1 Organic disorder of excessive somnolence [Organic hypersomnia]
   EXCLUDES *hypersomnia NOS (780.54)*
   hypersomnia not due to a substance or known physiological condition (307.43-307.44)
   hypersomnia with sleep apnea NOS (780.53)

327.10 Organic hypersomnia, unspecified

327.11 Idiopathic hypersomnia with long sleep time

327.12 Idiopathic hypersomnia without long sleep time

327.13 Recurrent hypersomnia
   Kleine-Levin syndrome
   Menstrual related hypersomnia

327.14 Hypersomnia due to medical condition classified elsewhere
   Code first underlying condition
   EXCLUDES *hypersomnia due to mental disorder (327.15)*

327.15 Hypersomnia due to mental disorder
   Code first mental disorder
   EXCLUDES *alcohol induced hypersomnia (291.82)*
   drug induced hypersomnia (292.85)

327.19 Other organic hypersomnia

√5ᵗʰ 327.2 Organic sleep apnea
   EXCLUDES *Cheyne-Stokes breathing (786.04)*
   hypersomnia with sleep apnea NOS (780.53)
   insomnia with sleep apnea NOS (780.51)
   sleep apnea in newborn (770.81-770.82)
   sleep apnea NOS (780.57)

327.20 Organic sleep apnea, unspecified

327.21 Primary central sleep apnea

327.22 High altitude periodic breathing

327.23 Obstructive sleep apnea (adult) (pediatric)
   G47.33 Obstructive sleep apnea (adult) (pediatric)   **I-10**

327.24 Idiopathic sleep related nonobstructive alveolar hypoventilation
   Sleep related hypoxia

327.25 Congenital central alveolar hypoventilation syndrome

327.26 Sleep related hypoventilation/ hypoxemia in conditions classifiable elsewhere
   Code first underlying condition

327.27 Central sleep apnea in conditions classified elsewhere
   Code first underlying condition

327.29 Other organic sleep apnea

√5ᵗʰ 327.3 Circadian rhythm sleep disorder
   Organic disorder of sleep wake cycle
   Organic disorder of sleep wake schedule
   EXCLUDES *alcohol induced circadian rhythm sleep disorder (291.82)*
   circadian rhythm sleep disorder of nonorganic origin (307.45)
   disruption of 24 hour sleep wake cycle NOS (780.55)
   drug induced circadian rhythm sleep disorder (292.85)

327.30 Circadian rhythm sleep disorder, unspecified

327.31 Circadian rhythm sleep disorder, delayed sleep phase type

327.32 Circadian rhythm sleep disorder, advanced sleep phase type

327.33 Circadian rhythm sleep disorder, irregular sleep-wake type

327.34 Circadian rhythm sleep disorder, free-running type

327.35 Circadian rhythm sleep disorder, jet lag type

327.36 Circadian rhythm sleep disorder, shift work type

327.37 Circadian rhythm sleep disorder in conditions classified elsewhere
   Code first underlying condition

327.39 Other circadian rhythm sleep disorder

√5ᵗʰ 327.4 Organic parasomnia
   EXCLUDES *alcohol induced parasomnia (291.82)*
   drug induced parasomnia (292.85)
   parasomnia not due to a known physiological condition (307.47)

327.40 Organic parasomnia, unspecified

327.41 Confusional arousals

327.42 REM sleep behavior disorder

Nervous System and Sense Organs

327.43–331.5

327.43   Recurrent isolated sleep paralysis

327.44   *Parasomnia in conditions classified elsewhere*

     Code first underlying condition

327.49   Other organic parasomnia

√5ᵗʰ 327.5   Organic sleep related movement disorders

     EXCLUDES   *restless legs syndrome (333.94)*
                    sleep related movement disorder NOS (780.58)

327.51   Periodic limb movement disorder

     Periodic limb movement sleep disorder

327.52   Sleep related leg cramps

327.53   Sleep related bruxism

327.59   Other organic sleep related movement disorders

327.8   Other organic sleep disorders

     AHA: 2Q, '07, 6

HEREDITARY AND DEGENERATIVE DISEASES OF THE CENTRAL NERVOUS SYSTEM (330-337)

     EXCLUDES   *hepatolenticular degeneration (275.1)*
                    multiple sclerosis (340)
                    other demyelinating diseases of central nervous system (341.0-341.9)

√4ᵗʰ 330   Cerebral degenerations usually manifest in childhood

     Use additional code to identify associated mental retardation

330.0   Leukodystrophy

     Krabbe's disease   Pelizaeus-Merzbacher disease
     Leukodystrophy: Sulfatide lipidosis
         NOS
         globoid cell
         metachromatic
         sudanophilic

     DEF: Hereditary disease of arylsulfatase or cerebroside sulfatase; characterized by a diffuse loss of myelin in CNS; infantile form causes blindness, motor disturbances, rigidity, mental deterioration and, occasionally, convulsions.

330.1   Cerebral lipidoses

     Amaurotic (familial) idiocy
     Disease-
         Batten
         Jansky-Bielschowsky
         Kufs'
         Spielmeyer-Vogt
         Tay-Sachs
     Gangliosidosis

     DEF: Genetic disorder causing abnormal lipid accumulation in the reticuloendothelial cells of the brain.

330.2   *Cerebral degeneration in generalized lipidoses*

     Code first underlying disease, as:
         Fabry's disease (272.7)
         Gaucher's disease (272.7)
         Niemann-Pick disease (272.7)
         sphingolipidosis (272.7)

330.3   *Cerebral degeneration of childhood in other diseases classified elsewhere*

     Code first underlying disease, as:
         Hunter's disease (277.5)
         mucopolysaccharidosis (277.5)

330.8   Other specified cerebral degenerations in childhood

     Alpers' disease or gray-matter degeneration
     Infantile necrotizing encephalomyelopathy
     Leigh's disease
     Subacute necrotizing encephalopathy or encephalomyelopathy

     AHA: N-D, '85, 5

330.9   Unspecified cerebral degeneration in childhood

√4ᵗʰ 331   Other cerebral degenerations

     Use additional code, where applicable, to identify dementia:
         with behavioral disturbance (294.11)
         without behavioral disturbance (294.10)

331.0   Alzheimer's disease

     DEF: Diffuse atrophy of cerebral cortex; causing a progressive decline in intellectual and physical functions, including memory loss, personality changes and profound dementia.

     AHA: 4Q, '00, 41; 4Q, '99, 7; N-D, '84, 20

     G30.9 Alzheimer's disease unspecified   **I-10**

√5ᵗʰ 331.1   Frontotemporal dementia

     DEF: Rare, progressive degenerative brain disease, similar to Alzheimer's; cortical atrophy affects the frontal and temporal lobes.

     AHA: 4Q, '03, 57

331.11   Pick's disease

     DEF: A progressive frontotemporal dementia with asymmetrical atrophy of the frontal and temporal regions of the cerebral cortex, abnormal rounded brain cells called Pick cells with the presence of abnormal staining of protein (called tau); symptoms include prominent apathy, behavioral changes such as disinhibition and restlessness, echolalia, impairment of language, memory, and intellect, increased carelessness, poor personal hygiene, and decreased attention span.

331.19   Other frontotemporal dementia
     Frontal dementia

331.2   Senile degeneration of brain

     EXCLUDES   *senility NOS (797)*

331.3   Communicating hydrocephalus

     Secondary normal pressure hydrocephalus

     EXCLUDES   *congenital hydrocephalus (742.3)*
                    idiopathic normal pressure hydrocephalus (331.5)
                    normal pressure hydrocephalus (331.5)
                    spina bifida with hydrocephalus (741.0)

     DEF: Subarachnoid hemorrhage and meningitis causing excess buildup of cerebrospinal fluid in cavities due to nonabsorption of fluid back through fluid pathways.

     AHA: S-O, '85, 12

331.4   Obstructive hydrocephalus

     Acquired hydrocephalus NOS

     EXCLUDES   *congenital hydrocephalus (742.3)*
                    idiopathic normal pressure hydrocephalus (331.5)
                    normal pressure hydrocephalus (331.5)
                    spina bifida with hydrocephalus (741.0)

     DEF: Obstruction of cerebrospinal fluid passage from brain into spinal canal.

     AHA: 4Q, '03, 106; 1Q, '99, 9

     G91.1 Obstructive hydrocephalus   **I-10**

331.5   Idiopathic normal pressure hydrocephalus [INPH]

     Normal pressure hydrocephalus NOS

     EXCLUDES   *congenital hydrocephalus (742.3)*
                    secondary normal pressure hydrocephalus (331.3)
                    spina bifida with hydrocephalus (741.0)

     DEF: Abnormal increase of cerebrospinal fluid in the brain's ventricles; results in dementia, progressive mental impairment, gait disturbance, and impaired bladder control.

     AHA: 4Q, '07, 74

331.7 **Cerebral degeneration in diseases classified elsewhere**

Code first underlying disease, as:
    alcoholism (303.0-303.9)
    beriberi (265.0)
    cerebrovascular disease (430-438)
    congenital hydrocephalus (741.0, 742.3)
    myxedema (244.0-244.9)
    neoplastic disease (140.0-239.9)
    vitamin B12 deficiency (266.2)

EXCLUDES *cerebral degeneration in:*
        Jakob-Creutzfeldt disease
        ▶*(046.11-046.19)*◄
        progressive multifocal
            leukoencephalopathy (046.3)
        subacute spongiform encephalopathy
            (046.1)

✓5ᵗʰ **331.8 Other cerebral degeneration**

331.81 Reye's syndrome ℙ

DEF: Rare childhood illness, often developed after a viral upper respiratory infection; characterized by vomiting, elevated serum transaminase, changes in liver and other viscera; brain swelling, disturbances of consciousness and seizures; can be fatal.

331.82 Dementia with Lewy bodies
    Dementia with Parkinsonism
    Lewy body dementia
    Lewy body disease

DEF: A cerebral dementia with neurophysiologic changes, increased hippocampal volume, hypoperfusion in the occipital lobes, and beta amyloid deposits with neurofibrillarity tangles, atrophy of cortex and brainstem, hallmark neuropsychologic characteristics are fluctuating cognition with pronounced variation in attention and alertness; recurrent hallucinations; and parkinsonism.

AHA: 4Q, '03, 57

G31.83 Dementia with Lewy bodies I-10

331.83 Mild cognitive impairment, so stated

EXCLUDES *altered mental status (780.97)*
        cerebral degeneration (331.0-331.9)
        change in mental status (780.97)
        cognitive deficits following (late
            effects of) cerebral hemorr-
            hage or infarction (438.0)
        cognitive impairment due to
            intracranial or head injury
            (850-854, 959.01)
        cognitive impairment due to late
            effect of intracranial injury
            (907.0)
        ▶*cognitive impairment due to skull*
            fracture (800-801, 803-804)◄
        dementia (290.0-290.43, 294.8)
        mild memory disturbance (310.8)
        neurologic neglect syndrome (781.8)
        personality change, nonpsychotic
            (310.1)

AHA: 4Q, '06, 75

331.89 Other
    Cerebral ataxia

331.9 Cerebral degeneration, unspecified

✓4ᵗʰ **332 Parkinson's disease**

EXCLUDES *dementia with Parkinsonism (331.82)*

332.0 Paralysis agitans
    Parkinsonism or Parkinson's disease:
        NOS
        idiopathic
        primary

DEF: Form of parkinsonism; progressive, occurs in senior years; characterized by masklike facial expression; condition affects ability to stand erect, walk smoothly; weakened muscles, also tremble and involuntarily movement.

AHA: M-A, '87, 7

G20 Parkinson's disease I-10

332.1 Secondary Parkinsonism
    Neuroleptic-induced Parkinsonism
    Parkinsonism due to drugs

    Use additional E code to identify drug, if drug-induced

EXCLUDES *Parkinsonism (in):*
        Huntington's disease (333.4)
        progressive supranuclear palsy (333.0)
        Shy-Drager syndrome (333.0)
        syphilitic (094.82)

✓4ᵗʰ **333 Other extrapyramidal disease and abnormal movement disorders**

INCLUDES other forms of extrapyramidal, basal ganglia, or striatopallidal disease

EXCLUDES *abnormal movements of head NOS (781.0)*
        sleep related movement disorders (327.51-327.59)

333.0 Other degenerative diseases of the basal ganglia
    Atrophy or degeneration:
        olivopontocerebellar [Déjérine-Thomas syndrome]
        pigmentary pallidal [Hallervorden-Spatz disease]
        striatonigral
    Parkinsonian syndrome associated with:
        idiopathic orthostatic hypotension
        symptomatic orthostatic hypotension
    Progressive supranuclear ophthalmoplegia
    Shy-Drager syndrome

AHA: 3Q, '96, 8

333.1 Essential and other specified forms of tremor
    Benign essential tremor
    Familial tremor
    Medication-induced postural tremor

    Use additional E code to identify drug, if drug-induced

EXCLUDES *tremor NOS (781.0)*

333.2 Myoclonus
    Familial essential myoclonus
    ▶Palatal myoclonus◄

EXCLUDES ▶ *progressive myoclonic epilepsy (345.1)*
        Unverricht-Lundborg disease (345.1)◄

    Use additional E code to identify drug, if drug-induced

DEF: Spontaneous movements or contractions of muscles.

AHA: 3Q, '97, 4; M-A, '87, 12

333.3 Tics of organic origin

    Use additional E code to identify drug, if drug-induced

EXCLUDES *Gilles de la Tourette's syndrome (307.23)*
        habit spasm (307.22)
        tic NOS (307.20)

333.4 Huntington's chorea

DEF: Genetic disease characterized by chronic progressive men tal deterioration; dementia and death within 15 years of onset.

333.5 Other choreas
    Hemiballism(us)
    Paroxysmal choreo-athetosis

    Use additional E code to identify drug, if drug-induced

EXCLUDES *Sydenham's or rheumatic chorea (392.0-392.9)*

333.6 Genetic torsion dystonia
    Dystonia:
        deformans progressiva
        musculorum deformans
    (Schwalbe-) Ziehen-Oppenheim disease

DEF: Sustained muscular contractions, causing twisting and repetitive movements that result in abnormal postures of trunk and limbs; etiology unknown.

✓5ᵗʰ **333.7 Acquired torsion dystonia**

333.71 Athetoid cerebral palsy
    Double athetosis (syndrome)
    Vogt's disease

EXCLUDES *infantile cerebral palsy (343.0-343.9)*

AHA: 4Q, '06, 76-78

✓4ᵗʰ
✓5ᵗʰ Additional Digit Required   Unspecified Code   Other Specified Code   Manifestation Code   ▶◄ Revised Text   ● New Code   ▲ Revised Code Title

2010 ICD-9-CM   **October 2009 • Volume 1 – 93**

Nervous System and Sense Organs

331.7–333.71

Nervous System and Sense Organs

333.72–335.20

333.72 **Acute dystonia due to drugs**
Acute dystonic reaction due to drugs
Neuroleptic induced acute dystonia
Use additional E code to identify drug

> **EXCLUDES** blepharospasm due to drugs (333.85)
> orofacial dyskinesia due to drugs (333.85)
> secondary Parkinsonism (332.1)
> subacute dyskinesia due to drugs (333.85)
> tardive dyskinesia (333.85)

AHA: 4Q, '06, 76-78

333.79 **Other acquired torsion dystonia**
AHA: 4Q, '06, 76-78

√5th **333.8** **Fragments of torsion dystonia**
Use additional E code to identify drug, if drug-induced

333.81 **Blepharospasm**

> **EXCLUDES** blepharospasm due to drugs (333.85)

DEF: Uncontrolled winking or blinking due to orbicularis oculi muscle spasm.

333.82 **Orofacial dyskinesia**

> **EXCLUDES** orofacial dyskinesia due to drugs (333.85)

DEF: Uncontrolled movement of mouth or facial muscles.

333.83 **Spasmodic torticollis**

> **EXCLUDES** torticollis:
> NOS (723.5)
> hysterical (300.11)
> psychogenic (306.0)

DEF: Uncontrolled movement of head due to spasms of neck muscle.

333.84 **Organic writers' cramp**

> **EXCLUDES** pychogenic (300.89)

333.85 **Subacute dyskinesia due to drugs**
Blepharospasm due to drugs
Orofacial dyskinesia due to drugs
Tardive dyskinesia
Use additional E code to identify drug

> **EXCLUDES** acute dystonia due to drugs (333.72)
> acute dystonic reaction due to drugs (333.72)
> secondary Parkinsonism (332.1)

AHA: 4Q, '06, 76-78

333.89 **Other**

√5th **333.9** **Other and unspecified extrapyramidal diseases and abnormal movement disorders**

333.90 **Unspecified extrapyramidal disease and abnormal movement disorder**
Medication-induced movement disorders NOS
Use additional E code to identify drug, if drug-induced

333.91 **Stiff-man syndrome**

333.92 **Neuroleptic malignant syndrome**
Use additional E code to identify drug

> **EXCLUDES** neuroleptic induced Parkinsonism (332.1)

AHA: 4Q, '94, 37

333.93 **Benign shuddering attacks**
AHA: 4Q, '94, 37

333.94 **Restless legs syndrome [RLS]**
DEF: Neurological disorder of unknown etiology with an irresistible urge to move the legs, which may temporarily relieve the symptoms, is accompanied by motor restlessness and sensations of pain, burning, prickling, or tingling.
AHA: 4Q, '06, 79
TIP: Assign an additional code if the underlying cause of the RLS is specified (e.g., iron deficiency anemia).
G25.81 Restless legs syndrome ⓘ-10

333.99 **Other**
Neuroleptic-induced acute akathisia
Use additional E code to identify drug, if drug-induced
AHA: 4Q, '04, 95; 2Q, '04, 12; 4Q, '94, 37

√4th **334** **Spinocerebellar disease**

> **EXCLUDES** olivopontocerebellar degeneration (333.0)
> peroneal muscular atrophy (356.1)

334.0 **Friedreich's ataxia**
DEF: Genetic recessive disease of children; sclerosis of dorsal, lateral spinal cord columns; characterized by ataxia, speech impairment, swaying and irregular movements, with muscle paralysis, especially of lower limbs.

334.1 **Hereditary spastic paraplegia**

334.2 **Primary cerebellar degeneration**
Cerebellar ataxia:
Marie's
Sanger-Brown
Dyssynergia cerebellaris myoclonica
Primary cerebellar degeneration:
NOS
hereditary
sporadic
AHA: M-A, '87, 9

334.3 **Other cerebellar ataxia**
Cerebellar ataxia NOS
Use additional E code to identify drug, if drug-induced

334.4 **Cerebellar ataxia in diseases classified elsewhere**
Code first underlying disease, as:
alcoholism (303.0-303.9)
myxedema (244.0-244.9)
neoplastic disease (140.0-239.9)

334.8 **Other spinocerebellar diseases**
Ataxia-telangiectasia [Louis-Bar syndrome]
Corticostriatal-spinal degeneration

334.9 **Spinocerebellar disease, unspecified**

√4th **335** **Anterior horn cell disease**

335.0 **Werdnig-Hoffmann disease**
Infantile spinal muscular atrophy
Progressive muscular atrophy of infancy
DEF: Spinal muscle atrophy manifested in prenatal period or shortly after birth; symptoms include hypotonia, atrophy of skeletal muscle; death occurs in infancy.

√5th **335.1** **Spinal muscular atrophy**

335.10 **Spinal muscular atrophy, unspecified**

335.11 **Kugelberg-Welander disease**
Spinal muscular atrophy:
familial
juvenile
DEF: Hereditary; juvenile muscle atrophy; appears during first two decades of life; due to lesions of anterior horns of spinal cord; includes wasting, diminution of lower body muscles and twitching.

335.19 **Other**
Adult spinal muscular atrophy

√5th **335.2** **Motor neuron disease**

335.20 **Amyotrophic lateral sclerosis** Ⓐ
Motor neuron disease (bulbar) (mixed type)
AHA: 4Q, '95, 81

Ⓝ Newborn Age: 0   Ⓟ Pediatric Age: 0-17   Ⓜ Maternity Age: 12-55   Ⓐ Adult Age: 15-124

335.21 Progressive muscular atrophy
Duchenne-Aran muscular atrophy
Progressive muscular atrophy (pure)

335.22 Progressive bulbar palsy

335.23 Pseudobulbar palsy

335.24 Primary lateral sclerosis

335.29 Other

335.8 Other anterior horn cell diseases

335.9 Anterior horn cell disease, unspecified

√4ᵗʰ **336 Other diseases of spinal cord**

336.0 Syringomyelia and syringobulbia
AHA: 1Q, '89, 10

336.1 Vascular myelopathies
Acute infarction of spinal cord (embolic) (nonembolic)
Arterial thrombosis of spinal cord
Edema of spinal cord
Hematomyelia
Subacute necrotic myelopathy

336.2 Subacute combined degeneration of spinal cord in diseases classified elsewhere

Code first underlying disease, as:
pernicious anemia (281.0)
other vitamin B12 deficiency anemia (281.1)
vitamin B12 deficiency (266.2)

336.3 Myelopathy in other diseases classified elsewhere

Code first underlying disease, as:
myelopathy in neoplastic disease (140.0-239.9)

EXCLUDES *myelopathy in:*
intervertebral disc disorder (722.70-722.73)
spondylosis (721.1, 721.41-721.42, 721.91)

AHA: 3Q, '99, 5

336.8 Other myelopathy
Myelopathy:
drug-induced
radiation-induced

Use additonal E code to identify cause

336.9 Unspecified disease of spinal cord
Cord compression NOS
Myelopathy NOS

EXCLUDES *myelitis (323.02, 323.1, 323.2, 323.42, 323.52,*
323.63, 323.72, 323.82, 323.9)
spinal (canal) stenosis (723.0, 724.00-724.09)

√4ᵗʰ **337 Disorders of the autonomic nervous system**

INCLUDES disorders of peripheral autonomic, sympathetic,
parasympathetic, or vegetative system

EXCLUDES *familial dysautonomia [Riley-Day syndrome] (742.8)*

√5ᵗʰ **337.0 Idiopathic peripheral autonomic neuropathy**

337.00 Idiopathic peripheral autonomic neuropathy, unspecified

337.01 Carotid sinus syndrome
Carotid sinus syncope

DEF: Vagal activation caused by pressure on the
carotid sinus baroreceptors; sympathetic nerve
impulses may cause sinus arrest or AV block.
AHA: 4Q, '08, 101-102

337.09 Other idiopathic peripheral autonomic neuropathy
Cervical sympathetic dystrophy or paralysis

337.1 Peripheral autonomic neuropathy in disorders classified elsewhere

Code first underlying disease, as:
amyloidosis (277.30-277.39)
diabetes (249.6, 250.6)
AHA: ▶2Q, '09, 13;◀ 2Q, '93, 6; 3Q, '91, 9; N-D, '84, 9

√5ᵗʰ **337.2 Reflex sympathetic dystrophy**

DEF: Disturbance of the sympathetic nervous system
evidenced by sweating, pain, pallor and edema following
injury to nerves or blood vessels.
AHA: 4Q, '93, 24

337.20 Reflex sympathetic dystrophy, unspecified
Complex regional pain syndrome type I,
unspecified

337.21 Reflex sympathetic dystrophy of the upper limb
Complex regional pain syndrome type I of the
upper limb

337.22 Reflex sympathetic dystrophy of the lower limb
Complex regional pain syndrome type I of the
lower limb

337.29 Reflex sympathetic dystrophy of other specified site
Complex regional pain syndrome type I of other
specified site

337.3 Autonomic dysreflexia
Use additional code to identify the cause, such as:
pressure ulcer (707.00-707.09)
fecal impaction (560.39)
urinary tract infection (599.0)

DEF: Noxious stimuli evokes paroxysmal hypertension,
bradycardia, excess sweating, headache, pilomotor responses,
facial flushing, and nasal congestion due to uncontrolled
parasympathetic nerve response; occurs in patients with
spinal cord injury above sympathetic outflow tract (T_6).
AHA: 4Q, '98, 37

337.9 Unspecified disorder of autonomic nervous system

PAIN (338)

√4ᵗʰ **338 Pain, not elsewhere classified**
Use additional code to identify:
pain associated with psychological factors (307.89)

EXCLUDES *generalized pain (780.96)*
headache syndromes (339.00-339.89)
localized pain, unspecified type–code to pain by site
migraines (346.0-346.9)
pain disorder exclusively attributed to psychological
factors (307.80)
vulvar vestibulitis (625.71)
vulvodynia (625.70-625.79)

AHA: 2Q, '07, 12

TIP: Do not assign a 338 code if the pain is not specified as acute or
chronic, unless post-thoracotomy, postoperative, neoplasm related or
central pain syndrome.

338.0 Central pain syndrome
Déjérine-Roussy syndrome
Myelopathic pain syndrome
Thalamic pain syndrome (hyperesthetic)
AHA: 4Q, '06, 79-81

√5ᵗʰ **338.1 Acute pain**

338.11 Acute pain due to trauma
AHA: 1Q, '07, 7; 4Q, '06, 79-81

338.12 Acute post-thoracotomy pain
Post-thoracotomy pain NOS
AHA: 4Q, '06, 79-81

338.18 Other acute postoperative pain
Postoperative pain NOS
AHA: 2Q, '07, 11; 4Q, '06, 79-81
G89.18 Other acute postprocedural pain   I-10

338.19 Other acute pain
EXCLUDES *neoplasm related acute pain (338.3)*
AHA: 2Q, '07, 11; 4Q, '06, 79-81

√4ᵗʰ √5ᵗʰ Additional Digit Required   Unspecified Code   Other Specified Code   Manifestation Code   ▶◀ Revised Text   ● New Code   ▲ Revised Code Title

Nervous System and Sense Organs

335.21–338.19

Nervous System and Sense Organs

338.2–341.22

✓5th **338.2 Chronic pain**
> *EXCLUDES* *causalgia (355.9)*
> *lower limb (355.71)*
> *upper limb (354.4)*
> *chronic pain syndrome (338.4)*
> *myofascial pain syndrome (729.1)*
> *neoplasm related chronic pain (338.3)*
> *reflex sympathetic dystrophy (337.20-337.29)*

338.21 Chronic pain due to trauma
AHA: 4Q, '06, 79-81

338.22 Chronic post-thoracotomy pain
AHA: 4Q, '06, 79-81

338.28 Other chronic postoperative pain
AHA: 4Q, '06, 79-81
G89.28 Other chronic postprocedural pain `I-10`

338.29 Other chronic pain
AHA: 4Q, '06, 79-81

338.3 Neoplasm related pain (acute) (chronic)
Cancer associated pain
Pain due to malignancy (primary) (secondary)
Tumor associated pain
AHA: 2Q, '07, 11; 4Q, '06, 79-81
G89.3 Neoplasm related pain (acute) (chronic) `I-10`

338.4 Chronic pain syndrome
Chronic pain associated with significant psychosocial dysfunction
AHA: 2Q, '07, 11; 4Q, '06, 79-81
G89.4 Chronic pain syndrome `I-10`

OTHER HEADACHE SYNDROMES (339)

✓4th **339 Other headache syndromes**
> *EXCLUDES* *headache:*
> *NOS (784.0)*
> *due to lumbar puncture (349.0)*
> *migraine (346.0-346.9)*
AHA: ▶4Q, '08, 102-105◀

✓5th **339.0 Cluster headaches and other trigeminal autonomic cephalgias**
TACS

339.00 Cluster headache syndrome, unspecified
Ciliary neuralgia
Cluster headache NOS
Histamine cephalgia
Lower half migraine
Migrainous neuralgia

339.01 Episodic cluster headache

339.02 Chronic cluster headache

339.03 Episodic paroxysmal hemicrania
Paroxysmal hemicrania NOS

339.04 Chronic paroxysmal hemicrania

339.05 Short lasting unilateral neuralgiform headache with conjunctival injection and tearing
SUNCT

339.09 Other trigeminal autonomic cephalgias

✓5th **339.1 Tension type headache**
> *EXCLUDES* *tension headache NOS (307.81)*
> *tension headache related to psychological factors (307.81)*
AHA: ▶4Q, '08, 103◀

339.10 Tension type headache, unspecified

339.11 Episodic tension type headache

339.12 Chronic tension type headache

✓5th **339.2 Post-traumatic headache**
> **TIP:** Do not assign during the acute phase of the trauma (e.g., head injury). When assigning 339.2X, report also a late effect code (e.g., 907.0 for intracranial injury).

339.20 Post-traumatic headache, unspecified
AHA: ▶4Q, '08, 108◀

339.21 Acute post-traumatic headache

339.22 Chronic post-traumatic headache

339.3 Drug induced headache, not elsewhere classified
Medication overuse headache
Rebound headache

✓5th **339.4 Complicated headache syndromes**

339.41 Hemicrania continua

339.42 New daily persistent headache
NDPH

339.43 Primary thunderclap headache

339.44 Other complicated headache syndrome

✓5th **339.8 Other specified headache syndromes**

339.81 Hypnic headache

339.82 Headache associated with sexual activity
Orgasmic headache
Preorgasmic headache

339.83 Primary cough headache

339.84 Primary exertional headache

339.85 Primary stabbing headache

339.89 Other specified headache syndromes

OTHER DISORDERS OF THE CENTRAL NERVOUS SYSTEM (340-349)

340 Multiple sclerosis
Disseminated or multiple sclerosis:
NOS
brain stem
cord
generalized
G35 Multiple sclerosis `I-10`

✓4th **341 Other demyelinating diseases of central nervous system**

341.0 Neuromyelitis optica

341.1 Schilder's disease
Baló's concentric sclerosis
Encephalitis periaxialis:
concentrica [Baló's]
diffusa [Schilder's]
DEF: Chronic leukoencephalopathy of children and adolescents; symptoms include blindness, deafness, bilateral spasticity and progressive mental deterioration.

✓5th **341.2 Acute (transverse) myelitis**
> *EXCLUDES* *acute (transverse) myelitis (in) (due to):*
> *following immunization procedures (323.52)*
> *infection classified elsewhere (323.42)*
> *postinfectious (323.63)*
> *protozoal diseases classified elsewhere (323.2)*
> *rickettsial diseases classified elsewhere (323.1)*
> *toxic (323.72)*
> *viral diseases classified elsewhere (323.02)*
> *transverse myelitis NOS (323.82)*

341.20 Acute (transverse) myelitis NOS
AHA: 4Q, '06, 58-63

341.21 Acute (transverse) myelitis in conditions classified elsewhere
Code first underlying condition
AHA: 4Q, '06, 58-63

341.22 Idiopathic transverse myelitis
AHA: 4Q, '06, 58-63

`N` Newborn Age: 0   `P` Pediatric Age: 0-17   `M` Maternity Age: 12-55   `A` Adult Age: 15-124

341.8 Other demyelinating diseases of central nervous system
Central demyelination of corpus callosum
Central pontine myelinosis
Marchiafava (-Bignami) disease
AHA: N-D, '87, 6

341.9 Demyelinating disease of central nervous system, unspecified

✓4th **342 Hemiplegia and hemiparesis**
Note: This category is to be used when hemiplegia (complete) (incomplete) is reported without further specification, or is stated to be old or long-standing but of unspecified cause. The category is also for use in multiple coding to identify these types of hemiplegia resulting from any cause.

EXCLUDES   *congenital (343.1)*
hemiplegia due to late effect of cerebrovascular accident (438.20-438.22)
infantile NOS (343.4)

The following fifth-digits are for use with codes 342.0-342.9:
  0 affecting unspecified side
  1 affecting dominant side
  2 affecting nondominant side

AHA: 4Q, '94, 38

§ ✓5th **342.0 Flaccid hemiplegia**
[0-2]

§ ✓5th **342.1 Spastic hemiplegia**
[0-2]

§ ✓5th **342.8 Other specified hemiplegia**
[0-2]

§ ✓5th **342.9 Hemiplegia, unspecified**
[0-2]   **AHA:** 3Q, '06, 5; 4Q, '98, 87
G81.90 Hemiplegia unspecified affect unspecified side   [I-10]

✓4th **343 Infantile cerebral palsy**
INCLUDES   cerebral:
  palsy NOS
  spastic infantile paralysis
congenital spastic paralysis (cerebral)
Little's disease
paralysis (spastic) due to birth injury:
  intracranial
  spinal

EXCLUDES   *athetoid cerebral palsy (333.71)*
hereditary cerebral paralysis, such as:
  hereditary spastic paraplegia (334.1)
  Vogt's disease (333.71)
spastic paralysis specified as noncongenital or noninfantile (344.0-344.9)

343.0 Diplegic
Congenital diplegia
Congenital paraplegia
DEF: Paralysis affecting both sides of the body simultaneously.

343.1 Hemiplegic
Congenital hemiplegia
EXCLUDES   *infantile hemiplegia NOS (343.4)*

343.2 Quadriplegic
Tetraplegic

343.3 Monoplegic

343.4 Infantile hemiplegia
Infantile hemiplegia (postnatal) NOS

343.8 Other specified infantile cerebral palsy

343.9 Infantile cerebral palsy, unspecified
Cerebral palsy NOS
AHA: 4Q, '05, 89
G80.9 Cerebral palsy unspecified   [I-10]

✓4th **344 Other paralytic syndromes**
Note: This category is to be used when the listed conditions are reported without further specification or are stated to be old or long-standing but of unspecified cause. The category is also for use in multiple coding to identify these conditions resulting from any cause.

INCLUDES   paralysis (complete) (incomplete), except as classifiable to 342 and 343
EXCLUDES   *congenital or infantile cerebral palsy (343.0-343.9)*
hemiplegia (342.0-342.9)
congenital or infantile (343.1, 343.4)

✓5th **344.0 Quadriplegia and quadriparesis**
TIP: Assign also a code from subcategory 438.5 if late effect of CVA.

344.00 Quadriplegia unspecified
AHA: 4Q, '03, 103; 4Q, '98, 38
G82.50 Quadriplegia unspecified   [I-10]

344.01 C₁-C₄ complete

344.02 C₁-C₄ incomplete

344.03 C₅-C₇ complete

344.04 C₅-C₇ incomplete

344.09 Other
AHA: 1Q, '01, 12; 4Q, '98, 39

344.1 Paraplegia
Paralysis of both lower limbs
Paraplegia (lower)
AHA: 4Q, '03, 110; M-A, '87, 10
G82.20 Paraplegia unspecified   [I-10]

344.2 Diplegia of upper limbs
Diplegia (upper)
Paralysis of both upper limbs

✓5th **344.3 Monoplegia of lower limb**
Paralysis of lower limb
EXCLUDES   *monoplegia of lower limb due to late effect of cerebrovascular accident (438.40-438.42)*

344.30 Affecting unspecified side

344.31 Affecting dominant side

344.32 Affecting nondominant side

✓5th **344.4 Monoplegia of upper limb**
Paralysis of upper limb
EXCLUDES   *monoplegia of upper limb due to late effect of cerebrovascular accident (438.30-438.32)*

344.40 Affecting unspecified side

344.41 Affecting dominant side

344.42 Affecting nondominant side

344.5 Unspecified monoplegia

✓5th **344.6 Cauda equina syndrome**
DEF: Dull pain and paresthesias in sacrum, perineum and bladder due to compression of spinal nerve roots; pain radiates down buttocks, back of thigh, calf of leg and into foot with prickling, burning sensations.

344.60 Without mention of neurogenic bladder

344.61 With neurogenic bladder
Acontractile bladder
Autonomic hyperreflexia of bladder
Cord bladder
Detrusor hyperreflexia
AHA: M-J, '87, 12; M-A, '87, 10

✓5th **344.8 Other specified paralytic syndromes**

344.81 Locked-in state
DEF: State of consciousness where patients are paralyzed and unable to respond to environmental stimuli; patients have eye movements, and stimuli can enter the brain but patients unable to respond.
AHA: 4Q, '93, 24

§   Requires fifth digit. Valid digits are in [brackets] under each code. See category 342 for codes and definitions.

344.89   **Other specified paralytic syndrome**

AHA: 2Q, '99, 4

344.9   **Paralysis, unspecified**

✓4ᵗʰ **345**   **Epilepsy and recurrent seizures**

The following fifth-digit subclassification is for use with categories 345.0, .1, .4–.9:

   0   **without mention of intractable eilepsy**
   1   **with intractable epilepsy**
     ▶pharmacoresistant (pharmacologically resistant)
     poorly controlled
     refractory (medically)
     treatment resistant◀

EXCLUDES ▶*hippocampal sclerosis (348.81)*
     mesial temporal sclerosis (348.81)◀
     progressive myoclonic epilepsy (333.2)
     ▶*temporal sclerosis (348.81)*◀

DEF: Brain disorder characterized by electrical-like disturbances; may include occasional impairment or loss of consciousness, abnormal motor phenomena and psychic or sensory disturbances.

AHA: 1Q, '93, 24; 2Q, '92, 8; 4Q, '92, 23

§ ✓5ᵗʰ **345.0**   **Generalized nonconvulsive epilepsy**
[0-1]

  Absences: Pykno-epilepsy
    atonic   Seizures:
    typical   akinetic
  Minor epilepsy   atonic
  Petit mal

AHA: For code 345.00: 1Q, '04, 18

§ ✓5ᵗʰ **345.1**   **Generalized convulsive epilepsy**
[0-1]

  Epileptic seizures:
    clonic
    myoclonic
    tonic
    tonic-clonic
  Grand mal
  Major epilepsy
  ▶Progressive myoclonic epilepsy
  Unverricht-Lundborg disease◀

EXCLUDES *convulsions:*
    NOS (780.39)
    infantile (780.39)
    newborn (779.0)
    infantile spasms (345.6)

DEF: Convulsive seizures with tension of limbs (tonic) or rhythmic contractions (clonic).

AHA: 3Q, '97, 4

345.2   **Petit mal status**

Epileptic absence status

DEF: Minor myoclonic spasms and sudden momentary loss of consciousness in epilepsy.

345.3   **Grand mal status**

Status epilepticus NOS

EXCLUDES *epilepsia partialis continua (345.7)*
  status:
    psychomotor (345.7)
    temporal lobe (345.7)

DEF: Sudden loss of consciousness followed by generalized convulsions in epilepsy.

AHA: 3Q, '05, 12

G40.301 Gen idiopath epilep&epi syn not intractabl w/se I-10

§ ✓5ᵗʰ **345.4**   **Localization-related (focal) (partial) epilepsy and**
[0-1]   **epileptic syndromes with complex partial seizures**

  Epilepsy:
    limbic system
    partial:
      secondarily generalized
      with impairment of consciousness
      with memory and ideational disturbances
    psychomotor
    psychosensory
    temporal lobe
  Epileptic automatism

§ ✓5ᵗʰ **345.5**   **Localization-related (focal) (partial) epilepsy and**
[0-1]   **epileptic syndromes with simple partial seizures**

  Epilepsy:
    Bravais-Jacksonian NOS
    focal (motor) NOS
    Jacksonian NOS
    motor partial
    partial NOS:
      without impairment of consciousness
    sensory-induced
    somatomotor
    somatosensory
    visceral
    visual

§ ✓5ᵗʰ **345.6**   **Infantile spasms**
[0-1]

  Hypsarrhythmia
  Lightning spasms
  Salaam attacks

EXCLUDES *salaam tic (781.0)*

AHA: N-D, '84, 12

§ ✓5ᵗʰ **345.7**   **Epilepsia partialis continua**
[0-1]

  Kojevnikov's epilepsy

DEF: Continuous muscle contractions and relaxation; result of abnormal neural discharge.

§ ✓5ᵗʰ **345.8**   **Other forms of epilepsy and recurrent seizures**
[0-1]

  Epilepsy:
    cursive [running]
    gelastic

§ ✓5ᵗʰ **345.9**   **Epilepsy, unspecified**
[0-1]

  Epileptic convulsions, fits, or seizures NOS
  Recurrent seizures NOS
  Seizure disorder NOS

EXCLUDES *convulsion (convulsive) disorder (780.39)*
  convulsive seizure or fit NOS (780.39)
  recurrent convulsions (780.39)

AHA: 1Q, '08, 17; N-D, '87, 12; **For code 345.90:** ▶2Q, '09, 10;◀

G40.909 Epilepsy uns not intractbl w/o status epilepticus I-10

✓4ᵗʰ **346**   **Migraine**

EXCLUDES *headache:*
  NOS (784.0)
  syndromes (339.00-339.89)

AHA: 4Q, '08, 103, 105-107

The following fifth-digit subclassification is for use with category 346:

   0   **without mention of intractable migraine without**
      mention of status migrainosus
   1   **with intractable migraine, so stated without mention of**
      status migrainosus
   2   **without mention of intractable migraine with status**
      migrainosus
   3   **with intractable migraine, so stated, with status**
      migrainosus

DEF: Benign vascular headache of extreme pain; commonly associated with irritability, nausea, vomiting and often photophobia; premonitory visual hallucination of a crescent in the visual field (scotoma).

§ ✓5ᵗʰ **346.0**   **Migraine with aura**
[0-3]

  Basilar migraine
  Classic migraine
  Migraine preceded or accompanied by transient focal
    neurological phenomena
  Migraine triggered seizures
  Migraine with acute-onset aura
  Migraine with aura without headache (migraine
    equivalents)
  Migraine with prolonged aura
  Migraine with typical aura
  Retinal migraine

EXCLUDES *persistent migraine aura (346.5, 346.6)*

§ ✓5ᵗʰ **346.1**   **Migraine without aura**
[0-3]

  Common migraine

---

§   Requires fifth digit. Valid digits are in [brackets] under each code. See appropriate category for codes and definitions.

Ⓝ Newborn Age: 0   Ⓟ Pediatric Age: 0-17   Ⓜ Maternity Age: 12-55   Ⓐ Adult Age: 15-124

§ ✓5th **346.2 Variants of migraine, not elsewhere classified**
[0-3]   Abdominal migraine
Cyclical vomiting associated with migraine
Ophthalmoplegic migraine
Periodic headache syndromes in child or adolescent
EXCLUDES *cyclical vomiting NOS (536.2)*
psychogenic cyclical vomiting (306.4)

§ ✓5th **346.3 Hemiplegic migraine**
[0-3]   Familial migraine
Sporadic migraine

§ ✓5th **346.4 Menstrual migraine**   ♀
[0-3]   Menstrual headache
Menstrually related migraine
Premenstrual headache
Premenstrual migraine
Pure menstrual migraine

§ ✓5th **346.5 Persistent migraine aura without cerebral infarction**
[0-3]   Persistent migraine aura NOS

§ ✓5th **346.6 Persistent migraine aura with cerebral infarction**
[0-3]   **AHA: For code 346.60:** 4Q, '08, 108

TIP: Assign also a code for the specific type of cerebral infarction.

§ ✓5th **346.7 Chronic migraine without aura**
[0-3]   Transformed migraine without aura

§ ✓5th **346.8 Other forms of migraine**
[0-3]

§ ✓5th **346.9 Migraine, unspecified**
[0-3]   **AHA:** N-D, '85, 16

G43.90 Migraine unspecified not intractable   I-10

✓4th **347 Cataplexy and narcolepsy**
DEF: Cataplexy: Sudden onset of muscle weakness with loss of tone and strength; caused by aggressive or spontaneous emotions.
DEF: Narcolepsy: Brief, recurrent, uncontrollable episodes of sound sleep.

✓5th **347.0 Narcolepsy**

347.00 Without cataplexy
Narcolepsy NOS

347.01 With cataplexy

✓5th **347.1 Narcolepsy in conditions classified elsewhere**
Code first underlying condition

347.10 Without cataplexy

347.11 With cataplexy

✓4th **348 Other conditions of brain**

348.0 Cerebral cysts
Arachnoid cyst   Porencephaly, acquired
Porencephalic cyst   Pseudoporencephaly
EXCLUDES *porencephaly (congenital) (742.4)*

348.1 Anoxic brain damage
Use additional E code to identify cause
EXCLUDES *that occurring in:*
abortion (634-638 with .7, 639.8)
ectopic or molar pregnancy (639.8)
labor or delivery (668.2, 669.4)
that of newborn (767.0, 768.0-768.9, 772.1-772.2)

DEF: Brain injury due to lack of oxygen, other than birth trauma.

G93.1 Anoxic brain damage not elsewhere classified   I-10

348.2 Benign intracranial hypertension
Pseudotumor cerebri
EXCLUDES *hypertensive encephalopathy (437.2)*

DEF: Elevated pressure in brain due to fluid retention in brain cavities.

✓5th **348.3 Encephalopathy, not elsewhere classified**
AHA: 4Q, '03, 58; 3Q, '97, 4

348.30 Encephalopathy, unspecified

G93.40 Encephalopathy unspecified   I-10

348.31 Metabolic encephalopathy
Septic encephalopathy
EXCLUDES *toxic metabolic encephalopathy (349.82)*

TIP: Physician documentation may include "acute confusional state," usually denoting delirium secondary to the encephalopathy.

348.39 Other encephalopathy
EXCLUDES *encephalopathy:*
alcoholic (291.2)
hepatic (572.2)
hypertensive (437.2)
toxic (349.82)

348.4 Compression of brain
Compression } brain (stem)
Herniation
Posterior fossa compression syndrome
DEF: Elevated pressure in brain due to blood clot, tumor, fracture, abscess, other condition.
AHA: 4Q, '94, 37
TIP: Assign for Arnold-Chiari syndrome, Type I. For Type II, III, or IV, refer to categories 741 and 742.

348.5 Cerebral edema
DEF: Elevated pressure in the brain due to fluid retention in brain tissues.
G93.6 Cerebral edema   I-10

✓5th **348.8 Other conditions of brain**
AHA: S-O, '87, 9

● **348.81 Temporal sclerosis**
Hippocampal sclerosis
Mesial temporal sclerosis

● **348.89 Other conditions of brain**
Cerebral:
calcification
fungus

348.9 Unspecified condition of brain

✓4th **349 Other and unspecified disorders of the nervous system**
AHA: 4Q, '08, 109

349.0 Reaction to spinal or lumbar puncture
Headache following lumbar puncture
AHA: 2Q, '99, 9; 3Q, '90, 18
TIP: Assign when documentation indicates mitral valve stenosis or obstruction with no further specification of cause.
G97.1 Other reaction to spinal and lumbar puncture   I-10

349.1 Nervous system complications from surgically implanted device
EXCLUDES *immediate postoperative complications (997.00-997.09)*
mechanical complications of nervous system device (996.2)

349.2 Disorders of meninges, not elsewhere classified
Adhesions, meningeal   Meningocele, acquired
(cerebral) (spinal)   Pseudomeningocele,
Cyst, spinal meninges   acquired
AHA: 1Q, '06, 15; 2Q, '98, 18; 3Q, '94, 4

✓5th **349.3 Dural tear**

349.31 Accidental puncture or laceration of dura during a procedure
Incidental (inadvertent) durotomy
AHA: 4Q, '08, 109-110
TIP: Do not assign code 998.2 Accidental puncture or laceration during a procedure, for an incidental dural tear.

349.39 Other dural tear

✓5th **349.8 Other specified disorders of nervous system**

349.81 Cerebrospinal fluid rhinorrhea
EXCLUDES *cerebrospinal fluid otorrhea (388.61)*
DEF: Cerebrospinal fluid discharging from the nose; caused by fracture of frontal bone with tearing of dura mater and arachnoid.

✓5th Additional Digit Required   Unspecified Code   Other Specified Code   Manifestation Code   ►◄ Revised Text   ● New Code   ▲ Revised Code Title

Cranial Nerves

- Olfactory bulb (I)
- Optic nerve (II)
- Oculomotor nerve (III)
- Trochlear nerve (IV)
- Trigeminal nerve (V)
- Abducens nerve (VI)
- Facial nerve (VII)
- Vestibulocochlear nerve (VIII)
- Glossopharyngeal nerve (IX)
- Vagus nerve (X)
- Accessory nerve (XI)
- Hypoglossal nerve (XII)

Pons

Trigeminal and Facial Nerve Branches

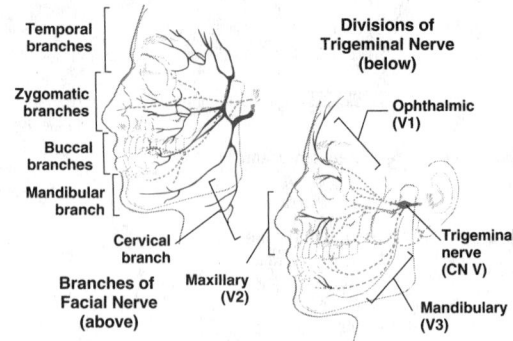

Temporal branches
Zygomatic branches
Buccal branches
Mandibular branch
Cervical branch

Branches of Facial Nerve (above)

Divisions of Trigeminal Nerve (below)

Ophthalmic (V1)
Trigeminal nerve (CN V)
Maxillary (V2)
Mandibulary (V3)

349.82 Toxic encephalopathy
Toxic metabolic encephalopathy

Use additional E code to identify cause

DEF: Brain tissue degeneration due to toxic substance.

AHA: 4Q, '93, 29

G92 Toxic encephalopathy   **I-10**

349.89 Other

349.9 Unspecified disorders of nervous system
Disorder of nervous system (central) NOS

DISORDERS OF THE PERIPHERAL NERVOUS SYSTEM (350-359)

EXCLUDES diseases of:
   acoustic [8th] nerve (388.5)
   oculomotor [3rd, 4th, 6th] nerves (378.0-378.9)
   optic [2nd] nerve (377.0-377.9)
   peripheral autonomic nerves (337.0-337.9)
   neuralgia
   neuritis   } NOS or "rheumatic" (729.2)
   radiculitis
   peripheral neuritis in pregnancy (646.4)

✓4th 350 Trigeminal nerve disorders
INCLUDES disorders of 5th cranial nerve

350.1 Trigeminal neuralgia
Tic douloureux   Trigeminal neuralgia NOS
Trifacial neuralgia

EXCLUDES postherpetic (053.12)

G50.0 Trigeminal neuralgia   **I-10**

350.2 Atypical face pain

350.8 Other specified trigeminal nerve disorders

350.9 Trigeminal nerve disorder, unspecified

✓4th 351 Facial nerve disorders
INCLUDES disorders of 7th cranial nerve
EXCLUDES that in newborn (767.5)

351.0 Bell's palsy
Facial palsy

DEF: Unilateral paralysis of face due to lesion on facial nerve; produces facial distortion.

G51.0 Bell's palsy   **I-10**

351.1 Geniculate ganglionitis
Geniculate ganglionitis NOS

EXCLUDES herpetic (053.11)

DEF: Inflammation of tissue at bend in facial nerve.

351.8 Other facial nerve disorders
Facial myokymia
Melkersson's syndrome

AHA: 3Q, '02, 13

351.9 Facial nerve disorder, unspecified

✓4th 352 Disorders of other cranial nerves

352.0 Disorders of olfactory [Ist] nerve

352.1 Glossopharyngeal neuralgia
DEF: Pain between throat and ear along petrosal and jugular ganglia.

AHA: 2Q, '02, 8

352.2 Other disorders of glossopharyngeal [9th] nerve

352.3 Disorders of pneumogastric [10th] nerve
Disorders of vagal nerve

EXCLUDES paralysis of vocal cords or larynx (478.30-478.34)

DEF: Nerve disorder affecting ear, tongue, pharynx, larynx, esophagus, viscera and thorax.

352.4 Disorders of accessory [11th] nerve
DEF: Nerve disorder affecting palate, pharynx, larynx, thoracic viscera, sternocleidomastoid and trapezius muscles.

352.5 Disorders of hypoglossal [12th] nerve
DEF: Nerve disorder affecting tongue muscles.

352.6 Multiple cranial nerve palsies
Collet-Sicard syndrome
Polyneuritis cranialis

352.9 Unspecified disorder of cranial nerves

✓4th 353 Nerve root and plexus disorders
EXCLUDES conditions due to:
   intervertebral disc disorders (722.0-722.9)
   spondylosis (720.0-721.9)
   vertebrogenic disorders (723.0-724.9)

353.0 Brachial plexus lesions
Cervical rib syndrome
Costoclavicular syndrome
Scalenus anticus syndrome
Thoracic outlet syndrome

EXCLUDES brachial neuritis or radiculitis NOS (723.4)
   that in newborn (767.6)

DEF: Acquired disorder in tissue along nerves in shoulder; causes corresponding motor and sensory dysfunction.

AHA: 3Q, '06, 12

353.1 Lumbosacral plexus lesions
DEF: Acquired disorder in tissue along nerves in lower back; causes corresponding motor and sensory dysfunction.

353.2 Cervical root lesions, not elsewhere classified

353.3 Thoracic root lesions, not elsewhere classified

353.4 Lumbosacral root lesions, not elsewhere classified

353.5 Neuralgic amyotrophy
Parsonage-Alden-Turner syndrome

Code first any associated underlying disease, such as:
   diabetes mellitus (249.6, 250.6)

353.6 Phantom limb (syndrome)
DEF: Abnormal tingling or a burning sensation, transient aches, and intermittent or continuous pain perceived as originating in the absent limb.

353.8 Other nerve root and plexus disorders

353.9 Unspecified nerve root and plexus disorder

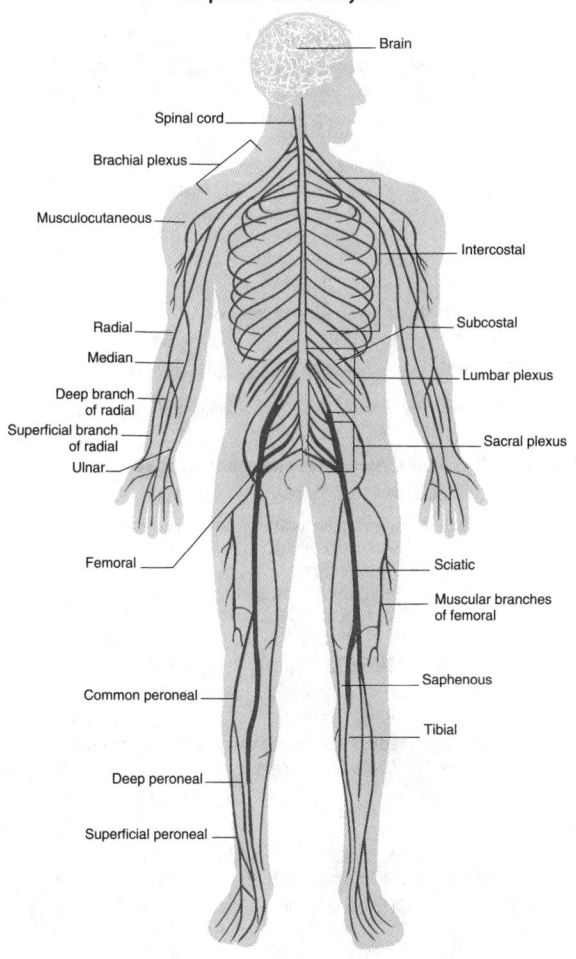

Peripheral Nervous System

Brain
Spinal cord
Brachial plexus
Musculocutaneous
Intercostal
Radial
Subcostal
Median
Lumbar plexus
Deep branch of radial
Superficial branch of radial
Ulnar
Sacral plexus
Femoral
Sciatic
Muscular branches of femoral
Common peroneal
Saphenous
Tibial
Deep peroneal
Superficial peroneal

✓4ᵗʰ **354　Mononeuritis of upper limb and mononeuritis multiplex**

DEF: Inflammation of a single nerve; known as mononeuritis multiplex when several nerves in unrelated body areas are affected.

354.0　**Carpal tunnel syndrome**
Median nerve entrapment
Partial thenar atrophy
DEF: Compression of median nerve by tendons; causes pain, tingling, numbness and burning sensation in hand.
G56.00 Carpal tunnel syndrome unspecified side　　I-10

354.1　**Other lesion of median nerve**
Median nerve neuritis

354.2　**Lesion of ulnar nerve**
Cubital tunnel syndrome
Tardy ulnar nerve palsy

354.3　**Lesion of radial nerve**
Acute radial nerve palsy
AHA: N-D, '87, 6

354.4　**Causalgia of upper limb**
Complex regional pain syndrome type II of the upper limb
EXCLUDES　causalgia:
　　NOS (355.9)
　　lower limb (355.71)
　　complex regional pain syndrome type II of the
　　　lower limb (355.71)
DEF: Peripheral nerve damage, upper limb; usually due to injury; causes burning sensation and trophic skin changes.

354.5　**Mononeuritis multiplex**
Combinations of single conditions classifiable to 354 or 355

354.8　**Other mononeuritis of upper limb**

354.9　**Mononeuritis of upper limb, unspecified**

✓4ᵗʰ　**355　Mononeuritis of lower limb**

355.0　**Lesion of sciatic nerve**
EXCLUDES　sciatica NOS (724.3)
DEF: Acquired disorder of sciatic nerve; causes motor and sensory dysfunction in back, buttock and leg.
AHA: 2Q, '89, 12

355.1　**Meralgia paresthetica**
Lateral cutaneous femoral nerve of thigh compression or syndrome
DEF: Inguinal ligament entraps lateral femoral cutaneous nerve; causes tingling, pain and numbness along outer thigh.

355.2　**Other lesion of femoral nerve**

355.3　**Lesion of lateral popliteal nerve**
Lesion of common peroneal nerve

355.4　**Lesion of medial popliteal nerve**

355.5　**Tarsal tunnel syndrome**
DEF: Compressed, entrapped posterior tibial nerve; causes tingling, pain and numbness in sole of foot.

355.6　**Lesion of plantar nerve**
Morton's metatarsalgia, neuralgia, or neuroma

✓5ᵗʰ　355.7　**Other mononeuritis of lower limb**

355.71　**Causalgia of lower limb**
EXCLUDES　causalgia:
　　NOS (355.9)
　　upper limb (354.4)
　　complex regional pain syndrome
　　　type II of upper limb (354.4)
DEF: Dysfunction of lower limb peripheral nerve, usually due to injury; causes burning pain and trophic skin changes.

355.79　**Other mononeuritis of lower limb**

355.8　**Mononeuritis of lower limb, unspecified**

355.9　**Mononeuritis of unspecified site**
Causalgia NOS
Complex regional pain syndrome NOS
EXCLUDES　causalgia:
　　lower limb (355.71)
　　upper limb (354.4)
　　complex regional pain syndrome:
　　　lower limb (355.71)
　　　upper limb (354.4)
G58.9 Mononeuropathy unspecified　　I-10

✓4ᵗʰ　**356　Hereditary and idiopathic peripheral neuropathy**

356.0　**Hereditary peripheral neuropathy**
Déjérine-Sottas disease

356.1　**Peroneal muscular atrophy**
Charcôt-Marie-Tooth disease
Neuropathic muscular atrophy
DEF: Genetic disorder, in muscles innervated by peroneal nerves; symptoms include muscle wasting in lower limbs and locomotor difficulties.

356.2　**Hereditary sensory neuropathy**
DEF: Inherited disorder in dorsal root ganglia, optic nerve, and cerebellum, causing sensory losses, shooting pains, and foot ulcers.

356.3　**Refsum's disease**
Heredopathia atactica polyneuritiformis
DEF: Genetic disorder of lipid metabolism; causes persistent, painful inflammation of nerves and retinitis pigmentosa.

356.4　**Idiopathic progressive polyneuropathy**

356.8　**Other specified idiopathic peripheral neuropathy**
Supranuclear paralysis

356.9　**Unspecified**
G60.9 Hereditary & idiopathic neuropathy unspecified　　I-10

Nervous System and Sense Organs

357–359.29

✓4th **357 Inflammatory and toxic neuropathy**

357.0 Acute infective polyneuritis
Guillain-Barré syndrome   Postinfectious polyneuritis

DEF: Guillain-Barré syndrome: acute demyelinatry polyneuropathy preceded by viral illness (i.e., herpes, cytomegalovirus [CMV], Epstein-Barr virus [EBV]) or a bacterial illness; areflexic motor paralysis with mild sensory disturbance and acellular rise in spinal fluid protein.

AHA: 2Q, '98, 12

357.1 Polyneuropathy in collagen vascular disease
Code first underlying disease, as:
disseminated lupus erythematosus (710.0)
polyarteritis nodosa (446.0)
rheumatoid arthritis (714.0)

357.2 Polyneuropathy in diabetes
Code first underlying disease (249.6, 250.6)

AHA: ▶2Q, '09, 13, 15;◀ 3Q, '08, 5; 4Q, '03, 105; 2Q, '92, 15; 3Q, '91, 9

357.3 Polyneuropathy in malignant disease
Code first underlying disease (140.0-208.9)

357.4 Polyneuropathy in other diseases classified elsewhere
Code first underlying disease, as:
amyloidosis (277.30-277.39)
beriberi (265.0)
chronic uremia (585.9)
deficiency of B vitamins (266.0-266.9)
diphtheria (032.0-032.9)
hypoglycemia (251.2)
pellagra (265.2)
porphyria (277.1)
sarcoidosis (135)
uremia NOS (586)

EXCLUDES *polyneuropathy in:*
herpes zoster (053.13)
mumps (072.72)

AHA: 2Q, '08, 8; 2Q, '98, 15

G63 Polyneuropathy in dz classified elsewhere   I-10

357.5 Alcoholic polyneuropathy

357.6 Polyneuropathy due to drugs
Use additional E code to identify drug

357.7 Polyneuropathy due to other toxic agents
Use additional E code to identify toxic agent

✓5th **357.8 Other**
AHA: 4Q, '02, 47; 2Q, '98, 12

357.81 Chronic inflammatory demyelinating polyneuritis
DEF: Inflammation of peripheral nerves resulting in destruction of myelin sheath; associated with diabetes mellitus, dysproteinemias, renal failure and malnutrition; symptoms are tingling, numbness, burning pain, diminished tendon reflexes, weakness of lower extremities.

357.82 Critical illness polyneuropathy
Acute motor neuropathy
DEF: An acute axonal neuropathy, both sensory and motor, that is associated with Systemic Inflammatory Response Syndrome (SIRS).
AHA: 4Q, '03, 111

357.89 Other inflammatory and toxic neuropathy

357.9 Unspecified

✓4th **358 Myoneural disorders**

✓5th **358.0 Myasthenia gravis**
DEF: Autoimmune disorder of acetylcholine at neuromuscular junction; causing fatigue of voluntary muscles.
AHA: 4Q, '03, 59

358.00 Myasthenia gravis without (acute) exacerbation
Myasthenia gravis NOS
G70.00 Myasthenia gravis w/o (acute)   I-10
exacerbation

358.01 Myasthenia gravis with (acute) exacerbation
Myasthenia gravis in crisis
AHA: 4Q, '07, 109; 1Q, '05, 4; 4Q, '04, 139

358.1 Myasthenic syndromes in diseases classified elsewhere
Eaton-Lambert syndrome from stated cause classified elsewhere
Code first underlying disease, as:
botulism (005.1, 040.41-040.42)
hypothyroidism (244.0-244.9)
malignant neoplasm (140.0-208.9)
pernicious anemia (281.0)
thyrotoxicosis (242.0-242.9)

358.2 Toxic myoneural disorders
Use additional E code to identify toxic agent

358.8 Other specified myoneural disorders

358.9 Myoneural disorders, unspecified
AHA: 2Q, '02, 16

✓4th **359 Muscular dystrophies and other myopathies**
EXCLUDES *idiopathic polymyositis (710.4)*

359.0 Congenital hereditary muscular dystrophy
Benign congenital myopathy
Central core disease
Centronuclear myopathy
Myotubular myopathy
Nemaline body disease
EXCLUDES *arthrogryposis multiplex congenita (754.89)*
DEF: Genetic disorder; causing progressive or nonprogressive muscle weakness.

359.1 Hereditary progressive muscular dystrophy
Muscular dystrophy: Muscular dystrophy:
NOS   Gower's
distal   Landouzy-Déjérine
Duchenne   limb-girdle
Erb's   ocular
fascioscapulohumeral   oculopharyngeal
DEF: Genetic degenerative, muscle disease; causes progressive weakness, wasting of muscle with no nerve involvement.

✓5th **359.2 Myotonic disorders**
EXCLUDES *periodic paralysis (359.3)*
DEF: Impaired movement due to spasmatic, rigid muscles.
AHA: 4Q, '07, 75

359.21 Myotonic muscular dystrophy
Dystrophia myotonica
Myotonia atrophica
Myotonic dystrophy
Proximal myotonic myopathy [PROMM]
Steinert's disease

359.22 Myotonia congenita
Acetazolamide responsive myotonia congenita
Dominant form [Thomsen's disease]
▶Myotonia levior◀
Recessive form [Becker's disease]

359.23 Myotonic chondrodystrophy
Congenital myotonic chondrodystrophy
Schwartz-Jampel disease

359.24 Drug induced myotonia
Use additional E code to identify drug

359.29 Other specified myotonic disorder
Myotonia fluctuans
Myotonia permanens
Paramyotonia congenita (of von Eulenburg)

N Newborn Age: 0   P Pediatric Age: 0-17   M Maternity Age: 12-55   A Adult Age: 15-124

359.3 Periodic paralysis
Familial periodic paralysis
Hypokalemic familial periodic paralysis
Hyperkalemic periodic paralysis
Hypokalemic periodic paralysis
Potassium sensitive periodic paralysis
EXCLUDES *paramyotonia congenita (of von Eulenburg) (359.29)*
DEF: Genetic disorder; characterized by rapidly progressive flaccid paralysis; attacks often occur after exercise or exposure to cold or dietary changes.

359.4 Toxic myopathy
Use additional E code to identify toxic agent
DEF: Muscle disorder caused by toxic agent.
AHA: 1Q, '88, 5

359.5 *Myopathy in endocrine diseases classified elsewhere*
Code first underlying disease, as:
Addison's disease (255.41)
Cushing's syndrome (255.0)
hypopituitarism (253.2)
myxedema (244.0-244.9)
thyrotoxicosis (242.0-242.9)
DEF: Muscle disorder secondary to dysfunction in hormone secretion.

359.6 *Symptomatic inflammatory myopathy in diseases classified elsewhere*
Code first underlying disease, as:
amyloidosis (277.30-277.39)
disseminated lupus erythematosus (710.0)
malignant neoplasm (140.0-208.9)
polyarteritis nodosa (446.0)
rheumatoid arthritis (714.0)
sarcoidosis (135)
scleroderma (710.1)
Sjögren's disease (710.2)

● √5th **359.7 Inflammatory and immune myopathies, NEC**
●   **359.71 Inclusion body myositis**
       IBM
●   **359.79 Other inflammatory and immune myopathies, NEC**
       Inflammatory myopathy NOS

√5th **359.8 Other myopathies**
    AHA: 4Q, '02, 47; 3Q, '90, 17

    359.81 Critical illness myopathy
       Acute necrotizing myopathy
       Acute quadriplegic myopathy
       Intensive care (ICU) myopathy
       Myopathy of critical illness

    359.89 Other myopathies
359.9 Myopathy, unspecified

DISORDERS OF THE EYE AND ADNEXA (360-379)
Use additional external cause code, if applicable, to identify the cause of the eye condition

√4th **360 Disorders of the globe**
INCLUDES disorders affecting multiple structures of eye

√5th **360.0 Purulent endophthalmitis**
EXCLUDES *bleb associated endophthalmitis (379.63)*

    360.00 Purulent endophthalmitis, unspecified
    360.01 Acute endophthalmitis
    360.02 Panophthalmitis
    360.03 Chronic endophthalmitis
    360.04 Vitreous abscess

√5th **360.1 Other endophthalmitis**
EXCLUDES *bleb associated endophthalmitis (379.63)*

    360.11 Sympathetic uveitis
      DEF: Inflammation of vascular layer of uninjured eye; follows injury to other eye.

Eye
Sclera, Cornea, Iris, Pupil, Anterior chamber, Posterior chamber, Ciliary body, Conjunctiva, Choroid (uvea), Vitreous body, Lamina cribosa, Optic nerve, Optic disk, Fovea, Retina, Lens, Hyaloid canal
Globe (Eyeball)

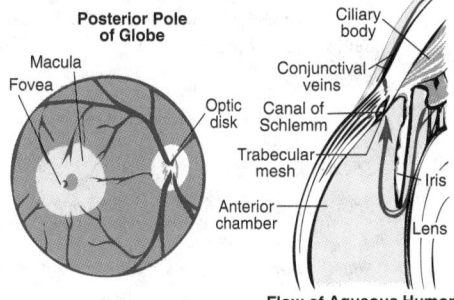

Posterior Pole of Globe
Macula, Fovea, Optic disk
Ciliary body, Conjunctival veins, Canal of Schlemm, Trabecular mesh, Anterior chamber, Iris, Lens
Flow of Aqueous Humor

    360.12 Panuveitis
      DEF: Inflammation of entire vascular layer of eye, including choroid, iris and ciliary body.

    360.13 Parasitic endophthalmitis NOS
      DEF: Parasitic infection causing inflammation of the entire eye.

    360.14 Ophthalmia nodosa
      DEF: Conjunctival inflammation caused by embedded hairs.

    360.19 Other
      Phacoanaphylactic endophthalmitis

√5th **360.2 Degenerative disorders of globe**
    AHA: 3Q, '91, 3

    360.20 Degenerative disorder of globe, unspecified

    360.21 Progressive high (degenerative) myopia
      Malignant myopia
      DEF: Severe, progressive nearsightedness in adults, complicated by serious disease of the choroid; leads to retinal detachment and blindness.

    360.23 Siderosis
      DEF: Iron pigment deposits within tissue of eyeball; caused by high iron content of blood.

    360.24 Other metallosis
      Chalcosis
      DEF: Metal deposits, other than iron, within eyeball tissues.

    360.29 Other
      EXCLUDES *xerophthalmia (264.7)*

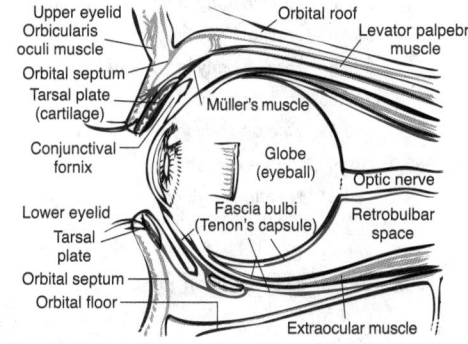

Adnexa
Upper eyelid, Orbicularis oculi muscle, Orbital septum, Tarsal plate (cartilage), Conjunctival fornix, Lower eyelid, Tarsal plate, Orbital septum, Orbital floor, Orbital roof, Levator palpebri muscle, Müller's muscle, Globe (eyeball), Optic nerve, Fascia bulbi (Tenon's capsule), Retrobulbar space, Extraocular muscle

Nervous System and Sense Organs

360.3–361.9

√5th **360.3 Hypotony of eye**

360.30 Hypotony, unspecified

DEF: Low osmotic pressure causing lack of tone, tension and strength.

360.31 Primary hypotony

360.32 Ocular fistula causing hypotony

DEF: Low intraocular pressure due to leak through abnormal passage.

360.33 Hypotony associated with other ocular disorders

360.34 Flat anterior chamber

DEF: Low pressure behind cornea, causing compression.

√5th **360.4 Degenerated conditions of globe**

360.40 Degenerated globe or eye, unspecified

360.41 Blind hypotensive eye
Atrophy of globe
Phthisis bulbi

DEF: Vision loss due to extremely low intraocular pressure.

360.42 Blind hypertensive eye
Absolute glaucoma

DEF: Vision loss due to painful, high intraocular pressure.

360.43 Hemophthalmos, except current injury

EXCLUDES traumatic (871.0-871.9, 921.0-921.9)

DEF: Pool of blood within eyeball, not from current injury.

360.44 Leucocoria

DEF: Whitish mass or reflex in the pupil behind lens; also called cat's eye reflex; often indicative of retinoblastoma.

√5th **360.5 Retained (old) intraocular foreign body, magnetic**

EXCLUDES current penetrating injury with magnetic foreign body (871.5)
retained (old) foreign body of orbit (376.6)

360.50 Foreign body, magnetic, intraocular, unspecified

360.51 Foreign body, magnetic, in anterior chamber

360.52 Foreign body, magnetic, in iris or ciliary body

360.53 Foreign body, magnetic, in lens

360.54 Foreign body, magnetic, in vitreous

360.55 Foreign body, magnetic, in posterior wall

360.59 Foreign body, magnetic, in other or multiple sites

√5th **360.6 Retained (old) intraocular foreign body, nonmagnetic**
Retained (old) foreign body:
NOS
nonmagnetic

EXCLUDES current penetrating injury with (nonmagnetic) foreign body (871.6)
retained (old) foreign body in orbit (376.6)

360.60 Foreign body, intraocular, unspecified

360.61 Foreign body in anterior chamber

360.62 Foreign body in iris or ciliary body

360.63 Foreign body in lens

360.64 Foreign body in vitreous

360.65 Foreign body in posterior wall

360.69 Foreign body in other or multiple sites

√5th **360.8 Other disorders of globe**

360.81 Luxation of globe

DEF: Displacement of eyeball.

360.89 Other

360.9 Unspecified disorder of globe

√4th **361 Retinal detachments and defects**

DEF: Light-sensitive layer at back of eye, separates from blood supply; disrupting vision.

√5th **361.0 Retinal detachment with retinal defect**
Rhegmatogenous retinal detachment

EXCLUDES detachment of retinal pigment epithelium (362.42-362.43)
retinal detachment (serous) (without defect) (361.2)

361.00 Retinal detachment with retinal defect, unspecified

361.01 Recent detachment, partial, with single defect

361.02 Recent detachment, partial, with multiple defects

361.03 Recent detachment, partial, with giant tear

361.04 Recent detachment, partial, with retinal dialysis
Dialysis (juvenile) of retina (with detachment)

361.05 Recent detachment, total or subtotal

361.06 Old detachment, partial
Delimited old retinal detachment

361.07 Old detachment, total or subtotal

√5th **361.1 Retinoschisis and retinal cysts**

EXCLUDES juvenile retinoschisis (362.73)
microcystoid degeneration of retina (362.62)
parasitic cyst of retina (360.13)

361.10 Retinoschisis, unspecified

DEF: Separation of retina due to degenerative process of aging; should not be confused with acute retinal detachment.

361.11 Flat retinoschisis

DEF: Slow, progressive split of retinal sensory layers.

361.12 Bullous retinoschisis

DEF: Fluid retention between split retinal sensory layers.

361.13 Primary retinal cysts

361.14 Secondary retinal cysts

361.19 Other
Pseudocyst of retina

361.2 Serous retinal detachment
Retinal detachment without retinal defect

EXCLUDES central serous retinopathy (362.41)
retinal pigment epithelium detachment (362.42-362.43)

√5th **361.3 Retinal defects without detachment**

EXCLUDES chorioretinal scars after surgery for detachment (363.30-363.35)
peripheral retinal degeneration without defect (362.60-362.66)

361.30 Retinal defect, unspecified
Retinal break(s) NOS

361.31 Round hole of retina without detachment

361.32 Horseshoe tear of retina without detachment
Operculum of retina without mention of detachment

361.33 Multiple defects of retina without detachment

√5th **361.8 Other forms of retinal detachment**

361.81 Traction detachment of retina
Traction detachment with vitreoretinal organization

361.89 Other
AHA: 3Q, '99, 12

361.9 Unspecified retinal detachment
AHA: N-D, '87, 10

| N Newborn Age: 0 | P Pediatric Age: 0-17 | M Maternity Age: 12-55 | A Adult Age: 15-124 |

√4ᵗʰ **362 Other retinal disorders**

     EXCLUDES   chorioretinal scars (363.30-363.35)
                      chorioretinitis (363.0-363.2)

√5ᵗʰ **362.0 Diabetic retinopathy**

     Code first diabetes (249.5, 250.5)

     DEF: Retinal changes in diabetes of long duration; causes hemorrhages, microaneurysms, waxy deposits and proliferative noninflammatory degenerative disease of retina.

     AHA: 4Q, '05, 65; 3Q, '91, 8

362.01 *Background diabetic retinopathy*
     Diabetic retinal microaneurysms
     Diabetic retinopathy NOS

362.02 *Proliferative diabetic retinopathy*
     DEF: Occurrence of the ischemic effects of vessel blockages result in neovascularization; new blood vessels begin to form to compensate for restricted blood flow; multiple areas of the retina and inner vitreous may be affected.
     AHA: 3Q, '96, 5

362.03 *Nonproliferative diabetic retinopathy NOS*

362.04 *Mild nonproliferative diabetic retinopathy*
     DEF: Early stages of degenerative condition of the retina due to diabetes; microaneurysm formation; small balloon-like swelling of the retinal vessels.

362.05 *Moderate nonproliferative diabetic retinopathy*
     DEF: Stage of degenerative condition of the retina due to diabetes with pronounced microaneurysms; vessel blockages can occur.

362.06 *Severe nonproliferative diabetic retinopathy*
     DEF: Stage of degenerative condition of the retina due to diabetes in which vascular breakdown in the retina results in multiple vascular blockages, or "beadings," with intraretinal hemorrhages.
     AHA: 4Q, '05, 67

362.07 *Diabetic macular edema*
     Note: Code 362.07 must be used with a code for diabetic retinopathy (362.01-362.06)
     Diabetic retinal edema
     DEF: Leakage from retinal blood vessels causes swelling of the macula and impaired vision; exudates or plaques may develop in the posterior pole of the retina due to the breakdown of retinal vasculature.

√5ᵗʰ **362.1 Other background retinopathy and retinal vascular changes**

362.10 Background retinopathy, unspecified
     AHA: 1Q, '06, 12

362.11 Hypertensive retinopathy
     DEF: Retinal irregularities caused by systemic hypertension.
     AHA: 3Q, '90, 3

362.12 Exudative retinopathy
     Coats' syndrome
     AHA: 3Q, '99, 12

362.13 Changes in vascular appearance
     Vascular sheathing of retina
     Use additional code for any associated atherosclerosis (440.8)

362.14 Retinal microaneurysms NOS
     DEF: Microscopic dilation of retinal vessels in nondiabetic.

362.15 Retinal telangiectasia
     DEF: Dilation of blood vessels of the retina.

362.16 Retinal neovascularization NOS
     Neovascularization: Neovascularization:
     choroidal   subretinal
     DEF: New and abnormal vascular growth in the retina.

362.17 Other intraretinal microvascular abnormalities
     Retinal sclerosis   Retinal varices

362.18 Retinal vasculitis
     Eales' disease   Retinal:
     Retinal: perivasculitis
     arteritis   phlebitis
     endarteritis
     DEF: Inflammation of retinal blood vessels.

√5ᵗʰ **362.2 Other proliferative retinopathy**
     AHA: ▶4Q, '08, 110-111◀

362.20 Retinopathy of prematurity, unspecified
     Retinopathy of prematurity NOS

362.21 Retrolental fibroplasia
     Cicatricial retinopathy of prematurity
     DEF: Fibrous tissue in vitreous, from retina to lens, causing blindness; associated with premature infants requiring high amounts of oxygen.

362.22 Retinopathy of prematurity, stage 0

362.23 Retinopathy of prematurity, stage 1

362.24 Retinopathy of prematurity, stage 2

362.25 Retinopathy of prematurity, stage 3

362.26 Retinopathy of prematurity, stage 4

362.27 Retinopathy of prematurity, stage 5

362.29 Other nondiabetic proliferative retinopathy
     AHA: 3Q, '96, 5

√5ᵗʰ **362.3 Retinal vascular occlusion**
     DEF: Obstructed blood flow to and from retina.

362.30 Retinal vascular occlusion, unspecified

362.31 Central retinal artery occlusion

362.32 Arterial branch occlusion

362.33 Partial arterial occlusion
     Hollenhorst plaque
     Retinal microembolism

362.34 Transient arterial occlusion
     Amaurosis fugax
     AHA: 1Q, '00, 16

362.35 Central retinal vein occlusion
     AHA: 2Q, '93, 6

362.36 Venous tributary (branch) occlusion

362.37 Venous engorgement
     Occlusion:
     incipient   } of retinal vein
     partial

√5ᵗʰ **362.4 Separation of retinal layers**
     EXCLUDES   retinal detachment (serous) (361.2)
                      rhegmatogenous (361.00-361.07)

362.40 Retinal layer separation, unspecified

362.41 Central serous retinopathy
     DEF: Serous-filled blister causing detachment of retina from pigment epithelium.

362.42 Serous detachment of retinal pigment epithelium
     Exudative detachment of retinal pigment epithelium
     DEF: Blister of fatty fluid causing detachment of retina from pigment epithelium.

362.43 Hemorrhagic detachment of retinal pigment epithelium
     DEF: Blood-filled blister causing detachment of retina from pigment epithelium.

√5ᵗʰ **362.5 Degeneration of macula and posterior pole**
     EXCLUDES   degeneration of optic disc (377.21-377.24)
                      hereditary retinal degeneration [dystrophy]
                       (362.70-362.77)

362.50 Macular degeneration (senile), unspecified

362.51 Nonexudative senile macular degeneration
     Senile macular degeneration:
     atrophic
     dry

√4ᵗʰ
√5ᵗʰ Additional Digit Required   Unspecified Code   Other Specified Code   Manifestation Code   ▶◀ Revised Text   ● New Code   ▲ Revised Code Title

2010 ICD-9-CM   **February 2009 • Volume 1 – 105**

362.52 **Exudative senile macular degeneration**
Kuhnt-Junius degeneration
Senile macular degeneration:
disciform
wet
DEF: Leakage in macular blood vessels with loss of visual acuity.

362.53 **Cystoid macular degeneration**
Cystoid macular edema
DEF: Retinal swelling and cyst formation in macula.

362.54 **Macular cyst, hole, or pseudohole**

362.55 **Toxic maculopathy**
Use additional E code to identify drug, if drug induced

362.56 **Macular puckering**
Preretinal fibrosis

362.57 **Drusen (degenerative)**
DEF: White, hyaline deposits on Bruch's membrane (lamina basalis choroideae).

√5ᵗʰ **362.6** **Peripheral retinal degenerations**
EXCLUDES hereditary retinal degeneration [dystrophy] (362.70-362.77)
retinal degeneration with retinal defect (361.00-361.07)

362.60 **Peripheral retinal degeneration, unspecified**

362.61 **Paving stone degeneration**
DEF: Degeneration of peripheral retina; causes thinning through which choroid is visible.

362.62 **Microcystoid degeneration**
Blessig's cysts   Iwanoff's cysts

362.63 **Lattice degeneration**
Palisade degeneration of retina
DEF: Degeneration of retina; often bilateral, usually benign; characterized by lines intersecting at irregular intervals in peripheral retina; retinal thinning and retinal holes may occur.

362.64 **Senile reticular degeneration**
DEF: Net-like appearance of retina; sign of degeneration.

362.65 **Secondary pigmentary degeneration**
Pseudoretinitis pigmentosa

362.66 **Secondary vitreoretinal degenerations**

√5ᵗʰ **362.7** **Hereditary retinal dystrophies**
DEF: Genetically induced progressive changes in retina.

362.70 **Hereditary retinal dystrophy, unspecified**

362.71 **Retinal dystrophy in systemic or cerebroretinal lipidoses**
Code first underlying disease, as:
cerebroretinal lipidoses (330.1)
systemic lipidoses (272.7)

362.72 **Retinal dystrophy in other systemic disorders and syndromes**
Code first underlying disease, as:
Bassen-Kornzweig syndrome (272.5)
Refsum's disease (356.3)

362.73 **Vitreoretinal dystrophies**
Juvenile retinoschisis

362.74 **Pigmentary retinal dystrophy**
Retinal dystrophy, albipunctate
Retinitis pigmentosa

362.75 **Other dystrophies primarily involving the sensory retina**
Progressive cone(-rod) dystrophy
Stargardt's disease

362.76 **Dystrophies primarily involving the retinal pigment epithelium**
Fundus flavimaculatus
Vitelliform dystrophy

362.77 **Dystrophies primarily involving Bruch's membrane**
Dystrophy:
hyaline
pseudoinflammatory foveal
Hereditary drusen

√5ᵗʰ **362.8** **Other retinal disorders**
EXCLUDES chorioretinal inflammations (363.0-363.2)
chorioretinal scars (363.30-363.35)

362.81 **Retinal hemorrhage**
Hemorrhage:
preretinal
retinal (deep) (superficial)
subretinal
AHA: 4Q, '96, 43

362.82 **Retinal exudates and deposits**

362.83 **Retinal edema**
Retinal:
cotton wool spots
edema (localized) (macular) (peripheral)
DEF: Retinal swelling due to fluid accumulation.

362.84 **Retinal ischemia**
DEF: Reduced retinal blood supply.

362.85 **Retinal nerve fiber bundle defects**

362.89 **Other retinal disorders**

362.9 **Unspecified retinal disorder**

√4ᵗʰ **363** **Chorioretinal inflammations, scars, and other disorders of choroid**

√5ᵗʰ **363.0** **Focal chorioretinitis and focal retinochoroiditis**
EXCLUDES focal chorioretinitis or retinochoroiditis in:
histoplasmosis (115.02, 115.12, 115.92)
toxoplasmosis (130.2)
congenital infection (771.2)

363.00 **Focal chorioretinitis, unspecified**
Focal:
choroiditis or chorioretinitis NOS
retinitis or retinochoroiditis NOS

363.01 **Focal choroiditis and chorioretinitis, juxtapapillary**

363.03 **Focal choroiditis and chorioretinitis of other posterior pole**

363.04 **Focal choroiditis and chorioretinitis, peripheral**

363.05 **Focal retinitis and retinochoroiditis, juxtapapillary**
Neuroretinitis

363.06 **Focal retinitis and retinochoroiditis, macular or paramacular**

363.07 **Focal retinitis and retinochoroiditis of other posterior pole**

363.08 **Focal retinitis and retinochoroiditis, peripheral**

√5ᵗʰ **363.1** **Disseminated chorioretinitis and disseminated retinochoroiditis**
EXCLUDES disseminated choroiditis or chorioretinitis in secondary syphilis (091.51)
neurosyphilitic disseminated retinitis or retinochoroiditis (094.83)
retinal (peri)vasculitis (362.18)

363.10 **Disseminated chorioretinitis, unspecified**
Disseminated:
choroiditis or chorioretinitis NOS
retinitis or retinochoroiditis NOS

363.11 **Disseminated choroiditis and, chorioretinitis posterior pole**

363.12 **Disseminated choroiditis and chorioretinitis, peripheral**

Ⓝ Newborn Age: 0   Ⓟ Pediatric Age: 0-17   Ⓜ Maternity Age: 12-55   Ⓐ Adult Age: 15-124

363.13 Disseminated choroiditis and chorioretinitis, generalized

Code first any underlying disease, as:
tuberculosis (017.3)

363.14 Disseminated retinitis and retinochoroiditis, metastatic

363.15 Disseminated retinitis and retinochoroiditis, pigment epitheliopathy

Acute posterior multifocal placoid pigment epitheliopathy

DEF: Widespread inflammation of retina and choroid; characterized by pigmented epithelium involvement.

√5th **363.2 Other and unspecified forms of chorioretinitis and retinochoroiditis**

EXCLUDES   panophthalmitis (360.02)
sympathetic uveitis (360.11)
uveitis NOS (364.3)

363.20 Chorioretinitis, unspecified

Choroiditis NOS   Uveitis, posterior NOS
Retinitis NOS

363.21 Pars planitis

Posterior cyclitis

DEF: Inflammation of peripheral retina and ciliary body; characterized by bands of white cells.

363.22 Harada's disease

DEF: Retinal detachment and bilateral widespread exudative choroiditis; symptoms include headache, vomiting, increased lymphocytes in cerebrospinal fluid; with temporary or permanent deafness.

√5th **363.3 Chorioretinal scars**

Scar (postinflammatory) (postsurgical) (posttraumatic):
choroid
retina

363.30 Chorioretinal scar, unspecified

363.31 Solar retinopathy

DEF: Retinal scarring caused by solar radiation.

363.32 Other macular scars

363.33 Other scars of posterior pole

363.34 Peripheral scars

363.35 Disseminated scars

√5th **363.4 Choroidal degenerations**

363.40 Choroidal degeneration, unspecified

Choroidal sclerosis NOS

363.41 Senile atrophy of choroid

DEF: Wasting away of choroid; due to aging.

363.42 Diffuse secondary atrophy of choroid

DEF: Wasting away of choroid in systemic disease.

363.43 Angioid streaks of choroid

DEF: Degeneration of choroid; characterized by dark brown steaks radiating from optic disk; occurs with pseudoxanthoma, elasticum or Paget's disease.

√5th **363.5 Hereditary choroidal dystrophies**

Hereditary choroidal atrophy:
partial [choriocapillaris]
total [all vessels]

363.50 Hereditary choroidal dystrophy or atrophy, unspecified

363.51 Circumpapillary dystrophy of choroid, partial

363.52 Circumpapillary dystrophy of choroid, total

Helicoid dystrophy of choroid

363.53 Central dystrophy of choroid, partial

Dystrophy, choroidal:
central areolar
circinate

363.54 Central choroidal atrophy, total

Dystrophy, choroidal:
central gyrate
serpiginous

363.55 Choroideremia

DEF: Hereditary choroid degeneration, occurs in first decade; characterized by constricted visual field and ultimately blindness in males; less debilitating in females.

363.56 Other diffuse or generalized dystrophy, partial

Diffuse choroidal sclerosis

363.57 Other diffuse or generalized dystrophy, total

Generalized gyrate atrophy, choroid

√5th **363.6 Choroidal hemorrhage and rupture**

363.61 Choroidal hemorrhage, unspecified

363.62 Expulsive choroidal hemorrhage

363.63 Choroidal rupture

√5th **363.7 Choroidal detachment**

363.70 Choroidal detachment, unspecified

363.71 Serous choroidal detachment

DEF: Detachment of choroid from sclera; due to blister of serous fluid.

363.72 Hemorrhagic choroidal detachment

DEF: Detachment of choroid from sclera; due to blood-filled blister.

363.8 Other disorders of choroid

363.9 Unspecified disorder of choroid

√4th **364 Disorders of iris and ciliary body**

√5th **364.0 Acute and subacute iridocyclitis**

Anterior uveitis
Cylitis   } acute, subacute
Iridocyclitis
Iritis

EXCLUDES   gonococcal (098.41)
herpes simplex (054.44)
herpes zoster (053.22)

364.00 Acute and subacute iridocyclitis, unspecified

364.01 Primary iridocyclitis

364.02 Recurrent iridocyclitis

364.03 Secondary iridocyclitis, infectious

364.04 Secondary iridocyclitis, noninfectious

Aqueous:
cells
fibrin
flare

364.05 Hypopyon

DEF: Accumulation of white blood cells between cornea and lens.

√5th **364.1 Chronic iridocyclitis**

EXCLUDES   posterior cyclitis (363.21)

364.10 Chronic iridocyclitis, unspecified

364.11 Chronic iridocyclitis in diseases classified elsewhere

Code first underlying disease, as:
sarcoidosis (135)
tuberculosis (017.3)

EXCLUDES   syphilitic iridocyclitis (091.52)

DEF: Persistent inflammation of iris and ciliary body; due to underlying disease or condition.

√5th **364.2 Certain types of iridocyclitis**

EXCLUDES   posterior cyclitis (363.21)
sympathetic uveitis (360.11)

364.21 Fuchs' heterochromic cyclitis

DEF: Chronic cyclitis characterized by differences in the color of the two irises; the lighter iris appears in the inflamed eye.

√4th
√5th   Additional Digit Required   Unspecified Code   Other Specified Code   Manifestation Code   ►◄ Revised Text   ● New Code   ▲ Revised Code Title

2010 ICD-9-CM   **Volume 1 – 107**

Nervous System and Sense Organs

364.22–364.82

364.22 Glaucomatocyclitic crises
DEF: An uncommon inflammatory unilateral eye condition, characteristic recurrent episodes of high intraocular pressure accompanied by mild inflammation.

364.23 Lens-induced iridocyclitis
DEF: Inflammation of iris; due to immune reaction to pro- teins in lens following trauma or other lens abnormality.

364.24 Vogt-Koyanagi syndrome
DEF: Uveomeningitis with exudative iridocyclitis and choroiditis; causes depigmentation of hair and skin, detached retina; tinnitus and loss of hearing.

364.3 Unspecified iridocyclitis
Uveitis NOS

√5ᵗʰ **364.4 Vascular disorders of iris and ciliary body**

364.41 Hyphema
Hemorrhage of iris or ciliary body
DEF: Hemorrhage in anterior chamber; also called hyphemia or "blood shot" eyes.

364.42 Rubeosis iridis
Neovascularization of iris or ciliary body
DEF: Blood vessel and connective tissue formation on surface of iris; symptomatic of diabetic retinopathy, central retinal vein occlusion and retinal detachment.

√5ᵗʰ **364.5 Degenerations of iris and ciliary body**

364.51 Essential or progressive iris atrophy

364.52 Iridoschisis
DEF: Splitting of the iris into two layers.

364.53 Pigmentary iris degeneration
Acquired heterochromia
Pigment dispersion syndrome } of iris
Translucency

364.54 Degeneration of pupillary margin
Atrophy of sphincter } of iris
Ectropion of pigment epithelium

364.55 Miotic cysts of pupillary margin
DEF: Serous-filled sacs in pupillary margin of iris.

364.56 Degenerative changes of chamber angle

364.57 Degenerative changes of ciliary body

364.59 Other iris atrophy
Iris atrophy (generalized) (sector shaped)

√5ᵗʰ **364.6 Cysts of iris, ciliary body, and anterior chamber**
EXCLUDES miotic pupillary cyst (364.55)
parasitic cyst (360.13)

364.60 Idiopathic cysts
DEF: Fluid-filled sacs in iris or ciliary body; unknown etiology.

364.61 Implantation cysts
Epithelial down-growth, anterior chamber
Implantation cysts (surgical) (traumatic)

364.62 Exudative cysts of iris or anterior chamber

364.63 Primary cyst of pars plana
DEF: Fluid-filled sacs of outermost ciliary ring.

364.64 Exudative cyst of pars plana
DEF: Protein, fatty-filled sacs of outermost ciliary ring; due to fluid lead from blood vessels.

√5ᵗʰ **364.7 Adhesions and disruptions of iris and ciliary body**
EXCLUDES flat anterior chamber (360.34)

364.70 Adhesions of iris, unspecified
Synechiae (iris) NOS

364.71 Posterior synechiae
DEF: Adhesion binding iris to lens.

364.72 Anterior synechiae
DEF: Adhesion binding the iris to cornea.

364.73 Goniosynechiae
Peripheral anterior synechiae
DEF: Adhesion binding the iris to cornea at the angle of the anterior chamber.

364.74 Pupillary membranes
Iris bombé
Pupillary:
    occlusion
    seclusion
DEF: Membrane traversing the pupil and blocking vision.

364.75 Pupillary abnormalities
Deformed pupil
Ectopic pupil
Rupture of sphincter, pupil

364.76 Iridodialysis
DEF: Separation of the iris from the ciliary body base; due to trauma or surgical accident.

364.77 Recession of chamber angle
DEF: Receding of anterior chamber angle of the eye; restricts vision.

√5ᵗʰ **364.8 Other disorders of iris and ciliary body**
AHA: 2Q, '07, 9

364.81 Floppy iris syndrome
Intraoperative floppy iris syndrome [IFIS]
Use additional E code to identify cause, such as:
    sympatholytics [antiadrenergics] causing
        adverse effect in therapeutic use
        (E941.3)
DEF: Condition complicating cataract surgery for patients who have received alpha blocker treatment for urinary retention problems; iris dilator muscle fails to dilate, and the iris may billow or flap.
AHA: 4Q, '07, 77, 79

364.82 Plateau iris syndrome
DEF: ▶A postoperative chronic angle-closure glaucoma characterized by closing of the anterior chamber angle secondary to a large or anteriorly positioned ciliary body that impairs the normal flow of aqueous fluid.◀
AHA: ▶4Q, '08, 112◀

▶**Plateau Iris Syndrome**◀

▶**Normal Aqueous Flow**◀

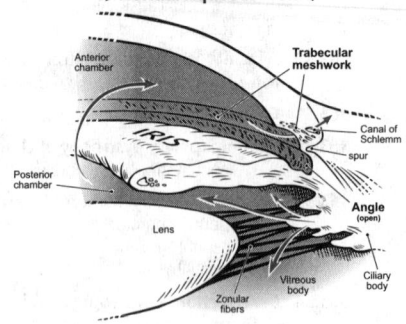

364.89 **Other disorders of iris and ciliary body**
Prolapse of iris NOS

EXCLUDES prolapse of iris in recent wound (871.1)

364.9 **Unspecified disorder of iris and ciliary body**

√4th **365** **Glaucoma**

EXCLUDES blind hypertensive eye [absolute glaucoma] (360.42)
congenital glaucoma (743.20-743.22)

DEF: Rise in intraocular pressure restricting blood flow; multiple causes.

√5th **365.0** **Borderline glaucoma [glaucoma suspect]**
AHA: 1Q, '90, 8

365.00 **Preglaucoma, unspecified**

365.01 **Open angle with borderline findings**
Open angle with:
borderline intraocular pressure
cupping of optic discs

DEF: Minor block of aqueous outflow from eye.

365.02 **Anatomical narrow angle**

365.03 **Steroid responders**

365.04 **Ocular hypertension**
DEF: High fluid pressure within eye; no apparent cause.

√5th **365.1** **Open-angle glaucoma**

365.10 **Open-angle glaucoma, unspecified**
Wide-angle glaucoma NOS

365.11 **Primary open angle glaucoma**
Chronic simple glaucoma
DEF: High intraocular pressure, despite free flow of aqueous.

365.12 **Low tension glaucoma**

365.13 **Pigmentary glaucoma**
DEF: High intraocular pressure; due to iris pigment granules blocking aqueous flow.

365.14 **Glaucoma of childhood**
Infantile or juvenile glaucoma

365.15 **Residual stage of open angle glaucoma**

√5th **365.2** **Primary angle-closure glaucoma**
DEF: ▶Glaucoma caused by a shift in the position of the iris of the eye that blocks the surface of the trabecular meshwork causing impairment of the normal flow of aqueous fluid.◀

365.20 **Primary angle-closure glaucoma, unspecified**

365.21 **Intermittent angle-closure glaucoma**
Angle-closure glaucoma:
interval
subacute
DEF: Recurring attacks of high intraocular pressure; due to blocked aqueous flow.

365.22 **Acute angle-closure glaucoma**
DEF: Sudden, severe rise in intraocular pressure due to blockage in aqueous drainage.

365.23 **Chronic angle-closure glaucoma**
AHA: 2Q, '98, 16

365.24 **Residual stage of angle-closure glaucoma**

▶Angle Closure Glaucoma◀

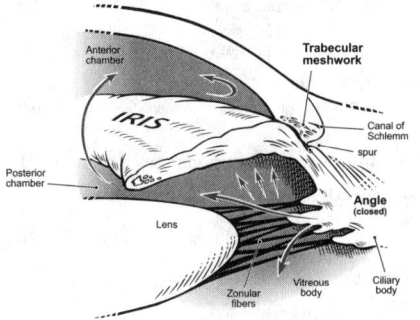

√5th **365.3** **Corticosteroid-induced glaucoma**
DEF: Elevated intraocular pressure; due to long-term corticosteroid therapy.

365.31 **Glaucomatous stage**

365.32 **Residual stage**

√5th **365.4** **Glaucoma associated with congenital anomalies, dystrophies, and systemic syndromes**

365.41 **Glaucoma associated with chamber angle anomalies**

365.42 **Glaucoma associated with anomalies of iris**

365.43 **Glaucoma associated with other anterior segment anomalies**

365.44 *Glaucoma associated with systemic syndromes*
Code first associated disease, as
neurofibromatosis (237.7)
Sturge-Weber (-Dimitri) syndrome (759.6)

√5th **365.5** **Glaucoma associated with disorders of the lens**

365.51 **Phacolytic glaucoma**
DEF: Elevated intraocular pressure; due to lens protein blocking aqueous flow.

365.52 **Pseudoexfoliation glaucoma**
DEF: Glaucoma characterized by small grayish particles deposited on the lens.

365.59 **Glaucoma associated with other lens disorders**

√5th **365.6** **Glaucoma associated with other ocular disorders**

365.60 **Glaucoma associated with unspecified ocular disorder**

365.61 **Glaucoma associated with pupillary block**
DEF: Acute, open-angle glaucoma caused by mature cataract; aqueous flow is blocked by lens material and macrophages.

365.62 **Glaucoma associated with ocular inflammations**

365.63 **Glaucoma associated with vascular disorders**

365.64 **Glaucoma associated with tumors or cysts**

365.65 **Glaucoma associated with ocular trauma**

√5th **365.8** **Other specified forms of glaucoma**

365.81 **Hypersecretion glaucoma**

365.82 **Glaucoma with increased episcleral venous pressure**

365.83 **Aqueous misdirection**
Malignant glaucoma
DEF: A form of secondary angle-closure glaucoma that occurs when aqueous humor flows into the posterior chamber of the eye (vitreous) rather than through the normal recycling channels.
AHA: 4Q, '02, 48

365.89 **Other specified glaucoma**
AHA: 2Q, '98, 16

365.9 **Unspecified glaucoma**
AHA: 3Q, '03, 14; 2Q, '01, 16
H40.9 Unspecified glaucoma   I-10

√4th **366** **Cataract**

EXCLUDES congenital cataract (743.30-743.34)
DEF: A variety of conditions that create a cloudy, or calcified lens that obstructs vision.

√5th **366.0** **Infantile, juvenile, and presenile cataract**

366.00 **Nonsenile cataract, unspecified**

366.01 **Anterior subcapsular polar cataract**
DEF: Defect within the front, center lens surface.

366.02 **Posterior subcapsular polar cataract**
DEF: Defect within the rear, center lens surface.

Nervous System and Sense Organs

366.03–367.51

Cataract

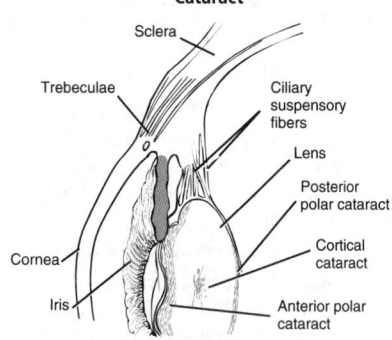

Sclera
Trebeculae
Ciliary suspensory fibers
Lens
Posterior polar cataract
Cortical cataract
Cornea
Iris
Anterior polar cataract

366.03 Cortical, lamellar, or zonular cataract
> **DEF:** Opacities radiating from center to edge of lens; appear as thin, concentric layers of lens.

366.04 Nuclear cataract

366.09 Other and combined forms of nonsenile cataract

√5ᵗʰ **366.1 Senile cataract**
> **AHA:** 3Q, '91, 9; S-0, '85, 10

366.10 Senile cataract, unspecified Ⓐ
> **AHA:** 1Q, '03, 5

366.11 Pseudoexfoliation of lens capsule Ⓐ

366.12 Incipient cataract Ⓐ
> Cataract: Cataract:
>   coronary   punctate
>   immature NOS   Water clefts
> **DEF:** Minor disorders of lens not affecting vision; due to aging.

366.13 Anterior subcapsular polar senile cataract Ⓐ

366.14 Posterior subcapsular polar senile cataract Ⓐ

366.15 Cortical senile cataract Ⓐ

366.16 Nuclear sclerosis Ⓐ
> Cataracta brunescens
> Nuclear cataract
> **AHA:** 4Q, '07, 79

366.17 Total or mature cataract Ⓐ

366.18 Hypermature cataract Ⓐ
> Morgagni cataract

366.19 Other and combined forms of senile cataract Ⓐ

√5ᵗʰ **366.2 Traumatic cataract**

366.20 Traumatic cataract, unspecified

366.21 Localized traumatic opacities
> Vossius' ring

366.22 Total traumatic cataract

366.23 Partially resolved traumatic cataract

√5ᵗʰ **366.3 Cataract secondary to ocular disorders**

366.30 Cataracta complicata, unspecified

366.31 Glaucomatous flecks (subcapsular)
> Code first underlying glaucoma (365.0-365.9)

366.32 Cataract in inflammatory disorders
> Code first underlying condition, as:
>   chronic choroiditis (363.0-363.2)

366.33 Cataract with neovascularization
> Code first underlying condition, as:
>   chronic iridocyclitis (364.10)

366.34 Cataract in degenerative disorders
> Sunflower cataract
> Code first underlying condition, as:
>   chalcosis (360.24)
>   degenerative myopia (360.21)
>   pigmentary retinal dystrophy (362.74)

√5ᵗʰ **366.4 Cataract associated with other disorders**

366.41 Diabetic cataract
> Code first diabetes (249.5, 250.5)
> **AHA:** 3Q, '91, 9; S-O, '85, 11

366.42 Tetanic cataract
> Code first underlying disease, as:
>   calcinosis (275.4)
>   hypoparathyroidism (252.1)

366.43 Myotonic cataract
> Code first underlying disorder (359.21, 359.23)

366.44 Cataract associated with other syndromes
> Code first underlying condition, as:
>   craniofacial dysostosis (756.0)
>   galactosemia (271.1)

366.45 Toxic cataract
> Drug-induced cataract
> Use additional E code to identify drug or other toxic substance

366.46 Cataract associated with radiation and other physical influences
> Use additional E code to identify cause

√5ᵗʰ **366.5 After-cataract**

366.50 After-cataract, unspecified
> Secondary cataract NOS

366.51 Soemmering's ring
> **DEF:** A donut-shaped lens remnant and a capsule behind the pupil as a result of cataract surgery or trauma.

366.52 Other after-cataract, not obscuring vision

366.53 After-cataract, obscuring vision

366.8 Other cataract
> Calcification of lens

366.9 Unspecified cataract
> H26.9 Unspecified cataract   I-10

√4ᵗʰ **367 Disorders of refraction and accommodation**

367.0 Hypermetropia
> Far-sightedness
> Hyperopia
> **DEF:** Refraction error, called also hyperopia, focal point is posterior to retina; abnormally short anteroposterior diameter or subnormal refractive power; causes farsightedness.

367.1 Myopia
> Near-sightedness
> **DEF:** Refraction error, focal point is anterior to retina; causes near-sightedness.

√5ᵗʰ **367.2 Astigmatism**

367.20 Astigmatism, unspecified

367.21 Regular astigmatism

367.22 Irregular astigmatism

√5ᵗʰ **367.3 Anisometropia and aniseikonia**

367.31 Anisometropia
> **DEF:** Eyes with refractive powers that differ by at least one diopter.

367.32 Aniseikonia
> **DEF:** Eyes with unequal retinal imaging; usually due to refractive error.

367.4 Presbyopia
> **DEF:** Loss of crystalline lens elasticity; causes errors of accommodation; due to aging.

√5ᵗʰ **367.5 Disorders of accommodation**

367.51 Paresis of accommodation
> Cycloplegia
> **DEF:** Partial paralysis of ciliary muscle; causing focus problems.

Ⓝ Newborn Age: 0   Ⓟ Pediatric Age: 0-17   Ⓜ Maternity Age: 12-55   Ⓐ Adult Age: 15-124

367.52　Total or complete internal ophthalmoplegia
　　　DEF: Total paralysis of ciliary muscle; large pupil incapable of focus.

367.53　Spasm of accommodation
　　　DEF: Abnormal contraction of ciliary muscle; causes focus problems.

√5ᵗʰ **367.8　Other disorders of refraction and accommodation**

367.81　Transient refractive change

367.89　Other
　　　Drug-induced ⎫ disorders of refraction and
　　　Toxic　　　⎭　　accommodation

367.9　Unspecified disorder of refraction and accommodation

√4ᵗʰ **368　Visual disturbances**
　　　EXCLUDES *electrophysiological disturbances (794.11-794.14)*

√5ᵗʰ **368.0　Amblyopia ex anopsia**
　　　DEF: Vision impaired due to disuse; esotropia often cause.

368.00　Amblyopia, unspecified

368.01　Strabismic amblyopia
　　　Suppression amblyopia

368.02　Deprivation amblyopia
　　　DEF: Decreased vision associated with suppressed retinal image of one eye.

368.03　Refractive amblyopia

√5ᵗʰ **368.1　Subjective visual disturbances**

368.10　Subjective visual disturbance, unspecified

368.11　Sudden visual loss

368.12　Transient visual loss
　　　Concentric fading　　　Scintillating scotoma

368.13　Visual discomfort
　　　Asthenopia　　　Photophobia
　　　Eye strain

368.14　Visual distortions of shape and size
　　　Macropsia　　　Micropsia
　　　Metamorphopsia

368.15　Other visual distortions and entoptic phenomena
　　　Photopsia　　　　Refractive:
　　　Refractive:　　　　polyopia
　　　　diplopia　　　Visual halos

368.16　Psychophysical visual disturbances
　　　Prosopagnosia
　　　Visual:
　　　　agnosia
　　　　disorientation syndrome
　　　　hallucinations
　　　　object agnosia

368.2　Diplopia
　　　Double vision
　　　H53.2　Diplopia　　　　　　　　　　　　　I-10

√5ᵗʰ **368.3　Other disorders of binocular vision**

368.30　Binocular vision disorder, unspecified

368.31　Suppression of binocular vision

368.32　Simultaneous visual perception without fusion

368.33　Fusion with defective stereopsis
　　　DEF: Faulty depth perception though normal ability to focus.

368.34　Abnormal retinal correspondence

√5ᵗʰ **368.4　Visual field defects**

368.40　Visual field defect, unspecified

368.41　Scotoma involving central area
　　　Scotoma:　　　　Scotoma:
　　　　central　　　　　paracentral
　　　　centrocecal
　　　DEF: Vision loss (blind spot) in central five degrees of visual field.

368.42　Scotoma of blind spot area
　　　Enlarged:　　　　Paracecal scotoma
　　　　angioscotoma
　　　　blind spot

368.43　Sector or arcuate defects
　　　Scotoma:　　　　Scotoma:
　　　　arcuate　　　　　Seidel
　　　　Bjerrum
　　　DEF: Arc-shaped blind spot caused by retinal nerve damage.

368.44　Other localized visual field defect
　　　Scotoma:　　　　Visual field defect:
　　　　NOS　　　　　　nasal step
　　　　ring　　　　　　peripheral

368.45　Generalized contraction or constriction

368.46　Homonymous bilateral field defects
　　　Hemianopsia (altitudinal) (homonymous)
　　　Quadrant anopia
　　　DEF: Disorders found in the corresponding vertical halves of the visual fields of both eyes.

368.47　Heteronymous bilateral field defects
　　　Hemianopsia:　　　Hemianopsia:
　　　　binasal　　　　　bitemporal
　　　DEF: Disorders in the opposite halves of the visual fields of both eyes.

√5ᵗʰ **368.5　Color vision deficiencies**
　　　Color blindness

368.51　Protan defect
　　　Protanomaly
　　　Protanopia
　　　DEF: Mild difficulty distinguishing green and red hues with shortened spectrum; sex-linked affecting one percent of males.

368.52　Deutan defect
　　　Deuteranomaly
　　　Deuteranopia
　　　DEF: Male-only disorder; difficulty in distinguishing green and red, no shortened spectrum.

368.53　Tritan defect
　　　Tritanomaly
　　　Tritanopia
　　　DEF: Difficulty in distinguishing blue and yellow; occurs often due to drugs, retinal detachment and central nervous system diseases.

368.54　Achromatopsia
　　　Monochromatism (cone) (rod)
　　　DEF: Complete color blindness; caused by disease, injury to retina, optic nerve or pathway.

368.55　Acquired color vision deficiencies

368.59　Other color vision deficiencies

√5ᵗʰ **368.6　Night blindness**
　　　Nyctalopia
　　　DEF: Nyctalopia: disorder of vision in dim light or night blindness.

368.60　Night blindness, unspecified

368.61　Congenital night blindness
　　　Hereditary night blindness
　　　Oguchi's disease

368.62　Acquired night blindness
　　　EXCLUDES *that due to vitamin A deficiency (264.5)*

368.63　Abnormal dark adaptation curve
　　　Abnormal threshold ⎫ of cones or rods
　　　Delayed adaptation　⎭

368.69　Other night blindness

Nervous System and Sense Organs

368.8–369.61

368.8 **Other specified visual disturbances**
Blurred vision NOS
AHA: 4Q, '02, 56

368.9 **Unspecified visual disturbance**
AHA: 3Q, '06, 22; 1Q, '04, 15

✓4th **369** **Blindness and low vision**
Note: Visual impairment refers to a functional limitation of the eye (e.g., limited visual acuity or visual field). It should be distinguished from visual disability, indicating a limitation of the abilities of the individual (e.g., limited reading skills, vocational skills), and from visual handicap, indicating a limitation of personal and socioeconomic independence (e.g., limited mobility, limited employability).

The levels of impairment defined in the table on this page are based on the recommendations of the WHO Study Group on Prevention of Blindness (Geneva, November 6-10, 1972; WHO Technical Report Series 518), and of the International Council of Ophthalmology (1976).

Note that definitions of blindness vary in different settings.

For international reporting WHO defines blindness as profound impairment. This definition can be applied to blindness of one eye (369.1, 369.6) and to blindness of the individual (369.0).

For determination of benefits in the U.S.A., the definition of legal blindness as severe impairment is often used. This definition applies to blindness of the individual only.

EXCLUDES *correctable impaired vision due to refractive errors (367.0-367.9)*

✓5th **369.0** **Profound impairment, both eyes**

369.00 **Impairment level not further specified**
Blindness:
NOS according to WHO definition
both eyes

369.01 **Better eye: total impairment; lesser eye: total impairment**

369.02 **Better eye: near-total impairment; lesser eye: not further specified**

369.03 **Better eye: near-total impairment; lesser eye: total impairment**

369.04 **Better eye: near-total impairment; lesser eye: near-total impairment**

369.05 **Better eye: profound impairment; lesser eye: not further specified**

369.06 **Better eye: profound impairment; lesser eye: total impairment**

369.07 **Better eye: profound impairment; lesser eye: near-total impairment**

369.08 **Better eye: profound impairment; lesser eye: profound impairment**

✓4th **369.1** **Moderate or severe impairment, better eye, profound impairment lesser eye**

369.10 **Impairment level not further specified**
Blindness, one eye, low vision other eye

369.11 **Better eye: severe impairment; lesser eye: blind, not further specified**

369.12 **Better eye: severe impairment; lesser eye: total impairment**

369.13 **Better eye: severe impairment; lesser eye: near-total impairment**

369.14 **Better eye: severe impairment; lesser eye: profound impairment**

369.15 **Better eye: moderate impairment; lesser eye: blind, not further specified**

369.16 **Better eye: moderate impairment; lesser eye: total impairment**

369.17 **Better eye: moderate impairment; lesser eye: near-total impairment**

369.18 **Better eye: moderate impairment; lesser eye: profound impairment**

✓5th **369.2** **Moderate or severe impairment, both eyes**

369.20 **Impairment level not further specified**
Low vision, both eyes NOS

369.21 **Better eye: severe impairment; lesser eye: not further specified**

369.22 **Better eye: severe impairment; lesser eye: severe impairment**

369.23 **Better eye: moderate impairment; lesser eye: not further specified**

369.24 **Better eye: moderate impairment; lesser eye: severe impairment**

369.25 **Better eye: moderate impairment; lesser eye: moderate impairment**

369.3 **Unqualified visual loss, both eyes**
EXCLUDES *blindness NOS:*
legal [U.S.A. definition] (369.4)
WHO definition (369.00)

369.4 **Legal blindness, as defined in U.S.A.**
Blindness NOS according to U.S.A. definition
EXCLUDES *legal blindness with specification of impairment level (369.01-369.08, 369.11-369.14, 369.21-369.22)*

H54.8 Legal blindness as defined in USA   I-10

✓5th **369.6** **Profound impairment, one eye**

369.60 **Impairment level not further specified**
Blindness, one eye

369.61 **One eye: total impairment; other eye: not specified**

Classification		LEVELS OF VISUAL IMPAIRMENT	Additional descriptors which may be encountered
"legal"	WHO	Visual acuity and/or visual field limitation (whichever is worse)	
(NEAR-) NORMAL VISION	NORMAL VISION	RANGE OF NORMAL VISION 20/10 20/13 20/16 20/20 20/25 2.0 1.6 1.25 1.0 0.8	
		NEAR-NORMAL VISION 20/30 20/40 20/50 20/60 0.7 0.6 0.5 0.4 0.3	
LOW VISION		MODERATE VISUAL IMPAIRMENT 20/70 20/80 20/100 20/125 20/160 0.25 0.20 0.16 0.12	Moderate low vision
		SEVERE VISUAL IMPAIRMENT 20/200 20/250 20/320 20/400 0.10 0.08 0.06 0.05 Visual field: 20 degrees or less	Severe low vision, "Legal" blindness
LEGAL BLINDNESS (U.S.A.) both eyes	BLINDNESS (WHO) one or both eyes	PROFOUND VISUAL IMPAIRMENT 20/500 20/630 20/800 20/1000 0.04 0.03 0.025 0.02 Count fingers at: less than 3m (10 ft.) Visual field: 10 degrees or less	Profound low vision, Moderate blindness
		NEAR-TOTAL VISUAL IMPAIRMENT Visual acuity: less than 0.02 (20/1000) Count fingers at: 1m (3 ft.) or less Hand movements: 5m (15 ft.) or less Light projection, light perception Visual field: 5 degrees or less	Severe blindness Near-total blindness
		TOTAL VISUAL IMPAIRMENT No light perception (NLP)	Total blindness

Visual acuity refers to best achievable acuity with correction.
Non-listed Snellen fractions may be classified by converting to the nearest decimal equivalent, e.g. 10/200 = 0.05, 6/30 = 0.20.
CF (count fingers) without designation of distance, may be classified to profound impairment.
HM (hand motion) without designation of distance, may be classified to near-total impairment.
Visual field measurements refer to the largest field diameter for a 1/100 white test object.

N Newborn Age: 0   P Pediatric Age: 0-17   M Maternity Age: 12-55   A Adult Age: 15-124

369.62　One eye: total impairment; other eye: near normal vision

369.63　One eye: total impairment; other eye: normal vision

369.64　**One eye: near-total impairment; other eye: not specified**

369.65　One eye: near-total impairment; other eye: near-normal vision

369.66　One eye: near-total impairment; other eye: normal vision

369.67　**One eye: profound impairment; other eye: not specified**

369.68　One eye: profound impairment; other eye: near-normal vision

369.69　One eye: profound impairment; other eye: normal vision

√5th 369.7　Moderate or severe impairment, one eye

369.70　**Impairment level not further specified**
Low vision, one eye

369.71　**One eye: severe impairment; other eye: not specified**

369.72　One eye: severe impairment; other eye: near-normal vision

369.73　One eye: severe impairment; other eye: normal vision

369.74　**One eye: moderate impairment; other eye: not specified**

369.75　One eye: moderate impairment; other eye: near-normal vision

369.76　One eye: moderate impairment; other eye: normal vision

369.8　Unqualified visual loss, one eye

369.9　**Unspecified visual loss**
AHA: 4Q, '02, 114; 3Q, '02, 20

√4th **370　Keratitis**

√5th 370.0　Corneal ulcer
EXCLUDES　that due to vitamin A deficiency (264.3)

370.00　**Corneal ulcer, unspecified**

370.01　**Marginal corneal ulcer**

370.02　**Ring corneal ulcer**

370.03　**Central corneal ulcer**

370.04　**Hypopyon ulcer**
Serpiginous ulcer
DEF: Corneal ulcer with an accumulation of pus in the eye's anterior chamber.

370.05　**Mycotic corneal ulcer**
DEF: Fungal infection causing corneal tissue loss.

370.06　**Perforated corneal ulcer**
DEF: Tissue loss through all layers of cornea.

370.07　**Mooren's ulcer**
DEF: Tissue loss, with chronic inflammation, at junction of cornea and sclera; seen in elderly.

√5th 370.2　Superficial keratitis without conjunctivitis
EXCLUDES　dendritic [herpes simplex] keratitis (054.42)

370.20　**Superficial keratitis, unspecified**

370.21　**Punctate keratitis**
Thygeson's superficial punctate keratitis
DEF: Formation of cellular and fibrinous deposits (keratic precipitates) on posterior surface; deposits develop after injury or iridocyclitis.

370.22　**Macular keratitis**
Keratitis:　　　　Keratitis:
areolar　　　　stellate
nummular　　　striate

370.23　**Filamentary keratitis**
DEF: Keratitis characterized by twisted filaments of mucoid material on the cornea's surface.

370.24　**Photokeratitis**
Snow blindness　　　Welders' keratitis
DEF: Painful, inflamed cornea; due to extended exposure to ultraviolet light.
AHA: 3Q, '96, 6

√5th 370.3　Certain types of keratoconjunctivitis

370.31　**Phlyctenular keratoconjunctivitis**
Phlyctenulosis
Use additional code for any associated tuberculosis (017.3)
DEF: Miniature blister on conjunctiva or cornea; associated with tuberculosis and malnutrition disorders.

370.32　**Limbar and corneal involvement in vernal conjunctivitis**
Use additional code for vernal conjunctivitis (372.13)
DEF: Corneal itching and inflammation in conjunctivitis; often limited to lining of eyelids.

370.33　**Keratoconjunctivitis sicca, not specified as Sjögren's**
EXCLUDES　Sjögren's syndrome (710.2)
DEF: Inflammation of conjunctiva and cornea; characterized by "horny" looking tissue and excess blood in these areas; decreased flow of lacrimal (tear) is a contributing factor.

370.34　**Exposure keratoconjunctivitis**
DEF: Incomplete closure of eyelid causing dry, inflamed eye.

370.35　**Neurotrophic keratoconjunctivitis**

√5th 370.4　Other and unspecified keratoconjunctivitis

370.40　**Keratoconjunctivitis, unspecified**
Superficial keratitis with conjunctivitis NOS

370.44　*Keratitis or keratoconjunctivitis in exanthema*
Code first underlying condition (050.0–052.9)
EXCLUDES　herpes simplex (054.43)
herpes zoster (053.21)
measles (055.71)

370.49　**Other**
EXCLUDES　epidemic keratoconjunctivitis (077.1)

√5th 370.5　Interstitial and deep keratitis

370.50　**Interstitial keratitis, unspecified**

370.52　**Diffuse interstitial keratitis**
Cogan's syndrome
DEF: Inflammation of cornea; with deposits in middle corneal layers; may obscure vision.

370.54　**Sclerosing keratitis**
DEF: Chronic corneal inflammation leading to opaque scarring.

370.55　**Corneal abscess**
DEF: Pocket of pus and inflammation on the cornea.

370.59　**Other**
EXCLUDES　disciform herpes simplex keratitis (054.43)
syphilitic keratitis (090.3)

√5th 370.6　Corneal neovascularization

370.60　**Corneal neovascularization, unspecified**

370.61　**Localized vascularization of cornea**
DEF: Limited infiltration of cornea by new blood vessels.

370.62　**Pannus (corneal)**
DEF: Buildup of superficial vascularization and granulated tissue under epithelium of cornea.
AHA: 3Q, '02, 20

370.63 Deep vascularization of cornea
> **DEF:** Deep infiltration of cornea by new blood vessels.

370.64 Ghost vessels (corneal)

370.8 Other forms of keratitis
> Code first underlying condition, such as:
> Acanthamoeba (136.21)
> Fusarium (118)
> **AHA:** ▶4Q, '08, 80-81;◀ 3Q, '94, 5

370.9 Unspecified keratitis

✓4th **371 Corneal opacity and other disorders of cornea**

✓5th **371.0 Corneal scars and opacities**
> **EXCLUDES** *that due to vitamin A deficiency (264.6)*

371.00 Corneal opacity, unspecified
> Corneal scar NOS

371.01 Minor opacity of cornea
> Corneal nebula

371.02 Peripheral opacity of cornea
> Corneal macula not interfering with central vision

371.03 Central opacity of cornea
> Corneal:
> leucoma ⎱ interfering with central
> macula ⎰ vision

371.04 Adherent leucoma
> **DEF:** Dense, opaque corneal growth adhering to the iris; also spelled as leukoma.

371.05 *Phthisical cornea*
> *Code first underlying tuberculosis (017.3)*

✓5th **371.1 Corneal pigmentations and deposits**

371.10 Corneal deposit, unspecified

371.11 Anterior pigmentations
> Stähli's lines

371.12 Stromal pigmentations
> Hematocornea

371.13 Posterior pigmentations
> Krukenberg spindle

371.14 Kayser-Fleischer ring
> **DEF:** Copper deposits forming ring at outer edge of cornea; seen in Wilson's disease and other liver disorders.

371.15 Other deposits associated with metabolic disorders

371.16 Argentous deposits
> **DEF:** Silver deposits in cornea.

✓5th **371.2 Corneal edema**

371.20 Corneal edema, unspecified

371.21 Idiopathic corneal edema
> **DEF:** Corneal swelling and fluid retention of unknown cause.

371.22 Secondary corneal edema
> **DEF:** Corneal swelling and fluid retention caused by an underlying disease, injury, or condition.

371.23 Bullous keratopathy
> **DEF:** Corneal degeneration; characterized by recurring, rupturing epithelial "blisters;" ruptured blebs expose corneal nerves; occurs in glaucoma, iridocyclitis and Fuchs' epithelial dystrophy.

371.24 Corneal edema due to wearing of contact lenses

✓5th **371.3 Changes of corneal membranes**

371.30 Corneal membrane change, unspecified

371.31 Folds and rupture of Bowman's membrane

371.32 Folds in Descemet's membrane

371.33 Rupture in Descemet's membrane

✓5th **371.4 Corneal degenerations**

371.40 Corneal degeneration, unspecified

371.41 Senile corneal changes
> Arcus senilis   Hassall-Henle bodies

371.42 Recurrent erosion of cornea
> **EXCLUDES** *Mooren's ulcer (370.07)*

371.43 Band-shaped keratopathy
> **DEF:** Horizontal bands of superficial corneal calcium deposits.

371.44 Other calcerous degenerations of cornea

371.45 Keratomalacia NOS
> **EXCLUDES** *that due to vitamin A deficiency (264.4)*
> **DEF:** Destruction of the cornea by keratinization of the epithelium with ulceration and perforation of the cornea; seen in cases of vitamin A deficiency.

371.46 Nodular degeneration of cornea
> Salzmann's nodular dystrophy

371.48 Peripheral degenerations of cornea
> Marginal degeneration of cornea [Terrien's]

371.49 Other
> Discrete colliquative keratopathy

✓5th **371.5 Hereditary corneal dystrophies**
> **DEF:** Genetic disorder; leads to opacities, edema or lesions of cornea.

371.50 Corneal dystrophy, unspecified

371.51 Juvenile epithelial corneal dystrophy

371.52 Other anterior corneal dystrophies
> Corneal dystrophy: Corneal dystrophy
> microscopic cystic   ring-like

371.53 Granular corneal dystrophy

371.54 Lattice corneal dystrophy

371.55 Macular corneal dystrophy

371.56 Other stromal corneal dystrophies
> Crystalline corneal dystrophy

371.57 Endothelial corneal dystrophy
> Combined corneal dystrophy
> Cornea guttata
> Fuchs' endothelial dystrophy

371.58 Other posterior corneal dystrophies
> Polymorphous corneal dystrophy

✓5th **371.6 Keratoconus**
> **DEF:** Bilateral bulging protrusion of anterior cornea; often due to noninflammatory thinning.

371.60 Keratoconus, unspecified

371.61 Keratoconus, stable condition

371.62 Keratoconus, acute hydrops

✓5th **371.7 Other corneal deformities**

371.70 Corneal deformity, unspecified

371.71 Corneal ectasia
> **DEF:** Bulging protrusion of thinned, scarred cornea.

371.72 Descemetocele
> **DEF:** Protrusion of Descemet's membrane into cornea.

371.73 Corneal staphyloma
> **DEF:** Protrusion of cornea into adjacent tissue.

✓5th **371.8 Other corneal disorders**

371.81 Corneal anesthesia and hypoesthesia
> **DEF:** Decreased or absent sensitivity of cornea.

371.82 Corneal disorder due to contact lens
> **EXCLUDES** *corneal edema due to contact lens (371.24)*
> **DEF:** Contact lens wear causing cornea disorder, excluding swelling.

N Newborn Age: 0   P Pediatric Age: 0-17   M Maternity Age: 12-55   A Adult Age: 15-124

371.89 Other

    AHA: 3Q, '99, 12

371.9 Unspecified corneal disorder

✓4th **372 Disorders of conjunctiva**

    EXCLUDES keratoconjunctivitis (370.3-370.4)

✓5th **372.0 Acute conjunctivitis**

    372.00 Acute conjunctivitis, unspecified

    372.01 Serous conjunctivitis, except viral

        EXCLUDES viral conjunctivitis NOS (077.9)

        AHA: 3Q, '08, 6

    372.02 Acute follicular conjunctivitis

        Conjunctival folliculosis NOS

        EXCLUDES conjunctivitis:

            adenoviral (acute follicular)
                (077.3)
            epidemic hemorrhagic (077.4)
            inclusion (077.0)
            Newcastle (077.8)
            epidemic keratoconjunctivitis (077.1)
            pharyngoconjunctival fever (077.2)

        DEF: Severe conjunctival inflammation with dense infiltrations of lymphoid tissues of inner eyelids; may be traced to a viral or chlamydial etiology.

    372.03 Other mucopurulent conjunctivitis

        Catarrhal conjunctivitis

        EXCLUDES blennorrhea neonatorum
                (gonococcal) (098.40)
            neonatal conjunctivitis(771.6)
            ophthalmia neonatorum NOS
                (771.6)

    372.04 Pseudomembranous conjunctivitis

        Membranous conjunctivitis

        EXCLUDES diphtheritic conjunctivitis (032.81)

        DEF: Severe inflammation of conjunctiva; false membrane develops on inner surface of eyelid; membrane can be removed without harming epithelium, due to bacterial infections, toxic and allergic factors, and viral infections.

    372.05 Acute atopic conjunctivitis

        DEF: Sudden, severe conjunctivitis due to allergens.

    372.06 Acute chemical conjunctivitis

        Acute toxic conjunctivitis

        Use additional E code to identify the chemical or toxic agent

        EXCLUDES burn of eye and adnexa
                (940.0-940.9)
            chemical corrosion injury of eye
                (940.2-940.3)

✓5th **372.1 Chronic conjunctivitis**

    372.10 Chronic conjunctivitis, unspecified

    372.11 Simple chronic conjunctivitis

    372.12 Chronic follicular conjunctivitis

        DEF: Persistent conjunctival inflammation with dense, localized infiltrations of lymphoid tissues of inner eyelids.

    372.13 Vernal conjunctivitis

        AHA: 3Q, '96, 8

    372.14 Other chronic allergic conjunctivitis

        AHA: 3Q, '96, 8

    372.15 Parasitic conjunctivitis

        Code first underlying disease, as:
            filariasis (125.0-125.9)
            mucocutaneous leishmaniasis (085.5)

✓5th **372.2 Blepharoconjunctivitis**

    372.20 Blepharoconjunctivitis, unspecified

    372.21 Angular blepharoconjunctivitis

        DEF: Inflammation at junction of upper and lower eyelids; may block lacrimal secretions.

372.22 Contact blepharoconjunctivitis

✓5th **372.3 Other and unspecified conjunctivitis**

    372.30 Conjunctivitis, unspecified

        H10.9 Unspecified conjunctivitis   I-10

    372.31 Rosacea conjunctivitis

        Code first underlying rosacea dermatitis (695.3)

    372.33 Conjunctivitis in mucocutaneous disease

        Code first underlying disease, as:
            erythema multiforme (695.10-695.19)
            Reiter's disease (099.3)

        EXCLUDES ocular pemphigoid (694.61)

    372.34 Pingueculitis

        EXCLUDES ► pinguecula (372.51)◄

        AHA: 4Q, '08, 112-113

    372.39 Other

        AHA: 2Q, '07, 9

✓5th **372.4 Pterygium**

    EXCLUDES pseudopterygium (372.52)

    DEF: Wedge-shaped, conjunctival thickening that advances from the inner corner of the eye toward the cornea.

    372.40 Pterygium, unspecified

    372.41 Peripheral pterygium, stationary

    372.42 Peripheral pterygium, progressive

    372.43 Central pterygium

    372.44 Double pterygium

    372.45 Recurrent pterygium

✓5th **372.5 Conjunctival degenerations and deposits**

    372.50 Conjunctival degeneration, unspecified

    372.51 Pinguecula

        EXCLUDES ► pingueculitis (372.34)◄

        DEF: Proliferative spot on the bulbar conjunctiva located near the sclerocorneal junction, usually on the nasal side; it is seen in elderly people.

    372.52 Pseudopterygium

        DEF: Conjunctival scar joined to the cornea; it looks like a pterygium but is not attached to the tissue.

    372.53 Conjunctival xerosis

        EXCLUDES conjunctival xerosis due to vitamin A
                deficiency (264.0, 264.1, 264.7)

        DEF: Dry conjunctiva due to vitamin A deficiency; related to Bitot's spots; may develop into xerophthalmia and keratomalacia.

    372.54 Conjunctival concretions

        DEF: Calculus or deposit on conjunctiva.

    372.55 Conjunctival pigmentations

        Conjunctival argyrosis

        DEF: Color deposits in conjunctiva.

    372.56 Conjunctival deposits

✓5th **372.6 Conjunctival scars**

    372.61 Granuloma of conjunctiva

    372.62 Localized adhesions and strands of conjunctiva

        DEF: Abnormal fibrous connections in conjunctiva.

    372.63 Symblepharon

        Extensive adhesions of conjunctiva

        DEF: Adhesion of the eyelids to the eyeball.

    372.64 Scarring of conjunctiva

        Contraction of eye socket (after enucleation)

✓5th **372.7 Conjunctival vascular disorders and cysts**

    372.71 Hyperemia of conjunctiva

        DEF: Conjunctival blood vessel congestion causing eye redness.

✓4th ✓5th Additional Digit Required   Unspecified Code   Other Specified Code   Manifestation Code   ►◄ Revised Text   ● New Code   ▲ Revised Code Title

2010 ICD-9-CM   **October 2009 · Volume 1 – 115**

372.72 Conjunctival hemorrhage
Hyposphagma
Subconjunctival hemorrhage

372.73 Conjunctival edema
Chemosis of conjunctiva
Subconjunctival edema
DEF: Fluid retention and swelling in conjunctival tissue.

372.74 Vascular abnormalities of conjunctiva
Aneurysm(ata) of conjunctiva

372.75 Conjunctival cysts
DEF: Abnormal sacs of fluid in conjunctiva.

✓5th **372.8 Other disorders of conjunctiva**

372.81 Conjunctivochalasis
DEF: Bilateral condition of redundant conjunctival tissue between globe and lower eyelid margin; may cover lower punctum, interferring with normal tearing.
AHA: 4Q, '00, 41

372.89 Other disorders of conjunctiva

372.9 Unspecified disorder of conjunctiva

✓4th **373 Inflammation of eyelids**

✓5th **373.0 Blepharitis**
EXCLUDES *blepharoconjunctivitis (372.20-372.22)*

373.00 Blepharitis, unspecified

373.01 Ulcerative blepharitis

373.02 Squamous blepharitis

✓5th **373.1 Hordeolum and other deep inflammation of eyelid**
DEF: Purulent, localized, staphylococcal infection in sebaceous glands of eyelids.

373.11 Hordeolum externum
Hordeolum NOS   Stye
DEF: Infection of the oil glands in the eyelash follicles.

373.12 Hordeolum internum
Infection of meibomian gland
DEF: Infection of the oil gland of the eyelid margin.

373.13 Abscess of eyelid
Furuncle of eyelid
DEF: Inflamed pocket of pus on the eyelid.

373.2 Chalazion
Meibomian (gland) cyst
EXCLUDES *infected meibomian gland (373.12)*
DEF: Chronic inflammation of the meibomian gland, causing an eyelid mass.

✓5th **373.3 Noninfectious dermatoses of eyelid**

373.31 Eczematous dermatitis of eyelid

373.32 Contact and allergic dermatitis of eyelid

373.33 Xeroderma of eyelid

373.34 Discoid lupus erythematosus of eyelid

373.4 Infective dermatitis of eyelid of types resulting in deformity
Code first underlying disease, as:
leprosy (030.0-030.9)
lupus vulgaris (tuberculous) (017.0)
yaws (102.0-102.9)

373.5 Other infective dermatitis of eyelid
Code first underlying disease, as:
actinomycosis (039.3)
impetigo (684)
mycotic dermatitis (110.0-111.9)
vaccinia (051.0)
postvaccination (999.0)
EXCLUDES *herpes:*
simplex (054.41)
zoster (053.20)

373.6 Parasitic infestation of eyelid
Code first underlying disease, as:
leishmaniasis (085.0-085.9)
loiasis (125.2)
onchocerciasis (125.3)
pediculosis (132.0)

373.8 Other inflammations of eyelids

373.9 Unspecified inflammation of eyelid

✓4th **374 Other disorders of eyelids**

✓5th **374.0 Entropion and trichiasis of eyelid**
DEF: Entropion: turning inward of eyelid edge toward eyeball.
DEF: Trichiasis: ingrowing eyelashes marked by irritation with possible distortion of sight.

374.00 Entropion, unspecified

374.01 Senile entropion   Ⓐ

374.02 Mechanical entropion

374.03 Spastic entropion

374.04 Cicatricial entropion

374.05 Trichiasis without entropion

✓5th **374.1 Ectropion**
DEF: Turning outward (eversion) of eyelid edge; exposes palpebral conjunctiva; dryness irritation result.

374.10 Ectropion, unspecified

374.11 Senile ectropion   Ⓐ

374.12 Mechanical ectropion

374.13 Spastic ectropion

374.14 Cicatricial ectropion

✓5th **374.2 Lagophthalmos**
DEF: Incomplete closure of eyes; causes dry eye and other complications.

374.20 Lagophthalmos, unspecified

374.21 Paralytic lagophthalmos

374.22 Mechanical lagophthalmos

374.23 Cicatricial lagophthalmos

✓5th **374.3 Ptosis of eyelid**

374.30 Ptosis of eyelid, unspecified
AHA: 2Q, '96, 11

374.31 Paralytic ptosis
DEF: Drooping of upper eyelid due to nerve disorder.

374.32 Myogenic ptosis
DEF: Drooping of upper eyelid due to muscle disorder.

374.33 Mechanical ptosis
DEF: Outside force causes drooping of upper eyelid.

374.34 Blepharochalasis
Pseudoptosis
DEF: Loss of elasticity, thickened or indurated skin of eyelids associated with recurrent episodes of idiopathic edema causing intracellular tissue atrophy.

Entropion and Ectropion

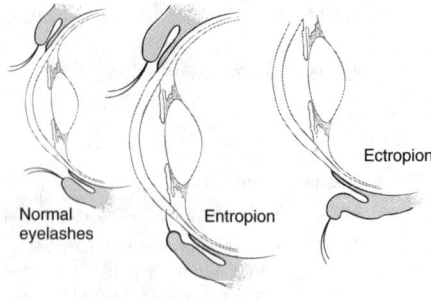

Normal eyelashes   Entropion   Ectropion

Ⓝ Newborn Age: 0   Ⓟ Pediatric Age: 0-17   Ⓜ Maternity Age: 12-55   Ⓐ Adult Age: 15-124

√5th **374.4** **Other disorders affecting eyelid function**

EXCLUDES   *blepharoclonus (333.81)*
blepharospasm (333.81)
facial nerve palsy (351.0)
third nerve palsy or paralysis (378.51-378.52)
tic (psychogenic) (307.20-307.23)
organic (333.3)

374.41 **Lid retraction or lag**

374.43 **Abnormal innervation syndrome**
Jaw-blinking
Paradoxical facial movements

374.44 **Sensory disorders**

374.45 **Other sensorimotor disorders**
Deficient blink reflex

374.46 **Blepharophimosis**
Ankyloblepharon
DEF: Narrowing of palpebral fissure horizontally; caused by laterally displaced inner canthi; either acquired or congenital.

√5th **374.5** **Degenerative disorders of eyelid and periocular area**

374.50 **Degenerative disorder of eyelid, unspecified**

374.51 *Xanthelasma*
Xanthoma (planum) (tuberosum) of eyelid
Code first underlying condition (272.0-272.9)
DEF: Fatty tumors of the eyelid linked to high fat content of blood.

374.52 **Hyperpigmentation of eyelid**
Chloasma
Dyspigmentation
DEF: Excess pigment of eyelid.

374.53 **Hypopigmentation of eyelid**
Vitiligo of eyelid
DEF: Lack of color pigment of the eyelid.

374.54 **Hypertrichosis of eyelid**
DEF: Excessive eyelash growth.

374.55 **Hypotrichosis of eyelid**
Madarosis of eyelid
DEF: Less than normal, or absent, eyelashes.

374.56 **Other degenerative disorders of skin affecting eyelid**

√5th **374.8** **Other disorders of eyelid**

374.81 **Hemorrhage of eyelid**
EXCLUDES   *black eye (921.0)*

374.82 **Edema of eyelid**
Hyperemia of eyelid
DEF: Swelling and fluid retention in eyelid.
AHA: ►4Q, '08, 131◄

374.83 **Elephantiasis of eyelid**
DEF: Filarial disease causing dermatitis and enlargement of eyelid.

374.84 **Cysts of eyelids**
Sebaceous cyst of eyelid

374.85 **Vascular anomalies of eyelid**

374.86 **Retained foreign body of eyelid**

374.87 **Dermatochalasis**
DEF: Acquired form of connective tissue disorder associated with decreased elastic tissue and abnormal elastin formation resulting in loss of elasticity of the skin of the eyelid, generally associated with aging.

374.89 **Other disorders of eyelid**

374.9 **Unspecified disorder of eyelid**

√4th **375** **Disorders of lacrimal system**

√5th **375.0** **Dacryoadenitis**

375.00 **Dacryoadenitis, unspecified**

Lacrimal System

375.01 **Acute dacryoadenitis**
DEF: Severe, sudden inflammation of the lacrimal gland.

375.02 **Chronic dacryoadenitis**
DEF: Persistent inflammation of the lacrimal gland.

375.03 **Chronic enlargement of lacrimal gland**

√5th **375.1** **Other disorders of lacrimal gland**

375.11 **Dacryops**
DEF: Overproduction and constant flow of tears; may cause distended lacrimal duct.

375.12 **Other lacrimal cysts and cystic degeneration**

375.13 **Primary lacrimal atrophy**

375.14 **Secondary lacrimal atrophy**
DEF: Wasting away of the lacrimal gland due to another disease.

375.15 **Tear film insufficiency, unspecified**
Dry eye syndrome
AHA: 3Q, '96, 6
DEF: Eye dryness and irritation from insufficient tear production.

375.16 **Dislocation of lacrimal gland**

√5th **375.2** **Epiphora**
DEF: Abnormal development of tears due to stricture of lacrimal passages.

375.20 **Epiphora, unspecified as to cause**

375.21 **Epiphora due to excess lacrimation**
DEF: Tear overflow due to overproduction.

375.22 **Epiphora due to insufficient drainage**
DEF: Tear overflow due to blocked drainage.

√5th **375.3** **Acute and unspecified inflammation of lacrimal passages**
EXCLUDES   *neonatal dacryocystitis (771.6)*

375.30 **Dacryocystitis, unspecified**

375.31 **Acute canaliculitis, lacrimal**

375.32 **Acute dacryocystitis**
Acute peridacryocystitis

375.33 **Phlegmonous dacryocystitis**
DEF: Infection of the tear sac with pockets of pus.

√5th **375.4** **Chronic inflammation of lacrimal passages**

375.41 **Chronic canaliculitis**

375.42 **Chronic dacryocystitis**

375.43 **Lacrimal mucocele**

√5th **375.5** **Stenosis and insufficiency of lacrimal passages**

375.51 **Eversion of lacrimal punctum**
DEF: Abnormal turning outward of the tear duct.

375.52 **Stenosis of lacrimal punctum**
DEF: Abnormal narrowing of the tear duct.

375.53 **Stenosis of lacrimal canaliculi**

375.54 **Stenosis of lacrimal sac**
DEF: Abnormal narrowing of the tear sac.

375.55 Obstruction of nasolacrimal duct, neonatal

> EXCLUDES congenital anomaly of nasolacrimal duct (743.65)

> **DEF:** Acquired, abnormal obstruction of tear drainage system from the eye to the nose; in an infant.

375.56 Stenosis of nasolacrimal duct, acquired

375.57 Dacryolith

> **DEF:** Concretion or stone anywhere in lacrimal system.

√5th **375.6 Other changes of lacrimal passages**

375.61 Lacrimal fistula

> **DEF:** Abnormal communication from the lacrimal system.

375.69 Other

√5th **375.8 Other disorders of lacrimal system**

375.81 Granuloma of lacrimal passages

> **DEF:** Abnormal nodules within lacrimal system.

375.89 Other

375.9 Unspecified disorder of lacrimal system

√4th **376 Disorders of the orbit**

√5th **376.0 Acute inflammation of orbit**

376.00 Acute inflammation of orbit, unspecified

376.01 Orbital cellulitis

> Abscess of orbit
> **DEF:** Infection of tissue between the orbital bone and eyeball.

376.02 Orbital periostitis

> **DEF:** Inflammation of connective tissue covering the orbital bone.

376.03 Orbital osteomyelitis

> **DEF:** Inflammation of the orbital bone.

376.04 Tenonitis

√5th **376.1 Chronic inflammatory disorders of orbit**

376.10 Chronic inflammation of orbit, unspecified

376.11 Orbital granuloma

> Pseudotumor (inflammatory) of orbit
> **DEF:** Abnormal nodule between orbital bone and eyeball.

376.12 Orbital myositis

> **DEF:** Painful inflammation of the muscles of the eye.

376.13 Parasitic infestation of orbit

> *Code first underlying disease, as:*
> hydatid infestation of orbit (122.3, 122.6, 122.9)
> myiasis of orbit (134.0)

√5th **376.2 Endocrine exophthalmos**

> *Code first underlying thyroid disorder (242.0-242.9)*

376.21 Thyrotoxic exophthalmos

> **DEF:** Painful inflammation of eye muscles.

376.22 Exophthalmic ophthalmoplegia

> **DEF:** Inability to rotate eye as a result of bulging eyes.

√5th **376.3 Other exophthalmic conditions**

376.30 Exophthalmos, unspecified

> **DEF:** Abnormal protrusion of eyeball.

376.31 Constant exophthalmos

> **DEF:** Continuous, abnormal protrusion or bulging of eyeball.

376.32 Orbital hemorrhage

> **DEF:** Bleeding behind the eyeball, causing it to bulge forward.

376.33 Orbital edema or congestion

> **DEF:** Fluid retention behind eyeball, causing forward bulge.

376.34 Intermittent exophthalmos

376.35 Pulsating exophthalmos

> **DEF:** Bulge or protrusion; associated with a carotid-cavernous fistula.

376.36 Lateral displacement of globe

> **DEF:** Abnormal displacement of the eyeball away from nose, toward temple.

√5th **376.4 Deformity of orbit**

376.40 Deformity of orbit, unspecified

376.41 Hypertelorism of orbit

> **DEF:** Abnormal increase in interorbital distance; associated with congenital facial deformities; may be accompanied by mental deficiency.

376.42 Exostosis of orbit

> **DEF:** Abnormal bony growth of orbit.

376.43 Local deformities due to bone disease

> **DEF:** Acquired abnormalities of orbit; due to bone disease.

376.44 Orbital deformities associated with craniofacial deformities

376.45 Atrophy of orbit

> **DEF:** Wasting away of bone tissue of orbit.

376.46 Enlargement of orbit

376.47 Deformity due to trauma or surgery

√5th **376.5 Enophthalmos**

> **DEF:** Recession of eyeball deep into eye socket.

376.50 Enophthalmos, unspecified as to cause

376.51 Enophthalmos due to atrophy of orbital tissue

376.52 Enophthalmos due to trauma or surgery

376.6 Retained (old) foreign body following penetrating wound of orbit

> Retrobulbar foreign body

√5th **376.8 Other orbital disorders**

376.81 Orbital cysts

> Encephalocele of orbit
> **AHA:** 3Q, '99, 13

376.82 Myopathy of extraocular muscles

> **DEF:** Disease in the muscles that control eyeball movement.

376.89 Other

376.9 Unspecified disorder of orbit

√4th **377 Disorders of optic nerve and visual pathways**

√5th **377.0 Papilledema**

377.00 Papilledema, unspecified

377.01 Papilledema associated with increased intracranial pressure

377.02 Papilledema associated with decreased ocular pressure

377.03 Papilledema associated with retinal disorder

377.04 Foster-Kennedy syndrome

> **DEF:** Retrobulbar optic neuritis, central scotoma and optic atrophy; caused by tumors in frontal lobe of brain that press downward.

√5th **377.1 Optic atrophy**

377.10 Optic atrophy, unspecified

377.11 Primary optic atrophy

> EXCLUDES neurosyphilitic optic atrophy (094.84)

377.12 Postinflammatory optic atrophy

> **DEF:** Adverse effect of inflammation causing wasting away of eye.

377.13 Optic atrophy associated with retinal dystrophies

> **DEF:** Progressive changes in retinal tissue due to metabolic disorder causing wasting away of eye.

N Newborn Age: 0   P Pediatric Age: 0-17   M Maternity Age: 12-55   A Adult Age: 15-124

377.14   **Glaucomatous atrophy [cupping] of optic disc**

377.15   **Partial optic atrophy**
Temporal pallor of optic disc

377.16   **Hereditary optic atrophy**
Optic atrophy: Optic atrophy:
    dominant hereditary   Leber's

✓5th **377.2   Other disorders of optic disc**

377.21   **Drusen of optic disc**

377.22   **Crater-like holes of optic disc**

377.23   **Coloboma of optic disc**
DEF: Ocular malformation caused by the failure of fetal fissure of optic stalk to close.

377.24   **Pseudopapilledema**

✓5th **377.3   Optic neuritis**
EXCLUDES   *meningococcal optic neuritis (036.81)*

377.30   **Optic neuritis, unspecified**

377.31   **Optic papillitis**
DEF: Swelling and inflammation of the optic disc.

377.32   **Retrobulbar neuritis (acute)**
EXCLUDES   *syphilitic retrobulbar neuritis (094.85)*
DEF: Inflammation of optic nerve immediately behind the eyeball.

377.33   **Nutritional optic neuropathy**
DEF: Malnutrition causing optic nerve disorder.

377.34   **Toxic optic neuropathy**
Toxic amblyopia
DEF: Toxic substance causing optic nerve disorder.

377.39   **Other**
EXCLUDES   *ischemic optic neuropathy (377.41)*

✓5th **377.4   Other disorders of optic nerve**

377.41   **Ischemic optic neuropathy**
DEF: Decreased blood flow affecting optic nerve.

377.42   **Hemorrhage in optic nerve sheaths**
DEF: Bleeding in meningeal lining of optic nerve.

377.43   **Optic nerve hypoplasia**
AHA: 4Q, '06, 81

377.49   **Other**
Compression of optic nerve

✓5th **377.5   Disorders of optic chiasm**

377.51   **Associated with pituitary neoplasms and disorders**
DEF: Abnormal pituitary growth causing disruption in nerve chain from retina to brain.

377.52   **Associated with other neoplasms**
DEF: Abnormal growth, other than pituitary, causing disruption in nerve chain from retina to brain.

377.53   **Associated with vascular disorders**
DEF: Vascular disorder causing disruption in nerve chain from retina to brain.

377.54   **Associated with inflammatory disorders**
DEF: Inflammatory disease causing disruption in nerve chain from retina to brain.

✓5th **377.6   Disorders of other visual pathways**

377.61   **Associated with neoplasms**

377.62   **Associated with vascular disorders**

377.63   **Associated with inflammatory disorders**

✓5th **377.7   Disorders of visual cortex**
EXCLUDES   *visual:*
agnosia (368.16)
hallucinations (368.16)
halos (368.15)

377.71   **Associated with neoplasms**

377.72   **Associated with vascular disorders**

377.73   **Associated with inflammatory**

377.75   **Cortical blindness**
DEF: Blindness due to brain disorder, rather than eye disorder.

377.9   **Unspecified disorder of optic nerve and visual pathways**

✓4th **378   Strabismus and other disorders of binocular eye movements**
EXCLUDES   *nystagmus and other irregular eye movements (379.50-379.59)*
DEF: Misalignment of the eyes due to imbalance in extraocular muscles.

✓5th **378.0   Esotropia**
Convergent concomitant strabismus
EXCLUDES   *intermittent esotropia (378.20-378.22)*
DEF: Visual axis deviation created by one eye fixing upon an image and the other eye deviating inward.

378.00   **Esotropia, unspecified**

378.01   **Monocular esotropia**

378.02   **Monocular esotropia with A pattern**

378.03   **Monocular esotropia with V pattern**

378.04   **Monocular esotropia with other noncomitancies**
Monocular esotropia with X or Y pattern

378.05   **Alternating esotropia**

378.06   **Alternating esotropia with A pattern**

378.07   **Alternating esotropia with V pattern**

378.08   **Alternating esotropia with other noncomitancies**
Alternating esotropia with X or Y pattern

✓5th **378.1   Exotropia**
Divergent concomitant strabismus
EXCLUDES   *intermittent exotropia (378.20, 378.23-378.24)*
DEF: Visual axis deviation created by one eye fixing upon an image and the other eye deviating outward.

378.10   **Exotropia, unspecified**

378.11   **Monocular exotropia**

378.12   **Monocular exotropia with A pattern**

378.13   **Monocular exotropia with V pattern**

378.14   **Monocular exotropia with other noncomitancies**
Monocular exotropia with X or Y pattern

378.15   **Alternating exotropia**

378.16   **Alternating exotropia with A pattern**

378.17   **Alternating exotropia with V pattern**

378.18   **Alternating exotropia with other noncomitancies**
Alternating exotropia with X or Y pattern

Eye Musculature

Superior rectus   Superior oblique
Lateral rectus   Medial rectus
Inferior oblique   Inferior rectus
Muscles and actions (right eye)

R.   L.
Monocular (one eye only) esotropia (inward)

Monocular exotropia (outward)

Monocular hypertropia (upward)

✓4th Additional Digit Required   Unspecified Code   Other Specified Code   Manifestation Code   ▶◀ Revised Text   ● New Code   ▲ Revised Code Title

2010 ICD-9-CM   **Volume 1 – 119**

✓5ᵗʰ **378.2 Intermittent heterotropia**

> **EXCLUDES** *vertical heterotropia (intermittent) (378.31)*
>
> **DEF:** Deviation of eyes seen only at intervals; it is also called strabismus.

378.20 Intermittent heterotropia, unspecified

> Intermittent: Intermittent:
> esotropia NOS   exotropia NOS

378.21 Intermittent esotropia, monocular

378.22 Intermittent esotropia, alternating

378.23 Intermittent exotropia, monocular

378.24 Intermittent exotropia, alternating

✓5ᵗʰ **378.3 Other and unspecified heterotropia**

378.30 Heterotropia, unspecified

378.31 Hypertropia

> Vertical heterotropia (constant) (intermittent)

378.32 Hypotropia

378.33 Cyclotropia

378.34 Monofixation syndrome

> Microtropia

378.35 Accommodative component in esotropia

✓5ᵗʰ **378.4 Heterophoria**

> **DEF:** Deviation occurring only when the other eye is covered.

378.40 Heterophoria, unspecified

378.41 Esophoria

378.42 Exophoria

378.43 Vertical heterophoria

378.44 Cyclophoria

378.45 Alternating hyperphoria

✓5ᵗʰ **378.5 Paralytic strabismus**

> **DEF:** Deviation of the eye due to nerve paralysis affecting muscle.

378.50 Paralytic strabismus, unspecified

378.51 Third or oculomotor nerve palsy, partial

> **AHA:** 3Q, '91, 9

378.52 Third or oculomotor nerve palsy, total

> **AHA:** 2Q, '89, 12

378.53 Fourth or trochlear nerve palsy

> **AHA:** 2Q, '01, 21

378.54 Sixth or abducens nerve palsy

> **AHA:** 2Q, '89, 12

378.55 External ophthalmoplegia

378.56 Total ophthalmoplegia

✓5ᵗʰ **378.6 Mechanical strabismus**

> **DEF:** Deviation of the eye due to an outside force upon the extraocular muscles.

378.60 Mechanical strabismus, unspecified

378.61 Brown's (tendon) sheath syndrome

> **DEF:** Congenital or acquired shortening of the anterior sheath of superior oblique muscle; eye is unable to move upward and inward; usually unilateral.

378.62 Mechanical strabismus from other musculofascial disorders

378.63 Limited duction associated with other conditions

✓5ᵗʰ **378.7 Other specified strabismus**

378.71 Duane's syndrome

> **DEF:** Congenital, affects one eye; due to abnormal fibrous bands attached to rectus muscle; inability to abduct affected eye with retraction of globe.

378.72 Progressive external ophthalmoplegia

> **DEF:** Paralysis progressing from one eye muscle to another.

378.73 Strabismus in other neuromuscular disorders

✓5ᵗʰ **378.8 Other disorders of binocular eye movements**

> **EXCLUDES** *nystagmus (379.50-379.56)*

378.81 Palsy of conjugate gaze

> **DEF:** Paralysis progressing from one eye muscle to another.

378.82 Spasm of conjugate gaze

> **DEF:** Muscle contractions impairing parallel movement of eye.

378.83 Convergence insufficiency or palsy

378.84 Convergence excess or spasm

378.85 Anomalies of divergence

378.86 Internuclear ophthalmoplegia

> **DEF:** Eye movement anomaly due to brainstem lesion.

378.87 Other dissociated deviation of eye movements

> Skew deviation

378.9 Unspecified disorder of eye movements

> Ophthalmoplegia NOS
> Strabismus NOS
>
> **AHA:** 2Q, '01, 21

✓4ᵗʰ **379 Other disorders of eye**

✓5ᵗʰ **379.0 Scleritis and episcleritis**

> **EXCLUDES** *syphilitic episcleritis (095.0)*

379.00 Scleritis, unspecified

> Episcleritis NOS

379.01 Episcleritis periodica fugax

> **DEF:** Hyperemia (engorgement) of the sclera and overlying conjunctiva characterized by a sudden onset and short duration.

379.02 Nodular episcleritis

> **DEF:** Inflammation of the outermost layer of the sclera, with formation of nodules.

379.03 Anterior scleritis

379.04 Scleromalacia perforans

> **DEF:** Scleral thinning, softening and degeneration; seen with rheumatoid arthritis.

379.05 Scleritis with corneal involvement

> Scleroperikeratitis

379.06 Brawny scleritis

> **DEF:** Severe scleral inflammation with thickening corneal margins.

379.07 Posterior scleritis

> Sclerotenonitis

379.09 Other

> Scleral abscess

✓5ᵗʰ **379.1 Other disorders of sclera**

> **EXCLUDES** *blue sclera (743.47)*

379.11 Scleral ectasia

> Scleral staphyloma NOS
>
> **DEF:** Protrusion of the contents of the eyeball where the sclera has thinned.

379.12 Staphyloma posticum

> **DEF:** Ring-shaped protrusion or bulging of sclera and uveal tissue at posterior pole of eye.

379.13 Equatorial staphyloma

> **DEF:** Ring-shaped protrusion or bulging of sclera and uveal tissue midway between front and back of eye.

379.14 Anterior staphyloma, localized

379.15 Ring staphyloma

379.16 Other degenerative disorders of sclera

379.19 Other

√5ᵗʰ **379.2 Disorders of vitreous body**

> **DEF:** Disorder of clear gel that fills space between retina and lens.

379.21 Vitreous degeneration
> Vitreous:
> cavitation
> detachment
> liquefaction

379.22 Crystalline deposits in vitreous
> Asteroid hyalitis
> Synchysis scintillans

379.23 Vitreous hemorrhage
> **AHA:** 3Q, '91, 15

379.24 Other vitreous opacities
> Vitreous floaters

379.25 Vitreous membranes and strands

379.26 Vitreous prolapse
> **DEF:** Slipping of vitreous from normal position.

379.29 Other disorders of vitreous
> **EXCLUDES** vitreous abscess (360.04)
> **AHA:** 1Q, '99, 11

√5ᵗʰ **379.3 Aphakia and other disorders of lens**
> **EXCLUDES** after-cataract (366.50-366.53)

379.31 Aphakia
> **EXCLUDES** cataract extraction status (V45.61)
> **DEF:** Absence of eye's crystalline lens.

379.32 Subluxation of lens

379.33 Anterior dislocation of lens
> **DEF:** Lens displaced toward iris.

379.34 Posterior dislocation of lens
> **DEF:** Lens displaced backward toward vitreous.

379.39 Other disorders of lens

√5ᵗʰ **379.4 Anomalies of pupillary function**

379.40 Abnormal pupillary function, unspecified

379.41 Anisocoria
> **DEF:** Unequal pupil diameter.

379.42 Miosis (persistent), not due to miotics
> **DEF:** Abnormal contraction of pupil less than 2 mil.

379.43 Mydriasis (persistent), not due to mydriatics
> **DEF:** Morbid dilation of pupil.

379.45 Argyll Robertson pupil, atypical
> Argyll Robertson phenomenon or pupil, nonsyphilitic
> **EXCLUDES** Argyll Robertson pupil (syphilitic) (094.89)
> **DEF:** Failure of pupil to respond to light; affects both eyes; may be caused by diseases such as syphilis of the central nervous system or miosis.

379.46 Tonic pupillary reaction
> Adie's pupil or syndrome

379.49 Other
> Hippus   Pupillary paralysis

√5ᵗʰ **379.5 Nystagmus and other irregular eye movements**

379.50 Nystagmus, unspecified
> **DEF:** Involuntary, rapid, rhythmic movement of eyeball; vertical, horizontal, rotatory or mixed; cause may be congenital, acquired, physiological, neurological, myopathic, or due to ocular diseases.
> **AHA:** 4Q, '02, 68; 2Q, '01, 21

379.51 Congenital nystagmus

379.52 Latent nystagmus

379.53 Visual deprivation nystagmus

379.54 Nystagmus associated with disorders of the vestibular system

379.55 Dissociated nystagmus

379.56 Other forms of nystagmus

379.57 Deficiencies of saccadic eye movements
> Abnormal optokinetic response
> **DEF:** Saccadic eye movements; small, rapid, involuntary movements by both eyes simultaneously, due to changing point of fixation on visualized object.

379.58 Deficiencies of smooth pursuit movements

379.59 Other irregularities of eye movements
> Opsoclonus

√5ᵗʰ **379.6 Inflammation (infection) of postprocedural bleb**
> Postprocedural blebitis

379.60 Inflammation (infection) of postprocedural bleb, unspecified
> **AHA:** 4Q, '06, 82

379.61 Inflammation (infection) of postprocedural bleb, stage 1
> **AHA:** 4Q, '06, 82

379.62 Inflammation (infection) of postprocedural bleb, stage 2
> **AHA:** 4Q, '06, 82

379.63 Inflammation (infection) of postprocedural bleb, stage 3
> Bleb associated endophthalmitis
> **AHA:** 4Q, '06, 82

379.8 Other specified disorders of eye and adnexa

√5ᵗʰ **379.9 Unspecified disorder of eye and adnexa**

379.90 Disorder of eye, unspecified

379.91 Pain in or around eye

379.92 Swelling or mass of eye

379.93 Redness or discharge of eye

379.99 Other ill-defined disorders of eye
> **EXCLUDES** blurred vision NOS (368.8)

DISEASES OF THE EAR AND MASTOID PROCESS (380-389)

> Use additional external cause code, if applicable, to identify the cause of the ear condition

√4ᵗʰ **380 Disorders of external ear**

√5ᵗʰ **380.0 Perichondritis and chondritis of pinna**
> Chondritis of auricle   Perichondritis of auricle

380.00 Perichondritis of pinna, unspecified

380.01 Acute perichondritis of pinna

380.02 Chronic perichondritis of pinna

380.03 Chondritis of pinna
> **DEF:** Infection that has progressed into the cartilage; presents as indurated and edematous skin over the pinna; vascular compromise occurs with tissue necrosis and deformity.
> **AHA:** 4Q, '04, 76

√5ᵗʰ **380.1 Infective otitis externa**

380.10 Infective otitis externa, unspecified
> Otitis externa (acute):
> NOS
> circumscribed
> diffuse
> hemorrhagica
> infective NOS

380.11 Acute infection of pinna
> **EXCLUDES** furuncular otitis externa (680.0)

Ear and Mastoid Process

Helix

Antihelix

Concha

External auditory meatus

Tragus

Mastoid process

Antitragus

380.12   **Acute swimmers' ear**
Beach ear
Tank ear
DEF: Otitis externa due to swimming.

380.13   *Other acute infections of external ear*
Code first underlying disease, as:
erysipelas (035)
impetigo (684)
seborrheic dermatitis (690.10-690.18)
EXCLUDES   *herpes simplex (054.73)*
herpes zoster (053.71)

380.14   **Malignant otitis externa**
DEF: Severe necrotic otitis externa; due to bacteria.

380.15   *Chronic mycotic otitis externa*
Code first underlying disease, as:
aspergillosis (117.3)
otomycosis NOS (111.9)
EXCLUDES   *candidal otitis externa (112.82)*

380.16   **Other chronic infective otitis externa**
Chronic infective otitis externa NOS

✓5th   **380.2**   **Other otitis externa**

380.21   **Cholesteatoma of external ear**
Keratosis obturans of external ear (canal)
EXCLUDES   *cholesteatoma NOS (385.30-385.35)*
postmastoidectomy (383.32)
DEF: Cystlike mass filled with debris, including cholesterol; rare, congenital condition.

380.22   **Other acute otitis externa**
Acute otitis externa:
actinic
chemical
contact
eczematoid
reactive

380.23   **Other chronic otitis externa**
Chronic otitis externa NOS

✓5th   **380.3**   **Noninfectious disorders of pinna**

380.30   **Disorder of pinna, unspecified**

380.31   **Hematoma of auricle or pinna**

380.32   **Acquired deformities of auricle or pinna**
EXCLUDES   *cauliflower ear (738.7)*
AHA: 3Q, '03, 12

380.39   **Other**
EXCLUDES   *gouty tophi of ear (274.81)*

380.4   **Impacted cerumen**
Wax in ear

✓5th   **380.5**   **Acquired stenosis of external ear canal**
Collapse of external ear canal

380.50   **Acquired stenosis of external ear canal, unspecified as to cause**

380.51   **Secondary to trauma**
DEF: Narrowing of the external ear canal; due to trauma.

380.52   **Secondary to surgery**
DEF: Postsurgical narrowing of the external ear canal.

380.53   **Secondary to inflammation**
DEF: Narrowing of the external ear canal; due to chronic inflammation.

✓5th   **380.8**   **Other disorders of external ear**

380.81   **Exostosis of external ear canal**

380.89   **Other**

380.9   **Unspecified disorder of external ear**

✓4th   **381**   **Nonsuppurative otitis media and Eustachian tube disorders**

✓5th   **381.0**   **Acute nonsuppurative otitis media**
Acute tubotympanic catarrh
Otitis media, acute or subacute:
catarrhal
exudative
transudative
with effusion
EXCLUDES   *otitic barotrauma (993.0)*

381.00   **Acute nonsuppurative otitis media, unspecified**

381.01   **Acute serous otitis media**
Acute or subacute secretory otitis media
DEF: Sudden, severe infection of the middle ear.

381.02   **Acute mucoid otitis media**
Acute or subacute seromucinous otitis media
Blue drum syndrome
DEF: Sudden, severe infection of the middle ear, with mucous.

381.03   **Acute sanguinous otitis media**
DEF: Sudden, severe infection of the middle ear, with blood.

381.04   **Acute allergic serous otitis media**

381.05   **Acute allergic mucoid otitis media**

381.06   **Acute allergic sanguinous otitis media**

✓5th   **381.1**   **Chronic serous otitis media**
Chronic tubotympanic catarrh

381.10   **Chronic serous otitis media, simple or unspecified**
DEF: Persistent infection of the middle ear, without pus.

381.19   **Other**
Serosanguinous chronic otitis media

✓5th   **381.2**   **Chronic mucoid otitis media**
Glue ear
EXCLUDES   *adhesive middle ear disease (385.10-385.19)*
DEF: Chronic condition; characterized by viscous fluid in middle ear; due to obstructed Eustachian tube.

381.20   **Chronic mucoid otitis media, simple or unspecified**

381.29   **Other**
Mucosanguinous chronic otitis media

381.3   **Other and unspecified chronic nonsuppurative otitis media**
Otitis media, chronic: Otitis media, chronic:
allergic   seromucinous
exudative   transudative
secretory   with effusion

381.4   **Nonsuppurative otitis media, not specified as acute or chronic**
Otitis media: Otitis media:
allergic   secretory
catarrhal   seromucinous
exudative   serous
mucoid   transudative
                 with effusion

√5th **381.5 Eustachian salpingitis**

381.50 Eustachian salpingitis, unspecified

381.51 Acute Eustachian salpingitis
DEF: Sudden, severe inflammation of the Eustachian tube.

381.52 Chronic Eustachian salpingitis
DEF: Persistent inflammation of the Eustachian tube.

√5th **381.6 Obstruction of Eustachian tube**
Stenosis
Stricture } of Eustachian tube

381.60 Obstruction of Eustachian tube, unspecified

381.61 Osseous obstruction of Eustachian tube
Obstruction of Eustachian tube from cholesteatoma, polyp, or other osseous lesion

381.62 Intrinsic cartilaginous obstruction of Eustachian tube
DEF: Blockage of Eustachian tube; due to cartilage overgrowth.

381.63 Extrinsic cartilaginous obstruction of Eustachian tube
Compression of Eustachian tube

381.7 Patulous Eustachian tube
DEF: Distended, oversized Eustachian tube.

√5th **381.8 Other disorders of Eustachian tube**

381.81 Dysfunction of Eustachian tube

381.89 Other

381.9 Unspecified Eustachian tube disorder

√4th **382 Suppurative and unspecified otitis media**

√5th **382.0 Acute suppurative otitis media**
Otitis media, acute:
necrotizing NOS
Otitis media, acute
purulent

382.00 Acute suppurative otitis media without spontaneous rupture of ear drum
DEF: Sudden, severe inflammation of middle ear, with pus.

382.01 Acute suppurative otitis media with spontaneous rupture of ear drum
DEF: Sudden, severe inflammation of middle ear, with pressure tearing ear drum tissue.

382.02 Acute suppurative otitis media in diseases classified elsewhere
Code first underlying disease, as:
influenza (487.8)
scarlet fever (034.1)

EXCLUDES postmeasles otitis (055.2)

382.1 Chronic tubotympanic suppurative otitis media
Benign chronic suppurative ottis media
Chronic tubotympanic disease } (with anterior perforation of ear drum)
DEF: Inflammation of tympanic cavity and auditory tube; with pus formation.

382.2 Chronic atticoantral suppurative otitis media
Chronic atticoantral disease
Persistent mucosal disease } (with posterior or superior maginal perforation of ear drum)
DEF: Inflammation of upper tympanic membrane and mastoid antrum with pus formation.

382.3 Unspecified chronic suppurative otitis media
Chronic purulent otitis media
EXCLUDES tuberculous otitis media (017.4)

382.4 Unspecified suppurative otitis media
Purulent otitis media NOS

382.9 Unspecified otitis media
Otitis media:
NOS
acute NOS
Otitis media:
chronic NOS
AHA: N-D, '84, 16
H66.93 Otitis media unspecified bilateral   **I-10**

√4th **383 Mastoiditis and related conditions**

√5th **383.0 Acute mastoiditis**
Abscess of mastoid
Empyema of mastoid

383.00 Acute mastoiditis without complications
DEF: Sudden, severe inflammation of mastoid air cells.

383.01 Subperiosteal abscess of mastoid
DEF: Pocket of pus within the mastoid bone.

383.02 Acute mastoiditis with other complications
Gradenigo's syndrome

383.1 Chronic mastoiditis
Caries of mastoid   Fistula of mastoid
EXCLUDES tuberculous mastoiditis (015.6)
DEF: Persistent inflammation of the mastoid air cells.

√5th **383.2 Petrositis**
Coalescing osteitis
Inflammation
Osteomyelitis } of petrous bone

383.20 Petrositis, unspecified

383.21 Acute petrositis
DEF: Sudden, severe inflammation of dense bone behind the ear.

383.22 Chronic petrositis
DEF: Persistent inflammation of dense bone behind the ear.

√5th **383.3 Complications following mastoidectomy**

383.30 Postmastoidectomy complication, unspecified

383.31 Mucosal cyst of postmastoidectomy cavity
DEF: Mucous-lined cyst cavity following removal of mastoid bone.

383.32 Recurrent cholesteatoma of postmastoidectomy cavity
DEF: Cystlike mass of cell debris in cavity following removal of mastoid bone.

383.33 Granulations of postmastoidectomy cavity
Chronic inflammation of postmastoidectomy cavity
DEF: Granular tissue in cavity following removal of mastoid bone.

√5th **383.8 Other disorders of mastoid**

383.81 Postauricular fistula
DEF: Abnormal passage behind mastoid cavity.

383.89 Other

383.9 Unspecified mastoiditis

√4th **384 Other disorders of tympanic membrane**

√5th **384.0 Acute myringitis without mention of otitis media**

384.00 Acute myringitis, unspecified
Acute tympanitis NOS
DEF: Sudden, severe inflammation of ear drum.

384.01 Bullous myringitis
Myringitis bullosa hemorrhagica
DEF: Type of viral otitis media characterized by the appearance of serous or hemorrhagic blebs on the tympanic membrane.

384.09 Other

384.1 Chronic myringitis without mention of otitis media
Chronic tympanitis
DEF: Persistent inflammation of ear drum; with no evidence of middle ear infection.

√4th
√5th Additional Digit Required   Unspecified Code   Other Specified Code   Manifestation Code   ▶◀ Revised Text   ● New Code   ▲ Revised Code Title

✓5th **384.2 Perforation of tympanic membrane**
Perforation of ear drum:
NOS
persistent posttraumatic
postinflammatory
EXCLUDES *otitis media with perforation of tympanic membrane (382.00-382.9)*
traumatic perforation [current injury] (872.61)

384.20 Perforation of tympanic membrane, unspecified

384.21 Central perforation of tympanic membrane

384.22 Attic perforation of tympanic membrane
Pars flaccida

384.23 Other marginal perforation of tympanic membrane

384.24 Multiple perforations of tympanic membrane

384.25 Total perforation of tympanic membrane

✓5th **384.8 Other specified disorders of tympanic membrane**

384.81 Atrophic flaccid tympanic membrane
Healed perforation of ear drum

384.82 Atrophic nonflaccid tympanic membrane

384.9 Unspecified disorder of tympanic membrane

✓4th **385 Other disorders of middle ear and mastoid**
EXCLUDES *mastoiditis (383.0-383.9)*

✓5th **385.0 Tympanosclerosis**

385.00 Tympanosclerosis, unspecified as to involvement

385.01 Tympanosclerosis involving tympanic membrane only
DEF: Tough, fibrous tissue impeding functions of ear drum.

385.02 Tympanosclerosis involving tympanic membrane and ear ossicles
DEF: Tough, fibrous tissue impeding functions of middle ear bones (stapes, malleus, incus).

385.03 Tympanosclerosis involving tympanic membrane, ear ossicles, and middle ear
DEF: Tough, fibrous tissue impeding functions of ear drum, middle ear bones and middle ear canal.

385.09 Tympanosclerosis involving other combination of structures

✓5th **385.1 Adhesive middle ear disease**
Adhesive otitis
Otitis media:
chronic adhesive
fibrotic
EXCLUDES *glue ear (381.20-381.29)*
DEF: Adhesions of middle ear structures.

385.10 Adhesive middle ear disease, unspecified as to involvement

385.11 Adhesions of drum head to incus

385.12 Adhesions of drum head to stapes

385.13 Adhesions of drum head to promontorium

385.19 Other adhesions and combinations

✓5th **385.2 Other acquired abnormality of ear ossicles**

385.21 Impaired mobility of malleus
Ankylosis of malleus

385.22 Impaired mobility of other ear ossicles
Ankylosis of ear ossicles, except malleus

385.23 Discontinuity or dislocation of ear ossicles
DEF: Disruption in auditory chain; created by malleus, incus and stapes.

385.24 Partial loss or necrosis of ear ossicles
DEF: Tissue loss in malleus, incus and stapes.

Middle and Inner Ear

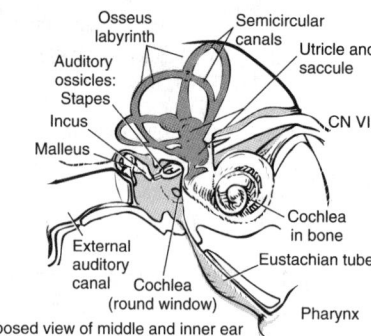

Exposed view of middle and inner ear

Cholesteatoma

✓5th **385.3 Cholesteatoma of middle ear and mastoid**
Cholesterosis
Epidermosis } of (middle) ear
Keratosis
Polyp
EXCLUDES *cholesteatoma:*
external ear canal (380.21)
recurrent of postmastoidectomy cavity (383.32)
DEF: Cystlike mass of middle ear and mastoid antrum filled with debris, including cholesterol.

385.30 Cholesteatoma, unspecified

385.31 Cholesteatoma of attic

385.32 Cholesteatoma of middle ear

385.33 Cholesteatoma of middle ear and mastoid
DEF: Cystlike mass of cell debris in middle ear and mastoid air cells behind ear.
AHA: 3Q, '00, 10

385.35 Diffuse cholesteatosis

✓5th **385.8 Other disorders of middle ear and mastoid**

385.82 Cholesterin granuloma
DEF: Granuloma formed of fibrotic tissue; contains cholesterol crystals surrounded by foreign-body cells; found in the middle ear and mastoid area.

385.83 Retained foreign body of middle ear
AHA: 3Q, '94, 7; N-D, '87, 9

385.89 Other

385.9 Unspecified disorder of middle ear and mastoid

N Newborn Age: 0   P Pediatric Age: 0-17   M Maternity Age: 12-55   A Adult Age: 15-124

✓4th **386 Vertiginous syndromes and other disorders of vestibular system**

EXCLUDES vertigo NOS (780.4)

AHA: M-A, '85, 12

✓5th **386.0 Ménière's disease**
Endolymphatic hydrops
Lermoyez's syndrome
Ménière's syndrome or vertigo

DEF: Distended membranous labyrinth of middle ear from endolymphatic hydrops; causes ischemia, failure of nerve function; hearing and balance dysfunction; symptoms include fluctuating deafness, ringing in ears and dizziness.

　386.00 **Ménière's disease, unspecified**
　　Ménière's disease (active)

　　H81.03 Ménière's disease bilateral 　I-10

　386.01 **Active Ménière's disease, cochleovestibular**

　386.02 **Active Ménière's disease, cochlear**

　386.03 **Active Ménière's disease, vestibular**

　386.04 **Inactive Ménière's disease**
　　Ménière's disease in remission

✓5th **386.1 Other and unspecified peripheral vertigo**

EXCLUDES epidemic vertigo (078.81)

　386.10 **Peripheral vertigo, unspecified**

　386.11 **Benign paroxysmal positional vertigo**
　　Benign paroxysmal positional nystagmus

　386.12 **Vestibular neuronitis**
　　Acute (and recurrent) peripheral vestibulopathy

　　DEF: Transient benign vertigo, unknown cause; characterized by response to caloric stimulation on one side, nystagmus with rhythmic movement of eyes; normal auditory function present.

　386.19 **Other**
　　Aural vertigo　　　　Otogenic vertigo

386.2 Vertigo of central origin
Central positional nystagmus
Malignant positional vertigo

✓5th **386.3 Labyrinthitis**

　386.30 **Labyrinthitis, unspecified**

　386.31 **Serous labyrinthitis**
　　Diffuse labyrinthitis

　　DEF: Inflammation of labyrinth; with fluid buildup.

　386.32 **Circumscribed labyrinthitis**
　　Focal labyrinthitis

　386.33 **Suppurative labyrinthitis**
　　Purulent labyrinthitis

　　DEF: Inflammation of labyrinth; with pus.

　386.34 **Toxic labyrinthitis**

　　DEF: Inflammation of labyrinth; due to toxic reaction.

　386.35 **Viral labyrinthitis**

✓5th **386.4 Labyrinthine fistula**

　386.40 **Labyrinthine fistula, unspecified**

　386.41 **Round window fistula**

　386.42 **Oval window fistula**

　386.43 **Semicircular canal fistula**

　386.48 **Labyrinthine fistula of combined sites**

✓5th **386.5 Labyrinthine dysfunction**

　386.50 **Labyrinthine dysfunction, unspecified**

　386.51 **Hyperactive labyrinth, unilateral**

　　DEF: Abnormal increased sensitivity of labyrinth to stimuli such as sound, pressure or gravitational change, affecting one ear.

　386.52 **Hyperactive labyrinth, bilateral**

　　DEF: Abnormal increased sensitivity of labyrinth to stimuli such as sound, pressure or gravitational change, affecting both ears.

　386.53 **Hypoactive labyrinth, unilateral**

　　DEF: Abnormal decreased sensitivity of labyrinth to stimuli such as sound, pressure or gravitational change, affecting one ear.

　386.54 **Hypoactive labyrinth, bilateral**

　　DEF: Abnormal decreased sensitivity of labyrinth to stimuli such as sound, pressure or gravitational change, affecting both ears.

　386.55 **Loss of labyrinthine reactivity, unilateral**

　　DEF: Decreased function of the labyrinth sensors, affecting one ear

　386.56 **Loss of labyrinthine reactivity, bilateral**

　　DEF: Decreased function of the labyrinth sensors, affecting both ears

　386.58 **Other forms and combinations**

386.8 Other disorders of labyrinth

386.9 Unspecified vertiginous syndromes and labyrinthine disorders

✓4th **387 Otosclerosis**

INCLUDES otospongiosis

DEF: Synonym for otospongiosis, spongy bone formation in the labyrinth bones of the ear; it causes progressive hearing impairment.

387.0 Otosclerosis involving oval window, nonobliterative

　DEF: Tough, fibrous tissue impeding functions of oval window.

387.1 Otosclerosis involving oval window, obliterative

　DEF: Tough, fibrous tissue blocking oval window.

387.2 Cochlear otosclerosis
Otosclerosis involving:
　otic capsule
　round window

　DEF: Tough, fibrous tissue impeding functions of cochlea.

387.8 Other otosclerosis

387.9 Otosclerosis, unspecified

✓4th **388 Other disorders of ear**

✓5th **388.0 Degenerative and vascular disorders of ear**

　388.00 **Degenerative and vascular disorders, unspecified**

　388.01 **Presbyacusis**

　　DEF: Progressive, bilateral perceptive hearing loss caused by advancing age; it is also known as presbycusis.

　388.02 **Transient ischemic deafness**

　　DEF: Restricted blood flow to auditory organs causing temporary hearing loss.

✓5th **388.1 Noise effects on inner ear**

　388.10 **Noise effects on inner ear, unspecified**

　388.11 **Acoustic trauma (explosive) to ear**
　　Otitic blast injury

　388.12 **Noise-induced hearing loss**

388.2 Sudden hearing loss, unspecified

✓5th **388.3 Tinnitus**

　DEF: Abnormal noises in ear; may be heard by others beside the affected individual; noises include ringing, clicking, roaring and buzzing.

　388.30 **Tinnitus, unspecified**

　388.31 **Subjective tinnitus**

　388.32 **Objective tinnitus**

✓5th **388.4 Other abnormal auditory perception**

　388.40 **Abnormal auditory perception, unspecified**

　388.41 **Diplacusis**

　　DEF: Perception of a single auditory sound as two sounds at two different levels of intensity.

　388.42 **Hyperacusis**

　　DEF: Exceptionally acute sense of hearing caused by such conditions as Bell's palsy; this term may also refer to painful sensitivity to sounds.

✓4th ✓5th **Additional Digit Required**　　**Unspecified Code**　　**Other Specified Code**　　**Manifestation Code**　　▶◀ Revised Text　　● New Code　　▲ Revised Code Title

2010 ICD-9-CM　　　　　　　　　　　　　　　　　　　　　　　　　　　**Volume 1 – 125**

Nervous System and Sense Organs

388.43–389.9

388.43 Impairment of auditory discrimination
DEF: Impaired ability to distinguish tone of sound.

388.44 Recruitment
DEF: Perception of abnormally increased loudness caused by a slight increase in sound intensity; it is a term used in audiology.

388.45 Acquired auditory processing disorder
Auditory processing disorder NOS
EXCLUDES central auditory processing disorder (315.32)
DEF: Difficulty in recognizing and interpreting sounds; a failure of the brain to process auditory information; due to neurological problems due to injury, infection, and degenerative conditions.
AHA: 4Q, '07, 79

388.5 Disorders of acoustic nerve
Acoustic neuritis
Degeneration
Disorder } of acoustic or eighth nerve
EXCLUDES acoustic neuroma (225.1)
syphilitic acoustic neuritis (094.86)
AHA: M-A, '87, 8

√5th 388.6 Otorrhea
388.60 Otorrhea, unspecified
Discharging ear NOS

388.61 Cerebrospinal fluid otorrhea
EXCLUDES cerebrospinal fluid rhinorrhea (349.81)
DEF: Spinal fluid leakage from ear.

388.69 Other
Otorrhagia

√5th 388.7 Otalgia
388.70 Otalgia, unspecified
Earache NOS

388.71 Otogenic pain

388.72 Referred pain

388.8 Other disorders of ear

388.9 Unspecified disorder of ear

√4th 389 Hearing loss
√5th 389.0 Conductive hearing loss
Conductive deafness
EXCLUDES mixed conductive and sensorineural hearing loss (389.20-389.22)
DEF: Dysfunction in sound-conducting structures of external or middle ear causing hearing loss.
AHA: 4Q, '07, 80; 4Q, '89, 5

389.00 Conductive hearing loss, unspecified

389.01 Conductive hearing loss, external ear

389.02 Conductive hearing loss, tympanic membrane

389.03 Conductive hearing loss, middle ear

389.04 Conductive hearing loss, inner ear

389.05 Conductive hearing loss, unilateral

389.06 Conductive hearing loss, bilateral
AHA: 4Q, '07, 81

389.08 Conductive hearing loss of combined types

√5th 389.1 Sensorineural hearing loss
Perceptive hearing loss or deafness
EXCLUDES abnormal auditory perception (388.40-388.44)
mixed conductive and sensorineural hearing loss (389.20-389.22)
psychogenic deafness (306.7)
DEF: Nerve conduction causing hearing loss.
AHA: 4Q, '07, 80; 4Q, '89, 5

389.10 Sensorineural hearing loss, unspecified
AHA: 1Q, '93, 29

389.11 Sensory hearing loss, bilateral

389.12 Neural hearing loss, bilateral

389.13 Neural hearing loss, unilateral

389.14 Central hearing loss

389.15 Sensorineural hearing loss, unilateral
AHA: 4Q, '06, 84

389.16 Sensorineural hearing loss, asymmetrical
AHA: 4Q, '06, 84

389.17 Sensory hearing loss, unilateral

389.18 Sensorineural hearing loss, bilateral
AHA: 4Q, '06, 84

√5th 389.2 Mixed conductive and sensorineural hearing loss
Deafness or hearing loss of type classifiable to 389.00-389.08 with type classifiable to 389.10-389.18
AHA: 4Q, '07, 80

389.20 Mixed hearing loss, unspecified

389.21 Mixed hearing loss, unilateral

389.22 Mixed hearing loss, bilateral

389.7 Deaf, non-speaking, not elsewhere classifiable

389.8 Other specified forms of hearing loss

389.9 Unspecified hearing loss
Deafness NOS
AHA: 1Q, '04, 15
H91.93 Unspecified hearing loss bilateral   I-10

7. DISEASES OF THE CIRCULATORY SYSTEM (390-459)

ACUTE RHEUMATIC FEVER (390-392)

DEF: Febrile disease occurs mainly in children or young adults following throat infection by group A *streptococci;* symptoms include fever, joint pain, lesions of heart, blood vessels and joint connective tissue, abdominal pain, skin changes, and chorea.

390 Rheumatic fever without mention of heart involvement
Arthritis, rheumatic, acute or subacute
Rheumatic fever (active) (acute)
Rheumatism, articular, acute or subacute
> **EXCLUDES**   *that with heart involvement (391.0-391.9)*

✓4ᵗʰ 391 Rheumatic fever with heart involvement
> **EXCLUDES**   *chronic heart diseases of rheumatic origin (393-398.99) unless rheumatic fever is also present or there is evidence of recrudescence or activity of the rheumatic process*

391.0 Acute rheumatic pericarditis
Rheumatic:
    fever (active) (acute) with pericarditis
    pericarditis (acute)
Any condition classifiable to 390 with pericarditis
> **EXCLUDES**   *that not specified as rheumatic (420.0-420.9)*

DEF: Sudden, severe inflammation of heart lining due to rheumatic fever.

391.1 Acute rheumatic endocarditis
Rheumatic:
    endocarditis, acute
    fever (active) (acute) with endocarditis or valvulitis
    valvulitis acute
Any condition classifiable to 390 with endocarditis or valvulitis
DEF: Sudden, severe inflammation of heart cavities due to rheumatic fever.

391.2 Acute rheumatic myocarditis
Rheumatic fever (active) (acute) with myocarditis
Any condition classifiable to 390 with myocarditis
DEF: Sudden, severe inflammation of heart muscles due to rheumatic fever.

391.8 Other acute rheumatic heart disease
Rheumatic:
    fever (active) (acute) with other or multiple types of heart involvement
    pancarditis, acute
Any condition classifiable to 390 with other or multiple types of heart involvement

391.9 Acute rheumatic heart disease, unspecified
Rheumatic:
    carditis, acute
    fever (active) (acute) with unspecified type of heart involvement
    heart disease, active or acute
Any condition classifiable to 390 with unspecified type of heart involvement

Sections of Heart Muscle

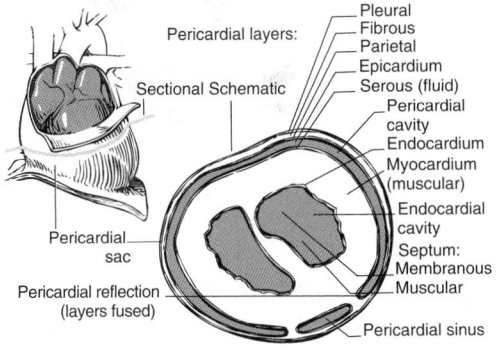

Pericardial layers:
Pleural
Fibrous
Parietal
Epicardium
Serous (fluid)

Sectional Schematic

Pericardial cavity
Endocardium
Myocardium (muscular)
Endocardial cavity
Septum:
  Membranous
  Muscular

Pericardial sac

Pericardial reflection (layers fused)

Pericardial sinus

✓4ᵗʰ 392 Rheumatic chorea
> **INCLUDES**   Sydenham's chorea
> **EXCLUDES**   *chorea: NOS (333.5) Huntington's (333.4)*

DEF: Childhood disease linked with rheumatic fever and streptococcal infections; symptoms include spasmodic, involuntary movements of limbs or facial muscles, psychic symptoms, and irritability.

392.0 With heart involvement
Rheumatic chorea with heart involvement of any type classifiable to 391

392.9 Without mention of heart involvement

CHRONIC RHEUMATIC HEART DISEASE (393-398)

393 Chronic rheumatic pericarditis
Adherent pericardium, rheumatic
Chronic rheumatic:
    mediastinopericarditis
    myopericarditis
> **EXCLUDES**   *pericarditis NOS or not specified as rheumatic (423.0-423.9)*

DEF: Persistent inflammation of heart lining due to rheumatic heart disease.

✓4ᵗʰ 394 Diseases of mitral valve
> **EXCLUDES**   *that with aortic valve involvement (396.0-396.9)*

394.0 Mitral stenosis
Mitral (valve):
    obstruction (rheumatic)
    stenosis NOS
DEF: Narrowing, of mitral valve between left atrium and left ventricle; due to rheumatic heart disease.

394.1 Rheumatic mitral insufficiency
Rheumatic mitral:
    incompetence
    regurgitation
> **EXCLUDES**   *that not specified as rheumatic (424.0)*

DEF: Malfunction of mitral valve between left atrium and left ventricle; due to rheumatic heart disease.
AHA: 2Q, '05, 14

394.2 Mitral stenosis with insufficiency
Mitral stenosis with incompetence or regurgitation
DEF: A narrowing or stricture of the mitral valve situated between the left atrium and left ventricle; valve does not completely close ,is insufficient (inadequate)in preventing regurgitation into the atrium; also called incompetence.
AHA: 1Q, '07, 11

394.9 Other and unspecified mitral valve diseases
Mitral (valve):
    disease (chronic)
    failure

✓4ᵗʰ 395 Diseases of aortic valve
> **EXCLUDES**   *that not specified as rheumatic (424.1) that with mitral valve involvement (396.0-396.9)*

395.0 Rheumatic aortic stenosis
Rheumatic aortic (valve) obstruction
DEF: Narrowing of the aortic valve; results in backflow into ventricle; due to rheumatic heart disease.
AHA: 4Q, '88, 8

395.1 Rheumatic aortic insufficiency
Rheumatic aortic:
    incompetence
    regurgitation
DEF: Malfunction of the aortic valve; results in backflow into left ventricle; due to rheumatic heart disease.

395.2 Rheumatic aortic stenosis with insufficiency
Rheumatic aortic stenosis with incompetence or regurgitation
DEF: Malfunction and narrowing, of the aortic valve; results in backflow into left ventricle; due to rheumatic heart disease.

395.9 Other and unspecified rheumatic aortic diseases
Rheumatic aortic (valve) disease

✓4ᵗʰ ✓5ᵗʰ   Additional Digit Required   Unspecified Code   Other Specified Code   Manifestation Code   ►◄ Revised Text   ● New Code   ▲ Revised Code Title

2010 ICD-9-CM   **Volume 1 – 127**

390–395.9

Circulatory System

396–402.91

✓4ᵗʰ **396 Diseases of mitral and aortic valves**

INCLUDES involvement of both mitral and aortic valves, whether specified as rheumatic or not

AHA: N-D, '87, 8

396.0 Mitral valve stenosis and aortic valve stenosis
Atypical aortic (valve) stenosis
Mitral and aortic (valve) obstruction (rheumatic)

396.1 Mitral valve stenosis and aortic valve insufficiency

396.2 Mitral valve insufficiency and aortic valve stenosis
AHA: ▶2Q, '09, 17; 1Q, '09, 18;◀2Q, '00, 16

396.3 Mitral valve insufficiency and aortic valve insufficiency
Mitral and aortic (valve):
incompetence
regurgitation
I08.0 Rheumatic d/o of both mitral & aortic valves I-10

396.8 Multiple involvement of mitral and aortic valves
Stenosis and insufficiency of mitral or aortic valve with stenosis or insufficiency, or both, of the other valve

396.9 Mitral and aortic valve diseases, unspecified

✓4ᵗʰ **397 Diseases of other endocardial structures**

397.0 Diseases of tricuspid valve
Tricuspid (valve) (rheumatic):
disease
insufficiency
obstruction
regurgitation
stenosis
DEF: Malfunction of the valve between right atrium and right ventricle; due to rheumatic heart disease.
AHA: 3Q, '06, 7; 2Q, '00, 16
I07.2 Rheumatic tricuspid stenosis and insufficiency I-10

397.1 Rheumatic diseases of pulmonary valve
EXCLUDES that not specified as rheumatic (424.3)

397.9 Rheumatic diseases of endocardium, valve unspecified
Rheumatic:
endocarditis (chronic)
valvulitis (chronic)
EXCLUDES that not specified as rheumatic (424.90-424.99)

✓4ᵗʰ **398 Other rheumatic heart disease**

398.0 Rheumatic myocarditis
Rheumatic degeneration of myocardium
EXCLUDES myocarditis not specified as rheumatic (429.0)
DEF: Chronic inflammation of heart muscle; due to rheumatic heart disease.

✓5ᵗʰ **398.9 Other and unspecified rheumatic heart diseases**

398.90 Rheumatic heart disease, unspecified
Rheumatic:
carditis
heart disease NOS
EXCLUDES carditis not specified as rheumatic (429.89)
heart disease NOS not specified as rheumatic (429.9)

398.91 Rheumatic heart failure (congestive)
Rheumatic left ventricular failure
DEF: Decreased cardiac output, edema and hypertension; due to rheumatic heart disease.
AHA: 2Q, '05, 14; 1Q, '95, 6; 3Q, '88, 3
I09.81 Rheumatic heart failure I-10

398.99 Other

HYPERTENSIVE DISEASE (401-405)

EXCLUDES that complicating pregnancy, childbirth, or the puerperium (642.0-642.9)
that involving coronary vessels (410.00-414.9)
AHA: 3Q, '90, 3; 2Q, '89, 12; S-O, '87, 9; J-A, '84, 11

✓4ᵗʰ **401 Essential hypertension**

INCLUDES high blood pressure
hyperpiesia
hyperpiesis
hypertension (arterial) (essential) (primary) (systemic)
hypertensive vascular:
degeneration
disease

EXCLUDES elevated blood pressure without diagnosis of hypertension (796.2)
pulmonary hypertension (416.0-416.9)
that involving vessels of:
brain (430-438)
eye (362.11)

DEF: Hypertension that occurs without apparent organic cause; idiopathic.
AHA: 2Q, '92, 5

401.0 Malignant
DEF: Severe high arterial blood pressure; results in necrosis in kidney, retina, etc.; hemorrhages occur and death commonly due to uremia or rupture of cerebral vessel.
AHA: M-J, '85, 19

401.1 Benign
DEF: Mildly elevated arterial blood pressure.

401.9 Unspecified
AHA: ▶1Q, '09, 18;◀2Q, '08, 16; 4Q, '05, 71; 3Q, '05, 8; 4Q, '04, 78; 4Q, '03, 105, 108, 111; 3Q, '03, 14; 2Q, '03, 16; 4Q, '97, 37
I10 Essential (primary) hypertension I-10

✓4ᵗʰ **402 Hypertensive heart disease**

INCLUDES hypertensive:
cardiomegaly
cardiopathy
cardiovascular disease
heart (disease) (failure)
any condition classifiable to 429.0-429.3, 429.8, 429.9 due to hypertension

Use additional code to specify type of heart failure (428.0-428.43), if known

AHA: 4Q, '02, 49; 2Q, '93, 9; N-D, '84, 18
TIP: Assign when a cardiac condition is stated (due to hypertension) or implied (hypertensive).

✓5ᵗʰ **402.0 Malignant**
402.00 Without heart failure
402.01 With heart failure
AHA: 4Q, '08, 180

✓5ᵗʰ **402.1 Benign**
402.10 Without heart failure
402.11 With heart failure

✓5ᵗʰ **402.9 Unspecified**
402.90 Without heart failure
I11.9 Hypertensive heart disease without heart failure I-10
402.91 With heart failure
AHA: 4Q, '02, 52; 1Q, '93, 19; 2Q, '89, 12

✓4ᵗʰ **403 Hypertensive chronic kidney disease**

INCLUDES   arteriolar nephritis
arteriosclerosis of:
    kidney
    renal arterioles
arteriosclerotic nephritis (chronic) (interstitial)
hypertensive:
    nephropathy
    renal failure
    uremia (chronic)
nephrosclerosis
renal sclerosis with hypertension

any condition classifiable to 585 with any condition classifiable to 401

EXCLUDES   *acute ►kidney◄ failure (584.5-584.9)*
renal disease stated as not due to hypertension
renovascular hypertension (405.0-405.9 with fifth-digit 1)

The following fifth-digit subclassification is for use with category 403:
  0 with chronic kidney disease stage I through stage IV, or unspecified
    Use additional code to identify the stage of chronic kidney disease (585.1-585.4, 585.9)
  1 with chronic kidney disease stage V or end stage renal disease
    Use additional code to identify the stage of chronic kidney disease (585.5, 585.6)

AHA: 4Q, '06, 84-86; 4Q, '05, 68; 4Q, '92, 22; 2Q, '92, 5

TIP: Assign whenever a patient has both chronic kidney disease and hypertension (presumed cause-and-effect relationship).

§ ✓5ᵗʰ **403.0 Malignant**
[0-1]

§ ✓5ᵗʰ **403.1 Benign**
[0-1]

§ ✓5ᵗʰ **403.9 Unspecified**
[0-1]   **AHA: For code 403.90:** 1Q, '08, 10 ;2Q, '07, 3; 4Q, '06, 86; **For code 403.91:** 1Q, '08, 7; 4Q, '05, 69; 1Q, '04, 14; 1Q, '03, 20; 2Q, '01, 11; 3Q, '91, 8

    I12.9 HTN CKD w/stage I thru IV CKD/UNS CKD   I-10

✓4ᵗʰ **404 Hypertensive heart and chronic kidney disease**

INCLUDES   disease:
    cardiorenal
    cardiovascular renal

any condition classifiable to 402 with any condition classifiable to 403

Use additional code to specify type of heart failure (428.0-428.43), if known

The following fifth-digit subclassification is for use with category 404:
  0 without heart failure and with chronic kidney disease stage I through stage IV, or unspecified
    Use additional code to identify the stage of chronic kidney disease (585.1-585.4, 585.9)
  1 with heart failure and with chronic kidney disease stage I through stage IV, or unspecified
    Use additional code to identify the stage of chronic kidney disease (585.1-585.4, 585.9)
  2 without heart failure and with chronic kidney disease stage V or end stage renal disease
    Use additional code to identify the stage of chronic kidney disease (585.5, 585.6)
  3 with heart failure and chronic kidney disease stage V or end stage renal disease
    Use additional code to identify the stage of chronic kidney disease (585.5, 585.6)

AHA: 4Q, '06, 84-86; 4Q, '05, 68; 4Q, '02, 49; 3Q, '90, 3; J-A, '84, 14

§ ✓5ᵗʰ **404.0 Malignant**
[0-3]

§ ✓5ᵗʰ **404.1 Benign**
[0-3]

§ ✓5ᵗʰ **404.9 Unspecified**
[0-3]   **I13.0** HTN heart & CKD HF & stage I thru IV CKD/UNS CKD   I-10

✓4ᵗʰ **405 Secondary hypertension**

DEF: High arterial blood pressure due to or with a variety of primary diseases, such as renal disorders, CNS disorders, endocrine, and vascular diseases.

AHA: 3Q, '90, 3; S-O, '87, 9, 11; J-A, '84, 14

✓5ᵗʰ **405.0 Malignant**

    405.01 Renovascular

    405.09 Other

✓5ᵗʰ **405.1 Benign**

    405.11 Renovascular

    405.19 Other

✓5ᵗʰ **405.9 Unspecified**

    405.91 Renovascular

    405.99 Other
      AHA: 3Q, '00, 4

ISCHEMIC HEART DISEASE (410-414)

INCLUDES   that with mention of hypertension

Use additional code to identify presence of hypertension (401.0-405.9)

AHA: 3Q, '91, 10; J-A, '84, 5

✓4ᵗʰ **410 Acute myocardial infarction**

INCLUDES   cardiac infarction
coronary (artery):
    embolism
    occlusion
    rupture
    thrombosis
infarction of heart, myocardium, or ventricle
rupture of heart, myocardium, or ventricle
ST elevation (STEMI) and non-ST elevation (NSTEMI) myocardial infarction

any condition classifiable to 414.1-414.9 specified as acute or with a stated duration of 8 weeks or less

The following fifth-digit subclassification is for use with category 410:
  0 episode of care unspecified
    Use when the source document does not contain sufficient information for the assigment of fifth-digit 1 or 2.
  1 initial episode of care
    Use fifth-digit 1 to designate the first episode of care (regardless of facility site) for a newly diagnosed myocardial infarction. The fifth-digit 1 is assigned regardless of the number of times a patient may be transferred during the initial episode of care.
  2 subsequent episode of care
    Use fifth-digit 2 to designate an episode of care following the initial episode when the patient is admitted for further observation, evaluation or treatment for a myocardial infarction that has received initial treatment, but is still less than 8 weeks old.

DEF: A sudden insufficiency of blood supply to an area of the heart muscle; usually due to a coronary artery occlusion.

AHA: 2Q, '06, 9; 4Q, '05, 69; 3Q, '01, 21; 3Q, '98, 15; 4Q, '97, 37; 3Q, '95, 9; 4Q, 92, 24; 1Q, '92, 10; 3Q, '91, 18; 1Q, '91, 14; 3Q, '89, 3

§ ✓5ᵗʰ **410.0 Of anterolateral wall**
[0-2]   ST elevation myocardial infarction (STEMI) of anterolateral wall
    AHA: For code 410.01: 4Q, '08, 72

§ ✓5ᵗʰ **410.1 Of other anterior wall**
[0-2]   Infarction:
    anterior (wall) NOS   ⎫ (with contiguous portion of
    anteroapical   ⎬   intraventricular
    anteroseptal   ⎭   septum)
  ST elevation myocardial infarction (STEMI) of other anterior wall
    AHA: For code 410.11: 3Q, '03, 10

§ ✓5ᵗʰ **410.2 Of inferolateral wall**
[0-2]   ST elevation myocardial infarction (STEMI) of inferolateral wall

---

§   Requires fifth digit. Valid digits are in [brackets] under each code. See appropriate category for codes and definitions.

✓4ᵗʰ
✓5ᵗʰ   **Additional Digit Required**   Unspecified Code   Other Specified Code   Manifestation Code   ►◄ Revised Text   ● New Code   ▲ Revised Code Title

2010 ICD-9-CM   **October 2009 • Volume 1 – 129**

Acute Myocardial Infarction

Anatomic Sites

Anterolateral 410.0
Other lateral 410.5
Posterobasal 410.6
Postero-lateral 410.5
Anteroseptal 410.1
Inferoposterior 410.3
Atrium only 410.8
Apical 410.1
Other and septum 410.4
Septum only
Papillary muscle

§ ✓5ᵗʰ **410.3 Of inferoposterior wall**
[0-2]   ST elevation myocardial infarction (STEMI) of inferoposterior wall

§ ✓5ᵗʰ **410.4 Of other inferior wall**
[0-2]   Infarction:
       diaphragmatic wall
       NOS   } (with contiguous portion of intraventricular
       inferior (wall) NOS   septum)
     ST elevation myocardial infarction (STEMI) of other inferior wall
     AHA: 1Q, '00, 7, 26; 4Q, '99, 9; 3Q, '97, 10; **For code 410.41:** 2Q, '01, 8, 9
     I21.19 STEMI invlv oth coronary artery of inferior wall   `I-10`

§ ✓5ᵗʰ **410.5 Of other lateral wall**
[0-2]   Infarction:
       apical-lateral
       basal-lateral
       high lateral
       posterolateral
     ST elevation myocardial infarction (STEMI) of other lateral wall

§ ✓5ᵗʰ **410.6 True posterior wall infarction**
[0-2]   Infarction:
       posterobasal
       strictly posterior
     ST elevation myocardial infarction (STEMI) of true posterior wall

§ ✓5ᵗʰ **410.7 Subendocardial infarction**
[0-2]   Non-ST elevation myocardial infarction (NSTEMI)
     Nontransmural infarction
     AHA: 1Q, '00, 7; **For code 410.71:** 4Q, '05, 71; 2Q, '05, 19
     I21.4 Non-ST elevation (NSTEMI) myocardial infarction   `I-10`

§ ✓5ᵗʰ **410.8 Of other specified sites**
[0-2]   Infarction of:
       atrium
       papillary muscle
       septum alone
     ST elevation myocardial infarction (STEMI) of other specified sites

§ ✓5ᵗʰ **410.9 Unspecified site**
[0-2]   Acute myocardial infarction NOS
     Coronary occlusion NOS
     Myocardial infarction NOS
     AHA: 1Q, '96, 17; 1Q, '92, 9; **For code 410.91:** 2Q, '05, 18; 3Q, '02, 5
     I21.3 ST elevation myocardial infarction of uns site   `I-10`

✓4ᵗʰ **411 Other acute and subacute forms of ischemic heart disease**
     AHA: 4Q, '94, 55; 3Q, '91, 24

411.0 Postmyocardial infarction syndrome
     Dressler's syndrome
     DEF: Complication developing several days/weeks after myocardial infarction; symptoms include fever, leukocytosis, chest pain, pericarditis, pleurisy, and pneumonitis; tendency to recur.

411.1 Intermediate coronary syndrome
     Impending infarction   Preinfarction syndrome
     Preinfarction angina   Unstable angina
     EXCLUDES   angina (pectoris) (413.9)
                      decubitus (413.0)
     DEF: A condition representing an intermediate stage between angina of effort and acute myocardial infarction. It is often documented by the physician as "unstable angina."
     AHA: 3Q, '07, 9; 4Q, '05, 105; 2Q, '04, 3; 1Q, '03, 12; 3Q, '01, 15; 2Q, '01, 7, 9; 4Q, '98, 86; 2Q, '96, 10; 3Q, '91, 24; 1Q, '91, 14; 3Q, '90, 6; 4Q, '89, 10
     TIP: Do not assign code 411.1 on the same episode of care as an acute myocardial infarction (category 410). Assign 411.1 for accelerated angina.
     I20.0 Unstable angina   `I-10`

✓5ᵗʰ **411.8 Other**
     AHA: 3Q, '91, 18; 3Q, '89, 4

411.81 Acute coronary occlusion without myocardial infarction
     Acute coronary (artery):
       embolism
       obstruction   } without or not resulting in myocardial infarction
       occlusion
       thrombosis
     EXCLUDES   obstruction without infarction due to atherosclerosis (414.00-414.07)
                    occlusion without infarction due to atherosclerosis (414.00-414.07)
     DEF: Interrupted blood flow to a portion of the heart; without tissue death.
     AHA: 3Q, '91, 24; 1Q, '91, 14

411.89 Other
     Coronary insufficiency (acute)
     Subendocardial ischemia
     AHA: 3Q, '01, 14; 1Q, '92, 9

412 Old myocardial infarction
     Healed myocardial infarction
     Past myocardial infarction diagnosed on ECG [EKG] or other special investigation, but currently presenting no symptoms
     AHA: 2Q, '03, 10; 2Q, '01, 9; 3Q, '98, 15; 2Q, '91, 22; 3Q, '90, 7
     TIP: Assign for any acute myocardial infarction stated to be older than 8 weeks.
     I25.2 Old myocardial infarction   `I-10`

✓4ᵗʰ **413 Angina pectoris**
     DEF: Severe constricting pain in the chest, often radiating from the precordium to the left shoulder and down the arm, due to ischemia of the heart muscle; usually caused by coronary disease; pain is often precipitated by effort or excitement.

413.0 Angina decubitus
     Nocturnal angina
     DEF: Angina occurring only in the recumbent position.

413.1 Prinzmetal angina
     Variant angina pectoris
     DEF: Angina occurring when patient is recumbent; associated with ST-segment elevations.
     AHA: 3Q, '06, 23

413.9 Other and unspecified angina pectoris
     Angina: Anginal syndrome
       NOS   Status anginosus
       cardiac   Stenocardia
       ►equivalent◄   Syncope anginosa
       of effort
     ►Use additional code(s) for symptoms associated with angina equivalent◄
     EXCLUDES   preinfarction angina (411.1)
     AHA: 2Q, '08, 16; 3Q, '02, 4; 3Q, '91, 16; 3Q, '90, 6
     TIP: For patients with both angina and coronary artery disease, sequence the CAD (subcategory 414.0) code first.
     I20.9 Angina pectoris unspecified   `I-10`

---

§   Requires fifth digit. Valid digits are in [brackets] under each code. See category 410 for codes and definitions.

N Newborn Age: 0   P Pediatric Age: 0-17   M Maternity Age: 12-55   A Adult Age: 15-124

√4ᵗʰ **414 Other forms of chronic ischemic heart disease**

> *EXCLUDES* *arteriosclerotic cardiovascular disease [ASCVD] (429.2)*
> *cardiovascular:*
> *arteriosclerosis or sclerosis (429.2)*
> *degeneration or disease (429.2)*

√5ᵗʰ **414.0 Coronary atherosclerosis**
Arteriosclerotic heart disease [ASHD]
Atherosclerotic heart disease
Coronary (artery):
arteriosclerosis
arteritis or endarteritis
atheroma
sclerosis
stricture

Use additional code, if applicable, to identify chronic total occlusion of coronary artery (414.2)

> *EXCLUDES* *embolism of graft (996.72)*
> *occlusion NOS of graft (996.72)*
> *thrombus of graft (996.72)*

DEF: A chronic condition marked by thickening and loss of elasticity of the coronary artery; caused by deposits of plaque containing cholesterol, lipid material and lipophages.
AHA: 2Q, '97, 13; 2Q, '95, 17; 4Q, '94, 49; 2Q, '94, 13; 1Q, '94, 6; 3Q, '90, 7

414.00 Of unspecified type of vessel, native or graft A
AHA: 1Q, '04, 24; 2Q, '03, 16; 3Q, '01, 15; 4Q, '99, 4; 3Q, '97, 15; 4Q, '96, 31

414.01 Of native coronary artery A
DEF: Plaque deposits in natural heart vessels.
AHA: ▶3Q, '08, 10;◀ 2Q, '08, 16; 3Q, '06, 25; 4Q, '05, 71; 2Q, '04, 3; 4Q, '03, 108; 3Q, '03, 9, 14; 3Q, '02, 4-9; 3Q, '01, 15; 2Q, '01, 8, 9; 3Q, '97, 15; 2Q, '96, 10; 4Q, '96, 31
TIP: Assign for documentation of CAD NOS in a patient with no history of coronary artery bypass procedure.
I25.10 ASHD of native cor artery w/o angina pectoris I-10

414.02 Of autologous vein bypass graft A
DEF: Plaque deposit in grafted vein originating within patient.

414.03 Of nonautologous biological bypass graft A
DEF: Plaque deposits in grafted vessel originating outside patient.

414.04 Of artery bypass graft A
Internal mammary artery
DEF: Plaque deposits in grafted artery originating within patient.
AHA: 4Q, '96, 31

414.05 Of unspecified type of bypass graft A
Bypass graft NOS
AHA: 3Q, '97, 15; 4Q, '96, 31

414.06 Of native coronary artery of transplanted heart
AHA: 4Q, '03, 60; 4Q, '02, 53

414.07 Of bypass graft (artery) (vein) of transplanted heart A

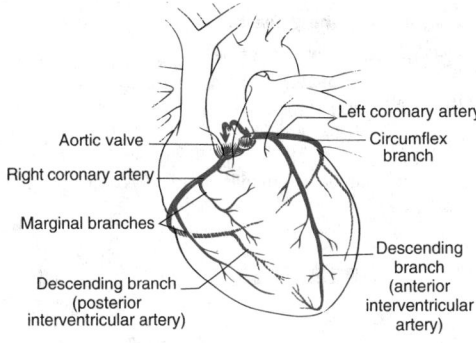

Arteries of the Heart

√5ᵗʰ **414.1 Aneurysm and dissection of heart**
AHA: 4Q, '02, 54

414.10 Aneurysm of heart (wall)
Aneurysm (arteriovenous):
mural
ventricular

414.11 Aneurysm of coronary vessels
Aneurysm (arteriovenous) of coronary vessels
DEF: Dilatation of all three-vessel wall layers forming a sac filled with blood.
AHA: 3Q, '03, 10; 1Q, '99, 17

414.12 Dissection of coronary artery
DEF: A tear in the intimal arterial wall of a coronary artery resulting in the sudden intrusion of blood within the layers of the wall.

414.19 Other aneurysm of heart
Arteriovenous fistula, acquired, of heart

414.2 Chronic total occlusion of coronary artery
Complete occlusion of coronary artery
Total occlusion of coronary artery
Code first coronary atherosclerosis (414.00-414.07)

> *EXCLUDES* *acute coronary occlusion with myo- cardial infarction (410.00-410.92)*
> *acute coronary occlusion without myocardial infarction (411.81)*

DEF: Complete blockage of coronary artery due to plaque accumulation over an extended period of time; results in substantial reduction of blood flow.
AHA: 4Q, '07, 82

414.3 Coronary atherosclerosis due to lipid rich plaque A
Code first coronary atherosclerosis (414.00-414.07)
AHA: ▶4Q, '08, 113◀

414.8 Other specified forms of chronic ischemic heart disease
Chronic coronary insufficiency
Ischemia, myocardial (chronic)
Any condition classifiable to 410 specified as chronic, or presenting with symptoms after 8 weeks from date of infarction

> *EXCLUDES* *coronary insufficiency (acute) (411.89)*

AHA: 3Q, '01, 15; 1Q, '92, 10; 3Q, '90, 7, 15; 2Q, '90, 19
I25.89 Other forms of chronic ischemic heart disease I-10

414.9 Chronic ischemic heart disease, unspecified
Ischemic heart disease NOS

Circulatory System

DISEASES OF PULMONARY CIRCULATION (415-417)

✓4th **415 Acute pulmonary heart disease**

415.0 Acute cor pulmonale

EXCLUDES   cor pulmonale NOS (416.9)

DEF: A heart-lung disease marked by dilation and failure of the right side of heart; due to pulmonary embolism; ventilatory function is impaired and pulmonary hypertension results.

✓5th **415.1 Pulmonary embolism and infarction**

Pulmonary (artery) (vein):   Pulmonary (artery) (vein):
  apoplexy   infarction (hemorrhagic)
  embolism   thrombosis

EXCLUDES ▸ chronic pulmonary embolism (416.2)
personal history of pulmonary embolism
    (V12.51) ◄
that complicating:
  abortion (634-638 with .6, 639.6)
  ectopic or molar pregnancy (639.6)
  pregnancy, childbirth, or the puerperium
    (673.0-673.8)

DEF: Embolism: Closure of the pulmonary artery or branch; due to thrombosis (blood clot).

DEF: Infarction: Necrosis of lung tissue; due to obstructed arterial blood supply, most often by pulmonary embolism.

AHA: 4Q, '90, 25

415.11 Iatrogenic pulmonary embolism and infarction

Use additional code for associated septic pulmonary embolism, if applicable, 415.12

AHA: 4Q, '95, 58

TIP: Do not assign additional code of 997.39 Other respiratory complications, with code 415.11.

415.12 Septic pulmonary embolism

Septic embolism NOS

Code first underlying infection, such as:
  septicemia (038.0-038.9)

EXCLUDES   septic arterial embolism (449)

AHA: 4Q, '07, 84-86

415.19 Other

I26.99 Other pulmonary embolism w/o acute `I-10`
cor pulmonale

✓4th **416 Chronic pulmonary heart disease**

416.0 Primary pulmonary hypertension

Idiopathic pulmonary arteriosclerosis
Pulmonary hypertension (essential) (idiopathic) (primary)

DEF: A rare increase in pulmonary circulation, often resulting in right ventricular failure or fatal syncope.

I27.0 Primary pulmonary hypertension `I-10`

416.1 Kyphoscoliotic heart disease

DEF: High blood pressure within the lungs as a result of curvature of the spine.

416.2 Chronic pulmonary embolism

Use additional code, if applicable, for associated
long-term (current) use of anticoagulants (V58.61)

EXCLUDES   personal history of pulmonary embolism
    (V12.51)

416.8 Other chronic pulmonary heart diseases

Pulmonary hypertension, secondary

I27.89 Other specified pulmonary heart diseases `I-10`

416.9 Chronic pulmonary heart disease, unspecified

Chronic cardiopulmonary disease
Cor pulmonale (chronic) NOS

✓4th **417 Other diseases of pulmonary circulation**

417.0 Arteriovenous fistula of pulmonary vessels

EXCLUDES   congenital arteriovenous fistula (747.3)

DEF: Abnormal communication between blood vessels within lung.

417.1 Aneurysm of pulmonary artery

EXCLUDES   congenital aneurysm (747.3)

Anatomy

Blood Flow

417.8 Other specified diseases of pulmonary circulation

Pulmonary:
  arteritis
  endarteritis
Rupture } of pulmonary vessel
Stricture

417.9 Unspecified disease of pulmonary circulation

OTHER FORMS OF HEART DISEASE (420-429)

✓4th **420 Acute pericarditis**

INCLUDES   acute:
  mediastinopericarditis
  myopericarditis
  pericardial effusion
  pleuropericarditis
  pneumopericarditis

EXCLUDES   acute rheumatic pericarditis (391.0)
postmyocardial infarction syndrome [Dressler's] (411.0)

DEF: Inflammation of the pericardium (heart sac); pericardial friction rub results from this inflammation and is heard as a scratchy or leathery sound.

420.0 Acute pericarditis in diseases classified elsewhere

Code first underlying disease, as:
  actinomycosis (039.8)
  amebiasis (006.8)
  chronic uremia (585.9)
  nocardiosis (039.8)
  tuberculosis (017.9)
  uremia NOS (586)

EXCLUDES   pericarditis (acute) (in):
  Coxsackie (virus) (074.21)
  gonococcal (098.83)
  histoplasmosis (115.0-115.9 with
    fifth-digit 3)
  meningococcal infection (036.41)
  syphilitic (093.81)

`N` Newborn Age: 0   `P` Pediatric Age: 0-17   `M` Maternity Age: 12-55   `A` Adult Age: 15-124

√5th **420.9 Other and unspecified acute pericarditis**

420.90 Acute pericarditis, unspecified

Pericarditis (acute):
NOS
infective NOS
sicca
AHA: 2Q, '89, 12

420.91 Acute idiopathic pericarditis

Pericarditis, acute:
benign
nonspecific
viral

420.99 Other

Pericarditis (acute):   Pericarditis (acute):
pneumococcal   suppurative
purulent   Pneumopyopericardium
staphylococcal   Pyopericardium
streptococcal

EXCLUDES *pericarditis in diseases classified elsewhere (420.0)*

√4th **421 Acute and subacute endocarditis**

DEF: Bacterial inflammation of the endocardium (intracardiac area); major symptoms include fever, fatigue, heart murmurs, splenomegaly, embolic episodes and areas of infarction.

421.0 Acute and subacute bacterial endocarditis

Endocarditis (acute)(chronic) (subacute):
bacterial
infective NOS
lenta
malignant
purulent
septic
ulcerative
vegetative
Infective aneurysm
Subacute bacterial endocarditis [SBE]

Use additional code to identify infectious organism [e.g., Streptococcus 041.0, Staphylococcus 041.1]

AHA: ▶4Q, '08, 73;◀ 1Q, '99, 12; 1Q, '91, 15

I33.0 Acute and subacute infective endocarditis   **I-10**

421.1 Acute and subacute infective endocarditis in diseases classified elsewhere

Code first underlying disease, as:
blastomycosis (116.0)
Q fever (083.0)
typhoid (fever) (002.0)

EXCLUDES *endocarditis (in):*
Coxsackie (virus) (074.22)
gonococcal (098.84)
histoplasmosis (115.0-115.9 with fifth-digit 4)
meningococcal infection (036.42)
monilial (112.81)

421.9 Acute endocarditis, unspecified

Endocarditis
Myoendocarditis   } acute or subacute
Periendocarditis

EXCLUDES *acute rheumatic endocarditis (391.1)*

Cardiac Tamponade

Normal   Cardiac Tamponade

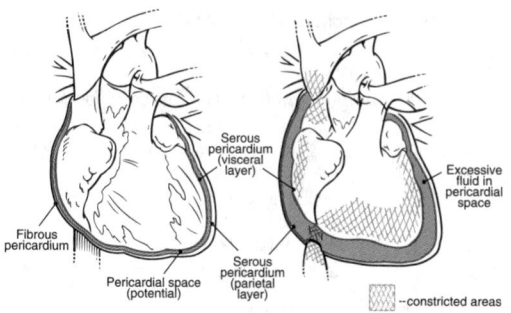

Serous pericardium (visceral layer)
Excessive fluid in pericardial space
Fibrous pericardium
Pericardial space (potential)
Serous pericardium (parietal layer)
▨ --constricted areas

√4th **422 Acute myocarditis**

EXCLUDES *acute rheumatic myocarditis (391.2)*

DEF: Acute inflammation of the muscular walls of the heart (myocardium).

422.0 Acute myocarditis in diseases classified elsewhere

Code first underlying disease, as:
myocarditis (acute):
influenzal (487.8)
tuberculous (017.9)

EXCLUDES *myocarditis (acute) (due to):*
aseptic, of newborn (074.23)
Coxsackie (virus) (074.23)
diphtheritic (032.82)
meningococcal infection (036.43)
syphilitic (093.82)
toxoplasmosis (130.3)

√5th **422.9 Other and unspecified acute myocarditis**

422.90 Acute myocarditis, unspecified

Acute or subacute (interstitial) myocarditis

422.91 Idiopathic myocarditis

Myocarditis (acute or subacute):
Fiedler's
giant cell
isolated (diffuse) (granulomatous)
nonspecific granulomatous

422.92 Septic myocarditis

Myocarditis, acute or subacute:
pneumococcal
staphylococcal

Use additional code to identify infectious organism [e.g., Staphylococcus 041.1]

EXCLUDES *myocarditis, acute or subacute:*
in bacterial diseases classified elsewhere (422.0)
streptococcal (391.2)

422.93 Toxic myocarditis

DEF: Inflammation of the heart muscle due to an adverse reaction to certain drugs or chemicals reaching the heart through the bloodstream.

422.99 Other

√4th **423 Other diseases of pericardium**

EXCLUDES *that specified as rheumatic (393)*

423.0 Hemopericardium

DEF: Blood in the pericardial sac (pericardium).

423.1 Adhesive pericarditis

Adherent pericardium   Pericarditis:
Fibrosis of pericardium   adhesive
Milk spots   obliterative
              Soldiers' patches

DEF: Two layers of serous pericardium adhere to each other by fibrous adhesions.

423.2 Constrictive pericarditis

Concato's disease
Pick's disease of heart (and liver)

DEF: Inflammation identified by a rigid, thickened and sometimes calcified pericardium; ventricles of the heart not adequately filled; congestive heart failure may result.

423.3 Cardiac tamponade

Code first the underlying cause

DEF: Life-threatening condition in which fluid or blood accumulates between the muscle of the heart (myocardium) and the outer sac (pericardium), resulting in compression of the heart, which decreases cardiac output.

AHA: 4Q, '07, 86, 87

423.8 Other specified diseases of pericardium

Calcification   } of pericardium
Fistula

AHA: 2Q, '89, 12

423.9 Unspecified disease of pericardium

AHA: 1Q, '07, 11

√4th √5th **Additional Digit Required**   **Unspecified Code**   **Other Specified Code**   **Manifestation Code**   ▶◀ Revised Text   ● New Code   ▲ Revised Code Title

Heart Valve Disorders

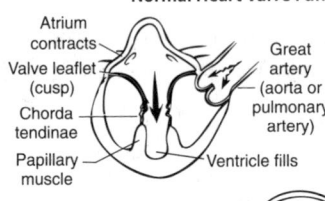

Valve stenosis (trouble opening)

Incompetent valve (trouble closing)

causes regurgitation (backflow of blood)

Insufficient valve (unable to close completely)

Shortened, fused chorda tendinae

Ventricular hypertrophy

Normal Heart Valve Function

Atrium contracts

Valve leaflet (cusp)

Chorda tendinae

Papillary muscle

Great artery (aorta or pulmonary artery)

Ventricle fills

Great vein (vena cava or pulmonary vein)

Atrium fills

Ventricle contracts

Great artery (blood to body or lungs)

✓4ᵗʰ 424 Other diseases of endocardium

> **EXCLUDES** bacterial endocarditis (421.0-421.9)
> rheumatic endocarditis (391.1, 394.0-397.9)
> syphilitic endocarditis (093.20-093.24)

424.0 Mitral valve disorders

Mitral (valve):
incompetence ⎫
insufficiency ⎬ NOS of specified cause, except
regurgitation ⎭   rheumatic

> **EXCLUDES** mitral (valve):
> disease (394.9)
> failure (394.9)
> stenosis (394.0)
> the listed conditions:
> specified as rheumatic (394.1)
> unspecified as to cause but with mention of:
> diseases of aortic valve (396.0-396.9)
> mitral stenosis or obstruction (394.2)

AHA: 3Q, '06, 7; 2Q, '00, 16; 3Q, '98, 11; N-D, '87, 8; N-D, '84, 8

I34.8 Other nonrheumatic mitral valve disorders `I-10`

424.1 Aortic valve disorders

Aortic (valve):
incompetence ⎫
insufficiency ⎬ NOS of specified cause, except
regurgitation ⎪   rheumatic
stenosis ⎭

> **EXCLUDES** hypertrophic subaortic stenosis (425.1)
> that specified as rheumatic (395.0-395.9)
> that of unspecified cause but with mention of
> diseases of mitral valve (396.0-396.9)

AHA: ▶4Q, '08, 179;◀ 4Q, '88, 8; N-D, '87, 8

424.2 Tricuspid valve disorders, specified as nonrheumatic

Tricuspid valve:
incompetence ⎫
insufficiency ⎬ of specified cause, except
regurgitation ⎪   rheumatic
stenosis ⎭

> **EXCLUDES** rheumatic or of unspecified cause (397.0)

424.3 Pulmonary valve disorders

Pulmonic: Pulmonic:
incompetence NOS   regurgitation NOS
insufficiency NOS   stenosis NOS

> **EXCLUDES** that specified as rheumatic (397.1)

✓5ᵗʰ 424.9 Endocarditis, valve unspecified

424.90 Endocarditis, valve unspecified, unspecified cause

Endocarditis (chronic):
NOS
nonbacterial thrombotic
Valvular:
incompetence ⎫
insufficiency ⎬ of unspecified valve,
regurgitation ⎪   unspecified cause
stenosis ⎭
Valvulitis (chronic)

I38 Endocarditis valve unspecified `I-10`

424.91 *Endocarditis in diseases classified elsewhere*

Code first underlying disease as:
atypical verrucous endocarditis
[Libman-Sacks] (710.0)
disseminated lupus erythematosus (710.0)
tuberculosis (017.9)

> **EXCLUDES** syphilitic (093.20-093.24)

424.99 Other

Any condition classifiable to 424.90 with specified cause, except rheumatic

> **EXCLUDES** endocardial fibroelastosis (425.3)
> that specified as rheumatic (397.9)

✓4ᵗʰ 425 Cardiomyopathy

> **INCLUDES** myocardiopathy

AHA: J-A, '85, 15

425.0 Endomyocardial fibrosis

425.1 Hypertrophic obstructive cardiomyopathy

Hypertrophic subaortic stenosis (idiopathic)

DEF: Cardiomyopathy marked by left ventricle hypertrophy, enlarged septum; results in obstructed blood flow.

425.2 Obscure cardiomyopathy of Africa

Becker's disease
Idiopathic mural endomyocardial disease

425.3 Endocardial fibroelastosis

Elastomyofibrosis

DEF: A condition marked by left ventricle hypertrophy and conversion of the endocardium into a thick fibroelastic coat; capacity of the ventricle may be reduced, but is often increased.

425.4 Other primary cardiomyopathies

Cardiomyopathy: Cardiomyopathy:
NOS   idiopathic
congestive   nonobstructive
constrictive   obstructive
familial   restrictive
hypertrophic   Cardiovascular collagenosis

AHA: 1Q, '07, 20; 2Q, '05, 14; 1Q, '00, 22; 4Q, '97, 55; 2Q, '90, 19

TIP: For congestive cardiomyopathy, assign first a code for the CHF (category 428) if the treatment is directed toward the CHF.

I42.8 Other cardiomyopathies `I-10`

425.5 Alcoholic cardiomyopathy

DEF: Heart disease as result of excess alcohol consumption.

AHA: S-O, '85, 15

425.7 *Nutritional and metabolic cardiomyopathy*

Code first underlying disease, as:
amyloidosis (277.30-277.39)
beriberi (265.0)
cardiac glycogenosis (271.0)
mucopolysaccharidosis (277.5)
thyrotoxicosis (242.0-242.9)

> **EXCLUDES** gouty tophi of heart (274.82)

Ⓝ Newborn Age: 0   Ⓟ Pediatric Age: 0-17   Ⓜ Maternity Age: 12-55   Ⓐ Adult Age: 15-124

425.8 *Cardiomyopathy in other diseases classified elsewhere*

Code first underlying disease, as:
Friedreich's ataxia (334.0)
myotonia atrophica (359.21)
progressive muscular dystrophy (359.1)
sarcoidosis (135)

EXCLUDES *cardiomyopathy in Chagas' disease (086.0)*

AHA: 2Q, '93, 9

I43 Cardiomyopathy in diseases classified elsewhere `I-10`

425.9 **Secondary cardiomyopathy, unspecified**

√4ᵗʰ 426 Conduction disorders

DEF: Disruption or disturbance in the electrical impulses that regulate heartbeats.

426.0 Atrioventricular block, complete
Third degree atrioventricular block

AHA: 2Q, '06, 14

TIP: Assign if documentation indicates intermittent complete heart block.

√5ᵗʰ 426.1 Atrioventricular block, other and unspecified

AHA: 2Q, '06, 14

TIP: Assign separate codes for each type of AV block documented.

426.10 Atrioventricular block, unspecified
Atrioventricular [AV] block (incomplete) (partial)

426.11 First degree atrioventricular block
Incomplete atrioventricular block, first degree
Prolonged P-R interval NOS

AHA: 2Q, '06, 14

I44.0 Atrioventricular block first degree `I-10`

426.12 Mobitz (type) II atrioventricular block
Incomplete atrioventricular block:
Mobitz (type) II
second degree, Mobitz (type) II

DEF: Impaired conduction of excitatory impulse from cardiac atrium to ventricle through AV node.

AHA: 2Q, '06, 14

426.13 Other second degree atrioventricular block
Incomplete atrioventricular block:
Mobitz (type) I [Wenckebach's]
second degree:
NOS
Mobitz (type) I
with 2:1 atrioventricular response [block]
Wenckebach's phenomenon

DEF: Wenckebach's phenomenon: impulses generated at constant rate to sinus node, P-R interval lengthens; results in cycle of ventricular inadequacy and shortened P-R interval; second-degree A-V block commonly called "Mobitz type 1."

426.2 Left bundle branch hemiblock
Block:
left anterior fascicular
left posterior fascicular

Nerve Conduction of the Heart

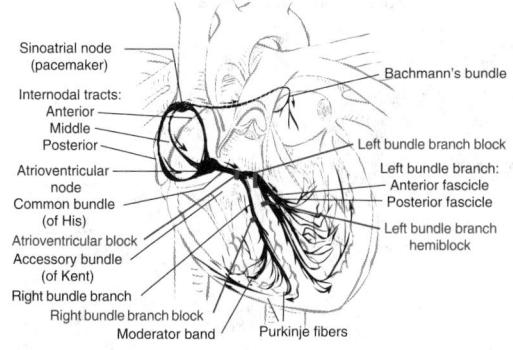

426.3 Other left bundle branch block
Left bundle branch block:
NOS
anterior fascicular with posterior fascicular
complete
main stem

I44.7 Left bundle-branch block unspecified `I-10`

426.4 Right bundle branch block

AHA: 3Q, '00, 3

I45.10 Unspecified right bundle-branch block `I-10`

√5ᵗʰ 426.5 Bundle branch block, other and unspecified

426.50 Bundle branch block, unspecified

426.51 Right bundle branch block and left posterior fascicular block

426.52 Right bundle branch block and left anterior fascicular block

426.53 Other bilateral bundle branch block
Bifascicular block NOS
Bilateral bundle branch block NOS
Right bundle branch with left bundle branch block (incomplete) (main stem)

426.54 Trifascicular block

426.6 Other heart block
Intraventricular block:
NOS
diffuse
myofibrillar
Sinoatrial block
Sinoauricular block

426.7 Anomalous atrioventricular excitation
Atrioventricular conduction:
accelerated
accessory
pre-excitation
Ventricular pre-excitation
Wolff-Parkinson-White syndrome

DEF: Wolff-Parkinson-White: normal conduction pathway is bypassed; results in short P-R interval on EKG; tendency to supraventricular tachycardia.

√5ᵗʰ 426.8 Other specified conduction disorders

426.81 Lown-Ganong-Levine syndrome
Syndrome of short P-R interval, normal QRS complexes, and supraventricular tachycardias

426.82 Long QT syndrome

DEF: Condition characterized by recurrent syncope, malignant arrhythmias, and sudden death; characteristic prolonged Q-T interval on electrocardiogram.

AHA: 4Q, '05, 72

426.89 Other
Dissociation:
atrioventricular [AV]
interference
isorhythmic
Nonparoxysmal AV nodal tachycardia

426.9 Conduction disorder, unspecified
Heart block NOS
Stokes-Adams syndrome

Normal and Long QT Electrocardiogram

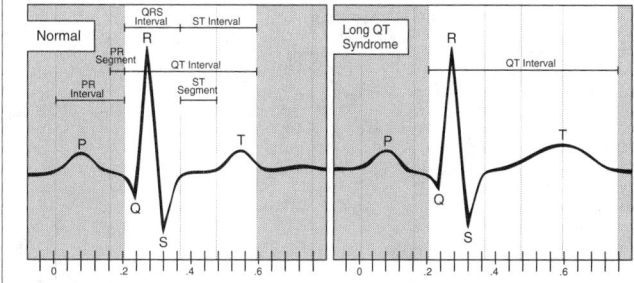

√4ᵗʰ / √5ᵗʰ Additional Digit Required | Unspecified Code | Other Specified Code | Manifestation Code | ▶◀ Revised Text | ● New Code | ▲ Revised Code Title

√4th **427 Cardiac dysrhythmias**

> **EXCLUDES** *that complicating:*
> *abortion (634-638 with .7, 639.8)*
> *ectopic or molar pregnancy (639.8)*
> *labor or delivery (668.1, 669.4)*
>
> **DEF:** Disruption or disturbance in the rhythm of heartbeats.
> **AHA:** J-A, '85, 15

427.0 Paroxysmal supraventricular tachycardia
> Paroxysmal tachycardia:
> atrial [PAT]
> atrioventricular [AV]
> junctional
> nodal
>
> **DEF:** Rapid atrial rhythm.

427.1 Paroxysmal ventricular tachycardia
> Ventricular tachycardia (paroxysmal)
> **DEF:** Rapid ventricular rhythm.
> **AHA:** ▶2Q, '09, 14;◀ 1Q, '08, 14; 2Q, '06, 15-16; 3Q, '95, 9; M-A, '86, 11
>
> **TIP:** If a ventricular tachycardia is documented as sustained or nonsustained but is induced during an EP study, assign 427.1.
>
> **I47.2** Ventricular tachycardia   `I-10`

427.2 Paroxysmal tachycardia, unspecified
> Bouveret-Hoffmann syndrome
> Paroxysmal tachycardia:
> NOS
> essential

√5th **427.3 Atrial fibrillation and flutter**
> **TIP:** Assign V58.61 Long-term (current) use of anticoagulants, as a secondary diagnosis if the patient is maintained on Coumadin.

    427.31 Atrial fibrillation
> > **DEF:** Irregular, rapid atrial contractions.
> > **AHA:** 4Q, '08, 135; 3Q, '05, 8; 4Q, '04, 78, 121; 3Q, '04, 7; 4Q, '03, 95, 105; 1Q, '03, 8; 2Q, '99, 17; 3Q, '95, 8
> >
> > **I48.0** Atrial fibrillation   `I-10`

    427.32 Atrial flutter
> > **DEF:** Regular, rapid atrial contractions.
> > **AHA:** 4Q, '03, 94
> >
> > **I48.1** Atrial flutter   `I-10`

√5th **427.4 Ventricular fibrillation and flutter**

    427.41 Ventricular fibrillation
> > **DEF:** Irregular, rapid ventricular contractions.
> > **AHA:** ▶2Q, '09, 14-15;◀ 3Q, '02, 5

    427.42 Ventricular flutter
> > **DEF:** Regular, rapid, ventricular contractions.

427.5 Cardiac arrest
> Cardiorespiratory arrest
> **AHA:** 3Q, '02, 5; 2Q, '00, 12; 3Q, '95, 8; 2Q, '88, 8
>
> **I46.9** Cardiac arrest cause unspecified   `I-10`

√5th **427.6 Premature beats**

    427.60 Premature beats, unspecified
> > Ectopic beats
> > Extrasystoles
> > Extrasystolic arrhythmia
> > Premature contractions or systoles NOS

    427.61 Supraventricular premature beats
> > Atrial premature beats, contractions, or systoles

    427.69 Other
> > Ventricular premature beats, contractions, or systoles
> > **AHA:** 4Q, '93, 42

√5th **427.8 Other specified cardiac dysrhythmias**

    427.81 Sinoatrial node dysfunction
> > Sinus bradycardia:
> > persistent
> > severe
> > Syndrome:
> > sick sinus
> > tachycardia-bradycardia
> >
> > **EXCLUDES** *sinus bradycardia NOS (427.89)*
> >
> > **DEF:** Complex cardiac arrhythmia; appears as severe sinus bradycardia, sinus bradycardia with tachycardia, or sinus bradycardia with atrioventricular block.
> > **AHA:** 3Q, '00, 8
> >
> > **I49.5** Sick sinus syndrome   `I-10`

    427.89 Other
> > Rhythm disorder:
> > coronary sinus
> > ectopic
> > nodal
> > Wandering (atrial) pacemaker
> >
> > **EXCLUDES** *carotid sinus syncope (337.0)*
> > *neonatal bradycardia (779.81)*
> > *neonatal tachycardia (779.82)*
> > *reflex bradycardia (337.0)*
> > *tachycardia NOS (785.0)*
> >
> > **I49.8** Other specified cardiac arrhythmias   `I-10`

427.9 Cardiac dysrhythmia, unspecified
> Arrhythmia (cardiac) NOS
> **AHA:** 2Q, '89, 10

√4th **428 Heart failure**
> Code, if applicable, heart failure due to hypertension first (402.0-402.9, with fifth-digit 1 or 404.0-404.9 with fifth-digit 1 or 3)
>
> **EXCLUDES** *following cardiac surgery (429.4)*
> *rheumatic (398.91)*
> *that complicating:*
> *abortion (634-638 with .7, 639.8)*
> *ectopic or molar pregnancy (639.8)*
> *labor or delivery (668.1, 669.4)*
>
> **AHA:** 4Q, '02, 49; 3Q, '98, 5; 2Q, '90, 16; 2Q, '90, 19; 2Q, '89, 10; 3Q, '88, 3

428.0 Congestive heart failure, unspecified
> Congestive heart disease
> Right heart failure (secondary to left heart failure)
>
> **EXCLUDES** *fluid overload NOS (276.6)*
>
> **DEF:** Mechanical inadequacy; caused by inability of heart to pump and circulate blood; results in fluid collection in lungs, hypertension, congestion and edema of tissue.
> **AHA:** ▶1Q, '09, 8, 18;◀ 4Q, '08, 72, 180, 182; 3Q, '08, 12; 3Q, '07, 9; 1Q, 07, 20; 3Q, '06, 7; 4Q, '05, 120; 3Q, '05, 8; 1Q, '05, 5, 9; 1Q, '05, 5, 9; 4Q, '04, 140; 3Q, '04, 7;4Q, '03, 109; 1Q, '03, 9; 4Q, '02, 52; 2Q, '01, 13; 4Q, '00, 48; 2Q, '00, 16; 1Q, '00, 22; 4Q, '99, 4; 1Q, '99, 11; 4Q, '97, 55; 3Q, '97, 10; 3Q, '96, 9; 3Q, '91, 18; 3Q, '91, 19; 2Q, '89, 12
>
> **TIP:** Assign additional code(s) from subcategory 428.2, 428.3, or 428.4 to specify the type of heart failure.
>
> **I50.9** Heart failure unspecified   `I-10`

Echocardiography of Heart Failure

Four-chamber echocardiograms, two-dimensional views.
LV: Left ventricle
RV: Right ventricle
RA: Right atrium
LA: Left atrium

Systolic dysfunction with dilated LV

Diastolic dysfunction with LV hypertrophy

N Newborn Age: 0   **P** Pediatric Age: 0-17   **M** Maternity Age: 12-55   **A** Adult Age: 15-124

428.1 Left heart failure

Acute edema of lung ⎫ with heart disease NOS or
Acute pulmonary edema ⎬ heart failure
Cardiac asthma
Left ventricular failure

DEF: Mechanical inadequacy of left ventricle; causing fluid in lungs.

✓5th **428.2 Systolic heart failure**

> EXCLUDES   *combined systolic and diastolic heart failure (428.40-428.43)*

DEF: Heart failure due to a defect in expulsion of blood caused by an abnormality in systolic function, or ventricular contractile dysfunction.

428.20 Unspecified

> I50.20 Unspecified systolic congestive heart   I-10
> failure

428.21 Acute

> I50.21 Acute systolic congestive heart failure   I-10

428.22 Chronic

> **AHA:** 4Q, '05, 120

428.23 Acute on chronic

> **AHA:** ▶1Q, '09, 8, 18;◀1Q, '03, 9

✓5th **428.3 Diastolic heart failure**

> EXCLUDES   *combined systolic and diastolic heart failure (428.40-428.43)*

DEF: Heart failure due to resistance to ventricular filling caused by an abnormality in the diastolic function.

428.30 Unspecified

> **AHA:** 4Q, '02, 52
>
> I50.30 Unspecified diastolic congestive heart   I-10
> failure

428.31 Acute

428.32 Chronic

> **AHA:** 3Q, '08, 12
>
> I50.32 Chronic diastolic congestive heart failure I-10

428.33 Acute on chronic

> **AHA:** 3Q, '08, 12; 1Q, '07, 20
>
> I50.33 Acute on chronic diastolic heart failure I-10

✓5th **428.4 Combined systolic and diastolic heart failure**

428.40 Unspecified

428.41 Acute

> **AHA:** 4Q, '04, 140

428.42 Chronic

428.43 Acute on chronic

> **AHA:** 3Q, '06, 7; 4Q, '02, 52

428.9 Heart failure, unspecified

Cardiac failure NOS
Heart failure NOS
Myocardial failure NOS
Weak heart

> **AHA:** 2Q, '89, 10; N-D, '85, 14

✓4th **429 Ill-defined descriptions and complications of heart disease**

429.0 Myocarditis, unspecified

Myocarditis
  NOS
  chronic (interstitial) ⎫ (with mention of
  fibroid   ⎬ arteriosclerosis)
  senile   ⎭

Use additional code to identify presence of arteriosclerosis

> EXCLUDES   *acute or subacute (422.0-422.9)*
>   *rheumatic (398.0)*
>   *acute (391.2)*
>   *that due to hypertension (402.0-402.9)*

429.1 Myocardial degeneration

Degeneration of heart or
  myocardium:
    fatty
    mural   ⎫ (with mention of
    muscular   ⎬ arteriosclerosis)
Myocardial: ⎪
  degeneration   ⎭
  disease

Use additional code to identify presence of arteriosclerosis

> EXCLUDES   *that due to hypertension (402.0-402.9)*

429.2 Cardiovascular disease, unspecified

Arteriosclerotic cardiovascular disease [ASCVD]
Cardiovascular arteriosclerosis
Cardiovascular:
  degeneration ⎫ (with mention of
  disease   ⎬ arteriosclerosis)
  sclerosis   ⎭

Use additional code to identify presence of arteriosclerosis

> EXCLUDES   *that due to hypertension (402.0-402.9)*

429.3 Cardiomegaly

Cardiac:
  dilatation
  hypertrophy
Ventricular dilatation

> EXCLUDES   *that due to hypertension (402.0-402.9)*
>
> I51.7 Cardiomegaly   I-10

429.4 Functional disturbances following cardiac surgery

Cardiac insufficiency ⎫ following cardiac surgery or
Heart failure   ⎬ due to presthesis
Postcardiotomy syndrome
Postvalvulotomy syndrome

> EXCLUDES   *cardiac failure in the immediate postoperative period (997.1)*
>
> **AHA:** 2Q, '02, 12; N-D, '85, 6

429.5 Rupture of chordae tendineae

> **DEF:** Torn tissue, between heart valves and papillary muscles.

429.6 Rupture of papillary muscle

> **DEF:** Torn muscle, between chordae tendineae and heart wall.

✓5th **429.7 Certain sequelae of myocardial infarction, not elsewhere classified**

Use additional code to identify the associated myocardial infarction:
  with onset of 8 weeks or less (410.00-410.92)
  with onset of more than 8 weeks (414.8)

> EXCLUDES   *congenital defects of heart (745, 746)*
>   *coronary aneurysm (414.11)*
>   *disorders of papillary muscle (429.6, 429.81)*
>   *postmyocardial infarction syndrome (411.0)*
>   *rupture of chordae tendineae (429.5)*

AHA: 3Q, '89, 5

429.71 Acquired cardiac septal defect   ▲

> EXCLUDES   *acute septal infarction (410.00-410.92)*
>
> **DEF:** Abnormal communication, between opposite heart chambers; due to defect of septum; not present at birth.

429.79 Other   ▲

Mural thrombus (atrial) (ventricular), acquired, following myocardial infarction

> **AHA:** 1Q, '92, 10

✓5th **429.8 Other ill-defined heart diseases**

429.81 Other disorders of papillary muscle

Papillary muscle:
  atrophy
  degeneration
  dysfunction
  incompetence
  incoordination
  scarring

✓4th ✓5th Additional Digit Required   Unspecified Code   Other Specified Code   Manifestation Code   ▶◀ Revised Text   ● New Code   ▲ Revised Code Title

2010 ICD-9-CM   **October 2009 • Volume 1 – 137**

Circulatory System

429.82 Hyperkinetic heart disease
DEF: Condition of unknown origin in young adults; marked by increased cardiac output at rest, increased rate of ventricular ejection; may lead to heart failure.

429.83 Takotsubo syndrome
Broken heart syndrome
Reversible left ventricular dysfunction following sudden emotional stress
Stress induced cardiomyopathy
Transient left ventricular apical ballooning syndrome
AHA: 4Q, '06, 87

429.89 Other
Carditis
EXCLUDES *that due to hypertension (402.0-402.9)*
AHA: 2Q, '06, 18; 3Q, '05, 14; 1Q, '92, 10

429.9 Heart disease, unspecified
Heart disease (organic) NOS
Morbus cordis NOS
EXCLUDES *that due to hypertension (402.0-402.9)*
AHA: ▶1Q, '09, 7;◀1Q, '93, 19
I51.9 Heart disease unspecified   I-10

CEREBROVASCULAR DISEASE (430-438)

INCLUDES with mention of hypertension (conditions classifiable to 401-405)
Use additional code to identify presence of hypertension
EXCLUDES *any condition classifiable to 430-434, 436, 437 occurring during pregnancy, childbirth, or the puerperium, or specified as puerperal (674.0)*
iatrogenic cerebrovascular infarction or hemorrhage (997.02)
AHA: 1Q, '93, 27; 3Q, '91, 10; 3Q, '90, 3; 2Q, '89, 8; M-A, '85, 6

430 Subarachnoid hemorrhage
Meningeal hemorrhage
Ruptured:
  berry aneurysm
  (congenital) cerebral aneurysm NOS
EXCLUDES *syphilitic ruptured cerebral aneurysm (094.87)*
AHA: 4Q, '04, 77
DEF: Bleeding in space between brain and lining.

431 Intracerebral hemorrhage
Hemorrhage (of):   Hemorrhage (of):
  basilar   internal capsule
  bulbar   intrapontine
  cerebellar   pontine
  cerebral   subcortical
  cerebromeningeal ventricular
  cortical   Rupture of blood vessel in brain
DEF: Bleeding within the brain.
AHA: 3Q, '07, 4; 4Q, '04, 77
I61.9 Nontraumatic intracerebral hemorrhage unspec   I-10

Berry Aneurysms

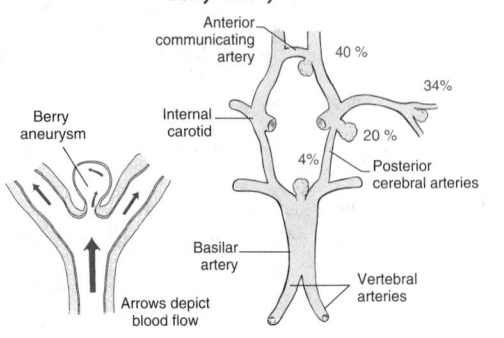

432 Other and unspecified intracranial hemorrhage
AHA: 4Q, '04, 7

432.0 Nontraumatic extradural hemorrhage
Nontraumatic epidural hemorrhage
DEF: Bleeding, nontraumatic, between skull and brain lining.

432.1 Subdural hemorrhage
Subdural hematoma, nontraumatic
DEF: Bleeding, between outermost and other layers of brain lining.

432.9 Unspecified intracranial hemorrhage
Intracranial hemorrhage NOS

433 Occlusion and stenosis of precerebral arteries
INCLUDES embolism
  narrowing   of basilar, carotid, and vertebral
  obstruction   arteries
  thrombosis
Use additional code, if applicable, to identify status post administration of tPA (rtPA) in a different facility within the last 24 hours prior to admission to current facility (V45.88)
EXCLUDES *insufficiency NOS of precerebral arteries (435.0-435.9)*

The following fifth-digit subclassification is for use with category 433:
  0 without mention of cerebral infarction
  1 with cerebral infarction

DEF: Blockage, stricture, arteries branching into brain.
AHA: 2Q, '95, 14; 3Q, '90, 16

§ **433.0 Basilar artery**
[0-1]

§ **433.1 Carotid artery**
[0-1]   **AHA:** 1Q, '00, 16; **For code 433.10:** 1Q, '06, 17; 1Q, '02, 7, 10
I65.29 Occlusion and stenosis of unspec carotid artery   I-10
I63.239 Cerebral infarct d/t usp occ/stenosis of uns carotid art   I-10
I63.449 Cerebral infarct d/t embo of uns cerebellar art   I-10

§ **433.2 Vertebral artery**
[0-1]

§ **433.3 Multiple and bilateral**
[0-1]   **AHA:** 2Q, '02, 19

§ **433.8 Other specified precerebral artery**
[0-1]

§ **433.9 Unspecified precerebral artery**
[0-1]   Precerebral artery NOS

434 Occlusion of cerebral arteries
Use additional code, if applicable, to identify status post administration of tPA (rtPA) in a different facility within the last 24 hours prior to admission to current facility (V45.88)

The following fifth-digit subclassification is for use with category 434:
  0 without mention of cerebral infarction
  1 with cerebral infarction

AHA: 2Q, '95, 14

§ **434.0 Cerebral thrombosis**
[0-1]   Thrombosis of cerebral arteries
AHA: For code 434.01: 4Q, '04, 77

Cerebrovascular Arteries

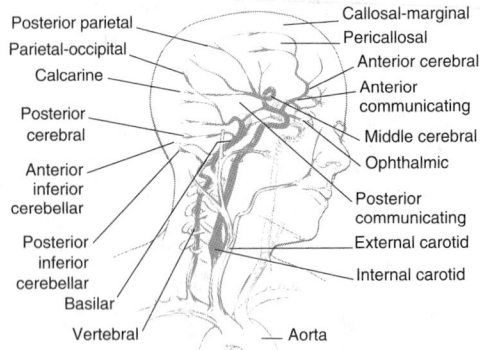

---

§   Requires fifth digit. Valid digits are in [brackets] under each code. See appropriate category for codes and definitions.

N Newborn Age: 0   P Pediatric Age: 0-17   M Maternity Age: 12-55   A Adult Age: 15-124

§ ✓5ᵗʰ **434.1 Cerebral embolism**
[0-1]
     AHA: For code 434.11: 4Q, '04, 77; 3Q, '97, 11

     I63.449 Cerebral infarct d/t embo of uns cerebellar art   I-10

§ ✓5ᵗʰ **434.9 Cerebral artery occlusion, unspecified**
[0-1]
     AHA: For code 434.91: 4Q, '08, 108; 3Q, '07, 9; 1Q, '07, 23; 4Q, '04, 77-78; 4Q, '98, 87

✓4ᵗʰ **435 Transient cerebral ischemia**

     INCLUDES cerebrovascular insufficiency (acute) with transient focal neurological signs and symptoms
insufficiency of basilar, carotid, and vertebral arteries
spasm of cerebral arteries

     EXCLUDES *acute cerebrovascular insufficiency NOS (437.1)*
that due to any condition classifiable to 433 (433.0-433.9)

     DEF: Temporary restriction of blood flow, to arteries branching into brain.

     435.0 Basilar artery syndrome

     435.1 Vertebral artery syndrome

     435.2 Subclavian steal syndrome

         DEF: Cerebrovascular insufficiency, due to occluded subclavian artery; symptoms include pain in mastoid and posterior head regions, flaccid paralysis of arm and diminished or absent radial pulse on affected side.

     435.3 Vertebrobasilar artery syndrome

         DEF: Transient ischemic attack; due to brainstem dysfunction; symptoms include confusion, vertigo, binocular blindness, diplopia, unilateral or bilateral weakness and paresthesis of extremities.
         AHA: 4Q, '95, 60

     435.8 Other specified transient cerebral ischemias

     435.9 Unspecified transient cerebral ischemia
         Impending cerebrovascular accident
         Intermittent cerebral ischemia
         Transient ischemic attack [TIA]

         AHA: N-D, '85, 12

         G45.9 Transient cerebral ischemic attack unspecified   I-10

436 Acute, but ill-defined, cerebrovascular disease
     Apoplexy, apoplectic:
         NOS
         attack
         cerebral
         seizure
     Cerebral seizure

     EXCLUDES *any condition classifiable to categories 430-435*
cerebrovascular accident (434.91)
CVA (ischemic) (434.91)
     embolic (434.11)
     hemorrhagic (430, 431, 432.0-432.9)
     thrombotic (434.01)
postoperative cerebrovascular accident (997.02)
stroke (ischemic) (434.91)
     embolic (434.11)
     hemorrhagic (430, 431, 432.0-432.9)
     thrombotic (434.01)

     AHA: 4Q, '04, 77; 4Q, '99, 3

     TIP: Do not assign when documentation indicates "CVA, stroke, or cerebral infarction." See instead default code 434.91.

✓4ᵗʰ **437 Other and ill-defined cerebrovascular disease**

     437.0 Cerebral atherosclerosis   A
         Atheroma of cerebral arteries
         Cerebral arteriosclerosis

         I67.2 Cerebral atherosclerosis   I-10

     437.1 Other generalized ischemic cerebrovascular disease
         Acute cerebrovascular insufficiency NOS
         Cerebral ischemia (chronic)

         AHA: ▶1Q, '09, 8◀

     437.2 Hypertensive encephalopathy

         DEF: Cerebral manifestations (such as visual disturbances and headache) due to high blood pressure.
         AHA: J-A, '84, 14

     437.3 Cerebral aneurysm, nonruptured
         Internal carotid artery, intracranial portion
         Internal carotid artery NOS

         EXCLUDES *congenital cerebral aneurysm, nonruptured (747.81)*
internal carotid artery, extracranial portion (442.81)

         AHA: ▶2Q, '09, 12◀

     437.4 Cerebral arteritis

         DEF: Inflammation of a cerebral artery or arteries.
         AHA: 4Q, '99, 21

     437.5 Moyamoya disease

         DEF: Cerebrovascular ischemia; vessels occlude and rupture causing tiny hemorrhages at base of brain; predominantly affects Japanese.

     437.6 Nonpyogenic thrombosis of intracranial venous sinus
         EXCLUDES *pyogenic (325)*

     437.7 Transient global amnesia

         DEF: Episode of short-term memory loss, not often recurrent; pathogenesis unknown; with no signs or symptoms of neurological disorder.
         AHA: 4Q, '92, 20

     437.8 Other

     437.9 Unspecified
         Cerebrovascular disease or lesion NOS

         AHA: ▶1Q, '09, 9◀

✓4ᵗʰ **438 Late effects of cerebrovascular disease**

     Note: This category is to be used to indicate conditions in 430-437 as the cause of late effects. The "late effects" include conditions specified as such, as sequelae, which may occur at any time after the onset of the causal condition.

     EXCLUDES *personal history of:*
cerebral infarction without residual deficits (V12.54)
PRIND [Prolonged reversible ischemic neurologic deficit] (V12.54)
RIND [Reversible ischemic neurological deficit] (V12.54)
transient ischemic attack [TIA] (V12.54)

     AHA: 3Q, '06, 3-4, 6; 4Q, '99, 4, 6, 7; 4Q, '98, 39, 88; 4Q, '97, 35, 37; 4Q, '92, 21;N-D,'86, 12; M-A, '86, 7
     TIP: Assign instead code V12.54 TIA and cerebral infarction without residual effects, if no residual deficits are present.

     438.0 Cognitive deficits

✓5ᵗʰ   **438.1 Speech and language deficits**

         438.10 Speech and language deficit, unspecified

         438.11 Aphasia

              DEF: Impairment or absence of the ability to communicate by speech, writing or signs or to comprehend the spoken or written language due to disease or injury to the brain.
              AHA: 4Q, '03, 105; 4Q, '97, 36

         438.12 Dysphasia

              DEF: Impaired speech; marked by inability to sequence language.
              AHA: 4Q, '99, 3, 9

         ● **438.13 Dysarthria**
         ● **438.14 Fluency disorder**
              Stuttering

         438.19 Other speech and language deficits

✓5ᵗʰ   **438.2 Hemiplegia/hemiparesis**

         DEF: Paralysis of one side of the body.

         438.20 Hemiplegia affecting unspecified side

              AHA: 4Q, '07, 94; 4Q, '03, 105; 4Q, '99, 3, 9

              I69.959 Hemipl & hemiparesis flw uns CVD affect uns side   I-10

         438.21 Hemiplegia affecting dominant side

         438.22 Hemiplegia affecting nondominant side

              AHA: 4Q, '03, 105; 1Q, '02, 16

---

§   Requires fifth digit. Valid digits are in [brackets] under each code. See category 434 for codes and definitions.

✓4ᵗʰ ✓5ᵗʰ Additional Digit Required	Unspecified Code	Other Specified Code	Manifestation Code	▶◀ Revised Text	● New Code	▲ Revised Code Title

√5ᵗʰ **438.3 Monoplegia of upper limb**

DEF: Paralysis of one limb or one muscle group.

438.30 Monoplegia of upper limb affecting unspecified side

438.31 Monoplegia of upper limb affecting dominant side

438.32 Monoplegia of upper limb affecting nondominant side

√5ᵗʰ **438.4 Monoplegia of lower limb**

438.40 Monoplegia of lower limb affecting unspecified side

438.41 Monoplegia of lower limb affecting dominant side

438.42 Monoplegia of lower limb affecting nondominant side

√5ᵗʰ **438.5 Other paralytic syndrome**

Use additional code to identify type of paralytic syndrome, such as:
locked-in state (344.81)
quadriplegia (344.00-344.09)

EXCLUDES late effects of cerebrovascular accident with:
hemiplegia/hemiparesis (438.20-438.22)
monoplegia of lower limb (438.40-438.42)
monoplegia of upper limb (438.30-438.32)

438.50 Other paralytic syndrome affecting unspecified side

438.51 Other paralytic syndrome affecting dominant side

438.52 Other paralytic syndrome affecting nondominant side

438.53 Other paralytic syndrome, bilateral

AHA: 4Q, '98, 39

438.6 Alterations of sensations

Use additional code to identify the altered sensation

438.7 Disturbances of vision

Use additional code to identify the visual disturbance
AHA: 4Q, '02, 56

√5ᵗʰ **438.8 Other late effects of cerebrovascular disease**

438.81 Apraxia

DEF: Inability to activate learned movements; no known sensory or motor impairment.

438.82 Dysphagia

Use additional code to identify the type of dysphagia, if known (787.20-787.29)
DEF: Inability or difficulty in swallowing.
AHA: 4Q, '07, 94
I69.991 Dysphagia following uns cerebrovascular disease | I-10 |

438.83 Facial weakness

Facial droop

438.84 Ataxia

AHA: 4Q, '02, 56

438.85 Vertigo

438.89 Other late effects of cerebrovascular disease

Use additional code to identify the late effect
AHA: ▶2Q, '09, 10;◀1Q, '05, 13; 4Q, '98, 39
TIP: Assign 438.89 and 728.87 Muscle weakness, for residual weakness secondary to late effect of CVA.
I69.998 Other sequelae flw uns cerebrovascular disease | I-10 |

438.9 Unspecified late effects of cerebrovascular disease

DISEASES OF ARTERIES, ARTERIOLES, AND CAPILLARIES (440-449)

√4ᵗʰ **440 Atherosclerosis**

INCLUDES arteriolosclerosis
arteriosclerosis (obliterans) (senile)
arteriosclerotic vascular disease
atheroma
degeneration:
arterial
arteriovascular
vascular
endarteritis deformans or obliterans
senile:
arteritis
endarteritis

EXCLUDES atheroembolism (445.01-445.89)
atherosclerosis of bypass graft of the extremities (440.30-440.32)

DEF: Stricture and reduced elasticity of artery; due to plaque deposits.

440.0 Of aorta | A |

AHA: 2Q, '93, 7; 2Q, '93, 8; 4Q, '88, 8

440.1 Of renal artery | A |

EXCLUDES atherosclerosis of renal arterioles (403.00-403.91)

√5ᵗʰ **440.2 Of native arteries of the extremities**

Use additional code, if applicable, to identify chronic total occlusion of artery of the extremities (440.4)

EXCLUDES atherosclerosis of bypass graft of the extremities (440.30-440.32)

AHA: 4Q, '94, 49; 4Q, '93, 27; 4Q, '92, 25; 3Q, '90, 15; M-A, '87, 6

TIP: Codes are listed in order of increasing severity; all patients who have gangrene (regardless of whether ulceration, rest pain, and/or intermittent claudication are present) are coded to 440.24. Patients without gangrene, but with ulceration (regardless of whether they also suffer from rest pain or intermittent claudication) are coded to 440.23.

440.20 Atherosclerosis of the extremities, unspecified | A |

I70.209 Uns atherosclero natv art of extrem uns extrem | I-10 |

440.21 Atherosclerosis of the extremities with intermittent claudication | A |

DEF: Atherosclerosis; marked by pain, tension and weakness after walking; no symptoms while at rest.
I70.219 Atherosclerosis native arteries ext interm claud uns ext | I-10 |

440.22 Atherosclerosis of the extremities with rest pain | A |

INCLUDES any condition classifiable to 440.21
DEF: Atherosclerosis, marked by pain, tension and weakness while at rest.

440.23 Atherosclerosis of the extremities with ulceration | A |

INCLUDES any condition classifiable to 440.21 and 440.22
Use additional code for any associated ulceration (707.10-707.9)
AHA: 4Q, '00, 44
I70.249 Atherosclero natv art lt leg ulceration uns site | I-10 |

440.24 Atherosclerosis of the extremities with gangrene | A |

INCLUDES any condition classifiable to 440.21, 440.22, and 440.23 with ischemic gangrene 785.4
Use additional code for any associated ulceration (707.10-707.9)
EXCLUDES gas gangrene (040.0)
AHA: 4Q, '03, 109; 3Q, '03, 14; 4Q, '95, 54; 1Q, '95, 11

440.29 Other | A |

N Newborn Age: 0   P Pediatric Age: 0-17   M Maternity Age: 12-55   A Adult Age: 15-124

Map of Major Arteries

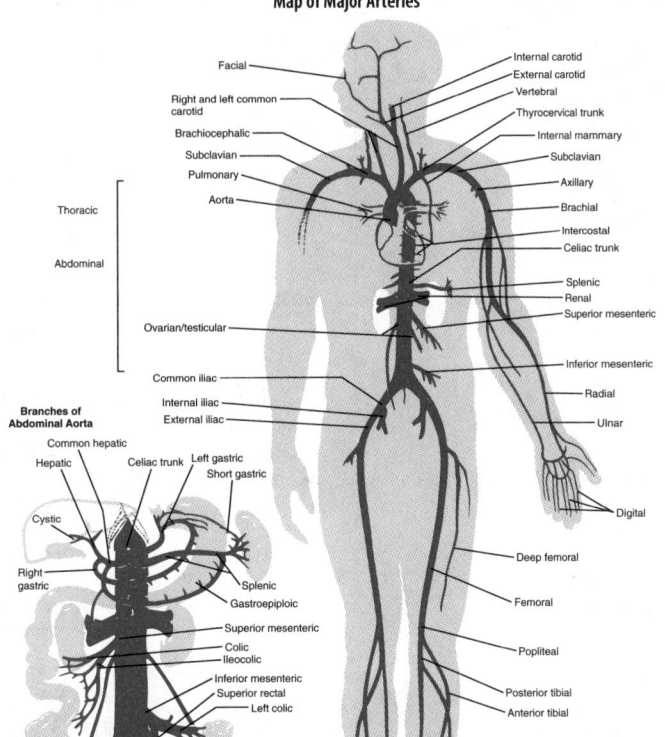

440.3 **Of bypass graft of extremities**
> EXCLUDES atherosclerosis of native arteries of the
> extremities (440.21-440.24)
> embolism [occlusion NOS] [thrombus] of graft
> (996.74)

AHA: 4Q, '94, 49

440.30 **Of unspecified graft** A

440.31 **Of autologous vein bypass graft** A

440.32 **Of nonautologous biological bypass graft** A

440.4 **Chronic total occlusion of artery of the extremities**
Complete occlusion of artery of the extremities
Total occlusion of artery of the extremities
Code first atherosclerosis of arteries of the extremities
(440.20-440.29, 440.30-440.32)
> EXCLUDES acute occlusion of artery of extremity
> (444.21-444.22)

AHA: 4Q, '07, 82

440.8 **Of other specified arteries** A
> EXCLUDES basilar (433.0)
> carotid (433.1)
> cerebral (437.0)
> coronary (414.00-414.07)
> mesenteric (557.1)
> precerebral (433.0-433.9)
> pulmonary (416.0)
> vertebral (433.2)

440.9 **Generalized and unspecified atherosclerosis** A
Arteriosclerotic vascular disease NOS
> EXCLUDES arteriosclerotic cardiovascular disease [ASCVD]
> (429.2)

I70.91 Generalized atherosclerosis I-10

441 **Aortic aneurysm and dissection**
> EXCLUDES syphilitic aortic aneurysm (093.0)
> traumatic aortic aneurysm (901.0, 902.0)

441.0 **Dissection of aorta**
DEF: Dissection or splitting of wall of the aorta; due to blood
entering through intimal tear or interstitial hemorrhage.
AHA: 4Q, '89, 10

441.00 **Unspecified site**

441.01 **Thoracic**
AHA: ▶1Q, '09, 16◀ 4Q, '07, 87

441.02 **Abdominal**

441.03 **Thoracoabdominal**

441.1 **Thoracic aneurysm, ruptured**

441.2 **Thoracic aneurysm without mention of rupture**
AHA: 3Q, '92, 10
I71.2 Thoracic aortic aneurysm without rupture I-10

441.3 **Abdominal aneurysm, ruptured**

441.4 **Abdominal aneurysm without mention of rupture**
AHA: 4Q, '00, 64; 1Q, '99, 15, 16, 17; 3Q, '92, 10
I71.4 Abdominal aortic aneurysm without rupture I-10

441.5 **Aortic aneurysm of unspecified site, ruptured**
Rupture of aorta NOS

441.6 **Thoracoabdominal aneurysm, ruptured**

441.7 **Thoracoabdominal aneurysm, without mention of rupture**
AHA: 2Q, '06, 16

441.9 **Aortic aneurysm of unspecified site without mention of rupture**
Aneurysm
Dilatation } of aorta
Hyaline necrosis

✓4th Additional Digit Required | Unspecified Code | Other Specified Code | Manifestation Code | ▶◀ Revised Text | ● New Code | ▲ Revised Code Title

Circulatory System

442–444.0

Thoracic and Abdominal Aortic Aneurysm

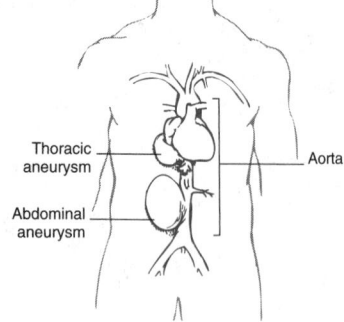

Thoracic aneurysm

Aorta

Abdominal aneurysm

✓4ᵗʰ **442 Other aneurysm**

INCLUDES   aneurysm (ruptured) (cirsoid) (false) (varicose) aneurysmal varix

EXCLUDES   arteriovenous aneurysm or fistula:
     acquired (447.0)
     congenital (747.60-747.69)
     traumatic (900.0-904.9)

DEF: Dissection or splitting of arterial wall; due to blood entering through intimal tear or interstitial hemorrhage.

442.0 Of artery of upper extremity

442.1 Of renal artery

442.2 Of iliac artery
     AHA: 1Q, '99, 16, 17

442.3 Of artery of lower extremity
     Aneurysm: Aneurysm:
        femoral artery   popliteal artery
     AHA: 2Q, '08, 13; 3Q, '02, 24-26; 1Q, '99, 16

✓5ᵗʰ **442.8 Of other specified artery**

     442.81 Artery of neck
         Aneurysm of carotid artery (common) (external) (internal, extracranial portion)

         EXCLUDES   internal carotid artery, intra- cranial portion (437.3)

     442.82 Subclavian artery

     442.83 Splenic artery

     442.84 Other visceral artery
         Aneurysm:
           celiac
           gastroduodenal
           gastroepiploic   ⎫
           hepatic   ⎬ artery
           pancreaticoduodenal   ⎭
           superior mesenteric

     442.89 Other
         Aneurysm:
           mediastinal artery
           spinal artery

         EXCLUDES   cerebral (nonruptured) (437.3)
                     congenital (747.81)
                     ruptured (430)
                     coronary (414.11)
                     heart (414.10)
                     pulmonary (417.1)

442.9 Of unspecified site

✓4ᵗʰ **443 Other peripheral vascular disease**

     443.0 Raynaud's syndrome
        Raynaud's:
          disease
          phenomenon (secondary)
        Use additional code to identify gangrene (785.4)
        DEF: Constriction of the arteries, due to cold or stress; bilateral ischemic attacks of fingers, toes, nose or ears; symptoms include pallor, paresthesia and pain.
        I73.00 Raynaud's syndrome without gangrene   **I-10**

443.1 Thromboangiitis obliterans [Buerger's disease]
     Presenile gangrene
     DEF: Inflammatory disease of extremity blood vessels, mainly the lower; occurs primarily in young men and leads to tissue ischemia and gangrene.

✓5ᵗʰ **443.2 Other arterial dissection**

     EXCLUDES   dissection of aorta (441.00-441.03)
                     dissection of coronary arteries (414.12)

     AHA: 4Q, '02, 54

     443.21 Dissection of carotid artery

     443.22 Dissection of iliac artery

     443.23 Dissection of renal artery

     443.24 Dissection of vertebral artery

     443.29 Dissection of other artery

✓5ᵗʰ **443.8 Other specified peripheral vascular diseases**

     443.81 Peripheral angiopathy in diseases classified elsewhere
         Code first underlying disease, as:
           diabetes mellitus (249.7, 250.7)
         AHA: 1Q, '04, 14; 3Q, '91, 10
         I79.8 Oth d/o art arterioles & cap in dz clas elsw **I-10**

     443.82 Erythromelalgia
         DEF: Rare syndrome of paroxysmal vasodilation; maldistribution of blood flow causes redness, pain, increased skin temperature, and burning sensations in various parts of the body.
         AHA: 4Q, '05, 73

     443.89 Other
         Acrocyanosis
         Acroparesthesia:
           simple [Schultze's type]
           vasomotor [Nothnagel's type]
         Erythrocyanosis

         EXCLUDES   chilblains (991.5)
                     frostbite (991.0-991.3)
                     immersion foot (991.4)
         AHA: 4Q, '07, 124
         I73.89 Other specified peripheral vascular dz   **I-10**

443.9 Peripheral vascular disease, unspecified
     Intermittent claudication NOS
     Peripheral:
       angiopathy NOS
       vascular disease NOS
     Spasm of artery

     EXCLUDES   atherosclerosis of the arteries of the extremities (440.20-440.22)
                     spasm of cerebral artery (435.0-435.9)
     AHA: 4Q, '92, 25; 3Q, '91, 10
     I73.9 Peripheral vascular disease unspecified   **I-10**

✓4ᵗʰ **444 Arterial embolism and thrombosis**

     INCLUDES   infarction:
                 embolic
                 thrombotic
         occlusion

     EXCLUDES   atheroembolism (445.01-445.89)
         that complicating:
           abortion (634-638 with .6, 639.6)
           ectopic or molar pregnancy (639.6)
           pregnancy, childbirth, or the pueperium (673.0-673.8)
           septic arterial embolism (449)
     AHA: 2Q, '92, 11; 4Q, '90, 27

     444.0 Of abdominal aorta
        Aortic bifurcation syndrome
        Aortoiliac obstruction
        Leriche's syndrome
        Saddle embolus
        AHA: 2Q, '93, 7; 4Q, '90, 27

   N   Newborn Age: 0   **P**   Pediatric Age: 0-17   **M**   Maternity Age: 12-55   **A**   Adult Age: 15-124

Arterial Diseases and Disorders

Lipids
Calcium deposits

Intimal
proliferation

Atherosclerosis
narrowing lumen

Thrombus (clot)
forming in lumen

Organization of
thrombus and
recanalization

Embolus
(from elsewhere)
occluding lumen

Aneurysm bypasses
lumen or...

...bulges from
arterial wall

Arteriovenous fistula

444.1 Of thoracic aorta
Embolism or thrombosis of aorta (thoracic)

☑5th **444.2 Of arteries of the extremities**
AHA: M-A, '87, 6

   444.21 Upper extremity

   444.22 Lower extremity
Arterial embolism or thrombosis:
  femoral
  peripheral NOS
  popliteal
   EXCLUDES *iliofemoral (444.81)*
AHA: 4Q, '07, 85; 3Q, '03, 10; 1Q, '03, 17; 3Q, '90, 16
I74.3 Embo & thromb of arteries of the low   [I-10]
extremities

☑5th **444.8 Of other specified artery**

   444.81 Iliac artery
AHA: 1Q, '03, 16

   444.89 Other
   EXCLUDES *basilar (433.0)*
carotid (433.1)
cerebral (434.0-434.9)
coronary (410.00-410.92)
mesenteric (557.0)
ophthalmic (362.30-362.34)
precerebral (433.0-433.9)
pulmonary (415.19)
renal (593.81)
retinal (362.30-362.34)
vertebral (433.2)

444.9 Of unspecified artery

☑4th **445 Atheroembolism**
  INCLUDES atherothrombotic microembolism
cholesterol embolism
AHA: 4Q, '02, 57

☑5th **445.0 Of extremities**

   445.01 Upper extremity

   445.02 Lower extremity

☑5th **445.8 Of other sites**

   445.81 Kidney
Use additional code for any associated acute
►kidney◄ failure or chronic kidney
disease (584, 585)

   445.89 Other site

☑4th **446 Polyarteritis nodosa and allied conditions**

   446.0 Polyarteritis nodosa
Disseminated necrotizing periarteritis
Necrotizing angiitis
Panarteritis (nodosa)
Periarteritis (nodosa)
DEF: Inflammation of small and mid-size arteries; symptoms
related to involved arteries in kidneys, muscles,
gastrointestinal tract and heart; results in tissue death.

   **446.1 Acute febrile mucocutaneous lymph node syndrome
[MCLS]**
Kawasaki disease
DEF: Acute febrile disease of children; marked by erythema of
conjunctiva and mucous membranes of upper respiratory
tract, skin eruptions and edema.

☑5th **446.2 Hypersensitivity angiitis**
   EXCLUDES *antiglomerular basement membrane disease
without pulmonary hemorrhage
(583.89)*

   446.20 Hypersensitivity angiitis, unspecified

   446.21 Goodpasture's syndrome
Antiglomerular basement membrane
antibody-mediated nephritis with
pulmonary hemorrhage
Use additional code to identify renal disease
(583.81)
DEF: Glomerulonephritis associated with hematuria,
progresses rapidly; results in death from renal
failure.

   446.29 Other specified hypersensitivity angiitis
AHA: 1Q, '95, 3

   446.3 Lethal midline granuloma
Malignant granuloma of face
DEF: Granulomatous lesion; in nose or paranasal sinuses; often
fatal; occurs chiefly in males.
AHA: 3Q, '00, 11

   446.4 Wegener's granulomatosis
Necrotizing respiratory granulomatosis
Wegener's syndrome
DEF: A disease occurring mainly in men; marked by
necrotizing granulomas and ulceration of the upper
respiratory tract; cause is a vasculitis affecting small vessels
due to an immune disorder.
AHA: 3Q, '00, 11

   446.5 Giant cell arteritis
Bagratuni's syndrome   Horton's disease
Cranial arteritis   Temporal arteritis
DEF: Inflammation of arteries; due to giant cells affecting
carotid artery branches, resulting in occlusion; symptoms
include fever, headache and neurological problems.
M31.6 Other giant cell arteritis   [I-10]

   446.6 Thrombotic microangiopathy
Moschcowitz's syndrome
Thrombotic thrombocytopenic purpura
DEF: Blockage of small blood vessels; due to hyaline deposits;
symptoms include purpura, CNS disorders; results in
protracted disease or rapid death.

   446.7 Takayasu's disease
Aortic arch arteritis
Pulseless disease
DEF: Progressive obliterative arteritis of brachiocephalic trunk,
left subclavian, and left common carotid arteries above aortic
arch; results in ischemia in brain, heart and arm.

☑4th **447 Other disorders of arteries and arterioles**

   447.0 Arteriovenous fistula, acquired
Arteriovenous aneurysm, acquired
   EXCLUDES *cerebrovascular (437.3)*
coronary (414.19)
pulmonary (417.0)
*surgically created arteriovenous shunt or
fistula:*
complication (996.1, 996.61-996.62)
status or presence (V45.11)
traumatic (900.0-904.9)
DEF: Communication between an artery and vein caused by
error in healing.

   447.1 Stricture of artery
AHA: 2Q, '93, 8; M-A, '87, 6
I77.1 Stricture of artery   [I-10]

☑4th ☑5th **Additional Digit Required**   Unspecified Code   Other Specified Code   Manifestation Code   ►◄ Revised Text   ● New Code   ▲ Revised Code Title

2010 ICD-9-CM   **October 2009 · Volume 1 – 143**

Circulatory System

447.2–452

447.2 Rupture of artery

Erosion

Fistula, except arteriovenous } of artery

Ulcer

     EXCLUDES *traumatic rupture of artery (900.0-904.9)*

447.3 Hyperplasia of renal artery

Fibromuscular hyperplasia of renal artery

     DEF: Overgrowth of cells in muscular lining of renal artery.

447.4 Celiac artery compression syndrome

Celiac axis syndrome

Marable's syndrome

447.5 Necrosis of artery

447.6 Arteritis, unspecified

Aortitis NOS   Endarteritis NOS

     EXCLUDES *arteritis, endarteritis:*

         aortic arch (446.7)

         cerebral (437.4)

         coronary (414.00-414.07)

         deformans (440.0-440.9)

         obliterans (440.0-440.9)

         pulmonary (417.8)

         senile (440.0-440.9)

      polyarteritis NOS (446.0)

      syphilitic aortitis (093.1)

     AHA: 1Q, '95, 3

447.8 Other specified disorders of arteries and arterioles

Fibromuscular hyperplasia of arteries, except renal

447.9 Unspecified disorders of arteries and arterioles

√4ᵗʰ **448 Disease of capillaries**

448.0 Hereditary hemorrhagic telangiectasia

Rendu-Osler-Weber disease

     DEF: Genetic disease with onset after puberty; results in multiple telangiectases, dilated venules on skin and mucous membranes; recurrent bleeding may occur.

448.1 Nevus, non-neoplastic

Nevus: Nevus:

   araneus   spider

   senile   stellar

     EXCLUDES *neoplastic (216.0-216.9)*

         port wine (757.32)

         strawberry (757.32)

     DEF: Enlarged or malformed blood vessels of skin; results in reddish swelling, skin patch, or birthmark.

448.9 Other and unspecified capillary diseases

Capillary:

   hemorrhage

   hyperpermeability

   thrombosis

     EXCLUDES *capillary fragility (hereditary) (287.8)*

449 Septic arterial embolism

Code first underlying infection, such as:

   infective endocarditis (421.0)

   lung abscess (513.0)

Use additional code to identify the site of the embolism (433.0-433.9, 444.0-444.9)

     EXCLUDES *septic pulmonary embolism (415.12)*

     AHA: 4Q, '07, 84-85

DISEASES OF VEINS AND LYMPHATICS, AND OTHER DISEASES OF CIRCULATORY SYSTEM (451-459)

√4ᵗʰ **451 Phlebitis and thrombophlebitis**

     INCLUDES endophlebitis

         inflammation, vein

         periphlebitis

         suppurative phlebitis

Use additional E code to identify drug, if drug-induced

     EXCLUDES *that complicating:*

         abortion (634-638 with .7, 639.8)

         ectopic or molar pregnancy (639.8)

         pregnancy, childbirth, or the puerperium (671.0-671.9)

     that due to or following:

         implant or catheter device (996.61-996.62)

         infusion, perfusion, or transfusion (999.2)

     DEF: Inflammation of a vein (phlebitis) with formation of a thrombus (thrombophlebitis).

     AHA: 1Q, '92, 16

     TIP: Do not assign an additional code from category 453 for thrombosis; if both conditions are present, assign only a code from category 451.

451.0 Of superficial vessels of lower extremities

Saphenous vein (greater) (lesser)

     AHA: 3Q, '91, 16

√5ᵗʰ **451.1 Of deep vessels of lower extremities**

     AHA: 3Q, '91, 16

     451.11 Femoral vein (deep) (superficial)

     451.19 Other

         Femoropopliteal vein

         Popliteal vein

         Tibial vein

451.2 Of lower extremities, unspecified

     AHA: 4Q, '04, 80

√5ᵗʰ **451.8 Of other sites**

     EXCLUDES *intracranial venous sinus (325)*

         nonpyogenic (437.6)

         portal (vein) (572.1)

     451.81 Iliac vein

     451.82 Of superficial veins of upper extremities

         Antecubital vein

         Basilic vein

         Cephalic vein

     451.83 Of deep veins of upper extremities

         Brachial vein

         Radial vein

         Ulnar vein

     451.84 Of upper extremities, unspecified

     451.89 Other

         Axillary vein

         Jugular vein

         Subclavian vein

         Thrombophlebitis of breast (Mondor's disease)

451.9 Of unspecified site

452 Portal vein thrombosis

Portal (vein) obstruction

     EXCLUDES *hepatic vein thrombosis (453.0)*

         phlebitis of portal vein (572.1)

     DEF: Formation of a blood clot in main vein of liver.

   N Newborn Age: 0   **P** Pediatric Age: 0-17   **M** Maternity Age: 12-55   **A** Adult Age: 15-124

Map of Major Veins

√4ᵗʰ **453 Other venous embolism and thrombosis**

　　EXCLUDES　*that complicating:*
　　　　　abortion (634-638 with .7, 639.8)
　　　　　ectopic or molar pregnancy (639.8)
　　　　　pregnancy, childbirth, or the puerperium
　　　　　　(671.0-671.9)

　　AHA: 1Q, '92, 16

453.0 Budd-Chiari syndrome
　　　Hepatic vein thrombosis
　　　DEF: Thrombosis or other obstruction of hepatic vein;
　　　symptoms include enlarged liver, extensive collateral vessels,
　　　intractable ascites and severe portal hypertension.

453.1 Thrombophlebitis migrans
　　　DEF: Slow, advancing thrombophlebitis; appearing first in one
　　　vein then another.

▲ **453.2 Of inferior vena cava**

453.3 Of renal vein

▲ √5ᵗʰ **453.4 Acute venous embolism and thrombosis of deep**
　　　vessels of lower extremity
　　　AHA: 3Q, '08,16

▲ 　　**453.40 Acute venous embolism and thrombosis of**
　　　　unspecified deep vessels of lower extremity
　　　　Deep vein thrombosis NOS
　　　　DVT NOS
　　　　I82.40 Embo & thrombo of uns deep veins　I-10
　　　　of lower extrem

▲ 　　**453.41 Acute venous embolism and thrombosis of**
　　　　deep vessels of proximal lower extremity
　　　　Femoral
　　　　Iliac
　　　　Popliteal
　　　　Thigh
　　　　Upper leg NOS
　　　　AHA: 4Q, '04, 79

▲ 　　**453.42 Acute venous embolism and thrombosis of**
　　　　deep vessels of distal lower extremity
　　　　Calf
　　　　Lower leg NOS
　　　　Peroneal
　　　　Tibial

● √5ᵗʰ **453.5 Chronic venous embolism and thrombosis of deep**
　　　vessels of lower extremity
　　　Use additional code, if applicable, for associated
　　　long-term (current) use of anticoagulants (V58.61)
　　　　EXCLUDES　*personal history of venous thrombosis and*
　　　　　embolism (V12.51)

● 　　**453.50 Chronic venous embolism and thrombosis of**
　　　　unspecified deep vessels of lower extremity

● 　　**453.51 Chronic venous embolism and thrombosis of**
　　　　deep vessels of proximal lower extremity

● 　　**453.52 Chronic venous embolism and thrombosis of**
　　　　deep vessels of distal lower extremity

● 　　**453.6 Venous embolism and thrombosis of superficial vessels**
　　　of lower extremity
　　　Saphenous vein (greater) (lesser)

● √5ᵗʰ **453.7 Chronic venous embolism and thrombosis of other**
　　　specified vessels
　　　Use additional code, if applicable, for associated
　　　long-term (current) use of anticoagulants (V58.61)
　　　　EXCLUDES　*personal history of venous thrombosis and*
　　　　　embolism (V12.51)

　　453.71 Chronic venous embolism and thrombosis of
　　　　superficial veins of upper extremity
　　　　Antecubital vein
　　　　Basilic vein
　　　　Cephalic vein

√4ᵗʰ
√5ᵗʰ　Additional Digit Required　　**Unspecified Code**　　　Other Specified Code　　　Manifestation Code　　　▶◀ Revised Text　　● New Code　　▲ Revised Code Title

2010 ICD-9-CM　　　　　　　　　　　　　　　　　　　　　　　　　　　　　　　**October 2009 • Volume 1 – 145**

Circulatory System

● **453.72** Chronic venous embolism and thrombosis of deep veins of upper extremity
Brachial vein
Radial vein
Ulnar vein

● **453.73** Chronic venous embolism and thrombosis of upper extremity, unspecified

● **453.74** Chronic venous embolism and thrombosis of axillary veins

● **453.75** Chronic venous embolism and thrombosis of subclavian veins

● **453.76** Chronic venous embolism and thrombosis of internal jugular veins

● **453.77** Chronic venous embolism and thrombosis of other thoracic veins
Brachiocephalic (innominate)
Superior vena cava

● **453.79** Chronic venous embolism and thrombosis of other specified veins

▲ √5th **453.8** Acute venous embolism and thrombosis of other specified veins
EXCLUDES cerebral (434.0-434.9)
coronary (410.00-410.92)
intracranial venous sinus (325)
nonpyogenic (437.6)
mesenteric (557.0)
portal (452)
precerebral (433.0-433.9)
pulmonary (415.19)

AHA: 3Q, '91, 16; M-A, '87, 6

● **453.81** Acute venous embolism and thrombosis of superficial veins of upper extremity
Antecubital vein
Basilic vein
Cephalic vein

● **453.82** Acute venous embolism and thrombosis of deep veins of upper extremity
Brachial vein   Ulnar vein
Radial vein

● **453.83** Acute venous embolism and thrombosis of upper extremity, unspecified

● **453.84** Acute venous embolism and thrombosis of axillary veins

● **453.85** Acute venous embolism and thrombosis of subclavian veins

● **453.86** Acute venous embolism and thrombosis of internal jugular veins

● **453.87** Acute venous embolism and thrombosis of other thoracic veins
Brachiocephalic (innominate)
Superior vena cava

● **453.89** Acute venous embolism and thrombosis of other specified veins
I82.89 Embolism and thrombosis of other [I-10] specified veins

453.9 **Of unspecified site**
Embolism of vein
Thrombosis (vein)

√4th **454** Varicose veins of lower extremities
EXCLUDES that complicating pregnancy, childbirth, or the puerperium (671.0)
DEF: Dilated leg veins; due to incompetent vein valves that allow reversed blood flow and cause tissue erosion or weakness of wall; may be painful.
AHA: 2Q, '91, 20

454.0 **With ulcer** [A]
Varicose ulcer (lower extremity, any part)
Varicose veins with ulcer of lower extremity [any part] or of unspecified site
Any condition classifiable to 454.9 with ulcer or specified as ulcerated
AHA: 4Q, '99, 18

454.1 **With inflammation** [A]
Stasis dermatitis
Varicose veins with inflammation of lower extremity [any part] or of unspecified site
Any condition classifiable to 454.9 with inflammation or specified as inflamed

454.2 **With ulcer and inflammation** [A]
Varicose veins with ulcer and inflammation of lower extremity [any part] or of unspecified site
Any condition classifiable to 454.9 with ulcer and inflammation

454.8 **With other complications**
Edema
Pain
Swelling
AHA: 4Q, '02, 58

454.9 **Asymptomatic varicose veins** [A]
Phlebectasia ⎫
Varicose veins ⎬ of lower extremity [any part] or of unspecified site
Varix ⎭
Varicose veins NOS
AHA: 4Q, '02, 58
TIP: Do not assign if patient seen for surgical treatment of varicose veins; query physician for specific symptom (inflammation, pain, edema, swelling).

√4th **455** Hemorrhoids
INCLUDES hemorrhoids (anus) (rectum)
piles
varicose veins, anus or rectum
EXCLUDES that complicating pregnancy, childbirth, or the puerperium (671.8)
DEF: Varicose condition of external hemorrhoidal veins causing painful swellings at the anus.

455.0 **Internal hemorrhoids without mention of complication**
AHA: 3Q, '05, 17
I84.21 Internal hemorrhoids without complication [I-10]

455.1 **Internal thrombosed hemorrhoids**

455.2 **Internal hemorrhoids with other complication**
Internal hemorrhoids: Internal hemorrhoids:
bleeding   strangulated
prolapsed   ulcerated
AHA: 3Q, '05, 17; 1Q, '03, 8
I84.111 Internal bleeding hemorrhoids [I-10]

455.3 **External hemorrhoids without mention of complication**
AHA: 1Q, '07, 13; 3Q, '05, 17
I84.22 External hemorrhoids without complicaton [I-10]

455.4 **External thrombosed hemorrhoids**

455.5 **External hemorrhoids with other complication**
External hemorrhoids:
bleeding
prolapsed
strangulated
ulcerated
AHA: 3Q, '05, 17; 1Q, '03, 8

455.6 **Unspecified hemorrhoids without mention of complication**
Hemorrhoids NOS

455.7 **Unspecified thrombosed hemorrhoids**
Thrombosed hemorrhoids, unspecified whether internal or external

455.8 **Unspecified hemorrhoids with other complication**
Hemorrhoids, unspecified whether internal or external:
bleeding
prolapsed
strangulated
ulcerated

455.9 **Residual hemorrhoidal skin tags**
Skin tags, anus or rectum

[N] Newborn Age: 0   [P] Pediatric Age: 0-17   [M] Maternity Age: 12-55   [A] Adult Age: 15-124

√4th 456 Varicose veins of other sites

456.0 Esophageal varices with bleeding
DEF: Distended, tortuous, veins of lower esophagus, usually due to portal hypertension.

456.1 Esophageal varices without mention of bleeding

√5th 456.2 Esophageal varices in diseases classified elsewhere
Code first underlying cause, as:
  cirrhosis of liver (571.0-571.9)
  portal hypertension (572.3)

  456.20 With bleeding
    AHA: N-D, '85, 14
    I85.11 Secondary esophageal varices with bleeding   I-10

  456.21 Without mention of bleeding
    AHA: 3Q, '05, 15; 2Q, '02, 4

456.3 Sublingual varices
DEF: Distended, tortuous veins beneath tongue.

456.4 Scrotal varices   ♂
Varicocele

456.5 Pelvic varices
Varices of broad ligament

456.6 Vulval varices   ♀
Varices of perineum
  EXCLUDES   *that complicating pregnancy, childbirth, or the puerperium (671.1)*

456.8 Varices of other sites
Varicose veins of nasal septum (with ulcer)
  EXCLUDES   *placental varices (656.7)*
    retinal varices (362.17)
    varicose ulcer of unspecified site (454.0)
    varicose veins of unspecified site (454.9)
AHA: 2Q, '02, 4

√4th 457 Noninfectious disorders of lymphatic channels

457.0 Postmastectomy lymphedema syndrome   A
Elephantiasis
Obliteration of lymphatic vessel } due to mastectomy
DEF: Reduced lymphatic circulation following mastectomy; symptoms include swelling of the arm on the operative side.
AHA: 2Q, '02, 12

457.1 Other lymphedema
Elephantiasis (nonfilarial) NOS   Lymphedema:
Lymphangiectasis   secondary
Lymphedema: Obliteration, lymphatic
  acquired (chronic)   vessel
  praecox
  EXCLUDES   *elephantiasis (nonfilarial):*
    congenital (757.0)
    eyelid (374.83)
    vulva (624.8)
DEF: Fluid retention due to reduced lymphatic circulation; due to other than mastectomy.
AHA: 3Q, '04, 5
I89.0 Lymphedema not elsewhere classified   I-10

457.2 Lymphangitis
Lymphangitis:
  NOS
  chronic
  subacute
  EXCLUDES   *acute lymphangitis (682.0-682.9)*

457.8 Other noninfectious disorders of lymphatic channels
Chylocele (nonfilarial)
Chylous:
  ascites
  cyst
Lymph node or vessel:
  fistula
  infarction
  rupture
  EXCLUDES   *chylocele:*
    filarial (125.0-125.9)
    tunica vaginalis (nonfilarial) (608.84)
AHA: 1Q, '04, 5; 3Q, '03, 17

457.9 Unspecified noninfectious disorder of lymphatic channels

√4th 458 Hypotension
INCLUDES   hypopiesis
EXCLUDES   *cardiovascular collapse (785.50)*
    maternal hypotension syndrome (669.2)
    shock (785.50-785.59)
    Shy-Drager syndrome (333.0)

458.0 Orthostatic hypotension
Hypotension:
  orthostatic (chronic)
  postural
DEF: Low blood pressure; occurs when standing.
AHA: 3Q, '00, 8; 3Q, '91, 9
I95.1 Orthostatic hypotension   I-10

458.1 Chronic hypotension
Permanent idiopathic hypotension
DEF: Persistent low blood pressure.

√5th 458.2 Iatrogenic hypotension
DEF: Abnormally low blood pressure; due to medical treatment.
AHA: 4Q, '03, 60; 3Q, '02, 12; 4Q, '95, 57

  458.21 Hypotension of hemodialysis
    Intra-dialytic hypotension
    AHA: 4Q, '03, 61

  458.29 Other iatrogenic hypotension
    Postoperative hypotension
    I95.81 Postprocedural hypotension   I-10

458.8 Other specified hypotension
AHA: 4Q, '97, 37

458.9 Hypotension, unspecified
Hypotension (arterial) NOS
I95.9 Hypotension unspecified   I-10

√4th 459 Other disorders of circulatory system

459.0 Hemorrhage, unspecified
Rupture of blood vessel NOS
Spontaneous hemorrhage NEC
  EXCLUDES   *hemorrhage:*
    gastrointestinal NOS (578.9)
    in newborn NOS (772.9)
    secondary or recurrent following trauma (958.2)
    traumatic rupture of blood vessel (900.0-904.9)
    nontraumatic hematoma of soft tissue (729.92)
AHA: 4Q, '90, 26
R58 Hemorrhage not elsewhere classified   I-10

√4th √5th   Additional Digit Required   Unspecified Code   Other Specified Code   Manifestation Code   ▶◀ Revised Text   ● New Code   ▲ Revised Code Title

2010 ICD-9-CM   **Volume 1 – 147**

Circulatory System

✓5ᵗʰ 459.1 Postphlebitic syndrome
Chronic venous hypertension due to deep vein thrombosis

> **EXCLUDES** *chronic venous hypertension without deep vein thrombosis (459.30-459.39)*

DEF: Various conditions following deep vein thrombosis; including edema, pain, stasis dermatitis, cellulitis, varicose veins and ulceration of the lower leg.
AHA: 4Q, '02, 58; 2Q, '91, 20

459.10 Postphlebitic syndrome without complications
Asymptomatic postphlebitic syndrome
Postphlebitic syndrome NOS

459.11 Postphlebitic syndrome with ulcer

459.12 Postphlebitic syndrome with inflammation

459.13 Postphlebitic syndrome with ulcer and inflammation

459.19 Postphlebitic syndrome with other complication

459.2 Compression of vein
Stricture of vein
Vena cava syndrome (inferior) (superior)

✓5ᵗʰ 459.3 Chronic venous hypertension (idiopathic)
Stasis edema

> **EXCLUDES** *chronic venous hypertension due to deep vein thrombosis (459.10-459.9)*
> *varicose veins (454.0-454.9)*

AHA: 4Q, '02, 59

459.30 Chronic venous hypertension without complications
Asymptomatic chronic venous hypertension
Chronic venous hypertension NOS

459.31 Chronic venous hypertension with ulcer
AHA: 4Q, '02, 43

459.32 Chronic venous hypertension with inflammation

459.33 Chronic venous hypertension with ulcer and inflammation

459.39 Chronic venous hypertension with other complication

✓5ᵗʰ 459.8 Other specified disorders of circulatory system

459.81 Venous (peripheral) insufficiency, unspecified
Chronic venous insufficiency NOS

Use additional code for any associated ulceration (707.10-707.9)

DEF: Insufficient drainage, venous blood, any part of body, results in edema or dermatosis.
AHA: 3Q, '04, 5; 2Q, '91, 20; M-A, '87, 6
TIP: Assign for stasis dermatitis without varicose veins or past DVT.
I87.2 Venous insufficiency (chronic) ▮ I-10
(peripheral)

459.89 Other
Collateral circulation (venous), any site
Phlebosclerosis
Venofibrosis

459.9 Unspecified circulatory system disorder

---

8. DISEASES OF THE RESPIRATORY SYSTEM (460-519)

Use additional code to identify infectious organism

ACUTE RESPIRATORY INFECTIONS (460-466)

EXCLUDES *pneumonia and influenza (480.0-488)*

460 Acute nasopharyngitis [common cold]
Coryza (acute)   Rhinitis:
Nasal catarrh, acute   acute
Nasopharyngitis: infective
  NOS
  acute
  infective NOS

EXCLUDES *nasopharyngitis, chronic (472.2)*
pharyngitis:
acute or unspecified (462)
chronic (472.1)
rhinitis:
allergic (477.0-477.9)
chronic or unspecified (472.0)
sore throat:
acute or unspecified (462)
chronic (472.1)

DEF: Acute inflammation of mucous membranes; extends from nares to pharynx.
AHA: 1Q, '88, 12

√4ᵗʰ 461 Acute sinusitis
INCLUDES abscess ⎫
empyema   ⎬ acute, of sinus (accessory)
infection   ⎪   (nasal)
inflammation ⎪
suppuration ⎭

EXCLUDES *chronic or unspecified sinusitis (473.0-473.9)*

461.0 Maxillary
Acute antritis

461.1 Frontal

461.2 Ethmoidal

461.3 Sphenoidal

461.8 Other acute sinusitis
Acute pansinusitis

461.9 Acute sinusitis, unspecified
Acute sinusitis NOS
J01.90 Acute sinusitis unspecified   **I-10**

462 Acute pharyngitis
Acute sore throat NOS
Pharyngitis (acute):
  NOS
  gangrenous
  infective
  phlegmonous
  pneumococcal
  staphylococca
  suppurative
  ulcerative
Sore throat (viral) NOS
Viral pharyngitis

EXCLUDES *abscess:*
peritonsillar [quinsy] (475)
pharyngeal NOS (478.29)
retropharyngeal (478.24)
chronic pharyngitis (472.1)
infectious mononucleosis (075)
that specified as (due to):
Coxsackie (virus) (074.0)
gonococcus (098.6)
herpes simplex (054.79)
influenza (487.1)
septic (034.0)
streptococcal (034.0)
AHA: 4Q, '99, 26; S-O, '85, 8
J02.9 Acute pharyngitis unspecified   **I-10**

Respiratory System

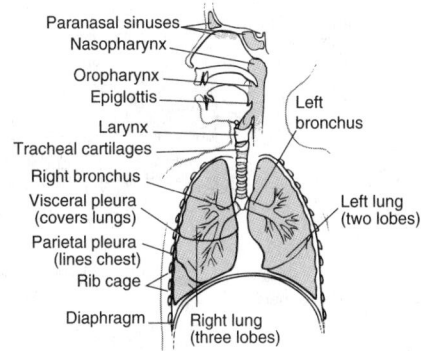

Paranasal sinuses
Nasopharynx
Oropharynx
Epiglottis
Larynx
Tracheal cartilages
Right bronchus
Visceral pleura (covers lungs)
Parietal pleura (lines chest)
Rib cage
Diaphragm
Left bronchus
Left lung (two lobes)
Right lung (three lobes)

463 Acute tonsillitis
Tonsillitis (acute):   Tonsillitis (acute):
  NOS   septic
  follicular   staphylococcal
  gangrenous   suppurative
  infective   ulcerative
  pneumococcal   viral

EXCLUDES *chronic tonsillitis (474.0)*
hypertrophy of tonsils (474.1)
peritonsillar abscess [quinsy] (475)
sore throat:
acute or NOS (462)
septic (034.0)
streptococcal tonsillitis (034.0)
AHA: N-D, '84, 16

√4ᵗʰ 464 Acute laryngitis and tracheitis
EXCLUDES *that associated with influenza (487.1)*
that due to Streptococcus (034.0)

√5ᵗʰ 464.0 Acute laryngitis
Laryngitis (acute):
  NOS
  edematous
  Hemophilus influenzae [H. influenzae]
  pneumococcal
  septic
  suppurative
  ulcerative
EXCLUDES *chronic laryngitis (476.0-476.1)*
influenzal laryngitis (487.1)
AHA: 4Q, '01, 42

464.00 Without mention of obstruction

464.01 With obstruction

√5ᵗʰ 464.1 Acute tracheitis
Tracheitis (acute):
  NOS
  catarrhal
  viral
EXCLUDES *chronic tracheitis (491.8)*

464.10 Without mention of obstruction

464.11 With obstruction

√5ᵗʰ 464.2 Acute laryngotracheitis
Laryngotracheitis (acute)
Tracheitis (acute) with laryngitis (acute)
EXCLUDES *chronic laryngotracheitis (476.1)*

464.20 Without mention of obstruction

464.21 With obstruction

√5ᵗʰ 464.3 Acute epiglottitis
Viral epiglottitis
EXCLUDES *epiglottitis, chronic (476.1)*

464.30 Without mention of obstruction

464.31 With obstruction

√4ᵗʰ Additional Digit Required   **Unspecified Code**   **Other Specified Code**   **Manifestation Code**   ▶◀ Revised Text   ● New Code   ▲ Revised Code Title
√5ᵗʰ
2010 ICD-9-CM   **Volume 1 – 149**

460–464.31

Upper Respiratory System

Paranasal sinuses drain into nose via ducts under nasal conchae

Frontal sinus

Olfactory bulb and nerves

Sphenoid sinus

Window in nasal septum reveals lateral nasal wall

Orifice of auditory tube

Nasal cavity from front

Soft palate

Naris

Epiglottis

Nasal conchae

Meati

Vocal cords

Septum

Larynx

Cricoid cartilage

Trachea

464.4 Croup
Croup syndrome

DEF: Acute laryngeal obstruction due to allergy, foreign body or infection; symptoms include barking cough, hoarseness and harsh, persistent high-pitched respiratory sound.

J05.0 Acute obstructive laryngitis [croup] `I-10`

√5ᵗʰ 464.5 Supraglottitis, unspecified
DEF: A rapidly advancing generalized upper respiratory infection of the lingual tonsillar area, epiglottic folds, false vocal cords, and the epiglottis; seen most commonly in children, but can affect people of any age.

AHA: 4Q, '01, 42

464.50 Without mention of obstruction
AHA: 4Q, '01, 43

464.51 With obstruction

√4ᵗʰ 465 Acute upper respiratory infections of multiple or unspecified sites
EXCLUDES upper respiratory infection due to:
influenza (487.1)
Streptococcus (034.0)

465.0 Acute laryngopharyngitis
DEF: Acute infection of the vocal cords and pharynx.

465.8 Other multiple sites
Multiple URI

AHA: 4Q, '07, 85

465.9 Unspecified site
Acute URI NOS
Upper respiratory infection (acute)

J06.9 Acute upper respiratory infection unspecified `I-10`

√4ᵗʰ 466 Acute bronchitis and bronchiolitis
INCLUDES that with:
bronchospasm
obstruction

466.0 Acute bronchitis
Bronchitis, acute or subacute:
fibrinous
membranous
pneumococcal
purulent
septic
viral
with tracheitis
Croupous bronchitis
Tracheobronchitis, acute

EXCLUDES acute bronchitis with chronic obstructive pulmonary disease (491.22)

DEF: Acute inflammation of main branches of bronchial tree due to infectious or irritant agents; symptoms include cough with a varied production of sputum, fever, substernal soreness, and lung rales.

AHA: 4Q, '04, 137; 1Q, '04, 3; 4Q, '02, 46; 4Q, '96, 28; 4Q, '91, 24; 1Q, '88, 12

TIP: If documented with COPD, assign only 491.22 Obstructive chronic bronchitis with acute bronchitis.

J20.9 Acute bronchitis unspecified `I-10`

√5ᵗʰ 466.1 Acute bronchiolitis
Bronchiolitis (acute)
Capillary pneumonia

DEF: Acute inflammation of main branches of bronchial tree due to infectious or irritant agents; symptoms include cough, tachycardia, and lung crackles.

466.11 Acute bronchiolitis due to respiratory syncytial virus (RSV)
AHA: 1Q, '05, 10; 4Q, '96, 27

J21.0 Acute bronchiolitis d/t resp syncytial virus `I-10`

466.19 Acute bronchiolitis due to other infectious organisms
Use additional code to identify organism

J21.8 Acute bronchiolitis d/t oth specified organisms `I-10`

OTHER DISEASES OF THE UPPER RESPIRATORY TRACT (470-478)

470 Deviated nasal septum
Deflected septum (nasal) (acquired)

EXCLUDES congenital (754.0)

√4ᵗʰ 471 Nasal polyps
EXCLUDES adenomatous polyps (212.0)

471.0 Polyp of nasal cavity
Polyp:
choanal

Polyp:
nasopharyngeal

471.1 Polypoid sinus degeneration
Woakes' syndrome or ethmoiditis

471.8 Other polyp of sinus
Polyp of sinus:
accessory
ethmoidal
maxillary
sphenoidal

471.9 Unspecified nasal polyp
Nasal polyp NOS

√4ᵗʰ 472 Chronic pharyngitis and nasopharyngitis
472.0 Chronic rhinitis
Ozena
Rhinitis:
NOS
atrophic
granulomatous

Rhinitis:
hypertrophic
obstructive
purulent
ulcerative

EXCLUDES allergic rhinitis (477.0-477.9)

DEF: Persistent inflammation of mucous membranes of nose.

472.1 Chronic pharyngitis
Chronic sore throat
Pharyngitis:
atrophic
granular (chronic)
hypertrophic

472.2 Chronic nasopharyngitis
EXCLUDES acute or unspecified nasopharyngitis (460)

DEF: Persistent inflammation of mucous membranes extending from nares to pharynx.

√4ᵗʰ 473 Chronic sinusitis
INCLUDES abscess
empyema
infection
suppuration

(chronic) of sinus
(accessory) (nasal)

EXCLUDES acute sinusitis (461.0-461.9)

473.0 Maxillary
Antritis (chronic)

J32.0 Chronic maxillary sinusitis `I-10`

473.1 Frontal

473.2 Ethmoidal
EXCLUDES Woakes' ethmoiditis (471.1)

473.3 Sphenoidal

N Newborn Age: 0   P Pediatric Age: 0-17   M Maternity Age: 12-55   A Adult Age: 15-124

Paranasal Sinuses

Frontal
Ethmoid
Sphenoid
Maxillary

Frontal

Ethmoid
Sphenoid

Maxillary

473.8 Other chronic sinusitis
Pansinusitis (chronic)

473.9 Unspecified sinusitis (chronic)
Sinusitis (chronic) NOS

J32.9 Chronic sinusitis unspecified   [I-10]

✓4ᵗʰ **474 Chronic disease of tonsils and adenoids**

✓5ᵗʰ **474.0 Chronic tonsillitis and adenoiditis**
EXCLUDES   *acute or unspecified tonsillitis (463)*
AHA: 4Q, '97, 38

474.00 Chronic tonsillitis

474.01 Chronic adenoiditis

474.02 Chronic tonsillitis and adenoiditis

✓5ᵗʰ **474.1 Hypertrophy of tonsils and adenoids**
Enlargement ⎫
Hyperplasia ⎬ of tonsils or adenoids
Hypertrophy ⎭

EXCLUDES   *that with:*
adenoiditis (474.01)
adenoiditis and tonsillitis (474.02)
tonsillitis (474.00)

474.10 Tonsils with adenoids
AHA: 2Q, '05, 16

474.11 Tonsils alone

474.12 Adenoids alone

474.2 Adenoid vegetations
DEF: Fungus-like growth of lymph tissue between the nares and pharynx.

474.8 Other chronic disease of tonsils and adenoids
Amygdalolith
Calculus, tonsil
Cicatrix of tonsil (and adenoid)
Tonsillar tag
Ulcer, tonsil

474.9 Unspecified chronic disease of tonsils and adenoids
Disease (chronic) of tonsils (and adenoid)

475 Peritonsillar abscess
Abscess of tonsil   Quinsy
Peritonsillar cellulitis
EXCLUDES   *tonsillitis:*
acute or NOS (463)
chronic (474.0)

J36 Peritonsillar abscess   [I-10]

✓4ᵗʰ **476 Chronic laryngitis and laryngotracheitis**

476.0 Chronic laryngitis
Laryngitis: Laryngitis:
catarrhal   sicca
hypertrophic

476.1 Chronic laryngotracheitis
Laryngitis, chronic, with tracheitis (chronic)
Tracheitis, chronic, with laryngitis
EXCLUDES   *chronic tracheitis (491.8)*
laryngitis and tracheitis, acute or unspecified (464.00-464.51)

✓4ᵗʰ **477 Allergic rhinitis**
INCLUDES allergic rhinitis (nonseasonal) (seasonal)
hay fever
spasmodic rhinorrhea
EXCLUDES   *allergic rhinitis with asthma (bronchial) (493.0)*
DEF: True immunoglobulin E (IgE)-mediated allergic reaction of nasal mucosa; seasonal (typical hay fever) or perennial (year-round allergens: dust, food, dander).

477.0 Due to pollen
Pollinosis

477.1 Due to food
AHA: 4Q, '00, 42

477.2 Due to animal (cat) (dog) hair and dander

477.8 Due to other allergen

477.9 Cause unspecified
AHA: 2Q, '97, 9

J30.9 Allergic rhinitis unspecified   [I-10]

✓4ᵗʰ **478 Other diseases of upper respiratory tract**

478.0 Hypertrophy of nasal turbinates
DEF: Overgrowth, enlargement of shell-shaped bones, in nasal cavity.

✓5ᵗʰ **478.1 Other diseases of nasal cavity and sinuses**
EXCLUDES   *varicose ulcer of nasal septum (456.8)*

478.11 Nasal mucositis (ulcerative)
Use additional E code to identify adverse effects of therapy, such as:
antineoplastic and immunosuppressive drugs (E930.7, E933.1)
radiation therapy (E879.2)
AHA: 4Q, '06, 88-90

478.19 Other diseases of nasal cavity and sinuses
Abscess   ⎫
Necrosis ⎬ of nose (septum)
Ulcer   ⎭
Cyst or mucocele of sinus (nasal)
Rhinolith
AHA: 4Q, '06, 88-90

J34.1 Cyst and mucocele of nose and nasal sinus   [I-10]

✓5ᵗʰ **478.2 Other diseases of pharynx, not elsewhere classified**

478.20 Unspecified disease of pharynx

478.21 Cellulitis of pharynx or nasopharynx

478.22 Parapharyngeal abscess

478.24 Retropharyngeal abscess
DEF: Purulent infection, behind pharynx and front of precerebral fascia.

478.25 Edema of pharynx or nasopharynx

478.26 Cyst of pharynx or nasopharynx

478.29 Other
Abscess of pharynx or nasopharynx
EXCLUDES   *ulcerative pharyngitis (462)*

✓5ᵗʰ **478.3 Paralysis of vocal cords or larynx**
DEF: Loss of motor ability of vocal cords or larynx; due to nerve or muscle damage.

478.30 Paralysis, unspecified
Laryngoplegia
Paralysis of glottis

478.31 Unilateral, partial

478.32 Unilateral, complete

478.33 Bilateral, partial

478.34 Bilateral, complete

478.4 Polyp of vocal cord or larynx
EXCLUDES   *adenomatous polyps (212.1)*

| ✓4ᵗʰ / ✓5ᵗʰ Additional Digit Required | Unspecified Code | Other Specified Code | Manifestation Code | ▶◀ Revised Text | ● New Code | ▲ Revised Code Title |

2010 ICD-9-CM   **Volume 1 – 151**

Respiratory System

473.8–478.4

478.5 Other diseases of vocal cords

Abscess
Cellulitis
Granuloma   } of vocal cords
Leukoplakia

Chorditis (fibrinous) (nodosa) (tuberosa)
Singers' nodes

478.6 Edema of larynx
Edema (of):   Edema (of):
glottis   supraglottic
subglottic

✓5th **478.7 Other diseases of larynx, not elsewhere classified**

478.70 Unspecified disease of larynx

478.71 Cellulitis and perichondritis of larynx
DEF: Inflammation of deep soft tissues or lining of bone of the larynx.

478.74 Stenosis of larynx

478.75 Laryngeal spasm
Laryngismus (stridulus)
DEF: Involuntary muscle contraction of the larynx.

478.79 Other
Abscess
Necrosis
Obstruction   } of larynx
Pachyderma
Ulcer
EXCLUDES ulcerative laryngitis (464.00-464.01)
AHA: 3Q, '91, 20

478.8 Upper respiratory tract hypersensitivity reaction, site unspecified
EXCLUDES hypersensitivity reaction of lower respiratory tract, as:
extrinsic allergic alveolitis (495.0-495.9)
pneumoconiosis (500-505)

478.9 Other and unspecified diseases of upper respiratory tract
Abcess
Cicatrix } of trachea

PNEUMONIA AND INFLUENZA (480-488)
EXCLUDES pneumonia:
allergic or eosinophilic (518.3)
aspiration:
NOS (507.0)
newborn (770.18)
solids and liquids (507.0-507.8)
congenital (770.0)
lipoid (507.1)
passive (514)
rheumatic (390)
ventilator-associated (997.31)

✓4th **480 Viral pneumonia**

480.0 Pneumonia due to adenovirus

480.1 Pneumonia due to respiratory syncytial virus
AHA: 4Q, '96, 28; 1Q, '88, 12

480.2 Pneumonia due to parainfluenza virus

480.3 Pneumonia due to SARS-associated coronavirus
DEF: A severe adult respiratory syndrome caused by the coronavirus, specified as inflammation of the lungs with consolidation.
AHA: 4Q, '03, 46-47

480.8 Pneumonia due to other virus not elsewhere classified
EXCLUDES congenital rubella pneumonitis (771.0)
influenza with pneumonia, any form (487.0)
pneumonia complicating viral diseases classified elsewhere (484.1-484.8)

480.9 Viral pneumonia, unspecified
AHA: 3Q, '98, 5

Lungs

Right Lung   Trachea   **Left Lung**
(Three Lobes)   Primary   **(Two Lobes)**
Bronchopulmonary   S1 S3   bronchus   Secondary bronchus
segments:
Upper lobe   S2   S1,2
S3 Upper
S5   S4 lobe
Middle   S5
lobe   S6
S4
S7,8
Lower   Lower
lobe   S8   S9 lobe
S7
Diaphragm   S9 S10 S10

481 Pneumococcal pneumonia [Streptococcus pneumoniae pneumonia]
Lobar pneumonia, organism unspecified
AHA: 2Q, '98, 7; 4Q, '92, 19; 1Q, '92, 18; 1Q, '91, 13; 1Q, '88, 13; M-A, '85, 6

✓4th **482 Other bacterial pneumonia**
AHA: 4Q, '93, 39

482.0 Pneumonia due to Klebsiella pneumoniae

482.1 Pneumonia due to Pseudomonas

482.2 Pneumonia due to Hemophilus influenzae [H. influenzae]
AHA: 2Q, '05, 19

✓5th **482.3 Pneumonia due to Streptococcus**
EXCLUDES Streptococcus pneumoniae (481)
AHA: 1Q, '88, 13

482.30 Streptococcus, unspecified

482.31 Group A

482.32 Group B

482.39 Other Streptococcus

✓5th **482.4 Pneumonia due to Staphylococcus**
AHA: 3Q, '91, 16

482.40 Pneumonia due to Staphylococcus, unspecified

482.41 Methicillin susceptible pneumonia due to Staphylococcus aureus
MSSA pneumonia
Pneumonia due to Staphylococcus aureus NOS
J15.21 Pneumonia due to staphylococcus   I-10
aureus

482.42 Methicillin resistant pneumonia due to Staphylococcus aureus
AHA: ▶4Q, '08, 69, 71, 72◀

482.49 Other Staphylococcus pneumonia

✓5th **482.8 Pneumonia due to other specified bacteria**
EXCLUDES pneumonia, complicating infectious disease classified elsewhere (484.1-484.8)
AHA: 3Q, '88, 11

482.81 Anaerobes
Bacteroides (melaninogenicus)
Gram-negative anaerobes

482.82 Escherichia coli [E. coli]

482.83 **Other gram-negative bacteria**
Gram-negative pneumonia NOS
Proteus
Serratia marcescens

EXCLUDES   *gram-negative anaerobes (482.81)*
Legionnaires' disease (482.84)

AHA: 2Q, '98, 5; 3Q, '94, 9

TIP: Do not assign based solely on laboratory findings of gram-negative bacteria on gram-stain. Physician substantiation is required.

J15.6 Pneumonia d/t oth aerobic Gram-negative bacteria `I-10`

482.84 **Legionnaires' disease**
DEF: Severe and often fatal infection by Legionella pneumophilia; symptoms include high fever, gastrointestinal pain, headache, myalgia, dry cough, and pneumonia; usually transmitted airborne via air conditioning systems.

AHA: 4Q, '97, 38

482.89 **Other specified bacteria**
AHA: 2Q, '97, 6

TIP: Do not assign based on documentation of "mixed bacterial pneumonia" or "gram-positive pneumonia." See instead 482.9.

482.9 **Bacterial pneumonia unspecified**
AHA: 2Q, '98, 6; 2Q, '97, 6; 1Q, '94, 17

J15.9 Unspecified bacterial pneumonia `I-10`

✓4th 483 **Pneumonia due to other specified organism**
AHA: N-D, '87, 5

TIP: Do not assign if pneumonia due to candidiasis; see code 112.4.

483.0 **Mycoplasma pneumoniae**
Eaton's agent
Pleuropneumonia-like organism [PPLO]

483.1 **Chlamydia**
AHA: 4Q, '96, 31

483.8 **Other specified organism**

✓4th 484 **Pneumonia in infectious diseases classified elsewhere**
EXCLUDES   *influenza with pneumonia, any form (487.0)*

484.1 *Pneumonia in cytomegalic inclusion disease*
Code first underlying disease (078.5)

484.3 *Pneumonia in whooping cough*
Code first underlying disease (033.0-033.9)

484.5 *Pneumonia in anthrax*
Code first underlying disease (022.1)

484.6 *Pneumonia in aspergillosis*
Code first underlying disease (117.3)
AHA: 4Q, '97, 40

484.7 *Pneumonia in other systemic mycoses*
Code first underlying disease
EXCLUDES   *pneumonia in:*
candidiasis (112.4)
coccidioidomycosis (114.0)
histoplasmosis (115.0-115.9 with fifth-digit 5)

484.8 *Pneumonia in other infectious diseases classified elsewhere*
Code first underlying disease, as:
Q fever (083.0)
typhoid fever (002.0)
EXCLUDES   *pneumonia in:*
actinomycosis (039.1)
measles (055.1)
nocardiosis (039.1)
ornithosis (073.0)
Pneumocystis carinii (136.3)
salmonellosis (003.22)
toxoplasmosis (130.4)
tuberculosis (011.6)
tularemia (021.2)
varicella (052.1)

485 **Bronchopneumonia, organism unspecified**
Bronchopneumonia: Pneumonia:
hemorrhagic   lobular
terminal   segmental
Pleurobronchopneumonia

EXCLUDES   *bronchiolitis (acute) (466.11-466.19)*
chronic (491.8)
lipoid pneumonia (507.1)

486 **Pneumonia, organism unspecified**
EXCLUDES   *hypostatic or passive pneumonia (514)*
influenza with pneumonia, any form (487.0)
inhalation or aspiration pneumonia due to foreign materials (507.0-507.8)
pneumonitis due to fumes and vapors (506.0)

AHA: 4Q, '08, 142; 4Q, '99, 6; 3Q, '99, 9; 3Q, '98, 7; 2Q, '98, 4, 5; 1Q, '98, 8; 3Q, '97, 9; 3Q, '94, 10; 3Q, '88, 11

TIP: Never assume a causal organism based on laboratory or radiology findings alone.

J18.9 Pneumonia unspecified organism `I-10`

✓4th 487 **Influenza**
▶Influenza caused by unspecified influenza virus◄
EXCLUDES   *Hemophilus influenzae [H. influenzae]:*
infection NOS (041.5)
▶*influenza due to 2009 H1N1 [swine] influenza virus (488.1)*
influenza due to identified avian influenza virus (488.0)
influenza due to identified novel H1N1 influenza virus (488.1)◄
laryngitis (464.00-464.01)
meningitis (320.0)

487.0 **With pneumonia**
Influenza with pneumonia, any form
Influenzal:
bronchopneumonia
pneumonia
Use additional code to identify the type of pneumonia (480.0-480.9, 481, 482.0-482.9, 483.0-483.8, 485)
AHA: 1Q, '06, 18; 2Q, '05, 18

487.1 **With other respiratory manifestations**
Influenza NOS
Influenzal:
laryngitis
pharyngitis
respiratory infection (upper) (acute)
DEF: Overgrowth, enlargement of shell-shaped bones, in nasal cavity.
AHA: 1Q, '06, 18; 2Q, '05, 18; 4Q, '99, 26
TIP: Selection of the principal diagnosis will be dependent on the circumstances of admission
J10.1 Influenza d/t oth influenza virus w/resp manifst `I-10`

487.8 **With other manifestations**
Encephalopathy due to influenza
Influenza with involvement of gastrointestinal tract
EXCLUDES   *"intestinal flu" [viral gastroenteritis] (008.8)*

▲ ✓4th 488 **Influenza due to certain identified influenza viruses**
EXCLUDES   ▶*influenza caused by unspecified influenza viruses (487.0-487.8)*◄

● 488.0 **Influenza due to identified avian influenza virus**
Avian influenza
Bird flu
Influenza A/H5N1
DEF: Infection caused by contact with bird influenza viruses; results in flu-like symptoms that may progress to other severe and life-threatening complications.
AHA: 4Q, '07, 87
TIP: Assign only if identified avian influenza virus is confirmed; coding may be based on provider diagnostic statement.

● 488.1 **Influenza due to identified novel H1N1 influenza virus**
2009 H1N1 [swine] influenza virus
Novel 2009 influenza H1N1
Novel H1N1 influenza
Novel influenza A/H1N1
Swine flu

✓4th ✓5th Additional Digit Required   Unspecified Code   Other Specified Code   Manifestation Code   ▶◄ Revised Text   ● New Code   ▲ Revised Code Title

2010 ICD-9-CM   **October 2009 • Volume 1 – 153**

Bronchioli and Alveoli

To trachea
Terminal bronchiolus
Pulmonary arteriole
Elastic fibers
Capillary network over all alveioli
Alveoli
Alveolus

Interrelationship Between Chronic Airway Obstruction, Chronic Bronchitis, and Emphysema

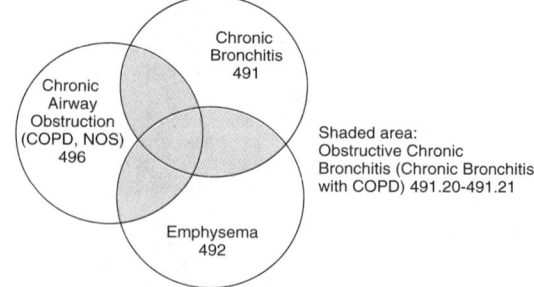

Chronic Bronchitis 491
Chronic Airway Obstruction (COPD, NOS) 496
Shaded area: Obstructive Chronic Bronchitis (Chronic Bronchitis with COPD) 491.20-491.21
Emphysema 492

CHRONIC OBSTRUCTIVE PULMONARY DISEASE AND ALLIED CONDITIONS (490-496)

AHA: 3Q, '88, 5

TIP: Due to the overlapping nature of conditions that make up COPD, it's essential that the coder review all instructional notes carefully.

490 Bronchitis, not specified as acute or chronic
Bronchitis NOS:
  catarrhal
  with tracheitis NOS
Tracheobronchitis NOS

EXCLUDES bronchitis:
  allergic NOS (493.9)
  asthmatic NOS (493.9)
  due to fumes and vapors (506.0)

J40 Bronchitis not specified as acute or chronic   I-10

✓4ᵗʰ 491 Chronic bronchitis
EXCLUDES *chronic obstructive asthma (493.2)*

491.0 Simple chronic bronchitis
Catarrhal bronchitis, chronic
Smokers' cough

J41.0 Simple chronic bronchitis

491.1 Mucopurulent chronic bronchitis
Bronchitis (chronic) (recurrent):
  fetid
  mucopurulent
  purulent

DEF: Chronic bronchial infection characterized by both mucus and pus secretions in the bronchial tree; recurs after asymptomatic periods; signs are coughing, expectoration and secondary changes in the lung.

AHA: 3Q, '88, 12

✓5ᵗʰ 491.2 Obstructive chronic bronchitis
Bronchitis:
  emphysematous
  obstructive (chronic) (diffuse)
Bronchitis with:
  chronic airway obstruction
  emphysema

EXCLUDES *asthmatic bronchitis (acute) NOS (493.9)*
  chronic obstructive asthma (493.2)

AHA: 3Q, '97, 9; 4Q, '91, 25; 2Q, '91, 21

491.20 Without exacerbation
Emphysema with chronic bronchitis

AHA: 3Q, '97, 9

491.21 With (acute) exacerbation
Acute exacerbation of chronic obstructive pulmonary disease [COPD]
Decompensated chronic obstructive pulmonary disease [COPD]
Decompensated chronic obstructive pulmonary disease [COPD] with exacerbation

EXCLUDES *chronic obstructive asthma with acute exacerbation (493.22)*

AHA: 1Q, '04, 3; 3Q, '02, 18, 19; 4Q, '01, 43; 2Q, '96, 10

J44.1 Chronic obst pulmonary disease with   I-10
exacerbation

491.22 With acute bronchitis
AHA: 3Q, '06, 20; 4Q, '04, 82

J44.0 Chronic obst pulm dz acute lower   I-10
respiratory inf

491.8 Other chronic bronchitis
Chronic:
  tracheitis
  tracheobronchitis

491.9 Unspecified chronic bronchitis
J42 Unspecified chronic bronchitis   I-10

✓4ᵗʰ 492 Emphysema
AHA: 2Q, '91, 21

492.0 Emphysematous bleb
Giant bullous emphysema
Ruptured emphysematous bleb
Tension pneumatocele
Vanishing lung

DEF: Formation of vesicle or bulla in emphysematous lung, more than one millimeter; contains serum or blood.

AHA: 2Q, '93, 3

492.8 Other emphysema
Emphysema (lung or pulmonary):
  NOS
  centriacinar
  centrilobular
  obstructive
  panacinar
  panlobular
  unilateral
  vesicular
MacLeod's syndrome
Swyer-James syndrome
Unilateral hyperlucent lung

EXCLUDES emphysema:
  with chronic bronchitis (491.20-491.22)
  compensatory (518.2)
  due to fumes and vapors (506.4)
  interstitial (518.1)
    newborn (770.2)
  mediastinal (518.1)
  surgical (subcutaneous) (998.81)
  traumatic (958.7)

AHA: ▶4Q, '08, 175;◀ 1Q, '05, 4; 4Q, '93, 41; J-A, '84, 17

J43.9 Emphysema unspecified   I-10

✓4ᵗʰ 493 Asthma
EXCLUDES *wheezing NOS (786.07)*

The following fifth-digit subclassification is for use with codes 493.0-493.2, 493.9:
  0 unspecified
  1 with status asthmaticus
  2 with (acute) exacerbation

DEF: Status asthmaticus: severe, intractable episode of asthma unresponsive to normal therapeutic measures.

AHA: 4Q, '04, 137; 4Q, '03, 62; 4Q, '01, 43; 4Q, '00, 42; 1Q, '91, 13; 3Q, '88, 9; J-A, '85, 8; N-D, '84, 17

TIP: If documentation indicates both exacerbation and status asthmaticus, assign only the code for status asthmaticus.

N Newborn Age: 0   P Pediatric Age: 0-17   M Maternity Age: 12-55   A Adult Age: 15-124

§ ✓5ᵗʰ **493.0 Extrinsic asthma**
[0-2]
     Asthma:
         allergic with stated cause
         atopic
         childhood
         hay
         platinum
     Hay fever with asthma

     EXCLUDES *asthma:*
         allergic NOS (493.9)
         detergent (507.8)
         miners' (500)
         wood (495.8)

     DEF: Transient stricture of airway diameters of bronchi; due to environmental factor; also called allergic (bronchial) asthma.

     J45.20 Mild intermittent asthma uncomplicated   I-10

§ ✓5ᵗʰ **493.1 Intrinsic asthma**
[0-2]
     Late-onset asthma

     DEF: Transient stricture, of airway diameters of bronchi; due to pathophysiological disturbances.

     AHA: 3Q, '88, 9; M-A, '85, 7

§ ✓5ᵗʰ **493.2 Chronic obstructive asthma**
[0-2]
     Asthma with chronic obstructive pulmonary disease [COPD]
     Chronic asthmatic bronchitis

     EXCLUDES *acute bronchitis (466.0)*
         chronic obstructive bronchitis (491.20-491.22)

     DEF: Persistent narrowing of airway diameters in the bronchial tree, restricting airflow and causing constant labored breathing.

     AHA: 2Q, '91, 21; 2Q, '90, 20; **For code 493.20:** 4Q, '03, 108; **For code 493.22:** ▶1Q, '09, 17;◀ 3Q, '06, 20

✓5ᵗʰ **493.8 Other forms of asthma**

     AHA: 4Q, '03, 62

     493.81 Exercise induced bronchospasm

     493.82 Cough variant asthma

§ ✓5ᵗʰ **493.9 Asthma, unspecified**
[0-2]
     Asthma (bronchial) (allergic NOS)
     Bronchitis:
         allergic
         asthmatic

     AHA: 4Q, '97, 40, **For code 493.90:** 4Q, '04, 137; 4Q, '03, 108; 4Q, '99, 25; 1Q, '97, 7; **For code 493.91:** 1Q, '05, 5; **For code 493.92:** 1Q, '03, 9

     J45.909 Unspecified asthma uncomplicated   I-10
     J45.901 Unspecified asthma with acute exacerbation   I-10

✓4ᵗʰ **494 Bronchiectasis**
     Bronchiectasis (fusiform) (postinfectious) (recurrent)
     Bronchiolectasis

     EXCLUDES *congenital (748.61)*
         tuberculous bronchiectasis (current disease) (011.5)

     DEF: Dilation of bronchi; due to infection or chronic conditions; causes decreased lung capacity and recurrent infections of lungs.

     AHA: 4Q, '00, 42

     494.0 Bronchiectasis without acute exacerbation

         J47.9 Bronchiectasis uncomplicated   I-10

     494.1 Bronchiectasis with acute exacerbation

✓4ᵗʰ **495 Extrinsic allergic alveolitis**

     INCLUDES allergic alveolitis and pneumonitis due to inhaled organic dust particles of fungal, thermophilic actinomycete, or other origin

     DEF: Pneumonitis due to particles inhaled into lung, often at workplace; symptoms include cough, chills, fever, increased heart and respiratory rates; develops within hours of exposure.

     495.0 Farmers' lung

     495.1 Bagassosis

     495.2 Bird-fanciers' lung
         Budgerigar-fanciers' disease or lung
         Pigeon-fanciers' disease or lung

     495.3 Suberosis
         Cork-handlers' disease or lung

     495.4 Malt workers' lung
         Alveolitis due to Aspergillus clavatus

     495.5 Mushroom workers' lung

     495.6 Maple bark-strippers' lung
         Alveolitis due to Cryptostroma corticale

     495.7 "Ventilation" pneumonitis
         Allergic alveolitis due to fungal, thermophilic actinomycete, and other organisms growing in ventilation [air conditioning] systems

     495.8 Other specified allergic alveolitis and pneumonitis
         Cheese-washers' lung
         Coffee workers' lung
         Fish-meal workers' lung
         Furriers' lung
         Grain-handlers' disease or lung
         Pituitary snuff-takers' disease
         Sequoiosis or red-cedar asthma
         Wood asthma

     495.9 Unspecified allergic alveolitis and pneumonitis
         Alveolitis, allergic (extrinsic)
         Hypersensitivity pneumonitis

496 Chronic airway obstruction, not elsewhere classified
     Note: This code is not to be used with any code from categories 491-493
     Chronic:
         nonspecific lung disease
         obstructive lung disease
         obstructive pulmonary disease [COPD] NOS

     EXCLUDES *chronic obstructive lung disease [COPD] specified (as) (with):*
         allergic alveolitis (495.0-495.9)
         asthma (493.20-493.22)
         bronchiectasis (494.0-494.1)
         bronchitis (491.20-491.22)
             with emphysema (491.20-491.22)
         decompensated (491.21)
         emphysema (492.0-492.8)

     AHA: ▶1Q, '09, 16;◀ 3Q, '07, 10; 4Q, '03, 109; 2Q, '00, 15; 2Q, '92, 16; 2Q, '91, 21; 3Q, '88, 56

     TIP: COPD is a nonspecific term that encompasses many different respiratory conditions; review medical record and query physician for more specific documentation of emphysema, bronchitis, asthma, etc.

     J44.9 Chronic obstructive pulmonary disease unspec   I-10

PNEUMOCONIOSES AND OTHER LUNG DISEASES DUE TO EXTERNAL AGENTS (500-508)

     DEF: Permanent deposits of particulate matter, within lungs; due to occupational or environmental exposure; results in chronic induration and fibrosis. (See specific listings in 500-508 code range)

500 Coal workers' pneumoconiosis   A
     Anthracosilicosis
     Anthracosis
     Black lung disease
     Coal workers' lung
     Miner's asthma

501 Asbestosis   A

502 Pneumoconiosis due to other silica or silicates
     Pneumoconiosis due to talc
     Silicotic fibrosis (massive) of lung
     Silicosis (simple) (complicated)

503 Pneumoconiosis due to other inorganic dust
     Aluminosis (of lung)
     Baritosis
     Bauxite fibrosis (of lung)
     Berylliosis
     Graphite fibrosis (of lung)
     Siderosis
     Stannosis

---

§   Requires fifth digit. Valid digits are in [brackets] under each code. See category 493 for codes and definitions.

✓4ᵗʰ Additional Digit Required   Unspecified Code   Other Specified Code   Manifestation Code   ▶◀ Revised Text   ● New Code   ▲ Revised Code Title
✓5ᵗʰ

504 Pneumonopathy due to inhalation of other dust
Byssinosis
Cannabinosis
Flax-dressers' disease
> EXCLUDES allergic alveolitis (495.0-495.9)
>   asbestosis (501)
>   bagassosis (495.1)
>   farmers' lung (495.0)

505 Pneumoconiosis, unspecified

✓4ᵗʰ 506 Respiratory conditions due to chemical fumes and vapors
Use additional E code to identify cause

506.0 Bronchitis and pneumonitis due to fumes and vapors
Chemical bronchitis (acute)
AHA: 3Q, '08, 7

506.1 Acute pulmonary edema due to fumes and vapors
Chemical pulmonary edema (acute)
> EXCLUDES acute pulmonary edema NOS (518.4)
>   chronic or unspecified pulmonary edema (514)
AHA: 3Q, '88, 4

506.2 Upper respiratory inflammation due to fumes and vapors
AHA: 3Q, '05, 10

506.3 Other acute and subacute respiratory conditions due to fumes and vapors

506.4 Chronic respiratory conditions due to fumes and vapors
Emphysema (diffuse) (chronic) ⎤ due to inhalation of
Obliterative bronchiolitis   ⎬ chemical
  (chronic) (subacute)   ⎪ fumes and
Pulmonary fibrosis (chronic)   ⎦ vapors

506.9 Unspecified respiratory conditions due to fumes and vapors
Silo-fillers' disease

✓4ᵗʰ 507 Pneumonitis due to solids and liquids
> EXCLUDES fetal aspiration pneumonitis (770.18)
AHA: 3Q, '91, 16

507.0 Due to inhalation of food or vomitus
Aspiration pneumonia (due to):
  NOS
  food (regurgitated)
  gastric secretions
  milk
  saliva
  vomitus
AHA: 1Q, '08, 18; 1Q, '89,10
TIP: Assign an additional code for pneumonia due to a specific organism if that documentation is provided in addition to aspiration pneumonia.
J69.0 Pneumonitis due to inhalation of food and vomit [I-10]

507.1 Due to inhalation of oils and essences
Lipoid pneumonia (exogenous)
> EXCLUDES endogenous lipoid pneumonia (516.8)

507.8 Due to other solids and liquids
Detergent asthma

✓4ᵗʰ 508 Respiratory conditions due to other and unspecified external agents
Use additional E code to identify cause

508.0 Acute pulmonary manifestations due to radiation
Radiation pneumonitis
AHA: 2Q, '88, 4

508.1 Chronic and other pulmonary manifestations due to radiation
Fibrosis of lung following radiation

508.8 Respiratory conditions due to other specified external agents

508.9 Respiratory conditions due to unspecified external agent

OTHER DISEASES OF RESPIRATORY SYSTEM (510-519)

✓4ᵗʰ 510 Empyema
Use additional code to identify infectious organism (041.0-041.9)
> EXCLUDES abscess of lung (513.0)
DEF: Purulent infection; within pleural space.

510.0 With fistula
Fistula: Fistula:
  bronchocutaneous   mediastinal
  bronchopleural   pleural
  hepatopleural   thoracic

Any condition classifiable to 510.9 with fistula
DEF: Purulent infection of respiratory cavity; with communication from cavity to another structure.

510.9 Without mention of fistula
Abscess: Pleurisy:
  pleura   septic
  thorax   seropurulent
Empyema (chest) (lung) (pleura) suppurative
Fibrinopurulent pleurisy   Pyopneumothorax
Pleurisy: Pyothorax
  purulent
AHA:4Q, '07, 113; 3Q, '94, 6
J86.9 Pyothorax without fistula [I-10]

✓4ᵗʰ 511 Pleurisy
> EXCLUDES pleurisy with mention of tuberculosis, current disease (012.0)
DEF: Inflammation of serous membrane of lungs and lining of thoracic cavity; causes exudation in cavity or membrane surface.

511.0 Without mention of effusion or current tuberculosis
Adhesion, lung or pleura   Pleurisy:
Calcification of pleura   NOS
Pleurisy (acute) (sterile):   pneumococcal
  diaphragmatic   staphylococcal
  fibrinous   streptococcal
  interlobar   Thickening of pleura
AHA: 3Q, '94, 5

511.1 With effusion, with mention of a bacterial cause other than tuberculosis
Pleurisy with effusion (exudative) (serous):
  pneumococcal
  staphylococcal
  streptococcal
  other specified nontuberculous bacterial cause

✓5ᵗʰ 511.8 Other specified forms of effusion, except tuberculous
> EXCLUDES traumatic (860.2-860.5, 862.29, 862.39)
AHA: ▶4Q, '08, 113-114;◀ 1Q, '97, 10

511.81 Malignant pleural effusion
Code first malignant neoplasm, if known
J91.0 Malignant pleural effusion [I-10]

511.89 Other specified forms of effusion, except tuberculous
Encysted pleurisy   Hydropneumothorax
Hemopneumothorax   Hydrothorax
Hemothorax

511.9 Unspecified pleural effusion
Pleural effusion NOS   Pleurisy:
Pleurisy: serous
  exudative   with effusion NOS
  serofibrinous
AHA: 2Q, '03, 7; 3Q, '91, 19; 4Q, '89, 11
TIP: Do not assign when the pleural effusion is a symptom of CHF and no therapeutic treatment (e.g., thoracentesis) is directed towards the pleural effusion.
J90 Pleural effusion not elsewhere classified [I-10]

✓4ᵗʰ 512 Pneumothorax
DEF: Collapsed lung; due to gas or air in pleural space.

512.0 Spontaneous tension pneumothorax
DEF: Leaking air from lung into lining causing collapse.
AHA: 3Q, '94, 5

Ⓝ Newborn Age: 0   Ⓟ Pediatric Age: 0-17   Ⓜ Maternity Age: 12-55   Ⓐ Adult Age: 15-124

512.1   Iatrogenic pneumothorax
Postoperative pneumothorax
DEF: Air trapped in the lining of the lung following surgery.
AHA: 4Q, '94, 40
TIP: Pneumothorax is a known risk associated with most thoracic surgery; do not assign based on radiology findings alone, without physician substantiation.
J95.81 Postprocedural pneumothorax   `I-10`

512.8   Other spontaneous pneumothorax
Pneumothorax: Pneumothorax:
  NOS   chronic
  acute
EXCLUDES   *pneumothorax:*
    congenital (770.2)
    traumatic (860.0-860.1, 860.4-860.5)
    tuberculous, current disease (011.7)
AHA: 2Q, '93, 3
J93.9 Pneumothorax unspecified   `I-10`

✓4ᵗʰ **513   Abscess of lung and mediastinum**

513.0   Abscess of lung
Abscess (multiple) of lung
Gangrenous or necrotic pneumonia
Pulmonary gangrene or necrosis
AHA: 4Q, '07, 85; 2Q, '98, 7

513.1   Abscess of mediastinum

514   Pulmonary congestion and hypostasis
Hypostatic:
  bronchopneumonia
  pneumonia
Passive pneumonia
Pulmonary congestion (chronic) (passive)
Pulmonary edema:
  NOS
  chronic
EXCLUDES   *acute pulmonary edema:*
    NOS (518.4)
    with mention of heart disease or failure (428.1)
    hypostatic pneumonia due to or specified as a specific type of pneumonia–code to the type of pneumonia (480.0-480.9, 481, 482.0-482.49, 483.0-483.8, 485, 486, 487.0)
DEF: Excessive retention of interstitial fluid in the lungs and pulmonary vessels; due to poor circulation.
AHA: 2Q, '98, 6; 3Q, '88, 5
J81.1 Chronic pulmonary edema   `I-10`

515   Postinflammatory pulmonary fibrosis
Cirrhosis of lung
Fibrosis of lung (atrophic)
  (confluent) (massive)   chronic or
  (perialveolar)   unspecified
  (peribronchial)
Induration of lung
DEF: Fibrosis and scarring of the lungs due to inflammatory reaction.
J84.1 Other interstitial pulmonary diseases w/fibrosis `I-10`

✓4ᵗʰ **516   Other alveolar and parietoalveolar pneumonopathy**

516.0   Pulmonary alveolar proteinosis
DEF: Reduced ventilation; due to proteinaceous deposits on alveoli; symptoms include dyspnea, cough, chest pain, weakness, weight loss, and hemoptysis.

516.1   Idiopathic pulmonary hemosiderosis
Essential brown induration of lung
Code first underlying disease (275.0)
DEF: Fibrosis of alveolar walls; marked by abnormal amounts hemosiderin in lungs; primarily affects children; symptoms include anemia, fluid in lungs, and blood in sputum; etiology unknown.

516.2   Pulmonary alveolar microlithiasis
DEF: Small calculi in pulmonary alveoli resembling sand-like particles on x-ray.

516.3   Idiopathic fibrosing alveolitis
Alveolar capillary block
Diffuse (idiopathic) (interstitial) pulmonary fibrosis
Hamman-Rich syndrome

516.8   Other specified alveolar and parietoalveolar pneumonopathies
Endogenous lipoid pneumonia
Interstitial pneumonia (desquamative) (lymphoid)
EXCLUDES   *lipoid pneumonia, exogenous or unspecified (507.1)*
AHA: 2Q, '06, 20; 1Q, '92, 12

516.9   Unspecified alveolar and parietoalveolar pneumonopathy

✓4ᵗʰ **517   Lung involvement in conditions classified elsewhere**
EXCLUDES   *rheumatoid lung (714.81)*

517.1   Rheumatic pneumonia
Code first underlying disease (390)

517.2   Lung involvement in systemic sclerosis
Code first underlying disease (710.1)

517.3   Acute chest syndrome
Code first sickle-cell disease in crisis (282.42, 282.62, 282.64, 282.69)
AHA: 4Q, '03, 51, 56

517.8   Lung involvement in other diseases classified elsewhere
Code first underlying disease, as:
  amyloidosis (277.30-277.39)
  polymyositis (710.4)
  sarcoidosis (135)
  Sjögren's disease (710.2)
  systemic lupus erythematosus (710.0)
EXCLUDES   *syphilis (095.1)*
AHA: 2Q, '03, 7

✓4ᵗʰ **518   Other diseases of lung**

518.0   Pulmonary collapse
Atelectasis
Collapse of lung
Middle lobe syndrome
EXCLUDES   *atelectasis:*
    congenital (partial) (770.5)
    primary (770.4)
    tuberculous, current disease (011.8)
AHA: 4Q, '90, 25
J98.11 Atelectasis   `I-10`

518.1   Interstitial emphysema
Mediastinal emphysema
EXCLUDES   *surgical (subcutaneous) emphysema (998.81)*
    that in fetus or newborn (770.2)
    traumatic emphysema (958.7)
DEF: Escaped air from the alveoli trapped in the interstices of the lung; trauma or cough may cause the disease.

518.2   Compensatory emphysema
DEF: Distention of all or part of the lung caused by disease processes or surgical intervention that decreased volume in another part of the lung; overcompensation reaction to the loss of capacity in another part of the lung.

518.3   Pulmonary eosinophilia
Eosinophilic asthma
Löffler's syndrome
Pneumonia:
  allergic
  eosinophilic
Tropical eosinophilia
DEF: Infiltration, into pulmonary parenchyma of eosinophilia; results in cough, fever, and dyspnea.

Respiratory System

512.1–518.3

✓4ᵗʰ
✓5ᵗʰ Additional Digit Required   ■ Unspecified Code   ■ Other Specified Code   ■ Manifestation Code   ►◄ Revised Text   ● New Code   ▲ Revised Code Title

2010 ICD-9-CM   **Volume 1 – 157**

518.4 Acute edema of lung, unspecified
Acute pulmonary edema NOS
Pulmonary edema, postoperative
  EXCLUDES pulmonary edema:
    acute, with mention of heart disease or
      failure (428.1)
    chronic or unspecified (514)
    due to external agents (506.0-508.9)
  DEF: Severe, sudden fluid retention within lung tissues.
  TIP: Do not assign separately if associated with CHF or heart
  disease; it is incorporated into those codes.

518.5 Pulmonary insufficiency following trauma and surgery
Adult respiratory distress syndrome
Pulmonary insufficiency following:
  shock
  surgery
  trauma
Shock lung
  EXCLUDES adult respiratory distress syndrome associated
      with other conditions (518.82)
    pneumonia:
      aspiration (507.0)
      hypostatic (514)
    respiratory failure in other conditions (518.81,
      518.83-518.84)
  AHA: 4Q, '04, 139; 3Q, '88, 3; 3Q, '88, 7; S-O, '87, 1
  J95.82 Postprocedural respiratory failure   I-10

518.6 Allergic bronchopulmonary aspergillosis
  DEF: Noninvasive hypersensitive reaction; due to allergic
  reaction to *Aspergillus fumigatus* (mold).
  AHA: 4Q, '97, 39

518.7 Transfusion related acute lung injury [TRALI]
  DEF: A relatively rare, but serious pulmonary complication of
  blood transfusion, with acute respiratory distress,
  noncardiogenic pulmonary edema, cyanosis, hypoxemia,
  hypotension, fever and chills.
  AHA: 4Q, '06, 91

✓5ᵗʰ **518.8 Other diseases of lung**

518.81 Acute respiratory failure
Respiratory failure NOS
  EXCLUDES acute and chronic respiratory failure
      (518.84)
    acute respiratory distress (518.82)
    chronic respiratory failure (518.83)
    respiratory arrest (799.1)
    respiratory failure, newborn (770.84)
  AHA: ▶2Q, '09, 11;◀1Q, '08, 18; 3Q, '07, 6; 2Q, '06,
  25; 4Q, '05, 96; 2Q, '05, 19; 1Q, '05, 3-8; 1Q, '05, 3–8;
  4Q, '04, 139; 1Q, '03, 15; 4Q, '98, 41; 3Q, '91, 14; 2Q,
  '91, 3; 4Q, '90, 25; 2Q, '90, 20; 3Q, '88, 7; 3Q, '88, 10;
  S-O, '87, 1
  TIP: If both respiratory failure and another acute
  condition are responsible for admission, either may
  be sequenced as principal diagnosis.
  J96.0 Acute respiratory failure   I-10

**518.82 Other pulmonary insufficiency, not
elsewhere classified**
Acute respiratory distress
Acute respiratory insufficiency
Adult respiratory distress syndrome NEC
  EXCLUDES adult respiratory distress syndrome
      associated with trauma and
      surgery (518.5)
    pulmonary insufficiency following
      trauma and surgery (518.5)
    respiratory distress:
      NOS (786.09)
      newborn (770.89)
      syndrome, newborn (769)
    shock lung (518.5)
  AHA: 4Q, '03, 105; 2Q, '91, 21; 3Q, '88, 7
  J80 Acute respiratory distress syndrome   I-10

518.83 Chronic respiratory failure
  AHA: 4Q, '05, 96; 4Q, '03, 103, 111
  J96.1 Chronic respiratory failure   I-10

518.84 Acute and chronic respiratory failure
Acute on chronic respiratory failure
  J96.2 Acute and chronic respiratory failure   I-10

**518.89 Other diseases of lung, not elsewhere
classified**
Broncholithiasis
Calcification of lung
Lung disease NOS
Pulmolithiasis
  DEF: Broncholithiasis: calculi in lumen of
  transbronchial tree.
  DEF: Pulmolithiasis: calculi in lung.
  AHA: 3Q, '90, 18; 4Q, '88, 6
  J98.4 Other disorders of lung   I-10

✓4ᵗʰ **519 Other diseases of respiratory system**

✓5ᵗʰ **519.0 Tracheostomy complications**

519.00 Tracheostomy complication, unspecified

519.01 Infection of tracheostomy
Use additional code to identify type of infection,
  such as:
    abscess or cellulitis of neck (682.1)
    septicemia (038.0-038.9)
Use additional code to identify organism
  (041.00-041.9)
  AHA: 4Q, '98, 41

519.02 Mechanical complication of tracheostomy
Tracheal stenosis due to tracheostomy

519.09 Other tracheostomy complications
Hemorrhage due to tracheostomy
Tracheoesophageal fistula due to tracheostomy

✓5ᵗʰ **519.1 Other diseases of trachea and bronchus, not elsewhere
classified**
  AHA: 3Q, '02, 18; 3Q, '88, 6

519.11 Acute bronchospasm
Bronchospasm NOS
  EXCLUDES acute bronchitis with bronchospasm
      (466.0)
    asthma (493.00-493.92)
    exercise induced bronchospasm
      (493.81)
  AHA: 4Q, '06, 92

519.19 Other diseases of trachea and bronchus
Calcification ⎫
Stenosis ⎬ of bronchus or trachea
Ulcer ⎭
  AHA: 4Q, '06, 92

519.2 Mediastinitis
  DEF: Inflammation of tissue between organs behind sternum.

**519.3 Other diseases of mediastinum, not elsewhere
classified**
Fibrosis ⎫
Hernia ⎬ of mediastinum
Retraction ⎭

519.4 Disorders of diaphragm
Diaphragmitis
Paralysis of diaphragm
Relaxation of diaphragm
  EXCLUDES congenital defect of diaphragm (756.6)
    diaphragmatic hernia (551-553 with .3)
    congenital (756.6)

**519.8 Other diseases of respiratory system, not
elsewhere classified**
  AHA: 4Q, '89, 12

519.9 Unspecified disease of respiratory system
Respiratory disease (chronic) NOS

N Newborn Age: 0   P Pediatric Age: 0-17   M Maternity Age: 12-55   A Adult Age: 15-124

9. DISEASES OF THE DIGESTIVE SYSTEM (520-579)

DISEASES OF ORAL CAVITY, SALIVARY GLANDS, AND JAWS (520-529)

✓4th **520 Disorders of tooth development and eruption**

520.0 Anodontia
Absence of teeth (complete) (congenital) (partial)
Hypodontia
Oligodontia
EXCLUDES acquired absence of teeth (525.10-525.19)

520.1 Supernumerary teeth
Distomolar
Fourth molar
Mesiodens
Paramolar
Supplemental teeth
EXCLUDES supernumerary roots (520.2)

520.2 Abnormalities of size and form
Concrescence ⎫
Fusion   ⎬ of teeth
Gemination ⎭

Dens evaginatus
Dens in dente
Dens invaginatus
Enamel pearls
Macrodontia
Microdontia
Peg-shaped [conical] teeth
Supernumerary roots
Taurodontism
Tuberculum paramolare
EXCLUDES that due to congenital syphilis (090.5)
tuberculum Carabelli, which is regarded as a normal variation

520.3 Mottled teeth
Mottling of enamel
Dental fluorosis
Nonfluoride enamel opacities

Digestive System

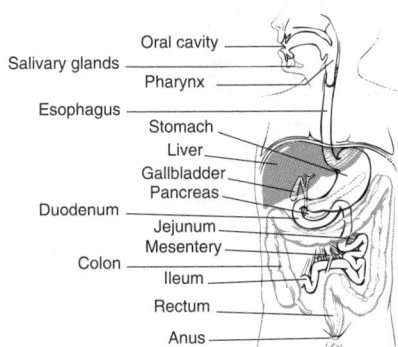

Oral cavity
Salivary glands
Pharynx
Esophagus
Stomach
Liver
Gallbladder
Pancreas
Duodenum
Jejunum
Mesentery
Colon
Ileum
Rectum
Anus

The Oral Cavity

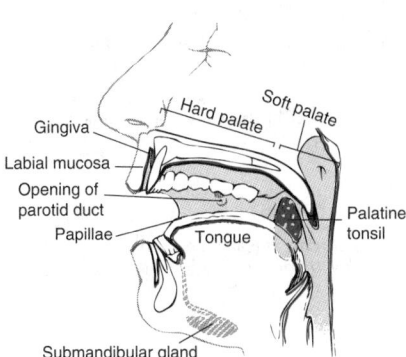

Gingiva
Hard palate
Soft palate
Labial mucosa
Opening of parotid duct
Papillae
Tongue
Palatine tonsil
Submandibular gland

Teeth

Labial frenulum
Mucosa
Vestibule
Gingiva
Upper lip
Hard palate
Uvula
Tongue
Enamel
Dentine
Gingiva (gum)
Root canal
Cementum
Section of molar
Soft palate
Maxillary view

Uvula
Tongue
Gingiva
Lower lip
Mucosa
Vestibule
Frenulum
Enamel
Pulp cavity
Dentin
Alveolar bone
Mandible
Section of incisor
Mandibulary view

520.4 Disturbances of tooth formation
Aplasia and hypoplasia of cementum
Dilaceration of tooth
Enamel hypoplasia (neonatal) (postnatal) (prenatal)
Horner's teeth
Hypocalcification of teeth
Regional odontodysplasia
Turner's tooth
EXCLUDES Hutchinson's teeth and mulberry molars in congenital syphilis (090.5)
mottled teeth (520.3)

520.5 Hereditary disturbances in tooth structure, not elsewhere classified
Amelogensis ⎫
Dentinogenesis ⎬ imperfecta
Odontogenesis ⎭

Dentinal dysplasia
Shell teeth

520.6 Disturbances in tooth eruption
Teeth:
   embedded
   impacted
   natal
   neonatal
   prenatal
   primary [deciduous]:
      persistent
      shedding, premature
Tooth eruption:
   late
   obstructed
   premature
EXCLUDES exfoliation of teeth (attributable to disease of surrounding tissues) (525.0-525.19)
AHA: 1Q, '06, 18; 2Q, '05, 15

520.7 Teething syndrome

520.8 Other specified disorders of tooth development and eruption
Color changes during tooth formation
Pre-eruptive color changes
EXCLUDES posteruptive color changes (521.7)

✓4th
✓5th
  Additional Digit Required   Unspecified Code   Other Specified Code   Manifestation Code   ▶◀ Revised Text   ● New Code   ▲ Revised Code Title
2010 ICD-9-CM   **Volume 1 – 159**

520–520.8

520.9 **Unspecified disorder of tooth development and eruption**

✓4th **521** **Diseases of hard tissues of teeth**

✓5th **521.0** **Dental caries**
AHA: 4Q, '01, 44

521.00 **Dental caries, unspecified**

521.01 **Dental caries limited to enamel**
Initial caries
White spot lesion

521.02 **Dental caries extending into dentine**

521.03 **Dental caries extending into pulp**

521.04 **Arrested dental caries**

521.05 **Odontoclasia**
Infantile melanodontia
Melanodontoclasia

EXCLUDES *internal and external resorption of teeth (521.40-521.49)*

DEF: A pathological dental condition described as stained areas, loss of tooth substance, and hypoplasia linked to nutritional deficiencies during tooth development and to cariogenic oral conditions.

521.06 **Dental caries pit and fissure**
Primary dental caries, pit and fissure origin

521.07 **Dental caries of smooth surface**
Primary dental caries, smooth surface origin

521.08 **Dental caries of root surface**
Primary dental caries, root surface

521.09 **Other dental caries**
AHA: 3Q, '02, 14

✓5th **521.1** **Excessive attrition (approximal wear) (occlusal wear)**

521.10 **Excessive attrition, unspecified**

521.11 **Excessive attrition, limited to enamel**

521.12 **Excessive attrition, extending into dentine**

521.13 **Excessive attrition, extending into pulp**

521.14 **Excessive attrition, localized**

521.15 **Excessive attrition, generalized**

✓5th **521.2** **Abrasion**
Abrasion:
dentifrice
habitual
occupational } of teeth
ritual
traditional
Wedge defect NOS

521.20 **Abrasion, unspecified**

521.21 **Abrasion, limited to enamel**

521.22 **Abrasion, extending into dentine**

521.23 **Abrasion, extending into pulp**

521.24 **Abrasion, localized**

521.25 **Abrasion, generalized**

✓5th **521.3** **Erosion**
Erosion of teeth:
NOS
due to:
medicine
persistent vomiting
idiopathic
occupational

521.30 **Erosion, unspecified**

521.31 **Erosion, limited to enamel**

521.32 **Erosion, extending into dentine**

521.33 **Erosion, extending into pulp**

521.34 **Erosion, localized**

521.35 **Erosion, generalized**

✓5th **521.4** **Pathological resorption**
DEF: Loss of dentin and cementum due to disease process.

521.40 **Pathological resorption, unspecified**

521.41 **Pathological resorption, internal**

521.42 **Pathological resorption, external**

521.49 **Other pathological resorption**
Internal granuloma of pulp

521.5 **Hypercementosis**
Cementation hyperplasia
DEF: Excess deposits of cementum, on tooth root.

521.6 **Ankylosis of teeth**
DEF: Adhesion of tooth to surrounding bone.

521.7 **Intrinsic posteruptive color changes**
Staining [discoloration] of teeth:
NOS
due to:
drugs
metals
pulpal bleeding

EXCLUDES *accretions [deposits] on teeth (523.6)*
extrinsic color changes (523.6)
pre-eruptive color changes (520.8)

✓5th **521.8** **Other specified diseases of hard tissues of teeth**

521.81 **Cracked tooth**

EXCLUDES *asymptomatic craze lines in enamel–omit code*
broken tooth due to trauma (873.63, 873.73)
fractured tooth due to trauma (873.63, 873.73)

521.89 **Other specified diseases of hard tissues of teeth**
Irradiated enamel
Sensitive dentin

521.9 **Unspecified disease of hard tissues of teeth**

✓4th **522** **Diseases of pulp and periapical tissues**

522.0 **Pulpitis**
Pulpal:
abscess
polyp
Pulpitis:
acute
chronic (hyperplastic) (ulcerative)
suppurative

522.1 **Necrosis of the pulp**
Pulp gangrene
DEF: Death of pulp tissue.

522.2 **Pulp degeneration**
Denticles
Pulp calcifications
Pulp stones

522.3 **Abnormal hard tissue formation in pulp**
Secondary or irregular dentin

522.4 **Acute apical periodontitis of pulpal origin**
DEF: Severe inflammation of periodontal ligament due to pulpal inflammation or necrosis.

522.5 **Periapical abscess without sinus**
Abscess:
dental
dentoalveolar

EXCLUDES *periapical abscess with sinus (522.7)*

522.6 **Chronic apical periodontitis**
Apical or periapical granuloma
Apical periodontitis NOS

Ⓝ Newborn Age: 0   Ⓟ Pediatric Age: 0-17   Ⓜ Maternity Age: 12-55   Ⓐ Adult Age: 15-124

522.7　Periapical abscess with sinus
Fistula:
alveolar process
dental

522.8　Radicular cyst
Cyst:
apical (periodontal)
periapical
radiculodental
residual radicular
EXCLUDES　*lateral developmental or lateral periodontal cyst (526.0)*
DEF: Cyst in tissue around tooth apex due to chronic infection of granuloma around root.

522.9　Other and unspecified diseases of pulp and periapical tissues

✓4th **523　Gingival and periodontal diseases**

✓5th **523.0　Acute gingivitis**
EXCLUDES　*acute necrotizing ulcerative gingivitis (101)*
herpetic gingivostomatitis (054.2)

523.00　Acute gingivitis, plaque induced
Acute gingivitis NOS

523.01　Acute gingivitis, non-plaque induced

✓5th **523.1　Chronic gingivitis**
Gingivitis (chronic):
desquamative
hyperplastic
simple marginal
ulcerative
EXCLUDES　*herpetic gingivostomatitis (054.2)*

523.10　Chronic gingivitis, plaque induced
Chronic gingivitis NOS
Gingivitis NOS

523.11　Chronic gingivitis, non-plaque induced

✓5th **523.2　Gingival recession**
Gingival recession (postinfective) (postoperative)

523.20　Gingival recession, unspecified

523.21　Gingival recession, minimal

523.22　Gingival recession, moderate

523.23　Gingival recession, severe

523.24　Gingival recession, localized

523.25　Gingival recession, generalized

✓5th **523.3　Aggressive and acute periodontitis**
Acute:
pericementitis
pericoronitis
EXCLUDES　*acute apical periodontitis (522.4)*
periapical abscess (522.5, 522.7)
DEF: Severe inflammation, of tissues supporting teeth.

523.30　Aggressive periodontitis, unspecified

523.31　Aggressive periodontitis, localized
Periodontal abscess

523.32　Aggressive periodontitis, generalized

523.33　Acute periodontitis

✓5th **523.4　Chronic periodontitis**
Chronic pericoronitis
Pericementitis (chronic)
Periodontitis:
NOS
complex
simplex
EXCLUDES　*chronic apical periodontitis (522.6)*

523.40　Chronic periodontitis, unspecified

523.41　Chronic periodontitis, localized

523.42　Chronic periodontitis, generalized

523.5　Periodontosis

523.6　Accretions on teeth
Dental calculus:
subgingival
supragingival
Deposits on teeth:
betel
materia alba
soft
tartar
tobacco
Extrinsic discoloration of teeth
EXCLUDES　*intrinsic discoloration of teeth (521.7)*
DEF: Foreign material on tooth surface, usually plaque or calculus.

523.8　Other specified periodontal diseases
Giant cell:
epulis
peripheral granuloma
Gingival:
cysts
enlargement NOS
fibromatosis
Gingival polyp
Periodontal lesions due to traumatic occlusion
Peripheral giant cell granuloma
EXCLUDES　*leukoplakia of gingiva (528.6)*

523.9　Unspecified gingival and periodontal disease
AHA: 3Q ,'02, 14

✓4th **524　Dentofacial anomalies, including malocclusion**

✓5th **524.0　Major anomalies of jaw size**
EXCLUDES　*hemifacial atrophy or hypertrophy (754.0)*
unilateral condylar hyperplasia or hypoplasia of mandible (526.89)

524.00　Unspecified anomaly
DEF: Unspecified deformity of jaw size.

524.01　Maxillary hyperplasia
DEF: Overgrowth or over development of upper jaw bone.

524.02　Mandibular hyperplasia
DEF: Overgrowth or over development of lower jaw bone.

524.03　Maxillary hypoplasia
DEF: Incomplete or underdeveloped, upper jaw bone.

524.04　Mandibular hypoplasia
DEF: Incomplete or underdeveloped, lower jaw bone.

524.05　Macrogenia
DEF: Enlarged, jaw, especially chin; affects bone, soft tissue, or both.

524.06　Microgenia
DEF: Underdeveloped mandible, characterized by an extremely small chin.

524.07　Excessive tuberosity of jaw
Entire maxillary tuberosity

524.09　Other specified anomaly

✓5th **524.1　Anomalies of relationship of jaw to cranial base**

524.10　Unspecified anomaly
Prognathism
Retrognathism
DEF: Prognathism: protrusion of lower jaw.
DEF: Retrognathism: jaw is located posteriorly to a normally positioned jaw; backward position of mandible.

524.11　Maxillary asymmetry
DEF: Absence of symmetry of maxilla.

524.12　Other jaw asymmetry

524.19　Other specified anomaly

✓4th ✓5th Additional Digit Required　　Unspecified Code　　　Other Specified Code　　　Manifestation Code　　▶◀ Revised Text　　● New Code　　▲ Revised Code Title
2010 ICD-9-CM　　　　　　　　　　　　　　　　　　　　　　　　　　　　　　　　　　　　　　　**Volume 1 – 161**

522.7–524.19

Angle's Classification of Malocclusion

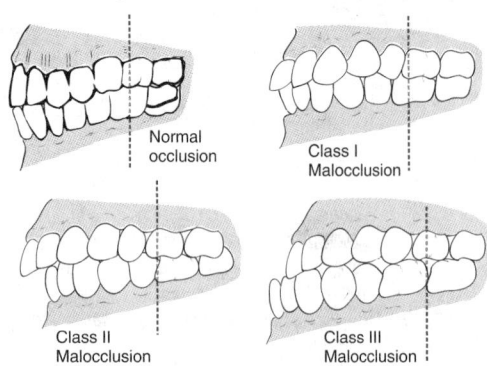

Normal occlusion

Class I Malocclusion

Class II Malocclusion

Class III Malocclusion

√5th **524.2 Anomalies of dental arch relationship**
Anomaly of dental arch
EXCLUDES hemifacial atrophy or hypertrophy (754.0)
soft tissue impingement (524.81-524.82)
unilateral condylar hyperplasia or hypoplasia
of mandible (526.89)

524.20 Unspecified anomaly of dental arch relationship

524.21 Malocclusion, Angle's class I
Neutro-occlusion

524.22 Malocclusion, Angle's class II
Disto-occlusion Division I
Disto-occlusion Division II

524.23 Malocclusion, Angle's class III
Mesio-occlusion

524.24 Open anterior occlusal relationship
Anterior open bite

524.25 Open posterior occlusal relationship
Posterior open bite

524.26 Excessive horizontal overlap
Excessive horizontal overjet

524.27 Reverse articulation
Anterior articulation
Crossbite
Posterior articulation

524.28 Anomalies of interarch distance
Excessive interarch distance
Inadequate interarch distance

524.29 Other anomalies of dental arch relationship
Other anomalies of dental arch

√5th **524.3 Anomalies of tooth position of fully erupted teeth**
EXCLUDES impacted or embedded teeth with abnormal
position of such teeth or adjacent teeth
(520.6)

524.30 Unspecified anomaly of tooth position
Diastema of teeth NOS
Displacement of teeth NOS
Transposition of teeth NOS

524.31 Crowding of teeth

524.32 Excessive spacing of teeth

524.33 Horizontal displacement of teeth
Tipped teeth
Tipping of teeth

524.34 Vertical displacement of teeth
Extruded tooth
Infraeruption of teeth
Intruded tooth
Supraeruption of teeth

524.35 Rotation of tooth/teeth

524.36 Insufficient interocclusal distance of teeth (ridge)
Lack of adequate intermaxillary vertical
dimension

524.37 Excessive interocclusal distance of teeth
Excessive intermaxillary vertical dimension
Loss of occlusal vertical dimension

524.39 Other anomalies of tooth position

524.4 Malocclusion, unspecified
DEF: Malposition of top and bottom teeth; interferes with
chewing.

√5th **524.5 Dentofacial functional abnormalities**

524.50 Dentofacial functional abnormality, unspecified

524.51 Abnormal jaw closure

524.52 Limited mandibular range of motion

524.53 Deviation in opening and closing of the mandible

524.54 Insufficient anterior guidance
Insufficient anterior occlusal guidance

524.55 Centric occlusion maximum intercuspation discrepancy
Centric occlusion of teeth discrepancy

524.56 Non-working side interference
Balancing side interference

524.57 Lack of posterior occlusal support

524.59 Other dentofacial functional abnormalities
Abnormal swallowing
Mouth breathing
Sleep postures
Tongue, lip, or finger habits

√5th **524.6 Temporomandibular joint disorders**
EXCLUDES current temporomandibular joint:
dislocation (830.0-830.1)
strain (848.1)

524.60 Temporomandibular joint disorders, unspecified
Temporomandibular joint-pain- dysfunction
syndrome [TMJ]

524.61 Adhesions and ankylosis (bony or fibrous)
DEF: Stiffening or union of temporomandibular joint
due to bony or fibrous union across joint.

524.62 Arthralgia of temporomandibular joint
DEF: Pain in temporomandibular joint; not
inflammatory in nature.

524.63 Articular disc disorder (reducing or non-reducing)

524.64 Temporomandibular joint sounds on opening and/or closing the jaw

524.69 Other specified temporomandibular joint disorders

√5th **524.7 Dental alveolar anomalies**

524.70 Unspecified alveolar anomaly

524.71 Alveolar maxillary hyperplasia
DEF: Excessive tissue formation in the dental alveoli
of upper jaw.

524.72 Alveolar mandibular hyperplasia
DEF: Excessive tissue formation in the dental alveoli
of lower jaw.

524.73 Alveolar maxillary hypoplasia
DEF: Incomplete or underdeveloped, alveolar tissue
of upper jaw.

524.74 Alveolar mandibular hypoplasia
DEF: Incomplete or underdeveloped, alveolar tissue
of lower jaw.

524.75 **Vertical displacement of alveolus and teeth**
Extrusion of alveolus and teeth

524.76 **Occlusal plane deviation**

524.79 Other specified alveolar anomaly

√5th 524.8 **Other specified dentofacial anomalies**

524.81 **Anterior soft tissue impingement**

524.82 **Posterior soft tissue impingement**

524.89 Other specified dentofacial anomalies

524.9 Unspecified dentofacial anomalies

√4th 525 **Other diseases and conditions of the teeth and supporting structures**

525.0 **Exfoliation of teeth due to systemic causes**
DEF: Deterioration of teeth and surrounding structures due to systemic disease.

√5th 525.1 **Loss of teeth due to trauma, extraction, or periodontal disease**
Code first class of edentulism (525.40-525.44, 525.50-525.54)
AHA: 4Q, '05, 74; 4Q, '01, 44

525.10 *Acquired absence of teeth, unspecified*
Tooth extraction status, NOS

525.11 *Loss of teeth due to trauma*

525.12 *Loss of teeth due to periodontal disease*

525.13 *Loss of teeth due to caries*

525.19 *Other loss of teeth*

√5th 525.2 **Atrophy of edentulous alveolar ridge**

525.20 Unspecified atrophy of edentulous alveolar ridge
Atrophy of the mandible NOS
Atrophy of the maxilla NOS

525.21 **Minimal atrophy of the mandible**

525.22 **Moderate atrophy of the mandible**

525.23 **Severe atrophy of the mandible**

525.24 **Minimal atrophy of the maxilla**

525.25 **Moderate atrophy of the maxilla**

525.26 **Severe atrophy of the maxilla**

525.3 **Retained dental root**

√5th 525.4 **Complete edentulism**
Use additional code to identify cause of edentulism (525.10-525.19)
AHA: 4Q, '05, 74

525.40 Complete edentulism, unspecified
Edentulism NOS

525.41 **Complete edentulism, class I**

525.42 **Complete edentulism, class II**

525.43 **Complete edentulism, class III**

525.44 **Complete edentulism, class IV**

√5th 525.5 **Partial edentulism**
Use additional code to identify cause of edentulism (525.10-525.19)
AHA: 4Q, '05, 74

525.50 Partial edentulism, unspecified

525.51 **Partial edentulism, class I**

525.52 **Partial edentulism, class II**

525.53 **Partial edentulism, class III**

525.54 **Partial edentulism, class IV**

√5th 525.6 **Unsatisfactory restoration of tooth**
Defective bridge, crown, fillings
Defective dental restoration
EXCLUDES *dental restoration status (V45.84)*
unsatisfactory endodontic treatment (526.61-526.69)

525.60 Unspecified unsatisfactory restoration of tooth
Unspecified defective dental restoration

525.61 **Open restoration margins**
Dental restoration failure of marginal integrity
Open margin on tooth restoration

525.62 **Unrepairable overhanging of dental restorative materials**
Overhanging of tooth restoration

525.63 **Fractured dental restorative material without loss of material**
EXCLUDES *cracked tooth (521.81)*
fractured tooth (873.63, 873.73)

525.64 **Fractured dental restorative material with loss of material**
EXCLUDES *cracked tooth (521.81)*
fractured tooth (873.63, 873.73)

525.65 **Contour of existing restoration of tooth biologically incompatible with oral health**
Dental restoration failure of periodontal anatomical integrity
Unacceptable contours of existing restoration
Unacceptable morphology of existing restoration

525.66 **Allergy to existing dental restorative material**
Use additional code to identify the specific type of allergy

525.67 **Poor aesthetics of existing restoration**
Dental restoration aesthetically inadequate or displeasing

525.69 Other unsatisfactory restoration of existing tooth

√5th 525.7 **Endosseous dental implant failure**

525.71 **Osseointegration failure of dental implant**
Failure of dental implant due to infection
Failure of dental implant due to unintentional loading
Failure of dental implant osseointegration due to premature loading
Failure of dental implant to osseointegrate prior to intentional prosthetic loading
Hemorrhagic complications of dental implant placement
Iatrogenic osseointegration failure of dental implant
Osseointegration failure of dental implant due to complications of systemic disease
Osseointegration failure of dental implant due to poor bone quality
Pre-integration failure of dental implant NOS
Pre-osseointegration failure of dental implant

525.72 **Post-osseointegration biological failure of dental implant**
Failure of dental implant due to lack of attached gingiva
Failure of dental implant due to occlusal trauma (caused by poor prosthetic design)
Failure of dental implant due to parafunctional habits
Failure of dental implant due to periodontal infection (peri-implantitis)
Failure of dental implant due to poor oral hygiene
Failure of dental implant to osseointegrate following intentional prosthetic loading
Iatrogenic post-osseointegration failure of dental implant
Post-osseointegration failure of dental implant due to complications of systemic disease

Digestive System

525.73–527.9

525.73 Post-osseointegration mechanic failure of dental implant
Failure of dental prosthesis causing loss of dental implant
Fracture of dental implant
Mechanical failure of dental implant NOS

> **EXCLUDES**   cracked tooth (521.81)
> fractured dental restorative material with loss of material (525.64)
> fractured dental restorative material without loss of material (525.63)
> fractured tooth (873.63, 873.73)

525.79 Other endosseous dental implant failure
Dental implant failure NOS

525.8 Other specified disorders of the teeth and supporting structures
Enlargement of alveolar ridge NOS
Irregular alveolar process

525.9 Unspecified disorder of the teeth and supporting structures

√4th **526 Diseases of the jaws**

526.0 Developmental odontogenic cysts
Cyst:
   dentigerous
   eruption
   follicular
   lateral developmental
   lateral periodontal
   primordial
Keratocyst

> **EXCLUDES**   radicular cyst (522.8)

526.1 Fissural cysts of jaw
Cyst:
   globulomaxillary
   incisor canal
   median anterior maxillary
   median palatal
   nasopalatine
   palatine of papilla

> **EXCLUDES**   cysts of oral soft tissues (528.4)

526.2 Other cysts of jaws
Cyst of jaw:
   NOS
   aneurysmal
   hemorrhagic
   traumatic

526.3 Central giant cell (reparative) granuloma

> **EXCLUDES**   peripheral giant cell granuloma (523.8)

526.4 Inflammatory conditions
Abscess
Osteitis   } of jaw (acute) (chronic)
Osteomyelitis (neonatal)   (suppurative)
Periostitis

Sequestrum of jaw bone

> **EXCLUDES**   alveolar osteitis (526.5)
> osteonecrosis of jaw (733.45)

526.5 Alveolitis of jaw
Alveolar osteitis
Dry socket
DEF: Inflammation, of alveoli or tooth socket.

√5th **526.6 Periradicular pathology associated with previous endodontic treatment**

526.61 Perforation of root canal space

526.62 Endodontic overfill

526.63 Endodontic underfill

526.69 Other periradicular pathology associated with previous endodontic treatment

√5th **526.8 Other specified diseases of the jaws**

526.81 Exostosis of jaw
Torus mandibularis
Torus palatinus
DEF: Spur or bony outgrowth on the jaw.

526.89 Other
Cherubism
Fibrous dysplasia   } of jaw(s)
Latent bone cyst
Osteoradionecrosis

Unilateral condylar hyperplasia or hypoplasia of mandible

526.9 Unspecified disease of the jaws

√4th **527 Diseases of the salivary glands**

527.0 Atrophy
DEF: Wasting away, necrosis of salivary gland tissue.

527.1 Hypertrophy
DEF: Overgrowth or overdeveloped salivary gland tissue.

527.2 Sialoadenitis
Parotitis:
   NOS
   allergic
   toxic
Sialoangitis
Sialodochitis

> **EXCLUDES**   epidemic or infectious parotitis (072.0-072.9)
> uveoparotid fever (135)

DEF: Inflammation of salivary gland.

527.3 Abscess

527.4 Fistula

> **EXCLUDES**   congenital fistula of salivary gland (750.24)

527.5 Sialolithiasis
Calculus   } of salivary gland or duct
Stone
Sialodocholithiasis

527.6 Mucocele
Mucous:
   extravasation cyst of salivary gland
   retention cyst of salivary gland
Ranula
DEF: Dilated salivary gland cavity filled with mucous.

527.7 Disturbance of salivary secretion
Hyposecretion
Ptyalism
Sialorrhea
Xerostomia

527.8 Other specified diseases of the salivary glands
Benign lymphoepithelial lesion of salivary gland
Sialectasia
Sialosis
Stenosis   } of salivary duct
Stricture

527.9 Unspecified disease of the salivary glands

N   Newborn Age: 0   P   Pediatric Age: 0-17   M   Maternity Age: 12-55   A   Adult Age: 15-124

✓4ᵗʰ **528 Diseases of the oral soft tissues, excluding lesions specific for gingiva and tongue**

✓5ᵗʰ **528.0 Stomatitis and mucositis (ulcerative)**

EXCLUDES   *cellulitis and abscess of mouth (528.3)*
diphtheritic stomatitis (032.0)
epizootic stomatitis (078.4)
gingivitis (523.0-523.1)
oral thrush (112.0)
Stevens-Johnson syndrome (695.13)
stomatitis:
  acute necrotizing ulcerative (101)
  aphthous (528.2)
  gangrenous (528.1)
  herpetic (054.2)
  Vincent's (101)

DEF: Stomatitis: Inflammation of oral mucosa; labial and buccal mucosa, tongue, palate, floor of the mouth, and gingivae.

AHA: 2Q, '99, 9

TIP: Do not assign if documented as fungal oral thrush, or as due to candidiasis. See instead 112.0.

528.00 Stomatitis and mucositis, unspecified
Mucositis NOS
Ulcerative mucositis NOS
Ulcerative stomatitis NOS
Vesicular stomatitis NOS
AHA: 4Q, '06, 88-90

528.01 Mucositis (ulcerative) due to antineoplastic therapy
Use additional E code to identify adverse effects of therapy, such as:
  antineoplastic and immunosuppressive drugs (E930.7, E933.1)
  radiation therapy (E879.2)
AHA: 4Q, '06, 88-90

528.02 Mucositis (ulcerative) due to other drugs
Use additional E code to identify drug
AHA: 4Q, '06, 88-90

528.09 Other stomatitis and mucositis (ulcerative)
AHA: 4Q, '06, 88-90

528.1 Cancrum oris
Gangrenous stomatitis
Noma
DEF: A severely gangrenous lesion of mouth due to fusospirochetal infection; destroys buccal, labial and facial tissues; can be fatal; found primarily in debilitated and malnourished children.

528.2 Oral aphthae
Aphthous stomatitis
Canker sore
Periadenitis mucosa necrotica recurrens
Recurrent aphthous ulcer
Stomatitis herpetiformis
EXCLUDES   *herpetic stomatitis (054.2)*
DEF: Small oval or round ulcers of the mouth marked by a grayish exudate and a red halo effect.

528.3 Cellulitis and abscess
Cellulitis of mouth (floor)
Ludwig's angina
Oral fistula
EXCLUDES   *abscess of tongue (529.0)*
cellulitis or abscess of lip (528.5)
fistula (of):
  dental (522.7)
  lip (528.5)
gingivitis (523.00-523.11)

528.4 Cysts
Dermoid cyst
Epidermoid cyst
Epstein's pearl   } of mouth
Lymphoepithelial cyst
Nasoalveolar cyst
Nasolabial cyst
EXCLUDES   *cyst:*
  gingiva (523.8)
  tongue (529.8)

528.5 Diseases of lips
Abscess
Cellulitis   } of lips
Fistula
Hypertrophy

Cheilitis:
  NOS
  angular
Cheilodynia
Cheilosis
EXCLUDES   *actinic cheilitis (692.79)*
congenital fistula of lip (750.25)
leukoplakia of lips (528.6)
AHA: S-O, '86, 10

528.6 Leukoplakia of oral mucosa, including tongue
Leukokeratosis of oral mucosa
Leukoplakia of:
  gingiva
  lips
  tongue
EXCLUDES   *carcinoma in situ (230.0, 232.0)*
leukokeratosis nicotina palati (528.79)
DEF: Thickened white patches of epithelium on mucous membranes of mouth.

✓5ᵗʰ **528.7 Other disturbances of oral epithelium, including tongue**
EXCLUDES   *carcinoma in situ (230.0, 232.0)*
leukokeratosis NOS (702.8)

528.71 Minimal keratinized residual ridge mucosa
Minimal keratinization of alveolar ridge mucosa

528.72 Excessive keratinized residual ridge mucosa
Excessive keratinization of alveolar ridge mucosa

528.79 Other disturbances of oral epithelium, including tongue
Erythroplakia of mouth or tongue
Focal epithelial hyperplasia of mouth or tongue
Leukoedema of mouth or tongue
Leukokeratosis nicotina palate
Other oral epithelium disturbances

528.8 Oral submucosal fibrosis, including of tongue

528.9 Other and unspecified diseases of the oral soft tissues
Cheek and lip biting
Denture sore mouth
Denture stomatitis
Melanoplakia
Papillary hyperplasia of palate
Eosinophilic granuloma
Irritative hyperplasia   } of oral mucosa
Pyogenic granuloma
Ulcer (traumatic)

✓4ᵗʰ **529 Diseases and other conditions of the tongue**

529.0 Glossitis
Abscess   } of tongue
Ulceration (traumatic)
EXCLUDES   *glossitis:*
  benign migratory (529.1)
  Hunter's (529.4)
  median rhomboid (529.2)
  Moeller's (529.4)

529.1 Geographic tongue
Benign migratory glossitis
Glossitis areata exfoliativa
DEF: Chronic glossitis; marked by filiform papillae atrophy and inflammation; no known etiology.

529.2 Median rhomboid glossitis
DEF: A noninflammatory, congenital disease characterized by rhomboid-like lesions at the middle third of the tongue's dorsal surface.

529.3 Hypertrophy of tongue papillae
Black hairy tongue
Coated tongue
Hypertrophy of foliate papillae
Lingua villosa nigra

529.4 Atrophy of tongue papillae
Bald tongue
Glazed tongue
Glossitis:
    Hunter's
    Moeller's
Glossodynia exfoliativa
Smooth atrophic tongue

529.5 Plicated tongue
Fissured }
Furrowed } tongue
Scrotal   }
EXCLUDES fissure of tongue, congenital (750.13)
DEF: Cracks, fissures or furrows, on dorsal surface of tongue.

529.6 Glossodynia
Glossopyrosis
Painful tongue
EXCLUDES glossodynia exfoliativa (529.4)

529.8 Other specified conditions of the tongue
Atrophy   }
Crenated }
Enlargement } (of) tongue
Hypertrophy }
Glossocele
Glossoptosis
EXCLUDES erythroplasia of tongue (528.79)
          leukoplakia of tongue (528.6)
          macroglossia (congenital) (750.15)
          microglossia (congenital) (750.16)
          oral submucosal fibrosis (528.8)

529.9 Unspecified condition of the tongue

DISEASES OF ESOPHAGUS, STOMACH, AND DUODENUM (530-538)

✓4ᵗʰ 530 Diseases of esophagus
EXCLUDES esophageal varices (456.0-456.2)

530.0 Achalasia and cardiospasm
Achalasia (of cardia)
Aperistalsis of esophagus
Megaesophagus
EXCLUDES congenital cardiospasm (750.7)
DEF: Failure of smooth muscle fibers to relax, at gastrointestinal junctures; such as esophagogastric sphincter when swallowing.

✓5ᵗʰ 530.1 Esophagitis
Esophagitis: Esphagitis:
    chemical   postoperative
    peptic   regurgitant
Use additional E code to identify cause, if induced by chemical
EXCLUDES tuberculous esophagitis (017.8)
AHA: 4Q, '93, 27; 1Q, '92, 17; 3Q, '91, 20
TIP: Do not assign if esophagitis due to candidiasis; see instead code 112.84.

530.10 Esophagitis, unspecified
Esophagitis NOS
AHA: 3Q, '05, 17

Esophagus

530.11 Reflux esophagitis
DEF: Inflammation of lower esophagus; due to regurgitated gastric acid.
AHA: 4Q, '95, 82
K21.0 Gastro-esophageal reflux disease w/esophagitis   `I-10`

530.12 Acute esophagitis
DEF: An acute inflammation of the mucous lining or submucosal coat of the esophagus.
AHA: 4Q, '01, 45

530.13 Eosinophilic esophagitis
AHA: ▶4Q, '08, 115-116◀

530.19 Other esophagitis
Abscess of esophagus
AHA: 3Q, '01, 10
K20 Esophagitis   `I-10`

✓5ᵗʰ 530.2 Ulcer of esophagus
Ulcer of esophagus:
    fungal
    peptic
Ulcer of esophagus due to ingestion of:
    aspirin
    chemicals
    medicines
Use additional E code to identify cause, if induced by chemical or drug
AHA: 4Q, '03, 63

530.20 Ulcer of esophagus without bleeding
Ulcer of esophagus NOS

530.21 Ulcer of esophagus with bleeding
EXCLUDES bleeding esophageal varices (456.0, 456.20)

530.3 Stricture and stenosis of esophagus
Compression of esophagus
Obstruction of esophagus
EXCLUDES congenital stricture of esophagus (750.3)
AHA: 2Q, '01, 4; 2Q, '97, 3; 1Q, '88, 13
TIP: If esophageal obstruction is due to impacted foreign body, such as meat or other substance, assign instead code 935.1.
K22.2 Esophageal obstruction   `I-10`

530.4 Perforation of esophagus
Rupture of esophagus
EXCLUDES traumatic perforation of esophagus (862.22, 862.32, 874.4-874.5)

530.5 Dyskinesia of esophagus
Corkscrew esophagus
Curling esophagus
Esophagospasm
Spasm of esophagus
EXCLUDES cardiospasm (530.0)
DEF: Difficulty performing voluntary esophageal movements.
AHA: 1Q, '88, 13; N-D, '84, 19

Ⓝ Newborn Age: 0   Ⓟ Pediatric Age: 0-17   Ⓜ Maternity Age: 12-55   Ⓐ Adult Age: 15-124

530.6   **Diverticulum of esophagus, acquired**
Diverticulum, acquired:
epiphrenic
pharyngoesophageal
pulsion
subdiaphragmatic
traction
Zenker's (hypopharyngeal)
Esophageal pouch, acquired
Esophagocele, acquired
EXCLUDES *congenital diverticulum of esophagus (750.4)*
AHA: J-F, '85, 3

530.7   **Gastroesophageal laceration-hemorrhage syndrome**
Mallory-Weiss syndrome
DEF: Laceration of distal esophagus and proximal stomach due to vomiting, hiccups or other sustained activity.

✓5ᵗʰ **530.8**   **Other specified disorders of esophagus**

530.81   **Esophageal reflux**
Gastroesophageal reflux
EXCLUDES *reflux esophagitis (530.11)*
DEF: Regurgitation of the gastric contents into esophagus and possibly pharynx.
AHA: 2Q, '01, 4; 1Q, '95, 7; 4Q, '92, 27
K21.9 Gastro-esophageal reflux dz w/o esophagitis   `I-10`

530.82   **Esophageal hemorrhage**
EXCLUDES *hemorrhage due to esophageal varices (456.0-456.2)*
AHA: 1Q, '05, 17

530.83   **Esophageal leukoplakia**

530.84   **Tracheoesophageal fistula**
EXCLUDES *congenital tracheoesophageal fistula (750.3)*

530.85   **Barrett's esophagus**
DEF: A metaplastic disorder in which specialized columnar epithelial cells replace the normal squamous epithelial cells; secondary to chronic gastroesophageal reflux damage to the mucosa; increases risk of developing adenocarcinoma.
AHA: 4Q, '03, 63
K22.7 Barrett's esophagus   `I-10`

530.86   **Infection of esophagostomy**
Use additional code to specify infection

530.87   **Mechanical complication of esophagostomy**
Malfunction of esophagostomy

530.89   **Other**
EXCLUDES *Paterson-Kelly syndrome (280.8)*

530.9   **Unspecified disorder of esophagus**

✓4ᵗʰ **531**   **Gastric ulcer**
INCLUDES ulcer (peptic):
prepyloric
pylorus
stomach
Use additional E code to identify drug, if drug-induced
EXCLUDES *peptic ulcer NOS (533.0-533.9)*

The following fifth-digit subclassification is for use with category 531:
0   **without mention of obstruction**
1   **with obstruction**

DEF: Destruction of tissue in lumen of stomach due to action of gastric acid and pepsin on gastric mucosa decreasing resistance to ulcers.
AHA: 1Q, '91, 15; 4Q, '90, 27

§ ✓5ᵗʰ **531.0**   **Acute with hemorrhage**
[0-1]   **AHA:** N-D, '84, 15

§ ✓5ᵗʰ **531.1**   **Acute with perforation**
[0-1]

§ ✓5ᵗʰ **531.2**   **Acute with hemorrhage and perforation**
[0-1]

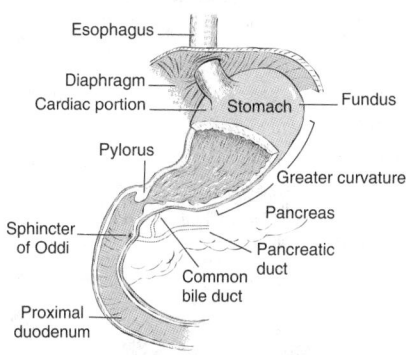

Stomach

Esophagus
Diaphragm
Cardiac portion — Stomach — Fundus
Pylorus
Greater curvature
Pancreas
Sphincter of Oddi
Pancreatic duct
Common bile duct
Proximal duodenum

§ ✓5ᵗʰ **531.3**   **Acute without mention of hemorrhage or perforation**
[0-1]

§ ✓5ᵗʰ **531.4**   **Chronic or unspecified with hemorrhage**
[0-1]   **AHA:** 4Q, '90, 22
K25.4 Chronic/unspec gastric ulcer w/hemorrhage   `I-10`

§ ✓5ᵗʰ **531.5**   **Chronic or unspecified with perforation**
[0-1]

§ ✓5ᵗʰ **531.6**   **Chronic or unspecified with hemorrhage and**
[0-1]   **perforation**

§ ✓5ᵗʰ **531.7**   **Chronic without mention of hemorrhage or**
[0-1]   **perforation**

§ ✓5ᵗʰ **531.9**   **Unspecified as acute or chronic, without mention**
[0-1]   **of hemorrhage or perforation**
K25.9 Gastric ulcer uns acute/chronic w/o hem/perf   `I-10`

✓4ᵗʰ **532**   **Duodenal ulcer**
INCLUDES erosion (acute) of duodenum
ulcer (peptic):
duodenum
postpyloric
Use additional E code to identify drug, if drug-induced
EXCLUDES *peptic ulcer NOS (533.0-533.9)*

The following fifth-digit subclassification is for use with category 532:
0   **without mention of obstruction**
1   **with obstruction**

DEF: Ulcers in duodenum due to action of gastric acid and pepsin on mucosa decreasing resistance to ulcers.
AHA: 4Q, '90, 27; 1Q, '91, 15

§ ✓5ᵗʰ **532.0**   **Acute with hemorrhage**
[0-1]   **AHA:** 4Q, '90, 22

§ ✓5ᵗʰ **532.1**   **Acute with perforation**
[0-1]

§ ✓5ᵗʰ **532.2**   **Acute with hemorrhage and perforation**
[0-1]

§ ✓5ᵗʰ **532.3**   **Acute without mention of hemorrhage or perforation**
[0-1]

§ ✓5ᵗʰ **532.4**   **Chronic or unspecified with hemorrhage**
[0-1]   **K26.4** Chronic/unspecified duodenal ulcer   `I-10`
w/hemorrhage

§ ✓5ᵗʰ **532.5**   **Chronic or unspecified with perforation**
[0-1]

§ ✓5ᵗʰ **532.6**   **Chronic or unspecified with hemorrhage and**
[0-1]   **perforation**

§ ✓5ᵗʰ **532.7**   **Chronic without mention of hemorrhage or**
[0-1]   **perforation**

§ ✓5ᵗʰ **532.9**   **Unspecified as acute or chronic, without mention**
[0-1]   **of hemorrhage or perfortaion**
K26.9 Duodenal ulcer uns acute/chronic w/o hem/perf   `I-10`

§   Requires fifth digit. Valid digits are in [brackets] under each code. See appropriate category for codes and definitions.

✓4ᵗʰ
✓5ᵗʰ
Additional Digit Required   Unspecified Code   Other Specified Code   Manifestation Code   ►◄ Revised Text   ● New Code   ▲ Revised Code Title
2010 ICD-9-CM   **Volume 1 – 167**

Digestive System

533–536.40

√4ᵗʰ **533 Peptic ulcer, site unspecified**

> **INCLUDES** gastroduodenal ulcer NOS
> peptic ulcer NOS
> stress ulcer NOS
>
> Use additional E code to identify drug, if drug-induced
>
> **EXCLUDES** peptic ulcer:
> duodenal (532.0-532.9)
> gastric (531.0-531.9)
>
> The following fifth-digit subclassification is for use with category 533:
> 0 without mention of obstruction
> 1 with obstruction
>
> **DEF:** Ulcer of mucous membrane of esophagus, stomach or duodenum due to gastric acid secretion.
> **AHA:** 1Q, '91, 15; 4Q, '90, 27

§ √5ᵗʰ **533.0 Acute with hemorrhage**
[0-1]

§ √5ᵗʰ **533.1 Acute with perforation**
[0-1]

§ √5ᵗʰ **533.2 Acute with hemorrhage and perforation**
[0-1]

§ √5ᵗʰ **533.3 Acute without mention of hemorrhage and perforation**
[0-1]

§ √5ᵗʰ **533.4 Chronic or unspecified with hemorrhage**
[0-1]

§ √5ᵗʰ **533.5 Chronic or unspecified with perforation**
[0-1]

§ √5ᵗʰ **533.6 Chronic or unspecified with hemorrhage and perforation**
[0-1]

§ √5ᵗʰ **533.7 Chronic without mention of hemorrhage or perforation**
[0-1]
> **AHA:** 2Q, '89, 16

§ √5ᵗʰ **533.9 Unspecified as acute or chronic, without mention of hemorrhage or perforation**
[0-1]

√4ᵗʰ **534 Gastrojejunal ulcer**

> **INCLUDES** ulcer (peptic) or erosion:
> anastomotic
> gastrocolic
> gastrointestinal
> gastrojejunal
> jejunal
> marginal
> stomal
>
> **EXCLUDES** primary ulcer of small intestine (569.82)
>
> The following fifth-digit subclassification is for use with category 534:
> 0 without mention of obstruction
> 1 with obstruction
>
> **AHA:** 1Q, '91, 15; 4Q, '90, 27

§ √5ᵗʰ **534.0 Acute with hemorrhage**
[0-1]

§ √5ᵗʰ **534.1 Acute with perforation**
[0-1]

§ √5ᵗʰ **534.2 Acute with hemorrhage and perforation**
[0-1]

§ √5ᵗʰ **534.3 Acute without mention of hemorrhage or perforation**
[0-1]

§ √5ᵗʰ **534.4 Chronic or unspecified with hemorrhage**
[0-1]

§ √5ᵗʰ **534.5 Chronic or unspecified with perforation**
[0-1]

§ √5ᵗʰ **534.6 Chronic or unspecified with hemorrhage and perforation**
[0-1]

§ √5ᵗʰ **534.7 Chronic without mention of hemorrhage or perforation**
[0-1]

§ √5ᵗʰ **534.9 Unspecified as acute or chronic, without mention of hemorrhage or perforation**
[0-1]

√4ᵗʰ **535 Gastritis and duodenitis**

> The following fifth-digit subclassification is for use with category 535:
> 0 without mention of hemorrhage
> 1 with hemorrhage
>
> **AHA:** 2Q, '92, 9; 4Q, '91, 25

§ √5ᵗʰ **535.0 Acute gastritis**
[0-1]
> **AHA:** 2Q, '92, 8; N-D, '86, 9

§ √5ᵗʰ **535.1 Atrophic gastritis**
[0-1]
> Gastritis:
> atrophic-hyperplastic
> chronic (atrophic)
> **DEF:** Inflammation of stomach, with mucous membrane atrophy and peptic gland destruction.
> **AHA:** 1Q, '94, 18
> **K29.50** Unspecified chronic gastritis without bleeding   I-10

§ √5ᵗʰ **535.2 Gastric mucosal hypertrophy**
[0-1]
> Hypertrophic gastritis

§ √5ᵗʰ **535.3 Alcoholic gastritis**
[0-1]

§ √5ᵗʰ **535.4 Other specified gastritis**
[0-1]
> Gastritis: Gastritis:
> allergic   superficial
> bile induced   toxic
> irritant
> **EXCLUDES** eosinophilic gastritis (535.7)
> **AHA:** 4Q, '90, 27

§ √5ᵗʰ **535.5 Unspecified gastritis and gastroduodenitis**
[0-1]
> **AHA:** For code 535.50: 3Q, '05, 17; 4Q, '99, 25

§ √5ᵗʰ **535.6 Duodenitis**
[0-1]
> **DEF:** Inflammation of intestine, between pylorus and jejunum.
> **AHA:** For code 535.60: 3Q, '05, 17
> **K29.80** Duodenitis without bleeding   I-10

§ √5ᵗʰ **535.7 Eosinophilic gastritis**
[0-1]
> **AHA:** 4Q, '08, 115-116

√4ᵗʰ **536 Disorders of function of stomach**

> **EXCLUDES** functional disorders of stomach specified as psychogenic (306.4)

536.0 Achlorhydria
> **DEF:** Absence of gastric acid due to gastric mucosa atrophy; unresponsive to histamines; also known as gastric anacidity.

536.1 Acute dilatation of stomach
> Acute distention of stomach

536.2 Persistent vomiting
> Cyclical vomiting
> Habit vomiting
> Persistent vomiting [not of pregnancy]
> Uncontrollable vomiting
> **EXCLUDES** ►bilious emesis (vomiting) (787.04)◄
> excessive vomiting in pregnancy (643.0-643.9)
> vomiting NOS (787.03)
> cyclical, associated with migraine (346.2)
> ►vomiting of fecal matter (569.87)◄

536.3 Gastroparesis
> Gastroparalysis
> Code first underlying disease, such as: diabetes mellitus (249.6, 250.6)
> **DEF:** Slight degree of paralysis within muscular coat of stomach.
> **AHA:** 4Q, '08, 94; 2Q, '04, 7; 2Q, '01, 4; 4Q, '94, 42

√5ᵗʰ **536.4 Gastrostomy complications**
> **AHA:** 4Q, '98, 42
> **TIP:** Do not assign code 997.4 Digestive system complications, for any gastrostomy complications.

536.40 Gastrostomy complication, unspecified

§ Requires fifth digit. Valid digits are in [brackets] under each code. See appropriate category for codes and definitions.

N Newborn Age: 0   P Pediatric Age: 0-17   M Maternity Age: 12-55   A Adult Age: 15-124

536.41 Infection of gastrostomy
Use additional code to specify type of infection,
such as:
abscess or cellulitis of abdomen (682.2)
septicemia (038.0-038.9)
Use additional code to identify organism
(041.00-041.9)
AHA: 4Q, '98, 42

536.42 Mechanical complication of gastrostomy

536.49 Other gastrostomy complications
AHA: 4Q, '98, 42

536.8 Dyspepsia and other specified disorders of function of stomach
Achylia gastrica
Hourglass contraction of stomach
Hyperacidity
Hyperchlorhydria
Hypochlorhydria
Indigestion
Tachygastria
EXCLUDES *achlorhydria (536.0)*
heartburn (787.1)
AHA: 2Q, '93, 6; 2Q, '89, 16; N-D, '84, 9
K30 Dyspepsia   I-10

536.9 Unspecified functional disorder of stomach
Functional gastrointestinal:
disorder
disturbance
irritation

✓4ᵗʰ 537 Other disorders of stomach and duodenum

537.0 Acquired hypertrophic pyloric stenosis
Constriction ⎫
Obstruction ⎬ of pylorus, acquired or adult
Stricture ⎭
EXCLUDES *congenital or infantile pyloric stenosis (750.5)*
AHA: 2Q, '01, 4; J-F, '85, 14

537.1 Gastric diverticulum
EXCLUDES *congenital diverticulum of stomach (750.7)*
DEF: Herniated sac or pouch, within stomach or duodenum.
AHA: J-F, '85, 4

537.2 Chronic duodenal ileus
DEF: Persistent obstruction between pylorus and jejunum.

537.3 Other obstruction of duodenum
Cicatrix ⎫
Stenosis ⎬ of duodenum
Stricture ⎪
Volvulus ⎭
EXCLUDES *congenital obstruction of duodenum (751.1)*

537.4 Fistula of stomach or duodenum
Gastrocolic fistula
Gastrojejunocolic fistula

537.5 Gastroptosis
DEF: Downward displacement of stomach.

Duodenum

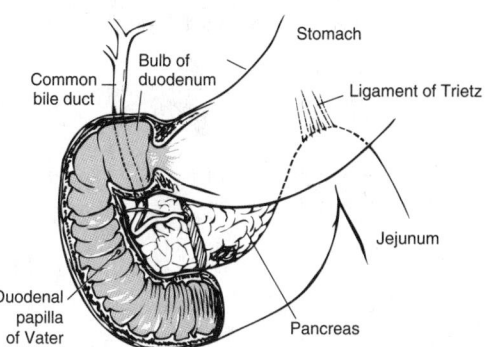

537.6 Hourglass stricture or stenosis of stomach
Cascade stomach
EXCLUDES *congenital hourglass stomach (750.7)*
hourglass contraction of stomach (536.8)

✓5ᵗʰ 537.8 Other specified disorders of stomach and duodenum
AHA: 4Q, '91, 25

537.81 Pylorospasm
EXCLUDES *congenital pylorospasm (750.5)*
DEF: Spasm of the pyloric sphincter.

537.82 Angiodysplasia of stomach and duodenum (without mention of hemorrhage)
AHA: 2Q, '07, 7; 3Q, '96, 10; 4Q, '90, 4

537.83 Angiodysplasia of stomach and duodenum with hemorrhage
DEF: Bleeding of stomach and duodenum due to vascular abnormalities.
AHA: 2Q, '07, 7

537.84 Dieulafoy lesion (hemorrhagic) of stomach and duodenum
DEF: An abnormally large and convoluted submucosal artery protruding through a defect in the mucosa in the stomach or intestines that can erode the epithelium causing hemorrhaging.
AHA: 4Q, '02, 60

537.89 Other
Gastric or duodenal:
prolapse
rupture
Intestinal metaplasia of gastric mucosa
Passive congestion of stomach
EXCLUDES *diverticula of duodenum (562.00-562.01)*
gastrointestinal hemorrhage (578.0-578.9)
AHA: 3Q, '05, 15; N-D, '84, 7
TIP: Assign for congestive portal gastropathy or portal hypertensive gastropathy.

537.9 Unspecified disorder of stomach and duodenum

538 Gastrointestinal mucositis (ulcerative)
Use additional E code to identify adverse effects of therapy, such as:
antineoplastic and immunosuppressive drugs (E930.7, E933.1)
radiation therapy (E879.2)
EXCLUDES *mucositis (ulcerative) of mouth and oral soft tissue (528.00- 528.09)*
AHA: 4Q, '06, 88-90

APPENDICITIS (540-543)

✓4ᵗʰ 540 Acute appendicitis
DEF: Inflammation of vermiform appendix due to fecal obstruction, neoplasm or foreign body of appendiceal lumen; causes infection, edema and infarction of appendiceal wall; may result in mural necrosis, and perforation.
AHA: N-D, '84, 19

540.0 With generalized peritonitis
Appendicitis ⎫ perforation ⎧ fulminating
(acute) ⎬ peritonitis (generalized) ⎨ gangrenous
with: ⎭ rupture ⎩ obstructive
Cecitis (acute) with perforation, peritonitis (generalized), rupture
Rupture of appendix
EXCLUDES *acute appendicitis with peritoneal abscess (540.1)*
K35.0 Acute appendicitis w/generalized peritonitis   I-10

540.1 With peritoneal abscess
Abscess of appendix
With generalized peritonitis
AHA: N-D, '84, 19

✓4ᵗʰ
✓5ᵗʰ Additional Digit Required   Unspecified Code   Other Specified Code   Manifestation Code   ▶◀ Revised Text   ● New Code   ▲ Revised Code Title
2010 ICD-9-CM   **Volume 1 – 169**

Digestive System

540.9–551.03

Appendix

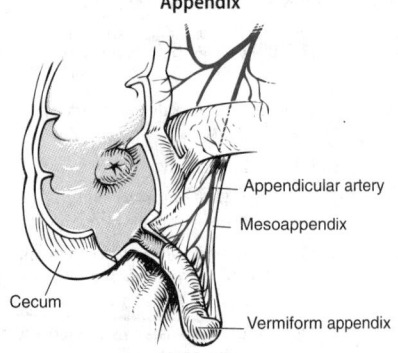

- Appendicular artery
- Mesoappendix
- Cecum
- Vermiform appendix

540.9   Without mention of peritonitis

Acute appendicitis without mention of perforation, peritonitis, or rupture:
- fulminating
- gangrenous
- inflamed
- obstructive

Acute cecitis without mention of perforation, peritonitis, or rupture

AHA: 1Q, '01, 15; 4Q, '97, 52

K35.9 Acute appednicitis unspecified   `I-10`

541   Appendicitis, unqualified

AHA: 2Q, '90, 26

TIP: Do not assign for normal appendix found at appendectomy. Assign instead symptom code (e.g., abdominal pain).

542   Other appendicitis

Appendicitis: Appendicitis:
- chronic   relapsing
- recurrent   subacute

EXCLUDES *hyperplasia (lymphoid) of appendix (543.0)*

AHA: 1Q, '01, 15

✓4ᵗʰ 543   Other diseases of appendix

543.0   Hyperplasia of appendix (lymphoid)

DEF: Proliferation of cells in appendix tissue.

Inguinal Hernias

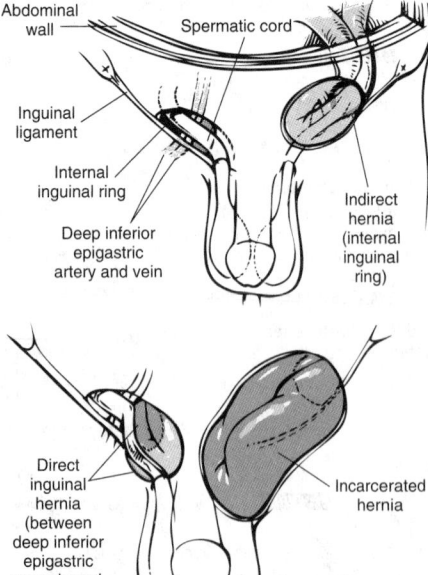

- Abdominal wall
- Spermatic cord
- Inguinal ligament
- Internal inguinal ring
- Deep inferior epigastric artery and vein
- Indirect hernia (internal inguinal ring)
- Direct inguinal hernia (between deep inferior epigastric vessels and rectus fascia)
- Incarcerated hernia

543.9   Other and unspecified   diseases of appendix

Appendicular or appendiceal:
- colic
- concretion
- fistula

Diverticulum
Fecalith
Intussusception } of appendix
Mucocele
Stercolith

HERNIA OF ABDOMINAL CAVITY (550-553)

INCLUDES   hernia:
- acquired
- congenital, except diaphragmatic or hiatal

✓4ᵗʰ 550   Inguinal hernia

INCLUDES   bubonocele
inguinal hernia (direct) (double) (indirect) (oblique) (sliding)
scrotal hernia

The following fifth-digit subclassification is for use with category 550:
- **0**   **unilateral or unspecified (not specified as recurrent)**
    Unilateral NOS
- **1**   **unilateral or unspecified, recurrent**
- **2**   **bilateral (not specified as recurrent)**
    Bilateral NOS
- **3**   **bilateral, recurrent**

DEF: Hernia protrusion of an abdominal organ or tissue through inguinal canal.

DEF: Indirect inguinal hernia: (external or oblique) leaves abdomen through deep inguinal ring, passes through inguinal canal lateral to the inferior epigastric artery.

DEF: Direct inguinal hernia: (internal) emerges between inferior epigastric artery and rectus muscle edge.

AHA: N-D, '85, 12

§   ✓5ᵗʰ   **550.0**   **Inguinal hernia, with gangrene**
[0-3]   Inguinal hernia with gangrene (and obstruction)

§   ✓5ᵗʰ   **550.1**   **Inguinal hernia, with obstruction, without mention**
[0-3]   **of gangrene**
      Inguinal hernia with mention of incarceration, irreducibility, or strangulation

§   ✓5ᵗʰ   **550.9**   **Inguinal hernia, without mention of obstruction**
[0-3]   **or gangrene**
      Inguinal hernia NOS

AHA: For code 550.91: 3Q, '03, 10; 1Q, '03, 4

K40.90 Uni ingin hernia w/o obst/gangrene not spec recur   `I-10`

✓4ᵗʰ 551   Other hernia of abdominal cavity, with gangrene

INCLUDES   *that with gangrene (and obstruction)*

✓5ᵗʰ 551.0   Femoral hernia with gangrene

551.00   Unilateral or unspecified (not specified as recurrent)
      Femoral hernia NOS with gangrene

551.01   Unilateral or unspecified, recurrent

551.02   Bilateral (not specified as recurrent)

551.03   Bilateral, recurrent

Hernias of Abdominal Cavity

- Hiatal hernia
- Diaphragm
- Epigastric hernia
- Incisional hernia
- Umbilical hernia
- Inguinal hernia

---

§   Requires fifth digit. Valid digits are in [brackets] under each code. See category 550 for codes and definitions.

Femoral Hernia

Diaphragmatic Hernias

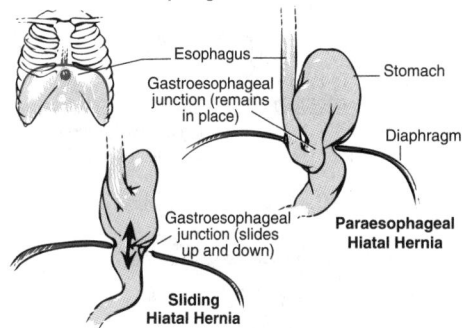

551.1   **Umbilical hernia with gangrene**
Parumbilical hernia specified as gangrenous

√5th **551.2**   **Ventral hernia with gangrene**

    551.20   Ventral, unspecified, with gangrene

    551.21   **Incisional, with gangrene**
Hernia:
postoperative   } specified as
recurrent, ventral   } gangrenous

    551.29   Other
Epigastric hernia specified as gangrenous

551.3   **Diaphragmatic hernia with gangrene**
Hernia:
hiatal (esophageal) (sliding)   } specified as
paraesophageal   } gangrenous
Thoracic stomach

    EXCLUDES   *congenital diaphragmatic hernia (756.6)*

551.8   Hernia of other specified sites, with gangrene
Any condition classifiable to 553.8 if specified as gangrenous

551.9   Hernia of unspecified site, with gangrene
Any condition classifiable to 553.9 if specified as gangrenous

√4th **552**   **Other hernia of abdominal cavity, with obstruction, but without mention of gangrene**

    EXCLUDES   *that with mention of gangrene (551.0-551.9)*

√5th **552.0**   **Femoral hernia with obstruction**
Femoral hernia specified as incarcerated, irreducible, strangulated, or causing obstruction

    552.00   **Unilateral or unspecified (not specified as recurrent)**

    552.01   **Unilateral or unspecified, recurrent**

    552.02   **Bilateral (not specified as recurrent)**

    552.03   **Bilateral, recurrent**

552.1   **Umbilical hernia with obstruction**
Parumbilical hernia specified as incarcerated, irreducible, strangulated, or causing obstruction

√5th **552.2**   **Ventral hernia with obstruction**
Ventral hernia specified as incarcerated, irreducible, strangulated, or causing obstruction

    552.20   Ventral, unspecified, with obstruction

    552.21   **Incisional, with obstruction**
Hernia:
postoperative   } specified as incarcerated,
recurrent,   } irreducible,
ventral   } strangulated, or
   } causing obstruction

        AHA: 3Q, '03, 11

    552.29   Other
Epigastric hernia specified as incarcerated, irreducible, strangulated, or causing obstruction

552.3   **Diaphragmatic hernia with obstruction**
Hernia:
hiatal (esophageal)   } specified as caracerated,
(sliding)   } irreducible, strangulated,
paraesophageal   } or causing obstruction
Thoracic stomach

    EXCLUDES   *congenital diaphragmatic hernia (756.6)*

552.8   Hernia of other specified sites, with obstruction
Any condition classifiable to 553.8 if specified as incarcerated, irreducible, strangulated, or causing obstruction

    EXCLUDES   *hernia due to adhesion with obstruction (560.81)*

    AHA: 1Q, '04, 10

552.9   Hernia of unspecified site, with obstruction
Any condition classifiable to 553.9 if specified as incarcerated, irreducible, strangulated, or causing obstruction

√4th **553**   **Other hernia of abdominal cavity without mention of obstruction or gangrene**

    EXCLUDES   *the listed conditions with mention of:*
gangrene (and obstruction) (551.0-551.9)
obstruction (552.0-552.9)

√5th **553.0**   **Femoral hernia**

    553.00   **Unilateral or unspecified (not specified as recurrent)**
Femoral hernia NOS

    553.01   **Unilateral or unspecified, recurrent**

    553.02   **Bilateral (not specified as recurrent)**

    553.03   **Bilateral, recurrent**

553.1   **Umbilical hernia**
Parumbilical hernia

    K42.9 Umbilical hernia without obstruction/gangrene   I-10

√5th **553.2**   **Ventral hernia**

    553.20   Ventral, unspecified

        AHA: 2Q, '06, 10; 3Q, '03, 6

    553.21   **Incisional**
Hernia:
postoperative
recurrent, ventral

        AHA: 3Q, '03, 6

        K43.91 Incisional hernia w/o obstruction or   I-10
gangrene

    553.29   Other
Hernia:
epigastric
spigelian

√4th
Additional Digit Required   Unspecified Code   Other Specified Code   Manifestation Code   ►◄ Revised Text   ● New Code   ▲ Revised Code Title

2010 ICD-9-CM   **Volume 1 – 171**

551.1–553.29

553.3 Diaphragmatic hernia

Hernia:
    hiatal (esophageal) (sliding)
    paraesophageal
Thoracic stomach

EXCLUDES   congenital:
         diaphragmatic hernia (756.6)
         hiatal hernia (750.6)
         esophagocele (530.6)

AHA: 2Q, '01, 6; 1Q, '00, 6

K44.9 Diaphragmatic hernia w/o obstruction/gangrene   I-10

553.8 Hernia of other specified sites

Hernia:
    ischiatic
    ischiorectal
    lumbar
    obturator
    pudendal
    retroperitoneal
    sciatic
Other abdominal hernia of specified site

EXCLUDES   vaginal enterocele (618.6)

553.9 Hernia of unspecified site

Enterocele
Epiplocele
Hernia:
    NOS
    interstitial
Hernia:
    intestinal
    intra-abdominal
Rupture (nontraumatic)
Sarcoepiplocele

NONINFECTIOUS ENTERITIS AND COLITIS (555-558)

✓4th 555 Regional enteritis

INCLUDES   Crohn's disease
              Granulomatous enteritis

EXCLUDES   ulcerative colitis (556)

DEF: Inflammation of intestine; classified to site.

TIP: Assign separate code for fistula, if present. Sequence 555 code as first-listed/principal diagnosis (if underlying cause of fistula).

555.0 Small intestine

Ileitis:
    regional
    segmental
    terminal
Regional enteritis or Crohn's disease of:
    duodenum
    ileum
    jejunum

555.1 Large intestine

Colitis:
    granulmatous
    regional
    transmural
Regional enteritis or Crohn's disease of:
    colon
    large bowel
    rectum

AHA: 3Q, '99, 8

555.2 Small intestine with large intestine

Regional ileocolitis

AHA: 1Q, '03, 18

Large Intestine

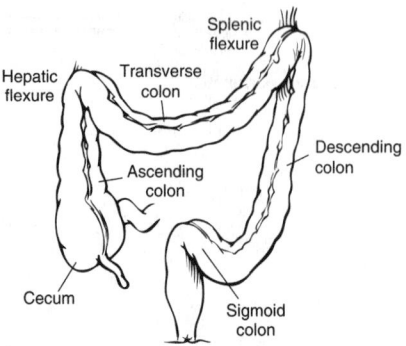

555.9 Unspecified site

Crohn's disease NOS
Regional enteritis NOS

AHA: ▶1Q, '09, 5;◀ 2Q, '05, 11; 3Q, '99, 8; 4Q, '97, 42; 2Q, '97, 3

K50.90 Crohns disease unspecified w/o complications   I-10

✓4th 556 Ulcerative colitis

DEF: Chronic inflammation of mucosal lining of intestinal tract; may be single area or entire colon.

AHA: 3Q, '99, 8

556.0 Ulcerative (chronic) enterocolitis

556.1 Ulcerative (chronic) ileocolitis

556.2 Ulcerative (chronic) proctitis

556.3 Ulcerative (chronic) proctosigmoiditis

556.4 Pseudopolyposis of colon

556.5 Left-sided ulcerative (chronic) colitis

556.6 Universal ulcerative (chronic) colitis

Pancolitis

556.8 Other ulcerative colitis

556.9 Ulcerative colitis, unspecified

Ulcerative enteritis NOS

AHA: 1Q, '03, 10

K51.90 Ulcerative colitis unspecified w/o complications   I-10

✓4th 557 Vascular insufficiency of intestine

EXCLUDES   necrotizing enterocolitis of the newborn (777.50-777.53)

DEF: Inadequacy of intestinal vessels.

557.0 Acute vascular insufficiency of intestine

Acute:
    hemorrhagic enterocolitis
    ischemic colitis, enteritis, or enterocolitis
    massive necrosis of intestine
Bowel infarction
Embolism of mesenteric artery
Fulminant enterocolitis
Hemorrhagic necrosis of intestine
Infarction of appendices epiploicae
Intestinal gangrene
Intestinal infarction (acute) (agnogenic) (hemorrhagic) (nonocclusive)
Mesenteric infarction (embolic) (thrombotic)
Necrosis of intestine
Terminal hemorrhagic enteropathy
Thrombosis of mesenteric artery

AHA: 2Q, '08, 15; 4Q, '01, 53

TIP: Do not assign an additional code for GI bleeding; it is inherent in 557.0.

K55.0 Acute vascular disorders of intestine   I-10

557.1 Chronic vascular insufficiency of intestine

Angina, abdominal
Chronic ischemic colitis, enteritis, or enterocolitis
Ischemic stricture of intestine
Mesenteric:
    angina
    artery syndrome (superior)
    vascular insufficiency

AHA: 3Q, '96, 9; 4Q, '90, 4; N-D, '86, 11; N-D, '84, 7

557.9 Unspecified vascular insufficiency of intestine

Alimentary pain due to vascular insufficiency
Ischemic colitis, enteritis, or enterocolitis NOS

K55.9 Vascular disorder of intestine unspecified   I-10

✓4th 558 Other and unspecified noninfectious gastroenteritis and colitis

EXCLUDES   infectious:
         colitis, enteritis, or gastroenteritis (009.0-009.1)
         diarrhea (009.2-009.3)

558.1 Gastroenteritis and colitis due to radiation

Radiation enterocolitis

558.2 Toxic gastroenteritis and colitis

Use additional E code to identify cause

558.3 Allergic gastroenteritis and colitis
Use additional code to identify type of food allergy
(V15.01-V15.05)

DEF: True immunoglobulin E (IgE)-mediated allergic reaction
of the lining of the stomach, intestines, or colon to food
proteins; causes nausea, vomiting, diarrhea, and abdominal
cramping.

AHA: ▶4Q, '08, 116;◀ 1Q, '03, 12; 4Q, '00, 42

✓5ᵗʰ **558.4 Eosinophilic gastroenteritis and colitis**
AHA: ▶4Q, '08, 116◀

558.41 Eosinophilic gastroenteritis
Eosinophilic enteritis
AHA: ▶4Q, '08, 116◀

558.42 Eosinophilic colitis
AHA: ▶4Q, '08, 115-116◀

**558.9 Other and unspecified noninfectious gastroenteritis
and colitis**

Colitis
Enteritis
Gastroenteritis ⎫
Ileitis   ⎬ NOS, dietetic, or noninfectious
Jejunitis
Sigmoiditis ⎭

AHA: 2Q, '08, 10; 1Q, '08, 10; 3Q, '99, 4, 6; N-D, '87, 7

K52.9 Noninfective gastroenteritis & colitis unspec   `I-10`

OTHER DISEASES OF INTESTINES AND PERITONEUM (560-569)

✓4ᵗʰ **560 Intestinal obstruction without mention of hernia**
EXCLUDES duodenum (537.2-537.3)
inguinal hernia with obstruction (550.1)
intestinal obstruction complicating hernia (552.0-552.9)
mesenteric:
embolism (557.0)
infarction (557.0)
thrombosis (557.0)
neonatal intestinal obstruction (277.01, 777.1-777.2,
777.4)

TIP: If intestinal obstruction is due to abdominal carcinomatosis or
Crohn's disease, sequence that condition first.

560.0 Intussusception
Intussusception (colon) (intestine) (rectum)
Invagination of intestine or colon
EXCLUDES intussusception of appendix (543.9)
DEF: Prolapse of a bowel section into adjacent section; occurs
primarily in children; symptoms include paroxysmal pain,
vomiting, presence of blood, and mucous passage from
rectum.
AHA: 4Q, '98, 82

560.1 Paralytic ileus
Adynamic ileus
Ileus (of intestine) (of bowel) (of colon)
Paralysis of intestine or colon
EXCLUDES gallstone ileus (560.31)
DEF: Obstruction of ileus due to inhibited bowel motility.
AHA: J-F, '87, 13
K56.0 Paralytic ileus   `I-10`

560.2 Volvulus
Knotting   ⎫
Strangulation ⎬ if intestine, bowel, or colon
Torsion   ⎬
Twist   ⎭
DEF: Entanglement of bowel; causes obstruction; may
compromise bowel circulation.

✓5ᵗʰ **560.3 Impaction of intestine**

560.30 Impaction of intestine, unspecified
Impaction of colon

560.31 Gallstone ileus
Obstruction of intestine by gallstone

Volvulus and Diverticulitis

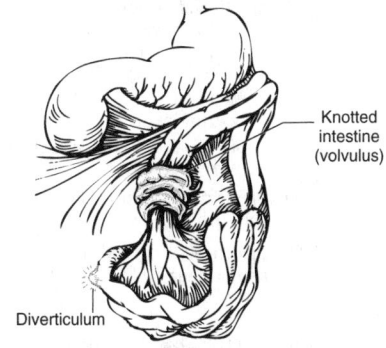

Knotted intestine (volvulus)

Diverticulum

560.39 Other
Concretion of intestine
Enterolith
Fecal impaction
AHA: 4Q, '98, 38
K56.4 Other impaction of intestine   `I-10`

✓5ᵗʰ **560.8 Other specified intestinal obstruction**

**560.81 Intestinal or peritoneal adhesions with
obstruction (postoperative) (postinfection)**
EXCLUDES adhesions without obstruction
(568.0)
DEF: Obstruction of peritoneum or intestine due to
abnormal union of tissues.
AHA: 4Q, '95, 55; 3Q, '95, 6; N-D, '87, 9
TIP: Do not assign additional code 997.4 Digestive
system complications.
K56.5 Intestinal adhes [bands] w/obst   `I-10`
(postproc) (postinfec)

560.89 Other
Acute pseudo-obstruction of intestine
Mural thickening causing obstruction
EXCLUDES ischemic stricture of intestine (557.1)
AHA: 2Q, '97, 3; 1Q, '88, 6

560.9 Unspecified intestinal obstruction
Enterostenosis ⎫
Obstruction   ⎪
Occlusion   ⎬ of intestine or colon
Stenosis   ⎪
Stricture   ⎭
EXCLUDES congenital stricture or stenosis of intestine
(751.1-751.2)
K56.60 Unspecified intestinal obstruction   `I-10`

✓4ᵗʰ **562 Diverticula of intestine**
Use additional code to identify any associated:
peritonitis (567.0-567.9)
EXCLUDES congenital diverticulum of colon (751.5)
diverticulum of appendix (543.9)
Meckel's diverticulum (751.0)
AHA: 4Q, '91, 25; J-F, '85, 1

✓5ᵗʰ **562.0 Small intestine**

**562.00 Diverticulosis of small intestine (without
mention of hemorrhage)**
Diverticulosis:
duodenum ⎫
ileum   ⎬ without mention of
jejunum ⎭ diverticulitis
DEF: Saclike herniations of mucous lining of small
intestine.

✓4ᵗʰ
✓5ᵗʰ **Additional Digit Required**   **Unspecified Code**   **Other Specified Code**   **Manifestation Code**   ▶◀ Revised Text   ● New Code   ▲ Revised Code Title
2010 ICD-9-CM   **February 2009 • Volume 1 – 173**

558.3–562.00

Digestive System

562.01–565.0

562.01 Diverticulitis of small intestine (without mention of hemorrhage)
Diverticulitis (with diverticulosis):
duodenum
ileum
jejunum
small intestine
DEF: Inflamed saclike herniations of mucous lining of small intestine

562.02 Diverticulosis of small intestine with hemorrhage

562.03 Diverticulitis of small intestine with hemorrhage

√5ᵗʰ **562.1 Colon**

562.10 Diverticulosis of colon (without mention of hemorrhage)
Diverticulosis:
NOS
intestine (large) } without metion of diverticulitis
Diverticular disease (colon)
DEF: Saclike herniations of mucous lining of large intestine.
AHA: 3Q, '05, 17; 3Q, '02, 15; 4Q, '90, 21; J-F, '85, 5
K57.90 Divrticulos intest part uns w/o perf/absc w/o bldg `I-10`

562.11 Diverticulitis of colon (without mention of hemorrhage)
Diverticulitis (with diverticulosis):
NOS
colon
intestine (large)
DEF: Inflamed saclike herniations of mucosal lining of large intestine.
AHA: 1Q, '96, 14; J-F, '85, 5
K57.92 Divrticulit intest part uns w/o perf/absc w/o bldg `I-10`

562.12 Diverticulosis of colon with hemorrhage

562.13 Diverticulitis of colon with hemorrhage

√4ᵗʰ **564 Functional digestive disorders, not elsewhere classified**
EXCLUDES functional disorders of stomach (536.0–536.9)
those specified as psychogenic (306.4)

√5ᵗʰ **564.0 Constipation**
AHA: 4Q, '01, 45

564.00 Constipation, unspecified
K59.00 Constipation unspecified `I-10`

564.01 Slow transit constipation
DEF: Delay in the transit of fecal material through the colon secondary to smooth muscle dysfunction or decreased peristaltic contractions along the colon: also called colonic inertia or delayed transit.

564.02 Outlet dysfunction constipation
DEF: Failure to relax the paradoxical contractions of the striated pelvic floor muscles during the attempted defecation.

564.09 Other constipation

564.1 Irritable bowel syndrome
Irritable colon
Spastic colon
DEF: Functional gastrointestinal disorder (FGID); symptoms: include diarrhea, constipation, abdominal pain; gas, distended abdomen, nausea, vomiting, emotional distress, and depression.
AHA: 1Q, '88, 6
K58.9 Irritable bowel syndrome without diarrhea `I-10`

564.2 Postgastric surgery syndromes
Dumping syndrome
Jejunal syndrome
Postgastrectomy syndrome
Postvagotomy syndrome
EXCLUDES malnutrition following gastrointestinal surgery (579.3)
postgastrojejunostomy ulcer (534.0–534.9)
AHA: 1Q, '95, 11

564.3 Vomiting following gastrointestinal surgery
Vomiting (bilious) following gastrointestinal surgery

564.4 Other postoperative functional disorders
Diarrhea following gastrointestinal surgery
EXCLUDES colostomy and enterostomy complications (569.60–569.69)

564.5 Functional diarrhea
EXCLUDES diarrhea:
NOS (787.91)
psychogenic (306.4)
DEF: Diarrhea with no detectable organic cause.

564.6 Anal spasm
Proctalgia fugax

564.7 Megacolon, other than Hirschsprung's
Dilatation of colon
EXCLUDES megacolon:
congenital [Hirschsprung's] (751.3)
toxic (556)
DEF: Enlarged colon; congenital or acquired; can occur acutely or become chronic.

√5ᵗʰ **564.8 Other specified functional disorders of intestine**
EXCLUDES malabsorption (579.0–579.9)
AHA: 1Q, '88, 6

564.81 Neurogenic bowel
DEF: Disorder of bowel due to spinal cord lesion above conus medullaris; symptoms include precipitous micturition, nocturia, headache, sweating, nasal obstruction and spastic contractions.
AHA: 1Q, '01, 12; 4Q, '98, 45

564.89 Other functional disorders of intestine
Atony of colon
DEF: Absence of normal bowel tone or strength.

564.9 Unspecified functional disorder of intestine

√4ᵗʰ **565 Anal fissure and fistula**

565.0 Anal fissure
EXCLUDES anal sphincter tear (healed) (non-traumatic) (old) (569.43)
traumatic (863.89, 863.99)
DEF: Ulceration of cleft at anal mucosa; causes pain, itching, bleeding, infection, and sphincter spasm; may occur with hemorrhoids.

Anal Fistula and Abscess

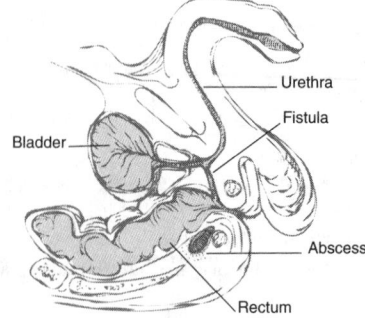

Bladder
Urethra
Fistula
Abscess
Rectum

565.1   **Anal fistula**

Fistula:
     anorectal
     rectal
     rectum to skin

> **EXCLUDES**   *fistula of rectum to internal organs—see*
>   *Alphabetic Index*
>   *ischiorectal fistula (566)*
>   *rectovaginal fistula (619.1)*

> **DEF:** Abnormal opening on cutaneous surface near anus; may lack connection with rectum.

> **AHA:** 1Q, '07, 13

566   **Abscess of anal and rectal regions**

Abscess:
     ischiorectal
     perianal
     perirectal
Cellulitis:
     anal
     perirectal
     rectal
Ischiorectal fistula

√4th **567**   **Peritonitis and retroperitoneal infections**

> **EXCLUDES**   *peritonitis:*
>   *benign paroxysmal (277.31)*
>   *pelvic, female (614.5, 614.7)*
>   *periodic familial (277.31)*
>   *puerperal ▶(670.8)◀*
>   *with or following:*
>   *abortion (634-638 with .0, 639.0)*
>   *appendicitis (540.0-540.1)*
>   *ectopic or molar pregnancy (639.0)*

> **DEF:** Inflammation of the peritoneal cavity.

   567.0   **Peritonitis in infectious diseases classified elsewhere**

> *Code first underlying disease*

> **EXCLUDES**   *peritonitis:*
>   *gonococcal (098.86)*
>   *syphilitic (095.2)*
>   *tuberculous (014.0)*

   567.1   **Pneumococcal peritonitis**

√5th **567.2**   **Other suppurative peritonitis**

> **AHA:** 4Q, '05, 74; 2Q, '01, 11, 12; 3Q, '99, 9; 2Q, '98, 19

     567.21   **Peritonitis (acute) generalized**

       Pelvic peritonitis, male

> **TIP:** For pelvic peritonitis in a female patient, refer to code 614.5.

     567.22   **Peritoneal abscess**

       Abscess (of):
         abdominopelvic
         mesenteric
         omentum
         peritoneum
         retrocecal
         subdiaphragmatic
         subhepatic
         subphrenic

> **K65.1** Peritoneal abscess   **I-10**

     567.23   **Spontaneous bacterial peritonitis**

> **EXCLUDES**   *bacterial peritonitis NOS (567.29)*

     567.29   **Other suppurative peritonitis**
       Subphrenic peritonitis

√5th **567.3**   **Retroperitoneal infections**

> **AHA:** 4Q, '05, 74

     567.31   **Psoas muscle abscess**

> **DEF:** Infection that extends into or around the psoas muscle that connects the lumbar vertebrae to the femur.

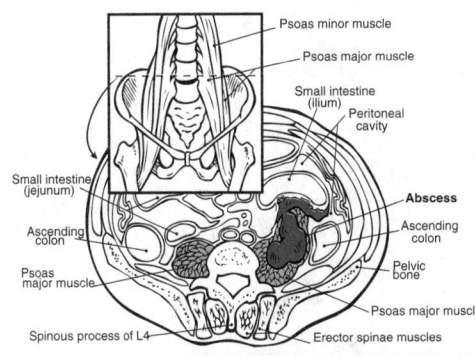

Psoas Muscle Abscess

Labels: Psoas minor muscle; Psoas major muscle; Small intestine (ilium); Peritoneal cavity; Abscess; Ascending colon; Pelvic bone; Psoas major muscle; Erector spinae muscles; Spinous process of L4; Psoas major muscle; Ascending colon; Small intestine (jejunum)

     567.38   **Other retroperitoneal abscess**

> **AHA:** 4Q, '05, 77

     567.39   **Other retroperitoneal infections**

√5th **567.8**   **Other specified peritonitis**

> **AHA:** 4Q, '05, 74

     567.81   **Choleperitonitis**
       Peritonitis due to bile

> **DEF:** Inflammation or infection due to presence of bile in the peritoneum resulting from rupture of the bile passages or gallbladder.

     567.82   **Sclerosing mesenteritis**
       Fat necrosis of peritoneum
       (Idiopathic) sclerosing mesenteric fibrosis
       Mesenteric lipodystrophy
       Mesenteric panniculitis
       Retractile mesenteritis

> **DEF:** Inflammatory processes involving the mesenteric fat; progresses to fibrosis and necrosis of tissue.

> **AHA:** 4Q, '05, 77

     567.89   **Other specified peritonitis**
       Chronic proliferative peritonitis
       Mesenteric saponification
       Peritonitis due to urine

   567.9   **Unspecified peritonitis**
     Peritonitis NOS
     Peritonitis of unspecified cause

> **AHA:** 1Q, '04, 10

√4th **568**   **Other disorders of peritoneum**

   568.0   **Peritoneal adhesions (postoperative) (postinfection)**
     Adhesions (of):
       abdominal (wall)
       diaphragm
       intestine
       male pelvis
       mesenteric
       omentum
       stomach
     Adhesive bands

> **EXCLUDES**   *adhesions:*
>   *pelvic, female (614.6)*
>   *with obstruction:*
>   *duodenum (537.3)*
>   *intestine (560.81)*

> **DEF:** Abnormal union of tissues in peritoneum.

> **AHA:** 3Q, '03, 7, 11; 4Q, '95, 55; 3Q, '95, 7; S-O, '85, 11

> **TIP:** Do not assign additional code 997.4 Digestive system complications.

> **K66.0** Peritoneal adhesns (postprocedural) (postinfection)   **I-10**

√5th **568.8**   **Other specified disorders of peritoneum**

     568.81   **Hemoperitoneum (nontraumatic)**

     568.82   **Peritoneal effusion (chronic)**

> **EXCLUDES**   *ascites NOS (789.51-789.59)*

> **DEF:** Persistent leakage of fluid within peritoneal cavity.

√4th √5th   Additional Digit Required   **Unspecified Code**   **Other Specified Code**   **Manifestation Code**   ▶◀ Revised Text   ● New Code   ▲ Revised Code Title

2010 ICD-9-CM   **October 2009 · Volume 1 – 175**

Rectum and Anus

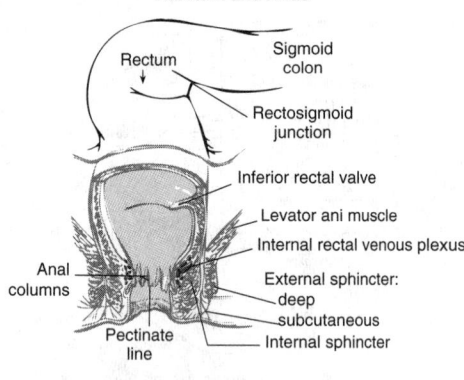

568.89   **Other**
Peritoneal:
   cyst
   granuloma

568.9   **Unspecified disorder of peritoneum**

✓4ᵗʰ **569** **Other disorders of intestine**

569.0   **Anal and rectal polyp**
Anal and rectal polyp NOS
EXCLUDES *adenomatous anal and rectal polyp (211.4)*

569.1   **Rectal prolapse**
Procidentia: Prolapse
   anus (sphincter)   anal canal
   rectum (sphincter)   rectal mucosa
Proctoptosis
EXCLUDES *prolapsed hemorrhoids (455.2, 455.5)*

569.2   **Stenosis of rectum and anus**
Stricture of anus (sphincter)

569.3   **Hemorrhage of rectum and anus**
EXCLUDES *gastrointestinal bleeding NOS (578.9)*
           melena (578.1)
AHA: 3Q, '05, 17
K62.5 Hemorrhage of anus and rectum   I-10

✓5ᵗʰ 569.4   **Other specified disorders of rectum and anus**

569.41   **Ulcer of anus and rectum**
Solitary ulcer } of anus (sphincter) or
Stercoral ulcer }   rectum (sphincter)

569.42   **Anal or rectal pain**
AHA: 1Q, '03, 8; 1Q, '96, 13

569.43   **Anal sphincter tear (healed) (old)**
Tear of anus, nontraumatic
Use additional code for any associated fecal
   incontinence (787.6)
EXCLUDES *anal fissure (565.0)*
           anal sphincter tear (healed) (old)
           complicating delivery (654.8)
AHA: 4Q, '07, 88

569.44   **Dysplasia of anus**
Anal intraepithelial neoplasia I and II (AIN I and II)
   (histologically confirmed)
Dysplasia of anus NOS
Mild and moderate dysplasia of anus
   (histologically confirmed)
EXCLUDES *abnormal results from anal cytologic*
           examination without
           histologic confirmation
           (796.70-796.79)
           anal intraepithelial neoplasia III
           (230.5, 230.6)
           carcinoma in situ of anus (230.5,
           230.6)
           HGSIL of anus (796.74)
           severe dysplasia of anus (230.5,
           230.6)
AHA: 4Q, '08, 117

569.49   **Other**
Granuloma } of rectum (sphincter)
Rupture   }
Hypertrophy of anal papillae
Proctitis NOS
EXCLUDES *fistula of rectum to:*
           internal organs–see Alphabetic
           Index
           skin (565.1)
           hemorrhoids (455.0-455.9)
           incontinence of sphincter ani (787.6)

569.5   **Abscess of intestine**
EXCLUDES *appendiceal abscess (540.1)*
K63.0 Abscess of intestine   I-10

✓5ᵗʰ 569.6   **Colostomy and enterostomy complications**
DEF: Complication in a surgically created opening, from
intestine to surface skin.
AHA: 4Q, '95, 58
TIP: Do not assign additional code 997.4 Digestive system
complications.

569.60   **Colostomy and enterostomy
complication, unspecified**

569.61   **Infection of colostomy or enterostomy**
Use additional code to identify organism
   (041.00-041.9)
Use additional code to specify type of infection,
   such as:
   abscess or cellulitis of abdomen (682.2)
   septicemia (038.0-038.9)

569.62   **Mechanical complication of colostomy and
enterostomy**
Malfunction of colostomy and enterostomy
AHA: 2Q, '05, 11 ; 1Q, '03, 10; 4Q, '98, 44

569.69   **Other complication**
Fistula
Hernia
Prolapse
AHA: 3Q, '98, 16

● ✓5ᵗʰ 569.7   **Complications of intestinal pouch**
● 569.71   **Pouchitis**
      Inflammation of internal ileoanal pouch
● 569.79   **Other complications of intestinal pouch**

✓5ᵗʰ 569.8   **Other specified disorders of intestine**
AHA: 4Q, '91, 25

569.81   **Fistula of intestine, excluding rectum and anus**
Fistula:
   abdominal wall
   enterocolic
   enteroenteric
   ileorectal
EXCLUDES *fistula of intestine to internal*
           organs–see Alphabetic Index
           persistent postoperative fistula
           (998.6)
AHA: 3Q, '99, 8

569.82   **Ulceration of intestine**
Primary ulcer of intestine
Ulceration of colon
EXCLUDES *that with perforation (569.83)*

569.83   **Perforation of intestine**

569.84   **Angiodysplasia of intestine (without mention
of hemorrhage)**
DEF: Small vascular abnormalities of the intestinal
tract without bleeding problems.
AHA: 3Q, '96, 10; 4Q, '90, 4; 4Q, '90, 21
TIP: Assign code 569.84 or 569.85 for documentation of either intestinal arteriovenous (AV) malformation or angiodysplasia.

Ⓝ Newborn Age: 0   Ⓟ Pediatric Age: 0-17   Ⓜ Maternity Age: 12-55   Ⓐ Adult Age: 15-124

569.85 Angiodysplasia of intestine with hemorrhage
> **DEF:** Small vascular abnormalities of the intestinal tract with bleeding problems.
> **AHA:** 3Q, '96, 9

569.86 Dieulafoy lesion (hemorrhagic) of intestine
> **AHA:** 4Q, '02, 60-61

● **569.87 Vomiting of fecal matter**

569.89 Other
> Enteroptosis
> Granuloma } of intestine
> Prolapse
> Pericolitis
> Perisigmoiditis
> Visceroptosis
>
> **EXCLUDES** gangrene of intestine, mesentery, or
>   omentum (557.0)
> hemorrhage of intestine NOS (578.9)
> obstruction of intestine (560.0-560.9)
>
> **AHA:** 3Q, '96, 9

569.9 Unspecified disorder of intestine

OTHER DISEASES OF DIGESTIVE SYSTEM (570-579)

570 Acute and subacute necrosis of liver
> Acute hepatic failure
> Acute or subacute hepatitis, not specified as infective
> Necrosis of liver (acute) (diffuse) (massive) (subacute)
> Parenchymatous degeneration of liver
> Yellow atrophy (liver) (acute) (subacute)
>
> **EXCLUDES** icterus gravis of newborn (773.0-773.2)
> serum hepatitis (070.2-070.3)
> that with:
>   abortion (634-638 with .7, 639.8)
>   ectopic or molar pregnancy (639.8)
>   pregnancy, childbirth, or the puerperium (646.7)
> viral hepatitis (070.0-070.9)
>
> **AHA:** 2Q, '05, 9; 1Q, '00, 22
>
> **K72.00** Acute and subacute hepatic failure without coma   `I-10`

✓4ᵗʰ **571 Chronic liver disease and cirrhosis**

     571.0 Alcoholic fatty liver   `A`

     571.1 Acute alcoholic hepatitis   `A`
> Acute alcoholic liver disease
> **AHA:** 2Q, '02, 4

     571.2 Alcoholic cirrhosis of liver   `A`
> Florid cirrhosis
> Laennec's cirrhosis (alcoholic)
> **DEF:** Fibrosis and dysfunction, of liver; due to alcoholic liver disease.
> **AHA:** 3Q, '07, 7; 2Q, '07, 6; 2Q, '02, 4; 1Q, '02, 3; N-D, '85, 14
> **TIP:** For a patient admitted for bleeding esophageal varices due to alcoholic liver cirrhosis, sequence the liver cirrhosis first.
> **K70.30** Alcoholic cirrhosis of liver without ascites   `I-10`

     571.3 Alcoholic liver damage, unspecified   `A`

✓5ᵗʰ **571.4 Chronic hepatitis**
> **EXCLUDES** viral hepatitis (acute) (chronic) (070.0-070.9)

     571.40 Chronic hepatitis, unspecified

     571.41 Chronic persistent hepatitis

     571.42 Autoimmune hepatitis
> **AHA:** 4Q, '08, 120

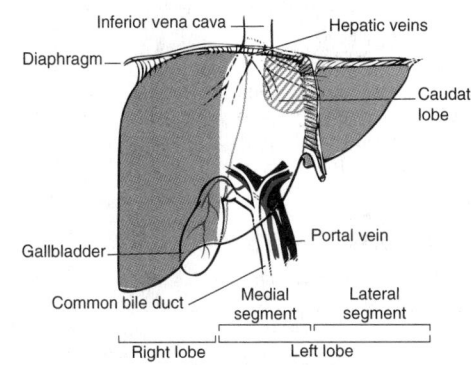

Liver

Inferior vena cava — Hepatic veins
Diaphragm —
Caudate lobe
Gallbladder — Portal vein
Common bile duct — Medial segment | Lateral segment
Right lobe — Left lobe

     571.49 Other
> Chronic hepatitis:
>   active
>   aggressive
> Recurrent hepatitis
> **AHA:** 3Q, '99, 19; N-D, '85, 14

     571.5 Cirrhosis of liver without mention of alcohol
> Cirrhosis of liver:
>   NOS
>   cryptogenic
>   macronodular
>   micronodular
>   posthepatitic
>   postnecrotic
> Healed yellow atrophy
>   (liver)
> Portal cirrhosis
> Code first, if applicable, viral hepatitis (acute) (chronic) (070.0-070.9)
> **DEF:** Fibrosis and dysfunction of liver; not alcohol related.
> **AHA:** 3Q, '07, 7; 2Q, '07, 5
> **TIP:** For a patient admitted for bleeding esophageal varices due to liver cirrhosis, sequence the liver cirrhosis first.

     571.6 Biliary cirrhosis
> Chronic nonsuppurative destructive cholangitis
> Cirrhosis:
>   cholangitic
>   cholestatic

     571.8 Other chronic nonalcoholic liver disease
> Chronic yellow atrophy (liver)
> Fatty liver, without mention of alcohol
> **AHA:** 2Q, '96, 12

     571.9 Unspecified chronic liver disease without mention of alcohol

✓4ᵗʰ **572 Liver abscess and sequelae of chronic liver disease**

     572.0 Abscess of liver
> **EXCLUDES** amebic liver abscess (006.3)

     572.1 Portal pyemia
> Phlebitis of portal vein
> Portal thrombophlebitis
> Pylephlebitis
> Pylethrombophlebitis
> **DEF:** Inflammation of portal vein or branches; may be due to intestinal disease; symptoms include fever, chills, jaundice, sweating, and abscess in various body parts.

▲ **572.2 Hepatic encephalopathy**
> ►Hepatic coma◄
> Hepatocerebral intoxication
> Portal-systemic encephalopathy
> **EXCLUDES** hepatic coma associated with viral
>   hepatitis—see category 070
> **AHA:** 2Q, '07, 5; 2Q, '05, 9; 1Q, '02, 3; 3Q, '95, 14
> **TIP:** Do not assign if hepatic coma is documented with viral hepatitis; see category 070 with fourth digit indicating hepatic coma.
> **K72.91** Hepatic failure unspecified with coma   `I-10`

✓4ᵗʰ Additional Digit Required   Unspecified Code   Other Specified Code   Manifestation Code   ►◄ Revised Text   ● New Code   ▲ Revised Code Title
✓5ᵗʰ

2010 ICD-9-CM   **October 2009 • Volume 1 – 177**

569.85–572.2

572.3 Portal hypertension

DEF: Abnormally high blood pressure in the portal vein.

AHA: 3Q, '05, 15

K76.6 Portal hypertension `I-10`

572.4 Hepatorenal syndrome

EXCLUDES *that following delivery (674.8)*

DEF: Hepatic and renal failure characterized by cirrhosis with ascites or obstructive jaundice, oliguria, and low sodium concentration.

AHA: 3Q, '93, 15

572.8 Other sequelae of chronic liver disease

✓4th **573 Other disorders of liver**

EXCLUDES *amyloid or lardaceous degeneration of liver (277.39)*
congenital cystic disease of liver (751.62)
glycogen infiltration of liver (271.0)
hepatomegaly NOS (789.1)
portal vein obstruction (452)

573.0 Chronic passive congestion of liver

DEF: Blood accumulation in liver tissue.

573.1 Hepatitis in viral diseases classified elsewhere

Code first underlying disease as:
Coxsackie virus disease (074.8)
cytomegalic inclusion virus disease (078.5)
infectious mononucleosis (075)

EXCLUDES *hepatitis (in):*
mumps (072.71)
viral (070.0-070.9)
yellow fever (060.0-060.9)

573.2 Hepatitis in other infectious diseases classified elsewhere

Code first underlying disease, as:
malaria (084.9)

EXCLUDES *hepatitis in:*
late syphilis (095.3)
secondary syphilis (091.62)
toxoplasmosis (130.5)

573.3 Hepatitis, unspecified

Toxic (noninfectious) hepatitis

Use additional E code to identify cause

AHA: 3Q, '98, 3, 4; 4Q, '90, 26

K75.9 Inflammatory liver disease unspecified `I-10`

573.4 Hepatic infarction

573.8 Other specified disorders of liver

Hepatoptosis

573.9 Unspecified disorder of liver

✓4th **574 Cholelithiasis**

The following fifth-digit subclassification is for use with category 574:
0 without mention of obstruction
1 with obstruction

§ ✓5th **574.0 Calculus of gallbladder with acute cholecystitis**
[0-1]

Biliary calculus ⎫
Calculus of cystic duct ⎬ with acute cholecystitis
Cholelithiasis ⎭

Any condition classifiable to 574.2 with acute cholecystitis

AHA: 4Q, '96, 32

K80.00 Calculus of GB w/acute cholecystitis w/o obst `I-10`

§ ✓5th **574.1 Calculus of gallbladder with other cholecystitis**
[0-1]

Biliary calculus ⎫
Calculus of cystic duct ⎬ with cholecystitis
Cholelithiasis ⎭

Cholecystitis with cholelithiasis NOS

Any condition classifiable to 574.2 with cholecystitis (chronic)

AHA: 3Q, '99, 9; 4Q, '96, 32, 69; 2Q, '96, 13; **For code 574.10:** 1Q, '03, 5

K80.10 Calculus of GB w/chronic cholecystitis w/o obst `I-10`

Gallbladder and Bile Ducts

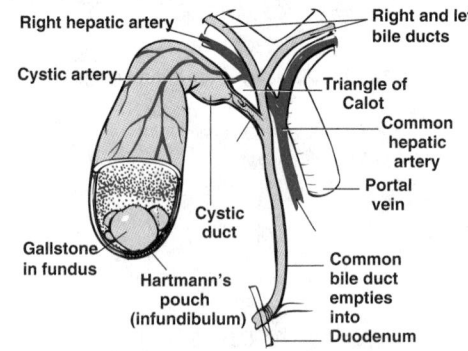

§ ✓5th **574.2 Calculus of gallbladder without mention of cholecystitis**
[0-1]

Biliary:
calculus NOS
colic NOS
Calculus of cystic duct
Cholelithiasis NOS
Colic (recurrent) of gallbladder
Gallstone (impacted)

AHA: For code 574.20: 1Q, '88, 14

K80.20 Calculus of GB w/o cholecystitis w/o obst `I-10`

§ ✓5th **574.3 Calculus of bile duct with acute cholecystitis**
[0-1]

Calculus of bile duct (any) ⎫
Choledocholithiasis ⎬ with acute cholecystitis

Any condition classifiable to 574.5 with acute cholecystitis

§ ✓5th **574.4 Calculus of bile duct with other cholecystitis**
[0-1]

Calculus of bile duct (any) ⎫
Choledocholithiasis ⎬ with cholecystitis (chronic)

Any condition classifiable to 574.5 with cholecystitis (chronic)

§ ✓5th **574.5 Calculus of bile duct without mention of cholecystitis**
[0-1]

Calculus of:
bile duct [any]
common duct
hepatic duct
Choledocholithiasis
Hepatic:
colic (recurrent)
lithiasis

AHA: 3Q, '94, 11

§ ✓5th **574.6 Calculus of gallbladder and bile duct with acute cholcystitis**
[0-1]

Any condition classifiable to 574.0 and 574.3

AHA: 4Q, '96, 32

§ ✓5th **574.7 Calculus of gallbladder and bile duct with other cholecytitis**
[0-1]

Any condition classifiable to 574.1 and 574.4

AHA: 4Q, '96, 32

§ ✓5th **574.8 Calculus of gallbladder and bile duct with acute and chronic cholcystitis**
[0-1]

Any condition classifiable to 574.6 and 574.7

AHA: 4Q, '96, 32

§ ✓5th **574.9 Calculus of gallbladder and bile duct without cholecystitis**
[0-1]

Any condition classifiable to 574.2 and 574.5

AHA: 4Q, '96, 32

§ Requires fifth digit. Valid digits are in [brackets] under each code. See category 574 for codes and definitions.

✓4ᵗʰ **575　Other disorders of gallbladder**

575.0　Acute cholecystitis

Abscess of gallbladder
Angiocholecystitis
Cholecystitis:
　emphysematous (acute)　⎫
　gangrenous　　　　　　　⎬ without mention of
　suppurative　　　　　　 ⎭　　calculus
Empyema of gallbladder
Gangrene of gallbladder

EXCLUDES *that with:*
　　　acute and chronic cholecystitis (575.12)
　　　choledocholithiasis (574.3)
　　　choledocholithiasis and cholelithiasis
　　　(574.6)
　　　cholelithiasis (574.0)

AHA: 3Q, '91, 17

TIP: Do not assign a separate cholecystitis code from category 575 with a code from category 574; cholecystitis is inherent.

K81.0 Acute cholecystitis　　　　　　　　　I-10

✓5ᵗʰ **575.1　Other cholecystitis**

Cholecystitis:　⎫
　NOS　　　　　⎬ without mention of calculus
　chronic　　　 ⎭

EXCLUDES *that with:*
　　　choledocholithiasis (574.4)
　　　choledocholithiasis and cholelithiasis
　　　(574.8)
　　　cholelithiasis (574.1)

AHA: 4Q, '96, 32

575.10　Cholecystitis, unspecified
　　　Cholecystitis NOS

575.11　Chronic cholecystitis
　　　K81.1 Chronic cholecystitis　　　　I-10

575.12　Acute and chronic cholecystitis
　　　AHA: 4Q, '97, 52; 4Q, '96, 32

575.2　Obstruction of gallbladder

Occlusion　⎫
Stenosis　 ⎬ of cystic duct or gallbladder without
Stricture　 ⎭　　mention of calculus

EXCLUDES *that with calculus (574.0-574.2 with*
　　　fifth-digit 1)

575.3　Hydrops of gallbladder
　Mucocele of gallbladder
　DEF: Serous fluid accumulation in bladder.
　AHA: 2Q, '89, 13

575.4　Perforation of gallbladder
　Rupture of cystic duct or gallbladder

575.5　Fistula of gallbladder
　Fistula:
　　cholecystoduodenal
　　cholecystoenteric

575.6　Cholesterolosis of gallbladder
　Strawberry gallbladder
　DEF: Cholesterol deposits in gallbladder tissue.
　AHA: 4Q, '90, 17

575.8　Other specified disorders of gallbladder

Adhesions　　　⎫
Atrophy　　　　 ⎪
Cyst　　　　　　⎬ of cystic duct or gallbladder
Hypertrophy　　⎪
Nonfunctioning ⎪
Ulcer　　　　　 ⎭

Biliary dyskinesia
EXCLUDES *Hartmann's pouch of intestine (V44.3)*
　　　nonvisualization of gallbladder (793.3)
AHA: 4Q, '90, 26; 2Q, '89, 13

575.9　Unspecified disorder of gallbladder

✓4ᵗʰ **576　Other disorders of biliary tract**

EXCLUDES *that involving the:*
　　　cystic duct (575.0-575.9)
　　　gallbladder (575.0-575.9)

576.0　Postcholecystectomy syndrome
　DEF: Jaundice or abdominal pain following cholecystectomy.
　AHA: 1Q, '88, 10
　TIP: Do not assign additional code 997.4 Digestive system complications.

576.1　Cholangitis

Cholangitis:　　　　　Cholangitis:
　NOS　　　　　　　　　recurrent
　acute　　　　　　　　 sclerosing
　ascending　　　　　　secondary
　chronic　　　　　　　 stenosing
　primary　　　　　　　suppurative

AHA: 2Q, '99, 13
K83.0 Cholangitis　　　　　　　　　I-10

576.2　Obstruction of bile duct

Occlusion　⎫
Stenosis　 ⎬ of bile duct, except cystic duct, without
Stricture　 ⎭　　mention of calculus

EXCLUDES *congenital (751.61)*
　　　that with calculus (574.3-574.5 with
　　　fifth-digit 1)

AHA: 3Q, '03, 17-18; 1Q, '01, 8; 2Q, '99, 13
K83.1 Obstruction of bile duct　　　　I-10

576.3　Perforation of bile duct
　Rupture of bile duct, except cystic duct

576.4　Fistula of bile duct
　Choledochoduodenal fistula

576.5　Spasm of sphincter of Oddi

576.8　Other specified disorders of biliary tract

Adhesions　　　⎫
Atrophy　　　　 ⎪
Cyst　　　　　　⎬ of bile duct (any)
Hypertrophy　　⎪
Nonfunctioning ⎪
Ulcer　　　　　 ⎭

EXCLUDES *congenital choledochal cyst (751.69)*
AHA: 3Q, '03, 17; 2Q, '99, 14

576.9　Unspecified disorder of biliary tract

✓4ᵗʰ **577　Diseases of pancreas**

577.0　Acute pancreatitis

Abscess of pancreas
Necrosis of pancreas:
　acute
　infective
Pancreatitis:
　NOS
　acute (recurrent)
　apoplectic
　hemorrhagic
　subacute
　suppurative

EXCLUDES *mumps pancreatitis (072.3)*
AHA: 3Q, '99, 9; 2Q, '98, 19; 2Q, '96, 13; 2Q, '89, 9
K85.0 Idiopathic acute pancreatitis　　I-10

577.1　Chronic pancreatitis

Chronic pancreatitis:
　NOS
　infectious
　interstitial
Pancreatitis:
　painless
　recurrent
　relapsing

AHA: 1Q, '01, 8; 2Q, '96, 13; 3Q, '94, 11
K86.1 Other chronic pancreatitis　　　I-10

577.2　Cyst and pseudocyst of pancreas
　K86.2 Cyst of pancreas　　　　　　I-10

✓4ᵗʰ ✓5ᵗʰ Additional Digit Required　　　**Unspecified Code**　　　**Other Specified Code**　　　**Manifestation Code**　　　▶◀ Revised Text　　　● New Code　　　▲ Revised Code Title

2010 ICD-9-CM　　　　　　　　　　　　　　　　　　　　　　　　　　　　　　**Volume 1 – 179**

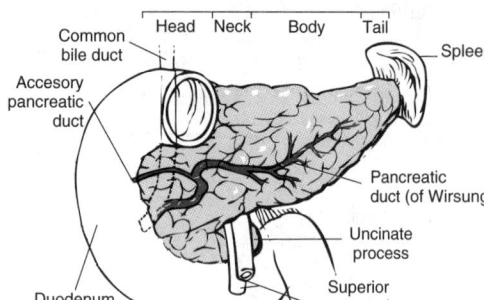

Pancreas

577.8 Other specified diseases of pancreas

Atrophy
Calculus } of pancreas
Cirrhosis
Fibrosis

Pancreatic:
infantilism
necrosis:
NOS
aseptic
fat
Pancreatolithiasis

EXCLUDES fibrocystic disease of pancreas (277.00-277.09)
islet cell tumor of pancreas (211.7)
pancreatic steatorrhea (579.4)

AHA: 1Q, '01, 8

577.9 Unspecified disease of pancreas

✓4ᵗʰ 578 Gastrointestinal hemorrhage

EXCLUDES that with mention of:
angiodysplasia of stomach and duodenum (537.83)
angiodysplasia of intestine (569.85)
diverticulitis, intestine:
large (562.13)
small (562.03)
diverticulosis, intestine:
large (562.12)
small (562.02)
gastritis and duodenitis (535.0-535.6)
ulcer:
duodenal, gastric, gastrojejuunal or peptic
(531.00-534.91)

AHA: 2Q, '92, 9; 4Q, '90, 20

578.0 Hematemesis
Vomiting of blood
AHA: 2Q, '02, 4

578.1 Blood in stool
Melena
EXCLUDES melena of the newborn (772.4, 777.3)
occult blood (792.1)
AHA: 2Q, '06, 17; 2Q, '92, 8
K92.1 Melena   **I-10**

578.9 Hemorrhage of gastrointestinal tract, unspecified
Gastric hemorrhage
Intestinal hemorrhage
AHA: 4Q, '06, 91; 3Q, '05, 17; N-D, '86, 9
TIP: Assign 578.9 if the physician does not establish a causal
link between GI bleeding and any possible causes found on
endoscopy.
K92.2 Gastrointestinal hemorrhage unspecified   **I-10**

✓4ᵗʰ 579 Intestinal malabsorption

579.0 Celiac disease
Celiac: Gee (-Herter) disease
crisis   Gluten enteropathy
infantilism   Idiopathic steatorrhea
rickets   Nontropical sprue
DEF: Malabsorption syndrome due to gluten consumption;
symptoms include fetid, bulky, frothy, oily stools; distended
abdomen, gas, asthenia, electrolyte depletion and vitamin B,
D and K deficiency.

579.1 Tropical sprue
Sprue:
NOS
tropical
Tropical steatorrhea
DEF: Diarrhea, occurs in tropics; may be due to enteric
infection and malnutrition.

579.2 Blind loop syndrome
Postoperative blind loop syndrome
DEF: Obstruction or impaired passage in small intestine due to
alterations, from strictures or surgery; causes stasis, abnormal
bacterial flora, diarrhea, weight loss, multiple vitamin
deficiency, and megaloblastic anemia.
TIP: Do not assign additional code 997.4 Digestive system
complications.

579.3 Other and unspecified postsurgical nonabsorption
Hypoglycemia } following gastrointestinal surgery
Malnutrition
AHA: 4Q, '03, 104

579.4 Pancreatic steatorrhea
DEF: Excess fat in feces due to absence of pancreatic juice in
intestine.

579.8 Other specified intestinal malabsorption
Enteropathy:
exudative
protein-losing
Steatorrhea (chronic)
AHA: 1Q, '88, 6

579.9 Unspecified intestinal malabsorption
Malabsorption syndrome NOS
AHA: 4Q, '04, 59

10. DISEASES OF THE GENITOURINARY SYSTEM (580-629)

NEPHRITIS, NEPHROTIC SYNDROME, AND NEPHROSIS (580-589)

> **EXCLUDES** *hypertensive chronic kidney disease (403.00-403.91, 404.00-404.93)*

☑️4th **580   Acute glomerulonephritis**

> **INCLUDES**   acute nephritis

DEF: Acute, severe inflammation in tuft of capillaries that filter the kidneys.

580.0   With lesion of proliferative glomerulonephritis
Acute (diffuse) proliferative glomerulonephritis
Acute poststreptococcal glomerulonephritis

580.4   With lesion of rapidly progressive glomerulonephritis
Acute nephritis with lesion of necrotizing glomerulitis
DEF: Acute glomerulonephritis; progresses to ESRD with diffuse epithelial proliferation.

☑️5th **580.8   With other specified pathological lesion in kidney**

580.81   *Acute glomerulonephritis in diseases classified elsewhere*

Code first underlying disease, as:
infectious hepatitis (070.0-070.9)
mumps (072.79)
subacute bacterial endocarditis (421.0)
typhoid fever (002.0)

580.89   Other
Glomerulonephritis, acute, with lesion of:
exudative nephritis
interstitial (diffuse) (focal) nephritis

580.9   Acute glomerulonephritis with unspecified pathological lesion in kidney

Glomerulonephritis
NOS
hemorrhagic
Nephritis
Nephropathy
} specified as acute

☑️4th **581   Nephrotic syndrome**

DEF: Disease process marked by symptoms such as; extensive edema, notable proteinuria, hypoalbuminemia, and susceptibility to intercurrent infections.

581.0   With lesion of proliferative glomerulonephritis

581.1   With lesion of membranous glomerulonephritis
Epimembranous nephritis
Idiopathic membranous glomerular disease
Nephrotic syndrome with lesion of:
focal glomerulosclerosis
sclerosing membranous glomerulonephritis
segmental hyalinosis

581.2   With lesion of membranoproliferative glomerulonephritis
Nephrotic syndrome with lesion (of):

endothelial
hypocomplementemic
persistent
lobular
mesangiocapillary
mixed membranous and
proliferative
} glomerulonephritis

DEF: Glomerulonephritis combined with clinical features of nephrotic syndrome; characterized by uneven thickening of glomerular capillary walls and mesangial cell increase; slowly progresses to ESRD.

581.3   With lesion of minimal change glomerulonephritis
Foot process disease
Lipoid nephrosis
Minimal change:
glomerular disease
glomerulitis
nephrotic syndrome
AHA: 1Q, '07, 23

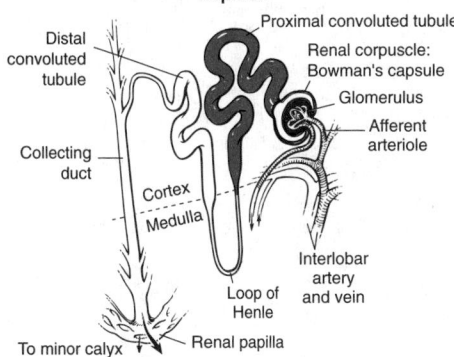

Kidney

Renal cortex — Fibrous capsule
Nephron
Medulla (pyramid)
Renal column
Renal sinus
Major calyx
Pelvis
Renal hilum
Minor calyx — Ureter

☑️5th **581.8   With other specified pathological lesion in kidney**

581.81   *Nephrotic syndrome in diseases classified elsewhere*

Code first underlying disease, as:
amyloidosis (277.30-277.39)
diabetes mellitus (249.4, 250.4)
tes mellitus (250.4)
malaria (084.9)
polyarteritis (446.0)
systemic lupus erythematosus (710.0)

> **EXCLUDES**   *nephrosis in epidemic hemorrhagic fever (078.6)*

AHA: 3Q, '91, 8, 12; S-O, '85, 3

581.89   Other
Glomerulonephritis with edema and lesion of:
exudative nephritis
interstitial (diffuse) (focal) nephritis

581.9   Nephrotic syndrome with unspecified pathological lesion in kidney
Glomerulonephritis with edema NOS
Nephritis:
nephrotic NOS
with edema NOS
Nephrosis NOS
Renal disease with edema NOS

☑️4th **582   Chronic glomerulonephritis**

> **INCLUDES**   chronic nephritis

DEF: Slow progressive type of nephritis characterized by inflammation of the capillary loops in the glomeruli of the kidney, which leads to renal failure.

582.0   With lesion of proliferative glomerulonephritis
Chronic (diffuse) proliferative glomerulonephritis

582.1   With lesion of membranous glomerulonephritis
Chronic glomerulonephritis:
membranous
sclerosing
Focal glomerulosclerosis
Segmental hyalinosis
AHA: S-O, '84, 16

Nephron

Distal convoluted tubule
Proximal convoluted tubule
Renal corpuscle:
Bowman's capsule
Glomerulus
Afferent arteriole
Collecting duct
Cortex
Medulla
Interlobar artery and vein
Loop of Henle
To minor calyx — Renal papilla

☑️4th
☑️5th
Additional Digit Required   **Unspecified Code**   **Other Specified Code**   **Manifestation Code**   ▶◀ Revised Text   ● New Code   ▲ Revised Code Title

2010 ICD-9-CM   **Volume 1 – 181**

580–582.1

Genitourinary System

582.2–584.6

582.2 With lesion of membranoproliferative glomerulonephritis
Chronic glomerulonephritis:
endothelial
hypocomplementemic persistent
lobular
membranoproliferative
mesangiocapillary
mixed membranous and proliferative
DEF: Chronic glomerulonephritis with mesangial cell proliferation.

582.4 With lesion of rapidly progressive glomerulonephritis
Chronic nephritis with lesion of necrotizing glomerulitis
DEF: Chronic glomerulonephritis rapidly progresses to ESRD; marked by diffuse epithelial proliferation.

√5th **582.8 With other specified pathological lesion in kidney**

582.81 Chronic glomerulonephritis in diseases classified elsewhere
Code first underlying disease, as:
amyloidosis (277.30-277.39)
systemic lupus erythematosus (710.0)

582.89 **Other**
Chronic glomerulonephritis with lesion of:
exudative nephritis
interstitial (diffuse) (focal) nephritis

582.9 Chronic glomerulonephritis with unspecified pathological lesion in kidney
Glomerulonephritis:
NOS
hemorrhagic   } specified as chronic
Nephritis
Nephropathy
AHA: 2Q, '01, 12

√4th **583 Nephritis and nephropathy, not specified as acute or chronic**
INCLUDES "renal disease" so stated, not specified as acute or chronic but with stated pathology or cause

583.0 With lesion of proliferative glomerulonephritis
Proliferative:
glomerulonephritis (diffuse) NOS
nephritis NOS
nephropathy NOS

583.1 With lesion of membranous glomerulonephritis
Membranous:
glomerulonephritis NOS
nephritis NOS
Membranous nephropathy NOS
DEF: Kidney inflammation or dysfunction with deposits on glomerular capillary basement membranes.
N05.2 Uns nephritic syndr w/ diffuse membranous gln I-10

583.2 With lesion of membranoproliferative glomerulonephritis
Membranoproliferative:
glomerulonephritis NOS
nephritis NOS
nephropathy NOS
Nephritis NOS, with lesion of:
hypocomplementemic
persistant
lobular
mesangiocapillary   } glomerulonephritis
mixed membranous and
proliferative
DEF: Kidney inflammation or dysfunction with mesangial cell proliferation.

583.4 With lesion of rapidly progressive glomerulonephritis
Necrotizing or rapidly progressive:
glomerulitis NOS
glomerulonephritis NOS
nephritis NOS
nephropathy NOS
Nephritis, unspecified, with lesion of necrotizing glomerulitis
DEF: Kidney inflammation or dysfunction; rapidly progresses to ESRD marked by diffuse epithelial proliferation.

583.6 With lesion of renal cortical necrosis
Nephritis, NOS
Nephropathy NS   } with (renal) cortical necrosis
Renal cortical necrosis NOS

583.7 With lesion of renal medullary necrosis
Nephritis, NOS   } with (renal) medullary
Nephropathy NOS   } [papillary] necrosis

√5th **583.8 With other specified pathological lesion in kidney**

583.81 Nephritis and nephropathy, not specified as acute or chronic, in diseases classified elsewhere
Code first underlying disease, as:
amyloidosis (277.30-277.39)
diabetes mellitus (249.4, 250.4)
gonococcal infection (098.19)
Goodpasture's syndrome (446.21)
systemic lupus erythematosus (710.0)
tuberculosis (016.0)
EXCLUDES *gouty nephropathy (274.10)*
syphilitic nephritis (095.4)
AHA: 2Q, '03, 7; 3Q, '91, 8; S-O, '85, 3

583.89 **Other**
Glomerulitis
Glomerulonephritis   } with lesions of:
Nephritis   exudative nephritis
Nephropathy   interstitial nephritis
Renal disease

583.9 With unspecified pathological lesion in kidney
Glomerulitis
Glomerulonephritis   } NOS
Nephritis
Nephropathy
EXCLUDES *nephropathy complicating pregnancy, labor,*
or the puerperium (642.0-642.9, 646.2)
renal disease NOS with no stated cause (593.9)

▲ √4th **584 Acute kidney failure**
INCLUDES ▶acute renal failure◀
EXCLUDES *following labor and delivery (669.3)*
posttraumatic (958.5)
that complicating:
abortion (634-638 with .3, 639.3)
ectopic or molar pregnancy (639.3)
DEF: State resulting from increasing urea and related substances from the blood (azotemia), often with urine output of less than 500 ml per day.
AHA: 1Q, '93, 18; 2Q, '92, 5; 4Q, '92, 22
TIP: Do not assign combination code for hypertensive renal disease unless chronic kidney disease is also present.

▲ **584.5 Acute kidney failure with lesion of tubular necrosis**
Lower nephron nephrosis
Renal failure with (acute) tubular necrosis
Tubular necrosis:
NOS
acute
DEF: Acute decline in kidney efficiency with destruction of tubules.
N17.0 Acute renal failure with tubular necrosis I-10

▲ **584.6 Acute kidney failure with lesion of renal cortical necrosis**
DEF: Acute decline in kidney efficiency with destruction of renal tissues that filter blood.

▲ **584.7 Acute kidney failure with lesion of renal medullary [papillary] necrosis**
Necrotizing renal papillitis
DEF: Acute decline in kidney efficiency with destruction of renal tissues that collect urine.

▲ **584.8 Acute kidney failure with other specified pathological lesion in kidney**
AHA: N-D, '85, 1

▲ **584.9 Acute kidney failure, unspecified**
Acute kidney injury (nontraumatic)
EXCLUDES *traumatic kidney injury (866.00-866.13)*
AHA: 4Q, '08, 192; 4Q, '07, 97; 2Q, '05, 18; 2Q, '03, 7; 1Q, '03, 22; 3Q, '02, 21, 28; 2Q, '01, 14; 1Q, '00, 22; 3Q, '96, 9; 4Q, '88, 1
N17.9 Acute renal failure unspecified   `I-10`

✓4ᵗʰ **585 Chronic kidney disease [CKD]**
Chronic uremia
Code first hypertensive chronic kidney disease, if applicable, (403.00-403.91, 404.00-404.93)
Use additional code to identify kidney transplant status, if applicable (V42.0)
Use additional code to identify manifestation as:
uremic:
neuropathy (357.4)
pericarditis (420.0)
AHA: 4Q, '06, 84-86; 4Q, '05, 68, 77; 1Q, '04, 5; 4Q, '03, 61, 111; 2Q, '03, 7; 2Q, '01, 12, 13; 1Q, '01, 3; 4Q, '98, 55; 3Q, '98, 6, 7; 2Q, '98, 20; 3Q, '96, 9; 1Q, '93, 18; 3Q, '91, 8; 4Q, '89, 1; N-D, '85, 15; S-O, '84, 3

585.1 Chronic kidney disease, Stage I
DEF: Some kidney damage; normal or slightly increased GFR (> 90).

585.2 Chronic kidney disease, Stage II (mild)
DEF: Kidney damage with mild decrease in GFR (60–89).

585.3 Chronic kidney disease, Stage III (moderate)
AHA: 4Q, '05, 69
DEF: Kidney damage with moderate decrease in GFR (30–59).
N18.3 Chronic kidney disease stage III moderate   `I-10`

585.4 Chronic kidney disease, Stage IV (severe)
DEF: Kidney damage with severe decrease in GFR (15–29).
N18.4 Chronic kidney disease stage IV severe   `I-10`

585.5 Chronic kidney disease, Stage V
EXCLUDES *chronic kidney disease, stage V requiring chronic dialysis (585.6)*
DEF: Kidney failure with GFR value of less than 15.

585.6 End stage renal disease
Chronic kidney disease requiring chronic dialysis
DEF: Federal government indicator of a stage V CKD patient undergoing treatment by dialysis or transplantation.
AHA: 4Q, '08, 193; 1Q, '08, 7; 4Q, '07, 86; 3Q, '07, 5, 9; 4Q, '06, 136; 4Q, '05, 79
N18.6 End stage renal disease   `I-10`

585.9 Chronic kidney disease, unspecified
Chronic renal disease
Chronic renal failure NOS
Chronic renal insufficiency
AHA: 1Q, '08, 10; 2Q, '07, 3; 4Q, '06, 86; 4Q, '05, 79
N18.9 Chronic kidney disease unspecified   `I-10`

586 Renal failure, unspecified
Uremia NOS
EXCLUDES *following labor and delivery (669.3)*
posttraumatic renal failure (958.5)
that complicating:
abortion (634-638 with .3, 639.3)
ectopic or molar pregnancy (639.3)
uremia:
extrarenal (788.9)
prerenal (788.9)
DEF: Renal failure: kidney functions cease; malfunction may be due to inability to excrete metabolized substances or retain level of electrolytes.
DEF: Uremia: excess urea, creatinine and other nitrogenous products of protein and amino acid metabolism in blood due to reduced excretory function in bilateral kidney disease; also called azotemia.
AHA: 3Q, '98, 6; 1Q, '93, 18; 1Q, '88, 3
N19 Unspecified renal failure   `I-10`

587 Renal sclerosis, unspecified
Atrophy of kidney
Contracted kidney
Renal:
cirrhosis
fibrosis

✓4ᵗʰ **588 Disorders resulting from impaired renal function**

588.0 Renal osteodystrophy
Azotemic osteodystrophy
Phosphate-losing tubular disorders
Renal:
dwarfism
infantilism
rickets
DEF: Condition resulting from chronic renal failure results in osteomalacia, osteoporosis or osteosclerosis; an abnormal level of phosphorus in the blood and impaired stimulation of the parathyroid.

588.1 Nephrogenic diabetes insipidus
EXCLUDES *diabetes insipidus NOS (253.5)*
DEF: Type of diabetes due to renal tubules inability to reabsorb water; not responsive to vasopressin; may develop into chronic renal insufficiency.

✓5ᵗʰ **588.8 Other specified disorders resulting from impaired renal function**
EXCLUDES *secondary hypertension (405.0-405.9)*

588.81 Secondary hyperparathyroidism (of renal origin)
Secondary hyperparathyroidism NOS
DEF: Parathyroid dysfunction caused by chronic renal failure; phosphate clearance is impaired, phosphate is released from bone, vitamin D is not produced, intestinal calcium absorption is low, and blood levels of calcium are lowered causing excessive production of parathyroid hormone.
AHA: 4Q, '04, 58-59
N25.81 Secondary hyperparathyroidism of renal origin   `I-10`

588.89 Other specified disorders resulting from impaired renal function
Hypokalemic nephropathy

588.9 Unspecified disorder resulting from impaired renal function

✓4ᵗʰ **589 Small kidney of unknown cause**

589.0 Unilateral small kidney

589.1 Bilateral small kidneys

589.9 Small kidney, unspecified

`✓4ᵗʰ`
`✓5ᵗʰ` **Additional Digit Required**   **Unspecified Code**   **Other Specified Code**   **Manifestation Code**   ▶◀ Revised Text   ● New Code   ▲ Revised Code Title

2010 ICD-9-CM   **October 2009 · Volume 1 – 183**

584.7–589.9

Genitourinary System

Genitourinary System

- Inferior vena cava
- Right kidney
- Anterior division of internal iliac artery
- Superior and Inferior vesicular arteries
- Ureteral orifice
- Urethra
- Aorta
- Left kidney
- Ureter
- Ovarian or testicular artery and vein
- Urinary bladder
- Urogenital diaphragm

OTHER DISEASES OF URINARY SYSTEM (590-599)

✓4ᵗʰ 590 Infections of kidney
Use additional code to identify organism, such as Escherichia coli [E. coli] (041.4)

✓5ᵗʰ 590.0 Chronic pyelonephritis
Chronic pyelitis
Chronic pyonephrosis
Code if applicable, any casual condition first

590.00 Without lesion of renal medullary necrosis

590.01 With lesion of renal medullary necrosis

✓5ᵗʰ 590.1 Acute pyelonephritis
Acute pyelitis
Acute pyonephrosis

590.10 Without lesion of renal medullary necrosis

590.11 With lesion of renal medullary necrosis

590.2 Renal and perinephric abscess
Abscess:
kidney
nephritic
perirenal
Carbuncle of kidney

590.3 Pyeloureteritis cystica
Infection of renal pelvis and ureter
Ureteritis cystica
DEF: Inflammation and formation of submucosal cysts in the kidney, pelvis, and ureter.

✓5ᵗʰ 590.8 Other pyelonephritis or pyonephrosis, not specified as acute or chronic

590.80 Pyelonephritis, unspecified
Pyelitis NOS
Pyelonephritis NOS
AHA: 1Q, '98, 10; 4Q, '97, 40
N11.9 Chronic tubulo-interstitial nephritis uns `I-10`

590.81 *Pyelitis or pyelonephritis in diseases classified elsewhere*
Code first underlying disease, as:
tuberculosis (016.0)

590.9 Infection of kidney, unspecified
EXCLUDES *urinary tract infection NOS (599.0)*

591 Hydronephrosis
Hydrocalycosis
Hydronephrosis
Hydroureteronephrosis
EXCLUDES *congenital hydronephrosis (753.29)*
hydroureter (593.5)
DEF: Distention of kidney and pelvis, with urine build-up due to ureteral obstruction; pyonephrosis may result.
AHA: 2Q, '98, 9
TIP: Hydronephrosis is not inherent in urinary obstructions and should be coded separately.
N13.30 Unspecified hydronephrosis `I-10`

✓4ᵗʰ 592 Calculus of kidney and ureter
EXCLUDES *nephrocalcinosis (275.4)*

592.0 Calculus of kidney
Nephrolithiasis NOS
Renal calculus or stone
Staghorn calculus
Stone in kidney
EXCLUDES *uric acid nephrolithiasis (274.11)*
AHA: 1Q, '00, 4
N20.0 Calculus of kidney `I-10`

592.1 Calculus of ureter
Ureteric stone
Ureterolithiasis
AHA: 2Q, '98, 9; 1Q, '98, 10; 1Q, '91, 11
N20.1 Calculus of ureter `I-10`

592.9 Urinary calculus, unspecified
AHA: 1Q, '98, 10; 4Q, '97, 40

✓4ᵗʰ 593 Other disorders of kidney and ureter

593.0 Nephroptosis
Floating kidney
Mobile kidney

593.1 Hypertrophy of kidney

593.2 Cyst of kidney, acquired
Cyst (multiple) (solitary) of kidney, not congenital
Peripelvic (lymphatic) cyst
EXCLUDES *calyceal or pyelogenic cyst of kidney (591)*
congenital cyst of kidney (753.1)
polycystic (disease of) kidney (753.1)
DEF: Abnormal, fluid-filled sac in the kidney, not present at birth.
AHA: 4Q, '90, 3
N28.1 Cyst of kidney acquired `I-10`

593.3 Stricture or kinking of ureter
Angulation ⎫
Constriction ⎬ of ureter (post-operative)
Stricture of pelviureteric junction
DEF: Stricture or knot in tube connecting kidney to bladder.
AHA: 2Q, '98, 9

593.4 Other ureteric obstruction
Idiopathic retroperitoneal fibrosis
Occlusion NOS of ureter
EXCLUDES *that due to calculus (592.1)*
AHA: 2Q, '97, 4

593.5 Hydroureter
EXCLUDES *congenital hydroureter (753.22)*
hydroureteronephrosis (591)

593.6 Postural proteinuria
Benign postural proteinuria
Orthostatic proteinuria
EXCLUDES *proteinuria NOS (791.0)*
DEF: Excessive amounts of serum protein in the urine caused by the body position, e.g., orthostatic and lordotic.

✓5ᵗʰ 593.7 Vesicoureteral reflux
DEF: Backflow of urine, from bladder into ureter due to obstructed bladder neck.
AHA: 4Q, '94, 42

593.70 Unspecified or without reflux nephropathy

593.71 With reflux nephropathy, unilateral

593.72 With reflux nephropathy, bilateral

593.73 With reflux nephropathy NOS

✓5ᵗʰ 593.8 Other specified disorders of kidney and ureter

593.81 Vascular disorders of kidney
Renal (artery):
embolism
hemorrhage
thrombosis
Renal infarction

N Newborn Age: 0   P Pediatric Age: 0-17   M Maternity Age: 12-55   A Adult Age: 15-124

593.82 **Ureteral fistula**
Intestinoureteral fistula
> **EXCLUDES** *fistula between ureter and female genital tract (619.0)*

DEF: Abnormal communication, between tube connecting kidney to bladder and another structure.

593.89 **Other**
Adhesions, kidney or ureter
Periureteritis
Polyp of ureter
Pyelectasia
Ureterocele
> **EXCLUDES** *tuberculosis of ureter (016.2)*
> *ureteritis cystica (590.3)*

593.9 **Unspecified disorder of kidney and ureter**
Acute renal disease
Acute renal insufficiency
Renal disease NOS
Salt-losing nephritis or syndrome
> **EXCLUDES** *chronic renal insufficiency (585.9)*
> *cystic kidney disease (753.1)*
> *nephropathy, so stated (583.0-583.9)*
> *renal disease:*
> *arising in pregnancy or the puerperium (642.1-642.2, 642.4-642.7, 646.2)*
> *not specified as acute or chronic, but with stated pathology or cause (583.0-583.9)*

AHA: 4Q, '05, 79; 1Q, '93, 17

N28.9 Disorder of kidney and ureter unspecified I-10

✓4ᵗʰ **594** **Calculus of lower urinary tract**

594.0 **Calculus in diverticulum of bladder**
DEF: Stone or mineral deposit in abnormal sac on the bladder wall.

594.1 **Other calculus in bladder**
Urinary bladder stone
> **EXCLUDES** *staghorn calculus (592.0)*

DEF: Stone or mineral deposit in bladder.

594.2 **Calculus in urethra**
DEF: Stone or mineral deposit in tube that empties urine from bladder.

594.8 **Other lower urinary tract calculus**
AHA: J-F, '85, 16

594.9 **Calculus of lower urinary tract, unspecified**
> **EXCLUDES** *calculus of urinary tract NOS (592.9)*

✓4ᵗʰ **595** **Cystitis**
> **EXCLUDES** *prostatocystitis (601.3)*

Use additional code to identify organism, such as Escherichia coli [E. coli] (041.4)

595.0 **Acute cystitis**
> **EXCLUDES** *trigonitis (595.3)*

DEF: Acute inflammation of bladder.
AHA: 2Q, '99, 15

N30.00 Acute cystitis without hematuria I-10

595.1 **Chronic interstitial cystitis**
Hunner's ulcer
Panmural fibrosis of bladder
Submucous cystitis
DEF: Inflamed lesion affecting bladder wall; symptoms include urinary frequency, pain on bladder filling, nocturia, and distended bladder.

595.2 **Other chronic cystitis**
Chronic cystitis NOS
Subacute cystitis
> **EXCLUDES** *trigonitis (595.3)*

DEF: Persistent inflammation of bladder.

Bladder
Anterior View

Lateral View

595.3 **Trigonitis**
Follicular cystitis
Trigonitis (acute) (chronic)
Urethrotrigonitis
DEF: Inflammation of the triangular area of the bladder called the trigonum vesicae.

595.4 *Cystitis in diseases classified elsewhere*
Code first underlying disease, as:
actinomycosis (039.8)
amebiasis (006.8)
bilharziasis (120.0-120.9)
Echinococcus infestation (122.3, 122.6)
> **EXCLUDES** *cystitis:*
> *diphtheritic (032.84)*
> *gonococcal (098.11, 098.31)*
> *monilial (112.2)*
> *trichomonal (131.09)*
> *tuberculous (016.1)*

✓5ᵗʰ 595.8 **Other specified types of cystitis**

595.81 **Cystitis cystica**
DEF: Inflammation of the bladder characterized by formation of multiple cysts.

595.82 **Irradiation cystitis**
Use additional E code to identify cause
DEF: Inflammation of the bladder due to effects of radiation.

595.89 **Other**
Abscess of bladder:
Cystitis:
bullous
emphysematous
glandularis

595.9 **Cystitis, unspecified**

Genitourinary System

596–598.1

✓4ᵗʰ **596 Other disorders of bladder**

Use additional code to identify urinary incontinence (625.6, 788.30-788.39)

AHA: M-A, '87, 10

596.0 Bladder neck obstruction

Contracture (acquired)
Obstruction (acquired) } of bladder neck or
Stenosis (acquired) vesicourethral orifice

EXCLUDES congenital (753.6)

DEF: Bladder outlet and vesicourethral obstruction; occurs as a consequence of benign prostatic hypertrophy or prostatic cancer; may also occur in either sex due to strictures, following radiation, cystoscopy, catheterization, injury, infection, blood clots, bladder cancer, impaction or disease compressing bladder neck.

AHA: 3Q, '02, 28; 2Q, '01, 14; N-D, '86, 10

N32.0 Bladder-neck obstruction I-10

596.1 Intestinovesical fistula

Fistula:
enterovesical
vesicocolic
vesicoenteric
vesicorectal

DEF: Abnormal communication, between intestine and bladder.

596.2 Vesical fistula, not elsewhere classified

Fistula:
bladder NOS
urethrovesical
vesicocutaneous
vesicoperineal

EXCLUDES fistula between bladder and female genital tract (619.0)

DEF: Abnormal communication between bladder and another structure.

596.3 Diverticulum of bladder

Diverticulitis
Diverticulum (acquired) (false) } of bladder

EXCLUDES that with calculus in diverticulum of bladder (594.0)

DEF: Abnormal pouch in bladder wall.

596.4 Atony of bladder

High compliance bladder
Hypotonicity
Inertia } of bladder

EXCLUDES neurogenic bladder (596.54)

DEF: Distended, bladder with loss of expulsive force; linked to CNS disease.

✓5ᵗʰ **596.5 Other functional disorders of bladder**

EXCLUDES cauda equina syndrome with neurogenic bladder (344.61)

596.51 Hypertonicity of bladder

Hyperactivity
Overactive bladder

DEF: Abnormal tension of muscular wall of bladder; may appear after surgery of voluntary nerve.

N32.81 Overactive bladder I-10

596.52 Low bladder compliance

DEF: Low bladder capacity; causes increased pressure and frequent urination.

596.53 Paralysis of bladder

DEF: Impaired bladder motor function due to nerve or muscle damage.

596.54 Neurogenic bladder NOS

DEF: Unspecified dysfunctional bladder due to lesion of central, peripheral nervous system; may result in incontinence, residual urine retention, urinary infection, stones and renal failure.

AHA: 1Q, '01, 12

N31.9 Neuromuscular dysfunction of bladder unspecified I-10

596.55 Detrusor sphincter dyssynergia

DEF: Instability of the urinary bladder sphincter muscle associated with urinary incontinence.

596.59 Other functional disorder of bladder

Detrusor instability

DEF: Detrusor instability: instability of bladder; marked by uninhibited contractions often leading to incontinence.

596.6 Rupture of bladder, nontraumatic

596.7 Hemorrhage into bladder wall

Hyperemia of bladder

EXCLUDES acute hemorrhagic cystitis (595.0)

596.8 Other specified disorders of bladder

Bladder: Bladder:
calcified hemorrhage
contracted hypertrophy

EXCLUDES cystocele, female (618.01-618.02, 618.09, 618.2-618.4)
hernia or prolapse of bladder, female (618.01-618.02, 618.09, 618.2-618.4)

AHA: J-F, '85, 8

596.9 Unspecified disorder of bladder

AHA: J-F, '85, 8

✓4ᵗʰ **597 Urethritis, not sexually transmitted, and urethral syndrome**

EXCLUDES nonspecific urethritis, so stated (099.4)

597.0 Urethral abscess

Abscess: Abscess of:
periurethral Cowper's gland
urethral (gland) Littré's gland
Abscess of: Periurethral cellulitis
bulbourethral gland

EXCLUDES urethral caruncle (599.3)

DEF: Pocket of pus in tube that empties urine from the bladder.

✓5ᵗʰ **597.8 Other urethritis**

597.80 Urethritis, unspecified

597.81 Urethral syndrome NOS

597.89 Other

Adenitis, Skene's glands
Cowperitis
Meatitis, urethral
Ulcer, urethra (meatus)
Verumontanitis

EXCLUDES trichomonal (131.02)

✓4ᵗʰ **598 Urethral stricture**

Use additional code to identify urinary incontinence (625.6, 788.30-788.39)

INCLUDES pinhole meatus
stricture of urinary meatus

EXCLUDES congenital stricture of urethra and urinary meatus (753.6)

DEF: Narrowing of tube that empties urine from bladder.

✓5ᵗʰ **598.0 Urethral stricture due to infection**

598.00 Due to unspecified infection

598.01 Due to infective diseases classified elsewhere

Code first underlying disease, as:
gonococcal infection (098.2)
schistosomiasis (120.0-120.9)
syphilis (095.8)

598.1 Traumatic urethral stricture

Stricture of urethra:
late effect of injury
postobstetric

EXCLUDES postoperative following surgery on genitourinary tract (598.2)

N Newborn Age: 0   P Pediatric Age: 0-17   M Maternity Age: 12-55   A Adult Age: 15-124

598.2 Postoperative urethral stricture
Postcatheterization stricture of urethra
AHA: 3Q, '97, 6

598.8 Other specified causes of urethral stricture
AHA: N-D, '84, 9

598.9 Urethral stricture, unspecified

√4ᵗʰ **599 Other disorders of urethra and urinary tract**

599.0 Urinary tract infection, site not specified
EXCLUDES *candidiasis of urinary tract (112.2)*
urinary tract infection of newborn (771.82)
Use additional code to identify organism, such as
Escherichia coli [E. coli] (041.4)
AHA: 3Q, '05, 12; 2Q, '04, 13; 4Q, '03, 79; 4Q, '99, 6; 2Q, '99,
15;1Q, '98, 5; 2Q, '96, 7; 4Q, '96, 33; 2Q, '95, 7; 1Q, '92, 13
TIP: Do not assign if UTI due to candidiasis; see code 112.2.
N39.0 Urinary tract infection site not specified   I-10

599.1 Urethral fistula
Fistula: Urinary fistula NOS
urethroperineal
urethrorectal
EXCLUDES *fistula:*
urethroscrotal (608.89)
urethrovaginal (619.0)
urethrovesicovaginal (619.0)
AHA: 3Q, '97, 6

599.2 Urethral diverticulum
DEF: Abnormal pouch in urethral wall.

599.3 Urethral caruncle
Polyp of urethra

599.4 Urethral false passage
DEF: Abnormal opening in urethra due to surgery; trauma or
disease.

599.5 Prolapsed urethral mucosa
Prolapse of urethra
Urethrocele
EXCLUDES *urethrocele, female (618.03, 618.09,*
618.2-618.4)

√5ᵗʰ **599.6 Urinary obstruction**
Use additional code to identify urinary incontinence
(625.6, 788.30-788.39)
EXCLUDES *obstructive nephropathy NOS (593.89)*
AHA: 4Q, '05, 80

599.60 Urinary obstruction, unspecified
Obstructive uropathy NOS
Urinary (tract) obstruction NOS
N13.9 Obstructive and reflux uropathy unspec I-10

**599.69 Urinary obstruction, not elsewhere
classified**
Code, if applicable, any causal condition first,
such as:
hyperplasia of prostate (600.0-600.9 with
fifth-digit 1)
AHA: 4Q, '06, 93

√5ᵗʰ **599.7 Hematuria**
Hematuria (benign) (essential)
EXCLUDES *hemoglobinuria (791.2)*
AHA: 4Q, '08, 121; 1Q, '00, 5; 3Q, '95, 8

599.70 Hematuria, unspecified
R31.9 Hematuria unspecified   I-10

599.71 Gross hematuria

599.72 Microscopic hematuria

√5ᵗʰ **599.8 Other specified disorders of urethra and urinary tract**
Use additional code to identify urinary incontinence
(625.6, 788.30-788.39), if present
EXCLUDES *symptoms and other conditions classifiable to*
788.0-788.2, 788.4-788.9, 791.0-791.9

599.81 Urethral hypermobility
DEF: Hyperactive urethra.

599.82 Intrinsic (urethral) sphincter deficiency [ISD]
DEF: Malfunctioning urethral sphincter.
AHA: 2Q, '96, 15

599.83 Urethral instability
DEF: Inconsistent functioning of urethra.

599.84 Other specified disorders of urethra
Rupture of urethra (nontraumatic)
Urethral:
cyst
granuloma
DEF: Rupture of urethra due to herniation or
breaking down of tissue; not due to trauma.
DEF: Urethral cyst: abnormal sac in urethra; usually
fluid filled.
DEF: Granuloma: inflammatory cells forming small
nodules in urethra.
AHA: ▶1Q, '09, 15◀

599.89 Other specified disorders of urinary tract

599.9 Unspecified disorder of urethra and urinary tract

DISEASES OF MALE GENITAL ORGANS (600-608)

√4ᵗʰ **600 Hyperplasia of prostate**
INCLUDES enlarged prostate
DEF: Fibrostromal proliferation in periurethral glands, causes blood in
urine; etiology unknown.
AHA: 3Q, '05, 20; 4Q, '00, 43; 3Q, '94, 12; 3Q, '92, 7; N-D, '86, 10

√5ᵗʰ **600.0 Hypertrophy (benign) of prostate**
Benign prostatic hypertrophy
Enlargement of prostate
Smooth enlarged prostate
Soft enlarged prostate
AHA: 4Q, '06, 93-95; 3Q, '05, 20; 4Q, '03, 63; 1Q, '03, 6; 3Q, '02,
28; 2Q, '01, 14

**600.00 Hypertrophy (benign) of prostate
without urinary obstruction and
other lower urinary tract symptoms [LUTS]**   A ♂
Hypertrophy (benign) of prostate NOS
N40.0 Enlarged prostate without LUTS   I-10

**600.01 Hypertrophy (benign) of prostate
with urinary obstruction and other lower
urinary tract symptoms [LUTS]**   A ♂
Hypertrophy (benign) of prostate with urinary
retention
Use additional code to identify symptoms:
incomplete bladder emptying (788.21)
nocturia (788.43)
straining on urination (788.65)
urinary frequency (788.41)
urinary hesitancy (788.64)
urinary incontinence (788.30-788.39)
urinary obstruction (599.69)
urinary retention (788.20)
urinary urgency (788.63)
weak urinary stream (788.62)
AHA: 4Q, '06, 93-95; 4Q, '03, 64

Male Pelvic Organs

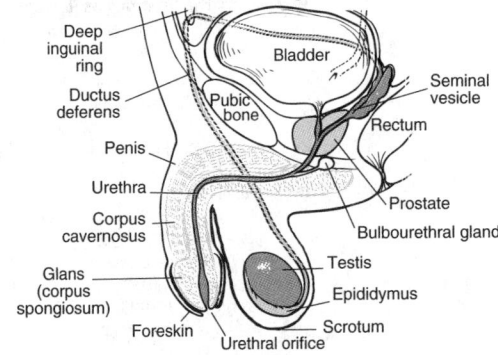

Deep inguinal ring
Ductus deferens
Penis
Urethra
Corpus cavernosus
Glans (corpus spongiosum)
Foreskin
Urethral orifice
Bladder
Pubic bone
Seminal vesicle
Rectum
Prostate
Bulbourethral gland
Testis
Epididymus
Scrotum

Genitourinary System

598.2–600.01

√5th **600.1 Nodular prostate**
Hard, firm prostate
Multinodular prostate
EXCLUDES *malignant neoplasm of prostate (185)*
DEF: Hard, firm nodule in prostate.
AHA: 4Q, '03, 63

600.10 Nodular prostate without urinary obstruction A ♂
Nodular prostate NOS

600.11 Nodular prostate with urinary obstruction A ♂
Nodular prostate with urinary retention

√5th **600.2 Benign localized hyperplasia of prostate**
Adenofibromatous hypertrophy of prostate
Adenoma of prostate
Fibroadenoma of prostate
Fibroma of prostate
Myoma of prostate
Polyp of prostate
EXCLUDES *benign neoplasms of prostate (222.2)*
hypertrophy of prostate (600.00-600.01)
malignant neoplasm of prostate (185)
DEF: Benign localized hyperplasia clearly defined epithelial tumor. .
AHA: 4Q, '06, 93-95; 4Q, '03, 63

600.20 Benign localized hyperplasia of prostate without urinary obstruction and other lower urinary tract symptoms [LUTS] A ♂
Benign localized hyperplasia of prostate NOS

600.21 Benign localized hyperplasia of prostate with urinary obstruction and other lower urinary tract symptoms [LUTS] A ♂
Benign localized hyperplasia of prostate with urinary retention
Use additional code to identify symptoms:
incomplete bladder emptying (788.21)
nocturia (788.43)
straining on urination (788.65)
urinary frequency (788.41)
urinary hesitancy (788.64)
urinary incontinence (788.30-788.39)
urinary obstruction (599.69)
urinary retention (788.20)
urinary urgency (788.63)
weak urinary stream (788.62)

600.3 Cyst of prostate A ♂
DEF: Sacs of fluid, which differentiate this from either nodular or adenomatous tumors.

√5th **600.9 Hyperplasia of prostate, unspecified**
Median bar
Prostatic obstruction NOS
AHA: 4Q, '06, 93-95; 4Q, '03, 63

600.90 Hyperplasia of prostate, unspecified, without urinary obstruction and other lower urinary tract symptoms [LUTS] A ♂
Hyperplasia of prostate NOS

600.91 Hyperplasia of prostate, unspecified with urinary obstruction and other lower urinary tract symptoms [LUTS] A ♂
Hyperplasia of prostate, unspecified, with urinary retention
Use additional code to identify symptoms:
incomplete bladder emptying (788.21)
nocturia (788.43)
straining on urination (788.65)
urinary frequency (788.41)
urinary hesitancy (788.64)
urinary incontinence (788.30-788.39)
urinary obstruction (599.69)
urinary retention (788.20)
urinary urgency (788.63)
weak urinary stream (788.62)

√4th **601 Inflammatory diseases of prostate**
Use additional code to identify organism, such as Staphylococcus (041.1), or Streptococcus (041.0)

601.0 Acute prostatitis A ♂
601.1 Chronic prostatitis A ♂
601.2 Abscess of prostate A ♂
601.3 Prostatocystitis A ♂
601.4 Prostatitis in diseases classified elsewhere A ♂
Code first underlying disease, as:
actinomycosis (039.8)
blastomycosis (116.0)
syphilis (095.8)
tuberculosis (016.5)
EXCLUDES *prostatitis:*
gonococcal (098.12, 098.32)
monilial (112.2)
trichomonal (131.03)

601.8 Other specified inflammatory diseases of prostate A ♂
Prostatitis:
cavitary
diverticular
granulomatous

601.9 Prostatitis, unspecified A ♂
Prostatitis NOS

√4th **602 Other disorders of prostate**

602.0 Calculus of prostate A ♂
Prostatic stone
DEF: Stone or mineral deposit in prostate.

602.1 Congestion or hemorrhage of prostate A ♂
DEF: Bleeding or fluid collection in prostate.

602.2 Atrophy of prostate A ♂

602.3 Dysplasia of prostate ♂
Prostatic intraepithelial neoplasia I (PIN I)
Prostatic intraepithelial neoplasia II (PIN II)
EXCLUDES *prostatic intraepithelial neoplasia III (PIN III) (233.4)*
DEF: Abnormality of shape and size of the intraepithelial tissues of the prostate; premalignant condition characterized by stalks and absence of a basilar cell layer; synonyms are intraductal dysplasia, large acinar atypical hyperplasia, atypical primary hyperplasia, hyperplasia with malignant changes, marked atypia, or duct-acinar dysplasia.
AHA: 4Q, '01, 46

602.8 Other specified disorders of prostate A ♂
Fistula
Infarction } of prostate
Stricture
Periprostatic adhesions

602.9 Unspecified disorder of prostate A ♂

√4th **603 Hydrocele**
INCLUDES hydrocele of spermatic cord, testis or tunica vaginalis
EXCLUDES *congenital (778.6)*
DEF: Circumscribed collection of fluid in tunica vaginalis, spermatic cord or testis.

603.0 Encysted hydrocele ♂
603.1 Infected hydrocele ♂
Use additional code to identify organism
603.8 Other specified types of hydrocele ♂
603.9 Hydrocele, unspecified ♂

Common Inguinal Canal Anomalies

✓4th **604 Orchitis and epididymitis**

Use additional code to identify organism, such as Escherichia coli [E. coli] (041.4), Staphylococcus (041.1), or Streptococcus (041.0)

604.0 Orchitis, epididymitis, and epididymo-orchitis, with abscess ♂

Abscess of epididymis or testis

✓5th **604.9 Other orchitis, epididymitis, and epididymo-orchitis, without mention of abscess**

604.90 Orchitis and epididymitis, unspecified ♂

604.91 Orchitis and epididymitis in diseases classified elsewhere ♂

Code first underlying disease, as:
diphtheria (032.89)
filariasis (125.0-125.9)
syphilis (095.8)

EXCLUDES *orchitis:*
gonococcal (098.13, 098.33)
mumps (072.0)
tuberculous (016.5)
tuberculous epididymitis (016.4)

604.99 Other ♂

605 Redundant prepuce and phimosis ♂
Adherent prepuce
Paraphimosis
Phimosis (congenital)
Tight foreskin

DEF: Constriction of preputial orifice causing inability of the prepuce to be drawn back over the glans; it may be congenital or caused by infection.

AHA: ▶3Q, '08, 9◀

✓4th **606 Infertility, male**

AHA: 2Q, '96, 9

606.0 Azoospermia A ♂
Absolute infertility
Infertility due to:
germinal (cell) aplasia
spermatogenic arrest (complete)

DEF: Absence of spermatozoa in the semen or inability to produce spermatozoa.

606.1 Oligospermia A ♂
Infertility due to:
germinal cell desquamation
hypospermatogenesis
incomplete spermatogenic arrest

DEF: Insufficient number of sperm in semen.

606.8 Infertility due to extratesticular causes A ♂
Infertility due to:
drug therapy
infection
obstruction of efferent ducts
radiation
systemic disease

606.9 Male infertility, unspecified A ♂

✓4th **607 Disorders of penis**

EXCLUDES *phimosis (605)*

607.0 Leukoplakia of penis ♂
Kraurosis of penis

EXCLUDES *carcinoma in situ of penis (233.5)*
erythroplasia of Queyrat (233.5)

DEF: White, thickened patches on glans penis.

607.1 Balanoposthitis ♂
Balanitis

Use additional code to identify organism

DEF: Inflammation of glans penis and prepuce.

607.2 Other inflammatory disorders of penis ♂
Abscess
Boil
Carbuncle } of corpus cavernosum or penis
Cellulitis
Cavernitis (penis)

Use additional code to identify organism

EXCLUDES *herpetic infection (054.13)*

607.3 Priapism ♂
Painful erection

DEF: Prolonged penile erection without sexual stimulation.

✓5th **607.8 Other specified disorders of penis**

607.81 Balanitis xerotica obliterans ♂
Induratio penis plastica

DEF: Inflammation of the glans penis, caused by stricture of the opening of the prepuce.

607.82 Vascular disorders of penis ♂
Embolism
Hematoma
  (nontraumatic) } of corpus cavernosum or penis
Hemorrhage
Thrombosis

607.83 Edema of penis ♂

DEF: Fluid retention within penile tissues.

607.84 Impotence of organic origin A ♂

EXCLUDES *nonorganic (302.72)*

DEF: Physiological cause interfering with erection.

AHA: 3Q, '91, 11

TIP: If impotence is a result of previous radical prostatectomy, assign also 997.99.

607.85 Peyronie's disease ♂

DEF: A severe curvature of the erect penis due to fibrosis of the cavernous sheaths.

AHA: 4Q, '03, 64

607.89 Other ♂
Atrophy
Fibrosis
   } of corpus cavernosum or penis
Hypertrophy
Ulcer (chronic)

607.9 Unspecified disorder of penis ♂

✓4th **608 Other disorders of male genital organs**

608.0 Seminal vesiculitis ♂
Abscess
Cellulitis } of seminal vesicle

Vesiculitis (seminal)

Use additional code to identify organism

EXCLUDES *gonococcal infection (098.14, 098.34)*

DEF: Inflammation of seminal vesicle.

608.1 Spermatocele ♂

DEF: Cystic enlargement of the epididymis or the testis; the cysts contain spermatozoa.

✓5th **608.2 Torsion of testis**

DEF: Twisted or rotated testis; may compromise blood flow.

608.20 Torsion of testis, unspecified ♂

AHA: 4Q, '06, 95

✓4th
✓5th
Additional Digit Required   Unspecified Code   Other Specified Code   Manifestation Code   ▶◀ Revised Text   ● New Code   ▲ Revised Code Title

2010 ICD-9-CM   **February 2009 • Volume 1 – 189**

Genitourinary System

608.21–610.9

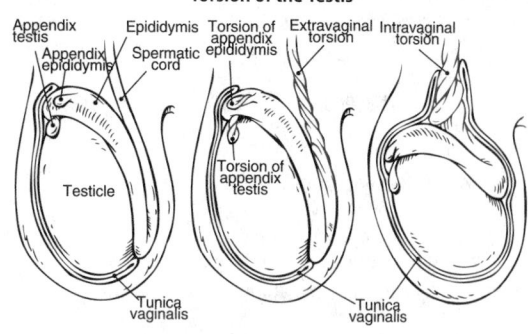

Torsion of the Testis

608.21 Extravaginal torsion of spermatic cord ♂

DEF: Torsion of the spermatic cord just below the tunica vaginalis attachments. .

AHA: 4Q, '06, 95

608.22 Intravaginal torsion of spermatic cord ♂

Torsion of spermatic cord NOS

DEF: Torsion within the tunica vaginalis also called the "bell-clapper" anomaly. It usually occurs in older children.

AHA: 4Q, '06, 95

608.23 Torsion of appendix testis ♂

DEF: Torsion of small solid projection of tissue on the upper outer surface of the testis (hydatid of Morgagni); a remnant of the embryologic mullerian duct.

AHA: 4Q, '06, 95

608.24 Torsion of appendix epididymis ♂

DEF: Torsion of small stalked appendage of the head of the epididymis (pedunculated hydatid); a detached embryologic efferent duct.

AHA: 4Q, '06, 95

608.3 Atrophy of testis ♂

608.4 Other inflammatory disorders of male genital organs ♂

Abscess

Boil   } of scrotum, spermatic cord, testis

Carbuncle   [except abscess], tunica

Cellulitis   vaginalis, or vas deferens

Vasitis

Use additional code to identify organism

EXCLUDES   abscess of testis (604.0)

✓5th **608.8 Other specified disorders of male genital organs**

608.81 Disorders of male genital organs in diseases classified elsewhere ♂

Code first underlying disease, as:
filariasis (125.0-125.9)
tuberculosis (016.5)

608.82 Hematospermia ♂

DEF: Presence of blood in the ejaculate; relatively common, affecting men of any age after puberty; cause is often the result of a viral or bacterial infection and inflammation.

AHA: 4Q, '01, 46

608.83 Vascular disorders ♂

Hematoma (non- ⎫ of seminal vessel, spermatic
   traumatic) ⎬ cord, testis, scrotum,
Hemorrhage ⎪ tunica vaginalis, or
Thrombosis ⎭ vas deferens
Hematocele NOS, male

AHA: 4Q, '03, 110

TIP: Assign for Fournier's gangrene, which is a result of an infection in the genital area.

608.84 Chylocele of tunica vaginalis ♂

DEF: Chylous effusion into tunica vaginalis; due to infusion of lymphatic fluids.

608.85 Stricture ♂

Stricture of:
spermatic cord
tunica vaginalis
vas deferens

608.86 Edema ♂

608.87 Retrograde ejaculation ♂

DEF: Condition where the semen travels to the bladder rather than out through the urethra due to damaged nerves causing the bladder neck to remain open during ejaculation.

AHA: 4Q, '01, 46

608.89 Other ♂

Atrophy ⎫ of seminal vessel, spermatic
Fibrosis ⎬ cord, testis, scrotum,
Hypertrophy ⎪ tunica vaginalis, or vas
Ulcer ⎭ deferens

EXCLUDES   atrophy of testis (608.3)

608.9 Unspecified disorder of male genital organs ♂

DISORDERS OF BREAST (610-612)

✓4th **610 Benign mammary dysplasias**

610.0 Solitary cyst of breast

Cyst (solitary) of breast

610.1 Diffuse cystic mastopathy Ⓐ

Chronic cystic mastitis
Cystic breast
Fibrocystic disease of
breast

DEF: Extensive formation of nodular cysts in breast tissue; symptoms include tenderness, change in size and hyperplasia of ductal epithelium.

AHA: 2Q, '06, 10

TIP: Assign in addition to screening mammography V code; is a normal variant, commonly found in normal breasts and not a pathological condition.

610.2 Fibroadenosis of breast

Fibroadenosis of breast:
NOS
chronic
cystic
diffuse
periodic
segmental

DEF: Non-neoplastic nodular condition of breast.

610.3 Fibrosclerosis of breast

DEF: Fibrous tissue in breast.

610.4 Mammary duct ectasia

Comedomastitis
Duct ectasia
Mastitis:
periductal
plasma cell

DEF: Atrophy of duct epithelium; causes distended collecting ducts of mammary gland; drying up of breast secretion, intraductal inflammation and periductal and interstitial chronic inflammatory reaction.

610.8 Other specified benign mammary dysplasias

Mazoplasia
Sebaceous cyst of breast

AHA: ▶2Q, '09, 9◀

610.9 Benign mammary dysplasia, unspecified

✓4ᵗʰ 611 Other disorders of breast

> **EXCLUDES** *that associated with lactation or the puerperium (675.0-676.9)*

611.0 Inflammatory disease of breast

Abscess (acute) (chronic) (nonpuerperal) of:
  areola
  breast
Mammillary fistula
Mastitis (acute) (subacute) (nonpuerperal):
  NOS
  infective
  retromammary
  submammary

> **EXCLUDES** *carbuncle of breast (680.2)*
> *chronic cystic mastitis (610.1)*
> *neonatal infective mastitis (771.5)*
> *thrombophlebitis of breast [Mondor's disease] (451.89)*

611.1 Hypertrophy of breast

Gynecomastia
Hypertrophy of breast:
  NOS
  massive pubertal

> **EXCLUDES** *breast engorgement in newborn (778.7)*
> *disproportion of reconstructed breast (612.1)*

611.2 Fissure of nipple

611.3 Fat necrosis of breast

Fat necrosis (segmental) of breast
Code first breast necrosis due to breast graft (996.79)

DEF: Splitting of neutral fats in adipose tissue cells as a result of trauma; a firm circumscribed mass is then formed in the breast.

611.4 Atrophy of breast

611.5 Galactocele

DEF: Milk-filled cyst in breast; due to blocked duct.

611.6 Galactorrhea not associated with childbirth

DEF: Flow of milk not associated with childbirth or pregnancy.

✓5ᵗʰ 611.7 Signs and symptoms in breast

611.71 Mastodynia

Pain in breast

611.72 Lump or mass in breast

AHA: 2Q, '03, 4-5

TIP: Do not assign if the underlying cause of the breast lump or mass is determined and documented during the episode of care.

611.79 Other

Induration of breast
Inversion of nipple
Nipple discharge
Retraction of nipple

✓5ᵗʰ 611.8 Other specified disorders of breast

AHA: 4Q, '08, 121-122

611.81 Ptosis of breast   A

> **EXCLUDES** *ptosis of native breast in relation to reconstructed breast (612.1)*

611.82 Hypoplasia of breast   A

Micromastia

> **EXCLUDES** ►*congenital absence of breast (757.6)*◄
> *hypoplasia of native breast in relation to reconstructed breast (612.1)*

611.83 Capsular contracture of breast implant   A

TIP: Do not assign additional code from category 996 Complications peculiar to certain specified procedures.

611.89 Other specified disorders of breast

Hematoma (nontraumatic) of breast
Infarction of breast
Occlusion of breast duct
Subinvolution of breast (postlactational) (postpartum)

611.9 Unspecified breast disorder

✓4ᵗʰ 612 Deformity and disproportion of reconstructed breast

AHA: 4Q, '08, 123

612.0 Deformity of reconstructed breast   A

Contour irregularity in reconstructed breast
Excess tissue in reconstructed breast
Misshapen reconstructed breast

612.1 Disproportion of reconstructed breast   A

Breast asymmetry between native breast and reconstructed breast
Disproportion between native breast and reconstructed breast

INFLAMMATORY DISEASE OF FEMALE PELVIC ORGANS (614-616)

Use additional code to identify organism, such as Staphylococcus (041.1), or Streptococcus (041.0)

> **EXCLUDES** *that associated with pregnancy, abortion, childbirth, or the puerperium (630-676.9)*

✓4ᵗʰ 614 Inflammatory disease of ovary, fallopian tube, pelvic cellular tissue, and peritoneum

> **EXCLUDES** *endometritis (615.0-615.9)*
> *major infection following delivery ►(670.0-670.8)◄*
> *that complicating:*
> *abortion (634-638 with .0, 639.0)*
> *ectopic or molar pregnancy (639.0)*
> *pregnancy or labor (646.6)*

614.0 Acute salpingitis and oophoritis   ♀

Any condition classifiable to 614.2, specified as acute or subacute

DEF: Acute inflammation, of ovary and fallopian tube.

614.1 Chronic salpingitis and oophoritis   ♀

Hydrosalpinx
Salpingitis:
  follicularis
  isthmica nodosa
Any condition classifiable to 614.2, specified as chronic

DEF: Persistent inflammation of ovary and fallopian tube.

614.2 Salpingitis and oophoritis not specified as acute, subacute, or chronic   ♀

Abscess (of):
  fallopian tube
  ovary
  tubo-ovarian
Oophoritis
Perioophoritis
Perisalpingitis
Pyosalpinx
Salpingitis
Salpingo-oophoritis
Tubo-ovarian inflammatory disease

> **EXCLUDES** *gonococcal infection (chronic) (098.37)*
> *acute (098.17)*
> *tuberculous (016.6)*

AHA: 2Q, '91, 5

614.3 Acute parametritis and pelvic cellulitis   ♀

Acute inflammatory pelvic disease
Any condition classifiable to 614.4, specified as acute

DEF: Parametritis: inflammation of the parametrium; pelvic cellulitis is a synonym for parametritis.

✓4ᵗʰ ✓5ᵗʰ Additional Digit Required   Unspecified Code   Other Specified Code   Manifestation Code   ►◄ Revised Text   ● New Code   ▲ Revised Code Title

2010 ICD-9-CM   **October 2009 · Volume 1 – 191**

614.4 Chronic or unspecified parametritis and pelvic cellulitis ♀
Abscess (of):
broad ligament
parametrium ⎫
pelvis, femal ⎬ chronic or NOS
pouch of Douglas ⎭
Chronic inflammatory pelvic disease
Pelvic cellulitis, female
EXCLUDES tuberculous (016.7)

614.5 Acute or unspecified pelvic peritonitis, female ♀
AHA: 4Q, '05, 74
TIP: For pelvic peritonitis in a male patient, refer to code 567.21.

614.6 Pelvic peritoneal adhesions, female (postoperative) (postinfection) ♀
Adhesions:
peritubal
tubo-ovarian
Use additional code to identify any associated infertility (628.2)
DEF: Fibrous scarring abnormally joining structures within abdomen.
AHA: 3Q, '03, 6; 1Q, '03, 4; 3Q, '95, 7; 3Q, '94, 12
N73.6 Female pelvic peritoneal adhesions (postinfective) **I-10**

614.7 Other chronic pelvic peritonitis, female ♀
EXCLUDES tuberculous (016.7)

614.8 Other specified inflammatory disease of female pelvic organs and tissues ♀

614.9 Unspecified inflammatory disease of female pelvic organs and tissues ♀
Pelvic infection or inflammation, female NOS
Pelvic inflammatory disease [PID]

√4ᵗʰ 615 Inflammatory diseases of uterus, except cervix
EXCLUDES following delivery ▶(670.0-670.8)◀
hyperplastic endometritis ▶(621.30-621.35)◀
that complicating:
abortion (634-638 with .0, 639.0)
ectopic or molar pregnancy (639.0)
pregnancy or labor (646.6)

615.0 Acute ♀
Any condition classifiable to 615.9, specified as acute or subacute

615.1 Chronic ♀
Any condition classifiable to 615.9, specified as chronic

615.9 Unspecified inflammatory disease of uterus ♀
Endometritis
Endomyometritis
Intrauterine infection
Metritis
Myometritis
Perimetritis
Pyometra
Uterine abscess
N71.9 Inflammatory disease of uterus unspecified **I-10**

√4ᵗʰ 616 Inflammatory disease of cervix, vagina, and vulva
EXCLUDES that complicating:
abortion (634-638 with .0, 639.0)
ectopic or molar pregnancy (639.0)
pregnancy, childbirth, or the puerperium (646.6)

616.0 Cervicitis and endocervicitis ♀
Cervicitis ⎫ with or without mention of
Endocervicitis ⎬ erosion or ectropion
Nabothian (gland) cyst or follicle
EXCLUDES erosion or ectropion without mention of cervicitis (622.0)
N72 Inflammatory disease of cervix uteri **I-10**

√5ᵗʰ 616.1 Vaginitis and vulvovaginitis
EXCLUDES vulvar vestibulitis (625.71)
DEF: Inflammation or infection of vagina or external female genitalia.

616.10 Vaginitis and vulvovaginitis, unspecified ♀
Vaginitis:
NOS
postirradiation
Vulvitis NOS
Vulvovaginitis NOS
Use additional code to identify organism, such as Escherichia coli [E. coli] (041.4), Staphylococcus (041.1), or Streptococcus (041.0)
EXCLUDES noninfective leukorrhea (623.5)
postmenopausal or senile vaginitis (627.3)

616.11 Vaginitis and vulvovaginitis in diseases classified elsewhere ♀
Code first underlying disease, as:
pinworm vaginitis (127.4)
EXCLUDES herpetic vulvovaginitis (054.11)
monilial vulvovaginitis (112.1)
trichomonal vaginitis or vulvovaginitis (131.01)

616.2 Cyst of Bartholin's gland ♀
Bartholin's duct cyst
DEF: Fluid-filled sac within gland of vaginal orifice.

616.3 Abscess of Bartholin's gland ♀
Vulvovaginal gland abscess

616.4 Other abscess of vulva ♀
Abscess ⎫
Carbuncle ⎬ of vulva
Furuncle ⎭

√5ᵗʰ 616.5 Ulceration of vulva

616.50 Ulceration of vulva, unspecified ♀
Ulcer NOS of vulva

616.51 Ulceration of vulva in diseases classified elsewhere ♀
Code first underlying disease, as:
Behçet's syndrome (136.1)
tuberculosis (016.7)
EXCLUDES vulvar ulcer (in):
gonococcal (098.0)
herpes simplex (054.12)
syphilitic (091.0)

√5ᵗʰ 616.8 Other specified inflammatory diseases of cervix, vagina, and vulva
EXCLUDES noninflammatory disorders of:
cervix (622.0-622.9)
vagina (623.0-623.9)
vulva (624.0-624.9)

616.81 Mucositis (ulcerative) of cervix, vagina, and vulva ♀
Use additional E code to identify adverse effects of therapy, such as:
antineoplastic and immunosuppressive drugs (E930.7, E933.1)
radiation therapy (E879.2)
AHA: 4Q, '06, 88-90

616.89 Other inflammatory disease of cervix, vagina and vulva ♀
Caruncle, vagina or labium
Ulcer, vagina
AHA: 4Q, '06, 88-90

616.9 Unspecified inflammatory disease of cervix, vagina, and vulva ♀

OTHER DISORDERS OF FEMALE GENITAL TRACT (617-629)

√4th 617 Endometriosis

617.0 Endometriosis of uterus   ♀
Adenomyosis
Endometriosis:
  cervix
  internal
  myometrium
EXCLUDES *stromal endometriosis (236.0)*
DEF: Aberrant uterine mucosal tissue; creating products of menses and inflamed uterine tissues.
AHA: 3Q, '92, 7
N80.0 Endometriosis of uterus   I-10

617.1 Endometriosis of ovary   ♀
Chocolate cyst of ovary
Endometrial cystoma of ovary
DEF: Aberrant uterine tissue; creating products of menses and inflamed ovarian tissues.
N80.1 Endometriosis of ovary   I-10

617.2 Endometriosis of fallopian tube   ♀
DEF: Aberrant uterine tissue; creating products of menses and inflamed tissues of fallopian tubes.

617.3 Endometriosis of pelvic peritoneum   ♀
Endometriosis:
  broad ligament
  cul-de-sac (Douglas')
  parametrium
  round ligament
DEF: Aberrant uterine tissue; creating products of menses and inflamed peritoneum tissues.

617.4 Endometriosis of rectovaginal septum and vagina   ♀
DEF: Aberrant uterine tissue; creating products of menses and inflamed tissues in and behind vagina.

617.5 Endometriosis of intestine   ♀
Endometriosis: Endometriosis:
  appendix   rectum
  colon
DEF: Aberrant uterine tissue; creating products of menses and inflamed intestinal tissues.

617.6 Endometriosis in scar of skin   ♀

617.8 Endometriosis of other specified sites   ♀
Endometriosis: Endometriosis:
  bladder   umbilicus
  lung   vulva

617.9 Endometriosis, site unspecified   ♀

√4th 618 Genital prolapse
Use additional code to identify urinary incontinence (625.6, 788.31, 788.33-788.39)
EXCLUDES *that complicating pregnancy, labor, or delivery (654.4)*

√5th 618.0 Prolapse of vaginal walls without mention of uterine prolapse
EXCLUDES *that with uterine prolapse (618.2-618.4)*
enterocele (618.6)
vaginal vault prolapse following hysterectomy (618.5)

618.00 Unspecified prolapse of vaginal walls   ♀
Vaginal prolapse NOS

618.01 Cystocele, midline   ♀
Cystocele NOS
DEF: Defect in the pubocervical fascia, the supportive layer of the bladder, causing bladder drop and herniated into the vagina along the midline.
N81.11 Cystocele midline   I-10

618.02 Cystocele, lateral   ♀
Paravaginal
DEF: Loss of support of the lateral attachment of the vagina at the arcus tendinous results in bladder drop; bladder herniates into the vagina laterally.

618.03 Urethrocele   ♀

618.04 Rectocele   ♀
Proctocele
N81.6 Rectocele   I-10

618.05 Perineocele   ♀

618.09 Other prolapse of vaginal walls without mention of uterine prolapse   ♀
Cystourethrocele

Female Genitourinary System

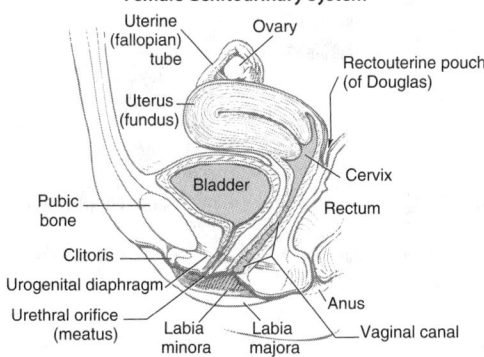

Common Sites of Endometriosis

Common sites of endometriosis, in descending order of frequency:
(1) ovary
(2) cul de sac
(3) utersacral ligaments
(4) broad ligaments
(5) fallopian tube
(6) uterovesical fold
(7) round ligament
(8) vermiform appendix
(9) vagina
(10) rectovaginal septum

Vaginal Midline Cystocele

Vaginal Lateral Cystocele

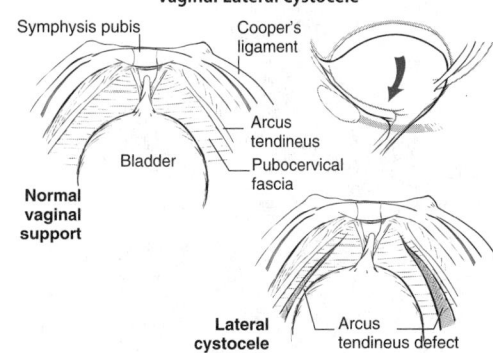

618.1 **Uterine prolapse without mention of vaginal wall prolapse** ♀
  Descensus uteri
  Uterine prolapse:
    NOS
    complete
    first degree
    second degree
    third degree
  EXCLUDES *that with mention of cystocele, urethrocele, or rectocele (618.2-618.4)*

618.2 **Uterovaginal prolapse, incomplete** ♀
  DEF: Downward displacement of uterus downward into vagina.
  N81.2 Incomplete uterovaginal prolapse `I-10`

618.3 **Uterovaginal prolapse, complete** ♀
  DEF: Downward displacement of uterus exposed within external genitalia.

618.4 **Uterovaginal prolapse, unspecified** ♀
  N81.4 Uterovaginal prolapse unspecified `I-10`

618.5 **Prolapse of vaginal vault after hysterectomy** ♀
  N99.3 Prolapse of vaginal vault after hysterectomy `I-10`

618.6 **Vaginal enterocele, congenital or acquired** ♀
  Pelvic enterocele, congenital or acquired
  DEF: Vaginal vault hernia formed by the loop of the small intestine protruding into the rectal vaginal pouch; can also accompany uterine prolapse or follow hysterectomy.
  N81.5 Vaginal enterocele `I-10`

618.7 **Old laceration of muscles of pelvic floor** ♀

√5th **618.8** **Other specified genital prolapse**
  618.81 **Incompetence or weakening of pubocervical tissue** ♀
  618.82 **Incompetence or weakening of rectovaginal tissue** ♀
  618.83 **Pelvic muscle wasting** ♀
    Disuse atrophy of pelvic muscles and anal sphincter
  618.84 **Cervical stump prolapse** ♀
    AHA: 4Q, '06, 97
  618.89 **Other specified genital prolapse** ♀

618.9 **Unspecified genital prolapse** ♀

√4th **619** **Fistula involving female genital tract**
  EXCLUDES *vesicorectal and intestinovesical fistula (596.1)*

619.0 **Urinary-genital tract fistula, female** ♀
  Fistula:
    cervicovesical
    ureterovaginal
    urethrovaginal
    urethrovesicovaginal
    uteroureteric
    uterovesical
    vesicocervicovaginal
    vesicovaginal

619.1 **Digestive-genital tract fistula, female** ♀
  Fistula:
    intestinouterine
    intestinovaginal
    rectovaginal
    rectovulval
    sigmoidovaginal
    uterorectal

619.2 **Genital tract-skin fistula, female** ♀
  Fistula:
    uterus to abdominal wall
    vaginoperineal

619.8 **Other specified fistulas involving female genital tract** ♀
  Fistula:
    cervix
    cul-de-sac (Douglas')
    uterus
    vagina
  DEF: Abnormal communication between female reproductive tract and skin.

619.9 **Unspecified fistula involving female genital tract** ♀

√4th **620** **Noninflammatory disorders of ovary, fallopian tube, and broad ligament**
  EXCLUDES *hydrosalpinx (614.1)*

620.0 **Follicular cyst of ovary** ♀
  Cyst of graafian follicle
  DEF: Fluid-filled, encapsulated cyst due to occluded follicle duct that secretes hormones into ovaries.
  N83.0 Follicular cyst of ovary `I-10`

620.1 **Corpus luteum cyst or hematoma** ♀
  Corpus luteum hemorrhage or rupture
  Lutein cyst
  DEF: Fluid-filled cyst due to serous developing from corpus luteum or clotted blood.
  N83.1 Corpus luteum cyst `I-10`

620.2 **Other and unspecified ovarian cyst** ♀
  Cyst:
    NOS
    corpus albicans
    retention NOS } of ovary
    serous
    theca-lutein
  Simple cystoma of ovary
  EXCLUDES *cystadenoma (benign) (serous) (220)*
    developmental cysts (752.0)
    neoplastic cysts (220)
    polycystic ovaries (256.4)
    Stein-Leventhal syndrome (256.4)
  N83.20 Unspecified ovarian cysts `I-10`

620.3 **Acquired atrophy of ovary and fallopian tube** ♀
  Senile involution of ovary

620.4 **Prolapse or hernia of ovary and fallopian tube** ♀
  Displacement of ovary and fallopian tube
  Salpingocele

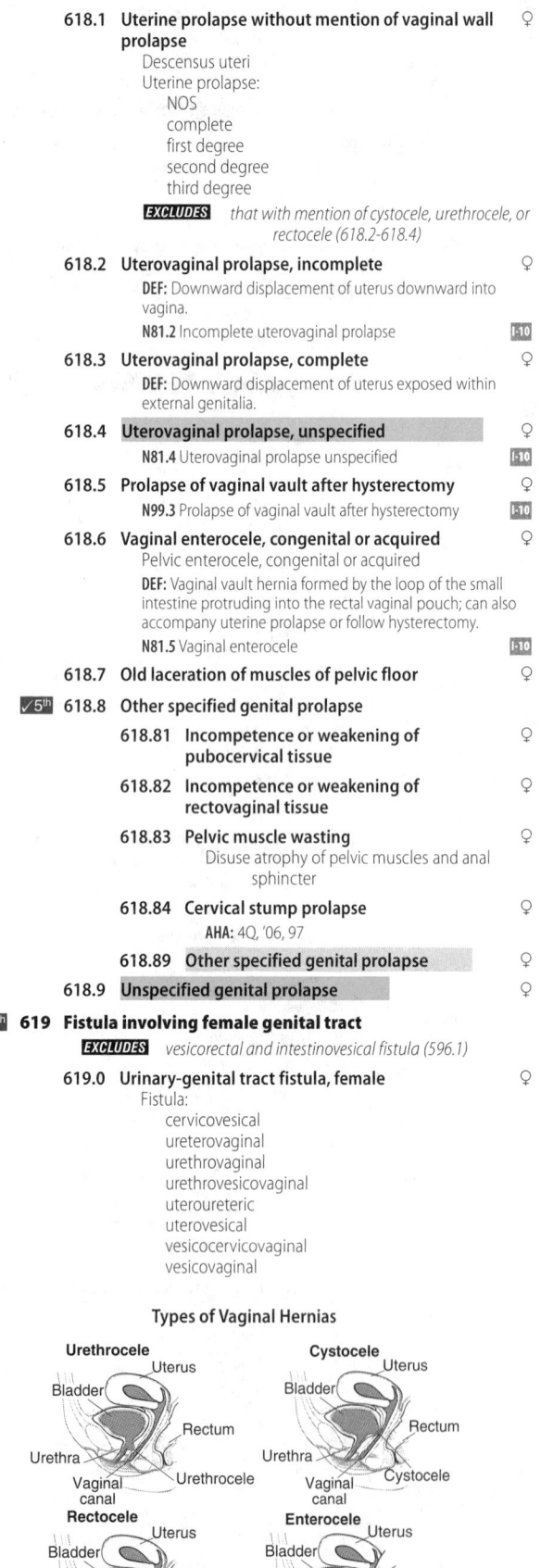

Types of Vaginal Hernias

Urethrocele
  Uterus
  Bladder
  Rectum
  Urethra
  Vaginal canal
  Urethrocele

Cystocele
  Uterus
  Bladder
  Rectum
  Urethra
  Vaginal canal
  Cystocele

Rectocele
  Uterus
  Bladder
  Rectum
  Urethra
  Vaginal canal
  Rectocele

Enterocele
  Uterus
  Bladder
  Rectum
  Urethra
  Vaginal canal
  Terminal ileum

Uterus and Ovaries
  Fundus of uterus
  Mesosalpinx
  Mesovarium
  Uterine (fallopian tube)
  Suspensory ligaments
  Ligament of ovary
  Body
  Ovary
  Uterosacral ligament
  Fimbria
  Cervix
  Ovary
  Vagina
  Broad ligament

N Newborn Age: 0   P Pediatric Age: 0-17   M Maternity Age: 12-55   A Adult Age: 15-124

620.5 Torsion of ovary, ovarian pedicle, or fallopian tube ♀
  Torsion:
    accessory tube
    hydatid of Morgagni

620.6 Broad ligament laceration syndrome ♀
  Masters-Allen syndrome

620.7 Hematoma of broad ligament ♀
  Hematocele, broad ligament
  DEF: Blood within peritoneal fold that supports uterus.

620.8 Other noninflammatory disorders of ovary, fallopian tube, and broad ligament ♀
  Cyst ⎫ of broad ligament or fallopian
  Polyp ⎬ tube

  Infarction ⎫
  Rupture ⎬ of ovary or fallopian tube
  Hematosalpinx ⎭
  EXCLUDES hematosalpinx in ectopic pregnancy (639.2)
       peritubal adhesions (614.6)
       torsion of ovary, ovarian pedicle, or fallopian
         tube (620.5)

620.9 Unspecified noninflammatory disorder of ovary, fallopian tube, and broad ligament ♀

✓4th **621 Disorders of uterus, not elsewhere classified**

621.0 Polyp of corpus uteri ♀
  Polyp:
    endometrium
    uterus NOS
  EXCLUDES cervical polyp NOS (622.7)
  N84.0 Polyp of corpus uteri I-10

621.1 Chronic subinvolution of uterus ♀
  EXCLUDES puerperal (674.8)
  DEF: Abnormal size of uterus after delivery; the uterus does
  not return to its normal size after the birth of a child.
  AHA: 1Q, '91, 11

621.2 Hypertrophy of uterus ♀
  Bulky or enlarged uterus
  EXCLUDES puerperal (674.8)

✓5th **621.3 Endometrial hyperplasia**
  DEF: Abnormal cystic overgrowth of endometrial tissue.

  621.30 Endometrial hyperplasia, unspecified ♀
    Endometrial hyperplasia NOS
    ▶Hyperplasia (adenomatous) (cystic)
       (glandular) of endometrium
    Hyperplastic endometritis◀

  621.31 Simple endometrial hyperplasia without atypia ♀
    EXCLUDES ▶ benign endometrial hyperplasia
         (621.34)◀

  621.32 Complex endometrial hyperplasia without atypia ♀
    EXCLUDES ▶ benign endometrial hyperplasia
         (621.34)◀

  621.33 Endometrial hyperplasia with atypia ♀
    EXCLUDES ▶ endometrial intraepithelial neoplasia
         [EIN] (621.35)◀

● **621.34 Benign endometrial hyperplasia** ♀
● **621.35 Endometrial intraepithelial neoplasia [EIN]** ♀
    EXCLUDES malignant neoplasm of
         endometrium with
         endometrial intraepithelial
         neoplasia [EIN] (182.0)

621.4 Hematometra ♀
  Hemometra
  EXCLUDES that in congenital anomaly (752.2-752.3)
  DEF: Accumulated blood in uterus.

621.5 Intrauterine synechiae ♀
  Adhesions of uterus
  Band(s) of uterus

621.6 Malposition of uterus ♀
  Anteversion ⎫
  Retroflexion ⎬ of uterus
  Retroversion ⎭
  EXCLUDES malposition complicating pregnancy, labor, or
       delivery (654.3-654.4)
       prolapse of uterus (618.1-618.4)

621.7 Chronic inversion of uterus ♀
  EXCLUDES current obstetrical trauma (665.2)
       prolapse of uterus (618.1-618.4)

621.8 Other specified disorders of uterus, not elsewhere classified ♀
  Atrophy, acquired ⎫
  Cyst ⎪
  Fibrosis NOS ⎬ of uterus
  Old laceration (postpartum) ⎪
  Ulcer ⎭
  EXCLUDES bilharzial fibrosis (120.0-120.9)
       endometriosis (617.0)
       fistulas (619.0-619.8)
       inflammatory diseases (615.0-615.9)

621.9 Unspecified disorder of uterus ♀

✓4th **622 Noninflammatory disorders of cervix**
  EXCLUDES abnormality of cervix complicating pregnancy, labor, or
       delivery (654.5-654.6)
       fistula (619.0-619.8)

622.0 Erosion and ectropion of cervix ♀
  Eversion ⎫
  Ulcer ⎬ of cervix
  EXCLUDES that in chronic cervicitis (616.0)
  DEF: Ulceration or turning outward of uterine cervix.

✓5th **622.1 Dysplasia of cervix (uteri)**
  EXCLUDES abnormal results from cervical cytologic
       examination without histologic
       confirmation (795.00-795.09)
       carcinoma in situ of cervix (233.1)
       cervical intraepithelial neoplasia III [CIN III]
         (233.1)
       HGSIL of cervix (795.04)
  DEF: Abnormal cell structures in portal between uterus and
  vagina.
  AHA: 1Q, '91, 11

  622.10 Dysplasia of cervix, unspecified ♀
    Anaplasia of cervix
    Cervical atypism
    Cervical dysplasia NOS

  622.11 Mild dysplasia of cervix ♀
    Cervical intraepithelial neoplasia I [CIN I]

  622.12 Moderate dysplasia of cervix ♀
    Cervical intraepithelial neoplasia II [CIN II]
    EXCLUDES carcinoma in situ of cervix (233.1)
         cervical intraepithelial neo-plasia III
           [CIN III] (233.1)
         severe dysplasia (233.1)

622.2 Leukoplakia of cervix (uteri) ♀
  EXCLUDES carcinoma in situ of cervix (233.1)
  DEF: Thickened, white patches on portal between uterus and
  vagina.

622.3 Old laceration of cervix ♀
  Adhesions ⎫
  Band(s) ⎬ of cervix
  Cicatrix (postpartum) ⎭
  EXCLUDES current obstetrical trauma (665.3)
  DEF: Scarring or other evidence of old wound on cervix.

Genitourinary System

622.4–625.2

622.4 Stricture and stenosis of cervix ♀
  Atresia (acquired)
  Contracture } of cervix
  Occlusion
  Pinpoint os uteri
  EXCLUDES *congenital (752.49)*
  that complicating labor (654.6)

622.5 Incompetence of cervix ♀
  EXCLUDES *complicating pregnancy (654.5)*
  that affecting fetus or newborn (761.0)
  DEF: Inadequate functioning of cervix; marked by abnormal widening during pregnancy; causing miscarriage.

622.6 Hypertrophic elongation of cervix ♀
  DEF: Overgrowth of cervix tissues extending down into vagina.

622.7 Mucous polyp of cervix ♀
  Polyp NOS of cervix
  EXCLUDES *adenomatous polyp of cervix (219.0)*

622.8 Other specified noninflammatory disorders of cervix ♀
  Atrophy (senile)
  Cyst } of cervix
  Fibrosis
  Hemorrhage
  EXCLUDES *endometriosis (617.0)*
  fistula (619.0-619.8)
  inflammatory diseases (616.0)

622.9 Unspecified noninflammatory disorder of cervix ♀

✓4ᵗʰ **623 Noninflammatory disorders of vagina**
  EXCLUDES *abnormality of vagina complicating pregnancy, labor, or delivery (654.7)*
  congenital absence of vagina (752.49)
  congenital diaphragm or bands (752.49)
  fistulas involving vagina (619.0-619.8)

623.0 Dysplasia of vagina ♀
  Mild and moderate dysplasia of vagina
  Vaginal intraepithelial neoplasia I and II [VAIN I and II]
  EXCLUDES *abnormal results from vaginal cytological examination without histologic confirmation (795.10-795.19)*
  carcinoma in situ of vagina (233.31)
  HGSIL of vagina (795.14)
  severe dysplasia of vagina (233.31)
  vaginal intraepithelial neoplasia III [VAIN III] (233.31)

623.1 Leukoplakia of vagina ♀
  DEF: Thickened white patches on vaginal canal.

623.2 Stricture or atresia of vagina ♀
  Adhesions (postoperative) (postradiation) of vagina
  Occlusion of vagina
  Stenosis, vagina
  Use additional E code to identify any external cause
  EXCLUDES *congenital atresia or stricture (752.49)*

623.3 Tight hymenal ring ♀
  Rigid hymen
  Tight hymenal ring } acquired or congenital
  Tight introitus
  EXCLUDES *imperforate hymen (752.42)*

623.4 Old vaginal laceration ♀
  EXCLUDES *old laceration involving muscles of pelvic floor (618.7)*
  DEF: Scarring or other evidence of old wound on vagina.

623.5 Leukorrhea, not specified as infective ♀
  Leukorrhea NOS of vagina
  Vaginal discharge NOS
  EXCLUDES *trichomonal (131.00)*
  DEF: Viscid whitish discharge, from vagina.

623.6 Vaginal hematoma ♀
  EXCLUDES *current obstetrical trauma (665.7)*

623.7 Polyp of vagina ♀

623.8 Other specified noninflammatory disorders of vagina ♀
  Cyst
  Hemorrhage } of vagina

623.9 Unspecified noninflammatory disorder of vagina ♀

✓4ᵗʰ **624 Noninflammatory disorders of vulva and perineum**
  EXCLUDES *abnormality of vulva and perineum complicating pregnancy, labor, or delivery (654.8)*
  condyloma acuminatum ▶(078.11)◀
  fistulas involving:
    perineum–see Alphabetic Index
    vulva (619.0-619.8)
  vulval varices (456.6)
  vulvar involvement in skin conditions (690-709.9)

✓5ᵗʰ **624.0 Dystrophy of vulva**
  EXCLUDES *carcinoma in situ of vulva (233.32)*
  severe dysplasia of vulva (233.32)
  vulvar intraepithelial neoplasia III [VIN III] (233.32)
  AHA: 4Q, '07, 90

  624.01 Vulvar intraepithelial neoplasia I [VIN I] ♀
    Mild dysplasia of vulva

  624.02 Vulvar intraepithelial neoplasia II [VIN II] ♀
    Moderate dysplasia of vulva
    AHA: 4Q, '07, 91

  624.09 Other dystrophy of vulva ♀
    Kraurosis of vulva
    Leukoplakia of vulva

624.1 Atrophy of vulva ♀

624.2 Hypertrophy of clitoris ♀
  EXCLUDES *that in endocrine disorders (255.2, 256.1)*

624.3 Hypertrophy of labia ♀
  Hypertrophy of vulva NOS
  DEF: Overgrowth of fleshy folds on either side of vagina.

624.4 Old laceration or scarring of vulva ♀
  DEF: Scarring or other evidence of old wound on external female genitalia.

624.5 Hematoma of vulva ♀
  EXCLUDES *that complicating delivery (664.5)*
  DEF: Blood in tissue of external genitalia.

624.6 Polyp of labia and vulva ♀

624.8 Other specified noninflammatory disorders of vulva and perineum ♀
  Cyst
  Edema } of vulva
  Stricture
  AHA: 1Q, '03, 13; 1Q, '95, 8

624.9 Unspecified noninflammatory disorder of vulva and perineum ♀

✓4ᵗʰ **625 Pain and other symptoms associated with female genital organs**

625.0 Dyspareunia ♀
  EXCLUDES *psychogenic dyspareunia (302.76)*
  DEF: Difficult or painful sexual intercourse.

625.1 Vaginismus ♀
  Colpospasm
  Vulvismus
  EXCLUDES *psychogenic vaginismus (306.51)*
  DEF: Vaginal spasms; due to involuntary contraction of musculature; prevents intercourse.

625.2 Mittelschmerz ♀
  Intermenstrual pain
  Ovulation pain
  DEF: Pain occurring between menstrual periods.

Ⓝ Newborn Age: 0   Ⓟ Pediatric Age: 0-17   Ⓜ Maternity Age: 12-55   Ⓐ Adult Age: 15-124

625.3 Dysmenorrhea ♀
Painful menstruation
EXCLUDES psychogenic dysmenorrhea (306.52)
AHA: 2Q, '94, 12
N94.6 Dysmenorrhea unspecified `I-10`

625.4 Premenstrual tension syndromes ♀
Menstrual molimen
Premenstrual dysphoric disorder
Premenstrual syndrome
Premenstrual tension NOS
EXCLUDES menstrual migraine (346.4)
AHA: 4Q, '03, 116

625.5 Pelvic congestion syndrome ♀
Congestion-fibrosis syndrome
Taylor's syndrome
DEF: Excessive accumulation of blood in vessels of pelvis; may occur after orgasm; causes abnormal menstruation, lower back pain and vaginal discharge.

625.6 Stress incontinence, female ♀
EXCLUDES mixed incontinence (788.33)
stress incontinence, male (788.32)
DEF: Involuntary leakage of urine due to insufficient sphincter control; occurs upon sneezing, laughing, coughing, sudden movement or lifting.
N39.3 Stress incontinence(female) (male) `I-10`

√5th **625.7 Vulvodynia**
DEF: ▶Vulvar pain without an identifiable cause that persists for three months or longer.◀
AHA: ▶4Q, '08, 124◀

625.70 Vulvodynia, unspecified ♀
Vulvodynia NOS

625.71 Vulvar vestibulitis ♀

625.79 Other vulvodynia ♀

625.8 Other specified symptoms associated with female genital organs ♀
AHA: N-D, '85, 16

625.9 Unspecified symptom associated with female genital organs ♀
AHA: 4Q, '06, 110
R39.8 Oth symptoms & signs involv genitourinary system `I-10`

√4th **626 Disorders of menstruation and other abnormal bleeding from female genital tract**
EXCLUDES menopausal and premenopausal bleeding (627.0)
pain and other symptoms associated with menstrual cycle (625.2-625.4)
postmenopausal bleeding (627.1)

626.0 Absence of menstruation ♀
Amenorrhea (primary) (secondary)

626.1 Scanty or infrequent menstruation ♀
Hypomenorrhea   Oligomenorrhea

626.2 Excessive or frequent menstruation ♀
Heavy periods   Menorrhagia
Menometrorrhagia   Plymenorrhea
EXCLUDES premenopausal (627.0)
that in puberty (626.3)
N92.0 Excess & frequent menstruation w/regular cycle `I-10`

626.3 Puberty bleeding ♀
Excessive bleeding associated with onset of menstrual periods
Pubertal menorrhagia

626.4 Irregular menstrual cycle ♀
Irregular: Irregular:
bleeding NOS   periods
menstruation

626.5 Ovulation bleeding ♀
Regular intermenstrual bleeding

626.6 Metrorrhagia ♀
Bleeding unrelated to menstrual cycle
Irregular intermenstrual bleeding

626.7 Postcoital bleeding ♀
DEF: Bleeding from vagina after sexual intercourse.

626.8 Other
Dysfunctional or functional uterine hemorrhage NOS
Menstruation:
retained
suppression of
N92.5 Other specified irregular menstruation `I-10`

626.9 Unspecified ♀

√4th **627 Menopausal and postmenopausal disorders**
EXCLUDES asymptomatic age-related (natural) postmenopausal status (V49.81)

627.0 Premenopausal menorrhagia ♀
Excessive bleeding associated with onset of menopause
Menorrhagia:
climacteric
menopausal
preclimacteric

627.1 Postmenopausal bleeding ♀
N95.0 Postmenopausal bleeding `I-10`

627.2 Symptomatic menopausal or female climacteric states ♀
Symptoms, such as flushing, sleeplessness, headache, lack of concentration, associated with the menopause

627.3 Postmenopausal atrophic vaginitis ♀
Senile (atrophic) vaginitis

627.4 Symptomatic states associated with artificial menopause ♀
Postartificial menopause syndromes
Any condition classifiable to 627.1, 627.2, or 627.3 which follows induced menopause
DEF: Conditions arising after hysterectomy.

627.8 Other specified menopausal and postmenopausal disorders ♀
EXCLUDES premature menopause NOS (256.31)

627.9 Unspecified menopausal and postmenopausal disorder ♀

√4th **628 Infertility, female**
INCLUDES primary and secondary sterility
DEF: Infertility: inability to conceive for at least one year with regular intercourse.
DEF: Primary infertility: occurring in patients who have never conceived.
DEF: Secondary infertility: occurring in patients who have previously conceived.
AHA: 2Q, '96, 9; 1Q, '95, 7

628.0 Associated with anovulation ♀
Anovulatory cycle
Use additional code for any associated Stein-Leventhal syndrome (256.4)

628.1 Of pituitary-hypothalamic origin ♀
Code first underlying cause, as:
adiposogenital dystrophy (253.8)
anterior pituitary disorder (253.0-253.4)

628.2 Of tubal origin ♀
Infertility associated with congenital anomaly of tube
Tubal:
block
occlusion
stenosis
Use additional code for any associated peritubal adhesions (614.6)

628.3 Of uterine origin ♀
Infertility associated with congenital anomaly of uterus
Nonimplantation
Use additional code for any associated tuberculous endometritis (016.7)

628.4   **Of cervical or vaginal origin**   ♀
Infertility associated with:
  anomaly of cervical mucus
  congenital structural anomaly
  dysmucorrhea

628.8   **Of other specified origin**   ♀

628.9   **Of unspecified origin**   ♀

√4th **629**   **Other disorders of female genital organs**

629.0   **Hematocele, female, not elsewhere classified**   ♀

    EXCLUDES   *hematocele or hematoma:*
        broad ligament (620.7)
        fallopian tube (620.8)
        that associated with ectopic pregnancy
          (633.00-633.91)
        uterus (621.4)
        vagina (623.6)
        vulva (624.5)

629.1   **Hydrocele, canal of Nuck**   ♀
Cyst of canal of Nuck (acquired)
  EXCLUDES   *congenital (752.41)*

√5th **629.2**   **Female genital mutilation status**   ♀
Female circumcision status
Female genital cutting
AHA: 4Q, '04, 88

  629.20   **Female genital mutilation status, unspecified**   ♀
Female genital cutting status, unspecified
Female genital mutilation status NOS

  629.21   **Female genital mutilation Type I status**   ♀
Clitorectomy status
Female genital cutting Type I status
DEF: Female genital mutilation involving clitorectomy, with part or all of the clitoris removed.

629.22   **Female genital mutilation Type II status**   ♀
Clitorectomy with excision of labia
  minora status
Female genital cutting Type II status
DEF: Female genital mutilation involving clitoris and the labia minora amputation.
AHA: 4Q, '04, 90

629.23   **Female genital mutilation Type III status**   ♀
Female genital cutting Type III status
Infibulation status
DEF: Female genital mutilation involving removal, most or all of the labia minora excised, labia majora incised which is then made into a hood of skin over the urethral and vaginal opening.
AHA: 4Q, '04, 90

629.29   **Other female genital mutilation status**   ♀
Female genital cutting Type IV status
Female genital mutilation Type IV status
Other female genital cutting status
AHA: 4Q, '06, 97

√5th **629.8**   **Other specified disorders of female genital organs**

629.81   **Habitual aborter without current pregnancy**   ♀
    EXCLUDES   *habitual aborter with current pregnancy (646.3)*
AHA: 4Q, '06, 98

629.89   **Other specified disorders of female genital organs**   ♀
AHA: 4Q, '06, 98

629.9   **Unspecified disorder of female genital organs**   ♀

Ⓝ Newborn Age: 0   Ⓟ Pediatric Age: 0-17   Ⓜ Maternity Age: 12-55   Ⓐ Adult Age: 15-124

11. COMPLICATIONS OF PREGNANCY, CHILDBIRTH, AND THE PUERPERIUM (630-679)

ECTOPIC AND MOLAR PREGNANCY (630-633)

Use additional code from category 639 to identify any complications

630 Hydatidiform mole   Ⓜ♀

Trophoblastic disease NOS
Vesicular mole

> **EXCLUDES**   chorioadenoma (destruens) (236.1)
> chorionepithelioma (181)
> malignant hydatidiform mole (236.1)

DEF: Abnormal product of pregnancy; marked by mass of cysts resembling bunch of grapes due to chorionic villi proliferation, and dissolution; must be surgically removed.

631 Other abnormal product of conception   Ⓜ♀

Blighted ovum
Mole:
   NOS
   carneous
   fleshy
   stone

632 Missed abortion   Ⓜ♀

Early fetal death before completion of 22 weeks' gestation with retention of dead fetus
Retained products of conception, not following spontaneous or induced abortion or delivery

> **EXCLUDES**   failed induced abortion (638.0-638.9)
> fetal death (intrauterine) (late) (656.4)
> missed delivery (656.4)
> that with abnormal product of conception (630, 631)

AHA: 1Q, '01, 5

002.1 Missed abortion   I-10

✓4ᵗʰ **633 Ectopic pregnancy**

INCLUDES   ruptured ectopic pregnancy

DEF: Fertilized egg develops outside uterus.

AHA: 4Q, '02, 61

✓5ᵗʰ **633.0 Abdominal pregnancy**

Intraperitoneal pregnancy

  633.00 Abdominal pregnancy without intrauterine pregnancy   Ⓜ♀

  633.01 Abdominal pregnancy with intrauterine pregnancy   Ⓜ♀

✓5ᵗʰ **633.1 Tubal pregnancy**

Fallopian pregnancy
Rupture of (fallopian) tube due to pregnancy
Tubal abortion

AHA: 2Q, '90, 27

  633.10 Tubal pregnancy without intrauterine pregnancy   Ⓜ♀

      000.1 Tubal pregnancy   I-10

  633.11 Tubal pregnancy with intrauterine pregnancy   Ⓜ♀

✓5ᵗʰ **633.2 Ovarian pregnancy**

  633.20 Ovarian pregnancy without intrauterine pregnancy   Ⓜ♀

  633.21 Ovarian pregnancy with intrauterine pregnancy   Ⓜ♀

✓5ᵗʰ **633.8 Other ectopic pregnancy**

Pregnancy:
  cervical
  combined
  cornual
  intraligamentous
  mesometric
  mural

  633.80 Other ectopic pregnancy without intrauterine pregnancy   Ⓜ♀

  633.81 Other ectopic pregnancy with intrauterine pregnancy   Ⓜ♀

✓5ᵗʰ **633.9 Unspecified ectopic pregnancy**

  633.90 Unspecified ectopic pregnancy without intrauterine pregnancy   Ⓜ♀

  633.91 Unspecified ectopic pregnancy with intrauterine pregnancy   Ⓜ♀

OTHER PREGNANCY WITH ABORTIVE OUTCOME (634-639)

The following fourth-digit subdivisions are for use with categories 634-638:

.0 Complicated by genital tract and pelvic infection
  Endometritis
  Salpingo-oophoritis
  Sepsis NOS
  Septicemia NOS
  Any condition classifiable to 639.0 with condition classifiable to 634-638
  EXCLUDES   urinary tract infection (634-638 with .7)

.1 Complicated by delayed or excessive hemorrhage
  Afibrinogenemia
  Defibrination syndrome
  Intravascular hemolysis
  Any condition classifiable to 639.1 with condition classifiable to 634-638

.2 Complicated by damage to pelvic organs and tissues
  Laceration, perforation, or tear of:
    bladder
    uterus
  Any condition classifiable to 639.2 with condition classifiable to 634-638

.3 Complicated by renal failure
  Oliguria
  Uremia
  Any condition classifiable to 639.3, with condition classifiable to 634-638

.4 Complicated by metabolic disorder
  Electrolyte imbalance with conditions classfiable to 634-638

.5 Complicated by shock
  Circulatory collapse
  Shock (postoperative) (septic)
  Any condition classifiable to 639.5 with condition classifiable to 634-638

.6 Complicated by embolism
  Embolism:
    NOS
    amniotic fluid
    pulmonary
  Any condition classifiable to 639.6, with condition classifiable to 634-638

.7 With other specified complications
  Cardiac arrest or failure
  Urinary tract infection
  Any condition classiable to 639.8 with condition classifiable to 634-638

.8 With unspecified complication

.9 Without mention of complication

§ ✓4ᵗʰ **634 Spontaneous abortion**

> Requires fifth-digit to identify stage:
> **0 unspecified**
> **1 incomplete**
> **2 complete**

INCLUDES   miscarriage
               spontaneous abortion

DEF: Spontaneous premature expulsion of the products of conception from the uterus.

AHA: 2Q, '91, 16

§§ ✓5ᵗʰ **634.0 Complicated by genital tract and pelvic infection**   Ⓜ♀
[0-2]

§§ ✓5ᵗʰ **634.1 Complicated by delayed or excessive hemorrhage**   Ⓜ♀
[0-2]   **AHA: For Code 634.11:** 1Q, '03, 6

§§ ✓5ᵗʰ **634.2 Complicated by damage to pelvic organs or tissues**   Ⓜ♀
[0-2]

§§ ✓5ᵗʰ **634.3 Complicated by renal failure**   Ⓜ♀
[0-2]

§§ ✓5ᵗʰ **634.4 Complicated by metabolic disorder**   Ⓜ♀
[0-2]

§   See beginning of section 634-639 for fourth-digit definitions.
§§ Requires fifth digit. Valid digits are in [brackets] under each code. See appropriate category for codes and definitions.

✓4ᵗʰ Additional Digit Required	Unspecified Code	Other Specified Code	Manifestation Code	▶◀ Revised Text	● New Code	▲ Revised Code Title

Ectopic Pregnancy Sites

§§ ✓5ᵗʰ **634.5** **Complicated by shock**   Ⓜ♀
[0-2]

§§ ✓5ᵗʰ **634.6** **Complicated by embolism**   Ⓜ♀
[0-2]

§§ ✓5ᵗʰ **634.7** **With other specified complications**   Ⓜ♀
[0-2]

§§ ✓5ᵗʰ **634.8** **With unspecified complication**   Ⓜ♀
[0-2]

§§ ✓5ᵗʰ **634.9** **Without mention of complication**   Ⓜ♀
[0-2]

§ ✓4ᵗʰ **635** **Legally induced abortion**

> Requires fifth-digit to identify stage:
> 0 unspecified
> 1 incomplete
> 2 complete

INCLUDES   abortion or termination of pregnancy:
     elective
     legal
     therapeutic

EXCLUDES   *menstrual extraction or regulation (V25.3)*

DEF: Intentional expulsion of products of conception from uterus performed by medical professionals inside boundaries of law.

AHA: 2Q, '94, 14

§§ ✓5ᵗʰ **635.0** **Complicated by genital tract and pelvic infection**   Ⓜ♀
[0-2]

§§ ✓5ᵗʰ **635.1** **Complicated by delayed or excessive**   Ⓜ♀
[0-2]   **hemorrhage**

§§ ✓5ᵗʰ **635.2** **Complicated by damage to pelvic organs**   Ⓜ♀
[0-2]   **or tissues**

§§ ✓5ᵗʰ **635.3** **Complicated by renal failure**   Ⓜ♀
[0-2]

§§ ✓5ᵗʰ **635.4** **Complicated by metabolic disorder**   Ⓜ♀
[0-2]

§§ ✓5ᵗʰ **635.5** **Complicated by shock**   Ⓜ♀
[0-2]

§§ ✓5ᵗʰ **635.6** **Complicated by embolism**   Ⓜ♀
[0-2]

§§ ✓5ᵗʰ **635.7** **With other specified complications**   Ⓜ♀
[0-2]

§§ ✓5ᵗʰ **635.8** **With unspecified complication**   Ⓜ♀
[0-2]

§§ ✓5ᵗʰ **635.9** **Without mention of complication**   Ⓜ♀
[0-2]   **AHA: For code 635.92:** 2Q, '94, 14

§ ✓4ᵗʰ **636** **Illegally induced abortion**

> Requires fifth-digit to identify stage:
> 0 unspecified
> 1 incomplete
> 2 complete

INCLUDES   abortion:
     criminal
     illegal
     self-induced

DEF: Intentional expulsion of products of conception from uterus; outside boundaries of law.

§§ ✓5ᵗʰ **636.0** **Complicated by genital tract and pelvic infection**   Ⓜ♀
[0-2]

§§ ✓5ᵗʰ **636.1** **Complicated by delayed or excessive**   Ⓜ♀
[0-2]   **hemorrhage**

§§ ✓5ᵗʰ **636.2** **Complicated by damage to pelvic organs**   Ⓜ♀
[0-2]   **or tissues**

§§ ✓5ᵗʰ **636.3** **Complicated by renal failure**   Ⓜ♀
[0-2]

§§ ✓5ᵗʰ **636.4** **Complicated by metabolic disorder**   Ⓜ♀
[0-2]

§§ ✓5ᵗʰ **636.5** **Complicated by shock**   Ⓜ♀
[0-2]

§§ ✓5ᵗʰ **636.6** **Complicated by embolism**   Ⓜ♀
[0-2]

§§ ✓5ᵗʰ **636.7** **With other specified complications**   Ⓜ♀
[0-2]

§§ ✓5ᵗʰ **636.8** **With unspecified complication**   Ⓜ♀
[0-2]

§§ ✓5ᵗʰ **636.9** **Without mention of complication**   Ⓜ♀
[0-2]

§ ✓4ᵗʰ **637** **Unspecified abortion**

> Requires fifth-digit to identify stage:
> 0 unspecified
> 1 incomplete
> 2 complete

INCLUDES   abortion NOS
     retained products of conception following abortion, not classifiable elsewhere

§§ ✓5ᵗʰ **637.0** **Complicated by genital tract and pelvic infection**   Ⓜ♀
[0-2]

§§ ✓5ᵗʰ **637.1** **Complicated by delayed or excessive**   Ⓜ♀
[0-2]   **hemorrhage**

§§ ✓5ᵗʰ **637.2** **Complicated by damage to pelvic organs**   Ⓜ♀
[0-2]   **or tissues**

§§ ✓5ᵗʰ **637.3** **Complicated by renal failure**   Ⓜ♀
[0-2]

§§ ✓5ᵗʰ **637.4** **Complicated by metabolic disorder**   Ⓜ♀
[0-2]

§§ ✓5ᵗʰ **637.5** **Complicated by shock**   Ⓜ♀
[0-2]

§§ ✓5ᵗʰ **637.6** **Complicated by embolism**   Ⓜ♀
[0-2]

§§ ✓5ᵗʰ **637.7** **With other specified complications**   Ⓜ♀
[0-2]

§§ ✓5ᵗʰ **637.8** **With unspecified complication**   Ⓜ♀
[0-2]

§§ ✓5ᵗʰ **637.9** **Without mention of complication**   Ⓜ♀
[0-2]

---

§   See beginning of section 634-639 for fourth-digit definitions.
§§   Requires fifth digit. Valid digits are in [brackets] under each code. See appropriate category for codes and definitions.

Ⓝ Newborn Age: 0   Ⓟ Pediatric Age: 0-17   Ⓜ Maternity Age: 12-55   Ⓐ Adult Age: 15-124

§ ✓4ᵗʰ **638 Failed attempted abortion**

> **INCLUDES** failure of attempted induction of (legal) abortion
> **EXCLUDES** *incomplete abortion (634.0-637.9)*
> **DEF:** Continued pregnancy despite an attempted legal abortion.

638.0 Complicated by genital tract and pelvic infection Ⓜ♀

638.1 Complicated by delayed or excessive hemorrhage Ⓜ♀

638.2 Complicated by damage to pelvic organs or tissues Ⓜ♀

638.3 Complicated by renal failure Ⓜ♀

638.4 Complicated by metabolic disorder Ⓜ♀

638.5 Complicated by shock Ⓜ♀

638.6 Complicated by embolism Ⓜ♀

638.7 With other specified complications Ⓜ♀

638.8 With unspecified complication Ⓜ♀

638.9 Without mention of complication Ⓜ♀

✓4ᵗʰ **639 Complications following abortion and ectopic and molar pregnancies**

> Note: This category is provided for use when it is required to classify separately the complications classifiable to the fourth-digit level in categories 634-638; for example:
>
> a) when the complication itself was responsible for an episode of medical care, the abortion, ectopic or molar pregnancy itself having been dealt with at a previous episode
>
> b) when these conditions are immediate complications of ectopic or molar pregnancies classifiable to 630-633 where they cannot be identified at fourth-digit level.

639.0 Genital tract and pelvic infection Ⓜ♀

Endometritis
Parametritis
Pelvic peritonitis } following conditions
Salpingitis   classifiable to 630-638
Salpingo-oophoritis
Sepsis NOS
Septicemia NOS

> **EXCLUDES** *urinary tract infection (639.8)*

639.1 Delayed or excessive hemorrhage Ⓜ♀

Afibrinogenemia } following conditions
Defibrination syndrome { classfiable to
Intravascular   630-638

639.2 Damage to pelvic organs and tissues Ⓜ♀

Laceration, perforation, or tear of:
bladder
bowel
broad ligament
cervix   } following conditions
periurethral tissue   classifiable to 630-638
uterus
vagina

▲ **639.3 Kidney failure** Ⓜ♀

Oliguria
Renal ▶(kidney):◀
failure (acute)   } following conditions
shutdown   classifiable to 630-638
tubular necrosis
Uremia

639.4 Metabolic disorders Ⓜ♀

Electrolyte imbalance following conditions classifiable to 630-638

639.5 Shock Ⓜ♀

Circulatory collapse } following conditions
Shock (postoperative) { classifiable to
(septic)   630-638

639.6 Embolism Ⓜ♀

Embolism:

NOS
air
amniotic fluid
blood-clot
fat   } following conditions
pulmonary   classifiable to 630-638
pyemic
septic
soap

639.8 Other specified complications following abortion or ectopic and molar pregnancy Ⓜ♀

Acute yellow atrophy or
necrosis of liver   } following conditons
Cardiac arrest or failure   classifiable to 630-638
Cerebral anoxia
Urinary tract infection

639.9 Unspecified complication following abortion or ectopic and molar pregnancy Ⓜ♀

Complication(s) not further specified following conditions classifiable to 630-638

COMPLICATIONS MAINLY RELATED TO PREGNANCY (640-649)

> **INCLUDES** the listed conditions even if they arose or were present during labor, delivery, or the puerperium

AHA: 2Q, '90, 11

The following fifth-digit subclassification is for use with categories 640-649 to denote the current episode of care. Valid fifth-digits are in [brackets] under each code.

0 unspecified as to episode of care or not applicable

1 delivered, with or without mention of antepartum condition
Antepartum condition with delivery
Delivery NOS (with mention of antepartum complication during current episode of care)
Intrapartum obstetric condition (with mention of antepartum complication during current episode of care)
Pregnancy, delivered (with mention of antepartum complication during current episode of care)

2 delivered, with mention of postpartum complication
Delivery with mention of puerperal complication during current episode of care

3 antepartum condition or complication
Antepartum obstetric condtion, not delivered during the current episode of care

4 postpartum condition of complication
Postpartum or puerperal obstetric condition or complication following delivery that occurred:
during previous episode of care
outside hospital, with subsequent admission for observation or care

✓4ᵗʰ **640 Hemorrhage in early pregnancy**

> **INCLUDES** hemorrhage before completion of 22 weeks' gestation

§§ ✓5ᵗʰ **640.0 Threatened abortion** Ⓜ♀
[0,1,3]

> **DEF:** Bloody discharge during pregnancy; cervix may be dilated and pregnancy is threatened, but the pregnancy is not terminated.

§§ ✓5ᵗʰ **640.8 Other specified hemorrhage in early pregnancy** Ⓜ♀
[0,1,3]

§§ ✓5ᵗʰ **640.9 Unspecified hemorrhage in early pregnancy** Ⓜ♀
[0,1,3]

✓4ᵗʰ **641 Antepartum hemorrhage, abruptio placentae, and placenta previa**

§ ✓5ᵗʰ **641.0 Placenta previa without hemorrhage** Ⓜ♀
[0,1,3]

Low impantation of placenta
Placenta previa noted: } without hemorrhage
during pregnancy
before labor (and delivered by
caesarean delivery

> **DEF:** Placenta implanted in lower segment of uterus; commonly causes hemorrhage in the last trimester of pregnancy.

§ See beginning of section 634-639 for fourth-digit definitions
§§ Requires fifth digit. Valid digits are in [brackets] under each code. See beginning of section 640-649 for codes and definitions.

✓4ᵗʰ Additional Digit Required   **Unspecified Code**   **Other Specified Code**   **Manifestation Code**   ▶◀ Revised Text   ● New Code   ▲ Revised Code Title
✓5ᵗʰ
2010 ICD-9-CM   **October 2009 · Volume 1 – 201**

Placenta Previa

Low (marginal) implantation

Partial placenta previa

Total placenta previa

Abruptio Placentae

Partial separation (concealed bleeding)

Partial separation (apparent hemorrhage)

Complete separation (concealed hemorrhage)

§ ✓5ᵗʰ **641.1 Hemorrhage from placenta previa**   Ⅿ♀
[0,1,3]
Low-lying placenta
Placenta previa
   incomplete
   marginal   NOS or with hemorrhage
   partial   (intrapartum)
   total

EXCLUDES   *hemorrhage from vasa previa (663.5)*

§ ✓5ᵗʰ **641.2 Premature separation of placenta**   Ⅿ♀
[0,1,3]
Ablatio placentae
Abruptio placentae
Accidental antepartum hemorrhage
Couvelaire uterus
Detachment of placenta (premature)
Premature separation of normally implanted placenta
DEF: Abruptio placentae: premature detachment of the placenta, characterized by shock, oliguria and decreased fibrinogen.
045.90 Premature sep of placenta unspec, uns trimester   Ⅰ-10

§ ✓5ᵗʰ **641.3 Antepartum hemorrhage associated**   Ⅿ♀
[0,1,3] **with coagulation defects**
Antepartum or intrapartum hemorrhage associated with:
   afibrinogenemia
   hyperfibrinolysis
   hypofibrinogenemia
EXCLUDES   *coagulation defects not associated with antepartum hemorrhage (649.3)*
DEF: Uterine hemorrhage prior to delivery.

§ ✓5ᵗʰ **641.8 Other antepartum hemorrhage**   Ⅿ♀
[0,1,3]
Antepartum or intrapartum hemorrhage associated with:
   trauma
   uterine leiomyoma

§ ✓5ᵗʰ **641.9 Unspecified antepartum hemorrhage**   Ⅿ♀
[0,1,3]
Hemorrhage:
   antepartum NOS
   intrapartum NOS
   of pregnancy NOS

✓4ᵗʰ **642 Hypertension complicating pregnancy, childbirth, and the puerperium**

§ ✓5ᵗʰ **642.0 Benign essential hypertension complicating**   Ⅿ♀
[0-4] **pregnancy, childbirth, and the puerperium**
Hypertension   specified as complicating, or as
  benign essential   reason for obstetric care
  chronic NOS   during pregnancy,
  essential   childbirth, or the
  pre-existing NOS   puerperium

010.02 Pre-exist essential hypertension comp childbirth   Ⅰ-10

§ ✓5ᵗʰ **642.1 Hypertension secondary to renal disease,**   Ⅿ♀
[0-4] **complicating pregnancy, childbirth, and the puerperium**
Hypertension secondary to renal disease, specified as complicating, or as a reason for obstetric care during pregnancy, childbirth, or the puerperium

§ ✓5ᵗʰ **642.2 Other pre-existing hypertension complicating**   Ⅿ♀
[0-4] **pregnancy, childbirth, and the puerperium**
Hypertensive   specified as complicating,
  chronic kidney disease   or as a reason for
  heart and chronic   obstetric care during
    kidney disease   pregnancy,
  heart disease   childbirth, or the
Malignant hypertension   puerperium

§ ✓5ᵗʰ **642.3 Transient hypertension of pregnancy**   Ⅿ♀
[0-4]
Gestational hypertension
Transient hypertension, so described, in pregnancy, childbirth, or the puerperium
AHA: 3Q, '90, 4
013.9 Gestatnl pg-inducd HTN w/o sig protnuria uns tri   Ⅰ-10

§ ✓5ᵗʰ **642.4 Mild or unspecified pre-eclampsia**   Ⅿ♀
[0-4]
Hypertension in pregnancy, childbirth, or the puerperium, not specified as pre-existing, with either albuminuria or edema, or both; mild or unspecified
Pre-eclampsia:
   NOS
   mild
Toxemia (pre-eclamptic):
   NOS
   mild
EXCLUDES   *albuminuria in pregnancy, without mention of hypertension (646.2)*
    edema in pregnancy, without mention of hypertension (646.1)
014.00 Mild pre-eclampsia unspecified trimester   Ⅰ-10

§ ✓5ᵗʰ **642.5 Severe pre-eclampsia**   Ⅿ♀
[0-4]
Hypertension in pregnancy, childbirth, or the puerperium, not specified as pre-existing, with either albuminuria or edema, or both; specified as severe
Pre-eclampsia, severe
Toxemia (pre-eclamptic), severe
AHA: N-D, '85, 3

§ ✓5ᵗʰ **642.6 Eclampsia**   Ⅿ♀
[0-4]
Toxemia:
   eclamptic
   with convulsions

§ ✓5ᵗʰ **642.7 Pre-eclampsia or eclampsia superimposed**   Ⅿ♀
[0-4] **on pre-existing hypertension**
Conditions classifiable to 642.4-642.6, with conditions classifiable to 642.0-642.2

§ ✓5ᵗʰ **642.9 Unspecified hypertension complicating**   Ⅿ♀
[0-4] **pregnancy, childbirth, or the puerperium**
Hypertension NOS, without mention of albuminuria or edema, complicating pregnancy, childbirth, or the puerperium
AHA: For code 642.94: ▶1Q, '09, 17◀

§   Requires fifth digit. Valid digits are in [brackets] under each code. See beginning of section 640-649 for codes and definitions.

Ⓝ Newborn Age: 0   Ⓟ Pediatric Age: 0-17   Ⓜ Maternity Age: 12-55   Ⓐ Adult Age: 15-124

✓4th **643 Excessive vomiting in pregnancy**

INCLUDES hyperemesis
vomiting:
persistent } arising during pregnancy
vicious
hyperemesis gravidarum

§ ✓5th **643.0 Mild hyperemesis gravidarum** M♀
[0,1,3] Hyperemesis gravidarum, mild or unspecified, starting before the end of the 22nd week of gestation

DEF: Detrimental vomiting and nausea.

§ ✓5th **643.1 Hyperemesis gravidarum with metabolic** M♀
[0,1,3] **disturbance**
Hyperemesis gravidarum, starting before the end of the 22nd week of gestation, with metabolic disturbance, such as:
carbohydrate depletion
dehydration
electrolyte imbalance

§ ✓5th **643.2 Late vomiting of pregnancy** M♀
[0,1,3] Excessive vomiting starting after 22 completed weeks of gestation

§ ✓5th **643.8 Other vomiting complicating pregnancy** M♀
[0,1,3] Vomiting due to organic disease or other cause, specified as complicating pregnancy, or as a reason for obstetric care during pregnancy

Use additional code to specify cause

§ ✓5th **643.9 Unspecified vomiting of pregnancy** M♀
[0,1,3] Vomiting as a reason for care during pregnancy, length of gestation unspecified

✓4th **644 Early or threatened labor**

§ ✓5th **644.0 Threatened premature labor** M♀
[0,3] Premature labor after 22 weeks, but before 37 completed weeks of gestation without delivery

EXCLUDES that occurring before 22 completed weeks of gestation (640.0)

060.00 Preterm labor without delivery unspec trimester I-10

§ ✓5th **644.1 Other threatened labor** M♀
[0,3] False labor:
NOS
after 37 completed weeks of } without delivery
gestation
Threatened labor NOS

§ ✓5th **644.2 Early onset of delivery** M♀
[0,1] Onset (spontaneous) of delivery } before 37 completed
Premature labor with onset of } weeks of
delivery } gestation

AHA: 2Q, '91, 16

TIP: Assign if an attempted termination of pregnancy results in a liveborn fetus.

060.14x0 Pt labor 3rd tri w/pt del 3rd tri not applic/uns I-10

✓4th **645 Late pregnancy**
AHA: 4Q, '00, 43; 4Q, '91, 26

§ ✓5th **645.1 Post term pregnancy** M♀
[0,1,3] Pregnancy over 40 completed weeks to 42 completed weeks gestation

048.0 Post-term pregnancy I-10

§ ✓5th **645.2 Prolonged pregnancy** M♀
[0,1,3] Pregnancy which has advanced beyond 42 completed weeks gestation

✓4th **646 Other complications of pregnancy, not elsewhere classified**
Use additional code(s) to further specify complication
AHA: 4Q, '95, 59

§ ✓5th **646.0 Papyraceous fetus** M♀
[0,1,3] **DEF:** Fetus that dies in the second trimester of pregnancy and is retained in the uterus, with subsequent atrophy and mummification; commonly occurs in twin pregnancy, nonviable fetus becomes compressed by growth of living twin.

§ ✓5th **646.1 Edema or excessive weight gain in** M♀
[0-4] **pregnancy, without mention of hypertension**
Gestational edema
Maternal obesity syndrome

EXCLUDES that with mention of hypertension (642.0-642.9)

§ ✓5th **646.2 Unspecified renal disease in pregnancy,** M♀
[0-4] **without mention of hypertension**
Albuminuria } in pregnancy or the
Nephropathy NOS } puerperium, without
Renal disease NOS } mention of
Uremia } hypertension

Gestational proteinuria

EXCLUDES that with mention of hypertension (642.0-642.9)

§ ✓5th **646.3 Habitual aborter** M♀
[0,1,3] EXCLUDES with current abortion (634.0-634.9)
without current pregnancy (629.81)

DEF: Three or more consecutive spontaneous abortions.

§ ✓5th **646.4 Peripheral neuritis in pregnancy** M♀
[0-4]

§ ✓5th **646.5 Asymptomatic bacteriuria in pregnancy** M♀
[0-4]

§ ✓5th **646.6 Infections of genitourinary tract in pregnancy** M♀
[0-4] Conditions classifiable to 590, 595, 597, 599.0, 616 complicating pregnancy, childbirth, or the puerperium
Conditions classifiable to 614.0-614.5, 614.7-614.9, 615 complicating pregnancy or labor

EXCLUDES major puerperal infection ▶(670.0-670.8)◀

AHA: For code 646.63: 4Q, '04, 90

023.90 Unspec GU tract infection in pregnancy uns tri I-10

§ ✓5th **646.7 Liver disorders in pregnancy** M♀
[0,1,3] Acute yellow atrophy of liver
(obstetric) (true) } of pregnancy
Icterus gravis
Necrosis of liver }

EXCLUDES hepatorenal syndrome following delivery (674.8)
viral hepatitis (647.6)

§ ✓5th **646.8 Other specified complications of pregnancy** M♀
[0-4] Fatigue during pregnancy
Herpes gestationis
Insufficient weight gain of pregnancy

AHA: 3Q, '98, 16; J-F, '85, 15

§ ✓5th **646.9 Unspecified complication of pregnancy** M♀
[0,1,3]

✓4th **647 Infectious and parasitic conditions in the mother classifiable elsewhere, but complicating pregnancy, childbirth, or the puerperium**

INCLUDES the listed conditions when complicating the pregnant state, aggravated by the pregnancy, or when a main reason for obstetric care

Use additional code(s) to further specify complication

EXCLUDES those conditions in the mother known or suspected to have affected the fetus (655.0-655.9)

§ ✓5th **647.0 Syphilis** M♀
[0-4] Conditions classifiable to 090-097

§ ✓5th **647.1 Gonorrhea** M♀
[0-4] Conditions classifiable to 098

§ ✓5th **647.2 Other venereal diseases** M♀
[0-4] Conditions classifiable to 099

§ ✓5th **647.3 Tuberculosis** M♀
[0-4] Conditions classifiable to 010-018

§ ✓5th **647.4 Malaria** M♀
[0-4] Conditions classifiable to 084

§ Requires fifth digit. Valid digits are in [brackets] under each code. See beginning of section 640-649 for codes and definitions.

Complications of Pregnancy, Childbirth & Puerperium

647.5–649.7

§ ✓5th **647.5 Rubella**   M♀
[0-4]   Conditions classifiable to 056

§ ✓5th **647.6 Other viral diseases**   M♀
[0-4]   Conditions classifiable to 042, 050-055, 057-079, 795.05,
        795.15, 796.75
    AHA: J-F, '85, 15
    TIP: Assign when pregnant patient has any HIV-related condition or is stated to have an asymptomatic HIV infection.
    098.52 Other viral diseases complicating childbirth   I-10

§ ✓5th **647.8 Other specified infectious and parasitic**   M♀
[0-4]   **diseases**

§ ✓5th **647.9 Unspecified infection or infestation**   M♀
[0-4]

✓4th **648 Other current conditions in the mother classifiable elsewhere, but complicating pregnancy, childbirth, or the puerperium**

    INCLUDES the listed conditions when complicating the pregnant state, aggravated by the pregnancy, or when a main reason for obstetric care

    Use additional code(s) to identify the condition

    EXCLUDES those conditions in the mother known or suspected to have affected the fetus (655.0-655.9)

§ ✓5th **648.0 Diabetes mellitus**   M♀
[0-4]   Conditions classifiable to 249, 250
    EXCLUDES gestational diabetes (648.8)
    AHA: 3Q, '91, 5, 11
    024.32 Uns pre-existing diabetes mellitus in childbirth   I-10

§ ✓5th **648.1 Thyroid dysfunction**   M♀
[0-4]   Conditions classifiable to 240-246

§ ✓5th **648.2 Anemia**   M♀
[0-4]   Conditions classifiable to 280-285
    AHA: For Code 648.22: 1Q, '02, 14; **For code 648.24:** ▶1Q, '09, 17◀
    TIP: Assign with fifth digit 2 for postpartum anemia.
    099.013 Anemia complicating pregnancy third trimester   I-10

§ ✓5th **648.3 Drug dependence**   M♀
[0-4]   Conditions classifiable to 304
    AHA: 2Q, '98, 13; 4Q, '88, 8

§ ✓5th **648.4 Mental disorders**   M♀
[0-4]   Conditions classifiable to 290-303, 305.0, 305.2-305.9,
        306-316, 317-319
    AHA: 2Q, '98, 13; 4Q, '95, 63
    099.314 Alcohol use complicating childbirth   I-10

§ ✓5th **648.5 Congenital cardiovascular disorders**   M♀
[0-4]   Conditions classifiable to 745-747

§ ✓5th **648.6 Other cardiovascular diseases**   M♀
[0-4]   Conditions classifiable to 390-398, 410-429
    EXCLUDES cerebrovascular disorders in the puerperium (674.0)
        peripartum cardiomyopathy (674.5)
        venous complications (671.0-671.9)
    AHA: 3Q, '98, 11

§ ✓5th **648.7 Bone and joint disorders of back, pelvis, and**   M♀
[0-4]   **lower limbs**
    Conditions classifiable to 720-724, and those classifiable to 711-719 or 725-738, specified as affecting the lower limbs

§ ✓5th **648.8 Abnormal glucose tolerance**   M♀
[0-4]   Conditions classifiable to 790.21-790.29
    Gestational diabetes
    Use additional code, if applicable, for associated long-term (current) insulin use (V58.67)
    DEF: Glucose intolerance arising in pregnancy, resolving at end of pregnancy.
    AHA: 3Q, '91, 5; **For code 648.83:** 4Q, '04, 56
    TIP: Do not assign if patient was diabetic before becoming pregnant; should never be assigned in combination with code 648.0X.
    024.429 Gestational diab mellitus childbirth uns cntrl   I-10

§ ✓5th **648.9 Other current conditions classifiable elsewhere**   M♀
[0-4]   Conditions classifiable to 440-459, 795.01-795.04, 795.06,
        795.10-795.14, 795.16, 796.70-796.74, 796.76
    Nutritional deficiencies [conditions classifiable to 260-269]
    AHA: 3Q, '06, 14; 4Q, '04, 88; N-D, '87, 10; **For code 648.91:** 1Q, '02, 14; **For code 648.93:** 4Q, '04, 90; **For code 648.94:** ▶1Q, '09, 17◀
    TIP: Assign for group B streptococcus carrier patients, along with code V02.51 Carrier or suspected carrier of infectious diseases.

✓4th **649 Other conditions or status of the mother complicating pregnancy, childbirth, or the puerperium**
    AHA: 4Q, '06, 99

§ ✓5th **649.0 Tobacco use disorder complicating pregnancy,**   M♀
[0-4]   **childbirth, or the puerperium**
    Smoking complicating pregnancy, childbirth, or the puerperium
    AHA: 4Q, '06, 99
    099.334 Smoking tobacco complicating childbirth   I-10

§ ✓5th **649.1 Obesity complicating pregnancy, childbirth,**   M♀
[0-4]   **or the puerperium**
    Use additional code to identify the obesity (278.00, 278.01)
    AHA: 4Q, '06, 99
    099.214 Obesity complicating childbirth   I-10

§ ✓5th **649.2 Bariatric surgery status complicating**   M♀
[0-4]   **pregnancy, childbirth, or the puerperium**
    Gastric banding status complicating pregnancy, childbirth, or the puerperium
    Gastric bypass status for obesity complicating pregnancy, childbirth, or the puerperium
    Obesity surgery status complicating pregnancy, childbirth, or the puerperium
    AHA: 4Q, '06, 99, 118

§ ✓5th **649.3 Coagulation defects complicating pregnancy,**   M♀
[0-4]   **childbirth, or the puerperium**
    Conditions classifiable to ▶286, 287, 289◀
    Use additional code to identify the specific coagulation defect ▶(286.0-286.9, 287.0-287.9, 289.0-289.9)◀
    EXCLUDES coagulation defects causing antepartum hemorrhage (641.3)
        postpartum coagulation defects (666.3)
    AHA: 4Q, '06, 99

§ ✓5th **649.4 Epilepsy complicating pregnancy, childbirth,**   M♀
[0-4]   **or the puerperium**
    Conditions classifiable to 345
    Use additional code to identify the specific type of epilepsy (345.00-345.91)
    EXCLUDES eclampsia (642.6)
    AHA: 4Q, '06, 99

§ ✓5th **649.5 Spotting complicating pregnancy**   M♀
[0,1,3]   **EXCLUDES** antepartum hemorrhage (641.0-641.9)
        hemorrhage in early pregnancy (640.0-640.9)
    AHA: 4Q, '06, 99

§ ✓5th **649.6 Uterine size date discrepancy**   M♀
[0-4]   **EXCLUDES** suspected problem with fetal growth not found (V89.04)
    AHA: 4Q, '06, 99

§ ✓5th **649.7 Cervical shortening**   M♀
[0,1,3]   **EXCLUDES** suspected cervical shortening not found (V89.05)
    DEF: A cervix that has shortened to < 25 mm in length by the 16th week of pregnancy; warning sign for impending premature delivery; treated by cervical cerclage placement or progesterone.
    AHA: 4Q, '08, 124-125; **For code 649.73:** 4Q, '08, 125

§   Requires fifth digit. Valid digits are in [brackets] under each code. See beginning of section 640-649 for codes and definitions.

N Newborn Age: 0   P Pediatric Age: 0-17   M Maternity Age: 12-55   A Adult Age: 15-124

NORMAL DELIVERY, AND OTHER INDICATIONS FOR CARE IN PREGNANCY, LABOR, AND DELIVERY (650-659)

The following fifth-digit subclassification is for use with categories 651-659 to denote the current episode of care. Valid fifth-digits are in [brackets] under each code.

- **0** unspecified as to episode of care or not applicable
- **1** delivered, with or without mention of antepartum condition
- **2** delivered, with mention of postpartum complication
- **3** antepartum condition or complication
- **4** postpartum condition or complication

650 Normal delivery　M♀

Delivery requiring minimal or no assistance, with or without episiotomy, without fetal manipulation [e.g., rotation version] or instrumentation [forceps] of spontaneous, cephalic, vaginal, full-term, single, live-born infant. This code is for use as a single diagnosis code and is not to be used with any other code in the range 630-676.

Use additional code to indicate outcome of delivery (V27.0)

> **EXCLUDES** *breech delivery (assisted) (spontaneous) NOS (652.2) delivery by vacuum extractor, forceps, cesarean section, or breech extraction, without specified complication (669.5-669.7)*

AHA: 2Q, '02, 10; 3Q, '01, 12; 3Q, '00, 5; 4Q, '95, 28, 59

TIP: Code 650 is to be assigned only for the episode of care during which the patient delivers and may be assigned if the patient is admitted for induction of labor.

O80 Encounter for full-term uncomplicated delivery　I-10

✓4th 651 Multiple gestation

§ ✓5th **651.0 Twin pregnancy**　M♀
[0,1,3]
> **EXCLUDES** *fetal conjoined twins (678.1)*
> **AHA:** 3Q, '06, 16
> **O30.009** Twin pregnancy unspecified, unspecified trimester　I-10

§ ✓5th **651.1 Triplet pregnancy**　M♀
[0,1,3]

§ ✓5th **651.2 Quadruplet pregnancy**　M♀
[0,1,3]

§ ✓5th **651.3 Twin pregnancy with fetal loss and**　M♀
[0,1,3] **retention of one fetus**
> Vanishing twin syndrome (651.33)

§ ✓5th **651.4 Triplet pregnancy with fetal loss and**　M♀
[0,1,3] **retention of one or more fetus(es)**

§ ✓5th **651.5 Quadruplet pregnancy with fetal loss**　M♀
[0,1,3] **and retention of one or more fetus(es)**

§ ✓5th **651.6 Other multiple pregnancy with fetal loss and**　M♀
[0,1,3] **retention of one or more fetus(es)**

§ ✓5th **651.7 Multiple gestation following (elective)**　M♀
[0,1,3] **fetal reduction**
> Fetal reduction of multiple fetuses reduced to single fetus
> **AHA:** 3Q, '06, 18; **For code 651.71:** 4Q, '05, 81

§ ✓5th **651.8 Other specified multiple gestation**　M♀
[0,1,3]

§ ✓5th **651.9 Unspecified multiple gestation**　M♀
[0,1,3]

✓4th 652 Malposition and malpresentation of fetus
Code first any associated obstructed labor (660.0)

§ ✓5th **652.0 Unstable lie**　M♀
[0,1,3] > **DEF:** Changing fetal position.

§ ✓5th **652.1 Breech or other malpresentation successfully**　M♀
[0,1,3] **converted to cephalic presentation**
> Cephalic version NOS

Malposition and Malpresentation

Breech
Mother's pelvis
Face (mentum)
Shoulder (arm prolapse)
Compound (extremity together with head)
Oblique

§ ✓5th **652.2 Breech presentation without mention of version**　M♀
[0,1,3]
> Breech delivery (assisted) (spontaneous) NOS
> Buttocks presentation
> Complete breech
> Frank breech
> **EXCLUDES** *footling presentation (652.8) incomplete breech (652.8)*
> **DEF:** Fetal presentation of buttocks or feet at birth canal.
> **O32.1xx0** Maternal care breech presentation not applic/uns　I-10

§ ✓5th **652.3 Transverse or oblique presentation**　M♀
[0,1,3]
> Oblique lie　　　Transverse lie
> **EXCLUDES** *transverse arrest of fetal head (660.3)*
> **DEF:** Delivery of fetus, shoulder first.

§ ✓5th **652.4 Face or brow presentation**　M♀
[0,1,3]
> Mentum presentation

§ ✓5th **652.5 High head at term**　M♀
[0,1,3]
> Failure of head to enter pelvic brim
> **O32.4xx0** Maternal care high head at term not applic/uns　I-10

§ ✓5th **652.6 Multiple gestation with malpresentation**　M♀
[0,1,3] **of one fetus or more**

§ ✓5th **652.7 Prolapsed arm**　M♀
[0,1,3]

§ ✓5th **652.8 Other specified malposition or malpresentation**　M♀
[0,1,3]
> Compound presentation

§ ✓5th **652.9 Unspecified malposition or malpresentation**　M♀
[0,1,3]

✓4th 653 Disproportion
Code first any associated obstructed labor (660.1)

§ ✓5th **653.0 Major abnormality of bony pelvis, not**　M♀
[0,1,3] **further specified**
> Pelvic deformity NOS

§ ✓5th **653.1 Generally contracted pelvis**　M♀
[0,1,3]
> Contracted pelvis NOS

§ ✓5th **653.2 Inlet contraction of pelvis**　M♀
[0,1,3]
> Inlet contraction (pelvis)

§ ✓5th **653.3 Outlet contraction of pelvis**　M♀
[0,1,3]
> Outlet contraction (pelvis)

§ ✓5th **653.4 Fetopelvic disproportion**　M♀
[0,1,3]
> Cephalopelvic disproportion NOS
> Disproportion of mixed maternal and fetal origin, with normally formed fetus
> **O33.4xx0** Mtrn care dispropor mtrn & fetal orig not applic　I-10

§ ✓5th **653.5 Unusually large fetus causing disproportion**　M♀
[0,1,3]
> Disproportion of fetal origin with normally formed fetus
> Fetal disproportion NOS
> **EXCLUDES** *that when the reason for medical care was concern for the fetus (656.6)*

---

§　Requires fifth digit. Valid digits are in [brackets] under each code. See beginning of section 640-649 for codes and definitions.

Complications of Pregnancy, Childbirth & Puerperium

653.6–655.9

Cephalopelvic Disproportion

Pubic symphysis

Ischial tuberosity

Contraction of pelvic outlet (from below)

Cephalopelvic disproportion due to: Contraction of pelvic inlet, or large fetus, or hydrocephalus

Pubic symphysis

Pelvic inlet from above

§ √5th **653.6** **Hydrocephalic fetus causing disproportion** Ⓜ♀
[0,1,3]   **EXCLUDES** *that when the reason for medical care was concern for the fetus (655.0)*

§ √5th **653.7** **Other fetal abnormality causing disproportion** Ⓜ♀
[0,1,3]   Fetal:
     ascites
     hydrops
     myelomeningocele
     sacral teratoma
     tumor
     EXCLUDES *conjoined twins causing disproportion (678.1)*

§ √5th **653.8** **Disproportion of other origin** Ⓜ♀
[0,1,3]   **EXCLUDES** *shoulder (girdle) dystocia (660.4)*

§ √5th **653.9** **Unspecified disproportion** Ⓜ♀
[0,1,3]

√4th **654** **Abnormality of organs and soft tissues of pelvis**
   INCLUDES the listed conditions during pregnancy, childbirth, or the puerperium
   Code first any associated obstructed labor (660.2)
   EXCLUDES *trauma to perineum and vulva complicating current delivery (664.0-664.9)*

§ √5th **654.0** **Congenital abnormalities of uterus** Ⓜ♀
[0-4]   Double uterus
     Uterus bicornis

§ √5th **654.1** **Tumors of body of uterus** Ⓜ♀
[0-4]   Uterine fibroids

§ √5th **654.2** **Previous cesarean delivery** Ⓜ♀
[0,1,3]   Uterine scar from previous cesarean delivery
     AHA: 1Q, '92, 8
     034.21 Maternal care for scar from prev cesarean del I-10

§ √5th **654.3** **Retroverted and incarcerated gravid uterus** Ⓜ♀
[0-4]   **DEF:** Retroverted: tilted back uterus; no change in angle of longitudinal axis.
     DEF: Incarcerated: immobile, fixed uterus.

§ √5th **654.4** **Other abnormalities in shape or position of gravid uterus and of neighboring structures** Ⓜ♀
[0-4]   Cystocele
     Pelvic floor repair
     Pendulous abdomen
     Prolapse of gravid uterus
     Rectocele
     Rigid pelvic floor

§ √5th **654.5** **Cervical incompetence** Ⓜ♀
[0-4]   Presence of Shirodkar suture with or without mention of cervical incompetence
     DEF: Abnormal cervix; tendency to dilate in second trimester; causes premature fetal expulsion.
     DEF: Shirodkar suture: purse-string suture used to artificially close incompetent cervix.

§ √5th **654.6** **Other congenital or acquired abnormality of cervix** Ⓜ♀
[0-4]   Cicatricial cervix
     Polyp of cervix
     Previous surgery to cervix
     Rigid cervix (uteri)
     Stenosis or stricture of cervix
     Tumor of cervix

§ √5th **654.7** **Congenital or acquired abnormality of vagina** Ⓜ♀
[0-4]   Previous surgery to vagina
     Septate vagina
     Stenosis of vagina (acquired) (congenital)
     Stricture of vagina
     Tumor of vagina

§ √5th **654.8** **Congenital or acquired abnormality of vulva** Ⓜ♀
[0-4]   Anal sphincter tear (healed) (old) complicating delivery
     Fibrosis of perineum
     Persistent hymen
     Previous surgery to perineum or vulva
     Rigid perineum
     Tumor of vulva
     EXCLUDES *anal sphincter tear (healed) (old) not associated with delivery (569.43)*
         varicose veins of vulva (671.1)
     AHA: 1Q, '03, 14

§ √5th **654.9** **Other and unspecified** Ⓜ♀
[0-4]   Uterine scar NEC

√4th **655** **Known or suspected fetal abnormality affecting management of mother**
   INCLUDES the listed conditions in the fetus as a reason for observation or obstetrical care of the mother, or for termination of pregnancy
   AHA: 3Q, '90, 4
   TIP: Only assign when the fetal condition affects the management of the mother. Assign on mother's chart when in utero procedures are performed on the fetus.

§ √5th **655.0** **Central nervous system malformation in fetus** Ⓜ♀
[0,1,3]   Fetal or suspected fetal:
     anencephaly
     hydrocephalus
     spina bifida (with myelomeningocele)

§ √5th **655.1** **Chromosomal abnormality in fetus** Ⓜ♀
[0,1,3]

§ √5th **655.2** **Hereditary disease in family possibly affecting fetus** Ⓜ♀
[0,1,3]

§ √5th **655.3** **Suspected damage to fetus from viral disease in the mother** Ⓜ♀
[0,1,3]   Suspected damage to fetus from maternal rubella

§ √5th **655.4** **Suspected damage to fetus from other disease in the mother** Ⓜ♀
[0,1,3]   Suspected damage to fetus from maternal:
     alcohol addiction
     listeriosis
     toxoplasmosis

§ √5th **655.5** **Suspected damage to fetus from drugs** Ⓜ♀
[0,1,3]

§ √5th **655.6** **Suspected damage to fetus from radiation** Ⓜ♀
[0,1,3]

§ √5th **655.7** **Decreased fetal movements** Ⓜ♀
[0,1,3]   **AHA:** 4Q, '97, 41

§ √5th **655.8** **Other known or suspected fetal abnormality, not elsewhere classified** Ⓜ♀
[0,1,3]   Suspected damage to fetus from:
     environmental toxins
     intrauterine contraceptive device
     AHA: 3Q, '06, 16, 18

§ √5th **655.9** **Unspecified** Ⓜ♀
[0,1,3]

---

§   Requires fifth digit. Valid digits are in [brackets] under each code. See beginning of section 640-649 for codes and definitions.

Ⓝ Newborn Age: 0   Ⓟ Pediatric Age: 0-17   Ⓜ Maternity Age: 12-55   Ⓐ Adult Age: 15-124

✓4ᵗʰ 656 Other known or suspected fetal and placental problems affecting management of mother

> **EXCLUDES** *fetal hematologic conditions (678.0)*
> *suspected placental problems not found (V89.02)*

§ **✓5ᵗʰ 656.0 Fetal-maternal hemorrhage** Ⓜ♀
[0,1,3]
Leakage (microscopic) of fetal blood into maternal circulation

§ **✓5ᵗʰ 656.1 Rhesus isoimmunization** Ⓜ♀
[0,1,3]
Anti-D [Rh] antibodies
Rh incompatibility
DEF: Antibodies developing against Rh factor; mother with Rh negative develops antibodies against Rh positive fetus.
036.0190 Mtrn care anti-D Rh antibods uns tri not applic I-10

§ **✓5ᵗʰ 656.2 Isoimmunization from other and unspecified** Ⓜ♀
[0,1,3] **blood-group incompatibility**
ABO isoimmunization
AHA: 4Q, '06, 135

§ **✓5ᵗʰ 656.3 Fetal distress** Ⓜ♀
[0,1,3]
Fetal metabolic acidemia
> **EXCLUDES** *abnormal fetal acid-base balance (656.8)*
> *abnormality in fetal heart rate or rhythm (659.7)*
> *fetal bradycardia (659.7)*
> *fetal tachycardia (659.7)*
> *meconium in liquor (656.8)*
DEF: Life-threatening disorder; fetal anoxia, hemolytic disease and other miscellaneous diseases cause fetal distress.
AHA: N-D, '86, 4

§ **✓5ᵗʰ 656.4 Intrauterine death** Ⓜ♀
[0,1,3]
Fetal death:
  NOS
  after completion of 22 weeks' gestation
  late
Missed delivery
> **EXCLUDES** *missed abortion (632)*

§ **✓5ᵗʰ 656.5 Poor fetal growth** Ⓜ♀
[0,1,3]
"Light-for-dates"
"Placental insufficiency"
"Small-for-dates"
036.5190 Mtrn care known/spct placental insuff uns tri I-10

§ **✓5ᵗʰ 656.6 Excessive fetal growth** Ⓜ♀
[0,1,3]
"Large-for-dates"
036.60x0 Mtrn care excess fetl grwth uns tri not applic I-10

§ **✓5ᵗʰ 656.7 Other placental conditions** Ⓜ♀
[0,1,3]
Abnormal placenta
Placental infarct
> **EXCLUDES** *placental polyp (674.4)*
> *placentitis (658.4)*

§ **✓5ᵗʰ 656.8 Other specified fetal and placental problems** Ⓜ♀
[0,1,3]
Abnormal acid-base balance
Intrauterine acidosis
Lithopedian
Meconium in liquor
Subchorionic hematoma
DEF: Lithopedion: Calcified fetus; not expelled by mother.
036.20x0 Mtrn care hydrops fetalis uns tri not applic/uns I-10

§ **✓5ᵗʰ 656.9 Unspecified fetal and placental problem** Ⓜ♀
[0,1,3]

✓4ᵗʰ 657 Polyhydramnios Ⓜ♀
[0,1,3]

§ **✓5ᵗʰ** Use 0 as fourth-digit for this category
Hydramnios
> **EXCLUDES** *suspected polyhydramnios not found (V89.01)*
DEF: Excess amniotic fluid.
AHA: 3Q, '06, 16; 4Q, '91, 26
040.9xx0 Polyhydramnios uns trimester not applicable/uns I-10

✓4ᵗʰ 658 Other problems associated with amniotic cavity and membranes

> **EXCLUDES** *amniotic fluid embolism (673.1)*
> *suspected problems with amniotic cavity and*
> *membranes not found (V89.01)*

§ **✓5ᵗʰ 658.0 Oligohydramnios** Ⓜ♀
[0,1,3]
Oligohydramnios without mention of rupture of membranes
DEF: Deficient amount of amniotic fluid.
AHA: 3Q, '06, 16
041.00x0 Oligohydramnios uns trimester not I-10
applicable/uns

§ **✓5ᵗʰ 658.1 Premature rupture of membranes** Ⓜ♀
[0,1,3]
Rupture of amniotic sac less than 24 hours prior to the onset of labor
AHA: For code 658.13: 1Q, '01, 5; 4Q, '98, 77
042.00 Prmat rom ool w/in 24 hrs of rup uns I-10
wks gestatn

§ **✓5ᵗʰ 658.2 Delayed delivery after spontaneous or** Ⓜ♀
[0,1,3] **unspecified rupture of membranes**
Prolonged rupture of membranes NOS
Rupture of amniotic sac 24 hours or more prior to the onset of labor

§ **✓5ᵗʰ 658.3 Delayed delivery after artificial rupture** Ⓜ♀
[0,1,3] **of membranes**

§ **✓5ᵗʰ 658.4 Infection of amniotic cavity** Ⓜ♀
[0,1,3]
Amnionitis
Chorioamnionitis
Membranitis
Placentitis
041.1090 Inf amniotic sac & memb uns, uns tri I-10
not applic/uns

§ **✓5ᵗʰ 658.8 Other** Ⓜ♀
[0,1,3]
Amnion nodosum
Amniotic cyst

§ **✓5ᵗʰ 658.9 Unspecified** Ⓜ♀
[0,1,3]

✓4ᵗʰ 659 Other indications for care or intervention related to labor and delivery, not elsewhere classified

§ **✓5ᵗʰ 659.0 Failed mechanical induction** Ⓜ♀
[0,1,3]
Failure of induction of labor by surgical or other instrumental methods

§ **✓5ᵗʰ 659.1 Failed medical or unspecified induction** Ⓜ♀
[0,1,3]
Failed induction NOS
Failure of induction of labor by medical methods, such as oxytocic drugs
061.9 Failed induction of labor unspecified I-10

§ **✓5ᵗʰ 659.2 Maternal pyrexia during labor, unspecified** Ⓜ♀
[0,1,3]
DEF: Fever during labor.
075.2 Pyrexia during labor not elsewhere classified I-10

§ **✓5ᵗʰ 659.3 Generalized infection during labor** Ⓜ♀
[0,1,3]
Septicemia during labor

§ **✓5ᵗʰ 659.4 Grand multiparity** Ⓜ♀
[0,1,3]
> **EXCLUDES** *supervision only, in pregnancy (V23.3)*
> *without current pregnancy (V61.5)*
DEF: Having borne six or more children previously.

§ **✓5ᵗʰ 659.5 Elderly primigravida** Ⓜ♀
[0,1,3]
First pregnancy in a woman who will be 35 years of age or older at expected date of delivery
> **EXCLUDES** *supervision only, in pregnancy (V23.81)*
AHA: 3Q, '01, 12
009.519 Supervisn of elderly primigravida I-10
uns trimester

---

§   Requires fifth digit. Valid digits are in [brackets] under each code. See beginning of section 640-649 for codes and definitions.

 Additional Digit Required   Unspecified Code   Other Specified Code   Manifestation Code   ▶◀ Revised Text   ● New Code   ▲ Revised Code Title

§ ✓5th **659.6 Elderly multigravida** Ⓜ♀
[0,1,3] Second or more pregnancy in a woman who will be 35 years of age or older at expected date of delivery

EXCLUDES *elderly primigravida 659.5*
supervision only, in pregnancy (V23.82)

AHA: 3Q, '01, 12

009.529 Supervisn of elderly multigravida uns trimester `I-10`

§ ✓5th **659.7 Abnormality in fetal heart rate or rhythm** Ⓜ♀
[0,1,3] Depressed fetal heart tones
Fetal:
bradycardia
tachycardia
Fetal heart rate decelerations
Non-reassuring fetal heart rate or rhythm

AHA: 4Q, '98, 48

076 Abn in fetal heart rate & rhythm comp L&D `I-10`

§ ✓5th **659.8 Other specified indications for care or** Ⓜ♀
[0,1,3] **intervention related to labor and delivery**
Pregnancy in a female less than 16 years old at expected date of delivery
Very young maternal age

AHA: 3Q, '01, 12

§ ✓5th **659.9 Unspecified indication for care or intervention** Ⓜ♀
[0,1,3] **related to labor and delivery**

COMPLICATIONS OCCURRING MAINLY IN THE COURSE OF LABOR AND DELIVERY (660-669)

The following fifth-digit subclassification is for use with categories 660-669 to denote the current episode of care. Valid fifth-digits are in [brackets] under each code.

0 unspecified as to episode of care or not applicable
1 delivered, with or without mention of antepartum condition
2 delivered, with mention of postpartum complication
3 antepartum condition or complication
4 postpartum condition or complication

✓4th **660 Obstructed labor**

AHA: 3Q, '95, 10

§ ✓5th **660.0 Obstruction caused by malposition of fetus at** Ⓜ♀
[0,1,3] **onset of labor**

Any condition classifiable to 652, causing obstruction during labor
Use additional code from 652.0-652.9 to identify condition

§ ✓5th **660.1 Obstruction by bony pelvis** Ⓜ♀
[0,1,3] Any condition classifiable to 653, causing obstruction during labor
Use additional code from 653.0-653.9 to identify condition

§ ✓5th **660.2 Obstruction by abnormal pelvic soft tissues** Ⓜ♀
[0,1,3] Prolapse of anterior lip of cervix
Any condition classifiable to 654, causing obstruction during labor
Use additional code from 654.0-654.9 to identify condition

§ ✓5th **660.3 Deep transverse arrest and persistent** Ⓜ♀
[0,1,3] **occipitoposterior position**

O64.0xx0 Obst labor incpl rotat of fetal head not applic `I-10`

§ ✓5th **660.4 Shoulder (girdle) dystocia** Ⓜ♀
[0,1,3] Impacted shoulders

DEF: Obstructed labor due to impacted fetal shoulders.

O66.0 Obstructed labor due to shoulder dystocia `I-10`

§ ✓5th **660.5 Locked twins** Ⓜ♀
[0,1,3]

§ ✓5th **660.6 Failed trial of labor, unspecified** Ⓜ♀
[0,1,3] Failed trial of labor, without mention of condition or suspected condition

§ ✓5th **660.7 Failed forceps or vacuum extractor,** Ⓜ♀
[0,1,3] **unspecified**
Application of ventouse or forceps, without mention of condition

§ ✓5th **660.8 Other causes of obstructed labor** Ⓜ♀
[0,1,3] Use additional code to identify condition

AHA: 4Q, '04, 88

§ ✓5th **660.9 Unspecified obstructed labor** Ⓜ♀
[0,1,3] Dystocia:
NOS
fetal NOS
maternal NOS

✓4th **661 Abnormality of forces of labor**

§ ✓5th **661.0 Primary uterine inertia** Ⓜ♀
[0,1,3] Failure of cervical dilation
Hypotonic uterine dysfunction, primary
Prolonged latent phase of labor

DEF: Lack of efficient contractions during labor causing prolonged labor.

O62.0 Primary inadequate contractions `I-10`

§ ✓5th **661.1 Secondary uterine inertia** Ⓜ♀
[0,1,3] Arrested active phase of labor
Hypotonic uterine dysfunction, secondary

O62.1 Secondary uterine inertia `I-10`

§ ✓5th **661.2 Other and unspecified uterine inertia** Ⓜ♀
[0,1,3] Atony of uterus without hemorrhage
Desultory labor
Irregular labor
Poor contractions
Slow slope active phase of labor

EXCLUDES *atony of uterus with hemorrhage (666.1)*
postpartum atony of uterus without hemorrhage (669.8)

§ ✓5th **661.3 Precipitate labor** Ⓜ♀
[0,1,3] **DEF:** Rapid labor and delivery.

§ ✓5th **661.4 Hypertonic, incoordinate, or prolonged** Ⓜ♀
[0,1,3] **uterine contractions**
Cervical spasm
Contraction ring (dystocia)
Dyscoordinate labor
Hourglass contraction of uterus
Hypertonic uterine dysfunction
Incoordinate uterine action
Retraction ring (Bandl's) (pathological)
Tetanic contractions
Uterine dystocia NOS
Uterine spasm

§ ✓5th **661.9 Unspecified abnormality of labor** Ⓜ♀
[0,1,3]

✓4th **662 Long labor**

§ ✓5th **662.0 Prolonged first stage** Ⓜ♀
[0,1,3]

§ ✓5th **662.1 Prolonged labor, unspecified** Ⓜ♀
[0,1,3]

§ ✓5th **662.2 Prolonged second stage** Ⓜ♀
[0,1,3]

§ ✓5th **662.3 Delayed delivery of second twin, triplet, etc.** Ⓜ♀
[0,1,3]

✓4th **663 Umbilical cord complications**

§ ✓5th **663.0 Prolapse of cord** Ⓜ♀
[0,1,3] Presentation of cord

DEF: Abnormal presentation of fetus; marked by protruding umbilical cord during labor; can cause fetal death.

§ ✓5th **663.1 Cord around neck, with compression** Ⓜ♀
[0,1,3] Cord tightly around neck

O69.1xx0 L&D comp by cord arnd neck with comprs not applic/uns `I-10`

---

§ Requires fifth digit. Valid digits are in [brackets] under each code. See beginning of section of 640-649 for codes and definitions.

Ⓝ Newborn Age: 0   Ⓟ Pediatric Age: 0-17   Ⓜ Maternity Age: 12-55   Ⓐ Adult Age: 15-124

§ ✓5ᵗʰ **663.2** **Other and unspecified cord entanglement,** Ⓜ♀
[0,1,3] **with compression**
Entanglement of cords of twins in mono-amniotic sac
Knot in cord (with compression)

§ ✓5ᵗʰ **663.3** **Other and unspecified cord entanglement,** Ⓜ♀
[0,1,3] **without mention of compression**
AHA: For code 663.31: 2Q, '03, 9

069.2xx0 L&D comp by oth cord entanglement not Ⓘ-10
applic/uns

§ ✓5ᵗʰ **663.4** **Short cord** Ⓜ♀
[0,1,3]

§ ✓5ᵗʰ **663.5** **Vasa previa** Ⓜ♀
[0,1,3] **DEF:** Abnormal presentation of fetus marked by blood vessels
of umbilical cord in front of fetal head.

§ ✓5ᵗʰ **663.6** **Vascular lesions of cord** Ⓜ♀
[0,1,3] Bruising of cord
Hematoma of cord
Thrombosis of vessels of cord

§ ✓5ᵗʰ **663.8** **Other umbilical cord complications** Ⓜ♀
[0,1,3] Velamentous insertion of umbilical cord

§ ✓5ᵗʰ **663.9** **Unspecified umbilical cord complication** Ⓜ♀
[0,1,3]

✓4ᵗʰ **664** **Trauma to perineum and vulva during delivery**
INCLUDES damage from instruments
that from extension of episiotomy
AHA: 1Q, '92, 11; N-D, '84, 10

§ ✓5ᵗʰ **664.0** **First-degree perineal laceration** Ⓜ♀
[0,1,4] Perineal laceration, rupture, or tear involving:
fourchette
hymen
labia
skin
vagina
vulva

070.0 First degree perineal laceration during delivery Ⓘ-10

§ ✓5ᵗʰ **664.1** **Second-degree perineal laceration** Ⓜ♀
[0,1,4] Perineal laceration, rupture, or tear (following episiotomy)
involving:
pelvic floor
perineal muscles
vaginal muscles
EXCLUDES that involving anal sphincter (664.2)
AHA: For code 664.11: ▶4Q, '08, 192◀

070.1 Second degree perineal laceration dur delivery Ⓘ-10

§ ✓5ᵗʰ **664.2** **Third-degree perineal laceration** Ⓜ♀
[0,1,4] Perineal laceration, rupture, or tear
(following episiotomy) involving:
anal sphincter
rectovaginal septum
sphincter NOS
EXCLUDES anal sphincter tear during delivery not
associated with third-degree perineal
laceration (664.6)
that with anal or rectal mucosal laceration
(664.3)

070.2 Third degree perineal laceration during delivery Ⓘ-10

§ ✓5ᵗʰ **664.3** **Fourth-degree perineal laceration** Ⓜ♀
[0,1,4] Perineal laceration, rupture, or tear as
classifiable to 664.2 and involving also:
anal mucosa
rectal mucosa

§ ✓5ᵗʰ **664.4** **Unspecified perineal laceration** Ⓜ♀
[0,1,4] Central laceration
AHA: 1Q, '92, 8

§ ✓5ᵗʰ **664.5** **Vulval and perineal hematoma** Ⓜ♀
[0,1,4] **AHA:** N-D, '84, 10

Perineal Lacerations

§ ✓5ᵗʰ **664.6** **Anal sphincter tear complicating delivery,** Ⓜ♀
[0,1,4] **not associated with third-degree perineal laceration**
EXCLUDES third-degree perineal laceration (664.2)
AHA: For code 664.61: 4Q, '07, 88, 90

§ ✓5ᵗʰ **664.8** **Other specified trauma to perineum and vulva** Ⓜ♀
[0,1,4] **AHA:** For code 664.81: 4Q, '07, 125
TIP: Assign when documentation indicates periurethral laceration only.

§ ✓5ᵗʰ **664.9** **Unspecified trauma to perineum and vulva** Ⓜ♀
[0,1,4]

✓4ᵗʰ **665** **Other obstetrical trauma**
INCLUDES damage from instruments

§ ✓5ᵗʰ **665.0** **Rupture of uterus before onset of labor** Ⓜ♀
[0,1,3]

§ ✓5ᵗʰ **665.1** **Rupture of uterus during labor** Ⓜ♀
[0,1] Rupture of uterus NOS

§ ✓5ᵗʰ **665.2** **Inversion of uterus** Ⓜ♀
[0,2,4]

§ ✓5ᵗʰ **665.3** **Laceration of cervix** Ⓜ♀
[0,1,4]

§ ✓5ᵗʰ **665.4** **High vaginal laceration** Ⓜ♀
[0,1,4] Laceration of vaginal wall or sulcus without mention of
perineal laceration

071.4 Obstetric high vaginal laceration alone Ⓘ-10

§ ✓5ᵗʰ **665.5** **Other injury to pelvic organs** Ⓜ♀
[0,1,4] Injury to:
bladder
urethra
AHA: M-A, '87, 10

071.5 Other obstetric injury to pelvic organs Ⓘ-10

§ ✓5ᵗʰ **665.6** **Damage to pelvic joints and ligaments** Ⓜ♀
[0,1,4] Avulsion of inner symphyseal cartilage
Damage to coccyx
Separation of symphysis (pubis)
AHA: N-D, '84, 12

§ ✓5ᵗʰ **665.7** **Pelvic hematoma** Ⓜ♀
[0,1,2,4] Hematoma of vagina

§ ✓5ᵗʰ **665.8** **Other specified obstetrical trauma** Ⓜ♀
[0-4]

§ ✓5ᵗʰ **665.9** **Unspecified obstetrical trauma** Ⓜ♀
[0-4]

✓4ᵗʰ **666** **Postpartum hemorrhage**
AHA: 1Q, '88, 14

§ ✓5ᵗʰ **666.0** **Third-stage hemorrhage** Ⓜ♀
[0,2,4] Hemorrhage associated with retained,
trapped, or adherent placenta
Retained placenta NOS

---

§ Requires fifth digit. Valid digits are in [brackets] under each code. See beginning of section 640-649 for codes and definitions.

| ✓4ᵗʰ ✓5ᵗʰ Additional Digit Required | Unspecified Code | Other Specified Code | Manifestation Code | ▶◀ Revised Text | ● New Code | ▲ Revised Code Title |

Complications of Pregnancy, Childbirth & Puerperium

666.1–670.8

§ ✓5ᵗʰ **666.1 Other immediate postpartum hemorrhage** Ⓜ♀
[0,2,4] Atony of uterus with hemorrhage
Hemorrhage within the first 24 hours following delivery of placenta
Postpartum atony of uterus with hemorrhage
Postpartum hemorrhage (atonic) NOS
> **EXCLUDES** *atony of uterus without hemorrhage (661.2)*
> *postpartum atony of uterus without hemorrhage (669.8)*

072.1 Other immediate postpartum hemorrhage Ⓘ-10

§ ✓5ᵗʰ **666.2 Delayed and secondary postpartum hemorrhage** Ⓜ♀
[0,2,4] Hemorrhage:
after the first 24 hours following delivery
associated with retained portions of placenta or membranes
Postpartum hemorrhage specified as delayed or secondary
Retained products of conception NOS, following delivery

§ ✓5ᵗʰ **666.3 Postpartum coagulation defects** Ⓜ♀
[0,2,4] Postpartum:
afibrinogenemia
fibrinolysis

✓4ᵗʰ **667 Retained placenta or membranes, without hemorrhage**
Requires fifth digit; valid digits are in [brackets] under each code. See beginning of section 660-669 for definitions.
DEF: Postpartum condition resulting from failure to expel placental membrane tissues due to failed contractions of uterine wall.
AHA: 1Q, '88, 14
TIP: A retained placenta is one that has not separated or been expelled within one hour after completion of the second stage of labor (birth of the fetus).

§ ✓5ᵗʰ **667.0 Retained placenta without hemorrhage** Ⓜ♀
[0,2,4] Placenta accreta
Retained placenta: } without hemorrhage
NOS
total

073.0 Retained placenta without hemorrhage Ⓘ-10

§ ✓5ᵗʰ **667.1 Retained portions of placenta or** Ⓜ♀
[0,2,4] **membranes, without hemorrhage**
Retained products of conception following delivery, without hemorrhage

✓4ᵗʰ **668 Complications of the administration of anesthetic or other sedation in labor and delivery**
> **INCLUDES** complications arising from the administration of a general or local anesthetic, analgesic, or other sedation in labor and delivery
> **EXCLUDES** *reaction to spinal or lumbar puncture (349.0)*
> *spinal headache (349.0)*
Use additional code(s) to further specify complication

§ ✓5ᵗʰ **668.0 Pulmonary complications** Ⓜ♀
[0-4] Inhalation (aspiration) of
stomach contents or secretions
Mendelson's syndrome
Pressure collapse of lung
} following anesthesia or other sedation in labor or delivery

§ ✓5ᵗʰ **668.1 Cardiac complications** Ⓜ♀
[0-4] Cardiac arrest or failure following anesthesia or other sedation in labor and delivery

§ ✓5ᵗʰ **668.2 Central nervous system complications** Ⓜ♀
[0-4] Cerebral anoxia following anesthesia or other sedation in labor and delivery

§ ✓5ᵗʰ **668.8 Other complications of anesthesia or other sedation in labor and delivery** Ⓜ♀
[0-4]
AHA: 2Q, '99, 9

§ ✓5ᵗʰ **668.9 Unspecified complication of anesthesia and other sedation** Ⓜ♀
[0-4]

✓4ᵗʰ **669 Other complications of labor and delivery, not elsewhere classified**

§ ✓5ᵗʰ **669.0 Maternal distress** Ⓜ♀
[0-4] Metabolic disturbance in labor and delivery

§ ✓5ᵗʰ **669.1 Shock during or following labor and delivery** Ⓜ♀
[0-4] Obstetric shock

§ ✓5ᵗʰ **669.2 Maternal hypotension syndrome** Ⓜ♀
[0-4] **DEF:** Low arterial blood pressure, in mother, during labor and delivery.

▲ § ✓5ᵗʰ **669.3 Acute kidney failure following labor and delivery** Ⓜ♀
[0,2,4]

§ ✓5ᵗʰ **669.4 Other complications of obstetrical surgery and procedures** Ⓜ♀
[0-4]
Cardiac:
arrest
failure
Cerebral anoxia
} following cesarean or other obstetrical surgery or procedure, including delivery NOS
> **EXCLUDES** *complications of obstetrical surgical wounds (674.1-674.3)*

§ ✓5ᵗʰ **669.5 Forceps or vacuum extractor delivery without mention of indication** Ⓜ♀
[0,1] Delivery by ventouse, without mention of indication

§ ✓5ᵗʰ **669.6 Breech extraction, without mention of indication** Ⓜ♀
[0,1]
> **EXCLUDES** *breech delivery NOS (652.2)*

§ ✓5ᵗʰ **669.7 Cesarean delivery, without mention of indication** Ⓜ♀
[0,1]
AHA: For code 669.71: 1Q, '01, 11
082 Encounter for cesarean delivery w/o indication Ⓘ-10

§ ✓5ᵗʰ **669.8 Other complications of labor and delivery** Ⓜ♀
[0-4] **AHA:** 4Q, '06, 135

§ ✓5ᵗʰ **669.9 Unspecified complication of labor and delivery** Ⓜ♀
[0-4]

COMPLICATIONS OF THE PUERPERIUM (670-677)

Note: Categories 671 and 673-676 include the listed conditions even if they occur during pregnancy or childbirth.

The following fifth-digit subclassification is for use with categories 670-676 to denote the current episode of care. Valid fifth-digits are in [brackets] under each code.
0 unspecified as to episode of care or not applicable
1 delivered, with or without mention of antepartum condition
2 delivered, with mention of postpartum complication
3 antepartum condition or complication
4 postpartum condition or complication

✓4ᵗʰ **670 Major puerperal infection**
> **EXCLUDES** *infection following abortion (639.0)*
> *minor genital tract infection following delivery (646.6)*
> *puerperal pyrexia NOS (672)*
> *puerperal fever NOS (672)*
> *puerperal pyrexia of unknown origin (672)*
> *urinary tract infection following delivery (646.6)*
DEF: Infection and inflammation, following childbirth.
AHA: 4Q, '91, 26; 2Q, '91, 7

▲ § ✓5ᵗʰ **670.0 Major puerperal infection, unspecified** Ⓜ♀
[0,2,4] **AHA: For code 670.02:** 3Q, '07, 8

● § ✓5ᵗʰ **670.1 Puerperal endometritis** Ⓜ♀
[0,2,4]

● § ✓5ᵗʰ **670.2 Puerperal sepsis** Ⓜ♀
[0,2,4] Puerperal pyemia

● § ✓5ᵗʰ **670.3 Puerperal septic thrombophlebitis** Ⓜ♀
[0,2,4]

● § ✓5ᵗʰ **670.8 Other major puerperal infection** Ⓜ♀
[0,2,4] Puerperal:
pelvic cellulitis
peritonitis
salpingitis

§ Requires fifth digit. Valid digits are in [brackets] under each code. See beginning of section 640-649 for codes and definitions.

Ⓝ Newborn Age: 0   Ⓟ Pediatric Age: 0-17   Ⓜ Maternity Age: 12-55   Ⓐ Adult Age: 15-124

✓4ᵗʰ **671 Venous complications in pregnancy and the puerperium**

> **EXCLUDES** ▶personal history of venous complications prior to pregnancy, such as:
> thrombophlebitis (V12.52)
> thrombosis and embolism (V12.51)◄

§ ✓5ᵗʰ **671.0 Varicose veins of legs**   Ⓜ♀
[0-4]   Varicose veins NOS
DEF: Distended, tortuous veins on legs associated with pregnancy.

§ ✓5ᵗʰ **671.1 Varicose veins of vulva and perineum**   Ⓜ♀
[0-4]   **DEF:** Distended, tortuous veins on external female genitalia associated with pregnancy.

§ ✓5ᵗʰ **671.2 Superficial thrombophlebitis**   Ⓜ♀
[0-4]   ▶Phlebitis NOS◄
Thrombophlebitis (superficial)
▶Thrombosis NOS◄

§ ✓5ᵗʰ **671.3 Deep phlebothrombosis, antepartum**   Ⓜ♀
[0,1,3]   Deep vein thrombosis antepartum
▶Use additional code to identify the deep vein thrombosis (453.40-453.42, 453.50-453.52, 453.72-453.79, 453.82-453.89)◄
▶Use additional code for long term (current) use of anticoagulants, if applicable (V58.61)◄

§ ✓5ᵗʰ **671.4 Deep phlebothrombosis, postpartum**   Ⓜ♀
[0,2,4]   Deep-vein thrombosis, postpartum
Pelvic thrombophlebitis, postpartum
Phlegmasia alba dolens (puerperal)
▶Use additional code to identify the deep vein thrombosis (453.40-453.42, 453.50-453.52, 453.72-453.79, 453.82-453.89)◄
▶Use additional code for long term (current) use of anticoagulants, if applicable (V58.61)◄

§ ✓5ᵗʰ **671.5 Other phlebitis and thrombosis**   Ⓜ♀
[0-4]   Cerebral venous thrombosis
Thrombosis of intracranial venous sinus

§ ✓5ᵗʰ **671.8 Other venous complications**   Ⓜ♀
[0-4]   Hemorrhoids

§ ✓5ᵗʰ **671.9 Unspecified venous complication**   Ⓜ♀
[0-4]

✓4ᵗʰ **672 Pyrexia of unknown origin during the puerperium**   Ⓜ♀
[0,2,4]

§ ✓5ᵗʰ   Use 0 as fourth-digit for this category

Postpartum fever NOS
Puerperal fever NOS
Puerperal pyrexia NOS
DEF: Fever of unknown origin experienced by the mother after childbirth.
AHA: 4Q, '91, 26
086.4 Pyrexia of unknown origin following delivery   Ⅰ-10

✓4ᵗʰ **673 Obstetrical pulmonary embolism**

INCLUDES pulmonary emboli in pregnancy, childbirth, or the puerperium, or specified as puerperal
EXCLUDES embolism following abortion (639.6)

§ ✓5ᵗʰ **673.0 Obstetrical air embolism**   Ⓜ♀
[0-4]   **DEF:** Sudden blocking of pulmonary artery with air or nitrogen bubbles during puerperium.

§ ✓5ᵗʰ **673.1 Amniotic fluid embolism**   Ⓜ♀
[0-4]   **DEF:** Sudden onset of pulmonary artery blockage from amniotic fluid entering the mother's circulation near the end of pregnancy due to strong uterine contractions.

§ ✓5ᵗʰ **673.2 Obstetrical blood-clot embolism**   Ⓜ♀
[0-4]   Puerperal pulmonary embolism NOS
AHA: For code 673.24: 1Q, '05, 6
DEF: Blood clot blocking artery in the lung; associated with pregnancy.
TIP: If a pregnant or postpartum patient develops a pulmonary embolism that progresses to acute respiratory failure, the code for the pregnancy/delivery complication (673.2X) should be sequenced first.

§ ✓5ᵗʰ **673.3 Obstetrical pyemic and septic embolism**   Ⓜ♀
[0-4]

§ ✓5ᵗʰ **673.8 Other pulmonary embolism**   Ⓜ♀
[0-4]   Fat embolism

✓4ᵗʰ **674 Other and unspecified complications of the puerperium, not elsewhere classified**

§ ✓5ᵗʰ **674.0 Cerebrovascular disorders in the puerperium**   Ⓜ♀
[0-4]   Any condition classifiable to 430-434, 436-437 occurring during pregnancy, childbirth, or the puerperium, or specified as puerperal
EXCLUDES intracranial venous sinus thrombosis (671.5)

§ ✓5ᵗʰ **674.1 Disruption of cesarean wound**   Ⓜ♀
[0,2,4]   Dehiscence or disruption of uterine wound
EXCLUDES uterine rupture before onset of labor (665.0)
uterine rupture during labor (665.1)

§ ✓5ᵗʰ **674.2 Disruption of perineal wound**   Ⓜ♀
[0,2,4]   Breakdown of perineum
Disruption of wound of:
episiotomy
perineal laceration
Secondary perineal tear
AHA: For code 674.24: 1Q, '97, 9

§ ✓5ᵗʰ **674.3 Other complications of obstetrical surgical wounds**   Ⓜ♀
[0,2,4]
Hematoma ⎫
Hemorrhage ⎬ of cesarean section or perineal
Infection ⎭ wound
EXCLUDES damage from instruments in delivery (664.0-665.9)
AHA: 2Q, '91, 7

§ ✓5ᵗʰ **674.4 Placental polyp**   Ⓜ♀
[0,2,4]

§ ✓5ᵗʰ **674.5 Peripartum cardiomyopathy**   Ⓜ♀
[0-4]   Postpartum cardiomyopathy
DEF: Any structural or functional abnormality of the ventricular myocardium, non-inflammatory disease of obscure or unknown etiology with onset during the postpartum period.
AHA: 4Q, '03, 65

§ ✓5ᵗʰ **674.8 Other**   Ⓜ♀
[0,2,4]   Hepatorenal syndrome, following delivery
Postpartum:
subinvolution of uterus
uterine hypertrophy
AHA: 3Q, '98, 16

§ ✓5ᵗʰ **674.9 Unspecified**   Ⓜ♀
[0,2,4]   Sudden death of unknown cause during the puerperium

✓4ᵗʰ **675 Infections of the breast and nipple associated with childbirth**

INCLUDES the listed conditions during pregnancy, childbirth, or the puerperium

§ ✓5ᵗʰ **675.0 Infections of nipple**   Ⓜ♀
[0-4]   Abscess of nipple

§ ✓5ᵗʰ **675.1 Abscess of breast**   Ⓜ♀
[0-4]   Abscess:
mammary
subareolar
submammary
purulent
retromammary
submammary

§ ✓5ᵗʰ **675.2 Nonpurulent mastitis**   Ⓜ♀
[0-4]   Lymphangitis of breast
Mastitis:
NOS
interstitial
parenchymatous

§   Requires fifth digit. Valid digits are in [brackets] under each code. See beginning of section 640-649 for codes and definitions.

§ ✓5ᵗʰ **675.8** **Other specified infections of the breast and** Ⓜ♀
[0-4] **nipple**

§ ✓5ᵗʰ **675.9** **Unspecified infection of the breast and nipple** Ⓜ♀
[0-4]

✓4ᵗʰ **676** **Other disorders of the breast associated with childbirth**
and disorders of lactation

[INCLUDES] the listed conditions during pregnancy, the
puerperium, or lactation

§ ✓5ᵗʰ **676.0** **Retracted nipple** Ⓜ♀
[0-4]

§ ✓5ᵗʰ **676.1** **Cracked nipple** Ⓜ♀
[0-4] Fissure of nipple

§ ✓5ᵗʰ **676.2** **Engorgement of breasts** Ⓜ♀
[0-4] **DEF:** Abnormal accumulation of milk in ducts of breast.

§ ✓5ᵗʰ **676.3** **Other and unspecified disorder of breast** Ⓜ♀
[0-4]

§ ✓5ᵗʰ **676.4** **Failure of lactation** Ⓜ♀
[0-4] Agalactia
DEF: Abrupt ceasing of milk secretion by breast.

§ ✓5ᵗʰ **676.5** **Suppressed lactation** Ⓜ♀
[0-4]

§ ✓5ᵗʰ **676.6** **Galactorrhea** Ⓜ♀
[0-4] [EXCLUDES] *galactorrhea not associated with childbirth*
(611.6)
DEF: Excessive or persistent milk secretion by breast; may be in
absence of nursing.

§ ✓5ᵗʰ **676.8** **Other disorders of lactation** Ⓜ♀
[0-4] Galactocele
DEF: Galactocele: Obstructed mammary gland, creating
retention cyst, results in milk-filled cysts enlarging mammary
gland.

Lactation Process: Ejection Reflex Arc

§ ✓5ᵗʰ **676.9** **Unspecified disorder of lactation** Ⓜ♀
[0-4]

677 **Late effect of complication of pregnancy, childbirth,** ♀
and the puerperium

Note: This category is to be used to indicate conditions in
632-648.9 and 651-676.9 as the cause of the late effect,
themselves classifiable elsewhere. The "late effects" include
conditions specified as such, or as sequelae, which may
occur at any time after puerperium.

Code first any sequelae

AHA: 1Q, '97, 9; 4Q, '94, 42

TIP: Sequence as a secondary diagnosis, after the code for the late
effect complication. May be assigned at any time after the initial postpartum period (six weeks following delivery).

OTHER MATERNAL AND FETAL COMPLICATIONS (678-679)

The following fifth-digit subclassification is for use with categories 678-679 to
denote the current episode of care. Valid fifth-digits are in [brackets] under each
code.

0 **unspecified as to episode of care or not applicable**
1 **delivered, with or without mention of antepartum condition**
2 **delivered, with mention of postpartum complication**
3 **antepartum condition or complication**
4 **postpartum condition or complication**

✓4ᵗʰ **678** **Other fetal conditions**

§ ✓5ᵗʰ **678.0** **Fetal hematologic conditions** Ⓜ♀
[0,1,3] Fetal anemia
Fetal thrombocytopenia
Fetal twin to twin transfusion
[EXCLUDES] *fetal and neonatal hemorrhage (772.0-772.9)*
fetal hematologic disorders affecting newborn
(776.0-776.9)
fetal-maternal hemorrhage (656.00-656.03)
isoimmunization incompatibility
(656.10-656.13, 656.20-656.23)
AHA: ▶4Q, '08, 125-127◀

§ ✓5ᵗʰ **678.1** **Fetal conjoined twins** Ⓜ♀
[0,1,3] **AHA:** ▶4Q, '08, 125-127◀

✓4ᵗʰ **679** **Complications of in utero procedures**
AHA: ▶4Q, '08, 127-128, 158◀

§ ✓5ᵗʰ **679.0** **Maternal complications from in utero procedure** Ⓜ♀
[0-4] [EXCLUDES] *maternal history of in utero procedure during*
previous pregnancy (V23.86)

§ ✓5ᵗʰ **679.1** **Fetal complications from in utero procedure** Ⓜ♀
[0-4] Fetal complications from amniocentesis
[EXCLUDES] *newborn affected by in utero procedure*
(760.61-760.64)
TIP: Assign only on the mother's record. Although there is a
fetal complication, it affects the mother's pregnancy.

---

§ Requires fifth digit. Valid digits are in [brackets] under each code. See beginning of section 640-649 for codes and definitions.

12. DISEASES OF THE SKIN AND SUBCUTANEOUS TISSUE (680-709)

INFECTIONS OF SKIN AND SUBCUTANEOUS TISSUE (680-686)

EXCLUDES *certain infections of skin classified under "Infectious and Parasitic Diseases," such as:*
erysipelas (035)
erysipeloid of Rosenbach (027.1)
herpes:
    simplex (054.0-054.9)
    zoster (053.0-053.9)
molluscum contagiosum (078.0)
viral warts ▶(078.10-078.19)◀

✓4ᵗʰ **680 Carbuncle and furuncle**

INCLUDES boil
    furunculosis

DEF: Carbuncle: necrotic boils in skin and subcutaneous tissue of neck or back mainly due to staphylococcal infection.

DEF: Furuncle: circumscribed inflammation of corium and subcutaneous tissue due to staphylococcal infection.

680.0 Face
Ear [any part]
Face [any part, except eye]
Nose (septum)
Temple (region)
EXCLUDES *eyelid (373.13)*
    lacrimal apparatus (375.31)
    orbit (376.01)

680.1 Neck

680.2 Trunk
Abdominal wall
Back [any part, except buttocks]
Breast
Chest wall
Flank
Groin
Pectoral region
Perineum
Umbilicus
EXCLUDES *buttocks (680.5)*
    external genital organs:
      female (616.4)
      male (607.2, 608.4)

680.3 Upper arm and forearm
Arm [any part, except hand]
Axilla
Shoulder

680.4 Hand
Finger [any]
Thumb
Wrist

680.5 Buttock
Anus
Gluteal region

680.6 Leg, except foot
Ankle
Hip
Knee
Thigh

680.7 Foot
Heel
Toe

680.8 Other specified sites
Head [any part, except face]
Scalp
EXCLUDES *external genital organs:*
    female (616.4)
    male (607.2, 608.4)

680.9 Unspecified site
Boil NOS
Carbuncle NOS
Furuncle NOS

Skin and Subcutaneous Layer

Hair follicle
Epidermis
Dermis
Hypodermis (subcutaneous layer)
Bulb
Sebaceous gland
Arrector pili muscle
Thick-skin epidermis
Hair shaft
Pacinian corpuscle
Hair matrix
Sweat (eccrine gland)
Sensory nerve
Blood vessels

✓4ᵗʰ **681 Cellulitis and abscess of finger and toe**

INCLUDES that with lymphangitis

Use additional code to identify organism, such as Staphylococcus (041.1)

DEF: Acute suppurative inflammation and edema in subcutaneous tissue or muscle of finger or toe.

AHA: 2Q, '91, 5; J-F, '87, 12

TIP: Coding of cellulitis due to superficial injury, burn, or frostbite requires two codes, one for the injury and one for the cellulitis. Sequencing depends on the circumstances of the admission.

✓5ᵗʰ 681.0 Finger

681.00 Cellulitis and abscess, unspecified
L03.019 Cellulitis of unspecified finger   I-10

681.01 Felon
Pulp abscess
Whitlow
EXCLUDES *herpetic whitlow (054.6)*
DEF: Painful abscess of fingertips caused by infection in the closed space of terminal phalanx.

681.02 Onychia and paronychia of finger
Panaritium   }
Perionychia   } of finger
DEF: Onychia: inflammation of nail matrix; causes nail loss.
DEF: Paronychia: inflammation of tissue folds around nail.

✓5ᵗʰ 681.1 Toe

681.10 Cellulitis and abscess, unspecified
AHA: 1Q, '05, 14
L03.039 Cellulitis of unspecified toe   I-10

681.11 Onychia and paronychia of toe
Panaritium   }
Perionychia   } of toe

681.9 Cellulitis and abscess of unspecified digit
Infection of nail NOS

✓4ᵗʰ **682 Other cellulitis and abscess**

INCLUDES abscess (acute
    cellulitis (diffuse)   } (with lymphangitis) except
    lymphangitis, acute   } of finger or toe

Use additional code to identify organism, such as Staphylococcus (041.1)

EXCLUDES *lymphangitis (chronic) (subacute) (457.2)*

DEF: Cellulitis: Acute suppurative inflammation of deep subcutaneous tissue and sometimes muscle due to infection of wound, burn or other lesion.

AHA: 2Q, '91, 5; J-F, '87, 12; S-O, '85, 10

TIP: Coding of cellulitis due to superficial injury, burn, or frostbite requires two codes, one for the injury and one for the cellulitis. Sequencing depends on the circumstances of the admission.

✓4ᵗʰ Additional Digit Required   **Unspecified Code**   **Other Specified Code**   **Manifestation Code**   ▶◀ Revised Text   ● New Code   ▲ Revised Code Title
✓5ᵗʰ
2010 ICD-9-CM   **October 2009 • Volume 1 – 213**

682.0   Face

Cheek, external	Nose, external
Chin	Submandibular
Forehead	Temple (region)

EXCLUDES   ear [any part] (380.10-380.16)
           eyelid (373.13)
           lacrimal apparatus (375.31)
           lip (528.5)
           mouth (528.3)
           nose (internal) (478.1)
           orbit (376.01)

L03.211 Cellulitis of face   `I-10`

682.1   Neck

L03.221 Cellulitis of neck   `I-10`

682.2   Trunk

Abdominal wall
Back [any part, except buttock]
Chest wall
Flank
Groin
Pectoral region
Perineum
Umbilicus, except newborn

EXCLUDES   anal and rectal regions (566)
           breast:
               NOS (611.0)
               puerperal (675.1)
           external genital organs:
               female (616.3-616.4)
               male (604.0, 607.2, 608.4)
           umbilicus, newborn (771.4)

AHA: 4Q, '98, 42

L03.319 Cellulitis of trunk unspecified   `I-10`

682.3   Upper arm and forearm

Arm [any part, except hand]
Axilla
Shoulder

EXCLUDES   hand (682.4)

AHA: 2Q, '03, 7

L03.113 Cellulitis of right upper limb   `I-10`

682.4   Hand, except fingers and thumb

Wrist

EXCLUDES   finger and thumb (681.00-681.02)

682.5   Buttock

Gluteal region

EXCLUDES   anal and rectal regions (566)

L03.317 Cellulitis of buttock   `I-10`

682.6   Leg, except foot

Ankle
Hip
Knee
Thigh

AHA: ▶1Q, '09, 10;◄ 3Q, '04, 5; 4Q, '03, 108

L03.115 Cellulitis of right lower limb   `I-10`

682.7   Foot, except toes

Heel

EXCLUDES   toe (681.10-681.11)

682.8   Other specified sites

Head [except face]
Scalp

EXCLUDES   face (682.0)

682.9   Unspecified site

Abscess NOS
Cellulitis NOS
Lymphangitis, acute NOS

EXCLUDES   lymphangitis NOS (457.2)

Lymphatic System of Head and Neck

Afferent vessels (in)
Blood vessels
Hilum
Efferent vessel (out)

Schematic of lymph node

Jugulodigastric
Superficial parotid
Submental
Occipital
Submandibular
Jugulomyohyoid
Anterior cervical

Lymphatic drainage of the head, neck, and face

683   Acute lymphadenitis

Abscess (acute)
Adenitis, acute   } lymph gland or node,
Lymphadenitis, acute   except mesenteric

Use additional code to identify organism, such as Staphylococcus (041.1)

EXCLUDES   enlarged glands NOS (785.6)
           lymphadenitis:
               chronic or subacute, except mesenteric (289.1)
               mesenteric (acute) (chronic) (subacute) (289.2)
               unspecified (289.3)

DEF: Acute inflammation of lymph nodes due to primary infection located elsewhere in the body.

684   Impetigo

Impetiginization of other dermatoses
Impetigo (contagiosa) [any site] [any organism]:
    bullous
    circinate
    neonatorum
    simplex
Pemphigus neonatorum

EXCLUDES   impetigo herpetiformis (694.3)

DEF: Infectious skin disease commonly occurring in children; caused by group A streptococci or *Staphylococcus aureus*; skin lesions usually appear on the face and consist of subcorneal vesicles and bullae that burst and form yellow crusts.

✓4th   685   Pilonidal cyst

`INCLUDES`   fistula   } coccygeal or pilonidal
           sinus

DEF: Hair-containing cyst or sinus in the tissues of the sacrococcygeal area; often drains through opening at the postanal dimple.

685.0   With abscess

685.1   Without mention of abscess

Stages of Pilonidal Disease

Normal follicle
Stretched follicle
Infected follicle
Acute abscess
Chronic abscess
Epithelial tube

`N` Newborn Age: 0   `P` Pediatric Age: 0-17   `M` Maternity Age: 12-55   `A` Adult Age: 15-124

✓4th **686** **Other local infections of skin and subcutaneous tissue**

Use additional code to identify any infectious organism
(041.0-041.8)

✓5th **686.0** **Pyoderma**

Dermatitis:
purulent
septic
suppurative

DEF: Nonspecific purulent skin disease related most to
furuncles, pustules, or possibly carbuncles.

686.00 **Pyoderma, unspecified**

686.01 **Pyoderma gangrenosum**

DEF: Persistent debilitating skin disease,
characterized by irregular, boggy, blue-red
ulcerations, with central healing and undermined
edges.
AHA: 4Q, '97, 42

686.09 **Other pyoderma**

686.1 **Pyogenic granuloma**

Granuloma:
septic
suppurative
telangiectaticum

EXCLUDES *pyogenic granuloma of oral mucosa (528.9)*

DEF: Solitary polypoid capillary hemangioma often asociated
with local irritation, trauma, and superimposed inflammation;
located on the skin and gingival or oral mucosa.

686.8 **Other specified local infections of skin and
subcutaneous tissue**

Bacterid (pustular)
Dermatitis vegetans
Ecthyma
Perlèche

EXCLUDES *dermatitis infectiosa eczematoides (690.8)
panniculitis (729.30-729.39)*

686.9 **Unspecified local infection of skin and
subcutaneous tissue**

Fistula of skin NOS
Skin infection NOS

EXCLUDES *fistula to skin from internal organs—see
Alphabetic Index*

OTHER INFLAMMATORY CONDITIONS OF SKIN AND
SUBCUTANEOUS TISSUE (690-698)

EXCLUDES *panniculitis (729.30-729.39)*

✓4th **690** **Erythematosquamous dermatosis**

EXCLUDES *eczematous dermatitis of eyelid (373.31)
parakeratosis variegata (696.2)
psoriasis (696.0-696.1)
seborrheic keratosis (702.11-702.19)*

✓5th **690.1** **Seborrheic dermatitis**

AHA: 4Q, '95, 58

690.10 **Seborrheic dermatitis, unspecified**

Seborrheic dermatitis NOS
L21.9 Seborrheic dermatitis unspecified   I-10

690.11 **Seborrhea capitis**   P

Cradle cap

690.12 **Seborrheic infantile dermatitis**   P

690.18 **Other seborrheic dermatitis**

690.8 **Other erythematosquamous dermatosis**

✓4th **691** **Atopic dermatitis and related conditions**

DEF: Atopic dermatitis: chronic, pruritic, inflammatory skin disorder
found on the face and antecubital and popliteal fossae; often
accompanied by allergic rhinitis, hay fever, asthma, and extreme
itching; also called allergic dermatitis, or disseminated neurodermatitis.

691.0 **Diaper or napkin rash**

Ammonia dermatitis
Diaper or napkin:
dermatitis
erythema
rash
Psoriasiform napkin eruption

691.8 **Other atopic dermatitis and
related conditions**

Atopic dermatitis
Besnier's prurigo
Eczema:
atopic
flexural
intrinsic (allergic)
Neurodermatitis:
atopic
diffuse (of Brocq)

✓4th **692** **Contact dermatitis and other eczema**

INCLUDES dermatitis:
NOS
contact
occupational
venenata
eczema (acute) (chronic):
NOS
allergic
erythematous
occupational

EXCLUDES *allergy NOS (995.3)
contact dermatitis of eyelids (373.32)
dermatitis due to substances taken internally
(693.0-693.9)
eczema of external ear (380.22)
perioral dermatitis (695.3)
urticarial reactions (708.0-708.9, 995.1)*

DEF: Contact dermatitis: acute or chronic dermatitis caused by initial
irritant effect of a substance, or by prior sensitization to a substance
coming once again in contact with skin.

692.0 **Due to detergents**

692.1 **Due to oils and greases**

692.2 **Due to solvents**

Dermatitis due to solvents of:
chlorocompound
cyclohexane
ester
glycol   } group
hydrocarbon
ketone

692.3 **Due to drugs and medicines in contact with skin**

Dermatitis (allergic) (contact) due to:
arnica
fungicides
iodine
keratolytics
mercurials
neomycin
pediculocides
phenols
scabicides
any drug applied to skin
Dermatitis medicamentosa due to drug applied to skin

Use additional E code to identify drug

EXCLUDES *allergy NOS due to drugs (995.27)
dermatitis due to ingested drugs (693.0)
dermatitis medicamentosa NOS (693.0)*

✓4th
✓5th Additional Digit Required   Unspecified Code   Other Specified Code   Manifestation Code   ►◄ Revised Text   ● New Code   ▲ Revised Code Title

2010 ICD-9-CM   **Volume 1 – 215**

Skin and Subcutaneous Tissue

692.4–692.89

692.4 Due to other chemical products
Dermatitis due to:
    acids
    adhesive plaster
    alkalis
    caustics
    dichromate
    insecticide
    nylon
    plastic
    rubber
AHA: ▶3Q, '08, 6-7;◀ 2Q, '89, 16

692.5 Due to food in contact with skin
Dermatitis, contact, due to:
    cereals
    fish
    flour
    fruit
    meat
    milk
EXCLUDES *dermatitis due to:*
    dyes (692.89)
    ingested foods (693.1)
    preservatives (692.89)

692.6 Due to plants [except food]
Dermatitis due to:
    lacquer tree [Rhus verniciflua]
    poison:
        ivy [Rhus toxicodendron]
        oak [Rhus diversiloba]
        sumac [Rhus venenata]
        vine [Rhus radicans]
    primrose [Primula]
    ragweed [Senecio jacobae]
    other plants in contact with the skin
EXCLUDES *allergy NOS due to pollen (477.0)*
    nettle rash (708.8)

√5ᵗʰ **692.7 Due to solar radiation**
EXCLUDES *sunburn due to other ultraviolet radiation*
    exposure (692.82)

692.70 Unspecified dermatitis due to sun

692.71 Sunburn
First degree sunburn
Sunburn NOS
AHA: 4Q, '01, 47
TIP: Do not assign if sunburn is due to tanning bed use; see instead code 692.82.

692.72 Acute dermatitis due to solar radiation
Acute solar skin damage NOS
Berloque dermatitis
Photoallergic response
Phototoxic response
Polymorphus light eruption
Use additional E code to identify drug, if drug induced
EXCLUDES *sunburn (692.71, 692.76-692.77)*
DEF: Berloque dermatitis: Phytophotodermatitis due to sun exposure after use of a product containing bergamot oil; causes red patches, that turn brown.
DEF: Photoallergic response: Dermatitis due to hypersensitivity to the sun; causes papulovesicular, eczematous or exudative eruptions.
DEF: Phototoxic response: Chemically induced sensitivity to sun causes burn-like reaction, occasionally vesiculation and subsequent hyperpigmentation.
DEF: Polymorphous light eruption: Inflammatory skin eruptions due to sunlight exposure; eruptions differ in size and shape.
DEF: Acute solar skin damage (NOS): Rapid, unspecified injury to skin from sun.

692.73 Actinic reticuloid and actinic granuloma
DEF: Actinic reticuloid: Dermatosis aggravated by light, causes chronic eczema-like eruption on exposed skin which extends to other unexposed surfaces; occurs in the eldery.
DEF: Actinic granuloma: Inflammatory response of skin to sun causing small nodule of microphages.

692.74 Other chronic dermatitis due to solar radiation
Chronic solar skin damage NOS
Solar elastosis
EXCLUDES *actinic [solar] keratosis (702.0)*
DEF: Solar elastosis: Premature aging of skin of light-skinned people; causes inelasticity, thinning or thickening, wrinkling, dryness, scaling and hyperpigmentation.
DEF: Chronic solar skin damage (NOS): Chronic skin impairment due to exposure to the sun, not otherwise specified.

692.75 Disseminated superficial actinic porokeratosis [DSAP]
DEF: Autosomal dominant skin condition occurring in skin that has been overexposed to the sun; characterized by superficial annular, keratotic, brownish-red spots or thickenings with depressed centers and sharp, ridged borders, may evolve into squamous cell carcinoma.
AHA: 4Q, '00, 43

692.76 Sunburn of second degree
AHA: 4Q, '01, 47
TIP: Do not assign if sunburn is due to tanning bed use; see instead code 692.82.

692.77 Sunburn of third degree
AHA: 4Q, '01, 47
TIP: Do not assign if sunburn is due to tanning bed use; see instead code 692.82.

692.79 Other dermatitis due to solar radiation
Hydroa aestivale
Photodermatitis   ⎫
Photosensitivity   ⎬ (due to sun)
                ⎭
Solar skin damage NOS

√5ᵗʰ **692.8 Due to other specified agents**

692.81 Dermatitis due to cosmetics

692.82 Dermatitis due to other radiation
Infrared rays
Light, except from sun
Radiation NOS
Tanning bed
Ultraviolet rays, except from sun
X-rays
EXCLUDES *solar radiation (692.70-692.79)*
AHA: 4Q, '01, 47; 3Q, '00, 5

692.83 Dermatitis due to metals
Jewelry

692.84 Due to animal (cat) (dog) dander
Due to animal (cat) (dog) hair

692.89 Other
Dermatitis due to:
    cold weather
    dyes
    hot weather
    preservatives
EXCLUDES *allergy (NOS) (rhinitis) due to animal*
    hair or dander (477.2)
    allergy to dust (477.8)
    sunburn (692.71, 692.76-692.77)

692.9   **Unspecified cause**
Dermatitis:
   NOS
   contact NOS
   venenata NOS
Eczema NOS
L23.9 Allergic contact dermatitis unspecified cause   `I-10`

✓4th **693**   **Dermatitis due to substances taken internally**
    EXCLUDES   *adverse effect NOS of drugs and medicines (995.20)*
       allergy NOS (995.3)
       contact dermatitis (692.0-692.9)
       urticarial reactions (708.0-708.9, 995.1)
    DEF: Inflammation of skin due to ingested substance.

693.0   **Due to drugs and medicines**
Dermatitis medicamentosa NOS
Use additional E code to identify drug
    EXCLUDES   *that due to drugs in contact with skin (692.3)*
    AHA: 2Q, '07, 8
    TIP: Assign for palmar plantar erythrodysesthesia (PPE) or hand-foot syndrome due to chemotherapy drugs.
    L27.0 Gen skin eruption d/t Rx & med taken internally   `I-10`

693.1   **Due to food**

693.8   **Due to other specified substances taken internally**

693.9   **Due to unspecified substance taken internally**
    EXCLUDES   *dermatitis NOS (692.9)*

✓4th **694**   **Bullous dermatoses**

694.0   **Dermatitis herpetiformis**
Dermatosis herpetiformis
Duhring's disease
Hydroa herpetiformis
    EXCLUDES   *herpes gestationis (646.8)*
       dermatitis herpetiformis:
         juvenile (694.2)
         senile (694.5)
    DEF: Chronic, multisystem disease manifested most in the cutaneous system; seen as an extremely pruritic eruption of various lesions that frequently heal leaving hyperpigmentation or hypopigmentation and occasionally scarring; usually associated with an asymptomatic gluten-sensitive enteropathy, and immunogenic factors.

694.1   **Subcorneal pustular dermatosis**
Sneddon-Wilkinson disease or syndrome
    DEF: Chronic relapses of sterile pustular blebs beneath the horny skin layer of the trunk and skin folds; resembles dermatitis herpetiformis.

694.2   **Juvenile dermatitis herpetiformis**
Juvenile pemphigoid

694.3   **Impetigo herpetiformis**
    DEF: Rare dermatosis associated with pregnancy; marked by itching pustules in third trimester, hypocalcemia, tetany, fever and lethargy; may result in maternal or fetal death.

694.4   **Pemphigus**
Pemphigus:
   NOS
   erythematosus
   foliaceus
   malignant
   vegetans
   vulgaris
    EXCLUDES   *pemphigus neonatorum (684)*
    DEF: Chronic, relapsing, sometimes fatal skin diseases; causes vesicles, bullae; autoantibodies against intracellular connections cause acantholysis.

694.5   **Pemphigoid**
Benign pemphigus NOS
Bullous pemphigoid
Herpes circinatus bullosus
Senile dermatitis herpetiformis

✓5th **694.6**   **Benign mucous membrane pemphigoid**
Cicatricial pemphigoid
Mucosynechial atrophic bullous dermatitis

694.60   **Without mention of ocular involvement**

694.61   **With ocular involvement**
Ocular pemphigus
    DEF: Mild self-limiting, subepidermal blistering of mucosa including the conjunctiva, seen predominantly in the elderly, produces adhesions and scarring.

694.8   **Other specified bullous dermatoses**
    EXCLUDES   *herpes gestationis (646.8)*

694.9   **Unspecified bullous dermatoses**

✓4th **695**   **Erythematous conditions**

695.0   **Toxic erythema**
Erythema venenatum

✓5th **695.1**   **Erythema multiforme**
Use additional code to identify associated manifestations, such as:
    arthropathy associated with dermatological disorders (713.3)
    conjunctival edema (372.73)
    conjunctivitis (372.04, 372.33)
    corneal scars and opacities (371.00-371.05)
    corneal ulcer (370.00-370.07)
    edema of eyelid (374.82)
    inflammation of eyelid (373.8)
    keratoconjunctivitis sicca (370.33)
    mechanical lagophthalmos (374.22)
    mucositis (478.11, 528.00, 538, 616.81)
    stomatitis (528.00)
    symblepharon (372.63)
Use additional E-code to identify drug, if drug-induced
Use additional code to identify percentage of skin exfoliation (695.50-695.59)
    EXCLUDES   *(Staphylococcal) scalded skin syndrome (695.81)*
    DEF: Symptom complex with varied skin eruption pattern of macular, bullous, papular, nodose, or vesicular lesions on the neck, face, and legs; gastritis and rheumatic pains; secondary to number of factors, including infections, ingestants, physical agents, malignancy and pregnancy.
    AHA: ▶4Q, '08, 128-130◀

695.10   **Erythema multiforme, unspecified**
Erythema iris
Herpes iris

695.11   **Erythema multiforme minor**

695.12   **Erythema multiforme major**

695.13   **Stevens-Johnson syndrome**

695.14   **Stevens-Johnson syndrome-toxic epidermal necrolysis overlap syndrome**
SJS-TEN overlap syndrome
    AHA: ▶4Q, '08, 131◀

695.15   **Toxic epidermal necrolysis**
Lyell's syndrome

695.19   **Other erythema multiforme**

695.2   **Erythema nodosum**
    EXCLUDES   *tuberculous erythema nodosum (017.1)*
    DEF: Panniculitis (an inflammatory reaction of the subcutaneous fat) of women, usually seen as a hypersensitivity reaction to infections, drugs, sarcoidosis, and specific enteropathies; the acute stage associated with fever, malaise, and arthralgia; the lesions are pink to blue in color as tender nodules and are found on the front of the legs below the knees.

695.3   **Rosacea**
Acne:
   erythematosa
   rosacea
Perioral dermatitis
Rhinophyma
    DEF: Chronic skin disease, usually of the face, characterized by persistent erythema and telangiectasis with acute episodes of edema, engorgement papules, and pustules.

✓4th ✓5th   Additional Digit Required   **Unspecified Code**   Other Specified Code   **Manifestation Code**   ▶◄ Revised Text   ● New Code   ▲ Revised Code Title

2010 ICD-9-CM   **February 2009 • Volume 1 – 217**

692.9–695.3

Skin and Subcutaneous Tissue

695.4–698.1

695.4 Lupus erythematosus

Lupus:
  erythematodes (discoid)
  erythematosus (discoid), not disseminated

EXCLUDES   *lupus (vulgaris) NOS (017.0)*
  systemic [disseminated] lupus erythematosus
  (710.0)

DEF: Group of connective tissue disorders occurring as various cutaneous diseases of unknown origin; it primarily affects women between the ages of 20 and 40.

✓5ᵗʰ **695.5 Exfoliation due to erythematous conditions according to extent of body surface involved**

Code first erythematous condition causing exfoliation, such as:
  Ritter's disease (695.81)
  (Staphylococcal) scalded skin syndrome (695.81)
  Stevens-Johnson syndrome (695.13)
  Stevens-Johnson syndrome-toxic epidermal
    necrolysis overlap syndrome (695.14)
  toxic epidermal necrolysis (695.15)

AHA: ▶4Q, '08, 128-131◀

695.50 Exfoliation due to erythematous condition involving less than 10 percent of body surface
Exfoliation due to erythematous condition NOS

695.51 Exfoliation due to erythematous condition involving 10-19 percent of body surface

695.52 Exfoliation due to erythematous condition involving 20-29 percent of body surface

695.53 Exfoliation due to erythematous condition involving 30-39 percent of body surface
AHA: ▶4Q, '08, 131◀

695.54 Exfoliation due to erythematous condition involving 40-49 percent of body surface

695.55 Exfoliation due to erythematous condition involving 50-59 percent of body surface

695.56 Exfoliation due to erythematous condition involving 60-69 percent of body surface

695.57 Exfoliation due to erythematous condition involving 70-79 percent of body surface

695.58 Exfoliation due to erythematous condition involving 80-89 percent of body surface

695.59 Exfoliation due to erythematous condition involving 90 percent or more of body surface

✓5ᵗʰ **695.8 Other specified erythematous conditions**

695.81 Ritter's disease
Dermatitis exfoliativa neonatorum
(Staphylococcal) Scalded skin syndrome
Use additional code to identify percentage of
  skin exfoliation (695.50-695.59)

DEF: Infectious skin disease of young children marked by eruptions ranging from a localized bullous to widespread of easily ruptured fine vesicles and bullae; results in exfoliation of large planes of skin and leaves raw areas.

695.89 Other
Erythema intertrigo
Intertrigo
Pityriasis rubra (Hebra)

EXCLUDES   *mycotic intertrigo (111.0-111.9)*
AHA: S-O, '86, 10

695.9 Unspecified erythematous condition
Erythema NOS
Erythroderma (secondary)

✓4ᵗʰ **696 Psoriasis and similar disorders**

696.0 Psoriatic arthropathy
DEF: Psoriasis associated with inflammatory arthritis; often involves interphalangeal joints.

696.1 Other psoriasis
Acrodermatitis continua
Dermatitis repens
Psoriasis:
  NOS
  any type, except arthropathic

EXCLUDES   *psoriatic arthropathy (696.0)*

L40.9 Psoriasis unspecified   `I-10`

696.2 Parapsoriasis
Parakeratosis variegata
Parapsoriasis lichenoides chronica
Pityriasis lichenoides et varioliformis
DEF: Erythrodermas similar to lichen, planus and psoriasis; symptoms include redness and itching; resistant to treatment.

696.3 Pityriasis rosea
Pityriasis circinata (et maculata)
DEF: Common, self-limited rash of unknown etiology marked by a solitary erythematous, salmon or fawn-colored herald plaque on the trunk, arms or thighs; followed by development of papular or macular lesions that tend to peel and form a scaly collarette.

696.4 Pityriasis rubra pilaris
Devergie's disease
Lichen ruber acuminatus
EXCLUDES   *pityriasis rubra (Hebra) (695.89)*
DEF: Inflammatory disease of hair follicles; marked by firm, red lesions topped by horny plugs; may form patches; occurs on fingers elbows, knees.

696.5 Other and unspecified pityriasis
Pityriasis:
  NOS
  alba
  streptogenes
EXCLUDES   *pityriasis:*
    simplex (690.18)
    versicolor (111.0)

696.8 Other

✓4ᵗʰ **697 Lichen**
EXCLUDES   *lichen:*
    obtusus corneus (698.3)
    pilaris (congenital) (757.39)
    ruber acuminatus (696.4)
    sclerosus et atrophicus (701.0)
    scrofulosus (017.0)
    simplex chronicus (698.3)
    spinulosus (congenital) (757.39)
    urticatus (698.2)

697.0 Lichen planus
Lichen: Lichen:
  planopilaris   ruber planus
DEF: Inflammatory, pruritic skin disease; marked by angular, flat-top, violet-colored papules; may be acute and widespread or chronic and localized.

697.1 Lichen nitidus
Pinkus' disease
DEF: Chronic, inflammatory, asymptomatic skin disorder, characterized by numerous glistening, flat-topped, discrete, skin-colored micropapules most often on penis, lower abdomen, inner thighs, wrists, forearms, breasts and buttocks.

697.8 Other lichen, not elsewhere classified
Lichen:
  ruber moniliforme
  striata

697.9 Lichen, unspecified

✓4ᵗʰ **698 Pruritus and related conditions**
EXCLUDES   *pruritus specified as psychogenic (306.3)*
DEF: Pruritus: Intense, persistent itching due to irritation of sensory nerve endings from organic or psychogenic causes.

698.0 Pruritus ani
Perianal itch

698.1 Pruritus of genital organs

698.2 Prurigo
Lichen urticatus
Prurigo:
NOS
Hebra's
mitis
simplex
Urticaria papulosa (Hebra)
EXCLUDES *prurigo nodularis (698.3)*

698.3 Lichenification and lichen simplex chronicus
Hyde's disease
Neurodermatitis (circumscripta) (local)
Prurigo nodularis
EXCLUDES *neurodermatitis, diffuse (of Brocq) (691.8)*
DEF: Lichenification: thickening of skin due to prolonged rubbing or scratching.
DEF: Lichen simplex chronicus: eczematous dermatitis, of face, neck, extremities, scrotum, vulva, and perianal region due to repeated itching, rubbing and scratching; spontaneous or evolves with other dermatoses.

698.4 Dermatitis factitia [artefacta]
Dermatitis ficta
Neurotic excoriation
Use additional code to identify any associated mental disorder
DEF: Various types of self-inflicted skin lesions characterized in appearance as an erythema to a gangrene.

698.8 Other specified pruritic conditions
Pruritus:
hiemalis
senilis
Winter itch

698.9 Unspecified pruritic disorder
Itch NOS
Pruritus NOS
L29.9 Pruritus unspecified   **I-10**

OTHER DISEASES OF SKIN AND SUBCUTANEOUS TISSUE
(700-709)
EXCLUDES *conditions confined to eyelids (373.0-374.9)*
congenital conditions of skin, hair, and nails (757.0-757.9)

700 Corns and callosities
Callus
Clavus
DEF: Corns: Conical or horny thickening of skin on toes, due to friction, pressure from shoes and hosiery; pain and inflammation may develop.
DEF: Callosities: Localized overgrowth (hyperplasia) of the horny epidermal layer due to pressure or friction.

√4ᵗʰ 701 Other hypertrophic and atrophic conditions of skin
EXCLUDES *dermatomyositis (710.3)*
hereditary edema of legs (757.0)
scleroderma (generalized) (710.1)

701.0 Circumscribed scleroderma
Addison's keloid
Dermatosclerosis, localized
Lichen sclerosus et atrophicus
Morphea
Scleroderma, circumscribed or localized
DEF: Thickened, hardened, skin and subcutaneous tissue; may involve musculoskeletal system.

701.1 Keratoderma, acquired
Acquired:
ichthyosis
keratoderma palmaris et plantaris
Elastosis perforans serpiginosa
Hyperkeratosis:
NOS
follicularis in cutem penetrans
palmoplantaris climacterica
Keratoderma:
climactericum
tylodes, progressive
Keratosis (blennorrhagica)
EXCLUDES *Darier's disease [keratosis follicularis] (congenital) (757.39)*
keratosis:
arsenical (692.4)
gonococcal (098.81)
AHA:4Q, '94, 48

701.2 Acquired acanthosis nigricans
Keratosis nigricans
DEF: Diffuse velvety hyperplasia of the spinous skin layer of the axilla and other body folds marked by gray, brown, or black pigmentation; in adult form often associated with malignant acanthosis nigricans in a benign, nevoid form relatively generalized.

701.3 Striae atrophicae
Atrophic spots of skin
Atrophoderma maculatum
Atrophy blanche (of Milian)
Degenerative colloid atrophy
Senile degenerative atrophy
Striae distensae
DEF: Bands of atrophic, depressed, wrinkled skin associated with stretching of skin from pregnancy, obesity, or rapid growth during puberty.

701.4 Keloid scar
Cheloid
Hypertrophic scar
Keloid
DEF: Overgrowth of scar tissue due to excess amounts of collagen during connective tissue repair; occurs mainly on upper trunk, face.

701.5 Other abnormal granulation tissue
Excessive granulation

701.8 Other specified hypertrophic and atrophic conditions of skin
Acrodermatitis atrophicans chronica
Atrophia cutis senilis
Atrophoderma neuriticum
Confluent and reticulate papillomatosis
Cutis laxa senilis
Elastosis senilis
Folliculitis ulerythematosa reticulata
Gougerot-Carteaud syndrome or disease
AHA: 1Q, '08, 7
TIP: Assign for nephrogenic fibrosing dermopathy (NFD) or nephrogenic systemic dermopathy (NSD), a systemic condition occurring only in patients with kidney disease.

701.9 Unspecified hypertrophic and atrophic conditions of skin
Atrophoderma
Skin tag

√4ᵗʰ 702 Other dermatoses
EXCLUDES *carcinoma in situ (232.0-232.9)*

702.0 Actinic keratosis
DEF: Wart-like growth, red or skin-colored; may form a cutaneous horn.
AHA: 1Q, '92, 18

√5ᵗʰ 702.1 Seborrheic keratosis
DEF: Common, benign, lightly pigmented, warty growth composed of basaloid cells.

702.11 Inflamed seborrheic keratosis
AHA: 4Q, '94, 48

702.19 Other seborrheic keratosis
Seborrheic keratosis NOS

702.8 Other specified dermatoses

✓4th 703 Diseases of nail
EXCLUDES congenital anomalies (757.5)
onychia and paronychia (681.02, 681.11)

703.0 Ingrowing nail
Ingrowing nail with infection
Unguis incarnatus
EXCLUDES infection, nail NOS (681.9)

703.8 Other specified diseases of nail
Dystrophia unguium
Hypertrophy of nail
Koilonychia
Leukonychia (punctata) (striata)
Onychauxis
Onychogryposis
Onycholysis

703.9 Unspecified disease of nail

✓4th 704 Diseases of hair and hair follicles
EXCLUDES congenital anomalies (757.4)

✓5th 704.0 Alopecia
EXCLUDES madarosis (374.55)
syphilitic alopecia (091.82)
DEF: Lack of hair, especially on scalp; often called baldness;
may be partial or total; occurs at any age.

704.00 Alopecia, unspecified
Baldness
Loss of hair

704.01 Alopecia areata
Ophiasis
DEF: Alopecia areata: usually reversible,
inflammatory, patchy hair loss found in beard or
scalp.
DEF: Ophiasis: alopecia areata of children; marked by
band around temporal and occipital scalp margins.

704.02 Telogen effluvium
DEF: Shedding of hair from premature telogen
development in follicles due to stress, including
shock, childbirth, surgery, drugs or weight loss.

704.09 Other
Folliculitis decalvans
Hypotrichosis:
NOS
postinfectional NOS
Pseudopelade

704.1 Hirsutism
Hypertrichosis:
NOS
lanuginosa, acquired
Polytrichia
EXCLUDES hypertrichosis of eyelid (374.54)
DEF: Excess hair growth; often in unexpected places and
amounts.

704.2 Abnormalities of the hair
Atrophic hair
Clastothrix
Fragilitas crinium
Trichiasis:
NOS
cicatrical
Trichorrhexis (nodosa)
EXCLUDES trichiasis of eyelid (374.05)

704.3 Variations in hair color
Canities (premature)
Grayness, hair (premature)
Heterochromia of hair
Poliosis:
NOS
circumscripta, acquired

704.8 Other specified diseases of hair and hair follicles
Folliculitis:
NOS
abscedens et suffodiens
pustular
Perifolliculitis:
NOS
capitis abscedens et suffodiens
scalp
Sycosis:
NOS
barbae [not parasitic]
lupoid
vulgaris

704.9 Unspecified disease of hair and hair follicles

✓4th 705 Disorders of sweat glands

705.0 Anhidrosis
Hypohidrosis
Oligohidrosis
DEF: Lack or deficiency of ability to sweat.

705.1 Prickly heat
Heat rash
Miliaria rubra (tropicalis)
Sudamina

✓5th 705.2 Focal hyperhidrosis
EXCLUDES generalized (secondary) hyperhidrosis (780.8)

705.21 Primary focal hyperhidrosis
Focal hyperhidrosis NOS
Hyperhidrosis NOS
Hyperhidrosis of:
axilla
face
palms
soles
DEF: A rare disorder of the sweat glands resulting in
excessive production of sweat; occurs in the
absence of any underlying condition, almost always
focal, confined to one or more specific areas of the
body.
AHA: 4Q, '04, 91

705.22 Secondary focal hyperhidrosis
Frey's syndrome
DEF: Secondary focal hyperhidrosis: a symptom of
an underlying disease process resulting in excessive
sweating beyond what the body requires to
maintain thermal control, confined to one or more
specific areas of the body.
DEF: Frey's syndrome: an auriculotemporal
syndrome due to lesion on the parotid gland;
characteristic redness and excessive sweating on
the cheek in connection with eating.
AHA: 4Q, '04, 91

✓5th 705.8 Other specified disorders of sweat glands

705.81 Dyshidrosis
Cheiropompholyx
Pompholyx
DEF: Vesicular eruption, on hands, feet causing
itching and burning.

705.82 Fox-Fordyce disease
DEF: Chronic, usually pruritic disease evidenced by
small follicular papular eruptions, especially in the
axillary and pubic areas; develops from the closure
and rupture of the affected apocrine glands'
intraepidermal portion of the ducts.

705.83 Hidradenitis
Hidradenitis suppurativa
DEF: Inflamed sweat glands.

705.89 Other

Bromhidrosis
Chromhidrosis
Granulosis rubra nasi
Urhidrosis

EXCLUDES *generalized hyperhidrosis (780.8)*
hidrocystoma (216.0-216.9)

DEF: Bromhidrosis: foul-smelling axillary sweat due to decomposed bacteria.

DEF: Chromhidrosis: secretion of colored sweat.

DEF: Granulosis rubra nasi: ideopathic condition of children; causes redness, sweating around nose, face and chin; tends to end by puberty.

DEF: Urhidrosis: urinous substance, such as uric acid, in sweat; occurs in uremia.

705.9 Unspecified disorder of sweat glands

Disorder of sweat glands NOS

✓4ᵗʰ 706 Diseases of sebaceous glands

706.0 Acne varioliformis

Acne:
frontalis
necrotica

DEF: Rare form of acne characterized by persistent brown papulo-pustules usually on the brow and temporoparietal part of the scalp.

706.1 Other acne

Acne: Acne:
NOS   vulgaris
conglobata   Blackhead
cystic   Comedo
pustular

EXCLUDES *acne rosacea (695.3)*

706.2 Sebaceous cyst

Atheroma, skin   Wen
Keratin cyst

DEF: Benign epidermal cyst, contains sebum and keratin; presents as firm, circumscribed nodule.

706.3 Seborrhea

EXCLUDES *seborrhea:*
capitis (690.11)
sicca (690.18)
seborrheic
dermatitis (690.10)
keratosis (702.11-702.19)

DEF: Seborrheic dermatitis marked by excessive secretion of sebum; the sebum forms an oily coating, crusts, or scales on the skin; it is also called hypersteatosis.

706.8 Other specified diseases of sebaceous glands

Asteatosis (cutis)
Xerosis cutis

706.9 Unspecified disease of sebaceous glands

✓4ᵗʰ 707 Chronic ulcer of skin

INCLUDES non-infected sinus of skin
non-healing ulcer

EXCLUDES *varicose ulcer (454.0, 454.2)*

AHA: 4Q, '04, 92

✓5ᵗʰ 707.0 Pressure ulcer

Bed sore
Decubitus ulcer
Plaster ulcer

Use additional code to identify pressure ulcer stage (707.20-707.25)

AHA: 4Q, '08, 132-133; 1Q, '04, 14; 4Q, '03, 110; 4Q, '99, 20; 1Q, '96, 15; 3Q, '90, 15; N-D, '87, 9

707.00 Unspecified site

707.01 Elbow

707.02 Upper back

Shoulder blades

Four Stages of Pressure Ulcers

First Stage
Persistent focal erythema

Second Stage
Partial thickness skin loss involving epidermis, dermis, or both

Third Stage
Full thickness skin loss extending through subcutaneous tissue

Fourth Stage
Necrosis of soft tissue extending to muscle and bone

707.03 Lower back

▶Coccyx◀
Sacrum

AHA: 3Q, '08, 17; 1Q, '05, 16

L89.159 Pressure ulcer of sacral region uns stage I-10

707.04 Hip

L89.209 Pressure ulcer of unspecified hip uns stage I-10

707.05 Buttock

L89.309 Pressure ulcer of unspecified buttock uns stage I-10

707.06 Ankle

707.07 Heel

AHA: 1Q, '05, 16

L89.609 Pressure ulcer of unspecified heel uns stage I-10

707.09 Other site

Head

L89.899 Pressure ulcer of other site unspecified stage I-10

✓5ᵗʰ 707.1 Ulcer of lower limbs, except pressure ulcer

Ulcer, chronic:
neurogenic ⎫
trophic   ⎬ of lower limb
            ⎭

Code, if applicable, any causal condition first:
atherosclerosis of the extremities with ulceration (440.23)
chronic venous hypertension with ulcer (459.31)
chronic venous hypertension with ulcer and inflammation (459.33)
diabetes mellitus (249.80-249.81, 250.80-250.83)
postphlebitic syndrome with ulcer (459.11)
postphlebitic syndrome with ulcer and inflammation (459.13)

AHA: 4Q, '00, 44; 4Q, '99, 15

707.10 Ulcer of lower limb, unspecified

AHA: 3Q, '04, 5; 4Q, '02, 43

L97.901 Non-prss chr ulcr uns part uns lw leg brkdwn skn I-10

707.11 Ulcer of thigh

Cutaneous Lesions

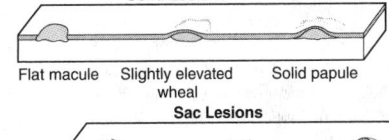

Skin and Subcutaneous Tissue

707.12–709.9

707.12 Ulcer of calf

> **L97.229** Non-press chronic ulcer left calf I-10
> w/uns severity

707.13 Ulcer of ankle

> **L97.309** Non-press chronic ulcer uns ankle I-10
> uns severity

707.14 Ulcer of heel and midfoot

> Plantar surface of midfoot

> **L97.409** Non-press chr ulcer uns heel & midft I-10
> uns sevrity

707.15 Ulcer of other part of foot

> Toes

> **L97.509** Non-press chr ulcer oth part uns ft I-10
> uns severity

707.19 Ulcer of other part of lower limb

> **L97.819** Non-press chr ulcer oth part rt low I-10
> leg uns sevr

√5th **707.2 Pressure ulcer stages**

> Code first site of pressure ulcer (707.00-707.09)

> **AHA:** ▶4Q, '08, 132-134◀

> **TIP:** If a pressure ulcer progresses during an admission from one stage to another, assign only the code for the higher stage.

707.20 Pressure ulcer, unspecified stage

> Healing pressure ulcer NOS
> Healing pressure ulcer, unspecified stage

707.21 Pressure ulcer stage I

> Healing pressure ulcer, stage I
> Pressure pre-ulcer skin changes limited to persistent focal erythema

707.22 Pressure ulcer stage II

> Healing pressure ulcer, stage II
> Pressure ulcer with abrasion, blister, partial thickness skin loss involving epidermis and/or dermis

707.23 Pressure ulcer stage III

> Healing pressure ulcer, stage III
> Pressure ulcer with full thickness skin loss involving damage or necrosis of subcutaneous tissue

707.24 Pressure ulcer stage IV

> Healing pressure ulcer, stage IV
> Pressure ulcer with necrosis of soft tissues through to underlying muscle, tendon, or bone

707.25 Pressure ulcer, unstageable

> **TIP:** Assign only if ulcer is covered by eschar, has been treated with skin or other graft, or is documented as a deep tissue injury but not documented as due to trauma.

707.8 Chronic ulcer of other specified sites

> Ulcer, chronic:
> neurogenic   } of other specified sites
> trophic

> **L98.499** Non-press chr ulcer skin oth sites uns severity I-10

707.9 Chronic ulcer of unspecified site

> Chronic ulcer NOS   Tropical ulcer NOS
> Trophic ulcer NOS   Ulcer of skin NOS

√4th **708 Urticaria**

> **EXCLUDES** edema:
> angioneurotic (995.1)
> Quincke's (995.1)
> hereditary angioedema (277.6)
> urticaria:
> giant (995.1)
> papulosa (Hebra) (698.2)
> pigmentosa (juvenile) (congenital) (757.33)

> **DEF:** Skin disorder marked by raised edematous patches of skin or mucous membrane with intense itching; also called hives.

708.0 Allergic urticaria

708.1 Idiopathic urticaria

708.2 Urticaria due to cold and heat

> Thermal urticaria

708.3 Dermatographic urticaria

> Dermatographia
> Factitial urticaria

708.4 Vibratory urticaria

708.5 Cholinergic urticaria

708.8 Other specified urticaria

> Nettle rash
> Urticaria:
> chronic
> recurrent periodic

708.9 Urticaria, unspecified

> Hives NOS

√4th **709 Other disorders of skin and subcutaneous tissue**

√5th **709.0 Dyschromia**

> **EXCLUDES** albinism (270.2)
> pigmented nevus (216.0-216.9)
> that of eyelid (374.52-374.53)

> **DEF:** Pigment disorder of skin or hair.

709.00 Dyschromia, unspecified

709.01 Vitiligo

> **DEF:** Persistent, progressive development of nonpigmented white patches on otherwise normal skin.

709.09 Other

709.1 Vascular disorders of skin

> Angioma serpiginosum
> Purpura (primary)annularis telangiectodes

709.2 Scar conditions and fibrosis of skin

> Adherent scar (skin)
> Cicatrix
> Disfigurement (due to scar)
> Fibrosis, skin NOS
> Scar NOS

> **EXCLUDES** keloid scar (701.4)

> **AHA:** N-D, '84, 19

709.3 Degenerative skin disorders

> Calcinosis: Degeneration, skin
> circumscripta   Deposits, skin
> cutis   Senile dermatosis NOS
> Colloid milium   Subcutaneous calcification

709.4 Foreign body granuloma of skin and subcutaneous tissue

> **EXCLUDES** residual foreign body without granuloma of skin and subcutaneous tissue (729.6)
> that of muscle (728.82)

709.8 Other specified disorders of skin

> Epithelial hyperplasia
> Menstrual dermatosis
> Vesicular eruption

> **DEF:** Epithelial hyperplasia: increased number of epitheleal cells.

> **DEF:** Vesicular eruption: liquid-filled structures appearing through skin.

> **AHA:** ▶4Q, '08, 99;◀ N-D, '87, 6

> **L98.8** Other spec disorders skin & subcutaneous tissue I-10

709.9 Unspecified disorder of skin and subcutaneous tissue

> Dermatosis NOS

---

13. DISEASES OF THE MUSCULOSKELETAL SYSTEM AND CONNECTIVE TISSUE (710-739)

Use additional external cause code, if applicable, to identify the cause of the musculoskeletal condition

The following fifth-digit subclassification is for use with categories 711-712, 715-716, 718-719, and 730:

0 site unspecified

1 shoulder region
Acromioclavicular joint(s)
Clavicle
Glenohumeral joint(s)
Scapula
Sternoclavicular joint(s)

2 upper arm
Elbow joint
Humerus

3 forearm
Radius
Ulna
Wrist joint

4 hand
Carpus
Metacarpus
Phalanges [fingers]

5 pelvic region and thigh
Buttock
Femur
Hip (joint)

6 lower leg
Fibula
Knee joint
Patella
Tibia

7 ankle and foot
Ankle joint
Digits [toes]
Metatarsus
Phalanges, foot
Tarsus
Other joints in foot

8 other specified sites
Head
Neck
Ribs
Skull
Trunk
Vertebral column

9 multiple sites

ARTHROPATHIES AND RELATED DISORDERS (710-719)

EXCLUDES　disorders of spine (720.0-724.9)

✓4th　710　Diffuse diseases of connective tissue

INCLUDES　all collagen diseases whose effects are not mainly confined to a single system

EXCLUDES　those affecting mainly the cardiovascular system, i.e., polyarteritis nodosa and allied conditions (446.0-446.7)

710.0　Systemic lupus erythematosus
Disseminated lupus erythematosus
Libman-Sacks disease

Use additional code to identify manifestation, as:
endocarditis (424.91)
nephritis (583.81)
chronic (582.81)
nephrotic syndrome (581.81)

EXCLUDES　lupus erythematosus (discoid) NOS (695.4)

DEF: A chronic multisystemic inflammatory disease affecting connective tissue; marked by anemia, leukopenia, muscle and joint pains, fever, rash of a butterfly pattern around cheeks and forehead area; of unknown etiology.

AHA: 2Q, '03, 7-8; 2Q, '97, 8

M32.9 Systemic lupus erythematosus unspecified　　I-10

710.1　Systemic sclerosis
Acrosclerosis
CRST syndrome
Progressive systemic sclerosis
Scleroderma

Use additional code to identify manifestation, as:
lung involvement (517.2)
myopathy (359.6)

EXCLUDES　circumscribed scleroderma (701.0)

DEF: Systemic disease, involving excess fibrotic collagen build-up; symptoms include thickened skin; fibrotic degenerative changes in various organs; and vascular abnormalities; condition occurs more often in females.

AHA: 1Q, '88, 6

710.2　Sicca syndrome
Keratoconjunctivitis sicca
Sjögren's disease

DEF: Autoimmune disease; associated with keratoconjunctivitis, laryngopharyngitis, rhinitis, dry mouth, enlarged parotid gland, and chronic polyarthritis.

710.3　Dermatomyositis
Poikilodermatomyositis
Polymyositis with skin involvement

DEF: Polymyositis characterized by flat-top purple papules on knuckles; upper eyelid rash, edema of eyelids and orbit area, red rash on forehead, neck, shoulders, trunk and arms; symptoms include fever, weight loss aching muscles; visceral cancer.

710.4　Polymyositis

DEF: Chronic, progressive, inflammatory skeletal muscle disease; causes weakness of limb girdles, neck, pharynx; may precede or follow scleroderma, Sjogren's disease, systemic lupus erythematosus, arthritis, or malignancy.

710.5　Eosinophilia myalgia syndrome
Toxic oil syndrome

Use additional E code to identify drug, if drug induced

DEF: Eosinophilia myalgia syndrome (EMS): inflammatory, multisystem fibrosis; associated with ingesting elementary L-tryptophan; symptoms include myalgia, weak limbs and bulbar muscles, distal sensory loss, areflexia, arthralgia, cough, fever, fatigue, skin rashes, myopathy, and eosinophil counts greater than 1000/microliter.

DEF: Toxic oil syndrome: syndrome similar to EMS due to ingesting contaminated cooking oil.

AHA: 4Q, '92, 21

710.8　Other specified diffuse diseases of connective tissue
Multifocal fibrosclerosis (idiopathic) NEC
Systemic fibrosclerosing syndrome

AHA: M-A, '87, 12

710.9　Unspecified diffuse connective tissue disease
Collagen disease NOS

✓4th　711　Arthropathy associated with infections

INCLUDES　arthritis
arthropathy 　　associated with conditions
polyarthritis 　　classifiable below
polyarthropathy

EXCLUDES　rheumatic fever (390)

The following fifth-digit subclassification is for use with category 711; valid digits are in [brackets] under each code. See list at beginning of chapter for definitions.

0 site unspecified
1 shoulder region
2 upper arm
3 forearm
4 hand
5 pelvic region and thigh
6 lower leg
7 ankle and foot
8 other specified sites
9 multiple sites

AHA: 1Q, '92, 17

§ ✓5th　711.0　Pyogenic arthritis
[0-9]　Arthritis or polyarthritis (due to):
coliform [Escherichia coli]
Hemophilus influenzae [H. influenzae]
pneumococcal
Pseudomonas
staphylococcal
streptococcal
Pyarthrosis

Use additional code to identify infectious organism (041.0-041.8)

DEF: Infectious arthritis caused by various bacteria; marked by inflamed synovial membranes, and purulent effusion in joints.

AHA: 1Q, '92, 16; 1Q, '91, 15

M00.869 Arthritis due to other bacteria unspecified knee　　I-10

---

§　Requires fifth digit. Valid digits are in [brackets] under each code. See beginning of section 710-739 for codes and defintions.

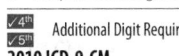

Additional Digit Required　　Unspecified Code　　Other Specified Code　　Manifestation Code　　▶◀ Revised Text　　● New Code　　▲ Revised Code Title

Joint Structures

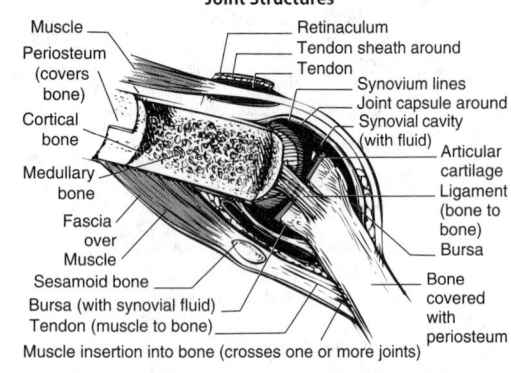

Muscle insertion into bone (crosses one or more joints)

§ ✓5ᵗʰ **711.1 Arthropathy associated with Reiter's disease and**
[0-9] **nonspecific urethritis**

Code first underlying disease as:
　nonspecific urethritis (099.4)
　Reiter's disease (099.3)

DEF: Reiter's disease: joint disease marked by diarrhea,
urethritis, conjunctivitis, keratosis and arthritis; of unknown
etiology; affects young males.

DEF: Urethritis: inflamed urethra.

§ ✓5ᵗʰ **711.2 Arthropathy in Behçet's syndrome**
[0-9] Code first underlying disease (136.1)

DEF: Behçet's syndrome: Chronic inflammatory disorder, of
unknown etiology; affects small blood vessels; causes ulcers
of oral and pharyngeal mucous membranes and genitalia,
skin lesions, retinal vasculitis, optic atrophy and severe uveitis.

§ ✓5ᵗʰ **711.3 Postdysenteric arthropathy**
[0-9] Code first underlying disease as:
　dysentery (009.0)
　enteritis, infectious (008.0-009.3)
　paratyphoid fever (002.1-002.9)
　typhoid fever (002.0)

EXCLUDES　salmonella arthritis (003.23)

§ ✓5ᵗʰ **711.4 Arthropathy associated with other bacterial diseases**
[0-9] Code first underlying disease as:
　diseases classifiable to 010-040, 090-099, except as in
　　711.1, 711.3, and 713.5
　leprosy (030.0-030.9)
　tuberculosis (015.0-015.9)

EXCLUDES　gonococcal arthritis (098.50)
　　meningococcal arthritis (036.82)

§ ✓5ᵗʰ **711.5 Arthropathy associated with other viral diseases**
[0-9] Code first underlying disease as:
　diseases classifiable to 045-049, 050-079, 480, 487
　O'nyong nyong (066.3)

EXCLUDES　that due to rubella (056.71)

§ ✓5ᵗʰ **711.6 Arthropathy associated with mycoses**
[0-9] Code first underlying disease (110.0-118)

§ ✓5ᵗʰ **711.7 Arthropathy associated with helminthiasis**
[0-9] Code first underlying disease as:
　filariasis (125.0-125.9)

§ ✓5ᵗʰ **711.8 Arthropathy associated with other infectious and**
[0-9] **parasitic diseases**

Code first underlying disease as:
　diseases classifiable to 080-088, 100-104, 130-136

EXCLUDES　arthropathy associated with sarcoidosis
　　(713.7)

AHA: 4Q, '91, 15; 3Q, '90, 14

§ ✓5ᵗʰ **711.9 Unspecified infective arthritis**
[0-9] Infective arthritis or polyarthritis (acute) (chronic)
　(subacute) NOS

✓4ᵗʰ **712 Crystal arthropathies**

INCLUDES　crystal-induced arthritis and synovitis
EXCLUDES　gouty arthropathy ▶(274.00-274.03)◀

DEF: Joint disease due to urate crystal deposit in joints or synovial
membranes.

The following fifth-digit subclassification is for use with category 712;
valid digits are in [brackets] under each code. See list at beginning of
chapter for definitions.

　0　site unspecified
　1　shoulder region
　2　upper arm
　3　forearm
　4　hand
　5　pelvic region and thigh
　6　lower leg
　7　ankle and foot
　8　other specified sites
　9　multiple sites

§ ✓5ᵗʰ **712.1 Chondrocalcinosis due to dicalcium**
[0-9] **phosphate crystals**

Chondrocalcinosis due to dicalcium phosphate crystals
　(with other crystals)
Code first underlying disease (275.4)

§ ✓5ᵗʰ **712.2 Chondrocalcinosis due to pyrophosphate crystals**
[0-9] Code first underlying disease (275.4)

§ ✓5ᵗʰ **712.3 Chondrocalcinosis, unspecified**
[0-9] Code first underlying disease (275.4)

§ ✓5ᵗʰ **712.8 Other specified crystal arthropathies**
[0-9]

§ ✓5ᵗʰ **712.9 Unspecified crystal arthropathy**
[0-9]

✓4ᵗʰ **713 Arthropathy associated with other disorders classified**
elsewhere

INCLUDES　arthritis　　　　　⎫ associated with
　　　　　arthropathy　　⎬ conditions
　　　　　polyarthritis　　⎬ classifiable
　　　　　polyarthropathy ⎭ below

713.0 Arthropathy associated with other endocrine and
metabolic disorders

Code first underlying disease as:
　acromegaly (253.0)
　hemochromatosis (275.0)
　hyperparathyroidism (252.00-252.08)
　hypogammaglobulinemia (279.00-279.09)
　hypothyroidism (243-244.9)
　lipoid metabolism disorder (272.0-272.9)
　ochronosis (270.2)

EXCLUDES　arthropathy associated with:
　　amyloidosis (713.7)
　　crystal deposition disorders, except gout
　　　(712.1-712.9)
　　diabetic neuropathy (713.5)
　　▶gout (274.00-274.03)◀

713.1 Arthropathy associated with gastrointestinal
conditions other than infections

Code first underlying disease as:
　regional enteritis (555.0-555.9)
　ulcerative colitis (556)

713.2 Arthropathy associated with hematological disorders

Code first underlying disease as:
　hemoglobinopathy (282.4-282.7)
　hemophilia (286.0-286.2)
　leukemia (204.0-208.9)
　malignant reticulosis (202.3)
　multiple myelomatosis (203.0)

EXCLUDES　arthropathy associated with Henoch-
　　Schönlein purpura (713.6)

§　Requires fifth digit. Valid digits are in [brackets] under each code. See beginning of section 710-739 for codes and defintions.

713.3 Arthropathy associated with dermatological disorders

Code first underlying disease as:
erythema multiforme (695.10-695.19)
erythema nodosum (695.2)
EXCLUDES psoriatic arthropathy (696.0)

713.4 Arthropathy associated with respiratory disorders

Code first underlying disease as:
diseases classifiable to 490-519
EXCLUDES arthropathy associated with respiratory
infections (711.0, 711.4-711.8)

713.5 Arthropathy associated with neurological disorders

Charcôt's arthropathy } associated with diseases
Neuropathic arthritis } classifiable elsewhere

Code first underlying disease as:
neuropathic joint disease [Charcôt's joints]:
NOS (094.0)
diabetic (249.6, 250.6)
syringomyelic (336.0)
tabetic [syphilitic] (094.0)

713.6 Arthropathy associated with hypersensitivity reaction

Code first underlying disease as:
Henoch (-Schönlein) purpura (287.0)
serum sickness (999.5)
EXCLUDES allergic arthritis NOS (716.2)

713.7 Other general diseases with articular involvement

Code first underlying disease as:
amyloidosis (277.30-277.39)
familial Mediterranean fever (277.31)
sarcoidosis (135)
AHA: 2Q, '97, 12

713.8 Arthropathy associated with other condition classifiable elsewhere

Code first underlying disease as:
conditions classifiable elsewhere except as in 711.1-
711.8, 712, and 713.0-713.7

✓4ᵗʰ 714 Rheumatoid arthritis and other inflammatory polyarthropathies

EXCLUDES rheumatic fever (390)
rheumatoid arthritis of spine NOS (720.0)
AHA: 2Q, '95, 3

714.0 Rheumatoid arthritis

Arthritis or polyarthritis:
atrophic
rheumatic (chronic)
Use additional code to identify manifestation, as:
myopathy (359.6)
polyneuropathy (357.1)
EXCLUDES juvenile rheumatoid arthritis NOS (714.30)
DEF: Chronic systemic disease principally of joints, manifested
by inflammatory changes in articular structures and synovial
membranes, atrophy, and loss in bone density.
AHA: 2Q, '06, 20; 1Q, '90, 5
M06.9 Rheumatoid arthritis unspecified   I-10

714.1 Felty's syndrome

Rheumatoid arthritis with splenoadenomegaly and
leukopenia
DEF: Syndrome marked by rheumatoid arthritis,
splenomegaly, leukopenia, pigmented spots on lower
extremity skin, anemia, and thrombocytopenia.

714.2 Other rheumatoid arthritis with visceral or systemic involvement

Rheumatoid carditis

✓5ᵗʰ 714.3 Juvenile chronic polyarthritis

DEF: Rheumatoid arthritis of more than one joint; lasts longer
than six weeks in age 17 or younger; symptoms include fever,
erythematous rash, weight loss, lymphadenopathy,
hepatosplenomegaly and pericarditis.

714.30 Polyarticular juvenile rheumatoid arthritis, chronic or unspecified

Juvenile rheumatoid arthritis NOS
Still's disease

714.31 Polyarticular juvenile rheumatoid arthritis, acute

714.32 Pauciarticular juvenile rheumatoid arthritis

714.33 Monoarticular juvenile rheumatoid arthritis

714.4 Chronic postrheumatic arthropathy

Chronic rheumatoid nodular fibrositis
Jaccoud's syndrome
DEF: Persistent joint disorder; follows previous rheumatic
infection.

✓5ᵗʰ 714.8 Other specified inflammatory polyarthropathies

714.81 Rheumatoid lung

Caplan's syndrome
Diffuse interstitial rheumatoid disease of lung
Fibrosing alveolitis, rheumatoid
DEF: Lung disorders associated with rheumatoid
arthritis.

714.89 Other

714.9 Unspecified inflammatory polyarthropathy

Inflammatory polyarthropathy or polyarthritis NOS
EXCLUDES polyarthropathy NOS (716.5)

✓4ᵗʰ 715 Osteoarthrosis and allied disorders

Note: Localized, in the subcategories below, includes bilateral
involvement of the same site.

INCLUDES arthritis or polyarthritis:
degenerative
hypertrophic
degenerative joint disease
osteoarthritis

EXCLUDES Marie-Strümpell spondylitis (720.0)
osteoarthrosis [osteoarthritis] of spine (721.0-721.9)

The following fifth-digit subclassification is for use with category 715;
valid digits are in [brackets] under each code. See list at beginning of
chapter for definitions.
0 site unspecified
1 shoulder region
2 upper arm
3 forearm
4 hand
5 pelvic region and thigh
6 lower leg
7 ankle and foot
8 other specified sites
9 multiple sites

§ ✓5ᵗʰ 715.0 Osteoarthrosis, generalized
[0,4,9]
Degenerative joint disease, involving multiple joints
Primary generalized hypertrophic osteoarthrosis
DEF: Chronic noninflammatory arthritis; marked by
degenerated articular cartilage and enlarged bone;
symptoms include pain and stiffness with activity.

§ ✓5ᵗʰ 715.1 Osteoarthrosis, localized, primary
[0-8]
Localized osteoarthropathy, idiopathic
M17.0 Bilateral primary osteoarthritis of knee   I-10

§ ✓5ᵗʰ 715.2 Osteoarthrosis, localized, secondary
[0-8]
Coxae malum senilis

§ ✓5ᵗʰ 715.3 Osteoarthrosis, localized, not specified whether
[0-8] **primary or secondary**
Otto's pelvis
AHA: For code 715.35: 3Q, '04, 12; 2Q, '04, 15; **For code 715.36:**
4Q, '03, 118; 2Q, '95, 5
M16.9 Osteoarthritis of hip unspecified   I-10

§ ✓5ᵗʰ 715.8 Osteoarthrosis involving, or with mention of
[0,9] **more than one site, but not specified as generalized**

§ ✓5ᵗʰ 715.9 Osteoarthrosis, unspecified whether
[0-8] **generalized or localized**
AHA: For code 715.90: 2Q, '97, 12
M19.90 Unspecified osteoarthritis unspecified site   I-10
M17.9 Osteoarthritis of knee unspecified   I-10

§ Requires fifth digit. Valid digits are in [brackets] under each code. See beginning of section 710-739 for codes and defintions.

Musculoskeletal System and Connective Tissue

716–717.9

√4th **716　Other and unspecified arthropathies**

> **EXCLUDES** cricoarytenoid arthropathy (478.79)

> The following fifth-digit subclassification is for use with category 716; valid digits are in [brackets] under each code. See list at beginning of chapter for definitions.
>
> 　0　site unspecified
> 　1　shoulder region
> 　2　upper arm
> 　3　forearm
> 　4　hand
> 　5　pelvic region and thigh
> 　6　lower leg
> 　7　ankle and foot
> 　8　other specified sites
> 　9　multiple sites

> **AHA:** 2Q, '95, 3

§ √5th **716.0　Kaschin-Beck disease**
[0-9]　　Endemic polyarthritis
　　　DEF: Chronic degenerative disease of spine and peripheral joints; occurs in eastern Siberian, northern Chinese, and Korean youth; may be a mycotoxicosis caused by eating cereals infected with fungus.

§ √5th **716.1　Traumatic arthropathy**
[0-9]　　**AHA: For Code 716.11:** 1Q, '02, 9; **For code 716.15:** ▶2Q, '09, 11◀

§ √5th **716.2　Allergic arthritis**
[0-9]　　**EXCLUDES** arthritis associated with Henoch-Schönlein purpura or serum sickness (713.6)

§ √5th **716.3　Climacteric arthritis**　　　　　　　♀
[0-9]　　Menopausal arthritis
　　　DEF: Ovarian hormone deficiency; causes pain in small joints, shoulders, elbows or knees; affects females at menopause; also called arthropathia ovaripriva.

§ √5th **716.4　Transient arthropathy**
[0-9]　　**EXCLUDES** palindromic rheumatism (719.3)

§ √5th **716.5　Unspecified polyarthropathy or polyarthritis**
[0-9]

§ √5th **716.6　Unspecified monoarthritis**
[0-8]　　Coxitis

§ √5th **716.8　Other specified arthropathy**
[0-9]

§ √5th **716.9　Arthropathy, unspecified**
[0-9]　　Arthritis ⎫
　　　　Arthropathy ⎬ (acute) (chronic) (subacute)
　　　　　　　　　⎭
　　　Articular rheumatism (chronic)
　　　Inflammation of joint NOS
　　　M12.9 Arthropathy unspecified　　　　I-10

√4th **717　Internal derangement of knee**
> **INCLUDES** degeneration ⎫
> 　　　　rupture, old ⎬ of articular cartilage or meniscus
> 　　　　tear, old ⎭　　of knee
>
> **EXCLUDES** acute derangement of knee (836.0-836.6)
> 　　　ankylosis (718.5)
> 　　　contracture (718.4)
> 　　　current injury (836.0-836.6)
> 　　　deformity (736.4-736.6)
> 　　　recurrent dislocation (718.3)

717.0　Old bucket handle tear of medial meniscus
　　Old bucket handle tear of unspecified cartilage

717.1　Derangement of anterior horn of medial meniscus

717.2　Derangement of posterior horn of medial meniscus

717.3　Other and unspecified derangement of medial meniscus
　　Degeneration of internal semilunar cartilage

√5th **717.4　Derangement of lateral meniscus**

　　717.40　Derangement of lateral meniscus, unspecified

　　717.41　Bucket handle tear of lateral meniscus

Disruption and Tears of Meniscus

Bucket-handle　　Flap-type　　Peripheral / Radial

Horizontal cleavage　　Vertical　　Congenital discoid meniscus

Internal Derangements of Knee

Disruptions of Cruciate Ligament — Anterior — Posterior
Chondromalacia of Patella — "Kissing" lesion of femur

717.42　Derangement of anterior horn of lateral meniscus

717.43　Derangement of posterior horn of lateral meniscus

717.49　Other

717.5　Derangement of meniscus, not elsewhere classified
　　Congenital discoid meniscus
　　Cyst of semilunar cartilage
　　Derangement of semilunar cartilage NOS

717.6　Loose body in knee
　　Joint mice, knee
　　Rice bodies, knee (joint)
　　DEF: The presence in the joint synovial area of a small, frequently calcified, loose body created from synovial membrane, organized fibrin fragments of articular cartilage or arthritis osteophytes.

717.7　Chondromalacia of patella
　　Chondromalacia patellae
　　Degeneration [softening] of articular cartilage of patella
　　DEF: Softened patella cartilage.
　　AHA: M-A, '85, 14; N-D, '84, 9

√5th **717.8　Other internal derangement of knee**

　　717.81　Old disruption of lateral collateral ligament

　　717.82　Old disruption of medial collateral ligament

　　717.83　Old disruption of anterior cruciate ligament

　　717.84　Old disruption of posterior cruciate ligament

　　717.85　Old disruption of other ligaments of knee
　　　　Capsular ligament of knee

　　717.89　Other
　　　　Old disruption of ligaments NOS

717.9　Unspecified internal derangement of knee
　　Derangement NOS of knee

---

§　Requires fifth digit. Valid digits are in [brackets] under each code. See beginning of section 710-739 for codes and definitions.

　N Newborn Age: 0　　　P Pediatric Age: 0-17　　　M Maternity Age: 12-55　　　A Adult Age: 15-124

✓4ᵗʰ 718 Other derangement of joint

> **EXCLUDES** current injury (830.0-848.9)
> jaw (524.60-524.69)

> The following fifth-digit subclassification is for use with category 718; valid digits are in [brackets] under each code. See list at beginning of chapter for definitions.
> 0 **site unspecified**
> 1 **shoulder region**
> 2 **upper arm**
> 3 **forearm**
> 4 **hand**
> 5 **pelvic region and thigh**
> 6 **lower leg**
> 7 **ankle and foot**
> 8 **other specified sites**
> 9 **multiple sites**

§ ✓5ᵗʰ **718.0 Articular cartilage disorder**
[0-5,7-9]   Meniscus:
disorder
rupture, old
tear, old
Old rupture of ligament(s) of joint NOS
> **EXCLUDES** articular cartilage disorder:
> in ochronosis (270.2)
> knee (717.0-717.9)
> chondrocalcinosis (275.4)
> metastatic calcification (275.4)

§ ✓5ᵗʰ **718.1 Loose body in joint**
[0-5,7-9]   Joint mice
> **EXCLUDES** knee (717.6)

> **DEF:** Calcified loose bodies in synovial fluid; due to arthritic osteophytes.
> **AHA: For code 718.17:** 2Q, '01, 15

§ ✓5ᵗʰ **718.2 Pathological dislocation**
[0-9]   Dislocation or displacement of joint, not recurrent and not current injury
Spontaneous dislocation (joint)

§ ✓5ᵗʰ **718.3 Recurrent dislocation of joint**
[0-9]   **AHA:** N-D, '87, 7

§ ✓5ᵗʰ **718.4 Contracture of joint**
[0-9]   **AHA:** 4Q, '98, 40
> **TIP:** Assign an additional code from category 438 if the contracture is a result of a CVA.

§ ✓5ᵗʰ **718.5 Ankylosis of joint**
[0-9]   Ankylosis of joint (fibrous) (osseous)
> **EXCLUDES** spine (724.9)
> stiffness of joint without mention of ankylosis (719.5)
> **DEF:** Immobility and solidification, of joint; due to disease, injury or surgical procedure.

§ ✓5ᵗʰ **718.6 Unspecified intrapelvic protrusion of acetabulum**
[0,5]   Protrusio acetabuli, unspecified
> **DEF:** Sinking of the floor of acetabulum; causing femoral head to protrude, limits hip movement; of unknown etiology.

§ ✓5ᵗʰ **718.7 Developmental dislocation of joint**
[0-9]   **EXCLUDES** congenital dislocation of joint (754.0-755.8)
> traumatic dislocation of joint (830-839)
> **AHA:** 4Q, '01, 48

§ ✓5ᵗʰ **718.8 Other joint derangement, not elsewhere classified**
[0-9]   Flail joint (paralytic)   Instability of joint
> **EXCLUDES** deformities classifiable to 736 (736.0-736.9)
> **AHA: For code 718.81:** 2Q, '00, 14
> **TIP:** Assign 718.81 for multidirectional shoulder instability.

§ ✓5ᵗʰ **718.9 Unspecified derangement of joint**
[0-5,7-9]   **EXCLUDES** knee (717.9)

Joint Derangements and Disorders

Loose body in joint · Dislocation of joint · Joint contracture · Ankylosis of joint · Synovial effusion (fluid) · Hemarthrosis (blood)

✓4ᵗʰ 719 Other and unspecified disorders of joint

> **EXCLUDES** jaw (524.60-524.69)

> The following fifth-digit subclassification is for use with codes 719.0-719.6, 719.8-719.9; valid digits are in [brackets] under each code. See list at beginning of chapter for definitions.
> 0 **site unspecified**
> 1 **shoulder region**
> 2 **upper arm**
> 3 **forearm**
> 4 **hand**
> 5 **pelvic region and thigh**
> 6 **lower leg**
> 7 **ankle and foot**
> 8 **other specified sites**
> 9 **multiple sites**

§ ✓5ᵗʰ **719.0 Effusion of joint**
[0-9]   Hydrarthrosis
Swelling of joint, with or without pain
> **EXCLUDES** intermittent hydrarthrosis (719.3)
> **M25.469** Effusion unspecified knee   I-10

§ ✓5ᵗʰ **719.1 Hemarthrosis**
[0-9]   **EXCLUDES** current injury (840.0-848.9)

§ ✓5ᵗʰ **719.2 Villonodular synovitis**
[0-9]   **DEF:** Overgrowth of synovial tissue, especially at knee joint; due to macrophage infiltration of giant cells in synovial villi and fibrous nodules.

§ ✓5ᵗʰ **719.3 Palindromic rheumatism**
[0-9]   Hench-Rosenberg syndrome
Intermittent hydrarthrosis
> **DEF:** Recurrent episodes of afebrile arthritis and periarthritis marked by their complete disappearance after a few days or hours; causes swelling, redness, and disability usually affecting only one joint; no known cause.

§ ✓5ᵗʰ **719.4 Pain in joint**
[0-9]   Arthralgia
> **AHA: For code 719.46:** 1Q, '01, 3
> **TIP:** Assign 719.46 for patellofemoral syndrome, a chronic knee pain common among athletes.
> **M25.519** Pain in unspecified shoulder   I-10
> **M25.552** Pain in left hip   I-10

§ ✓5ᵗʰ **719.5 Stiffness of joint, not elsewhere classified**
[0-9]

§ ✓5ᵗʰ **719.6 Other symptoms referable to joint**
[0-9]   Joint crepitus
Snapping hip
> **AHA:** 1Q, '94, 15; **For code 719.66:** 2Q, '07, 6
> **TIP:** Assign 719.66 for patellar clunk syndrome, which is a fibrous reaction caused by chronic pressure on the patella, S/P knee replacement surgery.

719.7 Difficulty in walking
> **EXCLUDES** abnormality of gait (781.2)
> **AHA:** 2Q, '04, 15; 4Q, '03, 66
> **R26.2** Difficulty in walking not elsewhere classified   I-10

§   Requires fifth digit. Valid digits are in [brackets] under each code. See beginning of section 710-739 for codes and defintions.

§ ✓5ᵗʰ **719.8** **Other specified disorders of joint**
[0-9]   Calcification of joint
     Fistula of joint
     EXCLUDES *temporomandibular joint-pain-dysfunction*
          syndrome [Costen's syndrome] (524.60)

§ ✓5ᵗʰ **719.9** **Unspecified disorder of joint**
[0-9]

DORSOPATHIES (720-724)

   EXCLUDES *curvature of spine (737.0-737.9)*
         osteochondrosis of spine (juvenile) (732.0)
         adult (732.8)

✓4ᵗʰ **720** **Ankylosing spondylitis and other inflammatory spondylopathies**

   720.0 **Ankylosing spondylitis**
       Rheumatoid arthritis of spine NOS
       Spondylitis:
         Marie-Strümpell
         rheumatoid
       DEF: Rheumatoid arthritis of spine and sacroiliac joints; fusion and deformity in spine follows; affects mainly males; cause unknown.

   720.1 **Spinal enthesopathy**
       Disorder of peripheral ligamentous or muscular attachments of spine
       Romanus lesion
       DEF: Tendinous or muscular vertebral bone attachment abnormality.

   720.2 **Sacroiliitis, not elsewhere classified**
       Inflammation of sacroiliac joint NOS
       DEF: Pain due to inflammation in joint, at juncture of sacrum and hip.

✓5ᵗʰ **720.8** **Other inflammatory spondylopathies**

     720.81 *Inflammatory spondylopathies in diseases classified elsewhere*
         Code first underlying disease as:
          tuberculosis (015.0)

     720.89 **Other**

   720.9 **Unspecified inflammatory spondylopathy**
       Spondylitis NOS

✓4ᵗʰ **721** **Spondylosis and allied disorders**
     DEF: Degenerative changes in spinal joint.
     AHA: 2Q, '89, 14

   721.0 **Cervical spondylosis without myelopathy**
       Cervical or cervicodorsal:
         arthritis
         osteoarthritis
         spondylarthritis

   721.1 **Cervical spondylosis with myelopathy**
       Anterior spinal artery compression syndrome
       Spondylogenic compression of cervical spinal cord
       Vertebral artery compression syndrome
       M47.12 Other spondylosis w/myelopathy cervical region   `I-10`

   721.2 **Thoracic spondylosis without myelopathy**
       Thoracic:
         arthritis
         osteoarthritis
         spondylarthritis

   721.3 **Lumbosacral spondylosis without myelopathy**
       Lumbar or lumbosacral:
         arthritis
         osteoarthritis
         spondylarthritis
       AHA: 4Q, '02, 107
       M47.817 Spondylosis w/o myelopath/radiculopath lumboscrl   `I-10`

✓5ᵗʰ **721.4** **Thoracic or lumbar spondylosis with myelopathy**

     721.41 **Thoracic region**
         Spondylogenic compression of thoracic spinal cord

     721.42 **Lumbar region**
         Spondylogenic compression of lumbar spinal cord

   721.5 **Kissing spine**
       Baastrup's syndrome
       DEF: Compression of spinous processes of adjacent vertebrae; due to mutual contact.

   721.6 **Ankylosing vertebral hyperostosis**

   721.7 **Traumatic spondylopathy**
       Kümmell's disease or spondylitis

   721.8 **Other allied disorders of spine**

✓5ᵗʰ **721.9** **Spondylosis of unspecified site**

     721.90 **Without mention of myelopathy**
       Spinal:
         arthritis (deformans) (degenerative) (hypertrophic)
         osteoarthritis NOS
       Spondylarthrosis NOS

     721.91 **With myelopathy**
         Spondylogenic compression of spinal cord NOS

✓4ᵗʰ **722** **Intervertebral disc disorders**
     AHA: 1Q, '88, 10

   722.0 **Displacement of cervical intervertebral disc without myelopathy**
       Neuritis (brachial) or radiculitis due to displacement or rupture of cervical intervertebral disc
       Any condition classifiable to 722.2 of the cervical or cervicothoracic intervertebral disc
       M50.20 Other cerv disc displacement uns cerv region   `I-10`

✓5ᵗʰ **722.1** **Displacement of thoracic or lumbar intervertebral disc without myelopathy**

     722.10 **Lumbar intervertebral disc without myelopathy**
       Lumbago or sciatica due to displacement of intervertebral disc
       Neuritis or radiculitis due to displacement or rupture of lumbar intervertebral disc
       Any condition classifiable to 722.2 of the lumbar or lumbosacral intervertebral disc
       AHA: ▶4Q, '08, 184;◀ 1Q, '07, 9; 3Q, '03, 12; 1Q, '03, 7; 4Q, '02, 107
       M51.26 Oth intervertebral disc displcmnt lumbar region   `I-10`

     722.11 **Thoracic intervertebral disc without myelopathy**
       Any condition classifiable to 722.2 of thoracic intervertebral disc

Normal Anatomy of Vertebral Disc

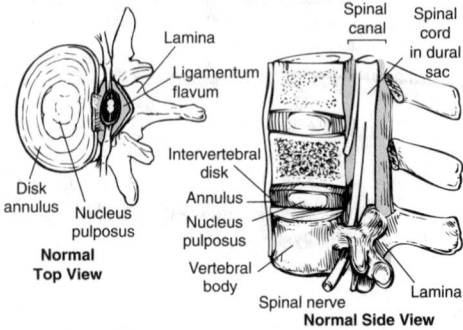

---

§   Requires fifth digit. Valid digits are in [brackets] under each code. See beginning of section 710-739 for codes and defintions.

Ⓝ Newborn Age: 0	Ⓟ Pediatric Age: 0-17	Ⓜ Maternity Age: 12-55	Ⓐ Adult Age: 15-124

Derangement of Vertebral Disc

Nucleus pulposus

Herniates through Annulus

Spinal cord

Spinal nerve

Spinal stenosis

Schmorl's nodule

Osteophyte

Folded or thickened ligamentum flavum

Collapsed disk

Laminectomy and/or diskectomy decompresses spinal canal

722.2   Displacement of intervertebral disc, site unspecified, without myelopathy
Discogenic syndrome NOS
Herniation of nucleus pulposus NOS
Intervertebral disc NOS:
   extrusion
   prolapse
   protrusion
   rupture
Neuritis or radiculitis due to displacement or rupture of intervertebral disc

√5ᵗʰ **722.3   Schmorl's nodes**
DEF: Irregular bone defect in the margin of the vertebral body; causes herniation into end plate of vertebral body.

722.30   Unspecified region

722.31   Thoracic region

722.32   Lumbar region

722.39   Other

722.4   Degeneration of cervical intervertebral disc
Degeneration of cervicothoracic intervertebral disc
M50.30 Other cerv disc degeneration uns cerv region   I-10

√5ᵗʰ **722.5   Degeneration of thoracic or lumbar intervertebral disc**

722.51   Thoracic or thoracolumbar intervertebral disc

722.52   Lumbar or lumbosacral intervertebral disc
AHA: 2Q, '06, 18; 4Q, '04, 133
M51.37 Oth intervertebral disc degen lumbosacral region   I-10

722.6   Degeneration of intervertebral disc, site unspecified
Degenerative disc disease NOS
Narrowing of intervertebral disc or space NOS

√5ᵗʰ **722.7   Intervertebral disc disorder with myelopathy**

722.70   Unspecified region

722.71   Cervical region

722.72   Thoracic region

722.73   Lumbar region

√5ᵗʰ **722.8   Postlaminectomy syndrome**
DEF: Spinal disorder due to spinal laminectomy surgery.
AHA: J-F, '87, 7
TIP: Assign if documentation indicates that scar tissue has formed following disc surgery.

722.80   Unspecified region

722.81   Cervical region

722.82   Thoracic region

722.83   Lumbar region
AHA: 2Q, '97, 15
M96.1 Postlaminectomy syndrome NEC   I-10

√5ᵗʰ **722.9   Other and unspecified disc disorder**
Calcification of intervertebral cartilage or disc
Discitis

722.90   Unspecified region
AHA: N-D, '84, 19

722.91   Cervical region

722.92   Thoracic region

722.93   Lumbar region
M51.86 Other intervertebral disc disorder lumbar region   I-10

√4ᵗʰ **723   Other disorders of cervical region**
EXCLUDES conditions due to:
   intervertebral disc disorders (722.0-722.9)
   spondylosis (721.0-721.9)
AHA: 3Q, '94, 14; 2Q, '89, 14

723.0   Spinal stenosis in cervical region
AHA: 4Q, '03, 101
M48.02 Spinal stenosis cervical region   I-10

723.1   Cervicalgia
Pain in neck
DEF: Pain in cervical spine or neck region.
M54.2 Cervicalgia   I-10

723.2   Cervicocranial syndrome
Barré-Liéou syndrome
Posterior cervical sympathetic syndrome
DEF: Neurologic disorder of upper cervical spine and nerve roots.

723.3   Cervicobrachial syndrome (diffuse)
DEF: Complex of symptoms due to scalenus anterior muscle compressing the brachial plexus; pain radiates from shoulder to arm or back of neck.
AHA: N-D, '85, 12

723.4   Brachial neuritis or radiculitis NOS
Cervical radiculitis
Radicular syndrome of upper limbs

723.5   Torticollis, unspecified
Contracture of neck
EXCLUDES congenital (754.1)
   due to birth injury (767.8)
   hysterical (300.11)
   ocular torticollis (781.93)
   psychogenic (306.0)
   spasmodic (333.83)
   traumatic, current (847.0)
DEF: Abnormally positioned neck relative to head; due to cervical muscle or fascia contractions; also called wryneck.
AHA: 2Q, '01, 21; 1Q, '95, 7

723.6   Panniculitis specified as affecting neck
DEF: Inflammation of the panniculus adiposus (subcutaneous fat) in the neck.

723.7   Ossification of posterior longitudinal ligament in cervical region

723.8   Other syndromes affecting cervical region
Cervical syndrome NEC
Klippel's disease
Occipital neuralgia
AHA: 1Q, '00, 7

723.9   Unspecified musculoskeletal disorders and symptoms referable to neck
Cervical (region) disorder NOS

Stenosis in Cervical Region

Spinal cord in fluid-filled Dural sac

Old displacement/ dislocation of C₁ on C₂

Posterior longitudinal ligament

Spinal cord

Spinal canal

Vertebral body

Torticollis

√4ᵗʰ
√5ᵗʰ   Additional Digit Required   Unspecified Code   Other Specified Code   Manifestation Code   ►◄ Revised Text   ● New Code   ▲ Revised Code Title
2010 ICD-9-CM   **Volume 1 – 229**

Musculoskeletal System and Connective Tissue

724–726.8

✓4ᵗʰ **724** **Other and unspecified disorders of back**

> *EXCLUDES*   collapsed vertebra (code to cause, e.g., osteoporosis, 733.00-733.09)
>   conditions due to:
>   intervertebral disc disorders (722.0-722.9)
>   spondylosis (721.0-721.9)

> AHA: 2Q, '89, 14

✓5ᵗʰ **724.0** **Spinal stenosis, other than cervical**

     724.00 **Spinal stenosis, unspecified region**

       M48.00 Spinal stenosis site unspecified   I-10

     724.01 **Thoracic region**

     724.02 **Lumbar region**

       AHA: ▶4Q, '08, 109;◀ 4Q, '07, 120; 1Q, '07, 10, 20; 4Q, '99, 13

       M48.06 Spinal stenosis lumbar region   I-10

     724.09 **Other**

724.1 **Pain in thoracic spine**

724.2 **Lumbago**
     Low back pain
     Low back syndrome
     Lumbalgia
     AHA: 2Q, '07, 11; N-D, '85, 12
     M54.5 Low back pain   I-10

724.3 **Sciatica**
     Neuralgia or neuritis of sciatic nerve
     EXCLUDES   specified lesion of sciatic nerve (355.0)
     AHA: 2Q, '89, 12
     M54.30 Sciatica unspecified side   I-10

724.4 **Thoracic or lumbosacral neuritis or radiculitis, unspecified**
     Radicular syndrome of lower limbs
     AHA: 2Q, '99, 3
     M51.14 Intervertebral disc d/o w/radiculopathy thoracic   I-10

724.5 **Backache, unspecified**
     Vertebrogenic (pain) syndrome NOS
     M54.9 Dorsalgia unspecified   I-10

724.6 **Disorders of sacrum**
     Ankylosis   } lumbosacral or sacroiliac (joint)
     Instability

✓5ᵗʰ **724.7** **Disorders of coccyx**

     724.70 **Unspecified disorder of coccyx**

     724.71 **Hypermobility of coccyx**

     724.79 **Other**
       Coccygodynia

724.8 **Other symptoms referable to back**
     Ossification of posterior longitudinal ligament NOS
     Panniculitis specified as sacral or affecting back

724.9 **Other unspecified back disorders**
     Ankylosis of spine NOS
     Compression of spinal nerve root NEC
     Spinal disorder NOS
     EXCLUDES   sacroiliitis (720.2)

RHEUMATISM, EXCLUDING THE BACK (725-729)

> *INCLUDES*   disorders of muscles and tendons and their attachments, and of other soft tissues

725 **Polymyalgia rheumatica**
     DEF: Joint and muscle pain, pelvis, and shoulder girdle stiffness, high sedimentation rate and temporal arteritis; occurs in elderly.
     M35.3 Polymyalgia rheumatica   I-10

✓4ᵗʰ **726** **Peripheral enthesopathies and allied syndromes**
     Note: Enthesopathies are disorders of peripheral ligamentous or muscular attachments.
     EXCLUDES   spinal enthesopathy (720.1)

726.0 **Adhesive capsulitis of shoulder**

✓5ᵗʰ **726.1** **Rotator cuff syndrome of shoulder and allied disorders**

     726.10 **Disorders of bursae and tendons in shoulder region, unspecified**
       Rotator cuff syndrome NOS
       Supraspinatus syndrome NOS
       AHA: 2Q, '01, 11
       M75.11 Rotator cuff syndrome right shoulder   I-10

     726.11 **Calcifying tendinitis of shoulder**

     726.12 **Bicipital tenosynovitis**

     726.19 **Other specified disorders**
       EXCLUDES   complete rupture of rotator cuff, nontraumatic (727.61)

726.2 **Other affections of shoulder region, not elsewhere classified**
     Periarthritis of shoulder
     Scapulohumeral fibrositis

✓5ᵗʰ **726.3** **Enthesopathy of elbow region**

     726.30 **Enthesopathy of elbow, unspecified**

     726.31 **Medial epicondylitis**

     726.32 **Lateral epicondylitis**
       Epicondylitis NOS
       Golfers' elbow
       Tennis elbow

     726.33 **Olecranon bursitis**
       Bursitis of elbow

     726.39 **Other**

726.4 **Enthesopathy of wrist and carpus**
     Bursitis of hand or wrist
     Periarthritis of wrist

726.5 **Enthesopathy of hip region**
     Bursitis of hip
     Gluteal tendinitis
     Iliac crest spur
     Psoas tendinitis
     Trochanteric tendinitis

✓5ᵗʰ **726.6** **Enthesopathy of knee**

     726.60 **Enthesopathy of knee, unspecified**
       Bursitis of knee NOS

     726.61 **Pes anserinus tendinitis or bursitis**
       DEF: Inflamed tendons of sartorius, gracilis and semitendinosus muscles of medial aspect of knee.

     726.62 **Tibial collateral ligament bursitis**
       Pellegrini-Stieda syndrome

     726.63 **Fibular collateral ligament bursitis**

     726.64 **Patellar tendinitis**

     726.65 **Prepatellar bursitis**
       AHA: 2Q, '06, 15

     726.69 **Other**
       Bursitis:
         infrapatellar
         subpatellar

✓5ᵗʰ **726.7** **Enthesopathy of ankle and tarsus**

     726.70 **Enthesopathy of ankle and tarsus, unspecified**
       Metatarsalgia NOS
       EXCLUDES   Morton's metatarsalgia (355.6)

     726.71 **Achilles bursitis or tendinitis**

     726.72 **Tibialis tendinitis**
       Tibialis (anterior) (posterior) tendinitis

     726.73 **Calcaneal spur**
       DEF: Overgrowth of calcaneous bone; causes pain on walking; due to chronic avulsion injury of plantar fascia from calcaneus.

     726.79 **Other**
       Peroneal tendinitis

726.8 **Other peripheral enthesopathies**

✓5th 726.9 Unspecified enthesopathy

726.90 **Enthesopathy of unspecified site**
Capsulitis NOS
Periarthritis NOS
Tendinitis NOS

726.91 **Exostosis of unspecified site**
Bone spur NOS
AHA: 2Q, '01, 15

✓4th 727 **Other disorders of synovium, tendon, and bursa**

✓5th 727.0 Synovitis and tenosynovitis

727.00 **Synovitis and tenosynovitis, unspecified**
Synovitis NOS
Tenosynovitis NOS
M65.9 Synovitis and tenosynovitis unspecified I-10

727.01 *Synovitis and tenosynovitis in diseases classified elsewhere*
Code first underlying disease as:
tuberculosis (015.0-015.9)
EXCLUDES *crystal-induced (275.4)*
gonococcal (098.51)
▶*gout (274.00-274.03)*◀
syphilitic (095.7)

727.02 **Giant cell tumor of tendon sheath**

727.03 **Trigger finger (acquired)**
DEF: Stenosing tenosynovitis or nodule in flexor tendon; cessation of flexion or extension movement in finger, followed by snapping into place.

727.04 **Radial styloid tenosynovitis**
de Quervain's disease

727.05 **Other tenosynovitis of hand and wrist**

727.06 **Tenosynovitis of foot and ankle**

727.09 **Other**

727.1 Bunion
DEF: Enlarged first metatarsal head due to inflamed bursa; results in laterally displaced great toe.

727.2 Specific bursitides often of occupational origin
Beat:
elbow
hand
knee
Chronic crepitant synovitis of wrist
Miners':
elbow
knee

727.3 **Other bursitis**
Bursitis NOS
EXCLUDES *bursitis:*
gonococcal (098.52)
subacromial (726.19)
subcoracoid (726.19)
subdeltoid (726.19)
syphilitic (095.7)
"frozen shoulder" (726.0)

Bunion

Normal metatarsophalangeal joint

Exostosis

Ganglia

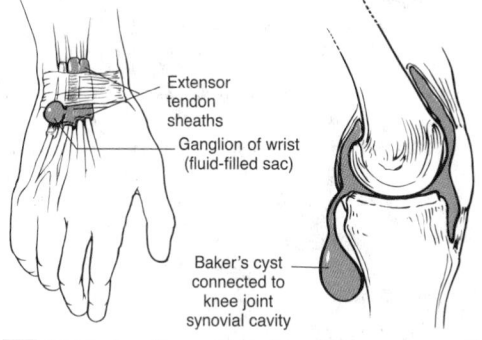

Extensor tendon sheaths

Ganglion of wrist (fluid-filled sac)

Baker's cyst connected to knee joint synovial cavity

✓5th 727.4 Ganglion and cyst of synovium, tendon, and bursa

727.40 **Synovial cyst, unspecified**
EXCLUDES *that of popliteal space (727.51)*
AHA: 2Q, '97, 6

727.41 **Ganglion of joint**

727.42 **Ganglion of tendon sheath**

727.43 **Ganglion, unspecified**

727.49 **Other**
Cyst of bursa

✓5th 727.5 Rupture of synovium

727.50 **Rupture of synovium, unspecified**

727.51 **Synovial cyst of popliteal space**
Baker's cyst (knee)

727.59 **Other**

✓5th 727.6 Rupture of tendon, nontraumatic

727.60 **Nontraumatic rupture of unspecified tendon**

727.61 **Complete rupture of rotator cuff**

727.62 **Tendons of biceps (long head)**

727.63 **Extensor tendons of hand and wrist**

727.64 **Flexor tendons of hand and wrist**

727.65 **Quadriceps tendon**

727.66 **Patellar tendon**

727.67 **Achilles tendon**

727.68 **Other tendons of foot and ankle**

727.69 **Other**

✓5th 727.8 Other disorders of synovium, tendon, and bursa

727.81 **Contracture of tendon (sheath)**
Short Achilles tendon (acquired)

727.82 **Calcium deposits in tendon and bursa**
Calcification of tendon NOS
Calcific tendinitis NOS
EXCLUDES *peripheral ligamentous or muscular attachments (726.0-726.9)*

727.83 **Plica syndrome**
Plica knee
DEF: A fold in the synovial tissue formed before birth, creating a septum between two pockets of synovial tissue; most common are the medial patellar plica and the suprapatellar plica. Plica syndrome, or plica knee, refers to symptomatic plica.
AHA: 4Q, '00, 44

727.89 **Other**
Abscess of bursa or tendon
EXCLUDES *xanthomatosis localized to tendons (272.7)*
AHA: 2Q, '89, 15

727.9 **Unspecified disorder of synovium, tendon, and bursa**

Musculoskeletal System and Connective Tissue

728–729.1

✓4ᵗʰ **728 Disorders of muscle, ligament, and fascia**
> EXCLUDES   enthesopathies (726.0-726.9)
> muscular dystrophies (359.0-359.1)
> myoneural disorders (358.00-358.9)
> myopathies (359.2-359.9)
> nontraumatic hematoma of muscle (729.92)
> old disruption of ligaments of knee (717.81-717.89)

728.0 Infective myositis
Myositis:
     purulent
     suppurative
> EXCLUDES   myositis:
>   epidemic (074.1)
>   interstitial (728.81)
>   syphilitic (095.6)
>   tropical (040.81)

DEF: Inflamed connective septal tissue of muscle.

✓5ᵗʰ **728.1 Muscular calcification and ossification**

728.10 Calcification and ossification, unspecified
Massive calcification (paraplegic)

728.11 Progressive myositis ossificans
DEF: Progressive myositic disease; marked by bony tissue formed by voluntary muscle; occurs among very young.

728.12 Traumatic myositis ossificans
Myositis ossificans (circumscripta)

728.13 Postoperative heterotopic calcification
DEF: Abnormal formation of calcium deposits in muscular tissue after surgery, marked by a corresponding loss of muscle tone and tension.

728.19 Other
Polymyositis ossificans

728.2 Muscular wasting and disuse atrophy, not elsewhere classified
Amyotrophia NOS
Myofibrosis
> EXCLUDES   neuralgic amyotrophy (353.5)
> pelvic muscle wasting and disuse atrophy (618.83)
> progressive muscular atrophy (335.0-335.9)

728.3 Other specific muscle disorders
Arthrogryposis
Immobility syndrome (paraplegic)
> EXCLUDES   arthrogryposis multiplex congenita (754.89)
> stiff-man syndrome (333.91)

728.4 Laxity of ligament

728.5 Hypermobility syndrome

728.6 Contracture of palmar fascia   A
Dupuytren's contracture
DEF: Dupuytren's contracture: flexion deformity of finger, due to shortened, thickened fibrosing of palmar fascia; cause unknown; associated with long-standing epilepsy.

✓5ᵗʰ **728.7 Other fibromatoses**

728.71 Plantar fascial fibromatosis
Contracture of plantar fascia
Plantar fasciitis (traumatic)
DEF: Plantar fascia fibromatosis; causes nodular swelling and pain; not associated with contractures.

728.79 Other
Garrod's or knuckle pads
Nodular fasciitis
Pseudosarcomatous fibromatosis (proliferative) (subcutaneous)
DEF: Knuckle pads: Pea-size nodules on dorsal surface of interphalangeal joints; new growth of fibrous tissue with thickened dermis and epidermis.

✓5ᵗʰ **728.8 Other disorders of muscle, ligament, and fascia**

728.81 Interstitial myositis
DEF: Inflammation of septal connective parts of muscle tissue.

728.82 Foreign body granuloma of muscle
Talc granuloma of muscle

728.83 Rupture of muscle, nontraumatic

728.84 Diastasis of muscle
Diastasis recti (abdomen)
> EXCLUDES   diastasis recti complicating pregnancy, labor, and delivery (665.8)

DEF: Muscle separation, such as recti abdominis after repeated pregnancies.

728.85 Spasm of muscle
M62.838 Other muscle spasm   I-10

728.86 Necrotizing fasciitis
Use additional code to identify:
    infectious organism (041.00-041.89)
    gangrene (785.4), if applicable
DEF: Fulminating infection begins with extensive cellulitis, spreads to superficial and deep fascia; causes thrombosis of subcutaneous vessels, and gangrene of underlying tissue.
AHA: 4Q, '95, 54

728.87 Muscle weakness (generalized)
> EXCLUDES   generalized weakness (780.79)

AHA: 1Q, '05, 13; 4Q, '03, 66
TIP: Assign an additional code from category 438 if the weakness is a result of a CVA.

728.88 Rhabdomyolysis
DEF: A disintegration or destruction of muscle; an acute disease characterized by the excretion of myoglobin into the urine.
AHA: 4Q, '03, 66

728.89 Other
Eosinophilic fasciitis
Use additional E code to identify drug, if drug induced
DEF: Eosinophilic fasciitis: inflammation of fascia of extremities associated with eosinophilia, edema, and swelling; occurs alone or as part of myalgia syndrome.
AHA: 3Q, '06, 13; 3Q, '02, 28; 2Q, '01, 14, 15

728.9 Unspecified disorder of muscle, ligament, and fascia
AHA: 4Q, '88, 11

✓4ᵗʰ **729 Other disorders of soft tissues**
> EXCLUDES   acroparesthesia (443.89)
> carpal tunnel syndrome (354.0)
> disorders of the back (720.0-724.9)
> entrapment syndromes (354.0-355.9)
> palindromic rheumatism (719.3)
> periarthritis (726.0-726.9)
> psychogenic rheumatism (306.0)

729.0 Rheumatism, unspecified and fibrositis
DEF: General term describes diseases of muscle, tendon, nerve, joint, or bone; symptoms include pain and stiffness.

729.1 Myalgia and myositis, unspecified
Fibromyositis NOS
DEF: Myalgia: muscle pain.
DEF: Myositis: inflamed voluntary muscle.
DEF: Fibromyositis: inflamed fibromuscular tissue.
M79.1 Myalgia   I-10

N Newborn Age: 0   P Pediatric Age: 0-17   M Maternity Age: 12-55   A Adult Age: 15-124

729.2 Neuralgia, neuritis, and radiculitis, unspecified

> EXCLUDES   *brachial radiculitis (723.4)*
> *cervical radiculitis (723.4)*
> *lumbosacral radiculitis (724.4)*
> *mononeuritis (354.0-355.9)*
> *radiculitis due to intervertebral disc*
> *involvement (722.0-722.2, 722.7)*
> *sciatica (724.3)*

> **DEF:** Neuralgia: paroxysmal pain along nerve; symptoms include brief pain and tenderness at point nerve exits.
> **DEF:** Neuritis: inflamed nerve, symptoms include paresthesia, paralysis and loss of reflexes at nerve site.
> **DEF:** Radiculitis: inflamed nerve root.

√5ᵗʰ 729.3 Panniculitis, unspecified

> **DEF:** Inflammatory reaction of subcutaneous fat; causes nodules; often develops in abdominal region.

729.30 Panniculitis, unspecified site

> Weber-Christian disease
> **DEF:** Febrile, nodular, nonsuppurative, relapsing inflammation of subcutaneous fat.

729.31 Hypertrophy of fat pad, knee

> Hypertrophy of infrapatellar fat pad

729.39 Other site

> EXCLUDES   *panniculitis specified as (affecting):*
> *back (724.8)*
> *neck (723.6)*
> *sacral (724.8)*

729.4 Fasciitis, unspecified

> EXCLUDES   *necrotizing fasciitis (728.86)*
> *nodular fasciitis (728.79)*

> **AHA:** 2Q, '94, 13

729.5 Pain in limb

> **AHA:** 2Q, '07, 11
> **M79.609** Pain in unspecified limb   **I-10**

729.6 Residual foreign body in soft tissue

> EXCLUDES   *foreign body granuloma:*
> *muscle (728.82)*
> *skin and subcutaneous tissue (709.4)*

√5ᵗʰ 729.7 Nontraumatic compartment syndrome

> Code first, if applicable, postprocedural complication (998.89)

> EXCLUDES   *compartment syndrome NOS (958.90)*
> *traumatic compartment syndrome (958.90-958.99)*

> **DEF:** Compression of nerves and blood vessels within an enclosed space, leading to impaired blood flow and muscle and nerve damage.

729.71 Nontraumatic compartment syndrome of upper extremity

> Nontraumatic compartment syndrome of shoulder, arm, forearm, wrist, hand, and fingers
> **AHA:** 4Q, '06, 100-102

729.72 Nontraumatic compartment syndrome of lower extremity

> Nontraumatic compartment syndrome of hip, buttock, thigh, leg, foot, and toes
> **AHA:** 4Q, '06, 100-102

729.73 Nontraumatic compartment syndrome of abdomen

> **AHA:** 4Q, '06, 100-102

729.79 Nontraumatic compartment syndrome of other sites

> **AHA:** 4Q, '06, 100-102

√5ᵗʰ 729.8 Other musculoskeletal symptoms referable to limbs

> **TIP:** Assign for pseudothrombophlebitis, which involves painful swelling of the lower extremity and mimics deep vein thrombosis (DVT).

729.81 Swelling of limb

> **AHA:** 4Q, '88, 6
> **TIP:** Assign for pseudothrombophlebitis, which involves painful swelling of the lower extremity and mimics deep vein thrombosis (DVT).

729.82 Cramp

729.89 Other

> EXCLUDES   *abnormality of gait (781.2)*
> *tetany (781.7)*
> *transient paralysis of limb (781.4)*

> **AHA:** 4Q, '88, 12
> **R29.898** Oth symptoms & signs involv   **I-10**
> musculoskeletal sys

√5ᵗʰ 729.9 Other and unspecified disorders of soft tissue

> **AHA:** ▶4Q, '08, 134-136◀

729.90 Disorders of soft tissue, unspecified

729.91 Post-traumatic seroma

> EXCLUDES   *seroma complicating a procedure (998.13)*

729.92 Nontraumatic hematoma of soft tissue

> Nontraumatic hematoma of muscle
> **AHA:** ▶4Q, '08, 135◀
> **TIP:** Assign an additional E code for a drug adverse effect if caused by Coumadin or other anticoagulants.

729.99 Other disorders of soft tissue

> Polyalgia

OSTEOPATHIES, CHONDROPATHIES, AND ACQUIRED MUSCULOSKELETAL DEFORMITIES (730-739)

√4ᵗʰ 730 Osteomyelitis, periostitis, and other infections involving bone

> EXCLUDES   *jaw (526.4-526.5)*
> *petrous bone (383.2)*

> Use additional code to identify organism, such as Staphylococcus (041.1)

> The following fifth-digit subclassification is for use with category 730; valid digits are in [brackets] under each code. See list at beginning of chapter for definitions.
> 0 site unspecified
> 1 shoulder region
> 2 upper arm
> 3 forearm
> 4 hand
> 5 pelvic region and thigh
> 6 lower leg
> 7 ankle and foot
> 8 other specified sites
> 9 multiple sites

> **DEF:** Osteomyelitis: bacterial inflammation of bone tissue and marrow.
> **DEF:** Periostitis: inflammation of specialized connective tissue; causes swelling of bone and aching pain.
> **AHA:** 4Q, '97, 43

§ √5ᵗʰ 730.0 Acute osteomyelitis
[0-9]

> Abscess of any bone except accessory sinus, jaw, or mastoid
> Acute or subacute osteomyelitis, with or without mention of periostitis
> Use additional code to identify major osseous defect, if applicable (731.3)
> **AHA:** 4Q, '06, 103; **For code 730.06:** 1Q, '02, 4; **For code 730.07:** 1Q, '04, 14

---

§   Requires fifth digit. Valid digits are in [brackets] under each code. See beginning of section 710-739 for codes and defintions.

√4ᵗʰ √5ᵗʰ Additional Digit Required   Unspecified Code   Other Specified Code   Manifestation Code   ▶◀ Revised Text   ● New Code   ▲ Revised Code Title

2010 ICD-9-CM   **February 2009 • Volume 1 – 233**

§ ✓5th **730.1 Chronic osteomyelitis**
[0-9]
Brodie's abscess
Chronic or old osteomyelitis, with or without mention of periostitis
Sequestrum of bone
Sclerosing osteomyelitis of Garré
Use additional code to identify major osseous defect, if applicable (731.3)
EXCLUDES *aseptic necrosis of bone (733.40-733.49)*
AHA: 4Q, '06, 103; **For code 730.17:** 3Q, '00, 4

§ ✓5th **730.2 Unspecified osteomyelitis**
[0-9]
Osteitis or osteomyelitis NOS, with or without mention of periostitis
Use additional code to identify major osseous defect, if applicable (731.3)
AHA: 4Q, '06, 103
M86.9 Osteomyelitis unspecified [I-10]

§ ✓5th **730.3 Periostitis without mention of osteomyelitis**
[0-9]
Abscess of periosteum } without mention of
Periostosis } osteomyelitis
EXCLUDES *that in secondary syphilis (091.61)*

§ ✓5th **730.7 *Osteopathy resulting from poliomyelitis***
[0-9] *Code first underlying disease (045.0-045.9)*

§ ✓5th **730.8 *Other infections involving bone in diseases classified elsewhere***
[0-9]
Code first underlying disease as:
tuberculosis (015.0-015.9)
typhoid fever (002.0)
EXCLUDES *syphilis of bone NOS (095.5)*
AHA: 2Q, '97, 16; 3Q, '91, 10

§ ✓5th **730.9 Unspecified infection of bone**
[0-9]

✓4th **731 Osteitis deformans and osteopathies associated with other disorders classified elsewhere**
DEF: Osteitis deformans: Bone disease marked by episodes of increased bone loss, excessive repair attempts; causes weakened, deformed bones with increased mass, bowed long bones, deformed flat bones, pain and pathological fractures; may be fatal if associated with congestive heart failure, giant cell tumors or bone sarcoma; also called Paget's disease.

731.0 Osteitis deformans without mention of bone tumor
Paget's disease of bone

731.1 Osteitis deformans in diseases classified elsewhere
Code first underlying disease as:
malignant neoplasm of bone (170.0-170.9)

731.2 Hypertrophic pulmonary osteoarthropathy
Bamberger-Marie disease
DEF: Clubbing, of fingers and toes; related to enlarged ends of long bones; due to chronic lung and heart disease.

731.3 Major osseous defects
Code first underlying disease, if known, such as:
aseptic necrosis (733.40-733.49)
malignant neoplasm of bone (170.0-170.9)
osteomyelitis (730.00-730.29)
osteoporosis (733.00-733.09)
peri-prosthetic osteolysis (996.45)
AHA: 4Q, '06, 103

731.8 Other bone involvement in diseases classified elsewhere
Code first underlying disease as:
diabetes mellitus (249.8, 250.8)
Use additional code to specify bone condition, such as:
acute osteomyelitis (730.00-730.09)
AHA: 1Q, '04, 14; 4Q, '97, 43; 2Q, '97, 16
TIP: For diabetic osteomyelitis, assign a total of three codes: 250.8X, 731.8, and a code from category 730.
M90.89 Osteopathy dz classified elsewhere multiple site [I-10]

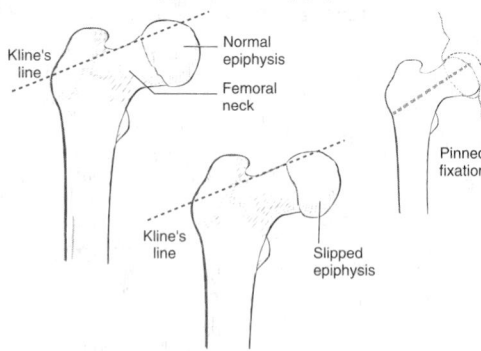

Slipped Femoral Epiphysis

✓4th **732 Osteochondropathies**
DEF: Conditions related to both bone and cartilage, or conditions in which cartilage is converted to bone (enchondral ossification).

732.0 Juvenile osteochondrosis of spine
Juvenile osteochondrosis (of):
marginal or vertebral epiphysis (of Scheuermann)
spine NOS
Vertebral epiphysitis
EXCLUDES *adolescent postural kyphosis (737.0)*

732.1 Juvenile osteochondrosis of hip and pelvis
Coxa plana
Ischiopubic synchondrosis (of van Neck)
Osteochondrosis (juvenile) of:
acetabulum
head of femur (of Legg-Calvé-Perthes)
iliac crest (of Buchanan)
symphysis pubis (of Pierson)
Pseudocoxalgia

732.2 Nontraumatic slipped upper femoral epiphysis
Slipped upper femoral epiphysis NOS

732.3 Juvenile osteochondrosis of upper extremity
Osteochondrosis (juvenile) of:
capitulum of humerus (of Panner)
carpal lunate (of Kienbock)
hand NOS
head of humerus (of Haas)
heads of metacarpals (of Mauclaire)
lower ulna (of Burns)
radial head (of Brailsford)
upper extremity NOS

732.4 Juvenile osteochondrosis of lower extremity, excluding foot
Osteochondrosis (juvenile) of:
lower extremity NOS
primary patellar center (of Köhler)
proximal tibia (of Blount)
secondary patellar center (of Sinding-Larsen)
tibial tubercle (of Osgood-Schlatter)
Tibia vara

732.5 Juvenile osteochondrosis of foot
Calcaneal apophysitis
Epiphysitis, os calcis
Osteochondrosis (juvenile) of:
astragalus (of Diaz)
calcaneum (of Sever)
foot NOS
metatarsal
second (of Freiberg)
fifth (of Iselin)
os tibiale externum (of Haglund)
tarsal navicular (of Köhler)

732.6 Other juvenile osteochondrosis
Apophysitis }
Epiphysitis } specified as juvenile, of other
Osteochondritis } site, or site NOS
Osteochondrosis }

732.7 Osteochondritis dissecans

§ Requires fifth digit. Valid digits are in [brackets] under each code. See beginning of section 710-739 for codes and defintions.

[N] Newborn Age: 0   [P] Pediatric Age: 0-17   [M] Maternity Age: 12-55   [A] Adult Age: 15-124

732.8   Other specified forms of osteochondropathy
Adult osteochondrosis of spine

732.9   Unspecified osteochondropathy

Apophysitis	} NOS
Epiphysitis	not specified as adult or
Osteochondritis	juvenile, of unspecified
Osteochondrosis	site

√4ᵗʰ **733   Other disorders of bone and cartilage**

EXCLUDES   bone spur (726.91)
cartilage of, or loose body in, joint (717.0-717.9, 718.0-718.9)
giant cell granuloma of jaw (526.3)
osteitis fibrosa cystica generalisata (252.01)
osteomalacia (268.2)
polyostotic fibrous dysplasia of bone (756.54)
prognathism, retrognathism (524.1)
xanthomatosis localized to bone (272.7)

√5ᵗʰ **733.0   Osteoporosis**
Use additional code to identify major osseous defect, if applicable (731.3)
Use additional code to identify personal history of pathologic (healed) fracture (V13.51)
DEF: Bone mass reduction that ultimately results in fractures after minimal trauma; dorsal kyphosis or loss of height often occur.
AHA: 4Q, '06, 103

733.00   Osteoporosis, unspecified
Wedging of vertebra NOS
AHA: 4Q, '07, 92;1Q, '07, 22; 3Q, '01, 19; 2Q, '98, 12
M81.8 Other osteoporosis w/o current pathological fx   **I-10**

733.01   Senile osteoporosis
Postmenopausal osteoporosis
AHA: 1Q, '07, 5, 6
M81.0 Age-related osteoporosis without current pathological fracture   **I-10**

733.02   Idiopathic osteoporosis

733.03   Disuse osteoporosis

733.09   Other
Drug-induced osteoporosis
Use additional E code to identify drug
AHA: 4Q, '03, 108
M81.6 Localized osteoporosis [Lequesne]   **I-10**

√5ᵗʰ **733.1   Pathologic fracture**
▶Chronic fracture◀
Spontaneous fracture
EXCLUDES   stress fracture (733.93-733.95)
traumatic fracture (800-829)
DEF: Fracture due to bone structure weakening by pathological processes (e.g., osteoporosis, neoplasms and osteomalacia).
AHA: 4Q, '08, 158; 1Q, '07, 3-4; 4Q, '93, 25; N-D, '86, 10; N-D, '85, 16
TIP: Assign only for newly diagnosed fractures; refer to V code aftercare categories if patient is receiving routine care during healing or recovery phase.

733.10   Pathologic fracture, unspecified site

733.11   Pathologic fracture of humerus

733.12   Pathologic fracture of distal radius and ulna
Wrist NOS

733.13   Pathologic fracture of vertebrae
Collapse of vertebra NOS
AHA: 3Q, '08, 4; 1Q, '07, 5, 6, 22; 3Q, '99, 5
TIP: Assign for a chronic vertebral pathological fracture for which the patient is receiving medication.
M48.53xA Collasped vertebra NEC cervicothorac initial enc   **I-10**

733.14   Pathologic fracture of neck of femur
Femur NOS
Hip NOS
AHA: 1Q, '01, 1; 1Q, '96, 16

733.15   Pathologic fracture of other specified part of femur
AHA: 2Q, '98, 12
M84.453A Pathological fracture, unspec femur, initial encounter for fx

733.16   Pathologic fracture of tibia or fibula
Ankle NOS

733.19   Pathologic fracture of other specified site

√5ᵗʰ **733.2   Cyst of bone**

733.20   Cyst of bone (localized), unspecified

733.21   Solitary bone cyst
Unicameral bone cyst

733.22   Aneurysmal bone cyst
DEF: Solitary bone lesion, bulges into periosteum; marked by calcified rim.

733.29   Other
Fibrous dysplasia (monostotic)
EXCLUDES   cyst of jaw (526.0-526.2, 526.89)
osteitis fibrosa cystica (252.01)
polyostotic fibrousdyplasia of bone (756.54)

733.3   Hyperostosis of skull
Hyperostosis interna frontalis
Leontiasis ossium
DEF: Abnormal bone growth on inner aspect of cranial bones.

√5ᵗʰ **733.4   Aseptic necrosis of bone**
Use additional code to identify major osseous defect, if applicable (731.3)
EXCLUDES   osteochondropathies (732.0-732.9)
DEF: Infarction of bone tissue due to a nonfectious etiology, such as a fracture, ischemic disorder or administration of immunosuppressive drugs; leads to degenerative joint disease or nonunion of fractures.
AHA: 4Q, '06, 103

733.40   Aseptic necrosis of bone, site unspecified

733.41   Head of humerus

733.42   Head and neck of femur
Femur NOS
EXCLUDES   Legg-Calvé-Perthes disease (732.1)
M87.256 Osteonecrosis due to previous trauma uns femur   **I-10**

733.43   Medial femoral condyle

733.44   Talus

733.45   Jaw
Use additional E code to identify drug, if drug-induced
EXCLUDES   osteoradionecrosis of jaw (526.89)
AHA: 4Q, '07, 91

733.49   Other

733.5   Osteitis condensans
Piriform sclerosis of ilium
DEF: Idiopathic condition marked by low back pain; associated with oval or triangular sclerotic, opaque bone next to sacroiliac joints in the ileum.

733.6   Tietze's disease
Costochondral junction syndrome
Costochondritis
DEF: Painful, idiopathic, nonsuppurative, swollen costal cartilage sometimes confused with cardiac symptoms because the anterior chest pain resembles that of coronary artery disease.
M94.0 Chondrocostal junction syndrome (Tietze dz)   **I-10**

733.7   Algoneurodystrophy
Disuse atrophy of bone
Sudeck's atrophy
DEF: Painful, idiopathic complex reflex sympathetic dystrophy, a chronic progressive disease characterized by severe pain, swelling, and changes in the skin..

√4ᵗʰ √5ᵗʰ   Additional Digit Required   Unspecified Code   Other Specified Code   Manifestation Code   ▶◀ Revised Text   ● New Code   ▲ Revised Code Title

2010 ICD-9-CM   **October 2009 • Volume 1 – 235**

Musculoskeletal System and Connective Tissue

733.8–736.02

✓5th **733.8** **Malunion and nonunion of fracture**
        AHA: 2Q, '94, 5

    733.81 **Malunion of fracture**

    733.82 **Nonunion of fracture**
        Pseudoarthrosis (bone)

✓5th **733.9** **Other unspecified disorders of bone and cartilage**
        AHA: ▶4Q, '08, 136-137◀

    733.90 **Disorder of bone and cartilage unspecified**

        M89.9 Disorder of bone, unspecified   I-10

    733.91 **Arrest of bone development or growth**
        Epiphyseal arrest

    733.92 **Chondromalacia**
        Chondromalacia:
          NOS
          localized, except patella
          systemic
          tibial plateau

        EXCLUDES   *chondromalacia of patella (717.7)*

        DEF: Articular cartilage softening.

    733.93 **Stress fracture of tibia or fibula**
        Stress reaction of tibia or fibula
        Use additional external cause code(s) to identify
          the cause of the stress fracture
        AHA: ▶4Q, '08, 158;◀ 4Q, '01, 48

    733.94 **Stress fracture of the metatarsals**
        Stress reaction of metatarsals
        Use additional external cause code(s) to identify
          the cause of the stress fracture
        AHA: ▶4Q, '08, 158;◀ 4Q, '01, 48

    733.95 **Stress fracture of other bone**
        Stress reaction of other bone
        Use additional external cause code(s) to identify
          the cause of the stress fracture

        EXCLUDES   *stress fracture of:*
             femoral neck (733.96)
             fibula (733.93)
             metatarsals (733.94)
             pelvis (733.98)
             shaft of femur (733.97)
             tibia (733.93)

        AHA: ▶4Q, '08, 158;◀ 4Q, '01, 48

    733.96 **Stress fracture of femoral neck**
        Stress reaction of femoral neck
        Use additional external cause code(s) to identify
          the cause of the stress fracture
        AHA: ▶4Q, '08, 158◀

    733.97 **Stress fracture of shaft of femur**
        Stress reaction of shaft of femur
        Use additional external cause code(s) to identify
          the cause of the stress fracture
        AHA: ▶4Q, '08, 158◀

    733.98 **Stress fracture of pelvis**
        Stress reaction of pelvis
        Use additional external cause code(s) to identify
          the cause of the stress fracture
        AHA: ▶4Q, '08, 158◀

    733.99 **Other**
        Diaphysitis
        Hypertrophy of bone
        Relapsing polychondritis
        AHA: J-F, '87, 14

734 **Flat foot**
    Pes planus (acquired)
    Talipes planus (acquired)

    EXCLUDES   *congenital (754.61)*
        rigid flat foot (754.61)
        spastic (everted) flat foot (754.61)

Acquired Deformities of Toe

Hallux valgus   Hallux varus

Hallux malleus (hammer of big toe)   Hammertoe

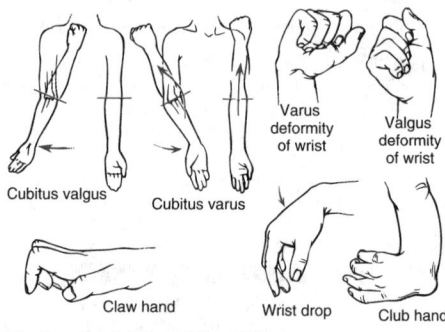

Acquired Deformities of Forearm

Varus deformity of wrist   Valgus deformity of wrist

Cubitus valgus   Cubitus varus

Claw hand   Wrist drop   Club hand

✓4th **735** **Acquired deformities of toe**

    EXCLUDES   *congenital (754.60-754.69, 755.65-755.66)*

    735.0 **Hallux valgus (acquired)**
        DEF: Angled displacement of the great toe, causing it to ride
        over or under other toes.

    735.1 **Hallux varus (acquired)**
        DEF: Angled displacement of the great toe toward the body
        midline, away from the other toes.

    735.2 **Hallux rigidus**
        DEF: Limited flexion movement at metatarsophalangeal joint
        of great toe; due to degenerative joint disease.

    735.3 **Hallux malleus**
        DEF: Extended proximal phalanx, flexed distal phalanges, of
        great toe; foot resembles claw or hammer.

    735.4 **Other hammer toe (acquired)**

    735.5 **Claw toe (acquired)**
        DEF: Hyperextended proximal phalanges, flexed middle and
        distal phalanges.

    735.8 **Other acquired deformities of toe**
        AHA: 4Q, '07, 123
        TIP: Assign for hallux limitus, a deformity of the first metatar-
        sophalangeal joint, which restricts the range of motion and
        can lead to stiffness and pain in the joint.

    735.9 **Unspecified acquired deformity of toe**

✓4th **736** **Other acquired deformities of limbs**

    EXCLUDES   *congenital (754.3-755.9)*

✓5th **736.0** **Acquired deformities of forearm, excluding fingers**

    736.00 **Unspecified deformity**
        Deformity of elbow, forearm, hand, or wrist
        (acquired) NOS

    736.01 **Cubitus valgus (acquired)**
        DEF: Deviation of the elbow away from the body
        midline upon extension; it occurs when the palm is
        turning outward.

    736.02 **Cubitus varus (acquired)**
        DEF: Elbow joint displacement angled laterally;
        when the forearm is extended, it is deviated toward
        the midline of the body; also called "gun stock"
        deformity.

N Newborn Age: 0   P Pediatric Age: 0-17   M Maternity Age: 12-55   A Adult Age: 15-124

736.03   Valgus deformity of wrist (acquired)
    DEF: Abnormal angulation away from the body midline.

736.04   Varus deformity of wrist (acquired)
    DEF: Abnormal angulation toward the body midline.

736.05   Wrist drop (acquired)
    DEF: Inability to extend the hand at the wrist due to extensor muscle paralysis

736.06   Claw hand (acquired)
    DEF: Flexion and atrophy of the hand and fingers; found in ulnar nerve lesions, syringomyelia, and leprosy.

736.07   Club hand, acquired
    DEF: Twisting of the hand out of shape or position; caused by the congenital absence of the ulna or radius.

736.09   Other

736.1   Mallet finger
    DEF: Permanently flexed distal phalanx.

√5ᵗʰ **736.2   Other acquired deformities of finger**

736.20   Unspecified deformity
    Deformity of finger (acquired) NOS

736.21   Boutonniere deformity
    DEF: A deformity of the finger caused by flexion of the proximal interphalangeal joint and hyperextension of the distal joint; also called buttonhole deformity.

736.22   Swan-neck deformity
    DEF: Flexed distal and hyperextended proximal interphalangeal joint.

736.29   Other
    EXCLUDES   trigger finger (727.03)
    AHA: 2Q, '05, 7; 2Q, '89, 13

√5ᵗʰ **736.3   Acquired deformities of hip**

736.30   Unspecified deformity
    Deformity of hip (acquired) NOS

736.31   Coxa valga (acquired)
    DEF: Increase of at least 140 degrees in the angle formed by the axis of the head and the neck of the femur, and the axis of its shaft.

736.32   Coxa vara (acquired)
    DEF: The bending downward of the neck of the femur: causing difficulty in movement; a right angle or less may be formed by the axis of the head and neck of the femur, and the axis of its shaft.

736.39   Other
    AHA: 2Q, '08, 4; 2Q, '91, 18
    TIP: Assign as principal diagnosis for follow-up visit for patient with hip methylmethacrylate cement spacer, following removal of infected joint prosthesis.

Deformities of Lower Limb

√5ᵗʰ **736.4   Genu valgum or varum (acquired)**

736.41   Genu valgum (acquired)
    DEF: Abnormally close together and an abnormally large space between the ankles; also called "knock-knees."

736.42   Genu varum (acquired)
    DEF: Abnormally separated knees and the inward bowing of the legs; it is also called "bowlegs."

736.5   Genu recurvatum (acquired)
    DEF: Hyperextended knees; also called "backknee."

736.6   Other acquired deformities of knee
    Deformity of knee (acquired) NOS

√5ᵗʰ **736.7   Other acquired deformities of ankle and foot**
    EXCLUDES   deformities of toe (acquired) (735.0-735.9)
            pes planus (acquired) (734)

736.70   Unspecified deformity of ankle and foot, acquired

736.71   Acquired equinovarus deformity
    Clubfoot, acquired
    EXCLUDES   clubfoot not specified as acquired (754.5-754.7)

736.72   Equinus deformity of foot, acquired
    DEF: A plantar flexion deformity that forces people to walk on their toes.

736.73   Cavus deformity of foot
    EXCLUDES   that with claw foot (736.74)
    DEF: Abnormally high longitudinal arch of the foot.

736.74   Claw foot, acquired
    DEF: High foot arch with hyperextended toes at metatarsophalangeal joint and flexed toes at distal joints; also called "main en griffe."

736.75   Cavovarus deformity of foot, acquired
    DEF: Inward turning of the heel from the midline of the leg and an abnormally high longitudinal arch.

736.76   Other calcaneus deformity

736.79   Other
    Acquired:
      pes   } not elsewhere classified
      talipes

√5ᵗʰ **736.8   Acquired deformities of other parts of limbs**

736.81   Unequal leg length (acquired)

736.89   Other
    Deformity (acquired):
      arm or leg, not elsewhere classified
      shoulder
    AHA: 2Q, '08, 5
    TIP: Assign as principal diagnosis for follow-up visit for patient with humeral methylmethacrylate cement spacer, following removal of infected joint prosthesis.

736.9   Acquired deformity of limb, site unspecified

√4ᵗʰ **737   Curvature of spine**
    EXCLUDES   congenital (754.2)

737.0   Adolescent postural kyphosis
    EXCLUDES   osteochondrosis of spine (juvenile) (732.0) adult (732.8)

√5ᵗʰ **737.1   Kyphosis (acquired)**

737.10   Kyphosis (acquired) (postural)
    M40.05 Postural kyphosis thoracolumbar region I-10

737.11   Kyphosis due to radiation

737.12   Kyphosis, postlaminectomy
    AHA: J-F, '87, 7
    M96.3 Postlaminectomy kyphosis   I-10

√4ᵗʰ Additional Digit Required   Unspecified Code   Other Specified Code   Manifestation Code   ►◄ Revised Text   ● New Code   ▲ Revised Code Title

2010 ICD-9-CM   **Volume 1 – 237**

Kyphosis and Lordosis

Kyphosis (hump)

Lordosis (concave)

737.19 Other

> **EXCLUDES** that associated with conditions classifiable elsewhere (737.41)

AHA: 1Q, '07, 20

√5ᵗʰ 737.2 Lordosis (acquired)

> **DEF:** Swayback appearance created by an abnormally increased spinal curvature; it is also referred to as "hollow back" or "saddle back."

737.20 Lordosis (acquired) (postural)

737.21 Lordosis, postlaminectomy

737.22 Other postsurgical lordosis

737.29 Other

> **EXCLUDES** that associated with conditions classifiable elsewhere (737.42)

√5ᵗʰ 737.3 Kyphoscoliosis and scoliosis

> **DEF:** Kyphoscoliosis: backward and lateral curvature of the spinal column; it is found in vertebral osteochondrosis.
>
> **DEF:** Scoliosis: an abnormal deviation of the spine to the left or right of the midline

737.30 Scoliosis [and kyphoscoliosis], idiopathic

> **AHA:** 3Q, '03, 19
>
> **M41.115** Juvenile idiopathic scoliosis thoracolumbar region [I-10]

737.31 Resolving infantile idiopathic scoliosis

737.32 Progressive infantile idiopathic scoliosis

> **AHA:** 3Q, '02, 12

737.33 Scoliosis due to radiation

737.34 Thoracogenic scoliosis

737.39 Other

> **EXCLUDES** that associated with conditions classifiable elsewhere (737.43) that in kyphoscoliotic heart disease (416.1)

AHA: 2Q, '02, 16

Scoliosis and Kyphoscoliosis

Scoliosis

Kyphoscoliosis

√5ᵗʰ 737.4 Curvature of spine associated with other conditions

> *Code first associated condition as:*
> Charcôt-Marie-Tooth disease (356.1)
> mucopolysaccharidosis (277.5)
> neurofibromatosis (237.7)
> osteitis deformans (731.0)
> osteitis fibrosa cystica (252.01)
> osteoporosis (733.00-733.09)
> poliomyelitis (138)
> tuberculosis [Pott's curvature] (015.0)

737.40 Curvature of spine, unspecified

737.41 Kyphosis

737.42 Lordosis

737.43 Scoliosis

737.8 Other curvatures of spine

737.9 Unspecified curvature of spine

> Curvature of spine (acquired) (idiopathic) NOS
> Hunchback, acquired
>
> **EXCLUDES** deformity of spine NOS (738.5)

√4ᵗʰ 738 Other acquired deformity

> **EXCLUDES** congenital (754.0-756.9, 758.0-759.9)
> dentofacial anomalies (524.0-524.9)

738.0 Acquired deformity of nose

> Deformity of nose (acquired)
> Overdevelopment of nasal bones
>
> **EXCLUDES** deflected or deviated nasal septum (470)

√5ᵗʰ 738.1 Other acquired deformity of head

738.10 Unspecified deformity

738.11 Zygomatic hyperplasia

> **DEF:** Abnormal enlargement of the zygoma (processus zygomaticus temporalis).

738.12 Zygomatic hypoplasia

> **DEF:** Underdevelopment of the zygoma (processus zygomaticus temporalis).

738.19 Other specified deformity

> **AHA:** 1Q, '06, 8; 2Q, '03, 13

738.2 Acquired deformity of neck

738.3 Acquired deformity of chest and rib

> Deformity:
> chest (acquired)
> rib (acquired)
> Pectus:
> carinatum, acquired
> excavatum, acquired

738.4 Acquired spondylolisthesis

> Degenerative spondylolisthesis
> Spondylolysis, acquired
>
> **EXCLUDES** congenital (756.12)
>
> **DEF:** Vertebra displaced forward over another; due to bilateral defect in vertebral arch, eroded articular surface of posterior facts and elongated pedicle between fifth lumbar vertebra and sacrum.
>
> **AHA:** 4Q, '07, 120; 1Q, '07, 10
>
> **M43.10** Spondylolisthesis site unspecified [I-10]

738.5 Other acquired deformity of back or spine

> Deformity of spine NOS
>
> **EXCLUDES** curvature of spine (737.0-737.9)
>
> **AHA:** 1Q, '08, 11
>
> **TIP:** Assign for post procedural flat back syndrome, which may be the result of a previous spinal fusion surgery. Do not assign a surgical complication code.

738.6 Acquired deformity of pelvis

> Pelvic obliquity
>
> **EXCLUDES** intrapelvic protrusion of acetabulum (718.6)
> that in relation to labor and delivery (653.0-653.4, 653.8-653.9)
>
> **DEF:** Pelvic obliquity: slanting or inclination of the pelvis at an angle between 55 and 60 degrees between the plane of the pelvis and the horizontal plane.

738.7 Cauliflower ear
> **DEF:** Abnormal external ear; due to injury, subsequent perichondritis.

738.8 Acquired deformity of other specified site
> Deformity of clavicle
> **AHA:** 2Q, '01, 15

738.9 Acquired deformity of unspecified site

√4th **739 Nonallopathic lesions, not elsewhere classified**
> **INCLUDES**   segmental dysfunction
>   somatic dysfunction
> **DEF:** Disability, loss of function or abnormality of a body part that is neither classifiable to a particular system nor brought about therapeutically to counteract another disease.

739.0 Head region
> Occipitocervical region

739.1 Cervical region
> Cervicothoracic region

739.2 Thoracic region
> Thoracolumbar region

739.3 Lumbar region
> Lumbosacral region

739.4 Sacral region
> Sacrococcygeal region
> Sacroiliac region

739.5 Pelvic region
> Hip region
> Pubic region

739.6 Lower extremities

739.7 Upper extremities
> Acromioclavicular region
> Sternoclavicular region

739.8 Rib cage
> Costochondral region
> Costovertebral region
> Sternochondral region

739.9 Abdomen and other
> **AHA:** 2Q, '89, 14

Musculoskeletal System and Connective Tissue

738.7–739.9

14. CONGENITAL ANOMALIES (740-759)

TIP: Codes from chapter 14 may be assigned throughout the life of the patient, whenever the congenital anomaly is diagnosed.

✓4ᵗʰ 740 Anencephalus and similar anomalies

740.0 Anencephalus
Acrania
Amyelencephalus
Hemicephaly
Hemianencephaly
DEF: Fetus without cerebrum, cerebellum and flat bones of skull.

740.1 Craniorachischisis
DEF: Congenital slit in cranium and vertebral column

740.2 Iniencephaly
DEF: Spinal cord passes through enlarged occipital bone (foramen magnum); absent vertebral bone layer and spinal processes; resulting in both reduction in number and proper fusion of the vertebrae.

✓4ᵗʰ 741 Spina bifida

EXCLUDES *spina bifida occulta (756.17)*

> The following fifth-digit subclassification is for use with category 741:
> **0 unspecified region**
> **1 cervical region**
> **2 dorsal [thoracic] region**
> **3 lumbar region**

DEF: Lack of closure of spinal cord's bony encasement; marked by cord protrusion into lumbosacral area; evident by elevated alpha-fetoprotein of amniotic fluid
AHA: 3Q, '94, 7
TIP: For Arnold-Chiari syndrome, Type I, refer to code 348.4.

§ ✓5ᵗʰ **741.0 With hydrocephalus**
[0-3]   Arnold-Chiari syndrome, type II
Chiari malformation, type II
Any condition classifiable to 741.9 with any condition classifiable to 742.3
AHA: 4Q, '97, 51; 4Q, '94, 37; S-O, '87, 10
Q05.4 Unspecified spina bifida with hydrocephalus   `I-10`

§ ✓5ᵗʰ **741.9 Without mention of hydrocephalus**
[0-3]   Hydromeningocele (spinal)
Hydromyelocele
Meningocele (spinal)
Meningomyelocele
Myelocele
Myelocystocele
Rachischisis
Spina bifida (aperta)
Syringomyelocele
Q05.8 Sacral spina bifida without hydrocephalus   `I-10`

Spina Bifida

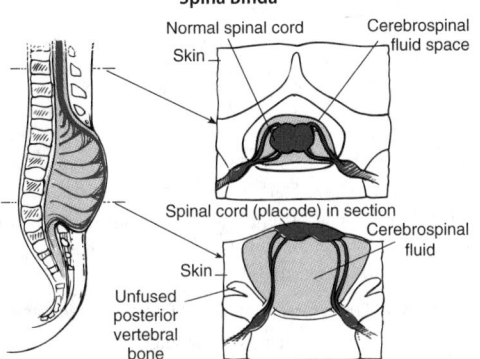

Normal spinal cord
Skin
Cerebrospinal fluid space

Spinal cord (placode) in section
Skin
Cerebrospinal fluid

Unfused posterior vertebral bone

Normal Ventricles and Hydrocephalus

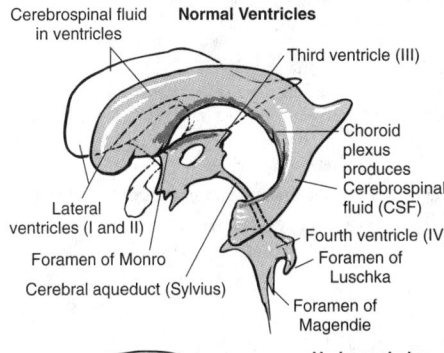

Cerebrospinal fluid in ventricles   **Normal Ventricles**
Third ventricle (III)
Choroid plexus produces Cerebrospinal fluid (CSF)
Lateral ventricles (I and II)
Foramen of Monro
Cerebral aqueduct (Sylvius)
Fourth ventricle (IV)
Foramen of Luschka
Foramen of Magendie

Hydrocephalus
Blockage of any CSF passage increases pressure in skull, which may push tissue through the Incisura tentorii or through the Foramen magnum
Enlarged ventricles

✓4ᵗʰ 742 Other congenital anomalies of nervous system

EXCLUDES *congenital central alveolar hypoventilation syndrome (327.25)*

742.0 Encephalocele
Encephalocystocele
Encephalomyelocele
Hydroencephalocele
Hydromeningocele, cranial
Meningocele, cerebral
Meningoencephalocele
DEF: Brain tissue protrudes through skull defect.
AHA: 4Q, '94, 37

742.1 Microcephalus
Hydromicrocephaly
Micrencephaly
DEF: Extremely small head or brain.

742.2 Reduction deformities of brain
Absence
Agenesis   } of part of brain
Aplasia
Hypoplasia

Agyria
Arhinencephaly
Holoprosencephaly
Microgyria
AHA: 3Q, '03, 15; 4Q, '94, 37
TIP: Assign for septo-optic dysplasia.

742.3 Congenital hydrocephalus
Aqueduct of Sylvius:
anomaly
obstruction, congenital
stenosis
Atresia of foramina of Magendie and Luschka
Hydrocephalus in newborn
EXCLUDES *hydrocephalus:*
acquired (331.3-331.4)
due to congenital toxoplasmosis (771.2)
with any condition classifiable to 741.9 (741.0)
DEF: Fluid accumulation within the skull; involves subarachnoid (external) or ventricular (internal) brain spaces.
AHA: 4Q, '05, 83
Q03.9 Congenital hydrocephalus unspecified   `I-10`

---

§   Requires fifth digit. Valid digits are in [brackets] under each code. See category 741 for codes and definitions.

| ✓4ᵗʰ ✓5ᵗʰ Additional Digit Required | Unspecified Code | Other Specified Code | Manifestation Code | ▶◀ Revised Text | ● New Code | ▲ Revised Code Title |

Congenital Anomalies

742.4–743.51

742.4   Other specified anomalies of brain
Congenital cerebral cyst
Macroencephaly
Macrogyria
Megalencephaly
Multiple anomalies of brain NOS
Porencephaly
Ulegyria
AHA: 1Q, '99, 9; 3Q, '92, 12

√5th   742.5   Other specified anomalies of spinal cord

742.51   Diastematomyelia
DEF: Congenital anomaly often associated with spina bifida; the spinal cord is separated into halves by a bony tissue resembling a "spike" (a spicule), each half surrounded by a dural sac.

742.53   Hydromyelia
Hydrorhachis
DEF: Dilated central spinal cord canal; characterized by increased fluid accumulation.

742.59   Other
Amyelia
Atelomyelia
Congenital anomaly of spinal meninges
Defective development of cauda equina
Hypoplasia of spinal cord
Myelatelia
Myelodysplasia
AHA: 2Q, '91, 14; 1Q, '89, 10
TIP: Assign for tethered spinal cord syndrome, regardless of when it is diagnosed.

742.8   Other specified anomalies of nervous system
Agenesis of nerve
Displacement of brachial plexus
Familial dysautonomia
Jaw-winking syndrome
Marcus-Gunn syndrome
Riley-Day syndrome
EXCLUDES   *neurofibromatosis (237.7)*

742.9   Unspecified anomaly of brain, spinal cord, and nervous system
Anomaly
Congenital:
  disease   of: brain
  lesion   nervous system
  Deformity   spinal cord

√4th   743   Congenital anomalies of eye

√5th   743.0   Anophthalmos
DEF: Complete absence of the eyes or the presence of vestigial eyes.

743.00   Clinical anophthalmos, unspecified
Agenesis
Cogenital absence   of eye
Anophthalmos NOS

743.03   Cystic eyeball, congenital

743.06   Cryptophthalmos
DEF: Skin is continuous over eyeball, results in apparent absence of eyelids.

√5th   743.1   Microphthalmos
Dysplasia
Hypoplasia   of eye
Rudimentary eye
DEF: Abnormally small eyeballs, may be opacities of cornea and lens, scarring of choroid and retina.

743.10   Microphthalmos, unspecified

743.11   Simple microphthalmos

743.12   Microphthalmos associated with other anomalies of eye and adnexa

√5th   743.2   Buphthalmos
Glaucoma:
  congenital
  newborn
Hydrophthalmos
EXCLUDES   *glaucoma of childhood (365.14)*
    traumatic glaucoma due to birth injury (767.8)
DEF: Distended, enlarged fibrous coats of eye; due to intraocular pressure of congenital glaucoma.

743.20   Buphthalmos, unspecified

743.21   Simple buphthalmos

743.22   Buphthalmos associated with other ocular anomalies
Keratoglobus,
  cogenital   associated with
Megalocornea   buphthalmos

√5th   743.3   Congenital cataract and lens anomalies
EXCLUDES   *infantile cataract (366.00-366.09)*
DEF: Opaque eye lens.

743.30   Congenital cataract, unspecified

743.31   Capsular and subcapsular cataract

743.32   Cortical and zonular cataract

743.33   Nuclear cataract

743.34   Total and subtotal cataract, congenital

743.35   Congenital aphakia
Congenital absence of lens

743.36   Anomalies of lens shape
Microphakia
Spherophakia

743.37   Congenital ectopic lens

743.39   Other

√5th   743.4   Coloboma and other anomalies of anterior segment
DEF: Coloboma: ocular tissue defect associated with defect of ocular fetal intraocular fissure; may cause small pit on optic disk, major defects of iris, ciliary body, choroid, and retina.

743.41   Anomalies of corneal size and shape
Microcornea
EXCLUDES   *that associated with buphthalmos (743.22)*

743.42   Corneal opacities, interfering with vision, congenital

743.43   Other corneal opacities, congenital

743.44   Specified anomalies of anterior chamber, chamber angle, and related structures
Anomaly:
  Axenfeld's
  Peters'
  Rieger's

743.45   Aniridia
DEF: Incompletely formed or absent iris; affects both eyes; dominant trait; also called congenital hyperplasia of iris.
AHA: 3Q, '02, 20

743.46   Other specified anomalies of iris and ciliary body
Anisocoria, congenital
Atresia of pupil
Coloboma of iris
Corectopia

743.47   Specified anomalies of sclera

743.48   Multiple and combined anomalies of anterior segment

743.49   Other

√5th   743.5   Congenital anomalies of posterior segment

743.51   Vitreous anomalies
Congenital vitreous opacity

743.52 **Fundus coloboma**
> **DEF:** Absent retinal and choroidal tissue; occurs in lower fundus; a bright white ectatic zone of exposed sclera extends into and changes the optic disk.

743.53 **Chorioretinal degeneration, congenital**

743.54 **Congenital folds and cysts of posterior segment**

743.55 **Congenital macular changes**

743.56 **Other retinal changes, congenital**
> **AHA:** 3Q, '99, 12

743.57 **Specified anomalies of optic disc**
> Coloboma of optic disc (congenital)

743.58 **Vascular anomalies**
> Congenital retinal aneurysm

743.59 **Other**

√5th 743.6 **Congenital anomalies of eyelids, lacrimal system, and orbit**

743.61 **Congenital ptosis**
> **DEF:** Drooping of eyelid.

743.62 **Congenital deformities of eyelids**
> Ablepharon
> Absence of eyelid
> Accessory eyelid
> Congenital:
>> ectropion
>> entropion
>
> **AHA:** 1Q, '00, 22
>
> **TIP:** Assign for epiblepharon, in which a redundant horizontal skin fold under the eyelid causes an abnormal vertical orientation of the eyelashes; may result in the eyelashes touching the eyeball.

743.63 **Other specified congenital anomalies of eyelid**
> Absence, agenesis, of cilia

743.64 **Specified congenital anomalies of lacrimal gland**

743.65 **Specified congenital anomalies of lacrimal passages**
> Absence, agenesis of:
>> lacrimal apparatus
>> punctum lacrimale
> Accessory lacrimal canal

743.66 **Specified congenital anomalies of orbit**

743.69 **Other**
> Accessory eye muscles

743.8 **Other specified anomalies of eye**
> **EXCLUDES** congenital nystagmus (379.51)
> ocular albinism (270.2)
> optic nerve hypoplasia (377.43)
> retinitis pigmentosa (362.74)

743.9 **Unspecified anomaly of eye**
> Congenital:
> anomaly NOS } of eye (any part)
> deformity NOS

√4th **744 Congenital anomalies of ear, face, and neck**
> **EXCLUDES** anomaly of:
> cervical spine (754.2, 756.10-756.19)
> larynx (748.2-748.3)
> nose (748.0-748.1)
> parathyroid gland (759.2)
> thyroid gland (759.2)
> cleft lip (749.10-749.25)

√5th 744.0 **Anomalies of ear causing impairment of hearing**
> **EXCLUDES** congenital deafness without mention of cause (389.0-389.9)

744.00 **Unspecified anomaly of ear with impairment of hearing**

744.01 **Absence of external ear**
> Absence of:
>> auditory canal (external)
>> auricle (ear) (with stenosis or atresia of auditory canal)

744.02 **Other anomalies of external ear with impairment of hearing**
> Atresia or stricture of auditory canal (external)

744.03 **Anomaly of middle ear, except ossicles**
> Atresia or stricture of osseous meatus (ear)

744.04 **Anomalies of ear ossicles**
> Fusion of ear ossicles

744.05 **Anomalies of inner ear**
> Congenital anomaly of:
>> membranous labyrinth
>> organ of Corti

744.09 **Other**
> Absence of ear, congenital

744.1 **Accessory auricle**
> Accessory tragus   Supernumerary:
> Polyotia   ear
> Preauricular appendage   lobule
> **DEF:** Redundant tissue or structures of ear.

√5th 744.2 **Other specified anomalies of ear**
> **EXCLUDES** that with impairment of hearing (744.00-744.09)

744.21 **Absence of ear lobe, congenital**

744.22 **Macrotia**
> **DEF:** Abnormally large pinna of ear.

744.23 **Microtia**
> **DEF:** Hypoplasia of pinna; associated with absent or closed auditory canal.

744.24 **Specified anomalies of Eustachian tube**
> Absence of Eustachian tube

744.29 **Other**
> Bat ear
> Darwin's tubercle
> Pointed ear
> Prominence of auricle
> Ridge ear
> **EXCLUDES** preauricular sinus (744.46)

744.3 **Unspecified anomaly of ear**
> Congenital:
> anomaly NOS } of ear, not elsewhere classified
> deformity NOS

√5th 744.4 **Branchial cleft cyst or fistula; preauricular sinus**

744.41 **Branchial cleft sinus or fistula**
> Branchial:
>> sinus (external) (internal)
>> vestige
> **DEF:** Cyst due to failed closure of embryonic branchial cleft.

744.42 **Branchial cleft cyst**

744.43 **Cervical auricle**

744.46 **Preauricular sinus or fistula**

744.47 **Preauricular cyst**

744.49 **Other**
> Fistula (of):
>> auricle, congenital
>> cervicoaural

744.5 **Webbing of neck**
> Pterygium colli
> **DEF:** Thick, triangular skinfold, stretches from lateral side of neck across shoulder; associated with Turner's and Noonan's syndromes.

√4th √5th Additional Digit Required   Unspecified Code   Other Specified Code   Manifestation Code   ▶◀ Revised Text   ● New Code   ▲ Revised Code Title

2010 ICD-9-CM   **Volume 1 – 243**

Congenital Anomalies

744.8–746.2

√5th **744.8 Other specified anomalies of face and neck**

744.81 Macrocheilia
Hypertrophy of lip, congenital
DEF: Abnormally large lips.

744.82 Microcheilia
DEF: Abnormally small lips.

744.83 Macrostomia
DEF: Bilateral or unilateral anomaly, of mouth due to malformed maxillary and mandibular processes; results in mouth extending toward ear.

744.84 Microstomia
DEF: Abnormally small mouth.

744.89 Other
EXCLUDES   *congenital fistula of lip (750.25)*
musculoskeletal anomalies (754.0-754.1, 756.0)

744.9 Unspecified anomalies of face and neck
Congenital:
anomaly NOS   } of face [any part] or neck [any
deformity NOS } part]

√4th **745 Bulbus cordis anomalies and anomalies of cardiac septal closure**

745.0 Common truncus
Absent septum   } between aorta and
Communication (abnormal) } pulmonary artery
Aortic septal defect
Common aortopulmonary trunk
Persistent truncus arteriosus

√5th **745.1 Transposition of great vessels**

745.10 Complete transposition of great vessels
Transposition of great vessels:
NOS
classical

745.11 Double outlet right ventricle
Dextratransposition of aorta
Incomplete transposition of great vessels
Origin of both great vessels from right ventricle
Taussig-Bing syndrome or defect

745.12 Corrected transposition of great vessels

745.19 Other

745.2 Tetralogy of Fallot
Fallot's pentalogy
Ventricular septal defect with pulmonary stenosis or atresia, dextraposition of aorta, and hypertrophy of right ventricle
EXCLUDES   *Fallot's triad (746.09)*
DEF: Obstructed cardiac outflow causes pulmonary stenosis, interventricular septal defect and right ventricular hypertrophy.

745.3 Common ventricle
Cor triloculare biatriatum
Single ventricle

Heart Defects

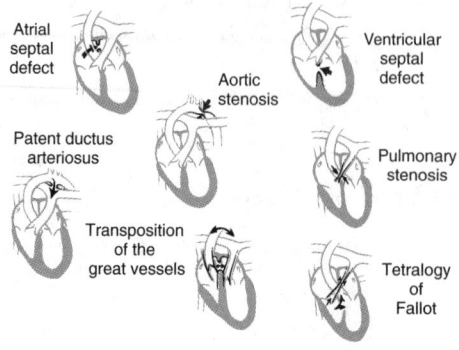

Atrial septal defect
Ventricular septal defect
Aortic stenosis
Patent ductus arteriosus
Pulmonary stenosis
Transposition of the great vessels
Tetralogy of Fallot

745.4 Ventricular septal defect
Eisenmenger's defect or complex
Gerbo dedefect
Interventricular septal defect
Left ventricular-right atrial communication
Roger's disease
EXCLUDES   *common atrioventricular canal type (745.69)*
single ventricle (745.3)
Q21.0 Ventricular septal defect   I-10

745.5 Ostium secundum type atrial septal defect
Defect:
atrium secundum
fossa ovalis
Lutembacher's syndrome
Patent or persistent:
foramen ovale
ostium secundum
DEF: Opening in atrial septum due to failure of the septum secundum and the endocardial cushions to fuse; there is a rim of septum surrounding the defect.
Q21.1 Atrial septal defect   I-10

√5th **745.6 Endocardial cushion defects**
DEF: Atrial and/or ventricular septal defects causing abnormal fusion of cushions in atrioventricular canal.

745.60 Endocardial cushion defect, unspecified type
DEF: Septal defect due to imperfect fusion of endocardial cushions.

745.61 Ostium primum defect
Persistent ostium primum
DEF: Opening in low, posterior septum primum; causes cleft in basal portion of atrial septum; associated with cleft mitral valve.

745.69 Other
Absence of atrial septum
Atrioventricular canal type ventricular septal defect
Common atrioventricular canal
Common atrium

745.7 Cor biloculare
Absence of atrial and ventricular septa
DEF: Atrial and ventricular septal defect; marked by heart with two cardiac chambers (one atrium, one ventricle), and one atrioventricular valve.

745.8 Other

745.9 Unspecified defect of septal closure
Septal defect NOS

√4th **746 Other congenital anomalies of heart**
EXCLUDES   *endocardial fibroelastosis (425.3)*

√5th **746.0 Anomalies of pulmonary valve**
EXCLUDES   *infundibular or subvalvular pulmonic stenosis (746.83)*
tetralogy of Fallot (745.2)

746.00 Pulmonary valve anomaly, unspecified

746.01 Atresia, congenital
Congenital absence of pulmonary valve

746.02 Stenosis, congenital
DEF: Stenosis of opening between pulmonary artery and right ventricle; causes obstructed blood outflow from right ventricle.

746.09 Other
Congenital insufficiency of pulmonary valve
Fallot's triad or trilogy

746.1 Tricuspid atresia and stenosis, congenital
Absence of tricuspid valve

746.2 Ebstein's anomaly
DEF: Malformation of the tricuspid valve characterized by septal and posterior leaflets attaching to the wall of the right ventricle; causing the right ventricle to fuse with the atrium into a large right atrium and a small ventricle; causes heart failure and abnormal cardiac rhythm.

746.3 Congenital stenosis of aortic valve
Congenital aortic stenosis

> *EXCLUDES*   *congenital:*
>   *subaortic stenosis (746.81)*
>   *supravalvular aortic stenosis (747.22)*

DEF: Stenosis of orifice of aortic valve; obstructs blood outflow from left ventricle.

AHA: 4Q, '88, 8

746.4 Congenital insufficiency of aortic valve
Bicuspid aortic valve
Congenital aortic insufficiency

DEF: Impaired functioning of aortic valve due to incomplete closure; causes backflow (regurgitation) of blood from aorta to left ventricle.

Q23.1 Congenital insufficiency of aortic valve   I-10

746.5 Congenital mitral stenosis
Fused commissure
Parachute deformity   } of mitral valve
Supernumerary cusps

DEF: Stenosis of left atrioventricular orifice.

AHA: 3Q, '07, 3

746.6 Congenital mitral insufficiency

DEF: Impaired functioning of mitral valve due to incomplete closure; causes backflow of blood from left ventricle to left atrium.

746.7 Hypoplastic left heart syndrome
Atresia, or marked hypoplasia, of aortic orifice or valve, with hypoplasia of ascending aorta and defective development of left ventricle (with mitral valve atresia)

√5ᵗʰ 746.8 Other specified anomalies of heart

    746.81 Subaortic stenosis

      DEF: Stenosis, of left ventricular outflow tract due to fibrous tissue ring or septal hypertrophy below aortic valve.

      AHA: 3Q, '07, 3

    746.82 Cor triatriatum

      DEF: Transverse septum divides left atrium due to failed resorption of embryonic common pulmonary vein; results in three atrial chambers.

    746.83 Infundibular pulmonic stenosis
      Subvalvular pulmonic stenosis

      DEF: Stenosis of right ventricle outflow tract within infundibulum due to fibrous diaphragm below valve or long, narrow fibromuscular channel.

    746.84 Obstructive anomalies of heart, not elsewhere classified
      Shone's syndrome
      Uhl's disease

      Use additional code for associated anomalies, such as:
        coarctation of aorta (747.10)
        congenital mitral stenosis (746.5)
        subaortic stenosis (746.81)

    746.85 Coronary artery anomaly
      Anomalous origin or communication of coronary artery
      Arteriovenous malformation of coronary artery
      Coronary artery:
        absence
        arising from aorta or pulmonary trunk
        single

      AHA: N-D, '85, 3

    746.86 Congenital heart block
      Complete or incomplete atrioventricular [AV] block

      DEF: Impaired conduction of electrical impulses; due to maldeveloped junctional tissue.

    746.87 Malposition of heart and cardiac apex
      Abdominal heart
      Dextrocardia
      Ectopia cordis
      Levocardia (isolated)
      Mesocardia

>   *EXCLUDES*   *dextrocardia with complete transposition of viscera (759.3)*

    746.89 Other
      Atresia
      Hypoplasia   } of cardiac vein

      Congenital:
        cardiomegaly
        diverticulum, left ventricle
        pericardial defect

      AHA: 3Q, '00, 3; 1Q, '99, 11; J-F, '85, 3

      TIP: Assign for Brugada syndrome, and also for congenital long QT syndrome. Additional codes may be required.

      Q24.8 Oth specified congenital malformations   I-10
      of heart

746.9 Unspecified anomaly of heart
Congenital:
  anomaly of heart NOS
  heart disease NOS

√4ᵗʰ 747 Other congenital anomalies of circulatory system

    747.0 Patent ductus arteriosus
      Patent ductus Botalli
      Persistent ductus arteriosus

      DEF: Open lumen in ductus arteriosus causes arterial blood recirculation in lungs; inhibits blood supply to aorta; symptoms such as shortness of breath more noticeable upon activity.

      Q25.0 Patent ductus arteriosus   I-10

  √5ᵗʰ 747.1 Coarctation of aorta

      DEF: Localized deformity of aortic media seen as a severe constriction of the vessel lumen; major symptom is high blood pressure in the arms and low pressure in the legs; may result in a CVA, rupture of the aorta, bacterial endocarditis or congestive heart failure.

    747.10 Coarctation of aorta (preductal) (postductal)
      Hypoplasia of aortic arch
      AHA: 3Q, '07, 3; 1Q, '99, 11; 4Q, '88, 8

    747.11 Interruption of aortic arch

  √5ᵗʰ 747.2 Other anomalies of aorta

    747.20 Anomaly of aorta, unspecified

    747.21 Anomalies of aortic arch
      Anomalous origin, right subclavian artery
      Dextraposition of aorta
      Double aortic arch
      Kommerell's diverticulum
      Overriding aorta
      Persistent:
        convolutions, aortic arch
        right aortic arch
      Vascular ring

>   *EXCLUDES*   *hypoplasia of aortic arch (747.10)*

      AHA: 1Q, '03, 15

    747.22 Atresia and stenosis of aorta
      Absence
      Aplasia
      Hypoplasia   } of aorta
      Stricture

      Supra (valvular)-aortic stenosis

>   *EXCLUDES*   *congenital aortic (valvular) stenosis or stricture, so stated (746.3)*
>   *hypoplasia of aorta in hypoplastic left heart syndrome (746.7)*

√4ᵗʰ **√5ᵗʰ**   Additional Digit Required   Unspecified Code   Other Specified Code   Manifestation Code   ▶◀ Revised Text   ● New Code   ▲ Revised Code Title

2010 ICD-9-CM   **Volume 1 – 245**

747.29   **Other**
Aneurysm of sinus of Valsalva
Congenital:
aneurysm ⎫
dilation ⎬ of aorta

747.3   **Anomalies of pulmonary artery**
Agenesis ⎫
Anomaly ⎪
Atresia   ⎬ of pulmonary artery
Coarctation ⎪
Hypoplasia ⎪
Stenosis ⎭

Pulmonary arteriovenous aneurysm
AHA: 1Q, '04, 16; 1Q, '94, 15; 4Q, '88, 8
Q25.7 Oth congenital malformations of pulmonary artery **I-10**

☑5ᵗʰ **747.4**   **Anomalies of great veins**

747.40   **Anomaly of great veins, unspecified**
Anomaly NOS of:
pulmonary veins
vena cava

747.41   **Total anomalous pulmonary venous connection**
Total anomalous pulmonary venous return [TAPVR]:
subdiaphragmatic
supradiaphragmatic

747.42   **Partial anomalous pulmonary venous connection**
Partial anomalous pulmonary venous return

747.49   **Other anomalies of great veins**
Absence   ⎫
Congenital   ⎬ of vena cava (inferior)
  stenosis   ⎭ (superior)
Persistent:
left posterior cardinal vein
left superior vena cava
Scimitar syndrome
Transposition of pulmonary veins NOS

747.5   **Absence or hypoplasia of umbilical artery**
Single umbilical artery

☑5ᵗʰ **747.6**   **Other anomalies of peripheral vascular system**
Absence ⎫
Anomaly ⎬ of artery or vein, NEC
Atresia   ⎭
Arteriovenous aneurysm (peripheral)
Arteriovenous malformation of the peripheral vascular system
Congenital:
aneurysm (peripheral)
phlebectasia
stricture, artery
varix
Multiple renal arteries
EXCLUDES   anomalies of:
      cerebral vessels (747.81)
      pulmonary artery (747.3)
    congenital retinal aneurysm (743.58)
    hemangioma (228.00-228.09)
    lymphangioma (228.1)

747.60   **Anomaly of the peripheral vascular system, unspecified site**

747.61   **Gastrointestinal vessel anomaly**
AHA: 3Q, '96, 10
TIP: Do not assign for gastric or intestinal AV malformation or angiodysplasia not stated to be congenital. See instead code 537.82, 537.83, 569.84, or 569.85.

747.62   **Renal vessel anomaly**

747.63   **Upper limb vessel anomaly**

Persistent Fetal Circulation

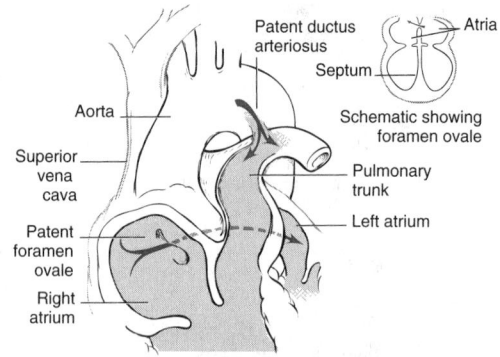

747.64   **Lower limb vessel anomaly**

747.69   **Anomalies of other specified sites of peripheral vascular system**

☑5ᵗʰ **747.8**   **Other specified anomalies of circulatory system**

747.81   **Anomalies of cerebrovascular system**
Arteriovenous malformation of brain
Cerebral arteriovenous aneurysm, congenital
Congenital anomalies of cerebral vessels
EXCLUDES   ruptured cerebral (arteriovenous) aneurysm (430)
Q28.3 Other malformations of cerebral vessels **I-10**

747.82   **Spinal vessel anomaly**
Arteriovenous malformation of spinal vessel
AHA: 3Q, '95, 5

747.83   **Persistent fetal circulation**   **N**
Persistent pulmonary hypertension
Primary pulmonary hypertension of newborn
DEF: A return to fetal circulation due to constriction of pulmonary arterioles and opening of the ductus arteriosus and foramen ovale, right-to-left shunting, oxygenation of the blood does not occur, and the lungs remain constricted after birth; is seen in term or post-term infants causes include asphyxiation, meconium aspiration syndrome, acidosis, sepsis, and developmental immaturity.
AHA: 4Q, '02, 62

747.89   **Other**
Aneurysm, congenital, specified site not elsewhere classified
EXCLUDES   congenital aneurysm:
    coronary (746.85)
    peripheral (747.6)
    pulmonary (747.3)
    retinal (743.58)
AHA: 4Q, '02, 63

747.9   **Unspecified anomaly of circulatory system**

☑4ᵗʰ **748**   **Congenital anomalies of respiratory system**
EXCLUDES   congenital central alveolar hypoventilation syndrome (327.25)
    congenital defect of diaphragm (756.6)

748.0   **Choanal atresia**
Atresia   ⎫
Congenital stenosis ⎬ of nares (anterior) (posterior)
DEF: Occluded posterior nares (choana), bony or membranous due to failure of embryonic bucconasal membrane to rupture.

748.1   **Other anomalies of nose**
Absent nose
Accessory nose
Cleft nose
Congenital:
deformity of nose
notching of tip of nose
perforation of wall of nasal sinus
Deformity of wall of nasal sinus
EXCLUDES   congenital deviation of nasal septum (754.0)

N Newborn Age: 0   **P** Pediatric Age: 0-17   **M** Maternity Age: 12-55   **A** Adult Age: 15-124

748.2   Web of larynx
Web of larynx:
NOS
glottic
subglottic

DEF: Malformed larynx; marked by thin, translucent, or thick, fibrotic spread between vocal folds; affects speech.

748.3   Other anomalies of larynx, trachea, and bronchus
Absence or agenesis of:
bronchus
larynx
trachea
Anomaly (of):
cricoid cartilage
epiglottis
thyroid cartilage
tracheal cartilage
Atresia (of):
epiglottis
glottis
larynx
trachea
Cleft thyroid, cartilage, congenital
Congenital:
dilation, trachea
stenosis:
larynx
trachea
tracheocele
Diverticulum:
bronchus
trachea
Fissure of epiglottis
Laryngocele
Posterior cleft of cricoid cartilage (congenital)
Rudimentary tracheal bronchus
Stridor, laryngeal, congenital

AHA: 1Q, '99, 14

Q32.4 Other congenital malformations of bronchus   I-10

748.4   Congenital cystic lung
Disease, lung:
cystic, congenital
polycystic, congenital
Honeycomb lung, congenital

EXCLUDES *acquired or unspecified cystic lung (518.89)*

DEF: Enlarged air spaces of lung parenchyma.

748.5   Agenesis, hypoplasia, and dysplasia of lung
Absence of lung (fissures) (lobe) (lobe)
Aplasia of lung
Hypoplasia of lung
Sequestration of lung

√5th **748.6   Other anomalies of lung**

748.60   Anomaly of lung, unspecified

748.61   Congenital bronchiectasis

748.69   Other
Accessory lung (lobe)
Azygos lobe (fissure), lung

748.8   Other specified anomalies of respiratory system
Abnormal communication between pericardial and pleural sacs
Anomaly, pleural folds
Atresia of nasopharynx
Congenital cyst of mediastinum

748.9   Unspecified anomaly of respiratory system
Anomaly of respiratory system NOS

Cleft Lip and Palate

Unilateral cleft lip
No cleft palate

Cleft lip with cleft alveolar ridge
No cleft palate

Unilateral cleft lip and cleft palate
Alveolar ridge
Cleft palate

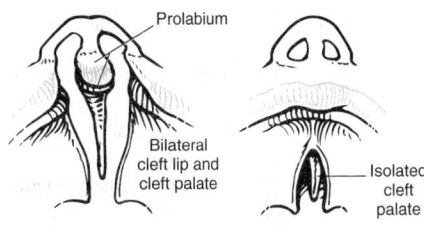
Prolabium
Bilateral cleft lip and cleft palate
Isolated cleft palate

√4th **749   Cleft palate and cleft lip**

√5th **749.0   Cleft palate**

749.00   Cleft palate, unspecified

749.01   Unilateral, complete

749.02   Unilateral, incomplete
Cleft uvula

749.03   Bilateral, complete

749.04   Bilateral, incomplete

√5th **749.1   Cleft lip**
Cheiloschisis
Congenital fissure of lip
Harelip
Labium leporinum

749.10   Cleft lip, unspecified

749.11   Unilateral, complete

749.12   Unilateral, incomplete

749.13   Bilateral, complete

749.14   Bilateral, incomplete

√5th **749.2   Cleft palate with cleft lip**
Cheilopalatoschisis

749.20   Cleft palate with cleft lip, unspecified

749.21   Unilateral, complete

749.22   Unilateral, incomplete

749.23   Bilateral, complete
AHA: 1Q, '96, 14

749.24   Bilateral, incomplete

749.25   Other combinations

√4th **750   Other congenital anomalies of upper alimentary tract**
EXCLUDES *dentofacial anomalies (524.0-524.9)*

750.0   Tongue tie
Ankyloglossia
DEF: Restricted tongue movement due to lingual frenum extending toward tip of tongue. Tongue may be fused to mouth floor affecting speech.

√5th **750.1   Other anomalies of tongue**

750.10   Anomaly of tongue, unspecified

750.11   Aglossia
DEF: Absence of tongue.

750.12   Congenital adhesions of tongue

Congenital Anomalies

750.13–751.4

750.13 **Fissure of tongue**
Bifid tongue
Double tongue

750.15 **Macroglossia**
Congenital hypertrophy of tongue

750.16 **Microglossia**
Hypoplasia of tongue

750.19 **Other**

√5th   750.2 **Other specified anomalies of mouth and pharynx**

750.21 **Absence of salivary gland**

750.22 **Accessory salivary gland**

750.23 **Atresia, salivary duct**
Imperforate salivary duct

750.24 **Congenital fistula of salivary gland**

750.25 **Congenital fistula of lip**
Congenital (mucus) lip pits

750.26 **Other specified anomalies of mouth**
Absence of uvula

750.27 **Diverticulum of pharynx**
Pharyngeal pouch

750.29 **Other specified anomalies of pharynx**
Imperforate pharynx

750.3 **Tracheoesophageal fistula, esophageal atresia and stenosis**
Absent esophagus
Atresia of esophagus
Congenital:
esophageal ring
stenosis of esophagus
stricture of esophagus
Congenital fistula:
esophagobronchial
esophagotracheal
Imperforate esophagus
Webbed esophagus

750.4 **Other specified anomalies of esophagus**
Dilatation, congenital ⎫
Displacement, congenital ⎪
Diverticulum ⎬ (of) esophagus
Duplication ⎪
Giant ⎭

Esophageal pouch
EXCLUDES *congenital hiatus hernia (750.6)*
AHA: J-F, '85, 3

750.5 **Congenital hypertrophic pyloric stenosis**
Congenital or infantile:
constriction ⎫
hypertrophy ⎪
spasm ⎬ of pylorus
stenosis ⎪
stricture ⎭

DEF: Obstructed pylorus due to overgrowth of pyloric muscle.
Q40.0 Congenital hypertrophic pyloric stenosis   I-10

750.6 **Congenital hiatus hernia**
Displacement of cardia through esophageal hiatus
EXCLUDES *congenital diaphragmatic hernia (756.6)*

750.7 **Other specified anomalies of stomach**
Congenital:
cardiospasm
hourglass stomach
Displacement of stomach
Diverticulum of stomach, congenital
Duplication of stomach
Megalogastria
Microgastria
Transposition of stomach

750.8 **Other specified anomalies of upper alimentary tract**

750.9 **Unspecified anomaly of upper alimentary tract**
Congenital:
anomaly NOS ⎫ of upper alimentary tract [any part,
deformity NOS ⎬ except tongue]

√4th   **751 Other congenital anomalies of digestive system**

751.0 **Meckel's diverticulum**
Meckel's diverticulum (displaced) (hypertrophic)
Persistent:
omphalomesenteric duct
vitelline duct

DEF: Malformed sacs or appendages of ileum of small intestine; can cause strangulation, volvulus and intussusception.
AHA: 1Q, '04, 10
TIP: Assign for mesodiverticular band, a fibrous band connecting the tip of the diverticulum to the mesentery; can cause small bowel herniation and obstruction.

751.1 **Atresia and stenosis of small intestine**   P
Atresia of:
duodenum
ileum
intestine NOS
Congenital:
absence ⎫
obstruction ⎬ of small intestine or intestine
stenosis ⎪   NOS
stricture ⎭

Imperforate jejunum

751.2 **Atresia and stenosis of large intestine rectum, and anal canal**   P
Absence:
anus (congenital)
appendix, congenital
large intestine, congenital
rectum
Atresia of:
anus
colon
rectum
Congenital or infantile:
obstruction of large intestine
occlusion of anus
stricture of anus
Imperforate:
anus
rectum
Stricture of rectum, congenital
AHA: 2Q, '98, 16

751.3 **Hirschsprung's disease and other congenital functional disorders of colon**
Aganglionosis
Congenital dilation of colon
Congenital megacolon
Macrocolon

DEF: Hirschsprung's disease: enlarged or dilated colon (megacolon), with absence of ganglion cells in the narrowed wall distally; causes inability to defecate.

751.4 **Anomalies of intestinal fixation**
Congenital adhesions:
omental, anomalous
peritoneal
Jackson's membrane
Malrotation of colon
Rotation of cecum or colon:
failure of
incomplete
insufficient
Universal mesentery

N   Newborn Age: 0   P   Pediatric Age: 0-17   M   Maternity Age: 12-55   A   Adult Age: 15-124

751.5   **Other anomalies of intestine**
Congenital diverticulum, colon
Dolichocolon
Duplication of:
    anus
    appendix
    cecum
    intestine
Ectopic anus
Megaloappendix
Megaloduodenum
Microcolon
Persistent cloaca
Transposition of:
    appendix
    colon
    intestine
AHA: 3Q, '02, 11; 3Q, '01, 8
Q43.9 Congenital malformation of intestine   **I-10**
unspecified

√5ᵗʰ 751.6   **Anomalies of gallbladder, bile ducts, and liver**

    751.60   **Unspecified anomaly of gallbladder, bile ducts, and liver**

    751.61   **Biliary atresia**   **P**
Congenital:
    absence
    hypoplasia   } of bile duct (common)
    obstruction   of passage
    stricture
AHA: S-O, '87, 8

    751.62   **Congenital cystic disease of liver**
Congenital polycystic disease of liver
Fibrocystic disease of liver

    751.69   **Other anomalies of gallbladder, bile ducts, and liver**
Absence of:
    gallbladder, congenital
    liver (lobe)
Accessory:
    hepatic ducts
    liver
Congenital:
    choledochal cyst
    hepatomegaly
Duplication of:
    biliary duct
    cystic duct
    gallbladder
    liver
Floating:
    gallbladder
    liver
Intrahepatic gallbladder
AHA: S-O, '87, 8

751.7   **Anomalies of pancreas**
Absence
Accessory
Agenesis   } (of) pancreas
Annular
Hypoplasia
Ectopic pancreatic tissue
Pancreatic heterotopia
EXCLUDES   *diabetes mellitus (249.0-249.9, 250.0-250.9)*
fibrocystic disease of pancreas (277.00-277.09)
neonatal diabetes mellitus (775.1)

751.8   **Other specified anomalies of digestive system**
Absence (complete) (partial) of alimentary tract NOS
Duplication   } of digestive organs NOS
Malposition, congenital
EXCLUDES   *congenital diaphragmatic hernia (756.6)*
congenital hiatus hernia (750.6)

751.9   **Unspecified anomaly of digestive system**
Congenital:
    anomaly NOS   } of digestive system NOS
    deformity NOS

√4ᵗʰ 752   **Congenital anomalies of genital organs**
EXCLUDES   *syndromes associated with anomalies in the number and form of chromosomes (758.0-758.9)*

752.0   **Anomalies of ovaries**   ♀
Absence, congenital
Accessory
Ectopic   } (of) ovary
Streak

√5ᵗʰ 752.1   **Anomalies of fallopian tubes and broad ligaments**

    752.10   **Unspecified anomaly of fallopian tubes and broad ligaments**   ♀

    752.11   **Embryonic cyst of fallopian tubes and broad ligaments**   ♀
Cyst: Cyst:
    epoophoron   parovarian
    fimbrial
AHA: S-O, '85, 13

    752.19   **Other**   ♀
Absence
Accessory   } (of) fallopian tube or broad ligament
Atresia

752.2   **Doubling of uterus**   ♀
Didelphic uterus
Doubling of uterus [any degree] (associated with doubling of cervix and vagina)

752.3   **Other anomalies of uterus**   ♀
Absence, congenital
Agenesis
Aplasia   } (of) uterus
Bicornuate
Uterus unicornis
Uterus with only one functioning horn
AHA: 3Q, '06, 18

√5ᵗʰ 752.4   **Anomalies of cervix, vagina, and external female genitalia**

    752.40   **Unspecified anomaly of cervix, vagina, and external female genitalia**   ♀

    752.41   **Embryonic cyst of cervix, vagina, and external female genitalia**   ♀
Cyst of: Cyst of:
    canal of Nuck,   vagina, embryonal
       congenital   vulva, congenital
    Gartner's duct
DEF: Embryonic fluid-filled cysts, of cervix, vagina or external female genitalia.

    752.42   **Imperforate hymen**   ♀
DEF: Complete closure of membranous fold around external opening of vagina.

    752.49   **Other anomalies of cervix, vagina, and external female genitalia**   ♀
Absence   } of cervix, clitoris, vagina, or vulva
Agenesis
Congenital stenosis or stricture of:
    cervical canal
    vagina
EXCLUDES   *double vagina associated with total duplication (752.2)*
AHA: 3Q, '06, 18

√5ᵗʰ 752.5   **Undescended and retractile testicle**
AHA: 4Q, '96, 33

    752.51   **Undescended testis**   ♂
Cryptorchism   Ectopic testis
Q53.20 Undescended testicle unspecified   **I-10**
bilateral

    752.52   **Retractile testis**   ♂

| √4ᵗʰ √5ᵗʰ Additional Digit Required | Unspecified Code | Other Specified Code | Manifestation Code | ►◄ Revised Text | ● New Code | ▲ Revised Code Title |

Congenital Anomalies

752.6–753.23

Hypospadias and Epispadias

Hypospadias
(ventral view)

Epispadias
(dorsal view)

✓5th 752.6 Hypospadias and epispadias and other penile anomalies

AHA: 4Q, '96, 34, 35

752.61 Hypospadias ♂

DEF: Abnormal opening of urethra on the ventral surface of the penis or perineum; also a rare defect of vagina.

AHA: 4Q, '03, 67-68; 3Q, '97, 6

Q54.1 Hypospadias penile [I-10]

752.62 Epispadias ♂
Anaspadias

DEF: Urethra opening on dorsal surface of penis; in females appears as a slit in the upper wall of urethra.

752.63 Congenital chordee ♂

DEF: Ventral bowing of penis due to fibrous band along corpus spongiosum; occurs with hypospadias.

752.64 Micropenis ♂

752.65 Hidden penis ♂

752.69 Other penile anomalies ♂

752.7 Indeterminate sex and pseudohermaphroditism
Gynandrism
Hermaphroditism
Ovotestis
Pseudohermaphroditism (male) (female)
Pure gonadal dysgenesis

EXCLUDES androgen insensitivity (259.50-259.52)
pseudohermaphroditism:
female, with adrenocortical disorder (255.2)
male, with gonadal disorder (257.8)
with specified chromosomal anomaly
(758.0-758.9)
testicular feminization syndrome
(259.50-259.52)

DEF: Pseudohermaphroditism: presence of gonads of one sex and external genitalia of other sex.

✓5th 752.8 Other specified anomalies of genital organs

EXCLUDES congenital hydrocele (778.6)
penile anomalies (752.61-752.69)
phimosis or paraphimosis (605)

752.81 Scrotal transposition ♂
AHA: 4Q, '03, 67-68

752.89 Other specified anomalies of genital organs
Absence of:
prostate
spermatic cord
vas deferens
Anorchism
Aplasia (congenital) of:
prostate
round ligament
testicle
Atresia of:
ejaculatory duct
vas deferens
Fusion of testes
Hypoplasia of testis
Monorchism
Polyorchism

752.9 Unspecified anomaly of genital organs
Congenital:
anomaly NOS } of genital organ, not
deformity NOS } elsewhere classified

✓4th 753 Congenital anomalies of urinary system

753.0 Renal agenesis and dysgenesis
Atrophy of kidney:
congenital
infantile
Congenital absence of kidney(s)
Hypoplasia of kidney(s)
Q60.2 Renal agenesis unspecified [I-10]

✓5th 753.1 Cystic kidney disease
EXCLUDES acquired cyst of kidney (593.2)
AHA: 4Q, '90, 3

753.10 Cystic kidney disease, unspecified
Q61.9 Cystic kidney disease unspecified [I-10]

753.11 Congenital single renal cyst

753.12 Polycystic kidney, unspecified type
Q61.3 Polycystic kidney unspecified [I-10]

753.13 Polycystic kidney, autosomal dominant
DEF: Slow progressive disease characterized by bilateral cysts causing increased kidney size and impaired function.

753.14 Polycystic kidney, autosomal recessive
DEF: Rare disease characterized by multiple cysts involving kidneys and liver, producing renal and hepatic failure in childhood or adolescence.

753.15 Renal dysplasia

753.16 Medullary cystic kidney
Nephronopthisis
DEF: Diffuse kidney disease results in uremia onset prior to age 20.

753.17 Medullary sponge kidney
DEF: Dilated collecting tubules; usually asymptomatic but calcinosis in tubules may cause renal insufficiency.

753.19 Other specified cystic kidney disease
Multicystic kidney

✓5th 753.2 Obstructive defects of renal pelvis and ureter
AHA: 4Q, '96, 35

753.20 Unspecified obstructive defect of renal pelvis and ureter

753.21 Congenital obstruction of ureteropelvic junction
DEF: Stricture at junction of ureter and renal pelvis.

753.22 Congenital obstruction of ureterovesical junction
Adynamic ureter
Congenital hydroureter
DEF: Stricture at junction of ureter and bladder.

753.23 Congenital ureterocele

753.29 Other
Q62.39 Other obstructive defects renal I-10
pelvis & ureter

753.3 Other specified anomalies of kidney
Accessory kidney
Congenital:
　calculus of kidney
　displaced kidney
Discoid kidney
Double kidney with double pelvis
Ectopic kidney
Fusion of kidneys
Giant kidney
Horseshoe kidney
Hyperplasia of kidney
Lobulation of kidney
Malrotation of kidney
Trifid kidney (pelvis)

AHA: 1Q, '07, 23

TIP: Assign for Finnish-type congenital nephrosis, along with
code 581.3 Nephrotic syndrome.

Q63.8 Oth specified congenital malformations of kidney I-10

753.4 Other specified anomalies of ureter
Absent ureter
Accessory ureter
Deviation of ureter
Displaced ureteric orifice
Double ureter
Ectopic ureter
Implantation, anomalous of ureter

753.5 Exstrophy of urinary bladder
Ectopia vesicae
Extroversion of bladder

DEF: Absence of lower abdominal and anterior bladder walls
with posterior bladder wall protrusion.

753.6 Atresia and stenosis of urethra and bladder neck
Congenital obstruction:
　bladder neck
　urethra
Congenital stricture of:
　urethra (valvular)
　urinary meatus
　vesicourethral orifice
Imperforate urinary meatus
Impervious urethra
Urethral valve formation

753.7 Anomalies of urachus
Cyst
Fistula　} (of) urachussinus
Patent
Persistent umbilical sinus

753.8 Other specified anomalies of bladder and urethra
Absence, congenital of:
　bladder
　urethra
Accessory:
　bladder
　urethra
Congenital:
　diverticulum of bladder
　hernia of bladder
　prolapse of:
　　bladder (mucosa)
　　urethra
　urethrorectal fistula
Double:
　urethra
　urinary meatus

753.9 Unspecified anomaly of urinary system
Congenital:
　anomaly NOS　} of urinary system [any part,
　deformity NOS　} 　　except urachus]

✓4th 754 Certain congenital musculoskeletal deformities
INCLUDES nonteratogenic deformities which are considered to
be due to intrauterine malposition and pressure

754.0 Of skull, face, and jaw
Asymmetry of face
Compression facies
Depressions in skull
Deviation of nasal septum, congenital
Dolichocephaly
Plagiocephaly
Potter's facies
Squashed or bent nose, congenital
EXCLUDES dentofacial anomalies (524.0-524.9)
syphilitic saddle nose (090.5)

754.1 Of sternocleidomastoid muscle
Congenital sternomastoid torticollis
Congenital wryneck
Contracture of sternocleidomastoid (muscle)
Sternomastoid tumor

754.2 Of spine
Congenital postural:
　lordosis
　scoliosis

✓5th 754.3 Congenital dislocation of hip
754.30 Congenital dislocation of hip, unilateral
Congenital dislocation of hip NOS

754.31 Congenital dislocation of hip, bilateral

754.32 Congenital subluxation of hip, unilateral
Congenital flexion deformity, hip or thigh
Predislocation status of hip at birth
Preluxation of hip, congenital

754.33 Congenital subluxation of hip, bilateral

754.35 Congenital dislocation of one hip with
subluxation of other hip

✓5th 754.4 Congenital genu recurvatum and bowing of long bones
of leg
754.40 Genu recurvatum
DEF: Backward curving of knee joint.

754.41 Congenital dislocation of knee (with genu
recurvatum)

754.42 Congenital bowing of femur

754.43 Congenital bowing of tibia and fibula

754.44 Congenital bowing of unspecified long
bones of leg

✓5th 754.5 Varus deformities of feet
EXCLUDES acquired (736.71, 736.75, 736.79)
754.50 Talipes varus
Congenital varus deformity of foot, unspecified
Pes varus
DEF: Inverted foot marked by outer sole resting on
ground.

754.51 Talipes equinovarus
Equinovarus (congenital)
DEF: Elevated, outward rotation of heel; also called
clubfoot.

754.52 Metatarsus primus varus
DEF: Malformed first metatarsal bone, with bone
angled toward body.

754.53 Metatarsus varus

754.59 Other
Talipes calcaneovarus

✓5th 754.6 Valgus deformities of feet
EXCLUDES valgus deformity of foot (acquired) (736.79)
754.60 Talipes valgus
Congenital valgus deformity of foot, unspecified

✓4th Additional Digit Required　　　Unspecified Code　　　Other Specified Code　　　Manifestation Code　　　▶◀ Revised Text　　　● New Code　　　▲ Revised Code Title
✓5th
2010 ICD-9-CM　　　**Volume 1 – 251**

753.29–754.60

754.61 **Congenital pes planus**
Congenital rocker bottom flat foot
Flat foot, congenital
EXCLUDES pes planus (acquired) (734)

754.62 **Talipes calcaneovalgus**

754.69 **Other**
Talipes:
equinovalgus
planovalgus

√5th 754.7 **Other deformities of feet**
EXCLUDES acquired (736.70-736.79)

754.70 **Talipes, unspecified**
Congenital deformity of foot NOS

754.71 **Talipes cavus**
Cavus foot (congenital)

754.79 **Other**
Asymmetric talipes
Talipes:
calcaneus
equinus

√5th 754.8 **Other specified nonteratogenic anomalies**

754.81 **Pectus excavatum**
Congenital funnel chest

754.82 **Pectus carinatum**
Congenital pigeon chest [breast]

754.89 **Other**
Club hand (congenital)
Congenital:
deformity of chest wall
dislocation of elbow
Generalized flexion contractures of lower limb
joints, congenital
Spade-like hand (congenital)

√4th 755 **Other congenital anomalies of limbs**
EXCLUDES those deformities classifiable to 754.0-754.8

√5th 755.0 **Polydactyly**

755.00 **Polydactyly, unspecified digits**
Supernumerary digits

755.01 **Of fingers**
Accessory fingers

755.02 **Of toes**
Accessory toes

√5th 755.1 **Syndactyly**
Symphalangy
Webbing of digits

755.10 **Of multiple and unspecified sites**

755.11 **Of fingers without fusion of bone**

755.12 **Of fingers with fusion of bone**

755.13 **Of toes without fusion of bone**

755.14 **Of toes with fusion of bone**

√5th 755.2 **Reduction deformities of upper limb**

755.20 **Unspecified reduction deformity of upper limb**
Ectromelia NOS }
Hemimelia NOS } of upper limb
Shortening of arm, congenital

755.21 **Transverse deficiency of upper limb**
Amelia of upper limb
Congenital absence of:
fingers, all (complete or partial)
forearm, including hand and fingers
upper limb, complete
Congenital amputation of upper limb
Transverse hemimelia of upper limb

755.22 **Longitudinal deficiency of upper limb, not elsewhere classified**
Phocomelia NOS of upper limb
Rudimentary arm

755.23 **Longitudinal deficiency, combined, involving humerus, radius, and ulna (complete or incomplete)**
Congenital absence of arm and forearm
(complete or incomplete) with or without
metacarpal deficiency and/or phalangeal
deficiency, incomplete
Phocomelia, complete, of upper limb

755.24 **Longitudinal deficiency, humeral, complete or partial (with or without distal deficiencies, incomplete)**
Congenital absence of humerus (with or
without absence of some [but not all]
distal elements)
Proximal phocomelia of upper limb

755.25 **Longitudinal deficiency, radioulnar, complete or partial (with or without distal deficiencies, incomplete)**
Congenital absence of radius and ulna (with or
without absence of some [but not all]
distal elements)
Distal phocomelia of upper limb

755.26 **Longitudinal deficiency, radial, complete or partial (with or without distal deficiencies, incomplete)**
Agenesis of radius
Congenital absence of radius (with or without
absence of some [but not all] distal
elements)

755.27 **Longitudinal deficiency, ulnar, complete or partial (with or without distal deficiencies, incomplete)**
Agenesis of ulna
Congenital absence of ulna (with or without
absence of some [but not all] distal
elements)

755.28 **Longitudinal deficiency, carpals or metacarpals, complete or partial (with or without incomplete phalangeal deficiency)**

755.29 **Longitudinal deficiency, phalanges, complete or partial**
Absence of finger, congenital
Aphalangia of upper limb, terminal, complete or
partial
EXCLUDES terminal deficiency of all five digits
(755.21)
transverse deficiency of phalanges
(755.21)

√5th 755.3 **Reduction deformities of lower limb**

755.30 **Unspecified reduction deformity of lower limb**
Ectromelia NOS }
Hemimelia NOS } of lower limb
Shortening of leg, congenital

755.31 **Transverse deficiency of lower limb**
Amelia of lower limb
Congenital absence of:
foot
leg, including foot and toes
lower limb, complete
toes, all, complete
Transverse hemimelia of lower limb

755.32 **Longitudinal deficiency of lower limb, not elsewhere classified**
Phocomelia NOS of lower limb

755.33 Longitudinal deficiency, combined, involving femur, tibia, and fibula (complete or incomplete)

Congenital absence of thigh and (lower) leg (complete or incomplete) with or without metacarpal deficiency and/or phalangeal deficiency, incomplete

Phocomelia, complete, of lower limb

755.34 Longitudinal deficiency, femoral, complete or partial (with or without distal deficiencies, incomplete)

Congenital absence of femur (with or without absence of some [but not all] distal elements)

Proximal phocomelia of lower limb

755.35 Longitudinal deficiency, tibiofibular, complete or partial (with or without distal deficiencies, incomplete)

Congenital absence of tibia and fibula (with or without absence of some [but not all] distal elements)

Distal phocomelia of lower limb

755.36 Longitudinal deficiency, tibia, complete or partial (with or without distal deficiencies, incomplete)

Agenesis of tibia

Congenital absence of tibia (with or without absence of some [but not all] distal elements)

755.37 Longitudinal deficiency, fibular, complete or partial (with or without distal deficiencies, incomplete)

Agenesis of fibula

Congenital absence of fibula (with or without absence of some [but not all] distal elements)

755.38 Longitudinal deficiency, tarsals or metatarsals, complete or partial (with or without incomplete phalangeal deficiency)

755.39 Longitudinal deficiency, phalanges, complete or partial

Absence of toe, congenital

Aphalangia of lower limb, terminal, complete or partial

> EXCLUDES   terminal deficiency of all five digits (755.31)
> transverse deficiency of phalanges (755.31)

755.4 Reduction deformities, unspecified limb

Absence, congenital (complete or partial) of limb NOS

Amelia
Ectromelia   } of unspecified limb
Hemimelia
Phocomelia

√5th **755.5 Other anomalies of upper limb, including shoulder girdle**

755.50 Unspecified anomaly of upper limb

755.51 Congenital deformity of clavicle

755.52 Congenital elevation of scapula

Sprengel's deformity

755.53 Radioulnar synostosis

DEF: Osseous adhesion of radius and ulna.

755.54 Madelung's deformity

DEF: Distal ulnar overgrowth or radial shortening; also called carpus curvus.

755.55 Acrocephalosyndactyly

Apert's syndrome

DEF: Premature cranial suture fusion (craniostenosis); marked by cone-shaped or pointed (acrocephaly) head and webbing of the fingers (syndactyly); similar to craniofacial dysostosis.

755.56 Accessory carpal bones

755.57 Macrodactylia (fingers)

DEF: Abnormally large fingers, toes.

755.58 Cleft hand, congenital

Lobster-claw hand

DEF: Extended separation between fingers into metacarpus; also may refer to large fingers and absent middle fingers of hand.

755.59 Other

Cleidocranial dysostosis

Cubitus:
valgus, congenital
varus, congenital

> EXCLUDES   club hand (congenital) (754.89)
> congenital dislocation of elbow (754.89)

√5th **755.6 Other anomalies of lower limb, including pelvic girdle**

755.60 Unspecified anomaly of lower limb

755.61 Coxa valga, congenital

DEF: Abnormally wide angle between the neck and shaft of the femur.

755.62 Coxa vara, congenital

DEF: Diminished angle between neck and shaft of femur.

755.63 Other congenital deformity of hip (joint)

Congenital anteversion of femur (neck)

> EXCLUDES   congenital dislocation of hip (754.30-754.35)

AHA: 1Q, '94, 15; S-O, '84, 15

Q65.9 Congenital deformity of hip   I-10
unspecified

755.64 Congenital deformity of knee (joint)

Congenital:
absence of patella
genu valgum [knock-knee]
genu varum [bowleg]
Rudimentary patella

755.65 Macrodactylia of toes

DEF: Abnormally large toes.

755.66 Other anomalies of toes

Congenital:
hallux valgus
hallux varus
hammer toe

755.67 Anomalies of foot, not elsewhere classified

Astragaloscaphoid synostosis
Calcaneonavicular bar
Coalition of calcaneus
Talonavicular synostosis
Tarsal coalitions

755.69 Other

Congenital:
angulation of tibia
deformity (of):
ankle (joint)
sacroiliac (joint)
fusion of sacroiliac joint

755.8 Other specified anomalies of unspecified limb

755.9 Unspecified anomaly of unspecified limb

Congenital:
anomaly NOS   } of unspecified limb
deformity NOS

> EXCLUDES   reduction deformity of unspecified limb (755.4)

√4th Additional Digit Required   Unspecified Code   Other Specified Code   Manifestation Code   ▶◀ Revised Text   ● New Code   ▲ Revised Code Title
√5th

2010 ICD-9-CM   **Volume 1 – 253**

Congenital Anomalies

756–756.73

✓4ᵗʰ **756 Other congenital musculoskeletal anomalies**

> **EXCLUDES** *congenital myotonic chondrodystrophy (359.23)*
> *those deformities classifiable to 754.0-754.8*

756.0 Anomalies of skull and face bones
Absence of skull bones
Acrocephaly
Congenital deformity of forehead
Craniosynostosis
Crouzon's disease
Hypertelorism
Imperfect fusion of skull
Oxycephaly
Platybasia
Premature closure of cranial sutures
Tower skull
Trigonocephaly

> **EXCLUDES** *acrocephalosyndactyly [Apert's syndrome]*
> *(755.55)*
> *dentofacial anomalies (524.0-524.9)*
> *skull defects associated with brain anomalies,*
> *such as:*
> *anencephalus (740.0)*
> *encephalocele (742.0)*
> *hydrocephalus (742.3)*
> *microcephalus (742.1)*

AHA: 3Q, '98, 9; 3Q, '96, 15

TIP: Assign for Nager syndrome (preaxial acrofacial dysostosis), along with codes for any additional features that are not captured in the code.

Q75.8 Other spec cong malformations skull & face bones ‖-10‖

✓5ᵗʰ **756.1 Anomalies of spine**

756.10 Anomaly of spine, unspecified

756.11 Spondylolysis, lumbosacral region
Prespondylolisthesis (lumbosacral)
> **DEF:** Bilateral or unilateral defect through the pars interarticularis of a vertebra causes spondylolisthesis.

756.12 Spondylolisthesis
> **DEF:** Downward slipping of lumbar vertebra over next vertebra; usually related to pelvic deformity.
> **Q76.2** Congenital spondylolisthesis ‖-10‖

756.13 Absence of vertebra, congenital

756.14 Hemivertebra
> **DEF:** Incomplete development of one side of a vertebra.

756.15 Fusion of spine [vertebra], congenital

756.16 Klippel-Feil syndrome
> **DEF:** Short, wide neck; limits range of motion due to ab-normal number of cervical vertebra or fused hemivertebrae.

756.17 Spina bifida occulta
> **EXCLUDES** *spina bifida (aperta) (741.0-741.9)*
> **DEF:** Spina bifida marked by a bony spinal canal defect without a protrusion of the cord or meninges; it is diagnosed by radiography and has no symptoms.

756.19 Other
Platyspondylia
Supernumerary vertebra

756.2 Cervical rib
Supernumerary rib in the cervical region
> **DEF:** Costa cervicalis: extra rib attached to cervical vertebra.

756.3 Other anomalies of ribs and sternum
Congenital absence of:
rib
sternum
Congenital:
fissure of sternum
fusion of ribs
Sternum bifidum
> **EXCLUDES** *nonteratogenic deformity of chest wall*
> *(754.81-754.89)*

756.4 Chondrodystrophy
Achondroplasia
Chondrodystrophia (fetalis)
Dyschondroplasia
Enchondromatosis
Ollier's disease
> **EXCLUDES** *congenital myotonic chondrodystrophy*
> *(359.23)*
> *lipochondrodystrophy [Hurler's syndrome]*
> *(277.5)*
> *Morquio's disease (277.5)*

DEF: Abnormal development of cartilage.

AHA: 2Q, '02, 16; S-O, '87, 10

TIP: Assign for Jeune's syndrome, and also for cartilage-hair syndrome (cartilage-hair hypoplasia).

✓5ᵗʰ **756.5 Osteodystrophies**

756.50 Osteodystrophy, unspecified

756.51 Osteogenesis imperfecta
Fragilitas ossium
Osteopsathyrosis
> **DEF:** A collagen disorder commonly characterized by brittle, osteoporotic, easily fractured bones, hypermobility of joints, blue sclerae, and a tendency to hemorrhage.

756.52 Osteopetrosis
> **DEF:** Abnormally dense bone, optic atrophy, hepatosplenomegaly, deafness; sclerosing depletes bone marrow and nerve foramina of skull; often fatal.

756.53 Osteopoikilosis
> **DEF:** Multiple sclerotic foci on ends of long bones, stippling in round, flat bones; identified by x-ray.

756.54 Polyostotic fibrous dysplasia of bone
> **DEF:** Fibrous tissue displaces bone results in segmented ragged-edge café-au-lait spots; occurs in girls of early puberty.

756.55 Chondroectodermal dysplasia
Ellis-van Creveld syndrome
> **DEF:** Inadequate enchondral bone formation; impaired development of hair and teeth, polydactyly, and cardiac septum defects.

756.56 Multiple epiphyseal dysplasia

756.59 Other
Albright (-McCune)-Sternberg syndrome

756.6 Anomalies of diaphragm
Absence of diaphragm
Congenital hernia:
diaphragmatic
foramen of Morgagni
Eventration of diaphragm
> **EXCLUDES** *congenital hiatus hernia (750.6)*

✓5ᵗʰ **756.7 Anomalies of abdominal wall**

756.70 Anomaly of abdominal wall, unspecified

756.71 Prune belly syndrome
Eagle-Barrett syndrome
Prolapse of bladder mucosa
> **DEF:** Prune belly syndrome: absence of lower rectus abdominis muscle and lower and medial oblique muscles; results in dilated bladder and ureters, dysplastic kidneys and hydronephrosis; common in male infants with undescended testicles.
> **AHA:** 4Q, '97, 44

● **756.72 Omphalocele**
Exomphalos
> **DEF:** Exomphalos: umbilical hernia prominent navel.
> **DEF:** Omphalocele: hernia of umbilicus due to impaired abdominal wall; results in membrane-covered intestine protruding through peritoneum and amnion.

● **756.73 Gastroschisis**
> **DEF:** Fissure of abdominal wall, results in protruding small or large intestine.

Ⓝ Newborn Age: 0   Ⓟ Pediatric Age: 0-17   Ⓜ Maternity Age: 12-55   Ⓐ Adult Age: 15-124

756.79 Other congenital anomalies of abdominal wall

> EXCLUDES   umbilical hernia (551-553 with .1)

√5th **756.8 Other specified anomalies of muscle, tendon, fascia, and connective tissue**

756.81 Absence of muscle and tendon
Absence of muscle (pectoral)

756.82 Accessory muscle

756.83 Ehlers-Danlos syndrome
DEF: Danlos syndrome: connective tissue disorder causes hyperextended skin and joints; results in fragile blood vessels with bleeding, poor wound healing and subcutaneous pseudotumors.

756.89 Other
Amyotrophia congenita
Congenital shortening of tendon
AHA: 3Q, '99, 16
TIP: Assign for Stickler's syndrome, a hereditary progressive arthro-ophthalmopathy, along with codes for the specific manifestations.

756.9 Other and unspecified anomalies of musculoskeletal system
Congenital:
anomaly NOS } of musculoskeletal system, not
deformity NOS } elsewhere classified

√4th **757 Congenital anomalies of the integument**

> INCLUDES   anomalies of skin, subcutaneous tissue, hair, nails, and breast

> EXCLUDES   hemangioma (228.00-228.09)
> pigmented nevus (216.0-216.9)

757.0 Hereditary edema of legs
Congenital lymphedema
Hereditary trophedema
Milroy's disease

757.1 Ichthyosis congenita
Congenital ichthyosis
Harlequin fetus
Ichthyosiform erythroderma
DEF: Overproduction of skin cells causes scaling of skin; may result in stillborn fetus or death soon after birth.

757.2 Dermatoglyphic anomalies
Abnormal palmar creases
DEF: Abnormal skin-line patterns of fingers, palms, toes and soles; initial finding of possible chromosomal abnormalities.

√5th **757.3 Other specified anomalies of skin**

757.31 Congenital ectodermal dysplasia
DEF: Tissues and structures originate in embryonic ectoderm; includes anhidrotic and hidrotic ectodermal dysplasia and EEC syndrome.

757.32 Vascular hamartomas
Birthmarks
Port-wine stain
Strawberry nevus
DEF: Benign tumor of blood vessels; due to malformed angioblastic tissues.
Q82.5 Congenital non-neoplastic nevus   I-10

757.33 Congenital pigmentary anomalies of skin
Congenital poikiloderma
Urticaria pigmentosa
Xeroderma pigmentosum
> EXCLUDES   albinism (270.2)
Q82.2 Mastocytosis   I-10

757.39 Other
Accessory skin tags, congenital
Congenital scar
Epidermolysis bullosa
Keratoderma (congenital)
> EXCLUDES   pilonidal cyst (685.0-685.1)
Q82.8 Other specified congenital   I-10
malformations of skin

757.4 Specified anomalies of hair
Congenital:
alopecia
atrichosis
beaded hair
hypertrichosis
monilethrix
Persistent lanugo

757.5 Specified anomalies of nails
Anonychia
Congenital:
clubnail
koilonychia
leukonychia
onychauxis
pachyonychia

▲ **757.6 Specified congenital anomalies of breast**
Accessory
►Congenital absent◄ } breast or nipple
Supernumerary
> EXCLUDES   absence of pectoral muscle (756.81)
> hypoplasia of breast (611.82)
> ►micromastia (611.82)◄

757.8 Other specified anomalies of the integument

757.9 Unspecified anomaly of the integument
Congenital:
anomaly NOS } of integument
deformity NOS }

√4th **758 Chromosomal anomalies**

> INCLUDES   syndromes associated with anomalies in the number and form of chromosomes

Use additional codes for conditions associated with the chromosomal anomalies

758.0 Down's syndrome
Mongolism
Translocation Down's syndrome
Trisomy:
21 or 22
G
Q90.9 Down's syndrome unspecified   I-10

758.1 Patau's syndrome
Trisomy:
13
D_1
DEF: Trisomy of 13th chromosome; characteristic failure to thrive, severe mental impairment, seizures, abnormal eyes, low-set ears and sloped forehead.

758.2 Edwards' syndrome
Trisomy:
18
E_3
DEF: Trisomy of 18th chromosome; characteristic mental and physical impairments; mainly affects females.

√5th **758.3 Autosomal deletion syndromes**

758.31 Cri-du-chat syndrome
Deletion 5p
DEF: Hereditary congenital syndrome caused by a microdeletion of short arm of chromosome 5; characterized by catlike cry in newborn, microencephaly, severe mental deficiency, and hypertelorism.

758.32 Velo-cardio-facial syndrome
Deletion 22q11.2
DEF: Microdeletion syndrome affecting multiple organs; characteristic cleft palate, heart defects, elongated face with almond-shaped eyes, wide nose, small ears, weak immune systems, weak musculature, hypothyroidism, short stature, and scoliosis; deletion at q11.2 on the long arm of the chromosome 22.

√4th Additional Digit Required   Unspecified Code   Other Specified Code   Manifestation Code   ►◄ Revised Text   ● New Code   ▲ Revised Code Title

758.33 Other microdeletions
Miller-Dieker syndrome
Smith-Magenis syndrome
DEF: Miller-Dieker syndrome: deletion from the short arm of chromosome 17; characteristic mental retardation, speech and motor development delays, neurological complications, and multiple abnormalities affecting the kidneys, heart, gastrointestinal tract; death in infancy or early childhood.
DEF: Smith-Magenis syndrome: deletion in a certain area of chromosome 17 that results in craniofacial changes, speech delay, hoarse voice, hearing loss and behavioral problems, such as self-destructive head banging, wrist biting, and tearing at nails.

758.39 Other autosomal deletions

758.4 Balanced autosomal translocation in normal individual

758.5 Other conditions due to autosomal anomalies
Accessory autosomes NEC

758.6 Gonadal dysgenesis
Ovarian dysgenesis
Turner's syndrome
XO syndrome
EXCLUDES *pure gonadal dysgenesis (752.7)*

758.7 Klinefelter's syndrome ♂
XXY syndrome
DEF: Impaired embryonic development of seminiferous tubes; results in small testes, azoospermia, infertility and enlarged mammary glands.

✓5ᵗʰ **758.8 Other conditions due to chromosome anomalies**

758.81 Other conditions due to sex chromosome anomalies

758.89 Other
Q99.8 Other specified chromosome abnormalities   I-10

758.9 Conditions due to anomaly of unspecified chromosome

✓4ᵗʰ **759 Other and unspecified congenital anomalies**

759.0 Anomalies of spleen
Aberrant
Absent } spleen
Accessory
Congenital splenomegaly
Ectopic spleen
Lobulation of spleen

759.1 Anomalies of adrenal gland
Aberrant
Absent } adrenal gland
Accessory
EXCLUDES *adrenogenital disorders (255.2)*
congenital disorders of steroid metabolism (255.2)

759.2 Anomalies of other endocrine glands
Absent parathyroid gland
Accessory thyroid gland
Persistent thyroglossal or thyrolingual duct
Thyroglossal (duct) cyst
EXCLUDES *congenital:*
goiter (246.1)
hypothyroidism (243)

759.3 Situs inversus
Situs inversus or transversus:
abdominalis
thoracis
Transposition of viscera:
abdominal
thoracic
EXCLUDES *dextrocardia without mention of complete transposition (746.87)*
DEF: Laterally transposed thoracic and abdominal viscera.

759.4 Conjoined twins
Craniopagus
Dicephalus
Pygopagus
Thoracopagus
Xiphopagus

759.5 Tuberous sclerosis
Bourneville's disease
Epiloia
DEF: Hamartomas of brain, retina and viscera, impaired mental ability, seizures and adenoma sebaceum.

759.6 Other hamartoses, not elsewhere classified
Syndrome:
Peutz-Jeghers
Sturge-Weber (-Dimitri)
von Hippel-Lindau
EXCLUDES *neurofibromatosis (237.7)*
DEF: Peutz-Jeghers: hereditary syndrome characterized by hamartomas of small intestine.
DEF: Sturge-Weber: congenital syndrome characterized by unilateral port-wine stain over trigeminal nerve, underlying meninges and cerebral cortex.
DEF: von Hipple-Lindau: hereditary syndrome of congenital angiomatosis of the retina and cerebellum.
AHA: 3Q, '92, 12

759.7 Multiple congenital anomalies, so described
Congenital:
anomaly, multiple NOS
deformity, multiple NOS

✓5ᵗʰ **759.8 Other specified anomalies**
AHA: S-O, '87, 9; S-O, '85, 11

759.81 Prader-Willi syndrome

759.82 Marfan syndrome
AHA: 3Q, '93, 11

759.83 Fragile X syndrome
AHA: 4Q, '94, 41

759.89 Other
Congenital malformation syndromes affecting multiple systems, not elsewhere classified
Laurence-Moon-Biedl syndrome
AHA: ▶3Q, '08, 3;◀ 3Q, '06, 21; 2Q, '05, 17; 2Q, '04, 12; 1Q, '01, 3; 3Q, '99, 17, 18; 3Q, '98, 8
TIP: Assign for the following syndromes: cardiofaciocutaneous (CFC), Borjeson-Forssman-Lehmann syndrome (BFLS), Alagille syndrome, startle disease, Alport's syndrome, branchio-oto-renal (BOR) syndrome, Costello syndrome, Williams syndrome, Antley-Bixler syndrome, and multiple pterygium syndrome. Assign additional codes for any documented manifestations.

759.9 Congenital anomaly, unspecified

N Newborn Age: 0   P Pediatric Age: 0-17   M Maternity Age: 12-55   A Adult Age: 15-124

15. CERTAIN CONDITIONS ORIGINATING IN THE PERINATAL PERIOD (760-779)

INCLUDES conditions which have their origin in the perinatal period, before birth through the first 28 days after birth, even though death or morbidity occurs later

Use additional code(s) to further specify condition

MATERNAL CAUSES OF PERINATAL MORBIDITY AND MORTALITY (760-763)

AHA: 2Q, '89, 14; 3Q, '90, 5

TIP: A newborn condition is clinically significant when it has implications for the newborn's *future* health care. This is an exception to the UHDDS guidelines.

✓4th **760 Fetus or newborn affected by maternal conditions which may be unrelated to present pregnancy**

INCLUDES the listed maternal conditions only when specified as a cause of mortality or morbidity of the fetus or newborn

EXCLUDES *maternal endocrine and metabolic disorders affecting fetus or newborn (775.0-775.9)*

AHA: 1Q, '94, 8; 2Q, '92, 12; N-D, '84, 11

TIP: Do not assign unless the mother's condition has actually affected the fetus or newborn.

760.0 Maternal hypertensive disorders
Fetus or newborn affected by maternal conditions classifiable to 642

760.1 Maternal renal and urinary tract diseases
Fetus or newborn affected by maternal conditions classifiable to 580-599

760.2 Maternal infections
Fetus or newborn affected by maternal infectious disease classifiable to 001-136 and 487, but fetus or newborn not manifesting that disease

EXCLUDES *congenital infectious diseases (771.0-771.8)*
maternal genital tract and other localized infections (760.8)

760.3 Other chronic maternal circulatory and respiratory diseases
Fetus or newborn affected by chronic maternal conditions classifiable to 390-459, 490-519, 745-748

760.4 Maternal nutritional disorders
Fetus or newborn affected by:
maternal disorders classifiable to 260-269
maternal malnutrition NOS

EXCLUDES *fetal malnutrition (764.10-764.29)*

760.5 Maternal injury
Fetus or newborn affected by maternal conditions classifiable to 800-995

✓5th **760.6 Surgical operation on mother and fetus**

EXCLUDES *cesarean section for present delivery (763.4)*
damage to placenta from amniocentesis, cesarean section, or surgical induction (762.1)

AHA: ▶4Q, '08, 137-138◀

TIP: These codes include existing conditions present at the time of birth that are related to procedures performed before the time of delivery.

760.61 Newborn affected by amniocentesis

EXCLUDES *fetal complications from amniocentesis (679.1)*

760.62 Newborn affected by other in utero procedure

EXCLUDES *fetal complications of in utero procedure (679.1)*

760.63 Newborn affected by other surgical operations on mother during pregnancy

EXCLUDES *newborn affected by previous surgical procedure on mother not associated with pregnancy (760.64)*

760.64 Newborn affected by previous surgical procedure on mother not associated with pregnancy

✓5th **760.7 Noxious influences affecting fetus or newborn via placenta or breast milk**
Fetus or newborn affected by noxious substance transmitted via placenta or breast milk

EXCLUDES *anesthetic and analgesic drugs administered during labor and delivery (763.5)*
drug withdrawal syndrome in newborn (779.5)

AHA: 3Q, '91, 21

760.70 Unspecified noxious substance
Fetus or newborn affected by:
Drug NEC

760.71 Alcohol
Fetal alcohol syndrome

760.72 Narcotics

760.73 Hallucinogenic agents

760.74 Anti-infectives
Antibiotics
Antifungals

760.75 Cocaine
AHA: 3Q, '94, 6; 2Q, '92, 12; 4Q, '91, 26
TIP: If documentation indicates drug withdrawal in the newborn, also assign code 779.5 Drug withdrawal syndrome in newborn.

760.76 Diethylstilbestrol [DES]
AHA: 4Q, '94, 45

760.77 Anticonvulsants N
Carbamazepine　　　Phenytoin
Phenobarbital　　　Valproic acid
AHA: 4Q, '05, 82

760.78 Antimetabolic agents N
Methotrexate
Retinoic acid
Statins
AHA: 4Q, '05, 82-83

760.79 Other
Fetus or newborn affected by:
immune sera ⎫ transmitted via
medicinal agents NEC ⎬ placenta
toxic substance NEC ⎭ or breast
P04.8 Newborn (suspected) affected by oth maternl noxious subst I-10

760.8 Other specified maternal conditions affecting fetus or newborn
Maternal genital tract and other localized infection affecting fetus or newborn, but fetus or newborn not manifesting that disease

EXCLUDES *maternal urinary tract infection affecting fetus or newborn (760.1)*

760.9 Unspecified maternal condition affecting fetus or newborn

✓4th **761 Fetus or newborn affected by maternal complications of pregnancy**

INCLUDES the listed maternal conditions only when specified as a cause of mortality or morbidity of the fetus or newborn

761.0 Incompetent cervix
DEF: Inadequate functioning of uterine cervix.

761.1 Premature rupture of membranes

Conditions in the Perinatal Period

761.2–763.83

761.2 Oligohydramnios

EXCLUDES *that due to premature rupture of membranes (761.1)*

DEF: Deficient amniotic fluid.

761.3 Polyhydramnios
Hydramnios (acute) (chronic)

DEF: Excess amniotic fluid.

761.4 Ectopic pregnancy
Pregnancy:
abdominal
intraperitoneal
tubal

761.5 Multiple pregnancy
Triplet (pregnancy)
Twin (pregnancy)

761.6 Maternal death

761.7 Malpresentation before labor
Breech presentation
External version
Oblique lie } before labor
Transverse lie
Unstable lie

761.8 Other specified maternal complications of pregnancy affecting fetus or newborn
Spontaneous abortion, fetus

761.9 Unspecified maternal complication of pregnancy affecting fetus or newborn

✓4ᵗʰ **762 Fetus or newborn affected by complications of placenta, cord, and membranes**

INCLUDES the listed maternal conditions only when specified as a cause of mortality or morbidity in the fetus or newborn

AHA: 1Q, '94, 8

762.0 Placenta previa N

DEF: Placenta developed in lower segment of uterus; causes hemorrhaging in last trimester.

762.1 Other forms of placental separation and hemorrhage N
Abruptio placentae
Antepartum hemorrhage
Damage to placenta from amniocentesis, cesarean section, or surgical induction
Maternal blood loss
Premature separation of placenta
Rupture of marginal sinus

762.2 Other and unspecified morphological and functional abnormalities of placenta N
Placental:
dysfunction
infarction
insufficiency

762.3 Placental transfusion syndromes N
Placental and cord abnormality resulting in twin-to-twin or other transplacental transfusion
Use additional code to indicate resultant condition in newborn:
fetal blood loss (772.0)
polycythemia neonatorum (776.4)

762.4 Prolapsed cord N
Cord presentation

762.5 Other compression of umbilical cord N
Cord around neck
Entanglement of cord
Knot in cord
Torsion of cord

AHA: 2Q, '03, 9

TIP: Assign only if the cord compression or entanglement was documented as having affected the fetus/newborn.

P02.5 Newborn (suspected) affected by oth compression I-10 umb cord

762.6 Other and unspecified conditions of umbilical cord N
Short cord
Thrombosis
Varices } of umbilical cord
Velamentous insertion
Vasa previa

EXCLUDES *infection of umbilical cord (771.4)*
single umbilical artery (747.5)

P02.69 Newborn (suspected) affected by oth cond I-10 umbil cord

762.7 Chorioamnionitis N
Amnionitis
Membranitis
Placentitis

DEF: Inflamed fetal membrane.

762.8 Other specified abnormalities of chorion and amnion N

762.9 Unspecified abnormality of chorion and amnion N

✓4ᵗʰ **763 Fetus or newborn affected by other complications of labor and delivery**

INCLUDES the listed conditions only when specified as a cause of mortality or morbidity in the fetus or newborn

EXCLUDES *newborn affected by surgical procedures on mother (760.61-760.64)*

AHA: 1Q, '94, 8

763.0 Breech delivery and extraction N

763.1 Other malpresentation, malposition, and disproportion during labor and delivery N
Fetus or newborn affected by:
abnormality of bony pelvis
contracted pelvis
persistent occipitoposterior position
shoulder presentation
transverse lie
Fetus or newborn affected by conditions classifiable to 652, 653, and 660

763.2 Forceps delivery N
Fetus or newborn affected by forceps extraction

763.3 Delivery by vacuum extractor N

763.4 Cesarean delivery N

EXCLUDES *placental separation or hemorrhage from cesarean section (762.1)*

763.5 Maternal anesthesia and analgesia N
Reactions and intoxications from maternal opiates and tranquilizers during labor and delivery

EXCLUDES *drug withdrawal syndrome in newborn (779.5)*

763.6 Precipitate delivery N
Rapid second stage

763.7 Abnormal uterine contractions N
Fetus or newborn affected by:
contraction ring
hypertonic labor
hypotonic uterine dysfunction
uterine inertia or dysfunction
Fetus or newborn affected by conditions classifiable to 661, except 661.3

✓5ᵗʰ **763.8 Other specified complications of labor and delivery affecting fetus or newborn**

AHA: 4Q, '98, 46

763.81 Abnormality in fetal heart rate or rhythm before the onset of labor N

763.82 Abnormality in fetal heart rate or rhythm during labor N

AHA: 4Q, '98, 46

763.83 Abnormality in fetal heart rate or rhythm, unspecified as to time of onset N

N Newborn Age: 0 P Pediatric Age: 0-17 M Maternity Age: 12-55 A Adult Age: 15-124

763.84　**Meconium passage during delivery**　　N

> **EXCLUDES**　meconium aspiration (770.11, 770.12)
> meconium staining (779.84)

DEF: Fetal intestinal activity that increases in response to a distressed state during delivery; anal sphincter relaxes, and meconium is passed into the amniotic fluid.

AHA: 4Q, '05, 83

TIP: If the meconium was documented as aspirated or had any effect on the newborn, see codes 770.11 and 770.12.

763.89　**Other specified complications of labor and delivery affecting fetus or newborn**　　N

Fetus or newborn affected by:
　abnormality of maternal soft tissues
　destructive operation on live fetus to facilitate delivery
　induction of labor (medical)
　other procedures used in labor and delivery
Fetus or newborn affected by other conditions classifiable to 650-669

763.9　**Unspecified complication of labor and delivery affecting fetus or newborn**　　N

OTHER CONDITIONS ORIGINATING IN THE PERINATAL PERIOD (764-779)

The following fifth-digit subclassification is for use with category 764 and codes 765.0-765.1 to denote birthweight:

0　unspecified [weight]
1　less than 500 grams
2　500-749 grams
3　750-999 grams
4　1,000-1,249 grams
5　1,250-1,499 grams
6　1,500-1,749 grams
7　1,750-1,999 grams
8　2,000-2,499 grams
9　2,500 grams and over

✓4th　**764**　**Slow fetal growth and fetal malnutrition**

AHA: ▶1Q, '09, 13◀ 3Q, '04, 4; 4Q, '02, 63; 1Q,'94, 8; 2Q, '91, 19; 2Q, '89, 15

§　✓5th　**764.0**　**"Light-for-dates" without mention of fetal malnutrition**　　N
[0-9]
Infants underweight for gestational age
"Small-for-dates"

P07.18 Other low birth weight newborn 2000-2499 grams　　I-10

§　✓5th　**764.1**　**"Light-for-dates" with signs of fetal malnutrition**　　N
[0-9]
Infants "light-for-dates" classifiable to 764.0, who in addition show signs of fetal malnutrition, such as dry peeling skin and loss of subcutaneous tissue

§　✓5th　**764.2**　**Fetal malnutrition without mention of "light-for-dates"**　　N
[0-9]
Infants, not underweight for gestational age, showing signs of fetal malnutrition, such as dry peeling skin and loss of subcutaneous tissue
Intrauterine malnutrition

§　✓5th　**764.9**　**Fetal growth retardation, unspecified**　　N
[0-9]
Intrauterine growth retardation
AHA: For code 764.97: 1Q, '97, 6

✓4th　**765**　**Disorders relating to short gestation and low birthweight**

> **INCLUDES**　the listed conditions, without further specification, as causes of mortality, morbidity, or additional care, in fetus or newborn

AHA: 1Q, '97, 6; 1Q, '94, 8; 2Q, '91, 19; 2Q, '89, 15

§　✓5th　**765.0**　**Extreme immaturity**　　N
[0-9]
Note: Usually implies a birthweight of less than 1000 grams.
Use additional code for weeks of gestation (765.20-765.29)
AHA: ▶1Q, '09, 13◀ 3Q, '04, 4; 4Q, '02, 63; **For code 765.03:** 4Q, '01, 51

§　✓5th　**765.1**　**Other preterm infants**　　N
[0-9]
Note: Usually implies a birthweight of 1000-2499 grams.
Prematurity NOS
Prematurity or small size, not classifiable to 765.0 or as "light-for-dates" in 764
Use additional code for weeks of gestation (765.20-765.29)
AHA: ▶1Q, '09, 13◀ 3Q, '04, 4; 4Q, '02, 63; **For code 765.10:** ▶1Q, '09, 15;◀ 1Q, '94, 14; **For code 765.17:** 4Q, '08, 139; 1Q, '97, 6; **For code 765.18:** 4Q, '02, 64

P07.10 Other low birth weight newborn uns weight　　I-10

✓5th　**765.2**　**Weeks of gestation**

AHA: 3Q, '04, 4; 4Q, '02, 63

TIP: Assign as an additional code with category 764 and codes from 765.0 and 765.1, as documented by the provider.

765.20　**Unspecified weeks of gestation**　　N

765.21　**Less than 24 completed weeks of gestation**　　N

765.22　**24 completed weeks of gestation**　　N

765.23　**25-26 completed weeks of gestation**　　N
AHA: ▶1Q, '09, 14◀

765.24　**27-28 completed weeks of gestation**　　N

765.25　**29-30 completed weeks of gestation**　　N
P07.31 Other preterm newborn 28-31 complete weeks　　I-10

765.26　**31-32 completed weeks of gestation**　　N
AHA: ▶1Q, '09, 14;◀ 4Q, '08, 139

765.27　**33-34 completed weeks of gestation**　　N

765.28　**35-36 completed weeks of gestation**　　N
AHA: 4Q, '02, 64
P07.32 Other preterm newborn 32-36 complete weeks　　I-10

765.29　**37 or more completed weeks of gestation**　　N

✓4th　**766**　**Disorders relating to long gestation and high birthweight**

> **INCLUDES**　the listed conditions, without further specification, as causes of mortality, morbidity, or additional care, in fetus or newborn

766.0　**Exceptionally large baby**　　N
Note: Usually implies a birthweight of 4500 grams or more.

766.1　**Other "heavy-for-dates" infants**　　N
Other fetus or infant "heavy-" or "large-for-dates" regardless of period of gestation
P08.1 Other heavy for gestational age newborn　　I-10

✓5th　**766.2**　**Late infant, not "heavy-for-dates"**
AHA: 2Q, '06, 12; 4Q, '03, 69
TIP: May be assigned based on gestational age alone, without documentation of any related specific condition or disorder.

766.21　**Post-term infant**　　N
Infant with gestation period over 40 completed weeks to 42 completed weeks
AHA: ▶1Q, '09, 12;◀
P08.21 Post-term newborn　　I-10

766.22　**Prolonged gestation of infant**　　N
Infant with gestation period over 42 completed weeks
Postmaturity NOS
AHA: ▶1Q, '09, 12◀

✓4th　**767**　**Birth trauma**

767.0　**Subdural and cerebral hemorrhage**　　N
Subdural and cerebral hemorrhage, whether described as due to birth trauma or to intrapartum anoxia or hypoxia
Subdural hematoma (localized)
Tentorial tear
Use additional code to identify cause

> **EXCLUDES**　intraventricular hemorrhage (772.10-772.14)
> subarachnoid hemorrhage (772.2)

§　Requires fifth digit. Valid digits are in [brackets] under each code. See beginning of section 764-779 for codes and definitions.

✓4th
✓5th　Additional Digit Required　　Unspecified Code　　Other Specified Code　　Manifestation Code　　▶◀ Revised Text　　● New Code　　▲ Revised Code Title

Conditions in the Perinatal Period

767.1–769

Epicranial Aponeurosis

✓5th **767.1**   **Injuries to scalp**
     AHA: 4Q, '03, 69

     767.11   **Epicranial subaponeurotic hemorrhage (massive)**   N
         Subgaleal hemorrhage
         DEF: A hemorrhage that occurs within the space between the galea aponeurotica, or epicranial aponeurosis, a thin tendinous structure that is attached to the skull laterally, and the periosteum of the skull.

     767.19   **Other injuries to scalp**   N
         Caput succedaneum
         Cephalhematoma
         Chignon (from vacuum extraction)
         P12.89 Other birth injuries to scalp   I-10

767.2   **Fracture of clavicle**   N

767.3   **Other injuries to skeleton**   N
     Fracture of:
         long bones
         skull
     EXCLUDES   *congenital dislocation of hip (754.30-754.35)*
                 fracture of spine, congenital (767.4)

767.4   **Injury to spine and spinal cord**   N
     Dislocation
     Fracture   } of spine or spinal cord due to
     Laceration   birth trauma
     Rupture

767.5   **Facial nerve injury**   N
     Facial palsy

767.6   **Injury to brachial plexus**   N
     Palsy or paralysis:
         brachial
         Erb (-Duchenne)
         Klumpke (-Déjérine)

767.7   **Other cranial and peripheral nerve injuries**   N
     Phrenic nerve paralysis

767.8   **Other specified birth trauma**   N
     Eye damage   Rupture of:
     Hematoma of: liver
         liver (subcapsular)   spleen
         testes   Scalpel wound
         vulva   Traumatic glaucoma
     EXCLUDES   *hemorrhage classifiable to 772.0-772.9*

767.9   **Birth trauma, unspecified**   N
     Birth injury NOS

✓4th **768**   **Intrauterine hypoxia and birth asphyxia**
     Use only when associated with newborn morbidity classifiable elsewhere
     EXCLUDES   *acidemia NOS of newborn (775.81)*
                 acidosis NOS of newborn (775.81)
                 cerebral ischemia NOS (779.2)
                 hypoxia NOS of newborn (770.88)
                 mixed metabolic and respiratory acidosis of newborn (775.81)
                 respiratory arrest of newborn (770.87)
     DEF: Oxygen intake insufficiency due to interrupted placental circulation or premature separation of placenta.
     AHA: 4Q, '92, 20

     768.0   **Fetal death from asphyxia or anoxia before onset of labor or at unspecified time**   N

     768.1   **Fetal death from asphyxia or anoxia during labor**   N

     768.2   **Fetal distress before onset of labor, in liveborn infant**   N
         Fetal metabolic acidemia before onset of labor, in liveborn infant

     768.3   **Fetal distress first noted during labor and delivery, in liveborn infant**   N
         Fetal metabolic acidemia first noted during labor and delivery, in liveborn infant

     768.4   **Fetal distress, unspecified as to time of onset, in liveborn infant**   N
         Fetal metabolic acidemia unspecified as to time of onset, in liveborn infant
         AHA: N-D, '86, 10

     768.5   **Severe birth asphyxia**   N
         Birth asphyxia with neurologic involvement
         EXCLUDES   *hypoxic-ischemic encephalopathy [HIE]*
                      ►*(768.70-768.73)*◄
         AHA: N-D, '86, 3

     768.6   **Mild or moderate birth asphyxia**   N
         Other specified birth asphyxia (without mention of neurologic involvement)
         EXCLUDES   *hypoxic-ischemic encephalopathy [HIE]*
                      ►*(768.70-768.73)*◄
         AHA: N-D, '86, 3

✓5th   **768.7**   **Hypoxic-ischemic encephalopathy [HIE]**
         AHA: 4Q, '06, 104

         ●   **768.70**   **Hypoxic-ischemic encephalopathy, unspecified**   N

         ●   **768.71**   **Mild hypoxic-ischemic encephalopathy**   N

         ●   **768.72**   **Moderate hypoxic-ischemic encephalopathy**   N

         ●   **768.73**   **Severe hypoxic-ischemic encephalopathy**   N

     768.9   **Unspecified birth asphyxia in liveborn infant**   N
         Anoxia   } NOS, in liveborn infant
         Asphyxia

769   **Respiratory distress syndrome**   N
     Cardiorespiratory distress syndrome of newborn
     Hyaline membrane disease (pulmonary)
     Idiopathic respiratory distress syndrome [IRDS or RDS] of newborn
     Pulmonary hypoperfusion syndrome
     EXCLUDES   *transient tachypnea of newborn (770.6)*
     DEF: Severe chest contractions upon air intake and expiratory grunting; infant appears blue due to oxygen deficiency and has rapid respiratory rate; formerly called hyaline membrane disease.
     AHA: 1Q, '89, 10; N-D, '86, 6
     TIP: Do not assign if documentation specifies Type II respiratory distress syndrome, which usually resolves within six to 24 hours after birth; see instead 770.6.
     P22.0 Respiratory distress syndrome of newborn   I-10

     N Newborn Age: 0   P Pediatric Age: 0-17   M Maternity Age: 12-55   A Adult Age: 15-124

✓4ᵗʰ **770**   **Other respiratory conditions of fetus and newborn**

770.0   **Congenital pneumonia**   N
Infective pneumonia acquired prenatally
> **EXCLUDES**   *pneumonia from infection acquired after birth (480.0-486)*

AHA: 1Q, '05, 10

✓5ᵗʰ **770.1**   **Fetal and newborn aspiration**
> **EXCLUDES**   *aspiration of postnatal stomach contents (770.85, 770.86)*
> *meconium passage during delivery (763.84)*
> *meconium staining (779.84)*

AHA: 4Q, '05, 83

770.10   **Fetal and newborn aspiration, unspecified**   N

770.11   **Meconium aspiration without respiratory symptoms**   N
Meconium aspiration NOS

770.12   **Meconium aspiration with respiratory symptoms**   N
Meconium aspiration pneumonia
Meconium aspiration pneumonitis
Meconium aspiration syndrome NOS

Use additional code to identify any secondary pulmonary hypertension (416.8), if applicable

DEF: Meconium aspiration syndrome: aspiration of fetal intestinal material during or prior to delivery, usually a complication of placental insufficiency, causing pneumonitis and bronchial obstruction (inflammatory reaction of lungs).

770.13   **Aspiration of clear amniotic fluid without respiratory symptoms**   N
Aspiration of clear amniotic fluid NOS

770.14   **Aspiration of clear amniotic fluid with respiratory symptoms**   N
Aspiration of clear amniotic fluid with pneumonia
Aspiration of clear amniotic fluid with pneumonitis

Use additional code to identify any secondary pulmonary hypertension (416.8), if applicable

770.15   **Aspiration of blood without respiratory symptoms**   N
Aspiration of blood NOS

770.16   **Aspiration of blood with respiratory symptoms**   N
Aspiration of blood with pneumonia
Aspiration of blood with pneumonitis

Use additional code to identify any secondary pulmonary hypertension (416.8), if applicable

770.17   **Other fetal and newborn aspiration without respiratory symptoms**   N

770.18   **Other fetal and newborn aspiration with respiratory symptoms**   N
Other aspiration pneumonia
Other aspiration pneumonitis

Use additional code to identify any secondary pulmonary hypertension (416.8), if applicable

770.2   **Interstitial emphysema and related conditions**   N
Pneumomediastinum
Pneumopericardium   } originating in the perinatal period
Pneumothorax

P25.0 Interstitial emphysema origin perinatal period   I-10

770.3   **Pulmonary hemorrhage**   N
Hemorrhage:
alveolar (lung)
intra-alveolar (lung)   } originating in the perinatal period
massive pulmonary

770.4   **Primary atelectasis**   N
Pulmonary immaturity NOS
DEF: Alveoli fail to expand causing insufficient air intake by newborn.

770.5   **Other and unspecified atelectasis**   N
Atelectasis:
NOS
partial   } originating in the perinatal period
secondary
Pulmonary collapse

770.6   **Transitory tachypnea of newborn**   N
Idiopathic tachypnea of newborn
Wet lung syndrome
> **EXCLUDES**   *respiratory distress syndrome (769)*

DEF: Quick, shallow breathing of newborn; short-term problem.
AHA: 4Q, '95, 4; 1Q, '94, 12; 3Q, '93, 7; 1Q, '89, 10; N-D, '86, 6
P22.1 Transient tachypnea of newborn   I-10

770.7   **Chronic respiratory disease arising in the perinatal period**
Bronchopulmonary dysplasia
Interstitial pulmonary fibrosis of prematurity
Wilson-Mikity syndrome
AHA: 2Q, '91, 19; N-D, '86, 11
P27.8 Other chronic resp dz origin perinatal period   I-10

✓5ᵗʰ **770.8**   **Other respiratory problems after birth**
> **EXCLUDES**   *mixed metabolic and respiratory acidosis of newborn (775.81)*

AHA: 4Q, '02, 65; 2Q, '98, 10; 2Q, '96, 10

770.81   **Primary apnea of newborn**   N
Apneic spells of newborn NOS
Essential apnea of newborn
Sleep apnea of newborn

DEF: Cessation of breathing when a neonate makes no respiratory effort for 15 seconds, resulting in cyanosis and bradycardia.
P28.3 Primary sleep apnea of newborn   I-10

770.82   **Other apnea of newborn**   N
Obstructive apnea of newborn

770.83   **Cyanotic attacks of newborn**   N

770.84   **Respiratory failure of newborn**   N
> **EXCLUDES**   *respiratory distress syndrome (769)*

AHA: ▶4Q, '08, 99◀

770.85   **Aspiration of postnatal stomach contents without respiratory symptoms**   N
Aspiration of postnatal stomach contents NOS
AHA: 4Q, '05, 83

770.86   **Aspiration of postnatal stomach contents with respiratory symptoms**   N
Aspiration of postnatal stomach contents with pneumonia
Aspiration of postnatal stomach contents with pneumonitis

Use additional code to identify any secondary pulmonary hypertension (416.8), if applicable
AHA: 4Q, '05, 83

770.87   **Respiratory arrest of newborn**   N
AHA: 4Q, '06, 104-106

770.88   **Hypoxemia of newborn**   N
Hypoxia NOS of newborn
AHA: 4Q, '06, 104-106

770.89   **Other respiratory problems after birth**   N
P28.89 Oth specified respiratory conditions of newborn   I-10

770.9   **Unspecified respiratory condition of fetus and newborn**   N

✓4ᵗʰ / ✓5ᵗʰ **Additional Digit Required**   **Unspecified Code**   **Other Specified Code**   **Manifestation Code**   ▶◀ Revised Text   ● New Code   ▲ Revised Code Title

2010 ICD-9-CM   **February 2009 · Volume 1 – 261**

Conditions in the Perinatal Period

770–770.9

Conditions in the Perinatal Period

771–773.0

✓4ᵗʰ **771　Infections specific to the perinatal period**

INCLUDES　infections acquired before or during birth or via the
umbilicus or during the first 28 days after birth

EXCLUDES　*congenital pneumonia (770.0)*
congenital syphilis (090.0-090.9)
infant botulism (040.41)
maternal infectious disease as a cause of mortality or
morbidity in fetus or newborn, but fetus or
newborn not manifesting the disease (760.2)
ophthalmia neonatorum due to gonococcus (098.40)
other infections not specifically classified to this category

AHA: N-D, '85, 4

771.0　Congenital rubella　　　　　　　　　　　　N
Congenital rubella pneumonitis

771.1　Congenital cytomegalovirus infection　　　N
Congenital cytomegalic inclusion disease

771.2　Other congenital infections　　　　　　　N
Congenital:　　　　　Congenital:
herpes simplex　　　toxoplasmosis
listeriosis　　　　　tuberculosis
malaria

771.3　Tetanus neonatorum　　　　　　　　　　N
Tetanus omphalitis

EXCLUDES　*hypocalcemic tetany (775.4)*

DEF: Severe infection of central nervous system; due to
exotoxin of tetanus bacillus from navel infection prompted by
nonsterile technique during umbilical ligation.

771.4　Omphalitis of the newborn　　　　　　　N
Infection:
navel cord
umbilical stump

EXCLUDES　*tetanus omphalitis (771.3)*

DEF: Inflamed umbilicus.

771.5　Neonatal infective mastitis　　　　　　　N

EXCLUDES　*noninfective neonatal mastitis (778.7)*

771.6　Neonatal conjunctivitis and dacryocystitis　N
Ophthalmia neonatorum NOS

EXCLUDES　*ophthalmia neonatorum due to gonococcus*
(098.40)

771.7　Neonatal Candida infection　　　　　　　N
Neonatal moniliasis
Thrush in newborn

✓5ᵗʰ **771.8　Other infection specific to the perinatal period**
Use additional code to identify organism (041.00-041.9)
AHA: 4Q, '02, 66

771.81　Septicemia [sepsis] of newborn　　　N
Use additional codes to identify severe sepsis
(995.92) and any associated acute organ
dysfunction, if applicable

AHA: 4Q, '08, 99

TIP: Assign instead of 038 or 995.91. Assign also a
code to identify severe sepsis (995.92) or any acute
organ dysfunction, or a code from category 041 to
specify the organism.

P36.9 Bacterial sepsis newborn unspecified　I-10

771.82　Urinary tract infection of newborn　　N

771.83　Bacteremia of newborn　　　　　　N

771.89　Other infections specific to the　　　N
perinatal period
Intra-amniotic infection of fetus NOS
Infection of newborn NOS

✓4ᵗʰ **772　Fetal and neonatal hemorrhage**

EXCLUDES　▶*fetal hematologic conditions complicating pregnancy*
(678.0)◄
hematological disorders of fetus and newborn
(776.0-776.9)

▲ **772.0　Fetal blood loss affecting newborn**　　　N
Fetal blood loss from:
cut end of co-twin's cord
placenta
ruptured cord
vasa previa
Fetal exsanguination
Fetal hemorrhage into:
co-twin
mother's circulation

✓5ᵗʰ **772.1　Intraventricular hemorrhage**
Intraventricular hemorrhage from any perinatal cause
AHA: 4Q, '01, 49; 3Q, '92, 8; 4Q, '88, 8

772.10　Unspecified grade　　　　　　　　N

772.11　Grade I　　　　　　　　　　　　N
Bleeding into germinal matrix

772.12　Grade II　　　　　　　　　　　N
Bleeding into ventricle

772.13　Grade III　　　　　　　　　　　N
Bleeding with enlargement of ventricle
AHA: 4Q, '01, 51

772.14　Grade IV　　　　　　　　　　　N
Bleeding into cerebral cortex

772.2　Subarachnoid hemorrhage　　　　　　　N
Subarachnoid hemorrhage from any perinatal cause

EXCLUDES　*subdural and cerebral hemorrhage (767.0)*

772.3　Umbilical hemorrhage after birth　　　　N
Slipped umbilical ligature

772.4　Gastrointestinal hemorrhage　　　　　　N

EXCLUDES　*swallowed maternal blood (777.3)*

772.5　Adrenal hemorrhage　　　　　　　　　N

772.6　Cutaneous hemorrhage　　　　　　　　N
Bruising
Ecchymoses
Petechiae　　　　　　　} in fetus or newborn
Superficial hematoma

P54.5 Neonatal cutaneous hemorrhage　　I-10

772.8　Other specified hemorrhage of fetus or　N
newborn

EXCLUDES　*hemorrhagic disease of newborn (776.0)*
pulmonary hemorrhage (770.3)

772.9　Unspecified hemorrhage of newborn　　N

✓4ᵗʰ **773　Hemolytic disease of fetus or newborn, due to**
isoimmunization

DEF: Hemolytic anemia of fetus or newborn due to maternal antibody
formation against fetal erythrocytes; infant blood contains
nonmaternal antigen.

TIP: Do not assign unless the physician substantiates confirmation by a
positive Coomb's (direct antibody or direct antiglobulin) test.

773.0　Hemolytic disease due to Rh isoimmunization　N
Anemia　　　　　　　　　] due to RH:
Erythroblastosis (fetalis)　　antibodies
Hemolytic disease (fetus)　} isoimmunization
(newborn)　　　　　　maternal/fetal
Jaundice　　　　　　　　incompatibility

Rh hemolytic disease
Rh isoimmunization

773.1 Hemolytic disease due to ABO isoimmunization   N
ABO hemolytic disease
ABO isoimmunization

Anemia	due to ABO:
Erythroblastosis (fetalis)	antibodies
Hemolytic disease (fetus)	isoimmunization
(newborn)	maternal/fetal
Jaundice	incompatibility

DEF: Incompatible Rh fetal-maternal blood grouping; prematurely destroys red blood cells; detected by Coombs test.
AHA: 3Q, '92, 8
P55.1 ABO isoimmunization of newborn   I-10

773.2 Hemolytic disease due to other and unspecified isoimmunization   N

Eythroblastosis (fetalis) (neonatorum) NOS
Hemolytic disease (fetus) (newborn) NOS
Jaundice or anemia due to other and unspecified blood-group incompatibility
AHA: 1Q, '94, 13
P55.9 Hemolytic disease of newborn unspecified   I-10

773.3 Hydrops fetalis due to isoimmunization   N
Use additional code to identify type of isoimmunization (773.0-773.2)
DEF: Massive edema of entire body and severe anemia; may result in fetal death or stillbirth.

773.4 Kernicterus due to isoimmunization   N
Use additional code to identify type of isoimmunization (773.0-773.2)
DEF: Complication of erythroblastosis fetalis associated with severe neural symptoms, high blood bilirubin levels and nerve cell destruction; results in bilirubin-pigmented gray matter of central nervous system.

773.5 Late anemia due to isoimmunization   N

✓4th **774 Other perinatal jaundice**

774.0 *Perinatal jaundice from hereditary hemolytic anemias*   N
Code first underlying disease (282.0-282.9)

774.1 Perinatal jaundice from other excessive hemolysis   N
Fetal or neonatal jaundice from:
bruising
drugs or toxins transmitted from mother
infection
polycythemia
swallowed maternal blood
Use additional code to identify cause
EXCLUDES *jaundice due to isoimmunization (773.0-773.2)*

774.2 Neonatal jaundice associated with preterm delivery   N
Hyperbilirubinemia of prematurity
Jaundice due to delayed conjugation associated with preterm delivery
AHA: 3Q, '91, 21
P59.0 Neonatal jaundice associated w/preterm delivery   I-10

✓5th **774.3 Neonatal jaundice due to delayed conjugation from other causes**

774.30 Neonatal jaundice due to delayed conjugation, cause unspecified   N
DEF: Jaundice of newborn with abnormal bilirubin metabolism; causes excess accumulated unconjugated bilirubin in blood.

774.31 *Neonatal jaundice due to delayed conjugation in diseases classified elsewhere*   N
Code first underlying diseases as:
congenital hypothyroidism (243)
Crigler-Najjar syndrome (277.4)
Gilbert's syndrome (277.4)

774.39 Other   N
Jaundice due to delayed conjugation from causes, such as:
breast milk inhibitors
delayed development of conjugating system

774.4 Perinatal jaundice due to hepatocellular damage   N
Fetal or neonatal hepatitis
Giant cell hepatitis
Inspissated bile syndrome

774.5 *Perinatal jaundice from other causes*   N
Code first underlying cause as:
congenital obstruction of bile duct (751.61)
galactosemia (271.1)
mucoviscidosis (277.00-277.09)

774.6 Unspecified fetal and neonatal jaundice   N
Icterus neonatorum
Neonatal hyperbilirubinemia (transient)
Physiologic jaundice NOS in newborn
EXCLUDES *that in preterm infants (774.2)*
AHA: 1Q, '94, 13; 2Q, '89, 15
P59.9 Neonatal jaundice unspecified   I-10

774.7 Kernicterus not due to isoimmunization   N
Bilirubin encephalopathy
Kernicterus of newborn NOS
EXCLUDES *kernicterus due to isoimmunization (773.4)*

✓4th **775 Endocrine and metabolic disturbances specific to the fetus and newborn**
INCLUDES transitory endocrine and metabolic disturbances caused by the infant's response to maternal endocrine and metabolic factors, its removal from them, or its adjustment to extrauterine existence

775.0 Syndrome of "infant of a diabetic mother"   N
Maternal diabetes mellitus affecting fetus or newborn (with hypoglycemia)
AHA: 1Q, '04, 7-8; 3Q, '91, 5
TIP: Do not assign if the infant has no manifestations or symptoms of the syndrome; refer instead to code V18.0 Family history, diabetes mellitus.
P70.1 Syndrome of infant of diabetic mother   I-10

775.1 Neonatal diabetes mellitus   N
Diabetes mellitus syndrome in newborn infant
AHA: 3Q, '91, 6

775.2 Neonatal myasthenia gravis   N

775.3 Neonatal thyrotoxicosis   N
Neonatal hyperthyroidism (transient)

775.4 Hypocalcemia and hypomagnesemia of newborn   N
Cow's milk hypocalcemia
Hypocalcemic tetany, neonatal
Neonatal hypoparathyroidism
Phosphate-loading hypocalcemia

775.5 Other transitory neonatal electrolyte disturbances   N
Dehydration, neonatal
AHA: 1Q, '05, 9
TIP: If the patient has neonatal hyperkalemia, assign also code 276.7 Hyperpotassemia.
P74.1 Dehydration of newborn   I-10

775.6 Neonatal hypoglycemia   N
EXCLUDES *infant of mother with diabetes mellitus (775.0)*
AHA: 1Q '94, 8
P70.4 Other neonatal hypoglycemia   I-10

775.7 Late metabolic acidosis of newborn   N

✓5th **775.8 Other neonatal endocrine and metabolic disturbances**

775.81 Other acidosis of newborn   N
Acidemia NOS of newborn
Acidosis of newborn NOS
Mixed metabolic and respiratory acidosis of newborn
AHA: 4Q, '06, 104-106

775.89 Other neonatal endocrine and metabolic disturbances   N
Amino-acid metabolic disorders described as transitory
AHA: 4Q, '06, 104-106

✓4th ✓5th **Additional Digit Required**   **Unspecified Code**   **Other Specified Code**   **Manifestation Code**   ►◄ Revised Text   ● New Code   ▲ Revised Code Title

Conditions in the Perinatal Period

775.9–778.8

775.9 Unspecified endocrine and metabolic disturbances specific to the fetus and newborn N

✓4ᵗʰ 776 Hematological disorders of newborn
> **INCLUDES** disorders specific to the newborn though possibly originating in utero
> **EXCLUDES** fetal hematologic conditions (678.0)

776.0 Hemorrhagic disease of newborn N
Hemorrhagic diathesis of newborn
Vitamin K deficiency of newborn
> **EXCLUDES** fetal or neonatal hemorrhage (772.0-772.9)

776.1 Transient neonatal thrombocytopenia N
Neonatal thrombocytopenia due to:
exchange transfusion
idiopathic maternal thrombocytopenia
isoimmunization
> **DEF:** Temporary decrease in blood platelets of newborn.
> **P61.0** Transient neonatal thrombocytopenia `I-10`

776.2 Disseminated intravascular coagulation in newborn N
> **DEF:** Disseminated intravascular coagulation of newborn: clotting disorder due to excess thromboplastic agents in blood as a result of disease or trauma; causes blood clotting within vessels and reduces available elements necessary for blood coagulation.

776.3 Other transient neonatal disorders of coagulation N
Transient coagulation defect, newborn

776.4 Polycythemia neonatorum N
Plethora of newborn
Polycythemia due to:
donor twin transfusion
maternal-fetal transfusion
> **DEF:** Abnormal increase of total red blood cells of newborn.

776.5 Congenital anemia N
Anemia following fetal blood loss
> **EXCLUDES** anemia due to isoimmunization (773.0-773.2, 773.5)
> hereditary hemolytic anemias (282.0-282.9)

776.6 Anemia of prematurity N
> **P61.2** Anemia of prematurity `I-10`

776.7 Transient neonatal neutropenia N
Isoimmune neutropenia
Maternal transfer neutropenia
> **EXCLUDES** congenital neutropenia (nontransient) (288.01)
> **DEF:** Decreased neutrophilic leukocytes in blood of newborn.

776.8 Other specified transient hematological disorders N
▲ **776.9 Unspecified hematological disorder specific to newborn** N

✓4ᵗʰ 777 Perinatal disorders of digestive system
> **INCLUDES** disorders specific to the fetus and newborn
> **EXCLUDES** intestinal obstruction classifiable to 560.0-560.9

777.1 Meconium obstruction N
Congenital fecaliths
Delayed passage of meconium
Meconium ileus NOS
Meconium plug syndrome
> **EXCLUDES** meconium ileus in cystic fibrosis (277.01)
> **DEF:** Meconium blocked digestive tract of newborn.

777.2 Intestinal obstruction due to inspissated milk N

777.3 Hematemesis and melena due to swallowed maternal blood N
Swallowed blood syndrome in newborn
> **EXCLUDES** that not due to swallowed maternal blood (772.4)

777.4 Transitory ileus of newborn N
> **EXCLUDES** Hirschsprung's disease (751.3)

✓5ᵗʰ 777.5 Necrotizing enterocolitis in newborn
> **DEF:** Serious intestinal infection and inflammation in preterm infants; severity is measured by stages and may progress to life-threatening perforation or peritonitis; resection surgical treatment may be necessary.
> **AHA:** 4Q, '08, 138-140

777.50 Necrotizing enterocolitis in newborn, unspecified N
Necrotizing enterocolitis in newborn, NOS

777.51 Stage I necrotizing enterocolitis in newborn N
▶Necrotizing enterocolitis without pneumatosis, without perforation◀
> **DEF:** Broad-spectrum symptoms with non-specific signs including feeding intolerance, sepsis, gastroenteritis, ileus, metabolic abnormalities.

777.52 Stage II necrotizing enterocolitis in newborn N
Necrotizing enterocolitis with pneumatosis, without perforation
> **DEF:** Proven NEC via abdominal radiographs showing intestinal dilatation and pneumatosis intestinalis

777.53 Stage III necrotizing enterocolitis in newborn N
Necrotizing enterocolitis with perforation
Necrotizing enterocolitis with pneumatosis and perforation
> **DEF:** Advanced stage in which infant demonstrates signs of bowel perforation, septic shock, metabolic acidosis, ascites, disseminated intravascular coagulopathy, neutropenia.
> **AHA:** 4Q, '08, 139

777.6 Perinatal intestinal perforation N
Meconium peritonitis

777.8 Other specified perinatal disorders of digestive system N

777.9 Unspecified perinatal disorder of digestive system N

778 Conditions involving the integument and temperature regulation of fetus and newborn

778.0 Hydrops fetalis not due to isoimmunization N
Idiopathic hydrops
> **EXCLUDES** hydrops fetalis due to isoimmunization (773.3)
> **DEF:** Edema of entire body, unrelated to immune response.

778.1 Sclerema neonatorum N
Subcutaneous fat necrosis
> **DEF:** Diffuse, rapidly progressing white, waxy, nonpitting hardening of tissue, usually of legs and feet, life-threatening; found in preterm or debilitated infants; unknown etiology.

778.2 Cold injury syndrome of newborn N

778.3 Other hypothermia of newborn N

778.4 Other disturbances of temperature regulation of newborn N
Dehydration fever in newborn
Environmentally-induced pyrexia
Hyperthermia in newborn
Transitory fever of newborn
> **P81.9** Disturbance of temp regulation newborn uns `I-10`

778.5 Other and unspecified edema of newborn N
Edema neonatorum

778.6 Congenital hydrocele N
Congenital hydrocele of tunica vaginalis
> **P83.5** Congenital hydrocele `I-10`

778.7 Breast engorgement in newborn N
Noninfective mastitis of newborn
> **EXCLUDES** infective mastitis of newborn (771.5)

778.8 Other specified conditions involving the integument of fetus and newborn N
Urticaria neonatorum
> **EXCLUDES** impetigo neonatorum (684)
> pemphigus neonatorum (684)
> **P83.8** Oth spec conditions integument specific newborn `I-10`

N Newborn Age: 0   P Pediatric Age: 0-17   M Maternity Age: 12-55   A Adult Age: 15-124

778.9 **Unspecified condition involving the integument and temperature regulation of fetus and newborn** N

✓4th **779** **Other and ill-defined conditions originating in the perinatal period**

779.0 **Convulsions in newborn** N

Fits ⎫
Seizures ⎭ in newborn

AHA: N-D, '84, 11

TIP: Clarify with the physician that convulsions are not actually infantile spasms; if so, refer to subcategory 345.6.

779.1 **Other and unspecified cerebral irritability in newborn** N

779.2 **Cerebral depression, coma, and other abnormal cerebral signs** N

Cerebral ischemia NOS of newborn
CNS dysfunction in newborn NOS

EXCLUDES cerebral ischemia due to birth trauma (767.0)
intrauterine cerebral ischemia (768.2-768.9)
intraventricular hemorrhage (772.10-772.14)

▲ ✓5th **779.3** **Disorder of stomach function and feeding problems in newborn**

AHA: 2Q, '89, 15

● **779.31** **Feeding problems in newborn** N

Slow feeding in newborn

EXCLUDES feeding problem in child over 28 days old (783.3)

P92.9 Feeding problem of newborn unspecified I-10

● **779.32** **Bilious vomiting in newborn** N

EXCLUDES bilious vomiting in child over 28 days old (787.04)

● **779.33** **Other vomiting in newborn** N

Regurgitation of food in newborn

EXCLUDES vomiting in child over 28 days old (536.2, 787.01-787.04)

● **779.34** **Failure to thrive in newborn** N

EXCLUDES failure to thrive in child over 28 days old (783.41)

779.4 **Drug reactions and intoxications specific to newborn** N

Gray syndrome from chloramphenicol administration in newborn

EXCLUDES fetal alcohol syndrome (760.71)
reactions and intoxications from maternal opiates and tranquilizers (763.5)

779.5 **Drug withdrawal syndrome in newborn** N

Drug withdrawal syndrome in infant of dependent mother

EXCLUDES fetal alcohol syndrome (760.71)

AHA: 3Q, '94, 6

TIP: If the infant is asymptomatic but has a positive drug screen (e.g., for cocaine), assign instead 760.75.

779.6 **Termination of pregnancy (fetus)** N

Fetal death due to:
induced abortion
termination of pregnancy

EXCLUDES spontaneous abortion (fetus) (761.8)

779.7 **Periventricular leukomalacia**

DEF: Necrosis of white matter adjacent to lateral ventricles with the formation of cysts; cause of PVL has not been firmly established, but thought to be related to inadequate blood flow in certain areas of the brain.

AHA: 4Q, '01, 50, 51

✓5th **779.8** **Other specified conditions originating in the perinatal period**

AHA: 4Q, '02, 67; 1Q, '94, 15

779.81 **Neonatal bradycardia** N

EXCLUDES abnormality in fetal heart rate or rhythm complicating labor and delivery (763.81-763.83)
bradycardia due to birth asphyxia (768.5-768.9)

P29.12 Neonatal bradycardia I-10

779.82 **Neonatal tachycardia** N

EXCLUDES abnormality in fetal heart rate or rhythm complicating labor and delivery (763.81-763.83)

779.83 **Delayed separation of umbilical cord** N

AHA: 4Q, '03, 71

779.84 **Meconium staining** N

EXCLUDES meconium aspiration (770.11, 770.12)
meconium passage during delivery (763.84)

AHA: 4Q, '05, 83, 88

P96.83 Meconium staining I-10

779.85 **Cardiac arrest of newborn** N

AHA: 4Q, '06, 104-106

779.89 **Other specified conditions originating in the perinatal period** N

Use additional code to specify condition

AHA: 1Q, '06, 18; 2Q, '05, 15; 1Q, '05, 9

P96.89 Oth spec conditions originating perinatal period I-10

779.9 **Unspecified condition originating in the perinatal period** N

Congenital debility NOS
Stillbirth NEC

✓4th ✓5th Additional Digit Required   Unspecified Code   Other Specified Code   Manifestation Code   ▶◀ Revised Text   ● New Code   ▲ Revised Code Title

2010 ICD-9-CM

October 2009 · Volume 1 – 265

16. SYMPTOMS, SIGNS, AND ILL-DEFINED CONDITIONS (780-799)

This section includes symptoms, signs, abnormal results of laboratory or other investigative procedures, and ill-defined conditions regarding which no diagnosis classifiable elsewhere is recorded.

Signs and symptoms that point rather definitely to a given diagnosis are assigned to some category in the preceding part of the classification. In general, categories 780-796 include the more ill-defined conditions and symptoms that point with perhaps equal suspicion to two or more diseases or to two or more systems of the body, and without the necessary study of the case to make a final diagnosis. Practically all categories in this group can be designated as "not otherwise specified," or as "unknown etiology," or as "transient." The Alphabetic Index should be consulted to determine which symptoms and signs are to be allocated here and which to more specific sections of the classification; the residual subcategories numbered .9 are provided for other relevant symptoms which cannot be allocated elsewhere in the classification.

The conditions and signs or symptoms included in categories 780-796 consist of: (a) cases for which no more specific diagnosis can be made even after all facts bearing on the case have been investigated; (b) signs or symptoms existing at the time of initial encounter that proved to be transient and whose causes could not be determined; (c) provisional diagnoses in a patient who failed to return for further investigation or care; (d) cases referred elsewhere for investigation or treatment before the diagnosis was made; (e) cases in which a more precise diagnosis was not available for any other reason; (f) certain symptoms which represent important problems in medical care and which it might be desired to classify in addition to a known cause.

SYMPTOMS (780-789)

AHA: 1Q, '91, 12; 2Q, '90, 3; 2Q, '90, 5; 2Q, '90, 15; M-A, '85, 3

✓4ᵗʰ **780 General symptoms**

  ✓5ᵗʰ **780.0 Alteration of consciousness**

      EXCLUDES ▶*alteration of consciousness due to:*
          intracranial injuries (850.0-854.19)
          skull fractures (800.00-801.99,
            803.00-804.99)◀
        coma:
          diabetic (249.2-249.3, 250.2-250.3)
          hepatic (572.2)
          originating in the perinatal period (779.2)

      AHA: 4Q, '92, 20

    780.01 Coma

      DEF: State of unconsciousness from which the patient cannot be awakened.
      AHA: 3Q, '96, 16

    780.02 Transient alteration of awareness

      DEF: Temporary, recurring spells of reduced consciousness.

    780.03 Persistent vegetative state

      DEF: Persistent wakefulness without consciousness due to nonfunctioning cerebral cortex.

    780.09 Other

      Drowsiness
      Semicoma
      Somnolence
      Stupor
      Unconsciousness

      R40.1 Stupor   `I-10`

  780.1 Hallucinations

    Hallucinations:
      NOS
      auditory
      gustatory
      olfactory
      tactile

    EXCLUDES *those associated with mental disorders, as*
        functional psychoses (295.0-298.9)
        organic brain syndromes (290.0-294.9,
          310.0-310.9)
        visual hallucinations (368.16)

    DEF: Perception of external stimulus in absence of stimulus; inability to distinguish between real and imagined.

780.2 Syncope and collapse

  Blackout
  Fainting
  (Near) (Pre) syncope
  Vasovagal attack

  EXCLUDES *carotid sinus syncope (337.0)*
    heat syncope (992.1)
    neurocirculatory asthenia (306.2)
    orthostatic hypotension (458.0)
    shock NOS (785.50)

  DEF: Sudden unconsciousness due to reduced blood flow to brain.
  AHA: 1Q, '02, 6; 3Q, '00, 12; 4Q, '95, 42; 3Q, '95, 14; N-D, '85, 12

  R55 Syncope and collapse   `I-10`

✓5ᵗʰ **780.3 Convulsions**

  EXCLUDES *convulsions:*
    epileptic (345.10-345.91)
    in newborn (779.0)

  DEF: Sudden, involuntary contractions of the muscles.
  AHA: 2Q, '97, 8; 1Q, '97, 12; 3Q, '94, 9; 1Q, '93, 24; 4Q, '92, 23; N-D, '87, 12

  780.31 Febrile convulsions (simple), unspecified

    Febrile seizure NOS
    AHA: 4Q, '97, 45

  780.32 Complex febrile convulsions

    Febrile seizure:
      atypical
      complex
      complicated

    EXCLUDES *status epilepticus (345.3)*
    AHA: 4Q, '06, 106

  780.39 Other convulsions

    Convulsive disorder NOS
    Fit NOS
    Recurrent convulsions NOS
    Seizure NOS

    AHA: 1Q, '08, 17; 3Q, '06, 22; 4Q, '04, 51; 1Q, '03, 7; 2Q, '99, 17; 4Q, '98, 39

    R56.9 Unspecified convulsions   `I-10`

780.4 Dizziness and giddiness

  Light-headedness
  Vertigo NOS

  EXCLUDES *Ménière's disease and other specified*
    vertiginous syndromes (386.0-386.9)

  DEF: Whirling sensations in head with feeling of falling.
  AHA: 2Q, '03, 11; 3Q, '00, 12; 2Q, '97, 9; 2Q, '91, 17

  R42 Dizziness and giddiness   `I-10`

✓5ᵗʰ **780.5 Sleep disturbances**

  EXCLUDES *circadian rhythm sleep disorders*
    (327.30-327.39)
    organic hypersomnia (327.10-327.19)
    organic insomnia (327.00-327.09)
    organic sleep apnea (327.20-327.29)
    organic sleep related movement disorders
      (327.51-327.59)
    parasomnias (327.40-327.49)
    that of nonorganic origin (307.40-307.49)

  AHA: 4Q, '05, 59

  780.50 Sleep disturbance, unspecified

  780.51 Insomnia with sleep apnea, unspecified

    DEF: Transient cessation of breathing disturbing sleep.

  780.52 Insomnia, unspecified

    DEF: Inability to maintain adequate sleep cycle.
    G47.00 Insomnia unspecified   `I-10`

  780.53 Hypersomnia with sleep apnea, unspecified

    DEF: Autonomic response inhibited during sleep; causes insufficient oxygen intake, acidosis and pulmonary hypertension.
    AHA: 1Q, '93, 28; N-D, '85, 4

  780.54 Hypersomnia, unspecified

    DEF: Prolonged sleep cycle.

✓4ᵗʰ Additional Digit Required   Unspecified Code   Other Specified Code   Manifestation Code   ▶◀ Revised Text   ● New Code   ▲ Revised Code Title
✓5ᵗʰ
2010 ICD-9-CM   **October 2009 • Volume 1 – 267**

Symptoms, Signs, and Ill-Defined Conditions

780.55–780.92

780.55   **Disruptions of 24 hour sleep wake cycle, unspecified**

780.56   **Dysfunctions associated with sleep stages or arousal from sleep**

780.57   **Unspecified sleep apnea**
> AHA: 1Q, '01, 6 ; 1Q, '97, 5; 1Q, '93, 28
>
> **G47.30** Sleep apnea unspecified   [I-10]

780.58   **Sleep related movement disorder, unspecified**
> **EXCLUDES**   restless legs syndrome (333.94)
>
> AHA: 4Q, '04, 95

780.59   **Other**

✓5ᵗʰ **780.6**   **Fever and other physiologic disturbances of temperature regulation**
> **EXCLUDES**   effects of reduced environmental temperature (991.0-991.9)
> effects of heat and light (992.0-992.9)
> fever, chills or hypothermia associated with confirmed infection–code to infection
>
> AHA: ▶4Q, '08,140-142;◀ 3Q, '05, 16; 3Q, '00,13; 4Q, '99, 26; 2Q, '91, 8

780.60   **Fever, unspecified**
> Chills with fever
> Fever NOS
> Fever of unknown origin (FUO)
> Hyperpyrexia NOS
> Pyrexia NOS
> Pyrexia of unknown origin
>
> **EXCLUDES**   chills without fever (780.64)
> neonatal fever (778.4)
> pyrexia of unknown origin (during):
> in newborn (778.4)
> labor (659.2)
> the puerperium (672)
>
> **R50.9** Fever unspecified   [I-10]

780.61   **Fever presenting with conditions classified elsewhere**
> Code first underlying condition when associated fever is present, such as with:
> leukemia (conditions classifiable to 204-208)
> neutropenia (288.00-288.09)
> sickle-cell disease (282.60-282.69)
>
> AHA: ▶4Q, '08, 142◀

780.62   **Postprocedural fever**
> **EXCLUDES**   postvaccination fever (780.63)
>
> **TIP:** Do not assign a code from category 998 for post-procedural fever.

780.63   **Postvaccination fever**
> Postimmunization fever

780.64   **Chills (without fever)**
> Chills NOS
>
> **EXCLUDES**   chills with fever (780.60)

780.65   **Hypothermia not associated with low environmental temperature**
> **EXCLUDES**   hypothermia:
> associated with low environmental temperature (991.6)
> due to anesthesia (995.89)
> of newborn (778.2, 778.3)

✓5ᵗʰ **780.7**   **Malaise and fatigue**
> **EXCLUDES**   debility, unspecified (799.3)
> fatigue (during):
> combat (308.0-308.9)
> heat (992.6)
> pregnancy (646.8)
> neurasthenia (300.5)
> senile asthenia (797)
>
> AHA: 4Q, '88, 12; M-A, '87, 8

780.71   **Chronic fatigue syndrome**
> **DEF:** Persistent fatigue, symptoms include weak muscles, sore throat, lymphadenitis, headache, depression and mild fever; no known cause; also called chronic mononucleosis, benign myalgic encephalomyelitis, Iceland disease and neurosthenia.
>
> AHA: 4Q, '98, 48

780.72   **Functional quadriplegia**
> Complete immobility due to severe physical disability or frailty
>
> **EXCLUDES**   hysterical paralysis (300.11)
> immobility syndrome (728.3)
> neurologic quadriplegia (344.00-344.09)
> quadriplegia NOS (344.00)
>
> **DEF:** ▶Inability to move due to another condition such as dementia, severe contractures, or arthritis, not a physiologic one; no mental ability to move independently; typically found in severely demented patients.◀
>
> AHA: ▶4Q, '08, 143◀
>
> **TIP:** The functional quadriplegic patient typically has severe dementia and the quadriplegia will be due to a nonneurologic condition.

780.79   **Other malaise and fatigue**
> Asthenia NOS
> Lethargy
> Postviral (asthenic) syndrome
> Tiredness
>
> **DEF:** Asthenia: Any weakness, lack of strength or loss of energy, especially neuromuscular.
> **DEF:** Lethargy: Listlessness, drowsiness, stupor and apathy.
> **DEF:** Malaise: Vague feeling of debility or lack of good health.
> **DEF:** Postviral (asthenic) syndrome: Listlessness, drowsiness, stupor and apathy; follows acute viral infection.
> **DEF:** Tiredness: General exhaustion or fatigue.
>
> AHA: 4Q, '04, 78; 1Q, '00, 6; 4Q, '99, 26
>
> **R53.83** Other fatigue   [I-10]

780.8   **Generalized hyperhidrosis**
> Diaphoresis   Secondary hyperhidrosis
> Excessive sweating
>
> **EXCLUDES**   focal (localized) (primary) (secondary) hyperhidrosis (705.21-705.22)
> Frey's syndrome (705.22)
>
> **DEF:** Excessive sweating, appears as droplets on skin; general or localized.
>
> **TIP:** Do not assign if documentation indicates a specific diagnosis of focal hyperhidrosis (primary or secondary); see subcategory 705.2.

✓5ᵗʰ **780.9**   **Other general symptoms**
> **EXCLUDES**   hypothermia:
> NOS (accidental) (991.6)
> due to anesthesia (995.89)
> of newborn (778.2-778.3)
> memory disturbance as part of a pattern of mental disorder
>
> AHA: 4Q, '02, 67; 4Q, '99, 10; 3Q, '93, 11; N-D, '85, 12

780.91   **Fussy infant (baby)**   [P]

780.92   **Excessive crying of infant (baby)**   [N]
> **EXCLUDES**   excessive crying of child, adolescent or adult (780.95)

[N] Newborn Age: 0   [P] Pediatric Age: 0-17   [M] Maternity Age: 12-55   [A] Adult Age: 15-124

780.93 Memory loss
Amnesia (retrograde)
Memory loss NOS

> **EXCLUDES** ▶ memory loss due to:
> intracranial injuries (850.0-854.19)
> skull fractures (800.00-801.99,
> 803.00-804.99)◄
> mild memory disturbance due to
> organic brain damage
> ▶(310.8)◄
> transient global amnesia (437.7)

AHA: 4Q, '03, 71

780.94 Early satiety

DEF: The premature feeling of being full; mechanism
of satiety is mutlifactorial.

AHA: 4Q, '03, 72

780.95 Excessive crying of child, adolescent, or adult

> **EXCLUDES** excessive crying of infant (baby)
> (780.92)

AHA: 4Q, '05, 89

780.96 Generalized pain
Pain NOS

AHA: 4Q, '06, 79-81

TIP: For pain syndromes, refer to category 338; if site
is specified, refer to index.

780.97 Altered mental status
Change in mental status

> **EXCLUDES** altered level of consciousness
> (780.01-780.09)
> altered mental status due to known
> condition–code to condition
> delirium NOS (780.09)

AHA: 4Q, '06, 107

R41.82 Altered mental status unspecified [I-10]

780.99 Other general symptoms

AHA: 4Q, '03, 103

√4ᵗʰ **781 Symptoms involving nervous and musculoskeletal
systems**

> **EXCLUDES** depression NOS (311)
> disorders specifically relating to:
> back (724.0-724.9)
> hearing (388.0-389.9)
> joint (718.0-719.9)
> limb (729.0-729.9)
> neck (723.0-723.9)
> vision (368.0-369.9)
> pain in limb (729.5)

781.0 Abnormal involuntary movements
Abnormal head movements Spasms NOS
Fasciculation Tremor NOS

> **EXCLUDES** abnormal reflex (796.1)
> chorea NOS (333.5)
> infantile spasms (345.60-345.61)
> spastic paralysis (342.1, 343.0-344.9)
> specified movement disorders classifiable to
> 333 (333.0-333.9)
> that of nonorganic origin (307.2-307.3)

R25.9 Unspecified abnormal involuntary movements [I-10]

781.1 Disturbances of sensation of smell and taste
Anosmia Parosmia
Parageusia

DEF: Anosmia: loss of sense of smell due to organic factors,
including loss of olfactory nerve conductivity, cerebral
disease, nasal fossae formation and peripheral olfactory nerve
diseases; can also be psychological disorder.

DEF: Parageusia: distorted sense of taste, or bad taste in
mouth.

DEF: Parosmia: distorted sense of smell.

781.2 Abnormality of gait
Gait: Gait:
ataxic spastic
paralytic staggering

> **EXCLUDES** ataxia:
> NOS (781.3)
> locomotor (progressive) (094.0)
> difficulty in walking (719.7)

DEF: Abnormal, asymmetric gait.

AHA: 2Q, '05, 6; 2Q, '04, 15

TIP: If the patient's gait abnormality is due to a joint problem,
refer to code 719.7 Difficulty in walking.

R26.9 Unspecified abnormalities of gait and mobility [I-10]

781.3 Lack of coordination
Ataxia NOS Muscular incoordination

> **EXCLUDES** ataxic gait (781.2)
> cerebellar ataxia (334.0-334.9)
> difficulty in walking (719.7)
> vertigo NOS (780.4)

AHA: 4Q, '04, 51; 3Q, '97, 12

781.4 Transient paralysis of limb
Monoplegia, transient NOS

> **EXCLUDES** paralysis (342.0-344.9)

781.5 Clubbing of fingers

DEF: Enlarged soft tissue of distal fingers.

781.6 Meningismus
Dupré's syndrome
Meningism

DEF: Condition with signs and symptoms that resemble
meningeal irritation; it is associated with febrile illness and
dehydration with no evidence of infection.

AHA: 3Q, '00,13; J-F, '87, 7

781.7 Tetany
Carpopedal spasm

> **EXCLUDES** tetanus neonatorum (771.3)
> tetany:
> hysterical (300.11)
> newborn (hypocalcemic) (775.4)
> parathyroid (252.1)
> psychogenic (306.0)

DEF: Nerve and muscle hyperexcitability; symptoms include
muscle spasms, twitching, cramps, laryngospasm with
inspiratory stridor, hyperreflexia and choreiform movements.

781.8 Neurologic neglect syndrome
Asomatognosia Left-sided neglect
Hemi-akinesia Sensory extinction
Hemi-inattention Sensory neglect
Hemispatial neglect Visuospatial neglect

AHA: 4Q, '94, 37

TIP: If documented as sequelae of a CVA, assign also a code
from category 438.

√5ᵗʰ **781.9 Other symptoms involving nervous and
musculoskeletal systems**

AHA: 4Q, '00, 45

781.91 Loss of height

> **EXCLUDES** osteoporosis (733.00-733.09)

781.92 Abnormal posture

781.93 Ocular torticollis

DEF: Abnormal head posture as a result of a
contracted state of cervical muscles to correct a
visual disturbance; either double vision or a visual
field defect.

AHA: 4Q, '02, 68

781.94 Facial weakness
Facial droop

> **EXCLUDES** facial weakness due to late effect of
> cerebrovascular accident
> (438.83)

AHA: 4Q, '03, 72

TIP: Do not assign if facial droop or weakness is due
to Bell's palsy; see instead code 351.0.

R29.810 Facial weakness [I-10]

Symptoms, Signs, and Ill-Defined Conditions

781.99–783.9

781.99　Other symptoms involving nervous and musculoskeletal systems

✓4th　**782**　**Symptoms involving skin and other integumentary tissue**
　　　EXCLUDES　*symptoms relating to breast (611.71-611.79)*

782.0　Disturbance of skin sensation
　　　Anesthesia of skin　　　Hypoesthesia
　　　Burning or prickling　　　Numbness
　　　　sensation　　　Paresthesia
　　　Hyperesthesia　　　Tingling
　　　R20.9 Unspecified disturbances of skin sensation　　I-10

782.1　Rash and other nonspecific skin eruption
　　　Exanthem
　　　EXCLUDES　*vesicular eruption (709.8)*
　　　AHA: 4Q, '08, 99

782.2　Localized superficial swelling, mass, or lump
　　　Subcutaneous nodules
　　　EXCLUDES　*localized adiposity (278.1)*

782.3　Edema
　　　Anasarca
　　　Dropsy
　　　Localized edema NOS
　　　EXCLUDES　*ascites (789.51-789.59)*
　　　　　　edema of:
　　　　　　　newborn NOS (778.5)
　　　　　　　pregnancy (642.0-642.9, 646.1)
　　　　　　fluid retention (276.6)
　　　　　　hydrops fetalis (773.3, 778.0)
　　　　　　hydrothorax (511.81-511.89)
　　　　　　nutritional edema (260, 262)
　　　DEF: Edema: excess fluid in intercellular body tissue.
　　　DEF: Anasarca: massive edema in all body tissues.
　　　DEF: Dropsy: serous fluid accumulated in body cavity or cellular tissue.
　　　DEF: Localized edema: edema in specific body areas.
　　　AHA: 2Q, '00, 18
　　　R60.9 Edema unspecified　　I-10

782.4　Jaundice, unspecified, not of newborn
　　　Cholemia NOS
　　　Icterus NOS
　　　EXCLUDES　*jaundice in newborn (774.0-774.7)*
　　　　　　due to isoimmunization (773.0-773.2, 773.4)
　　　DEF: Bilirubin deposits of skin, causing yellow cast.
　　　R17 Unspecified jaundice　　I-10

782.5　Cyanosis
　　　EXCLUDES　*newborn (770.83)*
　　　DEF: Deficient oxygen of blood; causes blue cast to skin.

✓5th　**782.6**　Pallor and flushing

　　　782.61　Pallor

　　　782.62　Flushing
　　　　　　Excessive blushing

782.7　Spontaneous ecchymoses
　　　Petechiae
　　　EXCLUDES　*ecchymosis in fetus or newborn (772.6)*
　　　　　　purpura (287.0-287.9)
　　　DEF: Hemorrhagic spots of skin; resemble freckles.

782.8　Changes in skin texture
　　　Induration　}　of skin
　　　Thickening

782.9　Other symptoms involving skin and integumentary tissues

✓4th　**783**　**Symptoms concerning nutrition, metabolism, and development**

783.0　Anorexia
　　　Loss of appetite
　　　EXCLUDES　*anorexia nervosa (307.1)*
　　　　　　loss of appetite of nonorganic origin (307.59)
　　　R63.0 Anorexia　　I-10

783.1　Abnormal weight gain
　　　EXCLUDES　*excessive weight gain in pregnancy (646.1)*
　　　　　　obesity (278.00)
　　　　　　　morbid (278.01)

✓5th　**783.2**　Abnormal loss of weight and underweight
　　　Use additional code to identify Body Mass Index (BMI), if known (V85.0-V85.54)
　　　AHA: 4Q, '00, 45

　　　783.21　Loss of weight
　　　　　　AHA: 4Q, '05, 96
　　　　　　R63.4 Abnormal weight loss　　I-10

　　　783.22　Underweight
　　　　　　AHA: 4Q, '05, 96

783.3　Feeding difficulties and mismanagement
　　　Feeding problem (elderly) (infant)
　　　EXCLUDES　*feeding disturbance or problems:*
　　　　　　in newborn ▶(779.31-779.34)◀
　　　　　　of nonorganic origin (307.50-307.59)
　　　AHA: 3Q, '97, 12

✓5th　**783.4**　Lack of expected normal physiological development in childhood
　　　EXCLUDES　*delay in sexual development and puberty (259.0)*
　　　　　　gonadal dysgenesis (758.6)
　　　　　　pituitary dwarfism (253.3)
　　　　　　slow fetal growth and fetal malnutrition (764.00-764.99)
　　　　　　specific delays in mental development (315.0-315.9)
　　　AHA: 4Q, '00, 45; 3Q, '97, 4

　　　783.40　Lack of normal physiological development, unspecified
　　　　　　Inadequate development
　　　　　　Lack of development

　　　783.41　Failure to thrive　　P
　　　　　　Failure to gain weight
　　　　　　EXCLUDES　*▶failure to thrive in newborn (779.34)◀*
　　　　　　DEF: Organic failure to thrive: acute or chronic illness that interferes with nutritional intake, absorption, metabolism excretion and energy requirements. Nonorganic FTT is symptom of neglect or abuse.
　　　　　　AHA: 1Q, '03, 12

　　　783.42　Delayed milestones　　P
　　　　　　Late talker
　　　　　　Late walker

　　　783.43　Short stature
　　　　　　Growth failure　　Lack of growth
　　　　　　Growth retardation　Physical retardation
　　　　　　DEF: Constitutional short stature: stature inconsistent with chronological age. Genetic short stature is when skeletal maturation matches chronological age.

783.5　Polydipsia
　　　Excessive thirst

783.6　Polyphagia
　　　Excessive eating
　　　Hyperalimentation NOS
　　　EXCLUDES　*disorders of eating of nonorganic origin (307.50-307.59)*

783.7　Adult failure to thrive　　A
　　　R62.7 Adult failure to thrive　　I-10

783.9　Other symptoms concerning nutrition, metabolism, and development
　　　Hypometabolism
　　　EXCLUDES　*abnormal basal metabolic rate (794.7)*
　　　　　　dehydration (276.51)
　　　　　　other disorders of fluid, electrolyte, and acid-base balance (276.0-276.9)
　　　AHA: 2Q, '04, 3

N Newborn Age: 0　　　P Pediatric Age: 0-17　　　M Maternity Age: 12-55　　　A Adult Age: 15-124

√4ᵗʰ **784 Symptoms involving head and neck**
> *EXCLUDES*   *encephalopathy NOS (348.30)*
> *specific symptoms involving neck classifiable to 723*
> *(723.0-723.9)*

784.0 Headache
Facial pain
Pain in head NOS
> *EXCLUDES*   *atypical face pain (350.2)*
> *migraine (346.0-346.9)*
> *tension headache (307.81)*

AHA: 3Q, '06, 22; 2Q, '06, 17; 3Q, '00, 13; 1Q, '90, 4; 3Q, '92, 14
TIP: Do not assign if headache syndrome has been diagnosed, refer to category 339.
R51 Headache   I-10

784.1 Throat pain
> *EXCLUDES*   *dysphagia (787.20-787.29)*
> *neck pain (723.1)*
> *sore throat (462)*
> *chronic (472.1)*

784.2 Swelling, mass, or lump in head and neck
Space-occupying lesion, intracranial NOS
AHA: 1Q, '03, 8

784.3 Aphasia
> *EXCLUDES*   *aphasia due to late effects of cerebrovascular*
> *disease (438.11)*
> *developmental aphasia (315.31)*

DEF: Inability to communicate through speech, written word, or sign language.
AHA: 4Q, '04, 78; 4Q, '98, 87; 3Q, '97, 12
R47.01 Aphasia   I-10

▲ √5ᵗʰ **784.4 Voice and resonance disorders**
▲   **784.40 Voice and resonance disorder, unspecified**

784.41 Aphonia
Loss of voice

● **784.42 Dysphonia**
Hoarseness

● **784.43 Hypernasality**

● **784.44 Hyponasality**

▲ **784.49 Other voice and resonance disorders**
Change in voice

√5ᵗʰ **784.5 Other speech disturbance**
> *EXCLUDES*   ►*speech disorder due to late effect of*
> *cerebrovascular accident*
> *(438.10-438.19)*◄
> *stammering and stuttering (307.0)*
> *that of nonorganic origin (307.0, 307.9)*

● **784.51 Dysarthria**
> *EXCLUDES*   *dysarthria due to late effect of*
> *cerebrovascular accident*
> *(438.13)*

● **784.59 Other speech disturbance**
Dysphasia
Slurred speech
Speech disturbance NOS
R47.89 Other speech disturbances   I-10

√5ᵗʰ **784.6 Other symbolic dysfunction**
> *EXCLUDES*   *developmental learning delays (315.0-315.9)*

784.60 Symbolic dysfunction, unspecified

784.61 Alexia and dyslexia
Alexia (with agraphia)
DEF: Alexia: Inability to understand written word due to central brain lesion.
DEF: Dyslexia: Ability to recognize letters but inability to read, spell, and write words; genetic.

784.69 Other
Acalculia
Agnosia
Agraphia NOS
Apraxia

784.7 Epistaxis
Hemorrhage from nose
Nosebleed
AHA: 3Q, '04, 7
R04.0 Epistaxis   I-10

784.8 Hemorrhage from throat
> *EXCLUDES*   *hemoptysis (786.3)*

√5ᵗʰ **784.9 Other symptoms involving head and neck**

784.91 Postnasal drip
AHA: 4Q, '06, 108

784.99 Other symptoms involving head and neck
Choking sensation
Feeling of foreign body in throat
Halitosis
Mouth breathing
Sneezing
> *EXCLUDES*   *foreign body in throat (933.0)*

AHA: 4Q, '06, 108

√4ᵗʰ **785 Symptoms involving cardiovascular system**
> *EXCLUDES*   *heart failure NOS (428.9)*

785.0 Tachycardia, unspecified
Rapid heart beat
> *EXCLUDES*   *neonatal tachycardia (779.82)*
> *paroxysmal tachycardia (427.0-427.2)*

DEF: Excessively rapid heart rate.
AHA: 2Q, '03, 11
R00.0 Tachycardia unspecified   I-10

785.1 Palpitations
Awareness of heart beat
> *EXCLUDES*   *specified dysrhythmias (427.0-427.9)*

R00.2 Palpitations   I-10

785.2 Undiagnosed cardiac murmurs
Heart murmurs NOS
AHA: 4Q, '92, 16
R01.1 Cardiac murmur unspecified   I-10

785.3 Other abnormal heart sounds
Cardiac dullness, increased or decreased
Friction fremitus, cardiac
Precordial friction

785.4 Gangrene
Gangrene: Gangrenous cellulitis
    NOS   Phagedena
    spreading cutaneous
Code first any associated underlying condition
> *EXCLUDES*   *gangrene of certain sites–see Alphabetic Index*
> *gangrene with atherosclerosis of the*
> *extremities (440.24)*
> *gas gangrene (040.0*

DEF: Gangrene: necrosis of skin tissue due to bacterial infection, diabetes, embolus and vascular supply loss.
DEF: Gangrenous cellulitis: group A streptococcal infection; begins with severe cellulitis, spreads to superficial and deep fascia; produces gangrene of underlying tissues.
AHA: 1Q, '04, 14; 3Q, '91, 12; 3Q, '90, 15; M-A, '86, 12
I96 Gangrene not elsewhere classified   I-10

√5ᵗʰ **785.5 Shock without mention of trauma**

785.50 Shock, unspecified
Failure of peripheral circulation
DEF: Peripheral circulatory failure due to heart insufficiencies.
AHA: 2Q, '96, 10

785.51 Cardiogenic shock
DEF: Shock syndrome: associated with myocardial infarction, cardiac tamponade and massive pulmonary embolism; symptoms include mental confusion, reduced blood pressure, tachycardia, pallor and cold, clammy skin.
AHA: 4Q, '08, 182; 3Q, '05, 14
R57.0 Cardiogenic shock   I-10

√4ᵗʰ Additional Digit Required   **Unspecified Code**   Other Specified Code   Manifestation Code   ►◄ Revised Text   ● New Code   ▲ Revised Code Title
√5ᵗʰ
2010 ICD-9-CM   **October 2009 • Volume 1 – 271**

Symptoms, Signs, and Ill-Defined Conditions

785.52–786.52

785.52 Septic shock
Shock:
   endotoxic
   gram-negative
Code first:
   systemic inflammatory response syndrome
     due to infectious process with organ
     dysfunction (995.92)

AHA: ►4Q, '08, 99;◄ 4Q, '06, 113; 2Q, '05, 18-19; 4Q, '03, 73, 79

TIP: The diagnosis of septic shock indicates the presence of severe sepsis; code 785.52 should not be assigned without first assigning code 995.92.

785.59 Other
Shock:
   hypovolemic
EXCLUDES   shock (due to):
     anesthetic (995.4)
     anaphylactic (995.0)
     due to serum (999.4)
     electric (994.8)
     following abortion (639.5)
     lightning (994.0)
     obstetrical (669.1)
     postoperative (998.0)
     traumatic (958.4)

AHA: 2Q, '00, 3

785.6 Enlargement of lymph nodes
Lymphadenopathy
"Swollen glands"
EXCLUDES   lymphadenitis (chronic) (289.1-289.3)
     acute (683)

R59.9 Enlarged lymph nodes unspecified   I-10

785.9 Other symptoms involving cardiovascular system
Bruit (arterial)
Weak pulse

✓4ᵗʰ 786 Symptoms involving respiratory system and other chest symptoms

✓5ᵗʰ 786.0 Dyspnea and respiratory abnormalities

786.00 Respiratory abnormality, unspecified

786.01 Hyperventilation
EXCLUDES   hyperventilation, psychogenic (306.1)
DEF: Rapid breathing causes carbon dioxide loss from blood.

786.02 Orthopnea
DEF: Difficulty breathing except in upright position.

786.03 Apnea
EXCLUDES   apnea of newborn (770.81, 770.82)
     sleep apnea (780.51, 780.53, 780.57)
DEF: Cessation of breathing.
AHA: 4Q, '98, 50

786.04 Cheyne-Stokes respiration
DEF: Rhythmic increase of depth and frequency of breathing with apnea; occurs in frontal lobe and diencephalic dysfunction.
AHA: 4Q, '98, 50

786.05 Shortness of breath
DEF: Inability to take in sufficient oxygen.
AHA: 4Q, '99, 25; 1Q, '99, 6; 4Q, '98, 50
R06.02 Shortness of breath   I-10

786.06 Tachypnea
EXCLUDES   transitory tachypnea of newborn (770.6)
DEF: Abnormal rapid respiratory rate; called hyperventilation.
AHA: 4Q, '98, 50

786.07 Wheezing
EXCLUDES   asthma (493.00-493.92)
DEF: Stenosis of respiratory passageway; causes whistling sound; due to asthma, coryza, croup, emphysema, hay fever, edema, and pleural effusion.
AHA: 4Q, '98, 50

786.09 Other
Respiratory:
   distress
   insufficiency
EXCLUDES   respiratory distress:
     following trauma and surgery (518.5)
     newborn (770.89)
     syndrome (newborn) (769)
     adult (518.5)
     respiratory failure (518.81, 518.83-518.84)
     newborn (770.84)
AHA: 4Q, '05, 90; 2Q, '98, 10; 1Q, '97, 7; 1Q, '90, 9
R06.82 Tachypnea not elsewhere classified   I-10

786.1 Stridor
EXCLUDES   congenital laryngeal stridor (748.3)
DEF: Obstructed airway causes harsh sound.

786.2 Cough
EXCLUDES   cough:
     psychogenic (306.1)
     smokers' (491.0)
     with hemorrhage (786.3)
AHA: 4Q, '99, 26
R05 Cough   I-10

786.3 Hemoptysis
Cough with hemorrhage
Pulmonary hemorrhage NOS
EXCLUDES   pulmonary hemorrhage of newborn (770.3)
DEF: Coughing up blood or blood-stained sputum.
AHA: 2Q, '06, 17; 4Q, '90, 26
R04.2 Hemoptysis   I-10

786.4 Abnormal sputum
Abnormal:
   amount
   color   } (of) sputum
   odor
Excessive

✓5ᵗʰ 786.5 Chest pain

786.50 Chest pain, unspecified
AHA: 1Q, '07, 19; 2Q, '06, 7; 1Q, '03, 6; 1Q, '02, 4; 4Q, '99, 25
R07.9 Chest pain unspecified   I-10

786.51 Precordial pain
DEF: Chest pain over heart and lower thorax.

786.52 Painful respiration
Pain:
   anterior chest wall
   pleuritic
Pleurodynia
EXCLUDES   epidemic pleurodynia (074.1)
AHA: N-D, '84, 17
TIP: Assign for musculoskeletal chest pain with no indication of underlying cause.
R07.1 Chest pain on breathing   I-10

N Newborn Age: 0   P Pediatric Age: 0-17   M Maternity Age: 12-55   A Adult Age: 15-124

786.59 **Other**
Discomfort ⎫
Pressure ⎬ in chest
Tightness ⎭

EXCLUDES *pain in breast (611.71)*

AHA: 1Q, '02, 6

TIP: Assign for chest pain due to anxiety, along with an additional code for anxiety. Chest pain is not integral to the diagnosis of anxiety.

R07.89 Other chest pain `I-10`

786.6 **Swelling, mass, or lump in chest**
EXCLUDES *lump in breast (611.72)*

R22.2 Localized swelling, mass, lump, trunk `I-10`

786.7 **Abnormal chest sounds**
Abnormal percussion, chest
Friction sounds, chest
Rales
Tympany, chest
EXCLUDES *wheezing (786.07)*

786.8 **Hiccough**
EXCLUDES *psychogenic hiccough (306.1)*

786.9 **Other symptoms involving respiratory system and chest**
Breath-holding spell

✓4ᵗʰ **787** **Symptoms involving digestive system**
EXCLUDES *constipation (564.00-564.09)*
pylorospasm (537.81)
congenital (750.5)

✓5ᵗʰ **787.0** **Nausea and vomiting**
Emesis
EXCLUDES *hematemesis NOS (578.0)*
vomiting:
bilious, following gastrointestinal surgery (564.3)
cyclical (536.2)
associated with migraine (346.2)
psychogenic (306.4)
excessive, in pregnancy (643.0-643.9)
▶*fecal matter (569.87)*◀
habit (536.2)
of newborn ▶*(779.32, 779.33)*◀
▶*persistent (536.2)*◀
psychogenic NOS (307.54)

AHA: M-A, '85, 11

787.01 **Nausea with vomiting**
AHA: 1Q, '03, 5
R11.0 Nausea with vomiting `I-10`

787.02 **Nausea alone**
AHA: 3Q, '00, 12; 2Q, '97, 9
R11.1 Nausea alone `I-10`

787.03 **Vomiting alone**

787.04 **Bilious emesis**
Bilious vomiting
EXCLUDES *bilious emesis (vomiting) in newborn (779.32)*

787.1 **Heartburn**
Pyrosis
Waterbrash
EXCLUDES *dyspepsia or indigestion (536.8)*
AHA: 2Q, '01, 6

✓5ᵗʰ **787.2** **Dysphagia**
Code first, if applicable, dysphagia due to late effect of cerebrovascular accident (438.82)
AHA: 4Q, '07, 92-94; 3Q, '07, 7; 4Q, '03, 103, 109; 2Q, '01, 4

787.20 **Dysphagia, unspecified**
Difficulty in swallowing NOS

787.21 **Dysphagia, oral phase**

787.22 **Dysphagia, oropharyngeal phase**
AHA: 4Q, '07, 94

Phases of Swallowing

Oral phase

Oropharyngeal phase

Pharyngeal phase

Pharyngeoesophageal phase

787.23 **Dysphagia, pharyngeal phase**

787.24 **Dysphagia, pharyngoesophageal phase**

787.29 **Other dysphagia**
Cervical dysphagia
Neurogenic dysphagia
R13.19 Other dysphagia `I-10`

787.3 **Flatulence, eructation, and gas pain**
Abdominal distention (gaseous)
Bloating
Tympanites (abdominal) (intestinal)
EXCLUDES *aerophagy (306.4)*
DEF: Flatulence: excess air or gas in intestine or stomach.
DEF: Eructation: belching, expelling gas through mouth.
DEF: Gas pain: gaseous pressure affecting gastrointestinal system.

787.4 **Visible peristalsis**
Hyperperistalsis
DEF: Increase in involuntary movements of intestines.

787.5 **Abnormal bowel sounds**
Absent bowel sounds
Hyperactive bowel sounds

787.6 **Incontinence of feces**
Encopresis NOS
Incontinence of sphincter ani
EXCLUDES *that of nonorganic origin (307.7)*
AHA: 1Q, '97, 9

787.7 **Abnormal feces**
Bulky stools
EXCLUDES *abnormal stool content (792.1)*
melena:
NOS (578.1)
newborn (772.4, 777.3)

✓5ᵗʰ **787.9** **Other symptoms involving digestive system**
EXCLUDES *gastrointestinal hemorrhage (578.0-578.9)*
intestinal obstruction (560.0-560.9)
specific functional digestive disorders:
esophagus (530.0-530.9)
stomach and duodenum (536.0-536.9)
those not elsewhere classified (564.00-564.9)

787.91 **Diarrhea**
Diarrhea NOS
AHA: 4Q, '08, 99; 4Q, '95, 54
R19.7 Diarrhea unspecified `I-10`

787.99 **Other**
Change in bowel habits
Tenesmus (rectal)
DEF: Tenesmus: Painful, ineffective straining at the rectum with limited passage of fecal matter.

√4ᵗʰ **788 Symptoms involving urinary system**

> **EXCLUDES** *hematuria (599.70-599.72)*
> *nonspecific findings on examination of the urine (791.0-791.9)*
> *small kidney of unknown cause (589.0-589.9)*
> *uremia NOS (586)*
> *urinary obstruction (599.60, 599.69)*

788.0 Renal colic

Colic (recurrent) of:
   kidney
   ureter

DEF: Kidney pain.

AHA: 3Q, '04, 8

TIP: Do not assign if renal colic is due to calculus; see category 592.

788.1 Dysuria

Painful urination
Strangury

√5ᵗʰ **788.2 Retention of urine**

Code, if applicable, any causal condition first, such as:
   hyperplasia of prostate (600.0-600.9 with fifth-digit 1)

DEF: Accumulation of urine in the bladder due to inability to void

788.20 Retention of urine, unspecified

AHA: 4Q, '06, 93, 95; 2Q, '04, 18; 3Q, '03, 12-13; 1Q, '03, 6; 3Q, '96, 10

R33.9 Retention of urine unspecified   I-10

788.21 Incomplete bladder emptying

AHA: 4Q, '06, 93

788.29 Other specified retention of urine

√5ᵗʰ **788.3 Urinary incontinence**

Code, if applicable, any causal condition first, such as:
   congenital ureterocele (753.23)
   genital prolapse (618.00-618.9)
   hyperplasia of prostate (600.0-600.9 with fifth-digit 1)

> **EXCLUDES** *functional urinary incontinence (788.91)*
> *that of nonorganic origin (307.6)*
> *urinary incontinence associated with cognitive impairment (788.91)*

AHA: 4Q, '06, 93; 4Q, '92, 22

788.30 Urinary incontinence, unspecified

Enuresis NOS

AHA: ►1Q, '09, 15◄

R32 Unspecified urinary incontinence   I-10

788.31 Urge incontinence

DEF: Inability to control urination, upon urge to urinate.

AHA: 1Q, '00, 19

788.32 Stress incontinence, male   ♂

> **EXCLUDES** *stress incontinence, female (625.6)*

DEF: Inability to control urination associated with weak sphincter in males.

788.33 Mixed incontinence, (male) (female)

Urge and stress

DEF: Urge, stress incontinence: involuntary discharge of urine due to anatomic displacement.

788.34 Incontinence without sensory awareness

DEF: Involuntary discharge of urine without sensory warning.

788.35 Post-void dribbling

DEF: Involuntary discharge of residual urine after voiding.

788.36 Nocturnal enuresis

DEF: Involuntary discharge of urine during the night.

788.37 Continuous leakage

DEF: Continuous, involuntary urine seepage.

788.38 Overflow incontinence

DEF: Leakage caused by pressure of retained urine in the bladder after the bladder has fully contracted due to weakened bladder muscles or an obstruction of the urethra.

788.39 Other urinary incontinence

√5ᵗʰ **788.4 Frequency of urination and polyuria**

Code, if applicable, any causal condition first, such as:
   hyperplasia of prostate (600.0-600.9 with fifth-digit 1)

788.41 Urinary frequency

Frequency of micturition

AHA: 4Q, '06, 93

788.42 Polyuria

DEF: Excessive urination.

788.43 Nocturia

DEF: Urination affecting sleep patterns.

AHA: 4Q, '06, 93

788.5 Oliguria and anuria

Deficient secretion of urine
Suppression of urinary secretion

> **EXCLUDES** *that complicating:*
> *abortion (634-638 with .3, 639.3)*
> *ectopic or molar pregnancy (639.3)*
> *pregnancy, childbirth, or the puerperium (642.0-642.9, 646.2)*

DEF: Oliguria: diminished urinary secretion related to fluid intake.

DEF: Anuria: lack of urinary secretion due to renal failure or obstructed urinary tract.

√5ᵗʰ **788.6 Other abnormality of urination**

Code, if applicable, any causal condition first, such as:
   hyperplasia of prostate (600.0-600.9 with fifth-digit 1)

788.61 Splitting of urinary stream

Intermittent urinary stream

788.62 Slowing of urinary stream

Weak stream

AHA: 4Q, '06, 93

788.63 Urgency of urination

> **EXCLUDES** *urge incontinence (788.31, 788.33)*

DEF: Feeling of intense need to urinate; abrupt sensation of imminent urination.

AHA: 4Q, '06, 93; 4Q, '03, 74

788.64 Urinary hesitancy

AHA: 4Q, '06, 93, 109

788.65 Straining on urination

AHA: 4Q, '06, 93, 109

788.69 Other

788.7 Urethral discharge

Penile discharge
Urethrorrhea

788.8 Extravasation of urine

DEF: Leaking or infiltration of urine into tissues.

√5ᵗʰ **788.9 Other symptoms involving urinary system**

AHA: 1Q, '05, 12; 4Q, '88, 1

788.91 Functional urinary incontinence

Urinary incontinence due to cognitive impairment, or severe physical disability or immobility

> **EXCLUDES** *urinary incontinence due to physiologic condition (788.30-788.39)*

AHA: 4Q, '08, 144-145

788.99 Other symptoms involving urinary system

Extrarenal uremia
Vesical:
   pain
   tenesmus

√4ᵗʰ **789　Other symptoms involving abdomen and pelvis**

> EXCLUDES　symptoms referable to genital organs:
> female (625.0-625.9)
> male (607.0-608.9)
> psychogenic (302.70-302.79)

> The following fifth-digit subclassification is to be used for codes 789.0. 789.3, 789.4, 789.6:
> 0　unspecified site
> 1　right upper quadrant
> 2　left upper quadrant
> 3　right lower quadrant
> 4　left lower quadrant
> 5　periumbilic
> 6　epigastric
> 7　generalized
> 9　other specified site
> 　　Multiple sites

§ √5ᵗʰ **789.0　Abdominal pain**
[0-7, 9]　　Cramps, abdominal
　　　AHA: 1Q, '95, 3; **For code 789.06:** 1Q, '02, 5
　　　R10.9 Unspecified abdominal pain　I-10
　　　R10.31 Right lower quadrant pain　I-10
　　　R10.13 Epigastric pain　I-10
　　　R10.84 Generalized abdominal pain　I-10

789.1　Hepatomegaly
　　　Enlargement of liver

789.2　Splenomegaly
　　　Enlargement of spleen

§ √5ᵗʰ **789.3　Abdominal or pelvic swelling, mass, or lump**
[0-7, 9]　　Diffuse or generalized swelling or mass:
　　　　abdominal NOS
　　　　umbilical
　　　EXCLUDES　abdominal distention (gaseous) (787.3)
　　　　　ascites (789.51-789.59)

§ √5ᵗʰ **789.4　Abdominal rigidity**
[0-7, 9]

√5ᵗʰ **789.5　Ascites**
　　　Fluid in peritoneal cavity
　　　DEF: Serous fluid effusion and accumulation in abdominal cavity.
　　　AHA: 4Q, '07, 95; 2Q, '05, 8; 4Q, '89, 11

　789.51　Malignant ascites
　　　Code first malignancy, such as:
　　　　malignant neoplasm of ovary (183.0)
　　　　secondary malignant neoplasm of retroperitoneum and peritoneum (197.6)
　　　AHA: 4Q, '07, 96
　　　R18.0 Malignant ascites　I-10

　789.59　Other ascites
　　　AHA: 4Q, '08, 99
　　　R18.8 Other ascites　I-10

§ √5ᵗʰ **789.6　Abdominal tenderness**
[0-7, 9]　　Rebound tenderness

● **789.7　Colic**
　　　Colic NOS
　　　Infantile colic
　　　EXCLUDES　colic in adult and child over 12 months old (789.0)
　　　　renal colic (788.0)

789.9　Other symtoms involving abdomen and pelvis
　　　Umbilical:
　　　　bleeding
　　　　discharge

NONSPECIFIC ABNORMAL FINDINGS (790-796)

AHA: 2Q, '90, 16

√4ᵗʰ **790　Nonspecific findings on examination of blood**

> EXCLUDES　abnormality of:
> platelets (287.0-287.9)
> thrombocytes (287.0-287.9)
> white blood cells (288.00-288.9)

√5ᵗʰ **790.0　Abnormality of red blood cells**

> EXCLUDES　anemia:
> congenital (776.5)
> newborn, due to isoimmunization (773.0-773.2, 773.5)
> of premature infant (776.6)
> other specified types (280.0-285.9)
> hemoglobin disorders (282.5-282.7)
> polycythemia:
> familial (289.6)
> neonatorum (776.4)
> secondary (289.0)
> vera (238.4)

　　　AHA: 4Q, '00, 46

　790.01　Precipitous drop in hematocrit
　　　Drop in hematocrit
　　　►Drop in hemoglobin◄
　　　TIP: Typically reported as a reason for encounter at a dialysis center.

　790.09　Other abnormality of red blood cells
　　　Abnormal red cell morphology NOS
　　　Abnormal red cell volume NOS
　　　Anisocytosis
　　　Poikilocytosis

790.1　Elevated sedimentation rate

√5ᵗʰ **790.2　Abnormal glucose**

> EXCLUDES　diabetes mellitus (249.00-249.91, 250.00-250.93)
> dysmetabolic syndrome X (277.7)
> gestational diabetes (648.8)
> glycosuria (791.5)
> hypoglycemia (251.2)
> that complicating pregnancy, childbirth, or puerperium (648.8)

　　　AHA: 4Q, '03, 74; 3Q, '91, 5
　　　TIP: These codes are typically assigned on encounters before a patient is diagnosed with diabetes mellitus.

　790.21　Impaired fasting glucose
　　　Elevated fasting glucose

　790.22　Impaired glucose tolerance test (oral)
　　　Elevated glucose tolerance test

　790.29　Other abnormal glucose
　　　Abnormal glucose NOS
　　　Abnormal non-fasting glucose
　　　Hyperglycemia NOS
　　　Pre-diabetes NOS
　　　AHA: 2Q, '05, 21
　　　R73.09 Other abnormal glucose　I-10

790.3　Excessive blood level of alcohol
　　　Elevated blood-alcohol
　　　AHA: S-O, '86, 3

790.4　Nonspecific elevation of levels of transaminase or lactic acid dehydrogenase [LDH]
　　　R74.0 Nonspecific elevation levels transaminase & LDH　I-10

790.5　Other nonspecific abnormal serum enzyme levels
　　　Abnormal serum level of:
　　　　acid phosphatase
　　　　alkaline phosphatase
　　　　amylase
　　　　lipase
　　　EXCLUDES　deficiency of circulating enzymes (277.6)
　　　R74.8 Abnormal levels of other serum enzymes　I-10

---

§　Requires fifth digit. Valid digits are in [brackets] under each code. See category 789 for codes and definitions.

790.6 Other abnormal blood chemistry
Abnormal blood level of:
cobalt
copper
iron
lead
lithium
magnesium
mineral
zinc
EXCLUDES abnormality of electrolyte or acid-base balance (276.0-276.9)
hypoglycemia NOS (251.2)
lead poisoning (984.0-984.9)
specific finding indicating abnormality of:
amino-acid transport and metabolism (270.0-270.9)
carbohydrate transport and metabolism (271.0-271.9)
lipid metabolism (272.0-272.9)
uremia NOS (586)

AHA: 4Q, '88, 1

TIP: If only azotemia is documented (indexed to 790.6), clarify with physician; if due to uremia or renal failure, code to those conditions instead.

R78.89 Finding oth spec substances not norm found blood   I-10

790.7 Bacteremia
EXCLUDES bacteremia of newborn (771.83)
septicemia (038)

Use additional code to identify organism (041)

DEF: Laboratory finding of bacteria in the blood in the absence of two or more signs of sepsis; transient in nature, progresses to septicemia with severe infectious process.

AHA: 2Q, '03, 7; 4Q, '93, 29; 3Q, '88, 12

TIP: If clinical signs or symptoms indicating systemic disease exist, query physician for the presence of sepsis; code to category 038 if documented.

790.8 Viremia, unspecified
DEF: Presence of a virus in the blood stream.
AHA: 4Q, '88, 10

√5th **790.9 Other nonspecific findings on examination of blood**
AHA: 4Q, '93, 29

790.91 Abnormal arterial blood gases

790.92 Abnormal coagulation profile
Abnormal or prolonged:
bleeding time
coagulation time
partial thromboplastin time [PTT]
prothrombin time [PT]
EXCLUDES coagulation (hemorrhagic) disorders (286.0-286.9)

R79.1 Abnormal coagulaton profile   I-10

790.93 Elevated prostate specific antigen, [PSA] A♂

790.94 Euthyroid sick syndrome
DEF: Transient alteration of thyroid hormone metabolism due to nonthyroid illness or stress.
AHA: 4Q, '97, 45

790.95 Elevated C-reactive protein [CRP]
DEF: Inflammation in an arterial wall results in elevated C-reactive protein (CRP) in the blood; CRP is a recognized risk factor in cardiovascular disease.

790.99 Other
AHA: 2Q, '03, 14

√4th **791 Nonspecific findings on examination of urine**
EXCLUDES hematuria NOS (599.70-599.72)
specific findings indicating abnormality of:
amino-acid transport and metabolism (270.0-270.9)
carbohydrate transport and metabolism (271.0-271.9)

791.0 Proteinuria
Albuminuria
Bence-Jones proteinuria
EXCLUDES postural proteinuria (593.6)
that arising during pregnancy or the puerperium (642.0-642.9, 646.2)
DEF: Excess protein in urine.
AHA: 3Q, '91, 8

791.1 Chyluria
EXCLUDES filarial (125.0-125.9)
DEF: Excess chyle in urine.

791.2 Hemoglobinuria
DEF: Free hemoglobin in blood due to rapid hemolysis of red blood cells.

791.3 Myoglobinuria
DEF: Myoglobin (oxygen-transporting pigment) in urine.

791.4 Biliuria
DEF: Bile pigments in urine.

791.5 Glycosuria
EXCLUDES renal glycosuria (271.4)
DEF: Sugar in urine.

791.6 Acetonuria
Ketonuria
DEF: Excess acetone in urine.

791.7 Other cells and casts in urine

791.9 Other nonspecific findings on examination of urine
Crystalluria
Elevated urine levels of:
17-ketosteroids
catecholamines
indolacetic acid
vanillylmandelic acid [VMA]
Melanuria
AHA: 1Q, '05, 12

√4th **792 Nonspecific abnormal findings in other body substances**
EXCLUDES that in chromosomal analysis (795.2)

792.0 Cerebrospinal fluid

792.1 Stool contents
Abnormal stool color   Occult stool
Fat in stool   Pus in stool
Mucus in stool
EXCLUDES blood in stool [melena] (578.1)
newborn (772.4, 777.3)
AHA: 2Q, '92, 9

792.2 Semen   ♂
Abnormal spermatozoa
EXCLUDES azoospermia (606.0)
oligospermia (606.1)

792.3 Amniotic fluid   M♀
DEF: Nonspecific abnormal findings in amniotic fluid.
AHA: N-D, '86, 4

792.4 Saliva
EXCLUDES that in chromosomal analysis (795.2)

792.5 Cloudy (hemodialysis) (peritoneal) dialysis effluent
AHA: 4Q, '00, 46

792.9 Other nonspecific abnormal findings in body substances
Peritoneal fluid
Pleural fluid
Synovial fluid
Vaginal fluids

▲ ✓4th **793 Nonspecific (abnormal) findings on radiological and other examination of body structure**

> **INCLUDES**   nonspecific abnormal findings of:
> thermography
> ultrasound examination [echogram]
> x-ray examination
>
> **EXCLUDES**   *abnormal results of function studies and radioisotope scans (794.0-794.9)*

793.0 Skull and head

> **EXCLUDES**   *nonspecific abnormal echoencephalogram (794.01)*
>
> **AHA:** 3Q, '06, 22

793.1 Lung field

> Coin lesion ⎱
> Shadow   ⎰ (of) lung
>
> **DEF:** Coin lesion of lung: coin-shaped, solitary pulmonary nodule.

793.2 Other intrathoracic organ

> Abnormal:
> echocardiogram
> heart shadow
> ultrasound cardiogram
> Mediastinal shift

793.3 Biliary tract

> Nonvisualization of gallbladder

793.4 Gastrointestinal tract

793.5 Genitourinary organs

> Filling defect:
> bladder
> kidney
> ureter

793.6 Abdominal area, including retroperitoneum

793.7 Musculoskeletal system

✓5th **793.8 Breast**

> **AHA:** 4Q, '01, 51

793.80 Abnormal mammogram, unspecified

793.81 Mammographic microcalcification

> **EXCLUDES**   *mammographic calcification (793.89)*
> *mammographic calculus (793.89)*
>
> **DEF:** Calcium and cellular debris deposits in the breast that cannot be felt but can be detected on a mammogram; can be a sign of cancer, benign conditions, or changes in the breast tissue as a result of inflammation, injury, or obstructed duct.

● **793.82 Inconclusive mammogram**

> Dense breasts NOS
> Inconclusive mammogram NEC
> Inconclusive mammography due to dense breasts
> Inconclusive mammography NEC

▲ **793.89 Other (abnormal) findings on radiological examination of breast**

> Mammographic calcification
> Mammographic calculus

✓5th **793.9 Other**

> **EXCLUDES**   *abnormal finding by radioisotope localization of placenta (794.9)*
>
> **TIP:** Sequence a code for the sign or symptom that was the reason for the imaging or radiological test first.

793.91 Image test inconclusive due to excess body fat

> Use additional code to identify Body Mass Index (BMI), if known (V85.0-V85.54)
>
> **AHA:** 4Q, '06, 109

▲ **793.99 Other nonspecific (abnormal) findings on radiological and other examinations of body structure**

> Abnormal:
> placental finding by x-ray or ultrasound method
> radiological findings in skin and subcutaneous tissue
>
> **AHA:** 4Q, '06, 109

✓4th **794 Nonspecific abnormal results of function studies**

> **INCLUDES**   radioisotope:
> scans
> uptake studies
> scintiphotography

✓5th **794.0 Brain and central nervous system**

794.00 Abnormal function study, unspecified

794.01 Abnormal echoencephalogram

794.02 Abnormal electroencephalogram [EEG]

794.09 Other

> Abnormal brain scan

✓5th **794.1 Peripheral nervous system and special senses**

794.10 Abnormal response to nerve stimulation, unspecified

794.11 Abnormal retinal function studies

> Abnormal electroretinogram [ERG]

794.12 Abnormal electro-oculogram [EOG]

794.13 Abnormal visually evoked potential

794.14 Abnormal oculomotor studies

794.15 Abnormal auditory function studies

> **AHA:** 1Q, '04, 15-16
>
> **TIP:** If the reason for the encounter was for a hearing examination, sequence a code from subcategory V72.1 first. When nonspecific hearing loss is documented, assign 389.9 instead of 794.15.

794.16 Abnormal vestibular function studies

794.17 Abnormal electromyogram [EMG]

> **EXCLUDES**   *that of eye (794.14)*

794.19 Other

794.2 Pulmonary

> Abnormal lung scan
> Reduced:
> ventilatory capacity
> vital capacity

✓5th **794.3 Cardiovascular**

794.30 Abnormal function study, unspecified

794.31 Abnormal electrocardiogram [ECG] [EKG]

> **EXCLUDES**   *long QT syndrome (426.82)*
>
> **R94.31** Abnormal electrocardiogram [ECG] [EKG]   `I-10`

794.39 Other

> Abnormal:
> ballistocardiogram
> phonocardiogram
> vectorcardiogram
>
> **R94.39** Abnormal result oth cardiovasculr function study   `I-10`

794.4 Kidney

> Abnormal renal function test

794.5 Thyroid

> Abnormal thyroid:
> scan
> uptake

794.6 Other endocrine function study

794.7 Basal metabolism

> Abnormal basal metabolic rate [BMR]

✓4th Additional Digit Required   Unspecified Code   Other Specified Code   Manifestation Code   ▶◀ Revised Text   ● New Code   ▲ Revised Code Title
✓5th

2010 ICD-9-CM   **October 2009 • Volume 1 – 277**

794.8 Liver
Abnormal liver scan
R94.5 Abnormal results of liver function studies [I-10]

794.9 Other
Bladder
Pancreas
Placenta
Spleen

√4th **795 Other and nonspecific abnormal cytological, histological, immunological and DNA test findings**

EXCLUDES abnormal cytologic smear of anus and anal HPV (796.70-796.79)
nonspecific abnormalities of red blood cells (790.01-790.09)

√5th **795.0 Abnormal Papanicolaou smear of cervix and cervical HPV**
Abnormal thin preparation smear of cervix
Abnormal cervical cytology

EXCLUDES abnormal cytologic smear of vagina and vaginal HPV (795.10-795.19)
carcinoma ▶in situ◀ of cervix (233.1)
cervical intraepithelial neoplasia I (CIN I) (622.11)
cervical intraepithelial neoplasia II (CIN II) (622.12)
cervical intraepithelial neoplasia III (CIN III) (233.1)
dysplasia (histologically confirmed) of cervix (uteri) NOS (622.10)
mild cervical dysplasia (histologically confirmed) (622.11)
moderate cervical dysplasia (histologically confirmed) (622.12)
severe cervical dysplasia (histologically confirmed) (233.1)

AHA: 4Q, '08, 145-146; 4Q, '02, 69

795.00 Abnormal glandular Papanicolaou smear of cervix ♀
Atypical endocervical cells NOS
Atypical endometrial cells NOS
Atypical cervical glandular cells NOS

795.01 Papanicolaou smear of cervix with atypical squamous cells of undetermined significance [ASC-US] ♀
AHA: 2Q, '06, 4

795.02 Papanicolaou smear of cervix with atypical squamous cells cannot exclude high grade squamous intraepithelial lesion [ASC-H] ♀

795.03 Papanicolaou smear of cervix with low grade squamous intraepithelial lesion [LGSIL] ♀

795.04 Papanicolaou smear of cervix with high grade squamous intraepithelial lesion [HGSIL] ♀

795.05 Cervical high risk human papillomavirus [HPV] DNA test positive ♀

795.06 Papanicolaou smear of cervix with cytologic evidence of malignancy ♀
AHA: 4Q, '06, 110

795.07 Satisfactory cervical smear but lacking transformation zone ♀

795.08 Unsatisfactory cervical cytology smear ♀
Inadequate cervical cytology sample
AHA: 2Q, '06, 4

795.09 Other abnormal Papanicolaou smear of cervix and cervical HPV ♀
Cervical low risk human papillomavirus (HPV) DNA test positive
Use additional code for associated human papillomavirus (079.4)

EXCLUDES encounter for Papanicolaou cervical smear to confirm findings of recent normal smear following initial abnormal smear (V72.32)

√5th **795.1 Abnormal Papanicolaou smear of vagina and vaginal HPV**
Abnormal thin preparation smear of vagina NOS
Abnormal vaginal cytology NOS
Use additional code to identify acquired absence of uterus and cervix, if applicable (V88.01-V88.03)

EXCLUDES abnormal cytologic smear of cervix and cervical HPV (795.00-795.09)
carcinoma in situ of vagina (233.31)
carcinoma in situ of vulva (233.32)
dysplasia (histologically confirmed) of vagina NOS (623.0, 233.31)
dysplasia (histologically confirmed) of vulva NOS (624.01, 624.02, 233.32)
mild vaginal dysplasia (histologically confirmed) (623.0)
mild vulvar dysplasia (histologically confirmed) (624.01)
moderate vaginal dysplasia (histologically confirmed) (623.0)
moderate vulvar dysplasia (histologically confirmed) (624.02)
severe vaginal dysplasia (histologically confirmed) (233.31)
severe vulvar dysplasia (histologically confirmed) (233.32)
vaginal intraepithelial neoplasia I (VAIN I) (623.0)
vaginal intraepithelial neoplasia II (VAIN II) (623.0)
vaginal intraepithelial neoplasia III (VAIN III) (233.31)
vulvar intraepithelial neoplasia I (VIN I) (624.01)
vulvar intraepithelial neoplasia II (VIN II) (624.02)
vulvar intraepithelial neoplasia III (VIN III) (233.32)

AHA: 4Q, '08, 145-148

795.10 Abnormal glandular Papanicolaou smear of vagina ♀
Atypical vaginal glandular cells NOS

795.11 Papanicolaou smear of vagina with atypical squamous cells of undetermined significance [ASC-US] ♀

795.12 Papanicolaou smear of vagina with atypical squamous cells cannot exclude high grade squamous intraepithelial lesion [ASC-H] ♀

795.13 Papanicolaou smear of vagina with low grade squamous intraepithelial lesion [LGSIL] ♀

795.14 Papanicolaou smear of vagina with high grade squamous intraepithelial lesion [HGSIL] ♀

795.15 Vaginal high risk human papillomavirus [HPV] DNA test positive ♀
EXCLUDES condyloma acuminatum (078.11)
genital warts (078.11)

795.16 Papanicolaou smear of vagina with cytologic evidence of malignancy ♀

795.18 Unsatisfactory vaginal cytology smear ♀
Inadequate vaginal cytology sample

795.19 Other abnormal Papanicolaou smear of vagina and vaginal HPV ♀
Vaginal low risk human papillomavirus (HPV) DNA test positive
Use additional code for associated human papillomavirus (079.4)

795.2 Nonspecific abnormal findings on chromosomal analysis
Abnormal karyotype

√5th **795.3 Nonspecific positive culture findings**
Positive culture findings in:
nose
throat
sputum
wound
EXCLUDES that of: .
blood (790.7-790.8)
urine (791.9)

795.31 Nonspecific positive findings for anthrax
Positive findings by nasal swab
AHA: 4Q, '02, 70
TIP: If the patient has been exposed only to anthrax, assign instead V01.81. If a patient has not been exposed but fears anthrax and tests negative, assign instead V71.82.

795.39 Other nonspecific positive culture findings
EXCLUDES ▶colonization status (V02.0-V02.9)◀

795.4 Other nonspecific abnormal histological findings

795.5 Nonspecific reaction to tuberculin skin test without active tuberculosis
Abnormal result of Mantoux test
PPD positive
Tuberculin (skin test):
positive
reactor

795.6 False positive serological test for syphilis
False positive Wassermann reaction

√5th **795.7 Other nonspecific immunological findings**
EXCLUDES abnormal tumor markers (795.81-795.89)
elevated prostate specific antigen [PSA] (790.93)
elevated tumor associated antigens (795.81-795.89)
isoimmunization, in pregnancy (656.1-656.2) affecting fetus or newborn (773.0-773.2)
AHA: 2Q, '93, 6

795.71 Nonspecific serologic evidence of human immunodeficiency virus [HIV]
Inclusive human immunodeficiency [HIV] test (adult) (infant)
Note: This code is **only** to be used when a test finding is reported as nonspecific. Asymptomatic positive findings are coded to V08. If any HIV infection symptom or condition is present, see code 042. Negative findings are not coded.
EXCLUDES acquired immunodeficiency syndrome [AIDS] (042)
asymptomatic human immunodeficiency virus, [HIV] infection status (V08)
HIV infection, symptomatic (042)
human immunodeficiency virus [HIV] disease (042)
positive (status) NOS (V08)
AHA: 2Q, '04, 11; 1Q, '93, 21; 1Q, '93, 22; 2Q, '92, 11; J-A, '87, 24

795.79 Other and unspecified nonspecific immunologoical findings
Raised antibody titer
Raised level of immunoglobulins

√5th **795.8 Abnormal tumor markers**
Elevated tumor associated antigens [TAA]
Elevated tumor specific antigens [TSA]
EXCLUDES elevated prostate specific antigen [PSA] (790.93)

795.81 Elevated carcinoembryonic antigen [CEA]
AHA: 4Q, '06, 111

795.82 Elevated cancer antigen 125 [CA 125] ♀
AHA: 4Q, '06, 111

795.89 Other abnormal tumor markers
AHA: 4Q, '06, 111

√4th **796 Other nonspecific abnormal findings**

796.0 Nonspecific abnormal toxicological findings
Abnormal levels of heavy metals or drugs in blood, urine, or other tissue
EXCLUDES excessive blood level of alcohol (790.3)
AHA: 1Q, '97, 16

796.1 Abnormal reflex

796.2 Elevated blood pressure reading without diagnosis of hypertension
Note: This category is to be used to record an episode of elevated blood pressure in a patient in whom no formal diagnosis of hypertension has been made, or as an incidental finding.
AHA: 2Q, '03, 11; 3Q, '90, 4; J-A, '84, 12
TIP: Assign an additional E code for poisoning or adverse effect of a drug if the documentation indicates it's the underlying cause of the elevated blood pressure.
R03.0 Elevated blood-pressure reading without dx HTN I-10

796.3 Nonspecific low blood pressure reading

796.4 Other abnormal clinical findings
AHA: 1Q, '97, 16

796.5 Abnormal finding on antenatal screening ♀ M
AHA: 4Q, '97, 46

796.6 Abnormal findings on neonatal screening N
EXCLUDES nonspecific serologic evidence of human immunodeficiency virus [HIV] (795.71)
AHA: 4Q, '04, 99

√5th **796.7 Abnormal cytologic smear of anus and anal HPV**
EXCLUDES abnormal cytologic smear of cervix and cervical HPV (795.00-795.09)
abnormal cytologic smear of vagina and vaginal HPV (795.10-795.19)
anal intraepithelial neoplasia I (AIN I) (569.44)
anal intraepithelial neoplasia II (AIN II) (569.44)
anal intraepithelial neoplasia III (AIN III) (230.5, 230.6)
carcinoma in situ of anus (230.5, 230.6)
dysplasia (histologically confirmed) of anus NOS (569.44)
mild anal dysplasia (histologically confirmed) (569.44)
moderate anal dysplasia (histologically confirmed) (569.44)
severe anal dysplasia (histologically confirmed) ▶(230.5, 230.6)◀
AHA: 4Q, '08, 117-119

796.70 Abnormal glandular Papanicolaou smear of anus
Atypical anal glandular cells NOS

796.71 Papanicolaou smear of anus with atypical squamous cells of undetermined significance [ASC-US]

796.72 Papanicolaou smear of anus with atypical squamous cells cannot exclude high grade squamous intraepithelial lesion [ASC-H]

796.73 Papanicolaou smear of anus with low grade squamous intraepithelial lesion [LGSIL]

796.74 Papanicolaou smear of anus with high grade squamous intraepithelial lesion [HGSIL]

Symptoms, Signs, and Ill-Defined Conditions

796.75–799.9

796.75 Anal high risk human papillomavirus [HPV] DNA test positive

796.76 Papanicolaou smear of anus with cytologic evidence of malignancy

796.77 Satisfactory anal smear but lacking transformation zone

796.78 Unsatisfactory anal cytology smear
Inadequate anal cytology sample

796.79 Other abnormal Papanicolaou smear of anus and anal HPV
Anal low risk human papillomavirus (HPV) DNA test positive
Use additional code for associated human papillomavirus (079.4)

796.9 Other

ILL-DEFINED AND UNKNOWN CAUSES OF MORBIDITY AND MORTALITY (797-799)

797 Senility without mention of psychosis
Frailty
Old age
Senescence
Senile asthenia
Senile:
debility
exhaustion
EXCLUDES senile psychoses (290.0-290.9)

√4ᵗʰ **798 Sudden death, cause unknown**

798.0 Sudden infant death syndrome   P
Cot death
Crib death
Sudden death of nonspecific cause in infancy
DEF: Death of infant under age one due to nonspecific cause.

798.1 Instantaneous death

798.2 Death occurring in less than 24 hours from onset of symptoms, not otherwise explained
Death known not to be violent or instantaneous, for which no cause could be discovered
Died without sign of disease

798.9 Unattended death
Death in circumstances where the body of the deceased was found and no cause could be discovered
Found dead

√4ᵗʰ **799 Other ill-defined and unknown causes of morbidity and mortality**

√5ᵗʰ 799.0 Asphyxia and hypoxemia
EXCLUDES asphyxia and hypoxemia (due to):
carbon monoxide (986)
hypercapnia (786.09)
inhalation of food or foreign body (932-934.9)
newborn (768.0-768.9)
traumatic (994.7)

799.01 Asphyxia
DEF: Lack of oxygen in inspired air, causing a deficiency of oxygen in tissues (hypoxia) and elevated levels of arterial carbon dioxide (hypercapnia).
AHA: 4Q, '05, 90

799.02 Hypoxemia
DEF: Deficient oxygenation of the blood.
AHA: 2Q, '06, 24, 25; 4Q, '05, 90
R09.02 Hypoxemia   I-10

799.1 Respiratory arrest
Cardiorespiratory failure
EXCLUDES cardiac arrest (427.5)
failure of peripheral circulation (785.50)
respiratory distress:
NOS (786.09)
acute (518.82)
following trauma and surgery (518.5)
newborn (770.89)
syndrome (newborn) (769)
adult (following trauma and surgery) (518.5)
other (518.82)
respiratory failure (518.81, 518.83-518.84)
newborn (770.84)
respiratory insufficiency (786.09)
acute (518.82)

▲ √5ᵗʰ 799.2 Signs and symptoms involving emotional state
EXCLUDES ▶anxiety (293.84, 300.00-300.09)
depression (311)◀

● 799.21 Nervousness
Nervous

● 799.22 Irritability
Irritable

● 799.23 Impulsiveness
Impulsive
EXCLUDES impulsive neurosis (300.3)

● 799.24 Emotional lability

● 799.25 Demoralization and apathy
Apathetic

● 799.29 Other signs and symptoms involving emotional state

799.3 Debility, unspecified
EXCLUDES asthenia (780.79)
nervous debility (300.5)
neurasthenia (300.5)
senile asthenia (797)

799.4 Cachexia
Wasting disease
Code first underlying condition, if known
DEF: General ill health and poor nutrition.
AHA: 3Q, '06, 14, 15; 3Q, '90, 17
TIP: Assign an additional code for any associated malnutrition, if documented.
R64 Cachexia   I-10

√5ᵗʰ 799.8 Other ill-defined conditions

799.81 Decreased libido   A
Decreased sexual desire
EXCLUDES psychosexual dysfunction with inhibited sexual desire (302.71)
AHA: 4Q, '03, 75

● 799.82 Apparent life threatening event in infant
ALTE
Apparent life threatening event in newborn and infant
Use additional code(s) for associated signs and symptoms
EXCLUDES signs and symptoms associated with a confirmed diagnosis–code to confirmed diagnosis

799.89 Other ill-defined conditions

799.9 Other unknown and unspecified cause
Undiagnosed disease, not specified as to site or system involved
Unknown cause of morbidity or mortality
AHA: 1Q, '98, .4; 1Q, '90, 20

N Newborn Age: 0   P Pediatric Age: 0-17   M Maternity Age: 12-55   A Adult Age: 15-124

Injury and Poisoning

17. INJURY AND POISONING (800-999)

Use E code(s) to identify the cause and intent of the injury or poisoning (E800-E999)

Note:

1. The principle of multiple coding of injuries should be followed wherever possible. Combination categories for multiple injuries are provided for use when there is insufficient detail as to the nature of the individual conditions, or for primary tabulation purposes when it is more convenient to record a single code; otherwise, the component injuries should be coded separately.

   Where multiple sites of injury are specified in the titles, the word "with" indicates involvement of both sites, and the word "and" indicates involvement of either or both sites. The word "finger" includes thumb.

2. Categories for "late effect" of injuries are to be found at 905-909.

FRACTURES (800-829)

EXCLUDES   malunion (733.81)
nonunion (733.82)
pathological or spontaneous fracture (733.10-733.19)
stress fractures (733.93-733.95)

The terms "condyle," "coronoid process," "ramus," and "symphysis" indicate the portion of the bone fractured, not the name of the bone involved.

The descriptions "closed" and "open" used in the fourth-digit subdivisions include the following terms:

closed (with or without delayed healing):
comminuted	impacted
depressed	linear
elevated	simple
fissured	slipped epiphysis
fracture NOS	spiral
greenstick	

open (with or without delayed healing):
compound	puncture
infected	with foreign body
missile	

Note: A fracture not indicated as closed or open should be classified as closed.

AHA: 4Q, '08, 158; 1Q, '07, 3-4; 4Q, '90, 26; 3Q, '90, 5; 3Q, '90, 13; 2Q, '90, 7; 2Q, '89, 15, S-O, '85, 3

TIP: Assign the acute fracture codes only while the patient is receiving active treatment for the fracture, such as during surgical care, an ED encounter, or evaluation and treatment by a new physician. Otherwise, refer to aftercare category V54.

FRACTURE OF SKULL (800-804)

INCLUDES ▶traumatic brain injury due to fracture of skull◀

The following fifth-digit subclassification is for use with the appropriate codes in category 800, 801, 803, and 804:
0 unspecified state of consciousness
1 with no loss of consciousness
2 with brief [less than one hour] loss of consciousness
3 with moderate [1-24 hours] loss of consciousness
4 with prolonged [more than 24 hours] loss of consciousness and return to pre-existing conscious level
5 with prolonged [more than 24 hours] loss of consciousness, without return to pre-existing conscious level
> Use fifth-digit 5 to designate when a patient is unconscious and dies before regaining consciousness, regardless of the duration of the loss of consciousness
6 with loss of consciousness of unspecified duration
9 with concussion, unspecified

✓4ᵗʰ 800 Fracture of vault of skull
     INCLUDES   frontal bone
                 parietal bone
     DEF: Fracture of bone that forms skull dome and protects brain.
     AHA: 4Q,'96, 36

§ ✓5ᵗʰ   **800.0 Closed without mention of intracranial injury**
         [0-6, 9]

§ ✓5ᵗʰ   **800.1 Closed with cerebral laceration and contusion**
         [0-6, 9]

§ ✓5ᵗʰ   **800.2 Closed with subarachnoid, subdural, and**
         [0-6, 9] **extradural hemorrhage**

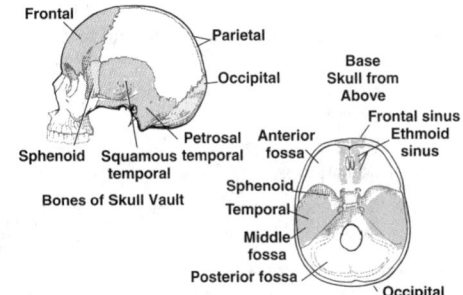

Skull

§ ✓5ᵗʰ   **800.3 Closed with other and unspecified intracranial hemorrhage**
         [0-6, 9]

§ ✓5ᵗʰ   **800.4 Closed with intracranial injury of other and unspecified nature**
         [0-6, 9]

§ ✓5ᵗʰ   **800.5 Open without mention of intracranial injury**
         [0-6, 9]

§ ✓5ᵗʰ   **800.6 Open with cerebral laceration and contusion**
         [0-6, 9]

§ ✓5ᵗʰ   **800.7 Open with subarachnoid, subdural, and extradural hemorrhage**
         [0-6, 9]

§ ✓5ᵗʰ   **800.8 Open with other and unspecified intracranial hemorrhage**
         [0-6, 9]

§ ✓5ᵗʰ   **800.9 Open with intracranial injury of other and unspecified nature**
         [0-6, 9]

✓4ᵗʰ 801 Fracture of base of skull
     INCLUDES   fossa:
                 anterior
                 middle
                 posterior
             occiput bone
             orbital roof
             sinus:
                 ethmoid
                 frontal
             sphenoid bone
             temporal bone
     DEF: Fracture of bone that forms skull floor.
     AHA: 4Q, '96, 36

§ ✓5ᵗʰ   **801.0 Closed without mention of intracranial injury**
         [0-6, 9]

§ ✓5ᵗʰ   **801.1 Closed with cerebral laceration and contusion**
         [0-6, 9]   **AHA: For code 801.15:** 4Q, '96, 36

§ ✓5ᵗʰ   **801.2 Closed with subarachnoid, subdural, and extradural hemorrhage**
         [0-6, 9]

§ ✓5ᵗʰ   **801.3 Closed with other and unspecified intracranial hemorrhage**
         [0-6, 9]

Fractures

✓4ᵗʰ Additional Digit Required	Unspecified Code	Other Specified Code	Manifestation Code	▶◀ Revised Text	● New Code	▲ Revised Code Title

800-801.3

§ ✓5th **801.4** **Closed with intracranial** injury of other and
[0-6, 9] **unspecified nature**

§ ✓5th **801.5** Open without mention of intracranial injury
[0-6, 9]

§ ✓5th **801.6** Open with cerebral laceration and contusion
[0-6, 9]

§ ✓5th **801.7** Open with subarachnoid, subdural, and
[0-6, 9] extradural hemorrhage

§ ✓5th **801.8** **Open with other and** unspecified intracranial
[0-6, 9] **hemorrhage**

§ ✓5th **801.9** **Open with intracranial** injury of other and
[0-6, 9] **unspecified nature**

✓4th **802** **Fracture of face bones**
AHA: 4Q, '96, 36

802.0 Nasal bones, closed
S02.2xxA Fracture nasal bones initial encounter closed fx   I-10

802.1 Nasal bones, open

✓5th **802.2** Mandible, closed
Inferior maxilla
Lower jaw (bone)

802.20 **Unspecified site**

802.21 Condylar process

802.22 Subcondylar

802.23 Coronoid process

802.24 **Ramus, unspecified**

802.25 Angle of jaw

802.26 Symphysis of body

802.27 Alveolar border of body

802.28 **Body, other and** unspecified

802.29 Multiple sites

✓5th **802.3** Mandible, open

802.30 **Unspecified site**

802.31 Condylar process

802.32 Subcondylar

802.33 Coronoid process

802.34 **Ramus, unspecified**

802.35 Angle of jaw

802.36 Symphysis of body

802.37 Alveolar border of body

802.38 **Body, other and** unspecified

802.39 Multiple sites

802.4 Malar and maxillary bones, closed
Superior maxilla
Upper jaw (bone)
Zygoma
Zygomatic arch
S02.40xA Fx malar max & zygoma uns initial enc closed fx   I-10

802.5 Malar and maxillary bones, open

Facial Fracture

802.6 Orbital floor (blow-out), closed
S02.3xxA Fracture orbital floor initial encounter clos fx   I-10

802.7 Orbital floor (blow-out), open

802.8 **Other facial bones, closed**
Alveolus
Orbit:
    NOS
    part other than roof or floor
Palate
EXCLUDES   orbital:
     floor (802.6)
     roof (801.0-801.9)
S02.89xA Fx oth skull & face bones initial enc closed fx   I-10

802.9 **Other facial bones, open**

✓4th **803** **Other and unqualified skull fractures**
INCLUDES   skull NOS
         skull multiple NOS
AHA: 4Q, '96, 36

§ ✓5th **803.0** Closed without mention of intracranial injury
[0-6, 9]

§ ✓5th **803.1** Closed with cerebral laceration and contusion
[0-6, 9]

§ ✓5th **803.2** Closed with subarachnoid, subdural, and
[0-6, 9] extradural hemorrhage

§ ✓5th **803.3** **Closed with other and** unspecified intracranial
[0-6, 9] **hemorrhage**

§ ✓5th **803.4** **Closed with intracranial** injury of other and
[0-6, 9] **unspecified nature**

§ ✓5th **803.5** Open without mention of intracranial injury
[0-6, 9]

§ ✓5th **803.6** Open with cerebral laceration and contusion
[0-6, 9]

§ ✓5th **803.7** Open with subarachnoid, subdural, and
[0-6, 9] extradural hemorrhage

§ ✓5th **803.8** **Open with other and** unspecified intracranial
[0-6, 9] **hemorrhage**

§ ✓5th **803.9** **Open with intracranial** injury of other and
[0-6, 9] **unspecified nature**

✓4th **804** **Multiple fractures involving skull or face with other bones**
AHA: 4Q, '96, 36

§ ✓5th **804.0** Closed without mention of intracranial injury
[0-6, 9]

§ ✓5th **804.1** Closed with cerebral laceration and contusion
[0-6, 9] AHA: For code 804.10: 1Q, '06, 6

§ ✓5th **804.2** Closed with subarachnoid, subdural, and
[0-6, 9] extradural hemorrhage

§ ✓5th **804.3** **Closed with other and** unspecified intracranial
[0-6, 9] **hemorrhage**

§ ✓5th **804.4** **Closed with intracranial** injury of other and
[0-6, 9] **unspecified nature**

§ ✓5th **804.5** Open without mention of intracranial injury
[0-6, 9]

§ ✓5th **804.6** Open with cerebral laceration and contusion
[0-6, 9]

§ ✓5th **804.7** Open with subarachnoid, subdural, and
[0-6, 9] extradural hemorrage

§ ✓5th **804.8** **Open with other and** unspecified intracranial
[0-6, 9] **hemorrhage**

§ ✓5th **804.9** **Open with intracranial** injury of other and
[0-6, 9] **unspecified nature**

§   Requires fifth digit. Valid digits are in [brackets] under each code. See beginning of section 800-804 for codes and definitions.

Injury and Poisoning

FRACTURE OF NECK AND TRUNK (805-809)

✓4th **805 Fracture of vertebral column without mention of spinal cord injury**

    INCLUDES   neural arch
                spine
                spinous process
                transverse process
                vertebra

The following fifth-digit subclassification is for use with codes 805.0-805.1:

  0 cervical vertebra, unspecified level
  1 first cervical vertebra
  2 second cervical vertebra
  3 third cervical vertebra
  4 fourth cervical vertebra
  5 fifth cervical vertebra
  6 sixth cervical vertebra
  7 seventh cervical vertebra
  8 multiple cervical vertebrae

§ ✓5th **805.0 Cervical, closed**
  [0-8]   Atlas
           Axis

      S12.101A Uns nondisplcd fx 2nd cerv vert initial enc closed fx   **I-10**

§ ✓5th **805.1 Cervical, open**
  [0-8]

805.2 Dorsal [thoracic], closed
    S22.008A Oth fx uns thoracic vertebra initial enc clos fx   **I-10**

805.3 Dorsal [thoracic], open

805.4 Lumbar, closed
    AHA: 1Q, '07, 7; 4Q, '99, 12
    S32.008A Oth fx uns lumbar vertebra initial enc closed fx   **I-10**

805.5 Lumbar, open

805.6 Sacrum and coccyx, closed
    S32.19xA Other fx of sacrum initial encounter closed fx   **I-10**

805.7 Sacrum and coccyx, open

805.8 Unspecified, closed

805.9 Unspecified, open

Vertebral Column

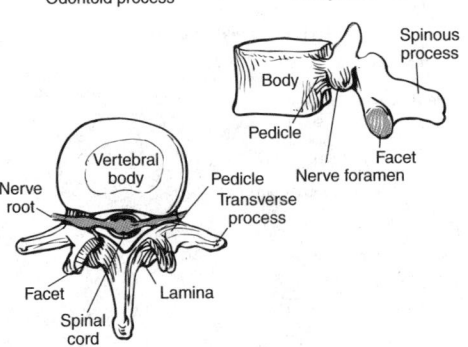

✓4th **806 Fracture of vertebral column with spinal cord injury**

    INCLUDES   any condition classifiable to 805 with:
           complete or incomplete transverse lesion (of cord)
           hematomyelia
           injury to:
               cauda equina
               nerve
           paralysis
           paraplegia
           quadriplegia
           spinal concussion

✓5th **806.0 Cervical, closed**

  806.00 C_1-C_4 level with unspecified spinal cord injury
      Cervical region NOS with spinal cord injury NOS

  806.01 C_1-C_4 level with complete lesion of cord

  806.02 C_1-C_4 level with anterior cord syndrome

  806.03 C_1-C_4 level with central cord syndrome

  806.04 C_1-C_4 level with other specified spinal cord injury
      C_1-C_4 level with:
        incomplete spinal cord lesion NOS
        posterior cord syndrome

  806.05 C_5-C_7 level with unspecified spinal cord injury

  806.06 C_5-C_7 level with complete lesion of cord

  806.07 C_5-C_7 level with anterior cord syndrome

  806.08 C_5-C_7 level with central cord syndrome

  806.09 C_5-C_7 level with other specified spinal cord injury
      C_5-C_7 level with:
        incomplete spinal cord lesion NOS
        posterior cord syndrome

✓5th **806.1 Cervical, open**

  806.10 C_1-C_4 level with unspecified spinal cord injury

  806.11 C_1-C_4 level with complete lesion of cord

  806.12 C_1-C_4 level with anterior cord syndrome

  806.13 C_1-C_4 level with central cord syndrome

  806.14 C_1-C_4 level with other specified spinal cord injury
      C_1-C_4 level with:
        incomplete spinal cord lesion NOS
        posterior cord syndrome

  806.15 C_5-C_7 level with unspecified spinal cord injury

  806.16 C_5-C_7 level with complete lesion of cord

  806.17 C_5-C_7 level with anterior cord syndrome

  806.18 C_5-C_7 level with central cord syndrome

  806.19 C_5-C_7 level with other specified spinal cord injury
      C_5-C_7 level with:
        incomplete spinal cord lesion NOS
        posterior cord syndrome

✓5th **806.2 Dorsal [thoracic], closed**

  806.20 T_1-T_6 level with unspecified spinal cord injury
      Thoracic region NOS with spinal cord injury NOS

  806.21 T_1-T_6 level with complete lesion of cord

  806.22 T_1-T_6 level with anterior cord syndrome

  806.23 T_1-T_6 level with central cord syndrome

  806.24 T_1-T_6 level with other specified spinal cord injury
      T_1-T_6 level with:
        incomplete spinal cord lesion NOS
        posterior cord syndrome

  806.25 T_7-T_{12} level with unspecified spinal cord injury

  806.26 T_7-T_{12} level with complete lesion of cord

  806.27 T_7-T_{12} level with anterior cord syndrome

---

§   Requires fifth digit. Valid digits are in [brackets] under each code. See category 805 for codes and definitions.

✓4th Additional Digit Required   **Unspecified Code**   **Other Specified Code**   **Manifestation Code**   ▶◀ Revised Text   ● New Code   ▲ Revised Code Title

✓5th

2010 ICD-9-CM   **Volume 1 – 283**

Injury and Poisoning

806.28–808.9

806.28 T₇-T₁₂ level with central cord syndrome

806.29 T₇-T₁₂ level with other specified spinal cord injury

T₇-T₁₂ level with:
incomplete spinal cord lesion NOS
posterior cord syndrome

✓5ᵗʰ **806.3** Dorsal [thoracic], open

806.30 T₁-T₆ level with unspecified spinal cord injury

806.31 T₁-T₆ level with complete lesion of cord

806.32 T₁-T₆ level with anterior cord syndrome

806.33 T₁-T₆ level with central cord syndrome

806.34 T₁-T₆ level with other specified spinal cord injury

T₁-T₆ level with:
incomplete spinal cord lesion NOS
posterior cord syndrome

806.35 T₇-T₁₂ level with unspecified spinal cord injury

806.36 T₇-T₁₂ level with complete lesion of cord

806.37 T₇-T₁₂ level with anterior cord syndrome

806.38 T₇-T₁₂ level with central cord syndrome

806.39 T₇-T₁₂ level with other specified spinal cord injury

T₇-T₁₂ level with:
incomplete spinal cord lesion NOS
posterior cord syndrome

806.4 Lumbar, closed
AHA: 4Q, '99, 11, 13

806.5 Lumbar, open

✓5ᵗʰ **806.6** Sacrum and coccyx, closed

806.60 With unspecified spinal cord injury

806.61 With complete cauda equina lesion

806.62 With other cauda equina injury

806.69 With other spinal cord injury

✓5ᵗʰ **806.7** Sacrum and coccyx, open

806.70 With unspecified spinal cord injury

806.71 With complete cauda equina lesion

806.72 With other cauda equina injury

806.79 With other spinal cord injury

806.8 Unspecified, closed

806.9 Unspecified, open

✓4ᵗʰ **807** Fracture of rib(s), sternum, larynx, and trachea

The following fifth-digit subclassification is for use with codes 807.0-807.1:

0 rib(s) unspecifed
1 one rib
2 two ribs
3 three ribs
4 four ribs
5 five ribs
6 six ribs
7 seven ribs
8 eight or more ribs
9 multiple ribs, unspecified

§ ✓5ᵗʰ **807.0** Rib(s), closed
[0-9]

S22.31xA Fracture rib right initial encounter closed fx I-10
S22.43xG Mx fx ribs bilat subseqnt enc fx delayed healing I-10

§ ✓5ᵗʰ **807.1** Rib(s), open
[0-9]

807.2 Sternum, closed
DEF: Break in flat bone (breast bone) in anterior thorax.

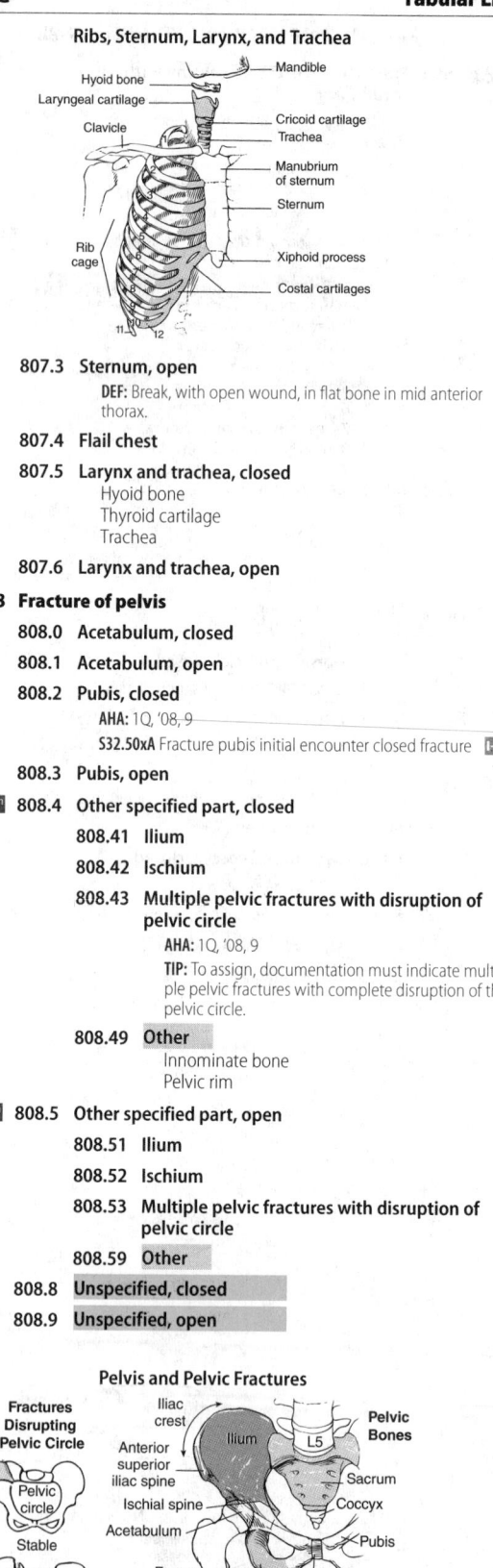

Ribs, Sternum, Larynx, and Trachea

807.3 Sternum, open
DEF: Break, with open wound, in flat bone in mid anterior thorax.

807.4 Flail chest

807.5 Larynx and trachea, closed
Hyoid bone
Thyroid cartilage
Trachea

807.6 Larynx and trachea, open

✓4ᵗʰ **808** Fracture of pelvis

808.0 Acetabulum, closed

808.1 Acetabulum, open

808.2 Pubis, closed
AHA: 1Q, '08, 9
S32.50xA Fracture pubis initial encounter closed fracture I-10

808.3 Pubis, open

✓5ᵗʰ **808.4** Other specified part, closed

808.41 Ilium

808.42 Ischium

808.43 Multiple pelvic fractures with disruption of pelvic circle
AHA: 1Q, '08, 9
TIP: To assign, documentation must indicate multiple pelvic fractures with complete disruption of the pelvic circle.

808.49 Other
Innominate bone
Pelvic rim

✓5ᵗʰ **808.5** Other specified part, open

808.51 Ilium

808.52 Ischium

808.53 Multiple pelvic fractures with disruption of pelvic circle

808.59 Other

808.8 Unspecified, closed

808.9 Unspecified, open

Pelvis and Pelvic Fractures

§ Requires fifth digit. Valid digits are in [brackets] under each code. See category 807 for codes and definitions.

Injury and Poisoning

✓4ᵗʰ **809 Ill-defined fractures of bones of trunk**

     INCLUDES   bones of trunk with other bones except those of skull and face
         multiple bones of trunk

     EXCLUDES   *multiple fractures of:*
         pelvic bones alone (808.0-808.9)
         ribs alone (807.0-807.1, 807.4)
         ribs or sternum with limb bones (819.0-819.1,
           828.0-828.1)
         skull or face with other bones (804.0-804.9)

     809.0   Fracture of bones of trunk, closed

     809.1   Fracture of bones of trunk, open

FRACTURE OF UPPER LIMB (810-819)

✓4ᵗʰ **810 Fracture of clavicle**

     INCLUDES   collar bone
         interligamentous part of clavicle

     The following fifth-digit subclassification is for use with category 810:
         0 unspecified part
           Clavicle NOS
         1 sternal end of clavicle
         2 shaft of clavicle
         3 acromial end of clavicle

§ ✓5ᵗʰ   **810.0**   **Closed**
         [0-3]

§ ✓5ᵗʰ   **810.1**   **Open**
         [0-3]

✓4ᵗʰ **811 Fracture of scapula**

     INCLUDES   shoulder blade

     The following fifth-digit subclassification is for use with category 811:
         0 unspecified part
         1 acromial process
           Acromion (process)
         2 coracoid process
         3 glenoid cavity and neck of scapula
         9 other

§ ✓5ᵗʰ   **811.0**   **Closed**
         [0-3, 9]

§ ✓5ᵗʰ   **811.1**   **Open**
         [0-3, 9]

✓4ᵗʰ **812 Fracture of humerus**

     ✓5ᵗʰ   **812.0**   **Upper end, closed**

         812.00   **Upper end, unspecified part**
             Proximal end   Shoulder

         812.01   **Surgical neck**
             Neck of humerus NOS

             S42.214A Uns nondsplcd fx surg neck rt   **I-10**
             humerus inital enc closed fx

         812.02   **Anatomical neck**

         812.03   **Greater tuberosity**

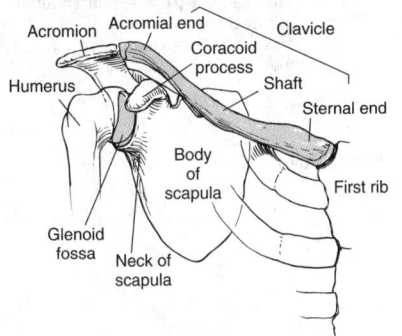

Right Clavicle and Scapula, Anterior View

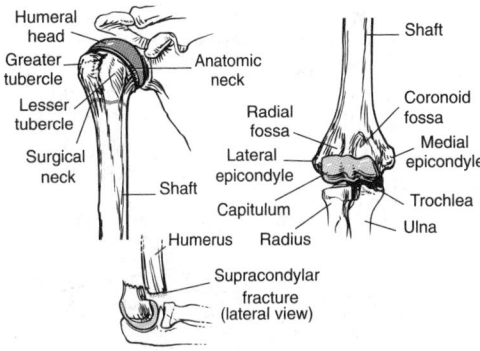

Right Humerus, Anterior View

         812.09   **Other**
             Head
             Lesser tuberosity
             Upper epiphysis

             S42.294A Oth nondsplcd fx up end rt humerus   **I-10**
             initial enc clos fx

✓5ᵗʰ   **812.1**   **Upper end, open**

         812.10   **Upper end, unspecified part**

         812.11   **Surgical neck**

         812.12   **Anatomical neck**

         812.13   **Greater tuberosity**

         812.19   **Other**

✓5ᵗʰ   **812.2**   **Shaft or unspecified part, closed**

         812.20   **Unspecified part of humerus**
             Humerus NOS
             Upper arm NOS

         812.21   **Shaft of humerus**
             AHA: 4Q, '05, 129; 3Q, '99, 14

✓5ᵗʰ   **812.3**   **Shaft or unspecified part, open**

         812.30   **Unspecified part of humerus**

         812.31   **Shaft of humerus**

✓5ᵗʰ   **812.4**   **Lower end, closed**
             Distal end of humerus
             Elbow

         812.40   **Lower end, unspecified part**

         812.41   **Supracondylar fracture of humerus**

         812.42   **Lateral condyle**
             External condyle

         812.43   **Medial condyle**
             Internal epicondyle

         812.44   **Lower end, unspecified part**
             Articular process NOS
             Lower epiphysis NOS

         812.49   **Other**
             Multiple fractures of lower end
             Trochlea

✓5ᵗʰ   **812.5**   **Lower end, open**

         812.50   **Lower end, unspecified part**

         812.51   **Supracondylar fracture of humerus**

         812.52   **Lateral condyle**

         812.53   **Medial condyle**

         812.54   **Condyle(s), unspecified**

         812.59   **Other**

✓4ᵗʰ **813 Fracture of radius and ulna**

     ✓5ᵗʰ   **813.0**   **Upper end, closed**
             Proximal end

         813.00   **Upper end of forearm, unspecified**

         813.01   **Olecranon process of ulna**

---

§   Requires fifth digit. Valid digits are in [brackets] under each code. See appropriate category for codes and definitions.

✓4ᵗʰ✓5ᵗʰ   Additional Digit Required   **Unspecified Code**   **Other Specified Code**   **Manifestation Code**   ▶◀ Revised Text   ● New Code   ▲ Revised Code Title

2010 ICD-9-CM   **Volume 1 – 285**

Injury and Poisoning

813.02–814.1

Right Radius and Ulna, Anterior View

813.02 Coronoid process of ulna

813.03 Monteggia's fracture
DEF: Fracture near the head of the ulnar shaft, causing dislocation of the radial head.

813.04 **Other and unspecified fractures of proximal end of ulna (alone)**
Multiple fractures of ulna, upper end

813.05 Head of radius

813.06 Neck of radius

813.07 **Other and unspecified fractures of proximal end of radius (alone)**
Multiple fractures of radius, upper end

813.08 Radius with ulna, upper end [any part]

√5th 813.1 Upper end, open

813.10 **Upper end of forearm, unspecified**

813.11 Olecranon process of ulna

813.12 Coronoid process of ulna

813.13 Monteggia's fracture

813.14 **Other and unspecified fractures of proximal end of ulna (alone)**

813.15 Head of radius

813.16 Neck of radius

813.17 **Other and unspecified fractures of proximal end of radius (alone)**

813.18 Radius with ulna, upper end [any part]

√5th 813.2 Shaft, closed

813.20 **Shaft, unspecified**

813.21 Radius (alone)

813.22 Ulna (alone)

813.23 Radius with ulna

√5th 813.3 Shaft, open

813.30 **Shaft, unspecified**

813.31 Radius (alone)

813.32 Ulna (alone)

813.33 Radius with ulna

√5th 813.4 Lower end, closed
Distal end

813.40 **Lower end of forearm, unspecified**

813.41 Colles' fracture
Smith's fracture
DEF: Break of lower end of radius; associated with backward movement of the radius lower section.

813.42 **Other fractures of distal end of radius (alone)**
Dupuytren's fracture, radius
Radius, lower end
DEF: Dupuytren's fracture: fracture and dislocation of the forearm; the fracture is of the radius above the wrist, and the dislocation is of the ulna at the lower end.
S52.501A Uns fx lower end rt radius initial enc closed fx   I-10

813.43 Distal end of ulna (alone)
Ulna:
head
lower end
lower epiphysis
styloid process

813.44 Radius with ulna, lower end
AHA: 1Q, '07, 7

▲ 813.45 Torus fracture of radius (alone)
EXCLUDES ▶torus fracture of radius and ulna (813.47)◀
AHA: 4Q, '02, 70

● 813.46 Torus fracture of ulna (alone)
EXCLUDES torus fracture of radius and ulna (813.47)

● 813.47 Torus fracture of radius and ulna

√5th 813.5 Lower end, open

813.50 **Lower end of forearm, unspecified**

813.51 Colles' fracture

813.52 **Other fractures of distal end of radius (alone)**

813.53 Distal end of ulna (alone)

813.54 Radius with ulna, lower end

√5th 813.8 Unspecified part, closed

813.80 **Forearm, unspecified**

813.81 **Radius (alone)**
AHA: 2Q, '98, 19

813.82 **Ulna (alone)**

813.83 **Radius with ulna**

√5th 813.9 Unspecified part, open

813.90 **Forearm, unspecified**

813.91 **Radius (alone)**

813.92 **Ulna (alone)**

813.93 **Radius with ulna**

√4th 814 **Fracture of carpal bone(s)**
The following fifth-digit subclassification is for use with category 814:
0 **carpal bone, unspecified**
Wrist NOS
1 navicular [scaphoid] of wrist
2 lunate [semilunar] bone of wrist
3 triquetral [cuneiform] bone of wrist
4 pisiform
5 trapezium bone [larger multangular]
6 trapezoid bone [smaller multangular]
7 capitate bone [os magnum]
8 hamate [unciform] bone
9 other

§ √5th 814.0 Closed
[0-9]

§ √5th 814.1 Open
[0-9]

§ Requires fifth digit. Valid digits are in [brackets] under each code. See category 814 for codes and definitions.

N Newborn Age: 0   P Pediatric Age: 0-17   M Maternity Age: 12-55   A Adult Age: 15-124

Hand Fractures

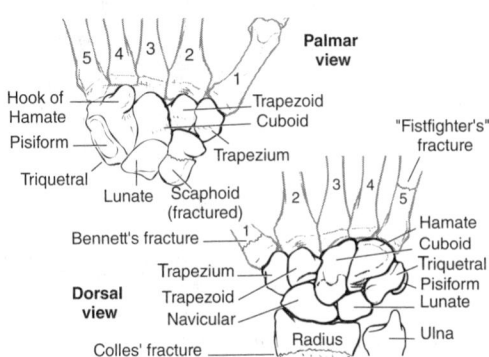

FRACTURE OF LOWER LIMB (820-829)

✓4ᵗʰ **820 Fracture of neck of femur**

  ✓5ᵗʰ **820.0 Transcervical fracture, closed**

    820.00 Intracapsular section, unspecified

    820.01 Epiphysis (separation) (upper)
      Transepiphyseal

    820.02 Midcervical section
      Transcervical NOS
      AHA: 3Q, '03, 12

    820.03 Base of neck
      Cervicotrochanteric section

    820.09 Other
      Head of femur
      Subcapital
      S72.064A Nondsplcd art fx head rt femur **I-10**
      initial enc closed fx

  ✓5ᵗʰ **820.1 Transcervical fracture, open**

    820.10 Intracapsular section, unspecified

    820.11 Epiphysis (separation) (upper)

    820.12 Midcervical section

    820.13 Base of neck

    820.19 Other

  ✓5ᵗʰ **820.2 Pertrochanteric fracture, closed**

    820.20 Trochanteric section, unspecified
      Trochanter:
        NOS
        greater
        lesser

    820.21 Intertrochanteric section

    820.22 Subtrochanteric section
      S72.25xA Nondsplcd subtrochant fx lt femur **I-10**
      inital enc closed fx

  ✓5ᵗʰ **820.3 Pertrochanteric fracture, open**

    820.30 Trochanteric section, unspecified

    820.31 Intertrochanteric section

    820.32 Subtrochanteric section

    820.8 Unspecified part of neck of femur, closed
      Hip NOS
      Neck of femur NOS
      S72.002A Fx uns part neck left femur initial enc clos fx **I-10**

    820.9 Unspecified part of neck of femur, open

✓4ᵗʰ **821 Fracture of other and unspecified parts of femur**

  ✓5ᵗʰ **821.0 Shaft or unspecified part, closed**

    821.00 Unspecified part of femur
      Thigh
      Upper leg
      EXCLUDES *hip NOS (820.8)*

    821.01 Shaft
      AHA: 1Q, '07, 4; 1Q, '99, 5
      S72.331A Displaced obl fx shaft rt femur initial **I-10**
      enc clos fx

  ✓5ᵗʰ **821.1 Shaft or unspecified part, open**

    821.10 Unspecified part of femur

    821.11 Shaft

  ✓5ᵗʰ **821.2 Lower end, closed**
      Distal end

    821.20 Lower end, unspecified part

    821.21 Condyle, femoral

✓4ᵗʰ **815 Fracture of metacarpal bone(s)**

  INCLUDES   hand [except finger]
        metacarpus

  The following fifth-digit subclassification is for use with category 815:
    0 metacarpal bone(s), site unspecified
    1 base of thumb [first] metacarpal
      Bennett's fracture
    2 base of other metacarpal bone(s)
    3 shaft of metacarpal bone(s)
    4 neck of metacarpal bone(s)
    9 multiple sites of metacarpus

§ ✓5ᵗʰ **815.0 Closed**
  [0-4, 9]

§ ✓5ᵗʰ **815.1 Open**
  [0-4, 9]

✓4ᵗʰ **816 Fracture of one or more phalanges of hand**

  INCLUDES   finger(s)   thumb

  The following fifth-digit subclassification is for use with category 816:
    0 phalanx or phalanges, unspecified
    1 middle or proximal phalanx or phalanges
    2 distal phalanx or phalanges
    3 multiple sites

  TIP: If phalangeal fracture(s) are due to crushing injury, sequence that code (927.3) first.

§ ✓5ᵗʰ **816.0 Closed**
  [0-3]

§ ✓5ᵗʰ **816.1 Open**
  [0-3]   **AHA: For code 816.12:** 4Q, '03, 77

✓4ᵗʰ **817 Multiple fractures of hand bones**

  INCLUDES   metacarpal bone(s) with phalanx or phalanges of same hand

  817.0 Closed

  817.1 Open

✓4ᵗʰ **818 Ill-defined fractures of upper limb**

  INCLUDES   arm NOS
        multiple bones of same upper limb

  EXCLUDES   *multiple fractures of:*
      metacarpal bone(s) with phalanx or phalanges
      (817.0-817.1)
      phalanges of hand alone (816.0-816.1)
      radius with ulna (813.0-813.9)

  818.0 Closed

  818.1 Open

✓4ᵗʰ **819 Multiple fractures involving both upper limbs, and upper limb with rib(s) and sternum**

  INCLUDES   arm(s) with rib(s) or sternum
        both arms [any bones]

  819.0 Closed

  819.1 Open

---

§   Requires fifth digit. Valid digits are in [brackets] under each code. See appropriate category for codes and definitions.

✓4ᵗʰ/✓5ᵗʰ Additional Digit Required   Unspecified Code   Other Specified Code   Manifestation Code   ▶◀ Revised Text   ● New Code   ▲ Revised Code Title

2010 ICD-9-CM   **Volume 1 – 287**

Right Femur, Anterior View

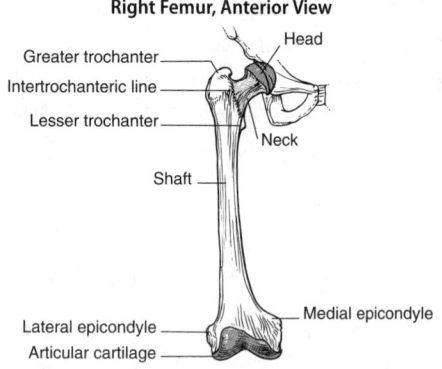

821.22	Epiphysis, lower (separation)
821.23	Supracondylar fracture of femur
821.29	Other

Multiple fractures of lower end

✓5th **821.3** **Lower end, open**

821.30	Lower end, unspecified part
821.31	Condyle, femoral
821.32	Epiphysis, lower (separation)
821.33	Supracondylar fracture of femur
821.39	Other

✓4th **822 Fracture of patella**

822.0 **Closed**

S82.001A Uns fx right patella initial encounter closed fx   I-10

822.1 **Open**

✓4th **823 Fracture of tibia and fibula**

> EXCLUDES   Dupuytren's fracture (824.4-824.5)
> ankle (824.4-824.5)
> radius (813.42, 813.52)
> Pott's fracture (824.4-824.5)
> that involving ankle (824.0-824.9)

The following fifth-digit subclassification is for use with category 823:
0 tibia alone
1 fibula alone
2 fibula with tibia

§ ✓5th **823.0** **Upper end, closed**
[0-2]   Head
Proximal end
Tibia:
   condyles
   tuberosity

S82.121A Displcd fx lat condyle rt tibia initial enc clos fx   I-10

§ ✓5th **823.1** **Upper end, open**
[0-2]

§ ✓5th **823.2** **Shaft, closed**
[0-2]

Right Tibia and Fibula, Anterior View

Torus Fracture

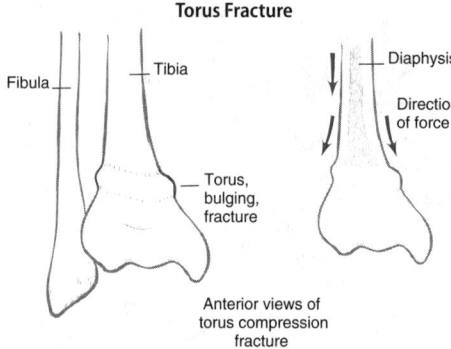

Anterior views of
torus compression
fracture

§ ✓5th **823.3** **Shaft, open**
[0-2]

§ ✓5th **823.4** **Torus fracture**
[0-2]   **DEF:** A bone deformity in children, occurring commonly in the tibia and fibula, in which the bone bends and buckles but does not fracture.
   AHA: 4Q, '02, 70

§ ✓5th **823.8** **Unspecified part, closed**
[0-2]   Lower leg NOS
   AHA: For code 823.82: 1Q, '97, 8

§ ✓5th **823.9** **Unspecified part, open**
[0-2]

✓4th **824 Fracture of ankle**

> **TIP:** If ankle fracture also includes syndesmotic injury, assign also code 845.03 Sprains and strains of tibiofibular (ligament), distal.

824.0 **Medial malleolus, closed**
Tibia involving:
   ankle
   malleolus
AHA: 1Q, '04, 9

824.1 **Medial malleolus, open**

824.2 **Lateral malleolus, closed**
Fibula involving:
   ankle
   malleolus
AHA: 2Q, '02, 3

824.3 **Lateral malleolus, open**

824.4 **Bimalleolar, closed**
Dupuytren's fracture, fibula
Pott's fracture
DEF: Bimalleolar, closed: Breaking of both nodules (malleoli) on either side of ankle joint, without an open wound.
DEF: Dupuytren's fracture (Pott's fracture): The breaking of the farthest end of the lower leg bone (fibula), with injury to the farthest end joint of the other lower leg bone (tibia).
S82.841A Displcd bimalleolar fx rt lw leg intial enc clos fx   I-10

824.5 **Bimalleolar, open**

824.6 **Trimalleolar, closed**
Lateral and medial malleolus with anterior or posterior lip of tibia
S82.855G Nondsplcd trimalleolr fx lt lw leg subsq clo   I-10
delay healing

824.7 **Trimalleolar, open**

824.8 **Unspecified, closed**
Ankle NOS
AHA: 3Q, '00, 12
S89.302A Uns physeal fx low end lt fibula initial enc clo fx   I-10

824.9 **Unspecified, open**

✓4th **825 Fracture of one or more tarsal and metatarsal bones**

825.0 **Fracture of calcaneus, closed**
Heel bone
Os calcis

825.1 **Fracture of calcaneus, open**

---

§   Requires fifth digit. Valid digits are in [brackets] under each code. See category 823 for codes and definitions.

Right Foot, Dorsal

✓5th **825.2 Fracture of other tarsal and metatarsal bones, closed**

    825.20 Unspecified bone(s) of foot [except toes]
        Instep

    825.21 Astragalus
        Talus

    825.22 Navicular [scaphoid], foot

    825.23 Cuboid

    825.24 Cuneiform, foot

    825.25 Metatarsal bone(s)

    825.29 Other
        Tarsal with metatarsal bone(s) only
        EXCLUDES *calcaneus (825.0)*

✓5th **825.3 Fracture of other tarsal and metatarsal bones, open**

    825.30 Unspecified bone(s) of foot [except toes]

    825.31 Astragalus

    825.32 Navicular [scaphoid], foot

    825.33 Cuboid

    825.34 Cuneiform, foot

    825.35 Metatarsal bone(s)

    825.39 Other

✓4th **826 Fracture of one or more phalanges of foot**
    INCLUDES toe(s)

    826.0 Closed

    826.1 Open

✓4th **827 Other, multiple, and ill-defined fractures of lower limb**
    INCLUDES leg NOS
              multiple bones of same lower limb
    EXCLUDES *multiple fractures of:*
              ankle bones alone (824.4-824.9)
              phalanges of foot alone (826.0-826.1)
              tarsal with metatarsal bones (825.29, 825.39)
              tibia with fibula (823.0-823.9 with fifth-digit 2)

    827.0 Closed

    827.1 Open

✓4th **828 Multiple fractures involving both lower limbs, lower with upper limb, and lower limb(s) with rib(s) and sternum**
    INCLUDES arm(s) with leg(s) [any bones]
              both legs [any bones]
              leg(s) with rib(s) or sternum

    828.0 Closed

    828.1 Open

✓4th **829 Fracture of unspecified bones**

    829.0 Unspecified bone, closed

    829.1 Unspecified bone, open

DISLOCATION (830-839)

    INCLUDES displacement
              subluxation

    EXCLUDES *congenital dislocation (754.0-755.8)*
              pathological dislocation (718.2)
              recurrent dislocation (718.3)

The descriptions "closed" and "open," used in the fourth-digit subdivisions, include the following terms:

closed: open:
  complete   compound
  dislocation NOS   infected
  partial   with foreign body
  simple
  uncomplicated

A dislocation not indicated as closed or open should be classified as closed.

AHA: 3Q, '90, 12

TIP: Do not assign if documentation indicates developmental dislocation; see instead subcategory 718.7.

✓4th **830 Dislocation of jaw**
    INCLUDES jaw (cartilage) (meniscus)
              mandible
              maxilla (inferior)
              temporomandibular (joint)

    830.0 Closed dislocation

    830.1 Open dislocation

✓4th **831 Dislocation of shoulder**
    EXCLUDES *sternoclavicular joint (839.61, 839.71)*
              sternum (839.61, 839.71)

    The following fifth-digit subclassification is for use with category 831:
    0 shoulder, unspecified
       Humerus NOS
    1 anterior dislocation of humerus
    2 posterior dislocation of humerus
    3 inferior dislocation of humerus
    4 acromioclavicular (joint)
       Clavicle
    9 other
       Scapula

    TIP: Do not assign if documentation indicates recurrent shoulder dislocation; see instead code 718.31.

§ ✓5th **831.0 Closed dislocation**
[0-4, 9]

§ ✓5th **831.1 Open dislocation**
[0-4, 9]

✓4th **832 Dislocation of elbow**

    The following fifth-digit subclassification is for use with
    ▶subcategories 832.0 and 832.1:◀
    0 elbow, unspecified
    1 anterior dislocation of elbow
    2 posterior dislocation of elbow
    3 medial dislocation of elbow
    4 lateral dislocation of elbow
    9 other

§ ✓5th **832.0 Closed dislocation**
[0-4, 9]

§ ✓5th **832.1 Open dislocation**
[0-4, 9]

●   **832.2 Nursemaid's elbow**
       Subluxation of radial head

---

§ Requires fifth digit. Valid digits are in [brackets] under each code. See appropriate category for codes and definitions.

| ✓4th ✓5th Additional Digit Required | Unspecified Code | Other Specified Code | Manifestation Code | ▶◀ Revised Text | ● New Code | ▲ Revised Code Title |

Injury and Poisoning

833–839.21

✓4th **833 Dislocation of wrist**

The following fifth-digit subclassification is for use with category 833:

0 **wrist unspecified part**
   Carpal (bone)
   Radius, distal end
1 **radioulnar (joint), distal**
2 **radiocarpal (joint)**
3 **midcarpal (joint)**
4 **carpometacarpal (joint)**
5 **metacarpal (bone), proximal end**
9 **other**
   Ulna, distal end

§ ✓5th **833.0 Closed dislocation**
   [0-5, 9]

§ ✓5th **833.1 Open dislocation**
   [0-5, 9]

✓4th **834 Dislocation of finger**

INCLUDES finger(s)
   phalanx of hand
   thumb

The following fifth-digit subclassification is for use with category 834:

0 **finger unspecified part**
1 **metacarpophalangeal (joint)**
   Metacarpal (bone), distal end
2 **interphalangeal (joint), hand**

§ ✓5th **834.0 Closed dislocation**
   [0-2]

§ ✓5th **834.1 Open dislocation**
   [0-2]

✓4th **835 Dislocation of hip**

The following fifth-digit subclassification is for use with category 835:

0 **dislocation of hip, unspecified**
1 **posterior dislocation**
2 **obturator dislocation**
3 **other anterior dislocation**

§ ✓5th **835.0 Closed dislocation**
   [0-3]

§ ✓5th **835.1 Open dislocation**
   [0-3]

✓4th **836 Dislocation of knee**

EXCLUDES dislocation of knee:
   old or pathological (718.2)
   recurrent (718.3)
   internal derangement of knee joint (717.0-717.5,
      717.8-717.9)
   old tear of cartilage or meniscus of knee (717.0-717.5,
      717.8-717.9)

836.0 Tear of medial cartilage or meniscus of knee, current
   Bucket handle tear:
   NOS   } current injury
   medial meniscus

836.1 Tear of lateral cartilage or meniscus of knee, current

836.2 Other tear of cartilage or meniscus of knee, current
   Tear of:
   cartilage (semilunar) } current injury, not
   meniscus   specified as
                             medial or lateral

836.3 Dislocation of patella, closed

836.4 Dislocation of patella, open

✓5th **836.5 Other dislocation of knee, closed**

   836.50 Dislocation of knee, unspecified

   836.51 Anterior dislocation of tibia, proximal end
      Posterior dislocation of femur, distal end

   836.52 Posterior dislocation of tibia, proximal end
      Anterior dislocation of femur, distal end

   836.53 Medial dislocation of tibia, proximal end

   836.54 Lateral dislocation of tibia, proximal end

   836.59 Other

✓5th **836.6 Other dislocation of knee, open**

   836.60 Dislocation of knee, unspecified

   836.61 Anterior dislocation of tibia, proximal end

   836.62 Posterior dislocation of tibia, proximal end

   836.63 Medial dislocation of tibia, proximal end

   836.64 Lateral dislocation of tibia, proximal end

   836.69 Other

✓4th **837 Dislocation of ankle**

INCLUDES astragalus
   fibula, distal end
   navicular, foot
   scaphoid, foot
   tibia, distal end

837.0 Closed dislocation

837.1 Open dislocation

✓4th **838 Dislocation of foot**

The following fifth-digit subclassification is for use with category 838:

0 **foot unspecified**
1 **tarsal (bone), joint unspecified**
2 **midtarsal (joint)**
3 **tarsometatarsal (joint)**
4 **metatarsal (bone), joint unspecified**
5 **metatarsophalangeal (joint)**
6 **interphalangeal (joint), foot**
9 **other**
   Phalanx of foot
   Toe(s)

§ ✓5th **838.0 Closed dislocation**
   [0-6, 9]

§ ✓5th **838.1 Open dislocation**
   [0-6, 9]

✓4th **839 Other, multiple, and ill-defined dislocations**

✓5th **839.0 Cervical vertebra, closed**
   Cervical spine
   Neck

   839.00 Cervical vertebra, unspecified

   839.01 First cervical vertebra

   839.02 Second cervical vertebra

   839.03 Third cervical vertebra

   839.04 Fourth cervical vertebra

   839.05 Fifth cervical vertebra

   839.06 Sixth cervical vertebra

   839.07 Seventh cervical vertebra

   839.08 Multiple cervical vertebrae

✓5th **839.1 Cervical vertebra, open**

   839.10 Cervical vertebra, unspecified

   839.11 First cervical vertebra

   839.12 Second cervical vertebra

   839.13 Third cervical vertebra

   839.14 Fourth cervical vertebra

   839.15 Fifth cervical vertebra

   839.16 Sixth cervical vertebra

   839.17 Seventh cervical vertebra

   839.18 Multiple cervical vertebrae

✓5th **839.2 Thoracic and lumbar vertebra, closed**

   839.20 Lumbar vertebra

   839.21 Thoracic vertebra
      Dorsal [thoracic] vertebra**

§ Requires fifth digit. Valid digits are in [brackets] under each code. See appropriate category for codes and definitions.

N Newborn Age: 0   P Pediatric Age: 0-17   M Maternity Age: 12-55   A Adult Age: 15-124

√5ᵗʰ **839.3 Thoracic and lumbar vertebra, open**

    839.30 **Lumbar vertebra**

    839.31 **Thoracic vertebra**

√5ᵗʰ **839.4 Other vertebra, closed**

    839.40 Vertebra, unspecified site
        Spine NOS

    839.41 **Coccyx**

    839.42 **Sacrum**
        Sacroiliac (joint)

    839.49 Other

√5ᵗʰ **839.5 Other vertebra, open**

    839.50 Vertebra, unspecified site

    839.51 **Coccyx**

    839.52 **Sacrum**

    839.59 Other

√5ᵗʰ **839.6 Other location, closed**

    839.61 **Sternum**
        Sternoclavicular joint

    839.69 Other
        Pelvis

√5ᵗʰ **839.7 Other location, open**

    839.71 **Sternum**

    839.79 Other

  839.8 **Multiple and ill-defined, closed**
    Arm
    Back
    Hand
    Multiple locations, except fingers or toes alone
    Other ill-defined locations
    Unspecified location

  839.9 **Multiple and ill-defined, open**

SPRAINS AND STRAINS OF JOINTS AND ADJACENT MUSCLES (840-848)

INCLUDES	avulsion	
	hemarthrosis	of:
	laceration	joint capsule
	rupture	ligament
	sprain	muscle
	strain	tendon
	tear	

EXCLUDES *laceration of tendon in open wounds (880-884 and 890-894 with .2)*

√4ᵗʰ **840 Sprains and strains of shoulder and upper arm**

  840.0 **Acromioclavicular (joint) (ligament)**

  840.1 **Coracoclavicular (ligament)**

  840.2 **Coracohumeral (ligament)**

  840.3 **Infraspinatus (muscle) (tendon)**

  840.4 **Rotator cuff (capsule)**
    EXCLUDES *complete rupture of rotator cuff, nontraumatic (727.61)*

  840.5 **Subscapularis (muscle)**

  840.6 **Supraspinatus (muscle) (tendon)**

  840.7 **Superior glenoid labrum lesion**
    SLAP lesion
    AHA: 4Q,'01, 52
    DEF: Detachment injury of the superior aspect of the glenoid labrum which is the ring of fibrocartilage attached to the rim of the glenoid cavity of the scapula.

  840.8 Other specified sites of shoulder and upper arm

  840.9 Unspecified site of shoulder and upper arm
    Arm NOS
    Shoulder NOS

√4ᵗʰ **841 Sprains and strains of elbow and forearm**

  841.0 **Radial collateral ligament**

  841.1 **Ulnar collateral ligament**

  841.2 **Radiohumeral (joint)**

  841.3 **Ulnohumeral (joint)**

  841.8 Other specified sites of elbow and forearm

  841.9 Unspecified site of elbow and forearm
    Elbow NOS

√4ᵗʰ **842 Sprains and strains of wrist and hand**

  √5ᵗʰ 842.0 **Wrist**

    842.00 Unspecified site

    842.01 **Carpal (joint)**

    842.02 **Radiocarpal (joint) (ligament)**

    842.09 Other
        Radioulnar joint, distal

  √5ᵗʰ 842.1 **Hand**

    842.10 Unspecified site

    842.11 **Carpometacarpal (joint)**

    842.12 **Metacarpophalangeal (joint)**

    842.13 **Interphalangeal (joint)**

    842.19 Other
        Midcarpal (joint)

√4ᵗʰ **843 Sprains and strains of hip and thigh**

  843.0 **Iliofemoral (ligament)**

  843.1 **Ischiocapsular (ligament)**

  843.8 Other specified sites of hip and thigh

  843.9 Unspecified site of hip and thigh
    Hip NOS   Thigh NOS

√4ᵗʰ **844 Sprains and strains of knee and leg**

  844.0 **Lateral collateral ligament of knee**

  844.1 **Medial collateral ligament of knee**

  844.2 **Cruciate ligament of knee**

  844.3 **Tibiofibular (joint) (ligament), superior**

  844.8 Other specified sites of knee and leg

  844.9 Unspecified site of knee and leg
    Knee NOS   Leg NOS

√4ᵗʰ **845 Sprains and strains of ankle and foot**

  √5ᵗʰ 845.0 **Ankle**

    845.00 Unspecified site
        AHA: 2Q, '02, 3

    845.01 **Deltoid (ligament), ankle**
        Internal collateral (ligament), ankle

    845.02 **Calcaneofibular (ligament)**

    845.03 **Tibiofibular (ligament), distal**
        AHA: 1Q, '04, 9

    845.09 Other
        Achilles tendon

  √5ᵗʰ 845.1 **Foot**

    845.10 Unspecified site

    845.11 **Tarsometatarsal (joint) (ligament)**

    845.12 **Metatarsophalangeal (joint)**

    845.13 **Interphalangeal (joint), toe**

    845.19 Other

√4ᵗʰ **846 Sprains and strains of sacroiliac region**

  846.0 **Lumbosacral (joint) (ligament)**

  846.1 **Sacroiliac ligament**

  846.2 **Sacrospinatus (ligament)**

  846.3 **Sacrotuberous (ligament)**

√4ᵗʰ √5ᵗʰ Additional Digit Required	Unspecified Code	Other Specified Code	Manifestation Code	▶◀ Revised Text	● New Code	▲ Revised Code Title

Injury and Poisoning

846.8–851.0

846.8 **Other specified sites of sacroiliac region**

846.9 **Unspecified site of sacroiliac region**

✓4ᵗʰ **847 Sprains and strains of other and unspecified parts of back**
> EXCLUDES lumbosacral (846.0)

847.0 **Neck**
Anterior longitudinal (ligament), cervical
Atlanto-axial (joints)
Atlanto-occipital (joints)
Whiplash injury
> EXCLUDES neck injury NOS (959.0)
> thyroid region (848.2)

> S13.4xxA Sprain ligaments cervical spine initial encounter I-10

847.1 **Thoracic**

847.2 **Lumbar**

847.3 **Sacrum**
Sacrococcygeal (ligament)

847.4 **Coccyx**

847.9 **Unspecified site of back**
Back NOS

✓4ᵗʰ **848 Other and ill-defined sprains and strains**

848.0 **Septal cartilage of nose**

848.1 **Jaw**
Temporomandibular (joint) (ligament)

848.2 **Thyroid region**
Cricoarytenoid (joint) (ligament) Thyroid cartilage
Cricothyroid (joint) (ligament)

848.3 **Ribs**
Chondrocostal (joint) } without mention of injury
Costal cartilage } to sternum

✓5ᵗʰ 848.4 **Sternum**

848.40 **Unspecified site**

848.41 **Sternoclavicular (joint) (ligament)**

848.42 **Chondrosternal (joint)**

848.49 **Other**
Xiphoid cartilage

848.5 **Pelvis**
Symphysis pubis
> EXCLUDES that in childbirth (665.6)

848.8 **Other specified sites of sprains and strains**

848.9 **Unspecified site of sprain and strain**

INTRACRANIAL INJURY, EXCLUDING THOSE WITH SKULL FRACTURE (850-854)

> INCLUDES ▶traumatic brain injury without skull fracture◀
> EXCLUDES intracranial injury with skull fracture (800-801 and
> 803-804, except .0 and .5)
> open wound of head without intracranial injury
> (870.0-873.9)
> skull fracture alone (800-801 and 803-804 with .0, .5)

Note: The description "with open intracranial wound," used in the
fourth-digit subdivisions, includes those specified as open or
with mention of infection or foreign body.

The following fifth-digit subclassification is for use with categories 851-854:
0 **unspecified state of consciousness**
1 **with no loss of consciousness**
2 **with brief [less than one hour] loss of consciousness**
3 **with moderate [1-24 hours] loss of consciousness**
4 **with prolonged [more than 24 hours] loss of consciousness and
return to pre-existing conscious level**
5 **with prolonged [more than 24 hours] loss of consciousness without
return to pre-existing conscious level**
> Use fifth-digit 5 to designate when a patient is unconscious and dies
> before regaining consciousness, regardless of the duration of the
> loss of consciousness
6 **with loss of consciousness of unspecified duration**
9 **with concussion, unspecified**

AHA: 1Q, '93, 22

TIP: If documentation specifies only "head injury," with no further specificity, and is self-limiting, assign instead code 959.01 Head injury,
unspecified.

850 Concussion
> INCLUDES commotio cerebri
> EXCLUDES concussion with:
> cerebral laceration or contusion (851.0-851.9)
> cerebral hemorrhage (852-853)
> head injury NOS (959.01)

AHA: 2Q, '96, 6; 4Q, '90, 24

TIP: When a patient is treated for symptoms within 24 to 48 hours of
the concussion, clarify with the physician whether the concussion is
still in the acute phase or is a postconcussion syndrome; if so, assign
instead code 310.2.

850.0 **With no loss of consciousness**
Concussion with mental confusion or disorientation,
without loss of consciousness

✓5ᵗʰ 850.1 **With brief loss of consciousness**
Loss of consciousness for less than one hour
AHA: 4Q, '03, 76; 1Q, '99, 10; 2Q, '92, 5

850.11 **With loss of consciousness of 30 minutes or
less**
> S06.0x1A Concussion w/loc 30 min/less initial I-10
> encounter

850.12 **With loss of consciousness from 31 to 59
minutes**

850.2 **With moderate loss of consciousness**
Loss of consciousness for 1-24 hours

850.3 **With prolonged loss of consciousness and return to
pre-existing conscious level**
Loss of consciousness for more than 24 hours with
complete recovery

850.4 **With prolonged loss of consciousness, without return
to pre-existing conscious level**

850.5 **With loss of consciousness of unspecified duration**
> S06.0x9A Concussion w/loc uns duration initial I-10
> encounter

850.9 **Concussion, unspecified**

✓4ᵗʰ **851 Cerebral laceration and contusion**
AHA: 4Q, '96, 36; 1Q, '93, 22; 4Q, '90, 24

§ ✓5ᵗʰ 851.0 **Cortex (cerebral) contusion without mention of**
[0-6, 9] **open intracranial wound**

---

§ Requires fifth digit. Valid digits are in [brackets] under each code. See beginning of section 850-854 for codes and definitions.

Ⓝ Newborn Age: 0   Ⓟ Pediatric Age: 0-17   Ⓜ Maternity Age: 12-55   Ⓐ Adult Age: 15-124

Brain

Corpus callosum
Cerebrum
Hypothalamus
Interventricular foramen
Fornix
Third ventricle
Pineal body
Optic chiasm
Hypophysis
Pons
Corpora quadrigemina
Cerebral aqueduct
Vermis
Mamillary body
Peduncle
Medulla oblangata
Fourth ventricle
Median aperture
Spinal cord

Precentral gyrus (motor)
Anterior horn of lateral ventricle
Intraventricular foramen
Third ventricle
Lateral sulcus
Central sulcus
Postcentral gyrus (sensory)
Body and posterior horn of lateral ventricle
Inferior horn of lateral ventricle
Cerebral aqueduct
Lateral aperture
Fourth ventricle
Median aperture

§ ✓5th **851.1** **Cortex (cerebral) contusion with open**
[0-6, 9] **intracranial wound**
　　　　　AHA: 1Q, '92, 9

§ ✓5th **851.2** **Cortex (cerebral) laceration without mention of**
[0-6, 9] **open intracranial wound**
　　　　　S06.5x0A Traumatic subdurl hemorrhage w/o　　[I-10]
　　　　　loc initial enc

§ ✓5th **851.3** **Cortex (cerebral) laceration with open**
[0-6, 9] **intracranial wound**

§ ✓5th **851.4** **Cerebellar or brain stem contusion without**
[0-6, 9] **mention of open intracranial wound**

§ ✓5th **851.5** **Cerebellar or brain stem contusion with open**
[0-6, 9] **intracranial wound**

§ ✓5th **851.6** **Cerebellar or brain stem laceration without**
[0-6, 9] **mention of open intracranial wound**

§ ✓5th **851.7** **Cerebellar or brain stem laceration with open**
[0-6, 9] **intracranial wound**

§ ✓5th **851.8** **Other and unspecified cerebral laceration and**
[0-6, 9] **contusion, without mention of open intracranial**
wound

　　　　　Brain (membrane) NOS
　　　　　AHA: 4Q, '96, 37

§ ✓5th **851.9** **Other and unspecified cerebral laceration and**
[0-6, 9] **contusion, with open intracranial wound**

✓4th **852** **Subarachnoid, subdural, and extradural hemorrhage,**
following injury
　　　　EXCLUDES Cerebral contusion or laceration (with hemorrhage)
　　　　　　　　　(851.0-851.9)
　　　　DEF: Bleeding from lining of brain; due to injury.

§ ✓5th **852.0** **Subarachnoid hemorrhage following injury**
[0-6, 9] **without mention of open intracranial wound**
　　　　　Middle meningeal hemorrhage following injury

§ ✓5th **852.1** **Subarachnoid hemorrhage following injury with**
[0-6, 9] **open intracranial wound**

§ ✓5th **852.2** **Subdural hemorrhage following injury without**
[0-6, 9] **mention of open intracranial wound**
　　　　　AHA: 4Q, '96, 43; **For codes 852.21-852.29:** 4Q, '07, 107

§ ✓5th **852.3** **Subdural hemorrhage following injury with**
[0-6, 9] **open intracranial wound**

§ ✓5th **852.4** **Extradural hemorrhage following injury without**
[0-6, 9] **mention of open intracranial wound**
　　　　　Epidural hematoma following injury

§ ✓5th **852.5** **Extradural hemorrhage following injury with**
[0-6, 9] **open intracranial wound**

✓4th **853** **Other and unspecified intracranial hemorrhage following**
injury

§ ✓5th **853.0** **Without mention of open intracranial wound**
[0-6, 9] 　Cerebral compression due to injury
　　　　　Intracranial hematoma following injury
　　　　　Traumatic cerebral hemorrhage
　　　　　AHA: 3Q, '90, 14

§ ✓5th **853.1** **With open intracranial wound**
[0-6, 9]

✓4th **854** **Intracranial injury of other and unspecified nature**
　　　　INCLUDES ▶injury:
　　　　　　　　brain NOS
　　　　　　　　cavernous sinus
　　　　　　　　intracranial
　　　　　　　　traumatic brain NOS◄
　　　　EXCLUDES any condition classifiable to 850-853
　　　　　　　　head injury NOS (959.01)
　　　　AHA: 1Q, '99, 10; 2Q, '92, 6
　　　　TIP: Assign a code from category 854 for traumatic brain injury (TBI)
　　　　with diffuse axonal injury (DAI), also known as a shear injury.

§ ✓5th **854.0** **Without mention of open intracranial wound**
[0-6, 9] 　**AHA: For code 854.00:** 2Q, '05, 6

§ ✓5th **854.1** **With open intracranial wound**
[0-6, 9]

INTERNAL INJURY OF THORAX, ABDOMEN, AND PELVIS (860-869)

　　　　INCLUDES blast injuries
　　　　　　　　blunt trauma
　　　　　　　　bruise
　　　　　　　　concussion injuries (except cerebral)
　　　　　　　　crushing　　　　　　　　　　　 of internal
　　　　　　　　hematoma　　　　　　　　　　organs
　　　　　　　　laceration
　　　　　　　　puncture
　　　　　　　　tear
　　　　　　　　traumatic rupture

　　　　EXCLUDES concussion NOS (850.0-850.9)
　　　　　　　　flail chest (807.4)
　　　　　　　　foreign body entering through orifice (930.0-939.9)
　　　　　　　　injury to blood vessels (901.0-902.9)

Note: The description "with open wound," used in the fourth-digit
subdivisions, includes those with mention of infection or
foreign body.

✓4th **860** **Traumatic pneumothorax and hemothorax**
　　　　DEF: Traumatic pneumothorax: air or gas leaking into pleural space of
　　　　lung due to trauma.
　　　　DEF: Traumatic hemothorax: blood buildup in pleural space of lung due
　　　　to trauma.
　　　　AHA: 2Q, '93, 4
　　　　TIP: If there's no mention of trauma associated with pneumothorax, see
　　　　instead category 512.

　　　　860.0 **Pneumothorax without mention of open wound into**
thorax
　　　　　　S27.0xxA Traumatic pneumothorax initial encounter　　[I-10]

　　　　860.1 **Pneumothorax with open wound into thorax**

　　　　860.2 **Hemothorax without mention of open wound into**
thorax

　　　　860.3 **Hemothorax with open wound into thorax**

　　　　860.4 **Pneumohemothorax without mention of open wound**
into thorax

　　　　860.5 **Pneumohemothorax with open wound into thorax**

§　Requires fifth digit. Valid digits are in [brackets] under each code. See beginning of section 850-854 for codes and definitions.

Injury and Poisoning

861–863.99

√4th **861 Injury to heart and lung**
EXCLUDES *injury to blood vessels of thorax (901.0-901.9)*

√5th **861.0 Heart, without mention of open wound into thorax**
AHA: 1Q, '92, 9

861.00 Unspecified injury

861.01 Contusion
Cardiac contusion
Myocardial contusion
DEF: Bruising within the pericardium with no mention of open wound.

861.02 Laceration without penetration of heart chambers
DEF: Tearing injury of heart tissue, without penetration of chambers; no open wound.

861.03 Laceration with penetration of heart chambers

√5th **861.1 Heart, with open wound into thorax**

861.10 Unspecified injury

861.11 Contusion

861.12 Laceration without penetration of heart chambers

861.13 Laceration with penetration of heart chambers

√5th **861.2 Lung, without mention of open wound into thorax**

861.20 Unspecified injury

861.21 Contusion
DEF: Bruising of lung without mention of open wound.
S27.321A Contusion of lung unilateral initial encounter   I-10

861.22 Laceration

√5th **861.3 Lung, with open wound into thorax**

861.30 Unspecified injury

861.31 Contusion

861.32 Laceration

√4th **862 Injury to other and unspecified intrathoracic organs**
EXCLUDES *injury to blood vessels of thorax (901.0-901.9)*

862.0 Diaphragm, without mention of open wound into cavity

862.1 Diaphragm, with open wound into cavity

√5th **862.2 Other specified intrathoracic organs, without mention of open wound into cavity**

862.21 Bronchus

862.22 Esophagus

862.29 Other
Pleura
Thymus gland

√5th **862.3 Other specified intrathoracic organs, with open wound into cavity**

862.31 Bronchus

862.32 Esophagus

862.39 Other

862.8 Multiple and unspecified intrathoracic organs, without mention of open wound into cavity
Crushed chest
Multiple intrathoracic organs

862.9 Multiple and unspecified intrathoracic organs, with open wound into cavity

√4th **863 Injury to gastrointestinal tract**
EXCLUDES *anal sphincter laceration during delivery (664.2)*
bile duct (868.0-868.1 with fifth-digit 2)
gallbladder (868.0-868.1 with fifth-digit 2)

863.0 Stomach, without mention of open wound into cavity

863.1 Stomach, with open wound into cavity

√5th **863.2 Small intestine, without mention of open wound into cavity**

863.20 Small intestine, unspecified site

863.21 Duodenum

863.29 Other

√5th **863.3 Small intestine, with open wound into cavity**

863.30 Small intestine, unspecified site

863.31 Duodenum

863.39 Other

√5th **863.4 Colon or rectum, without mention of open wound into cavity**

863.40 Colon, unspecified site

863.41 Ascending [right] colon

863.42 Transverse colon

863.43 Descending [left] colon

863.44 Sigmoid colon

863.45 Rectum

863.46 Multiple sites in colon and rectum

863.49 Other

√5th **863.5 Colon or rectum, with open wound into cavity**

863.50 Colon, unspecified site

863.51 Ascending [right] colon

863.52 Transverse colon

863.53 Descending [left] colon

863.54 Sigmoid colon

863.55 Rectum

863.56 Multiple sites in colon and rectum

863.59 Other

√5th **863.8 Other and unspecified gastrointestinal sites, without mention of open wound into cavity**

863.80 Gastrointestinal tract, unspecified site

863.81 Pancreas, head

863.82 Pancreas, body

863.83 Pancreas, tail

863.84 Pancreas, multiple and unspecified sites

863.85 Appendix

863.89 Other
Intestine NOS

√5th **863.9 Other and unspecified gastrointestinal sites, with open wound into cavity**

863.90 Gastrointestinal tract, unspecified site

863.91 Pancreas, head

863.92 Pancreas, body

863.93 Pancreas, tail

863.94 Pancreas, multiple and unspecified sites

863.95 Appendix

863.99 Other

§   Requires fifth digit. Valid digits are in [brackets] under each code. See appropriate category for codes and definitions.

N Newborn Age: 0   P Pediatric Age: 0-17   M Maternity Age: 12-55   A Adult Age: 15-124

✓4ᵗʰ **864 Injury to liver**

The following fifth-digit subclassification is for use with category 864:
- 0 unspecified injury
- 1 hematoma and contusion
- 2 laceration, minor
  Laceration involving capsule only, or without significant involvement of hepatic parenchyma [i.e., less than 1 cm deep]
- 3 laceration, moderate
  Laceration involving parenchyma but without major disruption of parenchyma [i.e., less than 10 cm long and less than 3 cm deep]
- 4 laceration, major
  Laceration with significant disruption of hepatic parenchyma [i.e., 10 cm long and 3 cm deep]
  Multiple moderate lacerations, with or without hematoma
  Stellate lacerations of liver
- 5 laceration, unspecified
- 9 other

§ ✓5ᵗʰ **864.0 Without mention of open wound into cavity**
[0-5, 9]

§ ✓5ᵗʰ **864.1 With open wound into cavity**
[0-5, 9]

✓4ᵗʰ **865 Injury to spleen**

The following fifth-digit subclassification is for use with category 865:
- 0 unspecified injury
- 1 hematoma without rupture of capsule
- 2 capsular tears, without major disruption of parenchyma
- 3 laceration extending into parenchyma
- 4 massive parenchymal disruption
- 9 other

§ ✓5ᵗʰ **865.0 Without mention of wound into cavity**
[0-4, 9]

§ ✓5ᵗʰ **865.1 With open wound into cavity**
[0-4, 9]

✓4ᵗʰ **866 Injury to kidney**
EXCLUDES *acute kidney injury (nontraumatic) (584.9)*

The following fifth-digit subclassification is for use with category 866:
- 0 unspecified injury
- 1 hematoma without rupture of capsule
- 2 laceration
- 3 complete disruption of kidney parenchyma

AHA: 4Q, '08, 192

§ ✓5ᵗʰ **866.0 Without mention of open wound into cavity**
[0-3]

§ ✓5ᵗʰ **866.1 With open wound into cavity**
[0-3]

✓4ᵗʰ **867 Injury to pelvic organs**
EXCLUDES *injury during delivery (664.0-665.9)*

867.0 Bladder and urethra, without mention of open wound into cavity
AHA: N-D, '85, 15
TIP: Assign for urethral injury due to senile patient's pulling out indwelling urinary catheter.
S37.20xA Unspecified injury of bladder initial encounter **I-10**

867.1 Bladder and urethra, with open wound into cavity

867.2 Ureter, without mention of open wound into cavity

867.3 Ureter, with open wound into cavity

867.4 Uterus, without mention of open wound into cavity ♀

867.5 Uterus, with open wound into cavity ♀

867.6 Other specified pelvic organs, without mention of open wound into cavity
Fallopian tube
Ovary
Prostate
Seminal vesicle
Vas deferens

867.7 Other specified pelvic organs, with open wound into cavity

867.8 Unspecified pelvic organ, without mention of open wound into cavity

867.9 Unspecified pelvic organ, with open wound into cavity

✓4ᵗʰ **868 Injury to other intra-abdominal organs**

The following fifth-digit subclassification is for use with category 868:
- 0 unspecified intra-abdominal organ
- 1 adrenal gland
- 2 bile duct and gallbladder
- 3 peritoneum
- 4 retroperitoneum
- 9 other and multiple intra-abdominal organs

§ ✓5ᵗʰ **868.0 Without mention of open wound into cavity**
[0-4, 9]

§ ✓5ᵗʰ **868.1 With open wound into cavity**
[0-4, 9]

✓4ᵗʰ **869 Internal injury to unspecified or ill-defined organs**
INCLUDES internal injury NOS
multiple internal injury NOS

869.0 Without mention of open wound into cavity

869.1 With open wound into cavity
AHA: 2Q, '89, 15

OPEN WOUND (870-897)

INCLUDES animal bite
avulsion
cut
laceration
puncture wound
traumatic amputation

EXCLUDES *burn (940.0-949.5)*
crushing (925-929.9)
puncture of internal organs (860.0-869.1)
superficial injury (910.0-919.9)
that incidental to:
dislocation (830.0-839.9)
fracture (800.0-829.1)
internal injury (860.0-869.1)
intracranial injury (851.0-854.1)

Note: The description "complicated" used in the fourth-digit subdivisions includes those with mention of delayed healing, delayed treatment, foreign body, or infection.

AHA: 4Q, '01, 52

TIP: Do not assign a code designated as "complicated" based only on physician documentation of complicated. For coding purposes, there must be indications of delayed healing, delayed treatment, infection, or foreign body.

OPEN WOUND OF HEAD, NECK, AND TRUNK (870-879)

✓4ᵗʰ **870 Open wound of ocular adnexa**

870.0 Laceration of skin of eyelid and periocular area

870.1 Laceration of eyelid, full-thickness, not involving lacrimal passages

870.2 Laceration of eyelid involving lacrimal passages

870.3 Penetrating wound of orbit, without mention of foreign body

870.4 Penetrating wound of orbit with foreign body
EXCLUDES *retained (old) foreign body in orbit (376.6)*

870.8 Other specified open wounds of ocular adnexa

870.9 Unspecified open wound of ocular adnexa

✓4ᵗʰ **871 Open wound of eyeball**
EXCLUDES *2nd cranial nerve [optic] injury (950.0-950.9)*
3rd cranial nerve [oculomotor] injury (951.0)

871.0 Ocular laceration without prolapse of intraocular tissue
DEF: Tear in ocular tissue without displacing structures.
AHA: 3Q, '96, 7

---

§ Requires fifth digit. Valid digits are in [brackets] under each code. See appropriate category for codes and definitions.

✓4ᵗʰ Additional Digit Required	Unspecified Code	Other Specified Code	Manifestation Code	►◄ Revised Text	● New Code	▲ Revised Code Title

Injury and Poisoning

871.1–873.9

871.1 Ocular laceration with prolapse or exposure of intraocular tissue

871.2 Rupture of eye with partial loss of intraocular tissue
DEF: Forcible tearing of eyeball, with tissue loss.

871.3 Avulsion of eye
Traumatic enucleation
DEF: Traumatic extraction of eyeball from socket.

871.4 Unspecified laceration of eye

871.5 Penetration of eyeball with magnetic foreign body
EXCLUDES retained (old) magnetic foreign body in globe (360.50-360.59)

871.6 Penetration of eyeball with (nonmagnetic) foreign body
EXCLUDES retained (old) (nonmagnetic) foreign body in globe (360.60-360.69)

871.7 Unspecified ocular penetration

871.9 Unspecified open wound of eyeball

√4th 872 **Open wound of ear**

√5th 872.0 External ear, without mention of complication
872.00 External ear, unspecified site
872.01 Auricle, ear
Pinna
DEF: Open wound of fleshy, outer ear.
872.02 Auditory canal
DEF: Open wound of passage from external ear to eardrum.

√5th 872.1 External ear, complicated
872.10 External ear, unspecified site
872.11 Auricle, ear
872.12 Auditory canal

√5th 872.6 Other specified parts of ear, without mention of complication
872.61 Ear drum
Drumhead
Tympanic membrane
872.62 Ossicles
872.63 Eustachian tube
DEF: Open wound of channel between nasopharynx and tympanic cavity.
872.64 Cochlea
DEF: Open wound of snail shell shaped tube of inner ear.
872.69 Other and multiple sites

√5th 872.7 Other specified parts of ear, complicated
872.71 Ear drum
872.72 Ossicles
872.73 Eustachian tube
872.74 Cochlea
872.79 Other and multiple sites

872.8 Ear, part unspecified, without mention of complication
Ear NOS

872.9 Ear, part unspecified, complicated

√4th 873 **Other open wound of head**

873.0 Scalp, without mention of complication
S01.01xA Laceration w/o foreign body scalp initial enc I-10

873.1 Scalp, complicated

√5th 873.2 Nose, without mention of complication
873.20 Nose, unspecified site
873.21 Nasal septum
DEF: Open wound between nasal passages.

873.22 Nasal cavity
DEF: Open wound of nostrils.
873.23 Nasal sinus
DEF: Open wound of mucous-lined respiratory cavities.
873.29 Multiple sites

√5th 873.3 Nose, complicated
873.30 Nose, unspecified site
873.31 Nasal septum
873.32 Nasal cavity
873.33 Nasal sinus
873.39 Multiple sites

√5th 873.4 Face, without mention of complication
873.40 Face, unspecified site
873.41 Cheek
873.42 Forehead
Eyebrow
AHA: 4Q, '96, 43
S01.81xA Laceration w/o FB other part head initial enc I-10
873.43 Lip
873.44 Jaw
873.49 Other and multiple sites

√5th 873.5 Face, complicated
873.50 Face, unspecified site
873.51 Cheek
873.52 Forehead
873.53 Lip
873.54 Jaw
873.59 Other and multiple sites

√5th 873.6 Internal structures of mouth, without mention of complication
873.60 Mouth, unspecified site
873.61 Buccal mucosa
DEF: Open wound of inside of cheek.
873.62 Gum (alveolar process)
873.63 Tooth (broken) (fractured) (due to trauma)
EXCLUDES cracked tooth (521.81)
AHA: 1Q, '04, 17
873.64 Tongue and floor of mouth
873.65 Palate
DEF: Open wound of roof of mouth.
873.69 Other and multiple sites

√5th 873.7 Internal structures of mouth, complicated
873.70 Mouth, unspecified site
873.71 Buccal mucosa
873.72 Gum (alveolar process)
873.73 Tooth (broken) (fractured) (due to trauma)
EXCLUDES cracked tooth (521.81)
AHA: 1Q, '04, 17
873.74 Tongue and floor of mouth
873.75 Palate
873.79 Other and multiple sites

873.8 Other and unspecified open wound of head without mention of complication
Head NOS

873.9 Other and unspecified open wound of head complicated

✓4th **874　Open wound of neck**

　✓5th **874.0　Larynx and trachea, without mention of complication**

　　　874.00　Larynx with trachea

　　　874.01　Larynx

　　　874.02　Trachea

　✓5th **874.1　Larynx and trachea, complicated**

　　　874.10　Larynx with trachea

　　　874.11　Larynx

　　　874.12　Trachea

　874.2　Thyroid gland, without mention of complication

　874.3　Thyroid gland, complicated

　874.4　Pharynx, without mention of complication
　　　Cervical esophagus

　874.5　Pharynx, complicated

　874.8　Other and unspecified parts, without mention of complication
　　　Nape of neck
　　　Supraclavicular region
　　　Throat NOS

　874.9　Other and unspecified parts, complicated

✓4th **875　Open wound of chest (wall)**
　　　EXCLUDES　open wound into thoracic cavity (860.0-862.9)
　　　　　　　traumatic pneumothorax and hemothorax (860.1,
　　　　　　　860.3, 860.5)

　　　AHA: 3Q, '95, 17; 3Q, '93, 17

　875.0　Without mention of complication

　875.1　Complicated

✓4th **876　Open wound of back**
　　　INCLUDES　loin
　　　　　　　lumbar region
　　　EXCLUDES　open wound into thoracic cavity (860.0-862.9)
　　　　　　　traumatic pneumothorax and hemothorax (860.1,
　　　　　　　860.3, 860.5)

　876.0　Without mention of complication

　876.1　Complicated

✓4th **877　Open wound of buttock**
　　　INCLUDES　sacroiliac region

　877.0　Without mention of complication

　877.1　Complicated

✓4th **878　Open wound of genital organs (external), including traumatic amputation**
　　　EXCLUDES　injury during delivery (664.0-665.9)
　　　　　　　internal genital organs (867.0-867.9)

　878.0　Penis, without mention of complication　♂

　878.1　Penis, complicated　♂

　878.2　Scrotum and testes, without mention of complication　♂

　878.3　Scrotum and testes, complicated　♂

　878.4　Vulva, without mention of complication　♀
　　　Labium (majus) (minus)

　878.5　Vulva, complicated　♀

　878.6　Vagina, without mention of complication　♀

　878.7　Vagina, complicated　♀

　878.8　Other and unspecified parts, without mention of complication

　878.9　Other and unspecified parts, complicated

✓4th **879　Open wound of other and unspecified sites, except limbs**

　879.0　Breast, without mention of complication

　879.1　Breast, complicated

879.2　Abdominal wall, anterior, without mention of complication
　　　Abdominal wall NOS
　　　Epigastric region
　　　Hypogastric region
　　　Pubic region
　　　Umbilical region
　　AHA: 2Q, '91, 22; 3Q, '90, 5
　　TIP: If the abdominal wall open wound results in aortic rupture, sequence code 902.0 first.

879.3　Abdominal wall, anterior, complicated

879.4　Abdominal wall, lateral, without mention of complication
　　　Flank
　　　Groin
　　　Hypochondrium
　　　Iliac (region)
　　　Inguinal region

879.5　Abdominal wall, lateral, complicated

879.6　Other and unspecified parts of trunk, without mention of complication
　　　Pelvic region
　　　Perineum
　　　Trunk NOS

879.7　Other and unspecified parts of trunk, complicated

879.8　Open wound(s) (multiple) of unspecified site(s) without mention of complication
　　　Multiple open wounds NOS
　　　Open wound NOS

879.9　Open wound(s) (multiple) of unspecified site(s), complicated

OPEN WOUND OF UPPER LIMB (880-887)

AHA: N-D, '85, 5
TIP: For degloving injuries, assign code for open wound of the specified site, most often involving extremities.

✓4th **880　Open wound of shoulder and upper arm**

　　　The following fifth-digit subclassification is for use with category 880:
　　　　0　shoulder region
　　　　1　scapular region
　　　　2　axillary region
　　　　3　upper arm
　　　　9　multiple sites

§ ✓5th **880.0　Without mention of complication**
　[0-3, 9]

§ ✓5th **880.1　Complicated**
　[0-3, 9]　**AHA:** For code 880.13: 2Q, '06, 7

§ ✓5th **880.2　With tendon involvement**
　[0-3, 9]

✓4th **881　Open wound of elbow, forearm, and wrist**

　　　The following fifth-digit subclassification is for use with category 881:
　　　　0　forearm
　　　　1　elbow
　　　　2　wrist

§ ✓5th **881.0　Without mention of complication**
　[0-2]

§ ✓5th **881.1　Complicated**
　[0-2]

§ ✓5th **881.2　With tendon involvement**
　[0-2]

✓4th **882　Open wound of hand except finger(s) alone**

　882.0　Without mention of complication

　882.1　Complicated
　　　AHA: ▶4Q, '08, 152◀

　882.2　With tendon involvement

§　Requires fifth digit. Valid digits are in [brackets] under each code. See appropriate category for codes and definitions.

✓4th ✓5th Additional Digit Required	Unspecified Code	Other Specified Code	Manifestation Code	▶◀ Revised Text	● New Code	▲ Revised Code Title

✓4ᵗʰ **883 Open wound of finger(s)**

> INCLUDES   fingernail
> thumb (nail)

883.0   Without mention of complication

883.1   Complicated

883.2   With tendon involvement

✓4ᵗʰ **884 Multiple and unspecified open wound of upper limb**

> INCLUDES   arm NOS
> multiple sites of one upper limb
> upper limb NOS

884.0   Without mention of complication

884.1   Complicated

884.2   With tendon involvement

✓4ᵗʰ **885 Traumatic amputation of thumb (complete) (partial)**

> INCLUDES   thumb(s) (with finger(s) of either hand)

885.0   Without mention of complication
> AHA: 1Q, '03, 7

885.1   Complicated

✓4ᵗʰ **886 Traumatic amputation of other finger(s) (complete) (partial)**

> INCLUDES   finger(s) of one or both hands, without mention of thumb(s)

886.0   Without mention of complication

886.1   Complicated

✓4ᵗʰ **887 Traumatic amputation of arm and hand (complete) (partial)**

887.0   Unilateral, below elbow, without mention of complication

887.1   Unilateral, below elbow, complicated

887.2   Unilateral, at or above elbow, without mention of complication

887.3   Unilateral, at or above elbow, complicated

887.4   Unilateral, level not specified, without mention of complication

887.5   Unilateral, level not specified, complicated

887.6   Bilateral [any level], without mention of complication
> One hand and other arm

887.7   Bilateral [any level], complicated

OPEN WOUND OF LOWER LIMB (890-897)
> AHA: N-D, '85, 5

✓4ᵗʰ **890 Open wound of hip and thigh**

890.0   Without mention of complication

890.1   Complicated

890.2   With tendon involvement

✓4ᵗʰ **891 Open wound of knee, leg [except thigh], and ankle**

> INCLUDES   leg NOS
> multiple sites of leg, except thigh
> EXCLUDES   that of thigh (890.0-890.2)
> with multiple sites of lower limb (894.0-894.2)

891.0   Without mention of complication
> S81.031A Puncture wound w/o FB rt knee initial encounter   I-10

891.1   Complicated

891.2   With tendon involvement

✓4ᵗʰ **892 Open wound of foot except toe(s) alone**

> INCLUDES   heel

892.0   Without mention of complication

892.1   Complicated

892.2   With tendon involvement

✓4ᵗʰ **893 Open wound of toe(s)**

> INCLUDES   toenail

893.0   Without mention of complication

893.1   Complicated
> AHA: ▶4Q, '08, 73◀

893.2   With tendon involvement

✓4ᵗʰ **894 Multiple and unspecified open wound of lower limb**

> INCLUDES   lower limb NOS
> multiple sites of one lower limb, with thigh

894.0   Without mention of complication

894.1   Complicated

894.2   With tendon involvement

✓4ᵗʰ **895 Traumatic amputation of toe(s) (complete) (partial)**

> INCLUDES   toe(s) of one or both feet

895.0   Without mention of complication

895.1   Complicated

✓4ᵗʰ **896 Traumatic amputation of foot (complete) (partial)**

896.0   Unilateral, without mention of complication

896.1   Unilateral, complicated

896.2   Bilateral, without mention of complication
> EXCLUDES   one foot and other leg (897.6-897.7)

896.3   Bilateral, complicated

✓4ᵗʰ **897 Traumatic amputation of leg(s) (complete) (partial)**

897.0   Unilateral, below knee, without mention of complication

897.1   Unilateral, below knee, complicated

897.2   Unilateral, at or above knee, without mention of complication

897.3   Unilateral, at or above knee, complicated

897.4   Unilateral, level not specified, without mention of complication

897.5   Unilateral, level not specified, complicated

897.6   Bilateral [any level], without mention of complication
> One foot and other leg

897.7   Bilateral [any level], complicated
> AHA: 3Q, '90, 5

INJURY TO BLOOD VESSELS (900-904)

> INCLUDES   arterial hematoma
> avulsion
> cut   of blood vessel
> laceration   secondary to
> rupture   other injuries,
> traumatic aneurysm or fistula   e.g.; fracture or
> (arteriovenous)   open wound

> EXCLUDES   accidental puncture or laceration during medical procedure (998.2)
> intracranial hemorrhage following injury (851.0-854.1)

> AHA: 3Q, '90, 5

✓4ᵗʰ **900 Injury to blood vessels of head and neck**

✓5ᵗʰ 900.0   Carotid artery

900.00   Carotid artery, unspecified

900.01   Common carotid artery

900.02   External carotid artery

900.03   Internal carotid artery

900.1   Internal jugular vein

✓5ᵗʰ 900.8   Other specified blood vessels of head and neck

900.81   External jugular vein
> Jugular vein NOS

900.82   Multiple blood vessels of head and neck

900.89   Other

N Newborn Age: 0   P Pediatric Age: 0-17   M Maternity Age: 12-55   A Adult Age: 15-124

900.9 Unspecified blood vessel of head and neck

✓4th **901 Injury to blood vessels of thorax**
        EXCLUDES traumatic hemothorax (860.2-860.5)

901.0 Thoracic aorta

901.1 Innominate and subclavian arteries

901.2 Superior vena cava

901.3 Innominate and subclavian veins

✓5th 901.4 Pulmonary blood vessels

        901.40 Pulmonary vessel(s), unspecified

        901.41 Pulmonary artery

        901.42 Pulmonary vein

✓5th 901.8 Other specified blood vessels of thorax

        901.81 Intercostal artery or vein

        901.82 Internal mammary artery or vein

        901.83 Multiple blood vessels of thorax

        901.89 Other
                Azygos vein
                Hemiazygos vein

901.9 Unspecified blood vessel of thorax

✓4th **902 Injury to blood vessels of abdomen and pelvis**

902.0 Abdominal aorta

✓5th 902.1 Inferior vena cava

        902.10 Inferior vena cava, unspecified

        902.11 Hepatic veins

        902.19 Other

✓5th 902.2 Celiac and mesenteric arteries

        902.20 Celiac and mesenteric arteries,
                unspecified

        902.21 Gastric artery

        902.22 Hepatic artery

        902.23 Splenic artery

        902.24 Other specified branches of celiac axis

        902.25 Superior mesenteric artery (trunk)

        902.26 Primary branches of superior mesenteric
                artery
                Ileocolic artery

        902.27 Inferior mesenteric artery

        902.29 Other

✓5th 902.3 Portal and splenic veins

        902.31 Superior mesenteric vein and primary
                subdivisions
                Ileocolic vein

        902.32 Inferior mesenteric vein

        902.33 Portal vein

        902.34 Splenic vein

        902.39 Other
                Cystic vein
                Gastric vein

✓5th 902.4 Renal blood vessels

        902.40 Renal vessel(s), unspecified

        902.41 Renal artery

        902.42 Renal vein

        902.49 Other
                Suprarenal arteries

✓5th 902.5 Iliac blood vessels

        902.50 Iliac vessel(s), unspecified

        902.51 Hypogastric artery

        902.52 Hypogastric vein

        902.53 Iliac artery

902.54 Iliac vein

902.55 Uterine artery   ♀

902.56 Uterine vein   ♀

902.59 Other

✓5th 902.8 Other specified blood vessels of abdomen and pelvis

        902.81 Ovarian artery   ♀

        902.82 Ovarian vein   ♀

        902.87 Multiple blood vessels of abdomen and pelvis

        902.89 Other

902.9 Unspecified blood vessel of abdomen and pelvis

✓4th **903 Injury to blood vessels of upper extremity**

✓5th 903.0 Axillary blood vessels

        903.00 Axillary vessel(s), unspecified

        903.01 Axillary artery

        903.02 Axillary vein

903.1 Brachial blood vessels

903.2 Radial blood vessels

903.3 Ulnar blood vessels

903.4 Palmar artery

903.5 Digital blood vessels

903.8 Other specified blood vessels of upper
        extremity
        Multiple blood vessels of upper extremity

903.9 Unspecified blood vessel of upper extremity

✓4th **904 Injury to blood vessels of lower extremity and unspecified
        sites**

904.0 Common femoral artery
        Femoral artery above profunda origin

904.1 Superficial femoral artery

904.2 Femoral veins

904.3 Saphenous veins
        Saphenous vein (greater) (lesser)

✓5th 904.4 Popliteal blood vessels

        904.40 Popliteal vessel(s), unspecified

        904.41 Popliteal artery

        904.42 Popliteal vein

✓5th 904.5 Tibial blood vessels

        904.50 Tibial vessel(s), unspecified

        904.51 Anterior tibial artery

        904.52 Anterior tibial vein

        904.53 Posterior tibial artery

        904.54 Posterior tibial vein

904.6 Deep plantar blood vessels

904.7 Other specified blood vessels of lower
        extremity
        Multiple blood vessels of lower extremity

904.8 Unspecified blood vessel of lower extremity

904.9 Unspecified site
        Injury to blood vessel NOS

LATE EFFECTS OF INJURIES, POISONINGS, TOXIC EFFECTS, AND OTHER EXTERNAL CAUSES (905-909)

Note: These categories are to be used to indicate conditions classifiable to 800-999 as the cause of late effects, which are themselves classified elsewhere. The "late effects" include those specified as such, or as sequelae, which may occur at any time after the acute injury.

√4th **905 Late effects of musculoskeletal and connective tissue injuries**

> AHA: 1Q, '95, 10; 2Q, '94, 3

905.0 **Late effect of fracture of skull and face bones**
> Late effect of injury classifiable to 800-804
> AHA: 3Q, '97, 12

905.1 **Late effect of fracture of spine and trunk without mention of spinal cord lesion**
> Late effect of injury classifiable to 805, 807-809
> AHA: 1Q, '07, 20

905.2 **Late effect of fracture of upper extremities**
> Late effect of injury classifiable to 810-819

905.3 **Late effect of fracture of neck of femur**
> Late effect of injury classifiable to 820

905.4 **Late effect of fracture of lower extremities**
> Late effect of injury classifiable to 821-827
> S79.001S Uns physeal fx upper end right femur sequela   I-10

905.5 **Late effect of fracture of multiple and unspecified bones**
> Late effect of injury classifiable to 828-829

905.6 **Late effect of dislocation**
> Late effect of injury classifiable to 830-839

905.7 **Late effect of sprain and strain without mention of tendon injury**
> Late effect of injury classifiable to 840-848, except tendon injury

905.8 **Late effect of tendon injury**
> Late effect of tendon injury due to:
> > open wound [injury classifiable to 880-884 with .2, 890-894 with .2]
> > sprain and strain [injury classifiable to 840-848]
> AHA: 2Q, '89, 13; 2Q, '89, 15

905.9 **Late effect of traumatic amputation**
> Late effect of injury classifiable to 885-887, 895-897
> > **EXCLUDES** *late amputation stump complication (997.60-997.69)*

√4th **906 Late effects of injuries to skin and subcutaneous tissues**

906.0 **Late effect of open wound of head, neck, and trunk**
> Late effect of injury classifiable to 870-879

906.1 **Late effect of open wound of extremities without mention of tendon injury**
> Late effect of injury classifiable to 880-884, 890-894 except .2

906.2 **Late effect of superficial injury**
> Late effect of injury classifiable to 910-919

906.3 **Late effect of contusion**
> Late effect of injury classifiable to 920-924

906.4 **Late effect of crushing**
> Late effect of injury classifiable to 925-929

906.5 **Late effect of burn of eye, face, head, and neck**
> Late effect of injury classifiable to 940-941
> AHA: 4Q, '04, 76

906.6 **Late effect of burn of wrist and hand**
> Late effect of injury classifiable to 944
> AHA: 4Q, '94, 22

906.7 **Late effect of burn of other extremities**
> Late effect of injury classifiable to 943 or 945
> AHA: 4Q, '94, 22

906.8 **Late effect of burns of other specified sites**
> Late effect of injury classifiable to 942, 946-947
> AHA: 4Q, '94, 22

906.9 **Late effect of burn of unspecified site**
> Late effect of injury classifiable to 948-949
> AHA: 4Q, '94, 22

√4th **907 Late effects of injuries to the nervous system**

907.0 **Late effect of intracranial injury without mention of skull fracture**
> Late effect of injury classifiable to 850-854
> AHA: ▶4Q, '08, 108;◀ 4Q, '03, 103; 3Q, '90, 14
> S06.2x1S Diffuse traumatic brain inj loc 30 min/less seq   I-10

907.1 **Late effect of injury to cranial nerve**
> Late effect of injury classifiable to 950-951

907.2 **Late effect of spinal cord injury**
> Late effect of injury classifiable to 806, 952
> AHA: 4Q, '03, 103; 4Q, '98, 38
> S34.114S Complete lesion L4 of lumbar spinal cord sequela   I-10

907.3 **Late effect of injury to nerve root(s), spinal plexus(es), and other nerves of trunk**
> Late effect of injury classifiable to 953-954
> AHA: 2Q, '07, 11

907.4 **Late effect of injury to peripheral nerve of shoulder girdle and upper limb**
> Late effect of injury classifiable to 955

907.5 **Late effect of injury to peripheral nerve of pelvic girdle and lower limb**
> Late effect of injury classifiable to 956

907.9 **Late effect of injury to other and unspecified nerve**
> Late effect of injury classifiable to 957

√4th **908 Late effects of other and unspecified injuries**

908.0 **Late effect of internal injury to chest**
> Late effect of injury classifiable to 860-862

908.1 **Late effect of internal injury to intra-abdominal organs**
> Late effect of injury classifiable to 863-866, 868

908.2 **Late effect of internal injury to other internal organs**
> Late effect of injury classifiable to 867 or 869

908.3 **Late effect of injury to blood vessel of head, neck, and extremities**
> Late effect of injury classifiable to 900, 903-904

908.4 **Late effect of injury to blood vessel of thorax, abdomen, and pelvis**
> Late effect of injury classifiable to 901-902

908.5 **Late effect of foreign body in orifice**
> Late effect of injury classifiable to 930-939

908.6 **Late effect of certain complications of trauma**
> Late effect of complications classifiable to 958

908.9 **Late effect of unspecified injury**
> Late effect of injury classifiable to 959
> AHA: 3Q, '00, 4

√4th **909 Late effects of other and unspecified external causes**

909.0 **Late effect of poisoning due to drug, medicinal or biological substance**
> Late effect of conditions classifiable to 960-979
> > **EXCLUDES** *late effect of adverse effect of drug, medicinal or biological substance (909.5)*
> AHA: 4Q, '03, 103

909.1 **Late effect of toxic effects of nonmedical substances**
> Late effect of conditions classifiable to 980-989

909.2 **Late effect of radiation**
> Late effect of conditions classifiable to 990

909.3 **Late effect of complications of surgical and medical care**
> Late effect of conditions classifiable to 996-999
> AHA: 1Q, '93, 29

909.4 **Late effect of certain other external causes**
> Late effect of conditions classifiable to 991-994

N Newborn Age: 0   P Pediatric Age: 0-17   M Maternity Age: 12-55   A Adult Age: 15-124

909.5   **Late effect of adverse effect of drug, medical or biological substance**

> *EXCLUDES*   *late effect of poisoning due to drug, medicinal or biological substance (909.0)*

> **AHA:** 4Q, '94, 48

909.9   **Late effect of other and unspecified external causes**

SUPERFICIAL INJURY (910-919)

> *EXCLUDES*   *burn (blisters) (940.0-949.5)*
> *contusion (920-924.9)*
> *foreign body:*
>   *granuloma (728.82)*
>   *inadvertently left in operative wound (998.4)*
>   *residual in soft tissue (729.6)*
> *insect bite, venomous (989.5)*
> *open wound with incidental foreign body (870.0-897.7)*

> **AHA:** 2Q, '89, 15

> **TIP:** Do not code separately when associated with more severe injuries of the same site.

√4th **910**   **Superficial injury of face, neck, and scalp except eye**

> *INCLUDES*   cheek
>   ear
>   gum
>   lip
>   nose
>   throat

> *EXCLUDES*   *eye and adnexa (918.0-918.9)*

910.0   **Abrasion or friction burn without mention of infection**
> S00.01xA Abrasion of scalp initial encounter   I-10

910.1   **Abrasion or friction burn, infected**

910.2   **Blister without mention of infection**

910.3   **Blister, infected**

910.4   **Insect bite, nonvenomous, without mention of infection**

910.5   **Insect bite, nonvenomous, infected**

910.6   **Superficial foreign body (splinter) without major open wound and without mention of infection**

910.7   **Superficial foreign body (splinter) without major open wound, infected**

910.8   **Other and unspecified superficial injury of face, neck, and scalp without mention of infection**

910.9   **Other and unspecified superficial injury of face, neck, and scalp, infected**

√4th **911**   **Superficial injury of trunk**

> *INCLUDES*   abdominal wall   interscapular region
>   anus   labium (majus) (minus)
>   back   penis
>   breast   perineum
>   buttock   scrotum
>   chest wall   testis
>   flank   vagina
>   groin   vulva

> *EXCLUDES*   *hip (916.0-916.9)*
> *scapular region (912.0-912.9)*

911.0   **Abrasion or friction burn without mention of infection**
> **AHA:** 3Q, '01, 10

911.1   **Abrasion or friction burn, infected**

911.2   **Blister without mention of infection**

911.3   **Blister, infected**

911.4   **Insect bite, nonvenomous, without mention of infection**

911.5   **Insect bite, nonvenomous, infected**

911.6   **Superficial foreign body (splinter) without major open wound and without mention of infection**

911.7   **Superficial foreign body (splinter) without major open wound, infected**

911.8   **Other and unspecified superficial injury of trunk without mention of infection**

911.9   **Other and unspecified superficial injury of trunk, infected**

√4th **912**   **Superficial injury of shoulder and upper arm**

> *INCLUDES*   axilla
>   scapular region

912.0   **Abrasion or friction burn without mention of infection**

912.1   **Abrasion or friction burn, infected**

912.2   **Blister without mention of infection**

912.3   **Blister, infected**

912.4   **Insect bite, nonvenomous, without mention of infection**

912.5   **Insect bite, nonvenomous, infected**

912.6   **Superficial foreign body (splinter) without major open wound and without mention of infection**

912.7   **Superficial foreign body (splinter) without major open wound, infected**

912.8   **Other and unspecified superficial injury of shoulder and upper arm without mention of infection**

912.9   **Other and unspecified superficial injury of shoulder and upper arm infected**

√4th **913**   **Superficial injury of elbow, forearm, and wrist**

913.0   **Abrasion or friction burn without mention of infection**

913.1   **Abrasion or friction burn, infected**

913.2   **Blister without mention of infection**

913.3   **Blister, infected**

913.4   **Insect bite, nonvenomous, without mention of infection**

913.5   **Insect bite, nonvenomous, infected**

913.6   **Superficial foreign body (splinter) without major open wound and without mention of infection**

913.7   **Superficial foreign body (splinter) without major open wound, infected**

913.8   **Other and unspecified superficial injury of elbow, forearm, and wrist without mention of infection**

913.9   **Other and unspecified superficial injury of elbow, forearm, and wrist, infected**

√4th **914**   **Superficial injury of hand(s) except finger(s) alone**

914.0   **Abrasion or friction burn without mention of infection**

914.1   **Abrasion or friction burn, infected**

914.2   **Blister without mention of infection**

914.3   **Blister, infected**

914.4   **Insect bite, nonvenomous, without mention of infection**

914.5   **Insect bite, nonvenomous, infected**

914.6   **Superficial foreign body (splinter) without major open wound and without mention of infection**

914.7   **Superficial foreign body (splinter) without major open wound, infected**

914.8   **Other and unspecified superficial injury of hand without mention of infection**

914.9   **Other and unspecified superficial injury of hand, infected**

√4th **915**   **Superficial injury of finger(s)**

> *INCLUDES*   fingernail
>   thumb (nail)

915.0   **Abrasion or friction burn without mention of infection**

915.1   **Abrasion or friction burn, infected**

915.2   **Blister without mention of infection**

915.3   **Blister, infected**

√4th Additional Digit Required   Unspecified Code   Other Specified Code   Manifestation Code   ▶◀ Revised Text   ● New Code   ▲ Revised Code Title

√5th

2010 ICD-9-CM   **Volume 1 – 301**

Injury and Poisoning

915.4–922.33

915.4 Insect bite, nonvenomous, without mention of infection

915.5 Insect bite, nonvenomous, infected

915.6 Superficial foreign body (splinter) without major open wound and without mention of infection

915.7 Superficial foreign body (splinter) without major open wound, infected

915.8 Other and unspecified superficial injury of fingers without mention of infection

    AHA: 3Q, '01, 10

915.9 Other and unspecified superficial injury of fingers, infected

√4th 916 **Superficial injury of hip, thigh, leg, and ankle**

916.0 Abrasion or friction burn without mention of infection

    S80.812A Abrasion left lower leg initial encounter   I-10

916.1 Abrasion or friction burn, infected

916.2 Blister without mention of infection

916.3 Blister, infected

916.4 Insect bite, nonvenomous, without mention of infection

916.5 Insect bite, nonvenomous, infected

916.6 Superficial foreign body (splinter) without major open wound and without mention of infection

916.7 Superficial foreign body (splinter) without major open wound, infected

916.8 Other and unspecified superficial injury of hip, thigh, leg, and ankle without mention of infection

916.9 Other and unspecified superficial injury of hip, thigh, leg, and ankle, infected

√4th 917 **Superficial injury of foot and toe(s)**

    INCLUDES heel
                 toenail

917.0 Abrasion or friction burn without mention of infection

917.1 Abrasion or friction burn, infected

917.2 Blister without mention of infection

917.3 Blister, infected

917.4 Insect bite, nonvenomous, without mention of infection

917.5 Insect bite, nonvenomous, infected

917.6 Superficial foreign body (splinter) without major open wound and without mention of infection

917.7 Superficial foreign body (splinter) without major open wound, infected

917.8 Other and unspecified superficial injury of foot and toes without mention of infection

    AHA: 1Q, '03, 13

917.9 Other and unspecified superficial injury of foot and toes infected

    AHA: 1Q, '03, 13

    TIP: Assign for hair strangulation of toe, with infection.

√4th 918 **Superficial injury of eye and adnexa**

    EXCLUDES burn (940.0-940.9)
                 foreign body on external eye (930.0-930.9)

918.0 Eyelids and periocular area
    Abrasion
    Insect bite
    Superficial foreign body (splinter)

918.1 Cornea
    Corneal abrasion
    Superficial laceration
    EXCLUDES corneal injury due to contact lens (371.82)

918.2 Conjunctiva

918.9 Other and unspecified superficial injuries of eye
    Eye (ball) NOS

√4th 919 **Superficial injury of other, multiple, and unspecified sites**

    EXCLUDES multiple sites classifiable to the same three-digit category (910.0-918.9)

919.0 Abrasion or friction burn without mention of infection

919.1 Abrasion or friction burn, infected

919.2 Blister without mention of infection

919.3 Blister, infected

919.4 Insect bite, nonvenomous, without mention of infection

919.5 Insect bite, nonvenomous, infected

919.6 Superficial foreign body (splinter) without major open wound and without mention of infection

919.7 Superficial foreign body (splinter) without major open wound, infected

919.8 Other and unspecified superficial injuries without mention of infection

919.9 Other and unspecified superficial injury, infected

CONTUSION WITH INTACT SKIN SURFACE (920-924)

    INCLUDES bruise   } without fracture or open
               hematoma   }   wound

    EXCLUDES concussion (850.0-850.9)
                 hemarthrosis (840.0-848.9)
                 internal organs (860.0-869.1)
                 that incidental to:
                     crushing injury (925-929.9)
                     dislocation (830.0-839.9)
                     fracture (800.0-829.1)
                     internal injury (860.0-869.1)
                     intracranial injury (850.0-854.1)
                     nerve injury (950.0-957.9)
                     open wound (870.0-897.7)

920 Contusion of face, scalp, and neck except eye(s)
    Cheek
    Ear (auricle)
    Gum
    Lip
    Mandibular joint area
    Nose
    Throat
    S00.33xA Contusion of nose initial encounter   I-10

√4th 921 **Contusion of eye and adnexa**

921.0 Black eye, not otherwise specified

921.1 Contusion of eyelids and periocular area

921.2 Contusion of orbital tissues

921.3 Contusion of eyeball

    TIP: If iridodialysis (rupture of the root of the iris) is present and is due to the eyeball contusion, assign also code 364.76.

921.9 Unspecified contusion of eye
    Injury of eye NOS

√4th 922 **Contusion of trunk**

922.0 Breast

922.1 Chest wall

    S20.212A Contusion left front wall thorax initial enc   I-10

922.2 Abdominal wall
    Flank
    Groin

√5th 922.3 Back

    AHA: 4Q, '96, 39

    922.31 Back

        EXCLUDES interscapular region (922.33)

        AHA: 3Q, '99, 14

    922.32 Buttock

    922.33 Interscapular region

N Newborn Age: 0   P Pediatric Age: 0-17   M Maternity Age: 12-55   A Adult Age: 15-124

922.4　**Genital organs**
　　　　Labium (majus) (minus)
　　　　Penis
　　　　Perineum
　　　　Scrotum
　　　　Testis
　　　　Vagina
　　　　Vulva

922.8　**Multiple sites of trunk**

922.9　**Unspecified part**
　　　　Trunk NOS

√4ᵗʰ **923　Contusion of upper limb**

√5ᵗʰ 923.0　**Shoulder and upper arm**

923.00　**Shoulder region**

923.01　**Scapular region**

923.02　**Axillary region**

923.03　**Upper arm**

923.09　**Multiple sites**

√5ᵗʰ 923.1　**Elbow and forearm**

923.10　**Forearm**

923.11　**Elbow**

√5ᵗʰ 923.2　**Wrist and hand(s), except finger(s) alone**

923.20　**Hand(s)**

923.21　**Wrist**

923.3　**Finger**
　　　　Fingernail
　　　　Thumb (nail)

923.8　**Multiple sites of upper limb**

923.9　**Unspecified part of upper limb**
　　　　Arm NOS

√4ᵗʰ **924　Contusion of lower limb and of other and unspecified sites**

√5ᵗʰ 924.0　**Hip and thigh**

924.00　**Thigh**
　　　　　AHA: ▶1Q, '09, 10◀

924.01　**Hip**
　　　　　S70.02xA Contusion of left hip initial encounter I-10

√5ᵗʰ 924.1　**Knee and lower leg**

924.10　**Lower leg**

924.11　**Knee**

√5ᵗʰ 924.2　**Ankle and foot, excluding toe(s)**

924.20　**Foot**
　　　　　Heel

924.21　**Ankle**

924.3　**Toe**
　　　　Toenail

924.4　**Multiple sites of lower limb**

924.5　**Unspecified part of lower limb**
　　　　Leg NOS

924.8　**Multiple sites, not elsewhere classified**
　　　　AHA: 1Q, '03, 7
　　　　S70.10xA Contusion of unspecified thigh initial encounter I-10

924.9　**Unspecified site**

CRUSHING INJURY (925-929)

Use additional code to identify any associated injuries, such as:
　　fractures (800-829)
　　internal injuries (860.0-869.1)
　　intracranial injuries (850.0-854.1)
　　AHA: 4Q, '03, 77; 2Q, '93, 7

√4ᵗʰ **925　Crushing injury of face, scalp, and neck**
　　　　Cheek　　　　　Pharynx
　　　　Ear　　　　　　Throat
　　　　Larynx

925.1　**Crushing injury of face and scalp**
　　　　Cheek
　　　　Ear

925.2　**Crushing injury of neck**
　　　　Larynx
　　　　Pharynx
　　　　Throat

√4ᵗʰ **926　Crushing injury of trunk**

926.0　**External genitalia**
　　　　Labium (majus) (minus)
　　　　Penis
　　　　Scrotum
　　　　Testis
　　　　Vulva

√5ᵗʰ 926.1　**Other specified sites**

926.11　**Back**

926.12　**Buttock**

926.19　**Other**
　　　　　Breast

926.8　**Multiple sites of trunk**

926.9　**Unspecified site**
　　　　Trunk NOS

√4ᵗʰ **927　Crushing injury of upper limb**

√5ᵗʰ 927.0　**Shoulder and upper arm**

927.00　**Shoulder region**

927.01　**Scapular region**

927.02　**Axillary region**

927.03　**Upper arm**

927.09　**Multiple sites**

√5ᵗʰ 927.1　**Elbow and forearm**

927.10　**Forearm**

927.11　**Elbow**

√5ᵗʰ 927.2　**Wrist and hand(s), except finger(s) alone**

927.20　**Hand(s)**

927.21　**Wrist**

927.3　**Finger(s)**
　　　　AHA: 4Q, '03, 77

927.8　**Multiple sites of upper limb**

927.9　**Unspecified site**
　　　　Arm NOS

√4ᵗʰ **928　Crushing injury of lower limb**

√5ᵗʰ 928.0　**Hip and thigh**

928.00　**Thigh**

928.01　**Hip**

√5ᵗʰ 928.1　**Knee and lower leg**

928.10　**Lower leg**

928.11　**Knee**

√5ᵗʰ 928.2　**Ankle and foot, excluding toe(s) alone**

928.20　**Foot**
　　　　　Heel

928.21　**Ankle**

---

§　Requires fifth digit. Valid digits are in [brackets] under each code. See appropriate category for codes and definitions.

√4ᵗʰ
√5ᵗʰ　Additional Digit Required　　Unspecified Code　　　Other Specified Code　　　Manifestation Code　　▶◀ Revised Text　　● New Code　　▲ Revised Code Title

Injury and Poisoning

928.3–941.5

928.3   Toe(s)

928.8   Multiple sites of lower limb

928.9   Unspecified site
        Leg NOS

✓4ᵗʰ **929 Crushing injury of multiple and unspecified sites**

929.0   Multiple sites, not elsewhere classified

929.9   Unspecified site

EFFECTS OF FOREIGN BODY ENTERING THROUGH ORIFICE (930-939)

EXCLUDES   foreign body:
      granuloma (728.82)
      inadvertently left in operative wound (998.4, 998.7)
      in open wound (800-839, 851-897)
      residual in soft tissues (729.6)
      superficial without major open wound (910-919 with .6 or .7)

✓4ᵗʰ **930 Foreign body on external eye**

EXCLUDES   foreign body in penetrating wound of:
      eyeball (871.5-871.6)
        retained (old) (360.5-360.6)
      ocular adnexa (870.4)
        retained (old) (376.6)

930.0   Corneal foreign body

930.1   Foreign body in conjunctival sac

930.2   Foreign body in lacrimal punctum

930.8   Other and combined sites

930.9   Unspecified site
        External eye NOS

931 Foreign body in ear
    Auditory canal   Auricle

932 Foreign body in nose
    Nasal sinus   Nostril

✓4ᵗʰ **933 Foreign body in pharynx and larynx**

933.0   Pharynx
        Nasopharynx
        Throat NOS

933.1   Larynx
        Asphyxia due to foreign body
        Choking due to:
          food (regurgitated)
          phlegm
        TIP: Assign for mucous plug causing asphyxia; otherwise, for tracheobronchial, refer to code 519.19 Other diseases of trachea and bronchus.

✓4ᵗʰ **934 Foreign body in trachea, bronchus, and lung**

934.0   Trachea

934.1   Main bronchus
        AHA: 3Q, '02, 18

934.8   Other specified parts
        Bronchioles
        Lung

934.9   Respiratory tree, unspecified
        Inhalation of liquid or vomitus, lower respiratory tract NOS

✓4ᵗʰ **935 Foreign body in mouth, esophagus, and stomach**

935.0   Mouth

935.1   Esophagus
        AHA: 1Q, '88, 13
        TIP: If esophageal obstruction is due to stenosis, caustic stricture (e.g., lye ingestion), or tumor, assign instead code 530.3.

935.2   Stomach

936 Foreign body in intestine and colon

937 Foreign body in anus and rectum
    Rectosigmoid (junction)

938 Foreign body in digestive system, unspecified
    Alimentary tract NOS   Swallowed foreign body

✓4ᵗʰ **939 Foreign body in genitourinary tract**

939.0   Bladder and urethra

939.1   Uterus, any part   ♀
        EXCLUDES   intrauterine contraceptive device:
            complications from (996.32, 996.65)
            presence of (V45.51)

939.2   Vulva and vagina   ♀

939.3   Penis   ♂

939.9   Unspecified site

BURNS (940-949)

INCLUDES   burns from:
      electrical heating appliance
      electricity
      flame
      hot object
      lightning
      radiation
      chemical burns (external) (internal)
      scalds

EXCLUDES   friction burns (910-919 with .0, .1)
      sunburn (692.71, 692.76-692.77)

AHA: 4Q, 94, 22; 2Q, '90, 7; 4Q, '88, 3; M-A, '86, 9

TIP: Nonhealing burns are coded as acute burns, as is necrosis of burned skin. Assign code 958.3 for any documented infected burn site.

✓4ᵗʰ **940 Burn confined to eye and adnexa**

940.0   Chemical burn of eyelids and periocular area

940.1   Other burns of eyelids and periocular area

940.2   Alkaline chemical burn of cornea and conjunctival sac

940.3   Acid chemical burn of cornea and conjunctival sac

940.4   Other burn of cornea and conjunctival sac

940.5   Burn with resulting rupture and destruction of eyeball

940.9   Unspecified burn of eye and adnexa

✓4ᵗʰ **941 Burn of face, head, and neck**

EXCLUDES   mouth (947.0)

The following fifth-digit subclassification is for use with category 941:
  0 face and head, unspecified site
  1 ear [any part]
  2 eye (with other parts of face, head, and neck)
  3 lip(s)
  4 chin
  5 nose (septum)
  6 scalp [any part]
      Temple (region)
  7 forehead and cheek
  8 neck
  9 multiple sites [except with eye] of face, head and neck

AHA: 4Q, '94, 22; M-A, '86, 9

§ ✓5ᵗʰ **941.0 Unspecified degree**
[0-9]

§ ✓5ᵗʰ **941.1 Erythema [first degree]**
[0-9]   AHA: For code 941.19: 3Q, '05, 10

§ ✓5ᵗʰ **941.2 Blisters, epidermal loss [second degree]**
[0-9]

§ ✓5ᵗʰ **941.3 Full-thickness skin loss [third degree NOS]**
[0-9]

§ ✓5ᵗʰ **941.4 Deep necrosis of underlying tissues [deep third degree] without mention of loss of a body part**
[0-9]

§ ✓5ᵗʰ **941.5 Deep necrosis of underlying tissues [deep third degree] with loss of a body part**
[0-9]

---

§   Requires fifth digit. Valid digits are in [brackets] under each code. See appropriate category for codes and definitions.

N Newborn Age: 0   P Pediatric Age: 0-17   M Maternity Age: 12-55   A Adult Age: 15-124

√4th **942 Burn of trunk**

> **EXCLUDES** *scapular region (943.0-943.5 with fifth-digit 6)*
>
> The following fifth-digit subclassificaiton is for use with category 942:
> 0 **trunk, unspecified site**
> 1 breast
> 2 chest wall, excluding breast and nipple
> 3 abdominal wall
>   Flank
>   Groin
> 4 back [any part]
>   Buttock
>   Interscapular region
> 5 genitalia
>   Labium (majus) (minus
>   Penis
>   Perineum
>   Scrotum
>   Testis
>   Vulva
> 9 other and multiple sites of trunk

AHA: 4Q, '94, 22; M-A, '86, 9

§ √5th **942.0 Unspecified degree**
    [0-5, 9]

§ √5th **942.1** Erythema [first degree]
    [0-5, 9]

§ √5th **942.2** Blisters, epidermal loss [second degree]
    [0-5, 9]

§ √5th **942.3** Full-thickness skin loss [third degree NOS]
    [0-5, 9]

§ √5th **942.4** Deep necrosis of underlying tissues [deep third
    [0-5, 9] degree] without mention of loss of a body part

§ √5th **942.5** Deep necrosis of underlying tissues [deep third
    [0-5, 9] degree] with loss of a body part

√4th **943 Burn of upper limb, except wrist and hand**

> The following fifth-digit subclassificaiton is for use with category 943:
> 0 **upper limb, unspecified site**
> 1 forearm
> 2 elbow
> 3 upper arm
> 4 axilla
> 5 shoulder
> 6 scapular region
> 9 multiple sites of upper limb, except wrist and hand

AHA: 4Q, '94, 22; M-A, '86, 9

§ √5th **943.0 Unspecified degree**
    [0-6, 9]

§ √5th **943.1** Erythema [first degree]
    [0-6, 9]

§ √5th **943.2** Blisters, epidermal loss [second degree]
    [0-6, 9]

§ √5th **943.3** Full-thickness skin loss [third degree NOS]
    [0-6, 9]

§ √5th **943.4** Deep necrosis of underlying tissues [deep third
    [0-6, 9] degree] without mention of loss of a body part

§ √5th **943.5** Deep necrosis of underlying tissues [deep third
    [0-6, 9] degree] with loss of a body part

√4th **944 Burn of wrist(s) and hand(s)**

> The following fifth-digit subclassificaiton is for use with category 944:
> 0 **hand, unspecified site**
> 1 single digit [finger (nail)] other than thumb
> 2 thumb (nail)
> 3 two or more digits, not including thumb
> 4 two or more digits including thumb
> 5 palm
> 6 back of hand
> 7 wrist
> 8 multiple sites of wrist(s) and hand(s)

§ √5th **944.0 Unspecified degree**
    [0-8]

§ √5th **944.1** Erythema [first degree]
    [0-8]

§ √5th **944.2** Blisters, epidermal loss [second degree]
    [0-8]

§ √5th **944.3** Full-thickness skin loss [third degree NOS]
    [0-8]

§ √5th **944.4** Deep necrosis of underlying tissues [deep third
    [0-8] degree] without mention of loss of a body part

§ √5th **944.5** Deep necrosis of underlying tissues [deep third
    [0-8] degree] with loss of a body part

√4th **945 Burn of lower limb(s)**

> The following fifth-digit subclassification is for use with category 945:
> 0 **lower limb [leg], unspecified site**
> 1 toe(s) (nail)
> 2 foot
> 3 ankle
> 4 lower leg
> 5 knee
> 6 thigh [any part]
> 9 multiple sites of lower limb(s)

AHA: 4Q, '94, 22; M-A, '86, 9

§ √5th **945.0 Unspecified degree**
    [0-6, 9]

§ √5th **945.1** Erythema [first degree]
    [0-6, 9]

§ √5th **945.2** Blisters, epidermal loss [second degree]
    [0-6, 9]

§ √5th **945.3** Full-thickness skin loss [third degree NOS]
    [0-6, 9]

§ √5th **945.4** Deep necrosis of underlying tissues [deep third
    [0-6, 9] degree] without mention of loss of a body part

§ √5th **945.5** Deep necrosis of underlying tissues [deep third
    [0-6, 9] degree] with loss of a body part

√4th **946 Burns of multiple specified sites**

> **INCLUDES** burns of sites classifiable to more than one three-digit
>   category in 940-945
> **EXCLUDES** *multiple burns NOS (949.0-949.5)*
> **AHA:** 4Q, '94, 22; M-A, '86, 9
> **TIP:** Only assign if the specific sites of the multiple burns are not speci-
> fied.

946.0 Unspecified degree

946.1 Erythema [first degree]

946.2 Blisters, epidermal loss [second degree]

946.3 Full-thickness skin loss [third degree NOS]

946.4 Deep necrosis of underlying tissues [deep third degree]
     without mention of loss of a body part

946.5 Deep necrosis of underlying tissues [deep third degree]
     with loss of a body part

√4th **947 Burn of internal organs**

> **INCLUDES** burns from chemical agents (ingested)
> **AHA:** 4Q, '94, 22; M-A, '86, 9

947.0 Mouth and pharynx
     Gum
     Tongue

947.1 Larynx, trachea, and lung

947.2 Esophagus

947.3 Gastrointestinal tract
     Colon   Small intestine
     Rectum   Stomach

947.4 Vagina and uterus ♀

947.8 Other specified sites

947.9 Unspecified site

---

§   Requires fifth digit. Valid digits are in [brackets] under each code. See appropriate category for codes and definitions.

√4th Additional Digit Required   Unspecified Code   Other Specified Code   Manifestation Code   ▶◀ Revised Text   ● New Code   ▲ Revised Code Title
√5th
2010 ICD-9-CM   **Volume 1 – 305**

Injury and Poisoning

948–952.03

Burns

Degrees of Burns

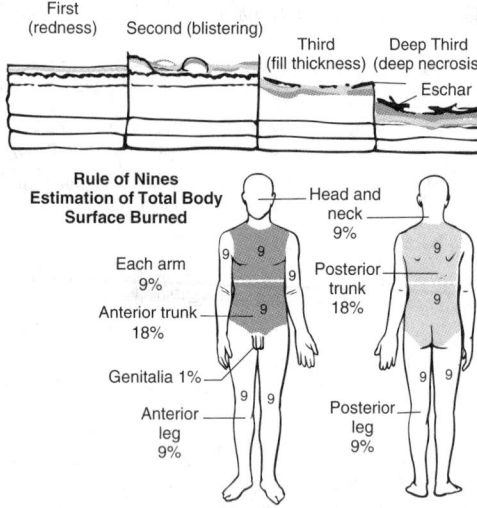

First (redness) Second (blistering) Third (fill thickness) Deep Third (deep necrosis) Eschar

Rule of Nines
Estimation of Total Body Surface Burned

Head and neck 9%
Each arm 9%
Posterior trunk 18%
Anterior trunk 18%
Genitalia 1%
Anterior leg 9%
Posterior leg 9%

✓4ᵗʰ **948 Burns classified according to extent of body surface involved**

Note: This category is to be used when the site of the burn is unspecified, or with categories 940-947 when the site is specified.

EXCLUDES *sunburn (692.71, 692.76-692.77)*

The following fifth-digit subclassification is for use with category 948 to indicate the percent of body surface with third degree burn; valid digits are in [brackets] under each code:

    0   **less than 10 percent or unspecified**
    1   **10-19%**
    2   **20-29%**
    3   **30-39%**
    4   **40-49%**
    5   **50-59%**
    6   **60-69%**
    7   **70-79%**
    8   **80-89%**
    9   **90% or more of body surface**

AHA: 4Q, '94, 22; 4Q, '88, 3; M-A, '86, 9; N-D, '84, 13

§ ✓5ᵗʰ **948.0**   **Burn [any degree] involving less than 10**
[0]   **percent of body surface**
         T31.0 Burns involving less than 10% of body surface   I-10

§ ✓5ᵗʰ **948.1**   **10-19 percent of body surface**
[0-1]

§ ✓5ᵗʰ **948.2**   **20-29 percent of body surface**
[0-2]

§ ✓5ᵗʰ **948.3**   **30-39 percent of body surface**
[0-3]

§ ✓5ᵗʰ **948.4**   **40-49 percent of body surface**
[0-4]

§ ✓5ᵗʰ **948.5**   **50-59 percent of body surface**
[0-5]

§ ✓5ᵗʰ **948.6**   **60-69 percent of body surface**
[0-6]

§ ✓5ᵗʰ **948.7**   **70-79 percent of body surface**
[0-7]

§ ✓5ᵗʰ **948.8**   **80-89 percent of body surface**
[0-8]

§ ✓5ᵗʰ **948.9**   **90 percent or more of body surface**
[0-9]

✓4ᵗʰ **949 Burn, unspecified**

INCLUDES   burn NOS
                multiple burns NOS

EXCLUDES *burn of unspecified site but with statement of the extent of body surface involved (948.0-948.9)*

AHA: 4Q, '94, 22; M-A, '86, 9

949.0   **Unspecified degree**

949.1   **Erythema [first degree]**

949.2   **Blisters, epidermal loss [second degree]**

949.3   **Full-thickness skin loss [third degree NOS]**

949.4   **Deep necrosis of underlying tissues [deep third degree] without mention of loss of a body part**

949.5   **Deep necrosis of underlying tissues [deep third degree] with loss of a body part**

INJURY TO NERVES AND SPINAL CORD (950-957)

INCLUDES   division of nerve
                lesion in continuity   (with open
                traumatic neuroma   wound)
                traumatic transient paralysis

EXCLUDES *accidental puncture or laceration during medical procedure (998.2)*

✓4ᵗʰ **950 Injury to optic nerve and pathways**

950.0   **Optic nerve injury**
         Second cranial nerve

950.1   **Injury to optic chiasm**

950.2   **Injury to optic pathways**

950.3   **Injury to visual cortex**

950.9   **Unspecified**
         Traumatic blindness NOS

✓4ᵗʰ **951 Injury to other cranial nerve(s)**

951.0   **Injury to oculomotor nerve**
         Third cranial nerve

951.1   **Injury to trochlear nerve**
         Fourth cranial nerve

951.2   **Injury to trigeminal nerve**
         Fifth cranial nerve

951.3   **Injury to abducens nerve**
         Sixth cranial nerve

951.4   **Injury to facial nerve**
         Seventh cranial nerve

951.5   **Injury to acoustic nerve**
         Auditory nerve
         Eighth cranial nerve
         Traumatic deafness NOS

951.6   **Injury to accessory nerve**
         Eleventh cranial nerve

951.7   **Injury to hypoglossal nerve**
         Twelfth cranial nerve

951.8   **Injury to other specified cranial nerves**
         Glossopharyngeal [9th cranial] nerve
         Olfactory [1st cranial] nerve
         Pneumogastric [10th cranial] nerve
         Traumatic anosmia NOS
         Vagus [10th cranial] nerve

951.9   **Injury to unspecified cranial nerve**

✓4ᵗʰ **952 Spinal cord injury without evidence of spinal bone injury**

✓5ᵗʰ **952.0**   **Cervical**

       952.00   **C$_1$-C$_4$ level with unspecified spinal cord injury**
                 Spinal cord injury, cervical region NOS

       952.01   **C$_1$-C$_4$ level with complete lesion of spinal cord**

       952.02   **C$_1$-C$_4$ level with anterior cord syndrome**

       952.03   **C$_1$-C$_4$ level with central cord syndrome**

§   Requires fifth digit. Valid digits are in [brackets] under each code. See appropriate category for codes and definitions.

N Newborn Age: 0   P Pediatric Age: 0-17   M Maternity Age: 12-55   A Adult Age: 15-124

Spinal Nerve Roots

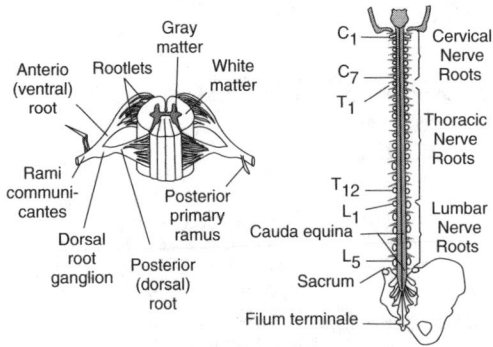

952.04 C₁-C₄ level with other specified spinal cord injury
Incomplete spinal cord lesion at C₁-C₄ level:
NOS
with posterior cord syndrome

952.05 C₅-C₇ level with unspecified spinal cord injury

952.06 C₅-C₇ level with complete lesion of spinal cord

952.07 C₅-C₇ level with anterior cord syndrome

952.08 C₅-C₇ level with central cord syndrome

952.09 C₅-C₇ level with other specified spinal cord injury
Incomplete spinal cord lesion at C₅-C₇ level:
NOS
with posterior cord syndrome

√5ᵗʰ 952.1 Dorsal [thoracic]

952.10 T₁-T₆ level with unspecified spinal cord injury
Spinal cord injury, thoracic region NOS

952.11 T₁-T₆ level with complete lesion of spinal cord

952.12 T₁-T₆ level with anterior cord syndrome

952.13 T₁-T₆ level with central cord syndrome

952.14 T₁-T₆ level with other specified spinal cord injury
Incomplete spinal cord lesion at T₁-T₆ level:
NOS
with posterior cord syndrome

952.15 T₇-T₁₂ level with unspecified spinal cord injury

952.16 T₇-T₁₂ level with complete lesion of spinal cord

952.17 T₇-T₁₂ level with anterior cord syndrome

952.18 T₇-T₁₂ level with central cord syndrome

952.19 T₇-T₁₂ level with other specified spinal cord injury
Incomplete spinal cord lesion at T₇-T₁₂ level:
NOS
with posterior cord syndrome

952.2 Lumbar

952.3 Sacral

952.4 Cauda equina

952.8 Multiple sites of spinal cord

952.9 Unspecified site of spinal cord

√4ᵗʰ **953 Injury to nerve roots and spinal plexus**

953.0 Cervical root

953.1 Dorsal root

953.2 Lumbar root

953.3 Sacral root

953.4 Brachial plexus

953.5 Lumbosacral plexus

953.8 Multiple sites

953.9 Unspecified site

√4ᵗʰ **954 Injury to other nerve(s) of trunk, excluding shoulder and pelvic girdles**

954.0 Cervical sympathetic

954.1 **Other sympathetic**
Celiac ganglion or plexus
Inferior mesenteric plexus
Splanchnic nerve(s)
Stellate ganglion

954.8 **Other specified nerve(s) of trunk**

954.9 **Unspecified nerve of trunk**

√4ᵗʰ **955 Injury to peripheral nerve(s) of shoulder girdle and upper limb**

955.0 Axillary nerve

955.1 Median nerve

955.2 Ulnar nerve

955.3 Radial nerve

955.4 Musculocutaneous nerve

955.5 Cutaneous sensory nerve, upper limb

955.6 Digital nerve

955.7 **Other specified nerve(s) of shoulder girdle and upper limb**

955.8 Multiple nerves of shoulder girdle and upper limb

955.9 **Unspecified nerve of shoulder girdle and upper limb**

√4ᵗʰ **956 Injury to peripheral nerve(s) of pelvic girdle and lower limb**

956.0 Sciatic nerve

956.1 Femoral nerve

956.2 Posterior tibial nerve

956.3 Peroneal nerve

956.4 Cutaneous sensory nerve, lower limb

956.5 **Other specified nerve(s) of pelvic girdle and lower limb**

956.8 Multiple nerves of pelvic girdle and lower limb

956.9 **Unspecified nerve of pelvic girdle and lower limb**

√4ᵗʰ **957 Injury to other and unspecified nerves**

957.0 Superficial nerves of head and neck

957.1 **Other specified nerve(s)**

957.8 Multiple nerves in several parts
Multiple nerve injury NOS

957.9 **Unspecified site**
Nerve injury NOS

CERTAIN TRAUMATIC COMPLICATIONS AND UNSPECIFIED INJURIES (958–959)

√4ᵗʰ **958 Certain early complications of trauma**
EXCLUDES *adult respiratory distress syndrome (518.5)*
flail chest (807.4)
post-traumatic seroma (729.91)
shock lung (518.5)
that occurring during or following medical procedures (996.0-999.9)

958.0 Air embolism
Pneumathemia
EXCLUDES *that complicating:*
abortion (634-638 with .6, 639.6)
ectopic or molar pregnancy (639.6)
pregnancy, childbirth, or the puerperium (673.0)

DEF: Arterial obstruction due to introduction of air bubbles into the veins following surgery or trauma.

√4ᵗʰ Additional Digit Required | Unspecified Code | Other Specified Code | Manifestation Code | ►◄ Revised Text | ● New Code | ▲ Revised Code Title

958.1 Fat embolism

> **EXCLUDES**   *that complicating:*
> *abortion (634-638 with .6, 639.6)*
> *pregnancy, childbirth, or the puerperium (673.8)*

> **DEF:** Arterial blockage due to the entrance of fat in circulatory system, after fracture of large bones or administration of corticosteroids.

958.2 Secondary and recurrent hemorrhage

958.3 Posttraumatic wound infection, not elsewhere classified

> **EXCLUDES**   *infected open wounds-code to complicated open wound of site*

> **AHA:** 4Q, '01, 53; S-O, '85, 10

> **TIP:** Do not assign if the infection is documented as due to cellulitis; see instead categories 681 and 682 and complicated wound codes.

958.4 Traumatic shock

> Shock (immediate) (delayed) following injury

> **EXCLUDES**   *shock:*
> *anaphylactic (995.0)*
> *due to serum (999.4)*
> *anesthetic (995.4)*
> *electric (994.8)*
> *following abortion (639.5)*
> *lightning (994.0)*
> *nontraumatic NOS (785.50)*
> *obstetric (669.1)*
> *postoperative (998.0)*

> **DEF:** Shock, immediate or delayed following injury.

958.5 Traumatic anuria

> Crush syndrome
> Renal failure following crushing

> **EXCLUDES**   *that due to a medical procedure (997.5)*

> **DEF:** Complete suppression of urinary secretion by kidneys due to trauma.

958.6 Volkmann's ischemic contracture

> Posttraumatic muscle contracture

> **DEF:** Muscle deterioration due to loss of blood supply from injury or tourniquet; causes muscle contraction and results in inability to extend the muscles fully.

958.7 Traumatic subcutaneous emphysema

> **EXCLUDES**   *subcutaneous emphysema resulting from a procedure (998.81)*

958.8 Other early complications of trauma

> **AHA:** 2Q, '92, 13

√5ᵗʰ 958.9 Traumatic compartment syndrome

> **EXCLUDES**   *nontraumatic compartment syndrome (729.71-729.79)*

> **DEF:** Compression of nerves and blood vessels within an enclosed space due to previous trauma, which leads to impaired blood flow and muscle and nerve damage.

> **TIP:** If the compartment syndrome is specified as chronic or exercise-induced, see instead subcategory 729.7.

> **958.90 Compartment syndrome, unspecified**
>> **AHA:** 4Q, '06, 100-102

> **958.91 Traumatic compartment syndrome of upper extremity**
>> Traumatic compartment syndrome of shoulder, arm, forearm, wrist, hand, and fingers
>> **AHA:** 4Q, '06, 100-102

> **958.92 Traumatic compartment syndrome of lower extremity**
>> Traumatic compartment syndrome of hip, buttock, thigh, leg, foot, and toes
>> **AHA:** 4Q, '06, 100-102

> **958.93 Traumatic compartment syndrome of abdomen**
>> **AHA:** 4Q, '06, 100-102

> **958.99 Traumatic compartment syndrome of other sites**
>> **AHA:** 4Q, '06, 100-102

√4ᵗʰ 959 Injury, other and unspecified

> **INCLUDES**   injury NOS
> **EXCLUDES**   *injury NOS of:*
> *blood vessels (900.0-904.9)*
> *eye (921.0-921.9)*
> *internal organs (860.0-869.1)*
> *intracranial sites (854.0-854.1)*
> *nerves (950.0-951.9, 953.0-957.9)*
> *spinal cord (952.0-952.9)*

√5ᵗʰ 959.0 Head, face and neck

> **959.01 Head injury, unspecified**
>> **EXCLUDES**   *concussion (850.1-850.9)*
>> *with head injury NOS (850.1-850.9)*
>> *head injury NOS with loss of consciousness (850.1-850.5)*
>> *specified head injuries (850.0-854.1)*
>> **AHA:** ▶4Q, '08, 108;◀ 4Q, '97, 46
>> **S09.90xA** Unspecified injury of head initial   **I-10** encounter

> **959.09 Injury of face and neck**
>> Cheek
>> Ear
>> Eyebrow
>> Lip
>> Mouth
>> Nose
>> Throat
>> **AHA:** 4Q, '97, 46

√5ᵗʰ 959.1 Trunk

> **EXCLUDES**   *scapular region (959.2)*
> **AHA:** 4Q, '03, 78; 1Q, '99, 10

> **959.11 Other injury of chest wall**
> **959.12 Other injury of abdomen**
> **959.13 Fracture of corpus cavernosum penis**   ♂
> **959.14 Other injury of external genitals**
> **959.19 Other injury of other sites of trunk**
>> Injury of trunk NOS

959.2 Shoulder and upper arm
> Axilla
> Scapular region

959.3 Elbow, forearm, and wrist
> **AHA:** 1Q, '97, 8

959.4 Hand, except finger

959.5 Finger
> Fingernail
> Thumb (nail)

959.6 Hip and thigh
> Upper leg

959.7 Knee, leg, ankle, and foot

959.8 Other specified sites, including multiple
> **EXCLUDES**   *multiple sites classifiable to the same four-digit category (959.0-959.7)*

959.9 Unspecified site

POISONING BY DRUGS, MEDICINAL AND BIOLOGICAL SUBSTANCES (960-979)

INCLUDES overdose of these substances
wrong substance given or taken in error

Use additional code to specify the effects of the poisoning

EXCLUDES *adverse effects ["hypersensitivity," "reaction," etc.] of correct substance properly administered. Such cases are to be classified according to the nature of the adverse effect, such as:*
adverse effect NOS (995.20)
allergic lymphadenitis (289.3)
aspirin gastritis (535.4)
blood disorders (280.0-289.9)
dermatitis:
   contact (692.0-692.9)
   due to ingestion (693.0-693.9)
nephropathy (583.9)
[The drug giving rise to the adverse effect may be identified by use of categories E930-E949.]
drug dependence (304.0-304.9)
drug reaction and poisoning affecting the newborn (760.0-779.9)
nondependent abuse of drugs (305.0-305.9)
pathological drug intoxication (292.2)

AHA: 2Q, '90, 11

TIP: Assign a poisoning code for interaction between prescribed drug and alcohol or prescribed drug and other nonprescribed drug or medicinal agent. Sequence poisoning code first, then code for manifestation of poisoning.

If respiratory failure is due to a poisoning, the poisoning code must be sequenced first.

√4ᵗʰ 960 Poisoning by antibiotics

EXCLUDES *antibiotics:*
   ear, nose, and throat (976.6)
   eye (976.5)
   local (976.0)

960.0 Penicillins
Ampicillin
Carbenicillin
Cloxacillin
Penicillin G

960.1 Antifungal antibiotics
Amphotericin B
Griseofulvin
Nystatin
Trichomycin
EXCLUDES *preparations intended for topical use (976.0-976.9)*

960.2 Chloramphenicol group
Chloramphenicol
Thiamphenicol

960.3 Erythromycin and other macrolides
Oleandomycin
Spiramycin

960.4 Tetracycline group
Doxycycline
Minocycline
Oxytetracycline

960.5 Cephalosporin group
Cephalexin
Cephaloglycin
Cephaloridine
Cephalothin

960.6 Antimycobacterial antibiotics
Cycloserine
Kanamycin
Rifampin
Streptomycin

960.7 Antineoplastic antibiotics
Actinomycin such as:
   Bleomycin
   Cactinomycin
   Dactinomycin
   Daunorubicin
   Mitomycin

960.8 Other specified antibiotics

960.9 Unspecified antibiotic

√4ᵗʰ 961 Poisoning by other anti-infectives

EXCLUDES *anti-infectives:*
   ear, nose, and throat (976.6)
   eye (976.5)
   local (976.0)

961.0 Sulfonamides
Sulfadiazine
Sulfafurazole
Sulfamethoxazole

961.1 Arsenical anti-infectives

961.2 Heavy metal anti-infectives
Compounds of:
   antimony
   bismuth
   lead
   mercury
EXCLUDES *mercurial diuretics (974.0)*

961.3 Quinoline and hydroxyquinoline derivatives
Chiniofon
Diiodohydroxyquin
EXCLUDES *antimalarial drugs (961.4)*

961.4 Antimalarials and drugs acting on other blood protozoa
Chloroquine
Cycloguanil
Primaquine
Proguanil [chloroguanide]
Pyrimethamine
Quinine

961.5 Other antiprotozoal drugs
Emetine

961.6 Anthelmintics
Hexylresorcinol
Piperazine
Thiabendazole

961.7 Antiviral drugs
Methisazone
EXCLUDES *amantadine (966.4)*
   cytarabine (963.1)
   idoxuridine (976.5)

961.8 Other antimycobacterial drugs
Ethambutol
Ethionamide
Isoniazid
Para-aminosalicylic acid derivatives
Sulfones

961.9 Other and unspecified anti-infectives
Flucytosine
Nitrofuran derivatives

√4ᵗʰ 962 Poisoning by hormones and synthetic substitutes

EXCLUDES *oxytocic hormones (975.0)*

962.0 Adrenal cortical steroids
Cortisone derivatives
Desoxycorticosterone derivatives
Fluorinated corticosteroids

962.1 Androgens and anabolic congeners
Methandriol
Nandrolone
Oxymetholone
Testosterone

√4ᵗʰ √5ᵗʰ Additional Digit Required   Unspecified Code   Other Specified Code   Manifestation Code   ▶◀ Revised Text   ● New Code   ▲ Revised Code Title

2010 ICD-9-CM   **Volume 1 – 309**

Injury and Poisoning

962.2–965.6

962.2 Ovarian hormones and synthetic substitutes
Contraceptives, oral
Estrogens
Estrogens and progestogens, combined
Progestogens

962.3 Insulins and antidiabetic agents
Acetohexamide
Biguanide derivatives, oral
Chlorpropamide
Glucagon
Insulin
Phenformin
Sulfonylurea derivatives, oral
Tolbutamide
AHA: 4Q, '93, 19; M-A, '85, 8

TIP: Assign only if documentation indicates overdose of insulin; if due to diabetic adjusting dosage, assign instead 250.8X or 249.8X and E932.3 for adverse reaction to insulin, if applicable.

962.4 Anterior pituitary hormones
Corticotropin
Gonadotropin
Somatotropin [growth hormone]

962.5 Posterior pituitary hormones
Vasopressin
EXCLUDES   *oxytocic hormones (975.0)*

962.6 Parathyroid and parathyroid derivatives

962.7 Thyroid and thyroid derivatives
Dextrothyroxin
Levothyroxine sodium
Liothyronine
Thyroglobulin

962.8 Antithyroid agents
Iodides
Thiouracil
Thiourea

962.9 Other and unspecified hormones and synthetic substitutes

963 Poisoning by primarily systemic agents

963.0 Antiallergic and antiemetic drugs
Antihistamines
Chlorpheniramine
Diphenhydramine
Diphenylpyraline
Thonzylamine
Tripelennamine
EXCLUDES   *phenothiazine-based tranquilizers (969.1)*

963.1 Antineoplastic and immunosuppressive drugs
Azathioprine
Busulfan
Chlorambucil
Cyclophosphamide
Cytarabine
Fluorouracil
Mercaptopurine
thio-TEPA
EXCLUDES   *antineoplastic antibiotics (960.7)*

963.2 Acidifying agents

963.3 Alkalizing agents

963.4 Enzymes, not elsewhere classified
Penicillinase

963.5 Vitamins, not elsewhere classified
Vitamin A
Vitamin D
EXCLUDES   *nicotinic acid (972.2)*
                vitamin K (964.3)

963.8 Other specified systemic agents
Heavy metal antagonists

963.9 Unspecified systemic agent

964 Poisoning by agents primarily affecting blood constituents

964.0 Iron and its compounds
Ferric salts
Ferrous sulfate and other ferrous salts

964.1 Liver preparations and other antianemic agents
Folic acid

964.2 Anticoagulants
Coumarin
Heparin
Phenindione
Warfarin sodium
AHA: 1Q, '94, 22

TIP: If documentation indicates an adverse reaction to Coumadin, assign instead manifestation (e.g., hematuria or epistaxis), code 790.92 if abnormal coagulation profile is documented, and E934.2.

964.3 Vitamin K [phytonadione]

964.4 Fibrinolysis-affecting drugs
Aminocaproic acid
Streptodornase
Streptokinase
Urokinase

964.5 Anticoagulant antagonists and other coagulants
Hexadimethrine
Protamine sulfate

964.6 Gamma globulin

964.7 Natural blood and blood products
Blood plasma
Human fibrinogen
Packed red cells
Whole blood
EXCLUDES   *transfusion reactions (999.4-999.8)*

964.8 Other specified agents affecting blood constituents
Macromolecular blood substitutes
Plasma expanders

964.9 Unspecified agent affecting blood constituents

965 Poisoning by analgesics, antipyretics, and antirheumatics
EXCLUDES   *drug dependence (304.0-304.9)*
                nondependent abuse (305.0-305.9)

965.0 Opiates and related narcotics

     965.00 Opium (alkaloids), unspecified
         AHA: 3Q, '07, 6

     965.01 Heroin
         Diacetylmorphine

     965.02 Methadone

     965.09 Other
         Codeine [methylmorphine]
         Meperidine [pethidine]
         Morphine
         AHA: 3Q, '07, 6

         T40.4x1A Poisoning oth synthetic narc accidnt I-10 initial enc

965.1 Salicylates
Acetylsalicylic acid [aspirin]
Salicylic acid salts
AHA: N-D, '94, 15

965.4 Aromatic analgesics, not elsewhere classified
Acetanilid
Paracetamol [acetaminophen]
Phenacetin [acetophenetidin]

965.5 Pyrazole derivatives
Aminophenazone [aminopyrine]
Phenylbutazone

965.6 Antirheumatics [antiphlogistics]
EXCLUDES   *salicylates (965.1)*
                steroids (962.0-962.9)
AHA: 4Q, '98, 50

N Newborn Age: 0   **P** Pediatric Age: 0-17   **M** Maternity Age: 12-55   **A** Adult Age: 15-124

965.61　**Propionic acid derivatives**
　　Fenoprofen
　　Flurbiprofen
　　Ibuprofen
　　Ketoprofen
　　Naproxen
　　Oxaprozin
　　AHA: 4Q, '98, 50

965.69　**Other antirheumatics**
　　Gold salts
　　Indomethacin

965.7　**Other non-narcotic analgesics**
　　Pyrabital

965.8　**Other specified analgesics and antipyretics**
　　Pentazocine

965.9　**Unspecified analgesic and antipyretic**

✓4th　**966　Poisoning by anticonvulsants and anti-Parkinsonism drugs**

966.0　**Oxazolidine derivatives**
　　Paramethadione
　　Trimethadione

966.1　**Hydantoin derivatives**
　　Phenytoin

966.2　**Succinimides**
　　Ethosuximide
　　Phensuximide

966.3　**Other and unspecified anticonvulsants**
　　Primidone
　　EXCLUDES　*barbiturates (967.0)*
　　　　　　　sulfonamides (961.0)

966.4　**Anti-Parkinsonism drugs**
　　Amantadine
　　Ethopropazine [profenamine]
　　Levodopa [L-dopa]

✓4th　**967　Poisoning by sedatives and hypnotics**
　　EXCLUDES　*drug dependence (304.0-304.9)*
　　　　　　　nondependent abuse (305.0-305.9)

967.0　**Barbiturates**
　　Amobarbital [amylobarbitone]
　　Barbital [barbitone]
　　Butabarbital [butabarbitone]
　　Pentobarbital [pentobarbitone]
　　Phenobarbital [phenobarbitone]
　　Secobarbital [quinalbarbitone]
　　EXCLUDES　*thiobarbiturate anesthetics (968.3)*

967.1　**Chloral hydrate group**

967.2　**Paraldehyde**

967.3　**Bromine compounds**
　　Bromide
　　Carbromal (derivatives)

967.4　**Methaqualone compounds**

967.5　**Glutethimide group**

967.6　**Mixed sedatives, not elsewhere classified**

967.8　**Other sedatives and hypnotics**

967.9　**Unspecified sedative or hypnotic**
　　Sleeping:
　　　drug
　　　pill　　} NOS
　　　tablet

✓4th　**968　Poisoning by other central nervous system depressants and anesthetics**
　　EXCLUDES　*drug dependence (304.0-304.9)*
　　　　　　　nondependent abuse (305.0-305.9)

968.0　**Central nervous system muscle-tone depressants**
　　Chlorphenesin (carbamate)
　　Mephenesin
　　Methocarbamol

968.1　**Halothane**

968.2　**Other gaseous anesthetics**
　　Ether
　　Halogenated hydrocarbon derivatives, except halothane
　　Nitrous oxide

968.3　**Intravenous anesthetics**
　　Ketamine
　　Methohexital [methohexitone]
　　Thiobarbiturates, such as thiopental sodium

968.4　**Other and unspecified general anesthetics**

968.5　**Surface [topical] and infiltration anesthetics**
　　Cocaine
　　Lidocaine [lignocaine]
　　Procaine
　　Tetracaine
　　AHA: 1Q, '93, 25

968.6　**Peripheral nerve- and plexus-blocking anesthetics**

968.7　**Spinal anesthetics**

968.9　**Other and unspecified local anesthetics**
　　T41.44xA Poisoning uns anesthetic undetermind initial enc　I-10

✓4th　**969　Poisoning by psychotropic agents**
　　EXCLUDES　*drug dependence (304.0-304.9)*
　　　　　　　nondependent abuse (305.0-305.9)

✓5th　969.0　**Antidepressants**

● 　969.00　**Antidepressant, unspecified**
　　　AHA: 3Q, '07, 6; #5, '94, 9; 3Q, '91, 14; N-D, '84, 14

● 　969.01　**Monoamine oxidase inhibitors**
　　　MAOI

● 　969.02　**Selective serotonin and norepinephrine reuptake inhibitors**
　　　SSNRI antidepressants
　　　TIP: Assign for serotonin syndrome due to poisoning, along with 333.99 and E854.0, for accidental poisoning.

● 　969.03　**Selective serotonin reuptake inhibitors**
　　　SSRI antidepressants
　　　TIP: Assign for serotonin syndrome due to poisoning, along with 333.99 and E854.0, for accidental poisoning.

● 　969.04　**Tetracyclic antidepressants**
● 　969.05　**Tricyclic antidepressants**
● 　969.09　**Other antidepressants**

969.1　**Phenothiazine-based tranquilizers**
　　Chlorpromazine
　　Fluphenazine
　　Prochlorperazine
　　Promazine

969.2　**Butyrophenone-based tranquilizers**
　　Haloperidol
　　Spiperone
　　Trifluperidol

969.3　**Other antipsychotics, neuroleptics, and major tranquilizers**

969.4　**Benzodiazepine-based tranquilizers**
　　Chlordiazepoxide
　　Diazepam
　　Flurazepam
　　Lorazepam
　　Medazepam
　　Nitrazepam
　　T42.4x1D Poisoning benzodiazepines accidental subseq enc　I-10

969.5　**Other tranquilizers**
　　Hydroxyzine
　　Meprobamate

Injury and Poisoning

969.6–974.2

969.6 Psychodysleptics [hallucinogens]
Cannabis (derivatives)
Lysergide [LSD]
Marihuana (derivatives)
Mescaline
Psilocin
Psilocybin

√5th 969.7 Psychostimulants
EXCLUDES central appetite depressants (977.0)

● 969.70 **Psychostimulant, unspecified**
AHA: 2Q, '03, 11

● 969.71 Caffeine

● 969.72 Amphetamines
Methamphetamines
TIP: Assign for overdose and poisoning of the club drug ecstasy.

● 969.73 Methylphenidate

● 969.79 **Other psychostimulants**

969.8 **Other specified psychotropic agents**

969.9 **Unspecified psychotropic agent**

√4th 970 **Poisoning by central nervous system stimulants**

970.0 Analeptics
Lobeline
Nikethamide

970.1 Opiate antagonists
Levallorphan
Nalorphine
Naloxone

970.8 **Other specified central nervous system stimulants**
AHA: 1Q, '05, 6

970.9 **Unspecified central nervous system stimulant**

√4th 971 **Poisoning by drugs primarily affecting the autonomic nervous system**

971.0 Parasympathomimetics [cholinergics]
Acetylcholine
Anticholinesterase:
organophosphorus
reversible
Pilocarpine

971.1 Parasympatholytics [anticholinergics and antimuscarinics] and spasmolytics
Atropine
Homatropine
Hyoscine [scopolamine]
Quaternary ammonium derivatives
EXCLUDES papaverine (972.5)

971.2 Sympathomimetics [adrenergics]
Epinephrine [adrenalin]
Levarterenol [noradrenalin]

971.3 Sympatholytics [antiadrenergics]
Phenoxybenzamine
Tolazolinehydrochloride

971.9 **Unspecified drug primarily affecting autonomic nervous system**

√4th 972 **Poisoning by agents primarily affecting the cardiovascular system**

972.0 Cardiac rhythm regulators
Practolol
Procainamide
Propranolol
Quinidine
EXCLUDES lidocaine (968.5)

972.1 Cardiotonic glycosides and drugs of similar action
Digitalis glycosides
Digoxin
Strophanthins

972.2 Antilipemic and antiarteriosclerotic drugs
Clofibrate
Nicotinic acid derivatives

972.3 Ganglion-blocking agents
Pentamethonium bromide

972.4 Coronary vasodilators
Dipyridamole
Nitrates [nitroglycerin]
Nitrites

972.5 **Other vasodilators**
Cyclandelate
Diazoxide
Papaverine
EXCLUDES nicotinic acid (972.2)

972.6 **Other antihypertensive agents**
Clonidine
Guanethidine
Rauwolfia alkaloids
Reserpine

972.7 Antivaricose drugs, including sclerosing agents
Sodium morrhuate
Zinc salts

972.8 Capillary-active drugs
Adrenochrome derivatives
Metaraminol

972.9 **Other and unspecified agents primarily affecting the cardiovascular system**

√4th 973 **Poisoning by agents primarily affecting the gastrointestinal system**

973.0 Antacids and antigastric secretion drugs
Aluminum hydroxide
Magnesium trisilicate
AHA: 1Q, '03, 19

973.1 Irritant cathartics
Bisacodyl
Castor oil
Phenolphthalein

973.2 Emollient cathartics
Dioctyl sulfosuccinates

973.3 **Other cathartics, including intestinal atonia drugs**
Magnesium sulfate

973.4 Digestants
Pancreatin
Papain
Pepsin

973.5 Antidiarrheal drugs
Kaolin
Pectin
EXCLUDES anti-infectives (960.0-961.9)

973.6 Emetics

973.8 **Other specified agents primarily affecting the gastrointestinal system**

973.9 **Unspecified agent primarily affecting the gastrointestinal system**

√4th 974 **Poisoning by water, mineral, and uric acid metabolism drugs**

974.0 Mercurial diuretics
Chlormerodrin
Mercaptomerin
Mersalyl

974.1 Purine derivative diuretics
Theobromine
Theophylline
EXCLUDES aminophylline [theophylline ethylenediamine] (975.7)
caffeine ►(969.71)◄

974.2 Carbonic acid anhydrase inhibitors
Acetazolamide

N Newborn Age: 0   P Pediatric Age: 0-17   M Maternity Age: 12-55   A Adult Age: 15-124

974.3 **Saluretics**
Benzothiadiazides
Chlorothiazide group

974.4 Other diuretics
Ethacrynic acid
Furosemide

974.5 **Electrolytic, caloric, and water-balance agents**

974.6 Other mineral salts, not elsewhere classified

974.7 **Uric acid metabolism drugs**
Allopurinol
Colchicine
Probenecid

✓4ᵗʰ 975 **Poisoning by agents primarily acting on the smooth and skeletal muscles and respiratory system**

975.0 **Oxytocic agents**
Ergot alkaloids
Oxytocin
Prostaglandins

975.1 **Smooth muscle relaxants**
Adiphenine
Metaproterenol [orciprenaline]
EXCLUDES *papaverine (972.5)*

975.2 **Skeletal muscle relaxants**

975.3 Other and unspecified drugs acting on muscles

975.4 **Antitussives**
Dextromethorphan
Pipazethate

975.5 **Expectorants**
Acetylcysteine
Guaifenesin
Terpin hydrate

975.6 **Anti-common cold drugs**

975.7 **Antiasthmatics**
Aminophylline [theophylline ethylenediamine]

975.8 Other and unspecified respiratory drugs

✓4ᵗʰ 976 **Poisoning by agents primarily affecting skin and mucous membrane, ophthalmological, otorhinolaryngological, and dental drugs**

976.0 **Local anti-infectives and anti-inflammatory drugs**

976.1 **Antipruritics**

976.2 **Local astringents and local detergents**

976.3 **Emollients, demulcents, and protectants**

976.4 Keratolytics, keratoplastics, other hair treatment drugs and preparations

976.5 Eye anti-infectives and other eye drugs
Idoxuridine

976.6 Anti-infectives and other drugs and preparations for ear, nose, and throat

976.7 **Dental drugs topically applied**
EXCLUDES *anti-infectives (976.0)*
local anesthetics (968.5)

976.8 Other agents primarily affecting skin and mucous membrane
Spermicides [vaginal contraceptives]

976.9 Unspecified agent primarily affecting skin and mucous membrane

✓4ᵗʰ 977 **Poisoning by other and unspecified drugs and medicinal substances**

977.0 **Dietetics**
Central appetite depressants

977.1 **Lipotropic drugs**

977.2 **Antidotes and chelating agents, not elsewhere classified**

977.3 **Alcohol deterrents**

977.4 **Pharmaceutical excipients**
Pharmaceutical adjuncts

977.8 Other specified drugs and medicinal substances
Contrast media used for diagnostic x-ray procedures
Diagnostic agents and kits

977.9 Unspecified drug or medicinal substance

✓4ᵗʰ 978 **Poisoning by bacterial vaccines**

978.0 **BCG**

978.1 **Typhoid and paratyphoid**

978.2 **Cholera**

978.3 **Plague**

978.4 **Tetanus**

978.5 **Diphtheria**

978.6 **Pertussis vaccine, including combinations with a pertussis component**

978.8 Other and unspecified bacterial vaccines

978.9 **Mixed bacterial vaccines, except combinations with a pertussis component**

✓4ᵗʰ 979 **Poisoning by other vaccines and biological substances**
EXCLUDES *gamma globulin (964.6)*

979.0 **Smallpox vaccine**

979.1 **Rabies vaccine**

979.2 **Typhus vaccine**

979.3 **Yellow fever vaccine**

979.4 **Measles vaccine**

979.5 **Poliomyelitis vaccine**

979.6 Other and unspecified viral and rickettsial vaccines
Mumps vaccine

979.7 **Mixed viral-rickettsial and bacterial vaccines, except combinations with a pertussis component**
EXCLUDES *combinations with a pertussis component (978.6)*

979.9 Other and unspecified vaccines and biological substances

TOXIC EFFECTS OF SUBSTANCES CHIEFLY NONMEDICINAL AS TO SOURCE (980-989)

Use additional code to specify the nature of the toxic effect
EXCLUDES *burns from chemical agents (ingested) (947.0-947.9)*
localized toxic effects indexed elsewhere (001.0-799.9)
respiratory conditions due to external agents (506.0-508.9)

✓4ᵗʰ 980 **Toxic effect of alcohol**

980.0 **Ethyl alcohol**
Denatured alcohol   Grain alcohol
Ethanol
Use additional code to identify any associated:
acute alcohol intoxication (305.0)
in alcoholism (303.0)
drunkenness (simple) (305.0)
pathological (291.4)
AHA: 3Q, '96, 16
T51.0x1A Toxic effect ethanol accidental initial encountr **I-10**

980.1 **Methyl alcohol**
Methanol
Wood alcohol

980.2 **Isopropyl alcohol**
Dimethyl carbinol
Isopropanol
Rubbing alcohol

980.3 **Fusel oil**
Alcohol:
amyl
butyl
propyl

980.8 Other specified alcohols

980.9 Unspecified alcohol

Injury and Poisoning

981–989.7

981 Toxic effect of petroleum products

Benzine   Petroleum:
Gasoline   ether
Kerosene   naphtha
Paraffin wax   spirit

✓4th 982 Toxic effect of solvents other than petroleum-based

982.0 Benzene and homologues

982.1 Carbon tetrachloride

982.2 Carbon disulfide

Carbon bisulfide

982.3 Other chlorinated hydrocarbon solvents

Tetrachloroethylene   Trichloroethylene

EXCLUDES *chlorinated hydrocarbon preparations other than solvents (989.2)*

AHA: ▶3Q, '08, 6-7◀

982.4 Nitroglycol

982.8 Other nonpetroleum-based solvents

Acetone

✓4th 983 Toxic effect of corrosive aromatics, acids, and caustic alkalis

983.0 Corrosive aromatics

Carbolic acid or phenol
Cresol

983.1 Acids

Acid:
hydrochloric
nitric
sulfuric

983.2 Caustic alkalis

Lye
Potassium hydroxide
Sodium hydroxide

983.9 Caustic, unspecified

✓4th 984 Toxic effect of lead and its compounds (including fumes)

INCLUDES that from all sources except medicinal substances

984.0 Inorganic lead compounds

Lead dioxide
Lead salts

984.1 Organic lead compounds

Lead acetate
Tetraethyl lead

984.8 Other lead compounds

984.9 Unspecified lead compound

✓4th 985 Toxic effect of other metals

INCLUDES that from all sources except medicinal substances

985.0 Mercury and its compounds

Minamata disease

985.1 Arsenic and its compounds

985.2 Manganese and its compounds

985.3 Beryllium and its compounds

985.4 Antimony and its compounds

985.5 Cadmium and its compounds

985.6 Chromium

985.8 Other specified metals

Brass fumes
Copper salts
Iron compounds
Nickel compounds

AHA: 1Q, '88, 5

TIP: Assign for aluminum overloading or excessive concentration of aluminum in the body, along with E879.1 if due to renal dialysis and E879.8 if due to total parenteral nutrition.

985.9 Unspecified metal

986 Toxic effect of carbon monoxide

Carbon monoxide from any source

✓4th 987 Toxic effect of other gases, fumes, or vapors

987.0 Liquefied petroleum gases

Butane
Propane

987.1 Other hydrocarbon gas

987.2 Nitrogen oxides

Nitrogen dioxide
Nitrous fumes

987.3 Sulfur dioxide

987.4 Freon

Dichloromonofluoromethane

987.5 Lacrimogenic gas

Bromobenzyl cyanide
Chloroacetophenone
Ethyliodoacetate

987.6 Chlorine gas

987.7 Hydrocyanic acid gas

987.8 Other specified gases, fumes, or vapors

Phosgene
Polyester fumes

987.9 Unspecified gas, fume, or vapor

AHA: 3Q, '05, 10

TIP: Assign for smoke inhalation, along with the appropriate E code describing the source of the smoke and fumes.

✓4th 988 Toxic effect of noxious substances eaten as food

EXCLUDES *allergic reaction to food, such as:*
gastroenteritis (558.3)
rash (692.5, 693.1)
food poisoning (bacterial) (005.0-005.9)
toxic effects of food contaminants, such as:
aflatoxin and other mycotoxin (989.7)
mercury (985.0)

988.0 Fish and shellfish

988.1 Mushrooms

988.2 Berries and other plants

988.8 Other specified noxious substances eaten as food

988.9 Unspecified noxious substance eaten as food

✓4th 989 Toxic effect of other substances, chiefly nonmedicinal as to source

989.0 Hydrocyanic acid and cyanides

Potassium cyanide
Sodium cyanide

EXCLUDES *gas and fumes (987.7)*

989.1 Strychnine and salts

989.2 Chlorinated hydrocarbons

Aldrin
Chlordane
DDT
Dieldrin

EXCLUDES *chlorinated hydrocarbon solvents (982.0-982.3)*

989.3 Organophosphate and carbamate

Carbaryl
Dichlorvos
Malathion
Parathion
Phorate
Phosdrin

989.4 Other pesticides, not elsewhere classified

Mixtures of insecticides

989.5 Venom

Bites of venomous snakes, lizards, and spiders
Tick paralysis

989.6 Soaps and detergents

989.7 Aflatoxin and other mycotoxin [food contaminants]

Ⓝ Newborn Age: 0   Ⓟ Pediatric Age: 0-17   Ⓜ Maternity Age: 12-55   Ⓐ Adult Age: 15-124

✓5th **989.8** Other substances, chiefly nonmedicinal as to source

    AHA: 4Q, '95, 60

  989.81 Asbestos

    EXCLUDES *asbestosis (501)*
    exposure to asbestos (V15.84)

  989.82 Latex

  989.83 Silicone

    EXCLUDES *silicone used in medical devices,*
    implants and grafts
    (996.00-996.79)

  989.84 Tobacco

  989.89 Other

989.9 Unspecified substance, chiefly nonmedicinal as to source

OTHER AND UNSPECIFIED EFFECTS OF EXTERNAL CAUSES (990-995)

990 Effects of radiation, unspecified

  Complication of:
    phototherapy
    radiation therapy
  Radiation sickness

  [The type of radiation giving rise to the adverse effect may be identified by use of the E codes.]

  EXCLUDES *specified adverse effects of radiation. Such conditions are to be classified according to the nature of the adverse effect, as:*
    burns (940.0-949.5)
    dermatitis (692.7-692.8)
    leukemia (204.0-208.9)
    pneumonia (508.0)
    sunburn (692.71, 692.76-692.77)

✓4th **991** Effects of reduced temperature

  991.0 Frostbite of face

  991.1 Frostbite of hand

  991.2 Frostbite of foot

  991.3 Frostbite of other and unspecified sites

  991.4 Immersion foot

    Trench foot

    DEF: Paresthesia, edema, blotchy cyanosis of foot, the skin is soft (macerated), pale and wrinkled, and the sole is swollen with surface ridging and following sustained immersion in water.

  991.5 Chilblains

    Erythema pernio
    Perniosis

    DEF: Red, swollen, itchy skin; follows damp cold exposure; also associated with pruritus and a burning feeling, in hands, feet, ears, and face in children, legs and toes in women, and hands and fingers in men.

  991.6 Hypothermia

    Hypothermia (accidental)

    EXCLUDES *hypothermia following anesthesia (995.89)*
    hypothermia not associated with low environmental temperature (780.65)

    DEF: Reduced body temperature due to low environmental temperatures.

  991.8 Other specified effects of reduced temperature

  991.9 Unspecified effect of reduced temperature

    Effects of freezing or excessive cold NOS

✓4th **992** Effects of heat and light

  EXCLUDES *burns (940.0-949.5)*
    diseases of sweat glands due to heat (705.0-705.9)
    malignant hyperpyrexia following anesthesia (995.86)
    sunburn (692.71, 692.76-692.77)

  992.0 Heat stroke and sunstroke

    Heat apoplexy   Siriasis
    Heat pyrexia   Thermoplegia
    Ictus solaris

    DEF: Headache, vertigo, cramps and elevated body temperature due to high environmental temperatures.

  992.1 Heat syncope

    Heat collapse

  992.2 Heat cramps

  992.3 Heat exhaustion, anhydrotic

    Heat prostration due to water depletion

    EXCLUDES *that associated with salt depletion (992.4)*

  992.4 Heat exhaustion due to salt depletion

    Heat prostration due to salt (and water) depletion

  992.5 Heat exhaustion, unspecified

    Heat prostration NOS

  992.6 Heat fatigue, transient

  992.7 Heat edema

    DEF: Fluid retention due to high environmental temperatures.

  992.8 Other specified heat effects

  992.9 Unspecified

✓4th **993** Effects of air pressure

  993.0 Barotrauma, otitic

    Aero-otitis media
    Effects of high altitude on ears

    DEF: Ringing ears, deafness, pain and vertigo due to air pressure changes.

  993.1 Barotrauma, sinus

    Aerosinusitis
    Effects of high altitude on sinuses

  993.2 Other and unspecified effects of high altitude

    Alpine sickness   Hypobaropathy
    Andes disease   Mountain sickness
    Anoxia due to high altitude

    AHA: 3Q, '88, 4

  993.3 Caisson disease

    Bends
    Compressed-air disease
    Decompression sickness
    Divers' palsy or paralysis

    DEF: Rapid reduction in air pressure while breathing compressed air; symptoms include skin lesions, joint pains, respiratory and neurological problems.

  993.4 Effects of air pressure caused by explosion

  993.8 Other specified effects of air pressure

  993.9 Unspecified effect of air pressure

✓4th **994** Effects of other external causes

  EXCLUDES *certain adverse effects not elsewhere classified (995.0-995.8)*

  994.0 Effects of lightning

    Shock from lightning
    Struck by lightning NOS

    EXCLUDES *burns (940.0-949.5)*

  994.1 Drowning and nonfatal submersion

    Bathing cramp
    Immersion

    AHA: 3Q, '88, 4

    TIP: When near-drowning results in acute respiratory edema, assign also code 518.5 Post-traumatic pulmonary insufficiency.

  994.2 Effects of hunger

    Deprivation of food
    Starvation

✓4th Additional Digit Required   Unspecified Code   Other Specified Code   Manifestation Code   ▶◀ Revised Text   ● New Code   ▲ Revised Code Title

2010 ICD-9-CM   **Volume 1 – 315**

Injury and Poisoning

994.3–995.55

994.3 Effects of thirst
Deprivation of water

994.4 Exhaustion due to exposure

994.5 Exhaustion due to excessive exertion
Exhaustion due to overexertion

994.6 Motion sickness
Air sickness   Travel sickness
Seasickness

994.7 Asphyxiation and strangulation
Suffocation (by):   Suffocation (by):
  bedclothes   plastic bag
  cave-in   pressure
  constriction   strangulation
  mechanical

EXCLUDES *asphyxia from:*
    carbon monoxide (986)
    inhalation of food or foreign body
      (932-934.9)
    other gases, fumes, and vapors
      (987.0-987.9)

994.8 Electrocution and nonfatal effects of electric current
Shock from electric current
Shock from electroshock gun (taser)
EXCLUDES *electric burns (940.0-949.5)*

994.9 Other effects of external causes
Effects of:
  abnormal gravitational [G] forces or states
  weightlessness

✓4th **995 Certain adverse effects not elsewhere classified**
EXCLUDES *complications of surgical and medical care (996.0-999.9)*

995.0 Other anaphylactic shock
Allergic shock   ⎫ NOS or due to adverse effect of
Anaphylactic   ⎬   correct medicinal
  reaction   substance properly
Anaphylaxis   ⎭   administered

Use additional E code to identify external cause, such as:
  adverse effects of correct medicinal substance
    properly administered [E930-E949]

EXCLUDES *anaphylactic reaction to serum (999.4)*
    anaphylactic shock due to adverse food
      reaction (995.60-995.69)

DEF: Immediate sensitivity response after exposure to specific antigen; results in life-threatening respiratory distress; usually followed by vascular collapse, shock , urticaria, angioedema and pruritus.
AHA: 4Q, '93, 30

995.1 Angioneurotic edema
Giant urticaria
EXCLUDES *urticaria:*
    due to serum (999.5)
    other specified (698.2, 708.0-708.9, 757.33)

DEF: Circulatory response of deep dermis, subcutaneous or submucosal tissues; causes localized edema and wheals.

✓5th **995.2 Other and unspecified adverse effect of drug, medicinal and biological substance (due) to correct medicinal substance properly administered**
Adverse effect   ⎫
Allergic reaction   ⎬ (due) to correct medicinal
Hypersensitivity   ⎬   substance properly
Idiosyncrasy   ⎭   administered
Drug:
  hypersensitivity NOS
  reaction NOS
EXCLUDES *pathological drug intoxication (292.2)*
AHA: 2Q, '97, 12; 3Q, '95, 13; 3Q, '92, 16

TIP: Codes from this subcategory should not be assigned for inpatient cases; their use is limited to certain outpatient cases in which there is no documentation of specific symptoms associated with the adverse effect.

995.20 Unspecified adverse effect of unspecified drug, medicinal and biological substance
AHA: 4Q, '06, 112

995.21 Arthus phenomenon
Arthus reaction
AHA: 4Q, '06, 112

995.22 Unspecified adverse effect of anesthesia
AHA: 4Q, '06, 112

995.23 Unspecified adverse effect of insulin
AHA: 4Q, '06, 112

995.24 Failed moderate sedation during procedure
Failed conscious sedation during procedure

995.27 Other drug allergy
Drug allergy NOS
Drug hypersensitivity NOS
AHA: 4Q, '06, 112

995.29 Unspecified adverse effect of other drug, medicinal and biological substance
AHA: 4Q, '06, 112

995.3 Allergy, unspecified
Allergic reaction NOS
Hypersensitivity NOS
Idiosyncrasy NOS
EXCLUDES *allergic reaction NOS to correct medicinal*
    substance properly administered
    (995.27)
    allergy to existing dental restorative materials
    (525.66)
    specific types of allergic reaction, such as:
      allergic diarrhea (558.3)
      dermatitis (691.0-693.9)
      hayfever (477.0-477.9)

995.4 Shock due to anesthesia
Shock due to anesthesia in which the correct substance was properly administered
EXCLUDES *complications of anesthesia in labor or delivery*
    (668.0-668.9)
    overdose or wrong substance given
    (968.0-969.9)
    postoperative shock NOS (998.0)
    specified adverse effects of anesthesia classified
    elsewhere, such as:
      anoxic brain damage (348.1)
      hepatitis (070.0-070.9), etc.
    unspecified adverse effect of anesthesia
    (995.22)

✓5th **995.5 Child maltreatment syndrome**
Use additional code(s), if applicable, to identify any associated injuries
Use additional E code to identify:
  nature of abuse (E960-E968)
  perpetrator (E967.0-E967.9)
AHA: 1Q, '98, 11

TIP: Although separate codes for any associated injuries should be assigned, codes from this subcategory may be assigned alone if there are no documented injuries or associated conditions.

995.50 Child abuse, unspecified   P

995.51 Child emotional/psychological abuse   P
AHA: 4Q, '96, 38, 40

995.52 Child neglect (nutritional)   P
AHA: 4Q, '96, 38, 40

995.53 Child sexual abuse   P
AHA: 4Q, '96, 39, 40

995.54 Child physical abuse   P
Battered baby or child syndrome
EXCLUDES *shaken infant syndrome (995.55)*
AHA: 3Q, '99, 14; 4Q, '96, 39, 40

995.55 Shaken infant syndrome   P
Use additional code(s) to identify any associated injuries
AHA: 4Q, '96, 40, 43

N Newborn Age: 0   P Pediatric Age: 0-17   M Maternity Age: 12-55   A Adult Age: 15-124

995.59 Other child abuse and neglect   P
Multiple forms of abuse

√5th **995.6 Anaphylactic shock due to adverse food reaction**
Anaphylactic reaction due to food
Anaphylactic shock due to nonpoisonous foods
AHA: 4Q, '93, 30
TIP: Codes from this subcategory may be assigned not only for anaphylactic shock, but also for any documentation of anaphylactic reaction to food.

995.60 Due to unspecified food

995.61 Due to peanuts

995.62 Due to crustaceans

995.63 Due to fruits and vegetables

995.64 Due to tree nuts and seeds
AHA: 1Q, '08, 12

995.65 Due to fish

995.66 Due to food additives

995.67 Due to milk products

995.68 Due to eggs

995.69 Due to other specified food

995.7 Other adverse food reactions, not elsewhere classified
Use additional code to identify the type of reaction, such as:
hives (708.0)
wheezing (786.07)
EXCLUDES *anaphylactic shock due to adverse food reaction (995.60-995.69)*
asthma (493.0, 493.9)
dermatitis due to food (693.1)
in contact with skin (692.5)
gastroenteritis and colitis due to food (558.3)
rhinitis due to food (477.1)

√5th **995.8 Other specified adverse effects, not elsewhere classified**

995.80 Adult maltreatment, unspecified   A
Abused person NOS
Use additional code to identify:
any associated injury
perpetrator (E967.0-E967.9)
AHA: 4Q, '96, 41, 43

995.81 Adult physical abuse   A
Battered:
person syndrome NEC
man
spouse
woman
Use additional code to identify:
any association injury
nature of abuse (E960-E968)
perpetrator (E967.0-E967.9)
AHA: 4Q, '96, 42, 43

995.82 Adult emotional/psychological abuse   A
Use additional E code to identify perpetrator (E967.0-E967.9)

995.83 Adult sexual abuse   A
Use additional code(s) to identify:
any associated injury
perpetrator (E967.0-E967.9)

995.84 Adult neglect (nutritional)   A
Use additional code(s) to identify:
intent of neglect (E904.0, E968.4)
perpetrator (E967.0-E967.9)

Continuum of Illness Due to Infection

Bacteremia ➡ Septicemia ➡ Sepsis
Severe Sepsis with Septic Shock ⬅ Severe Sepsis ⬅ Severe Sepsis

⬇

MODS (Multiple Organ Dysfunction Syndrome) ➡ Death

995.85 Other adult abuse and neglect   A
Multiple forms of abuse and neglect
Use additional code(s) to identify
any associated injury
intent of neglect (E904.0, E968.4)
nature of abuse (E960-E968)
perpetrator (E967.0-E967.9)

995.86 Malignant hyperthermia
Malignant hyperpyrexia due to anesthesia
AHA: 4Q, '98, 51

995.89 Other
Hypothermia due to anesthesia
AHA: 2Q, '04, 18; 3Q, '03, 12

√5th **995.9 Systemic inflammatory response syndrome (SIRS)**
DEF: Clinical response to infection or trauma that can trigger an acute inflammatory reaction and progresses to coagulation, impaired fibrinolysis, and organ failure; manifested by two or more of the following symptoms: fever, tachycardia, tachypnea, leukocytosis or leukopenia.
AHA: 4Q, '06, 113-116; 2Q, '04, 16; 4Q, '02, 71
TIP: Coding these conditions requires a minimum of two codes: the underlying cause (e.g., Infection or trauma) is sequenced first, followed by a code from subcategory 995.9.

995.90 Systemic inflammatory response syndrome, unspecified
SIRS NOS

995.91 Sepsis
Systemic inflammatory response syndrome due to infectious process without acute organ dysfunction
Code first underlying infection
EXCLUDES *sepsis with acute organ dysfunction (995.92)*
sepsis with multiple organ dysfunction (995.92)
severe sepsis (995.92)
AHA: 4Q, '08, 72; 4Q, '07, 86; 4Q, '06, 113-116; 2Q, '04, 16; 4Q, '03, 79

995.92 Severe sepsis
Sepsis with acute organ dysfunction
Sepsis with multiple organ dysfunction (MOD)
Systemic inflammatory response syndrome due to infectious process with acute organ dysfunction
Code first underlying infection
Use additional code to specify acute organ dysfunction, such as:
acute ▶kidney◀ failure (584.5-584.9)
acute respiratory failure (518.81)
critical illness myopathy (359.81)
critical illness polyneuropathy (357.82)
disseminated intravascular coagulopathy [DIC] (286.6)
encephalopathy (348.31)
hepatic failure (570)
septic shock (785.52)
AHA: 4Q, '08, 99; 4Q, '07, 97; 4Q, '06, 113-116; 2Q, '05, 18-19; 1Q, '05, 7; 1Q, '05, 7; 2Q, '04, 16; 4Q, '03, 73, 79
R65.21 Severe sepsis with septic shock   I-10

√4th Additional Digit Required   Unspecified Code   Other Specified Code   Manifestation Code   ▶◀ Revised Text   ● New Code   ▲ Revised Code Title

2010 ICD-9-CM   **October 2009 · Volume 1 – 317**

995.93 Systemic inflammatory response syndrome due to noninfectious process without acute organ dysfunction

Code first underlying conditions, such as:
acute pancreatitis (577.0)
trauma

> *EXCLUDES* *systemic inflammatory response syndrome due to noninfectious process with acute organ dysfunction (995.94)*

AHA: 4Q, '06, 113-116

995.94 Systemic inflammatory response syndrome due to noninfectious process with acute organ dysfunction

Code first underlying conditions, such as:
acute pancreatitis (577.0)
trauma

Use additional code to specify acute organ dysfunction, such as:
acute ►kidney◄ failure (584.5-584.9)
acute respiratory failure (518.81)
critical illness myopathy (359.81)
critical illness polyneuropathy (357.82)
disseminated intravascular coagulopathy [DIC] syndrome (286.6)
encephalopathy (348.31)
hepatic failure (570)

> *EXCLUDES* *severe sepsis (995.92)*

AHA: 4Q, '06, 113-116; 4Q, '03, 79

COMPLICATIONS OF SURGICAL AND MEDICAL CARE, NOT ELSEWHERE CLASSIFIED (996-999)

> *EXCLUDES* *adverse effects of medicinal agents (001.0-799.9, 995.0-995.8)*
> *burns from local applications and irradiation (940.0-949.5)*
> *complications of:*
> *conditions for which the procedure was performed*
> *surgical procedures during abortion, labor, and delivery (630-676.9)*
> *poisoning and toxic effects of drugs and chemicals (960.0-989.9)*
> *postoperative conditions in which no complications are present, such as:*
> *artificial opening status (V44.0-V44.9)*
> *closure of external stoma (V55.0-V55.9)*
> *fitting of prosthetic device (V52.0-V52.9)*
> *specified complications classified elsewhere*
> *anesthetic shock (995.4)*
> *electrolyte imbalance (276.0-276.9)*
> *postlaminectomy syndrome (722.80-722.83)*
> *postmastectomy lymphedema syndrome (457.0)*
> *postoperative psychosis (293.0-293.9)*
> *any other condition classified elsewhere in the Alphabetic Index when described as due to a procedure*

✓4ᵗʰ 996 Complications peculiar to certain specified procedures

> INCLUDES complications, not elsewhere classified, in the use of artificial substitutes [e.g., Dacron, metal, Silastic, Teflon] or natural sources [e.g., bone] involving:
> anastomosis (internal)
> graft (bypass) (patch)
> implant
> internal device:
> catheter
> electronic
> fixation
> prosthetic
> reimplant
> transplant

> *EXCLUDES* *accidental puncture or laceration during procedure (998.2)*
> *capsular contracture of breast implant (611.83)*
> *complications of internal anastomosis of:*
> *gastrointestinal tract (997.4)*
> *urinary tract (997.5)*
> *endosseous dental implant failures (525.71-525.79)*
> *intraoperative floppy iris syndrome [IFIS] (364.81)*
> *mechanical complication of respirator (V46.14)*
> *other specified complications classified elsewhere, such as:*
> *hemolytic anemia (283.1)*
> *functional cardiac disturbances (429.4)*
> *serum hepatitis (070.2-070.3)*

AHA: 1Q, '94, 3

✓5ᵗʰ 996.0 Mechanical complication of cardiac device, implant, and graft

Breakdown (mechanical) Obstruction, mechanical
Displacement   Perforation
Leakage   Protrusion

AHA: 2Q, '08, 9; 2Q, '93, 9

TIP: If the documentation indicates that the cardiac device (e.g., pacemaker, heart valve prosthesis) has reached its normally occurring end of life, do not assign a complication code; see instead subcategory V53.3.

996.00 Unspecified device, implant, and graft

996.01 Due to cardiac pacemaker (electrode)

AHA: 2Q, '06, 15; 2Q, '99, 11

T82.120A Displacement cardiac electrode [I-10] initial encounter

996.02 Due to heart valve prosthesis

996.03 Due to coronary bypass graft

> *EXCLUDES* *atherosclerosis of graft (414.02, 414.03)*
> *embolism [occlusion NOS] [thrombus] of graft (996.72)*

AHA: 2Q, '95, 17; N-D, '86, 5

996.04 Due to automatic implantable cardiac defibrillator

AHA: 2Q, '05, 3

996.09 Other

AHA: 2Q, '93, 9

996.1   Mechanical complication of other vascular device, implant, and graft

Mechanical complications involving:
    aortic (bifurcation) graft (replacement)
    arteriovenous:
        dialysis catheter }
        fistula   } surgically created
        shunt   }
    balloon (counterpulsation) device, intra-aortic
    carotid artery bypass graft
    femoral-popliteal bypass graft
    umbrella device, vena cava

> **EXCLUDES** atherosclerosis of biological graft
> (440.30-440.32)
> embolism [occlusion NOS] [thrombus] of
> (biological) (synthetic) graft (996.74)
> peritoneal dialysis catheter (996.56)

AHA: 1Q, '06, 10; 2Q, '05, 8; 1Q, '02, 13; 1Q, '95, 3

TIP: Assign for a nonmaturing AV fistula and also for postprocedural reduction in transjugular intrahepatic portosystemic shunt flow in a patient with a TIPS catheter.

T82.330A Leakage aortic bifurcation graft initial enc `I-10`

996.2   Mechanical complication of nervous system device, implant, and graft

Mechanical complications involving:
    dorsal column stimulator
    electrodes implanted in brain [brain "pacemaker"]
    peripheral nerve graft
    ventricular (communicating) shunt

AHA: 2Q, '99, 4; S-O, '87, 10

√5ᵗʰ 996.3   Mechanical complication of genitourinary device, implant, and graft

AHA: 3Q, '01, 13; S-O, '85, 3

996.30   Unspecified device, implant, and graft

996.31   Due to urethral [indwelling] catheter

996.32   Due to intrauterine contraceptive device ♀

996.39   Other

Cystostomy catheter
Prosthetic reconstruction of vas deferens
Repair (graft) of ureter without mention of resection

> **EXCLUDES** complications due to:
> external stoma of urinary tract
> (997.5)
> internal anastomosis of urinary
> tract (997.5)

√5ᵗʰ 996.4   Mechanical complication of internal orthopedic device, implant, and graft

Mechanical complications involving:
    external (fixation) device utilizing internal screw(s), pin(s) or other methods of fixation
    grafts of bone, cartilage, muscle, or tendon
    internal (fixation) device such as nail, plate, rod, etc.

Use additional code to identify prosthetic joint with mechanical complication (V43.60-V43.69)

> **EXCLUDES** complications of external orthopedic device,
> such as:
> pressure ulcer due to cast (707.00-707.09)

AHA: 4Q, '05, 91; 2Q, '99, 10; 2Q, '98, 19; 2Q, '96, 11; 3Q, '95, 16; N-D, '85, 11

TIP: Since these codes may be used for any joint device complications, assign an additional code from subcategory V43.6 to specify the joint involved.

996.40   Unspecified mechanical complication of internal orthopedic device, implant, and graft

996.41   Mechanical loosening of prosthetic joint
Aseptic loosening

AHA: 4Q, '05, 112

T84.031A Mech loosening int lt hip prosth jnt initial enc `I-10`

996.42   Dislocation of prosthetic joint
Instability of prosthetic joint
Subluxation of prosthetic joint

T84.020D Displacment internal right hip prosth `I-10`
subsqt enc

996.43   Broken prosthetic joint implant
Breakage (fracture) of prosthetic joint

996.44   Peri-prosthetic fracture around prosthetic joint

AHA: 4Q, '05, 93

996.45   Peri-prosthetic osteolysis
Use additional code to identify major osseous defect, if applicable (731.3)

AHA: 4Q, '06, 103

996.46   Articular bearing surface wear of prosthetic joint

996.47   Other mechanical complication of prosthetic joint implant
Mechanical complication of prosthetic joint NOS
►Prosthetic joint implant failure NOS◄

996.49   Other mechanical complication of other internal orthopedic device, implant, and graft
Breakage of internal fixation device in bone
Dislocation of internal fixation device in bone

> **EXCLUDES** mechanical complication of
> prosthetic joint implant
> (996.41-996.47)

√5ᵗʰ 996.5   Mechanical complication of other specified prosthetic device, implant, and graft

Mechanical complications involving:
    prosthetic implant in:
        bile duct
        breast
        chin
        orbit of eye
    nonabsorbable surgical material NOS
    other graft, implant, and internal device, not elsewhere classified

AHA: 1Q, '98, 11

996.51   Due to corneal graft

996.52   Due to graft of other tissue, not elsewhere classified

> **EXCLUDES** failure of artificial skin graft (996.55)
> failure of decellularized allodermis
> (996.55)
> sloughing of temporary skin
> allografts or xenografts
> (pigskin)–omit code

AHA: 1Q, '96, 10

996.53   Due to ocular lens prosthesis

> **EXCLUDES** contact lenses–code to condition

AHA: 1Q, '00, 9

996.54   Due to breast prosthesis
Breast capsule (prosthesis)
Mammary implant

AHA: 2Q, '98, 14; 3Q, '92, 4

TIP: If documentation indicates capsular contracture of breast implant, see instead code 611.83.

996.55   Due to artificial skin graft and decellularized allodermis
Dislodgement
Displacement
Failure
Non-adherence
Poor incorporation
Shearing

AHA: 4Q, '98, 52

996.56   Due to peritoneal dialysis catheter

> **EXCLUDES** mechanical complication of
> arteriovenous dialysis catheter
> (996.1)

AHA: 4Q, '98, 54

√4ᵗʰ Additional Digit Required   Unspecified Code   Other Specified Code   Manifestation Code   ►◄ Revised Text   ● New Code   ▲ Revised Code Title

2010 ICD-9-CM   **October 2009 • Volume 1 – 319**

996.1–996.56

Injury and Poisoning

996.57–996.75

996.57 Due to insulin pump
AHA: 4Q, '03, 81-82

996.59 Due to other implant and internal device, not elsewhere classified
Nonabsorbable surgical material NOS
Prosthetic implant in:
    bile duct
    chin
    orbit of eye
AHA: 2Q, '99, 13; 3Q, '94, 7
TIP: Assign for clogged biliary stent and also for nonfunctioning pressure equalization (PE) tubes.

✓5ᵗʰ **996.6 Infection and inflammatory reaction due to internal prosthetic device, implant, and graft**
Infection (causing   ⎫ due to (presence of) any device,
  obstruction)   ⎬   implant, and graft
Inflammation   ⎭ classifiable to 996.0-996.5

Use additional code to identify specified infections
AHA: 2Q, '89, 16; J-F, '87, 14

996.60 Due to unspecified device, implant, and graft

996.61 Due to cardiac device, implant, and graft
Cardiac pacemaker or defibrillator:
    electrode(s), lead(s)
    pulse generator
    subcutaneous pocket
Coronary artery bypass graft
Heart valve prosthesis

996.62 Due to other vascular device, implant, and graft
Arterial graft
Arteriovenous fistula or shunt
Infusion pump
Vascular catheter (arterial) (dialysis) (peripheral venous)

> **EXCLUDES**   infection due to:
>   *central venous catheter (999.31)*
>   *Hickman catheter (999.31)*
>   *peripherally inserted central cathe-*
>   *ter [PICC] (999.31)*
>   *portacath (port-a-cath) (999.31)*
>   *triple lumen catheter (999.31)*
>   *umbilical venous catheter (999.31)*

AHA: 4Q, '07, 86; 2Q, '04, 16; 1Q, '04, 5; 4Q, '03, 107, 111; 2Q, '03, 7; 2Q, '94, 13
T82.7xxA Inf & inflam react oth card vasc dev gft initial enc   `I-10`

996.63 Due to nervous system device, implant, and graft
Electrodes implanted in brain
Peripheral nerve graft
Spinal canal catheter
Ventricular (communicating) shunt (catheter)

996.64 Due to indwelling urinary catheter
Use additional code to identify specified infections, such as:
    cystitis (595.0-595.9)
    sepsis (038.0-038.9)
AHA: 3Q, '93, 6
T83.51xD Inf & inflam react indwll urinary cath subsq enc   `I-10`

996.65 Due to other genitourinary device implant, and graft
Intrauterine contraceptive device
AHA: 1Q, '00, 15

996.66 Due to internal joint prosthesis
Use additional code to identify infected prosthetic joint (V43.60-V43.69)
AHA: 2Q, '08, 3-5; 2Q, '07, 7; 4Q, '05, 91, 113; 2Q, '91, 18
TIP: Do not assign for the second admission of a staged procedure whereby the infected prosthesis has been previously removed and the patient now returns for placement of a new prosthesis; see instead codes from category 736.
T84.51xA Inf & inflam reaction int rt hip pros initial enc   `I-10`

996.67 Due to other internal orthopedic device, implant, and graft
Bone growth stimulator (electrode)
Internal fixation device (pin) (rod) (screw)

996.68 Due to peritoneal dialysis catheter
Exit-site infection or inflammation
AHA: 4Q, '98, 54

996.69 Due to other internal prosthetic device, implant, and graft
Breast prosthesis
Ocular lens prosthesis
Prosthetic orbital implant
AHA: 2Q, '08, 11; 4Q, '03, 108; 4Q, '98, 52

✓5ᵗʰ **996.7 Other complications of internal (biological) (synthetic) prosthetic device, implant, and graft**
Complication NOS   ⎫
Occlusion NOS   ⎪
Embolism   ⎪ due to (presence of) any device,
Fibrosis   ⎬   implant, and graft
Hemorrhage   ⎪ classifiable to 996.0-996.5
Pain   ⎪
Stenosis   ⎪
Thrombus   ⎭

Use additional code to identify complication, such as: pain due to presence of device, implant or graft (338.18-338.19, 338.28-338.29)
▶venous embolism and thrombosis (453.2-453.9)◀

> **EXCLUDES**   *disruption (dehiscence) of internal suture*
>   *material (998.31)*
>   *transplant rejection (996.8)*

AHA: 2Q, '07, 12; 4Q, '05, 94; 1Q, '89, 9; N-D, '86, 5

996.70 Due to unspecified device, implant, and graft

996.71 Due to heart valve prosthesis

996.72 Due to other cardiac device, implant, and graft
Cardiac pacemaker or defibrillator:
    electrode(s), lead(s)
    subcutaneous pocket
Coronary artery bypass (graft)

> **EXCLUDES**   *occlusion due to atherosclerosis*
>   *(414.02-414.06)*

AHA: 3Q, '08, 10; 3Q, '06, 8, 25; 3Q, '01, 20
TIP: Assign for in-stent stenosis of previously placed coronary artery stent.
T82.847A Pain cardiac prosth devc impl graft initial enc   `I-10`

996.73 Due to renal dialysis device, implant, and graft
AHA: 2Q, '91, 18
T82.858A Stenosis vasc prosth devc impl graft initial enc   `I-10`

996.74 Due to other vascular device, implant, and graft

> **EXCLUDES**   *occlusion of biological graft due to*
>   *atherosclerosis*
>   *(440.30-440.32)*

AHA: 1Q, '03, 16, 17

996.75 Due to nervous system device, implant, and graft

Ⓝ Newborn Age: 0   Ⓟ Pediatric Age: 0-17   Ⓜ Maternity Age: 12-55   Ⓐ Adult Age: 15-124

996.76   **Due to genitourinary device, implant, and graft**
     AHA: ▶1Q, '09, 15;◀ 1Q, '00, 15
     T83.83xA Hemorrhage GU prosth devc impl graft initial enc   `I-10`

996.77   **Due to internal joint prosthesis**
     Use additional code to identify prosthetic joint (V43.60-V43.69)
     AHA: 4Q, '05, 91
     T84.84xA Pain int ortho prosth devc impl gft initial enc   `I-10`

996.78   **Due to other internal orthopedic device, implant, and graft**
     AHA: 2Q, '03, 14

996.79   **Due to other internal prosthetic device, implant, and graft**
     AHA: 2Q, '04, 7; 1Q,'01, 8; 3Q, '95, 14; 3Q, '92, 4

√5ᵗʰ   **996.8**   **Complications of transplanted organ**
     Transplant failure or rejection
     Use additional code to identify nature of complication, such as:
       cytomegalovirus (CMV) infection (078.5)
       graft-versus-host disease (279.50-279.53)
       malignancy associated with organ transplant (199.2)
       post-transplant lymphoproliferative disorder (PTLD) (238.77)
     AHA: 4Q, '08, 82-83; 3Q, '01, 12; 3Q, '93, 3, 4; 2Q, '93, 11; 1Q, '93, 24
     TIP: Assign only if the complication affects the function of the transplanted organ. Assign also a code for the specific complication.

996.80   **Transplanted organ, unspecified**

996.81   **Kidney**
     AHA: 4Q, '08, 83; 3Q, '03, 16; 3Q, '98, 6, 7; 3Q, '94, 8; 2Q, '94, 9; 1Q, '93, 24
     TIP: Do not assign for chronic kidney disease (CKD) status following kidney transplant. The provider must indicate transplant failure, rejection, or other complication to support assignment of this code.
     T86.11 Kidney transplant rejection   `I-10`

996.82   **Liver**
     AHA: 4Q, '08, 82, 99; 3Q, '03, 17; 3Q, '98, 3, 4

996.83   **Heart**
     AHA: 3Q, '03, 16; 4Q, '02, 53; 3Q, '98, 5

996.84   **Lung**
     AHA: 2Q, '03, 12; 3Q, '98, 5

996.85   **Bone marrow**
     AHA: 4Q, '08, 91; 4Q, '90, 4

996.86   **Pancreas**

996.87   **Intestine**

996.89   **Other specified transplanted organ**
     AHA: 3Q, '94, 5

√5ᵗʰ   **996.9**   **Complications of reattached extremity or body part**

996.90   **Unspecified extremity**

996.91   **Forearm**

996.92   **Hand**

996.93   **Finger(s)**

996.94   **Upper extremity,** other and unspecified

996.95   **Foot and toe(s)**

996.96   **Lower extremity,** other and unspecified

996.99   **Other specified body part**

√4ᵗʰ   **997**   **Complications affecting specified body systems, not elsewhere classified**
     Use additional code to identify complications
     EXCLUDES   the listed conditions when specified as:
       causing shock (998.0)
       complications of:
         anesthesia:
           adverse effect (001.0-799.9, 995.0-995.8)
           in labor or delivery (668.0-668.9)
           poisoning (968.0-969.9)
         implanted device or graft (996.0-996.9)
         obstetrical procedures (669.0-669.4)
         reattached extremity (996.90-996.96)
         transplanted organ (996.80-996.89)
     AHA: 1Q, '94, 4; 1Q, '93, 26

√5ᵗʰ   **997.0**   **Nervous system complications**

997.00   **Nervous system complication, unspecified**

997.01   **Central nervous system complication**
     Anoxic brain damage
     Cerebral hypoxia
     EXCLUDES   cerebrovascular hemorrhage or infarction (997.02)
     AHA: 1Q, '07, 22; 1Q, '06, 15
     TIP: Assign for hyperperfusion syndrome, a complication of carotid endarterectomy.

997.02   **Iatrogenic cerebrovascular infarction or hemorrhage**
     Postoperative stroke
     AHA: 3Q, '06, 6; 2Q, '04, 8; 4Q, '95, 57
     TIP: Assign an additional code to specify the type of postoperative stroke involved.
     I97.810 Intraop cerebrvascular infarct during card surg   `I-10`

997.09   **Other nervous system complications**
     G97.0 Cerebrospinal fluid leak from spinal puncture   `I-10`

997.1   **Cardiac complications**
     Cardiac:
       arrest
       insufficiency   }   during or resulting from a procedure
     Cardiorespiratory failure
     Heart failure
     EXCLUDES   the listed conditions as long-term effects of cardiac surgery or due to the presence of cardiac prosthetic device (429.4)
     AHA: 4Q, '08, 179; 2Q, '02, 12
     I97.711 Intraoperative cardiac arrest during oth surgery   `I-10`

997.2   **Peripheral vascular complications**
     Phlebitis or thrombophlebitis during or resulting from a procedure
     EXCLUDES   the listed conditions due to:
       implant or catheter device (996.62)
       infusion, perfusion, or transfusion (999.2)
       complications affecting blood vessels (997.71-997.79)
     AHA: 1Q, '03, 6; 3Q, '02, 24-26
     T81.72xA Complication of vein following a procedure NEC init. enc   `I-10`

√4ᵗʰ √5ᵗʰ   Additional Digit Required   Unspecified Code   Other Specified Code   Manifestation Code   ▶◀ Revised Text   ● New Code   ▲ Revised Code Title

2010 ICD-9-CM   **October 2009 • Volume 1 – 321**

Injury and Poisoning

997.3–997.99

✓5ᵗʰ **997.3 Respiratory complications**

> **EXCLUDES** *iatrogenic [postoperative] pneumothorax (512.1)*
> *iatrogenic pulmonary embolism (415.11)*
> *Mendelson's syndrome in labor and delivery (668.0)*
> *specified complications classified elsewhere, such as:*
>   *adult respiratory distress syndrome (518.5)*
>   *pulmonary edema, postoperative (518.4)*
>   *respiratory insufficiency, acute, postoperative (518.5)*
>   *shock lung (518.5)*
>   *tracheostomy complications (519.00-519.09)*
>   *transfusion related acute lung injury [TRALI] (518.7)*

> **AHA:** 1Q, '97, 10; 2Q, '93, 3; 2Q, '93, 9; 4Q, '90, 25

997.31 Ventilator associated pneumonia
> ▶Ventilator associated pneumonitis◀
> Use additional code to identify organism
> **AHA:** 4Q, '08, 148-149
> **TIP:** Do not assign unless the provider has documented the relationship between the pneumonia and ventilation status.

997.39 Other respiratory complications
> Mendelson's syndrome resulting from a procedure
> Pneumonia (aspiration) resulting from a procedure
> **DEF:** Mendelson's syndrome: acid pneumonitis due to aspiration of gastric acids, may occur after anesthesia or sedation.
> **J95.4** Chem pneumonitis d/t anesthesia [Mendelson syndrm]   I-10

997.4 Digestive system complications
> Complications of:
>   intestinal (internal) anastomosis and bypass, not elsewhere classified, except that involving urinary tract
> Hepatic failure ⎫
> Hepatorenal syndrome ⎬ *specified as due to a*
> Intestinal obstruction NOS ⎭ *procedure*

> **EXCLUDES** *gastrostomy complications (536.40-536.49)*
> *specified gastrointestinal complications classified elsewhere, such as:*
>   *blind loop syndrome (579.2)*
>   *colostomy and enterostomy complications (569.60-569.69)*
>   ▶*complications of intestinal pouch (569.71-569.79)*◀
>   *gastrojejunal ulcer (534.0-534.9)*
>   *infection of esophagostomy (530.86)*
>   *infection of external stoma (569.61)*
>   *mechanical complication of esophagostomy (530.87)*
>   *pelvic peritoneal adhesions, female (614.6)*
>   *peritoneal adhesions (568.0)*
>   *peritoneal adhesions with obstruction (560.81)*
>   *postcholecystectomy syndrome (576.0)*
>   *postgastric surgery syndromes (564.2)*
>   ▶*pouchitis (569.71)*◀
>   *vomiting following gastrointestinal surgery (564.3)*

> **AHA:** 2Q, '01, 4-6; 3Q, '99, 4; 2Q, '99, 14; 3Q, '97, 7; 1Q, '97, 11; 2Q, '95, 7; 1Q, '93, 26; 3Q, '92, 15; 2Q, '89, 15; 1Q, '88, 14
> **K91.3** Postprocedural intestinal obstruction   I-10

997.5 Urinary complications
> Complications of:
>   external stoma of urinary tract
>   internal anastomosis and bypass of urinary tract, including that involving intestinal tract

> Oliguria or anuria ⎫
> Renal ▶(kidney):◀ ⎬ *specified as due to*
>   failure (acute) ⎬ *procedure*
>   insufficiency (acute) ⎬
> Tubular necrosis (acute) ⎭

> **EXCLUDES** *specified complications classified elsewhere, such as:*
> *postoperative stricture of:*
>   *ureter (593.3)*
>   *urethra (598.2)*

> **AHA:** 3Q, '03, 13; 3Q, '96, 10, 15; 4Q, '95, 73; 1Q, '92, 13; 2Q, '89, 16; M-A, '87, 10; S-O, '85, 3
> **TIP:** If a urinary tract infection is specified as a postoperative complication, assign both 997.5 and 599.0.
> **N99.0** Postprocedural (acute) (chronic) renal failure   I-10

✓5ᵗʰ **997.6 Amputation stump complication**
> **EXCLUDES** *admission for treatment for a current traumatic amputation–code to complicated traumatic amputation phantom limb (syndrome) (353.6)*

> **AHA:** 4Q, '95, 82

997.60 Unspecified complication

997.61 Neuroma of amputation stump
> **DEF:** Hyperplasia generated nerve cell mass following amputation.

997.62 Infection (chronic)
> Use additional code to identify the organism
> **AHA:** 1Q, '05, 15 4Q, '96, 46
> **TIP:** If cellulitis is specified as a manifestation of the infection, assign an additional code from category 681 or 682.
> **T87.43** Infection amputation stump right lower extremity   I-10

997.69 Other
> **AHA:** 1Q, '05, 15

✓5ᵗʰ **997.7 Vascular complications of other vessels**
> **EXCLUDES** *peripheral vascular complications (997.2)*

997.71 Vascular complications of mesenteric artery
> **AHA:** 4Q, '01, 53
> **TIP:** For postoperative mesenteric artery embolism, assign also code 557.0 Acute vascular insufficiency of intestine.

997.72 Vascular complications of renal artery

997.79 Vascular complications of other vessels

✓5ᵗʰ **997.9 Complications affecting other specified body systems, not elsewhere classified**
> **EXCLUDES** *specified complications classified elsewhere, such as:*
> *broad ligament laceration syndrome (620.6)*
> *postartificial menopause syndrome (627.4)*
> *postoperative stricture of vagina (623.2)*

997.91 Hypertension
> **EXCLUDES** *essential hypertension (401.0-401.9)*
> **AHA:** 4Q, '95, 57

997.99 Other
> Vitreous touch syndrome
> **DEF:** Vitreous touch syndrome: vitreous protruding through pupil and attaches to corneal epithelium; causes aqueous fluid in vitreous body; marked by corneal edema, loss of lucidity; complication of cataract surgery.
> **AHA:** 2Q, '94, 12; 1Q, '94, 17

Ⓝ Newborn Age: 0   Ⓟ Pediatric Age: 0-17   Ⓜ Maternity Age: 12-55   Ⓐ Adult Age: 15-124

✓4th 998 Other complications of procedures, not elsewhere classified
AHA: 1Q, '94, 4

998.0 Postoperative shock
Collapse NOS
Shock (endotoxic)
(hypovolemic septic) } during or resulting from a surgical procedure

EXCLUDES shock:
anaphylactic due to serum (999.4)
anesthetic (995.4)
electric (994.8)
following abortion (639.5)
obstetric (669.1)
traumatic (958.4)

✓5th 998.1 Hemorrhage or hematoma or seroma complicating a procedure
EXCLUDES hemorrhage, hematoma, or seroma:
complicating cesarean section or puerperal perineal wound (674.3)
due to implanted device or graft (996.70-996.79)

998.11 Hemorrhage complicating a procedure
AHA: 3Q, '03, 13; 1Q, '03, 4; 4Q, '97, 52; 1Q, '97, 10
I97.410 Intraop hemorrhage circ sys organ comp card cath I-10

998.12 Hematoma complicating a procedure
AHA: 3Q, '06, 12; 1Q, '03, 6; 3Q, '02, 24, 26

998.13 Seroma complicating a procedure
AHA: 4Q, '96, 46; 1Q, '93, 26; 2Q, '92, 15; S-O, '87, 8

998.2 Accidental puncture or laceration during a procedure
Accidental perforation by catheter or other instrument during a procedure on:
blood vessel
nerve
organ

EXCLUDES iatrogenic [postoperative] pneumothorax (512.1)
puncture or laceration caused by implanted device intentionally left in operation wound (996.0-996.5)
specified complications classified elsewhere, such as:
broad ligament laceration syndrome (620.6)
dural tear (349.31)
incidental durotomy (349.31)
trauma from instruments during delivery (664.0-665.9)

AHA: 2Q, '07, 9; 1Q, '06, 15; 3Q, '02, 24, 26; 3Q, '94, 6; 3Q, '90, 17; 3Q, '90, 18
I97.51 Accidentl punct lac circ sys organ dur circ proc I-10

✓5th 998.3 Disruption of wound
Dehiscence
Rupture } of operation wound
Disruption of any suture materials or other closure method

EXCLUDES disruption of:
cesarean wound (674.1)
perineal wound, puerperal (674.2)

AHA: 4Q, '08, 149-152; 4Q, '02, 73; 1Q, '93, 19

998.30 Disruption of wound, unspecified
Disruption of wound NOS

998.31 Disruption of internal operation (surgical) wound
Disruption or dehiscence of closure of:
fascia, superficial or muscular
internal organ
muscle or muscle flap
ribs or rib cage
skull or craniotomy
sternum or sternotomy
tendon or ligament
Deep disruption or dehiscence of operation wound NOS

EXCLUDES complications of internal anastomosis of:
gastrointestinal tract (997.4)
urinary tract (997.5)

998.32 Disruption of external operation (surgical) wound
Disruption of operation wound NOS
Disruption or dehiscence of closure of:
cornea
mucosa
skin
subcutaneous tissue
Full-thickness skin disruption or dehiscence
Superficial disruption or dehiscence of operation wound

AHA: 1Q, '06, 8; 1Q, '05, 11; 4Q, '03, 104, 106
T81.31xA Disruption ext operation wound NEC initial enc I-10

998.33 Disruption of traumatic injury wound repair
Disruption or dehiscence of closure of traumatic laceration (external) (internal)
AHA: 4Q, '08, 151, 152

998.4 Foreign body accidentally left during a procedure
Adhesions
Obstruction } due to foreign body accidentally left in operative wound or body cavity during a procedure
Perforation

EXCLUDES obstruction or perforation caused by implanted device intentionally left in body (996.0-996.5)

AHA: ▶1Q, '09,18◀ 1Q, '89, 9

✓5th 998.5 Postoperative infection
EXCLUDES bleb associated endophthalmitis (379.63)
infection due to:
implanted device (996.60-996.69)
infusion, perfusion, or transfusion (999.31-999.39)
postoperative obstetrical wound infection (674.3)

998.51 Infected postoperative seroma
Use additional code to identify organism
AHA: 4Q, '96, 46

998.59 Other postoperative infection
Abscess:
intra-abdominal
stitch } postoperative
subphrenic
wound
Septicemia
Use additional code to identify infection
AHA: 2Q, '06, 23; 4Q, '04, 76; 4Q, '03, 104, 106-107; 3Q, '98, 3; 3Q, '95, 5; 2Q, '95, 7; 3Q, '94, 6; 1Q, '93, 19; J-F, '87, 14

TIP: Do not assign if the infection is related to an internal prosthetic device, implant, or graft; see instead subcategory 996.6.

T81.4xxA Infection following procedure initial encounter I-10

998.6 Persistent postoperative fistula
AHA: J-F, '87, 14
T81.83xD Persistent postprocedural fistula subsequent enc I-10

Injury and Poisoning

998.7–999.6

998.7 Acute reaction to foreign substance accidentally left during a procedure
Peritonitis:
    aseptic
    chemical

√5th **998.8 Other specified complications of procedures, not elsewhere classified**
    AHA: 4Q, '94, 46; 1Q, '89, 9

    998.81 Emphysema (subcutaneous) (surgical) resulting from a procedure

    998.82 Cataract fragments in eye following cataract surgery

    998.83 Non-healing surgical wound
        AHA: 4Q, '96, 47

    998.89 Other specified complications
        AHA: ▶2Q, '09, 11;◀ 3Q, '06, 9; 3Q, '05, 16; 3Q, '99, 13; 2Q, '98, 16
        TIP: Assign for cases in which a procedure is performed on the wrong body site (e.g., right leg versus left leg), along with E876.5-E876.7.
        T81.89 Other complications of procedures NEC `I-10`

998.9 Unspecified complication of procedure, not elsewhere classified
Postoperative complication NOS
    EXCLUDES   complication NOS of obstetrical, surgery or procedure (669.4)
    AHA: 4Q, '93, 37

√4th **999 Complications of medical care, not elsewhere classified**
    INCLUDES   complications, not elsewhere classified, of:
        dialysis (hemodialysis) (peritoneal) (renal)
        extracorporeal circulation
        hyperalimentation therapy
        immunization
        infusion
        inhalation therapy
        injection
        inoculation
        perfusion
        transfusion
        vaccination
        ventilation therapy
    Use additional code, where applicable, to identify specific complication
    EXCLUDES   specified complications classified elsewhere such as:
        complications of implanted device (996.0-996.9)
        contact dermatitis due to drugs (692.3)
        dementia dialysis (294.8)
        transient (293.9)
        dialysis disequilibrium syndrome (276.0-276.9)
        poisoning and toxic effects of drugs and chemicals (960.0-989.9)
        postvaccinal encephalitis (323.51)
        water and electrolyte imbalance (276.0-276.9)

    999.0 Generalized vaccinia
        EXCLUDES   vaccinia not from vaccine (051.02)
        DEF: Skin eruption, self-limiting; follows vaccination; due to transient viremia with virus localized in skin.

    999.1 Air embolism
        Air embolism to any site following infusion, perfusion, or transfusion
        EXCLUDES   embolism specified as:
            complicating:
               abortion (634-638 with .6, 639.6)
               ectopic or molar pregnancy (639.6)
               pregnancy, childbirth, or the puerperium (673.0)
            due to implanted device (996.7)
            traumatic (958.0)

999.2 Other vascular complications
Phlebitis   ⎫
Thromboembolism   ⎬ following infusion, perfusion, or transfusion
Thrombophlebitis   ⎭
    EXCLUDES   extravasation of vesicant drugs (999.81, 999.82)
        the listed conditions when specified as:
            due to implanted device (996.61-996.62. 996.72-996.74)
            postoperative NOS (997.2, 997.71-997.79)
    AHA: 2Q, '97, 5
    TIP: Do not assign for IV infiltration; if the infiltration is severe enough to cause other complications, a code for the specific complication should be assigned. For chemotherapy extravasation, see code 999.81.
    T80.1xxA Vasc comp follw inf transfusn tx inj initial enc `I-10`

√5th **999.3 Other infection**
Infection   ⎫
Sepsis   ⎬ following infusion, injection, transfusion, or vaccination
Septicemia ⎭
Use additional code to identify the specified infection, such as:
    septicemia (038.0-038.9)
    EXCLUDES   the listed conditions when specified as:
        due to implanted device (996.60-996.69)
        postoperative NOS (998.51-998.59)
    AHA: 4Q, '07, 96; 2Q, '01, 11, 12; 2Q, '97, 5; J-F, '87, 14

    999.31 Infection due to central venous catheter
        Catheter-related bloodstream infection (CRBSI) NOS
        Infection due to:
            Hickman catheter
            peripherally inserted central catheter (PICC)
            portacath (port-a-cath)
            triple lumen catheter
            umbilical venous catheter
        EXCLUDES   infection due to:
            arterial catheter (996.62)
            catheter NOS (996.69)
            peripheral venous catheter (996.62)
            urinary catheter (996.64)
        AHA: 4Q, '08, 72, 193; 4Q, '07, 97
        T80.21xD Inf due to central venous cath subsequent enc `I-10`

    999.39 Infection following other infusion, injection, transfusion, or vaccination
        AHA: 4Q, '08, 99

999.4 Anaphylactic shock due to serum
Anaphylactic reaction due to serum
    EXCLUDES   shock:
        allergic NOS (995.0)
        anaphylactic:
            NOS (995.0)
            due to drugs and chemicals (995.0)
    DEF: Life-threatening hypersensitivity to foreign serum; causes respiratory distress, vascular collapse, and shock.

999.5 Other serum reaction
Intoxication by serum
Protein sickness
Serum rash
Serum sickness
Urticaria due to serum
    EXCLUDES   serum hepatitis (070.2-070.3)
    DEF: Serum sickness: Hypersensitivity to foreign serum; causes fever, hives, swelling, and lymphadenopathy.

999.6 ABO incompatibility reaction
Incompatible blood transfusion
Reaction to blood group incompatibility in infusion or transfusion
    EXCLUDES   ▶minor blood group antigens reactions (Duffy) (E) (K(ell)) (Kidd) (Lewis) (M) (N) (P) (S) (999.89)◀

N Newborn Age: 0   P Pediatric Age: 0-17   M Maternity Age: 12-55   A Adult Age: 15-124

999.7 **Rh incompatibility reaction**
       Elevation of Rh titer
       Reactions due to Rh factor in infusion or transfusion

✓5ᵗʰ 999.8 **Other infusion and transfusion reaction**
       EXCLUDES   postoperative shock (998.0)
                     transfusion related acute lung injury [TRALI]
                        (518.7)
       AHA: ▶4Q, '08, 152-155;◀ 3Q, '00, 9

       999.81 **Extravasation of vesicant chemotherapy**
               Infiltration of vesicant chemotherapy
               AHA: ▶4Q, '08, 155◀

       999.82 **Extravasation of other vesicant agent**
               Infiltration of other vesicant agent

       999.88 **Other infusion reaction**

       999.89 **Other transfusion reaction**
               Transfusion reaction NOS

               Use additional code to identify graft-versus-host
                   reaction (279.5)
               AHA: ▶4Q, '08, 99, 154◀

999.9 **Other and unspecified complications of medical care, not elsewhere classified**
       Complications, not elsewhere classified, of:
       electroshock
       inhalation   } therapy
       ultrasound
       ventilation
       Unspecified misadventure of medical care
       EXCLUDES   unspecified complication of:
                        phototherapy (990)
                        radiation therapy (999)
                        ventilator associated pneumonia (997.31)
       AHA: 3Q, '06, 25; 1Q, '03, 19; 2Q, '97, 5

SUPPLEMENTARY CLASSIFICATION OF FACTORS INFLUENCING HEALTH STATUS AND CONTACT WITH HEALTH SERVICES (V01-V89)

This classification is provided to deal with occasions when circumstances other than a disease or injury classifiable to categories 001-999 (the main part of ICD) are recorded as "diagnoses" or "problems." This can arise mainly in three ways:

a)   When a person who is not currently sick encounters the health services for some specific purpose, such as to act as a donor of an organ or tissue, to receive prophylactic vaccination, or to discuss a problem which is in itself not a disease or injury. This will be a fairly rare occurrence among hospital inpatients, but will be relatively more common among hospital outpatients and patients of family practitioners, health clinics, etc.

b)   When a person with a known disease or injury, whether it is current or resolving, encounters the health care system for a specific treatment of that disease or injury (e.g., dialysis for renal disease; chemotherapy for malignancy; cast change).

c)   When some circumstance or problem is present which influences the person's health status but is not in itself a current illness or injury. Such factors may be elicited during population surveys, when the person may or may not be currently sick, or be recorded as an additional factor to be borne in mind when the person is receiving care for some current illness or injury classifiable to categories 001-999.

In the latter circumstances the V code should be used only as a supplementary code and should not be the one selected for use in primary, single cause tabulations. Examples of these circumstances are a personal history of certain diseases, or a person with an artificial heart valve in situ.

AHA: J-F, '87, 8

PERSONS WITH POTENTIAL HEALTH HAZARDS RELATED TO COMMUNICABLE DISEASES (VO1-V06)

EXCLUDES *family history of infectious and parasitic diseases (V18.8)*
personal history of infectious and parasitic diseases (V12.0)

✓4th V01   Contact with or exposure to communicable diseases

TIP: Do not assign if the patient shows signs or symptoms of the disease to which he or she was exposed.

V01.0   Cholera
Conditions classifiable to 001

V01.1   Tuberculosis
Conditions classifiable to 010-018

V01.2   Poliomyelitis
Conditions classifiable to 045

V01.3   Smallpox
Conditions classifiable to 050

V01.4   Rubella
Conditions classifiable to 056

V01.5   Rabies
Conditions classifiable to 071

V01.6   Venereal diseases
Conditions classifiable to 090-099
AHA: 4Q, '07, 125

✓5th V01.7   Other viral diseases
Conditions classifiable to 042-078 and V08, except as above
AHA: 2Q, '92, 11

V01.71   Varicella

V01.79   Other viral diseases

✓5th V01.8   Other communicable diseases
Conditions classifiable to 001-136, except as above
AHA: J-A, '87, 24

V01.81   Anthrax
AHA: 4Q, '02, 70, 78

V01.82   Exposure to SARS-associated coronavirus
AHA: 4Q, '03, 46-47

V01.83   Escherichia coli (E. coli)

V01.84   Meningococcus
Z20.811 Contact with and exposure to meningococcus   ⌐I-10⌐

V01.89   Other communicable diseases

V01.9   Unspecified communicable diseases

✓4th V02   Carrier or suspected carrier of infectious diseases

INCLUDES   colonization status
AHA: 3Q, '95, 18; 3Q, '94, 4

V02.0   Cholera

V02.1   Typhoid

V02.2   Amebiasis

V02.3   Other gastrointestinal pathogens

V02.4   Diphtheria

✓5th V02.5   Other specified bacterial diseases

V02.51   Group B streptococcus
AHA: 3Q, '06, 14; 1Q, '02, 14; 4Q, '98, 56

V02.52   Other streptococcus

V02.53   Methicillin susceptible Staphylococcus aureus
MSSA colonization
AHA: ►4Q, '08, 69, 71, 156◄

V02.54   Methicillin resistant Staphylococcus aureus
MRSA colonization
AHA: ►4Q, '08, 69, 71, 72, 156◄

V02.59   Other specified bacterial diseases
Meningococcal
Staphylococcal

✓5th V02.6   Viral hepatitis
Hepatitis Australian-antigen [HAA] [SH] carrier
Serum hepatitis carrier

V02.60   Viral hepatitis carrier, unspecfied
AHA: 4Q, '97, 47

V02.61   Hepatitis B carrier
AHA: 4Q, '97, 47
Z22.51 Carrier of viral hepatitis B   ⌐I-10⌐

V02.62   Hepatitis C carrier
AHA: 4Q, '97, 47

V02.69   Other viral hepatitis carrier
AHA: 4Q, '97, 47

V02.7   Gonorrhea

V02.8   Other venereal diseases

V02.9   Other specified infectious organism
AHA: 3Q, '95, 18; 1Q, '93, 22; J-A, '87, 24

✓4th V03   Need for prophylactic vaccination and inoculation against bacterial diseases

EXCLUDES   *vaccination not carried out (V64.00-V64.09)*
vaccines against combinations of diseases (V06.0-V06.9)

V03.0   Cholera alone

V03.1   Typhoid-paratyphoid alone [TAB]

V03.2   Tuberculosis [BCG]

V03.3   Plague

V03.4   Tularemia

V03.5   Diphtheria alone

V03.6   Pertussis alone

V03.7   Tetanus toxoid alone

✓5th V03.8   Other specified vaccinations against single bacterial diseases

V03.81   Hemophilus influenza, type B [Hib]

V03.82   Streptococcus pneumoniae [pneumococcus]

V03.89   Other specified vaccination
AHA: 2Q, '00, 9
TIP: Assign for vaccination against Lyme disease.

V03.9   Unspecified single bacterial disease

√4ᵗʰ **V04 Need for prophylactic vaccination and inoculation against certain viral diseases**

> **EXCLUDES** *vaccines against combinations of diseases (V06.0-V06.9)*

V04.0 Poliomyelitis

V04.1 Smallpox

V04.2 Measles alone

V04.3 Rubella alone

V04.4 Yellow fever

V04.5 Rabies

V04.6 Mumps alone

V04.7 Common cold

√5ᵗʰ **V04.8** Other viral diseases

> AHA: 4Q, '03, 83

V04.81 Influenza

V04.82 Respiratory syncytial virus (RSV)

> AHA: ▶1Q, '09, 14◀

V04.89 Other viral diseases

> AHA: 2Q, '07, 9
>
> **TIP:** Assign for vaccination against human papilloma virus (HPV).

√4ᵗʰ **V05 Need for other prophylactic vaccination and inoculation against single diseases**

> **EXCLUDES** *vaccines against combinations of diseases (V06.0-V06.9)*

V05.0 Athropod-borne viral encephalitis

V05.1 Other arthropod-borne viral diseases

V05.2 Leshmaniasis

V05.3 Viral hepatitis

V05.4 Varicella

> Chickenpox

V05.8 Other specified disease

> AHA: 1Q, '01, 4; 3Q, '91, 20

V05.9 Unspecified single disease

√4ᵗʰ **V06 Need for prophylactic vaccination and inoculation against combinations of diseases**

> Note: Use additional single vaccination codes from categories V03-V05 to identify any vaccinations not included in a combination code.

V06.0 Cholera with typhoid-paratyphoid [cholera+TAB]

V06.1 Diphtheia-tetanus-pertussis, combined [DTP] [DTaP]

> AHA: 4Q, '03, 83; 3Q, '98, 13

V06.2 Diphtheria-tetanus-pertussis with typhoid-paratyphoid [DTP+TAB]

V06.3 Diphtheria-tetanus-pertussis with poliomyelitis [DTP+polio]

V06.4 Measles-mumps-rubella [MMR]

V06.5 Tetanus-diphtheria [Td] [DT]

> AHA: 4Q, '03, 83

V06.6 Streptococcus pneumoniae [pneumococcus] and influenza

V06.8 Other combinations

> **EXCLUDES** *multiple single vaccination codes (V03.0-V05.9)*
>
> AHA: 1Q, '94, 19

V06.9 Unspecified combined vaccine

PERSONS WITH NEED FOR ISOLATION, OTHER POTENTIAL HEALTH HAZARDS AND PROPHYLACTIC MEASURES (V07-V09)

√4ᵗʰ **V07 Need for isolation and other prophylactic measures**

> **EXCLUDES** *prophylactic organ removal (V50.41-V50.49)*

V07.0 Isolation

> Admission to protect the individual from his surroundings or for isolation of individual after contact with infectious diseases

V07.1 Desensitization to allergens

V07.2 Prophylactic immunotherapy

> Administration of:
> antivenin
> immune sera [gamma globulin]
> RhoGAM
> tetanus antitoxin

√5ᵗʰ **V07.3** Other prophylactic chemotherapy

V07.31 Prophylactic fluoride administration

V07.39 Other prophylactic chemotherapy

> **EXCLUDES** *maintenance chemotherapy following disease (V58.11)*

V07.4 Hormone replacement therapy (postmenopausal) SDx ♀

> **Z79.890** Hormone replacement therapy postmenopausal   I-10

√5ᵗʰ **V07.5** Prophylactic use of agents affecting estrogen receptors and estrogen levels

> Code first, if applicable:
> malignant neoplasm of breast (174.0-174.9, 175.0-175.9)
> malignant neoplasm of prostate (185)
>
> Use additional code, if applicable, to identify:
> estrogen receptor positive status (V86.0)
> family history of breast cancer (V16.3)
> genetic susceptibility to cancer (V84.01-V84.09)
> personal history of breast cancer (V10.3)
> personal history of prostate cancer (V10.46)
> postmenopausal status (V49.81)
>
> **EXCLUDES** *hormone replacement therapy (postmenopausal) (V07.4)*
>
> AHA: 4Q, '08, 156

V07.51 Prophylactic use of selective estrogen receptor modulators [SERMs]   SDx

> Prophylactic use of:
> raloxifene (Evista)
> tamoxifen (Nolvadex)
> toremifene (Fareston)
>
> **Z79.81** Long term (current) use agent affecting estrogen receptors   I-10

V07.52 Prophylactic use of aromatase inhibitors   SDx

> Prophylactic use of:
> anastrozole (Arimidex)
> ▶exemestane◀ (Aromasin)
> letrozole (Femara)

V07.59 Prophylactic use of other agents affecting estrogen receptors and estrogen levels   SDx

> Prophylactic use of:
> estrogen receptor downregulators
> fulvestrant (Faslodex)
> gonadotropin-releasing hormone (GnRH) agonist
> goserelin acetate (Zoladex)
> leuprolide acetate (leuprorelin) (Lupron)
> megestrol acetate (Megace)

V07.8 Other specified prophylactic measure

> AHA: 1Q, '92, 11
>
> **TIP:** Assign for patients having prophylactic breast removal because of a strong family history of breast cancer, along with code V16.3 Family history of breast cancer.

V07.9 Unspecified prophylactic measure

N Newborn Age: 0   P Pediatric Age: 0-17   M Maternity Age: 12-55   A Adult Age: 15-124   SDx Secondary Diagnosis   PDx Primary Diagnosis

V08 Asymptomatic human immunodeficiency virus [HIV] infection status

HIV positive NOS

Note: This code is only to be used when no HIV infection symptoms or conditions are present. If any HIV infection symptoms or conditions are present, see code 042.

> EXCLUDES   *AIDS (042)*
> *human immunodeficiency virus [HIV] disease (042)*
> *exposure to HIV (V01.79)*
> *nonspecific serologic evidence of HIV (795.71)*
> *symptomatic human immunodeficiency virus [HIV] infection (042)*

AHA: 2Q, '04, 11; 2Q, '99, 8; 3Q, '95, 18

Z21 Asymptomatic HIV infection status   I-10

√4ᵗʰ V09 Infection with drug-resistant microorganisms

Note: This category is intended for use as an additional code for infectious conditions classified elsewhere to indicate the presence of drug-resistance of the infectious organism.

AHA: 3Q, '94, 4; 4Q, '93, 22

V09.0 Infection with microorganisms resistant to penicillins   SDx

AHA: 2Q, '06, 16; 4Q, '03, 104, 106

V09.1 Infection with microorganisms resistant to cephalosporins and other B-lactam antibiotics   SDx

V09.2 Infection with microorganisms resistant to macrolides   SDx

V09.3 Infection with microorganisms resistant to tetracyclines   SDx

V09.4 Infection with microorganisms resistant to aminoglycosides   SDx

√5ᵗʰ V09.5 Infection with microorganisms resistant to quinolones and fluoroquinolones

V09.50 Without mention of resistance to multiple quinolones and fluoroquinoles   SDx

V09.51 With resistance to multiple quinolones and fluoroquinoles   SDx

V09.6 Infection with microorganisms resistant to sulfonamides   SDx

√5ᵗʰ V09.7 Infection with microorganisms resistant to other specified antimycobacterial agents

> EXCLUDES   *Amikacin (V09.4)*
> *Kanamycin (V09.4)*
> *Streptomycin [SM] (V09.4)*

V09.70 Without mention of resistance to multiple antimycobacterial agents   SDx

V09.71 With resistance to multiple antimycobacterial agents   SDx

√5ᵗʰ V09.8 Infection with microorganisms resistant to other specified drugs

Vancomycin (glycopeptide) intermediate staphylococcus aureus (VISA/GISA)
Vancomycin (glycopeptide) resistant enterococcus (VRE)
Vancomycin (glycopeptide) resistant staphylococcus aureus (VRSA/GRSA)

V09.80 Without mention of resistance to multiple drugs   SDx

V09.81 With resistance to multiple drugs   SDx

√5ᵗʰ V09.9 Infection with drug-resistant microorganisms, unspecified

Drug resistance, NOS

V09.90 Without mention of multiple drug resistance   SDx

Z16 Infection with drug resistant microorganisms   I-10

V09.91 With multiple drug resistance   SDx

Multiple drug resistance NOS

PERSONS WITH POTENTIAL HEALTH HAZARDS RELATED TO PERSONAL AND FAMILY HISTORY (V10-V19)

> EXCLUDES   *obstetric patients where the possibility that the fetus might be affected is the reason for observation or management during pregnancy (655.0-655.9)*

AHA: J-F, '87, 1

√4ᵗʰ V10 Personal history of malignant neoplasm

AHA: 4Q, '02, 80; 4Q, '98, 69; 1Q, '95, 4; 3Q, '92, 5; M-J, '85, 10; 2Q, '90, 9

TIP: Assign the codes in this category only for a personal history of primary malignancy (not metastatic malignancies).

√5ᵗʰ V10.0 Gastrointestinal tract

History of conditions classifiable to 140-159

> EXCLUDES   ▶ *personal history of malignant carcinoid tumor (V10.91)*
> *personal history of malignant neuroendocrine tumor (V10.91)* ◀

V10.00 Gastrointestinal tract, unspecified

V10.01 Tongue

V10.02 Other and unspecified oral cavity and pharynx

V10.03 Esophagus

V10.04 Stomach

V10.05 Large intestine

Z85.03 Personal hx prim malig neoplasm large intestine   I-10

AHA: 3Q, '99, 7; 1Q, '95, 4

V10.06 Rectum, rectosigmoid junction, and anus

V10.07 Liver

V10.09 Other

AHA: 4Q, '03, 111

√5ᵗʰ V10.1 Trachea, bronchus, and lung

History of conditions classifiable to 162

> EXCLUDES   ▶ *personal history of malignant carcinoid tumor (V10.91)*
> *personal history of malignant neuroendocrine tumor (V10.91)* ◀

V10.11 Bronchus and lung

V10.12 Trachea

√5ᵗʰ V10.2 Other respiratory and intrathoracic organs

History of conditions classifiable to 160, 161, 163-165

V10.20 Respiratory organ, unspecified

V10.21 Larynx

AHA: 4Q, '03, 108, 110

V10.22 Nasal cavities, middle ear, and accessory sinuses

V10.29 Other

V10.3 Breast

History of conditions classifiable to 174 and 175

AHA: 3Q, '07, 4; 1Q, '07, 6; 2Q, '03, 5; 4Q, '01, 66; 4Q, '98, 65; 4Q, '97, 50; 1Q, '91, 16; 1Q, '90, 21

Z85.3 Personal history primary malig neoplasm breast   I-10

√5ᵗʰ V10.4 Genital organs

History of conditions classifiable to 179-187

V10.40 Female genital organ, unspecfied   ♀

V10.41 Cervix uteri   ♀

AHA: 4Q, '07, 99

V10.42 Other parts of uterus   ♀

V10.43 Ovary   ♀

V10.44 Other female genital organs   ♀

V10.45 Male genital organ, unspecfied   ♂

V10.46 Prostate   ♂

AHA: ▶ 1Q, '09, 15 ◀

V10.47 Testis   ♂

Z85.47 Personal history primary malig neoplasm testis   I-10

√4ᵗʰ Additional Digit Required   Unspecified Code   Other Specified Code   Manifestation Code   ▶◀ Revised Text   ● New Code   ▲ Revised Code Title

2010 ICD-9-CM   October 2009 • Volume 1 – 329

V08–V10.47

V10.48	Epididymis	♂
V10.49	**Other male genital organs**	♂

✓5th **V10.5 Urinary organs**
History of conditions classifiable to 188 and 189

V10.50 Urinary organ, unspecified

V10.51 Bladder

V10.52 Kidney
> **EXCLUDES** *renal pelvis (V10.53)*
> AHA: 2Q, '04, 4

V10.53 Renal pelvis
> AHA: 4Q, '01, 55

V10.59 **Other**

✓5th **V10.6 Leukemia**
Conditions classifiable to 204-208
> **EXCLUDES** *leukemia in remission (204-208)*
> AHA: 2Q, '92, 13; 4Q, '91, 26; 4Q, '90, 3

V10.60 Leukemia, unspecified

V10.61 Lymphoid leukemia

V10.62 Myeloid leukemia

V10.63 Monocytic leukemia

V10.69 **Other**

✓5th **V10.7 Other lymphatic and hematopoietic neoplasms**
Conditions classifiable to 200-203
> **EXCLUDES** *listed conditions in 200-203 in remission*
> AHA: M-J, '85, 18

V10.71 **Lymphosarcoma and reticulosarcoma**

V10.72 **Hodgkin's disease**

V10.79 **Other**

✓5th **V10.8 Personal history of malignant neoplasm of other sites**
History of conditions classifiable to 170-173, 190-195
> **EXCLUDES** ▶ *personal history of malignant carcinoid tumor (V10.91)*
> *personal history of malignant neuroendocrine tumor (V10.91)*◀

V10.81 **Bone**
> AHA: 2Q, '03, 13

V10.82 **Malignant melanoma of skin**

V10.83 **Other malignant neoplasm of skin**

V10.84 **Eye**

V10.85 **Brain**
> AHA: 1Q, '01, 6

V10.86 **Other parts of the nervous system**
> **EXCLUDES** *peripheral sympathetic, and parasympathetic nerves (V10.89)*

V10.87 **Thyroid**

V10.88 **Other endocrine glands and related structures**

V10.89 **Other**

▲ ✓5th **V10.9 Other and unspecified personal history of malignant neoplasm**

● **V10.90 Personal history of unspecified malignant neoplasm**
Personal history of malignant neoplasm NOS
> **EXCLUDES** *personal history of malignant carcinoid tumor (V10.91)*
> *personal history of malignant neuroendocrine tumor (V10.91)*
> *personal history of Merkel cell carcinoma (V10.91)*

● **V10.91 Personal history of malignant neuroendocrine tumor**
Personal history of malignant carcinoid tumor NOS
Personal history of malignant neuroendocrine tumor NOS
Personal history of Merkel cell carcinoma NOS
> Code first any continuing functional activity, such as:
> carcinoid syndrome (259.2)

✓4th **V11 Personal history of mental disorder**

V11.0 **Schizophrenia**
> **EXCLUDES** *that in remission (295.0-295.9 with fifth-digit 5)*

V11.1 **Affective disorders**
Personal history of manic-depressive psychosis
> **EXCLUDES** *that in remission (296.0-296.6 with fifth-digit 5, 6)*

V11.2 **Neurosis**

V11.3 **Alcoholism**

V11.8 **Other mental disorders**

V11.9 **Unspecified mental disorder**

✓4th **V12 Personal history of certain other diseases**
> AHA: 3Q, '92, 11

✓5th **V12.0 Infectious and parasitic diseases**
> **EXCLUDES** *personal history of infectious diseases specific to a body system*

V12.00 Unspecified infectious and parasitic disease

V12.01 **Tuberculosis**

V12.02 **Poliomyelitis**
> **Z86.12** Personal history of poliomyelitis   **I-10**

V12.03 **Malaria**

V12.04 **Methicillin resistant Staphylococcus aureus**
MRSA
> AHA: 4Q, '08, 69, 71

V12.09 **Other**

V12.1 **Nutritional deficiency**

V12.2 **Endocrine, metabolic, and immunity disorders**
> **EXCLUDES** *history of allergy (V14.0-V14.9, V15.01-V15.09)*
> AHA: 3Q, '07, 5

V12.3 **Diseases of blood and blood-forming organs**

✓5th **V12.4 Disorders of nervous system and sense organs**

V12.40 Unspecified disorder of nervous system and sense organs

V12.41 **Benign neoplasm of the brain**
> AHA: 4Q, '97, 48
> **TIP:** Benign neoplasms of the brain are tracked separately because, besides being potentially life-threatening, they often recur and can be difficult to treat.

V12.42 **Infections of the central nervous system**
Encephalitis   Meningitis
> AHA: 4Q, '05, 95

V12.49 Other disorders of nervous system and sense organs
> AHA: 4Q, '98, 59

✓5th **V12.5 Diseases of circulatory system**
> **EXCLUDES** *old myocardial infarction (412)*
> *postmyocardial infarction syndrome (411.0)*
> AHA: 4Q, '95, 61

V12.50 Unspecified circulatory disease

V12.51 **Venous thrombosis and embolism**
Pulmonary embolism
> AHA: 3Q, '06, 12; 4Q, '03, 108; 1Q, '02, 15

Ⓝ Newborn Age: 0   Ⓟ Pediatric Age: 0-17   Ⓜ Maternity Age: 12-55   Ⓐ Adult Age: 15-124   **SDx** Secondary Diagnosis   **PDx** Primary Diagnosis

330 – Volume 1 • October 2009   **2010 ICD-9-CM**

V12.52   Thrombophlebitis

V12.53   Sudden cardiac arrest
Sudden cardiac death successfully resuscitated
AHA: 4Q, '07, 98

V12.54   Transient ischemic attack [TIA], and cerebral infarction without residual deficits
Prolonged reversible ischemic neurological deficit [PRIND]
Reversible ischemic neurologic deficit [RIND]
Stroke NOS without residual deficits

> **EXCLUDES** ▸ *history of traumatic brain injury (V15.52)*◂
> *late effects of cerebrovascular disease (438.0-438.9)*

AHA: 4Q, '07, 98

TIP: Assign for old CVA for which the patient has no residual deficits; if deficits are present, see category 438.

Z86.73 Personal hx TIA & cerebral infarct   I-10
w/o deficits

V12.59   Other
AHA: 2Q, '07, 3; 4Q, '99, 4; 4Q, '98, 88; 4Q, '97, 37

✓5ᵗʰ **V12.6**   Diseases of respiratory system
> **EXCLUDES** *tuberculosis (V12.01)*

V12.60   Unspecified disease of respiratory system

V12.61   Pneumonia (recurrent)
AHA: 4Q, '05, 95

V12.69   Other diseases of respiratory system

✓5ᵗʰ **V12.7**   Diseases of digestive system
AHA: 1Q, '95, 3; 2Q, '89, 16

V12.70   Unspecified digestive disease

V12.71   Peptic ulcer disease

V12.72   Colonic polyps
AHA: 3Q, '02, 15

Z86.010 Personal history of colonic polyps   I-10

V12.79   Other

✓4ᵗʰ **V13**   **Personal history of other diseases**

✓5ᵗʰ **V13.0**   Disorders of urinary system

V13.00   Unspecified urinary disorder

V13.01   Urinary calculi

V13.02   Urinary (tract) infection
AHA: 4Q, '05, 95

V13.03   Nephrotic syndrome
AHA: 4Q, '05, 95

V13.09   Other

V13.1   Trophoblastic disease   ♀
> **EXCLUDES** *supervision during a current pregnancy (V23.1)*

✓5ᵗʰ **V13.2**   Other genital system and obstetric disorders
> **EXCLUDES** *habitual aborter (646.3)*
> *without current pregnancy (629.81)*
> *supervision during a current pregnancy of a woman with poor obstetric history (V23.0-V23.9)*

V13.21   Personal history of pre-term labor   ♀
> **EXCLUDES** *current pregnancy with history of pre-term labor (V23.41)*

AHA: 4Q, '02, 78

V13.22   Personal history of cervical dysplasia   ♀
Personal history of conditions classifiable to 622.10-622.12
> **EXCLUDES** *personal history of malignant neoplasm of cervix uteri (V10.41)*

AHA: 4Q, '07, 98

V13.29   Other genital system and obstetric disorders   ♀

V13.3   Diseases of skin and subcutaneous tissue

V13.4   Arthritis

✓5ᵗʰ **V13.5**   Other musculoskeletal disorders
AHA: 4Q, '08, 158

TIP: Personal histories of pathological, stress, or traumatic fractures are separately classified because a patient with such a history is at much higher risk of refracture of the same site.

V13.51   Pathologic fracture
Healed pathologic fracture
> **EXCLUDES** *personal history of traumatic fracture (V15.51)*

V13.52   Stress fracture
Healed stress fracture
> **EXCLUDES** *personal history of traumatic fracture (V15.51)*

V13.59   Other musculoskeletal disorders

✓5ᵗʰ **V13.6**   Congenital malformations
AHA: 4Q, '98, 63

V13.61   Hypospadias   SDx ♂

V13.69   Other congenital malformations
AHA: 1Q, '04, 16

V13.7   Perinatal problems
> **EXCLUDES** *low birth weight status (V21.30-V21.35)*

V13.8   Other specified diseases

V13.9   Unspecified disease
AHA: 4Q, '06, 117

✓4ᵗʰ **V14**   **Personal history of allergy to medicinal agents**

V14.0   Penicillin   SDx
Z88.0 Allergy status to penicillin   I-10

V14.1   Other antibiotic agent   SDx

V14.2   Sulfonamides   SDx

V14.3   Other anti-infective agent   SDx

V14.4   Anesthetic age   SDx

V14.5   Narcotic agent   SDx

V14.6   Analgesic agent   SDx

V14.7   Serum or vaccine   SDx

V14.8   Other specified medicinal agents   SDx

V14.9   Unspecified medicinal agent   SDx

✓4ᵗʰ **V15**   **Other personal history presenting hazards to health**
> **EXCLUDES** *personal history of drug therapy (V87.41-V87.49)*

✓5ᵗʰ **V15.0**   Allergy, other than to medicinal agents
> **EXCLUDES** *allergy to food substance used as base for medicinal agent (V14.0-V14.9)*

AHA: 4Q, '00, 42, 49

TIP: A person who has had an allergic episode to a substance in the past should always be considered allergic to the substance.

V15.01   Allergy to peanuts   SDx
Z91.010 Allergy to peanuts   I-10

V15.02   Allergy to milk products   SDx
> **EXCLUDES** *lactose intolerance (271.3)*

AHA: 1Q, '03, 12

V15.03   Allergy to eggs   SDx

V15.04   Allergy to seafood   SDx
Seafood (octopus) (squid) ink
Shellfish

V15.05   Allergy to other foods   SDx
Food additives   Nuts other than peanuts

▲   **V15.06**   Allergy to insects and arachnids   SDx
Bugs
Insect bites and stings
Spiders

V15.07   Allergy to latex   SDx
Latex sensitivity

| ✓4ᵗʰ / ✓5ᵗʰ Additional Digit Required | Unspecified Code | Other Specified Code | Manifestation Code | ▸◂ Revised Text | ● New Code | ▲ Revised Code Title |

2010 ICD-9-CM   **October 2009 • Volume 1 – 331**

V12.52–V15.07

V15.08　Allergy to radiographic dye `SDx`
Contrast media used for diagnostic x-ray procedures

V15.09　Other allergy, other than to medicinal agents `SDx`

V15.1　Surgery to heart and great vessels `SDx`
EXCLUDES　*replacement by transplant or other means (V42.1-V42.2, V43.2-V43.4)*
AHA: 1Q, '04, 16

√5ᵗʰ **V15.2　Surgery to other organs**
EXCLUDES　*replacement by transplant or other means (V42.0-V43.8)*
AHA: 4Q, '08, 158

V15.21　Personal history of undergoing in utero procedure during pregnancy `SDx` ♀
AHA: 4Q, '08, 158

V15.22　Personal history of undergoing in utero procedure while a fetus `SDx`
AHA: 4Q, '08, 158

V15.29　Surgery to other organs `SDx`

V15.3　Irradiation `SDx`
Previous exposure to therapeutic or other ionizing radiation

√5ᵗʰ **V15.4　Psychological trauma**
EXCLUDES　*history of condition classifiable to 290-316 (V11.0-V11.9)*

V15.41　History of physical abuse `SDx`
Rape
AHA: 3Q, '99, 15

V15.42　History of emotional abuse `SDx`
Neglect
AHA: 3Q, '99, 15

V15.49　Other `SDx`
AHA: 3Q, '99, 15

√5ᵗʰ **V15.5　Injury**
AHA: 4Q, '08, 158

V15.51　Traumatic fracture `SDx`
Healed traumatic fracture
EXCLUDES　*personal history of pathologic and stress fracture (V13.51, V13.52)*
TIP: Personal histories of pathological, stress, or traumatic fractures are separately classified because a patient with such a history is at much higher risk of refracture of the same site.

● **V15.52　History of traumatic brain injury** `SDx`
EXCLUDES　*personal history of cerebrovascular accident (cerebral infarction) without residual deficits (V12.54)*

V15.59　Other injury `SDx`

V15.6　Poisoning `SDx`

V15.7　Contraception
EXCLUDES　*current contraceptive management (V25.0-V25.4)*
presence of intrauterine contraceptive device as incidental finding (V45.5)

√5ᵗʰ **V15.8　Other specified personal history presenting hazards to health**
EXCLUDES　*contact with and (suspected) exposure to:*
aromatic compounds and dyes (V87.11-V87.19)
arsenic and other metals (V87.01-V87.09)
molds (V87.31)
AHA: 4Q, '95, 62

● **V15.80　History of failed moderate sedation** `SDx`
History of failed conscious sedation

V15.81　Noncompliance with medical treatment `SDx`
EXCLUDES　*noncompliance with renal dialysis (V45.12)*
AHA: 3Q, '07, 9; 4Q, '06, 136; 2Q, '03, 7; 2Q, '01, 11, 12, 13; 2Q, '99, 17; 2Q, '97, 11; 1Q, '97, 12; 3Q, '96, 9

V15.82　History of tobacco use `SDx`
EXCLUDES　*tobacco dependence (305.1)*
AHA: ▶1Q, '09, 17◀
Z87.82 Personal history of nicotine dependence `I-10`

● **V15.83　Underimmunization status** `SDx`
Delinquent immunization status
Lapsed immunization schedule status

▲ **V15.84　Contact with and (suspected) exposure to asbestos** `SDx`

▲ **V15.85　Contact with and (suspected) exposure to potentially hazardous body fluids** `SDx`

▲ **V15.86　Contact with and (suspected) exposure to lead** `SDx`

V15.87　History of extracorporeal membrane oxygenation [ECMO] `SDx`
AHA: 4Q, '03, 84

V15.88　History of fall `SDx`
At risk for falling
AHA: 4Q, '05, 95
Z91.81 History of falling `I-10`

V15.89　Other `SDx`
EXCLUDES　*contact with and (suspected) exposure to other potentially hazardous:*
chemicals (V87.2)
substances (V87.39)
AHA: 3Q, '08, 7; 3Q, '07, 5; 1Q, '90, 21; N-D, '84, 12

V15.9　Unspecified personal history presenting hazards to health `SDx`

√4ᵗʰ **V16　Family history of malignant neoplasm**

V16.0　Gastrointestinal tract
Family history of condition classifiable to 140-159
AHA: 1Q, '99, 4
TIP: Family history of colon cancer is a condition that meets the criteria of "high risk" for a screening colonoscopy.

V16.1　Trachea, bronchus, and lung
Family history of condition classifiable to 162

V16.2　Other respiratory and intrathoracic organs
Family history of condition classifiable to 160-161, 163-165

V16.3　Breast
Family history of condition classifiable to 174
AHA: 4Q, '04, 107; 2Q, '03, 4; 2Q, '00, 8; 1Q, '92, 11
Z80.3 Family history of malignant neoplasm of breast `I-10`

√5ᵗʰ **V16.4　Genital organs**
Family history of condition classifiable to 179-187
AHA: 4Q, '97, 48

V16.40　Genital organ, unspecified

V16.41　Ovary

V16.42　Prostate
Z80.42 Family history of malignant neoplasm of prostate `I-10`

V16.43　Testis

V16.49　Other
AHA: 2Q, '06, 2

√5ᵗʰ **V16.5　Urinary organs**
Family history of condition classifiable to 188-189

V16.51　Kidney

V16.52　Bladder
AHA: 4Q, '07, 98

V16.59　Other

Ⓝ Newborn Age: 0　　Ⓟ Pediatric Age: 0-17　　Ⓜ Maternity Age: 12-55　　Ⓐ Adult Age: 15-124　　`SDx` Secondary Diagnosis　　`PDx` Primary Diagnosis

332 – Volume 1 · October 2009　　　　　　　　　　　　　　　　　　　　　　　**2010 ICD-9-CM**

V16.6 **Leukemia**
Family history of condition classifiable to 204-208

V16.7 **Other lymphatic and hematopoietic neoplasms**
Family history of condition classifiable to 200-203

V16.8 **Other specified malignant neoplasm**
Family history of other condition classifiable to 140-199

V16.9 **Unspecified malignant neoplasm**

√4th **V17 Family history of certain chronic disabling diseases**

V17.0 **Psychiatric condition**
EXCLUDES *family history of mental retardation (V18.4)*

V17.1 **Stroke (cerebrovascular)**
Z82.3 Family history of stroke   I-10

V17.2 **Other neurological diseases**
Epilepsy
Huntington's chorea

V17.3 **Ischemic heart disease**

√5th V17.4 **Other cardiovascular diseases**
AHA: 1Q, '04, 6

V17.41 **Family history of sudden cardiac death [SCD]**
EXCLUDES *family history of ischemic heart disease (V17.3)*
family history of myocardial infarction (V17.3)
AHA: 4Q, '07, 98

V17.49 **Family history of other cardiovascular diseases**
Family history of cardiovascular disease NOS

V17.5 **Asthma**

V17.6 **Other chronic respiratory conditions**

V17.7 **Arthritis**

√5th V17.8 **Other musculoskeletal diseases**

V17.81 **Osteoporosis**
AHA: 4Q, '05, 95

V17.89 **Other musculoskeletal diseases**

√4th **V18 Family history of certain other specific conditions**

V18.0 **Diabetes mellitus**
AHA: 1Q, '04, 8
TIP: Assign for a normal infant born to a diabetic mother who presents with no manifestations of the syndrome.

√5th V18.1 **Other endocrine and metabolic diseases**

V18.11 **Multiple endocrine neoplasia [MEN] syndrome**
AHA: 4Q, '07, 98, 100

V18.19 **Other endocrine and metabolic diseases**

V18.2 **Anemia**

V18.3 **Other blood disorders**

V18.4 **Mental retardation**

√5th V18.5 **Digestive disorders**

V18.51 **Colonic polyps**
EXCLUDES *family history of malignant neoplasm of gastrointestinal tract (V16.0)*
AHA: 4Q, '06, 117
Z83.71 Family history of colonic polyps   I-10

V18.59 **Other digestive disorders**

√5th V18.6 **Kidney diseases**

V18.61 **Polycystic kidney**

V18.69 **Other kidney diseases**

V18.7 **Other genitourinary diseases**

V18.8 **Infectious and parasitic diseases**

V18.9 **Genetic disease carrier**
AHA: 4Q, '05, 95

√4th **V19 Family history of other conditions**

V19.0 **Blindness or visual loss**

V19.1 **Other eye disorders**

V19.2 **Deafness or hearing loss**

V19.3 **Other ear disorders**

V19.4 **Skin conditions**

V19.5 **Congenital anomalies**

V19.6 **Allergic disorders**

V19.7 **Consanguinity**

V19.8 **Other condition**

PERSONS ENCOUNTERING HEALTH SERVICES IN CIRCUMSTANCES RELATED TO REPRODUCTION AND DEVELOPMENT (V20-V29)

√4th **V20 Health supervision of infant or child**

V20.0 **Foundling**   PDx P

V20.1 **Other healthy infant or child receiving care**   PDx P
Medical or nursing care supervision of healthy infant in cases of:
maternal illness, physical or psychiatric
socioeconomic adverse condition at home
too many children at home preventing or interfering with normal care
AHA: 1Q, '00, 25; 3Q, '89, 14

V20.2 **Routine infant or child health check**   PDx P
Developmental testing of infant or child
►Health check for child over 28 days old◄
Immunizations appropriate for age
Routine vision and hearing testing
Use additional code(s) to identify:
special screening examination(s) performed (V73.0-V82.9)
EXCLUDES ► *health check for child under 29 days old (V20.31-V20.32)*
newborn health supervision (V20.31-V20.32)◄
special screening for developmental handicaps (V79.3)
AHA: ►1Q, '09, 15;◄ 1Q, '04, 15

● √5th V20.3 **Newborn health supervision**
Health check for child under 29 days old
EXCLUDES *health check for child over 28 days old (V20.2)*

● V20.31 **Health supervision for newborn under 8 days old**   N PDx
Health check for newborn under 8 days old

● V20.32 **Health supervision for newborn 8 to 28 days old**   N PDx
Health check for newborn 8 to 28 days old
Newborn weight check

√4th **V21 Constitutional states in development**

V21.0 **Period of rapid growth in childhood**   SDx

V21.1 **Puberty**   SDx

V21.2 **Other adolecsence**   SDx

√5th V21.3 **Low birth weight status**
EXCLUDES *history of perinatal problems*
AHA: 4Q, '00, 51
TIP: There are no age restrictions on these V codes after the perinatal period; assign for patients without the initial condition who may continue to manifest the consequences of it.

V21.30 **Low birth weight status, unspecified**   SDx

V21.31 **Low birth weight status, less than 500 grams**   SDx

V21.32 **Low birth weight status, 500-999 grams**   SDx

V21.33 **Low birth weight status, 1000-1499 grams** SDx

V21.34 **Low birth weight status, 1500-1999 grams** SDx

V21.35 **Low birth weight status, 2000-2500 grams** SDx

√4th √5th Additional Digit Required   Unspecified Code   Other Specified Code   Manifestation Code   ►◄ Revised Text   ● New Code   ▲ Revised Code Title

2010 ICD-9-CM   October 2009 • Volume 1 – 333

V16.6–V21.35

V21.8 **Other specified constitutional states in development** `SDx`

V21.9 **Unspecified constitutional state in development** `SDx`

✓4th **V22** **Normal pregnancy**

> *EXCLUDES* *pregnancy examination or test, pregnancy unconfirmed (V72.40)*
>
> **AHA:** 4Q, '07, 125
>
> **TIP:** Do not assign with any code from chapter 11, "Complications of Pregnancy, Childbirth, and the Puerperium."

V22.0 **Supervision of normal first pregnancy** `PDx` ♀

> **AHA:** 3Q, '99, 16
>
> **Z34.00** Encounter suprvisn norm 1 pregnancy uns trimestr `I-10`

V22.1 **Supervision of other normal pregnancy** `PDx` ♀

> **AHA:** 3Q, '99, 16

V22.2 **Pregnant state, incidental** `SDx` ♀

> Pregnant state NOS

✓4th **V23** **Supervision of high-risk pregnancy**

> **AHA:** 1Q, '90, 10

V23.0 **Pregnancy with history of infertility** `M` ♀

V23.1 **Pregnancy with history of trophoblastic disease** `M` ♀

> Pregnancy with history of:
> hydatidiform mole
> vesicular mole
>
> *EXCLUDES* *that without current pregnancy (V13.1)*

V23.2 **Pregnancy with history of abortion** `M` ♀

> Pregnancy with history of conditions classifiable to 634-638
>
> *EXCLUDES* *habitual aborter:*
> *care during pregnancy (646.3)*
> *that without current pregnancy (629.81)*

V23.3 **Grand multiparity** `M` ♀

> *EXCLUDES* *care in relation to labor and delivery (659.4)*
> *that without current pregnancy (V61.5)*

✓5th **V23.4** **Pregnancy with other poor obstetric history**

> Pregnancy with history of other conditions classifiable to 630-676

V23.41 **Pregnancy with history of labor pre-term** `M` ♀

> **AHA:** 4Q, '02, 79

V23.49 **Pregnancy with other poor obstetric history** `M` ♀

V23.5 **Pregnancy with other poor reproductive history** `M` ♀

> Pregnancy with history of stillbirth or neonatal death

V23.7 **Insufficient prenatal care** `M` ♀

> History of little or no prenatal care

✓5th **V23.8** **Other high-risk pregnancy**

> **AHA:** 4Q, '08, 158; 4Q, '98, 56, 63

V23.81 **Elderly primigravida** `M` ♀

> First pregnancy in a woman who will be 35 years of age or older at expected date of delivery
>
> *EXCLUDES* *elderly primigravida complicating pregnancy (659.5)*

V23.82 **Elderly multigravida** `M` ♀

> Second or more pregnancy in a woman who will be 35 years of age or older at expected date of delivery
>
> *EXCLUDES* *elderly multigravida complicating pregnancy (659.6)*

V23.83 **Young primigravida** `M` ♀

> First pregnancy in a female less than 16 years old at expected date of delivery
>
> *EXCLUDES* *young primigravida complicating pregnancy (659.8)*

V23.84 **Young multigravida** `M` ♀

> Second or more pregnancy in a female less than 16 years old at expected date of delivery
>
> *EXCLUDES* *young multigravida complicating pregnancy (659.8)*

V23.85 **Pregnancy resulting from assisted reproductive technology** `M` ♀

> Pregnancy resulting from in vitro fertilization
>
> **AHA:** 4Q, '08, 160

V23.86 **Pregnancy with history of in utero procedure during previous pregnancy** `M` ♀

> *EXCLUDES* *management of pregnancy affected by in utero procedure during current pregnancy* ▶*(679.0-679.1)*◄
>
> **AHA:** 4Q, '08, 158, 160

V23.89 **Other high-risk pregnancy** `M` ♀

> **AHA:** 3Q, '06, 14

V23.9 **Unspecified high-risk pregnancy** `M` ♀

✓4th **V24** **Postpartum care and examination**

V24.0 **Immediately after delivery** `PDx` `M` ♀

> Care and observation in uncomplicated cases
>
> **AHA:** 3Q, '06, 11

V24.1 **Lactating mother** `PDx` ♀

> Supervision of lactation

V24.2 **Routine postpartum follow-up** `PDx` ♀

✓4th **V25** **Encounter for contraceptive management**

> **AHA:** 4Q, '92, 24

✓5th **V25.0** **General counseling and advice**

V25.01 **Prescription of oral contraceptives** ♀

V25.02 **Initiation of other contraceptive measures**

> Fitting of diaphragm
> Prescription of foams, creams, or other agents
>
> **AHA:** 3Q, '97, 7

V25.03 **Encounter for emergency contraceptive counseling and prescription**

> Encounter for postcoital contraceptive counseling and prescription
>
> **AHA:** 4Q, '03, 84

V25.04 **Counseling and instruction in natural family planning to avoid pregnancy**

> **AHA:** 4Q, '07, 99
>
> **Z30.02** Counsel & instruct natural family plan avoid pg `I-10`

V25.09 **Other**

> Family planning advice

V25.1 **Insertion of intrauterine contraceptive device** ♀

V25.2 **Sterilization**

> Admission for interruption of fallopian tubes or vas deferens

V25.3 **Menstrual extraction** ♀

> Menstrual regulation

✓5th **V25.4** **Surveillance of previously prescribed contraceptive methods**

> Checking, reinsertion, or removal of contraceptive device
> Repeat prescription for contraceptive method
> Routine examination in connection with contraceptive maintenance
>
> *EXCLUDES* *presence of intrauterine contraceptive device as incidental finding (V45.5)*

V25.40 **Contraceptive surveillance, unspecified**

V25.41 **Contraceptive pill** ♀

V25.42 **Intrauterine contraceptive device** ♀

> Checking, reinsertion, or removal of intrauterine device

V25.43 **Implantable subdermal contraceptive** ♀

`N` Newborn Age: 0   `P` Pediatric Age: 0-17   `M` Maternity Age: 12-55   `A` Adult Age: 15-124   `SDx` Secondary Diagnosis   `PDx` Primary Diagnosis

334 – Volume 1 · October 2009   **2010 ICD-9-CM**

V25.49 Other contraceptive method
AHA: 3Q, '97, 7

V25.5 Insertion of implantable subdermal contraceptive ♀
AHA: 3Q, '92, 9

V25.8 Other specified contraceptive management
Postvasectomy sperm count
EXCLUDES sperm count following sterilization reversal (V26.22)
sperm count for fertility testing (V26.21)
AHA: 3Q, '96, 9

V25.9 Unspecified contraceptive management

✓4th **V26** **Procreative management**

V26.0 Tuboplasty or vasoplasty after previous sterilization
AHA: 2Q, '95, 10
TIP: Assign for encounters for tubal ligation or vasectomy reversal procedures.

V26.1 Artificial insemination ♀

✓5th **V26.2** Investigation and testing
EXCLUDES postvasectomy sperm count (V25.8)
AHA: 4Q, '00, 56

V26.21 Fertility testing
Fallopian insufflation
Sperm count for fertility testing
EXCLUDES genetic counseling and testing (V26.31-V26.39)

V26.22 Aftercare following sterilization reversal
Fallopian insufflation following sterilization reversal
Sperm count following sterilization reversal

V26.29 Other investigation and testing
AHA: 2Q, '96, 9; N-D, '85, 15

✓5th **V26.3** Genetic counseling and testing
EXCLUDES fertility testing (V26.21)
nonprocreative genetic screening (V82.71, V82.79)
AHA: 4Q, '05, 96

V26.31 Testing of female for genetic disease carrier status ♀
AHA: 4Q, '06, 117

V26.32 Other genetic testing of female ♀
Use additional code to identify habitual aborter (629.81, 646.3)
AHA: 4Q, '06, 117
Z31.438 Encounter oth genetic test female procreative mngmnt I-10

V26.33 Genetic counseling

V26.34 Testing of male for genetic disease carrier status ♂
AHA: 4Q, '06, 117

V26.35 Encounter for testing of male partner of habitual aborter ♂
AHA: 4Q, '06, 117

V26.39 Other genetic testing of male ♂
AHA: 4Q, '06, 117

✓5th **V26.4** General counseling and advice

V26.41 Procreative counseling and advice using natural family planning
AHA: 4Q, '07, 99

V26.42 Encounter for fertility preservation counseling
Encounter for fertility preservation counseling prior to cancer therapy
Encounter for fertility preservation counseling prior to surgical removal of gonads

V26.49 Other procreative management, counseling and advice

✓5th **V26.5** Sterilization status

V26.51 Tubal ligation status SDx ♀
EXCLUDES infertility not due to previous tubal ligation (628.0-628.9)
Z98.51 Tubal ligation status I-10

V26.52 Vasectomy status SDx ♂

✓5th **V26.8** Other specified procreative management

V26.81 Encounter for assisted reproductive fertility procedure cycle PDx ♀
Patient undergoing in vitro fertilization cycle
Use additional code to identify the type of infertility
EXCLUDES pre-cycle diagnosis and testing—code to reason for encounter
AHA: 4Q, '07, 99

V26.82 Encounter for fertility preservation procedure PDx
Encounter for fertility preservation procedure prior to cancer therapy
Encounter for fertility preservation procedure prior to surgical removal of gonads

V26.89 Other specified procreative management

V26.9 Unspecified procreative management

✓4th **V27** **Outcome of delivery**
Note: This category is intended for the coding of the outcome of delivery on the mother's record.
AHA: 2Q, '91, 16
TIP: Assign on the maternal chart for every admission during which a delivery occurs.

V27.0 Single liveborn SDx M ♀
AHA: 4Q, '08, 192; 4Q, '05, 81; 2Q, '03, 9; 2Q, '02, 10; 1Q, '01, 10; 3Q, '00, 5; 4Q, '98, 77; 4Q, '95, 59; 1Q, '92, 9
Z37.0 Single live birth I-10

V27.1 Single stillborn SDx M ♀

V27.2 Twins, both liveborn SDx M ♀
Z37.2 Twins both liveborn I-10

V27.3 Twins, one liveborn and one stillborn SDx M ♀

V27.4 Twins, both stillborn SDx M ♀

V27.5 Other multiple birth, all liveborn SDx M ♀

V27.6 Other multiple birth, some liveborn SDx M ♀

V27.7 Other multiple birth, all stillborn SDx M ♀

V27.9 Unspecified outcome of delivery SDx M ♀
Single birth
Multiple birth } outcome to infant unspecified

✓4th **V28** **Encounter for antenatal screening of mother**
EXCLUDES abnormal findings on screening — code to findings
routine prenatal care (V22.0-V23.9)
suspected fetal conditions affecting management of pregnancy (655.00-655.93, 656.00-656.93, 657.00-657.03, 658.00-658.93)
suspected fetal conditions not found (V89.01-V89.09)
AHA: 4Q, '06, 117; 1Q, '04, 11

V28.0 Screening for chromosomal anomalies by amniocentesis M ♀

V28.1 Screening for raised alpha-fetoprotein levels in amniotic fluid M ♀

V28.2 Other screening based on amniocentesis M ♀

V28.3 Encounter for routine screening for malformation using ultrasonics ♀
Encounter for routine fetal ultrasound NOS
EXCLUDES encounter for fetal anatomic survey (V28.81)
genetic counseling and testing (V26.31-V26.39)

V28.4 Screening for fetal growth retardation using ultrasonics ♀

✓4th Additional Digit Required   Unspecified Code   Other Specified Code   Manifestation Code   ▶◀ Revised Text   ● New Code   ▲ Revised Code Title
✓5th

V28.5   Screening for isoimmunization   ♀

V28.6   Screening for Streptococcus B   Ⓜ♀
      AHA: 4Q, '97, 46

✓5ᵗʰ **V28.8**   Other specified antenatal screening
      AHA: ▶4Q, '08, 159;◀ 3Q, '99, 16

    V28.81   Encounter for fetal anatomic survey   Ⓜ♀

    V28.82   Encounter for screening for risk   Ⓜ♀
            of pre-term labor

    V28.89   Other specified antenatal screening   Ⓜ♀
            Chorionic villus sampling
            Genomic screening
            Nuchal transluceny testing
            Proteomic screening

V28.9   Unspecified antenatal screening   ♀

✓4ᵗʰ **V29**   **Observation and evaluation of newborns and infants for suspected condition not found**

    Note: This category is to be used for newborns, within the neonatal period, (the first 28 days of life) who are suspected of having an abnormal condition resulting from exposure from the mother or the birth process, but without signs or symptoms, and, which after examination and observation, is found not to exist.

    EXCLUDES   suspected fetal conditions not found (V89.01-V89.09)

    AHA: 1Q, '00, 25; 4Q, '94, 47; 1Q, '94, 9; 4Q, '92, 21

    TIP: Do not assign if the infant shows any signs or symptoms.

¹ **V29.0**   Observation for suspected infectious condition   Ⓝ
      AHA: 1Q, '01, 10

¹ **V29.1**   Observation for suspected neurological condition   Ⓝ

¹ **V29.2**   Observation for suspected respiratory condition   Ⓝ

¹ **V29.3**   Observation for suspected genetic or metabolic condition   Ⓝ
      AHA: 2Q, '05, 21; 4Q, '98, 59, 68

¹ **V29.8**   Observation for other specified suspected condition   Ⓝ
      AHA: 2Q, '03, 15

¹ **V29.9**   Observation for unspecified suspected condition   Ⓝ
      AHA: 1Q, '02, 6

LIVEBORN INFANTS ACCORDING TO TYPE OF BIRTH (V30-V39)

    Note: These categories are intended for the coding of liveborn infants who are consuming health care [e.g., crib or bassinet occupancy].

    The following fouth-digit subdivisions are for use with categories V30-V39

      ✓5ᵗʰ   **0**   **Born in hospital**   Ⓝ
          1   **Born before admission to hospital**   Ⓝ
          2   **Born outside hospital and not hospitalized**
    The following two fifth-digits are for use with the fourth-digit .0, Born in hospital:
          0   **delivered without mention of cesarean delivery**
          1   **delivered by cesarean delivery**

    AHA: 1Q, '01, 10

§ ✓4ᵗʰ **V30**   **Single liveborn**   PDx
      AHA: 2Q, '03, 9; 4Q, '98, 46, 59; 1Q, '94, 9; **For code V30.00:** 1Q, '04, 8, 16; 4Q, '03, 68; **For code V30.01:** 4Q, '05, 88; **For code V30.10:** 3Q, '06, 10
      Z38.00 Single liveborn infant delivered vaginally   I-10

§ ✓4ᵗʰ **V31**   **Twin, mate liveborn**   PDx
      AHA: 3Q, '92, 10
      Z38.31 Twin liveborn infant delivered by cesarean   I-10

§ ✓4ᵗʰ **V32**   Twin, mate stillborn   PDx

§ ✓4ᵗʰ **V33**   Twin, unspecified   PDx

§ ✓4ᵗʰ **V34**   Other multiple, mates all liveborn   PDx

§ ✓4ᵗʰ **V35**   Other multiple, mates all stillborn   PDx

§ ✓4ᵗʰ **V36**   Other multiple, mates live and stillborn   PDx

§ ✓4ᵗʰ **V37**   Other multiple, unspecified   PDx

§ ✓4ᵗʰ **V39**   Unspecified   PDx

PERSONS WITH A CONDITION INFLUENCING THEIR HEALTH STATUS (V40-V49)

    Note: These categories are intended for use when these conditions are recorded as "diagnoses" or "problems."

    TIP: Includes patients with a carrier status or who have sequelae or residual of a past condition or disease, which may affect current or future treatment.

✓4ᵗʰ **V40**   **Mental and behavioral problems**

    V40.0   Problems with learning

    V40.1   Problems with communication [including speech]

    V40.2   Other mental problems

    V40.3   Other behavioral problems

    V40.9   Unspecified mental or behavioral problem

✓4ᵗʰ **V41**   **Problems with special senses and other special functions**

    V41.0   Problems with sight

    V41.1   Other eye problems

    V41.2   Problems with hearing

    V41.3   Other ear problems

    V41.4   Problems with voice production

    V41.5   Problems with smell and taste

    V41.6   Problems with swallowing and mastication

    V41.7   Problems with sexual function
      EXCLUDES   marital problems (V61.10)
              psychosexual disorders (302.0-302.9)

    V41.8   Other problems with special functions

    V41.9   Unspecified problem with special functions

✓4ᵗʰ **V42**   **Organ or tissue replaced by transplant**
    INCLUDES   homologous or heterologous (animal) (human) transplant organ status

    AHA: 3Q, '98, 3, 4

    TIP: Do not assign if the patient has a complication of the transplanted organ; the code from subcategory 996.8 provides the information.

    V42.0   Kidney   SDx
      AHA: 1Q, '08, 10; 1Q, '03, 10; 3Q, '01, 12
      Z94.0 Kidney transplant status   I-10

    V42.1   Heart   SDx
      AHA: 3Q, '03, 16; 3Q, '01, 13

    V42.2   Heart valve   SDx

    V42.3   Skin   SDx

    V42.4   Bone   SDx

    V42.5   Cornea   SDx

    V42.6   Lung   SDx

    V42.7   Liver   SDx
      Z94.4 Liver transplant status   I-10

    ✓5ᵗʰ **V42.8**   Other specified organ or tissue
      AHA: 4Q, '98, 64; 4Q, '97, 49

        V42.81   Bone marrow   SDx

        V42.82   Peripheral stem cells   SDx

        V42.83   Pancreas   SDx
           AHA: 1Q, '03, 10; 2Q, '01, 16

---

¹   A code from the V30–V39 series may be sequenced before the V29 on the newborn medical record.
§   Require fourth and fifth digits. See beginning of section V30-V39 for codes and definitions.

Ⓝ Newborn Age: 0   Ⓟ Pediatric Age: 0-17   Ⓜ Maternity Age: 12-55   Ⓐ Adult Age: 15-124   SDx Secondary Diagnosis   PDx Primary Diagnosis

336 – Volume 1 • February 2009   2010 ICD-9-CM

V42.84	Intestines	`SDx`
	AHA: 4Q, '00, 48, 50	
V42.89	Other	`SDx`
V42.9	Unspecified organ or tissue	`SDx`

√4th **V43 Organ or tissue replaced by other means**

INCLUDES   organ or tissue assisted by other means
replacement of organ by:
    artificial device
    mechanical device
    prosthesis

EXCLUDES   *cardiac pacemaker in situ (V45.01)*
fitting and adjustment of prosthetic device (V52.0-V52.9)
renal dialysis status (V45.11)

V43.0	Eye globe	`SDx`
V43.1	Lens	`SDx`
	Pseudophakos	
	AHA: 4Q, '98, 65	

√5th **V43.2 Heart**
Fully implantable artificial heart
Heart assist device
AHA: 4Q, '03, 85

V43.21	Heart assist device	`SDx`
V43.22	Fully implantable artificial heart	

V43.3 Heart valve   `SDx`
AHA: 3Q, '06, 7; 3Q, '02, 13, 14

TIP: If the status post heart valve replacement information includes "porcine" or mention of other homologous or heterologous tissue, assign instead V42.2.

Z95.2 Presence of prosthetic heart valve   `I-10`

V43.4	Blood vessel	`SDx`
V43.5	Bladder	`SDx`

√5th **V43.6 Joint**
AHA: 4Q, '05, 91

V43.60	Unspecified joint	`SDx`
V43.61	Shoulder	`SDx`
V43.62	Elbow	`SDx`
V43.63	Wrist	`SDx`
V43.64	Hip	`SDx`

AHA: ►1Q, '09, 6;◄ 2Q, '08, 3-5; 3Q, '06, 4, 5; 4Q, '05, 93, 112; 2Q, '04, 15

Z96.641 Presence of right artificial hip joint   `I-10`

V43.65	Knee	`SDx`
	AHA: 3Q, '06, 5	
V43.66	Ankle	`SDx`
V43.69	Other	`SDx`
V43.7	Limb	`SDx`

√5th **V43.8 Other organ or tissue**

V43.81	Larynx	`SDx`
	AHA: 4Q, '95, 55	
V43.82	Breast	`SDx`
	AHA: 4Q, '95, 55	
	Z98.82 Breast implant status	`I-10`
V43.83	Artificial skin	`SDx`
V43.89	Other	`SDx`

√4th **V44 Artificial opening status**

EXCLUDES   *artificial openings requiring attention or management (V55.0-V55.9)*

TIP: Do not assign if the patient has a complication of the artificial opening, such as infection or obstruction; assign only the complication code.

V44.0	Tracheostomy	`SDx`
	AHA: 4Q, '03, 103, 107, 111; 1Q, '01, 6	
V44.1	Gastrostomy	`SDx`

AHA: 4Q, '03, 103, 107-108, 110; 1Q, '01, 12; 3Q, '97, 12; 1Q, '93, 26

V44.2	Ileostomy	`SDx`
V44.3	Colostomy	`SDx`
	AHA: 4Q, '03, 110	
	Z93.3 Colostomy status	`I-10`
V44.4	Other artificial opening of gastrointestinal tract	`SDx`

√5th **V44.5 Cystostomy**

V44.50	Cystostomy, unspecified	`SDx`
V44.51	Cutaneous-vesicostomy	`SDx`
V44.52	Appendico-vesicostomy	`SDx`
V44.59	Other cystostomy	`SDx`
V44.6	Other artificial opening of urinary tract	`SDx`

    Nephrostomy   Urethrostomy
    Ureterostomy

V44.7	Artificial vagina	`SDx`
V44.8	Other artificial opening status	`SDx`
V44.9	Unspecified artificial opening status	`SDx`

√4th **V45 Other postprocedural states**

EXCLUDES   *aftercare management (V51-V58.9)*
malfunction or other complication — code to condition

AHA: 4Q, '03, 85

√5th **V45.0 Cardiac device in situ**

EXCLUDES   *artificial heart (V43.22)*
heart assist device (V43.21)

V45.00	Unspecified cardiac device	`SDx`
V45.01	Cardiac pacemaker	`SDx`
V45.02	Automatic implantable cardiac defibrillator	`SDx`

Z95.810 Presence auto implantable cardiac defibrillator   `I-10`

V45.09	Other specified cardiac device	`SDx`

Carotid sinus pacemaker in situ

√5th **V45.1 Renal dialysis status**

EXCLUDES   *admission for dialysis treatment or session (V56.0)*

AHA: 4Q, '08, 157; 1Q, '08, 7; 4Q, '07, 86; 3Q, '07, 9; 4Q, '06, 136; 4Q, '05, 96; 2Q, '03, 7; 2Q, '01, 12, 13

V45.11 Renal dialysis status   `SDx`
Hemodialysis status
Patient requiring intermittent renal dialysis
Peritoneal dialysis status
Presence of arterial-venous shunt (for dialysis)
AHA: 4Q, '08, 157, 193

Z99.2 Dependence on renal dialysis   `I-10`

V45.12	Noncompliance with renal dialysis	`SDx`
V45.2	Presence of cerebrospinal fluid drainage device	`SDx`

Cerebral ventricle (communicating) shunt, valve, or device in situ

EXCLUDES   *malfunction (996.2)*

AHA: 4Q, '03, 106

V45.3 Intestinal bypass or anastomosis status   `SDx`

EXCLUDES   *bariatric surgery status (V45.86)*
gastric bypass status (V45.86)
obesity surgery status (V45.86)

V45.4 Arthrodesis status   `SDx`
AHA: N-D, '84, 18

TIP: If there is a complication of the fusion graft site that requires refusion or revision, assign instead a code from subcategory 996.4.

√5th **V45.5 Presence of contraceptive device**

EXCLUDES   *checking, reinsertion, or removal of device (V25.42)*
complication from device (996.32)
insertion of device (V25.1)

V45.51 Intrauterine contraceptive device   `SDx` ♀

Z97.5 Presence of intrauterine contraceptive device   `I-10`

√4th √5th Additional Digit Required   Unspecified Code   Other Specified Code   Manifestation Code   ►◄ Revised Text   ● New Code   ▲ Revised Code Title

2010 ICD-9-CM   **October 2009 · Volume 1 – 337**

V42.84–V45.51

V Codes

V45.52–V47.2

V45.52 Subdermal contraceptive implant   SDx

V45.59 **Other**   SDx

√5ᵗʰ **V45.6 States following surgery of eye and adnexa**

Cataract extraction ⎫
Filtering bleb   ⎬ state following eye
Surgical eyelid adhesion ⎭   surgery

> EXCLUDES aphakia (379.31)
>   artificial eye globe (V43.0)

AHA: 4Q, '98, 65; 4Q, '97, 49

V45.61 **Cataract extraction status**   SDx

Use additional code for associated artificial lens status (V43.1)

V45.69 **Other states following surgery of eye and adnexa** SDx

AHA: 2Q, '01, 16; 1Q, '98, 10; 4Q, '97, 19

√5ᵗʰ **V45.7 Acquired absence of organ**

AHA: 4Q, '98, 65; 4Q, '97, 50

V45.71 **Acquired absence of breast and nipple**

> EXCLUDES ▶congenital absence of breast and nipple (757.6)◀

AHA: 4Q, '08, 159; 4Q, '01, 66

V45.72 **Acquired absence of intestine (large)(small)**

V45.73 **Acquired absence of kidney**

V45.74 **Other parts of urinary tract**

Bladder
AHA: 4Q, '00, 51

V45.75 **Stomach**

AHA: 4Q, '00, 51

V45.76 **Lung**

AHA: 4Q, '00, 51

V45.77 **Genital organs**

> EXCLUDES acquired absence of cervix and uterus (V88.01-V88.03)
>   female genital mutilation status (629.20-629.29)

AHA: 1Q, '03, 13, 14; 4Q, '00, 51

V45.78 **Eye**

AHA: 4Q, '00, 51

V45.79 **Other acquired absence of organ**

AHA: 4Q, '00, 51

√5ᵗʰ **V45.8 Other postprocedural status**

V45.81 **Aortocoronary bypass status**   SDx

AHA: 4Q, '03, 105; 3Q, '01, 15; 3Q, '97, 16

V45.82 **Percutaneous transluminal coronary angioplasty status** SDx

V45.83 **Breast implant removal status**   SDx

AHA: 4Q, '95, 55

V45.84 **Dental restoration status**   SDx

Dental crowns status
Dental fillings status
AHA: 4Q, '01, 54

V45.85 **Insulin pump status**   SDx

V45.86 **Bariatric surgery status**   SDx

Gastric banding status
Gastric bypass status for obesity
Obesity surgery status

> EXCLUDES bariatric surgery status complicating pregnancy, childbirth or the puerperium (649.2)
>   intestinal bypass or anastomosis status (V45.3)

AHA: ▶2Q, '09, 10;◀ 4Q, '06, 118

Z98.84 Bariatric surgery status   I-10

V45.87 **Transplanted organ removal status**   SDx

Transplanted organ previously removed due to complication, failure, rejection or infection

> EXCLUDES encounter for removal of transplanted organ — code to complication of transplanted organ (996.80-996.89)

AHA: 4Q, '08, 157

V45.88 **Status post administration of tPA (rtPA) in a different facility within the last 24 hours prior to admission to current facility** SDx

Code first condition requiring tPA administration, such as:
acute cerebral infarction (433.0-433.9 with fifth-digit 1, 434.0-434.9 with fifth digit 1)
acute myocardial infarction (410.00-410.92)

AHA: 4Q, '08, 157

TIP: Assign only on receiving facility record; assign even if the patient is still receiving tPA at the time of transfer.

V45.89 **Other**   SDx

Presence of neuropacemaker or other electronic device

> EXCLUDES artificial heart valve in situ (V43.3)
>   vascular prosthesis in situ (V43.4)

AHA: 1Q, '95, 11

√4ᵗʰ **V46 Other dependence on machines and devices**

V46.0 **Aspirator**   SDx

√5ᵗʰ **V46.1 Respirator [Ventilator]**

Iron lung
AHA: 4Q, '05, 96; 4Q, '03, 103; 1Q, '01, 12; J-F, '87, 7 3

V46.11 **Dependence on respirator, status**   SDx

AHA: 4Q, '04, 100

Z99.11 Dependence on respirator ventilator status I-10

V46.12 **Encounter for respirator dependence during power failure** PDx

AHA: 4Q, '04, 100

V46.13 **Encounter for weaning from respirator [ventilator]** PDx

V46.14 **Mechanical complication of respirator [ventilator]**

Mechanical failure of respirator [ventilator]

V46.2 **Supplemental oxygen**   SDx

Long-term oxygen therapy
AHA: 4Q, '03, 108; 4Q, '02, 79

V46.3 **Wheelchair dependence**   SDx

Wheelchair confinement status

Code first cause of dependence, such as:
muscular dystrophy (359.1)
obesity (278.00, 278.01)

AHA: 4Q, '08, 157

V46.8 **Other enabling machines**   SDx

Hyperbaric chamber
Possum [Patient-Operated-Selector-Mechanism]

> EXCLUDES cardiac pacemaker (V45.0)
>   kidney dialysis machine (V45.11)

V46.9 **Unspecified machine dependence**

AHA: 4Q, '06, 117

√4ᵗʰ **V47 Other problems with internal organs**

V47.0 **Deficiencies of internal organs**

V47.1 **Mechanical and motor problems with internal organs**

V47.2 **Other cardiorespiratory problems**

Cardiovascular exercise intolerance with pain (with):
at rest
less than ordinary activity
ordinary activity

N Newborn Age: 0   P Pediatric Age: 0-17   M Maternity Age: 12-55   A Adult Age: 15-124   SDx Secondary Diagnosis   PDx Primary Diagnosis

338 – Volume 1 · October 2009   2010 ICD-9-CM

V47.3 **Other digestive problems**

V47.4 **Other urinary problems**

V47.5 **Other genital problems**

V47.9 **Unspecified**

✓4ᵗʰ **V48 Problems with head, neck, and trunk**

V48.0 Deficiencies of head

EXCLUDES *deficiencies of ears, eyelids, and nose (V48.8)*

V48.1 Deficiencies of neck and trunk

V48.2 Mechanical and motor problems with head

V48.3 Mechanical and motor problems with neck and trunk

V48.4 Sensory problem with head

V48.5 Sensory problem with neck and trunk

V48.6 Disfigurements of head

V48.7 Disfigurements of neck and trunk

V48.8 **Other problems with head, neck, and trunk**

V48.9 **Unspecified problem with head, neck, or trunk**

✓4ᵗʰ **V49 Other conditions influencing health status**

V49.0 Deficiencies of limbs

V49.1 Mechanical problems with limbs

V49.2 Motor problems with limbs

V49.3 Sensory problems with limbs

V49.4 Disfigurements of limbs

V49.5 **Other problems of limbs**

✓5ᵗʰ V49.6 Upper limb amputation status

AHA: 4Q, '05, 94; 4Q, '98, 42; 4Q, '94, 39

V49.60 **Unspecified level**

Z89.201 Acquired absence of right upper limb uns level   I-10

V49.61 Thumb

V49.62 Other finger(s)

AHA: 2Q, '05, 7

V49.63 Hand

V49.64 Wrist

Disarticulation of wrist

V49.65 Below elbow

V49.66 Above elbow

Disarticulation of elbow

V49.67 Shoulder

Disarticulation of shoulder

✓5ᵗʰ V49.7 Lower limb amputation status

AHA: 3Q, '06, 5; 4Q, '05, 94; 4Q, '98, 42; 4Q, '94, 39

V49.70 **Unspecified level**

V49.71 Great toe

V49.72 Other toe(s)

V49.73 Foot

V49.74 Ankle

Disarticulation of ankle

V49.75 Below knee

Z89.52 Acquired absence of left leg below knee   I-10

V49.76 Above knee

Disarticulation of knee

V49.77 Hip

Disarticulation of hip

✓5ᵗʰ V49.8 Other specified conditions influencing health status

AHA: 4Q, '00, 51

V49.81 Asymptomatic postmenopausal status (age-related) (natural)   A ♀

EXCLUDES *menopausal and premenopausal disorder (627.0-627.9)*
postsurgical menopause (256.2)
premature menopause (256.31)
symptomatic menopause (627.0-627.9)

AHA: 4Q, '02, 79; 4Q, '00, 54

V49.82 Dental sealant status   SDx

AHA: 4Q, '01, 54

V49.83 Awaiting organ transplant status   SDx

V49.84 Bed confinement status

AHA: 4Q, '05, 96

V49.85 Dual sensory impairment   SDx

Blindness with deafness
Combined visual hearing impairment

Code first:
hearing impairment (389.00-389.9)
visual impairment (369.00-369.9)

AHA: 4Q, '07, 100

V49.89 **Other specified conditions influencing health status**

AHA: 4Q, '05, 94

V49.9 **Unspecified**

PERSONS ENCOUNTERING HEALTH SERVICES FOR SPECIFIC PROCEDURES AND AFTERCARE (V50-V59)

Note: Categories V51-V59 are intended for use to indicate a reason for care in patients who may have already been treated for some disease or injury not now present, or who are receiving care to consolidate the treatment, to deal with residual states, or to prevent recurrence.

EXCLUDES *follow-up examination for medical surveillance following treatment (V67.0-V67.9)*

✓4ᵗʰ **V50 Elective surgery for purposes other than remedying health states**

V50.0 Hair transplant

V50.1 **Other plastic surgery for unacceptable cosmetic appearance**

Breast augmentation or reduction
Face-lift

EXCLUDES *encounter for breast reduction (611.1)*
plastic surgery following healed injury or operation (V51.0-V51.8)

V50.2 Routine or ritual circumcision   ♂

Circumcision in the absence of significant medical indication

V50.3 Ear piercing

✓5ᵗʰ V50.4 Prophylactic organ removal

EXCLUDES *organ donations (V59.0-V59.9)*
therapeutic organ removal — code to condition

AHA: 4Q, '94, 44

TIP: Assign an additional code, such as one from category V16 Family history of malignant neoplasm, to indicate the reason for the prophylactic organ removal.

V50.41 Breast

AHA: 4Q, '04, 107

V50.42 Ovary   ♀

V50.49 **Other**

V50.8 **Other**

Z40.8 Encounter for other prophylactic surgery   I-10

V50.9 **Unspecified**

✓4ᵗʰ / ✓5ᵗʰ   Additional Digit Required   Unspecified Code   Other Specified Code   Manifestation Code   ►◄ Revised Text   ● New Code   ▲ Revised Code Title

2010 ICD-9-CM   **Volume 1 – 339**

V47.3–V50.9

✓4ᵗʰ **V51 Aftercare involving the use of plastic surgery**
Plastic surgery following healed injury or operation
EXCLUDES cosmetic plastic surgery (V50.2)
plastic surgery as treatment for current condition or
injury — code to condition or injury
repair of scarred tissue — code to scar
AHA: 4Q, '08, 159

V51.0 Encounter for breast reconstruction PDx A
following mastectomy
EXCLUDES deformity and disproportion of reconstructed
breast (612.0-612.1)
AHA: 4Q, '08, 159-160

V51.8 Other aftercare involving the use of plastic surgery

✓4ᵗʰ **V52 Fitting and adjustment of prosthetic device and implant**
INCLUDES removal of device
EXCLUDES malfunction or complication of prosthetic device
(996.0-996.7)
status only, without need for care (V43.0-V43.8)
AHA: 4Q, '05, 94; 4Q, '95, 55 ; 1Q, '90, 7

V52.0 Artificial arm (complete) (partial)

V52.1 Artificial leg (complete) (partial)

V52.2 Artificial eye

V52.3 Dental prosthetic device

V52.4 Breast prosthesis and implant ♀
Elective implant exchange (different material) (different
size)
Removal of tissue expander without synchronous
insertion of permanent implant
EXCLUDES admission for initial breast implant insertion
for breast augmentation (V50.1)
complications of breast implant (996.54,
996.69, 996.79)
encounter for breast reconstruction following
mastectomy (V51.0)
AHA: 4Q, '95, 80, 81

V52.8 Other specified prosthetic device
AHA: 2Q, '02, 12, 16

V52.9 Unspecified prosthetic device

✓4ᵗʰ **V53 Fitting and adjustment of other device**
INCLUDES removal of device
replacement of device
EXCLUDES status only, without need for care (V45.0-V45.8)

✓5ᵗʰ **V53.0 Devices related to nervous system and special senses**
AHA: 4Q, '98, 66; 4Q, '97, 51

**V53.01 Fitting and adjustment of cerebral ventricular
(communicating) shunt**
AHA: 4Q, '97, 51

**V53.02 Neuropacemaker (brain) (peripheral nerve)
(spinal cord)**

**V53.09 Fitting and adjustment of other devices
related to nervous system and special
senses**
Auditory substitution device
Visual substitution device
AHA: 2Q, '99, 4

V53.1 Spectacles and contact lenses

V53.2 Hearing aid

✓5ᵗʰ **V53.3 Cardiac device**
Reprogramming
AHA: 3Q, '92, 3; 1Q, '90, 7; M-J, '87, 8 ; N-D, '84, 18
TIP: Assign for cardiac device replacement when the device
has reached normal end-of-life parameters.

V53.31 Cardiac pacemaker
EXCLUDES mechanical complication of cardiac
pacemaker (996.01)
AHA: 1Q, '02, 3

V53.32 Automatic implantable cardiac defibrillator
AHA: 3Q, '05, 8

V53.39 Other cardiac device
AHA: 2Q, '08, 9; 1Q, '07, 20

V53.4 Orthodontic devices

▲ ✓5ᵗʰ **V53.5 Other gastrointestinal appliance and device**
EXCLUDES colostomy (V55.3)
ileostomy (V55.2)
other artificial opening of digestive tract
(V55.4)

● **V53.50 Fitting and adjustment of intestinal appliance
and device**

● **V53.51 Fitting and adjustment of gastric lap band**

● **V53.59 Fitting and adjustment of other
gastrointestinal appliance and device**

V53.6 Urinary devices
Urinary catheter
EXCLUDES cystostomy (V55.5)
nephrostomy (V55.6)
ureterostomy (V55.6)
urethrostomy (V55.6)

V53.7 Orthopedic devices
Orthopedic: Orthopedic:
brace corset
cast shoes
EXCLUDES other orthopedic aftercare (V54)

V53.8 Wheelchair

✓5ᵗʰ **V53.9 Other and unspecified device**
AHA: 2Q, '03, 6

V53.90 Unspecified device

V53.91 Fitting and adjustment of insulin pump
Insulin pump titration

V53.99 Other device
AHA: ▶2Q, '09, 10◀

✓4ᵗʰ **V54 Other orthopedic aftercare**
EXCLUDES fitting and adjustment of orthopedic devices (V53.7)
malfunction of internal orthopedic device
(996.40-996.49)
other complication of nonmechanical nature
(996.60-996.79)
AHA: 4Q, '08, 158; 1Q, '07, 3-4; 3Q, '95, 3

✓5ᵗʰ **V54.0 Aftercare involving internal fixation device**
EXCLUDES malfunction of internal orthopedic device
(996.40-996.49)
other complication of nonmechanical nature
(996.60-996.79)
removal of external fixation device (V54.89)
AHA: 4Q, '03, 87

**V54.01 Encounter for removal of internal fixation
device**

**V54.02 Encounter for lengthening/adjustment of
growth rod**

**V54.09 Other aftercare involving internal fixation
device**

✓5ᵗʰ **V54.1 Aftercare for healing traumatic fracture**
EXCLUDES ▶ aftercare following joint replacement
(V54.81)◀
aftercare for amputation stump (V54.89)
AHA: 4Q, '02, 80
TIP: Assign for follow-up and treatment during the healing
phase of the fracture; an aftercare code should be used for all
subsequent encounters after the initial encounter for care of a
fracture.

**V54.10 Aftercare for healing traumatic fracture
of arm, unspecified**

**V54.11 Aftercare for healing traumatic fracture of
upper arm**

Ⓝ Newborn Age: 0 　 Ⓟ Pediatric Age: 0-17 　 Ⓜ Maternity Age: 12-55 　 Ⓐ Adult Age: 15-124 　 SDx Secondary Diagnosis 　 PDx Primary Diagnosis

340 – Volume 1 · October 2009 　　　　　　　　　　　　　　　　　　　　　 2010 ICD-9-CM

V54.12 Aftercare for healing traumatic fracture of lower arm
    AHA: 1Q, '07, 7

V54.13 Aftercare for healing traumatic fracture of hip
    AHA: ►1Q, '09, 6;◄ 4Q, '03, 103, 105; 2Q, '03, 16

V54.14 Aftercare for healing traumatic fracture of leg, unspecified

V54.15 Aftercare for healing traumatic fracture of upper leg
    EXCLUDES   aftercare for healing traumatic fracture of hip (V54.13)
    AHA: 3Q, '06, 6

V54.16 Aftercare for healing traumatic fracture of lower leg

V54.17 Aftercare for healing traumatic fracture of vertebrae

V54.19 Aftercare for healing traumatic fracture of other bone
    AHA: 1Q, '05, 13; 4Q, '02, 80

√5th **V54.2 Aftercare for healing pathologic fracture**
    EXCLUDES ► aftercare following joint replacement (V54.81)◄
    AHA: 4Q, '02, 80

V54.20 Aftercare for healing pathologic fracture of arm, unspecified

V54.21 Aftercare for healing pathologic fracture of upper arm

V54.22 Aftercare for healing pathologic fracture of lower arm

V54.23 Aftercare for healing pathologic fracture of hip

V54.24 Aftercare for healing pathologic fracture of leg, unspecified

V54.25 Aftercare for healing pathologic fracture of upper leg
    EXCLUDES   aftercare for healing pathologic fracture of hip (V54.23)

V54.26 Aftercare for healing pathologic fracture of lower leg

V54.27 Aftercare for healing pathologic fracture of vertebrae
    AHA: 1Q, '07, 6; 4Q, '03, 108

V54.29 Aftercare for healing pathologic fracture of other bone
    AHA: 4Q, '02, 80

√5th **V54.8 Other orthopedic aftercare**
    AHA: 3Q, '01, 19; 4Q, '99, 5

V54.81 Aftercare following joint replacement
    Use additional code to identify joint replacement site (V43.60-V43.69)
    AHA: ►1Q, '09, 6;◄ 3Q, '06, 4; 2Q, '04, 15; 4Q, '02, 80

V54.89 Other orthopedic aftercare
    Aftercare for healing fracture NOS

V54.9 Unspecified orthopedic aftercare

√4th **V55 Attention to artificial openings**
    INCLUDES   adjustment or repositioning of catheter
        closure
        passage of sounds or bougies
        reforming
        removal or replacement of catheter
        toilet or cleansing
    EXCLUDES   complications of external stoma (519.00-519.09, 569.60-569.69, 997.4, 997.5)
        status only, without need for care (V44.0-V44.9)

V55.0 Tracheostomy

V55.1 Gastrostomy
    AHA: 4Q, '99, 9; 3Q, '97, 7, 8; 1Q, '96, 14; 3Q, '95, 13
    TIP: Assign for gastrostomy or PEG tube that has been dislodged or clogged, for which simple irrigation or replacement is performed.

V55.2 Ileostomy

V55.3 Colostomy
    AHA: ►1Q, '09, 5;◄ 2Q, '05, 4; 3Q, '97, 9
    Z43.3 Encounter for attention to colostomy   **I-10**

V55.4 Other artificial opening of digestive tract
    AHA: 2Q, '05, 14; 1Q, '03, 10

V55.5 Cystostomy

V55.6 Other artificial opening of urinary tract
    Nephrostomy   Urethrostomy
    Ureterostomy

V55.7 Artificial vagina

V55.8 Other specified artificial opening

V55.9 Unspecified artificial opening

√4th **V56 Encounter for dialysis and dialysis catheter care**
    Use additional code to identify the associated condition
    EXCLUDES   dialysis preparation — code to condition
    AHA: 4Q, '98, 66; 1Q, '93, 29

V56.0 Extracorporeal dialysis   **PDx**
    Dialysis (renal) NOS
    EXCLUDES   dialysis status (V45.11)
    AHA: 4Q, '05, 79; 1Q, '04, 23; 4Q, '00, 40; 3Q, '98, 6; 2Q, '98, 20

V56.1 Fitting and adjustment of extracorporeal dialysis catheter
    Removal or replacement of catheter
    Toilet or cleansing
    Use additional code for any concurrent extracorporeal dialysis (V56.0)
    AHA: 2Q, '98, 20

V56.2 Fitting and adjustment of peritoneal dialysis catheter
    Use additional code for any concurrent peritoneal dialysis (V56.8)
    AHA: 4Q, '98, 55

√5th **V56.3 Encounter for adequacy testing for dialysis**
    AHA: 4Q, '00, 55

V56.31 Encounter for adequacy testing for hemodialysis

V56.32 Encounter for adequacy testing for peritoneal dialysis
    Peritoneal equilibration test

V56.8 Other dialysis
    Peritoneal dialysis
    AHA: 4Q, '98, 55

√4th **V57 Care involving use of rehabilitation procedures**
    Use additional code to identify underlying condition
    AHA: 3Q, '06, 3; 1Q, '02, 19; 3Q, '97, 12; 1Q, '90, 6; S-O, '86, 3
    TIP: Assign codes from this category for episodes of care related to rehabilitation.

V57.0 Breathing exercises   **PDx**

V57.1 Other physical therapy   **PDx**
    Therapeutic and remedial exercises, except breathing
    AHA: 3Q, '06, 4; 2Q, '04, 15; 4Q, '02, 56; 4Q, '99, 5

√5th **V57.2 Occupational therapy and vocational rehabilitation**

V57.21 Encounter for occupational therapy   **PDx**
    AHA: 4Q, '99, 7

V57.22 Encounter for vocational therapy   **PDx**

▲ **V57.3 Speech-language therapy**   **PDx**
    AHA: 4Q, '97, 36

V57.4 Orthoptic training   **PDx**

√5th **V57.8 Other specified rehabilitation procedure**

V57.81 Orthotic training   **PDx**
    Gait training in the use of artificial limbs

√4th √5th Additional Digit Required   Unspecified Code   Other Specified Code   Manifestation Code   ►◄ Revised Text   ● New Code   ▲ Revised Code Title

V57.89 Other   `PDx`

Multiple training or therapy

AHA: 4Q, '07, 94; 3Q, '06, 6; 4Q, '03, 105-106, 108; 2Q, '03, 16; 1Q '02, 16; 3Q, '01, 21; 3Q, '97, 11, 12; S-O, '86, 4

V57.9 Unspecified rehabilitation procedure   `PDx`

√4ᵗʰ **V58 Encounter for other and unspecified procedures and aftercare**

> **EXCLUDES** *convalescence and palliative care (V66)*

TIP: If a patient is admitted for both radiation therapy and chemotherapy, either code V58.0 or V58.11 may be sequenced as the principal diagnosis.

V58.0 Radiotherapy   `PDx`

Encounter or admission for radiotherapy

> **EXCLUDES** *encounter for radioactive implant — code to condition*
> *radioactive iodine therapy — code to condition*

AHA: 3Q, '92, 5; 2Q, '90, 7; J-F, '87, 13

Z51.0 Encounter for antineoplastic radiation therapy   `I-10`

√5ᵗʰ **V58.1 Encounter for antineoplastic chemotherapy and immunotherapy**

Encounter or admission for chemotherapy

> **EXCLUDES** *chemotherapy and immunotherapy for nonneoplastic conditions — code to condition*

AHA: 1Q, '04, 13; 2Q, '03, 16; 3Q, '93, 4; 2Q, '92, 6; 2Q, '91, 17; 2Q, '90, 7; S-O, '84, 5

V58.11 Encounter for antineoplastic chemotherapy   `PDx`

AHA: 4Q, '08, 82, 155; 4Q, '07, 104; 2Q, '06, 20-21; 4Q, '05, 98

Z51.11 Encounter for antineoplastic chemotherapy   `I-10`

V58.12 Encounter for antineoplastic immunotherapy   `PDx`

AHA: 4Q, '05, 98

V58.2 Blood transfusion, without reported diagnosis

√5ᵗʰ **V58.3 Attention to dressings and sutures**

Change or removal of wound packing

> **EXCLUDES** *attention to drains (V58.49)*
> *planned postoperative wound closure (V58.41)*

AHA: 2Q, '05, 14

V58.30 Encounter for change or removal of nonsurgical wound dressing

Encounter for change or removal of wound dressing NOS

AHA: 4Q, '06, 117

V58.31 Encounter for change or removal of surgical wound dressing

AHA: 4Q, '06, 117

Z48.01 Encounter change/removal surgical wound dressing   `I-10`

V58.32 Encounter for removal of sutures

Encounter for removal of staples

AHA: 4Q, '06, 117

Z48.02 Encounter for removal of sutures   `I-10`

√5ᵗʰ **V58.4 Other aftercare following surgery**

Note: Codes from this subcategory should be used in conjunction with other aftercare codes to fully identify the reason for the aftercare encounter

> **EXCLUDES** *aftercare following sterilization reversal surgery (V26.22)*
> *attention to artificial openings (V55.0-V55.9)*
> *orthopedic aftercare (V54.0-V54.9)*

AHA: 4Q, '99, 9; N-D, '87, 9

V58.41 Encounter for planned postoperative wound closure

> **EXCLUDES** *disruption of operative wound (998.31-998.32)*
> *encounter for dressings and suture aftercare (V58.30-V58.32)*

AHA: 4Q, '99, 15

V58.42 Aftercare following surgery for neoplasm

Conditions classifiable to 140-239

AHA: 4Q, '02, 80

V58.43 Aftercare following surgery for injury and trauma

Conditions classifiable to 800-999

> **EXCLUDES** *aftercare for healing traumatic fracture (V54.10-V54.19)*

AHA: 4Q, '02, 80

V58.44 Aftercare following organ transplant

Use additional code to identify the organ transplanted (V42.0-V42.9)

AHA: 4Q, '04, 101

V58.49 Other specified aftercare following surgery

Change or removal of drains

AHA: 1Q, '96, 8, 9

V58.5 Orthodontics

> **EXCLUDES** *fitting and adjustment of orthodontic device (V53.4)*

√5ᵗʰ **V58.6 Long-term (current) drug use**

> **EXCLUDES** *drug abuse and dependence complicating pregnancy (648.3-648.4)*
> *drug abuse (305.00-305.93)*
> *drug dependence (304.00-304.93)*
> *hormone replacement therapy (postmenopausal) (V07.4)*
> *prophylactic use of agents affecting estrogen receptors and estrogen levels (V07.51-V07.59)*

AHA: ▶4Q, '08, 159;◄ 4Q, '03, 85; 1Q, '02, 84; 3Q, '02, 15; 4Q, '95, 61

TIP: Do not assign for patients on detoxification drugs or maintenance programs to prevent withdrawal symptoms related to drug dependence; assign instead drug dependence code(s).

V58.61 Long-term (current) use of anticoagulants   `SDx`

> **EXCLUDES** *long-term (current) use of aspirin (V58.66)*

AHA: ▶4Q, '08, 135;◄ 3Q, '06, 13; 3Q, '04, 7; 4Q, '03, 108; 3Q, '02, 13-16; 1Q, '02, 15, 16

Z79.01 Long term (current) use of anticoagulants   `I-10`

V58.62 Long-term (current) use of antibiotics   `SDx`

AHA: 4Q, '98, 59

V58.63 Long-term (current) use of antiplatelets/ antithrombotics   `SDx`

> **EXCLUDES** *long-term (current) use of aspirin (V58.66)*

V58.64 Long-term (current) use of non-steroidal anti-inflammatories (NSAID)   `SDx`

> **EXCLUDES** *long-term (current) use of aspirin (V58.66)*

V58.65 Long-term (current) use of steroids   `SDx`

Z79.5 Long term (current) use of steroids   `I-10`

V58.66 Long-term (current) use of aspirin   `SDx`

AHA: 4Q, '04, 102

V58.67 Long-term (current) use of insulin   `SDx`

AHA: 4Q, '04, 55-56, 103

Z79.4 Long term (current) use of insulin   `I-10`

`N` Newborn Age: 0   `P` Pediatric Age: 0-17   `M` Maternity Age: 12-55   `A` Adult Age: 15-124   `SDx` Secondary Diagnosis   `PDx` Primary Diagnosis

342 – Volume 1 · February 2009   2010 ICD-9-CM

V58.69 Long-term (current) use of other `SDx`
medications
Other high-risk medications
Long term current use of methadone
Long term current use of opiate analgesic
AHA: 4Q, '08, 156; 2Q, '04, 10; 1Q, '04, 13;
1Q, '03, 11; 2Q, '00, 8; 3Q, '99, 13; 2Q, '99, 17;
1Q, '97, 12; 2Q, '96, 7

√5ᵗʰ **V58.7** Aftercare following surgery to specified body systems,
not elsewhere classified
Note: Codes from this subcategory should be used in
conjunction with other aftercare codes to fully
identify the reason for the aftercare encounter
EXCLUDES _aftercare following organ transplant (V58.44)_
aftercare following surgery for neoplasm
_(V58.42)_
AHA: 4Q, '03, 104; 4Q, '02, 80

V58.71 Aftercare following surgery of the sense
organs, NEC
Conditions classifiable to 360-379, 380-389

V58.72 Aftercare following surgery of the nervous
system, NEC
Conditions classifiable to 320-359
EXCLUDES _aftercare following surgery of the_
sense organs, NEC (V58.71)

V58.73 Aftercare following surgery of the
circulatory system, NEC
Conditions classifiable to 390-459
AHA: ▶2Q, '09, 12;◀ 4Q, '03, 105

V58.74 Aftercare following surgery of the
respiratory system, NEC
Conditions classifiable to 460-519

V58.75 Aftercare following surgery of the teeth, oral
cavity and digestive system, NEC
Conditions classifiable to 520-579
AHA: 2Q, '05, 14

V58.76 Aftercare following surgery of the
genitourinary system, NEC
Conditions classifiable to 580-629
EXCLUDES _aftercare following sterilization_
reversal (V26.22)
AHA: 1Q, '05, 11-12

V58.77 Aftercare following surgery of the skin and
subcutaneous tissue, NEC
Conditions classifiable to 680-709

V58.78 Aftercare following surgery of the
musculoskeletal system, NEC
Conditions classifiable to 710-739
EXCLUDES _orthopedic aftercare (V54.01-V54.9)_

√5ᵗʰ **V58.8** Other specified procedures and aftercare
AHA: 4Q, '94, 45; 2Q, '94, 8

V58.81 Fitting and adjustment of vascular catheter
Removal or replacement of catheter
Toilet or cleansing
EXCLUDES _complication of renal dialysis_
_(996.73)_
complication of vascular catheter
_(996.74)_
dialysis preparation — code to
condition
encounter for dialysis (V56.0-V56.8)
fitting and adjustment of dialysis
catheter (V56.1)

V58.82 Fitting and adjustment of nonvascular
catheter, NEC
Removal or replacement of catheter
Toilet or cleansing
EXCLUDES _fitting and adjustment of peritoneal_
dialysis catheter (V56.2)
fitting and adjustment of urinary
catheter (V53.6)

V58.83 Encounter for therapeutic drug monitoring
Use additional code for any associated long-
term (current) drug use (V58.61-V58.69)
EXCLUDES _blood-drug testing for medico- legal_
reasons (V70.4)
DEF: Drug monitoring: Measurement of the level of
a specific drug in the body or measurement of a
specific function to assess effectiveness of a drug.
AHA: 4Q, '08, 156; 2Q, '04, 10; 1Q, '04, 13;4Q, '03, 85;
4Q, '02, 84; 3Q, '02, 13-16

V58.89 Other specified aftercare `Other Specified Code`
AHA: 4Q, '98, 59

V58.9 Unspecified aftercare `Unspecified Code`

√4ᵗʰ **V59** Donors
EXCLUDES _examination of potential donor (V70.8)_
self-donation of organ or tissue — code to condition
AHA: 4Q, '95, 62; 1Q, '90, 10; N-D, '84,
TIP: Assign only for living donations to other individuals, not for
self-donation or for cadaveric donations.

√5ᵗʰ **V59.0** Blood
V59.01 Whole blood `PDx`
V59.02 Stem cells `PDx`
V59.09 Other `PDx`

V59.1 Skin `PDx`
V59.2 Bone `PDx`
V59.3 Bone marrow `PDx`
V59.4 Kidney `PDx`
V59.5 Cornea `PDx`
V59.6 Liver `PDx`

√5ᵗʰ **V59.7** Egg (oocyte) (ovum)
AHA: 4Q, '05, 99

V59.70 Egg (oocyte) (ovum) donor, unspecified `PDx` ♀
V59.71 Egg (oocyte) (ovum) donor, under `PDx` ♀
age 35, anonymous recipient
Egg donor, under age 35 NOS
V59.72 Egg (oocyte) (ovum) donor, under `PDx` ♀
age 35, designated recipient
V59.73 Egg (oocyte) (ovum) donor, age 35 `PDx` ♀
and over, anonymous recipient
Egg donor, age 35 and over NOS
V59.74 Egg (oocyte) (ovum) donor, age 35 `PDx` ♀
and over, designated recipient

V59.8 Other specified organ or tissue `PDx`
AHA: 3Q, '02, 20

V59.9 Unspecified organ or tissue `PDx`

PERSONS ENCOUNTERING HEALTH SERVICES IN OTHER
CIRCUMSTANCES (V60-V69)

√4ᵗʰ **V60** Housing, household, and economic circumstances

V60.0 Lack of housing `SDx`
Hobos
Social migrants
Tramps
Transients
Vagabonds

V60.1 Inadequate housing `SDx`
Lack of heating
Restriction of space
Technical defects in home preventing adequate care

V60.2 Inadequate material resources `SDx`
Economic problem
Poverty NOS

V60.3 Person living alone `SDx`

√4ᵗʰ √5ᵗʰ Additional Digit Required   Unspecified Code   Other Specified Code   Manifestation Code   ▶◀ Revised Text   ● New Code   ▲ Revised Code Title

2010 ICD-9-CM   **October 2009 • Volume 1 – 343**

V60.4 No other household member able to render care `SDx`
　　Person requiring care (has) (is):
　　　family member too handicapped, ill, or otherwise
　　　　unsuited to render care
　　　partner temporarily away from home
　　　temporarily away from usual place of abode
　　EXCLUDES *holiday relief care (V60.5)*

V60.5 Holiday relief care `SDx`
　　Provision of health care facilities to a person normally
　　　cared for at home, to enable relatives to take a
　　　vacation

V60.6 Person living in residential institution `SDx`
　　Boarding school resident

`√5th` **V60.8 Other specified housing or economic circumstances**

● 　　**V60.81 Foster care (status)** `SDx`

● 　　**V60.89 Other specified housing or economic** `SDx`
　　　　　circumstances

V60.9 Unspecified housing or economic `SDx`
　　　circumstance

`√4th` **V61 Other family circumstances**
　　INCLUDES when these circumstances or fear of them, affecting
　　　　the person directly involved or others, are
　　　　mentioned as the reason, justified or not, for
　　　　seeking or receiving medical advice or care
　　AHA: 1Q, '90, 9

`√5th` **V61.0 Family disruption**
　　AHA: 4Q, '08, 160

　　V61.01 Family disruption due to family member on
　　　　military deployment
　　　　Individual or family affected by other family
　　　　　member being on deployment
　　　　EXCLUDES ▶ *family disruption due to family*
　　　　　member on non-military
　　　　　extended absence from home
　　　　　(V61.08) ◀

　　V61.02 Family disruption due to return of family
　　　　member from military deployment
　　　　Individual or family affected by other family
　　　　　member having returned from
　　　　　deployment (current or past conflict)

　　V61.03 Family disruption due to divorce or legal
　　　　separation

　　V61.04 Family disruption due to parent-child
　　　　estrangement
　　　　EXCLUDES *other family estrangement (V61.09)*

　　V61.05 Family disruption due to child in welfare
　　　　custody

　　V61.06 Family disruption due to child in foster care or
　　　　in care of non-parental family member

● 　　**V61.07 Family disruption due to death of family**
　　　　member
　　　　EXCLUDES *bereavement (V62.82)*

● 　　**V61.08 Family disruption due to other extended**
　　　　absence of family member
　　　　EXCLUDES *family disruption due to family*
　　　　　member on military
　　　　　deployment (V61.01)

　　V61.09 Other family disruption
　　　　Family estrangement NOS

`√5th` **V61.1 Counseling for marital and partner problems**
　　EXCLUDES *problems related to:*
　　　psychosexual disorders (302.0-302.9)
　　　sexual function (V41.7)

　　V61.10 Counseling for marital and partner
　　　　problems, unspecified
　　　　Marital conflict
　　　　Marital relationship problem
　　　　Partner conflict
　　　　Partner relationship problem

V61.11 Counseling for victim of spousal and partner
　　abuse
　　EXCLUDES *encounter for treatment of current*
　　　injuries due to abuse
　　　(995.80-995.85)

V61.12 Counseling for perpetrator of spousal and
　　partner abuse

`√5th` **V61.2 Parent-child problems**

　　V61.20 Counseling for parent-child problem,
　　　　unspecified
　　　　Concern about behavior of child
　　　　Parent-child conflict
　　　　Parent-child relationship problem

　　V61.21 Counseling for victim of child abuse
　　　　Child battering　　　　Child neglect
　　　　EXCLUDES *current injuries due to abuse*
　　　　　(995.50-995.59)

　　V61.22 Counseling for perpetrator of parental child
　　　　abuse
　　　　EXCLUDES *counseling for non-parental abuser*
　　　　　(V62.83)

● 　　**V61.23 Counseling for parent-biological child**
　　　　problem
　　　　Concern about behavior of biological child
　　　　Parent-biological child conflict
　　　　Parent-biological child relationship problem

● 　　**V61.24 Counseling for parent-adopted child problem**
　　　　Concern about behavior of adopted child
　　　　Parent-adopted child conflict
　　　　Parent-adopted child relationship problem

● 　　**V61.25 Counseling for parent (guardian)-foster child**
　　　　problem
　　　　Concern about behavior of foster child
　　　　Parent (guardian)-foster child conflict
　　　　Parent (guardian)-foster child relationship
　　　　　problem

▲ 　　**V61.29 Other parent-child problems**
　　　　AHA: 3Q, '99, 16

V61.3 Problems with aged parents or in-laws

`√5th` **V61.4 Health problems within family**

　　V61.41 Alcoholism in family

● 　　**V61.42 Substance abuse in family**

　　V61.49 Other
　　　　Care of　　　⎫ sick or handicapped person in
　　　　Presence of　⎬ family or household

V61.5 Multiparity

V61.6 Illegitimacy or illegitimate pregnancy `M` `♀`

V61.7 Other unwanted pregnancy `M` `♀`

V61.8 Other specified family circumstances
　　Problems with family members NEC
　　Sibling relationship problem

V61.9 Unspecified family circumstance

`√4th` **V62 Other psychosocial circumstances**
　　INCLUDES those circumstances or fear of them, affecting the
　　　　person directly involved or others, mentioned
　　　　as the reason, justified or not, for seeking or
　　　　receiving medical advice or care
　　EXCLUDES *previous psychological trauma (V15.41-V15.49)*

V62.0 Unemployment `SDx`
　　EXCLUDES *circumstances when main problem is*
　　　economic inadequacy or poverty (V60.2)

V62.1 Adverse effects of work environment `SDx`

`N` Newborn Age: 0　　　　`P` Pediatric Age: 0-17　　　　`M` Maternity Age: 12-55　　　　`A` Adult Age: 15-124　　　　`SDx` Secondary Diagnosis　　　　`PDx` Primary Diagnosis

V62.2 Other occupational circumstances or maladjustment ✓5th
AHA: 4Q, '08, 160

V62.21 Personal current military deployment status A SDx
Individual (civilian or military) currently deployed in theater or in support of military war, peacekeeping and humanitarian operations

V62.22 Personal history of return from military deployment A SDx
Individual (civilian or military) with past history of military war, peacekeeping and humanitarian deployment (current or past conflict)

V62.29 Other occupational circumstances or maladjustment A SDx
Career choice problem
Dissatisfaction with employment
Occupational problem

V62.3 Educational circumstances SDx
Academic problem
Dissatisfaction with school environment
Educational handicap

V62.4 Social maladjustment SDx
Acculturation problem
Cultural deprivation
Political, religious, or sex discrimination
Social:
    isolation
    persecution

V62.5 Legal circumstances SDx
Imprisonment   Litigation
Legal investigation   Prosecution

V62.6 Refusal of treatment for reasons of religion or conscience SDx

V62.8 Other psychological or physical stress, not elsewhere classified ✓5th

V62.81 Interpersonal problems, not elsewhere classified SDx
Relational problem NOS

V62.82 Bereavement, uncomplicated SDx
EXCLUDES bereavement as adjustment reaction (309.0)
▶family disruption due to death of family member (V61.07)◀

V62.83 Counseling for perpetrator of physical/sexual abuse SDx
EXCLUDES counseling for perpetrator of parental child abuse (V61.22)
counseling for perpetrator of spousal and partner abuse (V61.12)

V62.84 Suicidal ideation
EXCLUDES suicidal tendencies (300.9)
DEF: Thoughts of committing suicide; no actual attempt of suicide has been made.
AHA: 4Q, '05, 96
TIP: Assign as a secondary diagnosis for patients who have not attempted suicide, and who may not be considered a suicide risk, but who have indicated thoughts about suicide.
R45.85 Suicidal ideation I-10

V62.89 Other SDx
Borderline intellectual functioning
Life circumstance problems
Phase of life problems
Religious or spiritual problem

V62.9 Unspecified psychosocial circumstance SDx

V63 Unavailability of other medical facilities for care ✓4th
AHA: 1Q, '91, 21

V63.0 Residence remote from hospital or other health care facility

V63.1 Medical services in home not available
EXCLUDES no other household member able to render care (V60.4)
AHA: 4Q, '01, 67; 1Q, '01, 12

V63.2 Person awaiting admission to adequate facility elsewhere

V63.8 Other specified reasons for unavailability of medical facilities
Person on waiting list undergoing social agency investigation

V63.9 Unspecified reason for unavailability of medical facilities

V64 Persons encountering health services for specific procedures, not carried out ✓4th

V64.0 Vaccination not carried out ✓5th
AHA: 4Q, '05, 99

V64.00 Vaccination not carried out, unspecified reason SDx

V64.01 Vaccination not carried out because of acute illness SDx

V64.02 Vaccination not carried out because of chronic illness or condition SDx

V64.03 Vaccination not carried out because of immune compromised state SDx

V64.04 Vaccination not carried out because of allergy to vaccine or component SDx
Z28.04 Immunization not carried out pt allergy vaccine I-10

V64.05 Vaccination not carried out because of caregiver refusal SDx
Guardian refusal   Parent refusal
EXCLUDES vaccination not carried out because of caregiver refusal for religious reasons (V64.07)
AHA: 1Q, '07, 12

V64.06 Vaccination not carried out because of patient refusal SDx

V64.07 Vaccination not carried out for religious reasons SDx

V64.08 Vaccination not carried out because patient had disease being vaccinated against SDx

V64.09 Vaccination not carried out for other reason SDx

V64.1 Surgical or other procedure not carried out because of contraindication SDx
TIP: Assign an additional code to indicate the contraindication (reason the surgery or other procedure was canceled).

V64.2 Surgical or other procedure not carried out because of patient's decision SDx
AHA: 2Q, '01, 8

V64.3 Procedure not carried out for other reasons SDx

V64.4 Closed surgical procedure converted to open procedure ✓5th
AHA: 4Q, '03, 87; 4Q, '98, 68; 4Q, '97, 52

V64.41 Laparoscopic surgical procedure converted to open procedure SDx

V64.42 Thoracoscopic surgical procedure converted to open procedure SDx

V64.43 Arthroscopic surgical procedure converted to open procedure SDx

V65 Other persons seeking consultation ✓4th

V65.0 Healthy person accompanying sick person
Boarder

✓4th ✓5th Additional Digit Required   Unspecified Code   Other Specified Code   Manifestation Code   ▶◀ Revised Text   ● New Code   ▲ Revised Code Title

2010 ICD-9-CM   **October 2009 · Volume 1 – 345**

☑5ᵗʰ V65.1 Person consulting on behalf of another person
Advice or treatment for nonattending third party
EXCLUDES concern (normal) about sick person in family
(V61.41-V61.49)
AHA: 4Q, '03, 84

▲ **V65.11 Pediatric pre-birth visit for expectant parent(s)**
Pre-adoption visit for adoptive parent(s)

V65.19 Other person consulting on behalf of another person

V65.2 Person feigning illness
Malingerer   Peregrinating patient
AHA: 3Q, '99, 20
TIP: Assign for patients engaged in what is documented as "drug- seeking behavior."

V65.3 Dietary surveillance and counseling
Dietary surveillance and counseling (in):
NOS
colitis
diabetes mellitus
food allergies or intolerance
gastritis
hypercholesterolemia
hypoglycemia
obesity
Use additional code to identify Body Mass Index (BMI), if known (V85.0-V85.54)
AHA: 4Q, '05, 96

☑5ᵗʰ V65.4 Other counseling, not elsewhere classified
Health:
advice
education
instruction
EXCLUDES counseling (for):
contraception (V25.40-V25.49)
genetic (V26.31-V26.39)
on behalf of third party (V65.11-V65.19)
procreative management (V26.41-V26.49)

V65.40 Counseling NOS

V65.41 Exercise counseling

V65.42 Counseling on substance use and abuse
Z71.6 Tobacco abuse counseling   I-10

V65.43 Counseling on injury prevention

V65.44 Human immunodeficiency virus [HIV] counseling

V65.45 Counseling on other sexually transmitted diseases

V65.46 Encounter for insulin pump training
Z71.82 Insulin pump counseling and training   I-10

V65.49 Other specified counseling
AHA: 4Q, '08, 156; 2Q, '00, 8

V65.5 Person with feared complaint in whom no diagnosis was made
Feared condition not demonstrated
Problem was normal state
"Worried well"

V65.8 Other reasons for seeking consultation
EXCLUDES specified symptoms
AHA: 3Q, '92, 4

V65.9 Unspecified reason for consultation

☑4ᵗʰ V66 Convalescence and palliative care

V66.0 Following surgery   PDx

V66.1 Following radiotherapy   PDx

V66.2 Following chemotherapy   PDx

V66.3 Following psychotherapy and other treatment for mental disorder   PDx

V66.4 Following treatment of fracture   PDx

V66.5 Following other treatment   PDx

V66.6 Following combined treatment   PDx

V66.7 Encounter for palliative care   SDx
End of life care
Hospice care
Terminal care
Code first underlying disease
AHA: 3Q, '08, 13; 2Q, '05, 9; 4Q, '03, 107; 1Q, '98, 11; 4Q, '96, 47, 48
TIP: Assign as secondary diagnosis when treatment is focused on management of pain and symptoms in a patient with an incurable disease.
Z51.5 Encounter for palliative care   I-10

V66.9 Unspecified convalescence   PDx
AHA: 4Q, '99, 8

☑4ᵗʰ V67 Follow-up examination
INCLUDES surveillance only following completed treatment
EXCLUDES surveillance of contraception (V25.40-V25.49)
AHA: 4Q, '08, 157; 2Q, '03, 5; 4Q, '94, 98

☑5ᵗʰ V67.0 Following surgery
AHA: 4Q, '00, 56; 4Q, '98, 69; 4Q, '97, 50; 2Q, '95, 8;1Q, '95, 4; 3Q, '92, 11

V67.00 Following surgery, unspecified

V67.01 Follow-up vaginal pap smear   ♀
Vaginal pap-smear, status-post hysterectomy for malignant condition
Use additional code to identify:
acquired absence of uterus (V88.01-V88.03)
personal history of malignant neoplasm (V10.40-V10.44)
EXCLUDES vaginal pap smear status-post hysterectomy for non-malignant condition (V76.47)
AHA: 4Q, '08, 157

V67.09 Following other surgery
EXCLUDES sperm count following sterilization reversal (V26.22)
sperm count for fertility testing (V26.21)
AHA: 3Q, '08, 6; 3Q, '03, 16; 3Q, '02, 15

V67.1 Following radiotherapy

V67.2 Following chemotherapy
Cancer chemotherapy follow-up

V67.3 Following psychotherapy and other treatment for mental disorder

V67.4 Following treatment of healed fracture
EXCLUDES current (healing) fracture aftercare (V54.0-V54.9)
AHA: ▶1Q, '09, 6;◀ 1Q, '90, 7

☑5ᵗʰ V67.5 Following other treatment

V67.51 Following completed treatment with high-risk medications, not elsewhere classified
EXCLUDES long-term (current) drug use (V58.61-V58.69)
AHA: 1Q, '99, 5, 6;4Q, '95, 61 ; 1Q, '90, 18

V67.59 Other

V67.6 Following combined treatment

V67.9 Unspecified follow-up examination

N Newborn Age: 0   P Pediatric Age: 0-17   M Maternity Age: 12-55   A Adult Age: 15-124   SDx Secondary Diagnosis   PDx Primary Diagnosis

346 – Volume 1 · October 2009   2010 ICD-9-CM

✓4ᵗʰ **V68 Encounters for administrative purposes**

✓5ᵗʰ   **V68.0 Issue of medical certificates**

   EXCLUDES *encounter for general medical examination (V70.0-V70.9)*

V68.01 Disability examination [PDx]
   Use additional code(s) to identify specific examination(s), screening and testing performed (V72.0-V82.9)
   AHA: 4Q, '07, 101

V68.09 Other issue of medical certificates [PDx]

V68.1 Issue of repeat prescriptions [PDx]
   Issue of repeat prescription for:
      appliance
      glasses
      medications
   EXCLUDES *repeat prescription for contraceptives (V25.41-V25.49)*

V68.2 Request for expert evidence [PDx]

✓5ᵗʰ   **V68.8 Other specified administrative purpose**

V68.81 Referral of patient without examination or treatment [PDx]

V68.89 Other [PDx]

V68.9 Unspecified administrative purpose [PDx]

✓4ᵗʰ **V69 Problems related to lifestyle**
   AHA: 4Q, '94, 48

V69.0 Lack of physical exercise

V69.1 Inappropriate diet and eating habits
   EXCLUDES *anorexia nervosa (307.1)*
      bulimia (783.6)
      malnutrition and other nutritional deficiencies (260-269.9)
      other and unspecified eating disorders (307.50-307.59)

V69.2 High-risk sexual behavior

V69.3 Gambling and betting
   EXCLUDES *pathological gambling (312.31)*

V69.4 Lack of adequate sleep
   Sleep deprivation
   EXCLUDES *insomnia (780.52)*

V69.5 Behavioral insomnia of childhood [P]
   DEF: Behaviors on the part of the child or caregivers that cause negative compliance with a child's sleep schedule; results in lack of adequate sleep.
   AHA: 4Q, '05, 99

V69.8 Other problems related to lifestyle
   Self-damaging behavior

V69.9 Problem related to lifestyle, unspecified

PERSONS WITHOUT REPORTED DIAGNOSIS ENCOUNTERED DURING EXAMINATION AND INVESTIGATION OF INDIVIDUALS AND POPULATIONS (V70-V82)

Note: Nonspecific abnormal findings disclosed at the time of these examinations are classifiable to categories 790-796.

✓4ᵗʰ **V70 General medical examination**
   Use additional code(s) to identify any special screening examination(s) performed (V73.0-V82.9)

V70.0 Routine general medical examination at a health care facility [PDx]
   Health checkup
   EXCLUDES *health checkup of infant or child ▶over 28 days old◀ (V20.2)*
      ▶health supervision of newborn 8 to 28 days old (V20.32)
      health supervision of newborn under 8 days old (V20.31)◀
      pre-procedural general physical examination (V72.83)

V70.1 General psychiatric examination, requested by the authority [PDx]

V70.2 General psychiatric examination, other and unspecified [PDx]

V70.3 Other medical examination for administrative purposes [PDx]
   General medical examination for:
      admission to old age home
      adoption
      camp
      driving license
      immigration and naturalization
      insurance certification
      marriage
      prison
      school admission
      sports competition
   EXCLUDES *attendance for issue of medical certificates (V68.0)*
      pre-employment screening (V70.5)
   AHA: 3Q, '08, 6; 1Q, '90, 6
   Z02.6 Encounter for exam for insurance purposes [I-10]

V70.4 Examination for medicolegal reasons [PDx]
   Blood-alcohol tests   Paternity testing
   Blood-drug tests
   EXCLUDES *examination and observation following:*
      accidents (V71.3, V71.4)
      assault (V71.6)
      rape (V71.5)

V70.5 Health examination of defined subpopulations [PDx]
   Armed forces personnel
   Inhabitants of institutions
   Occupational healthexaminations
   Pre-employment screening
   Preschool children
   Prisoners
   Prostitutes
   Refugees
   School children
   Students

V70.6 Health examination in population surveys [PDx]
   EXCLUDES *special screening (V73.0-V82.9)*

V70.7 Examination of participant in clinical trial
   Examination of participant or control in clinical research
   AHA: 2Q, '06, 5-6; 4Q, '01, 55

V70.8 Other specified general medical examinations [PDx]
   Examination of potential donor of organ or tissue

V70.9 Unspecified general medical examination [PDx]

✓4ᵗʰ **V71 Observation and evaluation for suspected conditions not found**
   INCLUDES This category is to be used when persons without a diagnosis are suspected of having an abnormal condition, without signs or symptoms, which requires study, but after examination and observation, is found not to exist. This category is also for use for administrative and legal observation status.
   EXCLUDES *suspected maternal and fetal conditions not found (V89.01-V89.09)*
   AHA: 4Q, '94, 47; 2Q, '90, 5; M-A, '87, 1
   TIP: Assign observation codes only as principal/first-listed diagnosis and only if there is no documentation of any signs or symptoms.

✓5ᵗʰ   **V71.0 Observation for suspected mental condition**

V71.01 Adult antisocial behavior [A] [PDx]
   Dyssocial behavior or gang activity in adult without manifest psychiatric disorder

V71.02 Childhood or adolescent antisocial behavior [PDx]
   Dyssocial behavior or gang activity in child or adolescent without manifest psychiatric disorder

V Codes

V71.09–V72.82

V71.09	**Other suspected mental condition**	PDx
V71.1	**Observation for suspected malignant neoplasm**	PDx
V71.2	**Observation for suspected tuberculosis**	PDx
V71.3	**Observation following accident at work**	PDx
V71.4	**Observation following other accident**	PDx

    Examination of individual involved in motor vehicle traffic accident

    AHA: 1Q, '06, 9

V71.5	**Observation following alleged rape or seduction**	PDx

    Examination of victim or culprit

V71.6	**Observation following other inflicted injury**	PDx

    Examination of victim or culprit

V71.7	**Observation for suspected cardiovascular disease**	PDx

    AHA: 1Q, '04, 6; 3Q, '90, 10; S-O, '87, 10

√5ᵗʰ **V71.8 Observation and evaluation for other specified suspected conditions**

    EXCLUDES   contact with and (suspected) exposure to (potentially) hazardous substances (V15.84-V15.86, V87.0-V87.31)

    AHA: 4Q, '00, 54 ; 1Q, '90, 19

    V71.81 Abuse and neglect   PDx

        EXCLUDES   adult abuse and neglect (995.80-995.85)
                 child abuse and neglect (995.50-995.59)

        AHA: 4Q, '00, 55

    V71.82 Observation and evaluation for suspected exposure to anthrax   PDx

        AHA: 4Q, '02, 70, 85

    V71.83 Observation and evaluation for suspected exposure to other biological agent   PDx

        AHA: 4Q, '03, 47

    V71.89 Other specified suspected conditions   PDx

        AHA: 3Q, '08, 7; 2Q, '03, 15

V71.9	**Observation for unspecified suspected condition**	PDx

    AHA: 1Q, '02, 6

√4ᵗʰ **V72 Special investigations and examinations**

    INCLUDES   routine examination of specific system

    Use additional code(s) to identify any special screening examination(s) performed (V73.0-V82.9)

    EXCLUDES   general medical examination (V70.0-V70.4)
               general screening examination of defined population groups (V70.5, V70.6, V70.7)
               ▶health supervision of newborn 8 to 28 days old (V20.32)
               health supervision of newborn under 8 days old (V20.31)◀
               routine examination of infant or child ▶over 28 days old (V20.2)◀

V72.0 Examination of eyes and vision

    AHA: 1Q, '04, 15

√5ᵗʰ **V72.1 Examination of ears and hearing**

    AHA: 1Q, '04, 15

    V72.11 Encounter for hearing examination following failed hearing screening

        AHA: 4Q, '06, 118

        Z01.110 Encounter hearing exam follow failed   I-10
             hearing scr

    V72.12 Encounter for hearing conservation and treatment

        AHA: 4Q, '07, 100

    V72.19 Other examination of ears and hearing

V72.2 Dental examination

√5ᵗʰ **V72.3 Gynecological examination**

    EXCLUDES   cervical Papanicolaou smear without general gynecological examination (V76.2)
               routine examination in contraceptive management (V25.40-V25.49)

    V72.31 Routine gynecological examination   ♀

        General gynecological examination with or without Papanicolaou cervical smear
        Pelvic examination (annual) (periodic)

        Use additional code to identify:
            human papillomavirus (HPV) screening (V73.81)
            routine vaginal Papanicolaou smear (V76.47)

        AHA: 2Q, '06, 2-3; 4Q, '05, 98

    V72.32 Encounter for Papanicolaou cervical smear to confirm findings of recent normal smear following initial abnormal smear   ♀

        AHA: 2Q, '06, 4

√5ᵗʰ **V72.4 Pregnancy examination or test**

    AHA: 4Q, '05, 98

    V72.40 Pregnancy examination or test, pregnancy unconfirmed   ♀

        Possible pregnancy, not (yet) confirmed

    V72.41 Pregnancy examination or test, negative result   ♀

    V72.42 Pregnancy examination or test, positive result   ♀ M

V72.5 Radiological examination, not elsewhere classified

    Routine chest x-ray

    EXCLUDES   ▶radiologic examinations as part of pre-procedural testing (V72.81-V72.84)◀

    AHA: 1Q, '90, 19

V72.6 Laboratory examination

    ▶Encounters for blood and urine testing◀

    AHA: 2Q, '06, 4; 1Q, '90, 22

    ● **V72.60 Laboratory examination, unspecified**

    ● **V72.61 Antibody response examination**

        Immunity status testing

        EXCLUDES   encounter for allergy testing (V72.7)

    ● **V72.62 Laboratory examination ordered as part of a routine general medical examination**

        Blood tests for routine general physical examination

    ● **V72.63 Pre-procedural laboratory examination**

        Blood tests prior to treatment or procedure
        Pre-operative laboratory examination

    ● **V72.69 Other laboratory examination**

V72.7 Diagnostic skin and sensitization tests

    Allergy tests
    Skin tests for hypersensitivity

    EXCLUDES   diagnostic skin tests for bacterial diseases (V74.0-V74.9)

√5ᵗʰ **V72.8 Other specified examinations**

    EXCLUDES   ▶pre-procedural laboratory examinations (V72.63)◀

    V72.81 Pre-operative cardiovascular examination

        Pre-procedural cardiovascular examination

        Z01.810 Encounter for preprocedural   I-10
             cardiovascular exam

    V72.82 Pre-operative respiratory examination

        Pre-procedural respiratory examination

        AHA: 3Q, '96, 14

N Newborn Age: 0   P Pediatric Age: 0-17   M Maternity Age: 12-55   A Adult Age: 15-124   SDx Secondary Diagnosis   PDx Primary Diagnosis

348 – Volume 1 · October 2009   2010 ICD-9-CM

V72.83 Other specified pre-operative examination
▶Examination prior to chemotherapy◀
Other pre-procedural examination
Pre-procedural general physical examination

EXCLUDES routine general medical examination
(V70.0)

AHA: 3Q, '96, 14

V72.84 Pre-operative examination, unspecified
Pre-procedural examination, unspecified

V72.85 Other specified examination
AHA: 4Q, '05, 96; 1Q, '04, 12

V72.86 Encounter for blood typing

V72.9 Unspecified examination
AHA: 4Q, '06, 117

✓4th **V73** Special screening examination for viral and chlamydial diseases
AHA: 1Q, '04, 11

V73.0 Poliomyelitis

V73.1 Smallpox

V73.2 Measles

V73.3 Rubella

V73.4 Yellow fever

V73.5 Other arthropod-borne viral diseases
Dengue fever
Hemorrhagic fever
Viral encephalitis:
mosquito-borne
tick-borne

V73.6 Trachoma

✓5th **V73.8** Other specified viral and chlamydial diseases

V73.81 Human papillomavirus [HPV]
AHA: 4Q, '07, 100

V73.88 Other specified chlamydial diseases
AHA: 4Q, '07, 124

V73.89 Other specified viral diseases

✓5th **V73.9** Unspecified viral and chlamydial disease

V73.98 Unspecified chlamydial disease

V73.99 Unspecified viral disease

✓4th **V74** Special screening examination for bacterial and spirochetal diseases

INCLUDES diagnostic skin tests for these diseases
AHA: 1Q, '04, 11

V74.0 Cholera

V74.1 Pulmonary tuberculosis

V74.2 Leprosy [Hansen's disease]

V74.3 Diphtheria

V74.4 Bacterial conjunctivitis

V74.5 Venereal disease
Screening for bacterial and spirochetal sexually
transmitted diseases
Screening for sexually transmitted diseases NOS

EXCLUDES special screening for nonbacterial sexually
transmitted diseases (V73.81-V73.89,
V75.4, V75.8)

AHA: 4Q, '07, 124

V74.6 Yaws

V74.8 Other specified bacterial and spirochetal diseases
Brucellosis
Leptospirosis
Plague
Tetanus
Whooping cough

V74.9 Unspecified bacterial and spirochetal disease

✓4th **V75** Special screening examination for other infectious diseases
AHA: 1Q, '04, 11

V75.0 Rickettsial diseases

V75.1 Malaria

V75.2 Leishmaniasis

V75.3 Trypanosomiasis
Chagas' disease
Sleeping sickness

V75.4 Mycotic infections

V75.5 Schistosomiasis

V75.6 Filariasis

V75.7 Intestinal helminthiasis

V75.8 Other specified parasitic infections

V75.9 Unspecified infectious disease

✓4th **V76** Special screening for malignant neoplasms
AHA: 1Q, '04, 11

TIP: Whenever a screening examination is performed, the screening
code is the first-listed code, regardless of the findings or any procedure
that is performed as a result of the findings.

V76.0 Respiratory organs

✓5th **V76.1** Breast
AHA: 4Q, '98, 67

V76.10 Breast screening, unspecified

V76.11 Screening mammogram for high-risk patient♀
AHA: 2Q, '03, 4

V76.12 Other screening mammogram
AHA: 2Q, '06, 10; 2Q, '03, 3-4

V76.19 Other screening breast examination

V76.2 Cervix ♀
Routine cervical Papanicolaou smear

EXCLUDES special screening for human papillomavirus
(V73.81)
that as part of a general gynecological
examination (V72.31)

V76.3 Bladder

✓5th **V76.4** Other sites

V76.41 Rectum

V76.42 Oral cavity

V76.43 Skin

V76.44 Prostate ♂
Z12.5 Encounter screening malignant I-10
neoplasm prostate

V76.45 Testis ♂

V76.46 Ovary ♀
AHA: 4Q, '00, 52

V76.47 Vagina ♀
Vaginal pap smear status-post hysterectomy for
non-malignant condition
Use additional code to identify acquired
absence of uterus (V88.01-V88.03)

EXCLUDES vaginal pap smear status-post
hysterectomy for malignant
condition (V67.01)

AHA: 4Q, '08, 157; 4Q, '00, 52

V76.49 Other sites
AHA: 1Q, '99, 4

✓5th **V76.5** Intestine
AHA: 4Q, '00, 52

V76.50 Intestine, unspecified

✓4th ✓5th Additional Digit Required | Unspecified Code | Other Specified Code | Manifestation Code | ▶◀ Revised Text | ● New Code | ▲ Revised Code Title

2010 ICD-9-CM | October 2009 • Volume 1 – 349

V76.51   **Colon**
    EXCLUDES   *rectum (V76.41)*
    AHA: 4Q, '01, 56
    Z12.11 Encounter screening malignant   **I-10**
    neoplasm of colon

V76.52   **Small intestine**

√5th   V76.8   **Other neoplasm**
    AHA: 4Q, '00, 52

V76.81   **Nervous system**

V76.89   **Other neoplasm**

V76.9   **Unspecified**

√4th   **V77**   **Special screening for endocrine, nutritional, metabolic, and immunity disorders**
    AHA: 1Q, '04, 11

V77.0   **Thyroid disorders**

V77.1   **Diabetes mellitus**

V77.2   **Malnutrition**

V77.3   **Phenylketonuria [PKU]**

V77.4   **Galactosemia**

V77.5   **Gout**

V77.6   **Cystic fibrosis**
    Screening for mucoviscidosis

V77.7   **Other inborn errors of metabolism**

V77.8   **Obesity**

√5th   V77.9   **Other and unspecified endocrine, nutritional, metabolic, and immunity disorders**
    AHA: 4Q, '00, 53

V77.91   **Screening for lipoid disorders**
    Screening for cholesterol level
    Screening for hypercholesterolemia
    Screening for hyperlipidemia

V77.99   **Other and unspecified endocrine nutritional metabolic and immunity disorders**

√4th   **V78**   **Special screening for disorders of blood and blood-forming organs**
    AHA: 1Q, '04, 11

V78.0   **Iron deficiency anemia**

V78.1   **Other and unspecified deficiency anemia**

V78.2   **Sickle cell disease or trait**

V78.3   **Other hemoglobinopathies**

V78.8   **Other disorders of blood and blood-forming organs**

V78.9   **Unspecified disorder of blood and blood-forming organs**

√4th   **V79**   **Special screening for mental disorders and developmental handicaps**
    AHA: 1Q, '04, 11

V79.0   **Depression**

V79.1   **Alcoholism**

V79.2   **Mental retardation**

V79.3   **Developmental handicaps in early childhood**

V79.8   **Other specified mental disorders and developmental handicaps**

V79.9   **Unspecified mental disorder and developmental handicap**

√4th   **V80**   **Special screening for neurological, eye, and ear diseases**
    AHA: 1Q, '04, 11

√5th   V80.0   **Neurological conditions**

●   V80.01   **Traumatic brain injury**

●   V80.09   **Other neurological conditions**

V80.1   **Glaucoma**

V80.2   **Other eye conditions**
    Screening for:
    cataract
    congenital anomaly of eye
    senile macular lesions
    EXCLUDES   *general vision examination (V72.0)*

V80.3   **Ear diseases**
    EXCLUDES   *general hearing examination (V72.11-V72.19)*

√4th   **V81**   **Special screening for cardiovascular, respiratory, and genitourinary diseases**
    AHA: 1Q, '04, 11

V81.0   **Ischemic heart disease**

V81.1   **Hypertension**

V81.2   **Other and unspecified cardiovascular conditions**

V81.3   **Chronic bronchitis and emphysema**

V81.4   **Other and unspecified respiratory conditions**
    EXCLUDES   *screening for:*
    lung neoplasm (V76.0)
    pulmonary tuberculosis (V74.1)

V81.5   **Nephropathy**
    Screening for asymptomatic bacteriuria

V81.6   **Other and unspecified genitourinary conditions**

√4th   **V82**   **Special screening for other conditions**
    AHA: 1Q, '04, 11

V82.0   **Skin conditions**

V82.1   **Rheumatoid arthritis**

V82.2   **Other rheumatic disorders**

V82.3   **Congenital dislocation of hip**

V82.4   **Maternal postnatal screening for chromosomal anomalies**   ♀
    EXCLUDES   *antenatal screening by amniocentesis (V28.0)*

V82.5   **Chemical poisoning and other contamination**
    Screening for:
    heavy metal poisoning
    ingestion of radioactive substance
    poisoning from contaminated water supply
    radiation exposure

V82.6   **Multiphasic screening**

√5th   V82.7   **Genetic screening**
    EXCLUDES   *genetic testing for procreative management (V26.31-V26.39)*

V82.71   **Screening for genetic disease carrier status**
    AHA: 4Q, '06, 118

V82.79   **Other genetic screening**
    AHA: 4Q, '06, 118

√5th   V82.8   **Other specified conditions**
    AHA: 4Q, '00, 53

V82.81   **Osteoporosis**
    Use additional code to identify:
    hormone replacement therapy (postmenopausal) status (V07.4)
    postmenopausal (age-related) (natural) status (V49.81)
    AHA: 4Q, '00, 54

V82.89   **Other specified conditions**

V82.9   **Unspecified condition**

N Newborn Age: 0   P Pediatric Age: 0-17   M Maternity Age: 12-55   A Adult Age: 15-124   **SDx** Secondary Diagnosis   **PDx** Primary Diagnosis

350 – Volume 1 • October 2009   **2010 ICD-9-CM**

GENETICS (V83-V84)

✓4th V83 Genetic carrier status

AHA: 4Q, '02, 79; 4Q, '01, 54

TIP: The patient does not have the disease or carry a risk of developing it, but may genetically pass it to offspring who then may develop it.

✓5th V83.0 Hemophilia A carrier

V83.01 Asymptomatic hemophilia A carrier

V83.02 Symptomatic hemophilia A carrier

✓5th V83.8 Other genetic carrier status

V83.81 Cystic fibrosis gene carrier

V83.89 Other genetic carrier status

✓4th V84 Genetic susceptibility to disease

INCLUDES confirmed abnormal gene

Use additional code, if applicable, for any associated family history of the disease (V16-V19)

AHA: 4Q, '04, 106

TIP: The patient has a gene that increases the risk of developing a specific disease; assign only as a secondary condition.

✓5th V84.0 Genetic susceptibility to malignant neoplasm

Code first, if applicable, any current malignant neoplasms (140.0-195.8, 200.0-208.9, 230.0-234.9)

Use additional code, if applicable, for any personal history of malignant neoplasm (V10.0-V10.9)

V84.01 Genetic susceptibility to malignant SDx neoplasm of breast

AHA: 4Q, '04, 107

Z15.01 Genetic susceptibility malignant I-10 neoplasm breast

V84.02 Genetic susceptibility to malignant SDx ♀ neoplasm of ovary

V84.03 Genetic susceptibility to malignant SDx ♂ neoplasm of prostate

V84.04 Genetic susceptibility to malignant SDx ♀ neoplasm of endometrium

V84.09 Genetic susceptibility to other SDx malignant neoplasm

✓5th V84.8 Genetic susceptibility to other disease

V84.81 Genetic susceptibility to multiple SDx endocrine neoplasia [MEN]

AHA: 4Q, '07, 100

V84.89 Genetic susceptibility to other disease SDx

BODY MASS INDEX (V85)

✓4th V85 Body Mass Index [BMI]

Kilograms per meters squared

Note: BMI adult codes are for use for persons over 20 years old

AHA: 4Q, '08, 191; 4Q, '05, 97

TIP: While BMI may be coded from dietician or other caregiver documentation, the diagnosis of being overweight or obese must be coded from physician documentation.

V85.0 Body Mass Index less than 19, adult SDx A

V85.1 Body Mass Index between 19-24, adult SDx A

✓5th V85.2 Body Mass Index between 25-29, adult

V85.21 Body Mass Index 25.0-25.9, adult SDx A

V85.22 Body Mass Index 26.0-26.9, adult SDx A

V85.23 Body Mass Index 27.0-27.9, adult SDx A

V85.24 Body Mass Index 28.0-28.9, adult SDx A

V85.25 Body Mass Index 29.0-29.9, adult SDx A

✓5th V85.3 Body Mass Index between 30-39, adult

V85.30 Body Mass Index 30.0-30.9, adult SDx A

V85.31 Body Mass Index 31.0-31.9, adult SDx A

V85.32 Body Mass Index 32.0-32.9, adult SDx A

V85.33 Body Mass Index 33.0-33.9, adult SDx A

V85.34 Body Mass Index 34.0-34.9, adult SDx A

V85.35 Body Mass Index 35.0-35.9, adult SDx A

V85.36 Body Mass Index 36.0-36.9, adult SDx A

V85.37 Body Mass Index 37.0-37.9, adult SDx A

V85.38 Body Mass Index 38.0-38.9, adult SDx A

V85.39 Body Mass Index 39.0-39.9, adult SDx A

V85.4 Body Mass Index 40 and over, adult SDx A

Z68.4 Body mass index BMI 40 or greater adult I-10

✓5th V85.5 Body Mass Index, pediatric

Note: BMI pediatric codes are for use for persons age 2-20 years old. These percentiles are based on the growth charts published by the Centers for Disease Control and Prevention (CDC)

AHA: 4Q, '06, 118

V85.51 Body Mass Index, pediatric, less SDx P than 5th percentile for age

V85.52 Body Mass Index, pediatric, 5th SDx P percentile to less than 85th percentile for age

V85.53 Body Mass Index, pediatric, 85th SDx P percentile to less than 95th percentile for age

V85.54 Body Mass Index, pediatric, SDx P greater than or equal to 95th percentile for age

Z68.54 Body mass index (BMI) ≥ 95% for age I-10

ESTROGEN RECEPTOR STATUS (V86)

✓4th V86 Estrogen receptor status

Code first malignant neoplasm of breast (174.0-174.9, 175.0-175.9)

AHA: 4Q, '06, 118

V86.0 Estrogen receptor positive status [ER+] SDx

V86.1 Estrogen receptor negative status [ER-] SDx

OTHER SPECIFIED PERSONAL EXPOSURES AND HISTORY PRESENTING HAZARDS TO HEALTH (V87)

✓4th V87 Other specified personal exposures and history presenting hazards to health

✓5th V87.0 Contact with and (suspected) exposure to hazardous metals

EXCLUDES exposure to lead (V15.86)

toxic effect of metals (984.0-985.9)

AHA: 4Q, '08, 158

V87.01 Arsenic

V87.09 Other hazardous metals

Chromium compounds

Nickel dust

✓5th V87.1 Contact with and (suspected) exposure to hazardous aromatic compounds

EXCLUDES toxic effects of aromatic compounds (982.0, 983.0)

AHA: 4Q, '08, 158

V87.11 Aromatic amines

V87.12 Benzene

V87.19 Other hazardous aromatic compounds

Aromatic dyes NOS

Polycyclic aromatic hydrocarbons

V87.2 Contact with and (suspected) exposure to other potentially hazardous chemicals

Dyes NOS

EXCLUDES exposure to asbestos (V15.84)

toxic effect of chemicals (980-989)

AHA: 4Q, '08, 158

| ✓4th ✓5th | Additional Digit Required | Unspecified Code | Other Specified Code | Manifestation Code | ►◄ Revised Text | ● New Code | ▲ Revised Code Title |

2010 ICD-9-CM **Volume 1 – 351**

√5ᵗʰ **V87.3 Contact with and (suspected) exposure to other potentially hazardous substances**

     EXCLUDES   *contact with and (suspected) exposure to potentially hazardous body fluids (V15.85)*
                      toxic effect of substances (980-989)

     V87.31 Exposure to mold

     V87.32 Contact with and (suspected) exposure to algae bloom

     V87.39 Contact with and (suspected) exposure to other potentially hazardous substances

√5ᵗʰ **V87.4 Personal history of drug therapy**

     EXCLUDES   *long-term (current) drug use (V58.61-V58.69)*
     AHA: 4Q, '08, 159

     V87.41 Personal history of antineoplastic chemotherapy   `SDx`

         Z92.6 Personal hx chemotherapy for   `I-10`
neoplastic disease

     V87.42 Personal history of monoclonal drug therapy   `SDx`

     V87.43 Personal history of estrogen therapy   `SDx`

     V87.44 Personal history of inhaled steroid therapy   `SDx`

     V87.45 Personal history of systemic steroid therapy   `SDx`

         Personal history of steroid therapy NOS

     V87.46 Personal history of immunosuppression therapy   `SDx`

         EXCLUDES   *personal history of steroid therapy (V87.44, V87.45)*

     V87.49 Personal history of other drug therapy   `SDx`

ACQUIRED ABSENCE OF OTHER ORGANS AND TISSUE (V88)

√4ᵗʰ **V88 Acquired absence of other organs and tissue**

√5ᵗʰ **V88.0 Acquired absence of cervix and uterus**
     AHA: 4Q, '08, 157

     V88.01 Acquired absence of both cervix and uterus   `SDx` ♀

         Acquired absence of uterus NOS
Status post total hysterectomy

     V88.02 Acquired absence of uterus with remaining cervical stump   `SDx` ♀

         Status post partial hysterectomy with remaining cervical stump

     V88.03 Acquired absence of cervix with remaining uterus   `SDx` ♀

OTHER SUSPECTED CONDITIONS NOT FOUND (V89)

√4ᵗʰ **V89 Other suspected conditions not found**

√5ᵗʰ **V89.0 Suspected maternal and fetal conditions not found**

     EXCLUDES   *known or suspected fetal anomalies affecting management of mother, not ruled out (655.00, 655.93, 656.00-656.93, 657.00-657.03, 658.00-658.93)*
                   newborn and perinatal conditions — code to condition

     AHA: 4Q, '08, 159

     TIP: These investigations are performed while the fetus is in utero; the codes should be assigned only on the mother's medical record.

     V89.01 Suspected problem with amniotic cavity and membrane not found   `M` ♀

         Suspected oligohydramnios not found
Suspected polyhydramnios not found

     V89.02 Suspected placental problem not found   `M` ♀

     V89.03 Suspected fetal anomaly not found   `M` ♀

     V89.04 Suspected problem with fetal growth not found   `M` ♀

     V89.05 Suspected cervical shortening not found   `M` ♀

     V89.09 Other suspected maternal and fetal condition not found   `M` ♀

N Newborn Age: 0   **P** Pediatric Age: 0-17   **M** Maternity Age: 12-55   **A** Adult Age: 15-124   **SDx** Secondary Diagnosis   **PDx** Primary Diagnosis

352 – Volume 1 • October 2009   **2010 ICD-9-CM**

SUPPLEMENTARY CLASSIFICATION OF EXTERNAL CAUSES OF INJURY AND POISONING ▶(E000-E999)◀

This section is provided to permit the classification of environmental events, circumstances, and conditions as the cause of injury, poisoning, and other adverse effects. Where a code from this section is applicable, it is intended that it shall be used in addition to a code from one of the main chapters of ICD-9-CM, indicating the nature of the condition. Certain other conditions which may be stated to be due to external causes are classified in Chapters 1 to 16 of ICD-9-CM. For these, the "E" code classification should be used as an additional code for more detailed analysis.

▶Machinery accidents [other than those connected with transport] are classifiable to category E919, in which the fourth digit allows a broad classification of the type of machinery involved. ◀

Categories for "late effects" of accidents and other external causes are to be found at E929, E959, E969, E977, E989, and E999.

▶EXTERNAL CAUSE STATUS (E000)◀

Note: A code from category E000 may be used in conjunction with the external cause code(s) assigned to a record to indicate the status of the person at the time the event occurred. A single code from category E000 should be assigned for an encounter.

- ✓4ᵗʰ **E000 External cause status**
-     **E000.0 Civilian activity done for income or pay**
  Civilian activity done for financial or other compensation
  EXCLUDES   *military activity (E000.1)*
-     **E000.1 Military activity**
  EXCLUDES   *activity of off-duty military personnel (E000.8)*
-     **E000.8 Other external cause status**
  Activity NEC
  Hobby not done for income
  Leisure activity
  Off-duty activity of military personnel
  Recreation or sport not for income or while a student
  Student activity
  Volunteer activity
  EXCLUDES   *civilian activity done for income or compensation (E000.0)*
            military activity (E000.1)
-     **E000.9 Unspecified external cause status**

▶ACTIVITY (E001-E030)◀

Note: Categories E001 to E030 are provided for use to indicate the activity of the person seeking healthcare for an injury or health condition, such as a heart attack while shoveling snow, which resulted from, or was contributed to, by the activity. These codes are appropriate for use for both acute injuries, such as those from chapter 17, and conditions that are due to the long-term, cumulative affects of an activity, such as those from chapter 13. They are also appropriate for use with external cause codes for cause and intent if identifying the activity provides additional information on the event.

These codes should be used in conjunction with other external cause codes for external cause status (E000) and place of occurrence (E849).

This section contains the following broad activity categories:

E001	Activities involving walking and running
E002	Activities involving water and water craft
E003	Activities involving ice and snow
E004	Activities involving climbing, rappelling, and jumping off
E005	Activities involving dancing and other rhythmic movement
E006	Activities involving other sports and athletics played individually
E007	Activities involving other sports and athletics played as a team or group
E008	Activities involving other specified sports and athletics
E009	Activity involving other cardiorespiratory exercise
E010	Activity involving other muscle strengthening exercises
E011	Activities involving computer technology and electronic devices
E012	Activities involving arts and handcrafts
E013	Activities involving personal hygiene and household maintenance
E014	Activities involving person providing caregiving
E015	Activities involving food preparation, cooking and grilling
E016	Activities involving property and land maintenance, building and construction
E017	Activities involving roller coasters and other types of external motion
E018	Activities involving playing musical instrument
E019	Activities involving animal care
E029	Other activity
E030	Unspecified activity

- ✓4ᵗʰ **E001 Activities involving walking and running**
  EXCLUDES   *walking an animal (E019.0)*
             walking or running on a treadmill (E009.0)
-     **E001.0 Walking, marching and hiking**
  Walking, marching and hiking on level or elevated terrain
  EXCLUDES   *mountain climbing (E004.0)*
-     **E001.1 Running**
- ✓4ᵗʰ **E002 Activities involving water and water craft**
  EXCLUDES   *activities involving ice (E003.0-E003.9)*
             boating and other watercraft transport accidents (E830-E838)
-     **E002.0 Swimming**
-     **E002.1 Springboard and platform diving**
-     **E002.2 Water polo**
-     **E002.3 Water aerobics and water exercise**
-     **E002.4 Underwater diving and snorkeling**
  SCUBA diving
-     **E002.5 Rowing, canoeing, kayaking, rafting and tubing**
  Canoeing, kayaking, rafting and tubing in calm and turbulent water
-     **E002.6 Water skiing and wake boarding**
-     **E002.7 Surfing, windsurfing and boogie boarding**
-     **E002.8 Water sliding**
-     **E002.9 Other activity involving water and watercraft**
  Activity involving water NOS
  Parasailing
  Water survival training and testing
- ✓4ᵗʰ **E003 Activities involving ice and snow**
  EXCLUDES   *shoveling ice and snow (E016.0)*
-     **E003.0 Ice skating**
  Figure skating (singles) (pairs)
  Ice dancing
  EXCLUDES   *ice hockey (E003.1)*
-     **E003.1 Ice hockey**
-     **E003.2 Snow (alpine) (downhill) skiing, snow boarding, sledding, tobogganing and snow tubing**
  EXCLUDES   *cross country skiing (E003.3)*
-     **E003.3 Cross country skiing**
  Nordic skiing
-     **E003.9 Other activity involving ice and snow**
  Activity involving ice and snow NOS
- ✓4ᵗʰ **E004 Activities involving climbing, rappelling, and jumping off**
  EXCLUDES   *hiking on level or elevated terrain (E001.0)*
             jumping rope (E006.5)
             sky diving (E840-E844)
             trampoline jumping (E005.3)
-     **E004.0 Mountain climbing, rock climbing and wall climbing**
-     **E004.1 Rappelling**
-     **E004.2 BASE jumping**
  Building, Antenna, Span, Earth jumping
-     **E004.3 Bungee jumping**
-     **E004.4 Hang gliding**
-     **E004.9 Other activity involving climbing, rappelling and jumping off**
- ✓4ᵗʰ **E005 Activities involving dancing and other rhythmic movement**
  EXCLUDES   *martial arts (E008.4)*
-     **E005.0 Dancing**
-     **E005.1 Yoga**

- E005.2 **Gymnastics**
  Rhythmic gymnastics
  EXCLUDES *trampoline (E005.3)*

- E005.3 **Trampoline**

- E005.4 **Cheerleading**

- E005.9 **Other activity involving dancing and other rhythmic movements**

- ✓4th **E006 Activities involving other sports and athletics played individually**
  EXCLUDES *dancing (E005.0)*
  gymnastic (E005.2)
  trampoline (E005.3)
  yoga (E005.1)

- E006.0 **Roller skating (inline) and skateboarding**

- E006.1 **Horseback riding**

- E006.2 **Golf**

- E006.3 **Bowling**

- E006.4 **Bike riding**
  EXCLUDES *transport accident involving bike riding (E800-E829)*

- E006.5 **Jumping rope**

- E006.6 **Non-running track and field events**
  EXCLUDES *running (any form) (E001.1)*

- E006.9 **Other activity involving other sports and athletics played individually**
  EXCLUDES *activities involving climbing, rappelling, and jumping (E004.0-E004.9)*
  activities involving ice and snow (E003.0-E003.9)
  activities involving walking and running (E001.0-E001.9)
  activities involving water and watercraft (E002.0-E002.9)

- ✓4th **E007 Activities involving other sports and athletics played as a team or group**
  EXCLUDES *ice hockey (E003.1)*
  water polo (E002.2)

- E007.0 **American tackle football**
  Football NOS

- E007.1 **American flag or touch football**

- E007.2 **Rugby**

- E007.3 **Baseball**
  Softball

- E007.4 **Lacrosse and field hockey**

- E007.5 **Soccer**

- E007.6 **Basketball**

- E007.7 **Volleyball (beach) (court)**

- E007.8 **Physical games generally associated with school recess, summer camp and children**
  Capture the flag
  Dodge ball
  Four square
  Kickball

- E007.9 **Other activity involving other sports and athletics played as a team or group**
  Cricket

- ✓4th **E008 Activities involving other specified sports and athletics**

- E008.0 **Boxing**

- E008.1 **Wrestling**

- E008.2 **Racquet and hand sports**
  Handball
  Racquetball
  Squash
  Tennis

- E008.3 **Frisbee**
  Ultimate frisbee

- E008.4 **Martial arts**
  Combatives

- E008.9 **Other specified sports and athletics activity**
  EXCLUDES *sports and athletics activities specified in categories E001-E007*

- ✓4th **E009 Activity involving other cardiorespiratory exercise**
  Activity involving physical training

- E009.0 **Exercise machines primarily for cardiorespiratory conditioning**
  Elliptical and stepper machines
  Stationary bike
  Treadmill

- E009.1 **Calisthenics**
  Jumping jacks
  Warm up and cool down

- E009.2 **Aerobic and step exercise**

- E009.3 **Circuit training**

- E009.4 **Obstacle course**
  Challenge course
  Confidence course

- E009.5 **Grass drills**
  Guerilla drills

- E009.9 **Other activity involving cardiorespiratory exercise**
  EXCLUDES *activities involving cardiorespiratory exercise specified in categories E001-E008*

- ✓4th **E010 Activity involving other muscle strengthening exercises**

- E010.0 **Exercise machines primarily for muscle strengthening**

- E010.1 **Push-ups, pull-ups, sit-ups**

- E010.2 **Free weights**
  Barbells
  Dumbbells

- E010.3 **Pilates**

- E010.9 **Other activity involving other muscle strengthening exercises**
  EXCLUDES *activities involving muscle strengthening specified in categories E001-E009*

- ✓4th **E011 Activities involving computer technology and electronic devices**
  EXCLUDES *electronic musical keyboard or instruments (E018.0)*

- E011.0 **Computer keyboarding**
  Electronic game playing using keyboard or other stationary device

- E011.1 **Hand held interactive electronic device**
  Cellular telephone and communication device
  Electronic game playing using interactive device
  EXCLUDES *electronic game playing using keyboard or other stationary device (E011.0)*

- E011.9 **Other activity involving computer technology and electronic devices**

- ✓4th **E012 Activities involving arts and handcrafts**
  EXCLUDES *activities involving playing musical instrument (E018.0-E018.3)*

- E012.0 **Knitting and crocheting**

- E012.1 **Sewing**

- E012.2 **Furniture building and finishing**
  Furniture repair

- E012.9 **Activity involving other arts and handcrafts**

- ✓4th **E013 Activities involving personal hygiene and household maintenance**
  EXCLUDES *activities involving cooking and grilling (E015.0-E015.9)*
  activities involving property and land maintenance, building and construction (E016.0-E016.9)
  activity involving persons providing caregiving (E014.0-E014.9)
  dishwashing (E015.0)
  food preparation (E015.0)
  gardening (E016.1)

- E013.0 **Personal bathing and showering**

- E013.1 **Laundry**

- E013.2 **Vacuuming**

✓4th Fourth-digit Required   ▶◀ Revised Text   ● New Code   ▲ Revised Code TitleDx

- E013.3 Ironing
- E013.4 Floor mopping and cleaning
- E013.5 Residential relocation
    Packing up and unpacking involved in moving to a new residence
- E013.8 Other personal hygiene activity
- E013.9 Other household maintenance
- ✓4ᵗʰ **E014 Activities involving person providing caregiving**
- E014.0 Caregiving involving bathing
- E014.1 Caregiving involving lifting
- E014.9 Other activity involving person providing caregiving
- ✓4ᵗʰ **E015 Activities involving food preparation, cooking and grilling**
- E015.0 Food preparation and clean up
    Dishwasing
- E015.1 Grilling and smoking food
- E015.2 Cooking and baking
    Use of stove, oven and microwave oven
- E015.9 Other activity involving cooking and grilling
- ✓4ᵗʰ **E016 Activities involving property and land maintenance, building and construction**
- E016.0 Digging, shoveling and raking
    Dirt digging
    Raking leaves
    Snow shoveling
- E016.1 Gardening and landscaping
    Pruning, trimming shrubs, weeding
- E016.2 Building and construction
- E016.9 Other activity involving property and land maintenance, building and construction
- ✓4ᵗʰ **E017 Activities involving roller coasters and other types of external motion**
- E017.0 Roller coaster riding
- E017.9 Other activity involving external motion
- ✓4ᵗʰ **E018 Activities involving playing musical instrument**
    Activity involving playing electric musical instrument
- E018.0 Piano playing
    Musical keyboard (electronic) playing
- E018.1 Drum and other percussion instrument playing
- E018.2 String instrument playing
- E018.3 Wind and brass instrument playing
- ✓4ᵗʰ **E019 Activities involving animal care**
    EXCLUDES horseback riding (E006.1)
- E019.0 Walking an animal
- E019.1 Milking an animal
- E019.2 Grooming and shearing an animal
- E019.9 Other activity involving animal care
- ✓4ᵗʰ **E029 Other activity**
- E029.0 Refereeing a sports activity
- E029.1 Spectator at an event
- E029.2 Rough housing and horseplay
- E029.9 Other activity
- **E030 Unspecified activity**

▶**TRANSPORT ACCIDENTS (E800-E848)**◀

DEFINITIONS AND EXAMPLES RELATED TO TRANSPORT ACCIDENTS

(a) A **transport accident** (E800-E848) is any accident involving a device designed primarily for, or being used at the time primarily for, conveying persons or goods from one place to another.

INCLUDES   accidents involving:
    aircraft and spacecraft (E840-E845)
    watercraft (E830-E838)
    motor vehicle (E810-E825)
    railway (E800-E807)
    other road vehicles (E826-E829)

In classifying accidents which involve more than one kind of transport, the above order of precedence of transport accidents should be used.

Accidents involving agricultural and construction machines, such as tractors, cranes, and bulldozers, are regarded as transport accidents only when these vehicles are under their own power on a highway [otherwise the vehicles are regarded as machinery]. Vehicles which can travel on land or water, such as hovercraft and other amphibious vehicles, are regarded as watercraft when on the water, as motor vehicles when on the highway, and as off-road motor vehicles when on land, but off the highway.

EXCLUDES   accidents:
    in sports which involve the use of transport but where the transport vehicle itself was not involved in the accident
    involving vehicles which are part of industrial equipment used entirely on industrial premises
    occurring during transportation but unrelated to the hazards associated with the means of transportation [e.g., injuries received in a fight on board ship; transport vehicle involved in a cataclysm such as an earthquake]
    to persons engaged in the maintenance or repair of transport equipment or vehicle not in motion, unlesss injured by another vehicle in motion

(b) A **railway accident** is a transport accident involving a railway train or other railway vehicle operated on rails, whether in motion or not.

EXCLUDES   accidents:
    in repair shops
    in roundhouse or on turntable
    on railway premises but not involving a train or other railway vehicle

(c) A **railway train** or **railway vehicle** is any device with or without cars coupled to it, desiged for traffic on a railway.

INCLUDES   interurban:
    electric car } (operated chiefly on its own
    street car   right-of-way, not open to
                        other traffic)
    railway train, any power [diesel] [electric] [steam]
    funicular
    monorail or two-rail
    subterranean or elevated
    other vehicle designed to run on a railway track

EXCLUDES   interurban electric cars [streetcars] specified to be operating on a right-of-way that forms part of the public street or highway [definition (h)]

(d) A **railway** or **railroad** is a right-of-way designed for traffic on rails, which is used by carriages or wagons transporting passengers or freight, and by other rolling stock, and which is not open to other public vehicular traffic.

(e) A **motor vehicle accident** is a transport accident involving a motor vehicle. It is defined as a motor vehicle traffic accident or as a motor vehicle nontraffic accident according to whether the accident occurs on a public highway or elsewhere.

EXCLUDES   injury or damage due to cataclysm
    injury or damage while a motor vehicle, not under its own power, is being loaded on, or unloaded from, another conveyance

---

✓4ᵗʰ Fourth-digit Required   ▶◀ Revised Text   ● New Code   ▲ Revised Code TitleDx

(f) A **motor vehicle traffic accident** is any motor vehicle accident occurring on a public highway [i.e., originating, terminating, or involving a vehicle partially on the highway]. A motor vehicle accident is assumed to have occurred on the highway unless another place is specified, except in the case of accidents involving only off-road motor vehicles which are classified as nontraffic accidents unless the contrary is stated.

(g) A **motor vehicle nontraffic accident** is any motor vehicle accident which occurs entirely in any place other than a public highway.

(h) A **public highway [trafficway]** or **street** is the entire width between property lines [or other boundary lines] of every way or place, of which any part is open to the use of the public for purposes of vehicular traffic as a matter of right or custom. A **roadway** is that part of the public highway designed, improved, and ordinarily used, for vehicular travel.

> **INCLUDES**   approaches (public) to:
> > docks
> > public building
> > station
>
> **EXCLUDES**   *driveway (private)*
> > *parking lot*
> > *ramp*
> > *roads in:*
> > > *airfield*
> > > *farm*
> > > *industrial premises*
> > > *mine*
> > > *private grounds*
> > > *quarry*

(i) A **motor vehicle** is any mechanically or electrically powered device, not operated on rails, upon which any person or property may be transported or drawn upon a highway. Any object such as a trailer, coaster, sled, or wagon being towed by a motor vehicle is considered a part of the motor vehicle.

> **INCLUDES**   automobile [any type]
> > bus
> > construction machinery, farm and industrial machinery, steam roller, tractor, army tank, highway grader, or similar vehicle on wheels or treads, while in transport under own power
> > fire engine (motorized)
> > motorcycle
> > motorized bicycle [moped] or scooter
> > trolley bus not operating on rails
> > truck
> > van
>
> **EXCLUDES**   *devices used solely to move persons or materials within the confines of a building and its premises, such as:*
> > *building elevator*
> > *coal car in mine*
> > *electric baggage or mail truck used solely within a railroad station*
> > *electric truck used solely within an industrial plant*
> > *moving overhead crane*

(j) A **motorcycle** is a two-wheeled motor vehicle having one or two riding saddles and sometimes having a third wheel for the support of a sidecar. The sidecar is considered part of the motorcycle.

> **INCLUDES**   motorized:
> > bicycle [moped]
> > scooter
> > tricycle

(k) An **off-road motor vehicle** is a motor vehicle of special design, to enable it to negotiate rough or soft terrain or snow. Examples of special design are high construction, special wheels and tires, driven by treads, or support on a cushion of air.

> **INCLUDES**   all terrain vehicle [ATV]
> > army tank
> > hovercraft, on land or swamp
> > snowmobile

(l) A **driver** of a motor vehicle is the occupant of the motor vehicle operating it or intending to operate it. A **motorcyclist** is the driver of a motorcycle. Other authorized occupants of a motor vehicle are **passengers**.

(m) An **other road vehicle** is any device, except a motor vehicle, in, on, or by which any person or property may be transported on a highway.

> **INCLUDES**   animal carrying a person or goods
> > animal-drawn vehicles
> > animal harnessed to conveyance
> > bicycle [pedal cycle]
> > streetcar
> > tricycle (pedal)
>
> **EXCLUDES**   *pedestrian conveyance [definition (q)]*

(n) A **streetcar** is a device designed and used primarily for transporting persons within a municipality, running on rails, usually subject to normal traffic control signals, and operated principally on a right-of-way that forms part of the traffic way. A trailer being towed by a streetcar is considered a part of the streetcar.

> **INCLUDES**   interurban or intraurban electric or streetcar, when specified to be operating on a street or public highway
> > tram (car)
> > trolley (car)

(o) A **pedal cycle** is any road transport vehicle operated solely by pedals.

> **INCLUDES**   bicycle
> > pedal cycle
> > tricycle
>
> **EXCLUDES**   *motorized bicycle [definition (j)]*

(p) A **pedal cyclist** is any person riding on a pedal cycle or in a sidecar attached to such a vehicle.

(q) A **pedestrian conveyance** is any human powered device by which a pedestrian may move other than by walking or by which a walking person may move another pedestrian.

> **INCLUDES**   baby carriage
> > coaster wagon
> > heelies, wheelies
> > ice skates
> > perambulator
> > pushcart
> > pushchair
> > roller skates
> > scooter
> > skateboard
> > skis
> > sled
> > wheelchair

(r) A **pedestrian** is any person involved in an accident who was not at the time of the accident riding in or on a motor vehicle, railroad train, streetcar, animal-drawn or other vehicle, or on a bicycle or animal.

> **INCLUDES**   person:
> > changing tire of vehicle
> > in or operating a pedestrian conveyance
> > making adjustment to motor of vehicle
> > on foot

(s) A **watercraft** is any device for transporting passengers or goods on the water.

(t) A **small boat** is any watercraft propelled by paddle, oars, or small motor, with a passenger capacity of less than ten.

> **INCLUDES**   boat NOS
> > canoe
> > coble
> > dinghy
> > punt
> > raft
> > rowboat
> > rowing shell
> > scull
> > skiff
> > small motorboat
>
> **EXCLUDES**   *barge*
> > *lifeboat (used after abandoning ship)*
> > *raft (anchored) being used as a diving platform*
> > *yacht*

✔4ᵗʰ Fourth-digit Required   ▶◀ Revised Text   ● New Code   ▲ Revised Code TitleDx

(u) An **aircraft** is any device for transporting passengers or goods in the air.

> INCLUDES   airplane [any type]
> balloon
> bomber
> dirigible
> glider (hang)
> military aircraft
> parachute

(v) A **commercial transport aircraft** is any device for collective passenger or freight transportation by air, whether run on commercial lines for profit or by government authorities, with the exception of military craft.

RAILWAY ACCIDENTS (E800–E807)

Note: For definitions of railway accident and related terms see definitions (a) to (d).

> EXCLUDES   *accidents involving railway train and:*
> *aircraft (E840.0-E845.9)*
> *motor vehicle (E810.0-E825.9)*
> *watercraft (E830.0-E838.9)*

The following fourth-digit subdivisions are for use with categories E800–E807 to identify the injured person:
  .0 **Railway employee**
       Any person who by virtue of his employment in connection with a railway, whether by the railway company or not, is at increased risk of involvement in a railway accident, such as:
       catering staff of train
       driver
       guard
       porter
       postal staff on train
       railway fireman
       shunter
       sleeping car attendant
  .1 **Passenger on railway**
       Any authorized person traveling on a train, except a railway employee.
       > EXCLUDES *intending passenger waiting at station (.8)*
       > *unauthorized rider on railway vehicle (.8)*
  .2 **Pedestrian**
       See definition (r)
  .3 **Pedal cyclist**
       See definition (p)
  .8 **Other specified person**
       Intending passenger or bystander waiting at station
       Unauthorized rider on railway vehicle
  .9 **Unspecified person**

§ ✓4ᵗʰ **E800 Railway accident involving collision with rolling stock**

> INCLUDES   collision between railway trains or railway vehicles, any kind
> collision NOS on railway
> derailment with antecedent collision with rolling stock or NOS

§ ✓4ᵗʰ **E801 Railway accident involving collision with other object**

> INCLUDES   collision of railway train with:
> buffers
> fallen tree on railway
> gates
> platform
> rock on railway
> streetcar
> other nonmotor vehicle
> other object
> EXCLUDES   *collision with:*
> *aircraft (E840.0-E842.9)*
> *motor vehicle (E810.0-E810.9, E820.0-E822.9)*

§ ✓4ᵗʰ **E802 Railway accident involving derailment without antecedent collision**

§ ✓4ᵗʰ **E803 Railway accident involving explosion, fire, or burning**

> EXCLUDES   *explosion or fire, with antecedent derailment (E802.0-E802.9)*
> *explosion or fire, with mention of antecedent collision (E800.0-E801.9)*

§ ✓4ᵗʰ **E804 Fall in, on, or from railway train**

> INCLUDES   fall while alighting from or boarding railway train
> EXCLUDES   *fall related to collision, derailment, or explosion of railway train (E800.0-E803.9)*

§ ✓4ᵗʰ **E805 Hit by rolling stock**

> INCLUDES   crushed
> injured
> killed   } by railway train or part
> knocked down
> run over
> EXCLUDES   *pedestrian hit by object set in motion by railway train (E806.0-E806.9)*

§ ✓4ᵗʰ **E806 Other specified railway accident**

> INCLUDES   hit by object falling in railway train
> injured by door or window on railway train
> nonmotor road vehicle or pedestrian hit by object set in motion by railway train
> railway train hit by falling:
> earth NOS
> rock
> tree
> other object
> EXCLUDES   *railway accident due to cataclysm (E908-E909)*

§ ✓4ᵗʰ **E807 Railway accident of unspecified nature**

> INCLUDES   found dead } on railway right-of-way NOS
> injured
> railway accident NOS

MOTOR VEHICLE TRAFFIC ACCIDENTS (E810-E819)

Note: For definitions of motor vehicle traffic accident, and related terms, see definitions (e) to (k).

> EXCLUDES   *accidents involving motor vehicle and aircraft (E840.0-E845.9)*

The following fourth-digit subdivisions are for use with categories E810-E819 to identify the injured person:
  .0 **Driver of motor vehicle other than motorcycle**
       See definition (l)
  .1 **Passenger in motor vehicle other than motorcycle**
       See definition (l)
  .2 **Motorcyclist**
       See definition (l)
  .3 **Passenger on motorcycle**
       See definition (l)
  .4 **Occupant of streetcar**
  .5 **Rider of animal; occupant of animal-drawn vehicle**
  .6 **Pedal cyclist**
       See definition (p)
  .7 **Pedestrian**
       See definition (r)
  .8 **Other specified person**
       Occupant of vehicle other than above
       Person in railway train involved in accident
       Unauthorized rider of motor vehicle
  .9 **Unspecified person**

§ ✓4ᵗʰ **E810 Motor vehicle traffic accident involving collision with train**

> EXCLUDES   *motor vehicle collision with object set in motion by railway train (E815.0-E815.9)*
> *railway train hit by object set in motion by motor vehicle (E818.0-E818.9)*

§ ✓4ᵗʰ **E811 Motor vehicle traffic accident involving re-entrant collision with another motor vehicle**

> INCLUDES   collision between motor vehicle which accidentally leaves the roadway then re-enters the same roadway, or the opposite roadway on a divided highway, and another motor vehicle
> EXCLUDES   *collision on the same roadway when none of the motor vehicles involved have left and re-entered the highway (E812.0-E812.9)*

§   Requires fourth-digit. See beginning of appropriate section for codes and definitions.

✓4ᵗʰ Fourth-digit Required   ▶◀ Revised Text   ● New Code   ▲ Revised Code TitleDx

E Codes

E812–E819

§ ✓4ᵗʰ **E812 Other motor vehicle traffic accident involving collision with motor vehicle**

    INCLUDES   collision with another motor vehicle parked, stopped, stalled, disabled, or abandoned on the highway

           motor vehicle collision NOS

    EXCLUDES   *collision with object set in motion by another motor vehicle (E815.0-E815.9)*

           re-entrant collision with another motor vehicle (E811.0-E811.9)

§ ✓4ᵗʰ **E813 Motor vehicle traffic accident involving collision with other vehicle**

    INCLUDES   collision between motor vehicle, any kind, and:

           other road (nonmotor transport) vehicle, such as:

                animal carrying a person

                animal-drawn vehicle

                pedal cycle

                streetcar

    EXCLUDES   *collision with:*

           object set in motion by nonmotor road vehicle (E815.0-E815.9)

           pedestrian (E814.0-E814.9)

           nonmotor road vehicle hit by object set in motion by motor vehicle (E818.0-E818.9)

§ ✓4ᵗʰ **E814 Motor vehicle traffic accident involving collision with pedestrian**

    INCLUDES   collision between motor vehicle, any kind, and pedestrian

           pedestrian dragged, hit, or run over by motor vehicle, any kind

    EXCLUDES   *pedestrian hit by object set in motion by motor vehicle (E818.0-E818.9)*

§ ✓4ᵗʰ **E815 Other motor vehicle traffic accident involving collision on the highway**

    INCLUDES   collision (due to loss of control) (on highway) between motor vehicle, any kind, and:

           abutment (bridge) (overpass)

           animal (herded) (unattended)

           fallen stone, traffic sign, tree, utility pole

           guard rail or boundary fence

           interhighway divider

           landslide (not moving)

           object set in motion by railway train or road vehicle (motor) (nonmotor)

           object thrown in front of motor vehicle

           other object, fixed, movable, or moving

           safety island

           temporary traffic sign or marker

           wall of cut made for road

    EXCLUDES   *collision with:*

           any object off the highway (resulting from loss of control) (E816.0-E816.9)

           any object which normally would have been off the highway and is not stated to have been on it (E816.0-E816.9)

           motor vehicle parked, stopped, stalled, disabled, or abandoned on highway (E812.0-E812.9)

           moving landslide (E909)

           motor vehicle hit by object:

           set in motion by railway train or road vehicle (motor) (nonmotor) (E818.0-E818.9)

           thrown into or on vehicle (E818.0-E818.9)

§ ✓4ᵗʰ **E816 Motor vehicle traffic accident due to loss of control, without collision on the highway**

    INCLUDES   motor vehicle:

           failing to make curve

           going out of control (due to):

           blowout

           burst tire

           driver falling asleep

           drive inattention

           excessive speed

           failure of mechanical part

           and: coliding with object off the highway / overturning / stopping abruptly off the highway

    EXCLUDES   *collision on highway following loss of control (E810.0-E815.9)*

           loss of control of motor vehicle following collision on the highway (E810.0-E815.9)

§ ✓4ᵗʰ **E817 Noncollision motor vehicle traffic accident while boarding or alighting**

    INCLUDES   fall down stairs of motor bus

           fall from car in street

           injured by moving part of the vehicle

           trapped by door of motor bus

           } while boarding or alighting

§ ✓4ᵗʰ **E818 Other noncollision motor vehicle traffic accident**

    INCLUDES   accidental poisoning from exhaust gas generated by

           breakage of any part of

           explosion of any part of

           fall, jump, or being accidentally pushed from

           fire starting in

           hit by object thrown into or on

           injured by being thrown against some part of, or object in

           injury from moving part of

           object falling in or on

           object thrown on

           } motor vehicle while in motion

           collision of railway train or road vehicle except motor vehicle, with object set in motion by motor vehicle

           motor vehicle hit by object set in motion by railway train or road vehicle (motor) (nonmotor)

           pedestrian, railway train, or road vehicle (motor) (nonmotor) hit by object set in motion by motor vehicle

    EXCLUDES   *collision between motor vehicle and:*

           object set in motion by railway train or road vehicle (motor) (nonmotor) (E815.0-E815.9)

           object thrown towards the motor vehicle (E815.0-E815.9)

           person overcome by carbon monoxide generated by stationary motor vehicle off the roadway with motor running (E868.2)

§ ✓4ᵗʰ **E819 Motor vehicle traffic accident of unspecified nature**

    INCLUDES   motor vehicle traffic accident NOS

           traffic accident NOS

---

§   Requires fourth-digit. See beginning of appropriate section for codes and definitions.

✓4ᵗʰ Fourth-digit Required   ▶◀ Revised Text   ● New Code   ▲ Revised Code TitleDx

MOTOR VEHICLE NONTRAFFIC ACCIDENTS (E820-E825)

Note: For definitions of motor vehicle nontraffic accident and related terms see definition (a) to (k).

INCLUDES accidents involving motor vehicles being used in recreational or sporting activities off the highway

collision and noncollision motor vehicle acci- dents occurring entirely off the highway

EXCLUDES *accidents involving motor vehicle and:*
aircraft (E840.0-E845.9)
watercraft (E830.0-E838.9)
accidents, not on the public highway, involving agricultural and construction machinery but not involving another motor vehicle (E919.0, E919.2, E919.7)

The following fourth-digit subdivisions are for use with categories E820-E825 to identify the injured person:

.0 Driver of motor vehicle other than motorcycle
See definition (l)

.1 Passenger in motor vehicle other than motorcycle
See definition (l)

.2 Motorcyclist
See definition (l)

.3 Passenger on motorcycle
See definition (l)

.4 Occupant of streetcar

.5 Rider of animal; occupant of animal-drawn vehicle ·

.6 Pedal cyclist
See definition (p)

.7 Pedestrian
See definition (r)

.8 Other specified person
Occupant of vehicle other than above
Person in railway train involved in accident
Unauthorized rider of motor vehicle

.9 Unspecified person

§ ✓4ᵗʰ **E820 Nontraffic accident involving motor-driven snow vehicle**

INCLUDES breakage of part of
fall from
hit by   } motor-driven snow
overturning of   vehicle (not on
run over or dragged by   public highway)

collision of motor-driven snow vehicle with:
animal (being ridden) (-drawn vehicle)
another off-road motor vehicle
other motor vehicle, not on public highway
railway train
other object, fixed or movable
injury caused by rough landing of motor-driven snow vehicle (after leaving ground on rough terrain)

EXCLUDES *accident on the public highway involving motor driven snow vehicle (E810.0-E819.9)*

§ ✓4ᵗʰ **E821 Nontraffic accident involving other off-road motor vehicle**

INCLUDES breakage of part of
fall from
hit by
overturning of   } off-road motorvehicle
run over or dragged by   except snow
thrown against some part   vehicle (not on
of or object in   public highway

collision with:
animal (being ridden) (-drawn vehicle)
another off-road motor vehicle, except snow vehicle
other motor vehicle, not on public highway
other object, fixed or movable

EXCLUDES *accident on public highway involving off-road motor vehicle (E810.0-E819.9)*
collision between motor driven snow vehicle and other off-road motor vehicle (E820.0-E820.9)
hovercraft accident on water (E830.0-E838.9)

§ ✓4ᵗʰ **E822 Other motor vehicle nontraffic accident involving collision with moving object**

INCLUDES collision, not on public highway, between motor vehicle, except off-road motor vehicle and:
animal
nonmotor vehicle
other motor vehicle, except off-road motor vehicle
pedestrian
railway train
other moving object

EXCLUDES *collision with:*
motor-driven snow vehicle (E820.0-E820.9)
other off-road motor vehicle (E821.0-E821.9)

§ ✓4ᵗʰ **E823 Other motor vehicle nontraffic accident involving collision with stationary object**

INCLUDES collision, not on public highway, between motor vehicle, except off-road motor vehicle, and any object, fixed or movable, but not in motion

§ ✓4ᵗʰ **E824 Other motor vehicle nontraffic accident while boarding and alighting**

INCLUDES fall   } while boarding or alighting
injury from oving part   from motor vehicle,
of motor vehicle   except off-road motor
trapped by door of   vehicle, not on public
motor vehhicle   highway

§ ✓4ᵗʰ **E825 Other motor vehicle nontraffic accident of other and unspecified nature**

INCLUDES accidental poisoning from
carbon monoxide
generated by
breakage of any part of
explosion of any part of
fall, jump, or being
accidentally pushed
from   } motor vehicle while in
fire starting in   motion, not on
hit by object thrown into,   public highway
towards, or on
injured by being thrown
against some part of,
or object in
injury from moving part of
object falling in or on

motor vehicle nontraffic accident NOS

EXCLUDES *fall from or in stationary motor vehicle (E884.9, E885.9)*
overcome by carbon monoxide or exhaust gas generated by stationary motor vehicle off the roadway with motor running (E868.2)
struck by falling object from or in stationary motor vehicle (E916)

§ Requires fourth-digit. See beginning of appropriate section for codes and definitions.

✓4ᵗʰ Fourth-digit Required   ►◄ Revised Text   ● New Code   ▲ Revised Code TitleDx

2010 ICD-9-CM   **E Codes – 7**

OTHER ROAD VEHICLE ACCIDENTS (E826-E829)

> Note: Other road vehicle accidents are transport accidents involving road vehicles other than motor vehicles. For definitions of other road vehicle and related terms see definitions (m) to (o).
>
> **INCLUDES**   accidents involving other road vehicles being used in recreational or sporting activities
>
> **EXCLUDES**   *collision of other road vehicle [any] with:*
> *aircraft (E840.0-E845.9)*
> *motor vehicle (E813.0-E813.9, E820.0-E822.9)*
> *railway train (E801.0-E801.9))*

The following fourth-digit subdivisions are for use with categories E826-E829 to identify the injured person:
- **.0 Pedestrian**
  See definition (r)
- **.1 Pedal cyclist**
  See definition (p)
- **.2 Rider of animal**
- **.3 Occupant of animal-drawn vehicle**
- **.4 Occupant of streetcar**
- **.8 Other specified person**
- **.9 Unspecified person**

§ ✓4ᵗʰ **E826 Pedal cycle accident**

[0-9]   **INCLUDES**   breakage of any part of pedal cycle
collision between pedal cycle and:
    animal (being ridden) (herded) (unattended)
    another pedal cycle
    any pedestrian
    nonmotor road vehicle
    other object, fixed, movable, or moving, not set in motion by motor vehicle, railway train, or aircraft
entanglement in wheel of pedal cycle
fall from pedal cycle
hit by object falling or thrown on the pedal cycle
pedal cycle accident NOS
pedal cycle overturned

§ ✓4ᵗʰ **E827 Animal-drawn vehicle accident**

[0,2,4,8,9]   **INCLUDES**   breakage of any part of vehicle
collision between animal-drawn vehicle and:
    animal (being ridden) (herded) (unattended)
    nonmotor road vehicle, except pedal cycle
    pedestrian, pedestrian conveyance, or pedestrian vehicle
    other object, fixed, movable, or moving, not set in motion by motor vehicle, railway train, or aircraft

fall from ⎤
knocked down by ⎥
overturning of ⎥ animal drawn vehicle
running over by ⎥
thrown from ⎦

EXCLUDES   *collision of animal-drawn vehicle with pedal cycle (E826.0-E826.9)*

§ ✓4ᵗʰ **E828 Accident involving animal being ridden**

[0,2,4,8,9]   **INCLUDES**   collision between animal being ridden and:
    another animal
    nonmotor road vehicle, except pedal cycle, and animal-drawn vehicle
    pedestrian, pedestrian conveyance, or pedestrian vehicle
    other object, fixed, movable, or moving, not set in motion by motor vehicle, railway train, or aircraft

fall from ⎤
knocked down by ⎥
thrown from ⎥ animal being ridden
trampled by ⎦
ridden animal stumbled and fell

EXCLUDES   *collision of animal being ridden with:*
animal-drawn vehicle (E827.0-E827.9)
pedal cycle (E826.0-E826.9)

§ ✓4ᵗʰ **E829 Other road vehicle accidents**

[0,4,8,9]   **INCLUDES**
accident while boarding or alighting from ⎤
blow from object in ⎥
breakage of any part of ⎥ streetcar
caught in door of ⎥ nonmotor road
derailment of ⎥ vehicle not
fall in, on, or from ⎥ classifiable to
fire in ⎦ E826-E828

collision between streetcar or nonmotor road vehicle, except as in E826-E828, and:
    animal (not being ridden)
    another nonmotor road vehicle not classifiable to E826-E828
    pedestrian
    other object, fixed, movable, or moving, not set in motion by motor vehicle, railway train, or aircraft
nonmotor road vehicle accident NOS
streetcar accident NOS

EXCLUDES   *collision with:*
animal being ridden (E828.0-E828.9)
animal-drawn vehicle (E827.0-E827.9)
pedal cycle (E826.0-E826.9)

WATER TRANSPORT ACCIDENTS (E830-E838)

> Note: For definitions of water transport accident and related terms see definitions (a), (s), and (t).
>
> **INCLUDES**   watercraft accidents in the course of recreational activities
>
> **EXCLUDES**   *accidents involving both aircraft, including objects set in motion by aircraft, and watercraft (E840.0-E845.9)*

The following fourth-digit subdivisions are for use with categories E830-E838 to identify the injured person:
- **.0 Occupant of small boat, unpowered**
- **.1 Occupant of small boat, powered**
  See definition (t)
  EXCLUDES *water skier (.4)*
- **.2 Occupant of other watercraft – crew**
  Persons:
      engaged in operation of watercraft
      providing passenger services [cabin attendants, ship's physician, catering personnel]
      working on ship during voyage in other capacity [musician in band, operators of shops and beauty parlors
- **.3 Occupant of other watercraft – other than crew**
  Passenger
  Occupant of lifeboat, other than crew, after abandoning ship
- **.4 Water skier**
- **.5 Swimmer**
- **.6 Dockers, stevedores**
  Longshoreman employed on the dock in loading and unloading ships
- ▶**.7 Occupant of military watercraft, any type**◀
- **.8 Other specified person**
  Immigration and custom officials on board ship
  Person:
      accompanying passenger or member of crew visiting boat
  Pilot (guiding ship into port)
- **.9 Unspecified person**

§ ✓4ᵗʰ **E830 Accident to watercraft causing submersion**

INCLUDES   submersion and drowning due to:
    boat overturning
    boat submerging
    falling or jumping from burning ship
    falling or jumping from crushed watercraft
    ship sinking
    other accident to watercraft

---

§   Requires fourth-digit. Valid digits are in [brackets] under each code. See beginning of appropriate section for codes and definitions.

✓4ᵗʰ Fourth-digit Required   ▶◀ Revised Text   ● New Code   ▲ Revised Code TitleDx

§ ✓4th **E831 Accident to watercraft causing other injury**

INCLUDES: any injury, except submersion and drowning, as a
result of an accident to watercraft
burned while ship on fire
crushed between ships in collision
crushed by lifeboat after abandoning ship
fall due to collision or other accident to watercraft
hit by falling object due to accident to watercraft
injured in watercraft accident involving collision
struck by boat or part thereof after fall or jump from
damaged boat

EXCLUDES: *burns from localized fire or explosion on board ship
(E837.0-E837.9)*

§ ✓4th **E832 Other accidental submersion or drowning in water
transport accident**

INCLUDES: submersion or drowning as a result of an accident
other than accident to the watercraft, such as:
fall:
from gangplank
from ship
overboard
thrown overboard by motion of ship
washed overboard

EXCLUDES: *submersion or drowning of swimmer or diver who
voluntarily jumps from boat not involved in an
accident (E910.0-E910.9)*

§ ✓4th **E833 Fall on stairs or ladders in water transport**

EXCLUDES: *fall due to accident to watercraft (E831.0-E831.9)*

§ ✓4th **E834 Other fall from one level to another in water transport**

EXCLUDES: *fall due to accident to watercraft (E831.0-E831.9)*

§ ✓4th **E835 Other and unspecified fall in water transport**

EXCLUDES: *fall due to accident to watercraft (E831.0-E831.9)*

§ ✓4th **E836 Machinery accident in water transport**

INCLUDES: injuries in water transport caused by:
deck
engine room
galley } machinery
laundry
loading

§ ✓4th **E837 Explosion, fire, or burning in watercraft**

INCLUDES: explosion of boiler on steamship
localized fire on ship

EXCLUDES: *burning ship (due to collision or explosion) resulting in:
submersion or drowning (E830.0-E830.9)
other injury (E831.0-E831.9)*

§ ✓4th **E838 Other and unspecified water transport accident**

INCLUDES: accidental poisoning by gases or fumes on ship
atomic power plant malfunction in watercraft
crushed between ship and stationary object [wharf]
crushed between ships without accident to watercraft
crushed by falling object on ship or while loading or
unloading
hit by boat while water skiing
struck by boat or part thereof (after fall from boat)
watercraft accident NOS

AIR AND SPACE TRANSPORT ACCIDENTS (E840-E845)

Note: For definition of aircraft and related terms see definitions (u)
and (v).

The following fourth-digit subdivisions are for use with categories
E840-E845 to identify the injured person. Valid fourth digits are in
[brackets] under codes E842-E845:

.0 **Occupant of spacecraft**

.1 **Occupant of military aircraft, any**
Crew in military aircraft [air force] [army] [national guard]
[navy]
Passenger (civilian) (military) in military aircraft [air force]
[army] [national guard] [navy]
Troops in military aircraft [air force] [army] [national guard]
[navy]

EXCLUDES: *occupants of aircraft operated under
jurisdiction of police departments (.5)
parachutist (.7)*

.2 **Crew of commercial aircraft (powered) in surface to surface
transport**

.3 **Other occupant of commercial aircraft (powered) in surface to
surface transport**
Flight personnel:
not part of crew
on familiarization flight
Passenger on aircraft (powered) NOS

.4 **Occupant of commercial aircraft (powered) in surface to air
transport**
Occupant [crew] [passenger] of aircraft (powered)
engaged in activities, such as:
aerial spraying (crops) (fire retardants)
air drops of emergency supplies
air drops of parachutists, except from military craft
crop dusting
lowering of construction material [bridge or telephone
pole]
sky writing

.5 **Occupant of other powered aircraft**
Occupant [crew] [passenger] of aircraft (powered)
engaged in activities, such as:
aerobatic flying
aircraft racing
rescue operation
storm surveillance
traffic surveillance
Occupant of private plane NOS

.6 **Occupant of unpowered aircraft, except parachutist**
Occupant of aircraft classifiable to E842

.7 **Parachutist (military) (other)**
Person making voluntary descent
EXCLUDES: *person making descent after accident to
aircraft (.1-.6)*

.8 **Ground crew, airline employee**
Persons employed at airfields (civil) (military) or launching
pads, not occupants of aircraft

.9 **Other person**

§ ✓4th **E840 Accident to powered aircraft at takeoff or landing**

INCLUDES: collision of aircraft with any
object, fixed, movable, or
moving
crash } while taking off or
explosion on aircraft landing
fire on aircraft
forced landing

§ ✓4th **E841 Accident to powered aircraft, other and unspecified**

INCLUDES: aircraft accident NOS
aircraft crash or wreck NOS
any accident to powered aircraft while in transit or
when not specified whether in transit, taking
off, or landing
collision of aircraft with another aircraft, bird, or any
object, while in transit
explosion on aircraft while in transit
fire on aircraft while in transit

§ Requires fourth-digit. See beginning of appropriate section for codes and definitions.

✓4th Fourth-digit Required   ►◄ Revised Text   ● New Code   ▲ Revised Code TitleDx

E Codes

§ ✓4ᵗʰ **E842 Accident to unpowered aircraft**

[6-9] **INCLUDES** any accident, except collision with powered aircraft, to:

balloon
glider
hang glider
kite carrying a person
hit by object falling from unpowered aircraft

§ ✓4ᵗʰ **E843 Fall in, on, or from aircraft**

[0-9] **INCLUDES** accident in boarding or alighting from aircraft, any kind

fall in, on, or from aircraft [any kind], while in transit, taking off, or landing, except when as a result of an accident to aircraft

§ ✓4ᵗʰ **E844 Other specified air transport accidents**

[0-9] **INCLUDES** hit by:
    aircraft
    object falling from aircraft
injury by or from:
    machinery of aircraft
    rotating propellar
    voluntary parachute descent
poisoning by carbon monoxide
    from aircraft while in transit
sucked into jet

    } without accident to aircraft

any accident involving other transport vehicle (motor) (nonmotor) due to being hit by object set in motion by aircraft (powered)

EXCLUDES air sickness (E903)
effects of:
    high altitude (E902.0-E902.1)
    pressure change (E902.0-E902.1)
injury in parachute descent due to accident to aircraft (E840.0-E842-9)

§ ✓4ᵗʰ **E845 Accident involving spacecraft**

[0,8,9] **INCLUDES** launching pad accident
EXCLUDES effects of weightlessness in spacecraft (E928.0)

VEHICLE ACCIDENTS NOT ELSEWHERE CLASSIFIABLE (E846-E848)

E846 Accidents involving powered vehicles used solely within the buildings and premises of industrial or commercial establishment

Accident to, on, or involving:
    battery powered airport passenger vehicle
    battery powered trucks (baggage) (mail)
    coal car in mine
    logging car
    self propelled truck, industrial
    station baggage truck (powered)
    tram, truck, or tub (powered) in mine or quarry
Collision with:
    pedestrian
    other vehicle or object within premises
Explosion of
Fall from
Overturning of
Struck by

    } powered vehicle, industrial or commercial

EXCLUDES accidental poisoning by exhaust gas from vehicle not elsewhere classifiable (E868.2)
injury by crane, lift (fork), or elevator (E919.2)

E847 Accidents involving cable cars not running on rails

Accident to, on, or involving:
    cable car, not on rails
    ski chair-lift
    ski-lift with gondola
    téléférique
Breakage of cable
Caught or dragged by
Fall or jump from
Object thrown from or in

    } cable car, not on rails

E848 Accidents involving other vehicles, not elsewhere classifiable

Accident to, on, or involving:
    ice yacht
    land yacht
    nonmotor, nonroad vehicle NOS

✓4ᵗʰ **E849 Place of occurrence**

The following category is for use to denote the place where the injury or poisoning occurred.

E849.0 Home

Apartment
Boarding house
Farm house
Home premises
House (residential)
Noninstitutional place of residence
Private:
    driveway
    garage
    garden
    home
    walk
Swimming pool in private house or garden
Yard of home

EXCLUDES *home under construction but not yet occupied (E849.3)*
institutional place of residence (E849.7)

E849.1 Farm

Farm:
    buildings
    land under cultivation

EXCLUDES *farm house and home premises of farm (E849.0)*

E849.2 Mine and quarry

Gravel pit
Sand pit
Tunnel under construction

E849.3 Industrial place and premises

Building under construction
Dockyard
Dry dock
Factory
    building
    premises
Garage (place of work)
Industrial yard
Loading platform (factory) (store)
Plant, industrial
Railway yard
Shop (place of work)
Warehouse
Workhouse

E849.4 Place for recreation and sport

Amusement park
Baseball field
Basketball court
Beach resort
Cricket ground
Fives court
Football field
Golf course
Gymnasium
Hockey field
Holiday camp
Ice palace
Lake resort
Mountain resort

Playground, including school
    playground
Public park
Racecourse
Resort NOS
Riding school
Rifle range
Seashore resort
Skating rink
Sports palace
Stadium
Swimming pool, public
Tennis court
Vacation resort

EXCLUDES *that in private house or garden (E849.0)*

E849.5 Street and highway

---

§ Requires fourth-digit. Valid digits are in [brackets] under each code. See beginning of appropriate section for codes and definitions.

E849.6 Public building

Building (including adjacent grounds) used by the general
public or by a particular group of the public, such as:
airport
bank
café
casino
church
cinema
clubhouse
courthouse
dance hall
garage building (for car storage)
hotel
market (grocery or other commodity)
movie house
music hall
nightclub
office
office building
opera house
post office
public hall
radio broadcasting station
restaurant
school (state) (public) (private)
shop, commercial
station (bus) (railway)
store
theater

EXCLUDES   home garage (E849.0)
                industrial building or workplace (E849.3)

E849.7 Residential institution

Children's home
Dormitory
Hospital
Jail
Old people's home
Orphanage
Prison
Reform school

E849.8 Other specified places

Beach NOS   Pond or pool (natural)
Canal   Prairie
Caravan site NOS   Public place NOS
Derelict house   Railway line
Desert   Reservoir
Dock   River
Forest   Sea
Harbor   Seashore NOS
Hill   Stream
Lake NOS   Swamp
Mountain   Trailer court
Parking lot   Woods
Parking place

E849.9 Unspecified place

ACCIDENTAL POISONING BY DRUGS, MEDICINAL SUBSTANCES, AND BIOLOGICALS (E850-E858)

INCLUDES   accidental overdose of drug, wrong drug given or
                taken in error, and drug taken inadvertently
                accidents in the use of drugs and biologicals in medi-
                cal and surgical procedures

EXCLUDES   administration with suicidal or homicidal intent or intent
                to harm, or in circumstances classifiable to
                E980-E989 (E950.0-E950.5, E962.0, E980.0-E980.5)
                correct drug properly administered in therapeutic or
                prophylactic dosage, as the cause of adverse effect
                (E930.0-E949.9)

See Alphabetic Index for more complete list of specific drugs to be
classified under the fourth-digit subdivisions. The American
Hospital Formulary numbers can be used to classify new
drugs listed by the American Hospital Formulary Service
(AHFS). See Appendix C.

✓4ᵗʰ **E850 Accidental poisoning by analgesics, antipyretics, and antirheumatics**

E850.0 Heroin
Diacetylmorphine

E850.1 Methadone

E850.2 Other opiates and related narcotics
Codeine [methylmorphine]
Meperidine [pethidine]
Morphine
Opium (alkaloids)

E850.3 Salicylates
Acetylsalicylic acid [aspirin]
Amino derivatives of salicylic acid
Salicylic acid salts

E850.4 Aromatic analgesics, not elsewhere classified
Acetanilid
Paracetamol [acetaminophen]
Phenacetin [acetophenetidin]

E850.5 Pyrazole derivatives
Aminophenazone [amidopyrine]
Phenylbutazone

E850.6 Antirheumatics [antiphlogistics]
Gold salts
Indomethacin
EXCLUDES   salicylates (E850.3)
                steroids (E858.0)

E850.7 Other non-narcotic analgesics
Pyrabital

E850.8 Other specified analgesics and antipyretics
Pentazocine

E850.9 Unspecified analgesic or antipyretic

E851 Accidental poisoning by barbiturates
Amobarbital [amylobarbitone]
Barbital [barbitone]
Butabarbital [butabarbitone]
Pentobarbital [pentobarbitone]
Phenobarbital [phenobarbitone]
Secobarbital [quinalbarbitone]
EXCLUDES   thiobarbiturates (E855.1)

✓4ᵗʰ **E852 Accidental poisoning by other sedatives and hypnotics**

E852.0 Chloral hydrate group

E852.1 Paraldehyde

E852.2 Bromine compounds
Bromides
Carbromal (derivatives)

E852.3 Methaqualone compounds

E852.4 Glutethimide group

E852.5 Mixed sedatives, not elsewhere classified

E852.8 Other specified sedatives and hypnotics

E852.9 Unspecified sedative or hypnotic
Sleeping:
  drug
  pill   } NOS
  tablet

✓4ᵗʰ **E853 Accidental poisoning by tranquilizers**

E853.0 Phenothiazine-based tranquilizers
Chlorpromazine   Prochlorperazine
Fluphenazine   Promazine

E853.1 Butyrophenone-based tranquilizers
Haloperidol   Trifluperidol
Spiperone

E853.2 Benzodiazepine-based tranquilizers
Chlordiazepoxide   Lorazepam
Diazepam   Medazepam
Flurazepam   Nitrazepam

E853.8 Other specified tranquilizers
Hydroxyzine   Meprobamate

E853.9 Unspecified tranquilizer

E Codes

E854–E862.9

✓4th **E854 Accidental poisoning by other psychotropic agents**

E854.0 Antidepressants
Amitriptyline
Imipramine
Monoamine oxidase [MAO] inhibitors

E854.1 Psychodysleptics [hallucinogens]
Cannabis derivatives   Mescaline
Lysergide [LSD]   Psilocin
Marihuana (derivatives)   Psilocybin

E854.2 Psychostimulants
Amphetamine
Caffeine
EXCLUDES *central appetite depressants (E858.8)*

E854.3 Central nervous system stimulants
Analeptics
Opiate antagonists

E854.8 Other psychotropic agents

✓4th **E855 Accidental poisoning by other drugs acting on central and autonomic nervous system**

E855.0 Anticonvulsant and anti-Parkinsonism drugs
Amantadine
Hydantoin derivatives
Levodopa [L-dopa]
Oxazolidine derivatives [paramethadione]
[trimethadione]
Succinimides

E855.1 Other central nervous system depressants
Ether
Gaseous anesthetics
Halogenated hydrocarbon derivatives
Intravenous anesthetics
Thiobarbiturates, such as thiopental sodium

E855.2 Local anesthetics
Cocaine   Procaine
Lidocaine [lignocaine]   Tetracaine

E855.3 Parasympathomimetics [cholinergics]
Acetylcholine   Anticholinesterase:
Anticholinesterase: reversible
organophosphorus   Pilocarpine

E855.4 Parasympatholytics [anticholinergics and antimuscarinics] and spasmolytics
Atropine   Hyoscine [scopolamine]
Homatropine   Quaternary ammonium
derivatives

E855.5 Sympathomimetics [adrenergics]
Epinephrine [adrenalin]
Levarterenol [noradrenalin]

E855.6 Sympatholytics [antiadrenergics]
Phenoxybenzamine
Tolazoline hydrochloride

E855.8 Other specified drugs acting on central and autonomic nervous systems

E855.9 Unspecified drug acting on central and autonomic nervous systems

E856 Accidental poisoning by antibiotics

E857 Accidental poisoning by other anti-infectives

✓4th **E858 Accidental poisoning by other drugs**

E858.0 Hormones and synthetic substitutes

E858.1 Primarily systemic agents

E858.2 Agents primarily affecting blood constituents

E858.3 Agents primarily affecting cardiovascular system

E858.4 Agents primarily affecting gastrointestinal system

E858.5 Water, mineral, and uric acid metabolism drugs

E858.6 Agents primarily acting on the smooth and skeletal muscles and respiratory system

E858.7 Agents primarily affecting skin and mucous membrane, ophthalmological, otorhinolaryngological, and dental drugs

E858.8 Other specified drugs
Central appetite depressants

E858.9 Unspecified drug

ACCIDENTAL POISONING BY OTHER SOLID AND LIQUID SUBSTANCES, GASES, AND VAPORS (E860-E869)

Note: Categories in this section are intended primarily to indicate the external cause of poisoning states classifiable to 980-989. They may also be used to indicate external causes of localized effects classifiable to 001-799.

✓4th **E860 Accidental poisoning by alcohol, not elsewhere classified**

E860.0 Alcoholic beverages
Alcohol in preparations intended for consumption

E860.1 Other and unspecified ethyl alcohol and its products
Denatured alcohol   Grain alcohol NOS
Ethanol NOS   Methylated spirit

E860.2 Methyl alcohol
Methanol   Wood alcohol

E860.3 Isopropyl alcohol
Dimethyl carbinol   Rubbing alcohol subsitute
Isopropanol   Secondary propyl alcohol

E860.4 Fusel oil
Alcohol: Alcohol:
amyl   propyl
butyl

E860.8 Other specified alcohols

E860.9 Unspecified alcohol

✓4th **E861 Accidental poisoning by cleansing and polishing agents, disinfectants, paints, and varnishes**

E861.0 Synthetic detergents and shampoos

E861.1 Soap products

E861.2 Polishes

E861.3 Other cleansing and polishing agents
Scouring powders

E861.4 Disinfectants
Household and other disinfectants not ordinarily used on the person
EXCLUDES *carbolic acid or phenol (E864.0)*

E861.5 Lead paints

E861.6 Other paints and varnishes
Lacquers   Paints, other than lead
Oil colors   White washes

E861.9 Unspecified

✓4th **E862 Accidental poisoning by petroleum products, other solvents and their vapors, not elsewhere classified**

E862.0 Petroleum solvents
Petroleum: Petroleum:
ether   naphtha
benzine

E862.1 Petroleum fuels and cleaners
Antiknock additives   Gasoline or petrol
to petroleum fuels   Kerosene
Gas oils
EXCLUDES *kerosene insecticides (E863.4)*

E862.2 Lubricating oils

E862.3 Petroleum solids
Paraffin wax

E862.4 Other specified solvents
Benzene

E862.9 Unspecified solvent

✓4th **E863 Accidental poisoning by agricultural and horticultural chemical and pharmaceutical preparations other than plant foods and fertilizers**

> EXCLUDES   plant foods and fertilizers (E866.5)

E863.0 Insecticides of organochlorine compounds

Benzene hexachloride	Dieldrin
Chlordane	Endrine
DDT	Toxaphene

E863.1 Insecticides of organophosphorus compounds

Demeton	Parathion
Diazinon	Phenylsulphthion
Dichlorvos	Phorate
Malathion	Phosdrin
Methyl parathion	

E863.2 Carbamates

Aldicarb	Propoxur
Carbaryl	

E863.3 Mixtures of insecticides

E863.4 Other and unspecified insecticides

Kerosene insecticides

E863.5 Herbicides

2, 4-Dichlorophenoxyacetic acid [2, 4-D]
2, 4, 5-Trichlorophenoxyacetic acid [2, 4, 5-T]
Chlorates
Diquat
Mixtures of plant foods and fertilizers with herbicides
Paraquat

E863.6 Fungicides

Organic mercurials (used in seed dressing)
Pentachlorophenols

E863.7 Rodenticides

Fluoroacetates	Warfarin
Squill and derivatives	Zinc phosphide
Thallium	

E863.8 Fumigants

Cyanides	Phosphine
Methyl bromide	

E863.9 Other and unspecified

✓4th **E864 Accidental poisoning by corrosives and caustics, not elsewhere classified**

> EXCLUDES   those as components of disinfectants (E861.4)

E864.0 Corrosive aromatics

Carbolic acid or phenol

E864.1 Acids

Acid:	Acid:
hydrochloric	sulfuric
nitric	

E864.2 Caustic alkalis

Lye

E864.3 Other specified corrosives and caustics

E864.4 Unspecified corrosives and caustics

✓4th **E865 Accidental poisoning from poisonous foodstuffs and poisonous plants**

> INCLUDES   any meat, fish, or shellfish
> plants, berries, and fungi eaten as, or in mistake for, food, or by a child

> EXCLUDES   anaphylactic shock due to adverse food reaction (995.60-995.69)
> food poisoning (bacterial) (005.0-005.9)
> poisoning and toxic reactions to venomous plants (E905.6-E905.7)

E865.0 Meat

E865.1 Shellfish

E865.2 Other fish

E865.3 Berries and seeds

E865.4 Other specified plants

E865.5 Mushrooms and other fungi

E865.8 Other specified foods

E865.9 Unspecified foodstuff or poisonous plant

✓4th **E866 Accidental poisoning by other and unspecified solid and liquid substances**

> EXCLUDES   these substances as a component of:
> medicines (E850.0-E858.9)
> paints (E861.5-E861.6)
> pesticides (E863.0-E863.9)
> petroleum fuels (E862.1)

E866.0 Lead and its compounds and fumes

E866.1 Mercury and its compounds and fumes

E866.2 Antimony and its compounds and fumes

E866.3 Arsenic and its compounds and fumes

E866.4 Other metals and their compounds and fumes

Beryllium (compounds)
Brass fumes
Cadmium (compounds)
Copper salts
Iron (compounds)
Manganese (compounds)
Nickel (compounds)
Thallium (compounds)

E866.5 Plant foods and fertilizers

> EXCLUDES   mixtures with herbicides (E863.5)

E866.6 Glues and adhesives

E866.7 Cosmetics

E866.8 Other specified solid or liquid substances

E866.9 Unspecified solid or liquid substance

E867 Accidental poisoning by gas distributed by pipeline

Carbon monoxide from incomplete combustion of piped gas
Coal gas NOS
Liquefied petroleum gas distributed through pipes (pure or mixed with air)
Piped gas (natural) (manufactured)

✓4th **E868 Accidental poisoning by other utility gas and other carbon monoxide**

E868.0 Liquefied petroleum gas distributed in mobile containers

Butane	⎫ or carbon monoxide
Liquefied hydrocarbon gas NOS	⎬ from incomplete conbustion of
Propane	⎭ these gases

E868.1 Other and unspecified utility gas

Acetylene	⎫ or carbon monoxide
Gas NOS used for lighting, heating, or cooking	⎬ from incomplete conbustion of
Water gas	⎭ these gases

E868.2 Motor vehicle exhaust gas

Exhaust gas from:
any type of combustion engine not in watercraft
farm tractor, not in transit
gas engine
motor pump
motor vehicle, not in transit

> EXCLUDES   poisoning by carbon monoxide from:
> aircraft while in transit (E844.0-E844.9)
> motor vehicle while in transit (E818.0-E818.9)
> watercraft whether or not in transit (E838.0-E838.9)

E868.3 Carbon monoxide from incomplete combustion of other domestic fuels

Carbon monoxide from incomplete combustion of:

coal	⎫
coke	⎬ in domestic stove or fireplace
kerosene	
wood	⎭

> EXCLUDES   carbon monoxide from smoke and fumes due to conflagration (E890.0-E893.9)

E868.8 Carbon monoxide from other sources
Carbon monoxide from:
blast furnace gas
incomplete combustion of fuels in industrial use
kiln vapor

E868.9 Unspecified carbon monoxide

☑4ᵗʰ **E869 Accidental poisoning by other gases and vapors**
EXCLUDES   *effects of gases used as anesthetics (E855.1, E938.2)*
fumes from heavy metals (E866.0-E866.4)
smoke and fumes due to conflagration or explosion
(E890.0-E899)

E869.0 Nitrogen oxides

E869.1 Sulfur dioxide

E869.2 Freon

E869.3 Lacrimogenic gas [tear gas]
Bromobenzyl cyanide
Chloroacetophenone
Ethyliodoacetate

E869.4 Second-hand tobacco smoke

E869.8 Other specified gases and vapors
Chlorine
Hydrocyanic acid gas

E869.9 Unspecified gases and vapors

MISADVENTURES TO PATIENTS DURING SURGICAL AND MEDICAL CARE (E870-E876)

EXCLUDES   *accidental overdose of drug and wrong drug given in*
error (E850.0-E858.9)
surgical and medical procedures as the cause of
abnormal reaction by the patient, without
mention of misadventure at the time of procedure
(E878.0-E879.9)

☑4ᵗʰ **E870 Accidental cut, puncture, perforation, or hemorrhage during medical care**

E870.0 Surgical operation

E870.1 Infusion or transfusion

E870.2 Kidney dialysis or other perfusion

E870.3 Injection or vaccination

E870.4 Endoscopic examination

E870.5 Aspiration of fluid or tissue, puncture, and catheterization
Abdominal paracentesis
Aspirating needle biopsy
Blood sampling
Lumbar puncture
Thoracentesis
EXCLUDES   *heart catheterization (E870.6)*

E870.6 Heart catheterization

E870.7 Administration of enema

E870.8 Other specified medical care

E870.9 Unspecified medical care

☑4ᵗʰ **E871 Foreign object left in body during procedure**

E871.0 Surgical operation

E871.1 Infusion or transfusion

E871.2 Kidney dialysis or other perfusion

E871.3 Injection or vaccination

E871.4 Endoscopic examination

E871.5 Aspiration of fluid or tissue, puncture, and catheterization
Abdominal paracentesis
Aspiration needle biopsy
Blood sampling
Lumbar puncture
Thoracentesis
EXCLUDES   *heart catheterization (E871.6)*

E871.6 Heart catheterization

E871.7 Removal of catheter or packing

E871.8 Other specified procedures

E871.9 Unspecified procedure

☑4ᵗʰ **E872 Failure of sterile precautions during procedure**

E872.0 Surgical operation

E872.1 Infusion or transfusion

E872.2 Kidney dialysis and other perfusion

E872.3 Injection or vaccination

E872.4 Endoscopic examination

E872.5 Aspiration of fluid or tissue, puncture, and catheterization
Abdominal paracentesis
Aspiration needle biopsy
Blood sampling
Lumbar puncture
Thoracentesis
EXCLUDES   *heart catheterization (E872.6)*

E872.6 Heart catheterization

E872.8 Other specified procedures

E872.9 Unspecified procedure

☑4ᵗʰ **E873 Failure in dosage**
EXCLUDES   *accidental overdose of drug, medicinal or*
biological substance (E850.0-E858.9)

E873.0 Excessive amount of blood or other fluid during transfusion or infusion

E873.1 Incorrect dilution of fluid during infusion

E873.2 Overdose of radiation in therapy

E873.3 Inadvertent exposure of patient to radiation during medical care

E873.4 Failure in dosage in electroshock or insulin-shock therapy

E873.5 Inappropriate [too hot or too cold] temperature in local application and packing

E873.6 Nonadministration of necessary drug or medicinal substance

E873.8 Other specified failure in dosage

E873.9 Unspecified failure in dosage

☑4ᵗʰ **E874 Mechanical failure of instrument or apparatus during procedure**

E874.0 Surgical operation

E874.1 Infusion and transfusion
Air in system

E874.2 Kidney dialysis and other perfusion

E874.3 Endoscopic examination

E874.4 Aspiration of fluid or tissue, puncture, and catheterization
Abdominal paracentesis   Lumbar puncture
Aspiration needle biopsy   Thoracentesis
Blood sampling
EXCLUDES   *heart catheterization (E874.5)*

E874.5 Heart catheterization

E874.8 Other specified procedures

E874.9 Unspecified procedure

☑4ᵗʰ **E875 Contaminated or infected blood, other fluid, drug, or biological substance**
INCLUDES   presence of:
bacterial pyrogens
endotoxin-producing bacteria
serum hepatitis-producing agent

E875.0 Contaminated substance transfused or infused

E875.1 Contaminated substance injected or used for vaccination

---

☑4ᵗʰ Fourth-digit Required   ▶◀ Revised Text   ● New Code   ▲ Revised Code TitleDx

E875.2 Contaminated drug or biological substance administered by other means

E875.8 Other

E875.9 Unspecified

✓4ᵗʰ **E876 Other and unspecified misadventures during medical care**

E876.0 Mismatched blood in transfusion

E876.1 Wrong fluid in infusion

E876.2 Failure in suture and ligature during surgical operation

E876.3 Endotracheal tube wrongly placed during anesthetic procedure

E876.4 Failure to introduce or to remove other tube or instrument
> *EXCLUDES* *foreign object left in body during procedure (E871.0-E871.9)*

▲ * E876.5 Performance of wrong operation (procedure) on correct patient
> ▶Wrong device implanted into correct surgical site◀
> *EXCLUDES* ▶*correct operation (procedure) performed on wrong body part (E876.7)*◀

● * E876.6 Performance of operation (procedure) on patient not scheduled for surgery
> Performance of operation (procedure) intended for another patient
> Performance of operation (procedure) on wrong patient

● * E876.7 Performance of correct operation (procedure) on wrong side/body part
> Performance of correct operation (procedure) on wrong side
> Performance of correct operation (procedure) on wrong site

E876.8 Other specified misadventures during medical care
> Performance of inappropriate treatment NEC

E876.9 Unspecified misadventure during medical care

SURGICAL AND MEDICAL PROCEDURES AS THE CAUSE OF ABNORMAL REACTION OF PATIENT OR LATER COMPLICATION, WITHOUT MENTION OF MISADVENTURE AT THE TIME OF PROCEDURE (E878-E879)

> *INCLUDES* procedures as the cause of abnormal reaction, such as:
> displacement or malfunction of prosthetic device
> hepatorenal failure, postoperative
> malfunction of external stoma
> postoperative intestinal obstruction
> rejection of transplanted organ

> *EXCLUDES* *anesthetic management properly carried out as the cause of adverse effect (E937.0-E938.9)*
> *infusion and transfusion, without mention of misadventure in the technique of procedure (E930.0-E949.9)*

✓4ᵗʰ **E878 Surgical operation and other surgical procedures as the cause of abnormal reaction of patient, or of later complication, without mention of misadventure at the time of operation**

E878.0 Surgical operation with transplant of whole organ
> Transplantation of: Transplantation of:
> heart   liver
> kidney

E878.1 Surgical operation with implant of artificial internal device
> Cardiac pacemaker
> Electrodes implanted in brain
> Heart valve prosthesis
> Internal orthopedic device

E878.2 Surgical operation with anastomosis, bypass, or graft, with natural or artificial tissues used as implant
> Anastomosis:
> arteriovenous
> gastrojejunal
> Graft of blood vessel, tendon, or skin
> *EXCLUDES* *external stoma (E878.3)*

E878.3 Surgical operation with formation of external stoma
> Colostomy   Gastrostomy
> Cystostomy   Ureterostomy
> Duodenostomy

E878.4 Other restorative surgery

E878.5 Amputation of limb(s)

E878.6 Removal of other organ (partial) (total)

E878.8 Other specified surgical operations and procedures

E878.9 Unspecified surgical operations and procedures

✓4ᵗʰ **E879 Other procedures, without mention of misadventure at the time of procedure, as the cause of abnormal reaction of patient, or of later complication**

E879.0 Cardiac catheterization

E879.1 Kidney dialysis

E879.2 Radiological procedure and radiotherapy
> *EXCLUDES* *radio-opaque dyes for diagnostic x-ray procedures (E947.8)*

E879.3 Shock therapy
> Electroshock therapy   Insulin-shock therapy

E879.4 Aspiration of fluid
> Lumbar puncture   Thoracentesis

E879.5 Insertion of gastric or duodenal sound

E879.6 Urinary catheterization

E879.7 Blood sampling

E879.8 Other specified procedures
> Blood transfusion

E879.9 Unspecified procedure

ACCIDENTAL FALLS (E880-E888)

> *EXCLUDES* *falls (in or from):*
> *burning building (E890.8, E891.8)*
> *into fire (E890.0-E899)*
> *into water (with submersion or drowning) (E910.0-E910.9)*
> *machinery (in operation) (E919.0-E919.9)*
> *on edged, pointed, or sharp object (E920.0-E920.9)*
> *transport vehicle (E800.0-E845.9)*
> *vehicle not elsewhere classifiable (E846-E848)*

✓4ᵗʰ **E880 Fall on or from stairs or steps**

E880.0 Escalator

E880.1 Fall on or from sidewalk curb
> *EXCLUDES* *fall from moving sidewalk (E885.9)*

E880.9 Other stairs or steps

✓4ᵗʰ **E881 Fall on or from ladders or scaffolding**

E881.0 Fall from ladder

E881.1 Fall from scaffolding

E882 Fall from or out of building or other structure
> Fall from: Fall from:
> balcony   turret
> bridge   viaduct
> building   wall
> flagpole   window
> tower   Fall through roof
> *EXCLUDES* *collapse of a building or structure (E916)*
> *fall or jump from burning building (E890.8, E891.8)*

---

* Wrong surgery edit applies.

☑4ᵗʰ E883 Fall into hole or other opening in surface

INCLUDES   fall into: fall into:
      cavity   shaft
      dock   swimming pool
      hole   tank
      pit   well
      quarry

EXCLUDES   *fall into water NOS (E910.9)*
      that resulting in drowning or submersion without
        mention of injury (E910.0-E910.9)

E883.0 Accident from diving or jumping into water [swimming pool]
    Strike or hit:
      against bottom when jumping or diving into water
      wall or board of swimming pool
      water surface
    EXCLUDES   *diving with insufficient air supply (E913.2)*
       effects of air pressure from diving (E902.2)

E883.1 Accidental fall into well

E883.2 Accidental fall into storm drain or manhole

E883.9 Fall into other hole or other opening in surface

☑4ᵗʰ E884 Other fall from one level to another

E884.0 Fall from playground equipment
    EXCLUDES   *recreational machinery (E919.8)*

E884.1 Fall from cliff

E884.2 Fall from chair

E884.3 Fall from wheelchair

E884.4 Fall from bed

E884.5 Fall from other furniture

E884.6 Fall from commode
    Toilet

E884.9 Other fall from one level to another
    Fall from: Fall from:
      embankment   stationary vehicle
      haystack   tree

☑4ᵗʰ E885 Fall on same level from slipping, tripping, or stumbling

E885.0 Fall from (nonmotorized) scooter

E885.1 Fall from roller skates
    Heelies
    In-line skates
    Wheelies

E885.2 Fall from skateboard

E885.3 Fall from skis

E885.4 Fall from snowboard

E885.9 Fall from other slipping, tripping, or stumbling
    Fall on moving sidewalk

☑4ᵗʰ E886 Fall on same level from collision, pushing, or shoving, by or with other person
    EXCLUDES   *crushed or pushed by a crowd or human stampede*
       (E917.1, E917.6)

E886.0 In sports
    Tackles in sports
    EXCLUDES   *kicked, stepped on, struck by object, in sports*
       (E917.0, E917.5)

E886.9 Other and unspecified
    Fall from collision of pedestrian (conveyance) with
      another pedestrian (conveyance)

E887 Fracture, cause unspecified

☑4ᵗʰ E888 Other and unspecified fall
    Accidental fall NOS
    Fall on same level NOS

E888.0 Fall resulting in striking against sharp object
    Use additional external cause code to identify object
      (E920)

E888.1 Fall resulting in striking against other object

E888.8 Other fall

E888.9 Unspecified fall
    Fall NOS

ACCIDENTS CAUSED BY FIRE AND FLAMES (E890-E899)

INCLUDES   asphyxia or poisoning due to conflagration or ignition
    burning by fire
    secondary fires resulting from explosion

EXCLUDES   *arson (E968.0)*
    fire in or on:
      machinery (in operation) (E919.0-E919.9)
      transport vehicle other than stationary vehicle
       (E800.0-E845.9)
      vehicle not elsewhere classifiable (E846-E848)

☑4ᵗʰ E890 Conflagration in private dwelling

INCLUDES   conflagration in:
      apartment
      boarding house
      camping place
      caravan
      farmhouse
      house
      lodging house
      mobile home
      private garage
      rooming house
      tenement
    conflagration originating from sources classifiable to
      E893-E898 in the above buildings

E890.0 Explosion caused by conflagration

E890.1 Fumes from combustion of polyvinylchloride [PVC] and similar material in conflagration

E890.2 Other smoke and fumes from conflagration
    Carbon monoxide ⎫
    Fumes NOS   ⎬ from conflagration in private building
    Smoke NOS   ⎭

E890.3 Burning caused by conflagration

E890.8 Other accident resulting from conflagration
    Collapse of   ⎫
    Fall from   ⎬ burning private building
    Hit by object falling from
    Jump from   ⎭

E890.9 Unspecified accident resulting from conflagration in private dwelling

☑4ᵗʰ E891 Conflagration in other and unspecified building or structure
    Conflagration in:
      barn
      church
      convalescent and other residential home
      dormitory of educational institution
      factory
      farm outbuildings
      hospital
      hotel
      school
      store
      theater
    Conflagration originating from sources classifiable to E893-E898, in
      the above buildings

E891.0 Explosion caused by conflagration

E891.1 Fumes from combustion of polyvinylchloride [PVC] and similar material in conflagration

E891.2 Other smoke and fumes from conflagration
    Carbon monoxide ⎫
    Fumes NOS   ⎬ from conflagration in private building or structure
    Smoke NOS   ⎭

E891.3 Burning caused by conflagration

E891.8 Other accident resulting from conflagration

Collapse of
Fall from   } burning private
Hit by object falling from   building or
Jump from   structure

E891.9 Unspecified accident resulting from conflagration of other and unspecified building or structure

E892 Conflagration not in building or structure

Fire (uncontrolled) (in) (of):
forest
grass
hay
lumber
mine
prairie
transport vehicle [any], except while in transit
tunnel

✓4th **E893 Accident caused by ignition of clothing**

EXCLUDES *ignition of clothing:*
from highly inflammable material (E894)
with conflagration (E890.0-E892)

E893.0 From controlled fire in private dwelling

Ignition of clothing from:
normal fire (charcoal) (coal)
(electric) (gas) (wood) in: } in private dwelling
brazier   (as listed in
fireplace   E890)
furnace
stove

E893.1 From controlled fire in other building or structure

Ignition of clothing from:
normal fire (charcoal) (coal)
(electric) (gas) (wood)
in: } in other building or
brazier   structure (as
fireplace   listed in E891)
furnace
stove

E893.2 From controlled fire not in building or structure

Ignition of clothing from:
bonfire (controlled)
brazier fire (controlled), not in building or structure
trash fire (controlled)

EXCLUDES *conflagration not in building (E892)*
trash fire out of control (E892)

E893.8 From other specified sources

Ignition of clothing from: Ignition of clothing from:
blowlamp   cigarette
blowtorch   lighter
burning bedspread   matches
candle   pipe
cigar   welding torch

E893.9 Unspecified source

Ignition of clothing (from controlled fire NOS) (in building NOS) NOS

E894 Ignition of highly inflammable material

Ignition of:
benzine
gasoline
fat
kerosene   } (with ignition of clothing)
paraffin
petrol

EXCLUDES *ignition of highly inflammable material with:*
conflagration (E890.0-E892)
explosion (E923.0-E923.9)

E895 Accident caused by controlled fire in private dwelling

Burning by (flame of) normal fire (charcoal) (coal) (electric) (gas) (wood) in:
brazier
fireplace   } in private dwelling (as
furnace   listed in E890)
stove

EXCLUDES *burning by hot objects not producing fire or flames (E924.0-E924.9)*
ignition of clothing from these sources (E893.0)
poisoning by carbon monoxide from incomplete combustion of fuel (E867-E868.9)
that with conflagration (E890.0-E890.9)

E896 Accident caused by controlled fire in other and unspecified building or structure

Burning by (flame of) normal fire (charcoal) (coal)(electric)(gas)(wood) in:
brazier
fireplace   } in other building or structure (as
furnace   listed in E891)
stove

EXCLUDES *burning by hot objects not producing fire or flames (E924.0-E924.9)*
ignition of clothing from these sources (E893.1)
poisoning by carbon monoxide from incomplete combustion of fuel (E867-E868.9)
that with conflagration (E891.0-E891.9)

E897 Accident caused by controlled fire not in building or structure

Burns from flame of:
bonfire
brazier fire, not in building or structure } controlled
trash fire

EXCLUDES *ignition of clothing from these sources (E893.2)*
trash fire out of control (E892)
that with conflagration (E892)

✓4th **E898 Accident caused by other specified fire and flames**

EXCLUDES *conflagration (E890.0-E892)*
that with ignition of:
clothing (E893.0-E893.9)
highly inflammable material (E894)

E898.0 Burning bedclothes

Bed set on fire NOS

E898.1 Other

Burning by: Burning by:
blowlamp   lamp
blowtorch   lighter
candle   matches
cigar   pipe
cigarette   welding torch
fire in room NOS

E899 Accident caused by unspecified fire

Burning NOS

ACCIDENTS DUE TO NATURAL AND ENVIRONMENTAL FACTORS (E900-E909)

✓4th **E900 Excessive heat**

E900.0 Due to weather conditions

Excessive heat as the external cause of:
ictus solaris
siriasis
sunstroke

E900.1 Of man-made origin

Heat (in):
boiler room
drying room
factory
furnace room
generated in transport vehicle
kitchen

E900.9 Of unspecified origin

☑4ᵗʰ **E901 Excessive cold**

E901.0 Due to weather conditions
Excessive cold as the cause of:
chilblains NOS
immersion foot

E901.1 Of man-made origin

Contact with or inhalation of:	Prolonged exposure in:
dry ice	deep freeze unit
liquid air	refrigerator
liquid hydrogen	
liquid nitrogen	

E901.8 Other specified origin

E901.9 Of unspecified origin

☑4ᵗʰ **E902 High and low air pressure and changes in air pressure**

E902.0 Residence or prolonged visit at high altitude
Residence or prolonged visit at high altitude as the cause of:
Acosta syndrome
Alpine sickness
altitude sickness
Andes disease
anoxia, hypoxia
barotitis, barodontalgia, barosinusitis, otitic barotrauma
hypobarism, hypobaropathy
mountain sickness
range disease

E902.1 In aircraft
Sudden change in air pressure in aircraft during ascent or descent as the cause of:
aeroneurosis
aviators' disease

E902.2 Due to diving

High air pressure from rapid descent in water	as the cause of: caisson disease
Reduction in atmospheric pressure while surfacing from deep water diving	divers' disease divers' palsy or paralysis

E902.8 Due to other specified causes
Reduction in atmospheric pressure while surfacing from underground

E902.9 Unspecified cause

E903 Travel and motion

☑4ᵗʰ **E904 Hunger, thirst, exposure, and neglect**

EXCLUDES *any condition resulting from homicidal intent (E968.0-E968.9)*
hunger, thirst, and exposure resulting from accidents connected with transport (E800.0-E848)

E904.0 Abandonment or neglect of infants and helpless persons

Exposure to weather conditions	resulting from abandonment or neglect
Hunger or thirst	

Desertion of newborn
Inattention at or after birth
Lack of care (helpless person) (infant)
EXCLUDES *criminal [purposeful] neglect (E968.4)*

E904.1 Lack of food
Lack of food as the cause of:
inanition
insufficient nourishment
starvation
EXCLUDES *hunger resulting from abandonment or neglect (E904.0)*

E904.2 Lack of water
Lack of water as the cause of:
dehydration
inanition
EXCLUDES *dehydration due to acute fluid loss (276.51)*

E904.3 Exposure (to weather conditions), not elsewhere classifiable
Exposure NOS
Humidity
Struck by hailstones
EXCLUDES *struck by lightning (E907)*

E904.9 Privation, unqualified
Destitution

☑4ᵗʰ **E905 Venomous animals and plants as the cause of poisoning and toxic reactions**

INCLUDES chemical released by animal
insects
release of venom through fangs, hairs, spines, tentacles, and other venom apparatus
EXCLUDES *eating of poisonous animals or plants (E865.0-E865.9)*

E905.0 Venomous snakes and lizards

Cobra	Mamba
Copperhead snake	Rattlesnake
Coral snake	Sea snake
Fer de lance	Snake (venomous)
Gila monster	Viper
Krait	Water moccasin

EXCLUDES *bites of snakes and lizards known to be nonvenomous (E906.2)*

E905.1 Venomous spiders
Black widow spider
Brown spider
Tarantula (venomous)

E905.2 Scorpion

E905.3 Hornets, wasps, and bees
Yellow jacket

E905.4 Centipede and venomous millipede (tropical)

E905.5 Other venomous arthropods
Sting of:
ant
caterpillar

E905.6 Venomous marine animals and plants
Puncture by sea urchin spine
Sting of:
coral
jelly fish
nematocysts
sea anemone
sea cucumber
other marine animal or plant
EXCLUDES *bites and other injuries caused by nonvenomous marine animal (E906.2-E906.8)*
bite of sea snake (venomous) (E905.0)

E905.7 Poisoning and toxic reactions caused by other plants
Injection of poisons or toxins into or through skin by plant thorns, spines, or other mechanisms
EXCLUDES *puncture wound NOS by plant thorns or spines (E920.8)*

E905.8 Other specified

E905.9 Unspecified
Sting NOS
Venomous bite NOS

☑4ᵗʰ **E906 Other injury caused by animals**

EXCLUDES *poisoning and toxic reactions caused by venomous animals and insects (E905.0-E905.9)*
road vehicle accident involving animals (E827.0-E828.9)
tripping or falling over an animal (E885.9)

E906.0 Dog bite

E906.1 Rat bite

E906.2 Bite of nonvenomous snakes and lizards

E906.3 Bite of other animal except arthropod
    Cats   Rodents, except rats
    Moray eel   Shark

E906.4 Bite of nonvenomous arthropod
    Insect bite NOS

E906.5 Bite by unspecified animal
    Animal bite NOS

E906.8 Other specified injury caused by animal
    Butted by animal
    Fallen on by horse or other animal, not being ridden
    Gored by animal
    Implantation of quills of porcupine
    Pecked by bird
    Run over by animal, not being ridden
    Stepped on by animal, not being ridden
      EXCLUDES *injury by animal being ridden (E828.0-E828.9)*

E906.9 Unspecified injury caused by animal

E907 Lightning
    EXCLUDES *injury from:*
        fall of tree or other object caused by lightning (E916)
        fire caused by lightning (E890.0-E892)

✓4ᵗʰ E908 Cataclysmic storms, and floods resulting from storms
    EXCLUDES *collapse of dam or man-made structure causing flood (E909.3)*

    E908.0 Hurricane
        Storm surge
        "Tidal wave" caused by storm action
        Typhoon

    E908.1 Tornado
        Cyclone
        Twisters

    E908.2 Floods
        Torrential rainfall
        Flash flood
        EXCLUDES *collapse of dam or man-made structure causing flood (E909.3)*

    E908.3 Blizzard (snow)(ice)

    E908.4 Dust storm

    E908.8 Other cataclysmic storms
        Cloudburst

    E908.9 Unspecified cataclysmic storms, and floods resulting from storms
        Storm NOS

✓4ᵗʰ E909 Cataclysmic earth surface movements and eruptions

    E909.0 Earthquakes

    E909.1 Volcanic eruptions
        Burns from lava
        Ash inhalation

    E909.2 Avalanche, landslide, or mudslide

    E909.3 Collapse of dam or man-made structure

    E909.4 Tidalwave caused by earthquake
        Tidalwave NOS
        Tsunami
        EXCLUDES *tidalwave caused by tropical storm (E908.0)*

    E909.8 Other cataclysmic earth surface movements and eruptions

    E909.9 Unspecified cataclysmic earth surface movements and eruptions

ACCIDENTS CAUSED BY SUBMERSION, SUFFOCATION, AND FOREIGN BODIES (E910-E915)

✓4ᵗʰ E910 Accidental drowning and submersion
    INCLUDES immersion
               swimmers' cramp
    EXCLUDES *diving accident (NOS) (resulting in injury except drowning) (E883.0)*
        diving with insufficient air supply (E913.2)
        drowning and submersion due to:
            cataclysm (E908-E909)
            machinery accident (E919.0-E919.9)
            transport accident (E800.0-E845.9)
        effect of high and low air pressure (E902.2)
        injury from striking against objects while in running water (E917.2)

    E910.0 While water-skiing
        Fall from water skis with submersion or drowning
        EXCLUDES *accident to water-skier involving a watercraft and resulting in submersion or other injury (E830.4, E831.4)*

    E910.1 While engaged in other sport or recreational activity with diving equipment
        Scuba diving NOS
        Skin diving NOS
        Underwater spear fishing NOS

    E910.2 While engaged in other sport or recreational activity without diving equipment
        Fishing or hunting, except from boat or with diving equipment
        Ice skating
        Playing in water
        Surfboarding
        Swimming NOS
        Voluntarily jumping from boat, not involved in accident, for swim NOS
        Wading in water
        EXCLUDES *jumping into water to rescue another person (E910.3)*

    E910.3 While swimming or diving for purposes other than recreation or sport
        Marine salvage
        Pearl diving
        Placement of fishing nets   } (with diving equipment)
        Rescue (attempt) of another person
        Underwater construction or repairs

    E910.4 In bathtub

    E910.8 Other accidental drowning or submersion
        Drowning in:
            quenching tank
            swimming pool

    E910.9 Unspecified accidental drowning or submersion
        Accidental fall into water NOS
        Drowning NOS

E911 Inhalation and ingestion of food causing obstruction of respiratory tract or suffocation
    Aspiration and inhalation of food [any] (into respiratory tract) NOS
    Asphyxia by
    Choked on   } food [including bone, seed in food, regurgitated food]
    Suffocation by
    Compression of trachea
    Interruption of respiration   } by food lodged in esophagus
    Obstruction of respiration
    Obstruction of pharynx by food (bolus)
    EXCLUDES *injury, except asphyxia and obstruction of respiratory passage, caused by food (E915)*
        obstruction of esophagus by food without mention of asphyxia or obstruction of respiratory passage (E915)

E912 Inhalation and ingestion of other object causing obstruction of respiratory tract or suffocation

Aspiration and inhalation of foreign body except food (into respiratory tract) NOS

Foreign object [bean] [marble] in nose

Obstruction of pharynx by foreign body

Compression

Interruption of respiration } by foreign body in esophagus

Obstruction of respiration

EXCLUDES *injury, except asphyxia and obstruction of respiratory passage, caused by foreign body (E915)*
obstruction of esophagus by foreign body without mention of asphyxia or obstruction in respiratory passage (E915)

✓4ᵗʰ E913 Accidental mechanical suffocation

EXCLUDES *mechanical suffocation from or by:*
accidental inhalation or ingestion of:
food (E911)
foreign object (E912)
cataclysm (E908-E909)
explosion (E921.0-E921.9, E923.0-E923.9)
machinery accident (E919.0-E919.9)

E913.0 In bed or cradle

EXCLUDES *suffocation by plastic bag (E913.1)*

E913.1 By plastic bag

E913.2 Due to lack of air (in closed place)

Accidentally closed up in refrigerator or other airtight enclosed space

Diving with insufficient air supply

EXCLUDES *suffocation by plastic bag (E913.1)*

E913.3 By falling earth or other substance

Cave-in NOS

EXCLUDES *cave-in caused by cataclysmic earth surface movements and eruptions (E909)*
struck by cave-in without asphyxiation or suffocation (E916)

E913.8 Other specified means

Accidental hanging, except in bed or cradle

E913.9 Unspecified means

Asphyxia, mechanical NOS

Strangulation NOS

Suffocation NOS

E914 Foreign body accidentally entering eye and adnexa

EXCLUDES *corrosive liquid (E924.1)*

E915 Foreign body accidentally entering other orifice

EXCLUDES *aspiration and inhalation of foreign body, any, (into respiratory tract) NOS (E911-E912)*

OTHER ACCIDENTS (E916-E928)

E916 Struck accidentally by falling object

Collapse of building, except on fire

Falling:
rock
snowslide NOS
stone
tree

Object falling from:
machine, not in operation
stationary vehicle

Code first:
collapse of building on fire (E890.0-E891.9)
falling object in:
cataclysm (E908-E909)
machinery accidents (E919.0-E919.9)
transport accidents (E800.0-E845.9)
vehicle accidents not elsewhere classifiable (E846-E848)
object set in motion by:
explosion (E921.0-E921.9, E923.0-E923.9)
firearm (E922.0-E922.9)
projected object (E917.0-E917.9)

✓4ᵗʰ E917 Striking against or struck accidentally by objects or persons

INCLUDES bumping into or
against
colliding with } object (moving) (projected) (stationary)
kicking against } pedestrian conveyance
stepping on } person
struck by

EXCLUDES *fall from:*
collision with another person, except when caused by a crowd (E886.0-E886.9)
stumbling over object (E885.9)
fall resulting in striking against object (E888.0, E888.1)
injury caused by:
assault (E960.0-E960.1, E967.0-E967.9)
cutting or piercing instrument (E920.0-E920.9)
explosion (E921.0-E921.9, E923.0-E923.9)
firearm (E922.0-E922.9)
machinery (E919.0-E919.9)
transport vehicle (E800.0-E845.9)
vehicle not elsewhere classifiable (E846-E848)

E917.0 In sports without subsequent fall

Kicked or stepped on during game (football) (rugby)

Struck by hit or thrown ball

Struck by hockey stick or puck

E917.1 Caused by a crowd, by collective fear or panic without subsequent fall

Crushed

Pushed } by crowd or human stampede

Stepped on

E917.2 In running water without subsequent fall

EXCLUDES *drowning or submersion (E910.0-E910.9)*
that in sports (E917.0, E917.5)

E917.3 Furniture without subsequent fall

EXCLUDES *fall from furniture (E884.2, E884.4-E884.5)*

E917.4 Other stationary object without subsequent fall

Bath tub
Fence
Lamp-post

E917.5 Object in sports with subsequent fall

Knocked down while boxing

E917.6 Caused by a crowd, by collective fear or panic with subsequent fall

E917.7 Furniture with subsequent fall

EXCLUDES *fall from furniture (E884.2, E884.4-E884.5)*

E917.8 Other stationary object with subsequent fall

Bath tub
Fence
Lamp-post

E917.9 Other striking against with or without subsequent fall

E918 Caught accidentally in or between objects

Caught, crushed, jammed, or pinched in or between moving or stationary objects, such as:
escalator
folding object
hand tools, appliances, or implements
sliding door and door frame
under packing crate
washing machine wringer

EXCLUDES *injury caused by:*
cutting or piercing instrument (E920.0-E920.9)
machinery (E919.0-E919.9)
►*mechanism or component of firearm and air gun (E928.7)*◄
transport vehicle (E800.0-E845.9)
vehicle not elsewhere classifiable (E846-E848)
struck accidentally by:
falling object (E916)
object (moving) (projected) (E917.0-E917.9)

√4ᵗʰ **E919 Accidents caused by machinery**

INCLUDES

burned by
caught in (moving parts of)
collapse of
crushed by
cut or pierced by
drowning or submersion
    caused by
expolosion of, on, in
fall from or into moving part
    of
fire starting in or on
mechanical suffocation
    caused by   } machinery (accident)
object falling from, on, in
    motion by
overturning of
pinned under
run over by
struck by
thrown from

caught between machinery and other object
machinery accident NOS

EXCLUDES   accidents involving machinery, not in operation (E884.9,
            E916-E918)
         injury caused by:
            electric current in connection with machinery
               (E925.0-E925.9)
            escalator (E880.0, E918)
            explosion of pressure vessel in connection with
               machinery (E921.0-E921.9)
            ►mechanism or component of firearm and air gun
               (E928.7)◄
            moving sidewalk (E885.9)
            powered hand tools, appliances, and implements
               (E916-E918, E920.0-E921.9, E923.0-E926.9)
            transport vehicle accidents involving machinery
               (E800.0-E848)
            poisoning by carbon monoxide generated by machine
               (E868.8)

E919.0 Agricultural machines

Animal-powered   Farm tractor
   agricultural machine   Harvester
Combine   Hay mower or rake
Derrick, hay   Reaper
Farm machinery NOS   Thresher

EXCLUDES   that in transport under own power on the
            highway (E810.0-E819.9)
            that being towed by another vehicle on the
             highway (E810.0-E819.9, E827.0-E827.9,
             E829.0-E829.9)
            that involved in accident classifiable to
             E820-E829 (E820.0-E829.9)

E919.1 Mining and earth-drilling machinery

Bore or drill (land) (seabed)
Shaft hoist
Shaft lift
Under-cutter

EXCLUDES   coal car, tram, truck, and tub in mine (E846)

E919.2 Lifting machines and appliances

Chain hoist
Crane
Derrick
Elevator (building) (grain)   } except in agricultural or
Forklift truck   mining
Lift   operations
Pulley block
Winch

EXCLUDES   that being towed by another vehicle on the
            highway (E810.0-E819.9, E827.0-E827.9,
             E829.0-829.9)
            that in transport under own power on the
             highway (E810.0-E819.9)
            that involved in accident classifiable to
             E820-E829 (E820.0-E829.9)

E919.3 Metalworking machines

Abrasive wheel   Metal:
Forging machine   milling machine
Lathe   power press
Mechanical shears   rolling-mill
Metal: sawing machine
   drilling machine

E919.4 Woodworking and forming machines

Band saw   Overhead plane
Bench saw   Powered saw
Circular saw   Radial saw
Molding machine   Sander

EXCLUDES   hand saw (E920.1)

E919.5 Prime movers, except electrical motors

Gas turbine
Internal combustion engine
Steam engine
Water driven turbine

EXCLUDES   that being towed by other vehicle on the
            highway (E810.0-E819.9, E827.0-E827.9,
             E829.0-E829.9)
            that in transport under own power on the
             highway (E810.0-E819.9)

E919.6 Transmission machinery

Transmission: Transmission:
   belt   pinion
   cable   pulley
   chain   shaft
   gear

E919.7 Earth moving, scraping, and other excavating machines

Bulldozer   Steam shovel
Road scraper

EXCLUDES   that being towed by other vehicle on the
            highway (E810.0-E819.9, E827.0-E827.9,
             E829.0-E829.9)
            that in transport under own power on the
             highway (E810.0-E819.9)

E919.8 Other specified machinery

Machines for manufacture of:
   clothing
   foodstuffs and beverages
   paper
Printing machine
Recreational machinery
Spinning, weaving, and textile machines

E919.9 Unspecified machinery

√4ᵗʰ **E920 Accidents caused by cutting and piercing instruments or objects**

INCLUDES

                                      edged
accidental injury (by) object   } pointed
                                       sharp

EXCLUDES   ►injury caused by mechanism or component of firearm
             and air gun (E928.7)◄

E920.0 Powered lawn mower

E920.1 Other powered hand tools

Any powered hand tool [compressed air] [electric]
   [explosive cartridge] [hydraulic power], such as:
   drill
   hand saw
   hedge clipper
   rivet gun
   snow blower
   staple gun

EXCLUDES   band saw (E919.4)
            bench saw (E919.4)

E920.2 Powered household appliances and implements

Blender   Electric:
Electric: knife
   beater or mixer   sewing machine
   can opener   Garbage disposal appliance
   fan

E920.3 Knives, swords, and daggers

E920.4 Other hand tools and implements

Axe	Paper cutter
Can opener NOS	Pitchfork
Chisel	Rake
Fork	Scissors
Hand saw	Screwdriver
Hoe	Sewing machine, not powered
Ice pick	Shovel
Needle (sewing)	

E920.5 Hypodermic needle
Contaminated needle
Needle stick

E920.8 Other specified cutting and piercing instruments or objects

Arrow	Nail
Broken glass	Plant thorn
Dart	Splinter
Edge of stiff paper	Tin can lid
Lathe turnings	

> **EXCLUDES** animal spines or quills (E906.8)
> flying glass due to explosion (E921.0-E923.9)

E920.9 Unspecified cutting and piercing instrument or object

✓4ᵗʰ E921 Accident caused by explosion of pressure vessel
> **INCLUDES** accidental explosion of pressure vessels, whether or not part of machinery
> **EXCLUDES** explosion of pressure vessel on transport vehicle (E800.0-E845.9)

E921.0 Boilers

E921.1 Gas cylinders
Air tank	Pressure gas tank

E921.8 Other specified pressure vessels
Aerosol can	Tin can lid
Automobile tire	

E921.9 Unspecified pressure vessel

✓4ᵗʰ E922 Accident caused by firearm, and air gun missile
> **EXCLUDES** ▶injury caused by mechanism or component of firearm and air gun (E928.7)◀

E922.0 Handgun
Pistol	Revolver

> **EXCLUDES** Verey pistol (E922.8)

E922.1 Shotgun (automatic)

E922.2 Hunting rifle

E922.3 Military firearms
Army rifle	Machine gun

E922.4 Air gun
BB gun	Pellet gun

E922.5 Paintball gun

E922.8 Other specified firearm missile
Verey pistol [flare]

E922.9 Unspecified firearm missile
Gunshot wound NOS
Shot NOS

✓4ᵗʰ E923 Accident caused by explosive material
> **INCLUDES** flash burns and other injuries resulting from explosion of explosive material
> ignition of highly explosive material with explosion
> **EXCLUDES** explosion:
> in or on machinery (E919.0-E919.9)
> on any transport vehicle, except stationary motor vehicle (E800.0-E848)
> with conflagration (E890.0, E891.0,E892)
> ▶injury caused by mechanism or component of firearm and air gun (E928.7)◀
> secondary fires resulting from explosion (E890.0-E899)

E923.0 Fireworks

E923.1 Blasting materials
Blasting cap	Dynamite
Detonator	Explosive [any] used in blasting operations

E923.2 Explosive gases
Acetylene	Fire damp
Butane	Gasoline fumes
Coal gas	Methane
Explosion in mine NOS	Propane

E923.8 Other explosive materials
Bomb	Torpedo
Explosive missile	Explosion in munitions:
Grenade	dump
Mine	factory
Shell	

E923.9 Unspecified explosive material
Explosion NOS

✓4ᵗʰ E924 Accident caused by hot substance or object, caustic or corrosive material, and steam
> **EXCLUDES** burning NOS (E899)
> chemical burn resulting from swallowing a corrosive substance (E860.0-E864.4)
> fire caused by these substances and objects (E890.0-E894)
> radiation burns (E926.0-E926.9)
> therapeutic misadventures (E870.0-E876.9)

E924.0 Hot liquids and vapors, including steam
Burning or scalding by:
boiling water
hot or boiling liquids not primarily caustic or corrosive
liquid metal
steam
other hot vapor
> **EXCLUDES** hot (boiling) tap water (E924.2)

E924.1 Caustic and corrosive substances
Burning by:
acid [any kind]
ammonia
caustic oven cleaner or other substance
corrosive substance
lye
vitriol

E924.2 Hot (boiling) tap water

E924.8 Other
Burning by:
heat from electric heating appliance
hot object NOS
light bulb
steam pipe

E924.9 Unspecified

✓4ᵗʰ E925 Accident caused by electric current
> **INCLUDES** electric current from exposed wire, faulty appliance, high voltage cable, live rail, or open electric socket as the cause of:
> burn
> cardiac fibrillation
> convulsion
> electric shock
> electrocution
> puncture wound
> respiratory paralysis
> **EXCLUDES** burn by heat from electrical appliance (E924.8)
> lightning (E907)

E925.0 Domestic wiring and appliances

E925.1 Electric power generating plants, distribution stations, transmission lines
Broken power line

E925.2 Industrial wiring, appliances, and electrical machinery
Conductors
Control apparatus
Electrical equipment and machinery
Transformers

E925.8 Other electric current
　　Wiring and appliances in or on:
　　　farm [not farmhouse]
　　　outdoors
　　　public building
　　　residential institutions
　　　schools

E925.9 Unspecified electric current
　　Burns or other injury from electric current NOS
　　Electric shock NOS
　　Electrocution NOS

✓4ᵗʰ **E926 Exposure to radiation**

> *EXCLUDES* *abnormal reaction to or complication of treatment*
> *without mention of misadventure (E879.2)*
> *atomic power plant malfunction in water transport*
> *(E838.0-E838.9)*
> *misadventure to patient in surgical and medical*
> *procedures (E873.2-E873.3)*
> *use of radiation in war operations (E996-E997.9)*

E926.0 Radiofrequency radiation

Overexposure to:　　　from:
　microwave radiation　high-powered radio and
　radar radiation　　　　television
　radiofrequency　　　　transmitters
　radiofrequency　　industrial radiofrequency
　radiation [any]　　　induction heaters
　　　　　　　　radar installations

E926.1 Infrared heaters and lamps
　　Exposure to infrared radiation from heaters and lamps as
　　　the cause of:
　　　blistering
　　　burning
　　　charring
　　　inflammatory change
　　　EXCLUDES *physical contact with heater or lamp (E924.8)*

E926.2 Visible and ultraviolet light sources
　　Arc lamps
　　Black light sources
　　Electrical welding arc
　　Oxygas welding torch
　　Sun rays
　　Tanning bed
　　EXCLUDES *excessive heat from these sources*
　　　　　　(E900.1-E900.9)

E926.3 X-rays and other electromagnetic ionizing radiation
　　Gamma rays
　　X-rays (hard) (soft)

E926.4 Lasers

E926.5 Radioactive isotopes
　　Radiobiologicals
　　Radiopharmaceuticals

E926.8 Other specified radiation
　　Artificially accelerated beams of ionized particles
　　　generated by:
　　　betatrons
　　　synchrotrons

E926.9 Unspecified radiation
　　Radiation NOS

✓4ᵗʰ **E927 Overexertion and strenuous and repetitive movements or
loads**

　▶Use additional code to identify activity (E001-E030)◀

E927.0 Overexertion from sudden strenuous movement
　　Sudden trauma from strenuous movement

E927.1 Overexertion from prolonged static position
　　Overexertion from maintaining prolonged positions, such
　　　as:
　　　holding
　　　sitting
　　　standing

E927.2 Excessive physical exertion from prolonged activity

E927.3 Cumulative trauma from repetitive motion
　　Cumulative trauma from repetitive movements

E927.4 Cumulative trauma from repetitive impact

**E927.8 Other overexertion and strenuous and repetitive
movements or loads**

**E927.9 Unspecified overexertion and strenuous and repetitive
movements or loads**

✓4ᵗʰ **E928 Other and unspecified environmental and accidental
causes**

E928.0 Prolonged stay in weightless environment
　　Weightlessness in spacecraft (simulator)

E928.1 Exposure to noise
　　Noise (pollution)
　　Sound waves
　　Supersonic waves

E928.2 Vibration

E928.3 Human bite

E928.4 External constriction caused by hair

E928.5 External constriction caused by other object

E928.6 Environmental exposure to harmful algae and toxins
　　Algae bloom NOS　　　　Florida red tide
　　Blue-green algae bloom　Harmful algae bloom
　　Brown tide　　　　　　Pfiesteria piscicida
　　Cyanobacteria bloom　　Red tide

● **E928.7 Mechanism or component of firearm and air gun**
　　Injury due to:
　　　explosion of gun parts
　　　recoil
　　Pierced, cut, crushed, or pinched by slide, trigger
　　　mechanism, scope, or other gun part
　　Powder burn from firearm or air gun
　　　EXCLUDES *accident caused by firearm and air gun missile*
　　　　　　(E922.0-E922.9)

E928.8 Other

E928.9 Unspecified accident
　　Accident NOS
　　Blow NOS　　　　　　} stated as accidentally
　　Casualty (not due to war)　　inflicted
　　Decapitation

　　Knocked down
　　Killed　　　　　　　stated as accidentally
　　Injury [any part of body, or　inflicted, but not
　　　unspecified]　　　　　otherwise
　　Mangled　　　　　　　specified
　　Wound
　　　EXCLUDES *fracture, cause unspecified (E887)*
　　　　　　injuries undetermined whether accidentally or
　　　　　　purposely inflicted (E980.0-E989)

LATE EFFECTS OF ACCIDENTAL INJURY (E929)

Note: This category is to be used to indicate accidental injury as
the cause of death or disability from late effects, which are
themselves classifiable elsewhere. The "late effects" include
conditions reported as such, or as sequelae which may occur
at any time after the attempted suicide or self-inflicted
injury.

✓4ᵗʰ **E929 Late effects of accidental injury**

> *EXCLUDES* *late effects of:*
> *surgical and medical procedures (E870.0-E879.9)*
> *therapeutic use of drugs and medicines*
> *(E930.0-E949.9)*

E929.0 Late effects of motor vehicle accident
　　Late effects of accidents classifiable to E810-E825

E929.1 Late effects of other transport accident
　　Late effects of accidents classifiable to E800-E807,
　　　E826-E838, E840-E848

E929.2 Late effects of accidental poisoning
　　Late effects of accidents classifiable to E850-E858,
　　　E860-E869

E929.3 Late effects of accidental fall
Late effects of accidents classifiable to E880-E888

E929.4 Late effects of accident caused by fire
Late effects of accidents classifiable to E890-E899

E929.5 Late effects of accident due to natural and environmental factors
Late effects of accidents classifiable to E900-E909

E929.8 Late effects of other accidents
Late effects of accidents classifiable to E910-E928.8

E929.9 Late effects of unspecified accident
Late effects of accidents classifiable to E928.9

DRUGS, MEDICINAL AND BIOLOGICAL SUBSTANCES CAUSING ADVERSE EFFECTS IN THERAPEUTIC USE (E930-E949)

INCLUDES correct drug properly administered in therapeutic or prophylactic dosage, as the cause of any adverse effect including allergic or hypersensitivity reactions

EXCLUDES *accidental overdose of drug and wrong drug given or taken in error (E850.0-E858.9)*
accidents in the technique of administration of drug or biological substance, such as accidental puncture during injection, or contamination of drug (E870.0-E876.9)
administration with suicidal or homicidal intent or intent to harm, or in circumstances classifiable to E950.0-E950.5, E962.0, E980.0-E980.5

See Alphabetic Index for more complete list of specific drugs to be classified under the fourth-digit subdivisions. The American Hospital Formulary numbers can be used to classify new drugs listed by the American Hospital Formulary Service (AHFS). See Appendix C.

✓4ᵗʰ **E930 Antibiotics**
EXCLUDES *that used as eye, ear, nose, and throat [ENT], and local anti-infectives (E946.0-E946.9)*

E930.0 Penicillins
Natural
Synthetic
Semisynthetic, such as:
  ampicillin
Semisynthetic, such as:
  cloxacillin
  nafcillin
  oxacillin

E930.1 Antifungal antibiotics
Amphotericin B
Griseofulvin
Hachimycin [trichomycin]
Nystatin

E930.2 Chloramphenicol group
Chloramphenicol
Thiamphenicol

E930.3 Erythromycin and other macrolides
Oleandomycin
Spiramycin

E930.4 Tetracycline group
Doxycycline
Minocycline
Oxytetracycline

E930.5 Cephalosporin group
Cephalexin
Cephaloglycin
Cephaloridine
Cephalothin

E930.6 Antimycobacterial antibiotics
Cycloserine
Kanamycin
Rifampin
Streptomycin

E930.7 Antineoplastic antibiotics
Actinomycins, such as:
  Bleomycin
  Cactinomycin
  Dactinomycin
  Daunorubicin
  Mitomycin
EXCLUDES *other antineoplastic drugs (E933.1)*

E930.8 Other specified antibiotics

E930.9 Unspecified antibiotic

✓4ᵗʰ **E931 Other anti-infectives**
EXCLUDES *ENT, and local anti-infectives (E946.0-E946.9)*

E931.0 Sulfonamides
Sulfadiazine
Sulfafurazole
Sulfamethoxazole

E931.1 Arsenical anti-infectives

E931.2 Heavy metal anti-infectives
Compounds of:
  antimony
  bismuth
  lead
  mercury
EXCLUDES *mercurial diuretics (E944.0)*

E931.3 Quinoline and hydroxyquinoline derivatives
Chiniofon
Diiodohydroxyquin
EXCLUDES *antimalarial drugs (E931.4)*

E931.4 Antimalarials and drugs acting on other blood protozoa
Chloroquine phosphate
Cycloguanil
Primaquine
Proguanil [chloroguanide]
Pyrimethamine
Quinine (sulphate)

E931.5 Other antiprotozoal drugs
Emetine

E931.6 Anthelmintics
Hexylresorcinol
Male fern oleoresin
Piperazine
Thiabendazole

E931.7 Antiviral drugs
Methisazone
EXCLUDES *amantadine (E936.4)*
cytarabine (E933.1)
idoxuridine (E946.5)

E931.8 Other antimycobacterial drugs
Ethambutol
Ethionamide
Isoniazid
Para-aminosalicylic acid derivatives
Sulfones

E931.9 Other and unspecified anti-infectives
Flucytosine
Nitrofuranderivatives

✓4ᵗʰ **E932 Hormones and synthetic substitutes**

E932.0 Adrenal cortical steroids
Cortisone derivatives
Desoxycorticosterone derivatives
Fluorinated corticosteroid

E932.1 Androgens and anabolic congeners
Nandrolone phenpropionate
Oxymetholone
Testosterone and preparations

E932.2 Ovarian hormones and synthetic substitutes
Contraceptives, oral
Estrogens
Estrogens and progestogens combined
Progestogens

E932.3 Insulins and antidiabetic agents
Acetohexamide
Biguanide derivatives, oral
Chlorpropamide
Glucagon
Insulin
Phenformin
Sulfonylurea derivatives, oral
Tolbutamide
EXCLUDES *adverse effect of insulin administered for shock therapy (E879.3)*

E932.4 Anterior pituitary hormones
Corticotropin
Gonadotropin
Somatotropin [growth hormone]

✓4ᵗʰ Fourth-digit Required   ▶◀ Revised Text   ● New Code   ▲ Revised Code TitleDx

E932.5 **Posterior pituitary hormones**
Vasopressin
EXCLUDES *oxytocic agents (E945.0)*

E932.6 **Parathyroid and parathyroid derivatives**

E932.7 **Thyroid and thyroid derivatives**
Dextrothyroxine
Levothyroxine sodium
Liothyronine
Thyroglobulin

E932.8 **Antithyroid agents**
Iodides
Thiouracil
Thiourea

E932.9 **Other and unspecified hormones and synthetic substitutes**

✓4ᵗʰ **E933 Primarily systemic agents**

E933.0 **Antiallergic and antiemetic drugs**
Antihistamines   Diphenylpyraline
Chlorpheniramine   Thonzylamine
Diphenhydramine   Tripelennamine
EXCLUDES *phenothiazine-based tranquilizers (E939.1)*

E933.1 **Antineoplastic and immunosuppressive drugs**
Azathioprine
Busulfan
Chlorambucil
Cyclophosphamide
Cytarabine
Fluorouracil
Mechlorethamine hydrochloride
Mercaptopurine
Triethylenethiophosphoramide [thio-TEPA]
EXCLUDES *antineoplastic antibiotics (E930.7)*

E933.2 **Acidifying agents**

E933.3 **Alkalizing agents**

E933.4 **Enzymes, not elsewhere classified**
Penicillinase

E933.5 **Vitamins, not elsewhere classified**
Vitamin A
Vitamin D
EXCLUDES *nicotinic acid (E942.2)*
vitamin K (E934.3)

E933.6 **Oral bisphosphonates**

E933.7 **Intravenous bisphosphonates**

E933.8 **Other systemic agents, not elsewhere classified**
Heavy metal antagonists

E933.9 **Unspecified systemic agent**

✓4ᵗʰ **E934 Agents primarily affecting blood constituents**

E934.0 **Iron and its compounds**
Ferric salts
Ferrous sulphate and other ferrous salts

E934.1 **Liver preparations and other antianemic agents**
Folic acid

E934.2 **Anticoagulants**
Coumarin
Heparin
Phenindione
Prothrombin synthesis inhibitor
Warfarin sodium

E934.3 **Vitamin K [phytonadione]**

E934.4 **Fibrinolysis-affecting drugs**
Aminocaproic acid   Streptokinase
Streptodornase   Urokinase

E934.5 **Anticoagulant antagonists and other coagulants**
Hexadimethrine bromide
Protamine sulfate

E934.6 **Gamma globulin**

E934.7 **Natural blood and blood products**
Blood plasma
Human fibrinogen
Packed red cells
Whole blood

E934.8 **Other agents affecting blood constituents**
Macromolecular blood substitutes

E934.9 **Unspecified agent affecting blood constituents**

✓4ᵗʰ **E935 Analgesics, antipyretics, and antirheumatics**

E935.0 **Heroin**
Diacetylmorphine

E935.1 **Methadone**

E935.2 **Other opiates and related narcotics**
Codeine [methylmorphine]
Meperidine [pethidine]
Morphine
Opium (alkaloids)

E935.3 **Salicylates**
Acetylsalicylic acid [aspirin]
Amino derivatives of salicylic acid
Salicylic acid salts

E935.4 **Aromatic analgesics, not elsewhere classified**
Acetanilid
Paracetamol [acetaminophen]
Phenacetin [acetophenetidin]

E935.5 **Pyrazole derivatives**
Aminophenazone [aminopyrine]
Phenylbutazone

E935.6 **Antirheumatics [antiphlogistics]**
Gold salts
Indomethacin
EXCLUDES *salicylates (E935.3)*
steroids (E932.0)

E935.7 **Other non-narcotic analgesics**
Pyrabital

E935.8 **Other specified analgesics and antipyretics**
Pentazocine

E935.9 **Unspecified analgesic and antipyretic**

✓4ᵗʰ **E936 Anticonvulsants and anti-Parkinsonism drugs**

E936.0 **Oxazolidine derivatives**
Paramethadione
Trimethadione

E936.1 **Hydantoin derivatives**
Phenytoin

E936.2 **Succinimides**
Ethosuximide
Phensuximide

E936.3 **Other and unspecified anticonvulsants**
Beclamide
Primidone

E936.4 **Anti-Parkinsonism drugs**
Amantadine
Ethopropazine [profenamine]
Levodopa [L-dopa]

✓4ᵗʰ **E937 Sedatives and hypnotics**

E937.0 **Barbiturates**
Amobarbital [amylobarbitone]
Barbital [barbitone]
Butabarbital [butabarbitone]
Pentobarbital [pentobarbitone]
Phenobarbital [phenobarbitone]
Secobarbital [quinalbarbitone]
EXCLUDES *thiobarbiturates (E938.3)*

E937.1 **Chloral hydrate group**

E937.2 **Paraldehyde**

E937.3 **Bromine compounds**
Bromide
Carbromal (derivatives)

E937.4 Methaqualone compounds

E937.5 Glutethimide group

E937.6 Mixed sedatives, not elsewhere classified

E937.8 Other sedatives and hypnotics

E937.9 Unspecified
Sleeping:
drug
pill } NOS
tablet

✓4th **E938 Other central nervous system depressants and anesthetics**

E938.0 Central nervous system muscle-tone depressants
Chlorphenesin (carbamate)
Mephenesin
Methocarbamol

E938.1 Halothane

E938.2 Other gaseous anesthetics
Ether
Halogenated hydrocarbon derivatives, except halothane
Nitrous oxide

E938.3 Intravenous anesthetics
Ketamine
Methohexital [methohexitone]
Thiobarbiturates, such as thiopental sodium

E938.4 Other and unspecified general anesthetics

E938.5 Surface and infiltration anesthetics
Cocaine
Lidocaine [lignocaine]
Procaine
Tetracaine

E938.6 Peripheral nerve- and plexus-blocking anesthetics

E938.7 Spinal anesthetics

E938.9 Other and unspecified local anesthetics

✓4th **E939 Psychotropic agents**

E939.0 Antidepressants
Amitriptyline
Imipramine
Monoamine oxidase [MAO] inhibitors

E939.1 Phenothiazine-based tranquilizers
Chlorpromazine   Prochlorperazine
Fluphenazine   Promazine
Phenothiazine

E939.2 Butyrophenone-based tranquilizers
Haloperidol
Spiperone
Trifluperidol

E939.3 Other antipsychotics, neuroleptics, and major tranquilizers

E939.4 Benzodiazepine-based tranquilizers
Chlordiazepoxide   Lorazepam
Diazepam   Medazepam
Flurazepam   Nitrazepam

E939.5 Other tranquilizers
Hydroxyzine
Meprobamate

E939.6 Psychodysleptics [hallucinogens]
Cannabis (derivatives) Mescaline
Lysergide [LSD]   Psilocin
Marihuana (derivatives) Psilocybin

E939.7 Psychostimulants
Amphetamine
Caffeine
EXCLUDES *central appetite depressants (E947.0)*

E939.8 Other psychotropic agents

E939.9 Unspecified psychotropic agent

✓4th **E940 Central nervous system stimulants**

E940.0 Analeptics
Lobeline
Nikethamide

E940.1 Opiate antagonists
Levallorphan
Nalorphine
Naloxone

E940.8 Other specified central nervous system stimulants

E940.9 Unspecified central nervous system stimulant

✓4th **E941 Drugs primarily affecting the autonomic nervous system**

E941.0 Parasympathomimetics [cholinergics]
Acetylcholine
Anticholinesterase:
organophosphorus
reversible
Pilocarpine

E941.1 Parasympatholytics [anticholinergics and antimuscarinics] and spasmolytics
Atropine
Homatropine
Hyoscine [scopolamine]
Quaternary ammonium derivatives
EXCLUDES *papaverine (E942.5)*

E941.2 Sympathomimetics [adrenergics]
Epinephrine [adrenalin]
Levarterenol [noradrenalin]

E941.3 Sympatholytics [antiadrenergics]
Phenoxybenzamine
Tolazolinehydrochloride

E941.9 Unspecified drug primarily affecting the autonomic nervous system

✓4th **E942 Agents primarily affecting the cardiovascular system**

E942.0 Cardiac rhythm regulators
Practolol   Propranolol
Procainamide   Quinidine

E942.1 Cardiotonic glycosides and drugs of similar action
Digitalis glycosides   Strophanthins
Digoxin

E942.2 Antilipemic and antiarteriosclerotic drugs
Cholestyramine   Nicotinic acid derivatives
Clofibrate   Sitosterols
EXCLUDES *dextrothyroxine (E932.7)*

E942.3 Ganglion-blocking agents
Pentamethonium bromide

E942.4 Coronary vasodilators
Dipyridamole   Nitrites
Nitrates [nitroglycerin] Prenylamine

E942.5 Other vasodilators
Cyclandelate   Hydralazine
Diazoxide   Papaverine

E942.6 Other antihypertensive agents
Clonidine   Rauwolfia alkaloids
Guanethidine   Reserpine

E942.7 Antivaricose drugs, including sclerosing agents
Monoethanolamine
Zinc salts

E942.8 Capillary-active drugs
Adrenochrome derivatives
Bioflavonoids
Metaraminol

E942.9 Other and unspecified agents primarily affecting the cardiovascular system

✓4th **E943 Agents primarily affecting gastrointestinal system**

E943.0 Antacids and antigastric secretion drugs
Aluminum hydroxide
Magnesium trisilicate

E943.1 Irritant cathartics
  Bisacodyl
  Castor oil
  Phenolphthalein

E943.2 Emollient cathartics
  Sodium dioctyl sulfosuccinate

E943.3 Other cathartics, including intestinal atonia drugs
  Magnesium sulfate

E943.4 Digestants
  Pancreatin
  Papain
  Pepsin

E943.5 Antidiarrheal drugs
  Bismuth subcarbonate Pectin or Kaolin
  EXCLUDES *anti-infectives (E930.0-E931.9)*

E943.6 Emetics

E943.8 Other specified agents primarily affecting the gastrointestinal system

E943.9 Unspecified agent primarily affecting the gastrointestinal system

✓4ᵗʰ **E944 Water, mineral, and uric acid metabolism drugs**

E944.0 Mercurial diuretics
  Chlormerodrin   Mercurophylline
  Mercaptomerin   Mersalyl

E944.1 Purine derivative diuretics
  Theobromine
  Theophylline
  EXCLUDES *aminophylline [theophylline ethylenediamine] (E945.7)*

E944.2 Carbonic acid anhydrase inhibitors
  Acetazolamide

E944.3 Saluretics
  Benzothiadiazides   Chlorothiazide group

E944.4 Other diuretics
  Ethacrynic acid   Furosemide

E944.5 Electrolytic, caloric, and water-balance agents

E944.6 Other mineral salts, not elsewhere classified

E944.7 Uric acid metabolism drugs
  Cinchophen and congeners
  Colchicine
  Phenoquin
  Probenecid

✓4ᵗʰ **E945 Agents primarily acting on the smooth and skeletal muscles and respiratory system**

E945.0 Oxytocic agents
  Ergot alkaloids
  Prostaglandins

E945.1 Smooth muscle relaxants
  Adiphenine
  Metaproterenol [orciprenaline]
  EXCLUDES *papaverine (E942.5)*

E945.2 Skeletal muscle relaxants
  Alcuronium chloride
  Suxamethonium chloride

E945.3 Other and unspecified drugs acting on muscles

E945.4 Antitussives
  Dextromethorphan
  Pipazethate hydrochloride

E945.5 Expectorants
  Acetylcysteine
  Cocillana
  Guaifenesin [glyceryl guaiacolate]
  Ipecacuanha
  Terpin hydrate

E945.6 Anti-common cold drugs

E945.7 Antiasthmatics
  Aminophylline [theophylline ethylenediamine]

E945.8 Other and unspecified respiratory drugs

✓4ᵗʰ **E946 Agents primarily affecting skin and mucous membrane, ophthalmological, otorhinolaryngological, and dental drugs**

E946.0 Local anti-infectives and anti-inflammatory drugs

E946.1 Antipruritics

E946.2 Local astringents and local detergents

E946.3 Emollients, demulcents, and protectants

E946.4 Keratolytics, kerstoplastics, other hair treatment drugs and preparations

E946.5 Eye anti-infectives and other eye drugs
  Idoxuridine

E946.6 Anti-infectives and other drugs and preparations for ear, nose, and throat

E946.7 Dental drugs topically applied

E946.8 Other agents primarily affecting skin and mucous membrane
  Spermicides

E946.9 Unspecified agent primarily affecting skin and mucous membrane

✓4ᵗʰ **E947 Other and unspecified drugs and medicinal substances**

E947.0 Dietetics

E947.1 Lipotropic drugs

E947.2 Antidotes and chelating agents, not elsewhere classified

E947.3 Alcohol deterrents

E947.4 Pharmaceutical excipients

E947.8 Other drugs and medicinal substances
  Contrast media used for diagnostic x-ray procedures
  Diagnostic agents and kits

E947.9 Unspecified drug or medicinal substance

✓4ᵗʰ **E948 Bacterial vaccines**

E948.0 BCG vaccine

E948.1 Typhoid and paratyphoid

E948.2 Cholera

E948.3 Plague

E948.4 Tetanus

E948.5 Diphtheria

E948.6 Pertussis vaccine, including combinations with a pertussis component

E948.8 Other and unspecified bacterial vaccines

E948.9 Mixed bacterial vaccines, except combinations with a pertussis component

✓4ᵗʰ **E949 Other vaccines and biological substances**
  EXCLUDES *gamma globulin (E934.6)*

E949.0 Smallpox vaccine

E949.1 Rabies vaccine

E949.2 Typhus vaccine

E949.3 Yellow fever vaccine

E949.4 Measles vaccine

E949.5 Poliomyelitis vaccine

E949.6 Other and unspecified viral and rickettsial vaccines
  Mumps vaccine

E949.7 Mixed viral-rickettsial and bacterial vaccines, except combinations with a pertussis component
  EXCLUDES *combinations with a pertussis component (E948.6)*

E949.9 Other and unspecified vaccines and biological substances

SUICIDE AND SELF-INFLICTED INJURY (E950-E959)

> **INCLUDES**   injuries in suicide and attempted suicide
> self-inflicted injuries specified as intentional

☑4ᵗʰ E950 Suicide and self-inflicted poisoning by solid or liquid substances

E950.0 Analgesics, antipyretics, and antirheumatics

E950.1 Barbiturates

E950.2 Other sedatives and hypnotics

E950.3 Tranquilizers and other psychotropic agents

E950.4 Other specified drugs and medicinal substances

E950.5 Unspecified drug or medicinal substance

E950.6 Agricultural and horticultural chemical and pharmaceutical preparations other than plant foods and fertilizers

E950.7 Corrosive and caustic substances
> Suicide and self-inflicted poisoning by substances classifiable to E864

E950.8 Arsenic and its compounds

E950.9 Other and unspecified solid and liquid substances

☑4ᵗʰ E951 Suicide and self-inflicted poisoning by gases in domestic use

E951.0 Gas distributed by pipeline

E951.1 Liquefied petroleum gas distributed in mobile containers

E951.8 Other utility gas

☑4ᵗʰ E952 Suicide and self-inflicted poisoning by other gases and vapors

E952.0 Motor vehicle exhaust gas

E952.1 Other carbon monoxide

E952.8 Other specified gases and vapors

E952.9 Unspecified gases and vapors

☑4ᵗʰ E953 Suicide and self-inflicted injury by hanging, strangulation, and suffocation

E953.0 Hanging

E953.1 Suffocation by plastic bag

E953.8 Other specified means

E953.9 Unspecified means

E954 Suicide and self-inflicted injury by submersion [drowning]

☑4ᵗʰ E955 Suicide and self-inflicted injury by firearms, air guns and explosives

E955.0 Handgun

E955.1 Shotgun

E955.2 Hunting rifle

E955.3 Military firearms

E955.4 Other and unspecified firearm
> Gunshot NOS
> Shot NOS

E955.5 Explosives

E955.6 Air gun
> BB gun
> Pellet gun

E955.7 Paintball gun

E955.9 Unspecified

E956 Suicide and self-inflicted injury by cutting and piercing instrument

☑4ᵗʰ E957 Suicide and self-inflicted injuries by jumping from high place

E957.0 Residential premises

E957.1 Other man-made structures

E957.2 Natural sites

E957.9 Unspecified

☑4ᵗʰ E958 Suicide and self-inflicted injury by other and unspecified means

E958.0 Jumping or lying before moving object

E958.1 Burns, fire

E958.2 Scald

E958.3 Extremes of cold

E958.4 Electrocution

E958.5 Crashing of motor vehicle

E958.6 Crashing of aircraft

E958.7 Caustic substances, except poisoning
> **EXCLUDES**   *poisoning by caustic substance (E950.7)*

E958.8 Other specified means

E958.9 Unspecified means

E959 Late effects of self-inflicted injury

> Note: This category is to be used to indicate circumstances classifiable to E950-E958 as the cause of death or disability from late effects, which are themselves classifiable elsewhere. The "late effects" include conditions reported as such, or as sequelae which may occur at any time after the attempted suicide or self-inflicted injury.

HOMICIDE AND INJURY PURPOSELY INFLICTED BY OTHER PERSONS (E960-E969)

> **INCLUDES**   injuries inflicted by another person with intent to injure or kill, by any means

> **EXCLUDES**   *injuries due to:*
> *legal intervention (E970-E978)*
> *operations of war (E990-E999)*
> *terrorism (E979)*

☑4ᵗʰ E960 Fight, brawl, rape

E960.0 Unarmed fight or brawl
> Beatings NOS
> Brawl or fight with hands, fists, feet
> Injured or killed in fight NOS
> **EXCLUDES**   *homicidal:*
> *injury by weapons (E965.0-E966, E969)*
> *strangulation (E963)*
> *submersion (E964)*

E960.1 Rape

E961 Assault by corrosive or caustic substance, except poisoning
> Injury or death purposely caused by corrosive or caustic substance, such as:
> acid [any]
> corrosive substance
> vitriol
> **EXCLUDES**   *burns from hot liquid (E968.3)*
> *chemical burns from swallowing a corrosive substance (E962.0-E962.9)*

☑4ᵗʰ E962 Assault by poisoning

E962.0 Drugs and medicinal substances
> Homicidal poisoning by any drug or medicinal substance

E962.1 Other solid and liquid substances

E962.2 Other gases and vapors

E962.9 Unspecified poisoning

E963 Assault by hanging and strangulation
> Homicidal (attempt):
> garrotting or ligature
> hanging
> strangulation
> suffocation

☑4ᵗʰ Fourth-digit Required   ▶◀ Revised Text   ● New Code   ▲ Revised Code TitleDx

E Codes

E964–E977

E964 Assault by submersion [drowning]

☑4ᵗʰ **E965 Assault by firearms and explosives**

E965.0 Handgun
    Pistol
    Revolver

E965.1 Shotgun

E965.2 Hunting rifle

E965.3 Military firearms

E965.4 Other and unspecified firearm

E965.5 Antipersonnel bomb

E965.6 Gasoline bomb

E965.7 Letter bomb

E965.8 Other specified explosive
    Bomb NOS (placed in):
        car
        house
    Dynamite

E965.9 Unspecified explosive

E966 Assault by cutting and piercing instrument
    Assassination (attempt), homicide (attempt) by any instrument
        classifiable under E920
    Homicidal:
        cut
        puncture   } any part of the body
        stab
    Stabbed any part of the body

☑4ᵗʰ **E967 Perpetrator of child and adult abuse**
    Note: Selection of the correct perpetrator code is based on the
        relationship between the perpetrator and the victim

E967.0 By father, stepfather, or boyfriend
    Male partner of child's parent or guardian

E967.1 By other specified person

E967.2 By mother, stepmother, or girlfriend
    Female partner of child's parent or guardian

E967.3 By spouse or partner
    Abuse of spouse or partner by ex-spouse or ex-partner

E967.4 By child

E967.5 By sibling

E967.6 By grandparent

E967.7 By other relative

E967.8 By non-related caregiver

E967.9 By unspecified person

☑4ᵗʰ **E968 Assault by other and unspecified means**

E968.0 Fire
    Arson
    Homicidal burns NOS
        EXCLUDES *burns from hot liquid (E968.3)*

E968.1 Pushing from a high place

E968.2 Striking by blunt or thrown object

E968.3 Hot liquid
    Homicidal burns by scalding

E968.4 Criminal neglect
    Abandonment of child, infant, or other helpless person
        with intent to injure or kill

E968.5 Transport vehicle
    Being struck by other vehicle or run down with intent to
        injure
    Pushed in front of, thrown from, or dragged by moving
        vehicle with intent to injure

E968.6 Air gun
    BB gun
    Pellet gun

E968.7 Human bite

E968.8 Other specified means

E968.9 Unspecified means
    Assassination (attempt) NOS
    Homicidal (attempt):
        injury NOS
        wound NOS
    Manslaughter (nonaccidental)
    Murder (attempt) NOS
    Violence, non-accidental

E969 Late effects of injury purposely inflicted by other person
    Note: This category is to be used to indicate circumstances
        classifiable to E960-E968 as the cause of death or disability
        from late effects, which are themselves classifiable
        elsewhere. The "late effects" include conditions reported as
        such, or as sequelae which may occur at any time after injury
        purposely inflicted by another person.

LEGAL INTERVENTION (E970-E978)

INCLUDES   injuries inflicted by the police or other law-enforcing
                agents, including military on duty, in the course
                of arresting or attempting to arrest lawbreakers,
                suppressing disturbances, maintaining order,
                and other legal action
                legal execution
EXCLUDES   *injuries caused by civil insurrections (E990.0-E999)*

E970 Injury due to legal intervention by firearms
    Gunshot wound
    Injury by:
        machine gun
        revolver
        rifle pellet or rubber bullet
        shot NOS

E971 Injury due to legal intervention by explosives
    Injury by:
        dynamite
        explosive shell
        grenade
        mortar bomb

E972 Injury due to legal intervention by gas
    Asphyxiation by gas
    Injury by tear gas
    Poisoning by gas

E973 Injury due to legal intervention by blunt object
    Hit, struck by:
        baton (nightstick)
        blunt object
        stave

**E974 Injury due to legal intervention by cutting and piercing
    instrument**
    Cut
    Incised wound
    Injured by bayonet
    Stab wound

E975 Injury due to legal intervention by other specified means
    Blow
    Manhandling

E976 Injury due to legal intervention by unspecified means

E977 Late effects of injuries due to legal intervention
    Note: This category is to be used to indicate circumstances
        classifiable to E970-E976 as the cause of death or disability
        from late effects, which are themselves classifiable
        elsewhere. The "late effects" include conditions reported as
        such, or as sequelae, which may occur at any time after the
        injury due to legal intervention.

E978 Legal execution

All executions performed at the behest of the judiciary or ruling authority [whether permanent or temporary] as:

asphyxiation by gas
beheading, decapitation (by guillotine)
capital punishment
electrocution
hanging
poisoning
shooting
other specified means

TERRORISM (E979)

☑4ᵗʰ **E979 Terrorism**

Injuries resulting from the unlawful use of force or violence against persons or property to intimidate or coerce a Government, the civilian population, or any segment thereof, in furtherance of political or social objective

E979.0 Terrorism involving explosion of marine weapons

Depth-charge
Marine mine
Mine NOS, at sea or in harbour
Sea-based artillery shell
Torpedo
Underwater blast

E979.1 Terrorism involving destruction of aircraft

Aircraft used as a weapon
Aircraft:
  burned
  exploded
  shot down
Crushed by falling aircraft

E979.2 Terrorism involving other explosions and fragments

Antipersonnel bomb (fragments)
Blast NOS
Explosion (of):
  artillery shell
  breech-block
  cannon block
  mortar bomb
  munitions being used in terrorism
  NOS
Fragments from:
  artillery shell
  bomb
  grenade
  guided missile
  land-mine
  rocket
  shell
  shrapnel
Mine NOS

E979.3 Terrorism involving fires, conflagration and hot substances

Burning building or structure:
  collapse of
  fall from
  hit by falling object in
  jump from
Conflagration NOS
Fire (causing):
  Asphyxia
  Burns
  NOS
  Other injury
Melting of fittings and furniture in burning
Petrol bomb
Smouldering building or structure

E979.4 Terrorism involving firearms

Bullet:
  carbine
  machine gun
  pistol
  rifle
  rubber (rifle)
Pellets (shotgun)

E979.5 Terrorism involving nuclear weapons

Blast effects
Exposure to ionizing radiation from nuclear weapon
Fireball effects
Heat from nuclear weapon
Other direct and secondary effects of nuclear weapons

E979.6 Terrorism involving biological weapons

Anthrax
Cholera
Smallpox

E979.7 Terrorism involving chemical weapons

Gases, fumes, chemicals
Hydrogen cyanide
Phosgene
Sarin

E979.8 Terrorism involving other means

Drowning and submersion
Lasers
Piercing or stabbing instruments
Terrorism NOS

E979.9 Terrorism, secondary effects

Note: This code is for use to identify conditions occurring subsequent to a terrorist attack not those that are due to the initial terrorist act

EXCLUDES *late effect of terrorist attack (E999.1)*

INJURY UNDETERMINED WHETHER ACCIDENTALLY OR PURPOSELY INFLICTED (E980-E989)

Note: Categories E980-E989 are for use when it is unspecified or it cannot be determined whether the injuries are accidental (unintentional), suicide (attempted), or assault.

☑4ᵗʰ **E980 Poisoning by solid or liquid substances, undetermined whether accidentally or purposely inflicted**

E980.0 Analgesics, antipyretics, and antirheumatics

E980.1 Barbiturates

E980.2 Other sedatives and hypnotics

E980.3 Tranquilizers and other psychotropic agents

E980.4 Other specified drugs and medicinal substances

E980.5 Unspecified drug or medicinal substance

E980.6 Corrosive and caustic substances

Poisoning, undetermined whether accidental or purposeful, by substances classifiable to E864

E980.7 Agricultural and horticultural chemical and pharmaceutical preparations other than plant foods and fertilizers

E980.8 Arsenic and its compounds

E980.9 Other and unspecified solid and liquid substances

☑4ᵗʰ **E981 Poisoning by gases in domestic use, undetermined whether accidentally or purposely inflicted**

E981.0 Gas distributed by pipeline

E981.1 Liquefied petroleum gas distributed in mobile containers

E981.8 Other utility gas

☑4ᵗʰ **E982 Poisoning by other gases, undetermined whether accidentally or purposely inflicted**

E982.0 Motor vehicle exhaust gas

E982.1 Other carbon monoxide

E982.8 Other specified gases and vapors

E982.9 Unspecified gases and vapors

☑4ᵗʰ Fourth-digit Required   ▶◀ Revised Text   ● New Code   ▲ Revised Code TitleDx

✓4ᵗʰ **E983 Hanging, strangulation, or suffocation, undetermined whether accidentally or purposely inflicted**

E983.0 Hanging

E983.1 Suffocation by plastic bag

E983.8 Other specified means

E983.9 Unspecified means

E984 Submersion [drowning], undetermined whether accidentally or purposely inflicted

✓4ᵗʰ **E985 Injury by firearms, air guns and explosives, undetermined whether accidentally or purposely inflicted**

E985.0 Handgun

E985.1 Shotgun

E985.2 Hunting rifle

E985.3 Military firearms

E985.4 Other and unspecified firearm

E985.5 Explosives

E985.6 Air gun
   BB gun   Pellet gun

E985.7 Paintball gun

E986 Injury by cutting and piercing instruments, undetermined whether accidentally or purposely inflicted

✓4ᵗʰ **E987 Falling from high place, undetermined whether accidentally or purposely inflicted**

E987.0 Residential premises

E987.1 Other man-made structures

E987.2 Natural sites

E987.9 Unspecified site

✓4ᵗʰ **E988 Injury by other and unspecified means, undetermined whether accidentally or purposely inflicted**

E988.0 Jumping or lying before moving object

E988.1 Burns, fire

E988.2 Scald

E988.3 Extremes of cold

E988.4 Electrocution

E988.5 Crashing of motor vehicle

E988.6 Crashing of aircraft

E988.7 Caustic substances, except poisoning

E988.8 Other specified means

E988.9 Unspecified means

E989 Late effects of injury, undetermined whether accidentally or purposely inflicted

   Note: This category is to be used to indicate circumstances classifiable to E980-E988 as the cause of death or disability from late effects, which are themselves classifiable elsewhere. The "late effects" include conditions reported as such, or as sequelae, which may occur at any time after injury, undetermined whether accidentally or purposely inflicted.

INJURY RESULTING FROM OPERATIONS OF WAR (E990-E999)

INCLUDES injuries to military personnel and civilians caused by war and civil insurrections and occurring during the time of war and insurrection, ▶and peacekeeping missions◀

EXCLUDES accidents during training of military personnel manufacture of war material and transport, unless attributable to enemy action

✓4ᵗʰ **E990 Injury due to war operations by fires and conflagrations**

INCLUDES asphyxia, burns, or other injury originating from fire caused by a fire-producing device or indirectly by any conventional weapon

E990.0 From gasoline bomb
   ▶Incendiary bomb◀

● E990.1 From flamethrower

● E990.2 From incendiary bullet

● E990.3 From fire caused indirectly from conventional weapon
   EXCLUDES fire aboard military aircraft (E994.3)

E990.9 From other and unspecified source

✓4ᵗʰ **E991 Injury due to war operations by bullets and fragments**

EXCLUDES ▶injury due to bullets and fragments due to war operations, but occurring after cessation of hostilities (E998.0)
injury due to explosion of artillery shells and mortars (E993.2)
injury due to explosion of improvised explosive device [IED] (E993.3-E993.5)
injury due to sea-based artillery shell (E992.3)◀

E991.0 Rubber bullets (rifle)

E991.1 Pellets (rifle)

E991.2 Other bullets
   Bullet [any, except rubber bullets and pellets]
   carbine
   machine gun
   pistol
   rifle
   shotgun

E991.3 Antipersonnel bomb (fragments)

● E991.4 Fragments from munitions
   Fragments from:
   artillery shell
   bombs, except antipersonnel
   detonation of unexploded ordnance [UXO]
   grenade
   guided missile
   land mine
   rockets
   shell

● E991.5 Fragments from person-borne improvised explosive device [IED]

● E991.6 Fragments from vehicle-borne improvised explosive device [IED]
   IED borne by land, air, or water transport vehicle

● E991.7 Fragments from other improvised explosive device [IED]
   Roadside IED

● E991.8 Fragments from weapons
   Fragments from:
   artillery
   autocannons
   automatic grenade launchers
   missile launchers
   mortars
   small arms

E991.9 Other and unspecified fragments
   Shrapnel ▶NOS◀

✓4ᵗʰ **E992 Injury due to war operations by explosion of marine weapons**

● E992.0 Torpedo

● E992.1 Depth charge

● E992.2 Marine mines
   Marine mines at sea or in harbor

● E992.3 Sea-based artillery shell

● E992.8 Other marine weapons

● E992.9 Unspecified marine weapon
   Underwater blast NOS

✓4ᵗʰ **E993 Injury due to war operations by other explosion**
   ▶Injuries due to direct or indirect pressure or air blast of an explosion occurring during war operations◀
   EXCLUDES ▶injury due to fragments resulting from an explosion (E991.0-E991.9)
   injury due to detonation of unexploded ordnance but occurring after cessation of hostilities (E998.0-E998.9)
   injury due to nuclear weapons (E996.0-E996.9)◀

- E993.0 **Aerial bomb**
- E993.1 **Guided missile**
- E993.2 **Mortar**
  - Artillery shell
- E993.3 **Person-borne improvised explosive device [IED]**
- E993.4 **Vehicle-borne improvised explosive device [IED]**
  - IED borne by land, air, or water transport vehicle
- E993.5 **Other improvised explosive device [IED]**
  - Roadside IED
- E993.6 **Unintentional detonation of own munitions**
  - Unintentional detonation of own ammunition (artillery) (mortars)
- E993.7 **Unintentional discharge of own munitions launch device**
  - Unintentional explosion of own:
    - autocannons
    - automatic grenade launchers
    - missile launchers
    - small arms
- E993.8 **Other specified explosion**
  - Bomb
  - Grenade
  - Land mine
- E993.9 **Unspecified explosion**
  - Air blast NOS
  - Blast NOS
  - Blast wave NOS
  - Blast wind NOS
  - Explosion NOS

✓4ᵗʰ **E994 Injury due to war operations by destruction of aircraft**

- E994.0 **Destruction of aircraft due to enemy fire or explosives**
  - Air to air missile
  - Explosive device placed on aircraft
  - Rocket propelled grenade [RPG]
  - Small arms fire
  - Surface to air missile
- E994.1 **Unintentional destruction of aircraft due to own onboard explosives**
- E994.2 **Destruction of aircraft due to collision with other aircraft**
- E994.3 **Destruction of aircraft due to onboard fire**
- E994.8 **Other destruction of aircraft**
- E994.9 **Unspecified destruction of aircraft**

✓4ᵗʰ **E995 Injury due to war operations by other and unspecified forms of conventional warfare**

- E995.0 **Unarmed hand-to-hand combat**
  - **EXCLUDES** *intentional restriction of airway (E995.3)*
- E995.1 **Struck by blunt object**
  - Baton (nightstick)
  - Stave
- E995.2 **Piercing object**
  - Bayonet
  - Knife
  - Sword
- E995.3 **Intentional restriction of air and airway**
  - Intentional submersion
  - Strangulation
  - Suffocation
- E995.4 **Unintentional drowning due to inability to surface or obtain air**
  - Submersion
- E995.8 **Other forms of conventional warfare**
- E995.9 **Unspecified form of conventional warfare**

✓4ᵗʰ **E996 Injury due to war operations by nuclear weapons**
  - ▶Dirty bomb NOS◀
  - **EXCLUDES** ▶*late effects of injury due to nuclear weapons (E999.0, E999.1)*◀

- E996.0 **Direct blast effect of nuclear weapon**
  - Injury to bodily organs due to blast pressure
- E996.1 **Indirect blast effect of nuclear weapon**
  - Injury due to being thrown by blast
  - Injury due to being struck or crushed by blast debris
- E996.2 **Thermal radiation effect of nuclear weapon**
  - Burns due to thermal radiation
  - Fireball effects
  - Flash burns
  - Heat effects
- E996.3 **Nuclear radiation effects**
  - Acute radiation exposure
  - Beta burns
  - Fallout exposure
  - Radiation sickness
  - Secondary effects of nuclear weapons
- E996.8 **Other effects of nuclear weapons**
- E996.9 **Unspecified effect of nuclear weapon**

✓4ᵗʰ **E997 Injury due to war operations by other forms of unconventional warfare**

- E997.0 **Lasers**
- E997.1 **Biological warfare**
- E997.2 **Gases, fumes, and chemicals**
- E997.3 **Weapon of mass destruction [WMD], unspecified**
- E997.8 **Other specified forms of unconventional warfare**
- E997.9 **Unspecified form of unconventional warfare**

✓4ᵗʰ **E998 Injury due to war operations but occurring after cessation of hostilities**
  - Injuries due to operations of war but occurring after cessation of hostilities by any means classifiable under E990-E997
  - Injuries by explosion of bombs or mines placed in the course of operations of war, if the explosion occurred after cessation of hostilities

- E998.0 **Explosion of mines**
- E998.1 **Explosion of bombs**
- E998.8 **Injury due to other war operations but occurring after cessation of hostilities**
- E998.9 **Injury due to unspecified war operations but occurring after cessation of hostilities**

✓4ᵗʰ **E999 Late effect of injury due to war operations and terrorism**
  - Note: This category is to be used to indicate circumstances classifiable to E979, E990-E998 as the cause of death or disability from late effects, which are themselves classifiable elsewhere. The "late effects" include conditions reported as such, or as sequelae, which may occur at any time after the injury, resulting from operations of war or terrorism

- E999.0 **Late effect of injury due to war operations**
- E999.1 **Late effect of injury due to terrorism**

Official ICD-9-CM Government Appendixes

MORPHOLOGY OF NEOPLASMS

The World Health Organization has published an adaptation of the International Classification of Diseases for oncology (ICD-O). It contains a coded nomenclature for the morphology of neoplasms, which is reproduced here for those who wish to use it in conjunction with Chapter 2 of the International Classification of Diseases, 9th Revision, Clinical Modification.

The morphology code numbers consist of five digits; the first four identify the histological type of the neoplasm and the fifth indicates its behavior. The one-digit behavior code is as follows:

/0   Benign
/1   Uncertain whether benign or malignant
      Borderline malignancy
/2   Carcinoma in situ
      Intraepithelial
      Noninfiltrating
      Noninvasive
/3   Malignant, primary site
/6   Malignant, metastatic site
      Secondary site
/9   Malignant, uncertain whether primary or metastatic site

In the nomenclature below, the morphology code numbers include the behavior code appropriate to the histological type of neoplasm, but this behavior code should be changed if other reported information makes this necessary. For example, "chordoma (M9370/3)" is assumed to be malignant; the term "benign chordoma" should be coded M9370/0. Similarly, "superficial spreading adenocarcinoma (M8143/3)" described as "noninvasive" should be coded M8143/2 and "melanoma (M8720/3)" described as "secondary" should be coded M8720/6.

The following table shows the correspondence between the morphology code and the different sections of Chapter 2:

Morphology Code		ICD-9-CM Chapter 2
Histology/Behavior		
Any M8000- M8004	0	210-229 Benign neoplasms
M8000- M8004	1	239 Neoplasms of unspecified nature
M8010+	1	235-238 Neoplasms of uncertain behavior
Any	2	230-234 Carcinoma in situ
Any	3	140-195 200-208 Malignant neoplasms, stated or presumed to be primary
Any	6	196-198 Malignant neoplasms, stated or presumed to be secondary

The ICD-O behavior digit /9 is inapplicable in an ICD context, since all malignant neoplasms are presumed to be primary (/3) or secondary (/6) according to other information on the medical record.the first-listed term of the full ICD-O morphology nomenclature appears against each code number in the list below. The ICD-9-CM Alphabetical Index (Volume 2), however, includes all the ICD-O synonyms as well as a number of other morphological names still likely to be encountered on medical records but omitted from ICD-O as outdated or otherwise undesirable.

A coding difficulty sometimes arises where a morphological diagnosis contains two qualifying adjectives that have different code numbers. An example is "transitional cell epidermoid carcinoma."

"Transitional cell carcinoma NOS" is M8120/3 and "epidermoid carcinoma NOS" is M8070/3. In such circumstances, the higher number (M8120/3 in this example) should be used, as it is usually more specific.

CODED NOMENCLATURE FOR MORPHOLOGY OF NEOPLASMS

M800	**Neoplasms NOS**
M8000/0	Neoplasm, benign
M8000/1	Neoplasm, uncertain whether benign or malignant
M8000/3	Neoplasm, malignant
M8000/6	Neoplasm, metastatic
M8000/9	Neoplasm, malignant, uncertain whether primary or metastatic
M8001/0	Tumor cells, benign
M8001/1	Tumor cells, uncertain whether benign or malignant
M8001/3	Tumor cells, malignant
M8002/3	Malignant tumor, small cell type
M8003/3	Malignant tumor, giant cell type
M8004/3	Malignant tumor, fusiform cell type

M801-M804	**Epithelial neoplasms NOS**
M8010/0	Epithelial tumor, benign
M8010/2	Carcinoma in situ NOS
M8010/3	Carcinoma NOS
M8010/6	Carcinoma, metastatic NOS
M8010/9	Carcinomatosis
M8011/0	Epithelioma, benign
M8011/3	Epithelioma, malignant
M8012/3	Large cell carcinoma NOS
M8020/3	Carcinoma, undifferentiated type NOS
M8021/3	Carcinoma, anaplastic type NOS
M8022/3	Pleomorphic carcinoma
M8030/3	Giant cell and spindle cell carcinoma
M8031/3	Giant cell carcinoma
M8032/3	Spindle cell carcinoma
M8033/3	Pseudosarcomatous carcinoma
M8034/3	Polygonal cell carcinoma
M8035/3	Spheroidal cell carcinoma
M8040/1	Tumorlet
M8041/3	Small cell carcinoma NOS
M8042/3	Oat cell carcinoma
M8043/3	Small cell carcinoma, fusiform cell type

M805-M808	**Papillary and squamous cell neoplasms**
M8050/0	Papilloma NOS (except Papilloma of urinary bladder M8120/1)
M8050/2	Papillary carcinoma in situ
M8050/3	Papillary carcinoma NOS
M8051/0	Verrucous papilloma
M8051/3	Verrucous carcinoma NOS
M8052/0	Squamous cell papilloma
M8052/3	Papillary squamous cell carcinoma
M8053/0	Inverted papilloma
M8060/0	Papillomatosis NOS
M8070/2	Squamous cell carcinoma in situ NOS
M8070/3	Squamous cell carcinoma NOS
M8070/6	Squamous cell carcinoma, metastatic NOS
M8071/3	Squamous cell carcinoma, keratinizing type NOS
M8072/3	Squamous cell carcinoma, large cell, nonkeratinizing type
M8073/3	Squamous cell carcinoma, small cell, nonkeratinizing type
M8074/3	Squamous cell carcinoma, spindle cell type
M8075/3	Adenoid squamous cell carcinoma
M8076/2	Squamous cell carcinoma in situ with questionable stromal invasion
M8076/3	Squamous cell carcinoma, microinvasive
M8080/2	Queyrat's erythroplasia
M8081/2	Bowen's disease
M8082/3	Lymphoepithelial carcinoma

M809-M811	**Basal cell neoplasms**
M8090/1	Basal cell tumor
M8090/3	Basal cell carcinoma NOS
M8091/3	Multicentric basal cell carcinoma
M8092/3	Basal cell carcinoma, morphea type
M8093/3	Basal cell carcinoma, fibroepithelial type
M8094/3	Basosquamous carcinoma
M8095/3	Metatypical carcinoma
M8096/0	Intraepidermal epithelioma of Jadassohn
M8100/0	Trichoepithelioma
M8101/0	Trichofolliculoma
M8102/0	Tricholemmoma
M8110/0	Pilomatrixoma

M812-M813	**Transitional cell papillomas and carcinomas**
M8120/0	Transitional cell papilloma NOS
M8120/1	Urothelial papilloma
M8120/2	Transitional cell carcinoma in situ
M8120/3	Transitional cell carcinoma NOS
M8121/0	Schneiderian papilloma
M8121/1	Transitional cell papilloma, inverted type
M8121/3	Schneiderian carcinoma
M8122/3	Transitional cell carcinoma, spindle cell type
M8123/3	Basaloid carcinoma
M8124/3	Cloacogenic carcinoma
M8130/3	Papillary transitional cell carcinoma

M814-M838	**Adenomas and adenocarcinomas**
M8140/0	Adenoma NOS
M8140/1	Bronchial adenoma NOS
M8140/2	Adenocarcinoma in situ
M8140/3	Adenocarcinoma NOS
M8140/6	Adenocarcinoma, metastatic NOS
M8141/3	Scirrhous adenocarcinoma
M8142/3	Linitis plastica
M8143/3	Superficial spreading adenocarcinoma
M8144/3	Adenocarcinoma, intestinal type
M8145/3	Carcinoma, diffuse type
M8146/0	Monomorphic adenoma
M8147/0	Basal cell adenoma
M8150/0	Islet cell adenoma
M8150/3	Islet cell carcinoma
M8151/0	Insulinoma NOS
M8151/3	Insulinoma, malignant
M8152/0	Glucagonoma NOS
M8152/3	Glucagonoma, malignant
M8153/1	Gastrinoma NOS
M8153/3	Gastrinoma, malignant
M8154/3	Mixed islet cell and exocrine adenocarcinoma
M8160/0	Bile duct adenoma
M8160/3	Cholangiocarcinoma
M8161/0	Bile duct cystadenoma
M8161/3	Bile duct cystadenocarcinoma
M8170/0	Liver cell adenoma
M8170/3	Hepatocellular carcinoma NOS
M8180/0	Hepatocholangioma, benign
M8180/3	Combined hepatocellular carcinoma and cholangiocarcinoma
M8190/0	Trabecular adenoma
M8190/3	Trabecular adenocarcinoma
M8191/0	Embryonal adenoma
M8200/0	Eccrine dermal cylindroma

M8200/3	Adenoid cystic carcinoma
M8201/3	Cribriform carcinoma
M8210/0	Adenomatous polyp NOS
M8210/3	Adenocarcinoma in adenomatous polyp
M8211/0	Tubular adenoma NOS
M8211/3	Tubular adenocarcinoma
M8220/0	Adenomatous polyposis coli
M8220/3	Adenocarcinoma in adenomatous polyposis coli
M8221/0	Multiple adenomatous polyps
M8230/3	Solid carcinoma NOS
M8231/3	Carcinoma simplex
M8240/1	Carcinoid tumor NOS
M8240/3	Carcinoid tumor, malignant
M8241/1	Carcinoid tumor, argentaffin NOS
M8241/3	Carcinoid tumor, argentaffin, malignant
M8242/1	Carcinoid tumor, nonargentaffin NOS
M8242/3	Carcinoid tumor, nonargentaffin, malignant
M8243/3	Mucocarcinoid tumor, malignant
M8244/3	Composite carcinoid
M8250/1	Pulmonary adenomatosis
M8250/3	Bronchiolo-alveolar adenocarcinoma
M8251/0	Alveolar adenoma
M8251/3	Alveolar adenocarcinoma
M8260/0	Papillary adenoma NOS
M8260/3	Papillary adenocarcinoma NOS
M8261/1	Villous adenoma NOS
M8261/3	Adenocarcinoma in villous adenoma
M8262/3	Villous adenocarcinoma
M8263/0	Tubulovillous adenoma
M8270/0	Chromophobe adenoma
M8270/3	Chromophobe carcinoma
M8280/0	Acidophil adenoma
M8280/3	Acidophil carcinoma
M8281/0	Mixed acidophil-basophil adenoma
M8281/3	Mixed acidophil-basophil carcinoma
M8290/0	Oxyphilic adenoma
M8290/3	Oxyphilic adenocarcinoma
M8300/0	Basophil adenoma
M8300/3	Basophil carcinoma
M8310/0	Clear cell adenoma
M8310/3	Clear cell adenocarcinoma NOS
M8311/1	Hypernephroid tumor
M8312/3	Renal cell carcinoma
M8313/0	Clear cell adenofibroma
M8320/3	Granular cell carcinoma
M8321/0	Chief cell adenoma
M8322/0	Water-clear cell adenoma
M8322/3	Water-clear cell adenocarcinoma
M8323/0	Mixed cell adenoma
M8323/3	Mixed cell adenocarcinoma
M8324/0	Lipoadenoma
M8330/0	Follicular adenoma
M8330/3	Follicular adenocarcinoma NOS
M8331/3	Follicular adenocarcinoma, well differentiated type
M8332/3	Follicular adenocarcinoma, trabecular type
M8333/0	Microfollicular adenoma
M8334/0	Macrofollicular adenoma
M8340/3	Papillary and follicular adenocarcinoma
M8350/3	Nonencapsulated sclerosing carcinoma
M8360/1	Multiple endocrine adenomas
M8361/1	Juxtaglomerular tumor
M8370/0	Adrenal cortical adenoma NOS
M8370/3	Adrenal cortical carcinoma
M8371/0	Adrenal cortical adenoma, compact cell type
M8372/0	Adrenal cortical adenoma, heavily pigmented variant

M8373/0	Adrenal cortical adenoma, clear cell type
M8374/0	Adrenal cortical adenoma, glomerulosa cell type
M8375/0	Adrenal cortical adenoma, mixed cell type
M8380/0	Endometrioid adenoma NOS
M8380/1	Endometrioid adenoma, borderline malignancy
M8380/3	Endometrioid carcinoma
M8381/0	Endometrioid adenofibroma NOS
M8381/1	Endometrioid adenofibroma, borderline malignancy
M8381/3	Endometrioid adenofibroma, malignant

M839-M842   **Adnexal and skin appendage neoplasms**

M8390/0	Skin appendage adenoma
M8390/3	Skin appendage carcinoma
M8400/0	Sweat gland adenoma
M8400/1	Sweat gland tumor NOS
M8400/3	Sweat gland adenocarcinoma
M8401/0	Apocrine adenoma
M8401/3	Apocrine adenocarcinoma
M8402/0	Eccrine acrospiroma
M8403/0	Eccrine spiradenoma
M8404/0	Hidrocystoma
M8405/0	Papillary hydradenoma
M8406/0	Papillary syringadenoma
M8407/0	Syringoma NOS
M8410/0	Sebaceous adenoma
M8410/3	Sebaceous adenocarcinoma
M8420/0	Ceruminous adenoma
M8420/3	Ceruminous adenocarcinoma

M843   **Mucoepidermoid neoplasms**

M8430/1	Mucoepidermoid tumor
M8430/3	Mucoepidermoid carcinoma

M844-M849   **Cystic, mucinous, and serous neoplasms**

M8440/0	Cystadenoma NOS
M8440/3	Cystadenocarcinoma NOS
M8441/0	Serous cystadenoma NOS
M8441/1	Serous cystadenoma, borderline malignancy
M8441/3	Serous cystadenocarcinoma NOS
M8450/0	Papillary cystadenoma NOS
M8450/1	Papillary cystadenoma, borderline malignancy
M8450/3	Papillary cystadenocarcinoma NOS
M8460/0	Papillary serous cystadenoma NOS
M8460/1	Papillary serous cystadenoma, borderline malignancy
M8460/3	Papillary serous cystadenocarcinoma
M8461/0	Serous surface papilloma NOS
M8461/1	Serous surface papilloma, borderline malignancy
M8461/3	Serous surface papillary carcinoma
M8470/0	Mucinous cystadenoma NOS
M8470/1	Mucinous cystadenoma, borderline malignancy
M8470/3	Mucinous cystadenocarcinoma NOS
M8471/0	Papillary mucinous cystadenoma NOS
M8471/1	Papillary mucinous cystadenoma, borderline malignancy
M8471/3	Papillary mucinous cystadenocarcinoma
M8480/0	Mucinous adenoma
M8480/3	Mucinous adenocarcinoma
M8480/6	Pseudomyxoma peritonei
M8481/3	Mucin-producing adenocarcinoma
M8490/3	Signet ring cell carcinoma
M8490/6	Metastatic signet ring cell carcinoma

M850-M854   **Ductal, lobular, and medullary neoplasms**

M8500/2	Intraductal carcinoma, noninfiltrating NOS
M8500/3	Infiltrating duct carcinoma
M8501/2	Comedocarcinoma, noninfiltrating
M8501/3	Comedocarcinoma NOS
M8502/3	Juvenile carcinoma of the breast
M8503/0	Intraductal papilloma
M8503/2	Noninfiltrating intraductal papillary adenocarcinoma
M8504/0	Intracystic papillary adenoma
M8504/2	Noninfiltrating intracystic carcinoma
M8505/0	Intraductal papillomatosis NOS
M8506/0	Subareolar duct papillomatosis
M8510/3	Medullary carcinoma NOS
M8511/3	Medullary carcinoma with amyloid stroma
M8512/3	Medullary carcinoma with lymphoid stroma
M8520/2	Lobular carcinoma in situ
M8520/3	Lobular carcinoma NOS
M8521/3	Infiltrating ductular carcinoma
M8530/3	Inflammatory carcinoma
M8540/3	Paget's disease, mammary
M8541/3	Paget's disease and infiltrating duct carcinoma of breast
M8542/3	Paget's disease, extramammary (except Paget's disease of bone)

M855   **Acinar cell neoplasms**

M8550/0	Acinar cell adenoma
M8550/1	Acinar cell tumor
M8550/3	Acinar cell carcinoma

M856-M858   **Complex epithelial neoplasms**

M8560/3	Adenosquamous carcinoma
M8561/0	Adenolymphoma
M8570/3	Adenocarcinoma with squamous metaplasia
M8571/3	Adenocarcinoma with cartilaginous and osseous metaplasia
M8572/3	Adenocarcinoma with spindle cell metaplasia
M8573/3	Adenocarcinoma with apocrine metaplasia
M8580/0	Thymoma, benign
M8580/3	Thymoma, malignant

M859-M867   **Specialized gonadal neoplasms**

M8590/1	Sex cord-stromal tumor
M8600/0	Thecoma NOS
M8600/3	Theca cell carcinoma
M8610/0	Luteoma NOS
M8620/1	Granulosa cell tumor NOS
M8620/3	Granulosa cell tumor, malignant
M8621/1	Granulosa cell-theca cell tumor
M8630/0	Androblastoma, benign
M8630/1	Androblastoma NOS
M8630/3	Androblastoma, malignant
M8631/0	Sertoli-Leydig cell tumor
M8632/1	Gynandroblastoma
M8640/0	Tubular androblastoma NOS
M8640/3	Sertoli cell carcinoma
M8641/0	Tubular androblastoma with lipid storage
M8650/0	Leydig cell tumor, benign
M8650/1	Leydig cell tumor NOS
M8650/3	Leydig cell tumor, malignant
M8660/0	Hilar cell tumor
M8670/0	Lipid cell tumor of ovary
M8671/0	Adrenal rest tumor

M868-M871   **Paragangliomas and glomus tumors**

M8680/1	Paraganglioma NOS
M8680/3	Paraganglioma, malignant
M8681/1	Sympathetic paraganglioma

M8682/1	Parasympathetic paraganglioma
M8690/1	Glomus jugulare tumor
M8691/1	Aortic body tumor
M8692/1	Carotid body tumor
M8693/1	Extra-adrenal paraganglioma NOS
M8693/3	Extra-adrenal paraganglioma, malignant
M8700/0	Pheochromocytoma NOS
M8700/3	Pheochromocytoma, malignant
M8710/3	Glomangiosarcoma
M8711/0	Glomus tumor
M8712/0	Glomangioma

M872-M879 Nevi and melanomas

M8720/0	Pigmented nevus NOS
M8720/3	Malignant melanoma NOS
M8721/3	Nodular melanoma
M8722/0	Balloon cell nevus
M8722/3	Balloon cell melanoma
M8723/0	Halo nevus
M8724/0	Fibrous papule of the nose
M8725/0	Neuronevus
M8726/0	Magnocellular nevus
M8730/0	Nonpigmented nevus
M8730/3	Amelanotic melanoma
M8740/0	Junctional nevus
M8740/3	Malignant melanoma in junctional nevus
M8741/2	Precancerous melanosis NOS
M8741/3	Malignant melanoma in precancerous melanosis
M8742/2	Hutchinson's melanotic freckle
M8742/3	Malignant melanoma in Hutchinson's melanotic freckle
M8743/3	Superficial spreading melanoma
M8750/0	Intradermal nevus
M8760/0	Compound nevus
M8761/1	Giant pigmented nevus
M8761/3	Malignant melanoma in giant pigmented nevus
M8770/0	Epithelioid and spindle cell nevus
M8771/3	Epithelioid cell melanoma
M8772/3	Spindle cell melanoma NOS
M8773/3	Spindle cell melanoma, type A
M8774/3	Spindle cell melanoma, type B
M8775/3	Mixed epithelioid and spindle cell melanoma
M8780/0	Blue nevus NOS
M8780/3	Blue nevus, malignant
M8790/0	Cellular blue nevus

M880 Soft tissue tumors and sarcomas NOS

M8800/0	Soft tissue tumor, benign
M8800/3	Sarcoma NOS
M8800/9	Sarcomatosis NOS
M8801/3	Spindle cell sarcoma
M8802/3	Giant cell sarcoma (except of bone M9250/3)
M8803/3	Small cell sarcoma
M8804/3	Epithelioid cell sarcoma

M881-M883 Fibromatous neoplasms

M8810/0	Fibroma NOS
M8810/3	Fibrosarcoma NOS
M8811/0	Fibromyxoma
M8811/3	Fibromyxosarcoma
M8812/0	Periosteal fibroma
M8812/3	Periosteal fibrosarcoma
M8813/0	Fascial fibroma
M8813/3	Fascial fibrosarcoma
M8814/3	Infantile fibrosarcoma
M8820/0	Elastofibroma
M8821/1	Aggressive fibromatosis
M8822/1	Abdominal fibromatosis
M8823/1	Desmoplastic fibroma
M8830/0	Fibrous histiocytoma NOS

M8830/1	Atypical fibrous histiocytoma
M8830/3	Fibrous histiocytoma, malignant
M8831/0	Fibroxanthoma NOS
M8831/1	Atypical fibroxanthoma
M8831/3	Fibroxanthoma, malignant
M8832/0	Dermatofibroma NOS
M8832/1	Dermatofibroma protuberans
M8832/3	Dermatofibrosarcoma NOS

M884 Myxomatous neoplasms

M8840/0	Myxoma NOS
M8840/3	Myxosarcoma

M885-M888 Lipomatous neoplasms

M8850/0	Lipoma NOS
M8850/3	Liposarcoma NOS
M8851/0	Fibrolipoma
M8851/3	Liposarcoma, well differentiated type
M8852/0	Fibromyxolipoma
M8852/3	Myxoid liposarcoma
M8853/3	Round cell liposarcoma
M8854/3	Pleomorphic liposarcoma
M8855/3	Mixed type liposarcoma
M8856/0	Intramuscular lipoma
M8857/0	Spindle cell lipoma
M8860/0	Angiomyolipoma
M8860/3	Angiomyoliposarcoma
M8861/0	Angiolipoma NOS
M8861/1	Angiolipoma, infiltrating
M8870/0	Myelolipoma
M8880/0	Hibernoma
M8881/0	Lipoblastomatosis

M889-M892 Myomatous neoplasms

M8890/0	Leiomyoma NOS
M8890/1	Intravascular leiomyomatosis
M8890/3	Leiomyosarcoma NOS
M8891/1	Epithelioid leiomyoma
M8891/3	Epithelioid leiomyosarcoma
M8892/1	Cellular leiomyoma
M8893/0	Bizarre leiomyoma
M8894/0	Angiomyoma
M8894/3	Angiomyosarcoma
M8895/0	Myoma
M8895/3	Myosarcoma
M8900/0	Rhabdomyoma NOS
M8900/3	Rhabdomyosarcoma NOS
M8901/3	Pleomorphic rhabdomyosarcoma
M8902/3	Mixed type rhabdomyosarcoma
M8903/0	Fetal rhabdomyoma
M8904/0	Adult rhabdomyoma
M8910/3	Embryonal rhabdomyosarcoma
M8920/3	Alveolar rhabdomyosarcoma

M893-M899 Complex mixed and stromal neoplasms

M8930/3	Endometrial stromal sarcoma
M8931/1	Endolymphatic stromal myosis
M8932/0	Adenomyoma
M8940/0	Pleomorphic adenoma
M8940/3	Mixed tumor, malignant NOS
M8950/3	Mullerian mixed tumor
M8951/3	Mesodermal mixed tumor
M8960/1	Mesoblastic nephroma
M8960/3	Nephroblastoma NOS
M8961/3	Epithelial nephroblastoma
M8962/3	Mesenchymal nephroblastoma
M8970/3	Hepatoblastoma
M8980/3	Carcinosarcoma NOS
M8981/3	Carcinosarcoma, embryonal type
M8982/3	Myoepithelioma
M8990/0	Mesenchymoma, benign
M8990/1	Mesenchymoma NOS
M8990/3	Mesenchymoma, malignant
M8991/3	Embryonal sarcoma

M900-M903 Fibroepithelial neoplasms

M9000/0	Brenner tumor NOS
M9000/1	Brenner tumor, borderline malignancy

M9000/3	Brenner tumor, malignant
M9010/0	Fibroadenoma NOS
M9011/0	Intracanalicular fibroadenoma NOS
M9012/0	Pericanalicular fibroadenoma
M9013/0	Adenofibroma NOS
M9014/0	Serous adenofibroma
M9015/0	Mucinous adenofibroma
M9020/0	Cellular intracanalicular fibroadenoma
M9020/1	Cystosarcoma phyllodes NOS
M9020/3	Cystosarcoma phyllodes, malignant
M9030/0	Juvenile fibroadenoma

M904 Synovial neoplasms

M9040/0	Synovioma, benign
M9040/3	Synovial sarcoma NOS
M9041/3	Synovial sarcoma, spindle cell type
M9042/3	Synovial sarcoma, epithelioid cell type
M9043/3	Synovial sarcoma, biphasic type
M9044/3	Clear cell sarcoma of tendons and aponeuroses

M905 Mesothelial neoplasms

M9050/0	Mesothelioma, benign
M9050/3	Mesothelioma, malignant
M9051/0	Fibrous mesothelioma, benign
M9051/3	Fibrous mesothelioma, malignant
M9052/0	Epithelioid mesothelioma, benign
M9052/3	Epithelioid mesothelioma, malignant
M9053/0	Mesothelioma, biphasic type, benign
M9053/3	Mesothelioma, biphasic type, malignant
M9054/0	Adenomatoid tumor NOS

M906-M909 Germ cell neoplasms

M9060/3	Dysgerminoma
M9061/3	Seminoma NOS
M9062/3	Seminoma, anaplastic type
M9063/3	Spermatocytic seminoma
M9064/3	Germinoma
M9070/3	Embryonal carcinoma NOS
M9071/3	Endodermal sinus tumor
M9072/3	Polyembryoma
M9073/1	Gonadoblastoma
M9080/0	Teratoma, benign
M9080/1	Teratoma NOS
M9080/3	Teratoma, malignant NOS
M9081/3	Teratocarcinoma
M9082/3	Malignant teratoma, undifferentiated type
M9083/3	Malignant teratoma, intermediate type
M9084/0	Dermoid cyst
M9084/3	Dermoid cyst with malignant transformation
M9090/0	Struma ovarii NOS
M9090/3	Struma ovarii, malignant
M9091/1	Strumal carcinoid

M910 Trophoblastic neoplasms

M9100/0	Hydatidiform mole NOS
M9100/1	Invasive hydatidiform mole
M9100/3	Choriocarcinoma
M9101/3	Choriocarcinoma combined with teratoma
M9102/3	Malignant teratoma, trophoblastic

M911 Mesonephromas

M9110/0	Mesonephroma, benign
M9110/1	Mesonephric tumor
M9110/3	Mesonephroma, malignant
M9111/1	Endosalpingioma

M912-M916 Blood vessel tumors

M9120/0	Hemangioma NOS
M9120/3	Hemangiosarcoma
M9121/0	Cavernous hemangioma
M9122/0	Venous hemangioma
M9123/0	Racemose hemangioma
M9124/3	Kupffer cell sarcoma
M9130/0	Hemangioendothelioma, benign

M9130/1	Hemangioendothelioma NOS	M9320/0	Odontogenic myxoma	M9534/0	Angiomatous meningioma
M9130/3	Hemangioendothelioma, malignant	M9321/0	Odontogenic fibroma NOS	M9535/0	Hemangioblastic meningioma
M9131/0	Capillary hemangioma	M9330/0	Ameloblastic fibroma	M9536/0	Hemangiopericytic meningioma
M9132/0	Intramuscular hemangioma	M9330/3	Ameloblastic fibrosarcoma	M9537/0	Transitional meningioma
M9140/3	Kaposi's sarcoma	M9340/0	Calcifying epithelial odontogenic	M9538/1	Papillary meningioma
M9141/0	Angiokeratoma		tumor	M9539/3	Meningeal sarcomatosis
M9142/0	Verrucous keratotic hemangioma				

M935-M937 Miscellaneous tumors

M954-M957 Nerve sheath tumor

M9150/0	Hemangiopericytoma, benign	M9350/1	Craniopharyngioma	M9540/0	Neurofibroma NOS
M9150/1	Hemangiopericytoma NOS	M9360/1	Pinealoma	M9540/1	Neurofibromatosis NOS
M9150/3	Hemangiopericytoma, malignant	M9361/1	Pineocytoma	M9540/3	Neurofibrosarcoma
M9160/0	Angiofibroma NOS	M9362/3	Pineoblastoma	M9541/0	Melanotic neurofibroma
M9161/1	Hemangioblastoma	M9363/0	Melanotic neuroectodermal tumor	M9550/0	Plexiform neurofibroma
		M9370/3	Chordoma	M9560/0	Neurilemmoma NOS

M917 Lymphatic vessel tumors

M938-M948 Gliomas

M9170/0	Lymphangioma NOS	M9380/3	Glioma, malignant	M9560/1	Neurinomatosis
M9170/3	Lymphangiosarcoma	M9381/3	Gliomatosis cerebri	M9560/3	Neurilemmoma, malignant
M9171/0	Capillary lymphangioma	M9382/3	Mixed glioma	M9570/0	Neuroma NOS
M9172/0	Cavernous lymphangioma	M9383/1	Subependymal glioma		

M958 Granular cell tumors and alveolar soft part sarcoma

M9173/0	Cystic lymphangioma	M9384/1	Subependymal giant cell astrocytoma		
M9174/0	Lymphangiomyoma	M9390/0	Choroid plexus papilloma NOS	M9580/0	Granular cell tumor NOS
M9174/1	Lymphangiomyomatosis	M9390/3	Choroid plexus papilloma, malignant	M9580/3	Granular cell tumor, malignant
M9175/0	Hemolymphangioma	M9391/3	Ependymoma NOS	M9581/3	Alveolar soft part sarcoma

M918-M920 Osteomas and osteosarcomas

M959-M963 Lymphomas, NOS or diffuse

		M9392/3	Ependymoma, anaplastic type	M9590/0	Lymphomatous tumor, benign
M9180/0	Osteoma NOS	M9393/1	Papillary ependymoma	M9590/3	Malignant lymphoma NOS
M9180/3	Osteosarcoma NOS	M9394/1	Myxopapillary ependymoma	M9591/3	Malignant lymphoma, non Hodgkin's type
M9181/3	Chondroblastic osteosarcoma	M9400/3	Astrocytoma NOS		
M9182/3	Fibroblastic osteosarcoma	M9401/3	Astrocytoma, anaplastic type	M9600/3	Malignant lymphoma, undifferentiated cell type NOS
M9183/3	Telangiectatic osteosarcoma	M9410/3	Protoplasmic astrocytoma		
M9184/3	Osteosarcoma in Paget's disease of bone	M9411/3	Gemistocytic astrocytoma	M9601/3	Malignant lymphoma, stem cell type
		M9420/3	Fibrillary astrocytoma	M9602/3	Malignant lymphoma, convoluted cell type NOS
M9190/0	Juxtacortical osteosarcoma	M9421/3	Pilocytic astrocytoma		
M9191/0	Osteoid osteoma NOS	M9422/3	Spongioblastoma NOS	M9610/3	Lymphosarcoma NOS
M9200/0	Osteoblastoma	M9423/3	Spongioblastoma polare	M9611/3	Malignant lymphoma, lymphoplasma-cytoid type

M921-M924 Chondromatous neoplasms

		M9430/3	Astroblastoma		
M9210/0	Osteochondroma	M9440/3	Glioblastoma NOS	M9612/3	Malignant lymphoma, immunoblastic type
M9210/1	Osteochondromatosis NOS	M9441/3	Giant cell glioblastoma		
M9220/0	Chondroma NOS	M9442/3	Glioblastoma with sarcomatous component	M9613/3	Malignant lymphoma, mixed lympho-cytic-histiocytic NOS
M9220/1	Chondromatosis NOS				
M9220/3	Chondrosarcoma NOS	M9443/3	Primitive polar spongioblastoma	M9614/3	Malignant lymphoma, centroblas-tic-centrocytic, diffuse
M9221/0	Juxtacortical chondroma	M9450/3	Oligodendroglioma NOS		
M9221/1	Juxtacortical chondrosarcoma	M9451/3	Oligodendroglioma, anaplastic type	M9615/3	Malignant lymphoma, follicular center cell NOS
M9230/0	Chondroblastoma NOS	M9460/3	Oligodendroblastoma		
M9230/3	Chondroblastoma, malignant	M9470/3	Medulloblastoma NOS	M9620/3	Malignant lymphoma, lymphocytic, well differentiated NOS
M9240/3	Mesenchymal chondrosarcoma	M9471/3	Desmoplastic medulloblastoma		
M9241/0	Chondromyxoid fibroma	M9472/3	Medullomyoblastoma	M9621/3	Malignant lymphoma, lymphocytic, intermediate differentiation NOS
		M9480/3	Cerebellar sarcoma NOS		

M925 Giant cell tumors

		M9481/3	Monstrocellular sarcoma	M9622/3	Malignant lymphoma, centrocytic
M9250/1	Giant cell tumor of bone NOS			M9623/3	Malignant lymphoma, follicular center cell, cleaved NOS

M949-M952 Neuroepitheliomatous neoplasms

M9250/3	Giant cell tumor of bone, malignant				
M9251/1	Giant cell tumor of soft parts NOS			M9630/3	Malignant lymphoma, lymphocytic, poorly differentiated NOS
M9251/3	Malignant giant cell tumor of soft parts	M9490/0	Ganglioneuroma		
		M9490/3	Ganglioneuroblastoma	M9631/3	Prolymphocytic lymphosarcoma

M926 Miscellaneous bone tumors

		M9491/0	Ganglioneuromatosis	M9632/3	Malignant lymphoma, centroblastic type NOS
M9260/3	Ewing's sarcoma	M9500/3	Neuroblastoma NOS		
M9261/3	Adamantinoma of long bones	M9501/3	Medulloepithelioma NOS	M9633/3	Malignant lymphoma, follicular center cell, noncleaved NOS
M9262/0	Ossifying fibroma	M9502/3	Teratoid medulloepithelioma		

M927-M934 Odontogenic tumors

		M9503/3	Neuroepithelioma NOS		
M9270/0	Odontogenic tumor, benign	M9504/3	Spongioneuroblastoma	**M964**	**Reticulosarcomas**
M9270/1	Odontogenic tumor NOS	M9505/1	Ganglioglioma	M9640/3	Reticulosarcoma NOS
M9270/3	Odontogenic tumor, malignant	M9506/0	Neurocytoma	M9641/3	Reticulosarcoma, pleomorphic cell type
M9271/0	Dentinoma	M9507/0	Pacinian tumor	M9642/3	Reticulosarcoma, nodular
M9272/0	Cementoma NOS	M9510/3	Retinoblastoma NOS		

M965-M966 Hodgkin's disease

M9273/0	Cementoblastoma, benign	M9511/3	Retinoblastoma, differentiated type	M9650/3	Hodgkin's disease NOS
M9274/0	Cementifying fibroma	M9512/3	Retinoblastoma, undifferentiated type	M9651/3	Hodgkin's disease, lymphocytic pre-dominance
M9275/0	Gigantiform cementoma	M9520/3	Olfactory neurogenic tumor		
M9280/0	Odontoma NOS	M9521/3	Esthesioneurocytoma	M9652/3	Hodgkin's disease, mixed cellularity
M9281/0	Compound odontoma	M9522/3	Esthesioneuroblastoma	M9653/3	Hodgkin's disease, lymphocytic deple-tion NOS
M9282/0	Complex odontoma	M9523/3	Esthesioneuroepithelioma		
M9290/0	Ameloblastic fibro-odontoma			M9654/3	Hodgkin's disease, lymphocytic deple-tion, diffuse fibrosis

M953 Meningiomas

M9290/3	Ameloblastic odontosarcoma				
M9300/0	Adenomatoid odontogenic tumor	M9530/0	Meningioma NOS	M9655/3	Hodgkin's disease, lymphocytic deple-tion, reticular type
M9301/0	Calcifying odontogenic cyst	M9530/1	Meningiomatosis NOS		
M9310/0	Ameloblastoma NOS	M9530/3	Meningioma, malignant	M9656/3	Hodgkin's disease, nodular sclerosis NOS
M9310/3	Ameloblastoma, malignant	M9531/0	Meningotheliomatous meningioma		
M9311/0	Odontoameloblastoma	M9532/0	Fibrous meningioma		
M9312/0	Squamous odontogenic tumor	M9533/0	Psammomatous meningioma		

M9657/3	*Hodgkin's disease, nodular sclerosis, cellular phase*
M9660/3	*Hodgkin's paragranuloma*
M9661/3	*Hodgkin's granuloma*
M9662/3	*Hodgkin's sarcoma*

M969 — **Lymphomas, nodular or follicular**

M9690/3	*Malignant lymphoma, nodular NOS*
M9691/3	*Malignant lymphoma, mixed lympho-cytic-histiocytic, nodular*
M9692/3	*Malignant lymphoma, centroblas-tic-centrocytic, follicular*
M9693/3	*Malignant lymphoma, lymphocytic, well differentiated, nodular*
M9694/3	*Malignant lymphoma, lymphocytic, intermediate differentiation, nodular*
M9695/3	*Malignant lymphoma, follicular center cell, cleaved, follicular*
M9696/3	*Malignant lymphoma, lymphocytic, poorly differentiated, nodular*
M9697/3	*Malignant lymphoma, centroblastic type, follicular*
M9698/3	*Malignant lymphoma, follicular center cell, noncleaved, follicular*

M970 — **Mycosis fungoides**

M9700/3	*Mycosis fungoides*
M9701/3	*Sezary's disease*

M971-M972 — **Miscellaneous reticuloendothelial neoplasms**

M9710/3	*Microglioma*
M9720/3	*Malignant histiocytosis*
M9721/3	*Histiocytic medullary reticulosis*
M9722/3	*Letterer-Siwe's disease*

M973 — **Plasma cell tumors**

M9730/3	*Plasma cell myeloma*

M9731/0	*Plasma cell tumor, benign*
M9731/1	*Plasmacytoma NOS*
M9731/3	*Plasma cell tumor, malignant*

M974 — **Mast cell tumors**

M9740/1	*Mastocytoma NOS*
M9740/3	*Mast cell sarcoma*
M9741/3	*Malignant mastocytosis*

M975 — **Burkitt's tumor**

M9750/3	*Burkitt's tumor*

M980-M994 — **Leukemias NOS**

M9800/3	Leukemias NOS
M9800/3	*Leukemia NOS*
M9801/3	*Acute leukemia NOS*
M9802/3	*Subacute leukemia NOS*
M9803/3	*Chronic leukemia NOS*
M9804/3	*Aleukemic leukemia NOS*

M981 — **Compound leukemias**

M9810/3	*Compound leukemia*

M982 — **Lymphoid leukemias**

M9820/3	*Lymphoid leukemia NOS*
M9821/3	*Acute lymphoid leukemia*
M9822/3	*Subacute lymphoid leukemia*
M9823/3	*Chronic lymphoid leukemia*
M9824/3	*Aleukemic lymphoid leukemia*
M9825/3	*Prolymphocytic leukemia*

M983 — **Plasma cell leukemias**

M9830/3	*Plasma cell leukemia*

M984 — **Erythroleukemias**

M9840/3	*Erythroleukemia*
M9841/3	*Acute erythremia*
M9842/3	*Chronic erythremia*

M985 — **Lymphosarcoma cell leukemias**

M9850/3	*Lymphosarcoma cell leukemia*

M986 — **Myeloid leukemias**

M9860/3	*Myeloid leukemia NOS*
M9861/3	*Acute myeloid leukemia*
M9862/3	*Subacute myeloid leukemia*
M9863/3	*Chronic myeloid leukemia*
M9864/3	*Aleukemic myeloid leukemia*
M9865/3	*Neutrophilic leukemia*
M9866/3	*Acute promyelocytic leukemia*

M987 — **Basophilic leukemias**

M9870/3	*Basophilic leukemia*

M988 — **Eosinophilic leukemias**

M9880/3	*Eosinophilic leukemia*

M989 — **Monocytic leukemias**

M9890/3	*Monocytic leukemia NOS*
M9891/3	*Acute monocytic leukemia*
M9892/3	*Subacute monocytic leukemia*
M9893/3	*Chronic monocytic leukemia*
M9894/3	*Aleukemic monocytic leukemia*

M990-M994 — **Miscellaneous leukemias**

M9900/3	*Mast cell leukemia*
M9910/3	*Megakaryocytic leukemia*
M9920/3	*Megakaryocytic myelosis*
M9930/3	*Myeloid sarcoma*
M9940/3	*Hairy cell leukemia*

M995-M997 — **Miscellaneous myeloproliferative and lymphoproliferative disorders**

M9950/1	*Polycythemia vera*
M9951/1	*Acute panmyelosis*
M9960/1	*Chronic myeloproliferative disease*
M9961/1	*Myelosclerosis with myeloid metapla-sia*
M9962/1	*Idiopathic thrombocythemia*
M9970/1	*Chronic lymphoproliferative disease*

Appendix B: Glossary of Mental Disorders

APPENDIX B
WAS OFFICIALLY DELETED
OCTOBER 1, 2004

CLASSIFICATION OF DRUGS BY AMERICAN HOSPITAL FORMULARY SERVICE LIST NUMBER AND THEIR ICD-9-CM EQUIVALENTS

The coding of adverse effects of drugs is keyed to the continually revised Hospital Formulary of the American Hospital Formulary Service (AHFS) published under the direction of the American Society of Hospital Pharmacists.

The following section gives the ICD-9-CM diagnosis code for each AHFS list.

	AHFS* List	ICD-9-CM Diagnosis Code
4:00	ANTIHISTAMINE DRUGS	963.0
8:00	ANTI-INFECTIVE AGENTS	
8:04	Amebacides	961.5
	hydroxyquinoline derivatives	961.3
	arsenical anti-infectives	961.1
	quinoline derivatives	961.3
8:12.04	Antifungal Antibiotics	960.1
	nonantibiotics	961.9
8:12.06	Cephalosporins	960.5
8:12.08	Chloramphenicol	960.2
8:12.12	The Erythromycins	960.3
8:12.16	The Penicillins	960.0
8:12.20	The Streptomycins	960.6
8:12.24	The Tetracyclines	960.4
8:12.28	Other Antibiotics	960.8
	antimycobacterial antibiotics	960.6
	macrolides	960.3
8:16	Antituberculars	961.8
	antibiotics	960.6
8:18	Antivirals	961.7
8:20	Plasmodicides (antimalarials)	961.4
8:24	Sulfonamides	961.0
8:26	The Sulfones	961.8
8:28	Treponemicides	961.2
8:32	Trichomonacides	961.5
	hydroxyquinoline derivatives	961.3
	nitrofuran derivatives	961.9
8:36	Urinary Germicides	961.9
	quinoline derivatives	961.3
8:40	Other Anti-Infectives	961.9
10:00	ANTINEOPLASTIC AGENTS	963.1
	antibiotics	960.7
	progestogens	962.2
12:00	AUTONOMIC DRUGS	
12:04	Parasympathomimetic (Cholinergic) Agents	971.0
12:08	Parasympatholytic (Cholinergic Blocking Agents	971.1
12:12	Sympathomimetic (Adrenergic) Agents	971.2
12:16	Sympatholytic (Adrenergic Blocking) Agents	971.3
12:20	Skeletal Muscle Relaxants	975.2
	central nervous system	
	muscle-tone depressants	968.0
16:00	BLOOD DERIVATIVES	964.7
20:00	BLOOD FORMATION AND COAGULATION	
20:04	Antianemia Drugs	964.1
20:04.04	Iron Preparations	964.0
20:04.08	Liver and Stomach Preparations	964.1
20:12.04	Anticoagulants	964.2
20:12.08	Antiheparin Agents	964.5
20:12.12	Coagulants	964.5
20:12.16	Hemostatics	964.5
	capillary-active drugs	972.8
	fibrinolysis-affecting agents	964.4
	natural products	964.7
24:00	CARDIOVASCULAR DRUGS	
24:04	Cardiac Drugs	972.9
	cardiotonic agents	972.1
	rhythm regulators	972.0
24:06	Antilipemic Agents	972.2
	thyroid derivatives	962.7

	AHFS* List	ICD-9-CM Diagnosis Code
24:08	Hypotensive Agents	972.6
	adrenergic blocking agents	971.3
	ganglion-blocking agents	972.3
	vasodilators	972.5
24:12	Vasodilating Agents	972.5
	coronary	972.4
	nicotinic acid derivatives	972.2
24:16	Sclerosing Agents	972.7
28:00	CENTRAL NERVOUS SYSTEM DRUGS	
28:04	General Anesthetics	968.4
	gaseous anesthetics	968.2
	halothane	968.1
	intravenous anesthetics	968.3
28:08	Analgesics and Antipyretics	965.9
	antirheumatics	965.61-965.69
	aromatic analgesics	965.4
	non-narcotics NEC	965.7
	opium alkaloids	965.00
	heroin	965.01
	methadone	965.02
	specified type NEC	965.09
	pyrazole derivatives	965.5
	salicylates	965.1
	specified type NEC	965.8
28:10	Narcotic Antagonists	970.1
28:12	Anticonvulsants	966.3
	barbiturates	967.0
	benzodiazepine-based tranquilizers	969.4
	bromides	967.3
	hydantoin derivatives	966.1
	oxazolidine derivative	966.0
	succinimides	966.2
28:16.04	Antidepressants	969.0
28:16.08	Tranquilizers	969.5
	benzodiazepine-based	969.4
	butyrophenone-based	969.2
	major NEC	969.3
	phenothiazine-based	969.1
28:16.12	Other Psychotherapeutic Agents	969.8
28:20	Respiratory and Cerebral Stimulants	970.9
	analeptics	970.0
	anorexigenic agents	977.0
	psychostimulants	969.7
	specified type NEC	970.8
28:24	Sedatives and Hypnotics	967.9
	barbiturates	967.0
	benzodiazepine-based tranquilizers	969.4
	chloral hydrate group	967.1
	glutethamide group	967.5
	intravenous anesthetics	968.3
	methaqualone	967.4
	paraldehyde	967.2
	phenothiazine-based tranquilizers	969.1
	specified type NEC	967.8
	thiobarbiturates	968.3
	tranquilizer NEC	969.5
36:00	DIAGNOSTIC AGENTS	977.8
40:00	ELECTROLYTE, CALORIC, AND WATER BALANCE AGENTS NEC	974.5
40:04	Acidifying Agents	963.2
40:08	Alkalinizing Agents	963.3
40:10	Ammonia Detoxicants	974.5
40:12	Replacement Solutions NEC	974.5
	plasma volume expanders	964.8
40:16	Sodium-Removing Resins	974.5
40:18	Potassium-Removing Resins	974.5
40:20	Caloric Agents	974.5
40:24	Salt and Sugar Substitutes	974.5

AHFS* List		ICD-9-CM Diagnosis Code	AHFS* List		ICD-9-CM Diagnosis Code
40:28	Diuretics NEC	974.4	68:18	Gonadotropins	962.4
	carbonic acid anhydrase inhibitors	974.2	68:20	Insulins and Antidiabetic Agents	962.3
	mercurials	974.0	68:20.08	Insulins	962.3
	purine derivatives	974.1	68:24	Parathyroid	962.6
	saluretics	974.3	68:28	Pituitary	
40:36	Irrigating Solutions	974.5		anterior	962.4
40:40	Uricosuric Agents	974.7		posterior	962.5
44:00	ENZYMES NEC	963.4	68:32	Progestogens	962.2
	fibrinolysis-affecting agents	964.4	68:34	Other Corpus Luteum Hormones	962.2
	gastric agents	973.4	68:36	Thyroid and Antithyroid	
48:00	EXPECTORANTS AND COUGH PREPARATIONS			antithyroid	962.8
	antihistamine agents	963.0		thyroid	962.7
	antitussives	975.4	72:00	LOCAL ANESTHETICS NEC	968.9
	codeine derivatives	965.09		topical (surface) agents	968.5
	expectorants	975.5		infiltrating agents (intradermal)	
	narcotic agents NEC	965.09		(subcutaneous) (submucosal)	968.5
52:00	EYE, EAR, NOSE, AND THROAT PREPARATIONS			nerve blocking agents (peripheral)	
52:04	Anti-Infectives			(plexus) (regional)	968.6
	ENT	976.6		spinal	968.7
	ophthalmic	976.5	76:00	OXYTOCICS	975.0
52:04.04	Antibiotics		78:00	RADIOACTIVE AGENTS	990
	ENT	976.6	80:00	SERUMS, TOXOIDS, AND VACCINES	
	ophthalmic	976.5	80:04	Serums	979.9
52:04.06	Antivirals			immune globulin (gamma) (human)	964.6
	ENT	976.6	80:08	Toxoids NEC	978.8
	ophthalmic	976.5		diphtheria	978.5
52:04.08	Sulfonamides			and tetanus	978.9
	ENT	976.6		with pertussis component	978.6
	ophthalmic	976.5		tetanus	978.4
52:04.12	Miscellaneous Anti-Infectives			and diphtheria	978.9
	ENT	976.6		with pertussis component	978.6
	ophthalmic	976.5	80:12	Vaccines NEC	979.9
52:08	Anti-Inflammatory Agents			bacterial NEC	978.8
	ENT	976.6		with other bacterial component	978.9
	ophthalmic	976.5		pertussis component	978.6
52:10	Carbonic Anhydrase Inhibitors	974.2		viral and rickettsial component	979.7
52:12	Contact Lens Solutions	976.5		rickettsial NEC	979.6
52:16	Local Anesthetics	968.5		with bacterial component	979.7
52:20	Miotics	971.0		pertussis component	978.6
52:24	Mydriatics			viral component	979.7
	adrenergics	971.2		viral NEC	979.6
	anticholinergics	971.1		with bacterial component	979.7
	antimuscarinics	971.1		pertussis component	978.6
	parasympatholytics	971.1		rickettsial component	979.7
	spasmolytics	971.1	84:00	SKIN AND MUCOUS MEMBRANE PREPARATIONS	
	sympathomimetics	971.2	84:04	Anti-Infectives	976.0
52:28	Mouth Washes and Gargles	976.6	84:04.04	Antibiotics	976.0
52:32	Vasoconstrictors	971.2	84:04.08	Fungicides	976.0
52:36	Unclassified Agents		84:04.12	Scabicides and Pediculicides	976.0
	ENT	976.6	84:04.16	Miscellaneous Local Anti-Infectives	976.0
	ophthalmic	976.5	84:06	Anti-Inflammatory Agents	976.0
56:00	GASTROINTESTINAL DRUGS		84:08	Antipruritics and Local Anesthetics	
56:04	Antacids and Absorbents	973.0		antipruritics	976.1
56:08	Anti-Diarrhea Agents	973.5		local anesthetics	968.5
56:10	Antiflatulents	973.8	84:12	Astringents	976.2
56:12	Cathartics NEC	973.3	84:16	Cell Stimulants and Proliferants	976.8
	emollients	973.2	84:20	Detergents	976.2
	irritants	973.1	84:24	Emollients, Demulcents, and Protectants	976.3
56:16	Digestants	973.4	84:28	Keratolytic Agents	976.4
56:20	Emetics and Antiemetics		84:32	Keratoplastic Agents	976.4
	antiemetics	963.0	84:36	Miscellaneous Agents	976.8
	emetics	973.6	86:00	SPASMOLYTIC AGENTS	975.1
56:24	Lipotropic Agents	977.1		antiasthmatics	975.7
60:00	GOLD COMPOUNDS	965.69		papaverine	972.5
64:00	HEAVY METAL ANTAGONISTS	963.8		theophyllin	974.1
68:00	HORMONES AND SYNTHETIC SUBSTITUTES		88:00	VITAMINS	
68:04	Adrenals	962.0	88:04	Vitamin A	963.5
68:08	Androgens	962.1			
68:12	Contraceptives	962.2			
68:16	Estrogens	962.2			

AHFS* List		ICD-9-CM Diagnosis Code
88:08	Vitamin B Complex	963.5
	hematopoietic vitamin	964.1
	nicotinic acid derivatives	972.2
88:12	Vitamin C	963.5

AHFS* List		ICD-9-CM Diagnosis Code
88:16	Vitamin D	963.5
88:20	Vitamin E	963.5
88:24	Vitamin K Activity	964.3
88:28	Multivitamin Preparations	963.5
92:00	UNCLASSIFIED THERAPEUTIC AGENTS	977.8

* American Hospital Formulary Service

CLASSIFICATION OF INDUSTRIAL ACCIDENTS ACCORDING TO AGENCY

Annex B to the Resolution concerning Statistics of Employment Injuries adopted by the Tenth International Conference of Labor Statisticians on 12 October 1962

1 MACHINES

11 *Prime-Movers, except Electrical Motors*
111 *Steam engines*
112 *Internal combustion engines*
119 *Others*
12 *Transmission Machinery*
121 *Transmission shafts*
122 *Transmission belts, cables, pulleys, pinions, chains, gears*
129 *Others*
13 *Metalworking Machines*
131 *Power presses*
132 *Lathes*
133 *Milling machines*
134 *Abrasive wheels*
135 *Mechanical shears*
136 *Forging machines*
137 *Rolling-mills*
139 *Others*
14 *Wood and Assimilated Machines*
141 *Circular saws*
142 *Other saws*
143 *Molding machines*
144 *Overhand planes*
149 *Others*
15 *Agricultural Machines*
151 *Reapers (including combine reapers)*
152 *Threshers*
159 *Others*
16 *Mining Machinery*
161 *Under-cutters*
169 *Others*
19 *Other Machines Not Elsewhere Classified*
191 *Earth-moving machines, excavating and scraping machines, except means of transport*
192 *Spinning, weaving and other textile machines*
193 *Machines for the manufacture of food- stuffs and beverages*
194 *Machines for the manufacture of paper*
195 *Printing machines*
199 *Others*

2 MEANS OF TRANSPORT AND LIFTING EQUIPMENT

21 *Lifting Machines and Appliances*
211 *Cranes*
212 *Lifts and elevators*
213 *Winches*
214 *Pulley blocks*
219 *Others*
22 *Means of Rail Transport*
221 *Inter-urban railways*
222 *Rail transport in mines, tunnels, quarries, industrial establishments, docks, etc.*
229 *Others*
23 *Other Wheeled Means of Transport, Excluding Rail Transport*
231 *Tractors*
232 *Lorries*
233 *Trucks*
234 *Motor vehicles, not elsewhere classified*
235 *Animal-drawn vehicles*
236 *Hand-drawn vehicles*
239 *Others*
24 *Means of Air Transport*
25 *Means of Water Transport*
251 *Motorized means of water transport*
252 *Non-motorized means of water transport*
26 *Other Means of Transport*
261 *Cable-cars*
262 *Mechanical conveyors, except cable-cars*
269 *Others*

3 OTHER EQUIPMENT

31 *Pressure Vessels*
311 *Boilers*
312 *Pressurized containers*
313 *Pressurized piping and accessories*
314 *Gas cylinders*
315 *Caissons, diving equipment*
319 *Others*
32 *Furnaces, Ovens, Kilns*
321 *Blast furnaces*
322 *Refining furnaces*
323 *Other furnaces*
324 *Kilns*
325 *Ovens*
33 *Refrigerating Plants*
34 *Electrical Installations, Including Electric Motors, but Excluding Electric Hand Tools*
341 *Rotating machines*
342 *Conductors*
343 *Transformers*
344 *Control apparatus*
349 *Others*
35 *Electric Hand Tools*
36 *Tools, Implements, and Appliances, Except Electric Hand Tools*
361 *Power-driven hand tools, except electrichand tools*
362 *Hand tools, not power-driven*
369 *Others*
37 *Ladders, Mobile Ramps*
38 *Scaffolding*
39 *Other Equipment, Not Elsewhere Classified*

4 MATERIALS, SUBSTANCES AND RADIATIONS

41 *Explosives*
42 *Dusts, Gases, Liquids and Chemicals, Excluding Explosives*
421 *Dusts*
422 *Gases, vapors, fumes*
423 *Liquids, not elsewhere classified*
424 *Chemicals, not elsewhere classified*
43 *Flying Fragments*
44 *Radiations*
441 *Ionizing radiations*
449 *Others*
49 *Other Materials and Substances Not Elsewhere Classified*

5 WORKING ENVIRONMENT

51 *Outdoor*
511 *Weather*
512 *Traffic and working surfaces*
513 *Water*
519 *Others*
52 *Indoor*
521 *Floors*
522 *Confined quarters*
523 *Stairs*
524 *Other traffic and working surfaces*
525 *Floor openings and wall openings*
526 *Environmental factors (lighting, ventilation, temperature, noise, etc.)*
529 *Others*
53 *Underground*
531 *Roofs and faces of mine roads and tunnels, etc.*
532 *Floors of mine roads and tunnels, etc.*
533 *Working-faces of mines, tunnels, etc.*
534 *Mine shafts*
535 *Fire*
536 *Water*
539 *Others*

6 OTHER AGENCIES, NOT ELSEWHERE CLASSIFIED

61 *Animals*
611 *Live animals*
612 *Animal products*
69 *Other Agencies, Not Elsewhere Classified*

7 AGENCIES NOT CLASSIFIED FOR LACK OF SUFFICIENT DATA

LIST OF THREE-DIGIT CATEGORIES

1. INFECTIOUS AND PARASITIC DISEASES

Intestinal infectious diseases (001-009)
001 Cholera
002 Typhoid and paratyphoid fevers
003 Other salmonella infections
004 Shigellosis
005 Other food poisoning (bacterial)
006 Amebiasis
007 Other protozoal intestinal diseases
008 Intestinal infections due to other organisms
009 Ill-defined intestinal infections

Tuberculosis (010-018)
010 Primary tuberculous infection
011 Pulmonary tuberculosis
012 Other respiratory tuberculosis
013 Tuberculosis of meninges and central nervous system
014 Tuberculosis of intestines, peritoneum, and mesenteric glands
015 Tuberculosis of bones and joints
016 Tuberculosis of genitourinary system
017 Tuberculosis of other organs
018 Miliary tuberculosis

Zoonotic bacterial diseases (020-027)
020 Plague
021 Tularemia
022 Anthrax
023 Brucellosis
024 Glanders
025 Melioidosis
026 Rat-bite fever
027 Other zoonotic bacterial diseases

Other bacterial diseases (030-042)
030 Leprosy
031 Diseases due to other mycobacteria
032 Diphtheria
033 Whooping cough
034 Streptococcal sore throat and scarlatina
035 Erysipelas
036 Meningococcal infection
037 Tetanus
038 Septicemia
039 Actinomycotic infections
040 Other bacterial diseases
041 Bacterial infection in conditions classified elsewhere and of unspecified site

Human immunodeficiency virus (042)
042 Human immunodeficiency virus [HIV] disease

Poliomyelitis and other non-arthropod-borne viral diseases and prion diseases of central nervous system (045-049)
045 Acute poliomyelitis
046 Slow virus infections and prion diseases of central nervous system
047 Meningitis due to enterovirus
048 Other enterovirus diseases of central nervous system
049 Other non-arthropod-borne viral diseases of central nervous system

Viral diseases generally accompanied by exanthem (050-058)
050 Smallpox
051 Cowpox and paravaccinia
052 Chickenpox
053 Herpes zoster
054 Herpes simplex
055 Measles
056 Rubella
057 Other viral exanthemata
058 Other human herpesvirus

059 Other poxvirus infections

Arthropod-borne viral diseases (060-066)
060 Yellow fever
061 Dengue
062 Mosquito-borne viral encephalitis
063 Tick-borne viral encephalitis
064 Viral encephalitis transmitted by other and unspecified arthropods
065 Arthropod-borne hemorrhagic fever
066 Other arthropod-borne viral diseases

Other diseases due to viruses and Chlamydiae (070-079)
070 Viral hepatitis
071 Rabies
072 Mumps
073 Ornithosis
074 Specific diseases due to Coxsackievirus
075 Infectious mononucleosis
076 Trachoma
077 Other diseases of conjunctiva due to viruses and Chlamydiae
078 Other diseases due to viruses and Chlamydiae
079 Viral infection in conditions classified elsewhere and of unspecified site

Rickettsioses and other arthropod-borne diseases (080-088)
080 Louse-borne [epidemic] typhus
081 Other typhus
082 Tick-borne rickettsioses
083 Other rickettsioses
084 Malaria
085 Leishmaniasis
086 Trypanosomiasis
087 Relapsing fever
088 Other arthropod-borne diseases

Syphilis and other venereal diseases (090-099)
090 Congenital syphilis
091 Early syphilis, symptomatic
092 Early syphilis, latent
093 Cardiovascular syphilis
094 Neurosyphilis
095 Other forms of late syphilis, with symptoms
096 Late syphilis, latent
097 Other and unspecified syphilis
098 Gonococcal infections
099 Other venereal diseases

Other spirochetal diseases (100-104)
100 Leptospirosis
101 Vincent's angina
102 Yaws
103 Pinta
104 Other spirochetal infection

Mycoses (110-118)
110 Dermatophytosis
111 Dermatomycosis, other and unspecified
112 Candidiasis
114 Coccidioidomycosis
115 Histoplasmosis
116 Blastomycotic infection
117 Other mycoses
118 Opportunistic mycoses

Helminthiases (120-129)
120 Schistosomiasis [bilharziasis]
121 Other trematode infections
122 Echinococcosis
123 Other cestode infection
124 Trichinosis
125 Filarial infection and dracontiasis
126 Ancylostomiasis and necatoriasis
127 Other intestinal helminthiases
128 Other and unspecified helminthiases
129 Intestinal parasitism, unspecified

Other infectious and parasitic diseases (130-136)
130 Toxoplasmosis
131 Trichomoniasis
132 Pediculosis and phthirus infestation
133 Acariasis
134 Other infestation
135 Sarcoidosis
136 Other and unspecified infectious and parasitic diseases

Late effects of infectious and parasitic diseases (137-139)
137 Late effects of tuberculosis
138 Late effects of acute poliomyelitis
139 Late effects of other infectious and parasitic diseases

2. NEOPLASMS

Malignant neoplasm of lip, oral cavity, and pharynx (140-149)
140 Malignant neoplasm of lip
141 Malignant neoplasm of tongue
142 Malignant neoplasm of major salivary glands
143 Malignant neoplasm of gum
144 Malignant neoplasm of floor of mouth
145 Malignant neoplasm of other and unspecified parts of mouth
146 Malignant neoplasm of oropharynx
147 Malignant neoplasm of nasopharynx
148 Malignant neoplasm of hypopharynx
149 Malignant neoplasm of other and ill-defined sites within the lip, oral cavity, and pharynx

Malignant neoplasm of digestive organs and peritoneum (150-159)
150 Malignant neoplasm of esophagus
151 Malignant neoplasm of stomach
152 Malignant neoplasm of small intestine, including duodenum
153 Malignant neoplasm of colon
154 Malignant neoplasm of rectum, rectosigmoid junction, and anus
155 Malignant neoplasm of liver and intrahepatic bile ducts
156 Malignant neoplasm of gallbladder and extrahepatic bile ducts
157 Malignant neoplasm of pancreas
158 Malignant neoplasm of retroperitoneum and peritoneum
159 Malignant neoplasm of other and ill-defined sites within the digestive organs and peritoneum

Malignant neoplasm of respiratory and intrathoracic organs (160-165)
160 Malignant neoplasm of nasal cavities, middle ear, and accessory sinuses
161 Malignant neoplasm of larynx
162 Malignant neoplasm of trachea, bronchus, and lung
163 Malignant neoplasm of pleura
164 Malignant neoplasm of thymus, heart, and mediastinum
165 Malignant neoplasm of other and ill-defined sites within the respiratory system and intrathoracic organs

Malignant neoplasm of bone, connective tissue, skin, and breast (170-176)
170 Malignant neoplasm of bone and articular cartilage
171 Malignant neoplasm of connective and other soft tissue
172 Malignant melanoma of skin
173 Other malignant neoplasm of skin
174 Malignant neoplasm of female breast
175 Malignant neoplasm of male breast

176   Kaposi's sarcoma

Malignant neoplasm of genitourinary organs (179-189)

179   Malignant neoplasm of uterus, part unspecified
180   Malignant neoplasm of cervix uteri
181   Malignant neoplasm of placenta
182   Malignant neoplasm of body of uterus
183   Malignant neoplasm of ovary and other uterine adnexa
184   Malignant neoplasm of other and unspecified female genital organs
185   Malignant neoplasm of prostate
186   Malignant neoplasm of testis
187   Malignant neoplasm of penis and other male genital organs
188   Malignant neoplasm of bladder
189   Malignant neoplasm of kidney and other unspecified urinary organs

Malignant neoplasm of other and unspecified sites (190-199)

190   Malignant neoplasm of eye
191   Malignant neoplasm of brain
192   Malignant neoplasm of other and unspecified parts of nervous system
193   Malignant neoplasm of thyroid gland
194   Malignant neoplasm of other endocrine glands and related structures
195   Malignant neoplasm of other and ill-defined sites
196   Secondary and unspecified malignant neoplasm of lymph nodes
197   Secondary malignant neoplasm of respiratory and digestive systems
198   Secondary malignant neoplasm of other specified sites
199   Malignant neoplasm without specification of site

Malignant neoplasm of lymphatic and hematopoietic tissue (200-208)

200   Lymphosarcoma and reticulosar-coma and other specified malignant tumors of lymphatic tissue
201   Hodgkin's disease
202   Other malignant neoplasm of lymphoid and histiocytic tissue
203   Multiple myeloma and immunoproliferative neoplasms
204   Lymphoid leukemia
205   Myeloid leukemia
206   Monocytic leukemia
207   Other specified leukemia
208   Leukemia of unspecified cell type

Neuroendocrine tumors (209)

209   Neuroendocrine tumors

Benign neoplasms (210-229)

210   Benign neoplasm of lip, oral cavity, and pharynx
211   Benign neoplasm of other parts of digestive system
212   Benign neoplasm of respiratory and intrathoracic organs
213   Benign neoplasm of bone and articular cartilage
214   Lipoma
215   Other benign neoplasm of connective and other soft tissue
216   Benign neoplasm of skin
217   Benign neoplasm of breast
218   Uterine leiomyoma
219   Other benign neoplasm of uterus
220   Benign neoplasm of ovary

221   Benign neoplasm of other female genital organs
222   Benign neoplasm of male genital organs
223   Benign neoplasm of kidney and other urinary organs
224   Benign neoplasm of eye
225   Benign neoplasm of brain and other parts of nervous system
226   Benign neoplasm of thyroid gland
227   Benign neoplasm of other endocrine glands and related structures
228   Hemangioma and lymphangioma, any site
229   Benign neoplasm of other and unspecified sites

Carcinoma in situ (230-234)

230   Carcinoma in situ of digestive organs
231   Carcinoma in situ of respiratory system
232   Carcinoma in situ of skin
233   Carcinoma in situ of breast and genitourinary system
234   Carcinoma in situ of other and unspecified sites

Neoplasms of uncertain behavior (235-238)

235   Neoplasm of uncertain behavior of digestive and respiratory systems
236   Neoplasm of uncertain behavior of genitourinary organs
237   Neoplasm of uncertain behavior of endocrine glands and nervous system
238   Neoplasm of uncertain behavior of other and unspecified sites and tissues

Neoplasms of unspecified nature (239)

239   Neoplasm of unspecified nature

3. ENDOCRINE, NUTRITIONAL AND METABOLIC DISEASES, AND IMMUNITY DISORDERS

Disorders of thyroid gland (240-246)

240   Simple and unspecified goiter
241   Nontoxic nodular goiter
242   Thyrotoxicosis with or without goiter
243   Congenital hypothyroidism
244   Acquired hypothyroidism
245   Thyroiditis
246   Other disorders of thyroid

Diseases of other endocrine glands (249-259)

249   Secondary diabetes mellitus
250   Diabetes mellitus
251   Other disorders of pancreatic internal secretion
252   Disorders of parathyroid gland
253   Disorders of the pituitary gland and its hypothalamic control
254   Diseases of thymus gland
255   Disorders of adrenal glands
256   Ovarian dysfunction
257   Testicular dysfunction
258   Polyglandular dysfunction and related disorders
259   Other endocrine disorders

Nutritional deficiencies (260-269)

260   Kwashiorkor
261   Nutritional marasmus
262   Other severe protein-calorie malnutrition
263   Other and unspecified protein-calorie malnutrition
264   Vitamin A deficiency
265   Thiamine and niacin deficiency states
266   Deficiency of B-complex components
267   Ascorbic acid deficiency
268   Vitamin D deficiency
269   Other nutritional deficiencies

Other metabolic disorders and immnity disorders (270-279)

270   Disorders of amino-acid transport and metabolism
271   Disorders of carbohydrate transport and metabolism
272   Disorders of lipoid metabolism
273   Disorders of plasma protein metabolism
274   Gout
275   Disorders of mineral metabolism
276   Disorders of fluid, electrolyte, and acid-base balance
277   Other and unspecified disorders of metabolism
278   Overweight, obesity and other hyperalimentation
279   Disorders involving the immune mechanism

4. DISEASES OF BLOOD AND BLOOD-FORMING ORGANS (280-289)

280   Iron deficiency anemias
281   Other deficiency anemias
282   Hereditary hemolytic anemias
283   Acquired hemolytic anemias
284   Aplastic anemia
285   Other and unspecified anemias
286   Coagulation defects
287   Purpura and other hemorrhagic conditions
288   Diseases of white blood cells
289   Other diseases of blood and blood-forming organs

5. MENTAL DISORDERS

Organic psychotic conditions (290-294)

290   Senile and presenile organic psychotic conditions
291   Alcoholic psychoses
292   Drug psychoses
293   Transient organic psychotic conditions
294   Other organic psychotic conditions (chronic)

Other psychoses (295-299)

295   Schizophrenic psychoses
296   Affective psychoses
297   Paranoid states
298   Other nonorganic psychoses
299   Psychoses with origin specific to childhood

Neurotic disorders, personality disorders, and other nonpsychotic mental disorders (300-316)

300   Neurotic disorders
301   Personality disorders
302   Sexual and gender identity disorders
303   Alcohol dependence syndrome
304   Drug dependence
305   Nondependent abuse of drugs
306   Physiological malfunction arising from mental factors
307   Special symptoms or syndromes, not elsewhere classified
308   Acute reaction to stress
309   Adjustment reaction
310   Specific nonpsychotic mental disorders following organic brain damage
311   Depressive disorder, not elsewhereclassified
312   Disturbance of conduct, not elsewhere classified
313   Disturbance of emotions specific tochildhood and adolescence
314   Hyperkinetic syndrome of childhood
315   Specific delays in development
316   Psychic factors associated with diseases classified elsewhere

Mental retardation (317-319)

317   Mild mental retardation
318   Other specified mental retardation

319   Unspecified mental retardation

6. DISEASES OF THE NERVOUS SYSTEM AND SENSE ORGANS

Inflammatory diseases of the central nervous system (320-326)

320   Bacterial meningitis
321   Meningitis due to other organisms
322   Meningitis of unspecified cause
323   Encephalitis, myelitis, and encephalomyelitis
324   Intracranial and intraspinal abscess
325   Phlebitis and thrombophlebitis of intracranial venous sinuses
326   Late effects of intracranial abscess or pyogenic infection

Organic Sleep Disorders (327)

327   Organic sleep disorders

Hereditary and degenerative diseases of the central nervous system (330-337)

330   Cerebral degenerations usually manifest in childhood
331   Other cerebral degenerations
332   Parkinson's disease
333   Other extrapyramidal diseases and abnormal movement disorders
334   Spinocerebellar disease
335   Anterior horn cell disease
336   Other diseases of spinal cord
337   Disorders of the autonomic nervous system

Pain (338)

338   Pain, not elsewhere classified

Other headache syndromes (339)

339   Other headache syndromes

Other disorders of the central nervous system (340-349)

340   Multiple sclerosis
341   Other demyelinating diseases of central nervous system
342   Hemiplegia and hemiparesis
343   Infantile cerebral palsy
344   Other paralytic syndromes
345   Epilepsy and recurrent seizures
346   Migraine
347   Cataplexy and narcolepsy
348   Other conditions of brain
349   Other and unspecified disorders of the nervous system

Disorders of the peripheral nervous system (350-359)

350   Trigeminal nerve disorders
351   Facial nerve disorders
352   Disorders of other cranial nerves
353   Nerve root and plexus disorders
354   Mononeuritis of upper limb and mononeuritis multiplex
355   Mononeuritis of lower limb
356   Hereditary and idiopathic peripheral neuropathy
357   Inflammatory and toxic neuropathy
358   Myoneural disorders
359   Muscular dystrophies and other myopathies

Disorders of the eye and adnexa (360-379)

360   Disorders of the globe
361   Retinal detachments and defects
362   Other retinal disorders
363   Chorioretinal inflammations and scars and other disorders of choroid
364   Disorders of iris and ciliary body
365   Glaucoma
366   Cataract
367   Disorders of refraction and accommodation
368   Visual disturbances

369   Blindness and low vision
370   Keratitis
371   Corneal opacity and other disorders of cornea
372   Disorders of conjunctiva
373   Inflammation of eyelids
374   Other disorders of eyelids
375   Disorders of lacrimal system
376   Disorders of the orbit
377   Disorders of optic nerve and visual pathways
378   Strabismus and other disorders of binocular eye movements
379   Other disorders of eye

Diseases of the ear and mastoid process (380-389)

380   Disorders of external ear
381   Nonsuppurative otitis media and Eustachian tube disorders
382   Suppurative and unspecified otitis media
383   Mastoiditis and related conditions
384   Other disorders of tympanic membrane
385   Other disorders of middle ear and mastoid
386   Vertiginous syndromes and other disorders of vestibular system
387   Otosclerosis
388   Other disorders of ear
389   Hearing loss

7. DISEASES OF THE CIRCULATORY SYSTEM

Acute rheumatic fever (390-392)

390   Rheumatic fever without mention of heart involvement
391   Rheumatic fever with heart involvement
392   Rheumatic chorea

Chronic rheumatic heart disease (393-398)

393   Chronic rheumatic pericarditis
394   Diseases of mitral valve
395   Diseases of aortic valve
396   Diseases of mitral and aortic valves
397   Diseases of other endocardial structures
398   Other rheumatic heart disease

Hypertensive disease (401-405)

401   Essential hypertension
402   Hypertensive heart disease
403   Hypertensive kidney disease
404   Hypertensive heart and kidney disease
405   Secondary hypertension

Ischemic heart disease (410-414)

410   Acute myocardial infarction
411   Other acute and subacute form of ischemic heart disease
412   Old myocardial infarction
413   Angina pectoris
414   Other forms of chronic ischemic heart disease

Diseases of pulmonary circulation (415-417)

415   Acute pulmonary heart disease
416   Chronic pulmonary heart disease
417   Other diseases of pulmonary circulation

Other forms of heart disease (420-429)

420   Acute pericarditis
421   Acute and subacute endocarditis
422   Acute myocarditis
423   Other diseases of pericardium
424   Other diseases of endocardium
425   Cardiomyopathy
426   Conduction disorders
427   Cardiac dysrhythmias
428   Heart failure
429   Ill-defined descriptions and complications of heart disease

Cerebrovascular disease (430-438)

430   Subarachnoid hemorrhage
431   Intracerebral hemorrhage

432   Other and unspecified intracranial hemorrhage
433   Occlusion and stenosis of precerebral arteries
434   Occlusion of cerebral arteries
435   Transient cerebral ischemia
436   Acute but ill-defined cerebrovascular disease
437   Other and ill-defined cerebrovascular disease
438   Late effects of cerebrovascular disease

Diseases of arteries, arterioles, and capillaries (440-449)

440   Atherosclerosis
441   Aortic aneurysm and dissection
442   Other aneurysm
443   Other peripheral vascular disease
444   Arterial embolism and thrombosis
445   Atheroembolism
446   Polyarteritis nodosa and allied conditions
447   Other disorders of arteries and arterioles
448   Diseases of capillaries
449   Septic arterial embolism

Diseases of veins and lymphatics, and other diseases of circulatory system (451-459)

451   Phlebitis and thrombophlebitis
452   Portal vein thrombosis
453   Other venous embolism and thrombosis
454   Varicose veins of lower extremities
455   Hemorrhoids
456   Varicose veins of other sites
457   Noninfective disorders of lymphatic channels
458   Hypotension
459   Other disorders of circulatory system

8. DISEASES OF THE RESPIRATORY SYSTEM

Acute respiratory infections (460-466)

460   Acute nasopharyngitis [common cold]
461   Acute sinusitis
462   Acute pharyngitis
463   Acute tonsillitis
464   Acute laryngitis and tracheitis
465   Acute upper respiratory infections of multiple or unspecified sites
466   Acute bronchitis and bronchiolitis

Other diseases of upper respiratory tract (470-478)

470   Deviated nasal septum
471   Nasal polyps
472   Chronic pharyngitis and nasopharyngitis
473   Chronic sinusitis
474   Chronic disease of tonsils and adenoids
475   Peritonsillar abscess
476   Chronic laryngitis and aryngotracheitis
477   Allergic rhinitis
478   Other diseases of upper respiratory tract

Pneumonia and influenza (480-488)

480   Viral pneumonia
481   Pneumococcal pneumonia [Streptococcus pneumoniae pneumonia]
482   Other bacterial pneumonia
483   Pneumonia due to other specified organism
484   Pneumonia in infectious diseases classified elsewhere
485   Bronchopneumonia, organism unspecified
486   Pneumonia, organism unspecified
487   Influenza
488   Influenza due to certain identified influenza viruses

Chronic obstructive pulmonary disease and allied conditions (490-496)

490   Bronchitis, not specified as acute or chronic
491   Chronic bronchitis
492   Emphysema
493   Asthma
494   Bronchiectasis

495 Extrinsic allergic alveolitis
496 Chronic airways obstruction, not elsewhere classified

Pneumoconioses and other lung diseases due to external agents (500-508)
500 Coal workers' pneumoconiosis
501 Asbestosis
502 Pneumoconiosis due to other silica or silicates
503 Pneumoconiosis due to other inorganic dust
504 Pneumopathy due to inhalation of other dust
505 Pneumoconiosis, unspecified
506 Respiratory conditions due to chemical fumes and vapors
507 Pneumonitis due to solids and liquids
508 Respiratory conditions due to other and unspecified external agents

Other diseases of respiratory system (510-519)
510 Empyema
511 Pleurisy
512 Pneumothorax
513 Abscess of lung and mediastinum
514 Pulmonary congestion and hypostasis
515 Postinflammatory pulmonary fibrosis
516 Other alveolar and parietoalveolar pneumopathy
517 Lung involvement in conditions classified elsewhere
518 Other diseases of lung
519 Other diseases of respiratory system

9. DISEASES OF THE DIGESTIVE SYSTEM

Diseases of oral cavity, salivary glands, and jaws (520-529)
520 Disorders of tooth development and eruption
521 Diseases of hard tissues of teeth
522 Diseases of pulp and periapical tissues
523 Gingival and periodontal diseases
524 Dentofacial anomalies, including malocclusion
525 Other diseases and conditions of the teeth and supporting structures
526 Diseases of the jaws
527 Diseases of the salivary glands
528 Diseases of the oral soft tissues, excluding lesions specific for gingiva and tongue
529 Diseases and other conditions of the tongue

Diseases of esophagus, stomach, and duodenum (530-538)
530 Diseases of esophagus
531 Gastric ulcer
532 Duodenal ulcer
533 Peptic ulcer, site unspecified
534 Gastrojejunal ulcer
535 Gastritis and duodenitis
536 Disorders of function of stomach
537 Other disorders of stomach and duodenum
538 Gastrointestinal mucositis (ulcerative)

Appendicitis (540-543)
540 Acute appendicitis
541 Appendicitis, unqualified
542 Other appendicitis
543 Other diseases of appendix

Hernia of abdominal cavity (550-553)
550 Inguinal hernia
551 Other hernia of abdominal cavity, with gangrene
552 Other hernia of abdominal cavity, with ob-struction, but without mention of gangrene
553 Other hernia of abdominal cavity without mention of obstruction or gangrene

Noninfective enteritis and colitis (555-558)
555 Regional enteritis
556 Ulcerative colitis
557 Vascular insufficiency of intestine
558 Other noninfective gastroenteritis and colitis

Other diseases of intestines and peritoneum (560-569)
560 Intestinal obstruction without mention of hernia
562 Diverticula of intestine
564 Functional digestive disorders, not elsewhere classified
565 Anal fissure and fistula
566 Abscess of anal and rectal regions
567 Peritonitis and retroperitoneal infections
568 Other disorders of peritoneum
569 Other disorders of intestine

Other diseases of digestive system (570-579)
570 Acute and subacute necrosis of liver
571 Chronic liver disease and cirrhosis
572 Liver abscess and sequelae of chronic liver disease
573 Other disorders of liver
574 Cholelithiasis
575 Other disorders of gallbladder
576 Other disorders of biliary tract
577 Diseases of pancreas
578 Gastrointestinal hemorrhage
579 Intestinal malabsorption

10. DISEASES OF THE GENITOURINARY SYSTEM

Nephritis, nephrotic syndrome, and nephrosis (580-589)
580 Acute glomerulonephritis
581 Nephrotic syndrome
582 Chronic glomerulonephritis
583 Nephritis and nephropathy, not specified as acute or chronic
584 Acute kidney failure
585 Chronic kidney disease (CKD)
586 Renal failure, unspecified
587 Renal sclerosis, unspecified
588 Disorders resulting from impaired renal function
589 Small kidney of unknown cause

Other diseases of urinary system (590-599)
590 Infections of kidney
591 Hydronephrosis
592 Calculus of kidney and ureter
593 Other disorders of kidney and ureter
594 Calculus of lower urinary tract
595 Cystitis
596 Other disorders of bladder
597 Urethritis, not sexually transmitted, and urethral syndrome
598 Urethral stricture
599 Other disorders of urethra and urinary tract

Diseases of male genital organs (600-608)
600 Hyperplasia of prostate
601 Inflammatory diseases of prostate
602 Other disorders of prostate
603 Hydrocele
604 Orchitis and epididymitis
605 Redundant prepuce and phimosis
606 Infertility, male
607 Disorders of penis
608 Other disorders of male genital organs

Disorders of breast (610-612)
610 Benign mammary dysplasias
611 Other disorders of breast
612 Deformity and disproportion of reconstructed breast

Inflammatory disease of female pelvic organs (614-616)
614 Inflammatory disease of ovary, fallopian tube, pelvic cellular tissue, and peritoneum
615 Inflammatory diseases of uterus, except cervix
616 Inflammatory disease of cervix, vagina, and vulva

Other disorders of female genital tract (617-629)
617 Endometriosis
618 Genital prolapse
619 Fistula involving female genital tract
620 Noninflammatory disorders of ovary, fallopian tube, and broad ligament
621 Disorders of uterus, not elsewhere classified
622 Noninflammatory disorders of cervix
623 Noninflammatory disorders of vagina
624 Noninflammatory disorders of vulva and perineum
625 Pain and other symptoms associated with female genital organs
626 Disorders of menstruation and other abnormal bleeding from female genital tract
627 Menopausal and postmenopausal disorders
628 Infertility, female
629 Other disorders of female genital organs

11. COMPLICATIONS OF PREGNANCY, CHILDBIRTH AND THE PUERPERIUM

Ectopic and molar pregnancy and other pregnancy with abortive outcome (630-639)
630 Hydatidiform mole
631 Other abnormal product of conception
632 Missed abortion
633 Ectopic pregnancy
634 Spontaneous abortion
635 Legally induced abortion
636 Illegally induced abortion
637 Unspecified abortion
638 Failed attempted abortion
639 Complications following abortion and ectopic and molar pregnancies

Complications mainly related to pregnancy (640-649)
640 Hemorrhage in early pregnancy
641 Antepartum hemorrhage, abruptio placentae, and placenta previa
642 Hypertension complicating pregnancy, childbirth, and the puerperium
643 Excessive vomiting in pregnancy
644 Early or threatened labor
645 Prolonged pregnancy
646 Other complications of pregnancy, not elsewhere classified
647 Infective and parasitic conditions in the mother classifiable elsewhere but complicating pregnancy, childbirth, and the puerperium
648 Other current conditions in the mother classifiable elsewhere but complicating pregnancy, childbirth, and the puerperium
649 Other conditions or status of the mother complicating pregnancy, childbirth, or puerperium

Normal delivery, and other indications for care in pregnancy, labor, and delivery (650-659)
650 Normal delivery
651 Multiple gestation
652 Malposition and malpresentation of fetus
653 Disproportion
654 Abnormality of organs and soft tissues of pelvis
655 Known or suspected fetal abnormality affecting management of mother

656	Other fetal and placental problems affecting management of mother
657	Polyhydramnios
658	Other problems associated with amniotic cavity and membranes
659	Other indications for care or intervention related to labor and delivery and not elsewhere classified

Complications occurring mainly in the course of labor and delivery (660-669)

660	Obstructed labor
661	Abnormality of forces of labor
662	Long labor
663	Umbilical cord complications
664	Trauma to perineum and vulva during delivery
665	Other obstetrical trauma
666	Postpartum hemorrhage
667	Retained placenta or membranes, without hemorrhage
668	Complications of the administration of anesthetic or other sedation in labor and delivery
669	Other complications of labor and delivery, not elsewhere classified

Complications of the puerperium (670-679)

670	Major puerperal infection
671	Venous complications in pregnancy and the puerperium
672	Pyrexia of unknown origin during the puerperium
673	Obstetrical pulmonary embolism
674	Other and unspecified complications of the puerperium, not elsewhere classified
675	Infections of the breast and nipple associated with childbirth
676	Other disorders of the breast associated with childbirth, and disorders of lactation
677	Late effect of complication of pregnancy, childbirth, and the puerperium
678	Other fetal conditions
679	Complications of in utero procedures

12. DISEASES OF THE SKIN AND SUBCUTANEOUS TISSUE

Infections of skin and subcutaneous tissue (680-686)

680	Carbuncle and furuncle
681	Cellulitis and abscess of finger and toe
682	Other cellulitis and abscess
683	Acute lymphadenitis
684	Impetigo
685	Pilonidal cyst
686	Other local infections of skin and subcutaneous tissue

Inflammatory conditions of skin and subcutaneous tissue (690-698)

690	Erythematosquamous dermatosis
691	Atopic dermatitis and related conditions
692	Contact dermatitis and other eczema
693	Dermatitis due to substances taken internally
694	Bullous dermatoses
695	Erythematous conditions
696	Psoriasis and similar disorders
697	Lichen
698	Pruritus and related conditions

Other diseases of skin and subcutaneous tissue (700-709)

700	Corns and callosities
701	Other hypertrophic and atrophic conditions of skin
702	Other dermatoses
703	Diseases of nail
704	Diseases of hair and hair follicles
705	Disorders of sweat glands
706	Diseases of sebaceous glands
707	Chronic ulcer of skin
708	Urticaria
709	Other disorders of skin and subcutaneous tissue

13. DISEASES OF THE MUSCULOSKELETAL SYSTEM AND CONNECTIVE TISSUE

Arthropathies and related disorders (710-719)

710	Diffuse diseases of connective tissue
711	Arthropathy associated with infections
712	Crystal arthropathies
713	Arthropathy associated with other disorders classified elsewhere
714	Rheumatoid arthritis and other inflammatory polyarthropathies
715	Osteoarthrosis and allied disorders
716	Other and unspecified arthropathies
717	Internal derangement of knee
718	Other derangement of joint
719	Other and unspecified disorder of joint

Dorsopathies (720-724)

720	Ankylosing spondylitis and other inflammatory spondylopathies
721	Spondylosis and allied disorders
722	Intervertebral disc disorders
723	Other disorders of cervical region
724	Other and unspecified disorders of back

Rheumatism, excluding the back (725-729)

725	Polymyalgia rheumatica
726	Peripheral enthesopathies and allied syndromes
727	Other disorders of synovium, tendon, and bursa
728	Disorders of muscle, ligament, and fascia
729	Other disorders of soft tissues

Osteopathies, chondropathies, and acquired musculoskeletal deformities (730-739)

730	Osteomyelitis, periostitis, and other infections involving bone
731	Osteitis deformans and osteopathies associated with other disorders classified elsewhere
732	Osteochondropathies
733	Other disorders of bone and cartilage
734	Flat foot
735	Acquired deformities of toe
736	Other acquired deformities of limbs
737	Curvature of spine
738	Other acquired deformity
739	Nonallopathic lesions, not elsewhere classified

14. CONGENITAL ANOMALIES

740	Anencephalus and similar anomalies
741	Spina bifida
742	Other congenital anomalies of nervous system
743	Congenital anomalies of eye
744	Congenital anomalies of ear, face, and neck
745	Bulbus cordis anomalies and anomalies of cardiac septal closure
746	Other congenital anomalies of heart
747	Other congenital anomalies of circulatory system
748	Congenital anomalies of respiratory system
749	Cleft palate and cleft lip
750	Other congenital anomalies of upper alimentary tract
751	Other congenital anomalies of digestive system
752	Congenital anomalies of genital organs
753	Congenital anomalies of urinary system
754	Certain congenital musculoskeletal deformities
755	Other congenital anomalies of limbs
756	Other congenital musculoskeletal anomalies
757	Congenital anomalies of the integument
758	Chromosomal anomalies
759	Other and unspecified congenital anomalies

15. CERTAIN CONDITIONS ORIGINATING IN THE PERINATAL PERIOD

Maternal causes of perinatal morbidity and mortality (760-763)

760	Fetus or newborn affected by maternal conditions which may be unrelated to present pregnancy
761	Fetus or newborn affected by maternal complications of pregnancy
762	Fetus or newborn affected by complications of placenta, cord, and membranes
763	Fetus or newborn affected by other complications of labor and delivery

Other conditions originating in the perinatal period (764-779)

764	Slow fetal growth and fetal malnutrition
765	Disorders relating to short gestation and unspecified low birthweight
766	Disorders relating to long gestation and high birthweight
767	Birth trauma
768	Intrauterine hypoxia and birth asphyxia
769	Respiratory distress syndrome
770	Other respiratory conditions of fetus and newborn
771	Infections specific to the perinatal period
772	Fetal and neonatal hemorrhage
773	Hemolytic disease of fetus or newborn, due to isoimmunization
774	Other perinatal jaundice
775	Endocrine and metabolic disturbances specific to the fetus and newborn
776	Hematological disorders of newborn
777	Perinatal disorders of digestive system
778	Conditions involving the integument and temperature regulation of fetus and newborn
779	Other and ill-defined conditions originating in the perinatal period

16. SYMPTOMS, SIGNS, AND ILL-DEFINED CONDITIONS

Symptoms (780-789)

780	General symptoms
781	Symptoms involving nervous and musculoskeletal systems
782	Symptoms involving skin and other integumentary tissue
783	Symptoms concerning nutrition, metabolism, and development
784	Symptoms involving head and neck
785	Symptoms involving cardiovascular system
786	Symptoms involving respiratory system and other chest symptoms
787	Symptoms involving digestive system
788	Symptoms involving urinary system
789	Other symptoms involving abdomen and pelvis

Nonspecific abnormal findings (790-796)

790	Nonspecific findings on examination of blood
791	Nonspecific findings on examination of urine
792	Nonspecific abnormal findings in other body substances
793	Nonspecific (abnormal) findings on radiological and other examination of body structure
794	Nonspecific abnormal results of function studies

795   Nonspecific abnormal histological and immunological findings
796   Other nonspecific abnormal findings

Ill-defined and unknown causes of morbidity and mortality (797-799)
797   Senility without mention of psychosis
798   Sudden death, cause unknown
799   Other ill-defined and unknown causes of morbidity and mortality

17. INJURY AND POISONING

Fracture of skull (800-804)
800   Fracture of vault of skull
801   Fracture of base of skull
802   Fracture of face bones
803   Other and unqualified skull fractures
804   Multiple fractures involving skull or face with other bones

Fracture of spine and trunk (805-809)
805   Fracture of vertebral column without mention of spinal cord lesion
806   Fracture of vertebral column with spinal cord lesion
807   Fracture of rib(s), sternum, larynx, and trachea
808   Fracture of pelvis
809   Ill-defined fractures of bones of trunk

Fracture of upper limb (810-819)
810   Fracture of clavicle
811   Fracture of scapula
812   Fracture of humerus
813   Fracture of radius and ulna
814   Fracture of carpal bone(s)
815   Fracture of metacarpal bone(s)
816   Fracture of one or more phalanges of hand
817   Multiple fractures of hand bones
818   Ill-defined fractures of upper limb
819   Multiple fractures involving both upper limbs, and upper limb with rib(s) and sternum

Fracture of lower limb (820-829)
820   Fracture of neck of femur
821   Fracture of other and unspecified parts of femur
822   Fracture of patella
823   Fracture of tibia and fibula
824   Fracture of ankle
825   Fracture of one or more tarsal and metatarsal bones
826   Fracture of one or more phalanges of foot
827   Other, multiple, and ill-defined fractures of lower limb
828   Multiple fractures involving both lower limbs, lower with upper limb, and lower limb(s) with rib(s) and sternum
829   Fracture of unspecified bones

Dislocation (830-839)
830   Dislocation of jaw
831   Dislocation of shoulder
832   Dislocation of elbow
833   Dislocation of wrist
834   Dislocation of finger
835   Dislocation of hip
836   Dislocation of knee
837   Dislocation of ankle
838   Dislocation of foot
839   Other, multiple, and ill-defined dislocations

Sprains and strains of joints and adjacent muscles (840-848)
840   Sprains and strains of shoulder and upper arm
841   Sprains and strains of elbow and forearm
842   Sprains and strains of wrist and hand
843   Sprains and strains of hip and thigh
844   Sprains and strains of knee and leg

845   Sprains and strains of ankle and foot
846   Sprains and strains of sacroiliac region
847   Sprains and strains of other and unspecified parts of back
848   Other and ill-defined sprains and strains

Intracranial injury, excluding those with skull fracture (850-854)
850   Concussion
851   Cerebral laceration and contusion
852   Subarachnoid, subdural, and extradural hemorrhage, following injury
853   Other and unspecified intracranial hemorrhage following injury
854   Intracranial injury of other and unspecified nature

Internal injury of chest, abdomen, and pelvis (860-869)
860   Traumatic pneumothorax and hemothorax
861   Injury to heart and lung
862   Injury to other and unspecified intrathoracic organs
863   Injury to gastrointestinal tract
864   Injury to liver
865   Injury to spleen
866   Injury to kidney
867   Injury to pelvic organs
868   Injury to other intra-abdominal organs
869   Internal injury to unspecified or ill-defined organs

Open wound of head, neck, and trunk (870-879)
870   Open wound of ocular adnexa
871   Open wound of eyeball
872   Open wound of ear
873   Other open wound of head
874   Open wound of neck
875   Open wound of chest (wall)
876   Open wound of back
877   Open wound of buttock
878   Open wound of genital organs (external), including traumatic amputation
879   Open wound of other and unspecified sites, except limbs

Open wound of upper limb (880-887)
880   Open wound of shoulder and upper arm
881   Open wound of elbow, forearm, and wrist
882   Open wound of hand except finger(s) alone
883   Open wound of finger(s)
884   Multiple and unspecified open wound of upper limb
885   Traumatic amputation of thumb (complete) (partial)
886   Traumatic amputation of other finger(s) (complete) (partial)
887   Traumatic amputation of arm and hand (complete) (partial)

Open wound of lower limb (890-897)
890   Open wound of hip and thigh
891   Open wound of knee, leg [except thigh], and ankle
892   Open wound of foot except toe(s) alone
893   Open wound of toe(s)
894   Multiple and unspecified open wound of lower limb
895   Traumatic amputation of toe(s) (complete) (partial)
896   Traumatic amputation of foot (complete) (partial)
897   Traumatic amputation of leg(s) (complete) (partial)

Injury to blood vessels (900-904)
900   Injury to blood vessels of head and neck
901   Injury to blood vessels of thorax
902   Injury to blood vessels of abdomen and pelvis

903   Injury to blood vessels of upper extremity
904   Injury to blood vessels of lower extremity and unspecified sites

Late effects of injuries, poisonings, toxic effects, and other external causes (905-909)
905   Late effects of musculoskeletal and connective tissue injuries
906   Late effects of injuries to skin and subcutaneous tissues
907   Late effects of injuries to the nervous system
908   Late effects of other and unspecified injuries
909   Late effects of other and unspecified external causes

Superficial injury (910-919)
910   Superficial injury of face, neck, and scalp except eye
911   Superficial injury of trunk
912   Superficial injury of shoulder and upper arm
913   Superficial injury of elbow, forearm, and wrist
914   Superficial injury of hand(s) except finger(s) alone
915   Superficial injury of finger(s)
916   Superficial injury of hip, thigh, leg, and ankle
917   Superficial injury of foot and toe(s)
918   Superficial injury of eye and adnexa
919   Superficial injury of other, multiple, and unspecified sites

Contusion with intact skin surface (920-924)
920   Contusion of face, scalp, and neck except eye(s)
921   Contusion of eye and adnexa
922   Contusion of trunk
923   Contusion of upper limb
924   Contusion of lower limb and of other and unspecified sites

Crushing injury (925-929)
925   Crushing injury of face, scalp, and neck
926   Crushing injury of trunk
927   Crushing injury of upper limb
928   Crushing injury of lower limb
929   Crushing injury of multiple and unspecified sites

Effects of foreign body entering through orifice (930-939)
930   Foreign body on external eye
931   Foreign body in ear
932   Foreign body in nose
933   Foreign body in pharynx and larynx
934   Foreign body in trachea, bronchus, and lung
935   Foreign body in mouth, esophagus, and stomach
936   Foreign body in intestine and colon
937   Foreign body in anus and rectum
938   Foreign body in digestive system, unspecified
939   Foreign body in genitourinary tract

Burns (940-949)
940   Burn confined to eye and adnexa
941   Burn of face, head, and neck
942   Burn of trunk
943   Burn of upper limb, except wrist and hand
944   Burn of wrist(s) and hand(s)
945   Burn of lower limb(s)
946   Burns of multiple specified sites
947   Burn of internal organs
948   Burns classified according to extent of body surface involved
949   Burn, unspecified

Injury to nerves and spinal cord (950-957)
950   Injury to optic nerve and pathways
951   Injury to other cranial nerve(s)
952   Spinal cord injury without evidence of spinal bone injury

953	Injury to nerve roots and spinal plexus
954	Injury to other nerve(s) of trunk excluding shoulder and pelvic girdles
955	Injury to peripheral nerve(s) of shoulder girdle and upper limb
956	Injury to peripheral nerve(s) of pelvic girdle and lower limb
957	Injury to other and unspecified nerves

Certain traumatic complications and unspecified injuries (958-959)

958	Certain early complications of trauma
959	Injury, other and unspecified

Poisoning by drugs, medicinals and biological substances (960-979)

960	Poisoning by antibiotics
961	Poisoning by other anti-infectives
962	Poisoning by hormones and synthetic substitutes
963	Poisoning by primarily systemic agents
964	Poisoning by agents primarily affecting blood constituents
965	Poisoning by analgesics, antipyretics, and antirheumatics
966	Poisoning by anticonvulsants and anti-Parkinsonism drugs
967	Poisoning by sedatives and hypnotics
968	Poisoning by other central nervous system depressants and anesthetics
969	Poisoning by psychotropic agents
970	Poisoning by central nervous system stimulants
971	Poisoning by drugs primarily affecting the autonomic nervous system
972	Poisoning by agents primarily affecting the cardiovascular system
973	Poisoning by agents primarily affecting the gastrointestinal system
974	Poisoning by water, mineral, and uric acid metabolism drugs
975	Poisoning by agents primarily acting on the smooth and skeletal muscles and respiratory system
976	Poisoning by agents primarily affecting skin and mucous membrane, ophthalmological, otorhinolaryngological, and dental drugs
977	Poisoning by other and unspecified drugs and medicinals
978	Poisoning by bacterial vaccines
979	Poisoning by other vaccines and biological substances

Toxic effects of substances chiefly nonmedicinal as to source (980-989)

980	Toxic effect of alcohol
981	Toxic effect of petroleum products
982	Toxic effect of solvents other than petroleum-based
983	Toxic effect of corrosive aromatics, acids, and caustic alkalis
984	Toxic effect of lead and its compounds (including fumes)
985	Toxic effect of other metals
986	Toxic effect of carbon monoxide
987	Toxic effect of other gases, fumes, or vapors
988	Effect of noxious substances eaten as food
989	Toxic effect of other substances, chiefly nonmedicinal as to source

Other and unspecified effects of external causes (990-995)

990	Effects of radiation, unspecified
991	Effects of reduced temperature
992	Effects of heat and light
993	Effects of air pressure
994	Effects of other external causes

995	Certain adverse effects, not elsewhere classified

Complications of surgical and medical care, not elsewhere classified (996-999)

996	Complications peculiar to certain specified procedures
997	Complications affecting specified body systems, not elsewhere classified
998	Other complications of procedures, not elsewhere classified
999	Complications of medical care, not elsewhere classified

SUPPLEMENTARY CLASSIFICATION OF FACTORS INFLUENCING HEALTH STATUS AND CONTACT WITH HEALTH SERVICES

Persons with potential health hazards related to communicable diseases (V01-V09)

V01	Contact with or exposure to communicable diseases
V02	Carrier or suspected carrier of infectious diseases
V03	Need for prophylactic vaccination and inoculation against bacterial diseases
V04	Need for prophylactic vaccination and inoculation against certain viral diseases
V05	Need for other prophylactic vaccination and inoculation against single diseases
V06	Need for prophylactic vaccination and inoculation against combinations of diseases
V07	Need for isolation and other prophylactic measures
V08	Asymptomatic human immunodeficiency virus [HIV] infection status
V09	Infection with drug-resistant microorganisms

Persons with potential health hazards related to personal and family history (V10-V19)

V10	Personal history of malignant neoplasm
V11	Personal history of mental disorder
V12	Personal history of certain other diseases
V13	Personal history of other diseases
V14	Personal history of allergy to medicinal agents
V15	Other personal history presenting hazards to health
V16	Family history of malignant neoplasm
V17	Family history of certain chronic disabling diseases
V18	Family history of certain other specific conditions
V19	Family history of other conditions

Persons encountering health services in circumstances related to reproduction and development (V20-V29)

V20	Health supervision of infant or child
V21	Constitutional states in development
V22	Normal pregnancy
V23	Supervision of high-risk pregnancy
V24	Postpartum care and examination
V25	Encounter for contraceptive management
V26	Procreative management
V27	Outcome of delivery
V28	Antenatal screening
V29	Observation and evaluation of newborns and infants for suspected condition not found

Liveborn infants according to type of birth (V30-V39)

V30	Single liveborn
V31	mate liveborn
V32	Twin, mate stillborn
V33	Twin, unspecified
V34	Other multiple, mates all liveborn
V35	Other multiple, mates all stillborn
V36	Other multiple, mates live- and stillborn

V37	Other multiple, unspecified
V39	Unspecified

Persons with a condition influencing their health status (V40-V49)

V40	Mental and behavioral problems
V41	Problems with special senses and other special functions
V42	Organ or tissue replaced by transplant
V43	Organ or tissue replaced by other means
V44	Artificial opening status
V45	Other postprocedural states
V46	Other dependence on machines
V47	Other problems with internal organs
V48	Problems with head, neck, and trunk
V49	Other conditions influencing health status

Persons encountering health services for specific procedures and aftercare (V50-V59)

V50	Elective surgery for purposes other than remedying health states
V51	Aftercare involving the use of plastic surgery
V52	Fitting and adjustment of prosthetic device
V53	Fitting and adjustment of other device
V54	Other orthopedic aftercare
V55	Attention to artificial openings
V56	Encounter for dialysis and dialysis catheter care
V57	Care involving use of rehabilitation procedures
V58	Encounter for other and unspecified procedures and aftercare
V59	Donors

Persons encountering health services in other circumstances (V60-V69)

V60	Housing, household, and economic circumstances
V61	Other family circumstances
V62	Other psychosocial circumstances
V63	Unavailability of other medical facilities for care
V64	Persons encountering health services for specific procedures, not carried out
V65	Other persons seeking consultation
V66	Convalescence and palliative care
V67	Follow-up examination
V68	Encounters for administrative purposes
V69	Problems related to lifestyle

Persons without reported diagnosis encountered during examination and investigation of individuals and populations (V70-V82)

V70	General medical examination
V71	Observation and evaluation for suspected conditions not found
V72	Special investigations and examinations
V73	Special screening examination for viral and chlamydial diseases
V74	Special screening examination for bacterial and spirochetal diseases
V75	Special screening examination for other infectious diseases
V76	Special screening for malignant neoplasms
V77	Special screening for endocrine, nutritional, metabolic, and immunity disorders
V78	Special screening for disorders of blood and blood-forming organs
V79	Special screening for mental disorders and developmental handicaps
V80	Special screening for neurological, eye, and ear diseases
V81	Special screening for cardiovascular, respiratory, and genitourinary diseases
V82	Special screening for other conditions

Genetics (V83-V84)

V83	Genetic carrier status

V84   Genetic susceptibility to disease

Body mass index (V85)
V85   Body Mass Index

Estrogen receptor status (V86)
V86   Estrogen receptor status

Other specified personal exposures and history presenting hazards to health (V87)
V87   Other specified personal exposures and history presenting hazards to health

Acquired absence of other organs and tissue (V88)
V88   Acquired absence of other organs and tissue

Other suspected conditions not found (V89)
V89   Other suspected conditions not found

SUPPLEMENTARY CLASSIFICATION OF EXTERNAL CAUSES OF INJURY AND POISONING

External Cause Status (E000)
E000   External cause status

Activity (E001-E030)
E001   Activities involving walking and running
E002   Activities involving water and water craft
E003   Activities involving ice and snow
E004   Activities involving climbing, rappelling, and jumping off
E005   Activities involving dancing and other rhythmic movement
E006   Activities involving other sports and athletics played individually
E007   Activities involving other sports and athletics played as a team or group
E008   Activities involving other specified sports and athletics
E009   Activity involving other cardiorespiratory exercise
E010   Activity involving other muscle strengthening exercises
E011   Activities involving computer technology and electronic devices
E012   Activities involving arts and handcrafts
E013   Activities involving personal hygiene and household maintenance
E014   Activities involving person providing caregiving
E015   Activities involving food preparation, cooking and grilling
E016   Activities involving property and land maintenance, building and construction
E017   Activities involving roller coasters and other types of external motion
E018   Activities involving playing musical instrument
E019   Activities involving animal care
E029   Other activity
E030   Unspecified activity

Transport Accidents (E800-E848)

Railway accidents (E800-E807)
E800   Railway accident involving collision with roling stock
E801   Railway accident involving collision with other object
E802   Railway accident involving derailment without antecedent collision
E803   Railway accident involving explosion, fire, or burning
E804   Fall in, on, or from railway train
E805   Hit by rolling stock
E806   Other specified railway accident
E807   Railway accident of unspecified nature

Motor vehicle traffic accidents (E810-E819)
E810   Motor vehicle traffic accident involving collision with train
E811   Motor vehicle traffic accident involving re-entrant collision with another motor vehicle
E812   Other motor vehicle traffic accident involving collision with another motor vehicle
E813   Motor vehicle traffic accident involving collision with other vehicle
E814   Motor vehicle traffic accident involving collision with pedestrian
E815   Other motor vehicle traffic accident involving collision on the highway
E816   Motor vehicle traffic accident due to loss of control, without collision on the highway
E817   Noncollision motor vehicle traffic accident while boarding or alighting
E818   Other noncollision motor vehicle traffic accident
E819   Motor vehicle traffic accident of unspecified nature

Motor vehicle nontraffic accidents (E820-E825)
E820   Nontraffic accident involving motor-driven snow vehicle
E821   Nontraffic accident involving other off-road motor vehicle
E822   Other motor vehicle nontraffic accident involving collision with moving object
E823   Other motor vehicle nontraffic accident involving collision with stationary object
E824   Other motor vehicle nontraffic accident while boarding and alighting
E825   Other motor vehicle nontraffic accident of other and unspecified nature

Other road vehicle accidents (E826-E829)
E826   Pedal cycle accident
E827   Animal-drawn vehicle accident
E828   Accident involving animal being ridden
E829   Other road vehicle accidents

Water transport accidents (E830-E838)
E830   Accident to watercraft causing submersion
E831   Accident to watercraft causing other injury
E832   Other accidental submersion or drowning in water transport accident
E833   Fall on stairs or ladders in water transport
E834   Other fall from one level to another in water transport
E835   Other and unspecified fall in water transport
E836   Machinery accident in water transport
E837   Explosion, fire, or burning in watercraft
E838   Other and unspecified water transport accident

Air and space transport accidents (E840-E845)
E840   Accident to powered aircraft at takeoff or landing
E841   Accident to powered aircraft, other and unspecified
E842   Accident to unpowered aircraft
E843   Fall in, on, or from aircraft
E844   Other specified air transport accidents
E845   Other involving spacecraft

Vehicle accidents, not elsewhere classfiable (E846-E849)
E846   Accidents involving powered vehicles used solely within the buildings and premises of an industrial or commercial establishment
E847   Accidents involving cable cars not running on rails
E848   Accidents involving other vehicles, not elsewhere classifiable
E849   Place of occurrence

Accidental poisoning by drugs, medicinal substances, and biologicals (E850-E858)
E850   Accidental poisoning by analgesics, antipyretics, and antirheumatics
E851   Accidental poisoning by barbiturates
E852   Accidental poisoning by other sedatives and hypnotics
E853   Accidental poisoning by tranquilizers
E854   Accidental poisoning by other psychotropic agents
E855   Accidental poisoning by other drugs acting on central and autonomic nervous systems
E856   Accidental poisoning by antibiotics
E857   Accidental poisoning by anti-infectives
E858   Accidental poisoning by other drugs

Accidental poisoning by other solid and liquid substances, gases, and vapors (E860-E869)
E860   Accidental poisoning by alcohol, not elsewhere classified
E861   Accidental poisoning by cleansing and polishing agents, disinfectants, paints, and varnishes
E862   Accidental poisoning by petroleum products, other solvents and their vapors, not elsewhere classified
E863   Accidental poisoning by agricultural and horticultural chemical and pharmaceutical preparations other than plant foods and fertilizers
E864   Accidental poisoning by corrosives and caustics, not elsewhere classified
E865   Accidental poisoning from poisonous foodstuffs and poisonous plants
E866   Accidental poisoning by other and unspecified solid and liquid substances
E867   Accidental poisoning by gas distributed by pipeline
E868   Accidental poisoning by other utility gas and other carbon monoxide
E869   Accidental poisoning by other gases and vapors

Misadventures to patients during surgical and medical care (E870-E876)
E870   Accidental cut, puncture, perforation, or hemorrhage during medical care
E871   Foreign object left in body during procedure
E872   Failure of sterile precautions during procedure
E873   Failure in dosage
E874   Mechanical failure of instrument or apparatus during procedure
E875   Contaminated or infected blood, other fluid, drug, or biological substance
E876   Other and unspecified misadventures during medical care

Surgical and medical procedures as the cause of abnormal reaction of patient or later complication, without mention of misadventure at the time of procedure (E878-E879)
E878   Surgical operation and other surgical procedures as the cause of abnormal reaction of patient, or of later complication, without mention of misadventure at the time of operation
E879   Other procedures, without mention of misadventure at the time of procedure, as the cause of abnormal reaction of patient, or of later complication

Accidental falls (E880-E888)
E880   Fall on or from stairs or steps
E881   Fall on or from ladders or scaffolding
E882   Fall from or out of building or other structure
E883   Fall into hole or other opening in surface
E884   Other fall from one level to another